S0-BXL-590

DIRECTORY OF AMERICAN FIRMS OPERATING IN FOREIGN COUNTRIES

15th Edition

VOLUME 1

Part One - Alphabetical Index of
American Corporations
Pages: 1 - 324

Part Two - Alphabetical Index of
American Corporations by Country

Albania to Ecuador
Pages: 327 – 1118

UNIWORLD BUSINESS PUBLICATIONS, INC.
257 Central Park West, Suite 10A
New York, NY 10024-4110
Tel: (212) 496-2448
Fax: (212) 769-0413
uniworldbp@aol.com
www.uniworldbp.com

First Edition	1954
Second Edition	1957
Third Edition	1959
Fourth Edition	1961
Fifth Edition	1964
Sixth Edition	1966
Seventh Edition	1969
Eighth Edition	1975
Ninth Edition	1979
Tenth Edition	1984
Eleventh Edition	1987
Twelfth Edition	1991
Thirteenth Edition	1994
Fourteenth Edition	1996
Fifteenth Edition	1999

Uniworld Business Publications, Inc.
257 Central Park West
New York, New York 10024
uniworldbp@aol.com
www.uniworldbp.com

Printed in the United States of America

INTRODUCTION

Since it was first published in 1955, *Directory of American Firms Operating in Foreign Countries* has been an authoritative source of information on American firms which have branches, subsidiaries, or affiliates outside the United States. Designed to aid anyone interested in American business activities abroad, it is the only reference work of its kind. The Directory has been used by public, university, business, government and special libraries, banks, accounting, brokerage and investment firms, manufacturers, transportation companies, advertising and personnel agencies, researchers, embassies and many governmental agencies dealing with commerce, trade and foreign relations.

The 15th edition contains 2,450 U.S. firms with nearly 30,000 branches, subsidiaries and affiliates in 190 countries.

The Directory consists of three volumes.

Volume 1 - **Part One**: lists, in alphabetical order, American firms that have operations abroad. Each entry contains the company's U.S. address, telephone/fax, and principal product/service, and lists the foreign countries in which it has a branch, subsidiary, or affiliate. Some key personnel are noted, when provided: Chief Executive Officer (CEO), International Operations or Foreign Operations Officer (FO), and Human Resources Director (HR). These titles are meant to be generic and are assigned to the names given to us as the Chief Executive, the person in charge of Foreign Operations and the senior Human Resources officer. Also the web site address, annual revenue and number of employees are included, when available.

Volume 1 - **Part Two,** and **Volumes 2** and **3:** contain listings by country from Albania to Zimbabwe of the American firms' foreign operations. Each country listing includes, alphabetically, the name of the U.S. parent firm, address, telephone/fax, web site address, principal product/service, and the name and address of its branch, subsidiary, or affiliate in that country. With the 15th edition we have included the telephone/fax numbers and principal contact officer, when provided by the American parent.

U.S. Direct Investment Abroad

The overseas companies in this specialized listing are those in which American Firms have a substantial direct capital investment and which have been identified by the parent as a wholly or partially owned subsidiary, affiliate or branch. Franchises, representatives and non-commercial enterprises or institutions, such as hospitals, schools, etc., financed or operated by American philanthropic or religious organizations, are not included.

U.S. direct investment in foreign countries has continued to increase at 11% for 1996 and 1997, down slightly from the 14% increase reported for 1995. Although this investment trend has remained significantly positive, the number of U.S. companies with foreign operations captured by our research has remained constant at approximately 2,500; however, the number of foreign subsidiaries, branches and affiliates of those U.S. companies has grown from 18,000 in our 14th edition to nearly 30,000. These data and our empirical experience indicate significant consolidation, through merger and acquisition.

U.S. Direct Investment Abroad - Top Countries
(Historical-cost basis in $ Billions)
U.S. Bureau of Economic Analysis, 1998

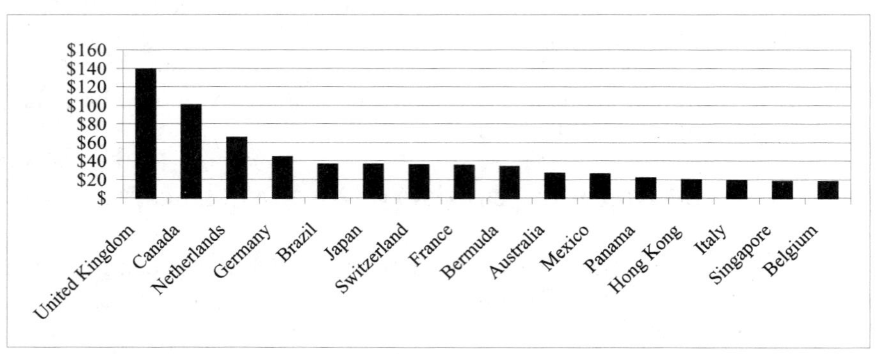

U.S. Direct Investment Abroad - by Region
(Historical-cost basis in $ Billions)
U.S. Bureau of Economic Analysis, 1998

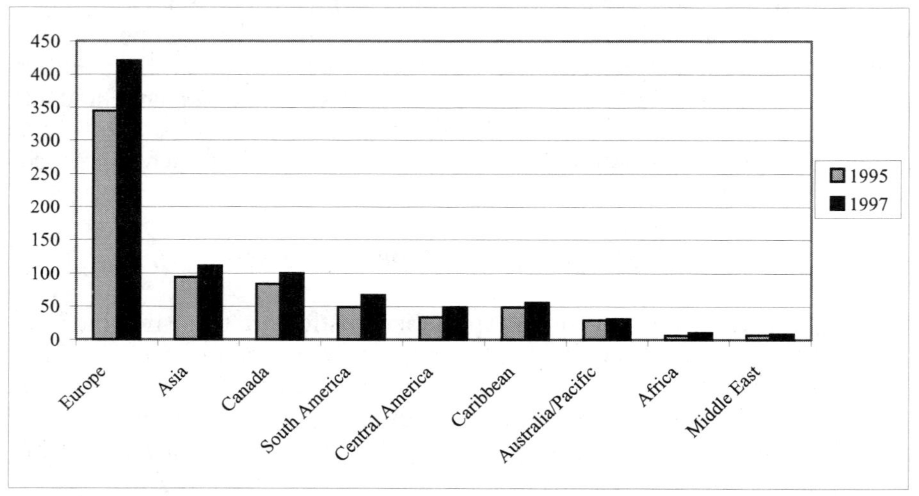

Source and Accuracy of Listings

In preparing the 1999 - 15th edition, 550 new companies have been added, and over 600 firms which were dissolved, no longer maintain operations abroad or were acquired, have been deleted. The primary sources of information were questionnaires completed by the U.S. parent company, and private and public sources developed over 40 years of publication, including extensive review of the financial media.

Direct telephone and telefax contacts were used extensively for verification and clarification. Each firm in the previous edition was sent an announcement of the new revised edition, along with a print-out of its former entry, and asked to provide current data. It was stated that if we did not receive a response from a firm, and there was no evidence that it had gone out of business, the previous entry would be carried forward to this edition.

The aim of this listing is to provide accurate, up-to-date listings. However, the Editor and Publisher cannot guarantee that the information received from a company or other source as the basis for an entry is correct. In addition, the designations and listings are not to be considered definitive as to legal status or the relationship between the American and the foreign firms.

As extensive as this compilation may be it does not claim to be all-inclusive. It contains only what has been disclosed to us. Also, in a directory of this scope some inaccuracies are inevitable. It would be appreciated if the reader noting such would inform us so corrections can be made in future editions.

Acknowledgments

Our sincere appreciation is extended to all company representatives who cooperated so generously in providing information for this directory, and to everyone who assisted in its preparation: Associate Editor Lynn Sherwood, Associate Publisher Debra Lipian, Book Designer David Bornstein, and research interns Taneika and Shameika Taylor.

Barbara D. Fiorito, Editor
Uniworld Business Publications, Inc.

Company Designations

Abbreviation	Term	Country
AB	Aktiebolag	Sweden
AG	Aktiengesellschaft	Austria, Germany, Switzerland
AS	Anonim Sirketi	Turkey
A/S	Aktieselskab	Denmark
	Aksjeselskap	Norway
BV	Beslotene Vennootschap	Netherlands
CA	Compania Anonima	Venezuela
CIE	Compagnie	Belgium, France
CO/Co.	Company	Canada, England, U.S.
CORP/Corp.	Corporation	England, U.S.
GmbH	Gesellschaft mit beschrankter Haftung	Austria, Germany
INC/Inc.	Incorporated	Canada, England, U.S.
KG	Kommanditgesellschaft	Germany
KK	Kabushiki Kaisha	Japan
LTD/Ltd.	Limited	Canada, England, U.S.
MIJ	Maatschappij	Netherlands
NV	Naamloze Vennoostchap	Belgium, Netherlands
OY	Osakeyhtio	Finland
P/L	Proprietary Limited	Australia
PLC	Public Limited Company	England, Scotland
PT	Perusahaan Terbatas	Indonesia
SA	Sociedad Anonima	Argentina, Brazil, Colombia, Spain, Venezuela
	Societe Anonyme	Belgium, France, Switzerland
SARL	Societe Anonoyme a Responsabilite Limitee	Belgium, France, Switzerland
SPA	Societa per Azioni	Italy
Sp z o.o	Spolka Odpowiedzialnoscia	Poland
SPRL	Societe de Personnes a Responsabilite Limitee	Belgium
SRL	Societa a Responsabilita Limitata	Italy

Abbreviations Used in This Report

A/C .... Air Conditioning
Access .... Accessories
Adv .... Advertising
Affil .... Affiliate(d)
Agcy .... Agent/Agency
Agric .... Agriculture
Apt .... Apartment
Arch .... Architect(ural)
Assur .... Assurance
Auto .... Automotive
Aux .... Auxiliary
Av/Ave .... Avenida/Avenue
Bil .... Billion
Bldg .... Building
Blvd .... Boulevard
Bus .... Business
CEO .... Chief Executive Officer
Chem .... Chemical
Chmn .... Chairman
Cir .... Circulation
Co .... Company
Col .... Colonia
Com .... Components
Coml .... Commercial
Commun .... Communications
Conslt .... Consultant/Consulting
Constr .... Construction
Corp .... Corporate/Corporation
Cust .... Customer
Dept .... Department
Devel .... Development
Diag .... Diagnostic
Dir. .... Director
Dist .... District
Distr .... Distributor/Distribution
Div .... Division
Divers .... Diversified
Dom .... Domestic
Econ .... Economics
Educ .... Education
Elec .... Electric(al)
Electr .... Electronic(s)
Emp .... Employee(s)
Eng .... Engineer(ing)
Envi .... Environmental
Equip .... Equipment
EVP .... Executive Vice President
Exch .... Exchange
Exec .... Executive
Exp .... Export(er)
Explor .... Exploration
Fax .... Facsimile
Fin .... Financial/Finance
Fl .... Floor
FO .... Foreign Operation(s) Officer
For .... Foreign
Frt .... Freight
Furn .... Furniture
Fwdg .... Forwarding
Gds .... Goods
Gen .... General
Hdqtrs/HQ .... Headquarters
Hdwe .... Hardware
Hwy .... Highway
Hos .... Hospital
HR .... Human Resources Officer
Hydr .... Hydraulic(s)
Imp .... Import(er)
Inc .... Incorporated
Ind .... Industrial/Industry
Inf .... Information
Ins .... Insurance
Inspc .... Inspect(ion)
Instru .... Instrument
Intl .... International
Invest .... Investment
JV .... Joint Venture
Lab .... Laboratory
Liq .... Liquid
Ltd .... Limited
Mach .... Machine(ry)
Maint .... Maintenance
Mat .... Material
Mdse .... Merchandise
Mdsng .... Merchandising
Meas .... Measurement
Med .... Medical
Mfg .... Manufacturing
Mfr .... Manufacture(r)
Mgmt .... Management
Mgn .... Managing
Mgr. .... Manager

Mil .... Million
Mkt .... Market
Mktg .... Marketing
Mng Dir .... Managing Director
Mng Ptrn .... Managing Partner
Mng. .... Managing
Nat .... Natural
NE .... Northeast
No/N .... North
NW .... Northwest
Oper .... Operation
Orgn .... Organization(al)
Pass .... Passenger
Petrol .... Petroleum
Pharm .... Pharmaceutical(s)
Plt .... Plant
Prdt .... Product(s)
Pres .... President
Prin .... Principal
Print .... Printing
Proc .... Process(ing)
Prod .... Production
Prog .... Programming
Pte/Prt. .... Private
Ptnr .... Partner
Pty .... Proprietary
Pub .... Publisher/Publishing
R&D .... Research & Development
Rd .... Road
Recre .... Recreation(al)
Refrig .... Refrigeration
Reg .... Regional
Reins .... Reinsurance
Rel .... Relations
Rep .... Representative
Ret .... Retail(er)
Rfg .... Refining
Ry .... Railway
Sci .... Scientific
SE .... Southeast
Serv .... Service(s)
So/S .... South
Spec .... Special(ty)/Specialized
St/Str .... Street
Sta .... Station
Ste .... Suite
Str .... Strasse
Sub .... Subsidiary
Super .... Supervision
Svce .... Service(s)
SVP .... Senior Vice President
SW .... Southwest
Sys .... System
Tech .... Technical/Technology
Tel .... Telephone
Telecom .... Telecommunications
Temp .... Temperature
Trans .... Transmission
Transp .... Transport(ation)
TV .... Television
VP .... Vice President
Whl .... Wholesale(r)
Whse .... Warehouse

Notes on Alphabetizing

Alphabetizing in this directory is by computer sort which places numerals before letters; and, among names, places special characters before numbers and letters in the following order: blanks, ampersands, plus signs, dashes, periods and slashes. For example, 3Z Co. precedes A Z Co., which precedes, in the following order, A&Z Co., A+Z Co., A-Z Co., A.Z. Co., A/Z Co., A1Z Co. and AZ Co.

Names such as The Jones Corp., Charles Jones Inc., and L.M. Jones & Co., are alphabetized conventionally: all will be found under J. Names which consist of initials only (e.g., LFM Co.) are in strict alphabetical order : Lewis., LFM Co., Lintz Inc.

While the custom in most countries is to place company designations (Co., Inc., etc.) at the end of the firm's name, that is not always the case. For example, Finland's "Oy" and Sweden's "AB" sometimes appear at the end and sometimes at the beginning of the company's name; in this directory they have been disregarded in alphabetizing.

Table of Contents – Volume 1

PART **ONE**

DIRECTORY OF
AMERICAN FIRMS
OPERATING IN
FOREIGN COUNTRIES
15th Edition

ALPHABETICAL INDEX OF AMERICAN CORPORATIONS

3COM CORPORATION

5400 Bayfront Plaza

Santa Clara, CA 95052-8145

Tel: (408) 764-5000 Fax: (408) 764-5001

CEO: Eric A. Benhamou

FO: William G. Marr

HR: Debra Engel, VP

Web site: www.3com.com

Emp: 3,072

Develop/mfr. computer networking products & systems.

Argentina, Australia, Austria, Brazil, Bulgaria, Canada, Chile, China (PRC), Colombia, Costa Rica, Czech Republic, England, U.K., France, Germany, Hong Kong, Hungary, India, Indonesia, Ireland, Israel, Japan, Malaysia, Mexico, New Zealand, Pakistan, Peru, Philippines, Poland, Saudi Arabia, Singapore, Slovakia, South Africa, South Korea, Spain, Switzerland, Taiwan (ROC), Thailand, Turkey, United Arab Emirates, Venezuela

3D LABS INC., LTD.

181 Metro Drive, Ste. 520

San Jose, CA 95110

Tel: (408) 436-3455 Fax: (408) 436-3458

CEO: Osman Kent, Pres.

FO: Thomas S. Donohue, VP

Web site: www.3dlabs.com

Emp: 100 Rev: $61 mil.

Produces 3D grahics accelorators chips for the PC computer platform.

England, U.K., Japan, Taiwan (ROC)

3D/INTERNATIONAL INC.

1900 West Loop South

Houston, TX 77027

Tel: (713) 871-7000 Fax: (713) 871-7456

CEO: John Murph, Pres.

HR: Jill Hardegree

Web site: www.3di.com

Design, management & environmental services.

Hong Kong, Saudi Arabia

3M

3M Center

St. Paul, MN 55144-1000

Tel: (612) 733-1110 Fax: (612) 733-9973

CEO: Livio D. DeSimone, Chmn.

FO: Ronald O. Baukol, EVP

HR: M. Kay Grenz, VP

Web site: www.mmm.com

Emp: 75,639 Rev: $15,070 mil.

Mfr. diversified products for industry, health care, imaging, communications, transport, safety, consumer, etc.

Argentina, Australia, Austria, Belgium, Brazil, Canada, Chile, China (PRC), Colombia, Costa Rica, Czech Republic, Denmark, Dominican Republic, Ecuador, Egypt, El Salvador, England, U.K., Fiji, Finland, France, Germany, Greece, Guatemala, Hong Kong, Hungary, India, Indonesia, Ireland, Israel, Italy, Jamaica, Japan, Kenya, Malaysia, Mexico, Morocco, Netherlands, New Zealand, Norway, Pakistan, Panama, Papua New Guinea, Peru, Philippines, Poland, Portugal, Russia, Singapore, South Africa, South Korea, Spain, Sri Lanka, Sweden, Switzerland, Taiwan (ROC), Thailand, Trinidad & Tobago, Turkey, Ukraine, United Arab Emirates, Uruguay, Venezuela, Vietnam, Zimbabwe

A.B. DICK CO.

5700 West Rouhy Ave.

Niles, IL 60714

Tel: (847) 779-1900 Fax: (847) 647-8369

CEO: Gerald McConnell, Pres.

FO: William Pesch

Web site: www.abdick.com

Emp: 1,500 Rev: $334 mil.

Mfr./sales automation systems.

Belgium, Canada, England, U.K., Malaysia

AAF INTERNATIONAL (American Air Filter)

215 Central Ave., PO Box 35690

Louisville, KY 40232-5690

Tel: (502) 637-0011 Fax: (502) 637-0321

CEO: Robert Brymer, Pres.

HR: Fred Zepp

Web site: www.aafintl.com

Emp: 5,100

Mfr. air filtration/pollution control & noise control equipment.

Brazil, Canada, England, U.K., France, Germany,

India, Japan, Mexico, Netherlands, Singapore, South Africa, Spain, Sweden, Switzerland

AAF-McQUAY INC.

111 South Calvert Street, Ste. 2800

Baltimore, MD 21202

Tel: (410) 528-2755 Fax: (410) 528-2797

CEO: Joseph Hunter, Pres.

HR: Gary Boyd

Web site: www.mcquay.com

Emp: 7,100

Mfr. air quality control products: heating, ventilating, air-conditioning & filtration products & services.

Australia, Austria, Canada, England, U.K., France, Germany, Greece, Italy, Mexico, Netherlands, Singapore, Spain, Turkey, Venezuela

AAR CORPORATION

One AAR Place, 1100 North Wood Dale Road

Wood Dale, IL 60191

Tel: (630) 227-2000 Fax: (630) 227-2562

CEO: David P. Storch, Pres.

FO: Ira A. Eichner, Chrm.

HR: Robert Naughton

Web site: www.aarcorp.com

Emp: 2,800

Aviation repair & supply provisioning; aircraft sales & leasing.

Belgium, England, U.K., France, Germany, Israel, Netherlands, Singapore, Wales, U.K.

ABBOTT LABORATORIES

One Abbott Park Road

Abbott Park, IL 60064-3500

Tel: (847) 937-6100 Fax: (847) 937-1511

CEO: Dwane Burnham, Chmn.

FO: Robert L. Parkman

HR: Ellen Walvoord

Web site: www.abbott.com

Emp: 50,000

Development/mfr./sale diversified health care products & services.

Argentina, Australia, Brazil, Canada, England, U.K., France, Germany, Ireland, Italy, Japan, Mexico, Netherlands, Russia, Switzerland, Thailand, Vietnam

ABF FREIGHT SYSTEM INC.

3801 Old Greenwood Road

Fort Smith, AR 72903

Tel: (501) 785-8928 Fax: (501) 785-8927

CEO: David Stubblefield

FO: Richard Coelho

HR: Dan Griesse

Emp: 12,000

Motor carrier.

Canada, Mexico

ABM, INC.

50 Fremont Street, #2600

San Francisco, CA 94105

Tel: (415) 597-4500 Fax: (415) 597-7160

CEO: William Steele, Pres.

HR: Donna Dell

Emp: 41,000

Building cleaning & maintenance services.

Canada

ABRASIVE TECHNOLOGY INC.

8400 Green Meadows Drive

Westerville, OH 43081

Tel: (614) 548-4100 Fax: (614) 548-7617

CEO: Loyal M. Peterman

FO: John Fuquay

HR: Bonnie Licis

Web site: www.abrasive-tech.com

Mfr. diamond & CBN tooling: bits, blades, drills, wheels, belts, discs.

Canada, Spain

ACADEMIC PRESS INC.

6277 Sea Harbor Drive

Orlando, FL 32887

Tel: (407) 345-2000 Fax: (407) 345-8388

CEO: Brian Kanez, Pres.

Web site: www.academicpress.com

Emp: 400

Publisher of educational & scientific books.

Czech Republic, Denmark, Egypt, England, U.K., France, Germany, Greece, Italy, Japan, Netherlands, Poland, South Africa, Spain

ACC CORPORATION

400 West Ave.

Rochester, NY 14611

Tel: (716) 987-3000 Fax: (716) 987-3499

CEO: Steve Dubnik, Pres.

FO: Chris Bantoft, Pres.

HR: Laurie Wiest

Web site: www.acccorp.com

Emp: 1,400 Rev: $372.6 mil.

Long distance & telecommunications services.

Canada, England, U.K., Germany

ACCELERATION INTERNATIONAL CORP.

475 Metro Place North

Dublin, OH 43017

Tel: (614) 764-7000 Fax: (614) 764-7198

CEO: Thomas Friedberg, Pres.

HR: Bryce Farmer

Emp: 140

Insurance holding company.

England, U.K.

ACCLAIM ENTERTAINMENT, INC.

1 Acclaim Plaza

Glen Cove, NY 11542

Tel: (516) 656-5000 Fax: (516) 656-2031

CEO: Gregory Fischbach, Pres.

Web site: www.acclaim-music.com

Emp: 194

Mfr. video games.

Canada, England, U.K., France, Germany, Japan

ACCO USA INC.

300 Tower Parkway

Lincoln, IL 60069

Tel: (847) 541-9500 Fax: (847) 478-0073

CEO: Bruce Gescheider, Pres.

HR: Erica Smith

Emp: 950

Paper fasteners & clips, metal fasteners, binders & staplers.

Australia, Canada, England, U.K., France, Germany, Jamaica, Japan, Mexico, Netherlands, New Zealand, Venezuela

ACCOUNTANTS ON CALL

Park 80 West, Plaza 2, 9th Fl.

Saddle Brook, NJ 07663

Tel: (201) 843-0006 Fax: (201) 843-4936

CEO: Stewart C . Libes, Pres.

Web site: www.aocnet.com

Full-service staffing & executive search firm specializing in accounting & financial personnel.

Canada, England, U.K.

ACCURIDE INTERNATIONAL, INC.

12311 Shoemaker Ave.

Santa Fe Springs, CA 90670-4721

Tel: (562) 903-0200 Fax: (562) 903-0208

CEO: Scott Jordan, Pres.

HR: Robert Morris

Web site: www.accuride.com

Mfr. drawer slides.

England, U.K., Germany, Japan, Mexico

ACE CONTROLS INC.

23435 Industrial Park Drive

Farmington Hills, MI 48024

Tel: (248) 476-0213 Fax: (248) 276-2470

CEO: William J. Chorkey

FO: Joel D. Colliau

Web site: www.aceshocks.com

Emp: 165

Industry hydraulic shock absorbers, cylinders, valves & automation controls.

England, U.K., Germany, Japan

ACHESON COLLOIDS CO.

511 Fort Street, PO Box 611747

Port Huron, MI 48061-1747

Tel: (810) 984-5581 Fax: (810) 984-1446

CEO: Michael Porter, Pres.

FO: Herbert A. Hoover

Emp: 850 Rev: $130 mil.

Chemicals, chemical preparations, paints & lubricating oils.

Australia, Belgium, Brazil, Canada, England, U.K., France, Germany, Japan, Netherlands, Spain

ACME UNITED CORPORATION

75 Kings Highway Cutoff

Fairfield, CT 06430-5340

Tel: (203) 332-7330 Fax: (203) 576-0007

CEO: Walter C. Johnsen, Pres.

FO: Brian S. Olsen

HR: Ralph Mastrony

Web site: www.acu.com

Emp: 433 Rev: $47 mil.

Mfr. surgical & medical instruments, pharmaceutical supplies.

Canada, England, U.K., Germany

ACTION INSTRUMENTS INC.

8601 Aero Drive

San Diego, CA 92123

Tel: (619) 279-5726 Fax: (619) 279-6290

CEO: James Pinto, Pres.

FO: Nick Holman

HR: Michelle Johnson

Emp: 260

Mfr. electronic instruments & industrial measurements computers.

England, U.K., France, Germany

ACTIVISION

3100 Ocean Park Boulevard

Santa Monica, CA 90405

Tel: (310) 255-2000 Fax: (310) 255-2100

CEO: Robert Kotick

FO: Brian Kelly, Pres.

HR: Page Morris

Web site: www.activision.com

Emp: 438

Development/mfr. entertainment software & video games.

Australia, England, U.K., Germany, Japan

ACXIOM CORPORATION

301 Industrial Boulevard

Conway, AR 72033-2000

Tel: (501) 336-1000 Fax: (501) 336-3919

CEO: Charles D. Mrogan, Jr., Chmn.

FO: Roger S. Kline, COO

HR: Cindy Childers

Web site: www.acxiom.com

Emp: 3,600 Rev: $465.1 mil.

Data warehouser, database manager, & other marketing information services.

England, U.K., Malaysia

ADAMS RITE MANUFACTURING COMPANY

4040 South Capital Ave., PO Box 1301

City of Industry, CA 91749

Tel: (562) 699-0511 Fax: (562) 699-5094

CEO: P. D. Adams

FO: Victor A. Vininski

HR: Ana Artavia

Web site: www.adamsrite.com

Emp: 240

Mfr. architectural hardware.

England, U.K.

ADAMS USA (DIV. WARNER LAMBERT)

201 Tabor Road

Morris Plains, NJ 07950

Tel: (973) 540-2000 Fax: (973) 540-2313

CEO: John Craig, Pres.

HR: Raymond Fino, VP

Emp: 2,500

Mfr./distribution & sale of chewing gum.

Canada, Peru, Venezuela

ADAPTEC INC.

691 South Milpitas Boulevard

Milpitas, CA 95035

Tel: (408) 945-8600 Fax: (408) 262-2533

CEO: Larry Boucher, Pres.

Web site: www.adaptec.com

Design/mfr./marketing hardware & software solutions.

Belgium, Germany, Japan, Singapore

ADC TELECOMMUNICATIONS INC.

PO Box 1101

Minneapolis, MN 55440-1101

Tel: (612) 938-8080 Fax: (612) 946-3292

CEO: William J. Cadogan, Pres.

HR: Laura Owen

Web site: www.adc.com

Emp: 6,000

Mfr. telecommunications equipment.

Canada, England, U.K., Mexico, Singapore, Venezuela

ADEMCO INTERNATIONAL

165 Eileen Way

Syosset, NY 11791

Tel: (516) 921-6704 Fax: (516) 496-8306

CEO: Roger Fradin, Pres.

FO: Alan Wachtel

Web site: www.ademcoint.com

Emp: 1,850

Mfr. security, fire & burglary systems & products.

Australia, Canada, England, U.K., Germany, Hong Kong, Italy, Poland, Scotland, U.K., Spain

ADESA CORPORATION

310 East 96 Street, Ste. 40

Indianapolis, IN 46240

Tel: (317) 815-1100 Fax: (317) 815-0500

CEO: James Hallett, Pres.

Emp: 1,700

Motor vehicles, automotive services & trucking.

Canada

ADOBE AIR INC.

500 South 15th Street

Phoenix, AZ 85034

Tel: (602) 257-0060 Fax: (602) 257-1349

CEO: Ron Rosin, Pres.

HR: Diane Allen

Mfr. evaporative air coolers and portable electric heaters.

Mexico

ADVANCE MACHINE COMPANY

14600 21st Ave. North

Plymouth, MN 55447

Tel: (612) 745-3500 Fax: (612) 745-3866

CEO: Ole Jakobsen, Acting Chmn.

FO: Jim Nelson

HR: Kenneth Frideres

Web site: www.advmac.com

Emp: 750

Industrial floor cleaning equipment.

Canada

ADVANCE PUBLICATIONS, INC.

950 Fingerboard Road

Staten Island, NY 10305

Tel: (718) 981-1234 Fax: (718) 981-1415

CEO: Donald E. Newhouse, Pres.

FO: Didier Guerin, Pres., Intl.

Web site: www.advance.net

Emp: 24,000

Publishing company (Glamour, Vogue, GQ, Architectural Digest) & cable TV operations.

England, U.K., France

ADVANCED LOGIC RESEARCH INC.

9401 Jeronimo Road

Irvine, CA 92718

Tel: (714) 581-6770 Fax: (714) 581-9240

CEO: Gene Lu, Pres.

HR: Angela Massours

Emp: 670

Computers

England, U.K., Germany, Singapore

ADVANCED MICRO DEVICES INC.

PO Box 3453

Sunnyvale, CA 94088-3000

Tel: (408) 732-2400 Fax: (408) 982-6164

CEO: Richard Previte, Pres.

HR: Stanley Winvick

Web site: www.amd.com

Mfr. integrated circuits for communications & computation industry.

England, U.K., Japan, Malaysia, Singapore, Thailand

ADVANCED PRODUCTS COMPANY

33 Defco Park Road

North Haven, CT 06473

Tel: (203) 239-3341 Fax: (203) 234-7233

CEO: Nancy Nicholson, Pres.

FO: Peter G. Amos, VP

HR: Joyce Abramczyk

Web site: www.advpro.com

Emp: 110

Mfr. Metallic & PTFE seals & gaskets.

Belgium, England, U.K., France, Germany

ADVANTICA RESTAURANT GROUP, INC.

203 East Main Street

Spartanburg, SC 29319

Tel: (864) 597-8000 Fax: (864) 597-7538

CEO: James B. Adamson, Pres.

HR: Stephen W. Wood

Emp: 90,000

Restaurants

Canada

ADYNO NOBEL

50 South Main Street, 11th Fl., Crossroads Tower
Salt Lake City, UT 84144
Tel: (801) 364-4800 Fax: (801) 328-6525
CEO: Doug Jackson
HR: Earl J. Banner
Mfr. explosive supplies, accessories for industrial and military applications; aluminum granules.
Brazil, Canada, Chile, Mexico, Peru

AEC INC.
801 AEC Drive
Wood Dale, IL 60191
Tel: (708) 595-1090 Fax: (708) 595-6641
CEO: Bruce Remen, Pres.
FO: Joe Prestinario
HR: Bob Zega
Emp: 500
Mfr./service auxiliary equipment for plastics industry.
England, U.K., Japan, Sweden

AERO SYSTEMS AVIATION CORPORATION
PO Box 52-2221
Miami, FL 33152
Tel: (305) 871-1300 Fax: (305) 8841400
CEO: Jack Stabile, Pres.
FO: Colin J.Devellerez
HR: R. Edward Holmes
Emp: 250
Aviation equipment sales & service systems.
England, U.K., Singapore

AEROFIN CORPORATION
4621 Murray Place, PO Box 10819
Lynchburg, VA 24506
Tel: (804) 845-7081 Fax: (804) 528-6242
CEO: K. H. Johnstone
FO: D. L. Corell
HR: J. Dearing
Emp: 280
Mfr. heat exchangers.
Canada

AEROGLIDE CORPORATION
PO Box 29505
Raleigh, NC 27626-0505
Tel: (919) 851-2000 Fax: (919) 851-6029
CEO: J. Fredrick Kelly, Jr.
FO: Thomas Mix
HR: D. A Humphries
Web site: www.aeroglide.com
Emp: 130
Mfr. rotary dryers, dehydrators, roasters, grain & coffee dryers.
Colombia

AEROMARITIME, INC.
4115 Pleasant Valley Drive
Chantilly, VA 22021
Tel: (703) 631-3111 Fax: (703) 631-3144
CEO: Eugene Courson, Pres.
Web site: www.aeromar.com
Military electronics.
England, U.K., Israel

AERONAUTICAL INSTRUMENTS & RADIO COMPANY
234 Garibaldi Ave.
Lodi, NJ 07644
Tel: (973) 473-0034 Fax: (973) 473-8748
CEO: H. J. Burke, Pres.
FO: M. C. Leblanc
HR: Evo Nicoletti
Mfr. aeronautical instruments.
Germany, Portugal, Thailand

AEROQUIP-VICKERS
3000 Strayer, PO Box 50
Maumee, OH 43537-0050
Tel: (419) 867-2200 Fax: (419) 867-2390
CEO: Darryl F. Allen, Pres.
HR: Debra G. Schaefer
Emp: 15,923
Mfr. engineering components and systems for industry.
Australia, Belgium, Brazil, Canada, England, U.K., Finland, France, Germany, Hong Kong, India, Italy, Japan, Mexico, Norway, Singapore, Spain, Sweden, Wales, U.K.

AEROVOX INC.
740 Bellville Road
New Bedford, MA 02745
Tel: (508) 994-9661 Fax: (508) 910-3123

CEO: Robert Elliott, Pres.

HR: Frank Zych

Web site: www.aerovox.com

Emp: 1,500 Rev: $120 mil.

Manufacturer of capcitors for electrical & electronic applications.

England, U.K.

AFRIDI & ANGELL

230 Park Ave.

New York, NY 10169

Tel: (212) 697-0300 Fax: (212) 697-0385

CEO: Mark A. Haddad, Mng. Prtn.

Web site: www.afridi.com

International law firm.

Lebanon, Pakistan, United Arab Emirates

AGCO CORPORATION

4830 River Green Parkway

Duluth, GA 30096-2568

Tel: (770) 813-9200 Fax: (770) 813-6038

CEO: Robert J. Ratliff, Chmn.

HR: John Broadwell

Web site: www.agcocorp.com

Emp: 6,600 Rev: $3,224.4 mil.

Mfr. farm equipment & machinery.

Canada

AIR EXPRESS INTERNATIONAL CORPORATION

120 Tokeneke Road, PO Box 1231

Darien, CT 06820

Tel: (203) 655-7900 Fax: (203) 655-5779

CEO: Guenter Rohrmann, Pres.

FO: Stephen C. Schwark, VP

HR: Billie Raisides, Dir.

Web site: www.aeilogistics.com

Emp: 7,419 Rev: $1,546 mil.

Air freight forwarder.

Algeria, Angola, Argentina, Australia, Austria, Bahrain, Bangladesh, Belgium, Bolivia, Botswana, Bulgaria, Burkina Faso, Burundi, Cameroon, Canada, Chile, China (PRC), Colombia, Costa Rica, Cyprus, Czech Republic, Denmark, Dominican Republic, Ecuador, Egypt, El Salvador, England, U.K., Ethiopia, Fiji, Finland, France, Germany, Greece, Guatemala, Haiti, Honduras, Hong Kong, Hungary, Iceland, India, Indonesia, Ireland, Israel, Italy, Jamaica, Japan, Jordan, Kenya, Kuwait, Lebanon, Liberia, Luxembourg, Malawi, Malaysia, Mexico, Morocco, Mozambique, Nepal, Netherlands, New Zealand, Nicaragua, Nigeria, Northern Ireland, U.K., Norway, Oman, Pakistan, Panama, Papua New Guinea, Paraguay, Peru, Philippines, Poland, Portugal, Qatar, Russia, Saudi Arabia, Scotland, U.K., Singapore, South Africa, South Korea, Spain, Sri Lanka, Sudan, Sweden, Switzerland, Taiwan (ROC), Thailand, Trinidad & Tobago, Tunisia, Turkey, Ukraine, United Arab Emirates, Uruguay, Venezuela, Vietnam, Wales, U.K., Yemen, Zambia, Zimbabwe

AIR PRODUCTS AND CHEMICALS, INC.

7201 Hamilton Boulevard

Allentown, PA 18195-1501

Tel: (610) 481-4911 Fax: (610) 481-5900

CEO: Harold A. Wagner, Pres.

FO: Christopher A. Loyd, VP

HR: Joseph P. McAndrew, VP

Emp: 15,200

Mfr. industry gases & related equipment, spec. chemicals, environmental/energy systems.

Belgium, Brazil, Canada, England, U.K., France, Germany, Hong Kong, Ireland, Japan, Malaysia, Mexico, Netherlands, Norway, South Korea, Spain, Taiwan (ROC)

AIR SEA PACKING

43-42 10th Street

Long Island City, NY 11101

Tel: (718) 937-6800 Fax: (718) 937-9646

CEO: Martin Weston, Pres.

Air & sea freight.

England, U.K., France

AIR WATER TECHNOLOGY RESEARCH-COTTRELL

PO Box 1500

Somerville, NJ 08876

Tel: (908) 685-4000 Fax: (908) 685-4050

CEO: Mallet Thierry

HR: Joan Quinn

Emp: 800

Mfr. air pollution control equipment & systems; technology services.

Belgium, Germany, Thailand

AIRBORNE EXPRESS

3101 Western Ave., PO Box 662

Seattle, WA 98111

Tel: (206) 285-4600 Fax: (206) 281-3937

CEO: Robert G. Brazier

FO: John J. Cella

HR: Dick Goodwin

Emp: 5,624 Rev: $2,912.4 mil.

Air transport services.

Australia, England, U.K., Hong Kong, Japan, New Zealand, Singapore, Taiwan (ROC)

AIRPORT GROUP INTERNATIONAL INC.

330 North Brand Blvd., Ste. 300

Glendale, CA 91203

Tel: (818) 409-7500 Fax: (818) 409-7979

CEO: Patrick Cowell, Pres.

FO: Thomas Farrell

HR: Charles Newman, VP

Emp: 1,300

Airport planning, development & management; airline services.

Canada, England, U.K.

AIRTOUCH COMMUNICATIONS, INC.

One California Street

San Francisco, CA 94111

Tel: (415) 658-2000 Fax: (415) 658-2034

CEO: Sam Ginn, Chmn.

FO: Louis C. Golm, Pres. Intl.

HR: Brian R. Jones, SVP

Web site: www.airtouch.com

Emp: 8,000 Rev: $3,594 mil.

Global wireless communications company with interests in cellular, paging, & personal communications services.

Belgium, Germany, India, Italy, Japan, Netherlands, Poland, Portugal, Romania, South Korea, Spain, Sweden

AJAX MAGNETHERMIC CORPORATION

1745 Overland Ave. NE, PO Box 991

Warren, OH 44482

Tel: (330) 372-8511 Fax: (330) 372-8644

CEO: Frank J. Spalla, Pres.

FO: Timothy J. Logan

HR: Jim Trepka

Emp: 750

Mfr. induction heating & melting equipment.

Canada, England, U.K., Japan

AJAY LEISURE PRODUCTS INC.

1501 E. Wisconsin Street

Delavan, WI 53115

Tel: (414) 728-5521 Fax: (414) 728-8119

CEO: Chuck Yahn, Pres.

FO: Peter Kowal

HR: Vicky Allison

Emp: 350

Mfr. golf bags.

Mexico

AKIN, GUMP, STRAUSS, HAUER & FELD LLP

1333 New Hampshire Ave., N.W.

Washington, DC 20036

Tel: (202) 877-4000 Fax: (202) 887-4288

CEO: R. Bruce McLean, Chmn.

HR: Laurel Digweed, Adm.

Web site: www.akingump.com

Emp: 1,700 Rev: $246 mil.

International law firm.

Belgium, England, U.K., Russia

AKRON BRASS COMPANY

1450 Spruce Street

Wooster, OH 44691

Tel: (330) 264-5678 Fax: (330) 264-2944

CEO: William Hamilton, Pres.

Emp: 270

Irrigation systems.

Canada

ALADDIN INDUSTRIES INC.

703 Murfreesboro Road

Nashville, TN 37210

Tel: (615) 748-3000 Fax: (615) 748-3070

CEO: Fred R. Meyer, Chmn. & Pres.

Emp: 1,300

Mfr. vacuum insulated products, insulated food containers & servers.

Australia, Brazil, England, U.K., France

ALADDIN PETROLEUM CORPORATION

221 S. Broadway, Petroleum Bldg.

Wichita, KS 67202

Tel: (316) 265-9602 Fax: (316) 265-7014

CEO: Gary Gensch, Pres.

Emp: 56

Oil exploration.

Brazil

ALAMO RENT A CAR

110 Southeast Sixth Street

Fort Lauderdale, FL 33301

Tel: (954) 522-0000 Fax: (954) 220-0120

CEO: William Lobeck

Web site: www.alamo.com

Car rentals.

Belgium, Canada, Channel Islands, U.K., Czech Republic, England, U.K., Germany, Greece, Ireland, Malta, Mexico, Netherlands, Northern Ireland, U.K., Portugal, Scotland, U.K., Slovakia, Switzerland, Wales, U.K.

ALARON INC.

1026 Doris Road, PO Box 215287

Auburn Hills, MI 48326

Tel: (248) 340-7500 Fax: (248) 340-7555

CEO: Robert Bourque, Pres.

FO: H. K. Law

HR: Gerald M. Milkovich

Web site: www.alaron.com

Emp: 50

Distributor of consumer electronic products.

Hong Kong

ALBANY INTERNATIONAL CORPORATION

PO Box 1907

Albany, NY 12201

Tel: (518) 445-2200 Fax: (518) 445-2265

CEO: Francis I. McKone, Pres.

FO: Thomas H. Richardson, SVP

HR: Robert M. Seraphin

Emp: 5,400 Rev: $500 mil.

Mfr. broadwoven & engineered fabrics, plastic products, filtration media.

Australia, Brazil, Canada, England, U.K., Finland, France, Germany, Italy, Japan, Mexico, Netherlands, Norway, Scotland, U.K., South Africa, Sweden, Switzerland

ALBEMARLE CORPORATION

451 Florida Ave.

Baton Rouge, LA 70801

Tel: (504) 388-8011 Fax: (504) 388-7686

CEO: Richard Betlem, Pres.

Chemical company.

Belgium, China (PRC), England, U.K., France, Hong Kong, Japan, Singapore

ALBERTO-CULVER COMPANY

2525 Armitage Ave.

Melrose Park, IL 60160

Tel: (708) 450-3000 Fax: (708) 450-3354

CEO: Howard B. Bernick, Chmn.

FO: John G. Horsman, Jr.

HR: Doug Meneely

Mfr./marketing personal care & beauty products, household & grocery products & institutional food products.

Australia, Belgium, Canada, England, U.K., France, Guatemala, Hong Kong, Italy, Mexico, Netherlands, Scotland, U.K., Sweden, Venezuela, Wales, U.K.

ALCO CONTROLS DIV EMERSON ELECTRIC

PO Box 411400

St. Louis, MO 63141

Tel: (314) 569-4500 Fax: (314) 567-2101

CEO: Kei Pang, Pres.

FO: George Middendorf

Emp: 1,800

Mfr. A/C & refrigerator flow controls.

Canada, Germany

ALCOA (ALUMINUM CO OF AMERICA)

Alcoa Bldg., 425 Sixth Ave.

Pittsburgh, PA 15219-1850

Tel: (412) 553-4545 Fax: (412) 553-4498

CEO: Paul H. O'Neill, Chmn.

FO: L. Patrick Hassey, Pres. Europe

HR: Robert F. Slagle, EVP

Emp: 76,800 Rev: $13,000 mil.

World's leading producer of aluminum & alumina; mining, refining, smelting, fabricating & recycling.

Argentina, Australia, Bahrain, Brazil, Canada, Chile, China (PRC), Colombia, England, U.K., Germany, Guinea, Hungary, India, Ireland, Italy, Jamaica, Japan, Malaysia, Mexico, Netherlands, Norway, Peru, Russia, Singapore, Spain, Surinam

ALCOA FUJIKURA LTD.

105 Westpark Drive

Brentwood, TN 37027

Tel: (615) 370-2100 Fax: (615) 370-2180

CEO: Robert S. Hughes

FO: Jack D. Jenkins

HR: James R. Michaud

Emp: 34,000

Mfr. optical groundwire, tube cable, fiber optic connectors & automotive wiring harnesses.

Canada, Germany, Japan, Mexico

ALCOA STEAMSHIP CO., INC.

1501 Alcoa Bldg., 24th Fl.

Pittsburgh, PA 15219

Tel: (412) 553-2545 Fax: (412) 553-2624

CEO: Merv Thede, Pres.

Ship owners/operators.

Surinam, Trinidad & Tobago

ALCONE MARKETING GROUP

15 Whatney

Irvine, CA 92618

Tel: (949) 770-4400 Fax: (949) 770-2308

CEO: Matthew R. Alcone, Chmn.

Web site: www.alconemarketing.com

Emp: 959 Rev: $197 mil.

Sales promotion & marketing services agencies.

Australia, England, U.K.

ALLEGHENY LUDLUM CORP.

1000 Six PPG Place

Pittsburgh, PA 15222

Tel: (412) 394-2805 Fax: (412) 394-2800

CEO: Richard Simmons, Chmn.

HR: B. Paul Mickey

Emp: 2,000

Steel & alloys.

Canada

ALLEGHENY TELEDYNE INC.

1000 Six PPG Place

Pittsburgh, PA 15222

Tel: (412) 394-2800 Fax: (412) 394-2805

CEO: Richard P. Simmons, Pres.

FO: Donald P. Rice, Pres.

Emp: 18,000

Diversified mfr.: aviation & electronics, specialty metals, industrial & consumer products.

Australia, Belgium, Brazil, England, U.K., France, Germany, Hong Kong, Israel, Italy, Japan, Malaysia, Mexico, Russia, Singapore, South Korea, Spain, Taiwan (ROC), Ukraine

ALLEGIANCE HEALTHCARE CORPORATION

1430 Waukegan Road

McGaw Park, IL 60085

Tel: (847) 689-8410 Fax: (847) 578-4437

CEO: Lester B. Knight, Chmn.

FO: David Imperiali, VP Intl.

HR: Robert B. DeBaun, VP

Web site: www.allegiance.net

Emp: 19,500 Rev: $4,350 mil.

Manufactures & distributes medical, surgical, respiratory therapy & laboratory products.

Belgium, Canada, England, U.K., France, Germany, Italy, Malta, Mexico, Netherlands, Spain, Switzerland

ALLEN TELECOM

25101 Chagrin Boulevard

Beachwood, OH 44122-5619

Tel: (216) 765-5818 Fax: (216) 765-0410

CEO: Robert G. Paul, Pres.

FO: Erik H. Van Der Kaay, EVP

HR: Peter G. de Villiers, VP

Web site: www.allentele.com

Emp: 3,300 Rev: $432.5 mil

Mfr. communications equipment, automotive bodies and parts, electronic components.

Argentina, Australia, Austria, Brazil, Canada, China (PRC), England, U.K., France, Germany, Hong Kong, India, Italy, Netherlands, Peru, Singapore, Taiwan (ROC)

ALLEN-BRADLEY COMPANY, INC.

1201 South Second Street

Milwaukee, WI 53204

Tel: (414) 382-2000 Fax: (414) 382-4444

CEO: Don Davis, CEO

FO: Jeff Banasznski, SVP

HR: Roger A. Jackson

Emp: 14,000 Rev: $2,500 mil.

Mfr. electrical controls & information devices.

Australia, Belgium, Brazil, Canada, China (PRC), Denmark, England, U.K., France, Germany, Hong Kong, India, Italy, Japan, Mexico, Netherlands, New Zealand, Russia, South Korea, Spain, Sweden, Switzerland, Taiwan (ROC), Thailand, United Arab Emirates, Venezuela

ALLENBERG COTTON CO., INC.

PO Box 3254

Cordova, TN 38018-3254

Tel: (901) 383-5000 Fax: (901) 383-5010

CEO: Joseph Nicosia, Pres.

Emp: 100

Raw cotton.

Germany, Mexico

ALLERGAN INC.

2525 Dupont Drive, PO Box 19534

Irvine, CA 92713-9534

Tel: (714) 246-4500 Fax: (714) 246-6987

CEO: David Pyott, Pres.

FO: Jacqueline J. Schiavo, VP

HR: Richard J. Hilles

Emp: 5,000 Rev: $900 mil.

Mfr. therapeutic eye care products, skin & neural care pharmaceuticals.

Argentina, Australia, Belgium, Brazil, Canada, England, U.K., France, Germany, Hong Kong, Ireland, Italy, Japan, South Africa, Spain

ALLIANCE CAPITAL MANAGEMENT L.P.

1345 Ave. of the Americas

New York, NY 10105

Tel: (212) 969-1000 Fax: (212) 969-2229

CEO: John D. Carifa, Pres.

HR: Rosanne Peress

Web site: www.alliancecapital.com

Emp: 1,500

Fund manager for large organizations.

Australia, Bahrain, Brazil, Canada, France, India, Japan, Luxembourg, Poland, Singapore, Turkey

ALLIEDSIGNAL INC.

101 Columbia Road, PO Box 2245

Morristown, NJ 07962-2245

Tel: (973) 455-2000 Fax: (973) 455-4807

CEO: Lawrence A. Bossidy, Pres.

FO: Paul R. Schindler

HR: Donald J. Redlinger

Web site: www.alliedsignal.com

Emp: 87,500 Rev: $12,000 mil.

Mfr. aerospace & automotive products, engineered materials.

Australia, Belgium, Brazil, Canada, China (PRC), England, U.K., France, Germany, Greece, Hong Kong, Ireland, Italy, Japan, Mexico, New Zealand, Poland, Portugal, Singapore, Spain

ALLIEDSIGNAL TECHNICAL SERVICES CORPORATION

One Bendix Road

Ellicott City, MD 21045

Tel: (410) 964-7000 Fax: (410) 730-6775

CEO: Ivan Stern, Pres.

HR: Linda Crouch

Web site: www.alliedsignal.com

Emp: 7,300

Technical services.

Saudi Arabia

ALLIEDSIGNAL, INC. - AUTOMOTIVE PRODUCTS GROUP

105 Pawtucket Ave.

Rumford, RI 02916-2422

Tel: (401) 434-7000 Fax: (401) 431-3670

CEO: Greg Perry

FO: Mark R. Marutiak

HR: Joe Grand

Web site: www.alliedsignal.com

Emp: 80,000

Mfr. spark plugs, filters, brakes.

Argentina, Brazil, Canada, France, Japan, Mexico, New Zealand, South Africa, Spain, Sweden, Venezuela, Wales, U.K.

THE ALLSTATE CORPORATION

Allstate Plaza, 2775 Sanders Road

Northbrook, IL 60062-6127

Tel: (847) 402-5000 Fax: (847) 836-3998

CEO: Edward M. Liddy, Pres.

FO: Michael J. McCabe, SVP

HR: Joan M. Crockett, SVP

Web site: www.allstate.com
Emp: 51,000
Personal property, auto & life insurance.
Canada, Germany, South Korea

ALLTEL INFORMATION SERVICES INC.
4001 Rodney Parham Road
Little Rock, AR 72212-2496
Tel: (501) 905-8000 Fax: (501) 220-4723
CEO: Scott Ford, Pres.
HR: James R. Hillis
Web site: www.alltel.com
Emp: 8,000
Full range outsourcing services.
England, U.K., Hong Kong, India

ALOETTE COSMETICS INC.
1301 Wrights Lane East
West Chester, PA 19380
Tel: (610) 692-0600 Fax: (610) 692-2334
CEO: Patricia J. Defibaugh
HR: Janet Bizal
Emp: 25
Drugs, proprietaries & sundries.
Canada

ALPHA INDUSTRIES INC.
20 Sylvan Road
Woburn, MA 01801
Tel: (781) 935-5150 Fax: (781) 824-4543
CEO: Thomas C. Leonard, Pres.
FO: David J. Aldrich, VP
HR: George LeVan, Mgr.
Web site: www.alphaind.com
Emp: 840 Rev: $117 mil.
Mfr. electronic & microwave components.
England, U.K., Germany

ALPHA WIRE COMPANY
711 Lidgerwood Ave.
Elizabeth, NJ 07207
Tel: (908) 925-8000 Fax: (908) 925-6923
CEO: Paul M. Schlessman
FO: Evan Jarrett
HR: Christine Birkner
Web site: www.alphawire.com
Emp: 125
Mfr. wire, cable & tubing products.
England, U.K.

ALPHARMA INC.
One Executive Drive, 4th Fl.
Fort Lee, NJ 07024
Tel: (201) 947-7774 Fax: (201) 947-5541
CEO: Einar W. Sissener, Chmn.
FO: Gert W. Munthe, Pres.
HR: Maj Bjerre, VP
Web site: www.alphapharm.com
Emp: 2,600 Rev: $500 mil.
Development/manufacture specialty human pharmaceuticals & animal health products.
Denmark, Indonesia, Norway, Singapore

ALPINE ENGINEERED PRODUCTS INC.
PO Box 2225
Pompano Beach, FL 33061
Tel: (954) 781-3333 Fax: (954) 973-2644
CEO: Ron Donnini, Pres.
HR: Kris Tubridy
Web site: www.2alpineng.com.
Emp: 500
Fabricated plate.
Belgium, Canada, England, U.K.

ALTEC INDUSTRIES INC.
210 Inverness Center Drive
Birmingham, AL 35242
Tel: (205) 991-7733 Fax: (205) 991-9993
CEO: Lee J. Styslinger, III
FO: Walter Scott Wilson
HR: Jack Frantz
Emp: 1,700
Mfr. truck mounted aerial lifts & pole erection derricks.
Canada

ALTHEIMER & GRAY
10 South Wacker Drive, Ste. 4000
Chicago, IL 60606-7482
Tel: (312) 715-4000 Fax: (312) 715-4800
CEO: Terry Schlade, Mng. Prtn.
FO: L. B. Goldman & J. E. Carroll
Emp: 422
International law firm.

Czech Republic, Poland, Slovakia, Turkey, Ukraine

ALVEY INC.

9301 Olive Boulevard
St. Louis, MO 63132
Tel: (314) 993-4700 Fax: (314) 995-2400
CEO: Stephen J. O'Neill, Pres.
HR: John Amato
Web site: www.alvey.com
Emp: 800

Mfr./sales automatic case palletizers, package & pallet conveyor systems.

Australia, Belgium, Brazil, Canada, Japan, Mexico, New Zealand, Philippines, Venezuela

AMATEX CORPORATION

1030 Standbridge Street
Norristown, PA 19404
Tel: (610) 277-6100 Fax: (610) 277-6106
CEO: R. C. Howard, Pres.
Emp: 275

Mfr. textile, fiberglass products.

Mexico, Sudan

AMBAC ASSURANCE CORPORATION

One State Street Plaza
New York, NY 10004
Tel: (212) 668-0340 Fax: (212) 509-9109
CEO: John W. Uhlein, III, Mng. Dir.
FO: Michael J. Maguire, Mng. Dir.
HR: Grey Bienstock
Web site: www.ambac.com
Emp: 340 Rev: $381.8 mil.

Reinsurance company.

Australia, England, U.K., France, Spain

AMCOL INTERNATIONAL CORPORATION

1500 West Shure Drive
Arlington Heights, IL 60004
Tel: (847) 394-8730 Fax: (847) 506-6199
CEO: John Hughes
FO: John Maginot
HR: Steve Alexander
Web site: www.amcol.com
Emp: 1,500 Rev: $477 mil.

Bentonite mining, mfr. specialty chemicals, environmental products.

Australia, England, U.K.

AMDAHL CORPORATION

1250 East Arques Ave., PO Box 3470
Sunnyvale, CA 94088-3470
Tel: (408) 746-6000 Fax: (408) 773-0833
CEO: David D. Wright, Pres.
FO: Orval J. Nutt
HR: Anthony M. Pozos
Web site: www.amdahl.com
Emp: 5,600

Development/mfr. large scale computers, software, data storage products, information-technology solutions & support.

Australia, Austria, Belgium, Canada, Denmark, England, U.K., France, Germany, Hong Kong, Ireland, Italy, Luxembourg, Netherlands, New Zealand, Norway, Portugal, Scotland, U.K., Singapore, South Africa, Spain, Sweden, Switzerland, Thailand

AMERACE / EAGLE INDUSTRIES

2 N. Riverside Plaza, #1160
Chicago, IL 60606
Tel: (312) 906-8700 Fax: (312) 906-8372
CEO: William Hall, Pres.
Emp: 2,000

Chemicals, rubber products, plastics, electrical components & controls.

Canada, England, U.K., France, Japan, Luxembourg

AMERADA HESS CORPORATION

1185 Ave. of the Americas
New York, NY 10036
Tel: (212) 997-8500 Fax: (212) 536-8390
CEO: John B. Hess, Chmn.
FO: W. Laidlaw, Pres.
HR: Neal Gelfand, SVP
Web site: www.hess.com
Emp: 9,200 Rev: $8,234 mil

Crude oil & natural gas.

Canada, Denmark, England, U.K., Gabon, Norway

AMERCO

1325 Airmotive Way, Ste. 100
Reno, NV 89502-3239
Tel: (702) 688-6300 Fax: (702) 688-6338
CEO: Edward J. Shoen, Chmn. & Pres.

HR: Henry P. Kelly, VP

Web site: www.uhaul.com

Emp: 14,400 Rev: $1,425 mil.

Truck rental (U-Haul), moving supplies, storage facilities, short-term property-casualty insurance & life, health & annuity-type insurance products.

Canada

AMERCORD

Industrial Blvd. PO Box 458

Lumber City, GA 31549

Tel: (912) 363-4371 Fax: (912) 363-4991

CEO: Bill Winspear, Pres.

Emp: 250

Forestry; mfr. steel, tire cord.

Japan, Mexico, Venezuela

AMEREX USA INC.

350 Fifth Ave.

New York, NY 10016

Tel: (212) 967-3330 Fax: (212) 967-3330

CEO: Fred Shvetz, Pres.

FO: Alexander E. Shvetz

Emp: 100

General merchandise.

Japan

AMERICA ONLINE, INC.

2200 AOL Way

Dulles, VA 20166

Tel: (703) 453-4000 Fax: (703) 265-5769

CEO: Stephen M. Case, Chmn.

FO: Robert W. Pittman, Pres.

HR: Mark Stavish, SVP

Web site: www.aol.com

Emp: 8,500 Rev: $2,600 mil

Internet service provider.

Canada, England, U.K., France, Germany, Japan, Sweden

AMERICAN & EFIRD INC.

PO Box 507

Mt. Holly, NC 28120

Tel: (704) 827-4311 Fax: (704) 822-6054

CEO: Fred Jackson, Pres.

HR: Robert Edwards, Jr.

Emp: 2,478

Mfr. industrial thread, yarn & consumer sewing products.

Canada, Chile, Costa Rica, Dominican Republic, England, U.K., Hong Kong, Mexico, Singapore, South Korea, Venezuela

AMERICAN AIRLINES INC.

4333 Amon Carter Boulevard

Ft. Worth, TX 76155

Tel: (817) 963-1234 Fax: (817) 967-9641

CEO: Donald J. Carty, Chmn.

FO: Bella D. Goren, Pres. AMR Intl.

HR: A. Jane Allison, VP

Web site: www.amrcorp.com

Emp: 90,600 Rev: $18,570 mil.

Air transport services.

Australia, Bahamas, Barbados, Bermuda, Brazil, Canada, Dominican Republic, England, U.K., France, Germany, Haiti, Hong Kong, Italy, Jamaica, Japan, Mexico, Netherlands, New Zealand, Philippines, Poland, Saudi Arabia, Singapore, South Korea, Spain, Sweden, Switzerland, Taiwan (ROC), Thailand, Venezuela

AMERICAN AMICABLE LIFE INSURANCE COMPANY

American-Amicable Bldg.

Waco, TX 76703

Tel: (254) 297-2777 Fax: (254) 297-2733

CEO: Lanny Peavy, Pres.

HR: DeiAnna Duncan

Emp: 350

Life, accident & health insurance.

England, U.K., Germany, Japan

AMERICAN APPRAISAL ASSOCIATES INC.

411 E. Wisconsin Ave.

Milwaukee, WI 53202

Tel: (414) 271-7240 Fax: (414) 271-1041

CEO: Ronald M. Goergen, Pres.

HR: Nanette Wellstein

Emp: 585

Valuation consulting services.

Canada, Czech Republic, England, U.K., Hong Kong, Hungary, Italy, Japan, Mexico, Morocco, Poland, Portugal, Russia, Spain, Taiwan (ROC), Thailand

AMERICAN BANKERS INSURANCE GROUP, INC.

11222 Quail Roost Drive
Miami, FL 33157-6596
Tel: (305) 253-2244 Fax: (305) 252-6987
CEO: Gerald N. Gaston
FO: R. Kirk Landon, Chmn.
HR: Phillip Sharkey, SVP
Web site: www.abig.com
Emp: 2,943 Rev: $1,621 MIL.
Insurance.
Canada, England, U.K.

AMERICAN BILTRITE INC.

57 River Street
Wellesley Hills, MA 02181
Tel: (781) 237-6655 Fax: (781) 237-6880
CEO: Roger S. Marcus, Chmn.
FO: Richard G. Marcus, Pres.
HR: Bonnie Posnak, Dir.
Web site: www.abitape.com
Emp: 3,030 Rev: $418 mil.
Mfr. industrial rubber & plastic products.
Belgium, Canada, Guatemala, Honduras, Singapore

ABC, INC.

77 West 66th Street
New York, NY 10023
Tel: (212) 456-7777 Fax: (212) 456-6384
CEO: Robert Iger, Pres.
FO: Herbert Granath, Int'l TV
HR: Jeff Rosen, VP
Emp: 12,000
Radio/TV production & broadcasting.
Colombia, Ecuador, France, Germany, Japan, Lebanon, Venezuela

AMERICAN BUILDINGS COMPANY

1150 State Docks Road
Eufaula, AL 36072-0800
Tel: (334) 687-2032 Fax: (334) 667-8315
CEO: Robert T. Ammerman, Pres.
FO: Joel R. Voelkert, Pres.
HR: Byron L. Brumfield, VP
Web site: www.ambldgs.com
Emp: 900 Rev: $323 mil.
Metal buildings.
China (PRC)

AMERICAN BUREAU OF SHIPPING

2 World Trade Center, 106th Fl.
New York, NY 10048
Tel: (212) 839-5000 Fax: (212) 839-5209
CEO: Frank J. Iarossi, Chmn.
FO: Andrew V. Pistena, SVP
Emp: 1,500 Rev: $77 mil.
Classification/certification of ships & offshore structures, development & technical assistance.
Brazil, England, U.K., Greece, Japan, Singapore, United Arab Emirates

AMERICAN BUSINESS PRODUCTS, INC.

2100 Riveredge Pkwy., Ste. 1200
Atlanta, GA 30328
Tel: (770) 953-8300 Fax: (770) 952-2343
CEO: Larry Gellerstedt, Pres.
FO: Ingo Hafner, Mng. Prtn.
HR: Barbara Tolleson
Emp: 3,200 Rev: $500 mil.
Supplies printing, book printing, label production & extrusion coating for flexable packaging.
Germany

AMERICAN COMMERCIAL INC.

25 Enterprise Ave.
Secaucus, NJ 07094
Tel: (201) 867-9210 Fax: (201) 867-0457
CEO: Ray Dingman
HR: Tony Santarelli
Emp: 150
Dinnerware, crystal & gifts.
Japan

AMERICAN EXPRESS COMPANY

American Express Tower, World Financial Center
New York, NY 10285-4765
Tel: (212) 640-2000 Fax: (212) 619-9802
CEO: Harvey Golub, Chmn.
FO: James M. Cracchiolo, Pres. Int'l
HR: Ursula F. Fairbairn, EVP
Web site: www.americanexpress.com
Emp: 73,620 Rev: $17,760 mil.
Travel, travelers cheques, charge card & financial services.

Argentina, Bahrain, Belgium, Brazil, Brunei, Canada, Channel Islands, U.K., Chile, Czech Republic, Egypt, England, U.K., Finland, France, Germany, Greece, Hungary, Ireland, Italy, Japan, Malaysia, Mexico, New Zealand, Norway, Panama, Poland, Russia, Scotland, U.K., Slovakia, Spain, Sweden, Switzerland, Taiwan (ROC), Thailand, Uruguay, Vietnam, Wales, U.K.

AMERICAN FAMILY LIFE ASSURANCE COMPANY of COLUMBUS (AFLAC)

American Family Center, 1932 Wynnton Road

Columbus, GA 31999

Tel: (706) 323-3431 Fax: (706) 324-6330

CEO: Daniel P. Amos

FO: Minoru Nakai, Pres. Intl.

HR: Angie Hart, VP HR

Web site: www.aflac.com

Emp: 4,032 Rev: $7,251 mil.

Insurance & TV broadcasting.

Japan

AMERICAN GENERAL CORPORATION

2929 Allen Parkway

Houston, TX 77019-2155

Tel: (713) 522-1111 Fax: (713) 523-8531

CEO: Robert M. Devlin, Chmn.

FO: James S. D'Agostino, Jr., Pres.

HR: Jo Ann Waddell, VP

Web site: www.agc.com

Emp: 16,200 Rev: $8,827 mil.

Financial services & holding company.

Canada

AMERICAN GREETINGS CORPORATION

One American Road

Cleveland, OH 44144-2398

Tel: (216) 252-7300 Fax: (216) 252-6777

CEO: Morry Weiss, Chmn.

FO: Hans Haacke, VP

Emp: 21,000 Rev: $1,000 mil.

Mfr./distributor greeting cards, gift wrappings, tags, seals, ribbons & party goods.

Brazil, Canada, England, U.K., Mexico

AMERICAN HOME PRODUCTS CORPORATION

Five Giralda Farms

Madison, NJ 07940-0874

Tel: (973) 660-5000 Fax: (973) 660-6048

CEO: John R. Stafford, Chmn.

FO: John B. Adams, VP Corp. Dev.

HR: René R. Lewin, VP

Web site: www.ahp.com

Emp: 64,000 Rev: $13,000 mil

Mfr. pharmaceutical, animal health care & crop protection products.

Argentina, Australia, Brazil, Canada, China (PRC), England, U.K., France, Germany, Ireland, Italy, Mexico, Philippines, Taiwan (ROC), Venezuela

AMERICAN INTERNATIONAL GROUP INC.

70 Pine Street

New York, NY 10270

Tel: (212) 770-7000 Fax: (212) 509-9705

CEO: M. R. Greenberg, Chmn.

FO: Evan Greenberg, COO

HR: Axel I. Freundman, SVP

Web site: www.aig.com

Emp: 40,000 Rev: $27,000 mil.

Worldwide insurance and financial services.

Australia, Bermuda, Brazil, Canada, Colombia, Cyprus, England, U.K., France, Germany, Guatemala, Haiti, Hong Kong, Ivory Coast, Jamaica, Japan, New Zealand, Philippines, Switzerland, Taiwan (ROC), Thailand, Uganda, Vietnam

AMERICAN LOCKER GROUP INC.

15 West Second Street

Jamestown, NY 14702

Tel: (716) 664-9600 Fax: (716) 483-2822

CEO: Roy Glosser, Pres.

HR: Carol Derr

Emp: 200 Rev: $12 mil.

Mfr. coin-operated locks, office furniture.

Brazil, Canada, England, U.K.

AMERICAN MANAGEMENT SYSTEMS, INC.

4050 Legato Road

Fairfax, VA 22033

Tel: (703) 267-8000 Fax: (703) 267-5067

CEO: Paul A. Brands, Chmn.

FO: James Sheaffer

HR: Judith D.Tinelli, VP

Web site: www.amsinc.com

Emp: 7,570 Rev: $870 mil.

Systems integration & consulting.

Australia, Belgium, Canada, England, U.K., France, Germany, Italy, Mexico, Netherlands, Poland, Portugal, Spain, Sweden, Switzerland

AMERICAN METER COMPANY

300 Welsh Road, Bldg. #1

Horsham, PA 19044-2234

Tel: (215) 830-1800 Fax: (215) 830-1890

CEO: Harry Skilton

Measure & control services for natural gas industry.

Denmark, England, U.K., Netherlands

AMERICAN OPTICAL CORPORATION

853 Camino Del Mar, Ste. 200

Del Mar, CA 92014

Tel: (619) 509-9899 Fax: (619) 509-9898

CEO: Jeremy Bishop, Pres.

Emp: 5,000 Rev: $200 mil

Mfr. opthalmic lenses & frames, custom molded products, specialty lenses.

Brazil, Canada, England, U.K., France, Mexico, Singapore, Switzerland, Zimbabwe

AMERICAN PRECISION INDUSTRIES INC.

2777 Walden Ave.

Buffalo, NY 14225

Tel: (716) 684-9700 Fax: (716) 684-2129

CEO: Kurt Wiedenhaupt, Pres.

FO: Richard S. Warzala, Corp. VP

HR: James R. Schwinger, VP

Web site: www.apicorporate.com

Emp: 1,900 Rev: $184 mil.

Mfr. heat transfer equipment, motion control devices,coils, capacitors, electro-mechanical clutches & brakes.

Canada, China (PRC), England, U.K., France, Germany, Japan, Netherlands, Poland, Sweden, Switzerland

AMERICAN PRESIDENT LINES LTD

1111 Broadway

Oakland, CA 94607

Tel: (510) 272-8000 Fax: (510) 272-7941

CEO: Timothy Rhein, Pres

HR: Mike Mahr

Intermodal shipping services.

Canada, Hong Kong, Japan, Pakistan, Philippines, Russia, Singapore, South Korea, Taiwan (ROC), Thailand, Vietnam

AMERICAN RE-INSURANCE COMPANY

555 College Road East

Princeton, NJ 08543

Tel: (609) 243-4200 Fax: (609) 243-4257

CEO: Edward Noonan, Pres.

HR: Robert Humes

Emp: 1,000

Reinsurance.

Australia, Canada, Chile, Colombia, England, U.K., Singapore

AMERICAN SAFETY RAZOR CO.

PO Box 500

Staunton, VA 24401

Tel: (540) 248-8000 Fax: (540) 248-0522

CEO: William Weathersty, Pres.

HR: Reggie Ryals

Mfr. private-label & branded shaving razors & blades & cotton swabs.

Canada, England, U.K., Israel

AMERICAN SOFTWARE, INC.

470 East Paces Fery Road, NE

Atlanta, GA 30305

Tel: (404) 261-4381 Fax: (404) 264-5514

CEO: Thomas L. Newberry, Chmn.

HR: Kevin Burdett, Dir.

Web site: www.amsoftware.com

Emp: 600 Rev: $85 mil

Mfr./sales of financial control software & systems.

Australia, England, U.K., Japan

AMERICAN STANDARD INC.

One Centennial Ave.

Piscataway, NJ 08855-6820

Tel: (732) 980-3000 Fax: (732) 980-6118

CEO: Emmanuel A. Kampouris

HR: Helene Zeicher

Emp: 36,000 Rev: $4,000 mil.

Mfr. heating, plumbing & sanitary equipment,

china, earthenware.

Austria, Belgium, Brazil, Bulgaria, Canada, Costa Rica, Czech Republic, Dominican Republic, England, U.K., France, Germany, Guatemala, Israel, Italy, Mexico, Netherlands, Philippines, Thailand

AMERICAN TELESOURCE INTERNATIONAL, INC. (ATSI)

12500 Network Blvd., Ste. 407

San Antonio, TX 78249

Tel: (210) 558-6090 Fax: (210) 558-6095

CEO: Arthur L. Smith, Pres.

FO: Jesus Enriquez

HR: Arnold Cardenas

Web site: www.atsi.net

Emp: 615 Rev: $30 mil.

Long distance communications, payphones & private satellite communications networks.

Mexico

AMERICAN TOOL COMPANIES INC.

8400 LakeView Pkwy., #400

Kenosha, WI 53142

Tel: (847) 478-1090 Fax: (847) 478-1090

CEO: Allen Petersen, Pres,

FO: Dennis Jacobson

HR: Ben Kaplan

Emp: 1,500

Mfr. hand tools, cutting tools & power tool accessories.

Australia, Canada, Denmark, Taiwan (ROC)

AMERICAN UNIFORM COMPANY

PO Box 2130

Cleveland, TN 37311

Tel: (423) 476-6561 Fax: (423) 559-3855

CEO: Gary K. Smith, Pres.

HR: Jimmy R. Kibler

Emp: 1,680

Mfr. work clothing, uniforms.

Canada, Italy

AMERITECH CORPORATION

30 South Wacker Drive

Chicago, IL 60606

Tel: (312) 750-5000 Fax: (312) 207-0016

CEO: Richard C. Notebaert, Chmn. & Pres.

FO: Timothy J. Cawley, Pres. Europe

HR: Walter M. Oliver, SVP

Web site: www.ameritech.com

Emp: 75,000

Provides security systems & telecommunications services.

Belgium, Denmark, Hungary, Norway

AMERON INC.

245 South Los Robles Ave.

Pasadena, CA 91109-7007

Tel: (626) 683-4000 Fax: (626) 683-4060

CEO: James S. Marlen, Pres.

HR: George J. Fischer, SVP

Emp: 2,700 Rev: $400 mil.

Mfr. steel pipe systems, concrete products, traffic & lighting poles, protective coatings.

Brazil, Colombia, France, Germany, Mexico, Netherlands, Saudi Arabia, Spain

AMES TEXTILE CORPORATION

710 Chelmsford Street

Lowell, MA 01851

Tel: (508) 458-3321 Fax: (508) 441-9808

CEO: Edward B. Stevens

Emp: 1,000

Textile products.

England, U.K., France, Netherlands

AMETEK INC.

4 Station Square

Paoli, PA 19301

Tel: (610) 647-2121 Fax: (610) 296-3412

CEO: Walter E. Blankley, Chmn.

HR: Monica Haley

Web site: www.ametek.com

Emp: 6,300

Mfr. instruments, electric motors & engineered materials.

Canada, China (PRC), Czech Republic, Denmark, England, U.K., France, Germany, Italy, Singapore, Taiwan (ROC)

AMMIRATI PURIS LINTAS

One Dag Hammarskjold Plaza

New York, NY 10017

Tel: (212) 605-8000 Fax: (212) 605-4705

CEO: Martin F. Puris, Chmn.

FO: Maxwell J. Gosling

HR: Don Parker

Web site: www.interpublic.com

Emp: 9,296 Rev: $854 mil.

International advertising agency.

Argentina, Australia, Austria, Bangladesh, Belgium, Brazil, Canada, Chile, China (PRC), Colombia, Costa Rica, Czech Republic, Denmark, Dominican Republic, Ecuador, Egypt, El Salvador, England, U.K., Finland, France, Germany, Ghana, Greece, Guatemala, Honduras, Hong Kong, Hungary, India, Indonesia, Israel, Italy, Ivory Coast, Japan, Kenya, Lebanon, Malaysia, Mexico, Myanmar, Namibia, Netherlands, New Zealand, Nicaragua, Nigeria, Pakistan, Panama, Peru, Philippines, Poland, Portugal, Romania, Russia, Singapore, South Africa, South Korea, Spain, Sri Lanka, Sweden, Switzerland, Taiwan (ROC), Thailand, Trinidad & Tobago, Turkey, United Arab Emirates, Uruguay, Vietnam, Zambia, Zimbabwe

AMOCO CHEMICAL COMPANY

200 East Randolph Drive

Chicago, IL 60601

Tel: (312) 856-3200 Fax: (312) 856-2460

CEO: William Lowrie, Pres.

Mfr./sale petrol based chemicals, plastics, chemicals/plastic products

Belgium, Brazil, Germany, South Korea, Switzerland, Taiwan (ROC)

AMOCO OIL COMPANY

200 East Randolph Drive

Chicago, IL 60601

Tel: (312) 856-5111 Fax: (312) 856-2454

CEO: H. Lawrence Fuller, Chmn.

FO: John L. Carl, EVP

HR: R. Wayne Anderson, SVP

Emp: 43,205 Rev: $30,000 mil.

Petroleum mfr. & refining.

Azerbaijan, Brazil, England, U.K., Russia

AMP INC.

470 Friendship Road, PO Box 3608

Harrisburg, PA 17105-3608

Tel: (717) 564-0100 Fax: (717) 780-6130

CEO: Robert Ripp, Chmn.

HR: Donald Prowell

Emp: 46,500 Rev: $5,750 mil.

Develop/mfr. electronic & electrical connection products & systems.

Argentina, Australia, Austria, Belgium, Brazil, Canada, China (PRC), Croatia, Czech Republic, Denmark, Egypt, England, U.K., Estonia, Finland, France, Germany, Greece, Hong Kong, Hungary, India, Ireland, Israel, Italy, Japan, Lithuania, Malaysia, Mexico, Netherlands, New Zealand, Norway, Philippines, Poland, Portugal, Russia, Singapore, Slovakia, Slovenia, South Africa, South Korea, Spain, Sweden, Switzerland, Taiwan (ROC), Thailand, Turkey, Vietnam

AMPACET CORPORATION

660 White Plains Road

Tarrytown, NY 10591-5130

Tel: (914) 631-6600 Fax: (914) 631-7197

CEO: David S. Weil, Pres.

FO: Howard W. England, SVP

Web site: www.ampacet.com

Mfr. color and additive concentrates for the plastics industry.

Belgium, Canada, Italy, Luxembourg, Malaysia

AMPCO METAL INC.

1745 S. 38th Street, PO Box 2004

Milwaukee, WI 53201

Tel: (414) 645-3750 Fax: (414) 645-3225

CEO: Robert Darling, Pres.

FO: Luis Bento

HR: Jim Darling

Emp: 435

Mfr./distributor/sale cast & wrought copper-based alloys.

England, U.K., France, Netherlands, Portugal, Switzerland

AMPEX CORPORATION

500 Broadway

Redwood City, CA 94063-3199

Tel: (650) 367-2011 Fax: (650) 367-4669

CEO: Edward J. Bramson, Chmn.

FO: Robert L. Atchison

HR: Richard J. Jacquet

Web site: www.ampex.com

Emp: 2,800 Rev: $80 mil.

Mfr. extremely high-performance digital data storage, data retrieval & image processing systems for a broad range of corporate scientific &

government applications.

England, U.K., France, Germany, Hong Kong, Italy, Japan, Spain, Sweden, Switzerland

AMPHENOL PRODUCTS

1925A Ohio Street

Lisle, IL 60532

Tel: (630) 960-1010 Fax: (630) 810-5640

CEO: Don Duda, Gen. Mgr.

Emp: 400

Electric interconnect/penetrate systems & assemblies.

Austria, Canada, England, U.K., France, Germany, Hong Kong, India, Italy, Japan, Netherlands, Sweden

AMSTED INDUSTRIES INC.

205 North Michigan

Chicago, IL 60601

Tel: (312) 645-1700 Fax: (312) 819-8429

CEO: Gordon R. Lohman, Chmn.

FO: Arthur W. Goetschel, Pres.

HR: Arthur M. Meske, Dir.

Web site: www.amsted.com

Emp: 8,500 Rev: $1,100 mil.

Privately-held, diversified manufacturer of products for the construction & building markets, general industry & the railroads.

Australia, Belgium, Canada, England, U.K., Italy, Japan, Spain

AMWAY CORPORATION

7575 Fulton Street East

Ada, MI 49355-0001

Tel: (616) 787-6000 Fax: (616) 787-6177

CEO: Dick DiVos, Pres.

FO: Dave Braum, VP

Web site: www.amway.com

Emp: 12,500 Rev: $3,900 mil.

Mfr./sale home care, personal care, nutrition & houseware products.

Australia, Austria, Belgium, Brazil, Canada, England, U.K., France, Germany, Guatemala, Hong Kong, Hungary, Indonesia, Italy, Japan, Macau, Malaysia, Mexico, Netherlands, New Zealand, Panama, Poland, Portugal, South Korea, Spain, Switzerland, Taiwan (ROC), Thailand

ANACOMP INC.

PO Box 509005

San Diego, CA 92150

Tel: (619) 679-9797 Fax: (619) 748-9482

CEO: Ralph Koehrer, Pres.

FO: Gary Roth

HR: Greg Armstrong

Emp: 4,200 Rev: $500 mil.

Mfr. electronic computing equipment.

Belgium, Brazil, England, U.K., France, Germany, Netherlands

ANADARKO PETROLEUM CORP.

17001 Northchase Drive

Houston, TX 77060

Tel: (281) 875-1101 Fax: (281) 874-3316

CEO: Robert J. Allison, Jr., Pres.

Emp: 1,000 Rev: $434 mil.

Energy

England, U.K.

ANALOG DEVICES INC.

1 Technology Way, Box 9106

Norwood, MA 02062

Tel: (781) 329-4700 Fax: (781) 326-8703

CEO: Jerald Fishman, Pres.

HR: Ross Brown, VP

Emp: 5,000

Mfr. integrated circuits & related devices.

Belgium, Denmark, England, U.K., France, Germany, India, Ireland, Israel, Italy, Japan, Netherlands, South Korea, Sweden, Switzerland

ANALOGIC CORPORATION

8 Centennial Drive

Peabody, MA 01960

Tel: (978) 977-3000 Fax: (978) 977-6811

CEO: Bernard M. Gordon, Chmn.

FO: Bruce R. Rusch, Pres.

HR: John W. Kirby

Emp: 1,400

Conceive/design/mfr. precision measure, signal processing & imaging equipment for medical, scientific, industry & communications.

China (PRC), Denmark, England, U.K.

ANALYSIS & TECHNOLOGY INC.

PO Box 220, Route 2

N. Stonington, CT 06359

Tel: (860) 599-3910 Fax: (860) 599-6510

CEO: Gary P. Bennett

HR: Stephen E. Johnston

Web site: www.aati.com

Emp: 1,750 Rev: $160 mil.

Commercial physical research, computer systems design, management services.

Australia

ANALYSTS INTERNATIONAL CORPORATION

7615 Metro Boulevard

Minneapolis, MN 55439

Tel: (612) 835-5900 Fax: (612) 897-4555

CEO: Frederick W. Lang, Chmn.

FO: Victor C. Benda, Pres.

HR: Lori Buegler

Web site: www.analysts.com

Emp: 5,300 Rev: $23 mil.

Provides computer software-related services -- including systems analysis and design, programming, and Y2K remediation.

Canada

ANAMET INC.

698 South Main Street

Waterbury, CT 06706

Tel: (203) 574-8500 Fax: (203) 573-1505

CEO: Michael Cloney, Pres.

Emp: 1,300

Mfr. industrial machinery, wiring devices, measure & control devices.

Canada, England, U.K., France, Mexico, Netherlands

ANAREN MICROWAVE INC.

6635 Kirkville Road

East Syracuse, NY 13057

Tel: (315) 432-8909 Fax: (315) 432-9121

CEO: Hugh A. Hair, Chmn.

FO: Robert Andrews

HR: Michelle Strobeck

Web site: www.anaren.com

Emp: 276 Rev: $37 mil.

Mfr./services microwave components.

England, U.K.

ANCHOR HOCKING CORPORATION

519 Pierce Ave., PO Box 600

Lancaster, OH 43130-0600

Tel: (740) 687-2111 Fax: (740) 687-2543

CEO: Mark Eichhorn, Pres.

HR: Karl Salmon

Emp: 12,200

Mfr. glassware & dinnerware plastic products.

Canada, England, U.K.

ANCHOR LABORATORIES INC.

2621 N. Belt Highway

St. Joseph, MO 64501

Tel: (816) 233-1385 Fax: (816) 233-1385

CEO: Finton Molloy, Pres.

Emp: 450

Vaccines & serums.

Mexico

ANDATACO CORPORATION

10140 Mesa Rim Road

San Diego, CA 92121

Tel: (619) 453-9191 Fax: (619) 453-9328

CEO: David Sykes, Pres.

HR: Kilgaya Bowman

Emp: 110

Mfr. computer peripherals.

Japan

ANDERSEN CONSULTING

100 South Wacker Drive, Ste. 1059

Chicago, IL 60606

Tel: (311) 123-7271 Fax: (312) 507-7965

CEO: George T. Shaheen

FO: David W. Andrews

HR: Carol E. Meyer

Web site: www.ac.com

Emp: 53,000 Rev: $6,647 mil.

Provides management & technology consulting services.

Argentina, Australia, Austria, Belgium, Brazil, Canada, China (PRC), Colombia, Czech Republic, Denmark, England, U.K., Finland, France, Germany, Greece, Hong Kong, Hungary, India, Indonesia, Ireland, Italy, Japan, Luxembourg, Malaysia, Mexico, Netherlands, New Zealand, Nigeria, Norway, Philippines, Poland, Portugal, Russia, Saudi Arabia, Singapore, Slovakia, South Africa, South Korea, Spain, Sweden, Switzerland,

Taiwan (ROC), Venezuela

ANDERSON & LEMBKE

135 Main Street, 21st Fl.

San Francisco, CA 94105

Tel: (415) 357-3400 Fax: (415) 357-3553

CEO: Mike Windsor, Pres.

Web site: www.anderson-lembke.com

Emp: 233 Rev: $30 mil.

Full service, business-to-business advertising & marketing services.

Hong Kong, Netherlands

ANDREW CORPORATION

10500 West 153rd Street

Orland Park, IL 60462

Tel: (708) 349-3300 Fax: (708) 349-5410

CEO: Floyd L. English, Chmn.

FO: John R.D. Dickson, VP

HR: Roger Blaylock, Mgr.

Web site: www.andrew.com

Emp: 4,227 Rev: $869.5 mil.

Mfr. antenna systems, coaxial cable, electronic communications & network connectivity systems.

Australia, Brazil, Canada, China (PRC), England, U.K., France, Germany, Hong Kong, Indonesia, Italy, Japan, Malaysia, Mexico, Russia, Saudi Arabia, Scotland, U.K., Singapore, South Africa, Spain, Sweden, Switzerland, Thailand

ANDREWS & KURTH LLP

600 Travis Street, Ste. 4200

Houston, TX 77002

Tel: (713) 220-4200 Fax: (713) 220-4285

CEO: Howard Ayers

HR: Deborah Ganjevi, Dir.

Web site: www.andrewskurth.com

Emp: 875 Rev: $100 mil.

International law firm.

England, U.K.

ANEMOSTAT PRODUCTS

888 North Keyser Ave.

Scranton, PA 18501

Tel: (717) 346-6586 Fax: (717) 342-8559

CEO: Don Halloran, V.P.

FO: T. Molineux

HR: Eleanor Petrauskas

Emp: 800

Mfr. air diffusers, grilles & related equipment for A/C, heating & ventilation.

Australia, Egypt, France, Germany, Japan, Qatar

ANGELICA CORPORATION

424 South Woods Mill Road, #300

Chesterfield, MO 63017-3406

Tel: (314) 854-3800 Fax: (314) 854-3890

CEO: Don Hubble, Pres.

FO: Lawrence J. Young

HR: Jill Witter

Emp: 9,711

Mfr., marketing & sales of uniforms.

Canada, England, U.K.

ANHEUSER-BUSCH INTERNATIONAL INC.

One Busch Place

St. Louis, MO 63118-1852

Tel: (314) 577-2000 Fax: (314) 577-2900

CEO: August A. Busch III, Pres. & Chmn.

FO: John H. Purnell, A-B Intl.

HR: William L. Rammes, VP

Web site: www.anheuser-busch.com

Emp: 24,326 Rev: $ 11,066 mil.

Malt production, aluminum beverage containers, rice milling, real estate development, metalized & paper label printing, railcar repair & theme-park facilities.

Brazil, China (PRC), England, U.K., Japan, Mexico, Philippines

ANIXTER INTERNATIONAL INC..

4711 Golf Road

Skokie, IL 60076

Tel: (847) 677-2600 Fax: (708) 677-9480

CEO: Robert Grubbs, Pres.

HR: Patricia Garland

Emp: 3,635 Rev: $2,805.2 mil.

Distributor wiring systems/products for voice, video, data and power applications.

Belgium, Canada, England, U.K., France, Norway, Poland, Spain, Switzerland, Taiwan (ROC)

ANSELL EDMONT INDUSTRIAL INC.

1300 Walnut Street

Coshocton, OH 43812

Tel: (614) 622-4311 Fax: (614) 622-9611

CEO: William Reed, Pres.

FO: Yuan Beaudoin

HR: R. K. Davis

Emp: 1,634

Mfr. industrial gloves, rubber and plastic products, protective clothing.

Belgium, Canada

K-2, INC.

4900 South Eastern Ave.

Los Angeles, CA 90040

Tel: (213) 724-2800 Fax: (213) 724-8174

CEO: B. I. Forester, Chmn.

HR: Michelle Jurado

Emp: 2,500

Mfr. sporting goods, recreational & industrial products.

Australia, England, U.K., Germany, Hong Kong, Norway

AON CORPORATION

123 North Wacker Drive

Chicago, IL 60606

Tel: (312) 701-3000 Fax: (312) 701-3100

CEO: Patrick G. Ryan, Chmn.

HR: Virginia Schooley, Dir.

Web site: www.aon.com

Emp: 33,000 Rev: $18,891 mil.

Insurance brokers worldwide; underwrites accident & health insurance, specialty & professional insurance; & provides risk management consultation.

Antigua, Argentina, Aruba, Australia, Austria, Bahrain, Barbados, Belgium, Belize, Bermuda, Bolivia, Botswana, Brazil, British Virgin Islands, Canada, Cayman Islands, Channel Islands, U.K., Chile, China (PRC), Colombia, Costa Rica, Cyprus, Czech Republic, Denmark, Dominican Republic, Ecuador, El Salvador, England, U.K., Fiji, Finland, France, French Antilles, Germany, Greece, Grenada, Guam, Guatemala, Guyana, Haiti, Honduras, Hong Kong, Hungary, India, Indonesia, Ireland, Isle of Man, Italy, Japan, Kazakhstan, Kenya, Kuwait, Lebanon, Lesotho, Luxembourg, Malaysia, Malta, Mexico, Morocco, Myanmar, Netherlands, Netherlands Antilles, New Zealand, Nicaragua, Nigeria, Northern Mariana Islands, Norway, Oman, Pakistan, Panama, Papua New Guinea, Paraguay, Peru, Philippines, Poland, Portugal, Romania, Russia, Saudi Arabia, Scotland, U.K., Singapore, Slovakia, Solomon Islands, South Africa, South Korea, Spain, Swaziland, Sweden, Switzerland, Taiwan (ROC), Thailand, Tunisia, Turkey, Turks & Caicos Islands, Uganda, Ukraine, United Arab Emirates, Uruguay, Uzbekistan, Vanuatu, Venezuela, Vietnam, Wales, U.K., Zambia, Zimbabwe

AP AUTOMOTIVE SYSTEMS, INC.

315 Matzinger Road

Toledo, OH 43612

Tel: (419) 727-5000 Fax: (419) 727-5025

CEO: T. Bernander

FO: B. Rosa

HR: J. Ulery

Emp: 3,000 Rev: $650 mil.

Mfr. auto parts & accessories.

Netherlands, Sweden

APPLE COMPUTER INC.

One Infinite Loop

Cupertino, CA 95014

Tel: (831) 996-1010 Fax: (831) 974-2113

CEO: Steve Jobs

FO: Timothy Cook, SVP

HR: Debbie Rau, VP

Web site: www.apple.com

Emp: 10,176 Rev: $7,081 mil.

Personal computers, peripherals & software.

Australia, Austria, Belgium, Brazil, Canada, China (PRC), England, U.K., France, Germany, Hong Kong, India, Ireland, Italy, Japan, Mexico, Netherlands, Philippines, Poland, Russia, Singapore, Spain, Sweden, Taiwan (ROC), Ukraine

APPLIED MAGNETICS CORPORATION

75 Robin Hill Road

Goleta, CA 93117

Tel: (805) 683-5353 Fax: (805) 967-8227

CEO: Craig D. Crisman, Pres.

HR: Randy Berg

Emp: 5,500

Mfr. magnetic recording heads.

Ireland, Malaysia, Singapore, South Korea

APPLIED MATERIALS, INC.

3050 Bowers Ave.

Santa Clara, CA 95054-3299

Tel: (408) 727-5555 Fax: (408) 727-9943

CEO: James C. Morgan, Chmn.

FO: Sasson Somekh, SVP

HR: Dana C. Ditmore, Grp. VP

Web site: www.appliedmaterials.com

Emp: 13,924 Rev: $4,074 mil.

Supplies manufacturing systems/services to semiconductor industry.

Belgium, China (PRC), England, U.K., France, Germany, Ireland, Israel, Italy, Japan, Netherlands, Scotland, U.K., Singapore, South Korea, Taiwan (ROC), Thailand

APPLIED POWER INC.

13000 W. Silver Spring Drive

Butler, WI 53007

Tel: (414) 781-6600 Fax: (414) 781-0629

CEO: Richard G. Sim, Pres.

HR: Louis E. Font

Emp: 2,840 Rev: $425.8 mil.

Mfr. hi-pressure tools, vibration control products, electrical tools, consumables, technical furniture & enclosures.

Australia, Brazil, Canada, China (PRC), England, U.K., France, Germany, Italy, Japan, Mexico, Netherlands, Russia, Singapore, South Korea, Spain

APPLIED SYSTEMS INC.

200 Applied Parkway

University Park, IL 60466

Tel: (708) 534-5575 Fax: (708) 534-5943

CEO: James P. Kellner, Chmn.

FO: John H. Carruth, EVP

HR: Janet Van Haren, Mgr.

Web site: www.appliedsystems.com

Emp: 1,100 Rev: $76 mil.

Computer systems, peripherals & software.

Canada, England, U.K.

ARAMARK CORPORATION

1101 Market Street

Philadelphia, PA 19107-2988

Tel: (215) 238-3000 Fax: (215) 238-3333

CEO: William Leonard, Pres.

HR: Brian Mulvaney

Emp: 133,000

Diversified managed services.

Belgium, Canada, England, U.K., Germany, Japan, South Korea, Spain

ARBOR ACRES FARM INC.

439 Marlborough Road

Glastonbury, CT 06033

Tel: (860) 633-4681 Fax: (860) 633-2433

CEO: Dr. Colin Baxter-Jones, Pres.

Emp: 750

Producers of male & female broiler breeders, commercial egg layers.

Argentina, Belgium, Brazil, Chile, Colombia, Ecuador, France, Greece, India, Indonesia, Ireland, Italy, Japan, Mexico, Netherlands, Nigeria, Peru, South Korea, Spain, Taiwan (ROC), Thailand, Venezuela, Zambia, Zimbabwe

ARCADIA AMERICAN REALTY CORPORATION

77 Park Ave.

New York, NY 10016

Tel: (212) 481-6265 Fax:

CEO: Jeffrey S. Becker

FO: Dick Leong & Laraine Fox

Emp: 7

Commercial & residential realty sales.

Hong Kong

ARCHER-DANIELS-MIDLAND COMPANY

4666 Faries Parkway

Decatur, IL 62526

Tel: (217) 424-5200 Fax: (217) 424-6196

CEO: Allen Andreas, Pres.

FO: Paul B. Mulhollem, VP

HR: Sheila Witts-Mannweiler, Dir.

Web site: www.admworld.com

Emp: 23,132 Rev: $16,109 mil.

Grain processing: flours, grains, oils & flax fibre.

Australia, Brazil, England, U.K., Hong Kong, Japan, Netherlands

ATLANTIC RICHFIELD COMPANY (ARCO)

515 South Flower Street

Los Angeles, CA 90071-2256

Tel: (213) 486-3511 Fax: (213) 486-2063

CEO: Michael R. Bowlin, Chmn. & Pres.

HR: J. H. Kelly

Web site: www.arco.com

Emp: 25,000

Petroleum & natural gas, chemicals & service stations.

Australia, Brazil, Canada, China (PRC), England, U.K., France, Germany, Hong Kong, Indonesia, Japan, Netherlands, New Zealand, Qatar, Russia, Singapore

ARCO CHEMICAL COMPANY

3801 West Chester Pike

Newtown Square, PA 19073-2387

Tel: (610) 359-2000 Fax: (610) 359-2722

CEO: Anthony G. Fernandes, Chmn.

FO: Lyndon E. Stanton, VP Europe

HR: Francis W. Welsh, VP

Web site: www.arcochem.com

Emp: 4,000 Rev: $2,022 mil

Mfr. propylene oxide, a chemical used for flexible foam products, coatings/paints & solvents/inks.

Austria, Belgium, Brazil, China (PRC), England, U.K., France, Germany, Hong Kong, Indonesia, Italy, Japan, Netherlands, Russia, Singapore, Spain, Taiwan (ROC), Thailand

ARDENT SOFTWARE, INC.

50 Washington Street

Westboro, MA 01581-1021

Tel: (508) 366-3888 Fax: (508) 366-3669

CEO: Peter Gyenes, Chmn.

FO: Corneilus P. McMullan, VP

HR: Sally N. Burke, Dir.

Web site: www.ardentsoftware.com

Emp: 570 Rev: $107 mil.

Publisher of database and file management software.

Australia, England, U.K., France, Germany, Japan, Malaysia, New Zealand, South Africa

ARENT FOX KINTNER PLOTKIN & KAHN, PLC

1050 Connecticut Ave., N.W.

Washington, DC 20036-5339

Tel: (202) 857-6000 Fax: (202) 857-6395

CEO: Christopher Smith

HR: Nancy Andriuk

Web site: www.arentfox.com

Emp: 250

International law firm.

Hungary, Saudi Arabia

ARGO INTERNATIONAL CORPORATION

140 Franklin Street

New York, NY 10013

Tel: (212) 431-1700 Fax: (212) 431-2206

CEO: John Calicchio, Chmn.

FO: John Santa Croce, Pres.

HR: John Sobieski

Emp: 290

Distributor electrical spare parts.

Argentina, Italy, Singapore

ARGOSY INTERNATIONAL (USA) INC.

225 West 34th Street

New York, NY 10122

Tel: (212) 268-0003 Fax: (212) 268-0336

CEO: Paul Marks, President

FO: Jen Chang, Gen. Mgr.

Emp: 16 Rev: $5 mil.

Mfr. & distributor specialty chemicals serving aerospace, automotive, marine & general industry.

Taiwan (ROC)

ARKANSAS BEST CORPORATION

3801 Old. Greenwood Road

Ft. Smith, AR 72903

Tel: (501) 785-6000 Fax: (501) 494-6658

CEO: Robert A. Young, III

FO: Larry R. Scott, EVP

HR: Kelli Wheeler, Mgr.

Web site: www.arkbest.com

Emp: 14,747 Rev: $1,644 mil.

Trucking, automotive supplies, service repair, bldg management, data processing services.

Canada

ARKWRIGHT

PO Box 9198

Waltham, MA 02254-9198

Tel: (781) 890-9300 Fax: (781) 890-0075

CEO: William J. Poutsiaka

FO: Wolfgang F. Friedel

HR: Enzo Rebula

Emp: 1,200

Property insurance & risk management services.

England, U.K.

ARMSTRONG ENGINEERING ASSOCIATES INC.

PO Box 566

West Chester, PA 19380

Tel: (610) 436-6080 Fax: (610) 436-0374

CEO: Richard Armstrong, VP

Emp: 75

Heat exchangers & process equipment for chemicals plants & oil refineries.

Scotland, U.K., Singapore

ARMSTRONG INTERNATIONAL INC.

816 Maple Street, PO Box 408

Three Rivers, MI 49093

Tel: (616) 273-1415 Fax: (616) 278-6555

CEO: M. H. Armstrong, Chmn.

FO: R. E. Masnari

HR: Ken Clay, VP

Emp: 800

Mfr. steam specialty products: traps, air vents, liquid drainers, strainers, valves, etc.

Belgium, Canada

ARMSTRONG WORLD INDUSTRIES INC.

PO Box 3001, 313 W. Liberty Street

Lancaster, PA 17604-3001

Tel: (717) 397-0611 Fax: (717) 396-2787

CEO: George A. Lorch, Chmn.

FO: Marc R. Olivie, Pres.

HR: Douglas L. Boles, SVP

Web site: www.armstrong.com

Emp: 10,600 Rev: $2,200 mil.

Mfr. & marketing interior furnishings & specialty products for bldg, auto & textile industry.

Australia, Bermuda, Canada, China (PRC), England, U.K., France, Germany, Hong Kong, India, Italy, Japan, Mexico, Netherlands, Russia, Singapore, South Korea, Spain, Switzerland, Thailand

ARNOLD & PORTER

555 12th Street, N.W.

Washington, DC 20004-1202

Tel: (202) 942-5000 Fax: (202) 942-5999

CEO: Michael N. Sohn, Chmn..

HR: Elizabeth Respess, Dir., HR

Emp: 1,020

International law firm.

England, U.K., Turkey

ARO INTERNATIONAL CORPORATION

One Aro Center

Bryan, OH 43506

Tel: (419) 636-4242 Fax: (419) 633-1674

CEO: Dennis Weaver, VP

FO: H. S. Ormsbee

HR: L. D. Babcock

Emp: 1,823

Mfr. cylinders, valves & pumps.

Belgium, Brazil, England, U.K., Germany, Venezuela

AROMACHEM

599 Johnson Ave.

Brooklyn, NY 11237

Tel: (718) 497-4664 Fax: (718) 821-2193

CEO: Philip Rosner, Pres.

HR: David R. Weisman

Emp: 200

Essential oils & extracts, perfumes & flavor material, aromatic chemicals.

Australia, Canada, England, U.K., France, Hong Kong, Indonesia, Japan, Mexico, New Zealand, South Korea, Spain, Thailand, Venezuela

ARROW COMPANY

48 West 38th Street

New York, NY 10018

Tel: (212) 984-8900 Fax: (212) 984-8940

CEO: Bryan Marsal, Pres.

Men's apparel.

Hong Kong

ARROW ELECTRONICS INC.

25 Hub Drive

Melville, NY 11747

Tel: (516) 391-4200 Fax: (516) 391-8919

CEO: Stephen P. Kaufman, Chmn.

HR: Tom Hallam

Emp: 8,000

Distributor of electronic components.

England, U.K., France, Germany, Hong Kong, Italy

ARROW MFG. CO., INC.

567 52nd Street

West New York, NJ 07093

Tel: (201) 867-4833 Fax: (201) 867-1596

CEO: Alan Weill, Pres.

HR: Derry Ziotas

Emp: 150

Mfr. plastic products, cosmetic & jewelry boxes.

Canada

ARTHUR ANDERSEN & COMPANY

33 West Monroe Street

Chicago, IL 60603

Tel: (312) 372-7100 Fax: (312) 507-0123

CEO: James Kackley

FO: John Mott

HR: Gary A. Beu

Web site: www.arthurandersen.com

Emp: 104,500 Rev: $11,300 mil.

Accounting & audit, tax & management consulting services.

Argentina, Australia, Austria, Bahrain, Belgium, Bermuda, Brazil, Brunei, Bulgaria, Canada, Cayman Islands, Channel Islands, U.K., China (PRC), Colombia, Croatia, Czech Republic, Denmark, Ecuador, Egypt, England, U.K., Estonia, Fiji, Finland, France, Germany, Greece, Guatemala, Hong Kong, Hungary, India, Indonesia, Ireland, Israel, Italy, Japan, Jordan, Kazakhstan, Kuwait, Latvia, Lebanon, Lithuania, Luxembourg, Malaysia, Mexico, Morocco, Netherlands, Netherlands Antilles, New Zealand, Nigeria, Norway, Oman, Palestine, Peru, Philippines, Poland, Portugal, Qatar, Romania, Russia, Saudi Arabia, Scotland, U.K., Singapore, Slovakia, South Africa, South Korea, Spain, Sweden, Switzerland, Syria, Taiwan (ROC), Thailand, Turkey, Ukraine, United Arab Emirates, Uzbekistan, Venezuela, Vietnam, Yemen

ARTOS ENGINEERING CO., INC.

W228 N2792 Duplainville Road

Waukesha, WI 53186

Tel: (414) 524-6600 Fax: (414) 524-0400

CEO: Larry Czernejewski, Pres.

Emp: 270

Mfr. metalworking machinery.

England, U.K., Italy, Netherlands

ARVIN INDUSTRIES INC.

One Noblitt Plaza, Box 3000

Columbus, IN 47202-3000

Tel: (812) 379-3000 Fax: (812) 379-3688

CEO: Bryon O. Pond, Chmn.

FO: V. William Hunt, Pres.

HR: Raymond P. Mack, VP, HR

Web site: www.arvin.com

Emp: 14,340 Rev: $2,300 mil.

Mfr. of automotive exhaust systems & ride control products.

Argentina, Canada, Germany, Japan, Mexico, Netherlands, South Africa, Spain, Venezuela

ASARCO INC.

180 Maiden Lane

New York, NY 10038

Tel: (212) 510-2000 Fax: (212) 510-1855

CEO: Richard de J. Osborne, Chmn.

FO: Francis R. McAllister, Pres.

HR: David B. Woodbury, VP

Web site: www.asarco.com

Emp: 11,800 Rev: $2,721 mil.

Nonferrous metals, specialty chemicals, minerals, mfr. industrial products, environmental services.

Australia, Canada, China (PRC), England, U.K., France, Germany, Hong Kong, Italy, Japan, Malaysia, Mexico, Netherlands, Papua New Guinea, Peru, Singapore, Spain, Sweden, Switzerland, Taiwan (ROC)

ASCOM HASLER MAILING SYSTEMS INC.

19 Forest Parkway, PO Box 858

Shelton, CT 06484-0904

Tel: (203) 926-1087 Fax: (203) 929-6084

CEO: Michael A. Allocca, Pres.

FO: Fran Dubkowski

HR: Louise Bruno

Emp: 300

Mfr. gummed tape dispensers, postal meters and scales, mailing machines.

Canada, England, U.K.

ASGROW SEED COMPANY LLC

4140 114th Street, PO Box 7570

Des Moines, IA 50322-7570

Tel: (515) 331-7100 Fax: (515) 331-7147

CEO: John A. Schillinger, Co-Pres.

FO: Jim Fetrow

HR: Darrell Bonner

Web site: www.asgrow.com

Emp: 750 Rev: $300 mil.

Breeders, producers & marketers of hybrid corn, hybrid sorghum, hybrid sunflower & proprietary soybeans.

France, Germany, Italy, Mexico, Spain

ASHLAND OIL INC.

1000 Ashland Drive

Russell, KY 41169

Tel: (606) 329-3333 Fax: (606) 329-5274

CEO: John R. Hall, Chmn.

FO: John D. van Meter

HR: Philip W. Block

Web site: www.ashland.com

Emp: 37,200 Rev: $13,2080 mil.

Petroleum exploration, refining & transportation; mfr. chemicals, oils & lubricants.

Australia, Brazil, Canada, Denmark, England, U.K., France, Germany, Hong Kong, Italy, Japan, Mexico, Netherlands, Portugal, Saudi Arabia, South Korea, Spain, Sweden, Switzerland

ASHWORTH BROTHERS INC.

89 Globe Mills Ave., PO Box 670

Fall River, MA 02722-0670

Tel: (508) 674-4693 Fax: (508) 675-9622

CEO: Rex Richie, Pres.

HR: Tom Shelhamer

Emp: 500

Flexible & metallic card clothing.

Canada

ASKO INC.

501 West 7th Ave., PO Box 355

Homestead, PA 15120

Tel: (412) 461-4110 Fax: (412) 461-5400

CEO: William H. Rackoff, Pres.

FO: A. C. Metzelaar

HR: Robert Thomas

Emp: 200

Mfr. industrial knives & saws for metal industrial.

Mexico, Netherlands

ASSOCIATED HYGENIC PRODUCTS

4455 River Green Parkway

Duluth, GA 30136

Tel: (770) 497-9800 Fax: (770) 623-8887

CEO: Peter Chang, Pres.

HR: Carlos Furgiuele

Emp: 250

Mfr. sanitary paper products.

Canada

ASSOCIATED MERCHANDISING CORPORATION

1440 Broadway

New York, NY 10018

Tel: (212) 596-4000 Fax: (212) 575-2993

CEO: Richard Kuzmich, Pres.

FO: William Dillon

HR: Barbara Dugan, VP

Emp: 1,200 Rev: $900 mil.

Retail service organization; apparel, shoes and accessories.

China (PRC), Denmark, England, U.K., France, Germany, Greece, Hong Kong, India, Israel, Italy, Japan, Philippines, Portugal, Singapore, South Korea, Spain, Sri Lanka, Taiwan (ROC), Turkey, Uruguay

ASSOCIATED METALS & MINERALS CORPORATION

3 North Corporate Park Drive

White Plains, NY 10604

Tel: (914) 251-5400 Fax: (914) 251-1073

CEO: Sal Purpuro, Pres.

Emp: 200

Metals & ores.

Argentina, Brazil, Germany, Japan

ASSOCIATED PRESS INC.

50 Rockefeller Plaza

New York, NY 10020-1605

Tel: (212) 621-1500 Fax: (212) 621-5447

CEO: Louis D. Boccardi, Pres.

FO: Claude E. Erbsen, VP

HR: James M. Donna, VP

Web site: www.ap.com

Emp: 3,500 Rev: $441 mil.

News gathering agency.

Australia, Belgium, Brazil, Canada, Denmark, Egypt, England, U.K., France, Germany, Hong Kong, India, Italy, Japan, Kenya, Lebanon,

Malaysia, Mexico, Norway, Peru, Portugal, Sweden, Switzerland, Turkey, Uruguay, Venezuela, Vietnam

ASSOCIATED SPRING

80 Scott Swamp Road

Farmington, CT 06032

Tel: (860) 678-0700 Fax: (860) 409-4611

CEO: T. E. Martin, Pres.

HR: Jim Majka

Emp: 2,700

Mfr. precision springs & stampings.

Mexico, Singapore

ASSOCIATES FIRST CAPITAL CORPORATION

250 E. Carpenter Freeway

Irving, TX 75062-2729

Tel: (972) 652-4000 Fax: (972) 652-7420

CEO: Keith W. Hughes, Chmn.

FO: Wilfred Y. Horie, EVP

HR: Michael E. McGill, EVP

Web site: www.theassociates.com

Emp: 22,600 Rev: $8,279 mil.

Consumer financial services.

Canada, Channel Islands, U.K., Costa Rica, England, U.K., Japan, Mexico, Northern Ireland, U.K., Scotland, U.K., Taiwan (ROC), Wales, U.K.

AST RESEARCH INC.

16215 Alton Parkway, PO Box 19658

Irvine, CA 92713-9658

Tel: (949) 727-4141 Fax: (949) 727-8584

CEO: Soon- Taek Kim, Pres.

HR: Leslie Catton, Mgr.

Web site: www.ast.com

Emp: 4,151 Rev: $2,104 mil.

Design/development/mfr. hi-performance desktop, server & notebook computers.

Australia, Belgium, Canada, China (PRC), Denmark, England, U.K., Finland, France, Germany, Hong Kong, Ireland, Italy, Japan, Malaysia, Netherlands, New Zealand, Norway, Pakistan, Scotland, U.K., Singapore, South Korea, Sweden, Switzerland, Taiwan (ROC), United Arab Emirates

ASTEA INTERNATIONAL, INC.

455 Business Center Drive

Horsham, PA 19044

Tel: (215) 682-2500 Fax: (215) 682-2515

CEO: Zack b. Bergreen, Chmn.

FO: Per Edstrom

HR: Eileen Pierson, Dir.

Web site: www.astea.com

Emp: 568 Rev: $61 mil.

Produces computer software that assists to automate and manage field service, sales and customer support operations.

Australia, England, U.K., France, Israel, Netherlands, New Zealand, Sweden

ASTRONAUTICS CORPORATION OF AMERICA

PO Box 523

Milwaukee, WI 53201-0523

Tel: (414) 447-8200 Fax: (414) 447-8231

CEO: R. E. Zelazo

FO: Dan Wade

HR: H. Russek

Web site: www.astronautics.com

Emp: 2,500

Design/development/mfr. aircraft instruments, avionics, electronics systems, vehicle electronics & computer maintenance service.

England, U.K., Israel, Russia

AT&T CORPORATION

32 Ave. of the Americas

New York, NY 10013-2412

Tel: (212) 387-5400 Fax: (908) 221-1211

CEO: C. Michael Armstrong, Chmn.

FO: R. C. Mark Baker, EVP Int'l.

HR: Harold W. Burlingame, EVP

Web site: www.att.com

Emp: 127,800 Rev: $51,319 mil.

Telecommunications

Australia, Brazil, Canada, Egypt, England, U.K., Greece, Hong Kong, Ireland, Italy, Japan, Mexico, Poland, Russia, Singapore, South Korea, Spain, Sweden, Taiwan (ROC), Thailand, Ukraine, Vietnam

ATKINSON CONSTRUCTION

1100 Grundy Lane

San Bruno, CA 94066

Tel: (650) 876-0400 Fax: (650) 876-1143

CEO: Jack J. Agresti, Vice Chmn.

Emp: 2,800

Construction.

Canada, Venezuela

ATLANTIC MUTUAL COS

100 Wall Street

New York, NY 10005

Tel: (212) 943-1800 Fax: (212) 428-6566

CEO: Klaus Dorfi, Pres.

Insurance.

Canada

ATLANTIC VENEER CORPORATION

PO Box 660

Beaufort, NC 28516-0660

Tel: (252) 728-3169 Fax: (252) 728-4906

CEO: Karl H. Moehring, Chmn.

HR: Ed Nelson

Emp: 2,100

Wood veneer & plywood mill.

Brazil

ATLAS VAN LINES INC.

1212 St. George Road

Evansville, IN 47711-2336

Tel: (812) 424-4326 Fax: (812) 421-7125

CEO: Wally Saubert

HR: Pat Walter, AVP

Web site: www.atlasvanlines.com

Emp: 750 Rev: $490 mil.

Trucking, freight transport.

Canada

ATTACHMATE CORPORATION

3617 131st Ave. S.E.

Bellevue, WA 98006-1332

Tel: (425) 644-4010 Fax: (425) 747-9924

CEO: Frank Pritt

FO: William E. Boisvert, Pres.

Web site: www.attachmate.com

Emp: 1,600

Mfr. connectivity software.

Australia, Belgium, Canada, Denmark, England, U.K., Finland, France, Germany, Hong Kong, Italy, Japan, Malaysia, Mexico, Netherlands, Norway, Portugal, Singapore, South Africa, Spain, Sweden, Switzerland

ATWOOD OCEANICS, INC.

PO Box 218350

Houston, TX 77218

Tel: (281) 492-2929 Fax: (281) 578-3253

CEO: John R. Irwin

FO: Larry P. Till

HR: Bill Sullens

Emp: 225 Rev: $89 mil.

Offshore drilling for gas and oil.

Australia, Cayman Islands, Malaysia, Panama

THE AUSTIN COMPANY

3650 Mayfield Road

Cleveland, OH 44121

Tel: (216) 382-6600 Fax: (216) 291-6684

CEO: J. William Melsop, Pres.

HR: Dennis M. Raymond

Emp: 2,000 Rev: $1,600 mil.

Consulting, design, engineering & construction.

Australia, Brazil, England, U.K., Netherlands

AUTO-TROL TECHNOLOGY CORPORATION

12500 North Washington Street

Denver, CO 80241-2400

Tel: (303) 452-4919 Fax: (303) 252-2249

CEO: Howard B. Hillman, Pres.

FO: Kenneth M. Dedeluk

HR: Lisa Jayne

Web site: www.auto-trol.com

Emp: 250 Rev: $19 mil.

Develops, markets & integrates computer-based solutions for industrial companies & government agencies worldwide.

Australia, Canada, England, U.K., Germany

AUTODESK INC.

111 McInnis Parkway

San Rafael, CA 94903

Tel: (415) 507-5000 Fax: (415) 507-6112

CEO: Eric Herr, Pres.

HR: Steve McMahon, VP

Web site: www.autodesk.com

Emp: 1,272

Develop/marketing/support computer-aided design, engineering, scientific & multimedia software

products.

Argentina, Australia, Austria, Belgium, Brazil, Canada, China (PRC), Czech Republic, England, U.K., France, Germany, Hong Kong, Hungary, India, Ireland, Israel, Italy, Japan, Mexico, Netherlands, Poland, Portugal, Russia, Singapore, South Africa, South Korea, Spain, Sweden, Switzerland, Taiwan (ROC), United Arab Emirates, Venezuela

AUTOMATIC DATA PROCESSING INC.

One ADP Boulevard

Roseland, NJ 07068

Tel: (973) 994-5000 Fax: (973) 994-5387

CEO: Arthur F. Weinbach, Chmn.

FO: G. Harry Durity, VP

HR: Richard C. Berke, VP

Web site: www.adp.com

Emp: 34,000 Rev: $4,800 mil.

Data processing services.

Brazil, Canada, England, U.K., France, Germany, Italy, Netherlands, Spain

AUTOMATIC SWITCH CO. (ASCO)

50-60 Hanover Road

Florham Park, NJ 07932

Tel: (973) 966-2000 Fax: (973) 966-2628

CEO: Randy P. Smith, Chmn. & Pres.

FO: Horst Braumann, Intl.

HR: Chris Walsh

Emp: 2,500

Mfr. solenoid valves, emergency power controls, pressure & temp. switches.

Australia, Belgium, Brazil, Canada, China (PRC), Czech Republic, England, U.K., France, Germany, Hong Kong, Hungary, India, Indonesia, Italy, Japan, Malaysia, Mexico, Netherlands, Poland, Portugal, Singapore, South Africa, South Korea, Spain, Sweden, Switzerland, Taiwan (ROC), Thailand, Turkey, United Arab Emirates

AUTOMATION DEVICES INC.

7050 West Ridge Road

Fairview, PA 16415-2028

Tel: (814) 474-5561 Fax: (814) 474-2131

CEO: Larry Smith, Pres.

HR: Jim Lohse

Mfr. industrial machinery, relays and controls.

Canada

AUTOSPLICE INC.

10121 Barnes Canyon Road

San Diego, CA 92121

Tel: (619) 535-0077 Fax: (619) 535-0130

CEO: Don Eisenberg, Pres.

FO: Terry Green, Dir. Int'l.

HR: Anita Ruka

Emp: 200 Rev: $35 mil.

Mfr. electronic components.

Brazil, Germany, Japan, Singapore

AVCO FINANCIAL SERVICES INC.

600 Anton Blvd., PO Box 5011

Costa Mesa, CA 92628-5011

Tel: (714) 435-1200 Fax: (714) 445-7722

CEO: Warren R. Lyons

FO: Eugene R. Schutt

Web site: www.avco.textron.com

Emp: 8,500 Rev: $7,700 mil.

Financial services, loans and insurance.

Australia, Canada, England, U.K., France, Hong Kong, India, New Zealand, Spain, Sweden

AVERY DENNISON CORPORATION

150 N. Orange Grove Blvd.

Pasadena, CA 91103

Tel: (626) 304-2000 Fax: (626) 792-7312

CEO: Philip M. Neal, Pres.

FO: Stephanie A. Streeter, VP

HR: J. Terry Schuler, VP

Web site: www.averydennison.com

Emp: 16,200 Rev: $3,346 mil.

Mfr. pressure-sensitive adhesives & materials, office products, labels, tags, retail systems, Carter's Ink & specialty chemicals.

Argentina, Australia, Austria, Belgium, Brazil, Canada, Chile, China (PRC), Colombia, Denmark, England, U.K., Finland, France, Germany, Hong Kong, Ireland, Italy, Japan, Mexico, Netherlands, Norway, South Africa, South Korea, Spain, Sweden, Switzerland, Wales, U.K.

AVIS, INC.

900 Old Country Road.

Garden City, NY 11530

Tel: (516) 222-3000 Fax: (516) 222-4381

CEO: Craig Hoenshell, Chmn.

FO: Michael Collins, VP

HR: Don Korn

Web site: www.avis.com

Emp: 21,000 Rev: $3,000 mil.

Car rental services.

Argentina, Australia, Bahamas, Brazil, Canada, Chile, Costa Rica, Ecuador, Guatemala, Haiti, Hong Kong, Indonesia, Jamaica, Malaysia, New Zealand, Pakistan, Panama, Peru, Philippines, Poland, Singapore, South Korea, Thailand, Uruguay, Venezuela

AVMARK INC.

1815 North Ft. Myer Drive, Ste.1000

Arlington, VA 22209

Tel: (703) 528-5610 Fax: (703) 528-3689

CEO: Barbara L. Beyer, Pres.

FO: Barbara L. Beyer

Emp: 42

Aviation consult, aircraft appraisal, aviation related publications.

England, U.K.

AVNET INC.

2211 South 47th Street

Phoenix, AR 85034

Tel: (602) 643-2000 Fax: (602) 643-4670

CEO: Roy Vallee

FO: Keith Williams

HR: Robert Zierk

Web site: www.avnet.com

Emp: 9,000

Distributor electronic components, computers & peripherals.

Australia, England, U.K., France, Germany, Hong Kong, Ireland, Italy, New Zealand, Sweden

AVON PRODUCTS INC.

1345 Ave. of the Americas

New York, NY 10105-0196

Tel: (212) 282-5000 Fax: (212) 282-6049

CEO: Charles R. Perrin

FO: Edwina Jung, COO

HR: Jill Kanin-Lovers, SVP

Web site: www.avon.com

Emp: 34,995 Rev: $5,080 mil.

Mfr./distributor beauty & related products, fashion jewelry, gifts & collectibles.

Argentina, Australia, Austria, Bolivia, Brazil, Canada, Chile, China (PRC), Croatia, Czech Republic, Dominican Republic, Ecuador, El Salvador, England, U.K., Finland, France, Germany, Guatemala, Honduras, Hong Kong, Hungary, India, Indonesia, Ireland, Italy, Japan, Malaysia, Mexico, Netherlands, New Zealand, Nicaragua, Panama, Paraguay, Peru, Philippines, Poland, Portugal, Russia, Senegal, Slovakia, South Africa, Spain, Sweden, Taiwan (ROC), Thailand, Turkey, Uruguay, Venezuela

AVX CORPORATION

PO Box 867

Myrtle Beach, SC 29578

Tel: (803) 448-9411 Fax: (803) 448-7139

CEO: John Gilbertson, Pres.

HR: Kathryn Byrd

Mfr. multilayer ceramic capacitors.

El Salvador, England, U.K., France, Hong Kong, Israel, Mexico, Northern Ireland, U.K.

AXCIOM CORPORATION

301 Industrial Boulevard

Conway, AR 72030-7168

Tel: (501) 336-1000 Fax:

CEO: Charles Morgan, Jr., Pres.

Emp: 2,500

Information retrieval services.

England, U.K.

AXENT TECHNOLOGIES, INC.

2400 Research Boulevard, Ste. 200

Rickville, MD 20850

Tel: (301) 258-5043 Fax: (301) 330-5756

CEO: John C. Becker, Pres.

FO: Marc S. Shinbrood, SVP

Web site: www.axent.com

Emp: 392 Rev: $42 mil.

Designs and supplies security management software .

Belgium, England, U.K., France, Germany, Netherlands, Sweden

AYDIN CORPORATION

700 Dresher Road

Horsham, PA 19044

Tel: (215) 657-7510 Fax: (215) 657-3830

CEO: I. Gary Bard, Chmn.

FO: Randy Ayoob, VP

Web site: www.aydin.com

Emp: 1,500 Rev: $115.4 mil.

Designs/manufactures products & systems for the acquisition & distribution of information over electronic communications media.

England, U.K., Turkey

AZON CORPORATION

720 Azon Road

Johnson City, NY 13790-1799

Tel: (607) 797-2368 Fax: (607) 797-4506

CEO: William L. Bordages, Pres.

HR: Valerie Allen

Web site: www.azon.com

Emp: 930

Mfr. paper, office equipment, films & photo equipment.

Belgium, Canada, France, Hong Kong, Hungary

B

B&P PROCESS EQUIPMENT AND SYSTEMS

1000 Hess Ave.

Saginaw, MI 48601

Tel: (517) 752-4121 Fax: (517) 757-1301

CEO: Ray Miller, Pres.

HR: Gena Kwaiser

Emp: 85

Food & chemicals processing.

England, U.K.

BABY TOGS INC.

460 West 34rd Street

New York, NY 10017

Tel: (212) 868-2100 Fax: (212) 947-2039

CEO: Jack Sitt, Pres.

Emp: 100

Mfr./importers of infants dresses & suits.

Philippines

BACARDI CORPORATION

PO Box G 3549

San Juan, PR 00936-3549

Tel: (809) 788-1500 Fax: (809) 245-0422

CEO: Roberto Del Rosal, Pres.

FO: Mario S. Belaval

Emp: 1,200 Rev: $398 mil.

Distiller & exporter of blended liquors.

Brazil

BADGER METER INC.

4545 W. Brown Deer Road, PO Box 23099

Milwaukee, WI 53223-0099

Tel: (414) 355-0400 Fax: (414) 371-5956

CEO: James C. Forbes

FO: Theodore N. Townsend

HR: Ronald H. Dix

Web site: www.badgermeter.com

Emp: 850 Rev: $130 mil.

Liquid meters & controls.

Germany

BAILEY-FISCHER & PORTER COMPANY

125 East County Line Road

Warminster, PA 18974

Tel: (215) 674-6000 Fax: (215) 441-5280

CEO: Gordon Woolbert, VP

HR: Judith Blake

Emp: 550

Design/mfr. measure, recording & control instruments & systems; mfr. industrial glass products.

Australia, Austria, Belgium, Canada, England, U.K., Finland, France, Germany, Italy, Mexico, Netherlands, Spain, Sweden

BAIN & CO., INC.

Two Copley Place

Boston, MA 02116

Tel: (617) 572-2000 Fax: (617) 572-2427

CEO: Orit Gadiesh, Chmn.

FO: David Bechhofer

HR: Elizabeth Corcoran

Web site: www.bain.com

Emp: 1,300 Rev: $480 mil.

Strategic management consulting services.

Australia, Belgium, Canada, England, U.K., France, Germany, Hong Kong, Italy, Japan, Mexico, Russia, Singapore, South Korea, Spain, Sweden, Switzerland, Ukraine

BAKER & BOTTS LLP

910 Louisiana Street, One Shell Plaza, Ste. 3000

Houston, TX 77002-4995

Tel: (713) 229-1234 Fax: (713) 229-1522

CEO: Richard C. Johnson, Mng. Prtn.

Web site: www.bakerbotts.com

Emp: 500

International law firm.

England, U.K., Russia

BAKER & McKENZIE

One Prudential Plaza, 130 East Randolph Drive, Ste. 2500

Chicago, IL 60601

Tel: (312) 861-8000 Fax: (312) 861-2899

CEO: John C. Klotsche, Chmn.

FO: Teresa A. Townsend

HR: Jennifer Pingolt

Web site: www.bakerinfo.com

Emp: 6,700 Rev: $785 mil.

International legal services.

Argentina, Australia, Azerbaijan, Belgium, Brazil, Canada, Chile, China (PRC), Colombia, Czech Republic, Egypt, England, U.K., France, Germany, Hong Kong, Hungary, Indonesia, Italy, Japan, Kazakhstan, Mexico, Netherlands, Philippines, Poland, Russia, Saudi Arabia, Singapore, Spain, Sweden, Switzerland, Taiwan (ROC), Thailand, Ukraine, Venezuela, Vietnam

MICHAEL BAKER CORPORATION

PO Box 12259

Pittsburgh, PA 15231

Tel: (412) 269-6300 Fax: (412) 269-6097

CEO: Charles I. Homan, Pres.

FO: Rodney Levett-Prinsep, SVP

HR: Kimberly W. Foltz, VP

Web site: www.mbakercorp.com

Emp: 3,700 Rev: $418 mil.

Engineering & construction operations & technical services.

England, U.K., Mexico

BAKER HUGHES INCORPORATED

3900 Essex Lane, Ste. 1200

Houston, TX 77027

Tel: (713) 439-8600 Fax: (713) 439-8699

CEO: Max L. Lukens, Chmn.

FO: Andrew J. Szescila, SVP

HR: Nicole Boisburn, Mgr.

Web site: www.bakerhughes.com

Emp: 21,500 Rev: $3,685 mil.

Develop & apply technology to drill, complete & produce oil and natural gas wells; provide separation systems to petroleum, municipal, continuous process & mining industries.

Algeria, Angola, Argentina, Australia, Azerbaijan, Bolivia, Brazil, Brunei, Cameroon, Canada, Chile, China (PRC), Colombia, Congo, Denmark, Ecuador, Egypt, England, U.K., France, Gabon, Germany, Hong Kong, Indonesia, Italy, Malaysia, Mexico, Netherlands, Nigeria, Norway, Oman, Pakistan, Peru, Qatar, Russia, Saudi Arabia, Scotland, U.K., Singapore, Syria, Thailand, Trinidad & Tobago, United Arab Emirates, Venezuela

J.T. BAKER INC.

222 Red School Lane

Phillipsburg, NJ 08865

Tel: (908) 859-2151 Fax: (908) 859-9318

CEO: Daniel Mulholland, Pres.

FO: C. A. Schluter

HR: Robert A. Book

Emp: 905

Mfr./sale/services lab & process chemicals.

Canada, England, U.K., Germany, Mexico, Netherlands, Singapore, Venezuela

BAKER PETROLITE CORPORATION

3900 Essex Lane

Houston, TX 77027

Tel: (713) 599-7400 Fax: (713) 599-7592

CEO: Glen Bassett, Pres.

Emp: 1,755

Mfr./prod specialty chemical treating programs, performance-enhancing additives & related equipment & services.

Austria, Canada, Ecuador, England, U.K., France, Germany, Indonesia, Italy, Japan, Malaysia, Mexico, Norway, Saudi Arabia, Singapore, Spain, Trinidad & Tobago

BALDWIN PIANO & ORGAN COMPANY

422 Wards Corder Road

Loveland, OH 45140-8390

Tel: (513) 576-4500 Fax: (513) 576-4636

CEO: Karen Hendricks, Pres.

HR: Jerri Hall,

Emp: 1,300

Mfr. pianos, organs, and clocks.

Mexico

BALDWIN TECHNOLOGY CO., INC.

One Norwalk West, 40 Richards Ave.

Norwalk, CT 06854

Tel: (203) 838-7470 Fax: (203) 852-7040

CEO: Gerald A. Nathe, Pres. & Chmn.

FO: Roger Johansson

HR: John Lawlor

Web site: www.baldwintech.com

Emp: 1,060 Rev: $28 mil.

Mfr./services material handling, accessories, control & prepress equipment for print industry.

Australia, China (PRC), England, U.K., France, Germany, Hong Kong, Ireland, Japan, Netherlands, Sweden

BALFOUR MACLAINE CORPORATION

61 Broadway, Ste. 2700

New York, NY 10006-3704

Tel: (212) 269-0800 Fax: (212) 514-7636

CEO: John D. Coffin

HR: A. J. Wilford

Emp: 100

Commodity brokers.

England, U.K.

BALL CORPORATION

345 South High Street

Muncie, IN 47305

Tel: (765) 747-6100 Fax: (765) 747-6203

CEO: George A. Sissel, Pres.

HR: Stephen Bolander

Emp: 13,000

Mfr. metal beverage & food containers, glass containers, aerospace systems & services.

Canada

BALSA ECUADOR LUMBER CORPORATION

10 Fairway Court, PO Box 195

Northvale, NJ 07647

Tel: (201) 767-1400 Fax: (201) 387-6631

CEO: Jack Kohn, Pres.

Light lumber.

Ecuador

BALTIMORE AIRCOIL CO., INC.

7595 Montevideo Road

Jessup, MD 20794

Tel: (410) 799-6200 Fax: (410) 799-6416

CEO: Matthew J. McKenna

FO: J. Joseph Willmott

HR: James R. Kieselhorst

Emp: 1,758

Mfr. evaporative cooling & heat transfer equipment for A/C, refrigeration & industrial process cooling.

Australia, Belgium, England, U.K., Japan, Switzerland

BANANA REPUBLIC

2 Harrison Street

San Francisco, CA 94105

Tel: (415) 777-0250 Fax: (415) 960-0322

CEO: Michael Dadario, EVP

Sales/distribution of clothing, shoes & handbags.

Canada

BAND-IT IDEX CORPORATION

4799 Dahlia Street

Denver, CO 80216

Tel: (303) 320-4555 Fax: (303) 333-6549

CEO: Pete Merkel, Pres.

HR: Sharon Church

Emp: 175

Mfr. pressure clamps.

England, U.K., Singapore

BANDAG INC.

2905 NW Highway 61

Muscatine, IA 52761

Tel: (319) 262-1400 Fax: (319) 262-1252

CEO: Martin G. Carver, Chmn.

FO: Donald F. Chester, SVP

HR: Mel Hershey

Emp: 2,360 Rev: $590 mil.

Mfr./sale retread tires.

Belgium, Brazil, Canada, India, Malaysia, Mexico, Netherlands, New Zealand, Sweden, Switzerland

THE BANK OF NEW YORK

48 Wall Street

New York, NY 10286

Tel: (212) 495-1784 Fax: (212) 495-2546

CEO: Thomas A. Renyi, Chmn. & Pres.

FO: Alan R. Griffith

HR: Thomas Angers

Web site: www.bankofny.com

Emp: 16,000

Banking servces.

Argentina, Australia, Belgium, Brazil, Canada, Cayman Islands, China (PRC), Egypt, England, U.K., France, Germany, Hong Kong, India, Indonesia, Ireland, Italy, Japan, Lebanon, Mexico, Netherlands Antilles, Philippines, Russia, Singapore, South Korea, Spain, Taiwan (ROC), Thailand, Turkey, United Arab Emirates, Uruguay, Venezuela

BANKAMERICA CORPORATION

555 California Street

San Francisco, CA 94104

Tel: (415) 622-3530 Fax: (415) 622-8467

CEO: David A. Coulter, Chmn.

FO: Michael J. Murray, Pres.

HR: Kathleen J. Burke

Web site: www.bankamerica.com

Emp: 90,500 Rev: $ 23,585 mil.

Financial services.

Argentina, Australia, Bahamas, Belgium, Brazil, Canada, Cayman Islands, Channel Islands, U.K., Chile, China (PRC), Colombia, England, U.K., France, Germany, Greece, Hong Kong, India, Indonesia, Ireland, Italy, Japan, Macau, Malaysia, Mexico, Netherlands, Pakistan, Panama, Philippines, Poland, Russia, Singapore, South Africa, South Korea, Spain, Switzerland, Taiwan (ROC), Thailand, United Arab Emirates, Venezuela, Vietnam

BANKBOSTON CORPORATION

100 Federal Street, PO Box 1788

Boston, MA 02110

Tel: (617) 434-2200 Fax: (617) 434-7547

CEO: Charles K. Gifford, Chmn.

FO: Bradford H. Warner, VC

HR: Helen G. Drinan, EVP

Web site: www.bankboston.com

Emp: 21,500 Rev: $69,000 mil.

Banking & insurance services.

Argentina, Bahamas, Brazil, Channel Islands, U.K., Chile, China (PRC), Colombia, England, U.K., France, Germany, Hong Kong, India, Indonesia, Japan, Mexico, Nigeria, Panama, Peru, Philippines, Poland, Portugal, Singapore, South Korea, Taiwan (ROC), Uruguay

BANKERS TRUST COMPANY

280 Park Ave.

New York, NY 10017

Tel: (212) 250-2500 Fax: (212) 250-2440

CEO: Frank N. Newman, Chmn.

FO: B.J. Kingdom

HR: Mark Bieler, EVP

Web site: www.bankerstrust.com

Emp: 18,200 Rev: $12,176 mil.

Banking & investment services.

Argentina, Australia, Bahamas, Bahrain, Belgium, Brazil, Canada, Cayman Islands, Channel Islands, U.K., Chile, China (PRC), Colombia, Czech Republic, Denmark, Egypt, England, U.K., France, Germany, Greece, Hong Kong, Hungary, India, Indonesia, Ireland, Italy, Ivory Coast, Japan, Luxembourg, Malaysia, Mexico, Netherlands, New Zealand, Nigeria, Panama, Peru, Philippines, Poland, Portugal, Scotland, U.K., Singapore, South Africa, South Korea, Spain, Sri Lanka, Switzerland, Taiwan (ROC), Thailand, Tunisia, Turkey, Venezuela, Yugoslavia

C.R. BARD INC.

730 Central Ave.

Murray Hill, NJ 07974

Tel: (908) 277-8000 Fax: (908) 277-8078

CEO: William J. Longfield, Chmn.

FO: Timothy M. Ring, Intl.

HR: Hope Greenfield

Web site: www.crbard.com

Emp: 9,500

Mfr. health care products.

Australia, Belgium, Canada, England, U.K., France, Germany, Hong Kong, India, Ireland, Italy, Japan, Netherlands, Portugal, Singapore, Spain

THE BARDEN CORPORATION

200 Park Ave., PO Box 2449

Danbury, CT 06813-2449

Tel: (203) 744-2211 Fax: (203) 744-3756

CEO: John A. McCloskey

HR: Donald E. Rowland

Emp: 1,300 Rev: $98 mil.

Precision ball bearings.

Brazil, England, U.K.

BARNES GROUP INC.

123 Main Street
Bristol, CT 06011-0489
Tel: (860) 583-7070 Fax: (860) 589-3507
CEO: Theodore E. Martin, Pres.
HR: John Arrington, SVP
Web site: www.barnesgroupinc.com
Emp: 4,200 Rev: $40.4 mil.
Mfr. steel springs, metal parts & supplies.
Brazil, Canada, England, U.K., France, Mexico, Singapore

BARNWELL INDUSTRIES INC.

1100 Alakea Street, Ste. 2900
Honolulu, HI 96813-2833
Tel: (808) 531-8400 Fax: (808) 531-7181
CEO: Morton H. Kinzler, Chmn.
FO: James H. Boyle, VP
HR: Margaret A. Mangan, AVP
Web site: www.brninc.con
Emp: 32 Rev: $14.8
Holding company: exploration/development gas & oil, drill water systems, farming/marketing papayas.
Canada, Israel

BARRINGER TECHNOLOGIES INC.

219 South Street
New Providence, NJ 07974
Tel: (908) 665-8200 Fax: (908) 665-8298
CEO: Stanley S. Binder, Chmn.
FO: K. Mason Schecter, VP
Web site: www.barringer.com
Emp: 119 Rev: $23 mil.
Physical research & testing, engineering services, oil & gas exploration.
Canada, England, U.K., France, Malaysia

BARRY CONTROLS INC.

40 Guest Street, PO Box 9105
Brighton, MA 02135-9105
Tel: (617) 787-1555 Fax: (617) 254-7381
CEO: N/A
Emp: 1,157
Mfr./sale vibration isolation mounting devices.
England, U.K., Germany

R.G. BARRY CORPORATION

13405 Yarmouth Road NW
Pickerington, OH 43147
Tel: (614) 864-6400 Fax: (614) 864-9787
CEO: Gordon Zacks, Pres.
FO: C. Galvis, EVP
HR: Drew Williams
Web site: www.rgbarry.com
Emp: 3,300 Rev: $150.0 mil.
Mfr. slippers & footwear.
China (PRC), England, U.K., France, Mexico, Wales, U.K.

BARRY-WEHMILLER COMPANIES, INC.

8020 Forsyth Boulevard
Clayton, MO 63105
Tel: (314) 862-8000 Fax: (314) 862-8858
CEO: Robert H. Chapman, Pres.
FO: Carlos A. Scheer
HR: Charles H. Borchelt
Web site: www.barry-wehmiller.com
Emp: 1,500 Rev: $260 mil
Mfr. of packaging automation equipment for filling, closing, conveying, cartoning, shrink wrapping & case packing plus systems integration.
England, U.K.

BARTON BRANDS LTD

55 East Monroe Street
Chicago, IL 60603
Tel: (312) 346-9200 Fax: (312) 855-1220
CEO: Alexander Berk, Pres.
FO: Paul Kraus
Emp: 515
Bourbon & blended whiskey.
England, U.K.

BASE TEN SYSTEMS INC.

One Electronics Drive
Trenton, NJ 08619
Tel: (609) 586-7010 Fax: (609) 586-1593
CEO: Thomas Gardner, Pres.
Emp: 160
Mfr. proprietary control systems, flight test systems, communications products.
Belgium, England, U.K., Germany, Ireland

BASSETT MIRROR CO., INC.

PO Box 627
Basset, VA 24055
Tel: (540) 629-3341 Fax: (540) 629-3709
CEO: William B. Morten, Pres.
Emp: 550
Mfr. glass products, metal & upholstered household furniture.
Canada

BATES WORLDWIDE INC.
405 Lexington Ave.
New York, NY 10174
Tel: (212) 297-7000 Fax: (212) 986-0270
CEO: Michael Bungey, Chmn.
FO: Ian Smith, Pres. Intl.
HR: Anne Melanson, EVP
Web site: www.batesww.com
Emp: 7,011 Rev: $520 mil.
Advertising, marketing, public relations & media consulting.
Argentina, Australia, Austria, Bangladesh, Belarus, Belgium, Brazil, Bulgaria, Cambodia, Canada, Chile, China (PRC), Colombia, Costa Rica, Croatia, Czech Republic, Denmark, Dominican Republic, Ecuador, Egypt, El Salvador, England, U.K., Estonia, Finland, France, Germany, Greece, Guatemala, Hong Kong, Hungary, India, Indonesia, Ireland, Israel, Italy, Japan, Jordan, Laos, Latvia, Lebanon, Lithuania, Macedonia, Malaysia, Mexico, Myanmar, Netherlands, New Zealand, Norway, Pakistan, Panama, Peru, Philippines, Poland, Portugal, Romania, Russia, Saudi Arabia, Singapore, Slovenia, South Africa, South Korea, Spain, Sri Lanka, Sweden, Switzerland, Taiwan (ROC), Thailand, Tunisia, Turkey, Ukraine, United Arab Emirates, Uruguay, Venezuela, Vietnam, Yugoslavia

BATTELLE MEMORIAL INSTITUTE
505 King Ave.
Columbus, OH 43201-2693
Tel: (614) 424-6424 Fax: (614) 424-3260
CEO: Dr. Douglas E. Olesen
HR: John Neale
Emp: 8,500
Tech. development, commercialization & management.
England, U.K., Germany, Switzerland

BATTENFELD GREASE & OIL CORP. OF NY
1174 Erie Ave., Box 728
North Tonawanda, NY 14120-0728
Tel: (716) 695-2100 Fax: (716) 695-0367
CEO: John A. Bellanti, Sr., Pres.
FO: Paul P. Converso, VP Mktg.
Web site: www.battenfeld-grease.com
Emp: 160 Rev: $30 mil.
Mfr. petrol products, lubricating greases & oils.
Canada

BAUSCH & LOMB INC.
One Bausch & Lomb Place
Rochester, NY 14604-2701
Tel: (716) 338-6000 Fax: (716) 338-6007
CEO: William M. Carpenter, Pres.
HR: Daryl M. Dickson, SVP
Web site: www.bausch.com
Emp: 13,000 Rev: $1,900 mil.
Mfr. vision care products & accessories & hearing aids.
Australia, Austria, Bermuda, Brazil, Canada, China (PRC), Colombia, Denmark, England, U.K., Finland, France, Germany, Greece, Hong Kong, India, Ireland, Italy, Japan, Malaysia, Mexico, Netherlands, New Zealand, Norway, Philippines, Portugal, Scotland, U.K., Singapore, South Korea, Spain, Sweden, Switzerland, Taiwan (ROC), Turkey, Venezuela

BAX GLOBAL CORPORATION
16808 Armstrong Ave., PO Box 19571
Irvine, CA 92623
Tel: (714) 752-4000 Fax: (714) 852-1488
CEO: C. Robert Campbell
FO: Steve Dearnley, Pres.
HR: Jay Arnold, VP
Web site: www.bax.com
Emp: 7,300
Air freight forwarder.
Australia, Belgium, Brazil, Canada, Chile, China (PRC), Denmark, England, U.K., Estonia, France, Germany, Hong Kong, India, Ireland, Italy, Japan, Malawi, Malaysia, Mexico, Netherlands, New Zealand, Philippines, Portugal, Scotland, U.K., Singapore, South Africa, South Korea, Spain, Sweden, Switzerland, Taiwan (ROC), Wales, U.K., Zambia, Zimbabwe

J.H. BAXTER & COMPANY

1700 S. El Camino Real, Ste. 200

San Mateo, CA 94402-5902

Tel: (650) 349-0201 Fax: (650) 570-6878

CEO: Rick Baxter, Pres.

HR: Ms. Chiye Horiye

Emp: 300

Pressure treated poles, piling & lumber.

Canada

BAXTER HEALTHCARE CORPORATION

One Baxter Parkway

Deerfield, IL 60015

Tel: (847) 948-2000 Fax: (847) 948-3948

CEO: Harry M. J. Kraemer, Jr., Pres

FO: Carlos del Salto, SVP

HR: Michael J. Tucker, SVP

Web site: www.baxter.com

Emp: 40,900 Rev: $6,700 mil.

Pharmaceutical preparations, surgical/medical instruments & cardiovascular products.

Australia, Austria, Barbados, Belgium, Brazil, Canada, Colombia, Costa Rica, Czech Republic, Denmark, Dominican Republic, England, U.K., Finland, France, Germany, Greece, Hong Kong, Hungary, Ireland, Italy, Japan, Malaysia, Malta, Mexico, Netherlands, Netherlands Antilles, New Zealand, Norway, Panama, Poland, Russia, Singapore, South Korea, Spain, Sweden, Switzerland, Taiwan (ROC), Venezuela

BBDO WORLDWIDE

1285 Ave. of the Americas

New York, NY 10019

Tel: (212) 459-5000 Fax: (212) 459-6645

CEO: Allen Rosenshine, Chmn.

Web site: www.bbdo.com

Emp: 13,354 Rev: $1,467 mil.

Multinational group of advertising agencies.

Argentina, Australia, Austria, Belgium, Brazil, Canada, Chile, China (PRC), Colombia, Costa Rica, Croatia, Czech Republic, Denmark, Egypt, Finland, France, Germany, Greece, Hong Kong, Hungary, India, Indonesia, Israel, Italy, Kuwait, Lebanon, Mexico, Netherlands, New Zealand, Norway, Panama, Peru, Philippines, Poland, Portugal, Romania, Russia, Saudi Arabia, Singapore, Slovakia, South Korea, Spain, Sweden, Taiwan (ROC), Thailand, Turkey, United Arab Emirates, Venezuela

BCS, INC.

8745 Remmet Ave.

Canoga Park, CA 91304

Tel: (888) 286-7188 Fax: (800) 500-4483

CEO: Jonathan Manhan, Pres.

FO: Larry Manhan, CEO

Electronic recycling services, buying and selling surplus inventories and equipment.

Mexico

BDO SEIDMAN, LLP

Two Prudential Plaza, 180 N. Stetson Ave., Ste. 2300

Chicago, IL 60601

Tel: (312) 240-1236 Fax: (312) 240-3329

CEO: Daniel Pavelich, Chmn.

HR: Warren Holmes

Web site: www.bdo.com

Emp: 16,022 Rev: $1,450 mil.

International accounting & financial consulting firm.

Argentina, Australia, Austria, Bahamas, Belgium, Brazil, British Virgin Islands, Bulgaria, Canada, Channel Islands, U.K., Chile, China (PRC), Colombia, Cyprus, Czech Republic, Denmark, Ecuador, Egypt, England, U.K., Fiji, Finland, France, Germany, Gibraltar, Greece, Guatemala, Hong Kong, Hungary, Iceland, India, Indonesia, Ireland, Isle of Man, Israel, Italy, Japan, Jordan, Kuwait, Lebanon, Luxembourg, Malaysia, Malta, Mauritius, Mexico, Morocco, Namibia, Netherlands, Netherlands Antilles, New Zealand, Norway, Oman, Pakistan, Palestine, Peru, Philippines, Poland, Portugal, Russia, Saudi Arabia, Senegal, Singapore, Slovakia, South Africa, South Korea, Spain, Sweden, Switzerland, Taiwan (ROC), Thailand, Tunisia, Turkey, Turkmenistan, Ukraine, United Arab Emirates, Uruguay, Vanuatu, Venezuela, Zambia, Zimbabwe

BEA SYSTEMS, INC.

2315 North First Street

St. Jose, CA 95131

Tel: (408) 570-8000 Fax: (408) 570-8091

CEO: William T. Coleman III, Chmn.

FO: Edward W. Scott Jr., EVP

Web site: www.beasys.com

Emp: 800 Rev: $157 mil.

Develops communications management software & provider of software consulting services.

Australia, Belgium, Brazil, Canada, China (PRC), Denmark, England, U.K., Finland, France, Germany, Hong Kong, Italy, Japan, Mexico, Netherlands, New Zealand, Norway, Singapore, South Africa, South Korea, Spain, Sweden, Switzerland, Taiwan (ROC), Thailand

D. D. BEAN & SONS COMPANY

Peterborough Road, PO Box 348

Jaffrey, NH 03452

Tel: (603) 532-8311 Fax: (603) 532-7361

CEO: Delcie D. Bean, Pres.

FO: Mark C. Bean

Emp: 250

Mfr. paper book & wooden stick matches.

Canada, Jamaica

BEAR STEARNS & CO., INC.

245 Park Ave.

New York, NY 10167

Tel: (212) 272-2000 Fax: (212) 272-3092

CEO: James E. Cayne, Pres.

FO: Jeffrey C. Bernstein

HR: Steven A. Lacoff

Web site: www.bearstearns.com

Emp: 8,000 Rev: $6,700 mil.

Investment banking, securities broker/dealer & investment advisory services.

Argentina, Brazil, China (PRC), England, U.K., France, Hong Kong, Ireland, Japan, Singapore, Switzerland

BEARIUM METALS CORPORATION

4106 South Creek Road

Chattanooga, TN 37406

Tel: (423) 622-9991 Fax: (423) 622-9991

CEO: J. W. Adams, Pres.

Emp: 75

Bearium metal alloys.

Canada, France

BECHTEL GROUP INC.

50 Beale Street, PO Box 3965

San Francisco, CA 94105-1895

Tel: (415) 768-1234 Fax: (415) 768-9038

CEO: Riley P. Bechtel, Chmn.

FO: Adrian Zaccaria, Pres.

HR: Granville H. Bowie, SVP HR

Web site: www.bechtel.com

Emp: 30,000 Rev: $11,329 mil.

General contractors in engineering & construction.

Algeria, Argentina, Australia, Azerbaijan, Belgium, Bolivia, Brazil, Canada, Chile, China (PRC), Egypt, England, U.K., France, Germany, Hong Kong, India, Indonesia, Japan, Jordan, Kuwait, Malaysia, Mexico, Netherlands, New Zealand, Nigeria, Oman, Peru, Philippines, Russia, Saudi Arabia, Singapore, South Africa, South Korea, Spain, Switzerland, Taiwan (ROC), Tanzania, Thailand, Trinidad & Tobago, Turkey, United Arab Emirates, Venezuela, Vietnam, Zambia

BECKER & POLIAKOFF, P.A.

Emerald Lake Corporate Park, 3111 Stirling Road

Fort Lauderdale, FL 33312

Tel: (954) 987-7550 Fax: (954) 985-4176

CEO: Gary Poliakoff

Emp: 57

Law firm; advice & assistance with foreign investments.

China (PRC), Czech Republic

BECKETT BROWN INTERNATIONAL

Three Church Circle, Ste. 207

Annapolis, MD 21401

Tel: (410) 315-7995 Fax: (410) 315-8882

CEO: Richard Beckett, Pres.

FO: Dave Bresett

HR: Lisa Tucker

Web site: www.beckettbrown.com

Emp: 125

Security company.

China (PRC), Hong Kong, Singapore, South Korea

BECKMAN COULTER

4300 Harbor Boulevard

Fullerton, CA 92835

Tel: (714) 871-4848 Fax: (714) 773-8898

CEO: John P. Wareham, Pres.

FO: A.Torrellas/B. Tatarion

HR: F. Mares

Emp: 5,900

Develop/mfr./marketing automated systems & supplies for biological analysis.

Australia, Austria, Canada, England, U.K., France, Germany, Hong Kong, Ireland, Italy, Japan, Mexico, Netherlands, Poland, Singapore, South Africa, Spain, Sweden, Switzerland, Taiwan (ROC)

BECTON DICKINSON AND COMPANY

One Becton Drive

Franklin Lakes, NJ 07417-1880

Tel: (201) 847-6800 Fax: (201) 847-6475

CEO: Clateo Castellini, Chmn.

HR: Rosemary Mede

Emp: 18,500 Rev: $2,000 mil.

Mfr./sale medical supplies, devices & diagnostic systems.

Brazil, Canada, France, Japan, Mexico, Singapore

BEL FUSE INC.

198 Van Vorst Street

Jersey City, NJ 07302

Tel: (201) 432-0463 Fax: (201) 432-9542

CEO: Daniel Bernstein, Pres.

FO: Dennis Ackerman

HR: Miriam Martinez

Emp: 724

Mfr. electronic components for networking, fuses, delay lines, hybrids & magnetic products.

Hong Kong, Macau

BELCO OIL & GAS CORPORATION

767 Fifth Ave., 46th Floor

New York, NY 10153

Tel: (212) 644-2200 Fax: (212) 644-2230

CEO: Robert Belfer

Emp: 3,070

Exploration & production of crude oil & natural gas.

Canada, Ecuador, Peru

BELDEN WIRE & CABLE COMPANY

2200 US Highway South, PO Box 1980

Richmond, IN 47374

Tel: (765) 983-5200 Fax: (765) 983-5294

CEO: Peter Wickman, Pres.

Web site: www.belden.com

Mfr. electronic wire & cable products.

Canada

BELL & HOWELL COMPANY

5215 Old Orchard Road

Skokie, IL 60077

Tel: (847) 470-7100 Fax: (847) 470-9625

CEO: James Roemer, Chmn.

HR: Marie Rubly, VP

Web site: www.bellhowell.com

Emp: 4,000

Diversified information products & services.

Australia, Belgium, Canada, England, U.K., France, Japan

BELL ATLANTIC CORPORATION

1095 Ave. of the Americas

New York, NY 10036

Tel: (212) 395-2121 Fax: (212) 395-1285

CEO: Raymond W. Smith, Chmn.

FO: John F. Killian, Pres. Intl.

HR: Donald J. Sacco, EVP

Web site: www.bellatlantic.com

Emp: 140,000 Rev: $30,000 mil.

Telecommunications.

Czech Republic, England, U.K., Greece, India, Indonesia, Italy, Japan, Mexico, New Zealand, Philippines, Slovakia, Thailand

BELL HELICOPTER TEXTRON INC.

PO Box 482

Fort Worth, TX 76101

Tel: (817) 280-2011 Fax: (817) 280-2321

CEO: Terry D. Stinson, Pres.

FO: Fred N. Huggard, Sr. VP

HR: George Metzger

Emp: 7,800

Mfr./sale/service helicopters, air cushion vehicles and rocket engines.

Brazil, Canada, Netherlands

BELL POLE LTD

PO Box 2786

New Brighton, MN 55112

Tel: (612) 633-4334 Fax: (612) 633-8852

CEO: Merton Bell, Pres.

Emp: 150

Mfr. poles.

Canada

BELL SPORTS INC.

6350 San Ignacio Ave.

San Jose, CA 95119

Tel: (408) 574-3400 Fax: (408) 224-9129

CEO: Mary George, Pres.

Emp: 600

Mfr. bicycle and automotive racing helmets and accessories.

France

BELLSOUTH INTERNATIONAL

1155 Peachtree Street NE, Ste. 400

Atlanta, GA 30367

Tel: (404) 249-4800 Fax: (404) 249-4880

CEO: Charles C. Miller III, Pres.

HR: John Haseldon

Web site: www.bellsouth.com

Emp: 81,000 Rev: $20,561 mil.

Mobile communications, telecommunications network systems.

Argentina, Australia, Brazil, Chile, China (PRC), Denmark, Ecuador, England, U.K., France, Germany, Hong Kong, India, Israel, New Zealand, Nicaragua, Panama, Peru, Uruguay, Venezuela

BELVEDERE COMPANY

One Belvedere Boulevard

Belvedere, IL 61008-8596

Tel: (815) 544-3131 Fax:

CEO: Martin Holmes, Pres.

Emp: 202

Mfr. beauty salon equipment.

Mexico

BEMIS CO., INC.

222 South 9th Street, Ste. 2300

Minneapolis, MN 55402-4099

Tel: (612) 376-3000 Fax: (612) 376-3180

CEO: John Roe

HR: Lawrence E. Schwanke

Emp: 7,855

Mfr. flexible packaging, specialty coated & graphics products.

Belgium, Canada, Germany

BEN & JERRY'S HOMEMADE INC.

30 Community Drive

South Burlington, VT 05403-6828

Tel: (802) 651-9600 Fax: (802) 651-9647

CEO: Ben Cohen, Chmn.

FO: Bruce Bowman, COO

HR: Richard Doran, Dir.

Web site: www.benjerry.com

Premium ice cream.

Canada, England, U.K., France, Israel, Netherlands, Russia

BENEFICIAL CORPORATION

301 N. Walnut Street

Wilmington, DE 19801

Tel: (302) 425-2500 Fax: (302) 425-2518

CEO: Finn M. W. Caspersen, Chmn.

FO: David J. Farris, Pres. & COO

HR: Challis M. Lowe, EVP HR

Web site: www.bnlcorp.com

Emp: 10,200 Rev: $2,956 mil.

Consumer financial, banking, and insurance services.

England, U.K., Germany, Ireland

BENJAMIN MOORE & COMPANY

51 Chestnut Ridge Road

Montvale, NJ 07645

Tel: (201) 573-9600 Fax: (201) 573-9046

CEO: Richard Roob, Chmn.

HR: Charles Vail

Emp: 1,200

Mfr. paints and varnishes.

Canada, New Zealand

BENSHAW INC.

1659 East Sutter Road

Glenshaw, PA 15116

Tel: (412) 487-8235 Fax: (412) 487-4201

CEO: Fran X. Livingston, Mgr.

FO: Ron Vines

Emp: 95

Mfr. solid state A/C motor controls.

Canada

BENTLY NEVADA CORPORATION

1617 Water Street, PO Box 157

Minden, NV 89423

Tel: (702) 782-3611 Fax: (702) 782-9259

CEO: Roger Harker, Pres.

FO: Steven Riggs

Emp: 900 Rev: $57 mil.

Electronic monitoring systems.

Argentina, Australia, Brazil, Canada, Chile, China (PRC), Colombia, England, U.K., France, Germany, Greece, India, Japan, Kuwait, Malaysia, Mexico, Netherlands, New Zealand, Nigeria, Norway, Saudi Arabia, Singapore, South Africa, South Korea, Taiwan (ROC), United Arab Emirates, Venezuela

BERGEN BRUNSWIG CORPORATION

4000 Metropolitan Drive

Orange, CA 92868-3598

Tel: (714) 385-4000 Fax: (714) 385-1442

CEO: Robert E. Martini, Chmn.

FO: Donald R. Roden, Pres.

HR: Carol E. Scherman, EVP

Web site: www.bergenbrunswig.com

Emp: 5,000 Rev: $12,000 mil

Wholesale pharmaceutical distributor supplying drugs and medical/surgical supplies to managed care facililties and hospitals.

Guam, Mexico

LOUIS BERGER INTERNATIONAL INC.

100 Halsted Street

East Orange, NJ 07019

Tel: (201) 678-1960 Fax: (201) 672-4284

CEO: Derish M. Wolff

HR: Richard Bergailo

Web site: www.louisberger.com

Emp: 1,700

Consulting engineers, architects, economists & planners.

Albania, Angola, Argentina, Armenia, Bangladesh, Belarus, Benin, Bolivia, Bosnia-Herzegovina, Burkina Faso, Burundi, Cambodia, Cameroon, Canada, Central African Republic, Chad, China (PRC), Cyprus, Dem. Rep. of Congo, Egypt, El Salvador, England, U.K., Ethiopia, France, Ghana, Greece, Grenada, Guinea, Honduras, Hong Kong, Hungary, India, Indonesia, Ivory Coast, Jamaica, Japan, Kazakhstan, Kenya, Lebanon, Madagascar, Malaysia, Mali, Mexico, Morocco, Mozambique, Nepal, Nicaragua, Niger, Nigeria, Pakistan, Panama, Paraguay, Peru, Philippines, Qatar, Romania, Russia, Senegal, Singapore, South Africa, South Korea, Sweden, Taiwan (ROC), Tanzania, Thailand, Turkey, Uganda, Uruguay, Vietnam, Zambia, Zimbabwe

BERNARD HODES GROUP

555 Madison Ave.

New York, NY 10022

Tel: (212) 935-4000 Fax: (212) 755-7324

CEO: Bernard Hodes, Pres.

Web site: www.hodes.com

Emp: 1,059 Rev: $130.7 mil.

Multinational recruitment agency.

Canada, England, U.K., Hong Kong

THE BERRY COMPANY

3170 Kettering Blvd.

Dayton, OH 45439

Tel: (937) 296-2121 Fax: (937) 296-2037

CEO: Elmer Smith, Pres.

FO: Smith

HR: Lynn Strassberg

Emp: 1,900

Advertising agency.

Sweden

BESSEMER GROUP, INC.

630 Fifth Ave., 39th Fl.

New York, NY 10022

Tel: (212) 708-9100 Fax: (212) 265-5826

CEO: Stuart Janney, Chmn.

FO: John Whitmore, Pres.

HR: Mary Martinez

Emp: 45

Consumer goods retail financing.

China (PRC)

BESSER COMPANY

801 Johnson Street, PO Box 336

Alpena, MI 49707

Tel: (517) 354-4111 Fax: (517) 354-3120

CEO: James C. Park, Pres.

FO: Kevin L. Curtis

HR: Joseph A. Cercone

Emp: 600

Mfr. equipment for concrete products industry; complete turnkey services.

Australia, Canada

BEST FORM, INC.

136 Madison Ave.

New York, NY 10016

Tel: (212) 696-1110 Fax: (212) 532-5708

CEO: Eric Wiseman, Pres.

Mfr. foundation garments.

Colombia, Germany, Venezuela

BEST LOCK CORPORATION

6161 East 75th Street

Indianapolis, IN 46250

Tel: (317) 849-2250 Fax: (317) 841-9852

CEO: Russell Best, Pres.

Emp: 900

Mfr. locking systems.

Canada

BEST WESTERN INTERNATIONAL

6201 North 24th Place

Phoenix, AZ 85106

Tel: (602) 957-4200 Fax: (602) 957-5740

CEO: Jerry Manion, COO

HR: Vicky Winston

International hotel chain.

Argentina, Aruba, Austria, Bahamas, Bahrain, Belgium, Botswana, Brazil, Canada, Cayman Islands, Chile, Costa Rica, Cyprus, Czech Republic, Denmark, Ecuador, Egypt, El Salvador, England, U.K., Finland, France, Germany, Greece, Guatemala, Honduras, Hungary, India, Indonesia, Ireland, Israel, Italy, Japan, Malaysia, Mauritius, Mexico, Myanmar, Netherlands, Norway, Pakistan, Panama, Portugal, Reunion, Russia, Scotland, U.K., Seychelles, Spain, Sri Lanka, Sweden, Switzerland, Thailand, Venezuela

BESTFOODS, INC.

700 Sylvan Ave., International Plaza

Englewood Cliffs, NJ 07632-9976

Tel: (201) 894-4000 Fax: (201) 894-2186

CEO: Charles R. Shoemate, Chmn.

FO: Alain Labergère, Pres. Europe

HR: Richard P. Bergeman, SVP

Web site: www.bestfoods.com

Emp: 44,200 Rev: $8,400 mil.

Consumer foods products; corn refining.

Argentina, Austria, Belgium, Bolivia, Brazil, Bulgaria, Canada, Chile, China (PRC), Colombia, Costa Rica, Czech Republic, Denmark, Dominican Republic, Ecuador, England, U.K., Finland, France, Germany, Greece, Guatemala, Hong Kong, Hungary, India, Indonesia, Ireland, Israel, Italy, Japan, Jordan, Kenya, Malaysia, Malta, Mexico, Morocco, Netherlands, New Zealand, Nigeria, Norway, Pakistan, Paraguay, Peru, Philippines, Poland, Portugal, Romania, Russia, Saudi Arabia, Singapore, Slovenia, South Africa, South Korea, Spain, Sri Lanka, Sweden, Switzerland, Taiwan (ROC), Thailand, Tunisia, Turkey, Uruguay, Venezuela, Vietnam, Wales, U.K., Yugoslavia

BETSEY JOHNSON INC.

498 Seventh Ave., 21st Fl.

New York, NY 10018

Tel: (212) 244-0843 Fax: (212) 244-0855

CEO: Betsey Johnson, Pres.

Fashion clothing line.

England, U.K.

BETZDEARBORN

4636 Somerton Road, PO Box 3002

Trevose, PA 19053-6783

Tel: (215) 953-2568 Fax: (215) 953-5524

CEO: William R. Cook, Pres. & Chmn.

FO: Larry V. Rankin, SVP Corp. Dev.

HR: June B. Barry

Web site: www.betzdearborn.com

Emp: 6,400 Rev: $1,300 mil.

Mfr. water/wastewater and process system treatment chemicals and services.

Argentina, Australia, Austria, Belgium, Brazil, Canada, Chile, Colombia, Denmark, Ecuador, England, U.K., Finland, France, Germany, Hong Kong, India, Indonesia, Ireland, Italy, Japan, Malaysia, Mexico, Netherlands, Norway, Peru, Poland, Portugal, Singapore, South Africa, South Korea, Spain, Sweden, Taiwan (ROC), Thailand, Uruguay, Venezuela

BEVERLY ENTERPRISES INC.

1200 South Waldron Road

Ft. Smith, AR 72903

Tel: (501) 452-6712 Fax: (501) 452-5131

CEO: David R. Banks, Pres.

Emp: 109,000

Nursing homes, retirement living centers, pharmacies.

Japan

BICKLEY INC.

PO Box 369

Bensalem, PA 19020

Tel: (215) 638-4500 Fax: (215) 638-4334

CEO: Vincent P. Harris

FO: Frederik C. Sas

HR: Harry K. Brown

Web site: www.ceramics.com/bickley

Emp: 50

Mfr. high temp. furnaces.

China (PRC)

BIJUR LUBRICATING CORPORATION

50 Kocher Drive

Bennington, VT 05201-1994

Tel: (802) 447-2174 Fax: (802) 447-1365

CEO: Carl Goodwin, Pres.

FO: Carl Goodwin

HR: Roger Yamamoto

Web site: www.bijur.com

Emp: 350

Design/mfr. centralized lubrication equipment for industrial machinery.

China (PRC), France, Ireland, Switzerland

BINDICATOR

1915 Dove Street

Port Huron, MI 48060

Tel: (810) 987-2700 Fax: (810) 987-4476

CEO: Norman F. Marsh, Pres.

FO: Carrie E. Blackmer

HR: Monica Boudreau

Emp: 90 Rev: $18 mil.

Mfr. level control instruments for measuring solids and liquids.

China (PRC)

SAMUEL BINGHAM COMPANY

127 East Lake Street, Ste. 300

Bloomgindale, IL 60108

Tel: (630) 924-9250 Fax: (630) 924-0469

CEO: Larry Ekstrom, Pres.

HR: Steve Stelter

Web site: www.binghamrollers.com

Emp: 600

Print and industrial rollers and inks.

Canada, Chile, Ecuador, Finland, Indonesia, Israel, Jamaica, Kenya, Mexico, New Zealand, Nigeria, Peru, Singapore, South Africa, Sri Lanka, Switzerland, Trinidad & Tobago, Turkey, Venezuela, Zambia

BINGHAM DANA LLP

150 Federal Street

Boston, MA 02110

Tel: (617) 951-8000 Fax: (617) 951-8736

CEO: Jay S. Zimmerman, Mng. Prtn.

HR: Lynn A. Carroll

Web site: www.bingham.com

Emp: 688

Law firm.

England, U.K.

BINKS MFG. COMPANY

9201 West Belmont Ave.

Franklin Park, IL 60131

Tel: (708) 671-3000 Fax: (708) 671-6489

CEO: Richard Kodrick

FO: John Baur

Emp: 1,600

Mfr. of spray painting and finishing equipment.

Australia, Belgium, Canada, England, U.K., France, Germany, Italy, Japan, Mexico, South Africa, Sweden

BINNEY & SMITH INC.

1100 Church Lane, PO Box 431

Easton, PA 18044-0431

Tel: (610) 253-6271 Fax: (610) 250-5768

CEO: Richard S. Gurin, Pres.

FO: Graham Wyles

HR: David Burford

Emp: 1,742

Mfr. rayons, art supplies and craft kits.

Australia, Canada, England, U.K., France, Mexico

BIO-RAD LABORATORIES INC.

1000 Alfred Nobel Drive

Hercules, CA 94547

Tel: (510) 724-7000 Fax: (510) 724-3167

CEO: David Schwartz, Pres.

HR: Chris Crispel

Emp: 2,300 Rev: $419 mil.

Mfr. life science research products, clinical diagnostics, analytical instruments.

Australia, Austria, Belgium, Canada, China (PRC), Denmark, England, U.K., France, Germany, Hong Kong, Israel, Italy, Japan, Netherlands, New

Zealand, Spain, Sweden, Switzerland

BIOMATRIX INC.

65 Railroad Ave.

Ridgefield, NJ 07657

Tel: (201) 945-9550 Fax: (201) 945-0363

CEO: Endre A. Balazs, MD

FO: Johaan W. Scheidt, VP

HR: Nina Esaki, Dir. HR

Web site: www.biomatrix.com

Emp: 220 Rev: $11 mil.

Mfr. hylan biological polymers for therapeutic medical and skin care products.

Canada, England, U.K., France, Hong Kong, Sweden, Switzerland

BIOWHITTAKER INC.

8830 Biggs Ford Road

Walkersville, MD 21793

Tel: (301) 898-7025 Fax: (301) 845-6099

CEO: Noel L. Buterbaugh, Pres.

HR: Rich Patchak

Emp: 510

Mfr. cell culture products, endotoxin detection assays.

England, U.K.

BIRD MACHINE CORPORATION

PO Box 9103

South Walpole, MA 02071

Tel: (508) 668-0400 Fax: (508) 668-6855

CEO: Tim Davis, Pres.

HR: Tim McGowan

Web site: www.Baker Hughes.com

Emp: 800 Rev: $220 mil.

Mfr. of liquid solid separation equipment.

Canada, Germany

BISSELL INC.

2345 Walker Road, NW

Grand Rapids, MI 49504

Tel: (616) 453-4451 Fax: (616) 453-1383

CEO: Mark J. Bissell, Pres.

HR: Tom McInerney

Emp: 2,000

Mfr. home care products.

France, Ireland

BIW CABLE SYSTEMS INC.

22 Joseph E. Warner Boulevard

N. Dighton, MA 02764-O6O4

Tel: (508) 822-5444 Fax: (508) 822-1944

CEO: Dimitri Naistrellis, Pres.

HR: Deb Shell

Emp: 207

Mfr. Electric wire, cable, cable assemblies and connectors.

Canada

BLACK & DECKER CORPORATION

701 E. Joppa Road

Towson, MD 21286

Tel: (410) 716-3900 Fax: (410) 716-2933

CEO: Nolan D. Archibald,

FO: A. van Schijndel & R. Thomas

HR: Leonard A.Strom

Web site: www.blackanddecker.com

Emp: 28,600 Rev: $5,000 mil.

Mfr. power tools and accessories, security hardware, small appliances, fasteners, information systems & services.

Australia, Austria, Belgium, Brazil, Canada, Chile, Denmark, England, U.K., Finland, France, Germany, Italy, Japan, Liechtenstein, Mexico, Netherlands, New Zealand, Norway, Singapore, Spain, Sweden, Switzerland, Venezuela

BLACK & VEATCH INTERNATIONAL

8400 Ward Pkwy., PO Box 8405

Kansas City, MO 64114

Tel: (913) 339-2000 Fax: (913) 339-2934

CEO: P. J. Adam, Chmn.

FO: John H. Robinson, Jr.

Emp: 8,000 Rev: $1,800 mil.

Engineering, architectural and construction services.

Australia, Egypt, England, U.K., Hong Kong, Japan, Poland, Thailand, Turkey, Wales, U.K.

BLACK BOX CORPORATION

1000 Park Drive

Lawrence, PA 15055

Tel: (724) 746-5500 Fax: (724) 746-0746

CEO: Jeffery M. Boetticher

FO: R. Croft

HR: Marisa Warford

Web site: www.blackbox.com

Emp: 950 Rev: $275 mil.

Direct marketer and technical service provider of communications, networking and related computer connectivity products.

Australia, Belgium, Brazil, Canada, England, U.K., France, Germany, Italy, Japan, Mexico, Netherlands, Spain, Switzerland

BLACK CLAWSON COMPANY

405 Lexington Ave., 61st Fl.

New York, NY 10174

Tel: (212) 916-8000 Fax: (212) 916-8057

CEO: Carl Landegger, Chmn.

Emp: 2,000

Paper and pulp mill machinery.

England, U.K., France, India, South Africa

THE BLACKSTONE GROUP INC.

360 North Michigan Ave.

Chicago, IL 60601

Tel: (312) 419-0400 Fax: (312) 419-8419

CEO: Ashref A. Hashim

Emp: 65

Marketing research, business consulting, engineering design & software.

India

BLACKSTONE MFG. CO., INC.

4630 West Harrison Ave.

Chicago, IL 60644

Tel: (773) 378-7800 Fax: (773) 378-8194

CEO: Bob Magasi, Mgr.

Emp: 350

Automotive products.

Mexico

BLAKESLEE

1844 South Laramie Ave.

Chicago, IL 60804

Tel: (708) 656-0660 Fax: (708) 656-0017

CEO: Erik O. Vilen

FO: Pirjo Stafseth

HR: Gary Stafseth

Emp: 205 Rev: $20 mil.

Food mixers, food preparation equipment and commercial dishwashers.

Canada

BLISS & LAUGHLIN STEEL COMPANY

281 East 155th Street

Harvey, IL 60426

Tel: (708) 333-1220 Fax:

CEO: Thomas Tyrell, Pres

Mfr. steel bars for industrial use.

Canada

H&R BLOCK, INC.

4400 Main Street

Kansas City, MO 64111

Tel: (816) 753-6900 Fax: (816) 753-8628

CEO: Frank Salizzoni, Pres.

FO: Ozzie Wenich, SVP & CFO

HR: Doug Waltman, VP

Web site: www.hrblock.com

Emp: 4,700

Tax preparation services & software, financial products and services & mortgage loans.

Australia, Bermuda, Canada, England, U.K., New Zealand

BLOOMBERG L.P.

499 Park Ave.

New York, NY 10022

Tel: (212) 318-2000 Fax: (212) 940-1954

CEO: Michael R. Bloomberg, Pres.

FO: Susan Friedlander, COO

HR: Lori Riordan

Web site: www.bloomberg.com

Emp: 4,000

Publishes magazines and provides TV, radio and newspaper wire services.

Argentina, Brazil, Chile, England, U.K., Hong Kong, Japan

BLOUNT INC.

4520 Executive Park Drive

Montgomery, AL 36116-1602

Tel: (334) 244-4000 Fax: (334) 271-8130

CEO: John M. Panettiere

HR: D. Joseph McInnes

Web site: www.blount.com

Emp: 5,700 Rev: $500 mil.

Mfr. cutting chain & equipment, timber harvest/handling equipment, sporting ammo, riding mowers.

Belgium, Brazil, Canada, England, U.K., Germany, Japan, Sweden

BLUE BIRD CORPORATION

3920 Arkwright Road, PO Box 7839

Macon, GA 31210

Tel: (912) 757-7100 Fax: (912) 474-9131

CEO: Paul Glaske, Pres.

FO: Mark Welden

HR: Rick Hudson

Emp: 2,800

Mfr./sale/services buses, parts and accessories.

Canada, Mexico

BLUE CROSS AND BLUE SHIELD ASSOC.

225 N. Michigan Ave.

Chicago, IL 60601-7680

Tel: (312) 297-6000 Fax: (312) 297-6609

CEO: Raymond P. McCaskey, Chmn.

FO: Patrick G. Hays, Pres.

Web site: www.bluecares.com

Emp: 15,000 Rev: $75,000 mil.

Provides health care coverage through indemnity insurance, HMO's and Medicare programs.

Jamaica, Japan, Mexico

BMC INDUSTRIES INC.

One Meridian Crossings, Ste. 850

Minneapolis, MN 55423

Tel: (612) 851-6000 Fax: (612) 851-6065

CEO: Paul B. Burke, Pres.

HR: Jim Brewer, Director

Web site: www.bmcind.com

Emp: 3,000 Rev: $320 mil,

Design/mfr./marketing precision etched products, electroformed components, special printed circuits, ophthalmic devices.

Germany, Hungary

BOART LONGYEAR CO.

2340 West 1700 South

Salt Lake City, UT 84104

Tel: (801) 972-6430 Fax: (801) 977-3372

CEO: Rich Swayne, Pres.

HR: W. Weston

Emp: 2,000 Rev: $290 mil.

Mfr. diamond drills, concrete cutting equipment and drill services.

Australia, Canada, Chile, Costa Rica, France, Germany, Mexico, Netherlands, New Zealand, Philippines, Spain

THE BOEING COMPANY

7755 East Marginal Way South

Seattle, WA 98108

Tel: (206) 655-2121 Fax: (206) 655-6300

CEO: Philip M. Condit, Chmn.

FO: Harry Stonecipher, Pres.

Web site: www.boeing.com.

Rev: $22 mil.

World's largest aerospace company; mfr. military and commercial aircraft, missiles and sattelite launch vehicles.

Australia, England, U.K., France, Germany

BOGUE ELECTRIC MFG. COMPANY

100 Pennsylvania Ave.

Paterson, NJ 07509

Tel: (973) 523-2200 Fax: (973) 278-8468

CEO: A. Sabbatino

FO: K. Wray

HR: R. Lanza

Web site: www.Bogueelectric.com

Emp: 50 Rev: $3 mil.

Electrical equipment, power supplies, battery chargers and micro projector controlled motors.

Italy

BOISE CASCADE CORPORATION

1111 West Jefferspm Street, PO Box 50

Boise, ID 83728-0001

Tel: (208) 384-6161 Fax: (208) 384-7189

CEO: George J. Harad, Chmn.

FO: Terry R. Lock, Sr. VP, Intl.

HR: J. Michael Gwartney, VP

Web site: www.bc.com

Emp: 17,200

Mfr./distributor paper and paper products, building products, office products.

Australia, Canada, China (PRC), England, U.K., France, Germany, Mexico, Netherlands

BOND FOUNDRY & MACHINE COMPANY

230 South Penn Street

Manheim, PA 17545

Tel: (717) 665-2275 Fax: (717) 665-3336

CEO: Louis Bond, Pres.

Emp: 50

Transmission appliances.

Canada

BOOK-OF-THE-MONTH CLUB INC.

1271 Ave. of the Americas

New York, NY 10020

Tel: (212) 522-4200 Fax: (212) 522-0303

CEO: George Artandi, Pres.

Web site: www.bomc.com

Emp: 700

Retail books to mail subscribers; phonograph records, art and reading courses.

Canada

BOOLE & BABBAGE, INC.

3131 Zanker Road

San Jose, CA 95134

Tel: (408) 526-3000 Fax: (408) 526-3055

CEO: Paul Newton, Pres.

FO: Han Bruggeling

HR: Victoria Reader

Web site: www.boole.com

Emp: 645

Develop/support enterprise automation & systems management software.

Austria, Belgium, Denmark, England, U.K., Finland, France, Germany, Ireland, Italy, Netherlands, Spain, Sweden, Switzerland

BOOZ ALLEN & HAMILTON INC.

8283 Greensboro Drive

McLean, VA 22102

Tel: (703) 902-5000 Fax: (703) 902-3333

CEO: William F. Stasior, Chmn.

FO: Ralph W. Shrader, Pres.

HR: Joni Bessler

Web site: www.bah.com

Emp: 8,000 Rev: $1,400 mil.

International management and technology consultants.

Argentina, Australia, Austria, Brazil, Canada, Chile, China (PRC), Colombia, England, U.K., France, Germany, Hong Kong, India, Indonesia, Italy, Japan, Mexico, Netherlands, New Zealand, Panama, Peru, Poland, Russia, Singapore, South Africa, South Korea, Spain, Switzerland, Thailand, Ukraine, United Arab Emirates, Venezuela

BORDEN INC.

180 East Broad Street

Columbus, OH 43215-3799

Tel: (614) 225-4000 Fax: (614) 220-6453

CEO: C. Robert Kidder, Chmn.

HR: Nancy A. Reardon, SVP

Emp: 12,000 Rev: $3.4 mil.

Mfr. Packaged foods, consumer adhesives, housewares and industrial chemicals.

Argentina, Australia, Belgium, Brazil, Canada, Colombia, Denmark, Ecuador, England, U.K., France, Ireland, Italy, Malaysia, Philippines, Spain, Uruguay

BORG-WARNER AUTOMOTIVE INC.

200 S. Michigan Ave.

Chicago, IL 60604

Tel: (312) 322-8500 Fax: (312) 461-0507

CEO: John F. Fiedler, Chmn.

HR: Geraldine Kinsella

Emp: 7,300

Mfr. automotive components; provider of security services.

Canada, China (PRC), Germany, Italy, Japan, Mexico, South Korea, Wales, U.K.

BORG-WARNER SECURITY CORPORATION

200 S. Michigan Ave.

Chicago, IL 60604

Tel: (312) 322-8500 Fax: (312) 322-8398

CEO: J. Joe Adorjan, Pres.

HR: Angela D'Aversa

Emp: 87,000

Security services.

Canada, England, U.K.

BOSE CORPORATION

The Mountain

Framingham, MA 01701-9168

Tel: (508) 879-7330 Fax: (508) 766-7543

CEO: Sherwin Greenblatt, Pres.

FO: Nic Merks

HR: John Coleman

Emp: 4,500

Mfr. quality audio equipment/speakers.

Australia, Belgium, Canada, Denmark, England, U.K., France, Germany, Ireland, Italy, Japan, Mexico, Netherlands, Norway, Switzerland

BOSS MANUFACTURING COMPANY

221 West First Street

Kewanee, IL 61443

Tel: (309) 852-2131 Fax: (309) 852-0848

CEO: Ken Fristed, Pres.

HR: Beverly J. Williams

Emp: 800

Safety products, protective clothing and sport/work gloves.

Canada, Mexico

THE BOSTON CONSULTING GROUP

Exchange Place, 31st Floor

Boston, MA 02109

Tel: (617) 973-1200 Fax: (617) 973-1339

CEO: Carl Stern, Pres.

Web site: www.bcg.com

Management consulting company.

Argentina, Australia, Austria, Belgium, Brazil, Canada, China (PRC), England, U.K., Finland, France, Germany, Hong Kong, Hungary, India, Indonesia, Italy, Japan, Malaysia, Mexico, Netherlands, New Zealand, Norway, Poland, Portugal, Russia, Singapore, South Korea, Spain, Sweden, Switzerland, Thailand

BOSTON GEAR

14 Hayward Street

North Quincy, MA 02171

Tel: (617) 328-3300 Fax: (617) 479-6238

CEO: Roger Pennycook, Pres.

Web site: www.Boston.Gear.Industry.Net

Mfr. car bearings and electrical products.

Canada

BOSTON SCIENTIFIC CORPORATION

One Scientific Place

Natick, MA 01760-1537

Tel: (508) 650-8000 Fax: (508) 650-8923

CEO: Peter M. Nicholas, Pres. & Chmn.

FO: James M. Corbett, Pres., Int'l.

HR: Robert G. MacLean, SVP

Web site: www.bsci.com

Emp: 10,000 Rev: $1,800 mil.

Mfr./distributes medical devices for use in minimally invasive surgeries.

Argentina, Australia, Austria, Canada, Denmark, England, U.K., France, Germany, Hong Kong, Ireland, Italy, Japan, Netherlands, Norway, Portugal, Singapore, South Korea, Spain, Sweden, Switzerland, Taiwan (ROC)

BOURNS INC.

1200 Columbia Ave.

Riverside, CA 92507

Tel: (909) 781-5500 Fax: (909) 781-5273

CEO: Gordon Bourns

Emp: 4,500 Rev: $350 mil.

Mfr. resistive components and networks, precision potentiometers, panel controls, switches and transducers.

Costa Rica, England, U.K., France, Germany, Hong Kong, Ireland, Mexico, Netherlands, Scotland, U.K., Singapore, South Korea, Switzerland, Taiwan (ROC)

BOWATER INC.

55 East Camperdown Way

Greenville, SC 29601

Tel: (864) 271-7733 Fax: (864) 282-9482

CEO: Arnold Nemirow, Chmn. & Pres.

HR: David F. Frisch, VP

Web site: www.bowater.com

Emp: 5,000 Rev: $1,485 mil.

Paper manufacturing.

Canada, Singapore

BOWEN TOOLS INC.

PO Box 3186

Houston, TX 77253-3186

Tel: (713) 868-8888 Fax: (713) 868-8775

CEO: Gary W. Stratulate, Pres.

HR: Jean Ferraro

Emp: 525

Mfr. drilling & specialty tools for oil/gas industry.

Canada, Netherlands, Scotland, U.K., Singapore

BOWES INDUSTRIES

5902 East 34th Street

Indianapolis, IN 46218

Tel: (317) 547-5245 Fax: (317) 545-7683

CEO: Wayne Smith, Pres.

Emp: 100

Mfr. automotive accessories.

Canada

BOWMAR INSTRUMENT CORPORATION

3601 East University Drive

Phoenix, AZ 85034

Tel: (602) 437-1520 Fax: (602) 437-9120

CEO: Hamid R. Shokrgozar, Pres.

Web site: www.whitemicro.com

Emp: 200 Rev: $27 mil.

Mfr. of high density memory modules and micro processor MCMs; state of the art micro-electronics devices.

England, U.K.

BOWNE INTERNATIONAL INC.

345 Hudson Street

New York, NY 10014

Tel: (212) 924-5500 Fax: (212) 229-3420

CEO: Carl J. Crosetto, Pres.

FO: William Penders, Mng. Dir.

Emp: 5,000

Financial printing and foreign language translation, localization (software), internet design and maintenance and facilities management.

Argentina, England, U.K., France, Germany, Hong Kong, Indonesia, Mexico, Singapore

BOXLIGHT CORPORATION

19332 Powder Hill Place

Poulsbo, WA 98370

Tel: (360) 779-7901 Fax: (360) 779-3299

CEO: Herb Myers, Pres.

HR: Rebecca Chadbourne

Web site: www.boxlight.com

Emp: 168

Mfr./sales/rentals of LCD panels and overhead, computer-based projection/presentation systems.

Belgium, England, U.K., Netherlands, Saudi Arabia, South Africa

BOYDEN CONSULTING CORPORATION

100 Park Ave., 34th Floor

New York, NY 10017

Tel: (212) 980-6534 Fax: (212) 980-6147

CEO: John Slosar, Pres.

Web site: www.boyden.com

Emp: 250

Executive search.

Argentina, Australia, Belgium, Brazil, Canada, Chile, China (PRC), Colombia, Czech Republic, Denmark, England, U.K., Finland, France, Germany, Greece, Hong Kong, India, Indonesia, Italy, Japan, Malaysia, Mexico, Netherlands, New Zealand, Norway, Peru, Philippines, Poland, Portugal, Russia, Singapore, South Africa, South Korea, Spain, Sweden, Switzerland, Taiwan (ROC), Thailand, United Arab Emirates, Venezuela

BOZELL WORLDWIDE

40 West 23rd Street

New York, NY 10010

Tel: (212) 727-5000 Fax: (212) 645-9173

CEO: David A. Bell

FO: Brian Tucker

Web site: www.bozell.com

Emp: 3,093 Rev: $404 mil.

Advertising, marketing, public relations and media consulting.

Argentina, Australia, Austria, Belgium, Brazil, Canada, Chile, China (PRC), Colombia, Czech Republic, Denmark, Ecuador, Egypt, England, U.K., Finland, France, Germany, Greece, Hong Kong, Hungary, Iceland, India, Indonesia, Israel, Italy, Japan, Kuwait, Malaysia, Mexico, Netherlands, New Zealand, Panama, Peru, Philippines, Poland, Portugal, Russia, Saudi Arabia, Singapore, South Africa, South Korea, Spain, Sri Lanka, Sweden, Switzerland, Taiwan (ROC), Thailand, Trinidad & Tobago, Turkey, United Arab Emirates, Venezuela

W. H. BRADY CO.

6555 W. Good Hope Road

Milwaukee, WI 53223

Tel: (414) 358-6600 Fax:

CEO: Katherine M. Hudson, Pres.

HR: Michael O. Oliver, VP

Web site: www.whbrady.com

Emp: 2,500 Rev: $426 mil.

Mfr. industrial ID for wire marking, circuit boards; facility ID, signage, printing systems & software.

Australia, Belgium, Brazil, Canada, England, U.K., France, Germany, Hong Kong, Italy, Japan, Malaysia, Singapore, South Korea, Sweden, Taiwan (ROC)

BRAND FARRAR BUXBAUM LLP

515 Flower Street, Ste. 3500

Los Angeles, CA 90017-2201

Tel: (213) 228-0288 Fax: (213) 426-6222

CEO: David Farrar, Sr. Prtn.

International law firm specializing in cross-border disputes and business transactions; intellectual property.

China (PRC), Hong Kong, Mongolia

BRANSON ULTRASONICS CORPORATION

41 Eagle Road

Danbury, CT 06813-1961

Tel: (203) 796-0400 Fax: (203) 796-2285

CEO: Charles Nims

FO: Charles Nims

HR: Freda Peters

Emp: 2,050

Mfr. plastics assembly equipment, ultrasonic cleaning equipment.

Argentina, Australia, Brazil, Canada, Chile, China (PRC), Colombia, Denmark, England, U.K., Finland, France, Germany, Hong Kong, India, Israel, Italy, Japan, Malaysia, Mexico, New Zealand, Pakistan, Peru, Philippines, Portugal, Singapore, South Africa, South Korea, Spain, Switzerland, Taiwan (ROC), Thailand, Turkey, Venezuela

C.F. BRAUN & COMPANY

4175 Whitmore Lake Road

Ann Arbor, MI 48105

Tel: (734) 663-1040 Fax: (734) 663-1403

CEO: Hugh A. Baird

FO: Frank S. Burroughs

HR: David K. Gillies

Engineering/construction/management for energy and power industrial.

Canada, England, U.K., Saudi Arabia

W. BRAUN COMPANY

300 North Canal Street

Chicago, IL 60606

Tel: (312) 346-6500 Fax: (312) 346-9643

CEO: Ed Rappaport, Pres.

FO: Larry Taylor

HR: Joan Corman

Emp: 180

Design/mfr./supply packaging.

Canada, Italy, Mexico

BRIDGE INFORMATION SYSTEMS INC.

717 Office Parkway

St. Louis, MO 63141

Tel: (314) 567-8300 Fax: (314) 432-5391

CEO: Tom Wendel, Chmn.

FO: Richard M. Hurwitz

HR: Peggy Hohl

Emp: 375

Investor information services.

England, U.K.

BRIGGS & STRATTON CORPORATION

PO Box 702

Milwaukee, WI 53201

Tel: (414) 259-5333 Fax: (414) 259-9594

CEO: F. P. Stratton, Jr.

FO: Hugo A. Keltz

HR: Gerald E. Zitzer

Emp: 7,660

Mfr. engines.

Australia, China (PRC), England, U.K., France, Germany, New Zealand, Sweden

BRINK'S INC.

Thorndal Circle

Darien, CT 06820

Tel: (203) 662-7800 Fax: (203) 662-7968

CEO: Michael Dan, Pres.

FO: J. T. Walsh

HR: Charles Tischer

Web site: www.brinks.com

Emp: 14,500

Security transportation.

Brazil, Canada, England, U.K., France, Israel, Italy, Spain

BRISTOL BABCOCK INC.

1100 Buckingham Street

Watertown, CT 06795

Tel: (203) 575-3000 Fax: (203) 575-3170

CEO: Gregory A. Altman

HR: Irene Jalbert

Emp: 1,200

Mfr. process control instruments and SCADA systems.

Canada, England, U.K., France, Mexico

BRISTOL-MYERS SQUIBB COMPANY

345 Park Ave.

New York, NY 10154

Tel: (212) 546-4000 Fax: (212) 546-4020

CEO: Charles A. Heimbold, Jr., Chmn.

FO: Stephen E. Bear, Pres. Intl.

HR: Charles G. Tharp, SVP

Web site: www.bms.com

Emp: 53,000 Rev: $16,700 mil.

Pharmaceutical and food preparations, medical and surgical instruments.

Argentina, Australia, Austria, Belgium, Brazil, Bulgaria, Canada, Chile, China (PRC), Colombia, Costa Rica, Czech Republic, Denmark, Dominican Republic, Ecuador, Egypt, El Salvador, England, U.K., Finland, France, Germany, Greece, Guam, Guatemala, Honduras, Hong Kong, Hungary, Iceland, Indonesia, Ireland, Israel, Italy, Jamaica, Japan, Kazakhstan, Malaysia, Mexico, Morocco, Netherlands, New Zealand, Nicaragua, Norway, Oman, Pakistan, Panama, Peru, Philippines, Poland, Portugal, Romania, Russia, Saudi Arabia, Singapore, South Africa, South Korea, Spain, Sweden, Switzerland, Taiwan (ROC), Thailand, Trinidad & Tobago, Tunisia, Ukraine, Venezuela, Vietnam, Wales, U.K.

BRK BRANDS/FIRST ALERT, INC.

3901 Liberty Street Road

Aurora, IL 60504-8122

Tel: (630) 851-7330 Fax: (630) 851-1331

CEO: Michael Paxton, Pres.

HR: Ms. C. Keeley

Emp: 4,200

Mfr. smoke detectors, fire extinguishers, lights, timers & sensor systems.

Australia, Canada, England, U.K., Mexico

BROBECK PHLEGER & HARRISON

Spear Street Tower, One Market Plaza

San Francisco, CA 94105

Tel: (415) 442-0900 Fax: (415) 442-1010

CEO: Karen Johnson McQuen, Mng. Prtn.

FO: John W. Larson

Emp: 700

International law joint venture.

Czech Republic, England, U.K.

BRODART COMPANY

500 Arch Street

Williamsport, PA 17705

Tel: (717) 326-2461 Fax: (717) 326-3039

CEO: Joseph Largen, Pres.

FO: Joseph Largen

HR: Tim Gage

Web site: www.brodart.com

Emp: 1,220

Mfr./distributor/services library books, supplies, furniture and automation products.

Canada

BROOKE NEW VALLEY CORPORATION

100 Southeast Second Street, 32nd Fl.

Miami, FL 33131

Tel: (305) 579-8000 Fax: (305) 579-8001

CEO: Bennett S. LeBow, Chmn. & Pres.

FO: Ronald S. Fulford

HR: Lynn Cordova, Dir.

Web site: www.liggett.net

Emp: 1,500 Rev: $389.6 mil.

Holding company with investments in securities, commercial real estate and tobacco.

Russia

BROOKS INSTRUMENT DIVISION

407 West Vine Street

Hatfield, PA 19440

Tel: (215) 362-3500 Fax: (215) 362-3745

CEO: Gene Perkins, Acting Pres.

FO: Joseph Vaszily

HR: Gene DeLallo

Web site: www.brooksinstrument.com

Emp: 900

Mfr. flowmeters and parts.

Japan, Netherlands

BROWN & ROOT INC.

4100 Clinton Drive

Houston, TX 77020-6299

Tel: (713) 676-3011 Fax: (713) 676-8532

CEO: Larry Pope, Pres.

FO: K.N.Henry/R.M.Bunker

HR: Lawrence Pope

Emp: 35,000

Engineering, construction and maintenance.

Australia, Azerbaijan, Bahrain, Brazil, Canada, China (PRC), Egypt, England, U.K., Hong Kong, India, Indonesia, Japan, Malaysia, Mexico, Netherlands, Saudi Arabia, Scotland, U.K., South Korea, Turkey, Venezuela

BROWN & SHARPE MFG. COMPANY

Precision Park, 200 Frenchtown Road

North Kingstown, RI 02852-1700

Tel: (401) 886-2000 Fax: (401) 886-2762

CEO: Frank Curtin, Pres.

FO: Frank Curtin

HR: Ralph Chase

Mfr./sale/services metrology equipment & precision tools.

Switzerland

BROWN & WOOD

One World Trade Center, 59th Fl.

New York, NY 10048

Tel: (212) 839-5300 Fax: (212) 839-5599

CEO: Thomas R. Smith, Jr.

FO: Ross Kauffman, Ptnr.

Emp: 300

Legal services.

Brazil, England, U.K., Hong Kong, Japan

BROWN BROTHERS HARRIMAN & COMPANY

59 Wall Street

New York, NY 10005

Tel: (212) 483-1818 Fax: (212) 493-8526

CEO: Anthony Enders, Mng. Prtn.

HR: Edwin F. Stabbert

Emp: 1,500

Financial services.

Cayman Islands, Channel Islands, U.K., England, U.K., France, Japan, Luxembourg, Switzerland

BROWN GROUP INC.

8300 Maryland Ave.

St. Louis, MO 63105

Tel: (314) 854-4000 Fax: (314) 854-4274

CEO: B. A. Bridgewater, Jr.

FO: Arthur G. Croci

HR: Steven D. Scanlan

Web site: www.browngroup.com

Emp: 14,000 Rev: $1,000 mil.

Mfr./sale footwear.

Brazil, France, Hong Kong, Italy, Taiwan (ROC)

BROWN-FORMAN CORPORATION

PO Box 1080

Louisville, KY 40201-1080

Tel: (502) 585-1100 Fax: (502) 774-7876

CEO: Owsley Brown, II

FO: E. Peter Rutledge

HR: Russell C. Buzby

Web site: www.brown-forman.com

Emp: 7,500 Rev: $1,700 mil.

Mfr./distributor distilled spirits, wine, china, crystal, silverware and luggage.

Brazil, Canada, Ireland

BROWNING CORPORATION

1 Browning Place

Morgan, UT 84050

Tel: (801) 876-2711 Fax: (801) 876-3331

CEO: Don W. Gobel, Pres.

HR: David Rich

Emp: 500

Sales/distribution of port firearms, fishing rods, etc.

Canada

BROWNING-FERRIS INDUSTRIES INC.

757 North Eldridge Parkway

Houston, TX 77079

Tel: (281) 870-8100 Fax: (281) 870-7844

CEO: Bruce Ranck, Pres.

HR: Kim Clarke, Div. VP

Waste management.

Canada

BRUNSWICK CORPORATION

1 Northfield Court

Lake Forest, IL 60045-4811

Tel: (847) 735-4700 Fax: (847) 735-4765

CEO: J. F. Reichert

Web site: www.brunswickcorp.com

Emp: 20,000

Mfr. recreational boats, marine engines, bowling centers & equipment, fishing equipment, defense/aerospace.

Belgium, Canada, Japan, Mexico, Switzerland

BRUSH WELLMAN INC.

17876 St. Clair Ave.
Cleveland, OH 44110
Tel: (216) 486-4200 Fax: (216) 383-4091
CEO: Gordon D. Harnett, Pres.
FO: Craig B. Harlan
HR: Daniel A. Skoch, VP
Web site: www.brushwellman.com
Emp: 2,100

Mfr. beryllium, beryllium alloys and ceramics, specialty metal systems and precious metal products.

England, U.K., Germany, Japan, Singapore

BRY-AIR INC.

10793 Street, Rt. 37 West
Sunbury, OH 43074
Tel: (740) 965-2974 Fax: (740) 965-5470
CEO: Paul D. Griesse
FO: Guy Griesse, VP Mktg.
Web site: www.bry-air.thomasregister.com
Emp: 360

Mfr. industrial dehumidifiers/auxiliary equipment for plastics industrial.

India, Malaysia

BT ALEX BROWN INC.

One South Street
Baltimore, MD 21202
Tel: (410) 727-1700 Fax: (410) 783-3356
CEO: Ted Virtue, Pres.
FO: Rodney A. McLauchlan
HR: Sherry Edelstein. Dir.
Web site: www.alexbrown.com
Emp: 2,500

Provides financial services to institutional and individual investors and investment banking services to corporate and municipal clients.

England, U.K., Japan, Switzerland

BTG, INC.

3877 Fairfax Ridge Road
Fairfax, VA 22030-7448
Tel: (703) 383-8000 Fax: (703) 383-8999
CEO: Edward H. Bersoff, Chmn. & Pres.
HR: Karen Wall, VP
Web site: www.btg.com
Emp: 1,319 Rev: $590 mil.

Provides system integration and adaptation services.

England, U.K., Germany

BTU INTERNATIONAL

23 Esquire Road
North Billerica, MA 01862
Tel: (508) 667-4111 Fax: (508) 667-9068
CEO: Paul J. van der Wansem
FO: Santo Di Naro
HR: Don Masson
Emp: 300 Rev: $45 mil.

Mfr. of industrial furnaces.

China (PRC), England, U.K., Singapore

BUCK CONSULTANTS INC.

One Pennsylvania Plaza
New York, NY 10119
Tel: (212) 330-1000 Fax: (212) 695-4184
CEO: Joseph Locicero, Chmn.
HR: William M. Brackley
Emp: 1,401

Employee benefit, actuarial and compensation consulting services.

Australia, Belgium, Canada, England, U.K., Hong Kong, Mexico

BUCKHORN INC.

55 West Techne Center Drive
Milford, OH 45150
Tel: (513) 831-4402 Fax: (513) 831-5474
CEO: William J. Tonachio, Gen. Mgr.
FO: Neville Jarvis
HR: Nancy J. Cuzzort
Emp: 300

Mfr. of reusable plastic packaging systems, plastic containers and pallets and project management services.

Canada, England, U.K.

BUCYRUS INTERNATIONAL, INC.

1100 Milwaukee Ave.
South Milwaukee, WI 53172
Tel: (414) 768-4000 Fax: (414) 768-4474
CEO: Willard R. Hildebrand, Pres.
FO: Timothy W. Sullivan, VP

HR: Chuck Murray

Emp: 1,250 Rev: $240 mil.

Mfr. of surface mining equipment, primarily walking draglines, electric mining shovels and blast hole drills.

Australia, Brazil, Canada, Cayman Islands, Chile, China (PRC), England, U.K., India, Mauritius, South Africa

BUDGET RENT A CAR CORPORATION

4225 Naperville Road

Lisle, IL 60532

Tel: (630) 955-1900 Fax: (630) 955-7799

CEO: Mr. Sandy Miller, Chmn.

FO: John Kennedy, Pres. Intl.

HR: Vicki Pyne, VP

Web site: www.budgetrentacar.com

Emp: 24,500 Rev: $2,700 mil.

Car and truck rental system.

Anguilla, Argentina, Aruba, Australia, Austria, Bahamas, Bahrain, Belgium, Belize, Brazil, Bulgaria, Canada, Chile, Colombia, Costa Rica, Croatia, Cyprus, Czech Republic, Denmark, Dominican Republic, Ecuador, Egypt, England, U.K., India, Ireland, Israel, Japan, Kenya, Malaysia, Malta, Mexico, New Caledonia, New Zealand, Qatar, Romania, Russia, Saudi Arabia, Singapore, Thailand, Turkey, Zimbabwe

BULAB HOLDINGS INC.

1256 N. McLean Blvd

Memphis, TN 38108

Tel: (901) 278-0330 Fax: (901) 276-5343

CEO: Robert H. Buckman

HR: Mark Koskiniemi

Web site: www.buckman.com

Emp: 1,270 Rev: $193 mil.

Biological products; chemicals & chemical preparations.

Argentina, Australia, Austria, Belgium, Brazil, Canada, England, U.K., Germany, Italy, Japan, Mexico, Monaco, Portugal, Singapore, South Africa, Spain, Sweden

BULOVA CORPORATION

One Bulova Ave.

Woodside, NY 11377-7874

Tel: (718) 204-3300 Fax: (718) 204-3546

CEO: Herbert C. Hofmann, Pres.

FO: Warren J. Neitzel

HR: Eleanor Smith

Emp: 500

Mfr. timepieces, watches and clocks, watch parts, batteries and precision defense products.

Canada, Hong Kong

BURLINGTON INDUSTRIES INC.

3330 W. Friendly Ave., PO Box 21207

Greensboro, NC 27420

Tel: (336) 379-2000 Fax: (336) 379-4943

CEO: George W. Henderson, Chmn.

HR: William McLaughlin

Emp: 26,000

Mfr./marketing textiles.

Mexico

BURLINGTON NORTHERN SANTA FE CORP.

3800 Continental Plaza, 777 Main St.

Fort Worth, TX 76102-5384

Tel: (817) 333-2000 Fax: (817) 333-2377

CEO: Robert D. Krebs, Chmn.

FO: Matthew Rose, SVP

HR: R. Gardner, VP

Web site: www.bnsf.com

Emp: 44,500

Rail services.

Canada

BURLINGTON RESOURCES

5051 Westheimer, Ste. 1400

Houston, TX 77056

Tel: (713) 624-9000 Fax: (713) 624-9645

CEO: Robert Shackouls, Chmn.

Emp: 750

Oil and gas exploration.

England, U.K., Venezuela

LEO BURNETT CO., INC.

35 West Wacker Drive

Chicago, IL 60601

Tel: (312) 220-5959 Fax: (312) 220-6533

CEO: Richard B. Fizdale, Chmn.

FO: Kerry M. Rubie, Vice Chmn.

HR: Tom Nossem

Web site: www.leoburnett.com

Emp: 8,000 Rev: $878 mil.

International advertising agency.

Argentina, Australia, Austria, Bahrain, Bangladesh, Belgium, Brazil, Bulgaria, Canada, Chile, Colombia, Costa Rica, Czech Republic, Denmark, Dominican Republic, Ecuador, Egypt, El Salvador, England, U.K., Estonia, France, Germany, Greece, Guatemala, Honduras, Hong Kong, Hungary, India, Indonesia, Ireland, Israel, Italy, Japan, Kazakhstan, Kuwait, Lebanon, Lithuania, Malaysia, Mexico, Myanmar, Netherlands, New Zealand, Nicaragua, Norway, Pakistan, Panama, Paraguay, Peru, Philippines, Poland, Portugal, Romania, Saudi Arabia, Singapore, Slovakia, Slovenia, South Korea, Spain, Sweden, Switzerland, Taiwan (ROC), Thailand, Turkey, United Arab Emirates, Uruguay, Venezuela, Vietnam

BURNS & ROE ENTERPRISES, INC.

800 Kinderkamack Road

Oradell, NJ 07649

Tel: (201) 986-4000 Fax: (201) 986-4118

CEO: K. Keith Roe

FO: Dennis E. Dugan

HR: James Santora

Emp: 2,000

Engineering and construction.

Australia, Russia, Taiwan (ROC)

BURR-BROWN RESEARCH CORPORATION

6730 S. Tucson Blvd.

Tucson, AZ 85706

Tel: (520) 746-1111 Fax: (520) 746-7211

CEO: Syrus Madavi, Pres.

FO: Mel Jordan

Emp: 1,500

Electronic components and systems modules.

Austria, Belgium, England, U.K., France, Germany, Italy, Japan, Netherlands, Scotland, U.K., Sweden, Switzerland

BURSON-MARSTELLER

230 Park Ave.

New York, NY 10003-1566

Tel: (212) 614-4000 Fax: (212) 614-4262

CEO: James H. Dowling

HR: John A. Mitchell

Web site: www.bm.com

Emp: 2,400

Public relations/public affairs consultants.

Argentina, Australia, Austria, Belgium, Brazil, Canada, Chile, China (PRC), Colombia, Czech Republic, Denmark, England, U.K., France, Germany, Hong Kong, Hungary, India, Indonesia, Italy, Japan, Malaysia, Mexico, Netherlands, New Zealand, Norway, Poland, Portugal, Russia, Singapore, South Korea, Spain, Sweden, Switzerland, Thailand, Venezuela

BUSSMANN

PO Box 14460

St. Louis, MO 63178-4460

Tel: (314) 394-2877 Fax: (314) 527-1405

CEO: Barry McHone, Pres.

Mfr. electronic fuses and circuit breakers.

Denmark, England, U.K., Mexico

BUTLER AUTOMATIC INC.

480 Neponset Street

Canton, MA 02021

Tel: (781) 828-5450 Fax: (781) 828-2715

CEO: Andrew Butler, Pres.

HR: Jean Faknham

Emp: 280

Mfr. web press equipment.

Switzerland

BUTLER INTERNATIONAL

110 Summit Ave.

Montvale, NJ 07645

Tel: (201) 573-8000 Fax: (201) 573-9723

CEO: Edward M. Kopko, Chmn. & Pres.

Web site: www.butlerintl.com

Emp: 6,000 Rev: $423.0 mil

Leading supplier of skilled technical personnel.

England, U.K., French Antilles, Indonesia, South Africa

BUTLER MANUFACTURING COMPANY

Penn Valley Park, PO Box 419917

Kansas City, MO 64141-0917

Tel: (816) 968-3000 Fax: (816) 968-3279

CEO: Robert H. West, Chmn.

FO: Clyde E. Wills, Pres. Int'l.

HR: Kip Rosner, VP

Emp: 5,117 Rev: $925 mil.

Pre-engineered steel structural systems, curtain wall and electrical distributor systems.

Brazil, Canada, China (PRC), Saudi Arabia, Scotland, U.K.

BUTTERICK CO., INC.

161 Ave. of the Americas

New York, NY 10013

Tel: (212) 620-2500 Fax: (212) 620-2746

CEO: Jay Stein, Pres.

FO: John E. Lehmann

HR: Ruth Rowan

Web site: www.butterick.com

Emp: 500

Sewing patterns.

Australia, Canada, England, U.K., France, Italy, New Zealand, South Africa

BWI KARTRIDG PAK

807 W. Kimberly Road

Davenport, IA 52808

Tel: (319) 391-1100 Fax: (319) 391-0017

CEO: Barry Shoulders

FO: Scott Scriven, Dir.

HR: Richard Davis

Emp: 150 Rev: $30 mil.

Meat packaging and aerosol filling equipment.

England, U.K.

C

C-COR ELECTRONICS INC.

60 Decibel Road

State College, PA 16801

Tel: (814) 238-2461 Fax: (814) 238-4065

CEO: Richard E. Perry

FO: David J. Eng

HR: Edwin Childs

Web site: www.c-cor.com

Emp: 1,200 Rev: $132 mil.

Design/mfr. amplifiers, fiber optics electronic equipment for data and cable TV systems.

Canada, Chile, Hong Kong, Netherlands

CABLE DATA INC.

11020 Sun Center Drive

Ranch Cordova, CA 95670

Tel: (916) 636-4501 Fax: (916) 636-5750

CEO: Michael McGrail, Pres.

FO: Mike Frampton

HR: Randy Gorrell

Emp: 2,565

Management/services software & hardware for cable TV, satellite & telecommunications industrial.

England, U.K.

CABLETRON SYSTEMS, INC.

35 Industrial Way, PO Box 5005

Rochester, NH 03866-5005

Tel: (603) 332-9400 Fax: (603) 337-3007

CEO: John D'Auguste, Pres.

HR: Linda Pepin

Emp: 4,870

Develop/mfr./marketing/install/support local & wide area network connectivity hardware & software.

Australia, Brazil, England, U.K., Poland, Singapore

CABOT CORPORATION

75 State Street

Boston, MA 02109-1807

Tel: (617) 345-0100 Fax: (617) 342-6103

CEO: Kenneth Burnes, Pres.

Emp: 5,400 Rev: $1,000 mil.

Mfr. carbon blacks, plastics; oil & gas, information systems.

Argentina, Australia, Belgium, Brazil, Colombia, England, U.K., France, Germany, Italy, Japan, Malaysia, Netherlands, Spain, Sweden, Switzerland

CACI INTERNATIONAL INC.

1100 Nort Glebe Road

Arlington, VA 22201

Tel: (703) 841-7800 Fax: (703) 841-7882

CEO: J.P. London, Chmn.

FO: Ronald R. Ross, Pres.

HR: William J. Clancy Jr., SVP

Web site: www.caci.com

Emp: 3,700 Rev: $326 mil.

Provides simulation technology/software and designs factories, computer networks, and communications systems for military, electronic commerce digital document management, logistics and Y2K remediation.

Canada, England, U.K., France, Germany,

Scotland, U.K.

CADILLAC PLASTIC & CHEMICAL COMPANY

143 Indusco Court

Troy, MI 48083

Tel: (248) 205-3100 Fax: (248) 205-3187

CEO: Kent Diarragh, Pres.

Emp: 1,400

Distributor plastic basic shapes.

Australia, Canada, England, U.K.

CADWALADER, WICKERSHAM & TAFT

100 Maden Lane

New York, NY 10038-4818

Tel: (212) 504-6000 Fax: (212) 504-6666

CEO: David Strumeyer

FO: Mitchell Wallsh

HR: Anita Howell

Web site: www.cadwalader.com

Emp: 500 Rev: $142 mil.

International law firm.

England, U.K.

CAHILL GORDON & REINDEL

80 Pine Street

New York, NY 10005

Tel: (212) 701-3000 Fax: (212) 269-5420

CEO: Mary Forcellon

HR: Mary Forcellon

Emp: 602 Rev: $136 mil.

Law firm.

France

CALBIOCHEM-NOVABIOCHEM CORPORATION

PO Box 12087

La Jolla, CA 92039

Tel: (619) 450-9600 Fax: (619) 452-3552

CEO: Steve Papadopoulos, Pres.

HR: Lee Hart

Mfr. biochemicals, immunochemicals and reagents.

England, U.K., Germany, Switzerland

CALCOMP INC.

2411 West La Palma Ave.

Anaheim, CA 92801

Tel: (714) 821-2000 Fax: (714) 821-2832

CEO: John Batterton, Pres.

FO: W. Rohloff & D. Lightfoot

HR: K. Coleman

Emp: 1,125

Mfr. computer graphics peripherals.

Australia, Austria, Belgium, Canada, England, U.K., France, Germany, Hong Kong, Italy, Japan, Mexico, Netherlands, Norway, Spain, Sweden, Switzerland

CALED CHEMICAL

26 Hanes Drive

Wayne, NJ 07470

Tel: (973) 696-7575 Fax: (973) 696-4790

CEO: Jack Belluscio

FO: J. Lakritz & W. Bernard

HR: Patrick Wiseman

Emp: 144

Mfr. dry cleaning chemicals and machine filters, laundry detergents, fabric protectors, flame retardants.

Canada

CALGON CARBON CORPORATION

Calgon Carbon Drive

Pittsburgh, PA 15230

Tel: (412) 787-6700 Fax: (412) 787-4541

CEO: Thomas A. McConomy, Pres.

FO: Robert van Haute

HR: Robert Courson

Emp: 1,100

Mfr. activated carbon, related systems & services.

Germany

CALGON CORPORATION

PO Box 1346

Pittsburgh, PA 15230

Tel: (412) 494-8000 Fax: (412) 494-8104

CEO: James Heagle, Pres.

FO: Manjeri S. Raman

HR: Vaughn L. Swope

Emp: 1,100

Mfr. cosmetic, personal care & water treatment products.

Belgium, Canada, England, U.K., Japan, Mexico, Saudi Arabia, South Africa, Venezuela

CALIFORNIA BUFF CO., INC.

1612 N. Indiana Street
Los Angeles, CA 90063
Tel: (213) 268-7884 Fax: (213) 268-8529
CEO: Natan Leisorek
FO: Elias Leisorek
Emp: 250
Mfr. buffs, satin finishing wheels, abrasive wheels, and cotton polishing.
Mexico

CALIFORNIA CEDAR PRODUCTS COMPANY

PO Box 528
Stockton, CA 95201
Tel: (209) 944-5800 Fax: (209) 944-9072
CEO: Philip C. Berolzheimer, Pres.
HR: Lee Thomas
Emp: 600
Incense-cedar products.
England, U.K., Japan

CALIFORNIA MICROWAVE INC.

555 Twin Dolphin Drive, Ste. 650
Redwood City, CA 94065
Tel: (650) 596-9000 Fax: (650) 596-6600
CEO: Philip Otto, Pres.
Emp: 2,300 Rev: $450 mil.
Telecommunications.
New Zealand, Portugal, Spain

CALIFORNIA PELLET MILL COMPANY (CPM)

1114 East Wabash Ave.
Crawfordsville, IN 47933
Tel: (765) 362-2600 Fax: (765) 362-7551
CEO: E. J. Elliott, Pres.
FO: Jack Hilliker
Mfr. machinery for pelleting.
Brazil, England, U.K., France, Germany, Ireland, Netherlands, Singapore

CALLAWAY GOLF CO.

2285 Rutherford Road
Carlsbad, CA 92008
Tel: (760) 931-1771 Fax: (760) 931-8013
CEO: Ely Callaway, Chmn.
HR: Elizabeth O'Mea
Mfr./sales of golf clubs.
England, U.K.

CALMAQUIP ENGINEERING CORPORATION

7240 NW 12th Street
Miami, FL 33121
Tel: (305) 592-4510 Fax: (305) 593-9618
CEO: Raul Gutierrez, Pres.
FO: Benjamin L. Sadler, Jr.
Emp: 100
Engineering
Canada, Costa Rica, Dominican Republic, Ecuador, Honduras, Panama, Saudi Arabia

CALTEX PETROLEUM CORPORATION

125 East John Carpenter Fwy.
Irving, TX 75062-2794
Tel: (972) 830-1000 Fax: (972) 830-1081
CEO: David Law-Smith, Chmn.
FO: Guy J. Camarata
HR: Stephen H. Nichols, VP
Web site: www.caltex.com
Emp: 7,500 Rev: $18,357 mil.
Petroleum products.
Australia, Bahrain, China (PRC), Egypt, England, U.K., Hong Kong, Indonesia, Japan, Kenya, Malawi, Malaysia, New Zealand, Pakistan, Philippines, Reunion, Saudi Arabia, Singapore, South Africa, South Korea, Taiwan (ROC), Tanzania, Thailand, Uganda, United Arab Emirates, Vietnam, Zambia, Zimbabwe

CALVIN KLEIN, INC.

205 West 39th Street, 5th Fl.
New York, NY 10018
Tel: (212) 719-2600 Fax: (212) 768-8922
CEO: Barry Schwartz, Chmn.
FO: Gabriella Forte, Pres.
HR: Christine Fortney
Emp: 900
Mfr. of high quality clothing and accessories
France, Hong Kong, Italy, Japan

CAMBREX CORP.

1 Meadowlands Plaza
East Rutherford, NJ 07063

Tel: (201) 804-3000 Fax: (201) 804-9852

CEO: James A. Mack, Pres.

FO: Claes Glassell, Pres. Int'l.

HR: Steven M. Klosk. EVP Adm.

Web site: www.cambex.com

Emp: 1,700 Rev: $385 mil.

Mfg. Bulf active chemicals for pharmaceuticals.

Belgium, China (PRC), England, U.K., Germany, India, Italy, Mexico, Sweden

CAMBRIDGE WIRE CLOTH COMPANY

105 Goodwill Road, PO Box 399

Cambridge, MD 21613

Tel: (410) 228-3000 Fax: (410) 228-6752

CEO: Dwaine Marshall, Pres.

Emp: 315

Mfr. industrial wire cloth, wire conveyor belting and industrial mesh.

Australia, Brazil, Mexico

CAMCO INC.

7030 Ardmore Street

Houston, TX 77021

Tel: (713) 747-4000 Fax: (713) 747-6751

CEO: Rene Huck, Pres.

HR: Terry Woodall, Dir.

Emp: 1,400

Oil field equipment for well drilling and production.

Canada, England, U.K., Indonesia, Nigeria, Singapore, United Arab Emirates, Venezuela

CAMP HEALTHCARE, INC.

PO Box 89

Jackson, MI 49204

Tel: (517) 787-1600 Fax: (517) 789-3388

CEO: Noel Murphy, Pres.

HR: Jo Boleratz

Emp: 510

Mfr. orthotics and prosthetics.

Canada

CAMPBELL SOUP COMPANY

Campbell Place

Camden, NJ 08103-1799

Tel: (609) 342-4800 Fax: (609) 342-3878

CEO: Dale Morrison, Pres.

HR: Stephen R. Armstrong

Emp: 43,256

Food products.

Argentina, Australia, Belgium, Canada, England, U.K., France, Hong Kong, Japan, Mexico, Spain

CANBERRA-PACKARD INDUSTRIES

800 Research Parkway

Meriden, CT 06450

Tel: (203) 238-2351 Fax: (203) 235-1347

CEO: George Serran, Pres.

FO: Emery G. Olcott, Pres.

Web site: www.packard.com

Emp: 1,750

Mfr. instruments for nuclear research.

Australia, Austria, Belgium, Denmark, England, U.K., France, Germany, Italy, Japan, Netherlands, Sweden, Switzerland

CANDELA LASER CORPORATION

530 Boston Post Road

Wayland, MA 01778

Tel: (508) 358-7400 Fax: (508) 358-5602

CEO: Gerard E. Puorro

FO: Kenji Shimuzu

HR: Rachel Dupuis

Emp: 150

Mfr./services medical laser systems.

Japan, Netherlands

CANNY BOWEN INC.

200 Park Ave.

New York, NY 10166

Tel: (212) 949-6611 Fax: (212) 949-5191

CEO: David R. Peasback

Emp: 50

Executive search firm.

England, U.K.

CAPITAL CONTROLS CO., INC.

3000 Advance Lane, PO Box 211

Colmar, PA 18915-0211

Tel: (215) 997-4000 Fax: (215) 997-4062

CEO: Mike Ashley, Pres.

Emp: 175

Mfr./services water disinfecting products and systems.

England, U.K.

THE CAPITAL GROUP COS INC.

333 South Hope
Los Angeles, CA 90071
Tel: (213) 486-9200 Fax: (213) 486-9557
CEO: Larry Clemmensen, Pres.
Emp: 3,000
Investment management.
England, U.K., Switzerland

CAPITAL ONE FINANCIAL CORPORATION

2980 Fairview Park Drive, Ste. 1300
Falls Church, VA 22042-4525
Tel: (703) 205-1000 Fax: (703) 205-1090
CEO: Richard D. Fairbank, Chmn.
FO: Nigel W. Morris, Pres.
HR: Dennis H. Liberson, SVP
Web site: www.capitalone.com
Emp: 7,550 Rev: $1,700 mil.
Holding company for credit card companies.
Canada, England, U.K.

CARANA CORPORATION

4350 N. Fairfax Drive, Ste. 500
Arlington, VA 22203
Tel: (703) 243-1700 Fax: (703) 243-0471
CEO: Carlos Torres, Pres.
FO: Eduardo Tugendhat
HR: Elizabeth Cobb
Emp: 50
Foreign trade consulting.
Bolivia, Kazakhstan, Poland, Russia

CARAVAN TOURS INC.

401 North Michigan Ave.
Chicago, IL 60611
Tel: (312) 321-9800 Fax: (312) 321-9810
CEO: T. Dennis Duffy, Pres.
FO: Tom Duffy
Tour operator.
England, U.K.

CARBOLINE COMPANY

350 Hanley Industrial Court
St. Louis, MO 63144
Tel: (314) 644-1000 Fax: (314) 644-4617
CEO: Sherwin L. Steinberg, Pres.
FO: James N. Webster
HR: Patricia Henderson
Emp: 550
Mfr. coatings, sealants.
Argentina, Australia, Barbados, Brazil, Canada, Ecuador, Egypt, England, U.K., France, Germany, Guatemala, India, Indonesia, Italy, Jamaica, Japan, Mexico, Netherlands, New Zealand, Norway, Oman, Panama, Peru, Philippines, Poland, Singapore, South Africa, South Korea, Spain, Taiwan (ROC), Thailand, Trinidad & Tobago, United Arab Emirates, Venezuela

CARBONE OF AMERICA

215 Stackpole Street
Saint Marys, PA 15857
Tel: (814) 781-1234 Fax: (814) 781-8455
CEO: Edward Stumpfs, Pres.
Emp: 1,000
Carbon and graphite specialties.
Canada

CARGILL, INC.

15407 McGinty Road
Minnetonka, MN 55440-5625
Tel: (612) 742-7575 Fax: (612) 742-7393
CEO: Ernest S. Micek, Chmn.
FO: Warren R. Staley, Pres.
HR: Nancy Siska, SVP
Web site: www.cargill.com
Emp: 79,000 Rev: $56,000 mil.
Food products, feeds, animal products.
Argentina, Australia, Belgium, Brazil, Canada, Chile, Colombia, England, U.K., France, Guatemala, Honduras, Hong Kong, Indonesia, Japan, Mexico, Netherlands, Peru, Poland, Singapore, Spain, Switzerland, Taiwan (ROC), Thailand, Venezuela, Vietnam

CARIBINER INTERNATIONAL, INC.

16 West 61st Street
New York, NY 10023
Tel: (212) 541-5300 Fax: (212) 541-5384
CEO: Raymond S. Ingleby, Chmn.
FO: Brian Shepherd, EVP
HR: Monique Bautista, Dir.
Web site: www.caribiner.com
Emp: 3,680 Rev: $342 mil.
Plans & produces meetings, events, and media

campaigns: creates film/video presentations; supports in-house communications & training programs: and supplies audio-visual equipment.

Australia, England, U.K., Hong Kong, Mexico, New Zealand, United Arab Emirates

CARLISLE SYNTEC SYSTEMS

PO Box 7000

Carlisle, PA 17013

Tel: (717) 245-7000   Fax: (717) 245-9107

CEO: John Altmeyer, Pres.

FO: Frank Meehan

HR: Doug Freeman

Emp: 1,150

Mfr. elastomeric roofing & waterproofing systems.

Belgium, Canada, England, U.K., France, Russia, Spain

CARLSON MARKETING GROUP

Carlson Parkway, PO Box 59159

Minneapolis, MN 55459

Tel: (612) 550-4520   Fax: (612) 550-4580

CEO: James J. Ryan, Pres.

Web site: www.cmgcarlson.com

Emp: 2,896   Rev: $285 mil.

Marketing services agency.

Belgium, Canada, England, U.K., Japan, New Zealand, Singapore

CARPCO INC.

4120 Haines Street

Jacksonville, FL 32206

Tel: (904) 353-3681   Fax: (904) 353-8705

CEO: Frank S. Knoll, Pres.

Emp: 66

Design/mfr. separation equipment for mining, recycling & research; testing & flowsheet design.

England, U.K.

CARPENTER TECHNOLOGY CORPORATION

101 W. Bern Street, PO Box 14662

Reading, PA 19612-4662

Tel: (610) 208-2000   Fax: (610) 208-3214

CEO: Robert W. Cardy, Pres.

FO: W. J. Keaveney

HR: R. W. Lodge

Emp: 4,200

Mfr. specialty steels & structural ceramics for casting industrial.

Belgium, Canada, England, U.K., France, Germany, Italy, Mexico, Taiwan (ROC)

CARRIER CORPORATION

One Carrier Place

Farmington, CT 06034-4015

Tel: (860) 674-3000   Fax: (860) 679-3010

CEO: John R. Lord, Chmn.

Web site: www.carrier.com

Emp: 30,000

Mfr./distributor/services A/C, heating & refrigeration equipment.

Argentina, Australia, Austria, Bahrain, Belgium, Brazil, Brunei, Bulgaria, Canada, Chile, China (PRC), Colombia, Egypt, England, U.K., Finland, France, Germany, Hong Kong, India, Italy, Japan, Kuwait, Liechtenstein, Malaysia, Mexico, Netherlands, New Zealand, Norway, Papua New Guinea, Philippines, Poland, Portugal, Russia, Saudi Arabia, Singapore, South Korea, Spain, Sweden, Switzerland, Taiwan (ROC), Thailand, United Arab Emirates, Venezuela, Vietnam

J.C. CARTER COMPANY

671 W. 17th Street

Costa Mesa, CA 92627

Tel: (714) 548-3421   Fax: (714) 752-2997

CEO: Michael Lipscomb,Pres.

HR: Helen Crichton

Emp: 275

Mfr. aerospace valves & pumps, cryogenic pumps.

Japan

CARTER-WALLACE INC.

1345 Ave. of the Americas

New York, NY 10105

Tel: (212) 339-5000   Fax: (212) 339-5100

CEO: Henry H. Hoyt, Jr., Chmn.

FO: Ralph Levine, Pres. COO

HR: Thomas B. Moorhead, VP

Emp: 3,350   Rev: $662 mil.

Mfr. personal care products and pet products.

Australia, Canada, England, U.K., France, Italy, Mexico, New Zealand, Spain

CASAS INTERNATIONAL BROKERAGE INC.

10030 Marconi Drive
San Diego, CA 92173-3255
Tel: (619) 661-6162 Fax: (619) 661-6800
CEO: Sylvia Casas-Jolliffe
FO: Mayo Obregon
HR: John E. Jolliffe
Emp: 145
Customhouse brokerage, freight forwarding, warehousing, import/export.
Mexico

CASCADE CORPORATION

201st Ave.
Portland, OR 97201
Tel: (503) 669-6300 Fax: (503) 669-6321
CEO: Robert Warren, Jr., Pres.
HR: Gregory S. Anderson
Web site: www.cascor.com
Emp: 865
Mfr. hydraulic forklift truck attachments.
Australia, Canada, England, U.K., France, Germany, Japan, Netherlands

CASE CORPORATION

700 State Street
Racine, WI 53404
Tel: (414) 636-6011 Fax: (414) 636-0200
CEO: Jean-Pierre Rosso, Chmn.
FO: Steven G. Lamb, Pres.
HR: Marc J. Castor, VP
Web site: www.casecorp.com
Emp: 18,000 Rev: $6,000 mil.
Mfr./sale agricultural and construction equipment.
Australia, Austria, Brazil, China (PRC), England, U.K., France, Germany, Mexico, Singapore, Uzbekistan

CASHCO INC.

PO Box 6
Ellsworth, KS 67439-0006
Tel: (913) 472-4461 Fax: (913) 472-3539
CEO: Phillip G. Rogers
FO: John C. Reid
HR: Dale L. Shepherd
Emp: 156
Mfr. pressure regulators and control valves.
Canada

A.M. CASTLE & COMPANY

3400 N. Wolf Road
Franklin Park, IL 60131
Tel: (784) 755-7111 Fax: (784) 455-7136
CEO: R. G. Mork, Pres.
HR: Paul Winsauer
Emp: 1,200
Metals distribution.
Canada, Netherlands

CAT PUMPS

1681 94th Lane NE
Minneapolis, MN 55449-4324
Tel: (612) 780-5440 Fax: (612) 780-2958
CEO: Steve Bruggeman, Pres.
Emp: 150
Mfr./distributor pumps.
Belgium, England, U.K., Germany, Switzerland

CATERPILLAR INC.

100 NE Adams Street
Peoria, IL 61629-6105
Tel: (309) 675-1000 Fax: (309) 675-1182
CEO: Donald V. Fites, Chmn.
HR: Alan J. Rassi, VP HR
Web site: www.cat.com
Emp: 65,000 Rev: $18.9 bil.
Mfr. earth/material-handling and construction machinery and equipment and engines.
Australia, Belgium, Bermuda, Brazil, Canada, Channel Islands, U.K., Chile, China (PRC), Denmark, England, U.K., France, Germany, Guatemala, Hong Kong, Hungary, India, Indonesia, Ireland, Italy, Japan, Kazakhstan, Malaysia, Mexico, Netherlands, Northern Ireland, U.K., Norway, Poland, Portugal, Russia, Singapore, South Africa, Spain, Sweden, Switzerland, Turkey, Turkmenistan, United Arab Emirates, Vietnam

L.D. CAULK COMPANY

PO Box 359
Milford, DE 19963
Tel: (302) 422-4511 Fax: (302) 422-5719
CEO: Brian Melonakos, VP
HR: Sally Paull
Emp: 2,500
Dental material.
Brazil, Canada

C.B. RICHARD ELLIS

533 South Fremont Ave.

Los Angeles, CA 90071-1712

Tel: (213) 613-3123 Fax: (213) 613-3535

CEO: James J. Didion, Chmn.

FO: Gary J. Beban, Pres.

HR: Nancy Morris

Web site: www.cbrichardellis.com

Emp: 9,000 Rev: $818 mil.

Commercial real estate services.

Argentina, Australia, Austria, Belgium, Botswana, Brazil, Canada, China (PRC), England, U.K., France, Germany, Hong Kong, Hungary, India, Indonesia, Italy, Japan, Mexico, Netherlands, New Zealand, Portugal, Scotland, U.K., Singapore, South Africa, Spain, Switzerland, Taiwan (ROC), Thailand, Turkey, Zimbabwe

CBI COMPANY

1501 North Division Street

Plainfield, IL 60544

Tel: (815) 241-7546 Fax: (815) 439-6010

CEO: Gerald Glenn, Pres.

HR: Steve Glenn

Emp: 11,000

Holding company: metal plate fabricating, construction, oil and gas drilling.

Argentina, Australia, Brazil, Canada, England, U.K., Germany, Indonesia, Netherlands, Philippines, Saudi Arabia, Singapore, South Africa, South Korea, United Arab Emirates, Venezuela

CCH INC.

2700 Lake Cook Road

Riverwoods, IL 60015

Tel: (847) 267-7000 Fax: (800) 224-8299

CEO: Hugh Yarrington, Pres. & Chmn.

HR: Don Cervantes

Emp: 5,700

Tax & business law information, software & services.

Australia, Canada, England, U.K., Germany, Japan, New Zealand, Singapore

CCI TRIAD

6207 Beecave Road

Austin, TX 78746

Tel: (510) 449-0606 Fax: (512) 328-8209

CEO: Glenn Stats, Pres.

Emp: 1,500

Information retrieval systems.

Canada, England, U.K.

CCS INTERNATIONAL LTD

360 Madison Ave., 6th Fl.

New York, NY 10017

Tel: (212) 557-3040 Fax: (212) 983-1278

CEO: Ed Sklar, Pres.

FO: Steven Heller

HR: Tom Felice

Emp: 150

Mfr. electronic security products.

England, U.K.

CDI CORPORATION

1717 Arch Street, 35th Fl.

Philadelphia, PA 19103

Tel: (215) 569-2200 Fax: (215) 569-1300

CEO: Mitch Weinick

FO: Christian M. Hoechst

HR: Wyman Lee

Emp: 24,000

Engineering, technical and temporary personnel services.

Canada, England, U.K.

CDM INTERNATIONAL INC.

Ten Cambridge Center

Cambridge, MA 02142

Tel: (617) 252-8000 Fax: (617) 577-7504

CEO: Thomas Furman, Pres.

FO: Frederick J. Holland

HR: M. Allen

Emp: 2,300

Consulting engineers.

Egypt, Hong Kong, Jordan, Oman, Philippines, Singapore, Taiwan (ROC), Thailand, Turkey

CEILCOTE AIR POLLUTION CONTROL

14955 Sprague Road

Strongsville, OH 44136

Tel: (440) 243-0700 Fax: (440) 234-3486

CEO: George R. Bent

FO: Torrey N. Foster

Emp: 420

Mfr. corrosion-resistant material, air pollution control equipment, construction services.

Australia, Canada, England, U.K., Germany, Japan, Mexico, New Zealand, Singapore

CELITE CORPORATION

PO Box 519

Lompoc, CA 93438

Tel: (805) 735-7791 Fax: (805) 735-5699

CEO: William J. Woods, Jr., Pres.

Mining/process diatomaceous earth (diatomite).

Canada, England, U.K., France, Hong Kong, Italy, Mexico

CENDANT CORPORATION

6 Sylvan Way

Parsippany, NJ 07054

Tel: (973) 428-9700 Fax: (973) 496-5902

CEO: Henry R. Silverman

HR: Tom Christopoul, EVP

Web site: www.cendant.com

Emp: 34,000 Rev: $5,300 mil.

Membership-based, direct marketer offering shopping/travel/insurance and dining discount programs

Canada, Hong Kong, India, Japan, Malaysia, Russia, South Africa, Thailand

CENTERCORE INC.

1355 West Front Street

Plainfield, NJ 07063

Tel: (908) 561-7662 Fax: (908) 561-3442

CEO: Paul Allegreto

HR: Richard Thornton

Emp: 300

Design/mfr. modular office workstations.

England, U.K.

CENTOCOR INC.

200 Great Valley Parkway

Malvern, PA 19355-1307

Tel: (610) 651-6000 Fax: (610) 651-6100

CEO: David P. Holveck

FO: Martin R. Page, SVP

HR: Michael P. Melore

Web site: www.centocor.com

Emp: 650 Rev: $201 mil.

Develop/mfr./marketing diagnostic & therapeutic products for human health care.

England, U.K., Japan, Netherlands

CENTRAL GULF LINES INC.

650 Poydras Street

New Orleans, LA 70130

Tel: (504) 529-5461 Fax: (504) 529-5745

CEO: Erik F. Johnsen

FO: Erik L. Johnsen

HR: Lawrence Tizzard

Emp: 130

Steamship service.

Netherlands, Singapore

CENTRAL NATIONAL-GOTTESMAN INC.

3 Manhattanville Road

Purchase, NY 10577-2110

Tel: (914) 696-9000 Fax: (914) 696-1066

CEO: James G. Wallach

HR: Louise Roberts Caputo

Emp: 800 Rev: $1,500 mil.

Worldwide sales pulp and paper products.

Argentina, Australia, Austria, Brazil, China (PRC), Colombia, England, U.K., France, Hong Kong, Indonesia, Italy, Japan, Malaysia, Mexico, Netherlands, Philippines, Singapore, Spain, Taiwan (ROC), Thailand, Venezuela

CENTURY 21 REAL ESTATE CORPORATION

6 Sylvan Way

Parsippany, NJ 07054-3826

Tel: (973) 496-5722 Fax: (973) 496-5527

CEO: Robert Moles, Pres.

FO: C. Javier Parraga, VP

HR: Andrea Jestin

Web site: www.century21.com

Emp: 110,00

Real estate.

Australia, Belgium, Canada, Costa Rica, England, U.K., France, Hong Kong, Indonesia, Israel, Japan, Mexico, New Zealand, Philippines, Singapore, South Korea, Spain, Taiwan (ROC)

CERDIAN CORPORATION

8100 34th Ave. South

Minneapolis, MN 55425

Tel: (612) 853-8100 Fax: (612) 853-4068

CEO: Lawrence Perlman, Chmn. & Pres.

HR: Ron James, EVP

Web site: www.ceridian.com

Emp: 8,000 Rev: $1,050 mil.

Provides diversified information services.

Canada, England, U.K.

CERTRON CORPORATION

1545 Sawtelle Blvd.

Los Angeles, CA 90025

Tel: (310) 914-0300 Fax: (310) 914-0310

CEO: Marshall I. Kass, Chmn.

FO: Jonathan E. Kass, Pres.

HR: Jesse A. Lopez, Dir.

Web site: www.certron.com

Emp: 56 Rev: $5 mil.

Mfr./distributor magnetic audio/video tapes & disks.

Mexico

CH2M HILL INC.

6060 South Willow Drive

Greenwood Village, CO 80111

Tel: (303) 771-0900 Fax: (303) 770-2616

CEO: Philip G. Hall, Chmn.

FO: Ralph R. Peterson

HR: F. K. Berry

Emp: 7,000 Rev: $900 mil.

Consulting engineers, planners, economists and scientists.

Argentina, Australia, Brazil, Canada, China (PRC), Czech Republic, Egypt, England, U.K., Hong Kong, Hungary, Japan, Jordan, Kazakhstan, Malaysia, New Zealand, Peru, Poland, Russia, Saudi Arabia, South Korea, Sri Lanka, Taiwan (ROC), Thailand, Trinidad & Tobago, Turkey, Ukraine

CHADBOURNE & PARKE LLP

30 Rockefeller Plaza

New York, NY 10112-0127

Tel: (212) 408-5100 Fax: (212) 541-5369

CEO: Charles K. O'Neill, Opers. Ptnr.

FO: Aniello Bianco, Mng. Dir.

Emp: 280

International law firm.

Australia, Belarus, England, U.K., Japan, Kazakhstan

THE CHAMBERS COMPANY

1010 North Charles Street

Baltimore, MD 21201

Tel: (410) 727-4535 Fax: (410) 727-6982

CEO: Robert A.Hickman

FO: J. H. L. Chambers II

HR: Mary Dircks

Emp: 62

Interior design and architectural services.

Bahamas

CHAMPION INTERNATIONAL CORPORATION

One Champion Plaza

Stamford, CT 06921

Tel: (213) 358-7000 Fax: (213) 358-2975

CEO: Richard E. Olson, Chmn.

FO: Rocky Wade, VP

HR: Paul Record

Emp: 24,600 Rev: $6,000 mil.

Manufacture and sale of pulp and paper.

Belgium, Brazil, Canada, Indonesia, Japan, Mexico, Singapore

CHAMPION PARTS REBUILDERS INC.

751 Roosevelt Road

Glen Ellyn, IL 60137

Tel: (630) 942-8317 Fax: (630) 942-0334

CEO: Jerry Bragiel, Pres.

HR: Barbara Wander

Emp: 2,500

Remanufacture of automotive, truck and tractor parts.

Canada

CHARTER BEHAVIORAL CORPORATION

577 Mulberry Street, PO Box 209

Macon, GA 31298

Tel: (912) 742-1161 Fax: (912) 751-2909

CEO: Edwin Crawford, Pres.

FO: Michael E. Wellons

HR: Ms. Renee Eversole

Emp: 3,500

International hospital management.

England, U.K.

CHASAN INTERNATIONAL INC.

1251 Ave. of the Americas

New York, NY 10020

Tel: (212) 719-1320 Fax: (212) 768-0190

CEO: Alan D. Chasan, Pres.

FO: Alan D. Chasan

Emp: 5

Real estate development & investment management.

Spain

THE CHASE MANHATTAN CORPORATION

World Headquarters, 270 Park Ave.

New York, NY 10017

Tel: (212) 270-6000 Fax: (212) 622-9030

CEO: Walter V. Shipley, Chmn.

FO: W. B. Harrison, Jr., EVP, Intl.

HR: John J. Farrell

Web site: www.chase.com

Emp: 69,000 Rev: $30,000 mil.

International banking and financial services.

Argentina, Australia, Austria, Bahamas, Bahrain, Barbados, Belgium, Brazil, British Virgin Islands, Cameroon, Canada, Channel Islands, U.K., Chile, China (PRC), Colombia, Czech Republic, Denmark, Dominican Republic, Ecuador, Egypt, England, U.K., Finland, France, Germany, Greece, Guatemala, Guyana, Honduras, Hong Kong, India, Indonesia, Ireland, Italy, Ivory Coast, Japan, Jordan, Kenya, Lebanon, Liberia, Luxembourg, Malaysia, Mexico, Netherlands, Netherlands Antilles, New Zealand, Nigeria, Northern Ireland, U.K., Norway, Pakistan, Panama, Paraguay, Peru, Philippines, Poland, Portugal, Qatar, Romania, Russia, Saudi Arabia, Senegal, Singapore, South Africa, South Korea, Spain, Sudan, Sweden, Switzerland, Taiwan (ROC), Thailand, Trinidad & Tobago, Tunisia, Turkey, United Arab Emirates, Uzbekistan, Venezuela, Vietnam

CHATTEM INC.

1715 West 38th Street

Chattanooga, TN 37409

Tel: (423) 821-4571 Fax: (423) 821-6132

CEO: Zan Guerry, Chmn.

FO: Robert E. Bosworth

HR: Wanda Neidig

Emp: 345

Mfr. health & beauty aids.

Canada, England, U.K.

CHECK TECHNOLOGY CORPORATION

12500 Whitewater Drive

Minnetonka, MN 55343-9420

Tel: (612) 939-9000 Fax: (612) 939-1151

CEO: Jay Herman, Pres.

HR: Rebecca Wagner

Emp: 175

Mfr. computer-controlled check/coupon print systems.

Australia, England, U.K., France, Spain

CHECKPOINT SYSTEMS, INC.

101 Wolf Drive

Thorofare, NJ 08086

Tel: (609) 848-1800 Fax: (609) 848-0957

CEO: Kevin P. Dowd, Pres.

FO: Lukas A. Geiges, SVP Intl.

Emp: 2,500 Rev: $290 mil.

Mfr. test, measurement and closed-circuit television systems.

Canada, England, U.K.

CHEMDYE INTERNATIONAL INC.

51 East 42nd Street, Ste. 1612

New York, NY 10017

Tel: (212) 687-3034 Fax: (212) 983-0491

CEO: B. L. Schmidt, Pres.

Emp: 300

Mfr. rubber products.

Germany

CHEMINEER INC.

PO Box 1123

Dayton, OH 45401-1123

Tel: (937) 454-3200 Fax: (937) 454-3379

CEO: Leonard Graziano, Pres.

FO: David Barke

HR: Ed Blohm

Emp: 780

Mfr. fluid agitators and static mixers for chemicals processing.

England, U.K.

THE CHEMITHON CORPORATION

5430 West Marginal Way, SW

Seattle, WA 98106

Tel: (206) 937-9954 Fax: (206) 932-3786

CEO: Kenneth B. Hohnstein

FO: Dr. Norman C. Foster

HR: Michelle Welch

Web site: www.chemithon.com.

Emp: 135

Mfr./services chemicals process equipment for detergent, specialty chemicals and power generation industries.

India

CHEMTEX INTERNATIONAL INC.

560 Lexington Ave.

New York, NY 10022

Tel: (212) 752-5220 Fax: (212) 752-0872

CEO: Julio J. Martinez

HR: Thomas McGannon, EVP

Emp: 900

Mfr. fibers & petrochemicals; engineering, procurement, construction, construction management.

China (PRC), India, Indonesia

THE CHERRY CORPORATION

3600 Sunset Ave., PO Box 718

Waukegan, IL 60087

Tel: (847) 662-9200 Fax: (847) 662-2990

CEO: Peter B. Cherry, Chmn.

Emp: 3,617

Mfr. electrical switches, electronic keyboards, controls & displays, semiconductors.

Australia, England, U.K., France, Germany, Hong Kong, India, Japan

CHESAPEAKE ENERGY CORP.

6104 North Western

Oklahoma City, OK 73118

Tel: (405) 848-8000 Fax: (405) 848-8588

CEO: Aubrey McClendon, Pres.

Rev: $50 mil.

Oil and natural gas.

Canada

CHESTERTON BINSWANGER INTERNATIONAL

Two Logan Square, 4th Floor

Philadelphia, PA 19103-2759

Tel: (215) 448-6000 Fax: (215) 448-6238

CEO: Frank G. Binswanger, Jr., Pres. & Chmn.

FO: Frank G. Binswanger, III

HR: Ellen Diorio

Emp: 4,300

Real estate & related services.

Argentina, Australia, Austria, Bahrain, Belgium, Brazil, Chile, Czech Republic, England, U.K., Finland, France, Germany, Hong Kong, Hungary, India, Indonesia, Italy, Japan, Malaysia, Mexico, Netherlands, Poland, Russia, Saudi Arabia, Singapore, Spain, Switzerland, Thailand, United Arab Emirates

A.W. CHESTERTON COMPANY

225 Fallon Road

Stoneham, MA 02180

Tel: (781) 438-7000 Fax: (781) 438-8971

CEO: James D. Chesterton, Pres.

FO: Stephen B. Chapman

HR: Rita Whelan

Web site: www.stoneham.chesterton.com

Emp: 1,700

Packing gaskets, sealing products systems, etc.

Australia, Canada, Chile, Germany, Ireland, Mexico

CHEVRON CHEMICAL COMPANY

6001 Bollinger Canyon Road., PO Box 5047

San Ramon, CA 94583-0947

Tel: (925) 842-1000 Fax: (925) 842-5775

CEO: Kenneth Derr, Pres.

FO: D.W. Callahan

HR: J. J. Ranslem

Web site: www.chevron.com

Emp: 4,900 Rev: $2,500 mil.

Mfr. chemicals.

Brazil, Canada, England, U.K., France, Germany, Japan, Mexico, Singapore, Switzerland, Vietnam

CHEVRON CORPORATION

575 Market Street

San Francisco, CA 94105

Tel: (415) 894-7700 Fax: (415) 894-2248

CEO: Kenneth T. Derr, Chmn.

FO: James N. Sullivan, VC

HR: Greg Matiuk

Web site: www.chevron.com

Emp: 38,000 Rev: $2,600 mil.

Oil exploration & production & petroleum products.

Brazil, Canada, Colombia, England, U.K., Indonesia, Saudi Arabia

CHICAGO METALLIC CORPORATION

4849 South Austin Ave.

Chicago, IL 60638

Tel: (708) 563-4600 Fax: (708) 563-4552

CEO: Larry Kinderman, Pres.

Steel and metal products.

Belgium, Singapore

CHICAGO RAWHIDE INDUSTRIES (CRI)

900 North State Street

Elgin, IL 60123

Tel: (847) 742-7840 Fax: (847) 742-7845

CEO: Z. J. Petkus, Pres.

FO: Frank Koenig

HR: Max Edwards

Emp: 2,000

Mfr. shaft and face seals.

Australia, Canada, England, U.K., Japan

CHICAGO RAWHIDE MFG. COMPANY

900 North State Street

Elgin, IL 60120

Tel: (847) 742-7840 Fax: (847) 742-7845

CEO: Gary Butcher, Pres.

FO: F. G. Auch

HR: F. Elegreet

Emp: 2,000

Seals & filters.

Australia, Canada, Japan, Mexico

CHIEF INDUSTRIES INC.

PO Box 2078

Grand Island, NE 68802-2078

Tel: (308) 382-8820 Fax: (308) 381-8475

CEO: Robert G. Eihusen, Chmn.

HR: Milt Ehly

Emp: 1,510

Mfr. grain bins, steel buildings, grain handling and drying equipment, elevator legs and components.

England, U.K.

CHIQUITA BRANDS INTERNATIONAL INC.

250 East Fifth Street

Cincinnati, OH 45202

Tel: (513) 784-8000 Fax: (513) 784-8030

CEO: Steven G. Warshaw, Pres. & COO

FO: Michael D. O'Brien, EVP

HR: Jean B. Lapointe, VP

Web site: www.chiquita.com

Emp: 39,000 Rev: $2,400 mil

Sale and distribution of bananas, fresh fruits and processed foods.

Australia, Canada, China (PRC), Colombia, Costa Rica, Ecuador, Germany, Honduras, Italy, Japan, Netherlands, Panama, Philippines

CHIRON CORPORATION

4560 Horton Street

Emeryville, CA 94608-2916

Tel: (510) 655-8730 Fax: (510) 655-9910

CEO: Sean Lance, Pres.

HR: J. Mike Smith

Emp: 6,000

Research/mfr./marketing therapeutics, vaccines, diagnostics, ophthalmic.

Australia, Austria, Belgium, Canada, England, U.K., France, Germany, Hong Kong, Italy, Japan, Mexico, Netherlands, Poland, Scotland, U.K., Singapore, South Korea, Spain, Sweden, Switzerland

THE CHRISTIAN SCIENCE PUBLISHING SOCIETY

1 Norway Street

Boston, MA 02115

Tel: (617) 450-2000 Fax: (617) 450-7575

CEO: John L. Selover

FO: John L. Selover

HR: Stephanie McNeil

Emp: 600

Publishing company.

China (PRC), England, U.K., France, Israel, Japan, Jordan, Mexico, Russia

CHRYSLER CORPORATION

1000 Chrysler Drive

Auburn Hills, MI 48326-2766

Tel: (248) 576-5741 Fax: (248) 512-5143

CEO: Robert Eaton

FO: Ted Cunningham

HR: Kathy Oswald

Web site: www.chrysler.com

Emp: 123,000

Mfr./marketing cars & light trucks, electronic & aerospace products & systems.

Austria, Canada, China (PRC), France, Germany, Mexico, Russia

CHRYSLER FINANCIAL CORPORATION

27777 Franklin Road

Southfield, MI 48034

Tel: (248) 948-3555 Fax: (248) 948-3987

CEO: Darrell Davis, Pres.

FO: Henry G. Spellman

HR: Linda Rumschlag

Web site: www.chrysler financial.com

Emp: 3,200

Financial services.

Canada, Mexico

THE CHUBB CORPORATION

15 Mountain View Road

Warren, NJ 07061-1615

Tel: (908) 580-2000 Fax: (908) 580-3606

CEO: Dean R. O'Hare, Chmn.

FO: Robert M. Lynyak

HR: Baxter Graham, SVP

Web site: www.chubb.com

Emp: 11,000 Rev: $6,550.0 mil

Holding company: property/casualty insurance.

Argentina, Australia, Belgium, Brazil, Canada, Chile, China (PRC), Colombia, Denmark, England, U.K., France, Germany, Hong Kong, India, Ireland, Italy, Japan, Mexico, Netherlands, Scotland, U.K., Singapore, South Korea, Spain, Sweden, Taiwan (ROC), Thailand, Venezuela

CHURCH & DWIGHT CO., INC.

469 North Harrison Street

Princeton, NJ 08543

Tel: (609) 683-5900 Fax: (609) 497-7177

CEO: Robert A. Davies, II, Pres

Emp: 900

Specialty chemicals and consumer products.

Canada, England, U.K.

CIBER, INC.

5251 DTC Parkway, Ste. 1400

Engelwood, CO 80111

Tel: (303) 220-0100 Fax: (303) 220-7100

CEO: Bobby G. Stevenson, Chmn.

FO: William E. Storrison

HR: Dave Plisko, Dir.

Web site: www.ciber.com

Emp: 5,700 Rev: $550 mil.

Provides software development and maintenance services, year 2000 support and information technology consulting.

Canada

CIGNA CORPORATION

One Liberty Place

Philadelphia, PA 19192

Tel: (215) 761-1000 Fax: (215) 761-5008

CEO: Wilson H. Taylor, Chmn.

HR: Donald M. Levinson

Emp: 50,600 Rev: $18,400 mil.

Insurance, invest, health care and other financial services.

Argentina, Australia, Austria, Bahamas, Belgium, Bermuda, Brazil, Canada, Channel Islands, U.K., Chile, Colombia, Denmark, Dominican Republic, Ecuador, England, U.K., France, Germany, Ghana, Greece, Hong Kong, Indonesia, Israel, Italy, Jamaica, Japan, Lebanon, Liberia, Malaysia, Mexico, Netherlands, Netherlands Antilles, New Zealand, Norway, Pakistan, Panama, Paraguay, Philippines, Poland, Portugal, Saudi Arabia, Scotland, U.K., Singapore, South Korea, Spain, Sweden, Switzerland, Taiwan (ROC), Thailand, Turkey, Venezuela, Vietnam

CINCINNATI INCORPORATED

PO Box 11111

Cincinnati, OH 45211

Tel: (513) 367-7100 Fax: (513) 367-7552

CEO: John Kahler, Pres.

HR: Blevins Heansley

Emp: 603

Mfr. metal forming machines.

Japan

CINCINNATI MILACRON INC.

4701 Marburg Ave.

Cincinnati, OH 45209

Tel: (513) 841-8100 Fax: (513) 841-8919

CEO: Daniel J. Meyer, Chmn.

HR: Theodore Mauser

Emp: 7,885 Rev: $1,000 mil.

Develop/mfr. technologies for metalworking & plastics processing industrial.

Austria, Brazil, England, U.K., France, Germany, Japan, Mexico, Netherlands

CINCOM SYSTEMS INC.

2300 Montana Ave.

Cincinnati, OH 45211

Tel: (513) 612-2300 Fax: (513) 481-8332

CEO: Thomas M. Nies, Chmn.

HR: Gerald Shawhan

Web site: www.cincom.com

Emp: 1,400 Rev: $200 mil.

Develop/distributor computer software.

Australia, Belgium, Brazil, Canada, Denmark, England, U.K., France, Germany, Hong Kong, Japan, Mexico, Monaco, Netherlands, New Zealand, Norway, Scotland, U.K., Singapore, Sweden, Switzerland

CINERGY CORP.

139 East Fourth Street

Cincinnati, OH 45202

Tel: (513) 421-9500 Fax: (513) 651-9196

CEO: Jackson H. Randolph, Chmn.

FO: James E. Rogers, Pres.

HR: Jerry W. Liggett, VP

Web site: www.cinergy.com

Emp: 7,000

Utility holding company - generates, transmits and distributes electricity and natural gas.

Argentina, England, U.K.

CIRCON ACMI

300 Stillwater Ave., PO Box 1971

Stamford, CT 06904-1971

Tel: (203) 357-8300 Fax: (203) 328-8789

CEO: Richard Auhll, Pres.

FO: D. Piggin & R. Devine

HR: Jon St. Clair

Emp: 786

Mfr./sale/services medical & surgical endoscopes, instruments & video systems.

France

CISCO SYSTEMS, INC.

170 Tasman Drive

San Jose, CA 95134-1706

Tel: (408) 526-4000 Fax: (408) 526-4100

CEO: John T. Chambers, Pres.

FO: Gary Daichendt, SVP

HR: Barbara Beck, SVP

Web site: www.cisco.com

Rev: $6,400 mil.

Develop/mfr./market computer hardware and software networking systems.

Argentina, Australia, Austria, Belgium, Brazil, Canada, Chile, China (PRC), Colombia, Costa Rica, Czech Republic, Denmark, England, U.K., Finland, France, Germany, Greece, Hong Kong, Hungary, India, Indonesia, Ireland, Israel, Italy, Japan, Malaysia, Mexico, Netherlands, New Zealand, Norway, Peru, Philippines, Poland, Portugal, Russia, Singapore, South Africa, South Korea, Spain, Sweden, Switzerland, Taiwan (ROC), Thailand, Turkey, United Arab Emirates, Venezuela

CITICORP

399 Park Ave.

New York, NY 10043

Tel: (212) 559-1000 Fax: (212) 527-2066

CEO: John S. Reed, Chmn.

FO: Mary Alice W. Taylor, EVP

HR: Lawrence R. Phillips, EVP

Web site: www.citibank.com

Emp: 93,000 Rev: $34,500 mil.

International banking and financial services.

Algeria, Argentina, Aruba, Australia, Bahamas, Bahrain, Bangladesh, Belgium, Bolivia, Brazil, Brunei, Canada, Cayman Islands, Channel Islands, U.K., Chile, China (PRC), Colombia, Costa Rica, Czech Republic, Dem. Rep. of Congo, Dominican Republic, Ecuador, Egypt, El Salvador, England, U.K., Finland, Gabon, Germany, Greece, Guam, Guatemala, Haiti, Honduras, Hong Kong, Hungary, India, Indonesia, Ireland, Israel, Italy, Ivory Coast, Jamaica, Japan, Jordan, Kazakhstan, Kenya, Malaysia, Mexico, Monaco, Morocco, Netherlands, New Zealand, Nigeria, Norway, Oman, Pakistan, Panama, Paraguay, Peru, Philippines, Poland, Portugal, Romania, Russia, Saudi Arabia, Scotland, U.K., Senegal, Singapore, Slovakia, South Africa, South Korea, Sri Lanka, Sudan, Switzerland, Taiwan (ROC), Tanzania, Thailand, Trinidad & Tobago, Tunisia, Turkey, United Arab Emirates, Uruguay, Venezuela, Vietnam, Zambia

CITRIX SYSTEMS, INC.

6400 NW 6th Way
Fort Lauderdale, FL 33309
Tel: (954) 267-3000 Fax: (954) 267-9319
CEO: Roger W. Roberts
FO: Michael Wendl, Mng. Dir.
HR: James J. Felcyn Jr., VP
Web site: www.citrix.com
Emp: 303 Rev: $124 mil.
Developer of computer software.
Australia, England, U.K., France, Germany

CKS GROUP, INC.

10441 Bandley Drive
Cupertino, CA 95014
Tel: (408) 366-5100 Fax: (408) 342-5420
CEO: Mark D. Kvamme, Chmn.
FO: Robert T. Clarkson, CKS Int'l.
HR: Steve Schier
Web site: www.cks.com
Emp: 641 Rev: $166.6 mil.
Design and implementation services for multimedia marketing programs.
France, Germany

CLARCOR INC.

2323 Sixth Street, PO Box 7007
Rockford, IL 61125
Tel: (815) 962-8867 Fax: (815) 962-0417
CEO: Norman E. Johnson, Pres.
FO: David J. Anderson
HR: David J. Lindsay, VP
Emp: 2,500
Mfr. filtration products and consumer packaging products.
Australia, Belgium, England, U.K., Hong Kong

CLAYTON INDUSTRIES

4213 N. Temple City Blvd.
El Monte, CA 91731
Tel: (626) 443-9381 Fax: (626) 442-1701
CEO: William Clayton, Jr., Pres.
HR: Boyd Calvin
Web site: www.clayton industries.com
Emp: 750
Mfr. steam generators, dynamometers and water treatment chemicals.
Belgium, Mexico

CLEARY GOTTLIEB STEEN & HAMILTON

One Liberty Plaza
New York, NY 10006
Tel: (212) 225-2000 Fax: (212) 225-3999
CEO: Ned B. Stiles, Mng. Ptnr.
FO: David Almquist
HR: Nancy Roberts, Dir.
Emp: 1,430 Rev: $341 mil.
International law firm.
Belgium, England, U.K., France, Germany, Hong Kong, Italy, Japan

CLEMENTINA-CLEMCO CORP.

1657 Rawlings Road
Burlingame, CA 94010
Tel: (650) 692-9080 Fax: (650) 697-0217
CEO: Mark Cleary, Pres.
Emp: 150
Blast cleaning equipment & systems, dust collection systems, coating & finishing systems, dry stripping facilities.
Australia, Germany, Singapore

CLEVELAND-CLIFFS INC.

1100 Superior Ave., 18th Floor
Cleveland, OH 44114
Tel: (216) 694-5700 Fax: (216) 694-4880
CEO: John S. Brinzo, Pres.
FO: John W. Sanders
HR: Richard F. Novak
Emp: 4,972
Iron, coal mining, and transportation.
Australia, Canada

CLIMAX MOLYBDENUM CORPORATION

1370 Washington Pike
Bridgeville, PA 15017
Tel: (412) 257-5181 Fax: (412) 257-5191
CEO: Milton Ward, Pres.
Emp: 4,900
Molybdenum, tungsten.
England, U.K., France, Germany, Japan

THE CLOROX COMPANY

1221 Broadway, PO Box 24305

Oakland, CA 94623-1305

Tel: (510) 271-7000 Fax: (510) 832-1463

CEO: G. Craig Sullivan, Pres. & Chmn.

FO: Richard T. Conti

HR: Janet M. Brady

Emp: 4,700 Rev: $1,000 mil.

Mfr. soap & detergents, and domestic consumer packaged products.

Argentina, Brazil, Canada, Cayman Islands, Chile, China (PRC), Colombia, Costa Rica, Dominican Republic, Egypt, Hong Kong, Malaysia, Mexico, Panama, Peru, Poland, Saudi Arabia, South Korea, Spain, Uruguay, Venezuela, Yemen

CMS ENERGY CORPORATION

Fairlane Plaza South, Ste. 1100, 330 Town Drive

Dearborn, MI 48126

Tel: (313) 436-9200 Fax: (313) 436-9225

CEO: William T. McCormick, Jr., Chrm

FO: James W. Cook, SVP

HR: John F. Drake, VP

Web site: www.cmsenergy.com

Emp: 9,659 Rev: $4,797 mil.

Independent power plant operator.

Argentina, Australia, Brazil, Colombia, Ecuador, Ghana, Morocco, Singapore, Turkey, Venezuela

CNA FINANCIAL CORPORATION

CNA Plaza

Chicago, IL 60685

Tel: (312) 822-5000 Fax: (312) 822-6419

CEO: Edward J. Noha, Chmn.

FO: Dennis H. Chookaszian, CEO

HR: Carol Dubnicki, SVP

Web site: www.can.com

Emp: 24,000 Rev: $17,000 mil.

Commercial property/casualty insurance policies.

Argentina, Australia, England, U.K., France, Germany, Hungary, Ireland, Italy

CNB INTERNATIONAL, INC.

171 Church Street, Ste. 140

Charleston, SC 29401

Tel: (843) 853-1250 Fax: (843) 937-8210

CEO: Tim Kelleher, Pres.

HR: Carol Rodgers

Web site: www.cnb-intl.com

Emp: 750

Mfr. Metal forming presses and aftermarket services.

Australia, England, U.K., India

COACH LEATHERWEAR CO.

516 West 34 Street

New York, NY 10001

Tel: (212) 594-1850 Fax: (212) 594-1682

CEO: Lou Frankfort, Pres.

FO: Cathy Burns

Mfr. and sales of high-quality leather products, including handbags and wallets.

England, U.K., Italy

THE COASTAL CORPORATION

Nine Greenway Plaza

Houston, TX 77046-0995

Tel: (713) 877-1400 Fax: (713) 877-6752

CEO: David A. Arledge, Pres. & Chmn.

FO: Jack C. Pester, SVP

HR: Ron Brownlee

Web site: www.coastalcorp.com

Emp: 13,000 Rev: $9,500 mil.

Oil refining, natural gas, related services; independent power production.

Aruba, Australia, Bermuda, Brazil, Canada, Chile, China (PRC), El Salvador, England, U.K., Estonia, Germany, Hungary, Indonesia, Peru, Philippines, Venezuela

COBE LABORATORIES INC.

1185 Oak Street

Lakewood, CO 80215

Tel: (303) 232-6800 Fax: (303) 231-4952

CEO: Mats Wahlstrom, Pres.

FO: Edward J. Giachetti, Sr.

HR: Teresa Blandford

Emp: 2,200

Mfr. medical equipment & supplies.

Australia, Belgium, Bermuda, Canada, England, U.K., France, Germany, Italy, Japan, Mexico, Netherlands, Singapore, South Korea

THE COCA-COLA COMPANY

P.O. Drawer 1734

Atlanta, GA 30301

Tel: (404) 676-2121 Fax: (404) 676-6792

CEO: M. Douglas Ivester, Chmn.

FO: William P. Casey, Pres.

Web site: www.coca-cola.com

Emp: 33,000 Rev: $4,000 mil.

Mfr./marketing/distributor soft drinks, syrups & concentrates, juice & juice-drink products.

Argentina, Australia, Belgium, Brazil, Canada, Chile, China (PRC), Colombia, Costa Rica, Denmark, Egypt, England, U.K., France, Germany, Guatemala, Guinea, Hong Kong, India, Indonesia, Israel, Italy, Japan, Kenya, Mexico, Netherlands, Nigeria, Norway, Philippines, Poland, Romania, Russia, South Africa, Spain, Sweden, Switzerland, Taiwan (ROC), Thailand, Turkey, Ukraine, Uruguay, Vietnam, Zambia

COEN CO., INC.

1510 Rollins Road

Burlingame, CA 94010

Tel: (650) 697-0440 Fax: (650) 686-5655

CEO: James H. White, Pres.

FO: W. A. Chapman

Emp: 300

Mfr. industrial burners.

Canada, Netherlands

COGNIZANT TECHNOLOGY SOLUTIONS CORPORATION

1700 Broadway, 26th Floor

New York, NY 10019

Tel: (212) 887-2385 Fax: (212) 887-2450

CEO: Wijeyaraj Mahadeva, Chmn.

FO: Lakshmi Narayanan, Pres.

Web site: www.dbss.com

Emp: 240 Rev: $25 mil.

Provides software development , application management, computer date corrections, and currency conversion.

Canada, England, U.K., India

COGSDILL TOOL PRODUCTS INC.

PO Box 7007

Camden, SC 29020

Tel: (803) 438-4000 Fax: (803) 438-5263

CEO: William Westerman, Pres.

HR: Barbara Walker

Emp: 200

Mfr. precision metalworking tools.

England, U.K.

COHERENT INC.

PO Box 54980

Santa Clara, CA 95056

Tel: (408) 764-4000 Fax: (408) 764-4800

CEO: Dr. Bernard Couillaud, Pres. & Chmn.

Emp: 1,325

Mfr. lasers for science, industrial & medical.

England, U.K., France, Germany, Hong Kong, Japan, Netherlands

COILCRAFT INC.

1102 Silver Lake Road

Cary, IL 60013

Tel: (847) 639-2361 Fax: (847) 639-1469

CEO: Thomas Liebman, Pres.

Emp: 1,300

Leaded & surface-mount coils & transformers.

Mexico, Taiwan (ROC)

COIN ACCEPTORS INC.

300 Hunter Ave.

St. Louis, MO 63124

Tel: (314) 725-0100 Fax: (314) 725-1243

CEO: Jack Thomas, Pres.

FO: Harold Tinsley

Emp: 1,100

Coin mechanisms for vending machinery.

Australia, England, U.K., Mexico

COLD SPRING GRANITE COMPANY

202 South 3rd Ave.

Cold Spring, MN 56320

Tel: (612) 685-3621 Fax: (612) 685-8490

CEO: Patrick Alexander, Pres.

FO: John Maile

HR: Chuck Gorres

Emp: 1,333

Granite quarrier and fabricator.

Canada

THE COLEMAN CO., INC.

3600 Hydraulic Street

Wichita, KS 67219

Tel: (316) 832-2653 Fax: (316) 832-3060

CEO: William Philips, VP

Emp: 3,000

Mfr./distributor/sales camping & outdoor recreation products.

Australia, Belgium, Brazil, Canada, England, U.K., Germany, Italy, Japan, Netherlands, Poland, United Arab Emirates

COLGATE-PALMOLIVE COMPANY

300 Park Ave.

New York, NY 10022

Tel: (212) 310-2000 Fax: (212) 310-2919

CEO: William Shanahan, Pres. & COO

HR: John Zoog, VP

Emp: 52,900

Mfr. pharmaceuticals, cosmetics, toiletries and detergents.

Algeria, Argentina, Australia, Austria, Belgium, Canada, Colombia, Costa Rica, Denmark, El Salvador, England, U.K., France, Germany, Greece, Guatemala, Guyana, Honduras, Hong Kong, India, Ireland, Italy, Ivory Coast, Jamaica, Japan, Kenya, Malaysia, Mexico, Morocco, Netherlands, New Zealand, Nicaragua, Panama, Peru, Philippines, Poland, Portugal, Russia, Senegal, Singapore, South Africa, Spain, Sweden, Switzerland, Thailand, Trinidad & Tobago, Uruguay, Venezuela, Vietnam, Zambia

COLLAGEN & COHESION

2500 Faber Place

Palo Alto, CA 94303

Tel: (650) 856-0200 Fax: (650) 856-0533

CEO: Gary Petersmeyer

HR: Deborah Webster

Emp: 465

Mfr. prod for repair/replacement of damaged human tissue.

England, U.K.

COLLINS & AIKMAN CORPORATION

701 McCullough Drive

Charlotte, NC 28262

Tel: (704) 547-8500 Fax: (704) 548-2081

CEO: Thomas E. Hannah, Pres.

HR: Harold R. Sunday, VP

Emp: 15,000 Rev: $1,600 mil.

Automotive interior systems and textile products.

Belgium, Mexico

COLSON INC.

3700 Airport Road

Jonesboro, AR 72401

Tel: (870) 932-4501 Fax: (870) 933-6612

CEO: James Blankenship, Pres.

Emp: 400

Mfr./sale casters.

Canada, China (PRC), Mexico

COLTEC INDUSTRIES INC.

2550 West Tyvola Road

Charlotte, NC 28217-4543

Tel: (704) 423-7000 Fax: (704) 423-7097

CEO: John W. Guffey, Jr., Pres.

HR: Roy S. Barr

Emp: 11,400

Mfr. aircraft landing gear and flight controls, water systems, engines, motor arms, valves, seals, etc.

Canada, Poland

COLUMBIA FOREST PRODUCTS, INC.

222 SW Columbia Street, Ste.1575

Portland, OR 97201-6600

Tel: (503) 224-5300 Fax: (503) 224-5294

CEO: Harry Demorest, Pres.

Mfr./sale plywood.

Canada

COLUMBIA PICTURES INDUSTRIES INC.

10202 West Washington Blvd.

Culver City, CA 90232

Tel: (310) 244-4000 Fax: (310) 244-2626

CEO: John Kalley, Pres.

HR: Gloria Weinstock

Web site: www.sony.com

Emp: 2,800

Producer and distributor of motion pictures.

Argentina, Australia, Austria, Belgium, Bolivia, Brazil, Chile, Colombia, Denmark, Dominican Republic, Ecuador, Egypt, England, U.K., Finland, France, Germany, Greece, Hong Kong, India, Israel, Italy, Japan, Kenya, Lebanon, Malaysia, Mexico, New Zealand, Norway, Panama, Peru, Philippines, Portugal, Singapore, Spain, Sweden, Switzerland, Taiwan (ROC), Thailand, Trinidad & Tobago, Uruguay, Venezuela

COLUMBIAN ROPE COMPANY

PO Box 270

Guntown, MS 38849-0270

Tel: (601) 348-2241 Fax: (601) 348-5749

CEO: Steve Ludt, Pres.

FO: Peter F. Metcalf

HR: Cherry Chester

Emp: 2,000

Mfr. rope, twine and industrial fiber products.

Canada, Philippines

COLUMBUS McKINNON CORPORATION

140 John James Audubon Pkwy.

Amherst, NY 14228-1197

Tel: (716) 689-5400 Fax: (716) 689-5644

CEO: H. P. Ladds, Jr.

FO: Craig P. Johnston

HR: Iivan Shawvan

Emp: 1,000

Mfr. chains, forgings, hoists, tire shredders and manipulators.

Canada, Zimbabwe

COMDATA NETWORK INC.

5301 Maryland Way

Brentwood, TN 37027

Tel: (615) 370-7000 Fax: (615) 370-7406

CEO: Tony Holcombe, Pres.

Web site: www.comdata.com

Emp: 1,900

Provides information services for the trucking industry, including long-distrance telecommunications services.

Canada

COMDISCO INC.

6111 N. River Road

Rosemont, IL 60018

Tel: (847) 698-3000 Fax: (847) 518-5440

CEO: Jack Slevan, Pres.

FO: Stephen W. Hamilton, EVP

HR: Lucie A. Buford

Rev: $2,819 mil.

Hi-tech asset and facility management and equipment leasing.

Australia, Austria, Canada, England, U.K., Finland, France, Germany, Japan, Netherlands, Singapore, Switzerland

COMERICA INCORPORATED

Comerica Tower, Detroit Center, 500 Woodward Ave.

Detroit, MI 48226

Tel: (313) 222-4000 Fax: (313) 965-4648

CEO: Eugene A. Miller, Chmn.

FO: Joseph J. Buttigieg ,III, EVP

HR: Richard A. Collister, EVP

Web site: www.comerica.com

Emp: 10,850 Rev: $ 3,100 mil.

Bank holding company; business & asset based lending, global finance & institutional trust & investment management services..

Canada, Mexico

COMMERCE GROUP CORP.

6001 N. 91st Street

Milwaukee, WI 53225-1795

Tel: (414) 462-5310 Fax: (414) 462-5312

CEO: Edward I. Machulak

FO: Edward L. Machulak

HR: Christine Wolski

Web site: www.execpc.com

Emp: 325

Gold mining.

El Salvador

COMMERCIAL INTERTECH CORPORATION

1775 Logan Ave., PO Box 239

Youngstown, OH 44501-0239

Tel: (330) 746-8011 Fax: (330) 746-1148

CEO: Paul J. Powers, Pres. & Chmn.

HR: John M. Savage

Emp: 4,000

Mfr. hydraulic components, pre-engineered buildings and stamped metal products.

Australia, Brazil, England, U.K., France, Germany, Italy, Japan, Luxembourg

COMMERCIAL METALS COMPANY

PO Box 1046

Dallas, TX 75221

Tel: (972) 689-4300 Fax: (972) 689-4320

CEO: Stanley A. Rabin, Pres.

FO: Walter Kammann

HR: Bert Romberg

Emp: 3,000

Metal collecting/processing, steel mills and metal trading.

Australia, Belgium, China (PRC), Hong Kong, Japan, Singapore, Switzerland

COMMUNICATIONS SYSTEMS INC.

213 S. Main Street

Hector, MN 55342

Tel: (320) 848-6231 Fax: (320) 848-2702

CEO: Curtis A. Sampson, Pres.

HR: Paul Hanson

Emp: 975

Mfr. telecommunications equipment.

Costa Rica, England, U.K.

COMPAQ COMPUTER CORPORATION

20555 State Highway 249, PO Box 692000

Houston, TX 77269-2000

Tel: (713) 370-0670 Fax: (713) 514-1740

CEO: Eckhard Pfeiffer, Pres.

FO: Andreas Barth, SVP

HR: Hans W. Gutsch, SVP

Web site: www.compaq.com

Emp: 32,656 Rev: $24,584 mil.

Develop/mfr. personal computers.

Argentina, Australia, Austria, Belgium, Brazil, Canada, Chile, China (PRC), Colombia, Czech Republic, Denmark, Ecuador, England, U.K., Finland, France, Germany, Hong Kong, Hungary, India, Ireland, Italy, Japan, Malaysia, Mexico, Netherlands, New Zealand, Norway, Poland, Portugal, Russia, Scotland, U.K., Singapore, South Africa, South Korea, Spain, Sweden, Switzerland, Taiwan (ROC), Thailand, United Arab Emirates, Venezuela

COMPUTER ASSOCIATES INTERNATIONAL INC.

One Computer Associates Plaza

Islandia, NY 11788

Tel: (516) 342-5224 Fax: (516) 342-5329

CEO: Charles B. Wang, Chmn.

FO: Sanjay Kumar, Pres. & COO

HR: Deborah Coughlin, SVP

Web site: www.cai.com

Emp: 11,000 Rev: $2,000 mil.

Integrated software for enterprise computing and information management, application development, manufacturing, financial applications and professional services.

Argentina, Australia, Austria, Bahrain, Belgium, Brazil, Canada, Chile, China (PRC), Colombia, Czech Republic, Denmark, England, U.K., Finland, France, Germany, Hong Kong, India, Indonesia, Ireland, Israel, Italy, Japan, Malaysia, Mexico, Netherlands, New Zealand, Norway, Philippines, Poland, Portugal, Russia, Singapore, South Africa, South Korea, Spain, Sweden, Switzerland, Taiwan (ROC), Thailand, Turkey, Venezuela

COMPUTER SCIENCES CORPORATION

2100 East Grand Ave.

El Segundo, CA 90245

Tel: (310) 615-0311 Fax: (310) 322-9768

CEO: Van Honeycutt, Chmn.

FO: Ronald W. Mackintosh

HR: Marvin Pulliam, VP

Web site: www.csc.com

Emp: 45,000 Rev: $5,616 mil.

Information technology services, management consulting, systems integration, outsourcing.

Belgium, Denmark, England, U.K., France, Germany, Netherlands

COMPUTERVISION/PARAMETRIC CORP.

128 Technology Drive

Waltham, MA 02453

Tel: (781) 275-1800 Fax: (781) 275-2670

CEO: Richard Harrison, Pres.

HR: Carl Ockerbloom

Web site: www.ptc.com

Emp: 2,400

Supplier of mechanical design automation & product data management software & services.

Australia, England, U.K., Germany, Hong Kong, Italy, Japan, Singapore

COMSAT CORPORATION

6560 Rock Spring Drive

Bethesda, MD 20817

Tel: (301) 214-3200 Fax: (301) 214-7100

CEO: Betty C. Alewine, Pres.

FO: Edwin I. Colodny, Chrm.

HR: Paul A. Jones, VP

Web site: www.comsat.com

Rev: $563 mil.

Provides global telecommunications services via satellite and develops advanced satellite networking technology.

Argentina, Bolivia, Brazil, China (PRC), Colombia, Guatemala, Hong Kong, India, Kazakhstan, Mexico, Peru, Russia, Turkey, Venezuela

COMSHARE INC.

3001 South State Street

Ann Arbor, MI 48108

Tel: (734) 994-4800 Fax: (734) 994-5895

CEO: Dennis Ganster, Chmn.

HR: Kevin McGrath

Emp: 1,000

Managerial application software.

Australia, Belgium, Canada, England, U.K., France, Germany, Netherlands

COMTEK INTERNATIONAL

43 Danbury Road

Wilton, CT 06897

Tel: (203) 834-1122 Fax: (203) 762-0773

CEO: Michael Tseytin

FO: Mark Logiurato

HR: Vikki Cirlson

Emp: 76

Produce international trade fairs.

Romania, Russia

CONAGRA INC.

One ConAgra Drive

Omaha, NE 68102-5001

Tel: (402) 595-4000 Fax: (402) 595-4595

CEO: Bruce C. Rohde, Pres. & Vice Chmn.

HR: Gerald B. Vernon, SVP

Web site: www.conagra.com

Emp: 82,000 Rev: $24,000 mil.

Prepared/frozen foods, grains, flour, animal feeds, agri chemicals, poultry, meat, dairy products, including Healthy Choice, Butterball and Hunt's.

Argentina, Australia, Belgium, Brazil, Bulgaria, Canada, Chile, China (PRC), Denmark, England, U.K., France, Germany, India, Japan, Malaysia, Mexico, Netherlands, New Zealand, Philippines, Portugal, Russia, Singapore, South Africa, South Korea, Spain, Switzerland, Taiwan (ROC), Turkey, Uruguay

CONAGRA PEAVEY COMPANY

730 Second Ave. South

Minneapolis, MN 55402

Tel: (612) 370-7500 Fax: (612) 370-7504

CEO: Jim Anderson, Pres.

HR: Laura Rosene

Emp: 5,500

Flour, feeds, seeds.

Argentina, Japan, Mexico, Netherlands, Switzerland

CONAIR CORPORATION

150 Milford Road

E. Windsor, NJ 08520

Tel: (609) 426-1300 Fax: (609) 426-8766

CEO: Leandro P. Rizzuto, Pres.

Emp: 2,000

Mfr. personal care & household appliances.

Canada, Costa Rica, Hong Kong, Taiwan (ROC)

CONCURRENT COMPUTER CORPORATION

2101 West Cypress Creek Road

Fort Lauderdale, FL 33309

Tel: (954) 974-1700 Fax: (954) 977-5580

CEO: Corky Siegel, Pres.

Emp: 1,800

Mfr. computer systems & software.

Ireland, Japan

CONDE NAST PUBLICATIONS INC.

350 Madison Ave.

New York, NY 10017

Tel: (212) 880-8800 Fax: (212) 880-8289

CEO: Samuel I. Newhouse, Jr., Chmn.

FO: Steven T. Florio, Pres. & CEO

HR: Benjamin Bogin

Emp: 1,100

Publishing company.

England, U.K., France

CONE MILLS CORPORATION

3101 N. Elm Street, PO Box 26540

Greensboro, NC 27415-6540

Tel: (336) 379-6220 Fax: (336) 379-6287

CEO: J. Patrick Danahy, Pres.

FO: Miguel G. Rubiera

HR: James S. Butner

Web site: www.cone.com

Emp: 6,000 Rev: $717 mil.

Mfr. denims, flannels, chamois & other fabrics.

Australia, Belgium, Hong Kong, Japan, Mexico, New Zealand, Singapore, South Korea, Thailand

CONOCO INC.

PO Box 2197

Houston, TX 77252

Tel: (281) 293-1000 Fax: (281) 293-1440

CEO: Archie Dunham, Pres.

Emp: 43,000

Oil, gas, coal, chemicals and minerals.

Argentina, Australia, Austria, Bahrain, Belgium, Brazil, Chad, Egypt, England, U.K., France, Germany, Indonesia, Ireland, Italy, Japan, Netherlands, Nigeria, Northern Ireland, U.K., Norway, Russia, Scotland, U.K., Singapore, Spain, Sweden, Switzerland, Tunisia, United Arab Emirates

CONSTRUCTION SPECIALTIES INC.

Headquarters, 3 Werner Way

Lebanon, NJ 08833

Tel: (908) 236-0800 Fax: (908) 236-0801

CEO: R. F. Dadd

FO: C. D. Van Koten, VP

HR: Lee DiRubbo

Web site: www.c-sgroup.com

Emp: 650

Mfr. architectural building products.

Canada, England, U.K., France

CONTAINER-STAPLING CORPORATION

27th and ICC Tracks

Herrin, IL 62948

Tel: (618) 942-2125 Fax: (618) 942-7700

CEO: Jean Cairatti, Mgr.

Emp: 250

Mfr. industrial stapling machines and supplies.

Belgium, Israel

CONTICO MANUFACTURING COMPANY

1101 Warson Road

St. Louis, MO 63132

Tel: (314) 997-5900 Fax: (314) 997-1270

CEO: Bill Miller, Chmn.

Emp: 2,200

Mfr. plastic tool boxes, storage bins/shelves, parts organizers, sporting goods.

England, U.K.

CONTINENTAL AIRLINES INC.

2929 Allen Parkway, Ste. 1501

Houston, TX 77019

Tel: (281) 834-5000 Fax: (281) 520-6329

CEO: Gordon Bethune, Chmn.

FO: Gregory Brenneman, Pres.

International airline carrier.

Belize, Brazil, Colombia, Costa Rica, Dominican Republic, Ecuador, El Salvador, England, U.K., France, Germany, Guatemala, Honduras, Italy, Mexico, Nicaragua, Panama, Peru, Portugal, Spain, Venezuela

CONTINENTAL CAN COMPANY

301 Merritt 7, 7 Corporate Park

Norwalk, CT 06856

Tel: (203) 750-5900 Fax: (203) 750-5908

CEO: Donald Bainton, Chmn.

HR: Ms. Linda Mumford

Packaging products and machinery, metal, plastic and paper containers.

Belgium, Bolivia, Brazil, England, U.K., Germany, Hong Kong, Indonesia, Kuwait, Mexico, Netherlands, Nigeria, Peru, Saudi Arabia, South Korea, Venezuela

CONTINENTAL CARBON COMPANY

333 Cyprus Run, Ste. 100

Houston, TX 77094

Tel: (281) 647-3700 Fax: (281) 647-3700

CEO: W. R. Toller

FO: J. E. Graves

Emp: 270

Mfr. carbon black.

Australia

CONTINENTAL INSURANCE COMPANY

333 South Wabash Ave.

Chicago, IL 60695

Tel: (312) 822-5000 Fax: (312) 822-6419

CEO: Phil Engo, Pres.

Emp: 12,500

Insurance services.

Australia, Belgium, Japan, Saudi Arabia

CONTROL DATA SYSTEMS INC.

4201 Lexington Ave.

North Arden Hills, MN 55126

Tel: (612) 415-2999 Fax: (612) 415-4891

CEO: James Ousley, Pres.

Web site: www.cdc.com

Emp: 1,900 Rev: $455 mil.

Computer peripherals and hardware.

Belgium, China (PRC), England, U.K., France, Germany, Italy, Japan, Malaysia, Netherlands, Singapore, South Korea, Spain, Sweden, Switzerland, Taiwan (ROC)

COOK INC.

925 South Curry Pike, PO Box 489

Bloomington, ID 47402

Tel: (812) 339-2235 Fax: (812) 339-8206

CEO: William A. Cook

Emp: 350

Instruments for cardiovascular diagnosis.

Denmark

COOPER INDUSTRIES INC.

6600 Travis Street, Ste. 5800

Houston, TX 77002

Tel: (713) 209-8400 Fax: (713) 209-8995

CEO: H. John Riley, Jr., Chmn.

FO: Ralph E. Jackson Jr., EVP

HR: Carl J. Plesnicher Jr., SVP

Web site: www.cooperindustries.com

Emp: 41,200 Rev: $5,289 mil.

Mfr./distributor electrical products, tools and hardware and automotive products.

Australia, Belgium, Brazil, Canada, Colombia, Denmark, England, U.K., France, Germany, India, Ireland, Italy, Malaysia, Mexico, Netherlands, Russia, Singapore, Spain, Sweden, Switzerland, Taiwan (ROC), Venezuela

COOPER TURBOCOMPRESSOR

3101 Broadway, PO Box 209

Buffalo, NY 14225-0209

Tel: (716) 896-6600 Fax: (716) 896-1233

CEO: E. Fred Minter, Pres.

Mfr. air & gas compressors.

Scotland, U.K.

COPELAND CORPORATION

1675 West Campbell Road

Sidney, OH 45365-0669

Tel: (937) 498-3011 Fax: (937) 498-3334

CEO: Tom Bettcher, Pres.

Web site: www.copeland-corp.com

Emp: 6,800

Producer of compressors and condensing units for commercial and residential air conditioning and refrigeration equipment.

Belgium, Canada

CORDIS CORPORATION

14201 Northwest 60th Street

Miami Lakes, FL 33014

Tel: (305) 824-2000 Fax: (305) 824-2747

CEO: Robert C. Strauss, Pres.

FO: Egbert Ratering

HR: Carolyn Donaldson

Emp: 3,600

Mfr. medical devices and systems.

Belgium, France, Netherlands

CORE LABORATORIES

5295 Hollister

Houston, TX 77042

Tel: (713) 460-9600 Fax: (713) 460-4389

CEO: David Demchur, Pres.

HR: Janelle Lerum

Emp: 900

Petroleum testing/analysis, analytical chemicals, laboratory and octane analysis instrumentation.

Australia, Canada, China (PRC), Colombia, Egypt, Indonesia, Malaysia, Mexico, Netherlands, New Zealand, Nigeria, Pakistan, Scotland, U.K., Singapore, United Arab Emirates, Venezuela

CORESTATES BANK

1500 Market Street

Philadelphia, PA 19101

Tel: (215) 973-3100 Fax: (215) 786-8899

CEO: Terrence A. Larsen

FO: Michael P. Heavener

HR: Vick Dewan

Web site: www.corestates.com

Emp: 19,000 Rev: $48,500 mil.

Primary international businesses; correspondent banking and trade services.

Argentina, Australia, Brazil, Chile, China (PRC), Colombia, England, U.K., France, Germany, Hong Kong, Indonesia, Italy, Japan, Malaysia, Mexico, Panama, Philippines, Singapore, South Korea, Spain, Taiwan (ROC), Thailand

CORNING HAZLETON INC.

9200 Leesburg Pike

Vienna, VA 22182

Tel: (703) 893-5400 Fax: (703) 759-6947

CEO: Joseph Herring, Pres.

Emp: 2,500

Contract research.

England, U.K., Germany, Japan

CORNING INC.

One Riverfront Plaza,

Corning, NY 14831

Tel: (607) 974-9000 Fax: (607) 974-8551

CEO: Roger G. Ackerman, Chmn.

FO: Larry Aiello Jr., SVP

HR: Pamela C. Schneider, VP

Web site: www.corning.com

Emp: 20,500 Rev: $4,090 mil.

Mfr. glass and specialty materials, consumer products; communications, laboratory services.

Australia, Belgium, Bermuda, Brazil, Canada, China (PRC), England, U.K., France, Germany, India, Italy, Japan, Malaysia, Singapore, South Korea, Wales, U.K.

COTY INC.

237 Park Ave.

New York, NY 10017

Tel: (212) 850-2300 Fax: (212) 850-2544

CEO: Jean-Andre Rougeot, Pres.

HR: Irene Harris

Web site: www.cotyinc.com

Fragrance, cosmetics and beauty treatments.

France

COUDERT BROTHERS

1114 Ave. of the Americas

New York, NY 10036-7794

Tel: (212) 626-4400 Fax: (212) 626-4210

CEO: Anthony Williams, Chmn.

HR: Dorothy McLeod, Dir.

Web site: www.coudert.com

Emp: 1,000 Rev: $141 mil.

International law firm.

Australia, Belgium, Brazil, Canada, China (PRC), England, U.K., France, Germany, Hong Kong, Hungary, Indonesia, Japan, Kazakhstan, Mexico, Russia, Singapore, Thailand, Vietnam

COULTER CORPORATION

PO Box 169015

Miami, FL 33116-9015

Tel: (305) 380-3800 Fax: (305) 380-8312

CEO: Ed Vivanco, Pres.

HR: Bill Furniss

Emp: 5,500

Mfr. blood analysis systems, flow cytometers, chemicals systems, scientific systems & reagents.

Australia, Brazil, Canada, England, U.K., France, Germany, Hong Kong, Italy, Japan, Kenya, Mexico, Netherlands, New Zealand, Portugal, South Africa, Spain, Turkey, United Arab Emirates, Venezuela

COVINGTON & BURLING

1201 Pennsylvania Ave., N.W.

Washington, DC 20044

Tel: (202) 662-6000 Fax: (202) 662-6291

CEO: Ralph Justus, CEO

HR: Donna Dennis, Dir.

Web site: www.cov.com

Emp: 850 Rev: $143 mil.

International law firm.

Belgium, England, U.K.

CRANE COMPANY

100 First Stamford Place

Stamford, CT 06907

Tel: (203) 363-7300 Fax: (203) 363-7359

CEO: Robert S. Evans, Chmn.

FO: L. Hill Clark, Pres. & COO

HR: Richard B. Phillips, VP

Emp: 11,000 Rev: $2,037

Diversified mfr./distributor engineered products for industrial.

Australia, Belgium, Canada, England, U.K., Germany, Spain

CRANE PUMPS & SYSTEMS, INC.

420 Third Street

Piqua, OH 45356

Tel: (937) 773-2442 Fax: (937) 773-2238

CEO: Lou Barlup, Pres.

FO: Bruce Lindhorst

Emp: 314

Mfr. water/waste water pumps and systems.

Colombia

CRAVATH, SWAINE & MOORE

Worldwide Plaza, 825 Eighth Ave.

New York, NY 10019-7475

Tel: (212) 474-1000 Fax: (212) 474-3700

CEO: Samuel C. Butler

HR: Margarette Luberda

Web site: www,cravath.com

Emp: 980 Rev: $273 mil.

International law firm.

England, U.K., Hong Kong

CRAWFORD FITTING COMPANY

29500 Solon

Solon, OH 44139

Tel: (440) 248-4600 Fax:

CEO: Joseph Callahan

Valves, tubes and fittings.

Australia

CRC PRESS INC.

2000 CorP.O.rate Boulevard, NW

Boca Raton, FL 33431

Tel: (561) 994-0555 Fax: (561) 997-0949

CEO: Dennis Buda, Pres.

HR: Karen Ansell

Emp: 205

Publishing: science, technical & medical books & journals.

England, U.K., Japan

CRITICARE SYSTEMS INC.

20925 Crossroads Circle

Waukesha, WI 53186

Tel: (414) 798-8282 Fax: (414) 798-8491

CEO: Gerhard J. Von der Ruhr, Pres.

Develop/mfr. diagnostic & therapeutic products.

Germany, Japan

CROMPTON & KNOWLES CORPORATION

1 Station Place Metro Center

Stamford, CT 06902

Tel: (203) 353-5400 Fax: (203) 353-5423

CEO: Vincent A. Calarco, Pres.

Web site: www.crompton-knowles.co

Emp: 1,300

Mfr. dyes, colors, flavors, fragrances, specialty chemicals and industrial products.

Belgium, Canada, England, U.K., Netherlands

CROSBY CORPORATION

PO Box 3128

Tulsa, OK 74101-3128

Tel: (918) 834-4611 Fax: (918) 832-0940

CEO: Larry Postelwait, Pres.

HR: Tom Rondot

Emp: 1,300

Mfr. machine tools, hardware, steel forgings.

Belgium, Canada, England, U.K.

A.T. CROSS COMPANY

One Albion Road

Lincoln, RI 02865

Tel: (401) 333-1200 Fax: (401) 334-2861

CEO: Russell A. Boss, Pres.

FO: Bradford R. Boss, Chrm.

Emp: 1,400

Mfr. writing instruments, leads, erasers and ink refills.

England, U.K., France, Germany, Ireland, Italy, Japan, Spain

CROSS-CULTURAL CONSULTING ASSOCIATES INC.

400 Alexander Park

Princeton, NJ 08540

Tel: (609) 514-3173 Fax: (609) 514-3411

CEO: Dean Foster, Chmn.

HR: Sheryl Foster

Emp: 10

Consulting and management training services.

England, U.K.

CROWELL & MORING

1001 Pennsylvania Ave., NW

Washington, DC 20004-2595

Tel: (202) 624-2500 Fax: (202) 628-5116

CEO: Herbert Martin, Mng. Prtn.

International law firm.

England, U.K.

CROWLEY MARITIME CORPORATION

155 Grand Ave.

Oakland, CA 94612

Tel: (510) 251-7500 Fax: (510) 251-7625

CEO: Tom Prowley, Pres.

Emp: 5,500

Marine transportation.

Canada, Indonesia, Singapore

CROWN ANDERSEN INC.

306 Dividend Drive

Peachtree City, GA 30269

Tel: (770) 486-2000 Fax: (770) 487-5066

CEO: Jack Brady

Emp: 96 Rev: $23 mil.

Holding company: design/mfr./install industry pollution control, heat recovery, air handling & waste systems.

Netherlands

CROWN CORK & SEAL COMPANY, INC.

One Crown Way

Philadelphia, PA 19154-4599

Tel: (215) 698-5100 Fax: (215) 698-5201

CEO: William J. Avery, Chmn.

FO: John Conway

HR: Fred Veil

Emp: 22,373

Mfr. cans, bottle caps; filling & packaging machinery.

Argentina, Belgium, Brazil, Canada, Chile, Colombia, Costa Rica, Dem. Rep. of Congo, Denmark, Ecuador, Ethiopia, France, Germany, Indonesia, Ireland, Italy, Kenya, Malaysia, Mexico, Morocco, Nigeria, Peru, Portugal, Singapore, South Africa, Spain, Thailand, Zambia, Zimbabwe

CROWN EQUIPMENT CORPORATION

40 South Washington Street

New Bremen, OH 45869

Tel: (419) 629-2311 Fax: (419) 629-2317

CEO: James F. Dicke, Pres.

FO: James D. Moran

Emp: 4,500

Mfr./sales/services forklift trucks, stackers.

Australia, Belgium, England, U.K., France, Germany, Ireland, New Zealand, Singapore

CSC COMPANY

9500 Arboretum Boulevard

Austin, TX 78759

Tel: (512) 345-5700 Fax: (512) 338-7041

CEO: Ronald Carroll, Pres.

HR: Debi Stafford

Emp: 1,200

Design and marketing software for insurance and financial services.

Australia, England, U.K., France, Germany, Japan, Netherlands

CSX CORPORATION

901 East Cary Street

Richmond, VA 23219-4031

Tel: (804) 782-1400 Fax: (804) 782-6747

CEO: John W. Snow, Chmn.

FO: Gerald L. Nichols, Vice Chrm.

HR: Linda Amato, Mgr.

Web site: www.csx.com

Provides freight delivery and contract logistics services.

Canada

CTS CORPORATION

905 Northwest Boulevard

Elkhart, IN 46514

Tel: (219) 293-7511 Fax: (219) 293-6146

CEO: Joseph Walker, Pres.

HR: James L. Cummins

Emp: 4,200

Mfr. electronic components.

Canada, Mexico, Scotland, U.K., Singapore, Taiwan (ROC)

CUBIC CORPORATION

9333 Balboa Ave., PO Box 85587

San Diego, CA 92123

Tel: (619) 277-6780 Fax: (619) 505-1523

CEO: Walter J. Zable, Chmn.

FO: Michael W. David, VP

HR: Bernie A. Kulchin

Web site: www.cubic.com

Emp: 3,500 Rev: $388.2 mil.

Automatic fare collection equipment, training systems.

Australia, Denmark, England, U.K., Hong Kong

CULLIGAN INTERNATIONAL COMPANY

One Culligan Parkway

Northbrook, IL 60062

Tel: (847) 205-6000 Fax: (847) 205-6030

CEO: Kenneth I. Wellings, Pres. Int'l

HR: Diane Frisch

Web site: www.culligan-man.com

Emp: 4,578 Rev: $506 mil.

Water treatment products and services.

Australia, Belgium, Canada, Czech Republic, England, U.K., France, Germany, Italy, Netherlands Antilles, Pakistan, Poland, Spain, Switzerland, United Arab Emirates

CUMMINS ENGINE CO., INC.

500 Jackson Street, PO Box 3005

Columbus, IN 47202-3005

Tel: (812) 377-5000 Fax: (812) 377-3334

CEO: James A. Henderson, Pres.

FO: Jack K. Edwards

HR: Kerry Dinneen

Emp: 23,500 Rev: $4,000 mil.

Mfr. diesel engines.

Australia, Belgium, Brazil, China (PRC), Colombia, England, U.K., France, Germany, India, Italy, Japan, Mexico, Russia, Singapore, Zimbabwe

CUMMINS SOUTHERN PLAINS INC.

600 North Watson Road

Arlington, TX 76011

Tel: (817) 640-6801 Fax: (817) 640-6852

CEO: Robert Gillikin, Pres.

HR: Don C. Watson

Emp: 750

Sales and service of diesel engines.

Venezuela

CUNA MUTUAL INSURANCE SOCIETY

5910 Mineral Point Road, PO Box 391

Madison, WI 53701

Tel: (608) 238-5851 Fax: (608) 238-0830

CEO: Michael Kitchen, Pres.

FO: Armando Teran

HR: Stanley Langfoss

Emp: 2,783

Insurance services.

Australia, Jamaica, Trinidad & Tobago

CURTIS, MALLET-PREVOST, COLT & MOSLE

101 Park Ave., 35th Floor

New York, NY 10178

Tel: (212) 696-6000 Fax: (212) 697-1559

CEO: George Kahale

International law firm.

Hong Kong

CURTISS-WRIGHT CORPORATION

1200 Wall Street West

Lyndhurst, NJ 07071

Tel: (201) 896-8400 Fax: (201) 438-5680

CEO: David Lasky, Chmn.

Emp: 1,600

Mfr. precision components and systems, engineered services to aerospace, flow control and marine industry.

Belgium, Canada, Denmark, England, U.K., France, Germany, Wales, U.K.

CYBEREX INC.

7171 Industrial Park Boulevard

Mentor, OH 44060

Tel: (440) 946-1783 Fax: (440) 946-5963

CEO: Larry Culp, Pres.

FO: Edward M. Meluch

HR: Kim Coleman

Web site: www.cyberex.com

Emp: 135

Mfr. uninterruptible power systems, line voltage regulators, static switches, power line filters.

Netherlands

CYBORG SYSTEMS INC.

2 N. Riverside Plaza

Chicago, IL 60606-0899

Tel: (312) 454-1865 Fax: (312) 454-0889

CEO: Steven Weinberg

FO: Michael D. Blair

HR: Patricia Christensen

Web site: www.cyborg,com

Emp: 600 Rev: $60 mil.

Develop/mfr. human resources, payroll and time/attendance software.

Canada, England, U.K., Singapore, South Africa

CYPRUS AMAX MINERALS COMPANY

9100 East Mineral Circle

Englewood, CO 80112

Tel: (303) 643-5000 Fax: (303) 643-5048

CEO: Milton H. Ward, Chmn. & Pres.

FO: Jeffrey G. Clevenger, EVP

Web site: www.cyprusamax.com

Emp: 10,000 Rev: $3,350.0 mil

Mining company supplying molybdenum (used in steelmaking).

Australia, Canada, Chile, England, U.K., Japan, Mexico, Netherlands, Panama, Peru, Russia, Zambia

D

D'ARCY MASIUS BENTON & BOWLES INC. (DMB&B)

1675 Broadway

New York, NY 10019

Tel: (212) 468-3622 Fax: (212) 468-2987

CEO: Arty Selkowitz, Chmn.

FO: John C. Ferries, Pres. Intl.

HR: Phil Bacher, SVP

Web site: www.dmbb.com

Emp: 6,878 Rev: $728.7 mil.

Full service international advertising and communications group.

Argentina, Australia, Austria, Belgium, Bolivia, Brazil, Canada, Chile, China (PRC), Colombia, Costa Rica, Czech Republic, Denmark, Dominican Republic, Ecuador, El Salvador, England, U.K., Finland, France, Germany, Greece, Guatemala, Hong Kong, Hungary, India, Indonesia, Ireland, Israel, Italy, Japan, Kazakhstan, Malaysia, Mexico, Netherlands, New Zealand, Norway, Pakistan, Peru, Philippines, Poland, Portugal, Romania, Russia, Saudi Arabia, Singapore, South Korea, Spain, Sweden, Switzerland, Taiwan (ROC), Thailand, Turkey, Ukraine, United Arab Emirates, Uruguay, Uzbekistan, Venezuela

D-M-E COMPANY

29111 Stephenson Highway

Madison Heights, MI 48071

Tel: (248) 398-6000 Fax: (248) 544-5705

CEO: Jerry Lirette, Pres.

FO: Dick Christopher

HR: Deb Ruwart

Emp: 1,300

Basic tooling for plastic molding and die casting.

Australia, Belgium, Brazil, Canada, England, U.K., France, Germany, Hong Kong, Israel, Italy, Japan, Malaysia, Mexico, Philippines, Portugal, Spain, Taiwan (ROC), Venezuela

DAKOTA MINING CORP.

410 17th Street, Ste. 2450

Denver, CO 80202

Tel: (303) 573-0221 Fax: (303) 573-1012

CEO: Alan R. Bell

FO: J. G. Kircher, VP

Emp: 100

Explores and operates gold properties

Mexico

DALLAS SEMICONDUCTOR CORPORATION

4401 South Beltway Parkway

Dallas, TX 75244-3292

Tel: (972) 371-4000 Fax: (972) 371-4956

CEO: C. Vin Prothro, Chmn.

FO: F.A. Scherpenberg, VP

HR: Gay Vencill, VP

Web site: www.dalsemi.com

Emp: 1,497 Rev: $368 mil.

Design/mfr. computer chips and chip-based subsystems.

England, U.K., France, Germany, Taiwan (ROC)

LEO A. DALY

8600 Indian Hills Drive

Omaha, NE 68114

Tel: (402) 391-8111 Fax: (402) 391-8564

CEO: Leo A. Daly, Pres.

FO: John L. Whisler

Emp: 730 Rev: $72 mil.

Planning, arch, engineering and interior design services.

Germany, Hong Kong, Spain, United Arab Emirates

DAMES & MOORE GROUP

911 Wilshire Boulevard

Los Angeles, CA 90017

Tel: (213) 683-1560 Fax: (213) 628-0015

CEO: Arthur C. Darrow, Pres.

FO: Peter G. Rowley, SVP

HR: Karen Bermeo, Mgr.

Web site: www.dames.com

Emp: 7,500 Rev: $1 bil.

Engineering, environmental and construction management services.

Australia, Canada, Chile, China (PRC), England, U.K., France, Germany, Hong Kong, Indonesia, Ireland, Italy, Japan, Lebanon, Malaysia, Netherlands, Philippines, Saudi Arabia, Scotland, U.K., Singapore, Spain, United Arab Emirates

DANA CORPORATION

4500 Door Street

Toledo, OH 43615

Tel: (419) 535-4500 Fax: (419) 535-4643

CEO: Southwood J. Morcott, Chmn.

FO: Marvin A. Franklin, Pres. Intl.

Web site: www.dana.com

Emp: 79,000 Rev: $11.9 mil.

Mfr./sales of automotive, heavy truck, off-highway, fluid & mechanical power components.

Argentina, Australia, Austria, Belgium, Brazil, Canada, China (PRC), Colombia, England, U.K., France, Germany, Hong Kong, India, Italy, Japan, Malaysia, Mexico, Netherlands, New Zealand, Poland, Singapore, South Korea, Spain, Sweden, Switzerland, Taiwan (ROC), Thailand, Uruguay, Venezuela

DANIEL INDUSTRIES INC.

9753 Pine Lake Drive, PO Box 55435

Houston, TX 77224

Tel: (713) 467-6000 Fax: (713) 827-3889

CEO: R. C. Lassiter, Chmn.

FO: Thomas A. Newton, Pres. & COO

HR: Michael T. Atkins, VP

Web site: www.danielind.com

Emp: 1,500 Rev: $275 mil.

Oil/gas equipment and systems; geophysical services.

Canada, England, U.K., Germany, Scotland, U.K.

DANIEL MANN JOHNSON & MENDENHALL

3250 Wilshire Blvd.

Los Angeles, CA 90010

Tel: (213) 381-3663 Fax: (213) 383-3656

CEO: Raymond W. Holdsworth

FO: Brian T. Harris

HR: Ron Deutch

Web site: www.dmjm.com

Emp: 1,157

Architects and engineers.

England, U.K., Kuwait, Philippines, Saudi Arabia, Taiwan (ROC), Thailand, Turkey, Vietnam

DARLING INTERNATIONAL INC.

251 O'Connor Ridge Blvd., Ste. 300

Irving, TX 55038

Tel: (972) 717-0300 Fax: (972) 717-1588

CEO: Dennis Longmire, Chmn.

Emp: 1,000

Animal by-products.

Canada

DATA DIMENSIONS, INC.

411 108th Street, Ste. 2100

Bellevue, WA 98004

Tel: (425) 688-1000 Fax: (425) 688-1099

CEO: Larry W. Martin, Chmn.

FO: John W. Cramer, EVP

HR: Michele Erwin, Dir.

Web site: www.data-dimensions.com

Emp: 450 Rev: $50 mil.

Provides computer systems consulting services to adapt computerized systems for year 2000 problems, and other data processing services.

England, U.K.

DATA GENERAL CORPORATION

4400 Computer Drive

Westboro, MA 01580

Tel: (508) 898-5000 Fax: (508) 366-1319

CEO: Ronald L. Skates

FO: Joseph Schwartz

HR: Jon Lane

Web site: www.dg.com

Emp: 7,100

Design, mfr. general purpose computer systems & peripheral products & services.

Australia, Austria, Belgium, Brazil, Canada, Chile, Denmark, England, U.K., Finland, France, Germany, Hong Kong, Ireland, Italy, Mexico, Netherlands, New Zealand, Norway, Peru, Portugal, Singapore, Spain, Sweden, Switzerland, Thailand, Venezuela

DATA I/O CORPORATION

10525 Willows Road, NE

Redmond, WA 98053

Tel: (425) 881-6444 Fax: (242) 582-1043

CEO: Dave Bullis, Pres.

FO: Horst Mader

HR: Susan Webber, VP

Emp: 550

Mfr. computer testing devices.

Canada, Germany, Japan

DATA RESEARCH ASSOCIATES, INC. (DRA)

1276 North Warson Road

St. Louis, MO 63132

Tel: (314) 432-1100 Fax: (314) 993-8927

CEO: Michael J. Mellinger, Chmn..

FO: Howard L. Wood, VC

HR: Maggie Bell, Mgr.

Web site: www.dra.com

Emp: 204 Rev: $35.4 mil.

Systems integrator for libraries and information providers.

Australia, Canada, France, Singapore

DATA TRANSLATION INC.

100 Locke Drive

Marlborough, MA 01752

Tel: (508) 481-3700 Fax: (508) 481-8620

CEO: Alfred A. Molinari, Jr., Pres.

FO: Joe Rushi

Emp: 230

Mfr. peripheral boards for image & array processing micro-computers.

England, U.K., Germany

DATAPRODUCTS CORPORATION

1757 Papo Kenyon Road

Simi Valley, CA 93063

Tel: (805) 578-4000 Fax: (805) 578-4001

CEO: Rick Roll, Pres. & COO

Emp: 3,354

Mfr. computer printers and supplies.

Australia, Austria, Canada, England, U.K., France, Germany, Hong Kong, Ireland, Italy, Mexico

DATASCOPE CORPORATION

14 Philips Parkway

Montvale, NJ 07645

Tel: (201) 391-8100 Fax: (201) 307-5400

CEO: Lawrence Saper

HR: James Cooper, VP

Web site: www.datascope.com

Emp: 1,300 Rev: $242 mil.

Mfr. medical devices.

Argentina, Canada, England, U.K., France, Germany, Netherlands

DATAWARE TECHNOLOGIES INC.

222 Third Street, Ste. 3300

Cambridge, MA 02142

Tel: (617) 621-0820 Fax: (617) 494-0740

CEO: Kurt Mueller, Pres.

FO: Jeffrey O. Nyweide

HR: Sue Martin

Web site: www.dataware.com

Emp: 200 Rev: $40 mil.

Multi-platform, multi-lingual software solutions & services for electronic information providers.

Australia, Canada, Denmark, England, U.K., France, Germany, Italy, Singapore, Sweden

DAVIS POLK & WARDWELL

450 Lexington Ave.

New York, NY 10017

Tel: (212) 450-4000 Fax: (212) 450-4800

CEO: Francis Morison, Mng. Prtn.

HR: Jeannie Gratta

Web site: www.dpw.com

Emp: 1,360 Rev: $390 mil.

International law firm.

England, U.K., France, Germany, Hong Kong, Japan

DAVIS WRIGHT TREMAINE

2600 Century Square, 1501 Fourth Ave.

Seattle, WA 98101

Tel: (206) 622-3150 Fax: (206) 628-7040

CEO: Bradley Diggs, Mng. Prtn.

Emp: 1,000

International law firm.

China (PRC)

DAY RUNNER, INC.

15295 Alton Parkway

Irvine, CA 92618

Tel: (714) 680-3500 Fax: (714) 680-0538

CEO: Mark A. Vidovich, Chmn.

FO: James E. Freeman Jr., COO

HR: Harold Pierce, Dir. HR

Web site: www.dayrunner.com

Emp: 1,146 Rev: $127.4 mil.

Mfg/distribution of paper-based organizers.

England, U.K., Hong Kong

DAY-GLO COLOR CORPORATION

4732 St. Clair Ave.

Cleveland, OH 44103

Tel: (216) 391-7070 Fax: (216) 391-7751

CEO: Chuck Pauli, Pres.

FO: Thomas J. Gray

Emp: 175

Fluorescent dyes and pigments.

Netherlands

DAYCO PRODUCTS INC.

1 Prestige Place, PO Box 1004

Miamisburg, OH 45342

Tel: (937) 226-7000 Fax: (937) 226-4689

CEO: Richard Bing, Pres.

FO: Richard Christian

HR: Steve Kerna, VP

Emp: 11,700

Diversified auto, industrial and household products.

Australia, Brazil, Canada, England, U.K., France, Germany, Mexico, Scotland, U.K., Sweden

DAYTON PROGRESS CORPORATION

500 Progress Road

Dayton, OH 45449

Tel: (937) 859-5111 Fax: (937) 859-5353

CEO: Thomas Fant, Pres.

Emp: 400

Punches, dies & guide bushings.

England, U.K.

DAYTON-WALTHER CORPORATION

PO Box 1022

Dayton, OH 45401

Tel: (937) 296-3113 Fax: (937) 297-3138

CEO: Fred Walther & E. M. Mitche

FO: R. E. Phillips

Emp: 2,500

Mfr. heavy duty components for truck/trailer chassis.

England, U.K., France, Mexico

DDB NEEDHAM WORLDWIDE INC.

437 Madison Ave.

New York, NY 10022

Tel: (212) 415-2000 Fax: (212) 415-3417

CEO: Keith Reinhard, Chmn.

Emp: 13,066 Rev: $1,591.2 mil.

Advertising agency.

Argentina, Australia, Austria, Bahrain, Belgium, Brazil, Bulgaria, Canada, Chile, China (PRC), Colombia, Costa Rica, Cyprus, Czech Republic, Denmark, Egypt, El Salvador, England, U.K., Estonia, Finland, France, Germany, Greece, Guatemala, Honduras, Hong Kong, Hungary, India, Ireland, Israel, Italy, Japan, Latvia, Lebanon, Macedonia, Malaysia, Mexico, Morocco, Netherlands, New Zealand, Norway, Panama, Peru, Philippines, Poland, Portugal, Romania, Russia, Saudi Arabia, Singapore, Slovakia, Slovenia, South Africa, South Korea, Spain, Sweden, Switzerland, Taiwan (ROC), Thailand, Tunisia, Turkey, Ukraine, United Arab Emirates, Uruguay, Venezuela, Yugoslavia

DE ZURIK, A Unit of General Signal

250 Riverside Ave. North

Sartell, MN 56377

Tel: (320) 259-2000 Fax: (320) 259-2227

CEO: Tom Frey

HR: Mike Kremier

Web site: www.dezurik.com

Mfr. manual, process & control valves.

Australia, Canada, England, U.K., India, Japan, Mexico, Singapore

DEBEVOISE & PLIMPTON

875 Third Ave.

New York, NY 10022

Tel: (212) 909-6000 Fax: (212) 909-6836

CEO: Barry R. Bryan, Presiding Prtn.

HR: Rachel B. Dressler

Web site: www.debevoise.com

Emp: 1,455 Rev: $226 mil.

International law firm.

England, U.K., France, Hong Kong, Hungary, Russia

DECHERT PRICE & RHOADS

4000 Bell Atlantic Tower, 1717 Arch Street

Philadelphia, PA 19103-2793

Tel: (215) 994-4000 Fax: (215) 994-2222

CEO: Barton J. Winokur, Chmn.

FO: Bernhard W. Witter, EVP

HR: Karen Suta, Dir.

Web site: www.dechert.com

Emp: 1,024 Rev: $161 mil.

International law firm.

Belgium, England, U.K., France

DECISION STRATEGIES INTERNATIONAL INC.

801 Second Ave.

New York, NY 10017-4706

Tel: (212) 599-9400 Fax: (212) 599-5288

CEO: Bart M. Schwartz, Chmn.

Emp: 40

Business intelligence & investigative consulting.

Italy

DEERE & COMPANY

One John Deere Road

Moline, IL 61265

Tel: (309) 765-8000 Fax: (309) 765-5772

CEO: Hans W. Becherer, Chmn.

FO: Nathan J. Jones, V.P.

HR: John K. Lawson, S.V.P.

Web site: www.deere.com

Emp: 35,500 Rev: $11,300 mil.

Mfr./sale agricultural, construction, utility, forestry and lawn, grounds care equipment.

Argentina, Canada, England, U.K., France, Germany, Italy, Mexico, South Africa, Spain, Sweden, Turkmenistan

DEERFIELD SPECIALTY PAPERS, INC.

PO Box 5437

Augusta, GA 30916-5437

Tel: (706) 798-1861 Fax: (706) 798-2270

CEO: Norman Baldrachi, Pres.

Emp: 700

Glassine papers.

Canada

DEKALB GENETICS CORP.

3100 Sycamore Road

DeKalb, IL 60115-9600

Tel: (815) 758-3461 Fax: (815) 758-3711

CEO: Bruce Bickner, Chmn.

FO: Dick Crowder, VP

HR: Jack McEnery, VP

Web site: www.dekalb.com

Emp: 2,000 Rev: $451 mil.

Develop/produce hybrid corn, sorghum, sunflower seed, varietal soybeans, alfalfa.

Argentina, Australia, Brazil, Canada, Chile, China (PRC), France, Italy, Mexico, South Africa, Spain, Thailand, Zimbabwe

DEL LABORATORIES INC.

565 Broad Hollow Road

Farmingdale, NY 11735

Tel: (516) 293-7070 Fax: (516) 293-1515

CEO: Dan K. Wassong, Chmn.

FO: William H. McMenemy, EVP

HR: Charles Schneck, Dir.

Web site: www.dellabs.com

Emp: 1,480 Rev: $263 mil.

Mfr. cosmetics, pharmaceuticals.

Canada

DELAVAN INC.

811 4th Street

West Des Moines, IA 50265-0100

Tel: (515) 274-1561 Fax: (515) 271-7204

CEO: James Baker, Pres.

HR: Laurie Engel

Emp: 800

Mfr. heating equipment, nozzles and hydraulic pumps.

England, U.K.

DELL COMPUTER CORPORATION

One Dell Way

Round Rock, TX 78682-2222

Tel: (512) 338-4400 Fax: (512) 728-3653

CEO: Michael S. Dell, Chmn.

FO: D. Keith Maxwell, VP Intl.

Web site: www.dell.com

Emp: 16,000 Rev: $12,300 mil.

Direct marketer & supplier of computer systems.

Australia, Austria, Belgium, Brazil, Canada, Chile, China (PRC), Czech Republic, Denmark, England, U.K., France, Germany, Hong Kong, India, Ireland, Japan, Malaysia, Mexico, Netherlands, New Zealand, Norway, Poland, Singapore, South Africa, South Korea, Spain, Sweden, Switzerland, Taiwan (ROC), Thailand

DELOITTE TOUCHE TOHMATSU INTERNATIONAL

PO Box 820

Wilton, CT 06897

Tel: (203) 761-3000 Fax: (203) 834-2200

CEO: J. Michael Cook, Pres.

FO: J. Thomas Presby

HR: Martyn Fisher

Web site: www.u.s.deloitte.com or www.dtti.com

Emp: 65,000 Rev: $7,400 mil.

Accounting, audit, tax and management consulting services.

Albania, Algeria, Angola, Argentina, Aruba, Australia, Austria, Bahamas, Bahrain, Barbados, Belgium, Belize, Bermuda, Bolivia, Botswana, Brazil, British Virgin Islands, Brunei, Bulgaria, Cameroon, Canada, Cayman Islands, Channel Islands, U.K., Chile, China (PRC), Colombia, Costa Rica, Cyprus, Czech Republic, Denmark, Dominican Republic, Ecuador, Egypt, England, U.K., Estonia, Fiji, Finland, France, Germany, Ghana, Gibraltar, Greece, Greenland, Guam, Guatemala, Guyana, Hong Kong, Hungary, Iceland, India, Indonesia, Ireland, Israel, Italy, Ivory Coast, Jamaica, Japan, Jordan, Kazakhstan, Kenya, Kuwait, Latvia, Lebanon, Lithuania, Luxembourg, Macau, Macedonia, Madagascar, Malawi, Malaysia, Malta, Mexico, Morocco, Mozambique, Netherlands, Netherlands Antilles, New Zealand, Nigeria, Northern Ireland, U.K., Northern Mariana Islands, Norway, Oman, Pakistan, Palau, Panama, Papua New Guinea, Paraguay, Peru, Philippines, Poland, Portugal, Qatar, Romania, Russia, San Marino, Saudi Arabia, Scotland, U.K., Singapore, Slovenia, South Africa, South Korea, Spain, Sweden, Switzerland, Syria, Taiwan (ROC), Thailand, Turkey, Uganda, Ukraine, United Arab Emirates, Uruguay, Uzbekistan, Venezuela, Vietnam, Wales, U.K., Yugoslavia, Zambia, Zimbabwe

DELPHI PACKARD ELECTRIC

408 Dana Street

Warren, OH 44486

Tel: (330) 373-2121 Fax: (330) 373-4888

CEO: David Heilman, Pres.

Mfr. ignition parts for automobiles.

Mexico

DELTA AIR LINES INC.

PO Box 20706

Atlanta, GA 30320-6001

Tel: (404) 715-2600 Fax: (404) 715-5494

CEO: Leo F. Mullin, Pres.

FO: Stephan Egli, VP

HR: Robert G. Adams, SVP

Web site: www.delta-air.com/index.html

Emp: 66,000 Rev: $14,000 mil.

Major worldwide airline; international air transport services.

Austria, Bahamas, Belgium, Bermuda, Bosnia-Herzegovina, Brazil, Canada, Cayman Islands, Croatia, Czech Republic, England, U.K., Finland, France, Germany, Greece, India, Ireland, Italy, Japan, Kenya, Mexico, Netherlands, Norway, Poland, Russia, Singapore, South Korea, Spain, Sweden, Switzerland, Turkey, Uganda, United Arab Emirates, Venezuela

DELUXE CORPORATION

3680 Victoria Street North

Shoreview, MN 55126-2966

Tel: (612) 483-7111 Fax: (612) 481-4163

CEO: John A. Blanchard, III, Chmn.

HR: Michael F. Reeves, VP

Web site: www.deluxe.com

Emp: 18,000 Rev: $1,900.0 mil.

Leading U.S. check printer and provider of electronic payment services.

Canada, England, U.K., India

DeMATTEIS CONSTRUCTION CORP.

820 Elmont Road

Elmont, NY 11003

Tel: (516) 285-5500 Fax: (516) 285-6950

CEO: Frederick DeMatteis, Chmn.

FO: Alfonso L. DeMatteis

HR: Albert Aboulafia

Web site: DEMATTEAB@aol.com

Emp: 1542 Rev: N/A

Real estate development and construction services.

China (PRC), Ireland, Vietnam

DENTSPLY INTERNATIONAL

570 West College Ave., PO Box 872

York, PA 17405-0872

Tel: (717) 845-7511 Fax: (717) 843-6357

CEO: John C. Miles, II

FO: Thomas L. Whiting, SVP

HR: Glenn K. Weirgarth, VP

Web site: www.dentsply.com

Emp: 5,300 Rev: $720 mil.

Mfr.& Distribution of dental supplies & equipment.

Argentina, Australia, Brazil, Canada, China (PRC), England, U.K., France, Germany, Hong Kong, India, Italy, Japan, Mexico, Philippines, Russia, South Africa, Switzerland, Taiwan (ROC), Thailand, Vietnam

DETROIT DIESEL CORPORATION

13400 Outer Drive West

Detroit, MI 48239

Tel: (313) 592-5000 Fax: (313) 592-5058

CEO: Chip McClure, Pres.

FO: Paul E. Moreton

HR: Paul F. Walters

Emp: 4,000

Mfr. diesel & aircraft engines, heavy-duty transmissions.

Canada, Switzerland

DEUTSCH COMPANY

2444 Wilshire Blvd

Santa Monica, CA 90403

Tel: (310) 453-0055 Fax:

CEO: Carl Deutsch

Electronic components.

France, Germany

DEVCON CORPORATION

30 Endicott Street

Danvers, MA 01923

Tel: (978) 777-1100 Fax: (978) 774-0516

CEO: David Parry, Pres.

Emp: 189

Mfr. filled epoxies, urethanes, adhesives and metal treatment products.

England, U.K., France, Germany, Ireland, Singapore

DEVELOPMENT ASSOCIATES INC.

1730 North Lynn Street

Arlington, VA 22209-2023

Tel: (703) 276-0677 Fax: (703) 276-0432

CEO: Peter B. Davis

FO: John H. Sullivan

HR: Sandy McKenzie

Emp: 223

Management consulting services.

Dominican Republic, Egypt, Jamaica, Lithuania, Nicaragua, Zimbabwe

DEWEY BALLANTINE LLP

1301 Ave. of the Americas

New York, NY 10019

Tel: (212) 259-8000 Fax: (212) 259-6333

CEO: Everett L. Jassy, Chmn.

HR: Kathleen Isaacs, Dir.

Web site: www.deweyballantine.com

Emp: 951 Rev: $228 mil.

International law firm.

Czech Republic, England, U.K., Hong Kong, Hungary, Poland

THE DEXTER CORPORATION

1 Elm Street

Windsor Locks, CT 06096

Tel: (860) 627-9051 Fax: (860) 627-7078

CEO: K. Grahame Walker, Chmn.

HR: Ellen C. Miles

Emp: 4,700

Mfr. nonwovens, polymer products, magnetic materials, biotechnology.

Australia, Belgium, Canada, China (PRC), England, U.K., France, Germany, Hong Kong, Italy, Japan, Malaysia, Mexico, Netherlands, New Zealand, Russia, Scotland, U.K., Singapore, Sweden, Switzerland, Venezuela, Wales, U.K.

DHL WORLDWIDE EXPRESS

333 Twin Dolphin Drive

Redwood City, CA 94065

Tel: (650) 593-7474 Fax: (650) 593-1689

CEO: Rob Kuijpers

FO: Jeff Corbett, SVP

HR: Garry Sellers, SVP

Web site: www.dhl.com

Emp: 50,000 Rev: $4,200 mil.

Worldwide air express carrier.

Albania, Algeria, Anguilla, Antigua, Argentina, Armenia, Aruba, Australia, Austria, Azerbaijan, Bahamas, Bahrain, Bangladesh, Barbados, Belarus, Belgium, Belize, Benin, Bermuda, Bolivia, Bosnia-Herzegovina, Botswana, Brazil, British Virgin Islands, Brunei, Bulgaria, Burkina Faso, Burundi, Cambodia, Cameroon, Canada, Cayman Islands, Chad, Channel Islands, U.K., Chile, China (PRC), Colombia, Congo, Costa Rica, Croatia, Cyprus, Czech Republic, Dem. Rep. of Congo, Denmark, Djibouti, Dominican Republic, Ecuador, Egypt, El Salvador, England, U.K., Estonia, Ethiopia, Fiji, Finland, France, French Antilles, French Polynesia, Gabon, Gambia, Georgia, Germany, Ghana, Gibraltar, Greece, Greenland, Grenada, Guam, Guatemala, Guinea, Guyana, Haiti, Honduras, Hong Kong, Hungary, Iceland, India, Indonesia, Iran, Ireland, Isle of Man, Israel, Italy, Ivory Coast, Jamaica, Japan, Jordan, Kazakhstan, Kenya, Kuwait, Laos, Latvia, Lebanon, Lesotho, Liberia, Libya, Liechtenstein, Lithuania, Luxembourg, Macau, Macedonia, Madagascar, Malawi, Malaysia, Mali, Malta, Mauritius, Mexico, Monaco, Mongolia, Morocco, Mozambique, Myanmar, Namibia, Nepal, Netherlands, Netherlands Antilles, New Caledonia, New Zealand, Nicaragua, Niger, Nigeria, North Korea, Northern Ireland, U.K., Northern Mariana Islands, Norway, Oman, Pakistan, Panama, Papua New Guinea, Paraguay, Peru, Philippines, Poland, Portugal, Qatar, Reunion, Romania, Russia, Saudi Arabia, Scotland, U.K., Senegal, Seychelles, Sierra Leone, Singapore, Slovakia, Slovenia, Solomon Islands, South Africa, South Korea, Spain, Sri Lanka, Sudan, Surinam, Swaziland, Sweden, Switzerland, Syria, Taiwan (ROC), Tajikistan, Tanzania, Thailand, Trinidad & Tobago, Turkey, Turkmenistan, Turks & Caicos Islands, Uganda, Ukraine, United Arab Emirates, Uruguay, Uzbekistan, Venezuela, Vietnam, Wales, U.K., Yemen, Yugoslavia, Zambia, Zimbabwe

DIAMOND CHAIN COMPANY

402 Kentucky Ave.

Indianapolis, IN 46225

Tel: (317) 638-6431 Fax: (317) 633-2243

CEO: Byron Speice, Chmn.

HR: Gary Adams

Mfr. roller chains.

Australia, England, U.K., India

DIAMOND POWER INTERNATIONAL, INC.

PO Box 415

Lancaster, OH 43130

Tel: (740) 687-6500 Fax: (740) 687-7430

CEO: David L. Keller, Pres.

FO: Jeff Koksal

HR: James R. Craft

Web site: www.diamondpower.com

Mfg. boiler cleaning equipment & ash handling systems: sootblowers, controls, diagnostics systems, gauges, OEM parts, rebuilds & field service.

Australia, Canada, China (PRC), Scotland, U.K.

DICTAPHONE CORPORATION

3191 Broadbridge Ave.

Stratford, CT 06497-2559

Tel: (203) 381-7000 Fax: (203) 381-7100

CEO: John Duerden, Pres.

HR: Anne Collins

Mfr./sale dictation, telephone answering and multi-channel voice communications recording systems.

Canada, England, U.K., Switzerland

DIEBOLD INC.

PO Box 8230

Canton, OH 44711

Tel: (330) 490-4000 Fax: (330) 490-3794

CEO: Robert W. Mahoney

FO: M. J. Hillock/E. N. Petersen

HR: Charles B. Scheurer, VP

Web site: www.interbold.com

Emp: 4,700

Mfr. automated banking systems; security services for banking industrial & related fields.

Germany, Hong Kong

DIETZGEN CORPORATION

1218 West Northwest Highway

Palatine, IL 60067

Tel: (847) 776-3500 Fax: (847) 776-3532

CEO: Larry Kujovich, Pres.

FO: Lory Galloway

HR: William J. Sullivan

Web site: www.dietzgen.com

Emp: 250

Mfr. reprographic & drafting media, accessories and supplies.

China (PRC), Mexico

DIGITAL EQUIPMENT CORPORATION

111 Powder Mill Road

Maynard, MA 01754

Tel: (978) 493-5111 Fax: (978) 493-7374

CEO: Eckhard Pfeiffer, Pres. & Chmn.

FO: Hans W. Dirkmann, VP

HR: Ilene B. Jacobs, VP

Web site: www.digital.com

Emp: 55,000 Rev: $13,100 mil.

Mfr. network computer systems, components, software and services.

Algeria, Australia, Austria, Belgium, Brazil, Bulgaria, Czech Republic, Denmark, England, U.K., Fiji, Finland, France, Germany, Greece, Hong Kong, Hungary, Iceland, India, Indonesia, Ireland, Israel, Italy, Japan, Luxembourg, Malaysia, Morocco, Netherlands, New Zealand, Norway, Philippines, Portugal, Romania, Singapore, Slovakia, South Africa, Spain, Sweden, Switzerland, Taiwan (ROC), Thailand, Venezuela

THE DII GROUP

6273 Monarch Park Place, Ste. 200

Niwot, CO 80503

Tel: (303) 652-2221 Fax: (303) 652-0602

CEO: Ron Budacz

Emp: 3,600 Rev: $335 mil.

Electronic subassemblies and components.

England, U.K., Ireland, Malaysia

DILLINGHAM CONSTRUCTION CORPORATION

5944 Inglewood Drive

Pleasanton, CA 94566

Tel: (925) 463-3300 Fax: (925) 463-1571

CEO: William Higgins, Pres.

HR: Howard Fallin

Emp: 1,200

General contracting.

Australia, Canada, Hong Kong, Pakistan

DIMON INCORPORATED

512 Bridge Street, PO Box 681

Danville, VA 24543-0681

Tel: (804) 792-7511 Fax: (804) 791-0377

CEO: Claude B. Owen, Jr., Chmn.

FO: Albert C. Monk, III, Pres.

HR: Richard D. O'Reilly, Sr. VP

Emp: 15,000 Rev: $2,500 mil.

One of world's largest importer and exporter of leaf tobacco and fresh cut flowers.

Brazil, Germany, Netherlands, Switzerland

DIODES, INC.

3050 East Hillcrest Drive, Ste. 200

Westlake Village, CA 91362

Tel: (805) 446-4800 Fax: (805) 446-4850

CEO: Michael A. Rosenberg, Pres.

HR: Patricia Friou

Web site: www.dides.com

Emp: 400 Rev: $65 mil.

Mfr. semiconductor devices.

China (PRC), Taiwan (ROC)

DIONEX CORPORATION

1228 Titan Way, PO Box 3603

Sunnyvale, CA 94088-3603

Tel: (408) 737-0700 Fax: (408) 730-9403

CEO: A. Blaine Bowman

Emp: 699

Develop/mfr./marketing/services chromatography systems & related products.

Austria, Belgium, Canada, England, U.K., France, Germany, Italy, Japan, Netherlands, Switzerland

WALT DISNEY COMPANY

500 South Buena Vista Street

Burbank, CA 91521

Tel: (818) 560-1000 Fax: (818) 560-1930

CEO: Michael D. Eisner, Chmn.

Emp: 120,000 Rev: $14,000 mil.

Film/TV production, theme parks, resorts, publishing, recording and retail stores.

Belgium, Brazil, Canada, China (PRC), Denmark, England, U.K., France, Germany, Italy, Japan, Portugal, Spain

DIXON TICONDEROGA COMPANY

195 International Parkway

Heathrow, FL 32746

Tel: (407) 829-9000 Fax: (407) 829-2574

CEO: Gino N. Pala, Pres.

HR: J. C. Walton

Emp: 980

Mfr./services writing implements and art supplies.

Canada, England, U.K., Mexico

DO ALL COMPANY

254 North Laurel Ave.

Des Plaines, IL 60016

Tel: (847) 803-7380 Fax: (847) 699-7524

CEO: Michael L. Wilkie, Pres.

HR: Kevin Hennessy

Emp: 300

Distributors of machinery tools, metal cutting tools, instruments and industrial supplies.

Australia, Belgium, England, U.K., Germany, Netherlands, Sweden

DOBOY PACKAGING MACHINERY INC.

869 South Knowles Ave.

New Richmond, WI 54017-1797

Tel: (715) 246-6511 Fax: (715) 246-6539

CEO: William Heilhecker, Pres.

FO: Jerry Klasen

HR: Candy Peterson

Emp: 675

Mfr. packaging machinery.

England, U.K., Germany, Singapore

DOLE FOOD COMPANY, INC.

31365 Oak Crest Drive

Westlake Village, CA 91361

Tel: (818) 879-6600 Fax: (818) 879-6615

CEO: David A. DeLorenzo, Pres. & COO

FO: W. F. Feeney, Pres. Eur.

HR: George R. Horne, VP

Web site: www.dole.com

Emp: 43,000

Produces/distributes fresh fruits and vegetables and canned juices and fruits.

England, U.K., Germany, Philippines, Thailand

DOMINICK & DOMINICK INC.

Financial Square, 32 Old Slip

New York, NY 10005

Tel: (212) 558-8800 Fax: (212) 248-0592

CEO: Paul M. Kennedy

Emp: 100

Investment brokers.

England, U.K., Germany, Switzerland

DOMINION RESOURCES, INC.

901 East Byrd Street, Ste. 1700

Richmond, VA 23219-6111

Tel: (804) 775-5700 Fax: (804) 775-5819

CEO: Thomas E. Capps, Pres. & Chmn.

FO: David L. Heavenridge, EVP

HR: Sally C. Smedley, Dir.

Web site: www.domres.com

Emp: 15,000 Rev: $7.5 mil.

Provides electrical power.

Argentina, Belize, Bolivia, England, U.K.

DONALDSON COMPANY, INC.

1400 West 94th Street

Minneapolis, MN 55431

Tel: (612) 887-3131 Fax: (612) 887-3155

CEO: William G. Van Dyke, Chmn.

FO: W. Cook & N. Priadka

HR: John E.Thames, VP

Web site: www.Donaldson.com

Emp: 7,000 Rev: $830 mil.

Mfr. filtration systems and replacement parts.

Australia, Belgium, China (PRC), England, U.K., France, Germany, Hong Kong, India, Indonesia, Japan, Mexico, Netherlands, South Africa, South Korea

DONALDSON, LUFKIN & JENRETTE, INC.

277 Park Ave.

New York, NY 10172

Tel: (212) 892-3000 Fax: (212) 892-7272

CEO: John S. Chalsty, Chmn.

FO: Joe. L. Roy, Pres.

HR: Gerald Rigg

Web site: www.dlj.com

Emp: 7,053 Rev: $4,640.5 mil.

Investment banking, capital markets, and financial services.

Argentina, Brazil, England, U.K., France, Hong Kong, India, Japan, Mexico, Switzerland

DONNA KARAN INTERNATIONAL INC.

550 Seventh Ave.
New York, NY 10018
Tel: (212) 789-1500 Fax: (212) 789-1682
CEO: John Idol, Pres.
Rev: $10 mil. (Intl.)
Design/mfr. activewear and DKNY clothing line.
England, U.K., Germany, Switzerland

R.R. DONNELLEY & SONS COMPANY

77 West Wacker Drive
Chicago, IL 60601-1696
Tel: (312) 326-8000 Fax: (312) 326-8543
CEO: William L. Davis, Chmn.
FO: James R. Donnelley
HR: Haven E. Cockerham, SVP
Web site: www.rrdonnelley.com
Emp: 26,000 Rev: $4,850 mil.
Commercial printing, allied communication services.
Argentina, Barbados, Brazil, China (PRC), England, U.K., France, Germany, Hong Kong, India, Ireland, Israel, Japan, Luxembourg, Mexico, Netherlands, Poland, Singapore, Taiwan (ROC), Thailand

DONNELLY CORPORATION

414 East 40th Street
Holland, MI 49423
Tel: (616) 786-7000 Fax: (616) 786-6034
CEO: J. Dwane Baumgardner, Chmn.
FO: Hans W. Huber, COO Europe
HR: Carol Kaplan
Web site: www.donnelly.com
Emp: 5,000 Rev: $671 mil.
Mfr. fabricated, molded & coated glass products for the automotive & electronics industries.
China (PRC), France, Germany, Ireland, Japan, Mexico, Portugal, Scotland, U.K., Spain, Sweden

DONOVAN LEISURE NEWTON & IRVINE

30 Rockefeller Plaza
New York, NY 10112
Tel: (212) 632-3000 Fax: (212) 632-3315
CEO: J. Peter Coll, Jr., Mng. Prtn.
Emp: 350
Law firm.
England, U.K., France

DOONEY & BOURKE

1 Regent Street
Norwalk, CT 06855
Tel: (203) 853-7515 Fax: (203) 838-7754
CEO: Peter Dooney, Chmn. & Pres.
Web site: www.dooney.com
Mfr./sales/distribution of fine leather handbags, wallets, belts and accessories.
Belgium, Canada, Italy, Spain

DOREMUS & CO., INC.

200 Varick Street
New York, NY 10271
Tel: (212) 366-3000 Fax: (212) 366-3629
CEO: Carl Anderson, Pres.
FO: Michael Callahan
HR: Rick Amato
Emp: 174 Rev: $29 mil.
Advertising & public relations.
England, U.K., Hong Kong

DORR-OLIVER INC.

612 Wheeler's Farm Road, PO Box 3819
Milford, CT 06460
Tel: (203) 876-5400 Fax: (203) 876-5432
CEO: Michael J. Smithlin, Pres.
HR: D. Oliver
Emp: 780
Mfr. process equipment for food, pulp & paper, mineral & chemicals industry; & municipal/industry waste treatment.
Australia, Belgium, Chile, England, U.K., France, Germany, Mexico, Netherlands

DORSEY & WHITNEY LLP

Pillsbury Center South, 220 S. Sixth Street
Minneapolis, MN 55402
Tel: (612) 340-2600 Fax: (612) 340-2868
CEO: Thomas O. Moe, Mng. Prtn.
HR: Joan F. Oygas
Web site: www.dorseylaw.com
Emp: 1,150
International law firm.
Belgium, England, U.K., Hong Kong

DOVER CORPORATION

280 Park Ave.

New York, NY 10017-1292

Tel: (212) 922-1640 Fax: (212) 922-1656

CEO: Gary L. Roubos, Chmn.

FO: John E. Pomeroy, Pres. Intl.

Web site: www.dovercorporation.com

Emp: 28,000 Rev: $3,500 mil.

Elevator manufacturer and holding company for varied industries.

Australia, Bahrain, Barbados, Bermuda, Canada, China (PRC), Costa Rica, Dominican Republic, Ecuador, Egypt, El Salvador, Germany, Guam, Guatemala, Hong Kong, Indonesia, Jamaica, Japan, Malaysia, Mexico, Myanmar, New Zealand, Pakistan, Panama, Philippines, Saudi Arabia, Singapore, South Korea, Taiwan (ROC), Thailand, United Arab Emirates, Venezuela

THE DOW CHEMICAL COMPANY

2030 Dow Center

Midland, MI 48674

Tel: (517) 636-1000 Fax: (517) 636-3228

CEO: William S. Stavropoulos, Pres.

HR: Larry Washington

Web site: www.atdow.com

Emp: 61,000 Rev: $20,000 mil.

Mfr. chemicals, plastics, pharmaceuticals, agricultural products, consumer products.

Argentina, Australia, Austria, Belgium, Brazil, Canada, Chile, Colombia, Costa Rica, Denmark, Ecuador, El Salvador, England, U.K., France, Germany, Guatemala, Hong Kong, India, Indonesia, Ivory Coast, Japan, Liberia, Luxembourg, Malaysia, Mexico, Morocco, Netherlands, Norway, Panama, Peru, Poland, Portugal, Russia, Saudi Arabia, Singapore, South Africa, South Korea, Spain, Sweden, Switzerland, Taiwan (ROC), Thailand, Venezuela

DOW CORNING CORPORATION

2220 West Salzburg Road, PO Box 1767

Midland, MI 48640

Tel: (517) 496-4000 Fax: (517) 496-6080

CEO: R. A. Hazleton, Chmn.

FO: D. C. Watters

HR: W. T. Gregory

Emp: 8,700 Rev: $2,000 mil.

Silicones, silicon chemicals, solid lubricants.

Argentina, Australia, Austria, Belgium, Brazil, Canada, Colombia, England, U.K., France, Germany, Greece, Hong Kong, Israel, Italy, Malaysia, Mexico, New Zealand, Philippines, Singapore, South Korea, Spain, Taiwan (ROC), Venezuela

DOW JONES & CO., INC.

200 Liberty Street

New York, NY 10281

Tel: (212) 416-2000 Fax: (212) 416-2655

CEO: Peter R. Kann, Chmn.

FO: Kenneth L. Burenga, Pres.

HR: James Schduto

Web site: www.wsj.com

Publishing and financial news services.

Belgium, England, U.K., Hong Kong

DRAFT WORLDWIDE

633 North St. Clair Street

Chicago, IL 60611-3211

Tel: (312) 944-3500 Fax: (312) 944-3566

CEO: Howard C. Draft, Chmn.

FO: Jordan H. Rednor

Web site: www.draftworldwide.com

Emp: 1,500 Rev: $142 mil.

Full service international advertising agency.

Brazil, England, U.K., Finland, France, Germany, Greece, Hong Kong, India, Israel, Italy, Japan, Macedonia, Malaysia, Portugal, Singapore, South Korea, Spain, Switzerland, Thailand

DRAKE BEAM MORIN INC.

101 Huntington Ave.

Boston, MA 02199

Tel: (617) 450-9860 Fax: (617) 267-2011

CEO: Craig Sawin, Pres.

FO: Brita Askey, VP

Web site: www.dbm.com

Emp: 410 Rev: $106 mil.

Human resource management consulting & training.

Argentina, Australia, Austria, Belgium, Brazil, Canada, Chile, Colombia, Denmark, England, U.K., Estonia, Finland, France, Germany, Greece, Hong Kong, Ireland, Israel, Italy, Japan, Malaysia, Mexico, Netherlands, New Zealand, Norway, Peru, Portugal, Scotland, U.K., Singapore, South Africa, South Korea, Spain, Sweden, Switzerland, Thailand, Turkey, Uruguay, Venezuela, Wales,

U.K.

DRAVO CORPORATION

11 Stanwix Street, 11th Fl.

Pittsburgh, PA 15222

Tel: (412) 995-5500   Fax: (412) 995-5570

CEO: Carl Gilbert, Pres.

FO: W. F. Thorbecke

HR: D. E. Snowberger

Emp: 14,000

Material handling equipment and process plants.

Australia, Canada, China (PRC), Hong Kong, Indonesia, Philippines, Saudi Arabia, Venezuela

DRESSER INDUSTRIES INC.

2001 Ross Ave., PO Box 718

Dallas, TX 75221-0718

Tel: (214) 740-6000   Fax: (214) 740-6584

CEO: William E. Bradford, Chmn.

FO: Donald C. Vaughn, Pres.

HR: Paul M. Bryant, VP

Web site: www.dresser.com

Emp: 31,300   Rev: $7,458 mil.

Diversified supplier of equipment & technical services to energy & natural resource industrial.

Australia, Austria, Belgium, Brazil, Canada, China (PRC), Costa Rica, England, U.K., France, Germany, Hong Kong, Italy, Japan, Mexico, Netherlands, Nigeria, Norway, Russia, Scotland, U.K., Singapore, South Africa, South Korea, Spain, Switzerland, Trinidad & Tobago, Tunisia, United Arab Emirates

DREVER COMPANY

PO Box 98, 380 Red Lion Road

Huntingdon, PA 19006-0098

Tel: (215) 947-3400   Fax: (215) 947-7934

CEO: J. R. Peterson, Pres.

FO: S. R. Peterson

HR: T. H. Paterson

Web site: www.drever.com

Emp: 190

Mfr. industrial furnaces.

Belgium, England, U.K., Italy

DRG INTERNATIONAL INC.

PO Box 1188

Mountainside, NJ 07092

Tel: (908) 233-2075   Fax: (908) 233-0758

CEO: Dr. Cyril E. Geacintov, Pres.

Emp: 85

Mfr./sale/service medical devices, diagnostic kits, clinical equipment.

Czech Republic, Germany, Poland, Russia

DRIVER-HARRIS COMPANY

308 Middlesex Street

Harrison, NJ 07029

Tel: (973) 483-4802   Fax: (973) 483-4806

CEO: Frank L. Driver, IV

FO: Frank L. Driver, IV

Emp: 158

Mfr. non-ferrous alloys.

England, U.K., Ireland

DU BOIS CHEMICAL

255 East 5th Street

Cincinnati, OH 45202-4799

Tel: (513) 762-6000   Fax: (513) 762-6030

CEO: Don Saunders

FO: Philip M. Sabatelli

Emp: 2,400

Mfr. specialty chemicals & maintenance products.

Canada, Dominican Republic, Mexico

E.I. DU PONT DE NEMOURS & COMPANY

1007 Market Street

Wilmington, DE 19898

Tel: (302) 774-1000   Fax: (302) 774-7321

CEO: John A. Krol, Chmn.

FO: Charles O. Holliday, Jr., CEO

HR: John D. Broyles, VP

Web site: www.dupont.com

Emp: 97,000

Mfr./sale diversified chemicals, plastics, specialty products and fibers.

Argentina, Australia, Belgium, Brazil, Canada, Colombia, England, U.K., Finland, France, Germany, Hong Kong, Ireland, Italy, Japan, Liberia, Mexico, Netherlands, New Zealand, Norway, Poland, Russia, Singapore, South Korea, Spain, Sweden, Switzerland, Taiwan (ROC), Thailand, Ukraine, Venezuela

DUKANE CORPORATION

2900 Dukane Drive

St. Charles, IL 60174

Tel: (630) 584-2300 Fax: (630) 584-2370

CEO: John McWilliam Stone, Jr.

HR: Robert Scarlet

Emp: 710

Mfr. facility intercommunications, optoelectronic device assembly, plastics welding, local area network equipment.

Canada

DUKE ENERGY CORPORATION

422 South Church Street

Charlotte, NC 28242

Tel: (704) 594-6200 Fax: (704) 382-3814

CEO: Paul M. Anderson, Pres. & COO

HR: James Pruett

Emp: 23,000 Rev: $16,300

Energy pipeliner, oil/gas exploration and production.

Canada, Ecuador, England, U.K., Norway, Saudi Arabia, Singapore

THE DUN & BRADSTREET CORPORATION

One Diamond Hill Road

Murray Hill, NJ 07974

Tel: (908) 665-5000 Fax: (908) 665-5524

CEO: Volney Taylor, Chmn.

FO: Michael R. Flock, Pres.

HR: Peter J. Ross, SVP

Web site: www.dnbcorp.com

Emp: 15,100 Rev: $2,154 mil.

Provides corporate credit, marketing & accounts-receivable management services & publishes credit ratings & financial information.

Australia, Austria, Belgium, Canada, Cyprus, Czech Republic, Denmark, England, U.K., Finland, France, Germany, Hong Kong, Hungary, Ireland, Israel, Italy, Japan, Netherlands, Norway, Poland, Portugal, Singapore, Spain, Sweden, Switzerland, Zimbabwe

DUNHAM-BUSH INC.

175 South Street

West Hartford, CT 06110

Tel: (860) 548-3780 Fax: (860) 548-1703

CEO: Mr. Yeo, Pres.

FO: Derek J. Smith

HR: R. O'Connell

Emp: 1,600

Industrial & commercial refrigeration, heating & A/C equipment.

Canada, England, U.K., Germany

DUNHILL INTERNATIONAL SEARCH

59 Elm Street, Ste. 520

New Haven, CT 06510

Tel: (203) 562-0511 Fax: (203) 562-2637

CEO: Donald J. Kaiser, Pres.

FO: James G. Kaiser

Emp: 300

International recruiting services: sales/marketing, accounting/finance, general managers.

Canada, Japan

DUO FASTENER CORP.

13951 South Quality Drive

Huntley, IL 60142

Tel: (847) 669-7300 Fax: (847) 669-7301

CEO: John A. Torstenson, Pres.

Emp: 950

Staplers, tackers and nailers.

Germany

DURACELL INTERNATIONAL INC.

Berkshire Industrial Park

Bethel, CT 06801

Tel: (203) 796-4000 Fax: (203) 796-4745

CEO: Peter Hoffman, Pres.

Emp: 7,700 Rev: $1,000 mil.

Mfr. batteries.

Argentina, Australia, Brazil, Chile, England, U.K., Hong Kong, Japan, Mexico, Poland

DURO-TEST CORPORATION

9 Law Drive

Fairfield, NJ 07004

Tel: (973) 808-1800 Fax: (973) 808-7107

CEO: Robert C. Sorensen

FO: Miguel Diaz

HR: Shirley Benson

Emp: 1,605

Mfr. fluorescent, incandescent & fluomeric lamps.

Canada, Japan, Mexico

DYN CORPORATION

2000 Edmund Halley Drive
Reston, VA 22091
Tel: (703) 264-0330 Fax: (703) 264-8600
CEO: Paul Lambardi, Pres.
HR: Roy Geiger
Emp: 16,000
Diversified technical services.
Germany, South Korea

DYNATECH CORPORATION
3 New England Executive Park
Burlington, MA 01803
Tel: (781) 272-6100 Fax: (781) 272-2304
CEO: John F. Reno, Chmn.
HR: John A. Mixon
Emp: 2,490
Develop/mfr. communications equipment.
Australia, Canada, Channel Islands, U.K., England, U.K., France, Germany, Hong Kong, Ireland, Italy, Japan

DYNEGY INC.
1000 Louisiana, Ste. 5800
Houston, TX 77002
Tel: (713) 507-6400 Fax: (713) 507-3871
CEO: Charles L. Watson, Chmn.
FO: James H. Current, Jr.
HR: Michael B. Barton, VP
Web site: www.dynegy.com
Emp: 1,400
Holding company that transports and markets energy to local utililties and industrial businesses.
Canada, England, U.K.

E

E-Z-EM INC.
717 Main Street
Westbury, NY 11590
Tel: (516) 333-8230 Fax: (516) 333-8278
CEO: Howard S. Stern, Chmn.
FO: Agustin V. Gago, VP Intl.
HR: Sandra D. Baron, VP HR
Web site: www.ezem.com
Emp: 911 Rev: $97 mil.
World's leading supplier of barium contrast media for medical imaging and accessories.
Belgium, Canada, England, U.K., Ireland, Japan, Netherlands

EA INTERNATIONAL, INC.
175 Middlesex Turnpike
Bedford, MA 01730
Tel: (781) 275-8846 Fax: (781) 275-7253
CEO: Edward M. Greco, Pres.
Web site: www.eaest.com
Emp: 500 Rev: $90 mil.
Environmental engineering, management and consulting.
Guam, Mexico

EAGLE ELECTRIC MFG. CO., INC.
45-31 Court Square
Long Island City, NY 11101
Tel: (718) 937-8000 Fax: (718) 482-0160
CEO: Neal W. Kluger
FO: Warren Cohen, Pres.
Emp: 2,100
Mfr. electrical wiring devices and switchgear.
Costa Rica, Philippines

THE EASTERN COMPANY
112 Bridge Street
Naugatuck, CT 06770
Tel: (203) 729-2255 Fax: (203) 723-8653
CEO: Len Legunza, Pres.
Emp: 704
Mfr. locks & security hardware.
Canada, Taiwan (ROC)

EASTMAN & BEAUDINE INC.

13355 Noel Road, Ste. 1370

Dallas, TX 75240

Tel: (972) 661-5520 Fax: (972) 980-8540

CEO: Bob Baudine, Pres.

Investments.

Belgium, Brazil, England, U.K., France, Japan, Netherlands

EASTMAN CHEMICAL

100 North Eastman Road

Kingsport, TN 37660

Tel: (423) 229-2000 Fax: (423) 229-1351

CEO: E. W. Davenport, Jr., Chmn.

FO: Roger K. Mowen, VP

HR: B. Fielding Rolston, VP Intl.

Web site: www.eastman.com

Emp: 17,000 Rev: $4,600 mil.

Mfr. plastics, chemicals, fibers.

Argentina, Australia, Brazil, Canada, China (PRC), Czech Republic, Denmark, England, U.K., France, Germany, Hong Kong, Hungary, India, Indonesia, Israel, Italy, Japan, Malaysia, Mexico, Netherlands, Poland, Singapore, South Africa, South Korea, Spain, Switzerland, Taiwan (ROC), Thailand, Turkey, United Arab Emirates, Venezuela

EASTMAN KODAK COMPANY

343 State Street

Rochester, NY 14650

Tel: (716) 724-4000 Fax: (716) 724-0663

CEO: George M.C. Fisher, Chmn.

HR: Michael P. Morley

Emp: 96,300 Rev: $13 bil.

Develop/mfr. photo & chemicals products, information management/video/copier systems, fibers/plastics for various industry.

Argentina, Australia, Austria, Belgium, Brazil, Canada, Chile, China (PRC), Colombia, Denmark, Dominican Republic, Egypt, England, U.K., Finland, France, Germany, Greece, Hong Kong, Hungary, India, Ireland, Italy, Japan, Kenya, Lebanon, Malaysia, Mexico, Netherlands, New Zealand, Norway, Pakistan, Panama, Peru, Philippines, Poland, Portugal, Russia, Scotland, U.K., Singapore, South Korea, Spain, Sweden, Switzerland, Taiwan (ROC), Thailand, Turkey, Ukraine, United Arab Emirates, Uruguay, Venezuela, Zimbabwe

EATON CORPORATION

1111 Superior Ave.

Cleveland, OH 44114

Tel: (216) 523-5000 Fax: (216) 479-7068

CEO: Alexander M. Cutler, Pres.

FO: Patrick X. Donovan, VP

Emp: 52,000 Rev: $6 bil.

Advanced technical products for transportation & industrial markets.

Argentina, Australia, Belgium, Brazil, Canada, Colombia, Costa Rica, England, U.K., France, Germany, Greece, Israel, Italy, Japan, Malaysia, Mexico, Monaco, New Zealand, Nigeria, Peru, Philippines, Singapore, Spain, Sweden, Thailand, Venezuela, Zambia

EATON CORP/CUTLER HAMMER

4201 North 27th Street

Milwaukee, WI 53216

Tel: (414) 449-6000 Fax: (414) 449-6221

CEO: Steve Cutler, Pres.

Emp: 38,000

Electric control apparatus, mfr. of advanced technologic products.

Australia, Brazil, Canada, Costa Rica, England, U.K., Germany, Italy, Malaysia, Mexico, New Zealand, Nigeria, Singapore, United Arab Emirates

EBSCO INDUSTRIES

5724 Highway 280 East

Birmingham, AL 35242-6818

Tel: (205) 991-6600 Fax: (205) 995-1586

CEO: Elton B. Stephens

HR: Patrick R. Sisbarro

Emp: 2,500

Serial pub/subscriptions, recreational & educational goods, mfr. sheet metal & wire products.

Germany

ECHLIN INC.

100 Double Beach Road

Branford, CT 06405

Tel: (203) 481-5751 Fax: (203) 481-6485

CEO: Larry W. McCurdy, Chmn.

FO: Larry Pavey

HR: Milton Makoski, SVP

Web site: www.echlin.com

Emp: 28,000

Supplies commercial vehicle components and auto fluid handling systems for the used car market

Australia, Brazil, Canada, China (PRC), England, U.K., Germany, South Africa, Venezuela

ECHO BAY MINES LTD.

6400 South Fidders Green Circle, Ste. 1000

Englewood, CO 80111

Tel: (303) 714-8600 Fax: (303) 714-8999

CEO: Robert Leclerc, Chmn.

Emp: 1,800

Gold and silver mining.

Canada

ECLIPSE INC.

1665 Elmwood Road

Rockford, IL 61103

Tel: (815) 877-3031 Fax: (815) 877-3336

CEO: Douglas Perks, Pres.

HR: Joan Linquist

Emp: 550

Mfr. industrial process heating equipment & systems.

Canada, England, U.K., Netherlands, Spain

ECOLAB INC.

Ecolab Center, 370 N. Wabasha Street

St. Paul, MN 55102

Tel: (612) 293-2233 Fax: (612) 225-3105

CEO: Allan L. Schuman, Pres.

FO: John P. Spooner, SVP Int'l

HR: Diana D. Lewis, VP HR

Web site: www.ecolab.com

Emp: 10,210 Rev: $1,640 mil.

Develop/mfr. premium cleaning, sanitizing and maintenance products and services for the hospitality, institutional, and residential markets.

Argentina, Australia, Austria, Barbados, Belgium, Brazil, Canada, Chile, China (PRC), Costa Rica, Czech Republic, Denmark, England, U.K., Finland, France, Germany, Greece, Guatemala, Honduras, Hong Kong, Hungary, Indonesia, Ireland, Italy, Jamaica, Japan, Kenya, Malaysia, Mexico, Morocco, Netherlands, New Zealand, Norway, Philippines, Poland, Portugal, Singapore, Slovenia, South Africa, South Korea, Spain, Sweden, Switzerland, Taiwan (ROC), Thailand, Turkey, Venezuela

ECOLOGY AND ENVIRONMENT INC.

368 Pleasant View Drive

Lancaster, NY 14086-1397

Tel: (716) 684-8060 Fax: (716) 684-0844

CEO: Gerhard J. Neumaier, Pres.

HR: Janet Steinbruckner, Dir. HR

Emp: 900 Rev: $59 mil.

Environmental, scientific & engineering consulting.

China (PRC), Germany, Hungary, Ireland, Mexico, Saudi Arabia, Venezuela

ECOWATER SYSTEMS INC.

1890 Woodlane Drive

Woodbury, MN 55125

Tel: (612) 739-5330 Fax: (612) 739-4547

CEO: Richard Elliott

FO: Fred C. Gedelman

HR: David S. Kell

Web site: www.ecowater.com

Emp: 509

Mfr. water treatment and purification products.

Belgium, Canada, China (PRC), England, U.K.

EDDIE BAUER INC.

15010 NE 36th Street

Redmont, WA 98052

Tel: (425) 882-6100 Fax: (425) 882-6383

CEO: Rick Fersch, Pres.

Web site: www.eddiebauer.com

Clothing retailer & mail order catalog company.

Canada, England, U.K., Germany, Japan

EDELMAN PUBLIC RELATIONS WORLDWIDE

200 East Randolph Drive, 63rd Floor

Chicago, IL 60601

Tel: (312) 240-3000 Fax: (312) 240-0596

CEO: Richard W. Edelman, Pres.

FO: Paul T. Bergevin, EVP

HR: Maria Laris, VP

Web site: www.edelman.com

Emp: 1,151 Rev: $122 mil.

International independent public relations firm.

Argentina, Australia, Belgium, Brazil, Canada, China (PRC), England, U.K., France, Germany, Hong Kong, Ireland, Italy, Malaysia, Mexico, Singapore, South Korea, Spain, Taiwan (ROC)

EDISON INTERNATIONAL

2244 Walnut Grove Ave.

Rosemead, CA 91770

Tel: (626) 302-1212 Fax: (626) 302-2517

CEO: John E. Bryson, Chmn.

FO: William J. Heller, SVP

HR: Lillian R. Gorman, VP

Web site: www.edisonx.com

Emp: 12,000 Rev: $9,200 mil

Utility holding company

Australia, England, U.K., Indonesia, Italy, Philippines, Spain, Thailand, Turkey

EDISON MISSION ENERGY

18101 Von Karman Ave., Ste. 1700

Irvine, CA 92612-1046

Tel: (714) 752-5588 Fax: (714) 752-5624

CEO: Edward R. Muller, Pres.

HR: Lynn M. Gardner

Web site: www.edisonx.com

Emp: 1,140 Rev: $975 mil.

Global power producer.

Australia, England, U.K., Indonesia, Italy, Philippines, Singapore, Spain, Turkey

EDO CORPORATION

60 East 42nd Street, Ste. 5010

New York, NY 10165

Tel: (212) 716-2000 Fax: (212) 716-2050

CEO: Frank Fariello, Pres.

Emp: 1,000

Mfr. aircraft parts and equipment.

Canada

J.D. EDWARDS & COMPANY

One Technology Way

Denver, CO 80237

Tel: (303) 334-4000 Fax: (303) 334-4970

CEO: C. Edward McVaney, Pres.

HR: Greg Dixon

Web site: www.jdedwards.com.

Computer software products.

Argentina, Australia, Austria, Belgium, Brazil, Canada, Chile, China (PRC), Colombia, Costa Rica, Czech Republic, Ecuador, Egypt, England, U.K., Finland, France, Germany, Greece, Hong Kong, Hungary, India, Indonesia, Ireland, Italy, Japan, Latvia, Malaysia, Mexico, Morocco, Netherlands, New Zealand, Peru, Philippines, Poland, Portugal, Russia, Saudi Arabia, Singapore, South Africa, South Korea, Spain, Sweden, Switzerland, Thailand, Ukraine, United Arab Emirates, Venezuela

EDWARDS SYSTEM TECHNOLOGY

90 Fieldston Court

Cheshire, CT 06410

Tel: (203) 699-3000 Fax: (203) 699-3031

CEO: Jay Twombly, VP

Emp: 3,500

Mfr. fire safety equipment, signaling systems.

Canada

EFCO

1800 NE Broadway Ave.

Des Moines, IA 50316-0386

Tel: (515) 266-1141 Fax: (515) 266-7970

CEO: Al Jennings, Pres.

FO: Bernie Savard

HR: Joe Michels

Emp: 800

Mfr. systems for concrete construction.

Argentina, Bolivia, Canada, Chile, Colombia, Costa Rica, Ecuador, England, U.K., Germany, Ireland, Mexico, Peru, Scotland, U.K., Taiwan (ROC), Venezuela

EG&G INC.

45 William Street

Wellesley, MA 02181-4078

Tel: (781) 237-5100 Fax: (781) 431-4114

CEO: John M. Kucharski

HR: Richard Walsh

Emp: 20,000

Diversified R/D, mfr. & services.

Australia, Belgium, Canada, China (PRC), Denmark, Egypt, England, U.K., Finland, France, Germany, India, Ireland, Italy, Japan, Netherlands, Norway, Philippines, Singapore, Sweden, Switzerland, Taiwan (ROC), Venezuela

EG&G SEALOL, INC.

50 Sharpe Drive

Cranston, RI 02920

Tel: (401) 463-8700 Fax: (401) 461-4310

CEO: Michael Galluccio, Mgr.

Emp: 600

Mfr. seals, joints and valves.

Germany, India, Italy, Japan

ELANCO ANIMAL HEALTH

Lilly Corporate Center

Indianapolis, IN 46206

Tel: (317) 276-3000 Fax: (317) 277-2012

CEO: Sidney Taruel, Pres.

Antibiotics and fine chemicals.

Hong Kong, Mexico

ELECTRIC FURNACE COMPANY

435 Wilson Street

Salem, OH 44460

Tel: (330) 332-4661 Fax: (330) 332-1853

CEO: Jacob O. Kamm, Pres.

HR: Vicki Sutter

Emp: 240

Mfr./design heat treating furnaces for metals industrial.

Canada, Germany

ELECTRO SCIENTIFIC INDUSTRIES, INC.

13900 NW Science Park Drive

Portland, OR 97229

Tel: (503) 641-4141 Fax: (503) 643-4873

CEO: Donald R. VanLuvanee, Pres.

HR: Robert C. Cimino, Dir.

Web site: www.elcsci.com

Emp: 900 Rev: $230 mil.

Mfg. Production and testing equpment used in manufacture of electronic components in pagers and cellular communication devices.

China (PRC), England, U.K., France, Germany, Hong Kong, Italy, Japan, Netherlands, Scotland, U.K., Singapore, South Korea

ELECTRO-SCIENCE LABORATORIES

416 East Church Road

King of Prussia, PA 19406

Tel: (610) 272-8000 Fax: (610) 272-6759

CEO: Michael A. Stein, Pres.

HR: Frank Goldburg

Emp: 95

Mfr. thick film materials & solder pastes.

England, U.K., France, Germany, Japan

ELECTROGLAS INC.

2901 Coronado Drive

Santa Clara, CA 95054

Tel: (408) 727-6500 Fax: (408) 982-8025

CEO: Curt Wozniak, Chmn.

Emp: 500

Mfr. semi-conductor test equipment, automatic wafer probers.

France, Germany, Hong Kong, Japan, Scotland, U.K., Singapore, South Korea, Taiwan (ROC)

ELECTRONIC ARTS INC.

1450 Fashion Island Boulevard

San Mateo, CA 94404

Tel: (650) 571-7171 Fax: (650) 286-5137

CEO: Lawrence F. Probst, III, Chmn.

FO: Mark S. Lewis, EVP Intl.

Web site: www.ea.com

Emp: 2,000 Rev: $900.0mil

Distribution and sales of entertainment software.

Australia, England, U.K., Germany

ELECTRONIC SPACE SYSTEMS CORPORATION (ESSCO)

Old Powder Mill Road

Concord, MA 01742-4697

Tel: (508) 369-7200 Fax: (508) 369-7641

CEO: Albert Cohen

FO: Albert Cohen, CEO

HR: Leo Clark, Sr.

Web site: www.esscoradomes.com

Emp: 150 Rev: $25 mil.

Design/mfr. radomes, antennas, radar, range reflectors, and satellite communications.

Ireland

THE EMBALMERS' SUPPLY COMPANY

1370 Honeyspot Road Ext

Stratford, CT 06497

Tel: (203) 375-2984 Fax: (203) 378-9160

CEO: Richard Beck, Pres.

Embalmers chemicals, equipment & supplies.

Canada

EMC CORP.

35 Parkwood Drive

Hopkinton, MA 01748-9103

Tel: (508) 435-1000 Fax: (508) 435-8884

CEO: Michael C. Ruettgers, Pres.

FO: Richard J. Lehane, SVP

Web site: www.emc.com

Emp: 6,300 Rev: $2,938 mil

Designs/supplies intelligent enterprise storage & retrieval technology for open systems, mainframes & midrange environments.

Australia, Austria, Belgium, Brazil, Canada, China (PRC), Denmark, England, U.K., France, Germany, Hong Kong, Ireland, Israel, Italy, Japan, Malaysia, Netherlands, New Zealand, Norway, Scotland, U.K., Singapore, South Africa, South Korea, Sweden, Switzerland, Taiwan (ROC), Thailand

EMCO WHEATON INC.

409A Airport Blvd

Morrisville, NC 27560

Tel: (919) 467-5878 Fax: (919) 467-7718

CEO: Joan Stalk, Pres.

Mfr. petroleum handling equipment.

Australia, Brazil, Canada, England, U.K., France, Germany, Japan

EMERSON & CUMMING SPECIALTY POLYMERS

46 Manning Road

Bellerica, MA 01821

Tel: (978) 436-9700 Fax: (978) 436-9701

CEO: Joseph McGonnell, Pres.

Mfr. specialty polymers.

Belgium, Japan

EMERSON ELECTRIC COMPANY

8000 West Florissant Ave., PO Box 4100

St. Louis, MO 63136

Tel: (314) 553-2000 Fax: (314) 553-3527

CEO: Charles F. Knight, Chmn.

HR: Charles T. Kelly, VP

Web site: www.emersonelectric.com

Emp: 100,000 Rev: $12,300 mil.

Electrical and electronic products, industrial components and systems, consumer, government and defense products.

Belgium, Canada, China (PRC), India, Ireland, Japan, Mexico, Philippines, Poland, Saudi Arabia, Slovakia, Thailand

EMERSON RADIO CORPORATION

9 Entin Road

Parsippany, NJ 07054

Tel: (973) 884-5800 Fax: (973) 428-2033

CEO: Marino Andriani, Pres.

FO: Kunio Takei

HR: Casper Kaffke

Emp: 850

Consumer electronics, radios, TV & VCR, tape recorders and players, computer products.

Canada, Hong Kong, South Korea, Taiwan (ROC)

EMERY WORLDWIDE

One Lagoon Drive, Ste. 400

Redwood City, CA 94065

Tel: (650) 596-9600 Fax: (650) 596-7901

CEO: David I. Beatson, Pres.

FO: Chutta Ratnathicam

HR: Don Fawcett

Web site: www.emeryworld.com

Freight transport, global logistics and air cargo.

Australia, Austria, Belgium, Canada, Chile, China (PRC), Denmark, England, U.K., Finland, France, Germany, Hong Kong, Hungary, Italy, Japan, Kuwait, Malaysia, Malta, Mexico, Netherlands, New Zealand, Philippines, Portugal, Singapore, South Africa, South Korea, Spain, Sri Lanka, Sweden, Switzerland, Thailand, Turkey

ENCYCLOPAEDIA BRITANNICA INC.

310 S. Michigan Ave.

Chicago, IL 60604

Tel: (312) 427-9700 Fax: (312) 294-2176

CEO: Don Yannias, Pres.

FO: Thomas Gies

HR: Karl Steinberg, SVP

Web site: www.E.B.com

Emp: 1,500 Rev: $586 mil.

Publishing; books.

Australia, Belgium, Brazil, Canada, England, U.K., France, Germany, Italy, Japan, Netherlands, Philippines, South Korea

ENDO LABORATORIES INC.

500 Endo Boulevard

Garden City, NY 11530

Tel: (516) 522-3300 Fax:

CEO: N. F. Reinert

FO: D. L. Rhoads

Emp: 1,030

Ethical pharmaceuticals.

Australia, Colombia, Mexico, Philippines

ENERPAC

13000 West Silver Spring Drive

Butler, WI 53007

Tel: (414) 781-6600 Fax: (414) 781-1049

CEO: Guus Boel, Chmn.

HR: Susan Gibbs

Emp: 900

Mfr./sale high pressure hydraulic maintenance tools.

England, U.K., France, India, Japan, Netherlands, Spain

ENGELHARD CORPORATION

101 Wood Ave. S., CN 770

Iselin, NJ 08830

Tel: (732) 205-5000 Fax: (732) 632-9253

CEO: Barry Terry, Pres.

HR: John Hess

Emp: 5,830

Mfr. pigments, additives, catalysts, chemicals, engineered materials.

Canada, China (PRC), England, U.K., France, Hong Kong, Italy, Japan, Mexico, Netherlands, Russia, Turkey

ENRON CORPORATION

1400 Smith Street

Houston, TX 77002-7361

Tel: (713) 853-6161 Fax: (713) 853-3129

CEO: Jeffrey Skilling, Pres.

FO: Rodney L. Gray, EVP Intl.

Web site: www.enron.com

Rev: $585 mil.

Exploration, production, transportation and distribution of integrated natural gas and electricity.

Argentina, Bolivia, Brazil, China (PRC), Colombia, England, U.K., India, Indonesia, Italy, Mozambique, Papua New Guinea, Philippines, Poland, Qatar, Russia, Singapore, South Africa, United Arab Emirates, Venezuela, Vietnam

ENSEARCH INTERNATIONAL DEVELOPMENT INC.

300 South St. Paul Street

Dallas, TX 75201

Tel: (214) 651-8700 Fax: (214) 670-2520

CEO: David Biegler, Pres.

FO: J. A. Boosey

HR: B. Dowling

Emp: 11,500

Diversified energy operations.

England, U.K., Switzerland

ENTERPRISES INTERNATIONAL INC.

PO Box 293

Hoquiam, WA 98550

Tel: (360) 533-6222 Fax: (360) 532-2792

CEO: Isabelle S. Lamb

FO: David E. Lamb

HR: Larry B. Lock

Emp: 708

Mfr./sale/services capital equipment for pulp, paper and newsprint industrial.

Canada, Netherlands, Switzerland

ENTHONE-OMI INTERNATIONAL

West Haven Industrial Park, PO Box 900

New Haven, CT 06516

Tel: (203) 934-8611 Fax: (203) 937-1680

CEO: Richard Fanelli, Pres.

Web site: www.enthone-omi.com

Emp: 125

Metal finishing chemicals and equipment.

India, Italy, Netherlands, Spain

A. EPSTEIN & SONS INTERNATIONAL

600 W. Fulton Street

Chicago, IL 60606-1199

Tel: (312) 454-9100 Fax: (312) 559-1217

CEO: Mickey Kupperman

HR: Michele DeClercq

Emp: 108

Engineering & construction.

England, U.K., France, Israel, Poland

EQUIFAX INC.

PO Box 4081

Atlanta, GA 30302

Tel: (404) 885-8000 Fax: (404) 888-5452

CEO: Tom F. Chapman

FO: Michael Shannon

HR: Russ Wise

Web site: www.equifax.com

Emp: 10,000

Information and knowledge-based solutions.

Argentina, Canada, Chile, England, U.K., France, Mexico, Netherlands, Spain

ERICO PRODUCTS INC.

34600 Solon Road

Cleveland, OH 44139

Tel: (440) 248-0100 Fax: (440) 248-0723

CEO: Jeff Church, Pres.

HR: D. Roebuck

Emp: 1,350

Mfr. electric welding apparatus & hardware, metal stampings, specialty fasteners.

Brazil, Canada, Chile, England, U.K., France, Germany, Italy, Mexico, Netherlands, Spain, Sweden

ERIE INTERNATIONAL LTD

4000 South 13th Street

Milwaukee, WI 53221

Tel: (414) 483-0524 Fax: (414) 483-6610

CEO: Joe Wilsted, Pres.

Emp: 200

Mfr. controls, valves.

Belgium, Canada

ERIEZ MAGNETICS

PO Box 10652

Erie, PA 16514

Tel: (814) 833-9881 Fax: (814) 833-3348

CEO: Chester F. Giermak, Pres.

FO: Tim Shuttleworth

HR: Raymond Cook

Emp: 480

Mfr. magnets, vibratory feeders, metal detectors, screeners/sizers, mining equipment, current separators.

Australia, Canada, Japan, Mexico, South Africa, Wales, U.K.

ERNST & YOUNG, LLP

787 Seventh Ave.

New York, NY 10019

Tel: (212) 773-3000 Fax: (212) 773-6350

CEO: Philip A. Laskawy, Chmn.

FO: Michael Henning, CEO Int'l.

HR: Thomas Hough

Web site: www.eyi.com

Emp: 79,500 Rev: $9,100.0 mil

Accounting and audit, tax and management consulting services.

Albania, Angola, Argentina, Aruba, Australia, Austria, Azerbaijan, Bahamas, Bahrain, Bangladesh, Barbados, Belgium, Bermuda, Bolivia, Botswana, Brazil, British Virgin Islands, Brunei, Bulgaria, Cambodia, Cameroon, Canada, Cayman Islands, Channel Islands, U.K., Chile, China (PRC), Colombia, Congo, Costa Rica, Cyprus, Czech Republic, Denmark, Djibouti, Dominican Republic, Ecuador, Egypt, El Salvador, England, U.K., Estonia, Fiji, Finland, France, Gabon, Germany, Ghana, Gibraltar, Greece, Guam, Guatemala, Guinea, Guyana, Honduras, Hong Kong, Hungary, Iceland, India, Indonesia, Ireland, Isle of Man, Israel, Italy, Ivory Coast, Jamaica, Japan, Jordan, Kazakhstan, Kenya, Kuwait, Latvia, Lebanon, Lesotho, Libya, Liechtenstein, Luxembourg, Malawi, Malaysia, Malta, Mauritius, Mexico, Morocco, Mozambique, Namibia, Netherlands, Netherlands Antilles, New Zealand, Nicaragua, Nigeria, Northern Ireland, U.K., Norway, Oman, Panama, Papua New Guinea, Paraguay, Peru, Philippines, Poland, Portugal, Qatar, Romania, Russia, Saudi Arabia, Scotland, U.K., Senegal, Singapore, Slovakia, Slovenia, South Africa, South Korea, Spain, Sri Lanka, Surinam, Swaziland, Sweden, Switzerland, Taiwan (ROC), Tanzania, Thailand, Trinidad & Tobago, Tunisia, Turkey, Uganda, Ukraine, United Arab Emirates, Uruguay, Venezuela, Vietnam, Wales, U.K., Yemen, Zambia, Zimbabwe

ESCO CORPORATION

2141 NW 25th Ave.

Portland, OR 97210

Tel: (503) 228-2141 Fax: (503) 778-6330

CEO: Steve Pratt, Pres.

FO: Mark Mallory, Mgr. Intl.

HR: Joe Smith

Emp: 1,550

Mfr. equipment for mining, construction and forestry industries.

Brazil, Canada, France, Singapore

ESCO ELECTRONICS CORP.

8888 Ladue Road, Ste. 200

St. Louis, MO 63124

Tel: (314) 213-7200 Fax: (314) 213-7250

CEO: Dennis J. Moore, Chmn.

Emp: 3,700 Rev: $500 mil.

Electronic subassemblies and components.

England, U.K., France, Germany, Ireland, Sweden

ESCO ENGINEERING INC.

25 North Street

Canton, MA 02021

Tel: (781) 828-7340 Fax: (781) 828-1714

CEO: Bassam E. Shalhoub, Pres.

Emp: 142

Water purification and sewage treatment.

Lebanon, Saudi Arabia

ESSEF CORPORATION

220 Park Drive

Chardon, OH 44024-1333

Tel: (440) 286-2200 Fax: (440) 286-2206

CEO: Thomas B. Waldin, Pres.

FO: Douglas J. Brittelle, EVP

HR: David Hillyer, Mgr.

Web site: www.essef.com

Emp: 2,100 Rev: $306 mil.

Mfr. non-metallic pressure vessels & related products.

Belgium, India, Italy, Spain, Taiwan (ROC)

ESSEX SPECIALTY PRODUCTS INC.

1250 Harmon Road

Auburn Hills, MI 48326

Tel: (248) 391-6300 Fax: (248) 391-6385

CEO: J. George Braendle

HR: Deborah M. French

Web site: www.dow.com

Emp: 500

Mfr. adhesives, sealants and structural reinforcement composites.

Switzerland

ESTEE LAUDER INTERNATIONAL INC.

767 Fifth Ave.

New York, NY 10153

Tel: (212) 572-4200 Fax: (212) 572-3941

CEO: Leonard Lauder, Chmn.

FO: Daniel Brestoe, Pres.

HR: Andrew Cavanaugh, SVP

Cosmetics, perfumes & Aveda hair care products.

Australia, Denmark, Japan, Poland, Russia, Sweden, Switzerland

ESTERLINE TECHNOLOGIES

10800 NE 8th Street, Ste. 600

Bellevue, WA 98004

Tel: (425) 453-9400 Fax: (425) 453-2916

CEO: Wendell P. Hurlbut, Chmn.

HR: Marcia Greenberg

Emp: 3,000

Mfr. equipment and instruments for industrial automation, precision measure, data acquisition.

England, U.K., France, Germany, Italy, Spain

ETEC SYSTEMS, INC.

26460 Corporate Ave.

Hayward, CA 94545

Tel: (510) 783-9210 Fax: (510) 887-2870

CEO: Stephen E. Cooper, Chmn.

FO: William D. Cole, VP

HR: Trisha A. Dohren, VP

Web site: www.etec.com

Emp: 902 Rev: $241 mil.

Mfr. of photolithography equipment used in semiconductor manufacturing.

France, Germany, Japan, South Korea, Taiwan (ROC)

ETHICON INC.

PO Box 151

Somerville, NJ 08876

Tel: (908) 218-0707 Fax: (908) 218-3373

CEO: F. G. Fitzpatrick

FO: W. A. Pence

Emp: 4,000

Surgical products.

Germany

ETHYL CORPORATION

330 South 4th Street, PO Box 2189

Richmond, VA 23219

Tel: (804) 788-5000 Fax: (804) 788-5688

CEO: Thomas E. Gottwald, Pres.

HR: Henry C. Page, Jr.

Emp: 1,500

Mfr. fuel & lubricant additives.

Belgium, Canada, England, U.K., Singapore

EURO RSCG Worldwide

350 Hudson Street

New York, NY 10014

Tel: (212) 886-2000 Fax: (212) 886-2016

CEO: Robert Schmetterer, Chmn.

Emp: 1,083 Rev: $952 mil.

International advertising agency group.

Argentina, Australia, Austria, Belgium, Brazil, Chile, Colombia, Czech Republic, Denmark, England, U.K., Finland, France, Germany, Greece, Hong Kong, Hungary, India, Indonesia, Israel, Italy, Japan, Malaysia, Mexico, Morocco, Netherlands, Norway, Paraguay, Peru, Philippines, Poland, Portugal, Singapore, South Korea, Spain, Sweden, Switzerland, Taiwan (ROC), Thailand, Uruguay, Venezuela

EVENFLO COMPANY, INC.

1000 Evenflo Drive

Canton, GA 30114

Tel: (770) 704-2000 Fax: (770) 704-2002

CEO: George Harris, Pres.

Mfr. of baby products.

Canada, Mexico, Philippines, Russia

EXCEL INDUSTRIES, INC.

1120 North Main Street

Elkhart, IN 46514

Tel: (219) 264-2131 Fax: (219) 264-2136

CEO: James O. Futterknecht, Jr., Chmn.

FO: Joseph A. Robinson, SVP

HR: Michael C. Paquette, V.P.

Web site: www.excelinc.com

Emp: 6,500 Rev: $962.3 mil.

Mfg. automotive, heavy truck, RV and bus components.

Brazil, Czech Republic, England, U.K., Germany, Mexico, Portugal, Spain

EXCELLON AUTOMATION

24751 Crenshaw Boulevard

Torrance, CA 90505

Tel: (310) 534-6300 Fax: (310) 534-6777

CEO: Richard Pinto, Pres.

FO: Richard Pinto

HR: C. Dzieminski

Emp: 450

PCB drilling and routing machines; optical inspection equipment.

England, U.K., Germany

EXCITE, INC.

555 Broadway

Redwood City, CA 94063

Tel: (650) 568-6000 Fax: (650) 568-6030

CEO: George Bell, Pres.

FO: Jed Simmons, Dir. Intl.

Web site: www.excite.com

Rev: $50 mil.

Online computer internet service provider.

England, U.K.

EXE TECHNOLOGIES, INC.

12740 Hillcrest Road

Dallas, TX 75230

Tel: (972) 233-3761 Fax: (972) 788-4208

CEO: Ray Hood, Pres.

HR: Pat Kyle

Web site: www.exe.com

Provides a complete line of supply chain management execution software for WMS.

Australia, England, U.K., Hong Kong, Indonesia, Japan, Malaysia, Philippines, Singapore, United Arab Emirates

EXIDE ELECTRONICS INTERNATIONAL CORPORATION

8521 Six Forks Road

Raleigh, NC 27615

Tel: (919) 870-3020 Fax: (919) 870-3100

CEO: Tom Gutierrez, Pres.

FO: Mark A. Ascolese, Group VP

HR: Irene Wong, VP

Web site: www.exide.com

Emp: 3000 Rev: $578 mil.

Mfr./services uninterruptible power systems.

Canada, Denmark, England, U.K., Finland, France, Germany, Norway, Poland, Sweden

EXOLON-ESK COMPANY

1000 East Niagara Street, PO Box 590

Tonawanda, NY 14151-0590

Tel: (716) 693-4550 Fax: (716) 693-0151

CEO: Robert Rieger, Pres.

HR: Ron E. Myers

Emp: 175

Mfr. fused aluminum oxide and silicon carbide abrasive grains.

Canada, Norway

EXPEDITORS INTERNATIONAL OF WASHINGTON INC.

999 Throd Ave., Ste. 2500

Seattle, WA 98104

Tel: (206) 674-3400 Fax: (206) 682-9777

CEO: Peter J. Rose, Chmn.

FO: Kevin M. Walsh, Pres.

HR: Michael Austin, VP

Web site: www.expd.com

Emp: 4,500 Rev: $954 mil.

Air/ocean freight forwarding, customs brokerage, international logistics solutions.

Australia, Austria, Bangladesh, Belgium, Canada, Chile, China (PRC), Cyprus, Ecuador, Egypt, England, U.K., Finland, Germany, Greece, Hong Kong, India, Indonesia, Italy, Japan, Kuwait, Lebanon, Malaysia, Mexico, Netherlands, New Zealand, Pakistan, Philippines, Portugal, Saudi Arabia, Scotland, U.K., Singapore, South Africa, South Korea, Spain, Sri Lanka, Sweden, Taiwan (ROC), Thailand, Turkey, United Arab Emirates

EXXON CORPORATION

225 E. John W. Carpenter Freeway

Irving, TX 75062-2298

Tel: (972) 444-1000 Fax: (972) 444-1882

CEO: Lee R. Raymond, Chmn.

FO: S. R. Gill, Pres. Int'l.

HR: T.J. Hearn, VP

Web site: www.exxon.com

Emp: 80,000 Rev: $120,279 mil.

Petroleum exploration, production, refining; mfr. petroleum & chemicals products; coal & minerals.

Angola, Argentina, Australia, Azerbaijan, Bahamas, Belgium, Bermuda, Bolivia, Brazil, Canada, Chad, Chile, China (PRC), Colombia, Congo, Egypt, El Salvador, England, U.K., France, French Antilles, Germany, Hong Kong, Hungary, Indonesia, Italy, Japan, Kazakhstan, Malaysia, Mexico, Netherlands, Nicaragua, Niger, Nigeria, Norway, Papua New Guinea, Peru, Russia, Saudi Arabia, Scotland, U.K., Singapore, Thailand, Trinidad & Tobago, Venezuela, Vietnam, Yemen

F

JOHN FABICK TRACTOR COMPANY

1 Fabick Drive

Fenton, MO 63026

Tel: (314) 343-5900 Fax: (314) 343-4910

CEO: Harry Fabick, Pres.

HR: James Lucas

Emp: 500

Wheel tractors, excavating and road building equipment.

Lebanon

FABREEKA INTERNATIONAL INC.

1023 Turnpike, PO Box 210

Stoughton, MA 02072

Tel: (781) 341-3655 Fax: (781) 341-3983

CEO: J. Patrick Norton

FO: Keith White

HR: Charles E. Bradley

Emp: 65

Mfr. vibration isolation materials; consulting & engineering services.

England, U.K.

FAEGRE & BENSON LLP

2200 Norwest Center, 90 South Seventh Street

Minneapolis, MN 55402-3901

Tel: (612) 336-3000 Fax: (612) 336-3026

CEO: Jim Stephenson, Mng. Prtn.

Web site: www.faegre.com

Emp: 658

International law firm.

England, U.K., Germany

FAHNESTOCK & COMPANY

125 Broad Street

New York, NY 10004

Tel: (212) 668-8000 Fax: (212) 344-9077

CEO: Albert Lowenthal, Pres.

Emp: 550

Security brokers and dealers.

Argentina, Venezuela

FAIRCHILD AEROSPACE CORP.

PO Box 790490

San Antonio, TX 78279-0490

Tel: (210) 824-9421 Fax: (210) 824-9476

CEO: Jim Robinson, Pres.

HR: Douglas Barnes

Emp: 1,200

Mfr. turboprop aircraft.

Germany, Poland

FAIRCHILD PUBLICATIONS INC.

7 West 34th Street

New York, NY 10001

Tel: (212) 630-4000 Fax: (212) 630-3563

CEO: Michael Cody, Pres.

Emp: 900

Publishers.

England, U.K., Japan

FAIRMONT TAMPER

415 North Main Street

Fairmont, MN 56031

Tel: (507) 235-3361 Fax: (507) 235-7370

CEO: G. Robert Newman, Pres.

HR: D. W. Bates

Emp: 950

Mfr./services railroad track maintenance-of-way equipment.

Australia, England, U.K.

THE FALK CORPORATION

3001 W. Canal Street, PO Box 492,

Milwaukee, WI 53208

Tel: (414) 238-4919 Fax: (414) 937-4359

CEO: Thomas L. Misiak, Pres.

FO: Donald L. Willis

HR: Candace Shabez

Web site: www.falkcorp.com

Emp: 1,500

Designers and manufacturers of power transmission equipment including gears, geared reducers & drives, couplings.

Brazil, Canada, Japan, Mexico

FANSTEEL INC.

1 Tantalum Place

North Chicago, IL 60064

Tel: (847) 689-4900 Fax: (847) 689-0307

CEO: William Jarosz, Pres.

HR: Michael Mocniak

Emp: 2,100

Mfr. refractory metals, cutting and mining tools and aerospace fabrications.

England, U.K., Japan

FARMLAND INDUSTRIES INC.

PO Box 7305

Kansas City, MO 64116

Tel: (816) 459-6000 Fax: (816) 459-6849

CEO: H. D. Cleberg

Food production & marketing.

Mexico, Switzerland

FARR COMPANY

2221 Park Place

El Segundo, CA 90245

Tel: (310) 536-6300 Fax: (310) 643-9086

CEO: Jack Meany, Chmn.

HR: Jan Peet

Emp: 575

Mfr. filtration equipment.

Canada, England, U.K.

FARREL CORPORATION

25 Main Street

Ansonia, CT 06401

Tel: (203) 736-5500 Fax: (203) 735-6267

CEO: Rolf K. Leibergesell, Pres. & Chmn.

HR: Elaine Fiordelisi

Emp: 600

Mfr. polymer processing equipment.

Australia, England, U.K., Germany

FATMAN INTERNATIONAL PRIVATE DETECTIVE AGENCY

6638 Cascade Road SE

Grand Rapids, MI 49546-6896

Tel: (616) 949-1790 Fax: (616) 949-4800

CEO: Theo R. Grevers, Pres.

FO: Theo R. Grevers

Web site: www.fatmanpi.com

Worldwide private investigators - private, civil, corporate and business.

Netherlands

FAXON CO., INC.

15 Southwest Park
Westwood, MA 02090
Tel: (781) 329-3350 Fax: (781) 329-9875
CEO: Dan Tonkery, Pres.
Emp: 1,000
Distributor books & periodicals.
Canada

FDX CORPORATION (FED EX)
2005 Corporate Ave., PO Box 727
Memphis, TN 38194
Tel: (901) 369-3600 Fax: (901) 395-2000
CEO: Frederick W. Smith, Chmn.
FO: Alan B. Graf, EVP
HR: Joseph C. McCarty, III, VP
Web site: www.fdxcorp.com
Emp: 126,000 Rev: $11,520 mil.
Package express delivery service.
Belgium, Brazil, England, U.K., France, Germany, Hong Kong, Japan, Netherlands, Russia, Singapore, Switzerland, Ukraine, Vietnam

FEDERAL-MOGUL CHAMPION SPARK PLUG COMPANY
900 Upton Ave.
Toledo, OH 43607
Tel: (419) 535-2567 Fax: (419) 535-2332
CEO: Joel M. Campbell, Pres.
FO: Sydney A. Allen
HR: John F. McAvoy
Emp: 8,000
Mfr. spark plugs, wiper blades and related products.
Australia, Belgium, Canada, England, U.K., Mexico, New Zealand, Venezuela

FEDERAL-MOGUL CORPORATION
26555 Northwestern Highway, PO Box 1966
Southfield, MI 48034
Tel: (248) 354-7700 Fax: (248) 354-8983
CEO: Richard A. Snell, Chmn.
FO: James B. Carano, VP
HR: Richard P. Randazzo, VP
Web site: www.federalmogul.com
Emp: 41,000 Rev: $5,000 mil.
Mfr./distributor precision parts for automobiles, trucks, farm and construction vehicles.
Argentina, Australia, Austria, Bahrain, Barbados, Belgium, Bolivia, Brazil, Canada, Cayman Islands, Chile, Costa Rica, Dominican Republic, Ecuador, England, U.K., France, Germany, Greece, Guatemala, Hong Kong, Italy, Japan, Malaysia, Mexico, Netherlands, New Zealand, Panama, Singapore, South Africa, Spain, Switzerland, Taiwan (ROC), Turkey, Uruguay, Venezuela

FERGUSON COMPANY
11820 Lockland Road
St. Louis, MO 63146-4281
Tel: (314) 567-3200 Fax: (314) 567-4701
CEO: Carl Olesky, Pres.
HR: Thomas J. Schreiber
Emp: 295
Mfr. indexing & transfer equipment, custom cams, parts handlers, rotary tables, link conveyors.
Belgium

FERREX INTERNATIONAL INC.
26 Broadway
New York, NY 10004
Tel: (212) 509-7030 Fax: (212) 344-4728
CEO: William J. Ferretti, Pres.
FO: H. Browne
Emp: 40
Mfr./distributor of road maintenance machinery, welding & industrial equipment & supplies.
England, U.K., Hong Kong, Monaco

FERRO CORPORATION
1000 Lakeside Ave.
Cleveland, OH 44114-1183
Tel: (216) 641-8580 Fax: (216) 696-5784
CEO: Hector R. Ortino, Pres.
FO: Joachim Roesser, Pres. Euro.
HR: Paul V. Richard, VP
Web site: www.ferro.com
Emp: 6,851 Rev: $1,381 mil.
Mfr. Specialty chemicals, coatings, plastics, colors, refractories.
Argentina, Australia, Belgium, Brazil, Canada, Denmark, Ecuador, Egypt, England, U.K., France, Germany, Greece, Guatemala, Hong Kong, Indonesia, Italy, Japan, Malaysia, Mexico, Myanmar, Netherlands, New Zealand, Nicaragua, Peru, Philippines, Portugal, Singapore, South Korea, Spain, Sweden, Taiwan (ROC), Thailand, Turkey, Venezuela

FERROFLUIDICS CORPORATION

40 Simon Street
Nashua, NH 03061
Tel: (603) 883-9800 Fax: (603) 883-2308
CEO: Paul Avery, Pres.
HR: Sue Brodie
Emp: 246

Mfr. rotary feedthrough designs, emission seals, automated crystal-growing systems, bearings, ferrofluids.

England, U.K., Germany, Japan

FIBRE METAL PRODUCTS INC.

PO Box 248
Concordville, PA 19331
Tel: (610) 459-5300 Fax: (610) 358-9138
CEO: Kenneth H. Huntoon, Pres.
FO: Ingemar H. Olsson
Emp: 275

Welding accessories and industrial safety equipment.

Mexico

FIDELITY INVESTMENTS

82 Devonshire Street
Boston, MA 02109
Tel: (617) 563-7000 Fax: (617) 476-6105
CEO: Edward C. Johnson, III, Chmn.
FO: James C. Curvey, Vice Chrm.
HR: Anthony J. Rucci, EVP
Web site: www.fidelity.com
Emp: 23,300 Rev: $5,080.4 mil.

Diversified financial services company offering investment management, retirement, brokerage, and shareholder services directly to individuals and institutions and through financial intermediaries.

Bermuda, Canada, Channel Islands, U.K., England, U.K., France, Germany, Hong Kong, Japan, Luxembourg, Netherlands, Sweden, Taiwan (ROC)

FIDUCIARY TRUST COMPANY OF NY

2 World Trade Center, 94th Fl.
New York, NY 10048
Tel: (212) 466-4100 Fax: (212) 313-2662
CEO: Anne Tatlock, Pres.
Emp: 380

Banking services.

Australia, England, U.K., Hong Kong, Japan, Switzerland

FileNET CORPORATION

3565 Harbor Boulevard
Costa Mesa, CA 92626
Tel: (714) 966-3400 Fax: (714) 966-3490
CEO: Lee D. Roberts, Pres.
FO: Lewis H. Carpenter, Jr., SVP
HR: Audrey N. Schaeffer, VP
Web site: www.filenet.com
Emp: 1,581 Rev: $251 mil.

Provides integrated document management (IDM) software and services for internet and client server-based imaging, workflow, cold and electronic document imanagement solutions.

Australia, Canada, England, U.K., France, Germany, Hong Kong, Ireland, Italy, Japan, Netherlands, Singapore, South Korea, Spain

FILON DIVISION

12333 S. Van Ness Ave.
Hawthorne, CA 90250
Tel: (213) 757-5141 Fax: (213) 241-5667
CEO: Mike McNerney
FO: Paul Hatton
HR: Mort Arnush
Emp: 700

Mfr. fiberglass reinforced plastic commercial/industrial panels.

Switzerland

FILTRA SYSTEMS/HYDROMATION

4000 Town Center, Ste. 1000
Southfield, MI 48075-1410
Tel: (248) 356-9090 Fax: (248) 356-2812
CEO: Jack R. Bratten, Pres.

Industrial filter systems.

Australia, Belgium, England, U.K., Japan

FINANCIAL GUARANTY INSURANCE COMPANY

115 Broadway
New York, NY 10006
Tel: (212) 312-3000 Fax: (212) 312-3093
CEO: Ann C. Stern, Pres.
FO: Patrick O'Sullivan

HR: Sunita Holzer

Emp: 179

Financial guaranty insurance.

England, U.K., France, Japan

FINNIGAN CORPORATION

355 River Oaks Parkway

San Jose, CA 95134-1991

Tel: (408) 433-4800 Fax: (408) 433-4823

CEO: Richard W. K. Chapman, Pres.

HR: Sherri Shood

Emp: 525

Mfr. mass spectrometers.

China (PRC), England, U.K., France, Germany, Italy, Japan, Netherlands, Sweden

FIREMENS INSURANCE COMPANY OF NEWARK

180 Maiden Lane

New York, NY 10038

Tel: (212) 440-3000 Fax: (212) 440-7130

CEO: Phil Engal, Pres.

Emp: 13,000

Fire, marine and casualty insurance.

Argentina, Brazil

FIRST AMERICAN FINANCIAL CORPORATION

114 East 5th Street

Santa Ana, CA 92701

Tel: (714) 558-3211 Fax: (714) 550-0762

CEO: Parker S. Kennedy, Pres.

FO: Donald Kennedy, Chrm.

Emp: 8,000

Title insurance.

England, U.K.

FIRST BRANDS CORPORATION

83 Wooster Heights Road, Bldg. 301

Danbury, CT 06813-1911

Tel: (203) 731-2300 Fax: (203) 731-2389

CEO: William V. Stephenson, Chmn.

FO: James S. Gracie, Int'l.

HR: Ronald F. Dainton, VP

Web site: www.firstbrands.com

Emp: 4,800 Rev: $1,204 mil.

Mfr. plastic wrap and bags, pet products, and re-usable cleaning cloth and pre-moistened toweling.

England, U.K., Hong Kong, Philippines

FIRST CHICAGO NBD CORPORATION

One First National Plaza

Chicago, IL 60670

Tel: (312) 732-4000 Fax: (312) 732-4000

CEO: Verne G. Istock

HR: Timothy P. Moen

Web site: www.fcnbd.com

Emp: 37,500

Financial products and services.

Argentina, Australia, Canada, China (PRC), England, U.K., Germany, Hong Kong, Japan, Mexico, Singapore, South Korea, Taiwan (ROC)

FIRST DATA CORPORATION

401 Hackensack Ave.

Hackensack, NJ 07601

Tel: (201) 525-4700 Fax: (201) 342-0401

CEO: Henry C. Duques, Chmn.

FO: Charles T. Fote, Pres. & COO

HR: Bob Bender, SVP

Web site: www.firstdatacorp.com

Emp: 36,000 Rev: $5,234 mil.

Information and transaction processing services.

Australia, England, U.K.

FIRST NATIONAL BANK OF CHICAGO

One First National Plaza

Chicago, IL 60670

Tel: (312) 732-4000 Fax: (312) 732-3620

CEO: Verne Istock, Pres.

FO: Alan Delp

HR: James Alex

Emp: 15,900

Financial services.

Australia, Canada, Channel Islands, U.K., England, U.K., Hong Kong, Japan, Mexico, Philippines, Singapore, South Korea, Spain, Switzerland

FIRST SPICE MIXING COMPANY

33-33 Greenpoint Ave.

Long Island City, NY 11101

Tel: (718) 361-2556 Fax: (718) 361-2515

CEO: Peter Epstein, Pres.

FO: Vicki Epstein

Emp: 75

Mfr. spices & seasonings.

Canada

FIRST UNION CORPORATION

One First Union Center

Charlotte, NC 28288-0013

Tel: (704) 374-6565 Fax: (704) 374-3425

CEO: Edward E. Crutchfield, Chmn.

FO: John R. Georgius, Pres.

HR: Don R. Johnson, EVP

Web site: www.firstunion.com

Emp: 47,096 Rev: $14,329 mil.

Banking, financial and insurance services.

Bahamas, Cayman Islands, England, U.K., Hong Kong, India, South Africa

FISCHBACH & MOORE INTERNATIONAL CORPORATION

675 Central Ave.

New Providence, NJ 07974

Tel: (908) 508-2600 Fax: (908) 508-2686

CEO: James Kimsey, Pres.

Emp: 5,000

General, mechanical and electrical construction.

Taiwan (ROC), Thailand

FISCHER IMAGING CORPORATION

12300 North Grant Street

Denver, CO 80241

Tel: (303) 452-6800 Fax: (303) 452-4335

CEO: Morgan W. Nields, Chmn.

FO: Mke Tesic, VP

HR: Gayle Landus, Dir.

Web site: www.fischerimaging.com

Emp: 416 Rev: $57 mil.

Mfr. x-ray equipment.

Australia, China (PRC), Denmark

FISERV INC.

PO Box 979, 255 Fiserv Drive

Brookfield, WI 53008-0979

Tel: (414) 879-5000 Fax: (414) 879-5013

CEO: George D. Dalton, Chmn.

FO: Leslie M. Muma, Pres.

HR: Jack P. Bucalo, SVP

Web site: www.fiserv.com

Emp: 10,090 Rev: $974 mil.

Data processing products and services for the financial industry.

Australia, Canada, England, U.K., Singapore, Thailand

FISHER SCIENTIFIC INC.

Liberty Lane

Hampton, NH 03842

Tel: (603) 929-5911 Fax: (603) 929-0222

CEO: Paul M. Montrone, Chmn.

FO: Denis N. Maiorani, Pres.

HR: Tom Rea, VP

Web site: www.fisher1.com

Emp: 6,800 Rev: $2,175 mil.

Mfr. science instruments & apparatus, chemicals, reagents.

Belgium, Brazil, Canada, Egypt, England, U.K., France, Germany, Japan, Malaysia, Mexico, Netherlands, Singapore, South Korea, Switzerland

FISHER-ROSEMOUNT

8000 Maryland Ave., Ste. 500

Clayton, MO 63105-4755

Tel: (314) 746-9900 Fax: (314) 746-9974

CEO: Larry Solley, Chmn.

HR: Susan Keck

Emp: 8,000

Mfr. industrial process control equipment.

Australia, Austria, Azerbaijan, Bangladesh, Belgium, Brazil, Brunei, Bulgaria, Canada, China (PRC), Czech Republic, Denmark, England, U.K., Finland, France, Germany, Greece, Hong Kong, Hungary, India, Indonesia, Ireland, Italy, Japan, Malaysia, Mexico, Netherlands, New Zealand, Norway, Pakistan, Philippines, Poland, Portugal, Russia, Saudi Arabia, Scotland, U.K., Singapore, Slovakia, South Africa, South Korea, Spain, Sri Lanka, Sweden, Switzerland, Thailand, United Arab Emirates

FLACK + KURTZ CONSULTING ENGINEERS, LLP

475 Fifth Ave.

New York, NY 10017

Tel: (212) 532-9600 Fax: (212) 689-7489

CEO: Norman Kurtz

FO: David Stillman

Web site: www.fk.com

Emp: 265

Consulting engineers for building services, ie., HVAC, electrical, lighting, plumbing/hydraulics, life safety, fire protection and telecommunications.

England, U.K., Hong Kong

FLAREGAS CORPORATION

100 Airport Executive Park, Ste. 103

Nanuet, NY 10954

Tel: (914) 352-8700 Fax: (914) 352-4464

CEO: Nicholas Sanderson, VP

Flare systems.

England, U.K.

C.B. FLEET CO., INC.

4615 Murray Place, PO Box 11349

Lynchburg, VA 24506

Tel: (804) 528-4000 Fax: (804) 847-4219

CEO: Doug Bellaire, Pres.

HR: Wayne Johnson

Web site: www.dewitt.com

Emp: 400

Mfr. pharmaceutical, health and beauty aids.

Australia, England, U.K., France, Singapore

FLEET NATIONAL BANK

50 Kennedy Plaza

Providence, RI 02903

Tel: (401) 278-5800 Fax: (401) 278-5801

CEO: Terrence Murray, Chmn.

HR: Anne Szostak

Emp: 21,500

Banking, financial services.

England, U.K.

FLEETWOOD ENTERPRISES, INC.

3125 Myers Street, PO Box 7638

Riverside, CA 92513-7638

Tel: (909) 351-3500 Fax: (909) 351-3724

CEO: Glenn F. Kummer, Pres. & COO

FO: Nelson W. Potter, EVP

Web site: www.Fleetwood.com

Emp: 18,000 Rev: $3,000 mil.

Manufacture homes and recreational vehicles.

Canada

FLEXTRONICS INC. INTERNATIONAL

2241 Lundy Ave.

San Jose, CA 95131-1822

Tel: (408) 428-1300 Fax: (408) 428-0420

CEO: William Mc Namara, Pres.

HR: Audrey Wheeler-Denning

Emp: 2,200

Contract manufacturer for electronics industry.

China (PRC), Hong Kong, Singapore

FLINT INK CORPORATION

25111 Glendale Ave.

Detroit, MI 48239-2689

Tel: (313) 538-6800 Fax: (313) 538-3538

CEO: Leonard D. Frescoln, Pres.

HR: Brett Green

Web site: www.flintink.com

Emp: 3,600

Manufacturer of printing inks and pigments.

Australia, Canada, Colombia, England, U.K., Ireland, Italy, Mexico, Netherlands, New Zealand, Spain, Sweden, Zimbabwe

FLIR SYSTEMS, INC.

16505 SW 72nd Ave.

Portland, OR 97224-1206

Tel: (503) 684-3731 Fax: (503) 684-5452

CEO: Robert P. Daltry, Chmn.

FO: J. Kenneth Stringer, Pres.

HR: Marti Bunyard, Dir.

Web site: www.flir.com

Emp: 652 Rev: $92 mil.

Designer, Mfr., & marketer of imaging systems for aircraft, shipping, defense and environmental protection indusrties.

England, U.K., Sweden

FLOW INTERNATIONAL CORPORATION

23500 64th Ave. S., PO Box 97040

Kent, WA 98064-9740

Tel: (253) 872-4900 Fax: (253) 813-3285

CEO: Ronald W. Tarrant, Pres.

HR: Beth Kanbel

Mfr. high-pressure waterjet cutting/cleaning equipment, powered scaffolding; concrete cleaning/removal.

Germany, Taiwan (ROC)

FLOWSERVE CORPORATION

222 W. Los Cloinas Blvd.

Irving, TX 75039

Tel: (972) 443-6500 Fax: (972) 443-6858

CEO: William M. Jordan, Pres.

FO: Curtis E. Daly

Web site: www.flowserve.com

Emp: 2,500

Mfr. chemicals equipment, pumps, valves, filters, fans and heat exchangers.

Australia, Belgium, Brazil, Canada, England, U.K., France, Germany, Ireland, Italy, Netherlands, Singapore, Venezuela

FLOWSERVE FLUID SEALING DIVISION

222 Los Colinas Blvd., Ste. 1500

Irving, TX 75039

Tel: (616) 381-2650 Fax: (616) 443-6800

CEO: George Shedlarski, Pres.

FO: Thomas E. Haan, VP

HR: Julie Trey, Dir. HR

Web site: www.flowserve.com

Emp: 2,100 Rev: $110 mil.

Mfr. mechanical seals, compression packings and auxiliaries.

Australia, Bahrain, Belgium, Brazil, Canada, England, U.K., Germany, India, Mexico, Netherlands, New Zealand, Singapore, South Korea

FLUKE CORPORATION

PO Box 9090

Everett, WA 98206-9090

Tel: (425) 347-6100 Fax: (425) 356-5116

CEO: William Parzybok

FO: Ronald Wambolt

HR: Patrick O'Hara

Web site: www.fluke.com

Emp: 2,400 Rev: $413 mil.

Mfr. electronic test tools.

Australia, Canada, China (PRC), Denmark, England, U.K., Finland, France, Germany, Italy, Japan, Malaysia, Netherlands, Norway, Singapore, South Korea, Spain, Sweden, Switzerland

FLUOR DANIEL INC.

3353 Michelson Drive

Irvine, CA 92698

Tel: (714) 975-2000 Fax: (714) 975-5271

CEO: James Stein, Pres. & COO

FO: Charles J. Bradley, Jr.

HR: Charles J. Bradley, Jr.

Web site: www.flourdaniel.com

Emp: 60,679 Rev: $14,200 mil.

Engineering & construction services.

Argentina, Australia, Canada, Chile, China (PRC), England, U.K., Germany, Hong Kong, Indonesia, Japan, Kuwait, Malaysia, Mexico, Netherlands, Philippines, Poland, Saudi Arabia, Singapore, South Africa, South Korea, Spain, Thailand, Venezuela

FMC - JETWAY SYSTEMS

1805 W. 2550 South, PO Box 9368

Ogden, UT 84401-3249

Tel: (801) 627-6600 Fax: (801) 629-3474

CEO: David L. Harmer

FO: Timothy J. Roberts

HR: Arthur Belinger

Emp: 600

Mfr. aircraft loading bridges and ground support equipment.

England, U.K., Hong Kong

FMC CORPORATION

200 E. Randolph Drive

Chicago, IL 60601

Tel: (312) 861-6000 Fax: (312) 861-6141

CEO: Robert N. Burt, Chmn.

FO: William F. Black, EVP

HR: Michael W. Murray

Emp: 21,344 Rev: $4,000 mil.

Produces chemicals & precious metals, mfr. machinery, equipment & systems for industrial, agricultural & government use.

Argentina, Australia, Austria, Belgium, Brazil, Canada, Chile, China (PRC), Denmark, Egypt, England, U.K., France, Gabon, Germany, Greece, Guatemala, Hong Kong, Indonesia, Ireland, Italy, Ivory Coast, Japan, Kenya, Malaysia, Mexico, Netherlands, Norway, Pakistan, Philippines, Poland, Russia, Saudi Arabia, Singapore, South Korea, Spain, Switzerland, Thailand, Turkey, Ukraine, United Arab Emirates, Uruguay, Venezuela

FMC CORPORATION MATERIAL HANDLING EQUIPMENT

57 Cooper Ave.

Homer City, PA 15748-1306

Tel: (724) 479-4500 Fax: (724) 479-3400

CEO: Steve Smith, VP

FO: Bill Walker

HR: Richard Schellinger

Emp: 460

Mfr. bulk material handling and automation equipment.

England, U.K., Hong Kong, Mexico

FOAMEX INTERNATIONAL

1000 Columbia Ave.

Linwood, PA 19061

Tel: (800) 776-3626 Fax: (610) 859-3085

CEO: Rolf Christensen, COO

Emp: 7,700

Mfr. polyurethane foam.

Brazil, Mexico

FOOT LOCKER USA

233 Broadway

New York, NY 10279

Tel: (212) 720-3700 Fax: (212) 553-2042

CEO: Jay Friedman, Pres.

Mfr./sales shoes and sneakers.

Australia, England, U.K., France, Germany, Italy, Japan, Luxembourg, Netherlands, Spain

FORD MOTOR COMPANY

The American Road

Dearborn, MI 48121

Tel: (313) 322-3000 Fax: (313) 322-9600

CEO: William Clay Ford, Jr., Chmn.

FO: Jacques A. Nasser, Pres.

Web site: www.ford.com

Emp: 332,700 Rev: $129,000 mil.

Mfr./sales motor vehicles.

Argentina, Australia, Austria, Belgium, Brazil, Canada, Denmark, England, U.K., Finland, France, Germany, Ireland, Italy, Japan, Malaysia, Mexico, Netherlands, New Zealand, Norway, Poland, Russia, Spain, Sweden, Switzerland, Taiwan (ROC), Venezuela, Vietnam

FOREST LABORATORIES INC.

909 Third Ave., 23rd Floor

New York, NY 10022

Tel: (212) 421-7850 Fax: (212) 750-9152

CEO: Howard Solomon, Pres.

Emp: 350

Pharmaceuticals.

England, U.K.

FOREST OIL CORPORATION

1600 Broadway, Ste. 2200

Denver, CO 80202

Tel: (303) 812-1400 Fax: (303) 812-1602

CEO: Robert Boswell, Pres.

HR: Kathryn Davis

Emp: 182

Crude oil and natural gas.

Canada, Turkey

FORMICA CORPORATION

10155 Reading Road

Cincinnati, OH 45241-4805

Tel: (513) 786-3400 Fax: (513) 786-3082

CEO: A.F. Young, Pres.

HR: Peter Olmsted, VP

Emp: 4,500

Mfr. decorative laminate, adhesives and solvents.

Netherlands

FORRESTER RESEARCH, INC.

1033 Massachusetts Ave.

Cambridge, MA 02138

Tel: (617) 497-7090 Fax: (617) 868-0577

CEO: George F. Colony, Chmn.

FO: Richard C. Belanger

Web site: www.forrester.com

Emp: 240 Rev: $40 mil.

Provides clients an analysis of the effect of changing technologies on their operations.

Australia, Brazil, France, Italy, Netherlands, South Africa, Spain

FORT JAMES CORPORATION

1650 Lake Cook Road

Deerfield, IL 60015

Tel: (847) 317-5000 Fax: (847) 236-3755

CEO: Michael T. Riordan, Pres.

FO: John Rowley, EVP

HR: Daniel J. Girvan, SVP

Web site: www.fortjames.com

Emp: 29,000 Rev: $7,259 mil.

Mfr./sales of consumer paper and packaging

products.

Belgium, Canada, China (PRC), Denmark, England, U.K., Estonia, Finland, France, Greece, Ireland, Italy, Russia, Spain, Turkey, Wales, U.K.

FORTÉ SOFTWARE, INC.

1800 Harrison Street

Oakland, CA 94612

Tel: (510) 869-3400 Fax: (510) 869-3480

CEO: Martin J. Sprinzen, Chmn.

FO: Michael Hedger, EVP

HR: Jackie Revas, Admin.

Web site: www.forte.com

Emp: 445 Rev: $71 mil.

Developer computer software applications.

Australia, Belgium, England, U.K., France, Germany, Netherlands, Switzerland

FORTUNE BRANDS

1700 East Putnam Ave.

Old Greenwich, CT 06870

Tel: (203) 698-5000 Fax: (203) 637-2580

CEO: John Ludes, Pres.

HR: Robert Garber, SVR, HR

Mfr. diversified consumer products including Masterbrand, Acco office products, Jim Bean distillery products, Footjoy and Titleist golf products.

Australia, England, U.K.

L.B. FOSTER COMPANY

415 Holiday Drive

Pittsburgh, PA 15220

Tel: (412) 928-3400 Fax: (412) 928-7891

CEO: Lee B. Foster, II, Pres.

FO: Stan L. Hasselbusch

HR: Linda M. Terpenning

Emp: 600 Rev: $220 mil

Mfr./sales of steel pipe, railroad rail, highway products and accessories.

England, U.K.

FOSTER WHEELER CORPORATION

Perryville Corporate Park

Clinton, NJ 08809-4000

Tel: (908) 730-4000 Fax: (908) 730-5300

CEO: Richard Swift, Pres.

FO: N. William Atwater, EVP

HR: James E. Schessler

Emp: 8,500

Manufacturing, engineering and construction.

Australia, Bermuda, Canada, England, U.K., France, Italy, Poland, Saudi Arabia, Spain, Turkey, Venezuela

FOUR WINDS INTERNATIONAL GROUP

1500 SW First Ave., Ste. 850

Portland, OR 97201-2013

Tel: (503) 241-2732 Fax: (503) 241-1829

CEO: Jerome Rose, Pres.

FO: Stephen C. Standring

Web site: www.vanlines.com.au

Emp: 1,512

Transportation of household goods and general cargo and third party logistics.

Australia, Bahrain, Canada, Egypt, England, U.K., Germany, Hong Kong, Japan, Malaysia, New Zealand, Philippines, Saudi Arabia, Singapore, South Korea, Sweden, Taiwan (ROC), Thailand, Zambia

FOWNES BROTHERS & CO., INC.

411 Fifth Ave.

New York, NY 10016

Tel: (212) 683-0150 Fax: (212) 683-2832

CEO: Thomas Gluckman, Pres.

HR: Arnold Jaffe

Emp: 2,000

Dress and sport gloves.

Philippines

FRANK RUSSELL COMPANY

909 A Street

Tacoma, WA 98402

Tel: (253) 572-9500 Fax: (253) 591-3495

CEO: Michael J. Phillips

FO: Len Brennan

HR: Ben Scott

Web site: www.russell.com

Emp: 1,400 Rev: $225 mil.

Investment management & asset strategy consulting.

Australia, Canada, England, U.K., France, Japan, Netherlands, New Zealand, Switzerland

FRANKEL & COMPANY

2 World Trade Center

New York, NY 10048-0002

Tel: (212) 488-0200 Fax: (212) 488-1800

CEO: Theodore J. Anderson, Jr.

HR: Elizabeth A. Hoefler

Emp: 200

Insurance brokers.

Brazil

FRANKLIN COVEY CO.

2200 W. Parkway Blvd.

Salt Lake City, UT 84119-2331

Tel: (801) 975-1776 Fax: (801) 977-1431

CEO: Hyrum W. Smith, CEO

FO: Jon H. Rowberry, Pres.

HR: Daken Tanner, Mgr.

Web site: www.franklinquest.com

Emp: 4,700 Rev: $430 mil.

Provides productivity and time management products and seminars.

Argentina, Australia, Bermuda, Canada, Colombia, England, U.K., Hong Kong, Indonesia, Ireland, Japan, Malaysia, Mexico, New Zealand, Nigeria, Philippines, Singapore, South Africa, South Korea, Thailand, Trinidad & Tobago, Venezuela

FRANKLIN ELECTRIC CO., INC.

400 East Spring Street

Bluffton, IN 46714-3798

Tel: (219) 824-2900 Fax: (219) 824-2909

CEO: William H. Lawson, Chmn.

FO: John B. Lindsay, Pres.

HR: Gary Ward, Dir.

Web site: www.fele.com

Emp: 2,300 Rev: $303.3 mil.

Mfr./distribute electric motors, submersible motors and controls.

Australia, Canada, Germany, Mexico, South Africa

THE FRANKLIN MINT

US Route 1

Franklin Center, PA 19091

Tel: (610) 459-6000 Fax: (610) 459-6880

CEO: Adam Burger, Pres.

FO: Donna Fisher

HR: John Candiello, VP

Emp: 4,500

Design/marketing collectibles & luxury items.

Australia, Austria, Belgium, Canada, England, U.K., France, Germany, Hong Kong, Japan, Malaysia, Netherlands, New Zealand, Spain, Sweden, Switzerland, Taiwan (ROC), Thailand

FRANKLIN RESOURCES, INC.

777 Mariners Island Blvd.

San Mateo, CA 94404

Tel: (415) 312-2000 Fax: (415) 312-3655

CEO: Charles B. Johnson, Pres.

FO: Rupert H. Johnson, Jr.

HR: Donna Ikeda, VP

Web site: www.frk.com

Emp: 6,400 Rev: $2,000 mil.

Global and domestic investment advisory and portfolio management.

Argentina, Australia, Austria, Bahamas, Brazil, Canada, England, U.K., France, Germany, Hong Kong, India, Italy, Japan, Luxembourg, Netherlands, Poland, Russia, Scotland, U.K., Singapore, South Africa, South Korea, Taiwan (ROC), United Arab Emirates, Vietnam

FREEPORT-McMoRAN COPPER & GOLD INC.

1615 Poydras Street

New Orleans, LA 70112

Tel: (504) 582-4000 Fax: (504) 582-4899

CEO: James R. Moffett, Chmn.

FO: W. Russell King, SVP Intl.

HR: Robert M. Gettys

Web site: www.fcx.com

Emp: 8,800

Natural resources exploration and processing.

Australia, Indonesia, Spain, Tunisia

FRIED, FRANK, HARRIS, SHRIVER & JACOBSON

One New York Plaza

New York, NY 10004-1980

Tel: (212) 859-8000 Fax: (212) 859-4000

CEO: Harvey Pitt & Peter Cobb, Co-Chairs

FO: Dennis Bunder

HR: Gayle George, Dir.

Web site: www.ffhsj.com

Emp: 1,035 Rev: $200 mil.

International law firm.

England, U.K., France

FRIES & FRIES INC.

110 East 70th Street

Cincinnati, OH 45216

Tel: (513) 948-8000 Fax:

CEO: Mike Davis, Pres.

Flavoring compounds for food and pharmaceutical industries.

England, U.K., Mexico

FRITZ COMPANIES INC.

706 Mission Street, Ste. 900

San Francisco, CA 94103

Tel: (415) 904-8360 Fax: (415) 904-8661

CEO: Lynn C. Fritz, Chmn.

FO: Dennis L. Pelino, Pres.

HR: Steve Enna, Dir. HR

Web site: www.fritz.com

Emp: 10,000 Rev: $1,300 mil.

Integrated transportation, sourcing, distribution & customs brokerage services.

Antigua, Argentina, Aruba, Australia, Austria, Azerbaijan, Bahamas, Bahrain, Bangladesh, Belgium, Belize, Bermuda, Bolivia, Botswana, Brazil, Cambodia, Cameroon, Canada, Central African Republic, Chad, Chile, China (PRC), Colombia, Congo, Costa Rica, Cyprus, Czech Republic, Denmark, Dominican Republic, Ecuador, Egypt, El Salvador, England, U.K., Fiji, Finland, France, Gabon, Germany, Greece, Grenada, Guam, Guatemala, Haiti, Honduras, Hong Kong, Hungary, India, Indonesia, Ireland, Israel, Italy, Ivory Coast, Jamaica, Japan, Jordan, Kazakhstan, Kenya, Kuwait, Latvia, Lebanon, Malawi, Malaysia, Malta, Mauritius, Mexico, Nepal, Netherlands, Netherlands Antilles, New Zealand, Nicaragua, Northern Ireland, U.K., Northern Mariana Islands, Norway, Oman, Pakistan, Panama, Paraguay, Peru, Philippines, Poland, Portugal, Qatar, Russia, Saudi Arabia, Scotland, U.K., Senegal, Singapore, Slovenia, South Africa, South Korea, Spain, Sri Lanka, Sweden, Switzerland, Syria, Taiwan (ROC), Tanzania, Thailand, Trinidad & Tobago, Turkey, Uganda, Ukraine, United Arab Emirates, Uruguay, Venezuela, Vietnam, Yemen, Zimbabwe

FSI INTERNATIONAL INC.

322 Lake Hazeltine Drive

Chaska, MN 55318

Tel: (612) 448-5440 Fax: (612) 448-2825

CEO: Joel A.Elftmann, Pres.

FO: J. Wayne Stewart, EVP

HR: Mark A. Ahmann, VP

Web site: www.fsi-intl.com

Emp: 1,360 Rev: $252 mil.

Manufacturing equipment for computer silicon wafers.

England, U.K., Germany, Italy, Japan, Scotland, U.K., South Korea

FUISZ TECHNOLOGIES LTD.

14555 Avion at Lakeside

Chantilly, VA 20151

Tel: (703) 995-2400 Fax: (703) 803-6460

CEO: Kenneth W. McVey, Pres.

FO: Paul Kennedy, Pres.

Web site: www.fuisz.com

Rev: $8.5 mil.

R&D/mfr. commercial pharmaceuticals.

France, Germany, Ireland, Italy

FULBRIGHT & JAWORSKI

1301 mCkINNEY Street, Ste. 5100

Houston, TX 77010

Tel: (713) 651-5151 Fax: (713) 651-5246

CEO: A.T. Blackshear Jr., Chmn.

HR: Jane Williams, Dir.

Web site: www.fulbright.com

Emp: 1,554 Rev: $265 mil.

International law firm.

England, U.K., Hong Kong

H.B. FULLER COMPANY

1200 Willow Lake Blvd.

Vadnais Heights, MN 55110

Tel: (612) 236-5900 Fax: (612) 236-5898

CEO: Walter Kissling, Pres.

FO: Jerald L. Scott, SVP

HR: James A. Metts, VP

Web site: www.hbfuller.com

Emp: 6,000 Rev: $1,307 mil.

Mfr./distributor adhesives, sealants, coatings, paints, waxes, sanitation chemicals.

Argentina, Australia, Austria, Belgium, Bolivia, Brazil, Canada, Chile, China (PRC), Colombia, Costa Rica, Dominican Republic, Ecuador, El Salvador, England, U.K., France, Germany, Guatemala, Honduras, Hong Kong, Indonesia, Italy, Japan, Malaysia, Mexico, Netherlands, New Zealand, Nicaragua, Panama, Peru, Philippines,

Poland, Scotland, U.K., Singapore, South Korea, Spain, Sweden, Switzerland, Taiwan (ROC), Thailand, United Arab Emirates, Uruguay, Venezuela

FULTON BOILER WORKS INC.

3981 Jefferson Street, PO Box 257
Pulaski, NY 13142
Tel: (315) 298-5121 Fax: (315) 298-6390
CEO: R. Bramley Palm
FO: Dennis Dauphin
Web site: www.fulton.Com
Emp: 350
Mfr. steam and hot water boilers.
England, U.K.

FURON COMPANY

29982 Ivy Glenn Drive
Laguna Niguel, CA 92677
Tel: (714) 831-5350 Fax: (714) 643-1548
CEO: Mike Hagan, Chmn.
HR: Kevin Krogmeier
Mfr. of industrial components.
Belgium, England, U.K., Netherlands

G

GAB BUSINESS SERVICES INC.

Linden Plaza, 9 Campus Drive
Parsippany, NJ 07054-4476
Tel: (973) 993-3400 Fax: (973) 993-9579
CEO: David McGirr
HR: Guy Pedelini
Emp: 8,500
Insurance adjustment.
Belgium, England, U.K.

GAF CORPORATION

1361 Alps Road
Wayne, NJ 07470
Tel: (973) 628-3000 Fax: (973) 628-3326
CEO: Samuel J. Heyman, Chmn.
FO: Sunil Kumar, Pres.
HR: John Sinnott, VP
Web site: www.gaf.com
Emp: 2,500 Rev: $900 mil.
Mfr. building materials.
Australia, Austria, Belgium, Brazil, Canada, England, U.K., France, Germany, Italy, Japan, Mexico, Netherlands, New Zealand, Singapore, South Africa, Spain, Sweden, Switzerland

GAFFNEY CLINE & ASSOCIATES INC.

PO Box 796309
Dallas, TX 75379
Tel: (972) 733-1183 Fax: (972) 380-0180
CEO: William Cline, Pres.
Consultants to energy and mineral industrial.
Australia, England, U.K., Singapore

LEWIS GALOOB TOYS INC.

500 Forbes Blvd.
S. San Francisco, CA 94080
Tel: (650) 952-1678 Fax: (650) 583-4996
CEO: Mark D. Goldman, Pres.
FO: Ronald D. Hirschfeld, EVP
HR: Celeste Silva
Web site: www.galoob.com
Emp: 216 Rev: $239.6 mil
Mfr. toys, games, dolls.
Canada, Hong Kong

GALVESTON-HOUSTON COMPANY.

4900 Woodway, PO Box 2207
Houston, TX 77056
Tel: (713) 966-2500 Fax: (713) 966-2575
CEO: Nathan M. Avery, Pres.
HR: Dennis G. Berryhill
Emp: 1,500
Mfr. industrial equipment.
England, U.K., France

GANNETT CO., INC.

1100 Wilson Blvd.
Arlington, VA 22234
Tel: (703) 284-6000 Fax: (703) 247-3294
CEO: Douglas McCorkindale, Pres.
FO: David Mazzarella
HR: Richard Clapp
Web site: www.gannett.com
Emp: 39,000
Newspaper publishing and broadcasting company.
England, U.K., Hong Kong, Switzerland

GANNETT FLEMING CORDDRY & CARPENTER INC.

PO Box 67100
Harrisburg, PA 17106
Tel: (717) 763-7211 Fax: (717) 763-8150
CEO: Ronald Drnevich, Pres.
FO: John G. Peterson
HR: Walter P. Buehler
Emp: 1,112
Engineering consulting services.
Cameroon, Chad, Guinea

THE GAP

1 Harrison Street
San Francisco, CA 94105
Tel: (650) 952-4400 Fax: (650) 952-5884
CEO: Donald Fisher, Chmn.
HR: Debbie Cowan
Clothing store chain.
Canada, England, U.K., France, Germany, Japan

GARCY CORPORATION

1400 North 25th Ave.
Melrose Park, IL 60160
Tel: (773) 261-1800 Fax: (708) 345-3823
CEO: A.R. Umans, Pres.
Emp: 200
Commercial furniture & supplies.
Spain

GARDERE & WYNNE, LLP

3000 Thanksgiving Tower, 1601 Elm Street
Dallas, TX 75201-4761
Tel: (214) 999-3000 Fax: (214) 999-4667
CEO: Lawrence Schoenbrun, Mng. Prtn.
HR: Terry Turner, Dir.
Web site: www.gardere.com
Emp: 683
International law firm.
Mexico

GARDNER-DENVER

1800 Gardner Expressway
Quincy, IL 62301
Tel: (217) 222-5400 Fax: (217) 228-8247
CEO: Ross Centanni, Pres.
Mfr. portable air compressors and related drilling accessories.
Australia, England, U.K.

GARLOCK SEALING TECHNOLOGIES

1666 Division Street
Palmyra, NY 14522
Tel: (315) 597-4811 Fax: (315) 597-3216
CEO: Keith Miller, Pres.
FO: Ted Bojanowski, VP
HR: Jim Erven
Web site: www.garlock-inc.com
Emp: 2,000
Mfr. of gaskets, packing, seals and expansion joints.
Australia, Brazil, Canada, England, U.K., France, Germany, Mexico, Singapore, South Korea

GARTNER GROUP, INC.

56 Top Gallant Road
Stamford, CT 06904-2212
Tel: (203) 316-1111 Fax: (203) 316-1100
CEO: Manuel A. Fernandez, Chmn.
FO: William T. Clifford, Pres.
HR: Alissa Danchig, Dir.
Web site: www.gartner.com
Emp: 2,800 Rev: $510 mil.
Information technology and research.
Australia, England, U.K.

THE GATES RUBBER COMPANY

990 S. Broadway, PO Box 5887
Denver, CO 80217-5887
Tel: (303) 744-1911 Fax: (303) 744-4000
CEO: C.C. Gates Chmn.
FO: J.H. Hodges, Pres.
HR: Gloria Koshio
Emp: 11,800 Rev: $1,000 mil.
Mfr. rubber tires/inner tubes & industrial belts & hose.
Australia, Belgium, Brazil, Canada, England, U.K., France, Germany, Japan, Mexico, Scotland, U.K., Singapore, Spain

GATX CAPITAL CORPORATION

Four Embarcadero Center, Ste. 2200
San Francisco, CA 94111
Tel: (415) 955-3200 Fax: (415) 955-3449
CEO: Ronald H. Zech, Chmn.

HR: Tracie Oliver, VP

Lease & loan financing, residual guarantees.

Australia, Canada, England, U.K., France, Germany, Hong Kong, Japan, Singapore

GATX LOGISTICS INC.

1301 Riverplace Boulevard, Ste. 1200

Jacksonville, FL 32207

Tel: (904) 396-2517 Fax: (904) 396-3984

CEO: Joe Nicosia, Pres.

FO: Bob Simcoe

HR: Ron Peterca

Web site: www.gatx.com

Emp: 3,000 Rev: $250 mil.

Warehouse-based third party logistics.

Chile, Mexico

GB ELECTRICAL INC.

6101 North Baker Road

Milwaukee, WI 53209

Tel: (414) 352-4160 Fax: (414) 228-1616

CEO: Ted Lecher, Pres.

HR: Rosemary Wallner

Emp: 357

Mfr./distributor electric consumable items & specialty tools.

Canada

GCA CORPORATION

PO Box 10010

Stamford, CT 06904

Tel: (203) 329-4100 Fax: (203) 329-4159

CEO: Michael Lockhart, Pres., Chmn.

FO: Michael Steir

HR: Gaspare Bellomo

Emp: 1,100

Mfr. imaging systems for semiconductor industrial.

England, U.K., France, Hong Kong, Japan

GE CAPITAL FLEET SERVICES

3 Capital Drive

Eden Prairie, MN 55344

Tel: (612) 828-1000 Fax: (612) 828-2010

CEO: Rick Smith, Pres.

HR: Sharon McKinney, VP

Emp: 3,100

Corporate vehicle leasing and services.

Belgium

GEMRUSA INC.

135 East 50th Street, Ste. 3E

New York, NY 10022

Tel: (212) 921-9888 Fax: (212) 921-9890

CEO: Mohammed Jabir

FO: Ahmed Imran

HR: Mohammed Hilal

Emp: 23

Wholesale jewelry, trading commodities.

Thailand, Vietnam

GENCOR INDUSTRIES INC.

5201 North Orange Blossom Trail

Orlando, FL 32810

Tel: (407) 290-6000 Fax: (407) 578-0577

CEO: E. J. Elliott, Pres.

Mfr. heat process systems, equipment, instrumentation & controls.

England, U.K.

GENCORP INC.

175 Ghent Road

Fairlawn, OH 44333-3300

Tel: (216) 869-4200 Fax: (216) 869-4211

CEO: John B. Yasinsky

Emp: 9,000

Mfr. aerospace/defense, automotive & polymer products.

Canada, Germany, Ireland

GENERAL AUTOMATION INC.

17731 Mitchell North

Irvine, CA 92714

Tel: (714) 250-4800 Fax: (714) 752-6772

CEO: Robert Bagby, Chmn.

Emp: 152

Mfr./sale/services computer hardware & software.

England, U.K.

GENERAL BINDING CORPORATION

One GBC Plaza

Northbrook, IL 60062

Tel: (847) 272-3700 Fax: (847) 272-1369

CEO: Govi C. Reddy, Pres.

FO: Elliott L. Smith

HR: Joseph J. LaPorte

Emp: 3,500

Binding and laminating equipment and associated supplies.

Australia, Canada, England, U.K., France, Germany, India, Italy, Japan, Mexico, Netherlands, New Zealand, Spain, Sweden, Switzerland

GENERAL CABLE CORPORATION

4 Tesseneer Drive

Highland Heights, KY 41076

Tel: (606) 572-8000 Fax: (606) 572-8444

CEO: Stephen Robinowitz, Pres.

FO: William M. Johnson

HR: Richard D. Foster

Web site: www.generalcable.com

Emp: 4,400 Rev: $1,100 mil.

Mfr. wire and cable.

Canada, England, U.K., Mexico

GENERAL CHEMICAL GROUP INC.

Liberty Lane

Hampton, NH 03842

Tel: (603) 929-2606 Fax: (603) 929-2404

CEO: Richard R. Russell, Pres.

FO: DeLyle W. Bloomquist, VP

Emp: 2,300 Rev: $700 mil.

Mfr./produce inorganic chemicals and soda ash.

Canada

GENERAL DATACOMM INC.

1579 Straits Turnpike, PO Box 1299

Middlebury, CT 06762-1299

Tel: (203) 574-1118 Fax: (203) 758-8507

CEO: Ross A. Belson, Pres.

HR: Joseph Williams

Mfr./sale/services transportation equipment for communications networks.

Australia, Belgium, Canada, England, U.K., France, Hong Kong, Mexico

GENERAL DYNAMICS CORPORATION

3190 Fairview Park Drive

Falls Church, VA 22042-4523

Tel: (703) 876-3000 Fax: (703) 876-3125

CEO: Nicholas D. Chabraja, Chmn.

FO: Michael W. Wynne, SVP

HR: W. Peter Wylie, VP

Web site: www.gendyn.com

Emp: 29,000 Rev: $4,062 mil.

Mfr. aerospace equipment, submarines, strategic systems, armored vehicles, defense support systems.

Bahrain, Belgium, Canada, Egypt, England, U.K., Germany, Greece, Israel, Japan, South Korea

GENERAL ELECTRIC CAPITAL CORPORATION

260 Long Ridge Road

Stamford, CT 06927

Tel: (203) 357-4000 Fax: (203) 357-6489

CEO: Gary C. Wendt, Chmn.

Emp: 65,000 Rev: $33,500 mil.

Financial, property/casualty insurance, computer sales and trailer leasing services.

Argentina, Australia, Canada, China (PRC), Denmark, England, U.K., France, Germany, Hong Kong, Ireland, Italy, Japan, Lebanon, Luxembourg, Malaysia, Mexico, New Zealand, Singapore, Spain

GENERAL ELECTRIC CO.

3135 Easton Turnpike

Fairfield, CT 06431

Tel: (203) 373-2211 Fax: (203) 373-3131

CEO: John F. Welch, Jr., Chmn.

FO: Paolo Fresco, VC

HR: William J. Conaty, SVP

Web site: www.ge.com

Emp: 216,000 Rev: $79,180 mil.

Diversified manufacturing, technology and services.

Algeria, Argentina, Australia, Austria, Belgium, Brazil, Canada, Chile, China (PRC), Czech Republic, Egypt, England, U.K., France, Germany, Greece, Hong Kong, Hungary, India, Indonesia, Iran, Ireland, Israel, Italy, Japan, Luxembourg, Malaysia, Mexico, Netherlands, Nigeria, Pakistan, Peru, Philippines, Poland, Portugal, Romania, Russia, Saudi Arabia, Singapore, Slovakia, South Africa, South Korea, Spain, Sweden, Switzerland, Taiwan (ROC), Thailand, Turkey, Ukraine, United Arab Emirates, Venezuela, Vietnam, Wales, U.K., Yugoslavia

GENERAL LATEX & CHEMICAL CORPORATION

675 Massachusetts Ave.

Cambridge, MA 02139

Tel: (617) 576-8000 Fax: (617) 876-1010

CEO: William H. Jefferson, Pres.

FO: Andrew McGann

Mfr. latex compounds & dispersions, urethane foam systems.

Canada

GENERAL MILLS INC.

1 General Mills Blvd., PO Box 1113

Minneapolis, MN 55440

Tel: (612) 540-2311 Fax: (612) 540-4925

CEO: Stephen W. Sanger, Pres.

FO: Raymon G. Viault

HR: Michael A. Peel

Emp: 10,000 Rev: $5,600 mil.

Mfr. consumer foods.

Canada, Netherlands, Switzerland

GENERAL MOTORS ACCEPTANCE CORPORATION

100 Renaissance Center

Detroit, MI 48243-7301

Tel: (313) 556-5000 Fax: (313) 556-5108

CEO: John D. Finnegan

FO: Richard J. S. Clout

HR: S. Edwards, Jr

Web site: www.gmac.com

Emp: 18,000

Automobile financing.

Australia, Austria, Belgium, Brazil, Chile, Colombia, Denmark, England, U.K., Finland, France, Germany, Hungary, Italy, Mexico, Netherlands, New Zealand, Norway, Portugal, Scotland, U.K., Spain, Sweden, Switzerland, Taiwan (ROC), Venezuela

GENERAL MOTORS CORPORATION

100 Renaissance Center

Detroit, MI 48243.7301

Tel: (313) 556-5000 Fax: (313) 556-5108

CEO: John F. Smith, Jr., Chmn.

FO: Louis R. Hughes, Pres. Intl.

HR: Richard G. LeFauve, SVP

Web site: www.gm.com

Emp: 608,000 Rev: $166,5 bil.

Mfr. full line vehicles, automotive electronics, commercial technologies, telecommunications, space, finance.

Argentina, Australia, Austria, Belgium, Brazil, Canada, Chile, Dem. Rep. of Congo, Denmark, Ecuador, Egypt, England, U.K., Finland, France, Germany, Greece, Hungary, Ireland, Italy, Japan, Kenya, Luxembourg, Mexico, Netherlands, New Zealand, Norway, Philippines, Poland, Portugal, Russia, Scotland, U.K., Singapore, South Africa, South Korea, Spain, Sweden, Switzerland, Tunisia, Ukraine, Uruguay, Venezuela, Yugoslavia

GENERAL REINSURANCE CORPORATION

695 East Main Street

Stamford, CT 06904-2350

Tel: (203) 328-5000 Fax: (203) 328-6423

CEO: Ronald E. Ferguson, Chmn.

FO: James E. Gustafson

HR: T. Hoffman, Jr.

Web site: www.genre.com

Emp: 3,870 Rev: $8,250 mil.

Reinsurance services worldwide.

Argentina, Australia, Austria, Bermuda, Brazil, Canada, China (PRC), Colombia, Denmark, England, U.K., France, Germany, Hong Kong, Ireland, Italy, Japan, Latvia, Lebanon, Mexico, New Zealand, Russia, Singapore, South Africa, South Korea, Spain, Switzerland, Taiwan (ROC)

GENERAL SEMICONDUCTOR, INC.

10 Melville Park Road.

Melville, NY 11747

Tel: (516) 847-3000 Fax:

CEO: Ronald A. Osterag, Chmn.

FO: Vincent M. Guerico, SVP

Web site: www.gensemi.com

Emp: 5,000 Rev: $380 mil.

Mfr. of low- and medium-current power rectifiers and transient voltage supressors.

China (PRC), England, U.K., France, Germany, Hong Kong, Ireland, Singapore, Taiwan (ROC)

GENERAL TIME CORPORATION

PO Box 4125

Norcross, GA 30091-4125

Tel: (770) 447-5300 Fax: (770) 242-4009

CEO: Fred Tistilli, Pres.

Mfr. Clocks & watches.

Canada

GENETICS INSTITUTE INC.

150 Cambridge Park Drive

Cambridge, MA 02140

Tel: (617) 876-1170 Fax: (617) 876-0388

CEO: Gabriel Schmergel

HR: Zoltan A. Csimma

Emp: 1,000

Develop/commercialize biopharmaceutical therapeutic products.

France, Japan

GENICOM CORPORATION

14800 Conference Center Drive, Ste. 400

Chantilly, VA 20151

Tel: (703) 802-9200 Fax: (703) 802-9039

CEO: Paul T. Winn

FO: Michael Du Rang

HR: Karen Morinelli

Emp: 2,600

Supplier of network systems, service & printer solutions.

Australia, Canada, England, U.K., France, Germany, Italy

GEO LOGISTICS

3205 South Martin Street

East Point, GA 11434

Tel: (404) 768-0000 Fax: (404) 859-8192

CEO: Tony Quinn, Pres.

HR: Louis Roden

Emp: 80

Forwarding and air freight agent.

England, U.K.

THE GEON COMPANY

One Geon Center

Avon Lake, OH 44012

Tel: (440) 930-1000 Fax: (440) 930-3551

CEO: William F. Patient, Chmn.

FO: Thomas A. Watermire, Pres.

Mfr. vinyl resins & compounds.

Australia, Canada

GEONEX CORPORATION

8950 9th Street North

St. Petersburg, FL 33702

Tel: (813) 578-0100 Fax: (813) 577-6946

CEO: Kenneth Mellen, Chmn.

Emp: 1,095

Geo-information services: mapping, resource interpretation, analysis, testing and data base management.

Brazil, Canada, Egypt, England, U.K., Pakistan

GEORGIA BONDED FIBERS INC.

1040 West 29th Street, PO Box 751

Buena Vista, VA 24416

Tel: (540) 261-2181 Fax: (540) 261-3784

CEO: James C. Kostelni, Pres.

FO: Mike Breton

HR: Brenda Clark

Emp: 200

Mfr. insole and luggage material.

Belgium, Italy, South Korea

GEORGIA GULF CORPORATION

400 Perimeter Center Terrace

Atlanta, GA 30346

Tel: (404) 395-4500 Fax: (404) 395-4529

CEO: Jerry R. Satrum

Emp: 1,146

Mfr./marketing commodity chemicals & polymers.

Canada, New Zealand

GEORGIA-PACIFIC GROUP

133 Peachtree Street NE, 41st Floor

Atlanta, GA 30303

Tel: (404) 652-4000 Fax: (404) 230-7008

CEO: Alston D. Correll, Chmn.

HR: James T. Wright, VP

Web site: www.gp.com

Emp: 46,000 Rev: $7,400 mil

Mfr./sales bldg. products including lumber, paper products, metal products, chemicals and plastics.

Canada

GERALD METALS INC.

6 High Ridge Park

Stamford, CT 06905

Tel: (203) 329-4700 Fax: (203) 609-8301

CEO: Gerald Leonard

Emp: 750

Minerals and metals.

Mexico

GERBER PRODUCTS COMPANY

445 State Street

Fremont, MI 49412

Tel: (616) 928-2000 Fax: (616) 928-2723

CEO: Alfred A. Piergallini, Pres.

FO: Donald L. Hanson

HR: Christina Kiley

Emp: 15,000

Mfr./distributor baby food and related products.

Canada, Costa Rica, Hong Kong, Mexico, Poland

GETZ BROS & CO., INC.

150 Post Street, Ste. 500

San Francisco, CA 94108-4750

Tel: (415) 772-5500 Fax: (415) 772-5659

CEO: Robert E. Brindley

FO: James J. Beeman

HR: Tracy Moore

Web site: www.getz.com

Emp: 2,390

Diversified manufacturing, marketing and distribution services and travel services.

Australia, China (PRC), England, U.K., Estonia, Finland, Hong Kong, Hungary, India, Japan, Latvia, Malaysia, Pakistan, Philippines, Poland, Singapore, South Africa, South Korea, Sri Lanka, Taiwan (ROC), Thailand, Vietnam

GIBSON GREETINGS INC.

2100 Section Road

Cincinnati, OH 45237

Tel: (513) 841-6600 Fax: (513) 841-6739

CEO: Frank O'Connell, Pres.

FO: P. M. Osman/F. B. Munoz

HR: Karen Kemp

Emp: 10,000

Design/mfr. greetings cards, gift wrap & trim, paper partywares, related specialty products.

England, U.K., Mexico

GIBSON, DUNN & CRUTCHER LLP

333 S. Grand Ave.

Los Angeles, CA 90071

Tel: (213) 229-7000 Fax: (213) 229-7520

CEO: Ronald S. Beard, Chmn.

FO: Joel Sanders, Mng. Ptnr.

HR: Patricia Cauldle

Web site: www.gdclaw.com

Emp: 1,750 Rev: $336 mil.

International law firm.

England, U.K., France, Hong Kong, Saudi Arabia

GIDDINGS & LEWIS INC.

142 Doty Street, PO Box 590

Fond du Lac, WI 54936-0590

Tel: (920) 921-9400 Fax: (920) 929-4522

CEO: M. L. Isles

HR: R. N. Kelley

Web site: www.giddings.com

Emp: 4,000

Mfr. machine tools, factory automation products and services.

England, U.K.

THE GILLETTE COMPANY

Prudential Tower Building

Boston, MA 02199

Tel: (617) 421-7000 Fax: (617) 421-7123

CEO: Alfred M. Zeien, Chmn.

FO: Jorgen Wedel, EVP Intl.

HR: Edward E. Guillet, VP

Web site: www.gillette.com

Emp: 44,000 Rev: $10,000 mil.

Develop/mfr. personal care/use products: blades & razors, toiletries, cosmetics, stationery.

Argentina, Australia, Austria, Bahamas, Belgium, Bermuda, Brazil, Canada, Cayman Islands, Chile, China (PRC), Colombia, Costa Rica, Czech Republic, Denmark, Dominican Republic, Ecuador, Egypt, El Salvador, England, U.K., Finland, France, Germany, Guatemala, Hong Kong, Hungary, India, Indonesia, Ireland, Italy, Jamaica, Japan, Kenya, Malaysia, Mexico, Morocco, Netherlands, New Zealand, Norway, Pakistan, Panama, Papua New Guinea, Peru, Philippines, Poland, Portugal, Russia, Singapore, South Africa, South Korea, Spain, Sweden, Switzerland, Taiwan (ROC), Thailand, Turkey, Uruguay, Venezuela, Zimbabwe

GILSON INC.

3000 W. Beltline Hwy, PO Box 620027

Middleton, WI 53562-0027

Tel: (608) 836-1551 Fax: (608) 831-4451

CEO: Warren Gilson, Pres.

FO: Eric Marteau D'Autry

HR: Rich Goninen

Emp: 275

Mfr. analytical/biomedical instruments.

France

GIRARD INDUSTRIES

6531 North Eldridge Pkwy.
Houston, TX 77041-3507
Tel: (713) 466-3100 Fax: (713) 466-8050
CEO: J. David Henry, III, Chmn.
Web site: www.girardind.com
Emp: 20

Mfr. internal pipeline cleaners, pipeline polly-pigs and related products.

Scotland, U.K.

P.H. GLATFELTER COMPANY

228 South Main Street
Spring Grove, PA 17362
Tel: (717) 225-4711 Fax: (717) 225-6834
CEO: George H. Glatfelter, Pres.
Emp: 3,100

Mfr. printing & specialty papers.

Australia, Canada

GLEASON CORPORATION

1000 University Ave.
Rochester, NY 14692
Tel: (716) 473-1000 Fax: (716) 461-4348
CEO: James S. Gleason, Chmn. & Pres.
HR: John B. Kodwels, VP
Web site: www.gleasoncorp.com
Emp: 2,656 Rev: $339 mil.

Mfr. gear making machine tools; tooling & services.

Belgium, China (PRC), England, U.K., Germany, India, Italy, Switzerland

GLENAYRE ELECTRONICS LTD.

1 Glenayre Way
Quincy, IL 62301
Tel: (217) 223-3211 Fax: (217) 223-3284
CEO: Gary B. Smith, Pres.
FO: Lee M. Ellison, SVP Intl.
HR: Beverley W. Cox, SVP
Rev: $349 mil.

Mfr. Infrastructure components and pagers.

Brazil, China (PRC), Czech Republic, England, U.K., Hong Kong, India, Japan, Netherlands, New Zealand, Philippines, Singapore, Taiwan (ROC), United Arab Emirates

GLENAYRE TECHNOLOGIES INC.

5935 Carnegie Boulevard
Charlotte, NC 28209
Tel: (704) 553-0038 Fax: (704) 553-0524
CEO: Chris Yunkon, Pres.
Emp: 1,400 Rev: $390 mil.

Mfr. automation systems.

England, U.K., Italy, Spain

GLOBAL MARINE INC

777 North Eldridge
Houston, TX 77079
Tel: (281) 496-8000 Fax: (281) 531-1260
CEO: C. Russell Luigs, Chmn.
Web site: www.glm.com
Emp: 1,700

Offshore contract drilling, turnkey drilling, oil & gas exploration & production.

Australia, Congo, England, U.K., Gabon, Indonesia, Nigeria, Scotland, U.K., Trinidad & Tobago, United Arab Emirates

GLOBAL SILVERHAWK

1000 Burnett Ave.
Concord, CA 94520
Tel: (510) 609-7080 Fax: (510) 609-7081
CEO: Daniel J. Randall, Pres.
FO: Michael Inglis
Web site: www.globalsilverhawk.com
Emp: 1,000

International moving & forwarding.

China (PRC), Ecuador, Egypt, England, U.K., Germany, Hong Kong, Indonesia, Italy, Japan, Kuwait, Malaysia, Philippines, Singapore, Thailand

GNM & ASSOCIATES INC

8630 Fenton Street, #820
Silver Spring, MD 20910
Tel: (301) 588-6110 Fax: (301) 588-6656
CEO: Gaetano N. Musto, Pres.
FO: Gaetano N. Musto
HR: William Musto
Emp: 54

Consulting engineers, architects & planners.

Italy

GODIVA CHOCOLATIER INC.

355 Lexington Ave.

New York, NY 10017

Tel: (212) 984-5900 Fax: (212) 984-5901

CEO: Craig Rydin, Pres.

HR: John Kessler

Mfr. chocolate candy, Biscotti dipping cookies and after-dinner coffees.

Australia, Belgium, Canada, France, Japan

GOLD STANDARD INC

712 Kearns Bldg.

Salt Lake City, UT 84101

Tel: (801) 328-4452 Fax: (801) 328-4457

CEO: Scott L. Smith, Pres.

Gold mining exploration.

Brazil, Uruguay

GOLDEN BOOKS PUBLISHING COMPANY

888 Seventh Ave.

New York, NY 10106

Tel: (212) 567-6700 Fax: (212) 567-6788

CEO: Richard E. Synder, Chmn.

FO: Andrew J. W. Low

HR: Michael Bruno, SVP

Emp: 1,200

Publishing children's and adult books, educational and electronic products.

Canada

GOLDMAN SACHS & COMPANY

85 Broad Street

New York, NY 10004

Tel: (212) 902-1000 Fax: (212) 902-3000

CEO: Jon C. Corzine, Chmn.

FO: Henry M. Paulson, Jr.

Web site: www.gs.com

Emp: 10,000

Investment bankers; securities broker dealers.

Australia, Brazil, Canada, Cayman Islands, China (PRC), England, U.K., France, Germany, Hong Kong, Italy, Japan, Mexico, Singapore, South Korea, Spain, Switzerland, Taiwan (ROC), Thailand

THE GOODYEAR TIRE & RUBBER COMPANY

1144 East Market Street

Akron, OH 44316

Tel: (330) 796-2121 Fax: (330) 796-1817

CEO: Samir F. Gibara, Chmn.

FO: William J. Sharp, Pres. Global

HR: Jesse T. Williams, Sr., VP

Web site: www.goodyear.com

Emp: 95,472 Rev: $13,155 mil.

Mfr. tires, automotive belts and hose, conveyor belts, chemicals; oil pipeline transmission.

Argentina, Australia, Brazil, Canada, Chile, China (PRC), Colombia, England, U.K., France, Germany, Greece, Guatemala, India, Indonesia, Italy, Jamaica, Japan, Luxembourg, Malaysia, Mexico, Morocco, New Zealand, Peru, Philippines, Poland, Russia, Singapore, Slovenia, South Africa, Sweden, Switzerland, Taiwan (ROC), Thailand, Turkey, Venezuela

W. L. GORE & ASSOCIATES, INC.

555 Paper Mill Road

Newark, DE 19711

Tel: (302) 738-4880 Fax: (302) 738-7710

CEO: Robert W. Gore, Pres.

Emp: 7,000 Rev: $1,200 mil.

Mfr. electronic, industrial filtration, medical and fabric products.

Germany, Scotland, U.K.

THE GORMAN-RUPP COMPANY

PO Box 1217

Mansfield, OH 44901

Tel: (419) 755-1011 Fax: (419) 755-1266

CEO: John A. Walter, Pres.

FO: Kim Arnold

HR: Lee Wilkins

Web site: www.gormanrupp.com

Emp: 1,000

Mfr. pumps and related equipment, waste water and environmental equipment.

Canada

GORTON'S

327 Main Street

Gloucester, MA 01930

Tel: (978) 283-3000 Fax: (978) 281-8295

CEO: Steve Warhover, Pres.

Emp: 1,000

Frozen fish.

Canada

GOSS INC.

700 Oakmont Lane
Westmont, IL 60559-5546
Tel: (630) 850-5600 Fax: (630) 850-6310
CEO: Robert Kuhn, CEO
FO: Frank J. McKay
Emp: 5,000
Mfr. printing equipment.
England, U.K., France, Germany

GOULDS PUMPS INC.

240 Fall Street
Seneca Falls, NY 13148
Tel: (315) 568-2811 Fax: (315) 568-2418
CEO: Richard LaBrecque, Pres.
FO: Ivergen Schulz
Emp: 3,750
Mfr. industrial and water systems pumps.
Brazil, Canada, Mexico, Philippines

GOW-MAC INSTRUMENT COMPANY

277 Broadhead Road
Bethlehem, PA 18017
Tel: (610) 954-9000 Fax: (610) 954-0599
CEO: Robert Mathieu, Pres.
FO: Feh-Min-Fan
Web site: www.gow-mac.com
Emp: 57
Mfr. analytical instruments
Ireland

GOYA FOODS, INC.

100 Seaview Drive
Secaucus, NJ 07096
Tel: (201) 348-4900 Fax: (201) 348-6609
CEO: Joseph A. Unanue, Pres.
FO: Conrad O. Colon, VP
HR: Karmen A. Reccico, Mgr.
Web site: www.goyafoods.com
Emp: 3,000
Produces canned and packaged Hispanic food products, fruit juices and frozen entrees.
Dominican Republic, Spain

GPU INTERNATIONAL, INC.

300 Madison Ave.
Morristown, NJ 07962-1911
Tel: (973) 455-8200 Fax: (973) 455-8582
CEO: Fred D. Hafer, Pres.
FO: Bruce L. Levy, Pres. Intl.
Web site: www.gpu.com
Emp: 9,300
Global electric energy company.
Australia, Bolivia, Canada, Colombia, England, U.K., Pakistan, Philippines, Portugal, Senegal, Spain, Turkey

W. R. GRACE & COMPANY

One Town Center Road, 1750 Clint Moore Road
Boca Raton, FL 33486-1010
Tel: (561) 362-2000 Fax: (561) 561-2193
CEO: Paul J. Norris, Pres. & CEO
HR: William Monroe, VP
Web site: www.grace.com
Emp: 6,300 Rev: $1,480 mil.
Mfr. specialty chemicals and materials: packaging, health care, catalysts, construction, water treatment/process.
Argentina, Australia, Belgium, Brazil, Canada, Chile, China (PRC), Colombia, England, U.K., France, Germany, Greece, Hong Kong, India, Indonesia, Ireland, Italy, Japan, Malaysia, Mexico, Netherlands, New Zealand, Peru, Philippines, Poland, Russia, Singapore, South Africa, South Korea, Spain, Sweden, Switzerland, Taiwan (ROC), Thailand, Venezuela, Vietnam

GRACO INC

4050 Olson Memorial Hwy, PO Box 1441
Minneapolis, MN 55440-1441
Tel: (612) 623-6000 Fax: (612) 623-6777
CEO: George Aristides, Chmn.
FO: R. A. Wagner/T. J. Fay
HR: Mike Galdonik
Web site: www.graco.com
Emp: 2,000
Mfr./sales of infant & juvenile products; services fluid handling equipment & systems.
Argentina, Belgium, Canada, Chile, Colombia, Czech Republic, Egypt, England, U.K., Finland, France, Germany, Hong Kong, Italy, Japan, Lebanon, Norway, Panama, Philippines, Poland, Saudi Arabia, South Africa, South Korea, Turkey, Uruguay

GRAHAM & JAMES LLP

One Maritime Plaza - Ste. 300

San Francisco, CA 94111-3404
Tel: (415) 954-0200 Fax: (415) 391-2493
CEO: Michael D. Levine, Mng. Ptnr.
HR: Lisa Dickinson, Mgr.
Web site: www.gj.com
Emp: 800 Rev: $132 mil.
International law firm.
Australia, Belgium, China (PRC), Czech Republic, England, U.K., Germany, Hong Kong, Indonesia, Italy, Japan, Kuwait, Romania, Saudi Arabia, Singapore, Taiwan (ROC), Thailand, Vietnam

GRANT THORNTON INTERNATIONAL

800 One Prudential Plaza, 130 E. Randolph Drive
Chicago, IL 60601-6050
Tel: (312) 856-0001 Fax: (312) 616-7052
CEO: Robert A. Kleckner, Chmn.
FO: Lou Fanchi
HR: Lauranne Cermak
Emp: 10,000
Accounting, audit, tax and management consulting services.
Argentina, Australia, Austria, Botswana, Canada, Chile, China (PRC), Cyprus, Czech Republic, Denmark, England, U.K., France, Germany, Greece, Hong Kong, Hungary, India, Ireland, Italy, Japan, Luxembourg, Malta, Morocco, New Zealand, Northern Ireland, U.K., Norway, Poland, Portugal, Scotland, U.K., Slovakia, South Africa, Spain, Switzerland, Taiwan (ROC), Thailand, Wales, U.K.

GRAPHIC CONTROLS CORPORATION

PO Box 1271
Buffalo, NY 14240
Tel: (716) 853-7500 Fax: (716) 847-7551
CEO: Duane B. Hopper, Pres.
HR: Jan Reicis
Emp: 1,400
Mfr. information, medical and physiological monitoring products.
Australia, Canada, Spain

GRAYBAR ELECTRIC CO., INC.

34 North Meramec Ave.
Clayton, MO 63105
Tel: (314) 512-9200 Fax: (314) 512-9216
CEO: Carl L. Hall, Pres.
FO: William R. Kuykendall, Intl.
Rev: N/A
Electrical com data distributor.
Chile, Mexico, Singapore

THE GREAT ATLANTIC & PACIFIC TEA COMPANY

2 Paragon Drive
Montvale, NJ 07645
Tel: (201) 573-9700 Fax: (201) 930-8144
CEO: Christian W. Haub, Pres.
FO: Peter J. O'Gorman, Intl
HR: H. N. Lewis, SVP
Web site: www.aptea.com
Emp: 80,000 Rev: $10,260 mil.
Supermarket chain
Canada

GREAT LAKES CHEMICAL CORPORATION

One Great Lakes Blvd.
W. Lafayette, IN 47906
Tel: (765) 497-6100 Fax: (765) 497-6123
CEO: Mark Bulriss, Pres.
HR: Mark Esselman
Emp: 8,000
Mfr. bromine & derivatives, furfural & derivatives.
England, U.K., France, Germany, Hong Kong, Hungary, Italy, Switzerland

GREAT WESTERN CHEMICAL & McCALL OIL CO.

808 SW Fifteenth Ave.
Portland, OR 97205
Tel: (503) 228-2600 Fax: (503) 221-5752
CEO: Robert McCall, Pres.
HR: Jill Epstein
Emp: 385
Industrial chemical distribution & logistics.
Canada, Mexico

HARBISON WALKER REFRACTORIES CO.

600 Grant Street
Pittsburgh, PA 15219
Tel: (412) 562-6200 Fax: (412) 562-6331
CEO: Juan Bravo, Pres.
HR: Peggy Groover

Emp: 1,750

Mfr. refractories and lime.

Canada, England, U.K.

GREENBERG, TRAURIG, HOFFMAN, LIPOFF, ROSEN & QUENTEL

1221 Brickell Ave.

Miami, FL 33131

Tel: (305) 579-0500 Fax: (305) 579-0717

CEO: Larry J. Hoffman

HR: Rozlyn M. Friedman, Dir.

Web site: www.gtlaw.com

Rev: $135 mil.

International law firm.

Brazil

GREENFIELD INDUSTRIES INC

470 Old Evans Road

Evans, GA 30809

Tel: (706) 863-7708 Fax: (706) 860-8559

CEO: Durwin Gilbreath, Pres.

FO: John Woodbridge

HR: Tim Furguson

Emp: 3,850

Mfr. high-speed rotary cutting tools.

England, U.K., Germany, Hong Kong

GREFCO, INC.

23705 Crenshaw Blvd., Ste. 101

Torrance, CA 90505

Tel: (310) 517-0700 Fax: (310) 517-0794

CEO: Glenn Jones, Pres.

Emp: 1,000

Filter powders.

Belgium, India, Mexico, Philippines

GREY ADVERTISING INC.

777 Third Ave.

New York, NY 10017

Tel: (212) 546-2000 Fax: (212) 546-1495

CEO: Edward H. Meyer, Chmn.

FO: John Shannon, Pres. Intl.

HR: David Kozel, VP

Web site: www.giworldwwide.com

Emp: 9,900 Rev: $858.8 mil.

International advertising agency.

Albania, Argentina, Australia, Austria, Bangladesh, Belgium, Bolivia, Brazil, Bulgaria, Cambodia, Canada, Chile, China (PRC), Colombia, Costa Rica, Croatia, Czech Republic, Denmark, Dominican Republic, Ecuador, El Salvador, England, U.K., Estonia, Finland, France, Germany, Ghana, Greece, Guatemala, Honduras, Hong Kong, Hungary, India, Indonesia, Ireland, Israel, Italy, Jamaica, Japan, Kenya, Kuwait, Latvia, Lebanon, Lithuania, Macedonia, Malaysia, Mauritius, Mexico, Morocco, Myanmar, Netherlands, New Zealand, Nicaragua, Nigeria, Norway, Pakistan, Panama, Peru, Philippines, Poland, Portugal, Romania, Russia, Saudi Arabia, Singapore, Slovakia, Slovenia, South Africa, South Korea, Spain, Sri Lanka, Sweden, Switzerland, Taiwan (ROC), Thailand, Trinidad & Tobago, Turkey, Ukraine, United Arab Emirates, Uruguay, Uzbekistan, Venezuela, Vietnam, Yugoslavia, Zimbabwe

GREYHOUND LINES INC.

PO Box 660362

Dallas, TX 75266

Tel: (972) 789-7000 Fax: (972) 789-7330

CEO: John W. Teets

HR: Robert Lang

Emp: 37,000

Mfr. consumer products, transportation, consumer and financial services.

Canada, England, U.K.

GRIFFIN WHEEL COMPANY

200 West Monroe Street

Chicago, IL 60606

Tel: (312) 346-3300 Fax: (312) 346-3373

CEO: William Demmert, Pres.

HR: Michael J. White

Emp: 1,040

Mfr. cast steel wheels & composition brake shoes for railroad freight cars & diesel locomotives.

Canada

GRIFFITH LABORATORIES INC

One Griffith Center

Alsip, IL 60658

Tel: (708) 371-0900 Fax: (708) 597-3294

CEO: Mr. Richard Buehl, Pres.

HR: Bob Ufferman

Web site: www.griffithlabs.com

Emp: 2,500

Industrial food ingredients and equipment.

Austria, Belgium, Canada, Colombia, Costa Rica, El Salvador, England, U.K., France, Germany, Guatemala, Honduras, Hong Kong, Ireland, Israel, Italy, Japan, Mexico, New Zealand, Panama, Peru, Philippines, Singapore, South Korea, Spain, Taiwan (ROC), Thailand

GROUNDWATER TECHNOLOGY INC

100 River Ridge Drive

Norwood, MA 02062

Tel: (781) 769-7600 Fax: (781) 769-7992

CEO: Walter Barber, Pres.

FO: Rick Lewis

Emp: 1,400

Industrial site cleanup, management & consulting.

Australia, Austria, Canada, England, U.K., Germany, Hungary, Italy, Netherlands, New Zealand

GRUMMAN INTERNATIONAL INC

South Oyster Bay Road

Bethpage, NY 11714

Tel: (516) 575-0574 Fax: (516) 575-8214

CEO: Kent Kresa, Pres.

Emp: 22,350

Mfr./sale aerospace products, aircraft, software, automated test equipment and C3 projects.

Singapore, South Korea

GTE CORPORATION

One Stamford Forum

Stamford, CT 06904

Tel: (203) 965-2000 Fax: (203) 965-2277

CEO: Charles R. Lee, Chmn.

FO: M. T. Masin, Pres. Intl.

HR: J. Randall MacDonald, EVP

Web site: www.gte.com

Emp: 114,000 Rev: $23,260 mil.

Electronic products, telecommunications systems, publishing and communications.

Algeria, Argentina, Australia, Austria, Belgium, Brazil, Cameroon, Canada, China (PRC), Colombia, Dominican Republic, England, U.K., France, Germany, Hong Kong, Hungary, India, Italy, Japan, Kenya, Lebanon, Malaysia, Mexico, Netherlands, Nigeria, Philippines, Poland, Saudi Arabia, Spain, Sri Lanka, Switzerland, Taiwan (ROC), Thailand, Venezuela

GTE DIRECTORIES CORPORATION

2200 West Airfield Drive

DFW Airport, TX 75261-9810

Tel: (972) 453-7000 Fax: (972) 453-7573

CEO: Earl Goode, Pres.

Emp: 6,000

Publishing telephone directories.

Canada, Costa Rica, Hong Kong, Indonesia, Panama, Philippines, Singapore, Sri Lanka, Venezuela

GTE INTERNETWORKING

150 Cambridge Park Drive

Cambridge, MA 02140

Tel: (617) 873-2000 Fax: (617) 873-2857

CEO: George Conrades, Pres.

HR: Susan Bowman

Web site: www.bbn.com

Emp: 3,200 Rev: $497 mil.

R/D computer, communications, acoustics technologies and internetworking services.

England, U.K., Italy

GUARDIAN ELECTRIC MFG. COMPANY

1425 Lake Ave.

Woodstock, IL 60098

Tel: (815) 337-0050 Fax: (815) 337-0377

CEO: Kevin Kelly, Pres.

FO: Nigel Bayliss

HR: Virginia Barns

Emp: 530

Mfr. industrial controls, electrical relays and switches.

England, U.K.

GUARDIAN INDUSTRIES CORPORATION

2300 Harmon Road

Auburn Hills, MI 48326-1714

Tel: (248) 340-1800 Fax: (248) 340-9988

CEO: William Davidson, Pres.

Emp: 3,900

Mfr. and fabricate flat glass products and insulation materials.

Australia

GUARDSMAN PRODUCTS/LILLY INDUSTRIES

PO Box 88010
Grand Rapids, MI 49518
Tel: (616) 940-2900 Fax: (616) 285-7870
CEO: Douglas Hume, Chmn. & Pres.
HR: Mary Thompson
Emp: 820
Mfr. custom industrial coatings, diversified consumer products.
England, U.K.

GUEST SUPPLY INC.
PO Box 902
Monmouth Junction, NJ 08852-0902
Tel: (609) 514-9696 Fax: (609) 514-2692
CEO: Clifford W. Stanley, Pres.
Emp: 350
Mfr. personal care & housekeeping products.
Canada, England, U.K., New Zealand

GUILFORD MILLS INC
PO Box 26969
Greensboro, NC 27419
Tel: (336) 316-4000 Fax: (336) 316-4059
CEO: Charles A. Hayes
HR: S. Richard Sargent
Emp: 4,000
Mfr. textiles.
England, U.K.

GULTON INDUSTRIES INC
212 Durham Ave.
Metuchen, NJ 08840
Tel: (732) 548-6500 Fax: (732) 548-6781
CEO: Larry Curtis, Pres.
Emp: 3,500
Electronic instruments, controls and communications equipment.
Canada, England, U.K., Germany, Switzerland

H

HACH COMPANY
PO Box 389
Loveland, CO 80539
Tel: (970) 669-3050 Fax: (303) 970-2932
CEO: Bruch Hach
FO: Russell E. Heston
HR: Randy Petersen
Emp: 723
Mfr./distributor water analysis and organic instruments, test kits and chemicals.
Belgium

HAEMONETICS CORPORATION
400 Wood Road
Braintree, MA 02184
Tel: (781) 848-7100 Fax: (781) 848-5106
CEO: John F. White, Pres.
FO: Jean Papillon, SVP
Web site: www.haemonetics.
Emp: 1,100 Rev: $275 mil.
Mfr. automated blood processing systems and blood products
Belgium, China (PRC), England, U.K., Hong Kong, Japan, Netherlands, Scotland, U.K., Sweden, Switzerland, Taiwan (ROC)

HALE AND DORR LLP
60 State Street
Boston, MA 02109
Tel: (617) 526-6000 Fax: (617) 526-5000
CEO: John D. Hamilton, Jr., Chrmn.
FO: John E. Colbert, Jr.
HR: Ann L. Hirsh, Dir.
Web site: www.haledorr.com
Emp: 922 Rev: $160.5 mil.
International law firm.
England, U.K.

HALLIBURTON COMPANY
500 North Akard Street, Ste. 3600
Dallas, TX 75201-3391
Tel: (214) 978-2600 Fax: (214) 978-2685
CEO: Richard B. Chaney, Chmn.
FO: David J. Lesar

HR: Celeste Colgan

Web site: www.halliburton.com

Emp: 70,000 Rev: 8.8 mil.

Energy, construction and insurance.

Argentina, Austria, Bahrain, Bolivia, Brazil, Brunei, Canada, Colombia, Congo, Costa Rica, Croatia, Denmark, Ecuador, Egypt, England, U.K., France, Germany, Greece, Guatemala, India, Italy, Japan, Kuwait, Malaysia, Mexico, Netherlands, New Zealand, Nigeria, Norway, Oman, Pakistan, Papua New Guinea, Peru, Philippines, Qatar, Romania, Russia, Saudi Arabia, Scotland, U.K., Singapore, South Africa, Surinam, Thailand, Trinidad & Tobago, Tunisia, Turkey, Turkmenistan, United Arab Emirates, Venezuela, Vietnam, Yemen

HALLMARK CARDS INC.

PO Box 419580

Kansas City, MO 64141

Tel: (816) 274-5100 Fax: (816) 274-5061

CEO: Irvine O. Hockaday, Pres.

FO: Keith Alm

HR: Ralph Christensen

Emp: 19,200 Rev: $3,600 mil.

Mfr. greeting cards and related products.

Australia, Belgium, Canada, England, U.K., France, Hong Kong, Japan, Mexico, Netherlands, New Zealand, Spain

HAMBRECHT & QUIST

One Bush Street

San Francisco, CA 94104

Tel: (415) 439-3000 Fax: (415) 439-3638

CEO: Daniel H. Case, III, Chmn.

FO: William S. McDermott

HR: K.C. Egan, Dir. HR

Web site: www.hamquist.com

Emp: 823 Rev: $346.2 mil.

Investment banking and venture capital services.

England, U.K., France, Hong Kong, Japan, Philippines, Singapore, Taiwan (ROC), Thailand

HAMLIN INC.

612 E. Lake Street

Lake Mills, WI 53551

Tel: (920) 648-3000 Fax: (920) 648-3001

CEO: Gerald W. Oesterreich, Pres.

FO: William W. Hanson

HR: Debra DiDonato

Emp: 1,400

Mfr. position sensors, switches and reed relays.

England, U.K., Germany

HANDLEMAN COMPANY

500 Kirts Boulevard

Troy, MI 48084

Tel: (248) 362-4400 Fax: (248) 362-3615

CEO: Frank M. Handleman, Pres.

FO: Lawrence Hicks

HR: Rodger D. Apple

Emp: 2,950

Distributor pre-recorded music, books, video cassettes and computer software.

Canada

HANDY & HARMAN

555 Theodore Fremd Ave.

Rye, NY 10580

Tel: (914) 921-5200 Fax: (914) 925-4496

CEO: Robert LeBlanc, Pres.

HR: Bernard Lishinsky

Emp: 4,711

Precious & specialty metals for industry, refining, scrap metal; diversified industrial mfr.

Canada, Denmark, England, U.K., Hong Kong, Japan, Singapore

HANGER ORTHOPEDIC GROUP, INC.

7700 Old Georgetown Road, 2nd Fl.

Bethesda, MD 20814

Tel: (301) 986-0701 Fax: (301) 986-0102

CEO: Ivan Sabel, Pres.

Manufacture and sales of artificial limbs.

Belgium, Netherlands

M.A. HANNA COMPANY

200 Public Square, Ste. 36-5000

Cleveland, OH 44114

Tel: (216) 589-4000 Fax: (216) 589-4200

CEO: Douglas J. McGregor, Chmn.

FO: Garth W. Henry

HR: Thomas H. Wilson

Emp: 6,400

Mfr. color and additive concentrates.

Belgium, France

HARBORLITE CORPORATION

PO Box 100

Vicksburg, MI 49097

Tel: (616) 649-1352 Fax: (616) 649-3707

CEO: William Woods, Pres.

HR: Ray Lacasse

Mining/process perlite filter media.

England, U.K., France

HARCO TECHNOLOGIES CORPORATION

1055 W. Smith Road

Medina, OH 44256

Tel: (330) 725-6681 Fax: (330) 723-0244

CEO: Neal Restivo

FO: David M. Hickey

HR: Stacie Dobson

Web site: www.corrpro.com

Emp: 1,000 Rev: $130 mil.

Full-services corrosion engineering, cathodic protection.

Canada, England, U.K., France, Hong Kong, Indonesia, Malaysia, Portugal, Saudi Arabia, Singapore, United Arab Emirates

HARCOURT BRACE & COMPANY

6277 Sea Harbor Drive

Orlando, FL 32887

Tel: (407) 345-2000 Fax: (407) 345-9354

CEO: Brian J. Knez, Pres.

HR: Ernest Urquhart, VP

Emp: 5,600

Book publishing, tests and related service, journals, facsimile reprints, management consult, operates parks/shows.

Argentina, Australia, Bahamas, Brazil, Canada, Colombia, Costa Rica, England, U.K., Hong Kong, India, Japan, Malaysia, Mexico, Singapore, South Korea, Taiwan (ROC)

HARCOURT GENERAL

27 Boylston Street

Chestnut Hill, MA 02167

Tel: (617) 232-8200 Fax: (617) 739-1395

CEO: Richard A. Smith, Pres.

HR: Gerald T. Hughes, VP

Web site: www.harcourt-general.com

Emp: 18,500 Rev: $3,600 mil.

Publishing, specialty retailing and professional services.

Canada, England, U.K.

HARLEY-DAVIDSON INTERNATIONAL

3700 West Juneau Ave.

Milwaukee, WI 53208

Tel: (414) 342-4680 Fax: (414) 343-4621

CEO: Rich Teerlink, Chmn.

HR: Pat Thompson

Mfr. motorcycles, recreational and commercial vehicles, parts and accessories.

England, U.K., Germany, Japan

HARMAN JBL INTERNATIONAL

800 Balboa Boulevard

Nothridge, CA 91329

Tel: (818) 895-8734 Fax: (818) 893-1531

CEO: Sidney Harman, Pres.

HR: Paula Stern

Web site: www.harman.com

Emp: 4,600

Mfr. audio and video equipment, loudspeakers and sound reinforcement equipment.

Denmark, England, U.K., France, Germany, Japan, Wales, U.K.

HARNISCHFEGER INDUSTRIES INC

PO Box 554

Milwaukee, WI 53201

Tel: (414) 797-6480 Fax: (414) 797-6573

CEO: Jeffrey T. Grade, Chmn.

FO: John N. Hanson, Pres. & COO

HR: Joseph A. Podawiltz, VP

Web site: www.harnischfeger.com

Emp: 15,000 Rev: $1,000 mil.

Mfr. mining and material handling equipment, papermaking machinery and computer systems.

Australia, Brazil, Canada, Chile, China (PRC), England, U.K., Finland, France, Germany, Italy, Japan, Mexico, Poland, Russia, Scotland, U.K., Singapore, South Africa, Sweden

THE HARPER GROUP

260 Townsend Street

San Francisco, CA 94107-1719

Tel: (415) 978-0600 Fax: (415) 978-0692

CEO: Peter Gibert, Chmn.

HR: Rae Fawcett

Web site: www.circleintl.com

Emp: 3,250 Rev: $5.7 mil.

Ocean/air freight forwarding, customs brokerage, packing and wholesale, logistics management and insurance.

Angola, Argentina, Australia, Austria, Bahamas, Bahrain, Bangladesh, Barbados, Belgium, Bolivia, Brazil, Brunei, Cambodia, Canada, Chile, China (PRC), Colombia, Costa Rica, Cyprus, Czech Republic, Denmark, Dominican Republic, Ecuador, Egypt, El Salvador, England, U.K., Fiji, Finland, France, French Antilles, French Guiana, Germany, Ghana, Greece, Guam, Guatemala, Haiti, Honduras, Hong Kong, Hungary, India, Indonesia, Ireland, Israel, Italy, Jamaica, Japan, Jordan, Kenya, Kuwait, Lebanon, Malawi, Malaysia, Mauritius, Mexico, Mongolia, Nepal, Netherlands, Netherlands Antilles, New Zealand, Nicaragua, Nigeria, Northern Ireland, U.K., Norway, Oman, Pakistan, Panama, Papua New Guinea, Paraguay, Peru, Philippines, Poland, Portugal, Qatar, Russia, Saudi Arabia, Scotland, U.K., Singapore, South Africa, South Korea, Spain, Sri Lanka, Sweden, Switzerland, Taiwan (ROC), Tanzania, Thailand, Trinidad & Tobago, Turkey, Ukraine, United Arab Emirates, Uruguay, Venezuela, Vietnam, Wales, U.K., Yemen, Zambia, Zimbabwe

HARRIS CALORIFIC COMPANY

2345 Murphy Boulevard

Gainesville, GA 30501

Tel: (770) 536-8801 Fax: (770) 536-0544

CEO: Peter Ullman, Pres.

HR: John Rodgers

Emp: 350

Mfr./sales of gas welding and cutting equipment.

France, Germany, Ireland, Italy

HARRIS CORPORATION

1025 West NASA Blvd.

Melbourne, FL 32919

Tel: (407) 727-9100 Fax: (407) 727-9344

CEO: Phillip W. Farmer, Chmn. & Pres.

FO: Wesley E. Cantrell, Pres. Int'l.

HR: Nick E. Heldreth, VP

Web site: www.harris.com

Emp: 29,000

Mfr. communications and information-handling equipment, including copying and fax systems.

Belgium, Brazil, Canada, China (PRC), Czech Republic, Denmark, England, U.K., France, Germany, Greece, Hong Kong, Hungary, India, Indonesia, Israel, Italy, Japan, Malaysia, Netherlands, New Zealand, Norway, Poland, Portugal, Russia, Singapore, South Africa, South Korea, Spain, Sweden, Switzerland, Taiwan (ROC), Thailand, Turkey

HARSCO CORPORATION

PO Box 8888

Camp Hill, PA 17001-8888

Tel: (717) 763-7064 Fax: (717) 763-6424

CEO: Derek C. Hathaway, Chmn.

HR: Richard C. Hawkins

Emp: 13,000

Metal reclamation and mill services, infrastructure and construction and process industry products.

Australia, Canada, England, U.K., Germany, Malaysia, Mexico

THE HARTFORD FINANCIAL SERVICES GROUP, INC.

Hartford Plaza

Hartford, CT 06115

Tel: (860) 547-5000 Fax: (860) 547-5817

CEO: Ramani Ayer, Chmn.

FO: John Donahue, Pres

HR: Helen G. Goodman

Web site: www.thehartford.com

Emp: 25,000

Financial services.

Belgium, Canada, China (PRC), England, U.K., Luxembourg, Netherlands, Spain

HARTFORD LIFE INTERNATIONAL, LTD.

200 Hopmeadow Street

Simsbury, CT 06070

Tel: (860) 843-8982 Fax: (860) 843-8981

CEO: Lon A. Smith, Pres.

FO: Bruce Gardner, Pres. Intl.

Life insurance and group life sales.

Argentina, Bermuda, Brazil, Uruguay

HARTFORD RE COMPANY

55 Farmington Ave., Ste. 800

Hartford, CT 06105

Tel: (860) 520-2700 Fax: (860) 520-2726

CEO: Dennis B. Zettervall

FO: Radha Krishnan, EVP

Reinsurance.

Canada, England, U.K., Germany, Hong Kong, Spain, Taiwan (ROC)

THE HARTFORD STEAM BOILER INSPECTION & INSURANCE COMPANY

One State Street, PO Box5024

Hartford, CT 06102-5024

Tel: (860) 722-1866 Fax: (860) 722-5770

CEO: Gordon W. Kreh, Pres.

FO: William A. Kerr

HR: Susan W. Ahrens

Web site: www.hsb.com

Emp: 2,200

Inspection and quality assurance and asbestos monitoring.

Canada, England, U.K., Hong Kong, Singapore, South Korea, Spain

HARTMARX CORPORATION

101 North Wacker Drive

Chicago, IL 60606

Tel: (312) 372-6300 Fax: (312) 984-6155

CEO: E. O. Hand, Chmn.

Emp: 7,600

Mfr./licensing men's & women's apparel.

Hong Kong, Japan

HARTWELL BROTHERS HANDLE COMPANY

PO Box 80327

Memphis, TN 38108

Tel: (901) 452-2191 Fax: (901) 452-0267

CEO: Michael Keathley, Pres.

FO: Ron Keathley

Emp: 300

Mfr. replacement tool handles.

Canada

HARVARD APPARATUS

84 October Hill Road

Holliston, MA 01746

Tel: (508) 893-8999 Fax: (508) 429-5732

CEO: Chane Graziano

Web site: www.harvardapparatus.com

Emp: 225

Mfr./sales life science research products.

Canada, England, U.K., France

HARVEST INTERNATIONAL INC

1155 Connecticut Ave. NW

Washington, DC 20036

Tel: (202) 467-8595 Fax: (202) 223-8598

CEO: Harvey Goldstein

FO: Anne Miniter McKay

Emp: 65

Business consultants.

Indonesia

HASBRO INDUSTRIES INC

1027 Newport Ave.

Pawtucket, RI 02861

Tel: (401) 725-8697 Fax: (401) 727-5099

CEO: Alan G. Hassenfeld, Chmn.

FO: Alfred J. Verrecchia, Pres.

HR: Jim Kershner

Web site: www.hasbro.com

Emp: 12,000 Rev: $3,100 mil.

Toys, games and dolls.

Canada, China (PRC), England, U.K., France, Germany, Greece, Japan, Poland, Portugal, Spain

HASTINGS MFG. COMPANY

325 North Hanover Street

Hastings, MI 49058

Tel: (616) 945-2491 Fax: (616) 945-4667

CEO: Mark & Andy Johnson, Co-Pres.

HR: Joe Bennett

Emp: 1,700

Mfr. piston rings, filters.

Canada

HATHAWAY CORPORATION

8228 Park Meadows Drive

Littleton, CO 80124

Tel: (303) 799-8200 Fax: (303) 799-8880

CEO: Eugene E. Prince, Pres.

FO: Richard D. Smith

HR: Tracy Montford

Emp: 350

Mfr. monitoring and test instrumentation and motors, optical encoders.

Northern Ireland, U.K.

HAYNES INTERNATIONAL INC

1020 W. Park Ave., PO Box 9013

Kokomo, IN 46904-9013

Tel: (765) 456-6000 Fax: (765) 456-6905

CEO: M. D. Austin

HR: F. J. LaRosa

Web site: www.haynesintl.com

Emp: 980

Mfr. cobalt and nickel-base alloys for aerospace and chemicals industry.

England, U.K., France

HAYSSEN, INC.

225 Spartangreen Blvd.

Duncan, SC 29334

Tel: (864) 486-4000 Fax: (864) 486-4333

CEO: Dan Jones, Pres.

HR: Paul Comer

Web site: www.barry-wehmiller.com

Emp: 560

Mfr. automatic packaging machinery.

England, U.K.

HAYWARD INDUSTRIAL PRODUCTS INC.

900 Fairmount Avenue

Elizabeth, NJ 07207

Tel: (908) 351-5400 Fax: (908) 351-7893

CEO: Robert Davis, Pres.

HR: Wayne Wilson

Mfr. industrial strainers.

Canada, England, U.K.

HDR, INC.

8404 Indian Hill Drive

Omaha, NE 68114

Tel: (402) 399-1000 Fax: (402) 399-1238

CEO: Richard R. Bell

FO: James Suttle

HR: Roger Parkins

Web site: www.hdrinc.com

Emp: 350

Consulting architects and engineers.

Mexico, Saudi Arabia

HEALTH-MOR INC

3500 Payne Ave.

Cleveland, OH 44114

Tel: (216) 432-1990 Fax: (216) 432-0013

CEO: Carl Young, Pres.

HR: Ellen Gordon

Emp: 550

Mfr. floor care products, metal tubing, specialty machinery, tools, dies.

Canada

HEALTHSOUTH CORPORATION

One HealthSouth Parkway

Birmingham, AL 35243

Tel: (205) 967-7116 Fax: (205) 969-4740

CEO: Richard M. Scrushy, Chmn.

FO: James P. Bennett, Pres.

Web site: www.healthsouth.com

Rev: $2,200 mil.

Provider of comphrehensive outpatient and rehabilitative healthcare services.

England, U.K.

HEAT TIMER SERVICE CORPORATION

10 Dwight Place

Fairfield, NJ 07006

Tel: (973) 575-4004 Fax: (973) 575-4052

CEO: Michael Pitonyak, Pres.

Emp: 50

Heating systems controls, smoke alarms, digital temp and set point controls.

Canada

HECKETT

PO Box 1071

Butler, PA 16001-1071

Tel: (724) 283-5741 Fax: (724) 283-2410

CEO: Fred Bruch, Pres.

HR: R. A. Imhof

Emp: 3,000

Metal reclamation and steel mill services.

Germany, India, Mexico, Netherlands, South Africa, Spain, Wales, U.K.

HECLA MINING COMPANY

6500 Mineral Drive

Coeur d'Alene, ID 83815-8788

Tel: (208) 769-4100 Fax: (208) 769-4107

CEO: Arthur Brown

HR: Jon Langstaff

Web site: www.hecla-mining.com

Emp: 1,265

Non-ferrous and industrial metals mining and manufacturing.

Mexico

HEIDRICK & STRUGGLES INC

Sears Tower, 233 South Wacker Drive

Chicago, IL 60606

Tel: (312) 496-1200 Fax: (312) 496-1290

CEO: Patrick Pittard, Pres.

FO: Gerard Clery-Melin

HR: Patty Vasquez

Web site: www.h-s.com

Emp: 1,276 Rev: $180 mil.

Executive search firm.

Argentina, Australia, Belgium, Brazil, Canada, Chile, Czech Republic, Denmark, England, U.K., Finland, France, Germany, Hong Kong, Italy, Japan, Mexico, Netherlands, Norway, Peru, Poland, Portugal, Russia, Singapore, Spain, Sweden, Switzerland, Venezuela

HEIL TRAILER INTERNATIONAL

PO Box 181100

Chattanooga, TN 37414

Tel: (423) 855-6386 Fax: (423) 855-3459

CEO: Robert Foster, Pres.

FO: Mahmood Kazi, VP Int'l.

HR: Linda Morrow

Web site: www.heiltrailer.com

Rev: $225 mil.

Mfr./sales of AP and SS tank trailers for liquid, powder, chemicals, asphalt and aircraft refuelers and modular bulk containers.

England, U.K., Thailand

HEIN-WERNER CORPORATION

PO Box 1606

Waukesha, WI 53187-1606

Tel: (414) 542-6611 Fax: (414) 542-4884

CEO: Joseph L. Dindorf, Pres.

Emp: 566

Mfr. auto body repair equipment, engine rebuilding & brake repair equipment, hydraulic cylinders.

England, U.K., France, Germany, Italy, Switzerland

H.J. HEINZ COMPANY

600 Grant Street

Pittsburgh, PA 15219

Tel: (412) 456-5700 Fax: (412) 456-6128

CEO: William R. Johnson, Pres & COO

FO: Malcolm Ritchie, EVP

HR: Gary Matson, Mgr.

Web site: www.heinz.com

Emp: 40,000 Rev: $9,209 mil.

Processed food products and nutritional services.

Australia, Belgium, Botswana, Canada, China (PRC), Ecuador, Egypt, England, U.K., France, Germany, Ghana, Greece, Hungary, India, Ireland, Italy, Ivory Coast, Japan, Netherlands, New Zealand, Poland, Portugal, Russia, South Korea, Spain, Taiwan (ROC), Thailand, Turkmenistan, Venezuela, Wales, U.K., Zimbabwe

HELLER FINANCIAL INC.

500 West Monroe Street

Chicago, IL 60661

Tel: (312) 441-7000 Fax: (312) 441-7256

CEO: Richard Almeida, Pres.

Financial services.

Australia, Chile, Czech Republic, Denmark, England, U.K., Italy, Netherlands, Poland, Singapore

HELLER, EHRMAN, WHITE & McAULIFFE

333 Bush Street, Ste. 3000

San Francisco, CA 94104-2878

Tel: (415) 772-6000 Fax: (415) 772-6268

CEO: Robert A. Rosenfeld, Chmn.

HR: David Sanders, Dir.

Web site: www.hewm.com

Emp: 1,015 Rev: $142 mil.

International law Firm.

Hong Kong, Singapore

HELMERICH & PAYNE INC

1579 East 21st Street

Tulsa, OK 74114

Tel: (918) 742-5531 Fax: (918) 743-2671

CEO: Hans Helmerich, Chmn.

HR: Todd Sprague

Emp: 1,700

Oil/gas exploration & drilling, real estate, mfr. gas

odorants.

Colombia, Ecuador, Gabon, Papua New Guinea, Trinidad & Tobago, Venezuela

HENNINGSEN FOODS, INC.

5 International Drive

Rye Brook, NY 10573

Tel: (914) 694-1000 Fax: (914) 935-0220

CEO: Gil Eckhoff, Pres.

FO: Roy N. Nevans

HR: Michael Paturzo

Emp: 300

Dehydrated egg, poultry and meat products.

England, U.K., Netherlands

HENRY VALVE COMPANY

3215 North Ave.

Melrose Park, IL 60160

Tel: (708) 344-1100 Fax: (708) 344-0026

CEO: Robert Henry, Pres.

Emp: 250

Mfr. components for commercial A/C and refrigeration systems.

Canada, Scotland, U.K.

HERCULES INC

Hercules Plaza, 1313 North Market Street

Wilmington, DE 19894-0001

Tel: (302) 594-5000 Fax: (302) 594-5400

CEO: R. Keith Elliott, Chmn.

FO: Dominick W. DiDonna, SVP

HR: John M. Bondur, VP

Web site: www.herc.com

Emp: 6,200 Rev: $1.87 bil.

Mfr. specialty chemicals, plastics, film and fibers, coatings, resins, food ingredients.

Australia, Austria, Bahamas, Belgium, Bermuda, Brazil, Canada, Chile, China (PRC), Czech Republic, Denmark, England, U.K., Finland, France, Germany, Hong Kong, India, Indonesia, Italy, Japan, Mexico, Netherlands, New Zealand, Pakistan, Philippines, Poland, Russia, Scotland, U.K., Singapore, South Korea, Spain, Sweden, Taiwan (ROC)

HERR-YOSS INDUSTRIES, INC.

PO Box 234

Pittsburgh, PA 15230

Tel: (724) 538-3180 Fax: (724) 538-0042

CEO: A. A. Fornataro

FO: A. A. Fornataro

HR: D. D. Struth

Web site: www.HerrYoss.Com

Emp: 400 Rev: $80 mil.

Design, engineer and manufacture metal finishing equipment.

England, U.K., Japan

HERSHEY FOODS CORPORATION

100 Crystal A Drive

Hershey, PA 17033

Tel: (717) 534-6799 Fax: (717) 534-6760

CEO: Kenneth L. Wolfe, Chmn.

FO: Patrice N. LeMaire, Pres. Intl.

HR: Sharon A. Lambly, VP

Web site: www.hersheys.com

Emp: 16,200 Rev: $4,302 mil.

Mfr. chocolate, food and confectionery products.

China (PRC), Germany, Italy, Japan, Russia

THE HERTZ CORPORATION

225 Brae Boulevard

Park Ridge, NJ 07656-0713

Tel: (201) 307-2000 Fax: (201) 307-2644

CEO: Frank A. Olson, Chmn.

Emp: 21,500 Rev: $3,900 mil.

Worldwide headquarters office for car rental, car leasing and equipment rental.

Belgium, England, U.K., France, Ireland, Netherlands

HETEROCHEMICAL CORPORATION

111 East Hawthorne Ave.

Valley Stream, NY 11580

Tel: (516) 561-8225 Fax: (516) 561-8413

CEO: Lynne Galler, Pres.

Chloride products and germicides, etc.

Netherlands

HEWITT ASSOCIATES LLC

100 Half Day Road

Lincolnshire, IL 60069

Tel: (847) 295-5000 Fax: (847) 295-7634

CEO: Dale L. Gifford

FO: Dan DeCanniere, COO

HR: David Wille, Dir. HR

Emp: 7,000 Rev: $708 mil.

Employee benefits consulting firm.

Argentina, Australia, Austria, Belgium, Brazil, Canada, Chile, China (PRC), Czech Republic, England, U.K., France, Germany, Hong Kong, India, Indonesia, Ireland, Italy, Japan, Mexico, Netherlands, New Zealand, Philippines, Poland, Singapore, Slovenia, Spain, Switzerland, Thailand, Venezuela

HEWLETT-PACKARD COMPANY

3000 Hanover Street

Palo Alto, CA 94304-0890

Tel: (650) 857-1501 Fax: (650) 857-7299

CEO: Lewis E. Platt, Chmn.

FO: Franz X. Nawratil, VP

HR: Susan D. Bowick, VP

Web site: www.hp.com

Emp: 121,900 Rev: $42,895 mil.

Mfr. computing, communications & measurement products & services.

Argentina, Australia, Austria, Belgium, Brazil, Canada, Chile, China (PRC), Colombia, Czech Republic, Denmark, England, U.K., Finland, France, Germany, Greece, Hong Kong, Hungary, India, Ireland, Italy, Japan, Malaysia, Mexico, Netherlands, New Zealand, Norway, Philippines, Poland, Portugal, Russia, Singapore, South Korea, Spain, Sweden, Switzerland, Taiwan (ROC), Thailand, Turkey, Ukraine, Venezuela, Vietnam

HEXCEL CORPORATION

5794 West Las Positas Blvd.

Pleasanton, CA 94588

Tel: (925) 847-9500 Fax: (925) 734-9042

CEO: John J. Lee

FO: Earl C. Vicars

HR: Jim Conzen

Emp: 2,100 Rev: $350 mil.

Honeycomb core materials, specialty chemicals, resins and epoxies.

Belgium, England, U.K., France, Japan

HICKS, MUSE, TATE & FURST INC.

200 Cresent Court, Ste. 1600

Dallas, TX 75201

Tel: (214) 740-7300 Fax: (214) 740-7313

CEO: Thomas O. Hicks, Chmn.

FO: John R. Muse, COO

Emp: 150

Investment company.

Mexico

HIGH VOLTAGE ENGINEERING COMPANY

401 Edgewater Place

Wakefield, MA 01880

Tel: (781) 224-1001 Fax: (781) 224-1001

CEO: Clifford Press, Pres.

Emp: 1,500

Holding company: industrial & scientific instruments.

England, U.K., Ireland, Netherlands

HIGHLANDS INSURANCE COMPANY

10370 Richmond Ave.

Houston, TX 77042-4123

Tel: (713) 952-9555 Fax: (713) 952-9977

CEO: Richard Haverland, Pres.

Emp: 740

Property and casualty insurance.

England, U.K.

HILLERICH & BRADSBY COMPANY INC

PO Box 35700

Louisville, KY 40232-5700

Tel: (502) 585-5226 Fax: (502) 585-1179

CEO: John A. Hillerich, III, Pres.

HR: Bill Becker

Emp: 770

Golf, baseball and softball equipment.

Canada, England, U.K., Japan

HILTON HOTELS CORPORATION

9336 Civic Center Drive

Beverly Hills, CA 90210

Tel: (310) 278-4321 Fax: (310) 205-7880

CEO: Stephen Bollenbach, Pres.

Emp: 50,000

International hotel chain: Hilton International, Vista Hotels and Hilton National Hotels.

Australia, Austria, Belgium, Brazil, Canada, China (PRC), Colombia, Cyprus, Czech Republic, Egypt, England, U.K., France, Germany, Greece, Guam, Hong Kong, Hungary, Indonesia, Israel, Italy, Japan, Kenya, Madagascar, Malaysia, Netherlands,

Nigeria, Saudi Arabia, Singapore, South Korea, Spain, Sri Lanka, Sudan, Switzerland, Taiwan (ROC), Thailand, Trinidad & Tobago, Tunisia, Turkey, United Arab Emirates, Venezuela

HLW INTERNATIONAL, LLP

115 Fifth Ave.

New York, NY 10003

Tel: (212) 353-4600 Fax: (212) 353-4666

CEO: Leevi Kiil

FO: Leevi Kiil

HR: Mary Jane Beatty

Web site: www.currently in preparation

Emp: 270 Rev: $40.3 mil.

Architecture, engineering, planning and interior design.

Belgium, China (PRC), England, U.K., Mexico

HOBART BROTHERS COMPANY

Hobart Square, 600 W Main Street

Troy, OH 45373-2928

Tel: (937) 332-4000 Fax: (937) 332-5194

CEO: William Zinno, VP

FO: I. C. Schwab

HR: R. N. White

Emp: 2,500

Mfr. arc/automatic welding systems, power systems, filler metals.

Canada, Chile, Cyprus, England, U.K., Singapore

HOCKMAN-LEWIS LTD

200 Executive Drive, Ste. 320

West Orange, NJ 07052

Tel: (973) 325-3838 Fax: (973) 325-7974

CEO: William S. Hockman, Chmn.

HR: Garrett E. Pearce, Pres.

Emp: 140

Export management.

Costa Rica, El Salvador, England, U.K., Guatemala, Singapore

HODGSON, RUSS, ANDREWS, WOODS & GOODYEAR, LLP

Ste. 1800, One M&T Plaza

Buffalo, NY 14203

Tel: (716) 856-4000 Fax: (716) 849-0349

CEO: Diane Bennett

International law firm.

Canada

HOGAN SYSTEMS INC.

5525 LBJ Freeway

Dallas, TX 75240

Tel: (972) 386-0020 Fax: (972) 386-0315

CEO: Michael H. Anderson

FO: John E. O'Malley

HR: Dan Johnson

Emp: 380

Sale/distribution integrated software.

Australia, England, U.K.

HOHENBERG BROS COMPANY

7101 Goodlett Farms Parkway

Cordova, TN 38018

Tel: (901) 937-4500 Fax: (901) 937-4464

CEO: Jim Echols, Pres.

HR: Craig Clemensen

Mfr. cotton.

Brazil

HOLIDAY INNS WORLDWIDE, INC.

3 Ravinia Drive, Ste. 2900

Atlanta, GA 30346-2149

Tel: (770) 604-2000 Fax: (770) 604-5403

CEO: Thomas Oliver

HR: Michael Rumke

Emp: 39,000

Hotels, restaurants and casinos.

Austria, Bahamas, Bahrain, Barbados, Belgium, Bermuda, Bolivia, Brazil, Canada, Dominican Republic, Egypt, France, Germany, Greece, Haiti, Honduras, Hong Kong, India, Italy, Jamaica, Japan, Jordan, Luxembourg, Malaysia, Mexico, Netherlands, Nigeria, Oman, Pakistan, Panama, Peru, Philippines, Poland, Saudi Arabia, Scotland, U.K., Singapore, Slovenia, South Africa, Spain, Sri Lanka, Switzerland, Taiwan (ROC), Thailand, Trinidad & Tobago, United Arab Emirates, Venezuela

HOLLAND & KNIGHT

400 North Ashley Dr., Ste. 2300,

Tampa, FL 33602

Tel: (813) 227-8500 Fax: (813) 229-0134

CEO: Bob Feagan

HR: Kathy Long

Web site: www.hlaw.com

Emp: 1,000 Rev: $170 mil.

International Law fir.

Mexico

HOLLINGSWORTH & VOSE COMPANY

112 Washington Street

East Walpole, MA 02032

Tel: (508) 668-0295 Fax: (508) 668-3557

CEO: Valentine Hollingsworth, III

HR: Tara Roth

Web site: www.hollingsworth-vose.com

Emp: 1,050

Mfr. technical & industrial papers & non-woven fabrics.

England, U.K., Mexico

HOLME ROBERTS & OWEN

1700 Lincoln Street, Ste. 4100

Denver, CO 80203

Tel: (303) 861-7000 Fax: (303) 866-0200

CEO: James Wadsworth, Mng. Prtn.

International law firm.

Russia

HOLMES & NARVER INC.

999 Town & Country Road

Orange, CA 92868-4786

Tel: (714) 567-2400 Fax: (714) 543-0955

CEO: Grant G. McCullagh

FO: Robert L. Murphy

HR: Jearl Joslin

Emp: 1,300

Arch/engineering, construction/construction management, O&M services.

Saudi Arabia

HOLOPHANE CORPORATION

250 East Broad Street, #1400

Columbus, OH 43215

Tel: (740) 345-9631 Fax: (740) 349-4426

CEO: John Dallepezze, Pres.

Mfr. industry, commercial, outdoor, roadway & emergency lighting fixtures; inverters, programmable controllers.

Canada, England, U.K., Mexico

THE HOME DEPOT INC.

2455 Paces Ferry Road, NW

Atlanta, GA 30339-4024

Tel: (770) 433-8211 Fax: (770) 431-2685

CEO: Arthur M. Blank, Pres

FO: Bill Peña, VP Intl.

HR: Steve Messana, SVP

Web site: www.homedepot.com

Emp: 130,000 Rev: $24,200 mil.

Home improvement warehouse-style, retail chain stores.

Canada, Chile

HOMESTAKE MINING COMPANY

650 California Street

San Francisco, CA 94108

Tel: (415) 981-8150 Fax: (415) 397-5038

CEO: Harry M. Conger, Chmn.

FO: Jack E. Thompson, Pres.

HR: Mary Schuba

Web site: www.homestake.com

Emp: 1,500 Rev: $700 mil.

Precious metal and mineral mining.

Australia, Canada, Chile

HONEYWELL INC.

PO Box 524

Minneapolis, MN 55440-0524

Tel: (612) 951-1000 Fax: (612) 951-3066

CEO: Michael R. Bonsignore, Chmn.

HR: Gary Schulke

Web site: www.honeywell.com

Emp: 50,000

Develop/mfr. controls for home and building, industry, space and aviation.

Argentina, Australia, Austria, Belgium, Brazil, Bulgaria, Canada, Chile, China (PRC), Czech Republic, Denmark, Egypt, England, U.K., Finland, France, Germany, Hong Kong, Hungary, India, Indonesia, Italy, Japan, Kuwait, Malaysia, Mexico, Netherlands, New Zealand, Norway, Oman, Poland, Portugal, Romania, Russia, Saudi Arabia, Singapore, Slovakia, South Africa, South Korea, Spain, Sweden, Switzerland, Taiwan (ROC), Thailand, Turkey, Ukraine, United Arab Emirates, Venezuela

HONEYWELL-MEASUREX DMC CORPORATION

PO Box 490

Gaithersburg, MD 20884

Tel: (301) 948-2450 Fax: (301) 670-0506

CEO: Greg Ayres, VP

FO: Brian Monti, VP Sales

HR: Walter Lachenmayr

Web site: www.honeywell.com

Emp: 210

Mfr. quality and process control gauges.

China (PRC), England, U.K., France, Germany, Singapore

HOOD SAILMAKERS INC.

23 Johnny Cake Hill

Middletown, RI 02842

Tel: (401) 849-9400 Fax: (401) 849-9700

CEO: John T. Woodhouse, III

Emp: 150

Mfr. yacht sails.

England, U.K., Ireland

HORWATH INTERNATIONAL

415 Madison Ave.

New York, NY 10017

Tel: (212) 838-5566 Fax: (212) 838-3636

CEO: Werner E. Rotach, Pres.

Emp: 7,800

Public accountants and auditors.

Argentina, Australia, Austria, Bahrain, Belgium, Bermuda, Brazil, Canada, Cayman Islands, Channel Islands, U.K., Chile, Cyprus, Czech Republic, Denmark, Dominican Republic, Egypt, England, U.K., Ethiopia, France, Germany, Greece, Guatemala, Haiti, Hong Kong, Hungary, India, Indonesia, Ireland, Israel, Italy, Jamaica, Japan, Kenya, Lebanon, Luxembourg, Malaysia, Malta, Mexico, Monaco, Morocco, Netherlands, New Zealand, Nigeria, Norway, Pakistan, Panama, Paraguay, Peru, Philippines, Portugal, Saudi Arabia, Singapore, Slovakia, South Africa, South Korea, Sri Lanka, Sweden, Switzerland, Thailand, Turkey, United Arab Emirates, Venezuela

HOSKINS MFG. COMPANY

10776 Hall Road, PO Box 218

Hamburg, MI 48139-0218

Tel: (810) 231-1900 Fax: (810) 231-4311

CEO: Jerome Reinke

FO: James Breen

HR: Larry Zak

Emp: 440

Mfr. electric resistance & specialty alloys.

Ireland

HOUGHTON INTERNATIONAL INC.

PO Box 930, Madison & Van Buren Avenues

Valley Forge, PA 19482-0930

Tel: (610) 666-4000 Fax: (610) 666-1376

CEO: William F. MacDonald, Jr.

HR: David Yoder

Emp: 1,200 Rev: $190 mil.

Mfr. specialty chemicals, hydraulic fluids & lubricants.

Australia, Brazil, Canada, China (PRC), Denmark, England, U.K., Finland, France, Hong Kong, India, Israel, Italy, Japan, Mexico, Netherlands, New Zealand, Norway, Singapore, South Africa, Sweden, Switzerland, Taiwan (ROC)

HOUSEHOLD INTERNATIONAL INC.

2700 Sanders Road

Prospect Heights, IL 60070

Tel: (847) 564-5000 Fax: (847) 205-7452

CEO: William F. Aldinger, Chmn.

FO: Lawrence N. Bangs

HR: Sue Keenan

Web site: www.household.com

Emp: 14,900 Rev: $5,503 mil

Consumer finance and credit card services

Canada, England, U.K.

HOUSTON INDUSTRIES INCORPORATED

1111 Louisiana Street

Houston, TX 77002

Tel: (713) 207-3000 Fax: (713) 207-0206

CEO: R. Steve Letbetter, Pres. & COO

FO: David H. Odorizzi, SVP

HR: Susan D. Fabre, VP

Web site: www.houind.com

Emp: 12,000 Rev: $6,000 mil.

Provides gas and electric services.

Argentina, Brazil, Colombia, India, Mexico

HOWDEN FAN COMPANY

PO Box 985

Buffalo, NY 14240

Tel: (716) 847-5121 Fax: (716) 847-5180

CEO: Tom Graziano, Pres.

FO: Linda M. Neureuter

HR: Robert Pfile

Emp: 1,350

Mfr. fans and air-handling units.

Canada, Mexico

HOWMEDICA INC.

359 Veterans Boulevard

Rutherford, NJ 07070

Tel: (201) 507-7300 Fax: (201) 935-4873

CEO: Jack O'Mahony, Pres.

Web site: www.howmedica.com

Emp: 2,000

Hospital, medical and dental supplies.

Australia, Austria, Belgium, Brazil, Canada, China (PRC), Denmark, England, U.K., Finland, France, Germany, Greece, Hong Kong, India, Indonesia, Ireland, Italy, Japan, Malaysia, Mexico, Netherlands, New Zealand, Norway, Pakistan, South Africa, South Korea, Spain, Sweden, Switzerland, Taiwan (ROC)

HOWMET CORPORATION

475 Steamboat Road, PO Box 1960

Greenwich, CT 06836-1960

Tel: (203) 661-4600 Fax: (203) 661-1134

CEO: David L. Squier

FO: Mark Lasker

HR: Mike Malady

Web site: www.howmet.com

Emp: 10,250

Mfr. precision investment castings, alloys, engineering and refurbishment.

Canada, England, U.K., France, Italy, Japan

HUBBARD FARMS INC.

PO Box 415

Walpole, NH 03431

Tel: (603) 756-3311 Fax: (603) 756-9034

CEO: John Gascoyne, Pres.

FO: Juan Solis

Emp: 800

Poultry breeding R&D, poultry foundation breeding stock.

England, U.K., Netherlands, Taiwan (ROC)

HUBBELL CORPORATION

584 Derby-Milford Road

Orange, CT 06477

Tel: (203) 799-4100 Fax: (203) 799-4208

CEO: G. Ratcliffe, Pres.

FO:

HR: George Zurman, VP

Emp: 5,860

Electrical wiring components.

England, U.K.

J.M. HUBER CORPORATION

333 Thornall Street

Edison, NJ 08818

Tel: (732) 549-8600 Fax: (732) 549-2239

CEO:

HR: Sharon Fruges

Web site: www.huber.com

Emp: 2,200

Crude oil, gas, carbon black, kaolin clay, rubber and paper pigments, timber and minerals.

Scotland, U.K., Singapore, Sweden, Venezuela

HUCK INTERNATIONAL INC.

3724 East Columbia Street

Tucson, AZ 85714-3415

Tel: (520) 747-9898 Fax: (520) 519-7440

CEO: Bruce Zorrich, Pres.

FO: Robert S. Levine

HR: Sandra Bailey

Emp: 1,100 Rev: $333 mil.

Mfr. aerospace fasteners.

Australia, Canada, England, U.K., France, Germany, Japan, Mexico, Singapore, Taiwan (ROC)

HUGHES ELECTRONICS

200 N. Sepulveda Blvd., PO Box 956

El Segundo, CA 90245-0956

Tel: (310) 662-9821 Fax: (310) 647-6213

CEO: Michael T. Smith

FO: Gareth C. C. Chang

HR: Sandra L. Sarrison

Emp: 15,000 Rev: $5,100 mil.

Mfr. electronics equipment and systems.

Belgium, Brazil, China (PRC), Indonesia, Japan, Mexico, Singapore, United Arab Emirates

HUGHES HUBBARD & REED LLP

One Battery Park Plaza

New York, NY 10004-1482
Tel: (212) 837-6000 Fax: (212) 422-4726
CEO: Charles H. Scherer, Mng. Ptnr.
FO: Alex H. Baum
HR: Joann M. Byrne
Web site: www.hugheshubbard.com
Emp: 815 Rev: $101 mil.
International law firm.
France

HUMPHREY PRODUCTS COMPANY
PO Box 2008
Kalamazoo, MI 49003
Tel: (616) 381-5500 Fax: (616) 381-4113
CEO: Randall M. Webber, Chmn.
FO: Robert A. Kirk
HR: Patrick Aldworth
Emp: 390
Mfr./sale/services pneumatic actuators & valves for factory automation, motion control, etc.
Canada

HUNKAR LABORATORIES INC.
7007 Valley Ave.
Cincinnati, OH 45244
Tel: (513) 272-0013 Fax:
CEO: Eric R. Thiemann
FO: Nicholas J. Hunkar
HR: Betty Meranda
Web site: www.hunkar.com
Process equipment for plastics industry.
England, U.K.

HUNT INTERNATIONAL COMPANY
2005 Market Street
Philadelphia, PA 19103
Tel: (215) 656-0300 Fax: (215) 656-3700
CEO: Don Thompson, Pres.
Emp: 2,100
Mfr. office supplies, arts and craft products and computer accessories.
Canada, England, U.K., Germany

HUNT OIL COMPANY
1445 Ross at Field
Dallas, TX 75202
Tel: (214) 978-8000 Fax: (214) 978-8888
CEO: Gary Hurford, Pres.
HR: Dick Ulrich
Petroleum exploration and production.
Canada, Yemen

HUNT SCREW & MFG. COMPANY
4117 North Kilpatrick Ave.
Chicago, IL 60641
Tel: (773) 283-6900 Fax: (773) 283-6068
CEO: Joseph Varey, Pres.
Emp: 76
Machine parts and components.
Ireland

HUNTON & WILLIAMS
951 East Byrd Street, East Tower
Richmond, VA 23219-4074
Tel: (804) 788-8200 Fax: (804) 788-8218
CEO: Thurston R. Moore, Mng. Prtn.
FO: John H. Wilson
HR: Barry D. Koval
Web site: www.hunton.com
Emp: 1,378 Rev: $220 mil.
Law firm.
Belgium, Hong Kong, Poland, Thailand

HUNTSMAN CORPORATION
500 Huntsman Way
Salt Lake City, UT 84108
Tel: (801) 532-5200 Fax: (801) 536-1581
CEO: Jon M. Huntsman, Chmn.
FO: Thomas H. Wood
HR: William Chapman
Emp: 9,500
Mfr./sales specialty chemicals, industrial chemicals and petrochemicals.
Australia, Belgium, Brazil, Canada, England, U.K., Germany, Mexico, Singapore, United Arab Emirates, Venezuela

HUSSMAN CORPORATION
12999 St. Charles Rock Road
Bridgeton, MO 63044
Tel: (314) 291-2000 Fax: (314) 291-5144
CEO: J. Larry Vowell, Pres.
HR: Janice Maple
Emp: 7,000

Mfr. refrigeration and environmental control systems for food industrial.

Canada

HUTCHINSON TECHNOLOGY INC.

40 West Highland Park

Hutchinson, MN 55350-9784

Tel: (320) 587-1900 Fax: (320) 587-1892

CEO: Wayne M. Fortun, Chmn.

HR: Rebecca A. Albrecht

Emp: 4,800

Mfr. suspension assembly components for rigid disk drives.

Netherlands, Singapore

HYATT INTERNATIONAL CORPORATION

200 West Madison Street

Chicago, IL 60606

Tel: (312) 750-1234 Fax: (312) 750-8578

CEO: Douglas G. Geoga, Pres.

FO: Tom O'Toole, VP

HR: Linda Olson, SVP

Web site: www.hyatt.com

Emp: 90,000 Rev: $3,400 mil.

International hotel management.

Argentina, Aruba, Australia, Azerbaijan, Canada, Cayman Islands, Chile, England, U.K., France, Germany, Guam, Guatemala, Hong Kong, Hungary, Indonesia, Japan, Jordan, Kazakhstan, Malaysia, Mexico, New Zealand, Philippines, Spain, Thailand, Yugoslavia

HYDE SPRING & WIRE COMPANY

14341 Schaefer Highway

Detroit, MI 48227

Tel: (313) 272-2201 Fax: (313) 272-2242

CEO: John Hyde, Pres.

Mfr. coil springs and wire.

Canada

HYDRIL COMPANY

3300 North Sam Houston Pkwy. East

Houston, TX 77032

Tel: (281) 449-2000 Fax: (281) 985-3295

CEO: Richard C. Seaver, Chmn.

HR: Michael Sanford, VP

Emp: 1,400

Oil field machinery, equipment and rubber goods.

Canada

I

IBM CORPORATION

New Orchard Road

Armonk, NY 10504

Tel: (914) 765-1900 Fax: (914) 765-7382

CEO: Louis V. Gerstner, Jr., Chmn.

FO: Samuel Palmisano, SVP

HR: J. Thomas Bouchard, SVP

Web site: www.ibm.com

Emp: 225,000269 Rev: $78,508 mil.

Information products, technology & services.

Albania, Angola, Argentina, Australia, Austria, Azerbaijan, Bahamas, Bahrain, Bangladesh, Belgium, Bermuda, Bolivia, Bosnia-Herzegovina, Botswana, Brazil, Brunei, Bulgaria, Canada, Chile, China (PRC), Colombia, Costa Rica, Croatia, Cyprus, Czech Republic, Dem. Rep. of Congo, Denmark, Ecuador, Egypt, England, U.K., Ethiopia, Finland, France, French Antilles, French Guiana, Germany, Greece, Guatemala, Guyana, Honduras, Hong Kong, Hungary, Iceland, India, Indonesia, Ireland, Israel, Italy, Japan, Jordan, Kenya, Kuwait, Latvia, Liberia, Macau, Macedonia, Malawi, Malaysia, Malta, Mexico, Morocco, Namibia, Netherlands, New Caledonia, New Zealand, Norway, Oman, Pakistan, Panama, Paraguay, Peru, Philippines, Poland, Portugal, Qatar, Romania, Russia, Senegal, Sierra Leone, Singapore, Slovakia, Slovenia, South Africa, South Korea, Spain, Sri Lanka, Sudan, Sweden, Switzerland, Taiwan (ROC), Thailand, Tunisia, Turkey, Turkmenistan, Ukraine, United Arab Emirates, Uruguay, Uzbekistan, Venezuela, Vietnam, Yemen, Yugoslavia, Zambia, Zimbabwe

IBP INC.

PO Box 515

Dakota City, NE 68731

Tel: (402) 494-2061 Fax: (402) 241-2068

CEO: Robert L. Peterson, Chmn.

FO: Richard L. Bond, COO

HR: Richard H. Jochum

Web site: www.ibpinc.com

Emp: 38,000 Rev: $13,259 mil.

Produce beef and pork, hides and associated products, animal feeds, pharmaceuticals.

Canada, China (PRC), England, U.K., Ireland, Japan, Mexico, South Korea, Taiwan (ROC)

ICC INDUSTRIES INC.

460 Park Ave.

New York, NY 10022

Tel: (212) 521-1700 Fax: (212) 521-1794

CEO: Dr. John J. Farber, Chmn.

HR: Frances Foti

Web site: www.iccchem.com

Emp: 450

Manufacturing and trading of chemicals, plastics and pharmaceuticals.

Belgium, China (PRC), England, U.K., France, Hong Kong, Isle of Man, Israel, Italy, Japan, Netherlands, Romania, Russia, Singapore, Switzerland

ICF KAISER INTERNATIONAL INC.

9300 Lee Highway

Fairfax, VA 22031

Tel: (703) 934-3600 Fax: (703) 934-9740

CEO: James O. Edwards, Chmn.

FO: Ralph Praccio

HR: Marcy Romm

Emp: 5,700

Engineering, construction & consulting services.

Australia, England, U.K., France, Mexico, Portugal, Russia, Taiwan (ROC)

ICN PHARMACEUTICALS, INC.

3300 Hyland Ave.

Costa Mesa, CA 92626

Tel: (714) 545-0100 Fax: (714) 641-7268

CEO: M. Panic & A. Jerney, Pres.

HR: Jack Sholl

Emp: 18,000

Mfr./distribute pharmaceuticals.

Russia

ICORE INTERNATIONAL INC.

180 North Wolfe Road

Sunnyvale, CA 94086

Tel: (408) 732-5400 Fax: (408) 720-8507

CEO: Tess Fagnant, EVP

Emp: 100

Harness and conduit systems, battery connectors, etc.

Germany

ICP

1815 West County Road 54

Tiffin, OH 44883

Tel: (419) 447-6216 Fax: (419) 447-1878

CEO: Dick Sandilands, EVP

FO: Neil Holloway

Emp: 64

Magazines/directories for computer software marketing.

England, U.K.

ICS INTERNATIONAL INC

125 Oak Street

Scranton, PA 18515

Tel: (717) 342-7701 Fax: (717) 343-0560

CEO: Robert V. Antonucci, Pres.

Emp: 600

Correspondence courses.

Australia, Canada, New Zealand, Philippines, Scotland, U.K., Singapore

IDEAL TAPE COMPANY

1400 Middlesex Street

Lowell, MA 01851

Tel: (978) 458-6833 Fax: (978) 458-0302

CEO: Dennis Burns, GM

HR: Bonnie Posnak, VP

Emp: 101

Pressure sensitive tapes.

Belgium

IDEX CORPORATION

630 Dundee Road, Ste. 400

Northbrook, IL 60062

Tel: (847) 498-7070 Fax: (847) 498-3940

CEO: Donald N. Boyce, Chmn.

FO: Frank J. Hansen, Pres.

HR: Jerry N. Derck, VP

Emp: 4,000 Rev: $487 mil.

Mfr. industrial pumps, lubrication systems, metal fabrication equipment, bending and clamping devices.

Australia, England, U.K., Ireland, Netherlands, Singapore

IHS (INFORMATION HANDLING SERVICES)

15 Inverness Way East

Englewood, CO 80112

Tel: (303) 397-2300 Fax: (303) 397-2633

CEO: Michael J. Timbers, Pres.

FO: Robert Wing

HR: Alice Di Fraia

Web site: www.his.com

Emp: 2,300

Leading provider of tecnical engineering information

England, U.K.

IKG INDUSTRIES

270 Terminal Ave.

Clark, NJ 07066

Tel: (732) 815-9500 Fax: (908) 815-9557

CEO: Jim Mitchell, Pres.

FO: J. R. Chwalek

HR: Laura Daubner

Emp: 750

Mfr. metal gratings.

Mexico

IKON OFFICE SOLUTIONS

70 Valley Stream Parkway

Malvern, PA 19355

Tel: (610) 296-8000 Fax: (610) 408-7022

CEO: John E. Stuart

FO: Jim Forese

HR: Beth Sexton

Web site: www.ikon.com

Emp: 40,000

Provider of office technology solutions.

Canada, Denmark, England, U.K., Germany, Mexico, Switzerland

ILC TECHNOLOGY INC.

399 Java Drive

Sunnyvale, CA 94089

Tel: (408) 745-7900 Fax: (408) 744-0829

CEO: Henry Baumgartner

FO: John Lucero

HR: Ron Fredianelli

Web site: www.ilct.com

Emp: 350

Mfr. specialty light sources for medical, industrial and scientific applications.

England, U.K.

ILLINOIS TOOL WORKS (ITW)

3600 West Lake Ave.

Glenview, IL 60025-5811

Tel: (847) 724-7500 Fax: (847) 657-4268

CEO: W. James Farrell, Pres.

HR: R. McCarthy

Emp: 20,000 Rev: $3,000 mil.

Mfr. gears, tools, fasteners, sealants, plastic and metal components for industrial, medical, etc.

Australia, Brazil, Canada, England, U.K., France, Germany, Ireland, Italy, Japan, Mexico, New Zealand, Spain, Taiwan (ROC), Venezuela

ILSCO CORPORATION

4730 Madison Road

Cincinnati, OH 45227-1426

Tel: (513) 533-6200 Fax: (513) 871-4084

CEO: David FitzGibbon

FO: Kim Wanamaker

HR: William Edwards

Emp: 800

Mfr. electrical connectors.

Canada

IMATION CORPORATION

1 Imation Place

Oakdale, MN 55128

Tel: (612) 704-4000 Fax: (612) 537-4675

CEO: William T. Monahan, Chmn.

Dry laser-imaging film systems.

Germany, Italy

IMC GLOBAL

2345 Waukegan Road, Ste. E-200

Bannockburn, IL 60015-5516

Tel: (847) 607-3000 Fax: (847) 607-3404

CEO: Robert E. Fowler

Emp: 1,800

Mfr. garden, nursery, farm supplies and fertilizers.

Canada

IMO INDUSTRIES INC.

9211 Forest Hill Ave.

Richmond, VA 23235

Tel: (804) 560-4070 Fax: (804) 560-4076

CEO: Phil Knisily, Pres.

HR: David C. Christensen

Mfr./support mechanical and electronic controls, engineered power products.

Australia, England, U.K., France, Germany, Italy, Japan, Singapore, Spain, Sweden, Switzerland

IMODCO INC.

27001 Agoura Road, #350

Calabasas Hills, CA 91301-5359

Tel: (818) 880-0300 Fax: (818) 880-0333

CEO: Louis H. Smulders

FO: Howard Kaplan

HR: Karen Abrams

Emp: 73

Turnkey supplier/contractor for offshore mooring systems for trading tankers, FSO's and FPSO's.

Singapore

IMPERIAL TOY CORPORATION

2060 East Seventh Street

Los Angeles, CA 90021

Tel: (213) 489-2100 Fax: (213) 489-4467

CEO: Fred Kort, Pres.

Emp: 100

Mfr. plastic toys and novelties.

Hong Kong

IMS INTERNATIONAL INC.

100 Campus Road

Totowa, NJ 07512

Tel: (973) 790-0700 Fax: (973) 956-5544

CEO: Lars H. Ericson

FO: Karl Adam

Emp: 2,500

Market research reports.

Australia, Germany, Italy, Japan, Netherlands, Spain, Switzerland, United Arab Emirates

InaCom CORPORATION

10810 Farnam Drive

Omaha, NE 68154

Tel: (402) 392-3900 Fax: (402) 392-3602

CEO: Bill L. Fairfield, Pres.

FO: Cris Freiwald, Pres. Int'l Div.

HR: Patti Honz, Dir. HR

Web site: www.inacom.com

Emp: 4,200 Rev: $3,896 mil.

Provider of technology management products and services; reselling microcomputer systems, work stations and networking and telecommunications equipment.

Brazil, Canada, Colombia, Ecuador, Mexico, Venezuela

INDEL-DAVIS INC.

4401 S. Jackson Ave.

Tulsa, OK 74107

Tel: (918) 587-2151 Fax: (918) 446-1583

CEO: C. O. Vogt, Pres.

FO: Dan Moore, VP

HR: Karen East

Emp: 130

Mfr. exploration supplies to seismic industrial.

Singapore

INDUCTOTHERM CORPORATION

10 Indel Ave., PO Box 157

Rancocas, NJ 08073-0157

Tel: (609) 267-9000 Fax: (609) 267-3537

CEO: John H. Mortimer, Pres.

FO: Bernard Raffner

HR: David Braddock, VP

Emp: 1,000

Mfr. induction melting furnaces.

Australia, Belgium, Brazil, England, U.K., France, Germany, India, Japan, Mexico, South Korea, Taiwan (ROC), Turkey

INDUSTRIAL ACOUSTICS COMPANY

1160 Commerce Ave.

Bronx, NY 10462

Tel: (718) 931-8000 Fax: (718) 863-1138

CEO: Martin Hirschorn, Chmn.

FO: John M. Handley

HR: Ray Svana

Emp: 800

Design/mfr. acoustic structures for sound conditioning and noise control.

England, U.K., Germany, Hong Kong

INFONET SERVICES CORPORATION

2100 East Grand Ave.

El Segundo, CA 90245

Tel: (310) 335-2600 Fax: (310) 335-4507

CEO: José Collanzo

Web site: www.infonet.com

Emp: 1,500 Rev: $250 mil.

Provider of Internet services and electronic messaging services.

Argentina, Australia, Austria, Belgium, Bolivia, Brazil, Canada, Chile, China (PRC), Colombia, Costa Rica, Czech Republic, Denmark, Dominican Republic, Ecuador, Egypt, England, U.K., Finland, France, Germany, Greece, Hong Kong, Hungary, Indonesia, Ireland, Israel, Italy, Japan, Luxembourg, Malaysia, Mexico, Netherlands, Norway, Peru, Philippines, Portugal, Russia, Singapore, South Africa, South Korea, Spain, Sri Lanka, Sweden, Switzerland, Taiwan (ROC), Thailand, Turkey, Venezuela

INFORMATION BUILDERS INC.

1250 Broadway

New York, NY 10001

Tel: (212) 736-4433 Fax: (212) 643-8105

CEO: Gerald D. Cohen, Pres.

FO: Bruce J. Wilson

Emp: 2,400

Develop/mfr./services computer software.

Australia, Belgium, England, U.K., France, Germany, Netherlands, Spain, Switzerland

INFORMATION MANAGEMENT RESOURCES, INC.

26750 us Highway. 19 North, Ste. 500

Clearwater, FL 33761

Tel: (727) 797-7080 Fax: (727) 791-8152

CEO: Satish K. Sanan, Chmn.

FO: John R. Hindman, COO

Web site: www.imr.com

Emp: 1,535 Rev: $84 mil.

Provides application software and outsourcing services to business.

Australia, Canada, England, U.K., France, India, Northern Ireland, U.K.

INFORMATION RESOURCES, INC.

150 N. Clinton St.

Chicago, IL 60661

Tel: (312) 726-1221 Fax: (312) 726-0360

CEO: Gian M. Fulgoni

FO: Randall S. Smith, Pres.

HR: Gary Newman, SVP

Web site: www.infores.com

Emp: 6,800 Rev: $460 mil.

Provides bar code scanner services for retail sales organizations; processes, analyzes and sells data from the huge database created from these services.

Argentina, Australia, Canada, Cyprus, England, U.K., France, Germany, Greece, Guatemala, India, Italy, Japan, Mexico, Netherlands, New Zealand, Peru, Poland, Sweden, Taiwan (ROC), Turkey, Venezuela

INFORMIX CORPORATION

4100 Bohannon Drive

Menlo Park, CA 95025

Tel: (650) 926-6300 Fax: (650) 926-6593

CEO: Robert J. Finocchio Jr., Chmn. & Pres.

FO: Richaed S. Snook, VP

HR: Susan Daniel, VP

Web site: www.informix.com

Emp: 3,500 Rev: $660 mil.

Designs & produces database management software, connectivity interfaces & gateways, and other computer applications.

Argentina, Australia, Austria, Belgium, Bolivia, Brazil, Canada, Chile, China (PRC), Colombia, Czech Republic, Denmark, England, U.K., France, Germany, Hong Kong, India, Ireland, Italy, Japan, Kazakhstan, Malaysia, Mexico, Netherlands, New Zealand, Norway, Peru, Philippines, Poland, Portugal, Russia, Singapore, Slovakia, South Africa, South Korea, Spain, Sweden, Switzerland, Taiwan (ROC), Thailand, Ukraine, United Arab Emirates, Venezuela

INGERSOLL MILLING MACHINE CO. INC.

707 Fulton Ave.

Rockford, IL 61103

Tel: (815) 987-6000 Fax: (815) 987-6725

CEO: Fred C. Wilson, Pres.

Emp: 2,500 Rev: $370 mil.

Automated production systems.

Brazil, France, Germany, Italy, Japan

INGERSOLL-RAND COMPANY

200 Chestnut Ridge Road

Woodcliff Lake, NJ 07675

Tel: (201) 573-0123 Fax: (201) 573-3172

CEO: James E. Perrella, Chmn.

FO: Paul L. Bergren, EVP

HR: Donald H. Rice, VP

Web site: www.ingersoll-rand.com

Emp: 46,600 Rev: $7,103 mil.

Mfr. compressors, rock drills, pumps, air tools, door hardware, ball bearings.

Australia, Austria, Belgium, Brazil, Canada, Chile, China (PRC), Colombia, England, U.K., France, Germany, Hong Kong, India, Ireland, Italy, Japan, Mexico, Netherlands, New Zealand, Norway, Philippines, Poland, Russia, Singapore, South Africa, Spain, Sweden, Switzerland, Taiwan (ROC), Venezuela

INGRAM MICRO INC.

PO Box 25125

Santa Ana, CA 92799

Tel: (714) 566-1000 Fax: (714) 566-7940

CEO: Jerre L. Stead, Chmn.

FO: Jeffrey Rodek, Pres. Intl.

HR: Dave Finley, SVP

Web site: www.ingrammicro.com

Emp: 12,000 Rev: $190.0 mil

Distribute computer systems, software and related products.

Argentina, Australia, Belgium, Canada, Denmark, Ecuador, England, U.K., France, Germany, Italy, Japan, Malaysia, Mexico, Netherlands, Norway, Singapore, Spain, Sweden

INLAND STEEL INDUSTRIES, INC.

30 West Monroe Street

Chicago, IL 60603

Tel: (312) 346-0300 Fax: (312) 899-3197

CEO: Robert J. Darnall, Pres. & Chmn.

FO: Franklyn H. Beal, Pres. Int'l.

HR: Morgan J. Burke, VP

Web site: www.inland.com

Emp: 8,500

Holding company for steel products.

China (PRC), Hong Kong, India, Mexico

INSTEEL INDUSTRIES INC.

1373 Boggs Drive

Mt. Airy, NC 27030

Tel: (336) 786-2141 Fax: (336) 786-2144

CEO: Howard O. Woltz, III, Chmn.

HR: Richard Starr

Emp: 1,013

Mfr. wire products.

Mexico

INSTINET

875 Third Ave.

New York, NY 10022

Tel: (212) 310-9500 Fax: (212) 832-5183

CEO: Luis Restrepo, Mgr.

Investment and brokerage.

Canada, England, U.K., France, Germany, Hong Kong, Japan, Switzerland

INSTRON CORPORATION

100 Royall Street

Canton, MA 02021-1089

Tel: (781) 828-2500 Fax: (781) 575-5751

CEO: James M. McConnell, Pres.

FO: Arthur Hindman, VP

HR: Jonathan Burr

Emp: 1,000 Rev: $125 mil.

Mfr. material testing instruments.

Argentina, Australia, Belgium, Brazil, Canada, China (PRC), England, U.K., France, Germany, Italy, Japan, South Korea, Spain, Sweden

INSTRUMENT SYSTEMS CORPORATION

100 Jericho Quadrangle

Jericho, NY 11753

Tel: (516) 938-5544 Fax: (516) 938-5564

CEO: Robert Balemian

Emp: 2,000

Electronic products, communications systems.

Canada

INSUL-8 CORPORATION

1417 Industrial Pkwy.

Harlan, IA 51537-2351

Tel: (712) 755-3050 Fax: (712) 755-3979

CEO: Lon Miller, Pres.

HR: Rogeen Smith

Emp: 70

Mfr. mobile electrification products; conductor bar & festoon equipment.

Australia, Canada, England, U.K.

INTEGRATED SILICON SOLUTION, INC.

2231 Lawson Lane

Santa Clara, CA 95054-3311

Tel: (408) 588-0800 Fax: (408) 588-0805

CEO: Jimmy S.M. Lee, Chmn.

FO: Kong-Yeu Han, EVP

HR: Ruth Hewson, Dir.

Web site: www.issiusa.com

Emp: 450 Rev: $108 mil.

Mfr. high-speed memory chips and RAMs.

China (PRC), Germany, Hong Kong, Japan, South Korea, Taiwan (ROC)

INTEGRATED SYSTEMS, INC.

201 Moffett Park Drive

Sunnyvale, CA 94089

Tel: (408) 542-1500 Fax: (408) 542-1950

CEO: David P. St. Charles, Pres.

FO: Karen D. Auerbach, VP

HR: Janice Waterman, VP

Web site: www.isi.com

Emp: 584 Rev: $121 mil.

Develops and markets computer software products and services.

Canada, England, U.K., Finland, France, Germany, India, Israel, Italy, Japan, South Korea, Sweden

INTEL CORPORATION

Robert Noyce Building, 2200 Mission College Blvd.

Santa Clara, CA 95052-8119

Tel: (408) 765-8080 Fax: (408) 765-1739

CEO: Andrew S. Grove, Chmn.

FO: Craig R. Barrett, Pres.

HR: Patricia Murray, V.P.

Web site: www.intel.com

Rev: $25,070 mil

Mfr. semiconductor, microprocessor and micro-communications components and systems.

Australia, Brazil, China (PRC), Denmark, England, U.K., France, Germany, Hong Kong, Israel, Italy, Japan, Netherlands, Russia, Singapore

INTELLI QUEST INFORMATION GROUP, INC.

1250 Cap[ital Texas Hwy., Bldg. 1, Ste. 600

Austin, TX 78746

Tel: (512) 329-0808 Fax: (512) 329-0888

CEO: Peter Zandan, Chmn.

FO: Brian Sharples, Pres.

HR: Bobbi Garrison, Dir.

Web site: www.intelliquest.com

Emp: 400 Rev: $36.5 mil.

Marketing research consultant to technology companies.

England, U.K.

INTER-CONTINENTAL HOTELS

1120 Ave. of the Americas

New York, NY 10036

Tel: (212) 852-6400 Fax: (212) 852-6494

CEO: J. P. Kuhlman, Chmn.

Web site: www.interconti.com

Worldwide hotel and resort accommodations.

Argentina, Australia, Austria, Belgium, Brazil, Canada, China (PRC), Colombia, Czech Republic, Dominican Republic, Egypt, El Salvador, England, U.K., Finland, France, Gabon, Germany, Greece, Honduras, Hong Kong, Hungary, India, Indonesia, Israel, Italy, Japan, Jordan, Kenya, Malaysia, Malta, Mexico, Netherlands, Nicaragua, Panama, Philippines, Russia, Saudi Arabia, Scotland, U.K., Singapore, South Africa, South Korea, Spain, Sri Lanka, Sweden, Switzerland, Turkey, Ukraine, Venezuela, Zimbabwe

INTER-TEL INC.

7300 W. Boston Street

Chandler, AZ 85226

Tel: (602) 961-9000 Fax: (602) 961-1370

CEO: Steven G. Mihaylo

HR: Ellen Munoz

Emp: 500

Design/mfr. business communications systems.

England, U.K., Japan

INTERCONEX, INC.

55 Hunter Lane

Elmsford, NY 10523-1317

Tel: (914) 347-6600 Fax: (914) 347-0129

CEO: Monika Adee, Pres.

Emp: 160

Freight forwarding.

China (PRC), England, U.K., Hong Kong, Singapore

INTERGEN (INTERNATIONAL GENERATING CO., LTD.)

One Bowdoin Square, 5th Fl.
Boston, MA 02114
Tel: (617) 747-1777 Fax: (617) 747-1778
CEO: Carlos Riva, Pres.

Global power and fuel asset development company; develops/owns/operates electric power plants and related distribution facilities.

England, U.K., Hong Kong

INTERGRAPH CORPORATION

One Madison Industrial Park
Huntsville, AL 35894-0001
Tel: (205) 730-2000 Fax: (205) 730-7898
CEO: James W. Meadlock, Chrmn.
FO: Manfred Wittler, EVP
HR: Milford B. French, VP
Web site: www.intergraph.com
Emp: 7,700 Rev: $1,124 mil.

Develop/mfr. interactive computer graphic systems.

Australia, Austria, Bahrain, Belgium, Brazil, Canada, China (PRC), Czech Republic, Denmark, Egypt, England, U.K., Finland, France, Germany, Greece, Hong Kong, Hungary, India, Indonesia, Ireland, Israel, Italy, Japan, Kuwait, Lebanon, Malaysia, Mexico, Netherlands, New Zealand, Norway, Oman, Pakistan, Poland, Portugal, Romania, Russia, Saudi Arabia, Singapore, South Korea, Spain, Sweden, Switzerland, Taiwan (ROC), Thailand, Turkey, United Arab Emirates, Venezuela, Vietnam

INTERIM SERVICES INC.

2050 Spectrum Boulevard
Fort Lauderdale, FL 33309
Tel: (954) 938-7600 Fax: (954) 938-7666
CEO: Raymond Marcy, Chmn. & Pres.
FO: Ronald de Heer, EVP Europe
HR: Robert Morgan, VP
Web site: www.interim.com
Emp: 400,000 Rev: $1,600.0 mil.

Provides temporary personnel placement and staffing.

Australia, Canada, England, U.K., France, Germany, Hong Kong, Italy, Netherlands, New Zealand, Scotland, U.K., Singapore, Spain

INTERMAGNETICS GENERAL CORPORATION

450 Old Niskayuna Road, PO Box 461
Latham, NY 12110-0461
Tel: (518) 782-1122 Fax: (518) 783-2601
CEO: Carl H. Rosner, Pres.
HR: Myron E. Leach
Emp: 490

Design/mfr. superconductive magnets, magnetic systems & conductors, cryogenic products, refrigerants.

England, U.K., France

INTERMEC TECHNOLOGIES CORPORATION

6001 36th Ave. West, PO Box 4280
Everett, WA 98203-9280
Tel: (425) 348-2600 Fax: (425) 355-9551
CEO: Michael Ohanian, President
FO: John Roberts
HR: Dan Kruger
Web site: www.intermec.com
Emp: 3,100 Rev: $636 mil.

Mfr./distributor automated data collection systems.

Australia, Austria, Belgium, Brazil, Canada, Chile, Cyprus, Denmark, England, U.K., Finland, France, Germany, Greece, Guatemala, Hong Kong, Hungary, Iceland, Ireland, Israel, Italy, Japan, Mexico, Netherlands, New Zealand, Norway, Singapore, South Africa, South Korea, Spain, Sweden, Switzerland, Taiwan (ROC), Thailand, Turkey, Yugoslavia

INTERMETRICS INC.

23 Fourth Ave.
Burlington, MA 01803-3303
Tel: (781) 221-6990 Fax: (781) 221-6991
CEO: Michael Alexander, Pres.
Emp: 590

Software & systems engineering services.

Japan

INTERMETRO INDUSTRIES CORPORATION

651 N. Washington Street
Wilkes-Barre, PA 18705
Tel: (717) 825-2741 Fax: (717) 823-0250
CEO: John G. Nackley, Chmn.
HR: Tom Dimmick

Mfr. storage/material handling products.

Canada

INTERNATIONAL CLOSEOUT EXCHANGE SYSTEMS INC.

220 W. 19th Street, #1200

New York, NY 10011

Tel: (212) 647-8901 Fax: (212) 647-8900

CEO: Henry Kauftheil, Pres.

FO: Sam Mizrahi

HR: Jerry Neeman

Emp: 37

Online service listing off-price merchandise.

England, U.K., Hong Kong, South Korea

INTERNATIONAL COMPONENTS CORPORATION

420 N. May Street

Chicago, IL 60622

Tel: (312) 829-2525 Fax: (312) 829-0213

CEO: James Gaza

FO: Stuart Oakes

HR: Mary Marshall

Emp: 930

Mfr./sale/services portable DC battery chargers.

Brazil, England, U.K., Germany, Hong Kong, India, Japan, Singapore, Sweden

INTERNATIONAL DAIRY QUEEN INC.

PO Box 39286

Minneapolis, MN 55439-0286

Tel: (612) 830-0200 Fax: (612) 830-0270

CEO: Michael P. Sullivan, Pres.

FO: Gil Stemmerman

HR: Signe Pagel

Emp: 400

Mfr./sales fast foods and treats.

Canada

INTERNATIONAL DIESEL ELECTRIC CO., INC.

100 Midland Ave.

Middletown, NY 10940

Tel: (914) 342-3994 Fax: (914) 342-4905

CEO: Mr. Rohr, Pres.

Engine generating equipment.

Israel

INTERNATIONAL ELECTRONICS INC.

427 Turnpike Street

Canton, MA 02021

Tel: (781) 821-5566 Fax: (781) 821-4443

CEO: John Waldstein, Chmn.

FO: Robin Hatherell, Dir.

Web site: www.ieib.com

Manufacture security devices.

Colombia, England, U.K.

INTERNATIONAL FILLER CORPORATION

50 Bridge Street

North Tonawanda, NY 14120

Tel: (716) 693-4040 Fax: (716) 693-3528

CEO: John F. Pond, Pres.

FO: John F. Pond

Web site: www.internationalfiller.com

Mfr. of powdered cellulose, cotton flock, synthetic clock, and sisal fibers.

Belgium, Canada

INTERNATIONAL FLAVORS & FRAGRANCES INC.

521 West 57th Street

New York, NY 10019-2960

Tel: (212) 765-5500 Fax: (212) 708-7132

CEO: Eugene P. Grisanti, Chmn. & Pres.

FO: David G. Bluestein

HR: Eric Campbell

Web site: www.iff.com

Emp: 4,639 Rev: $1,426.8 mil.

Design/mfr. flavors, fragrances & aroma chemicals.

Argentina, Australia, Brazil, Canada, Chile, China (PRC), Colombia, Egypt, England, U.K., France, Germany, Hong Kong, Hungary, Indonesia, Ireland, Italy, Japan, Kenya, Mexico, Netherlands, Norway, Philippines, Portugal, Singapore, South Africa, South Korea, Spain, Sweden, Switzerland, Thailand, Turkey, Venezuela, Vietnam

INTERNATIONAL GAME TECHNOLOGY INC.

9295 Prototype Drive

Reno, NV 89511

Tel: (702) 448-0100 Fax: (702) 448-1488

CEO: G. Thomas Baker, Pres.

HR: Randy Kirner, VP

Web site: www.igtgame.com

Emp: 2,600

Mfr. games, hobby goods; equipment leasing, amusements, computers.

Argentina, Australia, Brazil, Canada, Japan, Macau, Netherlands, New Zealand, Peru, South Africa

INTERNATIONAL LOTTERY & TOTALIZATOR SYSTEMS INC.

2131 Faraday Ave.

Carlsbad, CA 92008

Tel: (760) 931-4000 Fax: (760) 931-1789

CEO: M. Mark Michalko, Pres.

FO: Robert F. McPhail, VP

HR: Mary A. Lopez, Mgr.

Web site: www.ilts.com

Emp: 116 Rev: $11 mil.

Mfr. fluid meters, counting devices; radio/TV & electronic stores.

Australia, England, U.K.

INTERNATIONAL MULTIFOODS CORPORATION

Box 2942

Minneapolis, MN 55402

Tel: (612) 340-3300 Fax: (612) 594-3343

CEO: Gary Costley, Pres.

HR: Joyce Traver

Emp: 9,000

Food services, grain and feed and food products.

Canada, Venezuela

INTERNATIONAL NETWORK SERVICES

1213 Innsbruck Dr.

Sunnyvale, CA 94089

Tel: (408) 542-0100 Fax: (408) 542-0101

CEO: Donald K. McKinney, Chmn.

FO: Peter Licata, VP

HR: Steven R. Humphreys, VP

Web site: www.ins.com

Emp: 1,353 Rev: $170 mil.

Provides computer network support, designs networking systems, manages equipment purchase and performance.

Canada, England, U.K., Netherlands

INTERNATIONAL PAPER COMPANY

2 Manhattanville Road

Purchase, NY 10577

Tel: (914) 397-1500 Fax: (914) 397-1596

CEO: John T. Dillon, Chmn.

FO: Robert Amen, Pres. Intl.

HR: Robert M. Byrnes, SVP

Web site: www.ipaper.com

Emp: 82,000 Rev: $20,096 mil.

Mfr./distributor container board, paper, wood products.

Australia, Austria, Bahamas, Belgium, Bermuda, Canada, Colombia, Denmark, Dominican Republic, England, U.K., Finland, France, Germany, Hong Kong, Israel, Italy, Japan, Netherlands, Norway, Philippines, Poland, South Africa, South Korea, Spain, Sweden, Switzerland, Taiwan (ROC), Venezuela

INTERNATIONAL RECTIFIER CORPORATION

233 Kansas Street

El Segundo, CA 90245

Tel: (310) 322-3331 Fax: (310) 322-3332

CEO: Alex Lidow & Derek Lidow, Co-CEO's

FO: Robert J. Mueller, EVP

HR: Robert Collin, Dir.

Web site: www.irf.com

Emp: 4,385 Rev: $486 mil.

Mfr. power semiconductor components.

Austria, Canada, China (PRC), Czech Republic, Denmark, England, U.K., Finland, France, Germany, Hong Kong, India, Italy, Japan, Mexico, Poland, Russia, Singapore, South Korea, Sweden, Switzerland

INTERNATIONAL SPECIALTY PRODUCTS

1361 Alps Road

Wayne, NJ 07470

Tel: (973) 628-4000 Fax: (973) 628-3311

CEO: Samuel J. Heyman, Chmn.

FO: Peter R. Heinze, Pres. & COO

HR: James J. Strupp, VP

Web site: www.ispcorp.com

Emp: 2,675 Rev: $749.2 mil.

Mfr. specialty chemical products.

Argentina, Australia, Austria, Belgium, Brazil, Bulgaria, Canada, China (PRC), Colombia, Czech Republic, England, U.K., France, Germany, Hong Kong, Hungary, India, Indonesia, Italy, Japan, Malaysia, Mexico, Netherlands, New Zealand, Poland, Russia, Singapore, South Korea, Spain,

Sweden, Switzerland, Taiwan (ROC), Thailand, Turkey, Venezuela

INTERNATIONAL TANK TERMINALS LTD

321 St. Charles Ave.
New Orleans, LA 70130
Tel: (504) 586-8300 Fax: (504) 525-9537
CEO: Thomas E. Coleman, Pres.

Storage tank facilities.

Pakistan

INTERNATIONAL TECHNOLOGIES CORPORATION

2790 Mosside Boulevard
Monroeville, PA 15146
Tel: (412) 372-7701 Fax: (412) 373-7135
CEO: James L. Kirk, VP
Emp: 2,300

Environmental services.

Canada

INTERNATIONAL TECHNOLOGY CORPORATION

2790 Mosside Boulevard
Monroeville, PA 15146-2792
Tel: (412) 372-7701 Fax: (412) 373-7135
CEO: Anthony J. DeLuca, Pres.
FO: James R. Mahoney, SVP
HR: Ann P. Harris, VP
Web site: www.itcorporation.com
Emp: 4,595 Rev: $442.2 mil.

Hazardous waste clean-up services

Mexico, South Korea, Taiwan (ROC)

INTERNATIONAL VITAMIN CORPORATION OVERSEAS

500 Halls Mill Road
Freehold, NJ 07728
Tel: (732) 308-3000 Fax: (732) 308-9793
CEO: Joseph Edell, Pres.
FO: Peter Olesinski, Pres. Intl.
Emp: 500

Mfr./distributor vitamins & dietary supplements.

Israel

INTERVOICE INC.

17811 Waterview Pkwy.
Dallas, TX 75206
Tel: (972) 454-8000 Fax: (972) 454-8707
CEO: David Berger, Pres.
HR: Don Brown
Emp: 550

Mfr. voice automation systems.

France, Singapore

INTRACO CORPORATION

530 Stephenson Hwy.
Troy, MI 48083
Tel: (248) 585-6900 Fax: (248) 585-6920
CEO: Nicola Antakli, Pres.

Export management and marketing consultants.

Cyprus, Lebanon

INTRALOX INC.

PO Box 50699
New Orleans, LA 70150
Tel: (504) 733-0463 Fax: (504) 734-0063
CEO: Dan Waters, Mgr.
Emp: 400

Mfr. plastic, modular conveyor belts and accessories.

Denmark, England, U.K., Germany, Netherlands

INTRUSION-PREPAKT INC.

PO Box 360007
Cleveland, OH 44136
Tel: (440) 238-6950 Fax: (440) 572-5533
CEO: D. S. Daczko
FO: E. W. Bindhoff
HR: A. J. Lackner
Emp: 200

Contractor: preplaced aggregate concrete, concrete repairs, erosion control, underwater concrete, etc.

Hong Kong, Panama, Spain

INVACARE CORPORATION

One Invacare Way
Elyria, OH 44036
Tel: (440) 329-6000 Fax: (440) 366-6568
CEO: Gerald Blouch, Pres.
FO: Ray Wandell
HR: Larry Steward
Web site: www.invacare.com

Emp: 3,052

Mfr. home medical equipment, wheelchairs, respiratory care products, home care aids.

Canada, France, Germany

INVENTION SUBMISSION CORPORATION

217 Ninth Street

Pittsburgh, PA 15222

Tel: (412) 288-1300 Fax: (412) 288-1354

CEO: Martin Berger, Pres.

FO: Peter Geiringer

HR: Kim Bulter

Emp: 245

Inventor assistance services.

Australia, Canada, England, U.K.

IOMEGA CORPORATION

1821 West 4000 South

Roy, UT 84067

Tel: (801) 778-4494 Fax: (801) 778-3450

CEO: Kim B. Edwards, Pres.

FO: L. Scott Flaig, EVP

HR: Kevin O'Connor, VP

Web site: www.iomega.com

Emp: 1,135 Rev: $1,700 mil.

Mfr. data storage products.

Belgium, England, U.K., France, Germany

IONICS INC.

65 Grove Street

Watertown, MA 02172

Tel: (617) 926-2500 Fax: (617) 926-4304

CEO: Arthur Goldstein, Chmn.

HR: Marianne Manzon Winsser

Web site: www.ionics.com

Emp: 450

Mfr. desalination equipment.

England, U.K., France, Italy, Saudi Arabia, Spain

IPSEN INDUSTRIES INC.

PO Box 6266

Rockford, IL 61125

Tel: (815) 332-4941 Fax: (815) 332-4549

CEO: Mario Ciampini, Pres.

Emp: 370

Heat treating equipment.

England, U.K.

IRRIDELCO INTERNATIONAL CORPORATION

440 Sylvan Ave.

Englewood Cliffs, NJ 07632

Tel: (201) 569-3030 Fax: (201) 569-9237

CEO: Ronald Gilbert, Chmn.

HR: Harold McNamara, VP

Web site: www.irridelco.com

Mfr./distributor of the most comprehensive lines of mechanical and micro irrigation; pumps and irrigation systems.

Australia, Chile, Colombia, Costa Rica, Ecuador, France, Germany, Guatemala, Jordan, Mexico, Peru, Philippines, Venezuela, Zimbabwe

ITT CORPORATION

1330 Ave. of the Americas

New York, NY 10019-5490

Tel: (212) 258-1000 Fax: (212) 258-1297

CEO: Robert Bowlan, Pres.

FO: Rand Araskog, Chrm.

HR: Ralph W. Pausig

Emp: 120,000

Design/mfr. communications & electronic equipment, hotels, insurance.

Australia, Austria, Bahrain, Brazil, Chile, Colombia, Dem. Rep. of Congo, Ecuador, England, U.K., Finland, France, Germany, Greece, Hong Kong, India, Indonesia, Ivory Coast, Japan, Kenya, Malaysia, Mexico, Morocco, Netherlands, New Zealand, Nigeria, Norway, Peru, Saudi Arabia, Singapore, South Korea, Spain, Surinam, Sweden, Switzerland, Taiwan (ROC), Thailand, Tunisia, Turkey, Zambia

ITT FEDERAL SERVICES CORPORATION

1 Gateway Plaza, PO Box 15012

Colorado Springs, CO 80935-5012

Tel: (719) 591-3600 Fax: (719) 591-3698

CEO: John R. Spearing, Pres.

Emp: 4,500

Engineer/install/support communications & electronic systems.

Germany

ITT SHERATON CORPORATION

60 State Street

Boston, MA 02108

Tel: (617) 367-3600 Fax: (617) 367-5676

CEO: John Kapioltas, Chmn.

FO: Osvaldo Librizzi

Emp: 125,000 Rev: $3,200 mil.

Hotel operations.

Argentina, Australia, Austria, Bahrain, Bangladesh, Belgium, Benin, Brazil, Bulgaria, Canada, Chile, China (PRC), Costa Rica, Cyprus, Dem. Rep. of Congo, Denmark, Dominican Republic, Egypt, England, U.K., France, Gabon, Germany, Guatemala, Hong Kong, India, Israel, Italy, Japan, Kuwait, Luxembourg, Mexico, Morocco, New Zealand, Nigeria, Oman, Pakistan, Peru, Philippines, Portugal, Qatar, Saudi Arabia, Scotland, U.K., South Korea, Spain, Sweden, Switzerland, Syria, Taiwan (ROC), Thailand, Tunisia, Turkey, Uganda, United Arab Emirates, Venezuela, Yemen, Zimbabwe

ITW RANSBURG FINISHING SYSTEMS

4141 West 54th Street

Indianapolis, IN 46254

Tel: (317) 298-5000 Fax: (317) 298-5010

CEO: Rolan Kjosen, Pres.

FO: Dennis Stephens

HR: Lois Christopher

Web site: www.itwdema.com

Emp: 150

Mfr. rotary atomizers, electrostatic guns, paint finishing systems.

Australia, Brazil, England, U.K., France, Germany, Mexico

J

J.P. MORGAN & CO. INC.

60 Wall Street

New York, NY 10260-0060

Tel: (212) 483-2323 Fax: (212) 648-5209

CEO: Douglas A. Warner, III, Chmn.

FO: Roberto Mendoza, Vice Chrm.

HR: Herbert J. Hefke, Dir. HR

Web site: www.jpm.com

Emp: 16,943 Rev: $262,159 mil. (assets)

International banking services.

Argentina, Australia, Bahamas, Belgium, Bermuda, Brazil, Canada, Cayman Islands, Chile, China (PRC), Czech Republic, England, U.K., France, Germany, Hong Kong, India, Indonesia, Italy, Japan, Lebanon, Malaysia, Mexico, Netherlands, Nigeria, Peru, Philippines, Poland, Portugal, Russia, Singapore, South Africa, South Korea, Spain, Switzerland, Taiwan (ROC), Thailand, Venezuela

J. WALTER THOMPSON COMPANY

466 Lexington Ave.

New York, NY 10017

Tel: (212) 210-7000 Fax: (212) 210-6944

CEO: Christopher Jones, Chmn.

FO: Peter Schweitzer, Pres.

Web site: www.jwt.com

Emp: 7,294 Rev: $1,171 mil.

International advertising and marketing services.

Argentina, Australia, Austria, Bangladesh, Belgium, Bolivia, Brazil, Canada, Chile, China (PRC), Colombia, Costa Rica, Czech Republic, Denmark, Dominican Republic, Ecuador, El Salvador, England, U.K., Finland, France, Germany, Ghana, Greece, Guatemala, Honduras, Hong Kong, Hungary, India, Indonesia, Ireland, Israel, Italy, Jamaica, Japan, Malaysia, Mexico, Netherlands, New Zealand, Nicaragua, Nigeria, Pakistan, Panama, Paraguay, Peru, Philippines, Poland, Portugal, Romania, Russia, Singapore, Slovenia, South Africa, South Korea, Spain, Sri Lanka, Sweden, Switzerland, Taiwan (ROC), Thailand, Trinidad & Tobago, Turkey, Ukraine, Uruguay, Venezuela, Vietnam, Zimbabwe

J.C. PENNEY COMPANY, INC.

6501 Legacy Drive

Plano, TX 75024-3698

Tel: (972) 431-1000 Fax: (972) 431-1977

CEO: James E. Oesterreicher, Chmn.

FO: Thomas D. Hutchens, Pres.

HR: Gary L. Davis, SVP HR

Web site: www.jcpenney.com

Emp: 260,000 Rev: $30,546 mil.

Department stores.

Chile, Hong Kong, India, Japan, Mexico, Singapore, South Korea, Taiwan (ROC), Thailand

JACOBS ENGINEERING GROUP INC.

1111 S. Arroyo Parkway

Pasadena, CA 91105

Tel: (626) 578-3500 Fax: (626) 578-6916

CEO: Noel G. Watson, Pres.

FO: Richard J. Slater, VP

HR: William Gebhardt, VP

Web site: www.jacobs.com

Emp: 17,725 Rev: $1,781 mil.

Engineering, design and consulting; construction and construction management; process plant maintenance.

Chile, England, U.K., France, India, Ireland, Italy, Mexico, Scotland, U.K., Spain, United Arab Emirates

JAMESBURY CORPORATION

640 Lincoln Street

Worcester, MA 01605

Tel: (508) 852-0200 Fax: (508) 852-8172

CEO: John Quinlivan, Pres.

HR: R. Baum

Emp: 1,140

Mfr. valves and accessories.

Canada, England, U.K., Germany, Japan, Mexico, Singapore

JASON INC.

411 E. Wisconsin Ave.

Milwaukee, WI 53202

Tel: (414) 277-9300 Fax: (414) 277-9445

CEO: Vincent Martin, Chmn. & Pres.

Mfr./sales auto trim and finishing products.

Taiwan (ROC)

JDA SOFTWARE GROUP, INC.

11811 N. Tatum Boulevard, Ste. 2000

Phoenix, AZ 85028

Tel: (602) 404-5500 Fax: (602) 404-5520

CEO: Brent W. Lippman

FO: Hamish Brewer, SVP

HR: Judy Wieler, Dir.

Web site: www.jda.com

Emp: 683 Rev: $92 mil.

Developer of information management software for retail, merchandising, distribution and store management.

Australia, Canada, Chile, England, U.K., France, Germany, Mexico, Singapore, South Africa

JEFFERIES & COMPANY, INC.

11100 Santa Monica Boulevard

Los Angeles, CA 90025

Tel: (310) 445-1199 Fax: (310) 914-1173

CEO: Mike Klowden, Pres.
Mike Klowden, Pres.

Real estate and financial advisor.

Japan, Switzerland

JET-LUBE INC.

4849 Homestead

Houston, TX 77028

Tel: (713) 674-7617 Fax: (713) 678-4604

CEO: Larry J. Eubanks, Pres.

HR: Cheryl Dodds

Web site: www.jetlube.com

Emp: 71

Mfr. anti-seize compounds, thread sealants, lubricants, greases.

Canada, England, U.K., Scotland, U.K.

JETBORNE INC.

8361 NW 64th Street

Miami, FL 33166

Tel: (305) 591-2999 Fax: (305) 513-0050

CEO: E. Brodatch, Pres.

FO: Iain Sturrock

HR: Terry Barbash

Emp: 100

Aircraft sales, leasing, support.

England, U.K.

JEUNIQUE INTERNATIONAL INC.

19501 E. Walnut Drive

City of Industry, CA 91748

Tel: (909) 598-8598 Fax: (909) 594-8258

CEO: Mulford J. Nobbs, Chmn.

FO: Leon Dobrinski

HR: Sheila Nobbs

Emp: 148

Mfr./sale vitamins, food supplements, cosmetics and diet products.

Canada, Germany, Mexico, Netherlands, South Africa

JEWELWAY INTERNATIONAL INC.

5151 E. Broadway Blvd, #500

Tucson, AZ 85711

Tel: (520) 747-9900 Fax: (520) 747-4813

CEO: Bruce Canith

FO: Jamie Onate

Emp: 400

Sale fine jewelry via independent representatives.

Australia, Canada

JLG INDUSTRIES INC.

JLG Drive

McConnellsburg, PA 17233-9533

Tel: (717) 485-5161 Fax: (717) 485-6417

CEO: L. David Black, Chmn.

FO: Michael Swartz

HR: Samuel D. Swope, VP

Emp: 2,705

Mfr. aerial work platforms, truck-mounted cranes and custom hydraulic machinery.

Australia, Scotland, U.K.

JOHN HANCOCK MUTUAL LIFE INSURANCE COMPANY

200 Clarendon Street, PO Box 111

Boston, MA 02117

Tel: (617) 572-6000 Fax: (617) 572-8628

CEO: Stephen L. Brown

HR: Diane M. Capstaff

Web site: www.jhancock.com

Emp: 19,000 Rev: $36,000 mil.

Life insurance services.

Argentina, Belgium, Bermuda, Brazil, Canada, England, U.K., Vietnam

JOHNS MANVILLE CORPORATION

717 17th Street

Denver, CO 80202

Tel: (303) 978-2000 Fax: (303) 978-2318

CEO: Charles L. Henry, Pres. & Chmn.

HR: Ron L. Hammons

Web site: www.jm.com

Emp: 8,000 Rev: $1,600 mil.

Mfr. fiberglass insulation, roofing products & systems, fiberglass material & reinforcements, filtration mats.

Canada, England, U.K., Germany, Japan

JOHNNIE D. JOHNSON & CO., INC. (JDJ&CO)

50 Broad Street, Ste. 2000

New York, NY 10004

Tel: (212) 425-4848 Fax: (212) 425-4670

CEO: Johnnie D. Johnson

FO: Jacqueline A. Hoyte

HR: Sylvia R. Bruzzese

Web site: www.investor-relations.com

Emp: 25

Investor relations, consulting.

England, U.K.

JOHNSON & JOHNSON

One Johnson & Johnson Plaza

New Brunswick, NJ 08933

Tel: (732) 524-0400 Fax: (732) 214-0334

CEO: Ralph S. Larsen, Chmn.

FO: Ronald G. Gelbman

HR: Shelly Carpenter

Web site: www.jnj.com

Emp: 90,500 Rev: $22,600 mil.

Mfr./distributor/R&D pharmaceutical, health care and cosmetic products.

Angola, Argentina, Australia, Austria, Belgium, Brazil, Canada, Chile, China (PRC), Colombia, Costa Rica, Czech Republic, Denmark, Dominican Republic, Ecuador, Egypt, England, U.K., France, Germany, Greece, Guatemala, Hong Kong, Hungary, India, Indonesia, Ireland, Israel, Italy, Jamaica, Japan, Kenya, Malaysia, Mexico, Morocco, Mozambique, Netherlands, New Zealand, Nigeria, Pakistan, Panama, Peru, Philippines, Poland, Portugal, Russia, Scotland, U.K., Singapore, Slovenia, South Africa, South Korea, Spain, Sweden, Switzerland, Taiwan (ROC), Thailand, Trinidad & Tobago, Turkey, Ukraine, United Arab Emirates, Uruguay, Venezuela, Vietnam, Zambia, Zimbabwe

S C JOHNSON & SON INC.

1525 Howe Street

Racine, WI 53403

Tel: (414) 260-2000 Fax: (414) 260-2133

CEO: Willaim D. Perez, Pres.

FO: James F. Di Marco, SVP

HR: Gayle P. Kosterman, SVP

Web site: www.scjohnsonwax.com

Emp: 12,500 Rev: $5,000 mil.

Home, auto, commercial and personal care products and specialty chemicals.

Argentina, Australia, Austria, Belgium, Brazil, Canada, Chile, China (PRC), Colombia, Costa Rica, Cyprus, Czech Republic, Denmark, Dominican Republic, Ecuador, Egypt, England,

U.K., France, Germany, Ghana, Greece, Hong Kong, Hungary, India, Indonesia, Ireland, Italy, Ivory Coast, Japan, Kenya, Malaysia, Mexico, Netherlands, New Zealand, Nigeria, Norway, Philippines, Poland, Portugal, Russia, Saudi Arabia, Singapore, South Africa, South Korea, Spain, Sweden, Switzerland, Taiwan (ROC), Thailand, Turkey, Ukraine, Uruguay, Venezuela, Vietnam

JOHNSON CONTROLS INC.

5757 N. Green Bay Ave., PO Box 591
Milwaukee, WI 53201-0591
Tel: (414) 228-1200 Fax:
CEO: James H. Keyes
FO: Ronald M. Williams
HR: Susan Davis
Web site: www.johnsoncontrols.com
Emp: 74,000

Mfr. facility management & control systems, auto seating, & batteries..

Australia, Belgium, Canada, Czech Republic, England, U.K., France, Germany, Hong Kong, Hungary, India, Italy, Japan, Malaysia, Mexico, Netherlands, Norway, Poland, Russia, Scotland, U.K., Slovakia, South Africa, Spain, Switzerland

THE JOHNSON CORPORATION

805 Wood Street
Three Rivers, MI 49093
Tel: (616) 278-1715 Fax: (616) 273-2230
CEO: Rudi Leerentveld
FO: Tom Monroe, Jr.
HR: Andy Boyd
Web site: www.joco.com
Emp: 240

Mfr. rotary joints and siphon systems.

Canada, England, U.K., Netherlands

JOHNSON WORLDWIDE ASSOCIATES, INC.

1326 Willow Road
Sturtevant, WI 53177
Tel: (414) 884-1500 Fax: (414) 884-1600
CEO: Ronald C. Whitaker, Pres.
FO: Philippe Blime, VP
HR: Floyd Wilkinson, VP
Web site: www.jwa.com
Emp: 1,366 Rev: $303 mil.

Mfr. diving, fishing, boating & camping sports equipment.

Australia, Austria, Belgium, Canada, England, U.K., France, Germany, Hong Kong, Indonesia, Italy, Japan, Spain, Sweden, Switzerland

JOHNSTON PUMP COMPANY

800 Koomey Road
Brookshire, TX 77423
Tel: (281) 934-6009 Fax: (281) 934-6059
CEO: R. K. Elders, Pres.
FO: R. Mahajan
HR: S. Pagan-Amado
Web site: www.johnson.pump.com
Emp: 500

Mfr. vertical turbine pumps.

Singapore

JOMAC PRODUCTS INC.

863 Easton Road
Warrington, PA 18976
Tel: (215) 343-0800 Fax: (215) 343-0912
CEO: William S. Colehower
FO: James Podall
HR: Kevin J. Doran
Emp: 300

Mfr. industrial protective work gloves and industrial rainwear.

Canada

JONES & VINING INC.

60 Kendrick Street
Needham, MA 02194
Tel: (781) 433-2600 Fax: (781) 433-2610
CEO: Michael Ohayon, Pres.
HR: Charles Warren
Emp: 450

Mfr. plastic and wood products.

Canada, Taiwan (ROC), Thailand

JONES APPAREL GROUP INC.

250 Rittenhouse Circle
Bristol, PA 19007
Tel: (215) 785-4000 Fax: (215) 785-1795
CEO: Sidney Kimmel, Chmn.
Emp: 1,600

Mfr. women's apparel, knitting mills.

Canada, Hong Kong, Mexico

JONES CHEMICALS, INC.

80 Munson Street

LeRoy, NY 14482

Tel: (716) 768-6281 Fax: (716) 768-2632

CEO: Jeffrey W. Jones, Pres.

HR: Elizabeth DeFazio, VP

Emp: 450

Repackager of chlorine and other chemicals used in water purification.

Spain

JONES LANG WOOTTON

101 East 52nd Street

New York, NY 10022

Tel: (212) 688-8181 Fax: (212) 308-5199

CEO: Michael Dow, Mng. Prtn.

International marketing consultants, leasing agents and property management advisors.

Czech Republic, England, U.K., France, Germany, Hong Kong, Hungary, Indonesia, Ireland, Israel, Japan, Luxembourg, Malaysia, Netherlands, New Zealand, Philippines, Russia, Vietnam

JONES, DAY, REAVIS & POGUE

North Point, 901 Lakeside Ave.

Cleveland, OH 44114

Tel: (216) 586-3939 Fax: (216) 579-0212

CEO: Patrick F. McCartan, Mng. Ptnr.

FO: David F. Clossey

Web site: www.jonesday.com

Emp: 2,968 Rev: $490 mil.

International law firm.

Belgium, England, U.K., France, Germany, Hong Kong, India, Japan, Saudi Arabia, Switzerland, Taiwan (ROC)

JOSLYN HI-VOLTAGE CORPORATION

4000 East 116th Street

Cleveland, OH 44105

Tel: (216) 271-6600 Fax: (216) 341-3615

CEO: James Domo, Pres.

Web site: www.joslyn.hi-voltage.com

Emp: 2,000

High voltage switches, sectionalizers and reclosers for voltage through 230 KV.

Canada

JOSTEN'S INC.

5501 Norman Center

Minneapolis, MN 55437

Tel: (612) 830-3300 Fax: (612) 830-8432

CEO: Robert Buhrmaster, Pres.

Emp: 5,200

Class rings, school and graduation related products, awards and trophies.

Canada

JOY MINING AND MACHINERY

177 Thorn Hill Road

Warrendale, PA 15086-7527

Tel: (724) 779-4500 Fax: (724) 779-4507

CEO: Wayne Hunnell, Pres.

Emp: 5,705

Mfr. of underground mining equipment.

Australia, England, U.K., South Africa

K

K-SWISS INC.

20664 Bahama Street

Chatsworth, CA 91311

Tel: (818) 998-3388 Fax: (818) 773-2390

CEO: Steven Nichols, Pres.

Web site: www.kswiss.com

Emp: 250

Mfr. casual and athletic shoes, socks and leisure apparel.

Australia, Bermuda, Canada, England, U.K., Netherlands, Taiwan (ROC)

K-TEL INTERNATIONAL INC.

2605 Fernbrook Lane North

Plymouth, MN 55447

Tel: (612) 559-6800 Fax: (612) 559-6803

CEO: David Weiner, Pres.

Web site: www.k-tel.com

Emp: 140

Sale/distributor packaged consumer entertainment and convenience products.

England, U.K., Finland, Germany, Ireland, Spain

KAHLE ENGINEERING COMPANY

50 S. Center Street, Bldg 1

Orange, NJ 07050

Tel: (973) 678-2020 Fax: (973) 678-0326

CEO: Julie Logothetis, Pres.

FO: Russell Garofalo

Web site: www.kahleengineering.com

Emp: 50

Mfr. automatic assembly mach, medical/industrial products.

Italy

KAISER ALUMINUM & CHEMICAL CORPORATION

6177 Sunol Blvd.

Pleasanton, CA 94566

Tel: (925) 462-1122 Fax: (925) 484-2472

CEO: George T. Haymaker, Jr.

Web site: www.kaiseral.research.com

Emp: 10,815

Mfr. aluminum and aluminum products and chemicals.

Australia, Canada, Ghana, Jamaica, Wales, U.K.

KAISER ALUMINUM CORPORATION

5847 San Felipe, Ste. 2600

Houston, TX 77057-3010

Tel: (713) 267-3777 Fax: (713) 267-3701

CEO: George T. Haymaker, Jr., Chmn.

FO: Lawrence L. Watts, Pres. Intl.

HR: Steve Hart

Web site: www.kaiseral.com

Emp: 9,600 Rev: $2,300 mil.

Aluminum refining and manufacturing.

Australia, Canada, Ghana, Jamaica, Russia, Wales, U.K.

KAMAN CORPORATION

1332 Blue Hills Ave.

Bloomfield, CT 06002

Tel: (860) 243-7100 Fax: (860) 243-6365

CEO: Charles H. Kaman, Chmn.

FO: Huntington Hardisty

Web site: www.kaman.com

Emp: 4,318 Rev: $1,044.8 mil.

Aviation & aerospace products & services, musical instruments.

Australia, Canada, England, U.K.

KAMDEN INTERNATIONAL SHIPPING INC.

167-41 147th Ave.

Jamaica, NY 11434

Tel: (718) 553-8181 Fax: (718) 244-0030

CEO: Dennis M. Costin, Pres.

Emp: 102

Freight forwarding services.

Australia, Canada, England, U.K.

KANEB SERVICES INC.

2435 N. Central Expwy, 7th Fl.

Richardson, TX 75080

Tel: (972) 699-4000 Fax: (972) 699-4025

CEO: John R. Barnes

FO: John R. Barnes

HR: William Kettler

Emp: 1,642

Specialized industry services: leak sealing, on-site machining, safety testing, fire protection, etc.

England, U.K.

KAPPLER PROTECTIVE APPAREL & FABRICS

PO Box 490, 115 Grimes Drive

Guntersville, AL 35976

Tel: (205) 505-4005 Fax: (205) 505-4004

CEO: George Kappler, Pres.

HR: Teresa Walker

Web site: www.kappler.com

Emp: 1,500 Rev: $90 mil.

Mfr. of protective apparel & fabrics.

Canada, England, U.K., France, Germany, Mexico

KATHABAR SYSTEMS INC.

370 Campus Drive

Somerset, NJ 08873

Tel: (732) 356-6000 Fax: (732) 356-0643

CEO: Francis Drury, Pres.

FO: Joseph A. Pash

Mfr./distribute dehumidification equipment.

Japan, Netherlands

KATY INDUSTRIES INC.

6300 South Syracuse Way, Ste. 300

Englewood, CO 80111

Tel: (303) 290-9300 Fax: (303) 290-9344

CEO: John Pramn, Pres.

Emp: 2,015

Holding company.

Canada, England, U.K., France, Germany

KAUFMAN & BROAD HOME CORPORATION

10990 Wilshire Blvd.

Los Angeles, CA 90024

Tel: (310) 231-4000 Fax: (310) 231-4222

CEO: Bruce E. Karatz, Pres.

Emp: 900

Housing construction and financing.

Canada, France

KAVINOKY & COOK, LLP

120 Delaware Avenue

Buffalo, NY 14202

Tel: (716) 845-6000 Fax: (716) 845-6474

CEO: Samuel Shapiro, Mng. Prtn.

Law firm.

Canada

KAWNEER CO., INC.

555 Guthridge Court

Norcross, GA 30092

Tel: (770) 449-5555 Fax: (770) 734-1570

CEO: Denny Goode, Pres.

FO: Franz Kurvers

HR: Alan Beske

Emp: 4,000

Mfr. arch aluminum products for commercial construction.

Canada, England, U.K., France, Germany, Netherlands

KAYDON CORPORATION

19345 U.S. 19 North, #500

Clearwater, FL 34624

Tel: (813) 531-1101 Fax: (813) 530-9247

CEO: Lawrence J. Cawley, Pres.

Emp: 1,700

Design/mfr. custom engineered products: bearings, rings, seals, etc.

England, U.K., Mexico

KAYE, SCHOLER, FIERMAN, HAYS & HANDLER, LLP

425 Park Ave.

New York, NY 10022-3598

Tel: (212) 836-8000 Fax: (212) 836-8689

CEO: David Klingsberg, Mng. Prtn.

American and international law practice.

Hong Kong

KAYSER-ROTH CORPORATION

4905 Koger Blvd.

Greensboro, NC 27407

Tel: (336) 852-2030 Fax: (336) 632-1921

CEO: Kevin Toomey, Pres.

HR: Rae Mackall, VP

Emp: 8,000

Mfr. hosiery.

Germany

KCL CORPORATION

PO Box 629

Shelbyville, IN 46176

Tel: (317) 392-2521 Fax: (317) 392-4772

CEO: Robert Stollmeier, Pres.

HR: Robin Smith

Emp: 500

Mfr. plastic products.

Canada

A.T. KEARNEY INC.

222 West Adams Street

Chicago, IL 60606

Tel: (312) 648-0111 Fax: (312) 223-6200

CEO: Fred G. Steingraber

FO: Philip F. Banks

HR: William Seithel

Web site: www.atkearney.com

Emp: 2,200

Management consultants and executive search.

Argentina, Australia, Austria, Belgium, Brazil, Canada, China (PRC), Czech Republic, Denmark, England, U.K., Finland, France, Germany, Hong Kong, India, Indonesia, Italy, Japan, Malaysia, Netherlands, New Zealand, Norway, Poland, Portugal, Russia, Singapore, South Korea, Spain, Sweden, Switzerland, Turkey, Venezuela

KEARNEY-NATIONAL INC.

108 Corporate Park Drive, Ste 114

White Plains, NY 10604

Tel: (914) 694-6700 Fax: (914) 694-6513

CEO: Joseph L. Aurichio, Pres.

Emp: 2,200

Mfr. electrical power distributor equipment, elect/electronic components.

Canada

KEITHLEY INSTRUMENTS INC.

28775 Aurora Road

Cleveland, OH 44139

Tel: (440) 248-0400 Fax: (440) 248-6168

CEO: Joseph P. Keithley, Chmn.

FO: Hermann Hamm

HR: Phil Etsler, VP

Web site: www.keithley.com

Emp: 665

Mfr. electronic test/measure instruments, PC-based data acquisition hardware/software.

China (PRC), England, U.K., France, Germany, Italy, Japan, Netherlands, Switzerland

KELCO INDUSTRIES INC.

9210 Country Club Road

Woodstock, IL 60098

Tel: (815) 338-5521 Fax: (815) 338-6558

CEO: Kevin Kelly, Pres.

Alginate products.

Canada

KELLEY DRYE & WARREN LLP

101 Park Ave.

New York, NY 10178

Tel: (212) 808-7800 Fax: (212) 808-7898

CEO: Merrill B. Stone, Mgn. Prtn.

HR: Libby Yoskowitz, Mgr.

Web site: www.kelleydrye.com

Emp: 812 Rev: $111 mil.

International law firm.

Belgium, Hong Kong

KELLOGG COMPANY

One Kellogg Square, PO Box 3599

Battle Creek, MI 49016-3599

Tel: (616) 961-2000 Fax: (616) 961-2871

CEO: Arnold G. Langbo, Chmn. & Pres.

FO: Donald G. Fritz, EVP

HR: Robert L. Creviston, VP

Web site: www.kelloggs.com

Emp: 15,500 Rev: $6,000 mil.

Mfr. ready-to-eat cereals and convenience foods.

Argentina, Australia, Belgium, Brazil, Chile, Colombia, Denmark, England, U.K., Finland, France, Germany, Guatemala, Ireland, Italy, Japan, Latvia, Malaysia, Mexico, Netherlands, Norway, Portugal, Singapore, South Africa, South Korea, Spain, Sweden, Venezuela

THE M. W. KELLOGG COMPANY

601 Jefferson Ave.

Houston, TX 77002

Tel: (713) 753-5414 Fax: (713) 753-5628

CEO: Jack Stanley, Pres.

HR: Renee Guillory

Web site: www.kellogg.com

Emp: 4,000

Design, engineering, procurement and construction for process and energy industry.

China (PRC), England, U.K., Indonesia, Malaysia, Nigeria, Singapore

KELLWOOD COMPANY

600 Kellwood Pkwy.

Chesterfield, MO 63017

Tel: (314) 576-3100 Fax: (314) 576-3434

CEO: Hal J. Upbin, Pres. & COO

FO: James C. Jacobsen, VC

HR: Leon M. McWhite

Emp: 18,360 Rev: $1,520 mil.

Mfr./marketing/sale primarily women's apparel and recreational camping products.

Hong Kong

KELLY SERVICES, INC.

999 W. Big Beaver Road

Troy, MI 48084

Tel: (248) 362-4444 Fax: (248) 244-4154

CEO: Terence E. Adderley, Chmn.

FO: Alfredo Maselli, SVP

HR: Joanne Start

Web site: www.kellyservices.com

Emp: 750,000 Rev: $3,853 mil.

Temporary help placement.

Australia, Belgium, Canada, Denmark, England, U.K., France, Ireland, Italy, Luxembourg, Mexico, Netherlands, New Zealand, Norway, Russia, Scotland, U.K., Spain, Switzerland

KELSEY-HAYES COMPANY

12025 Tech Center Drive
Livonia, MI 48150
Tel: (734) 266-2600 Fax: (734) 266-4603
CEO: Steve Lunn, Pres.
Emp: 10,000
Automotive and aircraft parts.
Canada, Mexico, Venezuela

KENDA SYSTEMS INC.
One Stiles Road
Salem, NH 03079
Tel: (603) 898-7884 Fax: (603) 898-3016
CEO: Stephen Kenda, Pres.
FO: Ursula Brennan
HR: Matt Hanna
Web site: www.kenda.com
Emp: 600
Computer programming services.
England, U.K., Germany, Netherlands

THE KENDALL COMPANY
15 Hampshire Street
Mansfield, MA 02048
Tel: (508) 261-8000 Fax: (508) 261-8542
CEO: Richard J. Meelia, Pres.
FO: R. D. Dullien, Pres. Intl.
HR: P. A. Prue, VP
Emp: 8,500
Mfr. medical disposable products, home health care products and specialty adhesive products.
Australia, Canada, Chile, China (PRC), England, U.K., France, Germany, India, Italy, Japan, Malaysia, Mexico, Netherlands, Panama, Singapore, South Africa, Spain, Thailand, United Arab Emirates, Venezuela

KENNAMETAL INC.
State Rte. 981
Latrobe, PA 15650
Tel: (724) 539-5000 Fax: (724) 539-4710
CEO: Robert L. McGeehan, Pres.
FO: Derwin R. Gilbreath, VP
HR: Timothy D. Hudson, VP
Web site: www.kennametal.com
Emp: 7,500 Rev: $1,156.3 mil.
Tools, hard carbide & tungsten alloys for metalworking industry.
Argentina, Australia, Austria, Belgium, Brazil, Chile, China (PRC), Colombia, Czech Republic, Denmark, El Salvador, England, U.K., Finland, France, Germany, Greece, Hong Kong, Hungary, India, Indonesia, Italy, Japan, Malaysia, Mexico, Netherlands, Philippines, Poland, Portugal, Russia, Singapore, South Korea, Spain, Sweden, Switzerland, Taiwan (ROC), Thailand, Turkey, Venezuela

KENT-MOORE DIV
28635 Mound Road
Warren, MI 48092
Tel: (810) 574-2332 Fax: (313) 578-7375
CEO: Robert Kindig, Pres.
HR: Dave Mied
Emp: 1,136
Mfr. service equipment for auto, construction, recreational, military and agricultural vehicles.
Australia, Brazil, England, U.K., Germany, Japan, Spain, Switzerland

KEPNER-TREGOE INC.
PO Box 704
Princeton, NJ 08542-0740
Tel: (609) 921-2806 Fax: (609) 924-4978
CEO: T. Quinn Spitzer, Pres.
FO: Mike Freedman
HR: Angela Wittik
Emp: 200
Management consulting & training.
Australia, Canada, England, U.K., France, Germany, Hong Kong, Japan, Malaysia, Singapore, Switzerland, Thailand

KERR CORPORATION
1717 West Collins Ave.
Orange, CA 92867
Tel: (714) 516-7400 Fax: (714) 516-7648
CEO: Steve Semmelmayer, Pres.
FO: Garrett Sato
HR: John Trapani
Web site: www.Sybrondental.com/kerr/
Emp: 1,300 Rev: $200 mil.
Mfr. dental supplies, jewelry mfr. supplies & equipment.
Italy

KERR-McGEE CORPORATION

PO Box 25861
Oklahoma City, OK 73125
Tel: (405) 270-1313 Fax: (405) 270-3123
CEO: Luke R. Corbett
HR: Julius Hilburn
Emp: 4,000
Oil & gas exploration & production, industrial chemicals, coal.
Canada, China (PRC), England, U.K., Scotland, U.K.

KETCHUM PUBLIC RELATIONS
Six PPG Place
Pittsburgh, PA 15222
Tel: (412) 456-3885 Fax: (412) 456-3588
CEO: Michael J. Kaczmarski, CFO
Web site: www.ketchum.com
Emp: 1,200
Advertising and public relations.
England, U.K., Germany, Japan, Netherlands, Singapore

KEY TRONIC CORPORATION
PO Box 14687
Spokane, WA 99214-0687
Tel: (509) 928-8000 Fax: (509) 927-5248
CEO: Jack W. Oehlke
FO: Tony G. McVeigh
Web site: www.keytronic.com
Emp: 2,400 Rev: $184 mil.
Computers and peripherals.
Ireland

KIDDE-FENWAL, INC.
400 Main Street
Ashland, MA 01721
Tel: (508) 881-2000 Fax: (508) 881-6729
CEO: Richard Demarle, Pres.
FO: Lewis F. Clark, Jr
HR: Phil Mongada
Web site: www.kidde-fenwal.com
Emp: 1,150
Temperature controls, ignition systems, fire/smoke detection and suppression systems.
England, U.K., Japan

KILIAN MFG. COMPANY
PO Box 1008
Torrington, CT 06790
Tel: (860) 626-2000 Fax: (860) 496-3642
CEO: Al Nixon, Pres.
Mfr. ungrounded ball bearings.
Canada

KILPATRICK STOCKTON
1100 Peachtree Street, NE, Ste. 2800
Atlanta, GA 30309
Tel: (404) 815-6500 Fax: (404) 815-6555
CEO: Tim Carssow
HR: Allison Guphrie
Emp: 1,000 Rev: $125 mil.
International law firm.
Belgium, England, U.K., Sweden

KIMBALL INTERNATIONAL INC.
PO Box 460
Jasper, IN 47549
Tel: (812) 482-1600 Fax: (812) 482-8804
CEO: James Thyen,Pres.
FO: Anthony P. Habig
HR: Terry P. Wilson
Emp: 6,500
Mfr. office furniture & seating, pianos, wood veneers, plywood products.
Austria, England, U.K., Mexico

KIMBERLY-CLARK CORPORATION
351 Phelps Drive
Irving, TX 75038
Tel: (972) 281-1200 Fax: (972) 281-1435
CEO: Wayne R. Sanders, Chmn.
FO: John A. Van Steenberg, Pres.
HR: Bruce J. Olson, VP
Web site: www.kimberly-clark.com.
Emp: 57,000 Rev: $12,547 mil.
Mfr./sales/distribution of consumer tissue, household and personal care products.
Argentina, Australia, Austria, Bahrain, Belgium, Bermuda, Brazil, Canada, Chile, China (PRC), Colombia, Costa Rica, Czech Republic, El Salvador, England, U.K., Finland, France, Germany, Honduras, Hong Kong, Hungary, India, Indonesia, Ireland, Israel, Italy, Japan, Malaysia, Mexico, Netherlands, Panama, Peru, Philippines, Poland, Portugal, Russia, Saudi Arabia, Singapore,

Slovakia, South Africa, South Korea, Spain, Switzerland, Taiwan (ROC), Thailand, Venezuela

KINETICSYSTEMS CORPORATION

900 N. State Street
Lockport, IL 60441
Tel: (815) 838-0005 Fax: (815) 838-4424
CEO: James M. Stephenson, Pres.
FO: Roderick H. Wischermann
HR: Frank Kabellis
Emp: 110

Mfr. electronic data acquisition and process control systems.

Switzerland

KINKO'S, INC.

255 W. Stanley Ave.
Ventura, CA 93002-8000
Tel: (805) 652-4000 Fax: (805) 652-4347
CEO: Paul J. Orfalea, Chmn.
FO: Michael Cohn, Pres. Int'l.
HR: Adrianna Foss, VP
Web site: www.kinkos.com
Emp: 24,000 Rev: $1,500 mil.

Kinko's operates a 24-hour-a-day, global chain of photocopy stores.

Australia, Canada, China (PRC), England, U.K., Japan, Netherlands, South Korea

KINNEY SHOE CORPORATION

233 Broadway
New York, NY 10279
Tel: (212) 720-3700 Fax: (212) 720-4223
CEO: Carol Greer, Pres.
HR: Patricia Peck
Emp: 35,000

Mfr./sale footwear and apparel.

Canada

KIRBY BUILDING SYSTEMS INC.

124 Kirby Drive, PO Box 390
Portland, TN 37148
Tel: (615) 325-4165 Fax: (615) 231-3460
CEO: Thomas McCann, Pres.
HR: Charles Wilcox
Emp: 300

Steel building systems.

England, U.K., Kuwait

KIRKLAND & ELLIS

200 East Randolph Drive
Chicago, IL 60601
Tel: (312) 861-2000 Fax: (312) 861-2200
CEO: Douglas McLemore
FO: Douglas McLemore
HR: Sally Howard
Web site: www.kirkland.com
Emp: 504 Rev: $255 mil.

International law firm.

England, U.K.

KIRKWOOD INDUSTRIES INC.

4855 W. 130th Street
Cleveland, OH 44135-5182
Tel: (216) 267-6200 Fax: (216) 362-3804
CEO: Richard W. Klym, Pres.
HR: Eileen Amato
Emp: 750

Mfr. electrical components, commutators, mica insulation, slip rings and carbon brushes.

India, Mexico

KIRSCH

309 N. Prospect Street
Sturgis, MI 49091-0370
Tel: (616) 659-5100 Fax: (616) 659-5614
CEO: David Roberts, Pres.
FO: Ann Bakker
HR: Gene Frohriep
Emp: 2,600

Mfr. drapery hardware & accessories, wood shelving, woven wood shades, etc.

Canada, Germany, Italy, Spain

KNAPE & VOGT MFG. COMPANY

2700 Oak Industrial Drive, NE
Grand Rapids, MI 49505
Tel: (616) 459-3311 Fax: (616) 459-3290
CEO: Allan E. Perry, Pres.
FO: Anthony R. Taylor
HR: Peter Bilski, Dir.
Web site: www.kv.com
Emp: 1,100 Rev: $176.6 mil.

Builders hardware, closet & cabinet fixtures &

accessories.

Canada

LESTER B KNIGHT & ASSOC INC.

549 West Randolph Street

Chicago, IL 60661

Tel: (312) 346-2300 Fax: (312) 648-1085

CEO: Stephen C. Mitchell, Pres.

FO: Stephen C. Mitchell

HR: James A. Turner

Emp: 720

Architecture, engineering, planning, operations & management consulting.

Austria, Belgium, China (PRC), England, U.K., Finland, France, Germany, Hungary, Netherlands, Norway, South Korea, Switzerland

KNIGHT-RIDDER INC.

One Herald Plaza

Miami, FL 33132

Tel: (305) 376-3800 Fax: (305) 376-3828

CEO: John C. Fontaine

HR: Mary Jean Connors

Emp: 21,000

Newspaper publishing, business information services.

England, U.K., Hong Kong, Switzerland

KNOLL, INC.

1235 Water Street

East Greenville, PA 18041

Tel: (215) 679-7991 Fax: (215) 679-3904

CEO: John Lynch, Pres.

FO: Ed Goodwin

HR: Barbara Ellixson

Web site: www.knoll.com

Emp: 3,000

Mfr. and sale of office furnishings.

Argentina, Austria, Belgium, Canada, Colombia, England, U.K., France, Germany, Italy, Japan, Netherlands, Spain, Switzerland

KNOWLES ELECTRONICS INC.

1151 Maplewood Drive

Itasca, IL 60131

Tel: (630) 250-5100 Fax: (630) 250-0575

CEO: Reg Garrett, Pres.

HR: Ray Cabrera

Emp: 450

Microphones and loudspeakers.

England, U.K., Taiwan (ROC)

KOCH INDUSTRIES INC.

4111 East 37th Street North

Wichita, KS 67220-3203

Tel: (316) 828-5500 Fax: (316) 828-5950

CEO: William W. Hanna, Pres. & COO

FO: Joe W. Moeller, EVP Int'l.

HR: Paul Wheeler, VP

Web site: www.kochind.com

Emp: 12,800 Rev: $30,000 mil.

Oil, financial services, agriculture and Purina Mills animal feed.

Canada, England, U.K., France, Germany, Italy, Mexico, Netherlands, Singapore, South Africa, Switzerland, Venezuela

KOCH-GLITSCH, INC.

PO Box 660053

Dallas, TX 75266-0053

Tel: (214) 583-3000 Fax: (214) 583-3344

CEO: Robert Difulgentiz, Pres.

FO: James C. Spalding

HR: Chip Davis

Mfr./services mass transfer/chemicals separation equipment, process engineering.

Canada, England, U.K., France, Germany, Italy, Japan

KOCH-GLITSCH, INC. (KOCH INDUSTRIES)

PO Box 8127

Wichita, KS 67208

Tel: (316) 828-5110 Fax: (316) 828-5950

CEO: Robert A. DiFulgentiz, Pres.

FO: Urban E. Monsch

HR: Chip Davis

Emp: 450

Mass transfer products, static mixers and mist eliminator systems.

Canada, Israel, Italy

THE KOHLER COMPANY

444 Highland Drive

Kohler, WI 53044

Tel: (920) 457-4441 Fax: (920) 459-1274

CEO: Herbert V. Kohler, Jr., Chmn.

HR: James Sweet

Emp: 18,000 Rev: $2,210 mil.

Plumbing products, ceramic tile and stone, cabinetry, furniture, engines, generators, switch gear and hospitality.

Argentina, Australia, Canada, China (PRC), England, U.K., France, Hong Kong, Japan, Mexico, Singapore, South Korea, Taiwan (ROC)

KOHN PEDERSEN FOX ASSOCIATES PC

111 West 57th Street

New York, NY 10019

Tel: (212) 977-6500 Fax: (212) 956-2526

CEO: A. Eugene Kohn, Pres.

FO: Lee Polisano

HR: Susan Appel

Emp: 230

Architectural design.

England, U.K., Germany, Japan

KOLLMORGEN CORPORATION

1601 Trapelo Road

Waltham, MA 02154

Tel: (781) 890-5655 Fax: (781) 890-7150

CEO: Gideon Argov, Pres.

HR: James Geller

Emp: 2,000

Mfr. printed circuits, electric motors & controls, electro-optical instruments.

England, U.K., France, Ireland, Switzerland

KOMLINE-SANDERSON ENGINEERING CORPORATION

12 Holland Ave.

Peapack, NJ 07977

Tel: (908) 234-1000 Fax: (908) 234-9487

CEO: Russell M. Komline, Pres.

HR: Annette Oswald

Industrial and sanitary filtration systems, dryers and pumps.

Canada

KOPPERS INDUSTRIES INC.

Koppers Bldg, 437 Seventh Ave.

Pittsburgh, PA 15219

Tel: (412) 227-2000 Fax: (412) 227-2333

CEO: Walt Turner, Pres

HR: Richard E. Hawkins

Emp: 13,000

Construction materials and services; chemicals and building products.

Australia, Barbados, Brazil, Canada, Chile, Guatemala, Jamaica, Taiwan (ROC)

KORN/FERRY INTERNATIONAL

1800 Century Park East

Los Angeles, CA 90067

Tel: (310) 552-1834 Fax: (310) 553-6452

CEO: Michael D. Boxberger, Pres

FO: Man Jit Singh, VP

HR: Charles Rafowicz, Dir.

Web site: www.kornferry.com

Emp: 1,139 Rev: $315 mil.

Executive search; management consulting.

Argentina, Australia, Austria, Belgium, Brazil, Canada, Chile, China (PRC), Colombia, Czech Republic, Denmark, England, U.K., Finland, France, Germany, Greece, Hong Kong, Hungary, India, Italy, Japan, Luxembourg, Malaysia, Mexico, Netherlands, New Zealand, Norway, Peru, Poland, Romania, Russia, Singapore, Slovakia, South Korea, Spain, Sweden, Switzerland, Thailand, Turkey, Venezuela

KOSS CORPORATION

4129 N. Port Washington Ave.

Milwaukee, WI 53212-1052

Tel: (414) 964-5000 Fax: (414) 964-8615

CEO: Michael J. Koss, Pres

FO: Declan Hanley, VP Intl. Sales

HR: Cheryl Mike

Emp: 200 Rev: $396 mil.

Mfr. high fidelity stereophones, active noise cancellation headsets, audio-video loudspeakers, computer loudspeakers, and communications headsets.

Switzerland

KOSTER KEUNEN WAXES LTD

90 Bourne Blvd.

Sayville, NY 11782

Tel: (516) 589-0400 Fax: (516) 589-1232

CEO: Richard B. Koster, Pres.

Emp: 10

Mfr. waxes.

Netherlands

KPMG PEAT MARWICK LLP

Three Chestnut Ridge Road

Montvale, NJ 07645

Tel: (201) 307-7000 Fax: (201) 930-8617

CEO: Stephen G. Butler, Chmn.

FO: Sergio Ruiz-Mier

HR: Jorge Ribalaigua, Dir.

Web site: www.kpmg.com

Emp: 82,500 Rev: $9,200 mil.

Accounting and audit, tax and management consulting services.

Anguilla, Antigua, Argentina, Aruba, Australia, Austria, Bahamas, Bahrain, Bangladesh, Barbados, Belgium, Belize, Bermuda, Bolivia, Botswana, Brazil, British Virgin Islands, Brunei, Bulgaria, Burundi, Canada, Cayman Islands, Channel Islands, U.K., Chile, China (PRC), Colombia, Costa Rica, Croatia, Cyprus, Czech Republic, Denmark, Dominican Republic, Ecuador, Egypt, El Salvador, England, U.K., Estonia, Fiji, Finland, France, French Antilles, French Polynesia, Gambia, Germany, Ghana, Gibraltar, Greece, Guatemala, Guyana, Haiti, Honduras, Hong Kong, Hungary, Iceland, India, Indonesia, Iran, Ireland, Isle of Man, Israel, Italy, Jamaica, Japan, Jordan, Kazakhstan, Kenya, Kuwait, Latvia, Lebanon, Libya, Lithuania, Luxembourg, Macau, Malawi, Malaysia, Malta, Mauritius, Mexico, Morocco, Mozambique, Namibia, Netherlands, Netherlands Antilles, New Caledonia, New Zealand, Nicaragua, Nigeria, Northern Ireland, U.K., Norway, Oman, Pakistan, Palestine, Panama, Papua New Guinea, Peru, Philippines, Poland, Portugal, Romania, Russia, San Marino, Saudi Arabia, Scotland, U.K., Seychelles, Sierra Leone, Singapore, Slovakia, Slovenia, South Africa, South Korea, Spain, Sri Lanka, St. Lucia, Sudan, Surinam, Swaziland, Sweden, Switzerland, Taiwan (ROC), Thailand, Trinidad & Tobago, Tunisia, Turkey, Turks & Caicos Islands, Ukraine, United Arab Emirates, Uruguay, Uzbekistan, Vanuatu, Venezuela, Wales, U.K., Yemen, Yugoslavia, Zambia, Zimbabwe

KRAFT FOODS INTERNATIONAL, INC. (DIV. PHILIP MORRIS COS.)

800 Westchester Ave.

Rye Brook, NY 10573-1301

Tel: (914) 335-2500 Fax: (914) 335-7144

CEO: Robert A. Eckert, Pres.

FO: Miles L. Marsh

HR: John J. Tucker

Emp: 40,000

Processor, distributor and manufacturer of food products.

Australia, Austria, Brazil, Canada, England, U.K., Hong Kong, Philippines, Poland, Switzerland

KRAS CORPORATION

88 Topeth Road

Fairless Hills, PA 19030

Tel: (215) 736-0981 Fax: (215) 736-8953

CEO: Lawrence L. Plummer, Chmn.

FO: Anita Tracey

HR: Bonnie Bickel

Emp: 400

Mfr. precision tools and machinery for electronic and plastics industrial.

Belarus, Hong Kong

THE KROLL-O'GARA COMPANY

9113 Le Saint Drive

Fairfield, OH 45014

Tel: (513) 874-2112 Fax: (513) 874-2558

CEO: Jules B. Kroll, Chmn.

FO: Wilfred T. O'Gara, Pres.

HR: Carol Pelosi, Dir.

Web site: www.kroll-ogara.com

Emp: 913 Rev: $190.4 mil.

Security and consulting services and vechiles.

Australia, Brazil, China (PRC), England, U.K., France, Germany, Hong Kong, India, Italy, Japan, Mexico, Philippines, Russia, Singapore, Switzerland

KULICKE & SOFFA INDUSTRIES INC.

2101 Blair Mill Road

Willow Grove, PA 19090

Tel: (215) 784-6000 Fax: (215) 659-7588

CEO: C. Scott Kulicke

HR: Jack Laflin

Web site: www.kns.com

Emp: 2,300 Rev: $501 mil.

Semiconductor assembly systems and services.

Hong Kong, Ireland, Israel, Japan, Singapore, Spain, Switzerland

THE KULJIAN COMPANY

3624 Science Center

Philadelphia, PA 19104

Tel: (215) 243-1900 Fax: (215) 243-1909

CEO: Arthur Kuljian, Pres.

FO: John A. Burckhardt

HR: P. H. Jeryan

Emp: 145

Studies, design, engineering, construction management and site supervision.

England, U.K., Hong Kong, India, Jordan, Kenya, Saudi Arabia, Syria, Tanzania, Venezuela

KURT SALMON ASSOCIATES INC.

1355 Peachtree Street NE

Atlanta, GA 30309

Tel: (404) 892-0321 Fax: (404) 898-9590

CEO: David A. Cole

FO: Peter Brown

HR: Marian Crandall

Emp: 550

Management consulting: consumer products, retailing.

England, U.K., Germany, Hong Kong, Italy, Spain, Switzerland

KWIK LOK CORPORATION

PO Box 9548

Yakima, WA 98909

Tel: (509) 248-4770 Fax: (509) 457-6531

CEO: Jerre Paxton, Pres.

HR: James Forsythe

Emp: 350

Mfr. bag closing machinery.

Australia, Canada, Ireland, Japan

KWIK-SEW PATTERN CO., INC.

3000 Washington Ave. North

Minneapolis, MN 55411

Tel: (612) 521-7651 Fax: (612) 521-1662

CEO: Kerstin Martensson

Web site: www.kwiksew.com

Emp: 40

Mfr. patterns and instruction books for home sewing.

Australia, Canada, New Zealand

KYSOR INDUSTRIAL CORPORATION

10 Wright Street

Cadillac, MI 49601-9785

Tel: (616) 779-7500 Fax: (616) 775-5749

CEO: Tim Campbell, Pres.

FO: Timothy D. Peterson

Emp: 2,300

Mfr. commercial refrigeration, commercial vehicle components.

South Korea, Wales, U.K.

L

LA ROCHE INDUSTRIES INC.

1100 Johnson Ferry Road, NE

Atlanta, GA 30342

Tel: (404) 851-0300 Fax: (404) 851-0421

CEO: W. Walter LaRoche, III

FO: Harold W. Ingalls, VP

HR: Joseph Martucci, Dir.

Web site: www.larocheind.com

Emp: 1,100 Rev: $400 mil.

Produce and distribute organic and inorganic chemicals.

France, Germany

LADAS & PARRY

26 West 61st Street

New York, NY 10023

Tel: (212) 708-1800 Fax: (212) 246-8959

CEO: Chuck Bernstein, Mng. Prtn.

International law firm.

England, U.K., Germany

LAI WARD HOWELL INTERNATIONAL INC.

200 Park Ave., Ste. 3100

New York, NY 10016-0136

Tel: (212) 953-7900 Fax: (212) 953-7907

CEO: Robert L. Pearson

FO: Roderick C. Gow, EVP

HR: Jonathan M. Canger, VP

Web site: www.laix.com

Emp: 386 Rev: $62 mil.

International executive search firm.

Australia, Austria, Bulgaria, Canada, Colombia, Czech Republic, England, U.K., Finland, France, Germany, Hong Kong, Hungary, Ireland, Japan, Mexico, Netherlands, New Zealand, Norway, Poland, Romania, Russia, Singapore, South Africa, South Korea, Spain, Sweden, Switzerland, Taiwan (ROC), Venezuela

LAMSON & SESSIONS CO

25701 Science Park Drive

Cleveland, OH 44122

Tel: (216) 464-3400 Fax: (216) 464-1455

CEO: John B. Schulze, Pres.

HR: Chares E. Allen, SVP

Emp: 1,814

Mfr. thermoplastic electrical conduit and related products; products for transportation equipment industry.

Denmark, Germany

LAND O' LAKES, INC.

4001 Lexington Ave. North

Arden Hills, MN 55126

Tel: (612) 481-2222 Fax: (612) 481-2022

CEO: John E. Gherty, Pres.

FO: Duane Halverson, EVP

HR: Jack Martin, VP

Emp: 5,500

Produces butter, margarine, packaged milk, sour cream, snack dips and Alpine Lace cheeses and crop protection products.

Albania, Bulgaria, Jamaica, Mexico, Poland, Romania, Russia, Taiwan (ROC), Uganda, Ukraine

LANDAUER ASSOCIATES INC.

666 Fifth Ave., 25th Fl.

New York, NY 10103-0001

Tel: (212) 621-9500 Fax: (212) 621-9567

CEO: Steven Kaplan, Pres.

Real estate counseling services.

Australia

LANDAUER INC.

2 Science Road

Glenwood, IL 60425-1586

Tel: (708) 755-7000 Fax: (708) 755-7016

CEO: Thomas M. Fulton

Web site: www.laudauer.com

Emp: 260

Provider of radiation dosimetry services to hospitals, medical and dental offices, university and national laboratories, nuclear power plants and other industries.

England, U.K., Japan

LANDER CO., INC.

PO Box 9610

Englewood, NJ 07631

Tel: (201) 568-9700 Fax: (201) 568-1788

CEO: Michael A. Zeher

FO: Robert Pozil

HR: Sandy Kaufman

Emp: 300

Mfr. health and beauty aids, cosmetics and toiletries.

Canada

LANDIS GARDNER

20 East Sixth Street

Waynesboro, PA 17268-2050

Tel: (717) 762-2161 Fax: (717) 765-5143

CEO: Jim Herrman

FO: G. E. Miller

HR: L. R. McCleaf

Emp: 780

Mfr. precision cylindrical grinding machinery and double disc grinding.

China (PRC), England, U.K.

LANDOR ASSOCIATES

Klamath House, 1001 Front Street

San Francisco, CA 94111-1424

Tel: (415) 955-1400 Fax: (415) 955-1358

CEO: Clay Timon, Chmn.

FO: Kay Stout, Mng. Dir.

Web site: www.landor.com

International marketing consulting firm, focused on developing and maintaining brand identity.

China (PRC), England, U.K., France, Germany, Hong Kong, India, Italy, Japan, Mexico, Philippines, South Korea, Spain, Sweden, Taiwan (ROC), Thailand

LANDS' END INC.

1 Lands' End Lane

Dodgeville, WI 53595

Tel: (608) 935-9341 Fax: (608) 935-4260

CEO: Michael J. Smith, Pres.

FO: Frank A. Buettner, VP Int'l.

HR: Kelly A. Ritchie

Web site: www.landsend.com

Emp: 9,000 Rev: $1,264 mil.

Clothing, home furnishings and mail order catalog company.

England, U.K., Germany, Japan

LANGER BIOMECHANICS GROUP, INC.

450 Commack Road
Deer Park, NY 11729
Tel: (516) 667-1200 Fax: (516) 667-1203
CEO: Gary L. Grahn, Pres.
FO: Kenneth Granat, Chrm.
Web site: www.langerbiomechanics.com
Emp: 200 Rev: $10.5 mil.
Mfr. prescription foot orthotics and gait-related products.
Canada, England, U.K.

LANIER WORLDWIDE, INC.

2300 Parklake Drive, N.E.
Atlanta, GA 30345
Tel: (770) 496-9500 Fax: (770) 621-1535
CEO: Wesley Cantrell, Pres.
HR: Harley Ostin
Specialize in digital copiers and multi-functional systems.
Australia, Belgium, Bermuda, Canada, Chile, China (PRC), Colombia, Costa Rica, Denmark, Dominican Republic, El Salvador, England, U.K., France, Germany, Greece, Guatemala, Italy, Netherlands, Norway, Panama, Russia, Singapore, Spain, Switzerland

LANMAN & KEMP-BARCLAY & CO., INC.

25 Woodland Ave.
Westwood, NJ 07675
Tel: (201) 666-4990 Fax: (201) 666-5836
CEO: Stephen Cooper
FO: Servando Rodriguez
HR: Antonia Castro
Web site: www.lanman-and-kemp.com
Emp: 40 Rev: $4 mil.
Manufacturers toiletries, soap and cologne.
Colombia, Peru, Venezuela

LATHAM & WATKINS

633 West 5th Street, Ste. 4000,
Los Angeles, CA 90071-2007
Tel: (213) 485-1234 Fax: (213) 891-8763
CEO: Robert Dell, Gen. Ptnr.
HR: Charles Curtis, Dir.
Web site: www.lw.com
Emp: 750 Rev: $420 mil.
International law firm.
England, U.K., Hong Kong, Japan, Russia, Singapore

LAW INTERNATIONAL INC.

3 Ravinia Drive, Ste. 1830
Atlanta, GA 30346
Tel: (404) 396-8000 Fax: (404) 391-0291
CEO: Michael W. Montgomery
FO: Michael W. Montgomery
Emp: 130
Consulting engineers and architects.
Saudi Arabia, Spain

LAWSON MARDON WHEATON, INC.

1101 Wheaton Ave.
Milville, NJ 08332
Tel: (609) 825-1400 Fax: (609) 825-0146
CEO: Hank Carter
Emp: 6,000
Mfr. glass and plastic containers and plastic products.
Brazil, Canada, England, U.K., India, Mexico

LAWTER INTERNATIONAL INC.

8601 95th Street
Pleasant Prairie, WI 53158
Tel: (414) 947-7300 Fax: (414) 947-7328
CEO: John Jilek, Pres.
HR: Tina Lenartz
Emp: 336
Resins, pigments and coatings.
Belgium, Canada, England, U.K., Germany, Ireland, Taiwan (ROC)

LAYNE CHRISTIANSEN, INC.

1900 Shawnee Mission Pkwy.
Mission Woods, KS 66205
Tel: (913) 362-0510 Fax: (913) 362-0133
CEO: Andrew Schmidt, Pres.
HR: John Wright
Emp: 3,500
Contract drilling.
Chile

LE TOURNEAU COMPANY

PO Box 2307
Longview, TX 75606
Tel: (903) 237-7000 Fax: (903) 267-7032
CEO: Dan Eckermann, Pres.
FO: Richard A. Hemmelgarn
HR: Chuck Bellatti
Emp: 1,250
Mfr. heavy construction and mining machinery equipment.
Australia, Belgium, Brazil, Chile, Colombia, Egypt, England, U.K., India, Japan, Mexico, Netherlands, New Zealand, Norway, Paraguay, Philippines, South Africa, Spain, Sweden, Thailand, Turkey, Venezuela, Yugoslavia

LEACH INTERNATIONAL INC.
6900 Orangethorp Ave.
Buena Park, CA 90622-5032
Tel: (714) 739-0770 Fax: (714) 739-1713
CEO: Ernie Johnson, Pres.
FO: Ron P. Zimmerman
HR: Jim Owens
Emp: 450
Mfr. aerospace electromechanical & solid state components.
England, U.K., France, Germany

LEAR CORPORATION
21557 Telegraph Road
Southfield, MI 48086-5008
Tel: (248) 746-1500 Fax: (248) 746-1722
CEO: Kenneth L. Way, Chmn.
FO: Robert E. Rossiter, Pres. & COO
HR: Roger A. Jackson, SVP HR
Web site: www.lear.com
Emp: 51,000 Rev: $7,343 mil.
Mgf./dist. car seats worldwide.
Brazil, China (PRC), Germany, India, Italy, Mexico, Poland, Portugal, Thailand, Turkey

LEARNING COMPANY
1 Athenaeum Street
Cambridge, MA 02142
Tel: (617) 494-1200 Fax: (617) 494-1219
CEO: Kevin O'Leary, Pres.
Mfr./distribute productivity and educational software.
Australia, Canada, England, U.K., France, Germany, Ireland, Netherlands

LEARNING TREE INTERNATIONAL, INC.
6053 West Century Blvd.
Los Angeles, CA 90045-0028
Tel: (310) 417-9700 Fax: (310) 417-8684
CEO: David C. Collins, Chmn.
FO: Eric Garen, Pres.
HR: Mary Adams, VP Adm.
Web site: www.learningtree.com
Emp: 645 Rev: $164.5 mil.
Information technology training services.
Canada, England, U.K., France, Hong Kong, Japan, Sweden

LEARONAL INC.
272 Buffalo Ave.
Freeport, NY 11520
Tel: (516) 868-8800 Fax: (516) 868-8824
CEO: Ronald Ostrow, Pres.
FO: Richard Kessler, EVP & COO
Web site: www.learonal.com
Emp: 1,000 Rev: $241 mil.
Producer of specialty chemicals and coatings. Provides electroplating and chemical manufacturing services.
Brazil, England, U.K., France, Germany, Hong Kong, Italy, Japan, Malaysia, Philippines, Singapore, South Korea, Switzerland, Taiwan (ROC)

G. LEBLANC CORPORATION
7001 Leblanc Blvd., PO Box 1415
Kenosha, WI 53141-1415
Tel: (414) 658-1644 Fax: (414) 658-2824
CEO: Vito Pascucci
FO: Andris Kusietis
HR: Richard Lindquist
Web site: www.gleblanc.com
Mfr./sale/services musical wind instruments.
France

LeBOEUF, LAMB, GREENE & MacRAE LLP
125 West 55th Street, 12th Fl.
New York, NY 10019
Tel: (212) 424-8000 Fax: (212) 424-8500

CEO: Donald J. Greene

HR: Gerri Stone

Web site: www.llgm.com

Emp: 1,725 Rev: $226 mil.

International law firm.

Belgium, Brazil, England, U.K., France, Kazakhstan, Kirghizia, Russia, Uzbekistan

LEDERLE LABS

401 N. Middletown Road

Pearl River, NY 10965

Tel: (914) 732-5000 Fax: (914) 732-5600

CEO: R. P. Luciano

Antibiotics and pharmaceutical products.

Japan, Kenya

LEGG MASON, INC.

100 Light Street

Baltimore, MD 21202

Tel: (410) 539-0000 Fax: (410) 539-4175

CEO: Raymond A. Mason, Chmn., Pres.

FO: James W. Brinkley, SEVP

HR: Joseph Timmons, VP HR

Web site: www.leggmason.com

Emp: 3,460 Rev: $639.7 mil.

Financial services; securities brokerage and trading, investment management, institutional and individual clients, investment and commercial mortgage banking.

England, U.K., France, Switzerland

LEHMAN BROTHERS HOLDINGS INC.

Three World Financial Center

New York, NY 10285

Tel: (212) 526-7000 Fax: (212) 526-3738

CEO: Richard S. Fuld ,Jr., Chmn.

FO: Stephen M. Lessing

HR: Mary Anne Rasmussen

Web site: www.lehman.com

Emp: 8,350 Rev: $16,880 mil.

Financial services, securities and merchant banking services.

Argentina, Bahrain, Brazil, Canada, Chile, China (PRC), England, U.K., France, Germany, Hong Kong, India, Indonesia, Israel, Italy, Japan, Mexico, Singapore, South Korea, Spain, Switzerland, Taiwan (ROC), Thailand, United Arab Emirates, Uruguay

LEIGH PRODUCTS INC.

2627 East Beltline, SE

Grand Rapids, MI 49506

Tel: (616) 942-1440 Fax: (616) 942-2170

CEO: Jim Dahlke, Pres.

Emp: 1,156

Ceiling systems, ventilators, wire hardware.

Canada

LENNOX INDUSTRIES INC.

2100 Lake Park Blvd.

Richardson, TX 75080

Tel: (972) 497-5000 Fax: (214) 497-5159

CEO: Robert Schjerven, Pres.

Emp: 4,925

Mfr. A/C products, gas heating products.

Australia, England, U.K.

LESLIE FAY, INC.

1412 Broadway

New York, NY 10018

Tel: (212) 221-4000 Fax: (212) 221-4033

CEO: John J. Pomerantz, Chmn.

FO: John Ward, Pres.

HR: Warren Heaps

Emp: 3,500

Wearing apparel.

Canada

LEUCADIA NATIONAL CORPORATION

315 Park Ave. South

New York, NY 10010

Tel: (212) 460-1900 Fax: (212) 598-4869

CEO: Joseph S. Steinberg, Chmn.

Holding company: real estate, banking, insurance, equipment leasing, mfr. plastics, cable, sinks & cabinets.

Barbados, Belgium, Bolivia, Canada, El Salvador

LEVEL EXPORT CORPORATION

1460 Broadway

New York, NY 10018

Tel: (212) 354-2600 Fax: (212) 302-8421

CEO: A. Levys

Emp: 24

Chewing gum.

Spain

LEVI STRAUSS & COMPANY

1155 Battery Street, Levi's Plaza
San Francisco, CA 94111-1230
Tel: (415) 544-6000 Fax: (415) 501-3939
CEO: Robert D. Haas, Chmn.
FO: Peter A. Jacobi, Pres. & COO
HR: Donna J. Goya, SVP
Web site: www.levistrauss.com
Emp: 37,000 Rev: $6,900 mil.

Mfr./distributor casual wearing apparel.

Argentina, Australia, Belgium, Brazil, Canada, Czech Republic, Denmark, England, U.K., Finland, France, Germany, Greece, Hong Kong, Hungary, Ireland, Italy, Japan, Malaysia, Mexico, Netherlands, New Zealand, Norway, Philippines, Poland, Russia, Singapore, South Africa, Spain, Sweden, Switzerland, Turkey

LHS GROUP INC.

6 Concourse Pkwy., Ste. 2700
Atlanta, GA 30328
Tel: (770) 280-3000 Fax: (770) 280-3099
CEO: Hartmut Lademacher, Chmn. & CEO
FO: Paul Freeman, VP
HR: Vance Schaeffer
Web site: www.lhsgroup.com
Emp: 750 Rev: $105 mil.

Provides multilingual software for telecommunications carriers.

Colombia, Germany, Hong Kong, Malaysia, Switzerland

LIBERTY MUTUAL GROUP

175 Berkeley Street
Boston, MA 02117
Tel: (617) 357-9500 Fax: (617) 350-7648
CEO: Gary L. Countryman, Chmn.
FO: Edmund F. Kelly, Pres.
Web site: www.libertymutual. com
Emp: 20,000 Rev: $8,500 mil.

Provides workers' compensation insurance and operates physical rehabilitation centers and provides risk prevention management.

Argentina, Belgium, Bermuda, Brazil, Canada, France, Hong Kong, Ireland, Japan, Malaysia, Mexico, Scotland, U.K., South Africa, Venezuela

LIFE TECHNOLOGIES INC.

9800 Medical Center Drive
Rockville, MD 20850
Tel: (301) 840-8000 Fax: (301) 329-8635
CEO: Dr. Stark Thompson, Pres.
Emp: 1,300 Rev: $310 mil.

Biotechnology.

Australia, Austria, Belgium, China (PRC), Denmark, England, U.K., France, Germany, Hong Kong, India, Italy, Japan, Netherlands, New Zealand, Poland, Portugal, Spain, Sweden, Switzerland, Taiwan (ROC), Uruguay

LIGHTNIN

135 Mt. Read Blvd., PO Box 1370
Rochester, NY 14611
Tel: (716) 436-5550 Fax: (716) 436-5589
CEO: H. P. Engelbrecht, Pres.
HR: Gary Betters
Emp: 2,300

Mfr./sale/services industrial mixing machinery, aerators.

Australia, Canada, China (PRC), England, U.K., Mexico, Singapore

LIGHTOLIER

631 Airport Road
Fall River, MA 02720
Tel: (508) 679-8131 Fax: (508) 674-4710
CEO: Zia Eftekar, Pres.
HR: M. Geuss
Emp: 1,290

Mfr. lighting fixtures and portable lamps.

Canada, Mexico

ELI LILLY & COMPANY

Lilly Corporate Center
Indianapolis, IN 46285
Tel: (317) 276-2000 Fax: (317) 277-6579
CEO: Sidney Taurel, Pres.
FO: Gerhard N. Mayr, Pres. Int'l
HR: Pedro P. Granadillo, VP
Web site: www.lilly.com
Emp: 31,100 Rev: $8,518 mil.

Mfr. pharmaceuticals and animal health products.

Argentina, Australia, Austria, Belgium, Brazil, Bulgaria, Canada, Chile, China (PRC), Colombia, Croatia, Czech Republic, Denmark, Egypt,

England, U.K., Estonia, Finland, France, Germany, Greece, Hong Kong, Hungary, India, Indonesia, Ireland, Israel, Italy, Ivory Coast, Japan, Kazakhstan, Kenya, Latvia, Lebanon, Lithuania, Malaysia, Mexico, Morocco, Netherlands, New Zealand, Norway, Pakistan, Peru, Philippines, Poland, Portugal, Romania, Russia, Saudi Arabia, Singapore, Slovakia, Slovenia, South Africa, South Korea, Spain, Sweden, Switzerland, Taiwan (ROC), Thailand, Turkey, Ukraine, United Arab Emirates, Uzbekistan, Venezuela, Vietnam, Yugoslavia

LILLY INDUSTRIES INC.

733 S West Street
Indianapolis, IN 46225
Tel: (317) 687-6700 Fax: (317) 687-6710
CEO: Douglas W. Huemme, Chmn.
FO: Robert S. Bailey
HR: Barry Melnkovic
Emp: 1,242

Mfr. industrial finishes, coatings & fillers.

Canada, Germany, Malaysia, Taiwan (ROC)

LIMITORQUE

PO Box 11318
Lynchburg, VA 24506
Tel: (804) 528-4400 Fax: (804) 845-9736
CEO: Bill Friel, Chmn.
FO: Mike Knudsen
HR: Dave McIntosh
Emp: 500

Mfr./marketing/services electric valve actuators.

England, U.K., Singapore

THE LINCOLN ELECTRIC COMPANY

22801 St. Clair Ave.
Cleveland, OH 44117-1199
Tel: (216) 481-8100 Fax: (216) 486-8385
CEO: Anthony A. Massaro, Chmn.
FO: John H. Weaver, VP
HR: Raymond S. Vogt, VP
Web site: www.lincolnelectric.com
Emp: 6,100 Rev: $1,150 mil.

Mfr. arc welding and welding related products, oxy-fuel and thermal cutting equipment and integral AC motors.

Argentina, Australia, Bahrain, Belgium, Brazil, Canada, Chile, China (PRC), Colombia, England, U.K., France, Germany, India, Indonesia, Italy, Japan, Mexico, Netherlands, Norway, Peru, Philippines, Poland, Romania, Russia, Saudi Arabia, Scotland, U.K., Singapore, South Africa, Spain, Sweden, Thailand, Turkey, United Arab Emirates, Venezuela

LINCOLN INDUSTRIAL

1 Lincoln Way
St. Louis, MO 63120
Tel: (314) 679-4200 Fax: (800) 424-5359
CEO: Mark Schroepfer, Pres.
HR: Albert W. Adams
Web site: www.lincolnindustrial.com
Emp: 700

Lubrication equipment and materials dispensing equipment.

Germany

LINCOLN NATIONAL LIFE REINSURANCE

PO Box 7808
Ft. Wayne, IN 46801
Tel: (219) 455-2000 Fax: (219) 455-2738
CEO: Larry Rowland, Pres.
FO: John Cantrell
Emp: 600

Reinsurance.

Philippines

ARTHUR D. LITTLE, INC.

25 Acorn Park
Cambridge, MA 02140-2390
Tel: (617) 498-5000 Fax: (617) 498-7200
CEO: Charles R. LaMantia, Pres.
FO: Maurice J.L. Olivier
HR: Alan J. Friedman, SVP
Web site: www.adlittle.com
Emp: 3,300 Rev: $589 mil.

Management, environmental, health & safety consulting; technical & product development.

Argentina, Australia, Austria, Belgium, Brazil, Canada, Colombia, Czech Republic, Denmark, England, U.K., France, Germany, Hong Kong, India, Italy, Japan, Malaysia, Mexico, Netherlands, Norway, Portugal, Russia, Saudi Arabia, Singapore, South Korea, Spain, Sweden, Switzerland, United Arab Emirates, Venezuela

LITTON INDUSTRIES INC.

21240 Burbank Boulevard
Woodland Hills, CA 91367
Tel: (818) 598-5000 Fax: (818) 598-3313
CEO: Michael R. Brown, Pres.
HR: Nancy Gaymon, VP
Web site: www.litton.com
Emp: 34,800 Rev: $4.2 bil.
Shipbuilding, electronics, and information technology.
Canada, England, U.K., France, Germany, Italy, Japan, Switzerland

LITTON PRC INC.
1500 PRC Drive
McLean, VA 22102
Tel: (703) 556-1000 Fax: (703) 556-1174
CEO: Leonard Pomata, Pres.
FO: Austin Yerks
HR: Walter Goodlett, SVP
Web site: www.prc.com
Emp: 5,750
Computer systems and services.
Canada, England, U.K., Germany, South Korea

LITTON WINCHESTER ELECTRONICS
400 Park Road
Watertown, CT 06795-0500
Tel: (860) 945-5000 Fax: (860) 945-5191
CEO: A. J. Bernardini, Pres.
Emp: 500
Mfr. electrical and electronic connectors, PCB assemblies and hardware.
Japan, Scotland, U.K.

LIZ CLAIBORNE INC.
1441 Broadway, 22nd Fl.
New York, NY 10018
Tel: (212) 354-4900 Fax: (212) 626-1800
CEO: Paul R. Charron, Chmn.
Rev: $2,400 mil.
Apparel manufacturer.
Canada, England, U.K.

LNP ENGINEERING PLASTICS
475 Creamery Way
Exton, PA 19341
Tel: (610) 363-4500 Fax: (610) 363-4749
CEO: Richard Burns, Pres.
FO: Evan Ewan
HR: Donald Mattey
Web site: www.lnp.com
Emp: 750
Mfr. thermoplastic composites.
Netherlands, Singapore

LoBue ASSOCIATES, INC.
1771 East Flamingo Road, Ste. #219A
Las Vegas, NV 89119
Tel: (702) 989-6940 Fax: (702) 433-4021
CEO: Eric Berliner, Pres.
FO: Robert Andrzejewski
HR: Donna Ortenzi
Emp: 50
Management consulting services for financial services industry.
Hong Kong

LOCKHEED MARTIN CORPORATION
6801 Rockledge Drive
Bethesda, MD 20817
Tel: (301) 897-6000 Fax: (301) 897-6652
CEO: Vance D. Coffman, Chmn.
FO: Peter Teets, Pres
HR: Robert B. Corlett
Web site: www.imco.com
Emp: 170,000 Rev: $1,200. Mil.
Design/mfr./management systems in fields of space, defense, energy, electronics and technical services.
Australia, Austria, Bahrain, Belgium, Canada, China (PRC), Denmark, Egypt, England, U.K., Ethiopia, France, Germany, Greece, Guam, Hong Kong, Hungary, India, Indonesia, Ireland, Israel, Italy, Japan, Jordan, Kuwait, Malaysia, Mexico, Netherlands, New Zealand, Northern Ireland, U.K., Norway, Pakistan, Poland, Russia, Saudi Arabia, Singapore, South Korea, Spain, Sri Lanka, Sweden, Switzerland, Taiwan (ROC), Thailand, Turkey, Turkmenistan, United Arab Emirates, Venezuela

LOCTITE CORPORATION
10 Columbus Boulevard
Hartford, CT 06106
Tel: (203) 520-5000 Fax: (203) 520-5073
CEO: David Freeman, Chmn.
HR: Bruce Vakiener, EVP

Web site: www.loctite.com

Emp: 4,725 Rev: $789 mil.

Mfr./sale industrial adhesives and sealants.

Argentina, Australia, Austria, Belgium, Brazil, Bulgaria, Canada, Chile, China (PRC), Colombia, Costa Rica, Croatia, Czech Republic, Denmark, England, U.K., Estonia, Finland, France, Germany, Hong Kong, Hungary, India, Ireland, Italy, Japan, Malaysia, Mexico, Netherlands, New Zealand, Norway, Philippines, Poland, Romania, Russia, Singapore, Slovakia, Slovenia, South Africa, South Korea, Spain, Sweden, Taiwan (ROC), Thailand, Turkey, Venezuela, Vietnam, Yugoslavia

LOEWS HOTELS

667 Madison Ave.

New York, NY 10021-8087

Tel: (212) 545-2000 Fax: (212) 545-2525

CEO: James S. Tisch, Pres. & COO

FO: Jonathan M. Tisch

HR: Alan Momeyer, VP

Web site: www.loews.com

Emp: 35,000

Hotel chain.

Canada, Monaco

LORAL SPACE & COMMUNICATIONS LTD.

600 Third Ave.

New York, NY 10016

Tel: (212) 697-1105 Fax: (212) 338-5662

CEO: Bernard L. Schwartz, Chmn.

FO: Henry A. Radzikowski, VP

HR: Stephen L. Jackson

Web site: www.loral.com

Emp: 4,000 Rev: $1.3 mil.

Marketing coordination: defense electronics, communications systems.

Hong Kong, Japan, South Korea

LORD CORPORATION

2000 West Grandview Blvd

Erie, PA 16514

Tel: (814) 868-0924 Fax: (814) 486-4345

CEO: Charles Hora, Pres.

FO: Edward J. Sawyer

HR: Robert Busch

Emp: 2,000 Rev: $275 mil.

Adhesives, coatings, chemicals, film products.

Brazil, England, U.K., Germany, Japan, Mexico

LOUIS ALLIS COMPANY

PO Box 2020, 427 East Stewart

Milwaukee, WI 53201

Tel: (414) 481-6000 Fax: (414) 481-8895

CEO: Daniel Stetler, Pres.

FO: J. A. Westrich

Emp: 1,500

Electric motors, adjustable speed drives, generators and compressors.

France, Sweden, Switzerland

LOUISIANA-PACIFIC CORPORATION

111 S.W. Fifth Ave.

Portland, OR 97204-3601

Tel: (503) 221-0800 Fax: (503) 796-0204

CEO: Mark A. Suwyn, Chmn.

FO: J. Keith Matheney, VP

HR: Michael J. Tull, VP

Web site: www.lpcorp.com

Emp: 12,000 Rev: $ 2,403 mil.

Mfr. lumber and building products.

Canada, Ireland

LOWE & PARTNERS WORLDWIDE

1114 Ave. of the Americas

New York, NY 10036

Tel: (212) 403-6700 Fax: (212) 403-6710

CEO: Frank Lowe, Chmn.

Emp: 4,000 Rev: $496 mil.

International advertising agency network.

Argentina, Austria, Belgium, Brazil, Bulgaria, Canada, Colombia, Czech Republic, Denmark, England, U.K., Finland, France, Germany, Greece, Hong Kong, Hungary, India, Italy, Mexico, Netherlands, Poland, Portugal, Romania, Russia, Singapore, Slovakia, Slovenia, South Africa, Spain, Sweden, Switzerland, Turkey, Venezuela

LSB INDUSTRIES INC.

16 S Pennsylvania Ave.

Oklahoma City, OK 73107

Tel: (405) 235-4546 Fax: (405) 235-5067

CEO: Jack E. Golsen, VP

Emp: 2,000

Mfr. acids, agricultural and industrial chemicals.

Italy

LSI LOGIC CORPORATION

1551 McCarthy Blvd
Milpitas, CA 95035
Tel: (408) 433-8000 Fax: (408) 954-3220
CEO: Wilfred J. Corrigan, Chmn. & CEO
FO: Joe M. Zelayta, EVP
HR: Lewis C. Wallbridge, VP
Web site: www.lsilogic.com
Emp: 4,443 Rev: $1,290 mil.

Develop/mfr. semiconductors.

Australia, Canada, Denmark, England, U.K., France, Germany, Hong Kong, Israel, Italy, Japan, Netherlands, Singapore, South Korea, Switzerland, Taiwan (ROC)

LTV STEEL COMPANY

200 Public Square
Cleveland, OH 44114-2308
Tel: (216) 622-5000 Fax: (216) 622-1066
CEO: J. Peter Kelly, Pres.
HR: Robert W. Huenefeld
Emp: 1,400

Mfr. steel.

Japan

LTX CORPORATION

LTX Park, University Ave.
Westwood, MA 02090
Tel: (617) 461-1000 Fax: (617) 326-4883
CEO: Roger W. Blethen, Pres.
Emp: 950 Rev: $266 mil.

Design/mfr. computer-controlled semiconductor test systems.

England, U.K., France, Germany, Italy, Japan, Netherlands

THE LUBRIZOL CORPORATION

29400 Lakeland Blvd.
Wickliffe, OH 44092-2298
Tel: (440) 943-4200 Fax: (440) 943-5337
CEO: William G. Bares
FO: J.E. Hodge, VP Opers.
HR: Mark W. Meister, VP
Web site: www.lubrizol.com
Emp: 4,291 Rev: $1,674 mil.

Mfr. chemicals additives for lubricants & fuels.

Argentina, Australia, Austria, Belgium, Bolivia, Brazil, Canada, Chile, China (PRC), Colombia, Ecuador, Egypt, England, U.K., Finland, France, Germany, Greece, India, Indonesia, Italy, Japan, Mexico, Nigeria, Norway, Paraguay, Peru, Russia, Saudi Arabia, Singapore, South Africa, South Korea, Spain, Sweden, Switzerland, Taiwan (ROC), Thailand, Turkey, United Arab Emirates, Venezuela

LUCENT TECHNOLOGIES, INC.

600 Mountain Ave.
Murray Hill, NJ 07974-0636
Tel: (908) 582-3000 Fax: (908) 582-2110
CEO: Richard McGinn, Pres.
FO: Dan Stanzione, COO
Web site: www.lucent.com
Emp: 126,600 Rev: $26,360 mil.

Design/mfr. wide range of public and private networks, communication systems and software, data networking systems, business telephone systems and microelectronics components.

Argentina, Australia, Brazil, Brunei, Canada, China (PRC), England, U.K., France, Germany, Hong Kong, India, Indonesia, Ireland, Japan, Malaysia, Mexico, Netherlands, Philippines, Poland, Russia, Singapore, South Korea, Spain, Taiwan (ROC), Thailand, Vietnam

LUCKETT TOBACCOS INC.

222 South First Street, #403
Louisville, KY 40202
Tel: (502) 561-0070 Fax: (502) 584-1650
CEO: William R. Meyer, Pres.
Emp: 6

Wholesale tobacco, cigarette mfr. supplies & equipment.

Haiti

LUFKIN INDUSTRIES INC.

407 Kilen Street
Lufkin, TX 75901
Tel: (409) 634-2211 Fax: (409) 637-5474
CEO: Doug Smith, Pres.
Emp: 2,300

Mfr./distributor oilfield pumping equipment, industrial hardware, truck trailers, propulsion gears.

Canada

LUFKIN RULE COMPANY

PO Box 728

Apex, NC 27502

Tel: (919) 362-7510 Fax: (919) 387-2371

CEO: Dave Cartright, Pres.

HR: Matt Dudukovich

Mfr. measuring tapes & rulers, hand tools.

Netherlands, Venezuela

LYDALL INC.

1 Colonial Road

Manchester, CT 06040

Tel: (860) 646-1233 Fax: (860) 646-4917

CEO: Leonard R. Jaskol

FO: Jacques J. Wagner

HR: Mon Estey

Emp: 900

Mfr. converted paper products, paperboard, non-woven specialty media.

France, Japan

LYRIC HIGH FIDELITY INC.

1221 Lexington Ave.

New York, NY 10028

Tel: (212) 535-5710 Fax:

CEO: Michael Kay, Pres.

Electrical equipment.

Greece

M

M-I

PO Box 48242

Houston, TX 77242-2842

Tel: (713) 739-0222 Fax: (713) 308-9503

CEO: Lauren Carroll, Pres.

HR: William Berryhill

Emp: 1,000

Drilling fluids.

Argentina, Brazil, Cameroon, Colombia, Denmark, Egypt, England, U.K., Gabon, Indonesia, Ivory Coast, Netherlands, Oman, Scotland, U.K., Tunisia, United Arab Emirates, Venezuela

M/A-COM INC.

1011 Pawtucket Boulevard

Lowell, MA 01853

Tel: (978) 442-5000 Fax: (978) 442-5354

CEO: Richard Clark, Pres.

HR: Jim Sullivan

Mfr. electronic components and communications equipment.

Argentina, Brazil, Canada, England, U.K., Finland, France, Germany, Hong Kong, Hungary, India, Ireland, Israel, Italy, Japan, Netherlands, New Zealand, Poland, South Africa, South Korea, Sweden, Turkey

MacANDREWS & FORBES GROUP INC.

36 East 63rd Street

New York, NY 10021

Tel: (212) 688-9000 Fax: (212) 527-6301

CEO: Bruce Slovin, Pres.

Emp: 647

Jewelry, watches, chocolate, cocoa and cosmetics.

England, U.K.

MacDERMID INC.

245 Freight Street

Waterbury, CT 06702-0671

Tel: (203) 575-5700 Fax: (203) 575-7900

CEO: Daniel H. Leever, Pres.

FO: Michael A. Pfaff, VP

HR: Gary St. Pierre, Dir.

Web site: www.macd.com

Emp: 1,200 Rev: $314 mil.

Chemicals processing for metal industrial, plastics, electronics cleaners, strippers.

Australia, Canada, England, U.K., France, Germany, Hong Kong, Israel, Italy, Japan, Netherlands, New Zealand, Singapore, South Africa, South Korea, Spain, Switzerland, Taiwan (ROC)

THE MacNEAL-SCHWENDLER CORPORATION

815 Colorado Boulevard

Los Angeles, CA 90041

Tel: (213) 258-9111 Fax: (213) 259-3838

CEO: George Riordan, Chmn.

FO: Werner Pohl

HR: Rich Lander

Emp: 660

Develop/mfr.computer-aided engineering software & services, advanced materials technology & training.

China (PRC), England, U.K., France, Germany, Israel, Italy, Japan, Netherlands, Russia, Spain, Switzerland, Taiwan (ROC)

MACRO INTERNATIONAL INC.

11785 Beltsville Drive
Calverton, MD 20705-3119
Tel: (301) 572-0200 Fax: (301) 572-0999
CEO: Frank Quirk, Pres.
HR: Sally Brand
Emp: 300

Research, evaluation, marketing research, surveys, management consult/training, information systems.

Hungary, Poland

R.H. MACY & COMPANY INC.

151 West 34th Street
New York, NY 10001
Tel: (212) 695-4400 Fax: (212) 643-1307
CEO: James Gray, Pres.
HR: Brad Belz
Emp: 45,000

Department stores; importers.

Denmark, England, U.K., France, Hong Kong, Ireland, Israel, Italy, Japan, Philippines, South Korea, Spain

MADISON CABLE CORPORATION

125 Goddard Memorial Drive
Worcester, MA 01603
Tel: (508) 752-7320 Fax: (508) 752-4230
CEO: L. Gaviglia, Pres.
Web site: www.amp.com

Mfr. cable wiring.

Scotland, U.K.

MAGELLAN PETROLEUM CORPORATION

149 Durham Road, Oak Park #31
Madison, CT 06443-2664
Tel: (203) 245-8380 Fax: (203) 245-8380
CEO: Jim Joyce, Pres.

Oil and gas production and exploration.

Australia

MAGNETEK

26 Centry Blvd. #600
Nash, MI 37214
Tel: (615) 316-5100 Fax: (615) 316-5181
CEO: Ron Hoge
FO: Tim Perfetto
HR: Laurie Cheesborough
Emp: 1,650

Mfr. fractional horsepower electric motors.

England, U.K., Thailand

MAGNETIC METALS CORPORATION

Box 351
Camden, NJ 08105
Tel: (609) 964-7842 Fax: (609) 963-8569
CEO: Donald Walsh, Pres.
HR: J. Eisendgel
Emp: 500

Magnetic alloys, shields; laminations & special stampings.

Canada, Mexico

MAGNETROL INTERNATIONAL

5300 Belmont Road
Downers Grove, IL 60515-4499
Tel: (630) 969-4000 Fax: (630) 969-9489
CEO: Judy G. Stevenson
FO: Paul D. Myatt, Dir.
HR: Mary E. Saranczak
Web site: www.magnetrol.com
Emp: 345

Mfr. level and flow instrumentation.

Belgium, Canada, England, U.K., France, Germany, Italy

MAIDENFORM INC.

200 Madison Ave.
New York, NY 10016
Tel: (212) 592-0700 Fax: (212) 686-2087
CEO: Reznik Maurice, Pres.

Mfr. intimate apparel.

Costa Rica, Dominican Republic, Ireland, Jamaica, Mexico

MAINE PUBLIC SERVICE COMPANY

PO Box 1209
Presque Isle, ME 04769
Tel: (207) 768-5811 Fax: (207) 764-6586
CEO: Paul Cariani
HR: Michael Thibodeau

Emp: 162 Rev: $55 mil.

Electricity production and distribution.

Canada

MAKINO INC.

7680 Innovation Way, PO Box 8003

Mason, OH 45040-8003

Tel: (513) 573-7200 Fax: (513) 573-7360

CEO: Donald D. Bowers, Pres.

HR: Joan Firestone

Web site: www.makino.com

Emp: 310

Mfr. machine tools.

Japan, Singapore

MALLINCKRODT INC.

675 McDonnell Blvd., PO Box 5840

St. Louis, MO 63134

Tel: (314) 654-2000 Fax: (314) 654-3005

CEO: C. Ray Holman, Chmn.

HR: Bruce Crockett

Emp: 13,000

Mfr. specialty medical products.

Australia, Austria, Belgium, Canada, England, U.K., France, Germany, Ireland, Japan, Mexico, Netherlands, Spain

THE MANITOWOC CO., INC.

PO Box 66

Manitowoc, WI 54221-0066

Tel: (920) 684-4410 Fax: (920) 683-8129

CEO: Perry Growcock, Pres.

FO: Ron Schad/Stu Herrera

HR: Thomas Musial

Emp: 1,900

Mfr. cranes, ice-making machinery & contract products; ship repair & conversion.

England, U.K.

MANPOWER INTERNATIONAL INC.

5301 N. Ironwood Road, PO Box 2053

Milwaukee, WI 53201-2053

Tel: (414) 961-1000 Fax: (414) 961-7081

CEO: Mitchell S. Fromstein, Chmn.

FO: Jeffrey A. Joerres, SVP

HR: Sharon Rooney, Mgr.

Web site: www.manpower

Emp: 2,012,000 Rev: $7,258.5 mil.

Temporary help, contract service, training & testing.

Argentina, Australia, Austria, Belgium, Bolivia, Brazil, Canada, Chile, Czech Republic, Denmark, Ecuador, England, U.K., France, Germany, Hong Kong, Hungary, Ireland, Israel, Italy, Japan, Luxembourg, Mexico, Monaco, Netherlands, Netherlands Antilles, New Zealand, Norway, Panama, Paraguay, Peru, Portugal, Russia, Scotland, U.K., Singapore, Spain, Sweden, Switzerland, Taiwan (ROC), Uruguay, Venezuela, Wales, U.K.

MANUFACTURER'S SERVICES LTD.

200 Baker Ave.

Concord, MA 01742-2125

Tel: (978) 287-5630 Fax: (978) 287-5635

CEO: Kevin Melia

FO: Robert Donahue, EVP

Web site: www.manserve.com

Emp: 3,000 Rev: $562 mil.

Provides electronic manufacturing services to the medical, computer and peripherals industries.

Singapore, Spain

MANUGISTICS INC.

2115 East Jefferson Street

Rockville, MD 20852

Tel: (301) 984-5000 Fax: (301) 984-5094

CEO: William M. Gibson, Chmn.

HR: Carl DiPietro

Emp: 269

Computer software development services.

England, U.K.

MARCAM CORPORATION

95 Wells Ave.

Newton, MA 02459

Tel: (617) 965-0220 Fax: (617) 965-7273

CEO: Jonathan Crane, Chmn.

FO: David M. Stoner

HR: Harvey Jones, VP

Emp: 1,150

Applications software & services.

Australia, Belgium, England, U.K., France, Germany, Italy, Netherlands, Singapore

MARCO

2300 W. Commodore Way
Seattle, WA 98199
Tel: (206) 285-3200 Fax: (206) 286-8027
CEO: Peter G. Schmidt, Pres.
FO: Charles R. Hart
HR: H. T. Schlapp, Jr.
Web site: www.marco.com
Emp: 1,000
Shipbuilding and repair, commercial fishing equipment and systems and hydraulic pumps.
Chile, Peru

MARK IV INDUSTRIES INC.
501 John James Audubon Pkwy., PO Box 810
Amherst, NY 14226-0810
Tel: (716) 689-4972 Fax: (716) 689-1529
CEO: William P. Montague, Pres.
HR: Michelle Aquaillina
Web site: www.mark-iv.com
Emp: 17,000 Rev: $2,200 mil.
Mfr. diversified products: timers & controls, power equipment, loudspeaker systems, etc.
Argentina, Australia, Brazil, Canada, England, U.K., Finland, France, Germany, India, Italy, Japan, Mexico, Singapore, Spain, Sweden

MARKEM CORPORATION
150 Congress Street
Keene, NH 03431
Tel: (603) 352-1130 Fax: (603) 357-1835
CEO: Thomas P. Putnam, Pres.
HR: Peter Plante
Web site: www.markem.com.
Emp: 750
Mfr./sales of industrial marking, print machinery and hot stamping foils.
Canada, England, U.K., France, Germany, Italy, Japan, Malaysia, Mexico, Netherlands, Norway, Philippines, Singapore, Spain, Sweden, Switzerland, Uruguay

MARKET FACTS INC.
3040 Salt Creek Lane
Arlington Heights, IL 60005
Tel: (847) 590-7000 Fax: (847) 590-7010
CEO: Thomas H. Payne
HR: Charise Davis
Emp: 550
Market research services.
Canada

MARLEY COOLING TOWER COMPANY
7401 West 129th Street
Overland Park, KS 66213
Tel: (913) 664-7400 Fax: (913) 664-7641
CEO: Richard Landon, Pres.
FO: Richard Grindstaff, SVP
HR: Jim Way, VP
Web site: www.marleyct.com
Emp: 6,000
Cooling and heating towers and waste treatment systems.
Australia, England, U.K., France, Germany, India, Italy, Japan, Malaysia, Spain

MARRIOTT INTERNATIONAL INC.
1 Marriott Drive
Washington, DC 20058
Tel: (301) 380-3000 Fax: (301) 380-5181
CEO: J. Willard Marriott, Jr., Chmn.
HR: Clifford J. Ehrlich
Emp: 230,000
Lodging, contract food and beverage service, and restaurants.
Australia, Austria, Bahamas, Bermuda, Canada, Cayman Islands, Chile, China (PRC), Costa Rica, Ecuador, Egypt, El Salvador, England, U.K., France, Germany, Greece, Guatemala, Hong Kong, Hungary, Israel, Japan, Jordan, Lebanon, Malaysia, Mexico, Netherlands, Pakistan, Panama, Peru, Philippines, Poland, Russia, Saudi Arabia, Scotland, U.K., Singapore, Switzerland, Thailand, United Arab Emirates, Vietnam, Wales, U.K.

MARS INC.
6885 Elm Street
McLean, VA 22101-3810
Tel: (703) 821-4900 Fax: (703) 448-9678
CEO: Forrest E. Mars Jr.
FO: Michael Tolkowsky
Web site: www.mars.com
Emp: 28,000 Rev: $ 15,000 mil.
Mfr. candy, snack foods, rice products and cat food.
Australia, Belgium, England, U.K., Germany, Ghana, Netherlands, Ukraine

MARSH & McLENNAN COS INC.

1166 Ave. of the Americas
New York, NY 10036-2774
Tel: (212) 345-5000 Fax: (212) 345-4808
CEO: A. J. C. Smith, Chmn.
FO: Douglas C. Davis, VP
Web site: www.marshmac.com
Emp: 36,000 Rev: $6,000 mil.

Insurance agents/brokers, pension and investment management consulting services.

Argentina, Australia, Austria, Bahamas, Barbados, Belgium, Bermuda, Brazil, Canada, Cayman Islands, Channel Islands, U.K., Chile, China (PRC), Colombia, Czech Republic, Denmark, Dominican Republic, Ecuador, Egypt, El Salvador, England, U.K., Fiji, France, Germany, Greece, Guatemala, Honduras, Hong Kong, Hungary, Indonesia, Ireland, Israel, Italy, Jamaica, Japan, Kazakhstan, Kenya, Luxembourg, Malaysia, Mexico, Netherlands, New Zealand, Nigeria, Northern Ireland, U.K., Norway, Panama, Papua New Guinea, Peru, Philippines, Poland, Portugal, Romania, Russia, Scotland, U.K., Singapore, Slovakia, South Africa, South Korea, Spain, Sweden, Switzerland, Taiwan (ROC), Thailand, Turkey, United Arab Emirates, Uruguay, Venezuela, Vietnam, Wales, U.K.

MARSH BELLOFRAM

State Route 2, Box 305
Newell, WV 26050
Tel: (304) 387-1200 Fax: (304) 387-1212
CEO: Dennis R. Burns, Pres.
HR: Tony Ranalli
Web site: www.marshbellofram.com
Emp: 700

Distributor of pressure gauges, valves, etc.

England, U.K., Singapore

J B MARTIN COMPANY

10 East 53rd Street, #3100
New York, NY 10022
Tel: (212) 421-2020 Fax: (212) 421-1460
CEO: Loic De Kertanguy, Pres.
FO: Minos Samoladas
Emp: 700

Mfr./sale velvets.

Canada, Mexico

MARTIN, DROUGHT & TORRES, INC.

Nation's Bank Plaza, 25th Floor, 300 Convent Street
San Antonio, TX 78205
Tel: (210) 227-7591 Fax: (210) 227-7924
CEO: James Martin, Mng. Prtn.

International law firm.

Mexico

MARTIN-DECKER TOTCO INC.

1200 Cypress Creek Road
Cedar Park, TX 78613-3614
Tel: (512) 340-5000 Fax: (512) 340-5219
CEO: R. J. Gondek
FO: E. G. Hottle
HR: C. Taylor
Emp: 663

Mfr. oilfield and industry weight and measure systems.

Canada, Scotland, U.K., Singapore

MARY KAY COSMETICS INC.

16251 Nor Dallas Pkw
Dallas, TX 75248
Tel: (214) 630-8787 Fax: (214) 631-5938
CEO: Richard R. Rogers, Chmn.
FO: Gerald M. Allen
Emp: 1,225

Cosmetics and toiletries.

Argentina, Australia, Canada, Chile, Germany, Russia, Thailand

MASCO CORPORATION

21001 Van Born Road
Taylor, MI 48180
Tel: (313) 274-7400 Fax: (313) 374-6666
CEO: Raymond Kennedy, Pres.
HR: David G. Wesenberg
Emp: 51,300

Mfr. home improvement, building and home furnishings products.

Canada, Denmark, England, U.K., Germany, Hong Kong, Italy, Spain, Thailand

MASONITE CORPORATION

1 South Wacker Drive
Chicago, IL 60606
Tel: (312) 750-0900 Fax: (312) 750-0958
CEO: Manco Snapp, Pres.
HR: Phil Kohner

Emp: 5,200

Mfr. hardboard, softboard & molded products.

Ireland, South Africa

MASTERCARD INTERNATIONAL INC.

200 Purchase Street

Purchase, NY 10577

Tel: (914) 249-2000 Fax: (914) 249-5475

CEO: Robert W. Selander, Pres.

FO: William I. Jacobs, EVP

HR: Michael Michl, SVP

Web site: www.mastercard.com

Emp: 2,357 Rev: $1,090 mil.

Provides financial payment systems globally.

Australia, Belgium, Brazil, Canada, Chile, China (PRC), Colombia, France, Hong Kong, India, Japan, Mexico, Singapore, South Africa, South Korea, Taiwan (ROC), Thailand, United Arab Emirates, Venezuela

MATHESON GAS PRODUCTS

959 Rt. 46 East

Parsippany,, NJ 07054-0624

Tel: (973) 257-1100 Fax: (973) 257-9393

CEO: Donald Ramlow, Pres.

FO: Larry Wood

HR: Gerald Cantrella

Web site: www.mathesongas.com

Emp: 1,000

Mfr. specialty gases and equipment.

Canada

MATHEWS & CLARK COMMUNICATIONS

710 Lakeway, #170

Sunnyvale, CA 94086-4013

Tel: (408) 736-1120 Fax: (408) 736-2523

CEO: Walter H. Mathews, Chmn.

HR: S. Chandra

Public relations: hi-tech industry.

England, U.K., Netherlands

MATLACK SYSTEMS INC.

2200 Concord Pike, PO Box 8789

Wilmington, DE 19899

Tel: (302) 426-2700 Fax: (302) 426-3298

CEO: G. J. Trippitelli, Pres.

Bulk trucking & services.

Canada

MATTEL INC.

333 Continental Blvd.

El Segundo, CA 90245-5012

Tel: (310) 252-2000 Fax: (310) 252-2179

CEO: Jill E. Barand, Chmn.

FO: Astrid Autolitano, Pres. Intl.

HR: Alan Kaye, VP

Web site: www.mattelmedia.com

Emp: 25,000 Rev: $4,800 mil.

Mfr. toys, dolls, games, crafts and hobbies.

Australia, Canada, Chile, China (PRC), England, U.K., France, Germany, Hong Kong, Indonesia, Italy, Malaysia, Mexico, Netherlands, New Zealand, Singapore, Spain, Switzerland, Taiwan (ROC)

MAURICE PINCOFFS CO., INC.

2040 North Loop West, #200

Houston, TX 77018

Tel: (713) 681-5461 Fax: (713) 681-8521

CEO: John I. Griffin

FO: John Griffin

HR: Art Reese

Web site: www.pincoffs.com

Emp: 95

International marketing and distribution.

Canada, France, Taiwan (ROC)

MAXITROL COMPANY

23555 Telegraph Road, PO Box 2230

Southfield, MI 48037-2230

Tel: (248) 356-1400 Fax: (248) 356-0829

CEO: Frank Kern III, Chmn.

FO: Larry C. Koskela

Emp: 230

Mfr. gas pressure regulators, emergency shut-off valves, electronic temp controls.

Germany

MAXON CORPORATION

201 East 18th Street

Muncie, IN 47302

Tel: (765) 284-3304 Fax: (765) 286-8394

CEO: Charles Hetrick, Pres.

HR: D. A. Clevenger

Emp: 350

Industry combustion equipment and valves.

Belgium, England, U.K., Germany, Netherlands

MAXTOR CORPORATION

510 Cottonwood Drive

Milpitas, CA 95035-7403

Tel: (408) 432-1700 Fax: (408) 432-4510

CEO: Michael R. Cannon, Pres.

HR: Phil Duncan

Web site: www.maxtor.com

Emp: 4,700

Mfr., develops and markets hard disk drives for desktop computer systems.

Australia, England, U.K., France, Germany, Hong Kong, Ireland, Japan, Scotland, U.K., Singapore, South Korea, Taiwan (ROC)

MAXXAM INC.

5847 San Felipe, Ste. 2600

Houston, TX 77057

Tel: (713) 975-7600 Fax: (713) 267-3701

CEO: Charles E. Hurwitz, Chmn.

FO: John LaDuc, SVP

HR: Diane Dudley

Emp: 9,500

Holding company for aluminum and timber products and real estate industries.

Australia, England, U.K., Ghana, Jamaica

GEORGE S MAY INTERNATIONAL COMPANY

303 S Northwest Hwy.

Park Ridge, IL 60068-4255

Tel: (847) 825-8806 Fax: (847) 825-7937

CEO: Donald J. Fletcher

FO: Daniel Hostetler

HR: Judy Bell

Web site: www.georgesmay.com

Emp: 1,100 Rev: $110 mil.

Management consulting.

Canada, Italy

MAYER, BROWN & PLATT

190 S. LaSalle Street

Chicago, IL 60603

Tel: (312) 782-0600 Fax: (312) 701-7711

CEO: Robert Helman

HR: Lori Monthei, Dir.

Web site: www.mayerbrown.com

Emp: 643 Rev: $340 mil.

International law firm.

Belgium, England, U.K., Germany, Kazakhstan, Kirghizia, Mexico, Russia, Turkmenistan, Uzbekistan

MAYFRAN INTERNATIONAL

PO Box 43038

Cleveland, OH 44143

Tel: (440) 461-4100 Fax: (440) 461-5565

CEO: Bruce Terry, Pres.

Emp: 230

Mfr. conveyors for metal working and refuse.

Canada, Germany, Japan, Netherlands

MAYTAG CORPORATION

403 West Fourth Street North

Newton, IA 50208

Tel: (515) 792-8000 Fax: (515) 787-8376

CEO: William L. Beer, Pres.

FO: Carl R. Moe, Pres., Int'l.

HR: Jon O. Nicholas, VP

Web site: www.maytagcorp.com

Emp: 22,000

Mfr./sales of large appliances, ovens, dishwashers, refrigerators and washing machines.

Canada, China (PRC), England, U.K., Mexico

MBNA CORPORATION

1100 King Street

Wilmington, DE 19801

Tel: (302) 453-9930 Fax: (302) 432-3614

CEO: Alfred Lerner, Chmn.

FO: John R. Cochran, III, EVP

HR: Ken Pizer, EVP

Web site: www.mbnainternational.com

Emp: 20,000 Rev: $4,500. mil.

Credit card issuer dealing primarily with VISA and MasterCard, home equity loans and property and casualty insurance.

England, U.K.

McCALL PATTERN COMPANY

11 Penn Plaza

New York, NY 10001

Tel: (212) 465-6800 Fax: (212) 465-6831

CEO: Robert L. Hermann, Pres.

Emp: 1,000

Fashion patterns.

Australia, Canada, England, U.K., South Africa

McCANN-ERICKSON WORLDWIDE

750 Third Ave.

New York, NY 10017

Tel: (212) 984-3644 Fax: (212) 984-2629

CEO: John J. Donner, Jr., Chmn.

FO: Peter Kim

HR: Jan Wijting

Emp: 11,228 Rev: $1,670 mil.

International advertising/marketing services.

Argentina, Australia, Austria, Azerbaijan, Bangladesh, Barbados, Belgium, Bolivia, Brazil, Bulgaria, Cambodia, Cameroon, Canada, Chile, China (PRC), Colombia, Costa Rica, Croatia, Cyprus, Czech Republic, Denmark, Dominican Republic, Ecuador, El Salvador, England, U.K., Estonia, Ethiopia, Finland, France, Georgia, Germany, Ghana, Greece, Guatemala, Honduras, Hong Kong, Hungary, India, Indonesia, Ireland, Israel, Italy, Ivory Coast, Jamaica, Japan, Kazakhstan, Kenya, Laos, Latvia, Lithuania, Macedonia, Malawi, Malaysia, Mexico, Morocco, Mozambique, Myanmar, Namibia, Netherlands, New Zealand, Nicaragua, Nigeria, Northern Ireland, U.K., Norway, Pakistan, Panama, Paraguay, Peru, Philippines, Poland, Portugal, Romania, Russia, Scotland, U.K., Senegal, Singapore, Slovakia, Slovenia, South Africa, South Korea, Spain, Sri Lanka, Sweden, Switzerland, Taiwan (ROC), Tanzania, Thailand, Trinidad & Tobago, Turkey, Uganda, Ukraine, Uruguay, Uzbekistan, Venezuela, Vietnam, Wales, U.K., Yugoslavia, Zambia, Zimbabwe

McCORMICK & COMPANY, INC.

18 Loveton Circle

Sparks, MD 21152-6000

Tel: (410) 771-7301 Fax: (410) 527-8289

CEO: Robert J. Lawless

HR: Karen D. Weatherholtz

Emp: 7,600

Mfr./distribution/sale seasonings, flavorings, specialty foods.

Australia, Canada, China (PRC), El Salvador, England, U.K., Japan, Mexico, Singapore, Switzerland, Venezuela

McDERMOTT INTERNATIONAL INC.

1450 Poydras Street, PO Box 60035

New Orleans, LA 70160-0035

Tel: (504) 587-5400 Fax: (504) 587-6153

CEO: Roger E. Tetrault, Chmn.

FO: Richard T. Tyner, Pres. Int'l

HR: Kevin A. Blasini, Dir. HR

Web site: www.mcdermott.com

Emp: 24,700 Rev: $3,674 mil.

Engineering & construction.

Bangladesh, Canada, China (PRC), Egypt, England, U.K., India, Indonesia, Mexico, Qatar, Scotland, U.K., Singapore, Thailand, Turkey

McDERMOTT WILL & EMERY

227 W. Monroe Street

Chicago, IL 60606-5096

Tel: (312) 372-2000 Fax: (312) 984-7700

CEO: Lawrence Gerber, Mng. Prtn.

HR: Lori Cerone

Web site: www.mwe.com

Emp: 2,032 Rev: $334 mil.

International law firm.

Lithuania, Russia

McDONALD'S CORPORATION

Kroc Drive

Oak Brook, IL 60523

Tel: (630) 623-3000 Fax: (630) 623-7409

CEO: Jack M. Greenberg, Pres.

FO: James Cantalupo, Pres., Intl.

HR: Steve Russell

Rev: $30,000 mil.

Fast food chain stores.

Argentina, Australia, Austria, Belarus, Belgium, Brazil, Bulgaria, Canada, Chile, China (PRC), Colombia, Croatia, Czech Republic, Denmark, Egypt, England, U.K., Estonia, Fiji, Finland, France, Germany, Greece, Honduras, Hong Kong, Hungary, India, Indonesia, Ireland, Italy, Jamaica, Japan, Latvia, Lithuania, Malaysia, Mexico, Netherlands, New Zealand, Norway, Paraguay, Peru, Philippines, Poland, Portugal, Romania, Russia, Singapore, Slovakia, South Africa, South Korea, Spain, Sweden, Switzerland, Taiwan (ROC), Thailand, Uruguay, Venezuela, Yugoslavia

THE McGRAW-HILL COMPANIES

1221 Ave. of the Americas

New York, NY 10020

Tel: (212) 512-2000 Fax: (212) 512-2703

CEO: Joseph L. Dionne, Chmn.

FO: Harold McGraw III, Pres.

HR: Patrick Pavelski

Emp: 15,000 Rev: $2,000 mil.

Books, magazines, information systems, financial service, publishing and broadcast operations.

Australia, Belgium, Brazil, Canada, England, U.K., Germany, India, Japan, Mexico, New Zealand, Portugal

McGUIRE, WOODS, BATTLE & BOOTHE LLP

One James Center, 901 E. Cary Street

Richmond, VA 23219

Tel: (804) 775-1000 Fax: (804) 775-1061

CEO: Robert L. Burrus, Chmn.

FO: Curtin M. Coward, Pres. Int'l.

HR: Allison P. Koschak

Web site: www.mwbb.com

Emp: 1,103

International law firm.

Belgium, Kazakhstan, Russia

MCI INTERNATIONAL INC.

2 International Drive

Rye Brook, NY 10573

Tel: (914) 937-3444 Fax: (914) 934-6996

CEO: Seth D. Blumenfeld, Pres.

HR: Nicholas Marano

Telecommunications.

Argentina, Belgium, France, Germany, Italy, Japan, Poland, Sweden, Venezuela

McKESSON CORPORATION

One Post Street

San Francisco, CA 94104-5296

Tel: (415) 983-8300 Fax: (415) 983-8453

CEO: Mark A. Pulido, Pres.

HR: William A. Armstrong, VP

Emp: 11,000 Rev: $12,000 mil.

Wholesale distribution of pharmaceuticals, health and beauty care aids, and other non-durable consumer goods.

Canada, Mexico

McKINSEY & COMPANY

55 East 52nd Street

New York, NY 10022

Tel: (212) 446-7000 Fax: (212) 446-8575

CEO: Rajat Gupta, Mng. Dir.

FO: Trever MacMurray, Dir.

HR: Jerome Vascellaro, Dir.

Web site: www.mckinsey.com

Emp: 7,100 Rev: $2,200 mil.

Management and business consulting services.

Argentina, Australia, Austria, Belgium, Brazil, Canada, Chile, China (PRC), Colombia, Czech Republic, Denmark, England, U.K., Finland, France, Germany, Hong Kong, Hungary, India, Indonesia, Ireland, Italy, Japan, Malaysia, Mexico, Netherlands, Norway, Poland, Portugal, Russia, South Africa, South Korea, Spain, Sweden, Switzerland, Taiwan (ROC), Thailand, Turkey, Venezuela

JOHN J McMULLEN ASSOCIATES INC.

1 World Trade Center, Ste. 3000

New York, NY 10048

Tel: (212) 466-2200 Fax: (212) 466-2326

CEO: John J. McMullen

Emp: 150

Naval architects.

Germany

McNALLY PITTSBURG INC.

100 North Pine, PO Box 651

Pittsburg, KS 66762

Tel: (316) 231-3000 Fax: (316) 231-0343

CEO: George E. Nettels, Jr.

HR: Jim Fry

Emp: 1,239

Mfr./erection of coal processing plants and material handling systems.

Australia, India

MEAD CORPORATION

Courthouse Plaza, NE

Dayton, OH 45463

Tel: (937) 495-6323 Fax: (937) 461-2424

CEO: Jerome F. Tatar, Chmn.

FO: Raymond W. Lane, EVP

HR: Russell E. Kross, VP

Web site: www.mead.com

Emp: 16,500 Rev: $5,077 mil.

Mfr. paper, packaging, pulp, lumber and other

wood products, school and office products; electronic publishing and distribution.

Argentina, Australia, Austria, Brazil, Canada, Chile, England, U.K., France, Germany, Hong Kong, Italy, Japan, Mexico, Netherlands, Poland, South Korea, Spain

MEADOWCRAFT INC.

4700 Pinson Valley Pkwy.

Birmingham, AL 35215

Tel: (205) 853-2220 Fax: (205) 854-4054

CEO: William McCanna, Pres.

FO: Juan Zamarron

HR: Larry York, VP

Web site: www.meadowcraft.com

Casual, patio and indoor wrought iron furniture, garden accessories, cushions and umbrellas.

Mexico

MECHANICAL SYSTEMS INC.

4110 Romaine

Greensboro, NC 27407

Tel: (336) 292-4956 Fax: (336) 294-7182

CEO: Harvey Burd, Pres.

Mechanical and electrical contractors.

Malaysia, Saudi Arabia, Singapore

MEDAR INC.

38700 Grand River Ave.

Farmington Hills, MI 48335-1563

Tel: (248) 477-3900 Fax: (248) 477-8897

CEO: Charles Drake

HR: Terry Simmerman

Emp: 300

Mfr. machine vision-based inspection systems & resistance welding controls for industry manufacturers.

Canada, England, U.K.

MEDEX ASSISTANCE CORPORATION

9515 Deereco Road, 4th Fl.

Timonium, MD 21093

Tel: (410) 453-6300 Fax: (410) 453-6301

CEO: William Casey, Pres.

FO: Beni Gibson

HR: Laurie Kregecz

Emp: 50

Medical & travel related assistance service.

England, U.K.

MEDICUS GROUP INTERNATIONAL

1675 Broadway

New York, NY 10019

Tel: (212) 468-3100 Fax: (212) 468-3222

CEO: Glenn J. DeSimone, Chmn.

Emp: 598 Rev: $75.9 mil.

International healthcare agency network.

Australia, Belgium, Canada, England, U.K., France, Germany, Italy, Japan, Spain

MEDITE CORPORATION

7905 Agate Road

White City, OR 97503

Tel: (541) 826-2671 Fax: (541) 826-9334

CEO: Jerry Bramwell

FO: Rory Kirwin

Emp: 700

Mfr. medium density fiberboard.

Ireland

MEDTRONIC INC.

7000 Central Ave., NE

Minneapolis, MN 55432

Tel: (612) 574-4000 Fax: (612) 574-4879

CEO: William W. George, Pres.

FO: Arthur D. Collins Jr.

HR: Janet S. Fiola

Emp: 10,400

Mfr./sale/service electrotherapeutic medical devices.

Australia, Austria, Belgium, Brazil, Canada, England, U.K., France, Germany, Italy, Japan, Netherlands, Spain, Switzerland

MELLON BANK NA

One Mellon Bank Center

Pittsburgh, PA 15258

Tel: (412) 234-5000 Fax: (412) 236-1662

CEO: Frank V. Cahouet, Pres.

FO: Stewart E. Sutin

HR: D. Michael Roark

Emp: 24,000

Commercial and trade banking and foreign exchange.

Canada, England, U.K., Hong Kong, Ireland, Japan

MELROE COMPANY

112 North University Drive, PO Box 6019
Fargo, ND 58108-6019
Tel: (701) 241-8700 Fax: (701) 241-8704
CEO: Chuck Hoge, Pres.
FO: Chin Wah Ying
HR: Greg Schmalz
Emp: 1,800
Mfr. heavy equipment.
Belgium, Singapore

MEMC ELECTRONIC MATERIALS, INC.

501 Pearl Drive
St. Peters, MO 63376
Tel: (314) 279-5500 Fax: (314) 279-5158
CEO: Ludger H. Viefhues
FO: Klaus R. von Horde, Pres.
HR: Brad Eldredge, Dir.
Web site: www.memc.com
Emp: 7,700 Rev: $ 987 mil.
Mfg. & distribution of silicon wafers.
China (PRC), England, U.K., France, Germany, Italy, Japan, Malaysia, South Korea, Taiwan (ROC)

MEMOREX CORPORATION

10100 Pioneer Boulevard
Santa Fe Springs, CA 90670
Tel: (562) 906-2800 Fax: (562) 906-2848
CEO: Alan Yak
FO: Reto Braun
HR: Elvira M. Hernandez
Emp: 10,000
Magnetic recording tapes, etc.
Australia, Austria, Brazil, Canada, Denmark, England, U.K., Finland, France, Germany, Ireland, Japan, Mexico, Netherlands, Spain, Sweden, Switzerland, Venezuela

THE MENTHOLATUM CO., INC.

707 Sterling Drive
Orchard Park, NY 14127-1587
Tel: (716) 677-2500 Fax: (716) 674-3696
CEO: Masashi Yoshida, Pres.
FO: Francis Chan
HR: Janice Kwarta
Web site: www.mentholatum.com
Mfr./distributor proprietary medicines, drugs, OTC's.
Australia, Canada, China (PRC), Hong Kong, India, Indonesia, Japan, Malaysia, Nigeria, Scotland, U.K., South Africa, Taiwan (ROC), Thailand, Vietnam

MENTOR GRAPHICS/MICROTEC RESEARCH

880 Ridder Park Drive
San Jose, CA 95131
Tel: (408) 487-7000 Fax: (408) 487-7001
CEO: Walden Rhines, Pres.
Develop/mfr. software tools for embedded systems market.
Belgium, China (PRC), Denmark, Egypt, England, U.K., France, Germany, Japan, South Korea, Sweden

MERCER MANAGEMENT CONSULTING INC.

1166 Ave. of the Americas
New York, NY 10036
Tel: (212) 345-3400 Fax: (212) 345-7414
CEO: Jim Down, Pres.
HR: Scott Davenport
Emp: 4,000
Management consulting.
Brazil, England, U.K., France, Germany

MERCK & COMPANY, INC.

1 Merck Drive
Whitehouse Station, NJ 08889
Tel: (908) 423-1000 Fax: (908) 423-2592
CEO: Daniel Anstice, Pres.
HR: James Rancourt
Emp: 28,000
Pharmaceuticals, chemicals and biologicals.
Argentina, Australia, Austria, Belgium, Bermuda, Brazil, Canada, Colombia, Costa Rica, Denmark, Ecuador, England, U.K., Finland, France, Germany, Greece, Hong Kong, India, Italy, Japan, Jordan, Kenya, Lebanon, Mexico, Morocco, Netherlands, New Zealand, Nigeria, Pakistan, Peru, Poland, Portugal, Russia, South Africa, South Korea, Spain, Sweden, Switzerland, Ukraine, Venezuela, Vietnam

MERCURY INTERACTIVE CORPORATION

1325 Borregas Ave.

Sunnyvale, CA 94089

Tel: (408) 822-5200 Fax: (408) 822-5300

CEO: Amnon Landan, Pres. &CEO

FO: Moshe Egert, VP Intl.

HR: Bonnie Jones, Dir.

Web site: www.merc-int.com

Emp: 450 Rev: $75.0 mil.

Mfr. computer software to decipher and eliminate "bugs" from systems.

Australia, Belgium, England, U.K., France, Germany, Israel, Japan, Singapore, Sweden

MERIDIAN DATA INC.

5615 Scotts Valley Drive

Scotts Valley, CA 95062

Tel: (408) 438-3100 Fax: (408) 438-6816

CEO: J. Gianluca

FO: Charles Joseph

HR: A. Stellar

Emp: 58

Mfr. computer systems and equipment..

England, U.K.

MERIDIAN DIAGNOSTICS INC.

3471 River Hills Drive

Cincinnati, OH 45244

Tel: (513) 271-3700 Fax: (513) 271-3762

CEO: John A. Kraeutler, Pres.

HR: Marlene Cook

Emp: 160

Develop/mfr. immunodiagnostic test kits, reagents, bacteria/parasite collection & preservation systems.

Italy

MERISEL INC.

200 Continental Blvd.

El Segundo, CA 90245

Tel: (310) 615-3080 Fax: (310) 615-1238

CEO: Dwight A. Steffensen, Chmn.

HR: Carol Baker, VP

Emp: 2,200

Distributor software & hardware.

Canada

MERITOR AUTOMOTIVE, INC.

2135 W. Maple Road

Troy, MI 48084-7186

Tel: (248) 435-1000 Fax: (248) 435-1393

CEO: Larry D. Yost, Chmn.

HR: Gary L. Collins, SVP

Web site: www.meritorauto.com

Emp: 16,000 Rev: $3,300 mil.

Mfr./sales of light and heavy vehicle systems for trucks, cars and speciality vehicles.

Australia, Brazil, Canada, China (PRC), Czech Republic, India, Japan, Turkey

MERLE NORMAN COSMETICS INC.

9130 Bellance Ave.

Los Angeles, CA 90045

Tel: (310) 641-3000 Fax: (310) 641-7144

CEO: Art Armstrong, Pres.

Emp: 1,200

Mfr./sales/distribution of cosmetics.

Canada, Guatemala, Mexico, Saudi Arabia

MERRILL LYNCH & COMPANY, INC.

World Financial Center, North Tower

New York, NY 10281-1323

Tel: (212) 449-1000 Fax: (212) 449-2892

CEO: David H. Komansky, Chmn.

FO: Michael J. P. Marks

HR: Mary E. Taylor, SVP

Emp: 40,000 Rev: $16,000 mil.

Security brokers and dealers, investment and business services.

Argentina, Australia, Austria, Bahrain, Brazil, Canada, Cayman Islands, Chile, China (PRC), England, U.K., France, Germany, Greece, Hong Kong, India, Indonesia, Ireland, Isle of Man, Italy, Japan, Lebanon, Luxembourg, Mexico, Monaco, Netherlands, New Zealand, Panama, Peru, Poland, Singapore, South Africa, South Korea, Spain, Switzerland, Taiwan (ROC), Thailand, Turkey, United Arab Emirates, Uruguay, Venezuela

MESABA HOLDINGS, INC.

7501 26th Ave. South

Minneapolis, MN 55450

Tel: (612) 726-5151 Fax: (612) 726-1568

CEO: Bryan K. Bedord, Pres.

FO: F. Darryl Richardson, VP

HR: Dan F. Sheehan

Web site: www.mesaba.com

Emp: 2,000

Regional airline carrier.

Canada

METAL IMPROVEMENT COMPANY

10 Forest Ave.

Paramus, NJ 07652

Tel: (201) 843-7800 Fax: (201) 843-3460

CEO: Gerald Nachman, Pres.

FO: James Daly

Emp: 950

Mfr. shot peening.

Canada, England, U.K., France, Germany, Wales, U.K.

METALLURG INC.

6 East 43 Street

New York, NY 10017

Tel: (212) 687-9470 Fax: (212) 697-2874

CEO: Michael A. Standen, Pres.

HR: Mary B. Higgins

Emp: 2,000 Rev: $525 mil.

Mfr. ferrous & nonferrous alloys & metals.

Brazil, Canada, England, U.K., Germany, Japan, Sweden, Switzerland, Turkey

METAMOR WORLDWIDE, INC.

4400 P.O.st Oak Parkway, Ste. 1130

Houston, TX 77027-3413

Tel: (713) 961-3633 Fax: (713) 963-9711

CEO: Michael T. Willis, Chmn. & Pres.

HR: Roslyn Larkey, VP

Web site: www.metamor.com

Emp: 2,500 Rev: $1.1 mil.

Provider of information technology and staffing services.

England, U.K., India

METCALF & EDDY INTERNATIONAL INC.

30 Harvard Mill Square

Wakefield, MA 01880

Tel: (781) 246-5200 Fax: (781) 245-6293

CEO: Jake Vittands, Pres.

HR: Mary K. Flaherty

Emp: 2,700

Consulting engineers.

Egypt, Saudi Arabia

METHODE ELECTRONICS INC.

7444 West Wilson Ave.

Chicago, IL 60656

Tel: (708) 867-9600 Fax: (708) 867-9130

CEO: William J. McGinley

Web site: www.methode.com

Emp: 3,000

Mfr. electronic components.

Singapore

METRA TOOL COMPANY

5275 Cogswell Road

Wayne, MI 48184

Tel: (734) 729-6400 Fax: (313) 729-6446

CEO: Charles E. Cain, Pres.

FO: Barry A. Grussner

Emp: 23

Mfr. fastening tools, blueprint items.

Canada

METROPOLITAN LIFE INSURANCE COMPANY

1 Madison Ave.

New York, NY 10010-3603

Tel: (212) 578-3818 Fax: (212) 252-7294

CEO: Robert H. Benmosche, Pres.

FO: John H. Tweedie, EVP

HR: Patricia T. Cousey, AVP

Emp: 45,000

Insurance and retirement savings products and services.

Argentina, Brazil, Canada, China (PRC), England, U.K., Hong Kong, Indonesia, Mexico, Portugal, South Korea, Spain, Taiwan (ROC)

MICHAELS STORES INC.

PO Box 619566

Irving, TX 75261-9566

Tel: (972) 409-1300 Fax: (972) 409-1521

CEO: Michael Rouleau, Pres.

HR: Kevin Rutherford

Web site: www.michaels.com

Emp: 17,200 Rev: $1,500 mil.

Retail stores; hobby, arts and crafts.

Canada

MICOM COMMUNICATIONS CORPORATION

4100 Los Angeles Ave.
Simi Valley, CA 93063
Tel: (805) 583-8600 Fax: (805) 583-1997
CEO: Nancy Shemwell, Gen. Mgr.
FO: Ken Burrough
HR: Jesse Williams
Emp: 356
Mfr. integration products for shared-line communications.
England, U.K.

MICREL, INCORPORATED

1849 Fortune Drive
San Jose, CA 95131
Tel: (408) 944-0800 Fax: (408) 944-0970
CEO: Raymond D. Zinn, Chmn.
FO: Robert Whelton, EVP
HR: Barbara Jenkins, Dir.
Web site: www.micrel.com
Emp: 546 Rev: $104 mil.
Designer and mfr. of analog intergrated circuits.
England, U.K., South Korea

MICRION CORPORATION

One Corporation Way
Peabody, MA 01960-7990
Tel: (978) 531-6464 Fax: (978) 531-9648
CEO: Nicholas P. Economou, Pres.
FO: Billy W. Ward, SVP
HR: Sheryl Cheny, Dir
Web site: www.micrion.com
Emp: 253 Rev: $56 mil.
Design & mfr. of semiconductor equipment for focused beam wafer modification applications, mask repair systems, & micromachining systems.
England, U.K., Germany, Japan, Taiwan (ROC)

MICRO ABRASIVES CORPORATION

720 Southampton Road
Westfield, MA 01086-0669
Tel: (413) 562-3641 Fax: (413) 562-7409
CEO: Robert Nesin, Pres.
Web site: www.microgrit.com
Emp: 60
Precision abrasive powders and slurries.
India

MICRO AGE, INC.

200 South MicroAge Way
Tempe, AZ 85282-1896
Tel: (602) 366-2000 Fax: (602) 966-7339
CEO: Jeffrey D. McKeever, Chmn.
FO: Christopher J. Koziol, SVP
HR: Alan R. Lyons, VP
Web site: www.microage.com
Emp: 4,300 Rev: $4,400 mil.
Computer systems integrator, software products and telecommunications equipment.
Canada, Hungary, Russia

MICROCHIP TECHNOLOGY INC.

2355 West Chandler Boulevard
Chandler, AZ 85224
Tel: (602) 786-7200 Fax: (602) 899-9210
CEO: Steve Sanghi, Pres. & Chmn.
FO: Robert A. Lanford, VP Intl.
HR: Michael J. Jones, VP
Web site: www.microchip.com
Emp: 2,200 Rev: $334 mil.
Mfr. electronic subassemblies and components.
Canada, China (PRC), England, U.K., France, Germany, Hong Kong, India, Italy, Japan, Philippines, Russia, Singapore, South Korea, Taiwan (ROC), Thailand

MICROMERITICS INSTRUMENT CORPORATION

One Micromeritics Drive
Norcross, GA 30093-1877
Tel: (770) 662-3620 Fax: (770) 662-3696
CEO: Warren Hendrix, Pres.
FO: Robert Johnson, Intl.
Emp: 235
Mfr. analytical instruments.
Belgium, China (PRC), England, U.K., France, Germany, Italy

MICRON TECHNOLOGY, INC. (MTI)

8000 S. Federal Way
Boise, ID 83707-0006
Tel: (208) 368-4000 Fax: (208) 368-4435
CEO: Steven R. Appleton, Chmn. & Pres.
FO: Donald D. Baldwin, VP Sales

Web site: www.micron.com

Emp: 12,000

Mfr. random-access memory chips and semi-conductor memory components.

England, U.K., Japan, Singapore

MICROSEMI CORPORATION

2830 South Fairview Street

Santa Ana, CA 92704

Tel: (714) 979-8220 Fax: (714) 557-5989

CEO: Philip Frey, Jr., Pres.

FO: T. S. (Andy) Yuen

HR: James Thomas

Emp: 1,500

Mfr. seimconductors.

Hong Kong, Ireland

MICROSOFT CORPORATION

One Microsoft Way

Redmond, WA 98052-6399

Tel: (425) 882-8080 Fax: (425) 936-7329

CEO: William H. Gates, Chmn.

FO: Bernard P. Vargnes, EVP

HR: Michael Murray, VP

Web site: www.microsoft.com

Emp: 22,232 Rev: $11,358 mil.

Computer software, peripherals and services.

Argentina, Australia, Austria, Belgium, Brazil, Canada, Chile, China (PRC), Colombia, Costa Rica, Croatia, Czech Republic, Denmark, Dominican Republic, Ecuador, Egypt, El Salvador, England, U.K., Finland, France, Germany, Greece, Guatemala, Hong Kong, Hungary, India, Indonesia, Ireland, Israel, Italy, Ivory Coast, Japan, Malaysia, Mauritius, Mexico, Morocco, Netherlands, New Zealand, Norway, Panama, Peru, Philippines, Poland, Portugal, Russia, Saudi Arabia, Singapore, Slovakia, Slovenia, South Africa, South Korea, Spain, Sweden, Switzerland, Taiwan (ROC), Thailand, Turkey, United Arab Emirates, Uruguay, Venezuela, Vietnam

MIDLAND INC.

2248 Research Drive

Fort Wayne, IN 46808

Tel: (219) 484-8895 Fax: (219) 484-8892

CEO: J. Boersma, Pres.

HR: Susan Scribner

Emp: 30

Export management.

Belgium, Singapore

MILBANK, TWEED, HADLEY & McCLOY

1 Chase Manhattan Plaza

New York, NY 10005-1413

Tel: (212) 530-5000 Fax: (212) 530-5219

CEO: Mel Immergut, Chmn.

HR: Jane L. MacLennan, Dir.

Web site: www.milbank.com

Emp: 910 Rev: $205 mil.

International law practice.

England, U.K., Hong Kong, Indonesia, Japan, Russia, Singapore

MILLER ELECTRIC MFG. COMPANY

PO Box 1079

Appleton, WI 54912-1079

Tel: (920) 734-9821 Fax: (920) 735-4125

CEO: Kevin Wallis, Pres.

HR: Mike Weller

Emp: 1,570

Mfr. arc welding machines.

Italy

HERMAN MILLER INC.

8500 Byron Road

Zeeland, MI 49464

Tel: (616) 654-3000 Fax: (616) 654-5385

CEO: Michael Vollema, Pres.

FO: Robert Frey

HR: Rod McCowan

Web site: www.hermanmiller.com

Emp: 7,500 Rev: $1,500 mil.

Office furnishings.

Australia, Canada, England, U.K., France, Japan, Mexico, Switzerland

MILLIPORE CORPORATION, ANALYTICAL PRODUCT DIVISION

80 Ashby Road, PO Box 9125

Bedford, MA 01730

Tel: (781) 275-9200 Fax: (781) 533-3110

CEO: William Zadel, Pres.

HR: Jeff Gard

Web site: www.millipore.com

Emp: 3,500 Rev: $1,000 mil.

Mfr. flow and pressure measurement and control components; precision filters, hi-performance liquid chromatography instruments.

Australia, Austria, Belgium, Brazil, China (PRC), Denmark, England, U.K., Finland, India, Japan, Mexico, Norway, Singapore, South Korea, Spain

MILTON BRADLEY COMPANY

443 Shaker Road

East Longmeadow, MA 01028

Tel: (413) 525-6411 Fax: (413) 525-1767

CEO: David Wilson, Pres.

HR: Lawrence B. Rybacki

Emp: 3,867

Jigsaw puzzles, toys and games.

France

MILTON ROY COMPANY

14845 West 64th Ave., PO Box FH

Arvada, CO 80004

Tel: (303) 425-0800 Fax: (303) 425-0896

CEO: William Taylor, Pres.

Emp: 1,500

Medical & industry equipment, process control instruments.

England, U.K., France, Germany, Ireland, Japan

MINE SAFETY APPLIANCES COMPANY

121 Gamma Drive, RIDC Industrial Pk., PO Box 426

Pittsburgh, PA 15230

Tel: (412) 967-3000 Fax: (412) 967-3452

CEO: John T. Ryan III, Chmn.

FO: George W. Steggles, VP

HR: Donald E. Crean

Emp: 4,500 Rev: $400 mil.

Safety equipment, industry filters.

Australia, Brazil, Canada, Chile, France, Germany, India, Italy, Japan, Mexico, Netherlands, Peru, Scotland, U.K., Singapore, South Africa, Spain, United Arab Emirates, Zambia, Zimbabwe

MINERAIS U S INC.

105 Raider Boulevard, Ste. 104

Belle Mead, NJ 08502

Tel: (908) 874-7666 Fax: (908) 874-7725

CEO: J. C. Barton, Pres.

Emp: 12

Marketing/distributor ferro alloys, ores and minerals.

Luxembourg

MINTEQ INTERNATIONAL INC.

405 Lexington Ave., 19th Fl.

New York, NY 10174-1901

Tel: (212) 878-1800 Fax: (212) 878-1952

CEO: Anton Dulski, Pres.

HR: Steven R. Cozzetto, Dir.

Web site: www.mineralstech.com

Emp: 750 Rev: $196 mil.

Mfr./market specialty refractory and metallurgical products and application systems.

Australia, Belgium, Brazil, Canada, China (PRC), England, U.K., Germany, Ireland, Italy, Japan, Mexico, South Africa, South Korea, Spain

MISSION MFG. COMPANY

PO Box 40402

Houston, TX 77040

Tel: (713) 460-6200 Fax: (713) 460-6229

CEO: Olof Lundblad, Pres.

Oil field equipment.

Brazil, England, U.K.

MOBIL CORPORATION

3225 Gallows Road

Fairfax, VA 22037-0001

Tel: (703) 846-3000 Fax: (703) 846-4669

CEO: Lucio A. Noto, Chmn.

FO: Stephen D. Pryor, EVP Intl.

HR: James McEnerey

Web site: www.mobil.com

Emp: 42,000 Rev: $58,300 mil.

Petroleum and gas exploration and refining, mfr. petroleum products, chemicals and petrochemicals.

Angola, Australia, Austria, Azerbaijan, Belgium, Brazil, Cameroon, Canada, Central African Republic, Chile, China (PRC), Colombia, Cyprus, Dem. Rep. of Congo, Denmark, Ecuador, England, U.K., Ethiopia, Fiji, Finland, France, Germany, Ghana, Hong Kong, Indonesia, Italy, Japan, Kenya, Lebanon, Liberia, Macau, Madeira, Mexico, Morocco, Netherlands, New Caledonia, New Zealand, Nigeria, Norway, Papua New Guinea, Peru, Philippines, Poland, Portugal, Russia, Saudi Arabia, Sierra Leone, Singapore, Spain, Sudan,

Sweden, Switzerland, Taiwan (ROC), Thailand, Trinidad & Tobago, Turkey, Ukraine, United Arab Emirates, Venezuela, Vietnam, Zambia

MODINE MANUFACTURING COMPANY

1500 DeKoven Ave.

Racine, WI 53403

Tel: (414) 636-1200 Fax: (414) 636-1424

CEO: Donald Johnson, Pres.

HR: Roger L. Hetrick

Web site: www.modine.com

Emp: 4,400

Mfr. heat-transfer products.

Austria, Canada, Denmark, England, U.K., France, Germany, Hungary, Italy, Japan, Mexico, Netherlands, Poland, Spain, Sweden, Switzerland

MOEN INC.

25300 Al Moen Drive

North Olmstead, OH 44070

Tel: (440) 962-2000 Fax: (440) 962-2089

CEO: Bruce Carbonari, Pres.

HR: Kirk Hoffman

Emp: 2,850

Mfr./service plumbing products.

Canada

MOGUL CORPORATION

PO Box 200

Chagrin Falls, OH 44022

Tel: (440) 247-5000 Fax: (440) 247-3714

CEO: Monte Krier, Pres.

FO: James S. Wallis

Emp: 2,000

Water treatment chemicals, equipment.

Australia, Canada, Germany, Netherlands

MOLEX INC.

2222 Wellington Court

Lisle, IL 60532

Tel: (630) 969-4550 Fax: (630) 969-1352

CEO: Frederick A. Krehbiel, Chmn.

FO: J. Joseph King, EVP

HR: Kathi M. Regas, VP

Web site: www.molex.com

Emp: 12,455 Rev: $1,623 mil.

Mfr. electronic, electrical & fiber optic interconnection products & systems, switches, application tooling.

Brazil, Canada, China (PRC), England, U.K., France, Germany, India, Ireland, Italy, Japan, Malaysia, Mexico, Singapore, South Africa, South Korea, Taiwan (ROC), Thailand

MOMENTUM

79 Fifth Ave.

New York, NY 10003

Tel: (212) 367-4500 Fax: (212) 367-4501

CEO: Mark Dowley, Chmn.

Web site: www.mccann.com

Emp: 300 Rev: $36.3 mil

Marketing consulting services.

England, U.K.

MONARCH MACHINE TOOL COMPANY

PO Box 668

Sidney, OH 45365-1335

Tel: (937) 910-9300 Fax: (937) 492-7958

CEO: Richard Clemens, Pres.

Emp: 1,037

Mfr. metal cutting lathes, machining centers and coil processing equipment.

England, U.K., Germany

MONROE SYSTEMS FOR BUSINESS INC.

1 Stewart Court

Danville, NJ 07834

Tel: (973) 537-2700 Fax: (973) 989-8116

CEO: Jeffrey Picower, Pres.

HR: Janet Craig

Emp: 1,190

Mfr. business machines and calculators.

Venezuela

MONSANTO COMPANY

800 N. Lindbergh Boulevard

St. Louis, MO 63167

Tel: (314) 694-1000 Fax: (314) 694-7625

CEO: Robert B. Shapiro, Chmn.

HR: Donna Kindl

Web site: www.monsanto.com

Emp: 21,000 Rev: $8,000 mil.

Life sciences company focussing on agriculture, nutrition, pharmaceuticals, health and wellness and sustainable development.

Australia, Belgium, Brazil, Canada, England, U.K.,

France, Hong Kong, Japan, Mexico, Poland, Russia, Singapore, South Korea, Taiwan (ROC), Thailand, Ukraine, Venezuela, Wales, U.K.

MONTANA POWER COMPANY

40 East Broadway
Butte, MT 59701
Tel: (406) 723-5421 Fax: (406) 497-2083
CEO: Robert P. Gannon, Pres.
HR: Robert Cenek
Emp: 4,100
Energy, mining, telecommunications, electronics, waste management.
Canada

MONTGOMERY WARD & CO., INC.

One Montgomery Ward Plaza
Chicago, IL 60671
Tel: (312) 467-2000 Fax: (312) 467-4871
CEO: Roger V. Goddu, Chmn.
FO: Mike Edmonds
HR: Robert A. Kasenter, EVP
Web site: www.mward.com
Emp: 50,000
Retail merchandisers.
Hong Kong, Japan, South Korea, Taiwan (ROC)

MONTICELLO DRUG COMPANY

1604 Stockton Street
Jacksonville, FL 32204
Tel: (904) 384-3666 Fax: (904) 388-6307
CEO: Henry E. Dean, III, Pres.
Emp: 10
Cold preparations.
Mexico

MOOG INC.

Jamison Road
East Aurora, NY 14052-0018
Tel: (716) 652-2000 Fax: (716) 687-4457
CEO: Robert T. Brady, Pres.
FO: S. Huckvale/K. Smith
HR: Joe Green
Web site: www.moog.com
Emp: 3,000 Rev: $300 mil.
Mfr. precision control components & systems.
Australia, Brazil, Denmark, England, U.K., Finland, France, Germany, Hong Kong, India, Ireland, Italy, Japan, Philippines, South Korea, Sweden

MOORE PRODUCTS COMPANY

Sumneytown Pike
Spring House, PA 19477
Tel: (215) 646-7400 Fax: (215) 646-6212
CEO: William B. Moore, Pres.
FO: K.S. Herbst/F. J. Gonzalez
HR: James F. Douglass
Emp: 1,147
Mfr. process control instruments.
Australia, Canada, England, U.K., France, India, Italy, Japan, Mexico, Netherlands, Singapore

MOORE TOOL COMPANY

800 Union Ave., PO Box 4088
Bridgeport, CT 06607-0088
Tel: (203) 366-3224 Fax: (203) 366-5694
CEO: Newman Marsilius
FO: John A. Kelly, Jr.
HR: John C. Stawarky
Web site: www.mooretool.com
Emp: 450
Mfr. ultra precision machine tools and tooling.
Switzerland

MORGAN ADHESIVES COMPANY

4560 Darrow Road
Stow, OH 44224
Tel: (330) 688-1111 Fax: (330) 688-2540
CEO: Robert Hawthorne, Pres.
HR: Kathryn Burik
Emp: 981
Self-adhesive print stock and emblem materials.
Belgium, Canada

MORGAN STANLEY DEAN WITTER & CO.

1585 Broadway
New York, NY 10036
Tel: (212) 761-4000 Fax: (212) 761-0086
CEO: Philip J. Purcell, Chmn.
FO: John J. Mack, Pres.
HR: Michael Cunningham, SVP
Web site: www.msdw.com
Emp: 47,000 Rev: $27,100 mil

Securities and commodities brokerage, investment banking, money management, personal trusts.

Australia, Brazil, Canada, China (PRC), England, U.K., France, Germany, Hong Kong, India, Italy, Japan, Luxembourg, Mexico, Russia, Singapore, South Africa, South Korea, Spain, Switzerland, Taiwan (ROC)

MORGAN, LEWIS & BOCKIUS LLP

2000 One Logan Square

Philadelphia, PA 19103-6993

Tel: (215) 963-5000 Fax: (215) 963-5299

CEO: Francis M. Milone, Mng. Ptnr.

FO: Charles G. Lubar, Intl.

HR: Hy Rudin, Dir. HR

Web site: www.mlb.com

Emp: 2,300 Rev: $359 mil.

International law firm.

Belgium, England, U.K., Germany, Indonesia, Japan, Singapore

MORRISON & FOERSTER

425 Market Street

San Francisco, CA 94105

Tel: (415) 268-7000 Fax: (415) 268-7522

CEO: Stephen Dunham, Chmn.

FO: William I. Schwartz

HR: Kathleen Dykstra

Web site: www.mofo.com

Emp: 1,404 Rev: $242 mil.

International law firm.

Belgium, China (PRC), England, U.K., Hong Kong, Japan, Singapore

MORRISON KNUDSEN CORPORATION

1 Morrison Knudsen Plaza, PO Box 73

Boise, ID 83729

Tel: (208) 386-5000 Fax: (208) 386-7186

CEO: Robert A. Tinstman, Pres.

FO: Thomas H. Zarges, SVP

HR: Alvia L. Henderson, VP

Web site: www.mk.com

Emp: 8,900 Rev: $1,700 mil.

Design/construction for environmental, industrial, process, power and transportation markets.

Bosnia-Herzegovina, China (PRC), Denmark, Egypt, England, U.K., Germany, Hong Kong, Indonesia, Mexico, Paraguay, Peru, Philippines, Poland, Singapore, Taiwan (ROC), Thailand, Ukraine

MORTON INTERNATIONAL INC.

100 North Riverside Plaza

Chicago, IL 60606-1596

Tel: (312) 807-2000 Fax: (312) 807-3150

CEO: S. Jay Stewart, Chmn.

FO: William E. Johnson, Pres.

HR: Christopher K. Julsrud

Web site: www.mortonintl.com

Emp: 8,500 Rev: $2,575 mil.

Mfr. adhesives, coatings, finishes, specialty chemicals, advanced and electronic materials, salt, airbags.

Bahamas, Belgium, Brazil, Canada, England, U.K., France, Germany, Hong Kong, Italy, Japan, Mexico, Netherlands, Singapore, Spain, Taiwan (ROC)

MOSLER INC.

8509 Berk Boulevard

Hamilton, OH 45015

Tel: (513) 870-1900 Fax: (513) 870-1170

CEO: Michel Rapoport, Pres.

FO: James R. HusVar

HR: Al Rabasca

Emp: 2,500

Mfr. security products, systems, & services to financial, commercial, & government market.

Canada, Mexico, Philippines

MOTION PICTURE ASSN. OF AMERICA

1600 Eye Street, NW

Washington, DC 20006

Tel: (202) 293-1966 Fax: (202) 293-7674

CEO: Jack J. Valenti, Pres.

Web site: www.mpaa.org

Emp: 100

Motion picture trade association.

Belgium, Brazil, Canada, Italy, Singapore

MOTOROLA, INC.

1303 East Algonquin Road

Schaumburg, IL 60196

Tel: (847) 576-5000 Fax: (847) 538-5191

CEO: Christopher B. Galvin

FO: Merle L. Gilmore, EVP

HR: Glenn A. Gienko, EVP

Web site: www.mot.com

Emp: 150,000 Rev: $29,800 mil.

Mfr. communications equipment, semiconductors and cellular phones.

Argentina, Australia, Austria, Bangladesh, Belarus, Belgium, Brazil, Canada, Chile, China (PRC), Colombia, Costa Rica, Czech Republic, Denmark, Egypt, England, U.K., Finland, France, Germany, Greece, Guam, Hong Kong, Hungary, India, Indonesia, Ireland, Israel, Italy, Japan, Kazakhstan, Kuwait, Latvia, Malaysia, Mexico, Morocco, Netherlands, New Zealand, Norway, Peru, Philippines, Poland, Portugal, Romania, Russia, Singapore, South Africa, South Korea, Spain, Sri Lanka, Sweden, Switzerland, Taiwan (ROC), Thailand, Turkey, Ukraine, United Arab Emirates, Venezuela, Vietnam

MOUNT HOPE MACHINERY COMPANY

15 Fifth Street

Taunton, MA 02780

Tel: (508) 824-6994 Fax: (508) 822-3962

CEO: Neal August, Pres.

Emp: 200

Web control equipment for paper, plastics and textiles.

Germany, Scotland, U.K.

MPB CORPORATION

10 Precision Park Optical Ave.

Keene, NH 03431

Tel: (603) 352-0310 Fax: (603) 355-4554

CEO: Donna Demaling, Pres.

Emp: 1,925

Mfr./sales/distribution bearings, tape guides and systems for missiles, etc.

England, U.K., France, Germany

MPSI SYSTEMS INC.

8282 South Memorial Drive

Tulsa, OK 74133

Tel: (918) 877-6774 Fax: (918) 254-8764

CEO: Ronald G. Harper, Chmn.

HR: Bill Webb

Emp: 700

Computer software, information system services.

England, U.K.

MTS SYSTEMS CORPORATION

1400 Technology Drive

Eden Prairie, MN 55344-2290

Tel: (612) 937-4000 Fax: (612) 937-4515

CEO: Donald M. Sullivan, Pres.

FO: Chip Emery

HR: Bruce Hebeisen

Web site: www.mts.com

Emp: 1,400 Rev: $303 mil.

Develop/mfr. mechanical testing & simulation products & services, industry measure & automation instrumentation.

Canada, China (PRC), England, U.K., France, Germany, Hong Kong, Italy, Japan, Singapore, South Korea, Sweden

MUELLER INDUSTRIES, INC.

6799 Great Oaks Road, Ste. 200

Memphis, TN 38138

Tel: (901) 753-3200 Fax: (901) 753-3255

CEO: William D. O'Hagan

HR: Lowell Hill, VP

Emp: 3,500 Rev: $880 mil.

Mfr. plumbing and heating products, refrigeration and A/C components, copper and copper alloy and metal forgings and extrusions.

Canada, England, U.K.

MULTI GRAPHICS

431 Lakeview Court

Mt. Prospect, IL 60056

Tel: (847) 375-1700 Fax: (847) 375-1810

CEO: Thomas Rooney, Pres.

FO: David A. Roberts

HR: Ray Vogt

Emp: 3,200

Mfr./sale/service printing & print prod equipment, mailroom/bindery systems, services & supplies for graphics industry.

Australia, Belgium, Canada, England, U.K., France, Germany, Japan, Netherlands, Switzerland

MULTIWARE

PO Box 907

Brookfield, CT 06874

Tel: (203) 374-8000 Fax: (203) 374-3374

CEO: Mike Lofrumento, Sr., Pres.

Emp: 382

Mfr. applications development software.

Australia, Belgium, Brazil, Canada, Colombia,

England, U.K., Finland, France, Germany, Hong Kong, Hungary, Italy, Mexico, Netherlands, Norway, Portugal, Singapore, Spain, Sweden, Switzerland, Ukraine, Venezuela, Zimbabwe

MURPHY OIL CORPORATION

PO Box 7000

El Dorado, AR 71731-7000

Tel: (870) 862-6411 Fax: (870) 862-9057

CEO: Claiborne P. Deming, Pres

HR: G. L. Dilreath, Jr.

Emp: 1,767

Crude oil, natural gas, mfr. petroleum products.

Canada, England, U.K.

F.E. MYERS & COMPANY

1101 Myers Parkway

Ashland, OH 44805

Tel: (419) 289-1144 Fax: (419) 289-6658

CEO: Fred C. Lavender

HR: J. Michael Gerard

Emp: 600

Pumps, water systems, wastewater, industrial.

Canada

MYERS INTERNATIONAL INC.

1293 South Main Street

Akron, OH 44301

Tel: (330) 253-5592 Fax: (330) 253-0035

CEO: S. E. Myers

FO: Pablo W. Grollmus

HR: Tom Bruser

Web site: www.myerstiresupply.com

Emp: 1,000 Rev: $340 mil.

Mfr. tire retreading & maintenance equipment & supplies.

Canada

N

NABORS INDUSTRIES INC.

515 West Greens Road, #1200

Houston, TX 77067

Tel: (281) 874-0035 Fax: (281) 872-5205

CEO: Eugene M. Isenberg, Chmn.

FO: Siegfried Meissner, Pres.

HR: Daniel McLachlin, VP

Emp: 10,632 Rev: $1,029 mil.

Oil & gas drilling, petrol products.

Canada, Colombia, Gabon, Saudi Arabia, Scotland, U.K., United Arab Emirates, Venezuela, Yemen

NAC REINSURANCE CORPORATION

One Greenwich Plaza

Greenwich, CT 06836-2568

Tel: (203) 622-5200 Fax: (203) 622-1494

CEO: Ronald L. Bornhuetter, Chmn.

FO: Charles J. Catt, Pres.

HR: Celia R. Brown, VP

Web site: www/nacre.com

Emp: 311 Rev: $723.9 mil.

Provides property and casualty reinsurance.

Australia, Canada, England, U.K., Spain

NACCO INDUSTRIES INC.

5875 Landerbrook Drive

Mayfield Heights, OH 44124-4017

Tel: (440) 449-9600 Fax: (440) 449-9607

CEO: Alfred M. Rankin, Jr., Pres. & Chmn.

HR: Dean Tsipis, VP

Web site: www.nacco.com

Emp: 12,650 Rev: $2,250 mil.

Mining/marketing lignite & metals, mfr. forklift trucks & small electric appliances, specialty retailers.

Australia, Brazil, Canada, Italy, Japan, Mexico, Netherlands, Northern Ireland, U.K., Scotland, U.K.

NACCO MATERIAL HANDLING GROUP

PO Box 847

Danville, IL 61834

Tel: (217) 443-7000 Fax: (217) 437-4940

CEO: J. Phillip Frazier

FO: Robert E. Lange

HR: J. Richard Kenyon

Web site: 503-639

Emp: 5,000

Fork lifts, trucks, trailers, towing winches, personnel lifts and compaction equipment.

Australia, Brazil, England, U.K., Netherlands

NAI TECHNOLOGIES INC.

282 New York Ave.

Huntington, NY 11743

Tel: (516) 271-5685 Fax: (516) 385-0815

CEO: Robert A. Carlson, Chmn.

FO: Stan Kawtoski, VP

HR: Len Stanton, Dir.

Web site: www.naitech.com

Emp: 190 Rev: $52 mil.

Mfr. computers & peripherals, office machines, communications equipment.

Australia, Belgium, Denmark, England, U.K., France, Germany, Greece, Israel, Italy, Netherlands, Norway

NALCO CHEMICAL COMPANY

One Nalco Center

Naperville, IL 60563-1198

Tel: (630) 305-1000 Fax: (630) 305-2900

CEO: Edward J. Mooney, Chmn.

FO: W. Steven Weeber, EVP

HR: James S. Lambe, VP

Web site: www.nalco.com

Emp: 6,900 Rev: $1,434 mil.

Chemicals for water and waste water treatment, oil products and refining, industry processes; water and energy management service.

Argentina, Australia, Austria, Brazil, Canada, Chile, Colombia, England, U.K., Finland, France, Germany, Hong Kong, India, Indonesia, Italy, Jamaica, Japan, Mexico, Netherlands, New Zealand, Peru, Philippines, Saudi Arabia, Singapore, South Africa, South Korea, Spain, Surinam, Sweden, Taiwan (ROC), Thailand, Trinidad & Tobago, Venezuela

NAMCO CONTROLS CORPORATION

5335 Avion Park Drive

Highland Heights, OH 44103

Tel: (440) 460-1360 Fax: (440) 460-3800

CEO: Alex Joseph, Pres.

FO: Alex Joseph, Pres.

HR: Kelli Knaus

Emp: 190

Mfr. sensors, switches and encoders.

Germany

NANOMETRICS INC.

310 DeGuigne Drive

Sunnyvale, CA 94086-3906

Tel: (408) 746-1600 Fax: (408) 720-0196

CEO: Vincent Coates,CEO

FO: William Fate

HR: Agnes Francisco

Web site: www.nanometrics.com

Emp: 160 Rev: $37 mil.

Mfr. optical measurement and inspection systems for semiconductor industry.

Japan, South Korea, Taiwan (ROC)

THE NASH ENGINEERING COMPANY

3 Trefoil Drive

Trumbull, CT 06611

Tel: (203) 459-3900 Fax: (203) 459-3511

CEO: Dennis Campbell, Pres.

Emp: 900

Mfr. air & gas compressors, vacuum pumps.

Brazil, England, U.K., Germany, Singapore, South Korea, Sweden

NASHUA CORPORATION

44 Franklin Street, PO Box 2002

Nashua, NH 03061-2002

Tel: (603) 880-2323 Fax: (603) 880-5671

CEO: Gerald G. Garbacz, Chmn.

HR: Bruce T. Wright, VP

Web site: www.nashua.com

Emp: 1,811 Rev: $173 mil.

Mfg. Imaging supplies (printer cartridges, toners, developers), labels, and specialty coated papers.

Canada, England, U.K., Japan

NATCO

2950 North Loop West

Houston, TX 77092-8839

Tel: (713) 683-9292 Fax: (713) 683-6787

CEO: Nat Gregory

FO: Perry Helvey

HR: Al Smith

Emp: 1,100

Mfr./sale/service oil and gas products.

Canada, England, U.K., Japan, Singapore

NATIONAL CAR RENTAL SYSTEM, INC.

7700 France Ave. South

Minneapolis, MN 55435

Tel: (612) 830-2121 Fax: (612) 830-2921

CEO: Jeff Parell, Pres.

HR: Ed Jones

Emp: 19,500

Car rentals.

Canada, Chile, Denmark, Dominican Republic, Ecuador, Egypt, El Salvador, England, U.K., Finland, France, Germany, Greece, Guatemala, Ireland, Israel, Jamaica, Kuwait, Lebanon, Luxembourg, Malaysia, Mexico, Netherlands, New Zealand, Nigeria, Norway, Panama, Paraguay, Peru, Philippines, Poland, Saudi Arabia, Switzerland, United Arab Emirates, Venezuela, Zimbabwe

NATIONAL CHEMSEARCH CORPORATION

2727 Chemsearch Blvd.

Irving, TX 75061

Tel: (972) 438-0211 Fax: (972) 438-0186

CEO: Irvin L. Levy, Pres.

HR: Neil Thomas

Web site: www.nch.com

Emp: 5,500

Commercial chemical products.

Belgium, Brazil, Denmark, France, Hong Kong, Mexico, Singapore, Spain, Switzerland, Venezuela

NATIONAL DATA CORPORATION

National Data Plaza

Atlanta, GA 30329-2010

Tel: (404) 728-2000 Fax: (404) 728-2551

CEO: Robert A. Yellowlees, Chmn.

FO: David K. Hunt, Pres. & COO

HR: Donald L. Howard, VP

Web site: www.ndcorp.com

Emp: 6,100 Rev: $649 mil.

Information systems & services for retail, healthcare, government & corporate markets.

Canada, England, U.K., Germany, Italy, Japan, Spain

NATIONAL FORGE COMPANY

Front Street, Rt No 6

Irvine, PA 16329

Tel: (814) 563-7522 Fax: (814) 563-9209

CEO: G. Roger Clark, Pres.

FO: Brian McGuinness

HR: William D. Bailey

Emp: 762

Mfr. forged & cast steel.

England, U.K.

NATIONAL GYPSUM COMPANY

2001 Rexford Road

Charlotte, NC 28211

Tel: (704) 365-7300 Fax: (704) 365-7276

CEO: Tony Maraia, Pres.

HR: Abby Malkin

Emp: 6,000

Building products & services.

Australia, Belgium, Brazil, Canada, England, U.K., Italy, Japan, Netherlands, Spain

NATIONAL MACHINERY COMPANY

162 Greenfield Street, PO Box 747

Tiffin, OH 44883

Tel: (419) 447-5211 Fax: (419) 447-5299

CEO: Paul N. Aley, Pres.

FO: Gerhard Doll

HR: Larry Baker

Emp: 800 Rev: $50 mil.

Mfr. forging machinery.

Germany

NATIONAL MANUFACTURING CO., INC.

PO Box 577

Sterling, IL 61081

Tel: (815) 625-1320 Fax: (815) 625-1333

CEO: Keith W. Benson, III, Pres.

Emp: 1,000

Mfr. hardware.

Canada

NATIONAL PATENT DEVELOPMENT CORPORATION

9 West 57th Street

New York, NY 10019

Tel: (212) 230-9500 Fax: (212) 230-9545

CEO: J. I. Feldman, Pres.

Emp: 2,800

Mfr./distributor medical, health care & specialty products.

Japan, Russia

NATIONAL REFRACTORIES & MINERALS CO.

1852 Rutan Drive MINERAL

Livermore, CA 94550-7635

Tel: (925) 449-5010 Fax: (925) 455-8362

CEO: Charles C. Smith, Chmn.

HR: U.R.B. Pelletier, VP

Emp: 676 Rev: $116 mil.

Produces and distributes refractories and nonferrous metals.

Canada

NATIONAL SEMICONDUCTOR CORP.

2900 Semiconductor Drive., PO Box 58090

Santa Clara, CA 95052-8090

Tel: (408) 721-5000 Fax: (408) 739-9803

CEO: Brian L. Halla, Pres.

HR: Richard A. Wilson, VP

Web site: www.national.com

Emp: 13,700 Rev: $2,500 mil.

Produce system-on-a-chip solutions for the information highway.

Brazil, Germany, Hong Kong, Japan, Malaysia, Philippines, Scotland, U.K., Singapore

NATIONAL SERVICE INDUSTRIES INC.

1420 Peachtree Street NE

Atlanta, GA 30309

Tel: (404) 853-1000 Fax:

CEO: James Balloun, Pres.

HR: F Andrew Logue

Emp: 22,000

Mfr. lighting equipment, specialty chemicals; textile rental.

Belgium, Canada, France, Italy, Netherlands, Switzerland

NATIONAL STARCH & CHEMICAL COMPANY

10 Finderne Ave.

Bridgewater, NJ 08807-3300

Tel: (908) 685-5000 Fax: (908) 685-5005

CEO: James A. Kennedy, Pres.

FO: William H.Powell, EVP

HR: Robert B. Hennessy, VP

Web site: www.national starch.com

Emp: 8,500 Rev: $2,500 mil.

Mfr. adhesives & sealants, resins & specialty chemicals, electronic materials & adhesives, food products, industry starch.

Argentina, Australia, Belgium, Brazil, Canada, Chile, China (PRC), Colombia, Costa Rica, Czech Republic, Denmark, England, U.K., Finland, France, Germany, Hong Kong, Hungary, Indonesia, Ireland, Italy, Japan, Malaysia, Mexico, Netherlands, New Zealand, Norway, Philippines, Poland, Saudi Arabia, Singapore, South Africa, South Korea, Spain, Sweden, Switzerland, Taiwan (ROC), Thailand, Venezuela

NATIONAL UTILITY SERVICE INC.

One Maynard Drive, PO Box 712

Park Ridge, NJ 07656-0712

Tel: (201) 391-4300 Fax: (201) 391-8158

CEO: Sarkis Soultanian

FO: R. Ray Curbelo

HR: Brian Wells

Emp: 975

Utility rate consulting.

Australia, Belgium, Canada, England, U.K., France, Germany, Hong Kong, Italy, South Africa, Sweden

NATIONAL-OILWELL, INC.

PO Box 4638

Houston, TX 77210-4638

Tel: (713) 960-5100 Fax: (713) 960-5428

CEO: Joel V. Staff, Pres. & Chmn.

FO: Frederick W. Pheasey, EVP

HR: J. N. Gauche

Web site: www.natoil.com

Emp: 3,000 Rev: $1,000 mil.

Mfr./distributor oilfield drills and tubulars.

Australia, Canada, England, U.K., France, Russia, Scotland, U.K., Singapore, United Arab Emirates, Venezuela

NATIONAL-STANDARD COMPANY

1618 Terminal Road

Niles, MI 49120

Tel: (616) 683-8100 Fax: (616) 683-6249

CEO: M. B. Savitske

FO: N. J. Birch

HR: R. J. Vansteelandt

Emp: 2,700

Mfr. wire, wire related products, machinery & medical products.

England, U.K., Germany, India, Scotland, U.K., South Africa

NATIONSBANK CORPORATION

100 North Tryon Street, Corporate Center

Charlotte, NC 28255

Tel: (704) 386-5000 Fax: (704) 386-1709

CEO: Hugh L. McColl, Jr.

FO: Kenneth D. Lewis, Pres.

HR: Charles Blythe

Web site: www.nationsbank.com

Emp: 80,360 Rev: $24,477 mil.

Banking and financial services.

Bahamas, Cayman Islands, Colombia, England, U.K., Germany, Hong Kong, Japan, Mexico, Panama, Singapore, South Korea, Taiwan (ROC)

NATIONWIDE INSURANCE

One Nationwide Plaza

Columbus, OH 43215-2220

Tel: (614) 249-8221 Fax: (614) 249-0375

CEO: D. Richard McFerson, Chmn.

FO: James Brock

Emp: 26,000

Insurance services.

Germany

NAVISTAR INTERNATIONAL CORPORATION

455 North Cityfront Plaza Drive

Chicago, IL 60611

Tel: (312) 836-2000 Fax: (312) 837-2227

CEO: John R. Horne, Chmn., Pres.

FO: Dennis W. Webb, Int'l.

HR: Joseph V. Thompson

Web site: www.navistar.com

Emp: 16,000 Rev: $6,400 mil.

Mfr. medium and heavy trucks, diesel engines and school buses.

Canada, Mexico, South Africa, United Arab Emirates

NBD BANK

611 Woodward Ave.

Detroit, MI 48226

Tel: (313) 225-1000 Fax: (313) 225-2109

CEO: Verne Istock

FO: William R. Flynn

HR: Fred J. Johns

Emp: 10,384

Banking services.

Australia, Canada, England, U.K., Germany, Hong Kong, Japan

NCR (NATIONAL CASH REGISTER)

1700 South Patterson Blvd.

Dayton, OH 45479

Tel: (937) 445-5000 Fax: (937) 445-7042

CEO: Lars Nyberg, Chmn.

FO: Jose Luis Solla

HR: Richard H. Evans, SVP

Web site: www.ncr.com

Emp: 38,000 Rev: $6,500 mil.

Mfr. automated teller machines and high-performance stationary bar code scanners.

Australia, Austria, Canada, Cyprus, England, U.K., France, Germany, Hong Kong, Ireland, Italy, Japan, Netherlands, Poland, Singapore, South Africa, South Korea, Spain, Switzerland, Turkey, United Arab Emirates

NEAC COMPRESSOR

191 Howard Street

Franklin, PA 16323

Tel: (814) 437-3711 Fax: (814) 432-3334

CEO: U. Stork, Pres.

Emp: 2,400

Mfr. air tools and equipment.

Belgium, Canada, England, U.K., Germany, India, Italy, Mexico, South Africa

NELES-JAMESBURY INC.

40 Lincoln Street

Worcester, MA 01615

Tel: (508) 852-0200 Fax: (508) 852-8172

CEO: John Quinlivan, Pres.

HR: Shelly Houle, PR

Emp: 2,400 Rev: $300 mil.

Mfr. electronic subasemblies and components.

Finland, France, Italy, Singapore, Spain

NELSON INDUSTRIES INC.

Highway 51

W. Stoughton, WI 53589

Tel: (608) 873-4373 Fax: (608) 873-4166

CEO: R. J. Flowers, Pres.

Emp: 1,800

Mfr. automotive parts & accessories, industry machinery.

Canada, Mexico

NETMANAGE INC.

10725 N. De Anza Blvd.

Cupertino, CA 95014

Tel: (408) 973-7171 Fax: (408) 257-6405

CEO: Zvi Alon, Chmn.

FO: Patrick Linehan

HR: Patricia M. Roboostoff, SVP

Web site: www.netmanage.com

Emp: 440 Rev: $62 mil.

Develop/mfr. computer software applications & tools.

Belgium, England, U.K., France, Germany, Israel, Italy, Japan, Netherlands, Sweden

NETSCAPE COMMUNICATIONS

501 East Middlefield Road

Mountain View, CA 94043

Tel: (650) 254-1900 Fax: (650) 528-4124

CEO: Jim Barksdale, Pres.

HR: Kandis Malefyt

Mfr./distribute Internet-based commercial and consumer software applications.

Australia, Barbados, Brazil, Canada, Denmark, England, U.K., France, Germany, Hong Kong, Ireland, Italy, Japan, Netherlands, Singapore, Spain, Sweden, Switzerland

NETWORK ASSOCIATES

3935 Freedon Circle

Santa Clara, CA 95054

Tel: (408) 988-3832 Fax: (408) 970-9727

CEO: William L. Larson, Chmn.

FO: Dennis L. Cline, EVP

HR: Pat Schoof, Dir.

Web site: www.networkassociate.com

Emp: 1,600 Rev: $612 mil.

Designs and produces network security and network management software and hardware.

Australia, Canada, England, U.K., Finland, France, Germany, Ireland, Italy, Netherlands, Singapore, Spain, Sweden

NETWORK EQUIPMENT TECHNOLOGIES INC.

6500 Paseo Padre Pkwy.

Freemont, CA 94555

Tel: (510) 713-7300 Fax: (510) 574-4000

CEO: Daniel J. Warmenhoven, Chmn.

HR: Roger Barney

Emp: 1,000

Mfr./service networking products to info-intensive organizations.

England, U.K., France, Norway

NEUTROGENA CORPORATION

5760 West 96th Street

Los Angeles, CA 90045

Tel: (310) 642-1150 Fax: (310) 337-5564

CEO: Lloyd E. Cotsen

FO: Christian Bardin

HR: Lorraine King

Emp: 900

Mfr. facial cleansing, moisturizing products; body care, sun & hair care specialty products.

England, U.K., France, Germany, Mexico

NEVILLE CHEMICAL COMPANY

2800 Neville Road

Pittsburgh, PA 15225-1496

Tel: (412) 331-4200 Fax: (412) 777-4234

CEO: L. Van V. Dauler, Jr., Pres

HR: William Pesce

Emp: 460

Mfr. hydrocarbon resins.

Netherlands

NEW BRUNSWICK SCIENTIFIC CO., INC.

44 Talmadge Road, Box 4005

Edison, NJ 08818-4005

Tel: (732) 287-1200 Fax: (732) 287-4222

CEO: Ezra Weisman

FO: Bill Dunne

HR: Victoria Gustafson

Web site: www.nbsc.com

Emp: 392 Rev: $45 mil.

Mfr. research and production equipment for life sciences.

Belgium, China (PRC), England, U.K., France, Germany, Netherlands

NEW HAMPSHIRE BALL BEARINGS INC.

Route 202 South

Peterborough, NH 03458-0805

Tel: (603) 924-3311 Fax: (603) 924-6632

CEO: Gary C. Yomantas, Pres.

FO: Alistair Wem

HR: Richard Conner

Emp: 1,050

Mfr. bearings & bearing assemblies.

England, U.K.

NEW VALLEY BROOKE CORPORATION

100 SE Second Street, 32nd Fl.

Miami, FL 33131

Tel: (305) 579-8000 Fax: (305) 579-8001

CEO: Bennett LeBow, Pres.

HR: L. Cordova

Emp: 15

Holding company.

Russia

NEW YORK LIFE INSURANCE COMPANY

51 Madison Ave.

New York, NY 10010

Tel: (212) 576-7000 Fax: (212) 576-4291

CEO: Seymour Sternberg

FO: Gary Benanav

HR: George J. Trapp

Emp: 10,000

Insurance services.

Hong Kong

THE NEW YORK TIMES COMPANY

229 West 43rd Street

New York, NY 10036-3959

Tel: (212) 556-1234 Fax: (212) 556-7389

CEO: Russell T. Lewis, Pres.

HR: Cynthia H. Augustine, Sr. VP

Web site: www.nyt.com

Emp: 10,400

Diversified media company including newspapers, magazines, television and radio stations, and electronic information and publishing.

Canada, England, U.K., France, Italy

NEWAY MANUFACTURING INC.

1013 N. Shiawassee Street, PO Box 188

Corunna, MI 48817-0188

Tel: (517) 743-3458 Fax: (517) 743-5764

CEO: Justin Heffernan, Pres.

FO: Marvin J. Schultz

HR: Mary Eickholt

Emp: 35

Mfr. valve seat cutters & refacers.

Ireland

THE NEWELL COMPANY

29 E Stephenson Street

Freeport, IL 61032-0943

Tel: (815) 963-1010 Fax: (815) 489-8212

CEO: John J. McDonough, Vice. Chmn.

FO: Paul Perez, CEO Int'l

HR: Norma Connors, VP Int'l HR

Web site: www.newellco.com

Emp: 24,600 Rev: $3,234 mil

Mfr. Hardware, housewares, and office products.

Australia, Belgium, Canada, Colombia, England, U.K., France, Germany, Italy, Japan, Mexico, Portugal, Spain, Sweden, Venezuela

NEWMONT GOLD COMPANY

1700 Lincoln Street

Denver, CO 80203

Tel: (303) 863-7414 Fax: (303) 837-5837

CEO: Ronald C. Cambre, Chmn.

FO: David Francisco

HR: Steve Conte

Web site: www.newmont.corp

Emp: 6,100 Rev: $1,628 mil.

Gold mining.

Indonesia, Peru, Uzbekistan

NEWPORT CORPORATION

PO Box 19607

Irvine, CA 92606

Tel: (949) 863-3144 Fax: (949) 253-1800

CEO: Robert G. Deuster

HR: Ingrid Stern

Web site: www.newport.com

Mfr./distributor precision components & systems for laser/optical technology, vibration/motion measure & control.

Canada, France, Germany, Italy, Japan, Netherlands, Switzerland, Taiwan (ROC)

NEWSWEEK INTERNATIONAL INC.

251 West 57 Street

New York, NY 10019

Tel: (212) 445-4000 Fax: (212) 445-4120

CEO: Richard M. Smith, Pres.

FO: Michael Elliott

HR: Jean Barish

Emp: 320

Publishing.

Australia, England, U.K., France, Hong Kong, Japan

NEXT LEVEL SYSTEMS, INC.

2200 Bayberry Road

Hatboro, PA 19040

Tel: (215) 674-4800 Fax: (215) 443-9554

CEO: Donald Rumsfeld

Emp: 9,200

Mfr. broadband communications & power rectifying components.

England, U.K., France, Germany, Hong Kong, Ireland, Italy, Japan, Mexico, Singapore, Taiwan (ROC)

NIBCO INC.

500 Simpson Ave., PO Box 1167

Elkhart, IN 46515

Tel: (219) 295-3000 Fax: (219) 295-3307

CEO: Rex Martin, Chmn.

HR: Joe Gross, VP

Emp: 3,171

Mfr. fluid handling products for residential, commercial, industrial & fire protection markets.

Canada, Netherlands

NICHOLAS CRITELLI ASSOCIATES, P.C.

Ste. 500, 317 Sixth Ave.

Des Moines, IA 50309-4128

Tel: (515) 243-3122 Fax: (515) 243-3121

CEO: Nick Critelli, Mng. Prtn.

International law firm.

England, U.K.

NICHOLSON FILE COMPANY

PO Box 728

Apex, NC 27502

Tel: (919) 362-7500 Fax: (919) 783-2007

CEO: Richard Cartwright, Pres.

Mfr. files, rasps and saws.

Brazil, Italy

NICOLET INSTRUMENT CORPORATION

5225 Verona Road

Madison, WI 53711-4495

Tel: (608) 276-6100 Fax: (608) 276-6222

CEO: Fred Walder, Pres.

HR: Cory Erickson

Emp: 1,100

Mfr. infrared spectrometers and oscilloscopesand medical electro-diagnostic equipment.

Belgium, England, U.K., France, Germany, Japan

A .C. NIELSEN COMPANY

177 Broad Street

Stamford, CT 06901

Tel: (203) 961-3000 Fax: (203) 961-3190

CEO: Nicholas Trivisono

FO: Albert J. Kretch

Web site: www.acnielsen.com

Emp: 18,000

Market research.

Argentina, Australia, Austria, Belgium, Brazil, Canada, Colombia, Czech Republic, Denmark, England, U.K., Finland, France, Germany, Greece, Hungary, Ireland, Italy, Japan, Mexico, Netherlands, New Zealand, Norway, Portugal, South Korea, Spain, Sweden, Switzerland, Taiwan (ROC)

NIELSEN MEDIA RESEARCH

299 Park Ave.

New York, NY 10017

Tel: (212) 708-7500 Fax: (212) 708-7795

CEO: William G. Jacobi, Chmn.

FO: John A. Dimling, Pres.

HR: Anita Rubino

Web site: www.nielsenmedia.com

Emp: 3,200 Rev: $1,415 mil.

Measures TV audience size.

Canada

NIKE INC.

1 Bowerman Drive

Beaverton, OR 97005

Tel: (503) 671-6453 Fax: (503) 671-6300

CEO: Philip H. Knight, Chmn.

FO: Timothy J. Joyce, VP

HR: Jeffrey M. Cava, VP

Web site: www.info.nike.com

Emp: 21,000 Rev: $9,000 mil.

Mfr. athletic footwear, equipment and apparel.

Austria, Canada, England, U.K., Hong Kong, Netherlands, Vietnam

NOBLE DRILLING CORPORATION

10370 Richmond Ave., #400

Houston, TX 77042

Tel: (713) 974-3131 Fax: (713) 974-3181

CEO: James C. Day, Pres.

Emp: 1,800

Drilling contractor, engineering services.

Bermuda, Canada, Scotland, U.K., Venezuela

NORDSON CORPORATION

28601 Clemens Road

Westlake, OH 44145

Tel: (440) 892-1580 Fax: (440) 892-9507

CEO: Edward P. Campbell, Pres.

FO: Patrice Boyer, VP

HR: Bruce H. Fields, VP

Web site: www.nordson.com

Emp: 4,024 Rev: $637 mil.

Mfr. industry application equipment, sealants & packaging machinery.

Australia, Austria, Belgium, Brazil, Canada, China (PRC), Colombia, Czech Republic, Denmark, England, U.K., Finland, France, Germany, Hong Kong, India, Italy, Japan, Malaysia, Mexico, Netherlands, Norway, Poland, Portugal, Russia, Singapore, South Korea, Spain, Sweden, Switzerland, Taiwan (ROC), Thailand, Venezuela, Vietnam

NORFOLK SOUTHERN CORPORATION

Three Commercial Place

Norfolk, VA 23510-1291

Tel: (757) 629-2600 Fax: (757) 629-2798

CEO: David R. Goode, Pres.

HR: Charles Moorman

Emp: 32,500

Holding company: transportation.

Canada, England, U.K.

NORGREN

5400 S. Delaware Street

Littleton, CO 80120-1663

Tel: (303) 794-2611 Fax: (303) 795-9487

CEO: William Wolsky, Pres.

FO: Steve Lewis

HR: Francine Hammer

Web site: www.norgren.com

Emp: 700 Rev: $1,500 mil.

Mfr. pneumatic filters, regulators, lubricators, valves, automation systems, dryers, push-in fittings.

Australia, Austria, Belgium, Brazil, Canada, China (PRC), Denmark, England, U.K., France, Germany, Hong Kong, Hungary, India, Ireland, Italy, Japan, Malaysia, Mexico, Netherlands, New Zealand, Norway, Singapore, Spain, Sweden, Switzerland

NORRELL CORPORATION

3535 Piedmont Road, NE

Atlanta, GA 30305

Tel: (404) 240-3000 Fax: (404) 240-3312

CEO: C. Douglas Miller, Chmn.

FO: Eugene F. Obermeyer, Pres.

HR: Peter F. Rosen, VP

Web site: www.norrell.com

Emp: 236,000

Franchised temporary-help/workforce, short and long-term staffing services.

Canada

NORRISEAL CONTROLS

PO Box 40575

Houston, TX 77240

Tel: (713) 466-3552 Fax: (713) 896-7386

CEO: Wade Wnuk, Pres.

Emp: 300

Mfr. butterfly valves, fittings and plugs.

Canada

NORTEK INC.

50 Kennedy Plaza
Providence, RI 02903
Tel: (401) 751-1600 Fax: (401) 751-4610
CEO: Richard L. Bready, Chmn.
FO: Jeff Mattison
HR: Jane C. White
Emp: 7,650
Mfr. residential and commercial building products.
Canada, Hong Kong

NORTH AMERICAN REFRACTORIES COMPANY
1228 Euclid Ave., Ste. 500
Cleveland, OH 44115-1809
Tel: (216) 621-5200 Fax: (216) 621-8143
CEO: Jacob Mosser, Pres.
Emp: 1,600
Mfr. firebrick, refractories.
Canada

NORTH LILY MINING COMPANY
210-1800 Glenarm Place, #210
Denver, CO 80202
Tel: (303) 294-0427 Fax: (303) 293-2235
CEO: Anton R. Hendriksz
FO: Thomas L. Crom
Emp: 101
Mining gold, silver and copper.
Canada, Chile

NORTHERN TRUST CORPORATION
50 South LaSalle Street
Chicago, IL 60675
Tel: (312) 630-6000 Fax: (312) 444-3378
CEO: William A. Osborn
Emp: 7,500
Banking services.
Canada, Cayman Islands, England, U.K., Ireland, Singapore

NORTHROP GRUMMAN CORPORATION
1840 Century Park East
Los Angeles, CA 90067-2199
Tel: (310) 553-6262 Fax: (310) 201-3023
CEO: Kent Kresa, Chmn.
HR: Marvin Elkin, Corp. VP
Web site: www.northgrum.com
Emp: 52,000 Rev: $9,153 mil.
Advanced technology for aircraft, electronics, and technical support services.
Canada, Ireland, Singapore, Spain

NORTHSTAR CONSULARS/PINNACLE WORLDWIDE, INC.
1201 Marquette Ave., Ste. 300
Minneapolis, MN 55403
Tel: (612) 338-2215 Fax: (612) 338-2572
CEO: Joel McCarthy, Pres.
Web site: www.pinnacleww.com
Worldwide public relations organization.
Belgium, Egypt, Greece, Russia, Spain, Turkey

NORTHWEST AIRLINES CORPORATION
2700 Lone Oak Parkway
Eagan, MN 55121-3034
Tel: (612) 726-2111 Fax: (612) 727-6717
CEO: John H. Dasburg, Pres.
FO: Michael E. Levine, EVP
Web site: www.nwa.com
Rev: $10.8 ml
Airline passenger and cargo carrier.
China (PRC), Japan

NORTON COMPANY
1 New Bond Street
Worcester, MA 01606
Tel: (508) 795-5000 Fax: (508) 795-5741
CEO: Pierre-Andre de Chalendar, Pres.
HR: Mark Stacey
Emp: 24,400
Abrasives, drill bits, construction and safety products and plastics.
Algeria, Argentina, Australia, Belgium, Brazil, Canada, Chile, Denmark, England, U.K., France, Germany, Haiti, India, Ireland, Italy, Luxembourg, Mexico, Netherlands, New Zealand, Northern Ireland, U.K., Peru, Scotland, U.K., Singapore, Spain, Sweden, Venezuela

NORTON-PERFORMANCE PLASTICS CORPORATION
150 Dey Road
Wayne, NJ 07470

Tel: (973) 696-4700 Fax: (973) 696-4056

CEO: Robert C. Ayotte, Pres.

Emp: 2,000 Rev: $370 mil.

Mfr./sales teflon and plastic components.

England, U.K., France, Germany, Italy, Japan

NORWEST BANK MINNESOTA NA

Norwest Center, 6th and Marquette

Minneapolis, MN 55479-0095

Tel: (612) 667-8110 Fax: (612) 667-5185

CEO: Richard Kovacevich, Chmn.

Emp: 16,189

Banking services.

Brazil, Hong Kong, Taiwan (ROC)

NOVELL INC.

122 East 1700 Street

Provo, UT 84606

Tel: (801) 861-7000 Fax: (801) 861-5555

CEO: Eric E. Schmidt, Pres.

FO: Ron Heinz

Emp: 4,600 Rev: $1,000 mil.

Develop/mfr. networking software and related equipment.

Brazil, Canada, England, U.K., Poland

NOVELLUS SYSTEMS INC.

3970 North First Street

San Jose, CA 95154

Tel: (408) 943-9700 Fax: (408) 943-3422

CEO: Richard S. Hill, Chmn.

FO: Dr. Peter R. Hanley, EVP

HR: Dr. Linus F. Cordes, VP

Web site: www.novellus.com

Emp: 900 Rev: $460 mil.

Mfr. advanced processing systems used in fabrication of integrated circuits.

China (PRC), England, U.K., France, Germany, Ireland, Israel, Japan, Netherlands, Singapore, South Korea, Taiwan (ROC)

NOVO COMMUNICATIONS

520 Main Street

Fort Lee, NJ 07024

Tel: (201) 592-9044 Fax: (201) 592-5946

CEO: Christopher W. Preuster, Chmn.

Emp: 85

Storage, distribution and service of film and tape libraries.

Canada, England, U.K., Hong Kong, Netherlands

NRG GENERATING (US) INC

1221 Nicollet Ave., Ste. 700

Minneapolis, MN 55403

Tel: (612) 373-8834 Fax: (612) 373-8833

CEO: Paul Klenk, Mgr.

Electric power generation.

England, U.K.

NUMATICS INC.

1450 North Milford Road

Highland, MI 48357

Tel: (248) 887-4111 Fax: (248) 887-9190

CEO: John Welker, Pres.

FO: Lee King

HR: Larry Strauss

Web site: www.numatics.com

Emp: 725

Mfr. control valves and manifolds.

Canada, England, U.K., Germany, Mexico

NUTONE INC.

Madison and Red Bank Roads

Cincinnati, OH 45227-1599

Tel: (513) 527-5100 Fax: (513) 527-5130

CEO: Gregory E. Lawton

FO: Glen L. Bowler

HR: Robert L. Edge

Web site: www.nutone.com

Emp: 1,000

Mfr. residential specialty products and electrical appliances.

Canada

NVF COMPANY

1166 Yorklyn Road

Yorklyn, DE 19736

Tel: (302) 239-5281 Fax: (302) 239-4323

CEO: William Koles, Pres.

Emp: 6,300

Metal containers, steel products, laminated plastics and papers.

Argentina, Canada, France

O

OAKITE PRODUCTS, INC.

50 Valley Road

Berkeley Heights, NJ 07922-2798

Tel: (908) 464-6900 Fax: (908) 464-7914

CEO: Ronald Felber, Pres.

FO: Gregory V. Poff

HR: William Wenhold

Mfr. chemical products for industry cleaning and metal treating.

Argentina, Canada, Mexico

OBJECT DESIGN INC.

25 Mall Road

Burlington, MA 01803

Tel: (781) 674-5000 Fax: (781) 674-5010

CEO: Robert Goldman

Web site: www.odi.com

Emp: 270 Rev: $50 mil.

Developer of object-oriented database management systems software.

Australia, Belgium, Canada, England, U.K., France, Germany, Italy, Japan, Netherlands

OCCIDENTAL PETROLEUM CORPORATION

10889 Wilshire Blvd.

Los Angeles, CA 90024

Tel: (310) 208-8800 Fax: (310) 443-6690

CEO: Dr. Dale R. Laurance, Pres.

FO: Robert M. McGee, VP

HR: Richard W.Hallock, EVP

Web site: www.oxy.com

Emp: 12,380 Rev: $8,016il.

Petroleum and petroleum products, chemicals, plastics.

Albania, Angola, Bangladesh, Belgium, Bermuda, Bolivia, Brazil, Colombia, Congo, Ecuador, England, U.K., Gabon, Germany, India, Indonesia, Malaysia, Netherlands, New Zealand, Oman, Pakistan, Papua New Guinea, Peru, Philippines, Qatar, Russia, Saudi Arabia, Spain, Switzerland, Trinidad & Tobago, Tunisia, United Arab Emirates, Venezuela, Yemen

OCEAN ENERGY CORPORATION

1201 Louisiana Street, #1400

Houston, TX 77002

Tel: (713) 654-9110 Fax: (713) 653-3194

CEO: James Flores, Pres.

Emp: 200

Petroleum and natural gas and exploration services.

Canada

OCEANEERING INTERNATIONAL INC.

11911 FM 529

Houston, TX 77041

Tel: (713) 329-4500 Fax: (713) 329-4951

CEO: John R. Huff

FO: T. Jay Collins

HR: Sheila Jaynes

Emp: 2,000

Transportation equipment, underwater service to offshore oil and gas industry.

Angola, Australia, Brazil, Brunei, Canada, Colombia, Congo, Egypt, England, U.K., Gabon, India, Indonesia, Malaysia, Mexico, Nigeria, Norway, Oman, Papua New Guinea, Philippines, Qatar, Saudi Arabia, Scotland, U.K., Singapore, Spain, Switzerland, Thailand, Trinidad & Tobago, United Arab Emirates

ODETICS INC.

1515 South Manchester Ave.

Anaheim, CA 92802-2907

Tel: (714) 774-5000 Fax: (714) 780-7857

CEO: Joel Slutzky, Chmn.

HR: Cathy Steger

Emp: 470

Design/mfr. digital data management products for mass data storage, communications & video security markets.

England, U.K., Singapore

OEA INC.

34501 East Quincy Ave.

Aurora, CO 80015

Tel: (303) 693-1248 Fax: (303) 691-6991

CEO: C. B. Kafadar, Pres.

Emp: 775

Mfr. propellant & explosive actuated devices, automotive products.

France

OFFICE DEPOT, INC.

2200 Old Germantown Road
Delray Beach, FL 33445
Tel: (561) 278-4800 Fax: (561) 265-4406
CEO: David I. Fuente, Chmn.
FO: Richard M. Bennington, EVP
HR: Thomas Kroeger, EVP
Web site: www.officedepot.com
Emp: 35,000 Rev: $6,700 mil.
Discount office product retailer with warehouse-style superstores.
Colombia, France, Hungary, Israel, Japan, Mexico, Poland, Thailand

OFFICEMAX, INC.

3605 Warrensville Center Road
Shaker Heights, OH 44122-5203
Tel: (216) 921-6900 Fax: (216) 491-4040
CEO: Michael Feuer, Chmn.
FO: John C. Martin, Pres.
HR: Judith A. Shoulak
Web site: www.officemax.com
Emp: 32,000 Rev: $3,800 mil.
Office furnishings, printing and copying services and super center office stores.
Japan, Mexico

C.M. OFFRAY & SON INC.

360 Rt. 24
Chester, NJ 07930-0601
Tel: (908) 879-4700 Fax: (908) 543-4294
CEO: C. V. Offray, Jr., Pres.
FO: William Jjoos
Emp: 2,750
Mfr. narrow fabrics.
Canada, England, U.K., Ireland

OGDEN ENVIRONMENTAL & ENERGY SERVICES COMPANY

3211 Germantown Road
Fairfax, VA 22053
Tel: (703) 246-0500 Fax: (703) 246-0598
CEO: J. Mark Elliott, Pres.
FO: Jay Stewart
HR: Donald Laing
Emp: 1,500
Environmental & energy consulting services for commercial clients & government agencies.
Germany, Japan, Spain

OGILVY & MATHER WORLDWIDE

309 West 49th Street
New York, NY 10019
Tel: (212) 237-4000 Fax: (212) 237-5123
CEO: Shelly Lazarus, Chmn.
Emp: 6,800 Rev: $838 mil.
Advertising, marketing, public relations & consulting firm.
Argentina, Australia, Austria, Belgium, Botswana, Brazil, Bulgaria, Canada, Chile, China (PRC), Colombia, Costa Rica, Cyprus, Czech Republic, Denmark, Dominican Republic, Ecuador, El Salvador, England, U.K., Finland, France, Germany, Greece, Hong Kong, Hungary, India, Indonesia, Ireland, Italy, Japan, Kazakhstan, Kenya, Malaysia, Mexico, Mozambique, Netherlands, New Zealand, Nigeria, Norway, Pakistan, Paraguay, Philippines, Poland, Portugal, Romania, Russia, Singapore, Slovakia, Slovenia, South Africa, South Korea, Spain, Sweden, Switzerland, Taiwan (ROC), Thailand, Turkey, Uganda, Ukraine, Uruguay, Venezuela

OGLEBAY NORTON COMPANY

1100 Superior Ave., 20th Fl.
Cleveland, OH 44114-2598
Tel: (216) 861-3300 Fax: (216) 861-2863
CEO: John N. Lauer, Chmn. & Pres.
FO: T. J. Wojciechowski, VP
HR: Ronald J. Compiseno
Web site: www.oglebaynorton.com
Emp: 900 Rev: $145.0 mil.
Produces limestone & provides transport services & raw materials for the construction & steel industries.
Canada

OHAUS CORPORATION

29 Hanover Road, PO Box 900
Florham Park, NJ 07932-0900
Tel: (973) 377-9000 Fax: (973) 593-0359
CEO: Jim Ohaus, Pres.
Emp: 375
Mfr. balances and scales for labs, industry and education.
England, U.K., France, Germany, Italy, Japan, Mexico, Poland, South Korea, Spain

THE OHIO ART COMPANY

One Toy Street
Bryan, OH 43506
Tel: (419) 636-3141 Fax: (419) 636-7614
CEO: Martin L. Killgallon II
FO: Paul R. McCusty
HR: Cheryl Kimpel
Web site: www.world-of-toys.com
Emp: 303 Rev: $36.3 mil.

Mfg./distributes toys; provides custom metal lithography and moulded plastic products to other companies.

England, U.K.

OIL STATES INDUSTRIES

7701 South Cooper Street
Arlington, TX 76017
Tel: (817) 468-1400 Fax: (817) 468-6250
CEO: Howard Hughes, Pres.
HR: Matt Moody

Mfr., drilling and production machinery and supplies for oil/gas production.

Canada, England, U.K.

OIL-DRI CORPORATION OF AMERICA

410 North Michigan Ave., Ste. 400
Chicago, IL 60611
Tel: (312) 321-1515 Fax: (312) 321-1271
CEO: Daniel S. Jaffee, Pres.
FO: Norman B. Gershon, VP
HR: Karen Jaffee Cofsky, Dir. HR
Web site: www.
Emp: 665 Rev: $156.6 mil.

Oil & grease absorbents, soil conditioners, and other sorbent mineral products.

Canada, England, U.K., Switzerland

THE OILGEAR COMPANY

2300 S. 51st Street
Milwaukee, WI 53219
Tel: (414) 327-1700 Fax: (414) 327-0532
CEO: David A. Zuege
FO: Bert Bursch
HR: Thomas J. Price
Emp: 967

Mfr. hydraulic power transmission machinery.

Australia, Brazil, England, U.K., France, Germany, India, Italy, Japan, Mexico, South Korea, Spain, Taiwan (ROC)

OLIN CORPORATION

501 Merritt Seven
Norwalk, CT 06856-4500
Tel: (203) 750-3000 Fax: (203) 356-3065
CEO: Donald W. Griffin, Pres. & Chmn.
FO: William M. Smith
HR: Peter C. Kosche
Emp: 9,500 Rev: $2,000 mil.

Mfr. chemicals, metals, applied physics in electronics, defense & aerospace industry.

Australia, Belgium, Brazil, England, U.K., France, Germany, Ireland, Japan, Mexico, New Zealand, Singapore, South Africa, Taiwan (ROC), Venezuela

OLSTEN CORPORATION

175 Broad Hollow Road
Melville, NY 11747-8905
Tel: (516) 844-7800 Fax: (516) 844-7022
CEO: Frank N. Liguori,Chmn.
FO: Stuart Olsten, VC & Pres.
HR: Maureen Mc Gurl, SVP
Web site: www.olsten.com
Emp: 642,000 Rev: $4,113 mil.

Staffing, home health care & information technology services.

Argentina, Brazil, Canada, Chile, Denmark, England, U.K., Finland, France, Germany, Mexico, Norway, Spain, Sweden

OM GROUP, INC.

3800 Terminal Tower
Cleveland, OH 44113-2203
Tel: (216) 781-0083 Fax: (216) 781-0902
CEO: James P. Mooney, Chmn.
FO: Thomas E. Fleming
HR: Michael J. Scott
Emp: 425

Producer and marketer of metal-based specialty chemicals.

Finland, France, Germany, Japan

OMNICOM GROUP

437 Madison Ave.
New York, NY 10022
Tel: (212) 415-3600 Fax: (212) 415-3530

CEO: Bruce Crawford, Chmn.

FO: John D. Wren, Pres.

Emp: 37,637 Rev: $4,154.3 mil.

International network of advertising, marketing, direct mail, public relations and consulting services.

England, U.K., France, Lebanon, Singapore

ONAN CORPORATION

1400 73rd Ave. NE

Minneapolis, MN 55432

Tel: (612) 574-5000 Fax: (612) 574-5298

CEO: Jerry E. Johnson, Mgr.

FO: Michael Mitchell

HR: Katie Pearson

Emp: 3,500

Mfr. electric generators, controls & switchgears.

Australia, England, U.K., Japan, Singapore, South Korea

ONEIDA LTD

163-181 Kenwood Ave.

Oneida, NY 13421-2899

Tel: (315) 361-3000 Fax: (315) 361-3658

CEO: William D. Mathews, Chmn.

FO: Allan H. Conseur, Pres.

HR: Robert J. Houle, VP

Web site: www.oneida.com

Emp: 4,500 Rev: $443 mil.

Mfr. cutlery, hollowware, china, crystal.

Australia, Canada, Mexico

ONEIDA ROSTONE CORPORATION

104 South Warner Street

Oneida, NY 13421

Tel: (315) 363-7990 Fax: (315) 363-8519

CEO: David Harrington, Pres.

Emp: 500

Mfr. custom molded glass and reinforced thermoset polyester products.

Ireland

ONTARIO STONE CORPORATION

34301 Chardon Road, Ste. #5

Willoughby, OH 44094-8459

Tel: (440) 943-9556 Fax: (440) 631-1425

CEO: Carl Barricelli , Jr., Pres.

Emp: 90

Stone & brick.

Canada

OPPENHEIMER CASING COMPANY

PO Box 849

Champlain, NY 12919

Tel: (518) 298-5411 Fax: (518) 298-3152

CEO: M. Whig, Pres.

Emp: 1,300

Mfr. sausage casings.

Australia, England, U.K.

OPRYLAND MUSIC GROUP

65 Music Square West

Nashville, TN 37203

Tel: (615) 321-5000 Fax: (615) 327-0560

CEO: Jerry Bradley

FO: Marc Wood

Web site: www.acuffrose.com

Emp: 45

Music publisher.

England, U.K., Germany

OPTEK TECHNOLOGY, INC.

1215 West Crosby Road

Carrollton, TX 75006

Tel: (972) 323-2200 Fax: (972) 323-2208

CEO: Thomas R. Filesi, Pres.

HR: Clark Basinger

Web site: www.optekinc.com

Emp: 2,000 Rev: $90 mil.

Mfr. electronic components.

Mexico

OPTICAL COATING LABORATORY, INC. (OCLI)

2789 Northpoint Pkwy.

Santa Rosa, CA 95407-7397

Tel: (707) 545-6440 Fax: (707) 525-7410

CEO: Charles J. Abbe, Pres. & COO

FO: Klaus F. Derge

HR: Gary Hochman

Web site: www.ocli.com

Emp: 1,500 Rev: $217 mil.

Mfr. thin film precision coated optical devices.

France, Germany, Scotland, U.K., Spain

OPW FUELING COMPONENTS

PO Box 405003

Cincinnati, OH 45240-5003

Tel: (513) 870-3100 Fax: (513) 874-1231

CEO: David J. Ropp, Pres.

HR: Paul Green

Mfr. fueling and vapor recovery nozzles, service station equipment, aboveground storage tank equipment.

Brazil, Netherlands

ORACLE CORPORATION

500 Oracle Parkway

Redwood Shores, CA 94065

Tel: (415) 506-7000 Fax: (415) 506-7200

CEO: Lawrence J. Ellison, Chmn.

FO: Raymond J. Lane, EVP

Emp: 17,000 Rev: $3,000 mil.

Develop/manufacture software.

Austria, Brazil, Colombia, England, U.K., Finland, France, Germany, Italy, Mexico, Spain, Switzerland, Venezuela, Vietnam

ORCHID INTERNATIONAL

100 Winners Circle

Brentwood, TN 37027

Tel: (615) 661-4300 Fax: (615) 661-4359

CEO: Grant Bibby, Pres.

Emp: 160

Mfr. metal stampings and automation/robotics.

Canada

ORIEL INSTRUMENTS CORPORATION

150 Long Beach Boulevard

Stratford, CT 06615

Tel: (203) 377-8282 Fax: (203) 378-2457

CEO: Allen Smith, Pres.

HR: Debbie Bergren

Emp: 150

Mfr. optical goods.

England, U.K., France

ORION CAPITAL CORPORATION

9 Farm Springs Road

Farmington, CT 06032

Tel: (860) 674-6600 Fax:

CEO: Robert B. Sanborn, Pres.

Emp: 1,400

Holding company: insurance.

England, U.K.

ORION MARINE CORPORATION

79 West Monroe Street, Ste. 1105

Chicago, IL 60603

Tel: (312) 263-5153 Fax: (312) 263-4233

CEO: Peter K. Schauer

Emp: 20

Ocean transportation.

Georgia, Russia, Ukraine

ORION RESEARCH INC.

500 Cummings Court

Beverly, MA 01915

Tel: (978) 922-4400 Fax: (617) 242-7885

CEO: Jim Barbookles, Pres.

FO: David Knight

HR: Lance Solimini

Web site: www.orionres.com

Emp: 350

Mfr. laboratory and industrial products, measure and display instruments.

England, U.K., Hong Kong

ORYX ENERGY COMPANY

PO Box 2880

Dallas, TX 75221-2880

Tel: (214) 715-4000 Fax: (214) 715-3311

CEO: Robert L. Keiser, Chmn.

FO: Jerry W. Box, Pres. Intl.

HR: Fran G. Heartwell

Web site: www.oryx.com

Emp: 1,200

Oil and gas exploration and production.

Ecuador, England, U.K.

OSCAR MAYER & COMPANY

PO Box 7188

Madison, WI 53707

Tel: (608) 241-3311 Fax: (608) 242-6102

CEO: Richard Searer, Pres.

Emp: 13,800

Meat and food products.

Japan, Spain, Venezuela

OSMONICS INC.

5951 Clearwater Drive

Minnetonka, MN 55343-8995

Tel: (612) 933-2277 Fax: (612) 933-0141

CEO: D. Dean Spatz

FO: Ken E. Johdahl

HR: Howard W. Dicke

Emp: 915 Rev: $164 mil.

Mfr. fluid filtration and separation equipment and components.

Australia, Brazil, China (PRC), Denmark, England, U.K., France, Germany, Hong Kong, Indonesia, Italy, Japan, Mexico, Philippines, Singapore, Switzerland, Thailand

OSMOSE INTERNATIONAL INC.

980 Ellicott Street

Buffalo, NY 14209

Tel: (716) 882-5905 Fax: (716) 882-5139

CEO: Jim Spengler, Pres.

Emp: 600

Mfr. wood preservatives; maintenance and inspection utility poles, railroad track and marine piling.

Denmark, England, U.K., Mexico

OSRAM SYLVANIA CHEMICALS INC.

Hawes Street

Towanda, PA 18848

Tel: (717) 268-5000 Fax: (717) 268-5157

CEO: Dr. A. Alper, VP

Emp: 2,000 Rev: $330 mil.

Chemicals.

Belgium, Brazil, China (PRC), Germany, Hong Kong, Italy, Japan

OTIS ELEVATOR COMPANY

10 Farm Springs Road

Farmington, CT 06032

Tel: (860) 676-6000 Fax: (860) 676-5111

CEO: George David, Pres.

HR: W. Ferguson

Emp: 50,000 Rev: $4,500 mil.

Mfr. elevators and escalators.

Argentina, Australia, Austria, Belgium, Brazil, Canada, China (PRC), Czech Republic, Denmark, Egypt, England, U.K., Finland, France, Germany, Greece, Hong Kong, Hungary, India, Indonesia, Italy, Japan, Jordan, Kenya, Kuwait, Lebanon, Luxembourg, Malaysia, Mexico, Morocco, Netherlands, New Zealand, Philippines, Poland, Portugal, Russia, Saudi Arabia, Singapore, South Africa, South Korea, Spain, Sri Lanka, Sweden, Switzerland, Taiwan (ROC), Thailand, Turkey, Ukraine, Uruguay, Vietnam, Zimbabwe

OUTBOARD MARINE CORPORATION

100 Sea Horse Drive

Waukegan, IL 60085

Tel: (847) 689-6200 Fax: (847) 689-5555

CEO: David D. Jones Jr., Pres.

FO: John Anderson, Gen. Mgr.

HR: Kinberly K. Bors, VP

Web site: www.omc-online.com

Emp: 7,442 Rev: $980 mil.

Mfr./market marine engines, boats & accessories.

Australia, Brazil, Canada, Hong Kong, Mexico

OUTDOOR TECHNOLOGIES GROUP

1900 18th Street

Spirit Lake, IA 51360

Tel: (712) 336-1520 Fax: (712) 336-4183

CEO: Tom Bedell

FO: Mike Binder

HR: Mike Brenny

Emp: 1,400

Mfr. fishing rods, reels, lines & tackle, outdoor products, soft and hard baits.

Australia, Canada, England, U.K., Taiwan (ROC)

OVERHEAD DOOR CORPORATION

PO Box 809046

Dallas, TX 75380-9046

Tel: (972) 233-6611 Fax: (972) 991-4416

CEO: Brian J. Bolton

HR: Frank W. Rudolph, VP

Emp: 3,100

Mfr. building products, garage doors and automatic entrances and transportation industry products.

England, U.K.

OWENS-CORNING FIBERGLAS CORPORATION

Fiberglas Tower

Toledo, OH 43659

Tel: (419) 248-8000 Fax: (419) 248-6227

CEO: Glen H. Hiner, Chmn.

HR: Robert Lonergan, SVP

Web site: www.housenet.com

Emp: 17,000 Rev: $3,000 mil.

Mfr. insulation, building materials, glass fiber products.

Belgium, Brazil, Cayman Islands, Denmark, England, U.K., France, Germany, Italy, Netherlands, Norway, Saudi Arabia, Spain, Sweden

OWENS-ILLINOIS, INC.

One SeaGate, PO Box 1035

Toledo, OH 43666

Tel: (419) 247-5000 Fax: (419) 247-2839

CEO: Joseph H. Lemieux, Chmn.

FO: R. Scott Trumbull, EVP

HR: Gary Benjamin

Emp: 27,000 Rev: $3,900 mil.

Largest mfr. of glass containers in the US; plastic containers, compression-molded closures and dispensing systems.

Brazil, Canada, China (PRC), Colombia, Czech Republic, Ecuador, England, U.K., Estonia, Finland, Hungary, India, Italy, Peru, Poland, South Africa, Spain, Venezuela

OXFORD INDUSTRIES INC.

222 Piedmont Ave. NE

Atlanta, GA 30308

Tel: (404) 659-2424 Fax: (404) 525-3650

CEO: J. Hicks Lanier, Chmn. & Pres.

HR: Herb Kraft

Emp: 9,857

Design/mfr./marketing consumer apparel products.

Hong Kong, Mexico

P

PACCAR INTERNATIONAL

777 106th Ave. NE

Bellevue, WA 98004

Tel: (425) 468-7400 Fax: (428) 468-8216

CEO: Mark C. Pigott, Chmn.

FO: David J. Hovind, Pres.

HR: Laurie L. Baker, VP HR

Emp: 19,000 Rev: $6,752 mil.

Heavy duty dump trucks, military vehicles.

Bahrain, Belgium, China (PRC), England, U.K., Indonesia, Russia, Singapore, South Africa

PACIFIC ARCHITECTS & ENGINEERS INC.

1111 West Sixth Street - 4th Floor

Los Angeles, CA 90017-1876

Tel: (213) 481-2311 Fax: (213) 481-7189

CEO: Allen E. Shay, Chmn. & Pres.

FO: Barry C. Wright, SVP

HR: Gloria Martinez, HR Mgr.

Web site: www.pae.com

Emp: 5,000 Rev: $100 mil.

Technical engineering services.

Germany, Indonesia, Italy, Japan, Malaysia, Myanmar, New Zealand, Panama, Russia, Singapore, South Korea, Thailand, Vietnam

PACIFIC GAS & ELECTRIC COMPANY

77 Beale Street, PO Box 770000

San Francisco, CA 94177

Tel: (415) 973-7000 Fax: (415) 972-9577

CEO: Robert Goynn, Jr.

FO: Jerry R. McLeod

HR: Barbara Coull Williams

Emp: 26,780

Electric and natural gas service.

Canada

PACIFIC SCIENTIFIC COMPANY

620 Newport Center Drive, Ste.700

Newport Beach, CA 92660

Tel: (714) 720-1714 Fax: (714) 720-1083

CEO: Edgar S. Brower, Pres.

Emp: 1,848

Mfr. electrical equipment & safety equipment.

England, U.K., France, Germany

PACIFIC TELESIS GROUP

140 New Montgomery Street

San Francisco, CA 94105

Tel: (415) 394-3000 Fax: (415) 542-4221

CEO: Edward Mueller, Pres.

HR: Michael Rodriquez

Emp: 51,590

Telecommunications and information systems.

England, U.K., Japan, Malaysia, South Korea, Spain, Thailand

PACKARD BELL NEC, INC.

One Packard Bell Way
Sacramento, CA 95828-0903
Tel: (916) 388-0101 Fax: (916) 388-1109
CEO: Beny Alagem, Chmn. & Pres.
FO: Brent Cohen, Pres. Intl.
HR: Fred Philpott, VP
Web site: www.packardbell.com

Sales/distribution of home computers.

Australia, Brazil, China (PRC), France, Israel, Japan, Malaysia

PADCO INC.

2220 Elm Street SE
Minneapolis, MN 55414
Tel: (612) 378-7270 Fax: (612) 378-9388
CEO: Robert I. Janssen, Pres.
FO: Robert I. Janssen
HR: Chandra Meka
Emp: 120

Mfr. paint sundries.

Canada, Costa Rica, Germany, Mexico

PAINE WEBBER GROUP INC.

1285 Ave. of the Americas
New York, NY 10019
Tel: (212) 713-2000 Fax: (212) 586-8282
CEO: Donald B. Marron, Chmn.
Emp: 16,627

Stock brokerage & investment services.

England, U.K., Hong Kong, Japan, Switzerland

PALL CORPORATION

2200 Northern Boulevard
East Hills, NY 11548-1289
Tel: (516) 484-5400 Fax: (516) 484-5228
CEO: Eric Krasnoff, Chmn.
FO: Dereck T. D. Williams
HR: Pat Lowy
Web site: www.pall.com
Emp: 7,700

Specialty materials and engineering; filters & related fluid clarification equipment.

Australia, Austria, Canada, China (PRC), England, U.K., France, Germany, Hong Kong, India, Ireland, Italy, Japan, New Zealand, Norway, Poland, Russia, Singapore, South Korea, Spain, Sweden, Switzerland, Taiwan (ROC), Thailand

PALMS & COMPANY, INC. (U.S. FUR EXCHANGE)

515 Lake Street South, Bldg. #103
Kirkland, WA 98033
Tel: (425) 828-6774 Fax: (425) 827-5528
CEO: Dr. P. J. van de Waal-Palms, Pres.
HR: Anke van de Waal
Emp: 250 Rev: $3,000 mil.

Fur auctioning, distribution and sale; investment banking

Armenia, Azerbaijan, Belarus, Estonia, Georgia, Kazakhstan, Lithuania, Netherlands, Russia, Turkmenistan, Ukraine, Uzbekistan

PAN-AMERICAN LIFE INSURANCE CO.

Pan American Life Center, PO Box 60219
New Orleans, LA 70130-0219
Tel: (504) 566-1300 Fax: (504) 566-3600
CEO: John K. Roberts, Jr., Pres.
FO: W. Timothy Knechtel, EVP
HR: Vicki Cansler, SVP
Web site: www.palic.com
Emp: 800

Insurance services.

Colombia, Dominican Republic, Ecuador, El Salvador, Guatemala, Honduras, Panama

PANALARM DIV. AMETEK

7401 North Hamlin Ave.
Skokie, IL 60076
Tel: (847) 675-2500 Fax: (847) 675-3011
CEO: Roger Piegza, Pres.
FO: Frank Knopf
Emp: 300

Mfr. electrical alarm systems, temp monitors, display systems, sensors.

Canada, England, U.K.

PANAMETRICS

221 Crescent Street
Waltham, MA 02154
Tel: (781) 899-2719 Fax: (781) 899-1552
CEO: Dr. F. B. Sellers, Pres.
HR: Stacey Charbonneau
Web site: www.panametrics.com

Process/non-destructive test instrumentation.

Australia, Austria, Canada, Denmark, England, U.K., Finland, France, Germany, Greece, Iran, Ireland, Israel, Italy, Japan, Kuwait, Malaysia, Mexico, Netherlands, Norway, Philippines, South Africa, South Korea, Sweden, Taiwan (ROC), Thailand, United Arab Emirates, Vietnam

PANDUIT CORPORATION

17301 Ridgeland Ave.

Tinley Park, IL 60477-0981

Tel: (708) 532-1800 Fax: (708) 532-1811

CEO: J. J. Caveney, Pres.

FO: Bernard T. Westapher

Emp: 2,000

Mfr. electrical/electronic wiring components.

Australia, Austria, Belgium, Canada, China (PRC), England, U.K., France, Germany, Hong Kong, Italy, Japan, Mexico, Netherlands, Singapore, South Korea, Spain, Taiwan (ROC), Thailand, United Arab Emirates

PANELFOLD INC.

10700 NW 36th Ave.

Miami, FL 33167

Tel: (305) 688-3501 Fax: (305) 681-2153

CEO: Guy E. Dixon III

FO: Gerald E. Schimmel

HR: Marsha Kallstrom

Web site: www.panelfold.com

Emp: 200

Mfr. folding doors and partitions, operable and relocatable partition systems.

Canada

PAPER CONVERTING MACHINE COMPANY

PO Box 19005

Green Bay, WI 54307

Tel: (920) 494-5601 Fax: (920) 494-8865

CEO: Frederick W. Baer

HR: Steve Herzog

Emp: 940

Paper converting machinery.

England, U.K.

PARADYNE

8545 Ulmerton Road, PO Box 2826

Largo, FL 34294-2826

Tel: (813) 530-2000 Fax: (813) 530-2875

CEO: Andrew May, Pres.

HR: Cheryl Melio

Emp: 1,700

Mfr. data communications products.

Canada, England, U.K., Hong Kong, Japan

PARAMETRIC TECHNOLOGY CORPORATION

128 Technology Drive

Waltham, MA 02154

Tel: (781) 398-5000 Fax: (781) 398-5674

CEO: Steven Walske & Chmn.

FO: John D. McMahon, EVP

HR: Carl Ockerbloom

Web site: www.ptc.com

Emp: 600 Rev: 809 mil.

Mfr. CAD/CAM/CAE software.

Argentina, Australia, Austria, Belgium, Brazil, Canada, China (PRC), Czech Republic, Denmark, England, U.K., Finland, France, Germany, Hong Kong, India, Indonesia, Ireland, Israel, Italy, Japan, Malaysia, Netherlands, New Zealand, Norway, Portugal, Russia, Scotland, U.K., Singapore, Slovakia, South Africa, South Korea, Spain, Sweden, Switzerland, Taiwan (ROC), Thailand

PARAMOUNT PARKS

8620 Red Oak Blvd., Ste. 315

Charlotte, NC 28217

Tel: (704) 525-5250 Fax: (704) 525-2960

CEO: Jane Cooper, Pres.

Owns and operates theme parks and water parks.

Canada

PAREXEL INTERNATIONAL CORPORATION

195 West Street

Waltham, MA 02154

Tel: (781) 487-9900 Fax: (781) 487-0525

CEO: Josef H. von Rickenbach, Chmn.

FO: Taylor J. Crouch, SVP

HR: Geralyn Burke, Dir.

Web site: www.parexel.com

Emp: 2,400 Rev: $208 mil

Provides contract medical, biotechnology, and pharmaceutical research and consulting services.

Australia, Canada, Czech Republic, England, U.K., France, Germany, Hungary, Israel, Italy, Japan,

Lithuania, Netherlands, Norway, Poland, Russia, Spain, Sweden, Wales, U.K.

PARK ELECTROCHEMICAL CORPORATION

5 Dakota Drive

Lake Success, NY 11042

Tel: (516) 354-4100 Fax: (516) 354-4128

CEO: Brian Shora, Pres.

FO: Charles Carter

Emp: 900

Multi-layer laminate printed circuit materials, industry comps, plumbing hardware products.

England, U.K., France, Singapore

PARKER ABEX NWL CORPORATION

2222 Palmer Ave.

Kalamazoo, MI 49001

Tel: (616) 384-3400 Fax: (616) 743-2131

CEO: William Higley, Pres.

Emp: 13,000

Mfr. aerospace & automotive friction materials & equipment.

Canada, Germany, India, Mexico

PARKER DRILLING COMPANY

8 East Third Street

Tulsa, OK 74103-3637

Tel: (918) 585-8221 Fax: (918) 585-1058

CEO: Robert L. Parker, Jr., Pres.

FO: Ronnie McKenzie

HR: Susan McDonald

Emp: 1,283

Drilling contractor.

Argentina, Bolivia, Colombia, Ecuador, Indonesia, Kenya, Kuwait, New Zealand, Pakistan, Papua New Guinea, Peru, Russia, Singapore, Sudan, Yemen

PARKER HANNIFIN CORPORATION

17325 Euclid Ave.

Cleveland, OH 44112

Tel: (216) 896-3000 Fax: (216) 896-4000

CEO: Duane E. Collins, Pres.

FO: Stephen L. Hayes, VP

HR: Daniel T. Garey, VP

Web site: www.parker.com

Emp: 39,873 Rev: $4,633 mil.

Mfr. motion-control products.

Argentina, Australia, Austria, Belgium, Brazil, Canada, China (PRC), Czech Republic, Denmark, England, U.K., Finland, France, Germany, Hong Kong, Italy, Japan, Malaysia, Mexico, Netherlands, New Zealand, Norway, Philippines, Singapore, South Africa, South Korea, Spain, Sweden, United Arab Emirates, Venezuela

PARSONS & WHITTEMORE INC.

4 International Drive

Rye Brook, NY 10573

Tel: (914) 937-9009 Fax: (914) 937-2259

CEO: Arthur L. Schwartz, Pres.

HR: Richard C. Martin

Emp: 1,300

Pulp and paper mfr., construction pulp and paper mills, engineering.

Canada

PARSONS BRINCKERHOFF QUADE & DOUGLAS

250 West 34th Street, Penn Plaza

New York, NY 10119

Tel: (212) 465-5000 Fax: (212) 465-5096

CEO: Tom O'Neil, Pres.

HR: B. L. Culmer

Emp: 900

Engineering consultants, planners and architects.

Turkey

THE PARSONS CORPORATION

100 West Walnut Street

Pasadena, CA 91124

Tel: (626) 440-2000 Fax: (626) 440-2630

CEO: James McNulty, Pres.

Emp: 10,000

Engineering and construction.

England, U.K., Japan, Kuwait, Mexico, Philippines, Saudi Arabia, Venezuela

PARSONS ENERGY & CHEMICALS GROUP INC.

2675 Morgantown Road

Reading, PA 19607

Tel: (610) 855-2000 Fax: (610) 855-2001

CEO: James McNulty, Pres.

Web site: www.parsons.com

Emp: 4,000

Provide full engineer-procurement-construction services, studies and project and constructiion management for utilities and independent power producers worldwide.

Australia, Egypt, England, U.K.

PARSONS ENGINEERING SCIENCE INC.

100 West Walnut Street

Pasadena, CA 91124

Tel: (626) 440-2000 Fax: (626) 440-4919

CEO: Jim McNulty, Pres.

HR: Phil R. Williams

Emp: 10,000

Environmental engineering.

Bangladesh, England, U.K., Indonesia, Japan, Kuwait, Oman, Pakistan, Philippines, Sri Lanka, Taiwan (ROC), United Arab Emirates, Vietnam

PARSONS TRANSPORTATION GROUP

1133 15th Street NW

Washington, DC 20005

Tel: (202) 775-3300 Fax: (202) 775-3422

CEO: Robert S. O'Neil, Chmn.

FO: Michael D. Coleman

HR: Ross Tierno

Emp: 1,175

Consulting engineers.

Bolivia, China (PRC), England, U.K., Indonesia, Kuwait, Malawi, Nigeria, Pakistan, Philippines, Taiwan (ROC), Tanzania, Thailand, United Arab Emirates

PARTECH INTERNATIONAL

50 California Street

San Francisco, CA 94111-4624

Tel: (415) 788-2929 Fax: (415) 788-6763

CEO: Tom McKinley, Pres.

Invests in startup and growth companies in information technology, communications and healthcare.

France, Japan

PATAGONIA INC.

259 West Santa Clara Street

Ventura, CA 93001

Tel: (805) 643-8616 Fax: (805) 653-6355

CEO: Yvon Chouinard, Pres.

Outdoor clothing retail stores and mail-order catalogue company.

Canada

PATTERSON, BELKNAP, WEBB & TYLER

1133 Ave. of the Americas

New York, NY 10036

Tel: (212) 336-2000 Fax: (212) 336-2222

CEO: Stephen Schwarz, Mng. Prtn.

FO: Scott Horton

HR: Lois White

International law firm.

Russia

PAUL, WEISS, RIFKIND, WHARTON & GARRISON

1285 Ave. of the Americas

New York, NY 10019-6064

Tel: (212) 373-3000 Fax: (212) 373-2268

CEO: Emil Sommer

Web site: www.paulweiss.com

Emp: 850 Rev: $219 mil.

Law firm engaged in American and international law practice.

China (PRC), France, Hong Kong, Japan

PAXAR CORPORATION

105 Corporate Park Drive

White Plains, NY 10604

Tel: (914) 697-6800 Fax: (914) 696-4128

CEO: Arthur Hersheft, Chmn. & Pres.

Web site: www.paxar.com

Emp: 1,800

Mfr./sales/distribution of labels, hang tags, scanners, printing equipment and inks.

Australia, Canada, Mexico

PCA ELECTRONICS INC.

16799 Schoenborn Street

North Hills, CA 91343

Tel: (818) 892-0761 Fax: (818) 894-5791

CEO: Morris Weinberg, Pres.

HR: Tony Essman

Web site: www.pca.com

Emp: 40

Mfr./sales of electronic equipment.

Canada, England, U.K., France, Hong Kong, Israel, Mexico

PCS DATA CONVERSION

238 Main Street
Cambridge, MA 02142
Tel: (617) 354-7424 Fax: (617) 876-4711
CEO: N. K. Patni, Pres.
FO: M. R. Sattawala
Emp: 200
Software consulting & contract programing services.
India

THE PEELLE COMPANY

34 Central Ave.
Hauppauge, NY 11788-4734
Tel: (516) 231-6000 Fax: (516) 231-6059
CEO: Henry E. Peelle III
FO: Robert B. Peelle, Jr.
Emp: 160
Mfr./sales/service elevator, fire and specially engineered doors.
Canada

PEER INTERNATIONAL CORPORATION

810 Seventh Ave.
New York, NY 10019
Tel: (212) 265-3910 Fax: (212) 489-2465
CEO: Ralph Peer, Pres.
Music publishers.
Spain

PELLA CORPORATION

102 Main Street
Pella, IA 50129
Tel: (515) 628-1000 Fax: (515) 628-6070
CEO: Gary Christenson, Pres.
FO: Jim Danks
HR: Rich Allen
Web site: www.pella.com
Emp: 4,500 Rev: $6.0 mil.
Mfr. wood windows, glass sliding and folding doors.
Netherlands

PENFORD

777 108th Ave.
Bellevue, WA 98004-5193
Tel: (425) 462-6000 Fax: (425) 462-2819
CEO: Jeffrey Cook
Emp: 300
Mfr. food ingredients, nutritional supplements, spec. carbohydrate & synthetic polymer chemicals.
England, U.K., Finland

PENNZOIL COMPANY

700 Milam
Houston, TX 77002
Tel: (713) 546-4000 Fax: (713) 546-6589
CEO: James L. Pate, Chmn.
FO: Stephen D. Chesebro, Pres. & COO
HR: Darlene Cox, Dir.
Web site: www.pennzoil.com
Emp: 10,214 Rev: $2,511 mil.
Produce/refine/market oil, natural gas, sulfur.
Azerbaijan, Belgium, Netherlands

PENSKE CORPORATION

13400 Outer Drive West
Detroit, MI 48239
Tel: (313) 592-5000 Fax: (313) 592-5256
CEO: Roger Penske, Chmn.
Web site: www.detroitdiesel.com
Design and manufacture engines and operate truck leasing facilities.
England, U.K., Germany

PENTA SOFTWARE

107 Lakefront Drive
Hunt Valley, MD 21030
Tel: (410) 771-8973 Fax: (410) 771-4020
CEO: Frederick A. Ayres
Develop/support computer publishing systems
England, U.K., France, Germany

PENTAIR, INC.

1500 County Road, B2 West
St. Paul, MN 55113-3105
Tel: (612) 636-7920 Fax: (612) 636-5508
CEO: Winslow H. Buxton, Pres. & Chmn.
FO: Gerald C. Kitch, Pres., Int'l.
HR: Deb Knutson
Emp: 10,000 Rev: $1,500 mil.
Diversified manufacturer operating in electrical

and electronic enclosures, professional tools/equipment and water products.

Brazil, Canada, Germany, Wales, U.K.

PENTON MEDIA

1100 Superior Ave.

Cleveland, OH 44114-2543

Tel: (216) 696-7000 Fax: (216) 696-7648

CEO: Dan Ramella

HR: Bobbi Navarra

Emp: 1,349

Publishing industrial magazines.

England, U.K.

PEPPER, HAMILTON & SCHEETZ

18th & Arch Streets., Logan Square Ste. 3000

Philadelphia, PA 19103

Tel: (215) 981-4000 Fax: (215) 981-4750

CEO: James L. Murray, Mng. Prtn.

International law firm.

Russia

PEPSiCO INC.

700 Anderson Hill Road

Purchase, NY 10577-1444

Tel: (914) 253-2000 Fax: (914) 253-2070

CEO: Roger A. Enrico, Chmn.

FO: Peter M. Thompson, Pres.

HR: William R. Bensyl, SVP

Web site: www.pepsico.com

Emp: 142,000 Rev: $20,917 mil.

Beverages and snack foods.

Argentina, Australia, Bermuda, Canada, Chile, China (PRC), England, U.K., France, Germany, Greece, Guatemala, India, Ireland, Japan, Mexico, Netherlands, Netherlands Antilles, Pakistan, Philippines, Poland, Russia, Spain, Thailand, Turkey, Ukraine, Vietnam

PERFECSEAL COMPANY

9800 Bustleton Ave.

Philadelphia, PA 19115

Tel: (215) 673-4500 Fax: (215) 676-1311

CEO: Alan McClure, Pres.

FO: Robert R. Burgess

Emp: 520

Mfr. packaging materials and converted products for medical and pharmaceutical products.

Northern Ireland, U.K.

PERFECT CIRCLE SEALED POWER

PO Box 1208

Muskegon, MI 49443

Tel: (616) 722-1300 Fax: (616) 724-1940

CEO: Daniel Moody, Pres.

Gaskets, seals, packings, etc.

Brazil, Canada, Mexico

PERIPHONICS CORPORATION

4000 Veterans Highway

Bohemia, NY 11716

Tel: (516) 467-0500 Fax: (516) 737-8520

CEO: Peter J. Cohen, Pres.

HR: Janet Anderson

Emp: 425

Mfr. voice processing systems.

Canada, England, U.K., Germany, Hong Kong, Mexico, Singapore

THE PERKIN-ELMER CORPORATION

761 Main Ave.

Norwalk, CT 06859-0001

Tel: (203) 762-1000 Fax: (203) 762-4228

CEO: Tony L. White, Chmn. & Pres.

FO: Dr. Elaine J. Heron

HR: Rafael Garofalo, VP

Web site: www.perkin-elmer.com

Emp: 7,188 Rev: $1,531 mil.

Leading supplier of systems for life science research and related applications.

Algeria, Angola, Argentina, Australia, Austria, Bahrain, Bangladesh, Belgium, Bolivia, Brazil, Bulgaria, Canada, Chile, China (PRC), Colombia, Costa Rica, Croatia, Cyprus, Czech Republic, Denmark, Dominican Republic, Ecuador, Egypt, El Salvador, England, U.K., Finland, France, Germany, Greece, Guatemala, Honduras, Hong Kong, Hungary, India, Indonesia, Ireland, Israel, Italy, Japan, Jordan, Kuwait, Lebanon, Macedonia, Malaysia, Malta, Mexico, Morocco, Nepal, Netherlands, New Zealand, Norway, Pakistan, Panama, Paraguay, Peru, Philippines, Poland, Portugal, Qatar, Romania, Russia, Saudi Arabia, Singapore, Slovakia, Slovenia, South Africa, South Korea, Spain, Sri Lanka, Switzerland, Taiwan (ROC), Thailand, Tunisia, Turkey, United Arab Emirates, Uruguay, Venezuela, Vietnam, Zambia, Zimbabwe

PEROT SYSTEMS CORPORATION

12377 Merit Drive, Ste. 1100
Dallas, TX 75251
Tel: (972) 383-5600 Fax: (972) 455-4100
CEO: Ross Perot, Chmn. & Pres.
HR: Paul Turevon, Dir.
Web site: www.perotsystems.com
Emp: 5,400 Rev: $780 mil.

Provides computer services technology.

England, U.K.

PETERSON AMERICAN CORPORATION

21200 Telegraph Road
Southfield, MI 48086-5059
Tel: (248) 799-5400 Fax: (248) 357-3176
CEO: Eric C. Peterson
Web site: www.pspring.com
Emp: 1,000 Rev: $106 mil.

Mfr. springs & wire products, metal stampings.

Canada, England, U.K., Mexico

PETROLEUM HELICOPTERS INC.

2121 Airline Highway, Ste. 400
Metairie, LA 70001
Tel: (504) 828-3323 Fax: (504) 828-8333
CEO: C. Suggs
FO: Gary Weber
HR: Ed Gatza
Web site: www.Phihelico.com
Emp: 2,000

Aerial transportation and helicopter charter.

Ecuador, Trinidad & Tobago

PFAUDLER, INC.

1000 West Ave., PO Box 23600
Rochester, NY 14692-3600
Tel: (716) 235-1000 Fax: (716) 436-9644
CEO: Gerald L. Connelly, Pres.
HR: Bette Quinn
Web site: www.pfaudler.com
Emp: 1,280

Mfr. glass lined reactors, storage vessels and reglassing services.

Brazil, China (PRC), England, U.K., Germany, India, Mexico, Scotland, U.K.

PFIZER INC.

235 East 42nd Street
New York, NY 10017-5755
Tel: (212) 573-2323 Fax: (212) 573-7851
CEO: William C. Steere, Jr., Chmn.
FO: Robert Neimeth
HR: William J. Robison, SVP
Web site: www.pfizer.com
Emp: 49,200 Rev: $12,504 mil.

Research-based, global health care company.

Angola, Argentina, Australia, Austria, Bangladesh, Belgium, Bermuda, Brazil, Canada, Cayman Islands, Chile, China (PRC), Colombia, Costa Rica, Denmark, Ecuador, Egypt, England, U.K., Finland, France, Germany, Ghana, Greece, Hungary, India, Indonesia, Ireland, Italy, Japan, Kenya, Malaysia, Mexico, Morocco, Mozambique, Netherlands, New Zealand, Nigeria, Norway, Pakistan, Panama, Peru, Philippines, Poland, Portugal, Russia, Singapore, South Africa, South Korea, Spain, Sri Lanka, Sweden, Switzerland, Taiwan (ROC), Tanzania, Thailand, Turkey, Uganda, Venezuela, Zambia, Zimbabwe

PHARMACIA & UPJOHN

95 Corporate Drive, PO Box 6995
Bridgewater, NJ 08807
Tel: (908) 306-4400 Fax: (908) 306-4433
CEO: Fred Hassan, Pres.
FO: Carrie Smith Dox, SVP
HR: Paul Matson, SVP
Web site: www.pnu.com
Emp: 30,000 Rev: $6,500 mil.

Mfr. pharmaceuticals, agricultural products, industry chemicals

Argentina, Australia, Austria, Belgium, Brazil, Bulgaria, Canada, Chile, China (PRC), Colombia, Croatia, Czech Republic, Dem. Rep. of Congo, Denmark, Ecuador, England, U.K., Finland, France, Germany, Greece, Guatemala, Hong Kong, Hungary, India, Indonesia, Ireland, Italy, Japan, Malaysia, Malta, Mexico, Netherlands, New Zealand, Norway, Pakistan, Panama, Peru, Philippines, Poland, Portugal, Romania, Russia, Singapore, Slovakia, Slovenia, South Africa, South Korea, Spain, Sweden, Switzerland, Taiwan (ROC), Thailand, Turkey, Ukraine, Venezuela, Yugoslavia

PHD INC.

9009 Clubridge Drive
Fort Wayne, IN 46899

Tel: (219) 747-6151 Fax: (219) 747-6754

CEO: Joe Oberlin

FO: Erik Grotness

HR: Jerry Hannah

Web site: www.phdinc.com.

Emp: 419

Mfr. pneumatic and hydraulic products used in factory automation.

England, U.K., Germany

PHELPS DODGE CORPORATION

2600 North Central Ave.

Phoenix, AZ 85004-3089

Tel: (602) 234-8100 Fax: (602) 234-8337

CEO: Douglas C. Yearley, Chmn.

FO: Salvador A. Sanlley, Pres.

HR: Stuart L. Marcus, VP

Emp: 15,500 Rev: $3,800 mil.

Copper, minerals, metals & spec engineered products for transportation & electrical markets.

Australia, Austria, Belgium, Canada, Chile, Costa Rica, Ecuador, El Salvador, England, U.K., Germany, Greece, Guatemala, Honduras, Hong Kong, Hungary, India, Italy, Japan, Mexico, Panama, Peru, Philippines, South Africa, Spain, Thailand, Venezuela, Zambia

PHH VEHICLE MANAGEMENT SERVICES

307 International Circle

Hunt Valley, MD 21030

Tel: (410) 771-3600 Fax: (410) 771-2841

CEO: Mark Miller, Pres.

HR: Rita Ennis, VP

Web site: www.phh.com

Emp: 6,264 Rev: $1,284 mil.

Provides vehicle fleet management, corporate relocation, and mortgage banking services.

Canada, England, U.K., France, Germany, Ireland, Italy

PHILADELPHIA INTERNATIONAL INVESTMENT CORPORATION

FC 1-1-23-6, PO Box 7618

Philadelphia, PA 19101-7611

Tel: (215) 973-3817 Fax: (215) 786-6091

CEO: Mr. Donald Frankenfield, Pres.

Investments.

Germany

PHILIP MORRIS COMPANIES, INC.

120 Park Ave.

New York, NY 10017--559

Tel: (212) 880-5000 Fax: (212) 878-2167

CEO: Geoffrey C. Bible, Chmn.

FO: Marc S. Goldberg, SVP

HR: Timothy A. Sompolski, SVP

Web site: www.

Emp: 150,000 Rev: $72,000 mil.

Mfr. cigarettes, food products, beer.

Australia, Brazil, Hong Kong, Japan, Switzerland

PHILIP SERVICES CORP. INDUSTRIAL GROUP

5151 San Felipe Street, #1600

Houston, TX 77056-3609

Tel: (713) 623-8777 Fax: (713) 625-7085

CEO: Robert M. Chiste, Pres.

FO: Ayman Gabrian, Pres. Europe

HR: Larry Rose, VP

Web site: www.philipinc.com

Emp: 15,000 Rev: $3,200 mil.

Trucking, refuse systems, staffing and numerous industrial-oriented services.

Austria, Canada, England, U.K., Germany, Netherlands, Spain, Wales, U.K.

PHILIPP BROTHERS CHEMICALS INC.

1 Parker Plaza

Fort Lee, NJ 07029

Tel: (201) 944-6020 Fax: (201) 944-7916

CEO: J. C. Bendheim

HR: Maria Engel

Emp: 700

Mfr. industry and agricultural chemicals.

China (PRC), England, U.K., France, Japan, Switzerland

PHILIPS SEMICONDUCTORS

811 East Arquest Ave.

Sunnyvale, CA 94088-3409

Tel: (408) 991-2000 Fax: (408) 991-2311

CEO: Arthur Vanderpoel, Pres.

HR: Randy McMill

Web site: www.semiconductor.philips.com

Emp: 10,400

Solid state circuits.

Japan, Netherlands, Singapore, South Korea, Switzerland, Thailand, Turkey

PHILLIPS PETROLEUM COMPANY

Phillips Building, 411 S. Keeler Ave.

Bartlesville, OK 74004

Tel: (918) 661-6600 Fax: (918) 661-7636

CEO: Wayne W. Allen, Chmn.

FO: James J. Mulva, Pres.

HR: Don Kremer

Web site: www.phillips66.com

Emp: 17,000 Rev: $15,424 mil.

Crude oil, natural gas, liquified petroleum gas, gasoline and petro-chemicals.

Australia, Austria, Bahrain, Belgium, Bolivia, Brazil, Colombia, Costa Rica, Denmark, Egypt, England, U.K., France, Germany, Ghana, Hong Kong, India, Indonesia, Ireland, Italy, Ivory Coast, Japan, Lebanon, Mexico, Nigeria, Norway, Peru, Singapore, Spain, Sweden, Switzerland, United Arab Emirates, Venezuela

PHILLIPS-VAN HEUSEN COMPANY

1001 Frontier Road

Bridgewater, NJ 08807

Tel: (908) 685-0050 Fax: (908) 704-8022

CEO: Bruce J. Klatsky, Pres.

HR: Betty Chaves

Wearing apparel.

Mexico

PICKER INTERNATIONAL INC.

595 Miner Road

Highland Heights, OH 44143

Tel: (440) 473-3000 Fax: (440) 473-4844

CEO: Cary Nolan, Pres.

HR: Charles Woods

Web site: www.picker.com

Mfr. diagnostic medical machines.

Australia, Bangladesh, Canada, England, U.K., France, Germany, Japan

PICTURETEL CORPORATION

100 Minuteman Road

Andover, MA 01810

Tel: (978) 292-5000 Fax: (978) 292-3300

CEO: Bruce R. Bond, Chmn.

FO: David W. Grainger, VP

HR: Lawrence Bornstein, VP

Web site: www.picturetel.com

Emp: 1,544 Rev: $466 mil.

Mfr. video conferencing systems, network bridging & multiplexing products, system peripherals.

Australia, Brazil, Canada, China (PRC), England, U.K., France, Germany, Hong Kong, Italy, Japan, Malaysia, Mexico, Singapore, South Korea, Spain, Sweden, Switzerland

PIERCE & STEVENS CORPORATION

PO Box 1092

Buffalo, NY 14240

Tel: (716) 856-4910 Fax: (716) 856-9718

CEO: Michael Prude, Pres.

FO: David R. Peacock

HR: Gail Orffeo, VP

Emp: 250

Mfr. coatings, adhesives and specialty chemical for packaging and graphic arts..

Canada

PILGRIM'S PRIDE CORPORATION

110 South Texas Street

Pittsburgh, TX 75686-0093

Tel: (903) 855-1000 Fax: (903) 856-7505

CEO: David Van Hoose & COO

FO: Lindy M. Pilgrim, Pres.

HR: Ray Gameson, SVP

Web site: www.pilgrimspride.com

Emp: 13,000 Rev: $1,278 mil.

Broiler & egg production, poultry & livestock feed.

Mexico

PILLAR INDUSTRIES

N92 W 15800 Megal Drive

Menomonee Falls, WI 53051

Tel: (414) 255-6470 Fax: (414) 255-0359

CEO: Larry Katsoulis, Pres.

HR: Arlene Bussard

Emp: 162

Mfr. induction heating & melting equipment.

China (PRC), England, U.K., India, Japan, Singapore

PILLSBURY MADISON & SUTRO LLP

235 Montgomert Street

San Francisco, CA 94104

Tel: (415) 983-1000 Fax: (415) 983-1200

CEO: Alfred Pepin Jr., Chmn.

HR: Linda Rydingsword

Web site: www.pillsburylaw.com

Emp: 1,300 Rev: $216 mil.

International law firm.

Hong Kong, Japan

PINKERTON'S, INC.

15910 Ventura Boulevard, Ste. 900

Encino, CA 91436

Tel: (818) 380-8800 Fax: (818) 380-8515

CEO: Denis Brown, Pres.

HR: Gary Hasanenk

Web site: www.pinkertons.com

Emp: 50,000

Security solutions.

Canada, Czech Republic, England, U.K., Hong Kong, Japan, Malaysia, Philippines, Portugal, Scotland, U.K., Taiwan (ROC), Thailand

PIONEER HI-BRED INTERNATIONAL INC.

400 Locust Street, Ste. 800

Des Moines, IA 50309

Tel: (515) 248-4800 Fax: (515) 248-4999

CEO: Charles S. Johnson, Chmn.

HR: Karen Pedersen

Emp: 5,000

Agricultural chemicals, farm supplies, biological products, research.

Argentina, Australia, Brazil, Canada, Chile, Egypt, Ethiopia, France, Germany, Italy, Mexico, Spain, Thailand, Venezuela

PIONEER NATURAL RESOURCES CO.

5205 North O'Connor Boulevard

Irving, TX 75039

Tel: (972) 444-9001 Fax: (972) 444-4328

CEO: Scott Sheffields, Pres.

HR: Becky Plumlee

Oil and gas

Argentina, Canada

PIPER JAFFRAY COMPANIES INC.

222 South Ninth Street

Minneapolis, MN 55402-3804

Tel: (612) 342-6000 Fax: (612) 342-1040

CEO: Addison L. Piper, Chmn.

FO: Andrew S. Duff, Pres.

HR: Edward Caillier

Web site: www.piperjaffray.com

Emp: 3,300 Rev: $600 mil.

Investment Banking and securities brokerage services.

England, U.K.

PITNEY BOWES INC.

1 Elmcroft Road

Stamford, CT 06926-0700

Tel: (203) 356-5000 Fax: (203) 351-6835

CEO: Michael J. Critelli, Chmn.

FO: Murray Martin, Pres. Int'l.

HR: Johanna Torsone, VP

Web site: www.pitneybowes.com

Emp: 30,000 Rev: $4,100 mil.

Mfr. postage meters, mailroom equipment, copiers, bus supplies, bus services, facsimile systems and financial services.

Argentina, Australia, Austria, Brazil, Canada, Chile, England, U.K., Finland, France, Germany, Hong Kong, Italy, Japan, Sweden, Switzerland

PITT-DES MOINES INC.

10200 Grogans Mill Road, Ste. 300

The Woodlands, TX 77380

Tel: (281) 774-2200 Fax: (281) 774-2204

CEO: W. W. McKee, Pres.

FO: L. V. Scorsone

Emp: 2,210 Rev: $475 mil.

Mfr. water and petrol storage systems, low temp and cryogenic tanks and systems, waste water treatment facilities.

Venezuela

PITTSBURGH CORNING CORPORATION

800 Presque Isle Drive

Pittsburgh, PA 15239-2799

Tel: (724) 327-6100 Fax: (724) 327-9501

CEO: Donald Schlegel, Pres.

HR: Richard C. McPherson

Emp: 1,146

Mfr. glass block and cellular glass insulation.

Belgium, England, U.K., France, Japan,

Netherlands, Sweden, Switzerland

PITTSTON COMPANY

PO Box 4229

Glen Allen, VA 23058

Tel: (805) 553-3600 Fax: (805) 553-3753

CEO: Jamers R. Barker, Chmn.

FO: Michael T. Dan

HR: Frank T. Lennon, VP

Web site: www.pittston.com

Emp: 33,000

Trucking, warehousing and armored car service, home security systems

Australia, Brazil, Canada

PLAINS COTTON COOPERATIVE ASSOCIATES

3301 East 50th Street

Lubbock, TX 79408

Tel: (806) 763-8011 Fax: (806) 762-7335

CEO: Van May, Pres.

Emp: 125

Merchandisers of raw cotton to domestic and foreign textile mills.

Hong Kong, Japan, South Korea, Taiwan (ROC)

PLANET HOLLYWOOD INTERNATIONAL, INC.

8669 Commodity Circle

Orlando, FL 32819

Tel: (407) 363-7827 Fax: (407) 363-4862

CEO: Robert I. Earl, Pres.

FO: Thomas Avallone, EVP

HR: Lissa Bobet, Dir. HR

Web site: www.planethollywood.com

Emp: 9,100 Rev: $373.4 mil.

Theme-dining restaurant chain and merchandise retail stores.

Argentina, Australia, Brazil, Canada, China (PRC), Czech Republic, England, U.K., Finland, France, Germany, Guam, Hong Kong, Indonesia, Israel, Italy, Mexico, Netherlands, Philippines, Russia, Singapore, South Africa, Spain, Switzerland, Thailand

PLANTERS PEANUTS

100 DeForest Ave.

East Hanover, NJ 07936

Tel: (973) 682-5000 Fax: (973) 503-2153

CEO: Wynn Willard, Pres.

Emp: 1,200

Nut products, peanut oil and candy.

Canada

PLANTRONICS

337 Encinal Street

Santa Cruz, CA 95061-1802

Tel: (831) 426-5858 Fax: (831) 425-5198

CEO: Robert S. Cecil, Chmn.

FO: S. Kenneth Kannappan, Pres.

HR: Carol L. Maurer

Web site: www.plantronics.com

Emp: 1,817 Rev: $236 mil.

Mfr. communications equipment, electrical & electronic appliances & apparatus.

Canada, England, U.K., France, Germany, Italy, Mexico, Netherlands, Spain, Sweden, Switzerland

PLAYBOY ENTERPRISES INC.

680 North Lake Shore Drive

Chicago, IL 60611

Tel: (312) 751-8000 Fax: (312) 751-2818

CEO: Christie Hefner, Pres.

HR: Denise Bindelglass

Emp: 643

Publishing and entertainment.

Netherlands

PLAYSKOOL INC.

1027 Newport Ave., PO Box 1059

Pawtucket, RI 02862

Tel: (401) 431-8697 Fax: (401) 431-8466

CEO: Alan G. Hassenfeld

HR: Jim Kershner

Web site: www.hasbro.co

Emp: 800

Mfr. wooden/plastic preschool and riding toys.

Switzerland

PLAYTEX APPAREL INC.

700 Fairfield Ave.

Stamford, CT 06904

Tel: (203) 356-8000 Fax: (203) 356-8448

CEO: Haywood Gibson, Pres.

HR: Dawn Cross

Web site: www.saralee.com

Mfr. intimate apparel.

Australia, Canada, France, Italy, Mexico, Scotland, U.K., Spain

PLIBRICO COMPANY

1800 N. Kingsbury Street

Chicago, IL 60614

Tel: (773) 549-7014 Fax: (773) 549-0424

CEO: Scott A. Schaefer, Pres.

FO: R. W. Schaefer Jr.

Emp: 1,900

Refractories, engineering and construction.

Austria, Belgium, Canada, Denmark, England, U.K., France, Germany, Japan, Mexico, Netherlands, Spain, Sweden

POLAROID CORPORATION

549 Technology Square

Cambridge, MA 02139

Tel: (781) 386-2000 Fax: (781) 386-3276

CEO: Gary T. DiCamillo, CEO

Web site: www.polaroid.com

Emp: 13,000 Rev: $2,000 mil.

Photographic equipment & supplies, optical products.

Australia, Austria, Bahamas, Belgium, Brazil, Canada, Denmark, England, U.K., France, Germany, Hong Kong, Italy, Japan, Netherlands, New Zealand, Poland, Russia, Switzerland

POLICY MANAGEMENT SYSTEMS CORPORATION

PO Box 10

Columbia, SC 29202

Tel: (803) 735-4000 Fax: (803) 735-5544

CEO: G. Larry Wilson, Pres.

Emp: 4,000

Computer software, insurance industry support services.

Australia, Austria, Canada, England, U.K., Germany, Norway, Spain, Sweden

R.L. POLK & COMPANY

1155 Brewery Park Blvd.

Detroit, MI 48207-2697

Tel: (248) 728-7111 Fax: (248) 393-2860

CEO: Arthur L. Olsen, Pres

HR: Joan Miszak

Web site: www.polk.com

Emp: 3,000

Directories, direct mail advertising.

Australia, Barbados, Canada, England, U.K., Germany

POLYCHROME GRAPHICS

222 Bridge Plaza Southkodak

Fort Lee, NJ 07024

Tel: (201) 346-8800 Fax: (201) 346-8846

CEO: Thomas Bittner

Emp: 1,850

Metal offset plates, coating specialties, graphic arts films.

Australia, England, U.K., Germany, Mexico

POMEROY INC.

1899 Spindrift Drive

LaJolla, CA 92037

Tel: (619) 459-5960 Fax: (619) 459-1818

CEO: Rex D. Cross, Pres.

Mfr./sale of building hardware and sash balances.

Canada, England, U.K.

POPE & TALBOT INC.

1500 SW First Ave.

Portland, OR 97201

Tel: (503) 228-9161 Fax: (503) 220-2722

CEO: Peter T. Pope, Chmn.

FO: Abe Friesen

HR: Richard N. Moffitt

Emp: 3,188

Mfr. paper, pulp & wood products.

Canada

PORTA SYSTEMS CORPORATION

575 Underhill Boulevard

Syosset, NY 11791

Tel: (516) 364-9300 Fax: (516) 682-4655

CEO: Sy Joffe, Pres.

HR: Donna Landeck

Emp: 1,000

Design/mfr. protection, connection & testing equipment for telecommunications industry.

England, U.K.

PORTEC RAIL PRODUCTS INC.

122 W 22nd Street, #100

Oak Brook, IL 60521-1553

Tel: (630) 573-4619 Fax: (630) 573-4604

CEO: John Cooper, Pres.

HR: Michael Borneck

Emp: 550

Mfr. engineered products for construction equipment, material handling & railroad track components.

Canada, Wales, U.K.

PORTER PRECISION PRODUCTS COMPANY

2734 Banning Road

Cincinnati, OH 45239-5504

Tel: (513) 923-3777 Fax: (513) 923-1111

CEO: John F. Cipriani, Sr., Pres.

FO: D. J. Lionette

HR: Philip Vogt

Emp: 250

Mfr. piercing punches & die supplies for metal stamping & tool/die industry.

Canada, England, U.K., Germany

POTTERS INDUSTRIES INC.

PO Box 840

Valley Forge, PA 19482-0840

Tel: (610) 651-4700 Fax: (610) 408-9723

CEO: Jack I. Grams, Pres.

Emp: 636

Mfr. glass spheres for road marking & industry applications.

Australia, Brazil, England, U.K., France, Germany, Japan, Mexico

POWER TECHNOLOGIES INC.

1482 Erie Blvd., PO Box 1058

Schenectady, NY 12301

Tel: (518) 395-5000 Fax: (518) 346-2777

CEO: Steven J. Balser, Pres.

FO: Ian S. Grant

HR: Kathy Rose

Emp: 126

Power systems engineering, consulting, services & related control software; power quality hardware.

Australia, England, U.K., Malaysia, Spain

POWER-PACKER

North 22 West 23685 Richfield Parkway-West

Waukesha, WI 53188-1013

Tel: (414) 523-7600 Fax: (414) 523-7580

CEO: William J. Albrecht, Chmn.

HR: Ron Wieczorek

Emp: 303

Mfr. OEM hydraulic systems.

France, Netherlands, Spain

POWERS PROCESS CONTROLS

3400 Oakton Street

Skokie, IL 60076

Tel: (847) 673-6700 Fax: (847) 673-9044

CEO: William Boglia, Pres.

Emp: 2,800

Mfr./sales control devices.

Canada

PPG INDUSTRIES

One PPG Place

Pittsburgh, PA 15272

Tel: (412) 434-3131 Fax: (412) 434-2190

CEO: Raymond W. LeBoeuf, Chmn.

HR: R. L. Crane

Web site: www.ppg.com

Emp: 31,900 Rev: $7,400 mil.

Mfr. coatings, flat glass, fiber glass, chemicals. coatings.

Argentina, Australia, Brazil, Canada, China (PRC), England, U.K., France, Germany, Hong Kong, Ireland, Italy, Japan, Mexico, Netherlands, Philippines, South Korea, Spain, Taiwan (ROC), Thailand, Venezuela

PRAXAIR, INC.

39 Old Ridgebury Road

Danbury, CT 06810-5113

Tel: (203) 837-2000 Fax: (203) 837-2450

CEO: H. William Lichtenberger, Chmn.

FO: Gabriel Toledo, Pres. Europe

HR: Barbara R. Harris

Web site: www.praxair.com

Emp: 25,388 Rev: $4,735 mil.

Produces and distributes industrial and specialty gases.

Argentina, Austria, Belgium, Bolivia, Brazil, Canada, Chile, China (PRC), Colombia, Croatia, Ecuador, France, Germany, India, Israel, Italy, Japan, Mexico, Netherlands, Paraguay, Peru,

Poland, Portugal, Singapore, South Korea, Spain, Turkey, Uruguay, Venezuela

PRECISION CASTPARTS CORPORATION

4600 SE Harney Drive

Portland, OR 97206

Tel: (503) 777-3881 Fax: (503) 653-4817

CEO: W. C. McCormick, Pres.

HR: Mark Damien

Emp: 5,116

Mfr. metal castings.

France

PRECISION INTERCONNECT

16640 SW 72nd Ave.

Portland, OR 97224

Tel: (503) 620-9400 Fax: (503) 620-7131

CEO: Vic Petroff, Mgr.

Mfr., custom design and test interconnect systems for medical imaging and surgical device, catheter, and high performance data markets.

Germany, Japan, Scotland, U.K.

PRECISION VALVE CORPORATION

PO Box 309

Yonkers, NY 10702

Tel: (914) 969-6500 Fax: (914) 966-4428

CEO: Robert H. Abplanalp, Chmn.

FO: F. K. Langford

Emp: 600 Rev: $20 mil.

Mfr. aerosol valves.

Argentina, Australia, Brazil, Canada, England, U.K., France, Germany, India, Italy, Japan, Mexico, New Zealand, Singapore, South Africa, Spain, Venezuela

PREFORMED LINE PRODUCTS COMPANY

600 Beta Drive, PO Box 91129

Cleveland, OH 44101

Tel: (440) 461-5200 Fax: (440) 461-2918

CEO: Jon R. Ruhlman

FO: Gordon W.Meldrum, VP Int'l

HR: Robert Weber, VP Emp. Rel.

Emp: 2,000 Rev: $108 mil.

Mfr. pole line hardware for electrical transmission lines; splice closures & related products for telecommunications.

Australia, Brazil, Canada, China (PRC), England, U.K., Mexico, Scotland, U.K., South Africa, Spain

PREMARK INTERNATIONAL INC.

1717 Deerfield Road

Deerfield, IL 60015

Tel: (847) 405-6000 Fax: (847) 405-6013

CEO: James Ringler, Pres. & Chmn.

HR: Kirk Mueller, VP

Web site: www.premarkintl.com

Emp: 24,000

Mfr./sale plastic, diversified consumer & commercial products.

Argentina, Australia, Austria, Belgium, Brazil, Canada, Denmark, England, U.K., France, Germany, Greece, Hong Kong, Italy, Japan, Mexico, Netherlands, New Zealand, Philippines, Portugal, South Africa, South Korea, Spain, Switzerland, Thailand, Venezuela

PREMIX INC.

PO Box 281, Rt. 20, Harmon Road

North Kingsville, OH 44068-0281

Tel: (440) 224-2181 Fax: (440) 224-2766

CEO: Wilbur Shenk, Pres.

FO: Steve Searl

HR: Ken Lazo

Emp: 560

Mfr. molded fiber glass, reinforced thermoset molding compounds and plastic parts.

Australia, England, U.K., Japan, Mexico

PRESTOLITE ELECTRIC INC.

2100 Commonwealth Ave.

Ann Arbor, MI 48105

Tel: (734) 913-6600 Fax: (734) 913-6656

CEO: P. Kim Packard, Pres.

FO: Jerry Weisenauer

HR: Karen Oldham

Emp: 1,300

Mfr. alternators, DC motors, relays, switches.

England, U.K., Wales, U.K.

PRETTY PRODUCTS INC.

Cambridge Road

Coshocton, OH 43812

Tel: (614) 622-3522 Fax: (614) 622-4915

CEO: James R. Lockwood, Pres.

FO: James Sylvester

HR: Ed Salmon

Emp: 2,500 Rev: $250 mil.

Mfr. automotive accessories.

Canada

PRI AUTOMATION, INC.

805 Middlesex Turnpike

Billerica, MA 01821-3986

Tel: (978) 663-8555 Fax: (978) 663-9755

CEO: Mitchell G. Tyson, Pres.

FO: James Cameron

HR: Steven P. Wentzell, VP

Web site: www.pria.com

Emp: 1,103 Rev: $170 mil.

Provides factory automation systems for silicon chip makers.

England, U.K., France, Germany, Japan, Singapore, South Korea, Taiwan (ROC)

PRICEWATERHOUSECOOPERS LLP

1251 Ave. of the Americas

New York, NY 10020

Tel: (212) 596-7000 Fax: (212) 790-6620

CEO: James J. Schiro

FO: Geoffrey Johnson

HR: William O'Brien

Web site: www.pwcglobal.com

Emp: 60,000 Rev: $5,600 mil.

Accounting and auditing, tax and management, and human resource consulting services.

Antigua, Argentina, Australia, Austria, Azerbaijan, Bahamas, Bahrain, Barbados, Belarus, Belgium, Bermuda, Bolivia, Botswana, Brazil, British Virgin Islands, Brunei, Bulgaria, Cameroon, Canada, Cayman Islands, Channel Islands, U.K., Chile, China (PRC), Colombia, Congo, Costa Rica, Cyprus, Czech Republic, Dem. Rep. of Congo, Denmark, Dominican Republic, Ecuador, Egypt, El Salvador, England, U.K., Estonia, Fiji, Finland, France, Gabon, Germany, Ghana, Gibraltar, Greece, Guatemala, Guyana, Honduras, Hong Kong, Hungary, India, Indonesia, Ireland, Isle of Man, Israel, Italy, Ivory Coast, Jamaica, Japan, Kazakhstan, Kenya, Latvia, Lithuania, Luxembourg, Macau, Malawi, Malaysia, Malta, Mauritius, Mexico, Morocco, Namibia, Netherlands, Netherlands Antilles, New Caledonia, New Zealand, Nicaragua, Nigeria, Northern Ireland, U.K., Norway, Oman, Pakistan, Panama, Papua New Guinea, Paraguay, Peru, Philippines, Poland, Portugal, Qatar, Romania, Russia, Saudi Arabia, Scotland, U.K., Senegal, Singapore, Slovakia, South Africa, South Korea, Spain, St. Lucia, Swaziland, Sweden, Switzerland, Taiwan (ROC), Tanzania, Thailand, Trinidad & Tobago, Turkey, Uganda, Ukraine, United Arab Emirates, Uruguay, Venezuela, Vietnam, Wales, U.K., Zambia, Zimbabwe

PRIMAC COURIER INC.

333 Sylvan Ave.

Englewood Cliffs, NJ 07632

Tel: (201) 871-1800 Fax: (201) 871-3313

CEO: Mary Jane McLaughlin

FO: James Lafaso

HR: Hazel Decker

Emp: 50

Air courier services.

Canada

PRIMEX INTERNATIONAL TRADING CORPORATION

230 Fifth Avenue

New York, NY 10001

Tel: (212) 679-5060 Fax: (212) 686-9853

CEO: Ernest Paul, Chmn.

FO: Herb Briggs, VP Intl.

HR: Stewart Paul, COO

Emp: 125 Rev: $100 mil.

Coffee: import/export, consulting services.

Brazil

PRINCIPAL INTERNATIONAL INC.

711 High Street

Des Moines, IA 50392-9950

Tel: (515) 248-8288 Fax: (515) 248-8049

CEO: David J. Drury, Chmn.

FO: J. Barry Griswell, Pres.

HR: Thomas Gaard, SVP HR

Web site: www.principal.com

Emp: 17,000 Rev: $67,000 mil

Insurance and investment services.

Argentina, Chile, China (PRC), Hong Kong, Indonesia, Mexico, Spain

PRINTRONIX INC.

17500 Cartwright Road

Irvine, CA 92623-9559

Tel: (949) 863-1900 Fax: (949) 660-8682

CEO: Robert A. Kleist, Chmn.

FO: C. Victor Fitzsimmons, SVP

HR: Juli A. Mathews, VP

Web site: www.printronix.com

Emp: 922 Rev: $170.4 mil

Mfr. computer printers.

Austria, England, U.K., France, Germany, Netherlands, Singapore

PROCTER & GAMBLE COMPANY

One Procter & Gamble Plaza

Cincinnati, OH 45202

Tel: (513) 983-1100 Fax: (513) 562-4500

CEO: John E. Pepper, Chmn.

FO: Harald Einsmann, EVP

HR: Richard Antoine, SVP

Web site: www.pg.com

Emp: 110,000 Rev: $37.2 bil.

Personal care, food, laundry, cleaning and industry products.

Argentina, Australia, Austria, Belgium, Brazil, Bulgaria, Canada, Chile, China (PRC), Colombia, Costa Rica, Croatia, Denmark, Egypt, El Salvador, England, U.K., Estonia, Finland, France, Germany, Greece, Guatemala, Hungary, Indonesia, Ireland, Italy, Japan, Kazakhstan, Kenya, Latvia, Lebanon, Lithuania, Malaysia, Mexico, Morocco, Netherlands, New Zealand, Nigeria, Norway, Pakistan, Peru, Philippines, Poland, Portugal, Romania, Russia, Saudi Arabia, Singapore, Slovenia, South Africa, South Korea, Spain, Sweden, Switzerland, Taiwan (ROC), Thailand, Turkey, Ukraine, Uzbekistan, Venezuela, Vietnam, Yemen, Yugoslavia

PROCTER & GAMBLE PHARMACEUTICALS

17 Eaton Ave.

Norwich, NY 13815-1799

Tel: (607) 335-2111 Fax: (607) 335-2798

CEO: Anthony Sebitsky, Mgr.

FO: F. H. Kruse

HR: Stuart Spence

Emp: 2,750

Develop/manufacture pharmaceuticals, chemicals and health products.

Australia, Belgium, Colombia, England, U.K., Greece, Netherlands, Venezuela

PROCTOR & SCHWARTZ INC.

251 Gibraltar Road

Horsham, PA 19044

Tel: (215) 443-5200 Fax: (215) 443-5206

CEO: J. Kulkarni, Pres.

Emp: 572

Mfr. industry drying machinery for food, tobacco, chemical and textile industry.

Scotland, U.K., Spain

PRODUCTO/MOORE TOOL COMPANY, INC.

990 Housatonic Ave., PO Box 780

Bridgeport, CT 06601-0780

Tel: (203) 367-8675 Fax: (203) 366-5694

CEO: Newman Marsilius III, Pres.

FO: Richard Marsilius

HR: Martha Graham

Emp: 275

Mfr. machine tools, die sets and diemakers accessories.

Canada

THE PROGRESSIVE CORPORATION

6300 Wilson Mills Road

Mayfield Village, OH 44143

Tel: (440) 461-5000 Fax: (440) 603-4420

CEO: Peter B. Lewis, Chmn. & Pres.

FO: Robert J. McMillan, Mktg.

HR: Tiona M. Thompson

Web site: www.auto-insurance.com

Emp: 14,000 Rev: $7,500 mil

Provides non-standard auto coverage and standard and preferred auto coverage.

Canada

PROSERV INC.

1620 L Street, NW, Ste. 600

Washington, DC 20036

Tel: (202) 721-7200 Fax: (202) 721-7201

CEO: Donald Dell, Chmn.

HR: Julie Kennedy

Emp: 225

Sports marketing, management and consulting.

England, U.K., France, Italy

PROSKAUER ROSE LLP

1585 Broadway
New York, NY 10036
Tel: (212) 969-3000 Fax: (212) 969-2900
CEO: Stanley Komaroff, Chmn.
HR: Ann Bafkey, Dir.
Web site: www.proskauer.com
Emp: 1,200 Rev: $215 mil.

International law firm.

France

PROVIDENT COMPANIES, INC.

One Fountain Square
Chattanooga, TN 37402
Tel: (423) 755-1011 Fax: (423) 755-7013
CEO: J. Harold Chandler, Pres. & Chmn.
FO: George Shell SVP
HR: Kathy Schoeffler, SVP
Web site: www.providentcompanies.com
Emp: 5,500 Rev: $4,000 mil.

Sale of disability and life insurance products to individuals and groups.

Canada

PRUDENTIAL INSURANCE COMPANY OF AMERICA

751 Broad Street
Newark, NJ 07102-3777
Tel: (973) 802-6000 Fax: (973) 802-2812
CEO: Arthur F. Ryan, Chmn.
FO: K. Sakaguchi, Pres. Intl.
HR: Michele S. Darling, EVP
Web site: www.prudential.com
Emp: 80,000 Rev: $29,900 mil.

Sale of life insurance and provides financial services.

Belgium, Brazil, Canada, Hong Kong, Italy, Japan, Netherlands, South Korea, Taiwan (ROC)

PSDI MAXIMO

100 Crosby Drive
Bedford, MA 01730
Tel: (781) 280-2000 Fax: (781) 280-0200
CEO: Norman E. Drapeau, Jr., Pres.
FO: Ted Williams, SVP
HR: Robert Clancy, VP
Web site: www.psdi.com
Emp: 600 Rev: $112 mil.

Develops, markets and provides maintenance management software systems.

Argentina, Australia, Belgium, Canada, China (PRC), England, U.K., France, Germany, Hong Kong, India, Japan, Mexico, Netherlands, Sweden, Thailand

PSI NET (PERFORMANCE SYSTEMS INTERNATIONAL INC.)

510 Huntmar Park Drive
Herndon, VA 22170
Tel: (703) 904-4100 Fax: (703) 904-4200
CEO: William L. Schrader, Chmn. & Pres.
FO: Volker Klein, VP Europe
HR: William P. Cripe, VP
Web site: wwwpsi.net
Rev: $121.9 mil.

Internet service provider.

Belgium, Canada, England, U.K., France, Germany, Japan, Netherlands, Switzerland

PULSE ENGINEERING INC.

12220 World Trade Drive, P.O. 12235
San Diego, CA 92112
Tel: (619) 674-8100 Fax: (619) 674 8263
CEO: John Kowalski, Pres.

Engineer/mfr. OEM devices for local area network markets & major voice/data transmission systems.

Hong Kong, Ireland

PURE INDUSTRIES INC.

441 Hall Ave.
Saint Marys, PA 15857
Tel: (814) 781-1573 Fax: (814) 781-9262
CEO: F. S. Brown, Pres.
FO: C. B. Land
HR: Susan Georgino
Emp: 775

Mfr. carbon graphite and silicon carbide components.

England, U.K.

PUTNAM INVESTMENTS

1 Post Office Square
Boston, MA 02109
Tel: (617) 292-1000 Fax: (617) 292-1499
CEO: Lawrence Lasser, Pres.

Emp: 500

Money management; mutual funds, annuities and retirement plans.

England, U.K., Japan

PYRONICS INC.

17700 Miles Ave.

Cleveland, OH 44128

Tel: (216) 662-8800 Fax: (216) 663-8954

CEO: Edward M. Kuska, Pres.

HR: George Balk

Web site: www.pyronics.com

Emp: 49

Mfr. combustion equipment, gas & oil burners.

Belgium

QMS INC.

One Magnum Pass

Mobile, AL 36618

Tel: (205) 633-4300 Fax: (205) 633-4866

CEO: Ed Lucente, Chmn.

HR: Tom McGoogan, VP

Emp: 1,600

Mfr. monochrome and color computer printers.

Australia, Canada, England, U.K., France, Germany, Hong Kong, Japan, Netherlands, Sweden, Switzerland

QUAKER CHEMICAL CORPORATION

Elm & Lee Streets

Conshohocken, PA 19428-0809

Tel: (610) 832-4000 Fax: (610) 832-8682

CEO: Ronald J. Naples, Chmn.

HR: James A. Geier, VP

Web site: www.quakerchem.com

Emp: 871 Rev: $241 mil.

Mfr. chemical specialties; total fluid management services.

Australia, Brazil, China (PRC), England, U.K., France, Hong Kong, India, Japan, Mexico, Netherlands, South Africa, Spain, Venezuela

QUAKER FABRIC CORPORATION

941 Grinnell Street

Fall River, MA 02721

Tel: (508) 678-1951 Fax: (508) 679-2580

CEO: Larry Liebenow, Pres.

HR: Cynthia Gordon

Emp: 1,382

Mfr. upholstery fabrics and yarns.

Mexico

THE QUAKER OATS COMPANY

Quaker Tower, 321 North Clark Street

Chicago, IL 60610-4714

Tel: (312) 222-7111 Fax: (312) 222-8323

CEO: Robert S. Morrison, CEO

FO: Barbara Allen, EVP Int'l.

HR: Douglas Ralston

Web site: www.quakeroats.com

Emp: 21,000 Rev: $5,000 mil.

Mfr. foods and beverages.

Belgium, Brazil, Denmark, England, U.K., France, Italy, Malaysia, Netherlands, Venezuela

QUAKER STATE CORPORATION

225 E. John Carpenter Freeway

Irving, TX 75062

Tel: (972) 868-0400 Fax: (972) 868-0678

CEO: John D. Barr, Pres.

HR: Dave Loeser

Emp: 4,570

Mfr. motor oil, lubricants, automotive chemicals, waxes.

Canada, Japan

QUALCOMM INC.

6355 Lusk Boulevard

San Diego, CA 92121

Tel: (619) 587-1121 Fax: (619) 658-1434

CEO: Irwin M. Jacobs, COO

FO: Chris Simpson, VP Intl.

Emp: 3,500 Rev: $500 mil.

Digital wireless telecommunications systems.

Argentina, Brazil, Chile, India, Israel, Singapore, South Korea

QUALITROL CORPORATION

1385 Fairport Road

Fairport, NY 14450

Tel: (716) 586-1515 Fax: (716) 377-0220

CEO: Ron Meyer, Pres.

Mfr. Gauges and thermometers.

Germany

QUALITY SEMICONDUCTOR, INC.

851 Martin Ave.
Santa Clara, CA 95050
Tel: (408) 450-8000 Fax: (408) 496-0773
CEO: R. Paul Gopta
HR: David Zimmer, VP
Web site: www.qualitysemi.com.
Emp: 206 Rev: $63 mil.

Mfr./design/distribute high-performance logic, networking and memory semiconductor devices.

Australia, England, U.K.

K.J. QUINN & CO., INC.

34 Folly Mill Road, PO Box 158
Seabrook, NH 03874
Tel: (603) 474-5753 Fax: (603) 474-7122
CEO: Leigh Quinn, Pres.
HR: Elaine Warren

Mfr. spec coatings, adhesives, polyurethane polymers, shoe finishes, UV/EB cure coatings.

Italy

R

R&B FALCON CORPORATION

901 Threadneedle, Ste. 200
Houston, TX 77079
Tel: (281) 496-5000 Fax: (281) 496-4363
CEO: Steven Webster, Pres.
HR: Don L. McIntire
Web site: www.rbfalcon.com
Emp: 1,736

Offshore contract drilling.

Congo, England, U.K., India, Indonesia, Italy, Malaysia, Norway, South Korea, Tunisia, United Arab Emirates

RADIATION SYSTEMS INC.

1501 Moran Road
Sterling, VA 20166
Tel: (703) 450-5680 Fax: (703) 450-4706
CEO: Richard E.Thomas, Pres.
HR: Leo C. Flynn
Emp: 1,021

Design/mfr./install turn-key antenna systems.

England, U.K.

RADIATOR SPECIALTY COMPANY

PO Box 34689
Charlotte, NC 28234-6080
Tel: (704) 377-6555 Fax: (704) 334-9425
CEO: Alan Blumenthal
FO: John Rae
Emp: 650

Mfr. plumbing/heating supplies, automotive chemical specialties, molded rubber parts.

Canada

RADISSON HOTELS INTERNATIONAL

Carlson Pkwy., PO Box 59159
Minneapolis, MN 55459-8204
Tel: (612) 540-5526 Fax: (612) 449-3400
CEO: Brian Stage, Chmn.
HR: Sue Gordon
Emp: 74,000

Hotels and resorts.

Australia, Austria, Bahamas, Belgium, Canada, Cayman Islands, China (PRC), Czech Republic, Denmark, Egypt, England, U.K., Finland, France, Germany, Hungary, India, Indonesia, Israel, Italy, Jamaica, Japan, Malaysia, Malta, Mexico, Netherlands, Northern Ireland, U.K., Norway, Russia, Saudi Arabia, South Korea, Switzerland, Thailand, Turkey, Yemen

RADIUS INC.

460 East Middlefield Road
Mountainview, CA 94043
Tel: (650) 404-6000 Fax: (650) 404-6200
CEO: Mark Housley, Pres.
HR: Dawn Thompson
Emp: 350

Mfr. graphic interface cards, displays, accelerators and multiprocessing software.

Canada, England, U.K., France, Japan

RAIN BIRD SPRINKLER MFG. CORPORATION

145 North Grand Ave.
Glendora, CA 91741-2469
Tel: (626) 963-9311 Fax: (626) 963-4287
CEO: Anthony W. La Fetra, Pres.

FO: Jack D. Buzzard

Web site: www.rainbird.com

World's largest manufacturer of lawn sprinklers and irrigation systems equipment.

Australia, Canada, England, U.K., France, Germany, Mexico, Netherlands, Spain, Sweden, United Arab Emirates

RAINBOW TECHNOLOGIES INC.

50 Technology Drive

Irvine, CA 92618

Tel: (714) 454-2100 Fax: (714) 454-8557

CEO: Walter Straub, Pres.

Emp: 120

Mfr. computer related security products.

England, U.K., France, Germany

POLO RALPH LAUREN

650 Madison Ave.

New York, NY 10022

Tel: (212) 318-7000 Fax: (212) 888-5780

CEO: Ralph Lauren, Chmn.

FO: Michael J. Newman, COO

HR: Karen L. Rosenbach

Web site: www.ralphlaurenfragrance.com

Emp: 5,000 Rev: $1,000 mil.

Designs and markets clothing, bath and bedding and operates Polo Ralph Lauren and Polo Sport stores.

England, U.K.

RALSTON PURINA COMPANY

Checkerboard Square

St. Louis, MO 63164

Tel: (314) 982-1000 Fax: (314) 982-1211

CEO: Patrick McGinnis, CEO

Emp: 54,000 Rev: $7,000 mil.

Animal feed, cereals, food products.

Belgium, Brazil, Canada, France, Hungary, Italy, Mexico, Netherlands Antilles, Singapore, South Korea, Spain

RAMSEY TECHNOLOGY INC.

501 90th Ave. NW

Minneapolis, MN 55433

Tel: (612) 783-2500 Fax: (612) 780-2525

CEO: Lew Ribich, Pres.

FO: Gary Saunders

HR: Deb Erar

Emp: 670

Mfr. in-motion weighing, inspection, monitoring & control equipment for the process industry.

Australia, Canada, England, U.K., France, Germany, Italy, Mexico, Netherlands, South Africa, Spain

RANCO INC.

555 Metro Place North, PO Box 248

Dublin, OH 43017

Tel: (614) 873-9200 Fax: (614) 873-9290

CEO: Robert Stadaler, Pres.

HR: John Jenkins

Emp: 4,900

Mfr. controls for appliance, automotive, comfort, commercial and consumer markets.

Canada, England, U.K., France, Germany, Italy, Japan, Mexico

RAND McNALLY

8255 North Central Park Ave.

Skokie, IL 60076

Tel: (847) 329-8100 Fax: (847) 673-0539

CEO: Henry Feinberg, Pres.

FO: Dean H. Dussias

HR: Mary Lynn Smelinghoff

Emp: 1,100

Publishing, consumer software, information and retail.

Canada, England, U.K.

RAY & BERNDTSON, INC.

301 Commerce, Ste. 2300

Fort Worth, TX 76102

Tel: (817) 334-0500 Fax: (817) 334-0779

CEO: Paul R. Ray, Jr., Pres.

HR: Sandy Iwata

Web site: www.prb.com

Executive search, management audit and management consulting firm.

Argentina, Australia, Austria, Belgium, Brazil, Canada, China (PRC), Czech Republic, Denmark, England, U.K., Finland, France, Germany, Hong Kong, Hungary, India, Italy, Japan, Mexico, Netherlands, Norway, Poland, Portugal, Spain, Sweden, Switzerland, Venezuela

RAY BURNER COMPANY

401 Parr Boulevard
Richmond, CA 94801
Tel: (510) 236-4972 Fax: (510) 236-4083
CEO: Russell C. Westover, Chmn.
Emp: 100
Mfr. gas & oil burners, controls, oil pump sets, boilers.
Germany

RAYCHEM CORPORATION

300 Constitution Drive
Menlo Park, CA 94025-1164
Tel: (650) 361-3333 Fax: (650) 361-2108
CEO: Richard Kashnow,Chmn.
FO: L. Frans Berthels, SVP
HR: Tim Burch, VP
Web site: www.raychem.com
Emp: 9,036 Rev: $1,765 mil.
Develop/mfr./market materials science products for electronics, telecommunications & industry.
Argentina, Australia, Belgium, Brazil, Canada, Chile, China (PRC), Cyprus, Denmark, Egypt, England, U.K., Finland, France, Germany, Hong Kong, India, Ireland, Italy, Japan, Malaysia, Mexico, Netherlands, New Zealand, Norway, Pakistan, Peru, Portugal, Saudi Arabia, Scotland, U.K., Singapore, South Korea, Spain, Sweden, Switzerland, Taiwan (ROC), Thailand, Turkey, Venezuela

THE RAYMOND CORPORATION

S. Canal Street
Greene, NY 13778-0130
Tel: (607) 656-2311 Fax: (607) 656-9005
CEO: James J. Malvaso
Emp: 1,249
Mfr./designs material handling products including reach trucks, walkie pallet trucks, orderpickers and Swing-Reach® trucks.
Canada

RAYMOND JAMES FINANCIAL, INC.

880 Carillon Parkway
St. Petersburg, FL 33716
Tel: (813) 573-3800 Fax: (813) 573-8244
CEO: Thomas A. James, Chmn.
FO: Francis S. Godbold, Pres.
HR: Chris Whitman, SVP HR
Web site: www.rjf.com
Emp: 3,244 Rev: $927.6 mil.
Financial services; securities brokerage, asset management, and investment banking services.
Belgium, England, U.K., France, Germany, India, Luxembourg, Switzerland

RAYONIER INC.

1177 Summer Street
Stamford, CT 06904
Tel: (203) 348-7000 Fax: (203) 964-4528
CEO: Ronald M. Gross, Chmn.
HR: John O'Grady
Emp: 3,200
Chemicals cellulose, paper pulps, logs and lumber.
England, U.K.

RAYOVAC CORPORATION

601 Rayovac Drive
Madison, WI 53711
Tel: (608) 275-3340 Fax: (608) 275-4577
CEO: David A. Jones
FO: Roger Warren
Web site: www.rayovac.com
Emp: 2,500
Mfr. batteries & lighting devices.
Canada, England, U.K., Hong Kong

RAYTECH CORPORATION

Four Corporate Drive, Ste. 295
Shelton, CT 06484
Tel: (203) 925-8000 Fax: (203) 925-8088
CEO: Albert A. Canosa, Pres.
FO: Alfred Klee
Emp: 1,207
Mfr. friction components & products for automotive & construction industry.
Germany

RAYTHEON COMPANY

141 Spring Street
Lexington, MA 02173
Tel: (781) 862-6600 Fax: (781) 860-2172
CEO: Dennis J. Picard, Chmn.
FO: James E. Drumgool, VP Int'l.
HR: Gail Anderson, SVP
Web site: www.raytheon.com

Emp: 119,000 Rev: $13.6 bil.

Mfr. diversified electronics, appliances, aviation, energy and environmental products; publishing, industry and construction services.

Argentina, Australia, Belgium, Brazil, Canada, Chile, China (PRC), Czech Republic, Egypt, England, U.K., France, Germany, India, Indonesia, Italy, Japan, Jordan, Kuwait, Malaysia, Mexico, Netherlands, Russia, Saudi Arabia, Singapore, South Africa, South Korea, Spain, Switzerland, Thailand, Turkey, United Arab Emirates, Venezuela, Vietnam

RAYTHEON ENGINEERS & CONSTRUCTORS INC.

141 Spring Street

Lexington, MA 02173

Tel: (781) 862-6600 Fax: (781) 860-2172

CEO: Chuck Miller, Pres.

Emp: 2,000

Engineering and construction services to process industrial.

England, U.K., Italy, Netherlands

READER'S DIGEST ASSOCIATION INC.

Reader's Digest Rd.

Pleasantville, NY 10570

Tel: (914) 238-1000 Fax: (914) 238-4559

CEO: Thomas O. Ryder, Chmn.

HR: Gary Rich

Emp: 7,200

Publisher of magazines and books and direct mail marketer.

Australia, Belgium, Canada, Denmark, England, U.K., Finland, France, Germany, Hong Kong, Italy, Mexico, Netherlands, New Zealand, Portugal, Singapore, South Africa, Sweden, Switzerland

REAL ESTATE RESEARCH CORPORATION

1820 Ridge Ave.

Evanston, IL 60201

Tel: (847) 864-9000 Fax: (847) 864-9025

CEO: Pat Carraciolo, Pres.

HR: Mary Adams

Emp: 94

Real estate research and appraisal.

Saudi Arabia

RECKITT & COLMAN

1655 Valley Road

Wayne, NJ 07470

Tel: (973) 633-3600 Fax: (973) 633-3633

CEO: Joseph Healy, Pres.

Emp: 1,952

Mfr. household, personal care, woodworking and industrial products.

Australia, Canada, England, U.K., France, Germany, Philippines, Saudi Arabia, Taiwan (ROC), Thailand

RED WING SHOE CO., INC.

314 Main Street

Red Wing, MN 55066

Tel: (612) 388-8211 Fax: (612) 388-7415

CEO: W. J. Sweasy, Chmn.

FO: Joseph Goggin, Pres.

HR: Rich Chalmers

Web site: www.redwingshoe.com

Emp: 2,000

Leather tanning and finishing; mfr. footwear, retail shoe stores.

Canada, England, U.K., Mexico

REDKEN LABORATORIES INC.

575 Fifth Ave.

New York, NY 10017

Tel: (212) 818-1500 Fax: (212) 984-4776

CEO: Guy Peyrelongue, Pres.

Emp: 950

Mfr. hair and skin care products.

Australia, Canada, England, U.K., Germany, Japan, New Zealand

REEBOK INTERNATIONAL LTD

100 Technology Center Drive

Stoughton, MA 02072

Tel: (781) 401-5000 Fax: (781) 401-7402

CEO: Paul B. Fireman, Chmn.

FO: Paul R. Duncan, EVP

HR: James R. Jones III, SVP

Web site: www.reebok.com

Emp: 6,800

Mfr. athletic shoes including casual, dress golf and walking shoes.

Canada, England, U.K., France, Germany, Hong Kong, Italy, Portugal, Russia, Spain

REED TECHNOLOGY AND INFORMATION SERVICES

One Progress Drive

Horsham, PA 19044

Tel: (215) 643-5000 Fax: (215) 682-5300

CEO: Darryl Fisher, Pres.

HR: Diana Lande

Web site: www.reedtech.com

Emp: 850

Electronic publishing and information delivery services.

England, U.K.

REED TOOL CO

6501 Navigation Blvd.

Houston, TX 77001

Tel: (713) 924-5200 Fax: (713) 924-5667

CEO: Roy J. Caldwell, Pres.

HR: Tim Bruegger

Emp: 800

Mfr. rock bits for oil and gas exploration.

England, U.K., France, Italy, Netherlands, Russia, Scotland, U.K., Singapore, United Arab Emirates

REEVES BROTHERS INC.

PO Box 1898, Hwy. 29 South

Spartanburg, SC 29304

Tel: (864) 576-1210 Fax: (864) 595-2180

CEO: Doug Hart, Pres.

Printing blanket and industrial coated fabrics.

Italy

REFAC TECHNOLOGY DEVELOPMENT CORPORATION

122 East 42nd Street, #4000

New York, NY 10168

Tel: (212) 687-4741 Fax: (212) 949-8716

CEO: Robert L. Tuchman, Pres.

Emp: 18

Consults to international technology transfer, foreign trade, & power supplies firms.

Japan, Switzerland, Taiwan (ROC)

REFCO GROUP LTD

111 W Jackson Blvd, #1700

Chicago, IL 60604

Tel: (312) 930-6500 Fax: (312) 930-6534

CEO: Philip Bennett, Pres.

Web site: www.refco.com

Emp: 670

Commodity & security brokers, financial services.

Canada

REFLEXITE TECHNOLOGY

120 Darling Drive

Avon, CT 06001

Tel: (860) 676-7100 Fax: (860) 676-7199

CEO: Cecil Ursprung, Pres.

Emp: 350

Mfr. plastic film, sheet, materials & shapes, optical lenses.

Canada

REGAL WARE INC.

1675 Reigle Drive, PO Box 395

Kewaskum, WI 53040-0395

Tel: (414) 626-2121 Fax: (414) 626-8565

CEO: Jeffrey A. Reigle, Pres.

FO: Doug Reigel

HR: James Moran

Emp: 2,000

Mfr. cookware, small electrical appliances, water purification & filtration products for home.

Canada, Japan, South Korea

REGAL-BELOIT CORPORATION

200 State Street

Beloit, WI 53511-6254

Tel: (608) 364-8800 Fax: (608) 364-8818

CEO: James L. Packard, Pres.

FO: Henry W. Knueppel

HR: Fritz Hollenbach

Emp: 2,631

Mfr. power transmission equipment, perishable cutting tools.

England, U.K., Germany, Italy

REGENT SPORTS CORPORATION

PO Box 11357

Hauppauge, NY 11788

Tel: (516) 234-2800 Fax: (516) 234-2948

CEO: J. Lipman, Pres.

Emp: 650

Sporting goods.

Canada, Germany

RELIABILITY INC.

PO Box 218370

Houston, TX 77218-8370

Tel: (281) 492-0550 Fax: (281) 492-0615

CEO: Larry Edwards, Pres.

Emp: 443

Mfr. burn-in/memory test systems, DC/DC converters.

Costa Rica, Singapore

RELIANCE GROUP HOLDINGS, INC.

55 East 52nd Street

New York, NY 10055

Tel: (212) 909-1100 Fax: (212) 909-1864

CEO: Saul P. Steinberg, Chmn.

FO: Robert M. Steinberg, Pres.

HR: Joel H. Rothwax, VP

Web site: www.rgh.com

Emp: 5,800 Rev: $11,333 mil.

Financial and insurance management services.

Argentina, Canada, England, U.K., Germany, Hong Kong, Mexico, Netherlands, Singapore, South Africa, Spain, Sweden, Switzerland

RELTEC CORPORATION

5900 Landerbrook Drive, Ste.300

Mayfield Heights, OH 44124-4019

Tel: (440) 460-3600 Fax: (440) 460-3690

CEO: Richard Schwobe, Pres.

Emp: 980

Telecommunications equipment.

Canada, Mexico

REMEDY CORPORATION

1505 Salado Drive

Mountain View, CA 94043-1110

Tel: (650) 903-5200 Fax: (650) 903-9001

CEO: Lawrence L. Garlick, Chmn.

FO: Michael L. Dionne, SVP

Web site: www.remedy.com

Emp: 648 Rev: 129 mil.

Developer and marketer of computer applications for the operations management market.

England, U.K., France, Germany, Japan, Singapore

REMINGTON ARMS CO., INC.

870 Remington Drive

Madison, NC 27025

Tel: (336) 548-8700 Fax: (336) 548-7801

CEO: Tom Millner, Pres.

FO: G. Gravel, Intl.

HR: Celeste Graves

Emp: 2,850

Mfr. sporting firearms and ammunition.

Canada, Germany

REMINGTON PRODUCTS COMPANY, L.L.C.

60 Main Street

Bridgeport, CT 06604

Tel: (203) 367-4400 Fax:

CEO: Neil P. DeFeo

FO: G. Hoddinott, Europe

HR: Allen Lipson

Emp: 1,200 Rev: $250 mil.

Mfr. home appliances, electric shavers.

Australia, Canada, England, U.K., France, Germany, New Zealand

RENA-WARE DISTRIBUTORS INC.

PO Box 97050

Redmond, WA 98073

Tel: (425) 881-6171 Fax: (425) 882-7500

CEO: Russ Cylstra, Pres.

Web site: www.exec@renaware.com

Emp: 1,200

Cookware and china.

Australia, Belgium, Netherlands, Switzerland

RENAISSANCE HOTELS AND RESORTS

1 Marriott Drive

Washington, DC 20058

Tel: (301) 380-3000 Fax: (301) 380-5181

CEO: Robert Olesen, VP

Hotel and resort chain.

Australia, Austria, Brazil, Canada, Czech Republic, Dominican Republic, Egypt, England, U.K., France, Germany, Grenada, Hong Kong, India, Israel, Jamaica, Japan, Malaysia, Netherlands, Russia, Switzerland, Thailand, Turkey

RENDIC INTERNATIONAL CORPORATION

9100 South Dadeland Blvd., Ste 1800

Miami, FL 33156
Tel: (305) 670-0066 Fax: (305) 670-0060
CEO: Jerko E. Rendic, Pres.
Web site: www.flintink.com
Sales of printing inks, press equipment and supplies.
Argentina, Chile, Ecuador

THE RENDON GROUP INC.
2000 S. Street NW
Washington, DC 20009
Tel: (202) 745-4900 Fax: (202) 745-0215
CEO: John W. Rendon, Jr., Chmn.
FO: Sandra L. Libby
HR: Peggy Rainwater
Emp: 28
Public relations, print & video production, strategic communications.
England, U.K., Indonesia, Kuwait

REPLOGLE GLOBES INC.
2801 South 25th Ave.
Broadview, IL 60153-4589
Tel: (708) 343-0900 Fax: (708) 343-0923
CEO: William F. Nickels
FO: Christopher Severn
HR: Mike Trombley
Emp: 200
Mfr. geographical world globes.
Denmark

REPUBLIC NATIONAL BANK OF NEW YORK
452 Fifth Ave.
New York, NY 10018
Tel: (212) 525-5000 Fax: (212) 525-6996
CEO: Walter H. Weiner, Chmn.
Web site: www.rnb.com
Emp: 4,900
Banking services.
Argentina, Australia, Bahamas, Canada, Cayman Islands, Chile, England, U.K., Hong Kong, Italy, Japan, Panama, Singapore, Uruguay

RESPIRONICS INC.
1001 Murry Ridge Drive
Murrysville, PA 15668-8550
Tel: (724) 733-0200 Fax: (412) 733-0299
CEO: Gerald E. McGinnis, Chmn.
FO: Kam-Kwen Ng
HR: William Decker
Emp: 1,074
Design/mfr. patient ventilation medical products.
Hong Kong

REUBEN H. DONNELLY CORPORATION
287 Bowman Ave.
Purchase, NY 10577
Tel: (914) 933-6800 Fax: (914) 933-6544
CEO: Frank Noonan, Pres.
FO: William Gartland
HR: Tibor Taraba
Emp: 3,000
Telephone directories, direct mail, merchandising services.
England, U.K.

REVELL/MONOGRAM
8601 Waukegan Road
Morton Grove, IL 60053
Tel: (847) 966-3500 Fax: (784) 767-5857
CEO: Theodore J. Eischeid, Pres.
FO: Theodore J. Eischeid
HR: Lorraine Milius
Emp: 650
Mfr. plastic hobby kits.
Germany

REVLON INC.
625 Madison Ave.
New York, NY 10022
Tel: (212) 527-4000 Fax: (212) 527-4995
CEO: Jerry W. Levin, Chmn.
FO: Joseph Heid, Pres. Intl.
HR: Jenna Sheldon
Web site: www.revlon.com
Rev: $2,400 mil.
Mfr. cosmetics, fragrances, toiletries and beauty care products.
Argentina, Australia, Belgium, Bermuda, Brazil, Canada, England, U.K., France, Germany, Hong Kong, Ireland, Israel, Italy, Japan, Mexico, New Zealand, Singapore, Spain, Venezuela

REXALL SUNDOWN INC.
851 Broken Sound Parkway NW

Boca Raton, FL 33487

Tel: (561) 241-9400 Fax: (561) 995-0197

CEO: Christ Nast, Pres.

Vitamins, nutritional supplements and diet and weight management products.

Hong Kong, Mexico, South Korea

REXNORD CORPORATION

4701 West Greenfield Ave.

Milwaukee, WI 53214

Tel: (414) 643-3000 Fax: (414) 643-3078

CEO: James R. Swenson. Pres.

FO: P. C. Wallace

HR: J. B. Kurowski

Emp: 4,800 Rev: $525 mil.

Mfr. power transmission products.

Australia, Belgium, Brazil, Canada, China (PRC), England, U.K., France, Germany, Italy, Mexico, Singapore

REYNOLDS & REYNOLDS COMPANY

PO Box 2608

Dayton, OH 45401

Tel: (937) 443-2000 Fax: (937) 485-4230

CEO: David R. Holmes, Chmn.

HR: Tom Momchilov, VP HR

Web site: www.reyrey.com

Emp: 9,138 Rev: $1,385.7 mil.

Business forms, systems & EDP service.

Canada

REYNOLDS INTERNATIONAL INC.

6601 W. Broad Street, PO Box 27002

Richmond, VA 23261

Tel: (804) 281-2000 Fax: (804) 281-2245

CEO: Jeremiah J. Sheehan, Chmn.

Emp: 31,000

Mfr. aluminum primary and fabricated products, plastic and paper packaging and food service products; gold mining.

Australia, Canada, China (PRC), Russia, Switzerland, Thailand

RHEOMETRIC SCIENTIFIC INC.

1 Possumtown Road

Piscataway, NJ 08854

Tel: (732) 560-8550 Fax: (732) 560-7451

CEO: Alexander Giacco, Pres.

HR: Matthew Bilt

Emp: 250

Design/mfr. rheological instruments & systems.

England, U.K., France, Germany, Japan

RICE FOWLER

201 St. Charles Ave., 36th Fl.

New Orleans, LA 70170

Tel: (504) 523-2600 Fax: (504) 523-2705

CEO: L. J. Schilling

Emp: 72

Law firm specializing in maritime, insurance, int'l, environmental, oil/gas, transportation, bankruptcy & reorganization.

Colombia, England, U.K.

RICH PRODUCTS CORPORATION

1 West Ferry

Buffalo, NY 14213

Tel: (716) 878-8000 Fax: (716) 878-8266

CEO: Robert E. Rich, Jr., Pres.

FO: Richard Ferranti, Pres. Intl.

HR: Brian Townson

Emp: 7,000

Mfr. non-dairy products.

England, U.K., Hong Kong, Japan, Singapore

RIDGE TOOL COMPANY

400 Clark Street

Elyria, OH 44035

Tel: (440) 323-5581 Fax: (440) 329-4853

CEO: C. L. Mikovich

FO: T. McKane

Web site: www.ridgid.com

Emp: 900

Hand & power tools for working pipe, drain cleaning equipment, etc.

Australia, Belgium, Brazil, England, U.K., France, Germany, Hong Kong, Ireland, Italy, Japan, Sweden, Switzerland

RIEKE CORPORATION

500 West 7th Street

Auburn, IN 46706

Tel: (219) 925-3700 Fax: (219) 925-2493

CEO: Lynn Brooks

HR: Mary Woodcock

Emp: 792

Mfr. steel drum closures, plugs, seals, faucets, rings, combination pail spout & closure, etc.

Canada, Mexico

RIGHT MANAGEMENT CONSULTANTS, INC.

1818 Market Street, 14th Fl.

Philadelphia, PA 19103-3614

Tel: (215) 988-1588 Fax: (215) 988-9112

CEO: Richard J. Pinola

FO: Peter Doris, EVP

HR: Sally Barlow, Mgr. HR

Web site: www.right.com

Emp: 880 Rev: $125.8 mil.

Out placement & human resources consulting services.

Belgium, Canada, England, U.K., France, Germany, Japan, Norway, Scotland, U.K., Switzerland

RITTENHOUSE INC.

250 South Northwest Highway

Park Ridge, IL 60068

Tel: (847) 692-9130 Fax: (847) 692-9818

CEO: Andrew B. Albert, Pres.

Emp: 800

Mfr. papers & paper products, ribbon cartridges for printers, labels for weigh scale & bar code printers.

Canada

THE RITZ-CARLTON HOTEL COMPANY, L.L.C.

3413 Peachtree Road NE, Ste. 300

Atlanta, GA 30326

Tel: (404) 237-5500 Fax: (404) 365-9643

CEO: Horst Schulze, Pres.

HR: Leonardo Inghilleri, VP

5-star hotel and restaurant chain.

Australia, England, U.K., Germany, Hong Kong, Indonesia, Japan, Malaysia, Mexico, Singapore, South Korea, Spain

RIVERWOOD INTERNATIONAL CORPORATION

3350 Cumberland Circle, #1600

Atlanta, GA 30339

Tel: (770) 644-3000 Fax: (770) 644-2927

CEO: Stephen M. Humphrey, CEO

FO: Tony Orta

HR: Robert H. Burg

Web site: www.riverwood.com

Emp: 5,000 Rev: $1,140 mil.

Mfr. paperboard packaging & machinery.

Brazil

RIVIANA FOODS INC.

2777 Allen Parkway

Houston, TX 77019

Tel: (713) 529-3251 Fax: (713) 529-1661

CEO: Joseph A. Hafner, Jr., Pres.

FO: David Van Oss

HR: Jack Nolingberg

Emp: 2,500

Rice & rice by-products & pet foods.

Belgium, Costa Rica, England, U.K., Guatemala

RJR NABISCO INC.

1301 Ave. of the Americas

New York, NY 10019

Tel: (212) 258-5600 Fax: (212) 969-9173

CEO: Steven F. Goldstone, Chmn.

FO: Lionel L. Nowell III, SVP

HR: Gerald I. Angowitz, SVP

Web site: www.rjrnabisco.com

Emp: 80,400 Rev: $17,057 mil.

Mfr. consumer packaged food products & tobacco products.

Brazil, Canada, Chile, China (PRC), Costa Rica, Ecuador, England, U.K., France, Germany, Greece, Guatemala, Hong Kong, Hungary, Jamaica, Japan, Malaysia, Mexico, Netherlands, Nicaragua, Peru, Portugal, Russia, Spain, Sweden, Switzerland, Trinidad & Tobago, Ukraine, Uruguay, Venezuela

RMO INC.

650 West Colfax Ave.

Denver, CO 80204

Tel: (303) 534-8181 Fax: (303) 592-8209

CEO: Jody Whitson, Pres.

Emp: 300

Mfr. dental equipment & supplies.

France

RMS GROUP INC.

43-59 10th Street

Long Island City, NY 11101

Tel: (212) 684-5470 Fax: (212) 684-6019

CEO: Bill Suri

FO: Sandy Parmar

Emp: 150

Technology-transfer development and sales.

Denmark, India, Japan

ROADWAY EXPRESS INC.

1077 George Boulevard, PO Box 471

Akron, OH 44309

Tel: (330) 384-1717 Fax: (330) 258-6082

CEO: M. W. Wickham, Pres.

FO: J. D. S. Taley

Emp: 39,000

Motor carrier and long haul trucking.

Canada, Mexico

ROADWAY PACKAGE SYSTEM INC.

1000 Scott Drive

Moon Township, PA 15108

Tel: (412) 269-1000 Fax: (412) 269-0551

CEO: I. T. Hofmann

Emp: 15,000

Small package shipments.

Canada

ROBBINS & MYERS INC.

1400 Kettering Tower

Dayton, OH 45423-1400

Tel: (937) 222-2610 Fax: (937) 225-3355

CEO: Daniel W. Duval, Pres

HR: Robert Anderson

Emp: 2,300 Rev: $351 mil.

Mfr. progressing cavity pumps, valves and agitators.

Brazil, Canada, China (PRC), England, U.K., India, Mexico, Scotland, U.K., Singapore, Taiwan (ROC)

ROBERT HALF INTERNATIONAL INC.

2884 Sand Hill Road, #200

Menlo Park, CA 94025

Tel: (650) 234-6000 Fax: (415) 854-9735

CEO: Harold M. Messmer, Jr., Chmn.

FO: Robert W. Glass, SVP

Emp: 1,000 Rev: $1,300 mil.

World leader in personnel and specialized staffing services.

Belgium, Canada, England, U.K., France, Israel, Netherlands

ROBERTS PHARMACEUTICAL CORP.

Meridian Center II, 4 Industrial Way West

Eatontown, NJ 07724-2274

Tel: (732) 389-1182 Fax: (732) 389-1014

CEO: John T. Spitznagel, Pres.

Emp: 460

Lisense, acquire, develop and commercialize innovative pharmaceuticals.

Canada, England, U.K.

ROBERTS-GORDON INC.

1250 William Street, PO Box 44

Buffalo, NY 14240-0044

Tel: (716) 852-4400 Fax: (716) 852-0854

CEO: Paul A. Dines, Pres.

FO: Mark J. Dines

Emp: 100

Mfr. industry gas burners, industry space heaters, infrared radiant tube heaters.

Canada, England, U.K.

ROBERTSON CECO CORPORATION

5000 Executive Pkwy., Ste. 425

San Ramon, CA 94583

Tel: (510) 358-0330 Fax: (510) 244-6780

CEO: E. A. Roskovenski, Pres.

HR: Jack Eskew

Emp: 1,400

Mfr. pre-engineered metal buildings.

Australia, Canada

ROCHESTER GAUGES INC.

PO Box 29242

Dallas, TX 75229-0242

Tel: (972) 241-2161 Fax: (972) 620-1403

CEO: J. W. LaDue, Pres.

HR: Linda Miracle

Emp: 450

Liquid-level gauges, level switches, pressured gauges, electric panel gauges, etc.

Belgium, Mexico

ROCHESTER INSTRUMENT SYSTEMS INC.

255 North Union Street
Rochester, NY 14605
Tel: (716) 263-7700 Fax: (716) 262-4777
CEO: Gerald Schaefer, Pres.
FO: Dan Rogoff
HR: Rhonda Lander
Emp: 600

Mfr. electronic alarms and monitors including annunciators, event recorders, etc.

Canada, England, U.K.

ROCHESTER MIDLAND CORPORATION

PO Box 1515
Rochester, NY 14603
Tel: (716) 266-2250 Fax: (716) 467-4406
CEO: Harlan D. Calkins
FO: Glenn O. Stoudt
Emp: 1,300

Mfr. specialty chemicals for industry cleaning and maintenance, water treatment and personal hygiene.

Canada, England, U.K., Ireland

ROCK OF AGES CORPORATION

PO Box 482
Barre, VT 05641-0482
Tel: (802) 476-3115 Fax: (802) 476-3110
CEO: Kurt M. Swenson, Pres.
FO: Jon Gregory, Pres.
HR: George Anderson
Web site: www.rockofages.com
Emp: 785 Rev: $52 mil.

Quarrier; dimension granite blocks, memorials, and precision industrial granite.

Canada, Japan

THE ROCKPORT COMPANY

220 Donald J. Lynch Blvd.
Marlboro, MA 01752
Tel: (508) 485-2090 Fax: (508) 480-0012
CEO: Angel Martinez, Pres.
HR: Richard Roesler

Mfr./import dress and casual footwear.

Brazil, Indonesia, Italy, Slovenia, Taiwan (ROC)

ROCKWELL INTERNATIONAL CORPORATION

600 Anton Boulevard
Costa Mesa, CA 92626-7147
Tel: (714) 424-4200 Fax: (714) 424-4251
CEO: Don H. Davis Jr., Chmn.
FO: Jodie K. Glore, SVP
HR: Joel R. Stone, SVP
Web site: www.rockwell.com
Emp: 45,000 Rev: $7,800 mil.

Products & service for aerospace and defense, automotive, electronics, graphics & automation industry.

Argentina, Australia, Austria, Belgium, Brazil, Canada, Chile, China (PRC), Colombia, Czech Republic, Denmark, England, U.K., France, Germany, Ghana, Hong Kong, India, Indonesia, Ireland, Israel, Italy, Japan, Kenya, Malaysia, Mauritius, Mexico, Morocco, Netherlands, New Zealand, Philippines, Poland, Portugal, Russia, Saudi Arabia, Singapore, South Africa, South Korea, Spain, Sweden, Switzerland, Taiwan (ROC), Thailand, Turkey, United Arab Emirates, Venezuela, Wales, U.K., Zimbabwe

R.A. RODRIGUEZ INC.

20 Seaview Boulevard
Garden City, NY 11050
Tel: (516) 625-8080 Fax: (516) 621-2424
CEO: R. A. Rodriguez, Jr.
FO: Robert A. Rodriguez
HR: Peter M. Rodriguez
Web site: www.rodriguez-usa.com
Emp: 80

Distribution of ball and roller bearings, precision gears, mechanical systems and related products.

England, U.K., Germany, Mexico

ROGERS CORPORATION

One Technology Drive, PO Box 188
Rogers, CT 06263-0188
Tel: (203) 774-9605 Fax:
CEO: Walt Boomer
FO: William Schunmann, VP
HR: Jack Richie
Web site: www.rogers-corp.com
Emp: 1,000 Rev: $221 mil.

Mfr. specialty materials including elastomers, circuit laminates and moldable composites.

Belgium, Japan

ROHM AND HAAS COMPANY

100 Independence Mall West
Philadelphia, PA 19106
Tel: (215) 592-3000 Fax: (215) 592-3377
CEO: J. Lawrence Wilson, Chmn.
FO: John P. Mulroney, Pres.
HR: Marisa Guerin
Web site: www.rohmhaas.com
Emp: 11,592 Rev: $34000 mil.
Mfr. industrial & agricultural chemicals, plastics.
Argentina, Australia, Austria, Belgium, Brazil, Canada, Chile, China (PRC), Colombia, Costa Rica, England, U.K., France, Germany, Greece, Honduras, Hong Kong, India, Indonesia, Italy, Japan, Malaysia, Mexico, New Zealand, Pakistan, Peru, Philippines, Russia, Scotland, U.K., Singapore, South Africa, South Korea, Spain, Sweden, Taiwan (ROC), Thailand, United Arab Emirates, Uruguay

RONALD E. LAIS, INC.
136 South Imperial Highway
Anaheim, CA 92807-3943
Tel: (714) 937-1700 Fax: (714) 937-1900
CEO: Ronald E. Lais
International law firm.
Croatia, Germany, India

ROPAK CORPORATION
660 S. State College Boulevard
Fullerton, CA 92631-5138
Tel: (714) 870-9757 Fax: (714) 447-3871
CEO: James R. Connell
HR: Gary Montgomery
Emp: 988
Mfr. plastic containers.
Canada

THE ROUSE COMPANY
10275 Little Patuxent Pkwy.
Columbia, MD 21044-3456
Tel: (410) 992-6000 Fax: (410) 992-6363
CEO: Anthony Deering, Pres.
Emp: 5,400
Design, construction & management of retail centers.
Canada

ROWAN COMPANIES INC.
2800 Post Oak Boulevard
Houston, TX 77056-6196
Tel: (713) 621-7800 Fax: (713) 960-7560
CEO: Charles R. Palmer, Chmn.
FO: Robert J. Pedrett
HR: Bill Person
Emp: 2,000
Contract drilling and air charter service.
England, U.K., Indonesia, Netherlands, Singapore

ROWE INTERNATIONAL INC.
27 Druid Hill Drive
Parsippany, NJ 07054-1453
Tel: (973) 334-0973 Fax: (973) 334-0985
CEO: David Sadler, Pres.
Emp: 1,400
Vending machines, background music systems and jukeboxes; bill and coin changers.
England, U.K.

T. ROWE PRICE ASSOCIATES, INC.
100 East Pratt Street
Baltimore, MD 21202
Tel: (41) 034-5200 Fax: (410) 345-2394
CEO: George A. Roche, Chmn. & Pres.
HR: Andrew Goresh
Web site: www.troweprice.com
Emp: 3,000
Investment and portfolio asset management.
Argentina, England, U.K., Hong Kong, Japan, Singapore

ROYAL APPLIANCE MFG. COMPANY
650 Alpha Drive
Cleveland, OH 44143
Tel: (440) 449-6150 Fax: (440) 449-7806
CEO: Mike Merriman, Pres.
HR: Kim Araps
Emp: 700
Mfr. vacuum cleaners.
England, U.K., Germany

RPM INC.
PO Box 777
Medina, OH 44258
Tel: (330) 273-5090 Fax: (330) 225-8743
CEO: Jim Karman, Pres.

Web site: www.rpminc.com

Emp: 1,600

Mfr. protective coatings and paint.

Canada, Luxembourg

RUBBERMAID INC.

1147 Akron Road

Wooster, OH 44691

Tel: (330) 264-6464 Fax: (330) 287-2846

CEO: Wolfgang R. Schmitt, Chmn.

FO: Leavitt B. Ahrens, Jr., SVP

HR: David L. Robertson, SVP

Web site: www:rubbermaid.com

Emp: 12,000 Rev: $2,400 mil.

Mfr. rubber and plastic resin home, commercial and industry products.

Australia, Austria, Belgium, Canada, France, Germany, Hong Kong, Ireland, Japan, Luxembourg, Mexico, Netherlands, Poland, Singapore, South Korea, Spain

RUDER FINN INC.

301 East 57th Street

New York, NY 10022

Tel: (212) 593-6400 Fax: (212) 593-6397

CEO: Dr. Kathy Bloomgarden, Pres.

Web site: www.ruderfinn.com

Emp: 270

Public relations service and broadcast communications.

England, U.K., France, Japan, Sweden

RUSSELL CORPORATION

PO Box 272

Alexander City, AL 35011

Tel: (205) 329-4000 Fax: (205) 329-5799

CEO: Jack Ward, Pres.

Emp: 14,500

Mfr. athletic and leisure apparel.

Belgium, Scotland, U.K.

RUSSELL REYNOLDS ASSOCIATES INC.

200 Park Ave.

New York, NY 10166-0002

Tel: (212) 351-2000 Fax: (212) 370-0896

CEO: Hobson Brown, Jr.

HR: James Bagley

Web site: www.ressreyn.com

Emp: 600

Executive recruiting services.

Argentina, Australia, Belgium, Brazil, Canada, China (PRC), Denmark, England, U.K., France, Germany, Hong Kong, Italy, Japan, Mexico, Netherlands, Poland, Scotland, U.K., Singapore, Spain

RUSSIN & VECCHI L.L.P.

815 Connecticut Ave. NW, Ste. 650

Washington, DC 20006

Tel: (202) 822-6100 Fax: (202) 822-6101

CEO: Jonathan Russin

FO: Leonard A. Chinitz

Emp: 90

Law firm.

Dominican Republic, Myanmar, Russia, Taiwan (ROC), Thailand, Vietnam

RUST-OLEUM CORPORATION

11 Hawthorn Parkway

Vernon Hills, IL 60061

Tel: (847) 367-7700 Fax: (847) 816-2300

CEO: Michael Tellor, Pres.

FO: Frank W. Hendricks

Emp: 500

Rust preventive coatings.

Canada, Netherlands

RVSI/ACUITY/CiMatrix

5 Shawmut Road

Canton, MA 02021

Tel: (781) 821-0830 Fax: (781) 828-8942

CEO: Pat Costa, Chmn.

FO: Tom Smith

HR: Pat Green

Mfr. bar code scanners & data collection equipment.

Belgium, Canada, England, U.K., France, Germany

RYDER SYSTEM, INC.

3600 NW 82nd Ave.

Miami, FL 33166

Tel: (305) 593-3726 Fax: (305) 500-4129

CEO: M. Anthony Burns, Chmn., Pres.

FO: Edward M. Straw, Pres.

HR: Thomas E. McKinnon, EVP

Web site: www.ryder.com

Emp: 42,000 Rev: $5,000 mil.

Integrated logistics, full-service truck leasing, truck rental and public transportation services.

Argentina, Brazil, Canada, Germany, Mexico, Netherlands, Poland

S

S&C ELECTRIC COMPANY

6601 N Ridge Blvd.

Chicago, IL 60626-3997

Tel: (773) 338-1000 Fax: (773) 038-3657

CEO: John W. Estey, Pres.

FO: S.O. Palafox

HR: Vilma M. Bell, VP

Emp: 1,900

Mfr. high voltage power equipment..

Canada

S.G. COWEN & CO.

Financial Square

New York, NY 10005

Tel: (212) 495-6000 Fax: (212) 380-8212

CEO: Kurt Wellings, Pres.

Emp: 1,600

Securities research, trading, broker/dealer services; investment banking & asset management.

Canada, England, U.K., France, Japan, Switzerland

SAFETY-KLEEN CORPORATION

1301 Gervais Street

Columbia, SC 29201

Tel: (803) 933-4200 Fax: (803) 933-4345

CEO: Kenneth W. Winger, Pres.

FO: Michael J. Bragagnolo, EVP

HR: Bob Arquilla, VP Admin.

Web site: www.laidlawenv.com

Emp: 4,500 Rev: $678.6

Solvent based parts cleaning service; sludge/solvent recycling service.

Australia, Canada, England, U.K., France, Germany, Spain

SAFEWAY INC.

5918 Stoneridge Mall Road

Pleasantville, CA 94588

Tel: (510) 467-3000 Fax: (510) 467-3230

CEO: Steven A. Burd, Pres.

HR: Robert Carlson

Emp: 107,000

Food marketing.

Canada

SALOMON SMITH BARNEY HOLDINGS INC.

7 World Trade Center

New York, NY 10048

Tel: (212) 783-7000 Fax: (212) 783-2110

CEO: D. Maughan & J. Dimon, Co-Chairmen

Emp: 3,000

Securities dealers and underwriters.

England, U.K., Hong Kong, Japan

SAMEDAN OIL CORPORATION

110 West Broadway Street

Ardmore, OK 73402

Tel: (580) 223-4110 Fax: (580) 221-1384

CEO: Robert Kelley, Pres.

Emp: 501

Gas & oil exploration & production.

Canada, Tunisia

SAMSONITE CORPORATION

11200 East 45th Ave.

Denver, CO 80239-3018

Tel: (303) 373-2000 Fax: (303) 373-6300

CEO: Luc van Nevel

FO: Karleinz Tretter

HR: Kim Henry

Emp: 8,000 Rev: $800 mil.

Mfr. luggage and leather goods.

Belgium, Canada, Italy, Mexico

SANDUSKY INTERNATIONAL

615 W. Market Street, PO Box 5012

Sandusky, OH 44871-8012

Tel: (419) 626-5340 Fax: (419) 626-3339

CEO: Ed Ryan

FO: Dan Scott

HR: Glenn Holzhauser

Emp: 350

Mfr. roll shells for paper machines, centrifugal tubular products.

Scotland, U.K.

SANFORD CORPORATION

2711 Washington Boulevard
Bellwood, IL 60104
Tel: (708) 547-6650 Fax: (708) 547-6719
CEO: Robert Parker, Pres.
FO: Thomas H. Beyer, Pres. Int'l.
HR: Tim Jahnke
Emp: 5,000

Mfr. inks, writing, drawing and drafting instruments.

Canada

SANTILLANA PUBLISHING COMPANY, INC.

2105 N.W. 86th Ave.
Miami, FL 33122
Tel: (305) 591-9522 Fax: (305) 591-9145
CEO: Manuel G. Sandoval, Pres.
Web site: www.insite-network.com/santillana

Children and adult book publishing.

England, U.K., Spain

SARA LEE CORPORATION

3 First National Plaza
Chicago, IL 60602-4260
Tel: (312) 726-2600 Fax: (312) 558-4995
CEO: John H. Bryan, Chmn. & CEO
FO: C. Steven McMillan, Pres.
HR: Karen Batenic
Emp: 127,989 Rev: $18,600 mil.

Mfr./distributor food and consumer packaged goods, intimate apparel and knitwear.

Argentina, Australia, Belgium, Canada, China (PRC), England, U.K., France, Hungary, Indonesia, Ireland, Italy, Japan, Mexico, Netherlands, Philippines, Russia, Scotland, U.K., Singapore, South Africa, Spain, Uruguay

SARGENT & GREENLEAF, INC.

One Security Drive, PO Box 930
Nicholasville, KY 40340-0930
Tel: (606) 885-9411 Fax: (606) 885-3063
CEO: Jerry A. Morgan
FO: Thomas J. Leppert, IV
HR: Shirlean Herron
Web site: www.sglocks.com
Emp: 174

Mfr. hi-security locking mechanisms.

Switzerland

SARGENT MANUFACTURING COMPANY

100 Sargent Drive
New Haven, CT 06511
Tel: (203) 562-2151 Fax: (203) 776-5992
CEO: Thanasis Molokotos, Pres.
HR: Jack Dwyer
Web site: www.Sargentlock.com
Emp: 650

Mfr. architectural builders hardware, locks.

Canada

SAS INSTITUTE INC.

SAS Campus Drive
Cary, NC 27513
Tel: (919) 677-8000 Fax: (919) 677-8123
CEO: Dr. James Goodnight, Pres.
Web site: www.sas.com
Emp: 4,100

Mfr./distributes decision support software.

Argentina, Australia, Austria, Belgium, Brazil, Canada, China (PRC), Czech Republic, Denmark, England, U.K., Finland, France, Germany, Hong Kong, Hungary, India, Indonesia, Italy, Japan, Malaysia, Mexico, Netherlands, New Zealand, Norway, Philippines, Poland, Portugal, Russia, Singapore, Slovakia, Slovenia, South Africa, South Korea, Spain, Sweden, Switzerland, Taiwan (ROC), Thailand, Turkey, United Arab Emirates

W. B. SAUNDERS COMPANY

Curtis Center, Independence Square W
Philadelphia, PA 19106
Tel: (215) 238-7800 Fax: (215) 238-7883
CEO: Lewis Reines, Pres.
HR: Robert Thorne

Medical and technical book publishers.

Canada, England, U.K., Japan

SAVAIR INC.

33200 Freeway Drive
St. Clair Shores, MI 48082
Tel: (810) 296-7390 Fax: (810) 296-7305
CEO: E. A. Wolfbauer, Pres.
HR: R. Chaudhry

Emp: 250

Mfr. welding guns, air & hydraulic cylinders, clinch & pierce units.

England, U.K.

SAVANNAH INTERNATIONAL CORPORATION

4171 North Mesa, Bldg. D

El Paso, TX 79902-1433

Tel: (915) 796-7000 Fax: (915) 593-4289

CEO: Michael Mitchell, Pres.

FO: Hans Meinel

HR: Victor Rueda

Emp: 6,000

Mfr. wearing apparel.

Australia, England, U.K., Hong Kong, Ireland, Japan

SBC COMMUNICATIONS INC.

175 East Houston, PO Box 2933

San Antonio, TX 78299-2933

Tel: (210) 821-4105 Fax: (210) 351-5034

CEO: Edward E. Whitacre, Jr., Pres.

FO: Cliff Eason

HR: Cassandra C. Carr

Web site: www.sbc.com

Emp: 116,000 Rev: $25,000 mil.

Telecommunications.

Chile, China (PRC), England, U.K., France, Israel, Mexico, South Africa, South Korea, Switzerland, Taiwan (ROC)

SCANTRON CORPORATION

1361 Valencia Ave.

Tustin, CA 92680-6463

Tel: (714) 247-2700 Fax: (714) 247-0011

CEO: Thomas R. Hoag, Pres.

HR: Sherri McKaig

Web site: www.scantron.com

Emp: 540

Design/mfr. optical mark readers, test scoring & data entry equipment, scannable forms, computer products.

Switzerland

SCHENECTADY INTERNATIONAL INC.

PO Box 1046

Schenectady, NY 12301

Tel: (518) 370-4200 Fax: (518) 382-8129

CEO: Kenneth Pettersen

FO: Stephen M. Abba, VP

HR: J. Richard Wyles

Mfr. electrical insulating varnishes, enamels, phenolic resins, alkylphenols.

Australia, Brazil, Canada, England, U.K., France, India, Japan, Mexico, South Africa, Switzerland

SCHENKER INTERNATIONAL FORWARDERS INC.

150 Albany Ave.

Freeport, NY 11520

Tel: (516) 377-3000 Fax: (516) 377-3005

CEO: Robert Doernte, Pres.

HR: Susan Ferraro

Web site: www.schenkerusa.com

Freight forwarders.

Argentina, Australia, Austria, Belgium, Brazil, Canada, Chile, China (PRC), Colombia, Denmark, Egypt, England, U.K., Ethiopia, Finland, France, Germany, Greece, Guatemala, Hong Kong, Iceland, India, Iran, Ireland, Italy, Japan, Kenya, Macau, Malaysia, Malta, Mauritius, Mexico, Morocco, Netherlands, New Zealand, Norway, Poland, Portugal, Reunion, Russia, Saudi Arabia, Scotland, U.K., Singapore, South Africa, Spain, Sweden, Switzerland, Taiwan (ROC), Thailand, Turkey, Vietnam, Zambia, Zimbabwe

R.P. SCHERER CORPORATION

PO Box 7060

Troy, MI 48007-7060

Tel: (248) 649-0900 Fax: (248) 649-4238

CEO: Aleksandar Erdeljan, Pres.

FO: George L. Fotiades, COO

Web site: www.rpscherer.com

Emp: 3,500

Mfr. pharmaceuticals; soft gelatin and two-piece hard shell capsules.

Argentina, Australia, Brazil, Canada, England, U.K., France, Germany, Italy, Japan, South Korea

SCHERING-PLOUGH CORPORATION

1 Giralda Farms

Madison, NJ 07940-1000

Tel: (973) 822-7000 Fax: (973) 822-7048

CEO: Richard Jay Kogan, Chmn.

FO: Raul E. Cesan, EVP

HR: John Ryan

Web site: www.sch-plough.com

Emp: 22,700 Rev: $6,778 mil.

Proprietary drug and cosmetic products.

Argentina, Australia, Brazil, Canada, England, U.K., France, Hong Kong, India, Ireland, Japan, Kenya, New Zealand, Peru, Philippines, Ukraine

SCHLAGE LOCK COMPANY

2401 Bayshore Boulevard

San Francisco, CA 94134

Tel: (415) 467-1100 Fax: (415) 330-5530

CEO: Brian McNealy, Pres.

FO: Harlow Rothert

Emp: 2,800

Mfr. locks and builders hardware.

Australia, Canada, Mexico

SCHLEGEL SYSTEMS

1555 Jefferson Road, PO Box 23197

Rochester, NY 14692-3197

Tel: (716) 427-7200 Fax: (716) 427-7216

CEO: Wayne Bowser, CEO

FO: Robert Faircloth

HR: Gregory J. Murrer

Emp: 3,000 Rev: $150 mil.

Mfr. engineered perimeter sealing systems for residential & commercial construction; fibers; rubber product.

Australia, Belgium, Brazil, Canada, England, U.K., France, Germany, Ireland, Italy, Japan, Spain

SCHOLASTIC CORPORATION

555 Broadway

New York, NY 10012

Tel: (212) 343-6100 Fax: (212) 343-4712

CEO: Richard Robinson, Chmn.

FO: David J. Walsh, SVP

HR: Larry V. Holland, VP

Web site: www.scholastic.com

Emp: 4,000 Rev: $1,058 mil.

Publishing/distribution educational & children's magazines, books, software.

Australia, Canada, England, U.K., Hong Kong, India, Ireland, Mexico, New Zealand

SCHRADER BELLOWS DIV

257 Huddleston Ave.

Cuyahoga Falls, OH 44221

Tel: (330) 923-5202 Fax: (330) 426-3259

CEO: Larry Reinhart, Mgr.

HR: Keith Gregory

Emp: 4,000

Mfr. pneumatic and hydraulic valves and cylinders, FRL units and accessories..

Belgium, Brazil, Canada, England, U.K.

A .SCHULMAN INC.

3550 West Market Street

Akron, OH 44333

Tel: (330) 666-3751 Fax: (330) 668-7204

CEO: Terry L. Haines, Pres.

Emp: 1,763

Mfr./sale plastic resins & compounds.

Belgium, Canada, France, Germany, Mexico, Switzerland, Wales, U.K.

THE CHARLES SCHWAB CORPORATION

101 Montgomery Street

San Francisco, CA 94104

Tel: (415) 627-7000 Fax: (415) 627-8840

CEO: Charles R. Schwab, Chmn.

FO: Peter J. McIntosh, EVP

Web site: www.schawb.com

Emp: 12,700 Rev: $2,299 mil.

Financial services; discount brokerage, retirement accounts.

England, U.K.

SCI SYSTEMS INC.

PO Box 1000

Huntsville, AL 35807

Tel: (256) 882-4800 Fax: (256) 882-4804

CEO: A. Eugene Sapp, Jr.

Emp: 9,000

R/D & mfr. electronics systems for commerce, industry, aerospace, etc.

Canada, Ireland, Mexico, Scotland, U.K., Singapore, Thailand

SCIENCE MANAGEMENT CORPORATION

721 US Hwy 202/206

Bridgewater, NJ 08807-1760

Tel: (908) 722-0300 Fax: (908) 722-4150

CEO: James A. Skidmore, Jr., Pres.

FO: Frank S. Rathgeber

HR: Joseph Leone

Emp: 425

Human/management resources, information technology, engineering & technology services.

Belgium, Canada, England, U.K., France, Germany

SCIENTIFIC AMERICAN INC.

415 Madison Ave.

New York, NY 10017

Tel: (212) 754-0550 Fax: (212) 355-6245

CEO: Jo Rosler, Pres.

Emp: 230

Magazine and textbook publishing.

Netherlands

SCIENTIFIC-ATLANTA, INC.

1 Technology Pkwy South

Norcross, GA 30092-2967

Tel: (770) 903-5000 Fax: (770) 903-2967

CEO: James F. McDonald, Pres.

FO: Larry Enterline

HR: Brian C. Koenig

Web site: www.sciatl.com

Emp: 5,800

A leading supplier of broadband communications systems, satellite-based video, voice and data communications networks and worldwide customer service and support.

Argentina, Australia, Brazil, Canada, Chile, China (PRC), Denmark, England, U.K., Hong Kong, Italy, Japan, Mexico, Singapore

SCOTSMAN ICE SYSTEMS

775 Corporate Woods Pkwy.

Vernon Hills, IL 60061

Tel: (847) 215-4500 Fax: (847) 913-9844

CEO: Richard Osborne, Pres.

FO: E. Lanzani

Emp: 1,000

Mfr. ice machines & refrigerators, drink dispensers.

Italy

THE SCOTT & FETZER COMPANY

28800 Clemens Road

Westlake, OH 44145

Tel: (440) 892-3000 Fax: (440) 892-3060

CEO: Kenneth J. Semelsberger, Chmn.

HR: Dana Philiips

Emp: 17,000

Electrical and lighting fixtures and leisure products.

Canada, Sweden

SCOTTS COMPANY

14111 Scottslawn Road

Marysville, OH 43041

Tel: (937) 644-0011 Fax: (937) 644-7244

CEO: Charles Berger, Chmn., Pres.

Rev: $900 mil.

Leading U.S. maker of lawn and garden products.

Netherlands

SDI TECHNOLOGIES

PO Box 2001

Rahway, NJ 07065

Tel: (908) 574-9000 Fax: (908) 579-1716

CEO: Morris Franco, Pres.

FO: Edward Blanco

HR: Ms. G. Zamorski

Emp: 1,300

Radios and electronic products.

Hong Kong, Japan

SEA-LAND SERVICE INC.

6000 Carnegie Boulevard

Charlotte, NC 28209

Tel: (704) 571-2000 Fax: (704) 571-4693

CEO: John P. Clancey, Pres.

HR: William Ryan

Web site: www.sealand.com

Emp: 8,500 Rev: $3,750 mil.

Largest U.S-based containerized transport service; ships, railroads, barge lines and trucking operations.

Austria, Brazil, Canada, Costa Rica, Czech Republic, Denmark, Dominican Republic, Egypt, El Salvador, England, U.K., France, Germany, Greece, Guatemala, Haiti, Honduras, Hong Kong, India, Ireland, Italy, Jamaica, Japan, Malta, Mexico, Netherlands, Nicaragua, Norway, Panama, Philippines, Portugal, Russia, Saudi Arabia, Scotland, U.K., Singapore, Slovenia, South Korea, Spain, Sweden, Switzerland, Taiwan (ROC), Thailand, Trinidad & Tobago, United Arab Emirates, Yugoslavia

SEAGATE TECHNOLOGY, INC.

920 Disc Drive

Scotts Valley, CA 95066

Tel: (408) 438-6550 Fax: (408) 438-7205

CEO: Steve Luczo, Pres.,

FO: Bill Watkins, EVP

HR: Jerald Maurer, SVP

Web site: www.seagate.com

Emp: 86,000 Rev: $6,819 mil.

Develop computer technology, software and hardware.

Australia, Canada, China (PRC), England, U.K., France, Germany, Hong Kong, Indonesia, Ireland, Italy, Japan, Malaysia, Mexico, Netherlands, Northern Ireland, U.K., Scotland, U.K., Singapore, South Korea, Sweden, Taiwan (ROC), Thailand

SEALED AIR CORPORATION

Park 80 Plaza East

Saddle Brook, NJ 07662-5291

Tel: (201) 791-7600 Fax: (201) 703-4205

CEO: William V. Hickey, Pres. & COO

FO: T. J. Dermot Dunphy, Chmn.

HR: Mary A. Coventry, VP

Web site: www.sealedair.com

Emp: 1,600 Rev: $842.8 mil.

Mfr. protective and specialty packaging solutions for industrial, food and consumer products.

Australia, Belgium, Brazil, Canada, China (PRC), England, U.K., Finland, France, Germany, Hong Kong, India, Italy, Japan, Malaysia, Mexico, Netherlands, New Zealand, Norway, Philippines, Singapore, South Korea, Spain, Sweden, Taiwan (ROC), Thailand

SEAMAN CORPORATION

1000 Venture Boulevard

Wooster, OH 44691

Tel: (330) 262-1111 Fax: (330) 263-6950

CEO: Richard N. Seaman, Pres.

FO: John Hugon

Emp: 200

Mfr. vinyl coated fabrics, geomembranes, roofing, pre-engineered structures.

Australia, Belgium

SEAQUIST PERFECT DISPENSING

1160 North Silver Lake Road

Cary, IL 60013

Tel: (847) 639-2124 Fax: (847) 639-2142

CEO: Carl Siebel, Pres.

HR: Rob Revak

Web site: www.seaperf.com

Emp: 650

Mfr. and sale of dispensing systems; lotion pumps and spray-through overcaps.

Australia, Brazil, Canada, China (PRC), England, U.K., France, Germany, Ireland, Italy, Japan, Mexico, Spain, Switzerland

G.D. SEARLE & COMPANY

5200 Old Orchard Road

Skokie, IL 60077

Tel: (847) 982-7000 Fax: (847) 470-1480

CEO: Richard U. DeSchutter, Pres.

FO: Alan L. Heller, COO

HR: Ann K.M. Gualtier

Web site: www.searlehealthnet.com

Emp: 3,351 Rev: $2,407 mil.

Mfr. pharmaceuticals, health care, optical products and specialty chemicals.

Australia, Belgium, Brazil, Canada, Costa Rica, Czech Republic, Denmark, England, U.K., Finland, France, Germany, Greece, Hong Kong, India, Indonesia, Ireland, Italy, Japan, Malaysia, Mexico, Netherlands, New Zealand, Norway, Pakistan, Philippines, Portugal, Singapore, South Africa, South Korea, Spain, Sweden, Switzerland, Taiwan (ROC), Thailand, Venezuela

SEARS ROEBUCK & COMPANY

3333 Beverly Road

Hoffman Estates, IL 60179

Tel: (847) 286-2500 Fax: (800) 427-3049

CEO: Arthur Martinez

HR: Anthony Rucci

Web site: www.sears.com

Emp: 443,000

Diversified general merchandise.

Brazil, Canada, Guatemala, Honduras, Mexico, Panama, Peru, Spain, Venezuela

SEDGWICK, DETERT, MORAN & ARNOLD

One Embarcadero Center, 16th Fl.

San Francisco, CA 94111

Tel: (415) 781-7900 Fax: (415) 781-2635

CEO: David Bordon, Mng. Prtn.

International law firm.

Switzerland

SEI INVESTMENTS COMPANY

1 Freedom Valley Drive

Oaks, PA 19456-1100

Tel: (610) 676-1000 Fax: (610) 676-2995

CEO: Alfred P. West Jr., Chmn.

FO: Henry H. Greer, Pres. & COO

HR: Scott Budge, SVP

Web site: www.seic.com

Emp: 1,133 Rev: $293 mio.

Accounting, evaluation and financial automated systems and services.

Argentina, Canada, England, U.K., Hong Kong, South Africa, Switzerland

SELAS CORPORATION OF AMERICA

2034 S. Limekiln Pike

Dresher, PA 19025

Tel: (215) 646-6600 Fax: (215) 646-3536

CEO: Stephen F. Ryan, Pres.

FO: Christian Bailliart

HR: Robert W. Mason

Emp: 350

Mfr. heat treating equipment for metal, glass, ceramic & chemical industry.

France, Germany, Italy, Japan

SELFIX SEYMOUR INC.

4501 W. 47th Street

Chicago, IL 60632

Tel: (773) 890-1010 Fax: (312) 890-0523

CEO: Jeff Dolan, Pres.

HR: Bob Anderson

Emp: 425

Mfr. plastic household products.

Canada, England, U.K.

SEMTECH CORPORATION

652 Mitchell Road, PO Box 367

Newbury Park, CA 91320

Tel: (805) 498-2111 Fax: (805) 498-3804

CEO: John D. Poe, Chmn.

FO: Zenyk Horbowy, VP Oper.

HR: Georgeann Ballard, Mgr.

Web site: www.semtech.com

Emp: 586 Rev: $102 mil.

Mfr. silicon rectifiers, rectifier assemblies, capacitors, switching regulators, AC/DC converters.

England, U.K., France, Germany, Mexico, Scotland, U.K., Taiwan (ROC)

SENCO PRODUCTS INC.

8485 Broadwell Road

Cincinnati, OH 45244

Tel: (513) 388-2000 Fax: (513) 388-2026

CEO: William Hess, Pres.

FO: John H. Dean

HR: Rick Gerwe

Emp: 1,500

Mfr. industry nailers, staplers, fasteners & accessories.

England, U.K., Germany, Japan, Netherlands, South Korea

SENSORMATIC ELECTRONICS CORPORATION

951 Yamato Road

Boca Raton, FL 33431-0700

Tel: (561) 912-6000 Fax: (561) 989-7774

CEO: Robert A. Vanourek, Pres.

FO: Terry W. Price, SVP

HR: Edward J. O'Brien, VP

Web site: www.sensormatic.com

Emp: 6,500 Rev: $1,025.7 mil.

Electronic article surveillance equipment.

Austria, Belgium, Brazil, France, Germany, Ireland, Spain, Switzerland

SEQUA CORPORATION

200 Park Ave.

New York, NY 10166

Tel: (212) 986-5500 Fax: (212) 370-1969

CEO: John Quicke, Pres.

HR: Jesse Battino, VP

Emp: 9,000

Mfr. aerospace products & systems, machinery & metal coatings, spec chemicals, automotive products.

France, Wales, U.K.

SEQUENT COMPUTER SYSTEMS INC.

15450 SW Koll Pkwy.

Beaverton, OR 97006-6063

Tel: (503) 626-5700 Fax: (503) 578-9890

CEO: Karl C. Powell, Jr., Chmn.

FO: Ronald Wilson, VP

HR: Tom Magas

Web site: www.sequent.com

Emp: 2,818 Rev: $833.9 mil.

Mfr. symmetric multiprocessing technology computers.

Australia, Austria, Belgium, Canada, Czech Republic, England, U.K., France, Germany, Hong Kong, Italy, Japan, Netherlands, New Zealand, Scotland, U.K., Singapore, Switzerland

THE SERVICEMASTER COMPANY

One ServiceMaster Way

Downers Grove, IL 60515-1700

Tel: (630) 271-1300 Fax: (630) 271-2710

CEO: Carlos H. Cantu, Pres.

HR: Patricia Asp, VP

Web site: www.svm.com

Emp: 45,825 Rev: $3,962 mil.

Management service to health care, school and industry facilities; diversified residential and commercial services.

Australia, Austria, Belgium, Canada, Chile, Czech Republic, Denmark, Dominican Republic, England, U.K., Finland, Germany, Hong Kong, Indonesia, Ireland, Japan, Jordan, Lebanon, Malaysia, Mexico, Netherlands, Norway, Philippines, Saudi Arabia, Singapore, South Korea, Spain, Sweden, Taiwan (ROC), Turkey, United Arab Emirates

SERVO CORPORATION OF AMERICA

123 Frost Street

Westbury, NY 11590-5026

Tel: (516) 938-9700 Fax: (516) 938-9644

CEO: Stephen A. Barre, Pres.

Emp: 52

Electronic equipment.

Switzerland

SEWARD & KISSEL

One Battery Park Plaza, 21st Floor

New York, NY 10004

Tel: (212) 574-1200 Fax: (212) 480-8421

CEO: Peter Pront, Mng. Prtn.

International law firm.

Hungary

SEYFARTH, SHAW, FAIRWEATHER & GERALDSON

55 East Monroe Street, Ste. 4200

Chicago, IL 60601

Tel: (312) 346-8000 Fax: (312) 269-8869

CEO: Andrew R. Laidlaw, CEO

HR: Linda Phillips

Web site: www.seyfarth.com

Emp: 1,000 Rev: $130 mil.

International law firm

Belgium

SHAKESPEARE FISHING TACKLE GROUP

3801 Westmore Drive

Columbia, SC 29223

Tel: (803) 754-7000 Fax: (803) 754-7342

CEO: Scott Hogsett, Mgr.

Emp: 275

Mfr. fishing tackle.

Belgium, England, U.K., Germany, Hong Kong, Japan, Netherlands

SHARED MEDICAL SYSTEMS CORPORATION

51 Valley Stream Pkwy

Malvern, PA 19355

Tel: (215) 219-6300 Fax: (215) 219-3124

CEO: Marvin Cadwell, Pres.

FO: Guillermo Ramas

HR: Doug Lawrence

Emp: 4,000

Computer-based information processing for healthcare industry.

England, U.K., Germany, Ireland, Netherlands, Spain

THE SHARPER IMAGE CORPORATION

650 Davis Street

San Francisco, CA 94111

Tel: (415) 445-6000 Fax: (415) 781-5251

CEO: Richard Thalheimer, Chmn.

Web site: www.sharperimage.com

Specialty retailer of innovative products.

Australia, Japan, Saudi Arabia, South Korea, Switzerland

SHEAFFER PEN, INC.

301 Ave. H
Fort Madison, IA 52627
Tel: (319) 372-3300 Fax: (319) 372-7539
CEO: Owen Jones, Pres.
FO: Owen Jones, Pres.
HR: Walter Walz
Emp: 1,400

Mfr. writing instruments.

Canada, England, U.K., France, Germany, Italy, Netherlands

SHEARMAN & STERLING

599 Lexington Ave.
New York, NY 10022-6069
Tel: (212) 848-4000 Fax: (212) 848-7179
CEO: Stephen R. Volk
FO: David A. McCabe
HR: Georgia Gearty
Web site: www.shearman.com
Emp: 620 Rev: $356 mil.

Law firm engaged in general American and international financial and commercial practice.

Canada, China (PRC), England, U.K., France, Germany, Hong Kong, Hungary, Japan, Singapore, Taiwan (ROC), United Arab Emirates

SHELDAHL INC.

1150 Sheldahl Road
Northfield, MN 55057-9444
Tel: (507) 663-8000 Fax: (507) 663-8545
CEO: James E. Donaghy
FO: Edward L. Lundstrom, Pres.
HR: B. M. Brumbaugh
Web site: www.sheldahl.com
Emp: 1,250 Rev: $105 mil.

Mfr. electrical & electronic components & laminated plastic products/adhesive-based tapes & materials & adhesiveless Novaclad®.

China (PRC), France, Japan

SHELDON'S INC.

626 Center Street
Antigo, WI 54409-2496
Tel: (715) 623-2382 Fax: (715) 623-3001
CEO: J. M. Sheldon, Pres.
Emp: 500

Mfr. recreational fishing tackle.

France

SHERWIN-WILLIAMS CO., INC.

101 Prospect Ave., N.W.
Cleveland, OH 44115-1075
Tel: (216) 566-2000 Fax: (216) 566-3312
CEO: John G. Breen, Chmn.
FO: Thomas A. Commes, Pres.
HR: Thomas E. Hopkins, VP
Web site: www.sherwin-williams.com
Emp: 25,000 Rev: $3,000 mil.

Mfr. paint, wallcoverings and related products.

Brazil, Canada, Chile, England, U.K., Jamaica, Mexico, Panama

SHIPLEY CO., INC.

455 Forest Street
Marlborough, MA 01752
Tel: (508) 481-7950 Fax: (508) 485-9113
CEO: Richard Shipley, Pres.
FO: Michael S. Foster
Emp: 1,500 Rev: $400 mil.

Mfr. chemicals for printed circuit boards and microelectronic manufacturing.

Austria, England, U.K., France, Germany, Hong Kong, Japan

SHOOK, HARDY & BACON P.C.

1200 Main Street, 22nd Floor
Kansas City, MO 64105
Tel: (816) 474-6550 Fax: (816) 421-5547
CEO: Patrick McLarney, Mng. Prtn.

International law firm.

England, U.K., Italy, Switzerland

SHOREWOOD PACKAGING CORPORATION

277 Park Ave.
New York, NY 10172
Tel: (212) 371-1500 Fax: (212) 752-5610
CEO: Marc P. Shore, Pres.
Emp: 1,000

Mfr. packaging for video/music industry & consumer products.

Canada, England, U.K.

J.R. SHORT MILLING CO., INC.

500 West Madison Street

Chicago, IL 60661

Tel: (312) 559-5450 Fax: (312) 559-5455

CEO: Jeffrey R. Short, Jr., Pres.

FO: Allen T. Short

Mfr. corn & soybean products, snack pellet products.

Canada

SHURE BROS. INC.

222 Hartrey Ave.

Evanston, IL 60202-3696

Tel: (847) 866-2200 Fax: (847) 866-2279

CEO: S. Lamantia, Pres.

HR: Barbara Goff

Mfr. microphones, teleconferencing systems, circuitry products.

Mexico

SHUTTS & BOWEN

1500 Miami Center, 201 Biscayne Boulevard

Miami, FL 33131

Tel: (305) 358-6300 Fax: (305) 381-9982

CEO: Arnold Berman, Mng. Prtn.

International law firm.

England, U.K., Netherlands

SIDLEY & AUSTIN

One First National Plaza, Ste. 3940

Chicago, IL 60603

Tel: (312) 853-7000 Fax: (312) 853-7036

CEO: E. Eden Martin

HR: Claudia D. Kreditor

Web site: www.sidley.com

Emp: 1,952 Rev: $360 mil.

International law firm.

England, U.K., Japan, Singapore

SIGMA-ALDRICH CORPORATION

3050 Spruce Street

St. Louis, MO 63103

Tel: (314) 771-5765 Fax: (314) 771-5757

CEO: Dr. Carl T. Cori, Chmn.

FO: F. Wicks, Pres.

HR: Terry Colvin

Emp: 1,600

Chemicals and biochemicals, aluminum and structural steel components.

Israel

SIGNODE PACKAGING SYSTEMS

3610 West Lake Ave.

Glenview, IL 60025

Tel: (847) 724-6100 Fax: (847) 657-4392

CEO: Russell M. Flaum, Pres.

FO: Russell M. Flaum

Emp: 3,200

Mfr. packaging systems.

Belgium, Canada, France, Germany, Hong Kong, India, Japan, Kenya, Netherlands, Spain, Taiwan (ROC), Wales, U.K.

SILICON GRAPHICS INC.

2011 N. Shoreline Blvd.

Mountain View, CA 94043-1389

Tel: (650) 960-1980 Fax: (650) 961-0595

CEO: Richard E. Belluzzo, Chmn.

FO: Keith Watson, EVP Intl.Sales

HR: Kirt Froggatt, VP

Web site: www.sgi.com

Emp: 10,300 Rev: $3,000 mil.

Design/mfr. special-effects computer graphic systems and software.

Argentina, Australia, Belgium, Brazil, Brunei, Canada, China (PRC), Czech Republic, Denmark, England, U.K., France, Germany, Hong Kong, Hungary, Indonesia, Israel, Italy, Japan, Luxembourg, Malaysia, Mexico, Netherlands, New Zealand, Norway, Philippines, Singapore, South Africa, South Korea, Sweden, Switzerland, Thailand, Vietnam

SILICON STORAGE TECHNOLOGY, INC.

1171 Sonora Court

Sunnyvale, CA 94086

Tel: (408) 735-9110 Fax: (408) 735-9036

CEO: Bing Yeh, Pres.

FO: Joel J. Camarda, VP Opers.

HR: Humberto Chacon, Supervisor

Web site: www.ssti.com

Emp: 184 Rev: $75 mil.

Mfr. single power supply small ease-block flash memory components, and two-power supply MTP flash products, sold to the PC industry.

England, U.K., Japan

SILICONIX INC.

2201 Laurelwood Drive
Santa Clara, CA 95054
Tel: (408) 988-8000 Fax: (408) 970-3950
CEO: Dr. King Owyang, Pres.
HR: Diane Berg
Emp: 2,280
Semiconductor components.
France, Germany, Hong Kong, Israel, Wales, U.K.

THE SIMCO CO., INC.

2257 N. Penn Road
Hatfield, PA 19440-1998
Tel: (215) 248-2171 Fax:
CEO: Gary Swink
Emp: 400
Mfr. apparatus for electrostatic charge neutralization.
Japan, Netherlands

SIMON & SCHUSTER INC.

1230 Ave. of the Americas
New York, NY 10020
Tel: (212) 698-7000 Fax: (212) 698-7007
CEO: Jonathan Newcomb, Pres
Web site: www.SimonSays.com
Publishes and distributes hardcover and paperback books, audiobooks, software and educational textbooks.
Australia, Brazil, England, U.K., India, Japan, Mexico, Singapore

SIMPLEX

1 Simplex Plaza
Gardner, MA 01441-0001
Tel: (978) 632-2500 Fax: (978) 632-8027
CEO: Edward G. Watkins, Pres.
FO: Michael McBride
HR: bbo hutzel
Emp: 4,050
Mfr./sale/service fire alarm & time control systems.
Australia, Canada, England, U.K., Hong Kong

SIMPLICITY PATTERN CO., INC.

2 Park Ave.
New York, NY 10016
Tel: (212) 372-0500 Fax: (212) 372-0628
CEO: Cary Findley, Chmn.
HR: Sheila Kornbluh
Web site: www.simplicity.com
Dress patterns.
Australia, Canada, England, U.K., Germany, New Zealand, South Africa

J.R. SIMPLOT CO., INC.

One Capital Center,999 Main Street, Ste.#1300
Boise, ID 83702
Tel: (208) 336-2110 Fax: (208) 389-7515
CEO: Stephen A. Beebe, Pres.
HR: Ted Roper, VP
Web site: www.simplot.com
Emp: 12,000 Rev: $2,800 mil.
Fresh/frozen fruits & vegetables, animal feeds, fertilizers.
Australia, Canada, China (PRC), Germany, Mexico

SIMPSON INVESTMENT CO., INC.

1301 Fifth Ave., Ste. 2800
Seattle, WA 98101
Tel: (206) 224-5000 Fax: (206) 224-5060
CEO: F. C. Moseley, Chmn.
HR: Cliff Slade
Emp: 4,500 Rev: $1,500 mil.
Paper, pulp & saw mills, wood products.
Japan

SIMPSON THACHER & BARTLETT

425 Lexington Ave.
New York, NY 10017
Tel: (212) 455-2000 Fax: (212) 455-2502
CEO: Larry Magel, Exec. Dir.
HR: Eric Edelson
Web site: www.simpsonthacher.com
Emp: 450 Rev: $315 mil.
International law Firm.
England, U.K., Hong Kong, Japan, Singapore

SIMS MANUFACTURING CO., INC.

81 E Main Street
Rutland, MA 01543
Tel: (508) 886-6115 Fax: (508) 886-6713
CEO: Robert C. Silvia
Emp: 300 Rev: $25 mil.
Mfg. cabs and ROPS for off-highway vehicles.

machinery & equipment.

Canada

SIZZLER INTERNATIONAL

12655 West Jefferson Boulevard

Los Angeles, CA 90066

Tel: (310) 827-2300 Fax: (310) 822-5786

CEO: Christopher Thomas, Pres.

HR: Kate McGuigan

Sizzler and Kentucky Fried Chicken food chain restaurants

Australia

SKADDEN, ARPS, SLATE, MEAGHER & FLOM LLP

919 Third Ave.

New York, NY 10022

Tel: (212) 735-3000 Fax: (212) 735-2000

CEO: Robert C. Sheehan, Exec. Prtn.

HR: Laurel E. Henschel, Dir.

Web site: www.sasmf.com

Emp: 3,000 Rev: $826 mil.

American/International law practice.

Australia, Belgium, Canada, China (PRC), England, U.K., France, Germany, Hong Kong, Japan, Russia, Singapore

SKIDMORE OWINGS & MERRILL

224 S. Michigan Ave., Ste. 1000

Chicago, IL 60604-2707

Tel: (312) 554-9090 Fax: (312) 360-4545

CEO: John H. Winkler

FO: Joseph Dailey, CFO

HR: Geri Griffith, Dir. Personnel

Web site: www.som.com

Emp: 850 Rev: $88 mil.

Architectural and engineering services.

England, U.K., Hong Kong

SKYTEL INTERNATIONAL

PO Box 2469

Jackson, MS 39225

Tel: (601) 944-1300 Fax: (601) 944-3900

CEO: John Stupka, Pres.

HR: Bob Halbach

Emp: 625

Radio paging services & systems implementation.

Hong Kong, Malaysia, Mexico

SL INDUSTRIES, INC.

520 Fellowship Road, Ste. A114,

Mount Laurel, NJ 08054

Tel: (609) 727-1500 Fax: (609) 727-1683

CEO: Owen Farren, Chmn.

HR: Robin Konzelman, Dir.

Emp: 1,700 Rev: $116 mil.

Design & mfr. electronic protection and power fluctuation devices.

Mexico

SLANT/FIN CORPORATION

100 Forest Drive at East Hills

Greenvale, NY 11548

Tel: (516) 484-2600 Fax: (516) 484-5921

CEO: Donald Brown, Pres.

FO: Peter Tal

HR: Edward Sliwinski

Emp: 350

Mfr. heating & A/C systems & components.

Canada, Israel

SLOAN COMPANY

4835 Colt Street, Ste. B

Ventura, CA 93003-7744

Tel: (805) 875-1123 Fax: (805) 676-3206

CEO: James Sloan, Pres.

Mfr. indicator lights.

Switzerland

WILBUR SMITH ASSOCS

NationsBank Tower, PO Box 92

Columbia, SC 29202

Tel: (803) 758-4500 Fax: (803) 251-2064

CEO: R. A. Hubbard

FO: John W. Bonniville

HR: D. Dantzler

Emp: 662 Rev: $64 mil.

Consulting engineers.

Canada, China (PRC), England, U.K., Hong Kong, India, Thailand, Zimbabwe

A.O. SMITH CORPORATION

11270 West Park Place, PO Box 23972

Milwaukee, WI 53224

Tel: (414) 359-4000 Fax: (414) 359-4064

CEO: Robert J. O'Toole, Chmn. Pres.

FO: A.E. Medice (Europe) & M.J. Cole (Asia)

HR: Edward J. O'Connor, V.P. HR

Web site: www.aosmith.com

Emp: 8,500 Rev: $832 mil.

Auto and truck frames, motors, water heaters, storage/handling systems, plastics, railroad products.

Canada, China (PRC), England, U.K., Ireland, Mexico, Netherlands, Venezuela

SMITH INTERNATIONAL, INC.

16740 Hardy Street

Houston, TX 77032

Tel: (713) 443-3370 Fax: (713) 233-5996

CEO: Douglas L. Rock, Chmn. & Pres.

FO: Al Kite/Bryan Dudman

HR: Peter Nicholson, VP

Web site: www.smith.intl.com

Emp: 6,000 Rev: $1,000 mil.

Mfr. drilling tools and equipment and provides related services for the drilling, completion and production sectors of the petroleum and mining industries.

Australia, Brazil, Canada, France, Germany, Italy, Mexico, Netherlands, Scotland, U.K., Venezuela

THE J. M. SMUCKER COMPANY

One Strawberry Lane

Orrville, OH 44667-0280

Tel: (330) 682-3000 Fax: (330) 684-3370

CEO: Timothy P. Smucker, Chmn.

FO: Charles A. Laine, VP

HR: Robert E. Ellis, VP

Web site: www.smucker.com

Emp: 2,000 Rev: $600 mil.

Mfr. preserves, jellies, ice cream, toppings & peanut butter.

Australia, Canada

SNAP ON DIAGNOSTICS

420 Barclay Boulevard

Lincolnshire, IL 60069

Tel: (847) 478-0700 Fax: (847) 478-7308

CEO: James Lane, Pres.

FO: L. Lange, Supervisor

HR: Cherril Lange

Web site: www.snapon.com

Emp: 1,700 Rev: $230 mil.

Mfr. auto maintenence, diagnostic & emission testing equipment.

Australia, Austria, Belgium, Brazil, Canada, England, U.K., Germany, Mexico, Netherlands

SNAP-ON INC.

2801 80th Street

Kenosha, WI 53141-1410

Tel: (414) 656-5200 Fax: (414) 656-5577

CEO: Robert Cornog, Pres.

FO: Dan Craighead

HR: Donald Lyons

Emp: 7,343

Mfr. automotive & industry maintenance service tools..

Australia, Belgium, Canada, England, U.K., France, Germany, Greece, Japan, Mexico, Netherlands, Scotland, U.K., Singapore, Taiwan (ROC)

SNAP-TITE INC.

2930 W. 22nd Street, PO Box 5051

Erie, PA 16512

Tel: (814) 838-5700 Fax: (814) 838-6382

CEO: George Clark, Pres.

Develop/mfr. laboratory, scientific and research instrumentation.

France, Ireland

SOCOTAB LEAF TOBACCO CO., INC.

342 Madison Ave.

New York, NY 10173-0899

Tel: (212) 687-2590 Fax: (212) 983-6386

CEO: H. S. Wertheimer, Pres.

Emp: 31

Tobacco dealer.

Greece, Switzerland, Turkey

SOLECTRON CORPORATION

777 Gibraltar Drive

Milpitas, CA 95035

Tel: (408) 957-8500 Fax: (408) 956-6075

CEO: Koichi Nishimura, Chmn.

FO: David Kynaston, Pres. Europe

HR: Tom Morelli, VP

Web site: www.solectron.com

Emp: 18,000 Rev: $3,600 mil.

Provides contract manufacturing services to equipment manufacturers.

Brazil, China (PRC), France, Germany, Ireland, Japan, Malaysia, Mexico, Romania, Scotland, U.K., Sweden, Taiwan (ROC)

SONESTA INTERNATIONAL HOTELS CORPORATION

200 Clarendon Street

Boston, MA 02166

Tel: (617) 421-5400 Fax: (617) 421-5402

CEO: Roger P. Sonnabend. CEO

HR: Jacqueline Sonnabend

Web site: www.sonesta.com

Hotels, resorts, and Nile cruises..

Anguilla, Aruba, Bahrain, Bermuda, Chile, Egypt

SONOCO PRODUCTS COMPANY

North Second Street, PO Box 160

Hartsville, SC 29550

Tel: (803) 383-7000 Fax: (803) 383-7008

CEO: Charles W. Coker, Chmn.

FO: Peter C. Browning, Pres.

HR: Cynthia A. Hartley, V.P.

Web site: www.sonoco.com

Emp: 20,000 Rev: $2,800 mil.

Mfr. packaging for consumer & industrial market and recycled paperboard.

Argentina, Australia, Belgium, Brazil, Canada, China (PRC), Colombia, England, U.K., France, Germany, Greece, Hong Kong, Indonesia, Italy, Japan, Malaysia, Mexico, Netherlands, New Zealand, Northern Ireland, U.K., Norway, Scotland, U.K., Singapore, Spain, Switzerland, Taiwan (ROC), Thailand, Venezuela

SOUTHERN COMPANY

270 Peachtree Street

Atlanta, GA 30303

Tel: (404) 506-5000 Fax: (404) 506-0642

CEO: A. W. Dahlberg, Pres.

HR: Robert Bell

Web site: www.southernco.com

Electric utility.

Argentina, Bahamas, Brazil, Chile, England, U.K., Germany, Hong Kong, Pakistan, Philippines, Trinidad & Tobago

SOUTHWESTERN PETROLEUM CORPORATION

534 North Main

Fort Worth, TX 76106

Tel: (817) 332-2336 Fax: (817) 877-4047

CEO: Art Dickerson, Chmn.

HR: Rachel Newman

Emp: 150

Mfr. roofing/building maintenance products and industry lubricants.

Belgium, Canada

SPALDING ETONIC WORLDWIDE

425 Meadow Street

Chicopee, MA 01021

Tel: (413) 536-1200 Fax: (413) 535-2746

CEO: Kevin Martin, Pres.

Emp: 2,683

Mfr. sports equipment and infant and juvenile furniture and accessories.

Australia, Canada, England, U.K., France, Germany, Italy, Japan, New Zealand, Sweden

SPARKLER FILTERS INC.

PO Box 19

Conroe, TX 77305-0019

Tel: (409) 756-4471 Fax: (409) 539-1165

CEO: James T. Reneau, Jr.

FO: Jose M. Sentmanat

HR: Robert Thompson

Emp: 91

Mfr. liquid filtration systems.

Germany, Netherlands

SPARTAN CHEMICAL COMPANY

110 North Westwood Ave.

Toledo, OH 43607

Tel: (419) 531-5551 Fax: (419) 536-8423

CEO: Thomas J. Swigart, Chmn.

Emp: 200 Rev: $5,500 mil.

Mfr. soaps & detergents; industrial & specialty chemicals.

Brazil

SPARTAN INTERNATIONAL INC.

1845 Cedar Street

Holt, MI 48842

Tel: (517) 694-3911 Fax: (517) 694-7952

CEO: Brant Krauss

HR: Vicki Nichols

Emp: 285 Rev: $51 mil.

Plastic products and commercial printing.

Canada

SPECTOR GROUP

3111 New Hyde Park Road

North Hills, NY 11040

Tel: (516) 365-4240 Fax: (516) 365-3604

CEO: Michael H. Spector, Pres.

FO: Charles A. Croigny

Emp: 71

Arch and interior design services.

Belgium

SPEIZMAN INDUSTRIES INC.

508 West Fifth Street, PO Box 31215

Charlotte, NC 28231

Tel: (704) 372-3751 Fax: (704) 376-3153

CEO: Robert S. Speizman, Pres.

FO: Leana Stewart

Emp: 49

Sale/service textile machinery and components.

Canada, Mexico

SPENCER STUART & ASSOCIATES INC.

401 North Michigan Ave., Ste. 3400

Chicago, IL 60611

Tel: (312) 822-0080 Fax: (312) 822-0116

CEO: Joseph E. Griesedieck Jr.

FO: John Mumm, Mng. Dir.

HR: John Mumm, Mng. Dir.

Web site: www.spencerstuart.com

Emp: 240 Rev: $239 mil.

Executive recruitment firm.

Argentina, Australia, Austria, Belgium, Brazil, Canada, Chile, China (PRC), Colombia, Czech Republic, England, U.K., France, Germany, Hong Kong, Hungary, Italy, Japan, Mexico, Netherlands, Singapore, South Africa, Spain, Switzerland

SPERRY-SUN DRILLING

3000 North Sam Houston Pkwy. East

Houston, TX 77032

Tel: (281) 871-5100 Fax: (281) 871-5742

CEO: Rod Clark, Pres.

HR: Murray Colgen

Emp: 1,025

Oilfield service.

Saudi Arabia, United Arab Emirates

SPI PHARMACEUTICALS INC.

ICN Plaza, 3300 Hyland Ave.

Costa Mesa, CA 92626

Tel: (714) 545-0100 Fax: (714) 641-7215

CEO: Adam Terney, Pres.

FO: Bill MacDonald

HR: Cindy Burns

Emp: 6,072

Mfr. pharmaceuticals, biochemicals and radioactive materials.

Canada, Mexico, Netherlands, Spain, Yugoslavia

SPIRAX SARCO, INC.

1951 Glenwood Street, SW

Allentown, PA 18103

Tel: (610) 797-5860 Fax: (610) 433-1346

CEO: Anthony Mauriello, Pres..

HR: Sam Cappello, VP

Web site: www.spiraxsarco-usa.com

Emp: 3,500

Mfr. industrial steam system equipment, including valves, pumps, traps, controls, regulators, meter, filters and accessories.

Brazil

SPIROL INTERNATIONAL CORPORATION

30 Rock Ave.

Danielson, CT 06239

Tel: (203) 774-8571 Fax: (203) 774-0487

CEO: James C. Shaw

HR: Patricia Chenail, HR Mgr.

Web site: www.spirol.com

Emp: 500

Mfr. engineered fasteners, shims, automation equipment.

Canada, England, U.K., France, Mexico

SPRAGUE DEVICES INC.

PO Box 389

Michigan City, IN 46361

Tel: (219) 872-7295 Fax: (219) 879-6998

CEO: Jim Davis, Pres.

HR: Joe Algozine, Dir.

Emp: 282

Mfr. heavy duty windshield wiper/washer systems and components.

Mexico

SPRAYING SYSTEMS COMPANY

PO Box 7900

Wheaton, IL 60188

Tel: (630) 665-5000 Fax: (630) 260-0842

CEO: James Bramsen, Pres.

HR: Mr. Yehling

Emp: 1,000

Fabricated metal products.

Germany, Japan, Switzerland

SPRINGS INDUSTRIES INC.

205 N. White Street, PO Box 70

Fort Mill, SC 29716

Tel: (803) 547-1500 Fax: (803) 547-1772

CEO: Ms. Crandall Bowles, Pres.

FO: Derick S. Close, VP Int'l.Sales

HR: Mario Putzrath

Web site: www.springs.com

Emp: 24,500

Mfr. and sales of home furnishings, finished fabrics and industry textiles.

Canada, Hong Kong, Mexico

SPRINT INTERNATIONAL

World Headquarters, 2330 Shawnee Mission Parkway

Westwood, KS 66205

Tel: (913) 624-3000 Fax: (913) 624-3281

CEO: William T. Esrey, Chmn.

FO: Gary D. Forsee, Pres.

HR: I. Benjamin Watson

Emp: 50,000 Rev: $14,000 mil.

Telecommunications equipment & services.

Australia, Belgium, Brazil, Canada, England, U.K., Hong Kong, Italy, Japan, Mexico, Russia, South Korea, Vietnam

SPS TECHNOLOGIES INC.

301 Highland Avenue

Jenkintown, PA 19046-2630

Tel: (215) 517-2000 Fax: (215) 517-2032

CEO: Charles W. Grigg, Pres.

Emp: 4,500

Mfr. aerospace & industry fasteners, tightening systems, magnetic materials, superalloys.

Australia, Brazil, Canada, England, U.K., Germany, India, Ireland, Italy, Japan, Mexico, Spain

SPSS INC.

444 N. Michigan Ave.

Chicago, IL 60611

Tel: (312) 329-2400 Fax: (312) 329-3668

CEO: Jack Noonan, Pres.

FO: Ian S. Durrell

HR: Cynthia Schnierle

Emp: 325

Mfr. statistical software.

Australia, England, U.K., Germany, India, Japan, Netherlands, Singapore, Sweden

SPX CORPORATION

700 Terrace Point Drive, PO Box 3301

Muskegon, MI 49443-3301

Tel: (616) 724-5000 Fax: (616) 724-5720

CEO: John B. Blystone, Chmn.

FO: Thomas J. Riordan, Pres.

HR: Stephen A. Lison, VP

Web site: www.spx.com

Emp: 4,593 Rev: $922 mil.

Mfr. Auto parts, special service tools, engine & drive-train parts.

Australia, Brazil, Canada, England, U.K., France, Germany, Italy, Japan, Mexico, Netherlands, Singapore, Spain, Switzerland

SQUIRE, SANDERS & DEMPSEY

4900 Society Center, 127 Public Square

Cleveland, OH 44114-1304

Tel: (216) 479-8500 Fax: (216) 479-8780

CEO: R. Thomas Stanton, Chmn.

HR: Jeffrey P. Hunter

Web site: www.ssd.com

Emp: 1,200 Rev: $145 mil.

International law firm.

Belgium, Czech Republic, England, U.K., Hong Kong, Hungary, Russia, Slovakia, Spain, Taiwan (ROC), Ukraine

SRI INTERNATIONAL

333 Ravenswood Ave.
Menlo Park, CA 94025-3493
Tel: (650) 859-2000 Fax: (650) 326-5512
CEO: William P. Sommers, Chmn.
FO: Allen M. Phipps
HR: Stephen B. McElfresh
Emp: 2,321
International consulting & research.
Australia, England, U.K., Italy, Japan, South Korea, Switzerland

THE ST. PAUL COMPANIES, INC.
385 Washington Street
St. Paul, MN 55102
Tel: (612) 310-7911 Fax: (612) 310-8294
CEO: Douglas W. Leatherdale, Chmn.
FO: Patrick A. Thiele, Pres. Intl.
Web site: www.stpaul.com
Emp: 14,000 Rev: $6,200 mil.
Provides investment, insurance and reinsurance services.
Argentina, Australia, Austria, Belgium, Botswana, Brazil, Canada, Chile, Colombia, Cyprus, Denmark, Ecuador, England, U.K., Fiji, Finland, France, Germany, Ghana, Greece, Guam, Hong Kong, Hungary, Iceland, India, Indonesia, Ireland, Italy, Japan, Kenya, Latvia, Lesotho, Luxembourg, Malaysia, Mexico, Morocco, Netherlands, Netherlands Antilles, New Zealand, Nigeria, Norway, Oman, Panama, Papua New Guinea, Peru, Philippines, Poland, Portugal, Romania, Russia, Saudi Arabia, Sierra Leone, Singapore, South Africa, South Korea, Spain, Sri Lanka, Surinam, Sweden, Switzerland, Taiwan (ROC), Thailand, Trinidad & Tobago, Tunisia, Turkey, United Arab Emirates, Venezuela

STA-RITE INDUSTRIES INC.
293 Wright Street
Delavan, WI 53115
Tel: (414) 728-5551 Fax: (414) 728-7323
CEO: Jim Donnelly
FO: Danis Gagnon
HR: Tom Schumann
Web site: www.starite.com
Emp: 1,800 Rev: $306 mil.
Mfr. water pumps, filters and systems.
Australia, France, Germany, Italy, Mexico, New Zealand

STALEY MFG. COMPANY __ A.E.
RR 4, Box 950
Houlton, ME 04730
Tel: (207) 532-9523 Fax: (207) 532-2572
CEO: Larry H. Cunningham, Pres.
HR: Margaret Sue Cassidy
Emp: 1,500
Mfr corn products, food and industrial starches and corn sweeteners.
Thailand

STANDARD & POOR'S CORPORATION
25 Broadway
New York, NY 10004
Tel: (212) 208-8000 Fax: (212) 410-0200
CEO: Harold W. McGraw, III, Chmn.
HR: Pat Palvaski, Dir.
Investment, finance, economic, mutual funds data and marketing information.
Australia, Japan, Philippines, Taiwan (ROC)

STANDARD COMMERCIAL CORPORATION
PO Box 450
Wilson, NC 27893
Tel: (919) 291-5507 Fax: (919) 237-1109
CEO: Marvin W. Coghill, Pres.
Emp: 6,500
Leaf tobacco dealers/processors and wool processors.
Australia, Brazil, Canada, Denmark, England, U.K., Germany, Greece, Malawi, South Korea, Switzerland, Thailand, Turkey, Zimbabwe

STANDARD MICROSYSTEMS CORPORATION
80 Arkay Drive
Hauppauge, NY 11788
Tel: (516) 435-6000 Fax: (516) 273-5550
CEO: Paul Richman
Emp: 850 Rev: $342 mil.
Telecommunications systems.
England, U.K., France

STANDARD PRODUCTS COMPANY
2401 South Gulley Road
Dearborn, MI 48124
Tel: (313) 561-1100 Fax: (313) 561-6526

CEO: Ronald L. Roudebush, Vice Chmn.

FO: James F. Keys, EVP

HR: John C. Brandmahl, VP

Web site: www.stdproducts.com

Emp: 10,350 Rev: $1,108 mil.

Mfr. molded & extruded rubber & plastic products for automotive & appliance industry, retread tire industry.

Brazil, Canada, England, U.K., France, India, Japan, Mexico, Poland, South Korea, Wales, U.K.

STANDEX INTERNATIONAL CORPORATION

6 Manor Parkway

Salem, NH 03079

Tel: (603) 893-9701 Fax: (603) 893-7324

CEO: Edward J. Trainor, Pres.

FO: David R. Crichton, EVP

HR: James L. Mettling

Web site: www.standex.com

Emp: 5,500 Rev: $616 mil.

Mfr. diversified graphics, institutional, industry/electronic & consumer products.

Australia, Canada, England, U.K., France, Germany, Ireland, Italy, Mexico, Norway, Portugal, Singapore, Spain, Sweden

STANLEY BOSTITCH INC.

815 Briggs Street

East Greenwich, RI 02818

Tel: (401) 884-2500 Fax: (401) 885-6511

CEO: Raymond Martino, Pres.

FO: O. J. Penden

Emp: 3,000

Mfr. stapling machines, stapling supplies, fastening systems & wire.

Australia, Belgium, Canada, England, U.K., France, Germany, Mexico, Spain, Switzerland

STANLEY CONSULTANTS, INC.

Stanley Building, 225 Iowa Ave.

Muscatine, IA 52761-3764

Tel: (319) 264-6600 Fax: (319) 264-6658

CEO: Gregs G. Thomopulos

FO: James A. Hollatz, SVP Intl.

HR: Karen J. Diercks

Web site: www.stanleygroup.com

Emp: 539

Engineering, architectural, planning & management services.

Botswana, Egypt, Jamaica, Jordan, Kuwait, United Arab Emirates

THE STANLEY WORKS

1000 Stanley Drive, PO Box 7000

New Britain, CT 06053

Tel: (860) 225-5111 Fax: (860) 827-3987

CEO: John M. Trani, Chmn.

FO: Stef Kranendijk, Pres.

HR: Mark J. Mathieu, VP

Web site: www.stanleyworks.com

Emp: 18,000 Rev: $2,670 mil.

Mfr. hand tools & hardware.

Australia, Belgium, Brazil, Canada, Colombia, Denmark, England, U.K., Finland, France, Germany, Greece, Hong Kong, Italy, Mexico, Netherlands, New Zealand, Norway, Philippines, Poland, Portugal, Reunion, Singapore, Taiwan (ROC)

STAPLES, INC.

One Research Drive

Westborough, MA 01581

Tel: (508) 370-8500 Fax: (508) 370-8955

CEO: Thomas G. Stemberg, Chmn.

FO: John C. Bingleman, Pres.

HR: Susan S. Hoyt, EVP

Web site: www.staples.com

Emp: 30,000 Rev: $5,100 mil

Superstore for office supplies and equipment.

Canada, England, U.K., Germany

STAPLING MACHINES COMPANY

41 Pine Street

Rockaway, NJ 07866

Tel: (973) 627-4400 Fax: (973) 627-5355

CEO: Wade Howle, Pres.

HR: Tracy O'Leary

Emp: 76

Mfr. wirebound box making machinery for fruit/vegetable industry and industrial applications.

Netherlands

STARBUCKS COFFEE CORPORATION

PO Box 34067

Seattle, WA 98124

Tel: (206) 447-4127 Fax: (206) 682-7570

CEO: Howard Schultz, Chmn.

HR: Sharon Elliott, VP

Emp: 25,000 Rev: $1,000 mil.

Coffee bean retail store and coffee bars.

Canada, England, U.K., Japan, New Zealand, Philippines, Singapore, South Korea, Taiwan (ROC), Thailand

STATE FARM INSURANCE COMPANY

1 State Farm Plaza

Bloomington, IL 61710-0001

Tel: (309) 766-2311 Fax: (309) 766-6169

CEO: Edward B. Rust, Jr., Pres.

FO: Dr. Wayne W. Sorenson

HR: John Coffey, HR

Web site: www.statefarm.com

Sales of automobile, life, health and homeowners insurance.

Canada

STATE STREET BANK & TRUST COMPANY

225 Franklin Street

Boston, MA 02101

Tel: (617) 786-3000 Fax: (617) 654-3386

CEO: Marshall N. Carter, Chmn,

FO: Jacques-Philippe Marson

HR: Trevor Lukes, SVP

Web site: www.statestreet.com

Emp: 14,000

Banking & financial services.

Australia, Austria, Belgium, Canada, Cayman Islands, Chile, China (PRC), Denmark, England, U.K., France, Germany, Hong Kong, Japan, Luxembourg, Netherlands Antilles, New Zealand, Singapore, Taiwan (ROC), United Arab Emirates

STEARNS CATALYTIC DIV OF UNITED ENGINEERS & CONSTRUCTORS

30 S. 17th Street

Philadelphia, PA 19103

Tel: (215) 422-3000 Fax: (215) 422-4648

CEO: Shay D. Assad,Pres.

FO: W. J. Osborne

HR: J. W. Renouf

Emp: 945

Engineering & construction.

England, U.K.

STEBBINS ENGINEERING & MFG. COMPANY

363 Eastern Boulevard

Watertown, NY 13601

Tel: (315) 782-3000 Fax: (315) 782-0481

CEO: A. Calligrais, Pres.

Emp: 1,500

Engineering and construction.

Canada

STEELCASE INC.

901 44th Street SE

Grand Rapids, MI 49508

Tel: (616) 247-2710 Fax: (616) 248-7010

CEO: James Hackett, Pres.

FO: Jerry K Myers

HR: Roger Martin

Emp: 20,700

Mfr. office, computer-support & systems furniture.

France, Japan

STEINER COMPANY

One East Superior Street

Chicago, IL 60611

Tel: (312) 642-1242 Fax: (312) 642-0226

CEO: Guy Marchesi, Pres.

Emp: 20

Soap and towel dispensers.

France, Germany, Indonesia, Italy, Japan, Switzerland

STEINER CORPORATION

505 East South Temple Street

Salt Lake City, UT 84102

Tel: (801) 328-8831 Fax: (801) 363-5680

CEO: Richard R. Steiner, Pres.

FO: Marvin Priske

Emp: 9,000 Rev: $500 mil

Linen supply service.

Argentina, Australia, Brazil, Canada, England, U.K., France, Germany, Japan, Mexico, South Africa, Spain, Switzerland

STEINWAY & SONS

1 Steinway Place

Long Island City, NY 11105

Tel: (718) 721-2600 Fax: (718) 932-4332

CEO: Bruce Stevens

FO: Thomas Kurrer, Mng. Dir.

Web site: www.steinway.com

Emp: 1,000 Rev: $150 mil.

Mfr./mktg. pianos.

Germany, Japan

STEMCO INC.

PO Box 1989

Longview, TX 75606

Tel: (903) 758-9981 Fax: (903) 232-3508

CEO: Mike Leslie

FO: Jim Reis

HR: George Kerekes

Web site: www.stemco.com

Emp: 635

Mfr. seals, hubcaps, hubodometers and locking nuts for heavy duty trucks, buses, trailers.

Canada, England, U.K.

STEPAN COMPANY

22 West Frontage Road

Northfield, IL 60093

Tel: (847) 446-7500 Fax: (847) 501-2443

CEO: F. Quinn Stepan, Pres.

HR: Craig O. Gardiner

Mfr. basic intermediate chemicals.

Canada, Colombia, France, Hong Kong, Malaysia, Mexico

STEPTOE & JOHNSON

1330 Connecticut Aveue

Washington, DC 20036

Tel: (202) 429-3000 Fax: (202) 429-3902

CEO: Lon Bonknight, CEO

HR: Patrick Peters

Web site: www.steptoe.com

Emp: 650 Rev: $96 mil.

International law firm.

Kazakhstan, Russia, Ukraine

STERIS CORPORATION

5960 Heisley Road

Mentor, OH 44060

Tel: (440) 354-2600 Fax: (440) 639-4459

CEO: Will Sanford, Pres.

FO: James Dunlavey

HR: Rosanne Kay

Emp: 3,500 Rev: $500 mil.

Mfr. sterilization/infection control equipment, surgical tables, lighting systems for health, pharmaceutical & scientific industries.

Brazil, England, U.K., Finland, Hong Kong, Japan

STERLING SOFTWARE INC.

1800 Alexander Bell Drive

Reston, VA 22091

Tel: (703) 264-8000 Fax: (703) 264-0762

CEO: Sterling L. Williams, Jr.

FO: Clive Smith, VP Int'l.

Emp: 4,000 Rev: $600 mil.

Sales/service software products; technical services.

Australia, Brazil, Canada, England, U.K., France, Germany, Italy, Japan, Norway

STEWART & STEVENSON SERVICES INC.

2707 North Loop West

Houston, TX 77008

Tel: (713) 868-7700 Fax: (713) 868-7692

CEO: Robert L. Hargrave, Pres.

Emp: 2,400

Design/mfr. customized diesel power systems.

Venezuela

STIEFEL LABORATORIES INC.

255 Alhambra Circle, Ste. 1000

Coral Gables, FL 33134

Tel: (305) 443-3807 Fax: (305) 443-3467

CEO: Charles W. Stiefel, Pres.

FO: Herbert A. Stiefel

HR: Matt S. Pattullo

Emp: 1,460

Mfr. pharmaceuticals, dermatological specialties.

Argentina, Australia, Belgium, Brazil, Canada, Cayman Islands, Chile, Colombia, Egypt, England, U.K., France, Germany, Greece, Ireland, Italy, Japan, Mexico, Morocco, Pakistan, Philippines, Poland, Portugal, Singapore, South Africa, South Korea, Spain, Taiwan (ROC), Thailand, Venezuela

STOKES VACUUM INC.

5500 Tabor Road

Philadelphia, PA 19120

Tel: (215) 831-5400 Fax: (215) 831-5420

CEO: Joel McFadden

FO: Graham T. Legge

HR: James Hughes

Web site: www.stokesvac.com

Vacuum pumps and components, vacuum dryers, oil-upgrading equipment and metallizers.

Argentina, Australia, China (PRC), England, U.K., France, Hong Kong, India, Israel, Japan, Mexico, Peru, Philippines, Singapore, South Korea, Taiwan (ROC)

STONE & WEBSTER ENGINEERING CORPORATION

245 Summer Street

Boston, MA 02210-2288

Tel: (617) 589-5111 Fax: (617) 589-2156

CEO: H. Kerner Smith, Chmn.

FO: Faud Koseoglu

HR: Patrick Shields

Emp: 6,100 Rev: $1,322.5 mil.

Engineering, construction, environmental and management services.

Canada, England, U.K., Indonesia, Malaysia, Saudi Arabia, South Korea, Taiwan (ROC), Thailand

STONE CONTAINER CORPORATION

150 N. Michigan Ave.

Chicago, IL 60601-7568

Tel: (312) 346-6600 Fax: (312) 580-3486

CEO: Roger W. Stone, Chmn.

FO: John D. Bence, SVP

HR: Gayle M. Sparapani, VP

Web site: www.stonecontainer.com

Emp: 24,600 Rev: $4,850 mil.

Mfr. paper and paper packaging.

Argentina, Belgium, Canada, Chile, China (PRC), Colombia, Costa Rica, England, U.K., France, Germany, Japan, Mexico, Netherlands, Spain, Venezuela

STORAGE TECHNOLOGY CORPORATION

2270 S. 88th Street

Louisville, CO 80028-0001

Tel: (303) 673-5151 Fax: (303) 673-5019

CEO: David Weiss, Pres.

FO: Bruce Taafe, VP

HR: Laurie Dodd

Emp: 11,000

Mfr./market/service information, storage and retrieval systems.

Australia, Belgium, Canada, Denmark, England, U.K., Finland, France, Germany, Italy, Japan, Netherlands, Norway, Sweden, Switzerland

STOTSENBURG & STOTSENBURG

757 Third Avenue

New York, NY 10017

Tel: (212) 595-5963 Fax: (212) 755-6155

CEO: John C. Stotsenburg, Mng. Prtn.

International law firm.

England, U.K.

STREAM INTERNATIONAL

275 Dan Road

Canton, MA 02021

Tel: (781) 575-6800 Fax: (781) 575-6999

CEO: Stephen D. R. Moore, Chmn.

FO: Judith G. Salerno, Pres.

HR: Lewis Legon, VP

Web site: ww.steam.com

Emp: 5,000 Rev: $185 mil.

Provider of outsourced technical support for major computer industry companies.

England, U.K., France, Germany, Ireland, Japan, Netherlands

STRUCTURAL DYNAMICS RESEARCH CORPORATION

2000 Eastman Drive

Milford, OH 45150-2789

Tel: (513) 576-2400 Fax:

CEO: William Weyand

Web site: www.sdrc.com

Emp: 1,900 Rev: $351 mil.

Developer of software used in Modeling esting, drafting and manufacturing.

Australia, Brazil, Canada, China (PRC), England, U.K., France, Germany, India, Italy, Japan, Netherlands, Singapore, South Korea, Spain, Sweden, Switzerland

STUART ENTERTAINMENT INC.

3211 Nebraska Ave.

Council Bluffs, IA 51501

Tel: (712) 323-1488 Fax: (712) 323-3215

CEO: Timothy R. Stuart, Pres.

FO: Clement Chantiam, VP

HR: Victoria Lindsey

Web site: www.bingoking.com

Emp: 400 Rev: $125 mil.

Mfg. bingo equipment and supplies, lottery tickets & video gaming machines.

Brazil, Canada, Mexico

SUBMICRON SYSTEMS

6330 Hedgewood Drive, Ste. 150

Allentown, PA 18106

Tel: (610) 391-9200 Fax: (610) 391-1982

CEO: David J. Ferran, Pres.

FO: David W. Dedman, EVP

Web site: www.subm.com

Emp: 650 Rev: $97.9 mil.

Mfr./sales wet surface preparation and cleaning equipment.

France

SUDLER & HENNESSEY

1633 Broadway, 25th Fl.

New York, NY 10019

Tel: (212) 969-5800 Fax: (212) 969-5996

CEO: Jed A. Beitler, Pres.

FO: Brian Harris

HR: Rosa Lombardo

Emp: 370

Healthcare products advertising.

Australia, Canada, England, U.K., France, Germany, Italy, Japan, Switzerland

SUGHRUE, MION, ZINN, MACPEAK & SEAS PLLC

2100 Pennsylvania Ave., NW Ste. 800

Washington, DC 20037-3202

Tel: (202) 293-7060 Fax: (202) 293-7860

CEO: Neil Siegel, Mng. Ptnr.

FO: Jody Rosenberg, Dir.

HR: Susan Magee, Dir.

Web site: www.sughrue.com

Emp: 185

International law firm.

Japan

SULLAIR CORPORATION

3700 E. Michigan Blvd.

Michigan City, IN 46360

Tel: (219) 879-5451 Fax: (219) 874-1273

CEO: Ed Laprade, Pres.

HR: ST

Emp: 1,200

Refrigeration systems, vacuum pumps, generators, etc.

Argentina, Australia, Brazil, England, U.K., France, Germany, Hong Kong, Malaysia, Mexico, Netherlands, New Zealand, Norway, Peru, Singapore, Taiwan (ROC)

SULLIVAN & CROMWELL

125 Broad Street

New York, NY 10004-2498

Tel: (212) 558-4000 Fax: (212) 558-3588

CEO: Ricardo Mestres Jr.

HR: Maria S. Alkiewicz, Dir.

Web site: www.sullcrom.com

Emp: 2,000 Rev: $395 mil.

International law firm.

Australia, England, U.K., France, Germany, Hong Kong, Japan

SUMMIT INDUSTRIAL CORPORATION

600 Third Ave.

New York, NY 10016

Tel: (212) 490-1100 Fax: (212) 949-6328

CEO: P. M. Yen

FO: Leonard Chan

Pharmaceuticals, agricultural and chemical products.

Hong Kong, Japan, Malaysia, South Korea, Taiwan (ROC)

SUMMIT TECHNOLOGY INC.

21 Hickory Drive

Waltham, MA 02154

Tel: (781) 890-1234 Fax: (781) 890-0313

CEO: Vern Sharma, Pres.

Emp: 150

Mfr. medical lasers.

Ireland

SUN INTERNATIONAL, INC.

1415 East Sunrise Blvd.

Fort Lauderdale, FL 33304

Tel: (954) 713-2500 Fax: (954) 713-2019

CEO: Kevin Desanctis, Pres.

Emp: 7,000

Ownership, development and operation of resort complexes.

Bahamas

SUN MICROSYSTEMS, INC.

901 San Antonio Road

Palo Alto, CA 94303

Tel: (650) 960-1300 Fax: (650) 856-2114

CEO: Scott G. McNealy, Chmn. & Pres.

FO: Joseph P. Roebuck, VP

HR: Kenneth M. Alvares, VP

Web site: www.sun.com

Emp: 20,000 Rev: $8,000 mil.

Computer peripherals and programming services.

Brazil, England, U.K., France, Germany, Ireland, Italy, Netherlands, Spain, Sweden

SUNBEAM CORPORATION

1615 South Congress Ave.

Delray Beach, FL 33445

Tel: (561) 243-2100 Fax: (561) 243-2218

CEO: Jerry W. Levin, Pres.

HR: Gary Mask

Web site: www.sunbeam.com

Emp: 8,000

Mfr. household and personal grooming appliances.

Canada, Germany, Mexico

SUNDSTRAND CORPORATION

PO Box 7003

Rockford, IL 61125-7003

Tel: (815) 226-6000 Fax: (815) 226-2699

CEO: Robert H. Jenkins, Pres.

HR: Patrick Winn

Web site: www.snds.com

Emp: 10,300

Design/mfr. proprietary technology based components and sub-systems for aerospace industry.

Belgium, France, Japan, Singapore

SUNDT INTERNATIONAL

PO Box 26685

Tucson, AZ 85726

Tel: (520) 748-7555 Fax: (520) 747-9673

CEO: Wilson Sundt, Pres.

Holding company.

Australia, Philippines, Saudi Arabia

SUNKIST GROWERS INC.

14130 Riverside Drive

Van Nuys, CA 91423

Tel: (818) 986-4800 Fax: (818) 379-7405

CEO: Russell L. Hanlin, Pres.

HR: John R. McGovern, VP

Web site: www.sunkist.com

Emp: 800 Rev: $1,050 mil.

Fruits & vegetables.

Hong Kong, Japan, Switzerland

SUNRISE MEDICAL INC.

2382 Faraday Ave., Ste. 200

Carlsbad, CA 92008

Tel: (760) 930-1500 Fax: (760) 930-1580

CEO: Richard H. Chandler, Pres.

HR: Deborah Beasley

Emp: 3,500

Mfr. medical appliances & supplies, furniture.

Canada, England, U.K., Japan

SUNSHINE MINING & REFINING COMPANY

877 West Main Street, Ste. 600

Boise, ID 83702

Tel: (208) 345-0660 Fax: (208) 342-0004

CEO: John S. Simko, Pres. & Chmn.

FO: Harry F. Cougher, SVP

HR: Lawrence F. Jeffries

Web site: www.sunshinemining.com

Emp: 300 Rev: $28 mil.

Mines and refines silver, copper, antimony and lead.

Argentina

SUPERIOR GRAPHITE COMPANY

120 S. Riverside Plaza

Chicago, IL 60606

Tel: (312) 559-2999 Fax: (312) 559-9064

CEO: Peter Roy Carney, Chmn.

Emp: 270

Mfr. natural and synthetic graphites, electrodes, lubricants, suspensions, carbide and carbon.

Canada, England, U.K., Sweden

SUPERIOR INDUSTRIES INTERNATIONAL INC.

7800 Woodley Ave.

Van Nuys, CA 91406-1788

Tel: (818) 781-4973 Fax: (818) 780-5631

CEO: Louis L. Borick

HR: James L. Walker

Emp: 4,500

Mfr. cast aluminum auto wheels & auto accessories.

Hungary, Mexico

SUPERIOR TUBE COMPANY

3900 Germantown Pike

Collegeville, PA 19426

Tel: (610) 489-5200 Fax: (610) 489-5252

CEO: Donald C.Reilly, Pres.

Emp: 1,200

Seamless tubes.

England, U.K.

SUPRA PRODUCTS INC.

2611 Pringle Road SE

Salem, OR 97302-1594

Tel: (503) 581-9101 Fax: (503) 364-1285

CEO: Soren Vestergaard

FO: Greg Burge

HR: Michelle Neal

Emp: 185

Mfr. lockboxes.

Canada

SURGICAL APPLIANCE INDUSTRIES INC.

3960 Rosslyn Drive

Cincinnati, OH 45209

Tel: (513) 271-4594 Fax: (513) 271-4747

CEO: L. Thomas Applegate, Pres.

Emp: 560

Mfr. surgical appliances & supplies.

Canada

SWAN SALES CORPORATION

6223 W. Forest Home Ave.

Milwaukee, WI 53220

Tel: (414) 543-5555 Fax: (414) 543-5588

CEO: Heidi Schuster, Pres.

General merchandise.

Germany

SWECO INC.

7120 New Buffington Road, PO Box 1509

Florence, KY 41042-1509

Tel: (606) 727-5100 Fax: (606) 727-5106

CEO: David Hale, Pres.

HR: V. Danny Cripe

Emp: 350

Mfr. vibratory process and solids control equipment.

Belgium, Brazil, Canada, Mexico, Singapore

SWEETHEART CUP CO. INC.

10100 Reistertown Road

Owings Mills, MD 21117

Tel: (410) 363-1111 Fax: (410) 998-1828

CEO: Samuel N. Shapiro

Emp: 10,000

Paper cups, drinking straws, ice cream cones, packaging equipment, etc.

Netherlands

SWINTEK CORPORATION

320 West Commercial Ave.

Moonachie, NJ 07074

Tel: (201) 935-0115 Fax: (201) 935-6021

CEO: Dominick Vespia, Pres.

Mfr./sales office machines, communications equipment.

Canada

SYBASE, INC.

6475 Christie Ave.

Emeryville, CA 94608

Tel: (510) 922-3500 Fax: (510) 922-3210

CEO: Mitchell E. Kertzman, Chmn.

FO: Michael E. Regan, SVP

HR: Nita C. White-Ivy, VP

Web site: www.sybase.com

Emp: 5,216 Rev: $903.9 mil.

Design/mfg/distribution of database management systems, software development tools, connectivity products, consulting and technical support services..

Argentina, Australia, Austria, Belgium, Brazil, Chile, China (PRC), Cyprus, Czech Republic, Denmark, Ecuador, England, U.K., Finland, France, Germany, Hong Kong, India, Indonesia, Ireland, Italy, Japan, Malaysia, Mexico, Netherlands, New Zealand, Norway, Peru, Philippines, Poland, Portugal, Russia, Singapore, Slovakia, South Africa, South Korea, Spain, Sweden, Switzerland, Taiwan (ROC), Thailand, Turkey, United Arab Emirates, Venezuela

SYBRON INTERNATIONAL CORPORATION

411 E. Wisconsin Ave.
Milwaukee, WI 53202
Tel: (414) 274-6600 Fax: (414) 274-6561
CEO: Kenneth F. Yontz, Chmn.
HR: Eillen Short
Emp: 3,000

Mfr. products for laboratories, professional orthodontic & dental markets.

Australia, Canada, Channel Islands, U.K., Denmark, England, U.K., Germany, Hong Kong, Hungary, Italy, Japan, Mexico, Switzerland

SYMANTEC CORPORATION

10201 Torre Ave.
Cupertino, CA 95014-2132
Tel: (408) 253-9600 Fax: (408) 446-8129
CEO: Gordon E. Eubanks Jr., Pres.
FO: Dana E. Siebert, EVP
HR: Rebecca Ranninger, VP
Web site: www.symantec.com
Emp: 2,300 Rev: $578 mil.

Designs and produces PC network security and network management software and hardware.

Australia, Brazil, Canada, England, U.K., France, Germany, Hong Kong, Ireland, Italy, Japan, Malaysia, Mexico, Netherlands, New Zealand, Russia, Singapore, South Korea, Sweden, Switzerland, Taiwan (ROC)

SYMBOL TECHNOLOGIES, INC.

One Symbol Plaza
Holtsville, NY 11742-1300
Tel: (516) 738-2400 Fax: (516) 563-2831
CEO: Jerome Swartz, Pres.
FO: Tony Wilson
Web site: www.symbol.com

Mfr. bar code-driven data management systems, wireless LAN's, and Portable Shopping System™.

Australia, Austria, Canada, China (PRC), Denmark, England, U.K., France, Germany, Italy, Japan, Mexico, Netherlands, Singapore, South Africa, Spain

SYSCO CORPORATION

1390 Enclave Parkway
Houston, TX 77077-2099
Tel: (713) 672-8080 Fax: (713) 679-5483
CEO: Ken Spitler, Pres.
HR: Dana Richardson

North America's largest marketer/distributor of food service products.

Canada

SYSTEM INTEGRATORS INC.

PO Box 13626
Sacramento, CA 95853
Tel: (916) 929-9481 Fax: (916) 928-0414
CEO: Frank Washington, Pres.
FO: M. Lee/D. Livingstone
HR: Renae Herman
Emp: 229

Develop/marketing software for publishing and newspapers.

Australia, Denmark, England, U.K., France, Germany

SYSTEM SOFTWARE ASSOCIATES INC.

500 West Madison Street, Ste. 3200
Chicago, IL 60661
Tel: (312) 258-6000 Fax: (312) 474-7500
CEO: William Stuek, Pres.
FO: Roger Koniski, Pres. Europe
Web site: www.ssax.com
Emp: 2,000 Rev: $425 mil.

Mfr. computer software.

Argentina, Belgium, China (PRC), England, U.K., Finland, France, Spain

T

TAB PRODUCTS COMPANY

1400 Page Mill Road, PO Box 10269
Palo Alto, CA 94303
Tel: (650) 852-2400 Fax: (650) 852-2679
CEO: Philip Kantz
FO: Kurt Lein
HR: Wendi Hill
Web site: www.tabproducts.com
Emp: 1,200
Mfr. filing systems and electronic office products.
Australia, Canada, Netherlands

TACO INC.

1160 Cranston Street
Cranston, RI 02920
Tel: (401) 942-8000 Fax: (401) 942-8692
CEO: John Hazen White, Jr., Pres.
FO: Robert A. Sinclair
HR: Kyle Adamonis
Emp: 450
Mfr. HVAC pumps & equipment.
Canada, South Korea

TACONIC PLASTICS INC.

PO Box 69
Petersburg, NY 12138
Tel: (518) 658-3202 Fax: (518) 658-3204
CEO: Gerald Henry, Pres.
Emp: 142
Mfr. teflon/silicone-coated fiberglass fabrics, tapes and belts; specialty tapes and circuit board substrates.
England, U.K., France, Ireland, South Korea

TANDY CORPORATION

100 Throckmorton Street
Fort Worth, TX 76102
Tel: (817) 390-3700 Fax: (817) 415-2647
CEO: John V. Roach, Chmn.
FO: David Christopher, EVP
HR: George J. Berger, VP
Web site: www.tandy.com
Emp: 44,000 Rev: $5,372 mil.
Electronic & acoustic equipment.
Australia, Belgium, Canada, England, U.K., France, Germany, Hong Kong, Japan, South Korea, Taiwan (ROC)

TATE ACCESS FLOORS INC.

7510 Montevideo Road, PO Box 278
Jessup, MD 20794-0278
Tel: (410) 799-4200 Fax: (410) 799-4250
CEO: Daniel R. Baker
HR: Victoria Ramina
Emp: 395
Mfr. access flooring for computers & offices.
England, U.K.

TBWA INTERNATIONAL

180 Maiden Lane
New York, NY 10038
Tel: (212) 804-1000 Fax: (212) 804-1200
CEO: Willaim G. Tragos, Chmn.
FO: Robert Kuperman, Pres.
Emp: 5,265 Rev: $550.3 mil.
International full service advertising agency.
Argentina, Australia, Austria, Belgium, Brazil, Bulgaria, Canada, Chile, China (PRC), Croatia, Czech Republic, Denmark, England, U.K., Finland, France, Germany, Greece, Hong Kong, Hungary, Israel, Italy, Netherlands, Norway, Poland, Portugal, Romania, Singapore, Slovakia, South Africa, Spain, Switzerland, Thailand

TC INDUSTRIES

PO Box 477
Crystal Lake, IL 60039
Tel: (815) 459-2400 Fax: (815) 459-3303
CEO: Thomas Z. Hayward, Jr., Chmn.
HR: Hank Deveikis
Emp: 600
Mfr./sales of fabricated metal products.
Canada, England, U.K.

TEAM INC.

1019 S. Hood Street
Alvin, TX 77511
Tel: (281) 331-6154 Fax: (281) 331-4107
CEO: William A. Ryan, Chmn.
FO: Kenneth M. Tholan, COO
HR: Clark A. Ingram, VP
Web site: www.teamindustrialservices.com

Emp: 480 Rev: $46 mil.

Consulting, engineering & rental services.

Australia, Belgium, China (PRC), England, U.K., France, Mexico, Netherlands, Norway, Saudi Arabia, Singapore, Spain, Taiwan (ROC), Trinidad & Tobago

TECH DATA CORPORATION

5350 Tech Data Drive

Clearwater, FL 34620-3122

Tel: (813) 539-7429 Fax: (813) 538-7876

CEO: Anthony A. Ibarguen, Pres.

FO: James T. Pollard, EVP

HR: Lawrence W. Hamilton, SVP

Web site: www.techdata.com

Emp: 5,000

Distributor of computer systems, software and related equipment.

Brazil, Canada, France, Germany

TECH-SYM CORPORATION

10500 Westoffice Drive, #200

Houston, TX 77042-5391

Tel: (713) 785-7790 Fax: (713) 780-3524

CEO: J. Michael Camp, Pres.

FO: Richard F. Miles

HR: Paul L. Harp

Web site: www.syntron.com

Emp: 2,459 Rev: $294

Electronics, real estate, aeromechanics.

Azerbaijan, Chile, China (PRC), England, U.K., Germany, Russia, Scotland, U.K., Singapore, Ukraine

TECH/OPS SEVCON INC.

1 Beacon Street

Boston, MA 02108

Tel: (617) 523-2030 Fax: (617) 523-0073

CEO: Bernard F. Start

Emp: 214

Mfr. solid state controllers for electrical powered vehicles.

England, U.K., France, Wales, U.K.

TECHNITROL INC.

1210 Northbrook Drive, #385

Trevose, PA 19053

Tel: (215) 355-2900 Fax:

CEO: Thomas Flakoll, Pres.

HR: David W. Lacey, VP

Web site: www.technitrol.com

Emp: 14,400 Rev: $397 mil.

Mfr. of electronic components, electrical contacts, and other parts/materials.

Canada, China (PRC), England, U.K., France, Germany, Ireland, Malaysia, Mexico, Philippines, Poland, Spain, Taiwan (ROC), Thailand

TECHNOLOGY SOLUTIONS COMPANY (TSC)

205 N. Michigan Ave., Ste. 1500

Chicago, IL 60601

Tel: (312) 228-4500 Fax: (312) 228-4501

CEO: John T. Kohler, Pres.

FO: William H. Waltrip, Chmn.

HR: Angela Landry

Web site: www.techsol.com

Emp: 1,500

Designs computer information systems and strategic business and management consulting for major corporations.

Australia, Canada, Chile, Colombia, England, U.K., France, Germany, Mexico, Switzerland

TECUMSEH PRODUCTS COMPANY

100 E. Patterson Street

Tecumseh, MI 49286-1899

Tel: (517) 423-8411 Fax: (517) 423-8526

CEO: Todd W. Herrick, Chmn.

FO: Thomas A. Jacoby

HR: W. Stubbs

Emp: 15,000 Rev: $1,600 mil.

Mfr. refrigeration & A/C compressors & units, small engines, pumps.

Brazil, Canada, England, U.K., France, Germany, Italy, Thailand

TEKELEC

26580 West Agoura Road

Calabasas, CA 91302

Tel: (818) 880-5656 Fax: (818) 880-6993

CEO: Michael L. Margolis, Pres.

FO: Timo Nicholson, Intl. Mktg.

HR: Scott R. Gardner, VP

Web site: www.tekelec.com

Emp: 420

Mfr. telecommunications testing equipment.

Japan, South Africa, South Korea

TEKNIS CORPORATION

PO Box 3189

N. Attleboro, MA 02761

Tel: (508) 695-3591 Fax: (508) 699-6059

CEO: Harold H. Friedman

Sale advanced technical products, fiber optics, materials for semiconductor mfr., security holographics

Australia, England, U.K., France

TEKTRONIX INC.

2660 Southwest Parkway Ave., PO Box 1000

Wilsonville, OR 97070-1000

Tel: (503) 627-7111 Fax: (503) 627-2406

CEO: Jerome J. Meyer, Chmn.

FO: Richard H. Wills

HR: Jim Bloom, VP

Web site: www.tek.com

Emp: 8,0630 Rev: $2,086 mil.

Mfr. test & measure, visual systems/color printing & communications/video and networking products.

Australia, Austria, Belgium, Brazil, Canada, China (PRC), Denmark, England, U.K., Finland, France, Germany, Hong Kong, India, Indonesia, Ireland, Israel, Italy, Japan, Malaysia, Mexico, Netherlands, Norway, Scotland, U.K., Singapore, South Korea, Spain, Sweden, Switzerland, Taiwan (ROC)

TELAIR INTERNATIONAL

1950 Williams Drive

Oxnard, CA 93030

Tel: (805) 988-1902 Fax: (805) 983-2492

CEO: Bill Greer, Pres.

Emp: 250

Mfr./sale/service hot air & fuel valves, electro-mechanical actuators.

Germany

TELE-COMMUNICATIONS INC.

PO Box 5630

Denver, CO 80217-5630

Tel: (303) 267-5500 Fax: (303) 779-1228

CEO: John C. Malone, Chmn.

FO: Fred Vierra, CEO Intl.

HR: Grace de Latoure

Web site: www.tci.com

Largest cable television operator in the U.S.

Argentina, Brazil, England, U.K., France, Germany, Japan, Mexico, Spain

TELEDYNE WATER PIK

1730 East Prospect Road

Fort Collins, CO 80553-0001

Tel: (970) 484-1352 Fax: (970) 221-8715

CEO: Wayne Brothers, Pres.

HR: Pamela Allen

Emp: 100

Mfr. oral hygiene appliances, shower massage equipment, water filtration products.

Canada, Germany, Japan

TELEFLEX INC.

630 West Germantown Pike, Ste. 450

Plymouth Meeting, PA 19462

Tel: (215) 834-6301 Fax: (610) 834-8307

CEO: Leonard K. Black, Pres. & Chmn.

Emp: 1,432

Designs/mfr./market mechanical and electro-mechanical systems, measure systems.

Canada, England, U.K.

TELEMATICS INTERNATIONAL INC.

1201 Cypress Creek Road

Ft. Lauderdale, FL 33309

Tel: (954) 772-3070 Fax: (954) 351-4404

CEO: Israel Frieder, Pres.

Emp: 450

Design/mfr. data communication & networking products & systems.

England, U.K., France, Germany

TELEX COMMUNICATIONS INC.

9600 Aldrich Ave. South

Minneapolis, MN 55420

Tel: (612) 884-4051 Fax: (612) 884-0043

CEO: John Hale

FO: Michel Locquegnies

HR: Kathy Curran

Emp: 3,200

Mfr. communications, audio-visual and professional audio products.

Canada, England, U.K., Singapore

TELLABS INC.

4951 Indiana Ave. 6303788800
Lisle, IL 60532
Tel: (630) 378-8800 Fax: (630) 679-3010
CEO: Michael J. Birck, Pres.
FO: Jeffrey J. Wake
Emp: 2,600

Design/mfr./service voice/data transport & network access systems.

Argentina, Australia, Canada, China (PRC), England, U.K., Finland, Germany, Hong Kong, India, Ireland, Mexico, Singapore, South Korea, Spain, Sweden, United Arab Emirates

TELXON CORPORATION

3330 W. Market Street, PO Box 5582
Akron, OH 44334-0582
Tel: (330) 867-3700 Fax: (330) 869-2220
CEO: Frank Brick, Pres.
Emp: 1,600

Develop/mfr. portable computer systems & related equipment.

Australia, Belgium, Canada, England, U.K., France, Germany, Italy, Japan, Singapore, Spain

TEMPEL STEEL COMPANY

5215 Old Orchard
Skokie, IL 60077
Tel: (847) 581-9400 Fax: (847) 581-9025
CEO: Vincent Bonano, Chmn.
Emp: 600 Rev: $375 mil.

Metal stampings; specialty transformers; motors & generators.

Brazil

TEMPLE-INLAND INC.

303 S. Temple Drie
Diboll, TX 75941
Tel: (409) 829-5511 Fax: (409) 829-1537
CEO: Clifford J. Grum, Chmn.
FO: Bart J. Doney, EVP
HR: Dan Hackler, VP
Web site: www.templeinland.com
Emp: 15,000 Rev: $3,625 mil.

Mfr. paper, packaging, bldg products; financial services.

Argentina, Mexico

TENNANT COMPANY

701 North Lilac Drive
Minneapolis, MN 55440
Tel: (612) 513-2112 Fax: (612) 541-6137
CEO: Roger L. Hale, Pres.
FO: William Strang, VP
HR: Paul Brunelle
Web site: www.Tennantco.com
Emp: 1,800

Mfr. industry floor maintenance sweepers and scrubbers, floor coatings.

Australia, Brazil, Canada, Germany, Japan, Netherlands, Singapore

TENNECO AUTOMOTIVE

500 North Field Drive
Lake Forest, IL 60045
Tel: (847) 482-5241 Fax: (847) 482-5295
CEO: Thomas E. Evans
FO: K. Douglas Schultz
Emp: 8,000

Automotive parts, exhaust systems, service equipment.

Argentina, Australia, Austria, Belgium, Brazil, Canada, China (PRC), Czech Republic, Denmark, England, U.K., France, Germany, India, Italy, Japan, Mexico, New Zealand, Poland, Portugal, Singapore, South Africa, Spain, Sweden, Turkey

TENNECO INC.

1275 King Street
Greenwich, CT 06831
Tel: (203) 863-1000 Fax: (203) 863-1134
CEO: Dana G. Mead, Chmn.
FO: Paul T. Stecko, COO
HR: Barry R. Schuman, SVP
Web site: www.tenneco.com
Emp: 49,335 Rev: $7,220 mil.

Mfr. automotive products and packaging materials/containers.

Australia, Belgium, Brazil, Canada, Denmark, England, U.K., France, Germany, Japan, Netherlands, Poland, Spain, Sweden

TENNECO PACKAGING CORPORATION OF AMERICA

1900 West Field Court
Lake Forest, IL 60045

Tel: (847) 482-2000 Fax: (847) 482-2181

CEO: Paul Stecko, Pres.

HR: John Potempa, VP

Web site: www.tenneco

Emp: 14,000

Mfr. custom packaging, aluminum and plastic molded fibre, corrugated containers.

Belgium, Canada, China (PRC), Denmark, Egypt, England, U.K., France, Germany, Hungary, Italy, Japan, Netherlands, Poland, Romania, Scotland, U.K., Spain, Sweden, Switzerland, Wales, U.K.

TENNESSEE ASSOCIATES INTERNATIONAL

223 Associates Blvd., PO Box 710

Alcoa, TN 37701-0710

Tel: (423) 982-9514 Fax: (423) 982-1481

CEO: Gerald D. Sentell, Pres.

FO: Timothy R. Carpenter

Emp: 106

Management consulting services.

Argentina, Brazil, Canada, Colombia, England, U.K., Germany, Indonesia, Mexico, Philippines, Thailand, Venezuela

TERADYNE INC.

321 Harrison Ave.

Boston, MA 02118

Tel: (617) 482-2700 Fax: (617) 422-2910

CEO: George W. Chamillard, Pres.

HR: James Dawson, Dir.

Web site: www.teradyne.com

Emp: 6,300 Rev: $1,266 mil.

Mfr. electronic test equipment & blackplane connection systems.

England, U.K., France, Germany, Hong Kong, Ireland, Italy, Japan, Taiwan (ROC)

TESORO PETROLEUM CORPORATION

8700 Tesoro Drive

San Antonio, TX 78217

Tel: (210) 828-8484 Fax: (210) 828-8600

CEO: Bruce A. Smith, Pres.

FO: Robert W. Oliver

HR: Thomas E. Reardon

Emp: 800

Produce/refine/distributor oil and gas.

Argentina, Bolivia

TETRA TECH, INC.

670 N. Rosemead Blvd.

Pasadena, CA 91107

Tel: (626) 351-4664 Fax: (626) 351-1188

CEO: Li-San Hwang, Chmn.

FO: Charles R. Faust, EVP

HR: Richard A. Lemmon, VP

Web site: www.tetratech.com

Emp: 2,262 Rev: $246.8 mil.

Environmental engineering and consulting services.

Argentina, Czech Republic, India, Indonesia, Philippines

TEXACO INC.

2000 Westchester Ave.

White Plains, NY 10650

Tel: (914) 253-4000 Fax: (914) 253-7753

CEO: Peter I. Bijur, Chmn.

FO: Glenn F. Tilton, SVP Int'l.

HR: Janet Stoner, VP

Web site: www.texaco.com

Exploration/marketing crude oil, mfr. petro chemicals and products.

Angola, Australia, Bahamas, Belgium, Brazil, Costa Rica, Denmark, Dominican Republic, Ecuador, El Salvador, England, U.K., France, Greece, Guatemala, Guyana, Haiti, Hong Kong, Indonesia, Ireland, Ivory Coast, Jamaica, Japan, Nicaragua, Nigeria, Panama, Peru, Russia, Saudi Arabia, South Korea, Uruguay

TEXAS INSTRUMENTS INC.

8505 Forest Lane

Dallas, TX 75243

Tel: (214) 995-2011 Fax: (214) 995-4360

CEO: Thomas J. Engibous

HR: Steven Leven

Web site: www.ti.com

Emp: 44,000 Rev: $10,000 mil.

Mfr. semiconductor devices, electronic electro-mechanical systems, instruments and controls.

Argentina, Australia, Austria, Belgium, Brazil, Canada, China (PRC), Denmark, England, U.K., Finland, France, Germany, Hong Kong, Hungary, India, Indonesia, Ireland, Italy, Japan, Malaysia, Mexico, Netherlands, New Zealand, Philippines, Portugal, Singapore, South Korea, Spain, Sweden, Switzerland, Taiwan (ROC), Thailand

TEXAS REFINERY CORPORATION

840 North Main Street

Fort Worth, TX 76101

Tel: (817) 332-1161 Fax: (817) 332-2340

CEO: Jerry Hopkins, Chmn.

HR: Jim Peel

Emp: 500

Mfr. Building and maintenance products & spec lubricants.

Canada, Luxembourg, Mexico

TEXTRON INC.

40 Westminster Street

Providence, RI 02903

Tel: (401) 421-2800 Fax: (401) 421-2878

CEO: Lewis B. Campbell, Pres

FO: Gero Meyersiek, VP Intl.

HR: John D. Butler, EVP

Web site: www.textron.com

Emp: 64,000 Rev: $10,500 mil.

Mfr. aerospace, industry and consumer products (Bell Helicopter & Cessna Aircraft) and financial services.

Australia, Brazil, Canada, England, U.K., France, Germany, Hong Kong, Italy, Mexico, Singapore, Switzerland

THERM-O-DISC INC.

1320 S. Main Street

Mansfield, OH 44907-0538

Tel: (419) 525-8500 Fax: (419) 525-8282

CEO: James A. Knight, Pres.

FO: Carl Gigandet

HR: James Curry

Emp: 5,500

Mfr. thermostats, controls, sensor & thermal cutoffs, switches.

Canada, Hong Kong, Ireland, Japan, Netherlands

THERMADYNE INDUSTRIES INC.

101 South Hanley Road, #300

St. Louis, MO 63105

Tel: (314) 746-2197 Fax: (314) 746-2349

CEO: Randy Curran

FO: Andrew H. Johnston

HR: Tom Drury

Web site: www.thermadyne.com

Emp: 3,250

Mfr. welding, cutting, and safety products.

Argentina, Australia, Brazil, Canada, China (PRC), Costa Rica, England, U.K., France, Hong Kong, Indonesia, Italy, Japan, Malaysia, Mexico, Philippines, Singapore, South Africa, South Korea, Thailand, United Arab Emirates, Venezuela

THERMCO SYSTEMS INC.

1465 North Batavia Street

Orange, CA 92867

Tel: (714) 639-2340 Fax: (714) 532-2133

CEO: Jeff Kowalski, Pres.

FO: Alfred W. Giese

HR: Trish Smith, Dir.

Emp: 700

Microprocessor controlled diffusion furnace systems and vacuum/gas systems for semiconductor processing.

England, U.K., Germany, Hong Kong

THERMO BLACK CLAWSON

605 Clark Street

Middletown, OH 45042

Tel: (513) 424-7400 Fax: (513) 424-1168

CEO: William Fondow, Pres.

Manufactures & specializes in the brown-paper segment of the recycling market

China (PRC)

THERMO ELECTRIC COMPANY

109 North Fifth Street

Saddle Brook, NJ 07662

Tel: (201) 843-5800 Fax: (201) 843-7144

CEO: Paul F. Walter, Pres.

FO: G. J. D. de Graaff

HR: Wanda Ortiz

Emp: 550

Mfr. temp/measure control products.

Belgium, Canada, Denmark, England, U.K., France, Germany, Japan, Netherlands, Norway, Singapore, Switzerland

THERMO ELECTRON CORPORATION

81 Wyman Street

Waltham, MA 02254-9046

Tel: (781) 622-1000 Fax: (781) 622-1207

CEO: George N. Hatsopoulos, Chmn.

FO: Peter G. Pantazelos, EVP

HR: Anne Pol, VP

Web site: www.thermo.com

Emp: 2,700 Rev: $3,600 mil.

Develop/mfr./sale of process equipment &instruments for energy intensive & healthcare industries.

Brazil, Canada, England, U.K., Germany, Japan, Mexico, Netherlands

THERMON

100 Thermon Drive, PO Box 609

San Marcos, TX 78667-0609

Tel: (512) 396-5801 Fax: (512) 754-2425

CEO: Richard L. Burdick, Pres.

HR: Dee Dee Baen

Emp: 484

Mfr. steam and electric heat tracing systems, components and accessories.

Australia, England, U.K., France, Germany, India, Italy, Japan, Netherlands, Norway, South Korea

THETFORD CORPORATION

7101 Jackson Road, PO Box 1285

Ann Arbor, MI 48106

Tel: (734) 769-6000 Fax: (734) 769-2023

CEO: John R. Arlen

FO: George Strasburg

HR: Jack Quigley

Emp: 300

Mfr. sanitation products and chemicals.

Brazil, Canada, England, U.K., Germany, Netherlands

THOMAS & BETTS CORPORATION

8155 T&B Blvd.

Memphis, TN 38125

Tel: (901) 252-5000 Fax: (901) 685-1988

CEO: Clyde R. Moore, Pres.

HR: John Schierer
John Schierer

Emp: 8,000

Mfr. elect/electronic connectors & accessories.

Australia, Canada, England, U.K., France, Germany, Italy, Japan, Luxembourg, Mexico, Singapore, South Africa, Spain, Sweden

THOMAS BUILT BUSES INC.

1408 Courtesy Road, PO Box 2450

High Point, NC 27261

Tel: (336) 889-4871 Fax: (336) 889-2589

CEO: J. W. Thomas III

FO: Larry Bannon

HR: Rick Holbert

Emp: 1,375

Mfr. buses & bus chassis.

Canada, Mexico

THOMAS INDUSTRIES INC.

4360 Brownsboro Road, Ste. 300

Louisville, KY 40232

Tel: (502) 893-4600 Fax: (502) 893-4685

CEO: Timothy C. Brown, Chmn., Pres.

FO: Peter Bissinger, VP

HR: Gilbert R. Grady

Web site: www.thomasind.com

Emp: 3,300 Rev: $547 mil.

Mfr. lighting fixtures, compressors and vacuum pumps.

Canada, England, U.K., Germany

THOMAS PUBLISHING COMPANY

5 Penn Plaza

New York, NY 10007

Tel: (212) 695-0500 Fax: (212) 290-7362

CEO: Thomas Holst-Knudsen, Pres.

HR: Ivy Molofsky, Dir.

Web site: www.thomaspublishing.com

Emp: 500

Publishing magazines and directories.

Belgium, Brazil, France, Germany, Hong Kong, Japan

THOMPSON AIRCRAFT TIRE CORPORATION

7775 NW 12th Street

Miami, FL 33126

Tel: (305) 592-3530 Fax:

CEO: Jenny Bucher, Pres.

Emp: 300

Retread aircraft tires, aircraft wheel and brake servicing.

Belgium, Hong Kong

TIDELAND SIGNAL CORPORATION

4310 Directors Row, PO Box 52430

Houston, TX 77052-2430

Tel: (713) 681-6101 Fax: (713) 681-6233

CEO: H. J. Saenger, Pres.

Web site: www.tidelandsignal.com

Mfr./sale aids to navigation.

Canada, England, U.K., Singapore

TIDEWATER INC.

Tidewater Place, 1440 Canal Street

New Orleans, LA 70112

Tel: (504) 568-1010 Fax: (504) 566-4582

CEO: William O'Malley, Pres.

HR: Mary Torrens

Marine service and equipment to companies engaged in exploration, development and production of oil, gas and minerals.

Australia, Brazil, Egypt, Indonesia, Italy, Mexico, Netherlands, Nigeria, Scotland, U.K., Singapore, Trinidad & Tobago, United Arab Emirates, Venezuela

TIFFANY & COMPANY

727 Fifth Ave.

New York, NY 10022

Tel: (212) 755-8000 Fax: (212) 605-4465

CEO: William R. Chaney, Chmn.

FO: Yone Akiyama, VP Int'l.

HR: David Eisenhower, VP

Web site: www.tiffany.com

Emp: 4,360 Rev: $1,018 mil.

Mfr./retail fine jewelry, silverware, china, crystal, leather goods, etc.

Australia, Canada, England, U.K., Germany, Hong Kong, Italy, Japan, Singapore, South Korea, Switzerland, Taiwan (ROC)

THE TIMBERLAND COMPANY

200 Domain Drive

Stratham, NH 03885

Tel: (603) 772-9500 Fax: (603) 773-1640

CEO: Sidney Swartz, Chmn.

FO: Gordon N. Peterson

HR: Lisa Letizio

Emp: 6,500 Rev: $655.1 mil.

Design/mfr. footwear, apparel & accessories for men & women.

England, U.K., France, Germany, Italy, Spain

TIME WARNER INC.

75 Rockefeller Plaza

New York, NY 10019

Tel: (212) 484-8000 Fax: (212) 275-3046

CEO: Gerald M. Levin, Chmn.

FO: Richard D. Parsons, Pres.

HR: Carolyn McCandless, VP HR

Web site: www.timewarner.com

Emp: 67,900 Rev: $24,622 mil.

Communications, publishing and entertainment company.

Brazil, Canada, England, U.K., France, Germany, Italy, Japan, Mexico, Netherlands, South Korea

TIMEPLEX INC.

400 Chestnut Ridge Road, PO Box 1206

Woodcliff Lake, NJ 07675

Tel: (201) 391-1111 Fax: (201) 573-6470

CEO: Randy Phillips

Emp: 1,800

Mfr., sale & services data communications equipment.

England, U.K.

TIMES MIRROR COMPANY

220 W. First Street

Los Angeles, CA 90012

Tel: (213) 237-3700 Fax: (213) 237-3800

CEO: Mark H. Willes, Chmn. & Pres.

HR: James R. Simpson, SVP

Web site: www.tm.com

Emp: 21,500 Rev: $3,300 mil.

Periodical & book publishing, communications.

Canada, England, U.K., Germany

TIMET CORPORATION

1999 Broadway, #4300

Denver, CO 80202

Tel: (303) 296-5600 Fax: (303) 296-5650

CEO: Andrew Dixey, Pres.

Web site: www.timet.com

Emp: 1,100

Non-ferrous drawing & rolling, coal & other minerals, metals service centers.

England, U.K., France, Germany

TIMEX CORPORATION

Park Road Extension
Middlebury, CT 06762
Tel: (203) 573-5000 Fax: (203) 573-6901
CEO: C. Michael Jacobi, Pres.
Emp: 7,600
Mfr. watches, clocks, timing instruments.
Australia, Canada, France, Germany, Poland

THE TIMKEN COMPANY
1835 Dueber Ave. SW, PO Box 6927
Canton, OH 44706-2798
Tel: (330) 438-3000 Fax: (330) 471-4118
CEO: J. R. Timken, Jr., Pres.
FO: Jon T. Elsasser, Grp VP
HR: Stephen A. Perry, Sr. VP
Emp: 21,000
Mfr. tapered roller bearings and quality alloy steels.
Australia, Brazil, Canada, England, U.K., France, South Africa

TITAN INDUSTRIAL CORPORATION
555 Madison Ave., 10th Fl.
New York, NY 10022
Tel: (212) 421-6700 Fax: (212) 421-6708
CEO: Jerome A. Siegel, Pres.
Emp: 150
Import and export steel products.
England, U.K.

TITLEIST & FOOT-JOY WORLDWIDE
333 Bridge Street
Fairhaven, MA 02719
Tel: (508) 979-2000 Fax: (508) 979-3909
CEO: Wally Uihlein, Chmn.
HR: Dennis Doherty
Golf clubs, golf shoes and related golf products.
England, U.K.

TIW CORPORATION
12300 S. Main Street, PO Box 35729
Houston, TX 77235
Tel: (713) 729-2110 Fax: (713) 728-4767
CEO: Stephen R. Pearce, Pres.
FO: A. R. Fahim
HR: Wanda Parchmont
Emp: 346
Mfr. liner hanger equipment, production packers, safety & kelly valves.
Canada, Germany, Singapore

TJX COMPANIES INC.
770 Cochituate Road
Framingham, MA 01701
Tel: (508) 390-1000 Fax: (508) 390-2828
CEO: Bernard Cammarata, Pres.
HR: Mark O. Jacobson
Web site: www.tjx.com
Emp: 59,000 Rev: $7,300 mil.
Retail stores, catalog & mail order houses.
Canada, England, U.K., Ireland, Netherlands

TMP WORLDWIDE, INC.
1633 Broadway, 33rd Floor
New York, NY 10019
Tel: (212) 940-3900 Fax: (212) 940-7926
CEO: Andrew J. McKelvey
Emp: 2,900 Rev: $274.1 mil.
#1 Yellow Pages agency & a leader in the recruitment and interactive advertising fields.
Australia, Belgium, England, U.K., France, Italy, Japan, Netherlands, New Zealand, Scotland, U.K., Spain, Wales, U.K.

TODD COMBUSTION INC.
15 Progress Drive, PO Box 884
Shelton, CT 06484
Tel: (203) 925-0380 Fax: (203) 925-0384
CEO: Tim Lepczyk, Pres.
HR: Debbie Mattis
Emp: 125
Heating & pumping equipment.
Canada

TODD UNIFORM INC.
3668 S. Geyer Road
St. Louis, MO 63127
Tel: (314) 984-0365 Fax: (314) 984-5798
CEO: Bruce W. Main, Pres.
Emp: 2,700
Mfr. work apparel, suits and coats and industry laundering.
Canada

TOKHEIM CORPORATION

PO Box 360, 10501 Corporate Drive
Fort Wayne, IN 46845
Tel: (219) 470-4600 Fax: (219) 482-2677
CEO: Douglas K. Pinner, Chmn.
FO: Patrick J. Schultz, Dir.
HR: Timothy Eastom, VP
Emp: 4,300 Rev: $733 mil.
Mfr. gasoline service station dispensers, point of sale systems, card readers and RFID equipment.
Canada, Netherlands, South Africa

TOMMY HILFIGER SPORTSWEAR, INC.
25 West 39 Street
New York, NY 10018
Tel: (212) 840-8888 Fax: (212) 302-8718
CEO: Joel Horowitz
FO: Silas Chou, Chrm.
Clothing manufacturer and chain stores.
Canada, Hong Kong, Japan, Mexico, Netherlands, Panama

TOOTSIE ROLL INDUSTRIES INC.
7401 S. Cicero Ave.
Chicago, IL 60629
Tel: (773) 838-3400 Fax: (773) 838-3534
CEO: Melvin J. Gordon, Chmn.
FO: Ellen R. Gordon, Pres.
HR: Michael Hale, Dir.
Emp: 1,750 Rev: $375.6 mil.
Mfr. candies and chocolate products.
Canada, Cayman Islands, Hong Kong, Mexico

TOPFLIGHT CORPORATION
Box 2847
York, PA 17405-2847
Tel: (717) 227-5400 Fax: (717) 227-1415
CEO: Patrick Masterson
HR: R. Mumford
Web site: www.topflight.com
Emp: 350
Commercial printing and service paper.
Australia, Netherlands, Sweden, Switzerland, Venezuela

THE TOPPS CO., INC.
1 Whitehall Street
New York, NY 10004-2108
Tel: (212) 376-0300 Fax: (212) 376-0573
CEO: Arthur T. Shorin, Chmn.
FO: Michael P. Clancy, VP
HR: William G. O'Connor, VP
Web site: www.topps.com
Emp: 500 Rev: $241.3 mil.
Mfr. chewing gum & confections.
Argentina, Brazil, Canada, England, U.K., Ireland, Italy, Mexico

TORK INC.
1 Grove Street
Mount Vernon, NY 10550
Tel: (914) 664-3542 Fax: (914) 664-5052
CEO: Victoria White, Pres.
FO: R. Sam Shankar
HR: L. Caponigro
Emp: 248
Mfr. time & photoelectric controls.
Mexico

THE TORO COMPANY
8111 Lyndale Ave. South
Minneapolis, MN 55420
Tel: (612) 888-8801 Fax: (612) 887-8258
CEO: Kendrick B. Melrose
HR: Karen Meyer
Mfr. lawn/turf maintenance products and snow removal equipment.
Belgium, England, U.K.

TOTES INC.
9655 International Blvd., PO Box 465658
Cincinnati, OH 45246
Tel: (513) 682-8200 Fax: (513) 682-8602
CEO: Douglas Gernert, Pres.
HR: Linda Schmidt
Mfr. rubber & plastic footwear, slippers, umbrellas.
Canada

TOWER AUTOMOTIVE, INC.
1350 West Hamlin Road, PO Box 5011
Rochester Hills, MI 48308-5011
Tel: (248) 650-4100 Fax: (248) 650-7406
CEO: Dugald Campbell, Pres.
HR: Nancy Delaney
Rev: $1,200 mil.

Mfr. stamped and welded assemblies for vehicle body structures and suspension systems for auto makers.

Brazil, Canada

TOWERS PERRIN

335 Madison Ave.

New York, NY 10017-4605

Tel: (212) 309-3400 Fax: (212) 309-0975

CEO: John T. Lynch, Pres.

FO: John Kneen, Mng. Dir.

HR: Rollie Stichweh, Mng. Dir. HR

Web site: www.towers.com

Emp: 7,251 Rev: $991 mil.

Management consulting services.

Argentina, Australia, Belgium, Bermuda, Brazil, Canada, England, U.K., France, Germany, Hong Kong, Italy, Japan, Malaysia, Mexico, Netherlands, Portugal, Singapore, South Africa, South Korea, Spain, Switzerland, Venezuela

TOWNSEND ENGINEERING CO., INC.

2425 Hubbell Ave.

Des Moines, IA 50317

Tel: (515) 265-8181 Fax: (515) 263-3355

CEO: Ray T. Townsend, Pres.

Emp: 220

Mfr. machinery for food industry.

Netherlands

TOYS R US INC.

461 From Road

Paramus, NJ 07652

Tel: (201) 262-7800 Fax: (201) 262-8443

CEO: Robert Nakasone, Chmn.

Emp: 55,000

Retail stores: toys & games, sporting goods, computer software, books, records.

Australia, Canada, England, U.K., France, Germany, Hong Kong, Japan, Netherlands, Spain, Switzerland

TRACE MOUNTAIN PRODUCTS INC.

1040 East Brokaw Road

San Jose, CA 95131-2309

Tel: (408) 441-8040 Fax: (408) 441-3399

CEO: Dennis McDonnell, Chmn.

HR: Carol Din

Emp: 250

Mfr. diskette; tape duplication equipment.

Belgium, England, U.K., France

TRACOR INC.

6500 Tracor Lane

Austin, TX 78725-2000

Tel: (512) 926-2800 Fax: (512) 929-2241

CEO: George Melton, Pres.

Emp: 7,500

Time & frequency products, gas & liquid chromatographs, engineering service, ship repair.

Belgium, England, U.K., France, Germany, Israel, Mexico, Netherlands, Switzerland

TRAMMELL CROW COMPANY

2001 Ross Ave.

Dallas, TX 75201

Tel: (214) 863-3000 Fax: (214) 863-3125

CEO: George L. Lippe, Pres.

FO: Robert E. Sulentic, EVP

HR: Mary Jo Francis, VP

Web site: www.trammellcrow.com

Emp: 3,200

Commercial real estate management.

Canada, Spain

TRANE COMPANY

3600 Pammel Creek Road

La Crosse, WI 54601

Tel: (608) 787-2000 Fax: (608) 787-4990

CEO: James Schultz, EVP

FO: William Klug

Emp: 14,000

Mfr./distributor/service A/C systems and equipment.

Argentina, Australia, Austria, Belgium, Brazil, Croatia, Czech Republic, Egypt, England, U.K., France, Germany, Greece, Hong Kong, Hungary, India, Indonesia, Ireland, Italy, Japan, Malaysia, Mexico, Netherlands, Philippines, Portugal, Saudi Arabia, Scotland, U.K., Singapore, South Korea, Spain, Switzerland, Taiwan (ROC), Thailand, Turkey, United Arab Emirates, Venezuela

TRANS OCEAN OFFSHORE DRILLING

PO Box 2765

Houston, TX 77252-2765

Tel: (713) 871-7500 Fax: (713) 850-3711

CEO: W. Dennis Heagney, Chmn.

FO: Bob Browning

HR: Burt Crawford

Emp: 2,100 Rev: $54 mil.

Offshore oil well drilling.

Brazil, Egypt, Indonesia, Malaysia, Norway, Scotland, U.K., Singapore, United Arab Emirates

TRANS WORLD AIRLINES INC.

505 N. Sixth Street

St. Louis, MO 63101

Tel: (314) 589-3000 Fax: (314) 589-3129

CEO: Gerald L. Gitner, Chmn.

FO: Donald Casey, EVP Mktg.

HR: James F. Martin, S VP

Web site: www.twa.com

Emp: 22,321 Rev: $3,328 mil.

Air transport services.

Dominican Republic, Egypt, England, U.K., France, Germany, Greece, Israel, Italy, Jamaica, Japan, Mexico, Netherlands, Portugal, Spain, Sweden, Switzerland, Thailand

TRANS-LUX CORPORATION

110 Richards Ave.

Norwalk, CT 06854

Tel: (203) 853-4321 Fax: (203) 855-8636

CEO: Victor Liss

FO: Tibor Darany

HR: Richard Kramer

Web site: www.trans-lux com

Emp: 375

Mfr. moving-message displays.

Australia, Canada

TRANSAMERICA CORPORATION

600 Montgomery Street

San Francisco, CA 94111

Tel: (415) 983-4000 Fax: (415) 983-4400

CEO: Frank C. Herringer, Chmn.

FO: Richard N. Latzer, SVP

HR: Rona K. Pehrson, VP HR

Web site: www.transamerica.com

Emp: 8,700 Rev: $5,727 mil.

Life insurance, leasing, and commercial lending services.

Argentina, Australia, Belgium, Brazil, Canada, China (PRC), England, U.K., Germany, Hong Kong, India, Italy, Japan, New Zealand, Singapore, South Africa, South Korea

TRANSAMERICA OCCIDENTAL LIFE INSURANCE

Hill & Olive at 12th Street

Los Angeles, CA 90015

Tel: (213) 742-2111 Fax: (213) 742-4091

CEO: Thomas Cusack, Pres.

Emp: 4,500

Insurance services.

Canada, Hong Kong

TRANSILWRAP COMPANY, INC.

2828 N. Paulina Street, #100

Chicago, IL 60657-4012

Tel: (773) 296-1000 Fax: (773) 296-2007

CEO: Herbert Drower

Emp: 700 Rev: $160 mil.

Mfr. of printable plastic, laminating film and industrial films.

Canada

TRANSMATION INC.

977 Mt. Read Blvd.

Rochester, NY 14606

Tel: (716) 254-9000 Fax: (716) 254-0273

CEO: Eric McInroy, Pres.

HR: John DeVoldere

Emp: 220

Mfr. industry instruments, machinery and equipment.

Canada

TRANTER INC.

1054 Claussen Road, #314

Augusta, GA 30907

Tel: (706) 738-7900 Fax: (706) 738-6619

CEO: Ken Kaltz, Pres.

FO: Mariono Pelosi

HR: Don McLeod

Web site: www.tranter.com

Emp: 800

Mfr. heat exchangers.

Australia, Austria, Denmark, England, U.K., France, Germany, Italy, Netherlands, Spain, Sweden, Switzerland

TRAVELERS GROUP INC.

388 Greenwich Street
New York, NY 10013
Tel: (212) 816-8000 Fax: (212) 816-8915
CEO: Sanford I. Weill, Chmn.
HR: Barry L. Mannes, SVP
Web site: www.travelers.com
Emp: 68,000 Rev: $37,000 mil.
Provides insurance and financial services.
Belgium, Canada, England, U.K., Hong Kong, Japan, Singapore

TREDEGAR INDUSTRIES INC.

1100 Boulders Pkwy.
Richmond, VA 23225
Tel: (804) 330-1000 Fax:
CEO: John D. Gottwald
HR: Rick Woods
Emp: 5,000
Mfr. plastics and aluminum products; energy (oil and gas).
Netherlands

TREIBACHER SCHLEIFMITTEL CORPORATION

2000 College Ave.
Niagara Falls, NY 14305
Tel: (716) 286-1234 Fax:
CEO: Richard A. Davis, Pres.
Emp: 350
Mfr. abrasives.
Canada

TREMCO INC.

3735 Green Road
Beachwood, OH 44122-5718
Tel: (216) 292-5000 Fax: (216) 292-5134
CEO: Jeffrey L. Korach
Emp: 1,450
Mfr. protective coatings and sealants for building, maintenance and construction.
Canada, England, U.K.

TRICO PRODUCTS CORPORATION

817 Washington Street
Buffalo, NY 14203
Tel: (716) 852-5700 Fax: (716) 853-6242
CEO: Donald Fletcher, Pres.
HR: Greg Collins
Emp: 2,400
Mfr. windshield wiper systems and components.
Australia, England, U.K., Mexico

TRICON GLOBAL RESTAURANTS INC.

1441 Gardner Lane
Louisville, KY 40213
Tel: (502) 874-1000 Fax: (502) 874-8315
CEO: David Novak, Pres.
FO: Peter A. Bassi, Intl. Pres.
HR: Gregg R. Dedrick
Web site: www.triconglobal.com
KFC, Taco Bell and Pizza Hut restaurant food chains.
Australia, Belgium, Canada, China (PRC), England, U.K., Germany, Spain, Turkey

TRIMARK PICTURES

2644 30th Street
Santa Monica, CA 90405-3009
Tel: (310) 314-2000 Fax: (310) 399-3828
CEO: Mark Amin, Pres.
Distributor TV programs, broadcast management and consulting services.
Chile

TRIMBLE NAVIGATION LIMITED

645 N. Mary Ave.
Sunnyvale, CA 94088
Tel: (408) 481-8000 Fax: (408) 481-2000
CEO: Charles A. Trimble
Web site: www.trimble.com
Emp: 1,200 Rev: $272.3 mil.
Design/mfr. electronic geographic instrumentation.
Australia, Brazil, England, U.K., France, Germany, Italy, Japan, Mexico, New Zealand, Singapore, Spain

TRIMFIT INC.

10450 Drummond Road
Philadelphia, PA 19154
Tel: (215) 781-0600 Fax: (215) 632-6430
CEO: Arnold A. Kramer, Pres.
FO: Harry Schultz
Emp: 450

Mfr. hosiery.

Canada

TRINITY INDUSTRIES INC.

PO Box 568887

Dallas, TX 75356-8887

Tel: (214) 631-4420 Fax: (214) 589-8824

CEO: W. Ray Wallace, Pres.

Mfr. heavy metal products.

Mexico

TRION INC.

101 McNeil Road, PO Box 760

Sanford, NC 27331-0760

Tel: (919) 775-2201 Fax: (919) 774-8771

CEO: Steven Schneider, Pres.

HR: Gary Waters

Emp: 421

Mfr. air cleaners and electrostatic fluid depositors.

Canada, England, U.K., Germany

TRITON ENERGY LIMITED

6688 N. Central Expressway, #1400

Dallas, TX 75206-3925

Tel: (214) 691-5200 Fax: (214) 691-0340

CEO: Robert B. Holland, III

FO: Rick Stevens, VP

HR: Linda Smith

Web site: www.tritonenergy.com

Emp: 300 Rev: $150 mil.

Provider of oil and gas services to the energy industry.

Australia, England, U.K., France, New Zealand

TRU-WELD GRATING INC.

2000 Corporate Drive

Wexford, PA 15090

Tel: (724) 934-5320 Fax: (724) 934-5348

CEO: Martin M. Shaffer, Pres.

HR: Michelle Paulos

Emp: 175

Architectural metal work.

Canada

TRUE NORTH COMMUNICATIONS INC.

101 East Erie Street

Chicago, IL 60611

Tel: (312) 425-6000 Fax: (312) 425-6350

CEO: Bruce Mason

FO: Harry Reid, Pres. Intl.

HR: Paul Sollitto

Emp: 11,000 Rev: $1.2 bil.

Holding company, advertising agency.

Argentina, Australia, Austria, Belgium, Bermuda, Botswana, Brazil, Cambodia, Canada, Chile, China (PRC), Colombia, Costa Rica, Czech Republic, Denmark, Dominican Republic, Ecuador, Egypt, El Salvador, England, U.K., France, Gabon, Germany, Greece, Guatemala, Honduras, Hong Kong, Hungary, India, Indonesia, Italy, Jamaica, Japan, Jordan, Kenya, Kuwait, Lebanon, Malawi, Malaysia, Mauritius, Mexico, Myanmar, Namibia, Netherlands, New Zealand, Nicaragua, Norway, Pakistan, Panama, Paraguay, Peru, Philippines, Poland, Portugal, Russia, Saudi Arabia, Singapore, Slovakia, South Africa, South Korea, Spain, Sweden, Switzerland, Taiwan (ROC), Thailand, Trinidad & Tobago, Turkey, United Arab Emirates, Uruguay, Venezuela, Vietnam, Zambia, Zimbabwe

TRUE TEMPER CORPORATION

465 Railroad Ave., PO Box 8859

Camp Hill, PA 17011-8859

Tel: (717) 737-1500 Fax: (717) 730-2550

CEO: John M. Stoner, Jr.

Mfr. hand and edge tools, farm and garden tools, wheelbarrows.

Canada, Ireland

TRUE VISION CORPORATION

2500 Walsh Ave.

Santa Clara, CA 95051

Tel: (408) 562-4200 Fax: (408) 562-4066

CEO: Lou Doctor, Pres.

Emp: 200

Mfr. color video technology, video image hardware & accessories, display systems.

England, U.K., Taiwan (ROC)

TruServ CORPORATION

8600 West Bryn Mawr

Chicago, IL 60631-3505

Tel: (773) 695-5000 Fax: (773) 695-6541

CEO: Daniel A. Cotter, Chmn.

FO: Fred Kirst, VP

HR: Rob Ostrov, SVP

Web site: www.truserv.com

Emp: 5,800 Rev: $4,500 mil.

Dealer-owned, independent, hardware store cooperative.

England, U.K., France, Italy

TRW COMMERCIAL STEERING

800 Heath Street

Lafayette, IN 47904

Tel: (765) 423-5377 Fax: (765) 429-1868

CEO: Arvind M. Korde, Pres.

FO: R. I. Brettnacher

HR: G. K. Hale

Emp: 2,100

Mfr. steering gears, power steering pumps, columns, linkage.

Brazil

TRW INC.

1900 Richmond Road

Cleveland, OH 44124-3760

Tel: (216) 291-7000 Fax: (216) 291-7932

CEO: Joseph T. Gorman, Chmn.

FO: Richard D. McClain, VP

HR: Howard V. Knicely, EVP

Emp: 64,000 Rev: $9,000 mil.

Electric and energy-related products, automotive and aerospace products, tools and fasteners.

Australia, Austria, Brazil, Canada, England, U.K., France, Germany, Italy, Japan, Mexico, Northern Ireland, U.K., Singapore, Spain, Switzerland, Taiwan (ROC), United Arab Emirates

TULTEX CORPORATION

22 E. Church Street, PO Box 5191

Martinsville, VA 24115

Tel: (703) 632-2961 Fax: (703) 632-9123

CEO: Charles W. Davies, Pres.

FO: H. R. Badgett

HR: Ron Cox

Emp: 7,000

Mfr. sporting goods and apparel.

Canada

TURNER INTERNATIONAL INDUSTRIES INC.

375 Hudson Street

New York, NY 10014

Tel: (212) 229-6000 Fax: (212) 229-6418

CEO: Ellis T. Gravette, CEO

FO: Harold Parmelee, Pres.

HR: Robert G. Widing

Emp: 2,400 Rev: $2,000 mil.

General construction, construction management.

Belgium, Brazil, Singapore

TW METALS INC.

2211 Tubeway Ave.

Los Angeles, CA 90040

Tel: (213) 728-9101 Fax: (213) 728-5310

CEO: James F. Cameron, Chmn.

FO: George M. Supko

HR: Karen Diataledi

Emp: 575

Distributor pipe, tube, valves, fittings & flanges.

England, U.K., France

TWIN DISC INC.

1328 Racine Street

Racine, WI 53403-1758

Tel: (414) 638-4000 Fax: (414) 638-4482

CEO: Michael E. Batten, Pres.

FO: James McIndoe

HR: Arthur Zintek

Web site: www.twindisc.com

Emp: 1,400

Mfr. industry clutches, reduction gears and transmissions.

Australia, Belgium, Italy, Japan, New Zealand, Singapore, South Africa, Spain

TYCO INTERNATIONAL LTD.

One Tyco Park

Exeter, NH 03833

Tel: (603) 778-9700 Fax: (603) 778-7700

CEO: L. Dennis Kozlowski, Pres. & Chmn.

HR: Wendy Desmond, VP

Web site: www.tycoint.com

Emp: 75,000 Rev: $6,500 mil.

Mfr./sales fire & security systems, sprinkler systems, undersea fiber optic telecommuncations, printed circuit boards, pipe tubing and flow meters.

Austria, Bahrain, Belgium, Canada, Czech Republic, Denmark, Egypt, England, U.K., Finland, France, Germany, Greece, Hungary, Ireland, Isle of Man, Israel, Italy, Jordan, Kuwait,

Malta, Mexico, Netherlands, Nigeria, Northern Ireland, U.K., Norway, Oman, Poland, Qatar, Saudi Arabia, Scotland, U.K., South Africa, Spain, Sweden, Switzerland, Turkey, Wales, U.K.

TYCO PRESCHOOL INC.

200 Fifth Ave.

New York, NY 10010

Tel: (212) 620-8200 Fax: (212) 807-7183

CEO: Neil Friedman, Pres.

FO: Herb Whitson

Emp: 125

Distributor infant and preschool toys.

Hong Kong

W. S. TYLER INC.

8570 Tyler Road

Mentor, OH 44060

Tel: (440) 974-1047 Fax: (440) 974-0921

CEO: Larry Pope, Pres.

HR: Donald A. Whitehouse

Emp: 650

Mfr. vibrating screens, lab equipment & related screening media, crushing equipment.

Canada

TYSON FOODS INC.

PO Box 2020

Springdale, AR 72765-2020

Tel: (501) 290-4000 Fax: (501) 290-4061

CEO: Wayne Britt

FO: William Kuckuck, Pres. Int'l.

HR: William P. Jaycox, SVP

Web site: www.tyson.com

Emp: 59,400

Production/mfr./distributor poultry, beef, pork & seafood products.

Hong Kong, Japan, Singapore, South Korea

U

U.S. SAFETY

8101 Lenexa Drive

Lenexa, KS 66214

Tel: (913) 599-5555 Fax: (800) 252-5002

CEO: L. Alan Sankpill, Pres.

FO: Scott M. Wilson

HR: Mary Kay Manyon

Emp: 350

Design/development/mfr. personal protection equipment.

England, U.K.

U.S. SUMMIT CORPORATION

600 Third Ave.

New York, NY 10016

Tel: (212) 490-1100 Fax: (212) 557-3875

CEO: C. C. Wang,Pres.

FO: Leonard Chan

Marketing/distribution pharmaceuticals, chemicals.

Malaysia, Singapore, Taiwan (ROC), Thailand

U.S. SURGICAL CORPORATION

150 Glover Ave.

Norwalk, CT 06856

Tel: (203) 845-1000 Fax: (203) 847-0635

CEO: Howard Rosencrantz, Pres.

HR: David Renker

Web site: www.ussurg.com

Emp: 8,140

Mfr./development/market surgical staplers, laparoscopic instruments and sutures.

Australia, Austria, Belgium, Canada, England, U.K., France, Germany, Ireland, Italy, Netherlands, Russia, Spain, Switzerland

U.S. WHEAT ASSOCIATES

1620 I Street, NW

Washington, DC 20006

Tel: (202) 463-0999 Fax: (202) 785-1052

CEO: Alan Tracy, Pres.

HR: Kevin McGarry, VP

Market development for wheat products.

Chile, Egypt, Guatemala, India, Japan, Morocco, Netherlands, Philippines, South Korea, Taiwan

(ROC)

U.S. FILTER/WALLACE & TIERNAN

1901 West Garden Road
Vineland, NJ 08360
Tel: (609) 507-9000 Fax: (609) 507-4125
CEO: Joe Millen, Pres.
HR: Dorsett Bryant
Web site: www.usfwt.com
Mfr. disinfection and chemical feed equipment.
Canada, Germany

U.S. OFFICE PRODUCTS COMPANY

1025 Thomas Jefferson Street, NW, Ste. 600E
Washington, DC 20007
Tel: (202) 339-6700 Fax: (202) 339-6720
CEO: Jonathan J. Ledecky, Chmn.
FO: Robert M. Tank, VP
HR: Jim Foley
Web site: www.usop.com
Emp: 17,000
Sales and distribution of educational products, office supplies and office related services.
Australia, Canada, England, U.K., Indonesia, New Zealand, Philippines, Thailand

U.S. PLAYING CARD COMPANY

4590 Beech Street
Cincinnati, OH 45212-3497
Tel: (513) 396-5700 Fax: (513) 351-0131
CEO: Ronald C. Rule
HR: Louis Eichhold
Emp: 1,156
Mfr. playing cards and accessories and board games.
Canada, Spain

UNIFI INC.

7201 West Friendly Ave.
Greensboro, NC 27410-6237
Tel: (910) 294-4410 Fax: (910) 316-5422
CEO: William T. Kretzer, Pres.
Emp: 6,400
Yarn spinning mills, throwing/winding mills.
England, U.K., Ireland

UNIFIRST CORPORATION

68 Jonspin Road
Wilmington, MA 01887
Tel: (978) 658-8888 Fax: (978) 657-5663
CEO: Ronald D. Croatti, Pres.
FO: Bruce P. Boynton, VP Canada
HR: Michael McKinney, VP
Web site: www.unifirst.com
Emp: 7,000
Industrial launderers and sale/rental of uniform and work garments.
Canada, Sweden

UNIMIN CORPORATION

258 Elm Street
New Canaan, CT 06840
Tel: (203) 966-8880 Fax: (203) 966-3453
CEO: Kevin F. Crawford, Pres.
Emp: 1,300
Industrial sand, crushed stone, clay, non-metallic minerals.
Canada

UNION CAMP CORPORATION

1600 Valley Road
Wayne, NJ 07470
Tel: (973) 628-2000 Fax: (973) 628-2722
CEO: W. Craig McClelland, Chmn.
FO: Charles H. Greiner, Jr., EVP
HR: Jerome (Jerry) N. Carter, SVP
Web site: www.unioncamp.com
Emp: 19,000 Rev: $4,400 mil
Mfr. paper, packaging, chemicals and wood products.
Argentina, Brazil, Canada, Chile, China (PRC), Denmark, England, U.K., France, Germany, Ghana, Hong Kong, India, Ireland, Jamaica, Malaysia, Mexico, Netherlands, New Zealand, Nigeria, Philippines, Singapore, South Africa, Spain, Sweden, Turkey, Zimbabwe

UNION CARBIDE CORPORATION

39 Old Ridgebury Road
Danbury, CT 06817
Tel: (203) 794-2000 Fax: (203) 794-6269
CEO: William H. Joyce, Chmn.
HR: Malcolm A Kessinger, VP
Web site: www.unioncarbide.com
Emp: 11,000 Rev: $6,500 mil.
Mfr. industrial chemicals, plastics and resins.

Argentina, Australia, Austria, Bahrain, Belgium, Brazil, Canada, Chile, China (PRC), Colombia, Costa Rica, Ecuador, Egypt, England, U.K., France, Germany, Greece, Guatemala, Hong Kong, Indonesia, Italy, Japan, Jordan, Kuwait, Malaysia, Mexico, Morocco, New Zealand, Pakistan, Peru, Philippines, Russia, Singapore, South Africa, South Korea, Spain, Sri Lanka, Sweden, Switzerland, Taiwan (ROC), Thailand, Turkey, United Arab Emirates, Venezuela, Zimbabwe

UNION ELECTRIC STEEL CORPORATION

PO Box 465

Carnegie, PA 15106

Tel: (412) 429-7655 Fax: (412) 276-1711

CEO: Robert G. Carothers, Pres.

FO: Thomas J. Kelly

Emp: 601

Mfr. forged hardened steel rolls.

Belgium

UNION OIL INTERNATIONAL DIV

2141 Rosecrans Ave.

El Segundo, CA 90245

Tel: (310) 726-7600 Fax: (310) 726-7817

CEO: John Imle,Pres.

HR: L. R. McHodgkins

Emp: 19,399

Petroleum products, petrochemicals..

Australia, Benin, Brazil, Canada, Chile, Egypt, Hong Kong, Japan, Netherlands, Norway, Philippines, Scotland, U.K., Singapore, South Korea, Thailand

UNION PACIFIC CORPORATION

1717 Main Street, #5900

Dallas, TX 75201-4605

Tel: (214) 743-5600 Fax: (214) 743-5656

CEO: Richard K. Davidson, Chmn.

HR: Barb Schaefer

Emp: 47,000

Holding company: railroad, crude oil, natural gas, petroleum refining, metal mining service, real estate.

Canada, Japan, Mexico

UNION SPECIAL CORPORATION

One Union Special Plaza

Huntley, IL 60142

Tel: (847) 669-4345 Fax: (847) 669-3534

CEO: Terrance Hitpas, Pres.

HR: Mike Krizman

Web site: www.unionspecial.com

Emp: 1,290

Mfr. sewing machines.

Bangladesh, Belgium, Canada, Czech Republic, England, U.K., France, Germany, Hong Kong, India, Indonesia, Italy, Japan, Mexico, Philippines, Poland, Romania, Singapore, Slovakia, Vietnam

UNIROYAL CHEMICAL CO., INC.

World Headquarters, Benson Road

Middlebury, CT 06749

Tel: (203) 573-2000 Fax: (203) 573-2265

CEO: Vincent Colarco, Pres.

Emp: 49,241 Rev: $900 mil.

Tires, tubes and other rubber products, chemicals, plastics and textiles.

Argentina, Australia, Belgium, Brazil, Colombia, England, U.K., Germany, Hong Kong, Italy, Luxembourg, Mexico, Scotland, U.K., Spain

UNISOURCE WORLDWIDE, INC.

1100 Cassatt Ave.

Berwyn, PA 19312

Tel: (610) 296-4470 Fax: (610) 722-3400

CEO: Ray B. Mundt, Chmn.

FO: Charles F. White, Pres.

HR: Steve Becker, VP

Web site: www.unisourcelink.com

Emp: 14,000 Rev: $58.7 mil.

Distributor of paper and paper supply systems

Canada, Mexico

UNISYS CORPORATION.

PO Box 500, Union Meeting Road

Blue Bell, PA 19424

Tel: (215) 986-4011 Fax: (215) 986-6850

CEO: Lawrence A. Weinbach, Pres.

FO: Gerald A. Gagliardi, Pres. Intl.

HR: David O. Aker, VP

Web site: www.unisys.com

Emp: 32,000 Rev: $6,000 mil.

Mfr./marketing/servicing electronic information systems.

Australia, Austria, Belgium, Brazil, Canada, Denmark, England, U.K., Finland, France,

Germany, Hong Kong, Italy, Japan, Malaysia, Mexico, Netherlands, Norway, Philippines, Portugal, Singapore, South Africa, South Korea, Spain, Sweden, Switzerland, Taiwan (ROC), Turkey, Venezuela

UNITED AIRLINES INC.

PO Box 66100
Chicago, IL 60666
Tel: (847) 700-4000 Fax: (847) 952-7680
CEO: Gerald Greenwald, Chmn.
FO: Christopher D. Bowers, SVP Intl.
Web site: www.ual.com
Emp: 90,000 Rev: $11,000 mil.

Air transportation, passenger and freight.

Australia, Brazil, England, U.K., France, Germany, Japan, Poland, Singapore, South Korea, Sweden, Thailand

UNITED ASSET MANAGEMENT CORPORATION

One International Place, 44th Fl.
Boston, MA 02110
Tel: (617) 330-8900 Fax: (617) 330-1133
CEO: Norton H. Reamer, Chmn.
FO: Franklin H. Kettle
HR: Suzanne Meredith
Emp: 2,500 Rev: $940.0 mil

Investment management services.

Bahrain, Canada, England, U.K., Japan, Scotland, U.K., Singapore

UNITED CATALYSTS INC.

1600 West Hill Street
Louisville, KY 40210
Tel: (502) 634-7200 Fax: (502) 637-3732
CEO: C. Bert Knight, Pres.
FO: Alan Birch
Emp: 650

Mfr. catalysts for petroleum, chemical and food industry.

Belgium, Germany, India, Japan, Mexico

UNITED CENTRIFUGAL PUMPS INC.

222 W. Las Colinas Blvd.
Dallas, TX 75039
Tel: (408) 298-0123 Fax:
CEO: Bernard Rethore,Pres.

Mfr. pumps.

Lebanon, Netherlands

UNITED DESIGN CORPORATION

PO Box 1200
Noble, OK 73068
Tel: (405) 872-3468 Fax: (405) 360-4442
CEO: Jess Massien, Pres.
HR: Larry Feree
Emp: 700

Mfr. pottery products.

Canada

UNITED ELECTRIC CONTROLS COMPANY

PO Box 9143
Watertown, MA 02172-9143
Tel: (617) 926-1000 Fax: (617) 926-1000
CEO: David Reis
FO: Peter Godfrey
HR: Kelly Tonner
Emp: 400

Mfr./sale electro-mechanical & electronic controls & recorders.

Australia, England, U.K.

UNITED LABORATORIES INC.

320 Thirty-seventh Avenue
St. Charles, IL 60174
Tel: (630) 377-0900 Fax: (630) 377-0960
CEO: Nicholas J. Savaiano, Pres.
Emp: 430

Mfr. cleaning & sanitation products, chemicals.

Canada

UNITED PARCEL SERVICE OF AMERICA, INC.

55 Glenlake Parkway, NE
Atlanta, GA 30328
Tel: (404) 828-6000 Fax: (404) 828-6593
CEO: James P. Kelly
FO: Edward L. Schroeder, SVP
HR: Lea N. Soupata, SVP
Web site: www.ups.com
Emp: 330,000 Rev: $22,458 mil.

International package-delivery service.

Australia, Austria, Bahamas, Bahrain, Belgium,

Belize, Bermuda, Bolivia, Brazil, Bulgaria, Cayman Islands, Chile, China (PRC), Colombia, Costa Rica, Croatia, Cyprus, Czech Republic, Denmark, Dominican Republic, Ecuador, Egypt, El Salvador, England, U.K., Estonia, Finland, France, Germany, Ghana, Greece, Guatemala, Honduras, Hong Kong, Hungary, India, Indonesia, Ireland, Israel, Italy, Ivory Coast, Jamaica, Japan, Kenya, Kuwait, Latvia, Lebanon, Lithuania, Malaysia, Malta, Mexico, Morocco, Netherlands, Netherlands Antilles, Nicaragua, Nigeria, Norway, Panama, Paraguay, Peru, Philippines, Poland, Portugal, Qatar, Reunion, Romania, Russia, Saudi Arabia, Singapore, Slovakia, Slovenia, South Africa, South Korea, Sweden, Switzerland, Taiwan (ROC), Thailand, Turkey, Ukraine, United Arab Emirates, Uruguay, Venezuela, Zimbabwe

UNITED PRESS INTERNATIONAL

1400 I Street

Washington, DC 20005

Tel: (202) 898-8000 Fax: (202) 371-1239

CEO: James Adams, Pres.

Collection & distributor of news, newspictures, financial data.

Argentina, Australia, Brazil, Canada, England, U.K., Mexico

UNITED RENTALS INC.

4 Greenwich Office Park

Greenwich, CT 06830

Tel: (203) 622-3131 Fax: (203) 622-6080

CEO: Brad Jacobs, Pres.

Rev: $108 mil.

Equipment rental.

Canada

UNITED STATES SURGICAL CORPORATION

150 Glover Ave.

Norwalk, CT 06856

Tel: (203) 845-1000 Fax: (203) 845-4478

CEO: Leon C. Hirsch, Chmn.

FO: Turi Josefsen, Pres, Intl.

Web site: www.ussurg.com/public/Home-Page.html

Mfr./distribute surgical stapling instruments.

England, U.K.

UNITED STATES TRUST COMPANY OF NEW YORK

114 West 47th Street

New York, NY 10036

Tel: (212) 852-1000 Fax: (212) 852-1140

CEO: H. Marshall Schwarz, Chmn.

HR: Patricia McGuire, Mng. Dir.

Web site: www.ustrust.com

Emp: 1,510

Investment management company which also provides fiduciary and private banking services.

Cayman Islands

UNITED STATIONERS INC.

2200 East Golf Road

Des Plaines, IL 60016

Tel: (847) 699-5000 Fax: (847) 699-8046

CEO: Randall Larrimore, Pres.

Emp: 4,000

Wholesale office supplies.

Canada

UNITED TECHNOLOGIES CORPORATION

United Technologies Building

Hartford, CT 06101

Tel: (860) 728-7000 Fax: (860) 728-7979

CEO: George A. David, Chmn.

FO: Michael Blake, VP Intl.

HR: William L. Bucknall Jr., VP

Web site: www.utc.com

Emp: 180,100 Rev: $24,700 mil.

Mfr. aircraft engines, elevators, A/C, auto equipment, space and military electronic and rocket propulsion systems. Products include Pratt & Whitney, Otis elevators, Carrier heating and air conditioning and Sikorsky helicopters.

Argentina, Austria, Belgium, China (PRC), Denmark, England, U.K., France, Germany, Greece, Italy, Japan, Netherlands, Norway, Russia, Saudi Arabia, Scotland, U.K., Singapore, South Korea, Spain, Sweden, Switzerland, Venezuela

UNITED TOTE COMPANY

2311 South Seventh Ave.

Bozeman, MT 59715

Tel: (406) 582-4000 Fax: (406) 585-6609

CEO: Richard Haddrell, Pres.

FO: Linda Shelhamer

HR: Edward Neuman

Emp: 400

Design/mfr./operate pari-mutuel wagering systems.

Canada

UNITRODE CORPORATION

7 Continental Blvd.

Merrimack, NH 03054

Tel: (603) 424-2410 Fax: (603) 429-8771

CEO: Robert L. Gable

FO: K. Y. Chan

HR: Patrick Moquin

Web site: www.unitrode.com

Emp: 665 Rev: $177.6 mil.

Mfr. electronic components (analog/linear and mixed-signal)

England, U.K., Germany, Hong Kong, Italy, Singapore

UNIVAR CORPORATION

6100 Carillon Point

Kirkland, WA 98004

Tel: (425) 889-3400 Fax: (425) 889-4100

CEO: Paul Hough, Pres.

HR: Craig Lawson

Emp: 3,300

Industrial chemicals.

Canada, Netherlands

UNIVERSAL CORPORATION

PO Box 25099

Richmond, VA 23260

Tel: (804) 359-9311 Fax: (804) 254-3582

CEO: Henry Harrell, Pres.

FO: Harold W. Hamlett

HR: Brenda Riel

Holding company for tobacco and commodities.

Brazil, Canada, England, U.K., Greece, Hong Kong, Italy, Mexico, Netherlands, Philippines, South Korea, Switzerland, Thailand, Zimbabwe

UNIVERSAL FOODS CORPORATION

433 E. Michigan Street

Milwaukee, WI 53202

Tel: (414) 271-6755 Fax: (414) 347-4783

CEO: Kenneth Manning, Chmn.

HR: Tim Maguire

Emp: 5,000

Mfr. food products & food ingredients.

Canada, Costa Rica, England, U.K., Guatemala, Italy, Mexico

UNIVERSAL FOREST PRODUCTS INC.

2801 East Beltline Ave. NE

Grand Rapids, MI 49525

Tel: (616) 364-6161 Fax: (616) 364-5558

CEO: William G. Currie, Pres.

HR: James A. Overbeek

Emp: 1,950

Wood preservation services, structural wood, flooring, wood products.

Canada

UNIVERSAL INSTRUMENTS

90 Bevier Street, S. Dock

Binghamton, NY 13904

Tel: (607) 779-7522 Fax: (607) 779-7971

CEO: Gerhard Meese, Pres.

HR: Paul Slovodian, VP

Web site: www.dover.com

Emp: 1,700

Mfr./sales of instruments for electronic circuit assembly

Argentina, Australia, Brazil, Canada, China (PRC), Denmark, Egypt, England, U.K., Finland, France, Germany, Hong Kong, India, Ireland, Israel, Italy, Japan, Malaysia, Mexico, Norway, Philippines, Poland, Scotland, U.K., South Africa, South Korea, Spain, Sweden, Taiwan (ROC), Thailand, Turkey

UNIVERSAL WEATHER & AVIATION INC.

8787 Tallyho Road

Houston, TX 77061

Tel: (713) 944-1622 Fax: (713) 943-4650

CEO: Joe Rachelle, Pres.

Emp: 300

Airport transport services.

England, U.K., France, Italy, Mexico, Singapore

UNOCAL CORPORATION

PO Box 7600

Los Angeles, CA 90051

Tel: (213) 977-7600 Fax: (213) 726-7817

CEO: Roger C. Beach, Pres.

HR: David Demont

Emp: 15,005

Fully integrated high-tech energy resources development.

Azerbaijan, England, U.K., Singapore, Thailand, Vietnam

UNOVA INC.

360 North Crescent Drive

Beverly Hills, CA 90210-4287

Tel: (310) 888-2500 Fax: (310) 888-3848

CEO: Alton Brann, Pres.

Rev: $1.5 bil.

Automated data collection, mobile computing and manufacturing systems.

England, U.K., Germany

UNUM CORPORATION

2211 Congress Street

Portland, ME 04122

Tel: (207) 770-2211 Fax: (207) 770-4510

CEO: James F. Orr, III

FO: Thomas G. Brown, EVP

HR: Eileen C. Sarrar

Web site: www.unum.com

Emp: 7,200 Rev: $3,460 mil.

Disability and special risk insurance.

Argentina, Bermuda, Canada, England, U.K., Japan, Singapore

UOP INC.

25 E. Algonquin Road

Des Plaines, IL 60017

Tel: (847) 391-2000 Fax: (847) 391-2253

CEO: Michael Winfield,Pres.

HR: Ray Tutton

Emp: 11,800

Diversified research, development & mfr. of industry products & systems management studies & service.

Argentina, Australia, Bahrain, Belgium, Canada, Colombia, England, U.K., France, Germany, Hong Kong, Ireland, Japan, Kuwait, Saudi Arabia, Sweden

UPRIGHT INC.

1775 Park Street

Selma, CA 93662

Tel: (209) 891-5200 Fax: (209) 896-9012

CEO: Jim Dillon, Pres.

HR: Cathy Peppers

Emp: 750

Mfr. aluminum scaffolds & aerial lifts.

Ireland, Malaysia

UROPLASTY INC.

2718 Summer Street NE

Minneapolis, MN 55413-2820

Tel: (651) 378-1180 Fax: (651) 378-2027

CEO: Dan Holman, Pres.

FO: Marc Herregraven

Emp: 17

Mfr. urology products.

England, U.K., Netherlands

URS CORPORATION

100 California Street, Ste. 500

San Francisco, CA 94111-4529

Tel: (415) 774-2700 Fax: (415) 398-1904

CEO: Martin M. Koffel, Chmn.

FO: Irwin L. Rosenstein, VP

HR: Barbara Noel, Dir.

Web site: www.urscorp.com

Emp: 3,200 Rev: $400 mil.

Provides planning, design and construction management services, pollution control and hazardous waste management.

Hong Kong, Japan, Malaysia, Philippines, Turks & Caicos Islands

URSCHEL LABORATORIES INC.

2503 Calumet Ave., PO Box 2200

Valparaiso, IN 46384-2200

Tel: (219) 464-4811 Fax: (219) 462-3879

CEO: Robert R. Urschel, Chmn.

FO: Dave Steider

HR: Charles Parsons

Emp: 215

Design/mfr. precision food processing equipment.

Denmark, England, U.K., France, Germany, Japan, Netherlands, Portugal, Switzerland

US AIRWAYS, INC.

2345 Crystal Drive

Arlington, VA 22227
Tel: (703) 872-7000 Fax: (703) 294-5096
CEO: Rakesh Gangwal, Pres.
FO: Stephen M. Wolf, Chrm.
HR: John R. Long, III, EVP
Web site: www.usairways.com
Emp: 38,500 Rev: $8,500 mil.
Commercial airline.
France, Germany

U.S. FILTER CORPORATION
40-004 Cook Street
Palm Desert, CA 92211
Tel: (760) 340-0098 Fax: (760) 341-9368
CEO: Richard Heckmann, Pres.
HR: Rita Leduc
Emp: 130
Technical design and service water process systems.
France, Spain, Switzerland

US FILTER/MEMTEC AMERICA
2118 Greenspring Drive
Timonium, MD 21093
Tel: (410) 252-0800 Fax: (410) 252-6027
CEO: Ron Reilly, Pres.
HR: Kevin O'Neill
Emp: 1,550
Mfr. purification & separation systems & products.
Australia, England, U.K., France, Germany, Japan, Singapore

US WEST, INC.
7800 East Orchard Road, PO Box 6508
Englewood, CO 80155-6508
Tel: (303) 793-6500 Fax: (303) 793-6654
CEO: Richard D. McCormick, Chmn.
FO: Michael P. Glinsky, EVP
HR: Charles P. Russ, III
Emp: 2,800
Tele-communications provider; integrated communications services.
Belgium, Czech Republic, England, U.K., Hungary, India, Indonesia, Japan, Malaysia, Russia, Slovakia, Spain

USAA
900 Fredericksburg Road
San Antonio, TX 78288
Tel: (210) 498-2211 Fax: (210) 498-9940
CEO: Robert T. Herres, Chmn.
FO: William T. Flynn, III
HR: William B. Tracy
Emp: 15,700 Rev: $6,890 mil.
Provides financial services, life, property and casualty inurance and consumer sales services primarily to military and U.S. government personnel and their families.
England, U.K., Germany

USG CORPORATION
125 South Franklin Street
Chicago, IL 60606
Tel: (312) 606-4000 Fax: (312) 606-4093
CEO: William C. Foote, Chmn., Pres
HR: Hal Pendexter
Web site: www.usg.com
Emp: 14,200
Holding company for the building products industry.
Canada, Mexico

USX - U.S. STEEL GROUP
600 Grant Street
Pittsburgh, PA 15219-4776
Tel: (412) 391-8115 Fax: (412) 433-7519
CEO: Thomas J. Usher, Chmn.
HR: Dan D. Sandman, SVP
Web site: www.ussteel.com
Emp: 300 Rev: $6,800 mil
Steel production.
Canada, Mexico

USX-MARATHON GROUP
5555 San Felipe Road
Houston, TX 77056
Tel: (713) 629-6600 Fax: (713) 296-2952
CEO: Thomas J. Usher, Chmn.
FO: R. Keisler & W. Madison
HR: Daniel J. Sullenbarger, VP
Web site: www.marathon.com
Emp: 20,000 Rev: $15,500 mil.
Oil and gas exploration.
Canada, Egypt, England, U.K., Indonesia, Ireland, Netherlands, Norway, Scotland, U.K., Syria,

Tunisia

UTILICORPORATION UNITED INC.

PO Box 13287
Kansas City, MO 64199-3287
Tel: (816) 421-6600 Fax: (816) 472-6281
CEO: Richard C. Green, Jr., Chmn.
FO: Robert K. Green, Pres.
HR: Leo E. Morton, EVP
Emp: 3,022 Rev: $8,900 mil.

Electric and gas utility.

Australia, Canada, England, U.K., Jamaica, New Zealand

UTILX CORPORATION

22820 Russell Road, PO Box 97009
Kent, WA 98064-9709
Tel: (253) 395-0200 Fax: (253) 395-1040
CEO: Craig E. Davies, Pres.
FO: David Blaskowsky
HR: Ronald M. Dohr, VP
Emp: 980 Rev: $65 mil.

Mfr. utility construction machinery and guided boring systems and provides cable restoration services.

England, U.K.

UUNET

3060 Williams Drive
Fairfax, VA 22031-4648
Tel: (703) 206-5600 Fax: (703) 206-5601
CEO: Mark Spagnolo, Pres. & COO
FO: John Sidgmore, CEO
HR: Diana Lawrence, VP
Web site: www.worldcom.

World's largest Internet service provider; World Wide Web hosting services, security products and consulting services to businesses, professionals, and on-line service providers.

Belgium, Canada, England, U.K., France, Germany, Luxembourg, Netherlands, Sweden

V

VALENITE INC.

PO Box 9636
Madison Heights, MI 48071-9636
Tel: (248) 589-1000 Fax: (810) 597-4820
CEO: James Christie, Pres.
HR: Christine McDermott
Emp: 2,083

Cemented carbide, high speed steel, ceramic & diamond cutting tool products, etc.

Belgium, Canada, England, U.K., France, Germany, Italy, Japan, Mexico, Scotland, U.K., Spain, Switzerland, Taiwan (ROC)

VALHI INC.

5430 LBJ Freeway, Ste. 1700
Dallas, TX 75240
Tel: (972) 233-1700 Fax: (972) 375-0586
CEO: Harold Simmons, Pres. & Chmn.
HR: Keith Johnson
Emp: 12,000

Chemicals, hardware, sugar, mining.

Belgium, Canada, England, U.K., France, Germany, Norway, Scotland, U.K.

VALLEY FORGE CORPORATION

100 Smith Ranch Road, Ste. 326
San Rafael, CA 94903-1994
Tel: (415) 492-1500 Fax: (415) 492-0128
CEO: David R. Brining, Pres.
Emp: 470

Recreational goods, communications equipment, turbo actuators, switchgear & current-carrying devices.

Canada

VALMONT INDUSTRIES INC.

West Highway 275, PO Box 358
Valley, NE 68064-0358
Tel: (402) 359-2201 Fax: (402) 359-4948
CEO: Mogens Bay, Pres.
FO: E. Robert Meaney
Emp: 3,754

Mfr. irrigation systems, steel lighting, utility & communication poles.

China (PRC), France, Netherlands, Poland, Spain

VALSPAR CORPORATION

1101 South Third Street

Minneapolis, MN 55415-1259

Tel: (612) 332-7371 Fax: (612) 375-7723

CEO: Richard M. Rompala, Chmn.

FO: Rolf Engh, VP

HR: Gary E. Gardner, VP

Web site: www.valspar.com

Emp: 3,200 Rev: $1,017 mil.

Produce paint, varnish & allied products.

Australia, Canada, England, U.K., France, Germany, Norway, Singapore, South Africa

THE VANGUARD GROUP, INC.

100 Vanguard Boulevard

Malvern, PA 19355

Tel: (610) 648-6000 Fax: (610) 669-6605

CEO: John J. Brennan, Chmn. & Pres.

HR: K. Gubanich, Dir.

Web site: www.vanguard.com

Emp: 5,000 Rev: $1,600.0 mil

Mutual fund provider.

Australia

VANSTAR CORPORATION

1100 Abernathy Rd., Bldg. 500, Ste. 1200

Atlanta, GA 30328

Tel: (770) 522-4700 Fax: (770) 522-0695

CEO: William Y. Tauscher, Chmn.

HR: Wayne M. Keegan, SVP

Web site: www.vanstar.com

Emp: 7,000 Rev: $2,839 mil.

Provides computer services and products to major corporations.

Hong Kong, Luxembourg

VANTON PUMP & EQUIPMENT CORPORATION

201 Sweetland Ave.

Hillside, NJ 07205

Tel: (908) 688-4216 Fax: (908) 686-9314

CEO: Gerald Lewis

FO: Edward C. Hubert

Web site: www.vanton.com

Emp: 70

Mfr. non-metallic rotary, horizontal and vertical pumps and accessories for corrosive, abrasive and chemically pure fluids.

England, U.K.

VAPOR CORPORATION

6420 West Howard Street

Niles, IL 60714-3395

Tel: (847) 967-8300 Fax: (847) 965-9874

CEO: Keith H. Nippes, EVP

HR: Dennis E. Huebner

Emp: 570

Mfr. bus and rail transit automatic door systems, railcar/locomotive relays and contractors, vehicle ID systems.

Canada, England, U.K., Italy

VAREL INTERNATIONAL

9230 Denton Drive, PO Box 540157

Dallas, TX 75354-0157

Tel: (214) 351-6486 Fax: (214) 351-6438

CEO: J. Stobie/G. Phillips

FO: Glenn Phillips

HR: Sandy Wade

Emp: 1,055

Mfr. oil, mining, geophysical, water-well & construction equipment.

Australia, Canada, Mexico, United Arab Emirates

VARIAN ASSOCIATES INC.

3050 Hansen Way

Palo Alto, CA 94304-100

Tel: (650) 493-4000 Fax: (650) 424-5358

CEO: J. Tracy O'Rourke, Chmn.

FO: Richard A. Aurelio, EVP

HR: Ernest M. Felago, VP

Web site: www.varian.com

Emp: 6,500 Rev: $1,426 mil.

Mfr. microwave tubes & devices, analytical instruments, semiconductor process & medical equipment, vacuum systems.

Australia, Austria, Belgium, Brazil, Canada, China (PRC), Denmark, England, U.K., Finland, France, Germany, Hong Kong, India, Italy, Japan, Mexico, Netherlands, Singapore, South Korea, Sweden, Switzerland

VARLEN CORPORATION

PO Box 3089

Naperville, IL 60566-7089

Tel: (630) 420-0400 Fax: (630) 420-7123

CEO: Raymond Jean, Pres.

Emp: 2,000

Mfr. railroad and automotive products, tubular steel products, laboratory equipment, mold and die castings.

Germany

VEECO INSTRUMENTS INC.

Terminal Drive

Plainview, NY 11803

Tel: (516) 349-8300 Fax: (516) 349-9079

CEO: Edward H. Braun, Chmn.

FO: Emmanuel N. Lakios, EVP

HR: Wendy Hauge, Dir.

Web site: www.veeco.com

Emp: 595 Rev: $165 mil.

Mfr. surface profiler, atomic force microscopes, leak and plating thickness detectors and semiconductor products.

England, U.K., France, Germany, Hong Kong, Japan, Taiwan (ROC)

VEEDER-ROOT COMPANY

125 Powder Forest Drive, PO Box 2003

Simsbury, CT 06070-2003

Tel: (860) 651-2700 Fax: (860) 651-2704

CEO: H. Lawrence Clup, Chmn.

HR: Kenneth Deskus

Emp: 1,900

Mfr. counting, controlling and sensing devices.

Australia, Brazil, Canada, France, Germany, Scotland, U.K.

VELCON FILTERS INC.

4525 Centennial Blvd.

Colorado Springs, CO 80919-3350

Tel: (719) 531-5855 Fax: (719) 531-5690

CEO: David C. Taylor, Pres.

FO: Robin Mason

Emp: 340

Mfr./sale filters & filtration systems.

Canada, England, U.K., Germany, Singapore

VELSICOL CHEMICAL CORPORATION

10400 West Higgins Road, Ste. 600

Rosemont, IL 60018-3728

Tel: (847) 298-9000 Fax: (847) 298-9014

CEO: Arthur R. Sigel

FO: David Frederick

Web site: www.velsicol.com

Emp: 600

Produces high performance specialty chemicals based on benzoic acid and cyclo pentadiene.

Australia, England, U.K., Estonia, Philippines

VERITAS DGC INC.

3701 Kirby Drive

Houston, TX 77096

Tel: (713) 512-8300 Fax: (713) 512-8701

CEO: David B. Robson, Chmn.

FO: Stephen J. Ludlow, Pres.

HR: T. Scott Smith

Web site: www.veritasdgc.com

Emp: 3,500

Geophysical services.

England, U.K., Singapore

VERMEER MFG. COMPANY

PO Box 200

Pella, IA 50219-0200

Tel: (515) 628-3141 Fax: (515) 621-7730

CEO: Mary Andringa

FO: Sander DeHaan

HR: Kurt Langel

Web site: www.vermeermfg.com.

Emp: 2,000

Mfr. agricultural and construction equipment.

Netherlands

VERNAY LABORATORIES INC.

120 East South College Street

Yellow Springs, OH 45387

Tel: (937) 767-7261 Fax: (937) 767-1208

CEO: Tom Allen

Emp: 650

Mechanical products, specialty molded shapes, rubber goods.

Italy, Japan, Netherlands

VERSA PRODUCTS CO., INC.

22 Spring Valley Road

Paramus, NJ 07652

Tel: (201) 843-2400 Fax: (201) 843-2931

CEO: Karl L. Larsson, Pres.

HR: Theresa Halpin

Emp: 150

Mfr. pneumatic and hydraulic directional control valves.

Netherlands

VERTEX COMMUNICATIONS CORPORATION

2600 North Longview Street

Kilgore, TX 75662-6842

Tel: (903) 984-0555 Fax: (903) 984-1826

CEO: J. Rex Vardeman, Chmn.

FO: A. Don Branum, SVP

HR: Wilora Tucker, VP

Web site: www.vertencomm.com

Emp: 872 Rev: $92 mil.

High-tech holding company; microwave components, amplifiers, converters, terminal network workstations, voice, video and data applications.

Germany, Scotland, U.K., Singapore

VF CORPORATION

1047 North Park Road

Wyomissing, PA 19610

Tel: (610) 378-1151 Fax: (610) 378-9371

CEO: Mackey J. McDonald, Pres.

FO: Timothy A. Lambeth, Pres.

HR: Harold E. Addis

Web site: www.vfc.com

Emp: 63,000

Mfr./marketing apparel including Lee and Wrangler jeans, Jansport backpacks and Healthtex.

Belgium, France, Hong Kong

VIACOM INC.

1515 Broadway, 28th Fl.

New York, NY 10036-5794

Tel: (212) 258-6000 Fax: (212) 258-6358

CEO: Sumner M. Redstone, Chmn.

HR: William A. Roskin, SVP

Web site: www.viacom.com

Emp: 116,000 Rev: $13,000 mil.

Communications, publishing and entertainment.

Australia, Brazil, Canada, England, U.K., France, Germany, Japan, Mexico, Netherlands, Singapore, Switzerland

VIASOFT, INC.

3033 N. 44th Street

Phoenix, AZ 85018

Tel: (602) 952-0050 Fax: (602) 840-4068

CEO: Steven D. Whiteman, Chmn.

FO: Colin J. Reardon, SVP

HR: Nancy Mattson, Dir.

Web site: www.viasoft.com

Emp: 550 Rev: $115 mil.

Mainframe computer software, specializing in OnMark 2000 software.

Australia, England, U.K., Japan

VICON INDUSTRIES INC.

525 Broadhollow Road

Melville, NY 11747

Tel: (516) 293-2200 Fax: (516) 293-2627

CEO: Kenneth M. Darby, Chmn. & Pres.

Emp: 200

Mfr. radio/TV communications equipment.

England, U.K.

VICOR CORPORATION

23 Frontage Road

Andover, MA 01810

Tel: (978) 470-2900 Fax: (978) 475-6715

CEO: Patrizio Vinciarelli

Emp: 650

Mfr. electrical industry apparatus.

Germany

VICTAULIC INTERNATIONAL

4901 Kesslersville Road, PO Box 31

Easton, PA 18004-0031

Tel: (610) 559-3300 Fax: (610) 559-3608

CEO: Joseph M. Trachtenberg, Chmn.

HR: William J. Buss

Web site: www.victaulic.com

Emp: 1,700

Mfr. piping products: couplings, valves, fittings, etc.

Belgium, Canada

VIDEO DISPLAY CORPORATION

1868 Tucker Industrial Road

Tucker, GA 30084

Tel: (770) 938-2080 Fax: (770) 493-3903

CEO: Ronald Oraway, Pres.

Emp: 600

Mfr./rebuild/distribute video display components.

England, U.K.

VIDEOJET SYSTEMS INTERNATIONAL INC.

1500 Mittel Boulevard

Wood Dale, IL 60191

Tel: (630) 860-7300 Fax: (630) 616-3657

CEO: Henry J. Bode, Pres.

HR: Bruce Ralph, VP

Web site: www.videojet.com

Emp: 1,300 Rev: $260 mil.

Mfr. computer peripherals and hardware, state-of-the-art industrial ink jet marking and coding products.

England, U.K., France, Germany, Ireland, Japan, Netherlands, Singapore

THE VIKING CORPORATION

210 N. Industrial Park Road

Hastings, MI 49058

Tel: (616) 945-9501 Fax: (616) 945-9599

CEO: Paul Jordan, Pres.

FO: Albert Pillon

HR: George Hamaty

Emp: 270

Mfr. fire extinguishing equipment.

Canada, Luxembourg

VIKING ELECTRONICS

9250 Independence Ave.

Chatsworth, CA 91311

Tel: (818) 341-4330 Fax: (818) 882-5713

CEO: Jerry Eddis, Pres.

HR: Sally Bush

Emp: 300

Mfr./sales of electronic interconnect systems.

England, U.K.

VIKING OFFICE PRODUCTS

950 West 190th Street

Torrance, CA 90502

Tel: (310) 225-4500 Fax: (310) 324-2396

CEO: Bruce Nelson, Pres.

FO: Doug Ramsdale, EVP Europe

HR: Geri Rivers, Director

Web site: www.vikingop.com

Emp: 3,700 Rev: $1,500 mil.

International direct marketer of office products, computer supplies, business furniture and stationery.

Australia, Austria, England, U.K., France, Germany, Ireland, Italy, Netherlands

VINA USA, INC.

150 Fifth Ave., Ste. 205

New York, NY 10011

Tel: (212) 620-0320 Fax: (212) 620-0254

CEO: Tran Quoc Thinh, Pres.

Emp: 12 Rev: $28 mil.

Financial consulting and import/export to Vietnam.

Vietnam

VINSON & ELKINS LP

1001 Fannin Street First City Tower

Houston, TX 77002

Tel: (713) 758-2222 Fax: (713) 758-2346

CEO: Harry Reasoner, Mng. Prtn.

International law firm.

Russia

VISHAY INTERTECHNOLOGY INC.

63 Lincoln Highway

Malvern, PA 19355

Tel: (610) 644-1300 Fax: (610) 296-0657

CEO: Dr. Felix Zandmann, Chmn. & Pres.

HR: William Spires

Web site: www.vishay.com

Emp: 14,000

Mfr. resistors, strain gages, capacitors, inductors, printed circuit boards.

Canada, England, U.K., France, Germany, Israel, Japan, Singapore

VISIO CORPORATION

520 Pike Street, Ste. 1800

Seattle, WA 98101-4001

Tel: (206) 521-4500 Fax: (206) 521-4501

CEO: Jeremy A. Jaech, Chmn.

FO: Gary E. Gigot, SVP

HR: Susan Slaton, Dir.

Web site: www.visio.com

Emp: 355 Rev: $100 mil

Developer and supplier of computer software.

Australia, England, U.K., France, Germany, Ireland, Italy, Japan, Malaysia, Netherlands, Singapore, South Africa, South Korea, Switzerland

VITRAMON INC.

PO Box 544

Bridgeport, CT 06601

Tel: (203) 268-6261 Fax: (203) 261-4446

CEO: Everett Arndt, Pres.

Web site: www.vishay.com

Emp: 1,200 Rev: $95 mil.

Ceramic capacitors.

Australia, Brazil, England, U.K., Germany

VIVITAR CORPORATION

1280 Rancho Conejo Blvd

Newbury Park, CA 91320

Tel: (805) 498-7008 Fax: (805) 498-5086

CEO: Victor Chelnick

HR: Lana Ceco

Emp: 102

Mfr. photographic equipment, electronic supplies.

Canada, England, U.K., France, Germany, Japan, Netherlands

VLSI TECHNOLOGY INC.

1109 McKay Drive

San Jose, CA 95131

Tel: (408) 434-3000 Fax: (408) 434-7584

CEO: Alfred J. Stein, Chmn.

FO: John S. Hodgson, SVP

HR: Art Gemmell, VP

Web site: www.vlsi.com

Emp: 2,500 Rev: $713 mil.

Mfr. custom & standard integrated circuits for computing, communications & industry applications.

Canada, England, U.K., France, Germany, Italy, Japan, Singapore, South Korea, Taiwan (ROC)

VOLT INFORMATION SCIENCES, INC.

1221 Ave. of the Americas, 47th Fl.

New York, NY 10020-1579

Tel: (212) 704-2400 Fax: (212) 704-2424

CEO: William Shaw, Chmn. & Pres.

FO: Jerome Shaw, EVP

Web site: www.volt.com

Emp: 31,000 Rev: $39.9 mil.

Staffing services and telecommunication services.

Australia, Brazil, Canada, England, U.K., France, Germany, Israel, Netherlands, Spain, Sweden, Uruguay

VTEL (VIDEOTELECOM CORPORATION)

108 Wild Basin Road

Austin, TX 78746

Tel: (512) 314-2700 Fax: (512) 314-2792

CEO: Jerry Benson

FO: Richard Couchman

HR: Judy Wallace

Emp: 210

Design/mfr. long-distance interactive video communications products.

England, U.K.

VULCAN MATERIALS COMPANY

1 Metroplex Drive

Birmingham, AL 35209

Tel: (205) 877-3000 Fax: (205) 877-3094

CEO: Donald M. James, Chmn.

HR: Wayne Houston, VP

Web site: www.vulcanmaterials.com

Emp: 7,000 Rev: $1,700 mil.

Mfr. construction materials & industry chemicals.

Canada, Mexico

VWR CORPORATION

1310 Goshen Pkwy

West Chester, PA 19380

Tel: (610) 431-1700 Fax: (610) 436-1760

CEO: J. B. Harris, Pres.

HR: R. E. Hedwall

Emp: 1,100

Distributor industrial & laboratory equipment & supplies.

Canada

WABCO (WESTINGHOUSE AIR BRAKE COMPANY)

1001 Air Brake Ave.
Wilmerding, PA 15148
Tel: (412) 825-1000 Fax: (412) 825-1501
CEO: William E. Kassling, Chmn. & Pres.
Rev: $453.5 mil.

Transportation technologies; develops, manufactures, and markets electronic products and equipment.

Australia, Canada, France, India

WACHOVIA BANK OF GEORGIA NA

PO Box 4148
Atlanta, GA 30302-4148
Tel: (404) 332-5000 Fax: (404) 332-5735
CEO: D. Gary Thompson, Pres.
FO: W. W. Dunn
HR: J. Kenneth Torreyson
Emp: 5,000

Commercial banking.

Cayman Islands, England, U.K., Japan

WACHOVIA CORPORATION

PO Box 3099
Winston-Salem, NC 27150
Tel: (919) 770-5000 Fax: (919) 770-5931
CEO: Leslie M. Baker, Jr., Pres.
FO: Walter E. Leonard, Jr., SVP
HR: Hector McEachern, Dir.
Web site: www.wachovia.com
Emp: 20,000 Rev: $65,400 mil.

Commercial banking.

Brazil, Cayman Islands, England, U.K., Japan

WACKENHUT CORPORATION

4200 Wackenhut Drive, Ste. 100
Palm Beach Gardens, FL 33410
Tel: (561) 622-5656 Fax: (561) 691-6736
CEO: Richard R. Wackenhut, Chmn.
FO: Fernando Carrizosa, SVP
HR: Sandra Nusbaum, SVP
Web site: www.wackenhut.com
Emp: 56,000 Rev: $1,127

Security systems & services.

Argentina, Australia, Belize, Bolivia, Brazil, Cameroon, Canada, Central African Republic, Chile, China (PRC), Colombia, Costa Rica, Cyprus, Czech Republic, Dominican Republic, Ecuador, El Salvador, England, U.K., France, Gambia, Germany, Ghana, Greece, Guatemala, Honduras, Hong Kong, India, Ivory Coast, Japan, Jordan, Mexico, Morocco, Mozambique, Nicaragua, Pakistan, Panama, Paraguay, Peru, Russia, Saudi Arabia, Scotland, U.K., Sierra Leone, Thailand, Trinidad & Tobago, Uruguay, Venezuela

WAHL CLIPPER CORPORATION

2902 N. Locust Street
Sterling, IL 61081
Tel: (815) 625-6525 Fax: (815) 625-1193
CEO: J. F. Wahl
FO: G.S. Wahl, Pres.
Emp: 1,600

Mfr. hair clippers, beard and mustache trimmers, shavers, pet clippers and soldering irons.

Canada, China (PRC), England, U.K., Germany, Hungary, Japan

WAINOCO OIL CORPORATION

10000 Memorial Drive, Ste. 600
Houston, TX 77024
Tel: (713) 688-9600 Fax: (713) 688-0616
CEO: James R. Gibbs, Pres.
Emp: 400

Oil/gas exploration, development and production.

Canada

WAL-MART STORES INC.

702 SW 8th Street
Bentonville, AR 72716-8611
Tel: (501) 273-4000 Fax: (501) 273-8980
CEO: David D. Glass, Pres.
FO: Bob L. Martin, Pres. Int'l
Web site: www.wal-mart.com
Emp: 528,000

Retailer.

Argentina, Brazil, Canada, China (PRC), Germany, Indonesia, Mexico

WALBAR METALS INC.

Peabody Ind Center, PO Box 3369
Peabody, MA 01961-3369

Tel: (978) 532-2350 Fax: (978) 532-7501

CEO: Theunis Botha, Pres.

HR: Dennis Creekmore

Emp: 900

Mfr. turbine components for engines; repair & coating service.

Canada

WALBRO CORPORATION

6242 Garfield Ave.

Cass City, MI 48762

Tel: (517) 872-2131 Fax: (517) 872-4957

CEO: Frank Bauchiero, Pres.

Emp: 3,650

Mfr. motor vehicle accessories & parts.

Japan, Singapore

WALCO INTERNATIONAL INC.

15 W Putnam Ave.

Porterville, CA 93257-3627

Tel: (817) 781-3510 Fax: (817) 416-1235

CEO: Jim Robeson, Pres.

Emp: 650

Drugs, proprietaries & sundries, farm supplies, medical & hospital equipment.

Canada

WALKER, INC.

303 Second Street, Marathon Plaza, 3 North

San Francisco, CA 94107

Tel: (415) 495-8811 Fax: (415) 957-1711

CEO: Leonard Y. Liu, Pres. & Chmn.

FO: Yugn Lee, VP Asia Pacific

HR: Wallace Breitman, VP

Web site: www.walker.com.

Emp: 550 Rev: $75 mil.

Provider of premier financial software solutions for large and medium-size enterprises.

Australia, England, U.K., Singapore

WALL COLMONOY CORPORATION

30261 Stephenson Hwy

Madison Heights, MI 48071

Tel: (248) 585-6400 Fax: (248) 585-7960

CEO: Joseph Maria, Pres.

FO: Demetario Jaramillo

HR: Joseph Drobet

Emp: 350 Rev: $50 mil.

Mfr. hard-surfacing and brazing alloys, equipment and services.

Canada, France, Wales, U.K.

WALTER, CONSTON, ALEXANDER & GREEN, PC

90 Park Ave.

New York, NY 10016-1387

Tel: (212) 210-9400 Fax: (212) 210-9444

CEO: Aydin Caginalp, Mng. Prtn.

Web site: www.wcag.com

Emp: 158

International law firm.

Germany

WANG LABORATORIES INC.

600 Technology Park Drive

Billerica, MA 01821

Tel: (508) 967-5000 Fax: (508) 967-5911

CEO: Joseph M. Tucci, Chmn.

HR: Albert A. Notini, SVP

Mfr. computer information processing systems.

Australia, Austria, Belgium, Canada, England, U.K., Germany, Hong Kong, Japan, Netherlands, New Zealand, Poland, Singapore, Switzerland

WARBURG DILLON READ

535 Madison Ave.

New York, NY 10022

Tel: (212) 906-7000 Fax: (212) 759-3755

CEO: Franklin Hobbs, Chmn.

Emp: 600

Investment banking.

England, U.K.

WARNACO INC.

90 Park Ave.

New York, NY 10016

Tel: (212) 661-1300 Fax: (212) 687-0480

CEO: Linda J. Wachner, Chmn.. & Pres.

HR: Dick Mitchell

Web site: www.warnaco.com

Emp: 20,000 Rev: $1,400 mil.

Mfr./sales intimate apparel and men's and women's sportswear.

Austria, Belgium, Canada, China (PRC), Costa Rica, Dominican Republic, England, U.K., France,

Germany, Honduras, Ireland, Italy, Mexico, Netherlands, Philippines, Spain, Sri Lanka, Switzerland

WARNER BROS INTERNATIONAL TELEVISION

4000 Warner Boulevard, Bldg.170, 3rd Fl.

Burbank, CA 91522

Tel: (818) 954-6000 Fax: (818) 977-4040

CEO: Jeffrey R. Schlesinger, Pres.

FO: Dan Morita, Dir., Intl.

HR: G. Moody

Emp: 121

Distributor TV programming and theatrical features.

Australia, Canada, England, U.K., France, Israel, Italy, Japan, Mexico, Spain, Turkey

WARNER ELECTRIC BRAKE & CLUTCH COMPANY

449 Gardner Street

South Beloit, IL 61080

Tel: (815) 389-3771 Fax: (815) 389-2582

CEO: William W. Keefer

FO: Paul de Belay

Web site: www.warnernet.com

Emp: 1,826

Global supplier of Power Transmission and Motion Control Solution Systems; automotive, industry brakes, and clutches.

Australia, England, U.K., France, Germany, Hong Kong, India, Italy, Netherlands, Singapore, Spain, Sweden, Switzerland, Taiwan (ROC), Thailand

WARNER-JENKINSON CO. INC.

2526 Baldwin Street

St. Louis, MO 63106

Tel: (314) 889-7600 Fax: (314) 658-7305

CEO: Michael A. Wick, Pres.

FO: Joseph DeRotaeche

HR: Maurice Smith

Emp: 500

Mfr. synthetic & natural colors for food, drugs & cosmetics.

Australia, Canada, England, U.K., France, Hong Kong, Mexico, Netherlands

WARNER-LAMBERT COMPANY

201 Tabor Road

Morris Plains, NJ 07950-2693

Tel: (973) 540-2000 Fax: (973) 540-3761

CEO: Melvin R. Goodes, Chmn.

FO: E. Phillip Milhomme, VP

HR: Raymond M. Fino, VP

Web site: www.warner-lambert.com

Emp: 40,000 Rev: $8,100 mil.

Mfr. ethical and proprietary pharmaceuticals, confectionery and consumer products & pet care supplies.

Australia, Austria, Belgium, Brazil, Canada, Chile, Colombia, Dominican Republic, Ecuador, England, U.K., France, Germany, Greece, Guatemala, Hong Kong, India, Indonesia, Ireland, Italy, Japan, Mexico, New Zealand, Pakistan, Peru, Philippines, Poland, South Africa, Spain, Taiwan (ROC), Thailand, Uruguay, Venezuela

WASSERSTEIN PERELLA & CO., INC.

31 West 52nd Street

New York, NY 10019

Tel: (212) 969-2700 Fax: (212) 969-7969

CEO: Bruce Wasserstein, Pres.

FO: Frederic M. Seegal, Mng. Dir.

Web site: www.wassersteinperella.com

Investment banking and financial services.

England, U.K., France, Germany, Japan

WASTE MANAGEMENT, INC.

3003 Butterfield Road

Oak Brook, IL 60523-1100

Tel: (630) 572-8800 Fax: (630) 572-3094

CEO: Robert Steve Miller, Chmn.

FO: Edwin G. Falkman, Chrm. Int'l.

HR: Paul G. George, SVP

Web site: www.wastemanagement.com

Emp: 58,000 Rev: $9 mil.

Environmental services and disposal company; collection, processing, transfer and disposal facilities.

Argentina, Australia, Austria, Brazil, Denmark, England, U.K., Finland, Germany, Hong Kong, Indonesia, Israel, Italy, Netherlands, New Zealand, Singapore, Sweden, Switzerland, Thailand

WATERBURY FARREL TECHNOLOGIES

60 Fieldstone Court

Cheshire, CT 06410

Tel: (203) 272-3271 Fax: (203) 271-0487

CEO: Andre Mazarian, Pres.

HR: Jan Talmadge

Emp: 1,729

Machine tools and metal working machinery.

Belgium, England, U.K.

WATERS CORPORATION

34 Maple Street

Milford, MA 01757

Tel: (508) 478-2000 Fax: (508) 872-1990

CEO: Douglas A. Berthiaume, Pres.

HR: Edmund Henault

Emp: 2,000 Rev: $333 mil.

Mfr./distribute liquid chromatographic instruments and test and measurement equipment.

Australia, Austria, Belgium, Brazil, Canada, Chile, China (PRC), Colombia, Denmark, England, U.K., Finland, France, Germany, Italy, Japan, Malaysia, Netherlands, Singapore, South Korea, Spain, Sweden, Switzerland, Taiwan (ROC), Uruguay, Venezuela

WATKINS INC.

PO Box 5570

Winona, MN 55987

Tel: (507) 457-3300 Fax: (507) 452-6723

CEO: Mark Jacobs, Chmn.

HR: Dave Fricke

Emp: 270

Mfr. cosmetics, medicines, spices and extracts, household cleaning products.

Canada

WATKINS-JOHNSON COMPANY

3333 Hillview Ave.

Palo Alto, CA 94304-1204

Tel: (415) 493-4141 Fax: (415) 813-2402

CEO: Dr. W. Keith Kennedy, Jr., Pres

Web site: www.wj.com

Emp: 1,500 Rev: $291 mil.

Radio-frequency products for wireless infrastructure market and semiconductor manufacturing equipment.

Japan, Scotland, U.K.

WATLOW ELECTRIC MFG. COMPANY

12001 Lackland Road

St. Louis, MO 63146-4039

Tel: (314) 878-4600 Fax: (314) 434-1020

CEO: Gary M. Neal, Pres.

FO: W. Schaefer

Web site: www.watlow.com

Emp: 2,400

Mfr. electrical heating units, electronic controls, thermocouple wire, metal-sheathed cable, infrared sensors.

England, U.K., France, Germany, Italy, Mexico, Singapore, South Korea, Taiwan (ROC)

WATSON WYATT & COMPANY

6707 Democracy Blvd., Ste. 800

Bethesda, MD 20817

Tel: (301) 581-4600 Fax: (301) 581-4937

CEO: A. W. (Pete) Smith, Jr., CEO

FO: Paul R. Daoust, EVP

HR: Sally Egan, Dir.

Web site: www.watsonwyatt.com

Emp: 5,000 Rev: $512 mil.

Creates compensation and benefits programs for major corporations.

Argentina, Australia, Belgium, Brazil, Canada, China (PRC), Colombia, England, U.K., Germany, Hong Kong, India, Indonesia, Ireland, Italy, Jamaica, Japan, Malaysia, Mexico, Netherlands, New Zealand, Philippines, Portugal, Scotland, U.K., Singapore, South Africa, South Korea, Spain, Sri Lanka, Sweden, Switzerland, Taiwan (ROC), Thailand, Zimbabwe

WATTS INDUSTRIES, INC.

815 Chestnut Street

North Andover, MA 01845-6098

Tel: (978) 688-1811 Fax: (978) 688-5841

CEO: Timothy P. Horne, Chmn.

FO: David A. Bloss, Sr., Pres.

Web site: www.wattsind.com

Emp: 4,300 Rev: $720 mil.

Designs/mfr./sales of industry valves and safety control products.

Canada, China (PRC), England, U.K., France, Germany, Italy, Netherlands, Spain

WAXMAN INDUSTRIES INC.

24460 Aurora Road

Bedford Heights, OH 44146

Tel: (440) 439-1830 Fax: (440) 439-8678

CEO: Armond Waxman

FO: Melvin Waxman

HR: John S. Peters

Emp: 750 Rev: $120 mil.

Assemble/distributor plumbing, electrical and hardware products.

China (PRC), Taiwan (ROC)

WD-40 COMPANY

1061 Cudahy Place

San Diego, CA 92110-3998

Tel: (619) 275-1400 Fax: (619) 275-5823

CEO: Garry O. Ridge, Pres.

FO: William B. Noble, Mng. Dir.

HR: Mary Rudy

Emp: 167

Mfr. branded multiple-purpose lubrication, protection and general maintenance products.

Australia, Canada, England, U.K., Malaysia

WEATHERFORD INTERNATIONAL INC.

5 Post Oak Blvd, Ste. 1760

Houston, TX 77227-3415

Tel: (713) 287-8400 Fax: (713) 963-9785

CEO: Bernard J. Buroc-Danner, Chmn.

FO: Robert E. Hendrix

HR: John Nicholson

Web site: www.weatherford.com

Emp: 7,200 Rev: $892 mil.

Oilfield services, products & equipment; mfr. marine cranes for oil and gas industry.

Algeria, Angola, Argentina, Australia, Austria, Bolivia, Brazil, Canada, China (PRC), Colombia, Congo, Cyprus, Denmark, Egypt, England, U.K., France, Gabon, Germany, Hong Kong, India, Indonesia, Italy, Kazakhstan, Kuwait, Malaysia, Mexico, Netherlands, New Zealand, Nigeria, Norway, Oman, Pakistan, Qatar, Romania, Russia, Saudi Arabia, Scotland, U.K., Singapore, Syria, Thailand, Trinidad & Tobago, Tunisia, Turkey, United Arab Emirates, Venezuela, Vietnam

WEAVEXX

401 Highway 12 West

Starkville, MS 39759

Tel: (601) 323-4064 Fax: (601) 324-1400

CEO: David J. Dumbrell

HR: Deb Hadley

Emp: 150

Mfr. papermakers' felts.

Canada

JERVIS B. WEBB COMPANY

34375 West Twelve Mile Road

Farmington Hills, MI 48331

Tel: (248) 553-1220 Fax: (248) 553-1237

CEO: George H. Webb, Pres.

FO: Donald Sandusky

HR: Susan Webb

Emp: 2,000

Mfr. integrators of material handling systems.

Australia, Canada, England, U.K., India

WEBER MARKING SYSTEMS INC.

711 West Algonquin Road

Arlington Heights, IL 60005

Tel: (847) 364-8500 Fax: (847) 364-8575

CEO: Joseph A. Weber, Jr.

FO: William J. Darras

HR: Shirley Griffin

Emp: 640

Mfr. label printing systems and custom labels.

Canada, Germany, Japan, Scotland, U.K.

WEBER-STEPHEN PRODUCTS CO.

200 E. Daniels Road

Palatine, IL 60067-6266

Tel: (874) 934-5700 Fax: (847) 934-3153

CEO: James Stephen, Pres.

HR: Joseph Moore

Mfr./sales Weber cooking systems and barbeque and gas grills.

England, U.K., France, Germany

WEDCO INC.

PO Box 397

Bloomsbury, NJ 08804

Tel: (908) 479-4181 Fax: (908) 479-6622

CEO: Sylvia Pacholder, Pres.

HR: Sam Hines

Plastics grinding and related services, machinery and equipment for plastics industry.

Brazil, England, U.K., France, Netherlands, Sweden

WEIGHT WATCHERS INTERNATIONAL

175 Crossways Park West

Woodbury, NY 11797

Tel: (516) 390-1400 Fax: (516) 390-1763

CEO: Kent Kreh, Pres.

HR: Brian Powers

Weight loss programs.

Australia, England, U.K., Finland, France, Germany, Sweden, Switzerland

WEIL, GOTSHAL & MANGES LLP

767 5th Ave.

New York, NY 10153

Tel: (212) 310-8000 Fax: (212) 310-8007

CEO: Stephen J. Dannhauser, Exec. Ptnr.

FO: John W. Neary

HR: Donna Lang

Web site: www.weil.com

Emp: 675 Rev: $354 mil.

International law firm.

Belgium, Czech Republic, England, U.K., Hungary, Poland

WEIL-McLAIN

500 Blaine Street

Michigan City, IN 46360

Tel: (219) 879-6561 Fax: (219) 879-4025

CEO: Thomas O. May

HR: Eric L. Nelson

Emp: 650

Mfr. cast iron boilers and domestic hot water heaters.

Canada

WELBILT CORPORATION

225 High Ridge Road

Stamford, CT 06905

Tel: (203) 325-8300 Fax: (203) 325-9800

CEO: Andrew Roake, Pres.

HR: Susan Fegan

Emp: 2,700

Mfr. commercial foodservice equipment.

Canada, England, U.K., France, Germany

WELCH ALLYN INC. , DATA COLLECTION DIV

4341 State Street Road

Skaneateles Falls, NY 13153

Tel: (315) 685-8351 Fax: (315) 685-4091

CEO: Kevin R. Jost, VP

FO: C. N. Benoit

Emp: 340

Mfr. bar code data collection systems.

England, U.K., Hong Kong

WELCH'S INC.

555 Virginia Road

Concord, MA 01742

Tel: (508) 371-1000 Fax: (508) 371-2832

CEO: Daniel Dillon, Pres.

Emp: 145

Mfr. juices and grape jams and jellies.

Hong Kong, Japan

WELLMAN INC.

1040 Broad Street, #302

Shrewsbury, NJ 07702

Tel: (732) 542-7300 Fax: (732) 542-9344

CEO: Thomas M. Duff, Pres.

Emp: 3,600

Plastic recycler; mfr. polyester fibres & resins.

Germany, Ireland, Netherlands

WENDY'S INTERNATIONAL, INC.

428 West Dublin-Granville Roads

Dublin, OH 43017

Tel: (614) 764-3100 Fax: (614) 764-3459

CEO: Gordon Teter, Chmn. & Pres.

Fast food restaurant chain.

Argentina, Aruba, Bahamas, Cayman Islands, China (PRC), Dominican Republic, El Salvador, England, U.K., Greece, Guatemala, Honduras, Hungary, Indonesia, Italy, Japan, Kuwait, Mexico, New Zealand, Philippines, Saudi Arabia, South Korea, Switzerland, Taiwan (ROC), Thailand, Turkey, United Arab Emirates, Venezuela

WERNER INTERNATIONAL INC.

55 East 52 Street, 29th Fl.

New York, NY 10055-0002

Tel: (212) 909-1260 Fax: (212) 909-1273

CEO: Antonio Rigamonti, Pres.

FO: Paul Wierks

HR: Mary Gallagher

Management consultants to textile and retail apparel industry.

Belgium

WERTHEIM SCHRODER & CO., INC.

787 Seventh Ave.

New York, NY 10019

Tel: (212) 492-6000 Fax: (212) 492-7029

CEO: Steven Kotler

Emp: 1,000

Investment banking, security brokers.

England, U.K., France, Switzerland

WESCO DISTRIBUTION INC.

Four Station Square #700

Pittsburgh, PA 15219

Tel: (412) 454-2200 Fax: (412) 454-2505

CEO: Roy W. Haley, Pres.

HR: Michael Meghan

Emp: 3,300

Electronic equipment and parts.

Canada

WESLEY INTERNATIONAL INC.

1825 South Woodward

Bloomfield Hills, MI 48302

Tel: (248) 857-9959 Fax: (248) 333-3136

CEO: Delbert W. Mullens, Chmn.

Emp: 800 Rev: $95.000 mil.

Mfr. coatings and castings.

Canada

WESLEY-JESSEN CORPORATION

333 East Howard Ave.

Des Plains, IL 60018

Tel: (847) 294-3000 Fax: (847) 294-3434

CEO: Kevin J. Ryan, Pres.

FO: Richard G. Wright

Emp: 580

Contact lenses and accessories, ophthalmic and dermatology products.

Australia, Canada, England, U.K., Germany

THE WEST BEND COMPANY

400 Washington Street

West Bend, WI 53095

Tel: (414) 334-2311 Fax: (414) 334-6800

CEO: Thomas W. Kieckhafer, Pres.

HR: Larry Grescoviak

Emp: 2,800

Mfr. small electrical appliances, cookware, water distillers, timers.

Canada, Mexico

WEST CHEMICAL PRODUCTS INC.

1000 Herrontown Road

Princeton, NJ 08540

Tel: (609) 921-0501 Fax: (609) 924-4308

CEO: Elwood W. Phares II,Pres.

HR: Maurice H. Sterman

Sanitary equipment & supplies.

Argentina, Dominican Republic, Guatemala, Mexico, Philippines

THE WEST COMPANY, INC.

101 Gordon Drive, PO Box 645

Lionville, PA 19341-0645

Tel: (610) 594-2900 Fax: (610) 594-3014

CEO: William G. Little, Chmn.

FO: Jerry A. Elers, Pres. & COO

HR: George R. Bennyhoff, SVP

Web site: www.thewestcompany.com

Emp: 4,800 Rev: $453 mil.

Mfr. products for filling, sealing, dispensing & delivering needs of health care & consumer products markets.

Argentina, Australia, Brazil, China (PRC), Colombia, Denmark, England, U.K., France, Germany, India, Italy, Japan, Mexico, Singapore, South Korea, Spain, Thailand, Venezuela, Yugoslavia

WEST POINT STEVENS INC.

507 West 10th Street, PO Box 71

West Point, GA 31833

Tel: (706) 645-4000 Fax: (706) 645-4453

CEO: Holcombe Green, Jr., Chmn.

HR: Roy Fisher

Emp: 22,000

Industry household and apparel fabrics and bed and bath products.

Canada, England, U.K.

WEST STAFF SERVICES INC.

301 Lennon Lane

Walnut Creek, CA 94598-2453

Tel: (925) 930-5300 Fax: (925) 934-5489

CEO: W. Robert Stover, Chmn.

FO: Michael K. Phippen, Pres.

HR: Joe Coute, VP

Web site: www.westaff.com

Emp: 41,638 Rev: $577 mil.

Secretarial & clerical temporary service.

Australia, Denmark, England, U.K., New Zealand, Norway, Switzerland

WESTERN ATLAS INC.

10205 Westheimer

Houston, TX 77251-1407

Tel: (713) 972-4000 Fax: (713) 952-9837

CEO: John R. Russell, Pres.

FO: Damir S. Skerl, EVP Intl.

HR: Robert Mason, Dir.

Web site: www.waii.com

Emp: 10,600 Rev: $1,600 mil.

Full service to the oil industry.

Algeria, Angola, Argentina, Australia, Azerbaijan, Bahrain, Bangladesh, Bolivia, Brazil, Brunei, Canada, Chad, China (PRC), Colombia, Ecuador, Egypt, England, U.K., Ethiopia, France, Guatemala, Indonesia, Italy, Kazakhstan, Kuwait, Malaysia, Mexico, Netherlands, Niger, Nigeria, Norway, Oman, Pakistan, Peru, Qatar, Romania, Russia, Saudi Arabia, Scotland, U.K., Singapore, Syria, Thailand, Trinidad & Tobago, United Arab Emirates, Venezuela, Yemen

WESTERN DIGITAL CORPORATION

8105 Irvine Center Drive

Irvine, CA 92718

Tel: (949) 932-5000 Fax: (949) 932-6629

CEO: Charles A. Haggerty, Chmn.

FO: David W. Schafer, SVP

HR: Jack Van Berkel, VP

Web site: www.wdc.com

Emp: 13,000 Rev: $3,540 mil.

Mfr. hard disk drives, video graphics boards, VLSI.

England, U.K., France, Germany, Hong Kong, Japan, Singapore, South Korea, Taiwan (ROC)

WESTERN UNION

1 Mack Center Drive

Paramus, NJ 07657

Tel: (201) 986-5100 Fax: (201) 818-6611

CEO: Ed Fuhrman, Pres.

HR: Frederick Sharp

Emp: 1,800

Financial and messaging service.

Australia, England, U.K., Netherlands, Russia, Spain

WESTINGHOUSE ELECTRIC (CBS)

11 Stanwix Street

Pittsburgh, PA 15222-1384

Tel: (412) 244-2000 Fax: (412) 642-4650

CEO: Michael H. Jordan, Chmn.

HR: James S. Moore

Emp: 85,000 Rev: $8,000 mil.

TV/radio broadcasting, mfr. electronic systems for industry/defense, financial & environmental services.

Argentina, Australia, Brazil, Canada, England, U.K., Germany, Ireland, Mexico, Poland, Russia, Singapore, South Korea, Ukraine

WESTVACO CORPORATION

299 Park Ave.

New York, NY 10171

Tel: (212) 688-5000 Fax: (212) 318-5055

CEO: John A. Luke Jr., Chmn.

FO: Charles E. Johnson Jr., VP

HR: John D. Flyn, VP

Web site: www.westvaco.com

Emp: 13,370 Rev: $2,982 mil.

Mfr. paper, packaging, chemicals.

Australia, Belgium, Brazil, Canada, Hong Kong, Japan

WEYERHAEUSER COMPANY

PO Box 2999, 33663 Weyerhaeuser Way South, Federal Way,

Tacoma, WA 98003

Tel: (253) 924-2345 Fax: (253) 924-2685

CEO: Steven R. Rogel, Pres.

FO: William R. Corbin, EVP

HR: Steven R. Hill

Web site: www.weyerhaeuser.com

Emp: 35,800 Rev: $11,210 mil.

Wood & wood fiber products.

Belgium, Canada, England, U.K., Hong Kong, Italy, Japan, Russia, Thailand

WHATMAN INC.

9 Bridewell Place

Clifton, NJ 07014

Tel: (973) 773-5800 Fax: (973) 472-6949

CEO: Paul Seliskar, Pres.

HR: Louise Crandell

Emp: 130

Laboratory filter paper and chromatography products.

England, U.K.

WHIRLPOOL CORPORATION

2000 N. M-63

Benton Harbor, MI 49022-2692

Tel: (616) 923-5000 Fax: (616) 923-5443

CEO: David R. Whitwam, Chmn.

FO: Jeff M. Fettig, EVP

HR: Greg Lee, SVP

Web site: www.whirlpoolcorp.com

Emp: 39,000 Rev: $7,600 mil.

Mfr./market home appliances: Whirlpool, Roper, KitchenAid, Estate, and Inglis.

Argentina, Australia, Brazil, Canada, Cayman Islands, China (PRC), France, Germany, Hong Kong, India, Italy, Japan, Mexico, Netherlands, New Zealand, Singapore, Slovakia, South Africa, South Korea, Sweden, Taiwan (ROC), Thailand

WHITE & CASE LLP

1155 Ave. of the Americas

New York, NY 10036-2767

Tel: (212) 819-8200 Fax: (212) 354-8113

CEO: James B. Hurlock, Mng. Ptnr.

FO: James Lotchford, COO

HR: Rita Troiso

Web site: www.whitecase.com

Rev: $318 mil.

International law firm.

Belgium, Brazil, Czech Republic, England, U.K., Finland, France, Hong Kong, Hungary, India, Indonesia, Japan, Kazakhstan, Mexico, Poland, Russia, Saudi Arabia, Singapore, Slovakia, South Africa, Sweden, Thailand, Turkey, Uzbekistan, Vietnam

WHITEHALL-ROBINS INC.

1407 Cummings Drive, PO Box 26609

Richmond, VA 23261-6609

Tel: (804) 257-2000 Fax: (804) 257-2120

CEO: E. Claiborne Robins, Jr.

FO: J. Steven Cole

Web site: www.ahp.com/whitehall.htm

Emp: 2,000 Rev: $1,400 mil.

Mfr. ethical pharmaceuticals and consumer products.

Australia, Canada, Colombia, England, U.K., France, Germany, Greece, Guatemala, Italy, Japan, Mexico, Philippines, Switzerland, Taiwan (ROC), Venezuela

WHITING CORPORATION

15700 Lathrop Ave.

Harvey, IL 60426-5098

Tel: (708) 331-4000 Fax: (708) 785-0755

CEO: Jeffrey Kahn

FO: Casey Skorpinski

HR: Walter Zookopny

Web site: www.whitingcorp.com

Emp: 300

Mfr. EOT cranes, metallurgical & railroad shop equipment.

Canada, China (PRC)

W. A. WHITNEY COMPANY

650 Race Street, PO Box 1206

Rockford, IL 61105-1206

Tel: (815) 964-6771 Fax: (815) 964-3175

CEO: Joe Meyer, Pres.

FO: Michael Donnelly

HR: Wayne Perrett

Emp: 230

Mfr. hydraulic punch/plasma cutting metal fabricating equipment.

Canada, Italy, Mexico

WHITTMAN-HART, INC.

311 South Wacker Drive, Ste. 3500

Chicago, IL 60606-6618

Tel: (312) 922-9200 Fax: (312) 913-3020

CEO: Robert F. Bernard, Chmn.

FO: Edward V. Szofer, Pres.

HR: Janie Denman

Web site: www.whittman-hart.com

Emp: 1,900 Rev: $173 mil.

Provides information technology, including network design/management & the development of custom software.

England, U.K.

WILBUR-ELLIS COMPANY

PO Box 7454

San Francisco, CA 94120

Tel: (415) 772-4000 Fax: (415) 772-4011

CEO: Brayton Wilbur, Jr.

FO: Frank Brown

HR: Ofelia Lee, Mng. HR

Emp: 2,100

International merchants and distributors.

China (PRC), Hong Kong, Indonesia, Japan, Malaysia, Philippines, Singapore, South Africa, South Korea, Taiwan (ROC), Thailand

JOHN WILEY & SONS INC.

605 Third Ave.

New York, NY 10158-0012

Tel: (212) 850-6000 Fax: (212) 850-6088

CEO: Bradford Wiley II, Chmn.

FO: Stephen M. Smith, SVP

HR: William J. Arlington, SVP

Web site: www.wiley.com

Emp: 1,754

Publisher: print & electronic products for academic, professional, scientific, technical & consumer market.

Australia, Canada, England, U.K., Germany, Russia, Singapore

WILLAMETTE INDUSTRIES, INC.

1300 SW Fifth Ave., Ste. 3800

Portland, OR 97201

Tel: (503) 227-5581 Fax: (503) 273-5603

CEO: William Swindells, Chmn. & COO

FO: Duane C. McDougall, COO

HR: David W. Morthland, VP

Web site: www.wii.com

Emp: 13,800 Rev: $3,439 mil.

Mfr., sales and distribution of paper and wood products.

France, Ireland

WILLIAM E WRIGHT COMPANY

PO Box 398, 85 South Street

West Warren, MA 01092

Tel: (413) 436-7732 Fax: (413) 436-9785

CEO: Cal Gauss, Pres.

HR: Peter Zarrilla

Emp: 1,300

Tapes, braids, apparel and furnishing trims.

Canada

WILLIAM MORRIS AGENCY INC.

1325 Ave. of the Americas

New York, NY 10019

Tel: (212) 586-5100 Fax: (212) 246-3583

CEO: Norman Brokaw, Chmn.

FO: Walter Zifkin, CEO

Book, theatre, music, film, television and commercials agency.

England, U.K.

T.D. WILLIAMSON INC.

PO Box 2299

Tulsa, OK 74101

Tel: (918) 254-9400 Fax: (918) 254-9474

CEO: Richard B. Williamson, Chmn.

FO: Jean-Paul van Schandevijl

HR: David R. Miller

Emp: 515

Mfr. equipment/provide service for pipeline maintenance.

Belgium, England, U.K., Singapore

WILLKIE FARR & GALLAGHER

One Citicorp Center, 153 East 53rd Street

New York, NY 10022-4669

Tel: (212) 821-8000 Fax: (212) 821-8111

CEO: Henry J. Kennedy, Mng. Prtn.

International law firm.

England, U.K., France

WILMER, CUTLER & PICKERING

2445 M Street, N.W.

Washington, DC 20037-1420

Tel: (202) 663-6000 Fax: (202) 663-6363

CEO: William Pertstein, Chmn. & Mng. Prtn.

HR: Joan Taylor, Dir.

Emp: 600 Rev: $119 mil.

International law firm.

Belgium, England, U.K., Germany

WILSON, ELSER, MOSKOWITZ, EDELMAN & DICKER

150 East 42nd Street

New York, NY 10017

Tel: (212) 490-3000 Fax: (212) 490-3038
CEO: Thomas Wilson, Mng. Prtn.

International law firm.

England, U.K.

WILTEK INC.

542 Westport Ave.
Norwalk, CT 06851
Tel: (203) 853-7400 Fax: (203) 846-3177
CEO: David S.Teitelman, Pres.
FO: Ken Joyce
Emp: 38

Electronic messaging, integration software services.

England, U.K.

A. WIMPFHEIMER & BROS INC.

22 Bayview Ave., PO Box 472
Stonington, CT 06378
Tel: (860) 535-1050 Fax: (860) 535-4398
CEO: Jacques D. Wimpfheimer, Chmn.
Emp: 400

Mfr./sales/distribution of American velvets.

England, U.K.

WINDMERE-DURABLE HOLDINGS, INC.

5980 Miami Lakes Drive
Hialeah, FL 33014
Tel: (305) 362-2611 Fax: (305) 364-0635
CEO: David M. Friedson, Pres. & Chmn.
FO: Raymond So, SVP
HR: David Warren, Dir.
Web site: www.windmere.com
Emp: 12,000 Rev: $250 mil.

Mfr. fans, electronic housewares.

China (PRC), Hong Kong

WINDWAY CAPITAL CORPORATION

630 Riverfront Drive, PO Box 897
Sheboygan, WI 53082-0897
Tel: (920) 457-8600 Fax: (920) 457-8599
CEO: Terry J. Kohler, Pres.
Emp: 1,200

Mfr. canvas & plastic products, metal stampings.

Canada

WINN-DIXIE STORES, INC.

5050 Edgewood Court
Jacksonville, FL 32254-3699
Tel: (904) 783-5000 Fax: (904) 783-5294
CEO: A. Dano Davis, Chmn.
FO: James Kufeldt, Pres.
HR: L. H. May, VP
Web site: www.winn-dixie.com
Emp: 136,000 Rev: $13,218 mil.

Retail grocery chain and manufacturing, bottling and processing operations.

Bahamas

WINSTON & STRAWN

35 West Wacker Drive - Ste. 4200
Chicago, IL 60601-9703
Tel: (312) 558-5600 Fax: (312) 558-5700
CEO: James M. Neis, Mng. Prtn.
Web site: www.winston.com
Emp: 1,375 Rev: $213 mil.

International law firm.

France, Saudi Arabia, Switzerland

HARRY WINSTON INC.

718 Fifth Ave.
New York, NY 10019
Tel: (212) 245-2000 Fax:
CEO: Ronald Winston, Pres.
HR: Joanne Gendelman
Emp: 350

Diamonds and lapidary work.

France, Ireland, Ivory Coast, Japan, Switzerland

WINTHROP, STIMSON, PUTNAM & ROBERTS

One Battery Park Plaza, 31st Floor
New York, NY 10004-1490
Tel: (212) 858-1000 Fax: (212) 858-1500
CEO: John Pritchard, Mng. Ptnr.
FO: William M. Evarts, Jr.
HR: Robin Taub
Web site: www.winstim.com
Emp: 620 Rev: $102 mil.

International law firm.

Belgium, England, U.K., Hong Kong, Japan, Singapore

WIREMOLD CO. INC.

60 Woodlawn Street

West Hartford, CT 06110

Tel: (860) 233-6251 Fax: (860) 523-3699

CEO: Arthur P. Byrne

Emp: 1,300

Mfr. noncurrent-carrying wiring devices.

Canada

WISER OIL CO. INC.

8115 Preston Road, #400

Dallas, TX 75225

Tel: (214) 265-0080 Fax: (214) 373-3610

CEO: Andrew J. Shoup, Jr., Pres. &CEO

HR: Karin L. O'Connor

Emp: 150 Rev: $3.3 mil

Crude petroleum & natural gas, exploration services.

Canada

WITCO CORPORATION

One American Lane

Greenwich, CT 06831-2559

Tel: (203) 552-2000 Fax: (203) 552-3070

CEO: Dr. E. Gary Cook, Chmn.

FO: Roger L. Sharp, EVP

HR: Margaret M. Contessa

Web site: www.witco.com

Emp: 5,970 Rev: $2,200 mil.

Mfr. chemical and petroleum products.

Australia, Brazil, Canada, Colombia, Denmark, Ecuador, England, U.K., France, Germany, Israel, Italy, Mexico, Netherlands, Spain

WIX FILTRATION PRODUCTS

1301 E. Ozark Ave.

Gastonia, NC 28052

Tel: (704) 864-6711 Fax: (704) 864-1843

CEO: Terry McCormack, Pres.

FO: Dieter Daniel

HR: Glenn Parrish

Emp: 2,500 Rev: $500 mil.

Mfr. oil, air and fuel filters.

Australia, China (PRC), Poland, Venezuela

WOLFE AXELROD ASSOCIATES

420 Lexington Ave.

New York, NY 10170

Tel: (212) 370-4500 Fax: (212) 370-4505

CEO: Steven Axelrod, Pres.

Emp: 8

Financial public relations, investor relations.

Israel

WOMETCO ENTERPRISES INC.

3195 Ponce de Leon Boulevard

Coral Gables, FL 33134

Tel: (305) 529-1400 Fax: (305) 529-1499

CEO: Michael Brown, Pres.

HR: Marvin Krantz

Emp: 6,000

Television broadcasting, film distribution, bottling, vending machines.

Bahamas, Canada, Dominican Republic, Japan

WOODHEAD INDUSTRIES INC.

Three Parkway North, Ste. 550

Deerfield, IL 60015

Tel: (847) 236-9300 Fax: (847) 236-0503

CEO: C. Mark DeWinter, Chmn.

HR: Robert A. Moulton

Emp: 1,200

Develop/mfr./sale/distributor elect/electronic, fiber optic and ergonomic special-function, non-commodity products.

Canada, France, Germany, Italy, Japan, Mexico, Netherlands, Singapore, Wales, U.K.

WOODWARD GOVERNOR COMPANY

5001 North Second Street, PO Box 7001

Rockford, IL 61125-7001

Tel: (815) 877-7441 Fax: (815) 639-6033

CEO: John A. Halbrook, Pres.

FO: Charles Kovac

HR: Rick Holm

Web site: www.woodward.com

Emp: 3,200 Rev: $410 mil.

Mfr./service speed control devices and systems for aircraft turbines, industrial engines and turbines.

Australia, Brazil, Czech Republic, England, U.K., Germany, India, Japan, Netherlands, Poland, Singapore

WOOLRICH INC.

1 Mill Street

Woolrich, PA 17779

Tel: (717) 769-6464 Fax: (717) 769-6470

CEO: Roswell Brayton, Jr., Pres.

Emp: 2,600

Mfr. fabrics and apparel.

Hong Kong

WORCESTER CONTROLS CORPORATION

33 Lott Drive

Marlboro, MA 01752

Tel: (508) 481-4800 Fax: (508) 481-4454

CEO: R. Kozlowski, Pres.

Emp: 800

Mfr. ball valves and control devices.

England, U.K., France, Germany, Netherlands

WORLD COURIER INC.

1313 Fourth Ave.

New Hyde Park, NY 11041

Tel: (516) 354-2600 Fax: (516) 354-2644

CEO: James R. Berger, Pres.

HR: Grisel Vasquez

International courier service.

Argentina, Australia, Belgium, Bermuda, Brazil, Canada, Denmark, Ecuador, England, U.K., France, Greece, Guatemala, Hong Kong, Italy, Japan, Mexico, Netherlands, Nigeria, Norway, Panama, Paraguay, Peru, Philippines, Saudi Arabia, Singapore, South Africa, Spain, Sweden, Switzerland, Uruguay, Venezuela

WORLDCOM, INC.

515 East Amite Street

Jackson, MS 39201-2701

Tel: (601) 360-8600 Fax: (601) 360-8616

CEO: Bernard J. Ebbers, Pres.

HR: Nancy Scheidemantel

Web site: www.wcom.com

Rev: $7,350 mil.

Telecommunications company serving local, long distance and Internet customers domestically and internationally.

Australia, Belgium, England, U.K., France, Germany, Hong Kong, Ireland, Italy, Japan, Netherlands, Singapore, Sweden, Switzerland

WRIGHT LINE INC.

160 Gold Star Blvd

Worcester, MA 01606

Tel: (508) 852-4300 Fax: (508) 853-8904

CEO: Dave Logan

FO: James Ayre

HR: Bob Sawdon, VP

Emp: 525

Mfr. filing systems.

Australia, Canada, England, U.K., Germany

WM WRIGLEY JR. COMPANY

410 N. Michigan Ave.

Chicago, IL 60611-4287

Tel: (312) 644-2121 Fax: (312) 644-0353

CEO: William Wrigley, Pres.

FO: Philip G. Hamilton, VP

HR: David E. Boxell, VP

Web site: www.wrigley.com

Emp: 8,200 Rev: $1,937 mil.

Mfr. chewing gum.

Australia, Austria, Bulgaria, Canada, China (PRC), Czech Republic, England, U.K., Finland, France, Germany, Hong Kong, Hungary, India, Israel, Japan, Kenya, Malaysia, Netherlands, New Zealand, Norway, Papua New Guinea, Philippines, Poland, Romania, Russia, Singapore, Slovakia, Slovenia, Spain, Sweden, Taiwan (ROC)

WUNDERMAN CATO JOHNSON

675 Ave. of the Americas

New York, NY 10010-5104

Tel: (212) 941-3000 Fax: (212) 633-0957

CEO: Jay Bingle, Chmn.

FO: Janet Coombs, Pres.

HR: Rosamund Lyster, Vp

Web site: www.wcj.com

International advertising and marketing consulting firm.

Argentina, Australia, Belgium, Brazil, Canada, Chile, China (PRC), Colombia, Denmark, Finland, France, Germany, Greece, Guatemala, Hong Kong, Hungary, India, Japan, Mexico, Netherlands, New Zealand, Peru, Philippines, Singapore, South Africa, Spain, Taiwan (ROC), Thailand, Turkey, Venezuela, Zimbabwe

WWF PAPER CORPORATION

Two Bala Plaza

Bala Cynwyd, PA 19004

Tel: (610) 667-9210 Fax: (610) 667-1663

CEO: E. V. Furlong, Jr.

FO: E. V. Furlong, Jr.

HR: Gloria Gregg

Web site: www.wwfpaper.com

Emp: 350

Wholesale of fine papers.

Canada, England, U.K., Mexico

WYMAN-GORDON COMPANY

244 Worcester Street

N. Grafton, MA 01536-8001

Tel: (508) 839-4441 Fax: (508) 839-7500

CEO: David P. Gruber, Pres.

Emp: 3,000

Mfr. forging & investment casting components, composite airframe structures.

Scotland, U.K.

WYNN OIL COMPANY

1050 West Fifth Street

Azusa, CA 91702-9510

Tel: (626) 334-0231 Fax: (626) 334-1456

CEO: Dr. Mark S. Filowitz, Pres.

HR: Lynn Levoy

Web site: www.wynnoil.com

Emp: 475

Mfr. of specialty chemicals, equipment and related service programs for automotive and industrial markets.

Australia, Belgium, Canada, England, U.K., France, Germany, Mexico, South Africa

WYNN'S PRECISION INC.

104 Hartman Drive

Lebanon, TN 37087

Tel: (615) 444-0191 Fax: (615) 444-4072

CEO: John Helenda, Pres.

Emp: 1,100

Mfr. rings, seals and custom molded rubber products.

Canada, England, U.K.

X

XEROX CORPORATION

800 Long Ridge Road, PO Box 1600

Stamford, CT 06904

Tel: (203) 968-3000 Fax: (203) 968-4312

CEO: Paul A. Allaire, Chmn.

FO: Patricia M. Wallington, VP

HR: Hector J. Motroni, VP

Web site: www.xerox.com

Emp: 87,600 Rev: $17, 000 mil.

Mfr. document processing equipment, systems and supplies.

Algeria, Angola, Argentina, Australia, Austria, Bahrain, Belarus, Belgium, Benin, Botswana, Brazil, Burkina Faso, Burundi, Cameroon, Canada, Central African Republic, Chad, Chile, China (PRC), Colombia, Costa Rica, Cyprus, Czech Republic, Denmark, Djibouti, Dominican Republic, Ecuador, Egypt, El Salvador, England, U.K., Ethiopia, Finland, France, Gabon, Gambia, Germany, Ghana, Gibraltar, Greece, Guatemala, Guinea, Honduras, Hong Kong, India, Indonesia, Iran, Ireland, Israel, Italy, Ivory Coast, Jamaica, Japan, Jordan, Kenya, Kuwait, Latvia, Lebanon, Lesotho, Madagascar, Malaysia, Malta, Mauritius, Mexico, Morocco, Mozambique, Netherlands, Netherlands Antilles, New Zealand, Nicaragua, Nigeria, Norway, Oman, Panama, Paraguay, Peru, Philippines, Poland, Portugal, Qatar, Romania, Russia, Saudi Arabia, Senegal, Seychelles, Sierra Leone, Singapore, South Africa, South Korea, Spain, Sudan, Swaziland, Sweden, Switzerland, Syria, Taiwan (ROC), Tanzania, Thailand, Tunisia, Turkey, Uganda, Ukraine, United Arab Emirates, Uruguay, Uzbekistan, Venezuela, Vietnam, Yemen, Yugoslavia, Zambia, Zimbabwe

XILINX INC.

2100 Logic Drive

San Jose, CA 95124-3400

Tel: (408) 559-7778 Fax: (408) 559-7114

CEO: Willem P. Roelandts, Pres.

FO: Randy Ong, VP Intl.

HR: Ray E. Madorin

Web site: www.xilinx.com

Emp: 868 Rev: $615.0 mil.

Programmable logic & related development systems software.

Canada, England, U.K., France, Germany, Hong Kong, Ireland, Japan, South Korea

XTRA CORPORATION

60 State Street

Boston, MA 02109

Tel: (617) 367-5000 Fax: (617) 227-3173

CEO: Lewis Rubin, Pres.

FO: Frederick M. Gutterson, VP

HR: Jeffrey R. Blum, VP HR

Web site: www.xtracorp.com

Emp: 876 Rev: $435 mil.

Holding company: leasing.

Australia, Brazil, Canada, China (PRC), England, U.K., France, Germany, Hong Kong, India, Italy, Japan, Mexico, Singapore, South Korea, United Arab Emirates

XYLAN CORPORATION

26707 West Agoura Road

Calabasas, CA 91302

Tel: (818) 880-3500 Fax: (818) 880-3505

CEO: Steve Y. Kim, Chmn.

FO: Rene Arvin, VP

HR: Andrew Jentis, Dir.

Web site: www.xylan.com

Emp: 721 Rev: $211 mil.

Mfr. Campus data network switches.

Australia, Canada, Japan, Netherlands, Singapore, South Korea

YAHOO! INC.

3420 Central Expressway

Santa Clara, CA 95051

Tel: (408) 731-3300 Fax: (408) 731-3301

CEO: Timothy Koogle

FO: Jeffrey Mallett, COO

HR: Beth Haba

Web site: www.yahoo-inc.com

Internet media company providing specialized content, free electronic mail and community offerings and commerce.

Australia, Canada, China (PRC), Denmark, England, U.K., France, Germany, Ireland, Italy, Japan, Norway, South Korea, Sweden

YELLOW FREIGHT SYSTEM INC.

10990 Roe Ave., PO Box 7270

Overland Park, KS 66207

Tel: (913) 345-3000 Fax: (913) 344-3246

CEO: William Zollars, Pres.

FO: Jim Bramlett, VP

HR: Deborah Kass, SVP

Web site: www.yellowfreight.com

Emp: 24,000 Rev: $2,500 mil.

Commodity transportation.

Canada, Mexico

YORK INTERNATIONAL CORPORATION

PO Box 1592

York, PA 17405-1592

Tel: (717) 771-7890 Fax: (717) 771-6212

CEO: Robert N. Pokelwaldt, Chmn.

HR: Robert D. Chattin

Emp: 10,000

Mfr. A/C, heating and refrigeration systems and equipment.

Canada, Egypt, England, U.K., France, Germany, Hong Kong, Malaysia, Mexico, Netherlands, Saudi Arabia, Singapore, Taiwan (ROC), Ukraine, United Arab Emirates, Venezuela

YOUNG & RUBICAM INC.

285 Madison Ave.

New York, NY 10017

Tel: (212) 210-3000 Fax: (212) 370-3796

CEO: Peter Georgescu, Chmn.

FO: Ed Vick, COO

HR: Bob Wells, SVP

Web site: www.yr.com

Emp: 13,037 Rev: $1,383 mil.

Advertising, public relations, direct marketing and sales promotion, corporate & product ID management.

Argentina, Australia, Austria, Barbados, Belgium, Brazil, Bulgaria, Canada, Chile, China (PRC), Colombia, Costa Rica, Czech Republic, Denmark, Dominican Republic, El Salvador, England, U.K., Finland, France, Germany, Greece, Guatemala, Honduras, Hong Kong, Hungary, India, Indonesia, Italy, Japan, Kenya, Malaysia, Mexico, Netherlands, New Zealand, Nicaragua, Norway, Panama, Peru, Philippines, Poland, Portugal, Romania, Russia, Singapore, Slovenia, South

Africa, South Korea, Spain, Sweden, Switzerland, Taiwan (ROC), Thailand, Turkey, Ukraine, Uruguay, Venezuela, Zambia, Zimbabwe

YSI INC.

1725 Brannum Lane, PO Box 279
Yellow Springs, OH 45387
Tel: (937) 767-7241 Fax: (937) 767-9353
CEO: Malte von Matthiessen, Pres.
HR: Rick Omlor
Emp: 373

Mfr. analyzers, measure instruments & electrical components.

England, U.K., Japan

Z

H. B. ZACHRY COMPANY

527 Logwood, PO Box 21130
San Antonio, TX 78221-0130
Tel: (210) 475-8000 Fax: (210) 927-8060
CEO: H. B. Zachry, Jr.

Construction.

Saudi Arabia

ZEDTEC COMBUSTION SYSTEMS, INC.

Ste. 203, 3901 Washington Road
McMurray, PA 15317
Tel: (724) 942-3408 Fax: (724) 942-4747
CEO: Gordon Dickinson, Pres.

Mfr./sale/service combustion equipment for industrial furnaces in glass, forging heat treating, and aluminum industries.

England, U.K.

ZIEBART INTERNATIONAL CORPORATION

1290 East Maple Road
Troy, MI 48084
Tel: (810) 588-4100 Fax: (810) 588-0718
CEO: Thomas E. Wolfe, Pres.
FO: Gregory A. Longe
Web site: www.ziebart.com
Emp: 150

Automotive aftermarket services.

Canada, England, U.K., Japan

JOHN ZINK COMPANY

PO Box 21220
Tulsa, OK 74121-1220
Tel: (918) 234-1800 Fax: (918) 234-2700
CEO: David Coch, Pres.
HR: Jack Carter
Emp: 1,000

Mfr. flare systems, thermal oxidizers, vapor recovery systems, process heater burners.

England, U.K.

ZIPPERTUBING COMPANY

13000 S. Broadway, PO Box 61129
Los Angeles, CA 90061
Tel: (310) 527-0488 Fax: (310) 767-1714
CEO: Terry Plummer, Pres.
FO: Bruce Hoffine
Emp: 200

Mfr. zip-on plastic tubing, wire markers, pipe insulation, EMI shielding.

Germany, Japan, Switzerland

ZIPPO MANUFACTURING COMPANY

33 Barbour Street
Bradford, PA 16701
Tel: (814) 368-2700 Fax: (814) 368-2874
CEO: Michael A. Schuler, Pres.
HR: Robert Kaczmarek, VP
Emp: 1,200 Rev: $150 mil.

Mfr. petroleum products, windproof lighters, silverware, advertising specialties.

Canada

ZITEL CORPORATION

47211 Bayside Pkwy.
Fremont, CA 94538
Tel: (510) 440-9600 Fax: (510) 440-9696
CEO: Jack H. King, Pres.
Web site: www.zitel.com
Emp: 190

Mfr. computer peripherals and software.

England, U.K., France, Netherlands

ZOLLNER PISTON COMPANY

2425 S. Coliseum Blvd.
Ft. Wayne, IN 46803
Tel: (219) 426-8081 Fax: (219) 423-2141
CEO: John Ogden, Pres.

HR: Joe Cobb

Emp: 1,100

Mfr. pistons and related components.

Canada

ZOMAX OPTICAL MEDIA, INC.

5353 Nathan Lane

Plymouth, MN 55442

Tel: (612) 553-9300 Fax: (612) 553-0826

CEO: Phillip T. Levin, Chmn.

FO: Anthony Angelini, VP

HR: Gary Mittelbuscher, Mgr.

Web site: www.zomax.com

Emp: 400 Rev: $35.0 mil.

Mfr./sales CD-ROM's, digital video discs and cassettes.

Ireland

ZURN INDUSTRIES INC.

14801 Quorum Drive

Dallas, TX 75240-7584

Tel: (972) 560-2000 Fax: (972) 560-2246

CEO: Robert R. Womack, Pres.

HR: William Durbin

Web site: www.zurn.com

Emp: 3,000

Mfr./sale of plumbing products and HVAC equipment; resource and fire sprinkler system construction.

Canada, Mexico, Singapore

ZYCAD CORPORATION TSS

47100 Bayside Pkwy.

Fremont, CA 94538-9942

Tel: (510) 360-8100 Fax: (510) 623-4550

CEO: Phillips W. Smith

FO: John Walsh

Emp: 235

Design/development/mfr./market logic & fault simulation acceleration products; system engineering services.

England, U.K., France, Germany, Japan, Taiwan (ROC)

PART **TWO**

DIRECTORY OF
AMERICAN FIRMS
OPERATING IN
FOREIGN COUNTRIES
15th Edition

ALPHABETICAL INDEX OF AMERICAN CORPORATIONS BY COUNTRY

Albania

LOUIS BERGER INTERNATIONAL INC.

100 Halsted Street, East Orange, NJ, 07019

Tel: (201) 678-1960 Fax: (201) 672-4284 Web site: www.louisberger.com

Consulting engineers, architects, economists & planners.

Louis Berger International Inc., Ministry of Public Works, Territory Adjustment and Tourism, Shesi Skenderbej, Tirana, Albania

Tel: 355-42-305-22 Fax: 355-42-305-22

DELOITTE TOUCHE TOHMATSU INTERNATIONAL

PO Box 820, Wilton, CT, 06897

Tel: (203) 761-3000 Fax: (203) 834-2200 Web site: www.u.s.deloitte.com or www.dtti.com

Accounting, audit, tax and management consulting services.

Deloitte & Touche, The Albanian Trade Ctr., Tirana, Albania

DHL WORLDWIDE EXPRESS

333 Twin Dolphin Drive, Redwood City, CA, 94065

Tel: (650) 593-7474 Fax: (650) 593-1689 Web site: www.dhl.com

Worldwide air express carrier.

DHL Worldwide Express, Rruga Donika Kastrioti Vila 1/1, Tirana, Albania

Tel: 355-42-32817

ERNST & YOUNG, LLP

787 Seventh Ave., New York, NY, 10019

Tel: (212) 773-3000 Fax: (212) 773-6350 Web site: www.eyi.com

Accounting and audit, tax and management consulting services.

Ernst & Young International, Romeo Mitri Fiscal and Financial Consulting, Tirana, Albania

Tel: 355-42-27955 Fax: 355-42-27955

GREY ADVERTISING INC.

777 Third Ave., New York, NY, 10017

Tel: (212) 546-2000 Fax: (212) 546-1495 Web site: www.giworldwwide.com

International advertising agency.

Grey Tirana, Tirana, Albania

IBM CORPORATION

New Orchard Road, Armonk, NY, 10504

Tel: (914) 765-1900 Fax: (914) 765-7382 Web site: www.ibm.com

Information products, technology & services.

IBM Albanian Computers and Services, Rruga "Asim Zeneli" N.5/1, Tirana, Albania

LAND O' LAKES, INC.

4001 Lexington Ave. North, Arden Hills, MN, 55126

Tel: (612) 481-2222 Fax: (612) 481-2022

Produces butter, margarine, packaged milk, sour cream, snack dips and Alpine Lace cheeses and crop protection products.

Land O' Lakes, Inc., Albania

OCCIDENTAL PETROLEUM CORPORATION

10889 Wilshire Blvd., Los Angeles, CA, 90024

Tel: (310) 208-8800 Fax: (310) 443-6690 Web site: www.oxy.com

Petroleum and petroleum products, chemicals, plastics.

Occidental Albania Inc., Albania

Algeria

AIR EXPRESS INTERNATIONAL CORPORATION

120 Tokeneke Road, PO Box 1231, Darien, CT, 06820

Tel: (203) 655-7900 Fax: (203) 655-5779 Web site: www.aeilogistics.com

Air freight forwarder.

AEI - Algiers, c/o Master, 2 blvd Said Yacoub, Algiers, Algeria (Locations: Annaba, Constantine, Oran, Algeria)

Tel: 213-2-640-667 Fax: 213-2-619-381

BAKER HUGHES INCORPORATED

3900 Essex Lane, Ste. 1200, Houston, TX, 77027

Tel: (713) 439-8600 Fax: (713) 439-8699 Web site: www.bakerhughes.com

Develop & apply technology to drill, complete & produce oil and natural gas wells; provide separation systems to petroleum, municipal, continuous process & mining industries.

Baker Hughes Tools, B.P. 527, Hassi Messaoud, Wilaya de Ouargla, Algeria

Tel: 213-9-739129 Fax: 213-9-739130

BECHTEL GROUP INC.

50 Beale Street, PO Box 3965, San Francisco, CA, 94105-1895

Tel: (415) 768-1234 Fax: (415) 768-9038 Web site: www.bechtel.com

General contractors in engineering & construction.

Bechtel Inc., Villa Djenane, Mouhoub 11, Chemin Acklai, B.P. 62, El Biar, Algeria

CITICORP

399 Park Ave., New York, NY, 10043

Tel: (212) 559-1000 Fax: (212) 527-2066 Web site: www.citibank.com

International banking and financial services.

Citibank N.A., El Aurassi, Bld Frantz Fanon, Algiers, Algeria

Contact: Kamal Driss, Mgr.

COLGATE-PALMOLIVE COMPANY

300 Park Ave., New York, NY, 10022

Tel: (212) 310-2000 Fax: (212) 310-2919

Mfr. pharmaceuticals, cosmetics, toiletries and detergents.

Colgate-Palmolive Corp., 26 Blvd. Zirout Youcaf, B.P. 576, Algiers, Algeria

DELOITTE TOUCHE TOHMATSU INTERNATIONAL

PO Box 820, Wilton, CT, 06897

Tel: (203) 761-3000 Fax: (203) 834-2200 Web site: www.u.s.deloitte.com or www.dtti.com

Accounting, audit, tax and management consulting services.

Saba & Company, Algeria - Mail To: c/o Joseph M. Sanbar, Dammam, Saudi Arabia

DHL WORLDWIDE EXPRESS

333 Twin Dolphin Drive, Redwood City, CA, 94065

Tel: (650) 593-7474 Fax: (650) 593-1689 Web site: www.dhl.com

Worldwide air express carrier.

DHL Worldwide Express, 18 Ave. Franklin Roosevelt, Alger 16000, Algeria

Tel: 213-2-230031

DIGITAL EQUIPMENT CORPORATION

111 Powder Mill Road, Maynard, MA, 01754

Tel: (978) 493-5111 Fax: (978) 493-7374 Web site: www.digital.com

Mfr. network computer systems, components, software and services.

Digital Equipment Algeria, Hotel El Aurassi, Niveau C.Bureau 13, Blvd. Frantz Fanon, Algiers, Algeria

Tel: 213-2-639624 Fax: 213-2-637851

GENERAL ELECTRIC CO.

3135 Easton Turnpike, Fairfield, CT, 06431

Tel: (203) 373-2211 Fax: (203) 373-3131 Web site: www.ge.com

Diversified manufacturing, technology and services.

Nuovo Pignone, Bureau d'Alger, El-Biar, Algeria

Tel: 213-2-924072 Fax: 213-2-792715

GTE CORPORATION

One Stamford Forum, Stamford, CT, 06904

Tel: (203) 965-2000 Fax: (203) 965-2277 Web site: www.gte.com

Electronic products, telecommunications systems, publishing and communications.

GTE Intl., Factory Projects Organization, 2 rue Isodore Tachet, Algiers, Algeria

NORTON COMPANY

1 New Bond Street, Worcester, MA, 01606

Tel: (508) 795-5000 Fax: (508) 795-5741

Abrasives, drill bits, construction and safety products and plastics.

Norton Co., 1 Blvd. Anatole France, Algiers, Algeria

THE PERKIN-ELMER CORPORATION

761 Main Ave., Norwalk, CT, 06859-0001

Tel: (203) 762-1000 Fax: (203) 762-4228 Web site: www.perkin-elmer.com

Leading supplier of systems for life science research and related applications.

Perkin-Elmer, Algiers, Algeria

Tel: 213-2-748799 Fax: 213-2-748556

WEATHERFORD INTERNATIONAL INC.

5 Post Oak Blvd, Ste. 1760, Houston, TX, 77227-3415

Tel: (713) 287-8400 Fax: (713) 963-9785 Web site: www.weatherford.com

Oilfield services, products & equipment; mfr. marine cranes for oil and gas industry.

Weatherford Oil Tool GmbH, B.P. 143, Hassi Messaoud, Algeria

Tel: 213-2-91410-1213 Fax: 213-2-914141

Weatherford Oil Tool GmbH, 63 Blvd. Bougara, El Biar, Algiers, Algeria

Tel: 213-2-91410-1213 Fax: 213-2-914141

WESTERN ATLAS INC.

10205 Westheimer, Houston, TX, 77251-1407

Tel: (713) 972-4000 Fax: (713) 952-9837 Web site: www.waii.com

Full service to the oil industry.

Western Atlas Logging Services, BP 493, Hassi Messaoud, 30500 Algeria

Tel: 213-9-730461 Fax: 213-9-730462 Contact: S. O'Shaunessy, Bus. Mgr.

Western Geophysical Cei., 52, rue Ben Ben Abdella Ben Ali, Hydra, Algiers, Algeria

Tel: 213-2-692163 Fax: 213-2-591931 Contact: M. Gillespie, Res. Mgr.

XEROX CORPORATION

800 Long Ridge Road, PO Box 1600, Stamford, CT, 06904

Tel: (203) 968-3000 Fax: (203) 968-4312 Web site: www.xerox.com

Mfr. document processing equipment, systems and supplies.

Xerox Ltd., Zone d'Activité Lot No 4, Lotissement Djaffar, Slimane Route des Dunes, Chéagr, Algeria

Tel: 213-2-369744 Fax: 213-2-369694

Angola

AIR EXPRESS INTERNATIONAL CORPORATION

120 Tokeneke Road, PO Box 1231, Darien, CT, 06820

Tel: (203) 655-7900 Fax: (203) 655-5779 Web site: www.aeilogistics.com

Air freight forwarder.

AEI, c/o Jacto Carga Ltda., Av. dos Combatentes 42, Caixa Postal 16326, Luanda, Angola

AEI Express Cargo (Transitarios), Ltd., Edif. Presidente, Largo 4 de Fevereiro, 3, 4th Fl., Rm. 441, Luanda, Angola

Tel: 244-2-353-206 Fax: 244-2-353-206

BAKER HUGHES INCORPORATED

3900 Essex Lane, Ste. 1200, Houston, TX, 77027

Tel: (713) 439-8600 Fax: (713) 439-8699 Web site: www.bakerhughes.com

Develop & apply technology to drill, complete & produce oil and natural gas wells; provide separation systems to petroleum, municipal, continuous process & mining industries.

Baker Hughes Tools, Cabinda, Angola

Tel: 510-842-1111

Baker Hughes Tools, Rua ConSelheiro, Aires DeOmelas, No. 67, Luanda, Angola

Tel: 244-9-500835 Fax: 244-9-501926

LOUIS BERGER INTERNATIONAL INC.

100 Halsted Street, East Orange, NJ, 07019

Tel: (201) 678-1960 Fax: (201) 672-4284 Web site: www.louisberger.com

Consulting engineers, architects, economists & planners.

Louis Berger International Inc., c/o ENEP, Rua de Amilicar Cabral nº 35, 1º & 2º andar, CP 5667, Luanda, Angola

DELOITTE TOUCHE TOHMATSU INTERNATIONAL

PO Box 820, Wilton, CT, 06897

Tel: (203) 761-3000 Fax: (203) 834-2200 Web site: www.u.s.deloitte.com or www.dtti.com

Accounting, audit, tax and management consulting services.

Deloitte & Touche (Portugal), Angola - c/o Helder J. Varandas, Oporto, Portugal

ERNST & YOUNG, LLP

787 Seventh Ave., New York, NY, 10019

Tel: (212) 773-3000 Fax: (212) 773-6350 Web site: www.eyi.com

Accounting and audit, tax and management consulting services.

Ernst & Young, Rua Major Kanyangula, 59 - 1st Fl., DI, Luanda, Angola

Tel: 351-1-7912000 Fax: 351-1-7957587 Contact: Albino Jacinto

EXXON CORPORATION

225 E. John W. Carpenter Freeway, Irving, TX, 75062-2298

Tel: (972) 444-1000 Fax: (972) 444-1882 Web site: www.exxon.com

Petroleum exploration, production, refining; mfr. petroleum & chemicals products; coal & minerals.

Exxon - Exploration & Production, Angola

THE HARPER GROUP

260 Townsend Street, San Francisco, CA, 94107-1719

Tel: (415) 978-0600 Fax: (415) 978-0692 Web site: www.circleintl.com

Ocean/air freight forwarding, customs brokerage, packing and wholesale, logistics management and insurance.

Circle Freight International (Portugal), Rua Engracia Fragoso, 49 - 1 Andar, Luanda, Angola

Tel: 244-390-030 Fax: 244-391-444

Circle Freight Intl. (Portugal) Lda., Rua Engracia Fragoso 49, Luanda, Angola

IBM CORPORATION

New Orchard Road, Armonk, NY, 10504

Tel: (914) 765-1900 Fax: (914) 765-7382 Web site: www.ibm.com

Information products, technology & services.

IBM Angola, SRC, Rua Conselheiiro Julio de Vilhena 16, PO Box 6487, Luanda, Angola

Tel: 244-2-390489 Fax: 244-2-335257

JOHNSON & JOHNSON

One Johnson & Johnson Plaza, New Brunswick, NJ, 08933

Tel: (732) 524-0400 Fax: (732) 214-0334 Web site: www.jnj.com

Mfr./distributor/R&D pharmaceutical, health care and cosmetic products.

Johnson & Johnson (Angola) Lda., Caixa Postal 2862, Luanda, Angola

MOBIL CORPORATION

3225 Gallows Road, Fairfax, VA, 22037-0001

Tel: (703) 846-3000 Fax: (703) 846-4669 Web site: www.mobil.com

Petroleum and gas exploration and refining, mfr. petroleum products, chemicals and petrochemicals.

Mobil Oil Portuguesa, Caixa Postal 330, Luanda, Angola

OCCIDENTAL PETROLEUM CORPORATION

10889 Wilshire Blvd., Los Angeles, CA, 90024

Tel: (310) 208-8800 Fax: (310) 443-6690 Web site: www.oxy.com

Petroleum and petroleum products, chemicals, plastics.

Occidental Angola Inc., Angola

OCEANEERING INTERNATIONAL INC.

11911 FM 529, Houston, TX, 77041

Tel: (713) 329-4500 Fax: (713) 329-4951

Transportation equipment, underwater service to offshore oil and gas industry.

Oceaneering Intl. Inc., Cabinda & Luanda, Angola

THE PERKIN-ELMER CORPORATION

761 Main Ave., Norwalk, CT, 06859-0001

Tel: (203) 762-1000 Fax: (203) 762-4228 Web site: www.perkin-elmer.com

Leading supplier of systems for life science research and related applications.

Perkin-Elmer, Luanda, Angola

Tel: 244-233-2025 Fax: 244-233-5061

PFIZER INC.

235 East 42nd Street, New York, NY, 10017-5755

Tel: (212) 573-2323 Fax: (212) 573-7851 Web site: www.pfizer.com

Research-based, global health care company.

Pfizer Lda., Angola

TEXACO INC.

2000 Westchester Ave., White Plains, NY, 10650

Tel: (914) 253-4000 Fax: (914) 253-7753 Web site: www.texaco.com

Exploration/marketing crude oil, mfr. petro chemicals and products.

Texaco Petroleos de Angola SARL, Caixa Postal 5897, Luanda, Angola

WEATHERFORD INTERNATIONAL INC.

5 Post Oak Blvd, Ste. 1760, Houston, TX, 77227-3415

Tel: (713) 287-8400 Fax: (713) 963-9785 Web site: www.weatherford.com

Oilfield services, products & equipment; mfr. marine cranes for oil and gas industry.

Weatherford Intl. Inc., Cabinda, Angola

Tel: 44-1714-878-101x2379 Fax: 44-1714-878-101x2514

WESTERN ATLAS INC.

10205 Westheimer, Houston, TX, 77251-1407

Tel: (713) 972-4000 Fax: (713) 952-9837 Web site: www.waii.com

Full service to the oil industry.

Western Atlas Logging Services, Rua Duarte Lopez No. 27, Luanda, Angola, West Africa

Tel: 244-2-395-585 Fax: 244-2-395-691 Contact: Mike Grammer, Dist. Mgr.

Western Geophysical, Luanda Processing Ctr., c/o Western Atlas Logging Services, Rua Duarte Lopez No. 27, Luanda, Angola

Tel: 244-2-395-691 Fax: 244-2-395-691 Contact: Mike West, Mgr.

XEROX CORPORATION

800 Long Ridge Road, PO Box 1600, Stamford, CT, 06904

Tel: (203) 968-3000 Fax: (203) 968-4312 Web site: www.xerox.com

Mfr. document processing equipment, systems and supplies.

Xerox Angola Lda., Largo 4 Fevereiro Nr. 3, Sala 141, Luanda, Angola

Tel: 244-233-567-6 Fax: 244-233-567-7

Anguilla

BUDGET RENT A CAR CORPORATION

4225 Naperville Road, Lisle, IL, 60532

Tel: (630) 955-1900 Fax: (630) 955-7799 Web site: www.budgetrentacar.com

Car and truck rental system.

Budget Rent A Car, Airport, Stoney Ground, Anguilla, B.W.I.

Tel: 809-497-2217

DHL WORLDWIDE EXPRESS

333 Twin Dolphin Drive, Redwood City, CA, 94065

Tel: (650) 593-7474 Fax: (650) 593-1689 Web site: www.dhl.com

Worldwide air express carrier.

DHL Worldwide Express, Stoney Ground, Anguilla

Tel: 599-542-952

KPMG PEAT MARWICK LLP

Three Chestnut Ridge Road, Montvale, NJ, 07645

Tel: (201) 307-7000 Fax: (201) 930-8617 Web site: www.kpmg.com

Accounting and audit, tax and management consulting services.

KPMG Peat Marwick, Caribbean Commercial Centre, PO Box 136, The Valley, Anguilla

Tel: 809-497-5500 Fax: 809-497-3755 Contact: Claudel V.V. Romney, Sr. Ptnr.

SONESTA INTERNATIONAL HOTELS CORPORATION

200 Clarendon Street, Boston, MA, 02166

Tel: (617) 421-5400 Fax: (617) 421-5402 Web site: www.sonesta.com

Hotels, resorts, and Nile cruises..

Sonesta Hotel Anguilla, Rendez-vous Bay West, Anguilla , B.W.I.

Antigua

AON CORPORATION

123 North Wacker Drive, Chicago, IL, 60606

Tel: (312) 701-3000 Fax: (312) 701-3100 Web site: www.aon.com

Insurance brokers worldwide; underwrites accident & health insurance, specialty & professional insurance; & provides risk management consultation.

AON Worldwide / St. Georges Insurance Brokers Ltd., St. Georges St. (PO Box 490) St. John's, Antigua

Tel: 268-462-1307 Fax: 268-462-4684 Contact: Ernest Letby

DHL WORLDWIDE EXPRESS

333 Twin Dolphin Drive, Redwood City, CA, 94065

Tel: (650) 593-7474 Fax: (650) 593-1689 Web site: www.dhl.com

Worldwide air express carrier.

DHL Worldwide Express, PO Box 82, St. Johns, Antigua

Tel: 599-542-952

FRITZ COMPANIES INC.

706 Mission Street, Ste. 900, San Francisco, CA, 94103

Tel: (415) 904-8360 Fax: (415) 904-8661 Web site: www.fritz.com

Integrated transportation, sourcing, distribution & customs brokerage services.

Fritz Companies Inc., St. Johns, Antigua

KPMG PEAT MARWICK LLP

Three Chestnut Ridge Road, Montvale, NJ, 07645

Tel: (201) 307-7000 Fax: (201) 930-8617 Web site: www.kpmg.com

Accounting and audit, tax and management consulting services.

KPMG Peat Marwick, High & Market Sts., St. Johns, Antigua

PRICEWATERHOUSECOOPERS LLP

1251 Ave. of the Americas, New York, NY, 10020

Tel: (212) 596-7000 Fax: (212) 790-6620 Web site: www.pwcglobal.com

Accounting and auditing, tax and management, and human resource consulting services.

Price Waterhouse Ltd., Price Waterhouse Centre, 11 Old Parham Rd., PO Box 1531, St. Johns, Antigua

Tel: 809-462-3000 Fax: 809-462-1902

Argentina

3COM CORPORATION

5400 Bayfront Plaza, Santa Clara, CA, 95052-8145

Tel: (408) 764-5000 Fax: (408) 764-5001 Web site: www.3com.com

Develop/mfr. computer networking products & systems.

3Com Argentina, Alicia Moreau de Justo 170 - 3 er. piso, Buenos Aires 107, Argentina

Tel: 54-1-3123266 Fax: 54-1-314-3329

3M

3M Center, St. Paul, MN, 55144-1000

Tel: (612) 733-1110 Fax: (612) 733-9973 Web site: www.mmm.com

Mfr. diversified products for industry, health care, imaging, communications, transport, safety, consumer, etc.

3M Argentina SACIFIA, Los Arboles 842, 1686 Hurlingham, Buenos Aires, Argentina

Tel: 54-1-469-8200 Fax: 54-1-469-8261

ABBOTT LABORATORIES

One Abbott Park Road, Abbott Park, IL, 60064-3500

Tel: (847) 937-6100 Fax: (847) 937-1511 Web site: www.abbott.com

Development/mfr./sale diversified health care products & services.

Abbott Laboratories Argentina SRL, Buenos Aires, Argentina

AIR EXPRESS INTERNATIONAL CORPORATION

120 Tokeneke Road, PO Box 1231, Darien, CT, 06820

Tel: (203) 655-7900 Fax: (203) 655-5779 Web site: www.aeilogistics.com

Air freight forwarder.

Air Express International, c/o Aero Expreso International, Bernardo de Irigoyen 308 - 1&4 pisos, 1379 Buenos Aires, Argentina

Tel: 54-1-334-3023 Fax: 54-1-111339

ALCOA (ALUMINUM CO OF AMERICA)

Alcoa Bldg., 425 Sixth Ave., Pittsburgh, PA, 15219-1850

Tel: (412) 553-4545 Fax: (412) 553-4498

World's leading producer of aluminum & alumina; mining, refining, smelting, fabricating & recycling.

Alsud Argentina S.A. Industrial y Comercial, Buenos Aires, Argentina

Feroscar S.A. Industrial y Comercial, LaPlata, Argentina

ALLEN TELECOM

25101 Chagrin Boulevard, Beachwood, OH, 44122-5619

Tel: (216) 765-5818 Fax: (216) 765-0410 Web site: www.allentele.com

Mfr. communications equipment, automotive bodies and parts, electronic components.

Allen Telecom Inc. de Argentina, Condarco 3700, 1419 Buenos Aires, Argentina

Tel: 54-1-573-0633 Fax: 54-1-573-0656 Contact: Daniel Macchi

ALLERGAN INC.

2525 Dupont Drive, PO Box 19534, Irvine, CA, 92713-9534

Tel: (714) 246-4500 Fax: (714) 246-6987

Mfr. therapeutic eye care products, skin & neural care pharmaceuticals.

Allergan SAICyF, Buenos Aires, Argentina

ALLIEDSIGNAL, INC. - AUTOMOTIVE PRODUCTS GROUP

105 Pawtucket Ave., Rumford, RI, 02916-2422

Tel: (401) 434-7000 Fax: (401) 431-3670 Web site: www.alliedsignal.com

Mfr. spark plugs, filters, brakes.

Sogefi Argentina, Aguilar 3003, 1826 Remedios de Escalada San Martin, Buenos Aires, Argentina

Tel: 54-1-220-4608 Fax: 54-1-246-1576 Contact: Dante Cisilino

AMERICAN EXPRESS COMPANY

American Express Tower, World Financial Center, New York, NY, 10285-4765

Tel: (212) 640-2000 Fax: (212) 619-9802 Web site: www.americanexpress.com

Travel, travelers cheques, charge card & financial services.

American Express Argentina SA, Arenales 707, Buenos Aries, Argentina 1061

Tel: 54-1-312-0900 Fax: 54-1-315-1866 Contact: Alejandro Sanchez, Opers. Dir.

AMERICAN HOME PRODUCTS CORPORATION

Five Giralda Farms, Madison, NJ, 07940-0874

Tel: (973) 660-5000 Fax: (973) 660-6048 Web site: www.ahp.com

Mfr. pharmaceutical, animal health care & crop protection products.

American Home Products Corporation, Argentina

AMMIRATI PURIS LINTAS

One Dag Hammarskjold Plaza, New York, NY, 10017

Tel: (212) 605-8000 Fax: (212) 605-4705 Web site: www.interpublic.com

International advertising agency.

Ammirati Puris Lintas Argentina, Av. Leandro No. Alerri 1050 (1005) Buenos Airs, Argentina

Tel: 54-1-316-9600 Contact: Alberto Betancourt, Mng. Dir.

AMP INC.

470 Friendship Road, PO Box 3608, Harrisburg, PA, 17105-3608

Tel: (717) 564-0100 Fax: (717) 780-6130

Develop/mfr. electronic & electrical connection products & systems.

AMP SA Argentina CIYF, 4 de Febrero 2676, 1651 Villa San Andres, Buenos Aires, Argentina

ANDERSEN CONSULTING

100 South Wacker Drive, Ste. 1059, Chicago, IL, 60606

Tel: (311) 123-7271 Fax: (312) 507-7965 Web site: www.ac.com

Provides management & technology consulting services.

Andersen Consulting, MAIPU 1210, 8th Fl., 1006 Buenos Aires, Argentina

Tel: 54-1-318-8555 Fax: 54-1-3309-4455

AON CORPORATION

123 North Wacker Drive, Chicago, IL, 60606

Tel: (312) 701-3000 Fax: (312) 701-3100 Web site: www.aon.com

Insurance brokers worldwide; underwrites accident & health insurance, specialty & professional insurance; & provides risk management consultation.

AON Group Ltd. Argentina SA, San Martin 320-piso 3, 1004 Buenos Aires, Argentina SA

Tel: 54-1-394-7961 Fax: 54-1-322-2212 Contact: Martin Clover

AON Risk Services Argentina S.A., Juncal 1319, 1062 Buenos Aires, Argentina

Tel: 54-1-814-8000 Fax: 54-1-814-8003 Contact: Adrian Salbuchi

AON Warranty Services of Argentina, Cerito 1070, 11th Fl., Capital Federal, 1010, Buenos Aires, Argentina

Tel: 54-1-815-4045 Contact: Victor Honre

Reinsur-Howden Argentina, Av. Corrientes 880, piso 12, 1043, Buenos Aires, Argentina

Tel: 54-1-326-0052 Fax: 54-1-325-9153 Contact: M. Rodriguez

ARBOR ACRES FARM INC.

439 Marlborough Road, Glastonbury, CT, 06033

Tel: (860) 633-4681 Fax: (860) 633-2433

Producers of male & female broiler breeders, commercial egg layers.

Arbor Acres Argentina SA, Casilla de Correo 3262-1193, Buenos Aires, Argentina

ARGO INTERNATIONAL CORPORATION

140 Franklin Street, New York, NY, 10013

Tel: (212) 431-1700 Fax: (212) 431-2206

Distributor electrical spare parts.

Argo Intl. Corp., Paraguay 776, piso 6, 1057 Buenos Aires, Argentina

ARTHUR ANDERSEN & COMPANY

33 West Monroe Street, Chicago, IL, 60603

Tel: (312) 372-7100 Fax: (312) 507-0123 Web site: www.arthurandersen.com

Accounting & audit, tax & management consulting services.

Arthur Andersen & Co./Pistrelli, Diaz y Asociados, 25 de Mayo 487, 1st Fl., 1002 Buenos Aires, Argentina

Tel: 54-1-311-6644

Arthur Andersen & Company, MAIPU 1210, 8th Fl., 1006 Buenos Aires, Argentina

ARVIN INDUSTRIES INC.

One Noblitt Plaza, Box 3000, Columbus, IN, 47202-3000

Tel: (812) 379-3000 Fax: (812) 379-3688 Web site: www.arvin.com

Mfr. of automotive exhaust systems & ride control products.

Profile S.A., Cordoba, Argentina

ASSOCIATED METALS & MINERALS CORPORATION

3 North Corporate Park Drive, White Plains, NY, 10604

Tel: (914) 251-5400 Fax: (914) 251-1073

Metals & ores.

Asometa Compania Asociada de Metales y Minerales SRL, Lima 187, 1073 Buenos Aires, Argentina

AUTODESK INC.

111 McInnis Parkway, San Rafael, CA, 94903

Tel: (415) 507-5000 Fax: (415) 507-6112 Web site: www.autodesk.com

Develop/marketing/support computer-aided design, engineering, scientific & multimedia software products.

Autodesk Argentina, A. Moreau de Justo, 1148 PB 110, Pto. Madero, Cap. Fed., Argentina

Tel: 54-1-341-4555 Fax: 54-1-341-4600

AVERY DENNISON CORPORATION

150 N. Orange Grove Blvd., Pasadena, CA, 91103

Tel: (626) 304-2000 Fax: (626) 792-7312 Web site: www.averydennison.com

Mfr. pressure-sensitive adhesives & materials, office products, labels, tags, retail systems, Carter's Ink & specialty chemicals.

Avery Dennison Argentina, Argentina

AVIS, INC.

900 Old Country Road., Garden City, NY, 11530

Tel: (516) 222-3000 Fax: (516) 222-4381 Web site: www.avis.com

Car rental services.

Avis Corp., Sheraton Hotel, Galeria Commercial, Buenos Aires, Argentina

Avis Corp., Bulevar Martim 2451, Mar de Plata, Argentina

AVON PRODUCTS INC.

1345 Ave. of the Americas, New York, NY, 10105-0196

Tel: (212) 282-5000 Fax: (212) 282-6049 Web site: www.avon.com

Mfr./distributor beauty & related products, fashion jewelry, gifts & collectibles.

Cosmeticos Avon S.A.C.I., Martin Rodriguez 4013, 1644 Victoria, Partido de San Fernando, Prov. de Buenos Aires, Argentina

Tel: 54-1-746-8000 Fax: 54-1-746-8282 Contact: Jorge Martinez Quiroga, Dir.

BAKER & McKENZIE

One Prudential Plaza, 130 East Randolph Drive, Ste. 2500, Chicago, IL, 60601

Tel: (312) 861-8000 Fax: (312) 861-2899 Web site: www.bakerinfo.com

International legal services.

Baker & McKenzie, Av. Leandro N. Alem 1110, piso 13, 1001 Buenos Aires, Argentina

Tel: 54-1-310-2200 Fax: 54-1-310-2299

BAKER HUGHES INCORPORATED

3900 Essex Lane, Ste. 1200, Houston, TX, 77027

Tel: (713) 439-8600 Fax: (713) 439-8699 Web site: www.bakerhughes.com

Develop & apply technology to drill, complete & produce oil and natural gas wells; provide separation systems to petroleum, municipal, continuous process & mining industries.

Baker Oil Tools - South Region Office, Maipu 1300, piso 14, Buenos Aires, 1006, Argentina

Tel: 54-1-313-1244 Fax: 54-1-313-8385

Baker Transworld Argentina, Ruta 3 #3396, Bo. Industrial, Comodoro, Rivsdavia 9000, Argentina

Tel: 54-97-484666

THE BANK OF NEW YORK

48 Wall Street, New York, NY, 10286

Tel: (212) 495-1784 Fax: (212) 495-2546 Web site: www.bankofny.com

Banking servces.

The Bank of New York SA, 25 de Mayo 199, 1002 Buenos Aires, Argentina

Tel: 54-1-331-1111 Fax: 54-1-334-0634 Contact: Armincar Bosi, VP & Gen. Mgr.

BANKAMERICA CORPORATION

555 California Street, San Francisco, CA, 94104

Tel: (415) 622-3530 Fax: (415) 622-8467 Web site: www.bankamerica.com

Financial services.

Bank of America - Latin America/Canada Capital Markets Group, 555 - 25 de Mayo, piso 2, 1002 Buenos Aires, Argentina

Tel: 54-1-319-2616 Fax: 54-1-311-7294 Contact: Leopoldo E. Visini, EVP

Bank of America NT & SA - Representative & Branch Office, 537 - 25 de Mayo, piso 1, 1002 Buenos Aires, Argentina

Tel: 54-1-319-2699 Fax: 54-1-319-2645 Contact: Rodolfo Alborelli, SVP & Gen. Mgr.

BANKBOSTON CORPORATION

100 Federal Street, PO Box 1788, Boston, MA, 02110

Tel: (617) 434-2200 Fax: (617) 434-7547 Web site: www.bankboston.com

Banking & insurance services.

BancBoston - Buenos Aires, Florida 99, 1005 Buenos Aires, Argentina

Tel: 54-1-346-2000 Fax: 54-1-346-3209 Contact: Juan Carlos Raschi, Reg. Mgr.

BankBoston - Córdoba, Rivadavia 25, 5000 Córdoba, Pcia.de Córdoba, Argentina

Tel: 54-51-215469

BankBoston - Mar Del Plata, Independencia 1827/31, 7600 Mar del Plata, Pcia. de Buenos Aires, Argentina

Tel: 54-23-952221

BankBoston - Mendoza, Necochea 165, 5500 Mendoza, Argentina
Tel: 54-61-380024

BankBoston - Resistencia, J. B. Justo 171, 3500 Resistencia, Argentina
Tel: 54-722-29433

BankBoston - Rosario, Av. Córdoba 1201, 2000 Rosario, Pcia. De Santa Fe, Argentina
Tel: 54-41-247979

BankBoston - Tucumán, San Marin 736, 4000 Tucumán, Argentina
Tel: 54-81-311077

Boston Inversora De Valores S.A., Sarmiento 539, 10th Fl., 1041 Buenos Aires, Argentina
Tel: 54-1-394-2642 Fax: 54-1-323-4835

Boston Overseas Financial Corporation S.A., Sarmiento 539, 10th Fl., 1041 Buenos Aires, Argentina
Tel: 54-1-393-7869 Fax: 54-1-343-9652

First National Boston Compañia De Inversiones S.A., Sarmiento 539, 10th Fl., 1041 Buenos Aires, Argentina
Tel: 54-1-393-7869 Fax: 54-1-393-9652

Fundacion Banco De Boston, Av. Diag. R.S. Pena 567-8, 1352 Buenos Aires, Argentina
Tel: 54-1-343-2475 Fax: 54-1-342-9899

Inversora Diagonal S.A., Sarmiento 539, 10th Fl., 1041 Buenos Aires, Argentina
Tel: 54-1-393-7869 Fax: 54-1-393-9652

The Boston Investment Group S.A., Sarmiento 539, 10th Fl., 1041 Buenos Aires, Argentina
Tel: 54-1-393-7869 Fax: 54-1-393-9652

The First National Boston S.A. Asesores De Seguros, Sarmiento 539, 10th Fl., 1041 Buenos Aires, Argentina
Tel: 54-1-393-2997 Fax: 54-1-393-9652

BANKERS TRUST COMPANY

280 Park Ave., New York, NY, 10017
Tel: (212) 250-2500 Fax: (212) 250-2440 Web site: www.bankerstrust.com
Banking & investment services.

B.T. Rio de la Plata SACF, San Martin 140, 15th Fl., 1004 Buenos Aires, Argentina
Tel: 54-1-331-4740 Fax: 54-1-331-7735 Contact: Patricio E. Kelly, VP

BATES WORLDWIDE INC.

405 Lexington Ave., New York, NY, 10174
Tel: (212) 297-7000 Fax: (212) 986-0270 Web site: www.batesww.com
Advertising, marketing, public relations & media consulting.

Bates Consultant, Sinclair 2976, Planto Baja, C.P. 1425, Buenos Aires, Argentina

Bates Selective, Sinclair 2976 - Plao 4, C.P. 1425, Buenos Aires, Argentina

Verdino Bates Publicidad, Duncal 4695, 1425 Buenos Aires, Argentina
Tel: 54-1-777-3100 Fax: 54-1-7714070 Contact: A. Verdina, Pres.

BBDO WORLDWIDE

1285 Ave. of the Americas, New York, NY, 10019
Tel: (212) 459-5000 Fax: (212) 459-6645 Web site: www.bbdo.com
Multinational group of advertising agencies.

Ratta/BBDO, Buenos Aires, Argentina

BDO SEIDMAN, LLP

Two Prudential Plaza, 180 N. Stetson Ave., Ste. 2300, Chicago, IL, 60601
Tel: (312) 240-1236 Fax: (312) 240-3329 Web site: www.bdo.com
International accounting & financial consulting firm.

BDO Latin America Reg. Office, Av. Córdoba 1318-9th Fl., 1055 Buenos Aires, Argentina
Tel: 54-1-372-7132 Fax: 54-1-814-4502 Contact: Dr. Silvio Becher

Becher Lichtenstein y Asociados, Av. Córdoba 1318-9th Fl., 1055 Buenos Aires, Argentina

Tel: 54-1-372-7132 Fax: 54-1-814-4502 Contact: Dr. Silvio Becher

BEAR STEARNS & CO., INC.

245 Park Ave., New York, NY, 10167

Tel: (212) 272-2000 Fax: (212) 272-3092 Web site: www.bearstearns.com

Investment banking, securities broker/dealer & investment advisory services.

Bear Stearns Argentina Inc., c/o Quadrum Group, 25 de Mayo 516, piso 20, 1002 Buenos Aires, Argentina

Tel: 54-1-315-6493 Fax: 54-1-315-6495

BECHTEL GROUP INC.

50 Beale Street, PO Box 3965, San Francisco, CA, 94105-1895

Tel: (415) 768-1234 Fax: (415) 768-9038 Web site: www.bechtel.com

General contractors in engineering & construction.

Bechtel Inc., Av. L.. Alem 712, piso 5, 1001 Buenos Aires, Argentina

Tel: 54-1-315-8000 Fax: 54-1-315-0081

BELLSOUTH INTERNATIONAL

1155 Peachtree Street NE, Ste. 400, Atlanta, GA, 30367

Tel: (404) 249-4800 Fax: (404) 249-4880 Web site: www.bellsouth.com

Mobile communications, telecommunications network systems.

Compania de Radiocommunicaciones Moviles SA (CRM), Movicom, Tucuman 744, piso 2, 1049 Buenos Aires, Argentina

Tel: 54-1-321-5006 Fax: 54-1-321-0334

BENTLY NEVADA CORPORATION

1617 Water Street, PO Box 157, Minden, NV, 89423

Tel: (702) 782-3611 Fax: (702) 782-9259

Electronic monitoring systems.

Lix Klett SACI, Sarmiento 1236, Buenos Aires, Argentina

LOUIS BERGER INTERNATIONAL INC.

100 Halsted Street, East Orange, NJ, 07019

Tel: (201) 678-1960 Fax: (201) 672-4284 Web site: www.louisberger.com

Consulting engineers, architects, economists & planners.

Louis Berger International Inc., Cordoba 669, piso 13, Of. A, 1054 Buenos Aires, Argentina

Tel: 54-1-312-2211 Fax: 54-1-312-2503

BEST WESTERN INTERNATIONAL

6201 North 24th Place, Phoenix, AZ, 85106

Tel: (602) 957-4200 Fax: (602) 957-5740

International hotel chain.

Best Western Art Deco Hotel, Libertad 446, Buenos Aires 1012, Argentina

Tel: 54-1-384-5298

BESTFOODS, INC.

700 Sylvan Ave., International Plaza, Englewood Cliffs, NJ, 07632-9976

Tel: (201) 894-4000 Fax: (201) 894-2186 Web site: www.bestfoods.com

Consumer foods products; corn refining.

Refinerias de Maiz SAICF, Tucumán 117, 1341 Buenos Aires, Argentina

Tel: 54-1-318-7000 Fax: 54-1-318-7001 Contact: Oscar A. Imbellone, Pres.

BETZDEARBORN

4636 Somerton Road, PO Box 3002, Trevose, PA, 19053-6783

Tel: (215) 953-2568 Fax: (215) 953-5524 Web site: www.betzdearborn.com

Mfr. water/wastewater and process system treatment chemicals and services.

BetzDearborn Argentina, S.A., Av. Del Libertador, 8616, 1429 Beunos Aires, Argentina

BLOOMBERG L.P.

499 Park Ave., New York, NY, 10022

Tel: (212) 318-2000 Fax: (212) 940-1954 Web site: www.bloomberg.com

Publishes magazines and provides TV, radio and newspaper wire services.

Bloomberg L.P., Buenos Aires, Argentina

Tel: 54-1-321-7700

BOOZ ALLEN & HAMILTON INC.

8283 Greensboro Drive, McLean, VA, 22102

Tel: (703) 902-5000 Fax: (703) 902-3333 Web site: www.bah.com

International management and technology consultants.

Booz Allen & Hamilton Argentina S.A., Av. Libertador 498, 29th Fl., 1001 Buenos aires, Argentina

Tel: 54-1-325-7403 Fax: 54-1-325-7788

BORDEN INC.

180 East Broad Street, Columbus, OH, 43215-3799

Tel: (614) 225-4000 Fax: (614) 220-6453

Mfr. Packaged foods, consumer adhesives, housewares and industrial chemicals.

Cia. Casco S.I.A.C., Av. Libertador, 2740/70, 1st Fl., Olivos, Buenos Aires, 1636, Argentina

Tel: 54-1-334-1424 Fax: 54-1-331-2140

THE BOSTON CONSULTING GROUP

Exchange Place, 31st Floor, Boston, MA, 02109

Tel: (617) 973-1200 Fax: (617) 973-1339 Web site: www.bcg.com

Management consulting company.

The Boston Consulting Group, Bouchard 547-10o (1106) Buenos Aires, Argentina

Tel: 54-1-314-2228

BOSTON SCIENTIFIC CORPORATION

One Scientific Place, Natick, MA, 01760-1537

Tel: (508) 650-8000 Fax: (508) 650-8923 Web site: www.bsci.com

Mfr./distributes medical devices for use in minimally invasive surgeries.

Boston Scientific Argentina S.A., Vera 745, 1414 Buenos Aires, Argentina

Tel: 54-1-855-5555 Fax: 54-1-856-8525

BOWNE INTERNATIONAL INC.

345 Hudson Street, New York, NY, 10014

Tel: (212) 924-5500 Fax: (212) 229-3420

Financial printing and foreign language translation, localization (software), internet design and maintenance and facilities management.

DMV Trading, Parana 768, piso 8, 1017 Buenos Aires, Argentina

Tel: 54-1-815-0467 Fax: 54-1-811-6813 Contact: Diana Villars, Mgr.

BOYDEN CONSULTING CORPORATION

100 Park Ave., 34th Floor, New York, NY, 10017

Tel: (212) 980-6534 Fax: (212) 980-6147 Web site: www.boyden.com

Executive search.

Boyden Associates Ltd., Av. Cordoba 1255, piso 10o'B', (1055) Buenos Aires, Argentina

Tel: 54-1-815-2705

BOZELL WORLDWIDE

40 West 23rd Street, New York, NY, 10010

Tel: (212) 727-5000 Fax: (212) 645-9173 Web site: www.bozell.com

Advertising, marketing, public relations and media consulting.

Bozell Vazquez, Av. Callao 1046, 3rd Fl., (1023) Buenos Aires, Argentina

Tel: 54-1-815-4850 Fax: 54-1-814-0494 Contact: Jorge Vazquez, Pres.

BRANSON ULTRASONICS CORPORATION

41 Eagle Road, Danbury, CT, 06813-1961

Tel: (203) 796-0400 Fax: (203) 796-2285

Mfr. plastics assembly equipment, ultrasonic cleaning equipment.

Intersonic, Freire 2275 Unidad 14, 1428 Buenos Aires, Argentina

Tel: 54-1-543-2657 Fax: 54-1-543-0546

BRISTOL-MYERS SQUIBB COMPANY

345 Park Ave., New York, NY, 10154

Tel: (212) 546-4000 Fax: (212) 546-4020 Web site: www.bms.com

Pharmaceutical and food preparations, medical and surgical instruments.

Bristol-Myers Squibb - Argentina, Calle Pellegrini 1365-PB, Buenos Aires, Argentina

BUDGET RENT A CAR CORPORATION

4225 Naperville Road, Lisle, IL, 60532

Tel: (630) 955-1900 Fax: (630) 955-7799 Web site: www.budgetrentacar.com

Car and truck rental system.

Budget Rent A Car, Av. Santa Fe 869, Av. Scalabrini Ortiz 258-1058, Buenos Aires, Argentina

Tel: 54-1-311-9870

BULAB HOLDINGS INC.

1256 N. McLean Blvd, Memphis, TN, 38108

Tel: (901) 278-0330 Fax: (901) 276-5343 Web site: www.buckman.com

Biological products; chemicals & chemical preparations.

Laboratorios Buckman SA, Av. San Isidro 4602, piso 1, 1429 Buenos Aires, Argentina

Tel: 54-1-701-3684 Fax: 54-1-702-1060

LEO BURNETT CO., INC.

35 West Wacker Drive, Chicago, IL, 60601

Tel: (312) 220-5959 Fax: (312) 220-6533 Web site: www.leoburnett.com

International advertising agency.

Leo Burnett Co. Inc.-Sucursal Argentina, Carlos Pellegrini 1363, 1011 Buenos Aires, Argentina

BURSON-MARSTELLER

230 Park Ave., New York, NY, 10003-1566

Tel: (212) 614-4000 Fax: (212) 614-4262 Web site: www.bm.com

Public relations/public affairs consultants.

Burson-Marsteller Buenos Aires, Paseo Colon 275, piso 1, Capital Federal, CP 1063, Argentina

Tel: 54-1-342-8010 Fax: 54-1-342-8018

CABOT CORPORATION

75 State Street, Boston, MA, 02109-1807

Tel: (617) 345-0100 Fax: (617) 342-6103

Mfr. carbon blacks, plastics; oil & gas, information systems.

Cabot Argentina SAIyC, Sarmiento 930, piso 2, Buenos Aires, Argentina

CAMPBELL SOUP COMPANY

Campbell Place, Camden, NJ, 08103-1799

Tel: (609) 342-4800 Fax: (609) 342-3878

Food products.

Swift-Armour SA, Argentina

CARBOLINE COMPANY

350 Hanley Industrial Court, St. Louis, MO, 63144

Tel: (314) 644-1000 Fax: (314) 644-4617

Mfr. coatings, sealants.

Tintas Letta SAIC, Mendoza 1290, Villa Zagala 1651, PCIA de Buenos Aires, Argentina

CARGILL, INC.

15407 McGinty Road, Minnetonka, MN, 55440-5625

Tel: (612) 742-7575 Fax: (612) 742-7393 Web site: www.cargill.com

Food products, feeds, animal products.

Cargill SACI, Casilla de Correo 2495, 1000 Buenos Aires, Argentina

CARRIER CORPORATION

One Carrier Place, Farmington, CT, 06034-4015

Tel: (860) 674-3000 Fax: (860) 679-3010 Web site: www.carrier.com

Mfr./distributor/services A/C, heating & refrigeration equipment.

Carrier-Lix Klett SA, Av. Rivadavia 611, piso 6, Buenos Aires, Argentina

Tel: 54-1-345-1455 Fax: 54-1-331-7997

C.B. RICHARD ELLIS

533 South Fremont Ave., Los Angeles, CA, 90071-1712

Tel: (213) 613-3123 Fax: (213) 613-3535 Web site: www.cbrichardellis.com

Commercial real estate services.

CB Richard Ellis, Buenos Aires, Argentina

CBI COMPANY

1501 North Division Street, Plainfield, IL, 60544

Tel: (815) 241-7546 Fax: (815) 439-6010

Holding company: metal plate fabricating, construction, oil and gas drilling.

CBI Argentina SA, Salta 1212, 1872 Sarandi, Buenos Aires, Argentina

CENTRAL NATIONAL-GOTTESMAN INC.

3 Manhattanville Road, Purchase, NY, 10577-2110

Tel: (914) 696-9000 Fax: (914) 696-1066

Worldwide sales pulp and paper products.

Central National Argentina SRL, Bartolome Mitre 734, piso 8, 1036 Buenos Aires, Argentina

Tel: 54-1-343-7460 Fax: 54-1-342-2809 Contact: Pedro Auspitz

CH2M HILL INC.

6060 South Willow Drive, Greenwood Village, CO, 80111

Tel: (303) 771-0900 Fax: (303) 770-2616

Consulting engineers, planners, economists and scientists.

CH2M Hill, Buenos Aires, Argentina

Tel: 54-1-312-8008

THE CHASE MANHATTAN CORPORATION

World Headquarters, 270 Park Ave., New York, NY, 10017

Tel: (212) 270-6000 Fax: (212) 622-9030 Web site: www.chase.com

International banking and financial services.

The Chase Manhattan Bank, Buenos Aires Branch, Calle Arenales 707, piso 5, 1061 Buenos Aires, Argentina

Tel: 54-1-319-2400 Fax: 54-1-319-2404 Contact: Marcelo Eduardo Podestá

CHESTERTON BINSWANGER INTERNATIONAL

Two Logan Square, 4th Floor, Philadelphia, PA, 19103-2759

Tel: (215) 448-6000 Fax: (215) 448-6238

Real estate & related services.

Gimenez Zapiola SRL, Av. Dorcoba 1367, 1055 Buenos Aires, Argentina

THE CHUBB CORPORATION

15 Mountain View Road, Warren, NJ, 07061-1615

Tel: (908) 580-2000 Fax: (908) 580-3606 Web site: www.chubb.com

Holding company: property/casualty insurance.

Chubb Argentina de Seguros, SA, 25 de Mayo 537, 5th Fl., Buenos Aires, Argentina

Tel: 54-1-313-1404 Fax: 54-1-313-1365

CIGNA CORPORATION

One Liberty Place, Philadelphia, PA, 19192

Tel: (215) 761-1000 Fax: (215) 761-5008

Insurance, invest, health care and other financial services.

Insurance Co. of North America, Suipacha 268, 2 piso, 1355 Buenos Aires, Argentina

CINERGY CORP.

139 East Fourth Street, Cincinnati, OH, 45202

Tel: (513) 421-9500 Fax: (513) 651-9196 Web site: www.cinergy.com

Utility holding company - generates, transmits and distributes electricity and natural gas.

PSI Energy Argentina, Inc., Argentina

CISCO SYSTEMS, INC.

170 Tasman Drive, San Jose, CA, 95134-1706

Tel: (408) 526-4000 Fax: (408) 526-4100 Web site: www.cisco.com

Develop/mfr./market computer hardware and software networking systems.

Cisco Systems Argentina, Cerrito 1054, piso 9, (1010) Buenos Aires, Argentina

Tel: 54-1-811-7526 Fax: 54-1-811-7495 Contact: Javier Núñez

CITICORP

399 Park Ave., New York, NY, 10043

Tel: (212) 559-1000 Fax: (212) 527-2066 Web site: www.citibank.com

International banking and financial services.

Citibank N.A., Bartolome Mitre 502/530, Buenos Aires, Argentina 1036

Tel: 54-1-329-1000 Fax: 54-1-329-1029 Contact: Carlos Maria Fedrigotti, Pres.

Citibank N.A., Bouchard 547, 27th Fl., Buenos Aires 1106, Argentina

Contact: Emilio L. Arcani, Mgr.

Citicorp Banco de Inversion S.A., San Martin 140, piso 12, Buenos Aires, Argentina 1005

Tel: 54-1-329-1000 Contact: Elsa M. Esposito, Gen. Mgr.

THE CLOROX COMPANY

1221 Broadway, PO Box 24305, Oakland, CA, 94623-1305

Tel: (510) 271-7000 Fax: (510) 832-1463

Mfr. soap & detergents, and domestic consumer packaged products.

Clorox Argentina SA, Buenos Aires, Argentina

CMS ENERGY CORPORATION

Fairlane Plaza South, Ste. 1100, 330 Town Drive, Dearborn, MI, 48126

Tel: (313) 436-9200 Fax: (313) 436-9225 Web site: www.cmsenergy.com

Independent power plant operator.

CMS Energy, Alsina 495, piso 5, 1087 Capital Federal, Buenos Aires, Argentina

Tel: 54-1-342-3792 Fax: 54-1-331-8056

CNA FINANCIAL CORPORATION

CNA Plaza, Chicago, IL, 60685

Tel: (312) 822-5000 Fax: (312) 822-6419 Web site: www.can.com

Commercial property/casualty insurance policies.

Omega ART, Buenos Aires, Argentina

THE COCA-COLA COMPANY

P.O. Drawer 1734, Atlanta, GA, 30301

Tel: (404) 676-2121 Fax: (404) 676-6792 Web site: www.coca-cola.com

Mfr./marketing/distributor soft drinks, syrups & concentrates, juice & juice-drink products.

Coca-Cola FEMSA, S.A. de C.V., Buenos Aires, Argentina - All mail to U.S. address

Inti SA, Buenos Aires, Argentina - All mail to U.S. address

COLGATE-PALMOLIVE COMPANY

300 Park Ave., New York, NY, 10022

Tel: (212) 310-2000 Fax: (212) 310-2919

Mfr. pharmaceuticals, cosmetics, toiletries and detergents.

Colgate-Palmolive Ltda. SAI, Av. Antartida Argentina 2269, 1836 Llavollol, Buenos Aires, Argentina

COLUMBIA PICTURES INDUSTRIES INC.

10202 West Washington Blvd., Culver City, CA, 90232

Tel: (310) 244-4000 Fax: (310) 244-2626 Web site: www.sony.com

Producer and distributor of motion pictures.

Fox Films de la Argentina Inc., Lavalle 1876, Buenos Aires, Argentina

COMPAQ COMPUTER CORPORATION

20555 State Highway 249, PO Box 692000, Houston, TX, 77269-2000

Tel: (713) 370-0670 Fax: (713) 514-1740 Web site: www.compaq.com

Develop/mfr. personal computers.

Compaq Argentina, S.A., Av. del Libertador 238, (1638) Vincente Lopez, Buenos Aires, Argentina

Tel: 54-1-796-8100 Fax: 54-1-796-5151

COMPUTER ASSOCIATES INTERNATIONAL INC.

One Computer Associates Plaza, Islandia, NY, 11788

Tel: (516) 342-5224 Fax: (516) 342-5329 Web site: www.cai.com

Integrated software for enterprise computing and information management, application development, manufacturing, financial applications and professional services.

Computer Associates de Argentina SA, Av. Alicia Moreau de Justo 400 - 2 piso, 1107 Beunos Aires, Argentina

Tel: 54-1-317-1500

COMSAT CORPORATION

6560 Rock Spring Drive, Bethesda, MD, 20817

Tel: (301) 214-3200 Fax: (301) 214-7100 Web site: www.comsat.com

Provides global telecommunications services via satellite and develops advanced satellite networking technology.

COMSAT International, Buenos Aires, Argentina

CONAGRA INC.

One ConAgra Drive, Omaha, NE, 68102-5001

Tel: (402) 595-4000 Fax: (402) 595-4595 Web site: www.conagra.com

Prepared/frozen foods, grains, flour, animal feeds, agri chemicals, poultry, meat, dairy products, including Healthy Choice, Butterball and Hunt's.

ConAgra Inc., Buenos Aires, Argentina

CONAGRA PEAVEY COMPANY

730 Second Ave. South, Minneapolis, MN, 55402

Tel: (612) 370-7500 Fax: (612) 370-7504

Flour, feeds, seeds.

ConAgra SA, Buenos Aires, Argentina

CONOCO INC.

PO Box 2197, Houston, TX, 77252

Tel: (281) 293-1000 Fax: (281) 293-1440

Oil, gas, coal, chemicals and minerals.

PASA Petroquimica Argentina SA, Suipacha 1111, piso 11, Buenos Aires, Argentina

CORESTATES BANK

1500 Market Street, Philadelphia, PA, 19101

Tel: (215) 973-3100 Fax: (215) 786-8899 Web site: www.corestates.com

Primary international businesses; correspondent banking and trade services.

Corestates Bank, Lavalle 190, 2/F Ofic. D, Capital Federal, Buenos Aires, Argentina

CROWN CORK & SEAL COMPANY, INC.

One Crown Way, Philadelphia, PA, 19154-4599

Tel: (215) 698-5100 Fax: (215) 698-5201

Mfr. cans, bottle caps; filling & packaging machinery.

Crown Cork de Argentina SAIC, Laprida 4755, Villa Martell, Buenos Aires, Argentina

Crown Cork de Argentina SAIC, Casilla de Correo 3478, 1000 Buenos Aires, Argentina

D'ARCY MASIUS BENTON & BOWLES INC. (DMB&B)

1675 Broadway, New York, NY, 10019

Tel: (212) 468-3622 Fax: (212) 468-2987 Web site: www.dmbb.com

Full service international advertising and communications group.

Graffiti/DMB&B, Uruguay 1112, piso 4, 1016 Buenos Aires, Argentina

Tel: 54-1-815-0533 Fax: 54-1-811-1629 Contact: Eduardo Baca, Pres.

DANA CORPORATION

4500 Door Street, Toledo, OH, 43615

Tel: (419) 535-4500 Fax: (419) 535-4643 Web site: www.dana.com

Mfr./sales of automotive, heavy truck, off-highway, fluid & mechanical power components.

Dana Corporation, Buenos Aires, Argentina

DATASCOPE CORPORATION

14 Philips Parkway, Montvale, NJ, 07645

Tel: (201) 391-8100 Fax: (201) 307-5400 Web site: www.datascope.com

Mfr. medical devices.

InterVascular SA, Buenos Aires, Argentina

DDB NEEDHAM WORLDWIDE INC.

437 Madison Ave., New York, NY, 10022

Tel: (212) 415-2000 Fax: (212) 415-3417

Advertising agency.

Rainuzzo/DDB Worldwide, Buenos Aires, Argentina

DEERE & COMPANY

One John Deere Road, Moline, IL, 61265

Tel: (309) 765-8000 Fax: (309) 765-5772 Web site: www.deere.com

Mfr./sale agricultural, construction, utility, forestry and lawn, grounds care equipment.

Industrias John Deere Argentina SA, Casilla de Correo 30, 2000 Rosaria, Argentina

DEKALB GENETICS CORP.

3100 Sycamore Road, DeKalb, IL, 60115-9600

Tel: (815) 758-3461 Fax: (815) 758-3711 Web site: www.dekalb.com

Develop/produce hybrid corn, sorghum, sunflower seed, varietal soybeans, alfalfa.

DeKalb Argentina SA, Maipu 1252, piso 5, 1006 Buenos Aires, Argentina

Tel: 54-1-310-0900 Fax: 54-1-310-0912 Contact: H. Jorge Ghengo, President

DELOITTE TOUCHE TOHMATSU INTERNATIONAL

PO Box 820, Wilton, CT, 06897

Tel: (203) 761-3000 Fax: (203) 834-2200 Web site: www.u.s.deloitte.com or www.dtti.com

Accounting, audit, tax and management consulting services.

Deloitte & Touche, Sarmiento 624, 1041 Buenos Aires, Argentina

Deloitte & Touche (Mendoza), Av. Espana 1340, piso 12-Of. 16/18, 5500 Mendoza, Argentina

Deloitte & Touche (Rosario), Santa Fe 1219, piso 3, 2000 Rosario, Santa Fe, Argentina

DENTSPLY INTERNATIONAL

570 West College Ave., PO Box 872, York, PA, 17405-0872

Tel: (717) 845-7511 Fax: (717) 843-6357 Web site: www.dentsply.com

Mfr.& Distribution of dental supplies & equipment.

Dentsply Argentina SACI, General Enrique Martinez 657/61, 1426 Buenos Aires, Argentina

Tel: 54-1-555-0808

DHL WORLDWIDE EXPRESS

333 Twin Dolphin Drive, Redwood City, CA, 94065

Tel: (650) 593-7474 Fax: (650) 593-1689 Web site: www.dhl.com

Worldwide air express carrier.

DHL Worldwide Express, Moreno 963/67, Buenos Aires 1091, Argentina

Tel: 54-1-347-0600

DOMINION RESOURCES, INC.

901 East Byrd Street, Ste. 1700, Richmond, VA, 23219-6111

Tel: (804) 775-5700 Fax: (804) 775-5819 Web site: www.domres.com

Provides electrical power.

Dominion Resources, Buenos Aires, Argentina

DONALDSON, LUFKIN & JENRETTE, INC.

277 Park Ave., New York, NY, 10172

Tel: (212) 892-3000 Fax: (212) 892-7272 Web site: www.dlj.com

Investment banking, capital markets, and financial services.

Donaldson Lufkin & Jenrette Inc., Av. Bouchard #547 piso 11, Buenoa Aires 1106, Argentina

Tel: 54-1-315-3550

R.R. DONNELLEY & SONS COMPANY

77 West Wacker Drive, Chicago, IL, 60601-1696

Tel: (312) 326-8000 Fax: (312) 326-8543 Web site: www.rrdonnelley.com

Commercial printing, allied communication services.

R. R. Donnelley Financial, (JV) Editorial Atlantida Cochrane, Salta No. 596, 3rd Fl., Buenos Aires, 1074-Capital Federal, Argentina

Tel: 54-1-381-0913

THE DOW CHEMICAL COMPANY

2030 Dow Center, Midland, MI, 48674

Tel: (517) 636-1000 Fax: (517) 636-3228 Web site: www.atdow.com

Mfr. chemicals, plastics, pharmaceuticals, agricultural products, consumer products.

Indoquim SA, Av. L.N. Alem 896, 1001 Buenos Aires, Argentina

DOW CORNING CORPORATION

2220 West Salzburg Road, PO Box 1767, Midland, MI, 48640

Tel: (517) 496-4000 Fax: (517) 496-6080

Silicones, silicon chemicals, solid lubricants.

Dow Corning de Argentina SRL, El Cano 2853, 1355 Buenos Aires, Argentina

DRAKE BEAM MORIN INC.

101 Huntington Ave., Boston, MA, 02199

Tel: (617) 450-9860 Fax: (617) 267-2011 Web site: www.dbm.com

Human resource management consulting & training.

DBM Argentina/CNN Consultores, San Jose 777 (1076) Buenos Aires, Argentina

Tel: 54-1-382-9982 Fax: 54-1-382-9982

E.I. DU PONT DE NEMOURS & COMPANY

1007 Market Street, Wilmington, DE, 19898

Tel: (302) 774-1000 Fax: (302) 774-7321 Web site: www.dupont.com

Mfr./sale diversified chemicals, plastics, specialty products and fibers.

Ducilo SA, E. Madero 1020, 1106 Buenos Aires, Argentina

DURACELL INTERNATIONAL INC.

Berkshire Industrial Park, Bethel, CT, 06801

Tel: (203) 796-4000 Fax: (203) 796-4745

Mfr. batteries.

Duracell Argentina SA, Av. Coronel Roca 6757/67, 1439 Buenos Aires, Argentina

EASTMAN CHEMICAL

100 North Eastman Road, Kingsport, TN, 37660

Tel: (423) 229-2000 Fax: (423) 229-1351 Web site: www.eastman.com

Mfr. plastics, chemicals, fibers.

Eastman Chemical Argentina S.R.L., Av. Del Libertador 498, P21, 1001 Buenos Aires, Argentina

Tel: 54-1-320-800 Fax: 54-1-394-2076

Eastman Chemical Argentina SRL, Camino Santa Ana, S/N Parque, Industriale Zarate, 2800 Zarate, Buenos Aires, Argentina

Tel: 54-4-872-9900 Fax: 54-4-872-9930 Contact: James Ray, Mgr.

EASTMAN KODAK COMPANY

343 State Street, Rochester, NY, 14650

Tel: (716) 724-4000 Fax: (716) 724-0663

Develop/mfr. photo & chemicals products, information management/video/copier systems, fibers/plastics for various industry.

Kodak Argentina SAIC, Casilla de Correo Central 5200, 1000 Buenos Aires, Argentina

EATON CORPORATION

1111 Superior Ave., Cleveland, OH, 44114

Tel: (216) 523-5000 Fax: (216) 479-7068

Advanced technical products for transportation & industrial markets.

Eaton ICSA, Av. Cordoba 679, piso 3, 1365 Buenos Aires, Argentina

ECOLAB INC.

Ecolab Center, 370 N. Wabasha Street, St. Paul, MN, 55102

Tel: (612) 293-2233 Fax: (612) 225-3105 Web site: www.ecolab.com

Develop/mfr. premium cleaning, sanitizing and maintenance products and services for the hospitality, institutional, and residential markets.

Ecolab Ltd., Buenos Aires, Argentina

Tel: 54-1-229-6276

EDELMAN PUBLIC RELATIONS WORLDWIDE

200 East Randolph Drive, 63rd Floor, Chicago, IL, 60601

Tel: (312) 240-3000 Fax: (312) 240-0596 Web site: www.edelman.com

International independent public relations firm.

Edelman PR Worldwide, Salem Viale, Paraguay 610, piso 29, 1350 Capital Federal, Buenos Aires, Argentina

Tel: 54-1-315-4020 Fax: 54-1-311-7161 Contact: Alberto Salem, Pres.

J.D. EDWARDS & COMPANY

One Technology Way, Denver, CO, 80237

Tel: (303) 334-4000 Fax: (303) 334-4970 Web site: www.jdedwards.com.

Computer software products.

Application Software, S.A., Suipacha 1111 piso 11, Buenos Aires, Argentina

Tel: 54-1-315-2552 Fax: 54-1-315-1903

EFCO

1800 NE Broadway Ave., Des Moines, IA, 50316-0386

Tel: (515) 266-1141 Fax: (515) 266-7970

Mfr. systems for concrete construction.

EFCO, Rawson 2702 - 3C, Olivos, Buenos Aires, Argentina

ENRON CORPORATION

1400 Smith Street, Houston, TX, 77002-7361

Tel: (713) 853-6161 Fax: (713) 853-3129 Web site: www.enron.com

Exploration, production, transportation and distribution of integrated natural gas and electricity.

Enron Pipeline Co., Av. Eduardo Madero, 900, Fl. 18, 1106 Buenos Aires, Argentina

Tel: 54-1-315-1717

Transportadora de Gas del Sur S.A., Don Bosco 3672 piso 7, 1206 Buenos Aires, Argentina

Tel: 54-1-865-9069

EQUIFAX INC.

PO Box 4081, Atlanta, GA, 30302

Tel: (404) 885-8000 Fax: (404) 888-5452 Web site: www.equifax.com

Information and knowledge-based solutions.

Equifax South America, Tacuari 202, Pito 10, 1071 Buenos Aires, Argentina

Organizacion Veraz SA, Tacuari 202, piso 10, 1071 Buenos Aires, Argentina

ERNST & YOUNG, LLP

787 Seventh Ave., New York, NY, 10019

Tel: (212) 773-3000 Fax: (212) 773-6350 Web site: www.eyi.com

Accounting and audit, tax and management consulting services.

Henry Martin, Lisdero y Asociados, Maipu 942, 8th Fl., 1340 Buenos Aires, Argentina

Tel: 54-1-311-8162 Fax: 54-1-315-4948 Contact: O. Laratro/A.Lisdero

EURO RSCG Worldwide

350 Hudson Street, New York, NY, 10014

Tel: (212) 886-2000 Fax: (212) 886-2016

International advertising agency group.

Euro RSCG Argentina, Buenos Aires, Argentina

EXXON CORPORATION

225 E. John W. Carpenter Freeway, Irving, TX, 75062-2298

Tel: (972) 444-1000 Fax: (972) 444-1882 Web site: www.exxon.com

Petroleum exploration, production, refining; mfr. petroleum & chemicals products; coal & minerals.

Esso SA Petrolero Argentina, Carlos Maria Della Paolera 297/299, 1001 Buenos Aires, Argentina

Exxon Chemical - Campana Paramins Plant, Av. Ing. E Mitre 574, 2804 Campana, Pcia de Buenos Aires, Argentina

FAHNESTOCK & COMPANY

125 Broad Street, New York, NY, 10004

Tel: (212) 668-8000 Fax: (212) 344-9077

Security brokers and dealers.

Fahnestock & Co. Argentina, San Martin 551, piso 1, Office 1, Buenos Aires, Argentina

FEDERAL-MOGUL CORPORATION

26555 Northwestern Highway, PO Box 1966, Southfield, MI, 48034

Tel: (248) 354-7700 Fax: (248) 354-8983 Web site: www.federalmogul.com

Mfr./distributor precision parts for automobiles, trucks, farm and construction vehicles.

Federal-Mogul Distribuidora SAC, Buenos Aires, Argentina

In-De-Co., H. Minoli SAIC, Buenos Aires, Argentina

FERRO CORPORATION

1000 Lakeside Ave., Cleveland, OH, 44114-1183

Tel: (216) 641-8580 Fax: (216) 696-5784 Web site: www.ferro.com

Mfr. Specialty chemicals, coatings, plastics, colors, refractories.

Ferro Enamel Argentina SA, Casilla de Correo 2553, Correo Central, 1000 Buenos Aires, Argentina

Tel: 54-1-334-0618 Fax: 54-1-334-8001 Contact: C.M. Rosso, Mng. Dir.

Frit, Color, vedoc & Complas Plant, Gibraltar 1365, 1874 Villa Vominico, Prov. De Buenoa aires, Argentina

Tel: 54-1-204-2051 Fax: 54-1-205-2229

FIREMENS INSURANCE COMPANY OF NEWARK

180 Maiden Lane, New York, NY, 10038

Tel: (212) 440-3000 Fax: (212) 440-7130

Fire, marine and casualty insurance.

American Intl. Underwriters, Av. Pte. Roque S. Pena 648, Buenos Aires, Argentina

FIRST CHICAGO NBD CORPORATION

One First National Plaza, Chicago, IL, 60670

Tel: (312) 732-4000 Fax: (312) 732-4000 Web site: www.fcnbd.com

Financial products and services.

First National Bank of Chicago, Av. Alicia Moreau de Justo 1180, Of. 305, Dock 8. Puerto Madero, 1106 Buenos Aires, Argentina

Tel: 54-1-343-4800 Fax: 54-1-343-0500 Contact: Robert J. Trbovich, Head Southern Cone

FLUOR DANIEL INC.

3353 Michelson Drive, Irvine, CA, 92698

Tel: (714) 975-2000 Fax: (714) 975-5271 Web site: www.flourdaniel.com

Engineering & construction services.

Fluor Daniel - SADE, Edif. Perez Companc, Maipu 1 (at Riverside) piso 5, Buenos Aires, Argentina 1599

Tel: 54-1-347-1003 Fax: 54-1-347-1004

FMC CORPORATION

200 E. Randolph Drive, Chicago, IL, 60601

Tel: (312) 861-6000 Fax: (312) 861-6141

Produces chemicals & precious metals, mfr. machinery, equipment & systems for industrial, agricultural & government use.

FMC Argentina SA, Av. Madero 1020-22, 1106 Buenos Aires, Argentina

Minera del Altiplano SA, Argentina

FORD MOTOR COMPANY

The American Road, Dearborn, MI, 48121

Tel: (313) 322-3000 Fax: (313) 322-9600 Web site: www.ford.com

Mfr./sales motor vehicles.

Ford Motor Argentina SA, Casilla de Correo 696, Correo Central, 1000 Buenos Aires, Argentina

FRANKLIN COVEY CO.

2200 W. Parkway Blvd., Salt Lake City, UT, 84119-2331

Tel: (801) 975-1776 Fax: (801) 977-1431 Web site: www.franklinquest.com

Provides productivity and time management products and seminars.

Franklin Covey Argentina, Corientes 861, 5to. Piso, 2000 Rosario, Argentina

Tel: 54-41-408-765 Fax: 54-41-408-765

FRANKLIN RESOURCES, INC.

777 Mariners Island Blvd., San Mateo, CA, 94404

Tel: (415) 312-2000 Fax: (415) 312-3655 Web site: www.frk.com

Global and domestic investment advisory and portfolio management.

Templeton Asset Management Ltd., Argentina Branch Office, Ing. E. Butty 220, 11th Fl., Capital Federal, Buenos Aires, Argentina 1300

Tel: 54-1-313-0848 Fax: 54-1-313-0885 Contact: Michel Tulle, Mng. Dir.

FRITZ COMPANIES INC.

706 Mission Street, Ste. 900, San Francisco, CA, 94103

Tel: (415) 904-8360 Fax: (415) 904-8661 Web site: www.fritz.com

Integrated transportation, sourcing, distribution & customs brokerage services.

Fritz de Argentina SA, Paraguay 776, 1057 Buenos Aires, Argentina

H.B. FULLER COMPANY

1200 Willow Lake Blvd., Vadnais Heights, MN, 55110

Tel: (612) 236-5900 Fax: (612) 236-5898 Web site: www.hbfuller.com

Mfr./distributor adhesives, sealants, coatings, paints, waxes, sanitation chemicals.

H.B. Fuller Argentina, S.A.I.C., Parque Industrial de Pilar, Ruta 8 Km. 60 Calle 3, CP (1629) Pilar, Provincia de Buenos Aires, Argentina

Tel: 54-322-96112 Fax: 54-322-96-506

GENERAL ELECTRIC CAPITAL CORPORATION

260 Long Ridge Road, Stamford, CT, 06927

Tel: (203) 357-4000 Fax: (203) 357-6489

Financial, property/casualty insurance, computer sales and trailer leasing services.

Employers Reinsurance Corp. (ERC), Av. L. N. Alen 619 - piso 4, Buenos Aires, C.P. 1001, Argentina

Tel: 54-1-317-8774 Fax: 54-1-317-8793

GENERAL ELECTRIC CO.

3135 Easton Turnpike, Fairfield, CT, 06431

Tel: (203) 373-2211 Fax: (203) 373-3131 Web site: www.ge.com

Diversified manufacturing, technology and services.

General Electric Co.-Argentina, Argentina - All mail to U.S. address; phone (800) 626-2004 or (518) 438-6500

Contact: John McCarter, Pres.

GEPS Global Power Generation, Av. Leandro N. Alem 619, Buenos Aires 01001, Argentina

Tel: 54-1-313-2880

GETSCO, Av. Leandro N. Alem 619, Buenos Aires 01001, Argentina

Tel: 54-1-312-3155 Fax: 54-1-111-794

Nuovo Pignone, Liaison Office, Buenos Aires 01003, Argentina

Tel: 54-1-312-7707 Fax: 54-1-315-3273

GENERAL MOTORS CORPORATION

100 Renaissance Center, Detroit, MI, 48243.7301

Tel: (313) 556-5000 Fax: (313) 556-5108 Web site: www.gm.com

Mfr. full line vehicles, automotive electronics, commercial technologies, telecommunications, space, finance.

General Motors-Cidea (JV), Buenos Aires, Argentina

GENERAL REINSURANCE CORPORATION

695 East Main Street, Stamford, CT, 06904-2350

Tel: (203) 328-5000 Fax: (203) 328-6423 Web site: www.genre.com

Reinsurance services worldwide.

General Re Compañia de Reaseguros SA, Arenales 707 - 3 piso, 1061 Buenos Aires, Argentina

Tel: 54-1-313-3553 Fax: 54-1-313-4884 Contact: Dr. Alberto Alfonso Sáenz, Pres.

THE GILLETTE COMPANY

Prudential Tower Building, Boston, MA, 02199

Tel: (617) 421-7000 Fax: (617) 421-7123 Web site: www.gillette.com

Develop/mfr. personal care/use products: blades & razors, toiletries, cosmetics, stationery.

Compania Gillette de Argentina SA, Buenos Aires, Argentina

Sylvapen Distribuidora SACIyF, Buenos Aires, Argentina

THE GOODYEAR TIRE & RUBBER COMPANY

1144 East Market Street, Akron, OH, 44316

Tel: (330) 796-2121 Fax: (330) 796-1817 Web site: www.goodyear.com

Mfr. tires, automotive belts and hose, conveyor belts, chemicals; oil pipeline transmission.

Neumaticos Goodyear SA, Lavalle 341, 1047 Buenos Aires, Argentina (Location: Hurlingham, Argentina.)

W. R. GRACE & COMPANY

One Town Center Road, 1750 Clint Moore Road, Boca Raton, FL, 33486-1010

Tel: (561) 362-2000 Fax: (561) 561-2193 Web site: www.grace.com

Mfr. specialty chemicals and materials: packaging, health care, catalysts, construction, water treatment/process.

Grace Argentina SA, Casilla Correo 85, 1878 Quilmes, Prov. Buenos Aires, Argentina

Tel: 54-1-229-0100 Fax: 54-1-229-0192

GRACO INC

4050 Olson Memorial Hwy, PO Box 1441, Minneapolis, MN, 55440-1441

Tel: (612) 623-6000 Fax: (612) 623-6777 Web site: www.graco.com

Mfr./sales of infant & juvenile products; services fluid handling equipment & systems.

Jose Luis Marini Victorica, Intendente Nyer 924, 1643 Beccar/BS, Argentina

Tel: 54-1-742-0842 Fax: 54-1-742-0841 Contact: Jose Luis Marini

GRANT THORNTON INTERNATIONAL

800 One Prudential Plaza, 130 E. Randolph Drive, Chicago, IL, 60601-6050

Tel: (312) 856-0001 Fax: (312) 616-7052

Accounting, audit, tax and management consulting services.

Grant Thornton Intl, Maipu 1252 - 6 piso (1006) Buenos Aires, Argentina

Tel: 54-1-314-1441 Fax: 54-1-313-1036

GREY ADVERTISING INC.

777 Third Ave., New York, NY, 10017

Tel: (212) 546-2000 Fax: (212) 546-1495 Web site: www.giworldwwide.com

International advertising agency.

Casares, Grey y Asociados, Suipacha 780, 1008 Buenos Aires, Argentina

GTE CORPORATION

One Stamford Forum, Stamford, CT, 06904

Tel: (203) 965-2000 Fax: (203) 965-2277 Web site: www.gte.com

Electronic products, telecommunications systems, publishing and communications.

GTE Sylvania Argentina SA, Cuyo 3066, Martinez, Pdo. San Isidro, Prov. Buenos Aires, Argentina

HALLIBURTON COMPANY

500 North Akard Street, Ste. 3600, Dallas, TX, 75201-3391

Tel: (214) 978-2600 Fax: (214) 978-2685 Web site: www.halliburton.com

Energy, construction and insurance.

Halliburton Ltd., Avda Casiano Cases s/n, 4563 Genral Mosconi, Salta, Argentina

Tel: 54-875-81100 Fax: 54-875-81100

Halliburton Ltd., Canal 5 y Ruta 22, Col. Valentina, 8300 Neuquen, Argentina

Tel: 54-99-461-076 Fax: 54-99-461-068

Halliburton Ltd., Anchorena 1733, Lujon de Cuyo, Mendoza, Argentina

Tel: 54-61-980-716 Fax: 54-6-981-869

Halliburton Ltd., Pinedo y Ortega, Barrio Industrial, 9000 Comodoro Rivadavia, Chubut, Argentina

Tel: 54-974-74800 Fax: 54-974-69646

Halliburton Ltd., Canadon Secon 9013, Santa Cruz, Argentina

Tel: 54-61-250-4332 Fax: 54-61-250-4332

Halliburton Ltd., Maipu 942, piso 6, 1340 Buenos Aires, Argentina

Tel: 54-1-313-8411 Fax: 54-1-313-9527

HARCOURT BRACE & COMPANY

6277 Sea Harbor Drive, Orlando, FL, 32887

Tel: (407) 345-2000 Fax: (407) 345-9354

Book publishing, tests and related service, journals, facsimile reprints, management consult, operates parks/shows.

Harcourt Brace de Argentina, S.A., Paraguay, 2088, Buenos Aires 1121, Argentina

Tel: 54-1-962-7330 Fax: 54-1-962-7330 Contact: Luis Lorenzo

THE HARPER GROUP

260 Townsend Street, San Francisco, CA, 94107-1719

Tel: (415) 978-0600 Fax: (415) 978-0692 Web site: www.circleintl.com

Ocean/air freight forwarding, customs brokerage, packing and wholesale, logistics management and insurance.

Circle Freight Intl. Argentina SA, 25 de Mayo 596, 1002 Buenos Aires, Argentina

Tel: 54-1-313-6562 Fax: 54-1-313-6607

HARTFORD LIFE INTERNATIONAL, LTD.

200 Hopmeadow Street, Simsbury, CT, 06070

Tel: (860) 843-8982 Fax: (860) 843-8981

Life insurance and group life sales.

Itt Hartford, Maipu 241 (1084) Buenos Aires, Argentina

Tel: 54-1-328-8888 Fax: 54-1-320-3018 Contact: Orlando Terzano, Mng. Dir.

HEIDRICK & STRUGGLES INC

Sears Tower, 233 South Wacker Drive, Chicago, IL, 60606

Tel: (312) 496-1200 Fax: (312) 496-1290 Web site: www.h-s.com

Executive search firm.

Heidrick & Struggles Intl. Inc., Cerrito 1294 piso 10, 1010 Buenos Aires, Argentina

Tel: 54-1-816-2881 Fax: 54-1-816-2909

HEWITT ASSOCIATES LLC

100 Half Day Road, Lincolnshire, IL, 60069

Tel: (847) 295-5000 Fax: (847) 295-7634

Employee benefits consulting firm.

Hewitt Associates, Ave. Carlos Pellegrini, 125 6th Fl., 1009 Buenos Aires, Argentina

Tel: 54-1-393-3122

HEWLETT-PACKARD COMPANY

3000 Hanover Street, Palo Alto, CA, 94304-0890

Tel: (650) 857-1501 Fax: (650) 857-7299 Web site: www.hp.com

Mfr. computing, communications & measurement products & services.

Hewlett-Packard Argentina SA, Montaneses 2140/50, 1428 Buenos Aires, Argentina

Tel: 54-1-787-7100 Fax: 54-1-787-721

HONEYWELL INC.

PO Box 524, Minneapolis, MN, 55440-0524

Tel: (612) 951-1000 Fax: (612) 951-3066 Web site: www.honeywell.com

Develop/mfr. controls for home and building, industry, space and aviation.

Honeywell SAIC, Belgrano 1156, Buenos Aires, Argentina

HORWATH INTERNATIONAL

415 Madison Ave., New York, NY, 10017

Tel: (212) 838-5566 Fax: (212) 838-3636

Public accountants and auditors.

Canepa, Naser, Koes y Asociados, Cerrito 146, 1010 Buenos Aires, Argentina

HOUSTON INDUSTRIES INCORPORATED

1111 Louisiana Street, Houston, TX, 77002

Tel: (713) 207-3000 Fax: (713) 207-0206 Web site: www.houind.com

Provides gas and electric services.

NorAM, Argentina

Contact: Pastor Sanjurjo, VP

HYATT INTERNATIONAL CORPORATION

200 West Madison Street, Chicago, IL, 60606

Tel: (312) 750-1234 Fax: (312) 750-8578 Web site: www.hyatt.com

International hotel management.

Park Hyatt Buenos Aires Hotes, Posadas 1086/88, Buenos Aires 1011, Argentina

Tel: 54-1-321-1234 Fax: 54-1-321-1235

IBM CORPORATION

New Orchard Road, Armonk, NY, 10504

Tel: (914) 765-1900 Fax: (914) 765-7382 Web site: www.ibm.com

Information products, technology & services.

IBM Argentina SA, Pje. de las Catalinas 275, Argentina

INFONET SERVICES CORPORATION

2100 East Grand Ave., El Segundo, CA, 90245

Tel: (310) 335-2600 Fax: (310) 335-4507 Web site: www.infonet.com

Provider of Internet services and electronic messaging services.

Infonet Argentina - Sedeco S.A., Reconquista 1034, piso 4, 1003 Buenos Aires, Argentina

Tel: 54-1-315-2424 Fax: 54-1-313-7015

INFORMATION RESOURCES, INC.

150 N. Clinton St., Chicago, IL, 60661

Tel: (312) 726-1221 Fax: (312) 726-0360 Web site: www.infores.com

Provides bar code scanner services for retail sales organizations; processes, analyzes and sells data from the huge database created from these services.

CCR, Division Estudios Especiales, Blanco Encalada 3222, C.F. Buenos Aires, 1428 Argentina

Tel: 54-1-546-7100 Fax: 54-1-546-7147

INFORMIX CORPORATION

4100 Bohannon Drive, Menlo Park, CA, 95025

Tel: (650) 926-6300 Fax: (650) 926-6593 Web site: www.informix.com

Designs & produces database management software, connectivity interfaces & gateways, and other computer applications.

Informix Software Argentina, Bouchard Tower, Bouchard 547 29th Fl., 1106 Buenos Aires, Argentina

Tel: 54-1-310-8888

INGRAM MICRO INC.

PO Box 25125, Santa Ana, CA, 92799

Tel: (714) 566-1000 Fax: (714) 566-7940 Web site: www.ingrammicro.com

Distribute computer systems, software and related products.

Ingram Micro Inc., Argentina

Tel: 54-1-803-1430 Fax: 54-1-803-1378

INSTRON CORPORATION

100 Royall Street, Canton, MA, 02021-1089

Tel: (781) 828-2500 Fax: (781) 575-5751

Mfr. material testing instruments.

Instron Ltda., Virrey del Pino 4071, 1420 Buenos Aires, Argentina

INTER-CONTINENTAL HOTELS

1120 Ave. of the Americas, New York, NY, 10036

Tel: (212) 852-6400 Fax: (212) 852-6494 Web site: www.interconti.com

Worldwide hotel and resort accommodations.

Hotel Inter-Continental Buenos Aires, 809 Mareno St., 1091 Buenos Aires, Argentina

Tel: 54-1-340-7100 Fax: 54-1-340-7199

INTERNATIONAL FLAVORS & FRAGRANCES INC.

521 West 57th Street, New York, NY, 10019-2960

Tel: (212) 765-5500 Fax: (212) 708-7132 Web site: www.iff.com

Design/mfr. flavors, fragrances & aroma chemicals.

International Flavors & Fragrances SACyI, Parque Industrial OKS, Einstein 824, 1619 Garín, Buenos Aires, Argentina

INTERNATIONAL GAME TECHNOLOGY INC.

9295 Prototype Drive, Reno, NV, 89511

Tel: (702) 448-0100 Fax: (702) 448-1488 Web site: www.igtgame.com

Mfr. games, hobby goods; equipment leasing, amusements, computers.

IGT Argentina S.A., Sarmiento 944, 9 piso/20, 1041 Buenos Aires, Argentina

Tel: 54-1-393-3400

INTERNATIONAL SPECIALTY PRODUCTS

1361 Alps Road, Wayne, NJ, 07470

Tel: (973) 628-4000 Fax: (973) 628-3311 Web site: www.ispcorp.com

Mfr. specialty chemical products.

ISP Argentina S.A., Av. Córdoba 679, piso 5A, 1365 Buenoa Aires, Argentina

Tel: 54-1-314-8971 Fax: 54-1-314-8976

ITT SHERATON CORPORATION

60 State Street, Boston, MA, 02108

Tel: (617) 367-3600 Fax: (617) 367-5676

Hotel operations.

Buenos Aires Sheraton Hotel, San Martin 1225 at Plaza Fuerza Aerea, 1104 Buenos Aires, Argentina

J.P. MORGAN & CO. INC.

60 Wall Street, New York, NY, 10260-0060

Tel: (212) 483-2323 Fax: (212) 648-5209 Web site: www.jpm.com

International banking services.

J.P. Morgan Argentina Sociedad de Bolsa S.A., Corrientes 411, Buenos Aires, Argentina 1043

Tel: 54-1-809-8500 Fax: 54-1-325-8046 Contact: José McLoughlin, Gen. Mgr.

Morgan Guaranty Trust Co. Argentina, 25 de Mayo 182, 1002 Buenos Aires, Argentina

Tel: 54-1-325-8046

Morgan Guaranty Trust Company of New York, Corrientes 411, Buenos Aires, Argentina 1043

Tel: 54-1-325-8046

J. WALTER THOMPSON COMPANY

466 Lexington Ave., New York, NY, 10017

Tel: (212) 210-7000 Fax: (212) 210-6944 Web site: www.jwt.com

International advertising and marketing services.

JWT Argentina, Buenos Aires, Argentina

JOHN HANCOCK MUTUAL LIFE INSURANCE COMPANY

200 Clarendon Street, PO Box 111, Boston, MA, 02117

Tel: (617) 572-6000 Fax: (617) 572-8628 Web site: www.jhancock.com

Life insurance services.

Sud America Cia. de Seguros de Vida SA, Av. RS Pena 530, Buenos Aires, Argentina

JOHNSON & JOHNSON

One Johnson & Johnson Plaza, New Brunswick, NJ, 08933

Tel: (732) 524-0400 Fax: (732) 214-0334 Web site: www.jnj.com

Mfr./distributor/R&D pharmaceutical, health care and cosmetic products.

Cilag Farmaceutica SA, Janssen Farmaceutica SA,, Cassila de Correo 29, Suc. 28, 1428 Buenos Aires, Argentina

Johnson & Johnson de Argentina SACyI, Casilla 79, Fatima-Pilar 1629, Buenos Aires, Argentina

Johnson & Johnson Medical S.A., Buenos Aires, Argentina

S C JOHNSON & SON INC.

1525 Howe Street, Racine, WI, 53403

Tel: (414) 260-2000 Fax: (414) 260-2133 Web site: www.scjohnsonwax.com

Home, auto, commercial and personal care products and specialty chemicals.

S.C. Johnson & Son de Argentina S.A.I.C., Casilla de Correo 4747, Correo Central, 1000 Buenos Aires, Argentina

A.T. KEARNEY INC.

222 West Adams Street, Chicago, IL, 60606

Tel: (312) 648-0111 Fax: (312) 223-6200 Web site: www.atkearney.com

Management consultants and executive search.

A. T. Kearney Argentina S.A., Av. Alicia Moreau de Justo 550, piso 4, 1107 Buenos Aires, Argentina

Tel: 54-1-311-1614

KELLOGG COMPANY

One Kellogg Square, PO Box 3599, Battle Creek, MI, 49016-3599

Tel: (616) 961-2000 Fax: (616) 961-2871 Web site: www.kelloggs.com

Mfr. ready-to-eat cereals and convenience foods.

Kellogg Co. Argentina SACIF, Buenos Aires, Argentina (All inquiries to U.S. address)

KENNAMETAL INC.

State Rte. 981, Latrobe, PA, 15650

Tel: (724) 539-5000 Fax: (724) 539-4710 Web site: www.kennametal.com

Tools, hard carbide & tungsten alloys for metalworking industry.

Project Corporation de Argentina S.A., Mariano Pelliza 4063/65, 1605 Munro, Buenos Aires, Argentina

Tel: 54-1-756-0737 Fax: 54-1-756-0321

KIMBERLY-CLARK CORPORATION

351 Phelps Drive, Irving, TX, 75038

Tel: (972) 281-1200 Fax: (972) 281-1435 Web site: www.kimberly-clark.com.

Mfr./sales/distribution of consumer tissue, household and personal care products.

Kimberly-Clark Corp., Locations in Cordoba, Pilar, and San Luis, Argentina

KNOLL, INC.

1235 Water Street, East Greenville, PA, 18041

Tel: (215) 679-7991 Fax: (215) 679-3904 Web site: www.knoll.com

Mfr. and sale of office furnishings.

Interieur Forma SA, Av. Alicia Moreau de Justo 140, piso 2, 1107 Buenos Aires, Argentina

Tel: 54-1-313-3232 Fax: 54-1-313-0560 Contact: Susi Aczel, Dir.

THE KOHLER COMPANY

444 Highland Drive, Kohler, WI, 53044

Tel: (920) 457-4441 Fax: (920) 459-1274

Plumbing products, ceramic tile and stone, cabinetry, furniture, engines, generators, switch gear and hospitality.

Kohler Plumbing International, Buenos Aires, Argentina

KORN/FERRY INTERNATIONAL

1800 Century Park East, Los Angeles, CA, 90067

Tel: (310) 552-1834 Fax: (310) 553-6452 Web site: www.kornferry.com

Executive search; management consulting.

Korn/Ferry International, Av. Quintana 585, piso 6, 1129 Buenos Aires, Argentina

Tel: 54-1-804-0046 Fax: 54-1-804-7568

KPMG PEAT MARWICK LLP

Three Chestnut Ridge Road, Montvale, NJ, 07645

Tel: (201) 307-7000 Fax: (201) 930-8617 Web site: www.kpmg.com

Accounting and audit, tax and management consulting services.

KPMG Finsterbusch Pickenhayn Sibille, Av. Leandro N. Alem 1050, 5th Fl., Buenos Aires, 1001, Argentina

Tel: 54-1-313-9633 Fax: 54-1-311-7117 Contact: Juan Carlos Pickenhayn, Sr.Ptnr.

LEHMAN BROTHERS HOLDINGS INC.

Three World Financial Center, New York, NY, 10285

Tel: (212) 526-7000 Fax: (212) 526-3738 Web site: www.lehman.com

Financial services, securities and merchant banking services.

Lehman Brothers, 25 de Mayo 195/8th Fl., 1002 Buenos Aires, Argentina

Tel: 54-1-343-8368

LEVI STRAUSS & COMPANY

1155 Battery Street, Levi's Plaza, San Francisco, CA, 94111-1230

Tel: (415) 544-6000 Fax: (415) 501-3939 Web site: www.levistrauss.com

Mfr./distributor casual wearing apparel.

Levi Strauss & Company, Av. A. Moreau de dusto 400, piso 2, 1107 Capital Federal, Buenos aires, Argentina

Tel: 54-1-318-9600 Fax: 54-1-318-9620

LIBERTY MUTUAL GROUP

175 Berkeley Street, Boston, MA, 02117

Tel: (617) 357-9500 Fax: (617) 350-7648 Web site: www.libertymutual. com

Provides workers' compensation insurance and operates physical rehabilitation centers and provides risk prevention management.

Liberty Mutual Group, Buenos Aires, Argentina

ELI LILLY & COMPANY

Lilly Corporate Center, Indianapolis, IN, 46285

Tel: (317) 276-2000 Fax: (317) 277-6579 Web site: www.lilly.com

Mfr. pharmaceuticals and animal health products.

Eli Lilly Interamerica Inc., Av. Scalabrini Ortiz 3333, piso 5, 1425 Buenos Aires, Argentina

Tel: 54-1-807-3030 Fax: 54-1-806-9189

THE LINCOLN ELECTRIC COMPANY

22801 St. Clair Ave., Cleveland, OH, 44117-1199

Tel: (216) 481-8100 Fax: (216) 486-8385 Web site: www.lincolnelectric.com

Mfr. arc welding and welding related products, oxy-fuel and thermal cutting equipment and integral AC motors.

Lincoln Electric de Argentina, Esteban Adrogue 1107, ler piso, Of. 4, (1846) Adrogue - Buenoa Aires, Argentina

Tel: 54-1-214-2133 Fax: 54-1-293-2056 Contact: Javier Esteban Croce

ARTHUR D. LITTLE, INC.

25 Acorn Park, Cambridge, MA, 02140-2390

Tel: (617) 498-5000 Fax: (617) 498-7200 Web site: www.adlittle.com

Management, environmental, health & safety consulting; technical & product development.

Arthur D. Little de Argentina SA, Av. Leandro N. Alem 1110; piso 2, 1001 Buenos Aires, Argentina

Tel: 54-1-312-0060 Fax: 54-1-312-1018

LOCTITE CORPORATION

10 Columbus Boulevard, Hartford, CT, 06106

Tel: (203) 520-5000 Fax: (203) 520-5073 Web site: www.loctite.com

Mfr./sale industrial adhesives and sealants.

Loctite Argentina SA, Augustin de Elia 856, 1704 Ramos Mejia, Buenos Aires, Argentina

Tel: 54-1-656-5174 Fax: 54-5-656-5174 Contact: Paulo Eduardo Costa

LOWE & PARTNERS WORLDWIDE

1114 Ave. of the Americas, New York, NY, 10036

Tel: (212) 403-6700 Fax: (212) 403-6710

International advertising agency network.

Aguila & Baccetti S.A., Buenos Aires, Argentina

THE LUBRIZOL CORPORATION

29400 Lakeland Blvd., Wickliffe, OH, 44092-2298

Tel: (440) 943-4200 Fax: (440) 943-5337 Web site: www.lubrizol.com

Mfr. chemicals additives for lubricants & fuels.

Lubrizol Argentina, Buenos Aires, Argentina

Tel: 54-1-393-4843

LUCENT TECHNOLOGIES, INC.

600 Mountain Ave., Murray Hill, NJ, 07974-0636

Tel: (908) 582-3000 Fax: (908) 582-2110 Web site: www.lucent.com

Design/mfr. wide range of public and private networks, communication systems and software, data networking systems, business telephone systems and microelectronics components.

Lucent Technologies - Network Systems Argentina, Esmeralda 55, 1035 Buenos Aires, Argentina

Tel: 54-1-340-8600 Fax: 54-1-340-8666 Contact: Silvia Martinica, PR Mgr.

M-I

PO Box 48242, Houston, TX, 77242-2842

Tel: (713) 739-0222 Fax: (713) 308-9503

Drilling fluids.

Imco Services, Halliburton Argentina SA, Av. Leandro N. Alen 466, 1003 Buenos Aires, Argentina

M/A-COM INC.

1011 Pawtucket Boulevard, Lowell, MA, 01853

Tel: (978) 442-5000 Fax: (978) 442-5354

Mfr. electronic components and communications equipment.

Reycom, Bernarde de Irigoyen 972 60 A, 1304 Buenos Aires, Argentina

Tel: 54-1-300-2013

MANPOWER INTERNATIONAL INC.

5301 N. Ironwood Road, PO Box 2053, Milwaukee, WI, 53201-2053

Tel: (414) 961-1000 Fax: (414) 961-7081 Web site: www.manpower

Temporary help, contract service, training & testing.

Cotecsud SASE, Av. Maipu 942, 1340 Buenos Aires, Argentina

Tel: 54-1-311-6698 Fax: 54-1-311-7191

MARK IV INDUSTRIES INC.

501 John James Audubon Pkwy., PO Box 810, Amherst, NY, 14226-0810

Tel: (716) 689-4972 Fax: (716) 689-1529 Web site: www.mark-iv.com

Mfr. diversified products: timers & controls, power equipment, loudspeaker systems, etc.

Dayco Argentina S.A., Alvear 838, 1646 San Fernando, Pcia Buenos Aires, Argentina

Tel: 54-1-744-1477 Fax: 54-1-744-8653

Dayco Argentina S.A., 5123 Ferreira, Cordoba, Argentina

Tel: 54-51-978185 Fax: 54-51-977734

Dayco Argentina S.A./Mark IV Auto, 5123 Ferreira, Cordoba, Argentina

Tel: 54-51-978-185 Fax: 54-51-977-734

MARSH & McLENNAN COS INC.

1166 Ave. of the Americas, New York, NY, 10036-2774

Tel: (212) 345-5000 Fax: (212) 345-4808 Web site: www.marshmac.com

Insurance agents/brokers, pension and investment management consulting services.

Ayling Marsh & McLennan S.A., Florida 234, 6 piso, 1334 Buenos Aires, Argentina

Tel: 54-1-320-5800 Fax: 54-1-325-0666 Contact: Roberto C. Ayling

MARY KAY COSMETICS INC.

16251 Nor Dallas Pkw, Dallas, TX, 75248

Tel: (214) 630-8787 Fax: (214) 631-5938

Cosmetics and toiletries.

Mary Kay Cosmetics Argentina SA, Florida 633, piso 3, Buenos Aires, Argentina

McCANN-ERICKSON WORLDWIDE

750 Third Ave., New York, NY, 10017

Tel: (212) 984-3644 Fax: (212) 984-2629

International advertising/marketing services.

McCann-Erickson SA de Pulicidad, Reconquista 609, 1003 Buenos Aires, Argentina

McDONALD'S CORPORATION

Kroc Drive, Oak Brook, IL, 60523

Tel: (630) 623-3000 Fax: (630) 623-7409

Fast food chain stores.

McDonald's Corp., Argentina

MCI INTERNATIONAL INC.

2 International Drive, Rye Brook, NY, 10573

Tel: (914) 937-3444 Fax: (914) 934-6996

Telecommunications.

MCI Intl. Argentina SA, Viamonte 837, 2 piso, 1053 Buenos Aires, Argentina

McKINSEY & COMPANY

55 East 52nd Street, New York, NY, 10022

Tel: (212) 446-7000 Fax: (212) 446-8575 Web site: www.mckinsey.com

Management and business consulting services.

McKinsey & Company, Maipu 1210 - piso 4, 1006 Buenos Aires, Argentina

Tel: 54-1-318-3900 Fax: 54-1-318-3970

MEAD CORPORATION

Courthouse Plaza, NE, Dayton, OH, 45463

Tel: (937) 495-6323 Fax: (937) 461-2424 Web site: www.mead.com

Mfr. paper, packaging, pulp, lumber and other wood products, school and office products; electronic publishing and distribution.

Mead Packaging Argentina, Temple 2780 (1752) Loma del Mirador, Buenos Aires, Argentina

Tel: 54-1-482-1335 Fax: 54-1-484-9425 Contact: Steve Scherger, Pres.

MERCK & COMPANY, INC.

1 Merck Drive, Whitehouse Station, NJ, 08889

Tel: (908) 423-1000 Fax: (908) 423-2592

Pharmaceuticals, chemicals and biologicals.

Merck Sharp & Dohme (Argentina) SAIyC, Av. Libertador 1406/1410, Vicente Lopez, Buenos Aires, Argentina

MERRILL LYNCH & COMPANY, INC.

World Financial Center, North Tower, New York, NY, 10281-1323

Tel: (212) 449-1000 Fax: (212) 449-2892

Security brokers and dealers, investment and business services.

Merrill Lynch Argentina S.A., Torre Bouchard Bldg., Bouchard 547, 23rd Fl., 1106 Capital Federal, Buenos Aires, Argentina

Tel: 54-1-317-7603 Fax: 54-1-314-1739

Smith New Court Argentina, Maipu 1300, 16th Fl., 1006 Buenos Aires, Argentina

Tel: 54-1-315-2311 Fax: 54-1-312-9846

METROPOLITAN LIFE INSURANCE COMPANY

1 Madison Ave., New York, NY, 10010-3603

Tel: (212) 578-3818 Fax: (212) 252-7294

Insurance and retirement savings products and services.

Metropolitan Life Seguros de Retiro SA, 942 Madero Ave., 8 & 11th Fls., (1106) Capital Federal, Buenos Aires, Argentina

Tel: 54-1-318-1800 Fax: 54-1-318-1850 Contact: Oscar Schmidt, Dir. Gen.

Metropolitan Life Seguros de Vida SA, 942 Madero Ave., 8 & 11th Fls., (1106) Capital Federal, Buenos Aires, Argentina

Tel: 54-1-318-1800 Fax: 54-1-318-1850 Contact: Oscar Schmidt, Dir. Gen.

MICROSOFT CORPORATION

One Microsoft Way, Redmond, WA, 98052-6399

Tel: (425) 882-8080 Fax: (425) 936-7329 Web site: www.microsoft.com

Computer software, peripherals and services.

Microsoft de Argentina S.A., Bouchard 547, 4tp piso, 1106 Capital Federal, Argentina

Tel: 54-1-316-1900 Fax: 54-1-316-1921

MOTOROLA, INC.

1303 East Algonquin Road, Schaumburg, IL, 60196

Tel: (847) 576-5000 Fax: (847) 538-5191 Web site: www.mot.com

Mfr. communications equipment, semiconductors and cellular phones.

Motorola de Comercialzacion y Servicios de Argentina S.A., Maipu 1210 piso 7, 1006 Buenoa Aires, Argentina

Tel: 54-1-317-5300 Fax: 54-1-317-5311

NALCO CHEMICAL COMPANY

One Nalco Center, Naperville, IL, 60563-1198

Tel: (630) 305-1000 Fax: (630) 305-2900 Web site: www.nalco.com

Chemicals for water and waste water treatment, oil products and refining, industry processes; water and energy management service.

Nalco Argentina SA, Av. Leandro N. Alem 712, piso 10, Capital Federal, Buenos Aires, Argentina

Tel: 54-1-310-6666 Fax: 54-1-310-6600

NATIONAL STARCH & CHEMICAL COMPANY

10 Finderne Ave., Bridgewater, NJ, 08807-3300

Tel: (908) 685-5000 Fax: (908) 685-5005 Web site: www.national starch.com

Mfr. adhesives & sealants, resins & specialty chemicals, electronic materials & adhesives, food products, industry starch.

National Starch & Chemical SA, N. Avellaneda 1357, 1642 San Isidro, Argentina

Tel: 54-1-743-2066 Fax: 54-1-742-2971

A .C. NIELSEN COMPANY

177 Broad Street, Stamford, CT, 06901

Tel: (203) 961-3000 Fax: (203) 961-3190 Web site: www.acnielsen.com

Market research.

A.C. Nielsen (Argentina) SA, Riva Davia 620, 1002 Buenos Aires, Argentina

NORTON COMPANY

1 New Bond Street, Worcester, MA, 01606

Tel: (508) 795-5000 Fax: (508) 795-5741

Abrasives, drill bits, construction and safety products and plastics.

Abrasivos Norton SA, Los Patos 2175, 1283 Buenos Aires, Argentina

NVF COMPANY

1166 Yorklyn Road, Yorklyn, DE, 19736

Tel: (302) 239-5281 Fax: (302) 239-4323

Metal containers, steel products, laminated plastics and papers.

NVF Europe, Buenos Aires, Argentina

OAKITE PRODUCTS, INC.

50 Valley Road, Berkeley Heights, NJ, 07922-2798

Tel: (908) 464-6900 Fax: (908) 464-7914

Mfr. chemical products for industry cleaning and metal treating.

Oakite Argentina SA, Balcarce 880-piso 8, 1064 Buenos Aires, Argentina

Tel: 54-1-362-5775 Fax: 54-1-307-0765 Contact: Carlos Vallejos

OGILVY & MATHER WORLDWIDE

309 West 49th Street, New York, NY, 10019

Tel: (212) 237-4000 Fax: (212) 237-5123

Advertising, marketing, public relations & consulting firm.

Ogilvy & Mather, Buenos Aires, Argentina

OLSTEN CORPORATION

175 Broad Hollow Road, Melville, NY, 11747-8905

Tel: (516) 844-7800 Fax: (516) 844-7022 Web site: www.olsten.com

Staffing, home health care & information technology services.

Olsten Ready Office, Viamonde 1145, 6° piso, (10530 Buenos Aires, Argentina

Tel: 54-1-373-2000 Fax: 54-1-373-4707

OTIS ELEVATOR COMPANY

10 Farm Springs Road, Farmington, CT, 06032

Tel: (860) 676-6000 Fax: (860) 676-5111

Mfr. elevators and escalators.

Ascensores Otis SA, Av. Ing. Huergo 1039, 1107 Buenos Aires, Argentina

PARAMETRIC TECHNOLOGY CORPORATION

128 Technology Drive, Waltham, MA, 02154

Tel: (781) 398-5000 Fax: (781) 398-5674 Web site: www.ptc.com

Mfr. CAD/CAM/CAE software.

Parametric Technology Corporation, Alicia Moreau, De Justo 550, 2nd Fl., Buenes Aires 1107 Argentina

Tel: 54-1-310-0097 Fax: 54-1-310-0063

PARKER DRILLING COMPANY

8 East Third Street, Tulsa, OK, 74103-3637

Tel: (918) 585-8221 Fax: (918) 585-1058

Drilling contractor.

Parker Drilling Co. South America, 2827 Llames Massini, Bario Industrial, Comodoro Rividavia, Argentina

PARKER HANNIFIN CORPORATION

17325 Euclid Ave., Cleveland, OH, 44112

Tel: (216) 896-3000 Fax: (216) 896-4000 Web site: www.parker.com

Mfr. motion-control products.

Parker Hannifin Argentina SAIC, Av. Pte. Arturo U. Illia 2064, Villa Maipu, 1650 San Martin, Buenos Aires, Argentina

Tel: 54-1-752-4129 Fax: 54-1-752-3704

PEPSiCO INC.

700 Anderson Hill Road, Purchase, NY, 10577-1444

Tel: (914) 253-2000 Fax: (914) 253-2070 Web site: www.pepsico.com

Beverages and snack foods.

Pepsi Sacks Argentina SA, Argentina

Pepsi-Cola Argentina SACI, Argentina

THE PERKIN-ELMER CORPORATION

761 Main Ave., Norwalk, CT, 06859-0001

Tel: (203) 762-1000 Fax: (203) 762-4228 Web site: www.perkin-elmer.com

Leading supplier of systems for life science research and related applications.

Biosystems S.A., Viamonte 965, 5 piso, 1053 Buenos Aires, Argentina

Tel: 54-1-322-2080 Fax: 54-1-322-7751

Perkin-Elmer Argentina, Tronador 620 (1427), Capital Federal, Argentina

Tel: 54-1-554-4004 Fax: 54-1-554-2807 Contact: Alejandro Auffenfeld, Gen. Mgr.

PFIZER INC.

235 East 42nd Street, New York, NY, 10017-5755

Tel: (212) 573-2323 Fax: (212) 573-7851 Web site: www.pfizer.com

Research-based, global health care company.

Pfizer SACI, Argentina

PHARMACIA & UPJOHN

95 Corporate Drive, PO Box 6995, Bridgewater, NJ, 08807

Tel: (908) 306-4400 Fax: (908) 306-4433 Web site: www.pnu.com

Mfr. pharmaceuticals, agricultural products, industry chemicals

Laboratorios Upjohn Anodia SAIC, Avd. Del Libertador 2740, Olivos, 1636, Buenos Aires, Argentina

PIONEER HI-BRED INTERNATIONAL INC.

400 Locust Street, Ste. 800, Des Moines, IA, 50309

Tel: (515) 248-4800 Fax: (515) 248-4999

Agricultural chemicals, farm supplies, biological products, research.

Pioneer Argentina SA, Reconquista 672, 1003 Buenos Aires, Argentina

PIONEER NATURAL RESOURCES CO.

5205 North O'Connor Boulevard, Irving, TX, 75039

Tel: (972) 444-9001 Fax: (972) 444-4328

Oil and gas

Pioneer Natural Resources Co., Argentina

PITNEY BOWES INC.

1 Elmcroft Road, Stamford, CT, 06926-0700

Tel: (203) 356-5000 Fax: (203) 351-6835 Web site: www.pitneybowes.com

Mfr. postage meters, mailroom equipment, copiers, bus supplies, bus services, facsimile systems and financial services.

Pitney Bowes Argentina, Argentina - All mail to: Pitney Bowes Latin America, 2424 N. Federal Hwy., Ste 360, Boca Raton, FL 33431 U.S.A.

Tel: 54-1-347-2040 Fax: 54-1-347-2041 Contact: Joe Denaro, VP Latin America & Caribbean Emp: 75

PLANET HOLLYWOOD INTERNATIONAL, INC.

8669 Commodity Circle, Orlando, FL, 32819

Tel: (407) 363-7827 Fax: (407) 363-4862 Web site: www.planethollywood.com

Theme-dining restaurant chain and merchandise retail stores.

Planet Hollywood International, Inc., Buenos Aires, Argentina

PPG INDUSTRIES

One PPG Place, Pittsburgh, PA, 15272

Tel: (412) 434-3131 Fax: (412) 434-2190 Web site: www.ppg.com

Mfr. coatings, flat glass, fiber glass, chemicals. coatings.

PPG Industries Argentina S.A., Cerrito 740, 1307 Buenos Aires, Argentina

PRAXAIR, INC.

39 Old Ridgebury Road, Danbury, CT, 06810-5113

Tel: (203) 837-2000 Fax: (203) 837-2450 Web site: www.praxair.com

Produces and distributes industrial and specialty gases.

Praxair Argentina S.A., Saavedra 2953, 1618 El Talar, Buenos Aires, Argentina

Tel: 54-1-736-6100 Fax: 54-1-736-6133

PRECISION VALVE CORPORATION

PO Box 309, Yonkers, NY, 10702

Tel: (914) 969-6500 Fax: (914) 966-4428

Mfr. aerosol valves.

Valvulas Precision de Argentina SACI, Fondo de la Legua 936, 1640 Martinez, Buenos Aires, Argentina

PREMARK INTERNATIONAL INC.

1717 Deerfield Road, Deerfield, IL, 60015

Tel: (847) 405-6000 Fax: (847) 405-6013 Web site: www.premarkintl.com

Mfr./sale plastic, diversified consumer & commercial products.

Dart Argentina SA, Av. del Libertador 498, 1001 Buenos Aires, Argentina

Tupperware SA, Av. del Libertador 498, 1001 Buenos Aires, Argentina

PRICEWATERHOUSECOOPERS LLP

1251 Ave. of the Americas, New York, NY, 10020

Tel: (212) 596-7000 Fax: (212) 790-6620 Web site: www.pwcglobal.com

Accounting and auditing, tax and management, and human resource consulting services.

Price Waterhouse Ltd., Edif. Cordoba Office Ctr., Av. Figueroa Alcorta 185, piso 9, Of. "A", 5000 Cordoba, Argentina

Tel: 54-1-23-4789 Fax: 54-1-23-4822

Price Waterhouse Ltd., Cerrito 268, Casillo de Correo Central 896, 1000 Buenos Aires, Argentina

Tel: 54-1-381-8181 Fax: 54-1-382-2793

PRINCIPAL INTERNATIONAL INC.

711 High Street, Des Moines, IA, 50392-9950

Tel: (515) 248-8288 Fax: (515) 248-8049 Web site: www.principal.com

Insurance and investment services.

Ethika S.A., Sarmiento 663 piso 4, 1316 Capital Federal, Buenos Aires, Argentina

Tel: 54-1-348-0900 Fax: 54-1-348-0902 Contact: Pedro Borda, Mgr.

Principal Life, Sarmiento 663 piso,4 1316 Capital Federal, Buenos Aires, Argentina

Tel: 54-1-348-0900 Fax: 54-1-348-0902 Contact: Juan-Manuel Artola, Mgr.

Qualitas Médica, S.A., Sarmiento 663 piso,4 1316 Capital Federal, Buenos Aires, Argentina
Tel: 54-1-348-0900 Fax: 54-1-348-0902

PROCTER & GAMBLE COMPANY
One Procter & Gamble Plaza, Cincinnati, OH, 45202
Tel: (513) 983-1100 Fax: (513) 562-4500 Web site: www.pg.com
Personal care, food, laundry, cleaning and industry products.
P&G Interamericas, Inc., Suipacha #664, 2nd Fl., (1008) Buenos Aires, Argentina

PSDI MAXIMO
100 Crosby Drive, Bedford, MA, 01730
Tel: (781) 280-2000 Fax: (781) 280-0200 Web site: www.psdi.com
Develops, markets and provides maintenance management software systems.
PSDI - SOLA, Cerrito 1070, 2nd Fl., (1010) CF, Buenos Aires, Argentina
Tel: 54-1-811-4000 Fax: 54-1-928-4140 Contact: Clyde McArdle, Dir. LA Ops. Emp: 8

QUALCOMM INC.
6355 Lusk Boulevard, San Diego, CA, 92121
Tel: (619) 587-1121 Fax: (619) 658-1434
Digital wireless telecommunications systems.
Qualcomm Argentina, Buenos Aires, Argentina

RAY & BERNDTSON, INC.
301 Commerce, Ste. 2300, Fort Worth, TX, 76102
Tel: (817) 334-0500 Fax: (817) 334-0779 Web site: www.prb.com
Executive search, management audit and management consulting firm.
Ray & Berndtson, Av. Leandro N. Alem 896 130, Buenos Aires 1001, Argentina
Tel: 54-1-311-9670 Fax: 54-1-312-0206 Contact: Alberto Armoni, Mng. Ptnr.

RAYCHEM CORPORATION
300 Constitution Drive, Menlo Park, CA, 94025-1164
Tel: (650) 361-3333 Fax: (650) 361-2108 Web site: www.raychem.com
Develop/mfr./market materials science products for electronics, telecommunications & industry.
Raychem SAIC, Carlos Pellegrini 1363, 1101 Buenos Aires, Argentina

RAYTHEON COMPANY
141 Spring Street, Lexington, MA, 02173
Tel: (781) 862-6600 Fax: (781) 860-2172 Web site: www.raytheon.com
Mfr. diversified electronics, appliances, aviation, energy and environmental products; publishing, industry and construction services.
Raytheon International, Buenos Aires, Argentina

RELIANCE GROUP HOLDINGS, INC.
55 East 52nd Street, New York, NY, 10055
Tel: (212) 909-1100 Fax: (212) 909-1864 Web site: www.rgh.com
Financial and insurance management services.
Reliance National Compañía Argentina de Seguros S.A., Brown 250, 8000 Bahía Blanca, Argentina
Tel: 54-91-55-0074 Fax: 54-91-55-0074 Contact: Claudio Aguiar, Mgr.
Reliance National Compañia Argentina de Seguros, Ltd., Av. Leandro N. Alem No. 1002, piso 4, 1001 Buenos Aires, Argentina
Tel: 54-1-316-1817 Fax: 54-1-313-2706 Contact: Antohony Zinicola, Mgr.

RENDIC INTERNATIONAL CORPORATION
9100 South Dadeland Blvd., Ste 1800, Miami, FL, 33156
Tel: (305) 670-0066 Fax: (305) 670-0060 Web site: www.flintink.com
Sales of printing inks, press equipment and supplies.

Rendic International Corporation, Estados Unidos 4585 (1667) Tortuguitas, Buenos Aires, Argentina

REPUBLIC NATIONAL BANK OF NEW YORK

452 Fifth Ave., New York, NY, 10018

Tel: (212) 525-5000 Fax: (212) 525-6996 Web site: www.rnb.com

Banking services.

Republic National Bank of New York, Reconquista 100, Buenos Aires, Argentina 1003

Tel: 54-1-349-1600 Fax: 54-1-345-1692 Contact: Martin Benegas Lynch, Gen. Mgr.

REVLON INC.

625 Madison Ave., New York, NY, 10022

Tel: (212) 527-4000 Fax: (212) 527-4995 Web site: www.revlon.com

Mfr. cosmetics, fragrances, toiletries and beauty care products.

Revlon de Argentina SA, Chiclana 3311, Buenos Aires, Argentina

ROCKWELL INTERNATIONAL CORPORATION

600 Anton Boulevard, Costa Mesa, CA, 92626-7147

Tel: (714) 424-4200 Fax: (714) 424-4251 Web site: www.rockwell.com

Products & service for aerospace and defense, automotive, electronics, graphics & automation industry.

Rockwell Automation Argentina S.A., Ave. Cordoba 4970, 1414 Buenos Aires, Argentina

Tel: 54-1-776-1100 Fax: 54-1-773-5175

ROHM AND HAAS COMPANY

100 Independence Mall West, Philadelphia, PA, 19106

Tel: (215) 592-3000 Fax: (215) 592-3377 Web site: www.rohmhaas.com

Mfr. industrial & agricultural chemicals, plastics.

Rohm and Haas Latin America Inc., Carlos Pellegrini #149 - piso 7, 1009 Buenos Aires, Argentina

Tel: 54-1-328-0506

T. ROWE PRICE ASSOCIATES, INC.

100 East Pratt Street, Baltimore, MD, 21202

Tel: (41) 034-5200 Fax: (410) 345-2394 Web site: www.troweprice.com

Investment and portfolio asset management.

Rowe Price-Fleming International, Buenos Aires, Argentina

RUSSELL REYNOLDS ASSOCIATES INC.

200 Park Ave., New York, NY, 10166-0002

Tel: (212) 351-2000 Fax: (212) 370-0896 Web site: www.ressreyn.com

Executive recruiting services.

Russell Reynolds Associates Inc., Av. Pte. Roque Sáenz Peña 832 - 1 piso, (1388) Capital Federal, Buenos Aires, Argentina

Tel: 54-1-394-3051 Fax: 54-1-394-5267 Contact: Lorenzo Zavala

RYDER SYSTEM, INC.

3600 NW 82nd Ave., Miami, FL, 33166

Tel: (305) 593-3726 Fax: (305) 500-4129 Web site: www.ryder.com

Integrated logistics, full-service truck leasing, truck rental and public transportation services.

Ryder System, Inc., Av. Libertador 14, 799, Acasusso, 1640 Buenos Aires, Argentina

Tel: 54-1-733-2400 Fax: 54-1-733-2444

SARA LEE CORPORATION

3 First National Plaza, Chicago, IL, 60602-4260

Tel: (312) 726-2600 Fax: (312) 558-4995

Mfr./distributor food and consumer packaged goods, intimate apparel and knitwear.

House of Fuller/Sara Lee, Buenos Aires, Argentina

SAS INSTITUTE INC.

SAS Campus Drive, Cary, NC, 27513

Tel: (919) 677-8000 Fax: (919) 677-8123 Web site: www.sas.com

Mfr./distributes decision support software.

SAS Institute (Argentina) Inc., Buenos Aires, Argentina

Tel: 54-1-310-0076 Fax: 54-1-310-0098

SCHENKER INTERNATIONAL FORWARDERS INC.

150 Albany Ave., Freeport, NY, 11520

Tel: (516) 377-3000 Fax: (516) 377-3005 Web site: www.schenkerusa.com

Freight forwarders.

Schenker International Artentina SA, Tte Gral. J. D. Peron 949 piso 5, PO Box 2812, 1038 Cap Fed, Buenos Aires 1000, Argentina

Tel: 54-1-322-4500 Fax: 54-1-322-9208

R.P. SCHERER CORPORATION

PO Box 7060, Troy, MI, 48007-7060

Tel: (248) 649-0900 Fax: (248) 649-4238 Web site: www.rpscherer.com

Mfr. pharmaceuticals; soft gelatin and two-piece hard shell capsules.

R.P. Scherer Argentina SAIC, Av. Marquez 691, Villa Loma Hermosa 1657, Pdo. 3 de Febrero, Buenos Aires, Argentina

Tel: 54-1-769-0026 Fax: 54-1-11-2154 Contact: Jorge H. Castro, President Emp: 104

SCHERING-PLOUGH CORPORATION

1 Giralda Farms, Madison, NJ, 07940-1000

Tel: (973) 822-7000 Fax: (973) 822-7048 Web site: www.sch-plough.com

Proprietary drug and cosmetic products.

Plough Essex Argentina SAIC, Maipu 1300, 1006 Buenos Aires, Argentina

SCIENTIFIC-ATLANTA, INC.

1 Technology Pkwy South, Norcross, GA, 30092-2967

Tel: (770) 903-5000 Fax: (770) 903-2967 Web site: www.sciatl.com

A leading supplier of broadband communications systems, satellite-based video, voice and data communications networks and worldwide customer service and support.

Scientific-Atlanta Argentina, S.A., Carlos Pellegrini, 1149 piso 11, Capital Federal, 1011, Argentina

Tel: 54-1-325-2800 Fax: 54-1-325-5900

SEI INVESTMENTS COMPANY

1 Freedom Valley Drive, Oaks, PA, 19456-1100

Tel: (610) 676-1000 Fax: (610) 676-2995 Web site: www.seic.com

Accounting, evaluation and financial automated systems and services.

SEI Investments Argentina S.A., Sarmiento 663, piso 7, (1316) Capital Federal, Buenos aires, Argentina

Tel: 54-1-325-9970

SILICON GRAPHICS INC.

2011 N. Shoreline Blvd., Mountain View, CA, 94043-1389

Tel: (650) 960-1980 Fax: (650) 961-0595 Web site: www.sgi.com

Design/mfr. special-effects computer graphic systems and software.

Silicon Graphics, S.A., Ave. Alicia Moreau de Justo 270, 1 piso Dock 2, Puerto Madero, Cap. Fed., Buenos Aires, Argentina

Tel: 54-1-311-6666 Fax: 54-1-315-6320

SONOCO PRODUCTS COMPANY

North Second Street, PO Box 160, Hartsville, SC, 29550

Tel: (803) 383-7000 Fax: (803) 383-7008 Web site: www.sonoco.com

Mfr. packaging for consumer & industrial market and recycled paperboard.

Sonoco Argentina SA, Calle Ferre 3260-70, Villa Soldati, Pompeya, Buenos Aires, Argentina

SOUTHERN COMPANY

270 Peachtree Street, Atlanta, GA, 30303

Tel: (404) 506-5000 Fax: (404) 506-0642 Web site: www.southernco.com

Electric utility.

Southern Energy, Inc., Hidroelectrica Alicura, L.N. Alem 712-piso 7 (1001), Buenos Aires, Argentina

Tel: 54-1-312-7126 Contact: Richardo Falabella, Gen. Mgr.

SPENCER STUART & ASSOCIATES INC.

401 North Michigan Ave., Ste. 3400, Chicago, IL, 60611

Tel: (312) 822-0080 Fax: (312) 822-0116 Web site: www.spencerstuart.com

Executive recruitment firm.

Spencer Stuart & Associates Inc., Paraguay 577/10 "B", (1057) Capital Federal, Buenos Aires, Argentina

Tel: 54-1-313-2233 Fax: 54-1-313-2299 Contact: Ignacio Marseillan

THE ST. PAUL COMPANIES, INC.

385 Washington Street, St. Paul, MN, 55102

Tel: (612) 310-7911 Fax: (612) 310-8294 Web site: www.stpaul.com

Provides investment, insurance and reinsurance services.

St. Paul Argentina Compania de Seguros SA, Torre Intercontinental Plaza, Morena 877, piso 8 Buenos Aires 1091, Argentina

Tel: 54-1-344-2500 Fax: 54-1-344-2599 Contact: Andreas Koch, Mgr.

STEINER CORPORATION

505 East South Temple Street, Salt Lake City, UT, 84102

Tel: (801) 328-8831 Fax: (801) 363-5680

Linen supply service.

Alsco, Carlos Maria Alvear 1429, Buenos Aires, Argentina

STIEFEL LABORATORIES INC.

255 Alhambra Circle, Ste. 1000, Coral Gables, FL, 33134

Tel: (305) 443-3807 Fax: (305) 443-3467

Mfr. pharmaceuticals, dermatological specialties.

Laboratorios Stiefel Argentina, Amenabar 1595, piso 4 Of. 35/36, 1426 Buenos Aires, Argentina

STOKES VACUUM INC.

5500 Tabor Road, Philadelphia, PA, 19120

Tel: (215) 831-5400 Fax: (215) 831-5420 Web site: www.stokesvac.com

Vacuum pumps and components, vacuum dryers, oil-upgrading equipment and metallizers.

Pennwalt SAICyF, Av. Eduardo Madero 1020, 1106 Buenos Aires, Argentina

STONE CONTAINER CORPORATION

150 N. Michigan Ave., Chicago, IL, 60601-7568

Tel: (312) 346-6600 Fax: (312) 580-3486 Web site: www.stonecontainer.com

Mfr. paper and paper packaging.

Stone Container Corporation, Mendoza & Bernal (Buenos aires), Argentina

SULLAIR CORPORATION

3700 E. Michigan Blvd., Michigan City, IN, 46360

Tel: (219) 879-5451 Fax: (219) 874-1273

Refrigeration systems, vacuum pumps, generators, etc.

Sullair Argentina SA, Av. Rivadavia 324, 1822 Valentin Alsina, Buenos Aires, Argentina

SUNSHINE MINING & REFINING COMPANY

877 West Main Street, Ste. 600, Boise, ID, 83702

Tel: (208) 345-0660 Fax: (208) 342-0004 Web site: www.sunshinemining.com

Mines and refines silver, copper, antimony and lead.

Pirquitas Mine, Argentina

SYBASE, INC.

6475 Christie Ave., Emeryville, CA, 94608

Tel: (510) 922-3500 Fax: (510) 922-3210 Web site: www.sybase.com

Design/mfg/distribution of database management systems, software development tools, connectivity products, consulting and technical support services..

Sybase Argentina S.A., Reconquista 522, piso 10, Capital Federal 1005, Buenos Aires, Argentina

Tel: 54-1-393-0421 Fax: 54-1-326-7039

SYSTEM SOFTWARE ASSOCIATES INC.

500 West Madison Street, Ste. 3200, Chicago, IL, 60661

Tel: (312) 258-6000 Fax: (312) 474-7500 Web site: www.ssax.com

Mfr. computer software.

System Software Associates, Av. L. N. Alem 928 6º Fl., Buenos Aires, 1001, Argentina

Tel: 54-1-312-2028 Fax: 54-1-313-3310

TBWA INTERNATIONAL

180 Maiden Lane, New York, NY, 10038

Tel: (212) 804-1000 Fax: (212) 804-1200

International full service advertising agency.

Savaglio TBWA, Buenos Aires, Argentina

TELE-COMMUNICATIONS INC.

PO Box 5630, Denver, CO, 80217-5630

Tel: (303) 267-5500 Fax: (303) 779-1228 Web site: www.tci.com

Largest cable television operator in the U.S.

Cablevision SA, Buenos Aires, Argentina

TELLABS INC.

4951 Indiana Ave. 6303788800, Lisle, IL, 60532

Tel: (630) 378-8800 Fax: (630) 679-3010

Design/mfr./service voice/data transport & network access systems.

Tellabs Inc., Buenos Aires, Argentina

TEMPLE-INLAND INC.

303 S. Temple Drie, Diboll, TX, 75941

Tel: (409) 829-5511 Fax: (409) 829-1537 Web site: www.templeinland.com

Mfr. paper, packaging, bldg products; financial services.

Temple-Inland Inc., Buenos Aires, Argentina

TENNECO AUTOMOTIVE

500 North Field Drive, Lake Forest, IL, 60045

Tel: (847) 482-5241 Fax: (847) 482-5295

Automotive parts, exhaust systems, service equipment.

Monroe Argentina SA, Uruguay 2627, 2000 Rosario, Argentina

Tel: 54-41-321575 Fax: 54-41-321588 Contact: Pablo Perez, Mgr. Emp: 376

TENNESSEE ASSOCIATES INTERNATIONAL

223 Associates Blvd., PO Box 710, Alcoa, TN, 37701-0710

Tel: (423) 982-9514 Fax: (423) 982-1481

Management consulting services.

TAI Argentina, Arribenos 888, 1426 Buenos Aires, Argentina

TESORO PETROLEUM CORPORATION

8700 Tesoro Drive, San Antonio, TX, 78217

Tel: (210) 828-8484 Fax: (210) 828-8600

Produce/refine/distributor oil and gas.

Tesoro Argentina Petroleum Co., Argentina

TETRA TECH, INC.

670 N. Rosemead Blvd., Pasadena, CA, 91107

Tel: (626) 351-4664 Fax: (626) 351-1188 Web site: www.tetratech.com

Environmental engineering and consulting services.

Tetra Tech - Argentina, 144 - piso 6 1003, Buenos Aires, Argentina

Tel: 54-1-345-5410 Fax: 54-1-345-5420 Contact: Rene Altamitano

TEXAS INSTRUMENTS INC.

8505 Forest Lane, Dallas, TX, 75243

Tel: (214) 995-2011 Fax: (214) 995-4360 Web site: www.ti.com

Mfr. semiconductor devices, electronic electro-mechanical systems, instruments and controls.

Texas Instruments Argentina SAICF, Ruta Panamericana Km 25.500, Don Torcuato, Buenos Aires, Argentina

THERMADYNE INDUSTRIES INC.

101 South Hanley Road, #300, St. Louis, MO, 63105

Tel: (314) 746-2197 Fax: (314) 746-2349 Web site: www.thermadyne.com

Mfr. welding, cutting, and safety products.

Thermadyne Southern S.A., Rosario, Argentina

Tel: 54-1-555-927

THE TOPPS CO., INC.

1 Whitehall Street, New York, NY, 10004-2108

Tel: (212) 376-0300 Fax: (212) 376-0573 Web site: www.topps.com

Mfr. chewing gum & confections.

Topps Argentina S.A., Sinclair3139, 2nd Fl. "A" 1425- Capital Federal, Argentina

Tel: 54-1-778-9002 Fax: 54-1-778-9003

TOWERS PERRIN

335 Madison Ave., New York, NY, 10017-4605

Tel: (212) 309-3400 Fax: (212) 309-0975 Web site: www.towers.com

Management consulting services.

Towers, Perrin, Marcu & Associados, Av. Corrientes 316-6, piso 6, 1314 Buenos Aires, Argentina

Tel: 54-1-328-6475 Fax: 54-1-348-1012

TRANE COMPANY

3600 Pammel Creek Road, La Crosse, WI, 54601

Tel: (608) 787-2000 Fax: (608) 787-4990

Mfr./distributor/service A/C systems and equipment.

Trane de Argentina, Av. del Libertador 1254, 1638 Vicente Lopez, Buenos Aires, Argentina

TRANSAMERICA CORPORATION

600 Montgomery Street, San Francisco, CA, 94111

Tel: (415) 983-4000 Fax: (415) 983-4400 Web site: www.transamerica.com

Life insurance, leasing, and commercial lending services.

Transamerica Corporation, Buenos Aires, Argentina

Tel: 54-1-313-0525 Fax: 54-1-313-0519

TRUE NORTH COMMUNICATIONS INC.

101 East Erie Street, Chicago, IL, 60611

Tel: (312) 425-6000 Fax: (312) 425-6350

Holding company, advertising agency.

Pragma/FCB Publicidad SA, 1414 Capital Federal, Buenos Aires, Argentina

UNION CAMP CORPORATION

1600 Valley Road, Wayne, NJ, 07470

Tel: (973) 628-2000 Fax: (973) 628-2722 Web site: www.unioncamp.com

Mfr. paper, packaging, chemicals and wood products.

Puntapel, S.A., Av. Libertador Lopez, 1638 Vincente Lopez, Prov. Buenos Aires, Argentina

Tel: 54-1-718-0180 Fax: 54-1-718-0150

Union Camp Trading, S.A., Av. Brasil 160,, 1063 Buenos Aires, Argentina

Tel: 54-1-362-0833 Fax: 54-1-362-0724

Zucamor, S.A., Cno. Gral. Belgrano KM. 17, 1886 Ranelagh, Prov. Buenos Aires, Argentina

Tel: 54-1-258-8051 Fax: 54-1-258-1212

UNION CARBIDE CORPORATION

39 Old Ridgebury Road, Danbury, CT, 06817

Tel: (203) 794-2000 Fax: (203) 794-6269 Web site: www.unioncarbide.com

Mfr. industrial chemicals, plastics and resins.

Union Carbide Argenita SAICS, Leandro N. Alem 1060, piso 13, 1001 Buenos Aires, Argentina

UNIROYAL CHEMICAL CO., INC.

World Headquarters, Benson Road, Middlebury, CT, 06749

Tel: (203) 573-2000 Fax: (203) 573-2265

Tires, tubes and other rubber products, chemicals, plastics and textiles.

Uniroyal Quimica SAIC, Av. Ing. Huergo 1439, Buenos Aires, Argentina

UNITED PRESS INTERNATIONAL

1400 I Street, Washington, DC, 20005

Tel: (202) 898-8000 Fax: (202) 371-1239

Collection & distributor of news, newspictures, financial data.

UPI Inc., Av. Belgrano 271, 1092 Buenos Aires, Argentina

UNITED TECHNOLOGIES CORPORATION

United Technologies Building, Hartford, CT, 06101

Tel: (860) 728-7000 Fax: (860) 728-7979 Web site: www.utc.com

Mfr. aircraft engines, elevators, A/C, auto equipment, space and military electronic and rocket propulsion systems. Products include Pratt & Whitney, Otis elevators, Carrier heating and air conditioning and Sikorsky helicopters.

Ascensores Otis SA, Av. Ing. Huergo 1039, 1107 Buenos Aires, Argentina

UNIVERSAL INSTRUMENTS

90 Bevier Street, S. Dock, Binghamton, NY, 13904

Tel: (607) 779-7522 Fax: (607) 779-7971 Web site: www.dover.com

Mfr./sales of instruments for electronic circuit assembly

Jeren SRL, Buenos Aires, Argentina

Tel: 54-1-788-0566 Fax: 54-1-788-0563

UNUM CORPORATION

2211 Congress Street, Portland, ME, 04122

Tel: (207) 770-2211 Fax: (207) 770-4510 Web site: www.unum.com

Disability and special risk insurance.

Boston Compania Argentina de Seguros S.A., Suipacho 268, piso 44, 1355, Buenos Aires, Argentina

Tel: 54-1-394-6834 Fax: 54-1-394-0229 Contact: Horacio A. Sanchez Granel, Pres.

UOP INC.

25 E. Algonquin Road, Des Plaines, IL, 60017

Tel: (847) 391-2000 Fax: (847) 391-2253

Diversified research, development & mfr. of industry products & systems management studies & service.

UOP Inc., Canos Filtros, Johnson SA, Buenos Aires, Argentina

WACKENHUT CORPORATION

4200 Wackenhut Drive, Ste. 100, Palm Beach Gardens, FL, 33410

Tel: (561) 622-5656 Fax: (561) 691-6736 Web site: www.wackenhut.com

Security systems & services.

Search Organizacion de Seguridad SA, Tronador 543, 1427 Buenos Aires, Argentina

Tel: 54-1-554-2232 Fax: 54-1-554-2744

WAL-MART STORES INC.

702 SW 8th Street, Bentonville, AR, 72716-8611

Tel: (501) 273-4000 Fax: (501) 273-8980 Web site: www.wal-mart.com

Retailer.

Wal-Mart Stores Inc., Argentina

WASTE MANAGEMENT, INC.

3003 Butterfield Road, Oak Brook, IL, 60523-1100

Tel: (630) 572-8800 Fax: (630) 572-3094 Web site: www.wastemanagement.com

Environmental services and disposal company; collection, processing, transfer and disposal facilities.

Waste Management Intl. Ltd., Ave. Paseo Colon 221, 9th Fl., 1399 Buenos Aires, Argentina

WATSON WYATT & COMPANY

6707 Democracy Blvd., Ste. 800, Bethesda, MD, 20817

Tel: (301) 581-4600 Fax: (301) 581-4937 Web site: www.watsonwyatt.com

Creates compensation and benefits programs for major corporations.

Watson Wyatt Argentina, Av. Leandro N. Alem 790, piso 12, C.P. 1001, Buenos Aires, Argentina

Tel: 54-1-314-1029 Fax: 54-1-312-5862

WEATHERFORD INTERNATIONAL INC.

5 Post Oak Blvd, Ste. 1760, Houston, TX, 77227-3415

Tel: (713) 287-8400 Fax: (713) 963-9785 Web site: www.weatherford.com

Oilfield services, products & equipment; mfr. marine cranes for oil and gas industry.

Weatherford Intl., c/o Petro-Bach S.A., Florida 537, 1005 Buenos Aires, Argentina (Locations: Canadon Seco, Comodoro Rivadavia, Las Heras, Mendoza, Neuquen, Rincon de los Sauces, Rio Gallegos & Tartagal.)

Tel: 54-1-812-3516 Fax: 54-1-815-8496

WENDY'S INTERNATIONAL, INC.

428 West Dublin-Granville Roads, Dublin, OH, 43017

Tel: (614) 764-3100 Fax: (614) 764-3459

Fast food restaurant chain.

Wendy's International, Buenos Aires, Argentina

WEST CHEMICAL PRODUCTS INC.

1000 Herrontown Road, Princeton, NJ, 08540

Tel: (609) 921-0501 Fax: (609) 924-4308

Sanitary equipment & supplies.

West Chemical Products Argentina SA, Belgrano 407, piso 4, 1092 Buenos Aires, Argentina

THE WEST COMPANY, INC.

101 Gordon Drive, PO Box 645, Lionville, PA, 19341-0645

Tel: (610) 594-2900 Fax: (610) 594-3014 Web site: www.thewestcompany.com

Mfr. products for filling, sealing, dispensing & delivering needs of health care & consumer products markets.

West Argentina, Buenos Aires, Argentina

Tel: 54-1-849-0600

WESTERN ATLAS INC.

10205 Westheimer, Houston, TX, 77251-1407

Tel: (713) 972-4000 Fax: (713) 952-9837 Web site: www.waii.com

Full service to the oil industry.

Western Atlas Inc., Mexico 1651/1661, 1100 Buenos Aires, Argentina

Tel: 54-1-383-1106 Fax: 54-1-383-1194 Contact: D. Riley, Res. Mgr.

Western Atlas Logging Services, Hipolito Irigoyen 5551, Ruta No. 3, Barrio Industrial, 9000 Comodoro Rivadavia, Chubut, Argentina

Tel: 54-97-480-150 Fax: 54-97-480-150 Contact: D. Cabrera, Bus. Mgr.

Western Atlas Logging Services, Suipacha 268, piso, 1355 Buenos Aires, Argentina

Tel: 54-1-393-2294 Fax: 54-1-326-4627 Contact: Peter Manchester, Area Mgr.

WESTINGHOUSE ELECTRIC (CBS)

11 Stanwix Street, Pittsburgh, PA, 15222-1384

Tel: (412) 244-2000 Fax: (412) 642-4650

TV/radio broadcasting, mfr. electronic systems for industry/defense, financial & environmental services.

Westinghouse Electric Co. SA, Casilla de Correo 6, Buenos Aires, Argentina

WHIRLPOOL CORPORATION

2000 N. M-63, Benton Harbor, MI, 49022-2692

Tel: (616) 923-5000 Fax: (616) 923-5443 Web site: www.whirlpoolcorp.com

Mfr./market home appliances: Whirlpool, Roper, KitchenAid, Estate, and Inglis.

Whirlpool Argentina, Av. Crovara, 2550 - La Tablada - 1766, Buenos Aires, Argentina (Locations: Joinville, Manaus, Rio Claro, Sao Bernardo do Campo, Pernambuco, & San Luis, Argentina

Tel: 54-1-665-4889

WORLD COURIER INC.

1313 Fourth Ave., New Hyde Park, NY, 11041

Tel: (516) 354-2600 Fax: (516) 354-2644

International courier service.

World Courier SA Argentina, Av. Corrientes 327, piso 6, Buenos Aires, Argentina

WUNDERMAN CATO JOHNSON

675 Ave. of the Americas, New York, NY, 10010-5104

Tel: (212) 941-3000 Fax: (212) 633-0957 Web site: www.wcj.com

International advertising and marketing consulting firm.

Wunderman Cato Johnson, Aribeños 2841, Buenos Aires, Argentina

Tel: 54-1-784-0043 Fax: 54-1-793-7756 Contact: Karina Bertolasi, Gen. Mgr.

Wunderman Cato Johnson, Demaria 4412, Buenos Aires 1425, Argentina

Tel: 54-1-777-8500 Fax: 54-1-775-4919 Contact: Enrique Yuste, Gen. Mgr.

XEROX CORPORATION

800 Long Ridge Road, PO Box 1600, Stamford, CT, 06904

Tel: (203) 968-3000 Fax: (203) 968-4312 Web site: www.xerox.com

Mfr. document processing equipment, systems and supplies.

Xerox Argentina I.C.S.A., Rivadavia 2750, 3000 Santa Fe, Argentina

Xerox Argentina I.C.S.A., Provincias Unidas 923, 2000 Rosario, Argentina

Xerox Argentina I.C.S.A., 9 de Julio 1769, 5500 Mendoza, Argentina

Xerox Argentina I.C.S.A., Av. Independencia 2522, 7600 Mar del Plata, Buenos Aires, Mar del Plata, Argentina

Xerox Argentina I.C.S.A., C. Pellegrini 1244, 3400 Corrientes, Argentina

Xerox Argentina I.C.S.A., Colon 3995 Local 8, 5000 Cordoba, Argentina

Xerox Argentina I.C.S.A., Casilla De Correo 1664, Jaramillo 1595, 1429 Bueonos Aires, Argentina

Tel: 54-1-703-7700 Fax: 54-1-703-7701

YOUNG & RUBICAM INC.

285 Madison Ave., New York, NY, 10017

Tel: (212) 210-3000 Fax: (212) 370-3796 Web site: www.yr.com

Advertising, public relations, direct marketing and sales promotion, corporate & product ID management.

Young Rubicam de Argentina SA, Paseo Colon 275, piso 13, 1063 Buenos Aires, Argentina

Armenia

LOUIS BERGER INTERNATIONAL INC.

100 Halsted Street, East Orange, NJ, 07019

Tel: (201) 678-1960 Fax: (201) 672-4284 Web site: www.louisberger.com

Consulting engineers, architects, economists & planners.

CEPRA, c/o American University in Armenia, 40 Marshall Bargramian St., Yerevan, 375019, Armenia

Tel: 374-271-602 Fax: 374-151-048

DHL WORLDWIDE EXPRESS

333 Twin Dolphin Drive, Redwood City, CA, 94065

Tel: (650) 593-7474 Fax: (650) 593-1689 Web site: www.dhl.com

Worldwide air express carrier.

DHL Worldwide Express, Demirchian St. 36, Yerevan 375002, Armenia

Tel: 374-2-528058

PALMS & COMPANY, INC. (U.S. FUR EXCHANGE)

515 Lake Street South, Bldg. #103, Kirkland, WA, 98033

Tel: (425) 828-6774 Fax: (425) 827-5528

Fur auctioning, distribution and sale; investment banking

Palms & Co. (Armenia) Inc., Armenia - All mail to: PO Box 25, Lutsk-23 City Volyn Region, Ukraine 262023

Contact: Dr. Oleg Jourin

Aruba

AON CORPORATION

123 North Wacker Drive, Chicago, IL, 60606

Tel: (312) 701-3000 Fax: (312) 701-3100 Web site: www.aon.com

Insurance brokers worldwide; underwrites accident & health insurance, specialty & professional insurance; & provides risk management consultation.

AON Aruba, 31, A Wayaca, Oranjestad, Aruba

Tel: 297-8-31844 Fax: 297-8-38555 Contact: Peter den Dekker

BEST WESTERN INTERNATIONAL

6201 North 24th Place, Phoenix, AZ, 85106

Tel: (602) 957-4200 Fax: (602) 957-5740

International hotel chain.

BW Bucuti Beach Resort, LG Smith Blvd., #55B, Box 1299, Eagle Beach, Aruba

Tel: 297-8-31100

BW Manchebo Beach Resort, J.E. Irausquin Blvd., 55, Oranjestad, Aruba

Tel: 297-8-23444

BUDGET RENT A CAR CORPORATION

4225 Naperville Road, Lisle, IL, 60532

Tel: (630) 955-1900 Fax: (630) 955-7799 Web site: www.budgetrentacar.com

Car and truck rental system.

Budget Rent A Car, Kolibri Straat #1, Aruba

Tel: 297-8-28600

CITICORP

399 Park Ave., New York, NY, 10043

Tel: (212) 559-1000 Fax: (212) 527-2066 Web site: www.citibank.com

International banking and financial services.

Citibank N.A., Oranjestad, Aruba

THE COASTAL CORPORATION

Nine Greenway Plaza, Houston, TX, 77046-0995

Tel: (713) 877-1400 Fax: (713) 877-6752 Web site: www.coastalcorp.com

Oil refining, natural gas, related services; independent power production.

Coastal Aruba Fuels Company N.V., San Nicolas, Aruba

Coastal Aruba Refining Co. N.V., PO Box 2150, San Nicolas, Aruba

Coastal Petroleum Overseas N.V., San Nicolas, Aruba

DELOITTE TOUCHE TOHMATSU INTERNATIONAL

PO Box 820, Wilton, CT, 06897

Tel: (203) 761-3000 Fax: (203) 834-2200 Web site: www.u.s.deloitte.com or www.dtti.com

Accounting, audit, tax and management consulting services.

Deloitte & Touche, Fergusonstaat 58-60 (PO Box 1271), Oranjestad, Aruba

DHL WORLDWIDE EXPRESS

333 Twin Dolphin Drive, Redwood City, CA, 94065

Tel: (650) 593-7474 Fax: (650) 593-1689 Web site: www.dhl.com

Worldwide air express carrier.

DHL Worldwide Express, Cargo Bldg. Ctr., Bldg. D. Reina Beatrix Airport, Oranjestad, Aruba

Tel: 599-9-617472

ERNST & YOUNG, LLP

787 Seventh Ave., New York, NY, 10019

Tel: (212) 773-3000 Fax: (212) 773-6350 Web site: www.eyi.com

Accounting and audit, tax and management consulting services.

Moret Ernst & Young, Boerhaavesyraat 17, (PO Box 197) Oranjestad, Aruba

Tel: 297-8-24050 Fax: 297-8-26548

FRITZ COMPANIES INC.

706 Mission Street, Ste. 900, San Francisco, CA, 94103

Tel: (415) 904-8360 Fax: (415) 904-8661 Web site: www.fritz.com

Integrated transportation, sourcing, distribution & customs brokerage services.

Fritz Companies Inc., Aruba

HYATT INTERNATIONAL CORPORATION

200 West Madison Street, Chicago, IL, 60606

Tel: (312) 750-1234 Fax: (312) 750-8578 Web site: www.hyatt.com

International hotel management.

Hyatt Regency Aruba Resort & Casino, J. E. Irausquin Blvd. #85, Palm Beach, Aruba

Tel: 297-8-61234 Fax: 297-8-61682

KPMG PEAT MARWICK LLP

Three Chestnut Ridge Road, Montvale, NJ, 07645

Tel: (201) 307-7000 Fax: (201) 930-8617 Web site: www.kpmg.com

Accounting and audit, tax and management consulting services.

KPMG Croes & Croes Accountants, Emma Bldg. 2nd Fl., Caya GF (Betico) Croes 85, Oranjestad, Aruba

KPMG Peat Marwick, Wayaka 31D, Oranjestad, Aruba

Tel: 297-8-32098 Fax: 297-8-24378 Contact: Tico R. Croes, Sr. Ptnr.

SONESTA INTERNATIONAL HOTELS CORPORATION

200 Clarendon Street, Boston, MA, 02166

Tel: (617) 421-5400 Fax: (617) 421-5402 Web site: www.sonesta.com

Hotels, resorts, and Nile cruises..

Sonesta Hotel Aruba, LG Smith Blvd 82, Oranjestav, Aruba, AW

WENDY'S INTERNATIONAL, INC.

428 West Dublin-Granville Roads, Dublin, OH, 43017

Tel: (614) 764-3100 Fax: (614) 764-3459

Fast food restaurant chain.

Wendy's International, Oranjestad, Aruba

Australia

3COM CORPORATION

5400 Bayfront Plaza, Santa Clara, CA, 95052-8145

Tel: (408) 764-5000 Fax: (408) 764-5001 Web site: www.3com.com

Develop/mfr. computer networking products & systems.

3Com Australia, Level 13, 65 Berry St., North Sydney, NSW 2060, Australia

Tel: 61-2-9937-5000 Fax: 61-2-9956-6247

3Com Australia, Level 3, Waterfront Place, 1 Eagle St., Brisbane, Queensland 4000, Australia

Tel: 61-7-3360-0265 Fax: 61-7-3360-0269

3Com Australia, Level 11, Advance Bank Centre, 60 Marcus Clarke St., Canberra ACT 2600, Australia

Tel: 61-2-6243-5155 Fax: 61-2-6243-5127

3Com Australia, 473-479 Victoria St., West Melbourne, VIC 3003, Australia

Tel: 61-3-9934-8888 Fax: 61-3-9934-8880

3Com Australia, Level 13, 65 Berry St., North Sydney, NSW 2060, Australia

Tel: 61-2-9937-5000 Fax: 61-2-9956-6247

3Com Australia, Level 1, 420 St. Kilda Rd., Melbourne, VIC 3004, Australia

Tel: 61-3-9866-8022 Fax: 61-3-9866-8219

3Com New Zealand, Level 13, 65 Berry St., North Sydney, NSW 2060, Australia

Tel: 61-2-9937-5000 Fax: 61-2-9956-6247

3M

3M Center, St. Paul, MN, 55144-1000

Tel: (612) 733-1110 Fax: (612) 733-9973 Web site: www.mmm.com

Mfr. diversified products for industry, health care, imaging, communications, transport, safety, consumer, etc.

3M Australia, 24-30 Crittenden Rd., Findon SA 5023, Australia

Tel: 61-8-8202-6111

3M Australia, Corners of Blackburn & Ferntree Gully Roads, MT, Waverley, VIC 3149, Australia

Tel: 61-3-9265-4333

3M Australia, 4 Gould St., Osbourne Park, WA 6017, Australia

Tel: 61-9-9273-6666

3M Australia Pty. Ltd., United 14/16 Theodor St., Eagel Farm Qld 4009, Australia

Tel: 61-7-3246-1444

3M Australia Pty. Ltd. Head Office, 950 Pacific Hwy., Pymble, NSW 2073, Australia

Tel: 61-2-9498-9333 Fax: 800-800269

3M Automotive Industries Centre, 30 Green St., Thomastown, VIC 3074, Australia

Tel: 61-3-9466-1622 Fax: 61-3-9466-4145

3M Pharmaceuticals Pty. Ltd., 9-15 Chilvers Rd., Thornleigh, NSW 2120, Australia

Tel: 61-2-9875-6333 Fax: 61-2-9875-6416

AAF-McQUAY INC.

111 South Calvert Street, Ste. 2800, Baltimore, MD, 21202

Tel: (410) 528-2755 Fax: (410) 528-2797 Web site: www.mcquay.com

Mfr. air quality control products: heating, ventilating, air-conditioning & filtration products & services.

AAF Pty. Ltd., PO Box 423, St. Leonards, NSW 2065, Australia

ABBOTT LABORATORIES

One Abbott Park Road, Abbott Park, IL, 60064-3500

Tel: (847) 937-6100 Fax: (847) 937-1511 Web site: www.abbott.com

Development/mfr./sale diversified health care products & services.

Abbott Australasia Pty. Ltd., Cronulla, NSW, Australia

ACCO USA INC.

300 Tower Parkway, Lincoln, IL, 60069

Tel: (847) 541-9500 Fax: (847) 478-0073

Paper fasteners & clips, metal fasteners, binders & staplers.

Universal Tags Pty. Ltd., 62 Whiting St., Artarmon, NSW 2064, Australia

ACHESON COLLOIDS CO.

511 Fort Street, PO Box 611747, Port Huron, MI, 48061-1747

Tel: (810) 984-5581 Fax: (810) 984-1446

Chemicals, chemical preparations, paints & lubricating oils.

Acheson A.N.Z. Pty. Ltd., PO Box 48, Padstow, NSW 2211, Australia

ACTIVISION

3100 Ocean Park Boulevard, Santa Monica, CA, 90405

Tel: (310) 255-2000 Fax: (310) 255-2100 Web site: www.activision.com

Development/mfr. entertainment software & video games.

Activision Australia, Century Plaza, 41 Rawson St., Epping NSW 2121, Australia

Tel: 61-2-9869-0955 Fax: 61-2-9869-0977 Emp: 11

ADEMCO INTERNATIONAL

165 Eileen Way, Syosset, NY, 11791

Tel: (516) 921-6704 Fax: (516) 496-8306 Web site: www.ademcoint.com

Mfr. security, fire & burglary systems & products.

Admeco Australia Pty. Ltd., Unit 5, Riverside Centre, 24-28 River Rd. West, Parramatta, NSW 2150, Australia

Tel: 61-2-9842-9333 Fax: 61-2-9893-9480

AEROQUIP-VICKERS

3000 Strayer, PO Box 50, Maumee, OH, 43537-0050

Tel: (419) 867-2200 Fax: (419) 867-2390

Mfr. engineering components and systems for industry.

Vickers Systems Pty. Ltd., 169 Rosamond Rd., Maribyrnong, VIC 3034, Australia

AIR EXPRESS INTERNATIONAL CORPORATION

120 Tokeneke Road, PO Box 1231, Darien, CT, 06820

Tel: (203) 655-7900 Fax: (203) 655-5779 Web site: www.aeilogistics.com

Air freight forwarder.

AEI (Australia) Pty. Ltd. - Reg. Hdqtrs., Unit 20, 1st Fl., Discovery Cove, 1801 Botany Rd., Banksmeadow, Sydney NSW 2019, Australia (Locations: Adeliade, Brisbane, Cairna, Hobart, Melbourne, Perth.)

Tel: 61-2-9333-0600 Fax: 61-2-9333-0677

AIRBORNE EXPRESS

3101 Western Ave., PO Box 662, Seattle, WA, 98111

Tel: (206) 285-4600 Fax: (206) 281-3937

Air transport services.

Australian Airborne Pty. Ltd., 42 Church Rd., Mascot, NSW 2020, Australia

Australian Airborne Pty. Ltd., Unit 14, MIAC Bldg., PO Box 67, Tullamarine, VIC3043, Australia

ALADDIN INDUSTRIES INC.

703 Murfreesboro Road, Nashville, TN, 37210

Tel: (615) 748-3000 Fax: (615) 748-3070

Mfr. vacuum insulated products, insulated food containers & servers.

Aladdin Industries Pty. Ltd., 43-53 Bridge Rd., Stanmore, NSW 2048, Australia

ALBANY INTERNATIONAL CORPORATION

PO Box 1907, Albany, NY, 12201

Tel: (518) 445-2200 Fax: (518) 445-2265

Mfr. broadwoven & engineered fabrics, plastic products, filtration media.

Albany Felt Pty. Ltd., PO Box 417, Gosford, NSW 2250, Australia

ALBERTO-CULVER COMPANY

2525 Armitage Ave., Melrose Park, IL, 60160

Tel: (708) 450-3000 Fax: (708) 450-3354

Mfr./marketing personal care & beauty products, household & grocery products & institutional food products.

Alberto-Culver (Australia) Pty. Ltd., PO Box 253, Parramatta, NSW 2124, Australia

ALCOA (ALUMINUM CO OF AMERICA)

Alcoa Bldg., 425 Sixth Ave., Pittsburgh, PA, 15219-1850

Tel: (412) 553-4545 Fax: (412) 553-4498

World's leading producer of aluminum & alumina; mining, refining, smelting, fabricating & recycling.

Alcoa of Australia Ltd., Locations in Boddington, Huntly, Jarrahdale, Willowdale, Kwinana, Pinjarra, Point Henry and Wagerup Australia

ALCONE MARKETING GROUP

15 Whatney, Irvine, CA, 92618

Tel: (949) 770-4400 Fax: (949) 770-2308 Web site: www.alconemarketing.com

Sales promotion & marketing services agencies.

Alcone Marketing Group, 20/40 Yeo St., Neutral Bay 2089, Sydney, Australia

Tel: 61-2-9953-3243 Fax: 61-2-9953-0276 Contact: Cameron Parsons, Pres.

ALLEGHENY TELEDYNE INC.

1000 Six PPG Place, Pittsburgh, PA, 15222

Tel: (412) 394-2800 Fax: (412) 394-2805

Diversified mfr.: aviation & electronics, specialty metals, industrial & consumer products.

Teledyne Australia, Ground Fl., 285 Whitehorse Rd., Balwyn, VIC 3103, Australia

ALLEN TELECOM

25101 Chagrin Boulevard, Beachwood, OH, 44122-5619

Tel: (216) 765-5818 Fax: (216) 765-0410 Web site: www.allentele.com

Mfr. communications equipment, automotive bodies and parts, electronic components.

Allen Telecom (Australia) Pty. Ltd., Unit 7, Waverly Gate Business Park, 104-106 Ferntree Gully Rd., Oakleigh VIC 3166, Australia

Tel: 61-3-9548-7555 Fax: 61-3-9562-7155 Contact: Fraser Clayton

Allen Telecom (Australia) Pty. Ltd., Unit 7, Bankstown Office Ctr., 150 Canterbury Rd., Bankstown NSW 2200, Australia

Tel: 61-2-9793-9644 Fax: 61-2-9793-9747 Contact: Lindsay Patience

ALLEN-BRADLEY COMPANY, INC.

1201 South Second Street, Milwaukee, WI, 53204

Tel: (414) 382-2000 Fax: (414) 382-4444

Mfr. electrical controls & information devices.

Allen-Bradley Pty. Ltd., 37 Chapman St., PO Box 190, Blackburn, VIC3130, Australia

ALLERGAN INC.

2525 Dupont Drive, PO Box 19534, Irvine, CA, 92713-9534

Tel: (714) 246-4500 Fax: (714) 246-6987

Mfr. therapeutic eye care products, skin & neural care pharmaceuticals.

Allergan, Pharm. (Pty.) Ltd., Sydney, Australia

ALLIANCE CAPITAL MANAGEMENT L.P.

1345 Ave. of the Americas, New York, NY, 10105

Tel: (212) 969-1000 Fax: (212) 969-2229 Web site: www.alliancecapital.com

Fund manager for large organizations.

Alliance Capital Management, Sydney, Australia

ALLIEDSIGNAL INC.

101 Columbia Road, PO Box 2245, Morristown, NJ, 07962-2245

Tel: (973) 455-2000 Fax: (973) 455-4807 Web site: www.alliedsignal.com

Mfr. aerospace & automotive products, engineered materials.

Allied Corp. (Australia) Sales Ltd., 71 Queens Rd., Melbourne, VIC 3004, Australia

AlliedSignal Aerospace Co., Commerce House 1006, World Trade Centre, Melbourne, VIC3005, Australia

Bendix Mintex Pty. Ltd., Elizabeth St., PO Box 631, Ballarat, VIC 3350, Australia

Garrett Aerospace Pty. Ltd., Unit B, 1020 McEvory St., Waterloo, NSW 2017, Australia

Normalair-Garrett Mfg. (Pty.), King & Fraser Sts., Airport West, Melbourne, VIC 3042, Australia

ALVEY INC.

9301 Olive Boulevard, St. Louis, MO, 63132

Tel: (314) 993-4700 Fax: (314) 995-2400 Web site: www.alvey.com

Mfr./sales automatic case palletizers, package & pallet conveyor systems.

CBS Engineering Pty. Ltd. - Melbourne, 12/566 Gardeners Rd., Alexandria 2015, PO Box 473, Rosebery 2018, NSW Australia

Tel: 61-2-9693-1266 Fax: 61-2-9693-1315

CBS Engineering Pty. Ltd. - Sydney, 1/12 Summer Lane, Ringwood 3134, VIC, Australia

Tel: 61-3-9870-1122 Fax: 61-3-9870-1205

AMBAC ASSURANCE CORPORATION

One State Street Plaza, New York, NY, 10004

Tel: (212) 668-0340 Fax: (212) 509-9109 Web site: www.ambac.com

Reinsurance company.

MBIA-AMBAC International Mktg. Services Pty. Ltd., Level 29, The Chifley Tower, 2 Chifley Square, Sydney, Australia NSW 2000

Tel: 61-2-9375-2198 Fax: 61-2-9375-2119 Contact: Christopher Weeks, Dir.

AMCOL INTERNATIONAL CORPORATION

1500 West Shure Drive, Arlington Heights, IL, 60004

Tel: (847) 394-8730 Fax: (847) 506-6199 Web site: www.amcol.com

Bentonite mining, mfr. specialty chemicals, environmental products.

Volclay-Standard Pty. Ltd., PO Box 380, Crowie St., Greelong North VIC3215, Australia

Tel: 61-3-5278-2555 Fax: 61-2-5278-5833 Contact: Bill Lewis, Mng. Dir. Emp: 9

AMDAHL CORPORATION

1250 East Arques Ave., PO Box 3470, Sunnyvale, CA, 94088-3470

Tel: (408) 746-6000 Fax: (408) 773-0833 Web site: www.amdahl.com

Development/mfr. large scale computers, software, data storage products, information-technology solutions & support.

Amdahl Australia Pty. Ltd., 1 Pacific Hwy., North Sydney, NSW 2060, Australia

AMERICAN AIRLINES INC.

4333 Amon Carter Boulevard, Ft. Worth, TX, 76155

Tel: (817) 963-1234 Fax: (817) 967-9641 Web site: www.amrcorp.com

Air transport services.

American Airlines Inc., GPO Box 3261, Sydney, NSW 2001, Australia

AMERICAN HOME PRODUCTS CORPORATION

Five Giralda Farms, Madison, NJ, 07940-0874

Tel: (973) 660-5000 Fax: (973) 660-6048 Web site: www.ahp.com

Mfr. pharmaceutical, animal health care & crop protection products.

American Home Products Corporation, Sydney, Australia

AMERICAN INTERNATIONAL GROUP INC.

70 Pine Street, New York, NY, 10270

Tel: (212) 770-7000 Fax: (212) 509-9705 Web site: www.aig.com

Worldwide insurance and financial services.

Australian American Assurance Co. Ltd., 549 St. Kilda Rd., Melbourne, Vic. 3004, Australia

AMERICAN MANAGEMENT SYSTEMS, INC.

4050 Legato Road, Fairfax, VA, 22033

Tel: (703) 267-8000 Fax: (703) 267-5067 Web site: www.amsinc.com

Systems integration & consulting.

AMS Management Systems Australia Pty. Ltd., Karovel House, 92 Pitt St., Ste. 601, Level 6, Sydney, NSW 2000, Australia

Tel: 61-2-9238-7619 Fax: 61-2-9221-1987 Contact: Andrea Macarley

AMERICAN RE-INSURANCE COMPANY

555 College Road East, Princeton, NJ, 08543

Tel: (609) 243-4200 Fax: (609) 243-4257

Reinsurance.

American Re-Insurance Co., 28-34 O'Connell St., Sydney, NSW 2000, Australia

American Re-Insurance Co., 84 William St., Melbourne, VIC3000, Australia

AMERICAN SOFTWARE, INC.

470 East Paces Fery Road, NE, Atlanta, GA, 30305

Tel: (404) 261-4381 Fax: (404) 264-5514 Web site: www.amsoftware.com

Mfr./sales of financial control software & systems.

American Software, Sydney, Australia

AMERICAN TOOL COMPANIES INC.

8400 LakeView Pkwy., #400, Kenosha, WI, 53142

Tel: (847) 478-1090 Fax: (847) 478-1090

Mfr. hand tools, cutting tools & power tool accessories.

ATC Tools Australasia Pty. Ltd., 44 Rocco Dr., Scoresby, VIC 3179, Australia

AMMIRATI PURIS LINTAS

One Dag Hammarskjold Plaza, New York, NY, 10017

Tel: (212) 605-8000 Fax: (212) 605-4705 Web site: www.interpublic.com

International advertising agency.

Ammirati Puris Lintas, Level 12, 468 St. Kilda Rd., Melbourne, VIC 3004, Australia

Tel: 61-3-9820-9655 Fax: 61-3-9820-0464 Contact: Austin Begg, Mng. Dir.

Ammirati Puris Lintas Australia, 10th Fl., The Denison, 65 Berry St., PO Box 925 North Sydney, NSW 2059, Australia

Tel: 61-2-9925-1701 Fax: 61-9957-1959 Contact: Leigh Clapham, Mng. Dir.

Lintas Hakuhodo, PO Box 925, North Sydney 2059, Australia

Tel: 61-2-9925-1899 Fax: 61-2-9957-1959 Contact: Kazuto Miyakawa

Lintas Hakuhodo, Level 12, 468 St. Kilda Rd., Melbourne VIC 304, Australia

Tel: 61-3-9820-9655 Fax: 61-3-9820-0464 Contact: Austin Begg

Lintas Online, Level 7, 65 Berry St., North Sydney N.S.W. 2060, Australia

Tel: 61-2-9954-4088 Fax: 61-2-9954-3055 Contact: Gary Henstridge

Lintas Sprint, 7th Fl., 65 Berry St., North Sydney N.S.W. 2060, Australia

Tel: 61-2-9925-1700 Fax: 61-2-9957-5222 Contact: Robin Shuker

McSpedden Carey, 8th Fl., 65 Berry St., North Sydney, N.S.W. 2060, Australia

Tel: 61-2-9957-6777 Fax: 61-2-9922-7822 Contact: Leigh Clapham, Mng. Dir.

Merchant and Partners (Perth), 394 Stirling Highway, Claremont, W.A. 6010, Australia

Tel: 61-9-385-2300 Fax: 61-9-385-2335 Contact: Debra Neve

Merchant and Partners (Sydney), 332-334 Kent St., Sydney N.S.W. 2000, Australia

Tel: 61-2-9290-2166 Fax: 61-2-9269-1864 Contact: Dennis Merchant

Underline Design, 360 Pacific Highway, PO Box 1307, Crows Nest N.S.W. 2065, Australia

Tel: 61-2-9436-1144 Fax: 61-2-9429-7203 Contact: David Stewart, Mng. Dir.

AMP INC.

470 Friendship Road, PO Box 3608, Harrisburg, PA, 17105-3608

Tel: (717) 564-0100 Fax: (717) 780-6130

Develop/mfr. electronic & electrical connection products & systems.

Australian AMP Pty. Ltd., Sydney, Australia

Tel: 61-2-9840-8200

AMSTED INDUSTRIES INC.

205 North Michigan, Chicago, IL, 60601

Tel: (312) 645-1700 Fax: (312) 819-8429 Web site: www.amsted.com

Privately-held, diversified manufacturer of products for the construction & building markets, general industry & the railroads.

Baltimore Aircoil Ltd., 120 Wisemans Ferry Rd., Somersby NSW 2250, Australia

Tel: 61-4-340-1200 Fax: 61-4-340-1545 Contact: Brian S. Drew, Mng. Dir. Emp: 91

AMWAY CORPORATION

7575 Fulton Street East, Ada, MI, 49355-0001

Tel: (616) 787-6000 Fax: (616) 787-6177 Web site: www.amway.com

Mfr./sale home care, personal care, nutrition & houseware products.

Amway of Australia Pty. Ltd., 46 Carrington Rd., PO Box 202, Castle Hill, NSW 2154, Australia

ANALYSIS & TECHNOLOGY INC.

PO Box 220, Route 2, N. Stonington, CT, 06359

Tel: (860) 599-3910 Fax: (860) 599-6510 Web site: www.aati.com

Commercial physical research, computer systems design, management services.

Analysis & Technology Australia Pty. Ltd., Unite 4, 55 Townesvile St., Fyshwick A.C.T., Australia 2609

Tel: 61-6-280-7347 Fax: 61-6-280-7346 Contact: Paul Fothergill, Mgr. Emp: 15

ANDERSEN CONSULTING

100 South Wacker Drive, Ste. 1059, Chicago, IL, 60606

Tel: (311) 123-7271 Fax: (312) 507-7965 Web site: www.ac.com

Provides management & technology consulting services.

Andersen Consulting, 141 Walker St., North Sydney, New South Wales 2060, Australia

Tel: 61-2-9927-5000 Fax: 61-2-9954-3484

Andersen Consulting, 360 Elizabeth St., Melbourne, VIC 3000, Australia

Tel: 61-3-9286-7000 Fax: 61-3-9286-7100

ANDREW CORPORATION

10500 West 153rd Street, Orland Park, IL, 60462

Tel: (708) 349-3300 Fax: (708) 349-5410 Web site: www.andrew.com

Mfr. antenna systems, coaxial cable, electronic communications & network connectivity systems.

Andrew Australia, 153 Barry Rd., Campbellfield, VIC3061, Australia

Tel: 61-3-9357-9111 Fax: 61-3-9357-9110

ANEMOSTAT PRODUCTS

888 North Keyser Ave., Scranton, PA, 18501

Tel: (717) 346-6586 Fax: (717) 342-8559

Mfr. air diffusers, grilles & related equipment for A/C, heating & ventilation.

Anemostat Pty. Ltd., 5-15 Cotton Ave., PO Box 132, Bankstown, NSW 2200, Australia

K-2, INC.

4900 South Eastern Ave., Los Angeles, CA, 90040

Tel: (213) 724-2800 Fax: (213) 724-8174

Mfr. sporting goods, recreational & industrial products.

Shakespeare Australia Pty. Ltd., Sydney, Australia

AON CORPORATION

123 North Wacker Drive, Chicago, IL, 60606

Tel: (312) 701-3000 Fax: (312) 701-3100 Web site: www.aon.com

Insurance brokers worldwide; underwrites accident & health insurance, specialty & professional insurance; & provides risk management consultation.

AON Consulting, Maritime Ctr., 27th Fl., 201 Kent St., Sydney NSW 2000, Australia

Tel: 61-2-9240-0403 Fax: 61-2-9252-4724 Contact: Jacqui Ruz

AON Group Australia Ltd., Level 12, The Landmark, Sydney NSW 2000, Australia

Tel: 61-2-9650-0200 Fax: 61-2-9650-0210 Contact: Richard Martin

AON Risk Services Australia Ltd. Head Office, Level 19, 2 Market St., Sydney NSW 2000, Australia (Locations: Adelaide, Brisbane, Darwin, Melbourne, Perth.)

Tel: 61-2-9390-7800 Fax: 61-2-9283-3295 Contact: Robert G. Harrison

Pacific-Asia Warranty Services, 255 Whitehore Rd., Ste. 6, Balwyn VIC 3103, Australia

Tel: 61-3-9888-6966 Contact: Grant Burt

Southen Cross Underwriting Pty. Ltd., The Rialto Building, Melbourne, Australia

Tel: 61-3-9629-4355 Fax: 61-3-9629-4377 Contact: Larry Bartle

APPLE COMPUTER INC.

One Infinite Loop, Cupertino, CA, 95014

Tel: (831) 996-1010 Fax: (831) 974-2113 Web site: www.apple.com

Personal computers, peripherals & software.

Apple Computer Australia Pty. Ltd., 16 Rodborough Rd., Frenchs Forest, NSW 2086, Australia

Tel: 61-2-9452-8000 Fax: 61-2-9452-8160

Apple Computer Australia Pty. Ltd. - Melbourne Office, Level 2, 55 Southbank Blvd., Southbank VIC 3006, Australia (Locations: Brisbane, Canberra & Perth, Australia.)

Tel: 61-3-9694-2200 Fax: 61-3-9686-1252

APPLIED POWER INC.

13000 W. Silver Spring Drive, Butler, WI, 53007

Tel: (414) 781-6600 Fax: (414) 781-0629

Mfr. hi-pressure tools, vibration control products, electrical tools, consumables, technical furniture & enclosures.

Applied Power Australia, Block V, Unit 3, Regents Park Estate, 391 Park Rd., PO Box 261, Regents Park, NSW 2143, Australia

ARCHER-DANIELS-MIDLAND COMPANY

4666 Faries Parkway, Decatur, IL, 62526

Tel: (217) 424-5200 Fax: (217) 424-6196 Web site: www.admworld.com

Grain processing: flours, grains, oils & flax fibre.

ADM Australia (Pty.) Ltd., Sydney, Australia

ATLANTIC RICHFIELD COMPANY (ARCO)

515 South Flower Street, Los Angeles, CA, 90071-2256

Tel: (213) 486-3511 Fax: (213) 486-2063 Web site: www.arco.com

Petroleum & natural gas, chemicals & service stations.

Arco Coal Australia Inc., 10 Eagle St., Brisbane, Qld 4000, Australia

Curragh Queensland Mining Ltd., AMP Bldg., 10 Eagle St., Brisbane, Qld 4000, Australia

ARDENT SOFTWARE, INC.

50 Washington Street, Westboro, MA, 01581-1021

Tel: (508) 366-3888 Fax: (508) 366-3669 Web site: www.ardentsoftware.com

Publisher of database and file management software.

Ardent Software Ltd., Level 1, Philips House, 15 Blue St., North Sydney NSW 2060, Australia

Tel: 61-2-9900-5600 Fax: 61-2-9957-6749

ARMSTRONG WORLD INDUSTRIES INC.

PO Box 3001, 313 W. Liberty Street, Lancaster, PA, 17604-3001

Tel: (717) 397-0611 Fax: (717) 396-2787 Web site: www.armstrong.com

Mfr. & marketing interior furnishings & specialty products for bldg, auto & textile industry.

Armstrong World Industries Pty. Ltd., Sydney, NSW, Australia (All inquiries to U.S. address)

Armstrong-Nylex Pty. Ltd., Melbourne, Vic., Australia (All inquiries to U.S. address)

AROMACHEM

599 Johnson Ave., Brooklyn, NY, 11237

Tel: (718) 497-4664 Fax: (718) 821-2193

Essential oils & extracts, perfumes & flavor material, aromatic chemicals.

Aromachem (Australia) Pty. Ltd., PO Box 889, 155 Brougham St., Pott's Point, NSW 2001, Australia

ARTHUR ANDERSEN & COMPANY

33 West Monroe Street, Chicago, IL, 60603

Tel: (312) 372-7100 Fax: (312) 507-0123 Web site: www.arthurandersen.com

Accounting & audit, tax & management consulting services.

Arthur Andersen & Co., 141 Walker St., North Sydney. NSW 2060, Australia (Locations: Adelaide, Brisbane, & Perth, Australia.)

Tel: 61-2-9964-6000

Arthur Andersen & Co., The Tower, Melbourne Central, 360 Elizabeth St., Melbourne, VIC 3000, Australia

Tel: 61-2-9286-8000

ASARCO INC.

180 Maiden Lane, New York, NY, 10038

Tel: (212) 510-2000 Fax: (212) 510-1855 Web site: www.asarco.com

Nonferrous metals, specialty chemicals, minerals, mfr. industrial products, environmental services.

Asarco Australia Ltd., Wiluna Mine, WA, Australia

Asarco Australia Ltd., Jundee Mine, WA, Australia

Enthone-Omi Inc., Australia

MIM Holdings Ltd., Mt. Isa, Hilton, Collinsville, Oaky Creek, Newlands, Ravenswood & Tick Hill, Australia

ASHLAND OIL INC.

1000 Ashland Drive, Russell, KY, 41169

Tel: (606) 329-3333 Fax: (606) 329-5274 Web site: www.ashland.com

Petroleum exploration, refining & transportation; mfr. chemicals, oils & lubricants.

Ashland Pacific Pty. Ltd., PO Box 162, Chester Hill, NSW 2162, Australia

Valvoline (Australia) Pty. Ltd., Private Bag 2, Smithfield, NSW, Australia

ASSOCIATED PRESS INC.

50 Rockefeller Plaza, New York, NY, 10020-1605

Tel: (212) 621-1500 Fax: (212) 621-5447 Web site: www.ap.com

News gathering agency.

The Associated Press, 364 Sussex St., Box K35, Haymarket, Sydney, NSW 2001, Australia

Tel: 61-2-9262-2999

AST RESEARCH INC.

16215 Alton Parkway, PO Box 19658, Irvine, CA, 92713-9658

Tel: (949) 727-4141 Fax: (949) 727-8584 Web site: www.ast.com

Design/development/mfr. hi-performance desktop, server & notebook computers.

AST Australia, Unit 5, 706 Mobray Rd., Lane Cove, NSW 2066, Australia

Tel: 61-2-9952-6400

ASTEA INTERNATIONAL, INC.

455 Business Center Drive, Horsham, PA, 19044

Tel: (215) 682-2500 Fax: (215) 682-2515 Web site: www.astea.com

Produces computer software that assists to automate and manage field service, sales and customer support operations.

Astea International Inc., Level 1, 39-41 Chandos St., PO Box 539, St. Leonards, NSW 2065, Australia

Tel: 61-2-9436-0855 Fax: 61-2-9436-0823

AT&T CORPORATION

32 Ave. of the Americas, New York, NY, 10013-2412

Tel: (212) 387-5400 Fax: (908) 221-1211 Web site: www.att.com

Telecommunications

AT&T (Australia) Ltd., 21st Fl., CBA Centre, 60 Margaret St., Sydney, NSW 2000, Australia

ATTACHMATE CORPORATION

3617 131st Ave. S.E., Bellevue, WA, 98006-1332

Tel: (425) 644-4010 Fax: (425) 747-9924 Web site: www.attachmate.com

Mfr. connectivity software.

Attachmate Melbourne, Melbourne, Australia

Tel: 61-39-694-6711

Attachmate Sydney, Sydney, Australia

Tel: 61-2-9975-7188

ATWOOD OCEANICS, INC.

PO Box 218350, Houston, TX, 77218

Tel: (281) 492-2929 Fax: (281) 578-3253

Offshore drilling for gas and oil.

Atwood Oceanics Australia Pty. Ltd., 9/30 Dudley St., Melbourne, VIC 3003, Australia

Tel: 61-8-9331-2099 Fax: 61-8-9337-1383 Contact: Terry Vinton, Principal Emp: 180

THE AUSTIN COMPANY

3650 Mayfield Road, Cleveland, OH, 44121

Tel: (216) 382-6600 Fax: (216) 291-6684

Consulting, design, engineering & construction.

Austin (Australia) Pty. Ltd., 3 Bowen Crescent, 9th fl., Melbourne, VIC3004, Australia

Austin (Australia) Pty. Ltd., 52-56 Atchinson St., St. Leonards, NSW 2065, Australia

AUTO-TROL TECHNOLOGY CORPORATION

12500 North Washington Street, Denver, CO, 80241-2400

Tel: (303) 452-4919 Fax: (303) 252-2249 Web site: www.auto-trol.com

Develops, markets & integrates computer-based solutions for industrial companies & government agencies worldwide.

Auto-trol Australia, 2804 Northpoint, 100 Miller St., North Sydney, NSW 2060, Australia

Tel: 61-2-9923-2977 Fax: 61-2-9959-4758 Contact: Steve Hopkins Emp: 4

AUTODESK INC.

111 McInnis Parkway, San Rafael, CA, 94903

Tel: (415) 507-5000 Fax: (415) 507-6112 Web site: www.autodesk.com

Develop/marketing/support computer-aided design, engineering, scientific & multimedia software products.

Autodesk Australia Pty. Ltd., Level 4, 13-15 Lyonpark Rd., Locked Bag No. 35, North Ryde AUS-NSW, 2113, Australia

Tel: 61-2-9844-8000 Fax: 61-2-9844-8044

AUTOMATIC SWITCH CO. (ASCO)

50-60 Hanover Road, Florham Park, NJ, 07932

Tel: (973) 966-2000 Fax: (973) 966-2628

Mfr. solenoid valves, emergency power controls, pressure & temp. switches.

Ascomation Pty. Ltd., Allambie Grove Bus. Park, #12/25 Frenchs Forest Rd. E., Frenchs Forest NSW 2086, Australia

Tel: 61-2-9451-7077 Fax: 61-2-9451-9924 Contact: F. Hall

AVCO FINANCIAL SERVICES INC.

600 Anton Blvd., PO Box 5011, Costa Mesa, CA, 92628-5011

Tel: (714) 435-1200 Fax: (714) 445-7722 Web site: www.avco.textron.com

Financial services, loans and insurance.

Avco Financial Services Ltd., Level 12 255 George St., Sydney, New South Wales 2000, Australia

Tel: 61-2-9324-7000

AVERY DENNISON CORPORATION

150 N. Orange Grove Blvd., Pasadena, CA, 91103

Tel: (626) 304-2000 Fax: (626) 792-7312 Web site: www.averydennison.com

Mfr. pressure-sensitive adhesives & materials, office products, labels, tags, retail systems, Carter's Ink & specialty chemicals.

Dennison Marking Systems Pty. Ltd., 95 Bonds Rd., Punchbowl, NSW 2196, Australia

Fasson Pty. Ltd., Hewittson Rd., Elizabeth, WA 5113, Australia

AVIS, INC.

900 Old Country Road., Garden City, NY, 11530

Tel: (516) 222-3000 Fax: (516) 222-4381 Web site: www.avis.com

Car rental services.

Avis Rent a Car System Inc., 400 Elizabeth St., Melbourne, Australia

Avis Rent a Car System Inc., 86 Vic. Rd., Paramatta, Australia

Avis Rent a Car System Inc., 163 Mitchell St., Alexandria, Sydney, NSW, Australia

Avis Rent a Car System Inc., 46 Hill St., Perth Airport, Perth, Australia

Avis Rent a Car System Inc., Terminus St. & Hume Way, Liverpool, Australia

AVNET INC.

2211 South 47th Street, Phoenix, AR, 85034

Tel: (602) 643-2000 Fax: (602) 643-4670 Web site: www.avnet.com

Distributor electronic components, computers & peripherals.

Avnet VSI Electronics (Australia) Pty. Ltd., Unit C, 6-8 Lyon Park Rd., North Ryde, NSW 2113, Australia

AVON PRODUCTS INC.

1345 Ave. of the Americas, New York, NY, 10105-0196

Tel: (212) 282-5000 Fax: (212) 282-6049 Web site: www.avon.com

Mfr./distributor beauty & related products, fashion jewelry, gifts & collectibles.

Avon Products Pty. Ltd., PO Box 180, Dee Why, NSW 2099, Australia

Tel: 61-2-9936-7777 Fax: 61-2-9936-7610 Contact: Sandra Pascoe

BAILEY-FISCHER & PORTER COMPANY

125 East County Line Road, Warminster, PA, 18974

Tel: (215) 674-6000 Fax: (215) 441-5280

Design/mfr. measure, recording & control instruments & systems; mfr. industrial glass products.

Bailey-Fischer & Porter Pty. Ltd., 474-478 Princes Highway, Noble Park, VIC 3174, Australia

BAIN & CO., INC.

Two Copley Place, Boston, MA, 02116

Tel: (617) 572-2000 Fax: (617) 572-2427 Web site: www.bain.com

Strategic management consulting services.

Bain International Inc., Level 34, Chifley Tower, 2 Chifley Square, Sydney, NSW 2000, Australia

Tel: 61-2-9229-1600

BAKER & McKENZIE

One Prudential Plaza, 130 East Randolph Drive, Ste. 2500, Chicago, IL, 60601

Tel: (312) 861-8000 Fax: (312) 861-2899 Web site: www.bakerinfo.com

International legal services.

Baker & McKenzie, (Box R126, Royal Exchange PO) AMP Centre, 50 Bridge St., Sydney NSW, Australia

Tel: 61-2-9225-0200 Fax: 61-2-9223-7711

Baker & McKenzie, (PO Box 2119T, GPO Melbourne 3001), Level 39 Rialto, 525 Collins St., Melbourne, VIC 3000 Australia

Tel: 61-3 9617-4200 Fax: 61-3-9614-2103

BAKER HUGHES INCORPORATED

3900 Essex Lane, Ste. 1200, Houston, TX, 77027

Tel: (713) 439-8600 Fax: (713) 439-8699 Web site: www.bakerhughes.com

Develop & apply technology to drill, complete & produce oil and natural gas wells; provide separation systems to petroleum, municipal, continuous process & mining industries.

Baker Hughes S.A., Level 2, 222 LaTrobe St., Melbourne, VIC 3001, Australia

Tel: 61-8-9455-0155 Fax: 61-8-9455-1117

Baker Oil Tools (Australia) Pty. Ltd., GPO Box T1746, Perth, WA 6001, Australia

Baker Oil Tools (Australia) Pty. Ltd., 1-5 Bell St., Canning Vale, WA 6155, Australia

Tel: 61-8-9455-0155 Fax: 61-8-9455-7918

Baker Oil Tools (Australia) Pty. Ltd., 5 Stoneham St., Ste. 4, Belmont, WA 6104, Australia

Tel: 61-8-9478-0500 Fax: 61-8-9478-6155

Baker Oil Tools (Australia) Pty. Ltd., 23 Pambula St., Regency Park, Adelaide, South Australia 5010

Tel: 61-8-8243-2966 Fax: 61-8-8345-4778

Baker Oil Tools (Australia) Pty. Ltd., 1684 McKinnon Rd., Berrimah, NT 0828, Australia

Tel: 61-8-8932-3765 Fax: 61-8-8932-3124

BALDWIN TECHNOLOGY CO., INC.

One Norwalk West, 40 Richards Ave., Norwalk, CT, 06854

Tel: (203) 838-7470 Fax: (203) 852-7040 Web site: www.baldwintech.com

Mfr./services material handling, accessories, control & prepress equipment for print industry.

Baldwin Graphic Equipment Pty. Ltd., PO Box 1234, Rozelle NSW 2039, Australia

Tel: 61-2-9555-9975 Fax: 61-2-9555-8246 Contact: Peter Tkachuk, Mgr.

BALTIMORE AIRCOIL CO., INC.

7595 Montevideo Road, Jessup, MD, 20794

Tel: (410) 799-6200 Fax: (410) 799-6416

Mfr. evaporative cooling & heat transfer equipment for A/C, refrigeration & industrial process cooling.

Baltimore Aircoil Co., RMB 3977, Wiseman's Ferry Rd., Somersby via Gosford, NSW 2250, Australia

THE BANK OF NEW YORK

48 Wall Street, New York, NY, 10286

Tel: (212) 495-1784 Fax: (212) 495-2546 Web site: www.bankofny.com

Banking servces.

The Bank of New York, Level 4, 90 William St., Melbourne, VIC 3000, Australia

Tel: 61-3-9670-0944 Fax: 61-3-9670-9559

The Bank of New York, Level 15, 179 Elizabeth St., Sydney NSW 2000, Australia

Tel: 61-2-9267-2300 Fax: 61-2-9267-2101

BANKAMERICA CORPORATION

555 California Street, San Francisco, CA, 94104

Tel: (415) 622-3530 Fax: (415) 622-8467 Web site: www.bankamerica.com

Financial services.

Bank of America NT & SA & Bank of America Australia Ltd., Level 18, Bank of America Centre, 135 King St., Sydney, NSW 2000, Australia

Tel: 61-2-9931-4200 Fax: 61-2-9221-1023 Contact: Barry Brownjohn, SVP

BANKERS TRUST COMPANY

280 Park Ave., New York, NY, 10017

Tel: (212) 250-2500 Fax: (212) 250-2440 Web site: www.bankerstrust.com

Banking & investment services.

Bankers Trust Australia Pty. Ltd/BT Funds Management Ltd.., Level 15, The Chifley Tower, 2 Chfley Square, Sydney, NSW 2000, Australia

Tel: 61-2-9259-3555 Contact: Rob Ferguson, Mng. Dir. Emp: 1800

C.R. BARD INC.

730 Central Ave., Murray Hill, NJ, 07974

Tel: (908) 277-8000 Fax: (908) 277-8078 Web site: www.crbard.com

Mfr. health care products.

Bard Bio Spectrum Pty. Ltd., Unit 3/29-35, Gibbs St., Chatswood, NSW 2067, Australia

BATES WORLDWIDE INC.

405 Lexington Ave., New York, NY, 10174

Tel: (212) 297-7000 Fax: (212) 986-0270 Web site: www.batesww.com

Advertising, marketing, public relations & media consulting.

Consensus Research, Level 3, 107 Mount St., North Sydney, NSM 2060, Australia

Tel: 61-2-9778-7388 Contact: Alan Jacobs, Dir.

Expanded Media, 107 Mount St., North Sydney, NSW 2060, Australia

Tel: 61-2-9778-7159 Contact: Darryl Phillips, CEO

George Patterson Bates, Level 4, Comalco Place, 12 Creek St., Brisbane, Queensland 4000, Australia

Tel: 61-7-3218-1000 Fax: 61-7-3229-5505 Contact: Bob Vines, Mng. Dir.

George Patterson Bates, 161 Collins St., Melbourne, VIC 30000, Australia
Tel: 61-3-9287-1200 Fax: 61-3-9287-1400 Contact: H. McLennan, Dir.
George Patterson Bates, 107 Mount St., North Sydney, NSW 2060, Australia
Tel: 61-2-9778-7100 Contact: Alex Hamill, Chmn.
Harrow Media, 33 Ewell St., Balmain, NSW 2041, Australia
Tel: 61-2-9810-1688 Fax: 61-2-9810-2077 Contact: John Collingwood-Smith, Mgr.
Healthcom Gracie, Level 5, 73 Walker St., North Sydney, NSW 2060, Australia
Tel: 61-2-9955-9500 Fax: 61-2-9955-0464 Contact: Fiona Gracie, Mng. Dir.
HMA George Patterson, Level 1, 378 Clarendon St., Melbourne, VIC 3205, Australia
Tel: 61-3-9645-8644 Fax: 61-3-9686-6330 Contact: Iain Hunter, Dir.
HMA George Patterson, Level 16, 122 Arthur St., North Sydney, NSW 2060, Australia
Tel: 61-2-92-2-8700 Fax: 61-2-9202-8766 Contact: Mike Hyland, Mng.
Marketforce, 1314 Hay St., West Perth, WA 6005, Australia
Tel: 61-8-9322-1655 Contact: Howard Read, Chmn.
Navigator, 182 Cumberland St., The Rocks, NSW 2000, Australia
Tel: 61-2-9252-0691 Fax: 61-2-9252-0695 Contact: Susan Hunt, Mgr.
Pathfinder Strategies, Level 1, 150 William St., Sydney NSW 2011, Australia
Tel: 61-2-9356-1930 Fax: 61-2-9356-1931 Contact: Keith Santis, Dir.
The Campaign Palace, Level 13, 409 St Kilda Rd., Melbourne, VIC 3004, Australia
Tel: 61-3-9867-7877 Fax: 61-3-9867-5307 Contact: D. Speakman, CEO
The Direct Bond, Level 6, 100 Mount St., North Sydney, NSW 2060, Australia
Tel: 61-2-9867-5600 Contact: Ian Kennedy, Chmn.
Underline Design, Level 1, 360 Pacific Highway, Crows Nest, NSW 2065, Australia
Tel: 61-2-9436-1144 Fax: 61-2-9436-7203 Contact: David Stewart, Dir.
Zenith Media, 1st Fl., Como Centre, 666 Chapel St., South Yarra, VIC 3141, Australia
Tel: 61-3-9242-7922 Fax: 61-3-9242-7057

BAUSCH & LOMB INC.

One Bausch & Lomb Place, Rochester, NY, 14604-2701
Tel: (716) 338-6000 Fax: (716) 338-6007 Web site: www.bausch.com
Mfr. vision care products & accessories & hearing aids.
Bausch & Lomb (Australia) Pty. Ltd., Sydney, Australia

BAX GLOBAL CORPORATION

16808 Armstrong Ave., PO Box 19571, Irvine, CA, 92623
Tel: (714) 752-4000 Fax: (714) 852-1488 Web site: www.bax.com
Air freight forwarder.
BAX Global, PB 80, 85 O'Riordan St., Alexandria, NSW 2015, Australia
Tel: 61-2-9598-9000 Fax: 61-2-9669-1084

BAXTER HEALTHCARE CORPORATION

One Baxter Parkway, Deerfield, IL, 60015
Tel: (847) 948-2000 Fax: (847) 948-3948 Web site: www.baxter.com
Pharmaceutical preparations, surgical/medical instruments & cardiovascular products.
Baxter Healthcare Pty. Ltd., PO Box 88, Toongabbie, NSW 2146, Australia
Pacific Diagnostica Pty. Ltd., 8 Murdoch Circuit, Acacia Ridge, Qld 4110, Australia

BBDO WORLDWIDE

1285 Ave. of the Americas, New York, NY, 10019
Tel: (212) 459-5000 Fax: (212) 459-6645 Web site: www.bbdo.com
Multinational group of advertising agencies.
Clemenger BBDO, Melbourne, Australia
ustralia

BDO SEIDMAN, LLP

Two Prudential Plaza, 180 N. Stetson Ave., Ste. 2300, Chicago, IL, 60601

Tel: (312) 240-1236 Fax: (312) 240-3329 Web site: www.bdo.com

International accounting & financial consulting firm.

BDO Nelson Parkhill, (GPO Box 2551, Sydney, NSW 2001)Level 23, 2 Market St., Sydney, NSW 2000, Australia

Tel: 61-2-9286-5555 Fax: 61-2-9286-5892 Contact: Paul T.C. Wenham

BEA SYSTEMS, INC.

2315 North First Street, St. Jose, CA, 95131

Tel: (408) 570-8000 Fax: (408) 570-8091 Web site: www.beasys.com

Develops communications management software & provider of software consulting services.

BEA Systems Pty. Inc., Australia/Asia Pacific, Level 2, 27 Peel St., South Brisbane, Queensland 4101, Australia

Tel: 61-7-3255-0244 Fax: 61-7-3255-0441

BEA Systems Pty. Inc., Level 1, 25 Geils Court, Deakin ACT 2600, Australia

Tel: 61-2-6232-4149 Fax: 61-2-6232-4159

BEA Systems Pty. Inc., 367 Collins St., Melbourne VIC 3000, Australia

Tel: 61-3-9221-6145 Fax: 61-3-9221-6161

BEA Systems Pty. Inc., Technical Support Centre, 60 Miller St., Ste. 801, Level 8, North Sydney, NSW 2060, Australia

Tel: 61-2-9923-4088 Fax: 61-2-9923-4080

BECHTEL GROUP INC.

50 Beale Street, PO Box 3965, San Francisco, CA, 94105-1895

Tel: (415) 768-1234 Fax: (415) 768-9038 Web site: www.bechtel.com

General contractors in engineering & construction.

Bechtel International Corp., 2 Mill St., Perth, WA 6000, Australia

Tel: 61-9-481-4250 Fax: 61-9-481-4252

Bechtel International Corp., Level 14, 295 Ann St., Brisbane, Queensland, Australia

Tel: 61-7-3214-7400 Fax: 61-7-3214-7450

Bechtel Pacific Corp. Ltd., 4th Fl., 6 Riverside Quay, Southbank, Melbourne, VIC3006, Australia

Tel: 61-3-9284-4444 Fax: 61-3-9284-4599

BECKMAN COULTER

4300 Harbor Boulevard, Fullerton, CA, 92835

Tel: (714) 871-4848 Fax: (714) 773-8898

Develop/mfr./marketing automated systems & supplies for biological analysis.

Beckman Coulter Instruments (Australia) Pty. Ltd., 24 College St., Gladesville, NSW 2111, Australia

BELL & HOWELL COMPANY

5215 Old Orchard Road, Skokie, IL, 60077

Tel: (847) 470-7100 Fax: (847) 470-9625 Web site: www.bellhowell.com

Diversified information products & services.

Bell & Howell Australia Pty. Ltd., 9 Short St., Chatswood, NSW 2067, Australia

BELLSOUTH INTERNATIONAL

1155 Peachtree Street NE, Ste. 400, Atlanta, GA, 30367

Tel: (404) 249-4800 Fax: (404) 249-4880 Web site: www.bellsouth.com

Mobile communications, telecommunications network systems.

Link Telecommunications, 8th Fl., 600 St. Kilda Rd., Melbourne, VIC 3004, Australia

BENTLY NEVADA CORPORATION

1617 Water Street, PO Box 157, Minden, NV, 89423

Tel: (702) 782-3611 Fax: (702) 782-9259

Electronic monitoring systems.

Rotor Dynamics Pty. Ltd., 1 Millers Rd., PO Box 134, Altona, VIC 3018, Australia

Rotor Dynamics Pty. Ltd., 28 Oatley Ave., PO Box 64, Oatley, NSW 2223, Australia

BESSER COMPANY

801 Johnson Street, PO Box 336, Alpena, MI, 49707

Tel: (517) 354-4111 Fax: (517) 354-3120

Mfr. equipment for concrete products industry; complete turnkey services.

Besser Co. Pty. Ltd., Unit 2/23 Bearing Rd., Seven Hills, NSW 2147, Australia

BETZDEARBORN

4636 Somerton Road, PO Box 3002, Trevose, PA, 19053-6783

Tel: (215) 953-2568 Fax: (215) 953-5524 Web site: www.betzdearborn.com

Mfr. water/wastewater and process system treatment chemicals and services.

BetzDearborn Australia Pty. Ltd., 69-77 Williamson Rd., Ingleburn N.S.W., Australia 2565

BINKS MFG. COMPANY

9201 West Belmont Ave., Franklin Park, IL, 60131

Tel: (708) 671-3000 Fax: (708) 671-6489

Mfr. of spray painting and finishing equipment.

Binks-Bellows (Australia) Pty. Ltd., 57 By-the-Sea Rd., PO Box 338, Monavale, NSW 2103, Australia

BINNEY & SMITH INC.

1100 Church Lane, PO Box 431, Easton, PA, 18044-0431

Tel: (610) 253-6271 Fax: (610) 250-5768

Mfr. rayons, art supplies and craft kits.

Binney & Smith (Australia) Pty. Ltd., PO Box 684, Glen Waverly, VIC3150, Australia

BIO-RAD LABORATORIES INC.

1000 Alfred Nobel Drive, Hercules, CA, 94547

Tel: (510) 724-7000 Fax: (510) 724-3167

Mfr. life science research products, clinical diagnostics, analytical instruments.

Bio-Rad Laboratories Pty. Ltd., Melbourne & Syndey, Australia

BLACK & DECKER CORPORATION

701 E. Joppa Road, Towson, MD, 21286

Tel: (410) 716-3900 Fax: (410) 716-2933 Web site: www.blackanddecker.com

Mfr. power tools and accessories, security hardware, small appliances, fasteners, information systems & services.

Black & Decker Australia, Australia - All mail to U.S. address.

BLACK & VEATCH INTERNATIONAL

8400 Ward Pkwy., PO Box 8405, Kansas City, MO, 64114

Tel: (913) 339-2000 Fax: (913) 339-2934

Engineering, architectural and construction services.

GHD-Black & Veatch Pty. Ltd., PO Box 39, 39 Regent St., Railway Sq., Sydney, NSW 2000, Australia

BLACK BOX CORPORATION

1000 Park Drive, Lawrence, PA, 15055

Tel: (724) 746-5500 Fax: (724) 746-0746 Web site: www.blackbox.com

Direct marketer and technical service provider of communications, networking and related computer connectivity products.

Black Box Catalog Australia Pty. Ltd., 21-23 Maroondah Highway, Croydon, VIC 3136, Australia

Tel: 61-3-9874-7100 Fax: 61-3-970-2955 Contact: John Proctor, Gen. Mgr.

H&R BLOCK, INC.

4400 Main Street, Kansas City, MO, 64111

Tel: (816) 753-6900 Fax: (816) 753-8628 Web site: www.hrblock.com

Tax preparation services & software, financial products and services & mortgage loans.

H&R Block (Australia) Ltd., PO Box 147, Thornleigh, NSW 2120, Australia

Tel: 61-2-9875-3692 Fax: 61-2-9875-3796 Contact: Philip M. Hunt, Dir.

BOART LONGYEAR CO.

2340 West 1700 South, Salt Lake City, UT, 84104

Tel: (801) 972-6430 Fax: (801) 977-3372

Mfr. diamond drills, concrete cutting equipment and drill services.

Longyear Australia Pty. Ltd., 919-929 Marion Rd., Mitchell Park, SA 5043, Australia

THE BOEING COMPANY

7755 East Marginal Way South, Seattle, WA, 98108

Tel: (206) 655-2121 Fax: (206) 655-6300 Web site: www.boeing.com.

World's largest aerospace company; mfr. military and commercial aircraft, missiles and sattelite launch vehicles.

Boeing Company, Sydney, Australia

BOISE CASCADE CORPORATION

1111 West Jefferspm Street, PO Box 50, Boise, ID, 83728-0001

Tel: (208) 384-6161 Fax: (208) 384-7189 Web site: www.bc.com

Mfr./distributor paper and paper products, building products, office products.

Boise Cascade Office Products, Ltd., Melbourne, VIC, Australia

Boise Cascade Office Products, Ltd., Canberra and Sydney, New South Wales, Australia

BOOZ ALLEN & HAMILTON INC.

8283 Greensboro Drive, McLean, VA, 22102

Tel: (703) 902-5000 Fax: (703) 902-3333 Web site: www.bah.com

International management and technology consultants.

Booz Allen & Hamilton (Australia) Ltd., Level 7, 7 Macquarie Place, Sydney, NSW 2000, Australia

Tel: 61-2-9321-1900 Fax: 61-2-9321-1988

Booz Allen & Hamilton (Australia) Ltd., Level 53, 101 Collins St., Melbourne, VIC, 3000 Australia

Tel: 61-3-9221-1900 Fax: 61-3-9221-1980

BORDEN INC.

180 East Broad Street, Columbus, OH, 43215-3799

Tel: (614) 225-4000 Fax: (614) 220-6453

Mfr. Packaged foods, consumer adhesives, housewares and industrial chemicals.

Borden Chemical Australia Pty., 2-8 James St., Laverton North, VIC 3026, Australia

Tel: 61-3-9369-2377 Fax: 61-3-9360-9471

BOSE CORPORATION

The Mountain, Framingham, MA, 01701-9168

Tel: (508) 879-7330 Fax: (508) 766-7543

Mfr. quality audio equipment/speakers.

Bose Australia Inc., 1 Sorrell St., Parramatta, NSW 2150, Australia

THE BOSTON CONSULTING GROUP

Exchange Place, 31st Floor, Boston, MA, 02109

Tel: (617) 973-1200 Fax: (617) 973-1339 Web site: www.bcg.com

Management consulting company.

The Boston Consulting Group, Level 61, Governor Phillip Tower, One Farrer Place, Sydney, NSW 2000, Australia

Tel: 61-3-965-62100

The Boston Consulting Group, 101 Collins St., Level 52, Melbourne VIC 3000, Australia

Tel: 61-4-9377-2297

BOSTON SCIENTIFIC CORPORATION

One Scientific Place, Natick, MA, 01760-1537

Tel: (508) 650-8000 Fax: (508) 650-8923 Web site: www.bsci.com

Mfr./distributes medical devices for use in minimally invasive surgeries.

Boston Scientific Pty. Ltd., 4A Lord St., Botany, NSW 2019, Australia

Tel: 61-2-9316-4444 Fax: 61-2-9316-4177

BOYDEN CONSULTING CORPORATION

100 Park Ave., 34th Floor, New York, NY, 10017

Tel: (212) 980-6534 Fax: (212) 980-6147 Web site: www.boyden.com

Executive search.

Boyden Associates Intl., Level 11, Challis House, 4 Martin Place, Sydney, NSW 2000, Australia

Tel: 61-2-9221-8311

Boyden Associates Intl. Inc., 367 Collins, Level 27, Melbourne, VIC 3000, Australia

Tel: 61-3-9614-7222

BOZELL WORLDWIDE

40 West 23rd Street, New York, NY, 10010

Tel: (212) 727-5000 Fax: (212) 645-9173 Web site: www.bozell.com

Advertising, marketing, public relations and media consulting.

BCM Partnership (Bristow Cornwell Moreland), PO Box 1201; Fortitude Valley, QLD 4006, Australia

Tel: 61-7-3308-2000 Fax: 61-7-3308-2050 Contact: Bill Bristow, Mng. Dir.

Bozell Worldwide Pty. Ltd., Level 2, 2A Glen St., Milsons Point, Sydney, NSW 2061, Australia

Tel: 61-2-9957-3800 Fax: 61-2-9954-4472 Contact: Ken Kierman, Mng. Dir.

Charterhouse Pty. Ltd., 2 The Parade West, Kent Town, South Australia 5071, Kent Town, South Australia, 5067

Tel: 61-8-8363-2300 Fax: 61-8-8362-0492 Contact: Peter Simpson, CEO

Dornau Shearn Communications, Level 3, 468 St. Kilda Rd., Melbourne, VIC 3004, Australia

W. H. BRADY CO.

6555 W. Good Hope Road, Milwaukee, WI, 53223

Tel: (414) 358-6600 Fax: Web site: www.whbrady.com

Mfr. industrial ID for wire marking, circuit boards; facility ID, signage, printing systems & software.

Seton Australia Pty. Ltd., PO Box 4515, Milperra, NSW 1891, Australia

Tel: 61-2-9616-2222 Fax: 61-2-9602-4166 Contact: Keith Kaczanowsk, Gen. Mgr.

W.H. Brady Pty. Ltd., PO Box 4064, Milperra NSW 1891, Australia

Tel: 61-2-9616-2200 Fax: 61-2-9601-6048 Contact: Keith Kaczanowsk, Gen. Mgr.

BRANSON ULTRASONICS CORPORATION

41 Eagle Road, Danbury, CT, 06813-1961

Tel: (203) 796-0400 Fax: (203) 796-2285

Mfr. plastics assembly equipment, ultrasonic cleaning equipment.

Consolidated Ultrasonics Pty. Ltd., 4 Stanton Rd., Private Mail Bag, Seven Hills 2147, Australia

Tel: 61-2-9647-6033 Fax: 61-2-9674-6357

BRIGGS & STRATTON CORPORATION

PO Box 702, Milwaukee, WI, 53201

Tel: (414) 259-5333 Fax: (414) 259-9594

Mfr. engines.

Briggs & Stratton Australia Pty. Ltd., Australia - All mail to U.S. address.

BRISTOL-MYERS SQUIBB COMPANY

345 Park Ave., New York, NY, 10154

Tel: (212) 546-4000 Fax: (212) 546-4020 Web site: www.bms.com

Pharmaceutical and food preparations, medical and surgical instruments.

Australia/New Zealand Medical Affairs, Holland House, 2nd Fl., 492 St. Kilda Rd., Melbourne, Australia

Bristol-Myers Squibb - Perth Australia, 27 William St., Freemantle WA 6160, Australia

ConvaTec Australia, 606 Hawthorne Rd., Ground Fl., East Brighton, VIC, Australia

Zimmer Asian Division Office, Locked Bag. #310, Frenchs Forest NSW 10086, Australia

BRK BRANDS/FIRST ALERT, INC.

3901 Liberty Street Road, Aurora, IL, 60504-8122

Tel: (630) 851-7330 Fax: (630) 851-1331

Mfr. smoke detectors, fire extinguishers, lights, timers & sensor systems.

BRK Brands Pty. Ltd., Unit 7, Riverside Centre, 24-28 River Rd. W., Parramatta, NSW 2150, Australia

BROWN & ROOT INC.

4100 Clinton Drive, Houston, TX, 77020-6299

Tel: (713) 676-3011 Fax: (713) 676-8532

Engineering, construction and maintenance.

Brown & Root Pty., PO Box 118, Brisbane, Queensland 4001, Australia

Tel: 61-7-3211-3950 Fax: 61-7-3211-3952

Brown & Root Pty., Mitchell Rd., PO Box 982, Roma, Queensland 4455, Australia

Tel: 61-7-622-4588 Fax: 61-7-622-3674

Brown & Root Pty., Level 2 Santos Building, 101 Grenfell St., Adelaide, South Australia 5000

Tel: 61-8-224-7108 Fax: 61-8-224-7280

Brown & Root Pty., 306 St. Vincent St., Port Adelaide, South Australia 5015

Tel: 61-8-8341-1135 Fax: 61-8-8214-0118

Brown & Root Pty., 90 Talinga Rd., Cheltenham, VIC 3192, Carlton, Australia

Tel: 61-3-9683-7522 Fax: 61-3-9583-7588

Brown & Root Pty., PO Box 1202, Canning Vale, Western Australia 6005, Australia

Tel: 61-9-455-5200 Fax: 61-9-455-5300

Dawson Brown & Root Pty. Ltd., 40 St. George's Ter., Perth, WA 6000, Australia

Tel: 61-8-9278-4100 Fax: 61-8-9278-4200

BUCK CONSULTANTS INC.

One Pennsylvania Plaza, New York, NY, 10119

Tel: (212) 330-1000 Fax: (212) 695-4184

Employee benefit, actuarial and compensation consulting services.

Buck Consultants Pty. Ltd., 2nd Fl., 20 Clarke St., PO Box 412, Crows Nest, Sydney, NSW 2065, Australia

BUCYRUS INTERNATIONAL, INC.

1100 Milwaukee Ave., South Milwaukee, WI, 53172

Tel: (414) 768-4000 Fax: (414) 768-4474

Mfr. of surface mining equipment, primarily walking draglines, electric mining shovels and blast hole drills.

Bucyrus (Australia) Pty. Ltd., 9th Fl., GWA House, 10 Market St., Brisbane, QLD. 4000, Australia

Tel: 61-7-3215-8888 Fax: 61-7-3229-8165 Contact: Johan Nienaber, Mng. Dir.

BUDGET RENT A CAR CORPORATION

4225 Naperville Road, Lisle, IL, 60532

Tel: (630) 955-1900 Fax: (630) 955-7799 Web site: www.budgetrentacar.com

Car and truck rental system.

Budget Rent A Car, Kingsford Smith Intl Airport, 2020, Sydney, Australia

Tel: 61-2-9669-2077 Fax: 61-2-9669-6808

Budget Rent A Car, Level 2, 128 Joilmont Rd., East Melbourne, 3002, Australia

Tel: 61-3-9206-3636

BULAB HOLDINGS INC.

1256 N. McLean Blvd, Memphis, TN, 38108

Tel: (901) 278-0330 Fax: (901) 276-5343 Web site: www.buckman.com

Biological products; chemicals & chemical preparations.

Buckman Laboratories Pty. Ltd., East Bomen Rd., PO Box 1396, Wagga Wagga, NSW 2650, Australia

Tel: 61-6-921-3155 Fax: 61-6-921-3677

LEO BURNETT CO., INC.

35 West Wacker Drive, Chicago, IL, 60601

Tel: (312) 220-5959 Fax: (312) 220-6533 Web site: www.leoburnett.com

International advertising agency.

Leo Burnett Connaghan, 40 Miller St., North Sydney, NSW 2060, Australia

Leo Burnett Pty. Ltd., 225 Greenwich Hill Rd., Dulwich, Adelaide, SA 5065, Australia

Leo Burnett Pty. Ltd., 45 Black St., Milton, Qld 4064, Australia

Leo Burnett Pty. Ltd., 464 Kilda Rd., Melbourne, VIC 3004, Australia

BURNS & ROE ENTERPRISES, INC.

800 Kinderkamack Road, Oradell, NJ, 07649

Tel: (201) 986-4000 Fax: (201) 986-4118

Engineering and construction.

Burns & Roe Worley, 521 Pacific Highway, Level 2, PO Box 321, St. Leonards, NSW 2065, Sydney, Australia

Tel: 61-2-439-1288 Fax: 61-2-439-5374 Contact: Brett Jobson, Mgr.

BURSON-MARSTELLER

230 Park Ave., New York, NY, 10003-1566

Tel: (212) 614-4000 Fax: (212) 614-4262 Web site: www.bm.com

Public relations/public affairs consultants.

Burson-Marsteller Canberra, 17 Barry Drive, Turner, Australian Capital Territory, 2612, Australia

Tel: 61-6-257-3688 Fax: 61-6-257-3689

Burson-Marsteller Melbourne, Level 20, Southgate Tower West, 60 City Rd., Southbank, VIC 3006, Australia

Tel: 61-3-9685-8500 Fax: 61-3-9686-1275

Burson-Marsteller Sydney, "The Denison" Level 16, 65 Berry St., North Sydney, New South Wales 2060, Australia

Tel: 61-2-9928-1500 Fax: 61-2-9928-1557 Emp: 43

BUTTERICK CO., INC.

161 Ave. of the Americas, New York, NY, 10013

Tel: (212) 620-2500 Fax: (212) 620-2746 Web site: www.butterick.com

Sewing patterns.

Butterick Co. Pty. Ltd., 3712 MCL Ctr., Martin Place, Sydney, NSW 2000, Australia

CABLETRON SYSTEMS, INC.

35 Industrial Way, PO Box 5005, Rochester, NH, 03866-5005

Tel: (603) 332-9400 Fax: (603) 337-3007

Develop/mfr./marketing/install/support local & wide area network connectivity hardware & software.

Cabletron System, Unit 8, Allambie Grove Business Estate, 25 French's Forest Rd., French's Forest, NSW 2086, Australia

CABOT CORPORATION

75 State Street, Boston, MA, 02109-1807

Tel: (617) 345-0100 Fax: (617) 342-6103

Mfr. carbon blacks, plastics; oil & gas, information systems.

Australian Carbon Black Pty. Ltd., PO Box 19, Altona, VIC 3018, Australia

CADILLAC PLASTIC & CHEMICAL COMPANY

143 Indusco Court, Troy, MI, 48083

Tel: (248) 205-3100 Fax: (248) 205-3187

Distributor plastic basic shapes.

Cadillac Plastic (Australia) Pty. Ltd., Silverwater, NSW 2141, Australia

Cadillac Plastic (Australia) Pty. Ltd., PO Box 145, Ermington, NSW 2115, Australia

CALCOMP INC.

2411 West La Palma Ave., Anaheim, CA, 92801

Tel: (714) 821-2000 Fax: (714) 821-2832

Mfr. computer graphics peripherals.

CalComp Australia Pty. Ltd., 7-9 Bridge Rd., Unit 5, Stanmore, NSW 2048, Australia

CALTEX PETROLEUM CORPORATION

125 East John Carpenter Fwy., Irving, TX, 75062-2794

Tel: (972) 830-1000 Fax: (972) 830-1081 Web site: www.caltex.com

Petroleum products.

Caltex Oil (Australia) Pty. Ltd., 167 Kent St., Sydney, NSW 2000, Australia

Caltex Refining Co. Ltd., Solander St., Kurnell, NSW 2231, Australia

CAMBRIDGE WIRE CLOTH COMPANY

105 Goodwill Road, PO Box 399, Cambridge, MD, 21613

Tel: (410) 228-3000 Fax: (410) 228-6752

Mfr. industrial wire cloth, wire conveyor belting and industrial mesh.

Locker-Cambridge Metal Belt Co. Pty. Ltd., PO Box 181, 125 Chesterville Rd., Moorabbin, VIC 3195, Australia

CAMPBELL SOUP COMPANY

Campbell Place, Camden, NJ, 08103-1799

Tel: (609) 342-4800 Fax: (609) 342-3878

Food products.

Campbell's Australasia Pty. Ltd., Australia

CANBERRA-PACKARD INDUSTRIES

800 Research Parkway, Meriden, CT, 06450

Tel: (203) 238-2351 Fax: (203) 235-1347 Web site: www.packard.com

Mfr. instruments for nuclear research.

Canberra-Packard Pty. Ltd., Unit 1, 170 Forster Rd., Mt. Waverley, VIC 3149, Australia

CARBOLINE COMPANY

350 Hanley Industrial Court, St. Louis, MO, 63144

Tel: (314) 644-1000 Fax: (314) 644-4617

Mfr. coatings, sealants.

Vessey Chemicals Pty. Ltd., PO Box 644, Artarmon, NSW 2064, Australia

CARGILL, INC.

15407 McGinty Road, Minnetonka, MN, 55440-5625

Tel: (612) 742-7575 Fax: (612) 742-7393 Web site: www.cargill.com

Food products, feeds, animal products.

Cargill Oilseeds Australia, Baranbar St., Narrabri, NSW 2390, Australia

CARIBINER INTERNATIONAL, INC.

16 West 61st Street, New York, NY, 10023

Tel: (212) 541-5300 Fax: (212) 541-5384 Web site: www.caribiner.com

Plans & produces meetings, events, and media campaigns: creates film/video presentations; supports in-house communications & training programs: and supplies audio-visual equipment.

Caribiner Audio Visual Services, 42 Dickinson Ave., Artarmon NSW 2064, Australia

Tel: 61-2-9436-2611 Fax: 61-2-9906-3130

Caribiner Wavelength, Level 2, 384 Eastern Valley Way, East Roseville NSW 2069, Australia

Tel: 61-2-9417-1677 Fax: 61-2-9417-1330

Caribiner Wavelength, The George, 129 Fitzroy St., St. Kilda, VIC 3182, Australia

Tel: 61-3-9593-8955 Fax: 61-3-9593-8966

CARRIER CORPORATION

One Carrier Place, Farmington, CT, 06034-4015

Tel: (860) 674-3000 Fax: (860) 679-3010 Web site: www.carrier.com

Mfr./distributor/services A/C, heating & refrigeration equipment.

Carrier Air Conditioning Pty. Ltd., 120 Terry St., Rozelle, NSW 2039, Australia

Carrier Services Management Pty. Ltd., Sydney, NSW, Australia

Tel: 61-2-818-9700 Fax: 61-2-555-7376

Direct Engineering Services Pty. Ltd., 17 Roydhouse St., PO Box 71, Wembley, WA 6014, Australia

Portslade Pty. Ltd., Wembley, WA, Australia

CARTER-WALLACE INC.

1345 Ave. of the Americas, New York, NY, 10105

Tel: (212) 339-5000 Fax: (212) 339-5100

Mfr. personal care products and pet products.

Carter-Wallace (Australia) Pty. Ltd., 6 Aquatic Drive, Frenchs Forest, PO Box 216, Brookvale, NSW 2100, Australia

Tel: 61-2-9452-5233 Fax: 61-2-9452-3093

CASCADE CORPORATION

201st Ave., Portland, OR, 97201

Tel: (503) 669-6300 Fax: (503) 669-6321 Web site: www.cascor.com

Mfr. hydraulic forklift truck attachments.

Cascade Materials Handling (Australia) Pty. Ltd., 121 Long St., Smithfield, NSW 2164, Australia

CASE CORPORATION

700 State Street, Racine, WI, 53404

Tel: (414) 636-6011 Fax: (414) 636-0200 Web site: www.casecorp.com

Mfr./sale agricultural and construction equipment.

Austoft Industries Ltd., PO Box 932, Cummins St., Bundaberg, Queensland, Australia 4670

Tel: 61-7-1525-893 Fax: 61-7-1531-908 Contact: Bud Wolf, Gen. Mgr.

Case Corporation Pty. Ltd., 31-67 Kurrajong Ave., St. Mary's, New South Wales 2760, Australia

Tel: 61-7-2673-7777 Fax: 61-7-2833-1441 Contact: Philip E. Moore, V.P. & Gen. Mgr.

CATERPILLAR INC.

100 NE Adams Street, Peoria, IL, 61629-6105

Tel: (309) 675-1000 Fax: (309) 675-1182 Web site: www.cat.com

Mfr. earth/material-handling and construction machinery and equipment and engines.

Caterpillar of Australia Ltd., 1 Sharps Rd, Private Mail Bag 4, Tullamarine, VIC 3042, Australia

C.B. RICHARD ELLIS

533 South Fremont Ave., Los Angeles, CA, 90071-1712

Tel: (213) 613-3123 Fax: (213) 613-3535 Web site: www.cbrichardellis.com

Commercial real estate services.

CB Richard Ellis, Sydney, Australia

CB Richard Ellis, Melbourne, Australia

CB Richard Ellis, Locations in Adelaide, Brisbane, Cairns, Canberra, Double Bay, Gold Coast, Milton, and Perth, Australia

CBI COMPANY

1501 North Division Street, Plainfield, IL, 60544

Tel: (815) 241-7546 Fax: (815) 439-6010

Holding company: metal plate fabricating, construction, oil and gas drilling.

CBI Constructors Pty. Ltd., 52-54 Phillip St., Sydney, NSW 2000, Australia

CBI Constructors Pty. Ltd., 5th Ave., Blacktown, NSW 2145, Australia

CCH INC.

2700 Lake Cook Road, Riverwoods, IL, 60015

Tel: (847) 267-7000 Fax: (800) 224-8299

Tax & business law information, software & services.

CCH Australia Ltd., 36-52 Talavera Rd., North Ryde, NSW 2113, Australia

CEILCOTE AIR POLLUTION CONTROL

14955 Sprague Road, Strongsville, OH, 44136

Tel: (440) 243-0700 Fax: (440) 234-3486

Mfr. corrosion-resistant material, air pollution control equipment, construction services.

Transfield (TAS) Pty. Ltd., PO Box 563, Devonport, Tasmania, 7310, Australia

CENTRAL NATIONAL-GOTTESMAN INC.

3 Manhattanville Road, Purchase, NY, 10577-2110

Tel: (914) 696-9000 Fax: (914) 696-1066

Worldwide sales pulp and paper products.

Central National Australia Pty. Ltd., 2 Capital City Blvd., Wantirna, VIC 3152, Australia

Tel: 61-3-9800-1522 Fax: 61-3-9887-2196 Contact: Rob Glas

CENTURY 21 REAL ESTATE CORPORATION

6 Sylvan Way, Parsippany, NJ, 07054-3826

Tel: (973) 496-5722 Fax: (973) 496-5527 Web site: www.century21.com

Real estate.

Century 21 Australasia Pty. Ltd., Level 14, 221 Elizabeth St., Sydney, NSW 2000, Australia

Tel: 61-2-9283-4221 Fax: 61-2-9283-4041 Contact: Charles Tarbey, Mng. Ptnr.

CH2M HILL INC.

6060 South Willow Drive, Greenwood Village, CO, 80111

Tel: (303) 771-0900 Fax: (303) 770-2616

Consulting engineers, planners, economists and scientists.

CH2M Hill, Adelaide, Australia

Tel: 61-7-185-041

CH2M Hill, Melbourne, Australia
Tel: 61-3-9272-1555

CHADBOURNE & PARKE LLP
30 Rockefeller Plaza, New York, NY, 10112-0127
Tel: (212) 408-5100 Fax: (212) 541-5369
International law firm.
Chambers & Company, Level 43, ANZ Tower, 55 Collins St., Melbourne, 3000, Australia
Tel: 61-3-9654-1988 Fax: 61-3-965-3958 Contact: Robin H. Chambers, Ptnr.

THE CHASE MANHATTAN CORPORATION
World Headquarters, 270 Park Ave., New York, NY, 10017
Tel: (212) 270-6000 Fax: (212) 622-9030 Web site: www.chase.com
International banking and financial services.
The Chase Manhattan Bank, Melbourne Branch, Level 37, 530 Collins St., Melbourne, VIC 3000, Australia
Tel: 61-3-9612-3111 Fax: 61-3-9612-3222
The Chase Manhattan Bank, Sydney Branch, AAP Centre, Levels 32-37, 259 George St., (GPO Box 9816) Sydney, NSW 2000, Australia
Tel: 61-2-9250-4111 Fax: 61-2-9250-4554

CHECK TECHNOLOGY CORPORATION
12500 Whitewater Drive, Minnetonka, MN, 55343-9420
Tel: (612) 939-9000 Fax: (612) 939-1151
Mfr. computer-controlled check/coupon print systems.
Check Technology Pty. Ltd., 5/8 Leighton Place, Hornsby, NSW 2077, Australia

THE CHERRY CORPORATION
3600 Sunset Ave., PO Box 718, Waukegan, IL, 60087
Tel: (847) 662-9200 Fax: (847) 662-2990
Mfr. electrical switches, electronic keyboards, controls & displays, semiconductors.
Cherry Australia Pty. Ltd., 14/104 Ferntree Gully Rd., Oakleigh, VIC 3166, Australia

CHESTERTON BINSWANGER INTERNATIONAL
Two Logan Square, 4th Floor, Philadelphia, PA, 19103-2759
Tel: (215) 448-6000 Fax: (215) 448-6238
Real estate & related services.
Chesterton Intl. (NSW) Pty. Ltd., Level 16, 77 Castlereagh St., Sydney, NSW 2000, Australia

A.W. CHESTERTON COMPANY
225 Fallon Road, Stoneham, MA, 02180
Tel: (781) 438-7000 Fax: (781) 438-8971 Web site: www.stoneham.chesterton.com
Packing gaskets, sealing products systems, etc.
Chesterton Australia Pty. Ltd., PO Box 6467, Baulkham Hills Business Centre, Baulkham Hills, NSW 2153, Australia

CHICAGO RAWHIDE INDUSTRIES (CRI)
900 North State Street, Elgin, IL, 60123
Tel: (847) 742-7840 Fax: (847) 742-7845
Mfr. shaft and face seals.
CR Industries Pty. Ltd., 4 Shearson Crescent, Mentone, VIC 3194, Australia

CHICAGO RAWHIDE MFG. COMPANY
900 North State Street, Elgin, IL, 60120
Tel: (847) 742-7840 Fax: (847) 742-7845
Seals & filters.
CR Industrial Products Pty. Ltd., 25 Graham Rd., Clayton, South Melbourne, 3169, Australia

CHIQUITA BRANDS INTERNATIONAL INC.

250 East Fifth Street, Cincinnati, OH, 45202

Tel: (513) 784-8000 Fax: (513) 784-8030 Web site: www.chiquita.com

Sale and distribution of bananas, fresh fruits and processed foods.

Chiquita Brands International, Australia

CHIRON CORPORATION

4560 Horton Street, Emeryville, CA, 94608-2916

Tel: (510) 655-8730 Fax: (510) 655-9910

Research/mfr./marketing therapeutics, vaccines, diagnostics, ophthalmic.

Australia Diagnostics Corp. Pty. Ltd., 2 Keith Campbell Ct., Scoresby, VIC 3179, Australia

Chiron Mimotopes Pty. Ltd., PO Box 40, 11 Duerdin St., Clayton, VIC 3168, Australia

Chiron Vision Australia, PO Box 347, 25-27 Whiting St., Artarmon, NSW 2064, Australia

THE CHUBB CORPORATION

15 Mountain View Road, Warren, NJ, 07061-1615

Tel: (908) 580-2000 Fax: (908) 580-3606 Web site: www.chubb.com

Holding company: property/casualty insurance.

Chubb Insurance Co. Australia Ltd., Level 51, Rialto South Tower, 525 Collins St., Melbourne, VIC 3000, Australia

Tel: 61-3-9242-5111 Fax: 61-3-9629-7417

Chubb Insurance Co. Australia Ltd., Level 9, Exchange Place, The Esplanade #2, Perth, WA 6000, Australia

Tel: 61-8-9325-7788 Fax: 61-8-9325-7730

Chubb Insurance Co. Australia Ltd., Level 36, Tower Bldg., Australia Sq., 264-278 George St., Sydney, NSW 2000, Australia

Tel: 61-2-9273-0100 Fax: 61-2-9273-0101

CIGNA CORPORATION

One Liberty Place, Philadelphia, PA, 19192

Tel: (215) 761-1000 Fax: (215) 761-5008

Insurance, invest, health care and other financial services.

Cigna Insurance Australia Ltd., Cigna Bldg., 28-34 O'Connell St., GPO Box 4065, Sydney, NSW 2000, Australia

Cigna Intl. Investment Advisors Australia Ltd., 12th Fl., 28-34 O'Connell St., Sydney, Australia

Cigna Life Insurance Australia Ltd., Cigna Bldg., 28-34 O'Connell St., Sydney, NSW 2000, Australia

Crusader Insurance Co. of Australia Ltd., 28-34 O'Connell St., Sydney, NSW 2000, Australia

Esis Intl. Inc., 23-30 Bridge St., Sydney, NSW 2000, Australia

Intl. Rehabilitation Associates Pty. Ltd., Sydney, Australia

CINCOM SYSTEMS INC.

2300 Montana Ave., Cincinnati, OH, 45211

Tel: (513) 612-2300 Fax: (513) 481-8332 Web site: www.cincom.com

Develop/distributor computer software.

Cincom Systems Inc., Sydney, Australia

Cincom Systems Inc., Melbourne, Australia

CISCO SYSTEMS, INC.

170 Tasman Drive, San Jose, CA, 95134-1706

Tel: (408) 526-4000 Fax: (408) 526-4100 Web site: www.cisco.com

Develop/mfr./market computer hardware and software networking systems.

Cisco Systems Australia Pty., Ltd., Level 17, 99 Walker St., PO Box 469, North Sydney, NSW 2060, Australia

Tel: 61-2-9935-4100 Fax: 61-2-9957-4077 Contact: N/A

CITICORP

399 Park Ave., New York, NY, 10043

Tel: (212) 559-1000 Fax: (212) 527-2066 Web site: www.citibank.com

International banking and financial services.

Citibank IPB, 81 Flinders St., Adelaide SA 5000, Australia

Tel: 61-8-8213-0859 Fax: 61-8-8213-0841

Citibank IPB, 387 Victoria Ave., Chatswood NSW 2067, Australia

Tel: 61-2-9414-1510 Fax: 61-2-9414-1550

Citibank Ltd., 187 Little Bourke Steet, Melbourne VIC 3000, Australia

Tel: 61-3-9663-1566 Fax: 61-3-9662-1418

Citibank Ltd., 1 Margaret St., Sydney NSW 2000, Australia

Tel: 61-2-9239-4715 Fax: 61-2-9239-9707

Citibank Ltd., 225 St. George's Terrace, Perth WA 6000, Australia

Tel: 61-8-9426-6581 Fax: 61-8-9426-6585

Citibank Ltd., 199 Charlotte St., Brisbane QLD 4000, Australia

Tel: 61-7-3226-0256 Fax: 61-7-3226-0216

CITRIX SYSTEMS, INC.

6400 NW 6th Way, Fort Lauderdale, FL, 33309

Tel: (954) 267-3000 Fax: (954) 267-9319 Web site: www.citrix.com

Developer of computer software.

Citrix Systems Pty. Ltd., State Forest Building, 423 Pennant Hills Rd., Pennant Hills, NSW 2120, Australia

Tel: 61-2-9980-0800 Fax: 61-2-9980-6763

CLARCOR INC.

2323 Sixth Street, PO Box 7007, Rockford, IL, 61125

Tel: (815) 962-8867 Fax: (815) 962-0417

Mfr. filtration products and consumer packaging products.

Baldwin Filters (Australia) Pty. Ltd., 30 Third Ave., PO Box 563, Sunshine, VIC 3020, Australia

CLEMENTINA-CLEMCO CORP.

1657 Rawlings Road, Burlingame, CA, 94010

Tel: (650) 692-9080 Fax: (650) 697-0217

Blast cleaning equipment & systems, dust collection systems, coating & finishing systems, dry stripping facilities.

Clemco Intl. Sales Co., 5 Clyde St., PO Box 414, Rydalmere, NSW 2116, Australia

CLEVELAND-CLIFFS INC.

1100 Superior Ave., 18th Floor, Cleveland, OH, 44114

Tel: (216) 694-5700 Fax: (216) 694-4880

Iron, coal mining, and transportation.

Cliffs W. A. Mining Co. Pty. Ltd., 12 St. George's Terrace, Perth, WA 6000, Australia

Pickands Mather & Co. Intl., 7th Fl., ANZ Bank Bldg., Pitt & Hunter Sts., Sydney, NSW 2000, Australia

CMS ENERGY CORPORATION

Fairlane Plaza South, Ste. 1100, 330 Town Drive, Dearborn, MI, 48126

Tel: (313) 436-9200 Fax: (313) 436-9225 Web site: www.cmsenergy.com

Independent power plant operator.

CMS Energy Corporation, Australia

CNA FINANCIAL CORPORATION

CNA Plaza, Chicago, IL, 60685

Tel: (312) 822-5000 Fax: (312) 822-6419 Web site: www.can.com

Commercial property/casualty insurance policies.

C.N.A., 31 Queen St., Level 3, Melbourne, Australia VIC 3000

CNB INTERNATIONAL, INC.

171 Church Street, Ste. 140, Charleston, SC, 29401

Tel: (843) 853-1250 Fax: (843) 937-8210 Web site: www.cnb-intl.com

Mfr. Metal forming presses and aftermarket services.

Clearning International Pty. Ltd., PO Box 620, Adelaide, Marleston, South Australia 5033, Australia

Tel: 61-8-8234-0764 Fax: 61-8-8234-0764 Contact: John Harrison, Dir.

THE COASTAL CORPORATION

Nine Greenway Plaza, Houston, TX, 77046-0995

Tel: (713) 877-1400 Fax: (713) 877-6752 Web site: www.coastalcorp.com

Oil refining, natural gas, related services; independent power production.

Coastal Gas Australia Pty. Ltd., Melbourne, Australia

Coastal Oil & Gas Australia Pty. Ltd., Perth, WA, Australia

Coastal Petroleum Overseas N.V., Melbourne, Australia

COBE LABORATORIES INC.

1185 Oak Street, Lakewood, CO, 80215

Tel: (303) 232-6800 Fax: (303) 231-4952

Mfr. medical equipment & supplies.

COBE Australia, Sydney, Australia

THE COCA-COLA COMPANY

P.O. Drawer 1734, Atlanta, GA, 30301

Tel: (404) 676-2121 Fax: (404) 676-6792 Web site: www.coca-cola.com

Mfr./marketing/distributor soft drinks, syrups & concentrates, juice & juice-drink products.

Coca-Cola Amatil Ltd., 71 Macquarie St., Sydney, NSW 2000, Australia

Coca-Cola Southeast Asia Ltd., 9 Rodborough Rd., French's Forest, NSW 2086, Australia

COIN ACCEPTORS INC.

300 Hunter Ave., St. Louis, MO, 63124

Tel: (314) 725-0100 Fax: (314) 725-1243

Coin mechanisms for vending machinery.

Coin Acceptors, Sydney, Australia

THE COLEMAN CO., INC.

3600 Hydraulic Street, Wichita, KS, 67219

Tel: (316) 832-2653 Fax: (316) 832-3060

Mfr./distributor/sales camping & outdoor recreation products.

Australian Coleman Inc., 5 Hallstrom Pl., Wetherill Park, NSW 2164, Australia

COLGATE-PALMOLIVE COMPANY

300 Park Ave., New York, NY, 10022

Tel: (212) 310-2000 Fax: (212) 310-2919

Mfr. pharmaceuticals, cosmetics, toiletries and detergents.

Colgate-Palmolive Pty. Ltd., 345 George St., Sydney, NSW 2000, Australia

COLUMBIA PICTURES INDUSTRIES INC.

10202 West Washington Blvd., Culver City, CA, 90232

Tel: (310) 244-4000 Fax: (310) 244-2626 Web site: www.sony.com

Producer and distributor of motion pictures.

Fox Columbia Film Distributors Pty. Ltd., 404-523 George St., Sydney, NSW 2001, Australia

COMDISCO INC.

6111 N. River Road, Rosemont, IL, 60018

Tel: (847) 698-3000 Fax: (847) 518-5440

Hi-tech asset and facility management and equipment leasing.

Comdisco Australia Pty. Ltd., North Sydney, NSW, Australia

COMMERCIAL INTERTECH CORPORATION

1775 Logan Ave., PO Box 239, Youngstown, OH, 44501-0239

Tel: (330) 746-8011 Fax: (330) 746-1148

Mfr. hydraulic components, pre-engineered buildings and stamped metal products.

Commercial Hydraulics Pty. Ltd., PO Box 191, 265 Inglis St., Port Melbourne, VIC 3207, Australia

COMMERCIAL METALS COMPANY

PO Box 1046, Dallas, TX, 75221

Tel: (972) 689-4300 Fax: (972) 689-4320

Metal collecting/processing, steel mills and metal trading.

CMC (Australia) Pty. Ltd., PO Box 113, Horstville, Sydney, NSW 2220, Australia

COMPAQ COMPUTER CORPORATION

20555 State Highway 249, PO Box 692000, Houston, TX, 77269-2000

Tel: (713) 370-0670 Fax: (713) 514-1740 Web site: www.compaq.com

Develop/mfr. personal computers.

Compaq Computer Australia Pty., Ltd., Level 7, 18-20 Orion Rd., PO Box 1220, Lane Cove, NSW 2066, Australia

Tel: 61-2-9911-1999 Fax: 61-2-9911-1800

COMPUTER ASSOCIATES INTERNATIONAL INC.

One Computer Associates Plaza, Islandia, NY, 11788

Tel: (516) 342-5224 Fax: (516) 342-5329 Web site: www.cai.com

Integrated software for enterprise computing and information management, application development, manufacturing, financial applications and professional services.

Computer Associates Pty. Ltd., 407 Pacific Highway, Artamon, NSW 2064, Australia

Tel: 61-2-9937-0500

COMPUTERVISION/PARAMETRIC CORP.

128 Technology Drive, Waltham, MA, 02453

Tel: (781) 275-1800 Fax: (781) 275-2670 Web site: www.ptc.com

Supplier of mechanical design automation & product data management software & services.

Computervision Australia Ltd., 71 Longueville Rd., PO Box 1364, Lane Cove, NSW 2066, Australia

COMSHARE INC.

3001 South State Street, Ann Arbor, MI, 48108

Tel: (734) 994-4800 Fax: (734) 994-5895

Managerial application software.

Comshare Australia Pty. Ltd., Level 1, 12 Help St., Chatswood, NSW 2067, Australia

CONAGRA INC.

One ConAgra Drive, Omaha, NE, 68102-5001

Tel: (402) 595-4000 Fax: (402) 595-4595 Web site: www.conagra.com

Prepared/frozen foods, grains, flour, animal feeds, agri chemicals, poultry, meat, dairy products, including Healthy Choice, Butterball and Hunt's.

D.R. Johnson Group Pty. Ltd., Pymble Corporate Centre, PO Box 539, Pymble, NSW, 2073, Australia

CONE MILLS CORPORATION

3101 N. Elm Street, PO Box 26540, Greensboro, NC, 27415-6540

Tel: (336) 379-6220 Fax: (336) 379-6287 Web site: www.cone.com

Mfr. denims, flannels, chamois & other fabrics.

Bunge Textiles, 26 Peel St., Colingwood, VIC 3066, Australia

Tel: 61-39-416-0933 Fax: 61-39-416-1995

Bunge Textiles Pty. Ltd., 29 Cooper St., Surrey Hills NSW 2010, Sydney, Australia

Tel: 61-2-9281-0322 Fax: 61-2-9281-0557 Contact: Andrew Davis

CONOCO INC.

PO Box 2197, Houston, TX, 77252

Tel: (281) 293-1000 Fax: (281) 293-1440

Oil, gas, coal, chemicals and minerals.

Conoco Australia Ltd., PO Box 6008, Hay St., E. Perth, WA, Australia

Continental Oil Co. of Australia Ltd., IBM Ctr., 168 Kent St., Sydney, NSW 2000, Australia

CONTINENTAL CARBON COMPANY

333 Cyprus Run, Ste. 100, Houston, TX, 77094

Tel: (281) 647-3700 Fax: (281) 647-3700

Mfr. carbon black.

Continental Carbon Australia Pty. Ltd., Private Bag, Cronulla, NSW 2230, Australia

CONTINENTAL INSURANCE COMPANY

333 South Wabash Ave., Chicago, IL, 60695

Tel: (312) 822-5000 Fax: (312) 822-6419

Insurance services.

Phoenix Assurance Co. Ltd., 32/34 Bridge St., Sydney, NSW, Australia

COOPER INDUSTRIES INC.

6600 Travis Street, Ste. 5800, Houston, TX, 77002

Tel: (713) 209-8400 Fax: (713) 209-8995 Web site: www.cooperindustries.com

Mfr./distributor electrical products, tools and hardware and automotive products.

Cooper Automotive Pty. Ltd., 83 Bourke Rd., Alexandria, NSW 2015, Australia

Tel: 61-2-9669-3322

Cooper Hand Tools Div., Albury, NSW, Australia

Cooper Hand Tools Division, Tottenham, Vic., Australia

Crouse-Hinds Australia, 391 Park Rd., PO Box 257 Regents Park, Sydney, NSW 2143, Australia

Tel: 61-2-743-7000 Fax: 61-2-743-7069 Contact: Steven Hood

CORE LABORATORIES

5295 Hollister, Houston, TX, 77042

Tel: (713) 460-9600 Fax: (713) 460-4389

Petroleum testing/analysis, analytical chemicals, laboratory and octane analysis instrumentation.

Core Laboratories, PO Box 785, Cloverdale, Perth, WA 6105, Australia

CORESTATES BANK

1500 Market Street, Philadelphia, PA, 19101

Tel: (215) 973-3100 Fax: (215) 786-8899 Web site: www.corestates.com

Primary international businesses; correspondent banking and trade services.

Corestates Bank, 60 Pitt St., Level 5, Sydney, NSW 2000, Australia

CORNING INC.

One Riverfront Plaza,, Corning, NY, 14831

Tel: (607) 974-9000 Fax: (607) 974-8551 Web site: www.corning.com

Mfr. glass and specialty materials, consumer products; communications, laboratory services.

Corning Australia Pty. Ltd., Auburn, NSW, Australia

Optical Waveguides Australia Pty. Ltd., Melbourne, Australia

COUDERT BROTHERS

1114 Ave. of the Americas, New York, NY, 10036-7794

Tel: (212) 626-4400 Fax: (212) 626-4210 Web site: www.coudert.com

International law firm.

Coudert Brothers, State Bank Centre Ste. 2202, 52 Martin Pl., Sydney, NSW 2000, Australia

Tel: 61-2-9223-1488 Fax: 61-2-235-3877 Contact: Peter J. Norman

COULTER CORPORATION

PO Box 169015, Miami, FL, 33116-9015

Tel: (305) 380-3800 Fax: (305) 380-8312

Mfr. blood analysis systems, flow cytometers, chemicals systems, scientific systems & reagents.

Coulter Electronics Pty. Ltd., PO Box W386, Warringah Mall, NSW 2100, Australia

CRANE COMPANY

100 First Stamford Place, Stamford, CT, 06907

Tel: (203) 363-7300 Fax: (203) 363-7359

Diversified mfr./distributor engineered products for industrial.

Crane Australia Pty. Ltd., PO Box 101, Dunheved Circuit, St. Mary's, Sydney, NSW 2760, Australia

CRAWFORD FITTING COMPANY

29500 Solon, Solon, OH, 44139

Tel: (440) 248-4600 Fax:

Valves, tubes and fittings.

Australian Swagelok Pty. Ltd., 11 Stanley St., Peakhurst, NSW 2210, Australia

CROWN EQUIPMENT CORPORATION

40 South Washington Street, New Bremen, OH, 45869

Tel: (419) 629-2311 Fax: (419) 629-2317

Mfr./sales/services forklift trucks, stackers.

Crown Controls Australia Pty. Ltd., Cor. Cooper & Long Sts., Smithfield, NSW 2164, Australia

CSC COMPANY

9500 Arboretum Boulevard, Austin, TX, 78759

Tel: (512) 345-5700 Fax: (512) 338-7041

Design and marketing software for insurance and financial services.

Continuum (Australia) Ltd., 5th Fl., 100 Mount St., North Sydney, NSW 2060, Australia

CUBIC CORPORATION

9333 Balboa Ave., PO Box 85587, San Diego, CA, 92123

Tel: (619) 277-6780 Fax: (619) 505-1523 Web site: www.cubic.com

Automatic fare collection equipment, training systems.

Southern Cubic Pty. Ltd., Unit A 41-49, St. Hillers Rd., Auburn, NSW 2114, Australia

Tel: 61-2-9749-9105 Fax: 61-2-9749-9102 Contact: Thomas Walker, Gen. Mgr.

CULLIGAN INTERNATIONAL COMPANY

One Culligan Parkway, Northbrook, IL, 60062

Tel: (847) 205-6000 Fax: (847) 205-6030 Web site: www.culligan-man.com

Water treatment products and services.

Culligan Australia Pty. Ltd., 4B Lord St., Botany, NSW 2019, Australia

Tel: 61-2-9316-4142 Fax: 61-2-9316-4144

CUMMINS ENGINE CO., INC.

500 Jackson Street, PO Box 3005, Columbus, IN, 47202-3005

Tel: (812) 377-5000 Fax: (812) 377-3334

Mfr. diesel engines.

Cummins Diesel Australia, 2 Caribbean Dr., Scoresby, VIC 3179, Australia

CUNA MUTUAL INSURANCE SOCIETY

5910 Mineral Point Road, PO Box 391, Madison, WI, 53701

Tel: (608) 238-5851 Fax: (608) 238-0830

Insurance services.

Cuna Mutual Insurance Society, PO Box 1418, North Sydney, NSW 2060, Australia

CYPRUS AMAX MINERALS COMPANY

9100 East Mineral Circle, Englewood, CO, 80112

Tel: (303) 643-5000 Fax: (303) 643-5048 Web site: www.cyprusamax.com

Mining company supplying molybdenum (used in steelmaking).

Cyprus Amax Minerals Company, Sydney, Australia

D'ARCY MASIUS BENTON & BOWLES INC. (DMB&B)

1675 Broadway, New York, NY, 10019

Tel: (212) 468-3622 Fax: (212) 468-2987 Web site: www.dmbb.com

Full service international advertising and communications group.

DMB&B Pty. Ltd., 499 St. Kilda Rd., Melbourne, VIC 3004, Australia

DMB&B Weekes Morris Osborn, 349 Bulwara Rd., Ultimo NSW 2007, Australia

Tel: 61-2-9377-0000 Fax: 61-2-9377-0011 Contact: David Morris, Chmn.

D-M-E COMPANY

29111 Stephenson Highway, Madison Heights, MI, 48071

Tel: (248) 398-6000 Fax: (248) 544-5705

Basic tooling for plastic molding and die casting.

Amalgamated Diemould DME Pty. Ltd., 10 Warren Ave., Bankstown, NSW 2200, Australia

DAMES & MOORE GROUP

911 Wilshire Boulevard, Los Angeles, CA, 90017

Tel: (213) 683-1560 Fax: (213) 628-0015 Web site: www.dames.com

Engineering, environmental and construction management services.

Dames & Moore, 135 Wickham Ter., Brisbane, Qld 4004, Australia

Dames & Moore, South Shore Centre, 85 The Esplanade, South Perth, WA 6151, Australia

Dames & Moore, 187 Mulgrave Rd., 1st fl., Cairns, Qld 4870, Australia

Dames & Moore, Level 1, 41 McLaren St., PO Box 1529, North Sydney, NSW 2060, Australia

Dames & Moore, 10/636 St. Kilda Rd., South Melbourne, VIC 3004, Australia

Dames & Moore, 1st Fl., Arkaba House, The Esplanade, Darwin, NT 0800, Australia

Food & Agriculture Intl. Ltd., 11-13 Bentham St., Adelaide, SA 5000, Australia

Forestry Technical Services, Anutech Court, Daley & North Rds., Acton, ACT 2601, Australia

Hardcastle & Richards, 2/636 St. Kilda Rd., South Melbourne, VIC 3004, Australia

Hardcastle & Richards, 215 Argent St., Broken Hill, NSW 2880, Australia

Hardcastle & Richards, 1/3-5 Bennett St., East Perth, WA 6004, Australia

Hardcastle & Richards, 2/100 Christie St., St. Leonards, NSW 2065, Australia

DANA CORPORATION

4500 Door Street, Toledo, OH, 43615

Tel: (419) 535-4500 Fax: (419) 535-4643 Web site: www.dana.com

Mfr./sales of automotive, heavy truck, off-highway, fluid & mechanical power components.

Dana Corporation, Sydney, Australia

DATA GENERAL CORPORATION

4400 Computer Drive, Westboro, MA, 01580

Tel: (508) 898-5000 Fax: (508) 366-1319 Web site: www.dg.com

Design, mfr. general purpose computer systems & peripheral products & services.

Data General Australia Pty. Ltd., Sydney, Australia

DATA RESEARCH ASSOCIATES, INC. (DRA)

1276 North Warson Road, St. Louis, MO, 63132

Tel: (314) 432-1100 Fax: (314) 993-8927 Web site: www.dra.com

Systems integrator for libraries and information providers.

Data Research International (Australia) Pty. Ltd., Ste. 2, 1st Fl., 350 King Street, West Melbourne, VIC 3003, Australia

Tel: 61-3-9329-3800 Fax: 61-3-9329-3223

DATAPRODUCTS CORPORATION

1757 Papo Kenyon Road, Simi Valley, CA, 93063

Tel: (805) 578-4000 Fax: (805) 578-4001

Mfr. computer printers and supplies.

Dataproducts Corp., Pacific View Business Park, Unit 2/10, Rodborough Rd., Frenchs Forest, NSW 2086, Australia

DATAWARE TECHNOLOGIES INC.

222 Third Street, Ste. 3300, Cambridge, MA, 02142

Tel: (617) 621-0820 Fax: (617) 494-0740 Web site: www.dataware.com

Multi-platform, multi-lingual software solutions & services for electronic information providers.

Dataware Technologies Pty. Ltd., Triple M Tower #2102, 500 Oxford St., Bondi Junction, NSW 2022, Australia

DAYCO PRODUCTS INC.

1 Prestige Place, PO Box 1004, Miamisburg, OH, 45342

Tel: (937) 226-7000 Fax: (937) 226-4689

Diversified auto, industrial and household products.

Dayco Australia Pty. Ltd., Unit 2A, 16-18 Milford St., E. Victoria Park, WA 6106, Australia

Dayco PacificPty. Ltd., 1 Lenton Place, North Rocks, NSW 2151, Australia

DDB NEEDHAM WORLDWIDE INC.

437 Madison Ave., New York, NY, 10022

Tel: (212) 415-2000 Fax: (212) 415-3417

Advertising agency.

Ad.Link DDB Needham Pty. Ltd., 1109 Hay St., Perth, WA 6005, Australia

DDB Needham Brisbane Pty. Ltd., 2nd Fl., Revesby House, 282 Wickham St., Fortitude Valley, Brisbane, Qld 4006, Australia

DDB Needham Melbourne Pty. Ltd., 615 St. Kilda Rd., Melbourne, VIC 3004, Australia

DDB Needham Sydney Pty. Ltd., 10th Fl., 76 Berry St., North Sydney, NSW 2060, Australia

DDB Needham Worldwide Pty. Ltd., 615 St. Kilda Rd., Melbourne, VIC 3004, Australia

DDB Needham Worldwide Pty. Ltd., 10th Fl., 76 Berry St., North Sydney, NSW 2060, Australia

Leonardi & Curtis Advertising Pty. Ltd., 170 Bridport St., Albert Park, VIC 3206, Australia

Stokes King DDB Needham Pty. Ltd., 190 Fullarton Rd., Dulwich, Adelaide, SA 5065, Australia

DE ZURIK, A Unit of General Signal

250 Riverside Ave. North, Sartell, MN, 56377

Tel: (320) 259-2000 Fax: (320) 259-2227 Web site: www.dezurik.com

Mfr. manual, process & control valves.

DeZurik of Australia Pty. Ltd., 109 Whitehorse Rd., Ste. 7, Blackburn, VIC 3130, Australia

Tel: 61-3-9894-8888 Fax: 61-3-9894-8044

DEKALB GENETICS CORP.

3100 Sycamore Road, DeKalb, IL, 60115-9600

Tel: (815) 758-3461 Fax: (815) 758-3711 Web site: www.dekalb.com

Develop/produce hybrid corn, sorghum, sunflower seed, varietal soybeans, alfalfa.

DeKalb Shand Seed Co. Pty. Ltd., PO Box 967, Carrington Rd., Toowoomba, Qld 4350, Australia

DELL COMPUTER CORPORATION

One Dell Way, Round Rock, TX, 78682-2222

Tel: (512) 338-4400 Fax: (512) 728-3653 Web site: www.dell.com

Direct marketer & supplier of computer systems.

Dell Australia, Unit 3, 14 Aquatic Drive, Frenchs Forest NSW 2086, Australia

Tel: 61-2-9930-3355 Fax: 61-2-9930-3311 Contact: Gary Elliott, Mng. Dir.

Dell Australia, Ste. 9, 214 Bay St., Brighton VIC 3186, Australia

Tel: 61-3-9595-0223 Fax: 61-2-9596-0708 Contact: Gary Elliott, Mng. Dir.

DELOITTE TOUCHE TOHMATSU INTERNATIONAL

PO Box 820, Wilton, CT, 06897

Tel: (203) 761-3000 Fax: (203) 834-2200 Web site: www.u.s.deloitte.com or www.dtti.com

Accounting, audit, tax and management consulting services.

Deloitte Touche Tohmatsu, Grosvenor Place, PO Box N250, 225 George St., Sydney, NSW 2000, Australia (Locations: Adelaide, Alice Springs, Brisbane, Canberra, Melbourne, & Perth, Australia.)

DENTSPLY INTERNATIONAL

570 West College Ave., PO Box 872, York, PA, 17405-0872

Tel: (717) 845-7511 Fax: (717) 843-6357 Web site: www.dentsply.com

Mfr.& Distribution of dental supplies & equipment.

Dentsply (Australia) Pty. Ltd., 134 Charles St., West Perth, Western Australia 6005, Australia

Tel: 61-8-9227-6772

Dentsply (Australia) Pty. Ltd., The Lakes Business Park, 339 Pacific Highway, Crows Nest, New South Wales 2065, Australia

Tel: 61-2-9957-2555

Dentsply (Australia) Pty. Ltd., Unit 5, 10 Hudson Rd., Albion, Queensland 4010, Australia

Tel: 61-7-3263-3224

Dentsply (Australia) Pty. Ltd., 204-206 Gipps St., Abbotsford, VIC 3067 Australia

Tel: 61-3-9278-8200

THE DEXTER CORPORATION

1 Elm Street, Windsor Locks, CT, 06096

Tel: (860) 627-9051 Fax: (860) 627-7078

Mfr. nonwovens, polymer products, magnetic materials, biotechnology.

Dexter Nonwovens, 1 Bungan Lane (First Fl.), PO Box 874, Mona Vale, NSW 2103, Australia

DHL WORLDWIDE EXPRESS

333 Twin Dolphin Drive, Redwood City, CA, 94065

Tel: (650) 593-7474 Fax: (650) 593-1689 Web site: www.dhl.com

Worldwide air express carrier.

DHL Worldwide Express, Level 3, 15 Bourke Rd., Mascot, Sydney 2020, Australia

Tel: 61-2-9317-8333

DIAMOND CHAIN COMPANY

402 Kentucky Ave., Indianapolis, IN, 46225

Tel: (317) 638-6431 Fax: (317) 633-2243

Mfr. roller chains.

Shawman Pty. Ltd., 8 Dalwood Ave., Seaforth, NSW 2092, Australia

DIAMOND POWER INTERNATIONAL, INC.

PO Box 415, Lancaster, OH, 43130

Tel: (740) 687-6500 Fax: (740) 687-7430 Web site: www.diamondpower.com

Mfg. boiler cleaning equipment & ash handling systems: sootblowers, controls, diagnostics systems, gauges, OEM parts, rebuilds & field service.

Diamond Power Australia Pty. Ltd., 10 Hereford St., Berkeley Vale, NSW 2261, Australia

DIGITAL EQUIPMENT CORPORATION

111 Powder Mill Road, Maynard, MA, 01754

Tel: (978) 493-5111 Fax: (978) 493-7374 Web site: www.digital.com

Mfr. network computer systems, components, software and services.

Digital Equipment Corporation Pty. Ltd., 410 Concord Rd., Rhodes NSW 2138, Australia

Tel: 61-2-9561-5252 Fax: 61-2-9807-2666

DILLINGHAM CONSTRUCTION CORPORATION

5944 Inglewood Drive, Pleasanton, CA, 94566

Tel: (925) 463-3300 Fax: (925) 463-1571

General contracting.

Dillingham Construction Pty. Ltd., Ste. 801, 80 Alfred St., Milsons Pt., NSW 2061, Australia

DO ALL COMPANY

254 North Laurel Ave., Des Plaines, IL, 60016

Tel: (847) 803-7380 Fax: (847) 699-7524

Distributors of machinery tools, metal cutting tools, instruments and industrial supplies.

DoAll Australia Pty. Ltd., 13-15 Cann St., Guildford, NSW 2161, Australia

DONALDSON COMPANY, INC.

1400 West 94th Street, Minneapolis, MN, 55431

Tel: (612) 887-3131 Fax: (612) 887-3155 Web site: www.Donaldson.com

Mfr. filtration systems and replacement parts.

Donaldson Australasia Pty. Ltd., PO Box 153, Wyong, NSW 2259, Australia

Tel: 61-2-4352-2022 Fax: 61-2-4351-2036 Contact: Allen Redman

DORR-OLIVER INC.

612 Wheeler's Farm Road, PO Box 3819, Milford, CT, 06460

Tel: (203) 876-5400 Fax: (203) 876-5432

Mfr. process equipment for food, pulp & paper, mineral & chemicals industry; & municipal/industry waste treatment.

Dorr-Oliver Pty. Ltd., 1 Central Ave., Thornleigh, NSW 2120, Australia

DOVER CORPORATION

280 Park Ave., New York, NY, 10017-1292

Tel: (212) 922-1640 Fax: (212) 922-1656 Web site: www.dovercorporation.com

Elevator manufacturer and holding company for varied industries.

Australian Elevator, 14 Production Ave., PO Biox 295, Kogarah 2217, N.S.W., Australia

Tel: 61-2-588-7999 Fax: 61-2-588-3835

THE DOW CHEMICAL COMPANY

2030 Dow Center, Midland, MI, 48674

Tel: (517) 636-1000 Fax: (517) 636-3228 Web site: www.atdow.com

Mfr. chemicals, plastics, pharmaceuticals, agricultural products, consumer products.

Dow Chemical (Australia) Ltd., 1000 Miller St., N. Sydney, NSW 2060, Australia

DOW CORNING CORPORATION

2220 West Salzburg Road, PO Box 1767, Midland, MI, 48640

Tel: (517) 496-4000 Fax: (517) 496-6080

Silicones, silicon chemicals, solid lubricants.

Dow Corning Australia Pty. Ltd., 21 Tattersall Rd., Blacktown, NSW 2148, Australia

DRAKE BEAM MORIN INC.

101 Huntington Ave., Boston, MA, 02199

Tel: (617) 450-9860 Fax: (617) 267-2011 Web site: www.dbm.com

Human resource management consulting & training.

DBM Australia - Pacific Reg. Hdqtrs., Level 6, 100 Walker St., North Sydney, NSW 2060, Australia (Locations:Adelaide, Brisbane, Canberra, Darwin, Melbourne, Parrametta, Perth, Tasmania,Townsville.)

Tel: 61-2-9966-1600 Fax: 61-2-9966-1500

DRAVO CORPORATION

11 Stanwix Street, 11th Fl., Pittsburgh, PA, 15222

Tel: (412) 995-5500 Fax: (412) 995-5570

Material handling equipment and process plants.

Dravo Pty. Ltd., 30 Atchnson St., St. Leonards, NSW 2065, Australia

DRESSER INDUSTRIES INC.

2001 Ross Ave., PO Box 718, Dallas, TX, 75221-0718

Tel: (214) 740-6000 Fax: (214) 740-6584 Web site: www.dresser.com

Diversified supplier of equipment & technical services to energy & natural resource industrial.

Dresser Australia Pty. Ltd., 79 Spine St., Sumner Park, Qld. 4074 Australia

M-I Australia Pty. Ltd., 251 Adelaide Terrace, Perth, WA 6000, Australia

E.I. DU PONT DE NEMOURS & COMPANY

1007 Market Street, Wilmington, DE, 19898

Tel: (302) 774-1000 Fax: (302) 774-7321 Web site: www.dupont.com

Mfr./sale diversified chemicals, plastics, specialty products and fibers.

DuPont (Australia) Ltd., PO Box 930, N. Sydney, NSW 2060, Australia

THE DUN & BRADSTREET CORPORATION

One Diamond Hill Road, Murray Hill, NJ, 07974

Tel: (908) 665-5000 Fax: (908) 665-5524 Web site: www.dnbcorp.com

Provides corporate credit, marketing & accounts-receivable management services & publishes credit ratings & financial information.

Moody's Investors Service Pty. Ltd., Level 10, 55 Hunter St., Sydney, NSW 2000, Australia

Tel: 61-2-9270-8111

DURACELL INTERNATIONAL INC.

Berkshire Industrial Park, Bethel, CT, 06801

Tel: (203) 796-4000 Fax: (203) 796-4745

Mfr. batteries.

Duracell Australia Pty. Ltd., PO Box 146, North Ryde, NSW 2113, Australia

DYNATECH CORPORATION

3 New England Executive Park, Burlington, MA, 01803

Tel: (781) 272-6100 Fax: (781) 272-2304

Develop/mfr. communications equipment.

Dynatech Communications Australia, Chatswood, Australia

EASTMAN CHEMICAL

100 North Eastman Road, Kingsport, TN, 37660

Tel: (423) 229-2000 Fax: (423) 229-1351 Web site: www.eastman.com

Mfr. plastics, chemicals, fibers.

Eastman Chemical Ltd., Level 8, 15 Talavera Rd., North Ryde, N.S.W. 2113 Sydney, Australia

Tel: 61-2-9878-0014 Fax: 61-2-9870-4488 Contact: Darren Ackland

EASTMAN KODAK COMPANY

343 State Street, Rochester, NY, 14650

Tel: (716) 724-4000 Fax: (716) 724-0663

Develop/mfr. photo & chemicals products, information management/video/copier systems, fibers/plastics for various industry.

Kodak (Australasia) Pty. Ltd., PO Box 90, 173 Elizabeth St., Coburg, VIC 3058, Australia

Kodak (Australasia) Pty. Ltd., Also in Adelaide, Brisbane, Canberra, Hobart, Launceston, Newcastle, Perth, Sydney & Townsville, Australia

EATON CORPORATION

1111 Superior Ave., Cleveland, OH, 44114

Tel: (216) 523-5000 Fax: (216) 479-7068

Advanced technical products for transportation & industrial markets.

Eaton Pty. Ltd., 33-35 Garden St., Kilsyth, VIC 3137, Australia

EATON CORP/CUTLER HAMMER

4201 North 27th Street, Milwaukee, WI, 53216

Tel: (414) 449-6000 Fax: (414) 449-6221

Electric control apparatus, mfr. of advanced technologic products.

Cutler-Hammer Australia Pty. Ltd., PO Box 66, Concord West, NSW 2138, Australia

ECHLIN INC.

100 Double Beach Road, Branford, CT, 06405

Tel: (203) 481-5751 Fax: (203) 481-6485 Web site: www.echlin.com

Supplies commercial vehicle components and auto fluid handling systems for the used car market

Echlin Inc., Sydney, Australia

ECOLAB INC.

Ecolab Center, 370 N. Wabasha Street, St. Paul, MN, 55102

Tel: (612) 293-2233 Fax: (612) 225-3105 Web site: www.ecolab.com

Develop/mfr. premium cleaning, sanitizing and maintenance products and services for the hospitality, institutional, and residential markets.

Ecolab Ltd., Sydney, Australia

Tel: 61-2-9680-5444

EDELMAN PUBLIC RELATIONS WORLDWIDE

200 East Randolph Drive, 63rd Floor, Chicago, IL, 60601

Tel: (312) 240-3000 Fax: (312) 240-0596 Web site: www.edelman.com

International independent public relations firm.

Edelman PR Worldwide, Level 24, AGL Building 111 Pacific Highway, North Sydney, NSW 2060, Australia

Tel: 61-2-9936-5500 Fax: 61-2-6636-5555 Contact: Robyn Sefiani

Edelman Sydney Worldwide, Level 24, AGL Building 111 Pacific Highway, North Sydney, NSW 2060, Australia

Tel: 61-2-9936-5500 Fax: 61-2-9936-5555 Contact: John MacGregor, Mng. Dir.

EDISON INTERNATIONAL

2244 Walnut Grove Ave., Rosemead, CA, 91770

Tel: (626) 302-1212 Fax: (626) 302-2517 Web site: www.edisonx.com

Utility holding company

Edison Mission Energy, Sydney, Australia

EDISON MISSION ENERGY

18101 Von Karman Ave., Ste. 1700, Irvine, CA, 92612-1046

Tel: (714) 752-5588 Fax: (714) 752-5624 Web site: www.edisonx.com

Global power producer.

Mission Energy Holdings Pty. Ltd., Level 20, HWT Tower, 40 City Rd., South Melbourne 3205 VIC, Australia

Tel: 61-3-9696-6477 Fax: 61-3-9696-8420 Contact: Gregory C. Hoppe, Reg. VP & Dir.

J.D. EDWARDS & COMPANY

One Technology Way, Denver, CO, 80237

Tel: (303) 334-4000 Fax: (303) 334-4970 Web site: www.jdedwards.com.

Computer software products.

JDE Australia, 1060 Hay St., 2nd Fl., West Perth, WA, Australia

Tel: 61-9-322-2523 Fax: 61-9-322-2118

JDE Australia, 465 Auburn Rd., Hawthorne, VIC 3122, Melbourne, VIC, Australia 3004

Tel: 61-3-9823-5111 Fax: 61-3-9824-8392

JDE Australia, Hdqtrs., 230 Victoria Rd., 1st Fl., PO Box 782, Glensville, NSW, Australia 2111

Tel: 61-2-816-3100 Fax: 61-2-879-6429

EG&G INC.

45 William Street, Wellesley, MA, 02181-4078

Tel: (781) 237-5100 Fax: (781) 431-4114

Diversified R/D, mfr. & services.

EG&G Sealol (Australia) Pty. Ltd., Unit 1, 59 Alexander Ave., Taren Point, NSW 2229, Australia

ELECTRONIC ARTS INC.

1450 Fashion Island Boulevard, San Mateo, CA, 94404

Tel: (650) 571-7171 Fax: (650) 286-5137 Web site: www.ea.com

Distribution and sales of entertainment software.

Electronic Arts Ltd., Melbourne, Australia

EMC CORP.

35 Parkwood Drive, Hopkinton, MA, 01748-9103

Tel: (508) 435-1000 Fax: (508) 435-8884 Web site: www.emc.com

Designs/supplies intelligent enterprise storage & retrieval technology for open systems, mainframes & midrange environments.

EMC Computer Systems - Australia, Level 6/110 Walker St., North Sydney, NSW 2060, Australia

Tel: 61-2-9922-7888 Fax: 61-2-9922-4287

EMC Computer Systems - Australia, Level 8, 1 Collins St., Melbourne, VIC 3000, Australia

Tel: 61-3-9654-7755

EMC Computer Systems - Australia, Level 6, Advance Bank Centre, 60 Marcus Clarke St., Canberra ACT 2601, Australia

Tel: 61-2-6243-4810

EMCO WHEATON INC.

409A Airport Blvd, Morrisville, NC, 27560

Tel: (919) 467-5878 Fax: (919) 467-7718

Mfr. petroleum handling equipment.

Wheaton Australia Pty. Ltd., 4 Stanton Rd., PO Box 355, Seven Hills, NSW 2147, Australia

EMERY WORLDWIDE

One Lagoon Drive, Ste. 400, Redwood City, CA, 94065

Tel: (650) 596-9600 Fax: (650) 596-7901 Web site: www.emeryworld.com

Freight transport, global logistics and air cargo.

Emery Worldwide, 25-27 Tullamarine Park Rd., Tullamarine,VIC 3043, Australia

ENCYCLOPAEDIA BRITANNICA INC.

310 S. Michigan Ave., Chicago, IL, 60604

Tel: (312) 427-9700 Fax: (312) 294-2176 Web site: www.E.B.com

Publishing; books.

Encyclopaedia Britannica Inc., 12 Anella Ave., Castle Hill, NSW 2154, Australia

ENDO LABORATORIES INC.

500 Endo Boulevard, Garden City, NY, 11530

Tel: (516) 522-3300 Fax:

Ethical pharmaceuticals.

Endo Labs, PO Box 232, Gordon, NSW 2071, Australia

ERIEZ MAGNETICS

PO Box 10652, Erie, PA, 16514

Tel: (814) 833-9881 Fax: (814) 833-3348

Mfr. magnets, vibratory feeders, metal detectors, screeners/sizers, mining equipment, current separators.

Eriez Magnetics Pty. Ltd., PO Box 427, Fawkner, VIC 3060, Australia

ERNST & YOUNG, LLP

787 Seventh Ave., New York, NY, 10019

Tel: (212) 773-3000 Fax: (212) 773-6350 Web site: www.eyi.com

Accounting and audit, tax and management consulting services.

Ernst & Young, Waterfront Place, 1 Eagle St., Brisbane QLD 4000, Australia

Ernst & Young, 33 Argyle St., Parramatta NSW 2150, Australia

Ernst & Young, 120 Collins Stret, Melbourne VIC 3000, Australia

Tel: 61-3-9288-8000 Fax: 61-3-9654-6166 Contact: Trevor Tappenden

Ernst & Young, Corporate Centre One, 2 Corporate Court, Bundall QLD 4217, Australia

Ernst & Young, 2nd Fl., 9-11 Cavenaugh St., Darwin NT 0800, Australia

Ernst & Young, Ernst & Young House, 54 Marcus Clarke St., Canberra ACT 2600, Australia

Ernst & Young, 152 St. Georges Terrace, Perth WA 6000, Australia

Ernst & Young, The Ernst & Young Building, 321 Kent St., Sydney NSW 2000, Australia

Tel: 61-2-9248-4466 Fax: 61-2-9248-4190 Contact: Brian Schwartz

Ernst & Young, Level 21, 91 King Willaim St., Adelaide SA 5000, Australia

Tel: 61-8-8238-4120 Fax: 61-8-8410-4661 Contact: Philip Pledge

ESTEE LAUDER INTERNATIONAL INC.

767 Fifth Ave., New York, NY, 10153

Tel: (212) 572-4200 Fax: (212) 572-3941

Cosmetics, perfumes & Aveda hair care products.

Estee Lauder (Australia) Pty. Ltd., GPO Box 4307, Sydney, NSW 2001, Australia

EURO RSCG Worldwide

350 Hudson Street, New York, NY, 10014

Tel: (212) 886-2000 Fax: (212) 886-2016

International advertising agency group.

Euro RSCG Partnerships, Sydney, Australia

EXE TECHNOLOGIES, INC.

12740 Hillcrest Road, Dallas, TX, 75230

Tel: (972) 233-3761 Fax: (972) 788-4208 Web site: www.exe.com

Provides a complete line of supply chain management execution software for WMS.

EXE Technologies, Inc. Melbourne, 72 Market St., South Melbourne, VIC 3205, Australia

Tel: 61-3-9645-7100 Fax: 61-3-9645-7066

EXE Technologies, Inc. Sydney, 91 Phillip St., Ste. 23, Level 7, Parramatta, NSW 2150, Australia

Tel: 61-2-9893-1860 Fax: 61-2-9893-1836

EXPEDITORS INTERNATIONAL OF WASHINGTON INC.

999 Throd Ave., Ste. 2500, Seattle, WA, 98104

Tel: (206) 674-3400 Fax: (206) 682-9777 Web site: www.expd.com

Air/ocean freight forwarding, customs brokerage, international logistics solutions.

Expeditors International Pty. Ltd., PO Box 624, Mascot, NSW 2020, Australia (Locations: Eagle Farm, QLD; Tullamarine, VIC; Welshpool, WA;

EXXON CORPORATION

225 E. John W. Carpenter Freeway, Irving, TX, 75062-2298

Tel: (972) 444-1000 Fax: (972) 444-1882 Web site: www.exxon.com

Petroleum exploration, production, refining; mfr. petroleum & chemicals products; coal & minerals.

Delhi Petroleum Pty. Ltd., 360 Elizabeth St., Melbourne, Vic. 3000, Australia

Esso Australia Ltd., 360 Elizabeth St., Melbourne, Vic. 3000, Australia

Esso Australia Resources Ltd., 360 Elizabeth St., Melbourne, Vic. 3000, Australia

Exxon Chemical - Kemcor, Kororoit Rd., Altona, Australia

FAIRMONT TAMPER

415 North Main Street, Fairmont, MN, 56031

Tel: (507) 235-3361 Fax: (507) 235-7370

Mfr./services railroad track maintenance-of-way equipment.

Tamper Australia, PO Box 5287, Brandale, Qld 4500, Australia

FARREL CORPORATION

25 Main Street, Ansonia, CT, 06401

Tel: (203) 736-5500 Fax: (203) 735-6267

Mfr. polymer processing equipment.

A. Boninan & Co. Ltd., PO Box 21, Broadmeadow, NSW 2292, Australia

FEDERAL-MOGUL CHAMPION SPARK PLUG COMPANY

900 Upton Ave., Toledo, OH, 43607

Tel: (419) 535-2567 Fax: (419) 535-2332

Mfr. spark plugs, wiper blades and related products.

Champion Spark Plug Co. (Australia) Pty. Ltd., 83 Bourke Rd., Alexandria, NSW 2015, Australia

FEDERAL-MOGUL CORPORATION

26555 Northwestern Highway, PO Box 1966, Southfield, MI, 48034

Tel: (248) 354-7700 Fax: (248) 354-8983 Web site: www.federalmogul.com

Mfr./distributor precision parts for automobiles, trucks, farm and construction vehicles.

Federal-Mogul Pty. Ltd., Sydney, Australia

FERRO CORPORATION

1000 Lakeside Ave., Cleveland, OH, 44114-1183

Tel: (216) 641-8580 Fax: (216) 696-5784 Web site: www.ferro.com

Mfr. Specialty chemicals, coatings, plastics, colors, refractories.

Ferro Chemicals Division -Footscray Operation, 469 Somerville Rd., West Footscray, 3012, VIC, Australia

Tel: 61-3-314-6977 Fax: 61-3-314-5045

Ferro Chemicals Division -Geelong Plant, 39 Roseneath St., North Geelong, 3215, VIC, Australia

Tel: 61-5-278-7666 Fax: 61-5-278-5992

Ferro Corp. (Australia) Pty. Ltd., PO Box 231, 105-115 Cochranes Rd., Moorabbin, VIC 3189, Australia

Tel: 61-3-555-9466 Fax: 61-3-555-7812 Contact: David Moseley, Mng. Dir.

FIDUCIARY TRUST COMPANY OF NY

2 World Trade Center, 94th Fl., New York, NY, 10048

Tel: (212) 466-4100 Fax: (212) 313-2662

Banking services.

Fiduciary Trust (Intl.) SA, Sydney, Australia

FileNET CORPORATION

3565 Harbor Boulevard, Costa Mesa, CA, 92626

Tel: (714) 966-3400 Fax: (714) 966-3490 Web site: www.filenet.com

Provides integrated document management (IDM) software and services for internet and client server-based imaging, workflow, cold and electronic document imanagement solutions.

FileNET Corp. Pty. Ltd., Level 22, Australia Square, 264-278 George St., Sydney, NSW 2000, Australia

Tel: 61-2-9273-9900 Fax: 61-2-9273-9950 Contact: Anna Scorciapino, Mgr.

FILTRA SYSTEMS/HYDROMATION

4000 Town Center, Ste. 1000, Southfield, MI, 48075-1410

Tel: (248) 356-9090 Fax: (248) 356-2812

Industrial filter systems.

Hydromation Austral Pty. Ltd., PO Box 54, Colchester Rd., Bayswater, VIC 3153, Australia

FIRST CHICAGO NBD CORPORATION

One First National Plaza, Chicago, IL, 60670

Tel: (312) 732-4000 Fax: (312) 732-4000 Web site: www.fcnbd.com

Financial products and services.

First National Bank of Chicago, Level 4, 70 Hindmarsh Square, GPO Box 858, Adelaid, SA 5001, Adelaide, SA 5000, Australia

Tel: 61-8-8228-2222 Fax: 61-8-8223-2948 Contact: Kevin Osborn, Branch Manager

First National Bank of Chicago, Level 32, Margaret St., Sydney, NSW 2000, Australia

Tel: 61-2-9250-2100 Fax: 61-2-9223-1823 Contact: Kevin Osborn, Branch Manager

First National Bank of Chicago, Level 19, 90 Collins St., Melbourne, VIC 3000, Australia

Tel: 61-3-9650-1388 Fax: 61-3-9650-2721 Contact: Kevin Osborn, Branch Manager

FIRST DATA CORPORATION

401 Hackensack Ave., Hackensack, NJ, 07601

Tel: (201) 525-4700 Fax: (201) 342-0401 Web site: www.firstdatacorp.com

Information and transaction processing services.

FDR Australia, 229 Pacific Highway, North Sydney, NSW 2060 Australia

Tel: 61-2-9959-7333 Fax: 61-2-9929-7998 Contact: Greg Nash, Mng. Dir.

FIRST NATIONAL BANK OF CHICAGO

One First National Plaza, Chicago, IL, 60670

Tel: (312) 732-4000 Fax: (312) 732-3620

Financial services.

First Chicago Australia Ltd., First Chicago House, 33 Pitt St., GPO Box 4293, Sydney, NSW 2000, Australia

FISCHER IMAGING CORPORATION

12300 North Grant Street, Denver, CO, 80241

Tel: (303) 452-6800 Fax: (303) 452-4335 Web site: www.fischerimaging.com

Mfr. x-ray equipment.

Fischer Imaging Australia Pty. Ltd., 5 Fir St., Redwood Gardens Estate, Dingley, VIC 3172, Australia

Tel: 61-3-9551-8166

FISERV INC.

PO Box 979, 255 Fiserv Drive, Brookfield, WI, 53008-0979

Tel: (414) 879-5000 Fax: (414) 879-5013 Web site: www.fiserv.com

Data processing products and services for the financial industry.

Fiserv Australia Pty. Ltd., 100 Walker St., Ste. 13, Level 11, North Sydney, NSW 2060, Australia

FISHER-ROSEMOUNT

8000 Maryland Ave., Ste. 500, Clayton, MO, 63105-4755

Tel: (314) 746-9900 Fax: (314) 746-9974

Mfr. industrial process control equipment.

Fisher-Rosemount Pty. Ltd., 5 Cross St., East Brunswick, VIC 3058, Australia

Fisher-Rosemount Pty. Ltd., 141 Walcott St., Mt. Lawley, WA 6050, Australia

Fisher-Rosemount Pty. Ltd., 471 Mountain Highway, Bayswater, VIC 3153, Australia

Tel: 61-3-9721-0200 Fax: 61-3-9720-4215

Fisher-Rosemount Pty. Ltd., 102 Hassall St., Wetherill Park, NSW 2164, Australia

Southern Controls Pty. Ltd., 4 King St., Blackburn, VIC 3108, Australia

C.B. FLEET CO., INC.

4615 Murray Place, PO Box 11349, Lynchburg, VA, 24506

Tel: (804) 528-4000 Fax: (804) 847-4219 Web site: www.dewitt.com

Mfr. pharmaceutical, health and beauty aids.

DeWitt International (Australia) Pty. Ltd., 25 Macbeth St., Braeside, Vic. 3195, Australia

FLINT INK CORPORATION

25111 Glendale Ave., Detroit, MI, 48239-2689

Tel: (313) 538-6800 Fax: (313) 538-3538 Web site: www.flintink.com

Manufacturer of printing inks and pigments.

Flink Ink Corporation, 320 Curtin Ave. West, Eagle Farm, QllD 4007, Brisbane, Australia

Tel: 61-7-3868-3000 Fax: 61-7-3868-3003 Contact: Charles Miller, Pres. Asia/Pacific

Flink Ink Corporation, 18-20 Robert St., Rozelle, NSW 2039, Sydney, Australia

Tel: 61-2-9810-7022 Fax: 61-2-9818-5297 Contact: Charles Miller, Pres. Asia/Pacific

Flink Ink Corporation, Lot 19-20 Berends Drive, Dandenong South 3164, Melbourne, Australia

Tel: 61-2-9768-2444 Fax: 61-3-9768-2555 Contact: Charles Miller, Pres. Asia/Pacific

Flint Ink Corporation Australia Pty. Ltd., 1/96 Willarong Rd., Caringbah, N.S.W. 229, Australia

Tel: 61-2-9540-4866 Fax: 61-2-9540-4867 Contact: Charles Miller, Pres. Asia/Pacific

FLOWSERVE CORPORATION

222 W. Los Cloinas Blvd., Irving, TX, 75039

Tel: (972) 443-6500 Fax: (972) 443-6858 Web site: www.flowserve.com

Mfr. chemicals equipment, pumps, valves, filters, fans and heat exchangers.

Valtek Australia, 10 Thorogood St., Victoria Park, WA 6100, Australia

Valtek Australia, 14 Dalmore Dr., Scoresby, VIC 3179, Australia

Tel: 61-3-976-48522

FLOWSERVE FLUID SEALING DIVISION

222 Los Colinas Blvd., Ste. 1500, Irving, TX, 75039

Tel: (616) 381-2650 Fax: (616) 443-6800 Web site: www.flowserve.com

Mfr. mechanical seals, compression packings and auxiliaries.

Petch/Durametallic (Australia) Pty. Ltd., 24 Underwood Ave., PO Box 210, Botany, NSW 2019, Australia

FLUKE CORPORATION

PO Box 9090, Everett, WA, 98206-9090

Tel: (425) 347-6100 Fax: (425) 356-5116 Web site: www.fluke.com

Mfr. electronic test tools.

Fluke Electronics, Sydney, Australia

FLUOR DANIEL INC.

3353 Michelson Drive, Irvine, CA, 92698

Tel: (714) 975-2000 Fax: (714) 975-5271 Web site: www.flourdaniel.com

Engineering & construction services.

Fluor Daniel Australia Ltd., 616 St. Kilda Rd., GPO Box 1320L, Melbourne, Vic. 3001, Australia

Tel: 61-3-9268-6000 Fax: 61-3-9268-6001

Fluor Daniel Australia Ltd., 5th Fl., 22 Mount St., Perth, WA 6000, Australia

FMC CORPORATION

200 E. Randolph Drive, Chicago, IL, 60601

Tel: (312) 861-6000 Fax: (312) 861-6141

Produces chemicals & precious metals, mfr. machinery, equipment & systems for industrial, agricultural & government use.

FMC (Australia) Ltd., Sydney, Australia

FOOT LOCKER USA

233 Broadway, New York, NY, 10279

Tel: (212) 720-3700 Fax: (212) 553-2042

Mfr./sales shoes and sneakers.

Foot Locker, Avalon Mall 48 Kenmount Rd., St. John's, NF A1B1W3, Australia

Tel: 61-7-9739-7419

Foot Locker, Truro Mall 245 Robie St., Truro, NS B2N5N6, Australia

Tel: 61-9-2893-1373

Foot Locker, Highland Square 689 Westville Rd., New Glasgow, NS B2H2S, Australia

Tel: 61-9-2752-8675

Foot Locker, Mayflower Mall 800 Grand Lake Rd., Sydney, NS B1P6S, Australia

Tel: 61-9-2539-9599

Foot Locker, The Village Mall 430 Topsail Rd., St. John's, NF A1E4N, Australia

Tel: 61-7-9364-8872

Foot Locker, Valley Mall Mount Bernard & Harold Ave.,Cornerbrook, NF A2H6G1, Australia

Tel: 61-7-9639-1005

FORD MOTOR COMPANY

The American Road, Dearborn, MI, 48121

Tel: (313) 322-3000 Fax: (313) 322-9600 Web site: www.ford.com

Mfr./sales motor vehicles.

Ford Motor Co. of Australia Ltd., 1735 Sydney Rd., Campbell Field, VIC 3601, Australia

FORRESTER RESEARCH, INC.

1033 Massachusetts Ave., Cambridge, MA, 02138

Tel: (617) 497-7090 Fax: (617) 868-0577 Web site: www.forrester.com

Provides clients an analysis of the effect of changing technologies on their operations.

SPL - Chariot, 28 Riddell Parade, Elsternwick, VIC 3185, Australia
Tel: 61-3-9530-0481 Fax: 61-3-6532-8693 Contact: Michael McDeemott, Mgr.

FORTÉ SOFTWARE, INC.
1800 Harrison Street, Oakland, CA, 94612
Tel: (510) 869-3400 Fax: (510) 869-3480 Web site: www.forte.com
Developer computer software applications.
Forté Software Pty. Ltd., Ste. 1, Level 3, 100 Walker St., North Sydney, NSW 2060, Australia
Tel: 61-3-9684-7711 Fax: 61-3-9699-5477
Forté Software Pty. Ltd., IBM Tower, Level 10, 60 City Rd., Southgate VIC 3006, Australia
Tel: 61-2-9926-1400 Fax: 61-2-9926-1401

FORTUNE BRANDS
1700 East Putnam Ave., Old Greenwich, CT, 06870
Tel: (203) 698-5000 Fax: (203) 637-2580
Mfr. diversified consumer products including Masterbrand, Acco office products, Jim Bean distillery products, Footjoy and Titleist golf products.
Acco Australia Ltd., 27 Clarinda, Locked Bag 8, S. Oakleigh, VIC 3166, Australia

FOSTER WHEELER CORPORATION
Perryville Corporate Park, Clinton, NJ, 08809-4000
Tel: (908) 730-4000 Fax: (908) 730-5300
Manufacturing, engineering and construction.
Foster Wheeler Australia Pty. Ltd., 63 Wadham Parade, Mount Waverly, VIC 3149, Australia

FOUR WINDS INTERNATIONAL GROUP
1500 SW First Ave., Ste. 850, Portland, OR, 97201-2013
Tel: (503) 241-2732 Fax: (503) 241-1829 Web site: www.vanlines.com.au
Transportation of household goods and general cargo and third party logistics.
Four Winds International Australia, PO Box 259, Sydney, NSW 2145, Sudytslis, Australia
Tel: 61-2-9896-3811 Fax: 61-2-9896-4345 Contact: Sid Valleydam, Pres. Emp: 102

FRANK RUSSELL COMPANY
909 A Street, Tacoma, WA, 98402
Tel: (253) 572-9500 Fax: (253) 591-3495 Web site: www.russell.com
Investment management & asset strategy consulting.
Frank Russell Co. Pty. Ltd., GPO Box 5291, Sydney, NSW 2001, Australia
Tel: 61-2-9377-8200 Fax: 61-2-9251-5864 Contact: Meredith Brooks, Mng. Dir. Emp: 43

FRANKLIN COVEY CO.
2200 W. Parkway Blvd., Salt Lake City, UT, 84119-2331
Tel: (801) 975-1776 Fax: (801) 977-1431 Web site: www.franklinquest.com
Provides productivity and time management products and seminars.
Franklin Covey Australia, GPO Box 2769, Brisbane, QLD 4001, Australia
Tel: 61-7-3259-0222 Fax: 61-7-3369-7810
Franklin Covey Australia, Ste. 4602, Level 46, MLC Centre, 19-29 Martin Place, Sydney, NSW 2000, Australia
Tel: 61-2-9221-5311 Fax: 61-2-9221-7811
Franklin Covey Australia, Level 2, 492 St. Kilda Rd., Melbourne, VIC 3004, Australia
Tel: 61-3-9804-5099 Fax: 61-3-9804-5710

FRANKLIN ELECTRIC CO., INC.
400 East Spring Street, Bluffton, IN, 46714-3798
Tel: (219) 824-2900 Fax: (219) 824-2909 Web site: www.fele.com
Mfr./distribute electric motors, submersible motors and controls.
Franklin Electric (Australia) Pty. Ltd., Frankston Rd., PO Box 167, Dandenong, VIC 3175, Australia

THE FRANKLIN MINT

US Route 1, Franklin Center, PA, 19091

Tel: (610) 459-6000 Fax: (610) 459-6880

Design/marketing collectibles & luxury items.

Franklin Mint Pty. Ltd., 3 International Court, Caribbean Gardens, Scoresby, VIC. 3179, Australia

FRANKLIN RESOURCES, INC.

777 Mariners Island Blvd., San Mateo, CA, 94404

Tel: (415) 312-2000 Fax: (415) 312-3655 Web site: www.frk.com

Global and domestic investment advisory and portfolio management.

Templeton Investment Management (Australia), Ltd., Sydney, Australia

FREEPORT-McMoRAN COPPER & GOLD INC.

1615 Poydras Street, New Orleans, LA, 70112

Tel: (504) 582-4000 Fax: (504) 582-4899 Web site: www.fex.com

Natural resources exploration and processing.

Freeport of Australia Inc., PO Box 280, Collins St., Melbourne, VIC 3000, Australia

FRITZ COMPANIES INC.

706 Mission Street, Ste. 900, San Francisco, CA, 94103

Tel: (415) 904-8360 Fax: (415) 904-8661 Web site: www.fritz.com

Integrated transportation, sourcing, distribution & customs brokerage services.

Fritz Companies Inc., Adelaide, Bribbane, Burnie, Canberra, Hobart, Melbourne, Newcastle, Perth & Sydney, Australia

H.B. FULLER COMPANY

1200 Willow Lake Blvd., Vadnais Heights, MN, 55110

Tel: (612) 236-5900 Fax: (612) 236-5898 Web site: www.hbfuller.com

Mfr./distributor adhesives, sealants, coatings, paints, waxes, sanitation chemicals.

H.B. Fuller Co. Australia Pty. Ltd., 16-22 Red Gum Drive, Dandenong South, VIC 3175, Melbourne, Australia (Locations: Gladesville,NSW; Milperra, NSW; Welshpool, WA; Virginia, QLD; Somerton Park, SA..)

Tel: 61-3-9706-5733 Fax: 61-3-9797-6266

GAF CORPORATION

1361 Alps Road, Wayne, NJ, 07470

Tel: (973) 628-3000 Fax: (973) 628-3326 Web site: www.gaf.com

Mfr. building materials.

GAF (Australasia) Pty. Ltd., PO Box 18, N. Melbourne, VIC 3051, Australia

GAF Australia, PO Box 110, Beaconsfield, NSW 2015, Australia

GAFFNEY CLINE & ASSOCIATES INC.

PO Box 796309, Dallas, TX, 75379

Tel: (972) 733-1183 Fax: (972) 380-0180

Consultants to energy and mineral industrial.

Gaffney Cline & Assoc., 9th Fl., 2 O'Connell St., Sydney, NSW 2000, Australia

GARDNER-DENVER

1800 Gardner Expressway, Quincy, IL, 62301

Tel: (217) 222-5400 Fax: (217) 228-8247

Mfr. portable air compressors and related drilling accessories.

Gardner-Denver Mining & Construction, New South Wales, Australia

GARLOCK SEALING TECHNOLOGIES

1666 Division Street, Palmyra, NY, 14522

Tel: (315) 597-4811 Fax: (315) 597-3216 Web site: www.garlock-inc.com

Mfr. of gaskets, packing, seals and expansion joints.

Garlock Pty. Ltd., PO Box 54, Arncliffe, NSW 2205, Australia

Tel: 61-2-9597-4422 Fax: 61-2-9597-7729 Contact: Alan Haselden, Mng. Dir.

GARTNER GROUP, INC.

56 Top Gallant Road, Stamford, CT, 06904-2212

Tel: (203) 316-1111 Fax: (203) 316-1100 Web site: www.gartner.com

Information technology and research.

Gartner Group Pacific, 424 Upper Roma Street, 3rd Fl., Brisbane, QLD 4003, Australia

THE GATES RUBBER COMPANY

990 S. Broadway, PO Box 5887, Denver, CO, 80217-5887

Tel: (303) 744-1911 Fax: (303) 744-4000

Mfr. rubber tires/inner tubes & industrial belts & hose.

Gates Australia Pty. Ltd., 4-6 Conquest Way So., Hallam, Vic. 3803, Australia

GATX CAPITAL CORPORATION

Four Embarcadero Center, Ste. 2200, San Francisco, CA, 94111

Tel: (415) 955-3200 Fax: (415) 955-3449

Lease & loan financing, residual guarantees.

GATX/National Australia Bank, Level 25, NAB House, 255 George St., Sydney, NSW 2000, Australia

GENERAL BINDING CORPORATION

One GBC Plaza, Northbrook, IL, 60062

Tel: (847) 272-3700 Fax: (847) 272-1369

Binding and laminating equipment and associated supplies.

GBC Australia Pty. Ltd., PO Box 325, 19 Victoria Rd., Castle Hill, NSW 2154, Australia

GENERAL DATACOMM INC.

1579 Straits Turnpike, PO Box 1299, Middlebury, CT, 06762-1299

Tel: (203) 574-1118 Fax: (203) 758-8507

Mfr./sale/services transportation equipment for communications networks.

General DataComm Pty. Ltd., 275 Alfred St. North, North Sydney, NSW 2060, Australia

GENERAL ELECTRIC CAPITAL CORPORATION

260 Long Ridge Road, Stamford, CT, 06927

Tel: (203) 357-4000 Fax: (203) 357-6489

Financial, property/casualty insurance, computer sales and trailer leasing services.

Employers Reinsurance Corp. (ERC), Level 20, AMP Place, 10 Eagle St., Brisbane, QLD 4000, Australia

Tel: 61-7-3221-7911 Fax: 61-7-3221-7872

Employers Reinsurance Corp. (ERC), Level 12, 356 Collins St., Melbourne, VIC 3000, Australia

Tel: 61-3-9642-1122 Fax: 61-3-9642-1177

Employers Reinsurance Corp. (ERC), Level 34, Westpac Plaza, 60 Margaret St., Sydney, New South Wales 2000, Australia

Tel: 61-2-9394-2800 Fax: 61-2-9394-2822

GENERAL ELECTRIC CO.

3135 Easton Turnpike, Fairfield, CT, 06431

Tel: (203) 373-2211 Fax: (203) 373-3131 Web site: www.ge.com

Diversified manufacturing, technology and services.

GE Aircraft Engines, 15 Blue St., North Sydney 02060, Australia

Tel: 61-2-2957-9260

GE Capital Global Projects, Gellco Level 20, Sydney, NSW 2000, Australia

Tel: 61-2-2225-7913 Fax: 61-2-2233-6295

GE Capital Services GENSTAR container, 118 Mount St., 4th Fl., New South Wales 02060, Australia

Tel: 61-2-2959-3144

GE PC - Australia Pty. Ltd., 5/25 Isabella St., North Parramatt, NSW 02151, Australia

Tel: 61-2-9630-7529 Fax: 61-2-9630-7748

General Electric Co.-Australia, Australia, All mail to U.S. address; phone (800) 626-2004 or (518) 438-6500

GENERAL MOTORS ACCEPTANCE CORPORATION

100 Renaissance Center, Detroit, MI, 48243-7301

Tel: (313) 556-5000 Fax: (313) 556-5108 Web site: www.gmac.com

Automobile financing.

GMAC Australia, Also in Adelaide, Perth, Brisbane, Hobart, Sydney, Newcastle & Townsville, Australia

GMAC Australia, 499 St. Kilda Rd., PO Box 7425, Melbourne, VIC 3004, Australia

GENERAL MOTORS CORPORATION

100 Renaissance Center, Detroit, MI, 48243.7301

Tel: (313) 556-5000 Fax: (313) 556-5108 Web site: www.gm.com

Mfr. full line vehicles, automotive electronics, commercial technologies, telecommunications, space, finance.

General Motors-Holden's Ltd., GPO Box 1714, Melbourne, VIC 3001, Australia

GENERAL REINSURANCE CORPORATION

695 East Main Street, Stamford, CT, 06904-2350

Tel: (203) 328-5000 Fax: (203) 328-6423 Web site: www.genre.com

Reinsurance services worldwide.

Cologne Life Reinsurance Company of Australia Ltd., Level 14, 1 York St., Box N280, Grosvenor Place, Sydney NSW 2000, Australia

Tel: 61-2-9250-9700 Fax: 61-2-9252-3020 Contact: Roy E. Deane, Mng. Dir.

General and Cologne Reinsurance Australasia Ltd., Level 11, 12 Creek St., Brisbane QLD 4000, Australia

Tel: 61-7-3221-9611 Fax: 61-7-3221-6307 Contact: John R. Prout, Mgr.

General and Cologne Reinsurance Australasia Ltd., Level 22, 367 Collins St., Melbourne VIC 3000, Australia

Tel: 61-3-9620-4000 Fax: 61-3-9621-1599 Contact: David C. Duxson, Mgr.

General and Cologne Reinsurance Australasia Ltd., Level 22, 25 Grenfell St., Adelaide SA 5000, Australia

Tel: 61-8-8231-9099 Fax: 61-8-8231-9321 Contact: Richard Simpson, Mgr.

General and Cologne Reinsurance Australasia Ltd., Level 3, 55 St. Georges Terrace, Perth WA 6000, Australia

Tel: 61-8-9325-7711 Fax: 61-8-9221-1005 Contact: Derek W. Greengrass, Mgr.

General and Cologne Reinsurance Australasia Ltd., Level 13, 225 George St., Sydney, NSW 2000, Australia

Tel: 61-2-9336-8100 Fax: 61-2-9251-1665

GENICOM CORPORATION

14800 Conference Center Drive, Ste. 400, Chantilly, VA, 20151

Tel: (703) 802-9200 Fax: (703) 802-9039

Supplier of network systems, service & printer solutions.

Genicom Pty. Ltd., 175 Gibbes St., Unit 12, Chatswood, NSW 2067, Australia

Contact: Stuart Fathers

THE GEON COMPANY

One Geon Center, Avon Lake, OH, 44012

Tel: (440) 930-1000 Fax: (440) 930-3551

Mfr. vinyl resins & compounds.

The Geon Co., Altona & Mentone (Vic), Australia

GETZ BROS & CO., INC.

150 Post Street, Ste. 500, San Francisco, CA, 94108-4750

Tel: (415) 772-5500 Fax: (415) 772-5659 Web site: www.getz.com

Diversified manufacturing, marketing and distribution services and travel services.

Getz Bros. & Co. (Australia) Pty. Ltd., 16 Harker St., Burwood, VIC 3125, Australia

Tel: 61-3-9269-3100 Fax: 61-3-9269-3199 Contact: Paul Kelly, Gen. Mgr. Emp: 30

Innoka Pty. Ltd, 6/106 Old Pittwater Rd., Brookvale, NSW 2100, Australia

Tel: 61-2-9938-4111 Fax: 61-2-9938-4508 Contact: Victor Chua, Gen. Mgr. Emp: 100

Medtel, 5 Orion Rd., Lane Cove, NSW 2066, Australia

Tel: 61-2-9413-6222 Fax: 61-2-9418-7019 Contact: Graham Vale Emp: 100

THE GILLETTE COMPANY

Prudential Tower Building, Boston, MA, 02199

Tel: (617) 421-7000 Fax: (617) 421-7123 Web site: www.gillette.com

Develop/mfr. personal care/use products: blades & razors, toiletries, cosmetics, stationery.

Braun Industries Pty. Ltd., North Sydney, NSW, Australia

Contact: G. Bruce Dean

Gillette (Australia) Pty. Ltd., Scoresby, Australia

Gillette Management Pty. Ltd., Davidson, NSW, Australia

Gillette Services Pty. Ltd., Scoresby, Australia

Liquid Paper Export Pty. Ltd., Scoresby, Australia

Oral-B Laboratories Pty. Ltd., North Sydney, NSW, Australia

P.H. GLATFELTER COMPANY

228 South Main Street, Spring Grove, PA, 17362

Tel: (717) 225-4711 Fax: (717) 225-6834

Mfr. printing & specialty papers.

Ecusta Australia Pty. Ltd., 2-10 Amex Ave., Girraween, Sydney, NSW 2145, Australia

GLOBAL MARINE INC

777 North Eldridge, Houston, TX, 77079

Tel: (281) 496-8000 Fax: (281) 531-1260 Web site: www.glm.com

Offshore contract drilling, turnkey drilling, oil & gas exploration & production.

Global Marine Inc., Freemantle, Australia

GODIVA CHOCOLATIER INC.

355 Lexington Ave., New York, NY, 10017

Tel: (212) 984-5900 Fax: (212) 984-5901

Mfr. chocolate candy, Biscotti dipping cookies and after-dinner coffees.

Godiva Chocolatier, Inc., Sydney, Australia

GOLDMAN SACHS & COMPANY

85 Broad Street, New York, NY, 10004

Tel: (212) 902-1000 Fax: (212) 902-3000 Web site: www.gs.com

Investment bankers; securities broker dealers.

Goldman, Sachs Australia L.L.C., Level 48, Governor Phillip Tower, 1 Farrer Place, Sydney, NSW 2000, Australia

Tel: 61-2-9320-1000

THE GOODYEAR TIRE & RUBBER COMPANY

1144 East Market Street, Akron, OH, 44316

Tel: (330) 796-2121 Fax: (330) 796-1817 Web site: www.goodyear.com

Mfr. tires, automotive belts and hose, conveyor belts, chemicals; oil pipeline transmission.

Goodyear Australia Ltd., 11Grand Ave., Camellia, NSW 2142, Australia

GPU INTERNATIONAL, INC.

300 Madison Ave., Morristown, NJ, 07962-1911

Tel: (973) 455-8200 Fax: (973) 455-8582 Web site: www.gpu.com

Global electric energy company.

Solaris Power, Melbourne, Australia

W. R. GRACE & COMPANY

One Town Center Road, 1750 Clint Moore Road, Boca Raton, FL, 33486-1010

Tel: (561) 362-2000 Fax: (561) 561-2193 Web site: www.grace.com

Mfr. specialty chemicals and materials: packaging, health care, catalysts, construction, water treatment/process.

W.R. Grace Australia Ltd., 1126 Sydney Rd., Fawkner, VIC 3060, Australia

Tel: 61-3-9358-2244 Fax: 61-3-9357-3013

GRAHAM & JAMES LLP

One Maritime Plaza - Ste. 300, San Francisco, CA, 94111-3404

Tel: (415) 954-0200 Fax: (415) 391-2493 Web site: www.gj.com

International law firm.

Deacons Graham & James, Level 31, BankWest Tower, 1108 St. George's Terrace, Perth WA 6000, Australia

Tel: 61-9-426-3222 Fax: 61-9-324-1334 Contact: Michael Arnett

Deacons Graham & James, Gold Fields House, Circular Quay, Sydney NSW 2000, Australia

Tel: 61-2-9330-8000 Fax: 61-2-9330-8111 Contact: Martin Przybylski

Deacons Graham & James, 385 Bourke St., Melbourne VIC 3000, Australia

Tel: 61-3-9230-0411 Fax: 61-3-9230-0505 Contact: Robert Symons

Deacons Graham & James, Riverside Centre, 123 Eagle St., Brisbane QLD 4000, Australia

Tel: 61-7-3309-0888 Fax: 61-7-3309-0999 Contact: Donald R. Boyd

Deacons Graham & James, Level 9 National Mutual Centre, 15 London Circuit, Canberra ACT 2601, Australia

Tel: 61-6-274-0777 Fax: 61-6-274-0666 Contact: Mark Treffers

GRANT THORNTON INTERNATIONAL

800 One Prudential Plaza, 130 E. Randolph Drive, Chicago, IL, 60601-6050

Tel: (312) 856-0001 Fax: (312) 616-7052

Accounting, audit, tax and management consulting services.

Grant Thornton Intl, Level 5, Reserve Bank Bldg., King George Sq., 102 Adelaide St., GPO Box 1008, Brisbane QLD 4000, AS, Australia

Tel: 61-7-3221-8027 Fax: 61-7-3221-8895

Grant Thornton Intl, Level 15, B.T. Tower, 1 Market St., Sydney NSW 2000, Australia

Tel: 61-2-284-6666 Fax: 61-2-267-4000

Grant Thornton Intl, 67 Greenhill Rd., Wayville, GPO Box 1270, Adelaide SA 5001, Australia

Tel: 61-8-372-6666 Fax: 91-8-372-6677

Grant Thornton Intl, 500 Collins St., GPO Box 4369, Melbourne VIC 3000, Australia

Tel: 61-3-9614-1166 Fax: 61-3-9629-6752

Grant Thornton Intl, Level 6, 256 St. George's Terrace, POB 1213, Perth WA 6000, Australia

Tel: 61-9-481-1448 Fax: 61-9-481-0152

GRAPHIC CONTROLS CORPORATION

PO Box 1271, Buffalo, NY, 14240

Tel: (716) 853-7500 Fax: (716) 847-7551

Mfr. information, medical and physiological monitoring products.

Miller Graphic Controls Pty. Ltd., PO Box 199, Clifton Hill, VIC 3068, Australia

GREY ADVERTISING INC.

777 Third Ave., New York, NY, 10017

Tel: (212) 546-2000 Fax: (212) 546-1495 Web site: www.giworldwwide.com

International advertising agency.

Grey Australia, 470 St. Kilda Rd., 4th fl., Melbourne, VIC 3004, Australia

GROUNDWATER TECHNOLOGY INC

100 River Ridge Drive, Norwood, MA, 02062

Tel: (781) 769-7600 Fax: (781) 769-7992

Industrial site cleanup, management & consulting.

Groundwater Technology Inc., Unit 1, 410 Churchill Rd., Kilburn, SA 5084, Australia

Groundwater Technology Inc., 8/177 Beaver Rd., Northcote, VIC 3070, Australia

Groundwater Technology Inc., 3 Teakle Rd., Osborne Park, WA 6017, Australia

GTE CORPORATION

One Stamford Forum, Stamford, CT, 06904

Tel: (203) 965-2000 Fax: (203) 965-2277 Web site: www.gte.com

Electronic products, telecommunications systems, publishing and communications.

GTE, Sylvania Way, PO Box 450, Lisarow Gofford, NSW 2250, Australia

GUARDIAN INDUSTRIES CORPORATION

2300 Harmon Road, Auburn Hills, MI, 48326-1714

Tel: (248) 340-1800 Fax: (248) 340-9988

Mfr. and fabricate flat glass products and insulation materials.

Permaglass (Australia) Pty. Ltd., PO Box 339, Chring Bah, NSW 2229, Australia

Sydney Glass Co. Pty. Ltd., 578 Princes Hwy., St. Peters, NSW 2044, Australia

HALLMARK CARDS INC.

PO Box 419580, Kansas City, MO, 64141

Tel: (816) 274-5100 Fax: (816) 274-5061

Mfr. greeting cards and related products.

Hallmark Cards Australia Ltd., 611 Blackburn Rd., N. Clayton 3168, VIC, Australia

Tel: 61-3-9560-9033

HARCOURT BRACE & COMPANY

6277 Sea Harbor Drive, Orlando, FL, 32887

Tel: (407) 345-2000 Fax: (407) 345-9354

Book publishing, tests and related service, journals, facsimile reprints, management consult, operates parks/shows.

Harcourt Brace & Company Australia, Locked Bag 16, Marrickville, NSW 2204, Australia

Tel: 61-2-9517-8999 Fax: 61-2-9517-2249

HARNISCHFEGER INDUSTRIES INC

PO Box 554, Milwaukee, WI, 53201

Tel: (414) 797-6480 Fax: (414) 797-6573 Web site: www.harnischfeger.com

Mfr. mining and material handling equipment, papermaking machinery and computer systems.

Beloit International Pty. Ltd., Level 6, 100 Albert Rd., South Melbourne, VIC 3205, Australia

Harnischfeger of Australia Pty. Ltd., PO Box 231, East Brisbane, Qld 4169, Australia

Joy Manufacturing Co. Pty. Ltd., PO Box 178, Johnson Ave., Kurri Kurri, SNW 2327, Australia

Joy Manufacturing Co. Pty. Ltd., Vale Rd., PO Box 314, Moss Vale, NSW 2577, Australia

THE HARPER GROUP

260 Townsend Street, San Francisco, CA, 94107-1719

Tel: (415) 978-0600 Fax: (415) 978-0692 Web site: www.circleintl.com

Ocean/air freight forwarding, customs brokerage, packing and wholesale, logistics management and insurance.

Circle International (Australia) Pty. Ltd., 9-11 International Dr., Tullamarine, Vic. 3043, Australia

Tel: 61-3-933-54401 Fax: 61-3-9933-85263

Circle International (Australia) Pty. Ltd., Unit 8, Forwarders Complex, Perth International Airport, Newburn, Western Australia 6104

Circle International (Australia) Pty. Ltd., 1-3 Boronia Rd., Eagle Farm, Queensland 4007, Australia

Tel: 61-7-3860-4155 Fax: 61-7-3860-4157

Circle International (Australia) Pty. Ltd., 9-13 Underwood Ave., Botany, Sydney, NSW 2019, Australia

Tel: 61-2-666-5022 Fax: 61-2-316-5351

Circle International (Australia) Pty. Ltd., 2 Frank Collopy Court, Adelaide Airport, Adelaide, SA 5950, Australia

Tel: 61-8-234-4988 Fax: 61-8-234-4093

Circle International (Australia) Pty. Ltd., 9-11 International Drive, Tullamarine, Melbourne, VIC 3043, Australia

Tel: 61-3-933-54401 Fax: 61-3-933-85263

Circle International (Australia) Pty. Ltd., Grace Removals Bldg., Sheppard St., Hume, Canberra, ACT 2620, Australia

Tel: 61-6-260-1416 Fax: 61-6-260-1507

Circle International (Australia) Pty. Ltd., c/o T.A.C.S., 37 Dutton St., Cairns, Queensland 4870, Australia

Tel: 61-7-0312-055 Fax: 61-7-0312-070

HARSCO CORPORATION

PO Box 8888, Camp Hill, PA, 17001-8888

Tel: (717) 763-7064 Fax: (717) 763-6424

Metal reclamation and mill services, infrastructure and construction and process industry products.

Tamper (Australia) Pty. Ltd., 4 Strathwyn St., Strathpine, Qld 4500, Australia

Taylor-Wharton (Australia) Pty. Ltd., Unit 1, 882 Leslie Dr., Albury, NSW 2640, Australia

HEIDRICK & STRUGGLES INC

Sears Tower, 233 South Wacker Drive, Chicago, IL, 60606

Tel: (312) 496-1200 Fax: (312) 496-1290 Web site: www.h-s.com

Executive search firm.

Heidrick & Struggles Intl. Inc., Govenor Phillip Tower, 1 Farrer Place, Level 38, Sydney NSW 2000, Australia

Tel: 61-2-9247-9599 Fax: 61-2-9247-9117

H.J. HEINZ COMPANY

600 Grant Street, Pittsburgh, PA, 15219

Tel: (412) 456-5700 Fax: (412) 456-6128 Web site: www.heinz.com

Processed food products and nutritional services.

H.J. Heinz Australia Ltd., Doveton, Vic., Australia

HELLER FINANCIAL INC.

500 West Monroe Street, Chicago, IL, 60661

Tel: (312) 441-7000 Fax: (312) 441-7256

Financial services.

Heller Financial Inc., Sydney, Australia

HERCULES INC

Hercules Plaza, 1313 North Market Street, Wilmington, DE, 19894-0001

Tel: (302) 594-5000 Fax: (302) 594-5400 Web site: www.herc.com

Mfr. specialty chemicals, plastics, film and fibers, coatings, resins, food ingredients.

Australian Holdings Co. Ltd., 49-61 Stephen Rd., PO Box 59, Botany, NSW 2019, Australia

HEWITT ASSOCIATES LLC

100 Half Day Road, Lincolnshire, IL, 60069

Tel: (847) 295-5000 Fax: (847) 295-7634

Employee benefits consulting firm.

Hewitt Associates, Level 2, 395 Collins St., Melbourne, VIC 3000, Australia

Tel: 61-3-9614-6100

Hewitt Associates, Level 2, 88 George St., The Rocks, Sydney, NSW 2000, Australia

Tel: 61-2-9247-8066

HEWLETT-PACKARD COMPANY

3000 Hanover Street, Palo Alto, CA, 94304-0890

Tel: (650) 857-1501 Fax: (650) 857-7299 Web site: www.hp.com

Mfr. computing, communications & measurement products & services.

Hewlett-Packard Australia Ltd., 31-41 Joseph St., Blackburn, VIC 3130, Australia

HILTON HOTELS CORPORATION

9336 Civic Center Drive, Beverly Hills, CA, 90210

Tel: (310) 278-4321 Fax: (310) 205-7880

International hotel chain: Hilton International, Vista Hotels and Hilton National Hotels.

Hilton International Company, 14th Fl., Capital Centre, 255 Pitt St., Sydney, NSW 2000, Australia

HOGAN SYSTEMS INC.

5525 LBJ Freeway, Dallas, TX, 75240

Tel: (972) 386-0020 Fax: (972) 386-0315

Sale/distribution integrated software.

Hogan Systems Australia, 390 St. Kilda Rd., Melbourne, Vic. 3004, Australia

HOMESTAKE MINING COMPANY

650 California Street, San Francisco, CA, 94108

Tel: (415) 981-8150 Fax: (415) 397-5038 Web site: www.homestake.com

Precious metal and mineral mining.

Homestake Iron Ore Co. of Australia Ltd., PO Box 338, Norwood, SA 5067, Australia

HONEYWELL INC.

PO Box 524, Minneapolis, MN, 55440-0524

Tel: (612) 951-1000 Fax: (612) 951-3066 Web site: www.honeywell.com

Develop/mfr. controls for home and building, industry, space and aviation.

Honeywell Australia Ltd., 5 Thomas Holt Dr., PO Box 700, North Ryde, NSW 2113, Australia

HORWATH INTERNATIONAL

415 Madison Ave., New York, NY, 10017

Tel: (212) 838-5566 Fax: (212) 838-3636

Public accountants and auditors.

Horwath & Horwath Australia, 1 Market St., Sydney, NSW 2000, Australia

Howarth & Howarth, 99 Frome St., Adelaide, SA 5001, Australia

HOUGHTON INTERNATIONAL INC.

PO Box 930, Madison & Van Buren Avenues, Valley Forge, PA, 19482-0930

Tel: (610) 666-4000 Fax: (610) 666-1376

Mfr. specialty chemicals, hydraulic fluids & lubricants.

Houghton Australia Pty. Ltd., PO Box 29, Concord, Sydney, NSW 2137, Australia

Houghton Australia Pty. Ltd., 287 Wickham Rd., Melbourne, VIC 3189, Australia

HOWMEDICA INC.

359 Veterans Boulevard, Rutherford, NJ, 07070

Tel: (201) 507-7300 Fax: (201) 935-4873 Web site: www.howmedica.com

Hospital, medical and dental supplies.

Howmedica Asia Reg. Office/Australia, Sydney NSW, Australia

Tel: 61-2-9850-3900

HUCK INTERNATIONAL INC.

3724 East Columbia Street, Tucson, AZ, 85714-3415

Tel: (520) 747-9898 Fax: (520) 519-7440

Mfr. aerospace fasteners.

Huck Australia Pty. Ltd., 14 Viewtech Pl., Rowville, VIC 3178, Australia

HUNTSMAN CORPORATION

500 Huntsman Way, Salt Lake City, UT, 84108

Tel: (801) 532-5200 Fax: (801) 536-1581

Mfr./sales specialty chemicals, industrial chemicals and petrochemicals.

Huntsman Chemical Company Australia Ltd., Somerville Rd., PO Box 62, West Footscray, VIC 3012, Australia

Tel: 61-3-316-3333 Fax: 61-3-316-3212

HYATT INTERNATIONAL CORPORATION

200 West Madison Street, Chicago, IL, 60606

Tel: (312) 750-1234 Fax: (312) 750-8578 Web site: www.hyatt.com

International hotel management.

Grand Hyatt Melbourne Hotel, Melbourne, VIC, Australia

Hyatt Hotel Canberra Hotel, Yarralumla, A.C.T., Australia

Hyatt Regency Adelaide Hotel, North Terrace, Adelaide, S.A. 5000, Australia

Tel: 61-8-231-1234 Fax: 61-8-231-1120

Hyatt Regency Coolum Resort, PO Box 78, Warran Rd., Coolum Beach, Queensland 4573, Australia

Tel: 61-7-5446-1234 Fax: 61-7-5446-2957

Hyatt Regency Perth Hotel, Perth, Australia

Park Hyatt Sydney Hotel, 7 Hickson Rd., The Rocks, Sydney NSW 2000, Australia

Tel: 61-2-9241-1234 Fax: 61-2-9256-1555

IBM CORPORATION

New Orchard Road, Armonk, NY, 10504

Tel: (914) 765-1900 Fax: (914) 765-7382 Web site: www.ibm.com

Information products, technology & services.

IBM Australia Ltd., 2 Coonara Ave., PO Box 400, West Pennant Hills, NSW, Australia 2120

Tel: 61-2-9354-4000 Fax: 61-2-9354-7766

ICF KAISER INTERNATIONAL INC.

9300 Lee Highway, Fairfax, VA, 22031

Tel: (703) 934-3600 Fax: (703) 934-9740

Engineering, construction & consulting services.

Kaiser Engineers Pty. Ltd., 6th fl., QV.1 Bldg., 250 St. George's Terrace, Perth, WA 6000, Australia

ICS INTERNATIONAL INC

125 Oak Street, Scranton, PA, 18515

Tel: (717) 342-7701 Fax: (717) 343-0560

Correspondence courses.

ICS (Australasia) Pty. Ltd., Level 1, 1 Waltham St., Artarmon, NSW 2064, Australia

IDEX CORPORATION

630 Dundee Road, Ste. 400, Northbrook, IL, 60062

Tel: (847) 498-7070 Fax: (847) 498-3940

Mfr. industrial pumps, lubrication systems, metal fabrication equipment, bending and clamping devices.

Knight Equipment, Melbourne, Australia

ILLINOIS TOOL WORKS (ITW)

3600 West Lake Ave., Glenview, IL, 60025-5811

Tel: (847) 724-7500 Fax: (847) 657-4268

Mfr. gears, tools, fasteners, sealants, plastic and metal components for industrial, medical, etc.

W.A. Deutsher Pty. Ltd., PO Box 154, Melbourne, VIC 3189, Australia

IMO INDUSTRIES INC.

9211 Forest Hill Ave., Richmond, VA, 23235

Tel: (804) 560-4070 Fax: (804) 560-4076

Mfr./support mechanical and electronic controls, engineered power products.

Morse Controls Pty. Ltd., 1 McCabe Place, Chatswood, NSW 2067, Australia

IMS INTERNATIONAL INC.

100 Campus Road, Totowa, NJ, 07512

Tel: (973) 790-0700 Fax: (973) 956-5544

Market research reports.

Intercontinental Medical Statistics (Australasia) Pty. Ltd., PO Box 372, Crows Nest, NSW 2065, Australia

INDUCTOTHERM CORPORATION

10 Indel Ave., PO Box 157, Rancocas, NJ, 08073-0157

Tel: (609) 267-9000 Fax: (609) 267-3537

Mfr. induction melting furnaces.

Inductotherm (Melting) Pty. Ltd., PO Box 171, 62 Bardia Ave., Seaford, VIC 3198, Australia

INFONET SERVICES CORPORATION

2100 East Grand Ave., El Segundo, CA, 90245

Tel: (310) 335-2600 Fax: (310) 335-4507 Web site: www.infonet.com

Provider of Internet services and electronic messaging services.

Infonet Australasia - Melbourne, 35 Collins St., 32nd Fl., Melbourne, VIC 3000, Australia

Tel: 61-3-9693-4952 Fax: 61-3-9662-9246

INFORMATION BUILDERS INC.

1250 Broadway, New York, NY, 10001

Tel: (212) 736-4433 Fax: (212) 643-8105

Develop/mfr./services computer software.

Information Builders Pty. Ltd., Level 8, 90 Collins St., PO Box 18013, Melbourne, VIC 8003, Australia

INFORMATION MANAGEMENT RESOURCES, INC.

26750 us Highway. 19 North, Ste. 500, Clearwater, FL, 33761

Tel: (727) 797-7080 Fax: (727) 791-8152 Web site: www.imr.com

Provides application software and outsourcing services to business.

IMR Australia, Level 4, 55 Lavender Street, Milsons Point, NSW 2061, Australia

Tel: 61-2-6654-1736 Fax: 61-2-9922-2648

INFORMATION RESOURCES, INC.

150 N. Clinton St., Chicago, IL, 60661

Tel: (312) 726-1221 Fax: (312) 726-0360 Web site: www.infores.com

Provides bar code scanner services for retail sales organizations; processes, analyzes and sells data from the huge database created from these services.

Information Resources Australia Pty. Ltd., Level 4, 39-41 Chandos St., St. Leonards, NSW 2065, Australia (Location, Melbourne, Australia.)

Tel: 61-2-9439-8322 Fax: 61-2-9439-5127

INFORMIX CORPORATION

4100 Bohannon Drive, Menlo Park, CA, 95025

Tel: (650) 926-6300 Fax: (650) 926-6593 Web site: www.informix.com

Designs & produces database management software, connectivity interfaces & gateways, and other computer applications.

Informix Software Pty. Ltd., Levels 6/7, 50 Berry St., North Sydney, NSW 2060, Australia (Locations: Brisbane, Canberra, & Melbourne, Australia)

Tel: 61-2-99-28-1600

INGERSOLL-RAND COMPANY

200 Chestnut Ridge Road, Woodcliff Lake, NJ, 07675

Tel: (201) 573-0123 Fax: (201) 573-3172 Web site: www.ingersoll-rand.com

Mfr. compressors, rock drills, pumps, air tools, door hardware, ball bearings.

Club Car (Australia) Pty. Ltd., PO Box 500, Brookvale, NSW 2100, Australia

Tel: 61-2-9971-2956 Fax: 61-2-9982-1615 Contact: Gary Sanderson

Ingersoll-Rand (Australia) Ltd., 1 Harnett Drive, Seaford, VIC, Australia 3198

Tel: 61-3-9554-1600 Fax: 61-3-9791-1494

Ingersoll-Rand (Australia) Ltd., 80-100 Frankston Rd., Dandenong, VIC 3175, Australia

Tel: 61-3-794-1611 Fax: 61-3-791-1494

INGRAM MICRO INC.

PO Box 25125, Santa Ana, CA, 92799

Tel: (714) 566-1000 Fax: (714) 566-7940 Web site: www.ingrammicro.com

Distribute computer systems, software and related products.

Ingram Micro Inc., Sydney, Australia

INSTRON CORPORATION

100 Royall Street, Canton, MA, 02021-1089

Tel: (781) 828-2500 Fax: (781) 575-5751

Mfr. material testing instruments.

Instron Corp. Australia Pty., Factory 15, 15 Stud Rd., Bayswater, VIC 3153, Australia

Instron Corp. Australia Pty., 1st fl., 19-23 Bridge St., Pymble, NSW 2073, Australia

INSUL-8 CORPORATION

1417 Industrial Pkwy., Harlan, IA, 51537-2351

Tel: (712) 755-3050 Fax: (712) 755-3979

Mfr. mobile electrification products; conductor bar & festoon equipment.

Insul-8 (Australia) Pty. Ltd., PO Box 463, Dandenong, Vic. 3175, Australia

INTEL CORPORATION

Robert Noyce Building, 2200 Mission College Blvd., Santa Clara, CA, 95052-8119

Tel: (408) 765-8080 Fax: (408) 765-1739 Web site: www.intel.com

Mfr. semiconductor, microprocessor and micro-communications components and systems.

Intel Australia Pty. Ltd., Crows Nest, NSW, Australia

INTER-CONTINENTAL HOTELS

1120 Ave. of the Americas, New York, NY, 10036

Tel: (212) 852-6400 Fax: (212) 852-6494 Web site: www.interconti.com

Worldwide hotel and resort accommodations.

Hotel Inter-Continental Sydney, 117 Macquarie St., Sydney SNW 2000, Australia

Tel: 61-2-9230-0200 Fax: 61-2-9240-1240

Inter-Continental Hotels, 117 Macquarie St., Ste. 900, Sydney 2000, NSW, Australia

Tel: 61-2-9232-1199 Fax: 61-2-9251-6674

INTERGRAPH CORPORATION

One Madison Industrial Park, Huntsville, AL, 35894-0001

Tel: (205) 730-2000 Fax: (205) 730-7898 Web site: www.intergraph.com

Develop/mfr. interactive computer graphic systems.

Intergraph Asia-Pacific Inc. (Asia-Pacific Hdqtrs.), Level 4, 32 Walker St., North Sydney, Australia 2060

Tel: 61-2-9929-2888 Fax: 61-2-999-2788

Intergraph Corp. Pty. Ltd., Technology Park Unit 2, 4 Brodie Hall Dr., Bentley, WA 6102, Australia

Tel: 61-9-4723-2-66 Fax: 61-9-4723-267

Intergraph Corp. Pty. Ltd., 7th Fl., 126 Margaret St., Brisbane, Queensland, Australia 4000

Tel: 61-7-3229-8905 Fax: 61-7-3221-0787

Intergraph Corp. Pty. Ltd., Level 1, 19 Barry Drive, Turner Act 2601, Canberra, Australia 2601

Tel: 61-6-257-3066 Fax: 61-6-257-3103

Intergraph Public Safety Pty. Ltd., Level 4, 420 St. Kilda Rd., Melbourne, VIC, Australia 3004

Tel: 61-3-9292-9600 Fax: 61-3-9292-9301

INTERIM SERVICES INC.

2050 Spectrum Boulevard, Fort Lauderdale, FL, 33309

Tel: (954) 938-7600 Fax: (954) 938-7666 Web site: www.interim.com

Provides temporary personnel placement and staffing.

Michael Page Finance, The Octagon, Parramatta, New South Wales 2150, Australia

Tel: 61-2-993-7700

Michael Page Finance, The Octagon Parramatta, New South Wales 2150, Australia

Tel: 61-2-9893-7700

Michael Page Group, Level 19, 1 York St., Sydney, New South Wales 2000, Australia

Tel: 61-2-9254-0200

Michael Page Sales & Marketing, Level 18, 600 Bourke St., Melbourne, VIC 3000, Australia

Tel: 61-3-9600-1136

INTERMEC TECHNOLOGIES CORPORATION

6001 36th Ave. West, PO Box 4280, Everett, WA, 98203-9280

Tel: (425) 348-2600 Fax: (425) 355-9551 Web site: www.intermec.com

Mfr./distributor automated data collection systems.

Intermec Australia Pty. Ltd., 15 Stamford Rd., Oakleigh, VIC 3166, Australia

Tel: 61-3-9563-0000 Fax: 61-3-9563-4000

INTERNATIONAL FLAVORS & FRAGRANCES INC.

521 West 57th Street, New York, NY, 10019-2960

Tel: (212) 765-5500 Fax: (212) 708-7132 Web site: www.iff.com

Design/mfr. flavors, fragrances & aroma chemicals.

International Flavors & Fragrances Australia Pty. Ltd., 156 S. Creek Rd., Dee Why, NSW 2099, Australia

INTERNATIONAL GAME TECHNOLOGY INC.

9295 Prototype Drive, Reno, NV, 89511

Tel: (702) 448-0100 Fax: (702) 448-1488 Web site: www.igtgame.com

Mfr. games, hobby goods; equipment leasing, amusements, computers.

IGT (Australia) Pty. Ltd., 1 Rosebery Ave., Rosebery, N.S.W. 2018, Australia

Tel: 61-2-9931-3400 Fax: 61-2-9663-5359 Contact: Gary Garton, Executive Chmn. Emp: 287

IGT Australia, Unit 7, 104 Newmarket Rd., Windsor, QLD 4030, Australia

Tel: 61-7-3357-3600 Fax: 61-7-3357-3900

INTERNATIONAL LOTTERY & TOTALIZATOR SYSTEMS INC.

2131 Faraday Ave., Carlsbad, CA, 92008

Tel: (760) 931-4000 Fax: (760) 931-1789 Web site: www.ilts.com

Mfr. fluid meters, counting devices; radio/TV & electronic stores.

Intl. Totalizator Systems Australia Pty. Ltd., 31 Seven Hill Rd. N., Unit 1A, Seven Hills, NSW 2147, Australia

INTERNATIONAL PAPER COMPANY

2 Manhattanville Road, Purchase, NY, 10577

Tel: (914) 397-1500 Fax: (914) 397-1596 Web site: www.ipaper.com

Mfr./distributor container board, paper, wood products.

Ilford (Australia) Pty. Ltd., Cnr. Ferntree Gully & Forster, Mount Waverley, Vic, Australia

International Paper Co. Pty. Ltd., PO Box H3, Australia Sq., NSW, Australia

INTERNATIONAL SPECIALTY PRODUCTS

1361 Alps Road, Wayne, NJ, 07470

Tel: (973) 628-4000 Fax: (973) 628-3311 Web site: www.ispcorp.com

Mfr. specialty chemical products.

ISP (Australasia) Pty. Ltd., 1st Fl., 991 Whitehorse Rd., Box Hill 3128, VIC, Australia

Tel: 61-3-9899-5082 Fax: 61-3-9899-5102

INVENTION SUBMISSION CORPORATION

217 Ninth Street, Pittsburgh, PA, 15222

Tel: (412) 288-1300 Fax: (412) 288-1354

Inventor assistance services.

Invention Submission Corp., Level 5, Nauru House, 80 Collins St., Melbourne, VIC 3000, Australia

IRRIDELCO INTERNATIONAL CORPORATION

440 Sylvan Ave., Englewood Cliffs, NJ, 07632

Tel: (201) 569-3030 Fax: (201) 569-9237 Web site: www.irridelco.com

Mfr./distributor of the most comprehensive lines of mechanical and micro irrigation; pumps and irrigation systems.

IDC Australia, 685 Lower North East Rd., Paradise SA 5075, Australia

Tel: 61-8-8336-5247 Fax: 61-8-8336-3399 Contact: Ngo Van Do

ITT CORPORATION

1330 Ave. of the Americas, New York, NY, 10019-5490

Tel: (212) 258-1000 Fax: (212) 258-1297

Design/mfr. communications & electronic equipment, hotels, insurance.

Standard Telephones & Cables, 552-280 Botany Rd., Alexandria, NSW 2015, Australia

ITT SHERATON CORPORATION

60 State Street, Boston, MA, 02108

Tel: (617) 367-3600 Fax: (617) 367-5676

Hotel operations.

Sheraton Hotels in Australia, Kindersley House, 33 Bligh St., Sydney, NSW 2000, Australia

ITW RANSBURG FINISHING SYSTEMS

4141 West 54th Street, Indianapolis, IN, 46254

Tel: (317) 298-5000 Fax: (317) 298-5010 Web site: www.itwdema.com

Mfr. rotary atomizers, electrostatic guns, paint finishing systems.

ITW Finishing Systems & Products Pty. Ltd., PO Box 85, 23 Ashford Ave., Milperra, NSW 2214, Australia

J.P. MORGAN & CO. INC.

60 Wall Street, New York, NY, 10260-0060

Tel: (212) 483-2323 Fax: (212) 648-5209 Web site: www.jpm.com

International banking services.

J.P. Morgan Australia - Melburne Office, 333 Collins St., GPO Box 1888R, Melbourne, VIC 3000, Australia

Tel: 61-3-9623-9300

J.P. Morgan Australia Ltd., 1 O'Connell St., GPO Box 5248, Sydney, NSW 2001, Australia

Tel: 61-2-9551-6100

Morgan Guaranty Trust Co. of NY, 1 O'Connell St., GPO Box 5248, Sydney, NSW 2001, Australia

Tel: 61-2-9551-6100

Morgan Guaranty Trust Co. of NY, 333 Collins St., GPO Box 1888R, Melbourne, VIC 3000, Australia

Tel: 61-3-9623-9300

J. WALTER THOMPSON COMPANY

466 Lexington Ave., New York, NY, 10017

Tel: (212) 210-7000 Fax: (212) 210-6944 Web site: www.jwt.com

International advertising and marketing services.

J. Walter Thompson Australia, Sydney, Australia

JDA SOFTWARE GROUP, INC.

11811 N. Tatum Boulevard, Ste. 2000, Phoenix, AZ, 85028

Tel: (602) 404-5500 Fax: (602) 404-5520 Web site: www.jda.com

Developer of information management software for retail, merchandising, distribution and store management.

JDA Software Group, Inc., Level 1, 434 St. Kilda Rd., Melbourne, VIC 3004, Australia

Tel: 61-3-9243-5551 Fax: 61-3-9243-5510

JDA Software Group, Inc., Ste. 9, Level 11, 100 Walker St., North Sydney, NSW 2060, Australia

Tel: 61-2-9925-0911 Fax: 61-2-9925-0966

JEWELWAY INTERNATIONAL INC.

5151 E. Broadway Blvd, #500, Tucson, AZ, 85711

Tel: (520) 747-9900 Fax: (520) 747-4813

Sale fine jewelry via independent representatives.

Jewelway Australia Pty. Ltd., 6-10 O'Connell St., Sydney, NSW 2000, Australia

JLG INDUSTRIES INC.

JLG Drive, McConnellsburg, PA, 17233-9533

Tel: (717) 485-5161 Fax: (717) 485-6417

Mfr. aerial work platforms, truck-mounted cranes and custom hydraulic machinery.

JLG Industries (Australia) Pty. Ltd., PO Box 972, 11 Bolwarra Rd., Port Macquarie, NSW 2444, Australia

JOHNSON & JOHNSON

One Johnson & Johnson Plaza, New Brunswick, NJ, 08933

Tel: (732) 524-0400 Fax: (732) 214-0334 Web site: www.jnj.com

Mfr./distributor/R&D pharmaceutical, health care and cosmetic products.

Janssen-Cilag Pty. Ltd., Locked Bag 30, Post Office, Lane Cove, NSW 2066, Australia

Johnson & Johnson Medical Pty. Ltd., PO Box 134, North Ryde, NSW 2113, Australia

Johnson & Johnson Pacific Pty. Ltd., GPO 3331, Sydney, NSW 2001, Australia

Ortho-Clinical Diagnostics, Melbourne, Australia

Tasmanian Alkaloids Pty. Ltd., PO Box 130, Westbury, Tasmania 7303, Australia

S C JOHNSON & SON INC.

1525 Howe Street, Racine, WI, 53403

Tel: (414) 260-2000 Fax: (414) 260-2133 Web site: www.scjohnsonwax.com

Home, auto, commercial and personal care products and specialty chemicals.

S.C. Johnson & Son Pty. Ltd., Private Bag 22 PO, Lane Cove, N.S.W. 2066, Australia

JOHNSON CONTROLS INC.

5757 N. Green Bay Ave., PO Box 591, Milwaukee, WI, 53201-0591

Tel: (414) 228-1200 Fax: Web site: www.johnsoncontrols.com

Mfr. facility management & control systems, auto seating, & batteries..

Johnson Controls Australia Pty. Ltd., 25 O'Connell Terrace, Brown Hills, Qld 4006, Australia

Tel: 61-7-7257-1033 Fax: 61-7-7852-1430 Contact: Dave Miller, Branch Manager

Johnson Controls Australia Pty. Ltd., 126 Beaconsfield St., Siverwater, NSW 2128, Australia

Tel: 61-2-9735-7444 Fax: 61-2-9735-7466 Contact: Anthony Cavacuiti, Gen. Mgr.

JOHNSON WORLDWIDE ASSOCIATES, INC.

1326 Willow Road, Sturtevant, WI, 53177

Tel: (414) 884-1500 Fax: (414) 884-1600 Web site: www.jwa.com

Mfr. diving, fishing, boating & camping sports equipment.

JWA Australia, 65 Parramatta Rd., Silverwater Central, Silverwater NSW, 2128 Australia

Tel: 61-2-9748-0199 Fax: 61-2-9748-0803

Scubapro Australia, Unit 21, 380 Eastern Vally Way, Chatswood, NSW 2067, Australia

Tel: 61-2-941-71011 Fax: 61-2-941-1044

JOY MINING AND MACHINERY

177 Thorn Hill Road, Warrendale, PA, 15086-7527

Tel: (724) 779-4500 Fax: (724) 779-4507

Mfr. of underground mining equipment.

Joy Manufacturing Co. (Pty.) Ltd., Vale Rd., Moss Vale, NSW 2577, Australia

K-SWISS INC.

20664 Bahama Street, Chatsworth, CA, 91311

Tel: (818) 998-3388 Fax: (818) 773-2390 Web site: www.kswiss.com

Mfr. casual and athletic shoes, socks and leisure apparel.

K-Swiss Australia Pty. Ltd., 586 Swanston St., Carlton, Melbourne, Vic., Australia

KAISER ALUMINUM & CHEMICAL CORPORATION

6177 Sunol Blvd., Pleasanton, CA, 94566

Tel: (925) 462-1122 Fax: (925) 484-2472 Web site: www.kaiseral.research.com

Mfr. aluminum and aluminum products and chemicals.

Queensland Alumina Ltd., GPO Box 374, Brisbane, Qld. 4001, Australia

KAISER ALUMINUM CORPORATION

5847 San Felipe, Ste. 2600, Houston, TX, 77057-3010

Tel: (713) 267-3777 Fax: (713) 267-3701 Web site: www.kaiseral.com

Aluminum refining and manufacturing.

Queensland Alumina Ltd., Australia (QAL), Gladstone, Australia

KAMAN CORPORATION

1332 Blue Hills Ave., Bloomfield, CT, 06002

Tel: (860) 243-7100 Fax: (860) 243-6365 Web site: www.kaman.com

Aviation & aerospace products & services, musical instruments.

Kaman Aerospace Corp., Canberra, Australia

KAMDEN INTERNATIONAL SHIPPING INC.

167-41 147th Ave., Jamaica, NY, 11434

Tel: (718) 553-8181 Fax: (718) 244-0030

Freight forwarding services.

Kamden Intl. Shipping Pty. Ltd., PO Box 170, Melbourne Airport, VIC 3045, Australia

A.T. KEARNEY INC.

222 West Adams Street, Chicago, IL, 60606

Tel: (312) 648-0111 Fax: (312) 223-6200 Web site: www.atkearney.com

Management consultants and executive search.

A. T. Kearney Australia Pty. Ltd., 120 Collins St., Level 38, Melbourne, VIC 3000, Australia

Tel: 61-3-9653-3700

A. T. Kearney Australia Pty. Ltd., Level 44, Governor Phillip Tower, 1 Farrer Pl., Sydney, NSW 2000, Australia

Tel: 61-2-9259-1999

KELLOGG COMPANY

One Kellogg Square, PO Box 3599, Battle Creek, MI, 49016-3599

Tel: (616) 961-2000 Fax: (616) 961-2871 Web site: www.kelloggs.com

Mfr. ready-to-eat cereals and convenience foods.

Kellogg (Australia) Pty. Ltd., Botany (Sydney), Australia (All inquiries to U.S. address)

KELLY SERVICES, INC.

999 W. Big Beaver Road, Troy, MI, 48084

Tel: (248) 362-4444 Fax: (248) 244-4154 Web site: www.kellyservices.com

Temporary help placement.

Kelly Services (Australia) Ltd., 11 branches throughout Australia

Kelly Services (Australia) Ltd. (HQ), Level 21, 68 Pitt St., Sydney, NSW 2000, Australia

Tel: 61-2-9233-3933 Fax: 61-2-9233-2595

THE KENDALL COMPANY

15 Hampshire Street, Mansfield, MA, 02048

Tel: (508) 261-8000 Fax: (508) 261-8542

Mfr. medical disposable products, home health care products and specialty adhesive products.

Kendall Australasia Pty. Ltd., Locked Bag 2020, Land Cove, Sydney NSW 2066, Australia

Tel: 61-2-9418-9611 Fax: 61-2-9418-9622

KENNAMETAL INC.

State Rte. 981, Latrobe, PA, 15650

Tel: (724) 539-5000 Fax: (724) 539-4710 Web site: www.kennametal.com

Tools, hard carbide & tungsten alloys for metalworking industry.

Kennametal Australia Pty. Ltd. - Adelaide Office, Unit 2.937 Marion Rd., Mitchell Park, SA 5043, Australia

Tel: 61-8-296-9699 Fax: 61-8-298-2958

Kennametal Australia Pty. Ltd. - Head Office, 73 Banksia St., Private Bag 21, Botany, NSW 2019, Australia

Tel: 61-2-9666-6655 Fax: 61-2-9666-6202

Kennametal Australia Pty. Ltd. - Melbourne Office, 20 Garden Blvd., Redwood Gardens Estate, Dingly, VIC 3172, Australia

Tel: 61-3-9551-2011 Fax: 61-3-9951-7469

Kennametal Australia Pty. Ltd. - Perth Office, Unit 10/20 Milford St., East Victoris Park, WA 6102, Australia

Tel: 61-9-361-6888 Fax: 61-9-470-2934

KENT-MOORE DIV

28635 Mound Road, Warren, MI, 48092

Tel: (810) 574-2332 Fax: (313) 578-7375

Mfr. service equipment for auto, construction, recreational, military and agricultural vehicles.

Kent-Moore Australia Pty. Ltd., Unit 2, 8 Gladstone Rd., Castle Hill, NSW 2154, Australia

KEPNER-TREGOE INC.

PO Box 704, Princeton, NJ, 08542-0740

Tel: (609) 921-2806 Fax: (609) 924-4978

Management consulting & training.

Kepner-Tregoe (Australia) Pty. Ltd., 140 Arthur St., PO Box 1333, North Sydney, NSW 2059, Australia

KIMBERLY-CLARK CORPORATION

351 Phelps Drive, Irving, TX, 75038

Tel: (972) 281-1200 Fax: (972) 281-1435 Web site: www.kimberly-clark.com.

Mfr./sales/distribution of consumer tissue, household and personal care products.

Kimberly-Clark of Australia Pty. Ltd., 20 Alfred St., Milsons Point, NSW 2061, Australia

KINKO'S, INC.

255 W. Stanley Ave., Ventura, CA, 93002-8000

Tel: (805) 652-4000 Fax: (805) 652-4347 Web site: www.kinkos.com

Kinko's operates a 24-hour-a-day, global chain of photocopy stores.

Kinko's, 175 Liverpool St., Sydney NSW 2000, Australia

Tel: 61-2-9267-4255 Fax: 61-2-9267-4141

THE KOHLER COMPANY

444 Highland Drive, Kohler, WI, 53044

Tel: (920) 457-4441 Fax: (920) 459-1274

Plumbing products, ceramic tile and stone, cabinetry, furniture, engines, generators, switch gear and hospitality.

The Kohler Company Australia, Unit 7, 171-175 Newton Rd., Wetherill Park, NSW 2164, Australia

Tel: 61-2-9756-4920 Fax: 61-2-9756-4945 Contact: Glenn Sheargold, Branch Mgr.

KOPPERS INDUSTRIES INC.

Koppers Bldg, 437 Seventh Ave., Pittsburgh, PA, 15219

Tel: (412) 227-2000 Fax: (412) 227-2333

Construction materials and services; chemicals and building products.

Koppers Australia Pty. Ltd., 6th Fl., Gold Fields House, Sydney Cove, BPO 4192, Sydney, NSW, Australia

KORN/FERRY INTERNATIONAL

1800 Century Park East, Los Angeles, CA, 90067

Tel: (310) 552-1834 Fax: (310) 553-6452 Web site: www.kornferry.com

Executive search; management consulting.

Korn/Ferry International, Level 42, Nauru House, 80 Collins St., Melbourne, VIC 3000, Australia

Tel: 61-3-9654-4588 Fax: 61-3-9650-9161

Korn/Ferry International Pty. Ltd., 1 Alfred St., Sydney, NSW 2000, Australia

Tel: 61-2-9247-7941 Fax: 61-2-9251-2043

KPMG PEAT MARWICK LLP

Three Chestnut Ridge Road, Montvale, NJ, 07645

Tel: (201) 307-7000 Fax: (201) 930-8617 Web site: www.kpmg.com

Accounting and audit, tax and management consulting services.

KPMG, National Office, Level 26, The KPMG Centre, 45 Clarence St., Sydney NSW 2000, Australia (Locations: Melbourne, Perth, Canberra, Adelaide, Brisbane & Darwin, Australia)

Tel: 61-2-9335-7000 Fax: 61-2-9299-7077 Contact: John B. Harkness, Sr. Ptnr.

KRAFT FOODS INTERNATIONAL, INC. (DIV. PHILIP MORRIS COS.)

800 Westchester Ave., Rye Brook, NY, 10573-1301

Tel: (914) 335-2500 Fax: (914) 335-7144

Processor, distributor and manufacturer of food products.

Kraft Foods Australia & New Zealand, 850 Lorimer St., Port Melbourne, VIC 3207, Australia

THE KROLL-O'GARA COMPANY

9113 Le Saint Drive, Fairfield, OH, 45014

Tel: (513) 874-2112 Fax: (513) 874-2558 Web site: www.kroll-ogara.com

Security and consulting services and vechiles.

Kroll Associates (Australia) Pty. Ltd., Ground Fl., Watermark Building, 5-7 VIC Parade, Manly, Sydney, Australia 2095

Tel: 61-2-9977-0211 Fax: 61-2-9977-0255

KWIK LOK CORPORATION

PO Box 9548, Yakima, WA, 98909

Tel: (509) 248-4770 Fax: (509) 457-6531

Mfr. bag closing machinery.

Kwik-Sew Paterns (Australia) Inc., 6 Brixton Dr., Cheltenham, VIC 3192, Australia

KWIK-SEW PATTERN CO., INC.

3000 Washington Ave. North, Minneapolis, MN, 55411

Tel: (612) 521-7651 Fax: (612) 521-1662 Web site: www.kwiksew.com

Mfr. patterns and instruction books for home sewing.

Kwik-Sew Patterns (Australia) Inc., PO Box 111, Moorooka, Qld 4105, Australia

Tel: 61-7-3892-3966 Fax: 61-7-3892-4103 Contact: Kevin Houghton, Gen. Mgr.

LAI WARD HOWELL INTERNATIONAL INC.

200 Park Ave., Ste. 3100, New York, NY, 10016-0136

Tel: (212) 953-7900 Fax: (212) 953-7907 Web site: www.laix.com

International executive search firm.

LAI Ward Howell Intl., 44 Martin Place #102, Sydney, NSW 2000, Australia (Location in Melbourne, Australia)

LANDAUER ASSOCIATES INC.

666 Fifth Ave., 25th Fl., New York, NY, 10103-0001

Tel: (212) 621-9500 Fax: (212) 621-9567

Real estate counseling services.

Landauer Australia Pty. Ltd., MLC Centre #6102, 19-29 Martin Place, Sydney, NSW 2000, Australia

LANIER WORLDWIDE, INC.

2300 Parklake Drive, N.E., Atlanta, GA, 30345

Tel: (770) 496-9500 Fax: (770) 621-1535

Specialize in digital copiers and multi-functional systems.

Lanier (Australia) Pty. Ltd., 854 Lorimer St., Port Melbourne VIC 3207, Australia

Tel: 61-3-9676-1000 Fax: 61-3-9676-1010

LE TOURNEAU COMPANY

PO Box 2307, Longview, TX, 75606

Tel: (903) 237-7000 Fax: (903) 267-7032

Mfr. heavy construction and mining machinery equipment.

Blackwood Hodge (Australia) Pty. Ltd., Private Bag 66, Parramatta, NSW 2124, Australia

Marathon LeTourneau Australia Pty. Ltd., PO Box 1405, Milton, Qld 4064, Australia

LEARNING COMPANY

1 Athenaeum Street, Cambridge, MA, 02142

Tel: (617) 494-1200 Fax: (617) 494-1219

Mfr./distribute productivity and educational software.

Learning Company, Sydney, Australia

LENNOX INDUSTRIES INC.

2100 Lake Park Blvd., Richardson, TX, 75080

Tel: (972) 497-5000 Fax: (214) 497-5159

Mfr. A/C products, gas heating products.

Lennox Australia Pty. Ltd., PO Box 289, Mulgrave North, Vic. 3170, Australia

LEVI STRAUSS & COMPANY

1155 Battery Street, Levi's Plaza, San Francisco, CA, 94111-1230

Tel: (415) 544-6000 Fax: (415) 501-3939 Web site: www.levistrauss.com

Mfr./distributor casual wearing apparel.

Levi Strauss (Australia) Pty. Ltd., 41 McLaren St., PO Box 306, North Sydney, NSW 2060, Australia

Tel: 61-2-9922-5588 Fax: 61-2-9922-5598

LIFE TECHNOLOGIES INC.

9800 Medical Center Drive, Rockville, MD, 20850

Tel: (301) 840-8000 Fax: (301) 329-8635

Biotechnology.

Life Technologies, Sydney, Australia

LIGHTNIN

135 Mt. Read Blvd., PO Box 1370, Rochester, NY, 14611

Tel: (716) 436-5550 Fax: (716) 436-5589

Mfr./sale/services industrial mixing machinery, aerators.

Lightnin Mixers Pte. Ltd., Unit 5, Block C, 391 Park Rd., Regents Park, NSW 2143, Australia

ELI LILLY & COMPANY

Lilly Corporate Center, Indianapolis, IN, 46285

Tel: (317) 276-2000 Fax: (317) 277-6579 Web site: www.lilly.com

Mfr. pharmaceuticals and animal health products.

Eli Lilly Australia Pty. Ltd., 112 Wharf Rd., West Ryde, NSW 2114, Australia

Tel: 61-2-9325-4444 Fax: 61-2-9325-4400

THE LINCOLN ELECTRIC COMPANY

22801 St. Clair Ave., Cleveland, OH, 44117-1199

Tel: (216) 481-8100 Fax: (216) 486-8385 Web site: www.lincolnelectric.com

Mfr. arc welding and welding related products, oxy-fuel and thermal cutting equipment and integral AC motors.

The Lincoln Electric Co. (Australia) Pty. Ltd., 35 Bryant St., Padstow, NSW 2211, Australia

Tel: 61-2-9772-7222 Fax: 61-2-9792-1387 Contact: Robert J. Lee, Mng. Dir.

ARTHUR D. LITTLE, INC.

25 Acorn Park, Cambridge, MA, 02140-2390

Tel: (617) 498-5000 Fax: (617) 498-7200 Web site: www.adlittle.com

Management, environmental, health & safety consulting; technical & product development.

Arthur D. Little International, Inc., Level 38, Governor Phillip Tower, 1 Farrer Place, Sydney, NSW 2000, Australia

Tel: 61-2-9247-9955 Fax: 61-2-9247-3985

Arthur D. Little International, Inc., Level 11, 459 Collins St., Melbourne VIC 3000, Australia

Tel: 61-3-9649-7600 Fax: 61-3-9614-7349

LOCKHEED MARTIN CORPORATION

6801 Rockledge Drive, Bethesda, MD, 20817

Tel: (301) 897-6000 Fax: (301) 897-6652 Web site: www.imco.com

Design/mfr./management systems in fields of space, defense, energy, electronics and technical services.

Lockheed Aeronautical Systems, Manly 2095, New South Wales, Australia

Contact: F. Kasell, Mgr.

Lockheed Aeronautical Systems, 492 Maintenance Squadron, RAAF Edinburgh 5111, South Australia, Australia

Contact: J. Miller, Mgr.

Lockheed Martin Intl. Ltd., AMA House #3B, 42 Macquarie St., Level 3, Barton, ACT 2600, Australia

Contact: J. Osburnsen, Mng. Dir

LOCTITE CORPORATION

10 Columbus Boulevard, Hartford, CT, 06106

Tel: (203) 520-5000 Fax: (203) 520-5073 Web site: www.loctite.com

Mfr./sale industrial adhesives and sealants.

Loctite Australia Pty. Ltd., PO Box 2622, Tarren Point, NSW 2229, Australia

Tel: 61-2-9525-8366 Fax: 61-2-9525-5643

LSI LOGIC CORPORATION

1551 McCarthy Blvd, Milpitas, CA, 95035

Tel: (408) 433-8000 Fax: (408) 954-3220 Web site: www.lsilogic.com

Develop/mfr. semiconductors.

Reptechnic Pty. Ltd., 3/36 Bydown St., Neutral Bay, NSW 2089, Australia

Tel: 61-2-9953-9844 Fax: 61-2-9953-9683

THE LUBRIZOL CORPORATION

29400 Lakeland Blvd., Wickliffe, OH, 44092-2298

Tel: (440) 943-4200 Fax: (440) 943-5337 Web site: www.lubrizol.com

Mfr. chemicals additives for lubricants & fuels.

Lubrizol Australia, 28 River St., Silverwater, NSW 2141, Australia

Tel: 61-2-9648-5122

LUCENT TECHNOLOGIES, INC.

600 Mountain Ave., Murray Hill, NJ, 07974-0636

Tel: (908) 582-3000 Fax: (908) 582-2110 Web site: www.lucent.com

Design/mfr. wide range of public and private networks, communication systems and software, data networking systems, business telephone systems and microelectronics components.

Network Systems Australia/Global Pvt. Systems, (GPS) 231 Holt St., PO Box 37, Pikenba, Queensland, 4008 Australia

Tel: 61-7-3860-1200 Fax: 61-7-3860-1211 Contact: Richard Dall'Asen, Location Mgr.

Network Systems Australia/Global Pvt. Systems, 6-10 Talavera Rd., North Ryde NSW 2113, Sydney, Australia

Tel: 61-2-9352-9000 Fax: 61-2-9352-9111 Contact: Catherine Wu, PR Mgr.

MacDERMID INC.

245 Freight Street, Waterbury, CT, 06702-0671

Tel: (203) 575-5700 Fax: (203) 575-7900 Web site: www.macd.com

Chemicals processing for metal industrial, plastics, electronics cleaners, strippers.

MacDermid Australia Branch, 299 Canterbury Rd., Revesby, NSW 2212, Australia

Tel: 61-2-9792-1555 Fax: 61-2-9792-1969

MAGELLAN PETROLEUM CORPORATION

149 Durham Road, Oak Park #31, Madison, CT, 06443-2664

Tel: (203) 245-8380 Fax: (203) 245-8380

Oil and gas production and exploration.

Magellan Petroleum Australia Ltd., 99 Leichhardt St., Spring Hill, Brisbane, Qld 4000, Australia

MALLINCKRODT INC.

675 McDonnell Blvd., PO Box 5840, St. Louis, MO, 63134

Tel: (314) 654-2000 Fax: (314) 654-3005

Mfr. specialty medical products.

Mallinckrodt Medical Pty. Ltd., VIC, Australia

MANPOWER INTERNATIONAL INC.

5301 N. Ironwood Road, PO Box 2053, Milwaukee, WI, 53201-2053

Tel: (414) 961-1000 Fax: (414) 961-7081 Web site: www.manpower

Temporary help, contract service, training & testing.

Manpower Personnel Services, 34 Hunter St., Sydney, NSW 2000, Australia

Tel: 61-2-9246-8950 Fax: 61-2-9235-0097

MARCAM CORPORATION

95 Wells Ave., Newton, MA, 02459

Tel: (617) 965-0220 Fax: (617) 965-7273

Applications software & services.

Marcam Australia Pty. Ltd., 542 Station St. 2/F, Box Hill, Vic. 3128, Australia

MARK IV INDUSTRIES INC.

501 John James Audubon Pkwy., PO Box 810, Amherst, NY, 14226-0810

Tel: (716) 689-4972 Fax: (716) 689-1529 Web site: www.mark-iv.com

Mfr. diversified products: timers & controls, power equipment, loudspeaker systems, etc.

Dayco Pacific Pty. Ltd., 11 Dansu Court, Hallam, VIC 3803, Australia

Tel: 61-3-9796-4044 Fax: 61-3-9796-4544

MARLEY COOLING TOWER COMPANY

7401 West 129th Street, Overland Park, KS, 66213

Tel: (913) 664-7400 Fax: (913) 664-7641 Web site: www.marleyct.com

Cooling and heating towers and waste treatment systems.

Marley Temcel Australia Pty. Ltd., Unit 1/83 Bassett St., Mona Vale NSW 2103, Australia

Tel: 61-2-9979-8111 Fax: 61-2-9979-8866

MARRIOTT INTERNATIONAL INC.

1 Marriott Drive, Washington, DC, 20058

Tel: (301) 380-3000 Fax: (301) 380-5181

Lodging, contract food and beverage service, and restaurants.

Great Barrier Reef Resort, CNR Williams Esplanade & Velvers Rd., Palm Cove, Cairns Queensland, Australia 4879

Tel: 61-7-4055-3999 Fax: 61-7-4055-3902

MARS INC.

6885 Elm Street, McLean, VA, 22101-3810

Tel: (703) 821-4900 Fax: (703) 448-9678 Web site: www.mars.com

Mfr. candy, snack foods, rice products and cat food.

Master Foods Holdings Pty. Ltd., 29-37 Smith St., Matraville, NSW, Australia

Uncle Ben's of Australia Pty. Ltd., Kelly St., Wodonga, VIC 3690, Australia

MARSH & McLENNAN COS INC.

1166 Ave. of the Americas, New York, NY, 10036-2774

Tel: (212) 345-5000 Fax: (212) 345-4808 Web site: www.marshmac.com

Insurance agents/brokers, pension and investment management consulting services.

J&H Marsh & McLennan Pty. Ltd., 360 Collins St., Melbourne, VIC 3000, Australia

Tel: 61-39-268-7777 Fax: 61-39-670-1418 Contact: Alastair Mitchell

J&H Marsh & McLennan Pty. Ltd., 18 Paterson St., Lanceston, Tasmania 7250, Australia

Tel: 61-36-331-2166 Fax: 61-36-331-0870 Contact: Graeme Moore

J&H Marsh & McLennan Pty. Ltd., 250 St. George's Terrace, Perth. Western Australia 6000, Australia

Tel: 61-89-424-9888 Fax: 61-89-424-9898 Contact: Geoff Ferguson

J&H Marsh & McLennan Pty. Ltd., 7 Franklin Warf, Hobart, Tasmainia 7000, Australia

Tel: 61-36-234-4366 Fax: 61-36-231-1986 Contact: Robert Taylor

J&H Marsh & McLennan Pty. Ltd., Level 7, 167 Eagle St., Brisbane, Queensland 4000, Australia

Tel: 61-7-3221-3855 Fax: 61-7-3221-1739 Contact: Peter Forno

J&H Marsh & McLennan Pty. Ltd., 15 London Circuit, Canberra, Australian Capital Territory 2600, Australia
Australia

Tel: 61-2-6249-1422 Fax: 61-2-6249-1305 Contact: Angela Warnes

J&H Marsh & McLennan Pty. Ltd., 12 Pirie St., Adelaide, South Australia 5000, Australia

Tel: 61-8-8212-5481 Fax: 61-8-8212-6168 Contact: Dirk van Elst

J&H Marsh & McLennan Pty. Ltd., 60 Margaret St., Sydney, New South Wales 2000, Australia

Tel: 61-2-9375-0500 Fax: 61-2-9375-0400 Contact: John Richardson

MARY KAY COSMETICS INC.

16251 Nor Dallas Pkw, Dallas, TX, 75248

Tel: (214) 630-8787 Fax: (214) 631-5938

Cosmetics and toiletries.

Mary Kay Cosmetics Pty. Ltd., 551 Burwood Highway, Knoxfield, VIC 31801, Australia

MASTERCARD INTERNATIONAL INC.

200 Purchase Street, Purchase, NY, 10577

Tel: (914) 249-2000 Fax: (914) 249-5475 Web site: www.mastercard.com

Provides financial payment systems globally.

MasterCard International Inc., Level 10, 146 Arthur St., North Sydney, NSW 2060, Australia

MATTEL INC.

333 Continental Blvd., El Segundo, CA, 90245-5012

Tel: (310) 252-2000 Fax: (310) 252-2179 Web site: www.mattelmedia.com

Mfr. toys, dolls, games, crafts and hobbies.

Mattel Pty. Ltd., 55 Queensbridge St., South Melbourne, VIC 3205, Australia

MAXTOR CORPORATION

510 Cottonwood Drive, Milpitas, CA, 95035-7403

Tel: (408) 432-1700 Fax: (408) 432-4510 Web site: www.maxtor.com

Mfr., develops and markets hard disk drives for desktop computer systems.

Maxtor Dick Drives Pty. Ltd., 45-57 Grafton St., Ste. 103, Bondi Junction, SNW 2022, Australia

Tel: 61-2-9369-3662 Fax: 61-2-9369-2082

MAXXAM INC.

5847 San Felipe, Ste. 2600, Houston, TX, 77057

Tel: (713) 975-7600 Fax: (713) 267-3701

Holding company for aluminum and timber products and real estate industries.

Maxxam Inc., Sydney, Australia

McCALL PATTERN COMPANY

11 Penn Plaza, New York, NY, 10001

Tel: (212) 465-6800 Fax: (212) 465-6831

Fashion patterns.

McCall Pattern Co., Sydney, Australia

McCANN-ERICKSON WORLDWIDE

750 Third Ave., New York, NY, 10017

Tel: (212) 984-3644 Fax: (212) 984-2629

International advertising/marketing services.

McCann-Erickson Advertising Pty. Ltd., Northpoint, 100 Miller St., North Sydney, NSW 2060, Australia

McCORMICK & COMPANY, INC.

18 Loveton Circle, Sparks, MD, 21152-6000

Tel: (410) 771-7301 Fax: (410) 527-8289

Mfr./distribution/sale seasonings, flavorings, specialty foods.

McCormick Foods Australia Pty. Ltd., Private Bag 31, Clayton, VIC 3169, Australia

McDONALD'S CORPORATION

Kroc Drive, Oak Brook, IL, 60523

Tel: (630) 623-3000 Fax: (630) 623-7409

Fast food chain stores.

McDonald's Corp., Australia

THE McGRAW-HILL COMPANIES

1221 Ave. of the Americas, New York, NY, 10020

Tel: (212) 512-2000 Fax: (212) 512-2703

Books, magazines, information systems, financial service, publishing and broadcast operations.

McGraw-Hill Book Co. Australia Pty. Ltd., 4 Barcoo St., East Roseville, NSW 2026, Australia

McKINSEY & COMPANY

55 East 52nd Street, New York, NY, 10022

Tel: (212) 446-7000 Fax: (212) 446-8575 Web site: www.mckinsey.com

Management and business consulting services.

McKinsey & Co. Inc., 52 Martin Place, 24th Fl., Sydney, NSW 2000, Australia

Tel: 61-2-9232-4344 Fax: 61-2-9232-9815

McKinsey & Company, 1 Collins St., 13th Fl., Melbourne, VIC 3000, Australia

Tel: 61-3-9659-3100 Fax: 61-3-9659-3200

McKinsey & Company, Level 13, 225 St. Georges Terrace, Perth, Western Australia 6000, Australia

Tel: 61-8-9426-7400 Fax: 61-8-9426-7444

McNALLY PITTSBURG INC.

100 North Pine, PO Box 651, Pittsburg, KS, 66762

Tel: (316) 231-3000 Fax: (316) 231-0343

Mfr./erection of coal processing plants and material handling systems.

McNally Australia Pty. Ltd., Centre Court, 25 Paul St., North Ryde, NSW 2113, Australia

MEAD CORPORATION

Courthouse Plaza, NE, Dayton, OH, 45463

Tel: (937) 495-6323 Fax: (937) 461-2424 Web site: www.mead.com

Mfr. paper, packaging, pulp, lumber and other wood products, school and office products; electronic publishing and distribution.

Mead Packaging Pty. Ltd., Ste. 203, Ground Fl, 242-244 Beecroft Rd., Epping NSW 2121, Australia

Tel: 61-2-9869-3564 Fax: 61-2-9869-3587 Contact: Jonathan Cole, Gen. Mgr.

MEDICUS GROUP INTERNATIONAL

1675 Broadway, New York, NY, 10019

Tel: (212) 468-3100 Fax: (212) 468-3222

International healthcare agency network.

Medicus PDA & R&R, Sydney, Australia

Medicus PDA & R&R, Melbourne, Australia

MEDTRONIC INC.

7000 Central Ave., NE, Minneapolis, MN, 55432

Tel: (612) 574-4000 Fax: (612) 574-4879

Mfr./sale/service electrotherapeutic medical devices.

Medtronic Australasia, 50 Strathallen Ave., Northbridge, NSW 2063, Australia

MEMOREX CORPORATION

10100 Pioneer Boulevard, Santa Fe Springs, CA, 90670

Tel: (562) 906-2800 Fax: (562) 906-2848

Magnetic recording tapes, etc.

Memorex Pty. Ltd., 61 Barry St. Neutral Bay, NSW 2089, Australia

THE MENTHOLATUM CO., INC.

707 Sterling Drive, Orchard Park, NY, 14127-1587

Tel: (716) 677-2500 Fax: (716) 674-3696 Web site: www.mentholatum.com

Mfr./distributor proprietary medicines, drugs, OTC's.

Mentholatum Australia Pty. Ltd., 12 Janine St., Scoresby, VIC 3179, Australia

Tel: 61-3-9763-0322 Fax: 61-3-9763-2699

MERCK & COMPANY, INC.

1 Merck Drive, Whitehouse Station, NJ, 08889

Tel: (908) 423-1000 Fax: (908) 423-2592

Pharmaceuticals, chemicals and biologicals.

Merck, Sharp & Dohme (Australia) Pty. Ltd., 54-68 Ferndell St., Granville, NSW 2142, Australia

MERCURY INTERACTIVE CORPORATION

1325 Borregas Ave., Sunnyvale, CA, 94089

Tel: (408) 822-5200 Fax: (408) 822-5300 Web site: www.merc-int.com

Mfr. computer software to decipher and eliminate "bugs" from systems.

Mercury Interactive (Australia) Pty. Ltd., Level 11, 580 St. Kilda Rd., Melbourne, Australia VIC 3004

Tel: 61-3-9526-3640 Fax: 61-3-9526-3690

Mercury Interactive (Australia) Pty. Ltd., Currency House, Level 5, 23 Hunter St., Sydney, Australia NSW 2000

Tel: 61-2-9223-7666 Fax: 61-2-9223-7498

MERITOR AUTOMOTIVE, INC.

2135 W. Maple Road, Troy, MI, 48084-7186

Tel: (248) 435-1000 Fax: (248) 435-1393 Web site: www.meritorauto.com

Mfr./sales of light and heavy vehicle systems for trucks, cars and speciality vehicles.

Meritor Automotive, Inc., Australia

MERRILL LYNCH & COMPANY, INC.

World Financial Center, North Tower, New York, NY, 10281-1323

Tel: (212) 449-1000 Fax: (212) 449-2892

Security brokers and dealers, investment and business services.

Merrill Lynch International, Level 39, 120 Collins St., Melbourne, VIC 3000, Australia

Tel: 61-3-9659-2222

Merrill Lynch International, Starcourt Arcade, Mollesworth St., Lismore, New South Wales 2480, Australia

Tel: 61-2-6621-2389

Merrill Lynch International, 44 Brisbane St., Tamworth, New South Wales, Australia

Tel: 61-2-6766-8177

Merrill Lynch International, Level 32, 10 Eagle St., Brisbane, Queensland 40, Australia

Tel: 61-7-3210-0444 Fax: 61-7-3210-0093

Merrill Lynch International, Level 33, Exchange Plaza, 2 The Esplanade, Perth, Western Australia 6000

Tel: 61-8-9221-4600 Fax: 61-8-9221-4418

Merrill Lynch International, Level 49, MLC Centre, 19-29 Martin Place, Sydney, New South Wales 2000, Australia

Tel: 61-2-9225-6500

MICROSOFT CORPORATION

One Microsoft Way, Redmond, WA, 98052-6399

Tel: (425) 882-8080 Fax: (425) 936-7329 Web site: www.microsoft.com

Computer software, peripherals and services.

Microsoft Australia (Pty.), 65 Epping Rd., North Ryde, NSW 2113, Australia

Tel: 61-2-870-2200 Fax: 61-2-805-1108

Ninemsn Pty. Ltd., Sydney, Australia

HERMAN MILLER INC.

8500 Byron Road, Zeeland, MI, 49464

Tel: (616) 654-3000 Fax: (616) 654-5385 Web site: www.hermanmiller.com

Office furnishings.

Herman Miller Australia, 33 Russell St., Melbourne, VIC 3000, Australia

Tel: 61-3-9654-5522 Fax: 61-2-9654-5969

Herman Miller Australia, 139 Murray St., Level 3, Prymont, NSW 2009, Australia

Tel: 61-2-9552-2300 Fax: 61-2-9552-2676

MILLIPORE CORPORATION, ANALYTICAL PRODUCT DIVISION

80 Ashby Road, PO Box 9125, Bedford, MA, 01730

Tel: (781) 275-9200 Fax: (781) 533-3110 Web site: www.millipore.com

Mfr. flow and pressure measurement and control components; precision filters, hi-performance liquid chromatography instruments.

Millipore Pty. Ltd., Private Bag 18, 87-89 Mars Rd., Lane Cove, NSW 2066, Australia

MINE SAFETY APPLIANCES COMPANY

121 Gamma Drive, RIDC Industrial Pk., PO Box 426, Pittsburgh, PA, 15230

Tel: (412) 967-3000 Fax: (412) 967-3452

Safety equipment, industry filters.

MSA (Australia) Pty. Ltd., 137 Gilba Rd., PO Box 43, Wentworthville, NSW 2145, Australia

MINTEQ INTERNATIONAL INC.

405 Lexington Ave., 19th Fl., New York, NY, 10174-1901

Tel: (212) 878-1800 Fax: (212) 878-1952 Web site: www.mineralstech.com

Mfr./market specialty refractory and metallurgical products and application systems.

MINTEQ Australia Pty. Ltd., Office E, 1st Fl., 285 Pennant Hills Rd., Carlingford NSW 2118, Australia

Tel: 61-2-9872-5300 Fax: 61-2-9872-5175 Contact: James Robert Reid, Dir. Emp: 7

MOBIL CORPORATION

3225 Gallows Road, Fairfax, VA, 22037-0001

Tel: (703) 846-3000 Fax: (703) 846-4669 Web site: www.mobil.com

Petroleum and gas exploration and refining, mfr. petroleum products, chemicals and petrochemicals.

Petroleum Refineries (Australia) Pty. Ltd., PO Box 170, Port Adelaide SA, 5015, Australia

Tel: 61-8-8205-6888 Fax: 61-8-8205-6099

Petroleum Refineries (Australia) Pty. Ltd., PO Box 821, Morphett Vale SA, 5162, Australia

Tel: 61-8-8392-6222 Fax: 61-8-8382-0962

Petroleum Refineries (Australia) Pty. Ltd., GPO Box 2079, Darwin NT, 0801, Australia

Tel: 61-8-8981-5199 Fax: 61-8-8981-3236

Petroleum Refineries (Australia) Pty. Ltd., GPO Box 10A, Perth WA, 6000, Australia

Tel: 61-8-9320-5444 Fax: 61-8-9321-3054

Petroleum Refineries (Australia) Pty. Ltd., Levels 5 and 6, 53 Berry St., North Sydney NSW, 2000, Australia

Tel: 61-2-9962-2555

Petroleum Refineries (Australia) Pty. Ltd., 500 Lytton Rd., Morningside, QLD 4170, Australia

Tel: 61-7-3213-7888 Fax: 61-7-3213-7899

Petroleum Refineries (Australia) Pty. Ltd., GPO Box 4507, Melbourne VIC, 3001, Australia

Tel: 61-3-9252-3111 Fax: 61-3-9866-9079

MOGUL CORPORATION

PO Box 200, Chagrin Falls, OH, 44022

Tel: (440) 247-5000 Fax: (440) 247-3714

Water treatment chemicals, equipment.

Mogul Chemicals Pty. Ltd., 19-21 Hale St., Botany, NSW 2019, Australia

MONSANTO COMPANY

800 N. Lindbergh Boulevard, St. Louis, MO, 63167

Tel: (314) 694-1000 Fax: (314) 694-7625 Web site: www.monsanto.com

Life sciences company focussing on agriculture, nutrition, pharmaceuticals, health and wellness and sustainable development.

Monsanto Australia Ltd., PO Box 6051, St. Kilda Rd. Central, 12th Fl., Melbourne, VIC, 3004 Australia

Tel: 61-3-9522-7122

MOOG INC.

Jamison Road, East Aurora, NY, 14052-0018

Tel: (716) 652-2000 Fax: (716) 687-4457 Web site: www.moog.com

Mfr. precision control components & systems.

Moog Australia Pty. Ltd., Unit 1, 12-14 Miles St., Mulgrave, VIC 3170, Australia

MOORE PRODUCTS COMPANY

Sumneytown Pike, Spring House, PA, 19477

Tel: (215) 646-7400 Fax: (215) 646-6212

Mfr. process control instruments.

Moore Products Co. (Australia) Pty., Federation Business Centre, Unit 27, 198 Young St., Waterloo, NSW 2017, Australia

MORGAN STANLEY DEAN WITTER & CO.

1585 Broadway, New York, NY, 10036

Tel: (212) 761-4000 Fax: (212) 761-0086 Web site: www.msdw.com

Securities and commodities brokerage, investment banking, money management, personal trusts.

Morgan Stanley Australia Ltd., Level 33, The Chifley Tower, Sydney NSW 2000, Australia

Morgan Stanley Dean Witter Australia Ltd., Level 53, 101 Collins St., Melbourne, VIC, 3000, Australia

MOTOROLA, INC.

1303 East Algonquin Road, Schaumburg, IL, 60196

Tel: (847) 576-5000 Fax: (847) 538-5191 Web site: www.mot.com

Mfr. communications equipment, semiconductors and cellular phones.

Motorola Australia Pty. Ltd., Unit 10, 67 Parramatta Rd., Silverwater, NSW 2141, Sydney, Australia (Locations: Chatswood, Melbourne, Coopers Plains, Mawson Lakes, Perth, Fyshwick, & Adelaide, Australia.)

Tel: 61-2-9735-5900 Fax: 61-2-9748-4221

MULTI GRAPHICS

431 Lakeview Court, Mt. Prospect, IL, 60056

Tel: (847) 375-1700 Fax: (847) 375-1810

Mfr./sale/service printing & print prod equipment, mailroom/bindery systems, services & supplies for graphics industry.

AM Intl. Pty. Ltd., PO Box 200, Mulgrave North, VIC3170, Australia

MULTIWARE

PO Box 907, Brookfield, CT, 06874

Tel: (203) 374-8000 Fax: (203) 374-3374

Mfr. applications development software.

Sapphire Australia, 166 Pacific Hwy., Unit 4, North Sydney, NSW 2060, Australia

NAC REINSURANCE CORPORATION

One Greenwich Plaza, Greenwich, CT, 06836-2568

Tel: (203) 622-5200 Fax: (203) 622-1494 Web site: www/nacre.com

Provides property and casualty reinsurance.

NAC Reinsurnace International Ltd., Governor Phillip Tower, Level 21, 1, Farrer Place, Sydney, Australia NSW 2000

Tel: 61-2-2924-78222 Fax: 61-2-2924-78811 Contact: Scott Ryrie, Gen. Mgr. Emp: 6

NACCO INDUSTRIES INC.

5875 Landerbrook Drive, Mayfield Heights, OH, 44124-4017

Tel: (440) 449-9600 Fax: (440) 449-9607 Web site: www.nacco.com

Mining/marketing lignite & metals, mfr. forklift trucks & small electric appliances, specialty retailers.

NACCO Materials Handling Group, TD Wang, 1 Bulle Court Ave., Milperra, NSW 2214, PO Box 100 Panania, 2213, Australia

Tel: 61-2-795-3800 Fax: 61-2-771-1255

NACCO MATERIAL HANDLING GROUP

PO Box 847, Danville, IL, 61834

Tel: (217) 443-7000 Fax: (217) 437-4940 Web site: 503-639

Fork lifts, trucks, trailers, towing winches, personnel lifts and compaction equipment.

Hyster Australia Pty. Ltd., Ashford Ave., Milperra, NSW 2214, Australia

NAI TECHNOLOGIES INC.

282 New York Ave., Huntington, NY, 11743

Tel: (516) 271-5685 Fax: (516) 385-0815 Web site: www.naitech.com

Mfr. computers & peripherals, office machines, communications equipment.

NAI Technologies, Australia

NALCO CHEMICAL COMPANY

One Nalco Center, Naperville, IL, 60563-1198

Tel: (630) 305-1000 Fax: (630) 305-2900 Web site: www.nalco.com

Chemicals for water and waste water treatment, oil products and refining, industry processes; water and energy management service.

Nalco Australia, Anderson St., Botany, NSW 2019, Australia

Tel: 61-2-9316-3000 Fax: 61-2-9666-5292

NATIONAL GYPSUM COMPANY

2001 Rexford Road, Charlotte, NC, 28211

Tel: (704) 365-7300 Fax: (704) 365-7276

Building products & services.

Austin Australia Pty. Ltd., Melbourne, Australia

Austin Australia Pty. Ltd., Sydney, Australia

NATIONAL STARCH & CHEMICAL COMPANY

10 Finderne Ave., Bridgewater, NJ, 08807-3300

Tel: (908) 685-5000 Fax: (908) 685-5005 Web site: www.national starch.com

Mfr. adhesives & sealants, resins & specialty chemicals, electronic materials & adhesives, food products, industry starch.

National Starch & Chemical Pty. Ltd., 7-9 Stanton Rd., Seven Hills, Sydney NSW 2147, Australia (Locations: Tullamarine & Milperra, Australia.)

Tel: 61-2-9624-6022 Fax: 61-2-9624-1468

NATIONAL UTILITY SERVICE INC.

One Maynard Drive, PO Box 712, Park Ridge, NJ, 07656-0712

Tel: (201) 391-4300 Fax: (201) 391-8158

Utility rate consulting.

NUS International Pty. Ltd., 122-130 Arthur St., North Sydney, NSW 2060, Australia

NATIONAL-OILWELL, INC.

PO Box 4638, Houston, TX, 77210-4638

Tel: (713) 960-5100 Fax: (713) 960-5428 Web site: www.natoil.com

Mfr./distributor oilfield drills and tubulars.

National-Oilwell Pty. Ltd., Mine St., Redbank, Queensland, Australia 4301

Tel: 61-7-5575-5585 Fax: 61-7-5578-6319

NBD BANK

611 Woodward Ave., Detroit, MI, 48226

Tel: (313) 225-1000 Fax: (313) 225-2109

Banking services.

NBD Bank, 70 Hindmarsh Sq., 4/F, Adelaide, SA 5000, Australia

NBD Bank, Locations in Sydney and Melbourne, Australia

NCR (NATIONAL CASH REGISTER)

1700 South Patterson Blvd., Dayton, OH, 45479

Tel: (937) 445-5000 Fax: (937) 445-7042 Web site: www.ncr.com

Mfr. automated teller machines and high-performance stationary bar code scanners.

NCR Australia Pty. Ltd., 8-20 Napier St., North Sydney, Australia 2060

Tel: 61-2-9964-8318 Fax: 61-2-9964-8444 Contact: Ross Millar, Dir.

NCR Australia Pty. Ltd., 641 Wllington St., Perth WA 6000, Australia

Tel: 61-2-9327-3155 Fax: 61-2-9481-5581 Contact: Graham Griffiths

NETSCAPE COMMUNICATIONS

501 East Middlefield Road, Mountain View, CA, 94043

Tel: (650) 254-1900 Fax: (650) 528-4124

Mfr./distribute Internet-based commercial and consumer software applications.

Netscape Communications Australian Pty. Ltd., (Head Office) Level 1, The Tea House, 28 Clarendon St., South Melbourne, VIC 3205, Australia

Tel: 61-3-9693-7600 Fax: 61-3-9693-7699

Netscape Communications Australian Pty. Ltd., Level 14, 99 Walker St., North Sydney, NSW 2060, Australia

Tel: 61-2-9911-7770 Fax: 61-2-9911-7724

NETWORK ASSOCIATES

3935 Freedon Circle, Santa Clara, CA, 95054

Tel: (408) 988-3832 Fax: (408) 970-9727 Web site: www.networkassociate.com

Designs and produces network security and network management software and hardware.

Network Associates (Pty.) Ltd., Level 1, 500 Pacific Highway, St. Leonards, NSW 2065 Australia

Tel: 61-2-9437-5866 Fax: 61-2-9439-5166

THE NEWELL COMPANY

29 E Stephenson Street, Freeport, IL, 61032-0943

Tel: (815) 963-1010 Fax: (815) 489-8212 Web site: www.newellco.com

Mfr. Hardware, housewares, and office products.

The Newell Company, Sydney, Australia

NEWSWEEK INTERNATIONAL INC.

251 West 57 Street, New York, NY, 10019

Tel: (212) 445-4000 Fax: (212) 445-4120

Publishing.

Newsweek Inc., 100 Miller St., North Sydney, NSW 2060, Australia

A .C. NIELSEN COMPANY

177 Broad Street, Stamford, CT, 06901

Tel: (203) 961-3000 Fax: (203) 961-3190 Web site: www.acnielsen.com

Market research.

A.C. Nielsen Australia Pty. Ltd., 85 Epping Rd., North Ryde, NSW 2113, Australia

NORDSON CORPORATION

28601 Clemens Road, Westlake, OH, 44145

Tel: (440) 892-1580 Fax: (440) 892-9507 Web site: www.nordson.com

Mfr. industry application equipment, sealants & packaging machinery.

Nordson Australia Pty. Ltd., Unit 4, 6 Boden Rd., Seven Hills, NSW 2147, Australia

Tel: 61-2-9838-7144 Fax: 61-2-9838-7394

Nordson Australia Pty. Ltd., 373B Cross Rd., Edwardstown, SA 5039, Australia

Tel: 61-88-371-1545 Fax: 61-88-297-2256

Nordson Australia Pty. Ltd., 3 Harvton St., Stafford, Qld 4053, Australia

Tel: 61-7-3356-6000 Fax: 61-7-3356-9787

Nordson Australia Pty. Ltd., 4-5 Harnett Close, Mulgrave, VIC 3170, Australia

Tel: 61-3-9545-0388 Fax: 61-3-9545-0204

NORGREN

5400 S. Delaware Street, Littleton, CO, 80120-1663

Tel: (303) 794-2611 Fax: (303) 795-9487 Web site: www.norgren.com

Mfr. pneumatic filters, regulators, lubricators, valves, automation systems, dryers, push-in fittings.

IMI Norgren Pty. Ltd., 33 South Corporate Ave., Rowville, VIC 3178, Australia

Tel: 61-3-3921-30800 Fax: 61-3-3921-30890

NORTON COMPANY

1 New Bond Street, Worcester, MA, 01606
Tel: (508) 795-5000 Fax: (508) 795-5741
Abrasives, drill bits, construction and safety products and plastics.
Australian Abrasives Pty. Ltd., 302 Parramatta Rd., Auburn, NSW 2144, Australia
Christensen Inc., 424 North East Rd., Windsor Garden, 5087, Australia
Norton Pty. Ltd., 25 Nyrang St., Lidcombe, NSW 2141, Australia

OBJECT DESIGN INC.

25 Mall Road, Burlington, MA, 01803
Tel: (781) 674-5000 Fax: (781) 674-5010 Web site: www.odi.com
Developer of object-oriented database management systems software.
Object Design Pty. Ltd., Lvel 6, 390 St. Kilda Rd., Melbourne, VIC 3004, Australia
Tel: 61-3-9820-0095 Fax: 61-3-9820-0133

OCEANEERING INTERNATIONAL INC.

11911 FM 529, Houston, TX, 77041
Tel: (713) 329-4500 Fax: (713) 329-4951
Transportation equipment, underwater service to offshore oil and gas industry.
Oceaneering Intl. Inc., Karratha, Perth & Sale, Australia

OGILVY & MATHER WORLDWIDE

309 West 49th Street, New York, NY, 10019
Tel: (212) 237-4000 Fax: (212) 237-5123
Advertising, marketing, public relations & consulting firm.
Ogilvy & Mather, Sydney, Australia

THE OILGEAR COMPANY

2300 S. 51st Street, Milwaukee, WI, 53219
Tel: (414) 327-1700 Fax: (414) 327-0532
Mfr. hydraulic power transmission machinery.
Oilgear Towler Australia Pty. Ltd., 1A/45 Bay Rd., Taren Point, NSW 2229, Australia

OLIN CORPORATION

501 Merritt Seven, Norwalk, CT, 06856-4500
Tel: (203) 750-3000 Fax: (203) 356-3065
Mfr. chemicals, metals, applied physics in electronics, defense & aerospace industry.
Olin Australia Ltd., 64-66 Magnesium Dr., Crestmead, Qld 4132, Australia
Olin Australia Ltd., Level 2, 601 Pacific Hwy., PO Box 141, St. Leonards, NSW 2065, Australia
Olin Australia Ltd., PO Box 776, Hayes Rd., Pt. Henry, Geelong, VIC 3220, Australia

ONAN CORPORATION

1400 73rd Ave. NE, Minneapolis, MN, 55432
Tel: (612) 574-5000 Fax: (612) 574-5298
Mfr. electric generators, controls & switchgears.
Onan Australia, PO Box 100, 11 Manton St., Hindmarsh, SA 5007, Australia

ONEIDA LTD

163-181 Kenwood Ave., Oneida, NY, 13421-2899
Tel: (315) 361-3000 Fax: (315) 361-3658 Web site: www.oneida.com
Mfr. cutlery, hollowware, china, crystal.
Oneida Australia Inc. - Stanley Rogers & Sons/Westminster Ch, Sydney, Australia

OPPENHEIMER CASING COMPANY

PO Box 849, Champlain, NY, 12919

Tel: (518) 298-5411 Fax: (518) 298-3152

Mfr. sausage casings.

Galen Pharmaceuticals Pty. Ltd., 163 Port Hacking Rd., Miranda, NSW 2228, Australia

OSMONICS INC.

5951 Clearwater Drive, Minnetonka, MN, 55343-8995

Tel: (612) 933-2277 Fax: (612) 933-0141

Mfr. fluid filtration and separation equipment and components.

Osmonics, Doncaster East VIC, Australia

OTIS ELEVATOR COMPANY

10 Farm Springs Road, Farmington, CT, 06032

Tel: (860) 676-6000 Fax: (860) 676-5111

Mfr. elevators and escalators.

Otis Elevator Co. Pty. Ltd., PO Box 151, 50 Airds Rd., Minto, NSW 2566, Australia

OUTBOARD MARINE CORPORATION

100 Sea Horse Drive, Waukegan, IL, 60085

Tel: (847) 689-6200 Fax: (847) 689-5555 Web site: www.omc-online.com

Mfr./market marine engines, boats & accessories.

OMC Haynes Hunter, 16 Computer Drive, Yatala, Queensland, Australia

OUTDOOR TECHNOLOGIES GROUP

1900 18th Street, Spirit Lake, IA, 51360

Tel: (712) 336-1520 Fax: (712) 336-4183

Mfr. fishing rods, reels, lines & tackle, outdoor products, soft and hard baits.

Outdoor Technologies Group Australia (OTG Australia), Box 775 22/9 Powells Rd., Brookvale 2100 NSW Australia

Tel: 61-2-9905-5611 Fax: 61-2-9905-5528 Contact: Adrian Cronin, Mng. Dir. Emp: 19

PACKARD BELL NEC, INC.

One Packard Bell Way, Sacramento, CA, 95828-0903

Tel: (916) 388-0101 Fax: (916) 388-1109 Web site: www.packardbell.com

Sales/distribution of home computers.

Packard Bell NEC, Sydney, Australia

PALL CORPORATION

2200 Northern Boulevard, East Hills, NY, 11548-1289

Tel: (516) 484-5400 Fax: (516) 484-5228 Web site: www.pall.com

Specialty materials and engineering; filters & related fluid clarification equipment.

Pall Australia Ltd., 106 Talinga Rd., Cheltenham, Melbourne, VIC 3192, Australia

Tel: 61-39-584-8100 Fax: 61-39-584-6647

Pall Gelman Sciences, PO Box 4100, Lane Cove DC, Sydney, NSW 2066, Australia

Tel: 61-2-9428-2333 Fax: 61-2-9428-5610

PANAMETRICS

221 Crescent Street, Waltham, MA, 02154

Tel: (781) 899-2719 Fax: (781) 899-1552 Web site: www.panametrics.com

Process/non-destructive test instrumentation.

Panametrics Pty. Ltd., PO Box 234, Gymea N.S.W. 2227, Australia

Tel: 61-2-9525-4055 Fax: 61-2-9526-2776 Contact: Peter Wingrove

PANDUIT CORPORATION

17301 Ridgeland Ave., Tinley Park, IL, 60477-0981

Tel: (708) 532-1800 Fax: (708) 532-1811

Mfr. electrical/electronic wiring components.

Panduit Pty. Ltd., 30-36 Kitchen Rd., Dandenong, VIC 3164, Australia

PARAMETRIC TECHNOLOGY CORPORATION

128 Technology Drive, Waltham, MA, 02154

Tel: (781) 398-5000 Fax: (781) 398-5674 Web site: www.ptc.com

Mfr. CAD/CAM/CAE software.

Parametric Technology Australia Pty. Ltd., 382 Wellington Rd., Mulgrave, VIC, Melbourne 3170 Australia

Tel: 61-3-9561-4111 Fax: 61-3-9561-4166

Parametric Technology Australia Pty. Ltd., Level 3, 275 Alfred St., North Sydney, NSW Sydney 2060 Australia

Tel: 61-2-9955-2833 Fax: 61-2-9955-2854

PAREXEL INTERNATIONAL CORPORATION

195 West Street, Waltham, MA, 02154

Tel: (781) 487-9900 Fax: (781) 487-0525 Web site: www.parexel.com

Provides contract medical, biotechnology, and pharmaceutical research and consulting services.

PAREXEL International Pty. Ltd., Level 13, 15 Blue St., North Sydney, 2060 NSW, Australia

Tel: 61-2-995-47951 Fax: 61-2-995-47976

PARKER HANNIFIN CORPORATION

17325 Euclid Ave., Cleveland, OH, 44112

Tel: (216) 896-3000 Fax: (216) 896-4000 Web site: www.parker.com

Mfr. motion-control products.

Parker Hannifin (Australia) (Pty.) Ltd., 9 Carrington Rd., Castle Hill, NSW 2154, Australia

PARSONS ENERGY & CHEMICALS GROUP INC.

2675 Morgantown Road, Reading, PA, 19607

Tel: (610) 855-2000 Fax: (610) 855-2001 Web site: www.parsons.com

Provide full engineer-procurement-construction services, studies and project and constructiion management for utilities and independent power producers worldwide.

Parsons Energy & Chemicals Group Inc., Melbourne, Australia

PAXAR CORPORATION

105 Corporate Park Drive, White Plains, NY, 10604

Tel: (914) 697-6800 Fax: (914) 696-4128 Web site: www.paxar.com

Mfr./sales/distribution of labels, hang tags, scanners, printing equipment and inks.

Monarch Marking Systems Australia Pty. Ltd., PO Box 71, Lidcombe, 2141, Australia

PEPSiCO INC.

700 Anderson Hill Road, Purchase, NY, 10577-1444

Tel: (914) 253-2000 Fax: (914) 253-2070 Web site: www.pepsico.com

Beverages and snack foods.

PepsiCo Australia Pty. Ltd., Australia

THE PERKIN-ELMER CORPORATION

761 Main Ave., Norwalk, CT, 06859-0001

Tel: (203) 762-1000 Fax: (203) 762-4228 Web site: www.perkin-elmer.com

Leading supplier of systems for life science research and related applications.

Perkin-Elmer Applied Biosystems Div., VIC, Australia

Tel: 61-3-9212-8585 Fax: 61-3-9212-8502

PFIZER INC.

235 East 42nd Street, New York, NY, 10017-5755

Tel: (212) 573-2323 Fax: (212) 573-7851 Web site: www.pfizer.com

Research-based, global health care company.

Howmedica Investments Pty. Ltd., Australia

Pficonprod Pty. Ltd., Australia

Pfizer Agricare Pty. Ltd., Australia

Pfizer Pty Ltd., Australia

S.D. Investments Pty. Ltd., Australia

Valleylab Australia Pty. Ltd., Australia

PHARMACIA & UPJOHN

95 Corporate Drive, PO Box 6995, Bridgewater, NJ, 08807

Tel: (908) 306-4400 Fax: (908) 306-4433 Web site: www.pnu.com

Mfr. pharmaceuticals, agricultural products, industry chemicals

Pharmacia & Upjohn, 9/19-21 Malua St., Dolls Point, NSW 2219, Australia

Upjohn Pty. Ltd., 55-73 Kirby St., Rydalmere, NSW 2116, Australia

PHELPS DODGE CORPORATION

2600 North Central Ave., Phoenix, AZ, 85004-3089

Tel: (602) 234-8100 Fax: (602) 234-8337

Copper, minerals, metals & spec engineered products for transportation & electrical markets.

Phelps Dodge Exploration Corp., Sydney, Australia

PHILIP MORRIS COMPANIES, INC.

120 Park Ave., New York, NY, 10017--559

Tel: (212) 880-5000 Fax: (212) 878-2167 Web site: www.

Mfr. cigarettes, food products, beer.

Philip Morris Ltd. (Australia), 252 Chesterfield Rd., Moorabbin, VIC 3189, Australia

PHILLIPS PETROLEUM COMPANY

Phillips Building, 411 S. Keeler Ave., Bartlesville, OK, 74004

Tel: (918) 661-6600 Fax: (918) 661-7636 Web site: www.phillips66.com

Crude oil, natural gas, liquified petroleum gas, gasoline and petro-chemicals.

Phillips Australia Chemicals Pty. Ltd., Captain Cook Dr., Kurnell, NSW 2219, Australia

Phillips Petroleum Co., GPO 73A, Brisbane, Queensland 4001, Australia

PICKER INTERNATIONAL INC.

595 Miner Road, Highland Heights, OH, 44143

Tel: (440) 473-3000 Fax: (440) 473-4844 Web site: www.picker.com

Mfr. diagnostic medical machines.

Picker Ltd., Sydney, Australia

PICTURETEL CORPORATION

100 Minuteman Road, Andover, MA, 01810

Tel: (978) 292-5000 Fax: (978) 292-3300 Web site: www.picturetel.com

Mfr. video conferencing systems, network bridging & multiplexing products, system peripherals.

PictureTel Australia Pty. Ltd., 182 Blues Point Rd., Level 6, North Sydney NSW 2060, Australia (Locations: Brisbane, Canberra & Melbourne)

Tel: 61-2-9978-8000 Fax: 61-2-9978-8008

PIONEER HI-BRED INTERNATIONAL INC.

400 Locust Street, Ste. 800, Des Moines, IA, 50309

Tel: (515) 248-4800 Fax: (515) 248-4999

Agricultural chemicals, farm supplies, biological products, research.

Pioneer Hi-Bred Australia Pty. Ltd., Taylor St., Toowoomba, Qld. 4350, Australia

PITNEY BOWES INC.

1 Elmcroft Road, Stamford, CT, 06926-0700

Tel: (203) 356-5000 Fax: (203) 351-6835 Web site: www.pitneybowes.com

Mfr. postage meters, mailroom equipment, copiers, bus supplies, bus services, facsimile systems and financial services.

Pitney Bowes Australia Pty., Level 3, Unit 3, 14 Aquatic Drive, Frenchs Foret, NSW 2086, Australia

Tel: 61-2-9454-4310 Fax: 61-2-9454-4441 Contact: Alan Stearn, Mng. Dir. Emp: 200

PITTSTON COMPANY

PO Box 4229, Glen Allen, VA, 23058

Tel: (805) 553-3600 Fax: (805) 553-3753 Web site: www.pittston.com

Trucking, warehousing and armored car service, home security systems

Stawell Gold Mine/Silver Swan, Sydney, Australia

PLANET HOLLYWOOD INTERNATIONAL, INC.

8669 Commodity Circle, Orlando, FL, 32819

Tel: (407) 363-7827 Fax: (407) 363-4862 Web site: www.planethollywood.com

Theme-dining restaurant chain and merchandise retail stores.

Planet Hollywood International, Inc., Melbourne, Australia

Planet Hollywood International, Inc., Sydney, Australia

PLAYTEX APPAREL INC.

700 Fairfield Ave., Stamford, CT, 06904

Tel: (203) 356-8000 Fax: (203) 356-8448 Web site: www.saralee.com

Mfr. intimate apparel.

Playtex Pty. Ltd., 104 Briens Rd., Northmead, NSW 2152, Australia

Playtex Pty. Ltd., PO Box 66, Wentworthville, NSW 2145, Australia

POLAROID CORPORATION

549 Technology Square, Cambridge, MA, 02139

Tel: (781) 386-2000 Fax: (781) 386-3276 Web site: www.polaroid.com

Photographic equipment & supplies, optical products.

Polaroid Australia Pty. Ltd., Enden Park Estate 31, Waterloo Rd., North Ryde, NSW 2113, Australia

POLICY MANAGEMENT SYSTEMS CORPORATION

PO Box 10, Columbia, SC, 29202

Tel: (803) 735-4000 Fax: (803) 735-5544

Computer software, insurance industry support services.

Creative Computer Systems Pty. Ltd., 436 Kilda St., Melbourne, VIC 3004, Australia

Policy Management Systems Australia Pty. Ltd., 3 Byfield St., North Ryde, NSW 2113, Australia

R.L. POLK & COMPANY

1155 Brewery Park Blvd., Detroit, MI, 48207-2697

Tel: (248) 728-7111 Fax: (248) 393-2860 Web site: www.polk.com

Directories, direct mail advertising.

R.L. Polk & Co. (Australia) Pty. Ltd., 671 Gardeners Rd., Mascot (Sydney), NSW 2020, Australia

R.L. Polk & Co. (Australia) Pty. Ltd., 96 Herbert St., Northcote (Melbourne), VIC 3070, Australia

R.L. Polk & Co. Australia Pty. Ltd., 50 Sheppard St., Hume (Canberra), ACT 2620, Australia

POLYCHROME GRAPHICS

222 Bridge Plaza Southkodak, Fort Lee, NJ, 07024

Tel: (201) 346-8800 Fax: (201) 346-8846

Metal offset plates, coating specialties, graphic arts films.

Polychrome A.C.P. Ltd., 193 Bouverie St., Carlton, VIC 3053, Australia

POTTERS INDUSTRIES INC.

PO Box 840, Valley Forge, PA, 19482-0840

Tel: (610) 651-4700 Fax: (610) 408-9723

Mfr. glass spheres for road marking & industry applications.

Potters Industries Pty. Ltd., Lot 4, Boundary Rd., Laverton, VIC 3028, Australia

POWER TECHNOLOGIES INC.

1482 Erie Blvd., PO Box 1058, Schenectady, NY, 12301

Tel: (518) 395-5000 Fax: (518) 346-2777

Power systems engineering, consulting, services & related control software; power quality hardware.

PTI Australia, 30 Angliss St., Wilston, Brisbane, Qld 4051, Australia

PPG INDUSTRIES

One PPG Place, Pittsburgh, PA, 15272

Tel: (412) 434-3131 Fax: (412) 434-2190 Web site: www.ppg.com

Mfr. coatings, flat glass, fiber glass, chemicals. coatings.

Transitions Optical Pty. Ltd., PO Box 95, Lonsdale, South Australia, 5160 Australia

PRECISION VALVE CORPORATION

PO Box 309, Yonkers, NY, 10702

Tel: (914) 969-6500 Fax: (914) 966-4428

Mfr. aerosol valves.

Precision Valve Australia Pty. Ltd., PO Box 312, Williamson Rd., Ingleburn, NSW 2565, Australia

Precision Valve Corp., 1/57 Darling Point Rd., Darling Point, Sydney, NSW 2027, Australia

PREFORMED LINE PRODUCTS COMPANY

600 Beta Drive, PO Box 91129, Cleveland, OH, 44101

Tel: (440) 461-5200 Fax: (440) 461-2918

Mfr. pole line hardware for electrical transmission lines; splice closures & related products for telecommunications.

Preformed Line Products (Australia) Ltd., Sydney, Australia

PREMARK INTERNATIONAL INC.

1717 Deerfield Road, Deerfield, IL, 60015

Tel: (847) 405-6000 Fax: (847) 405-6013 Web site: www.premarkintl.com

Mfr./sale plastic, diversified consumer & commercial products.

Tupperware Australia Pty. Ltd., Private Bag 6, Hawthorn, VIC 3122, Australia

PREMIX INC.

PO Box 281, Rt. 20, Harmon Road, North Kingsville, OH, 44068-0281

Tel: (440) 224-2181 Fax: (440) 224-2766

Mfr. molded fiber glass, reinforced thermoset molding compounds and plastic parts.

CME (Composite Materials Engineering), 29 Stud Rd., Bayswater, VIC, Australia 3153

Tel: 61-3-729-4999 Fax: 61-3-720-6870 Contact: Michael Lewis, Gen. Mgr. Emp: 40

PRICEWATERHOUSECOOPERS LLP

1251 Ave. of the Americas, New York, NY, 10020

Tel: (212) 596-7000 Fax: (212) 790-6620 Web site: www.pwcglobal.com

Accounting and auditing, tax and management, and human resource consulting services.

Price Waterhouse Ltd., Level 6, Maritime Centre, 201 Kent St., GPO Box 4177, Sydney, NSW 2001, Australia

Tel: 61-2-9256-7000 Fax: 61-2-9256-7777

Price Waterhouse Ltd., 256 St. George's Terrace, 8th Fl., PO BOX 7118, Cloisters Square, Perth, WA 6850, Australia

Tel: 61-9-322-4911 Fax: 61-9-322-7006

Price Waterhouse Ltd., Price Waterhouse Centre, 215 Spring St., 5th Fl., GPO Box 2798Y, Melbourne, VIC 3001, Australia

Tel: 61-3-9666-6111 Fax: 61-3-9666-6444

Price Waterhouse Ltd., 75 Hindmarsh Square, 4th Fl., GPO Box 1219, Adelaide, SA 5001, Australia

Tel: 61-8-236-7000 Fax: 61-8-236-7005

Price Waterhouse Ltd., Level 11, Waterfront Place, 1 Eagle St., PO Box 7894, Brisbane, Qld 4001 Australia

Tel: 61-7-364-5666 Fax: 61-7-364-5877

Price Waterhouse Ltd., Price Waterhouse Centre, 19 Moore St., GPO Box 386, Canberra, ACT 2601, Australia

Tel: 61-6-276-0222 Fax: 61-6-276-0285

Price Waterhouse Ltd. - Australasian Office, Level 14, Maritime Centre, 201 Kent St., GPO Box 4177 Sydney, NSW 2001, Australia

Tel: 61-2-256-7000 Fax: 61-2-256-7777

PROCTER & GAMBLE COMPANY

One Procter & Gamble Plaza, Cincinnati, OH, 45202

Tel: (513) 983-1100 Fax: (513) 562-4500 Web site: www.pg.com

Personal care, food, laundry, cleaning and industry products.

P&G Australia Pty. Ltd., 99 Phillip St., Parramatta NSW, Australia 2150

PROCTER & GAMBLE PHARMACEUTICALS

17 Eaton Ave., Norwich, NY, 13815-1799

Tel: (607) 335-2111 Fax: (607) 335-2798

Develop/manufacture pharmaceuticals, chemicals and health products.

Norwich Eaton Pty. Ltd., 6th Fl., Lombard House, 781 Pacific Hwy., Chatswood, NSW, Australia

PSDI MAXIMO

100 Crosby Drive, Bedford, MA, 01730

Tel: (781) 280-2000 Fax: (781) 280-0200 Web site: www.psdi.com

Develops, markets and provides maintenance management software systems.

PSDI Australia Pty. Ltd. _ Head Office, 3/76 Berry St., North Sydney, NSW 2060, Australia (Locations: Brisbane & Melbourne)

Tel: 61-2-9463-7734 Fax: 61-2-9957-2669 Contact: Peter Boyd, Gen. Mgr. Emp: 32

QMS INC.

One Magnum Pass, Mobile, AL, 36618

Tel: (205) 633-4300 Fax: (205) 633-4866

Mfr. monochrome and color computer printers.

QMS Australia Pty. Ltd., 651 Canterbury Rd., Surrey Hills, Vic. 3127, Australia

QUAKER CHEMICAL CORPORATION

Elm & Lee Streets, Conshohocken, PA, 19428-0809

Tel: (610) 832-4000 Fax: (610) 832-8682 Web site: www.quakerchem.com

Mfr. chemical specialties; total fluid management services.

Quaker Chemical (Australasia) Pty. Ltd., 8 Abbott Rd., Seven Hills, NSW 2147, Australia

Contact: P. Amos, Mng. Dir.

QUALITY SEMICONDUCTOR, INC.

851 Martin Ave., Santa Clara, CA, 95050

Tel: (408) 450-8000 Fax: (408) 496-0773 Web site: www.qualitysemi.com.

Mfr./design/distribute high-performance logic, networking and memory semiconductor devices.

Quality Semiconductor - AWA Microelectronics, Sydney, Australia

RADISSON HOTELS INTERNATIONAL

Carlson Pkwy., PO Box 59159, Minneapolis, MN, 55459-8204

Tel: (612) 540-5526 Fax: (612) 449-3400

Hotels and resorts.

Radisson Hotels Australia, Locations in Cairms, Palm Meadows, Port Douglas, Dunsborough and Melbourne, Australia

Tel: 61-3-9322-8000 Fax: 61-3-9322-8888

Radisson Kestrel Hotel, 8-13 South Steyne, Manly NSW 2095, Australia

Tel: 61-2-9977-8866 Fax: 1-2-9977-8209

RAIN BIRD SPRINKLER MFG. CORPORATION

145 North Grand Ave., Glendora, CA, 91741-2469

Tel: (626) 963-9311 Fax: (626) 963-4287 Web site: www.rainbird.com

World's largest manufacturer of lawn sprinklers and irrigation systems equipment.

Rain Bird Australia Pty. Ltd., 1/96 Levanswell Rd., Morabbin, VIC 3189, Australia

RAMSEY TECHNOLOGY INC.

501 90th Ave. NW, Minneapolis, MN, 55433

Tel: (612) 783-2500 Fax: (612) 780-2525

Mfr. in-motion weighing, inspection, monitoring & control equipment for the process industry.

Ramsey Engineering Pty. Ltd., PO Box 228, 20-22 Box Rd., Caringbah, NSW 2229, Australia

RAY & BERNDTSON, INC.

301 Commerce, Ste. 2300, Fort Worth, TX, 76102

Tel: (817) 334-0500 Fax: (817) 334-0779 Web site: www.prb.com

Executive search, management audit and management consulting firm.

Ray & Berndtson, Level 29, 367 Collins St., Melbourne 3000, Australia

Tel: 61-3-9614-2845 Contact: Ian R. G. Knop, Mng. Ptnr.

Ray & Berndtson, Level 7, 7 Macquarie Place, Sydney 2000, Australia

Tel: 61-2-252-2393 Fax: 61-2-252-2606 Contact: Ian R. G. Knop, Mng. Ptnr.

RAYCHEM CORPORATION

300 Constitution Drive, Menlo Park, CA, 94025-1164

Tel: (650) 361-3333 Fax: (650) 361-2108 Web site: www.raychem.com

Develop/mfr./market materials science products for electronics, telecommunications & industry.

Raychem (Australia) Pty. Ltd., Also in Auburn (Sydney), Perth & Underwood (Brisbane), Australia

Raychem (Australia) Pty. Ltd., 600 Doncaster Rd. #2, Doncaster, Vic. 3108, Australia

Sigmaform Australia, 1/22 Collinsvale St., PO Box 547, Archerfield, Qld. 4108, Australia

RAYTHEON COMPANY

141 Spring Street, Lexington, MA, 02173

Tel: (781) 862-6600 Fax: (781) 860-2172 Web site: www.raytheon.com

Mfr. diversified electronics, appliances, aviation, energy and environmental products; publishing, industry and construction services.

Raytheon International, Sydney, Australia

READER'S DIGEST ASSOCIATION INC.

Reader's Digest Rd., Pleasantville, NY, 10570

Tel: (914) 238-1000 Fax: (914) 238-4559

Publisher of magazines and books and direct mail marketer.

Reader's Digest Services Pty. Ltd., 26-32 Waterloo St., Surry Hills, Sydney, NSW 2010, Australia

RECKITT & COLMAN

1655 Valley Road, Wayne, NJ, 07470

Tel: (973) 633-3600 Fax: (973) 633-3633

Mfr. household, personal care, woodworking and industrial products.

L&F Products Australia, 82 Hughes Ave., Ermington, NSW 2115, Australia

REDKEN LABORATORIES INC.

575 Fifth Ave., New York, NY, 10017

Tel: (212) 818-1500 Fax: (212) 984-4776

Mfr. hair and skin care products.

Redken Labs. Pty. Ltd., Unit C, 31-33 Sirius Rd., Lane Cove, NSW 2066, Australia

REMINGTON PRODUCTS COMPANY, L.L.C.

60 Main Street, Bridgeport, CT, 06604

Tel: (203) 367-4400 Fax:

Mfr. home appliances, electric shavers.

Remington Products Australia Pty. Ltd., 19 Overseas Drive, Nobel Park, VIC 3174, Australia

Tel: 61-3-9795-5622 Fax: 61-3-9795-4980 Contact: Graham Kimpton, VP & Gen. Mgr.

RENA-WARE DISTRIBUTORS INC.

PO Box 97050, Redmond, WA, 98073

Tel: (425) 881-6171 Fax: (425) 882-7500 Web site: www.exec@renaware.com

Cookware and china.

Rena-Ware Distributors Pty. Ltd., 161 Broadway, Sydney, NSW 2000, Australia

RENAISSANCE HOTELS AND RESORTS

1 Marriott Drive, Washington, DC, 20058

Tel: (301) 380-3000 Fax: (301) 380-5181

Hotel and resort chain.

Renaissance Sydney Hotel, Sydney, Australia

Tel: 61-2-9372-2233

REPUBLIC NATIONAL BANK OF NEW YORK

452 Fifth Ave., New York, NY, 10018

Tel: (212) 525-5000 Fax: (212) 525-6996 Web site: www.rnb.com

Banking services.

Republic Mase Bank Ltd., Sydney, Australia

REVLON INC.

625 Madison Ave., New York, NY, 10022

Tel: (212) 527-4000 Fax: (212) 527-4995 Web site: www.revlon.com

Mfr. cosmetics, fragrances, toiletries and beauty care products.

Revlon Australia Pty. Ltd., 100 Walker St., North Sydney, NSW 2060, Australia

REXNORD CORPORATION

4701 West Greenfield Ave., Milwaukee, WI, 53214

Tel: (414) 643-3000 Fax: (414) 643-3078

Mfr. power transmission products.

Rexnord Australia Pty. Ltd., PO Box 304, Padstow, NSW 2211, Australia

REYNOLDS INTERNATIONAL INC.

6601 W. Broad Street, PO Box 27002, Richmond, VA, 23261

Tel: (804) 281-2000 Fax: (804) 281-2245

Mfr. aluminum primary and fabricated products, plastic and paper packaging and food service products; gold mining.

Reynolds Australia Ltd., 8th Fl., Griffin Ctr., 28 Esplanade, Perth, WA 6000, Australia

RIDGE TOOL COMPANY

400 Clark Street, Elyria, OH, 44035

Tel: (440) 323-5581 Fax: (440) 329-4853 Web site: www.ridgid.com

Hand & power tools for working pipe, drain cleaning equipment, etc.

Ridge Tool Australia Pty. Ltd., PO Box 660, Somerton, MDC, VIC 3061, Australia

Tel: 61-3-9357-0877 Fax: 61-3-9357-0866

THE RITZ-CARLTON HOTEL COMPANY, L.L.C.

3413 Peachtree Road NE, Ste. 300, Atlanta, GA, 30326

Tel: (404) 237-5500 Fax: (404) 365-9643

5-star hotel and restaurant chain.

The Ritz-Carlton Double Bay (Sydney), Double Bay, NSW, 2028, Australia

Tel: 61-2-9362-4744

The Ritz-Carlton Sydney, 93 Macquarie St., Sydney, NSW, 2000, Australia

Tel: 61-2-9252-4600

ROBERTSON CECO CORPORATION

5000 Executive Pkwy., Ste. 425, San Ramon, CA, 94583

Tel: (510) 358-0330 Fax: (510) 244-6780

Mfr. pre-engineered metal buildings.

H.H. Robertson (Australia) Pty. Ltd., PO Box 254, Revesby, NSW 2212, Australia

ROCKWELL INTERNATIONAL CORPORATION

600 Anton Boulevard, Costa Mesa, CA, 92626-7147

Tel: (714) 424-4200 Fax: (714) 424-4251 Web site: www.rockwell.com

Products & service for aerospace and defense, automotive, electronics, graphics & automation industry.

Rockwell Australia Pty. Ltd.- Electronic Commerce, Level 18, 124 Walker St., North Sydney, NSW 2060, Australia

Tel: 61-2-9959-1888 Fax: 61-2-9959-1855

Rockwell Australia Pty. Ltd.- Semiconductor Systema, 51 Rawson St., Ste. 603, Epping, NSW 2121, Australia

Tel: 61-2-9869-4088 Fax: 61-2-9869-4077

Rockwell Automation Australia Pty. Ltd., Level 1, 9 Waterloo Rd., North Ryde, NSW 2113, Australia (Locations: Adelaide, Brisbane, Melbourne, & Perth, Australia.)

Tel: 61-2-9886-8888 Fax: 61-2-9886-8800

Rockwell Automation Australia Pty. Ltd., Wellington Centre, 1 Portrush Rd., PO Box 264, Payneham, S. Australia 5070, Australia

Tel: 61-8-8365-1002 Fax: 61-8-8365-0322

ROHM AND HAAS COMPANY

100 Independence Mall West, Philadelphia, PA, 19106

Tel: (215) 592-3000 Fax: (215) 592-3377 Web site: www.rohmhaas.com

Mfr. industrial & agricultural chemicals, plastics.

Rohm and Haas (Australia) Pty. Ltd., 969 Burke Rd., Camberwell, VIC 3124, Australia (Locations: Geelong-Point Henry, VIC; Sydney- Burwood, NA; Brisbane - Lutwyche, QLD, Australia.)

Tel: 61-3-9272-4222

RUBBERMAID INC.

1147 Akron Road, Wooster, OH, 44691

Tel: (330) 264-6464 Fax: (330) 287-2846 Web site: www:rubbermaid.com

Mfr. rubber and plastic resin home, commercial and industry products.

Rubbermaid, Melbourne, Australia

RUSSELL REYNOLDS ASSOCIATES INC.

200 Park Ave., New York, NY, 10166-0002

Tel: (212) 351-2000 Fax: (212) 370-0896 Web site: www.ressreyn.com

Executive recruiting services.

Russell Reynolds Associates Inc., Level 15, Bourke Place, 600 Bourke St., Melbourne, VIC 3000, Australia

Tel: 61-3-9603-1300 Fax: 61-3-9670-1600 Contact: Lynn R. Anderson

Russell Reynolds Associates Inc., Ste. 1902, A.M.P. Centre, 50 Bridge St., Sydney, NSW 2000, Australia

Tel: 61-2-9364-3100 Fax: 61-2-9233-3471 Contact: Lynn R. Anderson

SAFETY-KLEEN CORPORATION

1301 Gervais Street, Columbia, SC, 29201

Tel: (803) 933-4200 Fax: (803) 933-4345 Web site: www.laidlawenv.com

Solvent based parts cleaning service; sludge/solvent recycling service.

Worton Services (NZ) Ltd., PO Box 234, 1 Jumal Place, Smithfield, 2164 NSW, Australia

Worton Services Pty. Ltd., PO Box 234, 1 Jumal Place, Smithfield, NSW 2164, Australia

SARA LEE CORPORATION

3 First National Plaza, Chicago, IL, 60602-4260

Tel: (312) 726-2600 Fax: (312) 558-4995

Mfr./distributor food and consumer packaged goods, intimate apparel and knitwear.

KOSL Australia, PO Box 572, Gosford, NSW 2250, Australia

Nutri-Metics International, Sydney, Australia

Playtex (Pty.) Ltd., 104 Briens Rd., Northmead, NSW 2152, Australia

Sara Lee Holdings (Australia) Pty. Ltd., Level 12, 1 Pacific Hwy., North Sydney, NSW 2060, Australia

SAS INSTITUTE INC.

SAS Campus Drive, Cary, NC, 27513

Tel: (919) 677-8000 Fax: (919) 677-8123 Web site: www.sas.com

Mfr./distributes decision support software.

SAS Institute (Australia) Ltd., Lane Cove, NSW, Australia

Tel: 61-2-9428-0428 Fax: 61-2-9418-7211

SAVANNAH INTERNATIONAL CORPORATION

4171 North Mesa, Bldg. D, El Paso, TX, 79902-1433

Tel: (915) 796-7000 Fax: (915) 593-4289

Mfr. wearing apparel.

Farah Australia Pty. Ltd., PO Box 219, Waterloo, NSW 2017, Australia

Farah Mfg. Australia Pty. Ltd., PO Box M-4, Sydney Mail Exchange, Redfern, NSW, Australia

SCHENECTADY INTERNATIONAL INC.

PO Box 1046, Schenectady, NY, 12301

Tel: (518) 370-4200 Fax: (518) 382-8129

Mfr. electrical insulating varnishes, enamels, phenolic resins, alkylphenols.

Schenectady Australia Pty. Ltd., 72 Christie St., PO Box 515, St. Marys, NSW 2760, Australia

SCHENKER INTERNATIONAL FORWARDERS INC.

150 Albany Ave., Freeport, NY, 11520

Tel: (516) 377-3000 Fax: (516) 377-3005 Web site: www.schenkerusa.com

Freight forwarders.

Schenker International (Australia) Pty. Ltd., 72-80 Bourke Rd., Private Bag 53, Alexandria NSW 2015, Sydney, Australia

Tel: 61-2-9333-0333 Fax: 61-2-933-0496

Schenker International (Melbourne) Pty. Ltd., International Trade Park, 7 International Square, PO Box 1078, Melbourne Airport, VIC 3043, Tullamarine, Australia

Tel: 61-3-9339-0622 Fax: 61-3-9338-2834

R.P. SCHERER CORPORATION

PO Box 7060, Troy, MI, 48007-7060

Tel: (248) 649-0900 Fax: (248) 649-4238 Web site: www.rpscherer.com

Mfr. pharmaceuticals; soft gelatin and two-piece hard shell capsules.

R.P. Scherer Pty. Ltd., 217-221 Governor Rd., Braeside, VIC, 3195, Australia

Tel: 61-3-9586-1222 Fax: 61-3-9586-1200 Contact: Barrie P. Webb, Chmn. & CEO Emp: 223

SCHERING-PLOUGH CORPORATION

1 Giralda Farms, Madison, NJ, 07940-1000

Tel: (973) 822-7000 Fax: (973) 822-7048 Web site: www.sch-plough.com

Proprietary drug and cosmetic products.

Essex Labs Pty. Ltd., PO Box 231, Baulkham Hills, NSW 2153, Australia

Plough Australia Pty. Ltd., PO Box 130, North Ryde, NSW 2113, Australia

SCHLAGE LOCK COMPANY

2401 Bayshore Boulevard, San Francisco, CA, 94134

Tel: (415) 467-1100 Fax: (415) 330-5530

Mfr. locks and builders hardware.

R.B. Davies Pty. Ltd., 450 Illawarra Rd., Marrickville, NSW 2204, Australia

SCHLEGEL SYSTEMS

1555 Jefferson Road, PO Box 23197, Rochester, NY, 14692-3197

Tel: (716) 427-7200 Fax: (716) 427-7216

Mfr. engineered perimeter sealing systems for residential & commercial construction; fibers; rubber product.

Schelegel Pty. Ltd., 44-48 Riverside Rd., Chipping Norton, NSW 2170, Australia

SCHOLASTIC CORPORATION

555 Broadway, New York, NY, 10012

Tel: (212) 343-6100 Fax: (212) 343-4712 Web site: www.scholastic.com

Publishing/distribution educational & children's magazines, books, software.

Scholastic Australia Pty. Ltd., 14 Railway Crescent, Lisarow via Gosford, NSW 2250, Australia

Tel: 61-43-283-55 Contact: Ken Jolly, Mng. Dir.

SCIENTIFIC-ATLANTA, INC.

1 Technology Pkwy South, Norcross, GA, 30092-2967

Tel: (770) 903-5000 Fax: (770) 903-2967 Web site: www.sciatl.com

A leading supplier of broadband communications systems, satellite-based video, voice and data communications networks and worldwide customer service and support.

Scientific-Atlanta Pty. Ltd., Unit 2, 2 Awautic Drive, Frenches Forest, NSW 2086, Australia

Tel: 61-2-9452-3388 Fax: 61-2-9451-4432

SEAGATE TECHNOLOGY, INC.

920 Disc Drive, Scotts Valley, CA, 95066

Tel: (408) 438-6550 Fax: (408) 438-7205 Web site: www.seagate.com

Develop computer technology, software and hardware.

Seagate Technology Australia Pty. Ltd., 1st Fl., Lot 3 Walker Place, Wetherill Park NSW 2164, Australia

Tel: 61-2-9725-3366 Fax: 61-2-9725-4052 Emp: 10

SEALED AIR CORPORATION

Park 80 Plaza East, Saddle Brook, NJ, 07662-5291

Tel: (201) 791-7600 Fax: (201) 703-4205 Web site: www.sealedair.com

Mfr. protective and specialty packaging solutions for industrial, food and consumer products.

Sealed Air Australia Pty. Ltd., 3 Burrows Rd., Alexandria, NSW 2015, Australia

Tel: 61-2-9550-7888 Fax: 61-2-9550-1962

Trigon/Viskase Pty. Ltd., 415 Creek Rd., Mt. Gravatt East QLD, PO Box 2107, Mansfield QLD, Australia

Tel: 61-7-3347-1333 Fax: 61-7-3849-6955

SEAMAN CORPORATION

1000 Venture Boulevard, Wooster, OH, 44691

Tel: (330) 262-1111 Fax: (330) 263-6950

Mfr. vinyl coated fabrics, geomembranes, roofing, pre-engineered structures.

Vessel Engineering Services Pty. Ltd., Citicorp House, 217 George St., Brisbane, Qld 4000, Australia

SEAQUIST PERFECT DISPENSING

1160 North Silver Lake Road, Cary, IL, 60013

Tel: (847) 639-2124 Fax: (847) 639-2142 Web site: www.seaperf.com

Mfr. and sale of dispensing systems; lotion pumps and spray-through overcaps.

Seaquist-Valois Australia Pty. Ltd., Wetherill Park, Australia

G.D. SEARLE & COMPANY

5200 Old Orchard Road, Skokie, IL, 60077

Tel: (847) 982-7000 Fax: (847) 470-1480 Web site: www.searlehealthnet.com

Mfr. pharmaceuticals, health care, optical products and specialty chemicals.

Searle Australia Pty. Ltd., PO Box 1380, South 20 Clarke St., Crows Nest, NSW 2065, Australia

Tel: 61-2-9902-4500 Fax: 61-2-9438-4930

SEQUENT COMPUTER SYSTEMS INC.

15450 SW Koll Pkwy., Beaverton, OR, 97006-6063

Tel: (503) 626-5700 Fax: (503) 578-9890 Web site: www.sequent.com

Mfr. symmetric multiprocessing technology computers.

Sequent Computer Systems Australia, Ltd., 160 Pacific Highway North, Sydney NS 260, Australia

Tel: 61-2-9900-4600

Sequent Computer Systems Inc., Level 11, 580 St. Kilda Rd., PO Box 6505 St. Kilda Rd. Ctr., Melbourne, VIC 3004, Australia

Contact: Nick Lambert, Mng. Dir.

THE SERVICEMASTER COMPANY

One ServiceMaster Way, Downers Grove, IL, 60515-1700

Tel: (630) 271-1300 Fax: (630) 271-2710 Web site: www.svm.com

Management service to health care, school and industry facilities; diversified residential and commercial services.

Merry Maids, Sydney, Australia

ServiceMaster, Sydney, Australia

THE SHARPER IMAGE CORPORATION

650 Davis Street, San Francisco, CA, 94111

Tel: (415) 445-6000 Fax: (415) 781-5251 Web site: www.sharperimage.com

Specialty retailer of innovative products.

The Sharper Image, Shop 20, 8 Whiteman St., Southbank, VIC 3006, Crown Melbourne, Australia

Tel: 61-3-968-26655

The Sharper Image, 447 Chapel St., South Yarra 3141, Melbourne, Australia

Tel: 61-3-9826-0011

SILICON GRAPHICS INC.

2011 N. Shoreline Blvd., Mountain View, CA, 94043-1389

Tel: (650) 960-1980 Fax: (650) 961-0595 Web site: www.sgi.com

Design/mfr. special-effects computer graphic systems and software.

Silicon Graphics Pty. Ltd., 446 Victoria Rd., Gladesville NSW 2111, Australia

Tel: 61-2-879-9500 Fax: 61-2-879-6026 Contact: Brenda Hunter, Mgr.

SIMON & SCHUSTER INC.

1230 Ave. of the Americas, New York, NY, 10020

Tel: (212) 698-7000 Fax: (212) 698-7007 Web site: www.SimonSays.com

Publishes and distributes hardcover and paperback books, audiobooks, software and educational textbooks.

Prentice-Hall of Australia Pty. Ltd., PO Box 151, 7 Grosvenor Pl., Brookvale, NSW 2100, Australia

SIMPLEX

1 Simplex Plaza, Gardner, MA, 01441-0001

Tel: (978) 632-2500 Fax: (978) 632-8027

Mfr./sale/service fire alarm & time control systems.

Simplex, Units F & G, 140 Old Pittwater Rd., Brookvale, NSW 2100, Australia

SIMPLICITY PATTERN CO., INC.

2 Park Ave., New York, NY, 10016

Tel: (212) 372-0500 Fax: (212) 372-0628 Web site: www.simplicity.com

Dress patterns.

Simplicity Patterns Pty. Ltd., 95-99 Bonds Rd., Punchbowl, NSW 2196, Australia

J.R. SIMPLOT CO., INC.

One Capital Center,999 Main Street, Ste.#1300, Boise, ID, 83702

Tel: (208) 336-2110 Fax: (208) 389-7515 Web site: www.simplot.com

Fresh/frozen fruits & vegetables, animal feeds, fertilizers.

Simplot Australia (Pty.) Ltd., 1279 Nepean Highway, Cheltenham, PO Box 177, Southland Centre, VIC, Australia 3192

Tel: 61-3-9264-0444 Fax: 61-3-9264-0405

SIZZLER INTERNATIONAL

12655 West Jefferson Boulevard, Los Angeles, CA, 90066

Tel: (310) 827-2300 Fax: (310) 822-5786

Sizzler and Kentucky Fried Chicken food chain restaurants

Sizzler International (Asia Pacific), 1620 Edmonstone St., New Market, Queensland, Australia 4051

Tel: 61-7-3352-0800 Fax: 61-7-3352-0877 Contact: Kevin Perkins, Pres.

SKADDEN, ARPS, SLATE, MEAGHER & FLOM LLP

919 Third Ave., New York, NY, 10022

Tel: (212) 735-3000 Fax: (212) 735-2000 Web site: www.sasmf.com

American/International law practice.

Skadden, Arps, Slate, Meagher & Flom (International), Level 13, 131 Macquarie St., Sydney, New South Wales, 2000, Australia

Tel: 61-2-224-6000 Fax: 61-2-9253-6044 Contact: Ronald C. Barasch, Partner

SMITH INTERNATIONAL, INC.

16740 Hardy Street, Houston, TX, 77032

Tel: (713) 443-3370 Fax: (713) 233-5996 Web site: www.smith.intl.com

Mfr. drilling tools and equipment and provides related services for the drilling, completion and production sectors of the petroleum and mining industries.

Smith International Australia (Pty.) Ltd., Unit 2, 30 Canvale Rd., Canning Vale, Western Australia 6155, Australia

Tel: 61-9-455-7000 Contact: Barry Olson, Area Mgr.

THE J. M. SMUCKER COMPANY

One Strawberry Lane, Orrville, OH, 44667-0280

Tel: (330) 682-3000 Fax: (330) 684-3370 Web site: www.smucker.com

Mfr. preserves, jellies, ice cream, toppings & peanut butter.

Henry Jones Foods, 233 Cardigan St., Ste. 9, Level 2, Carlton, Vic. 3053, Australia

SNAP ON DIAGNOSTICS

420 Barclay Boulevard, Lincolnshire, IL, 60069

Tel: (847) 478-0700 Fax: (847) 478-7308 Web site: www.snapon.com

Mfr. auto maintenence, diagnostic & emission testing equipment.

Suntester (Australia) Pty. Ltd., PO Box 382, 31 Prince William Drive, Seven Hills, NSW 2147, Australia

Tel: 61-2-9837-9199 Fax: 61-2-9838-0241 Contact: Don Rotunda, Gen. Mgr.

SNAP-ON INC.

2801 80th Street, Kenosha, WI, 53141-1410

Tel: (414) 656-5200 Fax: (414) 656-5577

Mfr. automotive & industry maintenance service tools..

Snap-On Tools (Australia) Pty. Ltd., PO Box 663, Seven Hills, NSW 2147, Australia

Snap-On Tools (Australia) Pty. Ltd., Also in Brisbane, Adelaide, Perth, Sydney, Glen Waverley, Australia

SONOCO PRODUCTS COMPANY

North Second Street, PO Box 160, Hartsville, SC, 29550

Tel: (803) 383-7000 Fax: (803) 383-7008 Web site: www.sonoco.com

Mfr. packaging for consumer & industrial market and recycled paperboard.

Sonoco Australia Pty. Ltd. (IPD), Sydney Enfield Plant, 84-82 Cosgrove Rd., Enfield, New South Wales 2136, Australia

Tel: 61-2-742-5599

Sonoco Australia Pty. Ltd. (IPD), Ulverstone Plant, 9 Trevor St., Ulverstone, Tasmania 7315, Australia

Tel: 61-4-251-504

Sonoco Australia Pty. Ltd. (IPD), Wodonga Plant, 36 Moloney Drive, Wogonga, VIC 3690, Australia

Tel: 61-60-561588

Sonoco Pacific Pty. Ltd., PO Box 499, North Sydney, NSW 2059, Australia

Sunoco Australia Pty. Ltd.(IPD), Brisbane Plant, 19 Pritchard Rd., Virginia, Queensland 4014, Australia

Tel: 61-7-3865-1322

Sunoco Australia Pty. Ltd.(IPD), Melbourne Plant, 17-25 Templestowe Rd., Bulleen, VIC 3105, Australia

Tel: 61-3-9850-1291

SPALDING ETONIC WORLDWIDE

425 Meadow Street, Chicopee, MA, 01021

Tel: (413) 536-1200 Fax: (413) 535-2746

Mfr. sports equipment and infant and juvenile furniture and accessories.

Spalding Australia Pty. Ltd., 969 Burke Rd., Camberwell, VIC 3124, Australia

SPENCER STUART & ASSOCIATES INC.

401 North Michigan Ave., Ste. 3400, Chicago, IL, 60611

Tel: (312) 822-0080 Fax: (312) 822-0116 Web site: www.spencerstuart.com

Executive recruitment firm.

Spencer Stuart & Associates Inc., 44th Fl., 55 Collins St., Melbourne, VIC 3000, Australia

Tel: 61-3-9654-2155 Fax: 61-3-9654-4730 Contact: John Mumm

Spencer Stuart & Associates Inc., 6th Fl., Johnsons Building, Cnr. George & Grosvenor Sts., Sydney, NSW 2000, Australia

Tel: 61-2-9247-4031 Fax: 61-2-9251-3021 Contact: John Mumm

SPRINT INTERNATIONAL

World Headquarters, 2330 Shawnee Mission Parkway, Westwood, KS, 66205

Tel: (913) 624-3000 Fax: (913) 624-3281

Telecommunications equipment & services.

Sprint International Pty. Ltd., Level 8, Prudential Centre, 495 Victoria Ave., Chatswood, NSW 2067, Australia

SPS TECHNOLOGIES INC.

301 Highland Avenue, Jenkintown, PA, 19046-2630

Tel: (215) 517-2000 Fax: (215) 517-2032

Mfr. aerospace & industry fasteners, tightening systems, magnetic materials, superalloys.

Unbrako Pty. Ltd., PO Box 77, Norcal Rd., Nunawading, VIC 3131, Australia

SPSS INC.

444 N. Michigan Ave., Chicago, IL, 60611

Tel: (312) 329-2400 Fax: (312) 329-3668

Mfr. statistical software.

SPSS Australasia Pty. Ltd., 121 Walker St., North Sydney, NSW 2060, Australia

SPX CORPORATION

700 Terrace Point Drive, PO Box 3301, Muskegon, MI, 49443-3301

Tel: (616) 724-5000 Fax: (616) 724-5720 Web site: www.spx.com

Mfr. Auto parts, special service tools, engine & drive-train parts.

Power Team Australia, 3 Expo Ct., Mt. Waverly, VIC 3149, Australia

Robinair Australia, c/o Australian Automotive Group, Unit 2, Gladstone Rd., Castle Hill, NSW 2154, Australia

SPX Australia Pty. Ltd., Unit 2, 8 Gladstone Rd., Castle Hill, NSW 2154, Australia

SRI INTERNATIONAL

333 Ravenswood Ave., Menlo Park, CA, 94025-3493

Tel: (650) 859-2000 Fax: (650) 326-5512

International consulting & research.

Australian Artificial Intelligence Institution, 1 Grattan St., Carlton, VIC 3053, Australia

THE ST. PAUL COMPANIES, INC.

385 Washington Street, St. Paul, MN, 55102

Tel: (612) 310-7911 Fax: (612) 310-8294 Web site: www.stpaul.com

Provides investment, insurance and reinsurance services.

QBE Insurance Group Ltd., 82 Pitt St., Sydney, N.S.W. 2000, Australia

STA-RITE INDUSTRIES INC.

293 Wright Street, Delavan, WI, 53115

Tel: (414) 728-5551 Fax: (414) 728-7323 Web site: www.starite.com

Mfr. water pumps, filters and systems.

Onga Pty. Ltd., 2 Redwood Drive, Notling Hill, VIC 3168, Australia

Tel: 61-3-9574-4000 Fax: 61-3-9562-7237 Contact: Bela Kristof Emp: 215

STANDARD & POOR'S CORPORATION

25 Broadway, New York, NY, 10004

Tel: (212) 208-8000 Fax: (212) 410-0200

Investment, finance, economic, mutual funds data and marketing information.

Standard & Poor's Corp., 120 Collins St., Level 37, Melbourne, Australia 3000

Tel: 61-3-9250-4500 Fax: 61-3-9250-4803 Contact: Louise Griffith, Mgr.

STANDARD COMMERCIAL CORPORATION

PO Box 450, Wilson, NC, 27893

Tel: (919) 291-5507 Fax: (919) 237-1109

Leaf tobacco dealers/processors and wool processors.

Standard Wool Australia (Pty.) Ltd., Fremantle, Australia

STANDEX INTERNATIONAL CORPORATION

6 Manor Parkway, Salem, NH, 03079

Tel: (603) 893-9701 Fax: (603) 893-7324 Web site: www.standex.com

Mfr. diversified graphics, institutional, industry/electronic & consumer products.

Roehlen Industries (Melbourne), Pty. Ltd., PO Box 354, Mordialloc, VIC 3195, Australia

Tel: 61-3-9580-4155 Fax: 61-3-9580-2954 Contact: Trevor Kahl, Mgr.

STANLEY BOSTITCH INC.

815 Briggs Street, East Greenwich, RI, 02818

Tel: (401) 884-2500 Fax: (401) 885-6511

Mfr. stapling machines, stapling supplies, fastening systems & wire.

Stanley Bostitch Australia, PO Box 472, Auburn, NSW, 2144, Australia

THE STANLEY WORKS

1000 Stanley Drive, PO Box 7000, New Britain, CT, 06053

Tel: (860) 225-5111 Fax: (860) 827-3987 Web site: www.stanleyworks.com

Mfr. hand tools & hardware.

Stanley-Bostitch (Pty.) Ltd., PO Box 450, 47-55 Williamson Rd., Ingleburn, NSW 2565, Australia

The Stanley Works Pty. Ltd., PO Box 10, 8 Moncrief Rd., Nunawading, VIC 3131, Australia

STATE STREET BANK & TRUST COMPANY

225 Franklin Street, Boston, MA, 02101

Tel: (617) 786-3000 Fax: (617) 654-3386 Web site: www.statestreet.com

Banking & financial services.

State Street Australia Ltd., Level 64, MLC Centre, 19 Martin Pl., Sydney, NSW 2000, Australia

STEINER CORPORATION

505 East South Temple Street, Salt Lake City, UT, 84102

Tel: (801) 328-8831 Fax: (801) 363-5680

Linen supply service.

Alsco, PO Box 245, Alexandria, Sydney, NSW 2015, Australia

STERLING SOFTWARE INC.

1800 Alexander Bell Drive, Reston, VA, 22091

Tel: (703) 264-8000 Fax: (703) 264-0762

Sales/service software products; technical services.

Systems Sterling Intl. (Australia) Ltd., Level 14, Tower A, Zenith Centre, 821 Pacific Hwy., Chatswood, NSW 2067, Australia

STIEFEL LABORATORIES INC.

255 Alhambra Circle, Ste. 1000, Coral Gables, FL, 33134

Tel: (305) 443-3807 Fax: (305) 443-3467

Mfr. pharmaceuticals, dermatological specialties.

Stiefel Laboratories Pty. Ltd., Unit 14, 5 Salisbury Rd., Castle Hill, NSW 2154, Australia

STOKES VACUUM INC.

5500 Tabor Road, Philadelphia, PA, 19120

Tel: (215) 831-5400 Fax: (215) 831-5420 Web site: www.stokesvac.com

Vacuum pumps and components, vacuum dryers, oil-upgrading equipment and metallizers.

Sharples-Stokes Pty. Ltd., PO Box 2344, N. Parramatta, NSW 2151, Australia

STORAGE TECHNOLOGY CORPORATION

2270 S. 88th Street, Louisville, CO, 80028-0001

Tel: (303) 673-5151 Fax: (303) 673-5019

Mfr./market/service information, storage and retrieval systems.

Storage Technology Corp., 174 Pacific Hwy., St. Leonards, NSW 2065, Australia

STRUCTURAL DYNAMICS RESEARCH CORPORATION

2000 Eastman Drive, Milford, OH, 45150-2789

Tel: (513) 576-2400 Fax: Web site: www.sdrc.com

Developer of software used in Modeling esting, drafting and manufacturing.

SDRC Ltd., 28/2 Eastbourne Rd., Darling Point, NSM 2027, Australia

Tel: 61-2-9328-0416 Fax: 61-2-9328-0417

SUDLER & HENNESSEY

1633 Broadway, 25th Fl., New York, NY, 10019

Tel: (212) 969-5800 Fax: (212) 969-5996

Healthcare products advertising.

Sudler & Hennessey, Southgate Tower West, Level 20, 60 City Rd., South Melbourne, VIC 3205, Australia

Tel: 61-2-9699-928 Fax: 61-3-9699-5662 Contact: G. Walker, Gen. Mgr. & R. Schmidt, Dir.

Sudler & Hennessey, The Denison, Level 15, 65 Berry St., North Sydney, NSW 2060, Australia

Tel: 61-2-9931-6111 Fax: 61-2-9931-6162 Contact: David McLean, Mng. Dir.

SULLAIR CORPORATION

3700 E. Michigan Blvd., Michigan City, IN, 46360

Tel: (219) 879-5451 Fax: (219) 874-1273

Refrigeration systems, vacuum pumps, generators, etc.

Sullair Australia Ltd., 1 Windsor Rd., Penrose, Vineyard, NSW 2756, Australia

SULLIVAN & CROMWELL

125 Broad Street, New York, NY, 10004-2498

Tel: (212) 558-4000 Fax: (212) 558-3588 Web site: www.sullcrom.com

International law firm.

Sullivan & Cromwell, 101 Collins St., Melbourne, VIC 3000, Australia

SUNDT INTERNATIONAL

PO Box 26685, Tucson, AZ, 85726

Tel: (520) 748-7555 Fax: (520) 747-9673

Holding company.

Sundt Intl. Pty. Ltd., 12th Fl., Wynyard House, 291 George St., Sydney, NSW, Australia

SYBASE, INC.

6475 Christie Ave., Emeryville, CA, 94608

Tel: (510) 922-3500 Fax: (510) 922-3210 Web site: www.sybase.com

Design/mfg/distribution of database management systems, software development tools, connectivity products, consulting and technical support services..

Sybase Australia Pty. Ltd., Level 15, 201 Miller St., North Sydney NSW 2060, Australia

Tel: 61-2-9936-8800 Fax: 61-2-9936-8822

Sybase Australia Pty. Ltd., Macquarie Building, Level 3, Ste. 2, 55 Blackall St., Barton ACT 2600, Australia

Tel: 61-6-273-5233 Fax: 61-6-273-2399

Sybase Australia Pty. Ltd., Level 12, 636 St. Kilda Rd., Melbourne VIC 3004, Australia

Tel: 61-3-9520-4000 Fax: 61-3-6520-4022

SYBRON INTERNATIONAL CORPORATION

411 E. Wisconsin Ave., Milwaukee, WI, 53202

Tel: (414) 274-6600 Fax: (414) 274-6561

Mfr. products for laboratories, professional orthodontic & dental markets.

Kerr Australia Pty. Ltd., Unit 2, 11 Packard Ave., Castle Hill, NSW 2154, Australia

Ormco Pty. Ltd., Unit 2, 11 Packard Ave., Castle Hill, NSW 2154 Australia

SYMANTEC CORPORATION

10201 Torre Ave., Cupertino, CA, 95014-2132

Tel: (408) 253-9600 Fax: (408) 446-8129 Web site: www.symantec.com

Designs and produces PC network security and network management software and hardware.

Symantec Pty. Ltd. - Melbourne, Como Business Centre, 644 Chapel St., South Yarra VIC 3142, Australia

Tel: 61-3-9823-6233 Fax: 61-3-826-3638

Symantec Pty. Ltd. - Sydney, 408 Victoria Rd., Gladesville, NSW 2111, Australia

Tel: 61-2-9850-1000 Fax: 61-2-9850-1001

SYMBOL TECHNOLOGIES, INC.

One Symbol Plaza, Holtsville, NY, 11742-1300

Tel: (516) 738-2400 Fax: (516) 563-2831 Web site: www.symbol.com

Mfr. bar code-driven data management systems, wireless LAN's, and Portable Shopping System™.

Symbol Technologies Australia Pty. Ltd., 10th Fl., 432 St. Kilda Rd., Melbourne, VIC 3004, Australia

Tel: 61-3-9866-6044 Fax: 61-3-9866-6270

SYSTEM INTEGRATORS INC.

PO Box 13626, Sacramento, CA, 95853

Tel: (916) 929-9481 Fax: (916) 928-0414

Develop/marketing software for publishing and newspapers.

Australian System Integrators Pty. Ltd., 541 Kent St. 2/F, Sydney, NSW 2000, Australia

TAB PRODUCTS COMPANY

1400 Page Mill Road, PO Box 10269, Palo Alto, CA, 94303

Tel: (650) 852-2400 Fax: (650) 852-2679 Web site: www.tabproducts.com

Mfr. filing systems and electronic office products.

TAB Datafile, Unit 1/12 Frderick St., PO Box 70, St. Leonards NSW, Australia 2065

Tel: 61-2-9436-4000 Fax: 61-2-9436-4111

TANDY CORPORATION

100 Throckmorton Street, Fort Worth, TX, 76102

Tel: (817) 390-3700 Fax: (817) 415-2647 Web site: www.tandy.com

Electronic & acoustic equipment.

Tandy Australia Ltd., 91 Kurrajong Ave., PO Box 254, Mt. Druitt, NSW, Australia

TBWA INTERNATIONAL

180 Maiden Lane, New York, NY, 10038

Tel: (212) 804-1000 Fax: (212) 804-1200

International full service advertising agency.

Whybin TBWA, Melbourne, Australia

TEAM INC.

1019 S. Hood Street, Alvin, TX, 77511

Tel: (281) 331-6154 Fax: (281) 331-4107 Web site: www.teamindustrialservices.com

Consulting, engineering & rental services.

Team Inc. Europe B.V., Sydney, Australia

Tel: 61-2-9828-0288 Fax: 61-2-9604-2780

TECHNOLOGY SOLUTIONS COMPANY (TSC)

205 N. Michigan Ave., Ste. 1500, Chicago, IL, 60601

Tel: (312) 228-4500 Fax: (312) 228-4501 Web site: www.techsol.com

Designs computer information systems and strategic business and management consulting for major corporations.

TSC Australia, Level 20, 99 Walker Street, North Sydney, SNW, Australia 2060

Contact: Barry Evans

TEKNIS CORPORATION

PO Box 3189, N. Attleboro, MA, 02761

Tel: (508) 695-3591 Fax: (508) 699-6059

Sale advanced technical products, fiber optics, materials for semiconductor mfr., security holographics

Teknis Pty. Ltd., PO Box 45, Kingswood, SA 5062, Australia

TEKTRONIX INC.

2660 Southwest Parkway Ave., PO Box 1000, Wilsonville, OR, 97070-1000

Tel: (503) 627-7111 Fax: (503) 627-2406 Web site: www.tek.com

Mfr. test & measure, visual systems/color printing & communications/video and networking products.

Tektronix Australia Pty. Ltd., 80 Waterloo Rd., North Ryde (Sydney), NSW 1670, Australia Perth, Australia.)

Tel: 61-2-9888-0100 Fax: 61-2-9888-0125

Tektronix Australia Pty. Ltd., Locations: Adelaide, Balwyn Melbourne, Brisbane and Canberra, Australia.

TELLABS INC.

4951 Indiana Ave. 6303788800, Lisle, IL, 60532

Tel: (630) 378-8800 Fax: (630) 679-3010

Design/mfr./service voice/data transport & network access systems.

Tellabs Pty. Ltd., 37 Loyalty Rd., North Rocks, NSW 2151, Australia

TELXON CORPORATION

3330 W. Market Street, PO Box 5582, Akron, OH, 44334-0582

Tel: (330) 867-3700 Fax: (330) 869-2220

Develop/mfr. portable computer systems & related equipment.

Telxon Australia Pty. Ltd., 4 Cambridge St., Epping NSW 2121, Australia

TENNANT COMPANY

701 North Lilac Drive, Minneapolis, MN, 55440

Tel: (612) 513-2112 Fax: (612) 541-6137 Web site: www.Tennantco.com

Mfr. industry floor maintenance sweepers and scrubbers, floor coatings.

Tennant Co. Australia Pty. Ltd., Unit 2, Block Y, 391 Park Rd., Regents Park Estate, N.S.W. 2143, Australia

Tel: 61-2-9-743-7955 Fax: 61-2-9743-7956

TENNECO AUTOMOTIVE

500 North Field Drive, Lake Forest, IL, 60045

Tel: (847) 482-5241 Fax: (847) 482-5295

Automotive parts, exhaust systems, service equipment.

Monroe Australia Pty. Ltd., Springs-Alexandria, Australia 52 O'Riordan St., Alexandria NSW 2015, Australia

Tel: 61-2-9693-1411 Fax: 61-2-9693-5720 Contact: David Wiggins, Mgr. Emp: 115

Monroe Australia Pty. Ltd., 1326-1378 South Rd., Clovelly park 5042, Adelaide, SA, Australia

Tel: 61-8-8277-1711 Fax: 61-8-8276-1653 Contact: Jack Chyer, Mgr. Emp: 457

TENNECO INC.

1275 King Street, Greenwich, CT, 06831

Tel: (203) 863-1000 Fax: (203) 863-1134 Web site: www.tenneco.com

Mfr. automotive products and packaging materials/containers.

J.I. Case (Australia) Pty. Ltd., Windsor Rd., Northmead, NSW 2152, Australia

Monroe Australia Pty. Ltd., PO Box 61, St. Marys, SA 5042, Australia

Walker Australia Pty. Ltd., 29 Morrow Rd., O'Sullivan Beach, SA 5166, Australia

TEXACO INC.

2000 Westchester Ave., White Plains, NY, 10650

Tel: (914) 253-4000 Fax: (914) 253-7753 Web site: www.texaco.com

Exploration/marketing crude oil, mfr. petro chemicals and products.

Texaco Overseas Petroleum Co., GPO Box 4991, Sydney, NSW 2001, Australia

TEXAS INSTRUMENTS INC.

8505 Forest Lane, Dallas, TX, 75243

Tel: (214) 995-2011 Fax: (214) 995-4360 Web site: www.ti.com

Mfr. semiconductor devices, electronic electro-mechanical systems, instruments and controls.

Texas Instruments Australia Ltd., Central Park Business Ctr., 38 Gilby Rd., Mount Waverly, VIC 3149, Australia

Tel: 61-3-9538-5200

TEXTRON INC.

40 Westminster Street, Providence, RI, 02903

Tel: (401) 421-2800 Fax: (401) 421-2878 Web site: www.textron.com

Mfr. aerospace, industry and consumer products (Bell Helicopter & Cessna Aircraft) and financial services.

Avco Financial Services Ltd., 910 Pacific Hwy., Gordon, NSW 2072, Australia

Tel: 61-2-498-0222 Fax: 61-2-498-0387 Contact: John R. Bergin, SVP & Mng. Dir.

THERMADYNE INDUSTRIES INC.

101 South Hanley Road, #300, St. Louis, MO, 63105

Tel: (314) 746-2197 Fax: (314) 746-2349 Web site: www.thermadyne.com

Mfr. welding, cutting, and safety products.

Cigweld, Melbourne, Australia

Tel: 61-3-9487-1234

THERMON

100 Thermon Drive, PO Box 609, San Marcos, TX, 78667-0609

Tel: (512) 396-5801 Fax: (512) 754-2425

Mfr. steam and electric heat tracing systems, components and accessories.

Thermon Australia Pty. Ltd., 30 London Dr., PO Box 532, Bayswater, VIC 3153, Australia

THOMAS & BETTS CORPORATION

8155 T&B Blvd., Memphis, TN, 38125

Tel: (901) 252-5000 Fax: (901) 685-1988

Mfr. elect/electronic connectors & accessories.

Thomas & Betts Pty. Ltd., 10 Lucca Rd., Wyong North, NSW 2259, Australia

TIDEWATER INC.

Tidewater Place, 1440 Canal Street, New Orleans, LA, 70112

Tel: (504) 568-1010 Fax: (504) 566-4582

Marine service and equipment to companies engaged in exploration, development and production of oil, gas and minerals.

Tidewater Port Jackson Marine Pty. Ltd., 1st Fl., 391 Plummer St., Port Melbourne, VIC 3207, Australia

TIFFANY & COMPANY

727 Fifth Ave., New York, NY, 10022

Tel: (212) 755-8000 Fax: (212) 605-4465 Web site: www.tiffany.com

Mfr./retail fine jewelry, silverware, china, crystal, leather goods, etc.

Tiffany & Co. Australia, Chiffley Place, 2 Chiffley Square, Sydney NSW 2000, Australia

Tel: 61-2-2235-1777

Tiffany & Co. Australia, Melbourne Crown & Entertainment Complex, Shop 45, 8 Whitman St., Southbank, VIC 3006, Australia

Tel: 61-3-9682-8788

TIMEX CORPORATION

Park Road Extension, Middlebury, CT, 06762

Tel: (203) 573-5000 Fax: (203) 573-6901

Mfr. watches, clocks, timing instruments.

TMX Australia Ltd., 86 Derby St., Pascoe Vale, Coburg, VIC 3058, Australia

THE TIMKEN COMPANY

1835 Dueber Ave. SW, PO Box 6927, Canton, OH, 44706-2798

Tel: (330) 438-3000 Fax: (330) 471-4118

Mfr. tapered roller bearings and quality alloy steels.

Australian Timken Prop. Ltd., 101-199 Learmonth Rd., Ballarat, VIC 3350, Australia

TMP WORLDWIDE, INC.

1633 Broadway, 33rd Floor, New York, NY, 10019

Tel: (212) 940-3900 Fax: (212) 940-7926

#1 Yellow Pages agency & a leader in the recruitment and interactive advertising fields.

TMP Worldwide Australia, Locations in Brisbane, Adelaide, Canberra, Hobart, Melbourne, and Perth, Australia

TMP Worldwide Australia, 7-13 Parraween St., Cremorna NSW Sydney, Australia

Tel: 61-2-99-08-9011

TOPFLIGHT CORPORATION

Box 2847, York, PA, 17405-2847

Tel: (717) 227-5400 Fax: (717) 227-1415 Web site: www.topflight.com

Commercial printing and service paper.

Pacific Lables Pty. Ltd., 1615 Botany Rd., Botany, NSW 2019, Australia

TOWERS PERRIN

335 Madison Ave., New York, NY, 10017-4605

Tel: (212) 309-3400 Fax: (212) 309-0975 Web site: www.towers.com

Management consulting services.

Tillinghast-Towers Perrin, Level 22, 44 St. George's Terrace, Perth, WA 6000, Australia

Tillinghast-Towers Perrin, Level 10, 101 Collins St., Melbourne, VIC. 3000, Australia

Tel: 61-3-9270-8111 Fax: 61-3-9270-8199

Tillinghast-Towers Perrin, GPO Box 85, Brisbane, Qld 4001, Australia

Tillinghast-Towers Perrin, Leve 16 MLC Centre, 19-19 Martin Place, Sydney, NSW 2000, Australia

Tel: 61-2-9229-5111 Fax: 61-2-9221-4505

Total Risk Management - A Towers Perrin Company, Level 9, 12 Moore St., Canberra, ACT 2601, Australia

Tel: 61-2-218-6700 Fax: 61-2-218-6705

TOYS R US INC.

461 From Road, Paramus, NJ, 07652

Tel: (201) 262-7800 Fax: (201) 262-8443

Retail stores: toys & games, sporting goods, computer software, books, records.

Toys R Us (Australia) Pty. Ltd., 391 Park Rd, Regents Park, NSW 2143, Australia

TRANE COMPANY

3600 Pammel Creek Road, La Crosse, WI, 54601
Tel: (608) 787-2000 Fax: (608) 787-4990
Mfr./distributor/service A/C systems and equipment.

Trane Australia, 24-32 Forge St., Blacktown, NSW 2148, Australia

TRANS-LUX CORPORATION

110 Richards Ave., Norwalk, CT, 06854
Tel: (203) 853-4321 Fax: (203) 855-8636 Web site: www.trans-lux com
Mfr. moving-message displays.

Trans-Lux Pty. Ltd., 73 Broadmeadow Rd., Newcastle, NSW 2292, Australia

TRANSAMERICA CORPORATION

600 Montgomery Street, San Francisco, CA, 94111
Tel: (415) 983-4000 Fax: (415) 983-4400 Web site: www.transamerica.com
Life insurance, leasing, and commercial lending services.

Transamerica Corporation, Sydney, Australia
australia

Tel: 61-2-9957-1922 Fax: 61-2-9922-5414

TRANTER INC.

1054 Claussen Road, #314, Augusta, GA, 30907
Tel: (706) 738-7900 Fax: (706) 738-6619 Web site: www.tranter.com
Mfr. heat exchangers.

SWEP Heat Exchangers Pvt. Ltd., 2/2 Apollo St., Warriewood, NSW 2102, Australia

Tel: 61-2-9979-7239 Fax: 61-2-9979-7213

TRICO PRODUCTS CORPORATION

817 Washington Street, Buffalo, NY, 14203
Tel: (716) 852-5700 Fax: (716) 853-6242
Mfr. windshield wiper systems and components.

Trico Pty. Ltd., Princess Hwy., 820-850 Springvale, VIC 3171, Australia

TRICON GLOBAL RESTAURANTS INC.

1441 Gardner Lane, Louisville, KY, 40213
Tel: (502) 874-1000 Fax: (502) 874-8315 Web site: www.triconglobal.com
KFC, Taco Bell and Pizza Hut restaurant food chains.

Bell Taco Funding Syndicate, Australia

Pizza Hut Properties Ply. Ltd., Australia

TRIMBLE NAVIGATION LIMITED

645 N. Mary Ave., Sunnyvale, CA, 94088
Tel: (408) 481-8000 Fax: (408) 481-2000 Web site: www.trimble.com
Design/mfr. electronic geographic instrumentation.

Trimble Navigation Australia Pty. Ltd.., Level 1/123 Gotha St., Fortitude Valley, Queensland 4006, Australia

Tel: 61-7-3216-0044 Fax: 61-7-3216-0088

TRITON ENERGY LIMITED

6688 N. Central Expressway, #1400, Dallas, TX, 75206-3925
Tel: (214) 691-5200 Fax: (214) 691-0340 Web site: www.tritonenergy.com
Provider of oil and gas services to the energy industry.

Crusader Ltd., AMP Place, 12 Creek St., Brisbane, Qld 4000, Australia

TRUE NORTH COMMUNICATIONS INC.

101 East Erie Street, Chicago, IL, 60611

Tel: (312) 425-6000 Fax: (312) 425-6350

Holding company, advertising agency.

FCB Direct, Level 3, 137 Pyrmont St., Pyrmont, NSW 2009, Australia

FCB Direct, 580 St. Kilda Rd., Melbourne, VIC 3002, Australia

FCB/Hocking Advertising Pty. Ltd., 11-13 King William St., Adelaide, SA 5000, Australia

Foote, Cone & Belding (Melbourne), 580 St. Kuilda Rd., Melbourne, VIC 3004, Australia

TRW INC.

1900 Richmond Road, Cleveland, OH, 44124-3760

Tel: (216) 291-7000 Fax: (216) 291-7932

Electric and energy-related products, automotive and aerospace products, tools and fasteners.

TRW Australia Ltd., PO Box 43, Carrington Rd., Marrickville, NSW 2204, Australia (Locations: Melbourne, Perth.)

TWIN DISC INC.

1328 Racine Street, Racine, WI, 53403-1758

Tel: (414) 638-4000 Fax: (414) 638-4482 Web site: www.twindisc.com

Mfr. industry clutches, reduction gears and transmissions.

Twin Disc (Pacific) Pty. Ltd., 130a Radium St., Welshpool, WA 6106, Australia

Tel: 61-8-9451-9366 Fax: 61-8-9451-9318

Twin Disc (Pacific) Pty. Ltd., PO Box 442, Virginia, Qld 4014, Australia

Tel: 61-7-3265-1200 Fax: 61-7-3865-1371

U.S. SURGICAL CORPORATION

150 Glover Ave., Norwalk, CT, 06856

Tel: (203) 845-1000 Fax: (203) 847-0635 Web site: www.ussurg.com

Mfr./development/market surgical staplers, laparoscopic instruments and sutures.

Auto Suture Co. Australia, Australia - All mail to U.S. address.

Auto Suture Holdings Pty. Ltd., Australia - All mail to U.S. address.

U.S. OFFICE PRODUCTS COMPANY

1025 Thomas Jefferson Street, NW, Ste. 600E, Washington, DC, 20007

Tel: (202) 339-6700 Fax: (202) 339-6720 Web site: www.usop.com

Sales and distribution of educational products, office supplies and office related services.

Bookland Pty. Ltd. Div. Blue Star Office Products, Perth, Western Australia

MBE (Mail Boxes Etc.), 184 Blues Point Rd., McMahons Point, North Sydney, NSW 2061, Australia

Tel: 61-3-9922-2300 Fax: 61-3-9923-2280

MBE (Mail Boxes Etc.), 60 Liverpool St., Hobart TAS 7000, Australia

Tel: 61-3-6231-9990 Fax: 61-3-6231-9995

U.S. Office Products Australia, Sydney, Australia

UNION CARBIDE CORPORATION

39 Old Ridgebury Road, Danbury, CT, 06817

Tel: (203) 794-2000 Fax: (203) 794-6269 Web site: www.unioncarbide.com

Mfr. industrial chemicals, plastics and resins.

Union Carbide Australia Ltd., Malvern, Australia

Union Carbide Australia Ltd., PO Box 287, 1-7 Jordan St., Gladesville, NSW 2111, Australia

UNION OIL INTERNATIONAL DIV

2141 Rosecrans Ave., El Segundo, CA, 90245

Tel: (310) 726-7600 Fax: (310) 726-7817

Petroleum products, petrochemicals..

Union Oil Development Corp., 8-12 Bridge St., Sydney, NSW 2000, Australia

UNIROYAL CHEMICAL CO., INC.

World Headquarters, Benson Road, Middlebury, CT, 06749
Tel: (203) 573-2000 Fax: (203) 573-2265
Tires, tubes and other rubber products, chemicals, plastics and textiles.
Uniroyal Pty. Ltd., 1028-1042 South Rd., Edwardstown, SA 5039, Australia

UNISYS CORPORATION.

PO Box 500, Union Meeting Road, Blue Bell, PA, 19424
Tel: (215) 986-4011 Fax: (215) 986-6850 Web site: www.unisys.com
Mfr./marketing/servicing electronic information systems.
Future Systems Ltd., 44-52 The Terrace, Wellington, NSW 6000, Australia
Synercom Australia Pty. Ltd., 213 Miller St., North Sydney, NSW 2060, Australia
Unisys Australia Ltd., 30 Alfred St., PO Box 488, Milsons Pt., NSW 2067, Australia
Unisys New Zealand Ltd., Unisys House, 44-52 The Terrace, Wellington, NSW 6000, Australia

UNITED AIRLINES INC.

PO Box 66100, Chicago, IL, 60666
Tel: (847) 700-4000 Fax: (847) 952-7680 Web site: www.ual.com
Air transportation, passenger and freight.
United Airlines, 11 Barrack St., Sydney, NSW 2000, Australia

UNITED ELECTRIC CONTROLS COMPANY

PO Box 9143, Watertown, MA, 02172-9143
Tel: (617) 926-1000 Fax: (617) 926-1000
Mfr./sale electro-mechanical & electronic controls & recorders.
United Electric Controls (Australia) Pty. Ltd., Unit 2, 615 Warrigal Rd., Locked Bag 600, Ashburton, VIC 3147, Australia

UNITED PARCEL SERVICE OF AMERICA, INC.

55 Glenlake Parkway, NE, Atlanta, GA, 30328
Tel: (404) 828-6000 Fax: (404) 828-6593 Web site: www.ups.com
International package-delivery service.
UPS Pty. Ltd., 247 King St., Mascot, NSW 2020, Sydney, Australia
Tel: 61-2-9667-1333 Fax: 61-2-9313-1515

UNITED PRESS INTERNATIONAL

1400 I Street, Washington, DC, 20005
Tel: (202) 898-8000 Fax: (202) 371-1239
Collection & distributor of news, newspictures, financial data.
United Press Intl., 2 Holt St., Sydney, NSW 5336, Australia

UNIVERSAL INSTRUMENTS

90 Bevier Street, S. Dock, Binghamton, NY, 13904
Tel: (607) 779-7522 Fax: (607) 779-7971 Web site: www.dover.com
Mfr./sales of instruments for electronic circuit assembly
Vema International Pty. Ltd., Bayswater, VIC, Australia
Tel: 61-3-9729-8222 Fax: 61-3-9729-7971

UOP INC.

25 E. Algonquin Road, Des Plaines, IL, 60017
Tel: (847) 391-2000 Fax: (847) 391-2253
Diversified research, development & mfr. of industry products & systems management studies & service.
Bostik Australia Pty. Ltd., PO Box 60, Thomastown 3074, Australia
Bostrom Div. UOP Pty. Ltd., Melbourne, Australia

Johnson Screen Div. UOP Pty. Ltd., Kirrawee, Australia

US FILTER/MEMTEC AMERICA

2118 Greenspring Drive, Timonium, MD, 21093

Tel: (410) 252-0800 Fax: (410) 252-6027

Mfr. purification & separation systems & products.

Memtec Ltd., 1 Memtec Parkway, South Windsor, NSW 2756, Australia

UTILICORPORATION UNITED INC.

PO Box 13287, Kansas City, MO, 64199-3287

Tel: (816) 421-6600 Fax: (816) 472-6281

Electric and gas utility.

UtiliCorp United, Sydney, Australia

VALSPAR CORPORATION

1101 South Third Street, Minneapolis, MN, 55415-1259

Tel: (612) 332-7371 Fax: (612) 375-7723 Web site: www.valspar.com

Produce paint, varnish & allied products.

Valspar Inc., Sydney, Australia

THE VANGUARD GROUP, INC.

100 Vanguard Boulevard, Malvern, PA, 19355

Tel: (610) 648-6000 Fax: (610) 669-6605 Web site: www.vanguard.com

Mutual fund provider.

The Vanguard Group, Sydney, Australia

VAREL INTERNATIONAL

9230 Denton Drive, PO Box 540157, Dallas, TX, 75354-0157

Tel: (214) 351-6486 Fax: (214) 351-6438

Mfr. oil, mining, geophysical, water-well & construction equipment.

Varel Far East, 3 Rawlinson St., O'Connor, Perth, WA 6163, Australia

VARIAN ASSOCIATES INC.

3050 Hansen Way, Palo Alto, CA, 94304-100

Tel: (650) 493-4000 Fax: (650) 424-5358 Web site: www.varian.com

Mfr. microwave tubes & devices, analytical instruments, semiconductor process & medical equipment, vacuum systems.

Varian Techtron Pty. Ltd., 679 Springvale Rd., Mulgravia, VIC 3170, Australia (Location: Melbourne, Australia.)

VEEDER-ROOT COMPANY

125 Powder Forest Drive, PO Box 2003, Simsbury, CT, 06070-2003

Tel: (860) 651-2700 Fax: (860) 651-2704

Mfr. counting, controlling and sensing devices.

Veeder-Root (Australia) Pty. Ltd., 82 Herald St., Cheltenham, VIC 3192, Australia

VELSICOL CHEMICAL CORPORATION

10400 West Higgins Road, Ste. 600, Rosemont, IL, 60018-3728

Tel: (847) 298-9000 Fax: (847) 298-9014 Web site: www.velsicol.com

Produces high performance specialty chemicals based on benzoic acid and cyclo pentadiene.

Velsicol Australia Ltd., PO Box 349, 10 Williams St., Turramura, NSW 2074, Australia

Tel: 61-2-9488-9011 Contact: Ross J. Blackmore, Dir.

VIACOM INC.

1515 Broadway, 28th Fl., New York, NY, 10036-5794

Tel: (212) 258-6000 Fax: (212) 258-6358 Web site: www.viacom.com

Communications, publishing and entertainment.

Prentice Hall of Australia Pty. Ltd., PO Box 152, Brookvale, NSW 2100, Australia

Simon & Schuster Pty. Ltd., 408-426 Victoria Rd., Sydney, NSW 2111, Australia

Viacom Intl. Pty. Ltd., 16th Fl., St. Martin's Tower, 31 Market St., Sydney, NSW 2000, Australia

VIASOFT, INC.

3033 N. 44th Street, Phoenix, AZ, 85018

Tel: (602) 952-0050 Fax: (602) 840-4068 Web site: www.viasoft.com

Mainframe computer software, specializing in OnMark 2000 software.

Viasoft Pty. Ltd., PO Box 603, North Sydney, NSW 2059, Australia

VIKING OFFICE PRODUCTS

950 West 190th Street, Torrance, CA, 90502

Tel: (310) 225-4500 Fax: (310) 324-2396 Web site: www.vikingop.com

International direct marketer of office products, computer supplies, business furniture and stationery.

Viking Office Products Pty., 15-17 Loyalty Rd., North Rocks, N.S.W. 2151, Australia

Tel: 61-2-9848-4444 Fax: 61-2-9848-4[illegible]5 Contact: Anne Cashman, Mgr. Emp: 197

VISIO CORPORATION

520 Pike Street, Ste. 1800, Seattle, WA, 98101-4001

Tel: (206) 521-4500 Fax: (206) 521-4501 Web site: www.visio.com

Developer and supplier of computer software.

Visio International Pty. Incorporated, Aistralia/New Zealand, Level 17, 275 Alfred St., North Sydney NSW 2060, Australia

Tel: 61-2-9929-2399 Fax: 61-2-9929-2349

VITRAMON INC.

PO Box 544, Bridgeport, CT, 06601

Tel: (203) 268-6261 Fax: (203) 261-4446 Web site: www.vishay.com

Ceramic capacitors.

Vitramon Pty. Ltd., E58 Frederick, PO Box 140, Rockdale, NSW 2216, Australia

VOLT INFORMATION SCIENCES, INC.

1221 Ave. of the Americas, 47th Fl., New York, NY, 10020-1579

Tel: (212) 704-2400 Fax: (212) 704-2424 Web site: www.volt.com

Staffing services and telecommunication services.

Volt Autologic Pty. Ltd., 845 Pacific Highway, Ground Fl., Chatswood, NSW 2067, Australia

Tel: 61-2-9419-6766 Fax: 61-2-9419-6950

WABCO (WESTINGHOUSE AIR BRAKE COMPANY)

1001 Air Brake Ave., Wilmerding, PA, 15148

Tel: (412) 825-1000 Fax: (412) 825-1501

Transportation technologies; develops, manufactures, and markets electronic products and equipment.

Futuris Industrial Products, Melbourne, Australia

Futuris Industrial Products, Sydney, Australia

WACKENHUT CORPORATION

4200 Wackenhut Drive, Ste. 100, Palm Beach Gardens, FL, 33410

Tel: (561) 622-5656 Fax: (561) 691-6736 Web site: www.wackenhut.com

Security systems & services.

Wackenhut Australia Pty., Ltd., Level 18, National Mutual Building, 44 Market St., Sydney, NSW 2000 Australia

Tel: 61-2-299-8529 Fax: 61-2-299-8039

WALKER, INC.

303 Second Street, Marathon Plaza, 3 North, San Francisco, CA, 94107

Tel: (415) 495-8811 Fax: (415) 957-1711 Web site: www.walker.com.

Provider of premier financial software solutions for large and medium-size enterprises.

Walker Interactive Systems Pty Ltd., Level 11, 99 Walker St., North Sydney, NSW 2060, Australia

Tel: 61-2-9923-1311 Fax: 61-2-9923-2572 Contact: Mark Ellis, Dir. Emp: 4

WANG LABORATORIES INC.

600 Technology Park Drive, Billerica, MA, 01821

Tel: (508) 967-5000 Fax: (508) 967-5911

Mfr. computer information processing systems.

Wang Computer Pty. Ltd., 10-14 Paul St., Milsons Point, NSW 2061, Australia

WARNER BROS INTERNATIONAL TELEVISION

4000 Warner Boulevard, Bldg.170, 3rd Fl., Burbank, CA, 91522

Tel: (818) 954-6000 Fax: (818) 977-4040

Distributor TV programming and theatrical features.

Warner Bros. Pty. Ltd., Level 6, 116 Military Rd., Neutral Bay SNW 2089, Australia

Tel: 61-2-9495-3000 Fax: 61-2-9908-5500 Contact: Wayne Broun, VP Mng. Dir.

WARNER ELECTRIC BRAKE & CLUTCH COMPANY

449 Gardner Street, South Beloit, IL, 61080

Tel: (815) 389-3771 Fax: (815) 389-2582 Web site: www.warnernet.com

Global supplier of Power Transmission and Motion Control Solution Systems; automotive, industry brakes, and clutches.

Warner Electric Australia Pty. Ltd., United 1/11 Packard Ave., Castle Hill, N.S.W. 2154, Australia

Tel: 61-2-894-0133 Fax: 61-2-894-0368

WARNER-JENKINSON CO. INC.

2526 Baldwin Street, St. Louis, MO, 63106

Tel: (314) 889-7600 Fax: (314) 658-7305

Mfr. synthetic & natural colors for food, drugs & cosmetics.

Warner-Jenkinson Australia, Unit 17, 24-26 Carrick Dr., Tullamarine, VIC 3043, Australia

WARNER-LAMBERT COMPANY

201 Tabor Road, Morris Plains, NJ, 07950-2693

Tel: (973) 540-2000 Fax: (973) 540-3761 Web site: www.warner-lambert.com

Mfr. ethical and proprietary pharmaceuticals, confectionery and consumer products & pet care supplies.

Parke Davis/Consumer Healthcare, PO Box 42, Cawarra Rd., Caringbah, Sydney, NSW 2229, Australia

Contact: John Montgomery, Pres.

WASTE MANAGEMENT, INC.

3003 Butterfield Road, Oak Brook, IL, 60523-1100

Tel: (630) 572-8800 Fax: (630) 572-3094 Web site: www.wastemanagement.com

Environmental services and disposal company; collection, processing, transfer and disposal facilities.

Pacific Waste Management New South Wales. Ltd., 3 Burroway Rd., Homebush Bay, NSW 2127, PO Box 592, Sydney Mkts 2129, Australia

WATERS CORPORATION

34 Maple Street, Milford, MA, 01757

Tel: (508) 478-2000 Fax: (508) 872-1990

Mfr./distribute liquid chromatographic instruments and test and measurement equipment.

Waters Associates Pty. Ltd., 82-96 Myrtle St., Chippendale, Sydney, NSW 2008, Australia

WATSON WYATT & COMPANY

6707 Democracy Blvd., Ste. 800, Bethesda, MD, 20817

Tel: (301) 581-4600 Fax: (301) 581-4937 Web site: www.watsonwyatt.com

Creates compensation and benefits programs for major corporations.

Watson Wyatt & Co., 4th Fl., One Collins St., Melbourne, VIC 3000, Australia (Location: Sydney, Australia)

Tel: 61-3-9650-9133 Fax: 61-3-9654-8227 Contact: Andrew Dillon

WD-40 COMPANY

1061 Cudahy Place, San Diego, CA, 92110-3998

Tel: (619) 275-1400 Fax: (619) 275-5823

Mfr. branded multiple-purpose lubrication, protection and general maintenance products.

WD-40 Co. (Australia) Pty. Ltd., PO Box 649, Epping, NSW 2121, Australia

Contact: Geoffrey J. Holdsworth, Mng. Dir.

WEATHERFORD INTERNATIONAL INC.

5 Post Oak Blvd, Ste. 1760, Houston, TX, 77227-3415

Tel: (713) 287-8400 Fax: (713) 963-9785 Web site: www.weatherford.com

Oilfield services, products & equipment; mfr. marine cranes for oil and gas industry.

Weatherford Australia Pty. Ltd., Unit 14/2 Powell St., PO Box 157, Osborne Park, WA 6017, Australia (Offices: Darwin, Perth.)

Tel: 61-3-5143-2772 Fax: 61-3-5143-2770

JERVIS B. WEBB COMPANY

34375 West Twelve Mile Road, Farmington Hills, MI, 48331

Tel: (248) 553-1220 Fax: (248) 553-1237

Mfr. integrators of material handling systems.

Webb Conveyor Co. of Australia, PO Box 1063, Bundoora, VIC 3083, Australia

WEIGHT WATCHERS INTERNATIONAL

175 Crossways Park West, Woodbury, NY, 11797

Tel: (516) 390-1400 Fax: (516) 390-1763

Weight loss programs.

Weight Watchers International, Sydney, Australia

WESLEY-JESSEN CORPORATION

333 East Howard Ave., Des Plains, IL, 60018

Tel: (847) 294-3000 Fax: (847) 294-3434

Contact lenses and accessories, ophthalmic and dermatology products.

Barnes-Hind Pty. Ltd., 7 Dickson Ave., Artarmon, NSW 2064, Australia

THE WEST COMPANY, INC.

101 Gordon Drive, PO Box 645, Lionville, PA, 19341-0645

Tel: (610) 594-2900 Fax: (610) 594-3014 Web site: www.thewestcompany.com

Mfr. products for filling, sealing, dispensing & delivering needs of health care & consumer products markets.

West Pharmapackaging Pty. Ltd., Brookvale, Sydney, Australia

Tel: 61-2-9939-1199

WEST STAFF SERVICES INC.

301 Lennon Lane, Walnut Creek, CA, 94598-2453

Tel: (925) 930-5300 Fax: (925) 934-5489 Web site: www.westaff.com

Secretarial & clerical temporary service.

Western Personnel Services Pty. Ltd., PO Box 139, South Melbourne, Vic. 3205, Australia

WESTERN ATLAS INC.

10205 Westheimer, Houston, TX, 77251-1407

Tel: (713) 972-4000 Fax: (713) 952-9837 Web site: www.waii.com

Full service to the oil industry.

Western Atlas Logging Services, Darwin Offshore Logistics Base, Lot 4233 Pruen Rd., PO Box 352, Berrimah NT 0828, Australia

Tel: 61-8-8947-1282 Fax: 61-8-8947-2227 Contact: V. Merkulov, Service Mgr.

Western Atlas Logging Services, 2nd Level Sheraton Court, 207 Adelaide Terrace, East Perth 6004, Western Australia, Australia

Tel: 61-9-268-2682 Fax: 61-9-268-2600 Contact: James McDougall, Bus. Mgr.

Western Geophysical, 432 St. Kilda Rd., 9th Fl., Anl House, South Melbourne, VIC 3004, Australia

Tel: 61-3-9820-8700 Fax: 61-3-9820-8703 Contact: M.Giles, Mgr.

Western Geophysical - Adelaide Processing Center, 74 George St., Thebarton, South Australia 5031, Australia

Tel: 61-8-8234-5229 Fax: 61-8-8234-5876 Contact: M. Symonds, Mgr.

Western Geophysical, Far East & Australia HQ, 2nd Level, Sheraton Court, 207 Adeliade Terrace, East Perth 6004, Western Australia, Australia

Tel: 61-8-9268-2682 Fax: 61-8-9268-2600 Contact: S. Pickering, Area Mgr.

WESTERN UNION

1 Mack Center Drive, Paramus, NJ, 07657

Tel: (201) 986-5100 Fax: (201) 818-6611

Financial and messaging service.

Western Union Financial Services Intl., 259 George St., Sydney NSW 2000, Australia

WESTINGHOUSE ELECTRIC (CBS)

11 Stanwix Street, Pittsburgh, PA, 15222-1384

Tel: (412) 244-2000 Fax: (412) 642-4650

TV/radio broadcasting, mfr. electronic systems for industry/defense, financial & environmental services.

Tyree Industries Ltd., PO Box 315, Liverpool, NSW 2170, Australia

WESTVACO CORPORATION

299 Park Ave., New York, NY, 10171

Tel: (212) 688-5000 Fax: (212) 318-5055 Web site: www.westvaco.com

Mfr. paper, packaging, chemicals.

Westvaco Pacific Pty. Ltd., 2SM Bldg., 186 Blues Point Rd., North Sydney, NSW 2060, Australia

WHIRLPOOL CORPORATION

2000 N. M-63, Benton Harbor, MI, 49022-2692

Tel: (616) 923-5000 Fax: (616) 923-5443 Web site: www.whirlpoolcorp.com

Mfr./market home appliances: Whirlpool, Roper, KitchenAid, Estate, and Inglis.

Whirlpool Asia Ltd., Noble Park, Australia

WHITEHALL-ROBINS INC.

1407 Cummings Drive, PO Box 26609, Richmond, VA, 23261-6609

Tel: (804) 257-2000 Fax: (804) 257-2120 Web site: www.ahp.com/whitehall.htm

Mfr. ethical pharmaceuticals and consumer products.

Whitehall-Robins Pty. Ltd., 102 Bonds Rd., Punchbowl, NSW 2196, Australia

JOHN WILEY & SONS INC.

605 Third Ave., New York, NY, 10158-0012

Tel: (212) 850-6000 Fax: (212) 850-6088 Web site: www.wiley.com

Publisher: print & electronic products for academic, professional, scientific, technical & consumer market.

Jacaranda Wiley Ltd., 33 Park Rd., PO Box 1226, Milton, Qld. 4064, Australia

Tel: 61-7-385-9755 Fax: 61-7-3859-9715 Contact: Peter Donoughue, Mgr.

WITCO CORPORATION

One American Lane, Greenwich, CT, 06831-2559

Tel: (203) 552-2000 Fax: (203) 552-3070 Web site: www.witco.com

Mfr. chemical and petroleum products.

Witco Australia Pty. Ltd., 27-31 Doody St., Alexandria, NSW 2015, Australia

WIX FILTRATION PRODUCTS

1301 E. Ozark Ave., Gastonia, NC, 28052

Tel: (704) 864-6711 Fax: (704) 864-1843

Mfr. oil, air and fuel filters.

Wix Australia, 415 West Botany St., Rocksdale NSW 2216, Australia

Tel: 61-2-9587-7222 Fax: 61-2-9330-9300 Contact: Goff Collins, Gen. Mgr. Emp: 300

WOODWARD GOVERNOR COMPANY

5001 North Second Street, PO Box 7001, Rockford, IL, 61125-7001

Tel: (815) 877-7441 Fax: (815) 639-6033 Web site: www.woodward.com

Mfr./service speed control devices and systems for aircraft turbines, industrial engines and turbines.

Woodward Governor Company, PO Box 319, Unit 1-1, Wirega Ave., Kingsgrove, NSW 2208, Australia

Tel: 61-2-9758-2322 Fax: 61-2-9750-6272 Contact: Bob Thilmont Emp: 15

WORLD COURIER INC.

1313 Fourth Ave., New Hyde Park, NY, 11041

Tel: (516) 354-2600 Fax: (516) 354-2644

International courier service.

World Courier Australia Pty. Ltd., 23-25 O'Connell St., Sydney, NSW 2065, Australia

WORLDCOM, INC.

515 East Amite Street, Jackson, MS, 39201-2701

Tel: (601) 360-8600 Fax: (601) 360-8616 Web site: www.wcom.com

Telecommunications company serving local, long distance and Internet customers domestically and internationally.

WorldCom International, Sydney, Australia

WRIGHT LINE INC.

160 Gold Star Blvd, Worcester, MA, 01606

Tel: (508) 852-4300 Fax: (508) 853-8904

Mfr. filing systems.

Datafile Pty. Ltd., 19-21 Antoine St., Rydalmere, NSW 2116, Australia

WM WRIGLEY JR. COMPANY

410 N. Michigan Ave., Chicago, IL, 60611-4287

Tel: (312) 644-2121 Fax: (312) 644-0353 Web site: www.wrigley.com

Mfr. chewing gum.

The Wrigley Co. Pty. Ltd., PO Box 64, Hornsby, (Sydney) NSW 2078, Australia

WUNDERMAN CATO JOHNSON

675 Ave. of the Americas, New York, NY, 10010-5104

Tel: (212) 941-3000 Fax: (212) 633-0957 Web site: www.wcj.com

International advertising and marketing consulting firm.

Mosiaca Multicultural Marketing, "The Denison", Level 14, 65 Berry St., North Sydney, NSW 2060, Australia

Tel: 61-2-9931-6262 Fax: 61-2-9956-7607 Contact: Paula Masselos, Gen. Mgr.

Wunderman Cato Johnson, "The Denison", Level 14, 65 Berry St., North Sydney, NSW 2060, Australia

Tel: 61-2-9931-6262 Fax: 61-2-9956-7607 Contact: Peter Horovitz, Mng. Dir.

Wunderman Cato Johnson, Melbourne Office, 4th Fl., 21-31 Goodwood St., Richmond, VIC 3121 Australia

Tel: 61-3-9426-1555 Fax: 61-3-9426-1557 Contact: Peter Horovitz, Mng. Dir.

Wunderman Cato Johnson, Adeliade Office, 182-184 Fullarton Rd., 1st Fl., Dulwich, SA 5065, Australia

Tel: 61-8-8366-4777 Fax: 61-8-8333-2276 Contact: John Peters, Mng. Dir.

WYNN OIL COMPANY

1050 West Fifth Street, Azusa, CA, 91702-9510

Tel: (626) 334-0231 Fax: (626) 334-1456 Web site: www.wynnoil.com

Mfr. of specialty chemicals, equipment and related service programs for automotive and industrial markets.

Wynn's Australia Pty. Ltd., 1-3 Rodborough Rd., PO Box 96, French's Forest, NSW 2086, Australia

Tel: 61-2-9451-3444 Fax: 61-2-9975-1785 Contact: Kevin Plummer, Pres. Emp: 22

XEROX CORPORATION

800 Long Ridge Road, PO Box 1600, Stamford, CT, 06904

Tel: (203) 968-3000 Fax: (203) 968-4312 Web site: www.xerox.com

Mfr. document processing equipment, systems and supplies.

Fuji Xerox Australia Pty, Ltd., 101 Waterloo Rd., North Ryde NSW 2113, Australia

Tel: 61-2-9856-5000 Fax: 61-2-9856-5003

XTRA CORPORATION

60 State Street, Boston, MA, 02109

Tel: (617) 367-5000 Fax: (617) 227-3173 Web site: www.xtracorp.com

Holding company: leasing.

Xtra International, Sydney, Australia

XYLAN CORPORATION

26707 West Agoura Road, Calabasas, CA, 91302

Tel: (818) 880-3500 Fax: (818) 880-3505 Web site: www.xylan.com

Mfr. Campus data network switches.

Xylan Corporation, Australian Headquarters, Sydney, Australia

Tel: 61-2-9957-6561

YAHOO! INC.

3420 Central Expressway, Santa Clara, CA, 95051

Tel: (408) 731-3300 Fax: (408) 731-3301 Web site: www.yahoo-inc.com

Internet media company providing specialized content, free electronic mail and community offerings and commerce.

Yahoo! Inc., Ste. 10/Norberry Terrace, 177-199 Pacific Highway, North Sydney, NSW, Australia 2060

Tel: 61-2-9460-0328 Fax: 61-2-9460-0277

YOUNG & RUBICAM INC.

285 Madison Ave., New York, NY, 10017

Tel: (212) 210-3000 Fax: (212) 370-3796 Web site: www.yr.com

Advertising, public relations, direct marketing and sales promotion, corporate & product ID management.

Young & Rubicam Australia/New Zealand, 65 Berry St., 17th Fl., North Sydney, NSW 2060, Australia

Young & Rubicam Pty. Ltd., 182-184 Fullarton Rd., Dulwich, SA 5065, Australia

Austria

3COM CORPORATION

5400 Bayfront Plaza, Santa Clara, CA, 95052-8145

Tel: (408) 764-5000 Fax: (408) 764-5001 Web site: www.3com.com

Develop/mfr. computer networking products & systems.

3Com GmbH, Opernring 5/Top 412, A-1010 Vienna, Austria

Tel: 43-1-580-170 Fax: 43-1-580-17-20

3M

3M Center, St. Paul, MN, 55144-1000

Tel: (612) 733-1110 Fax: (612) 733-9973 Web site: www.mmm.com

Mfr. diversified products for industry, health care, imaging, communications, transport, safety, consumer, etc.

3M Osterreich GesmbH, Brunner Feldstrasse 63, A-2380 Perchtoldsdorf, Austria

Tel: 43-1-86-6860 Fax: 43-1-86-686-269

AAF-McQUAY INC.

111 South Calvert Street, Ste. 2800, Baltimore, MD, 21202

Tel: (410) 528-2755 Fax: (410) 528-2797 Web site: www.mcquay.com

Mfr. air quality control products: heating, ventilating, air-conditioning & filtration products & services.

AAF Luftreiningungsysteme GmbH, Weyrgasse 8/7, A-1030 Vienna, Austria

AIR EXPRESS INTERNATIONAL CORPORATION

120 Tokeneke Road, PO Box 1231, Darien, CT, 06820

Tel: (203) 655-7900 Fax: (203) 655-5779 Web site: www.aeilogistics.com

Air freight forwarder.

AEI / Cargoplan Speditiona GmbH, Objekt 630, Airport Vienna, A-1300 Vienna, Austria (Locations: Graz, Innsbruck, Linz, Salzburg)

Tel: 43-1-7007-3298 Fax: 43-1-7007-3399

ALLEN TELECOM

25101 Chagrin Boulevard, Beachwood, OH, 44122-5619

Tel: (216) 765-5818 Fax: (216) 765-0410 Web site: www.allentele.com

Mfr. communications equipment, automotive bodies and parts, electronic components.

A. Rohe GmbH, Scherbangasse 3, A-1230 Vienna, Austria

MIKOM - Austria, Vertriebs und Service GmbH, Himbergstrasse 7, 3 Steige, 2320 Wein-Schwechart, Austria

Tel: 43-1-706-3999 Fax: 43-1-707-4017

AMDAHL CORPORATION

1250 East Arques Ave., PO Box 3470, Sunnyvale, CA, 94088-3470

Tel: (408) 746-6000 Fax: (408) 773-0833 Web site: www.amdahl.com

Development/mfr. large scale computers, software, data storage products, information-technology solutions & support.

Amdahl Computersysteme GmbH, Palais Liechtenstein, Alserbachstrasse 16, A-1090 Vienna, Austria

Tel: 43-1-310-43000 Fax: 43-1-310-430010

AMERICAN STANDARD INC.

One Centennial Ave., Piscataway, NJ, 08855-6820

Tel: (732) 980-3000 Fax: (732) 980-6118

Mfr. heating, plumbing & sanitary equipment, china, earthenware.

Ideal Standard, Abteilung der Wabco-Westinghouse GmbH, Pasettistrasse 33-35, A-1200 Vienna, Austria

AMMIRATI PURIS LINTAS

One Dag Hammarskjold Plaza, New York, NY, 10017

Tel: (212) 605-8000 Fax: (212) 605-4705 Web site: www.interpublic.com

International advertising agency.

Ammirati Puris Lintas Austria, Prinz Eugenstrasse 8, A-1041 Vienna, Austria

Tel: 43-1-501120 Fax: 43-1-50112-207 Contact: Hannes Sonnberger

P.C.S. Salzburg, Ernst-Grein-Strasse 5, A-5026 Salzburg, Austria

Tel: 43-662-648635 Fax: 43-662-64864033 Contact: Guenther Hofmann, Mng. Dir.

AMP INC.

470 Friendship Road, PO Box 3608, Harrisburg, PA, 17105-3608

Tel: (717) 564-0100 Fax: (717) 780-6130

Develop/mfr. electronic & electrical connection products & systems.

AMP Osterreich Handelsges, MBH, Pilzgasse 31, A-1211 Vienna, Austria

Tel: 43-222-277-970

AMPHENOL PRODUCTS

1925A Ohio Street, Lisle, IL, 60532

Tel: (630) 960-1010 Fax: (630) 810-5640

Electric interconnect/penetrate systems & assemblies.

Amphenol GmbH, Tautenhayngasse 22, A-1150 Vienna, Austria

AMWAY CORPORATION

7575 Fulton Street East, Ada, MI, 49355-0001

Tel: (616) 787-6000 Fax: (616) 787-6177 Web site: www.amway.com

Mfr./sale home care, personal care, nutrition & houseware products.

Amway GmbH, Wienerstrasse 720, A-2203 Grossebersdorf, Austria

ANDERSEN CONSULTING

100 South Wacker Drive, Ste. 1059, Chicago, IL, 60606

Tel: (311) 123-7271 Fax: (312) 507-7965 Web site: www.ac.com

Provides management & technology consulting services.

Andersen Consulting, Jacquingasse 29, A-1030 Vienna, Austria

Tel: 43-1-799-1508 Fax: 43-1-799-1509

AON CORPORATION

123 North Wacker Drive, Chicago, IL, 60606

Tel: (312) 701-3000 Fax: (312) 701-3100 Web site: www.aon.com

Insurance brokers worldwide; underwrites accident & health insurance, specialty & professional insurance; & provides risk management consultation.

AON Jauch & Hübener, H.-Sattler-Gasse 8, A-5020, Salzburg, Austria

Tel: 43-662-870965 Fax: 43-662-878926 Contact: Randolf Fasching

AON Jauch & Hübener, M. Gaismayer-Strasse 11, A-6020, Innsbruck, Austria

Tel: 43-512-578579 Fax: 43-512-578589-14 Contact: Bernhard Rushwurm

AON Jauch & Hübener, Blechturmgasse 11, A-100, Vienna, Austria

Tel: 43-1-545-1686 Fax: 43-1-545-168644 Contact: Herald Berkovitch

APPLE COMPUTER INC.

One Infinite Loop, Cupertino, CA, 95014

Tel: (831) 996-1010 Fax: (831) 974-2113 Web site: www.apple.com

Personal computers, peripherals & software.

Apple Computer GmbH, Rotenturmstrasse 1-3 top 12, A-1010 Vienna, Austria

ARCO CHEMICAL COMPANY

3801 West Chester Pike, Newtown Square, PA, 19073-2387

Tel: (610) 359-2000 Fax: (610) 359-2722 Web site: www.arcochem.com

Mfr. propylene oxide, a chemical used for flexible foam products, coatings/paints & solvents/inks.

ARCO Chem Central Europe GmbH, Rotenturmstrasse 13, 1010 Vienna, Austria

Tel: 43-1-532-96-710 Fax: 43-1-532-9677

ARTHUR ANDERSEN & COMPANY

33 West Monroe Street, Chicago, IL, 60603

Tel: (312) 372-7100 Fax: (312) 507-0123 Web site: www.arthurandersen.com

Accounting & audit, tax & management consulting services.

Auditor Trehand GmbH, Teinfaltstrasse 8, A-1010 Vienna, Austria

Tel: 43-222-53133

AUTODESK INC.

111 McInnis Parkway, San Rafael, CA, 94903

Tel: (415) 507-5000 Fax: (415) 507-6112 Web site: www.autodesk.com

Develop/marketing/support computer-aided design, engineering, scientific & multimedia software products.

Autodesk Ges m.b.H., Traungasse 16, A-2600 Wels, Austria

Tel: 43-7242-68465 Fax: 43-7242-67994

AVERY DENNISON CORPORATION

150 N. Orange Grove Blvd., Pasadena, CA, 91103

Tel: (626) 304-2000 Fax: (626) 792-7312 Web site: www.averydennison.com

Mfr. pressure-sensitive adhesives & materials, office products, labels, tags, retail systems, Carter's Ink & specialty chemicals.

Fasson GmbH, Theresiengasse 58, A-1180 Vienna, Austria

AVON PRODUCTS INC.

1345 Ave. of the Americas, New York, NY, 10105-0196

Tel: (212) 282-5000 Fax: (212) 282-6049 Web site: www.avon.com

Mfr./distributor beauty & related products, fashion jewelry, gifts & collectibles.

Avon Cosmetics Vertriegsges m.b.H, Reisnerstrasse 55-57, A-1030 Vienna, Austria

Tel: 43-222-713-5552 Fax: 43-222-713-6886 Contact: Kevan-Walter Moorcroft, VP

BAILEY-FISCHER & PORTER COMPANY

125 East County Line Road, Warminster, PA, 18974

Tel: (215) 674-6000 Fax: (215) 441-5280

Design/mfr. measure, recording & control instruments & systems; mfr. industrial glass products.

Bailey-Fischer & Porter GmbH, Wiener Str. 17, A-2351 Wiener Neudorf, Austria

BAKER PETROLITE CORPORATION

3900 Essex Lane, Houston, TX, 77027

Tel: (713) 599-7400 Fax: (713) 599-7592

Mfr./prod specialty chemical treating programs, performance-enhancing additives & related equipment & services.

Petrolite HandelsGesmbH, Bruner Strasse 105, A-1210 Vienna, Austria

BATES WORLDWIDE INC.

405 Lexington Ave., New York, NY, 10174

Tel: (212) 297-7000 Fax: (212) 986-0270 Web site: www.batesww.com

Advertising, marketing, public relations & media consulting.

Dr. Puttner Bates, Wambachargasse 2, A-1130 Vienna, Austria

Tel: 43-1-801-0311 Fax: 43-1-801-0337 Contact: Dr. Gerhard Puttner, Chmn.

BAUSCH & LOMB INC.

One Bausch & Lomb Place, Rochester, NY, 14604-2701

Tel: (716) 338-6000 Fax: (716) 338-6007 Web site: www.bausch.com

Mfr. vision care products & accessories & hearing aids.

Bausch & Lomb GmbH, Vienna, Austria

BAXTER HEALTHCARE CORPORATION

One Baxter Parkway, Deerfield, IL, 60015

Tel: (847) 948-2000 Fax: (847) 948-3948 Web site: www.baxter.com

Pharmaceutical preparations, surgical/medical instruments & cardiovascular products.

Baxter GmbH, Franzosengraben 1D, A-1030 Vienna, Austria

Baxter Immuno AG, Richard Strauss Str. 33, A-1232 Vienna, Austria

BBDO WORLDWIDE

1285 Ave. of the Americas, New York, NY, 10019

Tel: (212) 459-5000 Fax: (212) 459-6645 Web site: www.bbdo.com

Multinational group of advertising agencies.

Team/BBDO, Vienna, Austria

BDO SEIDMAN, LLP

Two Prudential Plaza, 180 N. Stetson Ave., Ste. 2300, Chicago, IL, 60601

Tel: (312) 240-1236 Fax: (312) 240-3329 Web site: www.bdo.com

International accounting & financial consulting firm.

BDO Auxilia Treuhand GmbH, Herrengasse 2-4, A-1010 Vienna, Austria

Tel: 43-1-537-370 Fax: 43-1-537-3753 Contact: Werner Presoly

BECKMAN COULTER

4300 Harbor Boulevard, Fullerton, CA, 92835

Tel: (714) 871-4848 Fax: (714) 773-8898

Develop/mfr./marketing automated systems & supplies for biological analysis.

Beckman Coulter Instruments Austria GmbH, Handelskai 340, A-1020 Vienna, Austria

BEST WESTERN INTERNATIONAL

6201 North 24th Place, Phoenix, AZ, 85106

Tel: (602) 957-4200 Fax: (602) 957-5740

International hotel chain.

K+K Hotel Maria Theresia, Kirchberggasse -8, A-1070, Vienna, Austria

Parkhotel Kaserehof, Alpenstraffe 6, A-5020 Salzburg, Austria

Tel: 43-662-6-39-65

BESTFOODS, INC.

700 Sylvan Ave., International Plaza, Englewood Cliffs, NJ, 07632-9976

Tel: (201) 894-4000 Fax: (201) 894-2186 Web site: www.bestfoods.com

Consumer foods products; corn refining.

C.H. Knorr Nahrungsmittelfabrik GmbH, Kornstrasse 8, Postfach 168, A-4600 Wels, Austria

Tel: 43-7242-419-0 Fax: 43-7242-419-282 Contact: Gunter Rath, Mgr.

BETZDEARBORN

4636 Somerton Road, PO Box 3002, Trevose, PA, 19053-6783

Tel: (215) 953-2568 Fax: (215) 953-5524 Web site: www.betzdearborn.com

Mfr. water/wastewater and process system treatment chemicals and services.

BetzDearborn Ges.mbH, Storchengasse 1, 1150 Vienna, Austria

BIO-RAD LABORATORIES INC.

1000 Alfred Nobel Drive, Hercules, CA, 94547

Tel: (510) 724-7000 Fax: (510) 724-3167

Mfr. life science research products, clinical diagnostics, analytical instruments.

Bio-Rad Laboratories Inc., Vienna, Austria

BLACK & DECKER CORPORATION

701 E. Joppa Road, Towson, MD, 21286

Tel: (410) 716-3900 Fax: (410) 716-2933 Web site: www.blackanddecker.com

Mfr. power tools and accessories, security hardware, small appliances, fasteners, information systems & services.

Black & Decker Austria, Austria - All mail to U.S. address.

BOOLE & BABBAGE, INC.

3131 Zanker Road, San Jose, CA, 95134

Tel: (408) 526-3000 Fax: (408) 526-3055 Web site: www.boole.com

Develop/support enterprise automation & systems management software.

Boole & Babbage Osterreich GmbH, World Trade Ctr., A-1300 Vienna Airport, Austria

BOOZ ALLEN & HAMILTON INC.

8283 Greensboro Drive, McLean, VA, 22102

Tel: (703) 902-5000 Fax: (703) 902-3333 Web site: www.bah.com

International management and technology consultants.

Booz Allen & Hamilton GmbH, Kaerntner Ring 5-7, A-1010 Vienna, Austria

Tel: 43-1-513-5550 Fax: 43-1-513-4506

THE BOSTON CONSULTING GROUP

Exchange Place, 31st Floor, Boston, MA, 02109

Tel: (617) 973-1200 Fax: (617) 973-1339 Web site: www.bcg.com

Management consulting company.

The Boston Consulting Group, Parkring 10, A-1010 Vienna, Austria

Tel: 43-1-516-333

BOSTON SCIENTIFIC CORPORATION

One Scientific Place, Natick, MA, 01760-1537

Tel: (508) 650-8000 Fax: (508) 650-8923 Web site: www.bsci.com

Mfr./distributes medical devices for use in minimally invasive surgeries.

Boston Scientific GmbH, Handelskai 388/521/A, 1020 Vienna, Austria

Tel: 43-1-726-30-05 Fax: 43-1-726-30-05-15

BOZELL WORLDWIDE

40 West 23rd Street, New York, NY, 10010

Tel: (212) 727-5000 Fax: (212) 645-9173 Web site: www.bozell.com

Advertising, marketing, public relations and media consulting.

Bozell Hungary Kft, Stifgasse 15, A-1070 Vienna, Austria

Tel: 43-1-523-7304 Fax: 43-1-523-21-79-18

Bozell Kobza, Werbeagentur ges. m.b.H., Probusgaase 1, A-1190 Vienna, Austria

Tel: 43-1-379-110 Fax: 43-1-37-911-30 Contact: Rudy Kobza, Mng. Dir.

BRISTOL-MYERS SQUIBB COMPANY

345 Park Ave., New York, NY, 10154

Tel: (212) 546-4000 Fax: (212) 546-4020 Web site: www.bms.com

Pharmaceutical and food preparations, medical and surgical instruments.

ConvaTec Austria, Columbusgasse 4, A-1100 Vienna, Austria

Squibb Pharma - von Heyden GmbH, Mittersteig 10, Vienna, Austria

BUDGET RENT A CAR CORPORATION

4225 Naperville Road, Lisle, IL, 60532

Tel: (630) 955-1900 Fax: (630) 955-7799 Web site: www.budgetrentacar.com

Car and truck rental system.

Budget Rent A Car, Hilton Hotel Air terminal, Am Stadpark, 1030, Vienna, Austria

Tel: 43-1-714-6565

BULAB HOLDINGS INC.

1256 N. McLean Blvd, Memphis, TN, 38108

Tel: (901) 278-0330 Fax: (901) 276-5343 Web site: www.buckman.com

Biological products; chemicals & chemical preparations.

Buckman Laboratories GmbH, Wehlistrasse 29, A-1200 Vienna, Austria

Tel: 43-1-330-8102 Fax: 43-1-330-8103

LEO BURNETT CO., INC.

35 West Wacker Drive, Chicago, IL, 60601

Tel: (312) 220-5959 Fax: (312) 220-6533 Web site: www.leoburnett.com

International advertising agency.

Leo Burnett & Wirz, Vienna, Austria

BURR-BROWN RESEARCH CORPORATION

6730 S. Tucson Blvd., Tucson, AZ, 85706

Tel: (520) 746-1111 Fax: (520) 746-7211

Electronic components and systems modules.

Burr-Brown Research GmbH, Senefeldergasse 11, A-1100 Vienna, Austria

BURSON-MARSTELLER

230 Park Ave., New York, NY, 10003-1566

Tel: (212) 614-4000 Fax: (212) 614-4262 Web site: www.bm.com

Public relations/public affairs consultants.

Burson-Marsteller GmbH, Dornbacher Strasse 97, A-1170 Vienna, Austria

CALCOMP INC.

2411 West La Palma Ave., Anaheim, CA, 92801

Tel: (714) 821-2000 Fax: (714) 821-2832

Mfr. computer graphics peripherals.

CalComp GmbH, World Trade Ctr., Vienna Airport, Top Nr. 325, A-1300 Vienna-Flughafen, Austria

CANBERRA-PACKARD INDUSTRIES

800 Research Parkway, Meriden, CT, 06450

Tel: (203) 238-2351 Fax: (203) 235-1347 Web site: www.packard.com

Mfr. instruments for nuclear research.

Canberra-Packard GmbH, Josef Zapf Gasse 2, A-1210 Vienna, Austria

CARRIER CORPORATION

One Carrier Place, Farmington, CT, 06034-4015

Tel: (860) 674-3000 Fax: (860) 679-3010 Web site: www.carrier.com

Mfr./distributor/services A/C, heating & refrigeration equipment.

Carrier-Transex Kaelte-und Klimatechnik GmbH, Oberlaaerstrasse 282, A-1232 Vienna, Austria
Tel: 43-1-610-780 Fax: 43-1-610-7850

CASE CORPORATION

700 State Street, Racine, WI, 53404
Tel: (414) 636-6011 Fax: (414) 636-0200 Web site: www.casecorp.com
Mfr./sale agricultural and construction equipment.

Steyr Landmaschinentechnik AG, Steyrer Strasse 32, A-4300 Saint-Valentin, Austria
Tel: 43-7435-500242 Fax: 43-7435-54628

C.B. RICHARD ELLIS

533 South Fremont Ave., Los Angeles, CA, 90071-1712
Tel: (213) 613-3123 Fax: (213) 613-3535 Web site: www.cbrichardellis.com
Commercial real estate services.

CB Richard Ellis, Vienna, Austria

CENTRAL NATIONAL-GOTTESMAN INC.

3 Manhattanville Road, Purchase, NY, 10577-2110
Tel: (914) 696-9000 Fax: (914) 696-1066
Worldwide sales pulp and paper products.

VPI AG, Allgemeine Warenhandels-AG, Reichstratsstrasse 17, Postfach 26, A-1013, Vienna, Austria
Tel: 43-1-408-1533 Fax: 43-1-408-1533-13 Contact: Kurt Eder

THE CHASE MANHATTAN CORPORATION

World Headquarters, 270 Park Ave., New York, NY, 10017
Tel: (212) 270-6000 Fax: (212) 622-9030 Web site: www.chase.com
International banking and financial services.

Chase Manhattan Overseas Corporation, Rep. Office, Loewengasse 47/14, A-1030 Vienna, Austria

CHESTERTON BINSWANGER INTERNATIONAL

Two Logan Square, 4th Floor, Philadelphia, PA, 19103-2759
Tel: (215) 448-6000 Fax: (215) 448-6238
Real estate & related services.

Blumenauer Immobilien, Bauernmarkt 2, A-1010 Vienna, Austria

CHIRON CORPORATION

4560 Horton Street, Emeryville, CA, 94608-2916
Tel: (510) 655-8730 Fax: (510) 655-9910
Research/mfr./marketing therapeutics, vaccines, diagnostics, ophthalmic.

Ciba Corning Diagnostics GmbH, Traunstrasse 46, A-5026 Salzburg, Austria

CHRYSLER CORPORATION

1000 Chrysler Drive, Auburn Hills, MI, 48326-2766
Tel: (248) 576-5741 Fax: (248) 512-5143 Web site: www.chrysler.com
Mfr./marketing cars & light trucks, electronic & aerospace products & systems.

Eurostar GmbH, Graz, Austria

CIGNA CORPORATION

One Liberty Place, Philadelphia, PA, 19192
Tel: (215) 761-1000 Fax: (215) 761-5008
Insurance, invest, health care and other financial services.

Cigna Insurance Co. of Europe SA/NV, Alserbachstrasse 18, Postfach 4, A-1091 Vienna, Austria

CINCINNATI MILACRON INC.

4701 Marburg Ave., Cincinnati, OH, 45209
Tel: (513) 841-8100 Fax: (513) 841-8919
Develop/mfr. technologies for metalworking & plastics processing industrial.

Cincinnati Milacron Austria AG, Postfach 111, A-1231 Vienna, Austria

CISCO SYSTEMS, INC.

170 Tasman Drive, San Jose, CA, 95134-1706

Tel: (408) 526-4000 Fax: (408) 526-4100 Web site: www.cisco.com

Develop/mfr./market computer hardware and software networking systems.

Cisco Systems GmbH, World Trade Ctr., A-1300 Vienna Airport, Vienna, Austria

Tel: 43-1-7007-6776 Fax: 43-1-7007-6027 Contact: N/A

COLGATE-PALMOLIVE COMPANY

300 Park Ave., New York, NY, 10022

Tel: (212) 310-2000 Fax: (212) 310-2919

Mfr. pharmaceuticals, cosmetics, toiletries and detergents.

Colgate-Palmolive GmbH, Argentinierstrasse 22, A-1040 Vienna, Austria

COLUMBIA PICTURES INDUSTRIES INC.

10202 West Washington Blvd., Culver City, CA, 90232

Tel: (310) 244-4000 Fax: (310) 244-2626 Web site: www.sony.com

Producer and distributor of motion pictures.

Warner-Columbia Filmverleih GmbH, Postfach 115, A-1071 Vienna, Austria

COMDISCO INC.

6111 N. River Road, Rosemont, IL, 60018

Tel: (847) 698-3000 Fax: (847) 518-5440

Hi-tech asset and facility management and equipment leasing.

Comdisco Handelsgesellschaft mbH, Vienna, Austria

COMPAQ COMPUTER CORPORATION

20555 State Highway 249, PO Box 692000, Houston, TX, 77269-2000

Tel: (713) 370-0670 Fax: (713) 514-1740 Web site: www.compaq.com

Develop/mfr. personal computers.

Compaq Computer GmbH, Hietzinger Hauptstrasse 34, A 1130 Vienna, Austria

Tel: 43-1-878160 Fax: 43-1-878-1680

COMPUTER ASSOCIATES INTERNATIONAL INC.

One Computer Associates Plaza, Islandia, NY, 11788

Tel: (516) 342-5224 Fax: (516) 342-5329 Web site: www.cai.com

Integrated software for enterprise computing and information management, application development, manufacturing, financial applications and professional services.

Computer Associates Intl. GmbH, Wienerbergstrasse 3, A-1100 Vienna, Austria

Tel: 43-1-605-800

CONOCO INC.

PO Box 2197, Houston, TX, 77252

Tel: (281) 293-1000 Fax: (281) 293-1440

Oil, gas, coal, chemicals and minerals.

Conoco Austria Ltd., Postfach 6008, Hay St. E Perth, Wester, Austria

Conoco-Austria Mineraloel GmbH, A-5020 Salzburg, Austria

D'ARCY MASIUS BENTON & BOWLES INC. (DMB&B)

1675 Broadway, New York, NY, 10019

Tel: (212) 468-3622 Fax: (212) 468-2987 Web site: www.dmbb.com

Full service international advertising and communications group.

DMB&B GmbH, 17 Rotenturmstrasse, A-1010 Vienna, Austria

DANA CORPORATION

4500 Door Street, Toledo, OH, 43615

Tel: (419) 535-4500 Fax: (419) 535-4643 Web site: www.dana.com

Mfr./sales of automotive, heavy truck, off-highway, fluid & mechanical power components.

Dana Corporation, Graz, Austria

DATA GENERAL CORPORATION

4400 Computer Drive, Westboro, MA, 01580

Tel: (508) 898-5000 Fax: (508) 366-1319 Web site: www.dg.com

Design, mfr. general purpose computer systems & peripheral products & services.

Data General GmbH, Sechshauerstrasse 48, A-1150 Vienna, Austria

DATAPRODUCTS CORPORATION

1757 Papo Kenyon Road, Simi Valley, CA, 93063

Tel: (805) 578-4000 Fax: (805) 578-4001

Mfr. computer printers and supplies.

Dataproducts Handels GmbH, Hintere Zollamtsstr. 9/32, A-1030 Vienna, Austria

DDB NEEDHAM WORLDWIDE INC.

437 Madison Ave., New York, NY, 10022

Tel: (212) 415-2000 Fax: (212) 415-3417

Advertising agency.

Heye & Partner/Austria (DDB), Hietzinger Kai 169, A-1130 Vienna, Austria

DELL COMPUTER CORPORATION

One Dell Way, Round Rock, TX, 78682-2222

Tel: (512) 338-4400 Fax: (512) 728-3653 Web site: www.dell.com

Direct marketer & supplier of computer systems.

Dell Computer Ges. m.b.H., Hettenkofergasse 13, 1160 Vienna, Austria

Tel: 43-1-491-04 Fax: 43-1-491-04-80 Contact: Bruno Walter, Business Mgr.

DELOITTE TOUCHE TOHMATSU INTERNATIONAL

PO Box 820, Wilton, CT, 06897

Tel: (203) 761-3000 Fax: (203) 834-2200 Web site: www.u.s.deloitte.com or www.dtti.com

Accounting, audit, tax and management consulting services.

Deloitte & Touche Danubia Trehand GmbH, Akademiehof, Friedrichstrasse 10, A-1010 Vienna, Austria

Deloitte & Touche Salzburg BmbH, Innsbrucker Bundesstrasse 75, A-5020 Salzburg, Austria

Zolb, Bauer & Partner, Mildenburggasse 6, A-5020 Salzburg, Austria

DELTA AIR LINES INC.

PO Box 20706, Atlanta, GA, 30320-6001

Tel: (404) 715-2600 Fax: (404) 715-5494 Web site: www.delta-air.com/index.html

Major worldwide airline; international air transport services.

Delta Air Lines Inc., Vienna, Austria

DHL WORLDWIDE EXPRESS

333 Twin Dolphin Drive, Redwood City, CA, 94065

Tel: (650) 593-7474 Fax: (650) 593-1689 Web site: www.dhl.com

Worldwide air express carrier.

DHL Worldwide Express, Steingasse 6-8, Vienna 1030, Austria

Tel: 43-1-74481

DIGITAL EQUIPMENT CORPORATION

111 Powder Mill Road, Maynard, MA, 01754

Tel: (978) 493-5111 Fax: (978) 493-7374 Web site: www.digital.com

Mfr. network computer systems, components, software and services.

Digital Equipment Corporation GmbH, Gesellschaft m.b.H., Ziedlergasse 21, A-1230 Vienna, Austria

Tel: 43-1-866-300 Fax: 43-1-866-300

DIONEX CORPORATION

1228 Titan Way, PO Box 3603, Sunnyvale, CA, 94088-3603

Tel: (408) 737-0700 Fax: (408) 730-9403

Develop/mfr./marketing/services chromatography systems & related products.

Dionex Austria GmbH, Laxenburgerstrasse 220, A-1230 Wein, Austria

THE DOW CHEMICAL COMPANY

2030 Dow Center, Midland, MI, 48674

Tel: (517) 636-1000 Fax: (517) 636-3228 Web site: www.atdow.com

Mfr. chemicals, plastics, pharmaceuticals, agricultural products, consumer products.

Dow Chemical GmbH, Concordiapl. 2, A-1010 Vienna, Austria

DOW CORNING CORPORATION

2220 West Salzburg Road, PO Box 1767, Midland, MI, 48640

Tel: (517) 496-4000 Fax: (517) 496-6080

Silicones, silicon chemicals, solid lubricants.

Dow Corning GmbH, Mariahilferstrasse 180/4, A-1150 Vienna, Austria

DRAKE BEAM MORIN INC.

101 Huntington Ave., Boston, MA, 02199

Tel: (617) 450-9860 Fax: (617) 267-2011 Web site: www.dbm.com

Human resource management consulting & training.

DBM Karriereberatung GmbH - Europe, Schaaritzerstrasse 21 a, A-4020 Linz, Austria

Tel: 43-1-713-2811 Fax: 43-1-713-281133

DBM Karriereberatung GmbH - Europe, Hainburger Strasse 36, A-1030 Vienna, Austria

Tel: 43-1-713-2811 Fax: 43-1-713-281133

DRESSER INDUSTRIES INC.

2001 Ross Ave., PO Box 718, Dallas, TX, 75221-0718

Tel: (214) 740-6000 Fax: (214) 740-6584 Web site: www.dresser.com

Diversified supplier of equipment & technical services to energy & natural resource industrial.

Worthington GmbH, Industrietstrasse B-6, A-2345 Brunn-am-Gebirge, Austria

THE DUN & BRADSTREET CORPORATION

One Diamond Hill Road, Murray Hill, NJ, 07974

Tel: (908) 665-5000 Fax: (908) 665-5524 Web site: www.dnbcorp.com

Provides corporate credit, marketing & accounts-receivable management services & publishes credit ratings & financial information.

Dun & Bradstreet Information Services GmbH, Opernring 3-5, 1015 Vienna, Austria

Tel: 43-222-58-86-10

EASTMAN KODAK COMPANY

343 State Street, Rochester, NY, 14650

Tel: (716) 724-4000 Fax: (716) 724-0663

Develop/mfr. photo & chemicals products, information management/video/copier systems, fibers/plastics for various industry.

Kodak Fotoservice, Also in Dornbirn & Salzburg, Austria

Kodak Fotoservice, Albert Schweitzer-Gasse 4, A-1148 Vienna, Austria

Kodak GmbH, Albert Schweitzer-Gasse 4, A-1148 Vienna, Austria

ECOLAB INC.

Ecolab Center, 370 N. Wabasha Street, St. Paul, MN, 55102

Tel: (612) 293-2233 Fax: (612) 225-3105 Web site: www.ecolab.com

Develop/mfr. premium cleaning, sanitizing and maintenance products and services for the hospitality, institutional, and residential markets.

Ecolab Ltd., Vienna, Austria

Tel: 43-1-7152-550800

J.D. EDWARDS & COMPANY

One Technology Way, Denver, CO, 80237

Tel: (303) 334-4000 Fax: (303) 334-4970 Web site: www.jdedwards.com.

Computer software products.

J. D. Edwards Vienna, Top 532, World Trade Ctr., 1300 Vienna/Schwechat, Austria

Tel: 43-1-7007-6383 Fax: 43-1-7007-6387

EMC CORP.

35 Parkwood Drive, Hopkinton, MA, 01748-9103

Tel: (508) 435-1000 Fax: (508) 435-8884 Web site: www.emc.com

Designs/supplies intelligent enterprise storage & retrieval technology for open systems, mainframes & midrange environments.

EMC Computer Systems - Austria GmbH, Mariahelfer Strasse, 123/2/2, Vienna A-1060, Austria

Tel: 43-1-595-2550

EMERY WORLDWIDE

One Lagoon Drive, Ste. 400, Redwood City, CA, 94065

Tel: (650) 596-9600 Fax: (650) 596-7901 Web site: www.emeryworld.com

Freight transport, global logistics and air cargo.

Emery Worldwide, Intl Air Cargo Centre, Bldg. 250, Rm. F-180, Vienna Airport A-1300, Austria

ERNST & YOUNG, LLP

787 Seventh Ave., New York, NY, 10019

Tel: (212) 773-3000 Fax: (212) 773-6350 Web site: www.eyi.com

Accounting and audit, tax and management consulting services.

SOT Sud-Ost Treuhand AG, Praterstrasse 23, 1021 Vienna, Austria

Tel: 43-1-21170-1071 Fax: 43-1-2162077 Contact: Andreas Stefaner

EURO RSCG Worldwide

350 Hudson Street, New York, NY, 10014

Tel: (212) 886-2000 Fax: (212) 886-2016

International advertising agency group.

Euro RSCG, Vienna, Austria

EXPEDITORS INTERNATIONAL OF WASHINGTON INC.

999 Throd Ave., Ste. 2500, Seattle, WA, 98104

Tel: (206) 674-3400 Fax: (206) 682-9777 Web site: www.expd.com

Air/ocean freight forwarding, customs brokerage, international logistics solutions.

Austria Expeditors Speditions GmbH, Industriestr. 15, Objekt 6, A-2431 Enzersdorf/Fischa, Vienna, Austria (Office:Vienna International Airport)

Tel: 43-2230-2052 Fax: 43-2230-2052

FEDERAL-MOGUL CORPORATION

26555 Northwestern Highway, PO Box 1966, Southfield, MI, 48034

Tel: (248) 354-7700 Fax: (248) 354-8983 Web site: www.federalmogul.com

Mfr./distributor precision parts for automobiles, trucks, farm and construction vehicles.

Federal-Mogul Handels GmbH, Vienna, Austria

FISHER-ROSEMOUNT

8000 Maryland Ave., Ste. 500, Clayton, MO, 63105-4755

Tel: (314) 746-9900 Fax: (314) 746-9974

Mfr. industrial process control equipment.

Fisher Rosemount AG, Industrie-Zentrum No. Sud Strasse 2A, Obj. M29, Austria

FMC CORPORATION

200 E. Randolph Drive, Chicago, IL, 60601

Tel: (312) 861-6000 Fax: (312) 861-6141

Produces chemicals & precious metals, mfr. machinery, equipment & systems for industrial, agricultural & government use.

FMC Chemikalien GmbH, Vienna, Austria

FORD MOTOR COMPANY

The American Road, Dearborn, MI, 48121

Tel: (313) 322-3000 Fax: (313) 322-9600 Web site: www.ford.com

Mfr./sales motor vehicles.

Ford Motor Co. Austria KG, Fuerburgstrasse 51, Postfach 2, A-5021 Salzburg, Austria

THE FRANKLIN MINT

US Route 1, Franklin Center, PA, 19091

Tel: (610) 459-6000 Fax: (610) 459-6880

Design/marketing collectibles & luxury items.

Franklin Ming GmbH, Zillnerstr. 18, A-5020 Salzburg, Austria

FRANKLIN RESOURCES, INC.

777 Mariners Island Blvd., San Mateo, CA, 94404

Tel: (415) 312-2000 Fax: (415) 312-3655 Web site: www.frk.com

Global and domestic investment advisory and portfolio management.

Templeton Global Strategic Services GmbH, Vienna, Austria

Tel: 49-69-660-5911 Fax: 49-69-272-23120

FRITZ COMPANIES INC.

706 Mission Street, Ste. 900, San Francisco, CA, 94103

Tel: (415) 904-8360 Fax: (415) 904-8661 Web site: www.fritz.com

Integrated transportation, sourcing, distribution & customs brokerage services.

Fritz Companies Inc., Vienna, Austria

H.B. FULLER COMPANY

1200 Willow Lake Blvd., Vadnais Heights, MN, 55110

Tel: (612) 236-5900 Fax: (612) 236-5898 Web site: www.hbfuller.com

Mfr./distributor adhesives, sealants, coatings, paints, waxes, sanitation chemicals.

H.B. Fuller Austria GmbH, Kaplanstrasse 30, Postfach 214, 4600 Wels, Austria

Tel: 43-7242-4090 Fax: 43-7242-47296

GAF CORPORATION

1361 Alps Road, Wayne, NJ, 07470

Tel: (973) 628-3000 Fax: (973) 628-3326 Web site: www.gaf.com

Mfr. building materials.

GAF (Oesterreich) GmbH, Hietzinger Kai 101-105, A-1130 Vienna, Austria

GENERAL ELECTRIC CO.

3135 Easton Turnpike, Fairfield, CT, 06431

Tel: (203) 373-2211 Fax: (203) 373-3131 Web site: www.ge.com

Diversified manufacturing, technology and services.

General Electric Co.-Austria, Austria - All mail to U.S. address; phone (800) 626-2004 or (518) 438-6500

GENERAL MOTORS ACCEPTANCE CORPORATION

100 Renaissance Center, Detroit, MI, 48243-7301

Tel: (313) 556-5000 Fax: (313) 556-5108 Web site: www.gmac.com

Automobile financing.

General Motors Bank GmbH, Postfach 28, Landstrasser Hauptstr. 99, A-1031 Vienna, Austria

GENERAL MOTORS CORPORATION

100 Renaissance Center, Detroit, MI, 48243.7301

Tel: (313) 556-5000 Fax: (313) 556-5108 Web site: www.gm.com

Mfr. full line vehicles, automotive electronics, commercial technologies, telecommunications, space, finance.

General Motors Austria GmbH, Gross Enzerdorfer-Str. 59, A-1220 Vienna, Austria

GENERAL REINSURANCE CORPORATION

695 East Main Street, Stamford, CT, 06904-2350

Tel: (203) 328-5000 Fax: (203) 328-6423 Web site: www.genre.com

Reinsurance services worldwide.

Cologne Reinsurance Vienna, Renngasse 6-8, A-1010 Vienna, Austria

Tel: 43-1-536-860 Fax: 43-1-535-9443 Contact: Christof Goldi, Director

THE GILLETTE COMPANY

Prudential Tower Building, Boston, MA, 02199

Tel: (617) 421-7000 Fax: (617) 421-7123 Web site: www.gillette.com

Develop/mfr. personal care/use products: blades & razors, toiletries, cosmetics, stationery.

Braun Electric Austria GmbH, Vienna, Austria

Gillette GmbH, Vienna, Austria

GRANT THORNTON INTERNATIONAL

800 One Prudential Plaza, 130 E. Randolph Drive, Chicago, IL, 60601-6050

Tel: (312) 856-0001 Fax: (312) 616-7052

Accounting, audit, tax and management consulting services.

Jonasch Platzer/Grant Thornton, Henckellgasse 19, A-1140 Wein, Austria

Tel: 43-1-914-4256 Fax: 43-1-914-513513 Contact: Dr. Walter Platzer

GREY ADVERTISING INC.

777 Third Ave., New York, NY, 10017

Tel: (212) 546-2000 Fax: (212) 546-1495 Web site: www.giworldwwide.com

International advertising agency.

Grey Group Austria, Schonbrunner Str. 80, A-1050 Vienna, Austria

GRIFFITH LABORATORIES INC

One Griffith Center, Alsip, IL, 60658

Tel: (708) 371-0900 Fax: (708) 597-3294 Web site: www.griffithlabs.com

Industrial food ingredients and equipment.

Griffith Labs Inc., Vienna, Austria

Tel: 43-1-272-6212 Fax: 43-1-272-5993

GROUNDWATER TECHNOLOGY INC

100 River Ridge Drive, Norwood, MA, 02062

Tel: (781) 769-7600 Fax: (781) 769-7992

Industrial site cleanup, management & consulting.

Groundwater Technology Inc., Wehllstrasse 27 #1D, A-1200 Vienna, Austria

GTE CORPORATION

One Stamford Forum, Stamford, CT, 06904

Tel: (203) 965-2000 Fax: (203) 965-2277 Web site: www.gte.com

Electronic products, telecommunications systems, publishing and communications.

Herold Business Data, Vienna, Austria

HALLIBURTON COMPANY

500 North Akard Street, Ste. 3600, Dallas, TX, 75201-3391

Tel: (214) 978-2600 Fax: (214) 978-2685 Web site: www.halliburton.com

Energy, construction and insurance.

Halliburton Ltd., Postfach 107, A-1213, Vienna, Austria

Tel: 43-2246-4333 Fax: 43-2246-433315

THE HARPER GROUP

260 Townsend Street, San Francisco, CA, 94107-1719

Tel: (415) 978-0600 Fax: (415) 978-0692 Web site: www.circleintl.com

Ocean/air freight forwarding, customs brokerage, packing and wholesale, logistics management and insurance.

Star Pak Speditionsgesellschaft mbH, Air Cargo Bldg., Obj 263, PO Box 73, A-1300 Vienna Airport, Vienna, Austria

Tel: 43-1-7111-02095 Fax: 43-1-7111-5297

HERCULES INC

Hercules Plaza, 1313 North Market Street, Wilmington, DE, 19894-0001

Tel: (302) 594-5000 Fax: (302) 594-5400 Web site: www.herc.com

Mfr. specialty chemicals, plastics, film and fibers, coatings, resins, food ingredients.

Patex Chemie GmbH, Madlschenterweg 3, A-4050 Traun, Austria

HEWITT ASSOCIATES LLC

100 Half Day Road, Lincolnshire, IL, 60069

Tel: (847) 295-5000 Fax: (847) 295-7634

Employee benefits consulting firm.

Hewitt Associates, Röttig & Rutkowski, Ungargasse 15/5, A-1030 Vienna, Austria

Tel: 43-1-712-9981

HEWLETT-PACKARD COMPANY

3000 Hanover Street, Palo Alto, CA, 94304-0890

Tel: (650) 857-1501 Fax: (650) 857-7299 Web site: www.hp.com

Mfr. computing, communications & measurement products & services.

Hewlett-Packard GesmbH, Lieblgasse 1, A-1222 Vienna, Austria

HILTON HOTELS CORPORATION

9336 Civic Center Drive, Beverly Hills, CA, 90210

Tel: (310) 278-4321 Fax: (310) 205-7880

International hotel chain: Hilton International, Vista Hotels and Hilton National Hotels.

Hilton International Hotels, Vienna Plaza, Schottenring 11, A-1010 Vienna, Austria

HOLIDAY INNS WORLDWIDE, INC.

3 Ravinia Drive, Ste. 2900, Atlanta, GA, 30346-2149

Tel: (770) 604-2000 Fax: (770) 604-5403

Hotels, restaurants and casinos.

Holiday Inns Inc., Salurner Strasse 15, Postfach 97, A-6010 Innsbruck, Austria

HONEYWELL INC.

PO Box 524, Minneapolis, MN, 55440-0524

Tel: (612) 951-1000 Fax: (612) 951-3066 Web site: www.honeywell.com

Develop/mfr. controls for home and building, industry, space and aviation.

Honeywell Austria GmbH, Handelskai 388, A-1023 Vienna, Austria

HORWATH INTERNATIONAL

415 Madison Ave., New York, NY, 10017

Tel: (212) 838-5566 Fax: (212) 838-3636

Public accountants and auditors.

Horwath Consulting, Weimarer Strasse 5, A-1180 Vienna, Austria

I.B. Interfides Halvax, Himmer, Nidetzky & Partner, Grungasse 16, A-1052 Vienna, Austria

HOWMEDICA INC.

359 Veterans Boulevard, Rutherford, NJ, 07070

Tel: (201) 507-7300 Fax: (201) 935-4873 Web site: www.howmedica.com

Hospital, medical and dental supplies.

Howmedica Austria GmbH, Vienna, Austria

Tel: 43-1-545-1611

IBM CORPORATION

New Orchard Road, Armonk, NY, 10504

Tel: (914) 765-1900 Fax: (914) 765-7382 Web site: www.ibm.com

Information products, technology & services.

IBM Oesterreich Internationale Bueromaschinem GmbH, Obere Donaustrasse 95, A-1020 Vienna, Austria

Tel: 43-1-17060 Fax: 43-1-216-0886

INFONET SERVICES CORPORATION

2100 East Grand Ave., El Segundo, CA, 90245

Tel: (310) 335-2600 Fax: (310) 335-4507 Web site: www.infonet.com

Provider of Internet services and electronic messaging services.

Infonet Austria GmbH, Weidner Hauptstrasse 73, Postfach 60, A-1042 Vienna, Austria

Tel: 43-1-50-145 Fax: 43-1-50-260

INFORMIX CORPORATION

4100 Bohannon Drive, Menlo Park, CA, 95025

Tel: (650) 926-6300 Fax: (650) 926-6593 Web site: www.informix.com

Designs & produces database management software, connectivity interfaces & gateways, and other computer applications.

Informix Software GmbH, 10, Business Park Vienna, Wienerbergstr. 3/7.OG, A-1810 Vienna, Austria

Tel: 43-1-605620

INGERSOLL-RAND COMPANY

200 Chestnut Ridge Road, Woodcliff Lake, NJ, 07675

Tel: (201) 573-0123 Fax: (201) 573-3172 Web site: www.ingersoll-rand.com

Mfr. compressors, rock drills, pumps, air tools, door hardware, ball bearings.

Impco Voest-Alpine Pulping Technologies GmbH, Turmstrasse 44, Postfach 4, A-4031 Linz, Austria

Worthington GmbH, Industriestrasse B-6, A-2345 Brunn am Gebrige, Austria

INTER-CONTINENTAL HOTELS

1120 Ave. of the Americas, New York, NY, 10036

Tel: (212) 852-6400 Fax: (212) 852-6494 Web site: www.interconti.com

Worldwide hotel and resort accommodations.

Hotel Inter-Continental Wien, Johannesgasse 28, 1037 Vienna, Austria

Tel: 43-1-711-22 Fax: 43-1-713-4489

INTERGRAPH CORPORATION

One Madison Industrial Park, Huntsville, AL, 35894-0001

Tel: (205) 730-2000 Fax: (205) 730-7898 Web site: www.intergraph.com

Develop/mfr. interactive computer graphic systems.

Intergraph GmbH (Austria), Modecenterstrasse 14, Block A, 4 Stock, Vienna, Austria A-1030

Tel: 43-1-79-7350 Fax: 43-1-79-73535

INTERMEC TECHNOLOGIES CORPORATION

6001 36th Ave. West, PO Box 4280, Everett, WA, 98203-9280

Tel: (425) 348-2600 Fax: (425) 355-9551 Web site: www.intermec.com

Mfr./distributor automated data collection systems.

Intermec Strichcode Handelsges, Pottendorferstrasse 69, A-2523 Tattendorf, Austria

INTERNATIONAL PAPER COMPANY

2 Manhattanville Road, Purchase, NY, 10577

Tel: (914) 397-1500 Fax: (914) 397-1596 Web site: www.ipaper.com

Mfr./distributor container board, paper, wood products.

Ilford Anitec GmbH, Deutschstrasse 3, A-1232 Vienna, Austria

INTERNATIONAL RECTIFIER CORPORATION

233 Kansas Street, El Segundo, CA, 90245

Tel: (310) 322-3331 Fax: (310) 322-3332 Web site: www.irf.com

Mfr. power semiconductor components.

International Rectifiers - Austria, Hietziger Haupstrasse 37, A-1130 Vienna, Austria

Tel: 43-1-877-1261 Fax: 43-1-876-1413

INTERNATIONAL SPECIALTY PRODUCTS

1361 Alps Road, Wayne, NJ, 07470

Tel: (973) 628-4000 Fax: (973) 628-3311 Web site: www.ispcorp.com

Mfr. specialty chemical products.

ISP (Österreich) GmbH, Belvederegasse 18/1, A-1040 Vienna, Austria

Tel: 43-1-504-76210 Fax: 43-1-505-8944

ITT CORPORATION

1330 Ave. of the Americas, New York, NY, 10019-5490

Tel: (212) 258-1000 Fax: (212) 258-1297

Design/mfr. communications & electronic equipment, hotels, insurance.

ITT Austria Intl. Telephone Telegraphen GmbH, 75 Fresdner Strasse, A-1200 Vienna, Austria

ITT SHERATON CORPORATION

60 State Street, Boston, MA, 02108

Tel: (617) 367-3600 Fax: (617) 367-5676

Hotel operations.

Salzburg Sheraton Hotel, Auerspergstr. 4, A-5020 Salzburg, Austria

J. WALTER THOMPSON COMPANY

466 Lexington Ave., New York, NY, 10017

Tel: (212) 210-7000 Fax: (212) 210-6944 Web site: www.jwt.com

International advertising and marketing services.

Grill & Gull, Vienna, Austria

JOHNSON & JOHNSON

One Johnson & Johnson Plaza, New Brunswick, NJ, 08933

Tel: (732) 524-0400 Fax: (732) 214-0334 Web site: www.jnj.com

Mfr./distributor/R&D pharmaceutical, health care and cosmetic products.

Janssen & Cilag GmbH, Postfach 192, A-1232 Vienna, Austria

Johnson & Johnson GmbH, Weisshofweg 9, Postfach 80, A-5400 Hallein, Austria

Johnson & Johnson Medical GmbH, A-1232 Vienna, Austria

S C JOHNSON & SON INC.

1525 Howe Street, Racine, WI, 53403

Tel: (414) 260-2000 Fax: (414) 260-2133 Web site: www.scjohnsonwax.com

Home, auto, commercial and personal care products and specialty chemicals.

Johnson's Wax GmbH, Rennbhnweg 25, A-1222 Vienna, Austria

JOHNSON WORLDWIDE ASSOCIATES, INC.

1326 Willow Road, Sturtevant, WI, 53177

Tel: (414) 884-1500 Fax: (414) 884-1600 Web site: www.jwa.com

Mfr. diving, fishing, boating & camping sports equipment.

Scubapro Austria, Kinostrasse 21, A-5061 Salzburg-Glasenbach, Austria

Tel: 43-663-638467 Fax: 43-662-628468

A.T. KEARNEY INC.

222 West Adams Street, Chicago, IL, 60606

Tel: (312) 648-0111 Fax: (312) 223-6200 Web site: www.atkearney.com

Management consultants and executive search.

A. T. Kearney GmbH, Trattnerhof 1, A-1010 Vienna, Austria

Tel: 43-1-53-667

KENNAMETAL INC.

State Rte. 981, Latrobe, PA, 15650

Tel: (724) 539-5000 Fax: (724) 539-4710 Web site: www.kennametal.com

Tools, hard carbide & tungsten alloys for metalworking industry.

Kennametal Hertel, G. Beissteiner Vertriebs GmbH, A-2320 Schwechat/Vienna, Austria

Tel: 43-1-707-8471 Fax: 43-1-707-1918

KIMBALL INTERNATIONAL INC.

PO Box 460, Jasper, IN, 47549

Tel: (812) 482-1600 Fax: (812) 482-8804

Mfr. office furniture & seating, pianos, wood veneers, plywood products.

Bosendorfer L. Klavierfabrik AG, Bosendorferstrasse 12, A-1010 Vienna, Austria

KIMBERLY-CLARK CORPORATION

351 Phelps Drive, Irving, TX, 75038

Tel: (972) 281-1200 Fax: (972) 281-1435 Web site: www.kimberly-clark.com.

Mfr./sales/distribution of consumer tissue, household and personal care products.

Kimberly-Clark Corp., Vienna, Austria

LESTER B KNIGHT & ASSOC INC.

549 West Randolph Street, Chicago, IL, 60661

Tel: (312) 346-2300 Fax: (312) 648-1085

Architecture, engineering, planning, operations & management consulting.

Knight Wendling Consulting GesmbH, Maderstrasse 1, A-1040 Vienna, Austria

KNOLL, INC.

1235 Water Street, East Greenville, PA, 18041

Tel: (215) 679-7991 Fax: (215) 679-3904 Web site: www.knoll.com

Mfr. and sale of office furnishings.

Knoll International Austria GmbH, Bauernmarkt 12, A-1010 Vienna, Austria

KORN/FERRY INTERNATIONAL

1800 Century Park East, Los Angeles, CA, 90067

Tel: (310) 552-1834 Fax: (310) 553-6452 Web site: www.kornferry.com

Executive search; management consulting.

Korn/Ferry International, Dr. Karl-Lueger-Ring 8, A-1010 Vienna, Austria

Tel: 43-1-531-030 Fax: 43-1-531-0340

KPMG PEAT MARWICK LLP

Three Chestnut Ridge Road, Montvale, NJ, 07645

Tel: (201) 307-7000 Fax: (201) 930-8617 Web site: www.kpmg.com

Accounting and audit, tax and management consulting services.

KPMG Alpen-Treuhand GmbH, Gnsbacherstrasse 6, Innsbruck, A-6020, Austria

KPMG Austria WirtschaftsprDfungs-GmbH, Krassniggstra Klagenfurt, A-9020, Austria

KPMG Austria, WirtschaftsprDfungs GmbH, Kolingasse 19, Vienna A-1090, Austria

Tel: 43-1-313320 Fax: 43-1-313325 Contact: Robert Reiter, Ptnr.

KPMG Management Consulting GmbH, Grosse Mohrengase 1, Vienna A-1020, Austria

Mundus Treuhand-und, Revisionsges, mbH, Reichenhallerstrasse 6-8, Salzburg A-5020, Austria

THS Treuhand Salzburg GmbH, Nonntaler Hauptstra Salzburg, A-5020, Austria

KRAFT FOODS INTERNATIONAL, INC. (DIV. PHILIP MORRIS COS.)

800 Westchester Ave., Rye Brook, NY, 10573-1301

Tel: (914) 335-2500 Fax: (914) 335-7144

Processor, distributor and manufacturer of food products.

Kraft Jacobs Suchard, Jacobsgasse 3, A-1147 Vienna, Austria

LAI WARD HOWELL INTERNATIONAL INC.

200 Park Ave., Ste. 3100, New York, NY, 10016-0136

Tel: (212) 953-7900 Fax: (212) 953-7907 Web site: www.laix.com

International executive search firm.

LAI Ward Howell Intl., Mattiellistrasse 2-4, A-1040 Vienna, Austria

LIFE TECHNOLOGIES INC.

9800 Medical Center Drive, Rockville, MD, 20850

Tel: (301) 840-8000 Fax: (301) 329-8635

Biotechnology.

Life Technologies, Vienna, Austria

ELI LILLY & COMPANY

Lilly Corporate Center, Indianapolis, IN, 46285

Tel: (317) 276-2000 Fax: (317) 277-6579 Web site: www.lilly.com

Mfr. pharmaceuticals and animal health products.

Eli Lilly GmbH (Austria), Barichgasse 40-42, A-1030 Vienna, Austria

Tel: 43-1-711-780 Fax: 43-1-711-78286

ARTHUR D. LITTLE, INC.

25 Acorn Park, Cambridge, MA, 02140-2390

Tel: (617) 498-5000 Fax: (617) 498-7200 Web site: www.adlittle.com

Management, environmental, health & safety consulting; technical & product development.

Arthur D. Little Intl. GmbH, Palais Todesco, Kärntner Strasse 51, A-1015 Vienna, Austria
Tel: 43-1-515-4100 Fax: 43-1-515-4124

LOCKHEED MARTIN CORPORATION
6801 Rockledge Drive, Bethesda, MD, 20817
Tel: (301) 897-6000 Fax: (301) 897-6652 Web site: www.imco.com
Design/mfr./management systems in fields of space, defense, energy, electronics and technical services.
CalComp Ges, World Trade Ctr., Vienna Airport, Top Nr. 326, A-1300 Wien-Flughafen, Austria

LOCTITE CORPORATION
10 Columbus Boulevard, Hartford, CT, 06106
Tel: (203) 520-5000 Fax: (203) 520-5073 Web site: www.loctite.com
Mfr./sale industrial adhesives and sealants.
Loctite Europa Ges.m.b.H., Postfach 29, Akaziengasse 34, A-1234 Vienna, Austria

LOWE & PARTNERS WORLDWIDE
1114 Ave. of the Americas, New York, NY, 10036
Tel: (212) 403-6700 Fax: (212) 403-6710
International advertising agency network.
Lowe GGK Salzburg, Salzburg, Austria
Lowe GGK Wein, Vienna, Austria

THE LUBRIZOL CORPORATION
29400 Lakeland Blvd., Wickliffe, OH, 44092-2298
Tel: (440) 943-4200 Fax: (440) 943-5337 Web site: www.lubrizol.com
Mfr. chemicals additives for lubricants & fuels.
Lubrizol GmbH, Vienna, Austria
Tel: 43-1-597-3570

MALLINCKRODT INC.
675 McDonnell Blvd., PO Box 5840, St. Louis, MO, 63134
Tel: (314) 654-2000 Fax: (314) 654-3005
Mfr. specialty medical products.
Mallinckrodt Vertriebs GmbH, Wiener Neudorf, Austria

MANPOWER INTERNATIONAL INC.
5301 N. Ironwood Road, PO Box 2053, Milwaukee, WI, 53201-2053
Tel: (414) 961-1000 Fax: (414) 961-7081 Web site: www.manpower
Temporary help, contract service, training & testing.
Jade IAM GmbH, Zentagasse 47, A-1050 Vienna, Austria
Tel: 43-1-545-395477 Fax: 43-1-546-395579

MARRIOTT INTERNATIONAL INC.
1 Marriott Drive, Washington, DC, 20058
Tel: (301) 380-3000 Fax: (301) 380-5181
Lodging, contract food and beverage service, and restaurants.
Marriott Courtyard Linz, Europlatz 2, Linz, Austria 4020
Tel: 43-732-6959-0 Fax: 43-732-606090
Vienna Marriott Hotel, Vienna, Austria
Tel: 43-1-515-180

MARSH & McLENNAN COS INC.
1166 Ave. of the Americas, New York, NY, 10036-2774
Tel: (212) 345-5000 Fax: (212) 345-4808 Web site: www.marshmac.com
Insurance agents/brokers, pension and investment management consulting services.

Gradmann & Holler Kiefhaber GmbH, Paulanergrasse 15, A-1020 Vienna, Austria

Tel: 43-1-586-4977 Fax: 43-1-586-4932 Contact: Ernst Kiefhaber

McCANN-ERICKSON WORLDWIDE

750 Third Ave., New York, NY, 10017

Tel: (212) 984-3644 Fax: (212) 984-2629

International advertising/marketing services.

McCann-Erickson GmbH, Gregor Mendel-Strasse 50, Postfach 57, A-1191 Vienna 19, Austria

McDONALD'S CORPORATION

Kroc Drive, Oak Brook, IL, 60523

Tel: (630) 623-3000 Fax: (630) 623-7409

Fast food chain stores.

McDonald's Corp., Austria

Contact: Martin Knoll, Mgr.

McKINSEY & COMPANY

55 East 52nd Street, New York, NY, 10022

Tel: (212) 446-7000 Fax: (212) 446-8575 Web site: www.mckinsey.com

Management and business consulting services.

McKinsey & Company, Reichsratsstr. 7/1/12, 1010 Vienna, Austria

Tel: 43-1-40-88-2240 Fax: 43-1-408-9902

MEAD CORPORATION

Courthouse Plaza, NE, Dayton, OH, 45463

Tel: (937) 495-6323 Fax: (937) 461-2424 Web site: www.mead.com

Mfr. paper, packaging, pulp, lumber and other wood products, school and office products; electronic publishing and distribution.

Mead Coated Board Europe Kartonvertriebs AG, Alserbachstrasse 14-16, A1091, Vienna, Austria

Tel: 43-1-31005120 Fax: 43-1-310499 Contact: S. Nustret Kilerscioglu, Pres.

MEDTRONIC INC.

7000 Central Ave., NE, Minneapolis, MN, 55432

Tel: (612) 574-4000 Fax: (612) 574-4879

Mfr./sale/service electrotherapeutic medical devices.

Medtronic GesmbH, Handelskai 388/Top 852, A-1020 Vienna, Austria

MEMOREX CORPORATION

10100 Pioneer Boulevard, Santa Fe Springs, CA, 90670

Tel: (562) 906-2800 Fax: (562) 906-2848

Magnetic recording tapes, etc.

Memorex GmbH, Gottfried Kellergass 2/16, A-1030 Vienna, Austria

MERCK & COMPANY, INC.

1 Merck Drive, Whitehouse Station, NJ, 08889

Tel: (908) 423-1000 Fax: (908) 423-2592

Pharmaceuticals, chemicals and biologicals.

Merck, Sharp & Dohme GmbH, Spittelauer Lande 45, A-1090 Vienna, Austria

MERRILL LYNCH & COMPANY, INC.

World Financial Center, North Tower, New York, NY, 10281-1323

Tel: (212) 449-1000 Fax: (212) 449-2892

Security brokers and dealers, investment and business services.

Merrill Lynch Bank Austria AG, Bauernmarkt 2, A-1010, Vienna, Austria

Tel: 43-1-531-40 Fax: 43-1-535-0227

MICROSOFT CORPORATION

One Microsoft Way, Redmond, WA, 98052-6399

Tel: (425) 882-8080 Fax: (425) 936-7329 Web site: www.microsoft.com

Computer software, peripherals and services.

Microsoft Austria GmbH, Favoritenstrasse 321, A-1100 Vienna, Austria

Tel: 43-1-610-640 Fax: 43-1-610-64200

MILLIPORE CORPORATION, ANALYTICAL PRODUCT DIVISION

80 Ashby Road, PO Box 9125, Bedford, MA, 01730

Tel: (781) 275-9200 Fax: (781) 533-3110 Web site: www.millipore.com

Mfr. flow and pressure measurement and control components; precision filters, hi-performance liquid chromatography instruments.

Millipore GmbH, Heitzinger Hauptstrasse 145, A-1130 Vienna, Austria

MOBIL CORPORATION

3225 Gallows Road, Fairfax, VA, 22037-0001

Tel: (703) 846-3000 Fax: (703) 846-4669 Web site: www.mobil.com

Petroleum and gas exploration and refining, mfr. petroleum products, chemicals and petrochemicals.

Mobil Oil Austria AG, Postfach 33, Schwarzenberg Platz 3, A-1015 Vienna 1, Austria

MODINE MANUFACTURING COMPANY

1500 DeKoven Ave., Racine, WI, 53403

Tel: (414) 636-1200 Fax: (414) 636-1424 Web site: www.modine.com

Mfr. heat-transfer products.

Modine Handelsgesellschaft mbH, Industriestrasse B16 5 Stock, A-2345 Brunn/GEB, Austria

Modine Manufacturing Co., Berndorf, Austria

MOTOROLA, INC.

1303 East Algonquin Road, Schaumburg, IL, 60196

Tel: (847) 576-5000 Fax: (847) 538-5191 Web site: www.mot.com

Mfr. communications equipment, semiconductors and cellular phones.

Motorola GmbH, Hietzinger KAI 139, A-1131 Vienna, Austria

Tel: 43-1-878700 Fax: 43-1-878-70610

NALCO CHEMICAL COMPANY

One Nalco Center, Naperville, IL, 60563-1198

Tel: (630) 305-1000 Fax: (630) 305-2900 Web site: www.nalco.com

Chemicals for water and waste water treatment, oil products and refining, industry processes; water and energy management service.

Nalco Chemical GmbH, Scheydgasse 34-36, A-1210 Vienna, Austria

Tel: 43-1-270-2635 Fax: 43-1-270-2699

NCR (NATIONAL CASH REGISTER)

1700 South Patterson Blvd., Dayton, OH, 45479

Tel: (937) 445-5000 Fax: (937) 445-7042 Web site: www.ncr.com

Mfr. automated teller machines and high-performance stationary bar code scanners.

NCR Osterreich Geg. M.b.H., Storchesngasse 1, A1150 Vienna, Austria

Tel: 43-222-891-11-3300 Fax: 43-222-891-113109 Contact: Ferdinand Braun, Dir.

A .C. NIELSEN COMPANY

177 Broad Street, Stamford, CT, 06901

Tel: (203) 961-3000 Fax: (203) 961-3190 Web site: www.acnielsen.com

Market research.

A.C. Nielsen Co. GmbH, Moeringgasse 20, A-1150 Vienna 1, Austria

NIKE INC.

1 Bowerman Drive, Beaverton, OR, 97005

Tel: (503) 671-6453 Fax: (503) 671-6300 Web site: www.info.nike.com

Mfr. athletic footwear, equipment and apparel.

Nike Austria, Vienna, Austria

NORDSON CORPORATION

28601 Clemens Road, Westlake, OH, 44145

Tel: (440) 892-1580 Fax: (440) 892-9507 Web site: www.nordson.com

Mfr. industry application equipment, sealants & packaging machinery.

Nordson GesmbH (Austria), Concorde Business Park C2/13, A-2320 Schwechat, Austria

Tel: 43-1-707-5521 Fax: 43-1-707-5517

NORGREN

5400 S. Delaware Street, Littleton, CO, 80120-1663

Tel: (303) 794-2611 Fax: (303) 795-9487 Web site: www.norgren.com

Mfr. pneumatic filters, regulators, lubricators, valves, automation systems, dryers, push-in fittings.

IMI Norgren GmbH, Industriezentrum No-Sud, Strasse 2, A-2355 Wiener Neudorf, Austria

Tel: 43-2236-63520 Fax: 43-2236-6352020

OGILVY & MATHER WORLDWIDE

309 West 49th Street, New York, NY, 10019

Tel: (212) 237-4000 Fax: (212) 237-5123

Advertising, marketing, public relations & consulting firm.

Ogilvy & Mather, Vienna, Austria

ORACLE CORPORATION

500 Oracle Parkway, Redwood Shores, CA, 94065

Tel: (415) 506-7000 Fax: (415) 506-7200

Develop/manufacture software.

Oracle Datenbanksysteme GmbH, Schoepfleuthnergasse 25, A-1210 Vienna, Austria

OTIS ELEVATOR COMPANY

10 Farm Springs Road, Farmington, CT, 06032

Tel: (860) 676-6000 Fax: (860) 676-5111

Mfr. elevators and escalators.

Otis GmbH, Oberlaaer Strasse 282, A-1232 Vienna, Austria

PALL CORPORATION

2200 Northern Boulevard, East Hills, NY, 11548-1289

Tel: (516) 484-5400 Fax: (516) 484-5228 Web site: www.pall.com

Specialty materials and engineering; filters & related fluid clarification equipment.

Pall Austria Filter Ges.m.b.H, Wichtelgasse 57-59, Vienna A-1170, Austria

Tel: 43-1-491920 Fax: 43-1-491-9233

Pall Gelman Sciences, Wichtelgasse 57-59, Vienna A-1170, Austria

Tel: 43-1-491920 Fax: 43-1-491-9233

PANAMETRICS

221 Crescent Street, Waltham, MA, 02154

Tel: (781) 899-2719 Fax: (781) 899-1552 Web site: www.panametrics.com

Process/non-destructive test instrumentation.

Panametrics Messtechnik Gmbh, Waldgasse 39, A-1100 Vienna, Austria

Tel: 43-1-602-25-34 Fax: 43-1-602-25-34-11 Contact: Hans-Joachim Krech

PANDUIT CORPORATION

17301 Ridgeland Ave., Tinley Park, IL, 60477-0981

Tel: (708) 532-1800 Fax: (708) 532-1811

Mfr. electrical/electronic wiring components.

Panduit Corp., Zweigniederlassung Vienna, Erlachplatz 2-4, A-1100 Vienna, Austria

PARAMETRIC TECHNOLOGY CORPORATION

128 Technology Drive, Waltham, MA, 02154

Tel: (781) 398-5000 Fax: (781) 398-5674 Web site: www.ptc.com

Mfr. CAD/CAM/CAE software.

Parametric Technology Gesellschaft, Simmeringer Hauptstrasse 24, A-1110 Vienna, Austria

Tel: 43-1-7-40-40215 Fax: 43-1-7-40-40217

Parametric Technology Gesellschaft, Wiener Strasse 131, 4020 Linz, Austria

Tel: 43-732-333 42 05 Fax: 43-732-333 42 10

Parametric Technology Gesellschaft, Innsbrucker Bundesstrasse 40 A-5020 Salzburg, Austria

Tel: 43-662-439501 Fax: 43-662-43950180

Parametric Technology Gesellschaft, Vorarlberger Wirtschaftspark, A-6840 Gotzis, Austria

Tel: 43-5523-573700 Fax: 43-5523-573709

Parametric Technology Gesellschaft, Primoschgasse 3 A-9020 Klagenfurt, Austria

Tel: 43-463-3875-556 Fax: 43-463-3875-559

PARKER HANNIFIN CORPORATION

17325 Euclid Ave., Cleveland, OH, 44112

Tel: (216) 896-3000 Fax: (216) 896-4000 Web site: www.parker.com

Mfr. motion-control products.

Parker Ermeto GmbH, Badener Str. 12, Postfach 113, A-2700 Wiener Neustadt, Austria

Parker Hannifin NMF GbmH, Motion & Control, Handelskai 52, A-1200 Vienna, Austria

THE PERKIN-ELMER CORPORATION

761 Main Ave., Norwalk, CT, 06859-0001

Tel: (203) 762-1000 Fax: (203) 762-4228 Web site: www.perkin-elmer.com

Leading supplier of systems for life science research and related applications.

Perkin-Elmer GmbH, Weinerbergstraße 11b, A-1110, Vienna, Austria

Tel: 43-1-602-3101 Fax: 43-1-602-5174

PFIZER INC.

235 East 42nd Street, New York, NY, 10017-5755

Tel: (212) 573-2323 Fax: (212) 573-7851 Web site: www.pfizer.com

Research-based, global health care company.

Howmedica GmbH, Austria

Pfizer Corp. Austria GmbH, Mondscheingasse 16, 0171 Vienna, Austria

Tel: 43-1-52-1150 Fax: 43-1-526-9133

Pfizer Med-Inform Beratungs GmbH, Austria

PHARMACIA & UPJOHN

95 Corporate Drive, PO Box 6995, Bridgewater, NJ, 08807

Tel: (908) 306-4400 Fax: (908) 306-4433 Web site: www.pnu.com

Mfr. pharmaceuticals, agricultural products, industry chemicals

Pharmacia & Upjohn/Pharma-Handels-Geb.m.b.H., PB 297 Oberlaaer Str. 251, A-1100, Vienna, Austria

PHELPS DODGE CORPORATION

2600 North Central Ave., Phoenix, AZ, 85004-3089

Tel: (602) 234-8100 Fax: (602) 234-8337

Copper, minerals, metals & spec engineered products for transportation & electrical markets.

Phelps Dodge Eldra GmbH, Mureck, Austria

PHILIP SERVICES CORP. INDUSTRIAL GROUP

5151 San Felipe Street, #1600, Houston, TX, 77056-3609

Tel: (713) 623-8777 Fax: (713) 625-7085 Web site: www.philipinc.com

Trucking, refuse systems, staffing and numerous industrial-oriented services.

Industrial Services Philip Services (Europe), 317 Liebenauer Haupstrabe, Graz, Austria A-8041

Tel: 43-316-408-4706 Fax: 43-316-408-4750 Contact: Gernot Waltenstorfer

PHILLIPS PETROLEUM COMPANY

Phillips Building, 411 S. Keeler Ave., Bartlesville, OK, 74004

Tel: (918) 661-6600 Fax: (918) 661-7636 Web site: www.phillips66.com

Crude oil, natural gas, liquified petroleum gas, gasoline and petro-chemicals.

Phillips Petroleum Intl. Osthandel GmbH, Veithgasse 6, A-1030 Vienna, Austria

PITNEY BOWES INC.

1 Elmcroft Road, Stamford, CT, 06926-0700

Tel: (203) 356-5000 Fax: (203) 351-6835 Web site: www.pitneybowes.com

Mfr. postage meters, mailroom equipment, copiers, bus supplies, bus services, facsimile systems and financial services.

Pitney Bowes Austria Ges. m.b., Hosnedlgasse 35, Postfach 19, A-1221 Vienna, Austria

Tel: 43-1-2583621-0 Fax: 43-1-258362134 Contact: Gerhard Grill, Mng. Dir. Emp: 70

PLIBRICO COMPANY

1800 N. Kingsbury Street, Chicago, IL, 60614

Tel: (773) 549-7014 Fax: (773) 549-0424

Refractories, engineering and construction.

Austria-Plibrico Feuerfest-Engineering GmbH, Postfach 44, Hegelgasse 6, A-1015 Vienna 1, Austria

POLAROID CORPORATION

549 Technology Square, Cambridge, MA, 02139

Tel: (781) 386-2000 Fax: (781) 386-3276 Web site: www.polaroid.com

Photographic equipment & supplies, optical products.

Polaroid GmbH, Eitnergasse 13, A-1233 Vienna, Austria

POLICY MANAGEMENT SYSTEMS CORPORATION

PO Box 10, Columbia, SC, 29202

Tel: (803) 735-4000 Fax: (803) 735-5544

Computer software, insurance industry support services.

PMS Osterreich Gesmbh, Lannerweg 9, A-9201 Krumpendorf, Austria

PRAXAIR, INC.

39 Old Ridgebury Road, Danbury, CT, 06810-5113

Tel: (203) 837-2000 Fax: (203) 837-2450 Web site: www.praxair.com

Produces and distributes industrial and specialty gases.

SAID Verbrieb Technischer Gase GmbH, A-5120 St. Pantaleon, Trimmelkam, Austria

Tel: 43-6277-7447-0 Fax: 43-6277-7401

PREMARK INTERNATIONAL INC.

1717 Deerfield Road, Deerfield, IL, 60015

Tel: (847) 405-6000 Fax: (847) 405-6013 Web site: www.premarkintl.com

Mfr./sale plastic, diversified consumer & commercial products.

Dart Industries GmbH, Muhlgasse 58, A-2500 Baden, Austria

PRICEWATERHOUSECOOPERS LLP

1251 Ave. of the Americas, New York, NY, 10020

Tel: (212) 596-7000 Fax: (212) 790-6620 Web site: www.pwcglobal.com

Accounting and auditing, tax and management, and human resource consulting services.

Price Waterhouse Ltd., Bahnhofstrasse 10, A-6900 Bregenz, Austria

Tel: 43-7443-522-0 Fax: 43-7443-522-9

Price Waterhouse Ltd., Prinz-Eugen-Strasse 72, A-1040 Vienna, Austria

Tel: 43-1-501-88-0 Fax: 43-1-501-88-9

PRINTRONIX INC.

17500 Cartwright Road, Irvine, CA, 92623-9559

Tel: (949) 863-1900 Fax: (949) 660-8682 Web site: www.printronix.com

Mfr. computer printers.

Printronix Austria, Parkring 10/5, A-1010 Vienna, Austria

Tel: 43-1-516-333183 Fax: 43-1-516-333000

PROCTER & GAMBLE COMPANY

One Procter & Gamble Plaza, Cincinnati, OH, 45202

Tel: (513) 983-1100 Fax: (513) 562-4500 Web site: www.pg.com

Personal care, food, laundry, cleaning and industry products.

Procter & Gamble Austria GmbH, Mariahilfer Strasse 77-79, A-1060 Vienna, Austria

RADISSON HOTELS INTERNATIONAL

Carlson Pkwy., PO Box 59159, Minneapolis, MN, 55459-8204

Tel: (612) 540-5526 Fax: (612) 449-3400

Hotels and resorts.

Radisson SAS Hotels, Parkring 16, A-1010 Vienna, Austria(Locations in Salzburg)

Tel: 43-1-515-17-0 Fax: 43-1-512-22-16

Radisson SAS Hotels,

RAY & BERNDTSON, INC.

301 Commerce, Ste. 2300, Fort Worth, TX, 76102

Tel: (817) 334-0500 Fax: (817) 334-0779 Web site: www.prb.com

Executive search, management audit and management consulting firm.

Ray & Berndtson, Karntnerstrabe 49, Vienna A-1010, Austria

Tel: 43-1-599-99214 Fax: 43-1-599-99700 Contact: Joachim Zyla, Mng. Ptnr.

RENAISSANCE HOTELS AND RESORTS

1 Marriott Drive, Washington, DC, 20058

Tel: (301) 380-3000 Fax: (301) 380-5181

Hotel and resort chain.

Renaissance Penta Vienna Hotel, Vienna, Austria

Tel: 43-1-711-750

ROCKWELL INTERNATIONAL CORPORATION

600 Anton Boulevard, Costa Mesa, CA, 92626-7147

Tel: (714) 424-4200 Fax: (714) 424-4251 Web site: www.rockwell.com

Products & service for aerospace and defense, automotive, electronics, graphics & automation industry.

Rockwell Automation GmbH, Grottenhofstrasse 94, A-8052 Graz, Austria (Locations: Innsbruck, Linz, and Vienna, Austria.)

Tel: 43-316-287-3000 Fax: 43-316-287-30050

ROHM AND HAAS COMPANY

100 Independence Mall West, Philadelphia, PA, 19106

Tel: (215) 592-3000 Fax: (215) 592-3377 Web site: www.rohmhaas.com

Mfr. industrial & agricultural chemicals, plastics.

Rohm and Haas GmbH Austria, Diefenbachgasse 35-41, A-1150 Vienna, Austria

Tel: 43-1-894-17600

Shipley HMC Gmbh, Auhofstrasse 84, Stiege 3 Tur 39, A-1130 Vienna, Austria

Tel: 43-1-877-6024

RUBBERMAID INC.

1147 Akron Road, Wooster, OH, 44691

Tel: (330) 264-6464 Fax: (330) 287-2846 Web site: www:rubbermaid.com

Mfr. rubber and plastic resin home, commercial and industry products.

Dupol-Rubbermaid GmbH, Teisenbergg. 35, A-5013 Salzburg, Austria

SAS INSTITUTE INC.

SAS Campus Drive, Cary, NC, 27513

Tel: (919) 677-8000 Fax: (919) 677-8123 Web site: www.sas.com

Mfr./distributes decision support software.

SAS Institute (Austria) GmbH., Vienna, Austria

Tel: 43-1-5968-882-0 Fax: 43-1-5968-882-90

SCHENKER INTERNATIONAL FORWARDERS INC.

150 Albany Ave., Freeport, NY, 11520

Tel: (516) 377-3000 Fax: (516) 377-3005 Web site: www.schenkerusa.com

Freight forwarders.

Schenker & Co. AG, Lilienfelderstrasse 4, PO Box 37, St. Poelten, 3106 Austria

Tel: 43-2741-860 Fax: 43-2742-860-22

Schenker & Co. AG, PO Box 135, Vienna, A01110, Austria

Tel: 43-1-76086 Fax: 43-1-76086-449

SEA-LAND SERVICE INC.

6000 Carnegie Boulevard, Charlotte, NC, 28209

Tel: (704) 571-2000 Fax: (704) 571-4693 Web site: www.sealand.com

Largest U.S-based containerized transport service; ships, railroads, barge lines and trucking operations.

Paul Guenther GmbH & Co., Schwedenplatz 2, A-1010 Vienna, Austria

SENSORMATIC ELECTRONICS CORPORATION

951 Yamato Road, Boca Raton, FL, 33431-0700

Tel: (561) 912-6000 Fax: (561) 989-7774 Web site: www.sensormatic.com

Electronic article surveillance equipment.

Senelco GmbH & Co., Schwedenplatz 2, A-1010 Vienna, Austria

SEQUENT COMPUTER SYSTEMS INC.

15450 SW Koll Pkwy., Beaverton, OR, 97006-6063

Tel: (503) 626-5700 Fax: (503) 578-9890 Web site: www.sequent.com

Mfr. symmetric multiprocessing technology computers.

Sequent Computer Systems GmbH, Hütteldorferstrasse 81b/Stg.1, A-1150 Vienna, Austria

Tel: 43-1-982-75060 Fax: 43-1-982-750620

THE SERVICEMASTER COMPANY

One ServiceMaster Way, Downers Grove, IL, 60515-1700

Tel: (630) 271-1300 Fax: (630) 271-2710 Web site: www.svm.com

Management service to health care, school and industry facilities; diversified residential and commercial services.

ServiceMaster, Vienna, Austria

SHIPLEY CO., INC.

455 Forest Street, Marlborough, MA, 01752

Tel: (508) 481-7950 Fax: (508) 485-9113

Mfr. chemicals for printed circuit boards and microelectronic manufacturing.

Shipley HMC GmbH, Auhofstrasse 84, Stiege 3 Tur 39, A-1130 Vienna, Austria

Tel: 43-1-877-6024 Fax: 43-1-877-602424 Contact: A. K. Kostelecky, Mng. Dir.

SNAP ON DIAGNOSTICS

420 Barclay Boulevard, Lincolnshire, IL, 60069

Tel: (847) 478-0700 Fax: (847) 478-7308 Web site: www.snapon.com

Mfr. auto maintenence, diagnostic & emission testing equipment.

Sun Electric Austria GmbH, Hochtrasse 18-20, A-2380 Perchtoldsdorf, Austria

Tel: 43-222-865-97840 Fax: 43-222-865-9798429 Contact: H. Pechtl, Mng. Dir.

SPENCER STUART & ASSOCIATES INC.

401 North Michigan Ave., Ste. 3400, Chicago, IL, 60611

Tel: (312) 822-0080 Fax: (312) 822-0116 Web site: www.spencerstuart.com

Executive recruitment firm.

Spencer Stuart & Associates Inc., Innsbrucker Bundesstrasse 75, A-5020 Salzbug, Austria

Tel: 43-662-829775 Fax: 43-662-829774

Spencer Stuart & Associates Inc., Heiligenstaedterstrasse 51, A-1190 Vienna, Austria

Tel: 43-1-3688-7000 Fax: 43-1-3688-777 Contact: Reinhard Hager & Gerd Wilhelm

Spencer Stuart & Associates Inc., Claudiasrasse 14/III, A-6020 Innsbruck, Austria

Tel: 43-512-585052 Fax: 43-512-583213 Contact: Gerhard Oberhuber

THE ST. PAUL COMPANIES, INC.

385 Washington Street, St. Paul, MN, 55102

Tel: (612) 310-7911 Fax: (612) 310-8294 Web site: www.stpaul.com

Provides investment, insurance and reinsurance services.

Victoria Volksbanken Versicherungs A.G., Schottengasse 10, A-1013 Vienna, Austria

STATE STREET BANK & TRUST COMPANY

225 Franklin Street, Boston, MA, 02101

Tel: (617) 786-3000 Fax: (617) 654-3386 Web site: www.statestreet.com

Banking & financial services.

Euopean Direct Capital Management, Vienna, Austria

Tel: 43-22499-3200 Contact: Ivan Vohlmuth

SYBASE, INC.

6475 Christie Ave., Emeryville, CA, 94608

Tel: (510) 922-3500 Fax: (510) 922-3210 Web site: www.sybase.com

Design/mfg/distribution of database management systems, software development tools, connectivity products, consulting and technical support services..

Sybase Austria EDV, Floragasse 7/3, Q-1040 Vienna, Austria

Tel: 43-222-5048510-0 Fax: 43-222-5048510-33

SYMBOL TECHNOLOGIES, INC.

One Symbol Plaza, Holtsville, NY, 11742-1300

Tel: (516) 738-2400 Fax: (516) 563-2831 Web site: www.symbol.com

Mfr. bar code-driven data management systems, wireless LAN's, and Portable Shopping System™.

Symbol Technologies Austria GmbH, Prinz-Eugen Strasse 70, Ste. 3, 2. Haus, 5. Stock, 1040 Vienna, Austria

Tel: 43-1-505-5794 Fax: 43-1-505-3962

TBWA INTERNATIONAL

180 Maiden Lane, New York, NY, 10038

Tel: (212) 804-1000 Fax: (212) 804-1200

International full service advertising agency.

TBWA Werbegesellschaft, Vienna, Austria

TEKTRONIX INC.

2660 Southwest Parkway Ave., PO Box 1000, Wilsonville, OR, 97070-1000

Tel: (503) 627-7111 Fax: (503) 627-2406 Web site: www.tek.com

Mfr. test & measure, visual systems/color printing & communications/video and networking products.

Tektronix GmbH, Triester Straße 4, Wiener Neudorf A-2351, (Vienna) Austria

Tel: 43-2236-8092-224 Fax: 43-2236-8092-200

TENNECO AUTOMOTIVE

500 North Field Drive, Lake Forest, IL, 60045

Tel: (847) 482-5241 Fax: (847) 482-5295

Automotive parts, exhaust systems, service equipment.

Monroe Europe, Hildebrandgasse 25/5, Postfach 33, A-1180 Vienna, Austria

TEXAS INSTRUMENTS INC.

8505 Forest Lane, Dallas, TX, 75243

Tel: (214) 995-2011 Fax: (214) 995-4360 Web site: www.ti.com

Mfr. semiconductor devices, electronic electro-mechanical systems, instruments and controls.

Texas Instruments, Vienna, Austria

TRANE COMPANY

3600 Pammel Creek Road, La Crosse, WI, 54601

Tel: (608) 787-2000 Fax: (608) 787-4990

Mfr./distributor/service A/C systems and equipment.

Trane Austria, Office Ctr. SIG, Simmeringer Hauptstrasse 24, A-1110 Vienna, Austria

Trane Eastern Europe, Gartengasse 26, A-1050 Vienna, Austria

TRANTER INC.

1054 Claussen Road, #314, Augusta, GA, 30907

Tel: (706) 738-7900 Fax: (706) 738-6619 Web site: www.tranter.com

Mfr. heat exchangers.

SWEP Warmetauscher Austria GmbH, Kammeringstrasse 18, A-2353, Guntramsdorf, Austria

Tel: 43-2236-56623 Fax: 43-2236-56621

TRUE NORTH COMMUNICATIONS INC.

101 East Erie Street, Chicago, IL, 60611

Tel: (312) 425-6000 Fax: (312) 425-6350

Holding company, advertising agency.

Publicis/FCB, Spiegelgasse 1, A-1015 Vienna, Austria

TRW INC.

1900 Richmond Road, Cleveland, OH, 44124-3760

Tel: (216) 291-7000 Fax: (216) 291-7932

Electric and energy-related products, automotive and aerospace products, tools and fasteners.

TRW Intl. Services GmbH, Prinz Augenstrasse 8, A-1040 Vienna, Austria

TRW Repa GmbH, A-5082 Groedig, Austria

TYCO INTERNATIONAL LTD.

One Tyco Park, Exeter, NH, 03833

Tel: (603) 778-9700 Fax: (603) 778-7700 Web site: www.tycoint.com

Mfr./sales fire & security systems, sprinkler systems, undersea fiber optic telecommuncations, printed circuit boards, pipe tubing and flow meters.

Industrie Bedarfs Gesellschaft m.b.h., A-1230 Vienna, Eitnergasse 25, Austria

Tel: 43-1-865-5801 Fax: 43-1-86-55-805

U.S. SURGICAL CORPORATION

150 Glover Ave., Norwalk, CT, 06856

Tel: (203) 845-1000 Fax: (203) 847-0635 Web site: www.ussurg.com

Mfr./development/market surgical staplers, laparoscopic instruments and sutures.

Auto Suture (Austria) GmbH, Austria - All mail to U.S. address.

UNION CARBIDE CORPORATION

39 Old Ridgebury Road, Danbury, CT, 06817

Tel: (203) 794-2000 Fax: (203) 794-6269 Web site: www.unioncarbide.com

Mfr. industrial chemicals, plastics and resins.

Union Carbide Austria GmbH, Storchengasse 1, Postfach 315, A-1150 Vienna, Austria

UNISYS CORPORATION.

PO Box 500, Union Meeting Road, Blue Bell, PA, 19424

Tel: (215) 986-4011 Fax: (215) 986-6850 Web site: www.unisys.com

Mfr./marketing/servicing electronic information systems.

Unisys Osterreich GmbH, Mariahilferstr. 20, A-1071 Vienna, Austria

UNITED PARCEL SERVICE OF AMERICA, INC.

55 Glenlake Parkway, NE, Atlanta, GA, 30328

Tel: (404) 828-6000 Fax: (404) 828-6593 Web site: www.ups.com

International package-delivery service.

United Parcel Service Speditionsges.m.b.H., Am Concorde Park 1/B4, 2320 Schwechat, Austria

UNITED TECHNOLOGIES CORPORATION

United Technologies Building, Hartford, CT, 06101

Tel: (860) 728-7000 Fax: (860) 728-7979 Web site: www.utc.com

Mfr. aircraft engines, elevators, A/C, auto equipment, space and military electronic and rocket propulsion systems. Products include Pratt & Whitney, Otis elevators, Carrier heating and air conditioning and Sikorsky helicopters.

Freissler Otis GmbH, Oberlaaerstrasse, Postfach 104, A-1232 Vienna, Austria

VARIAN ASSOCIATES INC.

3050 Hansen Way, Palo Alto, CA, 94304-100

Tel: (650) 493-4000 Fax: (650) 424-5358 Web site: www.varian.com

Mfr. microwave tubes & devices, analytical instruments, semiconductor process & medical equipment, vacuum systems.

Varian GmbH, Eisgrubengassse 2, Postfach 14, A-2334 Vosendorf bei Vienna, Austria

VIKING OFFICE PRODUCTS

950 West 190th Street, Torrance, CA, 90502

Tel: (310) 225-4500 Fax: (310) 324-2396 Web site: www.vikingop.com

International direct marketer of office products, computer supplies, business furniture and stationery.

Viking Direkt GesmbH, Tragweiner Strasse 37, 4230 Pregarten, Austria

Tel: 43-723-65151 Fax: 43-723-651515 Contact: Rolf van Kaldekerken, Mgr. Emp: 31

WANG LABORATORIES INC.

600 Technology Park Drive, Billerica, MA, 01821

Tel: (508) 967-5000 Fax: (508) 967-5911

Mfr. computer information processing systems.

Wang GmbH, Linkewienzelle 234, A-1150 Vienna, Austria

WARNACO INC.

90 Park Ave., New York, NY, 10016

Tel: (212) 661-1300 Fax: (212) 687-0480 Web site: www.warnaco.com

Mfr./sales intimate apparel and men's and women's sportswear.

Warnaco, Vienna, Austria

WARNER-LAMBERT COMPANY

201 Tabor Road, Morris Plains, NJ, 07950-2693

Tel: (973) 540-2000 Fax: (973) 540-3761 Web site: www.warner-lambert.com

Mfr. ethical and proprietary pharmaceuticals, confectionery and consumer products & pet care supplies.

Substantia GmbH, Postfach 35, Ketzergasse 118, A-1234 Vienna, Austria

WASTE MANAGEMENT, INC.

3003 Butterfield Road, Oak Brook, IL, 60523-1100

Tel: (630) 572-8800 Fax: (630) 572-3094 Web site: www.wastemanagement.com

Environmental services and disposal company; collection, processing, transfer and disposal facilities.

Rudolf Beck & Söhne GmbH, Wolfholzgasse 9, 2345 Brunn/Gebirge, Austria

WATERS CORPORATION

34 Maple Street, Milford, MA, 01757

Tel: (508) 478-2000 Fax: (508) 872-1990

Mfr./distribute liquid chromatographic instruments and test and measurement equipment.

Waters Associates GmbH, Schonbachstrasse 13, A-1130 Vienna, Austria

WEATHERFORD INTERNATIONAL INC.

5 Post Oak Blvd, Ste. 1760, Houston, TX, 77227-3415

Tel: (713) 287-8400 Fax: (713) 963-9785 Web site: www.weatherford.com

Oilfield services, products & equipment; mfr. marine cranes for oil and gas industry.

Weatherford Oil Tool GmbH, Donaufelderstr. 36/II/4/12, A-1210 Vienna, Austria

WM WRIGLEY JR. COMPANY

410 N. Michigan Ave., Chicago, IL, 60611-4287

Tel: (312) 644-2121 Fax: (312) 644-0353 Web site: www.wrigley.com

Mfr. chewing gum.

Wrigley Austria GmbH, Josef Waach-Strasse 11, A-5023 Salzburg, Austria

XEROX CORPORATION

800 Long Ridge Road, PO Box 1600, Stamford, CT, 06904

Tel: (203) 968-3000 Fax: (203) 968-4312 Web site: www.xerox.com

Mfr. document processing equipment, systems and supplies.

Rank Xerox Gessellschaft M.B.H., Triester Str. 70, 1101 Vienna, Austria

Tel: 43-1-601970 Fax: 43-1-6019-7310

YOUNG & RUBICAM INC.

285 Madison Ave., New York, NY, 10017

Tel: (212) 210-3000 Fax: (212) 370-3796 Web site: www.yr.com

Advertising, public relations, direct marketing and sales promotion, corporate & product ID management.

Young & Rubicam GmbH, Marc Aurel-Strasse 4, Postfach 999, A-1011 Vienna, Austria

Azerbaijan

AMOCO OIL COMPANY

200 East Randolph Drive, Chicago, IL, 60601

Tel: (312) 856-5111 Fax: (312) 856-2454

Petroleum mfr. & refining.

Amoco Caspian Sea Petroleum Company, 11 Hassan Aliyev St., Baku, Azerbaijan

Tel: 99-412-989170

BAKER & McKENZIE

One Prudential Plaza, 130 East Randolph Drive, Ste. 2500, Chicago, IL, 60601

Tel: (312) 861-8000 Fax: (312) 861-2899 Web site: www.bakerinfo.com

International legal services.

Baker & McKenzie, The Landmark Bldg., 96 Nizami St., 6th Fl., Baku 370010 Azerbaijan

Tel: 99-412-98-24-80 Fax: 99-412-97-08-05

BAKER HUGHES INCORPORATED

3900 Essex Lane, Ste. 1200, Houston, TX, 77027

Tel: (713) 439-8600 Fax: (713) 439-8699 Web site: www.bakerhughes.com

Develop & apply technology to drill, complete & produce oil and natural gas wells; provide separation systems to petroleum, municipal, continuous process & mining industries.

Baker Oil Tools, 191/44 B. Safar Oflu St., Baku, 370000, Azerbaijan

Tel: 99-412-942941 Fax: 99-412-973004

BECHTEL GROUP INC.

50 Beale Street, PO Box 3965, San Francisco, CA, 94105-1895

Tel: (415) 768-1234 Fax: (415) 768-9038 Web site: www.bechtel.com

General contractors in engineering & construction.

Bechtel International Corp., 59 Suleyman Tagizade St., Baku, Azerbaijan

Tel: 99-412-936801 Fax: 99-412-936815 Contact: Chapay Sultanov

BROWN & ROOT INC.

4100 Clinton Drive, Houston, TX, 77020-6299

Tel: (713) 676-3011 Fax: (713) 676-8532

Engineering, construction and maintenance.

Brown & Root/Halliburton International Inc., 41 Bolshaya Krepostnaya St., Baku. Azerbaijan

Tel: 99-412-989344 Fax: 99-412-989344 Contact: Selcuk Guner, Reg. Mgr.

DHL WORLDWIDE EXPRESS

333 Twin Dolphin Drive, Redwood City, CA, 94065

Tel: (650) 593-7474 Fax: (650) 593-1689 Web site: www.dhl.com

Worldwide air express carrier.

DHL Worldwide Express, Tbilisi Ave., Palace of Sport, Entrance 7, Baku 370078, Azerbaijan

Tel: 99-4-8922-934714

ERNST & YOUNG, LLP

787 Seventh Ave., New York, NY, 10019

Tel: (212) 773-3000 Fax: (212) 773-6350 Web site: www.eyi.com

Accounting and audit, tax and management consulting services.

Ernst & Young Baku, 11 Mardanov Qardashlari St. 11, Apt. 32, Baku, Azerbaijan
Tel: 99-412-983385 Fax: 99-412-937312 Contact: Alum Bati

EXXON CORPORATION
225 E. John W. Carpenter Freeway, Irving, TX, 75062-2298
Tel: (972) 444-1000 Fax: (972) 444-1882 Web site: www.exxon.com
Petroleum exploration, production, refining; mfr. petroleum & chemicals products; coal & minerals.
Exxon Ventures, 1 Injasanat St., Baku, Azerbaijan
Tel: 99-412-988035 Contact: John Hoholick, Res. Mgr.

FISHER-ROSEMOUNT
8000 Maryland Ave., Ste. 500, Clayton, MO, 63105-4755
Tel: (314) 746-9900 Fax: (314) 746-9974
Mfr. industrial process control equipment.
Emerson F-R, The Landmark, Ste. 109 B, 2nd Fl., 96, Nizami St., 370000 Baku, Azerbaijan

FRITZ COMPANIES INC.
706 Mission Street, Ste. 900, San Francisco, CA, 94103
Tel: (415) 904-8360 Fax: (415) 904-8661 Web site: www.fritz.com
Integrated transportation, sourcing, distribution & customs brokerage services.
Fritz Companies Inc., Baku, Azerbaijan

HYATT INTERNATIONAL CORPORATION
200 West Madison Street, Chicago, IL, 60606
Tel: (312) 750-1234 Fax: (312) 750-8578 Web site: www.hyatt.com
International hotel management.
Hyatt Regency Baku Hotel, Bakuhanov St. 1, Baku, Azerbaijan
Tel: 99-412-981234 Fax: 99-412-980817

IBM CORPORATION
New Orchard Road, Armonk, NY, 10504
Tel: (914) 765-1900 Fax: (914) 765-7382 Web site: www.ibm.com
Information products, technology & services.
IBM AS/400 - Business Communications Ltd., 67, Nizami Str., Baku 370005 Azerbaijan
Tel: 99-412-989166 Fax: 99-412-933980
IBM PC - Dan Production and Commerce, Metabuat Cad. No. 29, Baku, Azerbaijan
Tel: 99-412-395172 Fax: 99-412-989775

McCANN-ERICKSON WORLDWIDE
750 Third Ave., New York, NY, 10017
Tel: (212) 984-3644 Fax: (212) 984-2629
International advertising/marketing services.
Yurd McCann-Erickson, Baku, Azerbaijan

MOBIL CORPORATION
3225 Gallows Road, Fairfax, VA, 22037-0001
Tel: (703) 846-3000 Fax: (703) 846-4669 Web site: www.mobil.com
Petroleum and gas exploration and refining, mfr. petroleum products, chemicals and petrochemicals.
Mobil Oil Azerbaijan, 19/13 Xanqani St., Block 4, Apt. 25, Baku, Azerbaijan
Tel: 99-412-932876 Fax: 99-412-873153-6523 Contact: Geoffrey B. Slater Res. Mgr.

PALMS & COMPANY, INC. (U.S. FUR EXCHANGE)
515 Lake Street South, Bldg. #103, Kirkland, WA, 98033
Tel: (425) 828-6774 Fax: (425) 827-5528
Fur auctioning, distribution and sale; investment banking

Palms & Co. (Azerbaijan) Inc., All mail to: PO Box 25, Lutsk-23 City Volyn Region, Ukraine 262023
Contact: Dr. Oleg Jourin

PENNZOIL COMPANY

700 Milam, Houston, TX, 77002
Tel: (713) 546-4000 Fax: (713) 546-6589 Web site: www.pennzoil.com
Produce/refine/market oil, natural gas, sulfur.
Pennzoil Caspian Corporation, "Old Intourist" Hotel, 63 Neftchiler Prospecti, Baku, Azerbaijan
Tel: 99-412-924007 Fax: 99-412-916788 Contact: Thomas Hickox, VP

PRICEWATERHOUSECOOPERS LLP

1251 Ave. of the Americas, New York, NY, 10020
Tel: (212) 596-7000 Fax: (212) 790-6620 Web site: www.pwcglobal.com
Accounting and auditing, tax and management, and human resource consulting services.
Price Waterhouse Ltd., Rasul Rza St., Bldg. No. 6, Apt. No. 33, 370000 Baku, Azerbaijan
Tel: 99-412-930700 Fax: 99-412-930700

TECH-SYM CORPORATION

10500 Westoffice Drive, #200, Houston, TX, 77042-5391
Tel: (713) 785-7790 Fax: (713) 780-3524 Web site: www.syntron.com
Electronics, real estate, aeromechanics.
Symtronix Baku, 10 Malaya Krepostnaya, St. 18, Baku, Azerbaijan 370004
Tel: 99-4-12-922505 Fax: 99-4-12-922505

UNOCAL CORPORATION

PO Box 7600, Los Angeles, CA, 90051
Tel: (213) 977-7600 Fax: (213) 726-7817
Fully integrated high-tech energy resources development.
Unocal Ltd., Mehdi Huseyin St. 1A, "Anba" Hotel, Baku, Azerbaijan
Tel: 99-412-989111 Fax: 99-412-989113 Contact: Wade Lundstrom, Res. Mgr.

WESTERN ATLAS INC.

10205 Westheimer, Houston, TX, 77251-1407
Tel: (713) 972-4000 Fax: (713) 952-9837 Web site: www.waii.com
Full service to the oil industry.
PetroAlliance Services Company Ltd., 7 Mamadaliev St., Apt. 5, Baku 370005, Azerbaijan
Tel: 99-412-936421 Fax: 99-412-934503

Bahamas

AMERICAN AIRLINES INC.

4333 Amon Carter Boulevard, Ft. Worth, TX, 76155

Tel: (817) 963-1234 Fax: (817) 967-9641 Web site: www.amrcorp.com

Air transport services.

American Airlines Inc., Nassau Intl Airport, PO Box N-3724, Nassau, Bahamas

AVIS, INC.

900 Old Country Road., Garden City, NY, 11530

Tel: (516) 222-3000 Fax: (516) 222-4381 Web site: www.avis.com

Car rental services.

Avis Rent a Car, Downtown W. Bay, PO Box N 8300, Nassau, Bahamas

Avis Rent a Car, Freeport Intl. Airport, Freeport, Bahamas

BANKAMERICA CORPORATION

555 California Street, San Francisco, CA, 94104

Tel: (415) 622-3530 Fax: (415) 622-8467 Web site: www.bankamerica.com

Financial services.

Bank America Trust & Banking Corp. Ltd., BankAmerica House, East Bay St., PO Box N-9100, Nassau, Bahamas

Tel: 242-393-7411 Fax: 242-393-3030 Contact: Jan Mezulanik, Mng Dir.

BANKBOSTON CORPORATION

100 Federal Street, PO Box 1788, Boston, MA, 02110

Tel: (617) 434-2200 Fax: (617) 434-7547 Web site: www.bankboston.com

Banking & insurance services.

BankBoston Trust Company (Bahamas) Ltd., Charlotte House, PO Box N-3930, Nassau, Bahamas

Tel: 809-322-8531 Fax: 809-328-2750

BANKERS TRUST COMPANY

280 Park Ave., New York, NY, 10017

Tel: (212) 250-2500 Fax: (212) 250-2440 Web site: www.bankerstrust.com

Banking & investment services.

Bankers Trust Company, Claughton House, PO Box N 3234, Nassau, Bahamas

BDO SEIDMAN, LLP

Two Prudential Plaza, 180 N. Stetson Ave., Ste. 2300, Chicago, IL, 60601

Tel: (312) 240-1236 Fax: (312) 240-3329 Web site: www.bdo.com

International accounting & financial consulting firm.

BDO Mann Judd, (PO Box N-10144) Ansbacher House, East St., Nassau, Bahamas

Tel: 242-325-6591 Fax: 242-325-6592 Contact: G. Cliffird Culmer

BEST WESTERN INTERNATIONAL

6201 North 24th Place, Phoenix, AZ, 85106

Tel: (602) 957-4200 Fax: (602) 957-5740

International hotel chain.

BW British Colonial Beach Resort, 1 Bay St., Nassau, Bahamas

Tel: 242-322-3301

BUDGET RENT A CAR CORPORATION

4225 Naperville Road, Lisle, IL, 60532

Tel: (630) 955-1900 Fax: (630) 955-7799 Web site: www.budgetrentacar.com

Car and truck rental system.

Budget Rent A Car, Central Hdqrs., Nassau, Bahamas

Tel: 242-323-7191

THE CHAMBERS COMPANY

1010 North Charles Street, Baltimore, MD, 21201

Tel: (410) 727-4535 Fax: (410) 727-6982

Interior design and architectural services.

The H. Chambers Co./House & Garden, Lyford Cay, PO Box N7776, Nassau, Bahamas

THE CHASE MANHATTAN CORPORATION

World Headquarters, 270 Park Ave., New York, NY, 10017

Tel: (212) 270-6000 Fax: (212) 622-9030 Web site: www.chase.com

International banking and financial services.

The Chase Manhattan Private Bank & Trust Co. (Bahamas) Ltd., PO Box N3708 Shirley and Charlotte Sts., Nassau, Bahamas

Tel: 242-356-1305 Fax: 242-325-1706

CIGNA CORPORATION

One Liberty Place, Philadelphia, PA, 19192

Tel: (215) 761-1000 Fax: (215) 761-5008

Insurance, invest, health care and other financial services.

Colina Insurance Co. Ltd., 12 Village Rd., PO Box N 4728, Nassau, Bahamas

CITICORP

399 Park Ave., New York, NY, 10043

Tel: (212) 559-1000 Fax: (212) 527-2066 Web site: www.citibank.com

International banking and financial services.

Citibank N.A., Citibank Bldg., PO Box N1576, Nassau, Bahamas

Contact: Carmen Butler, Mgr.

DELOITTE TOUCHE TOHMATSU INTERNATIONAL

PO Box 820, Wilton, CT, 06897

Tel: (203) 761-3000 Fax: (203) 834-2200 Web site: www.u.s.deloitte.com or www.dtti.com

Accounting, audit, tax and management consulting services.

Deloitte & Touche, PO Box F-43746, East Sunrise Highway, Freeport, Bahamas

Deloitte & Touche, PO Box N-7120, Dehands House, 2nd Terrace West, Collins Ave., Centerville, Nassau, Bahamas

DELTA AIR LINES INC.

PO Box 20706, Atlanta, GA, 30320-6001

Tel: (404) 715-2600 Fax: (404) 715-5494 Web site: www.delta-air.com/index.html

Major worldwide airline; international air transport services.

Delta Air Lines Inc., Nassau, Bahamas

Delta Air Lines Inc., Nassau, Bahamas

DHL WORLDWIDE EXPRESS

333 Twin Dolphin Drive, Redwood City, CA, 94065

Tel: (650) 593-7474 Fax: (650) 593-1689 Web site: www.dhl.com

Worldwide air express carrier.

DHL Worldwide Express, 157 Nassau St., PO Box N3735, Nassau, Bahamas

Tel: 809-325-8266

ERNST & YOUNG, LLP

787 Seventh Ave., New York, NY, 10019

Tel: (212) 773-3000 Fax: (212) 773-6350 Web site: www.eyi.com

Accounting and audit, tax and management consulting services.

Ernst & Young, Sassoon House, Shirley & Victoria, (PO Box N-3231) Nassau, Bahamas

Tel: 809-322-3805 Fax: 809-326-8180 Contact: Paul F. Clarke

EXXON CORPORATION

225 E. John W. Carpenter Freeway, Irving, TX, 75062-2298

Tel: (972) 444-1000 Fax: (972) 444-1882 Web site: www.exxon.com

Petroleum exploration, production, refining; mfr. petroleum & chemicals products; coal & minerals.

Esso Standard Oil S.A. Ltd., East Bay St., Nassau, Bahamas

FIRST UNION CORPORATION

One First Union Center, Charlotte, NC, 28288-0013

Tel: (704) 374-6565 Fax: (704) 374-3425 Web site: www.firstunion.com

Banking, financial and insurance services.

First Union National Bank, Bahamas

FRANKLIN RESOURCES, INC.

777 Mariners Island Blvd., San Mateo, CA, 94404

Tel: (415) 312-2000 Fax: (415) 312-3655 Web site: www.frk.com

Global and domestic investment advisory and portfolio management.

Templeton Global Advisors, Ltd., Nassau, Bahamas

FRITZ COMPANIES INC.

706 Mission Street, Ste. 900, San Francisco, CA, 94103

Tel: (415) 904-8360 Fax: (415) 904-8661 Web site: www.fritz.com

Integrated transportation, sourcing, distribution & customs brokerage services.

Fritz Companies Inc., Nassau, Bahamas

THE GILLETTE COMPANY

Prudential Tower Building, Boston, MA, 02199

Tel: (617) 421-7000 Fax: (617) 421-7123 Web site: www.gillette.com

Develop/mfr. personal care/use products: blades & razors, toiletries, cosmetics, stationery.

Oral-B Laboratories Freeport Ltd., Freeport, Bahamas

Oral-B Laboratories Nassau Ltd., Freeport, Bahamas

WECO Intl. Ltd., Freeport, Bahamas

HARCOURT BRACE & COMPANY

6277 Sea Harbor Drive, Orlando, FL, 32887

Tel: (407) 345-2000 Fax: (407) 345-9354

Book publishing, tests and related service, journals, facsimile reprints, management consult, operates parks/shows.

Harcourt Brace Carribean, c.o Academia, PO Box SS 6805, Nassau, Bahamas

Tel: 809-363-2043 Fax: 809-363-3844

THE HARPER GROUP

260 Townsend Street, San Francisco, CA, 94107-1719

Tel: (415) 978-0600 Fax: (415) 978-0692 Web site: www.circleintl.com

Ocean/air freight forwarding, customs brokerage, packing and wholesale, logistics management and insurance.

C. & B. Customs Brokerage, PO Box N 8678, Nassau, Bahamas

Tel: 809 393.3620 Fax: 809 393.5598

HERCULES INC

Hercules Plaza, 1313 North Market Street, Wilmington, DE, 19894-0001

Tel: (302) 594-5000 Fax: (302) 594-5400 Web site: www.herc.com

Mfr. specialty chemicals, plastics, film and fibers, coatings, resins, food ingredients.

Hercules Intl. Trade Corp. Ltd., 50 Shirley St., Nassau, Bahamas

HOLIDAY INNS WORLDWIDE, INC.

3 Ravinia Drive, Ste. 2900, Atlanta, GA, 30346-2149

Tel: (770) 604-2000 Fax: (770) 604-5403

Hotels, restaurants and casinos.

Holiday Inn, Freeport-Lucaya G.B., Lucaya Beach, Bahamas

IBM CORPORATION

New Orchard Road, Armonk, NY, 10504

Tel: (914) 765-1900 Fax: (914) 765-7382 Web site: www.ibm.com

Information products, technology & services.

IBM Products Distribution (Bahamas) Ltd., Bahamas

INTERNATIONAL PAPER COMPANY

2 Manhattanville Road, Purchase, NY, 10577

Tel: (914) 397-1500 Fax: (914) 397-1596 Web site: www.ipaper.com

Mfr./distributor container board, paper, wood products.

International Navigation Ltd., PO Box N-7790, Nassau, Bahamas

Winthrop Ltd., PO Box N-7790, Nassau, Bahamas

J.P. MORGAN & CO. INC.

60 Wall Street, New York, NY, 10260-0060

Tel: (212) 483-2323 Fax: (212) 648-5209 Web site: www.jpm.com

International banking services.

J.P.Morgan (Bahamas) Portfolio Co. Ltd., PO Box N 4899, Bahamas Financial Centre, Charlotte & Shirley Sts., Nassau, Bahamas

Tel: 242-326-5519

Morgan Guaranty Trust Co. of New York, IBM B1, Church & Ernest, PO Box 3935, Nassau, Bahamas

Tel: 242-326-5519

KPMG PEAT MARWICK LLP

Three Chestnut Ridge Road, Montvale, NJ, 07645

Tel: (201) 307-7000 Fax: (201) 930-8617 Web site: www.kpmg.com

Accounting and audit, tax and management consulting services.

KPMG Croes & Croes, 7th Fl. Centerville House, Collins Ave., Nassau, Bahamas

Tel: 242-322-8551 Fax: 242-326-5622 Contact: Michael H. Fielder, Sr. Ptnr.

KPMG Croes & Croes Accountants, 1st Fl., International Building, Freeport, Bahamas

MARRIOTT INTERNATIONAL INC.

1 Marriott Drive, Washington, DC, 20058

Tel: (301) 380-3000 Fax: (301) 380-5181

Lodging, contract food and beverage service, and restaurants.

Nassau Marriott Resort & Crystal Palace Casino, Nassau, New Providence, Bahamas

MARSH & McLENNAN COS INC.

1166 Ave. of the Americas, New York, NY, 10036-2774

Tel: (212) 345-5000 Fax: (212) 345-4808 Web site: www.marshmac.com

Insurance agents/brokers, pension and investment management consulting services.

J.S.Johnson & Co. Ltd., 34 Collins Ave., Nassau, Bahamas

Tel: 242-322-2341 Fax: 242-323-3720 Contact: Marvin V. Bethell

MORTON INTERNATIONAL INC.

100 North Riverside Plaza, Chicago, IL, 60606-1596

Tel: (312) 807-2000 Fax: (312) 807-3150 Web site: www.mortonintl.com

Mfr. adhesives, coatings, finishes, specialty chemicals, advanced and electronic materials, salt, airbags.

Morton Intl. Inc., Inagua, Bahamas

NATIONSBANK CORPORATION

100 North Tryon Street, Corporate Center, Charlotte, NC, 28255

Tel: (704) 386-5000 Fax: (704) 386-1709 Web site: www.nationsbank.com

Banking and financial services.

NationsBank Corp., Nassau, Bahamas (All mail to 901 Main St., Dallas, TX 75202)

POLAROID CORPORATION

549 Technology Square, Cambridge, MA, 02139

Tel: (781) 386-2000 Fax: (781) 386-3276 Web site: www.polaroid.com

Photographic equipment & supplies, optical products.

Polaroid Overseas Corp., PO Box 1046, Nassau, Bahamas

PRICEWATERHOUSECOOPERS LLP

1251 Ave. of the Americas, New York, NY, 10020

Tel: (212) 596-7000 Fax: (212) 790-6620 Web site: www.pwcglobal.com

Accounting and auditing, tax and management, and human resource consulting services.

Price Waterhouse Ltd., Providence House, East Hill St., PO Box N-3910, Nassau, Bahamas

Tel: 809-322-8543 Fax: 809-326-7308

RADISSON HOTELS INTERNATIONAL

Carlson Pkwy., PO Box 59159, Minneapolis, MN, 55459-8204

Tel: (612) 540-5526 Fax: (612) 449-3400

Hotels and resorts.

Radisson Cable Beach Casino and Golf Resort, PO Box N-4919, Nassau, Bahamas

Tel: 242-327-6000 Fax: 242-327-6987

Radisson Resort on Lucaya Beach, PO Box F2496, Royal Palm Way, Freeport, Bahamas

Radisson Xanadu Beach & Marina Resort, Sunken Treasure Dr., PO Box F2438, Freeport, Bahamas

REPUBLIC NATIONAL BANK OF NEW YORK

452 Fifth Ave., New York, NY, 10018

Tel: (212) 525-5000 Fax: (212) 525-6996 Web site: www.rnb.com

Banking services.

Republic National Bank of New York (Intl.) Ltd., Nassau, Bahamas

SOUTHERN COMPANY

270 Peachtree Street, Atlanta, GA, 30303

Tel: (404) 506-5000 Fax: (404) 506-0642 Web site: www.southernco.com

Electric utility.

Freeport Power Company, Port Authority Bldg., PO Box F-400888, Freeport, Bahamas

Tel: 242-351-3585 Contact: Larry Brantley, Pres.

SUN INTERNATIONAL, INC.

1415 East Sunrise Blvd., Fort Lauderdale, FL, 33304

Tel: (954) 713-2500 Fax: (954) 713-2019

Ownership, development and operation of resort complexes.

Bahamas Development Ltd., PO Box F 160, Freeport Grand Island, Bahamas

Britannia Towers, PO Box N 3707, Nassau, Bahamas

Paradise Enterprises Ltd., PO Box ES 6311, Nassau, Bahamas

Paradise Island Ltd., PO Box 4777, Nassau, Bahamas

TEXACO INC.

2000 Westchester Ave., White Plains, NY, 10650

Tel: (914) 253-4000 Fax: (914) 253-7753 Web site: www.texaco.com

Exploration/marketing crude oil, mfr. petro chemicals and products.

Texaco Bahamas Ltd., PO Box N 4807, Nassau, Bahamas

UNITED PARCEL SERVICE OF AMERICA, INC.

55 Glenlake Parkway, NE, Atlanta, GA, 30328

Tel: (404) 828-6000 Fax: (404) 828-6593 Web site: www.ups.com

International package-delivery service.

UPS / G.W.S. Worldwide Express, Airfreight Terminal, Cargo Bay E, PO Box F42533, Freeport, Bahamas

Tel: 242-352-3434 Fax: 242-352-7460

WENDY'S INTERNATIONAL, INC.

428 West Dublin-Granville Roads, Dublin, OH, 43017

Tel: (614) 764-3100 Fax: (614) 764-3459

Fast food restaurant chain.

Wendy's International, Bahamas

WINN-DIXIE STORES, INC.

5050 Edgewood Court, Jacksonville, FL, 32254-3699

Tel: (904) 783-5000 Fax: (904) 783-5294 Web site: www.winn-dixie.com

Retail grocery chain and manufacturing, bottling and processing operations.

Bahamas Supermarkets Ltd., Freeport & Nassau, Bahamas

The City Meat Markets Ltd., Freeport & Nassau, Bahamas

Winn-Dixie (Bahamas) Ltd., Freeport & Nassau, Bahamas

WOMETCO ENTERPRISES INC.

3195 Ponce de Leon Boulevard, Coral Gables, FL, 33134

Tel: (305) 529-1400 Fax: (305) 529-1499

Television broadcasting, film distribution, bottling, vending machines.

Caribbean Bottling Co. Ltd., PO Box N 1123, Nassau, Bahamas

Grand Bahama CATV Ltd., PO Box F 413, Freeport, Bahamas

Grand Bahamas Theatres Ltd., PO Box F 413, Freeport, Bahamas

Bahrain

AIR EXPRESS INTERNATIONAL CORPORATION

120 Tokeneke Road, PO Box 1231, Darien, CT, 06820

Tel: (203) 655-7900 Fax: (203) 655-5779 Web site: www.aeilogistics.com

Air freight forwarder.

AEI - Bahrain, c/o Intercol (International Agencies Co. Ltd.) Al Wazzan Building, 131, Al Khalifa Ave., PO Box 584, Manana, Bahrain

Tel: 973-728151 Fax: 973-321257

ALCOA (ALUMINUM CO OF AMERICA)

Alcoa Bldg., 425 Sixth Ave., Pittsburgh, PA, 15219-1850

Tel: (412) 553-4545 Fax: (412) 553-4498

World's leading producer of aluminum & alumina; mining, refining, smelting, fabricating & recycling.

Gulf Closures W.L.L., Manama, Bahrain

ALLIANCE CAPITAL MANAGEMENT L.P.

1345 Ave. of the Americas, New York, NY, 10105

Tel: (212) 969-1000 Fax: (212) 969-2229 Web site: www.alliancecapital.com

Fund manager for large organizations.

Alliance Capital Management, Bahrain

AMERICAN EXPRESS COMPANY

American Express Tower, World Financial Center, New York, NY, 10285-4765

Tel: (212) 640-2000 Fax: (212) 619-9802 Web site: www.americanexpress.com

Travel, travelers cheques, charge card & financial services.

Amex (Gulf States) EC (JV), Bahrain - All inquiries to U.S. address

AON CORPORATION

123 North Wacker Drive, Chicago, IL, 60606

Tel: (312) 701-3000 Fax: (312) 701-3100 Web site: www.aon.com

Insurance brokers worldwide; underwrites accident & health insurance, specialty & professional insurance; & provides risk management consultation.

A & A International, The Gulf Business Centre, Central Manama, Bahrain

Tel: 973-215275 Fax: 973-214641 Contact: Ken Mc Whinnie

ARTHUR ANDERSEN & COMPANY

33 West Monroe Street, Chicago, IL, 60603

Tel: (312) 372-7100 Fax: (312) 507-0123 Web site: www.arthurandersen.com

Accounting & audit, tax & management consulting services.

Arthur Andersen & Company, 6th Fl., BMB Ctr., Diplomatic Area, PO Box 20323, Manama, Bahrain

Tel: 973-530400

BANKERS TRUST COMPANY

280 Park Ave., New York, NY, 10017

Tel: (212) 250-2500 Fax: (212) 250-2440 Web site: www.bankerstrust.com

Banking & investment services.

Bankers Trust Company, PO Box 5905, Manama Centre, Manama, Bahrain

Tel: 973-229966 Fax: 973-229991 Contact: Nadim Zaman, VP Emp: 4

BEST WESTERN INTERNATIONAL

6201 North 24th Place, Phoenix, AZ, 85106
Tel: (602) 957-4200 Fax: (602) 957-5740
International hotel chain.

Baisan Tower, PO Box 15156, Manama, Bahrain

BROWN & ROOT INC.

4100 Clinton Drive, Houston, TX, 77020-6299
Tel: (713) 676-3011 Fax: (713) 676-8532
Engineering, construction and maintenance.

Brown & Root (Gulf) EC, PO Box 780, Manama, Bahrain

Brown & Root Middle East SA, PO Box 780, Manama, Bahrain

BUDGET RENT A CAR CORPORATION

4225 Naperville Road, Lisle, IL, 60532
Tel: (630) 955-1900 Fax: (630) 955-7799 Web site: www.budgetrentacar.com
Car and truck rental system.

Budget Rent A Car, PO Box 39, Manama, Bahrain
Tel: 973-534100

LEO BURNETT CO., INC.

35 West Wacker Drive, Chicago, IL, 60601
Tel: (312) 220-5959 Fax: (312) 220-6533 Web site: www.leoburnett.com
International advertising agency.

H & C Bahrain, Manama, Bahrain

Radius Advertising, PO Box 2915, Manama, Bahrain

CALTEX PETROLEUM CORPORATION

125 East John Carpenter Fwy., Irving, TX, 75062-2794
Tel: (972) 830-1000 Fax: (972) 830-1081 Web site: www.caltex.com
Petroleum products.

Caltex Bahrain, PO Box 25125, Awali, Bahrain

CARRIER CORPORATION

One Carrier Place, Farmington, CT, 06034-4015
Tel: (860) 674-3000 Fax: (860) 679-3010 Web site: www.carrier.com
Mfr./distributor/services A/C, heating & refrigeration equipment.

Carrier Intl. of Bahrain EC, Manama, Bahrain

THE CHASE MANHATTAN CORPORATION

World Headquarters, 270 Park Ave., New York, NY, 10017
Tel: (212) 270-6000 Fax: (212) 622-9030 Web site: www.chase.com
International banking and financial services.

The Chase Manhattan Bank, Bahrain Branch, Bahrain Commercial Complex, 4th Fl., PO Box 368, Manama, Bahrain
Tel: 973-53388 Fax: 973-535135

CHESTERTON BINSWANGER INTERNATIONAL

Two Logan Square, 4th Floor, Philadelphia, PA, 19103-2759
Tel: (215) 448-6000 Fax: (215) 448-6238
Real estate & related services.

Dabbagh Group Holding Co. Ltd., DHL Bldg. #14, PO Box 723, Manama, Bahrain

CITICORP

399 Park Ave., New York, NY, 10043

Tel: (212) 559-1000 Fax: (212) 527-2066 Web site: www.citibank.com

International banking and financial services.

Citibank N.A., Bab Al Bahrain Bldg., Government Rd., Fl. 1, Manama 548, Bahrain

Contact: Mohammed Al-Shroogi, Mgr.

COMPUTER ASSOCIATES INTERNATIONAL INC.

One Computer Associates Plaza, Islandia, NY, 11788

Tel: (516) 342-5224 Fax: (516) 342-5329 Web site: www.cai.com

Integrated software for enterprise computing and information management, application development, manufacturing, financial applications and professional services.

Computer Associates Middle East WLL, Ground Fl., Diplomat Tower, Bldge. 315, Rd. 1705, Blk 317, Manama, Bahrain

Tel: 973-537-977

CONOCO INC.

PO Box 2197, Houston, TX, 77252

Tel: (281) 293-1000 Fax: (281) 293-1440

Oil, gas, coal, chemicals and minerals.

Continental Oil Co. of Bahrain, PO Box 235, Manama, Bahrain

DDB NEEDHAM WORLDWIDE INC.

437 Madison Ave., New York, NY, 10022

Tel: (212) 415-2000 Fax: (212) 415-3417

Advertising agency.

DDB Bahrain, Mahooz, Bahrain

DELOITTE TOUCHE TOHMATSU INTERNATIONAL

PO Box 820, Wilton, CT, 06897

Tel: (203) 761-3000 Fax: (203) 834-2200 Web site: www.u.s.deloitte.com or www.dtti.com

Accounting, audit, tax and management consulting services.

Saba & Company, PO Box 421, Baharain Tower, 16th Fl., Al-Khalifa Rd., Manama, Bahrain

DHL WORLDWIDE EXPRESS

333 Twin Dolphin Drive, Redwood City, CA, 94065

Tel: (650) 593-7474 Fax: (650) 593-1689 Web site: www.dhl.com

Worldwide air express carrier.

DHL Worldwide Express, Um Al Hassan, PO Box 5741, Manama, Bahrain

Tel: 973-723636

DOVER CORPORATION

280 Park Ave., New York, NY, 10017-1292

Tel: (212) 922-1640 Fax: (212) 922-1656 Web site: www.dovercorporation.com

Elevator manufacturer and holding company for varied industries.

Abdul Aziz Eshaq Establishment, PO Box 5306, Manama, Bahrain

Tel: 973-254571 Fax: 973-272912

ERNST & YOUNG, LLP

787 Seventh Ave., New York, NY, 10019

Tel: (212) 773-3000 Fax: (212) 773-6350 Web site: www.eyi.com

Accounting and audit, tax and management consulting services.

Ernst & Young L.L.P., Bahrain

Tel: 973-535455 Fax: 973-535405

FEDERAL-MOGUL CORPORATION

26555 Northwestern Highway, PO Box 1966, Southfield, MI, 48034

Tel: (248) 354-7700 Fax: (248) 354-8983 Web site: www.federalmogul.com

Mfr./distributor precision parts for automobiles, trucks, farm and construction vehicles.

Federal-Mogul World Trade EC, Bahrain

FLOWSERVE FLUID SEALING DIVISION

222 Los Colinas Blvd., Ste. 1500, Irving, TX, 75039

Tel: (616) 381-2650 Fax: (616) 443-6800 Web site: www.flowserve.com

Mfr. mechanical seals, compression packings and auxiliaries.

Durametallic Middle East, PO Box 20611, Manama, Bahrain

FOUR WINDS INTERNATIONAL GROUP

1500 SW First Ave., Ste. 850, Portland, OR, 97201-2013

Tel: (503) 241-2732 Fax: (503) 241-1829 Web site: www.vanlines.com.au

Transportation of household goods and general cargo and third party logistics.

Four Winds Bahrain, PO Box 11131, Manama, Bahrain

Tel: 973-530212 Fax: 973-530212 Contact: Anter Sulton Faklroo, Mng. Dir.

FRITZ COMPANIES INC.

706 Mission Street, Ste. 900, San Francisco, CA, 94103

Tel: (415) 904-8360 Fax: (415) 904-8661 Web site: www.fritz.com

Integrated transportation, sourcing, distribution & customs brokerage services.

Fritz Companies Inc., Bahrain

GENERAL DYNAMICS CORPORATION

3190 Fairview Park Drive, Falls Church, VA, 22042-4523

Tel: (703) 876-3000 Fax: (703) 876-3125 Web site: www.gendyn.com

Mfr. aerospace equipment, submarines, strategic systems, armored vehicles, defense support systems.

GD Intl. Corp., Ste. 54, Diplomat Tower Bldg. 315, Rd. 1705, Block 317, Diplomatic area, Manama, Bahrain

HALLIBURTON COMPANY

500 North Akard Street, Ste. 3600, Dallas, TX, 75201-3391

Tel: (214) 978-2600 Fax: (214) 978-2685 Web site: www.halliburton.com

Energy, construction and insurance.

Halliburton Ltd., PO Box 515, Manama, Bahrain

Tel: 973-727102 Fax: 973-723437

THE HARPER GROUP

260 Townsend Street, San Francisco, CA, 94107-1719

Tel: (415) 978-0600 Fax: (415) 978-0692 Web site: www.circleintl.com

Ocean/air freight forwarding, customs brokerage, packing and wholesale, logistics management and insurance.

Circle Freight Intl. (Bahrain) Ltd., PO Box 5069, Manama, Bahrain

HOLIDAY INNS WORLDWIDE, INC.

3 Ravinia Drive, Ste. 2900, Atlanta, GA, 30346-2149

Tel: (770) 604-2000 Fax: (770) 604-5403

Hotels, restaurants and casinos.

Holiday Inn, PO Box 5831, Bahrain Intl. Airport, Manama, Bahrain

HORWATH INTERNATIONAL

415 Madison Ave., New York, NY, 10017

Tel: (212) 838-5566 Fax: (212) 838-3636

Public accountants and auditors.

Horwath, Abou Chakra & Co., Al-Mo'taz Bldg., Apt. 22, Al-Muthnna St., Manana, Bahrain

IBM CORPORATION

New Orchard Road, Armonk, NY, 10504

Tel: (914) 765-1900 Fax: (914) 765-7382 Web site: www.ibm.com

Information products, technology & services.

IBM - Bahrain Business Machines, Standard Chartered Bank Building, 7th Fl., Government Rd., Manama, Bahrain

Tel: 973-210880 Fax: 973-210576

INTERGRAPH CORPORATION

One Madison Industrial Park, Huntsville, AL, 35894-0001

Tel: (205) 730-2000 Fax: (205) 730-7898 Web site: www.intergraph.com

Develop/mfr. interactive computer graphic systems.

Intergraph Middle East Gulf EC, Bldg. 169, Rd. 1405, Block 314, PO Box 1715, Manama, Bahrain

Tel: 973-271900 Fax: 973-270241

ITT CORPORATION

1330 Ave. of the Americas, New York, NY, 10019-5490

Tel: (212) 258-1000 Fax: (212) 258-1297

Design/mfr. communications & electronic equipment, hotels, insurance.

Intl. Telephone & Telegraph Co. Ltd., Salahuddin Bldg., Al-Fateh Rd., PO Box 5473, Manama, Bahrain

ITT SHERATON CORPORATION

60 State Street, Boston, MA, 02108

Tel: (617) 367-3600 Fax: (617) 367-5676

Hotel operations.

Bahrain Sheraton, PO Box 30, Manama, Bahrain

KIMBERLY-CLARK CORPORATION

351 Phelps Drive, Irving, TX, 75038

Tel: (972) 281-1200 Fax: (972) 281-1435 Web site: www.kimberly-clark.com.

Mfr./sales/distribution of consumer tissue, household and personal care products.

Kimberly-Clark Corporation, East Riffa, Bahrain

KPMG PEAT MARWICK LLP

Three Chestnut Ridge Road, Montvale, NJ, 07645

Tel: (201) 307-7000 Fax: (201) 930-8617 Web site: www.kpmg.com

Accounting and audit, tax and management consulting services.

KPMG Fakhro, Chamber of Commerce & Industry Bldg., 5th Fl., Manama, Bahrain

Tel: 973-224807 Fax: 973-227443 Contact: Jamal Fakhro, Sr. Ptnr.

LEHMAN BROTHERS HOLDINGS INC.

Three World Financial Center, New York, NY, 10285

Tel: (212) 526-7000 Fax: (212) 526-3738 Web site: www.lehman.com

Financial services, securities and merchant banking services.

Lehman Brothers, Office No. 710, 7th Fl., Building 6, Rd. 1701, Area 317 - Diplomatic Area, Bahrain

Tel: 973-533076

THE LINCOLN ELECTRIC COMPANY

22801 St. Clair Ave., Cleveland, OH, 44117-1199

Tel: (216) 481-8100 Fax: (216) 486-8385 Web site: www.lincolnelectric.com

Mfr. arc welding and welding related products, oxy-fuel and thermal cutting equipment and integral AC motors.

The Lincoln Electric Company International, PO Box 11758, Manama, Bahrain

Tel: 973-3213643 Fax: 973-3213826 Contact: Ali Bazzi

LOCKHEED MARTIN CORPORATION

6801 Rockledge Drive, Bethesda, MD, 20817

Tel: (301) 897-6000 Fax: (301) 897-6652 Web site: www.imco.com

Design/mfr./management systems in fields of space, defense, energy, electronics and technical services.

Lockheed Aeronautical Systems, Manama, Bahrain (All inquiries to US office)

MERRILL LYNCH & COMPANY, INC.

World Financial Center, North Tower, New York, NY, 10281-1323

Tel: (212) 449-1000 Fax: (212) 449-2892

Security brokers and dealers, investment and business services.

Merrill Lynch International Bank, 4th Fl., Bahrain BMB Bldg., Diplomatic Area, PO Box 10399, Manama, Bahrain

Tel: 973-530260 Fax: 973-530245

PACCAR INTERNATIONAL

777 106th Ave. NE, Bellevue, WA, 98004

Tel: (425) 468-7400 Fax: (428) 468-8216

Heavy duty dump trucks, military vehicles.

Paccar AG, Al Hasan Bldg., Ste. 8, Diplomatic Area, Manama, Bahrain

Tel: 973-531014 Fax: 973-530587

THE PERKIN-ELMER CORPORATION

761 Main Ave., Norwalk, CT, 06859-0001

Tel: (203) 762-1000 Fax: (203) 762-4228 Web site: www.perkin-elmer.com

Leading supplier of systems for life science research and related applications.

Perkin-Elmer, Manama, Bahrain

Tel: 973-225547 Fax: 973-275819

PHILLIPS PETROLEUM COMPANY

Phillips Building, 411 S. Keeler Ave., Bartlesville, OK, 74004

Tel: (918) 661-6600 Fax: (918) 661-7636 Web site: www.phillips66.com

Crude oil, natural gas, liquified petroleum gas, gasoline and petro-chemicals.

Phillips Petroleum, Al-Andalus Bldg., PO Box 5485, Manama, Bahrain

PRICEWATERHOUSECOOPERS LLP

1251 Ave. of the Americas, New York, NY, 10020

Tel: (212) 596-7000 Fax: (212) 790-6620 Web site: www.pwcglobal.com

Accounting and auditing, tax and management, and human resource consulting services.

Price Waterhouse Ltd., Unitag House, 5th Fl., Government Rd., (PO Box 26403) Manama, Bahrain

Tel: 973-233266 Fax: 973-271459

SONESTA INTERNATIONAL HOTELS CORPORATION

200 Clarendon Street, Boston, MA, 02166

Tel: (617) 421-5400 Fax: (617) 421-5402 Web site: www.sonesta.com

Hotels, resorts, and Nile cruises..

Sonesta Hotel Bahrain, Bahrain

TYCO INTERNATIONAL LTD.

One Tyco Park, Exeter, NH, 03833

Tel: (603) 778-9700 Fax: (603) 778-7700 Web site: www.tycoint.com

Mfr./sales fire & security systems, sprinkler systems, undersea fiber optic telecommuncations, printed circuit boards, pipe tubing and flow meters.

Al Rawabie Trading, PO Box 28228, Bahrain

Tel: 973-263012 Fax: 973-261991

UNION CARBIDE CORPORATION

39 Old Ridgebury Road, Danbury, CT, 06817

Tel: (203) 794-2000 Fax: (203) 794-6269 Web site: www.unioncarbide.com

Mfr. industrial chemicals, plastics and resins.

Union Carbide (Europe) SA, PO Box 24, Manama, Bahrain

UNITED ASSET MANAGEMENT CORPORATION

One International Place, 44th Fl., Boston, MA, 02110

Tel: (617) 330-8900 Fax: (617) 330-1133

Investment management services.

Murray Johnstone Pvt. Investment, Ltd., PO Box 20257, Manama, Bahrain

Tel: 973-210362

UNITED PARCEL SERVICE OF AMERICA, INC.

55 Glenlake Parkway, NE, Atlanta, GA, 30328

Tel: (404) 828-6000 Fax: (404) 828-6593 Web site: www.ups.com

International package-delivery service.

United Parcel Service Bahrain, PO Box 113 Manama Centre, Manama, Bahrain

Tel: 973-223123 Fax: 973-224467

UOP INC.

25 E. Algonquin Road, Des Plaines, IL, 60017

Tel: (847) 391-2000 Fax: (847) 391-2253

Diversified research, development & mfr. of industry products & systems management studies & service.

Procon Inc., Bahrain

WESTERN ATLAS INC.

10205 Westheimer, Houston, TX, 77251-1407

Tel: (713) 972-4000 Fax: (713) 952-9837 Web site: www.waii.com

Full service to the oil industry.

Western Atlas Logging Services, Bldg. 20, Office 81 Bahrain Towers, Al Khalifa Rd., Manama 305, Bahrain

Tel: 973-212456 Fax: 973-215030 Contact: David C. Kellett, VP

XEROX CORPORATION

800 Long Ridge Road, PO Box 1600, Stamford, CT, 06904

Tel: (203) 968-3000 Fax: (203) 968-4312 Web site: www.xerox.com

Mfr. document processing equipment, systems and supplies.

Business International WLL, PO Box 585, Manama, Bahrain

Tel: 973-531977 Fax: 973-532016

Bangladesh

AIR EXPRESS INTERNATIONAL CORPORATION

120 Tokeneke Road, PO Box 1231, Darien, CT, 06820

Tel: (203) 655-7900 Fax: (203) 655-5779 Web site: www.aeilogistics.com

Air freight forwarder.

AEI Bangladesh Ltd., Ibrahim Chamber, 95 Motijheel Commercial Area, (Ground Fl.), Dhaka - 1000, Bangladesh (Locations: Chittagong, Gulshan, Kalyanpur, Khulnan, Narayangonj, Savar.)

Tel: 880-2-956-5114-17 Fax: 880-2-956-5112

AMMIRATI PURIS LINTAS

One Dag Hammarskjold Plaza, New York, NY, 10017

Tel: (212) 605-8000 Fax: (212) 605-4705 Web site: www.interpublic.com

International advertising agency.

Adcomm Ltd., 719 Satmasjid Rd., Dhanmondi, Shaka 1209, Bangladesh

Tel: 880-2-911-1918 Fax: 880-2-810-120 Contact: Geeteara Choudhury

BATES WORLDWIDE INC.

405 Lexington Ave., New York, NY, 10174

Tel: (212) 297-7000 Fax: (212) 986-0270 Web site: www.batesww.com

Advertising, marketing, public relations & media consulting.

ADCOMM Ltd., House 85, Rd. 6/A, Dhanmondi, Dhaka 1209, Bangladesh

Tel: 880-2-913-1595 Contact: G. S. Choudhury, Dir.

LOUIS BERGER INTERNATIONAL INC.

100 Halsted Street, East Orange, NJ, 07019

Tel: (201) 678-1960 Fax: (201) 672-4284 Web site: www.louisberger.com

Consulting engineers, architects, economists & planners.

Louis Berger International Inc., House No. 31, Rd. No. 1A, Block I, Banani, G.PO Box 4289, Dhaka 1000, Bangladesh

Tel: 880-1-885-201 Fax: 880-1-870-103

Louis Berger International Inc., PO Box 79, Nishindara Charamata, Bogra 5800, Bangladesh

Tel: 880-6204

LEO BURNETT CO., INC.

35 West Wacker Drive, Chicago, IL, 60601

Tel: (312) 220-5959 Fax: (312) 220-6533 Web site: www.leoburnett.com

International advertising agency.

Bitopi Advertising, Dhaka, Bangladesh

CITICORP

399 Park Ave., New York, NY, 10043

Tel: (212) 559-1000 Fax: (212) 527-2066 Web site: www.citibank.com

International banking and financial services.

Citibank N.A., Chamber Bldg., 122/124, Motijheel Commercial Area, Dhaka 1000, Bangladesh

DHL WORLDWIDE EXPRESS

333 Twin Dolphin Drive, Redwood City, CA, 94065

Tel: (650) 593-7474 Fax: (650) 593-1689 Web site: www.dhl.com

Worldwide air express carrier.

DHL Worldwide Express, Dhaka, Bangladesh

Tel: 880-2-988-1703

ERNST & YOUNG, LLP

787 Seventh Ave., New York, NY, 10019

Tel: (212) 773-3000 Fax: (212) 773-6350 Web site: www.eyi.com

Accounting and audit, tax and management consulting services.

S. F. Ahmed & Company, 128 New Eskaton Rd., Dhaka 1000, Bangladesh

Tel: 880-2-419938 Fax: 880-2-836979 Contact: F.U. Ahmed

EXPEDITORS INTERNATIONAL OF WASHINGTON INC.

999 Throd Ave., Ste. 2500, Seattle, WA, 98104

Tel: (206) 674-3400 Fax: (206) 682-9777 Web site: www.expd.com

Air/ocean freight forwarding, customs brokerage, international logistics solutions.

Expeditors (Bangladesh) Ltd., House No. 11,Road No. 11, Gulshan, Dhaka, 1212, Bangladesh

Tel: 880-2-872-187 Fax: 880-2-882-887

FISHER-ROSEMOUNT

8000 Maryland Ave., Ste. 500, Clayton, MO, 63105-4755

Tel: (314) 746-9900 Fax: (314) 746-9974

Mfr. industrial process control equipment.

Instrumentation Engineers Ltd., 3/3-C Purana Paltan, 1st Fl., GPO Box No. 2040, Dhaka 1000, Bangladesh

Tel: 880-2-862-555 Fax: 880-2-863-339

FRITZ COMPANIES INC.

706 Mission Street, Ste. 900, San Francisco, CA, 94103

Tel: (415) 904-8360 Fax: (415) 904-8661 Web site: www.fritz.com

Integrated transportation, sourcing, distribution & customs brokerage services.

Fritz Air Freight (Bangladesh) Ltd., Malik Chambers, 11/2 Toyenbee Circular Rd., Motjheel C.A., Dhaka 1000, Bangladesh (Office: Chittagong)

Fritz Ocean Freight (Bangladesh) Co. Ltd., Sultan Bldg. 2/F, 147 Motjheel C.A., Dhaka 1000, Bangladesh

GREY ADVERTISING INC.

777 Third Ave., New York, NY, 10017

Tel: (212) 546-2000 Fax: (212) 546-1495 Web site: www.giworldwwide.com

International advertising agency.

Grey Bangladesh, Dhaka, Bangladesh

THE HARPER GROUP

260 Townsend Street, San Francisco, CA, 94107-1719

Tel: (415) 978-0600 Fax: (415) 978-0692 Web site: www.circleintl.com

Ocean/air freight forwarding, customs brokerage, packing and wholesale, logistics management and insurance.

Wings Air Cargo/Ocean Freight Ltd., 58, Kamai Ataturk Ave., Banani C/A, Dhaka-1213, Bangladesh

Tel: 880-2-602-887 Fax: 880-2-883-024

Wings Air Cargo/Ocean Freight Ltd., 30, Agrabad C/A, 2nd Fl., Agrabad, Chittagong-4100, Bangladesh

Tel: 880-31-711-014 Fax: 880-31-710-127

IBM CORPORATION

New Orchard Road, Armonk, NY, 10504

Tel: (914) 765-1900 Fax: (914) 765-7382 Web site: www.ibm.com

Information products, technology & services.

IBM World Trade Corp., 14 Mohakhali Commercial Area, Pacific Centre, 6th Fl., Dhaka-1212, Bangladesh

Tel: 880-2-889783 Fax: 880-2-889788

ITT SHERATON CORPORATION

60 State Street, Boston, MA, 02108

Tel: (617) 367-3600 Fax: (617) 367-5676

Hotel operations.

Dhaka Sheraton Hotel, PO Box 504, Dhaka 2, Bangladesh

J. WALTER THOMPSON COMPANY

466 Lexington Ave., New York, NY, 10017

Tel: (212) 210-7000 Fax: (212) 210-6944 Web site: www.jwt.com

International advertising and marketing services.

Asiatic Marketing, Dhaka, Bangladesh

KPMG PEAT MARWICK LLP

Three Chestnut Ridge Road, Montvale, NJ, 07645

Tel: (201) 307-7000 Fax: (201) 930-8617 Web site: www.kpmg.com

Accounting and audit, tax and management consulting services.

Rahman Rahman Huq, 102 Agrabad Commercial Area, Chattagong, Bangladesh

Rahman Rahman Huq, 52 Motijeel Commercial Area, 2nd Fl., Dhaka 1000, Bangladesh

Tel: 880-2-956-1361 Fax: 880-2-995-0027 Contact: M. Saifur Rahman, Ptnr.

McCANN-ERICKSON WORLDWIDE

750 Third Ave., New York, NY, 10017

Tel: (212) 984-3644 Fax: (212) 984-2629

International advertising/marketing services.

Unitrend, Dhaka, Bangladesh

McDERMOTT INTERNATIONAL INC.

1450 Poydras Street, PO Box 60035, New Orleans, LA, 70160-0035

Tel: (504) 587-5400 Fax: (504) 587-6153 Web site: www.mcdermott.com

Engineering & construction.

J. Ray McDermott, S.A., Bangladesh

MOTOROLA, INC.

1303 East Algonquin Road, Schaumburg, IL, 60196

Tel: (847) 576-5000 Fax: (847) 538-5191 Web site: www.mot.com

Mfr. communications equipment, semiconductors and cellular phones.

Motorola South Asia Pte. Ltd., IQBAL Ctr., 6th Fl., 42 Kemal Ataturk Ave., Gulshan, Dhaka, Bangladesh

Tel: 880-2-857791 Fax: 880-2-813324

OCCIDENTAL PETROLEUM CORPORATION

10889 Wilshire Blvd., Los Angeles, CA, 90024

Tel: (310) 208-8800 Fax: (310) 443-6690 Web site: www.oxy.com

Petroleum and petroleum products, chemicals, plastics.

Occidental Bangladesh Inc., Bangladesh

PARSONS ENGINEERING SCIENCE INC.

100 West Walnut Street, Pasadena, CA, 91124

Tel: (626) 440-2000 Fax: (626) 440-4919

Environmental engineering.

Parsons Engineering Science Inc., Housing Settlement Directorate Bldg., 6/F, Segunbagicha, Dhaka, Bangladesh

THE PERKIN-ELMER CORPORATION

761 Main Ave., Norwalk, CT, 06859-0001

Tel: (203) 762-1000 Fax: (203) 762-4228 Web site: www.perkin-elmer.com

Leading supplier of systems for life science research and related applications.

Perkin-Elmer Bangladesh, Dhaka, Bangladesh

Tel: 880-2-956-9808 Fax: 880-2-956-4319

PFIZER INC.

235 East 42nd Street, New York, NY, 10017-5755

Tel: (212) 573-2323 Fax: (212) 573-7851 Web site: www.pfizer.com

Research-based, global health care company.

Pfizer Laboratories (Bangladesh) Ltd., Bangladesh

PICKER INTERNATIONAL INC.

595 Miner Road, Highland Heights, OH, 44143

Tel: (440) 473-3000 Fax: (440) 473-4844 Web site: www.picker.com

Mfr. diagnostic medical machines.

Picker Ltd., Bangladesh

UNION SPECIAL CORPORATION

One Union Special Plaza, Huntley, IL, 60142

Tel: (847) 669-4345 Fax: (847) 669-3534 Web site: www.unionspecial.com

Mfr. sewing machines.

JUKI Ltd., Sharif Plaza, 4th Fl., 39 Kamal Ataturk Ave., Banami, Dhaka-1213, Bangladesh

Tel: 880-2-988-4505 Fax: 880-2-988-4368

WESTERN ATLAS INC.

10205 Westheimer, Houston, TX, 77251-1407

Tel: (713) 972-4000 Fax: (713) 952-9837 Web site: www.waii.com

Full service to the oil industry.

Western Atlas Logging Services, House 43 Rd., 12 Baridhara, Dhaka, Bangladesh

Tel: 880-2-873-188 Fax: 880-2-873-188 Contact: M. Smart, Ops. Mgr.

Barbados

AMERICAN AIRLINES INC.

4333 Amon Carter Boulevard, Ft. Worth, TX, 76155

Tel: (817) 963-1234 Fax: (817) 967-9641 Web site: www.amrcorp.com

Air transport services.

American Airlines, Carlisle House Wharf, Bridgetown, Barbados

AON CORPORATION

123 North Wacker Drive, Chicago, IL, 60606

Tel: (312) 701-3000 Fax: (312) 701-3100 Web site: www.aon.com

Insurance brokers worldwide; underwrites accident & health insurance, specialty & professional insurance; & provides risk management consultation.

AON Insurance Managers (Barbados) Ltd.., Financial Services Ctr., St. Michael, Barbados

Tel: 246-436-4895 Fax: 246-436-9016 Contact: Ronald W. Jones

AON Worldwide John L. Sealy & Co, Ltd., 13, Pine Rd., St. Michael, Barbados

Tel: 246-427-6113 Fax: 246-427-6116 Contact: J, Sealy

BAXTER HEALTHCARE CORPORATION

One Baxter Parkway, Deerfield, IL, 60015

Tel: (847) 948-2000 Fax: (847) 948-3948 Web site: www.baxter.com

Pharmaceutical preparations, surgical/medical instruments & cardiovascular products.

Baxter Foreign Sale Cororation, Barbados

CARBOLINE COMPANY

350 Hanley Industrial Court, St. Louis, MO, 63144

Tel: (314) 644-1000 Fax: (314) 644-4617

Mfr. coatings, sealants.

Berger Paints Barbados Ltd., PO Box 218, Brandons, St. Michael, Bridgetown, Barbados

THE CHASE MANHATTAN CORPORATION

World Headquarters, 270 Park Ave., New York, NY, 10017

Tel: (212) 270-6000 Fax: (212) 622-9030 Web site: www.chase.com

International banking and financial services.

Chase Manhattan Bank N.A., Corner Broad & Nile St., PO Box 699, Bridgetown, Barbados

DELOITTE TOUCHE TOHMATSU INTERNATIONAL

PO Box 820, Wilton, CT, 06897

Tel: (203) 761-3000 Fax: (203) 834-2200 Web site: www.u.s.deloitte.com or www.dtti.com

Accounting, audit, tax and management consulting services.

Deloitte & Touche, PO Box 806E, Whitepark House, White Park Rd., Bridgetown, Barbados, BWI

DHL WORLDWIDE EXPRESS

333 Twin Dolphin Drive, Redwood City, CA, 94065

Tel: (650) 593-7474 Fax: (650) 593-1689 Web site: www.dhl.com

Worldwide air express carrier.

DHL Worldwide Express, Kendal Hill, Christchurch, Barbados

Tel: 809-429-4855

R.R. DONNELLEY & SONS COMPANY

77 West Wacker Drive, Chicago, IL, 60601-1696

Tel: (312) 326-8000 Fax: (312) 326-8543 Web site: www.rrdonnelley.com

Commercial printing, allied communication services.

R.R. Donnelley Financial, Bldg.18, Wildey Industrial Park, St. Michael, Bridgetown, Barbados

Tel: 246-431-6834

DOVER CORPORATION

280 Park Ave., New York, NY, 10017-1292

Tel: (212) 922-1640 Fax: (212) 922-1656 Web site: www.dovercorporation.com

Elevator manufacturer and holding company for varied industries.

Electric Sales & Service Co., Ltd., PO Box 79B, Webster Industrial Park, St. Michael, Barbados, W.I.

Tel: 809-426-0790 Fax: 809-426-0791

ECOLAB INC.

Ecolab Center, 370 N. Wabasha Street, St. Paul, MN, 55102

Tel: (612) 293-2233 Fax: (612) 225-3105 Web site: www.ecolab.com

Develop/mfr. premium cleaning, sanitizing and maintenance products and services for the hospitality, institutional, and residential markets.

Ecolab Ltd., Barbados

Tel: 246-428-1602

ERNST & YOUNG, LLP

787 Seventh Ave., New York, NY, 10019

Tel: (212) 773-3000 Fax: (212) 773-6350 Web site: www.eyi.com

Accounting and audit, tax and management consulting services.

Ernst & Young, Bush Hill, Bay St., (PO Box 261) Bridgetown, Barbados

Tel: 809-436-5138 Fax: 809427-5260 Contact: Ben L. Arrindell

FEDERAL-MOGUL CORPORATION

26555 Northwestern Highway, PO Box 1966, Southfield, MI, 48034

Tel: (248) 354-7700 Fax: (248) 354-8983 Web site: www.federalmogul.com

Mfr./distributor precision parts for automobiles, trucks, farm and construction vehicles.

Federal-Mogul World Trade Ltd. (FSC), Barbados

THE HARPER GROUP

260 Townsend Street, San Francisco, CA, 94107-1719

Tel: (415) 978-0600 Fax: (415) 978-0692 Web site: www.circleintl.com

Ocean/air freight forwarding, customs brokerage, packing and wholesale, logistics management and insurance.

Commercial Services Co. Ltd., Trident House, Lower Broad St., Bridgetown, Barbados, West Indies

Tel: 809-426-0320 Fax: 809-429-6204

HOLIDAY INNS WORLDWIDE, INC.

3 Ravinia Drive, Ste. 2900, Atlanta, GA, 30346-2149

Tel: (770) 604-2000 Fax: (770) 604-5403

Hotels, restaurants and casinos.

Holiday Inn, PO Box 639, Bridgetown, Barbados

KOPPERS INDUSTRIES INC.

Koppers Bldg, 437 Seventh Ave., Pittsburgh, PA, 15219

Tel: (412) 227-2000 Fax: (412) 227-2333

Construction materials and services; chemicals and building products.

Long Life Timbers Ltd., Bridgetown, Barbados

KPMG PEAT MARWICK LLP

Three Chestnut Ridge Road, Montvale, NJ, 07645

Tel: (201) 307-7000 Fax: (201) 930-8617 Web site: www.kpmg.com

Accounting and audit, tax and management consulting services.

KPMG Peat Marwick, Hastings, Christ Church, Bridgetown, Barbados

Tel: 246-427-52 Fax: 246-427-7123 Contact: Ken R. Hewitt, Sr. Ptnr.

LEUCADIA NATIONAL CORPORATION

315 Park Ave. South, New York, NY, 10010

Tel: (212) 460-1900 Fax: (212) 598-4869

Holding company: real estate, banking, insurance, equipment leasing, mfr. plastics, cable, sinks & cabinets.

Barbados Light & Power Co. Ltd., CPO Box 142, Bridgeton, Barbados

MARSH & McLENNAN COS INC.

1166 Ave. of the Americas, New York, NY, 10036-2774

Tel: (212) 345-5000 Fax: (212) 345-4808 Web site: www.marshmac.com

Insurance agents/brokers, pension and investment management consulting services.

CGM Insurance Brokers Ltd., CGM Building, Lower Collymore Rock, Bridgetown, Barbados West Indies

Tel: 246-426-1442 Fax: 246-426-7336 Contact: William Tomlin

J&H Marsh & McLennan (Barbados) Ltd., Whitepark House, White Park Rd., Bridgetown, Barbados West Indies

Tel: 809-436-9929 Fax: 809-436-9932 Contact: N/A

J&H Marsh & McLennan Management Services (Barbados) Ltd., Musson Building - 2nd Fl., Hincks St., Bridgetown, Barbados West Indies

Tel: 809-436-8921 Fax: 246-426-7336 Contact: N/A

McCANN-ERICKSON WORLDWIDE

750 Third Ave., New York, NY, 10017

Tel: (212) 984-3644 Fax: (212) 984-2629

International advertising/marketing services.

McCann-Erickson (Barbados), Nemwil House, Collymore Rock, St. Michael, Barbados

NETSCAPE COMMUNICATIONS

501 East Middlefield Road, Mountain View, CA, 94043

Tel: (650) 254-1900 Fax: (650) 528-4124

Mfr./distribute Internet-based commercial and consumer software applications.

Netscape Communications FSC Incorporated, Bridgetown, Barbados

R.L. POLK & COMPANY

1155 Brewery Park Blvd., Detroit, MI, 48207-2697

Tel: (248) 728-7111 Fax: (248) 393-2860 Web site: www.polk.com

Directories, direct mail advertising.

NDL Intl. Ltd., Bush Hill, Garrison, St. Michael, Barbados

PRICEWATERHOUSECOOPERS LLP

1251 Ave. of the Americas, New York, NY, 10020

Tel: (212) 596-7000 Fax: (212) 790-6620 Web site: www.pwcglobal.com

Accounting and auditing, tax and management, and human resource consulting services.

Price Waterhouse Ltd., Price Waterhouse Centre, Collymore Rock Rd., PO Box 634C, St. Michael, Bridgetown, Barbados

Tel: 809-436-7000 Fax: 809-429-3747

YOUNG & RUBICAM INC.

285 Madison Ave., New York, NY, 10017

Tel: (212) 210-3000 Fax: (212) 370-3796 Web site: www.yr.com

Advertising, public relations, direct marketing and sales promotion, corporate & product ID management.

Londsdale/Barbados, St. Michael, Barbados

Belarus

BATES WORLDWIDE INC.

405 Lexington Ave., New York, NY, 10174

Tel: (212) 297-7000 Fax: (212) 986-0270 Web site: www.batesww.com

Advertising, marketing, public relations & media consulting.

Bates Primary SSA, Svoboda Sq 17-1002, Minsk 22006, Belarus

Tel: 375-172-230-573 Contact: V. Pissaranko, Dir.

LOUIS BERGER INTERNATIONAL INC.

100 Halsted Street, East Orange, NJ, 07019

Tel: (201) 678-1960 Fax: (201) 672-4284 Web site: www.louisberger.com

Consulting engineers, architects, economists & planners.

Louis Berger S.A., Minsk, Belarus

Tel: 375-276-9259 Fax: 375-234-6522

CHADBOURNE & PARKE LLP

30 Rockefeller Plaza, New York, NY, 10112-0127

Tel: (212) 408-5100 Fax: (212) 541-5369

International law firm.

Borovtsox & Salei, 21 Chicherin St., Minsk 22009, Belarus

Tel: 375-172-394418 Fax: 375-172-394422 Contact: Valentin A. Borovtsov, Ptnr.

DHL WORLDWIDE EXPRESS

333 Twin Dolphin Drive, Redwood City, CA, 94065

Tel: (650) 593-7474 Fax: (650) 593-1689 Web site: www.dhl.com

Worldwide air express carrier.

DHL Worldwide Express, 18, Brestskaya St., Minsk 220099, Belarus

Tel: 375-17-278-4913

KRAS CORPORATION

88 Topeth Road, Fairless Hills, PA, 19030

Tel: (215) 736-0981 Fax: (215) 736-8953

Mfr. precision tools and machinery for electronic and plastics industrial.

InterKRAS, Belarus

McDONALD'S CORPORATION

Kroc Drive, Oak Brook, IL, 60523

Tel: (630) 623-3000 Fax: (630) 623-7409

Fast food chain stores.

McDonald's Corp., Minsk, Belarus

MOTOROLA, INC.

1303 East Algonquin Road, Schaumburg, IL, 60196

Tel: (847) 576-5000 Fax: (847) 538-5191 Web site: www.mot.com

Mfr. communications equipment, semiconductors and cellular phones.

Motorola Belarus, Hotel Orbita, Room 1205, 39 Pushkina Prospect, 220092 Minsk, Belarus

Tel: 375-172-577-347 Fax: 375-172-577-635

PALMS & COMPANY, INC. (U.S. FUR EXCHANGE)

515 Lake Street South, Bldg. #103, Kirkland, WA, 98033

Tel: (425) 828-6774 Fax: (425) 827-5528

Fur auctioning, distribution and sale; investment banking

Palms & Co. Inc., PO Box 97 Gomel 246050, Belarus

Tel: 375-232-534403 Contact: David Stickney Emp: 10

PRICEWATERHOUSECOOPERS LLP

1251 Ave. of the Americas, New York, NY, 10020

Tel: (212) 596-7000 Fax: (212) 790-6620 Web site: www.pwcglobal.com

Accounting and auditing, tax and management, and human resource consulting services.

Price Waterhouse Ltd., Nekrasova St. 7, Post Box 12, Minsk 220002, Belarus

Tel: 375-172-393323 Fax: 375-172-393371

XEROX CORPORATION

800 Long Ridge Road, PO Box 1600, Stamford, CT, 06904

Tel: (203) 968-3000 Fax: (203) 968-4312 Web site: www.xerox.com

Mfr. document processing equipment, systems and supplies.

Xerox Ltd., Minsk, Belarus

Belgium

3M

3M Center, St. Paul, MN, 55144-1000

Tel: (612) 733-1110 Fax: (612) 733-9973 Web site: www.mmm.com

Mfr. diversified products for industry, health care, imaging, communications, transport, safety, consumer, etc.

3M Belgium NV/SA, Hermeslann 7, B-1831 Diegem, Belgium

Tel: 32-2-722-5111 Fax: 32-2-720-0225

A.B. DICK CO.

5700 West Rouhy Ave., Niles, IL, 60714

Tel: (847) 779-1900 Fax: (847) 647-8369 Web site: www.abdick.com

Mfr./sales automation systems.

A. B. Dick Co., Brussels, Belgium

AAR CORPORATION

One AAR Place, 1100 North Wood Dale Road, Wood Dale, IL, 60191

Tel: (630) 227-2000 Fax: (630) 227-2562 Web site: www.aarcorp.com

Aviation repair & supply provisioning; aircraft sales & leasing.

AAR Engine Group International, Inc., Sabena Technical Dept. Bldg. 24/46, B-1930 Zaventem, Belgium

Tel: 32-2-723-4737 Fax: 32-2-7223-4090

ACHESON COLLOIDS CO.

511 Fort Street, PO Box 611747, Port Huron, MI, 48061-1747

Tel: (810) 984-5581 Fax: (810) 984-1446

Chemicals, chemical preparations, paints & lubricating oils.

SA Huileries du Marly NV, Blvd. Baudouin 20/21, B-1000 Brussels, Belgium

ADAPTEC INC.

691 South Milpitas Boulevard, Milpitas, CA, 95035

Tel: (408) 945-8600 Fax: (408) 262-2533 Web site: www.adaptec.com

Design/mfr./marketing hardware & software solutions.

Adaptec Europe SA, Dreve Richelle 161, Bldg. A, B-1410 Waterloo, Belgium

ADVANCED PRODUCTS COMPANY

33 Defco Park Road, North Haven, CT, 06473

Tel: (203) 239-3341 Fax: (203) 234-7233 Web site: www.advpro.com

Mfr. Metallic & PTFE seals & gaskets.

Advanced Products NV, Industrieterrin "Krekelenberg" Rupelweg, B-2850 Boom, Belgium

AEROQUIP-VICKERS

3000 Strayer, PO Box 50, Maumee, OH, 43537-0050

Tel: (419) 867-2200 Fax: (419) 867-2390

Mfr. engineering components and systems for industry.

Aeroquip Benelux NV, Industrieterrein Klein Gent, B-2200 Herentals, Belgium

AIR EXPRESS INTERNATIONAL CORPORATION

120 Tokeneke Road, PO Box 1231, Darien, CT, 06820

Tel: (203) 655-7900 Fax: (203) 655-5779 Web site: www.aeilogistics.com

Air freight forwarder.

AEI (Belgium) N.V.,S.A. - Reg. Hdqtrs., Building No. 720, B-1931 BRUCARGO, Brussels, Belgium (Locations: Antwerp, Liege)

Tel: 32-2-752-0211 Fax: 32-2-752-0413

AIR PRODUCTS AND CHEMICALS, INC.

7201 Hamilton Boulevard, Allentown, PA, 18195-1501

Tel: (610) 481-4911 Fax: (610) 481-5900

Mfr. industry gases & related equipment, spec. chemicals, environmental/energy systems.

Air Products SA, Chaussee de Wavre 1789, B-1160 Brussels, Belgium

AIR WATER TECHNOLOGY RESEARCH-COTTRELL

PO Box 1500, Somerville, NJ, 08876

Tel: (908) 685-4000 Fax: (908) 685-4050

Mfr. air pollution control equipment & systems; technology services.

Research-Cottrell Belgium SA, Chaussee Paul Houtart 88, B-7110 Houdeng Goegnies, Belgium

AIRTOUCH COMMUNICATIONS, INC.

One California Street, San Francisco, CA, 94111

Tel: (415) 658-2000 Fax: (415) 658-2034 Web site: www.airtouch.com

Global wireless communications company with interests in cellular, paging, & personal communications services.

Belgacom Mobile, S.A., Blvd Emile, Jacqmain, 157, 1210 Brussels, Belgium

Tel: 32-2-205-4000

AKIN, GUMP, STRAUSS, HAUER & FELD LLP

1333 New Hampshire Ave., N.W., Washington, DC, 20036

Tel: (202) 877-4000 Fax: (202) 887-4288 Web site: www.akingump.com

International law firm.

Akin Gump, Strauss, Hauer & Feld LLP, 65 Ave. Louise, PB #7 1050 Brussels, Belgium

Tel: 32-2-535-2911 Fax: 32-2-535-2900 Contact: Peter Verhaeghe

ALAMO RENT A CAR

110 Southeast Sixth Street, Fort Lauderdale, FL, 33301

Tel: (954) 522-0000 Fax: (954) 220-0120 Web site: www.alamo.com

Car rentals.

Alamo Rent A Car, Brussel National Airport, Arrivals Hall, 1930 Zaventem, Brussels, Belgium

ALBEMARLE CORPORATION

451 Florida Ave., Baton Rouge, LA, 70801

Tel: (504) 388-8011 Fax: (504) 388-7686

Chemical company.

Albemarle Corp., Brussels, Belgium

ALBERTO-CULVER COMPANY

2525 Armitage Ave., Melrose Park, IL, 60160

Tel: (708) 450-3000 Fax: (708) 450-3354

Mfr./marketing personal care & beauty products, household & grocery products & institutional food products.

Indola FIAC SA, Place E. Flagey 7, Bte. 1, B-1050 Brussels, Belgium

ALLEGHENY TELEDYNE INC.

1000 Six PPG Place, Pittsburgh, PA, 15222

Tel: (412) 394-2800 Fax: (412) 394-2805

Diversified mfr.: aviation & electronics, specialty metals, industrial & consumer products.

Teledyne Belgium, Airport Business Ctr., Vuurberg 80, B-1831 Diegam, Belgium

ALLEGIANCE HEALTHCARE CORPORATION

1430 Waukegan Road, McGaw Park, IL, 60085

Tel: (847) 689-8410 Fax: (847) 578-4437 Web site: www.allegiance.net

Manufactures & distributes medical, surgical, respiratory therapy & laboratory products.

Allegiance Sprl, Ave. Léon Champagne, 3, Saintes, Belgium

Tel: 32-2-391-0711 Fax: 32-2-391-0710 Contact: Andred Germaine, Mgr.

ALLEN-BRADLEY COMPANY, INC.

1201 South Second Street, Milwaukee, WI, 53204

Tel: (414) 382-2000 Fax: (414) 382-4444

Mfr. electrical controls & information devices.

Allen-Bradley Brussels, Weiveldlaan 4 1b. 34 & 35, B-1930 Nossegem-Zaventem, Belgium

ALLERGAN INC.

2525 Dupont Drive, PO Box 19534, Irvine, CA, 92713-9534

Tel: (714) 246-4500 Fax: (714) 246-6987

Mfr. therapeutic eye care products, skin & neural care pharmaceuticals.

Allergan Inc., Zaventem, Belgium

ALLIEDSIGNAL INC.

101 Columbia Road, PO Box 2245, Morristown, NJ, 07962-2245

Tel: (973) 455-2000 Fax: (973) 455-4807 Web site: www.alliedsignal.com

Mfr. aerospace & automotive products, engineered materials.

Bendix Wheels & Brakes Div., World Airways, Brussels Natl. Airport, B-1930 Zaventem, Belgium

NV Allied Chemical Intl. Corp., Ave. Louise 326, B-1050 Brussels, Belgium

NV AlliedSignal Intl. SA, Haasrode Research Park, Graumeer, B-3030 Heverlee, Belgium

ALPINE ENGINEERED PRODUCTS INC.

PO Box 2225, Pompano Beach, FL, 33061

Tel: (954) 781-3333 Fax: (954) 973-2644 Web site: www.2alpineng.com.

Fabricated plate.

Alpine Systems Corp., Brussels, Belgium

ALVEY INC.

9301 Olive Boulevard, St. Louis, MO, 63132

Tel: (314) 993-4700 Fax: (314) 995-2400 Web site: www.alvey.com

Mfr./sales automatic case palletizers, package & pallet conveyor systems.

Alvey Europe NV, Koningin Astridlaan 14, B-2660 Willebroek, Belgium

AMDAHL CORPORATION

1250 East Arques Ave., PO Box 3470, Sunnyvale, CA, 94088-3470

Tel: (408) 746-6000 Fax: (408) 773-0833 Web site: www.amdahl.com

Development/mfr. large scale computers, software, data storage products, information-technology solutions & support.

Amdahl Belgium SA/NV, Woluwe Garden, Woluwedal 26 #B4, B-1932 Sint-Stevens-Woluwe, Belgium

Tel: 33-1-47-65-7800

AMERICAN BILTRITE INC.

57 River Street, Wellesley Hills, MA, 02181

Tel: (781) 237-6655 Fax: (781) 237-6880 Web site: www.abitape.com

Mfr. industrial rubber & plastic products.

Ideal Tape Belgium, Industrie Zone, B-9600 Ronse, Belgium

Tel: 32-55-235151 Fax: 32-55-235161

AMERICAN EXPRESS COMPANY

American Express Tower, World Financial Center, New York, NY, 10285-4765

Tel: (212) 640-2000 Fax: (212) 619-9802 Web site: www.americanexpress.com

Travel, travelers cheques, charge card & financial services.

American Express Overseas Credit Corp. SA, Belgium - All inquiries to U.S. address

AMERICAN MANAGEMENT SYSTEMS, INC.

4050 Legato Road, Fairfax, VA, 22033

Tel: (703) 267-8000 Fax: (703) 267-5067 Web site: www.amsinc.com

Systems integration & consulting.

AMS Management Systems Europe SA/NV, Blvd. Emile Jacqmainlaan 159, 8th Fl., Brussels 1210, Belgium

Tel: 32-2-534-7831 Fax: 32-2-553-7731

AMERICAN STANDARD INC.

One Centennial Ave., Piscataway, NJ, 08855-6820

Tel: (732) 980-3000 Fax: (732) 980-6118

Mfr. heating, plumbing & sanitary equipment, china, earthenware.

Ideal Standard Europe, Blvd. du Souverain 348, B-1160 Brussels, Belgium

Ideal Standard SA, Div. of WABCO-Standard SA, Chaussee Paul Houtart 88, B-7070 Houdeng-Goegnies, Belgium

WABCO Belgium, Ave. Van Volxem 164-166, B-1190 Brussels, Belgium

AMERITECH CORPORATION

30 South Wacker Drive, Chicago, IL, 60606

Tel: (312) 750-5000 Fax: (312) 207-0016 Web site: www.ameritech.com

Provides security systems & telecommunications services.

Belgacom SA, Brussels, Belgium

AMMIRATI PURIS LINTAS

One Dag Hammarskjold Plaza, New York, NY, 10017

Tel: (212) 605-8000 Fax: (212) 605-4705 Web site: www.interpublic.com

International advertising agency.

Ammirati Puris Lintas Belgium, Swan House, Riverside Business Park - Unit G, Blvd. International 55, 1070 Brussels, Belgium

Tel: 32-2-556-4200 Fax: 32-2-523-2751 Contact: John Neirinckx

AMOCO CHEMICAL COMPANY

200 East Randolph Drive, Chicago, IL, 60601

Tel: (312) 856-3200 Fax: (312) 856-2460

Mfr./sale petrol based chemicals, plastics, chemicals/plastic products

Amoco Chemical Belgium NV, Belgium

Amoco Fina NV, Antwerp, Belgium

AMP INC.

470 Friendship Road, PO Box 3608, Harrisburg, PA, 17105-3608

Tel: (717) 564-0100 Fax: (717) 780-6130

Develop/mfr. electronic & electrical connection products & systems.

AMP Belgium, Brussels, Belgium

Tel: 32-3-719-2511

AMPACET CORPORATION

660 White Plains Road, Tarrytown, NY, 10591-5130

Tel: (914) 631-6600 Fax: (914) 631-7197 Web site: www.ampacet.com

Mfr. color and additive concentrates for the plastics industry.

Ampacet Belgium, 1, rue d'Ampacet, B-6780 Messancy, Belgium

Tel: 32-63-381300 Fax: 32-63-381393

AMSTED INDUSTRIES INC.

205 North Michigan, Chicago, IL, 60601

Tel: (312) 645-1700 Fax: (312) 819-8429 Web site: www.amsted.com

Privately-held, diversified manufacturer of products for the construction & building markets, general industry & the railroads.

Baltimore Aircoil International N.V., Industriepark, B-220 Heist-op-den-Berg, Belgium

Tel: 32-1-525-7700 Fax: 32-1-524-4779 Contact: John F. Carroll, Mng. Dir. Europe Emp: 313

AMWAY CORPORATION

7575 Fulton Street East, Ada, MI, 49355-0001

Tel: (616) 787-6000 Fax: (616) 787-6177 Web site: www.amway.com

Mfr./sale home care, personal care, nutrition & houseware products.

Amway Belgium Co., Ikaroslaan 4, B-1930 Zaventem, Belgium

ANACOMP INC.

PO Box 509005, San Diego, CA, 92150

Tel: (619) 679-9797 Fax: (619) 748-9482

Mfr. electronic computing equipment.

Anacomp SA, Ave. Lloyd George 7, B-1050 Brussels, Belgium

ANALOG DEVICES INC.

1 Technology Way, Box 9106, Norwood, MA, 02062

Tel: (781) 329-4700 Fax: (781) 326-8703

Mfr. integrated circuits & related devices.

Analog Devices Intl. Inc., Justitiesraat 18, B-2018 Antwerp, Belgium

ANDERSEN CONSULTING

100 South Wacker Drive, Ste. 1059, Chicago, IL, 60606

Tel: (311) 123-7271 Fax: (312) 507-7965 Web site: www.ac.com

Provides management & technology consulting services.

Andersen Consulting, Rue Royale 145, B-1000 Brussels, Belgium

Tel: 32-2-266-7211 Fax: 32-2-266-7233

ANIXTER INTERNATIONAL INC..

4711 Golf Road, Skokie, IL, 60076

Tel: (847) 677-2600 Fax: (708) 677-9480

Distributor wiring systems/products for voice, video, data and power applications.

Anixter Intl. Hdqtrs., Ave. de Tervueren 273, B-1150 Brussels, Belgium

ANSELL EDMONT INDUSTRIAL INC.

1300 Walnut Street, Coshocton, OH, 43812

Tel: (614) 622-4311 Fax: (614) 622-9611

Mfr. industrial gloves, rubber and plastic products, protective clothing.

Ansell Edmont Industrial Inc., Wijngaardvelt 34C, B-9300 Aalst, Belgium

AON CORPORATION

123 North Wacker Drive, Chicago, IL, 60606

Tel: (312) 701-3000 Fax: (312) 701-3100 Web site: www.aon.com

Insurance brokers worldwide; underwrites accident & health insurance, specialty & professional insurance; & provides risk management consultation.

AON Belgium NV, 153, rue Colonel Bourg, Brussels, Belgium

Tel: 32-2-730-9501 Fax: 32-2-730-9921 Contact: Pierre Derom

AON Belgium NV, 2A Potvlietlaan 2600, Antwerp, Belgium

Tel: 32-3-270-2411 Fax: 32-3-270-2455 Contact: Johan Willaert

AON Boels & Bégault, Blvd de la Sauvinière 68 Boite 32, Liège, Belgium

Tel: 32-4-232-3030 Fax: 32-4-223-2411 Contact: Guibert de Spirlet

AON Warranty Group Benelux, Kolonel Bourgstraat, 153, Brussels, Belgium

Tel: 32-2-73099-69 Contact: Marco Negegaal

London General Holdings, Ltd., Kolonel Bourgstraat, 153, Brussels, Belgium

Tel: 32-2-73099-69 Contact: Marco Negegaal

APPLE COMPUTER INC.

One Infinite Loop, Cupertino, CA, 95014

Tel: (831) 996-1010 Fax: (831) 974-2113 Web site: www.apple.com

Personal computers, peripherals & software.

Apple Computer SA, Rue Colonel Bourg 105A, B-1140 Brussels, Belgium

APPLIED MATERIALS, INC.

3050 Bowers Ave., Santa Clara, CA, 95054-3299

Tel: (408) 727-5555 Fax: (408) 727-9943 Web site: www.appliedmaterials.com

Supplies manufacturing systems/services to semiconductor industry.

Applied Materials S.A., Ave. Louise 120, 1050 Brussels, Belgium

Tel: 32-2-626-2390 Fax: 32-2-626-2399

ARAMARK CORPORATION

1101 Market Street, Philadelphia, PA, 19107-2988

Tel: (215) 238-3000 Fax: (215) 238-3333

Diversified managed services.

Aramark/Belgium, Place de l'Alma 3, Box 1, B-1200 Brussels, Belgium

Tel: 32-2-779-1555 Fax: 32-2-779-123 Contact: Christian Hock, Pres.

ARBOR ACRES FARM INC.

439 Marlborough Road, Glastonbury, CT, 06033

Tel: (860) 633-4681 Fax: (860) 633-2433

Producers of male & female broiler breeders, commercial egg layers.

Klavers PVBA, Koningsstraat 22A, B-2390 Ravels (Weelde), Belgium

ARCO CHEMICAL COMPANY

3801 West Chester Pike, Newtown Square, PA, 19073-2387

Tel: (610) 359-2000 Fax: (610) 359-2722 Web site: www.arcochem.com

Mfr. propylene oxide, a chemical used for flexible foam products, coatings/paints & solvents/inks.

ARCO Chemical Products Europe, Inc., Kuhlmannkaai 1, B-9042 Gent, Belgium

Tel: 32-9-341-1411

ARMSTRONG INTERNATIONAL INC.

816 Maple Street, PO Box 408, Three Rivers, MI, 49093

Tel: (616) 273-1415 Fax: (616) 278-6555

Mfr. steam specialty products: traps, air vents, liquid drainers, strainers, valves, etc.

Armstrong Machine Works SA, Parc Industriel des Hauts Sarts, Herstat, B-4040 Liege, Belgium

ARO INTERNATIONAL CORPORATION

One Aro Center, Bryan, OH, 43506

Tel: (419) 636-4242 Fax: (419) 633-1674

Mfr. cylinders, valves & pumps.

NV Aro SA, Eurolaan 3, B-2690 Temse, Belgium

ARTHUR ANDERSEN & COMPANY

33 West Monroe Street, Chicago, IL, 60603

Tel: (312) 372-7100 Fax: (312) 507-0123 Web site: www.arthurandersen.com

Accounting & audit, tax & management consulting services.

Arthur Andersen & Co./Maecel Asselberghs & Co., Ave. des Arts, 56, B1040 Brussels, Belgium (Locataions: Antwerp & Ghent, Belgium.)

Tel: 32-2-510-4211

ASSOCIATED PRESS INC.

50 Rockefeller Plaza, New York, NY, 10020-1605

Tel: (212) 621-1500 Fax: (212) 621-5447 Web site: www.ap.com

News gathering agency.

Associated Press (Belgium) SA, Blvd. Charlemagne 1, B-1040 Brussels, Belgium

Tel: 32-2-285-0112

AST RESEARCH INC.

16215 Alton Parkway, PO Box 19658, Irvine, CA, 92713-9658

Tel: (949) 727-4141 Fax: (949) 727-8584 Web site: www.ast.com

Design/development/mfr. hi-performance desktop, server & notebook computers.

AST Belgium, Prins Boudewijnlaan 17, Bus 3, B-2550 Kontich (Antwerp), Belgium

Tel: 32-3-450-8720

ATTACHMATE CORPORATION

3617 131st Ave. S.E., Bellevue, WA, 98006-1332

Tel: (425) 644-4010 Fax: (425) 747-9924 Web site: www.attachmate.com

Mfr. connectivity software.

Attachmate Brussels, Brussels, Belgium

Tel: 32-2-481-0750

AUTODESK INC.

111 McInnis Parkway, San Rafael, CA, 94903

Tel: (415) 507-5000 Fax: (415) 507-6112 Web site: www.autodesk.com

Develop/marketing/support computer-aided design, engineering, scientific & multimedia software products.

Autodesk B.V., Battelsesteenweg 455a, B-2800 Mechelen, Belgium

Tel: 32-15-281715 Fax: 32-15-280953

AUTOMATIC SWITCH CO. (ASCO)

50-60 Hanover Road, Florham Park, NJ, 07932

Tel: (973) 966-2000 Fax: (973) 966-2628

Mfr. solenoid valves, emergency power controls, pressure & temp. switches.

Asco/Joucomatic, Benelux N.V., Lusambostraat 53, B-1190, Brussels, Belgium

Tel: 32-2-333-0250 Fax: 32-2-333-0251 Contact: J. C. Serkumian

AVERY DENNISON CORPORATION

150 N. Orange Grove Blvd., Pasadena, CA, 91103

Tel: (626) 304-2000 Fax: (626) 792-7312 Web site: www.averydennison.com

Mfr. pressure-sensitive adhesives & materials, office products, labels, tags, retail systems, Carter's Ink & specialty chemicals.

Avery Office Products Benelux, Belgium

Fasson Industries NV, Tieblokkenlaan 1, B-2300 Turnhout, Belgium

Label Systems Benelux, Belgium

AXENT TECHNOLOGIES, INC.

2400 Research Boulevard, Ste. 200, Rickville, MD, 20850

Tel: (301) 258-5043 Fax: (301) 330-5756 Web site: www.axent.com

Designs and supplies security management software .

Axent Technologies BV, Antwerpsesteenweg 124, 2630 Aatselaar, Belgium

Tel: 32-3-877-1399 Fax: 32-3-877-1457

AZON CORPORATION

720 Azon Road, Johnson City, NY, 13790-1799

Tel: (607) 797-2368 Fax: (607) 797-4506 Web site: www.azon.com

Mfr. paper, office equipment, films & photo equipment.

Keuffel & Esser Intl. SA/NV, Route de Vieux Campinaire, ZI de Fleurus, B-6220 Hainaut, Belgium

BAILEY-FISCHER & PORTER COMPANY

125 East County Line Road, Warminster, PA, 18974

Tel: (215) 674-6000 Fax: (215) 441-5280

Design/mfr. measure, recording & control instruments & systems; mfr. industrial glass products.

Bailey-Fischer & Porter Belgium NV, Elektronikalaan 12-14, B-2610 Wilrijk, Belgium

BAIN & CO., INC.

Two Copley Place, Boston, MA, 02116

Tel: (617) 572-2000 Fax: (617) 572-2427 Web site: www.bain.com

Strategic management consulting services.

Bain & Co. Belgium Inc., Blue Tower 24th Fl., Ave. Louise 326, 1050 Brussels, Belgium

Tel: 32-2-626-2626

BAKER & McKENZIE

One Prudential Plaza, 130 East Randolph Drive, Ste. 2500, Chicago, IL, 60601

Tel: (312) 861-8000 Fax: (312) 861-2899 Web site: www.bakerinfo.com

International legal services.

Baker & McKenzie, 40 blvd du Regent - Regentlaan 40, 5th Fl., Brussels 1000, Belgium

Tel: 32-2- 506-3611 Fax: 32-2-511-6280

BALTIMORE AIRCOIL CO., INC.

7595 Montevideo Road, Jessup, MD, 20794

Tel: (410) 799-6200 Fax: (410) 799-6416

Mfr. evaporative cooling & heat transfer equipment for A/C, refrigeration & industrial process cooling.

Baltimore Aircoil Co., Industriepark, B-2200 Heist-op-den-Berg, Belgium

BANDAG INC.

2905 NW Highway 61, Muscatine, IA, 52761

Tel: (319) 262-1400 Fax: (319) 262-1252

Mfr./sale retread tires.

Bandag Europe NV, Industrieterrein, B-3650 Dilsen-Lanklaar, Belgium

Bandag NV, Zaventem, Belgium

THE BANK OF NEW YORK

48 Wall Street, New York, NY, 10286

Tel: (212) 495-1784 Fax: (212) 495-2546 Web site: www.bankofny.com

Banking servces.

The Bank of New York, Ave. des Arts 35 Kunstiaan, 1040 Brussels, Belgium

Tel: 32-2-545-8111 Fax: 32-2-545-8800

BANKAMERICA CORPORATION

555 California Street, San Francisco, CA, 94104

Tel: (415) 622-3530 Fax: (415) 622-8467 Web site: www.bankamerica.com

Financial services.

Bank of America NT & SA, Uitbreidingstraat 180, PO Box 6, B-2600 Antwerp, Belgium

Tel: 32-3-280-4211 Fax: 32-3-239-6109 Contact: Marcel Claes, VP

BANKERS TRUST COMPANY

280 Park Ave., New York, NY, 10017

Tel: (212) 250-2500 Fax: (212) 250-2440 Web site: www.bankerstrust.com

Banking & investment services.

Bankers Trust Co., Banque du Benelux SA, Rue des Colonies 40, B-1000 Brussels, Belgium

C.R. BARD INC.

730 Central Ave., Murray Hill, NJ, 07974

Tel: (908) 277-8000 Fax: (908) 277-8078 Web site: www.crbard.com

Mfr. health care products.

Bard Belgium NV, Ambachtenlaan 7, B-3030 Leuven, Belgium

BASE TEN SYSTEMS INC.

One Electronics Drive, Trenton, NJ, 08619

Tel: (609) 586-7010 Fax: (609) 586-1593

Mfr. proprietary control systems, flight test systems, communications products.

Base Ten Systems Ltd., Brussels, Belgium

BATES WORLDWIDE INC.

405 Lexington Ave., New York, NY, 10174

Tel: (212) 297-7000 Fax: (212) 986-0270 Web site: www.batesww.com

Advertising, marketing, public relations & media consulting.

Bates Belgium, 26 blvd General Jacques, 1050 Brussels, Belgium

Tel: 32-2-627-4711 Fax: 32-2-627-4779 Contact: Patrick Hanson-Lowe, Dir.

BAX GLOBAL CORPORATION

16808 Armstrong Ave., PO Box 19571, Irvine, CA, 92623

Tel: (714) 752-4000 Fax: (714) 852-1488 Web site: www.bax.com

Air freight forwarder.

BAX Global, Brucargo Bldg. 755, B-1931 Zaventem, Brussels, Belgium

Tel: 32-2-752-9550 Fax: 32-2-751-8532

BAXTER HEALTHCARE CORPORATION

One Baxter Parkway, Deerfield, IL, 60015

Tel: (847) 948-2000 Fax: (847) 948-3948 Web site: www.baxter.com

Pharmaceutical preparations, surgical/medical instruments & cardiovascular products.

Baxter R&D, Parc Industrial, rue du Progres 7, B-1400 Nivelles, Belgium

Baxter SA, Blvd. Rene Branquart 18, B-7860 Lessines, Belgium

Baxter Travenol NV, Industrielaan 6, B-1740 Ternat, Belgium

Baxter World Trade SA/Baxter SA, Ruye Colonel Bourg 105B, B-1140 Brussels, Belgium

Bentley Laboratories SA, 41 Gremstede St., Turnhout Belgium

BBDO WORLDWIDE

1285 Ave. of the Americas, New York, NY, 10019

Tel: (212) 459-5000 Fax: (212) 459-6645 Web site: www.bbdo.com

Multinational group of advertising agencies.

BBDO Belgium, Brussels, Belgium

BDO SEIDMAN, LLP

Two Prudential Plaza, 180 N. Stetson Ave., Ste. 2300, Chicago, IL, 60601

Tel: (312) 240-1236 Fax: (312) 240-3329 Web site: www.bdo.com

International accounting & financial consulting firm.

BDO Belgium G.I.E., Blvd de la Woluwe 60, B-1200 Brussels, Belgium

Tel: 32-2-778-0100 Fax: 32-2-771-5656 Contact: Frans J. Samyn

BEA SYSTEMS, INC.

2315 North First Street, St. Jose, CA, 95131

Tel: (408) 570-8000 Fax: (408) 570-8091 Web site: www.beasys.com

Develops communications management software & provider of software consulting services.

BEA Systems Europe N.V., European Hdqtrs., Excelsiorlaan 27, B-1930 Zaventem, Belgium

Tel: 32-2-714-0930 Fax: 32-2-725-0600

BECHTEL GROUP INC.

50 Beale Street, PO Box 3965, San Francisco, CA, 94105-1895

Tel: (415) 768-1234 Fax: (415) 768-9038 Web site: www.bechtel.com

General contractors in engineering & construction.

Bechtel International Corp., Postbus 269, B-9000 Ghent, Belgium

BELL & HOWELL COMPANY

5215 Old Orchard Road, Skokie, IL, 60077

Tel: (847) 470-7100 Fax: (847) 470-9625 Web site: www.bellhowell.com

Diversified information products & services.

Bell & Howell Benelux SA, Leuvensesteenweg 321, B-1940 St. Stevens Woluwe, Zaventem, Belgium

BEMIS CO., INC.

222 South 9th Street, Ste. 2300, Minneapolis, MN, 55402-4099

Tel: (612) 376-3000 Fax: (612) 376-3180

Mfr. flexible packaging, specialty coated & graphics products.

MACtac Europe SA, Blvd. Kennedy, B-7400 Soignies, Belgium

BEST WESTERN INTERNATIONAL

6201 North 24th Place, Phoenix, AZ, 85106

Tel: (602) 957-4200 Fax: (602) 957-5740

International hotel chain.

County House of Brussels, B-1180 Brussels, Belgium

BESTFOODS, INC.

700 Sylvan Ave., International Plaza, Englewood Cliffs, NJ, 07632-9976

Tel: (201) 894-4000 Fax: (201) 894-2186 Web site: www.bestfoods.com

Consumer foods products; corn refining.

Bestfoods Belgium, St. Pietersvliet 7 bus 1, B-2000 Antwepren, Belgium

Tel: 32-3-222-44-11 Fax: 32-2-231-93-19 Contact: Frederik Masselink, Mgr.

Bestfoods Europe sprl., 300 Ave. de Tervuren, Box 7, 1150 Brussels, Belgium

Tel: 32-2-761-09-11 Fax: 32-2-761-09-41 Contact: Alain Labergère, EVP

BETZDEARBORN

4636 Somerton Road, PO Box 3002, Trevose, PA, 19053-6783

Tel: (215) 953-2568 Fax: (215) 953-5524 Web site: www.betzdearborn.com

Mfr. water/wastewater and process system treatment chemicals and services.

BetzDearborn N.V., Toekomstlaan, 54 Industriepark, Wolfstee, 2200 Herentals, Belgium

Tel: 32-16-40-20-00 Fax: 32-16-40-00-87

BINKS MFG. COMPANY

9201 West Belmont Ave., Franklin Park, IL, 60131

Tel: (708) 671-3000 Fax: (708) 671-6489

Mfr. of spray painting and finishing equipment.

Binks Intl. SA, Chaussee de Bruxelles 684, B-1410 Waterloo, Belgium

BIO-RAD LABORATORIES INC.

1000 Alfred Nobel Drive, Hercules, CA, 94547

Tel: (510) 724-7000 Fax: (510) 724-3167

Mfr. life science research products, clinical diagnostics, analytical instruments.

Bio-Rad Laboratories Inc., Brussels & Ghent, Belgium

BLACK & DECKER CORPORATION

701 E. Joppa Road, Towson, MD, 21286

Tel: (410) 716-3900 Fax: (410) 716-2933 Web site: www.blackanddecker.com

Mfr. power tools and accessories, security hardware, small appliances, fasteners, information systems & services.

Black & Decker Belgium, Weihoek 1, 1930 Zaventem, Brussels, Belgium

Tel: 32-2-719-0711 Fax: 32-2-721-4045

BLACK BOX CORPORATION

1000 Park Drive, Lawrence, PA, 15055

Tel: (724) 746-5500 Fax: (724) 746-0746 Web site: www.blackbox.com

Direct marketer and technical service provider of communications, networking and related computer connectivity products.

Black Box Communications SA NV, Zaventem Business Park, Ikaroslaan 8, B-1930 Zaventem, Belgium

Tel: 32-2-725-8550 Fax: 32-2-725-9212 Contact: Pierre Carema, Gen. Mgr.

BLOUNT INC.

4520 Executive Park Drive, Montgomery, AL, 36116-1602

Tel: (334) 244-4000 Fax: (334) 271-8130 Web site: www.blount.com

Mfr. cutting chain & equipment, timber harvest/handling equipment, sporting ammo, riding mowers.

Blount Europe SA, Rue Buisson aux Loups 8, B-1400 Nivelles, Belgium

Tel: 32-67-887611 Fax: 32-67-210537 Contact: Jan Westland, Director

BOOLE & BABBAGE, INC.

3131 Zanker Road, San Jose, CA, 95134

Tel: (408) 526-3000 Fax: (408) 526-3055 Web site: www.boole.com

Develop/support enterprise automation & systems management software.

Boole & Babbage Belgium SA/NV, Excelsiorlaan 40, B-1930 Zaventem, Belgium

BORDEN INC.

180 East Broad Street, Columbus, OH, 43215-3799

Tel: (614) 225-4000 Fax: (614) 220-6453

Mfr. Packaged foods, consumer adhesives, housewares and industrial chemicals.

Borden Foods Belgium, Hogerheistraat 130, 1880 Ramsdonk, Belgium

Tel: 32-15-714-030

BOSE CORPORATION

The Mountain, Framingham, MA, 01701-9168

Tel: (508) 879-7330 Fax: (508) 766-7543

Mfr. quality audio equipment/speakers.

Bose NV, Essenestraat 16, B-1740 Ternat, Belgium

THE BOSTON CONSULTING GROUP

Exchange Place, 31st Floor, Boston, MA, 02109

Tel: (617) 973-1200 Fax: (617) 973-1339 Web site: www.bcg.com

Management consulting company.

The Boston Consulting Group, Blvd de I'Imperatrice, 13, 1000 Brussels, Belgium

Tel: 32-2-289-0202

BOXLIGHT CORPORATION

19332 Powder Hill Place, Poulsbo, WA, 98370

Tel: (360) 779-7901 Fax: (360) 779-3299 Web site: www.boxlight.com

Mfr./sales/rentals of LCD panels and overhead, computer-based projection/presentation systems.

Boxlight Europe -BPP BV/SA, Generaal de Wittelaan 9/14, B-2800 Mechelen, Belgium

Tel: 32-15-287-487 Fax: 32-15-287-499

BOYDEN CONSULTING CORPORATION

100 Park Ave., 34th Floor, New York, NY, 10017

Tel: (212) 980-6534 Fax: (212) 980-6147 Web site: www.boyden.com

Executive search.

Boyden Intl. SA, Ave. Franklin Roosevelt 81, B-1050 Brussels, Belgium

Tel: 32-2-644-2050

BOZELL WORLDWIDE

40 West 23rd Street, New York, NY, 10010

Tel: (212) 727-5000 Fax: (212) 645-9173 Web site: www.bozell.com

Advertising, marketing, public relations and media consulting.

Bozell Worldwide Brussels, Rue Gulledelle - No. 98, Woluwe-Saint-Lambert, 1200 Brussels, Belgium

Tel: 32-2-775-0222 Fax: 32-2-775-0220 Contact: Edward Brookshire, Mng. Dir.

W. H. BRADY CO.

6555 W. Good Hope Road, Milwaukee, WI, 53223

Tel: (414) 358-6600 Fax: Web site: www.whbrady.com

Mfr. industrial ID for wire marking, circuit boards; facility ID, signage, printing systems & software.

W.H. Brady N.V., Lindestraat 20, Industriepark C/3, B-9240 Zele, Belgium

Tel: 32-52-4578-11 Fax: 32-52-4578-12

BRISTOL-MYERS SQUIBB COMPANY

345 Park Ave., New York, NY, 10154

Tel: (212) 546-4000 Fax: (212) 546-4020 Web site: www.bms.com

Pharmaceutical and food preparations, medical and surgical instruments.

Bristol-Myers-European Community Affairs Office, Waterloo Office Park - Building #1, Drava Riojelle 61 Box 23/24, 1410 Waterloo, Belgium

ConvaTec Belgium, Chausse de la Hulpe 150, 1170 Brussels, Belgium

S.A. Bristol-Myers Belgium N.V., Chaussee de la Hulpe 185, 1170 Brussels, Belgium

UPASMedica, Rue Colonel Bourg 127-129, Brussels, Belgium

Zimmer S.A., Rue de la Petite Ile 5, 1070 Brussels, Belgium

BRUNSWICK CORPORATION

1 Northfield Court, Lake Forest, IL, 60045-4811

Tel: (847) 735-4700 Fax: (847) 735-4765 Web site: www.brunswickcorp.com

Mfr. recreational boats, marine engines, bowling centers & equipment, fishing equipment, defense/aerospace.

Mercury Marine Power-Europe Inc., Parc Industrial de Petit Rechain, B-4822 Verviers, Belgium

BUCK CONSULTANTS INC.

One Pennsylvania Plaza, New York, NY, 10119

Tel: (212) 330-1000 Fax: (212) 695-4184

Employee benefit, actuarial and compensation consulting services.

Buck Consultants SA, Rue de la Charite 15, B-1040 Brussels, Belgium

BUDGET RENT A CAR CORPORATION

4225 Naperville Road, Lisle, IL, 60532

Tel: (630) 955-1900 Fax: (630) 955-7799 Web site: www.budgetrentacar.com

Car and truck rental system.

Budget Rent A Car, Koouterveldstraat 4, 1831 Diegem- 1831, Brussels, Belgium

Tel: 32-2-751-5330 Fax: 32-2-721-5105

BULAB HOLDINGS INC.

1256 N. McLean Blvd, Memphis, TN, 38108

Tel: (901) 278-0330 Fax: (901) 276-5343 Web site: www.buckman.com

Biological products; chemicals & chemical preparations.

Buckman Laboratories SA, Wondelgemkaai 159, B-9000 Ghent, Belgium

Tel: 32-9-257-9211 Fax: 32-9-253-6295 Contact: Ismail Elmiligy, Gen. Mgr. Eur

LEO BURNETT CO., INC.

35 West Wacker Drive, Chicago, IL, 60601

Tel: (312) 220-5959 Fax: (312) 220-6533 Web site: www.leoburnett.com

International advertising agency.

Leo Burnett Worldwide Inc., Chaussee de la Hulpe 177, B-1170 Brussels, Belgium

BURR-BROWN RESEARCH CORPORATION

6730 S. Tucson Blvd., Tucson, AZ, 85706

Tel: (520) 746-1111 Fax: (520) 746-7211

Electronic components and systems modules.

Burr-Brown Intl. NV, Coghenlaan 118, B-1180 Brussels, Belgium

BURSON-MARSTELLER

230 Park Ave., New York, NY, 10003-1566

Tel: (212) 614-4000 Fax: (212) 614-4262 Web site: www.bm.com

Public relations/public affairs consultants.

Burson-Marsteller Brussels, Ave. Louise 225, Box 5, B-1050 Brussels, Belgium

Tel: 32-2-626-0640 Fax: 32-2-647-9530 Emp: 15

CABOT CORPORATION

75 State Street, Boston, MA, 02109-1807

Tel: (617) 345-0100 Fax: (617) 342-6103

Mfr. carbon blacks, plastics; oil & gas, information systems.

Cabot Belgium SA, Hanzestedenplaats, B-2000 Antwerp, Belgium

Cabot Belgium SA, Rue Emile Vandervelde 131, B-4431 Loncin, Belgium

CALCOMP INC.

2411 West La Palma Ave., Anaheim, CA, 92801

Tel: (714) 821-2000 Fax: (714) 821-2832

Mfr. computer graphics peripherals.

NV Calcomp SA, Ave. du Peage 105A, B-1932 Sint-Stevens Woluwe, Belgium

CALGON CORPORATION

PO Box 1346, Pittsburgh, PA, 15230

Tel: (412) 494-8000 Fax: (412) 494-8104

Mfr. cosmetic, personal care & water treatment products.

Chemviron Specialty Chemicals SA, Brusselsesteenweg 359, B-1900 Overijse, Belgium

CAMBREX CORP.

1 Meadowlands Plaza, East Rutherford, NJ, 07063

Tel: (201) 804-3000 Fax: (201) 804-9852 Web site: www.cambex.com

Mfg. Bulf active chemicals for pharmaceuticals.

BioWhittaker Europe, B-4800 Veriers, Parc Industriel de Petit Rechain, Belgium

Tel: 32-87-321611 Fax: 32-87-351967

CAMPBELL SOUP COMPANY

Campbell Place, Camden, NJ, 08103-1799

Tel: (609) 342-4800 Fax: (609) 342-3878

Food products.

NV Biscuits Delacre SA, Belgium

NV Campbell Food & Confectionery Coord. Center Europe SA, Belgium

CANBERRA-PACKARD INDUSTRIES

800 Research Parkway, Meriden, CT, 06450

Tel: (203) 238-2351 Fax: (203) 235-1347 Web site: www.packard.com

Mfr. instruments for nuclear research.

Canberra Semiconductor NV, Lammerdries 25, B-2430 Olen, Belgium

Canberra-Packard Benelux ND/SA, Research Parc, Pontbeeklaan 57, B-1730 Zellik, Belgium

CARGILL, INC.

15407 McGinty Road, Minnetonka, MN, 55440-5625

Tel: (612) 742-7575 Fax: (612) 742-7393 Web site: www.cargill.com

Food products, feeds, animal products.

Cargill NV, Muisbroeklaan Kaai 506, B-2030 Antwerp, Belgium

CARLISLE SYNTEC SYSTEMS

PO Box 7000, Carlisle, PA, 17013

Tel: (717) 245-7000 Fax: (717) 245-9107

Mfr. elastomeric roofing & waterproofing systems.

Carlisle SynTec Systems Benelux SA, Rue du Patinage 30, B-1990 Brussels, Belgium

CARLSON MARKETING GROUP

Carlson Parkway, PO Box 59159, Minneapolis, MN, 55459

Tel: (612) 550-4520 Fax: (612) 550-4580 Web site: www.cmgcarlson.com

Marketing services agency.

Carlson Marketing Group, Brussels, Belgium

CARPENTER TECHNOLOGY CORPORATION

101 W. Bern Street, PO Box 14662, Reading, PA, 19612-4662

Tel: (610) 208-2000 Fax: (610) 208-3214

Mfr. specialty steels & structural ceramics for casting industrial.

Carpenter Technology (Europe) SA, Blvd. Auguste Reyers 207-209, B-1040 Brussels, Belgium

CARRIER CORPORATION

One Carrier Place, Farmington, CT, 06034-4015

Tel: (860) 674-3000 Fax: (860) 679-3010 Web site: www.carrier.com

Mfr./distributor/services A/C, heating & refrigeration equipment.

NV Carrier SA, Chaussee de Mons 389, B-1070 Brussels, Belgium

Tel: 32-2-523-0170 Fax: 32-2-521-1353

CAT PUMPS

1681 94th Lane NE, Minneapolis, MN, 55449-4324

Tel: (612) 780-5440 Fax: (612) 780-2958

Mfr./distributor pumps.

NV Cat Pumps International SA, Gemzenstraat 2, Wilrijik, B-2610 Antwerp, Belgium

CATERPILLAR INC.

100 NE Adams Street, Peoria, IL, 61629-6105

Tel: (309) 675-1000 Fax: (309) 675-1182 Web site: www.cat.com

Mfr. earth/material-handling and construction machinery and equipment and engines.

Caterpillar Commercial N.V., Boite Postale 1, B-6200 Gosselies, Belgium

Caterpillar Group Services, N.V., Minervastraat 5, 1930 Zaventem, Belgium

Tel: 32-2-717-4611 Fax: 32-2-717-4600

C.B. RICHARD ELLIS

533 South Fremont Ave., Los Angeles, CA, 90071-1712

Tel: (213) 613-3123 Fax: (213) 613-3535 Web site: www.cbrichardellis.com

Commercial real estate services.

CB Richard Ellis, Brussels, Belgium

CENTURY 21 REAL ESTATE CORPORATION

6 Sylvan Way, Parsippany, NJ, 07054-3826

Tel: (973) 496-5722 Fax: (973) 496-5527 Web site: www.century21.com

Real estate.

Century 21 Benelux, De Hulsten 21, B-2980 Zoersel, Belgium

Tel: 32-3-309-2108 Contact: Rudy Guedens

CHAMPION INTERNATIONAL CORPORATION

One Champion Plaza, Stamford, CT, 06921

Tel: (213) 358-7000 Fax: (213) 358-2975

Manufacture and sale of pulp and paper.

Champion Intl. Europe Inc., Ave. de Tervuren 296, Brussels, Belgium

THE CHASE MANHATTAN CORPORATION

World Headquarters, 270 Park Ave., New York, NY, 10017

Tel: (212) 270-6000 Fax: (212) 622-9030 Web site: www.chase.com

International banking and financial services.

Banque de Commerce SA, Lange Gasthuisstraat 9, B-2000 Antwerp, Belgium

Chase Manhattan Bank SA, Ave. Rogier 14/15, Liege, Belgium

Chase Manhattan Bank SA, Notarisstraat 1, Ghent, Belgium

Chase Manhattan Bank SA - Brussels Branch, Blue Tower - 9th Fl., Box 51 - Ave. Louise 326, 1050 Brussels, Belgium

Tel: 32-2-629-5811 Fax: 32-2-629-5850

IDC-Belgium, Ave. des Arts 52, B-1040 Brussels, Belgium

CHESTERTON BINSWANGER INTERNATIONAL

Two Logan Square, 4th Floor, Philadelphia, PA, 19103-2759

Tel: (215) 448-6000 Fax: (215) 448-6238

Real estate & related services.

Chesterton Soprec SA, Treves Centre, 45 rue de Treves, B-1040 Brussels, Belgium

CHICAGO METALLIC CORPORATION

4849 South Austin Ave., Chicago, IL, 60638

Tel: (708) 563-4600 Fax: (708) 563-4552

Steel and metal products.

Chicago Metallic Continental NV, Oud Sluisstraat 5, B-2110 Wijnegem, Belgium

CHIRON CORPORATION

4560 Horton Street, Emeryville, CA, 94608-2916

Tel: (510) 655-8730 Fax: (510) 655-9910

Research/mfr./marketing therapeutics, vaccines, diagnostics, ophthalmic.

Ciba Corning Diagnostics SA/NV, Excelsiorlaan 49, B-1930 Zaventem, Belgium

THE CHUBB CORPORATION

15 Mountain View Road, Warren, NJ, 07061-1615

Tel: (908) 580-2000 Fax: (908) 580-3606 Web site: www.chubb.com

Holding company: property/casualty insurance.

Chubb Insurance Co. of Europe, SA, Twin House, rue Neerveld 107, B-1200 Brussels, Belgium

Tel: 32-2-778-0611 Fax: 32-3-778-0600

CIGNA CORPORATION

One Liberty Place, Philadelphia, PA, 19192

Tel: (215) 761-1000 Fax: (215) 761-5008

Insurance, invest, health care and other financial services.

Afia Life Insurance Co. SA/NV, Rue Belliard 9-11, B-1040 Brussels, Belgium

Cigna Insurance Co. of Europe SA/NV, Rue Belliard 9-11, B-1040 Brussels, Belgium

Cigna Reinsurance Co. SA/NV, Blvd. du Regent 37-40, B-1000 Brussels, Belgium

Esis Intl. Inc., Rue Beillard 9-11, B-1040 Brussels, Belgium

CINCOM SYSTEMS INC.

2300 Montana Ave., Cincinnati, OH, 45211

Tel: (513) 612-2300 Fax: (513) 481-8332 Web site: www.cincom.com

Develop/distributor computer software.

Cincom Systems Inc., Brussels, Belgium

CISCO SYSTEMS, INC.

170 Tasman Drive, San Jose, CA, 95134-1706

Tel: (408) 526-4000 Fax: (408) 526-4100 Web site: www.cisco.com

Develop/mfr./market computer hardware and software networking systems.

Cisco Systems Brussels, Complex Antares, 71 Ave. des Pleiades, 1200 Brussels, Belgium

Tel: 32-2-778-4200 Fax: 32-2-778-4300 Contact: N/A

CITICORP

399 Park Ave., New York, NY, 10043

Tel: (212) 559-1000 Fax: (212) 527-2066 Web site: www.citibank.com

International banking and financial services.

Citibank Belgium SA/NV, 263, Bd. General Jacques, Brussels 01050, Belgium

CLARCOR INC.

2323 Sixth Street, PO Box 7007, Rockford, IL, 61125

Tel: (815) 962-8867 Fax: (815) 962-0417

Mfr. filtration products and consumer packaging products.

Baldwin NV, Dijkstraat 1, B-2630 Aarstselaar, Belgium

CLAYTON INDUSTRIES

4213 N. Temple City Blvd., El Monte, CA, 91731

Tel: (626) 443-9381 Fax: (626) 442-1701 Web site: www.clayton industries.com

Mfr. steam generators, dynamometers and water treatment chemicals.

Clayton of Belgium NV, Rijksweg 30, B-2680 Bornem, Belgium

CLEARY GOTTLIEB STEEN & HAMILTON

One Liberty Plaza, New York, NY, 10006

Tel: (212) 225-2000 Fax: (212) 225-3999

International law firm.

Cleary, Gottlieb, Steen & Hamilton, Rue de la Loi 23, B-1040 Brussels, Belgium

COBE LABORATORIES INC.

1185 Oak Street, Lakewood, CO, 80215

Tel: (303) 232-6800 Fax: (303) 231-4952

Mfr. medical equipment & supplies.

COBE Laboratories Inc., Sterrebeekstraat 172, B-1930 Zaventem, Nossegem, Belgium

THE COCA-COLA COMPANY

P.O. Drawer 1734, Atlanta, GA, 30301

Tel: (404) 676-2121 Fax: (404) 676-6792 Web site: www.coca-cola.com

Mfr./marketing/distributor soft drinks, syrups & concentrates, juice & juice-drink products.

The Coca-Cola Co. (Belgium), Belgium - All mail to U.S. address.

THE COLEMAN CO., INC.

3600 Hydraulic Street, Wichita, KS, 67219

Tel: (316) 832-2653 Fax: (316) 832-3060

Mfr./distributor/sales camping & outdoor recreation products.

Coleman Europe, Bessenveldstraat 25, B-1831 Brussels, Belgium

COLGATE-PALMOLIVE COMPANY

300 Park Ave., New York, NY, 10022

Tel: (212) 310-2000 Fax: (212) 310-2919

Mfr. pharmaceuticals, cosmetics, toiletries and detergents.

Colgate-Palmolive SA, Blvd. de la Woluwe 58, B-1200 Brussels, Belgium

COLLINS & AIKMAN CORPORATION

701 McCullough Drive, Charlotte, NC, 28262

Tel: (704) 547-8500 Fax: (704) 548-2081

Automotive interior systems and textile products.

Painters Mill Belgium SA, Heistraat 80, B-2700 Sint-Niklaas, Belgium

COLUMBIA PICTURES INDUSTRIES INC.

10202 West Washington Blvd., Culver City, CA, 90232

Tel: (310) 244-4000 Fax: (310) 244-2626 Web site: www.sony.com

Producer and distributor of motion pictures.

Warner Columbia Films SNC, Rue Royale 326, B-1030 Brussels, Belgium

COMMERCIAL METALS COMPANY

PO Box 1046, Dallas, TX, 75221

Tel: (972) 689-4300 Fax: (972) 689-4320

Metal collecting/processing, steel mills and metal trading.

Cometals Intl. SA, Chaussee de la Hulpe 181, B-1170 Brussels, Belgium

COMPAQ COMPUTER CORPORATION

20555 State Highway 249, PO Box 692000, Houston, TX, 77269-2000

Tel: (713) 370-0670 Fax: (713) 514-1740 Web site: www.compaq.com

Develop/mfr. personal computers.

Compaq Computer N.V./S.A., Lozenberg 17, B-1932 Zaventem, Belgium

Tel: 32-2-716-9511 Fax: 32-2-725-2213

COMPUTER ASSOCIATES INTERNATIONAL INC.

One Computer Associates Plaza, Islandia, NY, 11788

Tel: (516) 342-5224 Fax: (516) 342-5329 Web site: www.cai.com

Integrated software for enterprise computing and information management, application development, manufacturing, financial applications and professional services.

Computer Associates S.A.-N.V., 34, blvd de la Woluwe, Woluwedal, B-1200 Brussels, Belgium

Tel: 32-2-773-2811

COMPUTER SCIENCES CORPORATION

2100 East Grand Ave., El Segundo, CA, 90245

Tel: (310) 615-0311 Fax: (310) 322-9768 Web site: www.csc.com

Information technology services, management consulting, systems integration, outsourcing.

CSC Computer Sciences NS/SA - Benelux Division, Ave. Lloyd George 7, B-1050 Brussels, Belgium

Contact: Malcolm Rudrum, Pres.

COMSHARE INC.

3001 South State Street, Ann Arbor, MI, 48108

Tel: (734) 994-4800 Fax: (734) 994-5895

Managerial application software.

Comshare BV, Leuvensesteenweg 392B, B-1932 St. Stevens Woluwe, Brussels, Belgium

CONAGRA INC.

One ConAgra Drive, Omaha, NE, 68102-5001

Tel: (402) 595-4000 Fax: (402) 595-4595 Web site: www.conagra.com

Prepared/frozen foods, grains, flour, animal feeds, agri chemicals, poultry, meat, dairy products, including Healthy Choice, Butterball and Hunt's.

ConAgra Europe B.V., Ave. Tervueren 168, B-1050 Brussels, Belgium

CONE MILLS CORPORATION

3101 N. Elm Street, PO Box 26540, Greensboro, NC, 27415-6540

Tel: (336) 379-6220 Fax: (336) 379-6287 Web site: www.cone.com

Mfr. denims, flannels, chamois & other fabrics.

Cone Mills Intl., Stephanie Square Business Centre, Ave. Louise 65, Boite 11, B-1050 Brussels, Belgium

CONOCO INC.

PO Box 2197, Houston, TX, 77252

Tel: (281) 293-1000 Fax: (281) 293-1440

Oil, gas, coal, chemicals and minerals.

Conoco Chemicals Europe SA, Rue Joseph Stevens 7, B-1000 Brussels, Belgium

Societe Europeenne des Carburants (SECA), Mechelsesteenweg 520, B-1800 Vilvoorde, Belgium

CONTAINER-STAPLING CORPORATION

27th and ICC Tracks, Herrin, IL, 62948

Tel: (618) 942-2125 Fax: (618) 942-7700

Mfr. industrial stapling machines and supplies.

Container-Stapling Corp., Driekoningenstraat 150, B-2700 St. Niklaas, Belgium

CONTINENTAL CAN COMPANY

301 Merritt 7, 7 Corporate Park, Norwalk, CT, 06856

Tel: (203) 750-5900 Fax: (203) 750-5908

Packaging products and machinery, metal, plastic and paper containers.

NV Cobelplast SA, Antwerpse Steenweg 8-10, B-9100 Loketen, Belgium

CONTINENTAL INSURANCE COMPANY

333 South Wabash Ave., Chicago, IL, 60695

Tel: (312) 822-5000 Fax: (312) 822-6419

Insurance services.

Phoenix Continental SA, Rue de La Loi 99-101, B-1040 Brussels, Belgium

CONTROL DATA SYSTEMS INC.

4201 Lexington Ave., North Arden Hills, MN, 55126

Tel: (612) 415-2999 Fax: (612) 415-4891 Web site: www.cdc.com

Computer peripherals and hardware.

Control Data Belgium, Inc., Ave. de la Metrologie, 4 Metrologielaan, Brussels 1130, Belgium

Tel: 32-2-247-9220 Fax: 32-2-247-9229

COOPER INDUSTRIES INC.

6600 Travis Street, Ste. 5800, Houston, TX, 77002

Tel: (713) 209-8400 Fax: (713) 209-8995 Web site: www.cooperindustries.com

Mfr./distributor electrical products, tools and hardware and automotive products.

Cooper Automotive, Aubange, Belgium

Cooper Automotive, Peronnes-lez-Binche, Belgium

COPELAND CORPORATION

1675 West Campbell Road, Sidney, OH, 45365-0669

Tel: (937) 498-3011 Fax: (937) 498-3334 Web site: www.copeland-corp.com

Producer of compressors and condensing units for commercial and residential air conditioning and refrigeration equipment.

Welkenraedt, Rue des Trois Boudons 127 B-4840 Welkenraedt, Belgium

CORDIS CORPORATION

14201 Northwest 60th Street, Miami Lakes, FL, 33014

Tel: (305) 824-2000 Fax: (305) 824-2747

Mfr. medical devices and systems.

Cordis Intl. SA, Ave. Louise 250, B-1050 Brussels, Belgium

CORNING INC.

One Riverfront Plaza,, Corning, NY, 14831

Tel: (607) 974-9000 Fax: (607) 974-8551 Web site: www.corning.com

Mfr. glass and specialty materials, consumer products; communications, laboratory services.

Pittsburgh Corning Europe NV, Brussels, Belgium

COUDERT BROTHERS

1114 Ave. of the Americas, New York, NY, 10036-7794

Tel: (212) 626-4400 Fax: (212) 626-4210 Web site: www.coudert.com

International law firm.

Coudert Brothers, Tour Louise 149, Ave. Louise - Box 8, B-1050 Brussels, Belgium

Tel: 32-2-542-1811 Fax: 32-2-542-188 Contact: Ingrid Bellander

COVINGTON & BURLING

1201 Pennsylvania Ave., N.W., Washington, DC, 20044

Tel: (202) 662-6000 Fax: (202) 662-6291 Web site: www.cov.com

International law firm.

Covington & Burling, Kuntslann Av. Des Arts 44/8, B-1040 Brussels, Belgium

Tel: 32-2-5495230

CRANE COMPANY

100 First Stamford Place, Stamford, CT, 06907

Tel: (203) 363-7300 Fax: (203) 363-7359

Diversified mfr./distributor engineered products for industrial.

Ferguson Machine Co. SA, Parc Industriel 33, B-1430 Braine le Chateau, Belgium

CROMPTON & KNOWLES CORPORATION

1 Station Place Metro Center, Stamford, CT, 06902

Tel: (203) 353-5400 Fax: (203) 353-5423 Web site: www.crompton-knowles.co

Mfr. dyes, colors, flavors, fragrances, specialty chemicals and industrial products.

Crompton & Knowles-Tertre SA, Rue de Progres 323, B-1000 Brussels, Belgium

CROSBY CORPORATION

PO Box 3128, Tulsa, OK, 74101-3128

Tel: (918) 834-4611 Fax: (918) 832-0940

Mfr. machine tools, hardware, steel forgings.

Crosby Europe NV, Leuvensebaan 49, B-2580 Antwerp, Belgium

CROWN CORK & SEAL COMPANY, INC.

One Crown Way, Philadelphia, PA, 19154-4599

Tel: (215) 698-5100 Fax: (215) 698-5201

Mfr. cans, bottle caps; filling & packaging machinery.

Crown Cork Co. (Belgium) NV, Place de l'Albertine 2, B-1000 Brussels, Belgium

CROWN EQUIPMENT CORPORATION

40 South Washington Street, New Bremen, OH, 45869

Tel: (419) 629-2311 Fax: (419) 629-2317

Mfr./sales/services forklift trucks, stackers.

Crown Handling NV, Kontichsesteenweg 57, B-2630 Aartselaar, Belgium

CULLIGAN INTERNATIONAL COMPANY

One Culligan Parkway, Northbrook, IL, 60062

Tel: (847) 205-6000 Fax: (847) 205-6030 Web site: www.culligan-man.com

Water treatment products and services.

Culligan NV, Culliganlaan 2, B-1920 Machelen Diegem, Belgium

CUMMINS ENGINE CO., INC.

500 Jackson Street, PO Box 3005, Columbus, IN, 47202-3005

Tel: (812) 377-5000 Fax: (812) 377-3334

Mfr. diesel engines.

Cummins Diesel NV, Blarenberglaan 4, Industriepark Noord 2, B-2800 Mechelen, Belgium

CURTISS-WRIGHT CORPORATION

1200 Wall Street West, Lyndhurst, NJ, 07071

Tel: (201) 896-8400 Fax: (201) 438-5680

Mfr. precision components and systems, engineered services to aerospace, flow control and marine industry.

Metal Improvement Co. Inc., Schurhavenveld 4056, B-3800 Sint-Truiden, Belgium

D'ARCY MASIUS BENTON & BOWLES INC. (DMB&B)

1675 Broadway, New York, NY, 10019

Tel: (212) 468-3622 Fax: (212) 468-2987 Web site: www.dmbb.com

Full service international advertising and communications group.

DMB&B SA, A.G. Bldg., Place du Champ de Mars 5, B-1050 Brussels, Belgium

D-M-E COMPANY

29111 Stephenson Highway, Madison Heights, MI, 48071

Tel: (248) 398-6000 Fax: (248) 544-5705

Basic tooling for plastic molding and die casting.

DME Europe, Industriepark Noord, B-2800 Mechelen, Belgium

DANA CORPORATION

4500 Door Street, Toledo, OH, 43615

Tel: (419) 535-4500 Fax: (419) 535-4643 Web site: www.dana.com

Mfr./sales of automotive, heavy truck, off-highway, fluid & mechanical power components.

Dana Corporation, Brussels, Belgium

DATA GENERAL CORPORATION

4400 Computer Drive, Westboro, MA, 01580

Tel: (508) 898-5000 Fax: (508) 366-1319 Web site: www.dg.com

Design, mfr. general purpose computer systems & peripheral products & services.

Data General SA, Blvd. du Souverain 191, B-1160 Brussels, Belgium

DDB NEEDHAM WORLDWIDE INC.

437 Madison Ave., New York, NY, 10022

Tel: (212) 415-2000 Fax: (212) 415-3417

Advertising agency.

DDB Denmark SA, Blvd. de la Cambre 33, B-1050 Brussels, Belgium

DECHERT PRICE & RHOADS

4000 Bell Atlantic Tower, 1717 Arch Street, Philadelphia, PA, 19103-2793

Tel: (215) 994-4000 Fax: (215) 994-2222 Web site: www.dechert.com

International law firm.

Dechert Price & Rhoads, 65 Ave. Louise, 1050 Brussels, Belgium

Tel: 32-2-535-5411 Fax: 32-2-535-5400

DELL COMPUTER CORPORATION

One Dell Way, Round Rock, TX, 78682-2222

Tel: (512) 338-4400 Fax: (512) 728-3653 Web site: www.dell.com

Direct marketer & supplier of computer systems.

Dell Computer NV/SA, Doornveld, Industrie Asse 3 nr 11 Bus 15/16, 1731 Asse-Zellik, Belgium

Tel: 32-2-481-9100 Fax: 32-2-419-299 Contact: Mathieu Loyen, Mng. Dir.

DELOITTE TOUCHE TOHMATSU INTERNATIONAL

PO Box 820, Wilton, CT, 06897

Tel: (203) 761-3000 Fax: (203) 834-2200 Web site: www.u.s.deloitte.com or www.dtti.com

Accounting, audit, tax and management consulting services.

Deloitte & Touche, Britselei 23-25, B-2000 Antwerp, Belgium

Deloitte & Touche, Brussels Airport Business Park, Berkenlaan 6, B-1831 Diegem, Belgium

DELTA AIR LINES INC.

PO Box 20706, Atlanta, GA, 30320-6001

Tel: (404) 715-2600 Fax: (404) 715-5494 Web site: www.delta-air.com/index.html

Major worldwide airline; international air transport services.

Delta Air Lines Inc., Brussels, Belgium

THE DEXTER CORPORATION

1 Elm Street, Windsor Locks, CT, 06096

Tel: (860) 627-9051 Fax: (860) 627-7078

Mfr. nonwovens, polymer products, magnetic materials, biotechnology.

Dexter Nonwovens, Ave. H. Debroux 15A, B-1160 Brussels, Belgium

The Dexter Corp., Ave. H. Debroux 15A, B-1160 Brussels, Belgium

DHL WORLDWIDE EXPRESS

333 Twin Dolphin Drive, Redwood City, CA, 94065

Tel: (650) 593-7474 Fax: (650) 593-1689 Web site: www.dhl.com

Worldwide air express carrier.

DHL Worldwide Express, Woluwelaan 151, Diegem 1831, Belgium

Tel: 32-2-715-5050

DIGITAL EQUIPMENT CORPORATION

111 Powder Mill Road, Maynard, MA, 01754

Tel: (978) 493-5111 Fax: (978) 493-7374 Web site: www.digital.com

Mfr. network computer systems, components, software and services.

Digital Equipment N.V./S.A., Luchtschipstraat 1, rue de l'Aeronef 1, B-1140 Evere, Belgium

Tel: 32-2-729-7111 Fax: 32-2-242-7560

DIONEX CORPORATION

1228 Titan Way, PO Box 3603, Sunnyvale, CA, 94088-3603

Tel: (408) 737-0700 Fax: (408) 730-9403

Develop/mfr./marketing/services chromatography systems & related products.

Dionex NV, Wayenborgstraat 14, Omega Business Park, B-2800 Mechelen, Belgium

WALT DISNEY COMPANY

500 South Buena Vista Street, Burbank, CA, 91521

Tel: (818) 560-1000 Fax: (818) 560-1930

Film/TV production, theme parks, resorts, publishing, recording and retail stores.

Walt Disney Production (Benelux) SA, Centre Intl. Rogier, Passage International 29, B-1000 Brussels, Belgium

DO ALL COMPANY

254 North Laurel Ave., Des Plaines, IL, 60016

Tel: (847) 803-7380 Fax: (847) 699-7524

Distributors of machinery tools, metal cutting tools, instruments and industrial supplies.

DoAll Belgium SPRL, Quai du Roi Albert 81, B-4020 Bressoux-Liege, Belgium

DONALDSON COMPANY, INC.

1400 West 94th Street, Minneapolis, MN, 55431

Tel: (612) 887-3131 Fax: (612) 887-3155 Web site: www.Donaldson.com

Mfr. filtration systems and replacement parts.

Donaldson Coordination Center, N.V., Interleuven laan 1, B-3001 Leuven, Belgium

Tel: 32-16-38-3811 Fax: 32-16-40-0077 Contact: Geert-Henk Touw

Donaldson Europe N.V., Interleuven laan 1, B-3001 Leuven, Belgium

Tel: 32-16-38-3811 Fax: 32-16-40-0077 Contact: Geert-Henk Touw

DOONEY & BOURKE

1 Regent Street, Norwalk, CT, 06855

Tel: (203) 853-7515 Fax: (203) 838-7754 Web site: www.dooney.com

Mfr./sales/distribution of fine leather handbags, wallets, belts and accessories.

Dooney & Bourke, Brussels, Belgium

DORR-OLIVER INC.

612 Wheeler's Farm Road, PO Box 3819, Milford, CT, 06460

Tel: (203) 876-5400 Fax: (203) 876-5432

Mfr. process equipment for food, pulp & paper, mineral & chemicals industry; & municipal/industry waste treatment.

Dorr-Oliver SA, Rue de l'Hopital 31, B-1000 Brussels, Belgium

DORSEY & WHITNEY LLP

Pillsbury Center South, 220 S. Sixth Street, Minneapolis, MN, 55402

Tel: (612) 340-2600 Fax: (612) 340-2868 Web site: www.dorseylaw.com

International law firm.

Dorsey & Whitney LLP, 35 Square De Meeûs,1000 Brussels, Belgium

Tel: 32-2-504-4611 Fax: 32-2-504-4646 Contact: Barry D. Glazer, Mng. Ptnr. Emp: 12

THE DOW CHEMICAL COMPANY

2030 Dow Center, Midland, MI, 48674

Tel: (517) 636-1000 Fax: (517) 636-3228 Web site: www.atdow.com

Mfr. chemicals, plastics, pharmaceuticals, agricultural products, consumer products.

Dow Chemical Europe SA, Blvd. de Waterloo 39, B-1000 Brussels, Belgium

DOW CORNING CORPORATION

2220 West Salzburg Road, PO Box 1767, Midland, MI, 48640

Tel: (517) 496-4000 Fax: (517) 496-6080

Silicones, silicon chemicals, solid lubricants.

Dow Corning Intl. Ltd., Chaussee de la Hulpe 154, B-1170 Brussels, Belgium

DOW JONES & CO., INC.

200 Liberty Street, New York, NY, 10281

Tel: (212) 416-2000 Fax: (212) 416-2655 Web site: www.wsj.com

Publishing and financial news services.

The Wall Street Journal/Europe, Hilton Tower, Blvd. de Waterloo 38, B-1000 Brussels, Belgium

DRAKE BEAM MORIN INC.

101 Huntington Ave., Boston, MA, 02199

Tel: (617) 450-9860 Fax: (617) 267-2011 Web site: www.dbm.com

Human resource management consulting & training.

DBM Belgium N.V., Dascottelei, 68 Bus 2, B-2100 Duerne (Antwerp), Belgium

Tel: 32-3-366-5499 Fax: 32-3-321-3880

DBM Belgium N.V., 40 rue de Bois Seigneur Isaac, B-1421 Braine Lâ Alleud, Brussels, Belgium

Tel: 32-2-387-2442 Fax: 32-2-387-2446

DRESSER INDUSTRIES INC.

2001 Ross Ave., PO Box 718, Dallas, TX, 75221-0718

Tel: (214) 740-6000 Fax: (214) 740-6584 Web site: www.dresser.com

Diversified supplier of equipment & technical services to energy & natural resource industrial.

Dresser Europe SA, Blvd. du Souverain 191, B-1160 Brussels, Belgium

Dresser Products NV, Halfstraat 70, B-2627 Antwerp, Belgium

DREVER COMPANY

PO Box 98, 380 Red Lion Road, Huntingdon, PA, 19006-0098

Tel: (215) 947-3400 Fax: (215) 947-7934 Web site: www.drever.com

Mfr. industrial furnaces.

Drever Intl. SA, Parc Industriel du Sart Tilman, B-4031 Liege, Belgium

Tel: 32-4-366-6262 Fax: 32-4-367-7678 Contact: Jean Marc Raick, Mng. Dir. Emp: 85

E.I. DU PONT DE NEMOURS & COMPANY

1007 Market Street, Wilmington, DE, 19898

Tel: (302) 774-1000 Fax: (302) 774-7321 Web site: www.dupont.com

Mfr./sale diversified chemicals, plastics, specialty products and fibers.

Du Pont de Nemours Belgium SA, Brussels, Belgium

THE DUN & BRADSTREET CORPORATION

One Diamond Hill Road, Murray Hill, NJ, 07974

Tel: (908) 665-5000 Fax: (908) 665-5524 Web site: www.dnbcorp.com

Provides corporate credit, marketing & accounts-receivable management services & publishes credit ratings & financial information.

Dun & Bradstreet Eurinform SA NV, Ave. des Pleiades 73, Plejadenlaan 73, B-1200 Brussels, Belgium

Tel: 32-2-778-7211

E-Z-EM INC.

717 Main Street, Westbury, NY, 11590

Tel: (516) 333-8230 Fax: (516) 333-8278 Web site: www.ezem.com

World's leading supplier of barium contrast media for medical imaging and accessories.

E-Z-EM Belgium B.V.B.A., Brussels, Belgium

EASTMAN & BEAUDINE INC.

13355 Noel Road, Ste. 1370, Dallas, TX, 75240

Tel: (972) 661-5520 Fax: (972) 980-8540

Investments.

Eastman & Beaudine Inc., Ave. de Broqueville 44, B-1200 Brussels, Belgium

EASTMAN KODAK COMPANY

343 State Street, Rochester, NY, 14650

Tel: (716) 724-4000 Fax: (716) 724-0663

Develop/mfr. photo & chemicals products, information management/video/copier systems, fibers/plastics for various industry.

NV Kodak SA, Steenstraat 20, B-1800 Koningslo-Vilvoorde, Belgium

EATON CORPORATION

1111 Superior Ave., Cleveland, OH, 44114

Tel: (216) 523-5000 Fax: (216) 479-7068

Advanced technical products for transportation & industrial markets.

Samuel Moore SA, Chaussee de Tiriemont 100, B-5800 Gembloux, Belgium

ECOLAB INC.

Ecolab Center, 370 N. Wabasha Street, St. Paul, MN, 55102

Tel: (612) 293-2233 Fax: (612) 225-3105 Web site: www.ecolab.com

Develop/mfr. premium cleaning, sanitizing and maintenance products and services for the hospitality, institutional, and residential markets.

Ecolab Ltd., Brussels, Belgium

Tel: 32-2-467-5111

ECOWATER SYSTEMS INC.

1890 Woodlane Drive, Woodbury, MN, 55125

Tel: (612) 739-5330 Fax: (612) 739-4547 Web site: www.ecowater.com

Mfr. water treatment and purification products.

Ecodyne SA, Geelfeweg 30A, B-2250 Olen, Belgium

Contact: Silvain Claeys, Gen. Mgr.

EDELMAN PUBLIC RELATIONS WORLDWIDE

200 East Randolph Drive, 63rd Floor, Chicago, IL, 60601

Tel: (312) 240-3000 Fax: (312) 240-0596 Web site: www.edelman.com

International independent public relations firm.

Edelman PR Worldwide, 20 rue des Deux Eglises, B-1000 Brussels, Belgium

Tel: 32-2-227-6170 Fax: 32-2-227-6189 Contact: Canstance Kann, Mng. Dir.

J.D. EDWARDS & COMPANY

One Technology Way, Denver, CO, 80237

Tel: (303) 334-4000 Fax: (303) 334-4970 Web site: www.jdedwards.com.

Computer software products.

J. D. Edwards & Company, CIM-Hardi Frankrijklei 119, 2000 Antwerp, 1130 Brussels, Belgium

Tel: 32-2-226-4090 Fax: 32-2-226-4206

EG&G INC.

45 William Street, Wellesley, MA, 02181-4078

Tel: (781) 237-5100 Fax: (781) 431-4114

Diversified R/D, mfr. & services.

EG&G Berthold Analytical Instruments, Vaartjijk 22, B-1800 Vilvoorde, Belgium

EMC CORP.

35 Parkwood Drive, Hopkinton, MA, 01748-9103

Tel: (508) 435-1000 Fax: (508) 435-8884 Web site: www.emc.com

Designs/supplies intelligent enterprise storage & retrieval technology for open systems, mainframes & midrange environments.

EMC Computer Systems - Holland, Imperiastraat 14, Zaventem B-1930, Belgium

Tel: 32-2-725-7425

EMERSON & CUMMING SPECIALTY POLYMERS

46 Manning Road, Bellerica, MA, 01821

Tel: (978) 436-9700 Fax: (978) 436-9701

Mfr. specialty polymers.

Grace NV, Nijverheidsstraat 7, B-2260 Westerloo, Belgium

EMERSON ELECTRIC COMPANY

8000 West Florissant Ave., PO Box 4100, St. Louis, MO, 63136

Tel: (314) 553-2000 Fax: (314) 553-3527 Web site: www.emersonelectric.com

Electrical and electronic products, industrial components and systems, consumer, government and defense products.

Emerson Electric Co., Ave. Adolphe Lacomle 52, B-1040 Brussels, Belgium

EMERY WORLDWIDE

One Lagoon Drive, Ste. 400, Redwood City, CA, 94065

Tel: (650) 596-9600 Fax: (650) 596-7901 Web site: www.emeryworld.com

Freight transport, global logistics and air cargo.

Emery Worldwide, Express Hub, Bldg. 724, B-1931 Brucargo, Brussels, Belgium

ENCYCLOPAEDIA BRITANNICA INC.

310 S. Michigan Ave., Chicago, IL, 60604

Tel: (312) 427-9700 Fax: (312) 294-2176 Web site: www.E.B.com

Publishing; books.

Encyclopaedia Britannica (Belgium) Ltd., Ave. Edouard Lacomble 21, B-1020 Brussels, Belgium

ERIE INTERNATIONAL LTD

4000 South 13th Street, Milwaukee, WI, 53221

Tel: (414) 483-0524 Fax: (414) 483-6610

Mfr. controls, valves.

Erie Controls-Europe NV, Herentals, Belgium

ERNST & YOUNG, LLP

787 Seventh Ave., New York, NY, 10019

Tel: (212) 773-3000 Fax: (212) 773-6350 Web site: www.eyi.com

Accounting and audit, tax and management consulting services.

Ernst & Young Tax Consultants, Ave. marcel Thiry 204, B-1200 Brussels, Belgium

Tel: 32-774-9339 Fax: 32-774-9390 Contact: Derek Gaw

ESSEF CORPORATION

220 Park Drive, Chardon, OH, 44024-1333

Tel: (440) 286-2200 Fax: (440) 286-2206 Web site: www.essef.com

Mfr. non-metallic pressure vessels & related products.

Structural Europe NV, Industriepark Wolfstee, B-2200 Herentals, Belgium

ETHYL CORPORATION

330 South 4th Street, PO Box 2189, Richmond, VA, 23219

Tel: (804) 788-5000 Fax: (804) 788-5688

Mfr. fuel & lubricant additives.

Ethyl Europe SA, Woluwe Garden, Woluwedal 26, B-1932 St. Stevens Woluwe, Belgium

EURO RSCG Worldwide

350 Hudson Street, New York, NY, 10014

Tel: (212) 886-2000 Fax: (212) 886-2016

International advertising agency group.

Equator, Brussels, Belgium

Euro RSCG United, Brussels, Belgium

Palmares, Brussels, Belgium

EXPEDITORS INTERNATIONAL OF WASHINGTON INC.

999 Throd Ave., Ste. 2500, Seattle, WA, 98104

Tel: (206) 674-3400 Fax: (206) 682-9777 Web site: www.expd.com

Air/ocean freight forwarding, customs brokerage, international logistics solutions.

Expeditors International NV, Noorderlaan 111, Box 12, 2nd Fl., Antwerp, B-2030, Belgium (Locations: Brucargo;

Tel: 32-3-544-9319 Fax: 32-3-544-9991

EXXON CORPORATION

225 E. John W. Carpenter Freeway, Irving, TX, 75062-2298

Tel: (972) 444-1000 Fax: (972) 444-1882 Web site: www.exxon.com

Petroleum exploration, production, refining; mfr. petroleum & chemicals products; coal & minerals.

Esso Inc., Blvd. du Souverain 280, B-1160 Brussels, Belgium

Exxon Chemical, Polderdijkweg 3, 2030 Antwerpen, Belgium

Exxon Chemical, Meerhout Polymers Plant, Biezenhoed 2, 2450 Meerhout, Belgium

Exxon Chemical/Antwerp Polymers Plant, Canada Straat 20 Haven 1007, 2070 Zwijndrecht, Belgium

FDX CORPORATION (FED EX)

2005 Corporate Ave., PO Box 727, Memphis, TN, 38194

Tel: (901) 369-3600 Fax: (901) 395-2000 Web site: www.fdxcorp.com

Package express delivery service.

Federal Express NV/SA, Brussels National Airport, B-1930 Zaventem, Belgium

Tel: 32-800-135055

FEDERAL-MOGUL CHAMPION SPARK PLUG COMPANY

900 Upton Ave., Toledo, OH, 43607

Tel: (419) 535-2567 Fax: (419) 535-2332

Mfr. spark plugs, wiper blades and related products.

Champion Spark Plug Europe SA, Kosterstraat 209, B-1920 Diegem, Belgium

FEDERAL-MOGUL CORPORATION

26555 Northwestern Highway, PO Box 1966, Southfield, MI, 48034

Tel: (248) 354-7700 Fax: (248) 354-8983 Web site: www.federalmogul.com

Mfr./distributor precision parts for automobiles, trucks, farm and construction vehicles.

Federal-Mogul, Kontich, Belgium

FERGUSON COMPANY

11820 Lockland Road, St. Louis, MO, 63146-4281

Tel: (314) 567-3200 Fax: (314) 567-4701

Mfr. indexing & transfer equipment, custom cams, parts handlers, rotary tables, link conveyors.

Ferguson Machine Co. SA, Parc Industriel 33, B-1440 Braine-le-Chateau, Belgium

FERRO CORPORATION

1000 Lakeside Ave., Cleveland, OH, 44114-1183

Tel: (216) 641-8580 Fax: (216) 696-5784 Web site: www.ferro.com

Mfr. Specialty chemicals, coatings, plastics, colors, refractories.

Ferro (Holland) B.V., Vossenstraat 65, 9210 Heusden, Belgium

Tel: 32-91-310561 Fax: 32-91-319367

FILTRA SYSTEMS/HYDROMATION

4000 Town Center, Ste. 1000, Southfield, MI, 48075-1410

Tel: (248) 356-9090 Fax: (248) 356-2812

Industrial filter systems.

Hydromation (Belgium) NV, Luikersteenweg, B-3700 Tongeren, Belgium

FISHER SCIENTIFIC INC.

Liberty Lane, Hampton, NH, 03842

Tel: (603) 929-5911 Fax: (603) 929-0222 Web site: www.fisher1.com

Mfr. science instruments & apparatus, chemicals, reagents.

Acros Organics, N.V., Geel West Zone 2, Janssen, Pharmaceuticalaan 3A, B-2440 Geel, Belgium

Tel: 32-14-575211 Fax: 32-14-593434

Fisher Scientific - Resco Trade N.V., Hoveniersstraat 34a, B-8500 Kortrijk, Belgium

Tel: 32-56-260260 Fax: 32-56-260-270

Fisher Scientific Europe, Geel West Zone 2, Janssen, Pharmaceuticalaan 3A, B-2440 Geel, Belgium

Tel: 32-14-575284 Fax: 32-14-575283

FISHER-ROSEMOUNT

8000 Maryland Ave., Ste. 500, Clayton, MO, 63105-4755

Tel: (314) 746-9900 Fax: (314) 746-9974

Mfr. industrial process control equipment.

Fisher Controls NV/SA, De Kleetlaan 4, B-1831, Diegem, Belgium

FLOWSERVE CORPORATION

222 W. Los Cloinas Blvd., Irving, TX, 75039

Tel: (972) 443-6500 Fax: (972) 443-6858 Web site: www.flowserve.com

Mfr. chemicals equipment, pumps, valves, filters, fans and heat exchangers.

SA Durco Europe NV, Parc Industrial, B-4822 Petit Rechain, Belgium

Tel: 32-2-702-9600

SA Durco NV, Rue de Geneve 6, B-1140 Brussels, Belgium

Tel: 32-2-8732-1411

FLOWSERVE FLUID SEALING DIVISION

222 Los Colinas Blvd., Ste. 1500, Irving, TX, 75039

Tel: (616) 381-2650 Fax: (616) 443-6800 Web site: www.flowserve.com

Mfr. mechanical seals, compression packings and auxiliaries.

Durametallic Benelux, Brugsesteenweg 591, B-9910 Ghent, Belgium

FMC CORPORATION

200 E. Randolph Drive, Chicago, IL, 60601

Tel: (312) 861-6000 Fax: (312) 861-6141

Produces chemicals & precious metals, mfr. machinery, equipment & systems for industrial, agricultural & government use.

FMC Europe SA, Ave. Louise 480, B-1050 Brussels, Belgium

Food Machinery Europe, Breedstraat 3, B-9100 Sint-Niklaas, Belgium

FORD MOTOR COMPANY

The American Road, Dearborn, MI, 48121

Tel: (313) 322-3000 Fax: (313) 322-9600 Web site: www.ford.com

Mfr./sales motor vehicles.

Ford Motor Co. (Belgium) NV, Kanaaldok 200, B-2030 Antwerp, Belgium

FORT JAMES CORPORATION

1650 Lake Cook Road, Deerfield, IL, 60015

Tel: (847) 317-5000 Fax: (847) 236-3755 Web site: www.fortjames.com

Mfr./sales of consumer paper and packaging products.

Fort James Corporation, Brussels, Belgium

Tel: 32-2-373-5811

FORTÉ SOFTWARE, INC.

1800 Harrison Street, Oakland, CA, 94612

Tel: (510) 869-3400 Fax: (510) 869-3480 Web site: www.forte.com

Developer computer software applications.

Forté Software SA/NV, Ave. dea Saisons, Jaargetijdenlaan 1000-102, box 30, 1050 Brussels, Belgium

Tel: 32-2-639-3993 Fax: 32-3-639-3944

THE FRANKLIN MINT

US Route 1, Franklin Center, PA, 19091

Tel: (610) 459-6000 Fax: (610) 459-6880

Design/marketing collectibles & luxury items.

Franklin Mint SA/NV, Ave. du Colvert 1, B-1170 Brussels, Belgium

FRITZ COMPANIES INC.

706 Mission Street, Ste. 900, San Francisco, CA, 94103

Tel: (415) 904-8360 Fax: (415) 904-8661 Web site: www.fritz.com

Integrated transportation, sourcing, distribution & customs brokerage services.

Fritz Companies Belgium NV, Brucargo Bldg 706, Rooms 7408-7409, B-1931 Brucargo, Belgium (Locations: Antwerp, Brussels, Rekkem & Temse)

Fritz Companies European Hdqtrs., Ankerrui 20, 7/F, B-2000 Antwerp, Belgium

H.B. FULLER COMPANY

1200 Willow Lake Blvd., Vadnais Heights, MN, 55110

Tel: (612) 236-5900 Fax: (612) 236-5898 Web site: www.hbfuller.com

Mfr./distributor adhesives, sealants, coatings, paints, waxes, sanitation chemicals.

EFTEC NV, Henry Fordlaan 1, B-3600 Genk, Belgium

Tel: 32-89-61-2786 Fax: 32-89-61-2793

H.B. Fuller Belgium NV/SA, Kontichsesteenweg 73, B-2630 Aartselaar, Belgium

Tel: 32-3-457-6802 Fax: 32-3-458-1190

FURON COMPANY

29982 Ivy Glenn Drive, Laguna Niguel, CA, 92677

Tel: (714) 831-5350 Fax: (714) 643-1548

Mfr. of industrial components.

Furon Samuel Moore, Chaussee de Tirlemot 100, B-5800 Gembloux, Belgium

Furon Seals NV/SA, Helststraat 51/7, B-2630 Aartselar, Belgium

GAB BUSINESS SERVICES INC.

Linden Plaza, 9 Campus Drive, Parsippany, NJ, 07054-4476

Tel: (973) 993-3400 Fax: (973) 993-9579

Insurance adjustment.

ITS Inc., Weber Bldg., Verbindingsdok Westkaai 26/30, B-2000 Antwerp, Belgium

GAF CORPORATION

1361 Alps Road, Wayne, NJ, 07470

Tel: (973) 628-3000 Fax: (973) 628-3326 Web site: www.gaf.com

Mfr. building materials.

GAF (Belgium) NV, Hodgkamerstraat 42, B-2700 Sint-Niklaas, Belgium

THE GATES RUBBER COMPANY

990 S. Broadway, PO Box 5887, Denver, CO, 80217-5887

Tel: (303) 744-1911 Fax: (303) 744-4000

Mfr. rubber tires/inner tubes & industrial belts & hose.

Gates Europe NV, Dr. Carlierlaan 30, B-9320 Erembodegen, Aalst, Belgium

GE CAPITAL FLEET SERVICES

3 Capital Drive, Eden Prairie, MN, 55344

Tel: (612) 828-1000 Fax: (612) 828-2010

Corporate vehicle leasing and services.

Avis Fleet Services Europe, Ave. des Communautes 5, B-1140 Brussels, Belgium

GENERAL DATACOMM INC.

1579 Straits Turnpike, PO Box 1299, Middlebury, CT, 06762-1299

Tel: (203) 574-1118 Fax: (203) 758-8507

Mfr./sale/services transportation equipment for communications networks.

General DataComm NV, Oude Arendonksebaan 117, B-2360 Oud-Turnhout, Belgium

GENERAL DYNAMICS CORPORATION

3190 Fairview Park Drive, Falls Church, VA, 22042-4523

Tel: (703) 876-3000 Fax: (703) 876-3125 Web site: www.gendyn.com

Mfr. aerospace equipment, submarines, strategic systems, armored vehicles, defense support systems.

Computer Systems and Communications, Building 2, Caserne Daumerie, Chievres Belgium 7950

Tel: 32-68-275155 Fax: 32-68-275196

General Dynamics Intl. Corp., Blvd. du Souverain 191, B-1160 Brussels, Belgium

GENERAL ELECTRIC CO.

3135 Easton Turnpike, Fairfield, CT, 06431

Tel: (203) 373-2211 Fax: (203) 373-3131 Web site: www.ge.com

Diversified manufacturing, technology and services.

GE Allplances, 5 Brussels 01200, Belgium

Tel: 32-2-775-9650

General Electric Co.-Belgium, Belgium - All mail to U.S. address; phone (800) 626-2004 or (518) 438-6500.

GENERAL MOTORS ACCEPTANCE CORPORATION

100 Renaissance Center, Detroit, MI, 48243-7301

Tel: (313) 556-5000 Fax: (313) 556-5108 Web site: www.gmac.com

Automobile financing.

GMAC, Twin House, Neerveldstraat 107, B-1220 Brussels, Belgium

GMAC Continental, Noorderlaan 139, B-2030 Antwerp, Belgium

GENERAL MOTORS CORPORATION

100 Renaissance Center, Detroit, MI, 48243.7301

Tel: (313) 556-5000 Fax: (313) 556-5108 Web site: www.gm.com

Mfr. full line vehicles, automotive electronics, commercial technologies, telecommunications, space, finance.

General Motors Continental SA, Noorderlaan 75, B-2000 Antwerp, Belgium

GEORGIA BONDED FIBERS INC.

1040 West 29th Street, PO Box 751, Buena Vista, VA, 24416

Tel: (540) 261-2181 Fax: (540) 261-3784

Mfr. insole and luggage material.

Bontex SA, Rue Slar, B-4801 Stembert, Belgium

THE GILLETTE COMPANY

Prudential Tower Building, Boston, MA, 02199

Tel: (617) 421-7000 Fax: (617) 421-7123 Web site: www.gillette.com

Develop/mfr. personal care/use products: blades & razors, toiletries, cosmetics, stationery.

Braun Belgium SA/NV, Zaventem, Belgium

Gillette Belgium SA/NV, Brussels, Belgium

Waterman Benelux SA, Brussels, Belgium

GLEASON CORPORATION

1000 University Ave., Rochester, NY, 14692

Tel: (716) 473-1000 Fax: (716) 461-4348 Web site: www.gleasoncorp.com

Mfr. gear making machine tools; tooling & services.

Gleason Works SA, Parc Industriel de Ghlin Baudour, B-7331 Baudour, Belgium

GODIVA CHOCOLATIER INC.

355 Lexington Ave., New York, NY, 10017

Tel: (212) 984-5900 Fax: (212) 984-5901

Mfr. chocolate candy, Biscotti dipping cookies and after-dinner coffees.

NV Biscuits Delacre SA, Brussels, Belgium

NV Godiva Belgium SA, Brussels, Belgium

Societe Francaise des Biscuits Delacre SA, Brussels, Belgium

W. R. GRACE & COMPANY

One Town Center Road, 1750 Clint Moore Road, Boca Raton, FL, 33486-1010

Tel: (561) 362-2000 Fax: (561) 561-2193 Web site: www.grace.com

Mfr. specialty chemicals and materials: packaging, health care, catalysts, construction, water treatment/process.

Grace N.V., City Ctr., Mechelssteenweg 136 bus 8, B-2018 Antwerpen, Belgium

Tel: 32-3-237-1010 Fax: 32-3-237-9200

GRACO INC

4050 Olson Memorial Hwy, PO Box 1441, Minneapolis, MN, 55440-1441

Tel: (612) 623-6000 Fax: (612) 623-6777 Web site: www.graco.com

Mfr./sales of infant & juvenile products; services fluid handling equipment & systems.

Graco NV, Industrieterrein-Oude Bunders, Slakweidestraat 31, B-3630 Maasmechelen, Belgium

GRAHAM & JAMES LLP

One Maritime Plaza - Ste. 300, San Francisco, CA, 94111-3404
Tel: (415) 954-0200 Fax: (415) 391-2493 Web site: www.gj.com
International law firm.
Graham & James/Taylor Joynson Garrett, 14 rue Montoyer, Brussels 1000, Belgium
Tel: 32-2-514-0402 Fax: 32-2-514-0088 Contact: John Grayston

GREFCO, INC.

23705 Crenshaw Blvd., Ste. 101, Torrance, CA, 90505
Tel: (310) 517-0700 Fax: (310) 517-0794
Filter powders.
Dicalite-Europe Nord SA, Ave. Louise 430, B-1050 Brussels, Belgium

GREY ADVERTISING INC.

777 Third Ave., New York, NY, 10017
Tel: (212) 546-2000 Fax: (212) 546-1495 Web site: www.giworldwwide.com
International advertising agency.
Grey Europe, Blvd. de la Woluwe 56, B-1200 Brussels, Belgium

GRIFFITH LABORATORIES INC

One Griffith Center, Alsip, IL, 60658
Tel: (708) 371-0900 Fax: (708) 597-3294 Web site: www.griffithlabs.com
Industrial food ingredients and equipment.
NV Griffith Laboratories SA, Wolfsteestraat Industriepark, Box 67, B-2410 Herentals, Belgium
Tel: 32-14-254-211 Fax: 32-14-220-053

GTE CORPORATION

One Stamford Forum, Stamford, CT, 06904
Tel: (203) 965-2000 Fax: (203) 965-2277 Web site: www.gte.com
Electronic products, telecommunications systems, publishing and communications.
Automatic Electric SA, Boomgaardstraat 22, B-2000 Antwerp, Belgium
GTE Sylvania NV, Frans Timmermansstraat 119, B-1730 Zellik, Belgium

HACH COMPANY

PO Box 389, Loveland, CO, 80539
Tel: (970) 669-3050 Fax: (303) 970-2932
Mfr./distributor water analysis and organic instruments, test kits and chemicals.
Hach Europe SA/NV, Boite Postale 229, B-5000 Namur 1, Belgium
Tel: 32-81-44-7171

HAEMONETICS CORPORATION

400 Wood Road, Braintree, MA, 02184
Tel: (781) 848-7100 Fax: (781) 848-5106 Web site: www.haemonetics.
Mfr. automated blood processing systems and blood products
Haemonetics Belgium SA-NV, Leuvensensteenweg 542, B.P. 14, Planet II Complex, 1930 Zaventem, Belgium
Tel: 32-2-720-7484 Fax: 32-2-720-7155

HALLMARK CARDS INC.

PO Box 419580, Kansas City, MO, 64141
Tel: (816) 274-5100 Fax: (816) 274-5061
Mfr. greeting cards and related products.
Hallmark Belgium N.V., Botermelkbaan 14, 2900 Schoten, Belgium
Tel: 32-3-68-51130

HANGER ORTHOPEDIC GROUP, INC.

7700 Old Georgetown Road, 2nd Fl., Bethesda, MD, 20814

Tel: (301) 986-0701 Fax: (301) 986-0102

Manufacture and sales of artificial limbs.

J.E. Hanger & Co. Ltd., Brussels, Belgium

M.A. HANNA COMPANY

200 Public Square, Ste. 36-5000, Cleveland, OH, 44114

Tel: (216) 589-4000 Fax: (216) 589-4200

Mfr. color and additive concentrates.

Wilson Color, 2 rue Melville Wilson, B-5330 Assesse, Belgium

THE HARPER GROUP

260 Townsend Street, San Francisco, CA, 94107-1719

Tel: (415) 978-0600 Fax: (415) 978-0692 Web site: www.circleintl.com

Ocean/air freight forwarding, customs brokerage, packing and wholesale, logistics management and insurance.

Circle Freight (Belgium) N.V., Verbindingsdok O.K. 17, Antwerp, B2000, Belgium

Tel: 32-3-231-6777 Fax: 32-2-225-0746

Circle Gilmex International NV/SA, Brucargo, Bldg., 729, 1931 Zaventem, Belgium

Tel: 32-2-752-9910 Fax: 32-2-751-7978

HARRIS CORPORATION

1025 West NASA Blvd., Melbourne, FL, 32919

Tel: (407) 727-9100 Fax: (407) 727-9344 Web site: www.harris.com

Mfr. communications and information-handling equipment, including copying and fax systems.

Harris Semiconductor, Mercure Ctr., rue de la Fusee 100, B-1130 Brussels, Belgium

Tel: 32-2-724-2111 Fax: 32-2-724-2205

THE HARTFORD FINANCIAL SERVICES GROUP, INC.

Hartford Plaza, Hartford, CT, 06115

Tel: (860) 547-5000 Fax: (860) 547-5817 Web site: www.thehartford.com

Financial services.

ZA Verzekerigen N.V., Laarstraat 16, 2610 Antwerp (Wilriji), Belgium

Tel: 32-3-825-0063 Fax: 32-3-825-0864 Contact: Bert Boulton, Mng. Dir.

HEIDRICK & STRUGGLES INC

Sears Tower, 233 South Wacker Drive, Chicago, IL, 60606

Tel: (312) 496-1200 Fax: (312) 496-1290 Web site: www.h-s.com

Executive search firm.

Heidrick & Struggles Intl. Inc., Ave. Lousie 81, Box 5, B-1050 Brussels. Belgium

Tel: 32-2-542-0750 Fax: 32-2-542-0752

H.J. HEINZ COMPANY

600 Grant Street, Pittsburgh, PA, 15219

Tel: (412) 456-5700 Fax: (412) 456-6128 Web site: www.heinz.com

Processed food products and nutritional services.

H.J. Heinz Branch Belgium, Brussels, Belgium

H.J. Heinz Northern Europe, Brussels, Belgium

HERCULES INC

Hercules Plaza, 1313 North Market Street, Wilmington, DE, 19894-0001

Tel: (302) 594-5000 Fax: (302) 594-5400 Web site: www.herc.com

Mfr. specialty chemicals, plastics, film and fibers, coatings, resins, food ingredients.

Hercules Chemicals, Doel, Belgium

Hercules Chemicals N.V., Industrieweg Chemicals Inc., PO Box 1, B-3583 Beringen, Belgium
Tel: 32-11-430111 Fax: 32-11-420361

S.A. Hercules Europe, N.V., Ave. de Tervuren 300, B-1150 Brussels, Belgium
Tel: 32-2-761-5511 Fax: 32-2-761-5555 Contact: Jan Noben

THE HERTZ CORPORATION

225 Brae Boulevard, Park Ridge, NJ, 07656-0713
Tel: (201) 307-2000 Fax: (201) 307-2644
Worldwide headquarters office for car rental, car leasing and equipment rental.

Hertz Rental Car, Brussels, Belgium

HEWITT ASSOCIATES LLC

100 Half Day Road, Lincolnshire, IL, 60069
Tel: (847) 295-5000 Fax: (847) 295-7634
Employee benefits consulting firm.

Hewitt Associates, Ave. des Cerisiers 15 bte 2, Kerselarenlaan 15 bus 2, 1030 Brussels, Belgium
Tel: 32-2-743-8611

HEWLETT-PACKARD COMPANY

3000 Hanover Street, Palo Alto, CA, 94304-0890
Tel: (650) 857-1501 Fax: (650) 857-7299 Web site: www.hp.com
Mfr. computing, communications & measurement products & services.

Hewlett-Packard Belgium SA/NV, Blvd. de las Woluwe, 100 Woluwedal, B-1200 Brussels, Belgium

HEXCEL CORPORATION

5794 West Las Positas Blvd., Pleasanton, CA, 94588
Tel: (925) 847-9500 Fax: (925) 734-9042
Honeycomb core materials, specialty chemicals, resins and epoxies.

Hexcel SA, Rue des 3 Bourdons 50, Parc Industriel, B-4840 Welkenraedt, Belgium

HILTON HOTELS CORPORATION

9336 Civic Center Drive, Beverly Hills, CA, 90210
Tel: (310) 278-4321 Fax: (310) 205-7880
International hotel chain: Hilton International, Vista Hotels and Hilton National Hotels.

Hilton International Hotels, 38 blvd de Waterloo, B-1000, Brussels, Belgium

HLW INTERNATIONAL, LLP

115 Fifth Ave., New York, NY, 10003
Tel: (212) 353-4600 Fax: (212) 353-4666 Web site: www.currently in preparation
Architecture, engineering, planning and interior design.

HLW International, LLP, Brussels, Belgium

HOLIDAY INNS WORLDWIDE, INC.

3 Ravinia Drive, Ste. 2900, Atlanta, GA, 30346-2149
Tel: (770) 604-2000 Fax: (770) 604-5403
Hotels, restaurants and casinos.

Holiday Inn SA, Boeveriestraat, B-2800 Brugge, Sauna, Belgium

HONEYWELL INC.

PO Box 524, Minneapolis, MN, 55440-0524
Tel: (612) 951-1000 Fax: (612) 951-3066 Web site: www.honeywell.com
Develop/mfr. controls for home and building, industry, space and aviation.

Honeywell Europe SA, Ave. du Bourget 3, B-1140 Brussels, Belgium

Honeywell SA, Ave. de Schiphol 3, B-1140 Brussels, Belgium

HORWATH INTERNATIONAL

415 Madison Ave., New York, NY, 10017

Tel: (212) 838-5566 Fax: (212) 838-3636

Public accountants and auditors.

Blanckaert, Missorten, Spaenhoven & Co., Meiseselaan 71, 1020 Brussels, Belgium

HOWMEDICA INC.

359 Veterans Boulevard, Rutherford, NJ, 07070

Tel: (201) 507-7300 Fax: (201) 935-4873 Web site: www.howmedica.com

Hospital, medical and dental supplies.

Howmedica Belgium, Zaventem, Belgium

Tel: 32-2-722-0356

HUGHES ELECTRONICS

200 N. Sepulveda Blvd., PO Box 956, El Segundo, CA, 90245-0956

Tel: (310) 662-9821 Fax: (310) 647-6213

Mfr. electronics equipment and systems.

Hughes Aircraft Intl. Service Co., Berkenlaan 1, B-1831 Diegem, Belgium

HUNTON & WILLIAMS

951 East Byrd Street, East Tower, Richmond, VA, 23219-4074

Tel: (804) 788-8200 Fax: (804) 788-8218 Web site: www.hunton.com

Law firm.

Hunton & Williams, Ave. Louise 326, B-1050 Brussels, Belgium

Tel: 32-2-643-5800 Fax: 32-2-643-5822 Contact: Lucas Berg Kamp, Mng. Ptnr. Emp: 15

HUNTSMAN CORPORATION

500 Huntsman Way, Salt Lake City, UT, 84108

Tel: (801) 532-5200 Fax: (801) 536-1581

Mfr./sales specialty chemicals, industrial chemicals and petrochemicals.

Huntsman Corporation Belgium N. V., Woluwe Office Garden, Woluwedal 26, B-1932, Zaventem, Belgium

Tel: 32-2-718-0120 Fax: 32-2-718-0211

IBM CORPORATION

New Orchard Road, Armonk, NY, 10504

Tel: (914) 765-1900 Fax: (914) 765-7382 Web site: www.ibm.com

Information products, technology & services.

Intl. Business Machines of Belgium SA, Square Victoria Regina 1, B-1210 Brussels, Belgium

Tel: 32-2-225-3333 Fax: 32-2-225-2473

ICC INDUSTRIES INC.

460 Park Ave., New York, NY, 10022

Tel: (212) 521-1700 Fax: (212) 521-1794 Web site: www.iccchem.com

Manufacturing and trading of chemicals, plastics and pharmaceuticals.

ICC Industries, Inc., Kardinaal Mercierlaan 32, B 3001 Heverlee, Belgium

Tel: 32-1-629-8040 Fax: 32-1-629-8041 Contact: Guy Roox

IDEAL TAPE COMPANY

1400 Middlesex Street, Lowell, MA, 01851

Tel: (978) 458-6833 Fax: (978) 458-0302

Pressure sensitive tapes.

Ideal Tape Co., Oswald Ponettestraat 45, B-9600 Ronse, Belgium

INDUCTOTHERM CORPORATION

10 Indel Ave., PO Box 157, Rancocas, NJ, 08073-0157

Tel: (609) 267-9000 Fax: (609) 267-3537

Mfr. induction melting furnaces.

Inducto Elphiac, Rue P.J. Antoine 79, B-4040 Herstal, Belgium

INFONET SERVICES CORPORATION

2100 East Grand Ave., El Segundo, CA, 90245

Tel: (310) 335-2600 Fax: (310) 335-4507 Web site: www.infonet.com

Provider of Internet services and electronic messaging services.

Infonet Belgium SA, 350/358 Ave. Louise, Box 11, Brussels, Belgium

Tel: 32-2-627-3811 Fax: 32-2-640-3638

INFORMATION BUILDERS INC.

1250 Broadway, New York, NY, 10001

Tel: (212) 736-4433 Fax: (212) 643-8105

Develop/mfr./services computer software.

Information Builders (Belgium), Blvd. Brand Whitlocklan 114, B-1200 Brussels, Belgium

INFORMIX CORPORATION

4100 Bohannon Drive, Menlo Park, CA, 95025

Tel: (650) 926-6300 Fax: (650) 926-6593 Web site: www.informix.com

Designs & produces database management software, connectivity interfaces & gateways, and other computer applications.

Informix Software NV/SA, Lozenberg 1, 1932 Zaventem, Belgium

Tel: 32-2-711-1111

INGERSOLL-RAND COMPANY

200 Chestnut Ridge Road, Woodcliff Lake, NJ, 07675

Tel: (201) 573-0123 Fax: (201) 573-3172 Web site: www.ingersoll-rand.com

Mfr. compressors, rock drills, pumps, air tools, door hardware, ball bearings.

Ingersoll-Rand Benelux, Produktieweg 10, B-2382 Zoeterwoude, Belgium

INGRAM MICRO INC.

PO Box 25125, Santa Ana, CA, 92799

Tel: (714) 566-1000 Fax: (714) 566-7940 Web site: www.ingrammicro.com

Distribute computer systems, software and related products.

Ingram Micro Inc., Leuvensesteenweg 11, 1932 Sint Stevens Woluwe, Brussels, Belgium

Tel: 32-2-722-7915 Fax: 32-2-725-2396

INSTRON CORPORATION

100 Royall Street, Canton, MA, 02021-1089

Tel: (781) 828-2500 Fax: (781) 575-5751

Mfr. material testing instruments.

Instrol Intl. Ltd., Mechelsesteenweg 326, B-2520 Edegem, Belgium

INTER-CONTINENTAL HOTELS

1120 Ave. of the Americas, New York, NY, 10036

Tel: (212) 852-6400 Fax: (212) 852-6494 Web site: www.interconti.com

Worldwide hotel and resort accommodations.

Europa Inter-Continental Brussels, Rue de la Loi 107, 1040 Brussels, Belgium

Tel: 32-2-230-1333 Fax: 32-2-230-3682

INTERGRAPH CORPORATION

One Madison Industrial Park, Huntsville, AL, 35894-0001

Tel: (205) 730-2000 Fax: (205) 730-7898 Web site: www.intergraph.com

Develop/mfr. interactive computer graphic systems.

Intergraph BENELUX BV, Tennessee House - Riverside Business Park, Internationalelaan 55, Brussels, Belgium B-1070

Tel: 32-2-52-62111 Fax: 32-2-52-62150

INTERMEC TECHNOLOGIES CORPORATION

6001 36th Ave. West, PO Box 4280, Everett, WA, 98203-9280

Tel: (425) 348-2600 Fax: (425) 355-9551 Web site: www.intermec.com

Mfr./distributor automated data collection systems.

Intermec Belgium, Bedrijfspark Heide 11, B-1780 Wemmel, Belgium

INTERNATIONAL FILLER CORPORATION

50 Bridge Street, North Tonawanda, NY, 14120

Tel: (716) 693-4040 Fax: (716) 693-3528 Web site: www.internationalfiller.com

Mfr. of powdered cellulose, cotton flock, synthetic clock, and sisal fibers.

International Filler of Belgium NV/SA, Eurolaan 5, Temse, Belgium B-9140

Tel: 32-3-711-1636 Fax: 32-3-771-3399 Contact: Daniel Van Ruyskensvelde

INTERNATIONAL PAPER COMPANY

2 Manhattanville Road, Purchase, NY, 10577

Tel: (914) 397-1500 Fax: (914) 397-1596 Web site: www.ipaper.com

Mfr./distributor container board, paper, wood products.

Aussedat Rey Belgium, Dobbelenberg 88, B-1300 Brussels, Belgium

Ilford Anitec NV/SA, Eigenlostraat 21, B-2700 Sint-Niklaas, Belgium

Ilford Photo SA, Ave. des Casemes 39, B-1040 Brussel, Belgium

International Paper (Europe) SA, Blvd. de la Woluwe 2, B-1150 Brussels, Belgium

Veratec SA, Blvd. de la Woluwe 56, B-1200 Brussels, Belgium

INTERNATIONAL SPECIALTY PRODUCTS

1361 Alps Road, Wayne, NJ, 07470

Tel: (973) 628-4000 Fax: (973) 628-3311 Web site: www.ispcorp.com

Mfr. specialty chemical products.

ISP (Belgium) NV, Hoogkamerstraat 42, B 9100, Sint-Niklaas, Belgium

Tel: 32-3-780-7200 Fax: 32-3-780-7314

IOMEGA CORPORATION

1821 West 4000 South, Roy, UT, 84067

Tel: (801) 778-4494 Fax: (801) 778-3450 Web site: www.iomega.com

Mfr. data storage products.

Iomega, Excelsiorlaan 39, Zaventem, B-1930 Brussels, Belgium

ITT SHERATON CORPORATION

60 State Street, Boston, MA, 02108

Tel: (617) 367-3600 Fax: (617) 367-5676

Hotel operations.

Sheraton Sales Center, Brussels Sheraton Hotel, Place Rogier 3, B-1000 Brussels, Belgium

J.P. MORGAN & CO. INC.

60 Wall Street, New York, NY, 10260-0060

Tel: (212) 483-2323 Fax: (212) 648-5209 Web site: www.jpm.com

International banking services.

Morgan Guaranty Trust Co., Frankrijklei 82, B-2000 Antwerp, Belgium

Morgan Guaranty Trust Co. of NY, Ave. des Arts 35, B-1040 Brussels, Belgium
Tel: 32-2-508-8211

J. WALTER THOMPSON COMPANY

466 Lexington Ave., New York, NY, 10017
Tel: (212) 210-7000 Fax: (212) 210-6944 Web site: www.jwt.com
International advertising and marketing services.
J. Walter Thompson Brussels, Brussels, Belgium

JOHN HANCOCK MUTUAL LIFE INSURANCE COMPANY

200 Clarendon Street, PO Box 111, Boston, MA, 02117
Tel: (617) 572-6000 Fax: (617) 572-8628 Web site: www.jhancock.com
Life insurance services.
John Hancock Intl. Services SA, Rue Montoyer 31, B-1040 Brussels, Belgium

JOHNSON & JOHNSON

One Johnson & Johnson Plaza, New Brunswick, NJ, 08933
Tel: (732) 524-0400 Fax: (732) 214-0334 Web site: www.jnj.com
Mfr./distributor/R&D pharmaceutical, health care and cosmetic products.
Cilag NV, Rue de la Fusee 66, B-1130 Brussels, Belgium
Cordis N.V., Zaventem, Belgium
Janssen Biotech NV, Lammerdries 55, B-2250 Olen, Belgium
Janssen Internationaal NV, Turnhoutseweg 30, B-2340 Beerse, Belgium
Janssen Pharmaceutica NV, Turnhoutseweg 30, B-2340 Beerse, Belgium
Janssen-Cilag N.V., Antwerp, Belgium
Ortho-Clinical Diagnostics NV, Antwerpseweg 19-21, B-2340 Beerse, Belgium

S C JOHNSON & SON INC.

1525 Howe Street, Racine, WI, 53403
Tel: (414) 260-2000 Fax: (414) 260-2133 Web site: www.scjohnsonwax.com
Home, auto, commercial and personal care products and specialty chemicals.
NV Johnson Wax Belgium SA, Noordkustlaan 16, Groot-Bijgaarden, B-1720 Brussels, Belgium

JOHNSON CONTROLS INC.

5757 N. Green Bay Ave., PO Box 591, Milwaukee, WI, 53201-0591
Tel: (414) 228-1200 Fax: Web site: www.johnsoncontrols.com
Mfr. facility management & control systems, auto seating, & batteries..
Johnson Controls SA/NV, Diegem Zuid-Pegasus Park, de Kleetlaan 2C, B1831 Diegem, Belgium
Tel: 32-2-711-4300 Fax: 32-2-725-7320 Contact: Rick Verheyden, Branch Mgr.

JOHNSON WORLDWIDE ASSOCIATES, INC.

1326 Willow Road, Sturtevant, WI, 53177
Tel: (414) 884-1500 Fax: (414) 884-1600 Web site: www.jwa.com
Mfr. diving, fishing, boating & camping sports equipment.
Scubapro Benelux, 51 Av. Prudent Bolslaan, B-1020 Brussels, Belgium
Tel: 32-2-426-8677 Fax: 32-2-426-8846

JONES, DAY, REAVIS & POGUE

North Point, 901 Lakeside Ave., Cleveland, OH, 44114
Tel: (216) 586-3939 Fax: (216) 579-0212 Web site: www.jonesday.com
International law firm.
Jones, Day, Reavis & Pogue, Ave. Louise 480, Louizalaan 480, Brussels, Belgium
Tel: 32-2-645-1411 Fax: 32-2-645-1445 Contact: Luc G. Houben, Partner Emp: 21

A.T. KEARNEY INC.

222 West Adams Street, Chicago, IL, 60606

Tel: (312) 648-0111 Fax: (312) 223-6200 Web site: www.atkearney.com

Management consultants and executive search.

A. T. Kearney N. V., Ave. des Arts 46, Kunstlaan, B-1040 Brussels, Belgium

Tel: 32-2-504-4811

KELLEY DRYE & WARREN LLP

101 Park Ave., New York, NY, 10178

Tel: (212) 808-7800 Fax: (212) 808-7898 Web site: www.kelleydrye.com

International law firm.

Kelley Drye & Warren LLP, 106 Ave. Louise, 1050 Brussels, Belgium

Tel: 32-2-646-1110 Fax: 32-2-640-0589

KELLOGG COMPANY

One Kellogg Square, PO Box 3599, Battle Creek, MI, 49016-3599

Tel: (616) 961-2000 Fax: (616) 961-2871 Web site: www.kelloggs.com

Mfr. ready-to-eat cereals and convenience foods.

Kellogg's Benelux, Zaventum, Belgium (All inquiries to U.S. address)

KELLY SERVICES, INC.

999 W. Big Beaver Road, Troy, MI, 48084

Tel: (248) 362-4444 Fax: (248) 244-4154 Web site: www.kellyservices.com

Temporary help placement.

Kelly Services Belgium, 63 Blvd Adolphe Max, 1000 Brussels, Belgium

Tel: 32-2-219-0909 Fax: 32-2-219-0910

KENNAMETAL INC.

State Rte. 981, Latrobe, PA, 15650

Tel: (724) 539-5000 Fax: (724) 539-4710 Web site: www.kennametal.com

Tools, hard carbide & tungsten alloys for metalworking industry.

Kennametal Hertel Belgium SA/NV, B-4040 Hertel, Belgium

Tel: 32-41-482734 Fax: 32-41-482814

KILPATRICK STOCKTON

1100 Peachtree Street, NE, Ste. 2800, Atlanta, GA, 30309

Tel: (404) 815-6500 Fax: (404) 815-6555

International law firm.

Kilpatrick Stockton, Brussels, Belgium

KIMBERLY-CLARK CORPORATION

351 Phelps Drive, Irving, TX, 75038

Tel: (972) 281-1200 Fax: (972) 281-1435 Web site: www.kimberly-clark.com.

Mfr./sales/distribution of consumer tissue, household and personal care products.

Kimberly-Clark Continental NV, Duffel, Belgium

LESTER B KNIGHT & ASSOC INC.

549 West Randolph Street, Chicago, IL, 60661

Tel: (312) 346-2300 Fax: (312) 648-1085

Architecture, engineering, planning, operations & management consulting.

Knight Wendling Consulting AG, Galerie Porte Louise 203, bte 1, B-1050 Brussels, Belgium

KNOLL, INC.

1235 Water Street, East Greenville, PA, 18041

Tel: (215) 679-7991 Fax: (215) 679-3904 Web site: www.knoll.com

Mfr. and sale of office furnishings.

Knoll Intl., Ave. Louise, Louisalaan 65, B-1050 Brussels, Belgium

KORN/FERRY INTERNATIONAL

1800 Century Park East, Los Angeles, CA, 90067
Tel: (310) 552-1834 Fax: (310) 553-6452 Web site: www.kornferry.com
Executive search; management consulting.
Korn/Ferry International SA, Ave. Louise 523, B-1050 Brussels, Belgium
Tel: 32-2-640-3240 Fax: 32-2-640-8382

KPMG PEAT MARWICK LLP

Three Chestnut Ridge Road, Montvale, NJ, 07645
Tel: (201) 307-7000 Fax: (201) 930-8617 Web site: www.kpmg.com
Accounting and audit, tax and management consulting services.
KPMG, Parc Industriel das Hauts Sarts, Lioge, B-4040, Belgium
KPMG, Kortrijksesteenweg 14-30, Gent-B-9000, Belgium
KPMG, Woluwe Office Park, rue Neerveld 101-103, Brussels B-1200, Belgium
Tel: 32-2-773-4300 Fax: 32-2-773-4399 Contact: Theo Erauw, Sr. Ptnr.
KPMG, Spoorweglaan 3, Antwerp, B-2610, Wilrijk, Belgium
KPMG European Hdqtrs., 54 Ave. Louise, Brussels B-1050, Belgium
Tel: 32-2-548-0909 Fax: 32-2-548-0909 Contact: Richard Ebling, Sr. Ptnr.

LANIER WORLDWIDE, INC.

2300 Parklake Drive, N.E., Atlanta, GA, 30345
Tel: (770) 496-9500 Fax: (770) 621-1535
Specialize in digital copiers and multi-functional systems.
Lanier Belgium N.V./S.A., De Villermontstraat 20A, 2550 Kontich, Belgium
Tel: 32-3-450-8911 Fax: 32-3-450-8905
Lanier Europe Coordination Center, Dreve de Willerieken 20, 1160 Brussels, Belgium
Tel: 32-2-658-2411 Fax: 32-2-675-4202

LAWTER INTERNATIONAL INC.

8601 95th Street, Pleasant Prairie, WI, 53158
Tel: (414) 947-7300 Fax: (414) 947-7328
Resins, pigments and coatings.
Lawter Chemicals SA, Toikomstlaan 18, B-9100 Lokeren, Belgium

LE TOURNEAU COMPANY

PO Box 2307, Longview, TX, 75606
Tel: (903) 237-7000 Fax: (903) 267-7032
Mfr. heavy construction and mining machinery equipment.
Bureau Technique Bia SA, Rameistraat 123, B-3090 Overijse, Belgium

LeBOEUF, LAMB, GREENE & MacRAE LLP

125 West 55th Street, 12th Fl., New York, NY, 10019
Tel: (212) 424-8000 Fax: (212) 424-8500 Web site: www.llgm.com
International law firm.
LeBoeuf, Lamb, Green & MacRae LLP, Ave. de arta 19H, 1040 Brussels, Belgium
Tel: 32-2-227-0900 Fax: 32-2-227-0909

LEUCADIA NATIONAL CORPORATION

315 Park Ave. South, New York, NY, 10010
Tel: (212) 460-1900 Fax: (212) 598-4869
Holding company: real estate, banking, insurance, equipment leasing, mfr. plastics, cable, sinks & cabinets.
Cornwed Plastics NV/SA, Ambachtenlaan 17, B-3030 Heverlee, Haasrode, Belgium

LEVI STRAUSS & COMPANY

1155 Battery Street, Levi's Plaza, San Francisco, CA, 94111-1230

Tel: (415) 544-6000 Fax: (415) 501-3939 Web site: www.levistrauss.com

Mfr./distributor casual wearing apparel.

Levi Strauss & Co, Europe, Middle East & Africa, Arnaut Fraiteur 15-23, 1050 Brussels, Belgium

Tel: 32-2-641-6011 Fax: 32-2-640-2997

Levi Strauss Belgium SA, Avignon 272, Atomium Square, Brussels International Trade Mart, Atrium 35B 93, 1020 Brussels, Belgium

Tel: 32-2-478-1012 Fax: 32-2-478-4231

LIBERTY MUTUAL GROUP

175 Berkeley Street, Boston, MA, 02117

Tel: (617) 357-9500 Fax: (617) 350-7648 Web site: www.libertymutual. com

Provides workers' compensation insurance and operates physical rehabilitation centers and provides risk prevention management.

Liberty Mutual Group, Brussels, Belgium

LIFE TECHNOLOGIES INC.

9800 Medical Center Drive, Rockville, MD, 20850

Tel: (301) 840-8000 Fax: (301) 329-8635

Biotechnology.

Life Technologies, Brussels, Belgium

ELI LILLY & COMPANY

Lilly Corporate Center, Indianapolis, IN, 46285

Tel: (317) 276-2000 Fax: (317) 277-6579 Web site: www.lilly.com

Mfr. pharmaceuticals and animal health products.

Eli Lilly Benelux SA, Rue de l'Etuve 52, B-1000 Brussels, Belgium

THE LINCOLN ELECTRIC COMPANY

22801 St. Clair Ave., Cleveland, OH, 44117-1199

Tel: (216) 481-8100 Fax: (216) 486-8385 Web site: www.lincolnelectric.com

Mfr. arc welding and welding related products, oxy-fuel and thermal cutting equipment and integral AC motors.

Lincoln Smitweld Belgium NV, Ave. Paul Gilsonlaan 470, B-1620 Drogenbos, Belgium

Tel: 32-2-377-0071 Fax: 32-2-378-1877 Contact: W. Fred Grifhorst, Mng. Dir.

ARTHUR D. LITTLE, INC.

25 Acorn Park, Cambridge, MA, 02140-2390

Tel: (617) 498-5000 Fax: (617) 498-7200 Web site: www.adlittle.com

Management, environmental, health & safety consulting; technical & product development.

Arthur D. Little International, Inc., Blvd. de la Woluwe 2, B-1150 Brussels, Belgium

Tel: 32-2-76-17333 Fax: 32-2-76-20758

LOCKHEED MARTIN CORPORATION

6801 Rockledge Drive, Bethesda, MD, 20817

Tel: (301) 897-6000 Fax: (301) 897-6652 Web site: www.imco.com

Design/mfr./management systems in fields of space, defense, energy, electronics and technical services.

Lockheed Aeronautical Systems, Postbus 2, 1820 Steenokker Zeel, Belgium

Tel: 32-2-752-4697

Lockheed International, Chaussee de la Hulpe 130, B-1050 Brussels, Belgium

Tel: 32-2-672-7250

LOCTITE CORPORATION

10 Columbus Boulevard, Hartford, CT, 06106

Tel: (203) 520-5000 Fax: (203) 520-5073 Web site: www.loctite.com

Mfr./sale industrial adhesives and sealants.

Loctite Belgium, Mechelsesteenweg 313, B-2550 Kontich, Belgium

Tel: 32-3-457-7833 Fax: 32-3-457-7960

LOWE & PARTNERS WORLDWIDE

1114 Ave. of the Americas, New York, NY, 10036

Tel: (212) 403-6700 Fax: (212) 403-6710

International advertising agency network.

Lowe Troost, Brussels, Belgium

THE LUBRIZOL CORPORATION

29400 Lakeland Blvd., Wickliffe, OH, 44092-2298

Tel: (440) 943-4200 Fax: (440) 943-5337 Web site: www.lubrizol.com

Mfr. chemicals additives for lubricants & fuels.

Lubrizol SA, Blvd. de la Woluwe 2, BP 9, B-1150 Brussels, Belgium

Tel: 32-2-762-1500

MAGNETROL INTERNATIONAL

5300 Belmont Road, Downers Grove, IL, 60515-4499

Tel: (630) 969-4000 Fax: (630) 969-9489 Web site: www.magnetrol.com

Mfr. level and flow instrumentation.

Magnetrol Intl. NV, Heikensstraat 6, B-9240 Zele, Belgium

Tel: 32-52-45-111 Fax: 32-52-0993 Contact: Paul D. Myatt, Dir. Worldwide Sales

MALLINCKRODT INC.

675 McDonnell Blvd., PO Box 5840, St. Louis, MO, 63134

Tel: (314) 654-2000 Fax: (314) 654-3005

Mfr. specialty medical products.

Mallinckrodt Inc., Brussels, Belgium

MANPOWER INTERNATIONAL INC.

5301 N. Ironwood Road, PO Box 2053, Milwaukee, WI, 53201-2053

Tel: (414) 961-1000 Fax: (414) 961-7081 Web site: www.manpower

Temporary help, contract service, training & testing.

Manpower (Belgium) SA, Rue du Commerce 20, 1040 Brussels, Belgium

MARCAM CORPORATION

95 Wells Ave., Newton, MA, 02459

Tel: (617) 965-0220 Fax: (617) 965-7273

Applications software & services.

Marcam Belgium NV, Imperiastraat 8, B-1930 Zaventem, Belgium

MARS INC.

6885 Elm Street, McLean, VA, 22101-3810

Tel: (703) 821-4900 Fax: (703) 448-9678 Web site: www.mars.com

Mfr. candy, snack foods, rice products and cat food.

Mars Chocolate Belgium SA, Rue des Palais 116, B-1030 Brussels, Belgium

MARSH & McLENNAN COS INC.

1166 Ave. of the Americas, New York, NY, 10036-2774

Tel: (212) 345-5000 Fax: (212) 345-4808 Web site: www.marshmac.com

Insurance agents/brokers, pension and investment management consulting services.

Henrijean Marsh McLennan S.A., Rue Fories 2, B8, B-4020 Liege, Belgium

Tel: 32-4-344-1844 Fax: 32-4-344-3416 Contact: N/A

Henrijean Marsh McLennan S.A., Uitbreidingstraat 180, 2600 Antwerpen, Belgium

Tel: 32-3-286-6411 Fax: 32-3-286-6562 Contact: Paul Bruyland

Henrijean Marsh McLennan S.A., Blvd. du Souverain 2, B-1170 Brussels, Belgium

Tel: 32-2-674-9611 Fax: 32-2-674-9920 Contact: Daniel Vanderlinden

MASTERCARD INTERNATIONAL INC.

200 Purchase Street, Purchase, NY, 10577

Tel: (914) 249-2000 Fax: (914) 249-5475 Web site: www.mastercard.com

Provides financial payment systems globally.

MasterCard International Inc., Europe, Chaussee de Tervuren 198 A, B-1410 Waterloo, Belgium

MAXON CORPORATION

201 East 18th Street, Muncie, IN, 47302

Tel: (765) 284-3304 Fax: (765) 286-8394

Industry combustion equipment and valves.

Maxon Intl. SA, Luchthavenlaan 16-18, B-1800 Vilvoorde, Belgium

MAYER, BROWN & PLATT

190 S. LaSalle Street, Chicago, IL, 60603

Tel: (312) 782-0600 Fax: (312) 701-7711 Web site: www.mayerbrown.com

International law firm.

Mayer, Brown & Platt, Square de Meeus 19/20, BTE.4, 1040 Brussels, Belgium

Tel: 32-2-512-9878 Fax: 32-2-511-3305

McCANN-ERICKSON WORLDWIDE

750 Third Ave., New York, NY, 10017

Tel: (212) 984-3644 Fax: (212) 984-2629

International advertising/marketing services.

McCann-Erickson Co. SA, Chaussee de la Hulpe 122, B-1050 Brussels, Belgium

Universal Advertising Team, Britselei 49, B-2000 Antwerp, Belgium

Universal Communication, Gorenenborgerlaan 22, B-2610 Wilrijk, Belgium

McDONALD'S CORPORATION

Kroc Drive, Oak Brook, IL, 60523

Tel: (630) 623-3000 Fax: (630) 623-7409

Fast food chain stores.

McDonald's Corp., Belgium

Contact: Marcus Hewson, Mgr.

THE McGRAW-HILL COMPANIES

1221 Ave. of the Americas, New York, NY, 10020

Tel: (212) 512-2000 Fax: (212) 512-2703

Books, magazines, information systems, financial service, publishing and broadcast operations.

DRI Europe Inc., Rue Camille Lemannier 1, B-1060 Brussels, Belgium

Standard & Poor's Intl. SA, 306 Ave. Charles Woest, B-1090 Brussels, Belgium

McGUIRE, WOODS, BATTLE & BOOTHE LLP

One James Center, 901 E. Cary Street, Richmond, VA, 23219

Tel: (804) 775-1000 Fax: (804) 775-1061 Web site: www.mwbb.com

International law firm.

McGuire, Woods, Battle & Boothe International LLP, 250 Ave. Louise, Bte. 64, 1050 Brussels, Belgium

Tel: 32-2-629-4211 Fax: 32-2-629-4222 Contact: Donald E. King, Mng. Ptnr.

MCI INTERNATIONAL INC.

2 International Drive, Rye Brook, NY, 10573

Tel: (914) 937-3444 Fax: (914) 934-6996

Telecommunications.

MCI Intl. Belgium SA/NV, 123-125 rue Colonel Bourg, B-1140 Brussels, Belgium

McKINSEY & COMPANY

55 East 52nd Street, New York, NY, 10022

Tel: (212) 446-7000 Fax: (212) 446-8575 Web site: www.mckinsey.com

Management and business consulting services.

McKinsey & Company, Ave. Louise 480 - B 22, B-1050 Brussels, Belgium

Tel: 32-2-645-4211 Fax: 32-2-645-4548

MEDICUS GROUP INTERNATIONAL

1675 Broadway, New York, NY, 10019

Tel: (212) 468-3100 Fax: (212) 468-3222

International healthcare agency network.

Medicus Advertising & Communications, Brussels, Belgium

MEDTRONIC INC.

7000 Central Ave., NE, Minneapolis, MN, 55432

Tel: (612) 574-4000 Fax: (612) 574-4879

Mfr./sale/service electrotherapeutic medical devices.

Medtronic Europe SA/NV, Woluwe Office Garden, Woluwedal 26, B-1932 Sint-Stevens-Woluwe, Belgium

MELROE COMPANY

112 North University Drive, PO Box 6019, Fargo, ND, 58108-6019

Tel: (701) 241-8700 Fax: (701) 241-8704

Mfr. heavy equipment.

Melroe Europe, J. Huysmanslaan 59, B-1651 Beersel (Lot), Belgium

MENTOR GRAPHICS/MICROTEC RESEARCH

880 Ridder Park Drive, San Jose, CA, 95131

Tel: (408) 487-7000 Fax: (408) 487-7001

Develop/mfr. software tools for embedded systems market.

Microtec Belgium, Brussels, Belgium

MERCK & COMPANY, INC.

1 Merck Drive, Whitehouse Station, NJ, 08889

Tel: (908) 423-1000 Fax: (908) 423-2592

Pharmaceuticals, chemicals and biologicals.

Merck, Sharp & Dohme Belgium, Chaussee de Waterloo 1135, B-1180 Brussels, Belgium

MERCURY INTERACTIVE CORPORATION

1325 Borregas Ave., Sunnyvale, CA, 94089

Tel: (408) 822-5200 Fax: (408) 822-5300 Web site: www.merc-int.com

Mfr. computer software to decipher and eliminate "bugs" from systems.

Mercury Interactive Benelux, Ambachtenlaan 13A, 3001 Leuven, Belgium

Tel: 32-16-396139 Fax: 32-16-396130

MICROMERITICS INSTRUMENT CORPORATION

One Micromeritics Drive, Norcross, GA, 30093-1877

Tel: (770) 662-3620 Fax: (770) 662-3696

Mfr. analytical instruments.

Micromeritics NV/SA, Excelsiorlaan 59, B-1930 Zaventem (Brussels), Belgium

MICROSOFT CORPORATION

One Microsoft Way, Redmond, WA, 98052-6399

Tel: (425) 882-8080 Fax: (425) 936-7329 Web site: www.microsoft.com

Computer software, peripherals and services.

Microsoft Belgium NV, Rue Colonel Bourgstraat 123-125, B-1140 Brussels, Belgium

Tel: 32-2-730-3911 Fax: 32-2-726-9609

MIDLAND INC.

2248 Research Drive, Fort Wayne, IN, 46808

Tel: (219) 484-8895 Fax: (219) 484-8892

Export management.

Midland Europe, Europark Noord 1, B-2700 Sint-Niklaas, Belgium

MILLIPORE CORPORATION, ANALYTICAL PRODUCT DIVISION

80 Ashby Road, PO Box 9125, Bedford, MA, 01730

Tel: (781) 275-9200 Fax: (781) 533-3110 Web site: www.millipore.com

Mfr. flow and pressure measurement and control components; precision filters, hi-performance liquid chromatography instruments.

Millipore Benelux SA/NV, Rue de la Fusee 60, B-1130 Brussels, Belgium

MINTEQ INTERNATIONAL INC.

405 Lexington Ave., 19th Fl., New York, NY, 10174-1901

Tel: (212) 878-1800 Fax: (212) 878-1952 Web site: www.mineralstech.com

Mfr./market specialty refractory and metallurgical products and application systems.

Minerals Technologies Europe N.V., Ikaros Business Park, Ikaroslaan 17, Box 27, B-1930 Zaventem, Belgium

Tel: 32-2-725-5160 Fax: 32-2-725-5226 Contact: David Rosenberg, VP Emp: 17

MOBIL CORPORATION

3225 Gallows Road, Fairfax, VA, 22037-0001

Tel: (703) 846-3000 Fax: (703) 846-4669 Web site: www.mobil.com

Petroleum and gas exploration and refining, mfr. petroleum products, chemicals and petrochemicals.

Mobil Brussels, Brussels, Belgium

MONSANTO COMPANY

800 N. Lindbergh Boulevard, St. Louis, MO, 63167

Tel: (314) 694-1000 Fax: (314) 694-7625 Web site: www.monsanto.com

Life sciences company focussing on agriculture, nutrition, pharmaceuticals, health and wellness and sustainable development.

Monsanto Co. Agricultural Group, Antwerp, Belgium

Monsanto Co. Chemical Group, Antwerp & Ghent, Belgium

Monsanto Europe NV, Antwerp Plant, Haven 627, Scheldelaan 460, 2040 Antwerp, Belgium

Tel: 32-3-568-5111 Contact: Chris Vaernewijck, Plant Mgr.

Monsanto Europe SA, BP 1, Ave. de Tervuren 270-272, B-1150 Brussels, Belgium

Monsanto Europe SA, Technical Centre, rue Laid Burniat, B-1348 Louvain-la-Neuve, Belgium

Tel: 32-10-47-1211 Contact: Colin A. Wiltshire,

MORGAN ADHESIVES COMPANY

4560 Darrow Road, Stow, OH, 44224

Tel: (330) 688-1111 Fax: (330) 688-2540

Self-adhesive print stock and emblem materials.

MACtac/Morgan Adhesives Ltd., Soigines, Belgium

MORGAN, LEWIS & BOCKIUS LLP

2000 One Logan Square, Philadelphia, PA, 19103-6993

Tel: (215) 963-5000 Fax: (215) 963-5299 Web site: www.mlb.com

International law firm.

Morgan, Lewis & Bockius LLP, 7 rue Guimard, B-1040, Brussels, Belgium

Tel: 32-2-512-5501 Fax: 32-2-512-5888 Contact: Howard M. Liebman, Mng. Ptnr. Emp: 16

MORRISON & FOERSTER

425 Market Street, San Francisco, CA, 94105

Tel: (415) 268-7000 Fax: (415) 268-7522 Web site: www.mofo.com

International law firm.

Morrison & Foerster, Ave. Moliere 262, B-1060 Brussels, Belgium

MORTON INTERNATIONAL INC.

100 North Riverside Plaza, Chicago, IL, 60606-1596

Tel: (312) 807-2000 Fax: (312) 807-3150 Web site: www.mortonintl.com

Mfr. adhesives, coatings, finishes, specialty chemicals, advanced and electronic materials, salt, airbags.

NV Morton Intl. SA, Locations in Kontich, and Kortenberg, Belgium

NV Morton Intl. SA, Chaussee de la Hulpe 130, B-1050 Brussels, Belgium

NV Morton Intl. SA, Wipstraat 5, B-2100 Brasschaat (Antwerp), Belgium

NV Morton Intl. SA, Gremelsloweg 120, B-3680 Maaseik, Belgium

MOTION PICTURE ASSN. OF AMERICA

1600 Eye Street, NW, Washington, DC, 20006

Tel: (202) 293-1966 Fax: (202) 293-7674 Web site: www.mpaa.org

Motion picture trade association.

Motion Picture Association Belgium, 6th Fl., 270-272 Ave. De Tervuren, B-1150 Brussels, Belgium

Tel: 32-2-778-2711 Fax: 32-2-778-2700 Contact: Chris Marcich

MOTOROLA, INC.

1303 East Algonquin Road, Schaumburg, IL, 60196

Tel: (847) 576-5000 Fax: (847) 538-5191 Web site: www.mot.com

Mfr. communications equipment, semiconductors and cellular phones.

Motorola NV/SA, Excelsiorlaan 89, B-1930 Zavendem (Keiberg) Belgium

Tel: 32-2-718-5411 Fax: 32-2-718-5599

MULTI GRAPHICS

431 Lakeview Court, Mt. Prospect, IL, 60056

Tel: (847) 375-1700 Fax: (847) 375-1810

Mfr./sale/service printing & print prod equipment, mailroom/bindery systems, services & supplies for graphics industry.

AM International SA/NV, Leuvensesteenweg 321, B-1932 St. Stevene-Wollwe, Zaventem, Belgium

MULTIWARE

PO Box 907, Brookfield, CT, 06874

Tel: (203) 374-8000 Fax: (203) 374-3374

Mfr. applications development software.

Dataleader NV, Rue de Bosquet 10, B-1180 Brussels, Belgium

NAI TECHNOLOGIES INC.

282 New York Ave., Huntington, NY, 11743

Tel: (516) 271-5685 Fax: (516) 385-0815 Web site: www.naitech.com

Mfr. computers & peripherals, office machines, communications equipment.

Evercom, Rue de Strasbourg 5, B-1130 Brussels, Belgium

Tel: 32-2-726-8414 Fax: 32-2-726-9225 Contact: Guy Zijlman

NATIONAL CHEMSEARCH CORPORATION

2727 Chemsearch Blvd., Irving, TX, 75061

Tel: (972) 438-0211 Fax: (972) 438-0186 Web site: www.nch.com

Commercial chemical products.

National Chemsearch Benelux SA, Rue de Bavay 109, B-1800 Vilvoorde, Belgium

NATIONAL GYPSUM COMPANY

2001 Rexford Road, Charlotte, NC, 28211

Tel: (704) 365-7300 Fax: (704) 365-7276

Building products & services.

NV Austin Belgium SA, Brussels, Belgium

NATIONAL SERVICE INDUSTRIES INC.

1420 Peachtree Street NE, Atlanta, GA, 30309

Tel: (404) 853-1000 Fax:

Mfr. lighting equipment, specialty chemicals; textile rental.

Zep Europe, Brussels, Belgium

NATIONAL STARCH & CHEMICAL COMPANY

10 Finderne Ave., Bridgewater, NJ, 08807-3300

Tel: (908) 685-5000 Fax: (908) 685-5005 Web site: www.national starch.com

Mfr. adhesives & sealants, resins & specialty chemicals, electronic materials & adhesives, food products, industry starch.

National Adhesives Corp., Brussels, Belgium

NATIONAL UTILITY SERVICE INC.

One Maynard Drive, PO Box 712, Park Ridge, NJ, 07656-0712

Tel: (201) 391-4300 Fax: (201) 391-8158

Utility rate consulting.

National Utility Service SA, Ave. Louise 221, PB 3, B-1050 Brussels, Belgium

NEAC COMPRESSOR

191 Howard Street, Franklin, PA, 16323

Tel: (814) 437-3711 Fax: (814) 432-3334

Mfr. air tools and equipment.

Chicago Pneumatic Tool Co. SA, Vuurberg 18, B-1920 Diegen-Machelen, Brussels, Belgium

NETMANAGE INC.

10725 N. De Anza Blvd., Cupertino, CA, 95014

Tel: (408) 973-7171 Fax: (408) 257-6405 Web site: www.netmanage.com

Develop/mfr. computer software applications & tools.

NetManage Benelux, Van Kerckhovenstraat 110, bus 208, 2880 Bomen, Belgium

Tel: 32-3-890-4710 Fax: 32-3-890-4714

NEW BRUNSWICK SCIENTIFIC CO., INC.

44 Talmadge Road, Box 4005, Edison, NJ, 08818-4005

Tel: (732) 287-1200 Fax: (732) 287-4222 Web site: www.nbsc.com

Mfr. research and production equipment for life sciences.

New Brunswick Scientific NV SA, Veldeke 1, B-1970 Wezembeek - Oppem, Belgium

Tel: 32-2-731-6787 Fax: 32-2-731-8130 Contact: Gerry Burgers, Gen. Mgr.

THE NEWELL COMPANY

29 E Stephenson Street, Freeport, IL, 61032-0943

Tel: (815) 963-1010 Fax: (815) 489-8212 Web site: www.newellco.com

Mfr. Hardware, housewares, and office products.

The Newell Company, Brussels, Belgium

NICOLET INSTRUMENT CORPORATION

5225 Verona Road, Madison, WI, 53711-4495

Tel: (608) 276-6100 Fax: (608) 276-6222

Mfr. infrared spectrometers and oscilloscopesand medical electro-diagnostic equipment.

Nicolet Instrument Benelux, Paul Humanslaan 105, BP 22, B-1200 Brussels, Belgium

A .C. NIELSEN COMPANY

177 Broad Street, Stamford, CT, 06901

Tel: (203) 961-3000 Fax: (203) 961-3190 Web site: www.acnielsen.com

Market research.

A.C. Nielsen Co. (Belgium) SA, Ave. des Arts 56, B-1040 Brussels, Belgium

NORDSON CORPORATION

28601 Clemens Road, Westlake, OH, 44145

Tel: (440) 892-1580 Fax: (440) 892-9507 Web site: www.nordson.com

Mfr. industry application equipment, sealants & packaging machinery.

Nordson Belgium NV, Industrieterrein Zaventem-Zuid, Hoge Wei 37, Weiveld, B-1930 Zaventem, Belgium

Tel: 32-2-720-9973 Fax: 32-2-720-7371

NORGREN

5400 S. Delaware Street, Littleton, CO, 80120-1663

Tel: (303) 794-2611 Fax: (303) 795-9487 Web site: www.norgren.com

Mfr. pneumatic filters, regulators, lubricators, valves, automation systems, dryers, push-in fittings.

IMI Norgren S.A./N.V., Rue de Trois Arbres 62, 1180 Bruxelles, Belgium

Tel: 32-2-376-6020 Fax: 32-2-376-2634

NORTHSTAR CONSULARS/PINNACLE WORLDWIDE, INC.

1201 Marquette Ave., Ste. 300, Minneapolis, MN, 55403

Tel: (612) 338-2215 Fax: (612) 338-2572 Web site: www.pinnacleww.com

Worldwide public relations organization.

Pinnacle Europe EEIG, Ave. Louise 149/34, B-1050 Brussels, Belgium

Tel: 32-2-535-9760 Fax: 32-2-535-7499

NORTON COMPANY

1 New Bond Street, Worcester, MA, 01606

Tel: (508) 795-5000 Fax: (508) 795-5741

Abrasives, drill bits, construction and safety products and plastics.

Norton Belgique SA, Allee Verte 11, B-1000 Brussels, Belgium

Norton SA/NV, Zone Industriel de Petit, Rechain, Ave. du Parc, B-4655 Chaineux, Belgium

OBJECT DESIGN INC.

25 Mall Road, Burlington, MA, 01803

Tel: (781) 674-5000 Fax: (781) 674-5010 Web site: www.odi.com

Developer of object-oriented database management systems software.

Object Design Inc., Haachtsesssteenweg 378 - 380, B-1910 Kampenhout, Belgium

Tel: 32-16-61-1016 Fax: 32-16-65-1913

OCCIDENTAL PETROLEUM CORPORATION

10889 Wilshire Blvd., Los Angeles, CA, 90024

Tel: (310) 208-8800 Fax: (310) 443-6690 Web site: www.oxy.com

Petroleum and petroleum products, chemicals, plastics.

Occidental Petroleum Belgium NV, Frankfyklei 39, B-2000 Antwerp, Belgium

OGILVY & MATHER WORLDWIDE

309 West 49th Street, New York, NY, 10019

Tel: (212) 237-4000 Fax: (212) 237-5123

Advertising, marketing, public relations & consulting firm.

HHD O&M, Brussels, Belgium

OLIN CORPORATION

501 Merritt Seven, Norwalk, CT, 06856-4500

Tel: (203) 750-3000 Fax: (203) 356-3065

Mfr. chemicals, metals, applied physics in electronics, defense & aerospace industry.

OCG Microelectric Materials NV, Keetberglaan 1A, Havennummer 1061, B-2070 Zwijndrecht, Belgium

Olin Europe SA, Excelsiorlaan 59, B-1930 Zaventem, Belgium

OSRAM SYLVANIA CHEMICALS INC.

Hawes Street, Towanda, PA, 18848

Tel: (717) 268-5000 Fax: (717) 268-5157

Chemicals.

Osram Sylvania Chemicals, Brussels, Belgium

OTIS ELEVATOR COMPANY

10 Farm Springs Road, Farmington, CT, 06032

Tel: (860) 676-6000 Fax: (860) 676-5111

Mfr. elevators and escalators.

NV Otis SA, Schepen A. Gossetlaan 17, B-1720 Dilbeek (Groot-Bijgaarden) Belgium

OWENS-CORNING FIBERGLAS CORPORATION

Fiberglas Tower, Toledo, OH, 43659

Tel: (419) 248-8000 Fax: (419) 248-6227 Web site: www.housenet.com

Mfr. insulation, building materials, glass fiber products.

European Owens-Corning Fiberglas (Belgium), Belgium

NV Owens-Corning SA, Battice, Belgium

PACCAR INTERNATIONAL

777 106th Ave. NE, Bellevue, WA, 98004

Tel: (425) 468-7400 Fax: (428) 468-8216

Heavy duty dump trucks, military vehicles.

Paccar AG, Rue St. Lambert 141, B-1200 Brussels, Belgium

PANDUIT CORPORATION

17301 Ridgeland Ave., Tinley Park, IL, 60477-0981

Tel: (708) 532-1800 Fax: (708) 532-1811

Mfr. electrical/electronic wiring components.

Panduit Belgium, Baron de Virolaan 2, B-1700 Dilbeek (Brussels), Belgium

PARAMETRIC TECHNOLOGY CORPORATION

128 Technology Drive, Waltham, MA, 02154

Tel: (781) 398-5000 Fax: (781) 398-5674 Web site: www.ptc.com

Mfr. CAD/CAM/CAE software.

Parametric Technology, Heizel Esplanade Box 40 B-1020 Brussels, Belgium

Tel: 32-2-4769648 Fax: 32-2-4769649

PARKER HANNIFIN CORPORATION

17325 Euclid Ave., Cleveland, OH, 44112

Tel: (216) 896-3000 Fax: (216) 896-4000 Web site: www.parker.com

Mfr. motion-control products.

Parker Hannifin SA/NV, Marcel Thiry Ct., Ave. Marcel Thiry 200D, B-1200 Brussels, Belgium

PENNZOIL COMPANY

700 Milam, Houston, TX, 77002

Tel: (713) 546-4000 Fax: (713) 546-6589 Web site: www.pennzoil.com

Produce/refine/market oil, natural gas, sulfur.

Duval Sales Intl. NV, Rubens Ctr. 33512 DSI B, Nationale Straat 5, B-2000 Antwerp, Belgium

THE PERKIN-ELMER CORPORATION

761 Main Ave., Norwalk, CT, 06859-0001

Tel: (203) 762-1000 Fax: (203) 762-4228 Web site: www.perkin-elmer.com

Leading supplier of systems for life science research and related applications.

Perkin-Elmer, Zaventem, Belgium

Tel: 32-2-712-5530 Fax: 32-2-725-4481

PFIZER INC.

235 East 42nd Street, New York, NY, 10017-5755

Tel: (212) 573-2323 Fax: (212) 573-7851 Web site: www.pfizer.com

Research-based, global health care company.

Cadsand Medica NV, Belgium

Pfizer European Service Center NV, Belgium

Pfizer Hospital Products (Belgium) NV, Belgium

Pfizer Research & Development Co. NV/SA (PDRCO), Belgium

Pfizer SA, Belgium

Roerig SA, Belgium

Societe Industrielle et Technique SA (INTEC), Belgium

PHARMACIA & UPJOHN

95 Corporate Drive, PO Box 6995, Bridgewater, NJ, 08807

Tel: (908) 306-4400 Fax: (908) 306-4433 Web site: www.pnu.com

Mfr. pharmaceuticals, agricultural products, industry chemicals

Pharmacia & Upjohn, Rijksweg 12, B-2870 Puurs, Belgium

PHELPS DODGE CORPORATION

2600 North Central Ave., Phoenix, AZ, 85004-3089

Tel: (602) 234-8100 Fax: (602) 234-8337

Copper, minerals, metals & spec engineered products for transportation & electrical markets.

Hudson Intl. Conductors Europe, Eeuwfeeststraat 2, B-2670 Puurs, Belgium

PHILLIPS PETROLEUM COMPANY

Phillips Building, 411 S. Keeler Ave., Bartlesville, OK, 74004

Tel: (918) 661-6600 Fax: (918) 661-7636 Web site: www.phillips66.com

Crude oil, natural gas, liquified petroleum gas, gasoline and petro-chemicals.

Phillips Petroleum Intl. Benelux SA, Steeweg op Brussels 355, B-1900 Overijse, Belgium

PITTSBURGH CORNING CORPORATION

800 Presque Isle Drive, Pittsburgh, PA, 15239-2799

Tel: (724) 327-6100 Fax: (724) 327-9501

Mfr. glass block and cellular glass insulation.

Pittsburgh Corning, Brussels, Belgium

PLIBRICO COMPANY

1800 N. Kingsbury Street, Chicago, IL, 60614

Tel: (773) 549-7014 Fax: (773) 549-0424

Refractories, engineering and construction.

Plibrico (Belgium) SA/NV, Rue Arthur Maes 65, B-1130 Brussels, Belgium

POLAROID CORPORATION

549 Technology Square, Cambridge, MA, 02139

Tel: (781) 386-2000 Fax: (781) 386-3276 Web site: www.polaroid.com

Photographic equipment & supplies, optical products.

Polaroid SA, Rue du Colonel Bourg 113, B-1140 Brussels, Belgium

PRAXAIR, INC.

39 Old Ridgebury Road, Danbury, CT, 06810-5113

Tel: (203) 837-2000 Fax: (203) 837-2450 Web site: www.praxair.com

Produces and distributes industrial and specialty gases.

Indugas N.V., Metropooldtraat 17, B-2900 Schoten, Belgium

Tel: 32-3-645-8900 Fax: 32-3-645-9086

Praxair N.V., Lammerdries 29, B-2250 Olen, Belgium

Tel: 32-1-424-7411 Fax: 32-1-422-5871

PREMARK INTERNATIONAL INC.

1717 Deerfield Road, Deerfield, IL, 60015

Tel: (847) 405-6000 Fax: (847) 405-6013 Web site: www.premarkintl.com

Mfr./sale plastic, diversified consumer & commercial products.

Dart Industries Belgium NV, Pierre Corneliskaai 35, Aalst, Belgium

PRICEWATERHOUSECOOPERS LLP

1251 Ave. of the Americas, New York, NY, 10020

Tel: (212) 596-7000 Fax: (212) 790-6620 Web site: www.pwcglobal.com

Accounting and auditing, tax and management, and human resource consulting services.

Price Waterhouse Ltd., Blvd. de la Woluwe 62, B-1200 Brussels, Belgium

Tel: 32-2-773-1211 Fax: 32-2-762-4565

Price Waterhouse Ltd., Place St. Lambert 14, B-1200 Brussels, Belgium

Tel: 32-2-773-4911 Fax: 32-2-762-5100

PROCTER & GAMBLE COMPANY

One Procter & Gamble Plaza, Cincinnati, OH, 45202

Tel: (513) 983-1100 Fax: (513) 562-4500 Web site: www.pg.com

Personal care, food, laundry, cleaning and industry products.

P&G Belgium, Temselaan 55, 1853 Strombeek-Bever, Brussels, Belgium (Location: Mechelen, Belgium.)

Tel: 32-2-456-4511 Fax: 32-2-456-4570

Procter & Gamble Benelux, Rue Philippe-le-Bon 1, B-1040 Brussels, Belgium

PROCTER & GAMBLE PHARMACEUTICALS

17 Eaton Ave., Norwich, NY, 13815-1799

Tel: (607) 335-2111 Fax: (607) 335-2798

Develop/manufacture pharmaceuticals, chemicals and health products.

Norwich Benelux SA, Rue de la Science 7, B-1040 Brussels, Belgium

PRUDENTIAL INSURANCE COMPANY OF AMERICA

751 Broad Street, Newark, NJ, 07102-3777

Tel: (973) 802-6000 Fax: (973) 802-2812 Web site: www.prudential.com

Sale of life insurance and provides financial services.

Le Rocher Compagnie de Reassurance SA, Arts Lux Bldg., Ave. des Arts 58, B-1040 Brussels, Belgium

PSDI MAXIMO

100 Crosby Drive, Bedford, MA, 01730

Tel: (781) 280-2000 Fax: (781) 280-0200 Web site: www.psdi.com

Develops, markets and provides maintenance management software systems.

PSDI Benelux NV, Kranenberg 6, 1731 Zellik, Belgium

Tel: 32-2-463-2233 Fax: 32-2-463-1706 Contact: Marcel van Velthoven, Gen. Mgr. Emp: 11

PSI NET (PERFORMANCE SYSTEMS INTERNATIONAL INC.)

510 Huntmar Park Drive, Herndon, VA, 22170

Tel: (703) 904-4100 Fax: (703) 904-4200 Web site: wwwpsi.net

Internet service provider.

PSINet Belgium S.P.R.L., 11, Ave. des Plélades, B-1200 Brussels, Belgium

Tel: 32-2-761-6500 Fax: 32-2-772-9234

PYRONICS INC.

17700 Miles Ave., Cleveland, OH, 44128

Tel: (216) 662-8800 Fax: (216) 663-8954 Web site: www.pyronics.com

Mfr. combustion equipment, gas & oil burners.

Pyronics Intl. SA, Zone Industriel de Jumet, 4-eme Rue, B-6040 Jumet, Belgium

Tel: 32-71-256-970 Fax: 32-71-256-979 Contact: Michael Debier, Mng. Dir.

THE QUAKER OATS COMPANY

Quaker Tower, 321 North Clark Street, Chicago, IL, 60610-4714

Tel: (312) 222-7111 Fax: (312) 222-8323 Web site: www.quakeroats.com

Mfr. foods and beverages.

Quaker Oats Europe Inc., 11-2 Ave. des Pleiades, B-1200 Brussels, Belgium

RADISSON HOTELS INTERNATIONAL

Carlson Pkwy., PO Box 59159, Minneapolis, MN, 55459-8204

Tel: (612) 540-5526 Fax: (612) 449-3400

Hotels and resorts.

Radisson SAS Hotel, Rue de Fosse-aux-Loups 47, B-1000 Brussels, Belgium (Location in Antwerpen)

Tel: 32-2-219-28-28 Fax: 32-2-219-6262

RALSTON PURINA COMPANY

Checkerboard Square, St. Louis, MO, 63164

Tel: (314) 982-1000 Fax: (314) 982-1211

Animal feed, cereals, food products.

Purina Protein Europe SA, Excelsionlaan 13, B-1930 Zaventem, Belgium

RAY & BERNDTSON, INC.

301 Commerce, Ste. 2300, Fort Worth, TX, 76102

Tel: (817) 334-0500 Fax: (817) 334-0779 Web site: www.prb.com

Executive search, management audit and management consulting firm.

Ray & Berndtson, Foutain Plaza Belgicastraat, 7 B-1930 Brussels, Belgium

Tel: 32-2-725-0004 Fax: 32-2-721-1004 Contact: D. Collet & F. Vaningelgem, Mng. Prtns.

RAYCHEM CORPORATION

300 Constitution Drive, Menlo Park, CA, 94025-1164

Tel: (650) 361-3333 Fax: (650) 361-2108 Web site: www.raychem.com

Develop/mfr./market materials science products for electronics, telecommunications & industry.

NV Raychem SA, Diestsesteenweg 692, B-3010 Kessel-lo, Belgium

Tel: 32-16-351-011 Fax: 32-16-351-696

RAYMOND JAMES FINANCIAL, INC.

880 Carillon Parkway, St. Petersburg, FL, 33716

Tel: (813) 573-3800 Fax: (813) 573-8244 Web site: www.rjf.com

Financial services; securities brokerage, asset management, and investment banking services.

Raymond James Benelux, 6 Ave. Lloyd George, 1000 Brussels, Belgium

Tel: 32-2-626-1060 Fax: 32-2-640-5560

RAYTHEON COMPANY

141 Spring Street, Lexington, MA, 02173

Tel: (781) 862-6600 Fax: (781) 860-2172 Web site: www.raytheon.com

Mfr. diversified electronics, appliances, aviation, energy and environmental products; publishing, industry and construction services.

Raytheon Overseas Ltd., Ave. Franklin D. Roosevelt 81, B-1050 Brussels, Belgium

READER'S DIGEST ASSOCIATION INC.

Reader's Digest Rd., Pleasantville, NY, 10570

Tel: (914) 238-1000 Fax: (914) 238-4559

Publisher of magazines and books and direct mail marketer.

Reader's Digest World Services SA, Quai du Hainaut 29, B-1080 Brussels, Belgium

RENA-WARE DISTRIBUTORS INC.

PO Box 97050, Redmond, WA, 98073

Tel: (425) 881-6171 Fax: (425) 882-7500 Web site: www.exec@renaware.com

Cookware and china.

Rena Ware Distributors SA, Rue de Brabant 62-66, B-1000 Brussels, Belgium

REVLON INC.

625 Madison Ave., New York, NY, 10022

Tel: (212) 527-4000 Fax: (212) 527-4995 Web site: www.revlon.com

Mfr. cosmetics, fragrances, toiletries and beauty care products.

Revlon SA, Ave. Michel-Ange 8, B-1040 Brussels, Belgium

REXNORD CORPORATION

4701 West Greenfield Ave., Milwaukee, WI, 53214

Tel: (414) 643-3000 Fax: (414) 643-3078

Mfr. power transmission products.

Rexnord Belgium N.V., Airport Ring Ctr., Maalbeekweg 17, B-1930 Zaventem, Belgium

RIDGE TOOL COMPANY

400 Clark Street, Elyria, OH, 44035

Tel: (440) 323-5581 Fax: (440) 329-4853 Web site: www.ridgid.com

Hand & power tools for working pipe, drain cleaning equipment, etc.

Ridge Tool Europe NV, Research Park Haasrode, 3001 Leuven, Belgium

Tel: 32-16-380-211 Fax: 32-16-381-210

RIGHT MANAGEMENT CONSULTANTS, INC.

1818 Market Street, 14th Fl., Philadelphia, PA, 19103-3614

Tel: (215) 988-1588 Fax: (215) 988-9112 Web site: www.right.com

Out placement & human resources consulting services.

Right Associates, Ave. Maurice 1, B-1050 Brussels, Belgium

Tel: 32-2-647-3120

Right Associates, Frankrijklei 107, 2000 Antwerp, Belgium

Tel: 32-2-226-3800

RIVIANA FOODS INC.

2777 Allen Parkway, Houston, TX, 77019

Tel: (713) 529-3251 Fax: (713) 529-1661

Rice & rice by-products & pet foods.

Boost Distribution CV, Oostakaai 16, PO Box 30, B-2170 Merksem, Belgium

ROBERT HALF INTERNATIONAL INC.

2884 Sand Hill Road, #200, Menlo Park, CA, 94025

Tel: (650) 234-6000 Fax: (415) 854-9735

World leader in personnel and specialized staffing services.

Robert Half Intl. Inc., Ghent, Belgium

Robert Half Intl. Inc., Charleroi, Belgium

Robert Half Intl. Inc., Fontaine Archer Van de Voorde, Ave. Louise 382, B-1050 Brussels, Belgium

Robert Half-Brussels, Ave. Louise 382, B-1050 Brussels, Belgium

ROCHESTER GAUGES INC.

PO Box 29242, Dallas, TX, 75229-0242

Tel: (972) 241-2161 Fax: (972) 620-1403

Liquid-level gauges, level switches, pressured gauges, electric panel gauges, etc.

Rochester Gauges Intl. SA, Chausse rue de Louvain 972, B-1140 Brussels, Belgium

ROCKWELL INTERNATIONAL CORPORATION

600 Anton Boulevard, Costa Mesa, CA, 92626-7147

Tel: (714) 424-4200 Fax: (714) 424-4251 Web site: www.rockwell.com

Products & service for aerospace and defense, automotive, electronics, graphics & automation industry.

Rockwell Automation European Hdqtrs. S.A./N.V., Ave. Herrmann Debroux, 46, 1160 Brussels, Belgium (Location: Diegem, Belgium.)

Tel: 32-2-663-0600 Fax: 32-2-663-0640

Rockwell Automation S.A./N.V., Control & Information Group, blvd de Souverain 68, 1170 Brussels, Belgium

Tel: 32-2-716-8411 Fax: 32-2-725-0724

ROGERS CORPORATION

One Technology Drive, PO Box 188, Rogers, CT, 06263-0188

Tel: (203) 774-9605 Fax: Web site: www.rogers-corp.com

Mfr. specialty materials including elastomers, circuit laminates and moldable composites.

Mektron NV, Afrikalaan 188, B-9000 Ghent, Belgium

Tel: 32-9-235-3611 Fax: 32-9-235-3658 Contact: Herman Van Lysebeth, Div. Mgr.

ROHM AND HAAS COMPANY

100 Independence Mall West, Philadelphia, PA, 19106

Tel: (215) 592-3000 Fax: (215) 592-3377 Web site: www.rohmhaas.com

Mfr. industrial & agricultural chemicals, plastics.

Rohm and Haas Benelux, Noorderlaan 111, B-2030 Antwerp, Belgium

Tel: 32-3-541-2880

RUBBERMAID INC.

1147 Akron Road, Wooster, OH, 44691

Tel: (330) 264-6464 Fax: (330) 287-2846 Web site: www:rubbermaid.com

Mfr. rubber and plastic resin home, commercial and industry products.

Rubbermaid Europe SA, Waterloo Office Park, Building K, 161 Dreve Richelle #34, B-1410 Waterloo, Brussels Belgium

Tel: 32-2-357-5151 Fax: 32-2-357-5161 Contact: David T. Gibbons, Pres.

RUSSELL CORPORATION

PO Box 272, Alexander City, AL, 35011

Tel: (205) 329-4000 Fax: (205) 329-5799

Mfr. athletic and leisure apparel.

Russell Intl. NV, Baron de Vironlaan 2, B-1710 Dilbeek, Brussels, Belgium

RUSSELL REYNOLDS ASSOCIATES INC.

200 Park Ave., New York, NY, 10166-0002

Tel: (212) 351-2000 Fax: (212) 370-0896 Web site: www.ressreyn.com

Executive recruiting services.

Russell Reynolds Associates Inc., Blouleard St. Michel 27, B-1040 Brussels, Belgium

Tel: 32-2-743-1220 Fax: 32-2-736-7380 Contact: Arthur Janta-Polzynski

RVSI/ACUITY/CiMatrix

5 Shawmut Road, Canton, MA, 02021

Tel: (781) 821-0830 Fax: (781) 828-8942

Mfr. bar code scanners & data collection equipment.

Computer Identics NV/SA, Veuvensesteenweg 510, Horizon Ctr., Bldg. C1, Box 14, B-1930 Zaventem, Belgium

SAMSONITE CORPORATION

11200 East 45th Ave., Denver, CO, 80239-3018

Tel: (303) 373-2000 Fax: (303) 373-6300

Mfr. luggage and leather goods.

Samsonite Europe NV, Westerring 17, B-9700 Oudenaarde, Belgium

SARA LEE CORPORATION

3 First National Plaza, Chicago, IL, 60602-4260

Tel: (312) 726-2600 Fax: (312) 558-4995

Mfr./distributor food and consumer packaged goods, intimate apparel and knitwear.

Hanes International NV, Vijfwindgatenstraat 21, B-9000 Ghent, Belgium

SAS INSTITUTE INC.

SAS Campus Drive, Cary, NC, 27513

Tel: (919) 677-8000 Fax: (919) 677-8123 Web site: www.sas.com

Mfr./distributes decision support software.

SAS Institute (Belgium) Inc., Tervuren, Belgium

Tel: 32-2-766-0700 Fax: 32-2-766-0777

SCHENKER INTERNATIONAL FORWARDERS INC.

150 Albany Ave., Freeport, NY, 11520

Tel: (516) 377-3000 Fax: (516) 377-3005 Web site: www.schenkerusa.com

Freight forwarders.

Schenker & Co NV, PO Box 706, Noorderlaan 139, Antwerpen 1931, Belgium

Tel: 32-2-751-9234 Fax: 32-2-751-9395

SCHLEGEL SYSTEMS

1555 Jefferson Road, PO Box 23197, Rochester, NY, 14692-3197

Tel: (716) 427-7200 Fax: (716) 427-7216

Mfr. engineered perimeter sealing systems for residential & commercial construction; fibers; rubber product.

NV Schlegel SA, Rochesterlaan 4, B-8470 Gistel, Belgium

SCHRADER BELLOWS DIV

257 Huddleston Ave., Cuyahoga Falls, OH, 44221

Tel: (330) 923-5202 Fax: (330) 426-3259

Mfr. pneumatic and hydraulic valves and cylinders, FRL units and accessories..

Schrader Bellows NV, Rue du Champ de la Couronne 29, B-1020 Brussels, Belgium

A .SCHULMAN INC.

3550 West Market Street, Akron, OH, 44333

Tel: (330) 666-3751 Fax: (330) 668-7204

Mfr./sale plastic resins & compounds.

NV A. Schulman Plastics SA, Pedro Colomalaan 25, Industriepark, B-2880 Bornem, Belgium

SCIENCE MANAGEMENT CORPORATION

721 US Hwy 202/206, Bridgewater, NJ, 08807-1760

Tel: (908) 722-0300 Fax: (908) 722-4150

Human/management resources, information technology, engineering & technology services.

SMC Intl. SA, Rue de Livourne 66, B-1050 Brussels, Belgium

SEALED AIR CORPORATION

Park 80 Plaza East, Saddle Brook, NJ, 07662-5291

Tel: (201) 791-7600 Fax: (201) 703-4205 Web site: www.sealedair.com

Mfr. protective and specialty packaging solutions for industrial, food and consumer products.

Sealed Air NV, Bergensesteenweg 709, B-1600 Sint Pieters Leeuw, Belgium

Tel: 32-2-360-2609 Fax: 32-2-360-3591

SEAMAN CORPORATION

1000 Venture Boulevard, Wooster, OH, 44691

Tel: (330) 262-1111 Fax: (330) 263-6950

Mfr. vinyl coated fabrics, geomembranes, roofing, pre-engineered structures.

ECC NV, Wilrijk, B-2610 Antwerp, Belgium

G.D. SEARLE & COMPANY

5200 Old Orchard Road, Skokie, IL, 60077

Tel: (847) 982-7000 Fax: (847) 470-1480 Web site: www.searlehealthnet.com

Mfr. pharmaceuticals, health care, optical products and specialty chemicals.

Continental Pharma Inc., Ave.de Tervuren 270-272, B-1150 Brussels, Belgium

Tel: 32-2-776-3611 Fax: 32-2-763-1168

SENSORMATIC ELECTRONICS CORPORATION

951 Yamato Road, Boca Raton, FL, 33431-0700

Tel: (561) 912-6000 Fax: (561) 989-7774 Web site: www.sensormatic.com

Electronic article surveillance equipment.

Senelco (Benelux) SA, Ave. du Roi Albert 177, B-1080 Brussels, Belgium

SEQUENT COMPUTER SYSTEMS INC.

15450 SW Koll Pkwy., Beaverton, OR, 97006-6063

Tel: (503) 626-5700 Fax: (503) 578-9890 Web site: www.sequent.com

Mfr. symmetric multiprocessing technology computers.

Sequent Computer Systems, Bessenveldstraat 25a, 1831 Diegem, Brussels, Belgium

Tel: 32-2-716-4805 Fax: 32-2-716-4727

THE SERVICEMASTER COMPANY

One ServiceMaster Way, Downers Grove, IL, 60515-1700

Tel: (630) 271-1300 Fax: (630) 271-2710 Web site: www.svm.com

Management service to health care, school and industry facilities; diversified residential and commercial services.

Terminix, Brussels, Belgium

SEYFARTH, SHAW, FAIRWEATHER & GERALDSON

55 East Monroe Street, Ste. 4200, Chicago, IL, 60601

Tel: (312) 346-8000 Fax: (312) 269-8869 Web site: www.seyfarth.com

International law firm

Seyfarth, Shaw, Fairweather & Geraldson, Ave. Louise 500, Box 8, 1050 Brussels, Belgium

Tel: 32-2-647-6025 Fax: 32-2-640-7071

SHAKESPEARE FISHING TACKLE GROUP

3801 Westmore Drive, Columbia, SC, 29223

Tel: (803) 754-7000 Fax: (803) 754-7342

Mfr. fishing tackle.

Noris Shakespeare SA, Rue du Parc 10, Parc Industrial, B-4430 Alleur, Belgium

SIGNODE PACKAGING SYSTEMS

3610 West Lake Ave., Glenview, IL, 60025

Tel: (847) 724-6100 Fax: (847) 657-4392

Mfr. packaging systems.

Signode Belgium/Signode Europa, E40 Business Park, Sterrebeekstraat 179, B-1930 Zaventem, Belgium

SILICON GRAPHICS INC.

2011 N. Shoreline Blvd., Mountain View, CA, 94043-1389

Tel: (650) 960-1980 Fax: (650) 961-0595 Web site: www.sgi.com

Design/mfr. special-effects computer graphic systems and software.

Silicon Graphics A, Brussels, Belgium

SKADDEN, ARPS, SLATE, MEAGHER & FLOM LLP

919 Third Ave., New York, NY, 10022

Tel: (212) 735-3000 Fax: (212) 735-2000 Web site: www.sasmf.com

American/International law practice.

Skadden, Arps, Slate, Meagher & Flom LLP, 523 Ave. Louise, Box 30, 1050, Brussels, Belgium

Tel: 32-2-648-7666 Fax: 32-2-640-3032 Contact: Barry E. Hawk, Partner

SNAP ON DIAGNOSTICS

420 Barclay Boulevard, Lincolnshire, IL, 60069

Tel: (847) 478-0700 Fax: (847) 478-7308 Web site: www.snapon.com

Mfr. auto maintenence, diagnostic & emission testing equipment.

Sun Electric (Belgium) NV, Gall Fortlei 24, B-2100 Deurne-Antwerp, Belgium

Tel: 32-14-232-611 Fax: 32-14-232-627 Contact: W.Sas, Mng. Dir.

SNAP-ON INC.

2801 80th Street, Kenosha, WI, 53141-1410

Tel: (414) 656-5200 Fax: (414) 656-5577

Mfr. automotive & industry maintenance service tools..

Snap-On Tools BV, KORE-Phase-10, Excelsiorlaan 44-46, B-1930 Zaventem, Belgium

Snap-On Tools BV, E-40 Business Park, Sterrebeekstraat 179/D/4, B-1930 Zaventem, Belgium

SONOCO PRODUCTS COMPANY

North Second Street, PO Box 160, Hartsville, SC, 29550

Tel: (803) 383-7000 Fax: (803) 383-7008 Web site: www.sonoco.com

Mfr. packaging for consumer & industrial market and recycled paperboard.

Eurocore, Zoning De Latour, B-6761 Virton, Belgium

Tel: 32-63-581986

Sonoco Europe, S.A. (IPD), Blvd du Souverain 100, Boite 3, B-1170 Brussels, Belgium

Tel: 32-2-672-4767

SOUTHWESTERN PETROLEUM CORPORATION

534 North Main, Fort Worth, TX, 76106

Tel: (817) 332-2336 Fax: (817) 877-4047

Mfr. roofing/building maintenance products and industry lubricants.

Southwestern Petroleum Europe SA, Boite Postale 3, B-2150 Oostmalle, Belgium

SPECTOR GROUP

3111 New Hyde Park Road, North Hills, NY, 11040

Tel: (516) 365-4240 Fax: (516) 365-3604

Arch and interior design services.

Spector Group/Croigny, Galerie Louise 43b, B-1050 Brussels, Belgium

SPENCER STUART & ASSOCIATES INC.

401 North Michigan Ave., Ste. 3400, Chicago, IL, 60611

Tel: (312) 822-0080 Fax: (312) 822-0116 Web site: www.spencerstuart.com

Executive recruitment firm.

Spencer Stuart & Associates Inc., Ave. e Tervueren 2, 1040 Brussels, Belgium

Tel: 32-2-732-2625 Fax: 32-2-732-1939 Contact: Peter Goossens

SPRINT INTERNATIONAL

World Headquarters, 2330 Shawnee Mission Parkway, Westwood, KS, 66205

Tel: (913) 624-3000 Fax: (913) 624-3281

Telecommunications equipment & services.

Global One (Europe), Park Atrium, rue des Colonies 11, B-1000 Brussels, Belgium

SQUIRE, SANDERS & DEMPSEY

4900 Society Center, 127 Public Square, Cleveland, OH, 44114-1304

Tel: (216) 479-8500 Fax: (216) 479-8780 Web site: www.ssd.com

International law firm.

Squire, Sanders & Dempsey, Ave. Louise, 165, Box 15, 1050 Brussels, Belgium

Tel: 322-627-1111 Fax: 322-627-1100 Contact: Brian N. Hartnett

THE ST. PAUL COMPANIES, INC.

385 Washington Street, St. Paul, MN, 55102

Tel: (612) 310-7911 Fax: (612) 310-8294 Web site: www.stpaul.com

Provides investment, insurance and reinsurance services.

Group AG, Blvd Emile Jacqmain 53, B-1000 Brussels, Belgium

STANLEY BOSTITCH INC.

815 Briggs Street, East Greenwich, RI, 02818

Tel: (401) 884-2500 Fax: (401) 885-6511

Mfr. stapling machines, stapling supplies, fastening systems & wire.

Stanley Bostitch Belgium, Kouterveldstraat 13, Diegem, Belgium

THE STANLEY WORKS

1000 Stanley Drive, PO Box 7000, New Britain, CT, 06053

Tel: (860) 225-5111 Fax: (860) 827-3987 Web site: www.stanleyworks.com

Mfr. hand tools & hardware.

Stanley Works Belgium NV, Dickstraat 9, B-9100 Lokeren, Belgium

STATE STREET BANK & TRUST COMPANY

225 Franklin Street, Boston, MA, 02101

Tel: (617) 786-3000 Fax: (617) 654-3386 Web site: www.statestreet.com

Banking & financial services.

State Street Bank & Trust Co., Rue Joseph II 36-38, B-1040 Brussels, Belgium

STIEFEL LABORATORIES INC.

255 Alhambra Circle, Ste. 1000, Coral Gables, FL, 33134

Tel: (305) 443-3807 Fax: (305) 443-3467

Mfr. pharmaceuticals, dermatological specialties.

Laboratoires Stiefel SA, 13-D Ambachtenlaan, B-3001 Leuven, Belgium

STONE CONTAINER CORPORATION

150 N. Michigan Ave., Chicago, IL, 60601-7568

Tel: (312) 346-6600 Fax: (312) 580-3486 Web site: www.stonecontainer.com

Mfr. paper and paper packaging.

Cartomills SA, Route de Douvrain 19, B-7410 Ghlin, Belgium (Location: Groot-Bijgaarden, belgium.)

STORAGE TECHNOLOGY CORPORATION

2270 S. 88th Street, Louisville, CO, 80028-0001

Tel: (303) 673-5151 Fax: (303) 673-5019

Mfr./market/service information, storage and retrieval systems.

Storage Technology (Belgium) NV/SA, Rue Hermesstraat 8A, B-1930 Zaventem, Belgium

SUNDSTRAND CORPORATION

PO Box 7003, Rockford, IL, 61125-7003

Tel: (815) 226-6000 Fax: (815) 226-2699 Web site: www.snds.com

Design/mfr. proprietary technology based components and sub-systems for aerospace industry.

Sundstrand Intl. Corp. SA, Woluwelaan, Box 1, B-1831 Diegem, Belgium

Tel: 32-2-725-4222 Fax: 32-2-725-3079

SWECO INC.

7120 New Buffington Road, PO Box 1509, Florence, KY, 41042-1509

Tel: (606) 727-5100 Fax: (606) 727-5106

Mfr. vibratory process and solids control equipment.

Sweco Europe SA, Parc Industriel, Chemin de la Ville 10, B-1400 Nivelles, Belgium

SYBASE, INC.

6475 Christie Ave., Emeryville, CA, 94608

Tel: (510) 922-3500 Fax: (510) 922-3210 Web site: www.sybase.com

Design/mfg/distribution of database management systems, software development tools, connectivity products, consulting and technical support services..

Sybase Belgium, Lozenberg 19, B-1932 Zaventem, Belgium

Tel: 32-2-716-8311 Fax: 32-2-725-6550

SYSTEM SOFTWARE ASSOCIATES INC.

500 West Madison Street, Ste. 3200, Chicago, IL, 60661

Tel: (312) 258-6000 Fax: (312) 474-7500 Web site: www.ssax.com

Mfr. computer software.

System Software Associates, Brussels, Belgium

TANDY CORPORATION

100 Throckmorton Street, Fort Worth, TX, 76102

Tel: (817) 390-3700 Fax: (817) 415-2647 Web site: www.tandy.com

Electronic & acoustic equipment.

Tandy Europe SA, Rue du Moulin a Papier 51, B-1160 Brussels, Belgium

TBWA INTERNATIONAL

180 Maiden Lane, New York, NY, 10038

Tel: (212) 804-1000 Fax: (212) 804-1200

International full service advertising agency.

TBWA, Brussels, Belgium

TEAM INC.

1019 S. Hood Street, Alvin, TX, 77511

Tel: (281) 331-6154 Fax: (281) 331-4107 Web site: www.teamindustrialservices.com

Consulting, engineering & rental services.

Team Inc. Europe B.V., Brussels, Belgium

Tel: 32-2-685-1722 Fax: 32-2-685-1723

TEKTRONIX INC.

2660 Southwest Parkway Ave., PO Box 1000, Wilsonville, OR, 97070-1000

Tel: (503) 627-7111 Fax: (503) 627-2406 Web site: www.tek.com

Mfr. test & measure, visual systems/color printing & communications/video and networking products.

Tektronix NV, Bedrijfspark Keiberg, Excelsiorlaan 3, Zaventem 1930 (Brussels), Belgium

Tel: 32-2-715-8970 Fax: 32-2-725-9953

TELXON CORPORATION

3330 W. Market Street, PO Box 5582, Akron, OH, 44334-0582

Tel: (330) 867-3700 Fax: (330) 869-2220

Develop/mfr. portable computer systems & related equipment.

Telxon Corp., Chaussee de la Hulpe 150, B-1170 Brussels, Belgium

TENNECO AUTOMOTIVE

500 North Field Drive, Lake Forest, IL, 60045

Tel: (847) 482-5241 Fax: (847) 482-5295

Automotive parts, exhaust systems, service equipment.

Monroe Belgium, Industriezone Noord/Oost, B-3800 St.Truiden, Belgium

Tel: 32-1-170-3111 Fax: 32-1-170-3306 Contact: Ronnie Leten, Mgr. Emp: 1277

Monroe Europe, Rue A. de Boeck 56, B-1140 Brussels, Belgium

TENNECO INC.

1275 King Street, Greenwich, CT, 06831

Tel: (203) 863-1000 Fax: (203) 863-1134 Web site: www.tenneco.com

Mfr. automotive products and packaging materials/containers.

Monroe Auto Equipment, Rue Auguste de Boeck 56, B-1140 Brussels, Belgium

Monroe Belgium NV, Industry Zone 1, B-3800 St. Truiden, Belgium

TENNECO PACKAGING CORPORATION OF AMERICA

1900 West Field Court, Lake Forest, IL, 60045

Tel: (847) 482-2000 Fax: (847) 482-2181 Web site: www.tenneco

Mfr. custom packaging, aluminum and plastic molded fibre, corrugated containers.

Ekco NV, Henry Fordlaan 60, B-3600 Genk, Belgium

Tenneco Packaging, Wellen, Belgium

TEXACO INC.

2000 Westchester Ave., White Plains, NY, 10650

Tel: (914) 253-4000 Fax: (914) 253-7753 Web site: www.texaco.com

Exploration/marketing crude oil, mfr. petro chemicals and products.

Texaco Belgium NV, Ave. Louise 149, B-1050 Brussels, Belgium

TEXAS INSTRUMENTS INC.

8505 Forest Lane, Dallas, TX, 75243

Tel: (214) 995-2011 Fax: (214) 995-4360 Web site: www.ti.com

Mfr. semiconductor devices, electronic electro-mechanical systems, instruments and controls.

Texas Instruments Ltd., Brussels, Belgium

THERMO ELECTRIC COMPANY

109 North Fifth Street, Saddle Brook, NJ, 07662

Tel: (201) 843-5800 Fax: (201) 843-7144

Mfr. temp/measure control products.

NV Telerex SA, Kouwenbergdreef 6, B-2230 Schilde, Belgium

THOMAS PUBLISHING COMPANY

5 Penn Plaza, New York, NY, 10007

Tel: (212) 695-0500 Fax: (212) 290-7362 Web site: www.thomaspublishing.com

Publishing magazines and directories.

IEN-Europe NV, Rue Verte 216, B-1210 Brussels, Belgium

THOMPSON AIRCRAFT TIRE CORPORATION

7775 NW 12th Street, Miami, FL, 33126

Tel: (305) 592-3530 Fax:

Retread aircraft tires, aircraft wheel and brake servicing.

Thompson Aircraft Tire Corp. Belgium SA, Route de Bavay 7230, Frameries, Belgium

TMP WORLDWIDE, INC.

1633 Broadway, 33rd Floor, New York, NY, 10019

Tel: (212) 940-3900 Fax: (212) 940-7926

#1 Yellow Pages agency & a leader in the recruitment and interactive advertising fields.

TMP Worldwide/RC&S Advertising, Woluwelaan 128, Diegem, Brussels, Belgium B-1831

THE TORO COMPANY

8111 Lyndale Ave. South, Minneapolis, MN, 55420

Tel: (612) 888-8801 Fax: (612) 887-8258

Mfr. lawn/turf maintenance products and snow removal equipment.

Toro Europe, Nijverheidsstraat 26, B-2431 Devel, Belgium

TOWERS PERRIN

335 Madison Ave., New York, NY, 10017-4605

Tel: (212) 309-3400 Fax: (212) 309-0975 Web site: www.towers.com

Management consulting services.

Towers, Perrin, Val d'Or, Gulledelle 94, B-1200 Brussels, Belgium

Tel: 32-2-775-8411 Fax: 32-2-775-8417

TRACE MOUNTAIN PRODUCTS INC.

1040 East Brokaw Road, San Jose, CA, 95131-2309

Tel: (408) 441-8040 Fax: (408) 441-3399

Mfr. diskette; tape duplication equipment.

Trace Mountain Europe, Wilrijkstraat 37-45, B-2140 Borgerhout, Belgium

TRACOR INC.

6500 Tracor Lane, Austin, TX, 78725-2000

Tel: (512) 926-2800 Fax: (512) 929-2241

Time & frequency products, gas & liquid chromatographs, engineering service, ship repair.

Olvis NV, Achterpad 13-15, B-2400 Mol, Belgium

TRANE COMPANY

3600 Pammel Creek Road, La Crosse, WI, 54601

Tel: (608) 787-2000 Fax: (608) 787-4990

Mfr./distributor/service A/C systems and equipment.

SA Trane, Ave. Tudesco 7, B-1160 Bruxelles, Belgium

TRANSAMERICA CORPORATION

600 Montgomery Street, San Francisco, CA, 94111

Tel: (415) 983-4000 Fax: (415) 983-4400 Web site: www.transamerica.com

Life insurance, leasing, and commercial lending services.

Transamerica Corporation, Antwerp, Belgium

Tel: 32-3-231-1146 Fax: 32-3-234-0623

TRAVELERS GROUP INC.

388 Greenwich Street, New York, NY, 10013

Tel: (212) 816-8000 Fax: (212) 816-8915 Web site: www.travelers.com

Provides insurance and financial services.

La Metropole Cie. Belge SA, Rue de la Loi 83-85, B-1040 Brussels, Belgium

TRICON GLOBAL RESTAURANTS INC.

1441 Gardner Lane, Louisville, KY, 40213

Tel: (502) 874-1000 Fax: (502) 874-8315 Web site: www.triconglobal.com

KFC, Taco Bell and Pizza Hut restaurant food chains.

Pizza Belgium SA, Belgium

TRUE NORTH COMMUNICATIONS INC.

101 East Erie Street, Chicago, IL, 60611

Tel: (312) 425-6000 Fax: (312) 425-6350

Holding company, advertising agency.

FCB Brussels, Gulledelle 98, 1200 Brussels, Belgium

TURNER INTERNATIONAL INDUSTRIES INC.

375 Hudson Street, New York, NY, 10014

Tel: (212) 229-6000 Fax: (212) 229-6418

General construction, construction management.

Turner Steiner Intl. SA, Ave. Louise 130A, B-1050 Brussels, Belgium

TWIN DISC INC.

1328 Racine Street, Racine, WI, 53403-1758

Tel: (414) 638-4000 Fax: (414) 638-4482 Web site: www.twindisc.com

Mfr. industry clutches, reduction gears and transmissions.

Twin Disc Intl. SA, Chaussee de Namur 54, B-1400 Nivelles, Belgium

Tel: 32-67-887-211 Fax: 32-67-887-333

TYCO INTERNATIONAL LTD.

One Tyco Park, Exeter, NH, 03833

Tel: (603) 778-9700 Fax: (603) 778-7700 Web site: www.tycoint.com

Mfr./sales fire & security systems, sprinkler systems, undersea fiber optic telecommuncations, printed circuit boards, pipe tubing and flow meters.

Keystone Valves and Controls, Tollaan, 105 A/B, B-1932 St. Stevens Woluwe, Belgium

Tel: 32-2-725-0090 Fax: 32-2-725-0734

U.S. SURGICAL CORPORATION

150 Glover Ave., Norwalk, CT, 06856

Tel: (203) 845-1000 Fax: (203) 847-0635 Web site: www.ussurg.com

Mfr./development/market surgical staplers, laparoscopic instruments and sutures.

Auto Suture Belgium BV, Belgium - All mail to U.S. address.

UNION CARBIDE CORPORATION

39 Old Ridgebury Road, Danbury, CT, 06817

Tel: (203) 794-2000 Fax: (203) 794-6269 Web site: www.unioncarbide.com

Mfr. industrial chemicals, plastics and resins.

UC Benelux NV, Atlantic House, Noorderlaan 147, B-2030 Antwerp, Belgium (Location: Vilvoorde)

UNION ELECTRIC STEEL CORPORATION

PO Box 465, Carnegie, PA, 15106

Tel: (412) 429-7655 Fax: (412) 276-1711

Mfr. forged hardened steel rolls.

Union Electric Steel NV, Albertkade 2, B-3980 Tessenderlo, Belgium

UNION SPECIAL CORPORATION

One Union Special Plaza, Huntley, IL, 60142

Tel: (847) 669-4345 Fax: (847) 669-3534 Web site: www.unionspecial.com

Mfr. sewing machines.

Union Special-Benelux NV/SA, Kazernestraat 90, B-1000 Brussels, Belgium

Tel: 32-2-513-5217 Fax: 32-2-514-2027

UNIROYAL CHEMICAL CO., INC.

World Headquarters, Benson Road, Middlebury, CT, 06749

Tel: (203) 573-2000 Fax: (203) 573-2265

Tires, tubes and other rubber products, chemicals, plastics and textiles.

Uniroyal Chemical Belgique SA, Rue Charles Lemaire 1, B-1160 Brussels, Belgium

UNISYS CORPORATION.

PO Box 500, Union Meeting Road, Blue Bell, PA, 19424

Tel: (215) 986-4011 Fax: (215) 986-6850 Web site: www.unisys.com

Mfr./marketing/servicing electronic information systems.

Unisys Belgium SA, Ave. du Bourget 20, B-1130 Brussels, Belgium

UNITED CATALYSTS INC.

1600 West Hill Street, Louisville, KY, 40210

Tel: (502) 634-7200 Fax: (502) 637-3732

Mfr. catalysts for petroleum, chemical and food industry.

Catalyst & Chemicals Europe SA, Place du Champ de Mars 2, B-1050 Brussels, Belgium

UNITED PARCEL SERVICE OF AMERICA, INC.

55 Glenlake Parkway, NE, Atlanta, GA, 30328

Tel: (404) 828-6000 Fax: (404) 828-6593 Web site: www.ups.com

International package-delivery service.

United Parcel Service Belgium NV, Woluwelaan 158, 1831 Diegem, Belgium

Tel: 32-800-12828

UPS Express Shop Brussels, Rue de Loi, Westraat 26, 1040 Brussels, Belgium

Tel: 32-2-230-4648

UNITED TECHNOLOGIES CORPORATION

United Technologies Building, Hartford, CT, 06101

Tel: (860) 728-7000 Fax: (860) 728-7979 Web site: www.utc.com

Mfr. aircraft engines, elevators, A/C, auto equipment, space and military electronic and rocket propulsion systems. Products include Pratt & Whitney, Otis elevators, Carrier heating and air conditioning and Sikorsky helicopters.

Ascenseurs Otis SA, Schepen A. Gossetlaan 17, B-1720 Dilbeek, Belgium

United Technologies Inc., Ave. Lloyd George 7, B-1050 Brussels, Belgium

UOP INC.

25 E. Algonquin Road, Des Plaines, IL, 60017

Tel: (847) 391-2000 Fax: (847) 391-2253

Diversified research, development & mfr. of industry products & systems management studies & service.

UOP Bostrom Belgium SA, Rue de l'Industrie, B-1400 Nivelles, Belgium

US WEST, INC.

7800 East Orchard Road, PO Box 6508, Englewood, CO, 80155-6508

Tel: (303) 793-6500 Fax: (303) 793-6654

Tele-communications provider; integrated communications services.

Telenet, Flanders, Brussels, Belgium

UUNET

3060 Williams Drive, Fairfax, VA, 22031-4648

Tel: (703) 206-5600 Fax: (703) 206-5601 Web site: www.worldcom.

World's largest Internet service provider; World Wide Web hosting services, security products and consulting services to businesses, professionals, and on-line service providers.

Uunet, Posthof. 3, B-2600 Antwerpen, Belgium

Tel: 32-3-285-6200 Fax: 32-3-281-4985 Contact: Lue Dierckx Emp: 60

VALENITE INC.

PO Box 9636, Madison Heights, MI, 48071-9636

Tel: (248) 589-1000 Fax: (810) 597-4820

Cemented carbide, high speed steel, ceramic & diamond cutting tool products, etc.

Valenite-Modco SARL, BP 216 Section 2, B-1180 Brussels Belgium

VALHI INC.

5430 LBJ Freeway, Ste. 1700, Dallas, TX, 75240

Tel: (972) 233-1700 Fax: (972) 375-0586

Chemicals, hardware, sugar, mining.

Kronos Europe Inc., Rue de l'Hopital 31, B-1000 Brussels, Belgium

Kronos SA/NV, Langerbruggekaai 10, B-9000 Ghent, Belgium

Kronos Worldwide Services SA/NV, Rue de l'Hopital 31, B-1000 Brussels, Belgium

VARIAN ASSOCIATES INC.

3050 Hansen Way, Palo Alto, CA, 94304-100

Tel: (650) 493-4000 Fax: (650) 424-5358 Web site: www.varian.com

Mfr. microwave tubes & devices, analytical instruments, semiconductor process & medical equipment, vacuum systems.

NV Varian Benelux SA, Excelsior 21, B-1930 Zaventem, Belgium

VF CORPORATION

1047 North Park Road, Wyomissing, PA, 19610

Tel: (610) 378-1151 Fax: (610) 378-9371 Web site: www.vfc.com

Mfr./marketing apparel including Lee and Wrangler jeans, Jansport backpacks and Healthtex.

VF Jeanswear, Dreve de Bonne Odeur, B-1160 Brussels, Belgium

VICTAULIC INTERNATIONAL

4901 Kesslersville Road, PO Box 31, Easton, PA, 18004-0031

Tel: (610) 559-3300 Fax: (610) 559-3608 Web site: www.victaulic.com

Mfr. piping products: couplings, valves, fittings, etc.

Victaulic-Europe, Industriepark Kwatrecht, Neerhonderd 37, B-9230 Wetteren, Belgium

WANG LABORATORIES INC.

600 Technology Park Drive, Billerica, MA, 01821

Tel: (508) 967-5000 Fax: (508) 967-5911

Mfr. computer information processing systems.

Wang Europe SA/NV, Ave. Louise 350, B-1050 Brussels, Belgium

WARNACO INC.

90 Park Ave., New York, NY, 10016

Tel: (212) 661-1300 Fax: (212) 687-0480 Web site: www.warnaco.com

Mfr./sales intimate apparel and men's and women's sportswear.

Warnaco, Brussels, Belgium

WARNER-LAMBERT COMPANY

201 Tabor Road, Morris Plains, NJ, 07950-2693

Tel: (973) 540-2000 Fax: (973) 540-3761 Web site: www.warner-lambert.com

Mfr. ethical and proprietary pharmaceuticals, confectionery and consumer products & pet care supplies.

Warner-Lambert Belgium, Excelsiorlaan 75-77, B-1930 Zaventem, Belgium

WATERBURY FARREL TECHNOLOGIES

60 Fieldstone Court, Cheshire, CT, 06410

Tel: (203) 272-3271 Fax: (203) 271-0487

Machine tools and metal working machinery.

Waterbury Farrel Div., J. Huysmanslaan 59, B-1660 Lot, Belgium

WATERS CORPORATION

34 Maple Street, Milford, MA, 01757

Tel: (508) 478-2000 Fax: (508) 872-1990

Mfr./distribute liquid chromatographic instruments and test and measurement equipment.

Waters Chromatography Div., Rue de la Russes 60, Raketstraat, B-1130 Brussels, Belgium

WATSON WYATT & COMPANY

6707 Democracy Blvd., Ste. 800, Bethesda, MD, 20817

Tel: (301) 581-4600 Fax: (301) 581-4937 Web site: www.watsonwyatt.com

Creates compensation and benefits programs for major corporations.

Watson Wyatt & Co., Av. Herrmann-Debroux, 52, 1160 Brussels, Belgium

Tel: 32-2-678-1550 Fax: 32-2-678-2883 Contact: Johan Heymans

WEIL, GOTSHAL & MANGES LLP

767 5th Ave., New York, NY, 10153

Tel: (212) 310-8000 Fax: (212) 310-8007 Web site: www.weil.com

International law firm.

Weil, Gotshal & Manges LLP, 81 Ave. Louise, Box 9-10, 1050 Brussels, Belgium

Tel: 32-2-543-7460 Fax: 32-2-543-7489 Contact: Steven E. Brummel, Ptnr.

WERNER INTERNATIONAL INC.

55 East 52 Street, 29th Fl., New York, NY, 10055-0002

Tel: (212) 909-1260 Fax: (212) 909-1273

Management consultants to textile and retail apparel industry.

Werner Intl., Woluwelaan 140B, B-1831 Diegem (Brussels) Belgium

WESTVACO CORPORATION

299 Park Ave., New York, NY, 10171

Tel: (212) 688-5000 Fax: (212) 318-5055 Web site: www.westvaco.com

Mfr. paper, packaging, chemicals.

Westvaco Europe SA, Ave. de Tervueren 296, B-1150 Brussels, Belgium

WEYERHAEUSER COMPANY

PO Box 2999, 33663 Weyerhaeuser Way South, Federal Way,, Tacoma, WA, 98003

Tel: (253) 924-2345 Fax: (253) 924-2685 Web site: www.weyerhaeuser.com

Wood & wood fiber products.

Weyerhaeuser Belgium SA, Rue de Praetere 214, B-1050 Brussels, Belgium

WHITE & CASE LLP

1155 Ave. of the Americas, New York, NY, 10036-2767

Tel: (212) 819-8200 Fax: (212) 354-8113 Web site: www.whitecase.com

International law firm.

White & Case LLP, 1 Place Madou, Box 34, 1210 Brussels, Belgium

Tel: 32-2-219-1620 Fax: 32-2-219-1626 Contact: Alasdair Bell

T.D. WILLIAMSON INC.

PO Box 2299, Tulsa, OK, 74101

Tel: (918) 254-9400 Fax: (918) 254-9474

Mfr. equipment/provide service for pipeline maintenance.

T.D. Williamson SA, Rue du Travail 6, B-1400 Nivelles, Belgium

WILMER, CUTLER & PICKERING

2445 M Street, N.W., Washington, DC, 20037-1420

Tel: (202) 663-6000 Fax: (202) 663-6363

International law firm.

Wilmer, Cutler & Pickering, Rue de la Roi 15, Wetstraat, B-1040 Brussels, Belgium

WINTHROP, STIMSON, PUTNAM & ROBERTS

One Battery Park Plaza, 31st Floor, New York, NY, 10004-1490

Tel: (212) 858-1000 Fax: (212) 858-1500 Web site: www.winstim.com

International law firm.

Winthrop, Stimson, Putnam & Roberts, Rue du Taciturne 42, B-1000 Brussels, Belgium

Tel: 32-2-230-1392 Fax: 32-2-230-9288

WORLD COURIER INC.

1313 Fourth Ave., New Hyde Park, NY, 11041

Tel: (516) 354-2600 Fax: (516) 354-2644

International courier service.

World Courier SA/NV, Jan Vranckystraat 6, B-3055 Neeryse, Belgium

WORLDCOM, INC.

515 East Amite Street, Jackson, MS, 39201-2701

Tel: (601) 360-8600 Fax: (601) 360-8616 Web site: www.wcom.com

Telecommunications company serving local, long distance and Internet customers domestically and internationally.

WorldCom International, Brussels, Belgium

WUNDERMAN CATO JOHNSON

675 Ave. of the Americas, New York, NY, 10010-5104

Tel: (212) 941-3000 Fax: (212) 633-0957 Web site: www.wcj.com

International advertising and marketing consulting firm.

Wunderman Cato Johnson, 1180 Brussels, Belgium

Tel: 32-2-375-6181 Fax: 32-2-372-0309 Contact: Henri Rysermans, Gen. Mgr.

WYNN OIL COMPANY

1050 West Fifth Street, Azusa, CA, 91702-9510

Tel: (626) 334-0231 Fax: (626) 334-1456 Web site: www.wynnoil.com

Mfr. of specialty chemicals, equipment and related service programs for automotive and industrial markets.

Wynn's Belgium NV, Industriepark West 46, B-9100 St. Niklaas, Belgium

Tel: 32-3-766-6020 Fax: 32-3-778-1656 Contact: Jozef van den bossche, Mng. Dir. Emp: 47

XEROX CORPORATION

800 Long Ridge Road, PO Box 1600, Stamford, CT, 06904

Tel: (203) 968-3000 Fax: (203) 968-4312 Web site: www.xerox.com

Mfr. document processing equipment, systems and supplies.

NV Rank Xerox SA, Wezembeekstraat, 5, 1930 Zaventem, Belgium

Tel: 32-2-716-6000 Fax: 32-2-716-6559

YOUNG & RUBICAM INC.

285 Madison Ave., New York, NY, 10017

Tel: (212) 210-3000 Fax: (212) 370-3796 Web site: www.yr.com

Advertising, public relations, direct marketing and sales promotion, corporate & product ID management.

Young & Rubicam SA, Dieweg 3B, B-1180 Brussels, Belgium

Belize

AON CORPORATION

123 North Wacker Drive, Chicago, IL, 60606

Tel: (312) 701-3000 Fax: (312) 701-3100 Web site: www.aon.com

Insurance brokers worldwide; underwrites accident & health insurance, specialty & professional insurance; & provides risk management consultation.

AON Worldwide / G.A. Roe & Sons (Insurance Services) Ltd., 6, Fort St., Belize City, Belize

Tel: 501-2-77493 Fax: 501-2-78617 Contact: C. Roe

BUDGET RENT A CAR CORPORATION

4225 Naperville Road, Lisle, IL, 60532

Tel: (630) 955-1900 Fax: (630) 955-7799 Web site: www.budgetrentacar.com

Car and truck rental system.

Budget Rent A Car, Psw Goldson International Airport, Belize City, Belize

Tel: 501-2-33986

CONTINENTAL AIRLINES INC.

2929 Allen Parkway, Ste. 1501, Houston, TX, 77019

Tel: (281) 834-5000 Fax: (281) 520-6329

International airline carrier.

Continental Airlines Inc., Belize City, Belize

DELOITTE TOUCHE TOHMATSU INTERNATIONAL

PO Box 820, Wilton, CT, 06897

Tel: (203) 761-3000 Fax: (203) 834-2200 Web site: www.u.s.deloitte.com or www.dtti.com

Accounting, audit, tax and management consulting services.

Deloitte & Touche, PO Box 1235, 40A Central America Blvd./Pine St., Belize City, Belize,CA

DHL WORLDWIDE EXPRESS

333 Twin Dolphin Drive, Redwood City, CA, 94065

Tel: (650) 593-7474 Fax: (650) 593-1689 Web site: www.dhl.com

Worldwide air express carrier.

DHL Worldwide Express, 38 New Rd., Belize City, Belize

Tel: 501-2-31070

DOMINION RESOURCES, INC.

901 East Byrd Street, Ste. 1700, Richmond, VA, 23219-6111

Tel: (804) 775-5700 Fax: (804) 775-5819 Web site: www.domres.com

Provides electrical power.

Dominion Resources, Belize City, Belize

FRITZ COMPANIES INC.

706 Mission Street, Ste. 900, San Francisco, CA, 94103

Tel: (415) 904-8360 Fax: (415) 904-8661 Web site: www.fritz.com

Integrated transportation, sourcing, distribution & customs brokerage services.

Fritz Companies Inc., Belize City, Belize

KPMG PEAT MARWICK LLP

Three Chestnut Ridge Road, Montvale, NJ, 07645

Tel: (201) 307-7000 Fax: (201) 930-8617 Web site: www.kpmg.com

Accounting and audit, tax and management consulting services.

KPMG Peat Marwick, Chartered Accountants, PO Box 756, 35A Regent St., Belize City, Belize

Tel: 501-2-76629 Fax: 501-2-76072 Contact: Stanley Ermeav, Sr., Partner

UNITED PARCEL SERVICE OF AMERICA, INC.

55 Glenlake Parkway, NE, Atlanta, GA, 30328

Tel: (404) 828-6000 Fax: (404) 828-6593 Web site: www.ups.com

International package-delivery service.

UPS / Trans-Express, 31 Freetown Rd., Belize City, Belize

Tel: 501-2-32929 Fax: 501-2-234482

WACKENHUT CORPORATION

4200 Wackenhut Drive, Ste. 100, Palm Beach Gardens, FL, 33410

Tel: (561) 622-5656 Fax: (561) 691-6736 Web site: www.wackenhut.com

Security systems & services.

Wackenhut Belize Ltd., PO Box 1930, #5784 Goldson, Belize City, Belize C.A.

Tel: 501-2-31419 Fax: 501-2-31683

Benin

LOUIS BERGER INTERNATIONAL INC.

100 Halsted Street, East Orange, NJ, 07019

Tel: (201) 678-1960 Fax: (201) 672-4284 Web site: www.louisberger.com

Consulting engineers, architects, economists & planners.

Louis Berger SA, PO Box 03-3057, Jericho, Cotonou, Benin

DHL WORLDWIDE EXPRESS

333 Twin Dolphin Drive, Redwood City, CA, 94065

Tel: (650) 593-7474 Fax: (650) 593-1689 Web site: www.dhl.com

Worldwide air express carrier.

DHL Worldwide Express, Lot No. 23 Patte D'Oie, 032147, Benin

Tel: 229-30-1314

ITT SHERATON CORPORATION

60 State Street, Boston, MA, 02108

Tel: (617) 367-3600 Fax: (617) 367-5676

Hotel operations.

Benin-Sheraton Hotel, Blvd de la Marina, B.P. 1901, Cotonous, Benin

UNION OIL INTERNATIONAL DIV

2141 Rosecrans Ave., El Segundo, CA, 90245

Tel: (310) 726-7600 Fax: (310) 726-7817

Petroleum products, petrochemicals..

Union Oil Co., B.P. 7600, Cotonous, Benin

XEROX CORPORATION

800 Long Ridge Road, PO Box 1600, Stamford, CT, 06904

Tel: (203) 968-3000 Fax: (203) 968-4312 Web site: www.xerox.com

Mfr. document processing equipment, systems and supplies.

Ets Kalaf Xerox, Carre 19 Ave., Monseigneur Steiniez, BP 06-2640, Cotonou, Benin

Tel: 229-315-434 Fax: 229-310-437

Bermuda

AMERICAN AIRLINES INC.

4333 Amon Carter Boulevard, Ft. Worth, TX, 76155

Tel: (817) 963-1234 Fax: (817) 967-9641 Web site: www.amrcorp.com

Air transport services.

American Airlines Inc., Queen St., Hamilton 5, Bermuda

AMERICAN INTERNATIONAL GROUP INC.

70 Pine Street, New York, NY, 10270

Tel: (212) 770-7000 Fax: (212) 509-9705 Web site: www.aig.com

Worldwide insurance and financial services.

AIU Ltd., 29 Richmond Rd., Pembroke 5, Bermuda

AON CORPORATION

123 North Wacker Drive, Chicago, IL, 60606

Tel: (312) 701-3000 Fax: (312) 701-3100 Web site: www.aon.com

Insurance brokers worldwide; underwrites accident & health insurance, specialty & professional insurance; & provides risk management consultation.

AON Group (Bermuda) Ltd., Craig Appin House 8, Wesley St., Hamilton HM 11, Bermuda

Tel: 44-1-295-2220 Fax: 44-1-296-4462 Contact: Pauline Richards

AON Insurance Managers (Bermuda) Ltd., Craig Appin House 8, Wesley St., Hamilton HM 11, Bermuda

Tel: 44-1-295-2220 Fax: 44-1-292-4910 Contact: Alan Cossar

AON Intermediaries (Bermuda) Ltd./ Aon Re (Bermuda) Ltd., Dorchester House 7, Church St., Hamilton HM 11, Bermuda

Tel: 44-1-295-0265 Fax: 44-1-292-3244 Contact: Joe Rego

ARMSTRONG WORLD INDUSTRIES INC.

PO Box 3001, 313 W. Liberty Street, Lancaster, PA, 17604-3001

Tel: (717) 397-0611 Fax: (717) 396-2787 Web site: www.armstrong.com

Mfr. & marketing interior furnishings & specialty products for bldg, auto & textile industry.

Armstrong FSC Ltd., Hamilton, Bermuda (All inquiries to U.S. address)

Liberty Commercial Services Ltd., Hamilton, Bermuda (All inquiries to U.S. address)

ARTHUR ANDERSEN & COMPANY

33 West Monroe Street, Chicago, IL, 60603

Tel: (312) 372-7100 Fax: (312) 507-0123 Web site: www.arthurandersen.com

Accounting & audit, tax & management consulting services.

Arthur Andersen & Co., Victoria Hall, 11 Victoria St. (PO Box HM 1553), Hamilton HMFX, Bermuda

Tel: 44-1-295-0001

BAUSCH & LOMB INC.

One Bausch & Lomb Place, Rochester, NY, 14604-2701

Tel: (716) 338-6000 Fax: (716) 338-6007 Web site: www.bausch.com

Mfr. vision care products & accessories & hearing aids.

Bausch & Lomb (Bermuda) Ltd., Hamilton, Bermuda

H&R BLOCK, INC.

4400 Main Street, Kansas City, MO, 64111

Tel: (816) 753-6900 Fax: (816) 753-8628 Web site: www.hrblock.com

Tax preparation services & software, financial products and services & mortgage loans.

Companion Insurance, Ltd. (Bermuda), Bermuda Commercial Bank Building, 44 Church St., Hamilton, Bermuda

CATERPILLAR INC.

100 NE Adams Street, Peoria, IL, 61629-6105

Tel: (309) 675-1000 Fax: (309) 675-1182 Web site: www.cat.com

Mfr. earth/material-handling and construction machinery and equipment and engines.

Caterpillar Insurance Co. Ltd., Hamilton, Bermuda

Depositary (Bermuda) Ltd., Hamilton, Bermuda

CIGNA CORPORATION

One Liberty Place, Philadelphia, PA, 19192

Tel: (215) 761-1000 Fax: (215) 761-5008

Insurance, invest, health care and other financial services.

Cigna Fund Managers Ltd., Victoria Hall, Victoria St., Hamilton, Bermuda

Cigna Intl. Asset Fund Ltd., Claredon House, Church St. West, Hamilton, Bermuda

Cigna Intl. Insurance Co. Ltd., Victoria Hall, Victoria St., Hamilton HM11, Bermuda

Cigna Intl. Insurance Managers Ltd., Victoria Hall, Victoria St., Hamilton HM11, Bermuda

Montgomery & Collins Intl. Ltd., Victoria Hall, Victoria St., Hamilton HM11, Bermuda

Riyad Insurance Co. Ltd., 30 Cedar Ave., Hamilton, Bermuda

THE COASTAL CORPORATION

Nine Greenway Plaza, Houston, TX, 77046-0995

Tel: (713) 877-1400 Fax: (713) 877-6752 Web site: www.coastalcorp.com

Oil refining, natural gas, related services; independent power production.

Coastal Offshore Insurance Ltd., Hamilton, Bermuda

COBE LABORATORIES INC.

1185 Oak Street, Lakewood, CO, 80215

Tel: (303) 232-6800 Fax: (303) 231-4952

Mfr. medical equipment & supplies.

Medical Intl. Ltd., Hamilton, Bermuda

CORNING INC.

One Riverfront Plaza,, Corning, NY, 14831

Tel: (607) 974-9000 Fax: (607) 974-8551 Web site: www.corning.com

Mfr. glass and specialty materials, consumer products; communications, laboratory services.

Teddington Co. Ltd., Hamilton, Bermuda

DELOITTE TOUCHE TOHMATSU INTERNATIONAL

PO Box 820, Wilton, CT, 06897

Tel: (203) 761-3000 Fax: (203) 834-2200 Web site: www.u.s.deloitte.com or www.dtti.com

Accounting, audit, tax and management consulting services.

Deloitte & Touche, PO BOX HM 1556, Corner House, Church & Parliment Sts., Hamilton HM 12, Bermuda

DELTA AIR LINES INC.

PO Box 20706, Atlanta, GA, 30320-6001

Tel: (404) 715-2600 Fax: (404) 715-5494 Web site: www.delta-air.com/index.html

Major worldwide airline; international air transport services.

Delta Air Lines Inc., Hamilton, Bermuda

DHL WORLDWIDE EXPRESS

333 Twin Dolphin Drive, Redwood City, CA, 94065

Tel: (650) 593-7474 Fax: (650) 593-1689 Web site: www.dhl.com

Worldwide air express carrier.

DHL Worldwide Express, 16 Church St., Hamilton HM11, Bermuda

Tel: 809-295-3300

DOVER CORPORATION

280 Park Ave., New York, NY, 10017-1292

Tel: (212) 922-1640 Fax: (212) 922-1656 Web site: www.dovercorporation.com

Elevator manufacturer and holding company for varied industries.

Bermuda Elevator Co., Ltd., 14 Dundonald St., PO Box HM1603, Hamilton HM09, Bermuda

Tel: 809-292-6459 Fax: 809-295-4062

ERNST & YOUNG, LLP

787 Seventh Ave., New York, NY, 10019

Tel: (212) 773-3000 Fax: (212) 773-6350 Web site: www.eyi.com

Accounting and audit, tax and management consulting services.

Ernst & Young, Reid Hall, 3 Reid St., (PO Box HM 463) Hamilton, HMBX Bermuda

Tel: 809-295-7000 Fax: 809-295-5193 Contact: Patrick L. Hackenberg

EXXON CORPORATION

225 E. John W. Carpenter Freeway, Irving, TX, 75062-2298

Tel: (972) 444-1000 Fax: (972) 444-1882 Web site: www.exxon.com

Petroleum exploration, production, refining; mfr. petroleum & chemicals products; coal & minerals.

Esso Trading Co. of Abu Dhabi, 25 Ferry Rd., St. George's GE 01, Bermuda

Exxon Financial Services Co. Ltd., 25 Ferry Rd., St. George's GE 01, Bermuda

Exxon Insurance Holdings Inc., 25 Ferry Rd., St. George's GE 01, Bermuda

Exxon Overseas Investment Corp., 25 Ferry Rd., St. George's GE 01, Bermuda

Mediterranean Standard Oil Co., 25 Ferry Rd., St. George's GE BX, Bermuda

FIDELITY INVESTMENTS

82 Devonshire Street, Boston, MA, 02109

Tel: (617) 563-7000 Fax: (617) 476-6105 Web site: www.fidelity.com

Diversified financial services company offering investment management, retirement, brokerage, and shareholder services directly to individuals and institutions and through financial intermediaries.

Fidelilty International Ltd., Pembroke Hall, 42 Crow Lane, Pembroke, HM19, Bermuda

Tel: 44-1-295-0665 Fax: 44-1-295-9373 Contact: Barry R. J. Bateman, Pres.

FOSTER WHEELER CORPORATION

Perryville Corporate Park, Clinton, NJ, 08809-4000

Tel: (908) 730-4000 Fax: (908) 730-5300

Manufacturing, engineering and construction.

York Jersey Liability Ltd., PO Box HM1826, Hamilton, Bermuda HMHX

FRANKLIN COVEY CO.

2200 W. Parkway Blvd., Salt Lake City, UT, 84119-2331

Tel: (801) 975-1776 Fax: (801) 977-1431 Web site: www.franklinquest.com

Provides productivity and time management products and seminars.

Franklin Covey Bermuda, 4 Dunscombe Rd., Warwick, Bermuda WK08, Bermuda

Tel: 441-236-0383 Fax: 441-236-0192

FRITZ COMPANIES INC.

706 Mission Street, Ste. 900, San Francisco, CA, 94103

Tel: (415) 904-8360 Fax: (415) 904-8661 Web site: www.fritz.com

Integrated transportation, sourcing, distribution & customs brokerage services.

Fritz Companies Inc., Hamilton, Bermuda

GENERAL REINSURANCE CORPORATION

695 East Main Street, Stamford, CT, 06904-2350

Tel: (203) 328-5000 Fax: (203) 328-6423 Web site: www.genre.com

Reinsurance services worldwide.

Cologne Reinsurance Company (Bermuda) Ltd., The Continental Building, Church St., PO 890, Hamilton HM DX, Bermuda

Tel: 44-1-295-8879 Fax: 44-1-295-7051 Contact: Niamh O'Riordan, Gen. Mgr.

THE GILLETTE COMPANY

Prudential Tower Building, Boston, MA, 02199

Tel: (617) 421-7000 Fax: (617) 421-7123 Web site: www.gillette.com

Develop/mfr. personal care/use products: blades & razors, toiletries, cosmetics, stationery.

Chancery Co. Ltd., Hamilton, Bermuda

HARTFORD LIFE INTERNATIONAL, LTD.

200 Hopmeadow Street, Simsbury, CT, 06070

Tel: (860) 843-8982 Fax: (860) 843-8981

Life insurance and group life sales.

The Hartford Management, Ltd., Crawford House, 50 Cedar Ave. (PO Box 2087), Hamilton, Bermuda HMHX

Tel: 44-1-295-5243 Fax: 44-1-295-4460 Contact: C. Robert Burns, Mng. Dir.

HERCULES INC

Hercules Plaza, 1313 North Market Street, Wilmington, DE, 19894-0001

Tel: (302) 594-5000 Fax: (302) 594-5400 Web site: www.herc.com

Mfr. specialty chemicals, plastics, film and fibers, coatings, resins, food ingredients.

Curtis Bay Insurance Co. Ltd., 30 Cedar Ave., PO Box HM 1179, Hamilton 5-24, Bermuda

HOLIDAY INNS WORLDWIDE, INC.

3 Ravinia Drive, Ste. 2900, Atlanta, GA, 30346-2149

Tel: (770) 604-2000 Fax: (770) 604-5403

Hotels, restaurants and casinos.

Holiday Inn, St. George, PO Box 59, Hamilton, Bermuda

HORWATH INTERNATIONAL

415 Madison Ave., New York, NY, 10017

Tel: (212) 838-5566 Fax: (212) 838-3636

Public accountants and auditors.

Arthur Morris & Co., Century House, Richmond Rd., Hamilton, Bermuda

IBM CORPORATION

New Orchard Road, Armonk, NY, 10504

Tel: (914) 765-1900 Fax: (914) 765-7382 Web site: www.ibm.com

Information products, technology & services.

WTC Insurance Corp. Ltd., Hamilton, Bermuda

INTERNATIONAL PAPER COMPANY

2 Manhattanville Road, Purchase, NY, 10577

Tel: (914) 397-1500 Fax: (914) 397-1596 Web site: www.ipaper.com

Mfr./distributor container board, paper, wood products.

Forest Insurance Ltd., Clarendon House, Church St. W, PO Box Hm 1022, Hamilton, Bermuda

J.P. MORGAN & CO. INC.

60 Wall Street, New York, NY, 10260-0060

Tel: (212) 483-2323 Fax: (212) 648-5209 Web site: www.jpm.com

International banking services.

Morgan Guaranty Finance Ltd., Crisson Bldg., Queen St., Hamilton 5, Bermuda

JOHN HANCOCK MUTUAL LIFE INSURANCE COMPANY

200 Clarendon Street, PO Box 111, Boston, MA, 02117

Tel: (617) 572-6000 Fax: (617) 572-8628 Web site: www.jhancock.com

Life insurance services.

John Hancock Insurance Co. of Bermuda Ltd., Reid House, Church St., Box HM 1826, Hamilton 5, Bermuda

K-SWISS INC.

20664 Bahama Street, Chatsworth, CA, 91311

Tel: (818) 998-3388 Fax: (818) 773-2390 Web site: www.kswiss.com

Mfr. casual and athletic shoes, socks and leisure apparel.

K-Swiss Intl. Ltd., Clarendon House, 2 Church St., Hamilton, Bermuda

KIMBERLY-CLARK CORPORATION

351 Phelps Drive, Irving, TX, 75038

Tel: (972) 281-1200 Fax: (972) 281-1435 Web site: www.kimberly-clark.com.

Mfr./sales/distribution of consumer tissue, household and personal care products.

Ridgeway Insurance Co. Ltd., Hamilton, Bermuda

KPMG PEAT MARWICK LLP

Three Chestnut Ridge Road, Montvale, NJ, 07645

Tel: (201) 307-7000 Fax: (201) 930-8617 Web site: www.kpmg.com

Accounting and audit, tax and management consulting services.

Butterfield & Steinhoff, Hamilton, Bermuda

KPMG Peat Marwick, Vallis Bldg., 58 Par-La-Ville Rd., Hamilton, HM11, Bermuda

Tel: 44-1-295-5063 Fax: 44-1-295-9132 Contact: Robert D. Steinhoff, Sr. Ptnr.

LANIER WORLDWIDE, INC.

2300 Parklake Drive, N.E., Atlanta, GA, 30345

Tel: (770) 496-9500 Fax: (770) 621-1535

Specialize in digital copiers and multi-functional systems.

Lanier Business Products Centre, PO Box PG 164, Paget PGBX, Bermuda

Tel: 44-1-295-0355 Fax: 44-1-292-4937

LIBERTY MUTUAL GROUP

175 Berkeley Street, Boston, MA, 02117

Tel: (617) 357-9500 Fax: (617) 350-7648 Web site: www.libertymutual. com

Provides workers' compensation insurance and operates physical rehabilitation centers and provides risk prevention management.

Liberty Mutual Group, Hamilton, Bermuda

MARRIOTT INTERNATIONAL INC.

1 Marriott Drive, Washington, DC, 20058

Tel: (301) 380-3000 Fax: (301) 380-5181

Lodging, contract food and beverage service, and restaurants.

Castle Harbour Marriott Resort, Tucker's Town, Bermuda

Tel: 44-1-293-2040

MARSH & McLENNAN COS INC.

1166 Ave. of the Americas, New York, NY, 10036-2774

Tel: (212) 345-5000 Fax: (212) 345-4808 Web site: www.marshmac.com

Insurance agents/brokers, pension and investment management consulting services.

J&H Marsh McLennan (Bermuda) Ltd., 11 Victoria St., Hamilton. HM HX, Bermuda

Tel: 44-1-292-4402 Fax: 44-1-292-1563 Contact: Andrew D. Carr

J&H Marsh McLennan Global Broking (Bermuda) Ltd., 8 Wesley St., PO Box HM 2444, Hamilton HM 11, Bermuda HMJX

Tel: 44-1-295-3545 Fax: 44-1-292-5731 Contact: Andrew D. Carr

J&H Marsh McLennan Management Services (Bermuda) Ltd., Craig Appin Building,Wesley St., Hamilton HM 11, Bermuda

Tel: 44-1-953-3454 Fax: 44-1-292-3796 Contact: Andrew D. Carr

MERCK & COMPANY, INC.

1 Merck Drive, Whitehouse Station, NJ, 08889

Tel: (908) 423-1000 Fax: (908) 423-2592

Pharmaceuticals, chemicals and biologicals.

Merck, Sharp & Dohme Ltd., Intl. Centre, PO Box 2000, Hamilton, Bermuda

NOBLE DRILLING CORPORATION

10370 Richmond Ave., #400, Houston, TX, 77042

Tel: (713) 974-3131 Fax: (713) 974-3181

Drilling contractor, engineering services.

Noble Drilling Intl. Ltd., Argyle House West, Cedar Ave., Hamilton, Bermuda

OCCIDENTAL PETROLEUM CORPORATION

10889 Wilshire Blvd., Los Angeles, CA, 90024

Tel: (310) 208-8800 Fax: (310) 443-6690 Web site: www.oxy.com

Petroleum and petroleum products, chemicals, plastics.

Occidental Ltd., Boyle Bldg., Church St., Hamilton, Bermuda

PEPSiCO INC.

700 Anderson Hill Road, Purchase, NY, 10577-1444

Tel: (914) 253-2000 Fax: (914) 253-2070 Web site: www.pepsico.com

Beverages and snack foods.

Anderson Hill Insurance Ltd., Bermuda

Pepsi-Cola (Bermuda) Ltd., Hamilton, Bermuda

Pepsi-Cola Intl. Ltd., Bermuda

PFIZER INC.

235 East 42nd Street, New York, NY, 10017-5755

Tel: (212) 573-2323 Fax: (212) 573-7851 Web site: www.pfizer.com

Research-based, global health care company.

The Kodiak Co. Ltd., Bermuda

PRICEWATERHOUSECOOPERS LLP

1251 Ave. of the Americas, New York, NY, 10020

Tel: (212) 596-7000 Fax: (212) 790-6620 Web site: www.pwcglobal.com

Accounting and auditing, tax and management, and human resource consulting services.

Price Waterhouse Ltd., Seven Reid St., PO Box HM 1624, Hamilton HMGX, Bermuda

Tel: 809-295-4271 Fax: 809-295-9797

REVLON INC.

625 Madison Ave., New York, NY, 10022

Tel: (212) 527-4000 Fax: (212) 527-4995 Web site: www.revlon.com

Mfr. cosmetics, fragrances, toiletries and beauty care products.

Revlon Mfr. Ltd., Hamilton, Bermuda

SONESTA INTERNATIONAL HOTELS CORPORATION

200 Clarendon Street, Boston, MA, 02166

Tel: (617) 421-5400 Fax: (617) 421-5402 Web site: www.sonesta.com

Hotels, resorts, and Nile cruises..

Sonesta Hotel Bermuda, PO Box 1070, Hamilton, Bermuda HMEX

TOWERS PERRIN

335 Madison Ave., New York, NY, 10017-4605

Tel: (212) 309-3400 Fax: (212) 309-0975 Web site: www.towers.com

Management consulting services.

Tillinghast - Towers Perrin, PO Box HM 1359, 30 Victoria St., Hamilton HM 12, Bermuda

Tel: 44-1-295-8863 Fax: 44-1-292-4237

TRUE NORTH COMMUNICATIONS INC.

101 East Erie Street, Chicago, IL, 60611

Tel: (312) 425-6000 Fax: (312) 425-6350

Holding company, advertising agency.

Aardvark Communications Ltd., DeCouto & Dunstan Bldg., 1st Fl., Victoria St., Hamilton HM HX, Bermuda

UNITED PARCEL SERVICE OF AMERICA, INC.

55 Glenlake Parkway, NE, Atlanta, GA, 30328

Tel: (404) 828-6000 Fax: (404) 828-6593 Web site: www.ups.com

International package-delivery service.

UPS / International Bonded Couriers of Bermuda, Ltd., Mechanics Building, 12 Church St., Hamilton, HM 11, Bermuda

Tel: 44-1-295-2467 Fax: 44-1-292-7422

UNUM CORPORATION

2211 Congress Street, Portland, ME, 04122

Tel: (207) 770-2211 Fax: (207) 770-4510 Web site: www.unum.com

Disability and special risk insurance.

UNUM International Ltd., Clarendon House, 2 Church St., PO Box HM 1022, Hamilton HMDX, Bermuda

Tel: 44-1-295-5950 Fax: 44-1-292-4720 Contact: Thomas G. Brown, Mng. Dir

WORLD COURIER INC.

1313 Fourth Ave., New Hyde Park, NY, 11041

Tel: (516) 354-2600 Fax: (516) 354-2644

International courier service.

World Courier Ltd., Dallas Bldg., Victoria St., Hamilton, Bermuda

Bolivia

AIR EXPRESS INTERNATIONAL CORPORATION

120 Tokeneke Road, PO Box 1231, Darien, CT, 06820

Tel: (203) 655-7900 Fax: (203) 655-5779 Web site: www.aeilogistics.com

Air freight forwarder.

Air Express Intl., c/o Remac Cargo/Deca Express, Mercado 1328, piso 4, Of. 408, La Paz, Bolivia

Tel: 591-2-365-083 Fax: 591-2-365-083

AON CORPORATION

123 North Wacker Drive, Chicago, IL, 60606

Tel: (312) 701-3000 Fax: (312) 701-3100 Web site: www.aon.com

Insurance brokers worldwide; underwrites accident & health insurance, specialty & professional insurance; & provides risk management consultation.

AON Worldwide / Kleffer & Asociados S.A., 2919, 6 de Agosta Av., La Paz, Bolivia

Tel: 591-2-433-434 Fax: 591-2-431-469 Contact: Jaime Trigo Flores

AVON PRODUCTS INC.

1345 Ave. of the Americas, New York, NY, 10105-0196

Tel: (212) 282-5000 Fax: (212) 282-6049 Web site: www.avon.com

Mfr./distributor beauty & related products, fashion jewelry, gifts & collectibles.

Productos Avon (Bolivia) Ltda., Av. Irala #452, Casilla Correo 2525, Santa Cruz, Bolivia

Tel: 5913-339-525 Fax: 591-2-339-570 Contact: Tania E. Mello, Mgr.

BAKER HUGHES INCORPORATED

3900 Essex Lane, Ste. 1200, Houston, TX, 77027

Tel: (713) 439-8600 Fax: (713) 439-8699 Web site: www.bakerhughes.com

Develop & apply technology to drill, complete & produce oil and natural gas wells; provide separation systems to petroleum, municipal, continuous process & mining industries.

Baker Hughes International Branche, Av. Grigota Esq. Av. Iberica, Santa Cruz, Bolivia

Tel: 591-33-553727 Fax: 591-33-553912

BECHTEL GROUP INC.

50 Beale Street, PO Box 3965, San Francisco, CA, 94105-1895

Tel: (415) 768-1234 Fax: (415) 768-9038 Web site: www.bechtel.com

General contractors in engineering & construction.

Bechtel International Corp., La Paz, Bolivia

LOUIS BERGER INTERNATIONAL INC.

100 Halsted Street, East Orange, NJ, 07019

Tel: (201) 678-1960 Fax: (201) 672-4284 Web site: www.louisberger.com

Consulting engineers, architects, economists & planners.

Louis Berger International Inc., Calle Capitan Ravelo, Psje. Isaac Eduardo 2654, La Paz, Bolivia

Tel: 591-33-58284 Fax: 591-33-91896

BESTFOODS, INC.

700 Sylvan Ave., International Plaza, Englewood Cliffs, NJ, 07632-9976

Tel: (201) 894-4000 Fax: (201) 894-2186 Web site: www.bestfoods.com

Consumer foods products; corn refining.

Maizena Comercial S.A., Parque Industrial Pl-11, Santa Cruz, Bolivia

Tel: 591-33-460888 Fax: 591-33-463941 Contact: Juan P. Irigoin, Mgr.

CARANA CORPORATION

4350 N. Fairfax Drive, Ste. 500, Arlington, VA, 22203

Tel: (703) 243-1700 Fax: (703) 243-0471

Foreign trade consulting.

CARANA Corp./Bolinvest, Av. Sanchez Lima 2400, Sopocachi, La Paz, Bolivia

CITICORP

399 Park Ave., New York, NY, 10043

Tel: (212) 559-1000 Fax: (212) 527-2066 Web site: www.citibank.com

International banking and financial services.

Citibank N.A., Av. Arce esq. Rosendo Gutierrez, Edif. Multicentro, La Paz, Bolivia

Tel: 591-2-430-099 Fax: 591-2-811-2894 Contact: Marcelo Cellerino, EVP

COLUMBIA PICTURES INDUSTRIES INC.

10202 West Washington Blvd., Culver City, CA, 90232

Tel: (310) 244-4000 Fax: (310) 244-2626 Web site: www.sony.com

Producer and distributor of motion pictures.

Distribuidores Asociados de Peliculas Ltda., Postosi 1007, La Paz, Bolivia

COMSAT CORPORATION

6560 Rock Spring Drive, Bethesda, MD, 20817

Tel: (301) 214-3200 Fax: (301) 214-7100 Web site: www.comsat.com

Provides global telecommunications services via satellite and develops advanced satellite networking technology.

COMSAT International, La Paz, Bolivia

CONTINENTAL CAN COMPANY

301 Merritt 7, 7 Corporate Park, Norwalk, CT, 06856

Tel: (203) 750-5900 Fax: (203) 750-5908

Packaging products and machinery, metal, plastic and paper containers.

Fabrica Boliviana de Envases SA, Casilla de Correos 1103, Cochababma, Bolivia

D'ARCY MASIUS BENTON & BOWLES INC. (DMB&B)

1675 Broadway, New York, NY, 10019

Tel: (212) 468-3622 Fax: (212) 468-2987 Web site: www.dmbb.com

Full service international advertising and communications group.

Ecco Publicidad Integral/DMB&B, Edif. Herrmann, piso 17, Casilla 335, La Paz, Bolivia

Tel: 591-2-372-746 Fax: 591-2-391-743 Contact: Maria Angelica K. de Calvo, Dir. Gen.

DELOITTE TOUCHE TOHMATSU INTERNATIONAL

PO Box 820, Wilton, CT, 06897

Tel: (203) 761-3000 Fax: (203) 834-2200 Web site: www.u.s.deloitte.com or www.dtti.com

Accounting, audit, tax and management consulting services.

Deloitte & Touche, Calle Mercado 1118, La Paz, Bolivia (Contact E.Roubik, Deloitte & Touche, Santiago, Chile

DHL WORLDWIDE EXPRESS

333 Twin Dolphin Drive, Redwood City, CA, 94065

Tel: (650) 593-7474 Fax: (650) 593-1689 Web site: www.dhl.com

Worldwide air express carrier.

DHL Worldwide Express, Av. 14 de Septiembre, Obrajes, La Paz, Bolivia

Tel: 591-2-785522

DOMINION RESOURCES, INC.

901 East Byrd Street, Ste. 1700, Richmond, VA, 23219-6111

Tel: (804) 775-5700 Fax: (804) 775-5819 Web site: www.domres.com

Provides electrical power.

Dominion Resources, LaPaz, Bolivia

EFCO

1800 NE Broadway Ave., Des Moines, IA, 50316-0386

Tel: (515) 266-1141 Fax: (515) 266-7970

Mfr. systems for concrete construction.

EFCO, Av. Espana 268, Santa Cruz de la Sierra, Bolivia

ENRON CORPORATION

1400 Smith Street, Houston, TX, 77002-7361

Tel: (713) 853-6161 Fax: (713) 853-3129 Web site: www.enron.com

Exploration, production, transportation and distribution of integrated natural gas and electricity.

Multicentro-Bloque, Edif. B., Av. Arce, esquina Rosendo Gutierrez, piso 10-Of. 1001, Bolivia

Transredes, Ave. Iberica #642, Barrio Las Palmas, Santa Cruz, Bolivia

Tel: 591-33-520008

ERNST & YOUNG, LLP

787 Seventh Ave., New York, NY, 10019

Tel: (212) 773-3000 Fax: (212) 773-6350 Web site: www.eyi.com

Accounting and audit, tax and management consulting services.

Berthin Ernst & Young, Torre B, piso 12, Calle Rosendo Gutierrez s/n y Av. Arce, Casilla No. 718, La Paz, Bolivia

Tel: 591-2-433372 Fax: 591-2-433-3105 Contact: Gonzalo Berthin

EXXON CORPORATION

225 E. John W. Carpenter Freeway, Irving, TX, 75062-2298

Tel: (972) 444-1000 Fax: (972) 444-1882 Web site: www.exxon.com

Petroleum exploration, production, refining; mfr. petroleum & chemicals products; coal & minerals.

Exxon - Exploration & Production, Bolivia

FEDERAL-MOGUL CORPORATION

26555 Northwestern Highway, PO Box 1966, Southfield, MI, 48034

Tel: (248) 354-7700 Fax: (248) 354-8983 Web site: www.federalmogul.com

Mfr./distributor precision parts for automobiles, trucks, farm and construction vehicles.

Federal-Mogul Boliviana SA, La Paz, Bolivia

FRITZ COMPANIES INC.

706 Mission Street, Ste. 900, San Francisco, CA, 94103

Tel: (415) 904-8360 Fax: (415) 904-8661 Web site: www.fritz.com

Integrated transportation, sourcing, distribution & customs brokerage services.

Fritz Companies Inc., La Paz & Santa Cruz, Bolivia

H.B. FULLER COMPANY

1200 Willow Lake Blvd., Vadnais Heights, MN, 55110

Tel: (612) 236-5900 Fax: (612) 236-5898 Web site: www.hbfuller.com

Mfr./distributor adhesives, sealants, coatings, paints, waxes, sanitation chemicals.

H.B. Fuller Bolivia, Ltda., Pje. Tejada Sorzano No. 2530, entre calles, Puerto Rico y Canada, PO Box 5629, La Paz, Bolivia

Tel: 591-2-26230 Fax: 591-2-26230

GPU INTERNATIONAL, INC.

300 Madison Ave., Morristown, NJ, 07962-1911

Tel: (973) 455-8200 Fax: (973) 455-8582 Web site: www.gpu.com

Global electric energy company.

GPU International, Santa Cruz, Sucre and Potosi, Bolivia

GREY ADVERTISING INC.

777 Third Ave., New York, NY, 10017

Tel: (212) 546-2000 Fax: (212) 546-1495 Web site: www.giworldwwide.com

International advertising agency.

Grey Bolivia, Lisimaco Gutierrez 394 Esquina Av. 20 de Octubre (Sopocachi), La Paz, Bolivia

HALLIBURTON COMPANY

500 North Akard Street, Ste. 3600, Dallas, TX, 75201-3391

Tel: (214) 978-2600 Fax: (214) 978-2685 Web site: www.halliburton.com

Energy, construction and insurance.

Halliburton Ltd., Casilla Postal 2529, Santa Cruz, Bolivia

Tel: 591-2-527167 Fax: 591-3-525418

THE HARPER GROUP

260 Townsend Street, San Francisco, CA, 94107-1719

Tel: (415) 978-0600 Fax: (415) 978-0692 Web site: www.circleintl.com

Ocean/air freight forwarding, customs brokerage, packing and wholesale, logistics management and insurance.

Circle Cargo Ltda., Av. 16 de Julio No 1490, Edif. Av., Po Box 534, La Paz, Bolivia

HOLIDAY INNS WORLDWIDE, INC.

3 Ravinia Drive, Ste. 2900, Atlanta, GA, 30346-2149

Tel: (770) 604-2000 Fax: (770) 604-5403

Hotels, restaurants and casinos.

Holiday Inn, Av. San Martin, 3 Anillo, Casilla de Correo 2966, Santa Cruz, Bolivia

IBM CORPORATION

New Orchard Road, Armonk, NY, 10504

Tel: (914) 765-1900 Fax: (914) 765-7382 Web site: www.ibm.com

Information products, technology & services.

IBM de Bolivia SA, La Paz, Bolivia

INFONET SERVICES CORPORATION

2100 East Grand Ave., El Segundo, CA, 90245

Tel: (310) 335-2600 Fax: (310) 335-4507 Web site: www.infonet.com

Provider of Internet services and electronic messaging services.

Infonet Bolivia, Av. Mariscal Santa Cruz, Edif. Hansa - piso 17 Of.8, PO Box 5755, La Paz, Bolivia

Tel: 591-2-315957 Fax: 591-2-314820

INFORMIX CORPORATION

4100 Bohannon Drive, Menlo Park, CA, 95025

Tel: (650) 926-6300 Fax: (650) 926-6593 Web site: www.informix.com

Designs & produces database management software, connectivity interfaces & gateways, and other computer applications.

Informix Software, Epsilon, av. Arce 2970, La Paz, Bolivia

Tel: 591-243-3099

J. WALTER THOMPSON COMPANY

466 Lexington Ave., New York, NY, 10017

Tel: (212) 210-7000 Fax: (212) 210-6944 Web site: www.jwt.com

International advertising and marketing services.

Fondo & Forma, La Paz, Bolivia

KPMG PEAT MARWICK LLP

Three Chestnut Ridge Road, Montvale, NJ, 07645

Tel: (201) 307-7000 Fax: (201) 930-8617 Web site: www.kpmg.com

Accounting and audit, tax and management consulting services.

KPMG Peat Marwick, Santa Cruz, Bolivia

KPMG Peat Marwick, Calle Capitán Ravelo 2131, La Pa, Bolivia

Tel: 591-2-372106 Fax: 591-2-372952 Contact: Drina Krsul, Ptnr.

KPMG Peat Marwick, Cochabamba, Bolivia

LEUCADIA NATIONAL CORPORATION

315 Park Ave. South, New York, NY, 10010

Tel: (212) 460-1900 Fax: (212) 598-4869

Holding company: real estate, banking, insurance, equipment leasing, mfr. plastics, cable, sinks & cabinets.

Cia. Boliviana de Energia Electrica SA, Plaza Venezuela, Casilla 353, La Paz, Bolivia

Empressa de Luz y Puerza Electrica de Oruro, Casilla 53, Oruro, Bolivia

THE LUBRIZOL CORPORATION

29400 Lakeland Blvd., Wickliffe, OH, 44092-2298

Tel: (440) 943-4200 Fax: (440) 943-5337 Web site: www.lubrizol.com

Mfr. chemicals additives for lubricants & fuels.

Lubrizol Bolivia, La Paz, Bolivia

MANPOWER INTERNATIONAL INC.

5301 N. Ironwood Road, PO Box 2053, Milwaukee, WI, 53201-2053

Tel: (414) 961-1000 Fax: (414) 961-7081 Web site: www.manpower

Temporary help, contract service, training & testing.

Manpower de Bolivia, Edidifio San Pablo. piso 3, Of. 305, Av. 16 de Julio, Casilla 8455, La Paz, Bolivia

Tel: 591-2-340100 Fax: 591-2-321133

McCANN-ERICKSON WORLDWIDE

750 Third Ave., New York, NY, 10017

Tel: (212) 984-3644 Fax: (212) 984-2629

International advertising/marketing services.

Nexus Comunicacion Total, La Paz, Bolivia

OCCIDENTAL PETROLEUM CORPORATION

10889 Wilshire Blvd., Los Angeles, CA, 90024

Tel: (310) 208-8800 Fax: (310) 443-6690 Web site: www.oxy.com

Petroleum and petroleum products, chemicals, plastics.

Occidental Boliviana Inc., Casilla 1296, Santa Cruz, Bolivia

PARKER DRILLING COMPANY

8 East Third Street, Tulsa, OK, 74103-3637

Tel: (918) 585-8221 Fax: (918) 585-1058

Drilling contractor.

Parker Drilling Co., Casilla 141, Santa Cruz, Bolivia

Parker Drilling Co. of Bolivia Inc., Calle Bolivar 530, piso 1, Santa Cruz, Bolivia

PARSONS TRANSPORTATION GROUP

1133 15th Street NW, Washington, DC, 20005

Tel: (202) 775-3300 Fax: (202) 775-3422

Consulting engineers.

De Leuw, Cather Intl. Ltd., Calle Otero de la Vega 552, La Paz, Bolivia

THE PERKIN-ELMER CORPORATION

761 Main Ave., Norwalk, CT, 06859-0001

Tel: (203) 762-1000 Fax: (203) 762-4228 Web site: www.perkin-elmer.com

Leading supplier of systems for life science research and related applications.

Beco International Ltda., Rosendo Gutierrez 608, piso 1, La Paz, Bolivia

Tel: 591-2-327-742 Fax: 591-2392-337 Contact: Adolf Gerke, Gen.Mgr.

PHILLIPS PETROLEUM COMPANY

Phillips Building, 411 S. Keeler Ave., Bartlesville, OK, 74004

Tel: (918) 661-6600 Fax: (918) 661-7636 Web site: www.phillips66.com

Crude oil, natural gas, liquified petroleum gas, gasoline and petro-chemicals.

Phillips Petroleum Co., Calle Tumusla 5444, Casilla 2846, Cochabamba, Bolivia

PRAXAIR, INC.

39 Old Ridgebury Road, Danbury, CT, 06810-5113

Tel: (203) 837-2000 Fax: (203) 837-2450 Web site: www.praxair.com

Produces and distributes industrial and specialty gases.

Praxair Boliva S.A., Plaza Isabel la Catolica 2498 - Murillo, La Paz, Bolivia

Tel: 591-2-34-0018 Fax: 591-2-39-1249

PRICEWATERHOUSECOOPERS LLP

1251 Ave. of the Americas, New York, NY, 10020

Tel: (212) 596-7000 Fax: (212) 790-6620 Web site: www.pwcglobal.com

Accounting and auditing, tax and management, and human resource consulting services.

Price Waterhouse Ltd./Moreno, Munoz y Cia, Calle 1 (Este) No. 9, Barrio Equipetrol, Casilla 568, Santa Cruz de la Sierra, Bolivia

Tel: 591-33-64050 Fax: 591-33-62436

Price Waterhouse Ltd./Moreno, Munoz y Cia, Av. Mariscal, Santa Cruz & Yanacocha, Edif. Hansa, POB 590, La Paz, Bolivia 591

Tel: 591-2-355027 Fax: 591-2-811-2752

TESORO PETROLEUM CORPORATION

8700 Tesoro Drive, San Antonio, TX, 78217

Tel: (210) 828-8484 Fax: (210) 828-8600

Produce/refine/distributor oil and gas.

Tesoro Bolivia Petroleum Co., Casilla 2449, Carretera Cochabamba KM 31/2, Santa Cruz, Bolivia

UNITED PARCEL SERVICE OF AMERICA, INC.

55 Glenlake Parkway, NE, Atlanta, GA, 30328

Tel: (404) 828-6000 Fax: (404) 828-6593 Web site: www.ups.com

International package-delivery service.

UPS / Jet Express Courier, Av. 16 de Julio 1479, Edif. San Pablo, piso 10, Of. 1003, La Paz, Bolivia

Tel: 591-2-327977 Fax: 591-2-393022

WACKENHUT CORPORATION

4200 Wackenhut Drive, Ste. 100, Palm Beach Gardens, FL, 33410

Tel: (561) 622-5656 Fax: (561) 691-6736 Web site: www.wackenhut.com

Security systems & services.

Wackenhut de Bolivia SA, Calle Abdon Saavedra, Esq. Rosendo Gutierrez 2310, Zona Sopocachi Casilla 11947, La Paz, Bolivia

Tel: 591-2-411313 Fax: 591-2-411323

WEATHERFORD INTERNATIONAL INC.

5 Post Oak Blvd, Ste. 1760, Houston, TX, 77227-3415

Tel: (713) 287-8400 Fax: (713) 963-9785 Web site: www.weatherford.com

Oilfield services, products & equipment; mfr. marine cranes for oil and gas industry.

Weatherford Intl. Inc., Santa Cruz, Bolivia

Tel: 591-33-532626 Fax: 591-33-534911

WESTERN ATLAS INC.

10205 Westheimer, Houston, TX, 77251-1407

Tel: (713) 972-4000 Fax: (713) 952-9837 Web site: www.waii.com

Full service to the oil industry.

Western Geophysical, Casilla de Correo 2497, Calle Colon 280, Santa Cruz, Bolivia

Tel: 591-33-34-814 Fax: 591-33-30-068 Contact: S. Gruber, Res. Mgr.

Bosnia-Herzegovina

LOUIS BERGER INTERNATIONAL INC.

100 Halsted Street, East Orange, NJ, 07019

Tel: (201) 678-1960 Fax: (201) 672-4284 Web site: www.louisberger.com

Consulting engineers, architects, economists & planners.

Louis Berger International Inc., European Commission. PHARE-OBNOVAm Vidiprivreda BiH Sarajevo, Hemlija Cemerlica 25, 71000,Sarajevo, Bosnia-Herzegovina

Tel: 38-771-61-23-66 Fax: 38-771-66-48-61

Louis Berger International Inc., Paromlinska b.b., 71000 Sarajevo, Bosnia-Herzegovina

Tel: 38-771-447-275 Fax: 38-771-447-420 Contact: George Milder

DELTA AIR LINES INC.

PO Box 20706, Atlanta, GA, 30320-6001

Tel: (404) 715-2600 Fax: (404) 715-5494 Web site: www.delta-air.com/index.html

Major worldwide airline; international air transport services.

Delta Air Lines Inc., Sarajevo, Bosnia-Herzegovina

DHL WORLDWIDE EXPRESS

333 Twin Dolphin Drive, Redwood City, CA, 94065

Tel: (650) 593-7474 Fax: (650) 593-1689 Web site: www.dhl.com

Worldwide air express carrier.

DHL Worldwide Express, Fra Andjela Zvizdovica 1, Sarajevo 71000, Bosnia-Herzegovina

Tel: 38-771-213900

IBM CORPORATION

New Orchard Road, Armonk, NY, 10504

Tel: (914) 765-1900 Fax: (914) 765-7382 Web site: www.ibm.com

Information products, technology & services.

IBM Bosnia - Herzegovina, Bosnian Business Systems (BBS), Kranjceviceva 39, 71000 Sarajevo, Bosnia-Herzegovina

Tel: 38-771-664-467 Fax: 38-771-214-269

MORRISON KNUDSEN CORPORATION

1 Morrison Knudsen Plaza, PO Box 73, Boise, ID, 83729

Tel: (208) 386-5000 Fax: (208) 386-7186 Web site: www.mk.com

Design/construction for environmental, industrial, process, power and transportation markets.

Morrison Knudsen Corporation, Sarajevo, Bosnia-Herzegovina

Botswana

AIR EXPRESS INTERNATIONAL CORPORATION

120 Tokeneke Road, PO Box 1231, Darien, CT, 06820

Tel: (203) 655-7900 Fax: (203) 655-5779 Web site: www.aeilogistics.com

Air freight forwarder.

AEI/Elliott International Pty. Ltd., United 4/B/2 Western Industrial Estate, PO Box 2044, Gaborone West, Botswana

AON CORPORATION

123 North Wacker Drive, Chicago, IL, 60606

Tel: (312) 701-3000 Fax: (312) 701-3100 Web site: www.aon.com

Insurance brokers worldwide; underwrites accident & health insurance, specialty & professional insurance; & provides risk management consultation.

Associated Insurance Brokers of Botswana (Pty.) Ltd., Charter House Phikwe Close, Selebi-Phikwe, Botswana

Tel: 267-810-910 Fax: 267-810-090 Contact: Pat Honnet

Associated Insurance Brokers of Botswana (Pty.) Ltd., 1st Fl., Autolot House Blue Jacket St., Francistown, Botswana

Tel: 267-212-191 Fax: 267-213-291 Contact: Pat Honnet

Associated Insurance Brokers of Botswana (Pty.) Ltd., 3rd Fl., Standard House, The Mall, Gaborone, Botswana

Tel: 267-351481 Fax: 367-314608 Contact: Pat Honnet

BEST WESTERN INTERNATIONAL

6201 North 24th Place, Phoenix, AZ, 85106

Tel: (602) 957-4200 Fax: (602) 957-5740

International hotel chain.

President Hotel, Botswana Rd., PO Box 200, Gaborone, Botwana

Thapama Hotel and Casino, Blue Jacket St., Francistown, Botswana

C.B. RICHARD ELLIS

533 South Fremont Ave., Los Angeles, CA, 90071-1712

Tel: (213) 613-3123 Fax: (213) 613-3535 Web site: www.cbrichardellis.com

Commercial real estate services.

CB Richard Ellis, Gaborone, Botswana

DELOITTE TOUCHE TOHMATSU INTERNATIONAL

PO Box 820, Wilton, CT, 06897

Tel: (203) 761-3000 Fax: (203) 834-2200 Web site: www.u.s.deloitte.com or www.dtti.com

Accounting, audit, tax and management consulting services.

Deloitte & Touche, Haskins St., Lot 6143, PO Box 834, Francistown, Bostwana

DHL WORLDWIDE EXPRESS

333 Twin Dolphin Drive, Redwood City, CA, 94065

Tel: (650) 593-7474 Fax: (650) 593-1689 Web site: www.dhl.com

Worldwide air express carrier.

DHL Worldwide Express, Barclays House, Khama Crescent, Gaborone, Botswana

Tel: 267-313894

ERNST & YOUNG, LLP

787 Seventh Ave., New York, NY, 10019

Tel: (212) 773-3000 Fax: (212) 773-6350 Web site: www.eyi.com

Accounting and audit, tax and management consulting services.

Ernst & Young, Finance House, Khama Crescent (PO Box 41015), Gaborone, Botswana

Tel: 267-74-078 Fax: 267-374-079 Contact: Francis Thomas

FRITZ COMPANIES INC.

706 Mission Street, Ste. 900, San Francisco, CA, 94103

Tel: (415) 904-8360 Fax: (415) 904-8661 Web site: www.fritz.com

Integrated transportation, sourcing, distribution & customs brokerage services.

Fritz Companies Inc., Botswana

GRANT THORNTON INTERNATIONAL

800 One Prudential Plaza, 130 E. Randolph Drive, Chicago, IL, 60601-6050

Tel: (312) 856-0001 Fax: (312) 616-7052

Accounting, audit, tax and management consulting services.

Acumen/Grant Thornton Intl, POB 1157, Embassy Chambers, First Fl., The Mall, Gaborone, Botswana

Tel: 267-352-313 Fax: 267-372-357 Contact: T.S. Rajaram Mohan

H.J. HEINZ COMPANY

600 Grant Street, Pittsburgh, PA, 15219

Tel: (412) 456-5700 Fax: (412) 456-6128 Web site: www.heinz.com

Processed food products and nutritional services.

H.J. Heinz (Botswana)(Pty.) Ltd., Gaborone, Botswana

Kgalagadi Soap Industries (Pty.) Ltd., Gaborone, Botswana

Refined Oil Products, Gaborone, Botswana

IBM CORPORATION

New Orchard Road, Armonk, NY, 10504

Tel: (914) 765-1900 Fax: (914) 765-7382 Web site: www.ibm.com

Information products, technology & services.

IBM Botswana, IBM Plaza, Haile Selassie Rd., Gaborone, Botswana

Tel: 267-30-1339 Fax: 267-30-1181

KPMG PEAT MARWICK LLP

Three Chestnut Ridge Road, Montvale, NJ, 07645

Tel: (201) 307-7000 Fax: (201) 930-8617 Web site: www.kpmg.com

Accounting and audit, tax and management consulting services.

KPMG, Professional House, BBS Mall, Broadhurst, Gaborone, Botswana

Tel: 267-31-2400 Fax: 267-37-5281 Contact: Tom Piper, Sr. Ptnr.

OGILVY & MATHER WORLDWIDE

309 West 49th Street, New York, NY, 10019

Tel: (212) 237-4000 Fax: (212) 237-5123

Advertising, marketing, public relations & consulting firm.

Ogilvy & Mather, Gabronne, Botswana

PRICEWATERHOUSECOOPERS LLP

1251 Ave. of the Americas, New York, NY, 10020

Tel: (212) 596-7000 Fax: (212) 790-6620 Web site: www.pwcglobal.com

Accounting and auditing, tax and management, and human resource consulting services.

Price Waterhouse Ltd., Finance House, 2nd Fl., Khama Crescent, (PO Box 1453) Gaborne, Botswana

Tel: 267-351081 Fax: 267-351668

Price Waterhouse Ltd., Stand 454/455, St.Patrick's St.,(PO Box 205) Francistown, Botswana

Tel: 267-213607 Fax: 267-212226

Price Waterhouse Ltd., Plot D18, The Mall, (PO Box 593) Maun, Botswana

Tel: 267-660506

Price Waterhouse Ltd./P-E Consulting Group, Finance House, 2nd Fl., Khama Crescent, (Private Bag 00290) Gaborne, Botswana

Tel: 267-351081 Fax: 267-351668

THE ST. PAUL COMPANIES, INC.

385 Washington Street, St. Paul, MN, 55102

Tel: (612) 310-7911 Fax: (612) 310-8294 Web site: www.stpaul.com

Provides investment, insurance and reinsurance services.

Botswana Insurance Company Ltd., Botswana Insurance House, The Main Mall, PO Box 715, Gaborone, Botswana

Tel: 267-360-0500 Fax: 267-372-867 Contact: Michael Hepburn, Chmn.

STANLEY CONSULTANTS, INC.

Stanley Building, 225 Iowa Ave., Muscatine, IA, 52761-3764

Tel: (319) 264-6600 Fax: (319) 264-6658 Web site: www.stanleygroup.com

Engineering, architectural, planning & management services.

Stanley Consultants Botswana Pty., Ltd., P/Bag 0085, Gaborone, Botswana

Tel: 267-303-441 Fax: 267-303-453

TRUE NORTH COMMUNICATIONS INC.

101 East Erie Street, Chicago, IL, 60611

Tel: (312) 425-6000 Fax: (312) 425-6350

Holding company, advertising agency.

Marketing Communications, Gaborone West, Phase 1, Plot 16739, Gaborone, Botswana

XEROX CORPORATION

800 Long Ridge Road, PO Box 1600, Stamford, CT, 06904

Tel: (203) 968-3000 Fax: (203) 968-4312 Web site: www.xerox.com

Mfr. document processing equipment, systems and supplies.

Xerotech (Pty.) Ltd., Main Mall, Botswana Rd., PB 0063, Gaborone, Botswana

Brazil

3COM CORPORATION

5400 Bayfront Plaza, Santa Clara, CA, 95052-8145

Tel: (408) 764-5000 Fax: (408) 764-5001 Web site: www.3com.com

Develop/mfr. computer networking products & systems.

3Com Do Brasil, Av. Carlos Gomes 1340 cjs., 401 e 402, Porto Alegra-RS 90480-00l, Brazil

Tel: 55-51-332-7959 Fax: 55-51-330-2917

3Com Do Brasil, Av. Engenheiro Domingos Ferreira, 2222, Salas 102/103, Empresarial Robert Gran, Boa Viagem-Recife-Pernambuco, CEP: 51021-040, Brazil

Tel: 55-81-466-1345 Fax: 55-81-465-8554

3Com Do Brasil, Av. Rio Branco, sala 1811/18° andar, Centro-Rio de Janeiro, 20090-003, Brazil

Tel: 55-21-518-1092 Fax: 55-21-518-1340

3Com Do Brasil, Rua Verbo Divino, 1661 1. Andar CJ.13, São Paulo, SP 04719-002, Brazil

Tel: 55-11-546-0869 Fax: 55-11-247-7399

3Com Do Brasil, Av. do Contorno, 5417-10° andar, Bairro Cruzeiro - Belo Horizonte, Minas Gerais - CEO 30.110-100, Brazil

Tel: 55-31-233-3180 Fax: 55-15-223-3585

3M

3M Center, St. Paul, MN, 55144-1000

Tel: (612) 733-1110 Fax: (612) 733-9973 Web site: www.mmm.com

Mfr. diversified products for industry, health care, imaging, communications, transport, safety, consumer, etc.

3M do Brasil Ltda., Via Anhanguera Km 110, 13170-970, Sumare, São Paulo, Brazil

Tel: 55-19-864-7000 Fax: 55-19-864-1206

AAF INTERNATIONAL (American Air Filter)

215 Central Ave., PO Box 35690, Louisville, KY, 40232-5690

Tel: (502) 637-0011 Fax: (502) 637-0321 Web site: www.aafintl.com

Mfr. air filtration/pollution control & noise control equipment.

AAF International, Av. Rouxinol 533/021, 04516-000 Moema, Brazil

Tel: 55-11-533-1360 Fax: 55-11-533-1360

ABBOTT LABORATORIES

One Abbott Park Road, Abbott Park, IL, 60064-3500

Tel: (847) 937-6100 Fax: (847) 937-1511 Web site: www.abbott.com

Development/mfr./sale diversified health care products & services.

Abbott Laboratories do Brazil Ltda., Rua Nova Iorque, 245, Brooklin, São Paulo, SP 04560-908 Brazil

Tel: 55-11-536-7000 Fax: 55-11-543-7063 Contact: Ramiro Zafra Emp: 1200

ACHESON COLLOIDS CO.

511 Fort Street, PO Box 611747, Port Huron, MI, 48061-1747

Tel: (810) 984-5581 Fax: (810) 984-1446

Chemicals, chemical preparations, paints & lubricating oils.

Acheson do Brazil Ltda., Rua Howard A. Acheson Jr., 279 Cotia, São Paulo, SP 06700-000, Brazil

Tel: 55-11-492-4000 Fax: 55-11-492-5433 Contact: J. Vasconcellos Emp: 58

ADYNO NOBEL

50 South Main Street, 11th Fl., Crossroads Tower, Salt Lake City, UT, 84144

Tel: (801) 364-4800 Fax: (801) 328-6525

Mfr. explosive supplies, accessories for industrial and military applications; aluminum granules.

Adyno Nobel Britanite Quimicas Ltda., Rua Brigadeiro Franco 1461, 80000 Curitiba PR, Brazil

AEROQUIP-VICKERS

3000 Strayer, PO Box 50, Maumee, OH, 43537-0050

Tel: (419) 867-2200 Fax: (419) 867-2390

Mfr. engineering components and systems for industry.

Aeroquip Vickers do Brasil, Caixa Postal 2536, 2001 Rio de Janeiro, Brazil

AIR PRODUCTS AND CHEMICALS, INC.

7201 Hamilton Boulevard, Allentown, PA, 18195-1501

Tel: (610) 481-4911 Fax: (610) 481-5900

Mfr. industry gases & related equipment, spec. chemicals, environmental/energy systems.

Air Products Gases Industriais Ltda., Praca Radialista Manoel de Nobrega 65, 02517 Casa Verde, São Paulo, SP, Brazil

Tel: 55-11-856-7999 Fax: 55-11-856-0801 Contact: Danilo Silva Costa

ALADDIN INDUSTRIES INC.

703 Murfreesboro Road, Nashville, TN, 37210

Tel: (615) 748-3000 Fax: (615) 748-3070

Mfr. vacuum insulated products, insulated food containers & servers.

M.A. Agostini S.A. (JV), Av. Automóvel Clube, 989, Rio de Janeiro, RJ 20761 Brazil

Tel: 55-21-201-5422 Fax: 55-21-241-3948 Contact: Luiz Carlos Frazão Bica, Pres. Emp: 700

ALADDIN PETROLEUM CORPORATION

221 S. Broadway, Petroleum Bldg., Wichita, KS, 67202

Tel: (316) 265-9602 Fax: (316) 265-7014

Oil exploration.

Comercial Exportadora M. Agostini, Travessa do Ouvidor 5, 7 andor, 20040 Rio de Janeiro, Brazil

ALBANY INTERNATIONAL CORPORATION

PO Box 1907, Albany, NY, 12201

Tel: (518) 445-2200 Fax: (518) 445-2265

Mfr. broadwoven & engineered fabrics, plastic products, filtration media.

Albany Internacional Filtros e Telas Indústria Ltda., Rua Colorado, 350, Indaial, SC 89130-000 Brazil

Tel: 55-47-333-1411 Fax: 55-47-333-1290 Contact: Bertil Engeh, Mg Dir Emp: 377

ALCOA (ALUMINUM CO OF AMERICA)

Alcoa Bldg., 425 Sixth Ave., Pittsburgh, PA, 15219-1850

Tel: (412) 553-4545 Fax: (412) 553-4498

World's leading producer of aluminum & alumina; mining, refining, smelting, fabricating & recycling.

Alcoa Alumínio S.A., Av. Maria Coelho Aguiar, 215, bloco C, 4o.andar, São Paulo, SP 05804-900 Brazil (Locations: Barueri, Cotia, Itapissuma, Queimados, São Caetano, Utinga, Salto, Turbarão and Valinhos Lages, Sorocaba, Pindamonhangaba and Pocos de Caldas, Brazil)

Tel: 55-11-545-4455 Fax: 55-11-545-6000 Contact: Fausto Penna Moreira Filho, Pres. Emp: 7290

Consórcio de Aluminio do Maranhão, São Luis, Brazil

ALLEGHENY TELEDYNE INC.

1000 Six PPG Place, Pittsburgh, PA, 15222

Tel: (412) 394-2800 Fax: (412) 394-2805

Diversified mfr.: aviation & electronics, specialty metals, industrial & consumer products.

Teledyne Brazil Comercio e Industria Ltda., Rua da Assembleja 10, Sala 1124, 20011-000 Rio de Janeiro, RJ, Brazil

Tel: 55-21-531-1722 Fax: 55-21-531-1277 Contact: James D. Martins, Mg. Dir. Emp: 10

ALLEN TELECOM

25101 Chagrin Boulevard, Beachwood, OH, 44122-5619

Tel: (216) 765-5818 Fax: (216) 765-0410 Web site: www.allentele.com

Mfr. communications equipment, automotive bodies and parts, electronic components.

Allen Telecom Brasil, Dias de Cruz, 445 Office 406, Meier, Rio de Janiero, 20720-012, Brazil

Tel: 55-21-595-2533 Fax: 55-21-595-4435 Contact: Carlos Machado

ALLEN-BRADLEY COMPANY, INC.

1201 South Second Street, Milwaukee, WI, 53204

Tel: (414) 382-2000 Fax: (414) 382-4444

Mfr. electrical controls & information devices.

Allen-Bradley Controles Electronicos Ltda., Rua Comendador Souza 194, Agua Branca, São Paulo, SP 05037-900 Brazil

Tel: 55-11-874-8800 Fax: 55-11-874-8970 Contact: Stanley Ribich, VP Emp: 250

ALLERGAN INC.

2525 Dupont Drive, PO Box 19534, Irvine, CA, 92713-9534

Tel: (714) 246-4500 Fax: (714) 246-6987

Mfr. therapeutic eye care products, skin & neural care pharmaceuticals.

Allergan-Lok Produtos Farmacêuticos Ltda., Av. Diederichsen, 1057, São Paulo, SP 04310-000, Brazil

Tel: 55-11-577-1799 Fax: 55-11-578-7883 Contact: Carlos Zalduondo, Gen'l Mgr Emp: 87

ALLIANCE CAPITAL MANAGEMENT L.P.

1345 Ave. of the Americas, New York, NY, 10105

Tel: (212) 969-1000 Fax: (212) 969-2229 Web site: www.alliancecapital.com

Fund manager for large organizations.

Alliance Capital Management, São Paulo, Brazil

ALLIEDSIGNAL INC.

101 Columbia Road, PO Box 2245, Morristown, NJ, 07962-2245

Tel: (973) 455-2000 Fax: (973) 455-4807 Web site: www.alliedsignal.com

Mfr. aerospace & automotive products, engineered materials.

Allied Chemical do Brasil, Av. Paulista 688, São Paulo, Brazil

AlliedSignal Aerospace Co., Rua Visconde de Piraja 430, 7-andar, Ipanema, 22410 Rio de Janeiro, Brazil

Garrett Equipamentos Ltda., Av. Julia Gaiolli 212/250, AMP da Rod. Pres. Duzra, 07210 Guarulhos, São Paulo, Brazil

Robert Bossy Freios Ltda., Rua João Felipe Zavier da Silva, 384, Campinas, SP 13001-970 Brazil , Brazil

Tel: 55-19-259-5100 Fax: 55-19-232-4644 Contact: Americo Nesti, Pres. Emp: 1691

ALLIEDSIGNAL, INC. - AUTOMOTIVE PRODUCTS GROUP

105 Pawtucket Ave., Rumford, RI, 02916-2422

Tel: (401) 434-7000 Fax: (401) 431-3670 Web site: www.alliedsignal.com

Mfr. spark plugs, filters, brakes.

Sogefi Industria do Autopecas Ltda., Av. Piraporinna 251, São Bernardo do Campo, São Paulo 09890, Brazil

Tel: 55-11-759-2400 Fax: 55-11-759-5959 Contact: Mario Milani

ALVEY INC.

9301 Olive Boulevard, St. Louis, MO, 63132

Tel: (314) 993-4700 Fax: (314) 995-2400 Web site: www.alvey.com

Mfr./sales automatic case palletizers, package & pallet conveyor systems.

PAVAX Comercial y Rep. LTDA., Rua Butanta, 461 cj 41, São Paulo 05424-140, Brazil

Tel: 55-11-813-4244 Fax: 55-11-867-8974

AMERICAN AIRLINES INC.

4333 Amon Carter Boulevard, Ft. Worth, TX, 76155

Tel: (817) 963-1234 Fax: (817) 967-9641 Web site: www.amrcorp.com

Air transport services.

American Airlines Inc., Rua Araújo, 216, 7º 9º10º andares, São Paulo, SP 01220-020 Brazil

Tel: 55-11-214-4000 Fax: 55-11-259-3470 Contact: Erli R. Rodrigues Emp: 330

AMERICAN BUREAU OF SHIPPING

2 World Trade Center, 106th Fl., New York, NY, 10048

Tel: (212) 839-5000 Fax: (212) 839-5209

Classification/certification of ships & offshore structures, development & technical assistance.

ABS America, Av. Venezuela 3, 8 andar, Rio de Janeiro, RJ 20081-310 Brazil

Tel: 55-21-253-8884 Fax: 55-21-263-4248 Contact: Jose Carlos Ferrera Emp: 50

AMERICAN EXPRESS COMPANY

American Express Tower, World Financial Center, New York, NY, 10285-4765

Tel: (212) 640-2000 Fax: (212) 619-9802 Web site: www.americanexpress.com

Travel, travelers cheques, charge card & financial services.

American Express do Brasil SA Turismo, Brazil - All inquiries to U.S. address

American Express do Brasil Servicos Internacionais Ltda., Brazil - All inquiries to U.S. address

American Express do Brasil Tempo & Cia. Inc., Av. Maria Coelho Aguiar, 215, Bloco F, 8o.andar, São Paulo, SP 05805-907 Brazil

Tel: 55-11-3741-5555 Fax: 55-11-3741-5453 Contact: Raul Rosenthal, Pres. Emp: 1250

AMERICAN GREETINGS CORPORATION

One American Road, Cleveland, OH, 44144-2398

Tel: (216) 252-7300 Fax: (216) 252-6777

Mfr./distributor greeting cards, gift wrappings, tags, seals, ribbons & party goods.

Requinte Indústrias Gráficas Ltda., Rua Budapeste, 502, São Paulo, SP 04250-000 Brazil

Tel: 55-11-947-4344 Fax: 55-11-947-4400 Contact: Salvador Ernesto P. Ronai, Chmn. Emp: 200

AMERICAN HOME PRODUCTS CORPORATION

Five Giralda Farms, Madison, NJ, 07940-0874

Tel: (973) 660-5000 Fax: (973) 660-6048 Web site: www.ahp.com

Mfr. pharmaceutical, animal health care & crop protection products.

American Home Products Corporation, Brazil

AMERICAN INTERNATIONAL GROUP INC.

70 Pine Street, New York, NY, 10270

Tel: (212) 770-7000 Fax: (212) 509-9705 Web site: www.aig.com

Worldwide insurance and financial services.

American Int'l Underwriters Representações S.A., Alameda Santos, 1787, 1o.ao 4o. andares, São Paulo, SP 01419-002 Brazil

Tel: 55-11-245-4777 Fax: 55-11-245-4700 Contact: Luiz Eduardo Pereria de Lucena, Pres. Emp: 400

AMERICAN LOCKER GROUP INC.

15 West Second Street, Jamestown, NY, 14702

Tel: (716) 664-9600 Fax: (716) 483-2822

Mfr. coin-operated locks, office furniture.

Malex do Brasil Ltda., Av. Washington Luis 4803, H, SP 04613 Brazil

Tel: 55-11-543-0488 Fax: 55-11-543-4493 Contact: Fernando Carneiro, D Emp: 30

AMERICAN OPTICAL CORPORATION

853 Camino Del Mar, Ste. 200, Del Mar, CA, 92014

Tel: (619) 509-9899 Fax: (619) 509-9898

Mfr. opthalmic lenses & frames, custom molded products, specialty lenses.

American Optical do Brasil, Rua Manoel Guedes, 504, 7o.andar, São Paulo, SP 04536-070 Brazil

Tel: 55-11-822-2455 Fax: 55-11-822-9301 Contact: Rodolfo C. Busch, Pres. Emp: 16

AMERICAN STANDARD INC.

One Centennial Ave., Piscataway, NJ, 08855-6820

Tel: (732) 980-3000 Fax: (732) 980-6118

Mfr. heating, plumbing & sanitary equipment, china, earthenware.

Ideal Standard Wabco Ind. e Com. Ltda., Via Anhanguera, Km. 106, Bloco A, Sumare, SP 13180-901 Brazil

Tel: 55-19-264-1950 Fax: 55-19-264-1719 Contact: Walter Klemens Schmidt, Mng. Dir. Emp: 360

AMERON INC.

245 South Los Robles Ave., Pasadena, CA, 91109-7007

Tel: (626) 683-4000 Fax: (626) 683-4060

Mfr. steel pipe systems, concrete products, traffic & lighting poles, protective coatings.

Amebras Indústria e Comércio Ltda.l, Rua Aurora, 983, 6o.andar, São Paulo, SP 01209-001 Brazil

Tel: 55-11-912-9655 Fax: 55-11-220-3190 Contact: Cesare Gutierrez, Pres. Emp: 35

AMMIRATI PURIS LINTAS

One Dag Hammarskjold Plaza, New York, NY, 10017

Tel: (212) 605-8000 Fax: (212) 605-4705 Web site: www.interpublic.com

International advertising agency.

Ammirati Puris Lintas Brazil, Rue Gomes de Carvalho, 1195-5º (Andar) 04547-004 São Paulo-SP, Brazil

Tel: 55-11-820-3600 Fax: 55-11-829-8821 Contact: Waltely Longo, Pres.

AMOCO CHEMICAL COMPANY

200 East Randolph Drive, Chicago, IL, 60601

Tel: (312) 856-3200 Fax: (312) 856-2460

Mfr./sale petrol based chemicals, plastics, chemicals/plastic products

Rhodiaco Industrias Quimicas Ltda., Brazil

AMOCO OIL COMPANY

200 East Randolph Drive, Chicago, IL, 60601

Tel: (312) 856-5111 Fax: (312) 856-2454

Petroleum mfr. & refining.

Amoco do Brasil Ltda., Rua Prof. Arthur Ramos, 183, 3o. andar, Sã0 Paulo, SP 01454-905 Brazil

Tel: 55-11-813-3833 Fax: 55-11-212-5126 Contact: Rubens Pelegrino, Pres. Emp: 7

AMP INC.

470 Friendship Road, PO Box 3608, Harrisburg, PA, 17105-3608

Tel: (717) 564-0100 Fax: (717) 780-6130

Develop/mfr. electronic & electrical connection products & systems.

AMP do Brazil Ltda., Rua Ado Benatti 53, CEP 05037 São Paulo, Brazil

Tel: 55-11-861-1311 Fax: 55-11-861-0397 Contact: Marco Antonio Ginciene Emp: 800

AMWAY CORPORATION

7575 Fulton Street East, Ada, MI, 49355-0001

Tel: (616) 787-6000 Fax: (616) 787-6177 Web site: www.amway.com

Mfr./sale home care, personal care, nutrition & houseware products.

Amway do Brasil Ltda., Av. Eng. Eusébio Stevaux 1257, 04696-000 São Paulo, Brazil

Tel: 55-11-548-2188 Fax: 55-11-541-9568 Contact: Danilo Saicali, Gen'l Mgr. Emp: 120

ANACOMP INC.

PO Box 509005, San Diego, CA, 92150

Tel: (619) 679-9797 Fax: (619) 748-9482

Mfr. electronic computing equipment.

Xidex do Brasil Ltda., Rua Montalverne, 1083, Jardim Piratininga, Osasco, SP 66230 Brazil Brazil

Tel: 55-11-707-5511 Fax: 55-11-707-8292 Contact: Magali Cardoso, VP

ANDERSEN CONSULTING

100 South Wacker Drive, Ste. 1059, Chicago, IL, 60606

Tel: (311) 123-7271 Fax: (312) 507-7965 Web site: www.ac.com

Provides management & technology consulting services.

Andersen Consulting, Praia de Botafogo, 300, 6º andar, 22250-040 Rio de Janeiro, RJ, Brazil

Tel: 55-21-559-9000 Fax: 55-21-551-7546

Andersen Consulting, Rua Alexandre Dumas, 2.051, 04717-004 São Paulo, SP, Brazil

Tel: 55-11-5188-3000 Fax: 55-11-5188-3200

ANDREW CORPORATION

10500 West 153rd Street, Orland Park, IL, 60462

Tel: (708) 349-3300 Fax: (708) 349-5410 Web site: www.andrew.com

Mfr. antenna systems, coaxial cable, electronic communications & network connectivity systems.

Andrew Industria e comercio Ltda., Av. Comendador Camilo Julio 1256, 18086,000 Sorocaba, SP 18105-000 Brazil

Tel: 55-15-238-4000 Fax: 55-15-238-4001 Emp: 104

ANHEUSER-BUSCH INTERNATIONAL INC.

One Busch Place, St. Louis, MO, 63118-1852

Tel: (314) 577-2000 Fax: (314) 577-2900 Web site: www.anheuser-busch.com

Malt production, aluminum beverage containers, rice milling, real estate development, metalized & paper label printing, railcar repair & theme-park facilities.

Budweiser Brasil Ltda., Brazil

AON CORPORATION

123 North Wacker Drive, Chicago, IL, 60606

Tel: (312) 701-3000 Fax: (312) 701-3100 Web site: www.aon.com

Insurance brokers worldwide; underwrites accident & health insurance, specialty & professional insurance; & provides risk management consultation.

AON Brasil Corretores de Seguros Ltda., Av. Indianopolis 1460/1500, São Paulo, Brazil

Tel: 55-11-577-1011 Fax: 55-11-5589-7904 Contact: Philip Krinker

AON Brasil Corretores de Seguros Ltda., 11, Rua do Mercado, 3 andar, Rio de Janeiro, Brazil

Tel: 55-21-262-1680 Fax: 55-21-262-6722 Contact: Peter D. Rees

AON Group Ltd., Av. Marechal Camara, Rio de Janeiro CEP 20020-080, Brazil

Tel: 55-21-220-5224 Fax: 55-21-220-5611 Contact: Gilberts R. Gama

AON Group Ltd. Brazil, 11 Rua do Mercado - 3 andar 20010 - 120 - RJ, Rio de Janeiro, Brazil

Tel: 55-21-262-1680 Fax: 55-21-262-6722 Contact: Carlos Alberto Caputo

Pilar Administradora E Corretora de Seguros S/C Ltda., São Paulo CEP 04548-050, Brazil

Tel: 55-11-822-7699 Fax: 55-11-820-8180 Contact: Joao Braga

APPLE COMPUTER INC.

One Infinite Loop, Cupertino, CA, 95014

Tel: (831) 996-1010 Fax: (831) 974-2113 Web site: www.apple.com

Personal computers, peripherals & software.

Apple Computer Brasil Ltda., Av. República do Líbano, 253, São Paulo, SP 04501-000 Brazil

Tel: 55-11-886-8010 Fax: 55-11-886-8001 Contact: Sidnei Brandão, Pres. Emp: 13

APPLIED POWER INC.

13000 W. Silver Spring Drive, Butler, WI, 53007

Tel: (414) 781-6600 Fax: (414) 781-0629

Mfr. hi-pressure tools, vibration control products, electrical tools, consumables, technical furniture & enclosures.

Power-Packer do Brasil Ltda., Rua Barao de Malgaco, 148 Real Parque, 05684 Morumbi São Paulo, Brazil

ARBOR ACRES FARM INC.

439 Marlborough Road, Glastonbury, CT, 06033

Tel: (860) 633-4681 Fax: (860) 633-2433

Producers of male & female broiler breeders, commercial egg layers.

Arbor Acres SA, Caixa Postal 400, 13500 Rio Claro, SP, Brazil

ARCHER-DANIELS-MIDLAND COMPANY

4666 Faries Parkway, Decatur, IL, 62526

Tel: (217) 424-5200 Fax: (217) 424-6196 Web site: www.admworld.com

Grain processing: flours, grains, oils & flax fibre.

Sadia Concordia SA Industria e Comercio, Brazil

ATLANTIC RICHFIELD COMPANY (ARCO)

515 South Flower Street, Los Angeles, CA, 90071-2256

Tel: (213) 486-3511 Fax: (213) 486-2063 Web site: www.arco.com

Petroleum & natural gas, chemicals & service stations.

AM PM Comestiveis Ltda., Praia do Flamengo 66, 22210 Rio de Janeiro, Brazil

ARCO CHEMICAL COMPANY

3801 West Chester Pike, Newtown Square, PA, 19073-2387

Tel: (610) 359-2000 Fax: (610) 359-2722 Web site: www.arcochem.com

Mfr. propylene oxide, a chemical used for flexible foam products, coatings/paints & solvents/inks.

ARCO Quimica do Brasil/SGS do Brasil S.A., Av. Vereador Alfredo das Neves 480, CEP 11095-510, Alemoa, Santos, Brazil

Tel: 55-13-230-3715

ARCO Quimica do Brazil Ltda., Av. Roque Petroni Jr., 999 cj 123, São Paulo, SP 04708-000, Brazil

Tel: 55-11-535-5673 Fax: 55-11-535-3321

ARO INTERNATIONAL CORPORATION

One Aro Center, Bryan, OH, 43506

Tel: (419) 636-4242 Fax: (419) 633-1674

Mfr. cylinders, valves & pumps.

Industria e Comercio Aro do Brazil Ltda., Av. Tiradentes 1525, 01102 São Paulo, Brazil

ARTHUR ANDERSEN & COMPANY

33 West Monroe Street, Chicago, IL, 60603

Tel: (312) 372-7100 Fax: (312) 507-0123 Web site: www.arthurandersen.com

Accounting & audit, tax & management consulting services.

Andersen Consulting S/C Ltda., **Rua Alexandre Dumas,1981, Praia de Botafogo, 300, 7§ andar, 22259-040 Rio de Janeiro, RJ Brazil (Location: São Paulo, SP, Brazil)**

Tel: 55-11-524-2444 Fax: 55-11-524-2747 Contact: Mario Fleck Emp: 850

Arthur Andersen S/C - Branco Advogados Associados, **Praia de Botafoga, 300-7§ andar, Caixa Postal 1/4, 20000-970, Rio de Janeiro, RJ, Brazil**

Tel: 55-21-559-4141

Arthur Andersen S/C - Branco Advogados Associados, **Rua Alexandre Dumas, 1981, Caixa Postal 1266, 01051-970, São Paulo - SP, Brazil (Locations: Salvador, BA; Belo Horozonte, MG; Campinas-SP; Porto Alegre-RS;Curitiba-PR; Ribeirao Preto SP, Brazil.)**

Tel: 55-11-524-2444

ASHLAND OIL INC.

1000 Ashland Drive, Russell, KY, 41169

Tel: (606) 329-3333 Fax: (606) 329-5274 Web site: www.ashland.com

Petroleum exploration, refining & transportation; mfr. chemicals, oils & lubricants.

Ashland Resinas Sinteticas Ltda., **Caixa Postal 1838, 13000 Campinas, SP, Brazil**

Tel: 55-19-240-1323 Fax: 55-19-240-2020 Contact: Ray Yeats, Gen'l Dir.

ASSOCIATED METALS & MINERALS CORPORATION

3 North Corporate Park Drive, White Plains, NY, 10604

Tel: (914) 251-5400 Fax: (914) 251-1073

Metals & ores.

Sociedade Comercio de Minerios e Metais Metalora Ltda., **Caixa Postal 3758, 20000 Rio de Janeiro, RJ, Brazil**

ASSOCIATED PRESS INC.

50 Rockefeller Plaza, New York, NY, 10020-1605

Tel: (212) 621-1500 Fax: (212) 621-5447 Web site: www.ap.com

News gathering agency.

Associated Press, **Av. Brasil, 500 sala 607, Rio de Janeiro, RJ 20940-070 Brazil**

Tel: 55-21-580-4442 Fax: 55-21-580-2309 Contact: Arnold Olmar Emp: 7

AT&T CORPORATION

32 Ave. of the Americas, New York, NY, 10013-2412

Tel: (212) 387-5400 Fax: (908) 221-1211 Web site: www.att.com

Telecommunications

AT&T Brasil Ltda., **Rua Lauro Muller, 116, grupo 3102, Botafogo, Rio de Janeiro, RJ 22290-160 Brazil**

Tel: 55-21-541-4944 Fax: 55-21-541-4697 Contact: Omar Carneiro de Cunha Emp: 400

ATLANTIC VENEER CORPORATION

PO Box 660, Beaufort, NC, 28516-0660

Tel: (252) 728-3169 Fax: (252) 728-4906

Wood veneer & plywood mill.

Atlantic Veneer do Brasil SA, **Caixa Postal 1115, 29000 Vitoria, ES, Brazil**

Carolina Industria e Comercio de Madeiras Tropicais Ltda, **Caixa Postal 86, 69100 Itacoatiara, Brazil**

Mato Grosso Madereira Industrial Ltda., **Av. Gov. Julio Jose Campos 5573, Varzea Grande, Mato Grosso, Brazil**

THE AUSTIN COMPANY

3650 Mayfield Road, Cleveland, OH, 44121

Tel: (216) 382-6600 Fax: (216) 291-6684

Consulting, design, engineering & construction.

Austin Brazil Projetos e Construções S.A., **Av. Paulista, 1439, 12o. andar, São Paulo, SP 01311-926 Brazil**

Tel: 55-11-285-0133 Fax: 55-11-289-3128 Contact: Marcelo Moreira Cesar, Dir. Emp: 450

AUTODESK INC.

111 McInnis Parkway, San Rafael, CA, 94903

Tel: (415) 507-5000 Fax: (415) 507-6112 Web site: www.autodesk.com

Develop/marketing/support computer-aided design, engineering, scientific & multimedia software products.

Autodesk Brazil, Rua Florida, 1758 - Andar 7 São Paulo, Brazil

Tel: 55-11-5505-0275 Fax: 55-11-5505-0232

AUTOMATIC DATA PROCESSING INC.

One ADP Boulevard, Roseland, NJ, 07068

Tel: (973) 994-5000 Fax: (973) 994-5387 Web site: www.adp.com

Data processing services.

ADP Systems Empresa de Computação, Rua Doutor Pedro Vicente, 205, São Paulo, SP 01109-010 Brazil

Tel: 55-11-225-7575 Fax: 55-11-225-8385 Contact: Carlos Mezer, VP

AUTOMATIC SWITCH CO. (ASCO)

50-60 Hanover Road, Florham Park, NJ, 07932

Tel: (973) 966-2000 Fax: (973) 966-2628

Mfr. solenoid valves, emergency power controls, pressure & temp. switches.

Ascoval Indústria e Comércio Ltda., Rodovia Presidente Castelo Branco Km. 20, Jardin Sta. Cecilia, Barueri, SP 06400, Brazil

Tel: 55-11-7295-5333 Fax: 55-11-421-5185 Contact: M. Vilela

AUTOSPLICE INC.

10121 Barnes Canyon Road, San Diego, CA, 92121

Tel: (619) 535-0077 Fax: (619) 535-0130

Mfr. electronic components.

Autosplice do Brasil Ind. e Com. Ltda., Rua Laguna 79, Jardim Platina, CEP 06273-140 Osasco, SP, Brazil

Tel: 55-11-706-4445 Fax: 55-11-706-4836 Contact: Bruno Busato, Mg. Dir.

AVERY DENNISON CORPORATION

150 N. Orange Grove Blvd., Pasadena, CA, 91103

Tel: (626) 304-2000 Fax: (626) 792-7312 Web site: www.averydennison.com

Mfr. pressure-sensitive adhesives & materials, office products, labels, tags, retail systems, Carter's Ink & specialty chemicals.

Avery Dennison Ltda., Rodovia Vinehedo-Viracopos Km. 177, Vinehedo, SP13280-000 Brazil

Tel: 55-19-876-5353 Fax: 55-19-876-5357 Contact: Joseph Venturini, Gen'l Mgr. Emp: 200

Dennison do Brazil Commercial Ltda., Av. Eng. Alberto G. Zagotis 254, Jurubatuba, 04675 São Paulo, Brazil

AVIS, INC.

900 Old Country Road., Garden City, NY, 11530

Tel: (516) 222-3000 Fax: (516) 222-4381 Web site: www.avis.com

Car rental services.

Avis, Automóveis de Aluguel Ltda., Rua Araujo, 232, 1o. andar, São Paulo, SP 01220-020 Brazil

Tel: 55-11-256-1180 Fax: 55-11-256-0824 Contact: Sergio Guanais, Dir.

AVON PRODUCTS INC.

1345 Ave. of the Americas, New York, NY, 10105-0196

Tel: (212) 282-5000 Fax: (212) 282-6049 Web site: www.avon.com

Mfr./distributor beauty & related products, fashion jewelry, gifts & collectibles.

Avon Cosméticos Ltda., Av. Interlagos, 4300, São Paulo, SP04660-907 Brazil

Tel: 55-11-546-7210 Fax: 55-11-546-7090 Contact: Ademar Serodio, Pres. Emp: 2393

BACARDI CORPORATION

PO Box G 3549, San Juan, PR, 00936-3549

Tel: (809) 788-1500 Fax: (809) 245-0422

Distiller & exporter of blended liquors.

Bacardi, Martini do Brasil Ind. e Com. Ltda., Av. Paulista, 2073, Cjto. Nacional Ed. Horsa, 16o. andar, São Paulo, SP 01311-300 Brazil

Tel: 55-11-287-8522 Fax: 55-11-288-7561 Contact: Paulo Sergio Rocha Serra Emp: 320

BAKER & McKENZIE

One Prudential Plaza, 130 East Randolph Drive, Ste. 2500, Chicago, IL, 60601

Tel: (312) 861-8000 Fax: (312) 861-2899 Web site: www.bakerinfo.com

International legal services.

Trench, Rossi e Watanabe, Av. Rio Branco, 1 - 19th Fl., Sec.B, (CP 1470) Rio de Janeiro, RJ Brazil

Tel: 55-21-516-4944 Fax: 55-21-516-6422

Trench, Rossi e Watanabe, Rua Martiniano de Carvalho, 1049 Paraiso (CP 2673) São Paulo CEP 0160-970, Brazil

Tel: 55-11-253-7999 Fax: 55-11-287-6967

Trench, Rossi e Watanabe, SCH - Q. 02 Liberty Mall, Torre A. conj. 1126, 70710-500 Brasilia D.F., Brazil

Tel: 55-61-327-3273 Fax: 55-61-327-3274 Contact: Tulio E. Coelho, Ptnr.

Veirano e Avogados Associados, Av. Nilo Peçanha, 50, 17o. andar, Rio de Janeiro, RJ 20044-900, Brazil

Tel: 55-21-282-1232 Fax: 55-21-262-4247 Contact: Ronaldo C. Veirano Emp: 88

BAKER HUGHES INCORPORATED

3900 Essex Lane, Ste. 1200, Houston, TX, 77027

Tel: (713) 439-8600 Fax: (713) 439-8699 Web site: www.bakerhughes.com

Develop & apply technology to drill, complete & produce oil and natural gas wells; provide separation systems to petroleum, municipal, continuous process & mining industries.

Baker Hughes do Brasil Ltda., Av. Marechal Camara, 160-salas 1833/34, Rio de Janeiro, RJ 20020-080, Brazil

Tel: 55-21-221-0383 Fax: 55-21-509-2090 Contact: Marco de Carvalho, Mgr.

Baker Hughes Equipamentos, Ltd., Rua Jesus Soares Pereira 592, Costa Do Sol, Macae, RJ 27923-370, Brazil

Tel: 55-24-7628445

BANDAG INC.

2905 NW Highway 61, Muscatine, IA, 52761

Tel: (319) 262-1400 Fax: (319) 262-1252

Mfr./sale retread tires.

Bandag do Brazil Ltda., Av. Mercedes Benz, 580, Campinas, SP 13055-720 Brazil

Tel: 55-19-245-5888 Fax: 55-19-245-5626 Contact: Fredeerico Kopittke, Gen'l Mgr.

THE BANK OF NEW YORK

48 Wall Street, New York, NY, 10286

Tel: (212) 495-1784 Fax: (212) 495-2546 Web site: www.bankofny.com

Banking servces.

Banco Credibanco SA, Av. Paulista 1294, 01310 Bela Vista, São Paulo, Brazil

Tel: 55-11-281-4777 Fax: 55-11-284-6903

BANKAMERICA CORPORATION

555 California Street, San Francisco, CA, 94104

Tel: (415) 622-3530 Fax: (415) 622-8467 Web site: www.bankamerica.com

Financial services.

BankAmerica Representação e Serviçõs Ltda., Rua Padre João Manoel 923, Andar 14, 01411-001 São Paulo, SP, Brazil

Tel: 55-11-3068-4800 Fax: 55-11-3068-4934 Contact: P.J Garrido, SVP & Country Mgr. Emp: 100

Multi-Banco SA, Rua Padre João Manoel 923, Andar 11, 01411-001, São Paulo, SP, Brazil

Tel: 55-11-3068-4803 Fax: 55-11-3068-4937 Contact: P.J. Garrido, SVP

BANKBOSTON CORPORATION

100 Federal Street, PO Box 1788, Boston, MA, 02110

Tel: (617) 434-2200 Fax: (617) 434-7547 Web site: www.bankboston.com

Banking & insurance services.

BankBoston - Brasilia, Edif. Federa o do ComErcio, 70300-500 Quadra 6 - Bloco A n 200, Brasilia DF, Brazil (Regional Offices: Belo Horizonte, Campinas, Curitiba, Porto Alegre.)

Tel: 55-61-321-7714 Fax: 55-61-224-9437

BankBoston - Rio De Janeiro, Av. Rio Branco, 110, 20040-001 - Centro, Rio de Janeiro - RJ, Brazil

Tel: 55-21-291-6123 Fax: 55-21-232-5120

BankBoston - São Paulo, Caixa Postal 8263, rue Libero Badaró 425, 01009-000 Centro, São Paulo, SP, Brazil

Tel: 55-11-3118-5144 Fax: 55-11-3118-5043 Contact: Henrique Meirelles, Gen. Mgr.

BANKERS TRUST COMPANY

280 Park Ave., New York, NY, 10017

Tel: (212) 250-2500 Fax: (212) 250-2440 Web site: www.bankerstrust.com

Banking & investment services.

Bankers Trust Company, Av. Rio Branco 123, andar 5, Salas 512/51, Rio de Janeiro, Brazil

Tel: 55-11-3178-3700 Fax: 55-11-3178-3867 Contact: Randolph Lewis Freiberg

Bankers Trust do Brasil Serviços Ltda., Av. Paulista, 2439, 13o. andar, cjto. 131, São Paulo, SP 01331-936 Brazil

Tel: 55-11-282-2577 Fax: 55-11-853-8837 Contact: Randolph L. Freiberg, Mg. Dir. Emp: 20

THE BARDEN CORPORATION

200 Park Ave., PO Box 2449, Danbury, CT, 06813-2449

Tel: (203) 744-2211 Fax: (203) 744-3756

Precision ball bearings.

Rodamentos Paulista RPL SA, Av. Queiroz Filho, 850/860, São Paulo, SP 05319 Brazil

Tel: 55-11-831-7755 Fax: 55-11-832-2042 Contact: J.D.M. Pereira, Mg.Dir. Emp: 25

BARNES GROUP INC.

123 Main Street, Bristol, CT, 06011-0489

Tel: (860) 583-7070 Fax: (860) 589-3507 Web site: www.barnesgroupinc.com

Mfr. steel springs, metal parts & supplies.

Stumpp & Schuele do Brasil Ind. e Com. Ltda., Rua Wallance Barnes, 301, Campinas, SP 13055-960 Brazil

Tel: 55-19-245-5071 Fax: 55-19-245-5272 Contact: Karl Paul Voetsch Mgr Emp: 224

BATES WORLDWIDE INC.

405 Lexington Ave., New York, NY, 10174

Tel: (212) 297-7000 Fax: (212) 986-0270 Web site: www.batesww.com

Advertising, marketing, public relations & media consulting.

Newcomm Bates, Av. Engl Luis Carlos Berrini, no 267-4 andar, Brooklin Novo-São Paulo, Brazil

Tel: 55-11-5505-3200 Contact: Roberto Justus, Pres.

BAUSCH & LOMB INC.

One Bausch & Lomb Place, Rochester, NY, 14604-2701

Tel: (716) 338-6000 Fax: (716) 338-6007 Web site: www.bausch.com

Mfr. vision care products & accessories & hearing aids.

BL Industria Ótica Ltda., Rua Leopolda, 351, Rio de Janeiro, RJ 20541 Brazil

Tel: 55-21-278-1622 Fax: 55-21-208-9299 Contact: Jorge Temer, Chmn

BAX GLOBAL CORPORATION

16808 Armstrong Ave., PO Box 19571, Irvine, CA, 92623

Tel: (714) 752-4000 Fax: (714) 852-1488 Web site: www.bax.com

Air freight forwarder.

BAX Global do Brasil Ltda., Estrada do Galeão, No. 2879, 3° Andar, Salas 306 A 310, Ilha do Governador, 21941-001, Rio de Janeiro, RJ, Brazil

Tel: 55-21-393-1811 Fax: 55-21-462-1082

BAX Global do Brasil Ltda., Rua Candido Vale, 319, 03068-010 -Tatuape, SP San Saulo, Brazil

Tel: 55-11-6941-7314 Fax: 55-11-6942-7461

BAXTER HEALTHCARE CORPORATION

One Baxter Parkway, Deerfield, IL, 60015

Tel: (847) 948-2000 Fax: (847) 948-3948 Web site: www.baxter.com

Pharmaceutical preparations, surgical/medical instruments & cardiovascular products.

Baxter Hospitalar Ltda., Av. Interlagos 3509, CEP 04661 Santo Amaro, São Paulo, SP04661-905 Brazil

Tel: 55-11-541-8922 Fax: 55-11-246-0519 Contact: Roberto Ferreira de M. Braga Emp: 290

BBDO WORLDWIDE

1285 Ave. of the Americas, New York, NY, 10019

Tel: (212) 459-5000 Fax: (212) 459-6645 Web site: www.bbdo.com

Multinational group of advertising agencies.

ALMAP/BBDO Cominicacoes, São Paulo, Brazil

BDO SEIDMAN, LLP

Two Prudential Plaza, 180 N. Stetson Ave., Ste. 2300, Chicago, IL, 60601

Tel: (312) 240-1236 Fax: (312) 240-3329 Web site: www.bdo.com

International accounting & financial consulting firm.

BDO Directa Auditores S/C, Rua Senador Felicio dos Santos, 392, 01511-010 São Paulo-SP, Brazil

Tel: 55-11-277-2199 Fax: 55-11-277-1534 Contact: Hans-Kurt Günther

BEA SYSTEMS, INC.

2315 North First Street, St. Jose, CA, 95131

Tel: (408) 570-8000 Fax: (408) 570-8091 Web site: www.beasys.com

Develops communications management software & provider of software consulting services.

BEA Systems, Inc., Aenida das Nações Unidas, 12551 - 23° & cj.2301, São Paulo - SP- Brazil

Tel: 55-11-3043-7350 Fax: 55-11-3043-7501

BEAR STEARNS & CO., INC.

245 Park Ave., New York, NY, 10167

Tel: (212) 272-2000 Fax: (212) 272-3092 Web site: www.bearstearns.com

Investment banking, securities broker/dealer & investment advisory services.

Bear Stearns do Brazil Ltda., Alameda Santos, 1940, 12th Fl., Ste. 1202, São Paulo, Brazil 01418-100

Tel: 55-11-289-2922 Fax: 55-11-285-5080 Contact: Philip Stratos, Mg. Dir. Emp: 15

BECHTEL GROUP INC.

50 Beale Street, PO Box 3965, San Francisco, CA, 94105-1895

Tel: (415) 768-1234 Fax: (415) 768-9038 Web site: www.bechtel.com

General contractors in engineering & construction.

Bechtel do Brasil Construções Ltda., Praia de Botofogo, 440, 22o.andar, Rio de Janeiro, RJ 22250-040 Brazil

Tel: 55-21-286-0690 Fax: 55-21-266-0698 Contact: João A. Magalhães, Pres. Emp: 20

Bechtel do Brasil Construções Ltda., Av. Dr. Chucri Zaidan, 920 5/6 andar, 04583-904 São Paulo, SP, Brazil

Tel: 55-11-3048-7656 Fax: 55-11-3048-7652

BECTON DICKINSON AND COMPANY

One Becton Drive, Franklin Lakes, NJ, 07417-1880

Tel: (201) 847-6800 Fax: (201) 847-6475

Mfr./sale medical supplies, devices & diagnostic systems.

Becton Dickinson Indústrias Cirúrgicas Ltda., Rua Alexandre Dumas 1976, 04717-004 São Paulo, Brazil

Tel: 55-11-545-9833 Fax: 55-11-247-8644 Contact: Aureo Nunes, Gen Mgr. Emp: 1500

BELL HELICOPTER TEXTRON INC.

PO Box 482, Fort Worth, TX, 76101

Tel: (817) 280-2011 Fax: (817) 280-2321

Mfr./sale/service helicopters, air cushion vehicles and rocket engines.

Rotobras Com. e Ind. de Helicópteros (Dealer), Rua Haroldo Paranhos, s/n, Aeroporto de Congonhas, São Paulo, SP 04357-060 Brazil

Tel: 55-11-531-5171 Fax: 55-11-531-6002 Contact: José Afonso Assumpção, Pres.

BELLSOUTH INTERNATIONAL

1155 Peachtree Street NE, Ste. 400, Atlanta, GA, 30367

Tel: (404) 249-4800 Fax: (404) 249-4880 Web site: www.bellsouth.com

Mobile communications, telecommunications network systems.

BCP Telecominicaçoes S.A., Rua Florida, 1970, São Paulo, SP, Brazil CEP 04565-001

Tel: 55-11-5509-6555 Fax: 55-11-5509-6257

BENTLY NEVADA CORPORATION

1617 Water Street, PO Box 157, Minden, NV, 89423

Tel: (702) 782-3611 Fax: (702) 782-9259

Electronic monitoring systems.

Engetec Indústria e Comércio Ltda., Rua do Paraíso, 139, 9o. andar, São Paulo, SP 04103-010 Brazil

Tel: 55-11-289-7575 Fax: 55-11-251-5267 Contact: Luiz Salgado Mendes Emp: 12

BEST WESTERN INTERNATIONAL

6201 North 24th Place, Phoenix, AZ, 85106

Tel: (602) 957-4200 Fax: (602) 957-5740

International hotel chain.

BW Sol Ipanema Hotel, Av. Vieria Souto 320, Rio de Janeiro, RJ 22420-000, Brazil

Tel: 55-21-523-0095

BESTFOODS, INC.

700 Sylvan Ave., International Plaza, Englewood Cliffs, NJ, 07632-9976

Tel: (201) 894-4000 Fax: (201) 894-2186 Web site: www.bestfoods.com

Consumer foods products; corn refining.

Refinacoes de Milho Brasil Ltda., Caixa Postal 19.100, 01065-970 São Paulo, Brazil

Tel: 55-11-5509-8122 Fax: 55-11-5506-2371 Contact: José Luis Fernández, Mgr.

Refinacoes de Milho Brazil Ltda., Praca da Republica 468, Caixa Postal 8151, São Paulo, SP 01045-908 Brazil

Tel: 55-11-224-5122 Fax: 55-11-223-0817 Contact: Sergio Bertone, Dir. Emp: 4000

BETZDEARBORN

4636 Somerton Road, PO Box 3002, Trevose, PA, 19053-6783

Tel: (215) 953-2568 Fax: (215) 953-5524 Web site: www.betzdearborn.com

Mfr. water/wastewater and process system treatment chemicals and services.

BetzDearborn Brasil LTDA., Rodovia Raposo Tavares, 22.901, Granja Vianna 06700-000, Cotia - SP, Brazil

Tel: 55-11-7923-1000 Fax: 55-11-492-7108

BLACK & DECKER CORPORATION

701 E. Joppa Road, Towson, MD, 21286

Tel: (410) 716-3900 Fax: (410) 716-2933 Web site: www.blackanddecker.com

Mfr. power tools and accessories, security hardware, small appliances, fasteners, information systems & services.

Black & Decker Brazil, Av. Industrial, 600, Santo André, SP 09080-500 Brazil

Tel: 55-11-411-9483 Fax: 55-11-440-2496 Contact: Brett Olson, Pres. Emp: 900

BLACK BOX CORPORATION

1000 Park Drive, Lawrence, PA, 15055

Tel: (724) 746-5500 Fax: (724) 746-0746 Web site: www.blackbox.com

Direct marketer and technical service provider of communications, networking and related computer connectivity products.

Black Box do Brasil, Av. Guido Caloi 1935, 05802-140 São Paulo, SP, Brazil

Tel: 55-11-5515-3400 Fax: 55-11-5515-0637 Contact: Moncyr Sampaio, Gen. Mgr.

BLOOMBERG L.P.

499 Park Ave., New York, NY, 10022

Tel: (212) 318-2000 Fax: (212) 940-1954 Web site: www.bloomberg.com

Publishes magazines and provides TV, radio and newspaper wire services.

Bloomberg L.P., São Paulo, Brazil

Tel: 55-11-3048-4500

BLOUNT INC.

4520 Executive Park Drive, Montgomery, AL, 36116-1602

Tel: (334) 244-4000 Fax: (334) 271-8130 Web site: www.blount.com

Mfr. cutting chain & equipment, timber harvest/handling equipment, sporting ammo, riding mowers.

Blount Industrial de Correntes Ltda., Rua Emilio Romani 1630, Area Sul-Cidade Industrial, 81450 Curitiba, Parana, Brazil

Tel: 55-41-316-5800 Fax: 55-41-316-5959 Contact: Vern Pearson, Gen. Mgr.

BOOZ ALLEN & HAMILTON INC.

8283 Greensboro Drive, McLean, VA, 22102

Tel: (703) 902-5000 Fax: (703) 902-3333 Web site: www.bah.com

International management and technology consultants.

Booz Allen & Hamilton do Brasil Consultores Ltda., Rua Gornes de Carvalho 1765, 5 andar, São Paulo, SP 04547-901 Brazil

Tel: 55-11-3049-4999 Fax: 55-11-820-6750 Contact: Oscar P. Bernardes, Pres.

BORDEN INC.

180 East Broad Street, Columbus, OH, 43215-3799

Tel: (614) 225-4000 Fax: (614) 220-6453

Mfr. Packaged foods, consumer adhesives, housewares and industrial chemicals.

Alba Quimica Ind. E Com. Ltda, Av. Maria Coelho Aguiar, 215, Bloco G - 1° andar, 05805-000 São Paulo, Brazil

Tel: 55-11-3741-1940 Fax: 55-11-3741-1659

THE BOSTON CONSULTING GROUP

Exchange Place, 31st Floor, Boston, MA, 02109

Tel: (617) 973-1200 Fax: (617) 973-1339 Web site: www.bcg.com

Management consulting company.

The Boston Consulting Group (Brasil) Ltda., Av. Nacões Unidas, 11.857-9o andar, 04578-000 São Paulo - SP, Brazil

Tel: 55-11-07-2020

BOYDEN CONSULTING CORPORATION

100 Park Ave., 34th Floor, New York, NY, 10017

Tel: (212) 980-6534 Fax: (212) 980-6147 Web site: www.boyden.com

Executive search.

Boyden do Brazil Ltda., Rua Alfredo Egidio de Souza Aranho 384, 7th Fl. Santo Amaro, 04726-170 São Paulo, Brazil

Tel: 55-11-523-6333

Boyden do Brazil Ltda., Rua Visconde de Piraja, 547 salsa 1026, Ipanema - Rio De Janiero, RJ 22420-003 Brazil

Tel: 55-21-511-0664

BOZELL WORLDWIDE

40 West 23rd Street, New York, NY, 10010

Tel: (212) 727-5000 Fax: (212) 645-9173 Web site: www.bozell.com

Advertising, marketing, public relations and media consulting.

Bozell Brazil, Rua General Jardim 482/13, Vila Buarque-CEP 01223-010, São Paulo, Brazil

Tel: 55-11-236-2988 Fax: 55-11-236-2990 Contact: Francisco Borghoff, Pres.

Norton Publicidade, SA, Av. Rio Branco, 128-4 Andar, Centro, CEP:20.040-002, Rio de Janeiro, Brazil

Quality Marketing Promocional, Rua Fradique Coutinho, 1639, São Paulo-SP, Brazil

Tel: 55-11-867-0700 Contact: Antonio Murena Jr.

Quality Marketing Promocional, Rua Fradique Coutinho, 1639, São Paulo-SP, Brazil

Tel: 55-11-867-0070 Fax: 55-11-867-0070

W. H. BRADY CO.

6555 W. Good Hope Road, Milwaukee, WI, 53223

Tel: (414) 358-6600 Fax: Web site: www.whbrady.com

Mfr. industrial ID for wire marking, circuit boards; facility ID, signage, printing systems & software.

W.H. Brady do Brasil Ltda., Centro Empresarial Alphaville, Av. Juruá, 105-Módulo 4, 06455-908 Barueri, São Paulo, Brazil

Tel: 55-11-7295-1235 Fax: 55-11-7295-0993

BRANSON ULTRASONICS CORPORATION

41 Eagle Road, Danbury, CT, 06813-1961

Tel: (203) 796-0400 Fax: (203) 796-2285

Mfr. plastics assembly equipment, ultrasonic cleaning equipment.

Eurosonics Tecnologia Industrial Ltda., Rua Vig. Taques Bittencourt 63, Santa Amaro, 04755 São Paulo, Brazil

Tel: 55-11-521-3199 Fax: 55-11-524-5778

BRINK'S INC.

Thorndal Circle, Darien, CT, 06820

Tel: (203) 662-7800 Fax: (203) 662-7968 Web site: www.brinks.com

Security transportation.

Brink's SA Transporte de Valores, Rua Joao Bricola 678, São Paulo, SP, Brazil

BRISTOL-MYERS SQUIBB COMPANY

345 Park Ave., New York, NY, 10154

Tel: (212) 546-4000 Fax: (212) 546-4020 Web site: www.bms.com

Pharmaceutical and food preparations, medical and surgical instruments.

Bristol-Myers Squibb Brasil SA, Rua Carlos Gomes, 924, San Amaro, São Paulo, SP 04743-903 Brazil
Tel: 55-11-522-8111 Fax: 55-11-548-2364 Contact: Andre Rodolfo Placco Attanasio Emp: 13520

BROWN & ROOT INC.
4100 Clinton Drive, Houston, TX, 77020-6299
Tel: (713) 676-3011 Fax: (713) 676-8532
Engineering, construction and maintenance.
Brown & Root do Brasil Servicos Maritimos Ltd., R. Senador Dantas 75, Rio de Janeiro, Brazil

BROWN & WOOD
One World Trade Center, 59th Fl., New York, NY, 10048
Tel: (212) 839-5300 Fax: (212) 839-5599
Legal services.
Brown & Wood, Rua da Consolação 247, 5º Andar, São Paulo, SP 01301-903 Brazil
Tel: 55-11-256-9785 Fax: 55-11-256-9785 Contact: Sandra L. Cervelim, Atty

BROWN GROUP INC.
8300 Maryland Ave., St. Louis, MO, 63105
Tel: (314) 854-4000 Fax: (314) 854-4274 Web site: www.browngroup.com
Mfr./sale footwear.
Pagoda Intl. Corp. do Brasil Ltda., Rua Carmo do Rio Verde 245, Santo Amaro, CEP 04729-010 São Paulo, Brazil
Tel: 55-11-524-9192 Fax: 55-11-523-7348 Contact: Andre Bruere, VP Emp: 22

BROWN-FORMAN CORPORATION
PO Box 1080, Louisville, KY, 40201-1080
Tel: (502) 585-1100 Fax: (502) 774-7876 Web site: www.brown-forman.com
Mfr./distributor distilled spirits, wine, china, crystal, silverware and luggage.
Brown-Forman Beverages Worldwide Ltda., 17th Fl., Ste. 178 Rua, Joaquim Floriana 72, Itaim Bibi, São Paulo, S.P., Brazil, 04534-000
Tel: 55-11-820-3521 Fax: 55-11-822-2154 Contact: Robert C. Collins, VP, Latin America Emp: 10

BUCYRUS INTERNATIONAL, INC.
1100 Milwaukee Ave., South Milwaukee, WI, 53172
Tel: (414) 768-4000 Fax: (414) 768-4474
Mfr. of surface mining equipment, primarily walking draglines, electric mining shovels and blast hole drills.
Bucyrus (Brasil) Ltd., Av. das Nacoes, 4069, Distrito Industrial, Prof. Jose Vieira de Mondonca, Caixa Postal 40, Vespasiano, MG, Brazil, CEP 33.200-000
Tel: 55-31-621-1899 Fax: 55-31-621-1817 Contact: Harry Looman, Gen. Mgr.

BUDGET RENT A CAR CORPORATION
4225 Naperville Road, Lisle, IL, 60532
Tel: (630) 955-1900 Fax: (630) 955-7799 Web site: www.budgetrentacar.com
Car and truck rental system.
Budget Rent A Car, Central Hdqrts., Rua Da Consolacao, 328-Loja, Brazil
Tel: 55-11-256-4355

BULAB HOLDINGS INC.
1256 N. McLean Blvd, Memphis, TN, 38108
Tel: (901) 278-0330 Fax: (901) 276-5343 Web site: www.buckman.com
Biological products; chemicals & chemical preparations.
Buckman Laboratórios Ltda., Caixa Postal 899, 13001-970 Campinas, SP Brazil
Tel: 55-19-864-1133 Fax: 55-19-864-1621 Contact: Alexandre M. Mesquita, Mgr.

LEO BURNETT CO., INC.

35 West Wacker Drive, Chicago, IL, 60601

Tel: (312) 220-5959 Fax: (312) 220-6533 Web site: www.leoburnett.com

International advertising agency.

Leo Burnett Publicidade Ltda., Av. Cidade Jardim 400, 01454 São Paulo, Brazil

BURSON-MARSTELLER

230 Park Ave., New York, NY, 10003-1566

Tel: (212) 614-4000 Fax: (212) 614-4262 Web site: www.bm.com

Public relations/public affairs consultants.

Burson-Marsteller São Paulo Ltda., Rus Jundai #50, 4th Fl., 01451 São Paulo, SP, Brazil

Tel: 55-11-887-4440 Fax: 55-11-887-4440 Emp: 25

BUTLER MANUFACTURING COMPANY

Penn Valley Park, PO Box 419917, Kansas City, MO, 64141-0917

Tel: (816) 968-3000 Fax: (816) 968-3279

Pre-engineered steel structural systems, curtain wall and electrical distributor systems.

Butler Do Brasil, Ltda., Av. Alvares Cabral, 1740, 2o Andar, Ed. Lucas Lopes - Sto. Agostinho, 30170-001 Belo Horizonte - MG Brazil

Tel: 55-31-291-7772 Fax: 55-31-291-6573 Contact: Charles E. Hatch, Mng. Dir.

CABLETRON SYSTEMS, INC.

35 Industrial Way, PO Box 5005, Rochester, NH, 03866-5005

Tel: (603) 332-9400 Fax: (603) 337-3007

Develop/mfr./marketing/install/support local & wide area network connectivity hardware & software.

Cabletron Systems do Brasil Ltda., Av. Paulista, 949, 7o.andar G72, São Paulo, SP 01311-917, Brazil

Tel: 55-11-251-3422 Fax: 55-11-251-3042 Contact: Eric J. Better, Dir. Emp: 35

CABOT CORPORATION

75 State Street, Boston, MA, 02109-1807

Tel: (617) 345-0100 Fax: (617) 342-6103

Mfr. carbon blacks, plastics; oil & gas, information systems.

Cabot do Brazil Ind. e Com. Ltda., Av. dos Eucaliptos, 88, São Paulo, SP 04517-900 Brazil

Tel: 55-11-536-0388 Fax: 55-11-542-6037 Contact: Chang Loo Sih, Pres. Emp: 112

CALIFORNIA PELLET MILL COMPANY (CPM)

1114 East Wabash Ave., Crawfordsville, IN, 47933

Tel: (765) 362-2600 Fax: (765) 362-7551

Mfr. machinery for pelleting.

Ingersol-Rand SA, CPM/Brazil Div., Av. Roberto de Jesus Alfonso 351, 14800 Araraquara, São Paulo, Brazil

CAMBRIDGE WIRE CLOTH COMPANY

105 Goodwill Road, PO Box 399, Cambridge, MD, 21613

Tel: (410) 228-3000 Fax: (410) 228-6752

Mfr. industrial wire cloth, wire conveyor belting and industrial mesh.

Cambridge do Brazil Ind. e Com. Ltda., Caixa Postal 1461, São Paulo, Brazil

CARBOLINE COMPANY

350 Hanley Industrial Court, St. Louis, MO, 63144

Tel: (314) 644-1000 Fax: (314) 644-4617

Mfr. coatings, sealants.

Sumare Industria Quimica SA, Caixa Postal 20971, 01491 São Paulo, SP, Brazil

CARGILL, INC.

15407 McGinty Road, Minnetonka, MN, 55440-5625

Tel: (612) 742-7575 Fax: (612) 742-7393 Web site: www.cargill.com

Food products, feeds, animal products.

Cargill Agricola SA, Rua Olavo Bilac, 157, São Paulo, SP 04671-900 Brazil

Tel: 55-11-546-3311 Fax: 55-11-546-3590 Contact: Henri Mathot, Pres. Emp: 1865

CARRIER CORPORATION

One Carrier Place, Farmington, CT, 06034-4015

Tel: (860) 674-3000 Fax: (860) 679-3010 Web site: www.carrier.com

Mfr./distributor/services A/C, heating & refrigeration equipment.

Carrier Transicold Brasil Ltda., Caxuas de Sol, Brazil

Springer Nordest SA, Rua Berto Cirio 521, Bairro São Luis, 92042 Canoas, Brazil

CASE CORPORATION

700 State Street, Racine, WI, 53404

Tel: (414) 636-6011 Fax: (414) 636-0200 Web site: www.casecorp.com

Mfr./sale agricultural and construction equipment.

Brastoft Maquinas e Sistemas Agroindustriais S/A, Rua Jose Coelho Prates Jr., 199, 13422-020 - Piracicaba - SP, Brazil

Tel: 55-19-422-1033 Fax: 55-19-422-1044 Contact: Sidney Macedo, Gen. Mgr.

Case do Brasil & Cia Ltda., Av. Jerome Case, 1951, Barrio Eden, 18087-370 Sococaba, SP Brazil

Tel: 55-15-225-2020 Fax: 55-15-225-2827 Contact: Gilberto P. da Costa, V.P. & Gen.Mgr. Emp: 400

CATERPILLAR INC.

100 NE Adams Street, Peoria, IL, 61629-6105

Tel: (309) 675-1000 Fax: (309) 675-1182 Web site: www.cat.com

Mfr. earth/material-handling and construction machinery and equipment and engines.

Caterpillar Brasil S.A., SBS Edif. Case de São Paulo, 9 andar, 70078 Brasilia, DF, Brazil

NOIL Participacoes e Comercio S.A., Rodovia Luiz de Queiroz Km 157, s/n, Piracicaba, SP 13420-900 Brazil

Brazil

L.D. CAULK COMPANY

PO Box 359, Milford, DE, 19963

Tel: (302) 422-4511 Fax: (302) 422-5719

Dental material.

Industrias Dentarias Caulk SA, Rua Darmstadt 401, 18-andar, Caixa Postal 15, Petropolis, RJ, Brazil

C.B. RICHARD ELLIS

533 South Fremont Ave., Los Angeles, CA, 90071-1712

Tel: (213) 613-3123 Fax: (213) 613-3535 Web site: www.cbrichardellis.com

Commercial real estate services.

CB Richard Ellis, Rio de Janeiro, Brazil

CB Richard Ellis, São Paulo, Brazil

CBI COMPANY

1501 North Division Street, Plainfield, IL, 60544

Tel: (815) 241-7546 Fax: (815) 439-6010

Holding company: metal plate fabricating, construction, oil and gas drilling.

CBI Construcues Ltda., Rua Evaristo de Veiga, Rio de Janeiro, Brazil

CENTRAL NATIONAL-GOTTESMAN INC.

3 Manhattanville Road, Purchase, NY, 10577-2110

Tel: (914) 696-9000 Fax: (914) 696-1066

Worldwide sales pulp and paper products.

Branac Papel e Celulose S.A., Rua Formosa 367, 15th Fl., São Paulo, SP 01049-000 Brazil
Tel: 55-11-250-2588 Fax: 55-11-224-9403 Contact: Antonio S. Rodriques do Prado Emp: 42

Branac Papel e Celulose S.A., Rua Teofilo Otoni 123-A, 6th Fl., 20090 Rio de Janeiro, RJ, Brazil
Tel: 55-21-223-4171 Fax: 55-21-233-5545 Contact: Jaime do Nascimento Brito

CH2M HILL INC.
6060 South Willow Drive, Greenwood Village, CO, 80111
Tel: (303) 771-0900 Fax: (303) 770-2616
Consulting engineers, planners, economists and scientists.

CH2M Hill, São Paulo, Brazil
Tel: 55-11-846-0101

CHAMPION INTERNATIONAL CORPORATION
One Champion Plaza, Stamford, CT, 06921
Tel: (213) 358-7000 Fax: (213) 358-2975
Manufacture and sale of pulp and paper.

Bamerindus Agro-Florestal/Champion International, Brazil

Champion Papel e Celulose Ltda., Rodovia SP 340 KM 171, Mogi Guaçu, SP 13840-970 Brazil
Tel: 55-19-861-8121 Fax: 55-19-861-1098 Contact: Ronaldo A.C. Pereira Emp: 2100

Industria de Papel Aropoti SA, Caix Postal 10, 128-40970 Mogiguacu, São Paulo, Brazil

Inpacel/Industria de Papel Arapoti S.A., Brazil

THE CHASE MANHATTAN CORPORATION
World Headquarters, 270 Park Ave., New York, NY, 10017
Tel: (212) 270-6000 Fax: (212) 622-9030 Web site: www.chase.com
International banking and financial services.

Banco Chase Manhattan S.A., Rua Verbo Divino 1400, São Paulo, Brazil 04719-002
Tel: 55-11-5180-4400 Fax: 55-11-5180-4510 Contact: Patrick Morin, Dir. & Pres.

Chase Manhattan Office for Southern Region, Rua Alvares Penteado, 131, Caixa Postal 30281, São Paulo, SP, Brazil

Chase Manhattan Office-Northern States, Rua do Ouvidor 98, Caixa Postal 221-ZC-00, Rio de Janeiro, Brazil

Manufacturers Hanover Arrandamento Mercantil, Praia do Botafago 228, 22250 Rio de Janeiro, Brazil

CHESTERTON BINSWANGER INTERNATIONAL
Two Logan Square, 4th Floor, Philadelphia, PA, 19103-2759
Tel: (215) 448-6000 Fax: (215) 448-6238
Real estate & related services.

Julio Bogoricin Imoveis, Av. Brasil 876 - Jd. America, 01430-000 São Paulo, Brazil

CHEVRON CHEMICAL COMPANY
6001 Bollinger Canyon Road., PO Box 5047, San Ramon, CA, 94583-0947
Tel: (925) 842-1000 Fax: (925) 842-5775 Web site: www.chevron.com
Mfr. chemicals.

Chevron do Brasil Ltda., Alameda dos Lupinás 512, Blocko B, 2o.andar, São Paulo 01059-970 Brazil
Tel: 55-11-579-9111 Fax: 55-11-577-1088 Contact: William E. Schulz, Pres. Emp: 260

CHEVRON CORPORATION
575 Market Street, San Francisco, CA, 94105
Tel: (415) 894-7700 Fax: (415) 894-2248 Web site: www.chevron.com
Oil exploration & production & petroleum products.

Asfaltos Chevron SA, Rua Ararai 35, Caixa Postal 12654, 04729 São Paulo, SP, Brazil

THE CHUBB CORPORATION

15 Mountain View Road, Warren, NJ, 07061-1615

Tel: (908) 580-2000 Fax: (908) 580-3606 Web site: www.chubb.com

Holding company: property/casualty insurance.

Chubb do Brasil Companhia de Seguros, Rua da Asembleia, 100-3 Andar, 2001-000 Rio de Janeior, RJ, Brazil

Tel: 55-21-276-3200 Fax: 55-21-276-3217

Chubb do Brasil Companhia de Seguros, Centro Empresarial de São Paulo, Rua Maria Coelho Aguiar, 215, Bl. F-4 Andar, 05805-900 São Paulo-SP, Brazil

Tel: 55-11-3741-2244 Fax: 55-11-246-0105

CIGNA CORPORATION

One Liberty Place, Philadelphia, PA, 19192

Tel: (215) 761-1000 Fax: (215) 761-5008

Insurance, invest, health care and other financial services.

Amazonas Seguradora SA, Av. Paulo de Frontin 628, 20001 Rio de Janeiro, Brazil

Cigna Brasil Emprendimentos Ltda., Av. Paulo de Frontin 628, 20262 Rio de Janiero, Brazil

Cigna Seguradora S.A., Rua Libero Badaró, 377, 15o. andar, São Paulo, SP 01009-000 Brazil

Tel: 55-11-232-1155 Fax: 55-11-605-8974 Contact: Robert G. Smith, Pres. Emp: 223

Cigna Seguradora SA, Av. Paulo de Frontin 628, 20001 Rio de Janeiro, Brazil

Sumare Processamento e Servicos SA, Av. Paulo de Frontin 628, Rio Comprido, 20262 Rio de Janeiro, Brazil

CINCINNATI MILACRON INC.

4701 Marburg Ave., Cincinnati, OH, 45209

Tel: (513) 841-8100 Fax: (513) 841-8919

Develop/mfr. technologies for metalworking & plastics processing industrial.

Genos Indústria e Comérico Ltda., Rua Armindo Hahne, 105, Osasco, SP 06210-096 Brazil

Tel: 55-11-703-7268 Fax: 55-11-702-8646 Contact: José Muliterno Celades, Pres. Emp: 120

CINCOM SYSTEMS INC.

2300 Montana Ave., Cincinnati, OH, 45211

Tel: (513) 612-2300 Fax: (513) 481-8332 Web site: www.cincom.com

Develop/distributor computer software.

Cincom Systems Inc., Av. República do Libano, 385, São Paulo, SO 04501-000 Brazil

Tel: 55-11-885-8877 Fax: 55-11-887-9225 Contact: Carlos Alberto Novais, Dir. Emp: 45

Cincom Systems Inc., Rio de Janeiro, Brazil

CISCO SYSTEMS, INC.

170 Tasman Drive, San Jose, CA, 95134-1706

Tel: (408) 526-4000 Fax: (408) 526-4100 Web site: www.cisco.com

Develop/mfr./market computer hardware and software networking systems.

Cisco Systems Do Brasil, Av. Naçoes Unidas, 12.995 Cj.132, 04578-000 Brooklin Novo, São Paulo - SP Brazil

Tel: 55-11-5505-4252 Fax: 55-11-5505-4901 Contact: N/A

CITICORP

399 Park Ave., New York, NY, 10043

Tel: (212) 559-1000 Fax: (212) 527-2066 Web site: www.citibank.com

International banking and financial services.

Banco Citibank SA, Ave. Paulista 1111, 17° andar, São Paulo, SP 01311-920 Brazil

Tel: 55-11-576-1000 Fax: 55-11-576-1402 Contact: Roberto V. do Valle, Pres. Emp: 2200

THE CLOROX COMPANY

1221 Broadway, PO Box 24305, Oakland, CA, 94623-1305

Tel: (510) 271-7000 Fax: (510) 832-1463

Mfr. soap & detergents, and domestic consumer packaged products.

Clorox do Brasil Ltda., Av. Brigadeiro Fairo Lima 2161, 5o.andar, sala 700, São Paulo, SP 01451-001 Brazil

Tel: 55-11-897-4700 Fax: 55-11-897-2701 Contact: Carlos Alcantara, Gen'l Mgr.

CMS ENERGY CORPORATION

Fairlane Plaza South, Ste. 1100, 330 Town Drive, Dearborn, MI, 48126

Tel: (313) 436-9200 Fax: (313) 436-9225 Web site: www.cmsenergy.com

Independent power plant operator.

Forca e Luz Cataguazes-Leopoldina, Brazil

THE COASTAL CORPORATION

Nine Greenway Plaza, Houston, TX, 77046-0995

Tel: (713) 877-1400 Fax: (713) 877-6752 Web site: www.coastalcorp.com

Oil refining, natural gas, related services; independent power production.

Coastal do Brasil Ltda., Rio de Janeiro, Brazil

THE COCA-COLA COMPANY

P.O. Drawer 1734, Atlanta, GA, 30301

Tel: (404) 676-2121 Fax: (404) 676-6792 Web site: www.coca-cola.com

Mfr./marketing/distributor soft drinks, syrups & concentrates, juice & juice-drink products.

Coca-Cola Industria e Com. Ltda., Av. Nilo Pecanha 50, andar 11, Caixa Postal 860, Rio de Janeiro, RJ, Brazil

THE COLEMAN CO., INC.

3600 Hydraulic Street, Wichita, KS, 67219

Tel: (316) 832-2653 Fax: (316) 832-3060

Mfr./distributor/sales camping & outdoor recreation products.

Coleman do Brasil Industrial e Com. Ltda., Av. Ireno da Silva Venancio 196, Bairro Angelo Vial, Votorantim/São Paulo, Brazil

COLUMBIA PICTURES INDUSTRIES INC.

10202 West Washington Blvd., Culver City, CA, 90232

Tel: (310) 244-4000 Fax: (310) 244-2626 Web site: www.sony.com

Producer and distributor of motion pictures.

Screen Gems-Columbia Pictures of Brazil Inc., Rua Joaquin Silva 98, Lapa, Caixa Postal 110, io de Janeiro, Brazil

COMMERCIAL INTERTECH CORPORATION

1775 Logan Ave., PO Box 239, Youngstown, OH, 44501-0239

Tel: (330) 746-8011 Fax: (330) 746-1148

Mfr. hydraulic components, pre-engineered buildings and stamped metal products.

Commercial Intertech do Brasil Ltda., Rua AMB do Brasil 251, 18120 Mairinque, SP, Brazil

COMPAQ COMPUTER CORPORATION

20555 State Highway 249, PO Box 692000, Houston, TX, 77269-2000

Tel: (713) 370-0670 Fax: (713) 514-1740 Web site: www.compaq.com

Develop/mfr. personal computers.

Compaq Computer Brasil Ind. e Com. Ltda., Rua Alexandre Dumas, 2220, São Paulo, SP 04717 Brazil

Tel: 55-11-246-7866 Fax: 55-11-524-8050 Contact: Jorge Schreurs, Pres. Emp: 403

COMPUTER ASSOCIATES INTERNATIONAL INC.

One Computer Associates Plaza, Islandia, NY, 11788

Tel: (516) 342-5224 Fax: (516) 342-5329 Web site: www.cai.com

Integrated software for enterprise computing and information management, application development, manufacturing, financial applications and professional services.

Computer Associates do Brasil Ltda., Av. Engenheiro Luiz Carlos Berrini 1253, 6/F, 04571-010 São Paulo, Brazil

Tel: 55-11-536-4366 Fax: 55-11-240-7001 Contact: Vincenzo Dragone Gen'l Mgr. Emp: 7500

COMSAT CORPORATION

6560 Rock Spring Drive, Bethesda, MD, 20817

Tel: (301) 214-3200 Fax: (301) 214-7100 Web site: www.comsat.com

Provides global telecommunications services via satellite and develops advanced satellite networking technology.

COMSAT International, Locations in Campinas, Rio de Janeiro and São Paulo, Brazil

CONAGRA INC.

One ConAgra Drive, Omaha, NE, 68102-5001

Tel: (402) 595-4000 Fax: (402) 595-4595 Web site: www.conagra.com

Prepared/frozen foods, grains, flour, animal feeds, agri chemicals, poultry, meat, dairy products, including Healthy Choice, Butterball and Hunt's.

ConAgra Inc., Brazil

CONOCO INC.

PO Box 2197, Houston, TX, 77252

Tel: (281) 293-1000 Fax: (281) 293-1440

Oil, gas, coal, chemicals and minerals.

Conoco Quimica do Brazil Ltda., Av. Paulista 1499, 13 andar, Conj 1301, 01311 São Paulo, SP, Brazil

CONTINENTAL AIRLINES INC.

2929 Allen Parkway, Ste. 1501, Houston, TX, 77019

Tel: (281) 834-5000 Fax: (281) 520-6329

International airline carrier.

Continental Airlines Inc., Brazil

CONTINENTAL CAN COMPANY

301 Merritt 7, 7 Corporate Park, Norwalk, CT, 06856

Tel: (203) 750-5900 Fax: (203) 750-5908

Packaging products and machinery, metal, plastic and paper containers.

Metalurgica Matarazzo SA, Caixa Postal 2400, 01000 São Paulo, Brazil

Shellmar Embalagem Moderna SA, Via Anchieta Km. 22, 09700 São Bernardo do Campo, Brazil

COOPER INDUSTRIES INC.

6600 Travis Street, Ste. 5800, Houston, TX, 77002

Tel: (713) 209-8400 Fax: (713) 209-8995 Web site: www.cooperindustries.com

Mfr./distributor electrical products, tools and hardware and automotive products.

Bussman do Brasil Ltda., Rodivia Santos Dumont, Km. 23, Cruz das almas, Itu - São Paulo - 13 300-000 Brazil

Tel: 55-11-7824-1856 Fax: 55-11-7824-1721

Cooper Hand Tools Div., Guarulhos,& Sococaba, São Paulo, Brazil

Cooper Hand Tools Div., Av. Liberdade, 4055, Ipiranga, Sorocaba, SP18087-170 Brazil

Tel: 55-15-225-2666 Fax: 55-15-225-1770 Contact: J. Duilio Justi, Gen'l Mgr. Emp: 400

Cooper Power Systems do Brasil Ltda., Rua Placido Vieira 79, Santo Amaro - São Paulo - SP Brazil

Tel: 55-11-524-4411 Fax: 55-11-524-1075

CORESTATES BANK

1500 Market Street, Philadelphia, PA, 19101

Tel: (215) 973-3100 Fax: (215) 786-8899 Web site: www.corestates.com

Primary international businesses; correspondent banking and trade services.

Corestates Bank, Rua Libero Badaro 377, 20 andar, CJ2009/10, 01009 São Paulo, Brazil

Tel: 55-11-607-4031 Fax: 55-11-607-9817 Contact: Sergio Carvalho, Dir. Emp: 5

CORNING INC.

One Riverfront Plaza,, Corning, NY, 14831

Tel: (607) 974-9000 Fax: (607) 974-8551 Web site: www.corning.com

Mfr. glass and specialty materials, consumer products; communications, laboratory services.

Corning Brasil Ind. e Com. Ltda., Av. Corning, 496, Suzano, SP 08613-370 Brazil

Tel: 55-11-476-3311 Fax: 55-11-476-1339 Contact: August Sá Pereira, Gen'l Mgr. Emp: 586

COUDERT BROTHERS

1114 Ave. of the Americas, New York, NY, 10036-7794

Tel: (212) 626-4400 Fax: (212) 626-4210 Web site: www.coudert.com

International law firm.

Coudert Brothers, c/o Machado, Meyer et al, Rua da Consolacao 247, 01301 São Paulo, SP, Brazil

COULTER CORPORATION

PO Box 169015, Miami, FL, 33116-9015

Tel: (305) 380-3800 Fax: (305) 380-8312

Mfr. blood analysis systems, flow cytometers, chemicals systems, scientific systems & reagents.

Coulter Electronics Industria e Commercio Ltda., Estrada do Mapua 591, Taquara, Jacarepagua, 22713 Rio de Janeiro, Brazil

CROWN CORK & SEAL COMPANY, INC.

One Crown Way, Philadelphia, PA, 19154-4599

Tel: (215) 698-5100 Fax: (215) 698-5201

Mfr. cans, bottle caps; filling & packaging machinery.

Crown Cork do Brazil SA, Rua Guaranta 468, Caixa Postal 10558, São Paulo, SP, Brazil

CUMMINS ENGINE CO., INC.

500 Jackson Street, PO Box 3005, Columbus, IN, 47202-3005

Tel: (812) 377-5000 Fax: (812) 377-3334

Mfr. diesel engines.

Cummins Brasil Ltda., Caixa Postal 13, 07270 Guaruchos, São Paulo, Brazil

Tel: 55-11-945-9811 Fax: 55-11-912-6296 Contact: Lucas Godinez, Pres. Emp: 1100

D'ARCY MASIUS BENTON & BOWLES INC. (DMB&B)

1675 Broadway, New York, NY, 10019

Tel: (212) 468-3622 Fax: (212) 468-2987 Web site: www.dmbb.com

Full service international advertising and communications group.

Salles/DMB&B, SCS Quadra 6 Bl.A., 157, Edif. Bandeirantes - sala 607, CEP 70300-910, Brasilia, DF Brazil

Tel: 55-61-226-2042 Fax: 55-61-226-1749 Contact: Monica Amaral Rebello, Mng. Dir.

Salles/Inter-Americana, R. Borges Lagoa 1328, 04038 São Paulo, SP, Brazil

D-M-E COMPANY

29111 Stephenson Highway, Madison Heights, MI, 48071

Tel: (248) 398-6000 Fax: (248) 544-5705

Basic tooling for plastic molding and die casting.

DME Polimold Ltda., Rua Vieira de Morais 311, Campo Belo, 04617 São Paulo, Brazil

DANA CORPORATION

4500 Door Street, Toledo, OH, 43615

Tel: (419) 535-4500 Fax: (419) 535-4643 Web site: www.dana.com

Mfr./sales of automotive, heavy truck, off-highway, fluid & mechanical power components.

Dana Corporation, Brazil

DATA GENERAL CORPORATION

4400 Computer Drive, Westboro, MA, 01580

Tel: (508) 898-5000 Fax: (508) 366-1319 Web site: www.dg.com

Design, mfr. general purpose computer systems & peripheral products & services.

Data General Ltda., Av. das Americas 4430, 22600 Barra da Tijuca, Rio de Janeiro, Brazil

DAYCO PRODUCTS INC.

1 Prestige Place, PO Box 1004, Miamisburg, OH, 45342

Tel: (937) 226-7000 Fax: (937) 226-4689

Diversified auto, industrial and household products.

Dayco do Brazil Ind. e Com. Ltda., Av. Marques de São Vincente 1205, Caixa Postal 4738, 01139 São Paulo, SP, Brazil

DDB NEEDHAM WORLDWIDE INC.

437 Madison Ave., New York, NY, 10022

Tel: (212) 415-2000 Fax: (212) 415-3417

Advertising agency.

DM9 DDB Needham, São Paulo, Brazil

DEKALB GENETICS CORP.

3100 Sycamore Road, DeKalb, IL, 60115-9600

Tel: (815) 758-3461 Fax: (815) 758-3711 Web site: www.dekalb.com

Develop/produce hybrid corn, sorghum, sunflower seed, varietal soybeans, alfalfa.

Braskalb Agropecuaria Brasileira Ltda., PO Box 1741 Rua Fernando Martini, 28, CEP 13073-060, Campinas, SP. Brazil

Tel: 55-19-243-5505 Fax: 55-19-243-0605 Contact: Jose Amauri Dimarzio, President

Sementes Selecionadas AD Ltd., Rodovia Assis Chateaubriand Km. 85, Caixa Postal 371, 14780 Barretos, SP, Brazil

DELL COMPUTER CORPORATION

One Dell Way, Round Rock, TX, 78682-2222

Tel: (512) 338-4400 Fax: (512) 728-3653 Web site: www.dell.com

Direct marketer & supplier of computer systems.

Dell Computer Company, Ltd., Brazil

DELOITTE TOUCHE TOHMATSU INTERNATIONAL

PO Box 820, Wilton, CT, 06897

Tel: (203) 761-3000 Fax: (203) 834-2200 Web site: www.u.s.deloitte.com or www.dtti.com

Accounting, audit, tax and management consulting services.

Deloitte Touche Tohmatsu, Av. Ipiranga, 32, 6o.andar, São Paulo ,SP 01046-010 Brazil

Tel: 55-11-257-0122 Fax: 55-11-258-8456 Contact: Jose B. Barretta, Mg. Ptnr.

Deloitte Touche Tohmatsu, Av. Presidente Wilson, 231-22, Andar, 20030-021 Rio de Janeiro, RJ, Brazil

DELTA AIR LINES INC.

PO Box 20706, Atlanta, GA, 30320-6001

Tel: (404) 715-2600 Fax: (404) 715-5494 Web site: www.delta-air.com/index.html

Major worldwide airline; international air transport services.

Delta Air Lines Inc., Locations in Fortaleza, Fliorianopolis and Porto Alegre, Brazil

DENTSPLY INTERNATIONAL

570 West College Ave., PO Box 872, York, PA, 17405-0872

Tel: (717) 845-7511 Fax: (717) 843-6357 Web site: www.dentsply.com

Mfr.& Distribution of dental supplies & equipment.

Dentsply Brazil, Rua Alice Herve 86, Bingen, 25665-010 Petropolis, RJ Brazil

Tel: 55-24-237-1262 Fax: 55-24-231-1137 Contact: Ricardo M. Filguriras, VP Emp: 800

DHL WORLDWIDE EXPRESS

333 Twin Dolphin Drive, Redwood City, CA, 94065

Tel: (650) 593-7474 Fax: (650) 593-1689 Web site: www.dhl.com

Worldwide air express carrier.

DHL Worldwide Express, Aveinda Vereador Jose Diniz 2421, São Paulo, SP 04603-001, Brazil

Tel: 55-11-536-2500

DIGITAL EQUIPMENT CORPORATION

111 Powder Mill Road, Maynard, MA, 01754

Tel: (978) 493-5111 Fax: (978) 493-7374 Web site: www.digital.com

Mfr. network computer systems, components, software and services.

Digital Equipment do Brasil Ltda., Av. Presidente Welson, 131, 26th Fl. Andar, CEP 20-030 Rio de Janeiro, Brazil

Tel: 55-21-277-6000 Fax: 55-21-262-0091

DIMON INCORPORATED

512 Bridge Street, PO Box 681, Danville, VA, 24543-0681

Tel: (804) 792-7511 Fax: (804) 791-0377

One of world's largest importer and exporter of leaf tobacco and fresh cut flowers.

Dimon do Brasil Tobacos Ltda., Rua Claudio Mandel 308, 96.880-000 Vera Cruz, Rio Grande do Sol, Brazil

Tel: 55-51-718-7100 Fax: 55-51-718-7119

WALT DISNEY COMPANY

500 South Buena Vista Street, Burbank, CA, 91521

Tel: (818) 560-1000 Fax: (818) 560-1930

Film/TV production, theme parks, resorts, publishing, recording and retail stores.

The Walt Disney Company (Brasil) Ltda., Rua General Jardim, 770, 12.o cj AB, São Paulo, SP 01223-010 Brazil

Tel: 55-11-257-4199 Fax: 55-11-258-3906 Contact: Elhanan Diesendruck, Pres. Emp: 27

DONALDSON, LUFKIN & JENRETTE, INC.

277 Park Ave., New York, NY, 10172

Tel: (212) 892-3000 Fax: (212) 892-7272 Web site: www.dlj.com

Investment banking, capital markets, and financial services.

Donaldson Lufkin & Jenrette Inc., Av. Brigadeiro Faria Lima, 1461-3rd Fl., 01481-900 São Paulo (SP) - Brazil

Tel: 55-11-817-2900

R.R. DONNELLEY & SONS COMPANY

77 West Wacker Drive, Chicago, IL, 60601-1696

Tel: (312) 326-8000 Fax: (312) 326-8543 Web site: www.rrdonnelley.com

Commercial printing, allied communication services.

Globo Cochrane Grafica Ltda., Rua Joana Foresto Storani, 676, Distrito Ind. CEP 13280-000, Vinhedo, São Paulo, SP Brazil

Tel: 55-11-287-4196 Fax: 55-11-285-3784 Contact: Jorge Planet, Pes. Emp: 300

R. R. Donnelley Financial, (JV) Cochrane International, Planet Consultores Associados, Rua Alfredo Trindade Moreira 37, Brooklin, São Paulo, SP CEP 04705-030, Brazil

Tel: 55-11-542-9916 Fax: 55-11-531-2810

THE DOW CHEMICAL COMPANY

2030 Dow Center, Midland, MI, 48674

Tel: (517) 636-1000 Fax: (517) 636-3228 Web site: www.atdow.com

Mfr. chemicals, plastics, pharmaceuticals, agricultural products, consumer products.

Cloroquim SA Ind. e Com., Praca do Patriarca, Predio Conde Matarazzo, São Paulo, SP, Brazil

Dow Quimica SA, Rua Alexandre Dumas, 1671, São Paulo, SP 04717-903 Brazil

Tel: 55-11-546-9122 Fax: 55-11-546-9385 Contact: Oscar Novo, Pres. Emp: 2300

DOW CORNING CORPORATION

2220 West Salzburg Road, PO Box 1767, Midland, MI, 48640

Tel: (517) 496-4000 Fax: (517) 496-6080

Silicones, silicon chemicals, solid lubricants.

Dow Corning do Brazil Ltda., Rua Francisco Tramontano, 100. 8o.andar, São Paulo, SP 06061-970 Brazil

Tel: 55-11-844-5199 Fax: 55-11-844-5727 Contact: Paulo A. Donatti, Dir. Emp: 90

DRAFT WORLDWIDE

633 North St. Clair Street, Chicago, IL, 60611-3211

Tel: (312) 944-3500 Fax: (312) 944-3566 Web site: www.draftworldwide.com

Full service international advertising agency.

DraftWorldwide, Av. Almirante Barroso, 139/10º Andar, 20013-005 Rio de Janeiro, Brazil

Tel: 55-21-532-3954 Fax: 55-21-532-3191 Contact: Pio Borges, Pres.

DraftWorldwide, Rua Padre Garcia Velbo, 73-1º Andar, 05421-030 Pinheiros, São Paulo, SP, Brazil

Tel: 55-11-815-9177 Fax: 55-11-815-9177 Contact: Pio Borges, Pres.

DRAKE BEAM MORIN INC.

101 Huntington Ave., Boston, MA, 02199

Tel: (617) 450-9860 Fax: (617) 267-2011 Web site: www.dbm.com

Human resource management consulting & training.

Drake Beam Morin do Brasil, Av. Eng. Luis Carlos Berrini 801, 2,5 & 6 andares, 04571-901 São Paulo, Brazil

Tel: 55-11-5503-3500 Fax: 55-11-5505-2957 Contact: Victoria C. Bloch, Dir. Emp: 18

Drake Beam Morin do Brasil, Av. Rio Branco, 89-21 andares, 20040-004 Rio de Janeiro - RJ, Brazil

Tel: 55-21-253-8481 Fax: 55-21-233-8007

DRESSER INDUSTRIES INC.

2001 Ross Ave., PO Box 718, Dallas, TX, 75221-0718

Tel: (214) 740-6000 Fax: (214) 740-6584 Web site: www.dresser.com

Diversified supplier of equipment & technical services to energy & natural resource industrial.

Dresser do Brasil Ltda., Rua Francisco Serrador 2, 20031 Rio de Janeiro, RJ, Brazil

Dresser Ind. e Com. Ltda., Estrada do Timbo, 126, Rio de Janeiro, RJ 21061 Brazil

Tel: 55-21-598-7722 Fax: 55-21-270-3487 Contact: Sergio Dabbur, Pres. Emp: 218

Dresser Industria e Com. Ltda., Jeffrey Equipamentos, Rua Dr. Cesar Castiglioni, 02515 São Paulo, Brazil

Masoneilan & Cia., Rua Hungaria 574, 01455 São Paulo, Brazil

Worthington do Brasil & Cia., Av. Suburbana 5451, 20751 Rio de Janeiro, RJ, Brazil

E.I. DU PONT DE NEMOURS & COMPANY

1007 Market Street, Wilmington, DE, 19898

Tel: (302) 774-1000 Fax: (302) 774-7321 Web site: www.dupont.com

Mfr./sale diversified chemicals, plastics, specialty products and fibers.

DuPont do Brazil SA, Rua de Consolacao 57, 1-andar, Caixa Postal 8112, São Paulo, SP, Brazil

DURACELL INTERNATIONAL INC.

Berkshire Industrial Park, Bethel, CT, 06801

Tel: (203) 796-4000 Fax: (203) 796-4745

Mfr. batteries.

Duracell Do Brasil Ind. e Com. Ltda., Av. Eng. Eusebio Stevaux 2105, São Paulo, SP 04696-000 Brazil Brazil

Tel: 55-11-521-2144 Fax: 55-11-521-1359 Contact: Luiz Carlos Sambo, Gen'l Mgr. Emp: 81

EASTMAN & BEAUDINE INC.

13355 Noel Road, Ste. 1370, Dallas, TX, 75240

Tel: (972) 661-5520 Fax: (972) 980-8540

Investments.

Eastman & Beaudine Inc., Rua Cardoso de Almeida 788 - conj. 53, 05013 São Paulo, Brazil

EASTMAN CHEMICAL

100 North Eastman Road, Kingsport, TN, 37660

Tel: (423) 229-2000 Fax: (423) 229-1351 Web site: www.eastman.com

Mfr. plastics, chemicals, fibers.

Eastman Chemical Brasileira Ltda., Av. Dr. Chucri Zaidan, 80, Bloco C-1 Andar, CJ.2C, CEP 04583-110 São Paulo - SP Brazil

Tel: 55-11-5506-9989 Fax: 55-11-5506-9262

EASTMAN KODAK COMPANY

343 State Street, Rochester, NY, 14650

Tel: (716) 724-4000 Fax: (716) 724-0663

Develop/mfr. photo & chemicals products, information management/video/copier systems, fibers/plastics for various industry.

Eastman Chemical Brasileira Ltda., Rua George Eastman 213, Caixa Postal 225, São Paulo, Brazil

Kodak Brasileira CIL, Rua George Eastman, 213, São Paulo, SP05690-900 Brazil

Tel: 55-11-845-2211 Fax: 55-11-844-5605 Contact: Gerald H. Greene Emp: 2700

Kodak Brasileira CIL, Also in Porto Alegre, Recife, Resende, Rio de Janeiro & San Jose dos Campos, Brazil

Kodak do Amazonas Ind. e Com. Ltda., Av. Maues 1330, 69000 Amazonas, Brazil

EATON CORPORATION

1111 Superior Ave., Cleveland, OH, 44114

Tel: (216) 523-5000 Fax: (216) 479-7068

Advanced technical products for transportation & industrial markets.

Eaton Corp. do Brazil, Almeda Franca 84, 04222 São Paulo, Brazil

Eaton Ltda., Rua Bela Cintra, 746, Ctjo. 31, São Paulo, SP 01415-902, Brazil , Brazil

Tel: 55-11-259-3955 Fax: 55-11-214-1090 Contact: Enrique Genaro Chenio, Mgr. Emp: 1075

Eaton S.A. Ind. de Pecas e Acessorios, Via Presidenta Dutra Km 325, São Jose dos Campos, SP, Brazil

Eaton-Yale & Towne Ltda., Div. Fuller, Av. Capuava 603, Santo Andre, SP, Brazil

EATON CORP/CUTLER HAMMER

4201 North 27th Street, Milwaukee, WI, 53216

Tel: (414) 449-6000 Fax: (414) 449-6221

Electric control apparatus, mfr. of advanced technologic products.

Eaton Corp. do Brasil, Rua Bela Cintra 746, 01415 São Paulo, Brazil

ECHLIN INC.

100 Double Beach Road, Branford, CT, 06405

Tel: (203) 481-5751 Fax: (203) 481-6485 Web site: www.echlin.com

Supplies commercial vehicle components and auto fluid handling systems for the used car market

Echlin Inc., Sao Paulo, Brazil

ECOLAB INC.

Ecolab Center, 370 N. Wabasha Street, St. Paul, MN, 55102

Tel: (612) 293-2233 Fax: (612) 225-3105 Web site: www.ecolab.com

Develop/mfr. premium cleaning, sanitizing and maintenance products and services for the hospitality, institutional, and residential markets.

Ecolab Química Ltda., Av. Brigadeiro Luiz Antonio, 3767 a 3779, São Paulo, SP 01401-001 Brazil

Tel: 55-11-886-2500 Fax: 55-11-885-8479 Contact: Richard G. Johnson, VP Emp: 300

EDELMAN PUBLIC RELATIONS WORLDWIDE

200 East Randolph Drive, 63rd Floor, Chicago, IL, 60601

Tel: (312) 240-3000 Fax: (312) 240-0596 Web site: www.edelman.com

International independent public relations firm.

Edelman do Brasil, Rua Joaquim Floriano, 820/834 - 19 andar, San Paulo - 04534-003, Brazil

Tel: 55-11-866-8400 Fax: 55-11-866-1230 Contact: Vivian Pinto Hirsch, Gen. Mgr.

J.D. EDWARDS & COMPANY

One Technology Way, Denver, CO, 80237

Tel: (303) 334-4000 Fax: (303) 334-4970 Web site: www.jdedwards.com.

Computer software products.

J. D. Edwards Brazil, Rua Quintana, 753 - 3o Andar, 04569-011, São Paulo, Brazil

Tel: 55-11-5505-3133 Fax: 55-11-5505-3168

EMC CORP.

35 Parkwood Drive, Hopkinton, MA, 01748-9103

Tel: (508) 435-1000 Fax: (508) 435-8884 Web site: www.emc.com

Designs/supplies intelligent enterprise storage & retrieval technology for open systems, mainframes & midrange environments.

EMC Computer Systems - Brasilia, Rua Geraldo Flausino, Gomes, 78 1st Fl., São Paulo (SP), Brazil

Tel: 55-11-5505-2646

EMCO WHEATON INC.

409A Airport Blvd, Morrisville, NC, 27560

Tel: (919) 467-5878 Fax: (919) 467-7718

Mfr. petroleum handling equipment.

Emco Wheaton Ind. & Com. SA, Caixa Postal 2602, ZC-00, Rio de Janeiro, Brazil

ENCYCLOPAEDIA BRITANNICA INC.

310 S. Michigan Ave., Chicago, IL, 60604

Tel: (312) 427-9700 Fax: (312) 294-2176 Web site: www.E.B.com

Publishing; books.

Encyclopaedia Britannica do Brasil Publicações Ltda., Rua Rego Freitas, 192, sala 1, São Paulo, SP 01220-907 Brazil

Tel: 55-11-224-8211 Fax: 55-11-221-8747 Contact: Luiz Carlos da S. Albuquerque Emp: 427

ENRON CORPORATION

1400 Smith Street, Houston, TX, 77002-7361

Tel: (713) 853-6161 Fax: (713) 853-3129 Web site: www.enron.com

Exploration, production, transportation and distribution of integrated natural gas and electricity.

Enron do Brasil Servicos Ltda., R. Helena No. 235, V. Olimpia, São Paulo, SP, Brazil

ERICO PRODUCTS INC.

34600 Solon Road, Cleveland, OH, 44139

Tel: (440) 248-0100 Fax: (440) 248-0723

Mfr. electric welding apparatus & hardware, metal stampings, specialty fasteners.

Erico do Brazil, Caixa Postal 30397, Av. Santa Marina 1.588, 05036 São Paulo, Brazil

ERNST & YOUNG, LLP

787 Seventh Ave., New York, NY, 10019

Tel: (212) 773-3000 Fax: (212) 773-6350 Web site: www.eyi.com

Accounting and audit, tax and management consulting services.

Ernst & Young, Av. Presidente Jusce Kubitscheck, 1830 Torre 1, Flores 3, 5-804543-900 São Paulo, Brazil

Ernst & Young, Av. Rio Branco, 128, 16th Fl., (Caixa Postal 4660) 20001-970 Rio de Janeiro, RJ Brazil

Tel: 55-21-203-2424 Fax: 55-21-224-2751 Contact: Jose Manuel R. da Silva

ESCO CORPORATION

2141 NW 25th Ave., Portland, OR, 97210

Tel: (503) 228-2141 Fax: (503) 778-6330

Mfr. equipment for mining, construction and forestry industries.

Maquinesco, Conjunto Nacional Edif. Horsa 1, Av. Paulista 2073, sala 1312, 01311 São Paulo, SP, Brazil

EURO RSCG Worldwide

350 Hudson Street, New York, NY, 10014

Tel: (212) 886-2000 Fax: (212) 886-2016

International advertising agency group.

Carillo Pastore Euro RSCG, São Paulo, Brazil

EXCEL INDUSTRIES, INC.

1120 North Main Street, Elkhart, IN, 46514

Tel: (219) 264-2131 Fax: (219) 264-2136 Web site: www.excelinc.com

Mfg. automotive, heavy truck, RV and bus components.

Dura Automotive Systems, Sao Paulo, Brazil

EXXON CORPORATION

225 E. John W. Carpenter Freeway, Irving, TX, 75062-2298

Tel: (972) 444-1000 Fax: (972) 444-1882 Web site: www.exxon.com

Petroleum exploration, production, refining; mfr. petroleum & chemicals products; coal & minerals.

Esso Brasileira de Petroleo Ltda., Av. Presidente Wilson 118, Rio de Janeiro, RJ 20020-030 Brazil

Tel: 55-21-277-2000 Fax: 55-21-227-2037 Contact: William A. Jackson, Pres. Emp: 1280

Exxon Quimica, Rua Campo da Ribeira 51, Ribeira - Ilha Governador, Rio de Janeiiro, Brazil 21930-080

Tel: 55-21-386-2270

THE FALK CORPORATION

3001 W. Canal Street, PO Box 492,, Milwaukee, WI, 53208

Tel: (414) 238-4919 Fax: (414) 937-4359 Web site: www.falkcorp.com

Designers and manufacturers of power transmission equipment including gears, geared reducers & drives, couplings.

PTI Brasil, Rua Jose Martins Coelho 300, 04461-050 São Paulo, Brazil

Tel: 55-11-882-1000 Fax: 55-11-548-1234 Contact: Claudio Bertolla, Pres. Emp: 233

FDX CORPORATION (FED EX)

2005 Corporate Ave., PO Box 727, Memphis, TN, 38194

Tel: (901) 369-3600 Fax: (901) 395-2000 Web site: www.fdxcorp.com

Package express delivery service.

Federal Express Corporation, Av. das Naçõs Unidas, 17891 São Paulo, SP 04795-100 Brazil

Tel: 55-11-5147300 Fax: 55-11-5147314 Contact: David B. Ogilvie, Gen. Mgr. Emp: 310

FEDERAL-MOGUL CORPORATION

26555 Northwestern Highway, PO Box 1966, Southfield, MI, 48034

Tel: (248) 354-7700 Fax: (248) 354-8983 Web site: www.federalmogul.com

Mfr./distributor precision parts for automobiles, trucks, farm and construction vehicles.

Federal-Mogul Comercio Internacional SA, São Paulo, Brazil

Glyco do Brasil, São Paulo, Brazil

FERRO CORPORATION

1000 Lakeside Ave., Cleveland, OH, 44114-1183

Tel: (216) 641-8580 Fax: (216) 696-5784 Web site: www.ferro.com

Mfr. Specialty chemicals, coatings, plastics, colors, refractories.

Ferro Enamel do Brazil Ind e Com. Ltda., Av. Senador Vergueiro 2720, Rudge Ramos, 09740 São Bernardo do Campo, São Paulo, Brazil (Office: Santa Catarina, Rio Claro.)

Tel: 55-11-455-2700 Fax: 55-11-455-2743 Contact: Larry Hall, Mng. Dir.

Nutriplant ICL, Caixa Postal 097, Av. Constante Pavan 1155, 13140 Paulina, São Paulo, Brazil

Tel: 55-11-450-3155 Fax: 55-11-450-3977

FIREMENS INSURANCE COMPANY OF NEWARK

180 Maiden Lane, New York, NY, 10038

Tel: (212) 440-3000 Fax: (212) 440-7130

Fire, marine and casualty insurance.

Firemen's Insurance Co. of Newark, NJ, Rua Senador Dantas 74, andar 9, ZC-06, Rio de Janeiro, RJ, Brazil

FISHER SCIENTIFIC INC.

Liberty Lane, Hampton, NH, 03842

Tel: (603) 929-5911 Fax: (603) 929-0222 Web site: www.fisher1.com

Mfr. science instruments & apparatus, chemicals, reagents.

Vidy Fabricação de Laboratórios, Rodovia Regis Bittencourt, 3360, Taboão da Serra, SP 06793-000 Brazilã

Tel: 55-11-491-5511 Fax: 55-11-491-3399 Contact: Charles Henri Stauffenegger, Chmn. Emp: 190

FISHER-ROSEMOUNT

8000 Maryland Ave., Ste. 500, Clayton, MO, 63105-4755

Tel: (314) 746-9900 Fax: (314) 746-9974

Mfr. industrial process control equipment.

Fisher Controls do Brasil Ltda., Rua Paes Leme 524, 05424 São Paulo, Brazil

FLOWSERVE CORPORATION

222 W. Los Cloinas Blvd., Irving, TX, 75039

Tel: (972) 443-6500 Fax: (972) 443-6858 Web site: www.flowserve.com

Mfr. chemicals equipment, pumps, valves, filters, fans and heat exchangers.

Valtek Brazil, Brazil

FLOWSERVE FLUID SEALING DIVISION

222 Los Colinas Blvd., Ste. 1500, Irving, TX, 75039

Tel: (616) 381-2650 Fax: (616) 443-6800 Web site: www.flowserve.com

Mfr. mechanical seals, compression packings and auxiliaries.

Durametallic do Brazil Ltda., Av. Casa Grande 1655, Diadema, SP09961-350 Brazil

Tel: 55-11-746-7877 Fax: 55-11-746-7014 Contact: Reginaldo T. Marques Emp: 116

FMC CORPORATION

200 E. Randolph Drive, Chicago, IL, 60601

Tel: (312) 861-6000 Fax: (312) 861-6141

Produces chemicals & precious metals, mfr. machinery, equipment & systems for industrial, agricultural & government use.

CBV Industria Mecanica SA, Brazil

FMC do Brazil Ind. e Com Ltda., Alameda Campinas, 462, 1o. andar, São Paulo, SP 01404-902 Brazil

Tel: 55-11-283-2722 Fax: 55-11-285-3601 Contact: Silvio Tichauer, Dir. Emp: 506

FMC-Kramer SA, Brazil

Jetway Systems Equipamentos Aeroportuarios Ltda., Brazil

FOAMEX INTERNATIONAL

1000 Columbia Ave., Linwood, PA, 19061

Tel: (800) 776-3626 Fax: (610) 859-3085

Mfr. polyurethane foam.

Foamex do Brasil, Rua Gilbergo Laste 110, 90850-300 Porto Alegre, RS, Brazil

FORD MOTOR COMPANY

The American Road, Dearborn, MI, 48121

Tel: (313) 322-3000 Fax: (313) 322-9600 Web site: www.ford.com

Mfr./sales motor vehicles.

Autolatina, Rua Professor Manoelito de Ornellas 303, 04719 São Paulo, Brazil

Ford do Brazil SA, Rua Profesor de Ornellas 303, 04799 São Paulo, Brazil

Tel: 55-11-5787970 Fax: 55-11-8489050 Contact: Ivan Fonseca e Silva, Pres. Emp: 17800

FORRESTER RESEARCH, INC.

1033 Massachusetts Ave., Cambridge, MA, 02138

Tel: (617) 497-7090 Fax: (617) 868-0577 Web site: www.forrester.com

Provides clients an analysis of the effect of changing technologies on their operations.

Intelligence Technologia S/C Ltda., Av. Nove de Julho, 5.617 - 7º -cj. 7A - CP 01407-200, São Paulo, Brazil

Tel: 55-11-3064-3558 Contact: Juliette Brown

FRANKEL & COMPANY

2 World Trade Center, New York, NY, 10048-0002

Tel: (212) 488-0200 Fax: (212) 488-1800

Insurance brokers.

Adams & Porter Sociedade de Corretagem de Seguros Ltda., Caixa Postal 30321, 01051 São Paulo, Brazil

Adams & Porter Sociedade de Corretagem de Seguros Ltda., Av. Beira Mar 200, 10 andar, 20021 Rio de Janeiro, Brazil

FRANKLIN RESOURCES, INC.

777 Mariners Island Blvd., San Mateo, CA, 94404

Tel: (415) 312-2000 Fax: (415) 312-3655 Web site: www.frk.com

Global and domestic investment advisory and portfolio management.

Templeton DO Brazil - Consultoria Financeira LTDA, Rio de Janeiro, Brazil

FRITZ COMPANIES INC.

706 Mission Street, Ste. 900, San Francisco, CA, 94103

Tel: (415) 904-8360 Fax: (415) 904-8661 Web site: www.fritz.com

Integrated transportation, sourcing, distribution & customs brokerage services.

Fritz do Brasil Transportes Interncionais Ltda., Rua Marcos Fernandes 146, Jardim da Saude, 04149-120 São Paulo, Brazil (Locations: Belo Horizonte, Blumenau, Campinas/Viracopos, Curitiba, Fortakeza, Franca, Manaus, Novo Hamburgo, Osasco, Porto Alegre, Recife, Rio de Janeiro, Salvador, Santos, Vitoria)

H.B. FULLER COMPANY

1200 Willow Lake Blvd., Vadnais Heights, MN, 55110

Tel: (612) 236-5900 Fax: (612) 236-5898 Web site: www.hbfuller.com

Mfr./distributor adhesives, sealants, coatings, paints, waxes, sanitation chemicals.

H.B. Fuller Brasil Ltda., Av. Brigadeiro Faria Lima, 1234 7.0 andar, CEP 01451-001, São Paulo, Brazil

Tel: 55-11-814-0933 Fax: 55-11-816-8003

H.B. Fuller Brasil Ltda., Rua Professor Joaquim Silva 669, Sorocaba, Caixa Postal 777, 18000 São Paulo, Brazil

Tel: 55-15-228-2500 Fax: 55-15-228-2364

H.B. Fuller Latin America, Mercosur Adhesives Division Office, Av. Brigadeiro Faria Lima, 1234 7.0 andar, CEP 01451-001, São Paulo SP, Brazil

Tel: 55-11-814-0933 Fax: 55-11-814-2471

GAF CORPORATION

1361 Alps Road, Wayne, NJ, 07470

Tel: (973) 628-3000 Fax: (973) 628-3326 Web site: www.gaf.com

Mfr. building materials.

GAF do Brasil Industria e Comercio Ltda., Rua Major Sertoria 212-2, andar, Caixa Postal 9693, 01222, São Paulo SP, Brazil

GARLOCK SEALING TECHNOLOGIES

1666 Division Street, Palmyra, NY, 14522

Tel: (315) 597-4811 Fax: (315) 597-3216 Web site: www.garlock-inc.com

Mfr. of gaskets, packing, seals and expansion joints.

Garlock do Brasil, Av. Bernardino de Campos, No. 98 5o Andar Conjunto B., Sâo Paulo, SP, Brazil

Tel: 55-11-884-9680

THE GATES RUBBER COMPANY

990 S. Broadway, PO Box 5887, Denver, CO, 80217-5887

Tel: (303) 744-1911 Fax: (303) 744-4000

Mfr. rubber tires/inner tubes & industrial belts & hose.

Gates do Brasil Ind. e Com. Ltda., Rua Cesario Alvim 602/634, Caixa Postal 10692, São Paulo 03054-900, Brazil

Tel: 55-11-291-8822 Fax: 55-11-2911700 Contact: William Wroblewski, Pres. Emp: 794

GENERAL ELECTRIC CO.

3135 Easton Turnpike, Fairfield, CT, 06431

Tel: (203) 373-2211 Fax: (203) 373-3131 Web site: www.ge.com

Diversified manufacturing, technology and services.

GE FANUC Automation, Av. Nove de Julho 5229, São Paulo - SP, CEP 01407, Brazil

Tel: 55-11-3067-8158 Fax: 55-11-3061-1455

General Electric do Brazil S.A., Rua Miguel Angelo, 37, PO Box 109 CEP 20785, Rio e Janiero, RJ 20785-220 Brazil

Tel: 55-21-201-8012 Fax: 55-21-281-9547 Contact: Kurt Josef Meier, Chmn. Emp: 2800

General Electric do Brazil S.A., Av. Nove de Julho, 5229, 8o. andar, São Paulo, SP 01407-907 Brazil

Tel: 55-11-3067-8050 Fax: 55-11-3067-8039 Contact: Kurt Josef Meier, Gen. Mgr. Emp: 2700

GEPS Global Power Generation, Claudio de Vasconcellos General Electric do Brazil S.A., Rio de Janeiro - RJ 20010-020, Brazil

Tel: 55-21-262-3644 Fax: 55-21-262-5087

GEVISA, Av. Mofarrej 592, São Paulo - SP 05311-000, Brazil (Office: Campinas - SP.)

Tel: 55-11-260-8211

GENERAL MOTORS ACCEPTANCE CORPORATION

100 Renaissance Center, Detroit, MI, 48243-7301

Tel: (313) 556-5000 Fax: (313) 556-5108 Web site: www.gmac.com

Automobile financing.

Financiadora GM, Alamedo Santos 647, São Paulo, SP, Brazil

GENERAL MOTORS CORPORATION

100 Renaissance Center, Detroit, MI, 48243.7301

Tel: (313) 556-5000 Fax: (313) 556-5108 Web site: www.gm.com

Mfr. full line vehicles, automotive electronics, commercial technologies, telecommunications, space, finance.

General Motors do Brasil, Av. Goiás, 1805, São Caetano do Sul, SP 09550-900 Brazil

il

Tel: 55-11-741-8229 Fax: 55-11-741-8572 Contact: André Beer, Pres. Emp: 19200

GENERAL REINSURANCE CORPORATION

695 East Main Street, Stamford, CT, 06904-2350

Tel: (203) 328-5000 Fax: (203) 328-6423 Web site: www.genre.com

Reinsurance services worldwide.

General & Cologne Re Brazil Ltda., Av. das Nações Unidas, 11.541, 14 andar - cj. 141, São Paulo - SP 04578-000, Brazil

Tel: 55-11-5506-3088 Fax: 55-11-5506-3630 Contact: Daniel Castillo, Mgr

GEONEX CORPORATION

8950 9th Street North, St. Petersburg, FL, 33702

Tel: (813) 578-0100 Fax: (813) 577-6946

Geo-information services: mapping, resource interpretation, analysis, testing and data base management.

Geonex Corp., Rua Martins Ferreira 79, Botafoga, Rio de Janeiro, RJ, Brazil

THE GILLETTE COMPANY

Prudential Tower Building, Boston, MA, 02199

Tel: (617) 421-7000 Fax: (617) 421-7123 Web site: www.gillette.com

Develop/mfr. personal care/use products: blades & razors, toiletries, cosmetics, stationery.

Braun do Brasil & Cia., São Paulo, Brazil

Contact: Eduardo V. Kello

Escovas Dentais do Brasil Ltda., Rio de Janeiro, Brazil

Fabrica Amazonense de Componentes Plasticos e Metalicos Ltda, Amazonas, Brazil

Felicitas Comercial e Cie., São Paulo, Brazil

Fortuna Comercial & Cia., Rio de Janeiro, Brazil

Gillette de Amazonia SA, Manaus, Amazonas, Brazil

Gillette do Brasil e Cia., Rio de Janeiro, Brazil

Gillette do Brasil e Cia., Rua Tito, 66, 4o. andar, São Paulo, SP 05051-000 Brazil

Tel: 55-11-263-4055 Fax: 55-11-864-3195 Contact: Alberto Tavares de Salles, Gen.Mgr. Emp: 77

Jafra Comercio, Participancoes e Servicos & Cie., San Paulo, Brazil

Ruby Participacoes Ltda., Rio de Janeiro, Brazil

Wilkinson Sword de Amazonia SA, Manaus, Amazonas, Brazil

GLENAYRE ELECTRONICS LTD.

1 Glenayre Way, Quincy, IL, 62301

Tel: (217) 223-3211 Fax: (217) 223-3284

Mfr. Infrastructure components and pagers.

Glenayre Electronics South America Ltda., 3rd Fl., Av. Paulista 1754, CEP 01310-200, São Paulo-SP, Brazil

Tel: 55-11-284-1922 Fax: 55-11-289-9370

GOLD STANDARD INC

712 Kearns Bldg., Salt Lake City, UT, 84101

Tel: (801) 328-4452 Fax: (801) 328-4457

Gold mining exploration.

Gold Standard Minas SA, Rua Joaquim Augusto de Andrade 257, Jardim das Americas, CEP 81520-010 Curitiba, Brazil

GOLDMAN SACHS & COMPANY

85 Broad Street, New York, NY, 10004

Tel: (212) 902-1000 Fax: (212) 902-3000 Web site: www.gs.com

Investment bankers; securities broker dealers.

Glodman, Sachs & Companhia, Av. Brigadeiro Faria Lima,1461-2o.andar-Cj.22, 01452-900 São Paulo, Brazil

Tel: 55-11-816-1036 Fax: 55-11-816-8256 Contact: Eduardo Gentil, VP Emp: 2

THE GOODYEAR TIRE & RUBBER COMPANY

1144 East Market Street, Akron, OH, 44316

Tel: (330) 796-2121 Fax: (330) 796-1817 Web site: www.goodyear.com

Mfr. tires, automotive belts and hose, conveyor belts, chemicals; oil pipeline transmission.

Goodyear do Brazil Produtos de Borracha Ltda., Av. Paulista 854, 01310 São Paulo, SP, Brazil (Locatons: Americana & Maua.)

Tel: 55-11-285-2244 Fax: 55-11-285-4001 Contact: John Charles Polhemus, Pres. Emp: 5700

GOULDS PUMPS INC.

240 Fall Street, Seneca Falls, NY, 13148

Tel: (315) 568-2811 Fax: (315) 568-2418

Mfr. industrial and water systems pumps.

Goulds Bombas e Equipamentos Ltda., Estrada ITU-Salto Km. 40, CXP 91 Salto, São Paulo, Brazil

W. R. GRACE & COMPANY

One Town Center Road, 1750 Clint Moore Road, Boca Raton, FL, 33486-1010

Tel: (561) 362-2000 Fax: (561) 561-2193 Web site: www.grace.com

Mfr. specialty chemicals and materials: packaging, health care, catalysts, construction, water treatment/process.

Grace Brasil Ltda., Av. Mofarrej, 619, São Paulo, SP 05311-902 Brazil

Tel: 55-11-833-2600 Fax: 55-11-832-2058 Contact: João Batista Rodrigues Aloe Emp: 1023

GREENBERG, TRAURIG, HOFFMAN, LIPOFF, ROSEN & QUENTEL

1221 Brickell Ave., Miami, FL, 33131

Tel: (305) 579-0500 Fax: (305) 579-0717 Web site: www.gtlaw.com

International law firm.

Greenberg, Traurig, Hoffman, Lipoff, Rosen & Quentel, Av. Paulista, No. 2006, Conjunto 509, 5 andar, São Paulo, SP Brazil

Tel: 55-11-288-7673 Fax: 55-11-283-4360

GREY ADVERTISING INC.

777 Third Ave., New York, NY, 10017

Tel: (212) 546-2000 Fax: (212) 546-1495 Web site: www.giworldwwide.com

International advertising agency.

Z+G Grey Comunicação Ltda., Av. Doutor Cadosa de Melo, 855, 11o. andar, São Paulo, SP 04548-005 Brazil

Tel: 55-11-822-4417 Fax: 55-11-828-0193 Contact: Sergio Guerreiro, Mg. Dir.

GTE CORPORATION

One Stamford Forum, Stamford, CT, 06904

Tel: (203) 965-2000 Fax: (203) 965-2277 Web site: www.gte.com

Electronic products, telecommunications systems, publishing and communications.

Automatic Electric do Brazil SA, Rua Conselheiro Crispiano 69, andar 6, São Paulo, SP, Brazil

GTE International Telecom Services, Rua 13 de Maio 238/240, Caixa Postal 9212, São Paulo, SP, Brazil

Sylvania Produtos Electricos Ltda., Rua Amoipira 157, São Paulo, SP, Brazil

HALLIBURTON COMPANY

500 North Akard Street, Ste. 3600, Dallas, TX, 75201-3391

Tel: (214) 978-2600 Fax: (214) 978-2685 Web site: www.halliburton.com

Energy, construction and insurance.

Halliburton Ltd., Rua do Rocio, 291 Conj. 12, Ed. Atrium III - Vila Olimpia, 04552-00, São Paulo, Brazil

Tel: 55-11-3040-0430 Fax: 55-11-3040-0431

Halliburton Ltd., Praia do Flamengo, 200, 23 Andar, 22210-020 Rio de Janeiro RJ, Brazil

Tel: 55-21-456-4343 Fax: 55-21-285-6399

Halliburton Ltd., Rodovia BR-235 KM4, 49160, NS Socorro, Aracaju, Brazil

Tel: 55-79-241-4847 Fax: 55-79-241-4847

Halliburton Ltd., Rua Jose Visc, s/n, 48.100-000, Catu BA, Brazil

Tel: 55-71-841-1311 Fax: 55-71-841-1812

HARCOURT BRACE & COMPANY

6277 Sea Harbor Drive, Orlando, FL, 32887

Tel: (407) 345-2000 Fax: (407) 345-9354

Book publishing, tests and related service, journals, facsimile reprints, management consult, operates parks/shows.

Harcourt Brace Brazil, Praia de Botofogo 252 B1 01/702, Rio de Janeiro 22250-040 R. J., Brazil

Tel: 55-21-553-1504 Fax: 55-21-553-1504 Contact: Ms. Adriana Motta Antonaccio

HARNISCHFEGER INDUSTRIES INC

PO Box 554, Milwaukee, WI, 53201

Tel: (414) 797-6480 Fax: (414) 797-6573 Web site: www.harnischfeger.com

Mfr. mining and material handling equipment, papermaking machinery and computer systems.

Beloit Industrial Ltda., Rua Olinto Lunardi 1400, 13067-200 Campinas, Brazil

Harnischfeger do Brazil Com. e Ind. Ltda., Av. Paulista 2202, andar 7, São Paulo, SP 01310-932, Brazil

Tel: 55-11-289-0855 Fax: 55-11-2881823 Contact: Jaime Carlos Julian Ronco Emp: 100

THE HARPER GROUP

260 Townsend Street, San Francisco, CA, 94107-1719

Tel: (415) 978-0600 Fax: (415) 978-0692 Web site: www.circleintl.com

Ocean/air freight forwarding, customs brokerage, packing and wholesale, logistics management and insurance.

Amazon Cargo c/o Amazoncargo Transporte Internacionais Ltda., Rua Dos Andradas, 387, Loja 1, Manaus, 69003-180, Brazil

Tel: 55-92-633-2737 Fax: 55-92-622-4052

Belo Horizonte (BHZ), Sonave Agencia Maritima, Av. Brasil, 84 6.0 Andar, Belo Harizonte, Minas Gerave, Brazil

Tel: 55-31-241-2900

Circle International, Rua Professora Heloisa Carneiro, 21, São Paulo, 04630.050, Brazil

Tel: 55-11-536-0599 Fax: 55-11--542-7113

Circle International, Rua Cardoso de Moraes, 61-conj. 1103/1105, Bonsucesso, 21032.000, Brazil

Tel: 55-21-260-6401 Fax: 55-21-290-8609

Circle International, c/o Pierri Sobrinho S.A, Av. Estados Unidos, 528, Salvador, 40010 010, Brazil

Tel: 55-71-242-9166 Fax: 55-71-243-0712

Circle International, Rue Professora Heloisa Carneiro, 21, São Paulo, 04630.050, Brazil

Tel: 55-11-536-0599 Fax: 55-11-542-7113

Circle International, Rua Bento Goncalves, 2310 S/104, Novo Hamburgo, RS, 93510-000, Brazil

Tel: 55-51-593-3277 Fax: 55-51-593-3277

Circle International, Rua Barao de Paranapanema, 146, Bloco B - 40xb0 andar, Sala 43, Conjunto 43, Campinas, 13026 100, Brazil

Tel: 55-19-2524-666 Fax: 55-19-2521-988

Circle International, c/o Pinho Comissaria de Despachos S/A, Rua Mal, Deodoro, 503 16 Andar, Curitiba, 80020,320, Brazil

Tel: 55-41-322-4241 Fax: 55-41-234-8357

Circle International, c/o Amazonas Doce Mar Ltda., Praca do Arsenal de Marinha, 35,9o. Andar Sala 904, Recife, 50030 360, Brazil

Tel: 55-81-224-9739 Fax: 55-81-224-9992

HARRIS CORPORATION

1025 West NASA Blvd., Melbourne, FL, 32919

Tel: (407) 727-9100 Fax: (407) 727-9344 Web site: www.harris.com

Mfr. communications and information-handling equipment, including copying and fax systems.

Harris do Brasil Ltda., Rua Gomes de Carvalho 1356, Ed. Mykonos, Conjunto 41, CEP 04547-005 São Paulo, Brazil

HARTFORD LIFE INTERNATIONAL, LTD.

200 Hopmeadow Street, Simsbury, CT, 06070

Tel: (860) 843-8982 Fax: (860) 843-8981

Life insurance and group life sales.

Icatu Hartford Seguros, Av. Presidente Wilson, 231-12o Andar, Centro, Rio de Janeiro, Brazil 20030=012

Tel: 55-21-292-3900 Fax: 55-21-532-0362 Contact: Nilton Molina, Mng. Dir.

HEIDRICK & STRUGGLES INC

Sears Tower, 233 South Wacker Drive, Chicago, IL, 60606

Tel: (312) 496-1200 Fax: (312) 496-1290 Web site: www.h-s.com

Executive search firm.

Heidrick & Struggles Intl. Inc., Rua das Nacoes Unidas 11.541, 11° andar, 04578-903 São Paulo, SP Brazil

Tel: 55-11-5504-4000

HERCULES INC

Hercules Plaza, 1313 North Market Street, Wilmington, DE, 19894-0001

Tel: (302) 594-5000 Fax: (302) 594-5400 Web site: www.herc.com

Mfr. specialty chemicals, plastics, film and fibers, coatings, resins, food ingredients.

Hercules Chemicals, Paulinia, Brazil

Hercules do Brazil Produtos Quimicos, Rua Mariana Correa, 562, São Paulo, SP 01444-900 Brazil

Tel: 55-11-280-6599 Fax: 55-11-853-1690 Contact: Juan Sabaté Pérez, Pres. Emp: 64

HEWITT ASSOCIATES LLC

100 Half Day Road, Lincolnshire, IL, 60069

Tel: (847) 295-5000 Fax: (847) 295-7634

Employee benefits consulting firm.

Hewitt Associates, Calcada das Orquideas, 186, Centro Comercial lphaville, Barueri, São Paulo, Brazil

Tel: 55-11-7295-3297

HEWLETT-PACKARD COMPANY

3000 Hanover Street, Palo Alto, CA, 94304-0890

Tel: (650) 857-1501 Fax: (650) 857-7299 Web site: www.hp.com

Mfr. computing, communications & measurement products & services.

Edisa Hewlett-Packard (EHP) SA, Rodovia Campinas-Paulina, Campinas, SP 13084-310 Brazil

Tel: 55-19-239-0044 Fax: 55-19-239-0044 Contact: Flavio Sehn, Pres. Emp: 121

HILTON HOTELS CORPORATION

9336 Civic Center Drive, Beverly Hills, CA, 90210

Tel: (310) 278-4321 Fax: (310) 205-7880

International hotel chain: Hilton International, Vista Hotels and Hilton National Hotels.

Hilton International Company, Rua Martins Fontes 330, 01050-000 São Paulo, SP, Brazil

HOHENBERG BROS COMPANY

7101 Goodlett Farms Parkway, Cordova, TN, 38018

Tel: (901) 937-4500 Fax: (901) 937-4464

Mfr. cotton.

Hohenberg SA, Comercio de Algodao, Rua Jose Bonifacio 278, Salas 406-407, São Paulo, SP, Brazil

HOLIDAY INNS WORLDWIDE, INC.

3 Ravinia Drive, Ste. 2900, Atlanta, GA, 30346-2149

Tel: (770) 604-2000 Fax: (770) 604-5403

Hotels, restaurants and casinos.

Holiday Inn, Av. Ana Costa 555, Santos, SP, Brazil

Holiday Inn, Rua Washington Luiz 399, Americana, SP, Brazil

Holiday Inn, Rua Aymores 501, Marilia, São Paulo, Brazil

Holiday Inn, Rua Alvares Cabral 1.120, Ribeirao Preto, Brazil

HONEYWELL INC.

PO Box 524, Minneapolis, MN, 55440-0524

Tel: (612) 951-1000 Fax: (612) 951-3066 Web site: www.honeywell.com

Develop/mfr. controls for home and building, industry, space and aviation.

Honeywell do Brasil & Cia., Rua Jose Alves da Cunha Lima 172, Butanta, 05360-050 São Paulo, Brazil

HORWATH INTERNATIONAL

415 Madison Ave., New York, NY, 10017

Tel: (212) 838-5566 Fax: (212) 838-3636

Public accountants and auditors.

Soteconti Auditores Independentes S/C, Av. Paulista 1754, 01310 São Paulo, SP, Brazil

HOUGHTON INTERNATIONAL INC.

PO Box 930, Madison & Van Buren Avenues, Valley Forge, PA, 19482-0930

Tel: (610) 666-4000 Fax: (610) 666-1376

Mfr. specialty chemicals, hydraulic fluids & lubricants.

E.F. Houghton do Brazil Ltda., Rua Alpont, 170, Mauá, SP 09390-1100 Brazil

Tel: 55-11-450-2133 Fax: 55-11-450-2216 Contact: Claiton E. Scalea, Pres.

HOUSTON INDUSTRIES INCORPORATED

1111 Louisiana Street, Houston, TX, 77002

Tel: (713) 207-3000 Fax: (713) 207-0206 Web site: www.houind.com

Provides gas and electric services.

NorAM, São Paulo, Brazil

Contact: Pastor Sanjurjo, VP

HOWMEDICA INC.

359 Veterans Boulevard, Rutherford, NJ, 07070

Tel: (201) 507-7300 Fax: (201) 935-4873 Web site: www.howmedica.com

Hospital, medical and dental supplies.

Howmedica Brazil, Guarulhos (SP), São Paulo, Brazil

Tel: 55-11-6464-7666

HUGHES ELECTRONICS

200 N. Sepulveda Blvd., PO Box 956, El Segundo, CA, 90245-0956

Tel: (310) 662-9821 Fax: (310) 647-6213

Mfr. electronics equipment and systems.

Hughes do Brazil Electronica, Ave. Rio Branco, 45-Sala 1305, Rio de Janeiro, RJ CEO 20090-003, Brazil

Tel: 55-21-439-4545 Fax: 55-21-439-1677

Hughes do Brazil Electronica, Av. Indianopolis, 3.096 Bloco B2 andar, Planato Paulista, São Paulo, SP CEP 04062-003, Brazil

Tel: 55-11-5582-0533 Fax: 55-11-5582-0576

HUNTSMAN CORPORATION

500 Huntsman Way, Salt Lake City, UT, 84108

Tel: (801) 532-5200 Fax: (801) 536-1581

Mfr./sales specialty chemicals, industrial chemicals and petrochemicals.

Huntsman de Brasil Participacoes Ltda., Av. Paulista, 807 Cj. 2314, 01311000, São Paulo, S.P., Brazil

Tel: 55-11-253-6448 Fax: 55-11-283-0623

IBM CORPORATION

New Orchard Road, Armonk, NY, 10504

Tel: (914) 765-1900 Fax: (914) 765-7382 Web site: www.ibm.com

Information products, technology & services.

IBM Brasil - Indústria Máquinas e Serviços Ltda., Av. Pasteur 138-146, 22290-900 Rio de Janeiro, Brazil

Tel: 55-11-546-5252 Fax: 55-11-546-5982 Contact: Giancarlo Gerli, Dir. Emp: 3500

IBM Brasil - Indústria Máquinas e Serviços Ltda., Rua Tutóia, 1157 - 19o. andar, São Paulo, SP 04007-900 Brazil

Tel: 55-11-886-3122 Fax: 55-11-886-3982 Contact: Giancarlo Gerli Emp: 3500

ILLINOIS TOOL WORKS (ITW)

3600 West Lake Ave., Glenview, IL, 60025-5811

Tel: (847) 724-7500 Fax: (847) 657-4268

Mfr. gears, tools, fasteners, sealants, plastic and metal components for industrial, medical, etc.

ITWSA Electronica e Plasticos Ltda., Av. Santa Catarina, 941 Aero Porto, São Paulo, SP, Brazil

InaCom CORPORATION

10810 Farnam Drive, Omaha, NE, 68154

Tel: (402) 392-3900 Fax: (402) 392-3602 Web site: www.inacom.com

Provider of technology management products and services; reselling microcomputer systems, work stations and networking and telecommunications equipment.

InaCom do Brasil, Rua Ingeniero Francisco Pita, Brito 779, 4th Fl., Local A, São Paulo, Brazil 04753080

Contact: Alan Sanchez, Mng. Ptnr.

INDUCTOTHERM CORPORATION

10 Indel Ave., PO Box 157, Rancocas, NJ, 08073-0157

Tel: (609) 267-9000 Fax: (609) 267-3537

Mfr. induction melting furnaces.

Inductotherm Industria e Comercio Ltda., Caixa Postal 143, Av. Roberto Gordon 455, 09990 Diadema, SP, Brazil

INFONET SERVICES CORPORATION

2100 East Grand Ave., El Segundo, CA, 90245

Tel: (310) 335-2600 Fax: (310) 335-4507 Web site: www.infonet.com

Provider of Internet services and electronic messaging services.

Infonet Brazil, Alameda Santos 705, 11th Fl., 01419 São Paulo - SP, Brazil

Tel: 55-11-284-2433 Fax: 56-11-284-2737

INFORMIX CORPORATION

4100 Bohannon Drive, Menlo Park, CA, 95025

Tel: (650) 926-6300 Fax: (650) 926-6593 Web site: www.informix.com

Designs & produces database management software, connectivity interfaces & gateways, and other computer applications.

Informix do Brasil, Rua Alexandre Dumas, 2200, Conj. 702, Sao Paulo, SP CEP 04717-910 Brazil (Locations: Brasilia & Rio de Janeiro, Brazil.)

Tel: 55-11-5181-8488

INGERSOLL MILLING MACHINE CO. INC.

707 Fulton Ave., Rockford, IL, 61103

Tel: (815) 987-6000 Fax: (815) 987-6725

Automated production systems.

Ingersoll Milling Machine Co. Inc., Brazil

INGERSOLL-RAND COMPANY

200 Chestnut Ridge Road, Woodcliff Lake, NJ, 07675

Tel: (201) 573-0123 Fax: (201) 573-3172 Web site: www.ingersoll-rand.com

Mfr. compressors, rock drills, pumps, air tools, door hardware, ball bearings.

Torrington Industria Y Comercio Ltda., Av. Dr. Cardoso De Mello, 1885, C.J. 11-1 andar - Vila Olimpia, CEP 04548 São Paulo, Brazil

Tel: 55-11-822-7400 Fax: 55-11-822-3924

INSTRON CORPORATION

100 Royall Street, Canton, MA, 02021-1089

Tel: (781) 828-2500 Fax: (781) 575-5751

Mfr. material testing instruments.

Equipamentes Cientificos Instron Ltda., Alameda Rio Negro 433, Predio 11, 2 andar, Sala 4, Alphaville Barveri, 06454-904 São Paulo, Brazil

Tel: 55-11-420-5324 Fax: 55-11-420-5326 Contact: George Glycerio, Gen Mgr

INTEL CORPORATION

Robert Noyce Building, 2200 Mission College Blvd., Santa Clara, CA, 95052-8119

Tel: (408) 765-8080 Fax: (408) 765-1739 Web site: www.intel.com

Mfr. semiconductor, microprocessor and micro-communications components and systems.

Intel Semicondutores do Brazil, Rue Florida, 1703-2 and CJ22, CEP 04565-001 San Paulo-SP, SP Brazil

Tel: 55-11-5505-2296

INTER-CONTINENTAL HOTELS

1120 Ave. of the Americas, New York, NY, 10036

Tel: (212) 852-6400 Fax: (212) 852-6494 Web site: www.interconti.com

Worldwide hotel and resort accommodations.

Hotel Inter-Continental São Paulo, Alameda Santos, 1123, 01419-001, São Paulo, SP Brazil

Tel: 55-11-3179-2600

INTERGRAPH CORPORATION

One Madison Industrial Park, Huntsville, AL, 35894-0001

Tel: (205) 730-2000 Fax: (205) 730-7898 Web site: www.intergraph.com

Develop/mfr. interactive computer graphic systems.

Sisgraph Ltda., Rua Estados Unidos 116, São Paulo, SP 01427-000 Brazil

Tel: 55-11-887-5300 Fax: 55-11-887-7763 Contact: Silvio Stewberg, Pres. Emp: 100

INTERMEC TECHNOLOGIES CORPORATION

6001 36th Ave. West, PO Box 4280, Everett, WA, 98203-9280

Tel: (425) 348-2600 Fax: (425) 355-9551 Web site: www.intermec.com

Mfr./distributor automated data collection systems.

Intermec do Brazil Technologia Ltda., Rua Barao do Flamengo, 32-4/F, 22220-8-080 Rio de Janeiro, Brazil (Locations: Santa Cecilia, São Paulo)

Tel: 55-21-556-5275 Fax: 55-21-556-1447

INTERNATIONAL COMPONENTS CORPORATION

420 N. May Street, Chicago, IL, 60622

Tel: (312) 829-2525 Fax: (312) 829-0213

Mfr./sale/services portable DC battery chargers.

International Components Corp. do Brasil Ltda., Fua Jesuino Marcondes Machado, 2322, Campinas, São Paulo, Brazil CEP 13092-321

INTERNATIONAL FLAVORS & FRAGRANCES INC.

521 West 57th Street, New York, NY, 10019-2960

Tel: (212) 765-5500 Fax: (212) 708-7132 Web site: www.iff.com

Design/mfr. flavors, fragrances & aroma chemicals.

I.F.F. Essencias e Fragrancias Ltda., Av. Brazil 22351, Caixa Postal 21670, ZC-27, Rio de Janeiro, RJ, Brazil

I.F.F. Essencias e Fragrancias Ltda., Av. Cauaxi, 65, Barrueri, SP 06454-020 Brazil

Tel: 55-11-726-3700 Fax: 55-11-421-3248 Contact: Carlos Armando Gaitan

I.F.F. Essencias e Fragrancias Ltda., Taubate, São Paulo, Brazil

INTERNATIONAL GAME TECHNOLOGY INC.

9295 Prototype Drive, Reno, NV, 89511

Tel: (702) 448-0100 Fax: (702) 448-1488 Web site: www.igtgame.com

Mfr. games, hobby goods; equipment leasing, amusements, computers.

IGT do Brazil Ltda., Rua Guararapes, 1.909-1.Andar-CJ.12, Brooklin Novo, São Paulo, SP, Brazil 04561-004

Tel: 55-11-505-4755

INTERNATIONAL SPECIALTY PRODUCTS

1361 Alps Road, Wayne, NJ, 07470

Tel: (973) 628-4000 Fax: (973) 628-3311 Web site: www.ispcorp.com

Mfr. specialty chemical products.

ISP do Brasil Ltda., Rua General Jardim, 633-1° Andar, 01271-900 São Paulo-SP, Brazil

Tel: 55-11-259-1422 Fax: 55-11-256-4037

ITT CORPORATION

1330 Ave. of the Americas, New York, NY, 10019-5490

Tel: (212) 258-1000 Fax: (212) 258-1297

Design/mfr. communications & electronic equipment, hotels, insurance.

Alfred Teves do Brazil Ind. e Com. Ltda., Rua 21 de Marco s/n, Varzia Paulista, SP, Brazil

Cia. Intl. de Importacao e Exportacao, Av. Rio Branco 99-101, Caixa Postal 430, ZC-21, Rio de Janeiro, RJ, Brazil

ITT SHERATON CORPORATION

60 State Street, Boston, MA, 02108

Tel: (617) 367-3600 Fax: (617) 367-5676

Hotel operations.

Petribu Sheraton Hotel, Av. Bernado Veira de Melo 1624, Piedade, 54410 Jaboatao dos Guararapes, Brazil

Sheraton Mofarrej Hotel & Towers, Alameda Santos 1437, São Paulo, Brazil

Tel: 55-11-253-5544 Fax: 55-11-289-8670 Contact: Alan Duggan Emp: 250

Sheraton Rio Hotel & Towers, Av. Niemeyer 121, 22450 Rio de Janeiro, Brazil

Tel: 55-21-274-1122 Fax: 55-21-239-5643 Contact: Hector Salanova, GenMgr

ITW RANSBURG FINISHING SYSTEMS

4141 West 54th Street, Indianapolis, IN, 46254

Tel: (317) 298-5000 Fax: (317) 298-5010 Web site: www.itwdema.com

Mfr. rotary atomizers, electrostatic guns, paint finishing systems.

ITW DeVilbiss Brazil, Rua Carmo do Rio Verde 144, 04729 São Paulo, Brazil

J.P. MORGAN & CO. INC.

60 Wall Street, New York, NY, 10260-0060

Tel: (212) 483-2323 Fax: (212) 648-5209 Web site: www.jpm.com

International banking services.

Banco J.P. Morgan, S.A - Rio de Janeiro Office, Praia de Botafogo, 228 - bloco A, 14th Fl. - Room 1405, 22250-040 Rio de Janeiro RJ, Brazil

Tel: 55-21-553-1142

Morgan Guaranty Trust Co., Av. Paulista, 1294, 7° andar, São Paulo, CEO 01310-915 SP, Brazil

Tel: 55-11-281-3700 Fax: 55-11-285-2676 Contact: Alfredo Gutiérrez, Gen. Mgr. Emp: 135

J. WALTER THOMPSON COMPANY

466 Lexington Ave., New York, NY, 10017

Tel: (212) 210-7000 Fax: (212) 210-6944 Web site: www.jwt.com

International advertising and marketing services.

CBBA Propaganda, São Paulo, Brazil

JWT Publicidade, São Paulo, Brazil

JOHN HANCOCK MUTUAL LIFE INSURANCE COMPANY

200 Clarendon Street, PO Box 111, Boston, MA, 02117

Tel: (617) 572-6000 Fax: (617) 572-8628 Web site: www.jhancock.com

Life insurance services.

John Hancock Services Internacionais Ltda., Sul America Com.Nacional de Seguros S.A., Rua Anchieta, 35-Pr.da Se, São Paulo, SP 01420 Brazil

Tel: 55-11-232-6131 Fax: 55-11-607-4507 Contact: Julio Bierrenbach, VP

Sul American Companhia Nacional de Seguros de Vida, Caixa Postal 971, Rio de Janeiro, RJ, Brazil

JOHNSON & JOHNSON

One Johnson & Johnson Plaza, New Brunswick, NJ, 08933

Tel: (732) 524-0400 Fax: (732) 214-0334 Web site: www.jnj.com

Mfr./distributor/R&D pharmaceutical, health care and cosmetic products.

Janssen-Cilag Farmaceutica Ltda., Caixa Postal 7136, CEP 01064-970 São Paulo, Brazil

Johnson & Johnson Professional Products Ltda., Caixa Postal 5030, CEP 01061-970 São Paulo, Brazil

Johnson & Johnson SA, Ind. e Com., Rua Gerivatiba, 207, Butanta, São Paulo, SP 05501-900 Brazil

Tel: 55-11-817-8122 Fax: 55-11-817-8678 Contact: Carlos Alberto Gottschalk, Pres. Emp: 3100

S C JOHNSON & SON INC.

1525 Howe Street, Racine, WI, 53403

Tel: (414) 260-2000 Fax: (414) 260-2133 Web site: www.scjohnsonwax.com

Home, auto, commercial and personal care products and specialty chemicals.

Companhias Ceras Johnson Limitada, Av. Comandante Guaranys, 599 Jacarepagua, Rio de Janeiro, RJ , Brazil
Brazil

Tel: 55-21-445-4455 Fax: 55-21-445-8280 Contact: Luiz Zunzunegui, Gen Mgr. Emp: 500

A.T. KEARNEY INC.

222 West Adams Street, Chicago, IL, 60606

Tel: (312) 648-0111 Fax: (312) 223-6200 Web site: www.atkearney.com

Management consultants and executive search.

A. T. Kearney Ltda., Rua Joaquim Floriano 72, Conj. 201, 04530-000 São Paulo, Brazil

Tel: 55-11-3040-6200

KELLOGG COMPANY

One Kellogg Square, PO Box 3599, Battle Creek, MI, 49016-3599

Tel: (616) 961-2000 Fax: (616) 961-2871 Web site: www.kelloggs.com

Mfr. ready-to-eat cereals and convenience foods.

Kellogg Brasil & CIA, Rua Geraldo Flausino Gomes, 78, São Paulo, SP 04575-060 Brazil (All inquiries to U.S. address)

Tel: 55-11-505-3033 Fax: 55-11-505-3821 Contact: Jorge Iglesias, Pres. Emp: 350

KENNAMETAL INC.

State Rte. 981, Latrobe, PA, 15650

Tel: (724) 539-5000 Fax: (724) 539-4710 Web site: www.kennametal.com

Tools, hard carbide & tungsten alloys for metalworking industry.

Project InLtd. do Brasil, Ltda., Joaquim do almeida 313, Mirandopolis, 04050-011 São Paulo, Brazil

Tel: 55-11-5585-2299 Fax: 55-11-5581-1152 Contact: Guillermo Maiztegui

KENT-MOORE DIV

28635 Mound Road, Warren, MI, 48092

Tel: (810) 574-2332 Fax: (313) 578-7375

Mfr. service equipment for auto, construction, recreational, military and agricultural vehicles.

Jurubatech Tecnologia Automotive Ltda., Av. Nossa Senhova do Sabara 4904, CEP 04447-021, São Paulo, SP, Brazil

KIMBERLY-CLARK CORPORATION

351 Phelps Drive, Irving, TX, 75038

Tel: (972) 281-1200 Fax: (972) 281-1435 Web site: www.kimberly-clark.com.

Mfr./sales/distribution of consumer tissue, household and personal care products.

K-C do Brasil, Locations in Porto Alegre, and Suzano, Brazil

KOPPERS INDUSTRIES INC.

Koppers Bldg, 437 Seventh Ave., Pittsburgh, PA, 15219

Tel: (412) 227-2000 Fax: (412) 227-2333

Construction materials and services; chemicals and building products.

Koppers Importadora Ltda., Caixa Postal 13.273, 02064 São Paulo, Brazil

KORN/FERRY INTERNATIONAL

1800 Century Park East, Los Angeles, CA, 90067

Tel: (310) 552-1834 Fax: (310) 553-6452 Web site: www.kornferry.com

Executive search; management consulting.

Korn/Ferry International Ltda., Condominio Transatlantico, Rua Verbo Divino 1488, 5/F Unidade 51A, 04719-904 São Paulo, Brazil

Tel: 55-11-5181-9200 Fax: 55-11-5181-6050 Contact: Paul C. Levinson, VP Emp: 900

Korn/Ferry International Ltda., Rio de Janeiro, Brazil

Tel: 55-21-518-1380 Fax: 55-21-518-1380

KPMG PEAT MARWICK LLP

Three Chestnut Ridge Road, Montvale, NJ, 07645

Tel: (201) 307-7000 Fax: (201) 930-8617 Web site: www.kpmg.com

Accounting and audit, tax and management consulting services.

KPMG Peat Marwick, Rua Dr. Renato Paes de Barros, 33, São Paulo 04530-904, Brazil

Tel: 55-11-3067-3000 Fax: 55-11-3067-3010 Contact: Derek T. Barnes, Ptnr.

KPMG Peat Marwick, Av.Tancredo Neves, 1672 Ed.Catabas Empresarial, 4th Fl-Grupo 401, Pituba, Salvador 41820-020, Brazil

KPMG Peat Marwick, Av. Rio Branco, 110, 41st Fl., Rio de Janeiro, 20040-001, Brazil

KPMG Peat Marwick, Rua Matias Cardisi, 63 - 8th Fl., Santo Agostinho, Belo Horizonte 30170-050, Brazil

KRAFT FOODS INTERNATIONAL, INC. (DIV. PHILIP MORRIS COS.)

800 Westchester Ave., Rye Brook, NY, 10573-1301

Tel: (914) 335-2500 Fax: (914) 335-7144

Processor, distributor and manufacturer of food products.

Kibon SA, Caixa Postal 30266, São Paulo, Brazil

Kraft Suchard Brasil Ltda., Rua Santo Arcadio, 290, São Paulo, SP 04707-901 Brazil

Tel: 55-11-536-3011 Fax: 55-11-531-4830 Contact: Dieter Zinner, Pres.

THE KROLL-O'GARA COMPANY

9113 Le Saint Drive, Fairfield, OH, 45014

Tel: (513) 874-2112 Fax: (513) 874-2558 Web site: www.kroll-ogara.com

Security and consulting services and vechiles.

Kroll Associates Brasil LTDA, Av. Nacoes Unidas 12551, 19 andar - Sala 1909, 004578-000 São Paulo/SP, Brazil

Tel: 305-789-7100 USA Fax: 305-789-7159 USA

O'Gara-Hess & Eisenhardt do Brasil Ltda., Av. Tambore, #1.393 - Alphaville, Barueri - SP, CEP 0654-000, Brazil

Tel: 55-11-7295-5133 Fax: 55-11-7295-5340 Contact: Marcos Aidukaitus, Gen. Mgr.

LAWSON MARDON WHEATON, INC.

1101 Wheaton Ave., Milville, NJ, 08332

Tel: (609) 825-1400 Fax: (609) 825-0146

Mfr. glass and plastic containers and plastic products.

Wheaton do Brazil SA Ind. e Com., Av. Jabaquara 2979, Caixa Postal 1461, 01000 São Paulo, SP, Brazil

LE TOURNEAU COMPANY

PO Box 2307, Longview, TX, 75606

Tel: (903) 237-7000 Fax: (903) 267-7032

Mfr. heavy construction and mining machinery equipment.

SRR-Equipamentos Ltda./Rimi Div., Av. Franklin Roosevelt 23, 20021 Rio de Janeiro, RJ, Brazil

LEAR CORPORATION

21557 Telegraph Road, Southfield, MI, 48086-5008

Tel: (248) 746-1500 Fax: (248) 746-1722 Web site: www.lear.com

Mgf./dist. car seats worldwide.

Probel, S.A., São Paulo & Porto Alegra, Brazil

LEARONAL INC.

272 Buffalo Ave., Freeport, NY, 11520

Tel: (516) 868-8800 Fax: (516) 868-8824 Web site: www.learonal.com

Producer of specialty chemicals and coatings. Provides electroplating and chemical manufacturing services.

Teenorvest Produtos Quimicos Ltda., Rua Oneda 40, Vila Armando Bondiolo, CEP 09895-280 São Bernardo do Campo, São Paulo, Brazil

Tel: 55-11-759-4422 Fax: 55-11-759-4949 Contact: Sergio Pereira, Pres.

LeBOEUF, LAMB, GREENE & MacRAE LLP

125 West 55th Street, 12th Fl., New York, NY, 10019

Tel: (212) 424-8000 Fax: (212) 424-8500 Web site: www.llgm.com

International law firm.

LeBoeuf, Lamb,Greene & MacRae LLP/Tavares Guerreiro Avogados, Av. Paulista, 1912-13 andar, São Paulo, SP 01310-200 Brazil

Tel: 55-11-287-4633 Fax: 55-11-283-1134

LEHMAN BROTHERS HOLDINGS INC.

Three World Financial Center, New York, NY, 10285

Tel: (212) 526-7000 Fax: (212) 526-3738 Web site: www.lehman.com

Financial services, securities and merchant banking services.

Lehman Brothers, Av. Brigadeiro Faria Lima, 1276-ED OS Bandirantes\Unidade 62, São Paulo, Brazil

Tel: 55-11-867-8545

LEVI STRAUSS & COMPANY

1155 Battery Street, Levi's Plaza, San Francisco, CA, 94111-1230

Tel: (415) 544-6000 Fax: (415) 501-3939 Web site: www.levistrauss.com

Mfr./distributor casual wearing apparel.

Levi Strauss do Brazil Industria e Comercio Ltda., Rodovia Raposo Tavares Km. 24, Rua Joao Paulo Ablas, nr 777, 5 Jardim da Gloria, Cotia- 06700 São Paulo, Brazil 01000

Tel: 55-11-492-3344 Fax: 55-11-492-3168 Contact: Isaac Sztutman, Gen Mgr. Emp: 700

LIBERTY MUTUAL GROUP

175 Berkeley Street, Boston, MA, 02117

Tel: (617) 357-9500 Fax: (617) 350-7648 Web site: www.libertymutual. com

Provides workers' compensation insurance and operates physical rehabilitation centers and provides risk prevention management.

Liberty Mutual Group, Rio de Janerio, Brazil

ELI LILLY & COMPANY

Lilly Corporate Center, Indianapolis, IN, 46285

Tel: (317) 276-2000 Fax: (317) 277-6579 Web site: www.lilly.com

Mfr. pharmaceuticals and animal health products.

Eli Lilly do Brazil Ltda., Av. Morumbi 8264, 04703-002 São Paulo, SP, Brazil

Tel: 55-11-532-6911 Fax: 55-11-531-0742

THE LINCOLN ELECTRIC COMPANY

22801 St. Clair Ave., Cleveland, OH, 44117-1199

Tel: (216) 481-8100 Fax: (216) 486-8385 Web site: www.lincolnelectric.com

Mfr. arc welding and welding related products, oxy-fuel and thermal cutting equipment and integral AC motors.

Lincoln Electric do Brasil, Rua Cuba 505, Penha CEP 21020160 Rio de Janeiro, RJ, Brazil

Tel: 55-21-290-3186 Contact: Rigerio Cassanova Nicolay

Lincoln Electric do Brasil Industria e Comercio Ltda., Rua Ricardo Cavatton 166, Agua Branca - CEP 05038-110, São Paulo - SP,Brazil

Tel: 55-11-861-0126 Fax: 55-11-861-4524 Contact: David Owens, Mng. Dir. Emp: 29

ARTHUR D. LITTLE, INC.

25 Acorn Park, Cambridge, MA, 02140-2390

Tel: (617) 498-5000 Fax: (617) 498-7200 Web site: www.adlittle.com

Management, environmental, health & safety consulting; technical & product development.

Arthur D. Little Ltda., Av. Brigadeiro Faria Lima 1478, 21 Andar, Jardim Paulistano, 01451-913 São Paulo, Brazil

Tel: 55-11-3039-1000 Fax: 55-11-813-0231

LOCTITE CORPORATION

10 Columbus Boulevard, Hartford, CT, 06106

Tel: (203) 520-5000 Fax: (203) 520-5073 Web site: www.loctite.com

Mfr./sale industrial adhesives and sealants.

Loctite Brasil Ltda., Av. Prof. Vernon Krieble 91, 06690-111 Itapevi, São Paulo, Brazil

Tel: 55-11-426-4011 Fax: 55-11-426-4820 Contact: Flavio T. Lacerda, Reg. Mgr. Emp: 280

LORD CORPORATION

2000 West Grandview Blvd, Erie, PA, 16514

Tel: (814) 868-0924 Fax: (814) 486-4345

Adhesives, coatings, chemicals, film products.

Lord Industrial Ltda., Via Anhanguera Km 63,5 Jundiai, SP 13213-180 Brazil

Tel: 55-11-732-7755 Fax: 55-11-732-3581 Contact: Robert J. Wasilenski, Reg Mgr. Emp: 42

LOWE & PARTNERS WORLDWIDE

1114 Ave. of the Americas, New York, NY, 10036

Tel: (212) 403-6700 Fax: (212) 403-6710

International advertising agency network.

Lowe Loducca, São Paulo, Brazil

THE LUBRIZOL CORPORATION

29400 Lakeland Blvd., Wickliffe, OH, 44092-2298

Tel: (440) 943-4200 Fax: (440) 943-5337 Web site: www.lubrizol.com

Mfr. chemicals additives for lubricants & fuels.

Lubrizol do Brasil Aditivos Ltda., Estrada Belford Roxo, 1375, Boa Esperanca Nova Iguacu, RJ 26110-260 Brazil

Tel: 55-21-761-1117 Fax: 55-21-761-4774 Contact: Gilson Luiz Maturity dos Santos Emp: 110

LUCENT TECHNOLOGIES, INC.

600 Mountain Ave., Murray Hill, NJ, 07974-0636

Tel: (908) 582-3000 Fax: (908) 582-2110 Web site: www.lucent.com

Design/mfr. wide range of public and private networks, communication systems and software, data networking systems, business telephone systems and microelectronics components.

Lucent Technologies Brazil, Rua Engenheiro Francisco Pita Brito #125, Edif. Herbert Levy, São Paolo, 04753-080 Brazil

Tel: 55-11-532-6400 Fax: 55-11-532-6405 Contact: Ana Rita Leivas, PR Mgr.

M-I

PO Box 48242, Houston, TX, 77242-2842

Tel: (713) 739-0222 Fax: (713) 308-9503

Drilling fluids.

Halliburton-IMCO do Brazil Servicos Com. e Ind. Ltda., Praca do Flamengo 200, Rio de Janeiro, Brazil

M/A-COM INC.

1011 Pawtucket Boulevard, Lowell, MA, 01853

Tel: (978) 442-5000 Fax: (978) 442-5354

Mfr. electronic components and communications equipment.

Hitech El. Indl Coml. Ltd., Rua Branco de Moraes 489 Ch. Santo Antonio, São Paulo 04718-101 SP Brazil

Tel: 55-11-882-4000

MANPOWER INTERNATIONAL INC.

5301 N. Ironwood Road, PO Box 2053, Milwaukee, WI, 53201-2053

Tel: (414) 961-1000 Fax: (414) 961-7081 Web site: www.manpower

Temporary help, contract service, training & testing.

Manpower Brazil, Etica Servicos Temporarios Ltda., Casa Central, Rua Jupi, 215, São Paulo, SP 04753, Brazil

Tel: 55-11-524-3830 Fax: 55-11-524-3830 Contact: Joao Renato de V. Pinheiro, Pres. Emp: 150

MARK IV INDUSTRIES INC.

501 John James Audubon Pkwy., PO Box 810, Amherst, NY, 14226-0810

Tel: (716) 689-4972 Fax: (716) 689-1529 Web site: www.mark-iv.com

Mfr. diversified products: timers & controls, power equipment, loudspeaker systems, etc.

Daytec S.A. J. V., Rodovia MG 050-Km 18.5, Distrito Industrial Renato Azeredo, 35675-000 Juatuba-MG, Brazil

Tel: 55-31-535-8800 Fax: 55-31-535-8830

Tecalon Brasileira de Auto PeAas S.A. J.V., Rua Rego Barros, No. 729/745 - Jd. Vila Formosa, CEP-03460-00, São Paulo, SP, Brazil

Tel: 55-11-918-9300 Fax: 55-11-271-1502

MARSH & McLENNAN COS INC.

1166 Ave. of the Americas, New York, NY, 10036-2774

Tel: (212) 345-5000 Fax: (212) 345-4808 Web site: www.marshmac.com

Insurance agents/brokers, pension and investment management consulting services.

J&H Marsh & McLennan Corretores de Seguros Ltda., Av. Rio Branco, 125, Rio de Janeiro, RJ 20040-006 Brazil

Tel: 55-21-297-5122 Fax: 55-21-221-2888 Contact: Francisco Rocha Emp: 130

J&H Marsh & McLennan Corretores de Seguros Ltda., Head Office - Av. Maria Coelho Aguiar, 215, Bloco F, 1st Fl., Jatdim São Luis, 05804-900 São Paulo, SP Brazil

Tel: 55-11-525-3622 Fax: 55-11-522-4060 Contact: Michael W. Liddee, Pres.

J&H Marsh McLennan Corretores de Seguros Ltda., Rua Visconde do Rosario, 3-cj. 1006/1010 Comercio, Salvador, Brazil 40015-050

Tel: 55-71-243-2200 Fax: 55-71-243-2345 Contact: Sergio Luiz Ribeiro Conde

J&H Marsh McLennan Corretores de Seguros Ltda., Rua Jose Paulina, 2236-7, cj. 73, 13013-002 Campinas, Brazil

Tel: 55-19-231-4977 Fax: 55-19-232-0662 Contact: Walmir Fernandes

J&H Marsh McLennan Corretores de Seguros Ltda., Rua 07 de Setembro 722, 6 andar, Porto Alegre, Brazil

Tel: 55-51-228-1858 Fax: 55-51-226-4855 Contact: Aristides Rezende

J&H Marsh McLennan Corretores de Seguros Ltda., Rua São Paulo, 409-cj. 1402/1404, 30179-130 Belo Horizonte, Minas Gerais, Brazil

Tel: 55-31-201-5233 Fax: 55-31-201-8400 Contact: Francisco A.V. Britto

MASTERCARD INTERNATIONAL INC.

200 Purchase Street, Purchase, NY, 10577

Tel: (914) 249-2000 Fax: (914) 249-5475 Web site: www.mastercard.com

Provides financial payment systems globally.

MasterCard International Inc., Edif. Plaza Centenario, Av. Das Nacoes Unidas, 12.995 - 17o. Andar - cj. 172, São Paulo - SP 04578- Brazil

McCANN-ERICKSON WORLDWIDE

750 Third Ave., New York, NY, 10017

Tel: (212) 984-3644 Fax: (212) 984-2629

International advertising/marketing services.

McCann-Erickson Publicidade Ltda., Rua Loefgren, 2527, São Paulo, SP 04040-033 Brazil

Tel: 55-11-576-3000 Fax: 55-11-549-5031 Contact: Jens Olesen, Pres. Emp: 400

McCann-Erickson Publicidade Ltda., Av. Almirante Barroso 63, 160/170 andares, 20031 Rio de Janeiro, Brazil

McDONALD'S CORPORATION

Kroc Drive, Oak Brook, IL, 60523

Tel: (630) 623-3000 Fax: (630) 623-7409

Fast food chain stores.

McDonald's Corp., Brazil

THE McGRAW-HILL COMPANIES

1221 Ave. of the Americas, New York, NY, 10020

Tel: (212) 512-2000 Fax: (212) 512-2703

Books, magazines, information systems, financial service, publishing and broadcast operations.

Makron Books do Brasil Editora Ltda., Rua Tabapua, 1348, São Paulo, SP 04533-004 Brazil

Tel: 55-11-829-1518 Fax: 55-11-829-4970 Contact: Milton Mira Assuncao Filho Emp: 100

McKINSEY & COMPANY

55 East 52nd Street, New York, NY, 10022

Tel: (212) 446-7000 Fax: (212) 446-8575 Web site: www.mckinsey.com

Management and business consulting services.

McKinsey & Company, Rua Alexaaandre Dumas, 1711, Edif. Birman 12, 12th Fl., São Paulo, SP 04717-004 Brazil

Tel: 55-11-5189-1400 Fax: 55-11-5189-1700 Contact: A.C. Reuter

MEAD CORPORATION

Courthouse Plaza, NE, Dayton, OH, 45463

Tel: (937) 495-6323 Fax: (937) 461-2424 Web site: www.mead.com

Mfr. paper, packaging, pulp, lumber and other wood products, school and office products; electronic publishing and distribution.

Mead Embalagens Ltda., Rua Tabapua, 41 2nd Fl., Itaim Bibi - 04533-010, São Paulo, Brazil

Tel: 55-11-851-1799 Fax: 55-11-851-0488 Contact: Fernando Silveira, Gen. Mgr. Emp: 7

MEDTRONIC INC.

7000 Central Ave., NE, Minneapolis, MN, 55432

Tel: (612) 574-4000 Fax: (612) 574-4879

Mfr./sale/service electrotherapeutic medical devices.

Biocardio Comercio e Representacoes Ltda., Praia do Flamengo, 66-B, Rio de Janeiro, RJ 22210-030 Brazil

Tel: 55-21-285-0736 Fax: 55-21-205-6094 Contact: Joaquim Cordeiro, Mgr.

MEMOREX CORPORATION

10100 Pioneer Boulevard, Santa Fe Springs, CA, 90670

Tel: (562) 906-2800 Fax: (562) 906-2848

Magnetic recording tapes, etc.

Memorex do Brazil, Productos de Precisao Ltda., Caixa Postal 5708, São Paulo, Brazil

MERCER MANAGEMENT CONSULTING INC.

1166 Ave. of the Americas, New York, NY, 10036

Tel: (212) 345-3400 Fax: (212) 345-7414

Management consulting.

Mercer MW Ltda., Av. Paulista, 949, 5o. andar, São Paulo, SP 01311-100 Brazil

Tel: 55-11-284-5600 Fax: 55-11-288-9763 Emp: 200

MERCK & COMPANY, INC.

1 Merck Drive, Whitehouse Station, NJ, 08889

Tel: (908) 423-1000 Fax: (908) 423-2592

Pharmaceuticals, chemicals and biologicals.

Merck Sharp & Dohme Industria Quimica e Farmaceutica Ltda., Av. Brig. Faria 1815, andar 12, Caixa Postal 8734, 01451 São Paulo, SP, Brazil

MERITOR AUTOMOTIVE, INC.

2135 W. Maple Road, Troy, MI, 48084-7186

Tel: (248) 435-1000 Fax: (248) 435-1393 Web site: www.meritorauto.com

Mfr./sales of light and heavy vehicle systems for trucks, cars and speciality vehicles.

Meritor Automotive, Inc., Brazil

MERRILL LYNCH & COMPANY, INC.

World Financial Center, North Tower, New York, NY, 10281-1323

Tel: (212) 449-1000 Fax: (212) 449-2892

Security brokers and dealers, investment and business services.

Merrill Lynch Brasil, Edif. Centro Cultural de Brasil, Av. Presidente Wilson, 231 c; 1801, 20030-021, Rio d Janeiro, RJ, Brazil

Tel: 55-21-3175-4078 Fax: 55-21-3175-4045 Contact: Eduardo Jorge Chame Saad Emp: 40

METALLURG INC.

6 East 43 Street, New York, NY, 10017

Tel: (212) 687-9470 Fax: (212) 697-2874

Mfr. ferrous & nonferrous alloys & metals.

Cia Industrial Fluminense, Rua Sete de Setembro 55-10 andar, 20050 Rio de Janeiro, RJ, Brazil

Companhia de Estanho Minas Brasil, Rua Sete de Setembro 55-10 andar, 20050 Rio de Janeiro, RJ, Brazil

Metallurg do Brasil Ltda., Rua Sete de Setembro 55-10 andar, 20050 Rio de Janeiro, RJ, Brazil

METROPOLITAN LIFE INSURANCE COMPANY

1 Madison Ave., New York, NY, 10010-3603

Tel: (212) 578-3818 Fax: (212) 252-7294

Insurance and retirement savings products and services.

Metropolitan Life Seguros e Previdencia Privada SA, Scritto, Cessao de Espace Svs., Rus Andre Fernandes, 187 CEP 04538-020, JD. Europa - San Paulo, Brazil

Tel: 55-11-881-4822 Fax: 55-11-881-7716 Contact: Thaddeus O. Burr, Pres.

MICROSOFT CORPORATION

One Microsoft Way, Redmond, WA, 98052-6399

Tel: (425) 882-8080 Fax: (425) 936-7329 Web site: www.microsoft.com

Computer software, peripherals and services.

Microsoft Brazil Ltda., Av. Rio Branco 1-15, andar CJ 1509, 20090-003 Rio de Janiero, Brazil

Tel: 55-11-5514-7100 Fax: 55-11-5514-7106

Microsoft Informatica Ltda., Av. dos Nacoes Unidas, 17891, São Paulo, SP 04795-100 Brazil

Tel: 55-11-5514-7100 Fax: 55-11-5514-7106 Contact: Mauro Mauratorio

MILLIPORE CORPORATION, ANALYTICAL PRODUCT DIVISION

80 Ashby Road, PO Box 9125, Bedford, MA, 01730

Tel: (781) 275-9200 Fax: (781) 533-3110 Web site: www.millipore.com

Mfr. flow and pressure measurement and control components; precision filters, hi-performance liquid chromatography instruments.

Millipore Ind. e Com. Ltda., Rua Prof. Campos de Oliveira 430, CEP 04675, São Paulo, Brazil

MINE SAFETY APPLIANCES COMPANY

121 Gamma Drive, RIDC Industrial Pk., PO Box 426, Pittsburgh, PA, 15230

Tel: (412) 967-3000 Fax: (412) 967-3452

Safety equipment, industry filters.

MSA do Brasil Ltda., Caixa Postal 376, 09900 Diadema, São Paulo, Brazil

Tel: 55-11-445-1499 Fax: 55-11-456-6433 Contact: Andre da Silva Emp: 250

MINTEQ INTERNATIONAL INC.

405 Lexington Ave., 19th Fl., New York, NY, 10174-1901

Tel: (212) 878-1800 Fax: (212) 878-1952 Web site: www.mineralstech.com

Mfr./market specialty refractory and metallurgical products and application systems.

Mintech Do Brasil Comercio Ltda., Av. Francisco Delgado, Duque, 2017, Tres Pocos, Volta Redonda, Brazil RT 27200-000

Tel: 55-11-575-8720 Fax: 55-11-549-2812 Contact: Ademir Marcos, Controller Emp: 10

MISSION MFG. COMPANY

PO Box 40402, Houston, TX, 77040

Tel: (713) 460-6200 Fax: (713) 460-6229

Oil field equipment.

TRW Mission Industrial Ltda., Rua Sargento Silvio Hollemback 151, Barros Filho, Rio de Janeiro, JR, Brazil

MOBIL CORPORATION

3225 Gallows Road, Fairfax, VA, 22037-0001

Tel: (703) 846-3000 Fax: (703) 846-4669 Web site: www.mobil.com

Petroleum and gas exploration and refining, mfr. petroleum products, chemicals and petrochemicals.

Mobil Oil do Brazil (Industria e Commercio) Ltda., Caixa Postal 8121, CEP 01001 São Paulo, SP, Brazil

MOLEX INC.

2222 Wellington Court, Lisle, IL, 60532

Tel: (630) 969-4550 Fax: (630) 969-1352 Web site: www.molex.com

Mfr. electronic, electrical & fiber optic interconnection products & systems, switches, application tooling.

Molex Inc., Manuas, Brazil

MONSANTO COMPANY

800 N. Lindbergh Boulevard, St. Louis, MO, 63167

Tel: (314) 694-1000 Fax: (314) 694-7625 Web site: www.monsanto.com

Life sciences company focussing on agriculture, nutrition, pharmaceuticals, health and wellness and sustainable development.

Monsanto Co. Agricultural Group, São Jose dos Campos, Brazil

Monsanto Co. Chemical Group, São Jose dos Campos, Brazil

Monsanto do Brasil Ltda., Edif. Passarelli, Rua Paes Leme 523, Caixa Postal 61535, 05424-904 Pinheiros, São Paulo, Brazil

Tel: 55-11-817-6233 Fax: 55-11-211-9922 Contact: Antonio Carlos A. de Queiroz Emp: 700

MOOG INC.

Jamison Road, East Aurora, NY, 14052-0018

Tel: (716) 652-2000 Fax: (716) 687-4457 Web site: www.moog.com

Mfr. precision control components & systems.

Moog do Brazil Controles Ltda., Rua Prof. Campos de Oliveira 338, Jurubatuba-Santo Amaro, São Paulo, Brazil

Tel: 55-11-523-8011 Fax: 55-11-524-2186 Contact: Johannes Luyten Emp: 23

MORGAN STANLEY DEAN WITTER & CO.

1585 Broadway, New York, NY, 10036

Tel: (212) 761-4000 Fax: (212) 761-0086 Web site: www.msdw.com

Securities and commodities brokerage, investment banking, money management, personal trusts.

Morgan Stanley do Brasil Ltda., Av. Roque Petroni Jr., 999. 13o. andar, São Paulo, SP 04707-910 Brazil

Tel: 55-11-532-2849 Fax: 55-11-532-2868 Contact: Francisco Gros

MORTON INTERNATIONAL INC.

100 North Riverside Plaza, Chicago, IL, 60606-1596

Tel: (312) 807-2000 Fax: (312) 807-3150 Web site: www.mortonintl.com

Mfr. adhesives, coatings, finishes, specialty chemicals, advanced and electronic materials, salt, airbags.

Morton Intl. Inc., São Paolo, Brazil

MOTION PICTURE ASSN. OF AMERICA

1600 Eye Street, NW, Washington, DC, 20006

Tel: (202) 293-1966 Fax: (202) 293-7674 Web site: www.mpaa.org

Motion picture trade association.

Associacao Brasileira Cinematografica, Rua Mexico 31/603, Rio de Janeiro, RJ 20013-144, Brazil

Tel: 55-21-240-2276 Fax: 55-21-240-3026 Contact: Steve Solot

MOTOROLA, INC.

1303 East Algonquin Road, Schaumburg, IL, 60196

Tel: (847) 576-5000 Fax: (847) 538-5191 Web site: www.mot.com

Mfr. communications equipment, semiconductors and cellular phones.

Motorola do Brasil Ltda., Rua Paes Leme, 524, 5o. andar, São Paulo, SP 05424-904 Brazil (Locations: Brasilia & Jaguariuna-SP, Brazil

Tel: 55-11-3030-5000 Fax: 55-11-815-2336 Contact: Flavio Grynszpan Emp: 80

MULTIWARE

PO Box 907, Brookfield, CT, 06874

Tel: (203) 374-8000 Fax: (203) 374-3374

Mfr. applications development software.

Planconsult, Rua Cardeal Arcoverde 620, 05408 São Paulo, SP, Brazil

NACCO INDUSTRIES INC.

5875 Landerbrook Drive, Mayfield Heights, OH, 44124-4017

Tel: (440) 449-9600 Fax: (440) 449-9607 Web site: www.nacco.com

Mining/marketing lignite & metals, mfr. forklift trucks & small electric appliances, specialty retailers.

Heister Brazil Ltd. Group, Caixa Postal 4151 (Av. Nacoes Unibas, 22.777, Santo Amaro CEP 04795-100, CEP 01061-970, São Paulo, Brazil

Tel: 55-11-548-3000 Fax: 55-11-524-4243

NACCO MATERIAL HANDLING GROUP

PO Box 847, Danville, IL, 61834

Tel: (217) 443-7000 Fax: (217) 437-4940 Web site: 503-639

Fork lifts, trucks, trailers, towing winches, personnel lifts and compaction equipment.

Companhia Hyster, Av. Nacoes Unidas 22.777, Caixa Postal 4151, 01000 São Paulo, Brazil

NALCO CHEMICAL COMPANY

One Nalco Center, Naperville, IL, 60563-1198

Tel: (630) 305-1000 Fax: (630) 305-2900 Web site: www.nalco.com

Chemicals for water and waste water treatment, oil products and refining, industry processes; water and energy management service.

Gamus Quimica, Ltda., Rua Alberto Spredemann, 329 Pomerode S.C., Brazil

Tel: 55-47-387-2000 Fax: 55-47-387-2000

Nalco Brazil Ltda., Av. das Nacoes Unidas 17.891, andar 11, Santo Amaro, São Paulo, SP, Brazil

Tel: 55-11-5514-7401 Fax: 55-11-523-3543

THE NASH ENGINEERING COMPANY

3 Trefoil Drive, Trumbull, CT, 06611

Tel: (203) 459-3900 Fax: (203) 459-3511

Mfr. air & gas compressors, vacuum pumps.

Nash do Brazil Bombas Ltda., Av. Mercedes Benz, 700 Districto Individual (Viiracopas) Co,pinas, SP, Brazil 13054-750

NATIONAL CHEMSEARCH CORPORATION

2727 Chemsearch Blvd., Irving, TX, 75061

Tel: (972) 438-0211 Fax: (972) 438-0186 Web site: www.nch.com

Commercial chemical products.

Natl. Chemsearch Ind. e Com. Ltda., Rua Tabatinguera 278, Caixa Postal 7023, São Paulo, SP, Brazil

NATIONAL GYPSUM COMPANY

2001 Rexford Road, Charlotte, NC, 28211

Tel: (704) 365-7300 Fax: (704) 365-7276

Building products & services.

Austin Brasil Projetos e Construcoes Ltd., São Paulo, Brazil

NATIONAL SEMICONDUCTOR CORP.

2900 Semiconductor Drive., PO Box 58090, Santa Clara, CA, 95052-8090

Tel: (408) 721-5000 Fax: (408) 739-9803 Web site: www.national.com

Produce system-on-a-chip solutions for the information highway.

National Semiconductores do Brasil Ltda., World Trade Ctr. 1801 Ave. das Nacoes, Unidas 12-551, 04578-903, São Paulo SP, Brazil

Tel: 55-11-3043-7451 Fax: 55-11-3043-7454 Contact: John Phelps, VP Emp: 10

NATIONAL STARCH & CHEMICAL COMPANY

10 Finderne Ave., Bridgewater, NJ, 08807-3300

Tel: (908) 685-5000 Fax: (908) 685-5005 Web site: www.national starch.com

Mfr. adhesives & sealants, resins & specialty chemicals, electronic materials & adhesives, food products, industry starch.

National Starch & Chemical Industrial Ltda., Rua Cenna Sbrighi, 27, 4o. andar, 05036-010 - São Paulo - SP, Brazil (Locations: Santa Catarina & Jardim Da Gloria-Cotia-SP, Brazil

Tel: 55-11-861-3355 Fax: 55-11-861-1473 Contact: Jose Valerio Emp: 300

NETSCAPE COMMUNICATIONS

501 East Middlefield Road, Mountain View, CA, 94043

Tel: (650) 254-1900 Fax: (650) 528-4124

Mfr./distribute Internet-based commercial and consumer software applications.

Netscape Communications do Brasil Ltda., 999-13 Andar, Morumbi Tower, São Paulo, SP Brazil

Tel: 55-11-532-2821 Fax: 55-11-532-2899

NICHOLSON FILE COMPANY

PO Box 728, Apex, NC, 27502

Tel: (919) 362-7500 Fax: (919) 783-2007

Mfr. files, rasps and saws.

Nicholson File do Brazil Ltda., Rua Florencio de Abrue 157, andar 1, Caixa Postal 4645, São Paulo, SP, Brazil

A .C. NIELSEN COMPANY

177 Broad Street, Stamford, CT, 06901

Tel: (203) 961-3000 Fax: (203) 961-3190 Web site: www.acnielsen.com

Market research.

AC Nielsen Ltda., Av. Bernardino de Campos 98-14, Paraiso, 04004 São Paolo, SP, Brazil

NORDSON CORPORATION

28601 Clemens Road, Westlake, OH, 44145

Tel: (440) 892-1580 Fax: (440) 892-9507 Web site: www.nordson.com

Mfr. industry application equipment, sealants & packaging machinery.

Nordson do Brasil Industria e Comercio Ltda., Alameda Aruana, 85 Tambore, CEP 06460-010 Barveri, SP, Brazil

Tel: 55-11-7295-2004 Fax: 55-11-7295-6698

NORGREN

5400 S. Delaware Street, Littleton, CO, 80120-1663

Tel: (303) 794-2611 Fax: (303) 795-9487 Web site: www.norgren.com

Mfr. pneumatic filters, regulators, lubricators, valves, automation systems, dryers, push-in fittings.

IMI Norgren Ltda., Av. Eng. Alberto de Zagottis, 696A - CEP04675 - 230, São Paulo SP, Brazil

Tel: 55-11-522-1066 Fax: 55-11-523-2259

NORTON COMPANY

1 New Bond Street, Worcester, MA, 01606

Tel: (508) 795-5000 Fax: (508) 795-5741

Abrasives, drill bits, construction and safety products and plastics.

Norton do Brazil SA Ind. e Com., Rua Dois No. 2363, Cidade Industrial, Belo Horizonte, Brazil

NORWEST BANK MINNESOTA NA

Norwest Center, 6th and Marquette, Minneapolis, MN, 55479-0095

Tel: (612) 667-8110 Fax: (612) 667-5185

Banking services.

Norwest Bank Minnesota NA, Cetenco Plaza, Av. Paulista 1842, Torre Norte, 1 andar, 01310 São Paulo, Brazil

Tel: 55-11-852-8093

NOVELL INC.

122 East 1700 Street, Provo, UT, 84606

Tel: (801) 861-7000 Fax: (801) 861-5555

Develop/mfr. networking software and related equipment.

Novell do Brasil Software Ltda., Alameda Ribeirao Preto, 130, 12o. andar, São Paulo, SP 01331-000 Brazil

Tel: 55-11-253-4866 Fax: 55-11-285-4847 Contact: Carlos Antonio da Costa Emp: 22

OCCIDENTAL PETROLEUM CORPORATION

10889 Wilshire Blvd., Los Angeles, CA, 90024

Tel: (310) 208-8800 Fax: (310) 443-6690 Web site: www.oxy.com

Petroleum and petroleum products, chemicals, plastics.

Eriez Produtos Magneticos e Metalurgicos, Av. Ipirange 318, Bloco B, andar 5, Caixa Postal 2632, 01046 São Paulo, SP, Brazil

Vulcan Material Plastico SA, Av. Rio Branco 156, andar 20, Caixa Postal 4400, ZC-21, Rio de Janeiro, RJ, Brazil

OCEANEERING INTERNATIONAL INC.

11911 FM 529, Houston, TX, 77041

Tel: (713) 329-4500 Fax: (713) 329-4951

Transportation equipment, underwater service to offshore oil and gas industry.

Oceaneering Intl. Inc., Rio de Janeiro, Brazil

OGILVY & MATHER WORLDWIDE

309 West 49th Street, New York, NY, 10019

Tel: (212) 237-4000 Fax: (212) 237-5123

Advertising, marketing, public relations & consulting firm.

Ogilvy & Mather Latin America, Av. Brigadeiro Faria Lima, 2000 Bolco B, 7th Fl., São Pulo SP 0148-900, Brazil

Standard, Ogilvy & Mather, São Paulo, Brazil

THE OILGEAR COMPANY

2300 S. 51st Street, Milwaukee, WI, 53219

Tel: (414) 327-1700 Fax: (414) 327-0532

Mfr. hydraulic power transmission machinery.

Oilgear do Brasil Hydraulica Ltda., Rua Cons. Antonio Carlos, 469, Jardim Campos Elizeos 13060--24 Campinas SP, Brazil

OLIN CORPORATION

501 Merritt Seven, Norwalk, CT, 06856-4500

Tel: (203) 750-3000 Fax: (203) 356-3065

Mfr. chemicals, metals, applied physics in electronics, defense & aerospace industry.

Olin Brazil Ltda., Av. Nacoes Unidas, 11857, 12o. andar, São Paulo, SP 04578-000 Brazil

Tel: 55-11-533-9383 Fax: 55-11-533-1950 Contact: Paolo Vodopivic, Pres. Emp: 120

OLSTEN CORPORATION

175 Broad Hollow Road, Melville, NY, 11747-8905

Tel: (516) 844-7800 Fax: (516) 844-7022 Web site: www.olsten.com

Staffing, home health care & information technology services.

Top Services, Alameda Joaquim Eugenio de Lima, 696 - 14 andar, 01403-000 - São Paulo, SP Brazil

Tel: 55-11-287-5044 Fax: 55-11-287-5863

OPW FUELING COMPONENTS

PO Box 405003, Cincinnati, OH, 45240-5003

Tel: (513) 870-3100 Fax: (513) 874-1231

Mfr. fueling and vapor recovery nozzles, service station equipment, aboveground storage tank equipment.

OPW Fueling Components Europe, Brazil

ORACLE CORPORATION

500 Oracle Parkway, Redwood Shores, CA, 94065

Tel: (415) 506-7000 Fax: (415) 506-7200

Develop/manufacture software.

Oracle do Brasil Sistemes Limitadas, Rua Jose Guerra, San Paulo, SP 04719-030 Brazil

Tel: 55-11-548-9111 Fax: 55-11-521-6386 Contact: Marcio Kaiser, Pres. Emp: 200

OSMONICS INC.

5951 Clearwater Drive, Minnetonka, MN, 55343-8995

Tel: (612) 933-2277 Fax: (612) 933-0141

Mfr. fluid filtration and separation equipment and components.

Osmonics Brazil, Rio de Janeiro, Brazil

OSRAM SYLVANIA CHEMICALS INC.

Hawes Street, Towanda, PA, 18848

Tel: (717) 268-5000 Fax: (717) 268-5157

Chemicals.

Osram Sylvania Chemicals, Brazil

OTIS ELEVATOR COMPANY

10 Farm Springs Road, Farmington, CT, 06032

Tel: (860) 676-6000 Fax: (860) 676-5111

Mfr. elevators and escalators.

Elevadores Otis SA, Estrada Particular Sadae Takagi 1775, Bairro Cooperativa, CEP 08960 S. Bernardo do Campo, SP, Brazil

Tel: 55-11-752-3222 Fax: 55-11-752-3296 Contact: Dieter Fanta, Pres.

OUTBOARD MARINE CORPORATION

100 Sea Horse Drive, Waukegan, IL, 60085

Tel: (847) 689-6200 Fax: (847) 689-5555 Web site: www.omc-online.com

Mfr./market marine engines, boats & accessories.

Outboard Marine Power, #170 Japium CEP 69078-000, Manaus, Amazonia, Brazil

OWENS-CORNING FIBERGLAS CORPORATION

Fiberglas Tower, Toledo, OH, 43659

Tel: (419) 248-8000 Fax: (419) 248-6227 Web site: www.housenet.com

Mfr. insulation, building materials, glass fiber products.

Fiberglas Fibras Ltda., Rio Claro, Brazil

OCFIBRAS Ltda. (Brasil), Guararema, Brazil

OWENS-ILLINOIS, INC.

One SeaGate, PO Box 1035, Toledo, OH, 43666

Tel: (419) 247-5000 Fax: (419) 247-2839

Largest mfr. of glass containers in the US; plastic containers, compression-molded closures and dispensing systems.

Companhia Industrial São Paulo e Rio (CISPER), Av. Nilo Pecanha, 11, 5o. andar, Rio de Janeiro, RJ 20020-100 Brazil

Tel: 55-21-297-4433 Fax: 55-21-220-3342 Contact: Jose Carlos Teixeira de Barcellos, Pres. Emp: 2000

PACKARD BELL NEC, INC.

One Packard Bell Way, Sacramento, CA, 95828-0903

Tel: (916) 388-0101 Fax: (916) 388-1109 Web site: www.packardbell.com

Sales/distribution of home computers.

Packard Bell NEC, São Paulo, Brazil

PARAMETRIC TECHNOLOGY CORPORATION

128 Technology Drive, Waltham, MA, 02154

Tel: (781) 398-5000 Fax: (781) 398-5674 Web site: www.ptc.com

Mfr. CAD/CAM/CAE software.

Parametric Technology Corporation, Av. das Nacoes Unidas, 12551, World Trade Ctr., 17th Fl., Ste. 37, Sau Paulo, Brazil CEP 04578-903

Tel: 55-11-893-7365 Fax: 55-11-893-7979

PARKER HANNIFIN CORPORATION

17325 Euclid Ave., Cleveland, OH, 44112

Tel: (216) 896-3000 Fax: (216) 896-4000 Web site: www.parker.com

Mfr. motion-control products.

Parker Hannifin Corp., Pneumatic Div., Ind. e Com. Ltda., Lucas Nogueira Garcez 2181, 123-000 Jacarei, SP, Brazil

Tel: 55-12-354-5100 Fax: 55-12-354-5266

Parker Hannifin Corp., Seal Div./Parker Hannifin Ind. e Com., Via Anhanguera, Km. 25.3, 05676 São Paulo, Brazil

Tel: 55-11-847-1222 Fax: 55-11-847-0817

Parker Hannifin Industria e Comercio Ltda./Irlemp Filter Div, Via Anhanguera, Km 25.5, Trevo Perus, 05276-000 São Paulo, Brazil

Tel: 55-11-847-1222 Fax: 55-11-1610

PENTAIR, INC.

1500 County Road, B2 West, St. Paul, MN, 55113-3105

Tel: (612) 636-7920 Fax: (612) 636-5508

Diversified manufacturer operating in electrical and electronic enclosures, professional tools/equipment and water products.

Invicta Delta, Caixa Postal 24, Av. Major Jose Levy Sobrinho 2500, Limeira, Brazil

PERFECT CIRCLE SEALED POWER

PO Box 1208, Muskegon, MI, 49443

Tel: (616) 722-1300 Fax: (616) 724-1940

Gaskets, seals, packings, etc.

Cia. Fabricadora de Pecas, Av. Alexandre de Gusmao 1395, Caixa Postal 366, Santo Andre, SP, Brazil

THE PERKIN-ELMER CORPORATION

761 Main Ave., Norwalk, CT, 06859-0001

Tel: (203) 762-1000 Fax: (203) 762-4228 Web site: www.perkin-elmer.com

Leading supplier of systems for life science research and related applications.

GENTEC Instrumentos Cientificos Ltda., Av. Marechal Camara, 160, Salas 1017 CEP 20020-080, Brazil

Tel: 55-21-532-3315 Fax: 55-21-220-0576

Perkin-Elmer Industria e Commercio Ltda., Rua Pageu 76, CEP 04139 São Paulo, SP, Brazil (Office: Puerto Allegro)

Tel: 55-11-5070--9600 Fax: 55-11-5070-9666 Contact: Rolando M. Ravasini, Mgr. Emp: 25

PFAUDLER, INC.

1000 West Ave., PO Box 23600, Rochester, NY, 14692-3600

Tel: (716) 235-1000 Fax: (716) 436-9644 Web site: www.pfaudler.com

Mfr. glass lined reactors, storage vessels and reglassing services.

Pfaudler Equipamentos Industriais Ltda., Caiza Postal 14, 12010-970 Taubate, SP, Brazil

Tel: 55-12-2326-244 Fax: 55-12-2326-301

PFIZER INC.

235 East 42nd Street, New York, NY, 10017-5755

Tel: (212) 573-2323 Fax: (212) 573-7851 Web site: www.pfizer.com

Research-based, global health care company.

Laboratorios Pfizer Ltda., Av. Presidente Tancredo de Almeida Neves, 1111, Guarulhos, SP 07190-916 Brazil

Tel: 55-11-964-7344 Fax: 55-11-964-7474 Contact: Ian Charles Read, Pres. Emp: 1100

PHARMACIA & UPJOHN

95 Corporate Drive, PO Box 6995, Bridgewater, NJ, 08807

Tel: (908) 306-4400 Fax: (908) 306-4433 Web site: www.pnu.com

Mfr. pharmaceuticals, agricultural products, industry chemicals

Pharmacia & Upjohn, Av. Das Nacoes Unidas, 12,995, 4 Andar, 04578-000, São Paulo, SP, Brazil

PHILIP MORRIS COMPANIES, INC.

120 Park Ave., New York, NY, 10017--559

Tel: (212) 880-5000 Fax: (212) 878-2167 Web site: www.

Mfr. cigarettes, food products, beer.

Philip Morris Mercosur Region, Rua Professor Manoelito de Omelas, 303, 04719-910 São Paulo SP, Brazil

Tel: 55-11-545-9300 Fax: 55-11-247-0326 Contact: Richard Sucre, Pres. Emp: 4700

PHILLIPS PETROLEUM COMPANY

Phillips Building, 411 S. Keeler Ave., Bartlesville, OK, 74004

Tel: (918) 661-6600 Fax: (918) 661-7636 Web site: www.phillips66.com

Crude oil, natural gas, liquified petroleum gas, gasoline and petro-chemicals.

Phillips Companhia de Carbonos Coloidais, Rua Algibebes 6/12, andar 8, Caixa Postal 948, Salvador, BA, Brazil

Phillips Produtos Petro-Quimicos "66" Ltda., Av. Brig. Luiz Antonio 1343, andar 5, Caixa Postal 30.818, 01317 São Paulo, SP, Brazil

PICTURETEL CORPORATION

100 Minuteman Road, Andover, MA, 01810

Tel: (978) 292-5000 Fax: (978) 292-3300 Web site: www.picturetel.com

Mfr. video conferencing systems, network bridging & multiplexing products, system peripherals.

PictureTel Brazil, Regus São Paulo, World Trade Ctr., Av. Das Nacoes Unidas, 12551, 17 andar - Room 17, Brooklin São Paulo CEP 04578-903, Brazil

Tel: 55-11-3043-7282 Fax: 55-11-3043-7802

PIONEER HI-BRED INTERNATIONAL INC.

400 Locust Street, Ste. 800, Des Moines, IA, 50309

Tel: (515) 248-4800 Fax: (515) 248-4999

Agricultural chemicals, farm supplies, biological products, research.

Pioneer Agricultura Ltda., Caixa Postal 89, 96800 Santa Cruz do Sul, RS, Brazil

Pioneer Sementes Ltda., Br. 471, Km. 49, Santa Cruz do Sul, 96800 Rio Grande do Sul, Brazil

Tel: 55-51-711-3733 Fax: 55-51-713-2373 Contact: Marlon Logan, Mgr. Emp: 220

PITNEY BOWES INC.

1 Elmcroft Road, Stamford, CT, 06926-0700

Tel: (203) 356-5000 Fax: (203) 351-6835 Web site: www.pitneybowes.com

Mfr. postage meters, mailroom equipment, copiers, bus supplies, bus services, facsimile systems and financial services.

Pitney Bowes Brazil, razil - All mail to: Pitney Bowes Latin America, 2424 N.Federal Hwy., Ste 360, Boca Raton, FL 33431 U.S.A.

Tel: 561-347-2040 Fax: 561-347-2041 Contact: Joe Denaro, VP Latin America & Caribbean Emp: 75

PITTSTON COMPANY

PO Box 4229, Glen Allen, VA, 23058

Tel: (805) 553-3600 Fax: (805) 553-3753 Web site: www.pittston.com

Trucking, warehousing and armored car service, home security systems

Brink's Seguranca e Transporte de Valores Ltda., Rua Felix Guilhem, 971, São Paulo, SP 05169-020 Brazil

Tel: 55-11-833-0144 Fax: 55-11-832-4993 Contact: Marcos Roberto Mazurek, Pres. Emp: 3300

PLANET HOLLYWOOD INTERNATIONAL, INC.

8669 Commodity Circle, Orlando, FL, 32819

Tel: (407) 363-7827 Fax: (407) 363-4862 Web site: www.planethollywood.com

Theme-dining restaurant chain and merchandise retail stores.

Planet Hollywood International, Inc., Rio de Janiero, Brazil

POLAROID CORPORATION

549 Technology Square, Cambridge, MA, 02139

Tel: (781) 386-2000 Fax: (781) 386-3276 Web site: www.polaroid.com

Photographic equipment & supplies, optical products.

Polaroid do Brasil Ltda., Av. Paulista, 1776, 11o. andar, São Paulo, SP 01310-921 Brazil

Tel: 55-11-285-6411 Fax: 55-11-287-5393 Contact: George Niemeyer, Pres. Emp: 50

POTTERS INDUSTRIES INC.

PO Box 840, Valley Forge, PA, 19482-0840

Tel: (610) 651-4700 Fax: (610) 408-9723

Mfr. glass spheres for road marking & industry applications.

Potters Industrial Ltda., Av. Prefeito Sa Lessa 381, 21530 Rio de Janeiro, RJ, Brazil

PPG INDUSTRIES

One PPG Place, Pittsburgh, PA, 15272

Tel: (412) 434-3131 Fax: (412) 434-2190 Web site: www.ppg.com

Mfr. coatings, flat glass, fiber glass, chemicals. coatings.

PPG Industrial do Brazil Ltda., PO Box 81, Via Anhanguera, Km 107, CEP 13170-970, Sumare, SP - Brazil

PRAXAIR, INC.

39 Old Ridgebury Road, Danbury, CT, 06810-5113

Tel: (203) 837-2000 Fax: (203) 837-2450 Web site: www.praxair.com

Produces and distributes industrial and specialty gases.

S.A. White Martins, Rua Mayrink Veiga, 9, 20090-050 Rio de Janeiro, Brazil

Tel: 55-21-588-6232 Fax: 55-21-588-6794

PRECISION VALVE CORPORATION

PO Box 309, Yonkers, NY, 10702

Tel: (914) 969-6500 Fax: (914) 966-4428

Mfr. aerosol valves.

Valvulas Precisho do Brazil Ltda., Rua Vincente Rodrigues da Silva, 641, Osasco, SP 06230-096 Brazil

Tel: 55-11-707-5911 Fax: 55-11-707-8797 Contact: Douglas Kielwagen, Mgr. Emp: 30

PREFORMED LINE PRODUCTS COMPANY

600 Beta Drive, PO Box 91129, Cleveland, OH, 44101

Tel: (440) 461-5200 Fax: (440) 461-2918

Mfr. pole line hardware for electrical transmission lines; splice closures & related products for telecommunications.

PLP-Produtos Para Linhas Preformados Ltd., Estrada Tenente Marques, 1112 Cajamar, SP 07750-000, São Paulo, Brazil

PREMARK INTERNATIONAL INC.

1717 Deerfield Road, Deerfield, IL, 60015

Tel: (847) 405-6000 Fax: (847) 405-6013 Web site: www.premarkintl.com

Mfr./sale plastic, diversified consumer & commercial products.

Dart do Brasil Industria e Comercio Ltda., Av. Doutor Chudi Zaidan, 86, 8o. andar, São Paulo, SP 04583-110 Brazil

Tel: 55-11-536-9595 Fax: 55-11-543-8689 Contact: Augustin Montreaux Emp: 287

PRICEWATERHOUSECOOPERS LLP

1251 Ave. of the Americas, New York, NY, 10020

Tel: (212) 596-7000 Fax: (212) 790-6620 Web site: www.pwcglobal.com

Accounting and auditing, tax and management, and human resource consulting services.

Price Waterhouse Ltd., Ed. Empresarial Ctr., Rua Padre Carapuceiro 733, 8th Fl., CP 317, 50001-970 Recife, PE Brazil

Tel: 55-81-326-7769 Fax: 55-81-465-1063

Price Waterhouse Ltd., Rua dos Inconfidentes 1190, 9th Fl., Caixa Postal 289, 30161-970 Belo Horizonte, MG Brazil

Tel: 55-31-261-6322 Fax: 55-31-261-6950

Price Waterhouse Ltd., SCS Setor Comercial Sul, Quadra 6, Ed. Bandeirantes, 4th Fl., CP 08850, 70312-970 Brasilia, Brazil

Tel: 55-61-224-8387 Fax: 55-61-226-7098

Price Waterhouse Ltd., Av. Almirante Barroso 139, 9th Fl., CP 949, 20001-970 Rio de Janeiro, RJ Brazil

Tel: 55-21-292-6112 Fax: 55-21-220-9812

Price Waterhouse Ltd., Ed. Independencia, Rua Gen. Jardim 36, CP 1978, São Paulo, SP 01223-906 Brazil

Tel: 55-11-236-3600 Fax: 55-11-259-1433 Contact: Paulo C. Estevao Netto Emp: 2000

PRIMEX INTERNATIONAL TRADING CORPORATION

230 Fifth Avenue, New York, NY, 10001

Tel: (212) 679-5060 Fax: (212) 686-9853

Coffee: import/export, consulting services.

Primex Internacional do Brasil Importação e Exportação Ltda., Rua Itápolis, 1172, Pacaembu, São Paulo, SP 01245-000 Brazil

Tel: 55-11-9257-7044 Fax: 55-11-259-1726 Contact: H.H. Figueiredo, Mg. Dir. Emp: 20

PROCTER & GAMBLE COMPANY

One Procter & Gamble Plaza, Cincinnati, OH, 45202

Tel: (513) 983-1100 Fax: (513) 562-4500 Web site: www.pg.com

Personal care, food, laundry, cleaning and industry products.

Proctor & Gamble do Brasil & Cia., Rua Quatá. 1177, São Paulo. SP 04546-045 Brazil

Tel: 55-11-828-3599 Fax: 55-11-828-3523 Contact: Fernando Aguirre, Pres. Emp: 1300

PRUDENTIAL INSURANCE COMPANY OF AMERICA

751 Broad Street, Newark, NJ, 07102-3777

Tel: (973) 802-6000 Fax: (973) 802-2812 Web site: www.prudential.com

Sale of life insurance and provides financial services.

Pruservicos Participacoes SA, c/o Grupa Atlantica Boavista, Av. Paulista 1415, 01311 São Paulo, Brazil

QUAKER CHEMICAL CORPORATION

Elm & Lee Streets, Conshohocken, PA, 19428-0809

Tel: (610) 832-4000 Fax: (610) 832-8682 Web site: www.quakerchem.com

Mfr. chemical specialties; total fluid management services.

Quaker Chemical Industria e Comercio Ltda., Av. Bernardino de Campos 98-9, São Paulo, SP, Brazil

Contact: Jose Luiz Bregolato, Mng. Dir.

Quaker Chemical Participacoes Ltda., Av. Bernardino de Campos, 98-9 Andar, São Paulo, Brazil

Contact: Jose Luiz Bregolato, Mng. Dir.

THE QUAKER OATS COMPANY

Quaker Tower, 321 North Clark Street, Chicago, IL, 60610-4714

Tel: (312) 222-7111 Fax: (312) 222-8323 Web site: www.quakeroats.com

Mfr. foods and beverages.

Produtos Alimenticios Quaker SA, Rua do Consolação 247, 10o.andar, São Paulo, SP 01301-903 Brazil

Tel: 55-11-259-1322 Fax: 55-11-255-6498 Contact: Jose Otavio Junqueira Franco Emp: 2500

QUALCOMM INC.

6355 Lusk Boulevard, San Diego, CA, 92121

Tel: (619) 587-1121 Fax: (619) 658-1434

Digital wireless telecommunications systems.

Qualcomm do Brasil, S.A., Av. Ibirapuera, 2657, São Paulo, SP 04029-200 Brazil

Tel: 55-11-536-9799 Fax: 55-11-241-0520 Contact: Rafael Steinhauser, Pres. Emp: 10

RALSTON PURINA COMPANY

Checkerboard Square, St. Louis, MO, 63164

Tel: (314) 982-1000 Fax: (314) 982-1211

Animal feed, cereals, food products.

Ralston Purina do Brazil Ltda., Av. das Naceos Unidas 13797, conj. Morumbi Bloco 111, 04794 São Paulo, Brazil

Tel: 55-11-536-3355 Fax: 55-11-542*1747 Contact: Astor Francisco Hanschild, Dir. Emp: 1100

RAY & BERNDTSON, INC.

301 Commerce, Ste. 2300, Fort Worth, TX, 76102

Tel: (817) 334-0500 Fax: (817) 334-0779 Web site: www.prb.com

Executive search, management audit and management consulting firm.

Ray & Berndtson, Av. Paulista, 1159 30 ander-Cj. 306, São Paulo 01311-200, Brazil

Tel: 55-11-5506-0166 Fax: 55-115506-6838 Contact: Winston Peglar

RAYCHEM CORPORATION

300 Constitution Drive, Menlo Park, CA, 94025-1164

Tel: (650) 361-3333 Fax: (650) 361-2108 Web site: www.raychem.com

Develop/mfr./market materials science products for electronics, telecommunications & industry.

Raychem Produtos Irradiados Ltda., Rua Paes Leme, 524, 7o. andar, São Paulo, SP 05424-010 Brazil

Tel: 55-11-816-0066 Fax: 55-11-816-0301 Contact: Dominique Einhorn, Pres. Emp: 62

RAYTHEON COMPANY

141 Spring Street, Lexington, MA, 02173

Tel: (781) 862-6600 Fax: (781) 860-2172 Web site: www.raytheon.com

Mfr. diversified electronics, appliances, aviation, energy and environmental products; publishing, industry and construction services.

Raytheon International, São Paulo, Brazil

RENAISSANCE HOTELS AND RESORTS

1 Marriott Drive, Washington, DC, 20058

Tel: (301) 380-3000 Fax: (301) 380-5181

Hotel and resort chain.

Renaissance Copabana Hotel, Rio de Janeiro, Brazil

Tel: 55-11-288-3860

Renaissance São Paulo Hotel, São Paulo, Brazil

Tel: 55-11-3069-2233

REVLON INC.

625 Madison Ave., New York, NY, 10022

Tel: (212) 527-4000 Fax: (212) 527-4995 Web site: www.revlon.com

Mfr. cosmetics, fragrances, toiletries and beauty care products.

Revlon, Brazil

REXNORD CORPORATION

4701 West Greenfield Ave., Milwaukee, WI, 53214

Tel: (414) 643-3000 Fax: (414) 643-3078

Mfr. power transmission products.

Rexnord Correntes SA, Caixa Postal 290, 93000 São Lepoldo, RS, Brazil

Tel: 55-11-592-6000 Fax: 55-11-592-2710 Contact: Jose Carlos Filo

RIDGE TOOL COMPANY

400 Clark Street, Elyria, OH, 44035

Tel: (440) 323-5581 Fax: (440) 329-4853 Web site: www.ridgid.com

Hand & power tools for working pipe, drain cleaning equipment, etc.

Ridgid Ferramentas e Maquinas Ltda., Av. Deputado Emilio Carlos, 1910, Caixa Postal 72, 06320-970 Carapicuiba, SP Brazil

Tel: 55-11-429-5522 Fax: 55-11-429-5745 Contact: Bradford L. Corson, Gen. Mgr. Emp: 27

RIVERWOOD INTERNATIONAL CORPORATION

3350 Cumberland Circle, #1600, Atlanta, GA, 30339

Tel: (770) 644-3000 Fax: (770) 644-2927 Web site: www.riverwood.com

Mfr. paperboard packaging & machinery.

Igaras Papeis e Embalagens Ltda., Rua do Rocio, 109, Vila Olimpia, São Paulo, SP04552-000

Brazil

Tel: 55-11-820-7377 Fax: 55-11-822-5497 Contact: Roberto Sanches, President Emp: 2600

RJR NABISCO INC.

1301 Ave. of the Americas, New York, NY, 10019

Tel: (212) 258-5600 Fax: (212) 969-9173 Web site: www.rjrnabisco.com

Mfr. consumer packaged food products & tobacco products.

Leite Gloria do Nordeste SA, Itapetinga, 45800 Bahia, Brazil

Prdts. Alimenticios Fleischmann y Royal Ltda., Av. Pedro II, 250 São Cristovao, Rio de Janeiro, RJ 20941-070 Brazil
Brazil

Tel: 55-21-574-1100 Fax: 55-21-589-2160 Contact: Freeman Brown, Pres. Emp: 6000

ROBBINS & MYERS INC.

1400 Kettering Tower, Dayton, OH, 45423-1400

Tel: (937) 222-2610 Fax: (937) 225-3355

Mfr. progressing cavity pumps, valves and agitators.

Robbins & Myers Brazil, São Paulo, Brazil

THE ROCKPORT COMPANY

220 Donald J. Lynch Blvd., Marlboro, MA, 01752

Tel: (508) 485-2090 Fax: (508) 480-0012

Mfr./import dress and casual footwear.

Rockport Brazil South, Rua Bage, 149 Bairro Boa Vista, 93, 41D-220, NovoHamburgo, RS, Brazil

Tel: 55-51-593-8502 Fax: 55-51-595-4380 Contact: Peter Dodge, Pres.

Rockport South American Industrial Ltda., Rua Doutor Julio Cardoso 2.273, 14400 Franca, SP, Brazil

ROCKWELL INTERNATIONAL CORPORATION

600 Anton Boulevard, Costa Mesa, CA, 92626-7147

Tel: (714) 424-4200 Fax: (714) 424-4251 Web site: www.rockwell.com

Products & service for aerospace and defense, automotive, electronics, graphics & automation industry.

Rockwell Automation do Brazil Ltda., Rua Tome de Souza 1065, 5o andar, Funcionarios, 30140-131 Belo Horizonte, MG, Brazil (Locations: Barueri, Campinas, Ribeirao Preto, Rio de Janeiro & São Paulo, São Leopoldo & Volta Redonda, Brazil.)

Tel: 55-31-227-4099 Fax: 55-31-227-4258

Rockwell Collins do Brazil Ltda., Av. Brig. Faria Lima, 1941- Sala 12, 12.227-901 - Jd. Cerere, São Paulo dos Campos, SP Brazil

Tel: 55-12-321-1633 Fax: 55-12-321-1901

Rockwell do Brasil Ind. e Com. Ltda. - Fumagalli Div., Sala A, Av. Major Jose Levy Sobrinho 2700,Limeira, SP13486-925, Brazil

Tel: 55-19-440-2132 Fax: 55-19-440-2222 Contact: Altimiro Boscoli, Dir. Emp: 1200

ROHM AND HAAS COMPANY

100 Independence Mall West, Philadelphia, PA, 19106

Tel: (215) 592-3000 Fax: (215) 592-3377 Web site: www.rohmhaas.com

Mfr. industrial & agricultural chemicals, plastics.

Rohm and Haas Quimica Ltda., Edif. Morumbi Office Tower, Av. Roque Petroni Jr., 999 - 9th Fl., CEP 04707-000 - So Paulo, Brazil (Locations: Paulina, Jacarei, SP, Brazil

Tel: 55-11-5097-9000 Fax: 55-11-421-4301 Contact: Carlos A. Estevez, Pres. Emp: 400

RUSSELL REYNOLDS ASSOCIATES INC.

200 Park Ave., New York, NY, 10166-0002

Tel: (212) 351-2000 Fax: (212) 370-0896 Web site: www.ressreyn.com

Executive recruiting services.

Russell Reynolds Associates Ltda., Av. Nações Unidas, 11857 - 12° andar - Conjunto 122, 04578-000 São Paulo - SP - Brazil

Tel: 55-11-5505-6165 Fax: 55-11-5505-6272 Contact: Fàtima Zorzato

RYDER SYSTEM, INC.

3600 NW 82nd Ave., Miami, FL, 33166

Tel: (305) 593-3726 Fax: (305) 500-4129 Web site: www.ryder.com

Integrated logistics, full-service truck leasing, truck rental and public transportation services.

Ryder System, Inc., Rua Tabapua, 145-11 andar, Itaim Bibi, São Paulo-SP 04533-010 Brazil

Tel: 55-11-820-8097 Fax: 55-11-820-8295

SAS INSTITUTE INC.

SAS Campus Drive, Cary, NC, 27513

Tel: (919) 677-8000 Fax: (919) 677-8123 Web site: www.sas.com

Mfr./distributes decision support software.

SAS Institute (Brazil) Inc., São Paulo, Brazil

Tel: 55-11-5505-5355 Fax: 55-11-5505-5302

SCHENECTADY INTERNATIONAL INC.

PO Box 1046, Schenectady, NY, 12301

Tel: (518) 370-4200 Fax: (518) 382-8129

Mfr. electrical insulating varnishes, enamels, phenolic resins, alkylphenols.

Schenectady Brasil Ltda., Rodovia Edgard Maximo Zambotto Km. 79, Ponte Alta, Caixa Postal 781, 12940-000 Atibaia, SP, Brazil

Tel: 55-78-71-1822 Fax: 55-78-71-0411 Contact: Adival S. de Freitas, Gen. Mgr. Emp: 90

SCHENKER INTERNATIONAL FORWARDERS INC.

150 Albany Ave., Freeport, NY, 11520

Tel: (516) 377-3000 Fax: (516) 377-3005 Web site: www.schenkerusa.com

Freight forwarders.

Schenker do Brasil Transportes Internacionais Ltds., R. Geraldo Flausino Gomes, No. 78, 12/13 andar, PO Box 2017, São Paulo, 04575, Brazil

Tel: 55-11-532-9000 Fax: 55-11-532-9100

R.P. SCHERER CORPORATION

PO Box 7060, Troy, MI, 48007-7060

Tel: (248) 649-0900 Fax: (248) 649-4238 Web site: www.rpscherer.com

Mfr. pharmaceuticals; soft gelatin and two-piece hard shell capsules.

R.P. Scherer do Brasil Encapsulacoes Ltda., Av. Jerome Case 1277, Zona Industrial, Sorocaba, SP, Brazil 18087-370

Tel: 55-15-2253060 Fax: 55-15-2252306 Contact: Henry Adler, Gen. Mgr. Emp: 117

SCHERING-PLOUGH CORPORATION

1 Giralda Farms, Madison, NJ, 07940-1000

Tel: (973) 822-7000 Fax: (973) 822-7048 Web site: www.sch-plough.com

Proprietary drug and cosmetic products.

Industria Quimica e Farmaceutica Schering SA, Rua Moraes e Silva 43, Caixa Postal 540, ZC-00, Rio de Janeiro, RJ, Brazil

SCHLEGEL SYSTEMS

1555 Jefferson Road, PO Box 23197, Rochester, NY, 14692-3197

Tel: (716) 427-7200 Fax: (716) 427-7216

Mfr. engineered perimeter sealing systems for residential & commercial construction; fibers; rubber product.

Schlegel do Brasil Industria e Comercio Ltda., Rua Itaquiti 301, 06400 Barueri, São Paulo, Brazil

Tel: 55-11-427-4200 Fax: 55-11-427-4833 Contact: Jose Carlo Filo Emp: 35

SCHRADER BELLOWS DIV

257 Huddleston Ave., Cuyahoga Falls, OH, 44221

Tel: (330) 923-5202 Fax: (330) 426-3259

Mfr. pneumatic and hydraulic valves and cylinders, FRL units and accessories..

Parker-Hannifin Industria e Comercio Ltda., Schrader Bellows Div., Av. Sumare 1529/1541, 05016 São Paulo, Brazil

SCIENTIFIC-ATLANTA, INC.

1 Technology Pkwy South, Norcross, GA, 30092-2967

Tel: (770) 903-5000 Fax: (770) 903-2967 Web site: www.sciatl.com

A leading supplier of broadband communications systems, satellite-based video, voice and data communications networks and worldwide customer service and support.

Scientific-Atlanta do Brasil Ltda., Rua do Rocio, 220, 6 andar, Conjunto 1, Villa dimpia, São Paulo, Brazil CP 04552904

Tel: 55-11-820-9154 Fax: 55-11-820-2514

SEA-LAND SERVICE INC.

6000 Carnegie Boulevard, Charlotte, NC, 28209

Tel: (704) 571-2000 Fax: (704) 571-4693 Web site: www.sealand.com

Largest U.S-based containerized transport service; ships, railroads, barge lines and trucking operations.

Sea-Land Services Ltda., Av. Nilo Pecanha 50, sala 1213, 20000 Rio de Janeiro, Brazil

Tel: 55-21-532-1196 Fax: 55-21-262-9618

SEALED AIR CORPORATION

Park 80 Plaza East, Saddle Brook, NJ, 07662-5291

Tel: (201) 791-7600 Fax: (201) 703-4205 Web site: www.sealedair.com

Mfr. protective and specialty packaging solutions for industrial, food and consumer products.

Sealed Air Brasil Ltda., Rua Eng. Francisco Azevedo, 243, Perdizes SP, CEP 05030010, Brazil

Tel: 55-11-871-1618 Fax: 55-11-873-1889

SEAQUIST PERFECT DISPENSING

1160 North Silver Lake Road, Cary, IL, 60013

Tel: (847) 639-2124 Fax: (847) 639-2142 Web site: www.seaperf.com

Mfr. and sale of dispensing systems; lotion pumps and spray-through overcaps.

Seaquist Valois do Brasil Ltda., São Paulo, Brazil

G.D. SEARLE & COMPANY

5200 Old Orchard Road, Skokie, IL, 60077

Tel: (847) 982-7000 Fax: (847) 470-1480 Web site: www.searlehealthnet.com

Mfr. pharmaceuticals, health care, optical products and specialty chemicals.

Searl do Brazil Ltda., Departamento Cientifico Rua Indenpendencia, 706 01524, Cambuci, São Paulo SP, Brazil

Tel: 55-11-915-8699 Fax: 55-11-273-8115

SEARS ROEBUCK & COMPANY

3333 Beverly Road, Hoffman Estates, IL, 60179

Tel: (847) 286-2500 Fax: (800) 427-3049 Web site: www.sears.com

Diversified general merchandise.

Sears Roebuck SA Com. e Ind., Caixa Postal 7146, Agua Branca, SP, Brazil

SENSORMATIC ELECTRONICS CORPORATION

951 Yamato Road, Boca Raton, FL, 33431-0700

Tel: (561) 912-6000 Fax: (561) 989-7774 Web site: www.sensormatic.com

Electronic article surveillance equipment.

Sensormatic Electronics Corporation, Brazil

SHERWIN-WILLIAMS CO., INC.

101 Prospect Ave., N.W., Cleveland, OH, 44115-1075

Tel: (216) 566-2000 Fax: (216) 566-3312 Web site: www.sherwin-williams.com

Mfr. paint, wallcoverings and related products.

Sherwin-Williams do Brasil I&E Ltda., Rua Garcia Lorca, 231, San Bernardo do Campo, SP 09701-970 Brazil

Tel: 55-11-457-4000 Fax: 55-11-457-4869 Contact: Claudio A. Geiger, Pres. Emp: 450

SILICON GRAPHICS INC.

2011 N. Shoreline Blvd., Mountain View, CA, 94043-1389

Tel: (650) 960-1980 Fax: (650) 961-0595 Web site: www.sgi.com

Design/mfr. special-effects computer graphic systems and software.

Silicon Graphics, Brazil

SIMON & SCHUSTER INC.

1230 Ave. of the Americas, New York, NY, 10020

Tel: (212) 698-7000 Fax: (212) 698-7007 Web site: www.SimonSays.com

Publishes and distributes hardcover and paperback books, audiobooks, software and educational textbooks.

Editora Prentice-Hall do Brazil Ltda., Travessa do Ouvidor 11/6, 20040 Rio de Janeiro, RJ, Brazil

SMITH INTERNATIONAL, INC.

16740 Hardy Street, Houston, TX, 77032

Tel: (713) 443-3370 Fax: (713) 233-5996 Web site: www.smith.intl.com

Mfr. drilling tools and equipment and provides related services for the drilling, completion and production sectors of the petroleum and mining industries.

Smith Internacional do Brazil Ltda., Rua Santa Luzia, 651-29th Fl., Ste. 2903, Rio de Janeiro, RJ 20030-040 Brazil

Tel: 55-21-240-8685 Fax: 55-21-262-9327 Contact: Jose Augusto Paes da Rosa Moreira Emp: 120

SNAP ON DIAGNOSTICS

420 Barclay Boulevard, Lincolnshire, IL, 60069

Tel: (847) 478-0700 Fax: (847) 478-7308 Web site: www.snapon.com

Mfr. auto maintenence, diagnostic & emission testing equipment.

Sun Electric do Brazil Com.e Ind. Ltda., Rua Juscelino Kubitscneck de Oliveria, 134500-000 Santa Barbara O'este, San Paulo, Brazil

Tel: 55-19-455-1800 Fax: 55-19-455-1040 Contact: Takaji Katayama, Mng. Dir.

SOLECTRON CORPORATION

777 Gibraltar Drive, Milpitas, CA, 95035

Tel: (408) 957-8500 Fax: (408) 956-6075 Web site: www.solectron.com

Provides contract manufacturing services to equipment manufacturers.

Solectron Corporation, Ambró Molina, 1090 Eugênio De Melo, 12247-000 São Paulo, Brazil

Tel: 55-12-380-7000 Fax: 55-12-380-7143

SONOCO PRODUCTS COMPANY

North Second Street, PO Box 160, Hartsville, SC, 29550

Tel: (803) 383-7000 Fax: (803) 383-7008 Web site: www.sonoco.com

Mfr. packaging for consumer & industrial market and recycled paperboard.

Sonoco do Brazil - Araucaria, Rua Francisco Knopik, 706-CIAR, 83706-550 Araucaria, Parana, Brazil

Tel: 55-41-843 2123

Sonoco do Brazil - Curitiba, Rua Emilio Romani, 1222-CIC, 81450-060, Curitiba, PR, Brazil

Tel: 55-41-347 1515

Sonoco do Brazil - Londrina, Ruo Noitibo, 157 - Villa Yara, 86027-000, Londrina, Parana, Brazil

Tel: 55-43-325 4626

Sonoco do Brazil - Poa, Av. Duque de Caxias, 445/455, 08550-000, Poa, São Paulo, Brazil

Tel: 55-11-463 2233

SOUTHERN COMPANY

270 Peachtree Street, Atlanta, GA, 30303

Tel: (404) 506-5000 Fax: (404) 506-0642 Web site: www.southernco.com

Electric utility.

Southern Energy, Inc., Rua da Candalaria 6S-1802, 20091-000, Rio de Janeiro, Brazil

Tel: 55-21-516-1459 Contact: Felicia Bellour, Dir.

SPARTAN CHEMICAL COMPANY

110 North Westwood Ave., Toledo, OH, 43607

Tel: (419) 531-5551 Fax: (419) 536-8423

Mfr. soaps & detergents; industrial & specialty chemicals.

Spartan do Brasil Produtos Quimicos Ltda., Rua Fernao Pompeo de Camargo, 1704, Campinas, SP 13036-321 Brazil

Tel: 55-19-231-9611 Fax: 55-19-232-7132 Contact: David J. Drake, Mg. Dir. Emp: 91

SPENCER STUART & ASSOCIATES INC.

401 North Michigan Ave., Ste. 3400, Chicago, IL, 60611

Tel: (312) 822-0080 Fax: (312) 822-0116 Web site: www.spencerstuart.com

Executive recruitment firm.

Spencer Stuart & Associates Inc., 10th Fl., Alameda Santos, 1787, 01419-010 São Paulo, SP Brazil

Tel: 55-11-284-0349 Fax: 55-11-289-1159 Contact: Rudolf Mayer-Singule

SPIRAX SARCO, INC.

1951 Glenwood Street, SW, Allentown, PA, 18103

Tel: (610) 797-5860 Fax: (610) 433-1346 Web site: www.spiraxsarco-usa.com

Mfr. industrial steam system equipment, including valves, pumps, traps, controls, regulators, meter, filters and accessories.

Spirax Sarco Industria e Comercia Ltda., Rod. Raposo Tavares, Km 31, Cotia, SP 06700-000 Brazil

Tel: 55-11-493-0633 Fax: 55-11-493-6094 Contact: Jose Roberto Vanorden Vieira, Pres. Emp: 250

SPRINT INTERNATIONAL

World Headquarters, 2330 Shawnee Mission Parkway, Westwood, KS, 66205

Tel: (913) 624-3000 Fax: (913) 624-3281

Telecommunications equipment & services.

Sprint Comunicacoes do Brasil Ltda., Rua Joaquim Floriano 72, Conj., São Paulo, SP 04534-000 Brazil

Tel: 55-11-820-2297 Fax: 55-11-822-6517 Contact: Francisco A. Loureiro Gen. Mgr. Emp: 10

SPS TECHNOLOGIES INC.

301 Highland Avenue, Jenkintown, PA, 19046-2630

Tel: (215) 517-2000 Fax: (215) 517-2032

Mfr. aerospace & industry fasteners, tightening systems, magnetic materials, superalloys.

Metalac SA Industria e Com., Caixa Postal 66181, 05389 São Paulo, SP, Brazil

Tel: 55-15-226-1011 Fax: 55-15-226-1286 Contact: Claudio de Araujo Pecanha Emp: 400

SPX CORPORATION

700 Terrace Point Drive, PO Box 3301, Muskegon, MI, 49443-3301

Tel: (616) 724-5000 Fax: (616) 724-5720 Web site: www.spx.com

Mfr. Auto parts, special service tools, engine & drive-train parts.

Jurubatech Tecnologia, Av. Nossa Senhora do Sabara 4901, Santa Amaro, São Paulo, SP 04447-021 Brazil

Tel: 55-11-246-4177 Fax: 55-11-246-2793 Contact: Leonard Higgins, Mg. Dir. Emp: 40

Robinair Brazil, c/o Jurubatech Tech. Automotiva Ltda., Av. Nossa Senhora do Sabara 5.753, 04685 Santo Amaro, Brazil

THE ST. PAUL COMPANIES, INC.

385 Washington Street, St. Paul, MN, 55102

Tel: (612) 310-7911 Fax: (612) 310-8294 Web site: www.stpaul.com

Provides investment, insurance and reinsurance services.

Grupo Bradesco de Seguros, Rua Barao de Itapagipe, 225-8° andar, 20.269-900, Rio Comprido, Rio de Janeiro, Brazil

STANDARD COMMERCIAL CORPORATION

PO Box 450, Wilson, NC, 27893

Tel: (919) 291-5507 Fax: (919) 237-1109

Leaf tobacco dealers/processors and wool processors.

Fumex Exportoras de Tabacos SA, Salvador, Bahia, Brazil

STANDARD PRODUCTS COMPANY

2401 South Gulley Road, Dearborn, MI, 48124

Tel: (313) 561-1100 Fax: (313) 561-6526 Web site: www.stdproducts.com

Mfr. molded & extruded rubber & plastic products for automotive & appliance industry, retread tire industry.

Standard Products Company, Rua Dr. Renaro Paes de Barros, 717 Conj. 112 - Itaim Bibi, São Paulo 04530-001 Brazil

Tel: 55-30-44-0113 Fax: 55-30-828-9150

Standard Products Company, Av. Manoel Vida, 1.000, Imaculada Conceição, Varginha, MG 37.062-460, Brazil

Tel: 55-35-219-4000 Fax: 55-35-219-4036

THE STANLEY WORKS

1000 Stanley Drive, PO Box 7000, New Britain, CT, 06053

Tel: (860) 225-5111 Fax: (860) 827-3987 Web site: www.stanleyworks.com

Mfr. hand tools & hardware.

Ferramentas Stanley S.A., Rua Araraf, 35, São Paulo, SP 04729-030, Brazil

Tel: 55-11-247-7744 Fax: 55-11-247-7121 Contact: Marcelo Guerra de Oliveira, Pres. Emp: 200

STEINER CORPORATION

505 East South Temple Street, Salt Lake City, UT, 84102

Tel: (801) 328-8831 Fax: (801) 363-5680

Linen supply service.

Toalheiro Brazil Ltda., ua Conde de Itu,875, Santa Amaro, São Paulo, SP 04741-001 Brazil

São Paulo, SP 04741-001 Brazil

Tel: 55-11-523-8722 Fax: 55-11-523-6961 Contact: Antonio Carlos de Camargo Emp: 900

Toalheiro Brazil Ltda., Rua Marques de Sabara 59, Rio de Janeiro, RJ. Brazil

STERIS CORPORATION

5960 Heisley Road, Mentor, OH, 44060

Tel: (440) 354-2600 Fax: (440) 639-4459

Mfr. sterilization/infection control equipment, surgical tables, lighting systems for health, pharmaceutical & scientific industries.

AMSCO Intl. Co., Rua Tabapuã 500-CJ51, 04533 São Paulo, Brazil

Tel: 55-11-542-3800 Contact: José Laranjeira, Gen'l Mgr Emp: 7

STERLING SOFTWARE INC.

1800 Alexander Bell Drive, Reston, VA, 22091

Tel: (703) 264-8000 Fax: (703) 264-0762

Sales/service software products; technical services.

Sterling Software do Brasil SA, Rua Quintana, 753, 2o. andar, São Paulo, SP 04569-011 Brazil

Tel: 55-11-505-3366 Fax: 55-11-505-1805 Contact: Alfredo Pinheiro, Mg. Dir. Emp: 25

STIEFEL LABORATORIES INC.

255 Alhambra Circle, Ste. 1000, Coral Gables, FL, 33134

Tel: (305) 443-3807 Fax: (305) 443-3467

Mfr. pharmaceuticals, dermatological specialties.

Laboratorios Stiefel Ltda., Av. Narain Singh 400, Bonnsucesso, Guarulhos, SP 07250-000 Brazil

Tel: 55-11-960-3111 Fax: 55-11-960-4152 Contact: Giovani Bastos, Mg. Dir. Emp: 300

STRUCTURAL DYNAMICS RESEARCH CORPORATION

2000 Eastman Drive, Milford, OH, 45150-2789

Tel: (513) 576-2400 Fax: Web site: www.sdrc.com

Developer of software used in Modeling esting, drafting and manufacturing.

SDRC do Brasil, Ltda. - South America Operation, Av. Roque Petroni Jr., 999, 13 andar, São Paulo - SP - Brazil CEP 04707-910

Tel: 55-11-532-2880 Fax: 55-11-532-2899

STUART ENTERTAINMENT INC.

3211 Nebraska Ave., Council Bluffs, IA, 51501

Tel: (712) 323-1488 Fax: (712) 323-3215 Web site: www.bingoking.com

Mfg. bingo equipment and supplies, lottery tickets & video gaming machines.

Stuart Entertainment do Brasil Ltda., Av. Paulista, 509, 6o. andar, São Paulo, SP 01311-000 Brazil

Tel: 55-11-284-8393 Fax: 55-11-284-6629 Contact: Kurt Armstrong, Int'l Sales Mgr. Emp: 2

SULLAIR CORPORATION

3700 E. Michigan Blvd., Michigan City, IN, 46360

Tel: (219) 879-5451 Fax: (219) 874-1273

Refrigeration systems, vacuum pumps, generators, etc.

Sullair SA, Alameda Joaquim Eugenio de Lima 680, 10 andar, 01403 São Paulo, Brazil

SUN MICROSYSTEMS, INC.

901 San Antonio Road, Palo Alto, CA, 94303

Tel: (650) 960-1300 Fax: (650) 856-2114 Web site: www.sun.com

Computer peripherals and programming services.

Sun Microsystems do Brasil Industria e Comercio Ltda., Rua Verbo Divino, 1488, São Paulo, SP 04719-904 Brazil

Tel: 55-11-524-8988 Fax: 55-11-547-0974 Contact: Dario Boralli, Dir. Emp: 16

SWECO INC.

7120 New Buffington Road, PO Box 1509, Florence, KY, 41042-1509

Tel: (606) 727-5100 Fax: (606) 727-5106

Mfr. vibratory process and solids control equipment.

Sweco Industrial Div., Belem, Brazil

SYBASE, INC.

6475 Christie Ave., Emeryville, CA, 94608

Tel: (510) 922-3500 Fax: (510) 922-3210 Web site: www.sybase.com

Design/mfg/distribution of database management systems, software development tools, connectivity products, consulting and technical support services..

Sybase do Brasil Software Ltda., Rua Bela Cintra, 967, Andar 9, São Paulo, 01415 905 SP Brazil

Tel: 55-11-214-4044 Fax: 55-11-214-0820

SYMANTEC CORPORATION

10201 Torre Ave., Cupertino, CA, 95014-2132

Tel: (408) 253-9600 Fax: (408) 446-8129 Web site: www.symantec.com

Designs and produces PC network security and network management software and hardware.

Symantec do Brazil, Av. Juruce, 302 -cj 11, São Paulo-SP 0408-011 Brazil

Tel: 55-11-5561-0284 Fax: 55-11-530-8869

TBWA INTERNATIONAL

180 Maiden Lane, New York, NY, 10038

Tel: (212) 804-1000 Fax: (212) 804-1200

International full service advertising agency.

TBWA Argentina, São Paulo, Brazil

TECH DATA CORPORATION

5350 Tech Data Drive, Clearwater, FL, 34620-3122

Tel: (813) 539-7429 Fax: (813) 538-7876 Web site: www.techdata.com

Distributor of computer systems, software and related equipment.

TD Brasil LTDA, Rua São Paulo, 137, 06465-130-Barueri-São Paulo, Brazil

Tel: 55-11-7295-8660 Fax: 55-11-7295-8666

TECUMSEH PRODUCTS COMPANY

100 E. Patterson Street, Tecumseh, MI, 49286-1899

Tel: (517) 423-8411 Fax: (517) 423-8526

Mfr. refrigeration & A/C compressors & units, small engines, pumps.

Sicom SA, Caixa Postal 54,São Carlos, SP 13560-900 Brazil

Tel: 55-16-271-1212 Fax: 55-16-272-7002 Contact: Wolfgang Rodolfo Falland, Chmn. Emp: 5000

TEKTRONIX INC.

2660 Southwest Parkway Ave., PO Box 1000, Wilsonville, OR, 97070-1000

Tel: (503) 627-7111 Fax: (503) 627-2406 Web site: www.tek.com

Mfr. test & measure, visual systems/color printing & communications/video and networking products.

Tektronix Industria e Com. Ltda., Av. Maria Coelho Aguiar, 215 - Bloco D - 1º Andar, São Paulo, SP 05805-000, Brazil

Tel: 55-11-3741-8360 Fax: 55-11-3741-7358 Emp: 40

Tektronix Industria e Com. Ltda., Rio de Janeiro, Brazil

TELE-COMMUNICATIONS INC.

PO Box 5630, Denver, CO, 80217-5630

Tel: (303) 267-5500 Fax: (303) 779-1228 Web site: www.tci.com

Largest cable television operator in the U.S.

Tele-Communications International Inc., São Paulo, Brazil

TEMPEL STEEL COMPANY

5215 Old Orchard, Skokie, IL, 60077

Tel: (847) 581-9400 Fax: (847) 581-9025

Metal stampings; specialty transformers; motors & generators.

Tempel do Brasil Industria e Comercio Ltda., Rua Engenheiro Eugenio Lorenzetti, 78, Ribeirao Pires, SP 09400-000 Brazil

Tel: 55-11-459-3866 Fax: 55-11-459-2211 Contact: Tell Fausto Ferrao, Pres. Emp: 300

TENNANT COMPANY

701 North Lilac Drive, Minneapolis, MN, 55440

Tel: (612) 513-2112 Fax: (612) 541-6137 Web site: www.Tennantco.com

Mfr. industry floor maintenance sweepers and scrubbers, floor coatings.

Equipamentos Tennant Ltda., Rua Alvares Cabral 871, No. 1001, 09980-160 Diadema, São Paulo, Brazil

Tel: 55-11-456-2655 Fax: 55-11-456-4160 Contact: Jeff Hanson, Gen Mgr.

TENNECO AUTOMOTIVE

500 North Field Drive, Lake Forest, IL, 60045

Tel: (847) 482-5241 Fax: (847) 482-5295

Automotive parts, exhaust systems, service equipment.

Monroe Auto Pecas (Brazil), Praca Vereadur Marcos Portiolli 26, 13800-970 Mogi Mirim, SP, Brazil

Tel: 55-19-860-5000 Fax: 55-19-862-3551 Contact: Ataide Nitta, Mgr. Emp: 705

Production de Elastomers Ltda., Rodivia Raposa Tarares Km. 36.5, 06700 Cotia, San Paulo, Brazil

Tel: 55-11-493-4282 Fax: 55-11-79-248-742 Contact: Atila Hevesy, Mgr. Emp: 550

TENNECO INC.

1275 King Street, Greenwich, CT, 06831

Tel: (203) 863-1000 Fax: (203) 863-1134 Web site: www.tenneco.com

Mfr. automotive products and packaging materials/containers.

J.I. Case do Brazil & Cia., Av. Jerome Case 1951, 18100 Sorocaba, São Paulo, Brazil

Monroe Auto Equipment, Rua Lavras 343, 30000 Bello Horizante, São Paulo, Brazil

Monroe Auto Pecas SA, Praca Vereador Marcos Portioli 26, 13800 Mogi Mirim, Brazil

TENNESSEE ASSOCIATES INTERNATIONAL

223 Associates Blvd., PO Box 710, Alcoa, TN, 37701-0710

Tel: (423) 982-9514 Fax: (423) 982-1481

Management consulting services.

Tennessee Associates do Brasil, Rua Augusta 2347, CJ 12, 01413-000 São Paulo, SP, Brazil

TEXACO INC.

2000 Westchester Ave., White Plains, NY, 10650

Tel: (914) 253-4000 Fax: (914) 253-7753 Web site: www.texaco.com

Exploration/marketing crude oil, mfr. petro chemicals and products.

Texaco Brazil SA, Rua Dom Gerardo 64, Caixa Postal 520, Rio de Janeiro, RJ, Brazil

TEXAS INSTRUMENTS INC.

8505 Forest Lane, Dallas, TX, 75243

Tel: (214) 995-2011 Fax: (214) 995-4360 Web site: www.ti.com

Mfr. semiconductor devices, electronic electro-mechanical systems, instruments and controls.

Texas Instrumentos Electronicos do Brazil Ltda., Rua Azarias de Melo 648/660, Caixa Postal 98886, 14100 Campinas, São Paulo, Brazil

Tel: 55-19-251-8144 Fax: 55-19-251-8321 Contact: Jose Nelson Salveti, Gen Mgr. Emp: 300

TEXTRON INC.

40 Westminster Street, Providence, RI, 02903

Tel: (401) 421-2800 Fax: (401) 421-2878 Web site: www.textron.com

Mfr. aerospace, industry and consumer products (Bell Helicopter & Cessna Aircraft) and financial services.

Mapri Textron Inc., Av Mofarrej, 971 V. Leopoldina, 05311-904, São Paulo, Brazil

Tel: 55-11-837-4000 Fax: 55-11-837-4134 Contact: Mario Borelli

THERMADYNE INDUSTRIES INC.

101 South Hanley Road, #300, St. Louis, MO, 63105

Tel: (314) 746-2197 Fax: (314) 746-2349 Web site: www.thermadyne.com

Mfr. welding, cutting, and safety products.

Thermadyne Do Brasil, São Paulo, Brazil

Tel: 55-11-744-3444

THERMO ELECTRON CORPORATION

81 Wyman Street, Waltham, MA, 02254-9046

Tel: (781) 622-1000 Fax: (781) 622-1207 Web site: www.thermo.com

Develop/mfr./sale of process equipment &instruments for energy intensive & healthcare industries.

Lodding do Brazil Ltda., Rua Domingos Jorge 676, 04761 São Paulo, Brazil

THETFORD CORPORATION

7101 Jackson Road, PO Box 1285, Ann Arbor, MI, 48106

Tel: (734) 769-6000 Fax: (734) 769-2023

Mfr. sanitation products and chemicals.

Thetford do Brazil, Av. Samuel Aisemberg 399, 09700 São Bernardo do Campo, São Paulo, Brazil

THOMAS PUBLISHING COMPANY

5 Penn Plaza, New York, NY, 10007

Tel: (212) 695-0500 Fax: (212) 290-7362 Web site: www.thomaspublishing.com

Publishing magazines and directories.

T/L Publicacoes Industriais Ltda, Caixa Postal 30.493, Rua Brigadeiro 356, 5 andar, 01000 São Paulo, SP, Brazil

Tel: 55-11-227-1022 Fax: 55-11-228-9373 Contact: R. Christopher Lund. Emp: 145

TIDEWATER INC.

Tidewater Place, 1440 Canal Street, New Orleans, LA, 70112

Tel: (504) 568-1010 Fax: (504) 566-4582

Marine service and equipment to companies engaged in exploration, development and production of oil, gas and minerals.

Pan Marine do Brasil Transportes Ltda., c/o Planave S.A., Rua Costa Ferreira 106, Centro, 20221 Rio de Janeiro, RJ, Brazil

Pan Marine do Brazil Transportes Ltda., Rodovia Arthur Bernardes 5511, Base do Tapana, Belem, Para, Brazil

TIME WARNER INC.

75 Rockefeller Plaza, New York, NY, 10019

Tel: (212) 484-8000 Fax: (212) 275-3046 Web site: www.timewarner.com

Communications, publishing and entertainment company.

Time-Life Internacional do Brasil Ltda., Rua da Assemblia 10, Rio de Janeiro, Brazil

THE TIMKEN COMPANY

1835 Dueber Ave. SW, PO Box 6927, Canton, OH, 44706-2798

Tel: (330) 438-3000 Fax: (330) 471-4118

Mfr. tapered roller bearings and quality alloy steels.

Timken do Brasil, Rua Engenheiro Mesquita Sampaio, São Paulo, SP 04711-000 Brazil

Tel: 55-11-247-1233 Fax: 55-11-522-7410 Contact: Georges Lammoglia, Pres.

THE TOPPS CO., INC.

1 Whitehall Street, New York, NY, 10004-2108

Tel: (212) 376-0300 Fax: (212) 376-0573 Web site: www.topps.com

Mfr. chewing gum & confections.

Topps do Brasil Ltda., Rua Carmo do Rio Verde, 241 conj. 41, VZ de Baixo, 04729-010 São Paulo, Brazil

Tel: 55-11-524-3483 Fax: 55-11-524-0182

TOWER AUTOMOTIVE, INC.

1350 West Hamlin Road, PO Box 5011, Rochester Hills, MI, 48308-5011

Tel: (248) 650-4100 Fax: (248) 650-7406

Mfr. stamped and welded assemblies for vehicle body structures and suspension systems for auto makers.

Metalurgica Caterina SA, São Paulo, Brazil

TOWERS PERRIN

335 Madison Ave., New York, NY, 10017-4605

Tel: (212) 309-3400 Fax: (212) 309-0975 Web site: www.towers.com

Management consulting services.

Tillinghast - Towers Perrin, Rua Dr. Eduardo de Souza Aranha 153-5, São Paulo, SP 04543-904 Brazil

Tel: 55-11-3040-3400 Fax: 55-11-829-5968 Contact: Aloisio Ferreira Emp: 50

Tillinghast - Towers Perrin, Av. Republica do Chile, 230, 18 andar - Centro, 20031-170-Rio de Janeiro, Brazil

Tel: 55-21-210-2101 Fax: 55-21-262-5246 Contact: Paulo Ferriera

TRANE COMPANY

3600 Pammel Creek Road, La Crosse, WI, 54601

Tel: (608) 787-2000 Fax: (608) 787-4990

Mfr./distributor/service A/C systems and equipment.

Trane do Brasil Ind. e Com. Ltda., Rua Elvira Ferraz 265 v. Olimpia, 04552-040 São Paulo, SP, Brazil

TRANS OCEAN OFFSHORE DRILLING

PO Box 2765, Houston, TX, 77252-2765

Tel: (713) 871-7500 Fax: (713) 850-3711

Offshore oil well drilling.

Sonat Offshore do Brasil Perfuracoes Martimas Ltda., Av. das Americas 679, Grupo 109, Dep. 22600-N, Barra de Tijuca, Rio de Janeiro, Brazil

Sonat Servicos Maritimos, Av. Prefeito Aristeu Ferreira da Silva, 265, Granja dos Cavaleiros, Macae, RJ 27901-970 Brazil

Tel: 55-24-762-6660 Fax: 55-24-762-9862 Contact: Bob Scott

TRANSAMERICA CORPORATION

600 Montgomery Street, San Francisco, CA, 94111

Tel: (415) 983-4000 Fax: (415) 983-4400 Web site: www.transamerica.com

Life insurance, leasing, and commercial lending services.

Transamerica Corporation, Rio de Janeiro, Brazil

Tel: 55-21-552-2255 Fax: 55-21-552-2971

TRIMBLE NAVIGATION LIMITED

645 N. Mary Ave., Sunnyvale, CA, 94088

Tel: (408) 481-8000 Fax: (408) 481-2000 Web site: www.trimble.com

Design/mfr. electronic geographic instrumentation.

Trimble Brasilia Limitada, Av. Presidente Wilson, 164 sala 120, 20030-020 Rio de Janeiro, RJ Brazil

Tel: 55-21-532-5473 Fax: 55-21-532-0532

TRUE NORTH COMMUNICATIONS INC.

101 East Erie Street, Chicago, IL, 60611

Tel: (312) 425-6000 Fax: (312) 425-6350

Holding company, advertising agency.

Giovanni/FCB, Praia de Botafogo #228, Ala A, 13º Andar, Rio de Janeiro, Brazil, CEP 22359-900

Giovanni/FCB, Rua Dr. Renato Paes de Barros #7, 5º Andar, São Paulo - S.P., Brazil, CEP 04530-001

Giovanni/FCB, SCS. Quadra 1, Bloco 1, Ed. Centre, Grupo 801, Brasilia/DF, Brazil, CEP 70300-500

Tel: 55-11-545-3193 Fax: 55-11-545-3320 Contact: Gustavo Cubas Ruiz Emp: 115

TRW COMMERCIAL STEERING

800 Heath Street, Lafayette, IN, 47904

Tel: (765) 423-5377 Fax: (765) 429-1868

Mfr. steering gears, power steering pumps, columns, linkage.

Industrias Gemmer do Brazil SA, Av. Rotary 825, São Bernardo do Camp, 09700 São Paulo, SP, Brazil

TRW INC.

1900 Richmond Road, Cleveland, OH, 44124-3760

Tel: (216) 291-7000 Fax: (216) 291-7932

Electric and energy-related products, automotive and aerospace products, tools and fasteners.

TRW Computadores, Rua Evaristo da Veiga 55, 22032 Rio de Janeiro, Brazil

TRW do Brasil S.A., Av. Joao Ramalho, 2000, Maua, SP 09371-903 Brazil

Tel: 55-11-416-4350 Fax: 55-11-416-4587 Contact: Jose Luiz Maria Emp: 3000

TRW Gemmer Thompson SA, Caixa Postal 8104, São Paulo, Brazil

TRW Mission Industria Ltda., Rua Sargento Silvio Hollenback 151, 20000 Rio de Janeiro, Brazil

TURNER INTERNATIONAL INDUSTRIES INC.

375 Hudson Street, New York, NY, 10014

Tel: (212) 229-6000 Fax: (212) 229-6418

General construction, construction management.

Turner Birmann Construction Management do Brasil S.A., Rua Alexandre Dumas, 2200, 8o. andar, São Paulo, SP 04717-004 Brazil

Tel: 55-11-521-7122 Fax: 55-11-548-4595 Contact: Joao Carlos Velloso Machado Emp: 50

UNION CAMP CORPORATION

1600 Valley Road, Wayne, NJ, 07470

Tel: (973) 628-2000 Fax: (973) 628-2722 Web site: www.unioncamp.com

Mfr. paper, packaging, chemicals and wood products.

Union Camp Corp. Chemical Products Div., Rua Francisco Cruz, 51524-C4117, 902 San Paulo, Brazil

Tel: 55-11-6914-5456 Fax: 55-11-6914-8926

UNION CARBIDE CORPORATION

39 Old Ridgebury Road, Danbury, CT, 06817

Tel: (203) 794-2000 Fax: (203) 794-6269 Web site: www.unioncarbide.com

Mfr. industrial chemicals, plastics and resins.

Union Carbide do Brazil Ltda., Rua Dr. Eduardo de Souza Aranha, 153, São Paulo, SP 04543-904 Brazil (Locations: Aratu, Cabo, & Cubatao)

Tel: 55-11-828-1133 Fax: 55-11-820-4050 Contact: Jean Daniel Peter, Pres. Emp: 650

UNION OIL INTERNATIONAL DIV

2141 Rosecrans Ave., El Segundo, CA, 90245

Tel: (310) 726-7600 Fax: (310) 726-7817

Petroleum products, petrochemicals..

Unionoil Exploracao de Petrolea Ltda., Praia do Flamengo 200, Rio de Janeiro, RJ, Brazil

UNIROYAL CHEMICAL CO., INC.

World Headquarters, Benson Road, Middlebury, CT, 06749

Tel: (203) 573-2000 Fax: (203) 573-2265

Tires, tubes and other rubber products, chemicals, plastics and textiles.

United States Rubber Intl. do Brazil SA, Rua Dona Veridiana 158, Caixa Postal 8041, São Paulo, SP, Brazil

UNISYS CORPORATION.

PO Box 500, Union Meeting Road, Blue Bell, PA, 19424

Tel: (215) 986-4011 Fax: (215) 986-6850 Web site: www.unisys.com

Mfr./marketing/servicing electronic information systems.

Unisys Electronica Ltda., Rua Teixeira de Freitas 31-14 andar, Rio de Janeiro, RJ 20021-350 Brazil

Tel: 55-21-217-1133 Fax: 55-21-221-9435 Contact: Robert Harvey Cook, Pres, Emp: 1700

UNITED AIRLINES INC.

PO Box 66100, Chicago, IL, 60666

Tel: (847) 700-4000 Fax: (847) 952-7680 Web site: www.ual.com

Air transportation, passenger and freight.

United Airlines, Av. Paulista, 777, 9o. andar, São Paulo, SP 01311-100 Brazil

Tel: 55-11-284-1326 Fax: 55-11-251-5955 Contact: Laurence Hughes, Gen. Dir. Emp: 240

UNITED PARCEL SERVICE OF AMERICA, INC.

55 Glenlake Parkway, NE, Atlanta, GA, 30328

Tel: (404) 828-6000 Fax: (404) 828-6593 Web site: www.ups.com

International package-delivery service.

UPS do Brasil & Cia., Rua Condessa do Pinhal, 158, Jardim Aeroporto, Campo Bello, São Paulo, SP CEP 04610-060, Brazil

Tel: 55-11-241-0122 Fax: 55-11-533-2363

UNITED PRESS INTERNATIONAL

1400 I Street, Washington, DC, 20005

Tel: (202) 898-8000 Fax: (202) 371-1239

Collection & distributor of news, newspictures, financial data.

UPI, Av. Paranapuan 1.793, 21910 Rio de Janeiro, RJ, Brazil

UNIVERSAL CORPORATION

PO Box 25099, Richmond, VA, 23260

Tel: (804) 359-9311 Fax: (804) 254-3582

Holding company for tobacco and commodities.

Tabacos Brasileiros Ltda., Caixa Postal 542, Blumenau, 89100 Santa Catarina, Brazil

UNIVERSAL INSTRUMENTS

90 Bevier Street, S. Dock, Binghamton, NY, 13904

Tel: (607) 779-7522 Fax: (607) 779-7971 Web site: www.dover.com

Mfr./sales of instruments for electronic circuit assembly

HITECH, São Paulo, Brazil

Tel: 55-11-5188-4000 Fax: 55-11-5188-4175

VARIAN ASSOCIATES INC.

3050 Hansen Way, Palo Alto, CA, 94304-100

Tel: (650) 493-4000 Fax: (650) 424-5358 Web site: www.varian.com

Mfr. microwave tubes & devices, analytical instruments, semiconductor process & medical equipment, vacuum systems.

Varian Ind. e Com. Ltda., Av. Dr. Cardoso de Melo 1644,São Paulo, SP 04548 -005 Brazil

Tel: 55-11-820-0444 Fax: 55-11-820-9350 Contact: Helio Ventura, Gen. Mgr. Emp: 45

VEEDER-ROOT COMPANY

125 Powder Forest Drive, PO Box 2003, Simsbury, CT, 06070-2003

Tel: (860) 651-2700 Fax: (860) 651-2704

Mfr. counting, controlling and sensing devices.

Veeder-Root do Brazil Com. e Ind. Ltda., Rua Ado Benatti 92, Caixa Postal 8343, 01051 São Paulo, Brazil

VIACOM INC.

1515 Broadway, 28th Fl., New York, NY, 10036-5794

Tel: (212) 258-6000 Fax: (212) 258-6358 Web site: www.viacom.com

Communications, publishing and entertainment.

Editora Prentice Hall do Brasil Ltda., Travessa do Ouvidor 11/6, 20040 Rio de Janeiro, Brazil

Viacom Video Audio Comunicacoes Ltda., Caixa Postal 51521, Alameda Jau 1742-11 andar, 01420 São Paulo, Brazil

VITRAMON INC.

PO Box 544, Bridgeport, CT, 06601

Tel: (203) 268-6261 Fax: (203) 261-4446 Web site: www.vishay.com

Ceramic capacitors.

Vitramon do Brasil Ltda., Rua Carmo do Rio Verde, 511, São Paulo, SP 04729-010 Brazil

Tel: 55-11-523-6333 Fax: 55-11-523-6041 Contact: Mario Alberto Diaz Medero Emp: 60

VOLT INFORMATION SCIENCES, INC.

1221 Ave. of the Americas, 47th Fl., New York, NY, 10020-1579

Tel: (212) 704-2400 Fax: (212) 704-2424 Web site: www.volt.com

Staffing services and telecommunication services.

Autologic Information International Latin America, Rua Fonseca Teles, 18, 20940-200, Rio de Janeiro, Brazil

Tel: 55-21-580-4213

WACHOVIA CORPORATION

PO Box 3099, Winston-Salem, NC, 27150

Tel: (919) 770-5000 Fax: (919) 770-5931 Web site: www.wachovia.com

Commercial banking.

Wachovia International Servicos Limitada, São Paulo, Brazil

WACKENHUT CORPORATION

4200 Wackenhut Drive, Ste. 100, Palm Beach Gardens, FL, 33410

Tel: (561) 622-5656 Fax: (561) 691-6736 Web site: www.wackenhut.com

Security systems & services.

GRW Ltda., Caixa Postal 2176, CEP 20001 São Paulo, Brazil

Pires Servicos de Seguranca Ltda., Rua Alfredo Pujol 1102, CEP 02017-902 Santana, São Paulo, Brazil

Tel: 55-11-959-1144 Fax: 55-11-267-3395

WAL-MART STORES INC.

702 SW 8th Street, Bentonville, AR, 72716-8611

Tel: (501) 273-4000 Fax: (501) 273-8980 Web site: www.wal-mart.com

Retailer.

Wal-Mart Brazil, Brazil

WARNER-LAMBERT COMPANY

201 Tabor Road, Morris Plains, NJ, 07950-2693

Tel: (973) 540-2000 Fax: (973) 540-3761 Web site: www.warner-lambert.com

Mfr. ethical and proprietary pharmaceuticals, confectionery and consumer products & pet care supplies.

Warner-Lambert Industria e Comercio Ltda., Rua Estrela D'Oeste, 701, Guarulhos,SP 07140-902, Brazil

Tel: 55-11-964-3211 Fax: 55-11-602-1693 Contact: Raul Norbeto Vazquez, Pres. Emp: 1200

WASTE MANAGEMENT, INC.

3003 Butterfield Road, Oak Brook, IL, 60523-1100

Tel: (630) 572-8800 Fax: (630) 572-3094 Web site: www.wastemanagement.com

Environmental services and disposal company; collection, processing, transfer and disposal facilities.

Sasa S.A., Estrada Municipal, 2200 Mato Dentro, Tremenbe SP, Caixa Postal 80, CEP 12120-000, Brazil

WATERS CORPORATION

34 Maple Street, Milford, MA, 01757

Tel: (508) 478-2000 Fax: (508) 872-1990

Mfr./distribute liquid chromatographic instruments and test and measurement equipment.

Waters Associates, Brazil

WATSON WYATT & COMPANY

6707 Democracy Blvd., Ste. 800, Bethesda, MD, 20817

Tel: (301) 581-4600 Fax: (301) 581-4937 Web site: www.watsonwyatt.com

Creates compensation and benefits programs for major corporations.

Watson Wyatt Brazil Ltda., Rua Arizona 1349, Ste. 141, Luxor Center, 04567-003, Sao Paulo, SP, Brazil

Tel: 55-11-5506-6334 Fax: 55-11-5506-2792 Contact: Giovani di Gesu

WEATHERFORD INTERNATIONAL INC.

5 Post Oak Blvd, Ste. 1760, Houston, TX, 77227-3415

Tel: (713) 287-8400 Fax: (713) 963-9785 Web site: www.weatherford.com

Oilfield services, products & equipment; mfr. marine cranes for oil and gas industry.

Weatherford Intl., c/o Seamar, Rua Uruguaiana 39-24 andar, 20050 Rio de Janeiro, Brazil (Caxias do Sul, Macae.)

Tel: 55-24-7734040

WEDCO INC.

PO Box 397, Bloomsbury, NJ, 08804

Tel: (908) 479-4181 Fax: (908) 479-6622

Plastics grinding and related services, machinery and equipment for plastics industry.

WEDCO America do Sul, Rua Paraiba, 476 - salas 14056, 30.130-140 Belo Horizonte-MG, Brazil

Tel: 55-31-261-8966 Fax: 55-31-261-8911 Contact: Paulo Cesar Palhares, Pres.

WEDCO Minerais Ltda., Rua Paraiba, 476 - salas 14056, 30.130-140 Belo Horizonte-MG, Brazil

Tel: 55-31-261-8966 Fax: 55-31-261-8911 Contact: Paulo Cesar Palhares, Pres.

THE WEST COMPANY, INC.

101 Gordon Drive, PO Box 645, Lionville, PA, 19341-0645

Tel: (610) 594-2900 Fax: (610) 594-3014 Web site: www.thewestcompany.com

Mfr. products for filling, sealing, dispensing & delivering needs of health care & consumer products markets.

West do Brazil, Av. Nossa Senhora das Gracas, 115, Bairro Serraria, 09980-000 Diadema -SP- Brazil

Tel: 55-11-445-4344 Fax: 55-11-456-5355 Contact: Ronaldo Gelain, Exec. Dir. Emp: 237

WESTERN ATLAS INC.

10205 Westheimer, Houston, TX, 77251-1407

Tel: (713) 972-4000 Fax: (713) 952-9837 Web site: www.waii.com

Full service to the oil industry.

SERMAR/Servicos de Geofisica Ltda., Praia de Botafogo 440, Andar 16, 22250-040 Rio de Janeiro, RJ, Brazil

Tel: 55-21-539-0342 Fax: 55-21-286-0546 Contact: J. Esteves, Res. Mgr.

Western Atlas Logging Services, Praia de Botafogo 440, Andar 16, 22250-040 Rio de Janeiro, RJ, Brazil

Tel: 55-21-539-0342 Fax: 55-21-286-0546 Contact: Juan J. Goicoechea, District Mgr.

WESTINGHOUSE ELECTRIC (CBS)

11 Stanwix Street, Pittsburgh, PA, 15222-1384

Tel: (412) 244-2000 Fax: (412) 642-4650

TV/radio broadcasting, mfr. electronic systems for industry/defense, financial & environmental services.

Westinghouse do Brasil Comercio e Servicos Ltda., Av. Alfredo Egidio de Souza Aranha, 75, cj.21 São Paulo, SP 04726-170 Brazil

Tel: 55-11-548-4005 Fax: 55-11-548-4929 Contact: Laurence Alan Rodriguez Emp: 2

WESTVACO CORPORATION

299 Park Ave., New York, NY, 10171

Tel: (212) 688-5000 Fax: (212) 318-5055 Web site: www.westvaco.com

Mfr. paper, packaging, chemicals.

Rigesa Ltda., Rua 13 de Maio 755, 13270 Valinhos, SP, Brazil

WHIRLPOOL CORPORATION

2000 N. M-63, Benton Harbor, MI, 49022-2692

Tel: (616) 923-5000 Fax: (616) 923-5443 Web site: www.whirlpoolcorp.com

Mfr./market home appliances: Whirlpool, Roper, KitchenAid, Estate, and Inglis.

Brasmotor (JV), Av. Brigadeiro Faria Lima, 2003 - 18° andar - Caixa Postal 8243 - São Paulo - SP CEP 01451-001, Brazil

Tel: 55-11-3039-5400 Fax: 55-11-3039-5566

Embraco SA, Rua Ruy Barbosa 1, Distrito Industrial, 89219 Joinville, Brazil

Multibras SA (JV), Edif. Plaza Centenário, Av. das Nações Unidas, 12.995 CEP 04578-000 - São Paulo - SP, Brazil

Tel: 55-11-5586-6100 Fax: 55-11-5586-6388

Whirlpool do Brasil Ltda., Av Brigadeiro Faria Lima 2003, 01415 São Paulo, Brazil

Tel: 55-11-814-7655 Fax: 55-11-814-9596 Contact: P. Daniel Miller, Pres.

WHITE & CASE LLP

1155 Ave. of the Americas, New York, NY, 10036-2767

Tel: (212) 819-8200 Fax: (212) 354-8113 Web site: www.whitecase.com

International law firm.

White & Case LLP, Edif. Plaza Centenario, 18° andar, Av. Das Nações Inidas, 12.995, 04578-000, São Paulo, SP Brazil

Tel: 55-11-5505-0170 Fax: 55-11-5505-0174

WITCO CORPORATION

One American Lane, Greenwich, CT, 06831-2559

Tel: (203) 552-2000 Fax: (203) 552-3070 Web site: www.witco.com

Mfr. chemical and petroleum products.

Witco do Brasil Ltda., Rua Verbp Divino, 1661, cjto.64, São Paulo, SP 04719-002 Brazil

Tel: 55-11-524-5409 Fax: 55-11-524-9984 Contact: Joao Teixeira Soares, Pres. Emp: 5

WOODWARD GOVERNOR COMPANY

5001 North Second Street, PO Box 7001, Rockford, IL, 61125-7001

Tel: (815) 877-7441 Fax: (815) 639-6033 Web site: www.woodward.com

Mfr./service speed control devices and systems for aircraft turbines, industrial engines and turbines.

Woodward Governor (Reguladores) Ltda., Rua Joaquin Norberto, 284, JD Santa Genebra, Caixa Postal 1785, CEP 13080-150, Campinas, SP, Brazil

Tel: 55-19-242-4788 Fax: 55-19-242-2992 Contact: Hugh Hiigel Emp: 60

WORLD COURIER INC.

1313 Fourth Ave., New Hyde Park, NY, 11041

Tel: (516) 354-2600 Fax: (516) 354-2644

International courier service.

World Courier do Brazil, Transportes Internacionais, São Paulo, Brazil

World Courier do Brazil, Transportes Internacionais, Rua Venezuela 3, salas 905/906, Rio de Janeiro, Brazil

WUNDERMAN CATO JOHNSON

675 Ave. of the Americas, New York, NY, 10010-5104

Tel: (212) 941-3000 Fax: (212) 633-0957 Web site: www.wcj.com

International advertising and marketing consulting firm.

ActionLine Telemarketing Do Brazil, Av. Paulista 1009 - 12th Fl., São Paulo SP Brazil

Tel: 55-11-5087-2700 Fax: 55-11-5087-2701 Contact: Emilio Cesio, Gen. Mgr.

Wunderman Cato Johnson, Rua Jundiai 50, 4 andar, 04001-140 São Paulo, SP Brazil

Tel: 55-11-885-1029 Fax: 55-11-887-7622 Contact: Eduardo Bicudo, Gen. Mgr.

Wunderman Cato Johnson, Rua Voluntarios da Patria, 45-Sala 507, CEP 22.270-000 Botafogo, Rio de Janeiro RJ Brazil

Tel: 55-21-286-9565 Fax: 55-21-286-7183 Contact: Estela Menezes, Off. Mgr.

XEROX CORPORATION

800 Long Ridge Road, PO Box 1600, Stamford, CT, 06904

Tel: (203) 968-3000 Fax: (203) 968-4312 Web site: www.xerox.com

Mfr. document processing equipment, systems and supplies.

Xerox De Chile, S.A., Av. Republica do Chile, 500/30, Centro-Rio de Janeiro/RJ, Brazil

Xerox De Chile, S.A., Av. Interlagos, 3501, São Paulo/SP, Brazil

Xerox do Brasil Ltda., Av. Rodrigues Alves, 261/279, Cais do Porto, Rio de Janeiro, RJ 20220-360 Brazil

Tel: 55-21-271-1212 Fax: 55-21-271-1646 Contact: Carlos Augusto Salles, Pres. Emp: 5000

XTRA CORPORATION

60 State Street, Boston, MA, 02109

Tel: (617) 367-5000 Fax: (617) 227-3173 Web site: www.xtracorp.com

Holding company: leasing.

Xtra International, Rio de Janeiro, Brazil

YOUNG & RUBICAM INC.

285 Madison Ave., New York, NY, 10017

Tel: (212) 210-3000 Fax: (212) 370-3796 Web site: www.yr.com

Advertising, public relations, direct marketing and sales promotion, corporate & product ID management.

Young & Rubicam do Brazil Ltda., Av. Brig. Faria Lima 2100, São Paulo, SP 01451-002 Brazil
Tel: 55-11-814-1022 Fax: 55-11-814-4812 Contact: Maria Cristina Carvalho Pinto

British Virgin Islands

AON CORPORATION

123 North Wacker Drive, Chicago, IL, 60606

Tel: (312) 701-3000 Fax: (312) 701-3100 Web site: www.aon.com

Insurance brokers worldwide; underwrites accident & health insurance, specialty & professional insurance; & provides risk management consultation.

AON Worldwide / Caribbean Insurers Ltd., Palm Grove Shopping Centre 1, Rd. Town, Tortola, BVI

Tel: 809-494-2728 Fax: 809-494-4393 Contact: C. Chippendale

BDO SEIDMAN, LLP

Two Prudential Plaza, 180 N. Stetson Ave., Ste. 2300, Chicago, IL, 60601

Tel: (312) 240-1236 Fax: (312) 240-3329 Web site: www.bdo.com

International accounting & financial consulting firm.

BDO Binder, PO Box 116, Creque Building, Main St., Rd. Town, Tortola, British Virgin Islands

Tel: 809-494-3783 Fax: 809-494-2220 Contact: Andrew D. Bickerton

THE CHASE MANHATTAN CORPORATION

World Headquarters, 270 Park Ave., New York, NY, 10017

Tel: (212) 270-6000 Fax: (212) 622-9030 Web site: www.chase.com

International banking and financial services.

Chase Manhattan Bank, British Virgin Islands

Tel: 809-494-2662 Fax: 809-494-2379

DELOITTE TOUCHE TOHMATSU INTERNATIONAL

PO Box 820, Wilton, CT, 06897

Tel: (203) 761-3000 Fax: (203) 834-2200 Web site: www.u.s.deloitte.com or www.dtti.com

Accounting, audit, tax and management consulting services.

Deloitte & Touche, Omar Hoge Building, 3rd Fl., Wickham's Cay I, Rd. Town, Tortola, BVI

DHL WORLDWIDE EXPRESS

333 Twin Dolphin Drive, Redwood City, CA, 94065

Tel: (650) 593-7474 Fax: (650) 593-1689 Web site: www.dhl.com

Worldwide air express carrier.

DHL Worldwide Express, Columbue Centre, Wickhams Cay PO Box 3255, Rd. Town, Tortola, British Virgin Islands

Tel: 809-494-4659

ERNST & YOUNG, LLP

787 Seventh Ave., New York, NY, 10019

Tel: (212) 773-3000 Fax: (212) 773-6350 Web site: www.eyi.com

Accounting and audit, tax and management consulting services.

Ernst & Young Trust Corporation (BVI) Ltd., G.E.U Dawson Bldg., Main St., (PO Box 3340) Rd. Town, Tortola, British Virgin Islands

Tel: 809-436-5138 Fax: 809-435-2079 Contact: Ben Arridell

KPMG PEAT MARWICK LLP

Three Chestnut Ridge Road, Montvale, NJ, 07645

Tel: (201) 307-7000 Fax: (201) 930-8617 Web site: www.kpmg.com

Accounting and audit, tax and management consulting services.

KPMG Peat Marwick, Tropic Isle Building, Rd. Town, Tortola, British Virgin Islands

Tel: 809-494-5800 Fax: 809-494-6565 Contact: Andrea J. Douglas, Ptnr.

PRICEWATERHOUSECOOPERS LLP

1251 Ave. of the Americas, New York, NY, 10020

Tel: (212) 596-7000 Fax: (212) 790-6620 Web site: www.pwcglobal.com

Accounting and auditing, tax and management, and human resource consulting services.

Price Waterhouse Ltd., Abbot Building, 2nd Fl., PO Box 933, Rd. Town, Tortola, BVI

Tel: 809-494-6122 Fax: 809-494-6124

Brunei

AMERICAN EXPRESS COMPANY

American Express Tower, World Financial Center, New York, NY, 10285-4765
Tel: (212) 640-2000 Fax: (212) 619-9802 Web site: www.americanexpress.com
Travel, travelers cheques, charge card & financial services.
American Express Intl. (Brunei) Sdn. Bhd., Brunei - All inquiries to U.S. address

ARTHUR ANDERSEN & COMPANY

33 West Monroe Street, Chicago, IL, 60603
Tel: (312) 372-7100 Fax: (312) 507-0123 Web site: www.arthurandersen.com
Accounting & audit, tax & management consulting services.
Arthur Andersen & Co./Hanafiah Raslan & Mohamad, Units 407-408 4th Fl. Komplek Jalan Sultan, PO Box 2470, Bandar Seri Begawan, 1924 Brunei Darussalam
Tel: 673-2-22-0564

BAKER HUGHES INCORPORATED

3900 Essex Lane, Ste. 1200, Houston, TX, 77027
Tel: (713) 439-8600 Fax: (713) 439-8699 Web site: www.bakerhughes.com
Develop & apply technology to drill, complete & produce oil and natural gas wells; provide separation systems to petroleum, municipal, continuous process & mining industries.
Baker Oil Tools, Lot 2769, Jalan Bolkiah, Seria, Kuala Belait 6008, Negara, Darussalam, Brunei
Tel: 673-3-226273 Fax: 673-2-224160

CARRIER CORPORATION

One Carrier Place, Farmington, CT, 06034-4015
Tel: (860) 674-3000 Fax: (860) 679-3010 Web site: www.carrier.com
Mfr./distributor/services A/C, heating & refrigeration equipment.
Q-Carrier (B) Sdn. Bhd., PO Box 116, Bandar Seria 7001, Bagawan, Brunei, Darussalem
Tel: 673-3-224126 Fax: 673-3-224127

CITICORP

399 Park Ave., New York, NY, 10043
Tel: (212) 559-1000 Fax: (212) 527-2066 Web site: www.citibank.com
International banking and financial services.
Citibank N.A., No. 12-15 Darussalam Complex, Jaltan Sultan, Bendar Seri Begaway 2085, Brunei
Contact: Hock Kian Cheng, Mgr.

DELOITTE TOUCHE TOHMATSU INTERNATIONAL

PO Box 820, Wilton, CT, 06897
Tel: (203) 761-3000 Fax: (203) 834-2200 Web site: www.u.s.deloitte.com or www.dtti.com
Accounting, audit, tax and management consulting services.
Deloitte & Touche, PO Box 1965, Bandar Seri Begawan 1919, Brunei Darussalam (see Head Office Singapore)

DHL WORLDWIDE EXPRESS

333 Twin Dolphin Drive, Redwood City, CA, 94065
Tel: (650) 593-7474 Fax: (650) 593-1689 Web site: www.dhl.com
Worldwide air express carrier.

DHL Worldwide Express, 3, SPG 27, Bangunan PIF, Jalan Gadong, Bandar Seri Begawan 3180, Brunei

Tel: 673-2-444982

ERNST & YOUNG, LLP

787 Seventh Ave., New York, NY, 10019

Tel: (212) 773-3000 Fax: (212) 773-6350 Web site: www.eyi.com

Accounting and audit, tax and management consulting services.

Ernst & Young, P.O Box 2162, Bandar Seri Begawan 1921, Negara Brunei Darussalam

Tel: 673-2-239139 Fax: 673-2-239142 Contact: James Low Tze Fatt

FISHER-ROSEMOUNT

8000 Maryland Ave., Ste. 500, Clayton, MO, 63105-4755

Tel: (314) 746-9900 Fax: (314) 746-9974

Mfr. industrial process control equipment.

AMPMO Services SDN Bhd., Lot. No. 4, G-22, Lorong Tengah, PO Box 473, Seria 7004, Negara Brunei Darussalam, Brunei

Tel: 673-3-224-147 Fax: 673-3-224-690

HALLIBURTON COMPANY

500 North Akard Street, Ste. 3600, Dallas, TX, 75201-3391

Tel: (214) 978-2600 Fax: (214) 978-2685 Web site: www.halliburton.com

Energy, construction and insurance.

Halliburton Ltd., PO Box 393, Duala Belait 6003, Brunei Darussalam, Brunei

Tel: 673-3-222-156 Fax: 673-3-224-665

THE HARPER GROUP

260 Townsend Street, San Francisco, CA, 94107-1719

Tel: (415) 978-0600 Fax: (415) 978-0692 Web site: www.circleintl.com

Ocean/air freight forwarding, customs brokerage, packing and wholesale, logistics management and insurance.

Circle Freight International (Brunei), Blk. C, No. 10 Beribi Industrial Complex 1, Jalan Gadong 3188, Negara Brunei Darussalam, Brunei

Tel: 673-2-449-278 Fax: 673-2-447-397

Circle Freight International (Brunei), Block C, No. 10, Beribi Industry Complex 1, Jalan Gadong, Bandar Seri Bagawan, Negara, Brunei

Tel: 673-2-449-278 Fax: 673-2-447-397

IBM CORPORATION

New Orchard Road, Armonk, NY, 10504

Tel: (914) 765-1900 Fax: (914) 765-7382 Web site: www.ibm.com

Information products, technology & services.

IBM Brunei Darussalam, IBM World Trade Corporation, RM 515 Plaza Athirah, JLN Tutong, Bandar Seri Begawan, Brunei Darussalam

Tel: 673-2-40660 Fax: 673-2-40662

KPMG PEAT MARWICK LLP

Three Chestnut Ridge Road, Montvale, NJ, 07645

Tel: (201) 307-7000 Fax: (201) 930-8617 Web site: www.kpmg.com

Accounting and audit, tax and management consulting services.

KPMG Peat Marwick, Brittania House, 38 Jalan Cator, Bandar Seri Begawan, 2085, Brunei Darussalam

LUCENT TECHNOLOGIES, INC.

600 Mountain Ave., Murray Hill, NJ, 07974-0636

Tel: (908) 582-3000 Fax: (908) 582-2110 Web site: www.lucent.com

Design/mfr. wide range of public and private networks, communication systems and software, data networking systems, business telephone systems and microelectronics components.

Lucent Technologies Brunei, Lalifuddin Complex, Blk. C, Lot 1150, Nos. 10-14, Simpang 168, Tungu Link Rd., Kg Pengkalan Gadong, Bandar Seri Begawan 3180, Darussalam, Brunei

Tel: 673-2-450-105 Fax: 673-2-450-106 Contact: Eu Meng Khng, PR Mgr.

OCEANEERING INTERNATIONAL INC.

11911 FM 529, Houston, TX, 77041

Tel: (713) 329-4500 Fax: (713) 329-4951

Transportation equipment, underwater service to offshore oil and gas industry.

Oceaneering Intl. Inc., Kuala Belait, Brunei

PRICEWATERHOUSECOOPERS LLP

1251 Ave. of the Americas, New York, NY, 10020

Tel: (212) 596-7000 Fax: (212) 790-6620 Web site: www.pwcglobal.com

Accounting and auditing, tax and management, and human resource consulting services.

Price Waterhouse Ltd., Kompleks Jalan Sultan, PO Box 2843, Bandar Seri Begawan 1928, Brunei Darussalam

Tel: 673-2-228593 Fax: 673-2-228594

SILICON GRAPHICS INC.

2011 N. Shoreline Blvd., Mountain View, CA, 94043-1389

Tel: (650) 960-1980 Fax: (650) 961-0595 Web site: www.sgi.com

Design/mfr. special-effects computer graphic systems and software.

FR Information Engineering, No. 16 Block Adek taman Alam, Bandar Seri Begawan, Brunei, Darrusalam

WESTERN ATLAS INC.

10205 Westheimer, Houston, TX, 77251-1407

Tel: (713) 972-4000 Fax: (713) 952-9837 Web site: www.waii.com

Full service to the oil industry.

Western Geophysical, c/o Dept. XGP/21, Brunei Shell Petroleum Company Sendirian Berhad, Seria 7082, Brunei Darussalam

Tel: 673-3-372-256 Fax: 673-3-372-040 Contact: M. Dwyer, Mgr.

Bulgaria

3COM CORPORATION

5400 Bayfront Plaza, Santa Clara, CA, 95052-8145

Tel: (408) 764-5000 Fax: (408) 764-5001 Web site: www.3com.com

Develop/mfr. computer networking products & systems.

3Com Bulgaria Ltd., James Baucher Blvd. 87, 5th Fl., Office 13, 1407 Sofia, Bulgaria

Tel: 359-2-962-5222 Fax: 359-2-962-4322

AIR EXPRESS INTERNATIONAL CORPORATION

120 Tokeneke Road, PO Box 1231, Darien, CT, 06820

Tel: (203) 655-7900 Fax: (203) 655-5779 Web site: www.aeilogistics.com

Air freight forwarder.

AEI / In Time Cargo Ltd., 12 Iskarsko Chaussee Blvd., 1592 Sofia, Bulgaria

Tel: 359-2-793-001 Fax: 359-2-793-740

AMERICAN STANDARD INC.

One Centennial Ave., Piscataway, NJ, 08855-6820

Tel: (732) 980-3000 Fax: (732) 980-6118

Mfr. heating, plumbing & sanitary equipment, china, earthenware.

Vidima-Ideal, Bulgaria

ARTHUR ANDERSEN & COMPANY

33 West Monroe Street, Chicago, IL, 60603

Tel: (312) 372-7100 Fax: (312) 507-0123 Web site: www.arthurandersen.com

Accounting & audit, tax & management consulting services.

Arthur Andersen Bulgaria, Ltd., 1, Bulgaria Square, PO Box 120, 1463 Sofia, Bulgaria

Tel: 359-2-546-181

BATES WORLDWIDE INC.

405 Lexington Ave., New York, NY, 10174

Tel: (212) 297-7000 Fax: (212) 986-0270 Web site: www.batesww.com

Advertising, marketing, public relations & media consulting.

S Team Bates Saatchi & Saatchi Advertising Balkans, 31, Evogi Georgiev St., Sofia 1000, Bulgaria

Tel: 359-2-963-1289 Contact: D. Sakan, Chmn.

BDO SEIDMAN, LLP

Two Prudential Plaza, 180 N. Stetson Ave., Ste. 2300, Chicago, IL, 60601

Tel: (312) 240-1236 Fax: (312) 240-3329 Web site: www.bdo.com

International accounting & financial consulting firm.

BDO Bulgaria OOD, Rakovski 145, ent. 5, V Fl., apart 6, 1000 Sofia, Bulgaria

Tel: 359-2-9805-600 Fax: 359-2-9805-600 Contact: Søren D. Sørensen

BESTFOODS, INC.

700 Sylvan Ave., International Plaza, Englewood Cliffs, NJ, 07632-9976

Tel: (201) 894-4000 Fax: (201) 894-2186 Web site: www.bestfoods.com

Consumer foods products; corn refining.

CPC Bulgaria Food., Bvd Buckston No. 31A, 1618 Sofia, Bulgaria

Tel: 359-2-559-749 Fax: 359-2-955-9340 Contact: Evgeni Mihov, Mgr.

BRISTOL-MYERS SQUIBB COMPANY

345 Park Ave., New York, NY, 10154

Tel: (212) 546-4000 Fax: (212) 546-4020 Web site: www.bms.com

Pharmaceutical and food preparations, medical and surgical instruments.

Bristol-Myers Squibb- Bulgaria, Sofia, Bulgaria

BUDGET RENT A CAR CORPORATION

4225 Naperville Road, Lisle, IL, 60532

Tel: (630) 955-1900 Fax: (630) 955-7799 Web site: www.budgetrentacar.com

Car and truck rental system.

Budget Rent A Car, 1 Vitosha Blvd, Sofia 1040, Bulgaria

Tel: 359-2-43331

LEO BURNETT CO., INC.

35 West Wacker Drive, Chicago, IL, 60601

Tel: (312) 220-5959 Fax: (312) 220-6533 Web site: www.leoburnett.com

International advertising agency.

Leo Burnett Advertising, Sofia, Bulgaria

CARRIER CORPORATION

One Carrier Place, Farmington, CT, 06034-4015

Tel: (860) 674-3000 Fax: (860) 679-3010 Web site: www.carrier.com

Mfr./distributor/services A/C, heating & refrigeration equipment.

Carrier Bulgaria, Sofia, Bulgaria

Tel: 359-2-687208 Fax: 359-2-683720

CONAGRA INC.

One ConAgra Drive, Omaha, NE, 68102-5001

Tel: (402) 595-4000 Fax: (402) 595-4595 Web site: www.conagra.com

Prepared/frozen foods, grains, flour, animal feeds, agri chemicals, poultry, meat, dairy products, including Healthy Choice, Butterball and Hunt's.

ConAgra Inc., Bulgaria

DDB NEEDHAM WORLDWIDE INC.

437 Madison Ave., New York, NY, 10022

Tel: (212) 415-2000 Fax: (212) 415-3417

Advertising agency.

Bulgaria/DDB, Sofia, Bulgaria

DELOITTE TOUCHE TOHMATSU INTERNATIONAL

PO Box 820, Wilton, CT, 06897

Tel: (203) 761-3000 Fax: (203) 834-2200 Web site: www.u.s.deloitte.com or www.dtti.com

Accounting, audit, tax and management consulting services.

Deloitte & Touche, 128, 8th Primorski Polk Blvd., Varna 9000, Bulgaria

Deloitte & Touche, 135-A Rakovski Str., 1000 Sofia, Bulgaria

IDOM Bulgaria Ltd., 135-A Rakovski Str., 1000 Sofia, Bulgaria

DHL WORLDWIDE EXPRESS

333 Twin Dolphin Drive, Redwood City, CA, 94065

Tel: (650) 593-7474 Fax: (650) 593-1689 Web site: www.dhl.com

Worldwide air express carrier.

DHL Worldwide Express, 10 Momina Cheshma Blvd., Droujba 2, Sofia 1582, Bulgaria

Tel: 359-2-429155

DIGITAL EQUIPMENT CORPORATION

111 Powder Mill Road, Maynard, MA, 01754

Tel: (978) 493-5111 Fax: (978) 493-7374 Web site: www.digital.com

Mfr. network computer systems, components, software and services.

Digital Equipment Bulgaria, #201-202, Interpred World Trade Ctr. Sofia, 36 Dragan Tzankov Blvd., 1057 Sofia, Bulgaria

Tel: 359-2-9161-3131 Fax: 359-2-973-3184

ERNST & YOUNG, LLP

787 Seventh Ave., New York, NY, 10019

Tel: (212) 773-3000 Fax: (212) 773-6350 Web site: www.eyi.com

Accounting and audit, tax and management consulting services.

Ernst & Young, 46 Albain, Sofia 1000, Bulgaria

Tel: 359-2-9920425 Fax: 359-2-492042 Contact: John M. Ayerst

FISHER-ROSEMOUNT

8000 Maryland Ave., Ste. 500, Clayton, MO, 63105-4755

Tel: (314) 746-9900 Fax: (314) 746-9974

Mfr. industrial process control equipment.

Process Control, Tzarichina Str. 1, 1505 Sofia, Bulgaria

GREY ADVERTISING INC.

777 Third Ave., New York, NY, 10017

Tel: (212) 546-2000 Fax: (212) 546-1495 Web site: www.giworldwwide.com

International advertising agency.

Grey Sofia, 5 Victor Hugo, 1124 Sofia, Bulgaria

HONEYWELL INC.

PO Box 524, Minneapolis, MN, 55440-0524

Tel: (612) 951-1000 Fax: (612) 951-3066 Web site: www.honeywell.com

Develop/mfr. controls for home and building, industry, space and aviation.

Honeywell Eood, 14 Iskarsko Shosse, BG-1592 Sofia, Bulgaria

IBM CORPORATION

New Orchard Road, Armonk, NY, 10504

Tel: (914) 765-1900 Fax: (914) 765-7382 Web site: www.ibm.com

Information products, technology & services.

IBM Bulgaria Ltd., 36 Dragan Tzankov Str., BG-1-4- Sofia, Bulgaria

Tel: 359-2-973-3171 Fax: 359-2-973-3163

INTERNATIONAL SPECIALTY PRODUCTS

1361 Alps Road, Wayne, NJ, 07470

Tel: (973) 628-4000 Fax: (973) 628-3311 Web site: www.ispcorp.com

Mfr. specialty chemical products.

ISP International Corporation, Trade Representation, bl. 13, Fl. 2, ap.4, Krasno Selo, JK. Beli Brezi, Sofia 1680 - Bulgaria

Tel: 359-2-581-5480 Fax: 359-2-581-5480

ITT SHERATON CORPORATION

60 State Street, Boston, MA, 02108

Tel: (617) 367-3600 Fax: (617) 367-5676

Hotel operations.

Sheraton Sofia Hotel Balkan, 5 Lenin Sq., BG-1000 Sofia, Bulgaria

KPMG PEAT MARWICK LLP

Three Chestnut Ridge Road, Montvale, NJ, 07645

Tel: (201) 307-7000 Fax: (201) 930-8617 Web site: www.kpmg.com

Accounting and audit, tax and management consulting services.

KPMG Bulgaria, 16 Slavyanska St., Sofia, 1000, Bulgaria

Tel: 359-2-98053 Fax: 359-2-980-0458

LAI WARD HOWELL INTERNATIONAL INC.

200 Park Ave., Ste. 3100, New York, NY, 10016-0136

Tel: (212) 953-7900 Fax: (212) 953-7907 Web site: www.laix.com

International executive search firm.

LAI Ward Howell Intl., 25A San Stefano St., BG-1504 Sofia, Bulgaria

LAND O' LAKES, INC.

4001 Lexington Ave. North, Arden Hills, MN, 55126

Tel: (612) 481-2222 Fax: (612) 481-2022

Produces butter, margarine, packaged milk, sour cream, snack dips and Alpine Lace cheeses and crop protection products.

Land O' Lakes, Inc., Bulgaria

ELI LILLY & COMPANY

Lilly Corporate Center, Indianapolis, IN, 46285

Tel: (317) 276-2000 Fax: (317) 277-6579 Web site: www.lilly.com

Mfr. pharmaceuticals and animal health products.

Eli Lilly (Suisse) S.A., Interpred World Trade Centre, Office Ste. No. 200, 36 Dragan Tzankov Blvd., BG-1057 Sofia, Bulgaria

Tel: 359-2-971-3397 Fax: 359-2-973-3169

LOCTITE CORPORATION

10 Columbus Boulevard, Hartford, CT, 06106

Tel: (203) 520-5000 Fax: (203) 520-5073 Web site: www.loctite.com

Mfr./sale industrial adhesives and sealants.

Loctite Roees Handelsges.m.b.H., Tsar Boris III Strasse 126, P.B. 55, BG - 1612 Sofia, Bulgaria

Tel: 359-2-558824 Fax: 359-2-558759

LOWE & PARTNERS WORLDWIDE

1114 Ave. of the Americas, New York, NY, 10036

Tel: (212) 403-6700 Fax: (212) 403-6710

International advertising agency network.

Lowe GGK Sofia, Sofia, Bulgaria

McCANN-ERICKSON WORLDWIDE

750 Third Ave., New York, NY, 10017

Tel: (212) 984-3644 Fax: (212) 984-2629

International advertising/marketing services.

P.B.I./ McCann-Erickson Sofia, Sofia, Bulgaria

McDONALD'S CORPORATION

Kroc Drive, Oak Brook, IL, 60523

Tel: (630) 623-3000 Fax: (630) 623-7409

Fast food chain stores.

McDonald's Corp., Bulgaria

OGILVY & MATHER WORLDWIDE

309 West 49th Street, New York, NY, 10019

Tel: (212) 237-4000 Fax: (212) 237-5123

Advertising, marketing, public relations & consulting firm.

Ogilvy & Mather, Sofia, Bulgaria

THE PERKIN-ELMER CORPORATION

761 Main Ave., Norwalk, CT, 06859-0001

Tel: (203) 762-1000 Fax: (203) 762-4228 Web site: www.perkin-elmer.com

Leading supplier of systems for life science research and related applications.

Perkin-Elmer, Sofia, Bulgaria

Tel: 359-2-958-1260 Fax: 359-2-958-1543

PHARMACIA & UPJOHN

95 Corporate Drive, PO Box 6995, Bridgewater, NJ, 08807

Tel: (908) 306-4400 Fax: (908) 306-4433 Web site: www.pnu.com

Mfr. pharmaceuticals, agricultural products, industry chemicals

Pharmacia & Upjohn, 1 Oborishte St., 1504 Sofia, Bulgaria

PRICEWATERHOUSECOOPERS LLP

1251 Ave. of the Americas, New York, NY, 10020

Tel: (212) 596-7000 Fax: (212) 790-6620 Web site: www.pwcglobal.com

Accounting and auditing, tax and management, and human resource consulting services.

Price Waterhouse Ltd., Stefan Karadja 10, 1000 Sofia, Bulgaria

Tel: 359-2-880122 Fax: 359-2-872461

PROCTER & GAMBLE COMPANY

One Procter & Gamble Plaza, Cincinnati, OH, 45202

Tel: (513) 983-1100 Fax: (513) 562-4500 Web site: www.pg.com

Personal care, food, laundry, cleaning and industry products.

Procter & Gamble Marketing S.R.L., Sofia, Bulgaria

TBWA INTERNATIONAL

180 Maiden Lane, New York, NY, 10038

Tel: (212) 804-1000 Fax: (212) 804-1200

International full service advertising agency.

TBWA Sofia, Sofia, Bulgaria

UNITED PARCEL SERVICE OF AMERICA, INC.

55 Glenlake Parkway, NE, Atlanta, GA, 30328

Tel: (404) 828-6000 Fax: (404) 828-6593 Web site: www.ups.com

International package-delivery service.

UPS Bulgaria, 12, Iskarsko Chausse Blvd., 1592 Sofia, Bulgaria

Tel: 359-2-793001 Fax: 359-2-79330124

WM WRIGLEY JR. COMPANY

410 N. Michigan Ave., Chicago, IL, 60611-4287

Tel: (312) 644-2121 Fax: (312) 644-0353 Web site: www.wrigley.com

Mfr. chewing gum.

Wrigley Bulgaria EOOD, Sofia, Bulgaria

YOUNG & RUBICAM INC.

285 Madison Ave., New York, NY, 10017

Tel: (212) 210-3000 Fax: (212) 370-3796 Web site: www.yr.com

Advertising, public relations, direct marketing and sales promotion, corporate & product ID management.

Adia Advertising, Sofia, Bulgaria

Burkina Faso

AIR EXPRESS INTERNATIONAL CORPORATION

120 Tokeneke Road, PO Box 1231, Darien, CT, 06820

Tel: (203) 655-7900 Fax: (203) 655-5779 Web site: www.aeilogistics.com

Air freight forwarder.

AEI/SDV Bobo Dioulasso, PO Box 319, Bobo Dioulasso, Burkina Faso

Tel: 226-971-212 Fax: 226-971-179

LOUIS BERGER INTERNATIONAL INC.

100 Halsted Street, East Orange, NJ, 07019

Tel: (201) 678-1960 Fax: (201) 672-4284 Web site: www.louisberger.com

Consulting engineers, architects, economists & planners.

Louis Berger International Inc., PO Box 5415 Ouagadougou, Burkina Faso

Tel: 226-302-917

Louis Berger International Inc., B.P. 129, Bobo-Dioulasso, Burkina Faso

Tel: 226-880-456 Fax: 226-880-456

DHL WORLDWIDE EXPRESS

333 Twin Dolphin Drive, Redwood City, CA, 94065

Tel: (650) 593-7474 Fax: (650) 593-1689 Web site: www.dhl.com

Worldwide air express carrier.

DHL Worldwide Express, Ave. de la Resistance du 17 Mai, 01 BP 3095, Immeuble CGP, Ouagadougou 01, Burkina Faso

Tel: 226-33-5171

XEROX CORPORATION

800 Long Ridge Road, PO Box 1600, Stamford, CT, 06904

Tel: (203) 968-3000 Fax: (203) 968-4312 Web site: www.xerox.com

Mfr. document processing equipment, systems and supplies.

Xero-Burkina, BP 3413, Zone Commerciale, Secteur 4, Ouagadougou, Burkina Faso

Tel: 226-306-125 Fax: 226-312-860

Burundi

AIR EXPRESS INTERNATIONAL CORPORATION

120 Tokeneke Road, PO Box 1231, Darien, CT, 06820

Tel: (203) 655-7900 Fax: (203) 655-5779 Web site: www.aeilogistics.com

Air freight forwarder.

AEI/Air Transit International (ATI), BP 6787, Bujumbura, Burundi

Tel: 257-21-8989 Fax: 257-21-8999

LOUIS BERGER INTERNATIONAL INC.

100 Halsted Street, East Orange, NJ, 07019

Tel: (201) 678-1960 Fax: (201) 672-4284 Web site: www.louisberger.com

Consulting engineers, architects, economists & planners.

Louis Berger International Inc., PO Box 6414, 5 Av. De Muyinga, Bujumbura, Burundi

Tel: 257-216-726 Fax: 257-216-725

DHL WORLDWIDE EXPRESS

333 Twin Dolphin Drive, Redwood City, CA, 94065

Tel: (650) 593-7474 Fax: (650) 593-1689 Web site: www.dhl.com

Worldwide air express carrier.

DHL Worldwide Express, Blvd de la Liberte, Bujumbura, Burundi

Tel: 257-223-425

KPMG PEAT MARWICK LLP

Three Chestnut Ridge Road, Montvale, NJ, 07645

Tel: (201) 307-7000 Fax: (201) 930-8617 Web site: www.kpmg.com

Accounting and audit, tax and management consulting services.

KPMG Klynveld, BP 2995, Bujumbura, Burundi

XEROX CORPORATION

800 Long Ridge Road, PO Box 1600, Stamford, CT, 06904

Tel: (203) 968-3000 Fax: (203) 968-4312 Web site: www.xerox.com

Mfr. document processing equipment, systems and supplies.

Gravimport Sprl, BP 156, Bujumbura, Burundi

Publigraphic Sprl, BP 73, Bujumbura, Burundi

Tel: 257-222-285 Fax: 257-226-953

Cambodia

BATES WORLDWIDE INC.

405 Lexington Ave., New York, NY, 10174

Tel: (212) 297-7000 Fax: (212) 986-0270 Web site: www.batesww.com

Advertising, marketing, public relations & media consulting.

Bates Cambodia, North Problem Insurance Park, No. 55, St. 178, Phnom Penh, Cambodia

Tel: 85-5-23-428-126 Contact: Herve Deville

LOUIS BERGER INTERNATIONAL INC.

100 Halsted Street, East Orange, NJ, 07019

Tel: (201) 678-1960 Fax: (201) 672-4284 Web site: www.louisberger.com

Consulting engineers, architects, economists & planners.

Louis Berger International Inc., PO Box 953, Phnom Penh, Cambodia

Tel: 85-5-23-361-104 Fax: 85-5-23-810-824

DHL WORLDWIDE EXPRESS

333 Twin Dolphin Drive, Redwood City, CA, 94065

Tel: (650) 593-7474 Fax: (650) 593-1689 Web site: www.dhl.com

Worldwide air express carrier.

DHL International (Cambodia) Pte. Ltd., 28, Monivong Blvd., Sangkat Sras Chark, Phnom Penh, Cambodia

Tel: 85-5-23-427726

ERNST & YOUNG, LLP

787 Seventh Ave., New York, NY, 10019

Tel: (212) 773-3000 Fax: (212) 773-6350 Web site: www.eyi.com

Accounting and audit, tax and management consulting services.

Ernst & Young / Phnom Penh, Mail c/o Ernst & Young Hong Kong, Wanchai, 26/F Great Eagle Centre, 23 Harbour Rd., Hong Kong

Tel: 84-8-44-7655 Fax: 84-8-44-7960 Contact: Gerard Holtzer

FRITZ COMPANIES INC.

706 Mission Street, Ste. 900, San Francisco, CA, 94103

Tel: (415) 904-8360 Fax: (415) 904-8661 Web site: www.fritz.com

Integrated transportation, sourcing, distribution & customs brokerage services.

Fritz Companies Inc., Phnom Penh, Cambodia

GREY ADVERTISING INC.

777 Third Ave., New York, NY, 10017

Tel: (212) 546-2000 Fax: (212) 546-1495 Web site: www.giworldwwide.com

International advertising agency.

Grey Cambodia, Phnom Penh, Cambodia

THE HARPER GROUP

260 Townsend Street, San Francisco, CA, 94107-1719

Tel: (415) 978-0600 Fax: (415) 978-0692 Web site: www.circleintl.com

Ocean/air freight forwarding, customs brokerage, packing and wholesale, logistics management and insurance.

Cambodia Company Ltd., 273-B rue 1, Sungkat Phsar Kandall 11, Phnom Penh, Cambodia

Tel: 85-5-23-62478 Fax: 85-5-23-62478

McCANN-ERICKSON WORLDWIDE

750 Third Ave., New York, NY, 10017

Tel: (212) 984-3644 Fax: (212) 984-2629

International advertising/marketing services.

McCann-Erickson Cambodia, Phnom Penh, Cambodia

TRUE NORTH COMMUNICATIONS INC.

101 East Erie Street, Chicago, IL, 60611

Tel: (312) 425-6000 Fax: (312) 425-6350

Holding company, advertising agency.

Prakit/FCB (Cambodia) Co., Ltd., #360 A Monivong Blvd., Sangkat Boeung Keng Kang, Phnom Penh City, Kampuchea, Cambodia

Cameroon

AIR EXPRESS INTERNATIONAL CORPORATION

120 Tokeneke Road, PO Box 1231, Darien, CT, 06820

Tel: (203) 655-7900 Fax: (203) 655-5779 Web site: www.aeilogistics.com

Air freight forwarder.

AEI/SDV Douala/STC, PO Box 215, Douala, Cameroon

Tel: 237-424-381 Fax: 237-425-253

BAKER HUGHES INCORPORATED

3900 Essex Lane, Ste. 1200, Houston, TX, 77027

Tel: (713) 439-8600 Fax: (713) 439-8699 Web site: www.bakerhughes.com

Develop & apply technology to drill, complete & produce oil and natural gas wells; provide separation systems to petroleum, municipal, continuous process & mining industries.

Baker Hughes Tools, B.P. 5074, Doula, Cameroon

Tel: 237-404277 Fax: 237-403349

Milchem Cameroon SARL, B.P. 5178, Douala, Cameroon

Milchem Minerals SABM, B.P. 5074, Douala, Cameroon

LOUIS BERGER INTERNATIONAL INC.

100 Halsted Street, East Orange, NJ, 07019

Tel: (201) 678-1960 Fax: (201) 672-4284 Web site: www.louisberger.com

Consulting engineers, architects, economists & planners.

Louis Berger International Inc., C/O Ingecam, B.P.5009-Nlongkak, Yaounde, Cameroon

Tel: 237-208920 Fax: 237-208920

THE CHASE MANHATTAN CORPORATION

World Headquarters, 270 Park Ave., New York, NY, 10017

Tel: (212) 270-6000 Fax: (212) 622-9030 Web site: www.chase.com

International banking and financial services.

Chase Bank Cameroon SA, B.P. 1132, 83 Blvd de la Liberte, Douala, Cameroon

DELOITTE TOUCHE TOHMATSU INTERNATIONAL

PO Box 820, Wilton, CT, 06897

Tel: (203) 761-3000 Fax: (203) 834-2200 Web site: www.u.s.deloitte.com or www.dtti.com

Accounting, audit, tax and management consulting services.

Akintola Williams & Co., SOCAR Bldg., Entrance C, Block A, 1st Flor, BP 5393, Douala, Cameroon

DHL WORLDWIDE EXPRESS

333 Twin Dolphin Drive, Redwood City, CA, 94065

Tel: (650) 593-7474 Fax: (650) 593-1689 Web site: www.dhl.com

Worldwide air express carrier.

DHL Worldwide Express, 244, blvd de la Liberte, BP 3582, Douala, Cameroon

Tel: 237-42-9882

ERNST & YOUNG, LLP

787 Seventh Ave., New York, NY, 10019

Tel: (212) 773-3000 Fax: (212) 773-6350 Web site: www.eyi.com

Accounting and audit, tax and management consulting services.

FFA Ernst & Young, 17 rue Ivy, B.P. 443, Douala, Cameroon

Tel: 237-42-89-18 Fax: 237-42-13-04 Contact: Claude Bouillot

FRITZ COMPANIES INC.

706 Mission Street, Ste. 900, San Francisco, CA, 94103

Tel: (415) 904-8360 Fax: (415) 904-8661 Web site: www.fritz.com

Integrated transportation, sourcing, distribution & customs brokerage services.

Fritz Companies Inc., Cameroon

GANNETT FLEMING CORDDRY & CARPENTER INC.

PO Box 67100, Harrisburg, PA, 17106

Tel: (717) 763-7211 Fax: (717) 763-8150

Engineering consulting services.

Gannett Fleming Transportation Engineers, B.P. 2063, Yaounde, Cameroon

GTE CORPORATION

One Stamford Forum, Stamford, CT, 06904

Tel: (203) 965-2000 Fax: (203) 965-2277 Web site: www.gte.com

Electronic products, telecommunications systems, publishing and communications.

GTE International Telecom Services, B.P. 509, Yaounde, Cameroon

M-I

PO Box 48242, Houston, TX, 77242-2842

Tel: (713) 739-0222 Fax: (713) 308-9503

Drilling fluids.

Halliburton-IMCO (Cameroon) SARL, Rue Jamot, Magazin de Cam, B.P. 5542 KDWA, Douala, Cameroon

McCANN-ERICKSON WORLDWIDE

750 Third Ave., New York, NY, 10017

Tel: (212) 984-3644 Fax: (212) 984-2629

International advertising/marketing services.

Nelson McCann, B.P. 12361, Douala, Cameroon

MOBIL CORPORATION

3225 Gallows Road, Fairfax, VA, 22037-0001

Tel: (703) 846-3000 Fax: (703) 846-4669 Web site: www.mobil.com

Petroleum and gas exploration and refining, mfr. petroleum products, chemicals and petrochemicals.

Mobil Oil, Blvd. du General Leclerc, B.P. 4058, Douala, Cameroon

PRICEWATERHOUSECOOPERS LLP

1251 Ave. of the Americas, New York, NY, 10020

Tel: (212) 596-7000 Fax: (212) 790-6620 Web site: www.pwcglobal.com

Accounting and auditing, tax and management, and human resource consulting services.

Price Waterhouse Ltd., Immeuble Le Cauris, rue Alfred Saker, (BP 5689) Akwa , Douala, Cameroon

Tel: 237-42-86-09 Fax: 237-42-86-09

WACKENHUT CORPORATION

4200 Wackenhut Drive, Ste. 100, Palm Beach Gardens, FL, 33410

Tel: (561) 622-5656 Fax: (561) 691-6736 Web site: www.wackenhut.com

Security systems & services.

Wackenhut Cameroon, B.P. 1387, Yaounde, Cameroon (Location: Douala, Cameroon.)

Tel: 237-20-1649 Fax: 237-20-7190

XEROX CORPORATION

800 Long Ridge Road, PO Box 1600, Stamford, CT, 06904

Tel: (203) 968-3000 Fax: (203) 968-4312 Web site: www.xerox.com

Mfr. document processing equipment, systems and supplies.

Unitraco, 4 rue Joss, BP 838, Douala, Cameroon

Canada

3COM CORPORATION

5400 Bayfront Plaza, Santa Clara, CA, 95052-8145

Tel: (408) 764-5000 Fax: (408) 764-5001 Web site: www.3com.com

Develop/mfr. computer networking products & systems.

3Com Canada Inc., Ste. 1600, 444 5th Ave. Southwest, Calgary, AB T2P 2T8, Canada

Tel: 403-265-3266 Fax: 403-265-3268

3Com Canada, Inc., Ste. 1810, Manulife Place, 10180 101st St., Edmonton, AB T5J 3S4, Canada

Tel: 403-423-3266 Fax: 403-423-2368

3Com Canada, Inc., 1405 Trans Canada Highway, Ste. 200, Dorval, PQ H9P 2V9, Canada

Tel: 514-683-3266 Fax: 514-683-5122

3Com Canada, Inc., 255 Albert St., Ste. 600, Ottawa, ON K1P 6A9, Canada

Tel: 613-566-7055 Fax: 613-233-9527

3Com Canada, Inc., 2225 Sheppard Ave., East, Atria 3, Ste. 1204, Toronto, ON M1J5C4, Canada

Tel: 416-498-3266 Fax: 416-498-1262

3Com Canada, Inc., 3665 Kingsway, Ste. 300, Vancouver, BC V5R 5W2, Canada

Tel: 604-434-3266 Fax: 604-434-3264

3M

3M Center, St. Paul, MN, 55144-1000

Tel: (612) 733-1110 Fax: (612) 733-9973 Web site: www.mmm.com

Mfr. diversified products for industry, health care, imaging, communications, transport, safety, consumer, etc.

3M Canada Inc., 1840 Oxford St. E., London, ON N5V 3R6, Canada

Contact: Robert J. Burgstahler

A.B. DICK CO.

5700 West Rouhy Ave., Niles, IL, 60714

Tel: (847) 779-1900 Fax: (847) 647-8369 Web site: www.abdick.com

Mfr./sales automation systems.

A. B. Dick Co., Toronto, ON, Canada

AAF INTERNATIONAL (American Air Filter)

215 Central Ave., PO Box 35690, Louisville, KY, 40232-5690

Tel: (502) 637-0011 Fax: (502) 637-0321 Web site: www.aafintl.com

Mfr. air filtration/pollution control & noise control equipment.

AAF International, 225, rue Guthrie, Dorval, PQ H5T IV8 Canada

Tel: 514-631-1036 Fax: 514-631-0855

AAF-McQUAY INC.

111 South Calvert Street, Ste. 2800, Baltimore, MD, 21202

Tel: (410) 528-2755 Fax: (410) 528-2797 Web site: www.mcquay.com

Mfr. air quality control products: heating, ventilating, air-conditioning & filtration products & services.

AAF-McQuay Canada Inc., 225 Ave. Guthrie, Pointe Claire Dorval, PQ H9P 2P5, Canada

ABBOTT LABORATORIES

One Abbott Park Road, Abbott Park, IL, 60064-3500

Tel: (847) 937-6100 Fax: (847) 937-1511 Web site: www.abbott.com

Development/mfr./sale diversified health care products & services.

Abbott Laboratories Ltd., Montreal, PQ, Canada

ABF FREIGHT SYSTEM INC.

3801 Old Greenwood Road, Fort Smith, AR, 72903

Tel: (501) 785-8928 Fax: (501) 785-8927

Motor carrier.

ABF Freight System Canada Ltd., Locations throughout Canada.

ABF Freight System Canada Ltd., 10765 Cote de Liesse Rd., Dorval, PQ H9P 2R9, Canada

ABM, INC.

50 Fremont Street, #2600, San Francisco, CA, 94105

Tel: (415) 597-4500 Fax: (415) 597-7160

Building cleaning & maintenance services.

American Building Maintenance of Canada Ltd., 1075 Clark Dr., Vancouver, BC V5L 3K2, Canada

Bradford Building Services Co. Ltd., 1075 Clark Dr., Vancouver, BC V5L 3K2, Canada

ABRASIVE TECHNOLOGY INC.

8400 Green Meadows Drive, Westerville, OH, 43081

Tel: (614) 548-4100 Fax: (614) 548-7617 Web site: www.abrasive-tech.com

Mfr. diamond & CBN tooling: bits, blades, drills, wheels, belts, discs.

Abrasive Technology NA Inc., 4145 Thimeus Blvd., St. Laurent, PQ H4R 2K7, Canada

ACC CORPORATION

400 West Ave., Rochester, NY, 14611

Tel: (716) 987-3000 Fax: (716) 987-3499 Web site: www.acccorp.com

Long distance & telecommunications services.

ACC TelEnterprises Ltd., 5343 Dundas St. W. #600, Etobicoke, ON M9B 6K5, Canada

Tel: 416-236-3636 Fax: 416-236-4749 Contact: Kevin Dickens, Pres. & CEO Emp: 500

ACCLAIM ENTERTAINMENT, INC.

1 Acclaim Plaza, Glen Cove, NY, 11542

Tel: (516) 656-5000 Fax: (516) 656-2031 Web site: www.acclaim-music.com

Mfr. video games.

Acclaim Canada Ltd., 208 Evans Ave., Toronto, ON M8Z 1J7, Canada

ACCO USA INC.

300 Tower Parkway, Lincoln, IL, 60069

Tel: (847) 541-9500 Fax: (847) 478-0073

Paper fasteners & clips, metal fasteners, binders & staplers.

Acco Canadian Co. Ltd., 501 McNicoll Ave., Willowdale, ON M2H 2E2, Canada

ACCOUNTANTS ON CALL

Park 80 West, Plaza 2, 9th Fl., Saddle Brook, NJ, 07663

Tel: (201) 843-0006 Fax: (201) 843-4936 Web site: www.aocnet.com

Full-service staffing & executive search firm specializing in accounting & financial personnel.

Accountants on Call, 1730-505 Burrurdst, Vancouver, BC V7X 1M4, Canada

Accountants on Call, Dominion Centre, Royal #2522, Royal Trust Tower, 77 King St. West, Toronto, ON M5K 1K2, Canada

Tel: 416-363-7747 Fax: 416-363-8499

ACHESON COLLOIDS CO.

511 Fort Street, PO Box 611747, Port Huron, MI, 48061-1747

Tel: (810) 984-5581 Fax: (810) 984-1446

Chemicals, chemical preparations, paints & lubricating oils.

Acheson Colloids (Canada) Ltd., PO Box 665, Brantford, ON N3T 5P9, Canada

ACME UNITED CORPORATION

75 Kings Highway Cutoff, Fairfield, CT, 06430-5340

Tel: (203) 332-7330 Fax: (203) 576-0007 Web site: www.acu.com

Mfr. surgical & medical instruments, pharmaceutical supplies.

Acme Ruler Ltd., 351 Foster St. S., Mount Forest, ON NO6 2L0, Canada

ADAMS USA (DIV. WARNER LAMBERT)

201 Tabor Road, Morris Plains, NJ, 07950

Tel: (973) 540-2000 Fax: (973) 540-2313

Mfr./distribution & sale of chewing gum.

Warner Lambert Ltd., 2200 Eglinton E, Scarborough, ON M1K 5C, Canada 9

ADC TELECOMMUNICATIONS INC.

PO Box 1101, Minneapolis, MN, 55440-1101

Tel: (612) 938-8080 Fax: (612) 946-3292 Web site: www.adc.com

Mfr. telecommunications equipment.

ADC Canada, 2147 de la Province, Longueuil, PQ J4G 1Y6, Canada

Tel: 514-677-9166 Fax: 514-677-1316

ADEMCO INTERNATIONAL

165 Eileen Way, Syosset, NY, 11791

Tel: (516) 921-6704 Fax: (516) 496-8306 Web site: www.ademcoint.com

Mfr. security, fire & burglary systems & products.

Ademco Group Canada, 2600 Skylark Ave., Bldg. 8, Ste. 201, Mississauga, ON L4W 5E7 Canada (Locations: Montreal, Toronto, Ottawa, Vancouver, Edmonton, Calgary, Winnepeg, & Halifax, Canada.)

Tel: 905-629-3606 Fax: 905-629-3635

ADESA CORPORATION

310 East 96 Street, Ste. 40, Indianapolis, IN, 46240

Tel: (317) 815-1100 Fax: (317) 815-0500

Motor vehicles, automotive services & trucking.

Adesa Canada Inc., 121 St. Pierre Rd., Vars, ON K0A 3H0, Canada

Montreal Auto Auction Ltd., 325 rue Norman, Lachine, PQ H8R 1A3, Canada

ADVANCE MACHINE COMPANY

14600 21st Ave. North, Plymouth, MN, 55447

Tel: (612) 745-3500 Fax: (612) 745-3866 Web site: www.advmac.com

Industrial floor cleaning equipment.

Advance Nilfisk Canada Ltd., 396 Watline Ave., Mississauga, ON L4Z 1X2, Canada

Tel: 905-712-3260

ADVANTICA RESTAURANT GROUP, INC.

203 East Main Street, Spartanburg, SC, 29319

Tel: (864) 597-8000 Fax: (864) 597-7538

Restaurants

Denny's of Canada Ltd., 116-01451 Shellbridge Way, Richmond, BC V6X 2W8, Canada

Tel: 604-270-8949 Contact: Rhonda J. Parish, Pres. Emp: 2

ADYNO NOBEL

50 South Main Street, 11th Fl., Crossroads Tower, Salt Lake City, UT, 84144

Tel: (801) 364-4800 Fax: (801) 328-6525

Mfr. explosive supplies, accessories for industrial and military applications; aluminum granules.

Adyno Nobel Canada Inc., 5090 Explorer Dr., Mississauga, ON L4W 4T9, Canada

AEROFIN CORPORATION

4621 Murray Place, PO Box 10819, Lynchburg, VA, 24506

Tel: (804) 845-7081 Fax: (804) 528-6242

Mfr. heat exchangers.

Aerofin Corp. Canada Ltd., 1020 Balmoral Rd., Cambridge, ON, Canada N1T 1A5

AEROQUIP-VICKERS

3000 Strayer, PO Box 50, Maumee, OH, 43537-0050

Tel: (419) 867-2200 Fax: (419) 867-2390

Mfr. engineering components and systems for industry.

Aeroquip (Canada) Ltd., 287 Bridgeland Ave., Toronto, ON M6A 1Z7, Canada

AGCO CORPORATION

4830 River Green Parkway, Duluth, GA, 30096-2568

Tel: (770) 813-9200 Fax: (770) 813-6038 Web site: www.agcocorp.com

Mfr. farm equipment & machinery.

Agco Canada Ltd., 515 Dewdney Ave., Regina, SK S4P 3Y3, Canada

Tel: 306-757-2681 Fax: 306-525-6446 Contact: Stan Jangula, Financial Services Mgr. Emp: 12

AIR EXPRESS INTERNATIONAL CORPORATION

120 Tokeneke Road, PO Box 1231, Darien, CT, 06820

Tel: (203) 655-7900 Fax: (203) 655-5779 Web site: www.aeilogistics.com

Air freight forwarder.

AEI Canada Inc., Custom Brokerage Services, 42885 Industrial Rd., Windsor, ON N9C 3R2, Canada

Tel: 519-972-1994

AEI Canada Inc. - Reg. Hdqtrs., 6575 Davand Drive, Mississauga, ON L5T 2M3, Canada (Locations: Alberta, Calgary; Fort Erie, ON; Halifax, Nova Scotia; Sarnia, ON; St. John's, Newfoundland; Vancouver, BC; & Winnipeg, MN, Canada)

Tel: 905-564-0564 Fax: 905-564-2345

AIR PRODUCTS AND CHEMICALS, INC.

7201 Hamilton Boulevard, Allentown, PA, 18195-1501

Tel: (610) 481-4911 Fax: (610) 481-5900

Mfr. industry gases & related equipment, spec. chemicals, environmental/energy systems.

Air Products Canada Ltd., 2090 Steeles Ave. E, Brampton, ON L6T 1A7, Canada

AIRPORT GROUP INTERNATIONAL INC.

330 North Brand Blvd., Ste. 300, Glendale, CA, 91203

Tel: (818) 409-7500 Fax: (818) 409-7979

Airport planning, development & management; airline services.

Airport Group Canada Inc., PO Box 6041, Toronto AMF, ON, Canada

AJAX MAGNETHERMIC CORPORATION

1745 Overland Ave. NE, PO Box 991, Warren, OH, 44482

Tel: (330) 372-8511 Fax: (330) 372-8644

Mfr. induction heating & melting equipment.

Ajax Magnethermic Canada, 333 Station St., Ajax, ON L1S 1S3, Canada

AKRON BRASS COMPANY

1450 Spruce Street, Wooster, OH, 44691

Tel: (330) 264-5678 Fax: (330) 264-2944

Irrigation systems.

Akron Mfg., Box 280, Aylmer, ON, Canada

ALAMO RENT A CAR

110 Southeast Sixth Street, Fort Lauderdale, FL, 33301

Tel: (954) 522-0000 Fax: (954) 220-0120 Web site: www.alamo.com

Car rentals.

Alamo Rent A Car, Carlingview Hotel, 221 Carlingview Drive, Toronto, ON Canada (Locations: Calgary, Montreal, Vancouver.)

ALBANY INTERNATIONAL CORPORATION

PO Box 1907, Albany, NY, 12201

Tel: (518) 445-2200 Fax: (518) 445-2265

Mfr. broadwoven & engineered fabrics, plastic products, filtration media.

Albany Canada, 649 Derwent Way, Annacis Industrial Estate, New Westminster, BC V3M 5P7, Canada

Albany Canada, 300 Westmount St., Cowansville, PQ J2K 1S9, Canada

Albany Intl. Engineered Systems Div., 805 Bancroft St., Pointe Claire, PQ H9R 4L6, Canada

Albany Papermaking Products Group, 1 North St., Perth, ON, Canada K7H 3E4

ALBERTO-CULVER COMPANY

2525 Armitage Ave., Melrose Park, IL, 60160

Tel: (708) 450-3000 Fax: (708) 450-3354

Mfr./marketing personal care & beauty products, household & grocery products & institutional food products.

Alberto-Culver Canada Inc., 506 Kipling Ave., Toronto, ON M8Z 5E2, Canada

ALCO CONTROLS DIV EMERSON ELECTRIC

PO Box 411400, St. Louis, MO, 63141

Tel: (314) 569-4500 Fax: (314) 567-2101

Mfr. A/C & refrigerator flow controls.

Alco Controls Div., Emerson Electric Co., 145 Sherwood Lane, Brantford, ON N3T 5S7, Canada

ALCOA (ALUMINUM CO OF AMERICA)

Alcoa Bldg., 425 Sixth Ave., Pittsburgh, PA, 15219-1850

Tel: (412) 553-4545 Fax: (412) 553-4498

World's leading producer of aluminum & alumina; mining, refining, smelting, fabricating & recycling.

DBM Industries, Ltd., Montreal, PQ, Canada

ALCOA FUJIKURA LTD.

105 Westpark Drive, Brentwood, TN, 37027

Tel: (615) 370-2100 Fax: (615) 370-2180

Mfr. optical groundwire, tube cable, fiber optic connectors & automotive wiring harnesses.

Alcoa Fujikura Ltd., Owen Sound, Canada

ALLEGHENY LUDLUM CORP.

1000 Six PPG Place, Pittsburgh, PA, 15222

Tel: (412) 394-2805 Fax: (412) 394-2800

Steel & alloys.

Jessop Steel Co., Wallaceburg, ON, Canada

ALLEGIANCE HEALTHCARE CORPORATION

1430 Waukegan Road, McGaw Park, IL, 60085

Tel: (847) 689-8410 Fax: (847) 578-4437 Web site: www.allegiance.net

Manufactures & distributes medical, surgical, respiratory therapy & laboratory products.

Allegiance Healthcare Canada Inc., 4 Robert Speck Parkway, Mississauga, ON, Canada

Tel: 905-281-6316 Fax: 905-281-6795 Contact: Gordon LaFortune, Mgr. Emp: 35

ALLEN TELECOM

25101 Chagrin Boulevard, Beachwood, OH, 44122-5619

Tel: (216) 765-5818 Fax: (216) 765-0410 Web site: www.allentele.com

Mfr. communications equipment, automotive bodies and parts, electronic components.

Allen Group/Ontario Ltd., 40 King St. W., Toronto, ON M5H 3Y2, Canada

Allen Telecom Canada Inc., 1815 Ironstone Manor, Unit 12, Pickering, ON L1W 3W9, Canada

Tel: 905-839-3474 Fax: 905-839-4663 Contact: Brenda Cannon, Off. Mgr.

ALLEN-BRADLEY COMPANY, INC.

1201 South Second Street, Milwaukee, WI, 53204

Tel: (414) 382-2000 Fax: (414) 382-4444

Mfr. electrical controls & information devices.

Allen-Bradley Canada Ltd., 135 Dundas St., Cambridge, ON N1R 5X1, Canada

ALLERGAN INC.

2525 Dupont Drive, PO Box 19534, Irvine, CA, 92713-9534

Tel: (714) 246-4500 Fax: (714) 246-6987

Mfr. therapeutic eye care products, skin & neural care pharmaceuticals.

Allergan Inc., Markham, ON, Canada

ALLIANCE CAPITAL MANAGEMENT L.P.

1345 Ave. of the Americas, New York, NY, 10105

Tel: (212) 969-1000 Fax: (212) 969-2229 Web site: www.alliancecapital.com

Fund manager for large organizations.

Alliance Capital Management, Toronto, ON Canada

ALLIEDSIGNAL INC.

101 Columbia Road, PO Box 2245, Morristown, NJ, 07962-2245

Tel: (973) 455-2000 Fax: (973) 455-4807 Web site: www.alliedsignal.com

Mfr. aerospace & automotive products, engineered materials.

Allied Chemical Canada Inc., 201 City Ctr. Dr., Mississauga, ON L5B 2T4, Canada

Barrday Inc., 75 Moorefield St., Cambridge, ON N1R 5W6, Canada

ALLIEDSIGNAL, INC. - AUTOMOTIVE PRODUCTS GROUP

105 Pawtucket Ave., Rumford, RI, 02916-2422

Tel: (401) 434-7000 Fax: (401) 431-3670 Web site: www.alliedsignal.com

Mfr. spark plugs, filters, brakes.

Fram Canada Ltd., PO Box 550, Stratford, ON, Canada

THE ALLSTATE CORPORATION

Allstate Plaza, 2775 Sanders Road, Northbrook, IL, 60062-6127

Tel: (847) 402-5000 Fax: (847) 836-3998 Web site: www.allstate.com

Personal property, auto & life insurance.

The Allstate Corporation, Toronto, ON, Canada

ALOETTE COSMETICS INC.

1301 Wrights Lane East, West Chester, PA, 19380

Tel: (610) 692-0600 Fax: (610) 692-2334

Drugs, proprietaries & sundries.

Aloette Cosmetics of Canada Inc., 89 Edilcan Dr., Concord, ON L4K 3S6, Canada

ALPINE ENGINEERED PRODUCTS INC.

PO Box 2225, Pompano Beach, FL, 33061

Tel: (954) 781-3333 Fax: (954) 973-2644 Web site: www.2alpineng.com.

Fabricated plate.

Alpine Systems Corp., 421 Rountree Dairy Rd., Woodbridge, ON L4L 8H1, Canada

ALTEC INDUSTRIES INC.

210 Inverness Center Drive, Birmingham, AL, 35242

Tel: (205) 991-7733 Fax: (205) 991-9993

Mfr. truck mounted aerial lifts & pole erection derricks.

Altec Industries Ltd., 831 Nipissing Rd., Milton, ON L9T 4Z4, Canada

ALVEY INC.

9301 Olive Boulevard, St. Louis, MO, 63132

Tel: (314) 993-4700 Fax: (314) 995-2400 Web site: www.alvey.com

Mfr./sales automatic case palletizers, package & pallet conveyor systems.

Pinnacle Automation Canada, 15-101 Don Quichotte, Ste. 603, Ile Perrot, PQ J7V 7X4, Canada

Tel: 514-453-3411 Fax: 514-453-6026

Pinnacle Automation Canada, #6 - 6620 Kitimat Rd., Mississauga, ON L5N 2B8, Canada

Tel: 905-858-0088 Fax: 905-858-0061

AMDAHL CORPORATION

1250 East Arques Ave., PO Box 3470, Sunnyvale, CA, 94088-3470

Tel: (408) 746-6000 Fax: (408) 773-0833 Web site: www.amdahl.com

Development/mfr. large scale computers, software, data storage products, information-technology solutions & support.

Amdahl Canada Ltd., 12 Concorde Place #100, North York, ON M3C 3R8, Canada (Locations: Calgary & Edmonton AB, Mississauga & Ottawa ON, Montreal & Quebec)

AMERACE / EAGLE INDUSTRIES

2 N. Riverside Plaza, #1160, Chicago, IL, 60606

Tel: (312) 906-8700 Fax: (312) 906-8372

Chemicals, rubber products, plastics, electrical components & controls.

Amerace Ltd., 10 Esna Park Dr., Markahan, ON, Canada

AMERADA HESS CORPORATION

1185 Ave. of the Americas, New York, NY, 10036

Tel: (212) 997-8500 Fax: (212) 536-8390 Web site: www.hess.com

Crude oil & natural gas.

Amerada Hess Canada Ltd., Western Canadian Place #1900, 700 9th Ave., Calgary, AB T2P 4B3, Canada

AMERCO

1325 Airmotive Way, Ste. 100, Reno, NV, 89502-3239

Tel: (702) 688-6300 Fax: (702) 688-6338 Web site: www.uhaul.com

Truck rental (U-Haul), moving supplies, storage facilities, short-term property-casualty insurance & life, health & annuity-type insurance products.

U-Haul International, Toronto, Canada

AMERICA ONLINE, INC.

2200 AOL Way, Dulles, VA, 20166

Tel: (703) 453-4000 Fax: (703) 265-5769 Web site: www.aol.com

Internet service provider.

America Online, Inc., Toronto, ON, Canada

AMERICAN & EFIRD INC.

PO Box 507, Mt. Holly, NC, 28120

Tel: (704) 827-4311 Fax: (704) 822-6054

Mfr. industrial thread, yarn & consumer sewing products.

Allied Thread Inc., 144 Port Royal W, Montreal, PQ H3L 3S9, Canada

AMERICAN AIRLINES INC.

4333 Amon Carter Boulevard, Ft. Worth, TX, 76155

Tel: (817) 963-1234 Fax: (817) 967-9641 Web site: www.amrcorp.com

Air transport services.

American Airlines Inc., Foster Bldg., 40 St. Clair Ave. W, Toronto, ON M4V 1M4, Canada

AMERICAN APPRAISAL ASSOCIATES INC.

411 E. Wisconsin Ave., Milwaukee, WI, 53202

Tel: (414) 271-7240 Fax: (414) 271-1041

Valuation consulting services.

American Appraisal Canada Ltd., 310 Front St. W., #800, Toronto, ON M5V 3B5, Canada

AMERICAN BANKERS INSURANCE GROUP, INC.

11222 Quail Roost Drive, Miami, FL, 33157-6596

Tel: (305) 253-2244 Fax: (305) 252-6987 Web site: www.abig.com

Insurance.

American Bankers Insurance Group, 40 Sheppard Ave. W #501, Willowdale, ON M2N 6K9, Canada

AMERICAN BILTRITE INC.

57 River Street, Wellesley Hills, MA, 02181

Tel: (781) 237-6655 Fax: (781) 237-6880 Web site: www.abitape.com

Mfr. industrial rubber & plastic products.

American Biltrite (Canada) Ltd., 200 Bank St., Sherbrooke, PQ J1H 4K3, Canada

AMERICAN EXPRESS COMPANY

American Express Tower, World Financial Center, New York, NY, 10285-4765

Tel: (212) 640-2000 Fax: (212) 619-9802 Web site: www.americanexpress.com

Travel, travelers cheques, charge card & financial services.

Amex Bank of Canada, Canada - All inquiries to U.S. address

Amex Canada Inc., Canada - All inquiries to U.S. address.

AMERICAN GENERAL CORPORATION

2929 Allen Parkway, Houston, TX, 77019-2155

Tel: (713) 522-1111 Fax: (713) 523-8531 Web site: www.agc.com

Financial services & holding company.

Financial Life Assurance Co. of Canada, 10 Four Seasons Pl., Etobicoke, ON M9B 6J2, Canada

AMERICAN GREETINGS CORPORATION

One American Road, Cleveland, OH, 44144-2398

Tel: (216) 252-7300 Fax: (216) 252-6777

Mfr./distributor greeting cards, gift wrappings, tags, seals, ribbons & party goods.

Carlton Canada, 1460 The Queensway, Toronto, ON M8Z 1S7, Canada

AMERICAN HOME PRODUCTS CORPORATION

Five Giralda Farms, Madison, NJ, 07940-0874

Tel: (973) 660-5000 Fax: (973) 660-6048 Web site: www.ahp.com

Mfr. pharmaceutical, animal health care & crop protection products.

American Home Products Corporation, Canada

AMERICAN INTERNATIONAL GROUP INC.

70 Pine Street, New York, NY, 10270

Tel: (212) 770-7000 Fax: (212) 509-9705 Web site: www.aig.com

Worldwide insurance and financial services.

AIU Canada Ltd., 145 Wellington St. W, Toronto, ON M5J 2R3, Canada

Commerce & Industry Insurance Co. of Canada, 145 Wellington St. W, Toronto, ON M5J 2R3, Canada

AMERICAN LOCKER GROUP INC.

15 West Second Street, Jamestown, NY, 14702

Tel: (716) 664-9600 Fax: (716) 483-2822

Mfr. coin-operated locks, office furniture.

Canadian Locker Co., 401 Mugget Ave., Agincourt, ON, Canada

AMERICAN MANAGEMENT SYSTEMS, INC.

4050 Legato Road, Fairfax, VA, 22033

Tel: (703) 267-8000 Fax: (703) 267-5067 Web site: www.amsinc.com

Systems integration & consulting.

AMS Management Systems Canada Inc., 1250 Rene Levesque West, Ste. 4500, Monteal, PQ H3B 4W8, Canada

Tel: 514-939-4662 Fax: 514-939-6015

AMS Management Systems Canada Inc., 2 Bloor St. West, Ste. 900, Toronto, ON, M4W 3E2 Canada

Tel: 416-960-6082 Fax: 416-960-9101

AMS Management Systems Canada Inc., Barrister House, 180 Elgin Sreet, Ste. 700, Ottawa, ON K2P 2K3, Canada

Tel: 613-232-7400 Fax: 613-232-0324 Contact: Linda Macpherson, Pres. Emp: 147

AMERICAN OPTICAL CORPORATION

853 Camino Del Mar, Ste. 200, Del Mar, CA, 92014

Tel: (619) 509-9899 Fax: (619) 509-9898

Mfr. opthalmic lenses & frames, custom molded products, specialty lenses.

AOCO Ltd., 80 Centurian Dr., Markham, ON L3R 8C1, Canada

AMERICAN PRECISION INDUSTRIES INC.

2777 Walden Ave., Buffalo, NY, 14225

Tel: (716) 684-9700 Fax: (716) 684-2129 Web site: www.apicorporate.com

Mfr. heat transfer equipment, motion control devices,coils, capacitors, electro-mechanical clutches & brakes.

Dustex of Canada Inc., 698 Wilson Ave., Kitchener, ON N2C 1H9, Canada

AMERICAN PRESIDENT LINES LTD

1111 Broadway, Oakland, CA, 94607

Tel: (510) 272-8000 Fax: (510) 272-7941

Intermodal shipping services.

American President Lines Ltd., 231 rue St. Jacques, Montreal, PQ H2Y 1M6, Canada

AMERICAN RE-INSURANCE COMPANY

555 College Road East, Princeton, NJ, 08543

Tel: (609) 243-4200 Fax: (609) 243-4257

Reinsurance.

American Re-Insurance Co., 20 Queen St. W, PO Box 65, Toronto, ON M3H 3R3, Canada

American Re-Insurance Co., 1001 Ouest Blvd. de Maisonneuve, Montreal, PQ H3A 3C8, Canada

AMERICAN SAFETY RAZOR CO.

PO Box 500, Staunton, VA, 24401

Tel: (540) 248-8000 Fax: (540) 248-0522

Mfr. private-label & branded shaving razors & blades & cotton swabs.

American Safety Razor Co., Newmarket, ON, Canada

Tel: 905-853-1600

AMERICAN STANDARD INC.

One Centennial Ave., Piscataway, NJ, 08855-6820

Tel: (732) 980-3000 Fax: (732) 980-6118

Mfr. heating, plumbing & sanitary equipment, china, earthenware.

American Standard Industrial Products (Div. of WABCO), 1 Blair Dr., Bramalea, ON L6T 2H4, Canada

American Standard-Canada, 80 Ward St., Toronto, ON M6H 4A7, Canada

AMERICAN TOOL COMPANIES INC.

8400 LakeView Pkwy., #400, Kenosha, WI, 53142

Tel: (847) 478-1090 Fax: (847) 478-1090

Mfr. hand tools, cutting tools & power tool accessories.

American Tool Companies, 5865 Coopers Ave., Mississauga, ON L4Z 1R9, Canada

AMERICAN UNIFORM COMPANY

PO Box 2130, Cleveland, TN, 37311

Tel: (423) 476-6561 Fax: (423) 559-3855

Mfr. work clothing, uniforms.

Canadian Uniform Ltd., 9697 St. Lawrence Blvd., Montreal, PQ H3L 2N2, Canada

AMETEK INC.

4 Station Square, Paoli, PA, 19301

Tel: (610) 647-2121 Fax: (610) 296-3412 Web site: www.ametek.com

Mfr. instruments, electric motors & engineered materials.

Ametek - Western Research, 8 Manning Close N.E., Calgary, AB T2E7N5, Canada

Tel: 403-235-8300 Fax: 403-248-3550

AMMIRATI PURIS LINTAS

One Dag Hammarskjold Plaza, New York, NY, 10017

Tel: (212) 605-8000 Fax: (212) 605-4705 Web site: www.interpublic.com

International advertising agency.

Ammirati Puris Lintas Canada, 181 Bay St., Ste. 1630, Toronto, ON, Canada M5J 2T3

Tel: 416-368-4400 Fax: 416-369-4404 Contact: Doug Robinson

AMP INC.

470 Friendship Road, PO Box 3608, Harrisburg, PA, 17105-3608

Tel: (717) 564-0100 Fax: (717) 780-6130

Develop/mfr. electronic & electrical connection products & systems.

AMP of Canada Ltd., Toronto, ON,Canada

AMPACET CORPORATION

660 White Plains Road, Tarrytown, NY, 10591-5130

Tel: (914) 631-6600 Fax: (914) 631-7197 Web site: www.ampacet.com

Mfr. color and additive concentrates for the plastics industry.

Ampacet Canada (Delta), 917 Cliveden Ave., Unit 103, Delta, BC V3M 5R6, Canada

Tel: 800-265-6712 Fax: 604-526-7322

Ampacet Canada (Kitchener), 101 Sasaga Drive, Kitchener, ON N2C 2G8, Canada

Tel: 800-265-6711 Fax: 519-748-5576

AMPHENOL PRODUCTS

1925A Ohio Street, Lisle, IL, 60532

Tel: (630) 960-1010 Fax: (630) 810-5640

Electric interconnect/penetrate systems & assemblies.

Amphenol Canada, 3285 Canvendish Blvd., Montreal, PQ H4B 2L9, Canada

Amphenol Canada, 44 Metropolitan Rd., Scarborough, ON M1R 2T9, Canada (Locations:Nepean, PQ; Renfrew, ON; & Richmond, BC, Canada.)

Tel: 416-291-4401

AMSTED INDUSTRIES INC.

205 North Michigan, Chicago, IL, 60601

Tel: (312) 645-1700 Fax: (312) 819-8429 Web site: www.amsted.com

Privately-held, diversified manufacturer of products for the construction & building markets, general industry & the railroads.

Griffin Canada, Inc., 1570 Ampere St., Ste. 504, Boucherville, PQ J4B 7L4, Canada

Tel: 514-641-7870 Fax: 514-641-0827 Contact: William J. Demmert, Pres. Emp: 13

AMWAY CORPORATION

7575 Fulton Street East, Ada, MI, 49355-0001

Tel: (616) 787-6000 Fax: (616) 787-6177 Web site: www.amway.com

Mfr./sale home care, personal care, nutrition & houseware products.

Amway of Canada Ltd., PO Box 5706, London, ON N6A 4S5, Canada

ANALYSTS INTERNATIONAL CORPORATION

7615 Metro Boulevard, Minneapolis, MN, 55439

Tel: (612) 835-5900 Fax: (612) 897-4555 Web site: www.analysts.com

Provides computer software-related services -- including systems analysis and design, programming, and Y2K remediation.

Analysts International Corporation, Toronto, ON, Canada

Tel: 877-603-3822

Analysts International Corporation, Ottawa, ON, Canada

Tel: 613-751-4445

ANAMET INC.

698 South Main Street, Waterbury, CT, 06706

Tel: (203) 574-8500 Fax: (203) 573-1505

Mfr. industrial machinery, wiring devices, measure & control devices.

Anamet Canada Inc., PO Box 50, Colborne, ON K0K 1S0, Canada

ANCHOR HOCKING CORPORATION

519 Pierce Ave., PO Box 600, Lancaster, OH, 43130-0600

Tel: (740) 687-2111 Fax: (740) 687-2543

Mfr. glassware & dinnerware plastic products.

Anchor Cap & Closure Corp. of Canada Ltd., 275 Wallace Ave., Toronto, ON M6P 3N3, Canada

Anchor Hocking Corp., 30 Industrial St., Toronto, ON M4G 1N9, Canada

ANDERSEN CONSULTING

100 South Wacker Drive, Ste. 1059, Chicago, IL, 60606

Tel: (311) 123-7271 Fax: (312) 507-7965 Web site: www.ac.com

Provides management & technology consulting services.

Andersen Consulting, 1900-79 Wellington St. West, Toronto, ON M5J1H1, Canada

Tel: 416-695-5050 Fax: 416-947-7950

ANDREW CORPORATION

10500 West 153rd Street, Orland Park, IL, 60462

Tel: (708) 349-3300 Fax: (708) 349-5410 Web site: www.andrew.com

Mfr. antenna systems, coaxial cable, electronic communications & network connectivity systems.

Andrew Canada Inc., 606 Beech St., Whitby, ON L1N 5S2, Canada

ANGELICA CORPORATION

424 South Woods Mill Road, #300, Chesterfield, MO, 63017-3406

Tel: (314) 854-3800 Fax: (314) 854-3890

Mfr., marketing & sales of uniforms.

Angelica Uniform of Canada Ltd., 35 Suntract Rd., Weston, ON M9N 2V8, Canada

Angelica-Whitewear Ltd., 5550 Fullum St., Montreal, PQ H2G 2H4, Canada

ANIXTER INTERNATIONAL INC..

4711 Golf Road, Skokie, IL, 60076

Tel: (847) 677-2600 Fax: (708) 677-9480

Distributor wiring systems/products for voice, video, data and power applications.

Anixter Canada, 33 City Centre Dr., Mississauga, ON L5B 2N5, Canada

ANSELL EDMONT INDUSTRIAL INC.

1300 Walnut Street, Coshocton, OH, 43812

Tel: (614) 622-4311 Fax: (614) 622-9611

Mfr. industrial gloves, rubber and plastic products, protective clothing.

Ansell Canada Inc., 105 Lauder, Cowansville, PQ J2K 2K8, Canada

AON CORPORATION

123 North Wacker Drive, Chicago, IL, 60606

Tel: (312) 701-3000 Fax: (312) 701-3100 Web site: www.aon.com

Insurance brokers worldwide; underwrites accident & health insurance, specialty & professional insurance; & provides risk management consultation.

AON B E P Inc., 1801 McGill College Ave., Ste. 1450, Montreal, PQ H3A 3P5, Canada

Tel: 514-982-4855 Fax: 514-288-0840 Contact: Andre Carignan

AON Consulting, Ste. 20 Bay St., Toronto, ON M5J 2N9, Canada (Locations: Edmonton, Winnipeg, & Calgary, Canada.)

Tel: 416-868-5942 Fax: 416-868-5958 Contact: Marilynne Madigan

AON Re (Canada) Inc., 999 West Hastings St., Ste. 1790, Vancouver, BC V6C 2W2, Canada

Tel: 604-684-3370 Fax: 604-684-3340 Contact: Vic Arnell

AON Reed Stenhouse, 125 9th Ave. S.E., Ste. 2700, Calgary, AB T2G 0P9, Canada

Tel: 403-267-7010 Fax: 403-261-0897 Contact: Mike Bagby

AON Reed Stenhouse, 44 Austin St., Ste. 201, St. John's ND A1B 4C2, Canada

Tel: 709-739-1000 Fax: 709-739-1001 Contact: Al Lorhan

AON Reed Stenhouse/Aon Parizeau, 900 Rene Levesque Blvd. East, Ste. 750, PO Box 1305, Quebec City, PQ G1K 7H6, Canada

Tel: 418-529-1234 Fax: 418-647-4976 Contact: Andre Soucisse

APPLE COMPUTER INC.

One Infinite Loop, Cupertino, CA, 95014

Tel: (831) 996-1010 Fax: (831) 974-2113 Web site: www.apple.com

Personal computers, peripherals & software.

Apple Canada, 7495 Birchmount Rd., Markham, ON L3R 5G2, Canada

APPLIED POWER INC.

13000 W. Silver Spring Drive, Butler, WI, 53007

Tel: (414) 781-6600 Fax: (414) 781-0629

Mfr. hi-pressure tools, vibration control products, electrical tools, consumables, technical furniture & enclosures.

GB Electrical Canada, 6615 Ordan Dr., Units 14-15, Mississauga, ON L5T 1X2, Canada

APPLIED SYSTEMS INC.

200 Applied Parkway, University Park, IL, 60466

Tel: (708) 534-5575 Fax: (708) 534-5943 Web site: www.appliedsystems.com

Computer systems, peripherals & software.

Applied Systems, 200 Watline Ave., Mississauga, ON L4Z 1P3, Canada

Tel: 905-507-9006 Fax: 905-507-4232

ARAMARK CORPORATION

1101 Market Street, Philadelphia, PA, 19107-2988

Tel: (215) 238-3000 Fax: (215) 238-3333

Diversified managed services.

Versa Services Ltd., 811 Islington Ave., Box 950, Station "U", Toronto, ON MBZ SY7, Canada

Tel: 416-253-3146 Fax: 416-255-5953 Contact: Peter McCawley, Pres.

ATLANTIC RICHFIELD COMPANY (ARCO)

515 South Flower Street, Los Angeles, CA, 90071-2256

Tel: (213) 486-3511 Fax: (213) 486-2063 Web site: www.arco.com

Petroleum & natural gas, chemicals & service stations.

ARCO Chemical Canada, 100 Consilium Place, Scarborough, ON M1H 3E3, Canada

ARKANSAS BEST CORPORATION

3801 Old. Greenwood Road, Ft. Smith, AR, 72903

Tel: (501) 785-6000 Fax: (501) 494-6658 Web site: www.arkbest.com

Trucking, automotive supplies, service repair, bldg management, data processing services.

ABF Freight System (BC) Ltd., 7890 Express St., Burnaby, BC V5A 1T4, Canada

ABF Freight System Canada Ltd., 81 The East Mall #105, Etobicoke, ON M8Z 5W3, Canada

ARMSTRONG INTERNATIONAL INC.

816 Maple Street, PO Box 408, Three Rivers, MI, 49093

Tel: (616) 273-1415 Fax: (616) 278-6555

Mfr. steam specialty products: traps, air vents, liquid drainers, strainers, valves, etc.

Armstrong Hunt Inc., 648 Moeller, Granby, PQ J2G 8E5, Canada

ARMSTRONG WORLD INDUSTRIES INC.

PO Box 3001, 313 W. Liberty Street, Lancaster, PA, 17604-3001

Tel: (717) 397-0611 Fax: (717) 396-2787 Web site: www.armstrong.com

Mfr. & marketing interior furnishings & specialty products for bldg, auto & textile industry.

Armstrong World Industries Ltd., Montreal, PQ, Canada (All inquiries to U.S. address)

AROMACHEM

599 Johnson Ave., Brooklyn, NY, 11237

Tel: (718) 497-4664 Fax: (718) 821-2193

Essential oils & extracts, perfumes & flavor material, aromatic chemicals.

Felton Intl. Inc., 601 Garyray Dr., Weston, ON M9L 1P9, Canada

Felton Intl. Inc., 5483 Royalmount Ave., Montreal, PQ H4P 1J3, Canada

ARROW MFG. CO., INC.

567 52nd Street, West New York, NJ, 07093

Tel: (201) 867-4833 Fax: (201) 867-1596

Mfr. plastic products, cosmetic & jewelry boxes.

Arrow Bingham Group Inc., 10 Fuller Rd., Ajax, ON L1S 3R2, Canada

ARTHUR ANDERSEN & COMPANY

33 West Monroe Street, Chicago, IL, 60603

Tel: (312) 372-7100 Fax: (312) 507-0123 Web site: www.arthurandersen.com

Accounting & audit, tax & management consulting services.

Arthur Andersen & Co., AETNA Tower, Ste. 1900, 79 Wellington St. West, Toronto, PQ M5J 1H1, Canada

Tel: 416-863-1540

Arthur Andersen & Co., 2700-600 de Maisonneuve Blvd. West, Montreal, PQ H3A 3J2, Canada

Tel: 514-848-1641

Arthur Andersen & Co., 45 St. Claire Ave. West, 12th Fl., (PO Box 29), Toronto-Dominion Centre, Toronto, ON M4V 3A7, Canada (Locations: Ottawa, Edmonton, Etobicoke, Calgary, Winnepeg, Vancouver, Mississaugua, Fredericton, Canada.)

Tel: 416-515-2424

Arthur Andersen & Co./Le Group Mallette Maheu, Ste. 1000, 5, Place Ville-Marie, Montreal, PQ H3B 4X3, Canada

Tel: 514-871-1850

ARVIN INDUSTRIES INC.

One Noblitt Plaza, Box 3000, Columbus, IN, 47202-3000

Tel: (812) 379-3000 Fax: (812) 379-3688 Web site: www.arvin.com

Mfr. of automotive exhaust systems & ride control products.

Arvin Automotive of Canada Ltd., 248 Bowes Rd., Concord, ON L4K 1B4, Canada

Arvin Automotive of Canada Ltd., 248 Bowes Rd., Concord, ON Canada L4K 1J9

Tel: 905-669-1080 Fax: 905-669-5543 Contact: Plato Rontis, Operations Mgr. Emp: 250

Arvin Ride and Motion Control Products Inc., 3560 Lake Shore Blvd. West, Toronto, ON M8W 1N6, Canada

Tel: 416-252-5111 Fax: 416-252-5529 Contact: Leigh Wright, VP & Gen. Mgr. Emp: 400

Arvin Ride Control Products Inc., 3560 Lake Shore Blvd. W., Etobicoke, ON M8W 1N6, Canada

ASARCO INC.

180 Maiden Lane, New York, NY, 10038

Tel: (212) 510-2000 Fax: (212) 510-1855 Web site: www.asarco.com

Nonferrous metals, specialty chemicals, minerals, mfr. industrial products, environmental services.

Asarco Inc., Aquarius Mine, Timmins, ON, Canada

Enthone-Omi Inc., Toronto, ON, Canada

ASCOM HASLER MAILING SYSTEMS INC.

19 Forest Parkway, PO Box 858, Shelton, CT, 06484-0904

Tel: (203) 926-1087 Fax: (203) 929-6084

Mfr. gummed tape dispensers, postal meters and scales, mailing machines.

Ascom Hasler Mailing Systems of Canada Ltd., 50 Riviera Dr., Markham, ON L3R 5M1, Canada

ASHLAND OIL INC.

1000 Ashland Drive, Russell, KY, 41169

Tel: (606) 329-3333 Fax: (606) 329-5274 Web site: www.ashland.com

Petroleum exploration, refining & transportation; mfr. chemicals, oils & lubricants.

Ashland Chemicals, Resins & Chemicals Div., 2620 Royal Windsor Dr., Mississauga, ON L5J 4E7, Canada

Valvoline Oil Canada, 905 Winston Churchill Blvd., Mississauga, ON, Canada

ASHWORTH BROTHERS INC.

89 Globe Mills Ave., PO Box 670, Fall River, MA, 02722-0670

Tel: (508) 674-4693 Fax: (508) 675-9622

Flexible & metallic card clothing.

Ashworth Card Clothing Co. Ltd., 316 St. Hubert St., Granby, PQ, Canada

Tel: 514-372-4747

ASSOCIATED HYGENIC PRODUCTS

4455 River Green Parkway, Duluth, GA, 30136

Tel: (770) 497-9800 Fax: (770) 623-8887

Mfr. sanitary paper products.

Associated Hygenic Products Ltd., 1185 Colborne St. E., Brantford, ON N3T 5N3, Canada

Tel: 519-759-5952

ASSOCIATED PRESS INC.

50 Rockefeller Plaza, New York, NY, 10020-1605

Tel: (212) 621-1500 Fax: (212) 621-5447 Web site: www.ap.com

News gathering agency.

Associated Press (Canada) Ltd., 36 King St. E., Toronto, ON M5C 2L9, Canada

Tel: 416-368-1388

ASSOCIATES FIRST CAPITAL CORPORATION

250 E. Carpenter Freeway, Irving, TX, 75062-2729

Tel: (972) 652-4000 Fax: (972) 652-7420 Web site: www.theassociates.com

Consumer financial services.

Associates First Capital Corporation, Montreal, PQ, Canada

Associates First Capital Corporation, Toronto, ON, Canada

AST RESEARCH INC.

16215 Alton Parkway, PO Box 19658, Irvine, CA, 92713-9658

Tel: (949) 727-4141 Fax: (949) 727-8584 Web site: www.ast.com

Design/development/mfr. hi-performance desktop, server & notebook computers.

AST Canada, 1405 Route Transcanadienne #200, Dorval, PQ H9P 2V9, Canada

Tel: 905-507-3278

AST Canada, 5600 Parkwood Way #550, Richmond, BC V6V 2M2, Canada

Tel: 905-507-3278

AST Canada, 255 Matheson Blvd. W., Mississauga, ON L5R 3G3, Canada

Tel: 905-507-3278

AT&T CORPORATION

32 Ave. of the Americas, New York, NY, 10013-2412

Tel: (212) 387-5400 Fax: (908) 221-1211 Web site: www.att.com

Telecommunications

AT&T Canada Inc., 3650 Victoria Park Ave. #700, Willowdale, ON M2H 3P7, Canada

ATKINSON CONSTRUCTION

1100 Grundy Lane, San Bruno, CA, 94066

Tel: (650) 876-0400 Fax: (650) 876-1143

Construction.

Comco Pipe & Supply Co., 5910 17th St. NW, Edmonton, AB T5J 2K1, Canada

Commonwealth Construction Co., 4599 Tillicum St., Burnaby, BC V5S 3J9, Canada

ATLANTIC MUTUAL COS

100 Wall Street, New York, NY, 10005

Tel: (212) 943-1800 Fax: (212) 428-6566

Insurance.

Focus Group Inc., 36 King St. E. #500, Toronto, ON M5C 1E5, Canada

ATLAS VAN LINES INC.

1212 St. George Road, Evansville, IN, 47711-2336

Tel: (812) 424-4326 Fax: (812) 421-7125 Web site: www.atlasvanlines.com

Trucking, freight transport.

Atlas Van Lines (Canada) Ltd., PO Box 970, Oakville, ON L6J 5M7, Canada

ATTACHMATE CORPORATION

3617 131st Ave. S.E., Bellevue, WA, 98006-1332

Tel: (425) 644-4010 Fax: (425) 747-9924 Web site: www.attachmate.com

Mfr. connectivity software.

Attachmate Canada, 3100 Steeles, AM, Ste. 302, Markham, ON, L3R 2T3, Canada

Attachmate Canada, 4240 Still Creek Drive, Ste. 400, Burnaby, BC V5C-6C6, Canada

AUTO-TROL TECHNOLOGY CORPORATION

12500 North Washington Street, Denver, CO, 80241-2400

Tel: (303) 452-4919 Fax: (303) 252-2249 Web site: www.auto-trol.com

Develops, markets & integrates computer-based solutions for industrial companies & government agencies worldwide.

Auto-trol Ltd., 2810 Matheson Blvd. East, Ste. 410, Mississauga, ON L4W 4X7, Canada

Tel: 905-624-5908 Fax: 905-624-1286 Contact: Kenneth M. Dedeluk Emp: 5

Auto-trol Technology Corporation, 1144 29th Ave., N.E., Ste. 300, Calgary, AB, Canada T2E 7PI

Tel: 403-250-1232 Fax: 403-250-1037 Contact: Kenneth M. Dedeluk Emp: 14

Auto-trol Technology Corporation, One Holiday St., East Tower, Ste. 115, Pointe Claire, PQ H9R 5N3, Canada

Tel: 514-426-2980 Fax: 514-426-2988 Contact: Kenneth M. Dedeluk Emp: 4

AUTODESK INC.

111 McInnis Parkway, San Rafael, CA, 94903

Tel: (415) 507-5000 Fax: (415) 507-6112 Web site: www.autodesk.com

Develop/marketing/support computer-aided design, engineering, scientific & multimedia software products.

Autodesk Canada Inc., 1 Holliday St., East Tower, 5th Fl., Point-Claire, PQ H9R 5N3, Canada

Tel: 514-697-0875 Fax: 514-697-4387

Autodesk Canada Inc., 4170 Still Creek Drive, Ste. 200, Burnaby, BC, V5C 6C6, Canada

Tel: 604-294-4902 Fax: 604-294-4926

Autodesk Canada Inc., 90 Allstate Pkwy., Markham, ON L3R 6H3, Canada

Tel: 905-946-0928 Fax: 905-946-0926

AUTOMATIC DATA PROCESSING INC.

One ADP Boulevard, Roseland, NJ, 07068

Tel: (973) 994-5000 Fax: (973) 994-5387 Web site: www.adp.com

Data processing services.

ADP Automotive Claims Service, 2150 Islington Ave., Etobicoke, ON M9P 3V4, Canada

ADP Dealer Services Ltd., 1210 Sheppard Ave. E., Toronto, ON M2K 1E3, Canada

ADP Independent Investors Communications Group, 1048 Ronsa Ct., Mississauga, ON L4W 4V6, Canada

Canadian ADP Services Ltd., 2150 Islington Ave., Etobicoke, ON M9P 3V4, Canada

AUTOMATIC SWITCH CO. (ASCO)

50-60 Hanover Road, Florham Park, NJ, 07932

Tel: (973) 966-2000 Fax: (973) 966-2628

Mfr. solenoid valves, emergency power controls, pressure & temp. switches.

Ascolectric Ltd., Airport Rd., PO Box 160, Brantford, ON N3T 5M8, Canada

Tel: 519-758-2700 Fax: 519-758-5540 Contact: D. Laackman, Mgr.

AUTOMATION DEVICES INC.

7050 West Ridge Road, Fairview, PA, 16415-2028

Tel: (814) 474-5561 Fax: (814) 474-2131

Mfr. industrial machinery, relays and controls.

Automation Devices (Canada) Ltd., 4700 Montrose Rd., Niagara Falls, ON L2H 1K3, Canada

AVCO FINANCIAL SERVICES INC.

600 Anton Blvd., PO Box 5011, Costa Mesa, CA, 92628-5011

Tel: (714) 435-1200 Fax: (714) 445-7722 Web site: www.avco.textron.com

Financial services, loans and insurance.

Avco Financial Services Canada Ltd., 201 Queens Ave., London, ON N6A 1J1, Canada

Tel: 519-672-4220

AVERY DENNISON CORPORATION

150 N. Orange Grove Blvd., Pasadena, CA, 91103

Tel: (626) 304-2000 Fax: (626) 792-7312 Web site: www.averydennison.com

Mfr. pressure-sensitive adhesives & materials, office products, labels, tags, retail systems, Carter's Ink & specialty chemicals.

Avery Labels Systems Inc., 35 McLachian Dr., Rexdale, ON M9W 1E4, Canada

Dennison Mfg. Canada Inc., 200 Base Line Rd., Bowmanville, ON L1C 1A2, Canada

AVIS, INC.

900 Old Country Road., Garden City, NY, 11530

Tel: (516) 222-3000 Fax: (516) 222-4381 Web site: www.avis.com

Car rental services.

Aviscar Inc., 1225 Metcalfe St., Montreal, PQ H3B 2V5, Canada

AVON PRODUCTS INC.

1345 Ave. of the Americas, New York, NY, 10105-0196

Tel: (212) 282-5000 Fax: (212) 282-6049 Web site: www.avon.com

Mfr./distributor beauty & related products, fashion jewelry, gifts & collectibles.

Avon Products Ltd., PO Box 8000, Pointe Claire-Dorvall, PQ H9R 4R3, Canada

AZON CORPORATION

720 Azon Road, Johnson City, NY, 13790-1799

Tel: (607) 797-2368 Fax: (607) 797-4506 Web site: www.azon.com

Mfr. paper, office equipment, films & photo equipment.

Azon Canada Inc., 6420 rue Abrams, Montreal, PQ, Canada H4L 4Y1

Tel: 514-335-3410

BAILEY-FISCHER & PORTER COMPANY

125 East County Line Road, Warminster, PA, 18974

Tel: (215) 674-6000 Fax: (215) 441-5280

Design/mfr. measure, recording & control instruments & systems; mfr. industrial glass products.

Bailey-Fischer & Porter (Canada) Ltd., 134 Norfinch Dr., Downsview, ON M3N 1X7, Canada

BAIN & CO., INC.

Two Copley Place, Boston, MA, 02116

Tel: (617) 572-2000 Fax: (617) 572-2427 Web site: www.bain.com

Strategic management consulting services.

Bain & Co. Canada Inc., 162 Cumberland St., Ste. 235, Toronto, ON M5R 3N5, Canada

Tel: 416-929-1888 Fax: 416-929-3470

BAKER & McKENZIE

One Prudential Plaza, 130 East Randolph Drive, Ste. 2500, Chicago, IL, 60601

Tel: (312) 861-8000 Fax: (312) 861-2899 Web site: www.bakerinfo.com

International legal services.

Baker & McKenzie, BCE Place, 181 Bay St., Ste. 2100, POB 874, Toronto, ON M5J 2T3 Canada

Tel: 416-863-1221 Fax: 416-863-6275

BAKER HUGHES INCORPORATED

3900 Essex Lane, Ste. 1200, Houston, TX, 77027

Tel: (713) 439-8600 Fax: (713) 439-8699 Web site: www.bakerhughes.com

Develop & apply technology to drill, complete & produce oil and natural gas wells; provide separation systems to petroleum, municipal, continuous process & mining industries.

Baker Oil Tools, 1300 401, 9th Ave. SW, Calgary, AB, T2P 3C5, Canada

Tel: 403-296-9600 Fax: 403-296-9699

Baker Oil Tools, 811 103 St., Fort St. John, BC V1J 5R, Canada

Tel: 250-785-3975 Fax: 250-785-5990

Baker Oil Tools, 620-1 Ave. East, Brooks, AB T1R 1C3 Canada

Tel: 403-362-4232 Fax: 403-362-8159

J.T. BAKER INC.

222 Red School Lane, Phillipsburg, NJ, 08865

Tel: (908) 859-2151 Fax: (908) 859-9318

Mfr./sale/services lab & process chemicals.

J.T. Baker, PO Box 355, Station A, Toronto, ON M5W 1C5, Canada

BAKER PETROLITE CORPORATION

3900 Essex Lane, Houston, TX, 77027

Tel: (713) 599-7400 Fax: (713) 599-7592

Mfr./prod specialty chemical treating programs, performance-enhancing additives & related equipment & services.

Petrolite Canada Inc., Nisku, AF, Canada: All mail to U.S. address.

BALL CORPORATION

345 South High Street, Muncie, IN, 47305

Tel: (765) 747-6100 Fax: (765) 747-6203

Mfr. metal beverage & food containers, glass containers, aerospace systems & services.

Ball Packaging Products Canada Inc., Mainway Dr., Burlington, ON L7M 1A3, Canada

BANANA REPUBLIC

2 Harrison Street, San Francisco, CA, 94105

Tel: (415) 777-0250 Fax: (415) 960-0322

Sales/distribution of clothing, shoes & handbags.

Banana Republic, Etobicoke, Canada

Banana Republic, Calgary, Canada

Banana Republic, Vancouver, BC, Canada

Banana Republic, Toronto, ON, Canada

Banana Republic, Edmondton, Canada

BANDAG INC.

2905 NW Highway 61, Muscatine, IA, 52761

Tel: (319) 262-1400 Fax: (319) 262-1252

Mfr./sale retread tires.

Bandag Canada Ltd., 5230 14th Ave., Shawinigan, PQ G9N 6V9, Canada

THE BANK OF NEW YORK

48 Wall Street, New York, NY, 10286

Tel: (212) 495-1784 Fax: (212) 495-2546 Web site: www.bankofny.com

Banking servces.

BNY Financial Corp. Canada, 500 Ouest Blvd. Rene-Levesque, Bureau 1400, Montreal, PQ H2Z 1W7, Canada

Tel: 514-397-9800

BANKAMERICA CORPORATION

555 California Street, San Francisco, CA, 94104

Tel: (415) 622-3530 Fax: (415) 622-8467 Web site: www.bankamerica.com

Financial services.

Bank of America Canada, 200 Front St. West, Ste. 2700, Toronto, ON M5V 3L2, Canada

Tel: 416-349-4100 Fax: 416-349-4285 Contact: Alfred P. Buhler, CEO

BANKERS TRUST COMPANY

280 Park Ave., New York, NY, 10017

Tel: (212) 250-2500 Fax: (212) 250-2440 Web site: www.bankerstrust.com

Banking & investment services.

Bankers Trust Co. Intl., 500 ouest, blvd, René-Lévesque, Bureau 1500, Montréal, PQ H2Z 1W7, Canada

Tel: 514-874-0781 Fax: 514-874-1218 Contact: Jacques Pinsonnault, Mng. Dir.

Bankers Trust Co. Intl., 2005, 421 7th Ave. S.W., Calgary, AB T2P 4K9, Canada

Tel: 403-233-2474 Fax: 403-266-6244 Contact: Calvin Schlenker, VP

BT Bank of Canada, Royal Bank Plaza, North Tower, Toronto, ON M5J 2J2, Canada

Tel: 416-865-0770 Fax: 416-865-0779 Contact: Harvey Naglie, Pres. & CEO

C.R. BARD INC.

730 Central Ave., Murray Hill, NJ, 07974

Tel: (908) 277-8000 Fax: (908) 277-8078 Web site: www.crbard.com

Mfr. health care products.

Bard Canada Inc., 2345 Stanfield Rd., Mississauga, ON L4Y 3Y3, Canada

BARNES GROUP INC.

123 Main Street, Bristol, CT, 06011-0489

Tel: (860) 583-7070 Fax: (860) 589-3507 Web site: www.barnesgroupinc.com

Mfr. steel springs, metal parts & supplies.

Associated Spring, Burlington, ON, Canada

Bowman Distribution, Concord (ON), Edmonton (AB), Moncton (NB) & St. Laurent (PQ), Canada

BARNWELL INDUSTRIES INC.

1100 Alakea Street, Ste. 2900, Honolulu, HI, 96813-2833

Tel: (808) 531-8400 Fax: (808) 531-7181 Web site: www.brninc.con

Holding company: exploration/development gas & oil, drill water systems, farming/marketing papayas.

Barnwell of Canada Ltd., 639 5th Ave. SW #1120, Calgary, AB T2P 0M9, Canada

Contact: James H. Boyle

BARRINGER TECHNOLOGIES INC.

219 South Street, New Providence, NJ, 07974

Tel: (908) 665-8200 Fax: (908) 665-8298 Web site: www.barringer.com

Physical research & testing, engineering services, oil & gas exploration.

Barringer Instruments Ltd., Mississauga, ON, Canada

Tel: 905-238-8837 Fax: 905-238-3018

BASSETT MIRROR CO., INC.

PO Box 627, Basset, VA, 24055

Tel: (540) 629-3341 Fax: (540) 629-3709

Mfr. glass products, metal & upholstered household furniture.

Roy Industries Ltd., 90 rue Marmette, Montmagny, PQ G5V 3S5, Canada

BATES WORLDWIDE INC.

405 Lexington Ave., New York, NY, 10174

Tel: (212) 297-7000 Fax: (212) 986-0270 Web site: www.batesww.com

Advertising, marketing, public relations & media consulting.

Armada Bates, Inc., 480 Boulevaard St. Laurent, Ste. 200, Montreal, PQ, H2Y 3Y7, Canada

Tel: 514-284-6191 Contact: Jacques Chalifour, Pres.

Bates Canada Inc., 2 St. Clair Ave. West, Toronto, ON, M4V 1LS, Canada

Tel: 416-925-8835 Fax: 416-925-1208 Contact: Patrick Knisley, Pres.

BATTENFELD GREASE & OIL CORP. OF NY

1174 Erie Ave., Box 728, North Tonawanda, NY, 14120-0728

Tel: (716) 695-2100 Fax: (716) 695-0367 Web site: www.battenfeld-grease.com

Mfr. petrol products, lubricating greases & oils.

Battenfeld Grease (Canada) Ltd., 68 Titan Rd., Toronto, ON M8Z 2J8, Canada

Tel: 416-239-1548 Fax: 416-239-3449 Contact: John A. Bellanti Emp: 25

BAUSCH & LOMB INC.

One Bausch & Lomb Place, Rochester, NY, 14604-2701

Tel: (716) 338-6000 Fax: (716) 338-6007 Web site: www.bausch.com

Mfr. vision care products & accessories & hearing aids.

Bausch & Lomb Canada Inc., Locations in Toronto, Ontario and Montreal, PQ, Canada

Charles River Canada, Inc., St. Constant, PQ, Canada

BAX GLOBAL CORPORATION

16808 Armstrong Ave., PO Box 19571, Irvine, CA, 92623

Tel: (714) 752-4000 Fax: (714) 852-1488 Web site: www.bax.com

Air freight forwarder.

BAX Global, 140 Thad Johnson Rd., Bay 2, Gloucester, ON K1V 0R4, Canada

Tel: 613-526-1684 Fax: 613-526-3844

BAX Global - Montreal, 768 Stuart Graham, Ste. 132, Montreal International Airport, Dorval, PQ H4Y 1E7, Canada

Tel: 514-636-6350 Fax: 514-636-6361

BAX Global - Toronto, 6400 Viking Drive, Air Cargo Bldg. "E", Pearson Int'l Airport, Mississauga, ON, L5P 1B2, Canada

Tel: 905-677-9067 Fax: 905-677-2152

BAX Global - Vancouver, 4831 "A" Miller Rd. #102, Richmond, BC, V7B 1Y1, Canada

Tel: 604-270-6282 Fax: 604-270-0327

J.H. BAXTER & COMPANY

1700 S. El Camino Real, Ste. 200, San Mateo, CA, 94402-5902

Tel: (650) 349-0201 Fax: (650) 570-6878

Pressure treated poles, piling & lumber.

J.H. Baxter & Co. Ltd., 361 Albert St., PO Box 278, Nanaimo, BC, Canada

BAXTER HEALTHCARE CORPORATION

One Baxter Parkway, Deerfield, IL, 60015

Tel: (847) 948-2000 Fax: (847) 948-3948 Web site: www.baxter.com

Pharmaceutical preparations, surgical/medical instruments & cardiovascular products.

Baxter Corp. (Eastern Region HQ), 6800 Trans Canada Hwy., Pointe Claire, PQ H9R 5L4, Canada

Baxter Corp. (Western Region HQ), 8590 Baxter Pl., Burnady, BC V5A 4T2, Canada

Baxter Diagnostics, 2360 Argentina Rd., Mississauga , ON L5N 5Z7, Canada

BBDO WORLDWIDE

1285 Ave. of the Americas, New York, NY, 10019

Tel: (212) 459-5000 Fax: (212) 459-6645 Web site: www.bbdo.com

Multinational group of advertising agencies.

BBDO Canada, Toronto, ON, Canada

Ross Roy Communications Canada, Windsor, ON,Canada

BDO SEIDMAN, LLP

Two Prudential Plaza, 180 N. Stetson Ave., Ste. 2300, Chicago, IL, 60601

Tel: (312) 240-1236 Fax: (312) 240-3329 Web site: www.bdo.com

International accounting & financial consulting firm.

BDO Dunwoody, PO Box 32, Royal Bank Plaza,33rd Fl., South Tower, 200 Bay St., Toronto, ON M5J 2J8, Canada

Tel: 416-865-0111 Fax: 416-367-3912 Contact: Peter E. Held

BEA SYSTEMS, INC.

2315 North First Street, St. Jose, CA, 95131

Tel: (408) 570-8000 Fax: (408) 570-8091 Web site: www.beasys.com

Develops communications management software & provider of software consulting services.

BEA Systems, Inc., 4255 Sherwoodtowne Blvd., Ste. 320, Mississauga (Toronto), ON L4Z1Y5, Canada

Tel: 905-277-4600 Fax: 905-277-2011

D. D. BEAN & SONS COMPANY

Peterborough Road, PO Box 348, Jaffrey, NH, 03452

Tel: (603) 532-8311 Fax: (603) 532-7361

Mfr. paper book & wooden stick matches.

D.D. Bean & Sons (Canada) Ltd., 1850 Union St., St. Cesaire, PQ J0L 1T0, Canada

BEARIUM METALS CORPORATION

4106 South Creek Road, Chattanooga, TN, 37406

Tel: (423) 622-9991 Fax: (423) 622-9991

Bearium metal alloys.

Gamma Foundries Ltd., 75 Newkirk Rd., Richmond Hill, ON L4C 3G4, Canada

BECHTEL GROUP INC.

50 Beale Street, PO Box 3965, San Francisco, CA, 94105-1895

Tel: (415) 768-1234 Fax: (415) 768-9038 Web site: www.bechtel.com

General contractors in engineering & construction.

Bechtel Canada Ltd., 10123 99th St., Edmonton, AB T5J 2P4, Canada

Bechtel International Corp., 12 Concorde Place, Ste. 200, North York, ON M3C 3T1, Canada

Tel: 416-441-4900 Fax: 416-441-4900

Bechtel International Corp., 500 Rene-Levesque Blvd., West Ste. 1503, Montreal, PQ H2Z1 W7, Canada

Tel: 514-871-1711 Fax: 514-871-1392

BECKMAN COULTER

4300 Harbor Boulevard, Fullerton, CA, 92835

Tel: (714) 871-4848 Fax: (714) 773-8898

Develop/mfr./marketing automated systems & supplies for biological analysis.

Beckman Coulter Instruments (Canada) Inc., 1045 Tristar Dr., Mississauga, ON L5T 1W5, Canada

BECTON DICKINSON AND COMPANY

One Becton Drive, Franklin Lakes, NJ, 07417-1880

Tel: (201) 847-6800 Fax: (201) 847-6475

Mfr./sale medical supplies, devices & diagnostic systems.

Becton Dickinson Canada, 2464 S. Sheridan Way, Mississauga, ON L5J 2M8, Canada

BELCO OIL & GAS CORPORATION

767 Fifth Ave., 46th Floor, New York, NY, 10153

Tel: (212) 644-2200 Fax: (212) 644-2230

Exploration & production of crude oil & natural gas.

Andex Oil Co. Ltd., 1300 700 Ninth Ave. SW, Calgary, AB T2P 3V4, Canada

BELDEN WIRE & CABLE COMPANY

2200 US Highway South, PO Box 1980, Richmond, IN, 47374

Tel: (765) 983-5200 Fax: (765) 983-5294 Web site: www.belden.com

Mfr. electronic wire & cable products.

Belden (Canada) Inc., 130 Willmott St., Cobourg, ON, Canada K9A 4M3

BELL & HOWELL COMPANY

5215 Old Orchard Road, Skokie, IL, 60077

Tel: (847) 470-7100 Fax: (847) 470-9625 Web site: www.bellhowell.com

Diversified information products & services.

Bell & Howell Ltd., 230 Barmac Dr., Weston, ON M9L 2X5, Canada

BELL HELICOPTER TEXTRON INC.

PO Box 482, Fort Worth, TX, 76101

Tel: (817) 280-2011 Fax: (817) 280-2321

Mfr./sale/service helicopters, air cushion vehicles and rocket engines.

Bell Helicopter Textron Canada Ltd., 12800 rue de L'Avenir, Mirabel, PQ, Canada J7J 1R4

Tel: 514-437-3400 Fax: 514-437-6010 Contact: Robert MaDonald, Pres.

BELL POLE LTD

PO Box 2786, New Brighton, MN, 55112

Tel: (612) 633-4334 Fax: (612) 633-8852

Mfr. poles.

Bell Pole Co. Ltd., PO Box 339, Lumby, BC, Canada

Tel: 250-547-2131 Contact: Ken Stewart, Pres.

BEMIS CO., INC.

222 South 9th Street, Ste. 2300, Minneapolis, MN, 55402-4099

Tel: (612) 376-3000 Fax: (612) 376-3180

Mfr. flexible packaging, specialty coated & graphics products.

Curwood Packaging (Canada) Ltd., 114 Armstrong Ave., Georgetown, ON L7G 4S2, Canada

MACtac Canada Ltd., 100 Kennedy Rd. S, Brampton, ON L6W 3E8, Canada

BEN & JERRY'S HOMEMADE INC.

30 Community Drive, South Burlington, VT, 05403-6828

Tel: (802) 651-9600 Fax: (802) 651-9647 Web site: www.benjerry.com

Premium ice cream.

Ben & Jerry's International, 255 East Knowlton Rd., Knowlton, PQ JOE-1V0, Canada

Tel: 514-242-1361

Ben & Jerry's International, 1316 De Maisonneauve St. West, Montreal, PQ H3G-2B, Canada

Tel: 514-286-6073

Ben & Jerry's International, 5582 Monkland Ave., Montreal, PQ H4A-1C, Canada

Tel: 514-488-6524

Ben & Jerry's International, 433 Place Jacques Cartier, Montreal, PQ H2Y-3B1, Canada

Tel: 514-876-4121

BENJAMIN MOORE & COMPANY

51 Chestnut Ridge Road, Montvale, NJ, 07645

Tel: (201) 573-9600 Fax: (201) 573-9046

Mfr. paints and varnishes.

Benjamin Moore & Co. Ltd., Mulock & Lloyd Aves., Toronto, ON, Canada

BENSHAW INC.

1659 East Sutter Road, Glenshaw, PA, 15116

Tel: (412) 487-8235 Fax: (412) 487-4201

Mfr. solid state A/C motor controls.

Benshaw Canada, Wallace Industrial Park, RR #1, Listowel, ON N4W 3G6, Canada

Tel: 519-291-5112

BENTLY NEVADA CORPORATION

1617 Water Street, PO Box 157, Minden, NV, 89423

Tel: (702) 782-3611 Fax: (702) 782-9259

Electronic monitoring systems.

Bently Nevada Canada Ltd., 70 Gibson Dr., Unit 4, Markham, ON L3R 2Z3, Canada

Bently Nevada Canada Ltd., PO Box 233, Nisku, AB T0C 2G0, Canada

LOUIS BERGER INTERNATIONAL INC.

100 Halsted Street, East Orange, NJ, 07019

Tel: (201) 678-1960 Fax: (201) 672-4284 Web site: www.louisberger.com

Consulting engineers, architects, economists & planners.

Louis Berger (Canada) Inc., Purdy's Wharf Business Centre, Ltd., 1959 Upper Water St.,#407, Halifax, NS B3J3N2 Canada

Tel: 902-423-1288 Fax: 902-422-2388

BERNARD HODES GROUP

555 Madison Ave., New York, NY, 10022

Tel: (212) 935-4000 Fax: (212) 755-7324 Web site: www.hodes.com

Multinational recruitment agency.

Bernard Hodes Advertising, Toronto, ON, Canada

BESSER COMPANY

801 Johnson Street, PO Box 336, Alpena, MI, 49707

Tel: (517) 354-4111 Fax: (517) 354-3120

Mfr. equipment for concrete products industry; complete turnkey services.

Besser Canada Ltd., 387 Orenda Rd., Bramalea, ON L6T 1G4, Canada

Proneq Industries Inc., 300 12th Ave., Ville des Laurentides, Quebec City, PQ J0R 1C0, Canada

BEST LOCK CORPORATION

6161 East 75th Street, Indianapolis, IN, 46250

Tel: (317) 849-2250 Fax: (317) 841-9852

Mfr. locking systems.

Best Universal Lock Ltd., 1155 Fewster Dr., Mississauga, ON L4W 1A2, Canada

Tel: 905-625-6941

BEST WESTERN INTERNATIONAL

6201 North 24th Place, Phoenix, AZ, 85106

Tel: (602) 957-4200 Fax: (602) 957-5740

International hotel chain.

Best Western Metro Inn, 212 Kingston Rd., Toronto, ON M1N 1T5, Canada

Tel: 416-267-1141

BESTFOODS, INC.

700 Sylvan Ave., International Plaza, Englewood Cliffs, NJ, 07632-9976

Tel: (201) 894-4000 Fax: (201) 894-2186 Web site: www.bestfoods.com

Consumer foods products; corn refining.

Bestfoods Foodservice Canada, 401 The West Mall, Etobiocoke, ON M9C 5H9, Canada

Tel: 416-620-2310 Fax: 416-620-3464 Contact: William N. Gallie, VP Mgr.

BETZDEARBORN

4636 Somerton Road, PO Box 3002, Trevose, PA, 19053-6783

Tel: (215) 953-2568 Fax: (215) 953-5524 Web site: www.betzdearborn.com

Mfr. water/wastewater and process system treatment chemicals and services.

BetzDearborn Canada, Inc., 3451 Erindale Station Rd., Mississauga, ON L5C 2S9, Canada

SAMUEL BINGHAM COMPANY

127 East Lake Street, Ste. 300, Bloomgindale, IL, 60108

Tel: (630) 924-9250 Fax: (630) 924-0469 Web site: www.binghamrollers.com

Print and industrial rollers and inks.

Bingham Company Canada Ltd., 52 Advance Rd., Toronto, ON M8Z 2T7, Canada

Tel: 416-239-8157

Samuel Bingham (Canada) Ltd., 13,100 Blvd. Metropolitain E, Montreal, PQ, Canada H1A 4A7

BINKS MFG. COMPANY

9201 West Belmont Ave., Franklin Park, IL, 60131

Tel: (708) 671-3000 Fax: (708) 671-6489

Mfr. of spray painting and finishing equipment.

Binks Mfg. Co., 14 Vansco Rd., Toronto, ON M8Z 5J5, Canada

BINNEY & SMITH INC.

1100 Church Lane, PO Box 431, Easton, PA, 18044-0431

Tel: (610) 253-6271 Fax: (610) 250-5768

Mfr. rayons, art supplies and craft kits.

Binney & Smith (Canada) Ltd., 15 Mary St. W, Lindsay, ON K9V 4R8, Canada

BIO-RAD LABORATORIES INC.

1000 Alfred Nobel Drive, Hercules, CA, 94547

Tel: (510) 724-7000 Fax: (510) 724-3167

Mfr. life science research products, clinical diagnostics, analytical instruments.

Bio-Rad Laboratories Ltd., Mississauga & Ottawa, Canada

BIOMATRIX INC.

65 Railroad Ave., Ridgefield, NJ, 07657

Tel: (201) 945-9550 Fax: (201) 945-0363 Web site: www.biomatrix.com

Mfr. hylan biological polymers for therapeutic medical and skin care products.

Biomatrix Medical Canada Inc., 275 Ave. Labrosse, Pointe-Clarie, PQ H9R 1A3, Canada

Tel: 514-697-8851 Fax: 514-697-3670 Contact: Danielle Grenon, Adm. Mgr. Emp: 74

BIRD MACHINE CORPORATION

PO Box 9103, South Walpole, MA, 02071

Tel: (508) 668-0400 Fax: (508) 668-6855 Web site: www.Baker Hughes.com

Mfr. of liquid solid separation equipment.

Bird Machine Co. of Canada Ltd., 2600 Wentz Ave., Saskatoon, SK 5K7 2L1, Canada

Tel: 306-931-0801 Fax: 306-931-2442 Contact: Bob Pritchers, Gen. Mgr. Emp: 40

BIW CABLE SYSTEMS INC.

22 Joseph E. Warner Boulevard, N. Dighton, MA, 02764-O6O4

Tel: (508) 822-5444 Fax: (508) 822-1944

Mfr. Electric wire, cable, cable assemblies and connectors.

BIW Cable Systems Inc., 1800 Ironstone Dr., Burlington, ON L7L SV3, Canada

BLACK & DECKER CORPORATION

701 E. Joppa Road, Towson, MD, 21286

Tel: (410) 716-3900 Fax: (410) 716-2933 Web site: www.blackanddecker.com

Mfr. power tools and accessories, security hardware, small appliances, fasteners, information systems & services.

Black & Decker Canada, Canada - All mail to U.S. address.

BLACK BOX CORPORATION

1000 Park Drive, Lawrence, PA, 15055

Tel: (724) 746-5500 Fax: (724) 746-0746 Web site: www.blackbox.com

Direct marketer and technical service provider of communications, networking and related computer connectivity products.

Black Box Canada Corp., Unit 13, 1111 Flint Rd., North York, ON M3J 3C7, Canada

Tel: 416-736-8000 Fax: 416-736-7348 Contact: Raymond Lau, Gen. Mgr.

BLAKESLEE

1844 South Laramie Ave., Chicago, IL, 60804

Tel: (708) 656-0660 Fax: (708) 656-0017

Food mixers, food preparation equipment and commercial dishwashers.

Blakeslee Food Service Equipment, Inc., 66 Crockford Blvd., Scarborough, ON MIR 3C3, Canada

BLISS & LAUGHLIN STEEL COMPANY

281 East 155th Street, Harvey, IL, 60426

Tel: (708) 333-1220 Fax:

Mfr. steel bars for industrial use.

Bliss & Laughlin Steel Co., Canada

H&R BLOCK, INC.

4400 Main Street, Kansas City, MO, 64111

Tel: (816) 753-6900 Fax: (816) 753-8628 Web site: www.hrblock.com

Tax preparation services & software, financial products and services & mortgage loans.

Cashplan Systems, Inc., #205, 3112 - 11th St., NE, Calgary, AB T2E 7J1, Canada

Contact: Arthur Arnott & Ozzie Wenich

H&R Block (Nova Scotia) Incorporated, 5445 Rainnie Drive, Halifax, NS B3J 1P8, Canada

Contact: James H. Ingraham

H&R Block Canada Incorporated, 340 Midpark Way SE, Ste. 200, Calgary, AB T2X 1P1, Canada

Tel: 403-254-8689 Fax: 403-254-9949 Contact: David T. Robottom

H&R Block Inc., 3440 Pharmacy, Scarborough, ON M1W 2P8, Canada

Two Dog Ranch Ltd., 525 South Terminal Ave., Namaino, BC V9R 5G1 Canada

Contact: J. Bonar Irving & Robert Newans

BLOUNT INC.

4520 Executive Park Drive, Montgomery, AL, 36116-1602

Tel: (334) 244-4000 Fax: (334) 271-8130 Web site: www.blount.com

Mfr. cutting chain & equipment, timber harvest/handling equipment, sporting ammo, riding mowers.

Blount Canada Ltd., 505 Edinburgh Rd. N, Guelph, ON N1H 6L4, Canada

Tel: 519-822-6870 Fax: 519-822-1450 Contact: Nicholas Galovich, Gen. Mgr.

Blount Holdings Ltd., 505 Edinburgh Rd. N, Guelph, ON N1H 6L4, Canada

Tel: 519-822-6870 Fax: 519-822-1450 Contact: Nicholas Galovich, Gen. Mgr.

BLUE BIRD CORPORATION

3920 Arkwright Road, PO Box 7839, Macon, GA, 31210

Tel: (912) 757-7100 Fax: (912) 474-9131

Mfr./sale/services buses, parts and accessories.

Canadian Blue Bird Sales Co., PO Box 880, Brantford, ON, Canada

BOART LONGYEAR CO.

2340 West 1700 South, Salt Lake City, UT, 84104

Tel: (801) 972-6430 Fax: (801) 977-3372

Mfr. diamond drills, concrete cutting equipment and drill services.

Canadian Longyear Ltd., PO Box 330, 1111 Main St. W, North Bay, ON P1B 8H6, Canada

N. Morissette Diamond Drilling Ltd., PO Box 789, Haileybury, ON P0J 1K0, Canada

BOISE CASCADE CORPORATION

1111 West Jefferspm Street, PO Box 50, Boise, ID, 83728-0001

Tel: (208) 384-6161 Fax: (208) 384-7189 Web site: www.bc.com

Mfr./distributor paper and paper products, building products, office products.

Boise Cascade Office Products, Ltd., Montreal, PQ, Canada

Boise Cascade Office Products, Ltd., Toronto, Canada

Boise Cascade Office Products, Ltd., Calgary, Canada

BOND FOUNDRY & MACHINE COMPANY

230 South Penn Street, Manheim, PA, 17545

Tel: (717) 665-2275 Fax: (717) 665-3336

Transmission appliances.

Bond Engineering Works Ltd., 35 Booth Ave., Toronto, ON M5M 2M3, Canada

BOOK-OF-THE-MONTH CLUB INC.

1271 Ave. of the Americas, New York, NY, 10020

Tel: (212) 522-4200 Fax: (212) 522-0303 Web site: www.bomc.com

Retail books to mail subscribers; phonograph records, art and reading courses.

Book-of-the-Month Club (Canada) Ltd., c/o O.E. McIntyre Ltd., 19 W. More Dr., Toronto, ON M9V 4M3, Canada

BOOZ ALLEN & HAMILTON INC.

8283 Greensboro Drive, McLean, VA, 22102

Tel: (703) 902-5000 Fax: (703) 902-3333 Web site: www.bah.com

International management and technology consultants.

Booz Allen & Hamilton Canada, 1200 McGill College, Ste. 1100, Montreal, PQ H3B 4G7, Canada

Tel: 514-875-8180 Fax: 514-393-9069

BORDEN INC.

180 East Broad Street, Columbus, OH, 43215-3799

Tel: (614) 225-4000 Fax: (614) 220-6453

Mfr. Packaged foods, consumer adhesives, housewares and industrial chemicals.

Borden Chemical Canada - Forest Products, 1550 Rand Ave., Vancouver, BC V6P 6C5, Canada

Tel: 604-261-9356 Fax: 604-263-2329

BORG-WARNER AUTOMOTIVE INC.

200 S. Michigan Ave., Chicago, IL, 60604

Tel: (312) 322-8500 Fax: (312) 461-0507

Mfr. automotive components; provider of security services.

Borg-Warner Automotive (Canada) Ltd., 385 Second Ave., Simcoe, ON N3Y 4L5, Canada

BORG-WARNER SECURITY CORPORATION

200 S. Michigan Ave., Chicago, IL, 60604

Tel: (312) 322-8500 Fax: (312) 322-8398

Security services.

Burns Intl. Security Services Ltd., 55 Bloor St. W #261, Toronto, ON M4W 1A5, Canada

Les Services de Protection Burns Intl. Ltee., 1075 Bay St., Toronto, ON M5S 2B1, Canada

BOSE CORPORATION

The Mountain, Framingham, MA, 01701-9168

Tel: (508) 879-7330 Fax: (508) 766-7543

Mfr. quality audio equipment/speakers.

Bose Ltd., Sainte-Marie, Beauce, PQ, Canada

Bose Ltd., 8-35 E. Beaver Creek Rd., Richmond Hill, ON L4B 1B3, Canada

BOSS MANUFACTURING COMPANY

221 West First Street, Kewanee, IL, 61443

Tel: (309) 852-2131 Fax: (309) 852-0848

Safety products, protective clothing and sport/work gloves.

Boss Canada, 53 Woodbridge Ave., Weston, ON L4L 2S6, Canada

THE BOSTON CONSULTING GROUP

Exchange Place, 31st Floor, Boston, MA, 02109

Tel: (617) 973-1200 Fax: (617) 973-1339 Web site: www.bcg.com

Management consulting company.

The Boston Consulting Group, BCE Place, 181 Bay St., Ste. 2400, PO Box 783, Toronto, ON M5J 2T3, Canada

Tel: 416-955-4200

BOSTON GEAR

14 Hayward Street, North Quincy, MA, 02171

Tel: (617) 328-3300 Fax: (617) 479-6238 Web site: www.Boston.Gear.Industry.Net

Mfr. car bearings and electrical products.

Boston Gear of Canada, Ltd., 2790 Slough St., Mississauga, ON L4T IG2, Canada

Tel: 905-625-1246

ESB Canada, Ltd., 104 58th Ave., SE, Calgary, AB T2H ON7, Canada

BOSTON SCIENTIFIC CORPORATION

One Scientific Place, Natick, MA, 01760-1537

Tel: (508) 650-8000 Fax: (508) 650-8923 Web site: www.bsci.com

Mfr./distributes medical devices for use in minimally invasive surgeries.

Boston Scientific Ltd., 350 Traders Blvd., East Mississauga, ON L4Z 1W7, Canada

Tel: 905-501-0350 Fax: 905-501-0440

BOWATER INC.

55 East Camperdown Way, Greenville, SC, 29601

Tel: (864) 271-7733 Fax: (864) 282-9482 Web site: www.bowater.com

Paper manufacturing.

Bowater/Mersey Paper Company, Ltd., 3691 Highway 3, PO Box 1150, Liverpool, NS, BOT 1KO Canada

Tel: 902-354-3411

BOWEN TOOLS INC.

PO Box 3186, Houston, TX, 77253-3186

Tel: (713) 868-8888 Fax: (713) 868-8775

Mfr. drilling & specialty tools for oil/gas industry.

Bowen Tools Ltd., North Bldg., 2nd Fl., 4080 78th Ave., Edmonton, BA T6B 3M8, Canada

BOWES INDUSTRIES

5902 East 34th Street, Indianapolis, IN, 46218

Tel: (317) 547-5245 Fax: (317) 545-7683

Mfr. automotive accessories.

Bowes Industries, 765 Woodward Ave., PO Box 3275, Station C, Hamilton, ON, Canada

Tel: 905-545-5865

BOYDEN CONSULTING CORPORATION

100 Park Ave., 34th Floor, New York, NY, 10017

Tel: (212) 980-6534 Fax: (212) 980-6147 Web site: www.boyden.com

Executive search.

Boyden Associates Ltd., 130 Adelaide St. West, Ste. 2000, Toronto ,ON M5H 3P5, Canada
Tel: 416-863-0153

Boyden Associates Ltd., 1250, blvd Rene-Levesque ouest, Bureau 4110, Montreal, PQ H3B 4W8, Canada
Tel: 514-935-4560

Boyden Associates Ltd., 2200, 520 - 5th Ave. SW, Calgary, AB T2P 3R7, Canada
Tel: 403-237-6603

Boyden Associates Ltd., 2610 Limestone Place, Coquitlam, BC V3E 2V1, Canada
Tel: 604-944-8081

BOZELL WORLDWIDE

40 West 23rd Street, New York, NY, 10010
Tel: (212) 727-5000 Fax: (212) 645-9173 Web site: www.bozell.com
Advertising, marketing, public relations and media consulting.

Bozell Worldwide, Canada Inc., 121 Bloor St., 10th Fl., Toronto, ON M4W 3M5, Canada
Tel: 416-961-9595 Fax: 416-961-9090 Contact: Liz Torleé, Pres.

Bozell Worldwide, Canada, Inc., 360 Notre Dame West, Ste. 500, Montreal, PQ H2Y 1T9 Canada
Tel: 514-281-1911 Fax: 514-281-9249 Contact: Liz Torleé, Pres.

W. H. BRADY CO.

6555 W. Good Hope Road, Milwaukee, WI, 53223
Tel: (414) 358-6600 Fax: Web site: www.whbrady.com
Mfr. industrial ID for wire marking, circuit boards; facility ID, signage, printing systems & software.

WHB Identification Solutions Inc., 56 Leek Crescent, Richmond Hill, ON L4B 1H1, Canada
Tel: 905-764-1717 Fax: 905-764-5557 Contact: Tracey Carpentier, VP & Gen. Mgr.

BRANSON ULTRASONICS CORPORATION

41 Eagle Road, Danbury, CT, 06813-1961
Tel: (203) 796-0400 Fax: (203) 796-2285
Mfr. plastics assembly equipment, ultrasonic cleaning equipment.

Branson Ultrasonics (Div. Of Emerson Electric Canada, Ltd.), 9999 Markham Rd., Dock 1 or 2, Markham, ON L3P 3J6, Canada
Tel: 905-475-4640 Fax: 905-475-4637

C.F. BRAUN & COMPANY

4175 Whitmore Lake Road, Ann Arbor, MI, 48105
Tel: (734) 663-1040 Fax: (734) 663-1403
Engineering/construction/management for energy and power industrial.

PCL-Braun-Simons Ltd., 1015 4th St. SW, Calgary, AB T2R 1J4, Canada

W. BRAUN COMPANY

300 North Canal Street, Chicago, IL, 60606
Tel: (312) 346-6500 Fax: (312) 346-9643
Design/mfr./supply packaging.

Braun Canada, 215 Shields Ct., Markham, ON L3R 8V2, Canada

BRINK'S INC.

Thorndal Circle, Darien, CT, 06820
Tel: (203) 662-7800 Fax: (203) 662-7968 Web site: www.brinks.com
Security transportation.

Brink's Canada, Toronto, ON, Canada
Contact: Gary K. Garton, Pres.

BRISTOL BABCOCK INC.

1100 Buckingham Street, Watertown, CT, 06795

Tel: (203) 575-3000 Fax: (203) 575-3170

Mfr. process control instruments and SCADA systems.

Bristol of Canada, 234 Attwell Dr., Rexdale, Toronto, ON M9W 5B3, Canada

BRISTOL-MYERS SQUIBB COMPANY

345 Park Ave., New York, NY, 10154

Tel: (212) 546-4000 Fax: (212) 546-4020 Web site: www.bms.com

Pharmaceutical and food preparations, medical and surgical instruments.

Bristol-Myers Squibb - Montreal, 2000 McGill College Ave., Montreal, PQ H3A 3H3,Canada

Bristol-Myers Squibb - Ontario, 2525 Queensview Drive, Ottawa, ON K2A 3YA Canada

Matrix (Canada), Canada - c/o Matrix USA, 30701 Carter St., Solon, Ohio 44139 USA

Mead Johnson of Canada, 231 Dundas St. East, Belleville, ON, Canada

Zimmer of Canada Ltd., 2323 Argentia Rd., Mississauga, ON, Canada

BRK BRANDS/FIRST ALERT, INC.

3901 Liberty Street Road, Aurora, IL, 60504-8122

Tel: (630) 851-7330 Fax: (630) 851-1331

Mfr. smoke detectors, fire extinguishers, lights, timers & sensor systems.

BRK Brands Canada, 6650 Finch Ave. W, Rexdale, ON M9W 5Y6, Canada

BRODART COMPANY

500 Arch Street, Williamsport, PA, 17705

Tel: (717) 326-2461 Fax: (717) 326-3039 Web site: www.brodart.com

Mfr./distributor/services library books, supplies, furniture and automation products.

Brodart Industries Canada, 109 Roy Blvd., Brantford, ON N3T 5N3, Canada

Brodart of Canada Ltd., 109 Roy Blvd., Brantford, ON N3T 5N3, Canada

Dart Realty, 109 Roy Blvd., Brantford, ON N3T 5N3, Canada

BROWN & ROOT INC.

4100 Clinton Drive, Houston, TX, 77020-6299

Tel: (713) 676-3011 Fax: (713) 676-8532

Engineering, construction and maintenance.

Brown & Root Ltd., PO Box 5588, Edmonton, AB T6C 4E9, Canada

Mid-Valley Industrial Services, 910 Rowntree Dairy Rd., Unit 27, Woodbridge, ON L4L 5W6, Canada

SRB Offshore Ltd., PO Box 9600, St. John's, NFA1A 3C1, Canada

BROWN-FORMAN CORPORATION

PO Box 1080, Louisville, KY, 40201-1080

Tel: (502) 585-1100 Fax: (502) 774-7876 Web site: www.brown-forman.com

Mfr./distributor distilled spirits, wine, china, crystal, silverware and luggage.

Canadian Mist Distillers Ltd., 202 MacDonald Rd., Collingwood, ON L9Y 4J2, Canada

BROWNING CORPORATION

1 Browning Place, Morgan, UT, 84050

Tel: (801) 876-2711 Fax: (801) 876-3331

Sales/distribution of port firearms, fishing rods, etc.

Browning Canada Sports Ltd., 5350 Ferrer St., Montreal, PQ H4P 1L9, Canada

Tel: 514-333-7261

BROWNING-FERRIS INDUSTRIES INC.

757 North Eldridge Parkway, Houston, TX, 77079

Tel: (281) 870-8100 Fax: (281) 870-7844

Waste management.

BFI Canada, 826 Felix Ave., Windsor, ON, Canada N9C 3K8

Tel: 519-258-2334

BRUNSWICK CORPORATION

1 Northfield Court, Lake Forest, IL, 60045-4811

Tel: (847) 735-4700 Fax: (847) 735-4765 Web site: www.brunswickcorp.com

Mfr. recreational boats, marine engines, bowling centers & equipment, fishing equipment, defense/aerospace.

Mercury Marine Ltd., 1156 Dundas Hwy. E, PO Box 488, Mississauga, ON L4Y 2CZ, Canada

BUCK CONSULTANTS INC.

One Pennsylvania Plaza, New York, NY, 10119

Tel: (212) 330-1000 Fax: (212) 695-4184

Employee benefit, actuarial and compensation consulting services.

GBB Buck Consultants Ltd., PO Box 15, 95 Wellington St. W, Toronto, ON M5J 2N7, Canada

BUCKHORN INC.

55 West Techne Center Drive, Milford, OH, 45150

Tel: (513) 831-4402 Fax: (513) 831-5474

Mfr. of reusable plastic packaging systems, plastic containers and pallets and project management services.

Buckhorn Canada, 8032 Torbrum Rd., Brampton, ON L6T 3T2, Canada

Tel: 905-971-6500 Fax: 905-791-9942 Contact: Jim Morrison, VP & Gen. Mgr. Emp: 12

BUCYRUS INTERNATIONAL, INC.

1100 Milwaukee Ave., South Milwaukee, WI, 53172

Tel: (414) 768-4000 Fax: (414) 768-4474

Mfr. of surface mining equipment, primarily walking draglines, electric mining shovels and blast hole drills.

Bucyrus Canada Ltd., 211A Amherst, Labrador City, ND A2V 2B7, Canada

Tel: 709-944-5899 Fax: 709-944-3339 Contact: Rene Turbide, Supervisor

BUDGET RENT A CAR CORPORATION

4225 Naperville Road, Lisle, IL, 60532

Tel: (630) 955-1900 Fax: (630) 955-7799 Web site: www.budgetrentacar.com

Car and truck rental system.

Budget Rent A Car, Lester B. Pearson International Airport, 5905 Campus Rd., Toronto, ON, Canada

Tel: 905-677-0840

Budget Rent A Car, Mirabel International Airport, Box 41, Montreal, PQ, Canada

Tel: 514-476-2687

Budget Rent A Car, Vancouver International Airport -V5C 4E4, Vancouver, BC, Canada

Tel: 604-668-7000

BULAB HOLDINGS INC.

1256 N. McLean Blvd, Memphis, TN, 38108

Tel: (901) 278-0330 Fax: (901) 276-5343 Web site: www.buckman.com

Biological products; chemicals & chemical preparations.

Buckman Laboratories of Canada Ltd., 351 Joseph Carrier Blvd., Vaudrevil, PQ J7V 5V5, Canada

Tel: 514-424-4404 Fax: 514-424-4294

BULOVA CORPORATION

One Bulova Ave., Woodside, NY, 11377-7874

Tel: (718) 204-3300 Fax: (718) 204-3546

Mfr. timepieces, watches and clocks, watch parts, batteries and precision defense products.

Bulova Watch Co. Ltd., 105 Bartley Dr., Toronto, ON M4A 1O8,Canada

BURLINGTON NORTHERN SANTA FE CORP.

3800 Continental Plaza, 777 Main St., Fort Worth, TX, 76102-5384

Tel: (817) 333-2000 Fax: (817) 333-2377 Web site: www.bnsf.com

Rail services.

Burlington Northern Canada, Winnipeg, MB, Canada

Burlington Northern Canada, Vancouver, BC, Canada

LEO BURNETT CO., INC.

35 West Wacker Drive, Chicago, IL, 60601

Tel: (312) 220-5959 Fax: (312) 220-6533 Web site: www.leoburnett.com

International advertising agency.

Leo Burnett Company, Toronto, Canada

Publicite Leo Burnett, Montreal, Canada

BURSON-MARSTELLER

230 Park Ave., New York, NY, 10003-1566

Tel: (212) 614-4000 Fax: (212) 614-4262 Web site: www.bm.com

Public relations/public affairs consultants.

Burson Marsteller, 80 Bloor St. W, Toronto, ON M5S 2V1, Canada

BUTLER MANUFACTURING COMPANY

Penn Valley Park, PO Box 419917, Kansas City, MO, 64141-0917

Tel: (816) 968-3000 Fax: (816) 968-3279

Pre-engineered steel structural systems, curtain wall and electrical distributor systems.

Butler Buildings (Canada), 3070 Mainway Drive, Unit 21, Burlington, ON L7M 1A3, Canada

Tel: 905-332-7786 Fax: 905-332-4060 Contact: William N. Evoy, Pres.

BUTTERICK CO., INC.

161 Ave. of the Americas, New York, NY, 10013

Tel: (212) 620-2500 Fax: (212) 620-2746 Web site: www.butterick.com

Sewing patterns.

Butterick Fashion Mktg. Co., 10 Butterick Rd., Toronto, ON M8W 3Z8, Canada

C-COR ELECTRONICS INC.

60 Decibel Road, State College, PA, 16801

Tel: (814) 238-2461 Fax: (814) 238-4065 Web site: www.c-cor.com

Design/mfr. amplifiers, fiber optics electronic equipment for data and cable TV systems.

C-Cor Electronics Canada Inc., 377 MacKenzie Ave., Ajax, ON L1S 2G2, Canada

Tel: 905-427-0366 Fax: 905-428-0927 Contact: Alan Hogg, Mgr.

CACI INTERNATIONAL INC.

1100 Nort Glebe Road, Arlington, VA, 22201

Tel: (703) 841-7800 Fax: (703) 841-7882 Web site: www.caci.com

Provides simulation technology/software and designs factories, computer networks, and communications systems for military, electronic commerce digital document management, logistics and Y2K remediation.

CACI International, Inc., Ottawa, ON, Canada

CADILLAC PLASTIC & CHEMICAL COMPANY

143 Indusco Court, Troy, MI, 48083

Tel: (248) 205-3100 Fax: (248) 205-3187

Distributor plastic basic shapes.

Cadillac Plastic (Canada) Ltd., 91 Ketfield St., Rexdale, ON M9W 5A4, Canada

CALCOMP INC.

2411 West La Palma Ave., Anaheim, CA, 92801

Tel: (714) 821-2000 Fax: (714) 821-2832

Mfr. computer graphics peripherals.

CalComp Canada, 401 Champagne Dr., Downsview, ON M3J 2C6, Canada

CALED CHEMICAL

26 Hanes Drive, Wayne, NJ, 07470

Tel: (973) 696-7575 Fax: (973) 696-4790

Mfr. dry cleaning chemicals and machine filters, laundry detergents, fabric protectors, flame retardants.

Caled Canada, 2241 Guenette, St. Laurent, PQ H4R 2E9, Canada

CALGON CORPORATION

PO Box 1346, Pittsburgh, PA, 15230

Tel: (412) 494-8000 Fax: (412) 494-8104

Mfr. cosmetic, personal care & water treatment products.

Calgon Canada Corp., 27 Finley Rd., Bramalea, ON L6T 1B2, Canada

CALMAQUIP ENGINEERING CORPORATION

7240 NW 12th Street, Miami, FL, 33121

Tel: (305) 592-4510 Fax: (305) 593-9618

Engineering

Calmaquip Canada Ltd., 2001 University, Montreal, PQ H3A 2A6, Canada

CAMCO INC.

7030 Ardmore Street, Houston, TX, 77021

Tel: (713) 747-4000 Fax: (713) 747-6751

Oil field equipment for well drilling and production.

Camco Ltd., PO Box 4416, Edmonton, AB T6E 4T5, Canada

Tel: 403-509-2363

CAMP HEALTHCARE, INC.

PO Box 89, Jackson, MI, 49204

Tel: (517) 787-1600 Fax: (517) 789-3388

Mfr. orthotics and prosthetics.

Camp Intl. Ltd., PO Box 495, 39 Davis St., Trenton, ON K8V 5R6, Canada

Tel: 613-392-6528

CAMPBELL SOUP COMPANY

Campbell Place, Camden, NJ, 08103-1799

Tel: (609) 342-4800 Fax: (609) 342-3878

Food products.

Campbell Soup Co. Ltd., Canada

CAPITAL ONE FINANCIAL CORPORATION

2980 Fairview Park Drive, Ste. 1300, Falls Church, VA, 22042-4525

Tel: (703) 205-1000 Fax: (703) 205-1090 Web site: www.capitalone.com

Holding company for credit card companies.

Capital One Inc., 350 Seventh Ave., SW, First Canadian Ctr., Ste. 1400, Calgary, AB, Canada T28 3N9

Tel: 703-205-1000 Fax: 703-205-1090 Contact: Carl Jentaft

CARBOLINE COMPANY

350 Hanley Industrial Court, St. Louis, MO, 63144

Tel: (314) 644-1000 Fax: (314) 644-4617

Mfr. coatings, sealants.

Corrosion Service Co. Ltd., 369 Rimrock Rd., Downsview, ON, Canada M3J 3G2

CARBONE OF AMERICA

215 Stackpole Street, Saint Marys, PA, 15857

Tel: (814) 781-1234 Fax: (814) 781-8455

Carbon and graphite specialties.

Carbone of America, 550 Evans Ave., Toronto, ON M8W 2V6, Canada

CARGILL, INC.

15407 McGinty Road, Minnetonka, MN, 55440-5625

Tel: (612) 742-7575 Fax: (612) 742-7393 Web site: www.cargill.com

Food products, feeds, animal products.

Cargill Ltd., 300-240 Graham Ave., Winnepeg, MB RC3C 4C5, Canada

CARLISLE SYNTEC SYSTEMS

PO Box 7000, Carlisle, PA, 17013

Tel: (717) 245-7000 Fax: (717) 245-9107

Mfr. elastomeric roofing & waterproofing systems.

Carlisle SynTec Systems Canada, 5940 Shawson Dr., Mississauga, ON L4W 3W5, Canada

Carlisle SynTec Systems Canada, Construction House, 2765 Oak St., Vancouver, BC V6H 2K3, Canada

Materiaux de Toiture Carlisle, 8300 Place Lorranie, Anjou, PQ H1J 1E6, Canada

CARLSON MARKETING GROUP

Carlson Parkway, PO Box 59159, Minneapolis, MN, 55459

Tel: (612) 550-4520 Fax: (612) 550-4580 Web site: www.cmgcarlson.com

Marketing services agency.

Carlson Marketing Group, Toronto, Canada

CARPENTER TECHNOLOGY CORPORATION

101 W. Bern Street, PO Box 14662, Reading, PA, 19612-4662

Tel: (610) 208-2000 Fax: (610) 208-3214

Mfr. specialty steels & structural ceramics for casting industrial.

Carpenter Technology (Canada) Ltd., 7464 Tranmere Dr., Unit 2, Mississauga, ON L5S 1K4, Canada

CARRIER CORPORATION

One Carrier Place, Farmington, CT, 06034-4015

Tel: (860) 674-3000 Fax: (860) 679-3010 Web site: www.carrier.com

Mfr./distributor/services A/C, heating & refrigeration equipment.

Carrier Canada Ltd., 1990 Minnesota Court #20, Mississauga, ON, Canada

Compu-Home Systems Inc., Toronto, ON, Canada

Temp Con Industries Inc., Vaudreuil, PQ, Canada

Werner's Wholesale Group Inc., 1345 Grant St., Vancouver, BC V5L 2X7, Canada

CARTER-WALLACE INC.

1345 Ave. of the Americas, New York, NY, 10105

Tel: (212) 339-5000 Fax: (212) 339-5100

Mfr. personal care products and pet products.

Carter-Horner, Inc., 5485 Ferrier St., Montreal, PQ H4P 1M6, Canada

Tel: 514-731-3931 Fax: 514-738-4124

Carter-Horner, Inc., 6600 Kitimat Rd., Mississauga, ON L5N 1L9, Canada

Tel: 905-826-6200 Fax: 905-826-0389

CASCADE CORPORATION

201st Ave., Portland, OR, 97201

Tel: (503) 669-6300 Fax: (503) 669-6321 Web site: www.cascor.com

Mfr. hydraulic forklift truck attachments.

Cascade Canada Inc., 5570 Timberlea Blvd., Mississauga, ON, Canada L4W 4M6

Tel: 905-629-7777

CASHCO INC.

PO Box 6, Ellsworth, KS, 67439-0006

Tel: (913) 472-4461 Fax: (913) 472-3539

Mfr. pressure regulators and control valves.

Cashco Canada Inc., 212 Wyecroft Rd., Oakville, ON L6K 3T9, Canada

A.M. CASTLE & COMPANY

3400 N. Wolf Road, Franklin Park, IL, 60131

Tel: (784) 755-7111 Fax: (784) 455-7136

Metals distribution.

Norton Steel Co. Ltd. of Canada, 190 rue Murray, Montreal, PQ H3C 2C8, Canada

CATERPILLAR INC.

100 NE Adams Street, Peoria, IL, 61629-6105

Tel: (309) 675-1000 Fax: (309) 675-1182 Web site: www.cat.com

Mfr. earth/material-handling and construction machinery and equipment and engines.

Caterpillar of Canada Ltd., PO Box 5000, Brampton, ON L6V 3Y4, Canada

L.D. CAULK COMPANY

PO Box 359, Milford, DE, 19963

Tel: (302) 422-4511 Fax: (302) 422-5719

Dental material.

L.D. Caulk Co. of Canada Ltd., 172 John St., Toronto, ON M5T 1X5, Canada

C.B. RICHARD ELLIS

533 South Fremont Ave., Los Angeles, CA, 90071-1712

Tel: (213) 613-3123 Fax: (213) 613-3535 Web site: www.cbrichardellis.com

Commercial real estate services.

CB Richard Ellis, 181 Bay St., Toronto, ON M5J 2T3, Canada

Tel: 416-368-4055

Richard Ellis of Canada, Locations in Calgary, Edmonton, Etobicoke, and Kitchener, Canada

Richard Ellis of Canada, Ste. 800, 1040 West Georgia St., V6B 4N9 Vancouver, BC, Canada

Tel: 604-687-7221

CBI COMPANY

1501 North Division Street, Plainfield, IL, 60544

Tel: (815) 241-7546 Fax: (815) 439-6010

Holding company: metal plate fabricating, construction, oil and gas drilling.

Horton CBI Ltd., 1801 McGill College Ave., Montreal, PQ, Canada

CCH INC.

2700 Lake Cook Road, Riverwoods, IL, 60015

Tel: (847) 267-7000 Fax: (800) 224-8299

Tax & business law information, software & services.

CCH Canadian Ltd., 6 Garamond Ct., Don Mills, ON M3C 1Z5, Canada

Les Publications CCH/FM Lte., 33 rue Racine, Farnham, PQ J2N 3A3, Canada

CCI TRIAD

6207 Beecave Road, Austin, TX, 78746

Tel: (510) 449-0606 Fax: (512) 328-8209

Information retrieval systems.

Triad Systems Canada Ltd., 30 Pennsylvania Ave. #3, Concord, ON L4K 4A5, Canada

CDI CORPORATION

1717 Arch Street, 35th Fl., Philadelphia, PA, 19103

Tel: (215) 569-2200 Fax: (215) 569-1300

Engineering, technical and temporary personnel services.

CDI Technical Services Ltd., One King St. W, Hamilton, ON L8P 1A4, Canada

Todays Temporary Ltd., 505 Consumers Rd., Willowdale, ON M2J 4V8, Canada

CEILCOTE AIR POLLUTION CONTROL

14955 Sprague Road, Strongsville, OH, 44136

Tel: (440) 243-0700 Fax: (440) 234-3486

Mfr. corrosion-resistant material, air pollution control equipment, construction services.

Ceilcote Canada, 7065 Fir Tree Dr., Mississauga, ON I5S 1G7, Canada

CELITE CORPORATION

PO Box 519, Lompoc, CA, 93438

Tel: (805) 735-7791 Fax: (805) 735-5699

Mining/process diatomaceous earth (diatomite).

Celite Canada Inc., 6 Eva Rd. #602, Etobicoke, ON M9C 2A8, Canada

CENDANT CORPORATION

6 Sylvan Way, Parsippany, NJ, 07054

Tel: (973) 428-9700 Fax: (973) 496-5902 Web site: www.cendant.com

Membership-based, direct marketer offering shopping/travel/insurance and dining discount programs

Europe Tax Free Shopping, Canada Tax Free Shopping, 33 Laird Drive, Toronto, ON M4G 359, Canada

Tel: 416-467-0947 Fax: 416-425-4858

CENTURY 21 REAL ESTATE CORPORATION

6 Sylvan Way, Parsippany, NJ, 07054-3826

Tel: (973) 496-5722 Fax: (973) 496-5527 Web site: www.century21.com

Real estate.

Century 21 Real Estate Canada Ltd., 1199 West Pender St., Ste. 700, Vancouver, BC V6E 2R1, Canada

Tel: 604-606-2100 Contact: Mr. U. Gary Charlwood

CERDIAN CORPORATION

8100 34th Ave. South, Minneapolis, MN, 55425

Tel: (612) 853-8100 Fax: (612) 853-4068 Web site: www.ceridian.com

Provides diversified information services.

Ceridian Canada, Ltd., 125 Gary St., Winnipeg, MB R3C3P1, Canada

Tel: 204-947-9400

CH2M HILL INC.

6060 South Willow Drive, Greenwood Village, CO, 80111

Tel: (303) 771-0900 Fax: (303) 770-2616

Consulting engineers, planners, economists and scientists.

CH2M Hill, Waterloo, ON, Canada

Tel: 519-579-3500

CH2M Hill, 255 Consumer Rd., North York, ON M2J 56B, Canada

Tel: 416-499-9000 Fax: 416-499-4687

CH2M Hill, Barrie, ON, Canada

Tel: 705-722-8800

CH2M Hill, London, ON, Canada

Tel: 519-858-8800

CH2M Hill, Ottawa, ON, Canada

Tel: 613-723-8700

CH2M Hill, Thorold, ON, Canada

Tel: 905-684-7425

CH2M Hill, Vancouver, BC, Canada

Tel: 604-684-3282

CH2M Hill, Calgary, AB, Canada

Tel: 403-237-9300

CH2M Hill Intl., 640 8th Ave. SW, Calgary, AB T2P 1G7, Canada

Tel: 403-237-8800

CHAMPION INTERNATIONAL CORPORATION

One Champion Plaza, Stamford, CT, 06921

Tel: (213) 358-7000 Fax: (213) 358-2975

Manufacture and sale of pulp and paper.

Champion International, Hinton, AB, Canada

Weldwood of Canada Ltd., 1055 W. Hastings St., PO Box 2179, Vancouver, BC V6B 3V8, Canada

CHAMPION PARTS REBUILDERS INC.

751 Roosevelt Road, Glen Ellyn, IL, 60137

Tel: (630) 942-8317 Fax: (630) 942-0334

Remanufacture of automotive, truck and tractor parts.

Champion Parts Rebuilders (Canada) Ltd., 224 Milvan Dr., Weston, ON M9L 24A, Canada

THE CHASE MANHATTAN CORPORATION

World Headquarters, 270 Park Ave., New York, NY, 10017

Tel: (212) 270-6000 Fax: (212) 622-9030 Web site: www.chase.com

International banking and financial services.

Chase Manhattan Canada Ltd., PO Box 301, Commerce Court Postal Station, Toronto, ON M5L 1G1, Canada

Chase Manhattan Canada Ltd., 333 Fifth Ave. SW, Calgary, AB T2P 3B6, Canada

Chase Manhattan Canada Ltd., 1 Place Ville Marie, Montreal, PQ H3B 3M9, Canada

Chase Manhattan Canada Ltd., PO Box 11581, Vancouver, BC V6B 4N4, Canada

The Chase Manhattan Bank of Canada, One First Canadian Place, 100 King St.,Ste. 6900, PO Box 106, Toronto, ON, Canada M5X 1A4

Tel: 416-216-4100 Fax: 416-216-4166

CHATTEM INC.

1715 West 38th Street, Chattanooga, TN, 37409

Tel: (423) 821-4571 Fax: (423) 821-6132

Mfr. health & beauty aids.

Chattem Canada Inc., 2220 Argentia Rd., Mississauga, ON L5N 2K7, Canada

CHECKPOINT SYSTEMS, INC.

101 Wolf Drive, Thorofare, NJ, 08086

Tel: (609) 848-1800 Fax: (609) 848-0957

Mfr. test, measurement and closed-circuit television systems.

Checkpoint Systems, Inc., Canada

CHESAPEAKE ENERGY CORP.

6104 North Western, Oklahoma City, OK, 73118

Tel: (405) 848-8000 Fax: (405) 848-8588

Oil and natural gas.

Ranger Oil Ltd., Calgary, AB, Canada

A.W. CHESTERTON COMPANY

225 Fallon Road, Stoneham, MA, 02180

Tel: (781) 438-7000 Fax: (781) 438-8971 Web site: www.stoneham.chesterton.com

Packing gaskets, sealing products systems, etc.

A.W. Chesterton Co., Burlington, ON, Canada

CHEVRON CHEMICAL COMPANY

6001 Bollinger Canyon Road., PO Box 5047, San Ramon, CA, 94583-0947

Tel: (925) 842-1000 Fax: (925) 842-5775 Web site: www.chevron.com

Mfr. chemicals.

Chevron Chemical (Canada) Ltd., 3228 S. Service Rd., Burlington, ON I7N 3H8, Canada

CHEVRON CORPORATION

575 Market Street, San Francisco, CA, 94105

Tel: (415) 894-7700 Fax: (415) 894-2248 Web site: www.chevron.com

Oil exploration & production & petroleum products.

Chevron Canada Ltd., 1050 W. Pender St., Vancouver, BC E6E 3T4, Canada

Chevron Standard Ltd., 400 5th Ave., Calgary, AB T2P 0L7, Canada

CHICAGO RAWHIDE INDUSTRIES (CRI)

900 North State Street, Elgin, IL, 60123

Tel: (847) 742-7840 Fax: (847) 742-7845

Mfr. shaft and face seals.

CR Canada Ltd., Park Rd. & Henry St., PO Box 70, Brantford, ON N3T 5M6, Canada

CHICAGO RAWHIDE MFG. COMPANY

900 North State Street, Elgin, IL, 60120

Tel: (847) 742-7840 Fax: (847) 742-7845

Seals & filters.

Chicago Rawhide Products Canada Ltd., PO Box 707, Brantford, ON, Canada

CHIQUITA BRANDS INTERNATIONAL INC.

250 East Fifth Street, Cincinnati, OH, 45202

Tel: (513) 784-8000 Fax: (513) 784-8030 Web site: www.chiquita.com

Sale and distribution of bananas, fresh fruits and processed foods.

Chiquita Brands Intenational, Canada

CHIRON CORPORATION

4560 Horton Street, Emeryville, CA, 94608-2916

Tel: (510) 655-8730 Fax: (510) 655-9910

Research/mfr./marketing therapeutics, vaccines, diagnostics, ophthalmic.

Chiron Vision Canada, 80 W. Beaver Creek #6, Richmond Hill, ON L4B 1H3, Canada

Ciba Corning Canada Inc., 90 Gough St., Unit #1, Markham, ON L3R 5V5, Canada

CHRYSLER CORPORATION

1000 Chrysler Drive, Auburn Hills, MI, 48326-2766

Tel: (248) 576-5741 Fax: (248) 512-5143 Web site: www.chrysler.com

Mfr./marketing cars & light trucks, electronic & aerospace products & systems.

Chrysler Canada Ltd., 2199 Chrysler Centre, Windsor, ON N9A 4H6, Canada

CHRYSLER FINANCIAL CORPORATION

27777 Franklin Road, Southfield, MI, 48034

Tel: (248) 948-3555 Fax: (248) 948-3987 Web site: www.chrysler financial.com

Financial services.

Chrysler Credit Canada Ltd., 4510 Rhodes Drive, Ste. 120, Windsor, ON N8W 5C2, Canada

Tel: 519-561-9210

THE CHUBB CORPORATION

15 Mountain View Road, Warren, NJ, 07061-1615

Tel: (908) 580-2000 Fax: (908) 580-3606 Web site: www.chubb.com

Holding company: property/casualty insurance.

Chubb Insurance Company of Canada, 3340 Petro Canada Centre, West Tower, 150-6 Ave., SW, Calgary, AB T1P 3Y7

Tel: 403-261-3881 Fax: 403-2269-2907

Chubb Insurance Company of Canada, 777 Dunsmuir St., Pacific Centre, Ste. 1800, Vancouver, BC V7Y 1K5, Canada

Tel: 604-685-2113 Fax: 604-685-3811

Chubb Insurance Company of Canada, One Financial Place, 1 Adelaide St. East, Toronto, ON M5C 2V9, Canada

Tel: 416-863-9=0550 Fax: 416-863-5010

Chubb Insurance Company of Canada, 1250 Rene-Levesque Blvd., West, 27th Fl., Montreal, PQ H3B 4W8, Canada

Tel: 514-938-4000 Fax: 514-938-2288

CHURCH & DWIGHT CO., INC.

469 North Harrison Street, Princeton, NJ, 08543

Tel: (609) 683-5900 Fax: (609) 497-7177

Specialty chemicals and consumer products.

Church & Dwight Ltd., 25 The Donway West, Don Mills, ON, Canada

CIBER, INC.

5251 DTC Parkway, Ste. 1400, Engelwood, CO, 80111

Tel: (303) 220-0100 Fax: (303) 220-7100 Web site: www.ciber.com

Provides software development and maintenance services, year 2000 support and information technology consulting.

Business Information Technology (BIT) of Canada, Inc., Canadian Headquarters, 4 Robert Speck Parkway, Ste. 360, Mississauga, ON L4Z 1S1, Canada (Offices: New Brunswick, Newfoundland, Prince Edward Island, Ontario, and Quebec, Canada.)

Tel: 905-279-7811 Fax: 905-279-5373

Business Information Technology (BIT) of Canada, Inc., 130 Slater St., Ste. 750, Ottawa, ON K1P 6E2, Canada

Tel: 613-598-4664 Fax: 613-594-8705

Business Information Technology (BIT) of Canada, Inc., 2000-1066 West Hastings St., Vancouver, BC V6E 3X2, Canada (Locations: Alberta, British Colombia, Manitoba, Northwest Territoies, Saskatchewan, and Yukon, Canada.)

Tel: 604-893-8308 Fax: 604-893-8309

CIGNA CORPORATION

One Liberty Place, Philadelphia, PA, 19192

Tel: (215) 761-1000 Fax: (215) 761-5008

Insurance, invest, health care and other financial services.

Cigna Insurance Co. of Canada, 100 Consilium Place #500, Scarborough, ON M1H 3E3, Canada

Cigna Life Insurance Co. of Canada, 20 Adelaide St. E #1200, Toronto, ON M5C 2T6, Canada

Connecticut General Life Insurance Co., 555 Younge St., Toronto, ON M7A 2H6, Canada

Life Insurance Co. of North America, 141 Adelaide St. W #709, Toronto, ON M5H 3L5, Canada

CINCOM SYSTEMS INC.

2300 Montana Ave., Cincinnati, OH, 45211

Tel: (513) 612-2300 Fax: (513) 481-8332 Web site: www.cincom.com

Develop/distributor computer software.

Cincom Systems Inc., Mississauga, ON, Canada

Cincom Systems Inc., Montreal, PQ, Canada

Cincom Systems Inc., Ottawa, ON, Canada

Cincom Systems Inc., Vancouver, BC, Canada

CISCO SYSTEMS, INC.

170 Tasman Drive, San Jose, CA, 95134-1706

Tel: (408) 526-4000 Fax: (408) 526-4100 Web site: www.cisco.com

Develop/mfr./market computer hardware and software networking systems.

Cisco Systems Canada Ltd., 150 York St., Ste. 600, Toronto, ON M5H 3S5, Canada

Tel: 416-216-8000 Fax: 416-216-8099 Contact: N/A

CITICORP

399 Park Ave., New York, NY, 10043

Tel: (212) 559-1000 Fax: (212) 527-2066 Web site: www.citibank.com

International banking and financial services.

Citibank N.A., 463 Dundas St. West, Toronto M5T 1GS, Canada

Tel: 416-977-7272 Fax: 416-977-8916

Citibank N.A., 612 Main St., Vancouver, BC V6A 2V3, Canada

Tel: 604-891-3333 Fax: 604-891-3300

CLEVELAND-CLIFFS INC.

1100 Superior Ave., 18th Floor, Cleveland, OH, 44114

Tel: (216) 694-5700 Fax: (216) 694-4880

Iron, coal mining, and transportation.

Adams Mine, PO Box 877, Kirkland Lake, ON P2N 3K7, Canada

Pickands Mather & Co., Wabush Mines, Wabush, LB, Canada

Pickands Mather & Co., Wabush Mines, Pointe Noire, PQ, Canada

Pickands Mather & Co., The Griffith Mine, Red Lake, ON, Canada

Sherman Mine, PO Box 217, Temagami, ON P0H 2H0, Canada

THE CLOROX COMPANY

1221 Broadway, PO Box 24305, Oakland, CA, 94623-1305

Tel: (510) 271-7000 Fax: (510) 832-1463

Mfr. soap & detergents, and domestic consumer packaged products.

Brita (Canada) Inc., Canada

The Clorox Co. of Canada Ltd., Moose Jaw, Toronto, ON, Canada

THE COASTAL CORPORATION

Nine Greenway Plaza, Houston, TX, 77046-0995

Tel: (713) 877-1400 Fax: (713) 877-6752 Web site: www.coastalcorp.com

Oil refining, natural gas, related services; independent power production.

Coastal Canada Petroleum, Inc., ON, Canada

Engage Energy Canada, L.P., Canada Trust Tower, Calgary, AB, Canada

Tel: 403-297-0333

Pétrochimie Coastal du Canada, 3500 Broadway St., Montreal, PQ, H1B5B4 Canada

Tel: 514-640-2200

COBE LABORATORIES INC.

1185 Oak Street, Lakewood, CO, 80215

Tel: (303) 232-6800 Fax: (303) 231-4952

Mfr. medical equipment & supplies.

COBE Canada Ltd., 80 Milner Ave., Scarborough, ON, M1S 3P8 Canada

THE COCA-COLA COMPANY

P.O. Drawer 1734, Atlanta, GA, 30301

Tel: (404) 676-2121 Fax: (404) 676-6792 Web site: www.coca-cola.com

Mfr./marketing/distributor soft drinks, syrups & concentrates, juice & juice-drink products.

Coca-Cola Beverages Canada, Canada - All mail to U.S. address.

COEN CO., INC.

1510 Rollins Road, Burlingame, CA, 94010

Tel: (650) 697-0440 Fax: (650) 686-5655

Mfr. industrial burners.

Coen Canada, 226 rue Roy, St. Eustache, PQ J7R 5R6, Canada

Tel: 450-472-7922

COGNIZANT TECHNOLOGY SOLUTIONS CORPORATION

1700 Broadway, 26th Floor, New York, NY, 10019

Tel: (212) 887-2385 Fax: (212) 887-2450 Web site: www.dbss.com

Provides software development , application management, computer date corrections, and currency conversion.

Cognizant Technology Solutions, Toronto, Canada

COLD SPRING GRANITE COMPANY

202 South 3rd Ave., Cold Spring, MN, 56320

Tel: (612) 685-3621 Fax: (612) 685-8490

Granite quarrier and fabricator.

Cold Spring Granite Canada Ltd., PO Box 730, Lac du Bonnet, MB R0E 1A0, Canada

THE COLEMAN CO., INC.

3600 Hydraulic Street, Wichita, KS, 67219

Tel: (316) 832-2653 Fax: (316) 832-3060

Mfr./distributor/sales camping & outdoor recreation products.

Canadian Coleman Co. Ltd., 15 N. Queen St., Toronto, ON, M8Z 2C1, Canada

COLGATE-PALMOLIVE COMPANY

300 Park Ave., New York, NY, 10022

Tel: (212) 310-2000 Fax: (212) 310-2919

Mfr. pharmaceuticals, cosmetics, toiletries and detergents.

Colgate-Palmolive Canada, 99 Vanderhoof Ave., Toronto, ON M4G 2M6, Canada

COLSON INC.

3700 Airport Road, Jonesboro, AR, 72401

Tel: (870) 932-4501 Fax: (870) 933-6612

Mfr./sale casters.

Colson Casters Ltd., 1600 Bishop St. N, Cambridge-Preston, ON N3H 4V6, Canada

COLTEC INDUSTRIES INC.

2550 West Tyvola Road, Charlotte, NC, 28217-4543

Tel: (704) 423-7000 Fax: (704) 423-7097

Mfr. aircraft landing gear and flight controls, water systems, engines, motor arms, valves, seals, etc.

Menasco Aerospace, 1400 S Service Way, Oakville, ON L6J 5Y7, Canada

COLUMBIA FOREST PRODUCTS, INC.

222 SW Columbia Street, Ste.1575, Portland, OR, 97201-6600

Tel: (503) 224-5300 Fax: (503) 224-5294

Mfr./sale plywood.

Columbia Forest Products, Inc., PO Box 10, Caste Postal 10, Hearst, ON POL 1NO, Canada,

Columbia Forest Products, Inc., 420 Notre Dame, St. Casimir, PQ GOA 3LO, Canada

COLUMBIAN ROPE COMPANY

PO Box 270, Guntown, MS, 38849-0270

Tel: (601) 348-2241 Fax: (601) 348-5749

Mfr. rope, twine and industrial fiber products.

Canada Cordage Inc., PO Box 158, Kitchener, ON N2G 3Y2, Canada

COLUMBUS McKINNON CORPORATION

140 John James Audubon Pkwy., Amherst, NY, 14228-1197

Tel: (716) 689-5400 Fax: (716) 689-5644

Mfr. chains, forgings, hoists, tire shredders and manipulators.

Columbus McKinnon Ltd., PO Box 1106, 10 Brook Rd. N, Cobourg, ON K9A 4W5, Canada

COMDATA NETWORK INC.

5301 Maryland Way, Brentwood, TN, 37027

Tel: (615) 370-7000 Fax: (615) 370-7406 Web site: www.comdata.com

Provides information services for the trucking industry, including long-distrance telecommunications services.

Permicom/Comdata, 161 Pennsylvania Ave., Ste. 5, Concord L4K 1C3, Toronto, Canada

Tel: 416-736-6665

COMDISCO INC.

6111 N. River Road, Rosemont, IL, 60018

Tel: (847) 698-3000 Fax: (847) 518-5440

Hi-tech asset and facility management and equipment leasing.

Comdisco Canada Ltd., Royal Bank Plaza, North Tower, 200 Bay St., Toronto, ON M5J 2J3, Canada

COMERICA INCORPORATED

Comerica Tower, Detroit Center, 500 Woodward Ave., Detroit, MI, 48226

Tel: (313) 222-4000 Fax: (313) 965-4648 Web site: www.comerica.com

Bank holding company; business & asset based lending, global finance & institutional trust & investment management services..

Comerica Bank - Canada, Ste. 2210, Royal Bank Plaza, South Tower, 200 Bay St., PO Box 61, Toronto, ON, Canada M5J 2j2

Tel: 416-367-3113 Contact: Philip Buxton

COMPAQ COMPUTER CORPORATION

20555 State Highway 249, PO Box 692000, Houston, TX, 77269-2000

Tel: (713) 370-0670 Fax: (713) 514-1740 Web site: www.compaq.com

Develop/mfr. personal computers.

Compaq Canada Inc., 45 Vogell Rd., Richmond Hill, ON L4B 3P6, Canada

Tel: 905-707-1715 Fax: 416-229-8898

COMPUTER ASSOCIATES INTERNATIONAL INC.

One Computer Associates Plaza, Islandia, NY, 11788

Tel: (516) 342-5224 Fax: (516) 342-5329 Web site: www.cai.com

Integrated software for enterprise computing and information management, application development, manufacturing, financial applications and professional services.

Computer Associates Canada Ltd., 5935 Airport Rd., Mississauga, ON L4V 1W5, Canada

Tel: 905-676-6700

COMSHARE INC.

3001 South State Street, Ann Arbor, MI, 48108

Tel: (734) 994-4800 Fax: (734) 994-5895

Managerial application software.

Comshare Ltd., 180 Attwell Dr., Ste. 300, Rexdale, ON M9W 6H4, Canada

CONAGRA INC.

One ConAgra Drive, Omaha, NE, 68102-5001

Tel: (402) 595-4000 Fax: (402) 595-4595 Web site: www.conagra.com

Prepared/frozen foods, grains, flour, animal feeds, agri chemicals, poultry, meat, dairy products, including Healthy Choice, Butterball and Hunt's.

ConAgra Grain, Toronto, ON, Canada

CONAIR CORPORATION

150 Milford Road, E. Windsor, NJ, 08520

Tel: (609) 426-1300 Fax: (609) 426-8766

Mfr. personal care & household appliances.

Conair Consumer Products Inc., 6707 Goreway Dr., Mississauga, ON L4V 1P7, Canada

CONSTRUCTION SPECIALTIES INC.

Headquarters, 3 Werner Way, Lebanon, NJ, 08833

Tel: (908) 236-0800 Fax: (908) 236-0801 Web site: www.c-sgroup.com

Mfr. architectural building products.

Construction Specialties Ltd., 895 Lakefront Promenade, Mississauga, ON L5E 2C2, Canada

Tel: 905-274-3611 Contact: Lloyd Johnson, Gen. Mgr.

COOPER INDUSTRIES INC.

6600 Travis Street, Ste. 5800, Houston, TX, 77002

Tel: (713) 209-8400 Fax: (713) 209-8995 Web site: www.cooperindustries.com

Mfr./distributor electrical products, tools and hardware and automotive products.

Cooper Industries (Canada) Inc., 308 Orenda Rd., Brampton, ON L6T 1G1, Canada

Cooper Lighting Div., Mississauga, ON, Canada

Crouse-Hinds Canada, 5925 Mc Laughlin Rd., Mississauga, ON L5R 1B8 , Canada (Locations: St. Johns, NFLD; Burlington ON; Burnaby, BC; Calgary, AB; Darthmouth, NS; Edmonton, AB; Guelph, ON; St. Laurent, PQ; Neuechatel, PQ; Sarnia, ON; Lively, ON; Winnipeg, MA.)

Tel: 905-507-4187 Fax: 905-501-4078

Kirsch Div., Repentigny, PQ, Canada

Moog Automotive, Cambridge, ON, Canada

COPELAND CORPORATION

1675 West Campbell Road, Sidney, OH, 45365-0669

Tel: (937) 498-3011 Fax: (937) 498-3334 Web site: www.copeland-corp.com

Producer of compressors and condensing units for commercial and residential air conditioning and refrigeration equipment.

Copeland Canada, 145 Sherwood Drive, Brantford, ON N3T 5S7, Canada

CORE LABORATORIES

5295 Hollister, Houston, TX, 77042

Tel: (713) 460-9600 Fax: (713) 460-4389

Petroleum testing/analysis, analytical chemicals, laboratory and octane analysis instrumentation.

Core Laboratories, 10946-89 Ave., Grande Prairie, AB T8V 4W4, Canada

Core Laboratories, 1540 25th Ave. NE, Calgary, AB T2E 7R2, Canada

Tel: 403-250-4000

Core Laboratories, 4777 93rd Ave., Edmonton, AB T6B 2T6, Canada

Core Laboratories, 463 Devonian St., PO Box 1370, Estevan, SK S4A 2K9, Canada

CORNING INC.

One Riverfront Plaza,, Corning, NY, 14831

Tel: (607) 974-9000 Fax: (607) 974-8551 Web site: www.corning.com

Mfr. glass and specialty materials, consumer products; communications, laboratory services.

Corning Canada Inc., Toronto, ON, Canada

COUDERT BROTHERS

1114 Ave. of the Americas, New York, NY, 10036-7794

Tel: (212) 626-4400 Fax: (212) 626-4210 Web site: www.coudert.com

International law firm.

Coudert Freres, 1000 de la Gauchetiere West, Ste. 2600, Montreal, PQ H3B 4W5, Canada

Tel: 514-399-1000 Fax: 514-399-1026

COULTER CORPORATION

PO Box 169015, Miami, FL, 33116-9015

Tel: (305) 380-3800 Fax: (305) 380-8312

Mfr. blood analysis systems, flow cytometers, chemicals systems, scientific systems & reagents.

Coulter Electronics of Canada Ltd., 905 Century Drive, Burlington, ON, Canada L7L 5J8

CRANE COMPANY

100 First Stamford Place, Stamford, CT, 06907

Tel: (203) 363-7300 Fax: (203) 363-7359

Diversified mfr./distributor engineered products for industrial.

Crane Canada Inc., PO Box 2700, St. Laurent, Montreal, PQ H4L 4Y7, Canada

Navend Ind. Co. Inc., 595 Middlefield Rd., Unit 20, Scarborough, ON M1V 3S2, Canada

CROMPTON & KNOWLES CORPORATION

1 Station Place Metro Center, Stamford, CT, 06902

Tel: (203) 353-5400 Fax: (203) 353-5423 Web site: www.crompton-knowles.co

Mfr. dyes, colors, flavors, fragrances, specialty chemicals and industrial products.

Crompton & Knowles of Canada Ltd., 1313 Kamato Rd., Mississauga, ON L4W 2M2, Canada

CROSBY CORPORATION

PO Box 3128, Tulsa, OK, 74101-3128

Tel: (918) 834-4611 Fax: (918) 832-0940

Mfr. machine tools, hardware, steel forgings.

Crosby Canada Ltd., 145 Heart Lake Rd. S, Brampton, ON L6W 3K3, Canada

CROWLEY MARITIME CORPORATION

155 Grand Ave., Oakland, CA, 94612

Tel: (510) 251-7500 Fax: (510) 251-7625

Marine transportation.

Arctic Transportation Ltd., 5240 Calgary Trail, Edmonton, AB T6H 5G8, Canada

Arctic Transportation Ltd., Esso Plaza E. Tower #1900, 425 First St. SW, Calgary, AB T2P 3L8, Canada

CROWN CORK & SEAL COMPANY, INC.

One Crown Way, Philadelphia, PA, 19154-4599

Tel: (215) 698-5100 Fax: (215) 698-5201

Mfr. cans, bottle caps; filling & packaging machinery.

Crown Cork & Seal Co. Ltd., 7900 Keele St., Concord, ON L4K 1B6, Canada

CSX CORPORATION

901 East Cary Street, Richmond, VA, 23219-4031

Tel: (804) 782-1400 Fax: (804) 782-6747 Web site: www.csx.com

Provides freight delivery and contract logistics services.

CSX Corporation, Toronto, ON, Canada

CTS CORPORATION

905 Northwest Boulevard, Elkhart, IN, 46514

Tel: (219) 293-7511 Fax: (219) 293-6146

Mfr. electronic components.

CTS of Canada Ltd., 80 Thomas St., Streetsville, ON L5M 1Y9, Canada

CULLIGAN INTERNATIONAL COMPANY

One Culligan Parkway, Northbrook, IL, 60062

Tel: (847) 205-6000 Fax: (847) 205-6030 Web site: www.culligan-man.com

Water treatment products and services.

Culligan of Canada Ltd., 2213 N. Sheridan Way, Sheridan Park, Mississauga, ON L5K 1A5, Canada

Tel: 905-822-1601 Fax: 905-822-1661

CURTISS-WRIGHT CORPORATION

1200 Wall Street West, Lyndhurst, NJ, 07071

Tel: (201) 896-8400 Fax: (201) 438-5680

Mfr. precision components and systems, engineered services to aerospace, flow control and marine industry.

Metal Improvement Co. Inc., 105 Alfred Kuehne Blvd., Brampton, ON L6T 4K3, Canada

CYBORG SYSTEMS INC.

2 N. Riverside Plaza, Chicago, IL, 60606-0899

Tel: (312) 454-1865 Fax: (312) 454-0889 Web site: www.cyborg,com

Develop/mfr. human resources, payroll and time/attendance software.

Cyborg Systems Canada Inc., 7030 Woodbine Ave., 5th Fl., Markham, ON, L3R 62G, Canada

Tel: 905-479-2969 Contact: Paul Martin

CYPRUS AMAX MINERALS COMPANY

9100 East Mineral Circle, Englewood, CO, 80112

Tel: (303) 643-5000 Fax: (303) 643-5048 Web site: www.cyprusamax.com

Mining company supplying molybdenum (used in steelmaking).

Cyprus Amax Minerals Company, Canada

D'ARCY MASIUS BENTON & BOWLES INC. (DMB&B)

1675 Broadway, New York, NY, 10019

Tel: (212) 468-3622 Fax: (212) 468-2987 Web site: www.dmbb.com

Full service international advertising and communications group.

DMB&B Canada Inc., 2 Bloor St. W, Toronto, ON, Canada M4W 3R3

D-M-E COMPANY

29111 Stephenson Highway, Madison Heights, MI, 48071

Tel: (248) 398-6000 Fax: (248) 544-5705

Basic tooling for plastic molding and die casting.

DME of Canada Ltd., 6210 Northwest Dr., Mississauga, ON, Canada

DAMES & MOORE GROUP

911 Wilshire Boulevard, Los Angeles, CA, 90017

Tel: (213) 683-1560 Fax: (213) 628-0015 Web site: www.dames.com

Engineering, environmental and construction management services.

Dames & Moore Canada, 1165 Franklin Blvd., Unit E, Cambridge, ON N1R 5S4, Canada

Dames & Moore Canada, 7560 Airport Rd., Mississauga, ON L4T 2H5, Canada

Norecol Dames & Moore, 1212 West Broadway #500, Vancouver, BC V6H 3V1, Canada

Norecol Dames & Moore, 201-1290 Broad St., Victoria, BC V8W 2A5, Canada

Norecol Dames & Moore, 13571 Commerce Pkwy. #250, Richmond, BC V6V 2R2, Canada

DANA CORPORATION

4500 Door Street, Toledo, OH, 43615

Tel: (419) 535-4500 Fax: (419) 535-4643 Web site: www.dana.com

Mfr./sales of automotive, heavy truck, off-highway, fluid & mechanical power components.

Dana Commercial Credit Canada Inc., 690 Darval Drive, Ste. 310, Oakville, ON LK6 3W7, Canada

Hayes-Dana Inc., PO Box 3029, St. Catherines, ON L2R 7K9, Canada

DANIEL INDUSTRIES INC.

9753 Pine Lake Drive, PO Box 55435, Houston, TX, 77224

Tel: (713) 467-6000 Fax: (713) 827-3889 Web site: www.danielind.com

Oil/gas equipment and systems; geophysical services.

Daniel Industries Canada, #114-4215-72 Ave. S.E., Calgary, AB T2C 2G5, Canada

Tel: 403-279-1879 Fax: 403-236-1337

DARLING INTERNATIONAL INC.

251 O'Connor Ridge Blvd., Ste. 300, Irving, TX, 55038

Tel: (972) 717-0300 Fax: (972) 717-1588

Animal by-products.

Darling Intl. of Canada Ltd., Park St., PO Box 97, Chatham, ON, Canada

Tel: 519-652-5751

DATA GENERAL CORPORATION

4400 Computer Drive, Westboro, MA, 01580

Tel: (508) 898-5000 Fax: (508) 366-1319 Web site: www.dg.com

Design, mfr. general purpose computer systems & peripheral products & services.

Data General (Canada) Ind., 2155 Leanne Blvd., Mississauga, ON L5K 2K8, Canada

DATA I/O CORPORATION

10525 Willows Road, NE, Redmond, WA, 98053

Tel: (425) 881-6444 Fax: (242) 582-1043

Mfr. computer testing devices.

Data I/O Canada, 6725 Airport Rd. #302, Mississauga, ON L4V 1V2, Canada

DATA RESEARCH ASSOCIATES, INC. (DRA)

1276 North Warson Road, St. Louis, MO, 63132

Tel: (314) 432-1100 Fax: (314) 993-8927 Web site: www.dra.com

Systems integrator for libraries and information providers.

DRA, 500 Place d' Armes, Ste. 2420, Montreal, PQ H2Y QW2, Canada

Tel: 514-350-4500 Fax: 514-350-5299

DATAPRODUCTS CORPORATION

1757 Papo Kenyon Road, Simi Valley, CA, 93063

Tel: (805) 578-4000 Fax: (805) 578-4001

Mfr. computer printers and supplies.

Dataproducts Canada, 15 W. Pearce St., Richmond Hill, ON L4B 1H6, Canada

DATASCOPE CORPORATION

14 Philips Parkway, Montvale, NJ, 07645

Tel: (201) 391-8100 Fax: (201) 307-5400 Web site: www.datascope.com

Mfr. medical devices.

Datascope Medical Products, Toronto, ON, Canada

DATAWARE TECHNOLOGIES INC.

222 Third Street, Ste. 3300, Cambridge, MA, 02142

Tel: (617) 621-0820 Fax: (617) 494-0740 Web site: www.dataware.com

Multi-platform, multi-lingual software solutions & services for electronic information providers.

Megalith Technologies Inc., One Antares Dr. #200, Nepean, ON K2E 8C4, Canada

DAYCO PRODUCTS INC.

1 Prestige Place, PO Box 1004, Miamisburg, OH, 45342

Tel: (937) 226-7000 Fax: (937) 226-4689

Diversified auto, industrial and household products.

Dayco Products Canada Inc., 46 Norelco Dr., Weston, ON M9L 1S3, Canada

DDB NEEDHAM WORLDWIDE INC.

437 Madison Ave., New York, NY, 10022

Tel: (212) 415-2000 Fax: (212) 415-3417

Advertising agency.

DDB Group/Heather Reid & Associates, Toronto, ON, Canada

Griffin Bacal Volny, Toronto, Canada

DE ZURIK, A Unit of General Signal

250 Riverside Ave. North, Sartell, MN, 56377

Tel: (320) 259-2000 Fax: (320) 259-2227 Web site: www.dezurik.com

Mfr. manual, process & control valves.

DeZurik Canada, 385 Franklin Blvd., PO Box 1300, Cambridge, ON N1R 5VS, Canada

Tel: 519-621-8980 Fax: 519-621-3006 Contact: Richard Hahn, VP Operations

DEERE & COMPANY

One John Deere Road, Moline, IL, 61265

Tel: (309) 765-8000 Fax: (309) 765-5772 Web site: www.deere.com

Mfr./sale agricultural, construction, utility, forestry and lawn, grounds care equipment.

John Deere Ltd., PO Box 1000, South Service Rd. at Hunter, Grimsby, ON L3M 4H5, Canada

DEERFIELD SPECIALTY PAPERS, INC.

PO Box 5437, Augusta, GA, 30916-5437

Tel: (706) 798-1861 Fax: (706) 798-2270

Glassine papers.

Deerfield Glassine Specialty Paper, Ltd., 845 Industrial Ave., Quebec City, PQ G1K 7K7, Canada

DEKALB GENETICS CORP.

3100 Sycamore Road, DeKalb, IL, 60115-9600

Tel: (815) 758-3461 Fax: (815) 758-3711 Web site: www.dekalb.com

Develop/produce hybrid corn, sorghum, sunflower seed, varietal soybeans, alfalfa.

DeKalb Canada, R.R. 5, 585 Riverview Dr., Chatham, ON N7M 5J5, Canada

Tel: 519-352-5310 Fax: 519-352-6259 Contact: Mike McGuire, Gen. Mgr.

DEL LABORATORIES INC.

565 Broad Hollow Road, Farmingdale, NY, 11735

Tel: (516) 293-7070 Fax: (516) 293-1515 Web site: www.dellabs.com

Mfr. cosmetics, pharmaceuticals.

Commerce Drug Canada Ltd., 25 Morrow Rd., Barrie, ON L4N 3V7, Canada

Del Laboratories (Canada) Ltd., 25 Morrow Rd., Barrie, ON L4N 3V7, Canada

The Theon Co. Ltd., 25 Morrow Rd., Barrie, ON L4N 3V7, Canada

DELL COMPUTER CORPORATION

One Dell Way, Round Rock, TX, 78682-2222

Tel: (512) 338-4400 Fax: (512) 728-3653 Web site: www.dell.com

Direct marketer & supplier of computer systems.

Dell Computer Corporation, Bow Valley Square IV, 250 6th Ave. Southwest, Ste. 1500, Calgary, AB T2P 3H7, Canada

Tel: 416-758-1425 Fax: 416-758-2100 Contact: Scott O'Hare, Mng. Dir.

Dell Computer Corporation, 155 Gordon Baker Rd., Ste. 501, North York, ON M2H 2NS, Canada

Tel: 416-758-1425 Fax: 416-758-2100 Contact: Scott O'Hare, Mng. Dir.

DELOITTE TOUCHE TOHMATSU INTERNATIONAL

PO Box 820, Wilton, CT, 06897

Tel: (203) 761-3000 Fax: (203) 834-2200 Web site: www.u.s.deloitte.com or www.dtti.com

Accounting, audit, tax and management consulting services.

Deloitte & Touche, 95 Wellington St. West, Ste. 1300, Toronto, ON M5J 2P4, Canada

Deloitte & Touche, 800 Sun Life Tower, Box 40, 150 King St. West, Toronto, ON M5H 1J9, Canada

Deloitte & Touche, 181 Bay St., Bay Wellington Tower -BCE Pl., Ste.1400, Toronto, ON M5J 2V1, Canada (Locations: Clagary, Edmonton, Hamilton, Hull, Ottawa, Sarnia, Saskatoon, Vancouver, & Winnipeg, Canada.)

Samson Belair/Deloitte & Touche, 1, Place Ville-Marie, Bureau 3000, Montreal, PQ H3B 4T9, Canada

DELTA AIR LINES INC.

PO Box 20706, Atlanta, GA, 30320-6001

Tel: (404) 715-2600 Fax: (404) 715-5494 Web site: www.delta-air.com/index.html

Major worldwide airline; international air transport services.

Delta Air Lines Inc., Locations in Calgary, Montreal, Toronto, Vancouver and Edmondton, Canada

DELUXE CORPORATION

3680 Victoria Street North, Shoreview, MN, 55126-2966

Tel: (612) 483-7111 Fax: (612) 481-4163 Web site: www.deluxe.com

Leading U.S. check printer and provider of electronic payment services.

Deluxe Corporation, 800 Cochrane Drive, Markham, ON L3R 8C9, Canada

DENTSPLY INTERNATIONAL

570 West College Ave., PO Box 872, York, PA, 17405-0872

Tel: (717) 845-7511 Fax: (717) 843-6357 Web site: www.dentsply.com

Mfr.& Distribution of dental supplies & equipment.

Dentsply Canada Ltd., 161 Vinyl Court, Woodbridge, ON L4L 4A3, Canada

Tel: 905-851-6060

DETROIT DIESEL CORPORATION

13400 Outer Drive West, Detroit, MI, 48239

Tel: (313) 592-5000 Fax: (313) 592-5058

Mfr. diesel & aircraft engines, heavy-duty transmissions.

Detroit Diesel of Canada Ltd., 150 Dufferin Ave. #701, London, ON, Canada

THE DEXTER CORPORATION

1 Elm Street, Windsor Locks, CT, 06096

Tel: (860) 627-9051 Fax: (860) 627-7078

Mfr. nonwovens, polymer products, magnetic materials, biotechnology.

D&S Plastics Intl., 625 Millway Blvd., Concord, ON L4K 3T9, Canada

Life Technologies Inc., 2270 Industrial St., Burlington, ON L7P 1A1, Canada

DHL WORLDWIDE EXPRESS

333 Twin Dolphin Drive, Redwood City, CA, 94065

Tel: (650) 593-7474 Fax: (650) 593-1689 Web site: www.dhl.com

Worldwide air express carrier.

DHL Worldwide Express, 6205 Airport Rd., Bldg. B, Ste. 400, Mississauga L4V 1E1, Canada

Tel: 416-240-9999

DIAMOND POWER INTERNATIONAL, INC.

PO Box 415, Lancaster, OH, 43130

Tel: (740) 687-6500 Fax: (740) 687-7430 Web site: www.diamondpower.com

Mfg. boiler cleaning equipment & ash handling systems: sootblowers, controls, diagnostics systems, gauges, OEM parts, rebuilds & field service.

Diamond Canapower Ltd., PO Box 5051, 3070 Mainway, Units 13 & 14, Burlington, ON L7R 4A7, Canada

Tel: 905-335-0321 Fax: 905-332-6399

DICTAPHONE CORPORATION

3191 Broadbridge Ave., Stratford, CT, 06497-2559

Tel: (203) 381-7000 Fax: (203) 381-7100

Mfr./sale dictation, telephone answering and multi-channel voice communications recording systems.

Dictaphone Canada Ltd., 630 E. Mail, Etobicoke, ON M9B 4B2, Canada

DILLINGHAM CONSTRUCTION CORPORATION

5944 Inglewood Drive, Pleasanton, CA, 94566

Tel: (925) 463-3300 Fax: (925) 463-1571

General contracting.

Delta Projects Ltd., Heritage Sq. Bldg., 8500 MacLeod Trail S, PO Box 5244, Sta. A, Calgary, AB, Canada

Dillingham Construction Ltd., PO Box 5507, Postal Section L, Edmondton, AB T6C 4E9, Canada

Dillingham Construction Ltd., 20 Brookshank Ave., N. Vancouver, BC V7J 2B8, Canada

DIONEX CORPORATION

1228 Titan Way, PO Box 3603, Sunnyvale, CA, 94088-3603

Tel: (408) 737-0700 Fax: (408) 730-9403

Develop/mfr./marketing/services chromatography systems & related products.

Dionex Canada Ltd., 586 Arus Rd., Ste. 4, Oakville, ON L6J 7S1 Canada

WALT DISNEY COMPANY

500 South Buena Vista Street, Burbank, CA, 91521

Tel: (818) 560-1000 Fax: (818) 560-1930

Film/TV production, theme parks, resorts, publishing, recording and retail stores.

Walt Disney Music of Canada Ltd., 270 Rexdale Blvd., Rexdale, ON M9W 1R2, Canada

DIXON TICONDEROGA COMPANY

195 International Parkway, Heathrow, FL, 32746

Tel: (407) 829-9000 Fax: (407) 829-2574

Mfr./services writing implements and art supplies.

Dixon Ticonderoga Company, 531 Davis Dr., Newmarket, ON L3Y 2P1, Canada

Dixon Ticonderoga Company, 1100 rue Bernard, Acton Vale, PQ J0H 1A0, Canada

DOONEY & BOURKE

1 Regent Street, Norwalk, CT, 06855

Tel: (203) 853-7515 Fax: (203) 838-7754 Web site: www.dooney.com

Mfr./sales/distribution of fine leather handbags, wallets, belts and accessories.

Jazz Ogilvy/Dooney & Bourke, 1307 rue St. Catherine Quest, Montreal, PQ, Canada

Tel: 514-842-7711

DOVER CORPORATION

280 Park Ave., New York, NY, 10017-1292

Tel: (212) 922-1640 Fax: (212) 922-1656 Web site: www.dovercorporation.com

Elevator manufacturer and holding company for varied industries.

Dover Corp. (Canada) Ltd., 1551 Caterpillar Rd., Mississauga, ON L4Y 2Z6, Canada

Tel: 905-949-6700

Dover Elevators, **19 Gates Drive, Charlottetown, P.E.I, Canada**

Tel: 902-566-5010

Dover Elevators, **2423 Holly Lane, Ottawa, ON K1V 7P2, Canada**

Tel: 613-731-0353

Dover Elevators, **Unit 3, 1440 Graham's Lane, Burlington, ON L7S 1W3, Canada**

Tel: 905-681-8180 Fax: 613-399-3070

Dover Elevators, **3935 Second Ave., Burnaby, BC V5C 3W9, Canada**

Tel: 604-294-2209 Fax: 604-294-2237

Dover Elevators, **Ste. 604, 10216-124th St., Edmonton, AB T5N 4A3, Canada**

Tel: 403-488-0976 Fax: 403-482-4151

Dover Elevators, **PO Box 506, Brockville, ON K6V 6K8, Canada**

Tel: 613-498-1698 Fax: 613-498-3984

Dover Elevators, **PO Box 23010, Belleville, ON K8P 5J3, Canada**

Tel: 613-969-7977 Fax: 613-399-3070

Dover Elevators, **Unit 4, 6320-11th St., S.E., Calgary, AB T2H 1L7, Canada**

Tel: 403-259-4183 Fax: 403-252-8722

THE DOW CHEMICAL COMPANY

2030 Dow Center, Midland, MI, 48674

Tel: (517) 636-1000 Fax: (517) 636-3228 Web site: www.atdow.com

Mfr. chemicals, plastics, pharmaceuticals, agricultural products, consumer products.

Dow Canada/Western Div., **PO Box 759, Fort Saskatchewan, AB T8L 2P4, Canada**

Dow Chemical of Canada Ltd., **PO Box 1012, Sarnia, ON N7T 7K7, Canada**

DOW CORNING CORPORATION

2220 West Salzburg Road, PO Box 1767, Midland, MI, 48640

Tel: (517) 496-4000 Fax: (517) 496-6080

Silicones, silicon chemicals, solid lubricants.

Dow Corning Canada Ltd., **6747 Campobello Rd., Mississauga, ON L5N 2M2, Canada**

DRAKE BEAM MORIN INC.

101 Huntington Ave., Boston, MA, 02199

Tel: (617) 450-9860 Fax: (617) 267-2011 Web site: www.dbm.com

Human resource management consulting & training.

Drake Beam Morin - Canada Inc., **77 Bloor St. W, Toronto, ON M5S 1M2, Canada (Locations: AB, Edmonton, Halifax, Hamilton, Markham, Mississauga, Ottawa, Regina, Saskatoon, Vancouver,& Winnipeg, Canada.)**

Tel: 416-922-7561 Fax: 416-922-6831

Drake Beam Morin - Montreal, Inc., **999 De Masionneuve Blvd., West, Ste. 600, Montreal, PQ H3A 3L4, Canada**

Tel: 514-843-6886 Fax: 514-845-8812

DRAVO CORPORATION

11 Stanwix Street, 11th Fl., Pittsburgh, PA, 15222

Tel: (412) 995-5500 Fax: (412) 995-5570

Material handling equipment and process plants.

Dravo of Canada Ltd., **4935 Kent St., Niagara Falls, ON L2H 1J6, Canada**

DRESSER INDUSTRIES INC.

2001 Ross Ave., PO Box 718, Dallas, TX, 75221-0718

Tel: (214) 740-6000 Fax: (214) 740-6584 Web site: www.dresser.com

Diversified supplier of equipment & technical services to energy & natural resource industrial.

Dresser Canada Ltd., **6688 Kitimat Rd., Mississauga, ON L5N 1P8, Canada**

Dresser Wheatley, 6875 9 St. N.E., Calgary, AB T2E 8R9, Canada
Tel: 403-730-9000 Fax: 403-730-9030 Contact: John W.H. Geddes, Pres.
M.W. Kellogg Co. Ltd., 500 4th Ave. SW, Calgary, AB T2P 2V6, Canada
Pleuger Canada Ltd., 4180 Dundas St. W, Toronto, ON, Canada

DU BOIS CHEMICAL
255 East 5th Street, Cincinnati, OH, 45202-4799
Tel: (513) 762-6000 Fax: (513) 762-6030
Mfr. specialty chemicals & maintenance products.
DuBois Chemicals of Canada Ltd., 2645 Royal Windsor Dr., Mississauga, ON L5J 1L1, Canada
Tel: 905-822-3511 Fax: 905-822-3797 Contact: David Cunningham

E.I. DU PONT DE NEMOURS & COMPANY
1007 Market Street, Wilmington, DE, 19898
Tel: (302) 774-1000 Fax: (302) 774-7321 Web site: www.dupont.com
Mfr./sale diversified chemicals, plastics, specialty products and fibers.
DuPont Canada Inc., Montreal, PQ, Canada

DUKANE CORPORATION
2900 Dukane Drive, St. Charles, IL, 60174
Tel: (630) 584-2300 Fax: (630) 584-2370
Mfr. facility intercommunications, optoelectronic device assembly, plastics welding, local area network equipment.
Dukane Canada, 461 Manitou Dr., Kitchener, ON N2C 1L5, Canada
Tel: 519-748-5352

DUKE ENERGY CORPORATION
422 South Church Street, Charlotte, NC, 28242
Tel: (704) 594-6200 Fax: (704) 382-3814
Energy pipeliner, oil/gas exploration and production.
Texas Eastern Exploration of Canada Ltd., 1502 49th St. SE, Calgary, AB, Canada

THE DUN & BRADSTREET CORPORATION
One Diamond Hill Road, Murray Hill, NJ, 07974
Tel: (908) 665-5000 Fax: (908) 665-5524 Web site: www.dnbcorp.com
Provides corporate credit, marketing & accounts-receivable management services & publishes credit ratings & financial information.
Moody's Canada Inc., BCE Place 181 Bay St., Ste. 1610, PO Box 753, Toronto, ON M5JT3 Canada

DUNHAM-BUSH INC.
175 South Street, West Hartford, CT, 06110
Tel: (860) 548-3780 Fax: (860) 548-1703
Industrial & commercial refrigeration, heating & A/C equipment.
Dunham-Bush Ltd., 140 Wendell Ave., Weston, ON, Canada

DUNHILL INTERNATIONAL SEARCH
59 Elm Street, Ste. 520, New Haven, CT, 06510
Tel: (203) 562-0511 Fax: (203) 562-2637
International recruiting services: sales/marketing, accounting/finance, general managers.
Dunhill of London, 159 Albert St., London, ON N5A 1L9, Canada

DURO-TEST CORPORATION
9 Law Drive, Fairfield, NJ, 07004
Tel: (973) 808-1800 Fax: (973) 808-7107
Mfr. fluorescent, incandescent & fluomeric lamps.

Duro-Test Canada Inc., 419 Attwell Dr., Rexdale, ON M9W 5W5, Canada
Tel: 416-675-1623 Fax: 416-675-8875 Contact: John Marshall, Gen. Mgr.

DYNATECH CORPORATION
3 New England Executive Park, Burlington, MA, 01803
Tel: (781) 272-6100 Fax: (781) 272-2304
Develop/mfr. communications equipment.
Dynatech Communications Ltd., Markham, ON, Canada
TTC Canada, Mississauga, ON, Canada

DYNEGY INC.
1000 Louisiana, Ste. 5800, Houston, TX, 77002
Tel: (713) 507-6400 Fax: (713) 507-3871 Web site: www.dynegy.com
Holding company that transports and markets energy to local utililties and industrial businesses.
Dynegy Canada, Inc., 350 Seventh Ave., S.W. , Ste. 2200, Calgary, AB T2P 3NG, Canada
Tel: 403-213-6000 Fax: 403-213-6005 Contact: Rod Wimer, Pres.

E-Z-EM INC.
717 Main Street, Westbury, NY, 11590
Tel: (516) 333-8230 Fax: (516) 333-8278 Web site: www.ezem.com
World's leading supplier of barium contrast media for medical imaging and accessories.
E-Z-EM Canada Inc., 11100 Colbert, Anjou, PQ H1J 2M9, Canada
Tel: 514-353-5820 Fax: 514-351-3450 Contact: Pierre-André Ouimet Emp: 200

THE EASTERN COMPANY
112 Bridge Street, Naugatuck, CT, 06770
Tel: (203) 729-2255 Fax: (203) 723-8653
Mfr. locks & security hardware.
Eberhard Hardware Ltd., PO Box 367, Tillsonburg, ON N4G 4H8, Canada

EASTMAN CHEMICAL
100 North Eastman Road, Kingsport, TN, 37660
Tel: (423) 229-2000 Fax: (423) 229-1351 Web site: www.eastman.com
Mfr. plastics, chemicals, fibers.
Eastman Chemical Canada, Inc., 11 Allstate Parkway, Ste. 430, Markham, ON L3R 9T8, Canada
Tel: 905-474-0101 Fax: 906474-1610
Eastman Chemical Canada, Inc., 15127 - 100th Ave., Ste. 204, Surrey, BC V3R 0N9, Canada
Tel: 604-582-6277 Fax: 604-583-6439 Contact: Gordon H. Burnham
Eastman Chemical Canada, Inc., 3100 Cote Vertu, Ste. 450, St. Laurent, PQ H4R 2J8, Canada
Tel: 514-332-5440 Fax: 514-332-4982

EASTMAN KODAK COMPANY
343 State Street, Rochester, NY, 14650
Tel: (716) 724-4000 Fax: (716) 724-0663
Develop/mfr. photo & chemicals products, information management/video/copier systems, fibers/plastics for various industry.
Eastmanchem Inc., 11 Allstate Pkwy., Markham, ON L3R 9T8, Canada
Eastmanchem Inc., Also in Vancouver & St. Laurent, Canada
Kodak Canada Inc., Also in Calgary, Edmonton, Vancouver, Winnipeg, Ottawa, Montreal & Ste. Foy, Canada
Kodak Canada Inc., 3500 Eglinton Ave. W, Toronto, ON M6M 1V3, Canada

EATON CORPORATION
1111 Superior Ave., Cleveland, OH, 44114
Tel: (216) 523-5000 Fax: (216) 479-7068
Advanced technical products for transportation & industrial markets.

Eaton Yale Ltd., 566 Riverview Dr., Chatham, ON N7M 5L9, Canada

EATON CORP/CUTLER HAMMER

4201 North 27th Street, Milwaukee, WI, 53216

Tel: (414) 449-6000 Fax: (414) 449-6221

Electric control apparatus, mfr. of advanced technologic products.

Eaton Yale Ltd., 45 Progress Ave., Scarborough, ON M1P 2Y6, Canada

ECHLIN INC.

100 Double Beach Road, Branford, CT, 06405

Tel: (203) 481-5751 Fax: (203) 481-6485 Web site: www.echlin.com

Supplies commercial vehicle components and auto fluid handling systems for the used car market

Echlin Canada, 6601 Goreway Drive, Mississauga, ON L4V 1V6, Canada

Tel: 905-405-0955

ECHO BAY MINES LTD.

6400 South Fidders Green Circle, Ste. 1000, Englewood, CO, 80111

Tel: (303) 714-8600 Fax: (303) 714-8999

Gold and silver mining.

Echo Bay Mines, 1210 Manulife Place, 10180 101st St., Edmonton, AB, T5J 354, Canada

Echo Bay Mines, Ste. 350, 66 Burrard St., Vancouver, BC, V6C 2XB, Canada

Tel: 604-662-4994

ECLIPSE INC.

1665 Elmwood Road, Rockford, IL, 61103

Tel: (815) 877-3031 Fax: (815) 877-3336

Mfr. industrial process heating equipment & systems.

Eclipse Combustion Ltd., 1145 Westport Crescent, Mississauga, ON L5T 1E8, Canada

ECOLAB INC.

Ecolab Center, 370 N. Wabasha Street, St. Paul, MN, 55102

Tel: (612) 293-2233 Fax: (612) 225-3105 Web site: www.ecolab.com

Develop/mfr. premium cleaning, sanitizing and maintenance products and services for the hospitality, institutional, and residential markets.

Ecolab Canada Ltd., 5105 Tomken Rd., Mississauga, ON, L4W 2X5, Canada

Tel: 905-238-0171 Fax: 905-238-2947

ECOWATER SYSTEMS INC.

1890 Woodlane Drive, Woodbury, MN, 55125

Tel: (612) 739-5330 Fax: (612) 739-4547 Web site: www.ecowater.com

Mfr. water treatment and purification products.

EcoWater Systems of Canada, 891 Rowntree Dairy Rd., Woodbridge, ON L4L 5W3, Canada

Contact: Al Dennis, Gen. Mgr.

EDDIE BAUER INC.

15010 NE 36th Street, Redmont, WA, 98052

Tel: (425) 882-6100 Fax: (425) 882-6383 Web site: www.eddiebauer.com

Clothing retailer & mail order catalog company.

Eddie Bauer Inc., Canada

EDELMAN PUBLIC RELATIONS WORLDWIDE

200 East Randolph Drive, 63rd Floor, Chicago, IL, 60601

Tel: (312) 240-3000 Fax: (312) 240-0596 Web site: www.edelman.com

International independent public relations firm.

Edelman Public Relations Canada, 2015 rue Peel, Ste. 500, Montreal, PQ H3A 1T8, Canada

Tel: 514-288-8290 Fax: 514-288-3479 Contact: Armand Torchia, Chmn.

Edelman Public Relations Canada, 214 King St. West, Ste. 600, Toronto, ON M5H 3S6 Canada
Tel: 416-979-1120 Fax: 416979-0176 Contact: Charles Fremes, Pres.

EDO CORPORATION
60 East 42nd Street, Ste. 5010, New York, NY, 10165
Tel: (212) 716-2000 Fax: (212) 716-2050
Mfr. aircraft parts and equipment.
Edo Canada Ltd., 1940 Centre Ave. NE, Calgary, AB T2E 0A7, Canada

J.D. EDWARDS & COMPANY
One Technology Way, Denver, CO, 80237
Tel: (303) 334-4000 Fax: (303) 334-4970 Web site: www.jdedwards.com.
Computer software products.
J. D. Edwards Ltd., 2225 Sheppard Ave. East, Ste. 700 Willowdale, ON M2J 5C2, Canada
Tel: 416-756-9393 Fax: 416-275-9399
J. D. Edwards Ltd., 425 - I St., S.W., Ste. 3400, Esso Plaza, Calgary, AB. T2P 3L8, Canada
Tel: 514-925-2600 Fax: 514-925-2626
J. D. Edwards Ltd., 400-66 Queen St., Ottawa, ON, Canada
Tel: 403-265-6080 Fax: 403-265-0389

EDWARDS SYSTEM TECHNOLOGY
90 Fieldston Court, Cheshire, CT, 06410
Tel: (203) 699-3000 Fax: (203) 699-3031
Mfr. fire safety equipment, signaling systems.
Edwards System Technology Intl., 6465 Airport Rd., Mississauga, ON L4Z 1E4, Canada

EFCO
1800 NE Broadway Ave., Des Moines, IA, 50316-0386
Tel: (515) 266-1141 Fax: (515) 266-7970
Mfr. systems for concrete construction.
EFCO Ltd., 527 E. Lake Blvd., PO Box 3682, Airdrie, AB T4B 2B8, Canada
EFCO Ltd., 30 Todd Rd., Georgetown, ON L7G 4R7, Canada

EG&G INC.
45 William Street, Wellesley, MA, 02181-4078
Tel: (781) 237-5100 Fax: (781) 431-4114
Diversified R/D, mfr. & services.
EG&G Canada Ltd., 22001 Dumberry Rd., Vaudreuil, PQ, Canada J7V 8P7
EG&G Canada Ltd./Instruments Div., 6535 Millcreek Dr., Unit 58, Mississauga, ON L5N 2M2, Canada
EG&G Sealol, 9379 Trans Canada Hwy., St. Laurent, PQ H4S 1V3, Canada
EG&G Sealol, 373 Vidal St S. #F, Sarnia, ON N7T 2V3, Canada
EG&G Sealol, 3424 78th Ave., Edmonton, AB T6B 2X9, Canada
Wallac Canada, 342 Aime-Vincent, Vaudreuil, PQ J7V 5V5, Canada

ELECTRIC FURNACE COMPANY
435 Wilson Street, Salem, OH, 44460
Tel: (330) 332-4661 Fax: (330) 332-1853
Mfr./design heat treating furnaces for metals industrial.
Canefco Ltd., 50 Milne Ave., Scarborough, ON M1L 1K3, Canada

THE EMBALMERS' SUPPLY COMPANY
1370 Honeyspot Road Ext, Stratford, CT, 06497
Tel: (203) 375-2984 Fax: (203) 378-9160
Embalmers chemicals, equipment & supplies.

Embalmers Supply Co. Canada Ltd., 42 Haas Rd., Rexdale, ON N9W 3A2, Canada

EMC CORP.

35 Parkwood Drive, Hopkinton, MA, 01748-9103

Tel: (508) 435-1000 Fax: (508) 435-8884 Web site: www.emc.com

Designs/supplies intelligent enterprise storage & retrieval technology for open systems, mainframes & midrange environments.

EMC Computer Systems - Canada, 275 Slatu St., Ottawa K1P 5H9, Canada

Tel: 613-233-2536

EMC Computer Systems - Canada, 2700 Matheson Blvd. East, Ste. 300, East Tower, Mississauga, ON L4W 4V9, Canada

Tel: 905-206-1580

EMC Computer Systems - Canada, 3773 Cote Vertu, Ste. 280, Ville St., St. Laurent, Montreal H4R 2M3, PQ, Canada

Tel: 514-856-6160

EMC Computer Systems - Canada, 2100 Bankers Hall, 855 2nd St., S.W. AB, Calgary T2P 4J9, Canada

Tel: 403-273-4824

EMCO WHEATON INC.

409A Airport Blvd, Morrisville, NC, 27560

Tel: (919) 467-5878 Fax: (919) 467-7718

Mfr. petroleum handling equipment.

Emco Wheaton Ltd., 136 The East Mall, Toronto, ON M8Z 5M2, Canada

EMERSON ELECTRIC COMPANY

8000 West Florissant Ave., PO Box 4100, St. Louis, MO, 63136

Tel: (314) 553-2000 Fax: (314) 553-3527 Web site: www.emersonelectric.com

Electrical and electronic products, industrial components and systems, consumer, government and defense products.

Emerson Electric Canada Ltd., 9999 Markum Rd., Markum, ON, L3P3J3 Canada

EMERSON RADIO CORPORATION

9 Entin Road, Parsippany, NJ, 07054

Tel: (973) 884-5800 Fax: (973) 428-2033

Consumer electronics, radios, TV & VCR, tape recorders and players, computer products.

Emerson Radio Canada Ltd., 6455 Vipond Dr., Mississauga, ON L5T 1S7, Canada

EMERY WORLDWIDE

One Lagoon Drive, Ste. 400, Redwood City, CA, 94065

Tel: (650) 596-9600 Fax: (650) 596-7901 Web site: www.emeryworld.com

Freight transport, global logistics and air cargo.

Canadian Freightways Ltd., 2100-78th Ave. NE, Calgary Intl. Airport, Calgary, AB T2E 6W6, Canada

ENCYCLOPAEDIA BRITANNICA INC.

310 S. Michigan Ave., Chicago, IL, 60604

Tel: (312) 427-9700 Fax: (312) 294-2176 Web site: www.E.B.com

Publishing; books.

Encyclopaedia Britannica Publications Ltd., 186 Shoemaker St., PO Box 9055, Kitchener, ON N2G 4Y1, Canada

ENGELHARD CORPORATION

101 Wood Ave. S., CN 770, Iselin, NJ, 08830

Tel: (732) 205-5000 Fax: (732) 632-9253

Mfr. pigments, additives, catalysts, chemicals, engineered materials.

Engelhard Canada Ltd., 195 Riviera Dr., Markham, ON L3R 5J61, Canada

ENTERPRISES INTERNATIONAL INC.

PO Box 293, Hoquiam, WA, 98550

Tel: (360) 533-6222 Fax: (360) 532-2792

Mfr./sale/services capital equipment for pulp, paper and newsprint industrial.

Gerrard-Ovalstrapping, 5330 South Service Rd., Burlington, ON L7L 5L1, Canada

EQUIFAX INC.

PO Box 4081, Atlanta, GA, 30302

Tel: (404) 885-8000 Fax: (404) 888-5452 Web site: www.equifax.com

Information and knowledge-based solutions.

Acrofax Inc., 7171 Jean Talon E., Anjou, PQ H1M 23N2, Canada

CBS Credit Bureau Services Ltd., 60 Bloor St. W. #1200, Toronto, ON M4W 3C1, Canada

Equifax Accounts Receivable Services Inc., 60 Bloor St. W. #1200, Toronto, ON M4W 3C1, Canada

Equifax Canada Inc., 7171 Jean Talon E., Anjou, PQ H1M 3N2, Canada

ERICO PRODUCTS INC.

34600 Solon Road, Cleveland, OH, 44139

Tel: (440) 248-0100 Fax: (440) 248-0723

Mfr. electric welding apparatus & hardware, metal stampings, specialty fasteners.

Erico Inc., 46 Ingram Dr., Toronto, ON M6M 2L6, Canada

ERIE INTERNATIONAL LTD

4000 South 13th Street, Milwaukee, WI, 53221

Tel: (414) 483-0524 Fax: (414) 483-6610

Mfr. controls, valves.

Erie Mfg. Co. (Canada) Ltd., Stouffville, ON, Canada

ERIEZ MAGNETICS

PO Box 10652, Erie, PA, 16514

Tel: (814) 833-9881 Fax: (814) 833-3348

Mfr. magnets, vibratory feeders, metal detectors, screeners/sizers, mining equipment, current separators.

Eriez of Canada Ltd., 200 Admiral Blvd., Mississauga, ON L5T 2N6, Canada

ERNST & YOUNG, LLP

787 Seventh Ave., New York, NY, 10019

Tel: (212) 773-3000 Fax: (212) 773-6350 Web site: www.eyi.com

Accounting and audit, tax and management consulting services.

Ernst & Young, Ernst & Young Tower, PO Box 251, Toronto-Dominion Ctr., Toronto, ON, M5K 1J7, Canada

Tel: 416-943-3146 Fax: 416-943-2201 Contact: Kerry Gray

ESCO CORPORATION

2141 NW 25th Ave., Portland, OR, 97210

Tel: (503) 228-2141 Fax: (503) 778-6330

Mfr. equipment for mining, construction and forestry industries.

ESCO Ltd., 1855 Kingsway Ave., Port Coquitlam, BC V3C 1T1, Canada

ETHYL CORPORATION

330 South 4th Street, PO Box 2189, Richmond, VA, 23219

Tel: (804) 788-5000 Fax: (804) 788-5688

Mfr. fuel & lubricant additives.

Ethyl Canada Inc., 350 Burnhamthorpe Rd. W, Mississauga, ON L5B 3J1, Canada

EVENFLO COMPANY, INC.

1000 Evenflo Drive, Canton, GA, 30114

Tel: (770) 704-2000 Fax: (770) 704-2002

Mfr. of baby products.

Evenflo Canada, 1171 Invicta Drive, Oakville, ON L6H 4MI, Canada

Tel: 905-337-2229 Contact: Tom Jorgensen, Dir.

EXIDE ELECTRONICS INTERNATIONAL CORPORATION

8521 Six Forks Road, Raleigh, NC, 27615

Tel: (919) 870-3020 Fax: (919) 870-3100 Web site: www.exide.com

Mfr./services uninterruptible power systems.

Exide Electronics, 380 Carlingview Drive, Etobicoke, ON, Canada M9W 5X9, Canada

Tel: 416-798-0112 Fax: 416-798-0062 Contact: Greg Bork

EXOLON-ESK COMPANY

1000 East Niagara Street, PO Box 590, Tonawanda, NY, 14151-0590

Tel: (716) 693-4550 Fax: (716) 693-0151

Mfr. fused aluminum oxide and silicon carbide abrasive grains.

Exolon-Esk Co. of Canada Ltd., PO Box 280, Thorold, ON L2V 3Z2, Canada

EXPEDITORS INTERNATIONAL OF WASHINGTON INC.

999 Throd Ave., Ste. 2500, Seattle, WA, 98104

Tel: (206) 674-3400 Fax: (206) 682-9777 Web site: www.expd.com

Air/ocean freight forwarding, customs brokerage, international logistics solutions.

EI Freight Canada Ltd., 6285 Northam Dr., Ste. 200, Mississauga, ON L4V 1X5, Canada

Tel: 905-673-0900 Fax: 905-673-0976

Expeditors Canada, Inc., Unit 230, 10691 Shellbridge Way, Richmond, BC V6X 2W8, Canada

Tel: 604-244-8543 Fax: 604-244-8503

EXXON CORPORATION

225 E. John W. Carpenter Freeway, Irving, TX, 75062-2298

Tel: (972) 444-1000 Fax: (972) 444-1882 Web site: www.exxon.com

Petroleum exploration, production, refining; mfr. petroleum & chemicals products; coal & minerals.

Exxon Chemical - Imperial Oil, Darthmouth Refinery, PO Box 1001, Darthmouth, NS BY2 3Z7, Canada

Exxon Chemical - Sarnia Chemical Plant, 1 Esso Chemical Drive, PO Box 3033, Sarnia, ON N7T 7Z4, Canada

Imperial Oil Ltd., 111 St. Clair Ave. W, Toronto, ON M5W 1K3, Canada

THE FALK CORPORATION

3001 W. Canal Street, PO Box 492,, Milwaukee, WI, 53208

Tel: (414) 238-4919 Fax: (414) 937-4359 Web site: www.falkcorp.com

Designers and manufacturers of power transmission equipment including gears, geared reducers & drives, couplings.

Falk of Canada Ltd., 45 Disco Rd., Etobicoke, ON M9W 1M2, Canada

Tel: 416-675-6071 Fax: 416-213-1020 Contact: Paul Harris

FARR COMPANY

2221 Park Place, El Segundo, CA, 90245

Tel: (310) 536-6300 Fax: (310) 643-9086

Mfr. filtration equipment.

Farr Co. Ltd., 2785 Francis Hughes Ave., Chomedey, Laval, PQ H7L 3J6, Canada

FAXON CO., INC.

15 Southwest Park, Westwood, MA, 02090

Tel: (781) 329-3350 Fax: (781) 329-9875

Distributor books & periodicals.

Faxon Canada Ltd., Routledge Rd., Hyde Park, ON NOM 1ZO, Canada

FEDERAL-MOGUL CHAMPION SPARK PLUG COMPANY

900 Upton Ave., Toledo, OH, 43607

Tel: (419) 535-2567 Fax: (419) 535-2332

Mfr. spark plugs, wiper blades and related products.

Champion Spark Plug Co. of Canada Ltd., PO Box 910, Windsor, ON, Canada

FEDERAL-MOGUL CORPORATION

26555 Northwestern Highway, PO Box 1966, Southfield, MI, 48034

Tel: (248) 354-7700 Fax: (248) 354-8983 Web site: www.federalmogul.com

Mfr./distributor precision parts for automobiles, trucks, farm and construction vehicles.

Federal-Mogul Canada Investment Co., Ontario, Canada

Federal-Mogul Canada Ltd., Locations: Calgary, Edmonton, Moncton, Montreal, Toronto, Vancouver & Winnipeg, Canada.

FERRO CORPORATION

1000 Lakeside Ave., Cleveland, OH, 44114-1183

Tel: (216) 641-8580 Fax: (216) 696-5784 Web site: www.ferro.com

Mfr. Specialty chemicals, coatings, plastics, colors, refractories.

Ferro Canada Ltd., Western Division, Gelcoats 8390, 124th St., Surrey, BC V3W 3X9, Canada

Tel: 604-599-4928 Fax: 604-594-0813 Contact: Chuck Handy, Bus. Mgr.

Ferro Industrial Products Ltd., 354 Davis Rd., Oakville, ON L6J 2X1, Canada

Tel: 905-845-4277 Fax: 905-845-9676 Contact: Henry Knoch, Adm. Mgr.

Ferro Quebec - Gelcoats, 3391, Route157, N.D. DuMont-Carmel, PQ, G0X 3J0, Canada

Tel: 819-378-6169 Fax: 819-378-7291 Contact: Remy Forget, Bus. Mgr.

Queen City Distributors Ltd., 49 Toro Rd., Downsview, ON M3J 2A4, Canada

Tel: 905-630-2110 Fax: 905-630-0667 Contact: Rick Craddock, Bus. Mgr.

FIDELITY INVESTMENTS

82 Devonshire Street, Boston, MA, 02109

Tel: (617) 563-7000 Fax: (617) 476-6105 Web site: www.fidelity.com

Diversified financial services company offering investment management, retirement, brokerage, and shareholder services directly to individuals and institutions and through financial intermediaries.

Fidelity Canada, Ltd., Canadian Hdqrts., E&Y Tower, 222 Bay St., Ste. 900, Toronto, ON M5K 1P1, Canada

Tel: 416-307-5300 Fax: 416-971-7678 Contact: Kevin J. Kelly, Pres.

Fidelity Investments Canada, Ltd., Locations in Halifax, Montreal, Ottawa, Vancourver and Winnipeg, Canada

FileNET CORPORATION

3565 Harbor Boulevard, Costa Mesa, CA, 92626

Tel: (714) 966-3400 Fax: (714) 966-3490 Web site: www.filenet.com

Provides integrated document management (IDM) software and services for internet and client server-based imaging, workflow, cold and electronic document imanagement solutions.

FileNET Canada, Inc., 4576 Yonge St., Ste. 512, North York, ON Canada M2N 6N4

Tel: 416-223-8400

FIRST CHICAGO NBD CORPORATION

One First National Plaza, Chicago, IL, 60670

Tel: (312) 732-4000 Fax: (312) 732-4000 Web site: www.fcnbd.com

Financial products and services.

First National Bank of Chicago, BCE Place, POBox 613, 161 Bay St., Ste. 4240, Toronto, ON M5J2S1, Canada

Tel: 416-865-0466 Fax: 416-363-7574 Contact: William Buchanan, President

FIRST NATIONAL BANK OF CHICAGO

One First National Plaza, Chicago, IL, 60670

Tel: (312) 732-4000 Fax: (312) 732-3620

Financial services.

First National Bank of Chicago (Canada), PO Box 448, Two First Canadian Place, Toronto, ON M5X 1E4, Canada

FIRST SPICE MIXING COMPANY

33-33 Greenpoint Ave., Long Island City, NY, 11101

Tel: (718) 361-2556 Fax: (718) 361-2515

Mfr. spices & seasonings.

First Spice Mixing Co. (Canada) Ltd., 98 Tycos Drive, Toronto, ON M6B 1V9, Canada

FISERV INC.

PO Box 979, 255 Fiserv Drive, Brookfield, WI, 53008-0979

Tel: (414) 879-5000 Fax: (414) 879-5013 Web site: www.fiserv.com

Data processing products and services for the financial industry.

Fiserv Solutions of Canada, Inc., 901 King St. West, 7th Fl., Toronto, ON M5V 3H5, Canada

FISHER SCIENTIFIC INC.

Liberty Lane, Hampton, NH, 03842

Tel: (603) 929-5911 Fax: (603) 929-0222 Web site: www.fisher1.com

Mfr. science instruments & apparatus, chemicals, reagents.

Fisher Scientific Ltd., 112 Colonnade Rd., Ottawa, ON K1G 4A9, Canada

Tel: 800-2FISHER Fax: 800-463-2996

FISHER-ROSEMOUNT

8000 Maryland Ave., Ste. 500, Clayton, MO, 63105-4755

Tel: (314) 746-9900 Fax: (314) 746-9974

Mfr. industrial process control equipment.

Fisher Controls Co. of Canada Ltd., PO Box 578, 1039 Dundas St., Woodstock, ON N4S 7Z6, Canada

Fisher Controls Co. of Canada Ltd., 360 Holiday Inn Dr., Cambridge, ON N3C 3Z9, Canada

Fisher Service Co., 2122 84th Ave., Edmonton, AB T6P 1K2, Canada

Spartan Controls Ltd., 11421 98th Ave., Grande Prairie, AB T8V 5S5, Canada

Tel: 403-539-1161 Fax: 403-532-2608

Spartan Controls Ltd., 10919 Alaska Rd., Fort St. John, BC V1J 6P3, Canada

Tel: 604-785-0285 Fax: 604-785-0280

Spartan Controls Ltd., Ste. 3, 350 MacAlpine Crescent, Fort McMurray, AB, Canada

Tel: 403-790-0440 Fax: 403-790-1535

Spartan Controls Ltd., 8225 Davies Rd., Edmonton, AB T6E 4N3, Canada

Tel: 403-468-5463 Fax: 403-465-2655

Spartan Controls Ltd., 305-27 St., S.E., Calgary, AB T2A 7V2, Canada

Tel: 403-207-0700 Fax: 403-207-0873

FLEETWOOD ENTERPRISES, INC.

3125 Myers Street, PO Box 7638, Riverside, CA, 92513-7638

Tel: (909) 351-3500 Fax: (909) 351-3724 Web site: www.Fleetwood.com

Manufacture homes and recreational vehicles.

Fleetwood Canada, Ltd., PO Box 485, Lindsay, ON K9V 5G4, Canada

Tel: 705-324-0095 Contact: Norm Smith, Div. Gen. Mgr.

FLINT INK CORPORATION

25111 Glendale Ave., Detroit, MI, 48239-2689

Tel: (313) 538-6800 Fax: (313) 538-3538 Web site: www.flintink.com

Manufacturer of printing inks and pigments.

Flink Ink Corporation of Canada, 704 Meridian Rd. N.E., Calgary, AB T2A 2N7, Canada

Tel: 403-272-4011 Fax: 403-248-4708 Contact: Daniel T. Keough, Pres.

Flint Ink Corporation of Canada, 9450 Tourlon, St. Leonard, PQ H1R 2J3, Canada

Tel: 514-852-6999 Fax: 514-852-4010 Contact: Daniel T. Keough, Pres.

Flint Ink Corporation of Canada, 800 Berry St., Winnipeg, MB R3H OS, Canada

Tel: 204-774-3571 Fax: 204-786-1310 Contact: Daniel T. Keough, Pres.

Flint Ink Corporation of Canada, 7978 82nd St., Ste. 100, Delta, BC V4G 1L8, Canada

Tel: 604-940-3880 Fax: 604-940-3881 Contact: Daniel T. Keough, Pres.

Flint Ink Corporation of Canada, 143 Stronach Crescent, London, ON N5V 3G5, Canada

Tel: 519-451-7620 Fax: 519-453-1604 Contact: Daniel T. Keough, Pres.

Flint Ink Corporation of Canada, 511 Millway Ave., Concord, ON L4K 3V4, Canada

Tel: 905-660-0360 Fax: 905-660-0364 Contact: Daniel T. Keough, Pres.

FLOWSERVE CORPORATION

222 W. Los Cloinas Blvd., Irving, TX, 75039

Tel: (972) 443-6500 Fax: (972) 443-6858 Web site: www.flowserve.com

Mfr. chemicals equipment, pumps, valves, filters, fans and heat exchangers.

Automax Controls, 3375 Laird Rd., Unit 4, Mississauga, ON L5L 5R7, Canada

Duriron Canada Inc., 120 Vinyl Ct., Wood Bridge, ON L4L 4A3, Canada

Tel: 905-856-8568

Duriron Canada Inc., 2160 Springer Ave., Burnaby, BC V5B 3M7, Canada

Valtek Controls Ltd., 9044 18th St., Edmonton, AB T6P 1K6, Canada

Tel: 403-449-4850

FLOWSERVE FLUID SEALING DIVISION

222 Los Colinas Blvd., Ste. 1500, Irving, TX, 75039

Tel: (616) 381-2650 Fax: (616) 443-6800 Web site: www.flowserve.com

Mfr. mechanical seals, compression packings and auxiliaries.

Durametallic Canada Inc., 130 Edward St., St. Thomas, ON N5P 1Z1, Canada

FLUKE CORPORATION

PO Box 9090, Everett, WA, 98206-9090

Tel: (425) 347-6100 Fax: (425) 356-5116 Web site: www.fluke.com

Mfr. electronic test tools.

Fluke Electronics Canada Inc., 400 Britannia Rd. E, Unit 1, Mississauga, ON L4Z 1X9, Canada

Tel: 905-890-7600 Fax: 905-890-6866

FLUOR DANIEL INC.

3353 Michelson Drive, Irvine, CA, 92698

Tel: (714) 975-2000 Fax: (714) 975-5271 Web site: www.flourdaniel.com

Engineering & construction services.

Fluor Daniel Canada Inc., 10101 Southport Rd. SW, Calgary, AB T2W 3N2, Canada

Fluor Daniel Wright/Wright Egineers Ltd., 1075 W. Georgia St. #500, Vancouver, BC V6E 4M7, Canada

FMC CORPORATION

200 E. Randolph Drive, Chicago, IL, 60601

Tel: (312) 861-6000 Fax: (312) 861-6141

Produces chemicals & precious metals, mfr. machinery, equipment & systems for industrial, agricultural & government use.

FMC of Canada Ltd., Toronto, ON, Canada

Marine Colloids Ltd., Canada

Mid-Atlantic Investments Ltd., Canada

FORD MOTOR COMPANY

The American Road, Dearborn, MI, 48121

Tel: (313) 322-3000 Fax: (313) 322-9600 Web site: www.ford.com

Mfr./sales motor vehicles.

Ford Motor Co. of Canada Ltd., PO Box 2000, Canadian Rd., Oakville, ON, Canada

FOREST OIL CORPORATION

1600 Broadway, Ste. 2200, Denver, CO, 80202

Tel: (303) 812-1400 Fax: (303) 812-1602

Crude oil and natural gas.

Caneagle Resources Corp., Calgary, AB, Canada (All mail to U.S. address)

Forest Canada I Development Ltd., Calgary, AB, Canada (All mail to U.S. address)

Forest Marketing Corp., Calgary, AB, Canada (All mail to U.S. address)

Forest Oil of Canada Ltd., Calgary, AB, Canada (All mail to U.S. address)

FORT JAMES CORPORATION

1650 Lake Cook Road, Deerfield, IL, 60015

Tel: (847) 317-5000 Fax: (847) 236-3755 Web site: www.fortjames.com

Mfr./sales of consumer paper and packaging products.

Fort James Corporation, Toronto, ON, Canada

Fort James Corporation, Edmonton, AB, Canada

FOSTER WHEELER CORPORATION

Perryville Corporate Park, Clinton, NJ, 08809-4000

Tel: (908) 730-4000 Fax: (908) 730-5300

Manufacturing, engineering and construction.

Foster Wheeler Ltd. (Canada), PO Box 3007, St. Catharines, ON L2R 7B7, Canada

FOUR WINDS INTERNATIONAL GROUP

1500 SW First Ave., Ste. 850, Portland, OR, 97201-2013

Tel: (503) 241-2732 Fax: (503) 241-1829 Web site: www.vanlines.com.au

Transportation of household goods and general cargo and third party logistics.

Four Winds Canada, 3016 21st St. NE, Calgary, AB T2E 6Z2, Canada

Tel: 403-250-7015 Fax: 403-250-1356 Contact: Paul Phone, Mgr. Emp: 150

FRANK RUSSELL COMPANY

909 A Street, Tacoma, WA, 98402

Tel: (253) 572-9500 Fax: (253) 591-3495 Web site: www.russell.com

Investment management & asset strategy consulting.

Frank Russell Canada Ltd., One First Canadian Place, 100 King St. West, Ste. 5900, Toronto, ON MSX 1E4 Canada

Tel: 416-362-8411 Fax: 416-362-4494 Contact: Craig Wainscott, Mng. Dir. Emp: 56

FRANKLIN COVEY CO.

2200 W. Parkway Blvd., Salt Lake City, UT, 84119-2331

Tel: (801) 975-1776 Fax: (801) 977-1431 Web site: www.franklinquest.com

Provides productivity and time management products and seminars.

Franklin Covey Canada, 1165 Franklin Blvd., Cambridge, ON N1R 8E1, Canada

Tel: 519-740-2580 Fax: 519-740-8833

Franklin Covey Canada, One First Canadian Place, Box 319, Street Level, Toronto, ON M5K 1E1, Canada

Tel: 416-362-7964 Fax: 416-362-0079

Franklin Covey Canada, Eaton Centre, 223, 751-3rd St., SW, Calgary, AL T2P 4K8, Canada

Tel: 403-262-6558 Fax: 403-262-6962

FRANKLIN ELECTRIC CO., INC.

400 East Spring Street, Bluffton, IN, 46714-3798

Tel: (219) 824-2900 Fax: (219) 824-2909 Web site: www.fele.com

Mfr./distribute electric motors, submersible motors and controls.

Franklin Electric of Canada Ltd., PO Box 5008, Strathroy, ON N7G 3J3, Canada

THE FRANKLIN MINT

US Route 1, Franklin Center, PA, 19091

Tel: (610) 459-6000 Fax: (610) 459-6880

Design/marketing collectibles & luxury items.

Franklin Mint Canada, 90 Royal Crest Ct., Markham, ON L3R 9T6, Canada

FRANKLIN RESOURCES, INC.

777 Mariners Island Blvd., San Mateo, CA, 94404

Tel: (415) 312-2000 Fax: (415) 312-3655 Web site: www.frk.com

Global and domestic investment advisory and portfolio management.

Templeton Management Ltd., Edmonton, AB, Canada

Tel: 800-387-0830

Templeton Management Ltd., Montreal, PQ, Canada

Tel: 800-387-0830

Templeton Management Ltd., Toronto, ON, Canada

Tel: 800-387-0830

Templeton Management Ltd., Vancouver, British Colombia, Canada

Tel: 800-387-0830

FRITZ COMPANIES INC.

706 Mission Street, Ste. 900, San Francisco, CA, 94103

Tel: (415) 904-8360 Fax: (415) 904-8661 Web site: www.fritz.com

Integrated transportation, sourcing, distribution & customs brokerage services.

Fritz Starber Inc., Head Office - Montreal, Canada (Locations: 40 in Canada)

H.B. FULLER COMPANY

1200 Willow Lake Blvd., Vadnais Heights, MN, 55110

Tel: (612) 236-5900 Fax: (612) 236-5898 Web site: www.hbfuller.com

Mfr./distributor adhesives, sealants, coatings, paints, waxes, sanitation chemicals.

H.B. Fuller Canada Inc., 880 Rangeview Dr., Mississauga, ON L5E 1G9, Canada

Tel: 905-274-1238 Fax: 905-274-5837

H.B. Fuller Canada Inc., 88 Industrial Blvd., Boucherville (Montreal), PQ J4B 2X2, Canada (Location: St. Andre Est, Quebec.)

Tel: 514-655-1324 Fax: 514-655-6380

GAF CORPORATION

1361 Alps Road, Wayne, NJ, 07470

Tel: (973) 628-3000 Fax: (973) 628-3326 Web site: www.gaf.com

Mfr. building materials.

GAF (Canada) Inc., 7575 Trans Canada Hwy., Ville St. Laurent, PQ 4HT IV6, Canada

GAF (Canada) Ltd., 1075 Queensway E, Mississauga, ON L4Y 4C1, Canada

LEWIS GALOOB TOYS INC.

500 Forbes Blvd., S. San Francisco, CA, 94080

Tel: (650) 952-1678 Fax: (650) 583-4996 Web site: www.galoob.com

Mfr. toys, games, dolls.

Galoob Toys Canada Inc., 400 Ambassador Drive, Mississauga, ON L5T 2J3, Canada

THE GAP

1 Harrison Street, San Francisco, CA, 94105

Tel: (650) 952-4400 Fax: (650) 952-5884

Clothing store chain.

The Gap, Canada

Canada

GARLOCK SEALING TECHNOLOGIES

1666 Division Street, Palmyra, NY, 14522

Tel: (315) 597-4811 Fax: (315) 597-3216 Web site: www.garlock-inc.com

Mfr. of gaskets, packing, seals and expansion joints.

Garlock of Canada Ltd., 2860 Plymouth Drive, Oakville, ON L6H 5S8, Canada

Tel: 905-829-3200 Fax: 905-829-3333 Contact: William Price, Pres.

Garlock of Canada Ltd. Textile Div., 4100 rue Garlock, Sherbrooke, PQ J1L 1W5, Canada

Tel: 819-563-8080 Fax: 819-563-5620 Contact: Gilles Vallee, VP, Gen. Mgr.

THE GATES RUBBER COMPANY

990 S. Broadway, PO Box 5887, Denver, CO, 80217-5887

Tel: (303) 744-1911 Fax: (303) 744-4000

Mfr. rubber tires/inner tubes & industrial belts & hose.

Gates Canada Inc., 300 Henry St., Brantford, ON N3T 5W1, Canada

GATX CAPITAL CORPORATION

Four Embarcadero Center, Ste. 2200, San Francisco, CA, 94111

Tel: (415) 955-3200 Fax: (415) 955-3449

Lease & loan financing, residual guarantees.

GATX Leasing National Ltd., PO Box 94, Sun Life Tower #2411, 150 King St. W, Toronto, ON, M5H 1J9 Canada

GB ELECTRICAL INC.

6101 North Baker Road, Milwaukee, WI, 53209

Tel: (414) 352-4160 Fax: (414) 228-1616

Mfr./distributor electric consumable items & specialty tools.

GB Electrical Inc., 6615 Ordan Dr., Unit 15, Mississauga, ON L5T 1X2, Canada

Tel: 905-564-5749

GENCORP INC.

175 Ghent Road, Fairlawn, OH, 44333-3300

Tel: (216) 869-4200 Fax: (216) 869-4211

Mfr. aerospace/defense, automotive & polymer products.

GenCorp, 100 Kennedy St., PO Box 1002, Welland, ON, Canada

GENERAL BINDING CORPORATION

One GBC Plaza, Northbrook, IL, 60062

Tel: (847) 272-3700 Fax: (847) 272-1369

Binding and laminating equipment and associated supplies.

GBC Canada Inc., 49 Railside Rd., Don Mills, ON M3A 1B3, Canada

GENERAL CABLE CORPORATION

4 Tesseneer Drive, Highland Heights, KY, 41076

Tel: (606) 572-8000 Fax: (606) 572-8444 Web site: www.generalcable.com

Mfr. wire and cable.

General Cable Canada Ltd., 345 Signet Dr., Weston, ON M9L 1V3, Canada

Tel: 416-741-0867 Fax: 416-741-7456 Contact: Les Kinch Emp: 14

GENERAL CHEMICAL GROUP INC.

Liberty Lane, Hampton, NH, 03842

Tel: (603) 929-2606 Fax: (603) 929-2404

Mfr./produce inorganic chemicals and soda ash.

General Chemical Group Inc., Toronto, ON, Canada

GENERAL DATACOMM INC.

1579 Straits Turnpike, PO Box 1299, Middlebury, CT, 06762-1299

Tel: (203) 574-1118 Fax: (203) 758-8507

Mfr./sale/services transportation equipment for communications networks.

General DataComm Ltd., 2255 Sheppard Ave. E #308W, Willowdale, ON M2J 4Y1, Canada

GENERAL DYNAMICS CORPORATION

3190 Fairview Park Drive, Falls Church, VA, 22042-4523

Tel: (703) 876-3000 Fax: (703) 876-3125 Web site: www.gendyn.com

Mfr. aerospace equipment, submarines, strategic systems, armored vehicles, defense support systems.

Computing Devices Canada, 3785 Richmond Rd., Neapean, ON, Canada

Tel: 613-596-7000 Fax: 613-596-7775 Contact: David E. Scott, Pres.

GENERAL ELECTRIC CAPITAL CORPORATION

260 Long Ridge Road, Stamford, CT, 06927

Tel: (203) 357-4000 Fax: (203) 357-6489

Financial, property/casualty insurance, computer sales and trailer leasing services.

Employers Reinsurance Corp. (ERC), Ste. 400, 200 Wellington St. West, PO Box 166, Toronto, ON M5V 3C7, Canada

Tel: 416-217-5555 Fax: 416-362-5556

GENERAL ELECTRIC CO.

3135 Easton Turnpike, Fairfield, CT, 06431

Tel: (203) 373-2211 Fax: (203) 373-3131 Web site: www.ge.com

Diversified manufacturing, technology and services.

GE Aircraft Engines, 2 blvd de L'Aeropo, Bromont, PQ J0E 1L0, Canada (Locations: Calgary, Mississauga)

Tel: 514-534-3270

GE FANUC Automation, Unit #170 6815 - 8th St. N.E., Calgary AB, T2E 7H7 Canada (Locations: St. Laurent, PQ; Mississauga, ON; Burnaby, BC, Canada)

Tel: 403-571-2314 Fax: 403-571-2333

GE International, 2300 Meadowvale Blvd., Mississauga, ON, Canada

Tel: 905-858-9009

General Electric - Canada, 107 Park St. North, Peterborough, ON K9J 7B5, Canada

Tel: 705-748-8486

General Electric Co. - CAMCO, Headquarters - 2645 Skylark Ave., Mississauga, ON, L4W 4H2, Canada (Locations: Montreal, Peterborough, Canada.)

Tel: 416-629-3000

GEPS Global Power Generation, 7420 St. Jacques St., Montreal PQ H4B 1W3, Canada (Locations: Edmonton, AB; Kamloops, BC; Winnipeg, MB, Canada.)

Tel: 514-340-5502

GENERAL LATEX & CHEMICAL CORPORATION

675 Massachusetts Ave., Cambridge, MA, 02139

Tel: (617) 576-8000 Fax: (617) 876-1010

Mfr. latex compounds & dispersions, urethane foam systems.

General Latex Canada Inc., 23 Chemin Handel #4B, Candiac, PQ JR5 1R7, Canada

General Latex Canada Inc., 68 Eastern Ave. E, Brampton, ON L6W 1X8, Canada

GENERAL MILLS INC.

1 General Mills Blvd., PO Box 1113, Minneapolis, MN, 55440

Tel: (612) 540-2311 Fax: (612) 540-4925

Mfr. consumer foods.

General Mills Canada Inc., 1330 Martin Grove Rd., Etobicoke, ON M9W 4X4, Canada

Tel: 416-743-8110 Contact: Christi Strauss

GENERAL MOTORS CORPORATION

100 Renaissance Center, Detroit, MI, 48243.7301

Tel: (313) 556-5000 Fax: (313) 556-5108 Web site: www.gm.com

Mfr. full line vehicles, automotive electronics, commercial technologies, telecommunications, space, finance.

Diesel Div. of GM Canada Ltd., PO Box 5160, London, ON N6A 4N5, Canada

Diesel Div. of GM Canada Ltd., 1000 Industrial Blvd., St. Eustache, PQ J7R 5A5, Canada

General Motors of Canada Ltd., 215 William St. E, Oshawa, ON L1G 1K7, Canada

GENERAL REINSURANCE CORPORATION

695 East Main Street, Stamford, CT, 06904-2350

Tel: (203) 328-5000 Fax: (203) 328-6423 Web site: www.genre.com

Reinsurance services worldwide.

Canadian Aircraft Insurance Group Toronto, Royal Bank Plaza, South Tower, 200 Bay St., Ste. 2450, Toronto, ON M5J 2J1, Canada

Tel: 416-865-0252 Fax: N/A Contact: Richard Neufeld, VP

Canadian Aircraft Insurance Group Vancouver, Stock Exchange Tower, 609 Granville St., Ste. 1290, Vancouver, BC V7Y 1C6, Canada

Tel: 604-669-6113 Contact: Geoffrey Watkins, VP

Cologne Reinsurance Company, 3650 Victoria Park Ave., Ste. 201, Toronto, ON M2H 3P7, Canada

Tel: 416-496-1148 Fax: 416-496-1089 Contact: Lorraine Williams, Agent

General Re Financial Products Toronto, 1 First Canadian Place, Ste. 5705, PO Box 471, Toronto, ON M5X 1E4, Canada

Tel: 416-360-2060 Fax: 416-360-2010 Contact: Sandra Taube-Godard

General Reinsurance Corporation Montreal, 1002 Sherbrooke West, Ste. 2000, Montreal, PQ H3A 3L6, Canada

Tel: 514-288-9667 Fax: 514-288-6751 Contact: Mark G. Schmitz, VP

GENERAL TIME CORPORATION

PO Box 4125, Norcross, GA, 30091-4125

Tel: (770) 447-5300 Fax: (770) 242-4009

Mfr. Clocks & watches.

Westclox Canada Ltd., Peterborough, ON, Canada

GENICOM CORPORATION

14800 Conference Center Drive, Ste. 400, Chantilly, VA, 20151

Tel: (703) 802-9200 Fax: (703) 802-9039

Supplier of network systems, service & printer solutions.

Genicom Canada Inc., 5420 Timberlea Blvd., Mississaugua, ON, L4W 2T7 Canada

Tel: 800-268-0464

THE GEON COMPANY

One Geon Center, Avon Lake, OH, 44012

Tel: (440) 930-1000 Fax: (440) 930-3551

Mfr. vinyl resins & compounds.

The Geon Co., Niagara Falls (ON) & Scotford (AB), Canada

GEONEX CORPORATION

8950 9th Street North, St. Petersburg, FL, 33702

Tel: (813) 578-0100 Fax: (813) 577-6946

Geo-information services: mapping, resource interpretation, analysis, testing and data base management.

Geonex Corp., 3883 Nashua Dr., Mississauga, ON L4V 1R3, Canada

GEORGIA GULF CORPORATION

400 Perimeter Center Terrace, Atlanta, GA, 30346

Tel: (404) 395-4500 Fax: (404) 395-4529

Mfr./marketing commodity chemicals & polymers.

Georgia Gulf Corp., Montreal (PQ) & Toronto (ON), Canada

GEORGIA-PACIFIC GROUP

133 Peachtree Street NE, 41st Floor, Atlanta, GA, 30303

Tel: (404) 652-4000 Fax: (404) 230-7008 Web site: www.gp.com

Mfr./sales bldg. products including lumber, paper products, metal products, chemicals and plastics.

Federal Packaging & Partitioning Co. Ltd., PO Box 148, Toronto, ON L1S 3C2, Canada

Georgia-Pacific Group, 525 Jean Paul Vincent, Longueuil, Canada

Tel: 514-670-7750

Georgia-Pacific Group, 6711 Mississauga Rd., Mississauga, ON L5N 2W3606, Canada

Tel: 905-813-8555

GERBER PRODUCTS COMPANY

445 State Street, Fremont, MI, 49412

Tel: (616) 928-2000 Fax: (616) 928-2723

Mfr./distributor baby food and related products.

Gerber (Canada) Inc., 56 Brockport Dr., Etobicoke, ON M9W 5N1, Canada

THE GILLETTE COMPANY

Prudential Tower Building, Boston, MA, 02199

Tel: (617) 421-7000 Fax: (617) 421-7123 Web site: www.gillette.com

Develop/mfr. personal care/use products: blades & razors, toiletries, cosmetics, stationery.

Braun Canada Ltd/Ltee., Mississauga, ON, Canada

Gillette Canada Inc., Kirkland, PQ, Canada

Jafra Intl. Inc., Markham, ON, Canada

Oral-B Laboratories Inc., Mississauga, ON, Canada

P.H. GLATFELTER COMPANY

228 South Main Street, Spring Grove, PA, 17362

Tel: (717) 225-4711 Fax: (717) 225-6834

Mfr. printing & specialty papers.

Ecusta Fibres Ltd., 346 Norquay Dr., Winkler, MB R6W 4B1, Canada

GODIVA CHOCOLATIER INC.

355 Lexington Ave., New York, NY, 10017

Tel: (212) 984-5900 Fax: (212) 984-5901

Mfr. chocolate candy, Biscotti dipping cookies and after-dinner coffees.

Godiva Chocolatier, Inc., Sherway Gardens, 25 The West Mall, Etobicoke, ON M9C 1B8, Canada

Tel: 415-622-1106

Godiva Chocolatier, Inc., Ogilvy's, 1307 St. Catherine St. West, Montreal, PQ H3G 1P7, Canada

Tel: 514-849-4789

GOLDEN BOOKS PUBLISHING COMPANY

888 Seventh Ave., New York, NY, 10106

Tel: (212) 567-6700 Fax: (212) 567-6788

Publishing children's and adult books, educational and electronic products.

Golden Books (Canada) Ltd., 200 Sheldon Dr., Cambridge, ON N1R 5X2, Canada

Tel: 519-623--3590 Fax: 519-623-3598 Contact: Frank R. White, Pres. Emp: 40

GOLDMAN SACHS & COMPANY

85 Broad Street, New York, NY, 10004

Tel: (212) 902-1000 Fax: (212) 902-3000 Web site: www.gs.com

Investment bankers; securities broker dealers.

Goldman Sachs Canada, 600 blvd de Maisonneuve Quest, Bureau 2350, Montreal, PQ H3A 3J2, Canada

Tel: 514-499-1510

Goldman, Sachs Canada, 150 King St. West, Ste. 1201, Toronto, ON M5H 1J9, Canada

Tel: 416-343-8900

Goldman, Sachs Canada, 200 Burrard St., 1630 Waterfront Centre, Vancouver, BC V6C 3L6, Canada

Tel: 604-257-1301

THE GOODYEAR TIRE & RUBBER COMPANY

1144 East Market Street, Akron, OH, 44316

Tel: (330) 796-2121 Fax: (330) 796-1817 Web site: www.goodyear.com

Mfr. tires, automotive belts and hose, conveyor belts, chemicals; oil pipeline transmission.

Goodyear Canada Inc., 10 Four Seasons Pl., Etobicoke, ON M9B 6G2, Canada (Locations: Bowmanville, ON; Collingwood, ON; Medicine Hat, AB; Napanee, ON; & Owen Sound,ON,Canada

Granford Mfg. Inc., Deregibus Blvd., St. Alphonse deGranby, PQ, Canada

THE GORMAN-RUPP COMPANY

PO Box 1217, Mansfield, OH, 44901

Tel: (419) 755-1011 Fax: (419) 755-1266 Web site: www.gormanrupp.com

Mfr. pumps and related equipment, waste water and environmental equipment.

Gorman-Rupp of Canada Ltd., 70 Burwell Rd., St. Thomas, ON N5P 3R7, Canada

Tel: 519-631-2870 Fax: 519-631-4624 Contact: Bill Horn, Gen. Mgr.

GORTON'S

327 Main Street, Gloucester, MA, 01930

Tel: (978) 283-3000 Fax: (978) 281-8295

Frozen fish.

Blue Water Seafood Ltd., 1640 Brandon Crescent, Lachine, Montreal, PQ H8T 2N1, Canada

GOULDS PUMPS INC.

240 Fall Street, Seneca Falls, NY, 13148

Tel: (315) 568-2811 Fax: (315) 568-2418

Mfr. industrial and water systems pumps.

Goulds Pumps Canada Inc., 185 Sheldon Dr., Cambridge, ON N1T 1A6, Canada

Goulds Pumps Canada Inc., 550 71st Ave., SE, Ste. 150, Calgary T2H 056, Canada

GPU INTERNATIONAL, INC.

300 Madison Ave., Morristown, NJ, 07962-1911

Tel: (973) 455-8200 Fax: (973) 455-8582 Web site: www.gpu.com

Global electric energy company.

GPU International, Vancouver, BC, Canada

W. R. GRACE & COMPANY

One Town Center Road, 1750 Clint Moore Road, Boca Raton, FL, 33486-1010

Tel: (561) 362-2000 Fax: (561) 561-2193 Web site: www.grace.com

Mfr. specialty chemicals and materials: packaging, health care, catalysts, construction, water treatment/process.

Grace Construction Products, 294 Clements Rd. West, Ajax, ON L1S 3C6 Canada

Tel: 905-683-8561 Fax: 905-683-5947

Grace Davison, 42 Fabre St., Valleyfield, PQ J6S 4K7, Canada

Tel: 514-373-4224 Fax: 514-373-7327

Grace Dearborn Inc., 3451 Erindale Station Rd., Mississauga, ON L5C 2S9, Canada

W.R. Grace & Co. of Canada Ltd., 294 Clements Rd. W, Ajax, ON L1S 3C6, Canada

W.R. Grace & Co. of Canada Ltd., Cryovac Div., 2365 Dixie Rd., Mississauga, ON L4Y 2A2, Canada

GRACO INC

4050 Olson Memorial Hwy, PO Box 1441, Minneapolis, MN, 55440-1441

Tel: (612) 623-6000 Fax: (612) 623-6777 Web site: www.graco.com

Mfr./sales of infant & juvenile products; services fluid handling equipment & systems.

Elfe Juvenile Products, 4580 Hickmore St., St.-Laurent, PQ H4T 1K2, Canada

Tel: 514-344-3533 Fax: 514-344-9296 Contact: Tracy McLeod

Graco Canada Inc., 3400 American Dr., Mississauga, ON L4V 1C1, Canada

GRANT THORNTON INTERNATIONAL

800 One Prudential Plaza, 130 E. Randolph Drive, Chicago, IL, 60601-6050

Tel: (312) 856-0001 Fax: (312) 616-7052

Accounting, audit, tax and management consulting services.

Doane Raymond Grant Thornton, Ste. 1900, 500-4th Ave. SW, Calgary, AB T2P 2V6, Canada

Tel: 403-260-2500 Fax: 403-260-2571 Contact: Michael J. Hudson

Doane Raymond Grant Thornton, Ste. 200, 888 St. Jean St., Quebec City, PQ G1R5H6, Canada

Tel: 418-647-3151 Fax: 418-647-5939 Contact: Roger Demers

Doane Raymond Grant Thornton, Ste. 1200, 350 Sparks St., Ottawa, ON K1R 7S8, Canada

Tel: 613-236-2211 Fax: 613-236-6104 Contact: Richard Baril

Doane Raymond Grant Thornton, Ste. 1900, 600 de La Gauchetiere St. West, Montreal, PQ H3B 4L8, Canada

Tel: 514-878-2691 Fax: 514-878-2127 Contact: Jacques Gilbert

Doane Raymond Grant Thornton, Ste. 1100, 2000 Barrington St., Cogswell Tower, PO Box 42, Halifax, NS B3J 2P8, Canada

Tel: 902-421-1734 Fax: 902-420-1068 Contact: Glenn R. Williams

Doane Raymond Grant Thornton, Ste. 500, 455 King St. West, Sherbrooke, PQ J1H 6G4, Canada

Tel: 819-822-4000 Fax: 819-821-3640 Contact: Nil Allaire

Doane Raymond Grant Thornton, Ste. 501, 199 Grafton St., PO Box 187, Charlottetown, PEI C1A7K4, Canada

Tel: 902-892-6547 Fax: 902-566-5358 Contact: J. Alan Long

Doane Raymond Grant Thornton, Ste. 2800, Royal Centre, 1055 W. Georgia St., PO Box 11177, Vancouver, BC V6E 4N3,Canada

Tel: 604-687-2711 Fax: 604-685-6569 Contact: David L. Merrell

Doane Raymond Grant Thornton, 350 Sparks St., Ste. 1200, Ottawa, ON K1R7S8, Canada

Tel: 613-236-2211 Fax: 613-236-6104 Contact: Richard Baril

Doane Raymond Grant Thornton, 19th Fl., South Tower, Royal Bank Plaza, 200 Bay St., Box 55, Toronto, ON M5J2P9, Canada

Tel: 416-366-0100 Fax: 416-360-4944 Contact: Howard Warren

Doane Raymond Grant Thornton, Ste. 1301, 10205-101 St., Edmonton, AB T5J2Z1, Canada

Tel: 403-422-7114 Fax: 403-426-3208 Contact: J. Albert Mondor

Grant Thornton Intl, No. America & Caribbean Divisional Office, 15 Gamelin Blvd., Ste. 400, Hull, PQ J8Y IV4, Canada

Tel: 819-770-9833 Fax: 819-770-4331 Contact: Jacques Carrière

GRAPHIC CONTROLS CORPORATION

PO Box 1271, Buffalo, NY, 14240

Tel: (716) 853-7500 Fax: (716) 847-7551

Mfr. information, medical and physiological monitoring products.

Graphic Controls Canada Ltd., Herbert St., Gananoque, ON K7G 2Y7, Canada

THE GREAT ATLANTIC & PACIFIC TEA COMPANY

2 Paragon Drive, Montvale, NJ, 07645

Tel: (201) 573-9700 Fax: (201) 930-8144 Web site: www.aptea.com

Supermarket chain

Great Atlantic & Pacific Tea Co., 5559 Dundas St. West, Etobike, ON M9B 1B9, Canada

Tel: 416-239-7171

GREAT WESTERN CHEMICAL & McCALL OIL CO.

808 SW Fifteenth Ave., Portland, OR, 97205

Tel: (503) 228-2600 Fax: (503) 221-5752

Industrial chemical distribution & logistics.

Great Western Chemical Co., 1599 Derwent Way, Annacis Island Delta, BC V3M 6K8, Canada

Great Western Chemical Co., Bay 11, 4155 75th Ave. SE, Calgary, AB T2C 2K8, Canada

HARBISON WALKER REFRACTORIES CO.

600 Grant Street, Pittsburgh, PA, 15219

Tel: (412) 562-6200 Fax: (412) 562-6331

Mfr. refractories and lime.

Harbison Walker Refractories, 234 Rosemont Ave., Weston, ON M9N 3C4, Canada

GREY ADVERTISING INC.

777 Third Ave., New York, NY, 10017

Tel: (212) 546-2000 Fax: (212) 546-1495 Web site: www.giworldwwide.com

International advertising agency.

Grey Canada, 1881 Yonge St., Toronto, ON M4S 3C4, Canada

GREYHOUND LINES INC.

PO Box 660362, Dallas, TX, 75266

Tel: (972) 789-7000 Fax: (972) 789-7330

Mfr. consumer products, transportation, consumer and financial services.

Brewster Transport Co. Ltd., PO Box 1140, Banff, AB, Canada T0L 0C0

Greyhound Computer of Canada Ltd., 181 University Ave., Toronto, ON M8S 3M7, Canada

Greyhound Lines of Canada Ltd., 877 Greyhound Way SW, Calgary, AB T3C 3V8, Canada

Motor Coach Industries Inc., 1149 St. Matthews Ave., Winnipeg, MB, R3G 0J8, Canada

GRIFFIN WHEEL COMPANY

200 West Monroe Street, Chicago, IL, 60606

Tel: (312) 346-3300 Fax: (312) 346-3373

Mfr. cast steel wheels & composition brake shoes for railroad freight cars & diesel locomotives.

Griffin Canada Inc., 1375 Brouillette St., St. Hyacinthe, PQ J2S 7B6, Canada

GRIFFITH LABORATORIES INC

One Griffith Center, Alsip, IL, 60658

Tel: (708) 371-0900 Fax: (708) 597-3294 Web site: www.griffithlabs.com

Industrial food ingredients and equipment.

The Griffith Laboratories Ltd., 757 Pharmacy Ave., Scarborough, ON M1L 3J8, Canada

Tel: 416-288-3050

GROUNDWATER TECHNOLOGY INC

100 River Ridge Drive, Norwood, MA, 02062

Tel: (781) 769-7600 Fax: (781) 769-7992

Industrial site cleanup, management & consulting.

Groundwater Technology Inc., 1500 Trinity Dr., Mississauga, ON L5T 1L6, Canada

Groundwater Technology Inc., 10200 Louis H. Lafontaine, Anjoy, PQ H1J 2T3, Canada

GTE CORPORATION

One Stamford Forum, Stamford, CT, 06904

Tel: (203) 965-2000 Fax: (203) 965-2277 Web site: www.gte.com

Electronic products, telecommunications systems, publishing and communications.

BC Telecom, Vancouver, BC, Canada

GTE Electrical Products, Mfg. plants & laboratories throughout Canada

Québec Tel Group, Inc., Rimouski, PQ, Canada

GTE DIRECTORIES CORPORATION

2200 West Airfield Drive, DFW Airport, TX, 75261-9810

Tel: (972) 453-7000 Fax: (972) 453-7573

Publishing telephone directories.

Dominion Directory Co. Ltd., 4400 Dominion St., Burnaby, BC V5G 4G4, Canada

GUEST SUPPLY INC.

PO Box 902, Monmouth Junction, NJ, 08852-0902

Tel: (609) 514-9696 Fax: (609) 514-2692

Mfr. personal care & housekeeping products.

Guest Intl. (Canada) Ltd., 55 Village Centre Place, Mississauga, ON L4Z 1V9, Canada

GULTON INDUSTRIES INC

212 Durham Ave., Metuchen, NJ, 08840

Tel: (732) 548-6500 Fax: (732) 548-6781

Electronic instruments, controls and communications equipment.

Gulton Industries (Canada) Ltd., 3451 Herbert St., Gananoque, ON K7G 2V1, Canada

HALLIBURTON COMPANY

500 North Akard Street, Ste. 3600, Dallas, TX, 75201-3391

Tel: (214) 978-2600 Fax: (214) 978-2685 Web site: www.halliburton.com

Energy, construction and insurance.

Halliburton Ltd., 1400 Tamarack Rd., Slave Lake, AB, TOG 2A2, Canada

Halliburton Ltd., Ste. 1000, 333-5th Ave. SW, Calgary, AB, T2P 3B6, Canada

Tel: 403-231-9300 Fax: 403-231-9420

HALLMARK CARDS INC.

PO Box 419580, Kansas City, MO, 64141

Tel: (816) 274-5100 Fax: (816) 274-5061

Mfr. greeting cards and related products.

Hallmark Cards Canada, 2 Hallcrown Pl., Willowdale, ON M2J 1P6, Canada

Tel: 416-492-1300

HANDLEMAN COMPANY

500 Kirts Boulevard, Troy, MI, 48084

Tel: (248) 362-4400 Fax: (248) 362-3615

Distributor pre-recorded music, books, video cassettes and computer software.

Handleman Co. of Canada Ltd., 10 Newgale Gate, Unit 1-4, Scarborough, ON M1X 1C5, Canada

HANDY & HARMAN

555 Theodore Fremd Ave., Rye, NY, 10580

Tel: (914) 921-5200 Fax: (914) 925-4496

Precious & specialty metals for industry, refining, scrap metal; diversified industrial mfr.

Handy & Harman of Canada Ltd., 290 Carlingview Dr., Rexdale, ON M9W 5G1, Canada

HARCO TECHNOLOGIES CORPORATION

1055 W. Smith Road, Medina, OH, 44256

Tel: (330) 725-6681 Fax: (330) 723-0244 Web site: www.corrpro.com

Full-services corrosion engineering, cathodic protection.

Corrpro Canada, Ste. 200, 807 Manning Rd., N.E., Calgary AB T2E 7M8, Canada

Tel: 403-235-6400 Fax: 403-272-9508 Contact: Dave Webster

Corrpro Canada Ottawa, Ste. 351, 5929L Jeaanne D'Arc Blvd., Orleans, ON K1C 7K2, Canada

Tel: 613-841-6045 Fax: 819-779-9053 Contact: Dr. Rejean J. H. Brousseau

HARCOURT BRACE & COMPANY

6277 Sea Harbor Drive, Orlando, FL, 32887

Tel: (407) 345-2000 Fax: (407) 345-9354

Book publishing, tests and related service, journals, facsimile reprints, management consult, operates parks/shows.

Harcourt Brace Canada Inc., 55 Horner Ave., Toronto, ON M8Z 4X6, Canada

HARCOURT GENERAL

27 Boylston Street, Chestnut Hill, MA, 02167

Tel: (617) 232-8200 Fax: (617) 739-1395 Web site: www.harcourt-general.com

Publishing, specialty retailing and professional services.

Holt Rinehart & Winston, 55 Horner Ave., Toronto, ON M8Z 4X6, Canada

W.B. Saunders & Co. Ltd., 1 Goldthorne Ave., Toronto, ON, Canada

HARNISCHFEGER INDUSTRIES INC

PO Box 554, Milwaukee, WI, 53201

Tel: (414) 797-6480 Fax: (414) 797-6573 Web site: www.harnischfeger.com

Mfr. mining and material handling equipment, papermaking machinery and computer systems.

Beloit Canada Ltd./Ltee., 1 Innovation Dr., Renfrew, ON K7V 4H4, Canada

Harnischfeger Corp. of Canada Ltd., 2 Lawsing Square #301, North York, ON M2J 4P8, Canada

Harnischfeger Corp. of Canada Ltd., 12391 No. 5 Rd., Richmond, BC, Canada V7A 4E9

Rader Canada Inc., PO Box 65567, Postal Station F, Vancouver, BC V5N 5K5, Canada

Rader Canada Inc., PO Box 925, Ville St. Laurent, Montreal, PQ H4L 4W3, Canada

THE HARPER GROUP

260 Townsend Street, San Francisco, CA, 94107-1719

Tel: (415) 978-0600 Fax: (415) 978-0692 Web site: www.circleintl.com

Ocean/air freight forwarding, customs brokerage, packing and wholesale, logistics management and insurance.

Circle Freight Intl. (Canada) Inc., Also in Montreal (PQ) & Vancouver (BC), Canada

Circle Intl. Freight (Canada) Ltd., PO Box 83, Toronto, ON L5P 1A2, Canada

Max Gruenhut Intl. (Canada), 81 Kelfield St., Unit 10, Rexdale, ON M9W 5A3, Canada

Max Gruenhut Intl. (Canada), Also in Montreal (PQ) & Vancouver (BC), Canada

HARRIS CORPORATION

1025 West NASA Blvd., Melbourne, FL, 32919

Tel: (407) 727-9100 Fax: (407) 727-9344 Web site: www.harris.com

Mfr. communications and information-handling equipment, including copying and fax systems.

Harris Canada Inc., 3 Hotel de Ville, Dollard des Ormeaux, PQ H9P 3G4, Canada

Tel: 415-421-8400

HARSCO CORPORATION

PO Box 8888, Camp Hill, PA, 17001-8888

Tel: (717) 763-7064 Fax: (717) 763-6424

Metal reclamation and mill services, infrastructure and construction and process industry products.

CapProducts of Canada, 25 Winnepeg St., Vanastra, ON N0M 1LO, Canada

THE HARTFORD FINANCIAL SERVICES GROUP, INC.

Hartford Plaza, Hartford, CT, 06115

Tel: (860) 547-5000 Fax: (860) 547-5817 Web site: www.thehartford.com

Financial services.

The Hartford Canada, 20 York Mills Rd., Willowdale, ON M2P 2C2, Canada

Tel: 416-218-1941 Fax: 416-733-1463 Contact: John Zink, Dir.

HARTFORD RE COMPANY

55 Farmington Ave., Ste. 800, Hartford, CT, 06105

Tel: (860) 520-2700 Fax: (860) 520-2726

Reinsurance.

Hartford Re Canada, 320 Bay St., Ste. 720, Toronto, ON M5H 4A6, Canada

Tel: 416-360-7721 Fax: 416-360-4099 Contact: Michael J. Rende, Gen. Mgr.

THE HARTFORD STEAM BOILER INSPECTION & INSURANCE COMPANY

One State Street, PO Box5024, Hartford, CT, 06102-5024

Tel: (860) 722-1866 Fax: (860) 722-5770 Web site: www.hsb.com

Inspection and quality assurance and asbestos monitoring.

The Boiler Inspection and Insurance Co. of Canada, 18 King St. E., Mezzanine, Toronto, ON M5C 1C4, Canada

HARTWELL BROTHERS HANDLE COMPANY

PO Box 80327, Memphis, TN, 38108

Tel: (901) 452-2191 Fax: (901) 452-0267

Mfr. replacement tool handles.

Elgin Handles Ltd., 21 Kains St., St. Thomas, ON N5P 1M8 Canada

Tel: 519-631-0330 Fax: 519-631-2001 Contact: Gary Keathley Emp: 40

HARVARD APPARATUS

84 October Hill Road, Holliston, MA, 01746

Tel: (508) 893-8999 Fax: (508) 429-5732 Web site: www.harvardapparatus.com

Mfr./sales life science research products.

Harvard Apparatus, Canada, 6010 Vanden Abeele St., Saint Laurent, PQ H4S 1R9, Canada

Tel: 514-335-0792 Fax: 514-335-3482 Contact: Robert Dinwoodie, Pres.

HASBRO INDUSTRIES INC

1027 Newport Ave., Pawtucket, RI, 02861

Tel: (401) 725-8697 Fax: (401) 727-5099 Web site: www.hasbro.com

Toys, games and dolls.

Hasbro Industries (Canada) Ltd., 2350 de la Province, Longueuil, PQ, Canada

HASTINGS MFG. COMPANY

325 North Hanover Street, Hastings, MI, 49058

Tel: (616) 945-2491 Fax: (616) 945-4667

Mfr. piston rings, filters.

Hastings Inc., 400 Huronia, Barrie, ON L5M 4V3, Canada

HAYWARD INDUSTRIAL PRODUCTS INC.

900 Fairmount Avenue, Elizabeth, NJ, 07207

Tel: (908) 351-5400 Fax: (908) 351-7893

Mfr. industrial strainers.

Hayward Canada, 1701 Flint Rd., North York, ON M3J 2W8, Canada

HEALTH-MOR INC

3500 Payne Ave., Cleveland, OH, 44114

Tel: (216) 432-1990 Fax: (216) 432-0013

Mfr. floor care products, metal tubing, specialty machinery, tools, dies.

HMI Inc., 34 Greensboro Dr., Rexdale, ON M9W 1E1, Canada

Tube-Fab Ltd., 15 Ellen St., Mississauga, ON L5M 2C1, Canada

HEAT TIMER SERVICE CORPORATION

10 Dwight Place, Fairfield, NJ, 07006

Tel: (973) 575-4004 Fax: (973) 575-4052

Heating systems controls, smoke alarms, digital temp and set point controls.

Steam & Industrial Equip. Co., 776 Halpern Ave., Dorval, PQ, Canada

HEIDRICK & STRUGGLES INC

Sears Tower, 233 South Wacker Drive, Chicago, IL, 60606

Tel: (312) 496-1200 Fax: (312) 496-1290 Web site: www.h-s.com

Executive search firm.

Heidrick & Struggles Intl. Inc., BCE Place, 161 Bay St., Ste. 2310, PO Box 601, Toronto, ON M5J 2S1, Canada

Tel: 416-361-4700 Fax: 416-361-4770

H.J. HEINZ COMPANY

600 Grant Street, Pittsburgh, PA, 15219

Tel: (412) 456-5700 Fax: (412) 456-6128 Web site: www.heinz.com

Processed food products and nutritional services.

H.J. Heinz Co. of Canada Ltd., North York, ON, Canada

Heinz Bakery Products, Mississauga, ON, Canada

Omstead Foods Ltd., Wheatley, ON, Canada

Shady Maple Farm Ltd., LaGuadeloupe, PQ, Canada

The Fitness Institute, Willowdale, ON, Canada

HENRY VALVE COMPANY

3215 North Ave., Melrose Park, IL, 60160

Tel: (708) 344-1100 Fax: (708) 344-0026

Mfr. components for commercial A/C and refrigeration systems.

Chil-Con Products, PO Box 1385, Brantford, ON, N3T 5T6 Canada

HERCULES INC

Hercules Plaza, 1313 North Market Street, Wilmington, DE, 19894-0001

Tel: (302) 594-5000 Fax: (302) 594-5400 Web site: www.herc.com

Mfr. specialty chemicals, plastics, film and fibers, coatings, resins, food ingredients.

Hercules Canada Ltd., Burlington, ON, Canada

Hercules Canada Ltd., Executive Centre, 4 Robert Speck Pkwy., Mississauga, ON, L4Z 1S1 Canada

Hercules Chemicals Ltd., St.-Jean, PQ, Canada

HEWITT ASSOCIATES LLC

100 Half Day Road, Lincolnshire, IL, 60069

Tel: (847) 295-5000 Fax: (847) 295-7634

Employee benefits consulting firm.

Coles Hewitt, Ste. 1400, 999 West Hasting St., Vancouver, BC V6C 2W2, Canada

Tel: 604-683-7311

Hewitt Associates, 25 Sheppard Ave. West, Toronto, ON M2N 6T1, Canada

Tel: 416-225-5001

Hewitt Associates, 1100 Rene-Levesque blvd West, Montreal, PQ, H3B 4N4 Canada

Tel: 514-878-3300

Hewitt Associates, 500 - Fourth Ave., SW, Ste. 1120, Calgary, AB T2P 2V6, Canada

Tel: 403-232-1188

HEWLETT-PACKARD COMPANY

3000 Hanover Street, Palo Alto, CA, 94304-0890

Tel: (650) 857-1501 Fax: (650) 857-7299 Web site: www.hp.com

Mfr. computing, communications & measurement products & services.

Hewlett-Packard (Canada) Ltd., 5150 Spectrum Way, Mississauga, ON L4W 5G1, Canada

HILLERICH & BRADSBY COMPANY INC

PO Box 35700, Louisville, KY, 40232-5700

Tel: (502) 585-5226 Fax: (502) 585-1179

Golf, baseball and softball equipment.

Hillerich & Bradsby Co. Ltd., 14 Arnold St., Wallaceburg, ON, N8A 3L7 Canada

HILTON HOTELS CORPORATION

9336 Civic Center Drive, Beverly Hills, CA, 90210

Tel: (310) 278-4321 Fax: (310) 205-7880

International hotel chain: Hilton International, Vista Hotels and Hilton National Hotels.

Edmonton Hilton, 10235 - 101st St., Edmonton, AB, T5J 3E9 Canada

Tel: 403-428-7111

Montreal Bonaventure Hilton, 1 Place Bonaventure, Montreal, Québec, H5A 1E4 Canada

Tel: 514-878-2332

Montreal Dorval Airport Hilton, 12505 Côte de Liesse, Dorval, Québec, Canada

Quebec Hilton, 1100, blvdother locations in René-Lévesque Est, C.P. 37120 PQ, Canada

Saint John Hilton, One Market Square, Saint John, New Brunswick, E2L 4Z6 Canada

Tel: 506-693-8484

Toronto Airport Hilton, 5875 Airport Rd., Mississauga, ON, L4V 1N1 Canada

Tel: 905-677-9900

Toronto Hilton, 145 Richmond St. West, Toronto, ON, M5H 2L2 Canada

Windsor Hilton, 277 Riverside Drive West, Windsor, ON, N9A 5K4, Canada

HOBART BROTHERS COMPANY

Hobart Square, 600 W Main Street, Troy, OH, 45373-2928

Tel: (937) 332-4000 Fax: (937) 332-5194

Mfr. arc/automatic welding systems, power systems, filler metals.

Hobart Brothers of Canada Ltd., 807 Pattulo Ave., Woodstock, ON, N4S 7W8 Canada

HODGSON, RUSS, ANDREWS, WOODS & GOODYEAR, LLP

Ste. 1800, One M&T Plaza, Buffalo, NY, 14203

Tel: (716) 856-4000 Fax: (716) 849-0349

International law firm.

Hodgson, Russ, Andrews, Woods & Goodyear, LLP, 3 Robert Speck Pkwy., Ste. 880, Mississauga, ON L4Z 2G5 Canada

Tel: 905-566-5061 Fax: 905-566-2049

HOLIDAY INNS WORLDWIDE, INC.

3 Ravinia Drive, Ste. 2900, Atlanta, GA, 30346-2149

Tel: (770) 604-2000 Fax: (770) 604-5403

Hotels, restaurants and casinos.

Holiday Inn, Armoury & Chestnut Sts., Toronto, ON M5G 1R1, Canada

Holiday Inn, 420 Sherbrooke St. W, Montreal, PQ, Canada

HOLOPHANE CORPORATION

250 East Broad Street, #1400, Columbus, OH, 43215

Tel: (740) 345-9631 Fax: (740) 349-4426

Mfr. industry, commercial, outdoor, roadway & emergency lighting fixtures; inverters, programmable controllers.

Holophane Canada Inc., 1620 Steeles Ave., Brampton, ON, L6T 1A5 Canada

THE HOME DEPOT INC.

2455 Paces Ferry Road, NW, Atlanta, GA, 30339-4024

Tel: (770) 433-8211 Fax: (770) 431-2685 Web site: www.homedepot.com

Home improvement warehouse-style, retail chain stores.

The Home Depot, Inc., 426 Ellesmere Rd., Scarborough, ON, M1R 4E7 Canada

Tel: 416-609-0852 Fax: 416-609-0819 Contact: Annette Verschuren, Pres., Canada

HOMESTAKE MINING COMPANY

650 California Street, San Francisco, CA, 94108

Tel: (415) 981-8150 Fax: (415) 397-5038 Web site: www.homestake.com

Precious metal and mineral mining.

Prime Resources Group, Canada

Contact: Walter T. Segsworth, Pres. Canada

Williams Mine, Canada

HONEYWELL INC.

PO Box 524, Minneapolis, MN, 55440-0524

Tel: (612) 951-1000 Fax: (612) 951-3066 Web site: www.honeywell.com

Develop/mfr. controls for home and building, industry, space and aviation.

Honeywell Ltd., 155 Gordon Baker Rd., North York, ON M2H 3N7, Canada

HORWATH INTERNATIONAL

415 Madison Ave., New York, NY, 10017

Tel: (212) 838-5566 Fax: (212) 838-3636

Public accountants and auditors.

Appel & Partners, 1 Westmount Square #200, Montreal, PQ H3Z 2P9, Canada

Orenstein & Partners, 595 Bay St. #300, Toronto, ON M5G 2C2, Canada

Tierney & White, 131 Water St. #214, Vancouver, BC V6B 4M3, Canada

HOUGHTON INTERNATIONAL INC.

PO Box 930, Madison & Van Buren Avenues, Valley Forge, PA, 19482-0930

Tel: (610) 666-4000 Fax: (610) 666-1376

Mfr. specialty chemicals, hydraulic fluids & lubricants.

E.F. Houghton & Co. of Canada Ltd., PO Box 113, Station D, Toronto, ON, M6P 3J5 Canada

HOUSEHOLD INTERNATIONAL INC.

2700 Sanders Road, Prospect Heights, IL, 60070

Tel: (847) 564-5000 Fax: (847) 205-7452 Web site: www.household.com

Consumer finance and credit card services

HFC of Canada, 101 Duncan Mill Rd., Ste. 500, North York, ON M3B 1Z3 Canada

HOWDEN FAN COMPANY

PO Box 985, Buffalo, NY, 14240

Tel: (716) 847-5121 Fax: (716) 847-5180

Mfr. fans and air-handling units.

Canadian Blower/Canada Pumps, 90 Woodside Ave., Kitchener, ON, N2G 4K1 Canada

Tel: 519-744-8111

HOWMEDICA INC.

359 Veterans Boulevard, Rutherford, NJ, 07070

Tel: (201) 507-7300 Fax: (201) 935-4873 Web site: www.howmedica.com

Hospital, medical and dental supplies.

Howmedica Canada, Guelph, Canada

Tel: 519-824-1140

HOWMET CORPORATION

475 Steamboat Road, PO Box 1960, Greenwich, CT, 06836-1960

Tel: (203) 661-4600 Fax: (203) 661-1134 Web site: www.howmet.com

Mfr. precision investment castings, alloys, engineering and refurbishment.

Howmet-Cercast, 3905 Industrial Blvd., Montreal North, PQ H1H 2Z2, Canada

Tel: 514-322-2371 Fax: 514-322-1340 Contact: Dieter Rupp, Sales Mgr. Emp: 265

HUCK INTERNATIONAL INC.

3724 East Columbia Street, Tucson, AZ, 85714-3415

Tel: (520) 747-9898 Fax: (520) 519-7440

Mfr. aerospace fasteners.

Huck Intl. Ltd., 6150 Kennedy Rd., Unit 10, Mississauga, ON L5T 2J4, Canada

HUMPHREY PRODUCTS COMPANY

PO Box 2008, Kalamazoo, MI, 49003

Tel: (616) 381-5500 Fax: (616) 381-4113

Mfr./sale/services pneumatic actuators & valves for factory automation, motion control, etc.

Humphrey Fluid Power Ltd., 570 Alden Rd., Unit 10, Markham, ON L3R 8N5, Canada

HUNT INTERNATIONAL COMPANY

2005 Market Street, Philadelphia, PA, 19103

Tel: (215) 656-0300 Fax: (215) 656-3700

Mfr. office supplies, arts and craft products and computer accessories.

Hunt (Canada) Intl., 5940 Ambler Dr., Mississauga, ON L4W 2N3, Canada

HUNT OIL COMPANY

1445 Ross at Field, Dallas, TX, 75202

Tel: (214) 978-8000 Fax: (214) 978-8888

Petroleum exploration and production.

Hunt Oil Co., 801 6th Ave. SW, Calgary, AB T2P 3W2, Canada

HUNTSMAN CORPORATION

500 Huntsman Way, Salt Lake City, UT, 84108

Tel: (801) 532-5200 Fax: (801) 536-1581

Mfr./sales specialty chemicals, industrial chemicals and petrochemicals.

Huntsman Corporation Canada Inc., 256 Victoria Rd. South, Guelph, ON N1E5R1, Canada
Tel: 519-824-3280 Fax: 519-824-4979

HUSSMAN CORPORATION
12999 St. Charles Rock Road, Bridgeton, MO, 63044
Tel: (314) 291-2000 Fax: (314) 291-5144
Mfr. refrigeration and environmental control systems for food industrial.
Hussman Canada, 58 Frank St., PO Box 550, Brantford, ON N3T 5R2, Canada
Tel: 519-756-6351 Contact: Brian Eves, Mgr.

HYATT INTERNATIONAL CORPORATION
200 West Madison Street, Chicago, IL, 60606
Tel: (312) 750-1234 Fax: (312) 750-8578 Web site: www.hyatt.com
International hotel management.
Hyatt Regency Vancouver Hotel, 655 Burrard St., Vancouver, BC V6C 2R7, Canada
Tel: 604-683-1234 Fax: 604-689-3707

HYDE SPRING & WIRE COMPANY
14341 Schaefer Highway, Detroit, MI, 48227
Tel: (313) 272-2201 Fax: (313) 272-2242
Mfr. coil springs and wire.
Hyde Spring & Wire Ltd., 366 Grand River Ave., Brantford, ON, Canada

HYDRIL COMPANY
3300 North Sam Houston Pkwy. East, Houston, TX, 77032
Tel: (281) 449-2000 Fax: (281) 985-3295
Oil field machinery, equipment and rubber goods.
Hydril Canadian Co. Ltd., 350 7th Ave. SW, Ste. 3000 Calgary, AB T2P 3N9, Canada
Tel: 403-531-1590 Fax: 403-955-2045

IBM CORPORATION
New Orchard Road, Armonk, NY, 10504
Tel: (914) 765-1900 Fax: (914) 765-7382 Web site: www.ibm.com
Information products, technology & services.
IBM Canada Ltd., 3600 Steeles Ave., East Markham, ON L3R 9Z7, Canada
Tel: 905-316-5000

IBP INC.
PO Box 515, Dakota City, NE, 68731
Tel: (402) 494-2061 Fax: (402) 241-2068 Web site: www.ibpinc.com
Produce beef and pork, hides and associated products, animal feeds, pharmaceuticals.
IBP Inc., Lakeside Farm Industries, Brooks, AB, Canada

ICS INTERNATIONAL INC
125 Oak Street, Scranton, PA, 18515
Tel: (717) 342-7701 Fax: (717) 343-0560
Correspondence courses.
ICS Canada Ltd., 9001 Avon Rd., Montreal West, PQ H4X 2G9, Canada

IKON OFFICE SOLUTIONS
70 Valley Stream Parkway, Malvern, PA, 19355
Tel: (610) 296-8000 Fax: (610) 408-7022 Web site: www.ikon.com
Provider of office technology solutions.
Ikon Office Solutions, 2405 St. Laurent Blvd., Unit A, Ottawa, ON K1G 5B4, Canada
Tel: 613-737-1179

Ikon Office Solutions, 6500 Viscount Rd., Mississauga, ON LAV 1H3, Canada

Tel: 905-677-0061 Fax: 905-677-7569

Ikon Office Solutions, 955 Green Valley Crescent, Ste. 190, Ottawa, ON K2C 3V4, Canada

Tel: 613-723-8141

Ikon Office Solutions, 2560 Mathe Blvd. East, Ste. 119, Mississauga, ON L4W 4Y9, Canada

Tel: 905-602-7333

ILLINOIS TOOL WORKS (ITW)

3600 West Lake Ave., Glenview, IL, 60025-5811

Tel: (847) 724-7500 Fax: (847) 657-4268

Mfr. gears, tools, fasteners, sealants, plastic and metal components for industrial, medical, etc.

Devon Corp., Scarborough, ON, Canada

ILSCO CORPORATION

4730 Madison Road, Cincinnati, OH, 45227-1426

Tel: (513) 533-6200 Fax: (513) 871-4084

Mfr. electrical connectors.

Ilsco of Canada Ltd., 1050 Lakeshore Rd. E, Mississauga, ON, Canada

Tel: 905-274-2341 Fax: 905-274-2689 Contact: Stan Szostak, Pres.

IMC GLOBAL

2345 Waukegan Road, Ste. E-200, Bannockburn, IL, 60015-5516

Tel: (847) 607-3000 Fax: (847) 607-3404

Mfr. garden, nursery, farm supplies and fertilizers.

Kalium Canada Ltd., 1801 Hamilton St., Regina, SK S4P 4B5, Canada

InaCom CORPORATION

10810 Farnam Drive, Omaha, NE, 68154

Tel: (402) 392-3900 Fax: (402) 392-3602 Web site: www.inacom.com

Provider of technology management products and services; reselling microcomputer systems, work stations and networking and telecommunications equipment.

InaCom Information Systems Ltd., 5155 Spectrum Way, Bldg. 16, Mississauga, ON L4W 5A1, Canada

Tel: 905-282-0883 Fax: 905-282-0886 Contact: Mike Abbott, Pres.

INFONET SERVICES CORPORATION

2100 East Grand Ave., El Segundo, CA, 90245

Tel: (310) 335-2600 Fax: (310) 335-4507 Web site: www.infonet.com

Provider of Internet services and electronic messaging services.

Infonet Canada -Teleglobe Canada, Inc., 70 York St., Ste. 1200, Toronto, ON, M5J 1S9 Canada

Tel: 416-365-3170 Fax: 416-365-0222

INFORMATION MANAGEMENT RESOURCES, INC.

26750 us Highway. 19 North, Ste. 500, Clearwater, FL, 33761

Tel: (727) 797-7080 Fax: (727) 791-8152 Web site: www.imr.com

Provides application software and outsourcing services to business.

IMR Canada, 190 Robert Speck Pkwy., Ste. 112, Mississaugua, ON LHZ 3K3, Canada

Tel: 605-275-3555 Fax: 605-275-5371

INFORMATION RESOURCES, INC.

150 N. Clinton St., Chicago, IL, 60661

Tel: (312) 726-1221 Fax: (312) 726-0360 Web site: www.infores.com

Provides bar code scanner services for retail sales organizations; processes, analyzes and sells data from the huge database created from these services.

Information Resources, 4711 Yonge St. Ste. 505, North York, ON M2P 1N6, Canada

Tel: 416-221-2100 Fax: 416-221-6157

INFORMIX CORPORATION

4100 Bohannon Drive, Menlo Park, CA, 95025

Tel: (650) 926-6300 Fax: (650) 926-6593 Web site: www.informix.com

Designs & produces database management software, connectivity interfaces & gateways, and other computer applications.

Informix Software, Inc., Ste. 1615, Box 31, 5149 Yonge St., North York, ON M2N 6L7, Canada (Locations: Montreal, Ottawa, Vancouver, Canada.)

Tel: 416-730-9009 Fax: 416-730-9467

INGERSOLL-RAND COMPANY

200 Chestnut Ridge Road, Woodcliff Lake, NJ, 07675

Tel: (201) 573-0123 Fax: (201) 573-3172 Web site: www.ingersoll-rand.com

Mfr. compressors, rock drills, pumps, air tools, door hardware, ball bearings.

IDP Brantford Canada Inc., Worthington Dr., PO Box 40, Brantford, ON N3T 5M5, Canada

Ingersoll-Rand Canada Inc., Air Compressor Group, 51 Worrcester Rd., Rexdale, ON M9W 4K2, Canada

Tel: 416-213-4552 Fax: 416-213-4560

INGRAM MICRO INC.

PO Box 25125, Santa Ana, CA, 92799

Tel: (714) 566-1000 Fax: (714) 566-7940 Web site: www.ingrammicro.com

Distribute computer systems, software and related products.

Ingram Micro Canada, Toronto, ON, Canada

INSTINET

875 Third Ave., New York, NY, 10022

Tel: (212) 310-9500 Fax: (212) 832-5183

Investment and brokerage.

Instinet, Toronto, ON, Canada

INSTRON CORPORATION

100 Royall Street, Canton, MA, 02021-1089

Tel: (781) 828-2500 Fax: (781) 575-5751

Mfr. material testing instruments.

Instron Canada Ltd., 969 Fraser Dr., Burlington, ON L7L 4X8, Canada

INSTRUMENT SYSTEMS CORPORATION

100 Jericho Quadrangle, Jericho, NY, 11753

Tel: (516) 938-5544 Fax: (516) 938-5564

Electronic products, communications systems.

Bedford Industries, 4750 Des Grandes Prairies Blvd., Montreal, PQ, Canada

White Electronic Development Corp., Mississauga, ON, Canada

INSUL-8 CORPORATION

1417 Industrial Pkwy., Harlan, IA, 51537-2351

Tel: (712) 755-3050 Fax: (712) 755-3979

Mfr. mobile electrification products; conductor bar & festoon equipment.

Insul-8 Corp. Ltd., 175 J. F. Kennedy Blvd., St. Jerome, PQ J7Y 4B5, Canada

INTEGRATED SYSTEMS, INC.

201 Moffett Park Drive, Sunnyvale, CA, 94089

Tel: (408) 542-1500 Fax: (408) 542-1950 Web site: www.isi.com

Develops and markets computer software products and services.

Integrated Systems, Inc., 300 March Rd., 4th Fl., Kanata, ON K2K 2E2, Canada

Tel: 613-599-4991 Fax: 613-599-5102

INTER-CONTINENTAL HOTELS

1120 Ave. of the Americas, New York, NY, 10036

Tel: (212) 852-6400 Fax: (212) 852-6494 Web site: www.interconti.com

Worldwide hotel and resort accommodations.

Hotel Inter-Continental Toronto, 220 Bloor St. West, Toronto, ON M5S 1TB, Canada

Tel: 416-960-5200 Fax: 416-960-8269

INTERGRAPH CORPORATION

One Madison Industrial Park, Huntsville, AL, 35894-0001

Tel: (205) 730-2000 Fax: (205) 730-7898 Web site: www.intergraph.com

Develop/mfr. interactive computer graphic systems.

Intergraph Canada Ltd., Ste. 407, 1959 Upper Water St., Halifax, NS B3J 3N2, Canada

Tel: 902-425-1142 Fax: 902-422-2388

Intergraph Canada Ltd., 2912 Memorial Dr. S.E., Calgary, AB TA2 7R9, Canada

Tel: 403-569-5500 Fax: 403-569-5801

Intergraph Canada Ltd., 1220 Boul Lebourneuf, Bureau 210, Quebec City, PQ G2K 2G4, Canada

Tel: 418-626-2405 Fax: 418-626-4214

Intergraph Canada Ltd., #100, 200 Malcolm St., Hull, PQ J8Y 3B5, Canada

Tel: 819-772-2040 Fax: 819-772-4449

Intergraph Canada Ltd., Ste. 250, 7070 Mississauga Rd., Mississauga, ON L5N 7G2, Canada

Tel: 905-812-9755 Fax: 905-812-9754

Intergraph Canada Ltd., #610, 4370 Dominion St., Burnaby, BC V5G 4L7, Canada

Tel: 604-412-3800 Fax: 604-433-1418

Intergraph Canada Ltd., #700 Sun Life Place, 10123 - 99 St., Edmonton, AB T5J 3H1, Canada

Tel: 403-424-7431 Fax: 403-424-9066

INTERIM SERVICES INC.

2050 Spectrum Boulevard, Fort Lauderdale, FL, 33309

Tel: (954) 938-7600 Fax: (954) 938-7666 Web site: www.interim.com

Provides temporary personnel placement and staffing.

Interim Personnel, 2100 Ellesmere Rd., Scarborough, ON, Canada

Tel: 416-431-6077

Interim Personnel, 120 Adelaide St. West, Ste. 2108, Toronto, ON, Canada

Tel: 416-863-9825

Interim Personnel, 1099 Kingston Rd., Ste. 230, Pickering, ON, Canada

Tel: 905-837-6060

Interim Personnel, 130 Albert St., Ste. 1007, Ottawa, ON, Canada

Tel: 613-237-7501

Interim Personnel, 419 King St. West, Oshawa, ON, Canada

Tel: 905-579-2911

Interim Personnel, 8 Nelson St., West Brampton, ON, Canada

Tel: 905-459-4755

Interim Personnel, Oxford Tower, Edmonton, AB, Canada

Tel: 403-423-2487

Interim Personnel, One City Centre Drive, Mississauga, ON, Canada

Tel: 905-566-1600

INTERMEC TECHNOLOGIES CORPORATION

6001 36th Ave. West, PO Box 4280, Everett, WA, 98203-9280

Tel: (425) 348-2600 Fax: (425) 355-9551 Web site: www.intermec.com

Mfr./distributor automated data collection systems.

Intermec Systems Corp., Toronto - Canada HQ -7065 Tranmere Drive, #3, Mississauga, ON L5S 1M2, Canada (Locations: Calgary, London, Montreal, Ottawa, Quebec & Vancouver, Canada.)

Tel: 905-673-9333 Fax: 905-673-3974

INTERMETRO INDUSTRIES CORPORATION

651 N. Washington Street, Wilkes-Barre, PA, 18705

Tel: (717) 825-2741 Fax: (717) 823-0250

Mfr. storage/material handling products.

Metropolitan Wire (Canada) Ltd., 3155 Orlando Dr., Mississauga, ON I4V 1C5, Canada

INTERNATIONAL DAIRY QUEEN INC.

PO Box 39286, Minneapolis, MN, 55439-0286

Tel: (612) 830-0200 Fax: (612) 830-0270

Mfr./sales fast foods and treats.

Orange Julius Canada Ltd., 5245 Harvester Rd., PO Box 430, Burlington, ON L7R 3Y3, Canada

INTERNATIONAL FILLER CORPORATION

50 Bridge Street, North Tonawanda, NY, 14120

Tel: (716) 693-4040 Fax: (716) 693-3528 Web site: www.internationalfiller.com

Mfr. of powdered cellulose, cotton flock, synthetic clock, and sisal fibers.

International Filler Corp. Ltd., Hamilton, ON, Canada

INTERNATIONAL FLAVORS & FRAGRANCES INC.

521 West 57th Street, New York, NY, 10019-2960

Tel: (212) 765-5500 Fax: (212) 708-7132 Web site: www.iff.com

Design/mfr. flavors, fragrances & aroma chemicals.

International Flavors & Fragrances Ltd., 6 Director Court, Unit 110, Woodbridge, ON L4L 3Z5, Canada

International Flavors & Fragrances Ltd., 7330 Keele St., Concord, ON L4K 1Z9, Canada

INTERNATIONAL GAME TECHNOLOGY INC.

9295 Prototype Drive, Reno, NV, 89511

Tel: (702) 448-0100 Fax: (702) 448-1488 Web site: www.igtgame.com

Mfr. games, hobby goods; equipment leasing, amusements, computers.

IGT Ltd., 1654 Field St., Winnipeg, MB R3E 3H8, Canada

Tel: 204-987-9060 Fax: 204-987-9069

IGT Ltd., 210-630 Tecumseh Rd. East, Windsor, ON, Canada N8X 4W2

IGT Ltd., #12 2020 White Birch Rd., Sydney, BC V8L 2RI, Canada

Tel: 250-656-6606

INTERNATIONAL MULTIFOODS CORPORATION

Box 2942, Minneapolis, MN, 55402

Tel: (612) 340-3300 Fax: (612) 594-3343

Food services, grain and feed and food products.

Robin Hood Multifoods Ltd., PO Box 4000, Station A, Willowdale, ON M2N 5T5, Canada

INTERNATIONAL NETWORK SERVICES

1213 Innsbruck Dr., Sunnyvale, CA, 94089

Tel: (408) 542-0100 Fax: (408) 542-0101 Web site: www.ins.com

Provides computer network support, designs networking systems, manages equipment purchase and performance.

International Network Services Canada, Ltd., The Exchange Tower, 130 King St. W, Ste. 1800, PO Box 427, Toronto, ON M5X 1E3, Canada

Tel: 416-945-6633 Fax: 416-947-0167

INTERNATIONAL PAPER COMPANY

2 Manhattanville Road, Purchase, NY, 10577

Tel: (914) 397-1500 Fax: (914) 397-1596 Web site: www.ipaper.com

Mfr./distributor container board, paper, wood products.

Anitec Image (Canada) Ltd., 2751 John St., Markham, ON, Canada

Ilford Photo (Canada) Ltd., 2751 John St., Markham, ON, Canada

International Paper Canada, Also in London ON, Burnaby BC, Edmonton AB, & Longueuil PQ, Canada

International Paper Canada Inc., 1210 Sheppard Ave. E, Willowdale, Toronto, ON, Canada

Veratec (Canada) Inc., 6 Curity Ave., Toronto, ON M5H 3E9, Canada

INTERNATIONAL RECTIFIER CORPORATION

233 Kansas Street, El Segundo, CA, 90245

Tel: (310) 322-3331 Fax: (310) 322-3332 Web site: www.irf.com

Mfr. power semiconductor components.

International Rectifiers - Canada, 15 Lincoln Court, Brampton ON L6T 3Z2, Canada

Tel: 905-453-2200 Fax: 905-453-1517

INTERNATIONAL SPECIALTY PRODUCTS

1361 Alps Road, Wayne, NJ, 07470

Tel: (973) 628-4000 Fax: (973) 628-3311 Web site: www.ispcorp.com

Mfr. specialty chemical products.

International Specialty Products, Pharmaceutical, Agricultural, Beverage Markets, 4055 Sladeview Cr. #7, Mississauga, ON L5L 5Y1 Canada

Tel: 905-607-2392 Fax: 905-607-9086

INTERNATIONAL TECHNOLOGIES CORPORATION

2790 Mosside Boulevard, Monroeville, PA, 15146

Tel: (412) 372-7701 Fax: (412) 373-7135

Environmental services.

OHM Remediation Services of Canada Ltd., 2192 Wyecroft Rd., Oakville, ON L6J 6L5, Canada

INVACARE CORPORATION

One Invacare Way, Elyria, OH, 44036

Tel: (440) 329-6000 Fax: (440) 366-6568 Web site: www.invacare.com

Mfr. home medical equipment, wheelchairs, respiratory care products, home care aids.

Invacare Canada, Inc., 5970 Chedworth Way, Mississauga, ON L5R 3T9, Canada

Tel: 905-890-8838 Fax: 905-890-5244

INVENTION SUBMISSION CORPORATION

217 Ninth Street, Pittsburgh, PA, 15222

Tel: (412) 288-1300 Fax: (412) 288-1354

Inventor assistance services.

Invention Submission Corp., 883 Hamilton St., Vancouver, BC V6B 2R7, Canada

Invention Submission Corp., 165 Matheson Blvd. E. #3, Mississauga, ON L4Z 3K2, Canada

Invention Submission Corp., 11012 MacLeod Trail S. #600, Calgary, AB T2J 6A5, Canada

ITT SHERATON CORPORATION

60 State Street, Boston, MA, 02108

Tel: (617) 367-3600 Fax: (617) 367-5676

Hotel operations.

Halifax Sheraton, 1919 Upper Water St., Halifax, NS B3J 3JS, Canada

Sheraton Hamilton, 116 King St. W, Hamilton, ON L8P 4V3, Canada

Sheraton Plaza Edmonton, 10010 104th St., Edmonton, AB T5J 0Z1, Canada

J.P. MORGAN & CO. INC.

60 Wall Street, New York, NY, 10260-0060

Tel: (212) 483-2323 Fax: (212) 648-5209 Web site: www.jpm.com

International banking services.

J. P. Morgan Canada, Royal Bank Plaza, South Tower, Ste. 2200, Toronto, ON M5J 2J2, Canada

Tel: 416-981-9200

J. P. Morgan Canada, 1501 McGill College Ave., Ste. 510, Montreal, PQ H3A 3M8, Canada

Tel: 514-840-1300

J. WALTER THOMPSON COMPANY

466 Lexington Ave., New York, NY, 10017

Tel: (212) 210-7000 Fax: (212) 210-6944 Web site: www.jwt.com

International advertising and marketing services.

Enterprise Toronto, Toronto, ON Canada

Groupaction Montreal, Montreal, ON Canada

J. Walter Thompson Co., Toronto, ON, Canada

JAMESBURY CORPORATION

640 Lincoln Street, Worcester, MA, 01605

Tel: (508) 852-0200 Fax: (508) 852-8172

Mfr. valves and accessories.

Jamesbury Canada, 1282 Algoma Rd., Ottawa, ON K1B 3W8, Canada

JDA SOFTWARE GROUP, INC.

11811 N. Tatum Boulevard, Ste. 2000, Phoenix, AZ, 85028

Tel: (602) 404-5500 Fax: (602) 404-5520 Web site: www.jda.com

Developer of information management software for retail, merchandising, distribution and store management.

JDA Software Canada Ltd., 2 Lansing Square, Ste. 904, North York, ON M2J 4P8, Canada

Tel: 416-490-9436 Fax: 416-490-8025

JDA Software Canada Ltd., 210, 7220 Fisher St., SE, Calgary, AB T2H 2H8, Canada

Tel: 403-255-9317 Fax: 403-252-9605

JET-LUBE INC.

4849 Homestead, Houston, TX, 77028

Tel: (713) 674-7617 Fax: (713) 678-4604 Web site: www.jetlube.com

Mfr. anti-seize compounds, thread sealants, lubricants, greases.

Jet-Lube of Canada Ltd., 3820 97th St., Edmonton, AB T6E 5S8, Canada

JEUNIQUE INTERNATIONAL INC.

19501 E. Walnut Drive, City of Industry, CA, 91748

Tel: (909) 598-8598 Fax: (909) 594-8258

Mfr./sale vitamins, food supplements, cosmetics and diet products.

Jeunique Intl. (Canada) Inc., 180 Admiral Blvd., Mississauga, ON L5T 2N6, Canada

JEWELWAY INTERNATIONAL INC.

5151 E. Broadway Blvd, #500, Tucson, AZ, 85711

Tel: (520) 747-9900 Fax: (520) 747-4813

Sale fine jewelry via independent representatives.

Jewelway Intl. Canada Inc., 101-12 Manning Close NE, Calgary, AB T2E 7N6, Canada

JOHN HANCOCK MUTUAL LIFE INSURANCE COMPANY

200 Clarendon Street, PO Box 111, Boston, MA, 02117

Tel: (617) 572-6000 Fax: (617) 572-8628 Web site: www.jhancock.com

Life insurance services.

Maritime Life Assurance Co., PO Box 1030, Halifax, NS B3S 2X5, Canada

JOHNS MANVILLE CORPORATION

717 17th Street, Denver, CO, 80202

Tel: (303) 978-2000 Fax: (303) 978-2318 Web site: www.jm.com

Mfr. fiberglass insulation, roofing products & systems, fiberglass material & reinforcements, filtration mats.

Johns Manville Canada Inc., 3625 Dufferin St. #402, North York, ON M3K 1NA, Canada

Johns Manville Canada Inc., 4704 58th St., Innisfail, AB T4G 1A2, Canada

JOHNSON & JOHNSON

One Johnson & Johnson Plaza, New Brunswick, NJ, 08933

Tel: (732) 524-0400 Fax: (732) 214-0334 Web site: www.jnj.com

Mfr./distributor/R&D pharmaceutical, health care and cosmetic products.

Janssen-Ortho Inc., 19 Green Belt Drive, Don Mills, ON M3C 1L9, Canada

Johnson & Johnson Inc., 2155 Blvd. Pie IX, Montreal, PQ H1V 2E4, Canada

Johnson & Johnson Medical Products, 1421 Lansdowne St. W, Peterborough, ON K9J 7B9, Canada

Johnson & Johnson Worldwide-Absorbent Products Research, 7101 Notre Dame St. E., Montreal, PQ H1N 2G4, Canada

LifeScan Canada Ltd., 234-4170 Still Creek Drive, Burnaby, BC V5C 6CS, Canada

McNeil Consumer Products Co., PO Box 1390, Guelph, ON N1H 7L4, Canada

Ortho-Clinical Diagnostics, Mississauga, ON, Canada

S C JOHNSON & SON INC.

1525 Howe Street, Racine, WI, 53403

Tel: (414) 260-2000 Fax: (414) 260-2133 Web site: www.scjohnsonwax.com

Home, auto, commercial and personal care products and specialty chemicals.

S.C. Johnson & Son Ltd., PO Box 520, Brantford, ON N3T 5R1, Canada

JOHNSON CONTROLS INC.

5757 N. Green Bay Ave., PO Box 591, Milwaukee, WI, 53201-0591

Tel: (414) 228-1200 Fax: Web site: www.johnsoncontrols.com

Mfr. facility management & control systems, auto seating, & batteries..

Johnson Controls Ltd., 7400 Birchmont Rd., Markham, ON L3R 5V4, Canada

Tel: 905-475-7610 Fax: 905-476-5404 Contact: Dave Glass, Area Gen. Mgr.

THE JOHNSON CORPORATION

805 Wood Street, Three Rivers, MI, 49093

Tel: (616) 278-1715 Fax: (616) 273-2230 Web site: www.joco.com

Mfr. rotary joints and siphon systems.

Johnson Canada, 3633 Boul. des Sources, Ste. 212, Dollard des Ormeaux, PQ H9B 2K4, Canada

JOHNSON WORLDWIDE ASSOCIATES, INC.

1326 Willow Road, Sturtevant, WI, 53177

Tel: (414) 884-1500 Fax: (414) 884-1600 Web site: www.jwa.com

Mfr. diving, fishing, boating & camping sports equipment.

JWA Canada, 4180 Harvester Rd., Burlington, ON L7L 6B6, Canada

Tel: 905-634-0023 Fax: 905-634-0261

Plastiques LPA, 471 Route 243, Mansonville, PQ J0E 1X0, Canada

Tel: 450-292-3574 Fax: 450-292-5098

Scubapro Canada, 125 Woodland Drive, Saltspring Island, BC V8K 1K1, Canada

Tel: 250-537-2511 Fax: 250-537-1985

JOMAC PRODUCTS INC.

863 Easton Road, Warrington, PA, 18976

Tel: (215) 343-0800 Fax: (215) 343-0912

Mfr. industrial protective work gloves and industrial rainwear.

Jomac Inc., PO Box 360, 10 Bachelder St., Beebe, PQ J0B 1EO, Canada

Jomac-Canada, 15 Main St., Beebe, PQ J0B 1EO, Canada

JONES & VINING INC.

60 Kendrick Street, Needham, MA, 02194

Tel: (781) 433-2600 Fax: (781) 433-2610

Mfr. plastic and wood products.

Formes United Inc., 101 Labelle Blvd., Ste. Therese de Blainville, PQ J7E 2X6, Canada

JONES APPAREL GROUP INC.

250 Rittenhouse Circle, Bristol, PA, 19007

Tel: (215) 785-4000 Fax: (215) 785-1795

Mfr. women's apparel, knitting mills.

Jones Apparel Group Canada Inc., 55-63 St. Regis Crescent N, Toronto, ON M3J 1Y9, Canada

JOSLYN HI-VOLTAGE CORPORATION

4000 East 116th Street, Cleveland, OH, 44105

Tel: (216) 271-6600 Fax: (216) 341-3615 Web site: www.joslyn.hi-voltage.com

High voltage switches, sectionalizers and reclosers for voltage through 230 KV.

Joslyn Canada Corporation, 1560 55c ave, Lachine, PQ H8T 3J5, Canada

Tel: 514-631-6145 Fax: 514-631-1215

JOSTEN'S INC.

5501 Norman Center, Minneapolis, MN, 55437

Tel: (612) 830-3300 Fax: (612) 830-8432

Class rings, school and graduation related products, awards and trophies.

Jostens Canada Ltd., 1051 King Edward St., Winnipeg, MB R3C 0R4, Canada

Tel: 204-633-9233 Contact: Bob Sigurdson, VP

K-SWISS INC.

20664 Bahama Street, Chatsworth, CA, 91311

Tel: (818) 998-3388 Fax: (818) 773-2390 Web site: www.kswiss.com

Mfr. casual and athletic shoes, socks and leisure apparel.

K-Swiss Canada, 2465 Dunwin Dr., Mississauga, ON L5L 1T1, Canada

KAISER ALUMINUM & CHEMICAL CORPORATION

6177 Sunol Blvd., Pleasanton, CA, 94566

Tel: (925) 462-1122 Fax: (925) 484-2472 Web site: www.kaiseral.research.com

Mfr. aluminum and aluminum products and chemicals.

Kaiser Aluminum & Chemical of Canada Ltd., London, ON, Canada

KAISER ALUMINUM CORPORATION

5847 San Felipe, Ste. 2600, Houston, TX, 77057-3010

Tel: (713) 267-3777 Fax: (713) 267-3701 Web site: www.kaiseral.com

Aluminum refining and manufacturing.

Kaiser Aluminum & Chemical of Canada Ltd., London, ON, Canada

KAMAN CORPORATION

1332 Blue Hills Ave., Bloomfield, CT, 06002

Tel: (860) 243-7100 Fax: (860) 243-6365 Web site: www.kaman.com

Aviation & aerospace products & services, musical instruments.

B & J Music Ltd. (Canada), Canada

Kaman Aircraft of Canada Ltd., St. Catharines, ON, Canada

Kanan Industrial Technologies, Ltd. (Canada), Canada

KAMDEN INTERNATIONAL SHIPPING INC.

167-41 147th Ave., Jamaica, NY, 11434

Tel: (718) 553-8181 Fax: (718) 244-0030

Freight forwarding services.

Kamden Intl. Shipping (Canada), Inc., PO Box 246-AMF, Lester B. Pearson Intl. Airport, Toronto, ON L5P IB1, Canada

KAPPLER PROTECTIVE APPAREL & FABRICS

PO Box 490, 115 Grimes Drive, Guntersville, AL, 35976

Tel: (205) 505-4005 Fax: (205) 505-4004 Web site: www.kappler.com

Mfr. of protective apparel & fabrics.

Kappler Canada Ltd., PO Box 1687, 20 Ryan Pl., Brantford, ON N3T 5V7, Canada

Tel: 519-752-4369 Fax: 519-752-2161 Contact: Sue Kalmar, Sales Mgr. Emp: 40

KATY INDUSTRIES INC.

6300 South Syracuse Way, Ste. 300, Englewood, CO, 80111

Tel: (303) 290-9300 Fax: (303) 290-9344

Holding company.

Bach-Simpson Ltd., PO Box 5484, London, ON N6A 4L6, Canada

Glit Canada, 400 Britannia Rd. E, Unit 5, Mississauga, ON L4Z 1X9, Canada

KAUFMAN & BROAD HOME CORPORATION

10990 Wilshire Blvd., Los Angeles, CA, 90024

Tel: (310) 231-4000 Fax: (310) 231-4222

Housing construction and financing.

Victoria Wood Development Corp., 1550 Kingston Rd., Pickering, ON L1V 1C3, Canada

KAVINOKY & COOK, LLP

120 Delaware Avenue, Buffalo, NY, 14202

Tel: (716) 845-6000 Fax: (716) 845-6474

Law firm.

Kavinoky & Cook, LLP, 207 Queen's Quay West, Ste. 455, POB 149, Toronto, ON M5J 1A7 Canada

Tel: 416- 203-0631 Fax: 416-203-0639

KAWNEER CO., INC.

555 Guthridge Court, Norcross, GA, 30092

Tel: (770) 449-5555 Fax: (770) 734-1570

Mfr. arch aluminum products for commercial construction.

Kawneer Co. Canada Ltd., 1051 Ellesmere Rd., Scarborough, ON M1P 2X1, Canada

KCL CORPORATION

PO Box 629, Shelbyville, IN, 46176

Tel: (317) 392-2521 Fax: (317) 392-4772

Mfr. plastic products.

KCL Promotional Packaging Products Ltd., 1320 Blundell Rd., Mississauga, ON L4Y 1M5, Canada

A.T. KEARNEY INC.

222 West Adams Street, Chicago, IL, 60606

Tel: (312) 648-0111 Fax: (312) 223-6200 Web site: www.atkearney.com

Management consultants and executive search.

A. T. Kearney Executive Search, 130 Adelaide St. West, Ste. 2710, Toronto, ON M5H 3P5, Canada

Tel: 416-947-1990

A. T. Kearney Ltd., Box 68, 20 Queen St. W. #2300, Toronto, ON M5H 3K3, Canada

Tel: 416-977-6886

LINX (Div. of A.T. Kearney Ltd.), Canada Post Place, 750 Heron Rd., Ste. E0161, Ottawa, ON K1V 1A7, Canada

Tel: 613-523-1300

KEARNEY-NATIONAL INC.

108 Corporate Park Drive, Ste 114, White Plains, NY, 10604

Tel: (914) 694-6700 Fax: (914) 694-6513

Mfr. electrical power distributor equipment, elect/electronic components.

Alomeg Div, Kearney National (Canada) Ltd., 90 Milvan Dr., Weston, ON M9L 1Z6, Canada

Kearney National (Canada) Ltd., 280 Speedvale Ave. W, Guelph, ON N1H 1C4, Canada

KELCO INDUSTRIES INC.

9210 Country Club Road, Woodstock, IL, 60098

Tel: (815) 338-5521 Fax: (815) 338-6558

Alginate products.

Scotia Marine Products, Lower Wood Harbour, NS, Canada

KELLY SERVICES, INC.

999 W. Big Beaver Road, Troy, MI, 48084

Tel: (248) 362-4444 Fax: (248) 244-4154 Web site: www.kellyservices.com

Temporary help placement.

Kelly Services (Canada) Ltd., 52 branches throughout Canada

Kelly Services (Canada) Ltd. (HQ), 1 University Ave. #300, Toronto, ON M5J 2P1, Canada

Tel: 416-368-1058 Fax: 416-368-3987

KELSEY-HAYES COMPANY

12025 Tech Center Drive, Livonia, MI, 48150

Tel: (734) 266-2600 Fax: (734) 266-4603

Automotive and aircraft parts.

Kelsey-Hayes Canada Ltd., Woodstock, ON, Canada

Kelsey-Hayes Canada Ltd., Windsor, ON, Canada

Kelsey-Hayes Canada Ltd., St. Catharines, ON, Canada

THE KENDALL COMPANY

15 Hampshire Street, Mansfield, MA, 02048

Tel: (508) 261-8000 Fax: (508) 261-8542

Mfr. medical disposable products, home health care products and specialty adhesive products.

Kendall Canada Inc., PO Box 570, Peterborough, ON K9J 6Z6, Canada

Tel: 705-749-9747

KEPNER-TREGOE INC.

PO Box 704, Princeton, NJ, 08542-0740

Tel: (609) 921-2806 Fax: (609) 924-4978

Management consulting & training.

Kepner-Tregoe Associates Ltd., 45 Sheppard Ave. E. #305, Willowdale, ON M2N 5W9, Canada

KERR-McGEE CORPORATION

PO Box 25861, Oklahoma City, OK, 73125

Tel: (405) 270-1313 Fax: (405) 270-3123

Oil & gas exploration & production, industrial chemicals, coal.

Kerr-McGee Canada Ltd., 250 6th Ave. SW, Calgary, AB T2P 3H7, Canada

KILIAN MFG. COMPANY

PO Box 1008, Torrington, CT, 06790

Tel: (860) 626-2000 Fax: (860) 496-3642

Mfr. ungrounded ball bearings.

Kilian Mfg. Corp. Ltd., 413 Horner Ave., Bldg. 703, Etobicoke, ON M8W 4W3, Canada

Kilian Mfg. Corp. Ltd., Toronto, ON, Canada

Tel: 905-890-2033

Kilian Mfg. Corp. Ltd., Montreal PQ, Canada

Tel: 514-631-6757

KIMBERLY-CLARK CORPORATION

351 Phelps Drive, Irving, TX, 75038

Tel: (972) 281-1200 Fax: (972) 281-1435 Web site: www.kimberly-clark.com.

Mfr./sales/distribution of consumer tissue, household and personal care products.

Kimberly-Clark of Canada Ltd., 365 Bloor St. E, Toronto, ON M4W 3L9, Canada

Scott Maritimes Ltd., Huntsville, ON, Canada

Scott Paper Ltd., New Glasgow, Nova Scotia, Canada

Spruce Falls Power & Paper Co. Ltd., Kapuskasing, ON, Canada

KINKO'S, INC.

255 W. Stanley Ave., Ventura, CA, 93002-8000

Tel: (805) 652-4000 Fax: (805) 652-4347 Web site: www.kinkos.com

Kinko's operates a 24-hour-a-day, global chain of photocopy stores.

Kinko's, Spring Garden Place, 1469 Brenton St., Halifax, NS B3J 3W7, Canada

Tel: 902-423-5500 Fax: 902-423-6556

Kinko's, 459 Bloor St., Toronto, ON M5S 1X9, Canada

Tel: 416-322-3455 Fax: 416-322-3136

Kinko's, 90 Dundas St. West, Mississauga, ON L5B 2T5, Canada

Tel: 905-306-0550 Fax: 905-306-0558

Kinko's, 5828 Macleod Trail South, Calgary, AB T2H OJ8, Canada

Tel: 403-258-0086 Fax: 403-258-0089

Kinko's, 1900 W. Broadway, Vancouver, BC V6J 1Z2, Canada

Tel: 604-734-2679 Fax: 604-734-2671

Kinko's, 170 University Ave. West, Waterloo, ON N2L E39, Canada

Tel: 519-746-3363 Fax: 519-746-8017

KINNEY SHOE CORPORATION

233 Broadway, New York, NY, 10279

Tel: (212) 720-3700 Fax: (212) 720-4223

Mfr./sale footwear and apparel.

Venator Group of Canada Ltd., 100 Mainshep Rd., Gerrard Square, Weston, ON M9M 1L5, Canada

Tel: 416-742-3590

KIRSCH

309 N. Prospect Street, Sturgis, MI, 49091-0370

Tel: (616) 659-5100 Fax: (616) 659-5614

Mfr. drapery hardware & accessories, wood shelving, woven wood shades, etc.

Kirsch Canada, 605 d'Iberville Blvd., Repentigny, PQ J6A 5H9, Canada

KNAPE & VOGT MFG. COMPANY

2700 Oak Industrial Drive, NE, Grand Rapids, MI, 49505

Tel: (616) 459-3311 Fax: (616) 459-3290 Web site: www.kv.com

Builders hardware, closet & cabinet fixtures & accessories.

Knape & Vogt Canada Ltd., Rexdale, ON, Canada

Knape & Vogt Canada Ltd., Quebec, Canada

KNOLL, INC.

1235 Water Street, East Greenville, PA, 18041

Tel: (215) 679-7991 Fax: (215) 679-3904 Web site: www.knoll.com

Mfr. and sale of office furnishings.

Klaus Neinkamper Ltd., 160 Pears Ave., Toronto, ON M5R 1T2, Canada

KOCH INDUSTRIES INC.

4111 East 37th Street North, Wichita, KS, 67220-3203

Tel: (316) 828-5500 Fax: (316) 828-5950 Web site: www.kochind.com

Oil, financial services, agriculture and Purina Mills animal feed.

Koch Canada, Calgary, AB, Canada

KOCH-GLITSCH, INC.

PO Box 660053, Dallas, TX, 75266-0053

Tel: (214) 583-3000 Fax: (214) 583-3344

Mfr./services mass transfer/chemicals separation equipment, process engineering.

Koch-Glitsch Canada Ltd., PO Box 880, 18 Dallas St., Uxbridge, ON L9P 2N2, Canada

Tel: 905-852-3381 Fax: 905-852-7821 Contact: Mike McGuire, Mgr.

KOCH-GLITSCH, INC. (KOCH INDUSTRIES)

PO Box 8127, Wichita, KS, 67208

Tel: (316) 828-5110 Fax: (316) 828-5950

Mass transfer products, static mixers and mist eliminator systems.

Koch Engineering Co. Ltd., 4750 Sheppard Ave. E, Agincourt, ON M1S 3V7, Canada

Tel: 416-293-3666 Fax: 416-293-6409

THE KOHLER COMPANY

444 Highland Drive, Kohler, WI, 53044

Tel: (920) 457-4441 Fax: (920) 459-1274

Plumbing products, ceramic tile and stone, cabinetry, furniture, engines, generators, switch gear and hospitality.

Kohler Ltd., 805 Education Rd., Cornwall, ON K6H 6C7, Canada

KOMLINE-SANDERSON ENGINEERING CORPORATION

12 Holland Ave., Peapack, NJ, 07977

Tel: (908) 234-1000 Fax: (908) 234-9487

Industrial and sanitary filtration systems, dryers and pumps.

KSE Ltd., Orenda Rd., Brampton, ON L6W 1W1, Canada

KOPPERS INDUSTRIES INC.

Koppers Bldg, 437 Seventh Ave., Pittsburgh, PA, 15219

Tel: (412) 227-2000 Fax: (412) 227-2333

Construction materials and services; chemicals and building products.

Koppers Intl. Canada Ltd., 10106 Shellbridge Way, Richmond, BC V6X 2W7, Canada

Koppers Products Ltd., 19 Meteor Dr., Rexdale, ON, Canada

Koppers-Hickson Canada Ltd., Meadowvale Corporate Centre, Plaza One, 2000 Agentia Rd., Mississauga, ON L5W 1P7, Canada

Sprout Waldron of Canada Ltd., 160 Roger St., Waterloo, ON N2J 1A9, Canada

Swanson Lumber Co. Ltd., 220-6325 103rd St., Edmonton, AB T6H 5H6, Canada

KORN/FERRY INTERNATIONAL

1800 Century Park East, Los Angeles, CA, 90067

Tel: (310) 552-1834 Fax: (310) 553-6452 Web site: www.kornferry.com

Executive search; management consulting.

Korn/Ferry International, Scotia Plaza #3918, 40 King St. W, Toronto, ON M5H 3Y2, Canada

Tel: 416-593-5776 Fax: 416-593-9350

KPMG PEAT MARWICK LLP

Three Chestnut Ridge Road, Montvale, NJ, 07645

Tel: (201) 307-7000 Fax: (201) 930-8617 Web site: www.kpmg.com

Accounting and audit, tax and management consulting services.

KPMG Peat Marwick, Scotia Plaza, Ste. 5400, 40 King St. West, ON M5H 322, Canada

Tel: 416-777-8000 Fax: 416-777-3969 Contact: D. Hugh Bessell, Ptnr.

KPMG Peat Marwick, Ste. 1600 Purdy's Warf Tower One, 1959 Upper Water St., Halifax, NS B3J 3N2, Canada

KPMG Peat Marwick, Ste. 1200 Bow Valley Square II, 205-5th Ave. SW, Calgary, AB T2P 4B9, Canada

KPMG Peat Marwick, #100-17410-107 Ave., Edmonton, AB T5J IE9, Canada

KPMG Peat Marwick, 777 Dunsmuir St., Vancouver BC V7Y 1K3 Canada

KPMG Peat Marwick, Bureau 400, 925 Chemin St. Louis, Quebec City, PQ, Canada

KPMG Peat Marwick, World Exchange Plaza, 45 O'Connor St., Ste.1000, Ottawa, ON K1P 1A4, Canada

KPMG Peat Marwick, Ste. 3300, Commerce Ct. West, 199 Bay St., Toronto ON M5L 1B2 Canada

KPMG Peat Marwick, Bureau 1900, 2000, Ave. Mc Gill College, PQ, Canada

KPMG Peat Marwick, Ste. 1100, Madison Centre, 4950 Yonge St, ON M2N 6K1, Canada

KPMG Peat Marwick, 2800/3000 Canada Trust Tower, 10104 - 103 Ave.., Edmonton, AB T5J 2V8 Canada

KRAFT FOODS INTERNATIONAL, INC. (DIV. PHILIP MORRIS COS.)

800 Westchester Ave., Rye Brook, NY, 10573-1301

Tel: (914) 335-2500 Fax: (914) 335-7144

Processor, distributor and manufacturer of food products.

Kraft Canada Inc., 95 Moatfield Drive, Don Mills, ON M3B 3L6, Canada

KWIK LOK CORPORATION

PO Box 9548, Yakima, WA, 98909

Tel: (509) 248-4770 Fax: (509) 457-6531

Mfr. bag closing machinery.

Kwik Lok Canada Ltd., 176 Sheldon Dr., Cambridge, ON N1R 7K1, Canada

KWIK-SEW PATTERN CO., INC.

3000 Washington Ave. North, Minneapolis, MN, 55411

Tel: (612) 521-7651 Fax: (612) 521-1662 Web site: www.kwiksew.com

Mfr. patterns and instruction books for home sewing.

Kwik-Sew Patterns (Canada) Ltd., 5035 Timberlea Blvd., Unit 7, Mississauga, ON L4W 2W9, Canada

Tel: 905-625-0135 Fax: 905-625-1290

LAI WARD HOWELL INTERNATIONAL INC.

200 Park Ave., Ste. 3100, New York, NY, 10016-0136

Tel: (212) 953-7900 Fax: (212) 953-7907 Web site: www.laix.com

International executive search firm.

Ward Howell Illsley Bourbonnais Inc., 131 Adelaide St. W. #1800, Toronto, ON M5H 3L5, Canada

Ward Howell Illsley Bourbonnais Inc., 141 Adelaide St. W, #1800, Toronto, ON M5H 3L5, Canada

Ward Howell Illsley Bourbonnais Inc., 420 McGill St. #400, Montreal, PQ H2Y 2G1, Canada

LANDER CO., INC.

PO Box 9610, Englewood, NJ, 07631

Tel: (201) 568-9700 Fax: (201) 568-1788

Mfr. health and beauty aids, cosmetics and toiletries.

Lander Co. Canada, 275 Finchdene Sq., Agincourt, ON M1S 3CS, Canada

Lander Co. Canada, Toronto, ON, Canada

LANGER BIOMECHANICS GROUP, INC.

450 Commack Road, Deer Park, NY, 11729

Tel: (516) 667-1200 Fax: (516) 667-1203 Web site: www.langerbiomechanics.com

Mfr. prescription foot orthotics and gait-related products.

The Langer Biomechanics Group of Canada/River Biomechanics, 29 Pemican Ct., Unit 3h, Toronto, ON M9M 2Z3, Canada

Tel: 416-744-8184 Fax: 416-744-0155 Contact: Rich Verman

LANIER WORLDWIDE, INC.

2300 Parklake Drive, N.E., Atlanta, GA, 30345

Tel: (770) 496-9500 Fax: (770) 621-1535

Specialize in digital copiers and multi-functional systems.

Lanier Canada, Inc., 5-2735 Matheson Blvd., E, Unit 5, Mississauga, ON L4W 4M8, Canada

Tel: 905-624-8440 Fax: 905-624-9570

Lanier Canada, Inc., 25 Royal Crest Court, Markham, ON L3R 9X4 , Canada

Tel: 905-513-8900 Fax: 905-513-9040

Lanier Canada, Inc., 15, rue De Valcourt, Gatineau, PQ J8T 8H1, Canada

Tel: 819-561-5521 Fax: 819-561-5595

Lanier Canada, Inc., #1-605 West Kent Ave. N., Vancouver, BC V6P 6T7, Canada

Tel: 604-323-1011 Fax: 604-323-1597

Lanier Canada, Inc., 1275 Hubrey Rd., PO Box 3143, London, ON N6A 4J4, Canada

Tel: 519-668-2230 Fax: 519-668-0166

Lanier Canada, Inc., 26-2015 32nd Ave., NE, Calgary, AB T2E 6Z3, Canada

Tel: 403-250-2679 Fax: 403-291-9506

LAWSON MARDON WHEATON, INC.

1101 Wheaton Ave., Milville, NJ, 08332

Tel: (609) 825-1400 Fax: (609) 825-0146

Mfr. glass and plastic containers and plastic products.

Wheaton Industries of Canada Ltd., Brampton, ON, Canada

LAWTER INTERNATIONAL INC.

8601 95th Street, Pleasant Prairie, WI, 53158

Tel: (414) 947-7300 Fax: (414) 947-7328

Resins, pigments and coatings.

Lawter Chemicals (Canada) Ltd., 29 Iron St., Rexdale, ON, Canada

LEARNING COMPANY

1 Athenaeum Street, Cambridge, MA, 02142

Tel: (617) 494-1200 Fax: (617) 494-1219

Mfr./distribute productivity and educational software.

Learning Company, Toronto, ON, Canada

LEARNING TREE INTERNATIONAL, INC.

6053 West Century Blvd., Los Angeles, CA, 90045-0028

Tel: (310) 417-9700 Fax: (310) 417-8684 Web site: www.learningtree.com

Information technology training services.

Learning Tree International Inc. (Canada), 1223 Michael St. North, Ste.110, Gloucester, ON K1J 7T2, Canada

Tel: 613-748-7520 Fax: 613-748-0479 Contact: David Booker, Pres. Emp: 34

LEHMAN BROTHERS HOLDINGS INC.

Three World Financial Center, New York, NY, 10285

Tel: (212) 526-7000 Fax: (212) 526-3738 Web site: www.lehman.com

Financial services, securities and merchant banking services.

Lehman Brothers, PO Box 444, The Exchange Tower, Ste. 3600, 130 King St. West, Toronto ON M5X 1E4, Canada

Tel: 416-955-1900 Fax: 416-955-1930

LEIGH PRODUCTS INC.

2627 East Beltline, SE, Grand Rapids, MI, 49506

Tel: (616) 942-1440 Fax: (616) 942-2170

Ceiling systems, ventilators, wire hardware.

Leigh Metal Products Ltd., 101 Brookside, London, ON, Canada

LESLIE FAY, INC.

1412 Broadway, New York, NY, 10018

Tel: (212) 221-4000 Fax: (212) 221-4033

Wearing apparel.

Leslie Fay Ltd., 1470 Peel St., Montreal, PQ, Canada

LEUCADIA NATIONAL CORPORATION

315 Park Ave. South, New York, NY, 10010

Tel: (212) 460-1900 Fax: (212) 598-4869

Holding company: real estate, banking, insurance, equipment leasing, mfr. plastics, cable, sinks & cabinets.

Domtech Holdings Inc., PO Box 220, 40 Davis St., Trenton, ON K8V 5R2, Canada

LEVI STRAUSS & COMPANY

1155 Battery Street, Levi's Plaza, San Francisco, CA, 94111-1230

Tel: (415) 544-6000 Fax: (415) 501-3939 Web site: www.levistrauss.com

Mfr./distributor casual wearing apparel.

Levi Strauss of Canada, 1725 16TH Ave., Richmond Hill, ON L4B 4C6, Canada

Tel: 905-763-4400 Fax: 905-763-4514

LIBERTY MUTUAL GROUP

175 Berkeley Street, Boston, MA, 02117

Tel: (617) 357-9500 Fax: (617) 350-7648 Web site: www.libertymutual. com

Provides workers' compensation insurance and operates physical rehabilitation centers and provides risk prevention management.

Liberty Mutual Group, Silver Springs Plaza, Unit #9, 5720 Silver Springs Blvd, N.E., Calgary AB T3B 4N7, Canada

Tel: 403-286-1155 Fax: 403-286-1393

Liberty Mutual Group, Tawa Centre, 3021 66th St., Edmonton, AB T6K 4B2, Canada

Tel: 403-490-1222 Fax: 403-490-1796

Liberty Mutual Group, Ste. 200, 1212-31 Ave. N.E., Calgary, AB T2E 7S8, Canada

Tel: 86-777-1677 Fax: 867-777-1662

Liberty Mutual Group, Ste. 402, 12220 Stony Plain Rd., Edmonton, AB T5N 4Y4, Canada

Tel: 403-482-6951 Fax: 403-423-0302

LIGHTNIN

135 Mt. Read Blvd., PO Box 1370, Rochester, NY, 14611

Tel: (716) 436-5550 Fax: (716) 436-5589

Mfr./sale/services industrial mixing machinery, aerators.

Greey-Lightnin, 100 Miranda Ave., Toronto, ON M6B 3W7, Canada

LIGHTOLIER

631 Airport Road, Fall River, MA, 02720

Tel: (508) 679-8131 Fax: (508) 674-4710

Mfr. lighting fixtures and portable lamps.

Canlyte/Lightolier, 3015 rue Louis A. Amos, Lachine, PQ H8T 1C4, Canada

ELI LILLY & COMPANY

Lilly Corporate Center, Indianapolis, IN, 46285

Tel: (317) 276-2000 Fax: (317) 277-6579 Web site: www.lilly.com

Mfr. pharmaceuticals and animal health products.

Eli Lilly & Co. (Canada) Ltd., 3650 Danforth Ave., Scarborough, ON M1N 2E8, Canada

Tel: 416-694-3221 Fax: 416-694-0487

LILLY INDUSTRIES INC.

733 S West Street, Indianapolis, IN, 46225

Tel: (317) 687-6700 Fax: (317) 687-6710

Mfr. industrial finishes, coatings & fillers.

Lilly Industries Inc., 65 Duke St., London, ON, Canada N6J 2X3

THE LINCOLN ELECTRIC COMPANY

22801 St. Clair Ave., Cleveland, OH, 44117-1199

Tel: (216) 481-8100 Fax: (216) 486-8385 Web site: www.lincolnelectric.com

Mfr. arc welding and welding related products, oxy-fuel and thermal cutting equipment and integral AC motors.

Lincoln Electric Co. of Canada Ltd., 179 Wicksteed Ave., Toronto, ON M4G 2B9, Canada (Locations: Calgary, AB; Edmonton, AB; Vancouver, BC; MB, WI; Maritimes, NS; Burlington, ON; & Montreal, QU, Canada.)

Tel: 416-421-2600 Fax: 416-421-3065 Contact: Richard J. Seif, Pres.

ARTHUR D. LITTLE, INC.

25 Acorn Park, Cambridge, MA, 02140-2390

Tel: (617) 498-5000 Fax: (617) 498-7200 Web site: www.adlittle.com

Management, environmental, health & safety consulting; technical & product development.

Arthur D. Little of Canada Ltd., 67 Yonge St. #400, Toronto, ON M5E 1J8, Canada

Tel: 416-361-1051 Fax: 416-361-1155

LITTON INDUSTRIES INC.

21240 Burbank Boulevard, Woodland Hills, CA, 91367

Tel: (818) 598-5000 Fax: (818) 598-3313 Web site: www.litton.com

Shipbuilding, electronics, and information technology.

Kester Solder Co. of Canada Ltd., 68 Prince Charles Rd., PO Box 474, Brantford, ON N3T 5N9, Canada

Litton Systems Canada, 25 City View Dr., Toronto, ON M9W 5A7, Canada

LITTON PRC INC.

1500 PRC Drive, McLean, VA, 22102

Tel: (703) 556-1000 Fax: (703) 556-1174 Web site: www.prc.com

Computer systems and services.

PSI (Public Safety Inc.), 405 The West Mall #700, Etobicoke, ON, Canada

LIZ CLAIBORNE INC.

1441 Broadway, 22nd Fl., New York, NY, 10018

Tel: (212) 354-4900 Fax: (212) 626-1800

Apparel manufacturer.

Liz Claiborne Inc., Toronto, ON, Canada

LOCKHEED MARTIN CORPORATION

6801 Rockledge Drive, Bethesda, MD, 20817

Tel: (301) 897-6000 Fax: (301) 897-6652 Web site: www.imco.com

Design/mfr./management systems in fields of space, defense, energy, electronics and technical services.

Airport Group Canada, Inc., PO Box 6041, Toronto AMF, ON L5P 1B2, Canada

Cal Comp Canada, Ltd., 120 Highway 15, Ste 206, Milihill Bldg., Ottawa, ON K2H 5Z1, Canada

CalComp Canada, 290-10991 Shellbridge Way, Richmond, BC V6X 3C6, Canada

Tel: 604-270-6276 Fax: 604-270-1329

CalComp Canada, 70 Hebb Drive, Ste. 8, RR #1, Dartmouth, NS B2W 3X7, Canada

Fax: 902-434-9592

CalComp Canada, East Tower #105, 1144 29th Ave., N.E., Calgary, AB 72E 7P1, Canada

Tel: 403-250-5555 Fax: 403-291-4102

Lockheed Aeronautical Systems, 3001 Solandt Rd., Ottawa, ON K1K 2M8, Canada

Tel: 613-991-9681 Fax: 613-998-8845 Contact: W. Sinyard

Lockheed Martin Canada, Inc., 3001 Solandt Rd., Kanata, ON K2K 2M8, Canada

Tel: 613-5993270 Fax: 613-5993282 Contact: L. Ashley, Pres.

LOCTITE CORPORATION

10 Columbus Boulevard, Hartford, CT, 06106

Tel: (203) 520-5000 Fax: (203) 520-5073 Web site: www.loctite.com

Mfr./sale industrial adhesives and sealants.

Loctite Canada Inc., 2225 Meadowpine Blvd., Mississauga, ON L5N 7P2, Canada

Tel: 905-814-6511 Fax: 905-814-5391

LOEWS HOTELS

667 Madison Ave., New York, NY, 10021-8087

Tel: (212) 545-2000 Fax: (212) 545-2525 Web site: www.loews.com

Hotel chain.

Loews Le Concorde, Quebec City, ON, Canada

Loews Vogue, Montreal, PQ, Canada

LOUISIANA-PACIFIC CORPORATION

111 S.W. Fifth Ave., Portland, OR, 97204-3601

Tel: (503) 221-0800 Fax: (503) 796-0204 Web site: www.lpcorp.com

Mfr. lumber and building products.

Louisiana-Pacific Canada Ltd., PO Box 2338, Mile 3 Alaskan Hwy., Dawson Creek, BC V1G 4P2, Canada

Tel: 250-782-1616

Louisiana-Pacific Canada Ltd., Pulp Mill, PO Box 900, Chetwynd, BC V0C 1J0, Canada

Tel: 250-788-7857

LOWE & PARTNERS WORLDWIDE

1114 Ave. of the Americas, New York, NY, 10036

Tel: (212) 403-6700 Fax: (212) 403-6710

International advertising agency network.

Bryant, Fulton & Shee, Vancouver, BC, Canada

Roche Macaulay & Partners, Toronto, ON, Canada

LSI LOGIC CORPORATION

1551 McCarthy Blvd, Milpitas, CA, 95035

Tel: (408) 433-8000 Fax: (408) 954-3220 Web site: www.lsilogic.com

Develop/mfr. semiconductors.

LSI Logic Corp. of Canada Inc., 260 Hearst Way, Ste. 400, Kanata, ON K2L 3H1, Canada

Tel: 613-592-1263 Fax: 613-592-3253

LSI Logic Corp. of Canada Inc., 755 St. Jean blvd Ste. 600, Pointe Claire, PQ H9R 5M9, Canada

Tel: 514-694-2417 Fax: 514-694-2699

LSI Logic Corp. of Canada, Inc., 401 The West Mall, Ste. 1110, Etobicoke (Toronto) ON M9C 5J5, Canada

Tel: 416-620-7400 Fax: 416-620-5005

THE LUBRIZOL CORPORATION

29400 Lakeland Blvd., Wickliffe, OH, 44092-2298

Tel: (440) 943-4200 Fax: (440) 943-5337 Web site: www.lubrizol.com

Mfr. chemicals additives for lubricants & fuels.

Lubrizol Canada Ltd., 5800 Thorold Stone Rd., Niagara Falls, ON L2E 6V2, Canada

LUCENT TECHNOLOGIES, INC.

600 Mountain Ave., Murray Hill, NJ, 07974-0636

Tel: (908) 582-3000 Fax: (908) 582-2110 Web site: www.lucent.com

Design/mfr. wide range of public and private networks, communication systems and software, data networking systems, business telephone systems and microelectronics components.

Lucent Technologies Reg. Customer Team, 3650 Victoria Park Ave., Ste. 700, Willowdale, ON M2H 3P7, Canada

Tel: 416-756-5085 Fax: 416756-5178 Contact: Valerie Vollenweider, PR Mgr.

LUFKIN INDUSTRIES INC.

407 Kilen Street, Lufkin, TX, 75901

Tel: (409) 634-2211 Fax: (409) 637-5474

Mfr./distributor oilfield pumping equipment, industrial hardware, truck trailers, propulsion gears.

Lufkin Machine Co. Ltd., Nisku Industrial Park, Edmonton, AB T0C 2G0, Canada

M/A-COM INC.

1011 Pawtucket Boulevard, Lowell, MA, 01853

Tel: (978) 442-5000 Fax: (978) 442-5354

Mfr. electronic components and communications equipment.

Cee-Jay Microsystems, Ltd., 5925 Airport Rd., Mississauga, ON L4V 1W1, Canada

Tel: 905-678-3188

MacDERMID INC.

245 Freight Street, Waterbury, CT, 06702-0671

Tel: (203) 575-5700 Fax: (203) 575-7900 Web site: www.macd.com

Chemicals processing for metal industrial, plastics, electronics cleaners, strippers.

MacDermid Chemicals Inc., 6535 Abrams St., St. Laurent, PQ H4S 9Z7, Canada

Tel: 514-745-7040 Fax: 514-745-7838

MacDermid Chemicals Inc., 4530 Fieldgate Dr., Mississauga, ON L4W 3W6, Canada

Tel: 905-624-1065 Fax: 906-624-6384

MAGNETIC METALS CORPORATION

Box 351, Camden, NJ, 08105

Tel: (609) 964-7842 Fax: (609) 963-8569

Magnetic alloys, shields; laminations & special stampings.

Magnetic Metals of Canada Ltd., 10 Spaulding Dr., Brantford, ON, Canada

MAGNETROL INTERNATIONAL

5300 Belmont Road, Downers Grove, IL, 60515-4499

Tel: (630) 969-4000 Fax: (630) 969-9489 Web site: www.magnetrol.com

Mfr. level and flow instrumentation.

Magnetrol Intl. Ltd., 6291-18 Dorman Rd., Mississagua, ON L4V 1H2, Canada

Tel: 905-678-2720 Fax: 905-678-7407 Contact: Kevin Martyn, Gen. Mgr.

MAINE PUBLIC SERVICE COMPANY

PO Box 1209, Presque Isle, ME, 04769

Tel: (207) 768-5811 Fax: (207) 764-6586

Electricity production and distribution.

Maine & New Brunswick Electrical Power Co. Ltd., Aroostook Junction, NB, Canada

MALLINCKRODT INC.

675 McDonnell Blvd., PO Box 5840, St. Louis, MO, 63134

Tel: (314) 654-2000 Fax: (314) 654-3005

Mfr. specialty medical products.

Mallinckrodt Medical Inc., Pointe Claire, PQ, Canada

MANPOWER INTERNATIONAL INC.

5301 N. Ironwood Road, PO Box 2053, Milwaukee, WI, 53201-2053

Tel: (414) 961-1000 Fax: (414) 961-7081 Web site: www.manpower

Temporary help, contract service, training & testing.

Manpower Services Ltd., Tchnical Office 55 Metcalfe Ste.800, K1P 6L5, Canada

Tel: 613-237-9070

Manpower Services Ltd., 20 Queen St. West, Ste. 2008 Box 22, Toronto, ON M5H 3R3, Canada

Tel: 416-977-1748 Fax: 416-977-0947

Manpower Services Ltd. - Canadian Head Office, 5090 Explorer Drive, 4th Fl. L4W 4X6, Canada

Tel: 905-624-4000 Fax: 905-624-3022

Manpower Services Ltd. - Edmonton, Toronto Dominion Tower, Edmonton Centre, Ste. 2101, T5J 2Z1, Canada

Tel: 403-420-0110 Fax: 403-424-0807

Manpower Services Ltd. - Saskatoon, 670-410 22nd St. East, S7K 5T6, Canada

Tel: 306-244-2088 Fax: 306-244-2099

Manpower Services Ltd. - Vancouver, 1290 Hornby St., V6Z 1W2, Canada

Tel: 604-682-1651 Fax: 604-669-5397

Manpower Services Ltd. - Winnipeg, Toronto Dominion Ctr., 1005-201 Portage Ave. R3B 3K6, Canada

Tel: 204-942-7800 Fax: 204-942-8870

MARK IV INDUSTRIES INC.

501 John James Audubon Pkwy., PO Box 810, Amherst, NY, 14226-0810

Tel: (716) 689-4972 Fax: (716) 689-1529 Web site: www.mark-iv.com

Mfr. diversified products: timers & controls, power equipment, loudspeaker systems, etc.

Dayco Ltd./Mark IV Industries Canada, Inc., 46 Norelco Drive, Weston, ON, M9L 1S3, Canada

Tel: 416-741-3900 Fax: 416-741-3816

MARKEM CORPORATION

150 Congress Street, Keene, NH, 03431

Tel: (603) 352-1130 Fax: (603) 357-1835 Web site: www.markem.com.

Mfr./sales of industrial marking, print machinery and hot stamping foils.

Markem Products Ltd., 9645 Cote de Liesse, Dorval, PQk H9P 1A3, Canada

Tel: 514-636-9455 Fax: 514-636-1460

Markem Products Ltd., 149 Manitou Drive, Kitchener, ON, N2C 1L4, Canada

Tel: 519-893-7055 Fax: 519-893-9461

MARKET FACTS INC.

3040 Salt Creek Lane, Arlington Heights, IL, 60005

Tel: (847) 590-7000 Fax: (847) 590-7010

Market research services.

Market Facts Canada Ltd., 77 Bloor St. W, Toronto, ON M5S 3A4, Canada

MARRIOTT INTERNATIONAL INC.

1 Marriott Drive, Washington, DC, 20058

Tel: (301) 380-3000 Fax: (301) 380-5181

Lodging, contract food and beverage service, and restaurants.

Fairfield Marriott Inn, 475 Yonge St., Toronto,ON M4Y 1X7 Canada

Tel: 416-924-0611 Fax: 416-924-5061

Marriott Courtyard Montreal, 410 Sherbrook St., O/W, Montreal, PQ, Canada

Tel: 514-844-8855 Fax: 514-844-0912

MARSH & McLENNAN COS INC.

1166 Ave. of the Americas, New York, NY, 10036-2774

Tel: (212) 345-5000 Fax: (212) 345-4808 Web site: www.marshmac.com

Insurance agents/brokers, pension and investment management consulting services.

J&H Marsh McLennan Ltd., 1801 Hollis St., Ste. 1300, Halifax, NS, B3J 3N4 Canada

Tel: 902-429-6710 Fax: 902-422-6843 Contact: Lloyd King

J&H Marsh McLennan Ltd., Canada Trust Tower, BCE Place, 161 Bay St., Toronto, ON M5J 2S4, Canada

Tel: 416-868-2600 Fax: 416-868-2526 Contact: Sheldon M. Rankin

J&H Marsh McLennan Ltd., 600 blvd de Maisonneuv, ouest, Montreal, PQ H3A 3J3 Canada

Tel: 514-285-5800 Fax: 514-285-4548 Contact: Alan Garner

J&H Marsh McLennan Ltd., Carling Executive Park, 1565 Carling Ave., Ste.600, Ottawa, ON K1Z 8R1 Canada

Tel: 613-725-5052 Fax: 613-725-1108 Contact: Mike Petersen

J&H Marsh McLennan Ltd., Bow Valley Square 3, 255 5th Ave. SW, Ste. 1000, Calgary, AB T2P 3G6 Canada

Tel: 403-290-7900 Fax: 403-261-9882 Contact: Peter Redmond

J&H Marsh McLennan Ltd., Montreal Trust Centre, 1300 - 510 Burrard St., Vancouver, BC V6C 3J2, Canada

Tel: 604-685-3765 Fax: 604-685-3112 Contact: Harry Richards

J B MARTIN COMPANY

10 East 53rd Street, #3100, New York, NY, 10022

Tel: (212) 421-2020 Fax: (212) 421-1460

Mfr./sale velvets.

J.B. Martin Canada Ltd., 445 rue St. Jacques, St. Jean, PQ J3B QM1, Canada

MARTIN-DECKER TOTCO INC.

1200 Cypress Creek Road, Cedar Park, TX, 78613-3614

Tel: (512) 340-5000 Fax: (512) 340-5219

Mfr. oilfield and industry weight and measure systems.

M/D Totco Inc., Bay 15, 2916 5th Ave. NE, Calgary, AB T2A 6K4, Canada

Tel: 403-569-2050

MARY KAY COSMETICS INC.

16251 Nor Dallas Pkw, Dallas, TX, 75248

Tel: (214) 630-8787 Fax: (214) 631-5938

Cosmetics and toiletries.

Mary Kay Cosmetics Inc., 5600 Ambler Dr., Mississauga, ON L4W 2K2, Canada

MASCO CORPORATION

21001 Van Born Road, Taylor, MI, 48180

Tel: (313) 274-7400 Fax: (313) 374-6666

Mfr. home improvement, building and home furnishings products.

Emco Ltd., PO Box 5252, London, ON N6A 4L6, Canada

Tel: 519-645-3900

Emco Ltd., 620 Richmond St., London, ON N6A 5J9, Canada

Tel: 519-645-3900

MASTERCARD INTERNATIONAL INC.

200 Purchase Street, Purchase, NY, 10577

Tel: (914) 249-2000 Fax: (914) 249-5475 Web site: www.mastercard.com

Provides financial payment systems globally.

MasterCard International Inc., Two First Canadian Place, Ste. 3680, Toronto, ON M5X 1B1, Canada

MATHESON GAS PRODUCTS

959 Rt. 46 East, Parsippany,, NJ, 07054-0624

Tel: (973) 257-1100 Fax: (973) 257-9393 Web site: www.mathesongas.com

Mfr. specialty gases and equipment.

Matheson Gas Products Canada, PO Box 89, Whitby, ON, Canada

ada

Tel: 905-668-3397 Fax: 905-668-6937

MATLACK SYSTEMS INC.

2200 Concord Pike, PO Box 8789, Wilmington, DE, 19899

Tel: (302) 426-2700 Fax: (302) 426-3298

Bulk trucking & services.

Matlack Inc., 17 Strathern Ave., Brampton, ON L6T 4P1, Canada

MATTEL INC.

333 Continental Blvd., El Segundo, CA, 90245-5012

Tel: (310) 252-2000 Fax: (310) 252-2179 Web site: www.mattelmedia.com

Mfr. toys, dolls, games, crafts and hobbies.

Mattel Holdings Ltd., 800 Islington Ave., Toronto, ON M8Z 4NZ, Canada

Mattel-Fisher Price Ltd., 6155 Fremont Blvd., Mississauga, ON L5R 3W2, Canada

MAURICE PINCOFFS CO., INC.

2040 North Loop West, #200, Houston, TX, 77018

Tel: (713) 681-5461 Fax: (713) 681-8521 Web site: www.pincoffs.com

International marketing and distribution.

Maurice Pincoffs Canada, 6050 Don Murie St., Niagara Falls, ON L2E 6X8, Canada

Tel: 905-353-8955 Fax: 905-353-8968 Contact: Kent Miller, Mgr. Emp: 25

GEORGE S MAY INTERNATIONAL COMPANY

303 S Northwest Hwy., Park Ridge, IL, 60068-4255

Tel: (847) 825-8806 Fax: (847) 825-7937 Web site: www.georgesmay.com

Management consulting.

George S May Intl. Co., 615 Rene Levesque #1100, Montreal, PQ H3B 1PS, Canada

MAYFRAN INTERNATIONAL

PO Box 43038, Cleveland, OH, 44143

Tel: (440) 461-4100 Fax: (440) 461-5565

Mfr. conveyors for metal working and refuse.

Mayfran Canada Ltd., 5955 Airport Rd., Mississauga, ON L4V 1R9, Canada

MAYTAG CORPORATION

403 West Fourth Street North, Newton, IA, 50208

Tel: (515) 792-8000 Fax: (515) 787-8376 Web site: www.maytagcorp.com

Mfr./sales of large appliances, ovens, dishwashers, refrigerators and washing machines.

Maytag International, 4151 North Service Rd., Burlington, ON L7R 4A8, Canada
Tel: 416-675-3977

McCALL PATTERN COMPANY
11 Penn Plaza, New York, NY, 10001
Tel: (212) 465-6800 Fax: (212) 465-6831
Fashion patterns.
McCall Pattern Co., 1406 Birchmount Rd., Scarborough, ON, Canada

McCANN-ERICKSON WORLDWIDE
750 Third Ave., New York, NY, 10017
Tel: (212) 984-3644 Fax: (212) 984-2629
International advertising/marketing services.
MacLaren McCann Canada, 40 St. Clair Ave. W, Toronto, ON M4V 1M6, Canada
McCann-Erickson Adv. of Canada Ltd., 10 Bay St., Toronto, ON M5S 1S8, Canada

McCORMICK & COMPANY, INC.
18 Loveton Circle, Sparks, MD, 21152-6000
Tel: (410) 771-7301 Fax: (410) 527-8289
Mfr./distribution/sale seasonings, flavorings, specialty foods.
McCormick Canada Inc., London, ON N6A 4Z2, Canada

McDERMOTT INTERNATIONAL INC.
1450 Poydras Street, PO Box 60035, New Orleans, LA, 70160-0035
Tel: (504) 587-5400 Fax: (504) 587-6153 Web site: www.mcdermott.com
Engineering & construction.
Babcock & Wilcox, 17611 105th Ave., 1st Fl., Edmonton, AB, Canada T5S 1T1
Tel: 403-489-0404 Fax: 403-489-4562 Contact: Richard Worden, Mgr.
Babcock & Wilcox, 2109 St. Regis blvd, Dollard-des-Ormeaux, PQ, Canada H0B 2M9
Tel: 514-685-4596 Fax: 514-685-4599 Contact: Partick Brouillette, Mgr.
Babcock & Wilcox, 479 Rothesay Ave., Saint John, NB E2J 2C6, Canada
Tel: 506-633-2880 Fax: 506-633-1353 Contact: George Thiessen, Mgr
Babcock & Wilcox, 11191 Coopersmith Place, Richmond, (Vancouver) BC, Canada
Tel: 604-275-4777 Fax: 604-275-6488 Contact: Mike Trivett, Mgr.
Babcock & Wilcox Intl., 581 Coronation Blvd., Cambridge, ON N1R 5V3, Canada
Tel: 519-621-2130 Fax: 519-622-7352 Contact: Ron Ojanpera, Dir.
Babcock & Wilcox Power Generation Group, 581 Coronation Blvd., Cambridge, ON N1R 5V3, Canada
Tel: 519-621-2130 Fax: 519-622-7352
Babcock & Wilcox Power Generation Group, PO Box 2320, 222 Service St., Highway 10 East, Melville, SK S0A 2P0, Canada
Tel: 306-728-3373 Fax: 306-728-3424

McDONALD'S CORPORATION
Kroc Drive, Oak Brook, IL, 60523
Tel: (630) 623-3000 Fax: (630) 623-7409
Fast food chain stores.
McDonald's Corp., Canada

THE McGRAW-HILL COMPANIES
1221 Ave. of the Americas, New York, NY, 10020
Tel: (212) 512-2000 Fax: (212) 512-2703
Books, magazines, information systems, financial service, publishing and broadcast operations.
DRI of Canada, 250 Bloor St. E, #405, Toronto, ON M4W 1F6, Canada
McGraw-Hill Ryerson Ltd., 300 Water St., Whitby, ON L1N 9B6, Canada

McKESSON CORPORATION

One Post Street, San Francisco, CA, 94104-5296

Tel: (415) 983-8300 Fax: (415) 983-8453

Wholesale distribution of pharmaceuticals, health and beauty care aids, and other non-durable consumer goods.

Medis Health & Pharmaceutical Services, Inc., 8625 Transcanada, Montreal, Canada

Tel: 514-745-2100

McKINSEY & COMPANY

55 East 52nd Street, New York, NY, 10022

Tel: (212) 446-7000 Fax: (212) 446-8575 Web site: www.mckinsey.com

Management and business consulting services.

McKinsey & Co. Inc., 175 Bloor St. East, North Tower, Ste. 1200, Toronto, ON M4W 3R8, Canada

Tel: 416-969-3700 Fax: 416-969-8980

McKinsey & Company, 1250, blvd René-Lévesque, Ouest, Bureau 4430, Montréal, PQ H3B 4W8, Canada

Tel: 514-939-6800 Fax: 514-939-6810

MEAD CORPORATION

Courthouse Plaza, NE, Dayton, OH, 45463

Tel: (937) 495-6323 Fax: (937) 461-2424 Web site: www.mead.com

Mfr. paper, packaging, pulp, lumber and other wood products, school and office products; electronic publishing and distribution.

Med Packaging (Canada) Ltd., 281 Fairall St., Ajax, ON LIS IR7, Canada

Tel: 905-683-2330 Fax: 905-683-5032 Contact: Ian Millar, Pres.

MEDAR INC.

38700 Grand River Ave., Farmington Hills, MI, 48335-1563

Tel: (248) 477-3900 Fax: (248) 477-8897

Mfr. machine vision-based inspection systems & resistance welding controls for industry manufacturers.

Medar Canada, 240 Cordova Rd., PO Box 858, Oshawa, ON L1H 7N1, Canada

MEDICUS GROUP INTERNATIONAL

1675 Broadway, New York, NY, 10019

Tel: (212) 468-3100 Fax: (212) 468-3222

International healthcare agency network.

Medicus Intercon, Toronto, ON, Canada

MEDTRONIC INC.

7000 Central Ave., NE, Minneapolis, MN, 55432

Tel: (612) 574-4000 Fax: (612) 574-4879

Mfr./sale/service electrotherapeutic medical devices.

Medtronic of Canada Ltd., 6733 Kitimat Rd., Mississauga, ON L5N 1W3, Canada

MELLON BANK NA

One Mellon Bank Center, Pittsburgh, PA, 15258

Tel: (412) 234-5000 Fax: (412) 236-1662

Commercial and trade banking and foreign exchange.

Mellon Bank Canada, 77 King St. W. #3200, Royal Trust Tower, Toronto, ON M5K 1KZ, Canada

RM Trust, 393 University Ave., 5th fl., Toronto, ON M5G 1E6, Canada

MEMOREX CORPORATION

10100 Pioneer Boulevard, Santa Fe Springs, CA, 90670

Tel: (562) 906-2800 Fax: (562) 906-2848

Magnetic recording tapes, etc.

Memtec Canada Ltd., 980 Dennison Rd., Unionville, Markham, ON, Canada

Tel: 905-477-7489

THE MENTHOLATUM CO., INC.

707 Sterling Drive, Orchard Park, NY, 14127-1587

Tel: (716) 677-2500 Fax: (716) 674-3696 Web site: www.mentholatum.com

Mfr./distributor proprietary medicines, drugs, OTC's.

The Mentholatum Co. of Canada Ltd., 20 Lewis St., Fort Erie, ON L7A 5M6, Canada

Tel: 905-871-1665 Fax: 905-871-2535

MERCK & COMPANY, INC.

1 Merck Drive, Whitehouse Station, NJ, 08889

Tel: (908) 423-1000 Fax: (908) 423-2592

Pharmaceuticals, chemicals and biologicals.

Merck, Sharp & Dohme of Canada Ltd., 16701 Trans-Canada Hwy., Kirkland, PQ H9H 3L1, Canada

MERISEL INC.

200 Continental Blvd., El Segundo, CA, 90245

Tel: (310) 615-3080 Fax: (310) 615-1238

Distributor software & hardware.

Merisel-Canada, 200 Ronson Drive, Etobicoke, ON M9W 529, Canada

Tel: 416-240-7012 Fax: 416-240-2610

MERITOR AUTOMOTIVE, INC.

2135 W. Maple Road, Troy, MI, 48084-7186

Tel: (248) 435-1000 Fax: (248) 435-1393 Web site: www.meritorauto.com

Mfr./sales of light and heavy vehicle systems for trucks, cars and speciality vehicles.

Meritor Automotive, Inc., Canada

MERLE NORMAN COSMETICS INC.

9130 Bellance Ave., Los Angeles, CA, 90045

Tel: (310) 641-3000 Fax: (310) 641-7144

Mfr./sales/distribution of cosmetics.

Merle Norman Cosmetics (Canada) Ltd., 346 Orenda, Bramalea, ON, Canada

MERRILL LYNCH & COMPANY, INC.

World Financial Center, North Tower, New York, NY, 10281-1323

Tel: (212) 449-1000 Fax: (212) 449-2892

Security brokers and dealers, investment and business services.

Merrill Lynch Canada Inc., Alberta Stock Exchange Tower, Ste. 1850, 300 5th Ave., S.W., Calgary AB T2P 3C4, Canada

Tel: 403-571-2890 Fax: 403-571-2895

Merrill Lynch Canada Inc., Place Montreal Trust, 1800 McGill College Ave., 25th Fl., Montreal, PQ H3A 3J6, Canada

Tel: 514-982-2700 Fax: 514-982-2729

Merrill Lynch Canada Inc., 200 King St. West, Toronto, ON, M5H 3W3, Canada

Tel: 416-586-6000 Fax: 416-586-6402

Merrill Lynch Canada Inc., Ste. 1550, Waterront Ctr., 200 Burrard St., Vancouver, BC V6C 3L6, Canada

Tel: 604-687-2663 Fax: 604-687-3663

Midland Walwyn, 181 Bay St., Toronto, ON M5J 2V8, Canada

Tel: 416-369-7400

MESABA HOLDINGS, INC.

7501 26th Ave. South, Minneapolis, MN, 55450

Tel: (612) 726-5151 Fax: (612) 726-1568 Web site: www.mesaba.com

Regional airline carrier.

Northwest Airlines, Montreal, PQ, Canada

METAL IMPROVEMENT COMPANY

10 Forest Ave., Paramus, NJ, 07652

Tel: (201) 843-7800 Fax: (201) 843-3460

Mfr. shot peening.

Metal Improvement Co., 105 Alfred Kuehne Blvd., Brampton, ON L6T 4K3, Canada

METALLURG INC.

6 East 43 Street, New York, NY, 10017

Tel: (212) 687-9470 Fax: (212) 697-2874

Mfr. ferrous & nonferrous alloys & metals.

Metallurg (Canada) Ltd., 40 University Ave. #1066, Toronto, ON M5J 1T1, Canada

METRA TOOL COMPANY

5275 Cogswell Road, Wayne, MI, 48184

Tel: (734) 729-6400 Fax: (313) 729-6446

Mfr. fastening tools, blueprint items.

Metra Tool Co., 10630 Tecumseh, Windsor, ON N8R 1A8, Canada

METROPOLITAN LIFE INSURANCE COMPANY

1 Madison Ave., New York, NY, 10010-3603

Tel: (212) 578-3818 Fax: (212) 252-7294

Insurance and retirement savings products and services.

Metropolitan Life Insurance Co. (La Metropolitaine), 99 Bank St. #100, Ottawa, ON K1P 5A3, Canada

Morguard Investments Ltd., One University Ave. #1500, Toronto, ON M5J 2V5, Canada

Tel: 416-862-3800 Fax: 416-862-3799 Contact: Antony K. Stephens, Chmn. & CEO

MICHAELS STORES INC.

PO Box 619566, Irving, TX, 75261-9566

Tel: (972) 409-1300 Fax: (972) 409-1521 Web site: www.michaels.com

Retail stores; hobby, arts and crafts.

Michaels of Canada Inc., 100 Alfred Kuehne Blvd., Brampton, ON L6T 4K4, Canada

MICRO AGE, INC.

200 South MicroAge Way, Tempe, AZ, 85282-1896

Tel: (602) 366-2000 Fax: (602) 966-7339 Web site: www.microage.com

Computer systems integrator, software products and telecommunications equipment.

MicroAge, Inc., 55 Director Court, Woodbridge, ON L4L 4S5, Canada

Tel: 905-264-8520

MICROCHIP TECHNOLOGY INC.

2355 West Chandler Boulevard, Chandler, AZ, 85224

Tel: (602) 786-7200 Fax: (602) 899-9210 Web site: www.microchip.com

Mfr. electronic subassemblies and components.

Microchip Technology Inc., 5925 Airport Rd., Ste. 200, Mississauga, ON L4V 1W1, Canada

Tel: 905-405-6279 Fax: 905-405-6253

MICROSOFT CORPORATION

One Microsoft Way, Redmond, WA, 98052-6399

Tel: (425) 882-8080 Fax: (425) 936-7329 Web site: www.microsoft.com

Computer software, peripherals and services.

Microsoft Canada Inc., 320 Matheson Blvd. W, Mississauga, ON L5R 3R1, Canada

Tel: 905-568-0434 Fax: 905-568-9641

HERMAN MILLER INC.

8500 Byron Road, Zeeland, MI, 49464

Tel: (616) 654-3000 Fax: (616) 654-5385 Web site: www.hermanmiller.com

Office furnishings.

Herman Miller Canada Ltd., 2360 Argentia Rd., Mississauga, ON L5N 4G9, Canada

MINE SAFETY APPLIANCES COMPANY

121 Gamma Drive, RIDC Industrial Pk., PO Box 426, Pittsburgh, PA, 15230

Tel: (412) 967-3000 Fax: (412) 967-3452

Safety equipment, industry filters.

Mine Safety Appliances Co. of Canada Ltd., 148 Norfinch Dr., Downsview, ON M3N 1X8, Canada

MINTEQ INTERNATIONAL INC.

405 Lexington Ave., 19th Fl., New York, NY, 10174-1901

Tel: (212) 878-1800 Fax: (212) 878-1952 Web site: www.mineralstech.com

Mfr./market specialty refractory and metallurgical products and application systems.

MINTEQ Canada Inc., 1870 Blvd. Des Sources, Pointe-Claire, PQ, H9R 5N4 Canada

Tel: 514-697-8260 Fax: 514-697-1163 Contact: Yves Dube, Dir. Emp: 74

MOBIL CORPORATION

3225 Gallows Road, Fairfax, VA, 22037-0001

Tel: (703) 846-3000 Fax: (703) 846-4669 Web site: www.mobil.com

Petroleum and gas exploration and refining, mfr. petroleum products, chemicals and petrochemicals.

Mobil Chemical Canada Ltd., Chemical Coatings Div., PO Box 200, West Hill, ON, Canada

Mobil Chemical Canada Ltd., Plastics Div., 321 University Ave., Belleville, ON K8M 5A2, Canada

Mobil Paint Co., 645 Coronation Dr., West Hill, ON, Canada

MODINE MANUFACTURING COMPANY

1500 DeKoven Ave., Racine, WI, 53403

Tel: (414) 636-1200 Fax: (414) 636-1424 Web site: www.modine.com

Mfr. heat-transfer products.

Modine Manufacturing Co., 51A Caldari Rd., Concord, ON, Canada

Tel: 905-738-6008

Modine of Canada Ltd., 151 Marycroft Ave., Woodbridge, ON L4L 5Y3, Canada

MOEN INC.

25300 Al Moen Drive, North Olmstead, OH, 44070

Tel: (440) 962-2000 Fax: (440) 962-2089

Mfr./service plumbing products.

Moen Canada, 2816 Bristol Circle, Oakville, ON L6H 5S7, Canada

Tel: 905-829-3400 Fax: 905-829-3500 Contact: Mike Dennis, Pres.

MOGUL CORPORATION

PO Box 200, Chagrin Falls, OH, 44022

Tel: (440) 247-5000 Fax: (440) 247-3714

Water treatment chemicals, equipment.

Mogul Canada, 2065 Dundas St. E, Unit 105, Mississauga, ON L4X 2W1, Canada

MOLEX INC.

2222 Wellington Court, Lisle, IL, 60532

Tel: (630) 969-4550 Fax: (630) 969-1352 Web site: www.molex.com

Mfr. electronic, electrical & fiber optic interconnection products & systems, switches, application tooling.

Molex Inc., Scarborough, ON, Canada

MONSANTO COMPANY

800 N. Lindbergh Boulevard, St. Louis, MO, 63167

Tel: (314) 694-1000 Fax: (314) 694-7625 Web site: www.monsanto.com

Life sciences company focussing on agriculture, nutrition, pharmaceuticals, health and wellness and sustainable development.

Monsanto - Morden Plant, Morden, MB, Canada

Contact: Dion N. Nagy, Plant Mgr.

Monsanto Canada, 2233 Argentia Rd., Mississauga, ON L5M 2C2, Canada

Tel: 905-814-9666 Fax: 905-814-9994 Contact: Brian Prendergast, President

Monsanto Co. Chemical Group, LaSalle, PQ, Canada

MONTANA POWER COMPANY

40 East Broadway, Butte, MT, 59701

Tel: (406) 723-5421 Fax: (406) 497-2083

Energy, mining, telecommunications, electronics, waste management.

Altana Exploration Co., 520 Britannia Bldg., 703 6th Ave. SW, Calgary, AB T2P 0T9, Canada

Canadian Montana Pipeline & Gas Co. Ltd., 520 Britannia Bldg., 703 6th Ave. SW, Calgary, AB T2P 0T9, Canada

Intercontinental Energy Corp., 520 Britannia Bldg., 703 6th Ave. SW, Calgary, AB T2P 0T9, Canada

MOORE PRODUCTS COMPANY

Sumneytown Pike, Spring House, PA, 19477

Tel: (215) 646-7400 Fax: (215) 646-6212

Mfr. process control instruments.

Moore Instruments Ltd., PO Box 370, Brampton, ON L6V 2L3, Canada

MORGAN ADHESIVES COMPANY

4560 Darrow Road, Stow, OH, 44224

Tel: (330) 688-1111 Fax: (330) 688-2540

Self-adhesive print stock and emblem materials.

MACtac of Canada Ltd., 100 Kennedy Rd., Brampton, ON, l6W 3E8, Canada

Tel: 905-459-3100 Fax: 905-459-8078

MORGAN STANLEY DEAN WITTER & CO.

1585 Broadway, New York, NY, 10036

Tel: (212) 761-4000 Fax: (212) 761-0086 Web site: www.msdw.com

Securities and commodities brokerage, investment banking, money management, personal trusts.

Morgan Stanley Canada Ltd., BCE Place, 181 Bay St. (PO Box 776), Toronto, ON M5J 2T3, Canada

Morgan Stanley Canada Ltd., 1501 McGill College Ave., Ste. 2310, Montreal, PQ H3A3M8, Canada

MORTON INTERNATIONAL INC.

100 North Riverside Plaza, Chicago, IL, 60606-1596

Tel: (312) 807-2000 Fax: (312) 807-3150 Web site: www.mortonintl.com

Mfr. adhesives, coatings, finishes, specialty chemicals, advanced and electronic materials, salt, airbags.

Morton Intl. Ltd., Locations in Brossard and Montreal, PQ, Canada

Morton Intl. Ltd., 430 Finley Ave., PO Box 100, Ajax, ON L1S 3C2, Canada

MOSLER INC.

8509 Berk Boulevard, Hamilton, OH, 45015

Tel: (513) 870-1900 Fax: (513) 870-1170

Mfr. security products, systems, & services to financial, commercial, & government market.

Mosler Canada, 280 Brittannia Rd. E, Mississauga, ON L4Z 1S6, Canada

MOTION PICTURE ASSN. OF AMERICA

1600 Eye Street, NW, Washington, DC, 20006

Tel: (202) 293-1966 Fax: (202) 293-7674 Web site: www.mpaa.org

Motion picture trade association.

Canadian Motion Picture Distributors Association (CMPDA), 22 St. Clair Ave. East, Ste. 1603, Toronto, ON, M4T 2S4, Canada

Tel: 416-961-1888 Fax: 416-968-1016 Contact: Doug Frith

MOTOROLA, INC.

1303 East Algonquin Road, Schaumburg, IL, 60196

Tel: (847) 576-5000 Fax: (847) 538-5191 Web site: www.mot.com

Mfr. communications equipment, semiconductors and cellular phones.

Motorola Canada Ltd., 4185 Stillcreek Drive, Burnaby, BC, Canada (Locations: Calgary, AB Canada)

Tel: 604-293-7602

MTS SYSTEMS CORPORATION

1400 Technology Drive, Eden Prairie, MN, 55344-2290

Tel: (612) 937-4000 Fax: (612) 937-4515 Web site: www.mts.com

Develop/mfr. mechanical testing & simulation products & services, industry measure & automation instrumentation.

MTS Testing Systems (Canada) Ltd., Plaza Four #100, 2000 Argentia Rd., Mississauga, ON L5N 1P7, Canada

MUELLER INDUSTRIES, INC.

6799 Great Oaks Road, Ste. 200, Memphis, TN, 38138

Tel: (901) 753-3200 Fax: (901) 753-3255

Mfr. plumbing and heating products, refrigeration and A/C components, copper and copper alloy and metal forgings and extrusions.

Streamline Cooper & Brass Ltd., 290 Ellor St., PO Box 5003, Strathray, ON, Canada

MULTI GRAPHICS

431 Lakeview Court, Mt. Prospect, IL, 60056

Tel: (847) 375-1700 Fax: (847) 375-1810

Mfr./sale/service printing & print prod equipment, mailroom/bindery systems, services & supplies for graphics industry.

AM Intl. Inc., 81 Curlew Dr., North York, ON M3A 2P8, Canada

MULTIWARE

PO Box 907, Brookfield, CT, 06874

Tel: (203) 374-8000 Fax: (203) 374-3374

Mfr. applications development software.

Computerlinks, 4946 Dundas St. W, Toronto, ON M9A 1B7, Canada

MURPHY OIL CORPORATION

PO Box 7000, El Dorado, AR, 71731-7000

Tel: (870) 862-6411 Fax: (870) 862-9057

Crude oil, natural gas, mfr. petroleum products.

Murphy Oil Co. Ltd., PO Box 2721, Station M, Calgary, AB T2P 3Y3, Canada

F.E. MYERS & COMPANY

1101 Myers Parkway, Ashland, OH, 44805

Tel: (419) 289-1144 Fax: (419) 289-6658

Pumps, water systems, wastewater, industrial.

The F.E. Myers Co., 808 Courtland Ave., Kitchener, ON, Canada

Emp: 25

MYERS INTERNATIONAL INC.

1293 South Main Street, Akron, OH, 44301

Tel: (330) 253-5592 Fax: (330) 253-0035 Web site: www.myerstiresupply.com

Mfr. tire retreading & maintenance equipment & supplies.

Myers Tire Supply (Canada) Ltd., 517 McCormick Blvd., London, ON H5W 4C8, Canada

Tel: 519-451-3430 Fax: 519-451-6843 Contact: Doug Young, Mgr. Emp: 50

NABORS INDUSTRIES INC.

515 West Greens Road, #1200, Houston, TX, 77067

Tel: (281) 874-0035 Fax: (281) 872-5205

Oil & gas drilling, petrol products.

Nabors Drilling Co. Ltd., PO Box 55, Nisku, AB T0C 2G0, Canada

NAC REINSURANCE CORPORATION

One Greenwich Plaza, Greenwich, CT, 06836-2568

Tel: (203) 622-5200 Fax: (203) 622-1494 Web site: www/nacre.com

Provides property and casualty reinsurance.

Encon Group Insurance Managers Inc., 350 Albert St., Ste. 700 Ottawa, OT KIR 1A4, Canada

Tel: 613-786-2000 Fax: 613-786-2001 Contact: Dennis Shillington, Pres.

NACCO INDUSTRIES INC.

5875 Landerbrook Drive, Mayfield Heights, OH, 44124-4017

Tel: (440) 449-9600 Fax: (440) 449-9607 Web site: www.nacco.com

Mining/marketing lignite & metals, mfr. forklift trucks & small electric appliances, specialty retailers.

Hamilton Beach/Proctor-Silex Inc., PO Box 1630, Picton, ON, K0K 2T0 Canada

Tel: 613-476-2191

NALCO CHEMICAL COMPANY

One Nalco Center, Naperville, IL, 60563-1198

Tel: (630) 305-1000 Fax: (630) 305-2900 Web site: www.nalco.com

Chemicals for water and waste water treatment, oil products and refining, industry processes; water and energy management service.

Nalco Canada, Inc., PO Box 5002, Burlington, ON L7R 3Y9, Canada

Tel: 905-632-8791 Fax: 905-333-6188

NASHUA CORPORATION

44 Franklin Street, PO Box 2002, Nashua, NH, 03061-2002

Tel: (603) 880-2323 Fax: (603) 880-5671 Web site: www.nashua.com

Mfg. Imaging supplies (printer cartridges, toners, developers), labels, and specialty coated papers.

Nashua Photo Ltd., 1725 Quebec Ave., Saskatoon, SK S7K 1V8, Canada

NATCO

2950 North Loop West, Houston, TX, 77092-8839

Tel: (713) 683-9292 Fax: (713) 683-6787

Mfr./sale/service oil and gas products.

NATCO Canada, PO Box 850, Station T, Calgary, AB T2H 2H3, Canada

NATIONAL CAR RENTAL SYSTEM, INC.

7700 France Ave. South, Minneapolis, MN, 55435
Tel: (612) 830-2121 Fax: (612) 830-2921
Car rentals.

Tilden Car Rental, 1485 Stanley St., Montreal, PQ H3A 1P6, Canada

NATIONAL DATA CORPORATION

National Data Plaza, Atlanta, GA, 30329-2010
Tel: (404) 728-2000 Fax: (404) 728-2551 Web site: www.ndcorp.com
Information systems & services for retail, healthcare, government & corporate markets.

NDC International Ltd., 1 Concorde Gate #700, Don Mills, ON M3C 3N6, Canada

NATIONAL GYPSUM COMPANY

2001 Rexford Road, Charlotte, NC, 28211
Tel: (704) 365-7300 Fax: (704) 365-7276
Building products & services.

The Austin Co. Ltd., Toronto, ON, Canada

NATIONAL MANUFACTURING CO., INC.

PO Box 577, Sterling, IL, 61081
Tel: (815) 625-1320 Fax: (815) 625-1333
Mfr. hardware.

National-Spar Inc., 600 Fenton Crescent, Swift Current, SK S9H 4J8, Canada

NATIONAL REFRACTORIES & MINERALS CO.

1852 Rutan Drive MINERAL, Livermore, CA, 94550-7635
Tel: (925) 449-5010 Fax: (925) 455-8362
Produces and distributes refractories and nonferrous metals.

National Refractories & Minerals Ltd., PO Box 488, Oakville, ON L6J 5A8, Canada

NATIONAL SERVICE INDUSTRIES INC.

1420 Peachtree Street NE, Atlanta, GA, 30309
Tel: (404) 853-1000 Fax:
Mfr. lighting equipment, specialty chemicals; textile rental.

Zep Alcare, Locations throughout Canada.

Zep Manufacturing Co. of Canada, Halifax (NS), Montreal (PQ) & Toronto, ON, Canada

NATIONAL STARCH & CHEMICAL COMPANY

10 Finderne Ave., Bridgewater, NJ, 08807-3300
Tel: (908) 685-5000 Fax: (908) 685-5005 Web site: www.national starch.com
Mfr. adhesives & sealants, resins & specialty chemicals, electronic materials & adhesives, food products, industry starch.

Nacan Products Ltd., 500 Keele St., Unit 104-109, Toronto, ON M6N 3C9, Canada (Locations: Surrey, BC; Collingwood, ON; Brantford, ON; Boucherville, PQ, Canada.)
Tel: 416-604-3930 Fax: 416-604-3927

NATIONAL UTILITY SERVICE INC.

One Maynard Drive, PO Box 712, Park Ridge, NJ, 07656-0712
Tel: (201) 391-4300 Fax: (201) 391-8158
Utility rate consulting.

National Utility Service (Canada) Ltd., 111 Gordon Baker Rd., North York, ON M2H 3R2, Canada

NATIONAL-OILWELL, INC.

PO Box 4638, Houston, TX, 77210-4638
Tel: (713) 960-5100 Fax: (713) 960-5428 Web site: www.natoil.com
Mfr./distributor oilfield drills and tubulars.

National-Oilwell Canada Ltd., PO Box 2097, 601 Industrial Rd., Brook, AB T1R1C7, Canada

Tel: 403-362-5164 Fax: 403-362-8456

National-Oilwell Canada Ltd., 2300 Bow Valley Square III, 255-5th Ave. W.W. Calgary, AB, Canada

Tel: 403-294-4500 Fax: 403-294-9166

NAVISTAR INTERNATIONAL CORPORATION

455 North Cityfront Plaza Drive, Chicago, IL, 60611

Tel: (312) 836-2000 Fax: (312) 837-2227 Web site: www.navistar.com

Mfr. medium and heavy trucks, diesel engines and school buses.

Navistar International Corporation Canada, 120 King St W, Hamilton, ON L8N 3S5, Canada

NBD BANK

611 Woodward Ave., Detroit, MI, 48226

Tel: (313) 225-1000 Fax: (313) 225-2109

Banking services.

NBD Bank Canada, Windsor, ON, Canada

NCR (NATIONAL CASH REGISTER)

1700 South Patterson Blvd., Dayton, OH, 45479

Tel: (937) 445-5000 Fax: (937) 445-7042 Web site: www.ncr.com

Mfr. automated teller machines and high-performance stationary bar code scanners.

NCR, 320 Front St. West, Toronto, ON M5V 3C4, Canada

Tel: 416-351-2066 Fax: 416-351-2122 Contact: Bob Angel, Dir.

NEAC COMPRESSOR

191 Howard Street, Franklin, PA, 16323

Tel: (814) 437-3711 Fax: (814) 432-3334

Mfr. air tools and equipment.

Chicago Pneumatic Tool Co. Ltd., 5895 Kennedy Rd., Mississauga, ON L4Z 2G3, Canada

NELSON INDUSTRIES INC.

Highway 51, W. Stoughton, WI, 53589

Tel: (608) 873-4373 Fax: (608) 873-4166

Mfr. automotive parts & accessories, industry machinery.

Nelson Muffler Canada Inc., 20579 Langley Bypass, Langley, BC V3A 5E8, Canada

NETSCAPE COMMUNICATIONS

501 East Middlefield Road, Mountain View, CA, 94043

Tel: (650) 254-1900 Fax: (650) 528-4124

Mfr./distribute Internet-based commercial and consumer software applications.

Netscape Communications, 79 Wellington St. West, 27th Fl., PO Box 148, Toronto-Dominion Ctr., Toronto, ON M5K 1H1, Canada

Tel: 416-814-3050 Fax: 416-814-9970

NETWORK ASSOCIATES

3935 Freedon Circle, Santa Clara, CA, 95054

Tel: (408) 988-3832 Fax: (408) 970-9727 Web site: www.networkassociate.com

Designs and produces network security and network management software and hardware.

Network Associates, 139 Main St., Unit 201, Unionville, ON L3R 2G6, Canada

Tel: 905-479-4189 Fax: 905-479-4540

THE NEW YORK TIMES COMPANY

229 West 43rd Street, New York, NY, 10036-3959

Tel: (212) 556-1234 Fax: (212) 556-7389 Web site: www.nyt.com

Diversified media company including newspapers, magazines, television and radio stations, and electronic information and publishing.

Donohue Malbaie Inc. (JV), 500 Sherbrooke West, Ste. 800, Montreal, PQ, Canada

Tel: 514-847-7700 Contact: Michael Desbiens, Pres.

THE NEWELL COMPANY

29 E Stephenson Street, Freeport, IL, 61032-0943

Tel: (815) 963-1010 Fax: (815) 489-8212 Web site: www.newellco.com

Mfr. Hardware, housewares, and office products.

Newell Industries Canada Inc., 387 Bloor St. E #202, Toronto, ON M4W 1H7, Canada

Newell Office Products of Canada Inc., 500 Esna Park Drive, Markham, ON, Canada L3R 1H5 Canada

NEWPORT CORPORATION

PO Box 19607, Irvine, CA, 92606

Tel: (949) 863-3144 Fax: (949) 253-1800 Web site: www.newport.com

Mfr./distributor precision components & systems for laser/optical technology, vibration/motion measure & control.

Newport Instruments Canada, Ltd., 2650 Meadowvale Blvd., Unit #3, Mississauga, ON L5N 6M5, Canada

Tel: 800-267-8999 Canada Fax: 905-567-0392 Contact: Dave Sandoz, Mgr.

NIBCO INC.

500 Simpson Ave., PO Box 1167, Elkhart, IN, 46515

Tel: (219) 295-3000 Fax: (219) 295-3307

Mfr. fluid handling products for residential, commercial, industrial & fire protection markets.

Nibco Canada Inc., 720 Cochrane Dr., Markham, ON L3R 8E1, Canada

A .C. NIELSEN COMPANY

177 Broad Street, Stamford, CT, 06901

Tel: (203) 961-3000 Fax: (203) 961-3190 Web site: www.acnielsen.com

Market research.

A.C. Nielsen of Canada, 160 McNabb St., Markham, ON L3R 4B8, Canada

Tel: 905-475-3344

NIELSEN MEDIA RESEARCH

299 Park Ave., New York, NY, 10017

Tel: (212) 708-7500 Fax: (212) 708-7795 Web site: www.nielsenmedia.com

Measures TV audience size.

Nielsen Media Research Canada, 160 McNabb St., Markham, ON L3R 4B 8, Canada

Tel: 905-475-9595 Fax: 905-475-7296

NIKE INC.

1 Bowerman Drive, Beaverton, OR, 97005

Tel: (503) 671-6453 Fax: (503) 671-6300 Web site: www.info.nike.com

Mfr. athletic footwear, equipment and apparel.

Nike Canada Ltd., 2445 Canoe Ave., Coquitlam, BC V3K 6A9, Canada

NOBLE DRILLING CORPORATION

10370 Richmond Ave., #400, Houston, TX, 77042

Tel: (713) 974-3131 Fax: (713) 974-3181

Drilling contractor, engineering services.

Noble Drilling (Canada) Ltd., 850, 506 3rd St. SW, Calgary, AB T2P 3E6, Canada

Noble Drilling (Canada) Ltd., 902 20th Ave., PO Box 80, Nisku, AB T0C 2G0, Canada

Noble Offshore Ltd., Baine Johnson Ctr, 10 Fort William Pl. 8th Fl., St. John's, NF A1C 1K4, Canada

NORDSON CORPORATION

28601 Clemens Road, Westlake, OH, 44145

Tel: (440) 892-1580 Fax: (440) 892-9507 Web site: www.nordson.com

Mfr. industry application equipment, sealants & packaging machinery.

Nordson Canada Ltd., 1585 Dagenais Blvd. W, Laval, PA H7L 5A3, Canada

Tel: 514-628-6770 Fax: 514-628-4414

Nordson Canada Ltd., 1211 Denison St., Markham, ON L3R 4B3, Canada

Tel: 905-475-6730 Fax: 905-475-8821

NORFOLK SOUTHERN CORPORATION

Three Commercial Place, Norfolk, VA, 23510-1291

Tel: (757) 629-2600 Fax: (757) 629-2798

Holding company: transportation.

North American Van Lines Canada Ltd., 850 Champlain Ave., Oshawa, ON L1J 8C3, Canada

NORGREN

5400 S. Delaware Street, Littleton, CO, 80120-1663

Tel: (303) 794-2611 Fax: (303) 795-9487 Web site: www.norgren.com

Mfr. pneumatic filters, regulators, lubricators, valves, automation systems, dryers, push-in fittings.

IMI Norgren Ltd., 3067 Jarrow Ave., Mississauga, ON L4X 2C6, Canada

Tel: 905-625-4060 Fax: 925-625-8273

NORRELL CORPORATION

3535 Piedmont Road, NE, Atlanta, GA, 30305

Tel: (404) 240-3000 Fax: (404) 240-3312 Web site: www.norrell.com

Franchised temporary-help/workforce, short and long-term staffing services.

Norrell Corporation, 4940 No. 3 Rd., Ste. 305, Richmond, Canada V6X3A5

Tel: 604-273-5474

Norrell Corporation, 1201-1166 Alberni St., Vancouver V6E3Z3, BC, Canada

Tel: 604-688-9556

NORRISEAL CONTROLS

PO Box 40575, Houston, TX, 77240

Tel: (713) 466-3552 Fax: (713) 896-7386

Mfr. butterfly valves, fittings and plugs.

W.C. Norris Co. Ltd., Edmonton, AB, Canada

NORTEK INC.

50 Kennedy Plaza, Providence, RI, 02903

Tel: (401) 751-1600 Fax: (401) 751-4610

Mfr. residential and commercial building products.

Broan Ltd., 1140 Tristar Dr., Mississauga, ON, Canada

NORTH AMERICAN REFRACTORIES COMPANY

1228 Euclid Ave., Ste. 500, Cleveland, OH, 44115-1809

Tel: (216) 621-5200 Fax: (216) 621-8143

Mfr. firebrick, refractories.

North American Refractories Co., PO Box 339, Caledonia, ON, Canada

NORTH LILY MINING COMPANY

210-1800 Glenarm Place, #210, Denver, CO, 80202

Tel: (303) 294-0427 Fax: (303) 293-2235

Mining gold, silver and copper.

International Mahogany Corp, 1090 West Georgia St. #1305, Vancouver, BC, Canada

NORTHERN TRUST CORPORATION

50 South LaSalle Street, Chicago, IL, 60675
Tel: (312) 630-6000 Fax: (312) 444-3378
Banking services.
The Northern Trust Co. of Canada, BCE Place, 161 Bay St. #4540, Toronto, ON M5J 2S1, Canada

NORTHROP GRUMMAN CORPORATION

1840 Century Park East, Los Angeles, CA, 90067-2199
Tel: (310) 553-6262 Fax: (310) 201-3023 Web site: www.northgrum.com
Advanced technology for aircraft, electronics, and technical support services.
Northrup Grumman-Canada Ltd., 777 Walker's Line, Burlington, ON L7N 2G1, Canada
Tel: 905-333-6000 Fax: 905-333-6050

NORTON COMPANY

1 New Bond Street, Worcester, MA, 01606
Tel: (508) 795-5000 Fax: (508) 795-5741
Abrasives, drill bits, construction and safety products and plastics.
Canadian Koebel Diamond Tools Ltd., 1 Towns Rd., Toronto, ON M8Z 1A2, Canada
Christiansen Diamond Products (Canada) Ltd., 16230-112 Ave., Edmonton, AB, Canada
Norton Chemical Process Products, 1170 Blair Rd., Burlington, ON L7M 1K9, Canada
Norton Co., 8001 Daly St., Niagara Falls, ON, Canada
Norton Co., PO Box 37, Cap de la Madeleine, PQ, Canada
Norton Co. of Canada Ltd., PO Box 908, Brantford, ON, Canada
Norton Co. of Canada Ltd., PO Box 3008, Station B, Hamilton, ON, Canada
Norton Research Corp. (Canada) Ltd., 8001 Daly St., Niagara Falls, ON, Canada
Norton Safety Products Ltd., 396 Humberline Dr., Rexdale, ON, Canada
Produits de Securite Norton (Que.) Ltee., 551 Gabriel St., St. Tite, PQ, Canada
Produits de Securite Norton (Que.) Ltee., Rachel St. E, Montreal, PQ, Canada

NOVELL INC.

122 East 1700 Street, Provo, UT, 84606
Tel: (801) 861-7000 Fax: (801) 861-5555
Develop/mfr. networking software and related equipment.
Novell Canada Ltd., 4100 Yonge St., Willowdale, ON L3R 8T3, Canada
Tel: 905-940-2670

NOVO COMMUNICATIONS

520 Main Street, Fort Lee, NJ, 07024
Tel: (201) 592-9044 Fax: (201) 592-5946
Storage, distribution and service of film and tape libraries.
Bonded Services Intl., 288 Judson St., Unit 10, Toronto, ON M8Z 5T6, Canada

NUMATICS INC.

1450 North Milford Road, Highland, MI, 48357
Tel: (248) 887-4111 Fax: (248) 887-9190 Web site: www.numatics.com
Mfr. control valves and manifolds.
Numatics Ltd., 363 Sovereign Rd., London, ON N6M 1A3, Canada
Tel: 519-452-1777 Fax: 519-452-3995

NUTONE INC.

Madison and Red Bank Roads, Cincinnati, OH, 45227-1599
Tel: (513) 527-5100 Fax: (513) 527-5130 Web site: www.nutone.com
Mfr. residential specialty products and electrical appliances.

NuTone Canada Inc., 6300 Tomken Rd., Mississauga, ON L5T IN2, Canada

Tel: 905-795-1808 Fax: 905-795-1567 Contact: Robert Lawton, Gen. Sales Mgr. Emp: 15

NVF COMPANY

1166 Yorklyn Road, Yorklyn, DE, 19736

Tel: (302) 239-5281 Fax: (302) 239-4323

Metal containers, steel products, laminated plastics and papers.

NVF Industries of Canada Ltd., Rexdale, ON, Canada

OAKITE PRODUCTS, INC.

50 Valley Road, Berkeley Heights, NJ, 07922-2798

Tel: (908) 464-6900 Fax: (908) 464-7914

Mfr. chemical products for industry cleaning and metal treating.

Oakite Products of Canada Ltd., 115 East Dr., Bramalea, ON L6T-IB7, Canada

Tel: 905-791-1628 Contact: Ross McLachlan

OBJECT DESIGN INC.

25 Mall Road, Burlington, MA, 01803

Tel: (781) 674-5000 Fax: (781) 674-5010 Web site: www.odi.com

Developer of object-oriented database management systems software.

Object Design Inc., Canada/Toronto Sales Office - 120 Eglinton Ave. E, Ste. 1000, Toronto, ON M4P 1E2, Canada

Tel: 416-544-8290 Fax: 416-544-8308

OCEAN ENERGY CORPORATION

1201 Louisiana Street, #1400, Houston, TX, 77002

Tel: (713) 654-9110 Fax: (713) 653-3194

Petroleum and natural gas and exploration services.

Ocean Energy Resources Canada Ltd., 350 7th Ave. SW, Calgary, AB T2P 3N9, Canada

OCEANEERING INTERNATIONAL INC.

11911 FM 529, Houston, TX, 77041

Tel: (713) 329-4500 Fax: (713) 329-4951

Transportation equipment, underwater service to offshore oil and gas industry.

Oceaneering Intl. Inc., Dartmouth, Nova Scotia, Canada

C.M. OFFRAY & SON INC.

360 Rt. 24, Chester, NJ, 07930-0601

Tel: (908) 879-4700 Fax: (908) 543-4294

Mfr. narrow fabrics.

Offray Ribbon Canada Inc., 160 Maden St., Valleyfield, PQ J6S 4V7, Canada

OGILVY & MATHER WORLDWIDE

309 West 49th Street, New York, NY, 10019

Tel: (212) 237-4000 Fax: (212) 237-5123

Advertising, marketing, public relations & consulting firm.

Ogilvy & Mather, Toronto, ON, Canada

OGLEBAY NORTON COMPANY

1100 Superior Ave., 20th Fl., Cleveland, OH, 44114-2598

Tel: (216) 861-3300 Fax: (216) 861-2863 Web site: www.oglebaynorton.com

Produces limestone & provides transport services & raw materials for the construction & steel industries.

Global Stone Corporation, 251 North Service Rd. West, Ste. 306, Oakville, ON, L6M 3E7, Canada

Tel: 905-815-1050

OIL STATES INDUSTRIES

7701 South Cooper Street, Arlington, TX, 76017

Tel: (817) 468-1400 Fax: (817) 468-6250

Mfr., drilling and production machinery and supplies for oil/gas production.

Oil States Industries Ltd., Toronto, Ontario, Canada

OIL-DRI CORPORATION OF AMERICA

410 North Michigan Ave., Ste. 400, Chicago, IL, 60611

Tel: (312) 321-1515 Fax: (312) 321-1271 Web site: www.

Oil & grease absorbents, soil conditioners, and other sorbent mineral products.

Favorite Products Co., Laval, PQ, Canada

OLSTEN CORPORATION

175 Broad Hollow Road, Melville, NY, 11747-8905

Tel: (516) 844-7800 Fax: (516) 844-7022 Web site: www.olsten.com

Staffing, home health care & information technology services.

Olsten Staffing Services, 839-5th Ave. SW, Atrium One, Ste. 100, Calgary, AB T2P 3C8, Canada

Tel: 403-237-7296 Fax: 403-233-2537

Olsten Staffing Services, 4711 Yonge St., North York, ON M2N 6K8, Canada

Olsten Staffing Services, 2000 rue Peel, Bureau 680, Montreal, PQ H3A 2W5, Canada

Tel: 514-847-0448 Fax: 514-847-0481

Olsten Staffing Services, 77 Bloor St. West, Ste. 1508, Toronto ON M5S 1M2, Canada

Tel: 416-964-9100 Fax: 416-964-0355

Olsten Staffing Services, #303 - Wesley Ave., Winnipeg, MB R3C 4C6, Canada

Tel: 204-949-3030 Fax: 204-949-3039

Olsten Staffing Services, 33 Charlotte St., 2nd Fl., St. John NB E2L 2H3, Canada

Tel: 506-636-9251

Olsten Staffing Services, 1470-1188 West Georgia St., Vancouver, BC V6E 4A2, Canada

Tel: 604-688-8367 Fax: 604-688-0961

Olsten Staffing Services, 5151 George St., Ste. 802, Haifax, NS B3J 1M5, Canada

Tel: 902-423-9111 Fax: 902-433-6609

ONEIDA LTD

163-181 Kenwood Ave., Oneida, NY, 13421-2899

Tel: (315) 361-3000 Fax: (315) 361-3658 Web site: www.oneida.com

Mfr. cutlery, hollowware, china, crystal.

Oneida Canada Inc., Canada

Tel: 905-356-1591

ONTARIO STONE CORPORATION

34301 Chardon Road, Ste. #5, Willoughby, OH, 44094-8459

Tel: (440) 943-9556 Fax: (440) 631-1425

Stone & brick.

Port Colborne Quarries Ltd., 1973 Chippawa, Port Colborne, ON L3K 5W1, Canada

ORCHID INTERNATIONAL

100 Winners Circle, Brentwood, TN, 37027

Tel: (615) 661-4300 Fax: (615) 661-4359

Mfr. metal stampings and automation/robotics.

Orchid Intl., 1060 Fountain St. N., Cambridge, ON N3H 4R7, Canada

OTIS ELEVATOR COMPANY

10 Farm Springs Road, Farmington, CT, 06032

Tel: (860) 676-6000 Fax: (860) 676-5111

Mfr. elevators and escalators.

Otis Canada Inc., 710 Doral Dr., PO Box 550, Oakville, ON L6J 5B7, Canada

OUTBOARD MARINE CORPORATION

100 Sea Horse Drive, Waukegan, IL, 60085

Tel: (847) 689-6200 Fax: (847) 689-5555 Web site: www.omc-online.com

Mfr./market marine engines, boats & accessories.

Outboard Marine Power Products Group, 1789 Stenson, Unit 7, Petersborough, ON K95 7B6, Canada

OUTDOOR TECHNOLOGIES GROUP

1900 18th Street, Spirit Lake, IA, 51360

Tel: (712) 336-1520 Fax: (712) 336-4183

Mfr. fishing rods, reels, lines & tackle, outdoor products, soft and hard baits.

Outdoor Technologies Canada (OTC), 815 Phillips St., Portage la Prairie, MB, Canada

OWENS-ILLINOIS, INC.

One SeaGate, PO Box 1035, Toledo, OH, 43666

Tel: (419) 247-5000 Fax: (419) 247-2839

Largest mfr. of glass containers in the US; plastic containers, compression-molded closures and dispensing systems.

Consumers Packaging Ltd., 777 Kipling Ave., Toronto, ON M8Z 5G6, Canada

PACIFIC GAS & ELECTRIC COMPANY

77 Beale Street, PO Box 770000, San Francisco, CA, 94177

Tel: (415) 973-7000 Fax: (415) 972-9577

Electric and natural gas service.

Alberta & Southern Gas Co. Ltd., 240 Fourth Ave. SW, #2900, Calgary, AB T2P 4L7, Canada

PADCO INC.

2220 Elm Street SE, Minneapolis, MN, 55414

Tel: (612) 378-7270 Fax: (612) 378-9388

Mfr. paint sundries.

Padco Ltd., 3440 Pharmacy Ave., Scarborough, ON M1W 2P8, Canada

PALL CORPORATION

2200 Northern Boulevard, East Hills, NY, 11548-1289

Tel: (516) 484-5400 Fax: (516) 484-5228 Web site: www.pall.com

Specialty materials and engineering; filters & related fluid clarification equipment.

Pall (Canada) Ltd., 3333 Cote Vertu, Ste. 305, St. Laurent, PQ H4R 1N1, Canada

Tel: 514-332-7255 Fax: 514-332-0996

Pall Canada Ltd., 7205 Millcreek Drive, Mississauga, ON L5N 3R3, Canada

Tel: 905-542-0330 Fax: 905-542-0331

Pall Gelman Sciences, 7205 Millcreek Drive, Mississauga, ON L5N 3R3, Canada

Tel: 905-542-0330 Fax: 905-542-0331

Pall Gelman Sciences, 2535 de Miniac, Ville St. Laurent, Montreal, H4S 1E5, Canada

Tel: 514-337-2744 Fax: 514-337-7114

PANALARM DIV. AMETEK

7401 North Hamlin Ave., Skokie, IL, 60076

Tel: (847) 675-2500 Fax: (847) 675-3011

Mfr. electrical alarm systems, temp monitors, display systems, sensors.

Willa Engineering, 422 Consumer Rd., North York, ON M2J 1P8, Canada
Tel: 416-499-4421

PANAMETRICS

221 Crescent Street, Waltham, MA, 02154
Tel: (781) 899-2719 Fax: (781) 899-1552 Web site: www.panametrics.com
Process/non-destructive test instrumentation.

In Tech Supplies Ltd., 140-8851 Beckwith Rd., Richmond, B.C. V6X 1V4 Canada
Tel: 604-276-8006 Fax: 604-276-8725

In Tech Supplies Ltd., 3528 78 Ave., Edmonton, AB T6B 2X9, Canada
Tel: 403-448-9575 Fax: 403-466-1280

Laser Fast, 450 Campbell St., Unit 7, Cobourg, ON K9A 4C4, Canada
Tel: 905-373-7433 Fax: 905-373-0597

Trikon Technologies, 6969 Trans Canada Highway, Ste. 127, Ville St. Laurent, PQ H4T 1V8, Canada
Tel: 514-339-5997 Fax: 514-339-5540

PANDUIT CORPORATION

17301 Ridgeland Ave., Tinley Park, IL, 60477-0981
Tel: (708) 532-1800 Fax: (708) 532-1811
Mfr. electrical/electronic wiring components.

Panduit Canada Ltd., 140 Amber St., Markham, ON L3R 3J8, Canada

PANELFOLD INC.

10700 NW 36th Ave., Miami, FL, 33167
Tel: (305) 688-3501 Fax: (305) 681-2153 Web site: www.panelfold.com
Mfr. folding doors and partitions, operable and relocatable partition systems.

Canuck Doors, Mississauga, ON, Canada

PARADYNE

8545 Ulmerton Road, PO Box 2826, Largo, FL, 34294-2826
Tel: (813) 530-2000 Fax: (813) 530-2875
Mfr. data communications products.

Paradyne Canada, 12831 230th St., Maple Ridge, BC V2X 0M4, Canada

Paradyne Canada, 100 York Blvd. #505, Richmond Hill, ON L4B 1J8, Canada
Tel: 905-709-5000

Paradyne Canada, 155 Glendeer Circle SE #105, Calgary, AB T2H 2S8, Canada

Paradyne Canada, 2075 University St. #1106, Montreal, PQ H3A 1K8, Canada

PARAMETRIC TECHNOLOGY CORPORATION

128 Technology Drive, Waltham, MA, 02154
Tel: (781) 398-5000 Fax: (781) 398-5674 Web site: www.ptc.com
Mfr. CAD/CAM/CAE software.

Parametric Technology (Canada) Ltd., The Number Five Donald Business Ctr., 5 Donald St., Ste. 200, Winnipeg, MB R3L 2T4 Canada
Tel: 204-284-0688 Fax: 204-284-0682

Parametric Technology (Canada) Ltd., 703 6th Ave. S.W., Ste. 330, Calgary, AB T2P 0T9 Canada
Tel: 403-509-2400 Fax: 403-509-2429

Parametric Technology (Canada) Ltd., 252 Pall Mall St., Ste. 300, London, ON, N6A 5P6 Canada
Tel: 519-679-1514 Fax: 519-679-3660

Parametric Technology (Canada) Ltd., Purdy's Wharf I.T. Centre, Ste. 401a, 1959 Upper Water St., Halifax, Nova Scotia, Canada
Tel: 902-420-0824 Fax: 902-420-0835

Parametric Technology (Canada) Ltd., 1511 Howe St., Ste. 500, Vancouver, B.C., V6Z 2P3 Canada
Tel: 604-691-1758 Fax: 604-691-1759

Parametric Technology (Canada) Ltd., 3333 Cote Vertu, Ste. 620, St. Laurent, PQ H4R 2N1 Canada

Tel: 514-333-4010 Fax: 514-333-6899

Parametric Technology (Canada) Ltd., 2630 Skymark Ave., Ste. 701, Mississauga, ON L4W 5A4 Canada

Tel: 905-602-4660 Fax: 905-602-4330

Parametric Technology Corp., 2430 Don Reid Drive, Ottawa, ON K1H 8P5 Canada

Tel: 613-739-5566 Fax: 613-739-8191

PARAMOUNT PARKS

8620 Red Oak Blvd., Ste. 315, Charlotte, NC, 28217

Tel: (704) 525-5250 Fax: (704) 525-2960

Owns and operates theme parks and water parks.

Paramount Canada's Wonderland®, 9580 Jane St., Vaughan, ON L68 1S6, Canada

PAREXEL INTERNATIONAL CORPORATION

195 West Street, Waltham, MA, 02154

Tel: (781) 487-9900 Fax: (781) 487-0525 Web site: www.parexel.com

Provides contract medical, biotechnology, and pharmaceutical research and consulting services.

PAREXEL International Ltd., 4263 Sherwoodtowne Blvd., Ste. 200, Mississauga, ON L4Z 2Y6, Canada

Tel: 905-814-5300 Fax: 905-814-5301

PARKER ABEX NWL CORPORATION

2222 Palmer Ave., Kalamazoo, MI, 49001

Tel: (616) 384-3400 Fax: (616) 743-2131

Mfr. aerospace & automotive friction materials & equipment.

Abex Industries Ltd., 50 Colborne St. E, Lindsay, ON K9V 4R8, Canada

Canparts Ltd., 177 Pinebush Rd., Cambridge, ON N1R 7H8, Canada

PARKER HANNIFIN CORPORATION

17325 Euclid Ave., Cleveland, OH, 44112

Tel: (216) 896-3000 Fax: (216) 896-4000 Web site: www.parker.com

Mfr. motion-control products.

Parker Hannifin Fluid Connectors Group, South Durham Rd., PO Box 158, Grimsby, ON L3M 4G4, Canada

Tel: 905-945-2274 Fax: 905-945-3946

Parker Hannifin Motion & Control Group, 530 Kipling Ave., Toronto, ON M8Z 5E6, Canada

Tel: 416-255-7371 Fax: 416-251-6890

Parker Hannifin Refrig. & Air Conditioning Group, 4943 Union St., Beamsville, ON L0R 1BO, Canada

Tel: 416-945-2274 Fax: 416-563-0919

Parker Hannifin Seal Group, 4120 Ridgeway Dr., Unit 35, Mississauga, ON L5L 5S9, Canada

Tel: 905-569-9100 Fax: 905-569-1022

PARSONS & WHITTEMORE INC.

4 International Drive, Rye Brook, NY, 10573

Tel: (914) 937-9009 Fax: (914) 937-2259

Pulp and paper mfr., construction pulp and paper mills, engineering.

St. Anne Nackawic Pulp Co. Ltd., Main Rd., Nackawic, NB E0H 1P0, Canada

Tel: 506-575-2000

St. Anne Pulp Sales Ltd., 250 Bloor St. E #1420, Toronto, ON M4W 1E6, Canada

Tel: 416-968-2900

PATAGONIA INC.

259 West Santa Clara Street, Ventura, CA, 93001

Tel: (805) 643-8616 Fax: (805) 653-6355

Outdoor clothing retail stores and mail-order catalogue company.

Patagonia, Inc., Canada

PAXAR CORPORATION

105 Corporate Park Drive, White Plains, NY, 10604

Tel: (914) 697-6800 Fax: (914) 696-4128 Web site: www.paxar.com

Mfr./sales/distribution of labels, hang tags, scanners, printing equipment and inks.

Monarch Marking Systems Ltd., 895 Brock Rd., Pickering, ON, Canada L1W 3C1

PCA ELECTRONICS INC.

16799 Schoenborn Street, North Hills, CA, 91343

Tel: (818) 892-0761 Fax: (818) 894-5791 Web site: www.pca.com

Mfr./sales of electronic equipment.

Canadian Source Corp., 907 St. Andrews St., New Westminster, BCV3M 1W1, Canada

Tel: 604-687-5285 Fax: 604-667-5295

Canadian Source Corp., 3775 14th Ave., Unit 15, Markham, ON L3R OH6, Canada

Tel: 905-415-1951 Fax: 905-415-1953

Canadian Source Corp., 148 Rene-Emard St., Ile-Perrot, PQ J7V 8V7, Canada

Tel: 514-457-5556 Fax: 514-457-5096

Canadian Source Corp., 273 Huntington Close, N.E., Calgary, AB T2K 5B4, Canada

Tel: 403-274-5211 Fax: 403-2745211

Canadian Source Corp., 17 Cherokee Bay, Winnipeg, MB R2J-2C4, Canada

Tel: 204-897-4401 Fax: 905-415-1953

THE PEELLE COMPANY

34 Central Ave., Hauppauge, NY, 11788-4734

Tel: (516) 231-6000 Fax: (516) 231-6059

Mfr./sales/service elevator, fire and specially engineered doors.

The Peelle Co. Ltd., 7415 Torbram Rd., Mississauga, ON L4T 1G8, Canada

PENTAIR, INC.

1500 County Road, B2 West, St. Paul, MN, 55113-3105

Tel: (612) 636-7920 Fax: (612) 636-5508

Diversified manufacturer operating in electrical and electronic enclosures, professional tools/equipment and water products.

Delta Intl. Machinery Corp., 644 Imperial Rd., Guelph, ON N1H 6M7, Canada

F.E. Myers Co., 269 Trillium Dr., PO Box 38, Kitchener, ON N2G 3W9, Canada

Lincoln Canada, 7017 Fir Tree Dr., Mississauga, ON L5S 1J7, Canada L5S 1J7

PEPSiCO INC.

700 Anderson Hill Road, Purchase, NY, 10577-1444

Tel: (914) 253-2000 Fax: (914) 253-2070 Web site: www.pepsico.com

Beverages and snack foods.

Hostess-FL NRO Ltd., Canada

Pepsi-Cola Canada (NRO) Ltd., Canada

Pepsi-Cola Canada Ltd., Canada

PERFECT CIRCLE SEALED POWER

PO Box 1208, Muskegon, MI, 49443

Tel: (616) 722-1300 Fax: (616) 724-1940

Gaskets, seals, packings, etc.

Perfect Circle, Victor Div. Hayes-Dana Ltd., St. Thomas, ON, Canada

PERIPHONICS CORPORATION

4000 Veterans Highway, Bohemia, NY, 11716

Tel: (516) 467-0500 Fax: (516) 737-8520

Mfr. voice processing systems.

Periphonics Corp., 151 Carlingview Dr., Rexdale, ON M9W 5S4, Canada

THE PERKIN-ELMER CORPORATION

761 Main Ave., Norwalk, CT, 06859-0001

Tel: (203) 762-1000 Fax: (203) 762-4228 Web site: www.perkin-elmer.com

Leading supplier of systems for life science research and related applications.

Perkin-Elmer - Applied Biosystems Division, Mississauga, ON, Canada

Tel: 905-821-8183 Fax: 905-821-8246

Perkin-Elmer Canada Ltd., 330 Cochrane Drive, Markham, ON L3R 8E5, Canada (Locations: Vancouver, Burlington, & Concord, Canada.)

Tel: 905-477-0176 Fax: 905-477-8220

PETERSON AMERICAN CORPORATION

21200 Telegraph Road, Southfield, MI, 48086-5059

Tel: (248) 799-5400 Fax: (248) 357-3176 Web site: www.pspring.com

Mfr. springs & wire products, metal stampings.

Peterson Spring of Canada Ltd. - Kingsville Plant, 208 Wigle Ave., Kingsville, ON N9Y 2J9 Canada

Tel: 519-733-2358 Fax: 519-733-3070 Contact: Guy Harrison

Peterson Spring of Canada Ltd. - Windsor Plant, 2992 Deziel Dr., Windsor, ON N8W 5A5, Canada

Tel: 519-948-3471 Fax: 519-948-6905 Contact: Doug Morris

PFIZER INC.

235 East 42nd Street, New York, NY, 10017-5755

Tel: (212) 573-2323 Fax: (212) 573-7851 Web site: www.pfizer.com

Research-based, global health care company.

Kirchimie Ltd., Canada

Pfizer C&G Inc., Canada

Pfizer Canada Inc., Toronto, Ontario, Canada

Pfizer Canada Inc., Canada

Pfizer Holding Ltd., Canada

Pfizer Hospital Products Ltd., Canada

Rogar/STB Inc., Canada

PHARMACIA & UPJOHN

95 Corporate Drive, PO Box 6995, Bridgewater, NJ, 08807

Tel: (908) 306-4400 Fax: (908) 306-4433 Web site: www.pnu.com

Mfr. pharmaceuticals, agricultural products, industry chemicals

Pharmacia & Upjohn, 5100 Spectrum Way, Mississauga, ON, LAW 5J5, Canada

Pharmacia & Upjohn Animal Health, 40 Centennital Rd., Orangeville, ON L9W 3T3, Canada

PHELPS DODGE CORPORATION

2600 North Central Ave., Phoenix, AZ, 85004-3089

Tel: (602) 234-8100 Fax: (602) 234-8337

Copper, minerals, metals & spec engineered products for transportation & electrical markets.

Accuride Canada Inc., PO Box 6280, Station D, London, ON N5W 5S1, Canada

Columbian Chemicals Co., Canada

Phelps Dodge Corp. of Canada Ltd., 120 Adelaide St. W #912, Toronto, ON M5H 1T1, Canada

PHH VEHICLE MANAGEMENT SERVICES

307 International Circle, Hunt Valley, MD, 21030

Tel: (410) 771-3600 Fax: (410) 771-2841 Web site: www.phh.com

Provides vehicle fleet management, corporate relocation, and mortgage banking services.

PHH Vehicle Management Services, 350 Burnhamthorpe Rd. West, Ste. 700, Mississauga, ON L5B 3P9, Canada

Tel: 905-270-8250

PHH Vehicle Management Services, 6363 Trans Canada Highway, Ste. 104, Ville St. Lauent, PQ H4T 129, Canada

Tel: 514-744-7250

PHH Vehicle Management Services, Harbour Centre, 555 W. Hastings St., Ste. 990, Vancouver, BC V6B 4N6, Canada

Tel: 604-681-5426

PHH Vehicle Management Services, Sun Life Plaza II, Ste. 2100, 140 4th Ave., SW, Calgary, AB T2P 3N3, Canada

Tel: 403-262-8980

PHILIP SERVICES CORP. INDUSTRIAL GROUP

5151 San Felipe Street, #1600, Houston, TX, 77056-3609

Tel: (713) 623-8777 Fax: (713) 625-7085 Web site: www.philipinc.com

Trucking, refuse systems, staffing and numerous industrial-oriented services.

Philip Services Corp. Industrial Group, 474 Southdown Rd., Mississauga, ON L5J 2Y4, Canada

Tel: 905-823-6880 Fax: 905-521-9182 Contact: Mike Smith

PICKER INTERNATIONAL INC.

595 Miner Road, Highland Heights, OH, 44143

Tel: (440) 473-3000 Fax: (440) 473-4844 Web site: www.picker.com

Mfr. diagnostic medical machines.

Picker Ltd., Toronto, Ontario, Canada

PICTURETEL CORPORATION

100 Minuteman Road, Andover, MA, 01810

Tel: (978) 292-5000 Fax: (978) 292-3300 Web site: www.picturetel.com

Mfr. video conferencing systems, network bridging & multiplexing products, system peripherals.

PictureTel Corporation, 675 Cochrane Drive, Ste. 302, east Tower, Markham, ON L3R 0B8, Canada

Tel: 905-474-4334 Fax: 905-474-1494

PIERCE & STEVENS CORPORATION

PO Box 1092, Buffalo, NY, 14240

Tel: (716) 856-4910 Fax: (716) 856-9718

Mfr. coatings, adhesives and specialty chemical for packaging and graphic arts..

Pierce & Stevens Canada Ltd., Catherine St. & Concession Rd., Fort Erie, ON, Canada

PINKERTON'S, INC.

15910 Ventura Boulevard, Ste. 900, Encino, CA, 91436

Tel: (818) 380-8800 Fax: (818) 380-8515 Web site: www.pinkertons.com

Security solutions.

Pinkerton Intl. Division, 1980 Sherbrooke St. W, #640, Montreal, PQ H3H 1E8, Canada

Tel: 514-935-2533 Fax: 514-935-7552 Contact: Paul St. Amour, Pres.

PIONEER HI-BRED INTERNATIONAL INC.

400 Locust Street, Ste. 800, Des Moines, IA, 50309

Tel: (515) 248-4800 Fax: (515) 248-4999

Agricultural chemicals, farm supplies, biological products, research.

Pioneer Hi-Bred Ltd., PO Box 30, Chatham, ON N7M 5L1, Canada

PIONEER NATURAL RESOURCES CO.

5205 North O'Connor Boulevard, Irving, TX, 75039

Tel: (972) 444-9001 Fax: (972) 444-4328

Oil and gas

Pioneer Natural Resources Co., Canada

PITNEY BOWES INC.

1 Elmcroft Road, Stamford, CT, 06926-0700

Tel: (203) 356-5000 Fax: (203) 351-6835 Web site: www.pitneybowes.com

Mfr. postage meters, mailroom equipment, copiers, bus supplies, bus services, facsimile systems and financial services.

Pitney Bowes Canada Ltd., 2200 Yonge St., Ste. 100, Toronto, ON, M4S 3E1, Canada

Tel: 416-489-2211 Fax: 416-484-3887 Contact: Fred Van Parys, Pres. & CEO Emp: 1400

PITTSTON COMPANY

PO Box 4229, Glen Allen, VA, 23058

Tel: (805) 553-3600 Fax: (805) 553-3753 Web site: www.pittston.com

Trucking, warehousing and armored car service, home security systems

Brinks' Canada Ltd., 55 Logan, Toronto, ON, Canada

Metropolitan Plt. Ltd., Montreal, PQ, Canada

Montreal Terminals Ltd., 10000 Notre Dame E, Montreal, PQ, Canada

PLANET HOLLYWOOD INTERNATIONAL, INC.

8669 Commodity Circle, Orlando, FL, 32819

Tel: (407) 363-7827 Fax: (407) 363-4862 Web site: www.planethollywood.com

Theme-dining restaurant chain and merchandise retail stores.

Planet Hollywood International, Inc., Locations in Toronto, Vancouver and Edmonton, Canada

PLANTERS PEANUTS

100 DeForest Ave., East Hanover, NJ, 07936

Tel: (973) 682-5000 Fax: (973) 503-2153

Nut products, peanut oil and candy.

Planters Nut & Chocolate Co. Ltd., 672 Dupont St., Toronto, ON, Canada

PLANTRONICS

337 Encinal Street, Santa Cruz, CA, 95061-1802

Tel: (831) 426-5858 Fax: (831) 425-5198 Web site: www.plantronics.com

Mfr. communications equipment, electrical & electronic appliances & apparatus.

Plantronics Canada Ltd., 1 Select Ave. #14, Scarborough, ON, Canada

PLAYTEX APPAREL INC.

700 Fairfield Ave., Stamford, CT, 06904

Tel: (203) 356-8000 Fax: (203) 356-8448 Web site: www.saralee.com

Mfr. intimate apparel.

Playtex Apparel Canada Ltd., 6343 Northam Dr., Airport Industrial Park, Malton, ON L4V 1N5, Canada

PLIBRICO COMPANY

1800 N. Kingsbury Street, Chicago, IL, 60614

Tel: (773) 549-7014 Fax: (773) 549-0424

Refractories, engineering and construction.

Plibrico (Canada) Ltd., PO Box 910, Burlington, ON L7R 3Y7, Canada

POLAROID CORPORATION

549 Technology Square, Cambridge, MA, 02139

Tel: (781) 386-2000 Fax: (781) 386-3276 Web site: www.polaroid.com

Photographic equipment & supplies, optical products.

Polaroid Corp. Ltd., 350 Carlingview Dr., Rexdale, ON, Canada

POLICY MANAGEMENT SYSTEMS CORPORATION

PO Box 10, Columbia, SC, 29202

Tel: (803) 735-4000 Fax: (803) 735-5544

Computer software, insurance industry support services.

Policy Management Systems Canada Ltd., Valhalla Executive Centre, 300 The East Mall #600, Islington, ON M9B 6B7, Canada

R.L. POLK & COMPANY

1155 Brewery Park Blvd., Detroit, MI, 48207-2697

Tel: (248) 728-7111 Fax: (248) 393-2860 Web site: www.polk.com

Directories, direct mail advertising.

B.C. Directories, 34 West 2nd Ave., Vancouver, BC V5Y 1B3, Canada

Blackburn/Polk Marketing Services Inc., 330 Front St. W. #1000, Toronto, ON M5V 3B7, Canada

Might Directories, PO Box 1005, Postal Station O, Toronto, ON M4A 2N4, Canada

R.L. Polk/King Kraft Div., 384 Neptune Crescent, London, ON N6M 1A1, Canada

Talbot Marketing, 220 Bartley Dr., Toronto, ON M4A 1G2, Canada

Talbot Marketing, 4474 Blakie Rd., Unit 130, Westminster, ON N6L 1G7, Canada

POMEROY INC.

1899 Spindrift Drive, LaJolla, CA, 92037

Tel: (619) 459-5960 Fax: (619) 459-1818

Mfr./sale of building hardware and sash balances.

Neeman Malek Unique Sash, 8301 Marcone ave, Ville D'Anjou, PQ, Canada

Tel: 514-493-1353 Fax: 514-493-0571 Contact: Neeman Malek, Dir.

POPE & TALBOT INC.

1500 SW First Ave., Portland, OR, 97201

Tel: (503) 228-9161 Fax: (503) 220-2722

Mfr. paper, pulp & wood products.

Pope & Talbot Ltd., PO Box 39, 570 68th Ave., Grand Forks, BC V0H 1H0, Canada

PORTEC RAIL PRODUCTS INC.

122 W 22nd Street, #100, Oak Brook, IL, 60521-1553

Tel: (630) 573-4619 Fax: (630) 573-4604

Mfr. engineered products for construction equipment, material handling & railroad track components.

Portec Ltd., 2044 32nd Ave., Lachine, PQ, Canada H8T 3H7

PORTER PRECISION PRODUCTS COMPANY

2734 Banning Road, Cincinnati, OH, 45239-5504

Tel: (513) 923-3777 Fax: (513) 923-1111

Mfr. piercing punches & die supplies for metal stamping & tool/die industry.

Porter Precision Products Canada Ltd., 45 Durward Pl., Waterloo, ON N2L 4E5, Canada

POWERS PROCESS CONTROLS

3400 Oakton Street, Skokie, IL, 60076

Tel: (847) 673-6700 Fax: (847) 673-9044

Mfr./sales control devices.

Powers Process Controls Ltd., 15 Torbarrie Rd., Downsview, ON, Canada

Tel: 905-238-4855 Contact: Ted Svetco, Mgr.

PPG INDUSTRIES

One PPG Place, Pittsburgh, PA, 15272

Tel: (412) 434-3131 Fax: (412) 434-2190 Web site: www.ppg.com

Mfr. coatings, flat glass, fiber glass, chemicals. coatings.

PPG Canada Inc., 834 Caledonia Rd., Toronto, ON M6B 3X9 Canada

PRAXAIR, INC.

39 Old Ridgebury Road, Danbury, CT, 06810-5113

Tel: (203) 837-2000 Fax: (203) 837-2450 Web site: www.praxair.com

Produces and distributes industrial and specialty gases.

Praxair Canada, Inc., 1 City Centre Drive, Ste. 1200, Mississauga, ON L5B 1M2, Canada

Tel: 905-803-1600 Fax: 905-803-1690

UCISCO, Inc., 1274 Lougar Ave., Clearwater, ON N7S 5N6, Canada

Tel: 519-332-0730 Fax: 519-332-0730

PRECISION VALVE CORPORATION

PO Box 309, Yonkers, NY, 10702

Tel: (914) 969-6500 Fax: (914) 966-4428

Mfr. aerosol valves.

Precision Valve Canada Ltd., 85 Fuller Rd., Ajax, ON L1S 2EI, Canada

PREFORMED LINE PRODUCTS COMPANY

600 Beta Drive, PO Box 91129, Cleveland, OH, 44101

Tel: (440) 461-5200 Fax: (440) 461-2918

Mfr. pole line hardware for electrical transmission lines; splice closures & related products for telecommunications.

Preformed Line Products (Canada) Ltd., Cambridge, ON, Canada

PREMARK INTERNATIONAL INC.

1717 Deerfield Road, Deerfield, IL, 60015

Tel: (847) 405-6000 Fax: (847) 405-6013 Web site: www.premarkintl.com

Mfr./sale plastic, diversified consumer & commercial products.

Premark Canada Inc., Toronto Dominion Bank Tower #2400, 66 Wellington St. W, Toronto, ON M5K 1E7, Canada

PRETTY PRODUCTS INC.

Cambridge Road, Coshocton, OH, 43812

Tel: (614) 622-3522 Fax: (614) 622-4915

Mfr. automotive accessories.

Pretty Ware Ltd., 40 Racine Rd., Toronto, ON, Canada

PRICEWATERHOUSECOOPERS LLP

1251 Ave. of the Americas, New York, NY, 10020

Tel: (212) 596-7000 Fax: (212) 790-6620 Web site: www.pwcglobal.com

Accounting and auditing, tax and management, and human resource consulting services.

Price Waterhouse Ltd., 1501 Toronto Dominion Tower, Edmonton Centre, Edmonton, AB T5J 2Z1, Canada

Tel: 403-493-8200 Fax: 403-428-8069

Price Waterhouse Ltd., Barrister House, 180 Elgin St., 11th Fl., Ottawa, ON K2P 2K3, Canada

Tel: 613-238-8200 Fax: 613-238-4798

Price Waterhouse Ltd., 1200 425 1st St. SW, Calgary, AB T2P 3V7, Canada

Tel: 403-267-1200 Fax: 403-233-0883

Price Waterhouse Ltd., 801 Hollis St., Ste. 900, Halifax, Nova Scotia B3J 3N4, Canada

Tel: 902-420-1900 Fax: 902-420-1755

Price Waterhouse Ltd., 1250 Boul. Rene-Levesque, Bureau 3500, Montreal, PQ H3B 2G4, Canada

Tel: 514-938-5600 Fax: 514-938-5709

Price Waterhouse Ltd., 2200 One Lombard Place, Winnipeg, MB R3B 0X7, Canada

Tel: 204-943-7321 Fax: 204-943-7774

Price Waterhouse Ltd., Tour de la Cite (Sainte-Foy), 870-2600 Blvd. Laurier, PQ, (Qc) GIV 4W2, Canada

Tel: 418-658-5782 Fax: 418-656-6640

Price Waterhouse Ltd., 601 West Hastings St., Ste. 1400, Vancouver, BC V6B 5A5, Canada

Tel: 604-682-4711 Fax: 604-662-5300

Price Waterhouse Ltd./ National Hdqtrs., One First Canadian Place, Ste. 3300, POB 190, Toronto, ON M5X 1H7, Canada

Tel: 416-863-1133 Fax: 416-365-8178

PRIMAC COURIER INC.

333 Sylvan Ave., Englewood Cliffs, NJ, 07632

Tel: (201) 871-1800 Fax: (201) 871-3313

Air courier services.

Primac Courier (Canada) Inc., 1157 Wellington St., Montreal, PQ H3C 2L8, Canada

Tel: 514-876-0040

Primac Courier (Canada) Inc., 2289 Fairview St., Unit 206, Burlington, ON L7R 2E3, Canada

Tel: 416-259-5400 Fax: 416-259-0651

PROCTER & GAMBLE COMPANY

One Procter & Gamble Plaza, Cincinnati, OH, 45202

Tel: (513) 983-1100 Fax: (513) 562-4500 Web site: www.pg.com

Personal care, food, laundry, cleaning and industry products.

Procter & Gamble Inc., 4711 Yonge St., North York, ON M2N 6K8, Canada (Locations: Belleville, Brockville, Hamilton & Weston, Canada.)

PRODUCTO/MOORE TOOL COMPANY, INC.

990 Housatonic Ave., PO Box 780, Bridgeport, CT, 06601-0780

Tel: (203) 367-8675 Fax: (203) 366-5694

Mfr. machine tools, die sets and diemakers accessories.

Producto Diemakers Supplies Ltd., 620 Supertest Rd., Unit 19, Downsview, ON M3J 2M8, Canada

Tel: 416-661-0555 Fax: 416-661-3708

THE PROGRESSIVE CORPORATION

6300 Wilson Mills Road, Mayfield Village, OH, 44143

Tel: (440) 461-5000 Fax: (440) 603-4420 Web site: www.auto-insurance.com

Provides non-standard auto coverage and standard and preferred auto coverage.

The Progressive Corp. of Canada, 200 Yorkland Blvd., 5th Fl., Willowdale, M2J 5C1 ON, Canada

Tel: 416-499-9947

PROVIDENT COMPANIES, INC.

One Fountain Square, Chattanooga, TN, 37402

Tel: (423) 755-1011 Fax: (423) 755-7013 Web site: www.providentcompanies.com

Sale of disability and life insurance products to individuals and groups.

Provident, 5420 North Service Rd., Box 5044, Burlington, ON L7R 4C1, Canada

Tel: 905-319-9501 Fax: 905-319-9490 Contact: George A. Shell, Jr., Dir., Canada Emp: 330

PRUDENTIAL INSURANCE COMPANY OF AMERICA

751 Broad Street, Newark, NJ, 07102-3777

Tel: (973) 802-6000 Fax: (973) 802-2812 Web site: www.prudential.com

Sale of life insurance and provides financial services.

Prudential Insurance Co. of America, 4 King St. W, Toronto, ON M5H 1B7, Canada

PSDI MAXIMO

100 Crosby Drive, Bedford, MA, 01730

Tel: (781) 280-2000 Fax: (781) 280-0200 Web site: www.psdi.com

Develops, markets and provides maintenance management software systems.

PSDI Canada Ltd., Burlington, ON, Canada

Tel: 905-336-8961 Fax: 905-336-8962 Contact: David Fisk, Mgr. Emp: 5

PSI NET (PERFORMANCE SYSTEMS INTERNATIONAL INC.)

510 Huntmar Park Drive, Herndon, VA, 22170

Tel: (703) 904-4100 Fax: (703) 904-4200 Web site: wwwpsi.net

Internet service provider.

ISTAR Internet Inc., 250 Albert St., Ste. 202, Ottawa, ON KIP 6MI, Canada

Tel: 613-780-2200 Fax: 613-780-6666

PSINet Ltd., 100 Shepard Ave., East, 6th Fl., North York, ON M2N 6NS, Canada

Tel: 416-228-3400 Fax: 416-223-0234

QMS INC.

One Magnum Pass, Mobile, AL, 36618

Tel: (205) 633-4300 Fax: (205) 633-4866

Mfr. monochrome and color computer printers.

QMS Canada Inc., Also in Toronto, Calgary, Ottawa, Quebec City, Winnipeg, Edmonton & Vancouver, Canada

QMS Canada Inc., 9630 Trans Canada Hwy., St. Laurent, PQ H4S 1V9, Canada

QUAKER STATE CORPORATION

225 E. John Carpenter Freeway, Irving, TX, 75062

Tel: (972) 868-0400 Fax: (972) 868-0678

Mfr. motor oil, lubricants, automotive chemicals, waxes.

Quaker State Inc., 1101 Blair Rd., Burlington, ON L7M 1T3, Canada

RADIATOR SPECIALTY COMPANY

PO Box 34689, Charlotte, NC, 28234-6080

Tel: (704) 377-6555 Fax: (704) 334-9425

Mfr. plumbing/heating supplies, automotive chemical specialties, molded rubber parts.

Radiator Specialty Co. Ltd., 1711 Amico Blvd., Mississauga, ON, Canada

RADISSON HOTELS INTERNATIONAL

Carlson Pkwy., PO Box 59159, Minneapolis, MN, 55459-8204

Tel: (612) 540-5526 Fax: (612) 449-3400

Hotels and resorts.

Radisson Hotel des Gouverneurs, 777 University St., Montreal, PQ H3C 3Z7, Canada

Tel: 514-879-1370 Fax: 514-879-1761

Radisson Plaza Hotel Admiral, 249 Queen's Quay West, Toronto, ON M5J 2N5, Canada

Tel: 416-203-3333 Fax: 416-203-3100

RADIUS INC.

460 East Middlefield Road, Mountainview, CA, 94043

Tel: (650) 404-6000 Fax: (650) 404-6200

Mfr. graphic interface cards, displays, accelerators and multiprocessing software.

Radius Inc. Canada, 250 The Esplanade #110, Toronto, ON M5A 1J2, Canada

RAIN BIRD SPRINKLER MFG. CORPORATION

145 North Grand Ave., Glendora, CA, 91741-2469

Tel: (626) 963-9311 Fax: (626) 963-4287 Web site: www.rainbird.com

World's largest manufacturer of lawn sprinklers and irrigation systems equipment.

Rain Bird Sprinkler Mfg. Co. (Canada) Ltd., 5337 180th St., Surrey, BC V3S 4K5, Canada

RALSTON PURINA COMPANY

Checkerboard Square, St. Louis, MO, 63164

Tel: (314) 982-1000 Fax: (314) 982-1211

Animal feed, cereals, food products.

Ralston Purina Canada Agri-Division, 404 Main St., Woodstock, ON N4S 7X5, Canada

Ralston Purina Canada Eveready Div., 2500 Royal Windsor Dr., Mississauga, ON L5J 1K8, Canada

Ralston Purina Canada Inc., 2500 Royal Windsor Dr., Mississauga, ON L5J 1K8, Canada

RAMSEY TECHNOLOGY INC.

501 90th Ave. NW, Minneapolis, MN, 55433

Tel: (612) 783-2500 Fax: (612) 780-2525

Mfr. in-motion weighing, inspection, monitoring & control equipment for the process industry.

Ramsey REC Ltd., 385 Enford Rd., Richmond Hill, ON L4C 3G2, Canada

RANCO INC.

555 Metro Place North, PO Box 248, Dublin, OH, 43017

Tel: (614) 873-9200 Fax: (614) 873-9290

Mfr. controls for appliance, automotive, comfort, commercial and consumer markets.

Ranco Controls Canada Ltd., 221 Evans Ave., Toronto, ON M8Z 1J5, Canada

RAND McNALLY

8255 North Central Park Ave., Skokie, IL, 60076

Tel: (847) 329-8100 Fax: (847) 673-0539

Publishing, consumer software, information and retail.

Allmaps Canada Ltd., 390 Steelcase Rd. E., Markham, ON L3R 1G2, Canada

RAY & BERNDTSON, INC.

301 Commerce, Ste. 2300, Fort Worth, TX, 76102

Tel: (817) 334-0500 Fax: (817) 334-0779 Web site: www.prb.com

Executive search, management audit and management consulting firm.

Ray & Berndtson, 710-1050 West Pender St., Vancouver, BC V6E 3S7, Canada

Tel: 604-685-0261 Fax: 604-684-7988 Contact: Kyle R. Mitchell, Mng. Ptnr.

Ray & Berndtson, 200 Bay St., Ste. 3150 South Tower, Toronto, ON M5J 2J3, Canada

Tel: 416-366-1990 Fax: 416-366-7353 Contact: W. Carl Lovas, Mng. Ptnr.

Ray & Berndtson, 155 Queen St., Ste. 900, Ottawa, ON K1P 6L1, Canada

Tel: 613-786-3191 Fax: 613-569-1661 Contact: Richard Morgan

Ray & Berndtson, 400 Fifth Ave. SW, Ste. 400, Calgary, AB T2P 0L6, Canada

Tel: 403-269-3277 Fax: 403-262-9347 Contact: Terry K. O'Callaghan

RAYCHEM CORPORATION

300 Constitution Drive, Menlo Park, CA, 94025-1164

Tel: (650) 361-3333 Fax: (650) 361-2108 Web site: www.raychem.com

Develop/mfr./market materials science products for electronics, telecommunications & industry.

Raychem Canada ltd., Also in Montreal PQ, Richmond (Vancouver) BC & Toronto, ON, Canada

Raychem Canada Ltd., 650 32nd ave, Ste. 505, Lachine, PQ H8T 3K5, Canada

Tel: 800-387-3993

THE RAYMOND CORPORATION

S. Canal Street, Greene, NY, 13778-0130

Tel: (607) 656-2311 Fax: (607) 656-9005

Mfr./designs material handling products including reach trucks, walkie pallet trucks, orderpickers and Swing-Reach® trucks.

The Raymond Corporation, 406 Elgin St., PO Box 1325, Brantford, ON N3T 5T6, Canada

Tel: 519-759-0358 Fax: 519-759-0360 Contact: James Locker, VP

RAYOVAC CORPORATION

601 Rayovac Drive, Madison, WI, 53711

Tel: (608) 275-3340 Fax: (608) 275-4577 Web site: www.rayovac.com

Mfr. batteries & lighting devices.

Rayovac Canada, 5448 Timberlea Blvd., Mississauga, ON L4W 2T7, Canada

Tel: 905-624-4448

RAYTHEON COMPANY

141 Spring Street, Lexington, MA, 02173

Tel: (781) 862-6600 Fax: (781) 860-2172 Web site: www.raytheon.com

Mfr. diversified electronics, appliances, aviation, energy and environmental products; publishing, industry and construction services.

D.C. Heath Canada Ltd., 100 Adelaide St. W #1600, Toronto, ON M5H 1S9, Canada

Raytheon Canada Ltd., 400 Phillip St., Waterloo, ON N2J 4K6, Canada

READER'S DIGEST ASSOCIATION INC.

Reader's Digest Rd., Pleasantville, NY, 10570

Tel: (914) 238-1000 Fax: (914) 238-4559

Publisher of magazines and books and direct mail marketer.

Reader's Digest, 215 Redfern Ave., Montreal, PQ H3Z 2V9, Canada

RECKITT & COLMAN

1655 Valley Road, Wayne, NJ, 07470

Tel: (973) 633-3600 Fax: (973) 633-3633

Mfr. household, personal care, woodworking and industrial products.

L&F Products Canada, 245 Edward St., Aurora, ON L4G 3M7, Canada

RED WING SHOE CO., INC.

314 Main Street, Red Wing, MN, 55066

Tel: (612) 388-8211 Fax: (612) 388-7415 Web site: www.redwingshoe.com

Leather tanning and finishing; mfr. footwear, retail shoe stores.

Red Wing Shoe Company (Canada) Ltd., 229 Queen St. E., Brampton, ON L6W 2B5, Canada

Tel: 905-454-1305 Contact: Joseph Goggin, President

REDKEN LABORATORIES INC.

575 Fifth Ave., New York, NY, 10017

Tel: (212) 818-1500 Fax: (212) 984-4776

Mfr. hair and skin care products.

Redken Laboratories (Canada) Ltd., 151 Carlingview Dr., Rexdale, ON M9W 5S4, Canada

REEBOK INTERNATIONAL LTD

100 Technology Center Drive, Stoughton, MA, 02072

Tel: (781) 401-5000 Fax: (781) 401-7402 Web site: www.reebok.com

Mfr. athletic shoes including casual, dress golf and walking shoes.

Reebok Canada Inc., 201 Earl Stewart Dr., Aurora, ON L4G 3H1, Canada

REFCO GROUP LTD

111 W Jackson Blvd, #1700, Chicago, IL, 60604

Tel: (312) 930-6500 Fax: (312) 930-6534 Web site: www.refco.com

Commodity & security brokers, financial services.

Refco Futures (Canada) Ltd., 1 First Canadian Pl., Toronto, ON M5X 1E2, Canada

REFLEXITE TECHNOLOGY

120 Darling Drive, Avon, CT, 06001

Tel: (860) 676-7100 Fax: (860) 676-7199

Mfr. plastic film, sheet, materials & shapes, optical lenses.

Reflexite Canada Inc., 6790 Kitimat Rd. #18, Mississauga, ON L5N 5L9, Canada

REGAL WARE INC.

1675 Reigle Drive, PO Box 395, Kewaskum, WI, 53040-0395

Tel: (414) 626-2121 Fax: (414) 626-8565

Mfr. cookware, small electrical appliances, water purification & filtration products for home.

Regal Ware Canada Inc., 10 Centennial Rd., Orangeville, ON L9W 1P8, Canada

REGENT SPORTS CORPORATION

PO Box 11357, Hauppauge, NY, 11788

Tel: (516) 234-2800 Fax: (516) 234-2948

Sporting goods.

Icon Sports Marketing, 37 Coulter Ave., St. Thomas, ON, N5R 5A5, Canada

Tel: 519-633-9907 Fax: 519-631-8386 Contact: Jamie Cickerman

RELIANCE GROUP HOLDINGS, INC.

55 East 52nd Street, New York, NY, 10055

Tel: (212) 909-1100 Fax: (212) 909-1864 Web site: www.rgh.com

Financial and insurance management services.

Reliance Insurance Company, 200 King St. West, Ste. 1906, Toronto, ON M5H 3T4, Canada

Tel: 416-581-0101

Reliance National Insurance Co., 1111 West Georgia St., Ste. 1330, Vancouver, BC V6E 4M3, Canada

Tel: 604-689-7359 Fax: 604-689-7322 Contact: B. Timothy Davies, VP

RELTEC CORPORATION

5900 Landerbrook Drive, Ste.300, Mayfield Heights, OH, 44124-4019

Tel: (440) 460-3600 Fax: (440) 460-3690

Telecommunications equipment.

Reltec Canada, 122 Edward St., St. Thomas, ON, Canada

Tel: 519-631-0999

REMINGTON ARMS CO., INC.

870 Remington Drive, Madison, NC, 27025

Tel: (336) 548-8700 Fax: (336) 548-7801

Mfr. sporting firearms and ammunition.

Remington Arms of Canada Ltd., 172 Sheldon Dr., Cambridge, ON, Canada

REMINGTON PRODUCTS COMPANY, L.L.C.

60 Main Street, Bridgeport, CT, 06604

Tel: (203) 367-4400 Fax:

Mfr. home appliances, electric shavers.

Remington Products (Canada), Inc., 475 Cochrane Drive, Unit #7, Markham, ON L3R 9R5, Canada

Tel: 905-470-9400 Fax: 905-470-9405 Contact: Perry R. Beadon, Gen. Mgr.

RENAISSANCE HOTELS AND RESORTS

1 Marriott Drive, Washington, DC, 20058

Tel: (301) 380-3000 Fax: (301) 380-5181

Hotel and resort chain.

Renaissance Edmonton Hotel, Edmonton, AB, Canada

Tel: 403-423-4811

Renaissance Vancouver Hotel, Vancouver, BC, Canada

Tel: 604-689-9211

REPUBLIC NATIONAL BANK OF NEW YORK

452 Fifth Ave., New York, NY, 10018

Tel: (212) 525-5000 Fax: (212) 525-6996 Web site: www.rnb.com

Banking services.

Republic National Bank of New York (Canada), Montreal, PQ & Toronto, ON, Canada

REVLON INC.

625 Madison Ave., New York, NY, 10022

Tel: (212) 527-4000 Fax: (212) 527-4995 Web site: www.revlon.com

Mfr. cosmetics, fragrances, toiletries and beauty care products.

Revlon Intl. Corp. (Canada), 2501 Stanfield Rd., Mississauga, ON L4Y 1R9, Canada

REXNORD CORPORATION

4701 West Greenfield Ave., Milwaukee, WI, 53214

Tel: (414) 643-3000 Fax: (414) 643-3078

Mfr. power transmission products.

Rexnord Canada Ltd., 81 Maybrook Dr., Scarborough, ON M1V 3Z2, Canada

REYNOLDS & REYNOLDS COMPANY

PO Box 2608, Dayton, OH, 45401

Tel: (937) 443-2000 Fax: (937) 485-4230 Web site: www.reyrey.com

Business forms, systems & EDP service.

Reynolds & Reynolds Co., Brampton, ON L6T 3X1, Canada

REYNOLDS INTERNATIONAL INC.

6601 W. Broad Street, PO Box 27002, Richmond, VA, 23261

Tel: (804) 281-2000 Fax: (804) 281-2245

Mfr. aluminum primary and fabricated products, plastic and paper packaging and food service products; gold mining.

Canadian Reynolds Metals Co. Ltd., 1420 Sherbrooke St. W, Montreal, PQ H3G 1K9, Canada

RIEKE CORPORATION

500 West 7th Street, Auburn, IN, 46706

Tel: (219) 925-3700 Fax: (219) 925-2493

Mfr. steel drum closures, plugs, seals, faucets, rings, combination pail spout & closure, etc.

Rieke Canada Ltd., 125 Orenda Rd., Brampton, ON L6W 1W3, Canada

RIGHT MANAGEMENT CONSULTANTS, INC.

1818 Market Street, 14th Fl., Philadelphia, PA, 19103-3614

Tel: (215) 988-1588 Fax: (215) 988-9112 Web site: www.right.com

Out placement & human resources consulting services.

Right Associates, 155 Queen St., Ste. 1308, Ottawa, ON K1P 6L1, Canada

Tel: 613-230-1311

Right Associates, 175 Bloor Street, East, Ste. 1801, Toronto, ON M4W 3R8, Canada

Tel: 416-926-1324

Right Associates, Ste. 1400, Bow Valley Square 1, 202 - 6th Ave. S.W., Calgary, AB T2P 2R9, Canada

Tel: 403-266-6690

Right Associates, 230-1100 Melville St., Vancouver, BC V6E 4A6, Canada

Tel: 604-669-1343

Right Associates, 300 Wellington Street, Ste. 101, London, ON N6B 2L5, Canada

Tel: 519-673-6375

Right Associates, 1, Place Ville Marie, Ste. 1414, Montreal, PQ H3B 2B2, Canada

Tel: 514-871-4778

Right Associates, 2366 Ave. C North, Saskatoon, SK S7L 5X5, Canada

Tel: 306-665-0404

Right Associates, 363 Broadway Ave., Ste. 1410, Winnipeg, MB R3C 3N9, Canada

Tel: 204-942-5511

Right Associates, 1020 Bayridge Drive, Kingston, ON K7P 2S2, Canada

Tel: 613-389-0595

Right Associates, Sun Life Place, Ste. 2320, 10123 99th St., Edmonton, AB T5J 3H1, Canada

Tel: 403-425-6220

RITTENHOUSE INC.

250 South Northwest Highway, Park Ridge, IL, 60068

Tel: (847) 692-9130 Fax: (847) 692-9818

Mfr. papers & paper products, ribbon cartridges for printers, labels for weigh scale & bar code printers.

Rittenhouse, 105 Gibson Dr., Markham, ON L3R 3K7, Canada

RJR NABISCO INC.

1301 Ave. of the Americas, New York, NY, 10019

Tel: (212) 258-5600 Fax: (212) 969-9173 Web site: www.rjrnabisco.com

Mfr. consumer packaged food products & tobacco products.

RJR-MacDonald Inc., 393 University Ave., Toronto, ON M5L 1K4, Canada

ROADWAY EXPRESS INC.

1077 George Boulevard, PO Box 471, Akron, OH, 44309

Tel: (330) 384-1717 Fax: (330) 258-6082

Motor carrier and long haul trucking.

Roadway Express (Canada) Inc., 1400 Inkster blvd, Winnepeg, MB R2X 1R1, Canada

Tel: 204-958-5006 Contact: A. Robinson, Mgr.

ROADWAY PACKAGE SYSTEM INC.

1000 Scott Drive, Moon Township, PA, 15108

Tel: (412) 269-1000 Fax: (412) 269-0551

Small package shipments.

Roadway Package System Ltd., PO Box 245, Malton, ON L4T 3B5, Canada

ROBBINS & MYERS INC.

1400 Kettering Tower, Dayton, OH, 45423-1400

Tel: (937) 222-2610 Fax: (937) 225-3355

Mfr. progressing cavity pumps, valves and agitators.

Robbins & Myers Canada Ltd., 8032 Torban Rd., Brampton, ON L6T 3T2, Canada

ROBERT HALF INTERNATIONAL INC.

2884 Sand Hill Road, #200, Menlo Park, CA, 94025

Tel: (650) 234-6000 Fax: (415) 854-9735

World leader in personnel and specialized staffing services.

Robert Half Intl. Inc., Locations in Ottawa and Toronto, Canada

Robert Half Intl. Inc., 603 7th Ave. SW, Calgary, AB T2P 2T5, Canada

Robert Half Intl. Inc., Locations in Mississauga, Montreal, North York and Vancouver, Canada

ROBERTS PHARMACEUTICAL CORP.

Meridian Center II, 4 Industrial Way West, Eatontown, NJ, 07724-2274

Tel: (732) 389-1182 Fax: (732) 389-1014

Lisense, acquire, develop and commercialize innovative pharmaceuticals.

Roberts Pharmaceutical Canada, Ltd., 400 Iroquiois Shore Rd., Oakville, ON L6H 1M5, Canada

Tel: 905-337-3538 Fax: 905-337-3539 Contact: Art Woodruff, Gen. Mgr. Emp: 80

ROBERTS-GORDON INC.

1250 William Street, PO Box 44, Buffalo, NY, 14240-0044

Tel: (716) 852-4400 Fax: (716) 852-0854

Mfr. industry gas burners, industry space heaters, infrared radiant tube heaters.

Roberts-Gordon Canada Inc., 241 South Service Rd. W, Grimsby, ON L3M 1Y7, Canada

ROBERTSON CECO CORPORATION

5000 Executive Pkwy., Ste. 425, San Ramon, CA, 94583

Tel: (510) 358-0330 Fax: (510) 244-6780

Mfr. pre-engineered metal buildings.

H.H. Robertson Inc., 61 Burford Rd., Hamilton, ON L8E 3C6, Canada

ROCHESTER INSTRUMENT SYSTEMS INC.

255 North Union Street, Rochester, NY, 14605

Tel: (716) 263-7700 Fax: (716) 262-4777

Mfr. electronic alarms and monitors including annunciators, event recorders, etc.

Rochester Instrument Systems Ltd., 915 Kipling Ave., Toronto, ON M8Z 5H4, Canada

ROCHESTER MIDLAND CORPORATION

PO Box 1515, Rochester, NY, 14603

Tel: (716) 266-2250 Fax: (716) 467-4406

Mfr. specialty chemicals for industry cleaning and maintenance, water treatment and personal hygiene.

Rochester Midland Ltd., 851 Progress Ct., Oakville, ON L6J 5A8, Canada

ROCK OF AGES CORPORATION

PO Box 482, Barre, VT, 05641-0482

Tel: (802) 476-3115 Fax: (802) 476-3110 Web site: www.rockofages.com

Quarrier; dimension granite blocks, memorials, and precision industrial granite.

Rock of Ages Canada Ltd., PO Box - CP 60, Beebe, PQ J0B 1E0, Canada

Tel: 819-876-2745 Fax: 819-876-2234 Contact: Donald Labone, Gen. Mgr. Emp: 120

ROCKWELL INTERNATIONAL CORPORATION

600 Anton Boulevard, Costa Mesa, CA, 92626-7147

Tel: (714) 424-4200 Fax: (714) 424-4251 Web site: www.rockwell.com

Products & service for aerospace and defense, automotive, electronics, graphics & automation industry.

Rockwell Automation Canada Inc., 11510-168th St., N.W., Edmonton, AL T5M 3T9, Canada

Tel: 403-489-2300 Fax: 403-486-7887

Rockwell Automation Canada Inc., 21 Frazee Ave., Dartmouth, NS B3B 1Z4, Canada

Tel: 902-468-2454 Fax: 902-468-3606

Rockwell Automation Canada Inc., 135 Dundas St., PO Box 843, Cambridge, ON N1R 5X1,Canada (Locations: Brampton; Brockville;Charlesbourg & Chicoutimi, QU;Calgary, Port Coquitlam, Edmonton, Darthmouth, Stoney Creek, Hanover, Kitchener, Laval, London, Mississauga, Montreal, Ottawa, etc.)

Tel: 519-623-1810 Fax: 519-623-8930

Rockwell Automation Canada Inc. Dodge, 296 Walker Drive, Bramalea, ON, L6T 4B3 Canada

Tel: 905-792-1739 Fax: 905-792-7728

Rockwell Automation Canada Inc. Sprecher + Schuh, 3610 Nashua Drive, Ste. 10, Mississauga, ON L4V 1L2, Canada

Tel: 905-677-7514 Fax: 905-677-7663

Rockwell Automation Canada, Inc., 427 Fitzwilliam St., Nanaimo, BC V9R 3A9, Canada

Tel: 250-741-8226 Fax: 250-753-4594

ROHM AND HAAS COMPANY

100 Independence Mall West, Philadelphia, PA, 19106

Tel: (215) 592-3000 Fax: (215) 592-3377 Web site: www.rohmhaas.com

Mfr. industrial & agricultural chemicals, plastics.

Rohm and Haas Canada Inc., 2 Manse Rd., West Hill, ON M1E 3T9, Canada

Tel: 416-284-4711

ROPAK CORPORATION

660 S. State College Boulevard, Fullerton, CA, 92631-5138

Tel: (714) 870-9757 Fax: (714) 447-3871

Mfr. plastic containers.

Ropak Canada Inc., Burlington Div., 1820 Ironside Dr., Burlington, ON, L7L 5V3, Canada

Ropak Canada Inc., Can-Am Div., PO Box 340, Springhill, NS B0M IX0, Canada

Ropak Canada Inc., Capilano Div., 1081 Cliveden Ave., Annacis Island, Delta, BC V3M 5VI, Canada

THE ROUSE COMPANY

10275 Little Patuxent Pkwy., Columbia, MD, 21044-3456

Tel: (410) 992-6000 Fax: (410) 992-6363

Design, construction & management of retail centers.

Rouse Service (Canada) Ltd., 25 The West Mall, Etobicoke, ON M9C 1B8, Canada

RPM INC.

PO Box 777, Medina, OH, 44258

Tel: (330) 273-5090 Fax: (330) 225-8743 Web site: www.rpminc.com

Mfr. protective coatings and paint.

RPM Canada, 12 Finley Rd., Bramalea, ON L6T 1A9, Canada

RUBBERMAID INC.

1147 Akron Road, Wooster, OH, 44691

Tel: (330) 264-6464 Fax: (330) 287-2846 Web site: www:rubbermaid.com

Mfr. rubber and plastic resin home, commercial and industry products.

Rubbermaid (Canada) Ltd., Mississauga, ON, Canada

RUSSELL REYNOLDS ASSOCIATES INC.

200 Park Ave., New York, NY, 10166-0002

Tel: (212) 351-2000 Fax: (212) 370-0896 Web site: www.ressreyn.com

Executive recruiting services.

Russell Reynolds Associates Ltda., Ste. 3500, Scotia Plaza, 40 King St. West, Toronto, ON M5H 3Y2, Canada

Tel: 416-364-3355 Fax: 416-364-5174 Contact: Richard C.E. Moore

RUST-OLEUM CORPORATION

11 Hawthorn Parkway, Vernon Hills, IL, 60061

Tel: (847) 367-7700 Fax: (847) 816-2300

Rust preventive coatings.

Rust-Oleum (Canada) Ltd., 590 Supertest Rd., Downsview, ON M3J 2M5, Canada

RVSI/ACUITY/CiMatrix

5 Shawmut Road, Canton, MA, 02021

Tel: (781) 821-0830 Fax: (781) 828-8942

Mfr. bar code scanners & data collection equipment.

Computer Identics Inc., 2275 Lakeshore Blvd. W. #518, Etobicoke, ON M8V 3Y3, Canada

RYDER SYSTEM, INC.

3600 NW 82nd Ave., Miami, FL, 33166

Tel: (305) 593-3726 Fax: (305) 500-4129 Web site: www.ryder.com

Integrated logistics, full-service truck leasing, truck rental and public transportation services.

Ryder System, Inc., 2233 Argentia Rd., Mississauga, ON L5N 2X7, Canada

Tel: 905-826-8777 Fax: 905-826-0079 Contact: Gordon Box

S&C ELECTRIC COMPANY

6601 N Ridge Blvd., Chicago, IL, 60626-3997

Tel: (773) 338-1000 Fax: (773) 038-3657

Mfr. high voltage power equipment..

S&C Electric Canada Ltd., 90 Belfield Rd., Toronto, ON M5W 1G4, Canada

Tel: 416-249-9171

S.G. COWEN & CO.

Financial Square, New York, NY, 10005

Tel: (212) 495-6000 Fax: (212) 380-8212

Securities research, trading, broker/dealer services; investment banking & asset management.

Cowen & Company, 67 Yonge St., Ste. 1202, Toronto, ON M5E 1J8 Canada

Tel: 416-362-2229 Fax: 416-362-5373 Contact: Rodney Vander Meersch, Mgr.

SAFETY-KLEEN CORPORATION

1301 Gervais Street, Columbia, SC, 29201

Tel: (803) 933-4200 Fax: (803) 933-4345 Web site: www.laidlawenv.com

Solvent based parts cleaning service; sludge/solvent recycling service.

Safety-Kleen Canada Ltd., 1110 Sherbrooke St. W, Montreal, PQ H3A 1G8, Canada

SAFEWAY INC.

5918 Stoneridge Mall Road, Pleasantville, CA, 94588

Tel: (510) 467-3000 Fax: (510) 467-3230

Food marketing.

Safeway Stores Canada, PO Box 864, Station M, Calgary, AB T2P 2J6, Canada

SAMEDAN OIL CORPORATION

110 West Broadway Street, Ardmore, OK, 73402

Tel: (580) 223-4110 Fax: (580) 221-1384

Gas & oil exploration & production.

Samedan Oil of Canada Inc., 2905-500 4th Ave. SW, Calgary, AB T2P 3E6, Canada

SAMSONITE CORPORATION

11200 East 45th Ave., Denver, CO, 80239-3018

Tel: (303) 373-2000 Fax: (303) 373-6300

Mfr. luggage and leather goods.

Samsonite Canada, 753 Ontario St., Stratford, ON N5A 9J9, Canada

SANFORD CORPORATION

2711 Washington Boulevard, Bellwood, IL, 60104

Tel: (708) 547-6650 Fax: (708) 547-6719

Mfr. inks, writing, drawing and drafting instruments.

Sanford Canada, 2670 Plymouth Drive, Oakville, ON L6H5R6, Canada

Tel: 905-829-5051 Fax: 905-829-3074

SARA LEE CORPORATION

3 First National Plaza, Chicago, IL, 60602-4260

Tel: (312) 726-2600 Fax: (312) 558-4995

Mfr./distributor food and consumer packaged goods, intimate apparel and knitwear.

Canadelle Inc., PO Box 850, St. Michel Station, Montreal, PQ H2A 3M3, Canada

Kiwi Canada, 1115 Guelph Line North, PO Box 5019, Station A, Burlington, ON L7R 3Z8, Canada

KOSL Canada, 379 Orenda Rd., Bramalee, ON L6T 1G6, Canada

Playtex Apparel Inc., 6363 Northam Dr., Airport Ind. Park, Malton, ON L4V 1N5, Canada

Tana-Canada, 8505 Dalton Rd., Montreal, PQ H4T 1V5, Canada

SARGENT MANUFACTURING COMPANY

100 Sargent Drive, New Haven, CT, 06511

Tel: (203) 562-2151 Fax: (203) 776-5992 Web site: www.Sargentlock.com

Mfr. architectural builders hardware, locks.

Sargent of Canada, 3475 14th Ave., Markham, ON L3R OH4, Canada

Tel: 705-742-3849 Fax: 705-748-4223 Contact: J. Haversat, Mng.Dir.& G.Erwin, Gen.Mgr. Emp: 18

SAS INSTITUTE INC.

SAS Campus Drive, Cary, NC, 27513

Tel: (919) 677-8000 Fax: (919) 677-8123 Web site: www.sas.com

Mfr./distributes decision support software.

SAS Institute (Canada) Inc., Montreal, PQ, Canada

Tel: 514-395-8922 Fax: 514-395-1303

SAS Institute (Canada) Inc., Vancouver, British Columba, Canada

Tel: 604-687-0334 Fax: 604-687-0336

SAS Institute (Canada) Inc., Calgary, AB, Canada

Tel: 403-265-5177 Fax: 403-265-5410

SAS Institute (Canada) Inc., Ottawa, ON, Canada

Tel: 613-231-8503 Fax: 613-231-8526

SAS Institute (Canada) Inc. (Hdqtrs.), 181 Bay St., BCE Place, Ste. 2120, PO Box 819, Toronto, ON M5J 2T3, Canada

Tel: 416-363-4424 Fax: 416-363-5399

W. B. SAUNDERS COMPANY

Curtis Center, Independence Square W, Philadelphia, PA, 19106

Tel: (215) 238-7800 Fax: (215) 238-7883

Medical and technical book publishers.

W.B. Saunders Co. Ltd., 55 Horner Ave., Toronto, ON M8Z 4X6, Canada

SCHENECTADY INTERNATIONAL INC.

PO Box 1046, Schenectady, NY, 12301

Tel: (518) 370-4200 Fax: (518) 382-8129

Mfr. electrical insulating varnishes, enamels, phenolic resins, alkylphenols.

Schenectady Canada Ltd., 319 Comstock Rd., Scarborough, ON M1L 2H3, Canada

SCHENKER INTERNATIONAL FORWARDERS INC.

150 Albany Ave., Freeport, NY, 11520

Tel: (516) 377-3000 Fax: (516) 377-3005 Web site: www.schenkerusa.com

Freight forwarders.

Schenker du Canada Limit Ue Station, Mirabel-Montreal Airport, Air Cargo Bldg., C#221-12005 rue Cargo A-3, PQ J7N, Mirabel, Canada

Tel: 514-476-3870 Fax: 514-4763860

Schenker of Canada Ltd., 9750-35th Ave., Edmonton, AB T6E 6J6, Canada

Tel: 403-463-4718 Fax: 403-462-2515

Schenker of Canada Ltd., 304 The East Mall, Ste. 100, Etobicoke, Toronto, ON M9B 6K3, Canada

Tel: 416-234-9300 Fax: 416-234-5635

Schenker of Canada Ltd., Ste. 130, 3015-12 St., NEPO, Calgary, AB T2E 7J2, Canada

Tel: 403-250-7313 Fax: 403-291-2583

Schenker of Canada Ltd., Toronto Airport, Air Cargo Bldg., Pearson Intl Airport, PO Box 127, Toronto, ON L5P 1A2,Canada

Tel: 416-234-9300

R.P. SCHERER CORPORATION

PO Box 7060, Troy, MI, 48007-7060

Tel: (248) 649-0900 Fax: (248) 649-4238 Web site: www.rpscherer.com

Mfr. pharmaceuticals; soft gelatin and two-piece hard shell capsules.

Pharmaphil, 3190 Devon Rd., Windsor, ON N8X 4L2, Canada

Tel: 519-969-7845 Fax: 519-969-0061 Contact: Alan Sine, Sterling Gabbitas Co-Managers Emp: 109

SCHERING-PLOUGH CORPORATION

1 Giralda Farms, Madison, NJ, 07940-1000

Tel: (973) 822-7000 Fax: (973) 822-7048 Web site: www.sch-plough.com

Proprietary drug and cosmetic products.

Schering Corp. Ltd., 3535 Tran-Canada Hwy., Point Claire, PQ H9R 1B4, Canada

SCHLAGE LOCK COMPANY

2401 Bayshore Boulevard, San Francisco, CA, 94134

Tel: (415) 467-1100 Fax: (415) 330-5530

Mfr. locks and builders hardware.

Schlage Lock Co. Ltd., 1290 Marine Dr. N, Vancouver, BC, Canada

SCHLEGEL SYSTEMS

1555 Jefferson Road, PO Box 23197, Rochester, NY, 14692-3197

Tel: (716) 427-7200 Fax: (716) 427-7216

Mfr. engineered perimeter sealing systems for residential & commercial construction; fibers; rubber product.

Schlegel Canada Inc., PO Box 218, 514 South Service Rd., Oakville, ON L6J 5A2, Canada

SCHOLASTIC CORPORATION

555 Broadway, New York, NY, 10012

Tel: (212) 343-6100 Fax: (212) 343-4712 Web site: www.scholastic.com

Publishing/distribution educational & children's magazines, books, software.

**Scholastic Canada Ltd., 9050 Yonge St., Richmond Hill, ON L4C 9S, Canada
6**

Tel: 905-883-5300 Contact: F.C.Larry Muller,Mng. Dir.

SCHRADER BELLOWS DIV

257 Huddleston Ave., Cuyahoga Falls, OH, 44221

Tel: (330) 923-5202 Fax: (330) 426-3259

Mfr. pneumatic and hydraulic valves and cylinders, FRL units and accessories..

Schrader Bellows, 530 Kipling Ave., Toronto, ON M8Z 5E6, Canada

A .SCHULMAN INC.

3550 West Market Street, Akron, OH, 44333

Tel: (330) 666-3751 Fax: (330) 668-7204

Mfr./sale plastic resins & compounds.

A. Schulman Canada Ltd., 400 S. Edgeware Rd., St. Thomas, ON N5P 3Z5, Canada

A. Schulman Canada Ltd., 5770 Hurontario St. #602, Mississauga, ON L5R 3G5, Canada

SCI SYSTEMS INC.

PO Box 1000, Huntsville, AL, 35807

Tel: (256) 882-4800 Fax: (256) 882-4804

R/D & mfr. electronics systems for commerce, industry, aerospace, etc.

Norlite Technology Inc., 4017 Carling Ave., Kanato, ON, Canada K2K 2A3, Canada

SCIENCE MANAGEMENT CORPORATION

721 US Hwy 202/206, Bridgewater, NJ, 08807-1760

Tel: (908) 722-0300 Fax: (908) 722-4150

Human/management resources, information technology, engineering & technology services.

SMC Management Services Group, 8 Canmotor Ave., Toronto, ON M8Z 4E5, Canada

SCIENTIFIC-ATLANTA, INC.

1 Technology Pkwy South, Norcross, GA, 30092-2967

Tel: (770) 903-5000 Fax: (770) 903-2967 Web site: www.sciatl.com

A leading supplier of broadband communications systems, satellite-based video, voice and data communications networks and worldwide customer service and support.

Scientific-Atlanta Canada Inc. (Nexus Div.), 7725 Lougheed Highway, Burnaby, BC V5A 4V8, Canada

Tel: 604-420-5322 Fax: 604-420-5941

Scientific-Atlanta Canada, Inc., Satellite TV Network Div., 120 Middlefield Rd., Unit 1, Scarborough, ON M1S 4M6, Canada

Tel: 416-299-6888 Fax: 416-299-7145

THE SCOTT & FETZER COMPANY

28800 Clemens Road, Westlake, OH, 44145

Tel: (440) 892-3000 Fax: (440) 892-3060

Electrical and lighting fixtures and leisure products.

SFZ Intl., c/o McMillan Binch, PO Box 38, Toronto, ON M51 2J7, Canada

SEA-LAND SERVICE INC.

6000 Carnegie Boulevard, Charlotte, NC, 28209

Tel: (704) 571-2000 Fax: (704) 571-4693 Web site: www.sealand.com

Largest U.S-based containerized transport service; ships, railroads, barge lines and trucking operations.

Intl. Sea-Land Shipping Service Ltd., PO Box 955, Montreal, PQ H2W 2N1, Canada

Intl. Sea-Land Shipping Service Ltd., 2010 Glen Dr., Vancouver, BC V5T 4B2, Canada

Intl. Sea-Land Shipping Service Ltd., 297 Rutherford Rd. S, Brampton, ON L6W 3J8, Canada

Intl. Sea-Land Shipping Service Ltd., 7403 Newman Blvd., Lasalle, PQ H8M 1X4, Canada

Intl. Sea-Land Shipping Service Ltd., 1401 W. Eighth Ave., Vancouver, BC V6H 1C9, Canada

SEAGATE TECHNOLOGY, INC.

920 Disc Drive, Scotts Valley, CA, 95066

Tel: (408) 438-6550 Fax: (408) 438-7205 Web site: www.seagate.com

Develop computer technology, software and hardware.

Seagate Softward Info Management Group, 1095 West Pender St., 4th Fl., Vancouver, BC V6E 2M6, Canada

Tel: 604-681-3435 Fax: 604-681-2934

SEALED AIR CORPORATION

Park 80 Plaza East, Saddle Brook, NJ, 07662-5291

Tel: (201) 791-7600 Fax: (201) 703-4205 Web site: www.sealedair.com

Mfr. protective and specialty packaging solutions for industrial, food and consumer products.

Sealed Air of Canada Ltd., 95 Glidden Rd., Brampton, ON L6T 2H8, Canada

Tel: 905-456-0701 Fax: 905-456-3870

SEAQUIST PERFECT DISPENSING

1160 North Silver Lake Road, Cary, IL, 60013

Tel: (847) 639-2124 Fax: (847) 639-2142 Web site: www.seaperf.com

Mfr. and sale of dispensing systems; lotion pumps and spray-through overcaps.

Seaquist Canada, 110 Snow blvd, Units 5-6, Concord, ON L4K 4B8, Canada

Tel: 905-660-0225 Fax: 905-650-0233 Contact: Geoff Wood Emp: 10

G.D. SEARLE & COMPANY

5200 Old Orchard Road, Skokie, IL, 60077

Tel: (847) 982-7000 Fax: (847) 470-1480 Web site: www.searlehealthnet.com

Mfr. pharmaceuticals, health care, optical products and specialty chemicals.

Searle Canada Inc., 400 Iroquois Shore Rd., Oakville, ON L6H 1M5, Canada

Tel: 905-844-1040 Fax: 905-844-7481

SEARS ROEBUCK & COMPANY

3333 Beverly Road, Hoffman Estates, IL, 60179

Tel: (847) 286-2500 Fax: (800) 427-3049 Web site: www.sears.com

Diversified general merchandise.

Simpson-Sears Ltd., 222 Jarvis St., Toronto, ON M5B 2B8, Canada

SEI INVESTMENTS COMPANY

1 Freedom Valley Drive, Oaks, PA, 19456-1100

Tel: (610) 676-1000 Fax: (610) 676-2995 Web site: www.seic.com

Accounting, evaluation and financial automated systems and services.

SEI Investments, 20 Queen St. W, Toronto, ON M5H 3R3, Canada

SEI Investments, Locations in Halifax, Montreal & Vancouver, Canada

SELFIX SEYMOUR INC.

4501 W. 47th Street, Chicago, IL, 60632

Tel: (773) 890-1010 Fax: (312) 890-0523

Mfr. plastic household products.

Selfix of Canada Ltd., 1822 Ellesmere Rd., Scarborough, ON M1H 2V5, Canada

SEQUENT COMPUTER SYSTEMS INC.

15450 SW Koll Pkwy., Beaverton, OR, 97006-6063

Tel: (503) 626-5700 Fax: (503) 578-9890 Web site: www.sequent.com

Mfr. symmetric multiprocessing technology computers.

Sequent Computer Systems (Canada) Ltd., 139 Woodmark Crescent SW, Calgary, AB T2P 2N9, Canada

Tel: 403-263-3019

Sequent Computer Systems (Canada) Ltd., 50 Burnhamthorpe Rd. W. #508, Mississauga, ON L5B 3C2, Canada

THE SERVICEMASTER COMPANY

One ServiceMaster Way, Downers Grove, IL, 60515-1700

Tel: (630) 271-1300 Fax: (630) 271-2710 Web site: www.svm.com

Management service to health care, school and industry facilities; diversified residential and commercial services.

Merry Maids, Toronto, ON, Canada

ServiceMaster LawnCare, Toronto, ON, Canada

SHEAFFER PEN, INC.

301 Ave. H, Fort Madison, IA, 52627

Tel: (319) 372-3300 Fax: (319) 372-7539

Mfr. writing instruments.

Sheaffer Pen, 6700 Century Rd. #104, Mississauga, ON L59 2V8, Canada

SHEARMAN & STERLING

599 Lexington Ave., New York, NY, 10022-6069

Tel: (212) 848-4000 Fax: (212) 848-7179 Web site: www.shearman.com

Law firm engaged in general American and international financial and commercial practice.

Shearman & Sterling, Commerce Court W. #4405, PO Box 247, Toronto, ON M5L 1E8, Canada

Tel: 416-360-8484 Fax: 416-360-2958 Contact: Brice T. Voran, Mng. Ptnr.

SHERWIN-WILLIAMS CO., INC.

101 Prospect Ave., N.W., Cleveland, OH, 44115-1075

Tel: (216) 566-2000 Fax: (216) 566-3312 Web site: www.sherwin-williams.com

Mfr. paint, wallcoverings and related products.

Sherwin-Williams Canada Inc., 180 Brunet Rd., Mississauga, ON L4Z 1T5, Canada

Fax: 905-5074198

SHOREWOOD PACKAGING CORPORATION

277 Park Ave., New York, NY, 10172

Tel: (212) 371-1500 Fax: (212) 752-5610

Mfr. packaging for video/music industry & consumer products.

Shorewood Packaging Corp. of Canada Ltd., 1625 Ouest rue Chabanel, Montreal, PQ H4N 2S7, Canada

J.R. SHORT MILLING CO., INC.

500 West Madison Street, Chicago, IL, 60661

Tel: (312) 559-5450 Fax: (312) 559-5455

Mfr. corn & soybean products, snack pellet products.

J.R. Short Canadian Mills Ltd., 70 Wicksteed Ave., Toronto, ON M4G 2B5, Canada M4G 2B5

SIGNODE PACKAGING SYSTEMS

3610 West Lake Ave., Glenview, IL, 60025

Tel: (847) 724-6100 Fax: (847) 657-4392

Mfr. packaging systems.

Signode Canada Ltd., 115 Ridgetop Rd., Scarborough, ON M1P 2K3, Canada

SILICON GRAPHICS INC.

2011 N. Shoreline Blvd., Mountain View, CA, 94043-1389

Tel: (650) 960-1980 Fax: (650) 961-0595 Web site: www.sgi.com

Design/mfr. special-effects computer graphic systems and software.

Silicon Graphics Canada Inc., 2550 Matheson Blvd., Ste. 130, Mississauga, ON L4W 4Z1, Canada

Tel: 905-625-4747 Fax: 905-625-4476

Silicon Graphics Canada, Inc., 875 Carling Ave., Ste. 210, Ottawa, ON K1S 5P1, Canada

Tel: 613-798-4747 Fax: 613-798-4749

Silicon Graphics Canada, Inc., 335-8th Ave., S.W., Ste 1430, Calgary, AB T2P 1C9, Canada

Tel: 403-269-5844 Fax: 403-269-6105

Silicon Graphics Canada, Inc., 4400 Dominion St., Ste. 105, Burnaby, BC V5G 4G3, Canada

Tel: 604-436-4747 Fax: 604-436-4745

Silicon Graphics Canada, Inc., 7405 Trans-Canada Highway, Ste. 150, St. Laurent, PQ H4T 1Z2, Canada

Tel: 514-745-2440 Fax: 514-745-2660

SIMPLEX

1 Simplex Plaza, Gardner, MA, 01441-0001

Tel: (978) 632-2500 Fax: (978) 632-8027

Mfr./sale/service fire alarm & time control systems.

Simplex, 6300 Viscount Rd., Mississauga, ON L4V 1H3, Canada

SIMPLICITY PATTERN CO., INC.

2 Park Ave., New York, NY, 10016

Tel: (212) 372-0500 Fax: (212) 372-0628 Web site: www.simplicity.com

Dress patterns.

Dominion Simplicity Patterns Ltd., 120 Mack Ave., Scarborough, ON M1L 2N3, Canada

J.R. SIMPLOT CO., INC.

One Capital Center,999 Main Street, Ste.#1300, Boise, ID, 83702

Tel: (208) 336-2110 Fax: (208) 389-7515 Web site: www.simplot.com

Fresh/frozen fruits & vegetables, animal feeds, fertilizers.

Simplot Canada Ltd., 1400 17th St. E., Brandon, MB R7A 7C4, Canada

SIMS MANUFACTURING CO., INC.

81 E Main Street, Rutland, MA, 01543

Tel: (508) 886-6115 Fax: (508) 886-6713

Mfg. cabs and ROPS for off-highway vehicles. machinery & equipment.

Sims Manufacturing Canada Ltd., 200 Moulinette Rd., Long Sault, ON K0C 1P0, Canada

Tel: 613-534-2289 Fax: 613-534-2182 Contact: Robert Leduc, Plant Mgr. Emp: 130

SKADDEN, ARPS, SLATE, MEAGHER & FLOM LLP

919 Third Ave., New York, NY, 10022

Tel: (212) 735-3000 Fax: (212) 735-2000 Web site: www.sasmf.com

American/International law practice.

Skadden, Arps, Slate, Meagher & Flom LLP, Ste. 1820, North Tower, PO Box 189, Royal Bank Plaza, M5J 2J4, Toronto, ON, Canada

Tel: 416-777-4700 Fax: 416-777-4747 Contact: Milton G. Strom, Partner

SLANT/FIN CORPORATION

100 Forest Drive at East Hills, Greenvale, NY, 11548

Tel: (516) 484-2600 Fax: (516) 484-5921

Mfr. heating & A/C systems & components.

Slant/Fin Ltd., 6450 Northan Dr., Mississauga, ON L4V 1H9, Canada

WILBUR SMITH ASSOCS

NationsBank Tower, PO Box 92, Columbia, SC, 29202

Tel: (803) 758-4500 Fax: (803) 251-2064

Consulting engineers.

Lawrence Flemming & Associates Ltd., 365 Evans Ave. #604, Toronto, ON M8Z 1K2, Canada

Tel: 416-252-5831 Fax: 416-253-9202

A.O. SMITH CORPORATION

11270 West Park Place, PO Box 23972, Milwaukee, WI, 53224

Tel: (414) 359-4000 Fax: (414) 359-4064 Web site: www.aosmith.com

Auto and truck frames, motors, water heaters, storage/handling systems, plastics, railroad products.

A.O. Smith Enterprises Ltd., 768 Erie St., Stratford, ON N5A 6T3, Canada

Tel: 519-271-5800 Contact: Katherine F. Berrill, Opers. Mgr.

SMITH INTERNATIONAL, INC.

16740 Hardy Street, Houston, TX, 77032

Tel: (713) 443-3370 Fax: (713) 233-5996 Web site: www.smith.intl.com

Mfr. drilling tools and equipment and provides related services for the drilling, completion and production sectors of the petroleum and mining industries.

Smith International Canada Ltd., Ste. 1600, 335 8th Ave., S.W., Calgary, AB T2P 1C9, Canada

Tel: 403-264-6077 Contact: Charles Beam, Pres.

THE J. M. SMUCKER COMPANY

One Strawberry Lane, Orrville, OH, 44667-0280

Tel: (330) 682-3000 Fax: (330) 684-3370 Web site: www.smucker.com

Mfr. preserves, jellies, ice cream, toppings & peanut butter.

J. M. Smucker Canada, 703 Evans Ave., Ste. 409, Toronto, ON, Canada

Tel: 416-695-2100

SNAP ON DIAGNOSTICS

420 Barclay Boulevard, Lincolnshire, IL, 60069

Tel: (847) 478-0700 Fax: (847) 478-7308 Web site: www.snapon.com

Mfr. auto maintenence, diagnostic & emission testing equipment.

Snap On Tools of Canada Ltd., 2325 Skymark Ave., Mississauga, ON L4W 5A9, Canada

Tel: 905-624-0066 Fax: 905-238-9658 Contact: Tommy Clark

SNAP-ON INC.

2801 80th Street, Kenosha, WI, 53141-1410

Tel: (414) 656-5200 Fax: (414) 656-5577

Mfr. automotive & industry maintenance service tools..

Snap-On Tools of Canada Ltd., Also in Calgary, Edmonton, Halifax, London, Chomedy Laval, Quebec City, Toronto, Vancouver, & Winnipeg, Canada.

Snap-On Tools of Canada Ltd., 2325 Skymark Ave., Mississauga, ON L4W 5A9, Canada

SONOCO PRODUCTS COMPANY

North Second Street, PO Box 160, Hartsville, SC, 29550

Tel: (803) 383-7000 Fax: (803) 383-7008 Web site: www.sonoco.com

Mfr. packaging for consumer & industrial market and recycled paperboard.

Coretech-Sonoco Ltd., 7420-A Bramalea Rd., Mississauga, ON, Canada L5S 1C5

Tel: 905-673-7373

Sonoco Containers, Inc., 6591 Kitimat Rd., Mississauga, ON L5N 3T4, Canada Mississauga, ON, Canada L5N 3T4

Tel: 905-858-7880

Sonoco Lmited, Other locations: Granby, PQ; Kingston, ON; Stephenville, Newfoundland; Moncton & St. John, NB; Nanaimo& Port Mellon, BC; Glen Miller, Whitby, ONT; Whitecourt, AB, Canada.

Sonoco Lmited (Paper), Terrebonne Plant, 25 rue Langlois, Terrebonne, PQ, Canada J6W 4H4

Tel: 514-471-4153

Sonoco Ltd., Edmonton Plant, 14069 - 128th Ave., N.W., Edmonton, AB, Canada

Tel: 403-451-2581

Sonoco Ltd., Brantford Plant, 33 Park Ave. East, Brantford, ON N3T 5T5, Canada

Tel: 519-752-6591

SOUTHWESTERN PETROLEUM CORPORATION

534 North Main, Fort Worth, TX, 76106

Tel: (817) 332-2336 Fax: (817) 877-4047

Mfr. roofing/building maintenance products and industry lubricants.

Southwestern Petroleum Canada Ltd., 87 West Dr., Brampton, ON L6T 2J6, Canada

SPALDING ETONIC WORLDWIDE

425 Meadow Street, Chicopee, MA, 01021

Tel: (413) 536-1200 Fax: (413) 535-2746

Mfr. sports equipment and infant and juvenile furniture and accessories.

Spalding Canada Ltd., 470 Norfinch Dr., Downsview, ON M3N 1Y4, Canada

SPARTAN INTERNATIONAL INC.

1845 Cedar Street, Holt, MI, 48842

Tel: (517) 694-3911 Fax: (517) 694-7952

Plastic products and commercial printing.

Spartan Plastics Canada Ltd., 1015 Green Valley Rd., London, ON N6A 4C2, Canada

Tel: 519-685-3690 Fax: 519-685-1117 Contact: Dave Angove Emp: 85

SPEIZMAN INDUSTRIES INC.

508 West Fifth Street, PO Box 31215, Charlotte, NC, 28231

Tel: (704) 372-3751 Fax: (704) 376-3153

Sale/service textile machinery and components.

Speizman Canada Inc., 5205 Boul. Metropolitain Est #3, Montreal, PQ H1R 1Z7, Canada

SPENCER STUART & ASSOCIATES INC.

401 North Michigan Ave., Ste. 3400, Chicago, IL, 60611

Tel: (312) 822-0080 Fax: (312) 822-0116 Web site: www.spencerstuart.com

Executive recruitment firm.

Spencer Stuart & Associates Inc., 1981 Ave. McGill College, Montreal, PQ H3A 2Y1, Canada

Tel: 514-288-3377 Fax: 514-288-4626 Contact: Andrew MacDougall

Spencer Stuart & Associates Inc., One University Ave., Ste. 801, Toronto, ON M5J 2P1 Canada

Tel: 416-361-0311 Fax: 416-361-6118 Contact: Andrew MacDougall

SPI PHARMACEUTICALS INC.

ICN Plaza, 3300 Hyland Ave., Costa Mesa, CA, 92626

Tel: (714) 545-0100 Fax: (714) 641-7215

Mfr. pharmaceuticals, biochemicals and radioactive materials.

ICN Canada Ltd., 1956 Bourdon St., St. Laurent, Montreal, PQ H4M 1V1, Canada

SPIROL INTERNATIONAL CORPORATION

30 Rock Ave., Danielson, CT, 06239

Tel: (203) 774-8571 Fax: (203) 774-0487 Web site: www.spirol.com

Mfr. engineered fasteners, shims, automation equipment.

Spirol Ind. Ltd., 3103 St. Etienne Blvd., Windsor, ON N8W 5B1, Canada

Tel: 519-974-3334 Fax: 519-974-6550 Contact: Tom Buchta, Gen. Mgr. Emp: 35

SPRINGS INDUSTRIES INC.

205 N. White Street, PO Box 70, Fort Mill, SC, 29716

Tel: (803) 547-1500 Fax: (803) 547-1772 Web site: www.springs.com

Mfr. and sales of home furnishings, finished fabrics and industry textiles.

Springs Canada Inc., 6345 Dixie Rd. #200, Mississauga, ON L5T 2K1, Canada

SPRINT INTERNATIONAL

World Headquarters, 2330 Shawnee Mission Parkway, Westwood, KS, 66205

Tel: (913) 624-3000 Fax: (913) 624-3281

Telecommunications equipment & services.

Sprint Communications Canada Inc., 43 Front St. E, 4th Fl., Toronto, ON M5E 1B3, Canada

SPS TECHNOLOGIES INC.

301 Highland Avenue, Jenkintown, PA, 19046-2630

Tel: (215) 517-2000 Fax: (215) 517-2032

Mfr. aerospace & industry fasteners, tightening systems, magnetic materials, superalloys.

Standco Inc., 101 Spinnaker Way, Concord, ON L4K 2T2, Canada

SPX CORPORATION

700 Terrace Point Drive, PO Box 3301, Muskegon, MI, 49443-3301

Tel: (616) 724-5000 Fax: (616) 724-5720 Web site: www.spx.com

Mfr. Auto parts, special service tools, engine & drive-train parts.

Automotive Diagnostics Canada, 221 Finchdene Sq., Scarborough, ON M1X 1B9, Canada

THE ST. PAUL COMPANIES, INC.

385 Washington Street, St. Paul, MN, 55102

Tel: (612) 310-7911 Fax: (612) 310-8294 Web site: www.stpaul.com

Provides investment, insurance and reinsurance services.

Seaboard Surety Company of Canada, 2 Bloor West, Toronto, ON, Canada M4W 3E2
Tel: 416-925-9360

STANDARD COMMERCIAL CORPORATION

PO Box 450, Wilson, NC, 27893
Tel: (919) 291-5507 Fax: (919) 237-1109
Leaf tobacco dealers/processors and wool processors.

Standard Commercial Tobacco Co. of Canada Ltd., Chatham, ON, Canada

STANDARD PRODUCTS COMPANY

2401 South Gulley Road, Dearborn, MI, 48124
Tel: (313) 561-1100 Fax: (313) 561-6526 Web site: www.stdproducts.com
Mfr. molded & extruded rubber & plastic products for automotive & appliance industry, retread tire industry.

Standard Products (Canada) Ltd., 346 Guelph St., Georgetown, ON L7G 4B5, Canada

Standard Products (Canada) Ltd., Head Office, 1030 Erie St., Stratford, ON N5A 6V7, Canada
Tel: 519-271-3360 Fax: 519-271-6692

STANDEX INTERNATIONAL CORPORATION

6 Manor Parkway, Salem, NH, 03079
Tel: (603) 893-9701 Fax: (603) 893-7324 Web site: www.standex.com
Mfr. diversified graphics, institutional, industry/electronic & consumer products.

Can-Am Casters & Wheels, 2884 Slough St., Mississauga, ON L4T 1G3, Canada
Tel: 905-673-9500 Fax: 905-673-5055 Contact: Barry Kent, Mgr.

STANLEY BOSTITCH INC.

815 Briggs Street, East Greenwich, RI, 02818
Tel: (401) 884-2500 Fax: (401) 885-6511
Mfr. stapling machines, stapling supplies, fastening systems & wire.

Stanley Bostitch Div. of Textron Canada Ltd., 19 Rangemore Rd., Toronto, ON M8Z 5H9, Canada

THE STANLEY WORKS

1000 Stanley Drive, PO Box 7000, New Britain, CT, 06053
Tel: (860) 225-5111 Fax: (860) 827-3987 Web site: www.stanleyworks.com
Mfr. hand tools & hardware.

Stanley Automatic Openers, PO Box 789, Windsor, ON N8W 5A7, Canada

Stanley Canada Inc., PO Box 66, Station B, Hamilton, ON L8L 7V2, Canada

Stanley Door Systems, 42 Queen Elizabeth Blvd., Toronto, ON M8Z 1M1, Canada

Stanley Hardware, PO Box 3001, Station B, Hamilton, ON L8L 7X9, Canada

Stanley Tools, 1100 Corporate Dr., Burlington, ON L7L 5R6, Canada

Stanley-Bostitch, 19 Rangemoor Rd., Toronto, ON M8Z 5H9, Canada

STAPLES, INC.

One Research Drive, Westborough, MA, 01581
Tel: (508) 370-8500 Fax: (508) 370-8955 Web site: www.staples.com
Superstore for office supplies and equipment.

Bureau En Gros, 200 blvd Greber, Gatineau, PQ J8T 6K2, Canada
Tel: 819-246-9470 Fax: 819-246-9535

Bureau En Gros, 565 blvd Lebourgneuf, Quebec City, PQ G2J 1R9, Canada
Tel: 418-622-5044 Fax: 418-622-6254

Business Depot Ltd., Cambridge Centre, 202 Brownlow Ave., Dartmouth, N.S., B3B 1T5, Canada
Tel: 902-468-3412 Fax: 902-468-2619

Business Depot Ltd., 5170 Dixie Rd., Mississauga, ON L4W 1E3, Canada
Tel: 905-602-5889 Fax: 905-602-5846

Business Depot Ltd., 2160 Steeles Ave. West, Concord, ON L4K 2Y7, Canada

Tel: 905-660-7051 Fax: 905-660-3893

Business Depot Ltd., 945 Eglinton Ave. East, Toronto, ON M4G 4B5, Canada

Tel: 416-696-0043 Fax: 416-696-1207

STARBUCKS COFFEE CORPORATION

PO Box 34067, Seattle, WA, 98124

Tel: (206) 447-4127 Fax: (206) 682-7570

Coffee bean retail store and coffee bars.

Starbucks Coffee Corp. (Reg. Office), 171 John St., Toronto, ON, Canada

Tel: 416-585-2575

STATE FARM INSURANCE COMPANY

1 State Farm Plaza, Bloomington, IL, 61710-0001

Tel: (309) 766-2311 Fax: (309) 766-6169 Web site: www.statefarm.com

Sales of automobile, life, health and homeowners insurance.

STATE FARM MUTUAL AUTO INS. CO., 100 Consilium Place, Ste. 102, Scarborough, ON MIH 3G9, Canada

Tel: 416-290-4100 Fax: 416-290-4719 Contact: Robert Cooke, Regional VP

STATE STREET BANK & TRUST COMPANY

225 Franklin Street, Boston, MA, 02101

Tel: (617) 786-3000 Fax: (617) 654-3386 Web site: www.statestreet.com

Banking & financial services.

CFDS Ltd./CFDS Investor Services, Ltd., Toronto, ON, Canada

Tel: 416-217-3407 Contact: Al O'Neal

State Street Trust Co. Canada, 100 King St. W. #3500, PO Box 23, Toronto, ON M5X 1A9, Canada

STEBBINS ENGINEERING & MFG. COMPANY

363 Eastern Boulevard, Watertown, NY, 13601

Tel: (315) 782-3000 Fax: (315) 782-0481

Engineering and construction.

Canadian Stebbins Engineering & Mfg. Co. Ltd., 2700 Lancaster Rd., Ottawa, ON K1B 4T7, Canada

Tel: 613-737-2800 Fax: 613-737-2801

Canadian Stebbins Engineering & Mfg. Co. Ltd., 2271 Rosser Ave., Burnabry, V5C 5E3 Vancouver, BC, Canada

Tel: 604-291-6491

STEINER CORPORATION

505 East South Temple Street, Salt Lake City, UT, 84102

Tel: (801) 328-8831 Fax: (801) 363-5680

Linen supply service.

Nelson's, 5 W. 4th Ave., Vancouver, BC V5Y 1G2, Canada

STEMCO INC.

PO Box 1989, Longview, TX, 75606

Tel: (903) 758-9981 Fax: (903) 232-3508 Web site: www.stemco.com

Mfr. seals, hubcaps, hubodometers and locking nuts for heavy duty trucks, buses, trailers.

Stemco Canada, 2860 Plymouth Drive, Oakville, ON L6H 5S8, Canada

Tel: 905-829-3200 Fax: 905-829-3333 Contact: Lynn Parsons

STEPAN COMPANY

22 West Frontage Road, Northfield, IL, 60093

Tel: (847) 446-7500 Fax: (847) 501-2443

Mfr. basic intermediate chemicals.

Stepan Canada, Rama Rd., Longford Mills, ON L0K 1L0, Canada

STERLING SOFTWARE INC.

1800 Alexander Bell Drive, Reston, VA, 22091

Tel: (703) 264-8000 Fax: (703) 264-0762

Sales/service software products; technical services.

Sterling Softward/Montreal Lab, 1180 Drummond St., Montreal, PQ H3G 2S1, Canada

Sterling Software Intl. Inc., 2235 Sheppard Ave. E #901, Willowdale, ON M2J 5A6, Canada

Sterling Software/AD Labs, 500-36 Antares Dr., Ottawa, ON K2E 7V2, Canada

STIEFEL LABORATORIES INC.

255 Alhambra Circle, Ste. 1000, Coral Gables, FL, 33134

Tel: (305) 443-3807 Fax: (305) 443-3467

Mfr. pharmaceuticals, dermatological specialties.

Stiefel Canada Inc., 6635 Henri Bourassa Blvd. West, Montreal, PQ H4R 1E1, Canada

STONE & WEBSTER ENGINEERING CORPORATION

245 Summer Street, Boston, MA, 02210-2288

Tel: (617) 589-5111 Fax: (617) 589-2156

Engineering, construction, environmental and management services.

Stone & Webster Canada Ltd., 2300 Yonge St., Toronto, ON M4P 2W6, Canada

STONE CONTAINER CORPORATION

150 N. Michigan Ave., Chicago, IL, 60601-7568

Tel: (312) 346-6600 Fax: (312) 580-3486 Web site: www.stonecontainer.com

Mfr. paper and paper packaging.

Macmillan Bathurst, 2070 Hadwen Rd., Mississauga, ON, Canada L5K 2C9 (Locations: Calgary Edmonton, Winnepeg, Darthmouth, Saint-Laurent, St. Johns, Regina, New Westminister, Canada.)

Stone Consolidated Inc., 800 Rene Levesque Blvd. W, Montreal, PQ, Canada H3C 2R5

STORAGE TECHNOLOGY CORPORATION

2270 S. 88th Street, Louisville, CO, 80028-0001

Tel: (303) 673-5151 Fax: (303) 673-5019

Mfr./market/service information, storage and retrieval systems.

StorageTek Canada Inc., 5580 Explorer Dr. #300, Mississauga, ON L4W 4Y1, Canada

STRUCTURAL DYNAMICS RESEARCH CORPORATION

2000 Eastman Drive, Milford, OH, 45150-2789

Tel: (513) 576-2400 Fax: Web site: www.sdrc.com

Developer of software used in Modeling esting, drafting and manufacturing.

Structural Dynamics Research Corporation (SDRC), 2018 Parklane Crescent, Burlington, ON L7M 3V6, Canada (Location: St. Catherines, ON.)

Tel: 905-319-6305 Fax: 905-335-2278

Structural Dynamics Research Corporation (SDRC), 1156 des Perdrix, Longueuil, PQ J4J5J8, Canada

Fax: 514-990-4421

STUART ENTERTAINMENT INC.

3211 Nebraska Ave., Council Bluffs, IA, 51501

Tel: (712) 323-1488 Fax: (712) 323-3215 Web site: www.bingoking.com

Mfg. bingo equipment and supplies, lottery tickets & video gaming machines.

Bazaar & Novelty, 301 Louth St., St. Catherines, ON L2S 3V6 Canada

Tel: 905-687-1700 Fax: 905-984-6377 Contact: Douglas Rye, Controller Emp: 400

Video King Gaming Systems, Inc., 1501 St. Mathews Ave., Winnipeg, MB R3G 3L3, Canada

Tel: 204-452-0100 Fax: 204-452-0600 Contact: Dan Free, VP - Electronics Div. Emp: 45

SUDLER & HENNESSEY

1633 Broadway, 25th Fl., New York, NY, 10019

Tel: (212) 969-5800 Fax: (212) 969-5996

Healthcare products advertising.

Sudler & Hennessey/Gall Inc., 60 Bloor St. W, Toronto, ON M4W 1J2, Canada

Tel: 416-961-7733 Fax: 416-961-8973 Contact: Bill Hambly, Mng. Dir.

SUNBEAM CORPORATION

1615 South Congress Ave., Delray Beach, FL, 33445

Tel: (561) 243-2100 Fax: (561) 243-2218 Web site: www.sunbeam.com

Mfr. household and personal grooming appliances.

Eddy Match Co. Ltd., 100 Crandall Ave., Pembroke, ON K8A 6x8, Canada

Sunbeam Corp. (Canada), 1040 Islington Ave., Toronto, ON M8Z 4R5, Canada

Sunbeam-Oster Inc., 350 Blvd. Industriel, St. Jean, PQ J3B 4S6, Canada

SUNRISE MEDICAL INC.

2382 Faraday Ave., Ste. 200, Carlsbad, CA, 92008

Tel: (760) 930-1500 Fax: (760) 930-1580

Mfr. medical appliances & supplies, furniture.

Sunrise Medical Canada, 265 Hood Rd., Unit 3, Markham, ON L3R 4N3, Canada L3R 4N3

SUPERIOR GRAPHITE COMPANY

120 S. Riverside Plaza, Chicago, IL, 60606

Tel: (312) 559-2999 Fax: (312) 559-9064

Mfr. natural and synthetic graphites, electrodes, lubricants, suspensions, carbide and carbon.

Superior Graphite Co., PO Box 20015, John Galt Postal Station, Cambridge, ON N1R 8C8, Canada

Tel: 519-650-1608 Fax: 519-650-1803

SUPRA PRODUCTS INC.

2611 Pringle Road SE, Salem, OR, 97302-1594

Tel: (503) 581-9101 Fax: (503) 364-1285

Mfr. lockboxes.

Supra Key Control Ltd., 2100 Thurston Dr., Unit 15, Ottawa, ON K1G 4K8, Canada

SURGICAL APPLIANCE INDUSTRIES INC.

3960 Rosslyn Drive, Cincinnati, OH, 45209

Tel: (513) 271-4594 Fax: (513) 271-4747

Mfr. surgical appliances & supplies.

Airway Surgical Appliances Ltd., 189 Colonnade Rd., Ottawa, ON K2E 7J4, Canada

SWECO INC.

7120 New Buffington Road, PO Box 1509, Florence, KY, 41042-1509

Tel: (606) 727-5100 Fax: (606) 727-5106

Mfr. vibratory process and solids control equipment.

Sweco Canada Inc., 40 Titan Rd., Toronto, ON M8Z 2J8, Canada

SWINTEK CORPORATION

320 West Commercial Ave., Moonachie, NJ, 07074

Tel: (201) 935-0115 Fax: (201) 935-6021

Mfr./sales office machines, communications equipment.

Swintek Canada Ltd., 15 W. Pearce St., Richmond Hill, ON, Canada

SYBRON INTERNATIONAL CORPORATION

411 E. Wisconsin Ave., Milwaukee, WI, 53202

Tel: (414) 274-6600 Fax: (414) 274-6561

Mfr. products for laboratories, professional orthodontic & dental markets.

Sybron Canada Ltd., PO Bag 900, Morrisburg, ON, Canada K0C 1X0

SYMANTEC CORPORATION

10201 Torre Ave., Cupertino, CA, 95014-2132

Tel: (408) 253-9600 Fax: (408) 446-8129 Web site: www.symantec.com

Designs and produces PC network security and network management software and hardware.

Symantec Canada Ltd., 895 Don Mills Rd., 500-2 Park Centre, Toronto, ON M3C 1W3, Canada

Tel: 416-441-3676 Fax: 416-441-0333

SYMBOL TECHNOLOGIES, INC.

One Symbol Plaza, Holtsville, NY, 11742-1300

Tel: (516) 738-2400 Fax: (516) 563-2831 Web site: www.symbol.com

Mfr. bar code-driven data management systems, wireless LAN's, and Portable Shopping System™.

Symbol Technologies Canada, Inc., 2450 Matheson Blvd. E., Mississauga, ON L4W 4Z2, Canada

Tel: 905-629-7226 Fax: 905-629-9765

Symbol Technologies, Inc., 4315 Canada Way, Burnaby, BC V5G 1J3, Canada

Symbol Technologies, Inc., 1565 Carling Ave., Ste. 112, Ottawa, ON, K1Z 8RI, Canada

Tel: 613-728-5800 Fax: 613-728-5465

Symbol Technologies, Inc., 6363 Transcanada Hwy., Ste. 201, St. Laurent, PQ H4T 1Z9, Canada

Tel: 514-747-7728 Fax: 514-747-7753

SYSCO CORPORATION

1390 Enclave Parkway, Houston, TX, 77077-2099

Tel: (713) 672-8080 Fax: (713) 679-5483

North America's largest marketer/distributor of food service products.

Strano Sysco Foodservice Ltd., PO Box 6000, Peterborough, ON K9J 7B1, Canada

Tel: 705-748-6701 Fax: 705-748-0025 Contact: Paul Strano, Jr., Pres.

TAB PRODUCTS COMPANY

1400 Page Mill Road, PO Box 10269, Palo Alto, CA, 94303

Tel: (650) 852-2400 Fax: (650) 852-2679 Web site: www.tabproducts.com

Mfr. filing systems and electronic office products.

TAB Datafile, Locations in Sainte-Foy and Villes St. Laurent, PQ, Canada

TAB Datafile, 130 Sparks Ave., Willowdale, ON M2H 2S4, Canada

Tel: 416-497-1552

TACO INC.

1160 Cranston Street, Cranston, RI, 02920

Tel: (401) 942-8000 Fax: (401) 942-8692

Mfr. HVAC pumps & equipment.

Taco Canada Ltd., 6180 Ordan Dr., Mississauga, ON L5T 2B3, Canada

TANDY CORPORATION

100 Throckmorton Street, Fort Worth, TX, 76102

Tel: (817) 390-3700 Fax: (817) 415-2647 Web site: www.tandy.com

Electronic & acoustic equipment.

Radio Shack Canada, PO Box 34000, 279 Bayview Drive, Barrie, ON L4M 4W5, Canada

TBWA INTERNATIONAL

180 Maiden Lane, New York, NY, 10038

Tel: (212) 804-1000 Fax: (212) 804-1200

International full service advertising agency.

TBWA Chiat/Day, Toronto, ON, Canada

TC INDUSTRIES

PO Box 477, Crystal Lake, IL, 60039

Tel: (815) 459-2400 Fax: (815) 459-3303

Mfr./sales of fabricated metal products.

TC Industries of Canada Ltd., 249 Speedvale Ave. W., Guelph, ON N1H 1C5, Canada

TECH DATA CORPORATION

5350 Tech Data Drive, Clearwater, FL, 34620-3122

Tel: (813) 539-7429 Fax: (813) 538-7876 Web site: www.techdata.com

Distributor of computer systems, software and related equipment.

Tech Data Canada, 4311 Viking Way, Unit 130, Richmond, BC V6V 2K9, Canada

Fax: 604-276-0834

Tech Data Canada, 6895 Columbus Rd., Mississauga, ON L5T 2G9, Canada

Fax: 905-795-2355 Contact: D. Reid, Pres.

TECHNITROL INC.

1210 Northbrook Drive, #385, Trevose, PA, 19053

Tel: (215) 355-2900 Fax: Web site: www.technitrol.com

Mfr. of electronic components, electrical contacts, and other parts/materials.

Pulse Engineering - Electronic Components, Ottawa, ON Canada

TECHNOLOGY SOLUTIONS COMPANY (TSC)

205 N. Michigan Ave., Ste. 1500, Chicago, IL, 60601

Tel: (312) 228-4500 Fax: (312) 228-4501 Web site: www.techsol.com

Designs computer information systems and strategic business and management consulting for major corporations.

TSC Canada, 90 Allstate Pkwy., Ste. 301, Markham, ON L3R 6H3, Canada

Tel: 905-944-5500 Fax: 905-944-5501 Contact: John Home

TECUMSEH PRODUCTS COMPANY

100 E. Patterson Street, Tecumseh, MI, 49286-1899

Tel: (517) 423-8411 Fax: (517) 423-8526

Mfr. refrigeration & A/C compressors & units, small engines, pumps.

Tecumseh Products of Canada Ltd., PO Box 2033, Terminal A, London, ON, Canada

TEKTRONIX INC.

2660 Southwest Parkway Ave., PO Box 1000, Wilsonville, OR, 97070-1000

Tel: (503) 627-7111 Fax: (503) 627-2406 Web site: www.tek.com

Mfr. test & measure, visual systems/color printing & communications/video and networking products.

Tektronix Canada Inc., 8666 Commerce Court, Burnaby (Vancouver) BC V5A 4N7, Canada

Tel: 604-420-2787 Fax: 604-420-2759

Tektronix Canada Inc., Locations: Calgary, Pointe Claire Locations in Montreal, Kanata (Ottawa), & Weston (Toronto), Canada)

TELEDYNE WATER PIK

1730 East Prospect Road, Fort Collins, CO, 80553-0001

Tel: (970) 484-1352 Fax: (970) 221-8715

Mfr. oral hygiene appliances, shower massage equipment, water filtration products.

Teledyne Water Pik Canada Ltd., 35 Grand Marshall Dr., Scarborough, ON M1B 5W9, Canada

TELEFLEX INC.

630 West Germantown Pike, Ste. 450, Plymouth Meeting, PA, 19462

Tel: (215) 834-6301 Fax: (610) 834-8307

Designs/mfr./market mechanical and electro-mechanical systems, measure systems.

Teleflex (Canada) Ltd., 1650 W. Second Ave., Vancouver, BC V6J 1H4, Canada

TELEX COMMUNICATIONS INC.

9600 Aldrich Ave. South, Minneapolis, MN, 55420

Tel: (612) 884-4051 Fax: (612) 884-0043

Mfr. communications, audio-visual and professional audio products.

Telex Communications Ltd. Canada, 705 Progress Ave., Unit 10, Scarborough, ON M1H 2X1, Canada

TELLABS INC.

4951 Indiana Ave. 6303788800, Lisle, IL, 60532

Tel: (630) 378-8800 Fax: (630) 679-3010

Design/mfr./service voice/data transport & network access systems.

Tellabs Communications Canada Ltd., 2433 Meadowvale Blvd., Mississauga, ON L5N 5S2, Canada

TELXON CORPORATION

3330 W. Market Street, PO Box 5582, Akron, OH, 44334-0582

Tel: (330) 867-3700 Fax: (330) 869-2220

Develop/mfr. portable computer systems & related equipment.

Telxon Canada Corp. Inc., 80 Microcourt #100, Markham, ON L3R 9Z5, Canada

TENNANT COMPANY

701 North Lilac Drive, Minneapolis, MN, 55440

Tel: (612) 513-2112 Fax: (612) 541-6137 Web site: www.Tennantco.com

Mfr. industry floor maintenance sweepers and scrubbers, floor coatings.

Tennant Co., 1329 Cardiff Blvd., Mississauga, ON L5S 1R2, Canada

Tel: 905-670-8599 Fax: 905-670-8547

TENNECO AUTOMOTIVE

500 North Field Drive, Lake Forest, IL, 60045

Tel: (847) 482-5241 Fax: (847) 482-5295

Automotive parts, exhaust systems, service equipment.

Tenneco Automotive, 1400 17th St. E., Owen Sound, ON M4K 5Z9, Canada

Tel: 519-376-9650 Fax: 519-376-9656 Contact: Roger Seabrook, Mgr. Emp: 274

Walker Canada, 500 Conestoga Blvd., Cambridge, ON N1R 7PG, Canada

Tel: 519-740-4411 Fax: 519-740-4430 Contact: John Sheridan, Mgr. Emp: 450

TENNECO INC.

1275 King Street, Greenwich, CT, 06831

Tel: (203) 863-1000 Fax: (203) 863-1134 Web site: www.tenneco.com

Mfr. automotive products and packaging materials/containers.

Tenneco Canada Inc., 2 Gibbs Rd., Etobicoke, ON M9B 1R1, Canada

TENNECO PACKAGING CORPORATION OF AMERICA

1900 West Field Court, Lake Forest, IL, 60045

Tel: (847) 482-2000 Fax: (847) 482-2181 Web site: www.tenneco

Mfr. custom packaging, aluminum and plastic molded fibre, corrugated containers.

PCA Canada, 3471 McNicoll Ave., Scarborough, ON M1V 4B8, Canada

TENNESSEE ASSOCIATES INTERNATIONAL

223 Associates Blvd., PO Box 710, Alcoa, TN, 37701-0710

Tel: (423) 982-9514 Fax: (423) 982-1481

Management consulting services.

Tennessee Associates Intl. Ltd., 3075 Ridgeway Dr. #8, Mississauga, ON L5L 5M6, Canada

TEXAS INSTRUMENTS INC.

8505 Forest Lane, Dallas, TX, 75243

Tel: (214) 995-2011 Fax: (214) 995-4360 Web site: www.ti.com

Mfr. semiconductor devices, electronic electro-mechanical systems, instruments and controls.

Texas Instruments Canada, 280 Centre St. East, Richmond Hill, ON L4C 1B1, Canada
Tel: 905-884-9181

TEXAS REFINERY CORPORATION

840 North Main Street, Fort Worth, TX, 76101
Tel: (817) 332-1161 Fax: (817) 332-2340
Mfr. Building and maintenance products & spec lubricants.
Texas Refinery Corp. of Canada Ltd., Canada - All mail to 840 North Main, Fort Worth, TX 76101

TEXTRON INC.

40 Westminster Street, Providence, RI, 02903
Tel: (401) 421-2800 Fax: (401) 421-2878 Web site: www.textron.com
Mfr. aerospace, industry and consumer products (Bell Helicopter & Cessna Aircraft) and financial services.
Avco Financial Services Canada Ltd., PO Box 5875, Terminal A, 201 Queens Ave., London, ON, Canada N6A 1J1
Tel: 519-672-4220 Fax: 519-660-2637 Contact: D. Murray Wallace, Pres.

THERM-O-DISC INC.

1320 S. Main Street, Mansfield, OH, 44907-0538
Tel: (419) 525-8500 Fax: (419) 525-8282
Mfr. thermostats, controls, sensor & thermal cutoffs, switches.
Therm-O-Disc Canada Ltd., 95 Edgeware Rd., St.Thomas, ON N5P 4C4, Canada

THERMADYNE INDUSTRIES INC.

101 South Hanley Road, #300, St. Louis, MO, 63105
Tel: (314) 746-2197 Fax: (314) 746-2349 Web site: www.thermadyne.com
Mfr. welding, cutting, and safety products.
Thermadyne Canada, Oakville, ON, Canada
Tel: 905-827-3648

THERMO ELECTRIC COMPANY

109 North Fifth Street, Saddle Brook, NJ, 07662
Tel: (201) 843-5800 Fax: (201) 843-7144
Mfr. temp/measure control products.
Thermo Electric (Canada) Ltd., c/o Electro Systems Group, 532 Berry St., Winnipeg, MB R3H 0R9, Canada
Thermo Electric (Canada) Ltd., 12 Rutherford Rd. S, Brampton, ON L6W 3J2, Canada
Thermo Electric (Canada) Ltd., 9655 45th Ave., Edmonton, AB T6E 5Z8, Canada
Thermo Electric (Canada) Ltd., 1234 Marine Dr. N, Vancouver, BC V7P 1T2, Canada
Thermo Electric (Canada) Ltd., 3005 DeBaene St., Ville St. Laurent, Montreal, PQ H4S 1K8, Canada

THERMO ELECTRON CORPORATION

81 Wyman Street, Waltham, MA, 02254-9046
Tel: (781) 622-1000 Fax: (781) 622-1207 Web site: www.thermo.com
Develop/mfr./sale of process equipment &instruments for energy intensive & healthcare industries.
Holcroft & Co. (Canada) Ltd., 94 Bessemer Ct., London, ON N6E 1K7, Canada
Thermo Electron (Canada) Inc., 6875 Bombardier St., St. Leonard, PQ H1P 3A1, Canada

THETFORD CORPORATION

7101 Jackson Road, PO Box 1285, Ann Arbor, MI, 48106
Tel: (734) 769-6000 Fax: (734) 769-2023
Mfr. sanitation products and chemicals.
Thetford Sanitation Ltd., 2299 Drew Rd., Unit 12, Mississauga, ON L5S 1A1, Canada

THOMAS & BETTS CORPORATION

8155 T&B Blvd., Memphis, TN, 38125

Tel: (901) 252-5000 Fax: (901) 685-1988

Mfr. elect/electronic connectors & accessories.

Thomas & Betts Ltd., PO Box 30700, Iberville, PQ J2X 2M9, Canada

THOMAS BUILT BUSES INC.

1408 Courtesy Road, PO Box 2450, High Point, NC, 27261

Tel: (336) 889-4871 Fax: (336) 889-2589

Mfr. buses & bus chassis.

Thomas Built Buses of Canada Ltd., PO Box 580, Woodstock, ON, Canada

THOMAS INDUSTRIES INC.

4360 Brownsboro Road, Ste. 300, Louisville, KY, 40232

Tel: (502) 893-4600 Fax: (502) 893-4685 Web site: www.thomasind.com

Mfr. lighting fixtures, compressors and vacuum pumps.

Lumec Inc., 618 Cure Boivin Blvd., Boisbrand, PQ J7G 2A7, Canada

Contact: J. F. Simard, Pres.

Thomas Lighting Inc., 189 Bullock Dr., Markham, ON L3P 1W4, Canada

Contact: Barry Thomson, Gen. Mgr.

TIDELAND SIGNAL CORPORATION

4310 Directors Row, PO Box 52430, Houston, TX, 77052-2430

Tel: (713) 681-6101 Fax: (713) 681-6233 Web site: www.tidelandsignal.com

Mfr./sale aids to navigation.

Tideland Signal Canada Ltd., 105-3650 Bonneville Pl., Burnaby, BC V3N 4T7, Canada

Tel: 604-421-0988 Fax: 604-421-0987

TIFFANY & COMPANY

727 Fifth Ave., New York, NY, 10022

Tel: (212) 755-8000 Fax: (212) 605-4465 Web site: www.tiffany.com

Mfr./retail fine jewelry, silverware, china, crystal, leather goods, etc.

Tiffany & Co. Canada, Holt Renfrew, 240 Sparks St., Ottawa, ON K1P 6G9, Canada

Tiffany & Co. Canada, Holt Renfrew, 1300 Sherbrook St. West, Montreal H3G 1H9, Canada

Tiffany & Co. Toronto, 85 Bloor St. West, Toronto, ON M5S 1M1 Canada

Tel: 416-921-3900

TIME WARNER INC.

75 Rockefeller Plaza, New York, NY, 10019

Tel: (212) 484-8000 Fax: (212) 275-3046 Web site: www.timewarner.com

Communications, publishing and entertainment company.

Little Brown & Co. (Canada) Ltd., 148 Yorkville Ave., Toronto, ON M5R 1CZ, Canada

Time Canada Ltd., 175 Bloor St. E, Toronto, ON M4W 3R8, Canada

TIMES MIRROR COMPANY

220 W. First Street, Los Angeles, CA, 90012

Tel: (213) 237-3700 Fax: (213) 237-3800 Web site: www.tm.com

Periodical & book publishing, communications.

Times Mirror Professional Publishing Ltd., 130 Flaska Dr., Markham, ON L6G 1B8, Canada

TM Learning International Inc., 207 Queens Quay W., Toronto, ON M5J 1A7, Canada

TIMEX CORPORATION

Park Road Extension, Middlebury, CT, 06762

Tel: (203) 573-5000 Fax: (203) 573-6901

Mfr. watches, clocks, timing instruments.

Timex Canada Inc., 445 Hood Rd., Markham, ON, Canada

THE TIMKEN COMPANY

1835 Dueber Ave. SW, PO Box 6927, Canton, OH, 44706-2798

Tel: (330) 438-3000 Fax: (330) 471-4118

Mfr. tapered roller bearings and quality alloy steels.

Canadian Timken Ltd., 1055 Talbot St., St. Thomas, ON N5P 1G5, Canada

TIW CORPORATION

12300 S. Main Street, PO Box 35729, Houston, TX, 77235

Tel: (713) 729-2110 Fax: (713) 728-4767

Mfr. liner hanger equipment, production packers, safety & kelly valves.

TIW Canada Ltd., 507 12th Ave., Nisky, AB T0C 2G0, Canada

TJX COMPANIES INC.

770 Cochituate Road, Framingham, MA, 01701

Tel: (508) 390-1000 Fax: (508) 390-2828 Web site: www.tjx.com

Retail stores, catalog & mail order houses.

Winners Apparel Ltd., 65 Densley Ave., Toronto, ON M6M 2P5, Canada

TODD COMBUSTION INC.

15 Progress Drive, PO Box 884, Shelton, CT, 06484

Tel: (203) 925-0380 Fax: (203) 925-0384

Heating & pumping equipment.

Todd Combusion Ltd., 585 Cure Boivin Blvd., Boisbriand, PQ J7G 2A8, Canada

TODD UNIFORM INC.

3668 S. Geyer Road, St. Louis, MO, 63127

Tel: (314) 984-0365 Fax: (314) 984-5798

Mfr. work apparel, suits and coats and industry laundering.

Todd Canada Inc., 80 Bramwin Ct., Brampton, ON L6T 5G2, Canada

TOKHEIM CORPORATION

PO Box 360, 10501 Corporate Drive, Fort Wayne, IN, 46845

Tel: (219) 470-4600 Fax: (219) 482-2677

Mfr. gasoline service station dispensers, point of sale systems, card readers and RFID equipment.

Tokheim & Gasboy of Canada Ltd., 5988 Ambler Dr., Mississauga, ON L4W 2P2, Canada

TOMMY HILFIGER SPORTSWEAR, INC.

25 West 39 Street, New York, NY, 10018

Tel: (212) 840-8888 Fax: (212) 302-8718

Clothing manufacturer and chain stores.

Tommy Hilfiger Sportswear, Ltd., PO Box 501, Ste. 1202, Toronto, ON, Canada

TOOTSIE ROLL INDUSTRIES INC.

7401 S. Cicero Ave., Chicago, IL, 60629

Tel: (773) 838-3400 Fax: (773) 838-3534

Mfr. candies and chocolate products.

Tootsie Roll of Canada Ltd., 137 Horner Ave., Etobicoke, ON M82 4Y1, Canada

Tel: 416-259-3415 Fax: 416-259-9844

THE TOPPS CO., INC.

1 Whitehall Street, New York, NY, 10004-2108

Tel: (212) 376-0300 Fax: (212) 376-0573 Web site: www.topps.com

Mfr. chewing gum & confections.

Topps Canada, 5409 Eglinton, Ave. W., Ste. 210, Etobicoke, ON M9C 5K6, Canada

Tel: 416-622-6425 Fax: 416-622-3023

TOTES INC.

9655 International Blvd., PO Box 465658, Cincinnati, OH, 45246

Tel: (513) 682-8200 Fax: (513) 682-8602

Mfr. rubber & plastic footwear, slippers, umbrellas.

Totes Canada Ltd., 77 Browns Lane, Etobicoke, ON M8W 4X5, Canada

TOWER AUTOMOTIVE, INC.

1350 West Hamlin Road, PO Box 5011, Rochester Hills, MI, 48308-5011

Tel: (248) 650-4100 Fax: (248) 650-7406

Mfr. stamped and welded assemblies for vehicle body structures and suspension systems for auto makers.

Tower Automotive, Inc., 421 Welham St., Barrie, ON, Canada

Tel: 705-733-2112 Fax: 705-733-2493 Contact: Neil Clark, Mgr.

TOWERS PERRIN

335 Madison Ave., New York, NY, 10017-4605

Tel: (212) 309-3400 Fax: (212) 309-0975 Web site: www.towers.com

Management consulting services.

Tillinghast-Towers Perrin, 1800 McGill College Ave., Montreal, PQ H3A 3J6, Canada

Tel: 514-982-9411 Fax: 514-982-9269

Tillinghast-Towers Perrin, 175 Bloor St. East, South Tower #1501, Toronto, ON M4W 3T6, Canada

Tel: 416-960-2700 Fax: 416-960-2819

Tillinghast-Towers Perrin, 3700, 150 6th Ave. SW, Calgary, AB T2P 3Y7, Canada

Tel: 403-261-1400 Fax: 403-237-6733

Towers Perrin, 1600-1100 Melville St., Ste. 1600, Vancouver, BC V6E 4A6, Canada

Tel: 604-691-1000 Fax: 604-691-1062

TOYS R US INC.

461 From Road, Paramus, NJ, 07652

Tel: (201) 262-7800 Fax: (201) 262-8443

Retail stores: toys & games, sporting goods, computer software, books, records.

Toys R Us (Canada) Ltd., 2777 Langstaff Rd., Concord, ON L4K 4M5, Canada

TRAMMELL CROW COMPANY

2001 Ross Ave., Dallas, TX, 75201

Tel: (214) 863-3000 Fax: (214) 863-3125 Web site: www.trammellcrow.com

Commercial real estate management.

Trammell Crow Company, British Columbia, Canada

Trammell Crow Company, Alberta, Canada

Trammell Crow Company, Prince Edward Island, Canada

Trammell Crow Company, Locations in Manitoba, Ontario, & Quebec, Canada

Trammell Crow Company, Saskatchewan, Canada

Trammell Crow Company, Nova Scotia, Canada

TRANS-LUX CORPORATION

110 Richards Ave., Norwalk, CT, 06854

Tel: (203) 853-4321 Fax: (203) 855-8636 Web site: www.trans-lux com

Mfr. moving-message displays.

Trans-Lux Canada Ltd., 5446 Gorvan Dr., Mississauga, ON L4W 3E8, Canada

TRANSAMERICA CORPORATION

600 Montgomery Street, San Francisco, CA, 94111

Tel: (415) 983-4000 Fax: (415) 983-4400 Web site: www.transamerica.com

Life insurance, leasing, and commercial lending services.

Transamerica Life Insurance Company of Canada, 300 Consilium Place, Scarborough, ON M1H 3G2, Canada

Tel: 416-290-6221

TRANSAMERICA OCCIDENTAL LIFE INSURANCE

Hill & Olive at 12th Street, Los Angeles, CA, 90015

Tel: (213) 742-2111 Fax: (213) 742-4091

Insurance services.

Transamerica Occidental Life Insurance Co., 300 Tonsilium Place, Scarborough, ON M1H 3G2 Canada

Tel: 416-290-6221

TRANSILWRAP COMPANY, INC.

2828 N. Paulina Street, #100, Chicago, IL, 60657-4012

Tel: (773) 296-1000 Fax: (773) 296-2007

Mfr. of printable plastic, laminating film and industrial films.

Transilwrap Company, Inc., 333 Finchdene Sq., Scarborough, ON M1X 1B9, Canada

Tel: 416-292-6000 Fax: 416-292-7399

TRANSMATION INC.

977 Mt. Read Blvd., Rochester, NY, 14606

Tel: (716) 254-9000 Fax: (716) 254-0273

Mfr. industry instruments, machinery and equipment.

Transmation (Canada) Inc., 5700 Timberlea Blvd., Mississauga, ON L4W 5B9, Canada

TRAVELERS GROUP INC.

388 Greenwich Street, New York, NY, 10013

Tel: (212) 816-8000 Fax: (212) 816-8915 Web site: www.travelers.com

Provides insurance and financial services.

Primerica Life Insurance Co., 350 Burnhamthorpe Rd., Mississauga, ON L4T 4J4, Canada

TREIBACHER SCHLEIFMITTEL CORPORATION

2000 College Ave., Niagara Falls, NY, 14305

Tel: (716) 286-1234 Fax:

Mfr. abrasives.

Treibacher Schleifmittel Corp., 3807 Stanley Ave., Niagara Falls, ON L2E 6T8, Canada

TREMCO INC.

3735 Green Road, Beachwood, OH, 44122-5718

Tel: (216) 292-5000 Fax: (216) 292-5134

Mfr. protective coatings and sealants for building, maintenance and construction.

Tremco Mfg. Co. Ltd., 220 Wicksteed Ave., Toronto, ON, Canada

Tel: 416-421-3300

TRICON GLOBAL RESTAURANTS INC.

1441 Gardner Lane, Louisville, KY, 40213

Tel: (502) 874-1000 Fax: (502) 874-8315 Web site: www.triconglobal.com

KFC, Taco Bell and Pizza Hut restaurant food chains.

KFC Canada (NRO) Ltd., Canada

TRIMFIT INC.

10450 Drummond Road, Philadelphia, PA, 19154

Tel: (215) 781-0600 Fax: (215) 632-6430

Mfr. hosiery.

Trimfit Co. Ltd., 240 Humberline Drive, Rexdale, ON M9W 5X1, Canada

Tel: 416-213-1400 Contact: Jack Osika, Pres.

TRION INC.

101 McNeil Road, PO Box 760, Sanford, NC, 27331-0760

Tel: (919) 775-2201 Fax: (919) 774-8771

Mfr. air cleaners and electrostatic fluid depositors.

Trion Canada Inc., 130 Otonabee Dr., Kitchener, ON N2C 1L6, Canada

TRU-WELD GRATING INC.

2000 Corporate Drive, Wexford, PA, 15090

Tel: (724) 934-5320 Fax: (724) 934-5348

Architectural metal work.

Tru-Weld Grating Ltd., PO Box 6778, Wetaskiwin, AB T9A 2G4, Canada

TRUE NORTH COMMUNICATIONS INC.

101 East Erie Street, Chicago, IL, 60611

Tel: (312) 425-6000 Fax: (312) 425-6350

Holding company, advertising agency.

FCB Direct, 151 Bloor St. West, 2nd Fl., Toronto, ON M5S 1SH, Canada

FCB Direct Montréal, 225 rue Roy East, Ste. 100, Montréal, PQ H2W 1M5, Canada

Generations Research Inc., 2345 Yonge St., Ste. 710, Toronto, ON M4P 2E5, Canada

Harrod & Mirlin/FCB, 245 Eglinton Ave. East, Ste. 300, Toronto, ON M4P 3C2, Canada

Provost/Ronalds-Reynolds, 1801 McGill College #660, Montreal, PQ H3A 1W3, Canada

TRUE TEMPER CORPORATION

465 Railroad Ave., PO Box 8859, Camp Hill, PA, 17011-8859

Tel: (717) 737-1500 Fax: (717) 730-2550

Mfr. hand and edge tools, farm and garden tools, wheelbarrows.

True Temper, #10 Shoreline Place, PO Box 239, Keswick, ON L4P 3E2, Canada

Tel: 905-989-2677 Fax: 905-989-2882

TRW INC.

1900 Richmond Road, Cleveland, OH, 44124-3760

Tel: (216) 291-7000 Fax: (216) 291-7932

Electric and energy-related products, automotive and aerospace products, tools and fasteners.

Nelson Stud Welding Div., TRW Canada Ltd., 2 Meridian Rd., Rexdale, ON, M9W 4Z7 Canada

TRW Canada Ltd., Thompson Products Div., PO Box 3004, St. Catharine's, ON L2R 7B5, Canada

TRW Data Systems, 270 Yorkland Blvd., Willowdale, ON M2J 1R8, Canada

TRW Electronics, Tuner Operations, 72 Gervais Dr., Don Mills, ON M3C 3H2, Canada

TRW Pleuger of Canada Ltd., 6650 Finch Ave., Rexdale, ON M9W 5Y6, Canada

TRW Reda Pump Co. of Canada, 324 Eighth Ave. SW, Calgary, AB T2P 2Z2, Canada

United-Carr Div. of TRW Canada Ltd., 455 Arvin Ave., Stoney Creek, ON L8G 4A2, Canada

TULTEX CORPORATION

22 E. Church Street, PO Box 5191, Martinsville, VA, 24115

Tel: (703) 632-2961 Fax: (703) 632-9123

Mfr. sporting goods and apparel.

Tultex Canada Inc., 11417 163rd St., Edmonton, AB T5M 3Y3, Canada

TYCO INTERNATIONAL LTD.

One Tyco Park, Exeter, NH, 03833

Tel: (603) 778-9700 Fax: (603) 778-7700 Web site: www.tycoint.com

Mfr./sales fire & security systems, sprinkler systems, undersea fiber optic telecommuncations, printed circuit boards, pipe tubing and flow meters.

Cantech Controls, 1916 - 27th Ave., N.E., Calgary, AB T2E 7A5, Canada

Tel: 403-250-9888 Fax: 403-291-5659

Kerwin Industries, 328 Sauiteaux Crescent, Winnipeg, MB R3J 3T2, Canada
Tel: 204-897-7444 Fax: 204-981-4064

Preston Phipps Inc., 763 Des Rocailles, Charlesburg Quest, PQ G1J 1A9, Canada
Tel: 418-628-6471 Fax: 418-628-8195

Preston Phipps Inc., 200 Tremblay Rd., Ottawa, ON K1G 3H5, Canada
Tel: 613-236-5774 Fax: 613-236-7612

Preston Phipps Inc., 6400 rue Vanden Abeele, St. Laurent, PQ H4S IR9, Canada
Tel: 514-333-5340 Fax: 514-333-6680

Preston Phipps Inc., 1 Market Square, 3rd Fl., St. John, NB E2L 4Z6, Canada
Tel: 506-658-0730 Fax: 506-658-0735

Preston Phipps Inc., 202 Brownlow Ave., Unit E, Bldg. E, Dartmouth, NS B3B IT5, Canada
Tel: 902-468-2004 Fax: 902-468-2109

Tyco Valves and Controls, 503 47th St. East, Saskatoon, SK S7K SB5, Canada
Tel: 306-242-6788 Fax: 306-242-5089

Tyco Valves and Controls, 4823 Sherbrooke St. West, Montreal, PQ H3Z 1G7, Canada
Tel: 514-935-6424 Fax: 514-935-1270

Tyco Valves and Controls, 216-3016 19th St., N.E., Calgary, AB T2E 6Y9, Canada
Tel: 403-250-1896 Fax: 403-291-0702

Tyco Valves and Controls, 470 Seaman St., Stoney Creek, ON L8E 2V9, Canada
Tel: 905-661-0434 Fax: 905-661-0445

Tyco Valves and Controls, 11340 120th St., Edmonton, AB TSG OW5, Canada
Tel: 403-452-9841 Fax: 403-452-9873

Tyco Valves and Controls, 11171 Horseshoe Way, Unit #3, Richmond, BC V7A 4S5, Canada
Tel: 604-272-5565 Fax: 604-272-5820

Wesco V.I. & C., 48 Pacific Ave., PO Box 2550, Station A, Sudbury, ON P3A 489, Canada
Tel: 705-673-1845 Fax: 705-673-4848

W. S. TYLER INC.

8570 Tyler Road, Mentor, OH, 44060
Tel: (440) 974-1047 Fax: (440) 974-0921

Mfr. vibrating screens, lab equipment & related screening media, crushing equipment.

W.S. Tyler Canada, PO Box 3006, St. Catharines, ON L2R 7B6, Canada
Tel: 905-688-2644

U.S. SURGICAL CORPORATION

150 Glover Ave., Norwalk, CT, 06856
Tel: (203) 845-1000 Fax: (203) 847-0635 Web site: www.ussurg.com

Mfr./development/market surgical staplers, laparoscopic instruments and sutures.

Auto Suture Co., Canada, Canada - All mail to U.S. address.

U.S. FILTER/WALLACE & TIERNAN

1901 West Garden Road, Vineland, NJ, 08360
Tel: (609) 507-9000 Fax: (609) 507-4125 Web site: www.usfwt.com

Mfr. disinfection and chemical feed equipment.

U.S. Filter/Wallace & Tiernan Canada, 250 Royal Crest Court, Markham, ON L3R 351, Canada
Tel: 905-944-2800 Fax: 905-474-1660 Contact: Cal Hooper

U.S. OFFICE PRODUCTS COMPANY

1025 Thomas Jefferson Street, NW, Ste. 600E, Washington, DC, 20007
Tel: (202) 339-6700 Fax: (202) 339-6720 Web site: www.usop.com

Sales and distribution of educational products, office supplies and office related services.

Arbuckle Foods, Inc., Vancouver, BC, Canada

Safari Coffee Company, Kelowna, BC, Canada

Take A Break Coffee Company, Ottawa, ON, Canada

Take A Break Coffee Company/Arbuckle Div., 575 West Hunt Club Rd., Nepean, ON K2G 5W5, Canada

Tel: 613-226-1414 Fax: 613-226-8114

U.S. Office Products Canada, Montreal, Canada

U.S. PLAYING CARD COMPANY

4590 Beech Street, Cincinnati, OH, 45212-3497

Tel: (513) 396-5700 Fax: (513) 351-0131

Mfr. playing cards and accessories and board games.

Intl. Playing Card Co. Ltd., 140 Renfrew Drive, Ste. 204, Markham, ON L3R 6B3, Canada

UNIFIRST CORPORATION

68 Jonspin Road, Wilmington, MA, 01887

Tel: (978) 658-8888 Fax: (978) 657-5663 Web site: www.unifirst.com

Industrial launderers and sale/rental of uniform and work garments.

Chinook Cleaners Ltd., 5702 60th St., Taber, AB, ON, Canada

Unifirst Canada Ltd., 2190 Winston Park Dr., Oakville, ON L6H 5W1, Canada

UNIMIN CORPORATION

258 Elm Street, New Canaan, CT, 06840

Tel: (203) 966-8880 Fax: (203) 966-3453

Industrial sand, crushed stone, clay, non-metallic minerals.

Unimin Canada Ltd., 5343 Dundas St. W. #400, Etobicoke, ON M9B 6K5, Canada

UNION CAMP CORPORATION

1600 Valley Road, Wayne, NJ, 07470

Tel: (973) 628-2000 Fax: (973) 628-2722 Web site: www.unioncamp.com

Mfr. paper, packaging, chemicals and wood products.

Bush Boake Allen Corp Ltd., 312 St. Patrick St., La Salle, PQ H8N 2H2, Canada

UNION CARBIDE CORPORATION

39 Old Ridgebury Road, Danbury, CT, 06817

Tel: (203) 794-2000 Fax: (203) 794-6269 Web site: www.unioncarbide.com

Mfr. industrial chemicals, plastics and resins.

Union Carbide Canada Ltd., Locations in Toronto, ON; Calgary and Red Deer, AB; Anjou, Boucherville, Montreal, QU; Canada

Union Carbide Canada Ltd., 1210 Sheppard Ave. E. #210, PO Box 38, Willowdale, ON M2K 1E3, Canada

UNION OIL INTERNATIONAL DIV

2141 Rosecrans Ave., El Segundo, CA, 90245

Tel: (310) 726-7600 Fax: (310) 726-7817

Petroleum products, petrochemicals..

Union Oil Co. of Canada Ltd., 335 Eighth Ave. SW, Calgary, AB T2P 2K6, Canada

UNION PACIFIC CORPORATION

1717 Main Street, #5900, Dallas, TX, 75201-4605

Tel: (214) 743-5600 Fax: (214) 743-5656

Holding company: railroad, crude oil, natural gas, petroleum refining, metal mining service, real estate.

Union Pacific Railroad, 6 Lansing Sq., Willowdale, ON M2J 1T5, Canada

Union Pacific Resources Inc., 205 5th Ave., Calgary, AB T2P 2V7, Canada

Union Pacific-Spokane Intl. Railroads, 717-304 Eighth Ave. SW, Calgary, AB, Canada

UNION SPECIAL CORPORATION

One Union Special Plaza, Huntley, IL, 60142

Tel: (847) 669-4345 Fax: (847) 669-3534 Web site: www.unionspecial.com

Mfr. sewing machines.

Union Special Canada, 5205 Metropolitan Blvd., Ste. 1, Montreal, Quebec H1R 1Z7, Canada

Tel: 514-329-4813 Fax: 514-329-4832 Contact: Jacques Briere, Mgr.

UNISOURCE WORLDWIDE, INC.

1100 Cassatt Ave., Berwyn, PA, 19312

Tel: (610) 296-4470 Fax: (610) 722-3400 Web site: www.unisourcelink.com

Distributor of paper and paper supply systems

Unisource Worldwide, Inc., Locations in Calgary and Edmonton, AB, Canada

Tel: 403-250-7850

Unisource Worldwide, Inc., Montreal, PQ, Canada

Tel: 514-367-3111

Unisource Worldwide, Inc., Prince George, BC, Canada

Tel: 604-563-0348

Unisource Worldwide, Inc., Victoria, BC, Canada

Tel: 604-652-3931

Unisource Worldwide, Inc., Locations in New Brunswick, New Foundland and Nova Scotia, Canada

Tel: 709-368-9353

Unisource Worldwide, Inc., Locations in London, Markham, Mississauga, ON, Canada

Tel: 905-276-8400

Unisource Worldwide, Inc., Quebec City, PQ, Canada

Tel: 418-681-4195

UNISYS CORPORATION.

PO Box 500, Union Meeting Road, Blue Bell, PA, 19424

Tel: (215) 986-4011 Fax: (215) 986-6850 Web site: www.unisys.com

Mfr./marketing/servicing electronic information systems.

Systemes Electroniques Parama, 6111 Royalmount, Montreal, PQ H4P 1K6, Canada

Unisys Canada Inc., 2001 Sheppard Ave E, Willowdale, ON M2J 4Z7, Canada

UNITED ASSET MANAGEMENT CORPORATION

One International Place, 44th Fl., Boston, MA, 02110

Tel: (617) 330-8900 Fax: (617) 330-1133

Investment management services.

Murray Johnstone Ltd., Richmond Hill, ON, Canada

Contact: Joseph R. Senecal, Pres.

Murray Johnstone Ltd., Toronto, ON, Canada

Contact: Graham S. Rennie, Pres.

UNITED DESIGN CORPORATION

PO Box 1200, Noble, OK, 73068

Tel: (405) 872-3468 Fax: (405) 360-4442

Mfr. pottery products.

United Design Canada Ltd., 10 Tidey St., Norwich, ON N0J 1P0, Canada

UNITED LABORATORIES INC.

320 Thirty-seventh Avenue, St. Charles, IL, 60174

Tel: (630) 377-0900 Fax: (630) 377-0960

Mfr. cleaning & sanitation products, chemicals.

United Laboratories of Canada Inc., 214 Dolomite Dr., Downsview, ON M3J 2N2, Canada

UNITED PRESS INTERNATIONAL

1400 I Street, Washington, DC, 20005

Tel: (202) 898-8000 Fax: (202) 371-1239

Collection & distributor of news, newspictures, financial data.

United Press Intl. Ltd., 366 Adelaide St. E, Toronto, ON M5A 1N4, Canada

UNITED RENTALS INC.

4 Greenwich Office Park, Greenwich, CT, 06830

Tel: (203) 622-3131 Fax: (203) 622-6080

Equipment rental.

BNR Equipment Ltd., 1182 Victoria St. North, North Kitchener, ON N2B 3C9, Canada

Tel: 519-578-4950

UNITED STATIONERS INC.

2200 East Golf Road, Des Plaines, IL, 60016

Tel: (847) 699-5000 Fax: (847) 699-8046

Wholesale office supplies.

United Stationers Canada Ltd., 60 Haist Ave., Unit 2, Woodridge, ON L4L 5V4, Canada

Tel: 905-856-8877

UNITED TOTE COMPANY

2311 South Seventh Ave., Bozeman, MT, 59715

Tel: (406) 582-4000 Fax: (406) 585-6609

Design/mfr./operate pari-mutuel wagering systems.

United Tote Canada Inc., 1391 St. James St. #15, Winnipeg, MB R3H 0Z1, Canada

UNIVAR CORPORATION

6100 Carillon Point, Kirkland, WA, 98004

Tel: (425) 889-3400 Fax: (425) 889-4100

Industrial chemicals.

Van Waters & Rogers Ltd., 9800 Van Horne Way, Richmond, BCV6X 1W5, Canada

UNIVERSAL CORPORATION

PO Box 25099, Richmond, VA, 23260

Tel: (804) 359-9311 Fax: (804) 254-3582

Holding company for tobacco and commodities.

Simcoe Leaf Tobacco Ltd., PO Box 280, Simcoe, ON N3Y 4L1, Canada

UNIVERSAL FOODS CORPORATION

433 E. Michigan Street, Milwaukee, WI, 53202

Tel: (414) 271-6755 Fax: (414) 347-4783

Mfr. food products & food ingredients.

Dyeco Ltd., River & Orchard Sts., Kingston, ON K7L 4X6, Canada

UNIVERSAL FOREST PRODUCTS INC.

2801 East Beltline Ave. NE, Grand Rapids, MI, 49525

Tel: (616) 364-6161 Fax: (616) 364-5558

Wood preservation services, structural wood, flooring, wood products.

USCI/Universal Forest Inc., 110 Montee Quay, St. Bernard de Lacolle, PQ, Canada

UNIVERSAL INSTRUMENTS

90 Bevier Street, S. Dock, Binghamton, NY, 13904

Tel: (607) 779-7522 Fax: (607) 779-7971 Web site: www.dover.com

Mfr./sales of instruments for electronic circuit assembly

Universal Instruments, Burlington, ON, Canada

Tel: 905-332-3773 Fax: 905-332-4045

Universal Instruments, Calgary, AB, Canada

Tel: 403-217-4413 Fax: 403-217-4423

Universal Instruments, Bromont, PQ, Canada

Tel: 514-534-4461 Fax: 514-534-4542

UNUM CORPORATION

2211 Congress Street, Portland, ME, 04122

Tel: (207) 770-2211 Fax: (207) 770-4510 Web site: www.unum.com

Disability and special risk insurance.

Duncanson & Holt Canada, Ltd., 33 Yonge St., Ste. 418, Toronto, ON M5E 189, Canada

Tel: 416-366-6480 Fax: 416-366-0430 Contact: Derrick J. Crawley, Pres.

UOP INC.

25 E. Algonquin Road, Des Plaines, IL, 60017

Tel: (847) 391-2000 Fax: (847) 391-2253

Diversified research, development & mfr. of industry products & systems management studies & service.

Flexonics Div., UOP Ltd., Brampton, ON, Canada

Forest Products Div., UOP Ltd., Rutherglen, ON, Canada

Forest Products Div., UOP Ltd., Mattawa, ON, Canada

Forest Products Div., UOP Ltd., North Bay, ON, Canada

Forest Products Div., UOP Ltd., Tee Lake, PQ, Canada

Forest Products Div., UOP Ltd., Deux Rivieres, PQ, Canada

Johnson Div., UOP Ltd., Ajax, ON, Canada

Shawinigan Procon Co., Toronto, ON, Canada

Shawinigan Procon Co., Calgary, AB, Canada

Wolverine Div., UOP Ltd., London, ON, Canada

USG CORPORATION

125 South Franklin Street, Chicago, IL, 60606

Tel: (312) 606-4000 Fax: (312) 606-4093 Web site: www.usg.com

Holding company for the building products industry.

Canadian Gypsum Co., 350 Burnhamthorpe Rd. W., 5th fl., Mississauga, ON L5B 3J1, Canada

USX - U.S. STEEL GROUP

600 Grant Street, Pittsburgh, PA, 15219-4776

Tel: (412) 391-8115 Fax: (412) 433-7519 Web site: www.ussteel.com

Steel production.

Met-Chem Canada Inc., 425 Blvd. de Maisonneuve W, Montreal, PQ H3A 3G5, Canada

USX-MARATHON GROUP

5555 San Felipe Road, Houston, TX, 77056

Tel: (713) 629-6600 Fax: (713) 296-2952 Web site: www.marathon.com

Oil and gas exploration.

Marathon Petroleum Canada Ltd., Calgary, AB, Canada

UTILICORPORATION UNITED INC.

PO Box 13287, Kansas City, MO, 64199-3287

Tel: (816) 421-6600 Fax: (816) 472-6281

Electric and gas utility.

West Kootenay Power Ltd., Waneta Plaza, 8100 Rock Island Hwy, Trail, BC V1R 4N7, Canada

UUNET

3060 Williams Drive, Fairfax, VA, 22031-4648

Tel: (703) 206-5600 Fax: (703) 206-5601 Web site: www.worldcom.

World's largest Internet service provider; World Wide Web hosting services, security products and consulting services to businesses, professionals, and on-line service providers.

Uunet Canada, Inc., 20 Bay St., Ste. 1300, Toronto, ON, M5J 2N8, Canada

Tel: 416-368-6621 Fax: 416-368-1350 Contact: Chris Scatliff, Pres.

Uunet Canada, Inc., 630, blvd, Réne-Lévesque Ouest, Bureau 2300, Montréal PQ H3B 1S6, Canada

Tel: 514-875-0010 Fax: 514-875-5735 Contact: Chris Scatliff, Pres. Emp: 130

VALENITE INC.

PO Box 9636, Madison Heights, MI, 48071-9636

Tel: (248) 589-1000 Fax: (810) 597-4820

Cemented carbide, high speed steel, ceramic & diamond cutting tool products, etc.

Valenite-Modco Ltd., 7675 Tranby Rd., Windsor, ON N8S 2B7, Canada

VALHI INC.

5430 LBJ Freeway, Ste. 1700, Dallas, TX, 75240

Tel: (972) 233-1700 Fax: (972) 375-0586

Chemicals, hardware, sugar, mining.

Kronos Canada Inc., 4 Place Ville Marie, Montreal, PQ H3B 4M5, Canada

Waterloo Furniture Components Ltd., 501 Manitou Dr., Kitchener, ON N2C 1L2, Canada

VALLEY FORGE CORPORATION

100 Smith Ranch Road, Ste. 326, San Rafael, CA, 94903-1994

Tel: (415) 492-1500 Fax: (415) 492-0128

Recreational goods, communications equipment, turbo actuators, switchgear & current-carrying devices.

Force 10 Marine Ltd., 23080 Hamilton Rd., Richmond, BC V6V 1C9, Canada

VALSPAR CORPORATION

1101 South Third Street, Minneapolis, MN, 55415-1259

Tel: (612) 332-7371 Fax: (612) 375-7723 Web site: www.valspar.com

Produce paint, varnish & allied products.

Valspar Inc., 645 Coronation Dr., Scarborough, ON M1E 4R6, Canada

Tel: 416-284-1681

VAPOR CORPORATION

6420 West Howard Street, Niles, IL, 60714-3395

Tel: (847) 967-8300 Fax: (847) 965-9874

Mfr. bus and rail transit automatic door systems, railcar/locomotive relays and contractors, vehicle ID systems.

Vapor Canada Inc., 10655 Henri-Bourassa W, Ville St. Laurent, Montreal, PQ H4S 1A1, Canada

Tel: 514-335-4200 Fax: 514-335-4201 Contact: Emmanuel Dictakis, EVP & Gen. Mgr.

VAREL INTERNATIONAL

9230 Denton Drive, PO Box 540157, Dallas, TX, 75354-0157

Tel: (214) 351-6486 Fax: (214) 351-6438

Mfr. oil, mining, geophysical, water-well & construction equipment.

Varel Canada Ltd., C2, 6215 3rd St. SE, Calgary, AB T2H 2L2, Canada

VARIAN ASSOCIATES INC.

3050 Hansen Way, Palo Alto, CA, 94304-100

Tel: (650) 493-4000 Fax: (650) 424-5358 Web site: www.varian.com

Mfr. microwave tubes & devices, analytical instruments, semiconductor process & medical equipment, vacuum systems.

Varian Canada Ltd., 45 River Dr., Georgetown, ON L7G 2J4, Canada

VEEDER-ROOT COMPANY

125 Powder Forest Drive, PO Box 2003, Simsbury, CT, 06070-2003

Tel: (860) 651-2700 Fax: (860) 651-2704

Mfr. counting, controlling and sensing devices.

Veeder-Root of Canada Ltd., 26 Fieldway Rd., Toronto, ON M8Z 3L2, Canada

VELCON FILTERS INC.

4525 Centennial Blvd., Colorado Springs, CO, 80919-3350

Tel: (719) 531-5855 Fax: (719) 531-5690

Mfr./sale filters & filtration systems.

3L Filters, 427 Elgin St. N, Cambridge, ON N1R 8G4, Canada

Velcon Canada, 1595 Bishop St., Cambridge, ON N1R 7J4, Canada

VIACOM INC.

1515 Broadway, 28th Fl., New York, NY, 10036-5794

Tel: (212) 258-6000 Fax: (212) 258-6358 Web site: www.viacom.com

Communications, publishing and entertainment.

Famous Players, 146 Bloor St. W, Toronto, ON M5S 1M4, Canada

Prentice Hall of Canada Inc., 1870 Birchmount Rd., Scarborough, ON M1P 2J7, Canada

Viacom Enterprises Canada, 45 Charles St. E, Toronto, ON M4Y 1S2, Canada

VICTAULIC INTERNATIONAL

4901 Kesslersville Road, PO Box 31, Easton, PA, 18004-0031

Tel: (610) 559-3300 Fax: (610) 559-3608 Web site: www.victaulic.com

Mfr. piping products: couplings, valves, fittings, etc.

Victaulic Co. of Canada, 65 Worcester Rd., Rexdale, ON M9W 5N7, Canada

THE VIKING CORPORATION

210 N. Industrial Park Road, Hastings, MI, 49058

Tel: (616) 945-9501 Fax: (616) 945-9599

Mfr. fire extinguishing equipment.

Viking Fire Protection Ltd., 3005 Pitfield Blvd., St. Laurent, PQ M4S 1H4, Canada

VISHAY INTERTECHNOLOGY INC.

63 Lincoln Highway, Malvern, PA, 19355

Tel: (610) 644-1300 Fax: (610) 296-0657 Web site: www.vishay.com

Mfr. resistors, strain gages, capacitors, inductors, printed circuit boards.

Techno Inc., 49 Bertal Rd., Toronto, ON M6M 4M5, Canada

VIVITAR CORPORATION

1280 Rancho Conejo Blvd, Newbury Park, CA, 91320

Tel: (805) 498-7008 Fax: (805) 498-5086

Mfr. photographic equipment, electronic supplies.

Vivitar Canada Ltd., 5211 Creekbank Rd., Mississauga, ON L4W 1R3, Canada

VLSI TECHNOLOGY INC.

1109 McKay Drive, San Jose, CA, 95131

Tel: (408) 434-3000 Fax: (408) 434-7584 Web site: www.vlsi.com

Mfr. custom & standard integrated circuits for computing, communications & industry applications.

VLSI Technology Inc., 5600 Parkwood Way, Ste. 415, Richmond, BC V6V 2M2, Canada

Tel: 604-231-8740 Fax: 604-231-8745

VOLT INFORMATION SCIENCES, INC.

1221 Ave. of the Americas, 47th Fl., New York, NY, 10020-1579

Tel: (212) 704-2400 Fax: (212) 704-2424 Web site: www.volt.com

Staffing services and telecommunication services.

Volt Autologic Inc., 833 Queens Way, Toronto, ON M8Z 1N6, Canada

VULCAN MATERIALS COMPANY

1 Metroplex Drive, Birmingham, AL, 35209

Tel: (205) 877-3000 Fax: (205) 877-3094 Web site: www.vulcanmaterials.com

Mfr. construction materials & industry chemicals.

Vulcan Materials Co., Vancouver, BC, Canada

VWR CORPORATION

1310 Goshen Pkwy, West Chester, PA, 19380

Tel: (610) 431-1700 Fax: (610) 436-1760

Distributor industrial & laboratory equipment & supplies.

VWR Scientific Canada Ltd., PO Box 20060, London, ON N6K 4G6, Canada

WABCO (WESTINGHOUSE AIR BRAKE COMPANY)

1001 Air Brake Ave., Wilmerding, PA, 15148

Tel: (412) 825-1000 Fax: (412) 825-1501

Transportation technologies; develops, manufactures, and markets electronic products and equipment.

Benn Iron Foundry, Wallaceburg, ON, Canada

Thermo Sealed Castings, Burlington, ON, Canada

Thermo Sealed Machining, Burlington, ON, Canada

Westinghouse Railway (Canada) Ltd., Stoney Creek, ON, Canada

WACKENHUT CORPORATION

4200 Wackenhut Drive, Ste. 100, Palm Beach Gardens, FL, 33410

Tel: (561) 622-5656 Fax: (561) 691-6736 Web site: www.wackenhut.com

Security systems & services.

Wackenhut of Canada Ltd., 180 Attwell Dr. #202, Toronto, ON M9W 6A9, Canada (Locations: Calgary, Edmonton, Medicine Hat & North York, Canada.)

Tel: 416-674-1300 Fax: 416-674-1301

WAHL CLIPPER CORPORATION

2902 N. Locust Street, Sterling, IL, 61081

Tel: (815) 625-6525 Fax: (815) 625-1193

Mfr. hair clippers, beard and mustache trimmers, shavers, pet clippers and soldering irons.

Wahl Clipper Corp. Ltd., 80 Orfus Rd., Toronto, ON M6A 1M7, Canada

WAINOCO OIL CORPORATION

10000 Memorial Drive, Ste. 600, Houston, TX, 77024

Tel: (713) 688-9600 Fax: (713) 688-0616

Oil/gas exploration, development and production.

Wainoco Oil Corp. Canada, 350 Seventh Ave. SW, Calgary, AB T2P 3N9, Canada

WAL-MART STORES INC.

702 SW 8th Street, Bentonville, AR, 72716-8611

Tel: (501) 273-4000 Fax: (501) 273-8980 Web site: www.wal-mart.com

Retailer.

Wal-Mart Stores Inc., Canada

WALBAR METALS INC.

Peabody Ind Center, PO Box 3369, Peabody, MA, 01961-3369

Tel: (978) 532-2350 Fax: (978) 532-7501

Mfr. turbine components for engines; repair & coating service.

Walbar Canada Inc., 1303 Aerowood Dr., Mississauga, ON L4W 2P6, Canada

WALCO INTERNATIONAL INC.

15 W Putnam Ave., Porterville, CA, 93257-3627

Tel: (817) 781-3510 Fax: (817) 416-1235

Drugs, proprietaries & sundries, farm supplies, medical & hospital equipment.

Province Livestock Supply Ltd., 2620 2nd Ave. N., Lethbridge, AB T1J 3Y7, Canada

Western Veterinary Supplies Ltd., 3026 2nd Ave. N., Lethbridge, AB T1H 0C6, Canada

WALL COLMONOY CORPORATION

30261 Stephenson Hwy, Madison Heights, MI, 48071

Tel: (248) 585-6400 Fax: (248) 585-7960

Mfr. hard-surfacing and brazing alloys, equipment and services.

Wall Colmonoy (Canada) Inc., 1575 Rossi Drive, Windsor, ON N9A 6J3, Canada

Tel: 519-737-9300 Fax: 519-737-9899 Contact: William P. Clark, Jr. Emp: 5

WANG LABORATORIES INC.

600 Technology Park Drive, Billerica, MA, 01821

Tel: (508) 967-5000 Fax: (508) 967-5911

Mfr. computer information processing systems.

Wang Laboratories (Canada) Ltd., 66 Leek Crescent, Wang Way, Richmond Hill, ON L4B 1J7, Canada

WARNACO INC.

90 Park Ave., New York, NY, 10016

Tel: (212) 661-1300 Fax: (212) 687-0480 Web site: www.warnaco.com

Mfr./sales intimate apparel and men's and women's sportswear.

Warnaco of Canada Ltd., 707 St. Lawrence St., Prescott, ON K0E IT0, Canada

WARNER BROS INTERNATIONAL TELEVISION

4000 Warner Boulevard, Bldg.170, 3rd Fl., Burbank, CA, 91522

Tel: (818) 954-6000 Fax: (818) 977-4040

Distributor TV programming and theatrical features.

Warner Bros. Intl. Television, 4576 Yonge St., 2nd Fl., North York, ON M2N 6P1, Canada

Tel: 416-250-8384 Fax: 416-250-8598 Contact: Robert Blair, Gen. Mgr.

WARNER-JENKINSON CO. INC.

2526 Baldwin Street, St. Louis, MO, 63106

Tel: (314) 889-7600 Fax: (314) 658-7305

Mfr. synthetic & natural colors for food, drugs & cosmetics.

Warner-Jenkinson (Canada) Ltd., PO Box 818, 30 River St., Kingston, ON K7L 4X6, Canada

WARNER-LAMBERT COMPANY

201 Tabor Road, Morris Plains, NJ, 07950-2693

Tel: (973) 540-2000 Fax: (973) 540-3761 Web site: www.warner-lambert.com

Mfr. ethical and proprietary pharmaceuticals, confectionery and consumer products & pet care supplies.

Adams Canada, Scarborough, ON, Canada

Contact: Eric Sorensen, Pres.

Warner-Lambert Canada Inc., 2200 Eglinton E, Toronto, ON M1L 2N3, Canada (Headquarters: Scarborough, Canada.)

Contact: Oliver Brandicourt, VP

WATERS CORPORATION

34 Maple Street, Milford, MA, 01757

Tel: (508) 478-2000 Fax: (508) 872-1990

Mfr./distribute liquid chromatographic instruments and test and measurement equipment.

Waters Associates Scientific Ltd., 6480 Viscount Rd., Mississauga, ON L4V 1H3, Canada

Waters Chromat. Div., 3688 Nashua Dr., Mississauga, ON L4V 1M5, Canada

WATKINS INC.

PO Box 5570, Winona, MN, 55987

Tel: (507) 457-3300 Fax: (507) 452-6723

Mfr. cosmetics, medicines, spices and extracts, household cleaning products.

Watkins Inc., 30-5 Scurfield Blvd., Winnipeg, MB R3Y 1G3, Canada

Contact: Richard C. Wantock

WATSON WYATT & COMPANY

6707 Democracy Blvd., Ste. 800, Bethesda, MD, 20817

Tel: (301) 581-4600 Fax: (301) 581-4937 Web site: www.watsonwyatt.com

Creates compensation and benefits programs for major corporations.

Watson Wyatt Canada, Ste. 1100, One Queen St., East, Toronto, ON M5C 2Y4, Canada (Locations: Montreal, Ottawa, Vancouver, Canada)

Tel: 416-862-0393 Fax: 416-366-9691

Watson Wyatt Canada, First Canadian Centre, 2700 West Tower, 350 7th Ave., S.W., Calgary AB T2P 3N9, Canada

Tel: 403-237-7373 Fax: 403-237-7862

WATTS INDUSTRIES, INC.

815 Chestnut Street, North Andover, MA, 01845-6098

Tel: (978) 688-1811 Fax: (978) 688-5841 Web site: www.wattsind.com

Designs/mfr./sales of industry valves and safety control products.

Ancon Industries, 5435 North Service Rd., Burlington, ON L7L 5H7, Canada

Enpoco Ltd., 5435 North Service Rd., Burlington, ON L7L 5H7, Canada

Epps Manufacturing Ltd., 5435 North Service Rd., Burlington, ON L7L 5H7, Canada

Watts Industries (Canada) Inc., 441 Hanlan Rd., Woodbridge, ON L4L 3T1, Canada

Watts Industries Inc., 5435 N. Service Rd., Burlington, ON L7L 5H7, Canada

WD-40 COMPANY

1061 Cudahy Place, San Diego, CA, 92110-3998

Tel: (619) 275-1400 Fax: (619) 275-5823

Mfr. branded multiple-purpose lubrication, protection and general maintenance products.

WD-40 Products (Canada) Ltd., PO Box 220, Etobicoke, ON M9C 4V3, Canada

WEATHERFORD INTERNATIONAL INC.

5 Post Oak Blvd, Ste. 1760, Houston, TX, 77227-3415

Tel: (713) 287-8400 Fax: (713) 963-9785 Web site: www.weatherford.com

Oilfield services, products & equipment; mfr. marine cranes for oil and gas industry.

Weatherford Intl. Inc., 14435 - 116 Ave., Edmonton, AB T5M 3E8 , Canada (Locations: Calgary, Darthmouth, Fort. St. John, Canada)

Tel: 403-250-3325 Fax: 403-291-4210

WEAVEXX

401 Highway 12 West, Starkville, MS, 39759

Tel: (601) 323-4064 Fax: (601) 324-1400

Mfr. papermakers' felts.

Lockport-Pacific Ltd., Vancouver, BC, Canada

Lockport-Warwick Ltd., Warwick, PQ, Canada

JERVIS B. WEBB COMPANY

34375 West Twelve Mile Road, Farmington Hills, MI, 48331

Tel: (248) 553-1220 Fax: (248) 553-1237

Mfr. integrators of material handling systems.

Jervis B. Webb Co. of Canada Ltd., 1647 Burlington St. E, Hamilton, ON L8H 7M5, Canada

WEBER MARKING SYSTEMS INC.

711 West Algonquin Road, Arlington Heights, IL, 60005

Tel: (847) 364-8500 Fax: (847) 364-8575

Mfr. label printing systems and custom labels.

Weber Marking Systems (Canada) Ltd., 2728 Slough St., Mississauga, ON L4T 1G3, Canada

WEIL-McLAIN

500 Blaine Street, Michigan City, IN, 46360

Tel: (219) 879-6561 Fax: (219) 879-4025

Mfr. cast iron boilers and domestic hot water heaters.

Weil-McLain, Div. Marley Canadian, Inc., A. Finley Rd., Brampton, ON L6T 1A9, Canada

Tel: 905-456-8300 Fax: 905-456-8582 Contact: Ron Elliott, Mgr. Emp: 11

WELBILT CORPORATION

225 High Ridge Road, Stamford, CT, 06905

Tel: (203) 325-8300 Fax: (203) 325-9800

Mfr. commercial foodservice equipment.

Garland Commercial Ranges Ltd., 1177 Kamato Rd., Mississauga, ON L4W 1K4, Canada

WESCO DISTRIBUTION INC.

Four Station Square #700, Pittsburgh, PA, 15219

Tel: (412) 454-2200 Fax: (412) 454-2505

Electronic equipment and parts.

Wesco Distribution Canada Inc., 3100 Steeles Ave E., Markham, ON L3R 8T3, Canada

WESLEY INTERNATIONAL INC.

1825 South Woodward, Bloomfield Hills, MI, 48302

Tel: (248) 857-9959 Fax: (248) 333-3136

Mfr. coatings and castings.

Wesley International Inc., Kitchener, Canada

WESLEY-JESSEN CORPORATION

333 East Howard Ave., Des Plains, IL, 60018

Tel: (847) 294-3000 Fax: (847) 294-3434

Contact lenses and accessories, ophthalmic and dermatology products.

Barnes-Hind Inc., 6535 Mill Creek Dr., Unit 67, Mississauga, ON L5N 2M2, Canada

THE WEST BEND COMPANY

400 Washington Street, West Bend, WI, 53095

Tel: (414) 334-2311 Fax: (414) 334-6800

Mfr. small electrical appliances, cookware, water distillers, timers.

West Bend of Canada, PO Box 6000, 191 John St., Barrie, ON L4M 4V3, Canada

WEST POINT STEVENS INC.

507 West 10th Street, PO Box 71, West Point, GA, 31833

Tel: (706) 645-4000 Fax: (706) 645-4453

Industry household and apparel fabrics and bed and bath products.

West Point Stevens Inc., Toronto, ON, Canada

WESTERN ATLAS INC.

10205 Westheimer, Houston, TX, 77251-1407

Tel: (713) 972-4000 Fax: (713) 952-9837 Web site: www.waii.com

Full service to the oil industry.

Western Atlas Logging Services, Canada Area Office, 1200, 505 - 3rd St. S.W., Calgary, AB T2P 3E6, Canada

Tel: 403-571-1000 Fax: 403-571-1050 Contact: G. Smith, VP

Western Geophysical, 2720 Fifth Ave. NE, Calgary, AB T2A 4V4, Canada
Tel: 403-272-9754 Fax: 403-272-5293 Contact: B. Drew, Mgr.

WESTINGHOUSE ELECTRIC (CBS)
11 Stanwix Street, Pittsburgh, PA, 15222-1384
Tel: (412) 244-2000 Fax: (412) 642-4650
TV/radio broadcasting, mfr. electronic systems for industry/defense, financial & environmental services.
Westinghouse Canada Inc., PO Box 510, Hamilton, ON L8N 3K2, Canada

WESTVACO CORPORATION
299 Park Ave., New York, NY, 10171
Tel: (212) 688-5000 Fax: (212) 318-5055 Web site: www.westvaco.com
Mfr. paper, packaging, chemicals.
Westvaco Canada Ltd., 5915 Airport Rd., Mississauga, ON L4V 1T1, Canada

WEYERHAEUSER COMPANY
PO Box 2999, 33663 Weyerhaeuser Way South, Federal Way,, Tacoma, WA, 98003
Tel: (253) 924-2345 Fax: (253) 924-2685 Web site: www.weyerhaeuser.com
Wood & wood fiber products.
Weyerhaeuser Canada Ltd., 1100 Melville, Vancouver, BC V6E 4A6, Canada
Tel: 604-691-2412

WHIRLPOOL CORPORATION
2000 N. M-63, Benton Harbor, MI, 49022-2692
Tel: (616) 923-5000 Fax: (616) 923-5443 Web site: www.whirlpoolcorp.com
Mfr./market home appliances: Whirlpool, Roper, KitchenAid, Estate, and Inglis.
Inglis Ltd., 1901 Minnesota Ct., Mississauga, ON L5N 3A7, Canada

WHITEHALL-ROBINS INC.
1407 Cummings Drive, PO Box 26609, Richmond, VA, 23261-6609
Tel: (804) 257-2000 Fax: (804) 257-2120 Web site: www.ahp.com/whitehall.htm
Mfr. ethical pharmaceuticals and consumer products.
Whitehall-Robins Co. Ltd., Mississauga, ON, Canada

WHITING CORPORATION
15700 Lathrop Ave., Harvey, IL, 60426-5098
Tel: (708) 331-4000 Fax: (708) 785-0755 Web site: www.whitingcorp.com
Mfr. EOT cranes, metallurgical & railroad shop equipment.
Whiting Equipment Ltd., 350 Alexander St., Welland, ON L3B 3B4, Canada
Tel: 905-732-7585

W. A. WHITNEY COMPANY
650 Race Street, PO Box 1206, Rockford, IL, 61105-1206
Tel: (815) 964-6771 Fax: (815) 964-3175
Mfr. hydraulic punch/plasma cutting metal fabricating equipment.
W.A. Whitney of Canada Ltd., 50 Paxman Rd., Unit 8, Etobicoke, ON M9C 1B7, Canada

JOHN WILEY & SONS INC.
605 Third Ave., New York, NY, 10158-0012
Tel: (212) 850-6000 Fax: (212) 850-6088 Web site: www.wiley.com
Publisher: print & electronic products for academic, professional, scientific, technical & consumer market.
John Wiley & Sons Canada Ltd., 22 Worcester Rd., Rexdale, ON M9W 1L1, Canada
Tel: 416-236-4433 Fax: 416-236-4447 Contact: Diane Wood, Pres.

WILLIAM E WRIGHT COMPANY

PO Box 398, 85 South Street, West Warren, MA, 01092

Tel: (413) 436-7732 Fax: (413) 436-9785

Tapes, braids, apparel and furnishing trims.

Wm. E. Wright Co. of Canada Ltd., 1123 Leslie St., Don Mills, ON M3C 2K1, Canada

WINDWAY CAPITAL CORPORATION

630 Riverfront Drive, PO Box 897, Sheboygan, WI, 53082-0897

Tel: (920) 457-8600 Fax: (920) 457-8599

Mfr. canvas & plastic products, metal stampings.

North Sails (Canada) Ltd., 11911 Machrina Way, Richmond, BC, Canada

North Sails Fogh Ltd., 2242 Lake Shore Blvd. W., Toronto, ON M8V 1A5, Canada

Vollrath of Canada Ltd., 5725 McLaughlin Rd., Mississauga, ON L5R 3K5, Canada

WIREMOLD CO. INC.

60 Woodlawn Street, West Hartford, CT, 06110

Tel: (860) 233-6251 Fax: (860) 523-3699

Mfr. noncurrent-carrying wiring devices.

Wiremold Canada Inc, 850 Gartshore St., Fergus, ON N1M 2W8, Canada

WISER OIL CO. INC.

8115 Preston Road, #400, Dallas, TX, 75225

Tel: (214) 265-0080 Fax: (214) 373-3610

Crude petroleum & natural gas, exploration services.

Wiser Oil Co. Canada Ltd., 645 7th Ave. SW, Calgary, AB T2P 4G8, Canada

Contact: Allan J. Simus, Pres.

WITCO CORPORATION

One American Lane, Greenwich, CT, 06831-2559

Tel: (203) 552-2000 Fax: (203) 552-3070 Web site: www.witco.com

Mfr. chemical and petroleum products.

Surpass Ltd., 250 Consumers Rd., Willowdale, ON M2J 4V6, Canada

Witco Canada Ltd., 2 Lansing Sq., Willowdale, ON M2J 4Z4, Canada

WOMETCO ENTERPRISES INC.

3195 Ponce de Leon Boulevard, Coral Gables, FL, 33134

Tel: (305) 529-1400 Fax: (305) 529-1499

Television broadcasting, film distribution, bottling, vending machines.

KVOS-TV, 1345 Burrard St., Vancouver, BC V6Z 2A2, Canada

Wometco (B.C.) Ltd., 2471 Viking Way, Richmond, BC V6V 1N3, Canada

Wometco Newfoundland Ltd., 60 O'Leary Ave., St. Johns, NF A1B 3V8, Canada

WOODHEAD INDUSTRIES INC.

Three Parkway North, Ste. 550, Deerfield, IL, 60015

Tel: (847) 236-9300 Fax: (847) 236-0503

Develop/mfr./sale/distributor elect/electronic, fiber optic and ergonomic special-function, non-commodity products.

Woodhead (Canada) Ltd., 1090 Brevik Pl., Mississauga, ON L4W 3Y5, Canada

WORLD COURIER INC.

1313 Fourth Ave., New Hyde Park, NY, 11041

Tel: (516) 354-2600 Fax: (516) 354-2644

International courier service.

World Courier of Canada Ltd., 212 N. Queen St., Etobicoke, ON, Canada

World Courier of Canada Ltd., 300 St. Sacrement St., Montreal, PQ, Canada

WRIGHT LINE INC.

160 Gold Star Blvd, Worcester, MA, 01606

Tel: (508) 852-4300 Fax: (508) 853-8904

Mfr. filing systems.

Datafile/Wright Line of Canada Ltd., 130 Sparks Ave., Willowdale, ON M2H 2S4, Canada

WM WRIGLEY JR. COMPANY

410 N. Michigan Ave., Chicago, IL, 60611-4287

Tel: (312) 644-2121 Fax: (312) 644-0353 Web site: www.wrigley.com

Mfr. chewing gum.

Wrigley Canada Inc., 1123 Leslie St., Don Mills, ON M3C 2K1, Canada

WUNDERMAN CATO JOHNSON

675 Ave. of the Americas, New York, NY, 10010-5104

Tel: (212) 941-3000 Fax: (212) 633-0957 Web site: www.wcj.com

International advertising and marketing consulting firm.

Wunderman Cato Johnson, 4100 Yonge St., Ste. 300, Tronto, ON M2P 2B5, Canada

Tel: 416-733-0015 Fax: 416-733-8447 Contact: Dan Plouffe, Pres.

WWF PAPER CORPORATION

Two Bala Plaza, Bala Cynwyd, PA, 19004

Tel: (610) 667-9210 Fax: (610) 667-1663 Web site: www.wwfpaper.com

Wholesale of fine papers.

WWF-Canada, Inc., 11970 Blvd. Albert-Hudon, Montreal-Nord H1G 3K3, PQ, Canada

Tel: 514-321-8820 Fax: 514-321-8341 Contact: Michael A. Catalfamo, VP, Gen. Mgr. Emp: 30

WWF-Canada, Inc., H.Q. Toronto Airport, 200-5925 Airport Rd., Mississauga, ON, LAV 1W1, Canada

Tel: 905-405-6288 Fax: 905-405-6264 Contact: Michael A. Catalfamo, VP, Gen. Mgr. Emp: 4

WYNN OIL COMPANY

1050 West Fifth Street, Azusa, CA, 91702-9510

Tel: (626) 334-0231 Fax: (626) 334-1456 Web site: www.wynnoil.com

Mfr. of specialty chemicals, equipment and related service programs for automotive and industrial markets.

Wynn's Canada, Ltd., 170 Traders Blvd. East, Mississauga, ON L4Z 1W7, Canada

Tel: 905-507-9966 Fax: 905-507-2265 Contact: David G. Formhals, V.P. & Gen. Mgr. Emp: 17

WYNN'S PRECISION INC.

104 Hartman Drive, Lebanon, TN, 37087

Tel: (615) 444-0191 Fax: (615) 444-4072

Mfr. rings, seals and custom molded rubber products.

Wynn's Precision Products Corp., Precision Drive, Orillia, ON L3V 2M3, Canada

XEROX CORPORATION

800 Long Ridge Road, PO Box 1600, Stamford, CT, 06904

Tel: (203) 968-3000 Fax: (203) 968-4312 Web site: www.xerox.com

Mfr. document processing equipment, systems and supplies.

Xerox Canada Itee, 3400 De Maisonneuve Blvd. West, Xerox Tower Ste. 900, Montreal, PQ H3Z 3G1, Canada

Tel: 514-939-3769

Xerox Canada Itee, 1901 Trans-Canada Highway, North Service Rd., Dorval, PQ H9P 1J1, Canada

Tel: 514-939-3769

Xerox Canada Ltd., 205-15 Innovation Blvd., Saskatoon, SK S7N 1X8, Canada

Tel: 306-652-9606

Xerox Canada Ltd., 2400 College Ave., Ste. 102, Regina, SK S4P 1C8, Canada

Tel: 306-525-9881

Xerox Canada Ltd., 165 Drive-In Rd., Sault Ste. Marie, ON P6B 5X5, Canada
Tel: 705-254-5887
Xerox Canada Ltd., 333 Preston St., Ottawa, ON K1S 5N4, Canada
Tel: 613-230-1002
Xerox Canada Ltd., 150 Dufferin Ave., 10th Fl., Ste. 1000, London, ON N6A 5N6, Canada
Tel: 519-679-3769
Xerox Canada Ltd., 45 Goderich Rd., Unit 11, Hamilton, ON, L8E 4W8, Canada
Tel: 905-560-5900
Xerox Canada Ltd., 33 Bloor St. East, Toronto, ON M4W 3H1, Canada
Tel: 416-229-3769
Xerox Canada Ltd., 1300, 112-4th Ave., S.W. Sun Life Plaza III, East Tower, Calgary, AB, Canada
Tel: 403-260-8800
Xerox Canada Ltd., 5925 Airport Rd., 3rd Fl., Mississauga, ON L4V 1W1, Canada
Tel: 416-229-3769
Xerox Canada Ltd., 1949 Upper Water St., 4th Fl., Halifax, NS, B3J 3N3, Canada
Tel: 902-425-6400
Xerox Canada Ltd., Franklin & 52nd Sts., Yellowknife, NWT, X1A 2N1, Canada
Tel: 403-873-6066
Xerox Canada Ltd., 5650 Yonge St., North York, ON M2M 4G7, Canada
Xerox Canada Ltd., Scotia Centre, Ste. 901, 235 Water St., St. John's, ND, A1C 1B5, Canada
Tel: 709-722-5370
Xerox Canada Ltd., 400 Main St., Saint John, NB, E2K 4N5, Canada
Tel: 506-647-1000
Xerox Canada Ltd., 895 Waverley St., Winnipeg, MB R3T 5P4, Canada
Tel: 204-488-5100
Xerox Canada Ltd., 975 Fort St., Victoria, B.C. V8V 3K3, Canada
Tel: 250-356-3200
Xerox Canada Ltd., 1900-200 Burrand St., Vancouver, BC V6C 3M3, Canada
Tel: 604-668-2300
Xerox Canada Ltd., 10180 - 101 St., 11th Fl., Edmonton, AB, Canada T5J 3S4
Xerox Canada Ltd., 3060 Caravelle Drive, Missisauga, ON, L4V IL7, Canada
Tel: 416-229-3769

XILINX INC.

2100 Logic Drive, San Jose, CA, 95124-3400
Tel: (408) 559-7778 Fax: (408) 559-7114 Web site: www.xilinx.com
Programmable logic & related development systems software.
Xilinx Inc., 34 Hampel Crescent, Stittsville, ON K2S 1E4, Canada

XTRA CORPORATION

60 State Street, Boston, MA, 02109
Tel: (617) 367-5000 Fax: (617) 227-3173 Web site: www.xtracorp.com
Holding company: leasing.
Xtra Lease (Canada) Ltd., Canada

XYLAN CORPORATION

26707 West Agoura Road, Calabasas, CA, 91302
Tel: (818) 880-3500 Fax: (818) 880-3505 Web site: www.xylan.com
Mfr. Campus data network switches.
Xylan Corporation, Canadian Headquarters, Woodbridge, ON, Canada (Location: Montreal,PQ Canada)
Tel: 905-264-2787

YAHOO! INC.

3420 Central Expressway, Santa Clara, CA, 95051

Tel: (408) 731-3300 Fax: (408) 731-3301 Web site: www.yahoo-inc.com

Internet media company providing specialized content, free electronic mail and community offerings and commerce.

Yahoo! Inc., 156 Front St., West, Ste. 400, Toronto, ON M5J 2L6, Canada

Tel: 416-596-5129 Fax: 416-340-6541

YELLOW FREIGHT SYSTEM INC.

10990 Roe Ave., PO Box 7270, Overland Park, KS, 66207

Tel: (913) 345-3000 Fax: (913) 344-3246 Web site: www.yellowfreight.com

Commodity transportation.

Yellow Freight System of British Columbia, Vancouver, BC, Canada

Yellow Freight System of Ontario, Locations in Alberta, Calgary, Montreal, Ottawa, Quebec City, & Toronto, Canada

YORK INTERNATIONAL CORPORATION

PO Box 1592, York, PA, 17405-1592

Tel: (717) 771-7890 Fax: (717) 771-6212

Mfr. A/C, heating and refrigeration systems and equipment.

York Air Conditioning Ltd., 375 Matheson Blvd. E, Mississauga, ON L4Z 1X8, Canada

YOUNG & RUBICAM INC.

285 Madison Ave., New York, NY, 10017

Tel: (212) 210-3000 Fax: (212) 370-3796 Web site: www.yr.com

Advertising, public relations, direct marketing and sales promotion, corporate & product ID management.

Saint-Jacques Vallee Y&R, 1600 Rene Levesque Blvd. West, Ste. 1800, Montreal, PQ H3H 1P9, Canada

Young & Rubicam Ltd., 60 Bloor St. W, Toronto, ON M4W 1J2, Canada

ZIEBART INTERNATIONAL CORPORATION

1290 East Maple Road, Troy, MI, 48084

Tel: (810) 588-4100 Fax: (810) 588-0718 Web site: www.ziebart.com

Automotive aftermarket services.

Ziebart Canada Inc., 131 Spinaker Way, Unit 2, Concord, ON L4K 2T2, Canada

Tel: 905-761-1870 Fax: 905-761-1872

ZIPPO MANUFACTURING COMPANY

33 Barbour Street, Bradford, PA, 16701

Tel: (814) 368-2700 Fax: (814) 368-2874

Mfr. petroleum products, windproof lighters, silverware, advertising specialties.

Zippo Mfg. Co. of Canada Ltd., 6158 Allendale Ave., Niagara Falls, ON L2E 6V9, Canada

Tel: 905-358-3674 Fax: 905-358-9419

ZOLLNER PISTON COMPANY

2425 S. Coliseum Blvd., Ft. Wayne, IN, 46803

Tel: (219) 426-8081 Fax: (219) 423-2141

Mfr. pistons and related components.

Zollner Canada Ltd., 475 Oak St. E., Leamington, ON N8H 3W2, Canada

ZURN INDUSTRIES INC.

14801 Quorum Drive, Dallas, TX, 75240-7584

Tel: (972) 560-2000 Fax: (972) 560-2246 Web site: www.zurn.com

Mfr./sale of plumbing products and HVAC equipment; resource and fire sprinkler system construction.

Zurn Industries Ltd., 35 Leading Rd., Etobicoke, ON, Canada M9V 4B7

Cayman Islands

AON CORPORATION

123 North Wacker Drive, Chicago, IL, 60606

Tel: (312) 701-3000 Fax: (312) 701-3100 Web site: www.aon.com

Insurance brokers worldwide; underwrites accident & health insurance, specialty & professional insurance; & provides risk management consultation.

AON Insurance Managers (Cayman) Ltd., 3rd Fl., Anderson Square, Grand Cayman, Cayman Islands, British West Indies

Tel: 345-945-2888 Fax: 345-945-2889 Contact: Peter Jones

ARTHUR ANDERSEN & COMPANY

33 West Monroe Street, Chicago, IL, 60603

Tel: (312) 372-7100 Fax: (312) 507-0123 Web site: www.arthurandersen.com

Accounting & audit, tax & management consulting services.

Arthur Andersen LLP, Harbour Centre, PO Box 1929, Grand Cayman, Cayman Islands, BWI

Tel: 345-949-9400

ATWOOD OCEANICS, INC.

PO Box 218350, Houston, TX, 77218

Tel: (281) 492-2929 Fax: (281) 578-3253

Offshore drilling for gas and oil.

Atwood Oceanics Pacific Ltd., c/o Maples & Calder, PO Box 309, Ugland House, George Town, Grand Cayman, Cayman Islands, B.W.I.

Contact: Michael A. Cardenas, Pres. & Mng. Dir. Emp: 200

THE BANK OF NEW YORK

48 Wall Street, New York, NY, 10286

Tel: (212) 495-1784 Fax: (212) 495-2546 Web site: www.bankofny.com

Banking servces.

BNY Fund Management (Cayman) Ltd., Anchorage Centre, PO Box 2634GT, Grand Cayman, Cayman Islands, B.W.I.

The Bank of New York, Cayman Islands - All mail to PO Box 11243, New York, NY 10259

The Bank of New York Trust Co. (Cayman) Ltd., Butterfield House, Fort St., PO Box 705, Grand Cayman, Cayman Islands

BANKAMERICA CORPORATION

555 California Street, San Francisco, CA, 94104

Tel: (415) 622-3530 Fax: (415) 622-8467 Web site: www.bankamerica.com

Financial services.

Bank of America NT & SA, Anchorage Centre, Fort St., PO Box 1078, Georgetown, Grand Cayman, Cayman Islands, BWI

Tel: 415-622-8514 Fax: 415-953-5346 Contact: H. Terry Cush, SVP

BankAmerica Trust & Banking Corp. (Cayman) Ltd., Fort St., PO Box 1092, Georgetown, Grand Cayman, Cayman Islands, BWI

Tel: 345-949-7888 Fax: 345-949-7883 Contact: Charles Farrington, Mng. Dir.

BANKERS TRUST COMPANY

280 Park Ave., New York, NY, 10017

Tel: (212) 250-2500 Fax: (212) 250-2440 Web site: www.bankerstrust.com

Banking & investment services.

Bankers Trust (Cayman) Intl. Ltd., PO Box 1967 George Town, GFK Bldg., 2nd Fl.,North Church St., George Town, Grand Cayman, Cayman Islands, B.W.I.

Tel: 809-949-8229 Fax: 809-949-7866 Contact: Tim Haddleton, VP

BEST WESTERN INTERNATIONAL

6201 North 24th Place, Phoenix, AZ, 85106

Tel: (602) 957-4200 Fax: (602) 957-5740

International hotel chain.

BW Sammy's Airport Inn, 23 Owen Roberts Drive, Grand Cayman, Cayman Islands, BWI

Tel: 345-945-2100

BROWN BROTHERS HARRIMAN & COMPANY

59 Wall Street, New York, NY, 10005

Tel: (212) 483-1818 Fax: (212) 493-8526

Financial services.

Brown Brothers Harriman & Co., PO Box 694, Grand Cayman, Cayman Islands, BWI

BUCYRUS INTERNATIONAL, INC.

1100 Milwaukee Ave., South Milwaukee, WI, 53172

Tel: (414) 768-4000 Fax: (414) 768-4474

Mfr. of surface mining equipment, primarily walking draglines, electric mining shovels and blast hole drills.

Equipment Assurance Ltd., PO Box 2322, One Cayman House, North Church St., Grand Cayman, Cayman Islands, B.W.I.

Tel: 809-949-8184 Fax: 809-949-7228 Contact: John E. Smith, Vice President

CITICORP

399 Park Ave., New York, NY, 10043

Tel: (212) 559-1000 Fax: (212) 527-2066 Web site: www.citibank.com

International banking and financial services.

Citibank N.A., Cayman Islands, BWI

THE CLOROX COMPANY

1221 Broadway, PO Box 24305, Oakland, CA, 94623-1305

Tel: (510) 271-7000 Fax: (510) 832-1463

Mfr. soap & detergents, and domestic consumer packaged products.

American Sanitary Co. (Overseas) Inc., Grand Cayman, Cayman Islands, BWI

Amesco Ltd., Grand Cayman, Cayman Islands

DELOITTE TOUCHE TOHMATSU INTERNATIONAL

PO Box 820, Wilton, CT, 06897

Tel: (203) 761-3000 Fax: (203) 834-2200 Web site: www.u.s.deloitte.com or www.dtti.com

Accounting, audit, tax and management consulting services.

Deloitte & Touche, One Capital Place, George Town, (PO Box 1787) Grand Cayman, Cayman Islands, BWI

DELTA AIR LINES INC.

PO Box 20706, Atlanta, GA, 30320-6001

Tel: (404) 715-2600 Fax: (404) 715-5494 Web site: www.delta-air.com/index.html

Major worldwide airline; international air transport services.

Delta Air Lines Inc., Grand Cayman, Cayman Islands

DHL WORLDWIDE EXPRESS

333 Twin Dolphin Drive, Redwood City, CA, 94065

Tel: (650) 593-7474 Fax: (650) 593-1689 Web site: www.dhl.com

Worldwide air express carrier.

DHL Worldwide Express, Unit 4, Dolphin Centre, Eastern Ave., Georgetown, Grand Cayman, Cayman Islands

Tel: 809-949-8575

ERNST & YOUNG, LLP

787 Seventh Ave., New York, NY, 10019

Tel: (212) 773-3000 Fax: (212) 773-6350 Web site: www.eyi.com

Accounting and audit, tax and management consulting services.

Ernst & Young, Anderson Square Bldg., Shedden Rd., (PO Box 510) George Town, Grand Cayman, Cayman Islands, BWI

Tel: 809-949-8444 Fax: 809-949-8004 Contact: Carlyle B. McLaughlin

FEDERAL-MOGUL CORPORATION

26555 Northwestern Highway, PO Box 1966, Southfield, MI, 48034

Tel: (248) 354-7700 Fax: (248) 354-8983 Web site: www.federalmogul.com

Mfr./distributor precision parts for automobiles, trucks, farm and construction vehicles.

Federal-Mogul Cayman Investment Co. Ltd., Cayman Islands, BWI

FIRST UNION CORPORATION

One First Union Center, Charlotte, NC, 28288-0013

Tel: (704) 374-6565 Fax: (704) 374-3425 Web site: www.firstunion.com

Banking, financial and insurance services.

First Union National Bank, Grand Cayman, Cayman Islands

THE GILLETTE COMPANY

Prudential Tower Building, Boston, MA, 02199

Tel: (617) 421-7000 Fax: (617) 421-7123 Web site: www.gillette.com

Develop/mfr. personal care/use products: blades & razors, toiletries, cosmetics, stationery.

Oral-B Laboratories Islands Ltd., Grand Cayman, Cayman Islands, BWI

GOLDMAN SACHS & COMPANY

85 Broad Street, New York, NY, 10004

Tel: (212) 902-1000 Fax: (212) 902-3000 Web site: www.gs.com

Investment bankers; securities broker dealers.

Goldman Sachs (Cayman) Trust, Ltd., PO Box 896, Harbour Centre, 2nd Fl., George Town, Grand Cayman, Cayman Islands, BWI

Tel: 345-949-6770

HORWATH INTERNATIONAL

415 Madison Ave., New York, NY, 10017

Tel: (212) 838-5566 Fax: (212) 838-3636

Public accountants and auditors.

Morris Brankin & Co., West Wind Bldg. 3rd Fl., Grand Cayman, Cayman Islands

HYATT INTERNATIONAL CORPORATION

200 West Madison Street, Chicago, IL, 60606

Tel: (312) 750-1234 Fax: (312) 750-8578 Web site: www.hyatt.com

International hotel management.

Hyatt Regency Grand Cayman Resort & Villas Resort, Seven Mile Beach, Grand Cayman Islands, BWI

Tel: 345-949-1234 Fax: 345-949-8528

J.P. MORGAN & CO. INC.

60 Wall Street, New York, NY, 10260-0060

Tel: (212) 483-2323 Fax: (212) 648-5209 Web site: www.jpm.com

International banking services.

Morgan Trust Company of the Cayman Islands Ltd., c/o CIBC Bank & Trust Company (Cayman) Ltd., PO Box 694, George Town, Grand Cayman, Cayman Islands

Tel: 809-849-8666

KPMG PEAT MARWICK LLP

Three Chestnut Ridge Road, Montvale, NJ, 07645

Tel: (201) 307-7000 Fax: (201) 930-8617 Web site: www.kpmg.com

Accounting and audit, tax and management consulting services.

KPMG Peat Marwick, The Genesis Bldg., George Town, Grand Cayman, Cayman Islands, BWI

Tel: 345-9494-800 Fax: 345-9497-164 Contact: Theo Bullmore, Sr. Ptnr.

MARRIOTT INTERNATIONAL INC.

1 Marriott Drive, Washington, DC, 20058

Tel: (301) 380-3000 Fax: (301) 380-5181

Lodging, contract food and beverage service, and restaurants.

Grand Cayman Marriott Beach Resort, Grand Cayman, Cayman Islands

Tel: 345-949-0088

MARSH & McLENNAN COS INC.

1166 Ave. of the Americas, New York, NY, 10036-2774

Tel: (212) 345-5000 Fax: (212) 345-4808 Web site: www.marshmac.com

Insurance agents/brokers, pension and investment management consulting services.

J&H Marsh & McLennan (Cayman Islands) Ltd., PO Box 1051, Barclays House, 3rd Fl., Sheddon Rd., Georgetown, Grand Cayman, Cayman Islands, BWI

Tel: 345-949-7988 Fax: 345-949-7849 Contact: Wayne A.M.Cowan

J&H Marsh & McLennan Management Services (Cayman) Ltd., Harbour Centre - Fourth Fl., North Church St., Georgetown, Grand Cayman, Cayman Islands, BWI

Tel: 809-949-7466 Fax: 809-949-8096 Contact: N/A

MERRILL LYNCH & COMPANY, INC.

World Financial Center, North Tower, New York, NY, 10281-1323

Tel: (212) 449-1000 Fax: (212) 449-2892

Security brokers and dealers, investment and business services.

Merrill Lynch Bank and Trust Co. (Cayman) Ltd., 4th Fl., Harbour Centre, North Church St., PO Box 1164 GT, Grand Cayman, Cayman Islands

Tel: 345-949-8206 Fax: 345-949-8895

NATIONSBANK CORPORATION

100 North Tryon Street, Corporate Center, Charlotte, NC, 28255

Tel: (704) 386-5000 Fax: (704) 386-1709 Web site: www.nationsbank.com

Banking and financial services.

NationsBank Corp., PO Box 1040, Georgetown, Grand Cayman, Cayman Islands, BWI

NORTHERN TRUST CORPORATION

50 South LaSalle Street, Chicago, IL, 60675

Tel: (312) 630-6000 Fax: (312) 444-3378

Banking services.

Cayman Island Branch of the Northern Trust Corp., PO Box 501, Georgetown, Cayman Islands, BWI

OWENS-CORNING FIBERGLAS CORPORATION

Fiberglas Tower, Toledo, OH, 43659

Tel: (419) 248-8000 Fax: (419) 248-6227 Web site: www.housenet.com

Mfr. insulation, building materials, glass fiber products.

Owens-Corning Cayman Ltd., Cayman Islands, BWI

PFIZER INC.

235 East 42nd Street, New York, NY, 10017-5755

Tel: (212) 573-2323 Fax: (212) 573-7851 Web site: www.pfizer.com

Research-based, global health care company.

Bay Ridge Enterprises Ltd., Cayman Islands, BWI

JAFCO Japan Health Care Investment Co. Ltd., Cayman Islands, BWI

PRICEWATERHOUSECOOPERS LLP

1251 Ave. of the Americas, New York, NY, 10020

Tel: (212) 596-7000 Fax: (212) 790-6620 Web site: www.pwcglobal.com

Accounting and auditing, tax and management, and human resource consulting services.

Price Waterhouse Ltd., First Home Tower, British-American Centre, Dr. Roy's Drive, Georgetown, POB 258, Grand Cayman, Cayman Islands, BWI

Tel: 809-949-7944 Fax: 809-949-7352

RADISSON HOTELS INTERNATIONAL

Carlson Pkwy., PO Box 59159, Minneapolis, MN, 55459-8204

Tel: (612) 540-5526 Fax: (612) 449-3400

Hotels and resorts.

Radisson Resort Grand Cayman, Seven Mile Beach, West Bay Rd., Grand Cayman, Cayman Islands, BWI

REPUBLIC NATIONAL BANK OF NEW YORK

452 Fifth Ave., New York, NY, 10018

Tel: (212) 525-5000 Fax: (212) 525-6996 Web site: www.rnb.com

Banking services.

Republic National Bank of New York (Cayman) Ltd., Georgetown, Grand Cayman, Cayman Islands, BWI

STATE STREET BANK & TRUST COMPANY

225 Franklin Street, Boston, MA, 02101

Tel: (617) 786-3000 Fax: (617) 654-3386 Web site: www.statestreet.com

Banking & financial services.

State Street Cayman Trust Co. Ltd., PO Box 2508-GT, Georgetown, Grand Cayman, Cayman Islands, BWI

STIEFEL LABORATORIES INC.

255 Alhambra Circle, Ste. 1000, Coral Gables, FL, 33134

Tel: (305) 443-3807 Fax: (305) 443-3467

Mfr. pharmaceuticals, dermatological specialties.

Caribbean Chemical Co. Ltd., PO Box 996GT, Grand Cayman, Cayman Islands

TOOTSIE ROLL INDUSTRIES INC.

7401 S. Cicero Ave., Chicago, IL, 60629

Tel: (773) 838-3400 Fax: (773) 838-3534

Mfr. candies and chocolate products.

World Trade & Marketing Ltd., PO Box 1751, Grand Cayman, Cayman Islands, BWI

UNITED PARCEL SERVICE OF AMERICA, INC.

55 Glenlake Parkway, NE, Atlanta, GA, 30328

Tel: (404) 828-6000 Fax: (404) 828-6593 Web site: www.ups.com

International package-delivery service.

UPS / CES Ltd./Sta-mar Enterprises, 225 Eastern Ave., Grand Cayman, Cayman Islands

Tel: 345-949-8771 Fax: 345-949-7447

UNITED STATES TRUST COMPANY OF NEW YORK

114 West 47th Street, New York, NY, 10036

Tel: (212) 852-1000 Fax: (212) 852-1140 Web site: www.ustrust.com

Investment management company which also provides fiduciary and private banking services.

United States Trust Company of New York (Grand Cayman), Ltd., PO Box 694, Grand Cayman, Cayman Islands, BWI

Tel: 345-92-126/7

WACHOVIA BANK OF GEORGIA NA

PO Box 4148, Atlanta, GA, 30302-4148

Tel: (404) 332-5000 Fax: (404) 332-5735

Commercial banking.

Wachovia Bank of Georgia N.A., Grand Cayman, Cayman Islands

WACHOVIA CORPORATION

PO Box 3099, Winston-Salem, NC, 27150

Tel: (919) 770-5000 Fax: (919) 770-5931 Web site: www.wachovia.com

Commercial banking.

WSH Holdings, Ltd., Grand Cayman, Cayman Islands

WENDY'S INTERNATIONAL, INC.

428 West Dublin-Granville Roads, Dublin, OH, 43017

Tel: (614) 764-3100 Fax: (614) 764-3459

Fast food restaurant chain.

Wendy's International, Grand Cayman, Cayman Islands

WHIRLPOOL CORPORATION

2000 N. M-63, Benton Harbor, MI, 49022-2692

Tel: (616) 923-5000 Fax: (616) 923-5443 Web site: www.whirlpoolcorp.com

Mfr./market home appliances: Whirlpool, Roper, KitchenAid, Estate, and Inglis.

South American Sales Co., Grand Cayman, Cayman Islands

Central African Republic

LOUIS BERGER INTERNATIONAL INC.

100 Halsted Street, East Orange, NJ, 07019

Tel: (201) 678-1960 Fax: (201) 672-4284 Web site: www.louisberger.com

Consulting engineers, architects, economists & planners.

Louis Berger International Inc., B.P. 2030, Bangui, Central African Republic

FRITZ COMPANIES INC.

706 Mission Street, Ste. 900, San Francisco, CA, 94103

Tel: (415) 904-8360 Fax: (415) 904-8661 Web site: www.fritz.com

Integrated transportation, sourcing, distribution & customs brokerage services.

Fritz Companies Inc., Central African Republic

MOBIL CORPORATION

3225 Gallows Road, Fairfax, VA, 22037-0001

Tel: (703) 846-3000 Fax: (703) 846-4669 Web site: www.mobil.com

Petroleum and gas exploration and refining, mfr. petroleum products, chemicals and petrochemicals.

Mobil Oil SA, B.P. 576, Bangui, Central African Republic

WACKENHUT CORPORATION

4200 Wackenhut Drive, Ste. 100, Palm Beach Gardens, FL, 33410

Tel: (561) 622-5656 Fax: (561) 691-6736 Web site: www.wackenhut.com

Security systems & services.

Wackenhut Intl. Inc., Multiservices Conseil Gerance, Rue Mgr. Grandin, B.P. 1567, Bangui, Central African Republic

Tel: 236-616450 Fax: 236-614991

XEROX CORPORATION

800 Long Ridge Road, PO Box 1600, Stamford, CT, 06904

Tel: (203) 968-3000 Fax: (203) 968-4312 Web site: www.xerox.com

Mfr. document processing equipment, systems and supplies.

Sodexafric, BP 254, Bangui, Central African Republic

Tel: 236-61-37-35 Fax: 236-61-65-00

Chad

LOUIS BERGER INTERNATIONAL INC.

100 Halsted Street, East Orange, NJ, 07019

Tel: (201) 678-1960 Fax: (201) 672-4284 Web site: www.louisberger.com

Consulting engineers, architects, economists & planners.

Louis Berger International Inc., Boite Postale 1191, N'Djamena, Chad

CONOCO INC.

PO Box 2197, Houston, TX, 77252

Tel: (281) 293-1000 Fax: (281) 293-1440

Oil, gas, coal, chemicals and minerals.

Continental Oil Co. of Chad, Boite Postale 694, N'Djamena, Chad

DHL WORLDWIDE EXPRESS

333 Twin Dolphin Drive, Redwood City, CA, 94065

Tel: (650) 593-7474 Fax: (650) 593-1689 Web site: www.dhl.com

Worldwide air express carrier.

DHL Worldwide Express, Ave. Felix Eboue, Rond Point de L'Union, PO Box 34, N'Djamena, Chad

Tel: 235-51-4372

EXXON CORPORATION

225 E. John W. Carpenter Freeway, Irving, TX, 75062-2298

Tel: (972) 444-1000 Fax: (972) 444-1882 Web site: www.exxon.com

Petroleum exploration, production, refining; mfr. petroleum & chemicals products; coal & minerals.

Exxon - Exploration & Production, Chad

FRITZ COMPANIES INC.

706 Mission Street, Ste. 900, San Francisco, CA, 94103

Tel: (415) 904-8360 Fax: (415) 904-8661 Web site: www.fritz.com

Integrated transportation, sourcing, distribution & customs brokerage services.

Fritz Companies Inc., Chad

GANNETT FLEMING CORDDRY & CARPENTER INC.

PO Box 67100, Harrisburg, PA, 17106

Tel: (717) 763-7211 Fax: (717) 763-8150

Engineering consulting services.

Gannett Fleming Transportation Engineers, c/o USAID, Boite Postale 413, N'Djamena, Chad

WESTERN ATLAS INC.

10205 Westheimer, Houston, TX, 77251-1407

Tel: (713) 972-4000 Fax: (713) 952-9837 Web site: www.waii.com

Full service to the oil industry.

Western Geophysical, Rue Saint Martin 2309, Porte 737 Klemat, N'Djamena, Chad

XEROX CORPORATION

800 Long Ridge Road, PO Box 1600, Stamford, CT, 06904

Tel: (203) 968-3000 Fax: (203) 968-4312 Web site: www.xerox.com

Mfr. document processing equipment, systems and supplies.

Ndjamena Xerox, BP 717, Ave. Charles De Gaulle, Ndjamena, Chad

Channel Islands, U.K.

ALAMO RENT A CAR

110 Southeast Sixth Street, Fort Lauderdale, FL, 33301

Tel: (954) 522-0000 Fax: (954) 220-0120 Web site: www.alamo.com

Car rentals.

Alamo Rent A Car, Falles Hire Cars, Airport Rd., Guernsey & Jersey, Channel Islands

AMERICAN EXPRESS COMPANY

American Express Tower, World Financial Center, New York, NY, 10285-4765

Tel: (212) 640-2000 Fax: (212) 619-9802 Web site: www.americanexpress.com

Travel, travelers cheques, charge card & financial services.

AEOCC Management Co. Ltd., Jersey, Channel Islands, U.K.

American Express Exposure Management Ltd., Jersey, Channel Islands, U.K.

American Express Overseas Credit Corp. Ltd., Jersey, Channel Islands, U.K.

Cardmember Financial Services Ltd., Jersey, Channel Islands, U.K.

AON CORPORATION

123 North Wacker Drive, Chicago, IL, 60606

Tel: (312) 701-3000 Fax: (312) 701-3100 Web site: www.aon.com

Insurance brokers worldwide; underwrites accident & health insurance, specialty & professional insurance; & provides risk management consultation.

AON Insurance Managers (Guernsey) Ltd., Maison Trinity, Trinity Square, Guernsey GY1 1LT, Channel Islands, UK

Tel: 44-1481-707909 Fax: 44-1481-710551 Contact: Barry Seymour

AON Insurance Managers (Jersey) Ltd., Jersey, Channel Islands, UK

Tel: 44-1481-707909 Fax: 44-1481-710551 Contact: Barry Seymour

ARTHUR ANDERSEN & COMPANY

33 West Monroe Street, Chicago, IL, 60603

Tel: (312) 372-7100 Fax: (312) 507-0123 Web site: www.arthurandersen.com

Accounting & audit, tax & management consulting services.

Arthur Andersen & Co., 4th Fl., Forum House, Grenville St., St.Helier, Jersey JEZ 4UF, Channel Islands, UK

Tel: 44-1534-89944

ASSOCIATES FIRST CAPITAL CORPORATION

250 E. Carpenter Freeway, Irving, TX, 75062-2729

Tel: (972) 652-4000 Fax: (972) 652-7420 Web site: www.theassociates.com

Consumer financial services.

Associates First Capital Corporation, St. Helier, Jersey, Channel Islands, U.K.

BANKAMERICA CORPORATION

555 California Street, San Francisco, CA, 94104

Tel: (415) 622-3530 Fax: (415) 622-8467 Web site: www.bankamerica.com

Financial services.

Bank of America NT & SA - Trust Services, Union House, Union St., PO Box 120, St. Helier, Jersey, Channel Islands, U.K.

Tel: 44-1534-874431 Fax: 44-1534-878546 Contact: K.A.M. Robinson, Mng. Dir.

BankAmerica Trust Co. (Jersey) Ltd., 11 Esplanade (PO Box 193), St. Helier, Jersey, Channel Islands, U.K.

Tel: 44-1534-875471 Fax: 44-1534-30062 Contact: Robert Gautier, VP

BANKBOSTON CORPORATION

100 Federal Street, PO Box 1788, Boston, MA, 02110

Tel: (617) 434-2200 Fax: (617) 434-7547 Web site: www.bankboston.com

Banking & insurance services.

BankBoston (Guernsey) Ltd., Ste. 9, Valley House, Hirzel St., St. Peter Port, Guernsey GY 1 NP, Channel Islands, U.K.

Tel: 44-2481-723721 Fax: 44-1481-724133

BANKERS TRUST COMPANY

280 Park Ave., New York, NY, 10017

Tel: (212) 250-2500 Fax: (212) 250-2440 Web site: www.bankerstrust.com

Banking & investment services.

Bankers Trust Company, 40 Esplanade, St. Helier, Jersey JE2 3QB, Channel Islands, U.K.

Tel: 44-1534-22500 Fax: 44-1534-38907 Contact: Tom Frost, VP

BT Trustees (Jersey) Ltd., PO Box 634, Kensington Chambers, 46-50 Kensington Pl., St. Helier, Jersey JE4 8YP, Channel Islands, U.K.

Tel: 44-1534-855200 Fax: 44-1534-885228 Contact: Paul James, Division Head

BDO SEIDMAN, LLP

Two Prudential Plaza, 180 N. Stetson Ave., Ste. 2300, Chicago, IL, 60601

Tel: (312) 240-1236 Fax: (312) 240-3329 Web site: www.bdo.com

International accounting & financial consulting firm.

BDO Carnaby Barrett, Seaton House, Seaton Place, St. Helier, Jersey, Channel Islands, UK

Tel: 44-1534-215665 Fax: 44-1534-21987 Contact: John B. Barrett

BDO Reads Ltd., Commerce House, St. Peter Port, Guernsey, Channel Islands, UK

Tel: 44-1481-724561 Fax: 44-1481-711657 Contact: John C. Rowe

BROWN BROTHERS HARRIMAN & COMPANY

59 Wall Street, New York, NY, 10005

Tel: (212) 483-1818 Fax: (212) 493-8526

Financial services.

BBH Advisory Services Ltd., Westbourne, The Grance, St. Peter Port, Guernsey, Channel Islands, U.K.

CATERPILLAR INC.

100 NE Adams Street, Peoria, IL, 61629-6105

Tel: (309) 675-1000 Fax: (309) 675-1182 Web site: www.cat.com

Mfr. earth/material-handling and construction machinery and equipment and engines.

DUECOSA Ltd., Channel Islands, U.K.

THE CHASE MANHATTAN CORPORATION

World Headquarters, 270 Park Ave., New York, NY, 10017

Tel: (212) 270-6000 Fax: (212) 622-9030 Web site: www.chase.com

International banking and financial services.

Chase Manhattan Bank & Trust Co. (C.I.) Ltd., PO Box 127, Grenville St., St. Helier, Jersey, Channel Islands, U.K.

Tel: 44-1534-626062 Fax: 44-1534-626301

The Chase Manhattan Bank,, PO Box 92, Albert House, South Esplanade, St. Peter Port, Guernsey, Channel Islands, U.K.

CIGNA CORPORATION

One Liberty Place, Philadelphia, PA, 19192

Tel: (215) 761-1000 Fax: (215) 761-5008

Insurance, invest, health care and other financial services.

Cigna Intl. Fund Managers (CI) Ltd., St. Julian's House, St. Peter Port, Guernsey, Channel Islands, U.K.

CITICORP

399 Park Ave., New York, NY, 10043

Tel: (212) 559-1000 Fax: (212) 527-2066 Web site: www.citibank.com

International banking and financial services.

Citibank N.A., PO Box 104, 38 Esplanade, St. Helier, Jersey, Channel Islands, UK

Contact: Alan Noble, Mgr.

DELOITTE TOUCHE TOHMATSU INTERNATIONAL

PO Box 820, Wilton, CT, 06897

Tel: (203) 761-3000 Fax: (203) 834-2200 Web site: www.u.s.deloitte.com or www.dtti.com

Accounting, audit, tax and management consulting services.

Deloitte & Touche - Gurensey, St. Peter's House, Le Bordage, St. Peter Port, Guernsey, GY1 3HW, Channel Islands, U.K.

Deloitte & Touche - Jersey, Lord Coutanche House, 66-68 Esplanade, (PO Box 403) St. Helier, Jersey, Channel Islands, U.K. JE2 3QB

DHL WORLDWIDE EXPRESS

333 Twin Dolphin Drive, Redwood City, CA, 94065

Tel: (650) 593-7474 Fax: (650) 593-1689 Web site: www.dhl.com

Worldwide air express carrier.

DHL Worldwide Express, Bays 10/13, States Aiport, Firest, Guernsey GY8 0DJ, Channel Islands, UK

Tel: 44-1481-36596 Fax: 44-1481-35948

DHL Worldwide Express, c/o Hi-Speed Freight Services Ltd., Gargo Area, States Airport, St. Peter, JE3 7BP, Jersey, Channel Islands, UK

Tel: 44-1534-43350 Fax: 44-1534-46124

DYNATECH CORPORATION

3 New England Executive Park, Burlington, MA, 01803

Tel: (781) 272-6100 Fax: (781) 272-2304

Develop/mfr. communications equipment.

Dynatech Data Communications Ltd., St. Peter Port, Guernsey, Channel Islands, U.K.

Dynatech Medical Products Ltd., St. Peter Port, Guernsey, Channel Islands, U.K.

ERNST & YOUNG, LLP

787 Seventh Ave., New York, NY, 10019

Tel: (212) 773-3000 Fax: (212) 773-6350 Web site: www.eyi.com

Accounting and audit, tax and management consulting services.

Ernst & Young, PO Box 621, Le Gallais Chambers, 54 Bath St., St. Helier, Jersey JE4 8YD, Channel Islands, U.K.

Tel: 44-1534-501315 Fax: 44-1534-23265 Contact: Paul Firth

Ernst & Young, 14 New St., St. Peter Port, Guernsey 9Y1 4LE, Channel Islands, U.K.

Tel: 44-1534-723232 Fax: 44-1534-710091 Contact: Russell Morris

FIDELITY INVESTMENTS

82 Devonshire Street, Boston, MA, 02109

Tel: (617) 563-7000 Fax: (617) 476-6105 Web site: www.fidelity.com

Diversified financial services company offering investment management, retirement, brokerage, and shareholder services directly to individuals and institutions and through financial intermediaries.

Fidelity International Ltd., Jersey, Channel Islands, U.K.

FIRST NATIONAL BANK OF CHICAGO

One First National Plaza, Chicago, IL, 60670

Tel: (312) 732-4000 Fax: (312) 732-3620

Financial services.

First National Bank of Chicago (CI) Ltd., St. Peter Port House, Saumarcz St., St. Peter Port, Guernsey, Channel Islands, U.K.

HORWATH INTERNATIONAL

415 Madison Ave., New York, NY, 10017

Tel: (212) 838-5566 Fax: (212) 838-3636

Public accountants and auditors.

Featherstone Toole & Co., 16 Dumaresq St., St. Heller, Jersey JE2 3RL, Channel Islands, U.K.

KPMG PEAT MARWICK LLP

Three Chestnut Ridge Road, Montvale, NJ, 07645

Tel: (201) 307-7000 Fax: (201) 930-8617 Web site: www.kpmg.com

Accounting and audit, tax and management consulting services.

KPMG, 38/39 The Esplanade, St. Helier, Jersey, JE4 8WQ, Channel Islands, U.K.

KPMG, Orbis House, 20 New St., St. Peter Port, Guernsey, GY1 4AN, Channel Islands, U.K.

Tel: 44-1481-721000 Fax: 44-1481-722373 Contact: Stepheen A. Matheson, Sr. Ptnr.

MARSH & McLENNAN COS INC.

1166 Ave. of the Americas, New York, NY, 10036-2774

Tel: (212) 345-5000 Fax: (212) 345-4808 Web site: www.marshmac.com

Insurance agents/brokers, pension and investment management consulting services.

J&H Marsh & McLennan Management Services (Guersney) Ltd., Hirzel Court, St. Peter Port, Guernsey, Channel Islands, U.K. GY1 3HH

Tel: 44-1481-728136 Fax: 44-1481-713617 Contact: John Copeland

PRICEWATERHOUSECOOPERS LLP

1251 Ave. of the Americas, New York, NY, 10020

Tel: (212) 596-7000 Fax: (212) 790-6620 Web site: www.pwcglobal.com

Accounting and auditing, tax and management, and human resource consulting services.

Price Waterhouse Ltd., Barclaytrust House, Les Echelons, South Esplanade, St. Peter Port, Guersey, Channel Islands, U.K.

Tel: 44-2481-720077 Fax: 44-2481-711267

Price Waterhouse Ltd., Eagle House, Don Rd., St. Helier, Jersey, Channel Islands, U.K.

Tel: 44-1534-74222 Fax: 44-1534-36790

SYBRON INTERNATIONAL CORPORATION

411 E. Wisconsin Ave., Milwaukee, WI, 53202

Tel: (414) 274-6600 Fax: (414) 274-6561

Mfr. products for laboratories, professional orthodontic & dental markets.

Sonning Medical Manufacturing Ltd., 4 La rue Martel, rue des Pres Trading Estate, St. Saviour, Jersey JE2 7QR, Channel Islands, U.K.

Chile

3COM CORPORATION

5400 Bayfront Plaza, Santa Clara, CA, 95052-8145

Tel: (408) 764-5000 Fax: (408) 764-5001 Web site: www.3com.com

Develop/mfr. computer networking products & systems.

3Com Chile, Huerfanos, No. 835, piso 21, Edif. Opera, Santiago, Chile

Tel: 56-2-633-9242 Fax: 56-2-633-8935

3M

3M Center, St. Paul, MN, 55144-1000

Tel: (612) 733-1110 Fax: (612) 733-9973 Web site: www.mmm.com

Mfr. diversified products for industry, health care, imaging, communications, transport, safety, consumer, etc.

3M Chile SA, Santa Isabel 1001, Providencia, Casilla 3068, Correo Central, Santiago, Chile

Tel: 56-2-410-3000 Fax: 56-2-204-8900

ADYNO NOBEL

50 South Main Street, 11th Fl., Crossroads Tower, Salt Lake City, UT, 84144

Tel: (801) 364-4800 Fax: (801) 328-6525

Mfr. explosive supplies, accessories for industrial and military applications; aluminum granules.

Adyno Nobel Chile Ltda., Malaga 89, piso 4, Las Condes, Santiago, Chile

AIR EXPRESS INTERNATIONAL CORPORATION

120 Tokeneke Road, PO Box 1231, Darien, CT, 06820

Tel: (203) 655-7900 Fax: (203) 655-5779 Web site: www.aeilogistics.com

Air freight forwarder.

AEI/Air Express International, c/o Decapack, Av. Oceanica 9452, PO Box 54T, Pudahuel, Santiago, Chile

Tel: 56-2-2707-800 Fax: 56-2-6010-867

ALCOA (ALUMINUM CO OF AMERICA)

Alcoa Bldg., 425 Sixth Ave., Pittsburgh, PA, 15219-1850

Tel: (412) 553-4545 Fax: (412) 553-4498

World's leading producer of aluminum & alumina; mining, refining, smelting, fabricating & recycling.

Alusud Embalajes Chile, Ltda., Santiago, Chile

AMERICAN & EFIRD INC.

PO Box 507, Mt. Holly, NC, 28120

Tel: (704) 827-4311 Fax: (704) 822-6054

Mfr. industrial thread, yarn & consumer sewing products.

Hilos A&E de Chile, Alberto Pepper 1610-Renca, Casilla 444-V, Santiago, Chile

AMERICAN EXPRESS COMPANY

American Express Tower, World Financial Center, New York, NY, 10285-4765

Tel: (212) 640-2000 Fax: (212) 619-9802 Web site: www.americanexpress.com

Travel, travelers cheques, charge card & financial services.

American Express Bank Ltd., Agustinas 1360, Santiago, Chile

Tel: 56-2-699-3919 Fax: 56-2-672-7686 Contact: Kenneth R. Gentile Barrera, Sr. Dir.

AMERICAN RE-INSURANCE COMPANY

555 College Road East, Princeton, NJ, 08543

Tel: (609) 243-4200 Fax: (609) 243-4257

Reinsurance.

Reaseguradora Bernardo O'Higgins, Huerfanos 1189, piso 5, Santiago, Chile

AMMIRATI PURIS LINTAS

One Dag Hammarskjold Plaza, New York, NY, 10017

Tel: (212) 605-8000 Fax: (212) 605-4705 Web site: www.interpublic.com

International advertising agency.

Ammirati Puris Lintas Chile, Av. Ricardo Lyon 1623, Providencia, Santiago, Chile

Tel: 56-1-115-0125 Fax: 56-2-204-7556 Contact: Claudi Meneghello

AON CORPORATION

123 North Wacker Drive, Chicago, IL, 60606

Tel: (312) 701-3000 Fax: (312) 701-3100 Web site: www.aon.com

Insurance brokers worldwide; underwrites accident & health insurance, specialty & professional insurance; & provides risk management consultation.

AON Claro, Santa Cruz SA, Hendaya 60, piso 7, Santiago, Chile

Tel: 56-2-331-5100 Fax: 56-2-331-5116 Contact: Carlos Bello

ARBOR ACRES FARM INC.

439 Marlborough Road, Glastonbury, CT, 06033

Tel: (860) 633-4681 Fax: (860) 633-2433

Producers of male & female broiler breeders, commercial egg layers.

Agricola Ariztia Ltda., Casilla 90, Melipilla, Chile

AVERY DENNISON CORPORATION

150 N. Orange Grove Blvd., Pasadena, CA, 91103

Tel: (626) 304-2000 Fax: (626) 792-7312 Web site: www.averydennison.com

Mfr. pressure-sensitive adhesives & materials, office products, labels, tags, retail systems, Carter's Ink & specialty chemicals.

Avery Dennison Chile, Chile

AVIS, INC.

900 Old Country Road., Garden City, NY, 11530

Tel: (516) 222-3000 Fax: (516) 222-4381 Web site: www.avis.com

Car rental services.

Avis Rent a Car System Inc., Elidoro Yanez 869, Santiago, Chile

AVON PRODUCTS INC.

1345 Ave. of the Americas, New York, NY, 10105-0196

Tel: (212) 282-5000 Fax: (212) 282-6049 Web site: www.avon.com

Mfr./distributor beauty & related products, fashion jewelry, gifts & collectibles.

Cosmeticos Avon S.A., Av. Central 350, Parque Indusrtial Aeropuerto, Quilicura, Santiago, Chile

Tel: 56-2-603-5372 Fax: 56-2-603-5355 Contact: Francis Guzman, Dir.

BAKER & McKENZIE

One Prudential Plaza, 130 East Randolph Drive, Ste. 2500, Chicago, IL, 60601

Tel: (312) 861-8000 Fax: (312) 861-2899 Web site: www.bakerinfo.com

International legal services.

Cruzat, Ortuzar & Mackenna (Baker McKenzie), Nueva Tajamar 481, Torre North, piso 21, Las Condes, Santiago, Chile

Tel: 56-2-367-7000 Fax: 56-2-362-9875 Contact: Carlos Cruzat, Ptnr.

BAKER HUGHES INCORPORATED

3900 Essex Lane, Ste. 1200, Houston, TX, 77027

Tel: (713) 439-8600 Fax: (713) 439-8699 Web site: www.bakerhughes.com

Develop & apply technology to drill, complete & produce oil and natural gas wells; provide separation systems to petroleum, municipal, continuous process & mining industries.

Baker Transworld Inc., L. Navarro 1066 ofc 401, Casilla 40-0, Punta Arenas, Chile

Tel: 56-61-241124 Fax: 56-61-248169

BANKAMERICA CORPORATION

555 California Street, San Francisco, CA, 94104

Tel: (415) 622-3530 Fax: (415) 622-8467 Web site: www.bankamerica.com

Financial services.

Bank of America - Latin America Area Office, Agustinas 1465, Santiago, Chile

Tel: 56-2-243-7000 Fax: 56-2-243-7230 Contact: Jaime J. Chocano, EVP

Bank of America NT & SA, Agustinas 1465, Santiago, Chile

Tel: 56-2-243-7210 Fax: 56-2-243-7393 Contact: Marco A. Gomez, SVP

BANKBOSTON CORPORATION

100 Federal Street, PO Box 1788, Boston, MA, 02110

Tel: (617) 434-2200 Fax: (617) 434-7547 Web site: www.bankboston.com

Banking & insurance services.

BankBoston - Santiago, Moneda 799, Casilla 1946, Correo Central, Santiago, Chile (Regional offices: Concepción, Valpariso, Viño Del Mar)

Tel: 56-2-686-0000 Fax: 56-2-686-0770 Contact: Jorge Ramirez, Gen. Mgr.

BANKERS TRUST COMPANY

280 Park Ave., New York, NY, 10017

Tel: (212) 250-2500 Fax: (212) 250-2440 Web site: www.bankerstrust.com

Banking & investment services.

Bankers Trust Company, Av. el Bosque, Sur 130 piso 5, Las Condes, Santiago, Chile

Tel: 56-2-203-1330 Fax: 56-2-203-1331 Contact: Patricio Parodi

Consorcio, Av. el Bosque, Sur 180 piso 3, Santiago, Chile

Tel: 56-2-230-4561 Fax: 56-2-230-4050 Contact: Guillermo Martinez Barros

BATES WORLDWIDE INC.

405 Lexington Ave., New York, NY, 10174

Tel: (212) 297-7000 Fax: (212) 986-0270 Web site: www.batesww.com

Advertising, marketing, public relations & media consulting.

Azocar, Morrison, Walker (AMW), Triana 873, Providenita, Santiago, Chile

Tel: 56-2-240-2700 Fax: 56-2-244-4991 Contact: P. Friedmann, Mgr.

BAX GLOBAL CORPORATION

16808 Armstrong Ave., PO Box 19571, Irvine, CA, 92623

Tel: (714) 752-4000 Fax: (714) 852-1488 Web site: www.bax.com

Air freight forwarder.

BAX Global, Las Urbinas 53, Office 103, Providencia, Santiago, Chile

Tel: 56-2-655-0377 Fax: 56-2-232-5832

BBDO WORLDWIDE

1285 Ave. of the Americas, New York, NY, 10019

Tel: (212) 459-5000 Fax: (212) 459-6645 Web site: www.bbdo.com

Multinational group of advertising agencies.

BBDO de Chile, Santiago, Chile

BDO SEIDMAN, LLP

Two Prudential Plaza, 180 N. Stetson Ave., Ste. 2300, Chicago, IL, 60601

Tel: (312) 240-1236 Fax: (312) 240-3329 Web site: www.bdo.com

International accounting & financial consulting firm.

BDO Jeria y Asociados, Monjitas 527 pisos 14-15, Casilla 3443 Santiago, Chile

Tel: 56-2-639-4063 Fax: 56-2-633-2875 Contact: Orlando Jeria

BECHTEL GROUP INC.

50 Beale Street, PO Box 3965, San Francisco, CA, 94105-1895

Tel: (415) 768-1234 Fax: (415) 768-9038 Web site: www.bechtel.com

General contractors in engineering & construction.

Bechtel International Corp., Nueva de Lyon 72, 4th Fl., Providencia, Santiago, Chile

Tel: 56-2-234-4747 Fax: 56-2-232-5208

BELLSOUTH INTERNATIONAL

1155 Peachtree Street NE, Ste. 400, Atlanta, GA, 30367

Tel: (404) 249-4800 Fax: (404) 249-4880 Web site: www.bellsouth.com

Mobile communications, telecommunications network systems.

BellSouth Chile, Av. El Bosque Norte 134, Las Condes, Santiago, Chile

Tel: 56-2-339-5000 Fax: 56-2-234-2215

BENTLY NEVADA CORPORATION

1617 Water Street, PO Box 157, Minden, NV, 89423

Tel: (702) 782-3611 Fax: (702) 782-9259

Electronic monitoring systems.

Turbomecanica Ltda., Casilla 90-C, Concepcion, Chile

BEST WESTERN INTERNATIONAL

6201 North 24th Place, Phoenix, AZ, 85106

Tel: (602) 957-4200 Fax: (602) 957-5740

International hotel chain.

BW Hotel Central, 21 De Mayo 425, Arica, Chile

Tel: 56-58-252-575

BESTFOODS, INC.

700 Sylvan Ave., International Plaza, Englewood Cliffs, NJ, 07632-9976

Tel: (201) 894-4000 Fax: (201) 894-2186 Web site: www.bestfoods.com

Consumer foods products; corn refining.

Industrias de Maiz y Alimentos S.A., Avda Vitacura 4380, Vitacura, Santiago, Chile

Tel: 56-2-290-0000 Fax: 56-2-228-4599 Contact: Luis E. Robles, Mgr.

BETZDEARBORN

4636 Somerton Road, PO Box 3002, Trevose, PA, 19053-6783

Tel: (215) 953-2568 Fax: (215) 953-5524 Web site: www.betzdearborn.com

Mfr. water/wastewater and process system treatment chemicals and services.

BetzDearborn de Chile Ltda., Avda La Travesia 6967, Parque Industrial Inverterra, Pudahuel, Santiago, Chile

SAMUEL BINGHAM COMPANY

127 East Lake Street, Ste. 300, Bloomgindale, IL, 60108

Tel: (630) 924-9250 Fax: (630) 924-0469 Web site: www.binghamrollers.com

Print and industrial rollers and inks.

Davis Graphics Ltda., Av. Ramon Freire 6588, Casilla 693, Santiago, Chile

BLACK & DECKER CORPORATION

701 E. Joppa Road, Towson, MD, 21286

Tel: (410) 716-3900 Fax: (410) 716-2933 Web site: www.blackanddecker.com

Mfr. power tools and accessories, security hardware, small appliances, fasteners, information systems & services.

Black & Decker Chile, Chile, All mail to U.S. address

BLOOMBERG L.P.

499 Park Ave., New York, NY, 10022

Tel: (212) 318-2000 Fax: (212) 940-1954 Web site: www.bloomberg.com

Publishes magazines and provides TV, radio and newspaper wire services.

Bloomberg L.P., Santiago, Chile

Tel: 56-2-639-7633

BOART LONGYEAR CO.

2340 West 1700 South, Salt Lake City, UT, 84104

Tel: (801) 972-6430 Fax: (801) 977-3372

Mfr. diamond drills, concrete cutting equipment and drill services.

Longyear Co., Casilla 15118, Las Dalias 2900, Macul, Santiago, Chile

BOOZ ALLEN & HAMILTON INC.

8283 Greensboro Drive, McLean, VA, 22102

Tel: (703) 902-5000 Fax: (703) 902-3333 Web site: www.bah.com

International management and technology consultants.

Booz Allen & Hamilton de Chile, Huerfanos 835 piso 21, Santiago, Chile

Tel: 56-2-639-4623 Fax: 56-2-633-4338

BOYDEN CONSULTING CORPORATION

100 Park Ave., 34th Floor, New York, NY, 10017

Tel: (212) 980-6534 Fax: (212) 980-6147 Web site: www.boyden.com

Executive search.

Boyden Associates Ltd., La Concepcion 81, Of. 607 Providencia, Santiago, Chile

Tel: 56-2-236-4293

BOZELL WORLDWIDE

40 West 23rd Street, New York, NY, 10010

Tel: (212) 727-5000 Fax: (212) 645-9173 Web site: www.bozell.com

Advertising, marketing, public relations and media consulting.

Unitros Chile S.A., Rapallo 4322, Las Condes, Santiago, Chile

Tel: 56-2-228-6016 Fax: 56-2-208-6727 Contact: Fernando Figueroa, Pres.

BRANSON ULTRASONICS CORPORATION

41 Eagle Road, Danbury, CT, 06813-1961

Tel: (203) 796-0400 Fax: (203) 796-2285

Mfr. plastics assembly equipment, ultrasonic cleaning equipment.

Codesonic, Santiago, Chile

Tel: 56-2-683-2889 Fax: 56-2-683-7254

BRISTOL-MYERS SQUIBB COMPANY

345 Park Ave., New York, NY, 10154

Tel: (212) 546-4000 Fax: (212) 546-4020 Web site: www.bms.com

Pharmaceutical and food preparations, medical and surgical instruments.

Bristol-Myers Squibb - Chile, Av. Balmaceda 2174, Santiago de Chile, Chile

BUCYRUS INTERNATIONAL, INC.

1100 Milwaukee Ave., South Milwaukee, WI, 53172

Tel: (414) 768-4000 Fax: (414) 768-4474

Mfr. of surface mining equipment, primarily walking draglines, electric mining shovels and blast hole drills.

Bucyrus International (Chile) Ltd., Av. Suecia 164 B, Providencia, Santiago, Chile

Tel: 56-2-2321166 Fax: 56-2-2326234 Contact: Jose Cuadrado, Gen. Mgr.

BUDGET RENT A CAR CORPORATION

4225 Naperville Road, Lisle, IL, 60532

Tel: (630) 955-1900 Fax: (630) 955-7799 Web site: www.budgetrentacar.com

Car and truck rental system.

Budget Rent A Car, Merino Benitez International Airport, Santiago, Chile

Tel: 56-2-26-901-384

LEO BURNETT CO., INC.

35 West Wacker Drive, Chicago, IL, 60601

Tel: (312) 220-5959 Fax: (312) 220-6533 Web site: www.leoburnett.com

International advertising agency.

Leo Burnett - Chile SA, Suecia 791, Santiago, Chile

BURSON-MARSTELLER

230 Park Ave., New York, NY, 10003-1566

Tel: (212) 614-4000 Fax: (212) 614-4262 Web site: www.bm.com

Public relations/public affairs consultants.

Burson-Marsteller, Av. El Bosque Norte 0440, Of. 404, Santiago, Chile

Tel: 56-2-203-5085 Fax: 56-2-203-5108 Emp: 16

C-COR ELECTRONICS INC.

60 Decibel Road, State College, PA, 16801

Tel: (814) 238-2461 Fax: (814) 238-4065 Web site: www.c-cor.com

Design/mfr. amplifiers, fiber optics electronic equipment for data and cable TV systems.

C-Cor Chile, Pedro DeValdivia, 1646 Providencia, Santiago, Chile

Tel: 56-2-340-7801 Fax: 56-2-274-4107 Contact: Steve Traynor, Mgr.

CARGILL, INC.

15407 McGinty Road, Minnetonka, MN, 55440-5625

Tel: (612) 742-7575 Fax: (612) 742-7393 Web site: www.cargill.com

Food products, feeds, animal products.

Cargill Chile Ltda., Fidel Oteiza 1921, piso 5, Santiago, Chile

CARRIER CORPORATION

One Carrier Place, Farmington, CT, 06034-4015

Tel: (860) 674-3000 Fax: (860) 679-3010 Web site: www.carrier.com

Mfr./distributor/services A/C, heating & refrigeration equipment.

Carrier Chile, Santiago de Chile

Tel: 56-2-553-3930 Fax: 56-2-553-3969

CATERPILLAR INC.

100 NE Adams Street, Peoria, IL, 61629-6105

Tel: (309) 675-1000 Fax: (309) 675-1182 Web site: www.cat.com

Mfr. earth/material-handling and construction machinery and equipment and engines.

Caterpillar Andes S.A., Santiago, Chile

THE CHASE MANHATTAN CORPORATION

World Headquarters, 270 Park Ave., New York, NY, 10017

Tel: (212) 270-6000 Fax: (212) 622-9030 Web site: www.chase.com

International banking and financial services.

Chase Manhattan Bank NA, Casilla 9192, Centro Comercial de la Merced, MacIver y Huerfanos, Santiago, Chile

The Chase Manhattan Bank, Santiago Branch, Agustinas 1235, piso 5, Santiago, Chile

Tel: 56-2-699-0068 Fax: 56-2-690-5177 Contact: Herman Isotta, Gen. Mgr.

CHESTERTON BINSWANGER INTERNATIONAL

Two Logan Square, 4th Floor, Philadelphia, PA, 19103-2759

Tel: (215) 448-6000 Fax: (215) 448-6238

Real estate & related services.

Fuenzalida Promotora Inmobilaria, Malaga 115, piso 2, Santiago, Chile

A.W. CHESTERTON COMPANY

225 Fallon Road, Stoneham, MA, 02180

Tel: (781) 438-7000 Fax: (781) 438-8971 Web site: www.stoneham.chesterton.com

Packing gaskets, sealing products systems, etc.

Chesterton International Chile Ltd., Concepcion, Chile

THE CHUBB CORPORATION

15 Mountain View Road, Warren, NJ, 07061-1615

Tel: (908) 580-2000 Fax: (908) 580-3606 Web site: www.chubb.com

Holding company: property/casualty insurance.

Chubb do Brasil Companhia de Seguros Generales, SA, Gertrudis Echnique 30-4 piso, Las Condes, Santiago, Chile

Tel: 56-1-206-2191 Fax: 56-2-206-2735

CIGNA CORPORATION

One Liberty Place, Philadelphia, PA, 19192

Tel: (215) 761-1000 Fax: (215) 761-5008

Insurance, invest, health care and other financial services.

Cigna Compania de Seguros (Chile) SA, Calle Nueva York 80, Casilla 493, Santiago, Chile

Cigna Compania de Seguros de Vida (Chile) SA, Calle Nueva York 80, Casilla 493, Santiago, Chile

Cigna Salud Isapre SA, Nueva York 80, piso 11, Casilla 493, Santiago, Chile

Esis Intl. Asesorias Ltda., Moneda 1123, Casilla 987, Santiago, Chile

Institucion de Salud Luis Pasteur SA, Almirante Lorenzo Gotuzzo 70, Santiago, Chile

Inversiones INA Ltda., Calle Nueva York 80, Santiago, Chile

CISCO SYSTEMS, INC.

170 Tasman Drive, San Jose, CA, 95134-1706

Tel: (408) 526-4000 Fax: (408) 526-4100 Web site: www.cisco.com

Develop/mfr./market computer hardware and software networking systems.

Cisco Systems Chile, Nueva Tajamar 555, Ofi. #1902, Las Condes, Santiago, Chile

Tel: 56-2-365-0655 Fax: 56-2-365-0653 Contact: N/A

CITICORP

399 Park Ave., New York, NY, 10043

Tel: (212) 559-1000 Fax: (212) 527-2066 Web site: www.citibank.com

International banking and financial services.

Citibank N.A., Providencia 2653, piso 3, Av. Andres Bello 2687, piso 7, Santiago, Chile

Tel: 56-2-338-3000 Fax: 56-2-338-3013 Contact: Ariel Sevi, Pres.

Citibank N.A., Ahumada 48, PO Box 2125, Santiago, Chile

Contact: Rodrigo Alvarez

THE CLOROX COMPANY

1221 Broadway, PO Box 24305, Oakland, CA, 94623-1305

Tel: (510) 271-7000 Fax: (510) 832-1463

Mfr. soap & detergents, and domestic consumer packaged products.

Clorox Chile Sa, Santiago, Chile

THE COASTAL CORPORATION

Nine Greenway Plaza, Houston, TX, 77046-0995

Tel: (713) 877-1400 Fax: (713) 877-6752 Web site: www.coastalcorp.com

Oil refining, natural gas, related services; independent power production.

Coastal Petroleum N. V., Santiago, Chile

THE COCA-COLA COMPANY

P.O. Drawer 1734, Atlanta, GA, 30301

Tel: (404) 676-2121 Fax: (404) 676-6792 Web site: www.coca-cola.com

Mfr./marketing/distributor soft drinks, syrups & concentrates, juice & juice-drink products.

The Coca-Cola Export Co., Casilla 3755, Santiago, Chile

COLUMBIA PICTURES INDUSTRIES INC.

10202 West Washington Blvd., Culver City, CA, 90232

Tel: (310) 244-4000 Fax: (310) 244-2626 Web site: www.sony.com

Producer and distributor of motion pictures.

Columbia Pictures of Chile Inc., Huerfanos 786, Casilla 9003, Santiago, Chile

COMPAQ COMPUTER CORPORATION

20555 State Highway 249, PO Box 692000, Houston, TX, 77269-2000

Tel: (713) 370-0670 Fax: (713) 514-1740 Web site: www.compaq.com

Develop/mfr. personal computers.

Compaq Computer de Chile, Av. 11 de Septiembre 1901- piso 1, Edif. Torreciudad, Providencia, Santiago, Chile

Tel: 56-2-200-8100 Fax: 56-2-252-0540

COMPUTER ASSOCIATES INTERNATIONAL INC.

One Computer Associates Plaza, Islandia, NY, 11788

Tel: (516) 342-5224 Fax: (516) 342-5329 Web site: www.cai.com

Integrated software for enterprise computing and information management, application development, manufacturing, financial applications and professional services.

Computer Associates de Chile Ltd., Av. Andres Bello 2777, Of. 1501, Edif. La Industria, Santiago, Chile

Tel: 56-2-203-3151

CONAGRA INC.

One ConAgra Drive, Omaha, NE, 68102-5001

Tel: (402) 595-4000 Fax: (402) 595-4595 Web site: www.conagra.com

Prepared/frozen foods, grains, flour, animal feeds, agri chemicals, poultry, meat, dairy products, including Healthy Choice, Butterball and Hunt's.

ConAgra Inc., Santiago, Chile

CORESTATES BANK

1500 Market Street, Philadelphia, PA, 19101

Tel: (215) 973-3100 Fax: (215) 786-8899 Web site: www.corestates.com

Primary international businesses; correspondent banking and trade services.

Corestates Bank, Amunategui 277, Of. 700, Santiago, Chile

CROWN CORK & SEAL COMPANY, INC.

One Crown Way, Philadelphia, PA, 19154-4599

Tel: (215) 698-5100 Fax: (215) 698-5201

Mfr. cans, bottle caps; filling & packaging machinery.

Crown Cork de Chile SAI, Camino de Milipilla 10, Santiago, Chile

CYPRUS AMAX MINERALS COMPANY

9100 East Mineral Circle, Englewood, CO, 80112

Tel: (303) 643-5000 Fax: (303) 643-5048 Web site: www.cyprusamax.com

Mining company supplying molybdenum (used in steelmaking).

Sociedad Chilena de Litio Ltda., Hendaya N 60, piso 3 er Of. 302, Las Condes, Santiago, Chile

Tel: 56-2-270-6500 Fax: 56-2-2706599

D'ARCY MASIUS BENTON & BOWLES INC. (DMB&B)

1675 Broadway, New York, NY, 10019

Tel: (212) 468-3622 Fax: (212) 468-2987 Web site: www.dmbb.com

Full service international advertising and communications group.

DMB&B, Kenedy Av. 5116, 4º piso, Vitacuram, Santiago de Chile

Tel: 56-2-242-1920 Fax: 56-2-242-1910 Contact: Juan Carlos Escobedo, Gen. Mgr.

DAMES & MOORE GROUP

911 Wilshire Boulevard, Los Angeles, CA, 90017

Tel: (213) 683-1560 Fax: (213) 628-0015 Web site: www.dames.com

Engineering, environmental and construction management services.

Dames & Moore, Av. 11 de Septiembre 1860, piso 17, Santiago, Chile

DATA GENERAL CORPORATION

4400 Computer Drive, Westboro, MA, 01580

Tel: (508) 898-5000 Fax: (508) 366-1319 Web site: www.dg.com

Design, mfr. general purpose computer systems & peripheral products & services.

Data General Chile Ltda., Suecia 392, Providencia, Santiago, Chile

DDB NEEDHAM WORLDWIDE INC.

437 Madison Ave., New York, NY, 10022

Tel: (212) 415-2000 Fax: (212) 415-3417

Advertising agency.

Zegers DDB Needham, Santiago, Chile

DEKALB GENETICS CORP.

3100 Sycamore Road, DeKalb, IL, 60115-9600

Tel: (815) 758-3461 Fax: (815) 758-3711 Web site: www.dekalb.com

Develop/produce hybrid corn, sorghum, sunflower seed, varietal soybeans, alfalfa.

Agricola Nacional S.A.C. el., Casilla 336, Correo 21, Almirante Pastene N. 300, Santiago, Chile

Tel: 56-2-235-2866 Fax: 56-2-235-8634 Contact: Dr. Fernando Martinez Perez-Canto

DELL COMPUTER CORPORATION

One Dell Way, Round Rock, TX, 78682-2222

Tel: (512) 338-4400 Fax: (512) 728-3653 Web site: www.dell.com

Direct marketer & supplier of computer systems.

Dell Computer De Chile Corp., Coyancura 2283, of. 302, Providencia, Santiago, Chile

Tel: 56-2-685-6800 Fax: 56-2-232-4290 Contact: Mario Henriguez, Mng. Dir.

DELOITTE TOUCHE TOHMATSU INTERNATIONAL

PO Box 820, Wilton, CT, 06897

Tel: (203) 761-3000 Fax: (203) 834-2200 Web site: www.u.s.deloitte.com or www.dtti.com

Accounting, audit, tax and management consulting services.

Deloitte & Touche, Mac Iver 225, (Casilla 3147) Santiago 1, Chile

DHL WORLDWIDE EXPRESS

333 Twin Dolphin Drive, Redwood City, CA, 94065

Tel: (650) 593-7474 Fax: (650) 593-1689 Web site: www.dhl.com

Worldwide air express carrier.

DHL Worldwide Express, San Francisco 301, Santiago, Chile

Tel: 56-2-638-4502

DORR-OLIVER INC.

612 Wheeler's Farm Road, PO Box 3819, Milford, CT, 06460

Tel: (203) 876-5400 Fax: (203) 876-5432

Mfr. process equipment for food, pulp & paper, mineral & chemicals industry; & municipal/industry waste treatment.

Dorr-Oliver de Chile Ltda., Casilla 14711, Moneda 1040, Santiago, Chile

THE DOW CHEMICAL COMPANY

2030 Dow Center, Midland, MI, 48674

Tel: (517) 636-1000 Fax: (517) 636-3228 Web site: www.atdow.com

Mfr. chemicals, plastics, pharmaceuticals, agricultural products, consumer products.

Dow Quimica Chilena SA, Suecia 281, Casilla 14590, Providencia, Santiago, Chile

DRAKE BEAM MORIN INC.

101 Huntington Ave., Boston, MA, 02199

Tel: (617) 450-9860 Fax: (617) 267-2011 Web site: www.dbm.com

Human resource management consulting & training.

DBM Chile, Av. Del Bosque Norte 0440, piso 13 Office 1302, Las Condes, Santiago de Chile, Santiago, Chile

Tel: 56-2-245-0707 Fax: 56-2-246-4035

DURACELL INTERNATIONAL INC.

Berkshire Industrial Park, Bethel, CT, 06801

Tel: (203) 796-4000 Fax: (203) 796-4745

Mfr. batteries.

Duracell Chile, Roman Diaz 1271, Providencia, Santiago, Chile

EASTMAN KODAK COMPANY

343 State Street, Rochester, NY, 14650

Tel: (716) 724-4000 Fax: (716) 724-0663

Develop/mfr. photo & chemicals products, information management/video/copier systems, fibers/plastics for various industry.

Kodak Chilena SAF, Alonso Ovalle 1180, Casilla 2797, Santiago, Chile

LOOK, Eleodoro Yanez 1804, Santiago, Chile

Muebles Andes, Rura 68 No. 6910, Casilla 547, Santiago, Chile

Nueva Vision, Hermando de Aguirre 939, Casilla 9727, Santiago, Chile

ECOLAB INC.

Ecolab Center, 370 N. Wabasha Street, St. Paul, MN, 55102

Tel: (612) 293-2233 Fax: (612) 225-3105 Web site: www.ecolab.com

Develop/mfr. premium cleaning, sanitizing and maintenance products and services for the hospitality, institutional, and residential markets.

Ecolab Ltd., Santiago, Chile

Tel: 56-2-738-6111

J.D. EDWARDS & COMPANY

One Technology Way, Denver, CO, 80237

Tel: (303) 334-4000 Fax: (303) 334-4970 Web site: www.jdedwards.com.

Computer software products.

Mekano, Dario Urzua 2165, Profidencia, Santiago, Chile

Tel: 56-2-233-4040 Fax: 56-2-232-3319

EFCO

1800 NE Broadway Ave., Des Moines, IA, 50316-0386

Tel: (515) 266-1141 Fax: (515) 266-7970

Mfr. systems for concrete construction.

EFCO, Av. General San Martin 7400, Quilicura, Santiago, Chile

EMERY WORLDWIDE

One Lagoon Drive, Ste. 400, Redwood City, CA, 94065

Tel: (650) 596-9600 Fax: (650) 596-7901 Web site: www.emeryworld.com

Freight transport, global logistics and air cargo.

Emery Worldwide de Chile, Emery House, Enrique Nercaseux 2380, Providencia, Santiago, Chile

EQUIFAX INC.

PO Box 4081, Atlanta, GA, 30302

Tel: (404) 885-8000 Fax: (404) 888-5452 Web site: www.equifax.com

Information and knowledge-based solutions.

Dicom SA, Miraflores 353, piso 8, Casilla 313-V, Santiago, Chile

Equifax de Chile SA, Amunategui 277, piso 3, Santiago, Chile

ERICO PRODUCTS INC.

34600 Solon Road, Cleveland, OH, 44139

Tel: (440) 248-0100 Fax: (440) 248-0723

Mfr. electric welding apparatus & hardware, metal stampings, specialty fasteners.

Erico-Chile Ltda., Grajales 2948, Casilla 16.666, Santiago, Chile

ERNST & YOUNG, LLP

787 Seventh Ave., New York, NY, 10019

Tel: (212) 773-3000 Fax: (212) 773-6350 Web site: www.eyi.com

Accounting and audit, tax and management consulting services.

Ernst & Young, Paseo Phillips 56, Casilla 50080 & 2186, Santiago, Chile

Tel: 56-2-6396125 Fax: 56-2-6383622 Contact: Juan de Dios Vergara

EURO RSCG Worldwide

350 Hudson Street, New York, NY, 10014

Tel: (212) 886-2000 Fax: (212) 886-2016

International advertising agency group.

Euro RSCG Chile, Santiago, Chile

EXPEDITORS INTERNATIONAL OF WASHINGTON INC.

999 Throd Ave., Ste. 2500, Seattle, WA, 98104

Tel: (206) 674-3400 Fax: (206) 682-9777 Web site: www.expd.com

Air/ocean freight forwarding, customs brokerage, international logistics solutions.

Expeditors Chile Transportes Internacionales Ltda., Av. Los Leones 382, Of. 602, Providencia, Santiago, Chile

Tel: 56-2-363-0699 Fax: 56-2-232-9958

EXXON CORPORATION

225 E. John W. Carpenter Freeway, Irving, TX, 75062-2298

Tel: (972) 444-1000 Fax: (972) 444-1882 Web site: www.exxon.com

Petroleum exploration, production, refining; mfr. petroleum & chemicals products; coal & minerals.

Compania Minera Disputada de Las Condes SA, Pedro de Valdivia 291, Santiago 9, Chile

Esso Chile Petrolera, San Antonio Chemical Plant, Barros Luco esq. 7 Norte, San Antonio, Chile

FEDERAL-MOGUL CORPORATION

26555 Northwestern Highway, PO Box 1966, Southfield, MI, 48034

Tel: (248) 354-7700 Fax: (248) 354-8983 Web site: www.federalmogul.com

Mfr./distributor precision parts for automobiles, trucks, farm and construction vehicles.

Federal-Mogul World Trade (Chile) Ltda., Santiago, Chile

FLUOR DANIEL INC.

3353 Michelson Drive, Irvine, CA, 92698

Tel: (714) 975-2000 Fax: (714) 975-5271 Web site: www.flourdaniel.com

Engineering & construction services.

Fluor Daniel Chile SA, Reyes Lavalle 3340, Las Condes, Santiago, Chile

Tel: 56-2-340-8000 Fax: 56-2-234-2853

FMC CORPORATION

200 E. Randolph Drive, Chicago, IL, 60601

Tel: (312) 861-6000 Fax: (312) 861-6141

Produces chemicals & precious metals, mfr. machinery, equipment & systems for industrial, agricultural & government use.

Minera FMC Ltda., Chile

FRITZ COMPANIES INC.

706 Mission Street, Ste. 900, San Francisco, CA, 94103

Tel: (415) 904-8360 Fax: (415) 904-8661 Web site: www.fritz.com

Integrated transportation, sourcing, distribution & customs brokerage services.

Fritz Chile SA, Av. Luis Thayer Ojeda 0115, Ofic. 1105, Santiago, Chile

H.B. FULLER COMPANY

1200 Willow Lake Blvd., Vadnais Heights, MN, 55110

Tel: (612) 236-5900 Fax: (612) 236-5898 Web site: www.hbfuller.com

Mfr./distributor adhesives, sealants, coatings, paints, waxes, sanitation chemicals.

H.B. Fuller Chile SA, Camino lo Espejo 1350, Casilla 50160-B Correo Central, Maipu-Santiago, Chile

Tel: 56-2-5578-720 Fax: 56-2-5574-522

GATX LOGISTICS INC.

1301 Riverplace Boulevard, Ste. 1200, Jacksonville, FL, 32207

Tel: (904) 396-2517 Fax: (904) 396-3984 Web site: www.gatx.com

Warehouse-based third party logistics.

Tatx Logistics Chile, Berlin No. 843, San Miguel, Santiago, Chile

GENERAL ELECTRIC CO.

3135 Easton Turnpike, Fairfield, CT, 06431

Tel: (203) 373-2211 Fax: (203) 373-3131 Web site: www.ge.com

Diversified manufacturing, technology and services.

General Electric de Chile S.A./GE International, Casilla 2103, Santiago, Chile

Tel: 56-2-555-3031 Fax: 56-2-555-0361

GETSCO, Av. Isidora Giyenechea 3356, Las Condes, Santiago, Chile

Tel: 56-2-233-2563

GENERAL MOTORS ACCEPTANCE CORPORATION

100 Renaissance Center, Detroit, MI, 48243-7301

Tel: (313) 556-5000 Fax: (313) 556-5108 Web site: www.gmac.com

Automobile financing.

GMAC Comercial Automotriz Chile SA, Once de Septiembre 2606, Casilla 366, Correo 21, Santiago, Chile

GENERAL MOTORS CORPORATION

100 Renaissance Center, Detroit, MI, 48243.7301

Tel: (313) 556-5000 Fax: (313) 556-5108 Web site: www.gm.com

Mfr. full line vehicles, automotive electronics, commercial technologies, telecommunications, space, finance.

General Motors Chile SA, Casilla 14370, Santiago, Chile

THE GILLETTE COMPANY

Prudential Tower Building, Boston, MA, 02199

Tel: (617) 421-7000 Fax: (617) 421-7123 Web site: www.gillette.com

Develop/mfr. personal care/use products: blades & razors, toiletries, cosmetics, stationery.

Inversiones Gilco (Chile) Ltda., Santiago, Chile

Oral-B Laboratories de Chile SA, Santiago, Chile

Productos Gillette Chile Ltda., Santiago, Chile

Publicidad Intensa Ltda., Santiago, Chile

Union Quimica Americana SA (UNISA), Santiago, Chile

THE GOODYEAR TIRE & RUBBER COMPANY

1144 East Market Street, Akron, OH, 44316

Tel: (330) 796-2121 Fax: (330) 796-1817 Web site: www.goodyear.com

Mfr. tires, automotive belts and hose, conveyor belts, chemicals; oil pipeline transmission.

Goodyear de Chile SAIC, Casilla 3607, Santiago, Chile

W. R. GRACE & COMPANY

One Town Center Road, 1750 Clint Moore Road, Boca Raton, FL, 33486-1010

Tel: (561) 362-2000 Fax: (561) 561-2193 Web site: www.grace.com

Mfr. specialty chemicals and materials: packaging, health care, catalysts, construction, water treatment/process.

Grace Quimica Cia. Ltd., Lago Rinihue, 02220 Lo Espejo, Santiago, Chile

Tel: 56-2-558-6641 Fax: 56-2-558-3938

GRACO INC

4050 Olson Memorial Hwy, PO Box 1441, Minneapolis, MN, 55440-1441

Tel: (612) 623-6000 Fax: (612) 623-6777 Web site: www.graco.com

Mfr./sales of infant & juvenile products; services fluid handling equipment & systems.

Silfa, Colon 1501, Independencia, Chile

Tel: 56-2-777-0416 Fax: 56-2-737-2727 Contact: Juan Pablo

GRANT THORNTON INTERNATIONAL

800 One Prudential Plaza, 130 E. Randolph Drive, Chicago, IL, 60601-6050

Tel: (312) 856-0001 Fax: (312) 616-7052

Accounting, audit, tax and management consulting services.

Grant Thornton Intl, Grant Thornton Bldg., Huerfanos No. 682, PO Box 3577, Santiago, Chile

Tel: 56-2-633-8669 Fax: 56-2-632-7359 Contact: Ramon A. Espejo

GRAYBAR ELECTRIC CO., INC.

34 North Meramec Ave., Clayton, MO, 63105

Tel: (314) 512-9200 Fax: (314) 512-9216

Electrical com data distributor.

Graybar International de Chile Limitada, El Juncal #111, Parque Industrial Portezuelo - Quilicura, Santiago, Chile

Tel: 56-2-747-1236 Fax: 56-2-747-1238

GREY ADVERTISING INC.

777 Third Ave., New York, NY, 10017

Tel: (212) 546-2000 Fax: (212) 546-1495 Web site: www.giworldwwide.com

International advertising agency.

Grey Chile, Ernesto Pinto Lagarrigue 148, Santiago, Chile

HARNISCHFEGER INDUSTRIES INC

PO Box 554, Milwaukee, WI, 53201

Tel: (414) 797-6480 Fax: (414) 797-6573 Web site: www.harnischfeger.com

Mfr. mining and material handling equipment, papermaking machinery and computer systems.

P & H Mining Equipment, Santiago, Chile

THE HARPER GROUP

260 Townsend Street, San Francisco, CA, 94107-1719

Tel: (415) 978-0600 Fax: (415) 978-0692 Web site: www.circleintl.com

Ocean/air freight forwarding, customs brokerage, packing and wholesale, logistics management and insurance.

The Harper Group Chile S.A., Av. Apoquindo 3076, Of. 801, Santiago, Chile

Tel: 56-1-141-9055 Fax: 56-1-242-9054

HEIDRICK & STRUGGLES INC

Sears Tower, 233 South Wacker Drive, Chicago, IL, 60606

Tel: (312) 496-1200 Fax: (312) 496-1290 Web site: www.h-s.com

Executive search firm.

Heidrick & Struggles Intl. Inc., Av. Andres Bello 2777, Oficiana 1503, Providencia Santiago, Chile

Tel: 56-2-203-3660 Fax: 56-2-203-3991

HELLER FINANCIAL INC.

500 West Monroe Street, Chicago, IL, 60661

Tel: (312) 441-7000 Fax: (312) 441-7256

Financial services.

Heller Financial Inc., Chile

HERCULES INC

Hercules Plaza, 1313 North Market Street, Wilmington, DE, 19894-0001

Tel: (302) 594-5000 Fax: (302) 594-5400 Web site: www.herc.com

Mfr. specialty chemicals, plastics, film and fibers, coatings, resins, food ingredients.

Hercules Chemicals Ltd., La Calera, Chile

HEWITT ASSOCIATES LLC

100 Half Day Road, Lincolnshire, IL, 60069

Tel: (847) 295-5000 Fax: (847) 295-7634

Employee benefits consulting firm.

Hewitt Associates Limitada, N.S. de los Angeles #112, El Golf, Santiago, Chile

Tel: 56-2-207-7104

HEWLETT-PACKARD COMPANY

3000 Hanover Street, Palo Alto, CA, 94304-0890

Tel: (650) 857-1501 Fax: (650) 857-7299 Web site: www.hp.com

Mfr. computing, communications & measurement products & services.

Hewlett-Packard SA, Av. Andres Bello 2777 - 24th Fl., Edif. de la Industria, Las Condes - Santiago, Chile

Tel: 56-2-230-1620 Fax: 56-2-203-3234

HOBART BROTHERS COMPANY

Hobart Square, 600 W Main Street, Troy, OH, 45373-2928

Tel: (937) 332-4000 Fax: (937) 332-5194

Mfr. arc/automatic welding systems, power systems, filler metals.

Hobart Brothers Co., Antonio Bellet 77, Office 1406, Providencia, Santiago, Chile

THE HOME DEPOT INC.

2455 Paces Ferry Road, NW, Atlanta, GA, 30339-4024

Tel: (770) 433-8211 Fax: (770) 431-2685 Web site: www.homedepot.com

Home improvement warehouse-style, retail chain stores.

The Home Depot Chile, S.A., Cerro Colorado, 5030, Ste. 410, Las Concles, Santiago, Chile

Tel: 56-2-362-1991 Contact: Bill Peña

HOMESTAKE MINING COMPANY

650 California Street, San Francisco, CA, 94108

Tel: (415) 981-8150 Fax: (415) 397-5038 Web site: www.homestake.com

Precious metal and mineral mining.

Agua de la Falda, SA, Santiago, Chile

HONEYWELL INC.

PO Box 524, Minneapolis, MN, 55440-0524

Tel: (612) 951-1000 Fax: (612) 951-3066 Web site: www.honeywell.com

Develop/mfr. controls for home and building, industry, space and aviation.

Honeywell SA, Eliodoro Yanez 2887, Santiago, Chile

HORWATH INTERNATIONAL

415 Madison Ave., New York, NY, 10017

Tel: (212) 838-5566 Fax: (212) 838-3636

Public accountants and auditors.

Horwath & Horwath-Macaya, Olate y Cia. Ltda., Agustinas #853, Of. 615, Santiago 1, Chile

HYATT INTERNATIONAL CORPORATION

200 West Madison Street, Chicago, IL, 60606

Tel: (312) 750-1234 Fax: (312) 750-8578 Web site: www.hyatt.com

International hotel management.

Hyatt Regency Santiago, Kennedy Ave. #4601, Santiago, Chile

Tel: 56-2-218-1234 Fax: 56-2-218-2513

IBM CORPORATION

New Orchard Road, Armonk, NY, 10504

Tel: (914) 765-1900 Fax: (914) 765-7382 Web site: www.ibm.com

Information products, technology & services.

IBM de Chile SAC, Av. Providencia 655, Santiago, Chile

Tel: 56-2-200-6000 Fax: 56-2-200-6999

INFONET SERVICES CORPORATION

2100 East Grand Ave., El Segundo, CA, 90245

Tel: (310) 335-2600 Fax: (310) 335-4507 Web site: www.infonet.com

Provider of Internet services and electronic messaging services.

Infonet Chile, Mardoqueo Fernandez 128 - Of. 901, Providencia,, Santiago, Chile

Tel: 56-2-368-9400 Fax: 56-2-368-9415

INFORMIX CORPORATION

4100 Bohannon Drive, Menlo Park, CA, 95025

Tel: (650) 926-6300 Fax: (650) 926-6593 Web site: www.informix.com

Designs & produces database management software, connectivity interfaces & gateways, and other computer applications.

Informix de Chile, Av. Pedro de Valdiva, 100 piso 17 y 18, Santiago, Chile

Tel: 56-2-334-4682

INGERSOLL-RAND COMPANY

200 Chestnut Ridge Road, Woodcliff Lake, NJ, 07675

Tel: (201) 573-0123 Fax: (201) 573-3172 Web site: www.ingersoll-rand.com

Mfr. compressors, rock drills, pumps, air tools, door hardware, ball bearings.

Ingersoll-Rand (Chile) Ltd., Av. El Bosque Norte 0107, Of. 41, Santiago, Chile

Tel: 56-2-242-9537 Fax: 56-2-242-9541

INTERMEC TECHNOLOGIES CORPORATION

6001 36th Ave. West, PO Box 4280, Everett, WA, 98203-9280

Tel: (425) 348-2600 Fax: (425) 355-9551 Web site: www.intermec.com

Mfr./distributor automated data collection systems.

Intermec Chile SA, Coronel #2330, Of. 11, Providencia Santiago, Chile

Tel: 56-2-234-1416 Fax: 56-2-233-7696

INTERNATIONAL FLAVORS & FRAGRANCES INC.

521 West 57th Street, New York, NY, 10019-2960

Tel: (212) 765-5500 Fax: (212) 708-7132 Web site: www.iff.com

Design/mfr. flavors, fragrances & aroma chemicals.

International Flavors & Fragrances (Chile), Santiago. Chile

IRRIDELCO INTERNATIONAL CORPORATION

440 Sylvan Ave., Englewood Cliffs, NJ, 07632

Tel: (201) 569-3030 Fax: (201) 569-9237 Web site: www.irridelco.com

Mfr./distributor of the most comprehensive lines of mechanical and micro irrigation; pumps and irrigation systems.

IDC Chile, Jose Manuel Infante 2296 Nunoa, Santiago, Chile

Tel: 56-2-341-1885 Fax: 56-2-364-0412 Contact: Juan Carlos Quezada

ITT CORPORATION

1330 Ave. of the Americas, New York, NY, 10019-5490

Tel: (212) 258-1000 Fax: (212) 258-1297

Design/mfr. communications & electronic equipment, hotels, insurance.

ITT Communicaciones Mundiales SA, Huerfanos 1546, Casilla 262-V, Santiago, Chile

ITT SHERATON CORPORATION

60 State Street, Boston, MA, 02108

Tel: (617) 367-3600 Fax: (617) 367-5676

Hotel operations.

Sheraton San Cristobal Hotel, Casilla 16058, Santiago, Chile

J.P. MORGAN & CO. INC.

60 Wall Street, New York, NY, 10260-0060

Tel: (212) 483-2323 Fax: (212) 648-5209 Web site: www.jpm.com

International banking services.

J.P. Morgan Chile Limitada, Alcantara 2000, Of. 1001, Las Condes, Santiago, Chile

Tel: 56-2-810-4900 Fax: 56-2-208-1022 Contact: Alfredo M. Irigoin, Mng. Dir.

J. WALTER THOMPSON COMPANY

466 Lexington Ave., New York, NY, 10017

Tel: (212) 210-7000 Fax: (212) 210-6944 Web site: www.jwt.com

International advertising and marketing services.

Azocar Morrison Walker (JWT), Santiago , Chile

J. Walter Thompson Chilena, Santiago, Chile

J.C. PENNEY COMPANY, INC.

6501 Legacy Drive, Plano, TX, 75024-3698

Tel: (972) 431-1000 Fax: (972) 431-1977 Web site: www.jcpenney.com

Department stores.

J. C. Penney Company, Inc., Alto Las Condes Mall, Av. Presidente Kennedy 9001, Santiago, Chile

JACOBS ENGINEERING GROUP INC.

1111 S. Arroyo Parkway, Pasadena, CA, 91105

Tel: (626) 578-3500 Fax: (626) 578-6916 Web site: www.jacobs.com

Engineering, design and consulting; construction and construction management; process plant maintenance.

Jacobs Engineering S.A., Puerto de Sol 55, 5th Fl., Las Condes, Santiago, Chile

Tel: 56-2-228-9596 Fax: 56-2-228-0686 Contact: Alan K. Crozier, Mgr.

JDA SOFTWARE GROUP, INC.

11811 N. Tatum Boulevard, Ste. 2000, Phoenix, AZ, 85028

Tel: (602) 404-5500 Fax: (602) 404-5520 Web site: www.jda.com

Developer of information management software for retail, merchandising, distribution and store management.

JDA Software Group, Inc., Av. Providencia 1806, piso 8, Santiago, Chile

Tel: 56-2-264-2650 Fax: 56-2-264-2654

JOHNSON & JOHNSON

One Johnson & Johnson Plaza, New Brunswick, NJ, 08933

Tel: (732) 524-0400 Fax: (732) 214-0334 Web site: www.jnj.com

Mfr./distributor/R&D pharmaceutical, health care and cosmetic products.

Johnson & Johnson de Chile SA, Clasificador 1333, Correo Central, Santiago, Chile

S C JOHNSON & SON INC.

1525 Howe Street, Racine, WI, 53403

Tel: (414) 260-2000 Fax: (414) 260-2133 Web site: www.scjohnsonwax.com

Home, auto, commercial and personal care products and specialty chemicals.

Quimica S.C. Johnson & Son Chilena S.A.C.I., Americo Vespucio Sur #942, Las Condes, Santiago, Chile

KELLOGG COMPANY

One Kellogg Square, PO Box 3599, Battle Creek, MI, 49016-3599

Tel: (616) 961-2000 Fax: (616) 961-2871 Web site: www.kelloggs.com

Mfr. ready-to-eat cereals and convenience foods.

Kellogg Chile SA, Santiago, Chile (All inquiries to U.S. address)

THE KENDALL COMPANY

15 Hampshire Street, Mansfield, MA, 02048

Tel: (508) 261-8000 Fax: (508) 261-8542

Mfr. medical disposable products, home health care products and specialty adhesive products.

Kendall International, Santiago, Chile

Tel: 56-2-734-9714 Fax: 56-2-736-9726

KENNAMETAL INC.

State Rte. 981, Latrobe, PA, 15650

Tel: (724) 539-5000 Fax: (724) 539-4710 Web site: www.kennametal.com

Tools, hard carbide & tungsten alloys for metalworking industry.

Project Chile, Av. Apoquindo 6275 Of. 8, Las Condes, Santiago, Chile

Tel: 56-2-246-0006 Fax: 56-2-246-9802 Contact: Pablo Rioseco

KIMBERLY-CLARK CORPORATION

351 Phelps Drive, Irving, TX, 75038

Tel: (972) 281-1200 Fax: (972) 281-1435 Web site: www.kimberly-clark.com.

Mfr./sales/distribution of consumer tissue, household and personal care products.

Forestal y Agricola Monte Aguila SA, Chile

Forestal y Industrial Santa Fe SA, Chile

KOPPERS INDUSTRIES INC.

Koppers Bldg, 437 Seventh Ave., Pittsburgh, PA, 15219

Tel: (412) 227-2000 Fax: (412) 227-2333

Construction materials and services; chemicals and building products.

Koppers Hickson (Chile) Ltd., Santiago, Chile

KORN/FERRY INTERNATIONAL

1800 Century Park East, Los Angeles, CA, 90067

Tel: (310) 552-1834 Fax: (310) 553-6452 Web site: www.kornferry.com

Executive search; management consulting.

Korn/Ferry International, Av. Libertador Bernardo O'Higgins 816, Santiago, Chile

Tel: 56-2-233-4155 Fax: 56-2-234-2784

KPMG PEAT MARWICK LLP

Three Chestnut Ridge Road, Montvale, NJ, 07645

Tel: (201) 307-7000 Fax: (201) 930-8617 Web site: www.kpmg.com

Accounting and audit, tax and management consulting services.

KPMG Peat Marwick, Miraflores 222, 9th Fl., Santiago, Chile

Tel: 56-2-639-4387 Fax: 56-2-639-4438 Contact: Miller A. Templeton, Ptnr.

LANIER WORLDWIDE, INC.

2300 Parklake Drive, N.E., Atlanta, GA, 30345

Tel: (770) 496-9500 Fax: (770) 621-1535

Specialize in digital copiers and multi-functional systems.

Lanier Chile, S.A., Av. Alemania 0350, Temuco, Chile

Tel: 56-45-239-096 Fax: 56-45-238-169

Lanier Chile, S.A., Agua Santa 77, Viña del Mar, Chile

Tel: 56-32-628-049 Fax: 56-32-665-068

Lanier Chile, S.A., Barros Arana 1538, Concepción, Chile

Tel: 56-41-236-801 Fax: 56-41-243-906

Lanier Chile, S.A., Pedro Pablo MuñozLa 570, Serna, Chile

Tel: 56-51-214875 Fax: 56-51-222243

Lanier Chile, S.A., Av. Ricardo Lyon 1660, PO Box 52640-Correo Central, Santiago, Chile

Tel: 56-2-204-0021 Fax: 56-2-225-2160

LAYNE CHRISTIANSEN, INC.

1900 Shawnee Mission Pkwy., Mission Woods, KS, 66205

Tel: (913) 362-0510 Fax: (913) 362-0133

Contract drilling.

Geotec Boyles Layne Christiansen SA, La Violetas 5931, Santiago, Chile

LE TOURNEAU COMPANY

PO Box 2307, Longview, TX, 75606

Tel: (903) 237-7000 Fax: (903) 267-7032

Mfr. heavy construction and mining machinery equipment.

Commercial Otero SA, La Bolsa 81, Casilla 2858 Correo Central, Santiago 1, Chile

LEHMAN BROTHERS HOLDINGS INC.

Three World Financial Center, New York, NY, 10285

Tel: (212) 526-7000 Fax: (212) 526-3738 Web site: www.lehman.com

Financial services, securities and merchant banking services.

Lehman Brothers, Gertrudes Echenique 30, Las Condes, Santiago, Chile

Tel: 56-2-207-1771

ELI LILLY & COMPANY

Lilly Corporate Center, Indianapolis, IN, 46285

Tel: (317) 276-2000 Fax: (317) 277-6579 Web site: www.lilly.com

Mfr. pharmaceuticals and animal health products.

Eli Lilly Chile S.A., San Eugenio 567, Santiago, Chile

Tel: 56-2-239-8952 Fax: 56-2-239-2814

THE LINCOLN ELECTRIC COMPANY

22801 St. Clair Ave., Cleveland, OH, 44117-1199

Tel: (216) 481-8100 Fax: (216) 486-8385 Web site: www.lincolnelectric.com

Mfr. arc welding and welding related products, oxy-fuel and thermal cutting equipment and integral AC motors.

Lincoln Electric Latin America, La Cascada 9393, Vitacura, Santiago, Chile

Tel: 56-2-243-0671

LOCTITE CORPORATION

10 Columbus Boulevard, Hartford, CT, 06106

Tel: (203) 520-5000 Fax: (203) 520-5073 Web site: www.loctite.com

Mfr./sale industrial adhesives and sealants.

Loctite Corporation Chile Ltda., Av. Pedro de Valdivia 6052, Macul, Santiago, Chile

Tel: 56-2-238-0055 Fax: 56-2-238-2588 Contact: Graciela Fernandez, Gen. Mgr.

THE LUBRIZOL CORPORATION

29400 Lakeland Blvd., Wickliffe, OH, 44092-2298

Tel: (440) 943-4200 Fax: (440) 943-5337 Web site: www.lubrizol.com

Mfr. chemicals additives for lubricants & fuels.

Lubrizol de Chile Ltda., Santiago, Chile

Tel: 56-2-233-6468

MANPOWER INTERNATIONAL INC.

5301 N. Ironwood Road, PO Box 2053, Milwaukee, WI, 53201-2053

Tel: (414) 961-1000 Fax: (414) 961-7081 Web site: www.manpower

Temporary help, contract service, training & testing.

Manpower de Chile Ltda., Estados Unidos 395, Santiago, Chile

Tel: 56-2-638-4774 Fax: 56-2-632-2598

MARCO

2300 W. Commodore Way, Seattle, WA, 98199

Tel: (206) 285-3200 Fax: (206) 286-8027 Web site: www.marco.com

Shipbuilding and repair, commercial fishing equipment and systems and hydraulic pumps.

Marco Chilena SA, Av. Andrew B. 2113, Clasificadar 116, Santiago, Chile

Tel: 56-2-231-0906 Fax: 56-2-231-9865 Contact: J. Michael Combes, Gen. Mgr. Emp: 650

MARRIOTT INTERNATIONAL INC.

1 Marriott Drive, Washington, DC, 20058

Tel: (301) 380-3000 Fax: (301) 380-5181

Lodging, contract food and beverage service, and restaurants.

Marriott de Chile Ltda., Aeropuerto Intl. Antonio Merino Benitez, Santiago, Chile

Tel: 56-2-3811500

MARSH & McLENNAN COS INC.

1166 Ave. of the Americas, New York, NY, 10036-2774

Tel: (212) 345-5000 Fax: (212) 345-4808 Web site: www.marshmac.com

Insurance agents/brokers, pension and investment management consulting services.

Claro J&H Marsh & McLennan S.A., Av. Americo Vespucio 100 pios 12 y 13, Las Condes, Santiago, Chile

Tel: 56-2-206-0115 Fax: 56-2-228-2211 Contact: Mario Claro

MARY KAY COSMETICS INC.

16251 Nor Dallas Pkw, Dallas, TX, 75248

Tel: (214) 630-8787 Fax: (214) 631-5938

Cosmetics and toiletries.

Mary Kay (Chile) Ltda., Europa 2035, Providencia, Santiago, Chile

MASTERCARD INTERNATIONAL INC.

200 Purchase Street, Purchase, NY, 10577

Tel: (914) 249-2000 Fax: (914) 249-5475 Web site: www.mastercard.com

Provides financial payment systems globally.

MasterCard International Inc., Miraflores 222, piso 29, Santiago, Chile

MATTEL INC.

333 Continental Blvd., El Segundo, CA, 90245-5012

Tel: (310) 252-2000 Fax: (310) 252-2179 Web site: www.mattelmedia.com

Mfr. toys, dolls, games, crafts and hobbies.

Mattel Chile SA, Av. Vicuna MacKenna 2301, Santiago, Chile

McCANN-ERICKSON WORLDWIDE

750 Third Ave., New York, NY, 10017

Tel: (212) 984-3644 Fax: (212) 984-2629

International advertising/marketing services.

McCann-Erickson SA de Publicidad, Eliodoro Yanez 2290, Casilla 2428, Providencia, Santiago, Chile

McDONALD'S CORPORATION

Kroc Drive, Oak Brook, IL, 60523

Tel: (630) 623-3000 Fax: (630) 623-7409

Fast food chain stores.

McDonald's Corp., Chile

McKINSEY & COMPANY

55 East 52nd Street, New York, NY, 10022

Tel: (212) 446-7000 Fax: (212) 446-8575 Web site: www.mckinsey.com

Management and business consulting services.

McKinsey & Company, Alcantara 200, 12th Fl., Auite 1201, Comuna d Las Condes, Santiago, Chile

Tel: 56-2-353-1800 Fax: 56-2-353-1801

MEAD CORPORATION

Courthouse Plaza, NE, Dayton, OH, 45463

Tel: (937) 495-6323 Fax: (937) 461-2424 Web site: www.mead.com

Mfr. paper, packaging, pulp, lumber and other wood products, school and office products; electronic publishing and distribution.

Mead Packaging Chile Limitada, Asturias No. 171, Of. 203 Las Condes, Santiago, Chile

Tel: 56-2-246-7534 Fax: 56-1-246-7532 Contact: F. Gardelman, Sales Mgr.

MERRILL LYNCH & COMPANY, INC.

World Financial Center, North Tower, New York, NY, 10281-1323

Tel: (212) 449-1000 Fax: (212) 449-2892

Security brokers and dealers, investment and business services.

Merrill Lynch Chile, S.A., Agustinas 640 Edif., Interamericana, 13th Fl., Santiago de Chile, Chile

Tel: 56-2-633-2214 Fax: 56-2-638-0513

MICROSOFT CORPORATION

One Microsoft Way, Redmond, WA, 98052-6399

Tel: (425) 882-8080 Fax: (425) 936-7329 Web site: www.microsoft.com

Computer software, peripherals and services.

Microsoft Chile, Av. Andres Bello #2777, piso, Edif. de la Industria, Providencia, Santiago, Chile

Tel: 56-2-330-6000 Fax: 56-2-218-5747

MINE SAFETY APPLIANCES COMPANY

121 Gamma Drive, RIDC Industrial Pk., PO Box 426, Pittsburgh, PA, 15230

Tel: (412) 967-3000 Fax: (412) 967-3452

Safety equipment, industry filters.

MSA de Chile Ltda., Casilla 16647, Santiago 9, Chile

MOBIL CORPORATION

3225 Gallows Road, Fairfax, VA, 22037-0001

Tel: (703) 846-3000 Fax: (703) 846-4669 Web site: www.mobil.com

Petroleum and gas exploration and refining, mfr. petroleum products, chemicals and petrochemicals.

COPEC Mobil Ltda., Correo Central 2060, Santiago, Chile

MOTOROLA, INC.

1303 East Algonquin Road, Schaumburg, IL, 60196

Tel: (847) 576-5000 Fax: (847) 538-5191 Web site: www.mot.com

Mfr. communications equipment, semiconductors and cellular phones.

Motorola Chile S.A., Av. Nueva Tajamar 481, Of. 1702, Las Condes, Santiago, Chile

Tel: 56-2-338-9000 Fax: 56-2-338-9090

NALCO CHEMICAL COMPANY

One Nalco Center, Naperville, IL, 60563-1198

Tel: (630) 305-1000 Fax: (630) 305-2900 Web site: www.nalco.com

Chemicals for water and waste water treatment, oil products and refining, industry processes; water and energy management service.

Nalco Productos Quimicos de Chile SA, Casilla 16477, Santiago 9, Chile

Tel: 56-2-624-6540 Fax: 56-2-624-6508

NATIONAL CAR RENTAL SYSTEM, INC.

7700 France Ave. South, Minneapolis, MN, 55435

Tel: (612) 830-2121 Fax: (612) 830-2921

Car rentals.

National Car Rental, Av. de la Concepcion 212, Santiago, Chile

NATIONAL STARCH & CHEMICAL COMPANY

10 Finderne Ave., Bridgewater, NJ, 08807-3300

Tel: (908) 685-5000 Fax: (908) 685-5005 Web site: www.national starch.com

Mfr. adhesives & sealants, resins & specialty chemicals, electronic materials & adhesives, food products, industry starch.

National Starch & Chemical SA, Serafin Zamora 221, Santiago, Chile

Tel: 56-2-557-4445 Fax: 56-2-538-2631

NORTH LILY MINING COMPANY

210-1800 Glenarm Place, #210, Denver, CO, 80202

Tel: (303) 294-0427 Fax: (303) 293-2235

Mining gold, silver and copper.

Minera Northern Resources Ltd., Av. El Bosque Sur 175, Providencia, Santiago, Chile

NORTON COMPANY

1 New Bond Street, Worcester, MA, 01606

Tel: (508) 795-5000 Fax: (508) 795-5741

Abrasives, drill bits, construction and safety products and plastics.

Christensen Diamond Products de Chile SA, Casilla 1150, Santiago, Chile

OGILVY & MATHER WORLDWIDE

309 West 49th Street, New York, NY, 10019

Tel: (212) 237-4000 Fax: (212) 237-5123

Advertising, marketing, public relations & consulting firm.

Northcote & Asociados (O&M), Santiago, Chile

OLSTEN CORPORATION

175 Broad Hollow Road, Melville, NY, 11747-8905

Tel: (516) 844-7800 Fax: (516) 844-7022 Web site: www.olsten.com

Staffing, home health care & information technology services.

Adyser, Rafel Cañas 224 Providencia, Santiago, Chile

Tel: 56-2-235-1525 Fax: 56-2-235-6127

PEPSiCO INC.

700 Anderson Hill Road, Purchase, NY, 10577-1444

Tel: (914) 253-2000 Fax: (914) 253-2070 Web site: www.pepsico.com

Beverages and snack foods.

Evercrisp Snack Products de Chile SA, Chile

Inversiones PFI Chile Ltda., Chile

THE PERKIN-ELMER CORPORATION

761 Main Ave., Norwalk, CT, 06859-0001

Tel: (203) 762-1000 Fax: (203) 762-4228 Web site: www.perkin-elmer.com

Leading supplier of systems for life science research and related applications.

Perkin-Elmer Chile Ltda., Av. Francisco Bilbao 882, Providencia Santiago, Chile

Tel: 56-2-665-1600 Fax: 56-2-269-8070

Weisser Analitica Ltda., 2001 Jose Domingo Canas, Santiago 9, Chile

Tel: 56-2-225-7266 Fax: 56-2-225-3181 Contact: Ricardo Weisser, Pres.

PFIZER INC.

235 East 42nd Street, New York, NY, 10017-5755

Tel: (212) 573-2323 Fax: (212) 573-7851 Web site: www.pfizer.com

Research-based, global health care company.

Roerig SA, Chile

PHARMACIA & UPJOHN

95 Corporate Drive, PO Box 6995, Bridgewater, NJ, 08807

Tel: (908) 306-4400 Fax: (908) 306-4433 Web site: www.pnu.com

Mfr. pharmaceuticals, agricultural products, industry chemicals

Upjohn Compania SA, Del Inca 4446, 4th Fl., Las Condes, Santiago, Chile

PHELPS DODGE CORPORATION

2600 North Central Ave., Phoenix, AZ, 85004-3089

Tel: (602) 234-8100 Fax: (602) 234-8337

Copper, minerals, metals & spec engineered products for transportation & electrical markets.

Compania Contractual Minera Candelaria, Copiapo, Chile

Phelps Dodge Exploration Corp., Santiago, Chile

Phelps Dodge Intl. Corp., Chile

Phelps Dodge Ojos del Salado Inc., Apaquindo 4499, Las Condes, Santiago, Chile

PIONEER HI-BRED INTERNATIONAL INC.

400 Locust Street, Ste. 800, Des Moines, IA, 50309

Tel: (515) 248-4800 Fax: (515) 248-4999

Agricultural chemicals, farm supplies, biological products, research.

Semillas Pioneer Chile Ltda., Las Bellotas 199, Santiago, Chile

PITNEY BOWES INC.

1 Elmcroft Road, Stamford, CT, 06926-0700

Tel: (203) 356-5000 Fax: (203) 351-6835 Web site: www.pitneybowes.com

Mfr. postage meters, mailroom equipment, copiers, bus supplies, bus services, facsimile systems and financial services.

Pitney Bowes Chile, Chile - All mail to: Pitney Bowes Latin America, 2424 N. Federal Hwy., Ste 360, Boca Raton, FL 33431 U.S.A.

Fax: 56-1-347-2041 Contact: Joe Denaro, VP Latin America & Caribbean Emp: 75

PRAXAIR, INC.

39 Old Ridgebury Road, Danbury, CT, 06810-5113

Tel: (203) 837-2000 Fax: (203) 837-2450 Web site: www.praxair.com

Produces and distributes industrial and specialty gases.

Praxair Chile S.A., Juana Weber 4725, Santiago, Chile

Tel: 56-2-779-5106 Fax: 56-2-779-1721

PRICEWATERHOUSECOOPERS LLP

1251 Ave. of the Americas, New York, NY, 10020

Tel: (212) 596-7000 Fax: (212) 790-6620 Web site: www.pwcglobal.com

Accounting and auditing, tax and management, and human resource consulting services.

Price Waterhouse Ltd., Edif. Espana, Huerfanos 863, 4th Fl., Casillo de Correo 3337, Santiago, Chile

Tel: 56-2-638-3032 Fax: 56-2-633-3329

Price Waterhouse Ltd., Anibal Pinto 215, 6th Fl., Of. 607, Casilla de Correo 705, Concepcion, Chile

Tel: 56-41-241772 Fax: 56-41-230154

PRINCIPAL INTERNATIONAL INC.

711 High Street, Des Moines, IA, 50392-9950

Tel: (515) 248-8288 Fax: (515) 248-8049 Web site: www.principal.com

Insurance and investment services.

BanRenta Compañía, Ave. Apoquindo 2942, Las Condes, Santiago, Chile

Tel: 56-2-231-0015 Fax: 56-2-246-0692 Contact: Francisco Mozo, Mgr.

PROCTER & GAMBLE COMPANY

One Procter & Gamble Plaza, Cincinnati, OH, 45202

Tel: (513) 983-1100 Fax: (513) 562-4500 Web site: www.pg.com

Personal care, food, laundry, cleaning and industry products.

P&G Chile Inc. Agencia, Av.Nueva Tajamar #481, Torre Sur-Of. 901, Las Comedes, Santiago, Chile

QUALCOMM INC.

6355 Lusk Boulevard, San Diego, CA, 92121

Tel: (619) 587-1121 Fax: (619) 658-1434

Digital wireless telecommunications systems.

Qualcomm Chile, Santiago, Chile

RAYCHEM CORPORATION

300 Constitution Drive, Menlo Park, CA, 94025-1164

Tel: (650) 361-3333 Fax: (650) 361-2108 Web site: www.raychem.com

Develop/mfr./market materials science products for electronics, telecommunications & industry.

Raychem Chile Ltda., Sucre 1073, Casilla 1140, Santiago, Chile

RAYTHEON COMPANY

141 Spring Street, Lexington, MA, 02173

Tel: (781) 862-6600 Fax: (781) 860-2172 Web site: www.raytheon.com

Mfr. diversified electronics, appliances, aviation, energy and environmental products; publishing, industry and construction services.

Raytheon International, Santiago, Chile

RENDIC INTERNATIONAL CORPORATION

9100 South Dadeland Blvd., Ste 1800, Miami, FL, 33156

Tel: (305) 670-0066 Fax: (305) 670-0060 Web site: www.flintink.com

Sales of printing inks, press equipment and supplies.

Rendic International Corporation, Americo Vespucio 2542, Comuna De Conchali Santiago, Chile

REPUBLIC NATIONAL BANK OF NEW YORK

452 Fifth Ave., New York, NY, 10018

Tel: (212) 525-5000 Fax: (212) 525-6996 Web site: www.rnb.com

Banking services.

Republic National Bank of New York, Huerfanos 1060, Santiago, Chile

RJR NABISCO INC.

1301 Ave. of the Americas, New York, NY, 10019

Tel: (212) 258-5600 Fax: (212) 969-9173 Web site: www.rjrnabisco.com

Mfr. consumer packaged food products & tobacco products.

Nabisco RoyalChile Ltda., Camino de Melipilla 13250, Santiago RM, Chile

ROCKWELL INTERNATIONAL CORPORATION

600 Anton Boulevard, Costa Mesa, CA, 92626-7147

Tel: (714) 424-4200 Fax: (714) 424-4251 Web site: www.rockwell.com

Products & service for aerospace and defense, automotive, electronics, graphics & automation industry.

Rockwell Automation Chile S.A., Av. Americo Vespucio Sur 100, Local 103, Las Condes, (Santiago) Chile

Tel: 56-2-207-3700 Fax: 56-2-207-6707

Rockwell Collins Chile S.A., A. Merino International Airport, LanChile Maintenance Base, Santiago, Chile

Tel: 56-2-601-8509 Fax: 56-2-601-9507

ROHM AND HAAS COMPANY

100 Independence Mall West, Philadelphia, PA, 19106

Tel: (215) 592-3000 Fax: (215) 592-3377 Web site: www.rohmhaas.com

Mfr. industrial & agricultural chemicals, plastics.

Rohm and Haas Chile Ltd., Casilla 131, Correo 35, Santiago, Chile

Tel: 56-2-2335781

SBC COMMUNICATIONS INC.

175 East Houston, PO Box 2933, San Antonio, TX, 78299-2933

Tel: (210) 821-4105 Fax: (210) 351-5034 Web site: www.sbc.com

Telecommunications.

VTR S.A., Santiago, Chile

SCHENKER INTERNATIONAL FORWARDERS INC.

150 Albany Ave., Freeport, NY, 11520

Tel: (516) 377-3000 Fax: (516) 377-3005 Web site: www.schenkerusa.com

Freight forwarders.

Schenker International Ltda, General del Canto, 421 piso 3, Casilla 319-V, Correo 21, Santiago 9, Chile

Tel: 56-2-236-3060 Fax: 56-2-236-3038

SCIENTIFIC-ATLANTA, INC.

1 Technology Pkwy South, Norcross, GA, 30092-2967

Tel: (770) 903-5000 Fax: (770) 903-2967 Web site: www.sciatl.com

A leading supplier of broadband communications systems, satellite-based video, voice and data communications networks and worldwide customer service and support.

Scientific-Atlanta Chile y Compania Limitada, Avda 11 de Septiembre 2155, Torre A Of. 1204, Santiago, Chile

Tel: 56-2-232-2681 Fax: 56-2-232-2681

THE SERVICEMASTER COMPANY

One ServiceMaster Way, Downers Grove, IL, 60515-1700

Tel: (630) 271-1300 Fax: (630) 271-2710 Web site: www.svm.com

Management service to health care, school and industry facilities; diversified residential and commercial services.

Merry Maids, Santiago, Chile

ServiceMaster, Santiago, Chile

SHERWIN-WILLIAMS CO., INC.

101 Prospect Ave., N.W., Cleveland, OH, 44115-1075

Tel: (216) 566-2000 Fax: (216) 566-3312 Web site: www.sherwin-williams.com

Mfr. paint, wallcoverings and related products.

Sherwin-Williams Chile, Santiago, Chile

Tel: 5-62-558-7733 Fax: 5-62-5585394 Contact: G. Paetz

SONESTA INTERNATIONAL HOTELS CORPORATION

200 Clarendon Street, Boston, MA, 02166

Tel: (617) 421-5400 Fax: (617) 421-5402 Web site: www.sonesta.com

Hotels, resorts, and Nile cruises..

Sonesta Hotel Santiago, Lux 2929, Las Condes, Santiago, Chile

SOUTHERN COMPANY

270 Peachtree Street, Atlanta, GA, 30303

Tel: (404) 506-5000 Fax: (404) 506-0642 Web site: www.southernco.com

Electric utility.

SEI Chile Ebelnor, S.A., Apoquindo 3721, Of. 114, Edif. "Torre Las Condes", Las Condes, Santiago, Chile

Tel: 56-2-206-3357 Contact: Mark Lynch, Gen. Mgr.

SPENCER STUART & ASSOCIATES INC.

401 North Michigan Ave., Ste. 3400, Chicago, IL, 60611

Tel: (312) 822-0080 Fax: (312) 822-0116 Web site: www.spencerstuart.com

Executive recruitment firm.

Spencer Stuart & Associates Inc., Marchant Perieria 201 - piso 9, Providencia, Santiago, Chile

Tel: 56-2-225-7303 Fax: 56-2-274-3935 Contact: Alfonso Mujica

THE ST. PAUL COMPANIES, INC.

385 Washington Street, St. Paul, MN, 55102

Tel: (612) 310-7911 Fax: (612) 310-8294 Web site: www.stpaul.com

Provides investment, insurance and reinsurance services.

Le Mans-ISE Compania de Seguros Generales S.A., Encomenderos 113, Las Condes, Santiago, Chile

STATE STREET BANK & TRUST COMPANY

225 Franklin Street, Boston, MA, 02101

Tel: (617) 786-3000 Fax: (617) 654-3386 Web site: www.statestreet.com

Banking & financial services.

State Street Bank & Trust Co., Santiago, Chile

STIEFEL LABORATORIES INC.

255 Alhambra Circle, Ste. 1000, Coral Gables, FL, 33134

Tel: (305) 443-3807 Fax: (305) 443-3467

Mfr. pharmaceuticals, dermatological specialties.

Laboratorios Stiefel de Chile & Cia. Ltda., Eleodoro Flores 2371, Nonoa, Santiago, Chile

STONE CONTAINER CORPORATION

150 N. Michigan Ave., Chicago, IL, 60601-7568

Tel: (312) 346-6600 Fax: (312) 580-3486 Web site: www.stonecontainer.com

Mfr. paper and paper packaging.

Stone Container Corporation, San Francisco (Santiago), Chile

SYBASE, INC.

6475 Christie Ave., Emeryville, CA, 94608

Tel: (510) 922-3500 Fax: (510) 922-3210 Web site: www.sybase.com

Design/mfg/distribution of database management systems, software development tools, connectivity products, consulting and technical support services..

Sybase Informatica Chile Ltda., Av. Providencia 1806, piso 6, Providencia, Santiago, Chile

Tel: 56-2-330-6700 Fax: 56-2-330-6800

TBWA INTERNATIONAL

180 Maiden Lane, New York, NY, 10038

Tel: (212) 804-1000 Fax: (212) 804-1200

International full service advertising agency.

Frederick y Valenzuela (TBWA), Santiago, Chile

TECH-SYM CORPORATION

10500 Westoffice Drive, #200, Houston, TX, 77042-5391

Tel: (713) 785-7790 Fax: (713) 780-3524 Web site: www.syntron.com

Electronics, real estate, aeromechanics.

Continental-Lensa S.A., El Rosal No. 5063, Hucchuraba, Santiago, Chile

Tel: 56-2-244-0086 Fax: 56-2-626-2315 Contact: Harald Weinreich

TECHNOLOGY SOLUTIONS COMPANY (TSC)

205 N. Michigan Ave., Ste. 1500, Chicago, IL, 60601

Tel: (312) 228-4500 Fax: (312) 228-4501 Web site: www.techsol.com

Designs computer information systems and strategic business and management consulting for major corporations.

TSC de Chile, Marchant Pereira, 201 piso 9 Profidencia, Santiago, Chile

Tel: 56-2-274-1020 Fax: 56-2-274-7955

TRIMARK PICTURES

2644 30th Street, Santa Monica, CA, 90405-3009

Tel: (310) 314-2000 Fax: (310) 399-3828

Distributor TV programs, broadcast management and consulting services.

Intl. Broadcast System Ltd., Av. Once de Septiembre 1860, Santiago, Chile

TRUE NORTH COMMUNICATIONS INC.

101 East Erie Street, Chicago, IL, 60611

Tel: (312) 425-6000 Fax: (312) 425-6350

Holding company, advertising agency.

IDB/FCB, S.A., Edif. Paseo Apoquindo, Av. Apoquindo 4499, piso 16, Las Condes, Santiago, Chile

U.S. WHEAT ASSOCIATES

1620 I Street, NW, Washington, DC, 20006

Tel: (202) 463-0999 Fax: (202) 785-1052

Market development for wheat products.

U.S. Wheat Associates Inc., Casilla 16616, Santiago 9, Chile

UNION CAMP CORPORATION

1600 Valley Road, Wayne, NJ, 07470

Tel: (973) 628-2000 Fax: (973) 628-2722 Web site: www.unioncamp.com

Mfr. paper, packaging, chemicals and wood products.

Union Camp Chile SA, Longitudinal Sur. Km. 75, Graneros, Rancagua, Chile

Tel: 56-72-471-212 Fax: 56-72-471-143

UNION CARBIDE CORPORATION

39 Old Ridgebury Road, Danbury, CT, 06817

Tel: (203) 794-2000 Fax: (203) 794-6269 Web site: www.unioncarbide.com

Mfr. industrial chemicals, plastics and resins.

Union Carbide Inter-America Inc., Av. Aponguindo 3076, Ofic. 701, Casilla 16706, Correo 9, Santiago, Chile

UNION OIL INTERNATIONAL DIV

2141 Rosecrans Ave., El Segundo, CA, 90245

Tel: (310) 726-7600 Fax: (310) 726-7817

Petroleum products, petrochemicals..

Moly Corp. Inc., Minera Union Oil Chile Ltda., Av. Providencia 1072, Torre A, Dento 1203, Santiago, Chile

UNITED PARCEL SERVICE OF AMERICA, INC.

55 Glenlake Parkway, NE, Atlanta, GA, 30328

Tel: (404) 828-6000 Fax: (404) 828-6593 Web site: www.ups.com

International package-delivery service.

UPS de Chile, Union Americana 221, Santiago, Chile

Tel: 56-2-680-1700 Fax: 56-2-680-1717

WACKENHUT CORPORATION

4200 Wackenhut Drive, Ste. 100, Palm Beach Gardens, FL, 33410

Tel: (561) 622-5656 Fax: (561) 691-6736 Web site: www.wackenhut.com

Security systems & services.

Wackenhut Chile SA, Av. Ejercito 171, Santiago, Chile (Locations: Concepcion & Antofagasta, Chile.)

Tel: 56-2-696-1683 Fax: 56-6-698-6217

WARNER-LAMBERT COMPANY

201 Tabor Road, Morris Plains, NJ, 07950-2693

Tel: (973) 540-2000 Fax: (973) 540-3761 Web site: www.warner-lambert.com

Mfr. ethical and proprietary pharmaceuticals, confectionery and consumer products & pet care supplies.

Empresas Warner-Lambert SA, Casilla 191-D, Santiago, Chile

WATERS CORPORATION

34 Maple Street, Milford, MA, 01757

Tel: (508) 478-2000 Fax: (508) 872-1990

Mfr./distribute liquid chromatographic instruments and test and measurement equipment.

Waters Associates, Santiago, Chile

WUNDERMAN CATO JOHNSON

675 Ave. of the Americas, New York, NY, 10010-5104

Tel: (212) 941-3000 Fax: (212) 633-0957 Web site: www.wcj.com

International advertising and marketing consulting firm.

Wunderman Cato Johnson, Roger de Flor 2996, Santiago, Chile

Tel: 56-2-231-6961 Fax: 56-2-232-7652 Contact: Oscar Gomezese, Gen. Mgr.

XEROX CORPORATION

800 Long Ridge Road, PO Box 1600, Stamford, CT, 06904

Tel: (203) 968-3000 Fax: (203) 968-4312 Web site: www.xerox.com

Mfr. document processing equipment, systems and supplies.

Xerox De Chile, S.A., Casilla Postal 2747, San Martin 880, 5 piso, Concepcion, Chile

Xerox De Chile, S.A., Casilla Postal 14889, Correo 21, Stgo., Alcantara #107, Las Condes, Santiago, Chile

Tel: 56-2-338-7000 Fax: 56-2-338-7432

Xerox De Chile, S.A., Cochrane 879, Valparaiso, Chile

Xerox De Chile, S.A., Casilla Postal 1076, Carrera 1807, Antofagasta, Chile

YOUNG & RUBICAM INC.

285 Madison Ave., New York, NY, 10017

Tel: (212) 210-3000 Fax: (212) 370-3796 Web site: www.yr.com

Advertising, public relations, direct marketing and sales promotion, corporate & product ID management.

Prolam/Young & Rubicam, Santiago, Chile

China (PRC)

3COM CORPORATION

5400 Bayfront Plaza, Santa Clara, CA, 95052-8145

Tel: (408) 764-5000 Fax: (408) 764-5001 Web site: www.3com.com

Develop/mfr. computer networking products & systems.

3Com Asia Ltd. - Beijing, RM 1656-1660, Office Tower, New Century Hotel, No. 6 Southern Rd., Capital Gym, Beijing 1000044, P.R.China (PRC)

Tel: 86-10-6849-2568 Fax: 86-10-6849-2789

3Com Asia Ltd. - Chengdu, Rm. 2405, Min-Shan Hotel Business Bldg., No. 55 Section, 2 Ren Min Nan Rd., Changdu 6100021, Sichuan Privince, China (PRC)

Tel: 86-28-558-3333 Fax: 86-28-557-3950

3Com Asia Ltd. - Guangzhou, c/o The Garden Hotel, Room 1013, Garden Tower, 368 Huanshi Dong Lu, Guangzhou 510064, China (PRC)

Tel: 86-20-8333-8999 Fax: 86-20-8384-9812

3Com Asia Ltd. - Shanghai, Room 2002, 20/F, Novel Plaza, No. 128 Nan Jing Rd. West, Shanghai 200003, China (PRC)

Tel: 86-21-63501581 Fax: 86-21-63501531

3M

3M Center, St. Paul, MN, 55144-1000

Tel: (612) 733-1110 Fax: (612) 733-9973 Web site: www.mmm.com

Mfr. diversified products for industry, health care, imaging, communications, transport, safety, consumer, etc.

3M China Ltd., 10F, New Town Mansion, 55 Loushanguan Rd., Shanghai 200335, China (PRC)

Tel: 86-21-6275-3535 Fax: 86-21-6275-2343

AIR EXPRESS INTERNATIONAL CORPORATION

120 Tokeneke Road, PO Box 1231, Darien, CT, 06820

Tel: (203) 655-7900 Fax: (203) 655-5779 Web site: www.aeilogistics.com

Air freight forwarder.

AEI Beijing Liaison Office, 1st Fl., Light Bldg., A-4 9th Block, Hepingli, Beijing 100013, China (PRC) (Locations: Changchun, Guangzhou, Pudong, Shanghai, Suzhou, Tainjin.)

Tel: 86-10-6424-2070-76 Fax: 86-10-6424-2069

ALBEMARLE CORPORATION

451 Florida Ave., Baton Rouge, LA, 70801

Tel: (504) 388-8011 Fax: (504) 388-7686

Chemical company.

Albemarle Corp., Beijing, China (PRC)

ALCOA (ALUMINUM CO OF AMERICA)

Alcoa Bldg., 425 Sixth Ave., Pittsburgh, PA, 15219-1850

Tel: (412) 553-4545 Fax: (412) 553-4498

World's leading producer of aluminum & alumina; mining, refining, smelting, fabricating & recycling.

Alcoa Shanghai Aluminum Products Co., Ltd., Shanghai, China (PRC)

Asian-American Containers Mfg. Co., Ltd., Tianjin, China (PRC)

ALLEN TELECOM

25101 Chagrin Boulevard, Beachwood, OH, 44122-5619

Tel: (216) 765-5818 Fax: (216) 765-0410 Web site: www.allentele.com

Mfr. communications equipment, automotive bodies and parts, electronic components.

Allen Telecom Beijing, CITIC - Bldg. 11-04 19 Juanguomenwai Ave., Beijing, China (PRC)

Tel: 86-10-6508-3088 Fax: 86-10-6508-3066 Contact: Harry Li

ALLEN-BRADLEY COMPANY, INC.

1201 South Second Street, Milwaukee, WI, 53204

Tel: (414) 382-2000 Fax: (414) 382-4444

Mfr. electrical controls & information devices.

Allen-Bradley Enterprise Xiamen Ltd., 38 Yue Hua Rd., Huli Ind. Dist., Xiamen, Fujian 361006, China (PRC)

ALLIEDSIGNAL INC.

101 Columbia Road, PO Box 2245, Morristown, NJ, 07962-2245

Tel: (973) 455-2000 Fax: (973) 455-4807 Web site: www.alliedsignal.com

Mfr. aerospace & automotive products, engineered materials.

AlliedSignal Aerospace Co., Lido Commercial Ctr., Block 2A, 5/F, Jichang Rd., Jiany Tai Rd., Beijing, China (PRC)

AMERICAN BUILDINGS COMPANY

1150 State Docks Road, Eufaula, AL, 36072-0800

Tel: (334) 687-2032 Fax: (334) 667-8315 Web site: www.ambldgs.com

Metal buildings.

American Buildings Co. (JV), Shanghai, China (PRC)

AMERICAN HOME PRODUCTS CORPORATION

Five Giralda Farms, Madison, NJ, 07940-0874

Tel: (973) 660-5000 Fax: (973) 660-6048 Web site: www.ahp.com

Mfr. pharmaceutical, animal health care & crop protection products.

American Home Products Corporation, China (PRC)

AMERICAN PRECISION INDUSTRIES INC.

2777 Walden Ave., Buffalo, NY, 14225

Tel: (716) 684-9700 Fax: (716) 684-2129 Web site: www.apicorporate.com

Mfr. heat transfer equipment, motion control devices,coils, capacitors, electro-mechanical clutches & brakes.

API Motion, China (PRC)

AMETEK INC.

4 Station Square, Paoli, PA, 19301

Tel: (610) 647-2121 Fax: (610) 296-3412 Web site: www.ametek.com

Mfr. instruments, electric motors & engineered materials.

AMEKAI Meters (XIAMEN), 1-2 Fl., Chuang Xin Bldg., Torch High Technology, Industrial Zone, Innovate City, Xiamen, Fujian, 361006 China (PRC)

Tel: 86-592-603-0565 Fax: 86-592-603-0570

Ametek Motors Shanghai Co. Ltd., #1 AMETEK Rd., Jiu Ting Economic Development Zone, Shanghai 201615, China (PRC)

Tel: 86-21-5763-2408 Fax: 86-21-5763-2411

Ametek Shanghai (SPL), Room 16B5, Harvest Bldg., #585 Long Hua Xi Rd., Shanghai 200232, China (PRC)

Tel: 86-21-6428-4067 Fax: 86-21-6487-5329

AMMIRATI PURIS LINTAS

One Dag Hammarskjold Plaza, New York, NY, 10017

Tel: (212) 605-8000 Fax: (212) 605-4705 Web site: www.interpublic.com

International advertising agency.

Ammarati Puris Lintas, 7th Fl., Olive Bldg., 620 Hua Shan Rd., Shanghai 200040, China (PRC)

Tel: 86-21-6248-4816 Fax: 86-21-6248-4808 Contact: David Taylor, Mng. Dir.

AMP INC.

470 Friendship Road, PO Box 3608, Harrisburg, PA, 17105-3608

Tel: (717) 564-0100 Fax: (717) 780-6130

Develop/mfr. electronic & electrical connection products & systems.

AMP Ltd., Locations in Hong Kong, Shanghai and Shunde, PRC, China (PRC)

ANALOGIC CORPORATION

8 Centennial Drive, Peabody, MA, 01960

Tel: (978) 977-3000 Fax: (978) 977-6811

Conceive/design/mfr. precision measure, signal processing & imaging equipment for medical, scientific, industry & communications.

Analogic Scientific, 3 Yanshan Rd., Shekou Shenzhen, Guangdong 518067, China (PRC)

ANDERSEN CONSULTING

100 South Wacker Drive, Ste. 1059, Chicago, IL, 60606

Tel: (311) 123-7271 Fax: (312) 507-7965 Web site: www.ac.com

Provides management & technology consulting services.

Andersen Consulting, 2nd Fl., Unisplendour Bldg., Tsinghua University, Beijing 100084, China (PRC)

Tel: 86-10-6254-3922 Fax: 86-10-6278-5989

ANDREW CORPORATION

10500 West 153rd Street, Orland Park, IL, 60462

Tel: (708) 349-3300 Fax: (708) 349-5410 Web site: www.andrew.com

Mfr. antenna systems, coaxial cable, electronic communications & network connectivity systems.

Andrew International, Unit 07, 10th Fl., East Ocean Centre, 24A Jianguomenwai Ave., 100022 Beijing, China (PRC)

Tel: 86-10-6515-5750 Fax: 86-10-6515-5751

Andrew International, Shanghai Rep. Office, Room 1601/1604, No. 129 Yan An Xi Rd., Shanghai Overseas Mansion, Shanghai, China (PRC) 200040

Tel: 86-21-6248-9093 Fax: 86-21-6249-9058

ANHEUSER-BUSCH INTERNATIONAL INC.

One Busch Place, St. Louis, MO, 63118-1852

Tel: (314) 577-2000 Fax: (314) 577-2900 Web site: www.anheuser-busch.com

Malt production, aluminum beverage containers, rice milling, real estate development, metalized & paper label printing, railcar repair & theme-park facilities.

Budweriser Wuhan International Brewing Co., Ltd., Wuhan, China (PRC)

AON CORPORATION

123 North Wacker Drive, Chicago, IL, 60606

Tel: (312) 701-3000 Fax: (312) 701-3100 Web site: www.aon.com

Insurance brokers worldwide; underwrites accident & health insurance, specialty & professional insurance; & provides risk management consultation.

AON China Representative Office, 2 Bei San Huan Rd. Ste. 1803, Beijing 100028, China (PRC)

Tel: 86-10-6460-3168 Fax: 86-10-6460-3169 Contact: David L.Y. Liu

AON/Bain Hogg Office, 305, Equatorial Hotel Office Buliding 65, Shanghai 200040, China (PRC)

Tel: 86-21-6248-1688 Fax: 86-21-6248-4919 Contact: Joseph Sitt

AON/Bain Hogg Office, 15th Fl., World Trade Ctr., Xinjiekou Nanjing 210005, China (PRC)
Tel: 86-25-471-1888 Fax: 86-25-470-2505 Contact: Clare WU

APPLE COMPUTER INC.

One Infinite Loop, Cupertino, CA, 95014
Tel: (831) 996-1010 Fax: (831) 974-2113 Web site: www.apple.com
Personal computers, peripherals & software.

Apple Computer International Ltd. - Beijing Office, 12/F Everbright Bldg., 6 Fu Xing Men Wai Street, Beijing 100045, China (PRC)
Tel: 86-10-6856-3330 Fax: 86-10-6856-1169 Contact: Vincent Tai, Gen. Mgr.

Apple Computer International Ltd. - Guangzhou Office, Room 2207, Dongshan Plaza, 69 Xianlie Road Centre, Guangzhou, 510095 China (PRC)
Tel: 86-20-8732-2228 Fax: 86-20-8732-2218 Contact: Vincent Tai, Gen. Mgr.

Apple Computer International Ltd. - Shanghai Office, 1913 Shanghai International Trade Center, 2200 Yan An Rd. West, Shanghai 200336, China (PRC)
Tel: 86-21-6278-0415 Fax: 86-21-6278-0412 Contact: Vincent Tai, Gen. Mgr.

APPLIED MATERIALS, INC.

3050 Bowers Ave., Santa Clara, CA, 95054-3299
Tel: (408) 727-5555 Fax: (408) 727-9943 Web site: www.appliedmaterials.com
Supplies manufacturing systems/services to semiconductor industry.

Applied Materials China - Beijing, Jia #10, Hui Xin Li, Xiao Guan, An Wai, Chao Yang Dist., Beijing 100029, China (PRC) (Locations: Tianjin & Wuxi, China (PRC))
Tel: 86-10-6496-7733 Fax: 86-10-6495-3170

Applied Materials China - Shanghai, 800 Yi Shan Rd., Shanghai 200233, China (PRC)
Tel: 86-21-6485-3332 Fax: 86-21-6485-2824

APPLIED POWER INC.

13000 W. Silver Spring Drive, Butler, WI, 53007
Tel: (414) 781-6600 Fax: (414) 781-0629
Mfr. hi-pressure tools, vibration control products, electrical tools, consumables, technical furniture & enclosures.

Shanghai Blackhawk Machinery Co. Ltd., China Record Bldg. #902, 811 Hengshan Rd., Shanghai, PRC

ATLANTIC RICHFIELD COMPANY (ARCO)

515 South Flower Street, Los Angeles, CA, 90071-2256
Tel: (213) 486-3511 Fax: (213) 486-2063 Web site: www.arco.com
Petroleum & natural gas, chemicals & service stations.

ARCO Asia-Pacific, Beijing, China (PRC)

Zhenhai Refining and Chemical Company, Shanghai, China (PRC)

ARCO CHEMICAL COMPANY

3801 West Chester Pike, Newtown Square, PA, 19073-2387
Tel: (610) 359-2000 Fax: (610) 359-2722 Web site: www.arcochem.com
Mfr. propylene oxide, a chemical used for flexible foam products, coatings/paints & solvents/inks.

ARCO Chemical China Ltd., 718 West Podium, Shanghai Centre, No. 1376, Nanjing Xi Lu, Shanghai, Post Code 200040, China (PRC)
Tel: 86-21-279-8830 Fax: 86-21-279-8831

ARMSTRONG WORLD INDUSTRIES INC.

PO Box 3001, 313 W. Liberty Street, Lancaster, PA, 17604-3001
Tel: (717) 397-0611 Fax: (717) 396-2787 Web site: www.armstrong.com
Mfr. & marketing interior furnishings & specialty products for bldg, auto & textile industry.

Armstrong Insulation (Panyu) Co. Ltd., Panyu, China (PRC) (All inquiries to U.S. address)

Armstrong Textile Rubber Products Co. Shanghai Ltd., Shanghai, China (PRC) (All inquiries to U.S. address)

Armstrong World Industries (China) Ltd., Shanghai, China (PRC) (All inquiries to U.S. address)

ARTHUR ANDERSEN & COMPANY

33 West Monroe Street, Chicago, IL, 60603

Tel: (312) 372-7100 Fax: (312) 507-0123 Web site: www.arthurandersen.com

Accounting & audit, tax & management consulting services.

Arthur Andersen & Co., China World Tower 1515-25, China World Trade Ctr., #1, Jian Guo Men Wai Av., Beijing 100004, PRC

Arthur Andersen & Co.,, 28/F., Shenzhen International Financial Bldg., 23 Jian She Rd., Shenzhen City, 518001 China (PRC)

Arthur Andersen (Shanghai) Bus. Consulting Co.,, 1590 Yan An Roas West, 7F, Tseng Chow Group Bldg., Shanghai 200052, China (PRC)

ASARCO INC.

180 Maiden Lane, New York, NY, 10038

Tel: (212) 510-2000 Fax: (212) 510-1855 Web site: www.asarco.com

Nonferrous metals, specialty chemicals, minerals, mfr. industrial products, environmental services.

Enthone-Omi Inc., China (PRC)

ASSOCIATED MERCHANDISING CORPORATION

1440 Broadway, New York, NY, 10018

Tel: (212) 596-4000 Fax: (212) 575-2993

Retail service organization; apparel, shoes and accessories.

Associated Merchandising Corp., 58 Mai Ming Rd. S., Shanghai, China (PRC)

AST RESEARCH INC.

16215 Alton Parkway, PO Box 19658, Irvine, CA, 92713-9658

Tel: (949) 727-4141 Fax: (949) 727-8584 Web site: www.ast.com

Design/development/mfr. hi-performance desktop, server & notebook computers.

AST China, Block A&B, 2&3/F, 133 Dong Ting Rd., T.E.D.A., Tianjin 300457, China (PRC)

Tel: 86-10-6849-8318

AUTODESK INC.

111 McInnis Parkway, San Rafael, CA, 94903

Tel: (415) 507-5000 Fax: (415) 507-6112 Web site: www.autodesk.com

Develop/marketing/support computer-aided design, engineering, scientific & multimedia software products.

Audodesk Far East Ltd., 1892-1893, Pana Tower, No. 128 Zhichun Rd., Beijing 100086, China (PRC)

Tel: 86-106-264-9581 Fax: 86-106-264-9584

AUTOMATIC SWITCH CO. (ASCO)

50-60 Hanover Road, Florham Park, NJ, 07932

Tel: (973) 966-2000 Fax: (973) 966-2628

Mfr. solenoid valves, emergency power controls, pressure & temp. switches.

Asco Asia, Beijing, c/o Emerson Electric China Holdings, 15/F Gateway Bldg., 10 Ya Bao Lu Rd., Chao Yang Dist., Beijing 100020, China (PRC)

Tel: 86-10-6-592-5321 Fax: 86-10-6-592-5320 Contact: Cui Weizhou

Asco Asia, Chengdu, c/o Emerson Electric Asia, Rm. 2004, Tong Mei Bldg., No. 76 Jianshe North Rd., Chengdu City, Sichuan, China (PRC)

Tel: 86-28-338-1496 Fax: 86-28-338-1494 Contact: Hu Yi

Asco Asia, Shanghai, c/o Emerson Electric China Holdings, Rm. 403-406, Man Po Intl. Bus. Ctr., 660 Xin Hua Rd., Shanghai 200052, China (PRC)

Tel: 86-22-6-282-6223 Fax: 86-21-6-282-6077 Contact: Tony Wong

AVERY DENNISON CORPORATION

150 N. Orange Grove Blvd., Pasadena, CA, 91103

Tel: (626) 304-2000 Fax: (626) 792-7312 Web site: www.averydennison.com

Mfr. pressure-sensitive adhesives & materials, office products, labels, tags, retail systems, Carter's Ink & specialty chemicals.

Avery Dennison China, China (PRC)

AVON PRODUCTS INC.

1345 Ave. of the Americas, New York, NY, 10105-0196

Tel: (212) 282-5000 Fax: (212) 282-6049 Web site: www.avon.com

Mfr./distributor beauty & related products, fashion jewelry, gifts & collectibles.

Avon Products (Guangzhou) Ltd., 2-3/F, 420-1 Huanshi Dong Rd., Guandzhou 510075, China (PRC)

Tel: 86-20-766-3536 Fax: 86-20-766-3531 Contact: Samantha Kong, Reg. Dir

Avon Products (Guangzhou) Ltd., 456 Wu Jing Rd., 9/F, Shanghai 200071, China (PRC)

Tel: 86-21-6356-6912 Fax: 86-21-6356-0403 Contact: Mike Gudgin, Reg. Dir.

BAKER & McKENZIE

One Prudential Plaza, 130 East Randolph Drive, Ste. 2500, Chicago, IL, 60601

Tel: (312) 861-8000 Fax: (312) 861-2899 Web site: www.bakerinfo.com

International legal services.

Baker & McKenzie, China World Tower, 1 Jianguomenwai Dajie, 100004 Beijing (Peking), China (PRC)

Tel: 86-10-6505-0591 Fax: 86-10-6505-2309

BAKER HUGHES INCORPORATED

3900 Essex Lane, Ste. 1200, Houston, TX, 77027

Tel: (713) 439-8600 Fax: (713) 439-8699 Web site: www.bakerhughes.com

Develop & apply technology to drill, complete & produce oil and natural gas wells; provide separation systems to petroleum, municipal, continuous process & mining industries.

Baker Hughes Inc., Room 531, Tanggu View Hotel, No.1, Zhabei Rd., Tanggu, Tianjin 300452, China (PRC)

Tel: 86-2-531-1935

Baker Hughes INTEQ, Room A-100, Tarim Hotel, Kola, Xinjiang 841000, China (PRC)

Tel: 86-996-217-3214 Fax: 86-996-217-3167

Baker Oil Tools, Ste. 1001, Consultec Bldg., B-12 Guang Hau Rd., Beijing, China (PRC)

Tel: 86-10-6505-2501 Fax: 86-10-6505-2831

Baker Oil Tools, Skekou Rep Office, 2/F Chiwan Bldg., Chiwan Petroleum Supply Base, Shekou, China (PRC)

Tel: 86-756-669-1294 Fax: 86-755-669-3852

BALDWIN TECHNOLOGY CO., INC.

One Norwalk West, 40 Richards Ave., Norwalk, CT, 06854

Tel: (203) 838-7470 Fax: (203) 852-7040 Web site: www.baldwintech.com

Mfr./services material handling, accessories, control & prepress equipment for print industry.

Baldwin Printing Control Equipment Co. Ltd., Rm. 115 - Juyuan Office Bldg., No. 33 Juer Alley, Jiaodaukou Nandajie St., Dongcheng Dist., Beijing 100009, China (PRC)

Tel: 86-10-6-407-0594 Fax: 86-10-6-407-0593 Contact: Yungyi Huang, Pres.

Baldwin Printing Control Equipment Co. Ltd., No. 38, Lane 339, Wu Zhong Rd., Min Hang Dist., Shanghai 201103, China (PRC)

Tel: 86-21-6464-9901 Fax: 86-21-6464-9934 Contact: Yungyi Huang, Pres.

THE BANK OF NEW YORK

48 Wall Street, New York, NY, 10286

Tel: (212) 495-1784 Fax: (212) 495-2546 Web site: www.bankofny.com

Banking servces.

The Bank of New York, Dynasty Business Ctr., Rm. 503, 457 Wulumuqi Rd. (N), Shanghai, China (PRC)

BANKAMERICA CORPORATION

555 California Street, San Francisco, CA, 94104

Tel: (415) 622-3530 Fax: (415) 622-8467 Web site: www.bankamerica.com

Financial services.

Bank of America NT & SA, Unit 22-23, 27/F China World Tower, China World Trade Centre, 1 Jian Guo Men Wai Ave., Beijing 100004, PRC

Tel: 86-10-505-3508 Fax: 86-10-505-3509 Contact: C.M. Pang, VP

BANKBOSTON CORPORATION

100 Federal Street, PO Box 1788, Boston, MA, 02110

Tel: (617) 434-2200 Fax: (617) 434-7547 Web site: www.bankboston.com

Banking & insurance services.

BankBoston - Beijing, 10D Citic Bldg., 19, Jianguomenwai Dajie, Beijing 100004, China (PRC)

Tel: 86-10-6593-1850 Fax: 86-10-6593-1852

BankBoston - Shanghai, Rm. 110, 11/F, Union Bldg., 100 Yan An Rd. East, Shanghai 200002, China (PRC)

Tel: 86-21-6321-2331 Fax: 86-21-6321-2353

BANKERS TRUST COMPANY

280 Park Ave., New York, NY, 10017

Tel: (212) 250-2500 Fax: (212) 250-2440 Web site: www.bankerstrust.com

Banking & investment services.

Bankers Trust Company, Beijing Luftthansa Ctr., Ste. 125, Ground Fl., 50 Liangmaqiao Rd., Chaoyang Dist., Beijing 100016, China (PRC)

Tel: 86-10-6463-8038 Fax: 86-10-6463-8037 Contact: Kingking Wong

R.G. BARRY CORPORATION

13405 Yarmouth Road NW, Pickerington, OH, 43147

Tel: (614) 864-6400 Fax: (614) 864-9787 Web site: www.rgbarry.com

Mfr. slippers & footwear.

R. G. Barry Corp., Block 4 2/F Processing Zone, Sha Tau Kok, Shenzhen City, China (PRC)

Tel: 86-755-535-1130 Fax: 86-755-535-1131

BATES WORLDWIDE INC.

405 Lexington Ave., New York, NY, 10174

Tel: (212) 297-7000 Fax: (212) 986-0270 Web site: www.batesww.com

Advertising, marketing, public relations & media consulting.

Bates Beijing, 23 Shul Zhui Zi, Chao Yang, Dist., Beijing, 100026 China (PRC)

Tel: 86-10-6598-8018 Contact: Jeffrey Yu, CEO

Bates Shanghai, Rms. 505-515, 5/F, Fu Xing Plaza, No. 109 Yan Dang Rd., Shanghai, 2000020, China (PRC)

Tel: 86-21-6356-2908 Contact: Jeffrey Yu, CEO

BAUSCH & LOMB INC.

One Bausch & Lomb Place, Rochester, NY, 14604-2701

Tel: (716) 338-6000 Fax: (716) 338-6007 Web site: www.bausch.com

Mfr. vision care products & accessories & hearing aids.

Bausch & Lomb Cina, Inc., Guangzhou, China (PRC)

Bausch & Lomb Cina, Inc., Bejing, China (PRC)

BAX GLOBAL CORPORATION

16808 Armstrong Ave., PO Box 19571, Irvine, CA, 92623

Tel: (714) 752-4000 Fax: (714) 852-1488 Web site: www.bax.com

Air freight forwarder.

BAX Global - Beijing, Bejing Leonardo Ctr., Rm. A101, No. 5 Wan Hong Rd., Da Shan Zi Huan Dao Dong, Chaoyang Dist., 100015, Beijing, China (PRC)

Tel: 86-10-64-65-0202 Fax: 86-10-64-35-1441

BAX Global - Shanghai, Lian Hang Commercial Bldg., Room 502/503, No.8, Lane 394, Yan An Xi Rd., Shanghai, 200040, China (PRC)

Tel: 86-21-6249-3093 Fax: 86-21-6249-1578

BBDO WORLDWIDE

1285 Ave. of the Americas, New York, NY, 10019

Tel: (212) 459-5000 Fax: (212) 459-6645 Web site: www.bbdo.com

Multinational group of advertising agencies.

BBDO/CNUAC, Beijing, China (PRC)

BDO SEIDMAN, LLP

Two Prudential Plaza, 180 N. Stetson Ave., Ste. 2300, Chicago, IL, 60601

Tel: (312) 240-1236 Fax: (312) 240-3329 Web site: www.bdo.com

International accounting & financial consulting firm.

BDO China, Beijing, Shanghai & Shenzhen, China (PRC) (Mail/Tel/Fax c/o Asia Pacific Office - Hong Kong (PRC))

Tel: 852-2541-5041 Fax: 852-2815-0002 Contact: Jennifer Y. Yip

BEA SYSTEMS, INC.

2315 North First Street, St. Jose, CA, 95131

Tel: (408) 570-8000 Fax: (408) 570-8091 Web site: www.beasys.com

Develops communications management software & provider of software consulting services.

BEA Systems Ltd. Beijing, 811, 8/F, Canway Bldg., 66 Nan Li Shi Lu, Beijing, 100045, China (PRC)

Tel: 86-10-6801-8877 Fax: 86-10-6804-2433

BEAR STEARNS & CO., INC.

245 Park Ave., New York, NY, 10167

Tel: (212) 272-2000 Fax: (212) 272-3092 Web site: www.bearstearns.com

Investment banking, securities broker/dealer & investment advisory services.

Bear Stearns & Co. Inc., Room 1710, Shanghai Intl Trade Ctr., 2200 Yan An Xi Rd. West, Shanghai 200335, China (PRC)

Tel: 86-21-6219-2642 Fax: 86-21-6219-7249

Bear Stearns & Co. Inc., Level 9, Units 23-24, China World Tower, #1 Jian Guo Men Wai Ave., Beijing 100004, China (PRC)

Tel: 86-10-6505-5101 Fax: 86-10-6505-5203

BECHTEL GROUP INC.

50 Beale Street, PO Box 3965, San Francisco, CA, 94105-1895

Tel: (415) 768-1234 Fax: (415) 768-9038 Web site: www.bechtel.com

General contractors in engineering & construction.

Bechtel International Corp., Room 501, Parkview Centre No. 2, Jiangtai Rd., Chao Yang Dist., Beijing 100016, China (PRC)

Tel: 86-10-6437-6669 Fax: 86-10-6437-6455

Bechtel International Corp., Kuen Yang International, Business Plaza Room 501, #798 Zhao Jia Bang Rd., Shanghai 200030, China (PRC)

Tel: 86-21-6473-5955 Fax: 86-21-6473-5992

BECKER & POLIAKOFF, P.A.

Emerald Lake Corporate Park, 3111 Stirling Road, Fort Lauderdale, FL, 33312

Tel: (954) 987-7550 Fax: (954) 985-4176

Law firm; advice & assistance with foreign investments.

Becker & Poliakoff, P.A., A-1 Unit, Room 1506, 371-375 Huan Shi Dong Rd., Guangzhou (Canton), Guangzhou, China (PRC)

BECKETT BROWN INTERNATIONAL

Three Church Circle, Ste. 207, Annapolis, MD, 21401

Tel: (410) 315-7995 Fax: (410) 315-8882 Web site: www.beckettbrown.com

Security company.

Beckett Brown International, Beijing, China (PRC)

Contact: Dave Bresett, VP Int'l.

BELLSOUTH INTERNATIONAL

1155 Peachtree Street NE, Ste. 400, Atlanta, GA, 30367

Tel: (404) 249-4800 Fax: (404) 249-4880 Web site: www.bellsouth.com

Mobile communications, telecommunications network systems.

BellSouth China Representative Office, Ste. S123, Beijing Lufthansa Centre, 50 Liangmaiqiao Rd., Chanoyang Dist., Beijing 100016, China (PRC)

Tel: 86-10-6465-1685 Fax: 86-10-6465-1686

BellSouth Shanghai Centre, Ltd., Ste. 431, 1376 Nanjing West Rd., Shanghai 200040 China (PRC)

Tel: 86-21-6279-8900 Fax: 86-21-6279-8910

Ji Tong - BellSouth Company, Beijing Gaode, Office Bldg. No. 11, North Third Ring Rd. West, Room 201-205, Haidian Dist., 100088 Beijing, China (PRC)

Tel: 86-10-6238-8708 Fax: 86-10-6238-8715

BENTLY NEVADA CORPORATION

1617 Water Street, PO Box 157, Minden, NV, 89423

Tel: (702) 782-3611 Fax: (702) 782-9259

Electronic monitoring systems.

Qing Hua Technical Services, Qing Hua Yuan, West Suburg, Beijing, China (PRC)

LOUIS BERGER INTERNATIONAL INC.

100 Halsted Street, East Orange, NJ, 07019

Tel: (201) 678-1960 Fax: (201) 672-4284 Web site: www.louisberger.com

Consulting engineers, architects, economists & planners.

Chelbi Eng. Consultants, Inc., Ding 28 Guozijian St., An Nei, Beijing 100007, China (PRC)

Tel: 86-10-6403-5968 Fax: 86-10-6403-1605

Louis Berger International Inc., Hunan Provincial Xiangtan-Leiyang Expressway Construction, Yangjia Garden Hotel, No.59 Xiangjian East Rd., Jiangdon Dist., Hengyang City 421002, Hunan Province, China (PRC)

Tel: 86-734-839-3061 Fax: 86-734-839-3060

Louis Berger International Inc., Tianhe Hotel, Shuangtaizi Dist., Panjin City, 124021 Liaoning Province, China (PRC)

Tel: 86-4271-398-2029 Fax: 86-4271-395-2031

Louis Berger International Inc., 70 Longhai Rd., Zhengzhou 450052, China (PRC)

Tel: 86-371-898-1035 Fax: 86-371-898-1035

Louis Berger International Inc., 52 Yanan Rd., Urumqi, Xinjiang 830001, China (PRC)

Tel: 86-373-287-4999 Fax: 86-373-287-4907

BESSEMER GROUP, INC.

630 Fifth Ave., 39th Fl., New York, NY, 10022

Tel: (212) 708-9100 Fax: (212) 265-5826

Consumer goods retail financing.

Bessemer Holdings Asia, Rm. 501, Dist. B, Yinhai Bldg., 250 Cao Xi Rd., Shanghai 200233, China (PRC)

Tel: 86-21-6482-7134 Contact: Michael Coorey, Pres.

BESTFOODS, INC.

700 Sylvan Ave., International Plaza, Englewood Cliffs, NJ, 07632-9976

Tel: (201) 894-4000 Fax: (201) 894-2186 Web site: www.bestfoods.com

Consumer foods products; corn refining.

Bestfoods Guangzhou Ltd., 2/F Block B, 170-174 Zhan Yi St., Lin He Rd. East, Tian He Dist., Guangzhou 510610, China (PRC)

Tel: 86-20-3880-3413 Fax: 86-20-3880-3422 Contact: Thin-Wai Chow, Chmn.

Bestfoods Shanghai Ltd., Room 8306, Bldg. A, Shanghai Jiahua Busines Centre, 808 Hongqiao Rd., Shanghai 200030, China (PRC)

Tel: 86-21-6486-8757 Fax: 86-21-6486-8894 Contact: J. Y. Yoo, Mgr.

CPC (Shandong) Foods Ltd., 89 Shui Ku Rd., Weifang Municipality 261052, Shandong Province, China (PRC) (PRC)

Tel: 86-536-832-9328 Fax: 86-536-832-9258 Contact: Levi Ying, Dir.

CPC Foods Co. Ltd. Beijing, 234 Nanding Rd., Yongdingmenwai, Fengtai Dist., Beijing 100075, China (PRC)

Tel: 86-10-6723-0010 Fax: 86-10-6723-8351 Contact: Jeffrey P. Reed, Chmn.

BICKLEY INC.

PO Box 369, Bensalem, PA, 19020

Tel: (215) 638-4500 Fax: (215) 638-4334 Web site: www.ceramics.com/bickley

Mfr. high temp. furnaces.

Bickley/Madam Du Hang, Rm. 10937, Xiyuan Hotel, No. 1 Sanlihe Rd., Beijing, China (PRC)

Tel: 86-10-6831-3388 Fax: 86-10-6834-5105 Contact: Madam Du Hang, Sales Rep. Emp: 2

BIJUR LUBRICATING CORPORATION

50 Kocher Drive, Bennington, VT, 05201-1994

Tel: (802) 447-2174 Fax: (802) 447-1365 Web site: www.bijur.com

Design/mfr. centralized lubrication equipment for industrial machinery.

Nanjing Bijur Machinery Products Ltd., 177 Xiaolingwe St., Nanjing 210014, China (PRC)

Tel: 86-25-4439440 Fax: 86-25-4432724 Contact: He Jian, Gen. Mgr. Emp: 120

BINDICATOR

1915 Dove Street, Port Huron, MI, 48060

Tel: (810) 987-2700 Fax: (810) 987-4476

Mfr. level control instruments for measuring solids and liquids.

Bindicator Shanghai, 28A Hai Xing Plaza, 1 Ryuhub (s) Rd., Shanghai, 200023 China (PRC)

Tel: 86-21-6418-5060 Fax: 86-21-6418-5059 Contact: Mdm Zhang, Gen. Mgr. Emp: 5

BIO-RAD LABORATORIES INC.

1000 Alfred Nobel Drive, Hercules, CA, 94547

Tel: (510) 724-7000 Fax: (510) 724-3167

Mfr. life science research products, clinical diagnostics, analytical instruments.

Bio-Rad Laboratories Inc., Beijing, China (PRC)

BOISE CASCADE CORPORATION

1111 West Jefferspm Street, PO Box 50, Boise, ID, 83728-0001

Tel: (208) 384-6161 Fax: (208) 384-7189 Web site: www.bc.com

Mfr./distributor paper and paper products, building products, office products.

Zhuhai Hiwin Boise Cascade Specialty Paper Co. Ltd., No. 9 Bldg., Nanshan Ind. Area, Zhuhai, Guangdong 519015, China (PRC)

Tel: 86-756-335-0611 Fax: 86-756-335-0911 Contact: Jim Kirby, Gen. Mgr.

BOOZ ALLEN & HAMILTON INC.

8283 Greensboro Drive, McLean, VA, 22102

Tel: (703) 902-5000 Fax: (703) 902-3333 Web site: www.bah.com

International management and technology consultants.

Booz Allen & Hamilton (China) Ltd., Ste. 510 Shanghai Centre, 1376 Nanjing Xi Lu, Shanghai 200040, China (PRC)

Tel: 86-21-6279-8500 Fax: 86-21-6279-8501

BORG-WARNER AUTOMOTIVE INC.

200 S. Michigan Ave., Chicago, IL, 60604

Tel: (312) 322-8500 Fax: (312) 461-0507

Mfr. automotive components; provider of security services.

Beijing-Warner Gear Co. Ltd., 2 Dingfuzhuang Xil, Chaoyang Dist., Beijing 1000024, China (PRC)

THE BOSTON CONSULTING GROUP

Exchange Place, 31st Floor, Boston, MA, 02109

Tel: (617) 973-1200 Fax: (617) 973-1339 Web site: www.bcg.com

Management consulting company.

The Boston Consulting Group, 2F, Olive L.V.O. Bldg., 620 Hua Shan Rd., Shanghai 200040, China (PRC)

Tel: 86-21-6248-5099

BOYDEN CONSULTING CORPORATION

100 Park Ave., 34th Floor, New York, NY, 10017

Tel: (212) 980-6534 Fax: (212) 980-6147 Web site: www.boyden.com

Executive search.

Boyden Associates Ltd., Ste. 435, East Tower, The Shanghai Centre, 1376 Nan Jing West Rd., Shanghai 200040, China (PRC)

Tel: 86-21-6279-8246

BOZELL WORLDWIDE

40 West 23rd Street, New York, NY, 10010

Tel: (212) 727-5000 Fax: (212) 645-9173 Web site: www.bozell.com

Advertising, marketing, public relations and media consulting.

Bozell China (Beijing), 5th Fl., Block B, Fu Hua Mansion, No.8 North St., Chao Yang Men, Dong Cheng Dist., Beijing 100027, China (PRC)

Tel: 86-10-6554-1350 Fax: 86-10-6554-1355 Contact: Wu Sui-ping, Mgr.

Bozell China (Guangzhou), 17-J Yue Hai Centre, 472 Huanshi Rd. East, Guangzhou 510075, China (PRC)

Tel: 86-20-8777-9688 Fax: 86-20-8760-9881 Contact: Elke Eskes-Frey, Dir.

Bozell China (Shanghai), Rooms C & D, 11th Fl., Golden Tower, Jiu An Plaza, 258 Tong Ren Rd., Shanghai 200040, China (PRC)

Tel: 86-21-6247-5769 Fax: 86-21-6247-5754 Contact: Sun Zhong (Steven), Mgr.

BRAND FARRAR BUXBAUM LLP

515 Flower Street, Ste. 3500, Los Angeles, CA, 90017-2201

Tel: (213) 228-0288 Fax: (213) 426-6222

International law firm specializing in cross-border disputes and business transactions; intellectual property.

Brand Farrar Buxbaum LLP, Ste. 2518, China World Trade Centre, No. 1 Jian Guo Men Wai Ave., Beijing (Peking), China (PRC)

Tel: 86-10-6505-2288 Fax: 86-10-6505-2638 Contact: Messrs. Farrar & Buxbaum, Sr. Partners

Brand Farrar Buxbaum LLP, Ste. 519, Foreign Trade Centre, 15 Hu Bing North Rd., Xiamen, China (PRC)

Tel: 86-592-506-3059 Fax: 86-592-511-1044 Contact: Messrs. Farrar & Buxbaum, Sr. Partners

Brand Farrar Buxbaum LLP, Ste. 2103A, Shenzhen Development Centre, Renmin Nan Lu, Shenzhen, P.R.C., Shanghai, China (PRC)

Tel: 86-755-229-8009 Fax: 86-755-229-8011 Contact: Messrs. Farrar & Buxbaum, Sr. Partners

Brand Farrar Buxbaum LLP, Ste. 1907, Astronautic Bldg., 525 Sichuan Bei Rd., Shanghai, China (PRC)

Tel: 86-21-6357-5676 Fax: 86-21-6357-5679 Contact: Messrs. Farrar & Buxbaum, Sr. Partners

Brand Farrar Buxbaum LLP, Ste. 512, China Hotel, Office Tower, Guangzhou (Canton), Guangzhou, China (PRC)

Tel: 86-20-8666-3388 Fax: 86-20-8668-1217 Contact: Messrs. Farrar & Buxbaum, Sr. Partners

BRANSON ULTRASONICS CORPORATION

41 Eagle Road, Danbury, CT, 06813-1961

Tel: (203) 796-0400 Fax: (203) 796-2285

Mfr. plastics assembly equipment, ultrasonic cleaning equipment.

Shanghai Branson Ultrasonics Co., Shanghai, China (PRC)

Tel: 86-21-640-87779 Fax: 86-21-643-33194

BRIGGS & STRATTON CORPORATION

PO Box 702, Milwaukee, WI, 53201

Tel: (414) 259-5333 Fax: (414) 259-9594

Mfr. engines.

Briggs & Stratton China, China (PRC) - All mail to U.S. address.

BRISTOL-MYERS SQUIBB COMPANY

345 Park Ave., New York, NY, 10154

Tel: (212) 546-4000 Fax: (212) 546-4020 Web site: www.bms.com

Pharmaceutical and food preparations, medical and surgical instruments.

Bristol-Myers Squibb - China (SASS), 1315 Jian Chuan Rd., Min Hang Dist., Shanghai, China (PRC)

Contact: Jack M. Wolinetz, Pres.

Bristol-Myers Squibb -Guangzhou China, No. 70 Mei Hua Lu, Guangzhou, Quangdong, PRC 510600, China (PRC)

Zimmer Shanghai, Shanghai, China (PRC)

BROWN & ROOT INC.

4100 Clinton Drive, Houston, TX, 77020-6299

Tel: (713) 676-3011 Fax: (713) 676-8532

Engineering, construction and maintenance.

Brown & Root Overseas Ltd., Lido Commercial Ctr., No. 303, 3rd Fl., Blk. A-2, Jichang Rd., Beijing, 100004, China (PRC)

Tel: 86-10-437-6662 Fax: 86-10-437-6331

China Brown & Root Marine Engineering & Construction Ltd., 401 Seaview Commercial Bldg., PO Box 328, Shekou, Shenzhen 518067, China (PRC)

Tel: 86-755-669-2470 Fax: 86-755-668-3061

COES-Brown & Root Marine Engineering & Construction Co. Ltd., PO Box 589, Tianjin 300452, Tianjin, China (PRC)

Tel: 86-22-531-1909 Fax: 86-22-531-6153

COESK-Taylor Diving Co., Rooms 912/914, 536 Bin Jiang Rd. E., Guangznou, Guangdong, China (PRC)

BTU INTERNATIONAL

23 Esquire Road, North Billerica, MA, 01862

Tel: (508) 667-4111 Fax: (508) 667-9068

Mfr. of industrial furnaces.

BTU China, Room 1125, Jingchao Mansion, #5 Nong Zhan Guan Nan Lu, Beijing, 100026, China (PRC)

BUCYRUS INTERNATIONAL, INC.

1100 Milwaukee Ave., South Milwaukee, WI, 53172

Tel: (414) 768-4000 Fax: (414) 768-4474

Mfr. of surface mining equipment, primarily walking draglines, electric mining shovels and blast hole drills.

Bacyrus International, Inc. (China), 8/F Office Tower, 2 Henderson Ctr., Beijing 18, Jianguomen Nei Ave., Dongcheng Dist., Beijing, China (PRC) 100005

Tel: 86-10-651-83110 Fax: 86-10-651-71532 Contact: John Oliver, Mng. Dir.

BURSON-MARSTELLER

230 Park Ave., New York, NY, 10003-1566

Tel: (212) 614-4000 Fax: (212) 614-4262 Web site: www.bm.com

Public relations/public affairs consultants.

Burson-Marsteller Beijng, 2/F Golden Brridge Plaza, 1A, Jiangguomenwai Ave., Beijing 100020, China (PRC)

Tel: 86-10-6507-9278 Fax: 86-10-6507-9278 Emp: 30

Burson-Marsteller Shanghai, Shainghai Overseas Chinese Mansion, Room 1908 129 Yan'An Rd. West, Shanghai 20040, China (PRC)

Tel: 86-21-6249-1640 Fax: 86-21-6249-1646 Emp: 20

BUTLER MANUFACTURING COMPANY

Penn Valley Park, PO Box 419917, Kansas City, MO, 64141-0917

Tel: (816) 968-3000 Fax: (816) 968-3279

Pre-engineered steel structural systems, curtain wall and electrical distributor systems.

Butler (Shanghai) Inc., Trimwell Industrial Park, 6th Fl., Yutang Raod, Songjiang, Shanghai, 201600, China (PRC)

Tel: 86-21-5774-1717 Fax: 86-21-5774-1823 Contact: Moufid A. Alossi, Pres. Asia/Pacific

CALTEX PETROLEUM CORPORATION

125 East John Carpenter Fwy., Irving, TX, 75062-2794

Tel: (972) 830-1000 Fax: (972) 830-1081 Web site: www.caltex.com

Petroleum products.

Caltex China Ltd., All mail to Caltex Oil Hong Kong, Box 147, Hong Kong (PRC)

CAMBREX CORP.

1 Meadowlands Plaza, East Rutherford, NJ, 07063

Tel: (201) 804-3000 Fax: (201) 804-9852 Web site: www.cambex.com

Mfg. Bulf active chemicals for pharmaceuticals.

Cambrex PRC, 6/F, Nan Wai Tan Bldg., 760 Zhong Shan Nan Rd., Shanghai 20010, China (PRC)

Tel: 86-21-6378-1230 Fax: 86-21-6378-6277

CARRIER CORPORATION

One Carrier Place, Farmington, CT, 06034-4015

Tel: (860) 674-3000 Fax: (860) 679-3010 Web site: www.carrier.com

Mfr./distributor/services A/C, heating & refrigeration equipment.

Shanghai Carrier Transicold Equipment Co. Ltd., Shanghai, China (PRC)

Shanghai Haoshen Carrier Air Conditioning, Ltd., Shanghai, China (PRC)

Shanghai Hezhong Carrier A/C Equipment Ltd., Shanghai, China (PRC)

Shanghai Tong Hui Carrier A/C Equipment Co. Ltd., Shanghai, China (PRC)

Shanghai Yileng Carrier Air Conditioning Equipment Co. Ltd., Shanghai, China (PRC)

Shenzhen Carrier Service Co., Shenzhen, China (PRC)

Tianjin Carrier A/C Equipment Co. Ltd., Tianjin Municipality, China (PRC)

Unified Marketing, Shanghai, China (PRC)

United Carrier Engineering & Services Co. Ltd., Shanghai, China (PRC)

CASE CORPORATION

700 State Street, Racine, WI, 53404

Tel: (414) 636-6011 Fax: (414) 636-0200 Web site: www.casecorp.com

Mfr./sale agricultural and construction equipment.

Liuzhou Case Liugong Construction Equipment Co. Lid., No. 1 Liutai Rd., Liuzhou, GuangXi, China (PRC) 545007

Tel: 86-772-388-6560 Fax: 86-772-388-6561 Contact: Pablo Toledo, Gen. Mgr.

CATERPILLAR INC.

100 NE Adams Street, Peoria, IL, 61629-6105

Tel: (309) 675-1000 Fax: (309) 675-1182 Web site: www.cat.com

Mfr. earth/material-handling and construction machinery and equipment and engines.

Caterpillar (China) Investment Co., Ltd., Shanghai, China (PRC)

Caterpillar Xuzhou Ltd., Xuzhou, China (PRC)

Guangzhou MaK Diesel Engine Ltd., Guangzhou, China (PRC)

C.B. RICHARD ELLIS

533 South Fremont Ave., Los Angeles, CA, 90071-1712

Tel: (213) 613-3123 Fax: (213) 613-3535 Web site: www.cbrichardellis.com

Commercial real estate services.

CB Richard Ellis, Beijing, China (PRC)

CB Richard Ellis, Locations in Guang/hou, Kowloon and Shanghai, China (PRC)

CENTRAL NATIONAL-GOTTESMAN INC.

3 Manhattanville Road, Purchase, NY, 10577-2110

Tel: (914) 696-9000 Fax: (914) 696-1066

Worldwide sales pulp and paper products.

CNG Beijing Rep Office, Hua-pu International Plaza, Ste. 815, No. 19, Chao Wai Ave., Beijing, China (PRC) 100020

Tel: 86-10-6599-2712 Fax: 86-10-6594-2711 Contact: Tiean Huang

CH2M HILL INC.

6060 South Willow Drive, Greenwood Village, CO, 80111

Tel: (303) 771-0900 Fax: (303) 770-2616

Consulting engineers, planners, economists and scientists.

CH2M Hill, Beijing, China (PRC)

Tel: 86-10-652-73603

THE CHASE MANHATTAN CORPORATION

World Headquarters, 270 Park Ave., New York, NY, 10017

Tel: (212) 270-6000 Fax: (212) 622-9030 Web site: www.chase.com

International banking and financial services.

The Chase Manhattan Bank, Beijing Rep. Office, 5/F Full Link Plaza, 18 Chaoyangmenwai Ave., Beijing 100020, China (PRC)

Tel: 86-10-6588-1039 Fax: 86-10-6588-1040

The Chase Manhattan Bank, Shanghai Rep. Office, Ste. 700A, Shanghai Centre, 1376 Nanjing Rd. West, Shanghai 200040, China (PRC)

Tel: 86-21-6279-7288 Fax: 86-21-6279-8101

The Chase Manhattan Bank, Tianjin Branch, Tianjin International Bldg., Room 1401, 75 Nanjing Rd., Tainjin 300050, China (PRC)

Tel: 86-22-2339-9111 Fax: 86-22-2339-8111

CHEMTEX INTERNATIONAL INC.

560 Lexington Ave., New York, NY, 10022

Tel: (212) 752-5220 Fax: (212) 752-0872

Mfr. fibers & petrochemicals; engineering, procurement, construction, construction management.

Chemtex Intl. Inc., Landmark Tower #2202, 8 Dongsanhuan North Rd., Beijing, China (PRC)

Contact: Sean Ma, Gen. Mgr.

CHIQUITA BRANDS INTERNATIONAL INC.

250 East Fifth Street, Cincinnati, OH, 45202

Tel: (513) 784-8000 Fax: (513) 784-8030 Web site: www.chiquita.com

Sale and distribution of bananas, fresh fruits and processed foods.

Chiquita Brands, China (PRC)

THE CHRISTIAN SCIENCE PUBLISHING SOCIETY

1 Norway Street, Boston, MA, 02115

Tel: (617) 450-2000 Fax: (617) 450-7575

Publishing company.

The Christian Science Monitor, 7-2-133 Jianguomenwai, Beijing, China (PRC)

Tel: 86-106-537-3125 Contact: Kevin Platt

CHRYSLER CORPORATION

1000 Chrysler Drive, Auburn Hills, MI, 48326-2766

Tel: (248) 576-5741 Fax: (248) 512-5143 Web site: www.chrysler.com

Mfr./marketing cars & light trucks, electronic & aerospace products & systems.

Beijing Jeep Corp. (JV), Beijing, China (PRC)

THE CHUBB CORPORATION

15 Mountain View Road, Warren, NJ, 07061-1615

Tel: (908) 580-2000 Fax: (908) 580-3606 Web site: www.chubb.com

Holding company: property/casualty insurance.

Federal Insurance Company, Rm. 2301, Full Link Plaza, No. 18, Chao Yang Men Wai Ave., Chao Yang Dist., Beijing, 1000020, China (PRC)

Tel: 86-10-6588-2050 Fax: 86-10-6588-2055

Federal Insurance Company, Chubb School of Insurance, Shanghai Univ. of Finance & Economics, 777 Guoding Rd., Shanghi, 100433, China (PRC)

Tel: 86-21-6511-4766 Fax: 86-21-6510-3923

Federal Insurance Company, 30/F, International Financial Bldg., 23 Jianshe Rd., Shenzhen, 518001, China (PRC)

Tel: 86-755-225-3324 Fax: 86-755-233-2164

CISCO SYSTEMS, INC.

170 Tasman Drive, San Jose, CA, 95134-1706

Tel: (408) 526-4000 Fax: (408) 526-4100 Web site: www.cisco.com

Develop/mfr./market computer hardware and software networking systems.

Cisco Systems (HK) Ltd., Beijing Office, Room 820, Jing Guang Centre, Hu Jia Lou, Chao Yang Qu, Beijing, PRC Post Code 100020, China (PRC)

Tel: 86-10-501-8888 x821 Fax: 861-501-3333-720 Contact: N/A

CITICORP

399 Park Ave., New York, NY, 10043

Tel: (212) 559-1000 Fax: (212) 527-2066 Web site: www.citibank.com

International banking and financial services.

Citibank N.A., 5th Fl., Shanghai Union Bldg., 100 Yanan Rd. East, Shanghai 200002, China (PRC)

THE CLOROX COMPANY

1221 Broadway, PO Box 24305, Oakland, CA, 94623-1305

Tel: (510) 271-7000 Fax: (510) 832-1463

Mfr. soap & detergents, and domestic consumer packaged products.

Clorox (Guangzhou) Co. Ltd., Taiping, China (PRC)

THE COASTAL CORPORATION

Nine Greenway Plaza, Houston, TX, 77046-0995

Tel: (713) 877-1400 Fax: (713) 877-6752 Web site: www.coastalcorp.com

Oil refining, natural gas, related services; independent power production.

Coastal Petroleum Overseas N.V., Shanghai, China (PRC)

THE COCA-COLA COMPANY

P.O. Drawer 1734, Atlanta, GA, 30301

Tel: (404) 676-2121 Fax: (404) 676-6792 Web site: www.coca-cola.com

Mfr./marketing/distributor soft drinks, syrups & concentrates, juice & juice-drink products.

Hainan Coca-Cola Bottler, China (PRC) - All mail to U.S. address.

Tianjin Coca-Cola Bottler, China (PRC) - All mail to U.S. address.

COLSON INC.

3700 Airport Road, Jonesboro, AR, 72401

Tel: (870) 932-4501 Fax: (870) 933-6612

Mfr./sale casters.

Colson Casters Ltd., China (PRC)

COMMERCIAL METALS COMPANY

PO Box 1046, Dallas, TX, 75221

Tel: (972) 689-4300 Fax: (972) 689-4320

Metal collecting/processing, steel mills and metal trading.

Cometals China Inc., Beijing Exhibition Hall, Nanlou Ermen 2107-2109, Beijing, China (PRC)

COMPAQ COMPUTER CORPORATION

20555 State Highway 249, PO Box 692000, Houston, TX, 77269-2000

Tel: (713) 370-0670 Fax: (713) 514-1740 Web site: www.compaq.com

Develop/mfr. personal computers.

Compaq Computer Corporation., No. 11 Bldg., Xi Yuan Hotel, No.1 San Li He Rd., Beijing 100044, China (PRC)

Tel: 86-10-6831-3399 Fax: 86-10-6834-6711

COMPUTER ASSOCIATES INTERNATIONAL INC.

One Computer Associates Plaza, Islandia, NY, 11788

Tel: (516) 342-5224 Fax: (516) 342-5329 Web site: www.cai.com

Integrated software for enterprise computing and information management, application development, manufacturing, financial applications and professional services.

Computer Associates (China) Ltd., Rm. 2401, Capital Mansion, No. 6 Xin Yuan Nan Rd., Chao Yang Dist., Beijing 100004, China (PRC)

Tel: 86-10-6466-1136

COMSAT CORPORATION

6560 Rock Spring Drive, Bethesda, MD, 20817

Tel: (301) 214-3200 Fax: (301) 214-7100 Web site: www.comsat.com

Provides global telecommunications services via satellite and develops advanced satellite networking technology.

COMSAT International, Locations in Beijing, Guangzhou and Shanghai, China (PRC)

CONAGRA INC.

One ConAgra Drive, Omaha, NE, 68102-5001

Tel: (402) 595-4000 Fax: (402) 595-4595 Web site: www.conagra.com

Prepared/frozen foods, grains, flour, animal feeds, agri chemicals, poultry, meat, dairy products, including Healthy Choice, Butterball and Hunt's.

ConAgra Inc., China (PRC)

CONTROL DATA SYSTEMS INC.

4201 Lexington Ave., North Arden Hills, MN, 55126

Tel: (612) 415-2999 Fax: (612) 415-4891 Web site: www.cdc.com

Computer peripherals and hardware.

Control Data China, Scite Tower, Room 12-07, 22 Jianguomenwau Dajia, Beijing 100004, China (PRC)

Tel: 86-10-65123717 Fax: 86-10-65124069

CORE LABORATORIES

5295 Hollister, Houston, TX, 77042

Tel: (713) 460-9600 Fax: (713) 460-4389

Petroleum testing/analysis, analytical chemicals, laboratory and octane analysis instrumentation.

China Corelab Ltd., 1 Shang Yie Warehouse, Unit D, Tai Zi Rd., CMSN Shekou Ind. Zone, Shenzhen, Shekou, China (PRC)

CORESTATES BANK

1500 Market Street, Philadelphia, PA, 19101

Tel: (215) 973-3100 Fax: (215) 786-8899 Web site: www.corestates.com

Primary international businesses; correspondent banking and trade services.

Corestates Bank, CSJ Conference Ctr. #905-906, Conference Mansion, 388 Zhejiang Mid-Road, Shanghai 200001, China (PRC)

CORNING INC.

One Riverfront Plaza,, Corning, NY, 14831

Tel: (607) 974-9000 Fax: (607) 974-8551 Web site: www.corning.com

Mfr. glass and specialty materials, consumer products; communications, laboratory services.

Intl. Hua-Mei Glass Engineering Co. Ltd., Beijing, China (PRC)

Shanghai Corning Engineering Corp. Ltd., Shanghai, China (PRC)

COUDERT BROTHERS

1114 Ave. of the Americas, New York, NY, 10036-7794

Tel: (212) 626-4400 Fax: (212) 626-4210 Web site: www.coudert.com

International law firm.

Coudert Brothers, Ste. 2708-9, Jing Guang Centre, Hu Jia Lou, Chao Yang Qu, Beijing 100020, China (PRC)

Tel: 86-10-6597-3851 Fax: 86-10-6597-8856

Coudert Brothers, Ste. 1804, Union Bldg., 100 Yanan Rd. East, Shanghai 200002, China (PRC)

CUMMINS ENGINE CO., INC.

500 Jackson Street, PO Box 3005, Columbus, IN, 47202-3005

Tel: (812) 377-5000 Fax: (812) 377-3334

Mfr. diesel engines.

Cummins Corp., Nationalities Cultural Palace, Room 304, Beijing, China (PRC)

D'ARCY MASIUS BENTON & BOWLES INC. (DMB&B)

1675 Broadway, New York, NY, 10019

Tel: (212) 468-3622 Fax: (212) 468-2987 Web site: www.dmbb.com

Full service international advertising and communications group.

DMB&B Ltd., Room 201, West Tower, Shanghai Universal Centre, 175 Xiang Yang Rd.South, Shanghai 200031, China (PRC)

Tel: 86-21-6472-9011 Fax: 86-21-6472-9173 Contact: Benny Hui, Gen. Mgr.

DMB&B Ltd., Room 1808, World Trade Centre Complex, South Tower, 371-375 Huan Shi Dong Lu, Guangzhou, 510095 China (PRC)

Tel: 86-20-8777-2908 Fax: 86-20-8778-5289 Contact: Li Ching Kit, Mng. Dir.

DMB&B Ltd., Room 601 North Bldg., EAS Tower, No. 21 Xiao Yun Rd., Sanyuan Dongqiao, Dong San Huan Beilu, Chaoyang District, Beijing 100027, China (PRC)

Tel: 86-10-6466-2225 Fax: 86-10-6462-3238 Contact: Chris Clarke, Mng. Dir.

DAMES & MOORE GROUP

911 Wilshire Boulevard, Los Angeles, CA, 90017

Tel: (213) 683-1560 Fax: (213) 628-0015 Web site: www.dames.com

Engineering, environmental and construction management services.

Dames & Moore, 509 Caoboa Rd., #06-09 New Caohejing Tower, Shanghai 200233, China (PRC)

DANA CORPORATION

4500 Door Street, Toledo, OH, 43615

Tel: (419) 535-4500 Fax: (419) 535-4643 Web site: www.dana.com

Mfr./sales of automotive, heavy truck, off-highway, fluid & mechanical power components.

Tianjin Wix Filter Corp. Ltd., Shin Yan Lou Hou Ce, Zhone Shan Men, He Dong Dist., Tianjin 300180, China (PRC)

DAVIS WRIGHT TREMAINE

2600 Century Square, 1501 Fourth Ave., Seattle, WA, 98101

Tel: (206) 622-3150 Fax: (206) 628-7040

International law firm.

Davis Wright Tremaine, Ste. 1008/1009, Jin Jiang Hotel, 59 Mao Ming Rd. South, Shanghai 200020, China (PRC)

DDB NEEDHAM WORLDWIDE INC.

437 Madison Ave., New York, NY, 10022

Tel: (212) 415-2000 Fax: (212) 415-3417

Advertising agency.

DDB Worldwide, Beijing, China (PRC)

DEKALB GENETICS CORP.

3100 Sycamore Road, DeKalb, IL, 60115-9600

Tel: (815) 758-3461 Fax: (815) 758-3711 Web site: www.dekalb.com

Develop/produce hybrid corn, sorghum, sunflower seed, varietal soybeans, alfalfa.

China National Seed Group Corporation, Jia 16, Xi-ba-He, Chao-Yang Dist., Beijing 100028, China (PRC)

Tel: 86-10-6420-1829 Fax: 86-10-6420-1820 Contact: He Zhong Hua, President

Seed Company of Xinjiang AIC Corporation, 31 Xi-Hou St., Urumqi 830002 Xinjiang, China (PRC)

Tel: 86-991-2619638 Fax: 86-991-2619066 Contact: Yan Xue Cheng, Gen. Mgr.

Shaanxi Province Seed Company, 11 Xi-Wu-Yuan, Xian, Shaanxi Province, China (PRC)

Tel: 86-29-7345784 Fax: 86-29-5264955 Contact: Zhuang Feng, Gen. Mgr.

DELL COMPUTER CORPORATION

One Dell Way, Round Rock, TX, 78682-2222

Tel: (512) 338-4400 Fax: (512) 728-3653 Web site: www.dell.com

Direct marketer & supplier of computer systems.

Dell Products (Europe) B.V., Section A, 3/F, Beijing Science Tech & Engineering Tower, No. 11, Baishiqiao Rd., Haidian Dist., Beijing 100081 China (PRC)

Tel: 86-10-68461122 Fax: 86-10-6846-7213 Contact: Liv Ling, Gen. Mgr.

Dell Products (Europe) B.V., Rm 2903, South Tower, Cuangzhou World Trade Centre Complex, 371-375 Huan Shi Dong Rd., Guangzhou, 510095, China (PRC)

Tel: 86-20-87609162 Fax: 86-20-87609151 Contact: Dick Lee, Gen. Mgr.

DELOITTE TOUCHE TOHMATSU INTERNATIONAL

PO Box 820, Wilton, CT, 06897

Tel: (203) 761-3000 Fax: (203) 834-2200 Web site: www.u.s.deloitte.com or www.dtti.com

Accounting, audit, tax and management consulting services.

Deloitte Touche Tohmatsu, Room 921, South Tower, World Trade Ctr. Complex, 371-375 Huan Shi Dong Rd., Guangzhou 510 060, China (PRC)

Deloitte Touche Tohmatsu, Ste. 806, Shenzhen Development Centre Bldg., Renminnan Rd., Shenzhen 518 001, China (PRC)

Deloitte Touche Tohmatsu, Rm 517-518, China World Twr, China World Trade Ctr, 1 Jianguo Men Wai Da Jei, Beijing 100 004, PRC

Deloitte Touche Tohmatsu Shanghai CPA Ltd., Ste. 4-6, 4th Fl., Central Place, 16 He Nan Rd. South, Shanghai 200 002, China (PRC)

DeMATTEIS CONSTRUCTION CORP.

820 Elmont Road, Elmont, NY, 11003

Tel: (516) 285-5500 Fax: (516) 285-6950 Web site: DEMATTEAB@aol.com

Real estate development and construction services.

DeMatteis Asia Ltd., China (PRC) - Contact: 102 EAB Plaza, Uniondale, NY 11556-0102 USA

Tel: 516-357-9000 Fax: 516-794-2448 Contact: John P.McInernery, VP

DENTSPLY INTERNATIONAL

570 West College Ave., PO Box 872, York, PA, 17405-0872

Tel: (717) 845-7511 Fax: (717) 843-6357 Web site: www.dentsply.com

Mfr.& Distribution of dental supplies & equipment.

Dentsply China, 1/F Block C, TEDA International Incubator Centre, No.5 Ave., TEDA 300457, Tianjin, China (PRC)

Tel: 86-22-2-532-9362

THE DEXTER CORPORATION

1 Elm Street, Windsor Locks, CT, 06096

Tel: (860) 627-9051 Fax: (860) 627-7078

Mfr. nonwovens, polymer products, magnetic materials, biotechnology.

Dexter Nonwovens, Room 1305, Astronautics Bldg., 222 Cao Xi Rd., Shanghai 200233, China (PRC)

The Dexter Corp., Room 1305, Astronautics Bldg., 222 Cao Xi Rd., Shanghai 200233, China (PRC)

DHL WORLDWIDE EXPRESS

333 Twin Dolphin Drive, Redwood City, CA, 94065

Tel: (650) 593-7474 Fax: (650) 593-1689 Web site: www.dhl.com

Worldwide air express carrier.

DHL Worldwide Express, 45 Xinyuan St., Chaoyang Dist., Beijing 100027, China (PRC)

Tel: 86-10-6466-2211

DIAMOND POWER INTERNATIONAL, INC.

PO Box 415, Lancaster, OH, 43130

Tel: (740) 687-6500 Fax: (740) 687-7430 Web site: www.diamondpower.com

Mfg. boiler cleaning equipment & ash handling systems: sootblowers, controls, diagnostics systems, gauges, OEM parts, rebuilds & field service.

Diamond Power Hubei Machine Co. Ltd., 251 Jing Yuan Rd., Jingshan, Hubei, China (PRC)

DIETZGEN CORPORATION

1218 West Northwest Highway, Palatine, IL, 60067

Tel: (847) 776-3500 Fax: (847) 776-3532 Web site: www.dietzgen.com

Mfr. reprographic & drafting media, accessories and supplies.

Shanghai Hong Ling-Dietzgen Paper Products, 645 Hong Zhong Rd., Ming Haug Dist., Shanghai 201103, China (PRC)

Tel: 86-21-6406-1122 Fax: 86-21-6406-0191

DIODES, INC.

3050 East Hillcrest Drive, Ste. 200, Westlake Village, CA, 91362

Tel: (805) 446-4800 Fax: (805) 446-4850 Web site: www.dides.com

Mfr. semiconductor devices.

Shanghai Kai Hong Electronics Co., Ltd., East of Xingqiao Town, Songjiang, Shanghai, China (PRC).

Tel: 86-21-9764-0435 Fax: 86-21-5764-0431 Contact: Joseph Liu Emp: 200

WALT DISNEY COMPANY

500 South Buena Vista Street, Burbank, CA, 91521

Tel: (818) 560-1000 Fax: (818) 560-1930

Film/TV production, theme parks, resorts, publishing, recording and retail stores.

Walt Disney Consumer Products, Asia/Pacific, Beijing, China (PRC)

Contact: John J. Feenie, EVP

DONALDSON COMPANY, INC.

1400 West 94th Street, Minneapolis, MN, 55431

Tel: (612) 887-3131 Fax: (612) 887-3155 Web site: www.Donaldson.com

Mfr. filtration systems and replacement parts.

Donaldson Filters Co., Ltd., No. 221, Xing Chuang Yi Lu, Wuxi-Singaport Industrial Park, Wuxi, Jiangsu, China (PRC)

Tel: 86-510-521-6010 Fax: 86-510-521-0542

Guilin Air King Enterprise Ltd., 15, Zhishan Rd., Guilin, China (PRC) 541002

Tel: 86-773-384-6379 Fax: 86-773-384-6360

R.R. DONNELLEY & SONS COMPANY

77 West Wacker Drive, Chicago, IL, 60601-1696

Tel: (312) 326-8000 Fax: (312) 326-8543 Web site: www.rrdonnelley.com

Commercial printing, allied communication services.

R. R. Donnelley Financial, Room 1809 Capitol Mansion No. 6 Xin Yuan Nan Lu, Chaoyang Dist., Beijing 1000, China (PRC)

Tel: 86-10-465-4783

Shenzhen Donnelley Bright Sun Printing Co. Ltd., Wu He Da Dao, Bantian Industrial zone, Longgang Dist., Guangdong Province, Shenzhen 5182129, China (PRC)

Tel: 86-755-889-2499

Shenzhen Donnelley Bright Sun Printing Co. Ltd., 2/F, 418Zhen Xing Rd., Shenzhen, Guangdong 518031, China (PRC)

DONNELLY CORPORATION

414 East 40th Street, Holland, MI, 49423

Tel: (616) 786-7000 Fax: (616) 786-6034 Web site: www.donnelly.com

Mfr. fabricated, molded & coated glass products for the automotive & electronics industries.

Donnelly Shanghai Fu Hua Window Systems Co., Ltd., 700 Yaohua Rd., PuDong, Shanghai, China (PRC)

DonnellyYantai Electronics, #9 NanShan Rd., Yantai City, ShanDong, Province 264001, China (PRC)

Shunde Donnelly Zhen Hua, 9, Ronggang Rd., Rongqi, Shunde, Guang Dong, China (PRC)

DOVER CORPORATION

280 Park Ave., New York, NY, 10017-1292

Tel: (212) 922-1640 Fax: (212) 922-1656 Web site: www.dovercorporation.com

Elevator manufacturer and holding company for varied industries.

Dover Elevator Systems, Inc., 2/F, Block B, Strong Office Bldg., 5 Wangjing Zhonghuan Nanlu, Chao Yang Dist., Beijing 100015, China (PRC)

Tel: 86-10-437-9812 Fax: 86-10-437-9820

DRAVO CORPORATION

11 Stanwix Street, 11th Fl., Pittsburgh, PA, 15222

Tel: (412) 995-5500 Fax: (412) 995-5570

Material handling equipment and process plants.

Dravo Corp., c/o East Asiatic Co., Minzu Wen Hua, Gong Ju, LaBu Xi, Dan, Beijing, China (PRC)

DRESSER INDUSTRIES INC.

2001 Ross Ave., PO Box 718, Dallas, TX, 75221-0718

Tel: (214) 740-6000 Fax: (214) 740-6584 Web site: www.dresser.com

Diversified supplier of equipment & technical services to energy & natural resource industrial.

Dresser Industrial Products b.v., Waukesha Engine Div - Xie-ma mail 9628, Beibei, Chongqing 630712, China (PRC)

Tel: 86-23-6821-2365 Fax: 86-23-6821-2365 Contact: Zhou Handong

Dresser Industrial Products b.v., Waukesha Engine Div - Xinmin Hutong #8-1133, Desheng Menwal St., Beijing, 100088, China (PRC)

Tel: 86-10-6235-5438 Fax: 86-10-6237-3100 Contact: Wu Zhengqi, Sr. Rep.

Dresser Roots/Dresser Industries Inc., CITIC Bldg., Ste. 2403, 19 Jianguomenwai Dagie, Beijing 100004, China (PRC)

EASTMAN CHEMICAL

100 North Eastman Road, Kingsport, TN, 37660

Tel: (423) 229-2000 Fax: (423) 229-1351 Web site: www.eastman.com

Mfr. plastics, chemicals, fibers.

Eastman Chemical (Beijing) Ltd., Office Unit 506, 5th Fl., Lido Commercial Bldg., Ji Chang Rd., Jiang Tai Rd., Beijing, China (PRC)

Tel: 86-10-6436-7376 Fax: 86-106436-7380 Contact: Andrew Yuen, Mgr.

Eastman Chemical (Shanghai) Ltd., Rm. 1612, Ruijing Bldg., 205 Mao Ming South Rd., Shanghai, China (PRC)

Tel: 86-21-6472-9777 Fax: 86-21-6472-3760 Contact: Tony Satterfield

EASTMAN KODAK COMPANY

343 State Street, Rochester, NY, 14650

Tel: (716) 724-4000 Fax: (716) 724-0663

Develop/mfr. photo & chemicals products, information management/video/copier systems, fibers/plastics for various industry.

Kodak (China) Ltd., Unit 1-2, Level 4, West Wing, China World Trade Ctr., 1 Jiangoomenwai Ave., Beijing 100004, PRC

ECHLIN INC.

100 Double Beach Road, Branford, CT, 06405

Tel: (203) 481-5751 Fax: (203) 481-6485 Web site: www.echlin.com

Supplies commercial vehicle components and auto fluid handling systems for the used car market

Echlin, Shanghai, China (PRC)

ECOLAB INC.

Ecolab Center, 370 N. Wabasha Street, St. Paul, MN, 55102

Tel: (612) 293-2233 Fax: (612) 225-3105 Web site: www.ecolab.com

Develop/mfr. premium cleaning, sanitizing and maintenance products and services for the hospitality, institutional, and residential markets.

Ecolab Ltd., Beijing, China (PRC)

Tel: 86-21-6275-0888

ECOLOGY AND ENVIRONMENT INC.

368 Pleasant View Drive, Lancaster, NY, 14086-1397

Tel: (716) 684-8060 Fax: (716) 684-0844

Environmental, scientific & engineering consulting.

Beijing YiYi Ecology and Environment Engineering Co. Ltd., 11A Xisi Bei 8 Tiao, Xicheng Dist., Beijing 100034, China (PRC)

ECOWATER SYSTEMS INC.

1890 Woodlane Drive, Woodbury, MN, 55125

Tel: (612) 739-5330 Fax: (612) 739-4547 Web site: www.ecowater.com

Mfr. water treatment and purification products.

EcoWater Systems Asia, 1336 Huashan Rd., Yu Jia Bldg., Ste. 17E, Shanghai, China (PRC) 200052

Tel: 86-21-6240-1366 Fax: 86-21-6240-1380 Contact: Alex Areces, VP Gen. Mgr. Asia Pacific

EDELMAN PUBLIC RELATIONS WORLDWIDE

200 East Randolph Drive, 63rd Floor, Chicago, IL, 60601

Tel: (312) 240-3000 Fax: (312) 240-0596 Web site: www.edelman.com

International independent public relations firm.

Edelman PR Worldwide, Hong Kong Macau Centre, 9th Fl., Office Tower, Dong Si Shi Tiao Jiao, Beijing 100027 China (PRC)

Tel: 86-10-6501-4285 Fax: 86-10-6501-4271 Contact: Timothy C. Heberlein, Gen. Mgr.

Edelman PR Worldwide, Room 3202, LT Square, 500 Chengdu North Rd., Shanghai 200003, China (PRC)

Tel: 86-21-6361-9485 Fax: 86-21-6361-9486 Contact: Jean Michel Dumont, Gen. Mgr.

Edelman PR Worldwide, Ste. 2804, Guangzhou International Electronic Bldg., 403 Huanshi Dong Lu, Guangzhou 510095, China (PRC)

Tel: 86-20-8732-2111 Fax: 86-20-8732-2119 Contact: Samuel Mak, Mng. Dir.

J.D. EDWARDS & COMPANY

One Technology Way, Denver, CO, 80237

Tel: (303) 334-4000 Fax: (303) 334-4970 Web site: www.jdedwards.com.

Computer software products.

Fujian Strong Systems Integration Ltd., 16F, Lippo Tianma Plaza, 1 North Wuyi Ave., Fuzjou, Fujian 3500001, China (PRC)

Tel: 86-591-337-0080

J. D. Edwards Shanghai, Dynasty Business Ctr., Ste. 611, No. 457 Wulumuqi Rd. North, Shanghai 2000040, China (PRC)

Tel: 86-12-6249-2708 Fax: 86-12-6249-2709

J. D. Edwards Shanghai, St. 611, Dynasty Business Ctr., No. 457 Wulumuqi Rd. North, China (PRC)

Tel: 86-21-6249-2708 Fax: 86-21-6249-2709

System-Pro Solutions Ltd, 3F JOS Bldg. Yongful Hotel, 45 Youngfu Rd., Guangzhou, China (PRC)

Tel: 86-20-8779-9442 Fax: 86-20-8779-9389

System-Pro Solutions Ltd., Dalu Hotel, 9th Fl., 69 Xizang Middle Rd., Shanghai 200003, China (PRC)

Tel: 86-21-6358-0399 Fax: 86-21-6359-9515

System-Pro Solutions Ltd., Bldg. 16, Cha Ci Xiao Qu, Dong Zhi Men Wai, Beijing 1000027, China (PRC)

Tel: 86-10-5463-4583 Fax: 86-10-6460-0242

EG&G INC.

45 William Street, Wellesley, MA, 02181-4078

Tel: (781) 237-5100 Fax: (781) 431-4114

Diversified R/D, mfr. & services.

EG&G China, Room 408, Scite Tower, 22 Jianguo Men Wai Da Jie, Beijing 100004, China (PRC)

EG&G Heimann Shenzhen Optoelectronics Ltd., Wearnes Technology Centre, Shenzhen Science & Industry Park, Shenzhen, Guangdong, China (PRC)

ELECTRO SCIENTIFIC INDUSTRIES, INC.

13900 NW Science Park Drive, Portland, OR, 97229

Tel: (503) 641-4141 Fax: (503) 643-4873 Web site: www.elcsci.com

Mfg. Production and testing equpment used in manufacture of electronic components in pagers and cellular communication devices.

Electro Scientific Industries China, Room 12, Unit 1, No. 6 Bldg., 23 Shijing Shan Rd., Beijing 100043, China (PRC)

Tel: 86-10-6884-3781 Fax: 86-10-6886-4045 Contact: Shi Baao Shan

EMC CORP.

35 Parkwood Drive, Hopkinton, MA, 01748-9103

Tel: (508) 435-1000 Fax: (508) 435-8884 Web site: www.emc.com

Designs/supplies intelligent enterprise storage & retrieval technology for open systems, mainframes & midrange environments.

EMC Computer Systems - Beijing Office, Room 953, New Century Office Tower, No. 6 Southern Rd., Capital Gym, Beijing 100044, China (PRC)

Tel: 86-10-6849-2058

EMERSON ELECTRIC COMPANY

8000 West Florissant Ave., PO Box 4100, St. Louis, MO, 63136

Tel: (314) 553-2000 Fax: (314) 553-3527 Web site: www.emersonelectric.com

Electrical and electronic products, industrial components and systems, consumer, government and defense products.

Emerson Electric Co., Suzhou, China (PRC)

EMERY WORLDWIDE

One Lagoon Drive, Ste. 400, Redwood City, CA, 94065

Tel: (650) 596-9600 Fax: (650) 596-7901 Web site: www.emeryworld.com

Freight transport, global logistics and air cargo.

Emery Worldwide, Rm. 770, Poly Plaza, 14 Dongzhimen Nandajie, Dongcheng Dist., Beijing 100 027, China (PRC)

Emery Worldwide, Rm. 1103, Rui Jun Bldg., 205 Mao Ming Nan Rd., Shanghai 200 020, China (PRC)

ENGELHARD CORPORATION

101 Wood Ave. S., CN 770, Iselin, NJ, 08830

Tel: (732) 205-5000 Fax: (732) 632-9253

Mfr. pigments, additives, catalysts, chemicals, engineered materials.

Engelhard Corporation, Room 207, 30 Si Nan Rd., Shanghai 200020, China (PRC)

Engelhard Corporation, 210 Tong Fu Xi Rd., 2/F, Guang Zhou, Guang Dong Province, Canton 510235, China (PRC)

ENRON CORPORATION

1400 Smith Street, Houston, TX, 77002-7361

Tel: (713) 853-6161 Fax: (713) 853-3129 Web site: www.enron.com

Exploration, production, transportation and distribution of integrated natural gas and electricity.

Enron International, Beining Silver Tower, 2 Dongsanhuan Beilu, Ste. 2512, Chaoyang Dist., Beijing, China (PRC) 100006

Tel: 86-10-6410-7455

Hainan Meinan Power Co., Haikou Intl Commercial Ctr., 38 Da Tong Rd., Rm. 809, Haikou, Hainan Province 570102, China (PRC)

Tel: 86-898-672-3140

ERNST & YOUNG, LLP

787 Seventh Ave., New York, NY, 10019

Tel: (212) 773-3000 Fax: (212) 773-6350 Web site: www.eyi.com

Accounting and audit, tax and management consulting services.

Ernst & Young, 10/F, Hong Kong Macau Centre, Dong Si Shi Tiao Li Jiao Qiao, Beijing, China (PRC) 100027

Tel: 852-2846-9959 Fax: 852-2840-0441 Contact: Alfred Shum

EXPEDITORS INTERNATIONAL OF WASHINGTON INC.

999 Throd Ave., Ste. 2500, Seattle, WA, 98104

Tel: (206) 674-3400 Fax: (206) 682-9777 Web site: www.expd.com

Air/ocean freight forwarding, customs brokerage, international logistics solutions.

EI Freight (HK) Ltd., Flat B, 8th Fl. Victory Mansion 2200 Kai Xuan Rd., Shanghai 200030, China (PRC) (Locations:Beijing, Dalian, Qingdao, Tianjin.)

EXXON CORPORATION

225 E. John W. Carpenter Freeway, Irving, TX, 75062-2298

Tel: (972) 444-1000 Fax: (972) 444-1882 Web site: www.exxon.com

Petroleum exploration, production, refining; mfr. petroleum & chemicals products; coal & minerals.

Esso - China/ Exxon Chemical, Jinzhou Juie Lubricant Additives Co. Ltd., No.2 Chongquing Rd., Guta Dist., Jarzhou City, Liaoning Province, Post Code 12001, China (PRC) (Operations: Shenzhen & Guangdong Province.)

FINNIGAN CORPORATION

355 River Oaks Parkway, San Jose, CA, 95134-1991

Tel: (408) 433-4800 Fax: (408) 433-4823

Mfr. mass spectrometers.

Finnigan MAT China Inc., B-7, Bai-Shi-Qiao-hu, Haidan, Beijing, China (PRC)

FIRST CHICAGO NBD CORPORATION

One First National Plaza, Chicago, IL, 60670

Tel: (312) 732-4000 Fax: (312) 732-4000 Web site: www.fcnbd.com

Financial products and services.

First National Bank of Chicago, CITIC Bldg., Ste. 1604, 19 Jianguomenwai Daijie, POBox 9031, Beijing, 100004 China (PRC)

Tel: 86-10-6500-3281 Fax: 86-10-6500-3166 Contact: Min-Hwa Hu, Branch Manager

FISCHER IMAGING CORPORATION

12300 North Grant Street, Denver, CO, 80241

Tel: (303) 452-6800 Fax: (303) 452-4335 Web site: www.fischerimaging.com

Mfr. x-ray equipment.

Fischer Imaging China, b07, Block H, 21, Century Hotel, No. 40 Liangmaqiao Rd., Chaoyang Districy, Beijing, China (PRC)

Tel: 86-10-6460-9911

FISHER-ROSEMOUNT

8000 Maryland Ave., Ste. 500, Clayton, MO, 63105-4755

Tel: (314) 746-9900 Fax: (314) 746-9974

Mfr. industrial process control equipment.

Beijing Rosemount Far East Instrument Company Ltd., No. 6 North St. Hepingli, Dong Cheng Dist., Beijing 100013, China (PRC)

Tel: 86-10-6428-2233 Fax: 86-21-6428-1512 Contact: Peter Hammond, Mgr.

Fisher Controls Hong Kong Ltd., 13th Fl., Gateway Bldg., No. 10 Yahao Rd., Chaoyang Dist., Beijing, 100020, China (PRC)

Tel: 86-10-6592-2528 Fax: 86-10-6592-5226

Fisher-Rosemount, Rm. 604, Tower 4, Dong Jun Plaza, 836 Dong Feng Rd. East, Guangzhou 510080, China (PRC)

Tel: 86-20-8767-6181 Fax: 86-20-8766-4874 Contact: Dick Wong, Mgr.

Fisher-Rosemount Pty. Ltd., 13th Fl., Gateway Bldg., No. 10 Yahao Rd., Chaoyang Dist., Beijing, 100020, China (PRC)

Tel: 86-10-6592-4528 Fax: 86-10-6592-5226 Contact: Minh Quan, Mgr.

Fisher-Rosemount Pty. Ltd., Rm. 404, Shangrila Golden Flower Hotel, 8 Chang Le Rd. (W), Xi'an, 710032, China (PRC)

Tel: 86-29-325-5563 Fax: 86-29-325-5076 Contact: Ron Wang, Mgr.

Fisher-Rosemount Pty. Ltd., Room 603, 605 Yin Du Hotel, No. 39 Xibei Rd., Urumqui, Xingjiang 830000, China (PRC)

Tel: 86-991-458-0603 Fax: 86-991-452-7551

Fisher-Rosemount Pty. Ltd., Room 1207 Foreign Trade Bldg., No. 210 Xi Yu Long St., Chengdu, Sichuan 610031, China (PRC)

Tel: 86-28-674-5622 Fax: 86-28-674-5173

Fisher-Rosemount Pty. Ltd., 20th Fl., Astronautics Bldg., No. 222, Cai Xi Rd., Shanghai, 200233, China (PRC)

Tel: 86-21-6482-2298 Fax: 86-21-6482-2300

Fisher-Rosemount Pty. Ltd., Room 3208, Development Centre Bldg., Renmingnan Rd., Shenzhen, 518001, China (PRC)

Tel: 86-755-223-7232 Fax: 86-755-223-6289 Contact: Oscar Wong, Mgr.

Lumax International Corp. Ltd., Fl. 2, No. 39 Haerbin Rd., Development Zone, Dalian, 116600, China (PRC)

Tel: 86-411-761-8011 Fax: 86-411-761-8015

Rosemount Shanghai Company Ltd., No. 1277 Xin Jin Qiao Rd., Jin Qiao Export Processing Zone, Pudong, Shanghai, 201206, China (PRC)

Tel: 86-21-5899-4415 Fax: 86-21-5899-4410 Contact: Patrick Lim, Mgr.

Star Controls Engineering Co. Pte. Ltd., 6D, Haixing Plaza 898 Xiexu Rd., Shanghai 200023, China (PRC)

Tel: 86-411-761-8011 Fax: 86-411-761-8015

Tianjin Fisher Controls Valve Co., Ltd., Jie Yuan Xi Rd., Nankai Dist., Tianjin, China (PRC)

Tel: 86-22-736-6613 Fax: 86-22-736-2238

FLEXTRONICS INC. INTERNATIONAL

2241 Lundy Ave., San Jose, CA, 95131-1822

Tel: (408) 428-1300 Fax: (408) 428-0420

Contract manufacturer for electronics industry.

Flextronics Computer (Shekou) Ltd., Nan Shan Bldg., Shekou, Shenzhen, China (PRC)

FLUKE CORPORATION

PO Box 9090, Everett, WA, 98206-9090

Tel: (425) 347-6100 Fax: (425) 356-5116 Web site: www.fluke.com

Mfr. electronic test tools.

Fluke International Corp., PO Box 9085, Beijing 100004 PRC, China (PRC)

Tel: 86-10-6512-3435 Fax: 86-10-6512-3437

FLUOR DANIEL INC.

3353 Michelson Drive, Irvine, CA, 92698

Tel: (714) 975-2000 Fax: (714) 975-5271 Web site: www.flourdaniel.com

Engineering & construction services.

Fluor Daniel China Inc., 2701 Landmark Bldg., 8 North Dongsanhuan Rd., Chaoyang Dist., Beijing 100004, China (PRC)

Tel: 86-10-6506-8015 Fax: 86-10-6506-8024

FMC CORPORATION

200 E. Randolph Drive, Chicago, IL, 60601

Tel: (312) 861-6000 Fax: (312) 861-6141

Produces chemicals & precious metals, mfr. machinery, equipment & systems for industrial, agricultural & government use.

FMC Asia Pacific Inc., CITIC Bldg. #604, 19 Jianguomen Wai Dajie, Beijing 100004, China (PRC)

FORT JAMES CORPORATION

1650 Lake Cook Road, Deerfield, IL, 60015

Tel: (847) 317-5000 Fax: (847) 236-3755 Web site: www.fortjames.com

Mfr./sales of consumer paper and packaging products.

Fort James Corporation, Shanghai, China (PRC)

FRITZ COMPANIES INC.

706 Mission Street, Ste. 900, San Francisco, CA, 94103

Tel: (415) 904-8360 Fax: (415) 904-8661 Web site: www.fritz.com

Integrated transportation, sourcing, distribution & customs brokerage services.

Fritz Air Freight, Room 1110-1111 City Hotel, 5-7 Shen Xi Rd. S, Shanghai 200020, China (PRC) (Locations: Beijing, Dalian, Fuzhou, Guangzhou, Harbin, Nanjing, Qingdao, Shenzhen, Tianjin, Wuhan, Wuxi, Xizmen, Yantai)

H.B. FULLER COMPANY

1200 Willow Lake Blvd., Vadnais Heights, MN, 55110

Tel: (612) 236-5900 Fax: (612) 236-5898 Web site: www.hbfuller.com

Mfr./distributor adhesives, sealants, coatings, paints, waxes, sanitation chemicals.

H.B. Fuller (China) Adhesives Ltd., 10 Bihua St., Jin Xiu Nan Lu, Guangzhou Economic & Technical Dept. Zone, Huanpu, Guangzhou 510730, China (PRC) (Locations: Beijing, Shanghai.)

Tel: 86-20-8221-4333 Fax: 86-20-8221-4818

GENERAL ELECTRIC CAPITAL CORPORATION

260 Long Ridge Road, Stamford, CT, 06927

Tel: (203) 357-4000 Fax: (203) 357-6489

Financial, property/casualty insurance, computer sales and trailer leasing services.

Employers Reinsurance Corp. (ERC), Lufthansa Centre C714, Chaoyang Dist., Beijing 1000016, China (PRC)

Tel: 86-10-6465-1068 Fax: 86-10-6465-1070

GENERAL ELECTRIC CO.

3135 Easton Turnpike, Fairfield, CT, 06431

Tel: (203) 373-2211 Fax: (203) 373-3131 Web site: www.ge.com

Diversified manufacturing, technology and services.

GE Capital Global Projects, Bldg. 3/F, Beijing 100004, China (PRC)

Tel: 86-10-500-6438

GE FANUC Automation, Unit 11B2, Block B, Shanghai 200232, China (PRC) (Locations: Beijing & Guangzhou, China (PRC)

Tel: 86-21-646-95883 Fax: 86-2-1648-79061

General Electric (USA) China, 4727 Zhen Nan Rd., Shanghai 201802 China (PRC)

Tel: 86-21-5912-7777 Fax: 86-21-5912-3434

General Electric (USA) China, 3rd Fl., Citic Bldg., Beijing 100004, China (PRC)

Tel: 86-10-6500-6438 Fax: 86-10-6512-7345

Nuovo Pignone, 19, Jian Guo Men Wal Ave., Beijing 100004, China (PRC)

Tel: 86-10-593-1826 Fax: 86-10-593-1830

GENERAL REINSURANCE CORPORATION

695 East Main Street, Stamford, CT, 06904-2350

Tel: (203) 328-5000 Fax: (203) 328-6423 Web site: www.genre.com

Reinsurance services worldwide.

Cologne Reinsurance Company, Shanghai Office, Ste. 508, West Tower, 1376 Nan Jung West Rd., Shanghai 200040, China (PRC)

Tel: 86-21-6279-7612 Fax: 86-21-6279-7599 Contact: Jeffrey Shaohui Pan

GENERAL SEMICONDUCTOR, INC.

10 Melville Park Road., Melville, NY, 11747

Tel: (516) 847-3000 Fax: Web site: www.gensemi.com

Mfr. of low- and medium-current power rectifiers and transient voltage supressors.

General Semiconductor - China, Manufacturing Facility - Tianjin, China (PRC)

Emp: 1,200

GETZ BROS & CO., INC.

150 Post Street, Ste. 500, San Francisco, CA, 94108-4750

Tel: (415) 772-5500 Fax: (415) 772-5659 Web site: www.getz.com

Diversified manufacturing, marketing and distribution services and travel services.

Getz Bros. & Co. (Guangzhou), Room 5A-7, 5/F Kang Long Office Ctr., Li Wan Rd., Guangzhou, China (PRC)

Tel: 86-20-813-6592 Fax: 86-20-813-6592 Contact: Yuen Tsuan Wai Emp: 30

Getz Bros. & Co. (Shanghai), 18139 Zhao Jia Bin Rd., Shanghai, China (PRC)

Tel: 86-21-646-66410 Fax: 86-21-646-63412 Contact: Peter Zhang Emp: 12

THE GILLETTE COMPANY

Prudential Tower Building, Boston, MA, 02199

Tel: (617) 421-7000 Fax: (617) 421-7123 Web site: www.gillette.com

Develop/mfr. personal care/use products: blades & razors, toiletries, cosmetics, stationery.

Gillette (Shanghai) Ltd., Shanghai, China (PRC)

Oral-B (Shanghai) Ltd., Shanghai, China (PRC)

Shenmei Daily Use Products Ltd. Co., Shenyang City, China (PRC)

GLEASON CORPORATION

1000 University Ave., Rochester, NY, 14692

Tel: (716) 473-1000 Fax: (716) 461-4348 Web site: www.gleasoncorp.com

Mfr. gear making machine tools; tooling & services.

Gleason Intl. Marketing Corp., Room 1310, Noble Tower, 22 Jianguo, Men Wai Dajie, Beijing 100004,China (PRC)

GLENAYRE ELECTRONICS LTD.

1 Glenayre Way, Quincy, IL, 62301

Tel: (217) 223-3211 Fax: (217) 223-3284

Mfr. Infrastructure components and pagers.

Glenayre Electronics, Inc., Beijing, Jing Bao Plaza, Rm. #404-414, #185 An Wai Da Jie, Dong Cheng Dist., Beijing, 100011, China (PRC)

Tel: 86-10-6425-6125 Fax: 86-10-6425-6199

Glenayre Electronics, Inc., Guangzhou, HongKong & Shanghai Bank Bldg., #706, 148 Dong Feng Xi Rd., Guangzhou 510170, China (PRC)

Tel: 86-20-8136-3888 Fax: 86-20-8136-4607

GLOBAL SILVERHAWK

1000 Burnett Ave., Concord, CA, 94520

Tel: (510) 609-7080 Fax: (510) 609-7081 Web site: www.globalsilverhawk.com

International moving & forwarding.

Global Silverhawk, Rm. 101, 780 Lane, No. 67 Hongzhong Rd., Honglu Huayuan, China (PRC) 20103

Contact: Clint Stevens, Gen. Mgr.

Global Silverhawk, International Distribution Ctr., Chas.Yang Port, No.1 Dongsihuan, Nanlu, 100023, Shibali Dain, Beijing, China (PRC)

Contact: Evan Wonacott, Gen. Mgr.

GOLDMAN SACHS & COMPANY

85 Broad Street, New York, NY, 10004

Tel: (212) 902-1000 Fax: (212) 902-3000 Web site: www.gs.com

Investment bankers; securities broker dealers.

Goldman Sachs (China) L.L.C., Unit 1102-04 Landmark Bldg., 8 North Dongsanhuan Rd., Chaoyang Dist., Beijing 100004, China (PRC)

Tel: 86-10-6501-2183

Goldman, Sachs (China) L.L.C., Ste. 505, Shanghai Centre, 1376 Nanjing Xi Lu, Shanghai 200040, China (PRC)

Tel: 86-21-6279-7261

THE GOODYEAR TIRE & RUBBER COMPANY

1144 East Market Street, Akron, OH, 44316

Tel: (330) 796-2121 Fax: (330) 796-1817 Web site: www.goodyear.com

Mfr. tires, automotive belts and hose, conveyor belts, chemicals; oil pipeline transmission.

Goodyear China -Tires, Quidao & Dalian China (PRC)

W. R. GRACE & COMPANY

One Town Center Road, 1750 Clint Moore Road, Boca Raton, FL, 33486-1010

Tel: (561) 362-2000 Fax: (561) 561-2193 Web site: www.grace.com

Mfr. specialty chemicals and materials: packaging, health care, catalysts, construction, water treatment/process.

Grace China Ltd., 30 Hong He Rd., Minhang Economic Zone, Shanghai, China (PRC)

Tel: 86-21-6430-0950 Fax: 86-21-6430-0425

GRAHAM & JAMES LLP

One Maritime Plaza - Ste. 300, San Francisco, CA, 94111-3404

Tel: (415) 954-0200 Fax: (415) 391-2493 Web site: www.gj.com

International law firm.

Graham & James LLP, Ste. 2002, CITIC Bldg., 19 Jianguomenwai Dajie, Beijing 100004, China (PRC)

Tel: 86-10-6507-8557 Fax: 86-10-6500-2557 Contact: David Livdahl

GRANT THORNTON INTERNATIONAL

800 One Prudential Plaza, 130 E. Randolph Drive, Chicago, IL, 60601-6050

Tel: (312) 856-0001 Fax: (312) 616-7052

Accounting, audit, tax and management consulting services.

Grant Thornton Beijing, Rm 1212 CVIK Tower, 22 Jianguomenwai Ave., Beijing 100004, China (PRC)

Tel: 86-10-512-2288 Fax: 86-10-512-3454 Contact: Hong Ying

GREY ADVERTISING INC.

777 Third Ave., New York, NY, 10017

Tel: (212) 546-2000 Fax: (212) 546-1495 Web site: www.giworldwwide.com

International advertising agency.

Grey China, Mapitol Mansion #1801, 6 Xin Yuan Nan Rd., Chao Yang Dist., Beijing 100004, China (PRC)

GTE CORPORATION

One Stamford Forum, Stamford, CT, 06904

Tel: (203) 965-2000 Fax: (203) 965-2277 Web site: www.gte.com

Electronic products, telecommunications systems, publishing and communications.

GTE China, Shanghai, Guangzhou and Beijing, China (PRC)

HAEMONETICS CORPORATION

400 Wood Road, Braintree, MA, 02184

Tel: (781) 848-7100 Fax: (781) 848-5106 Web site: www.haemonetics.

Mfr. automated blood processing systems and blood products

Haemonetics Shanghai, Rm. 1007, Shanghai Intl. Trade Ctr., Shanghai 200335 China (PRC)

Tel: 86-21-62950066 Fax: 86-21-62789380

HARNISCHFEGER INDUSTRIES INC

PO Box 554, Milwaukee, WI, 53201

Tel: (414) 797-6480 Fax: (414) 797-6573 Web site: www.harnischfeger.com

Mfr. mining and material handling equipment, papermaking machinery and computer systems.

Beloit Corporation/Joy Mining Machinery, China (PRC)

THE HARPER GROUP

260 Townsend Street, San Francisco, CA, 94107-1719

Tel: (415) 978-0600 Fax: (415) 978-0692 Web site: www.circleintl.com

Ocean/air freight forwarding, customs brokerage, packing and wholesale, logistics management and insurance.

Circle International, Rm. 1806, Block 10, No. 331, Dong Yuan Shan Chun, Pudong, Shanghai 200120, China (PRC)

Tel: 86-21-588-86329 Fax: 86-21-588-89054

HARRIS CORPORATION

1025 West NASA Blvd., Melbourne, FL, 32919

Tel: (407) 727-9100 Fax: (407) 727-9344 Web site: www.harris.com

Mfr. communications and information-handling equipment, including copying and fax systems.

Harris Semiconductor China Ltd., Room 4C, 4th Fl., Guo Men Bldg., 1 Zuo Jia Zhuang, Chao Yang Dist., Beijing, 100028 China (PRC)

Tel: 86-10-64606850 Fax: 86-10-6460-9262

Harris Semiconductor China Ltd., Rm. 3005 88 Tong Ren Rd., Shanghai, 20040 China (PRC)

Tel: 86-21-6247-7923 Fax: 86-21-6247-7926

THE HARTFORD FINANCIAL SERVICES GROUP, INC.

Hartford Plaza, Hartford, CT, 06115

Tel: (860) 547-5000 Fax: (860) 547-5817 Web site: www.thehartford.com

Financial services.

Hartford Fire Insurance Company, Xiamen Rep. Office, Rm. 606, Juati Commercial Bldg. No. 1226 Xiahe Rd., Xiamen 361004 China (PRC)

Tel: 86-592-516-1997 Fax: 86-592-516-1997 Contact: Hans Miller, Mng. Dir.

HASBRO INDUSTRIES INC

1027 Newport Ave., Pawtucket, RI, 02861

Tel: (401) 725-8697 Fax: (401) 727-5099 Web site: www.hasbro.com

Toys, games and dolls.

Hasbro Industries, Shanghei, China (PRC)

H.J. HEINZ COMPANY

600 Grant Street, Pittsburgh, PA, 15219

Tel: (412) 456-5700 Fax: (412) 456-6128 Web site: www.heinz.com

Processed food products and nutritional services.

Heinz-UFE Ltd., Guangzhou, China (PRC)

HERCULES INC

Hercules Plaza, 1313 North Market Street, Wilmington, DE, 19894-0001

Tel: (302) 594-5000 Fax: (302) 594-5400 Web site: www.herc.com

Mfr. specialty chemicals, plastics, film and fibers, coatings, resins, food ingredients.

Hercules Chemicals Ltd., Shanghai, China (PRC)

HERSHEY FOODS CORPORATION

100 Crystal A Drive, Hershey, PA, 17033

Tel: (717) 534-6799 Fax: (717) 534-6760 Web site: www.hersheys.com

Mfr. chocolate, food and confectionery products.

Hershey China, Shanghai, China (PRC)

HEWITT ASSOCIATES LLC

100 Half Day Road, Lincolnshire, IL, 60069

Tel: (847) 295-5000 Fax: (847) 295-7634

Employee benefits consulting firm.

Hewitt Associates, #C712B Office Bldg., Kempinski Hotel, Lufthansa Ctr., No. 50 Liangmaqiao Rd., Chaoyang Dist, Beijing 100016, China (PRC)

Tel: 86-10-6465-1027

Hewitt East Gate, Consulting Co. Ltd., 2nd Fl., Bldg. No.9, 500 Cao Bao Rd., Shanghai 200233, China (PRC)

Tel: 86-21-6451-5230

HEWLETT-PACKARD COMPANY

3000 Hanover Street, Palo Alto, CA, 94304-0890

Tel: (650) 857-1501 Fax: (650) 857-7299 Web site: www.hp.com

Mfr. computing, communications & measurement products & services.

China Hewlett-Packard Co. Ltd., 5-6/F West Wing, World Trade Ctr., 1 Jian Guo Men Wai Ave., Beijing, China (PRC)

HILTON HOTELS CORPORATION

9336 Civic Center Drive, Beverly Hills, CA, 90210

Tel: (310) 278-4321 Fax: (310) 205-7880

International hotel chain: Hilton International, Vista Hotels and Hilton National Hotels.

Beijing Hilton, 1 Dong Fang Rd., PO Box 4718, North Dong San Huan Rd., Chaoyang Dist. 100027 Beijing, China (PRC)

Tel: 86-10-466-2288

Shanghai Hilton, 250 Hua Shan Rd., 200040 Shanghai, China (PRC)

HLW INTERNATIONAL, LLP

115 Fifth Ave., New York, NY, 10003

Tel: (212) 353-4600 Fax: (212) 353-4666 Web site: www.currently in preparation

Architecture, engineering, planning and interior design.

HLW International, LLP, China (PRC)

HONEYWELL INC.

PO Box 524, Minneapolis, MN, 55440-0524

Tel: (612) 951-1000 Fax: (612) 951-3066 Web site: www.honeywell.com

Develop/mfr. controls for home and building, industry, space and aviation.

Honeywell China, Zhong Wei Ke Yi Bldg. 2/F, A34 Dong Huan Bei Ku, Chao Yang Dist., Beijing 100020, China (PRC)

Sinopec Honeywell Ltd., 5th Golden Peacock Arts World, Zhuangjiao Bldg., Hepingli, Chaoyang Dist., Beijing 100013, China (PRC)

HONEYWELL-MEASUREX DMC CORPORATION

PO Box 490, Gaithersburg, MD, 20884

Tel: (301) 948-2450 Fax: (301) 670-0506 Web site: www.honeywell.com

Mfr. quality and process control gauges.

Honeywell-Measurex DMC, 15th Fl., Han Wei Plaza, No. 7 Guanghua Rd., Chaoyang Dist., Beijing, 100020 China (PRC)

Tel: 86-10-6561-0208 Fax: 86-10-6561-0247 Contact: Andy Pei, Area Sales Mgr.

HOUGHTON INTERNATIONAL INC.

PO Box 930, Madison & Van Buren Avenues, Valley Forge, PA, 19482-0930

Tel: (610) 666-4000 Fax: (610) 666-1376

Mfr. specialty chemicals, hydraulic fluids & lubricants.

Houghton China Co. Ltd., 5th Subarea, Che Gong Miao Industrial Area, Shenzhen 518048, China (PRC)

HOWMEDICA INC.

359 Veterans Boulevard, Rutherford, NJ, 07070

Tel: (201) 507-7300 Fax: (201) 935-4873 Web site: www.howmedica.com

Hospital, medical and dental supplies.

Howmedica China, Beijing, China (PRC)

Tel: 86-10-6588-0288

HUGHES ELECTRONICS

200 N. Sepulveda Blvd., PO Box 956, El Segundo, CA, 90245-0956

Tel: (310) 662-9821 Fax: (310) 647-6213

Mfr. electronics equipment and systems.

Hughes Electronics Intl., Beijing Intl.Bldg., 21 Jianguomenwai Dajie, Beinjing, 100020, China (PRC)

Tel: 86-10-6532-1631 Fax: 86-10-6532-1898

Hughes Network Systems, Room 502, Ste. Tower, 22, Jianjuomenwai Dajie, Beijing, 100004, China (PRC)

Tel: 86-10-6512-2280 Fax: 86-10-6512-3593

Shanghai Hughes Network, No. 4 Bldg., Lane 20, Jinqiao Export Zone, Pudong, Shanghai 201206, China (PRC)

Tel: 86-21-5854-7938 Fax: 86-21-5854-8608

IBM CORPORATION

New Orchard Road, Armonk, NY, 10504

Tel: (914) 765-1900 Fax: (914) 765-7382 Web site: www.ibm.com

Information products, technology & services.

IBM China, IBM Shanghai Representative Office, Shanghai Centre, Ste. 507, 1376 Nanjing Xi Lu. Shanghai 20040, China (PRC)

Tel: 86-10-64376677 Fax: 86-10-64362870

IBM Rep Office, Lido Commercial Bldg., 3rd Fl., Jichang Rd., Jiangtai Rd., Beijing 100004, China (PRC)

Tel: 86-10-64376677 Fax: 86-10-64362870

IBP INC.

PO Box 515, Dakota City, NE, 68731

Tel: (402) 494-2061 Fax: (402) 241-2068 Web site: www.ibpinc.com

Produce beef and pork, hides and associated products, animal feeds, pharmaceuticals.

IBP Inc., East Jiao, Zhou City, China (PRC) (Locaton: Shanghai, China (PRC).)

Contact: Steve Langley, Sales Dir.

ICC INDUSTRIES INC.

460 Park Ave., New York, NY, 10022

Tel: (212) 521-1700 Fax: (212) 521-1794 Web site: www.iccchem.com

Manufacturing and trading of chemicals, plastics and pharmaceuticals.

Frutarom Flavors (Kunshan) Ltd., Dian Shan Hu Lake Town, Kunshan City, Jiangsu, China (PRC)

Tel: 86-520-748-1537 Fax: 86-520-748-1561

ICC Chemical Corporation, 16th Fl., Flat F, Hai Xing Plaza, 1 Rui Jin Rd. South, Lu Wan Dist., 20023 Shanghai, China (PRC)

Tel: 86-21-641-86078 Fax: 86-21-641-86060

ICC Chemical Corporation, Rm. 705, Songshan Hotel, 143 Zhongshan Rd., Dalian 116001, China (PRC)

Tel: 86-411-32-6371 Fax: 86-411-362-5142

INFONET SERVICES CORPORATION

2100 East Grand Ave., El Segundo, CA, 90245

Tel: (310) 335-2600 Fax: (310) 335-4507 Web site: www.infonet.com

Provider of Internet services and electronic messaging services.

Infonet China - Beijing, Ste. 1405, Scitech Tower, 22 Jianguomenwai Ave., Beijing 100004, China (PRC)

Tel: 86-10-6512-0952 Fax: 86-10-6512-0954

Infonet China - Guangzhou, Room 708, No. 2, Huangtian Zhijie Lujing Lu, Guangzhou, China (PRC) 510050

Tel: 86-20-350-0188 Fax: 86-20-357-3756

Infonet China - Shanghai, Ste. 11210, Donghu Hotel, Donghu Rd., Shanghia, China (PRC)

Tel: 86-21-641-58158 Fax: 86-21-641--58158

INFORMIX CORPORATION

4100 Bohannon Drive, Menlo Park, CA, 95025

Tel: (650) 926-6300 Fax: (650) 926-6593 Web site: www.informix.com

Designs & produces database management software, connectivity interfaces & gateways, and other computer applications.

Informix Software (China), Co. Ltd., Room 1461, Beijing New Century, Office Tower, No.6 Southern Rd., Capital Gymnasium, Beijing 100044, China (PRC) (Locations: Changsha, Chengdu, Guangzhou, Hangzhou, Shanghai, Shenyang, Wuhan & Xi'an, China)

Tel: 86-10-6849-2768

INGERSOLL-RAND COMPANY

200 Chestnut Ridge Road, Woodcliff Lake, NJ, 07675

Tel: (201) 573-0123 Fax: (201) 573-3172 Web site: www.ingersoll-rand.com

Mfr. compressors, rock drills, pumps, air tools, door hardware, ball bearings.

Beijing Ingersoll-Rand, 2/F, South Wing, Huapeng Mansion, 19 Dongsanhuan North Rd., Beijing 10004, Chaoyang Dist., Beijing 100020, China (PRC)

Tel: 86-10-6592-5086 Fax: 86-10-6592-5098

Shanghai Ingersoll-Rand Compressor Ltd., 16/B, Meike Mansion, 1 Tian Yao Qiao Rd., Xu Jia Hui, Shanghai 200030, China (PRC)

Tel: 86-21-6468-1081 Fax: 86-21-6468-1083

INLAND STEEL INDUSTRIES, INC.

30 West Monroe Street, Chicago, IL, 60603

Tel: (312) 346-0300 Fax: (312) 899-3197 Web site: www.inland.com

Holding company for steel products.

Shanghai Ryerson, Shanghai, China (PRC)

INSTRON CORPORATION

100 Royall Street, Canton, MA, 02021-1089

Tel: (781) 828-2500 Fax: (781) 575-5751

Mfr. material testing instruments.

Instron Corp. Beijing, Friendship Hotel, Room 60922, Block 9, Suyuan Garden, Beijing 100873, China (PRC)

INTEGRATED SILICON SOLUTION, INC.

2231 Lawson Lane, Santa Clara, CA, 95054-3311

Tel: (408) 588-0800 Fax: (408) 588-0805 Web site: www.issiusa.com

Mfr. high-speed memory chips and RAMs.

Integrated Silicon Solution, Inc., China Office, Shanghai, China (PRC)

Tel: 86-21-648-20697 Fax: 86-21-648-22286

Integrated Silicon Solution, Inc., China Office, Shenzhen, China (PRC)

Tel: 86-755-335-1929 Fax: 86-755-335-1929

Integrated Silicon Solution, Inc., China Office, Beijing, China (PRC)

Tel: 86-10-6275-3381 Fax: 86-10-6253-6841

Integrated Silicon Solution, Inc., China Office, HJiangsu, China (PRC)

Tel: 86-512-725-0384 Fax: 86-512-725-0536

INTEL CORPORATION

Robert Noyce Building, 2200 Mission College Blvd., Santa Clara, CA, 95052-8119

Tel: (408) 765-8080 Fax: (408) 765-1739 Web site: www.intel.com

Mfr. semiconductor, microprocessor and micro-communications components and systems.

Intel China, China (PRC)

INTER-CONTINENTAL HOTELS

1120 Ave. of the Americas, New York, NY, 10036

Tel: (212) 852-6400 Fax: (212) 852-6494 Web site: www.interconti.com

Worldwide hotel and resort accommodations.

Huiquan Dynasty Hotel, 9 Nanhai Rd., Quingdao, P. R. China (PRC)

Tel: 86-532-287-3366 Fax: 86-532-287-1122

Yinhe Dynasty Inter-Continental Chengdu, 99 Xia Xi Shun Cheng St., Chengdu 610016, China (PRC)

Tel: 86-28-661-8888 Fax: 86-28-674-8837

INTERCONEX, INC.

55 Hunter Lane, Elmsford, NY, 10523-1317

Tel: (914) 347-6600 Fax: (914) 347-0129

Freight forwarding.

Interconex China Ltd., Beijing, No. 9 Jianquo Mennei Dajie, International Hotel, Ste. 4022, Beijing, China (PRC)

Tel: 86-10-6525-4338 Fax: 86-10-6525-4338 Contact: Mike Johnsen

Interconex China Ltd., Shanghai, New Garden Hotel #2128, 1900 Hong Quio Lu, Shanghai 200335, China (PRC)

Tel: 86-21-6242-6810 Fax: 86-21-6242-6810 Contact: Gerald Liu

INTERGRAPH CORPORATION

One Madison Industrial Park, Huntsville, AL, 35894-0001

Tel: (205) 730-2000 Fax: (205) 730-7898 Web site: www.intergraph.com

Develop/mfr. interactive computer graphic systems.

Intergraph (Shenzhen) Company Ltd., 2809 Blk B, Tian An International Bldg., Remin South Rd., Shenzhen, China (PRC)

Tel: 86-775-2290069 Fax: 86-775-2171605

Intergraph China, Inc. - Beijing, Room 1201, The Gateway, 10 Yabao, Chaoyang Dist., Beijing, China (PRC) 100020

Tel: 86-10-6592-5270 Fax: 86-10-6592-5268

Intergraph China, Inc. - Shanghai, Room 5f-A Eastern Business Bldg., No. 586 Fan Yu Rd., Shanghai, China (PRC)

Tel: 86-21-6283-4365 Fax: 86-21-6283-4366

INTERNATIONAL FLAVORS & FRAGRANCES INC.

521 West 57th Street, New York, NY, 10019-2960

Tel: (212) 765-5500 Fax: (212) 708-7132 Web site: www.iff.com

Design/mfr. flavors, fragrances & aroma chemicals.

International Flavors & Fragrances (China), Beijing, China (PRC)

International Flavors & Fragrances (China), Xin'anjiang /(Hangzhou), China (PRC)

International Flavors & Fragrances (China), Guangzhou, China (PRC)

International Flavors & Fragrances (China), Shanghai, China (PRC)

INTERNATIONAL RECTIFIER CORPORATION

233 Kansas Street, El Segundo, CA, 90245

Tel: (310) 322-3331 Fax: (310) 322-3332 Web site: www.irf.com

Mfr. power semiconductor components.

International Rectifier Holdings Inc., Bldg. C #1205 Hui Yuan International Apartment, 8 Anli Rd., An Ding Men Wai, Beijing, China (PRC) 100101

Tel: 86-10-6499-1428 Fax: 86-10-6499-1428

International Rectifier Holdings Inc., Power IC Technology Ctr., 202 Zhuque St., Xian 710061, China (PRC)

Tel: 86-29-526-8274 Fax: 86-29-526-8274

International Rectifier Holdings Inc., IR Applications Ctr., PO Box 14, Shanghai University, 149 Rd., Shanghai 200072, China (PRC)

Tel: 86-21-5662-1235 Fax: 86-21-5690-4706

INTERNATIONAL SPECIALTY PRODUCTS

1361 Alps Road, Wayne, NJ, 07470

Tel: (973) 628-4000 Fax: (973) 628-3311 Web site: www.ispcorp.com

Mfr. specialty chemical products.

ISP (Hong Kong) Ltd., Chengdu Repesentative Office, Room 381, Jinjiang Hotel, 36 Renmin Nan Lu Er Duan, Chengdu 610012, China (PRC)

Tel: 86-28-557-2313 Fax: 86-28-557-2313

ISP (Hong Kong) Ltd., Shanghai Rep. Office, Room 702, Dynasty Business Ctr., 457 Wu Lu Mu Qi North Rd., Shanghai 200040, China (PRC)

Tel: 86-21-8249-3900 Fax: 86-21-6249-3908

ISP (Hong Kong) Ltd., Guangzhou Representative Office, Room 1911, Yi An Plaza, No. 38 Jianshe 6 Rd., Guangzhou, 510060, China (PRC)

Tel: 86-20-8384-7752 Fax: 86-20-8383-4851

ISP (Hong Kong) Ltd., Beijing Representative Office, Room 1607 Jing Tai Mansion, NO. 24 St. Jai Guo Men Wai, Beijing 100022, China (PRC)

Tel: 86-10-6515-6265 Fax: 86-10-6515-6267

ITT SHERATON CORPORATION

60 State Street, Boston, MA, 02108

Tel: (617) 367-3600 Fax: (617) 367-5676

Hotel operations.

Hua Ting Sheraton Hotel, Cao Xi Bei Lu, Shanghai, China (PRC)

The Great Wall Sheraton Hotel, North Donghuan Rd., Beijing, China (PRC)

J.P. MORGAN & CO. INC.

60 Wall Street, New York, NY, 10260-0060

Tel: (212) 483-2323 Fax: (212) 648-5209 Web site: www.jpm.com

International banking services.

J.P. Morgan & Co. - Representative Office, Shanghai Ctr., East Tower, Room 667, 1376 Nan Jing Rd. West, Shanghai 200040, China (PRC)

Tel: 86-21-6279-7301

J.P. Morgan & Company - Representative Office, 27th Fl., CITIC Bldg., No.19, Jianguomenwai Dajie, Beijing 100004, China (PRC)

Tel: 86-10-522-7488

J. WALTER THOMPSON COMPANY

466 Lexington Ave., New York, NY, 10017

Tel: (212) 210-7000 Fax: (212) 210-6944 Web site: www.jwt.com

International advertising and marketing services.

Bridge/J. Walter Thompson China, Beijing, China (PRC)

JOHNSON & JOHNSON

One Johnson & Johnson Plaza, New Brunswick, NJ, 08933

Tel: (732) 524-0400 Fax: (732) 214-0334 Web site: www.jnj.com

Mfr./distributor/R&D pharmaceutical, health care and cosmetic products.

Johnson & Johnson China Ltd., Shanghai J&J Ltd., Shatex Plaza 8/F, 88 Zunyi Rd. S., Changning Dist., Shanghai 200335, China (PRC)

Johnson & Johnson Medical Ltd., Shanghai, China (PRC)

LifeScan, Shanghai, China (PRC)

Shanghai Johnson & Johnson Ltd., Shanghai, China (PRC)

Xian-Janssen Pharmaceutical Ltd., 34 Wanshou Rd. N., Xian, Shaanxi Province, China (PRC)

S C JOHNSON & SON INC.

1525 Howe Street, Racine, WI, 53403

Tel: (414) 260-2000 Fax: (414) 260-2133 Web site: www.scjohnsonwax.com

Home, auto, commercial and personal care products and specialty chemicals.

Shanghai Johnson Ltd., 932 New Jin Qiao Rd., Pudong, Shanghai 201206, China (PRC)

A.T. KEARNEY INC.

222 West Adams Street, Chicago, IL, 60606

Tel: (312) 648-0111 Fax: (312) 223-6200 Web site: www.atkearney.com

Management consultants and executive search.

A .T. Kearney (Hong Kong) Ltd.., China World Trade Ctr., Room 1428-1430, No. 1 Jian Guo Men Wai Ave., Beijing 100004, China (PRC)

Tel: 86-10-6505-4627-30

KEITHLEY INSTRUMENTS INC.

28775 Aurora Road, Cleveland, OH, 44139

Tel: (440) 248-0400 Fax: (440) 248-6168 Web site: www.keithley.com

Mfr. electronic test/measure instruments, PC-based data acquisition hardware/software.

Keithley Instruments China, Holiday Inn Lido, Office Bldg. 404C, Beijing 100004, China (PRC)

THE M. W. KELLOGG COMPANY

601 Jefferson Ave., Houston, TX, 77002

Tel: (713) 753-5414 Fax: (713) 753-5628 Web site: www.kellogg.com

Design, engineering, procurement and construction for process and energy industry.

Kellogg China Inc., CITIC Bldg., Ste. 2403, 19 Jianguomenwai Dajie, Beijing, China (PRC)

THE KENDALL COMPANY

15 Hampshire Street, Mansfield, MA, 02048

Tel: (508) 261-8000 Fax: (508) 261-8542

Mfr. medical disposable products, home health care products and specialty adhesive products.

Kendall Yantai Medical Products Co. Ltd., 1 Tianchi Rd., Yantai Economic & Technical Development Zone, Yantai Shandong, China (PRC)

KENNAMETAL INC.

State Rte. 981, Latrobe, PA, 15650

Tel: (724) 539-5000 Fax: (724) 539-4710 Web site: www.kennametal.com

Tools, hard carbide & tungsten alloys for metalworking industry.

Kennametal Hardpoint Inc., Room 743, The Garden Hotel, Office Tower, No. 38, Huanshi Dong Lu, Guangzhou, China (PRC) 510064

Tel: 86-20-8384-4990 Fax: 86-20-8384-4003

Kennametal Hardpoint Inc., Room 1910, Shudu Mansion Hotel, No. 20, North 3rd. Shuwa St., Chengdu, Sichuan, China (PRC) 610016

Tel: 86-28-674-5402 Fax: 86-28-674-3563

Kennametal Hardpoint Inc., Room 502, Jin Tai Garden Bldg., 58 Mao Ming Rd. (S), Shanghai, China (PRC) 200020

Tel: 86-21-6472-3825 Fax: 86-21-6472-7543

Kennametal Hardpoint Inc. - Head Office, Room 1559, New Century Office Tower, No. 6, Southern Rd., Capital GYM, Beijing, China (PRC) 100044

Tel: 86-10-6849-2179 Fax: 86-10-6849-2178

KERR-McGEE CORPORATION

PO Box 25861, Oklahoma City, OK, 73125

Tel: (405) 270-1313 Fax: (405) 270-3123

Oil & gas exploration & production, industrial chemicals, coal.

Kerr-McGee China Petroleum Ltd., Ste. 1305-1314, Lucky Tower, Block B, 3 Dongsanhuan Beilu, Beijing 100027, China (PRC)

KIMBERLY-CLARK CORPORATION

351 Phelps Drive, Irving, TX, 75038

Tel: (972) 281-1200 Fax: (972) 281-1435 Web site: www.kimberly-clark.com.

Mfr./sales/distribution of consumer tissue, household and personal care products.

Kimberly-Clark (Guangzhou) Ltd., China (PRC)

Kimberly-Clark (Shanghai) Co. Ltd., China (PRC)

KINKO'S, INC.

255 W. Stanley Ave., Ventura, CA, 93002-8000

Tel: (805) 652-4000 Fax: (805) 652-4347 Web site: www.kinkos.com

Kinko's operates a 24-hour-a-day, global chain of photocopy stores.

Kinko's, A11 Xiang Jun Gei Li Dong, Sanhuan Rd., Chao Yang Dist., Beijing, 100020, China (PRC)

Tel: 86-10-6595-8050 Fax: 86-10-6596-8218

LESTER B KNIGHT & ASSOC INC.

549 West Randolph Street, Chicago, IL, 60661

Tel: (312) 346-2300 Fax: (312) 648-1085

Architecture, engineering, planning, operations & management consulting.

Lester B. Knight Intl. Corp. Inc., 902 Electric Power Bldg., 430 Xu Jia Hui Rd., Shanghai 200025, China (PRC)

THE KOHLER COMPANY

444 Highland Drive, Kohler, WI, 53044

Tel: (920) 457-4441 Fax: (920) 459-1274

Plumbing products, ceramic tile and stone, cabinetry, furniture, engines, generators, switch gear and hospitality.

Kohler Engines, China Office, Unit A914 Yin Hai Bldg., 250 Cao Xi Rd., Shanghai 200233, China (PRC)

Tel: 86-21-6482-1252 Fax: 82-21-6482-1255

Kohler Plumbing International, Fosham, China (PRC)

KORN/FERRY INTERNATIONAL

1800 Century Park East, Los Angeles, CA, 90067

Tel: (310) 552-1834 Fax: (310) 553-6452 Web site: www.kornferry.com

Executive search; management consulting.

Korn/Ferry International, Shanghai, China (PRC)

Tel: 86-21-62-79-8681 Fax: 86-21-62-79-8682

Korn/Ferry International, Landmark Bldg. #606, 8 N. Dongsamhuan Rd., Chao Yang Dist., Beijing 100004, China (PRC)

Tel: 86-10-6590-0961 Fax: 86-10-6590-0962

KPMG PEAT MARWICK LLP

Three Chestnut Ridge Road, Montvale, NJ, 07645

Tel: (201) 307-7000 Fax: (201) 930-8617 Web site: www.kpmg.com

Accounting and audit, tax and management consulting services.

KPMG Peat Marwick, Room 1603, Block A, Shenzhen Tian An, International Bldg., Renmin South Rd., Shenzhen, China (PRC)

KPMG Peat Marwick, Zone 3, Yantze New World Hotel, 2099 Yanan Xi Rd., Shanghai 200335, China (PRC)

KPMG Peat Marwick, 2609 Jing Guang Centre, Hu Jia Lou, Beijing, 100020, China (PRC)

THE KROLL-O'GARA COMPANY

9113 Le Saint Drive, Fairfield, OH, 45014

Tel: (513) 874-2112 Fax: (513) 874-2558 Web site: www.kroll-ogara.com

Security and consulting services and vechiles.

Kroll Associates (Asia) Ltd., Beijing Office, Ste. 1119, Goldland Bldg., Chaoyang Dist., Beijing, China (PRC) 100016

Tel: 86-10-6464-3898 Fax: 86-10-6464-3899

LANDIS GARDNER

20 East Sixth Street, Waynesboro, PA, 17268-2050

Tel: (717) 762-2161 Fax: (717) 765-5143

Mfr. precision cylindrical grinding machinery and double disc grinding.

Shanghai Machine Tool Works (SMTW), 1146 Jungong Rd., Shanghai 200093, China PRC

LANDOR ASSOCIATES

Klamath House, 1001 Front Street, San Francisco, CA, 94111-1424

Tel: (415) 955-1400 Fax: (415) 955-1358 Web site: www.landor.com

International marketing consulting firm, focused on developing and maintaining brand identity.

Landor Associates, c/o Arthur Andersen & Co., 19/F, Shui On Plaza, 333 Huai Hai Zhong Rd., Shanghai 200021, China (PRC)

Tel: 86-21-6386-6688 Fax: 86-21-6386-2288 Contact: Michelle Lee

LANIER WORLDWIDE, INC.

2300 Parklake Drive, N.E., Atlanta, GA, 30345

Tel: (770) 496-9500 Fax: (770) 621-1535

Specialize in digital copiers and multi-functional systems.

Beijing Lanuxum OA Group, No. 9, Maoling Ju, Muxidi, Haidian Dist., Beijing, China (PRC)

Tel: 86-10-685-15567 Fax: 86-10-685-71822

LEAR CORPORATION

21557 Telegraph Road, Southfield, MI, 48086-5008

Tel: (248) 746-1500 Fax: (248) 746-1722 Web site: www.lear.com

Mgf./dist. car seats worldwide.

Jiangxi Jiangling Lear, Interior Systems Co., China (PRC)

LEHMAN BROTHERS HOLDINGS INC.

Three World Financial Center, New York, NY, 10285

Tel: (212) 526-7000 Fax: (212) 526-3738 Web site: www.lehman.com

Financial services, securities and merchant banking services.

Lehman Brothers, Level 12, Unit 03, China World Trade Ctr., No.1 Jianguomenwai Ave., Beijing, China (PRC)

Tel: 86-10-505-0303

LIFE TECHNOLOGIES INC.

9800 Medical Center Drive, Rockville, MD, 20850

Tel: (301) 840-8000 Fax: (301) 329-8635

Biotechnology.

Life Technologies, China (PRC)

LIGHTNIN

135 Mt. Read Blvd., PO Box 1370, Rochester, NY, 14611

Tel: (716) 436-5550 Fax: (716) 436-5589

Mfr./sale/services industrial mixing machinery, aerators.

Lightnin China Mixers Ltd., 1/F, 18 485 Guiping Rd., Caohejing Hi-Tech Park, Shanghai 200233, China (PRC)

ELI LILLY & COMPANY

Lilly Corporate Center, Indianapolis, IN, 46285

Tel: (317) 276-2000 Fax: (317) 277-6579 Web site: www.lilly.com

Mfr. pharmaceuticals and animal health products.

Eli Lilly China Ltd., Shanghai & Suzhou, China (PRC)

THE LINCOLN ELECTRIC COMPANY

22801 St. Clair Ave., Cleveland, OH, 44117-1199

Tel: (216) 481-8100 Fax: (216) 486-8385 Web site: www.lincolnelectric.com

Mfr. arc welding and welding related products, oxy-fuel and thermal cutting equipment and integral AC motors.

Lincoln Electric Company (Shanghai) Welding Co., Ltd., Part A #2 Warehouse, 200 Fu Te Rd. (N), Wai Gao Qiano Free Trade Zone, Pudong, Shanghai 200133, China (PRC)

Tel: 86-21-5866-8666 Fax: 86-21-5866-7666 Contact: Dr. Yan Li, Plant Mgr.

The Lincoln Electric Company, First Fl., Extension 1, No. 325, Jie Fang Nan Lu, He Xi, Tianjin 300202, China (PRC)

Tel: 86-22-2831-4170 Fax: 86-22-2831-4179 Contact: Dai Shu Hua

The Lincoln Electric Company, A613. A614 Yin Hai Bldg., 250 Cao Xi Rd., Shanghai 200233, China (PRC)

Tel: 86-21-6-482-7154 Fax: 86-21-6-482-7166 Contact: Julius Wu

LOCKHEED MARTIN CORPORATION

6801 Rockledge Drive, Bethesda, MD, 20817

Tel: (301) 897-6000 Fax: (301) 897-6652 Web site: www.imco.com

Design/mfr./management systems in fields of space, defense, energy, electronics and technical services.

Lockheed Aircraft Service International, China Hotel, Rm. 1431, Apt. Bl D, Liu Hua Lu, Guangzhou 510015, China (PRC)

Tel: 86-20-657-9757 Fax: 86-20-666-1881 Contact: G. Lange, Mgr.

Lockheed Martin China Inc., 808-180 Beijing New Century Office Tower, No. 6 Southern Rd. Capital Gym, Beijing 100046 China (PRC)

Tel: 86-10-849-2126 Fax: 86-10-849-2125 Contact: J. Wang, VP

LOCTITE CORPORATION

10 Columbus Boulevard, Hartford, CT, 06106

Tel: (203) 520-5000 Fax: (203) 520-5073 Web site: www.loctite.com

Mfr./sale industrial adhesives and sealants.

Loctite (China) Co. Ltd., 8R, South Gate, Bldg. 7 Jin Long Garden, 68 Xinzhong Xi Jie, Gongti Bei Lu, 100027, China (PRC)

Tel: 86-10-6500-3566 Fax: 86-10-6552-7726 Contact: Geoff Zheng

Loctite (China) Company Ltd., Manufacturing Facility, Yantai Development zone, Shandong, China (PRC) 264006

Tel: 86-535-6637-2999 Fax: 86-535-6637-1999 Contact: Jin Wenhai, Nat'l Mgr.

THE LUBRIZOL CORPORATION

29400 Lakeland Blvd., Wickliffe, OH, 44092-2298

Tel: (440) 943-4200 Fax: (440) 943-5337 Web site: www.lubrizol.com

Mfr. chemicals additives for lubricants & fuels.

Lubrizol China Inc., Beijing, China (PRC)

Tel: 86-10-6467-3326

LUCENT TECHNOLOGIES, INC.

600 Mountain Ave., Murray Hill, NJ, 07974-0636

Tel: (908) 582-3000 Fax: (908) 582-2110 Web site: www.lucent.com

Design/mfr. wide range of public and private networks, communication systems and software, data networking systems, business telephone systems and microelectronics components.

Lucent Technologies China Company Ltd., CVIK Place, 22 Jian Guo Men Wai Ave., Beijing 100004, China (PRC)

Tel: 86-10-6522-5566 Fax: 86-10-6522-7743 Contact: H.T. Kung, PR Mgr.

Lucent Technologies Fiber Optic Cable Company Ltd., 9 Longqing St., Beijing Economic and Technological Development Zone, Beijing 100076, China (PRC)

Tel: 86-10-67881199 Fax: 86-10-67881402 Contact: Bernard Choo, Location Head

Lucent Technologies of Shanghai Ltd., 704 Yishan Rd., Shanghai, China (PRC) 200233

Tel: 86-21-6470-5858 Fax: 86-21-6470-0411 Contact: Nico Buijs, Location Head

Lucent Technologies of Tianjin Cable Co., Ltd., Yibai Rd., Canglian Zhuang, Hebei Dist., Tianjin, China (PRC) 300402

Tel: 86-22-630-8978 Fax: 86-22-630-6758 Contact: Charles Li, Location Mgr.

Lucent Technologies Qingdao Power Systems Company, Huite Industrial City, High Tech Park, Qingdao, Shandong Province, China (PRC) 266101

Tel: 86-10-6522-5566 Fax: 86-10-6522-7743 Contact: Rene Weaver, Location Head

Lucent Technologies Shanghai Fiber Optic Company Ltd., 15 Guijing Rd., Shanghai, China (PRC) 200233

Tel: 86-21-6485-2520 Fax: 86-21-6485-0939 Contact: Lee How Giap, Location Head

Qingdao Telecommunications Systems Ltd., Huite Industrial City, High Tech Park, Qingdao, Shandong Province, China (PRC) 266101

Tel: 86-532-8702000 Fax: 86-532-8701998 Contact: Mike Shen, Location Head

Shanghai Lucent Technologies Transmission Equipment Co., Ltd, Bldg. 10, 700 Yishan Rd., Shanghai, China (PRC) 200233
China (PRC)

Tel: 86-21-6483-6868 Fax: 86-21-6483-6688 Contact: Mynoon Doro, Location Head

THE MacNEAL-SCHWENDLER CORPORATION

815 Colorado Boulevard, Los Angeles, CA, 90041

Tel: (213) 258-9111 Fax: (213) 259-3838

Develop/mfr.computer-aided engineering software & services, advanced materials technology & training.

The MacNeal-Schwendler Co. Ltd., Xi-Yuan Hotel #5124, Erligou, Beijing 100046, China (PRC)

MARRIOTT INTERNATIONAL INC.

1 Marriott Drive, Washington, DC, 20058

Tel: (301) 380-3000 Fax: (301) 380-5181

Lodging, contract food and beverage service, and restaurants.

New World Courtyard Beijing, 3C Chongwenmen Wai St., Chongwen Dist., Beijing, China (PRC) 100062

Tel: 86-10-671-81188 Fax: 86-10-670-81808

New World Courtyard Qingdao, 39 Shandong Rd., Qingdao, Sahndong, China (PRC) 266071

Tel: 86-523-581-4688 Fax: 86-523-583-6777

New World Courtyard Shenyang, No. 2 Nanjing Nan St., Heping Dist., Shenyang, China (PRC) 110001

Tel: 86-24-238-69888 Fax: 86-24-238-60018

MARSH & McLENNAN COS INC.

1166 Ave. of the Americas, New York, NY, 10036-2774

Tel: (212) 345-5000 Fax: (212) 345-4808 Web site: www.marshmac.com

Insurance agents/brokers, pension and investment management consulting services.

J&H Marsh & McLennan Ltd., Room 612-613, 6th Fl., Office Tower II, Henderson Centre, Dongcheng Dist., Beijing 100005, China (PRC)

Tel: 86-10-6518-2675 Fax: 86-10-6518-3466 Contact: alice Chan

J&H Marsh & McLennan Ltd., Room 1306-1307, 13/F., South Tower, Hong Kong Plaza, No. 283 Huai Hai Zhong Rd., Shanghai 200021, China (PRC)

Tel: 86-21-6390-7288 Fax: 86-21-6390-7282 Contact: Jimmy Hung

MASTERCARD INTERNATIONAL INC.

200 Purchase Street, Purchase, NY, 10577

Tel: (914) 249-2000 Fax: (914) 249-5475 Web site: www.mastercard.com

Provides financial payment systems globally.

MasterCard International Inc., Room 901, Olympic Hotel Pte., Ltd., 52 Baishiqiao Rd., Haidian Dist., Beijing 10080, China (PRC)

MATTEL INC.

333 Continental Blvd., El Segundo, CA, 90245-5012

Tel: (310) 252-2000 Fax: (310) 252-2179 Web site: www.mattelmedia.com

Mfr. toys, dolls, games, crafts and hobbies.

Mattel, Beijing, China (PRC)

MAYTAG CORPORATION

403 West Fourth Street North, Newton, IA, 50208

Tel: (515) 792-8000 Fax: (515) 787-8376 Web site: www.maytagcorp.com

Mfr./sales of large appliances, ovens, dishwashers, refrigerators and washing machines.

Hefei Rongshida Group/Maytag, Beijing, China (PRC)

McCANN-ERICKSON WORLDWIDE

750 Third Ave., New York, NY, 10017

Tel: (212) 984-3644 Fax: (212) 984-2629

International advertising/marketing services.

McCann-Erickson Guangming, Room 5035, Peking Hotel, Beijing, China (PRC)

McCORMICK & COMPANY, INC.

18 Loveton Circle, Sparks, MD, 21152-6000

Tel: (410) 771-7301 Fax: (410) 527-8289

Mfr./distribution/sale seasonings, flavorings, specialty foods.

Shanghai McCormick Foods Company, Ltd., No. 791, Hong Mei Rd. South, Shanghai, China (PRC) 200237

McDERMOTT INTERNATIONAL INC.

1450 Poydras Street, PO Box 60035, New Orleans, LA, 70160-0035

Tel: (504) 587-5400 Fax: (504) 587-6153 Web site: www.mcdermott.com

Engineering & construction.

Babcock & Wilcox, Office Unit 418, Block A-1, Lido Commercial Bldg., Jichang Rd., Jiang Tai Rd., Beijing 100004, China (PRC)

Tel: 86-10-6437-8766 Fax: 86-10-6436-7697 Contact: Lila Chen, Dir.

Babcock & Wilcox Beijing Company Ltd., Bajiacock, West Suburb, PO Box 4354, Shijingshan Dist. 100043, Beijing, China (PRC)

Tel: 86-10-6886-1332 Fax: 86-10-6886-1336

McDONALD'S CORPORATION

Kroc Drive, Oak Brook, IL, 60523

Tel: (630) 623-3000 Fax: (630) 623-7409

Fast food chain stores.

McDonald's Corp., China (PRC)

McKINSEY & COMPANY

55 East 52nd Street, New York, NY, 10022

Tel: (212) 446-7000 Fax: (212) 446-8575 Web site: www.mckinsey.com

Management and business consulting services.

McKinsey & Company, 23/F Shui On Plaza, No. 333 Huai Hai Zhong Lu, Shanghai 200021, China (PRC)

Tel: 86-21-6385-8888 Fax: 86-21-6386-2000

McKinsey & Company, 7/F, No. 2 Citic Bldg., 19 Jianguomenwai Da Jie, Beijing, China (PRC)

Tel: 86-10-6500-5436 Fax: 86-10-6500-5478

MEMC ELECTRONIC MATERIALS, INC.

501 Pearl Drive, St. Peters, MO, 63376

Tel: (314) 279-5500 Fax: (314) 279-5158 Web site: www.memc.com

Mfg. & distribution of silicon wafers.

MEMC Electronic Materials, Inc., Shanghai Representative Office, Ste. 661, Shanghai Centre, 1376 Nanjing Xi Lu, Shanghai 200040 China (PRC)

Tel: 86-21-627-98931 Fax: 86-21-627-98941

THE MENTHOLATUM CO., INC.

707 Sterling Drive, Orchard Park, NY, 14127-1587

Tel: (716) 677-2500 Fax: (716) 674-3696 Web site: www.mentholatum.com

Mfr./distributor proprietary medicines, drugs, OTC's.

The Mentholatum (Zhongshan) Pharmaceuticals Co. Ltd., The Second Industrial Estates, Sam Heung, Zhongshan, Guangdong Province, China (PRC)

Tel: 86-760-6685596 Fax: 86-760-668-5433

MENTOR GRAPHICS/MICROTEC RESEARCH

880 Ridder Park Drive, San Jose, CA, 95131

Tel: (408) 487-7000 Fax: (408) 487-7001

Develop/mfr. software tools for embedded systems market.

Microtec China, China (PRC)

MERITOR AUTOMOTIVE, INC.

2135 W. Maple Road, Troy, MI, 48084-7186

Tel: (248) 435-1000 Fax: (248) 435-1393 Web site: www.meritorauto.com

Mfr./sales of light and heavy vehicle systems for trucks, cars and speciality vehicles.

Dura Auto Systems, China (PRC)

Meritor Automotive, Inc., China (PRC)

MERRILL LYNCH & COMPANY, INC.

World Financial Center, North Tower, New York, NY, 10281-1323

Tel: (212) 449-1000 Fax: (212) 449-2892

Security brokers and dealers, investment and business services.

Merrill Lynch International Inc., Ste. 3301-3302 China World Tower, China World Trade Ctr., 1 Jian Guo Men Wai Ave., Beijing 100004, P.R.C.

Tel: 86-10-6505-0290 Fax: 86-10-6505-0278

Merrill Lynch International Inc., Ste. 308 West Tower, Shanghai Ctr., 1276 Nanjing West Rd., Shanghai 2000040, China (PRC)

Tel: 86-21-6279-7032 Fax: 86-21-6279-7031

METROPOLITAN LIFE INSURANCE COMPANY

1 Madison Ave., New York, NY, 10010-3603

Tel: (212) 578-3818 Fax: (212) 252-7294

Insurance and retirement savings products and services.

Metropolitan Life Insurance Co., 1006 China World Trade Tower, No.1 Jian Guo Men Wai Ave., Beijing 100004, China (PRC)

Tel: 86-10-6505-05134 Fax: 86-10-6505-5136 Contact: Malone Ma, Chief Rep.

Metropolitan Life Insurance Company, Ste. 809-810, Overseas Chinese Mansion, 129 Yan'an West Rd., Shanghai 200040, China (PRC)

Tel: 86-21-6249-1350 Fax: 86-21-6249-1351 Contact: Kenneth Chao, Chief Rep.

MICROCHIP TECHNOLOGY INC.

2355 West Chandler Boulevard, Chandler, AZ, 85224

Tel: (602) 786-7200 Fax: (602) 899-9210 Web site: www.microchip.com

Mfr. electronic subassemblies and components.

Microchip Technology, Shanghai, Unit 406 of Shanghai Golden Bridge Bldg., 2077 Yan'an West Rd., Hong Qiao Dist., Shanghai, China (PRC)

Tel: 86-21-6275-5700 Fax: 86-21-6275-5060

MICROMERITICS INSTRUMENT CORPORATION

One Micromeritics Drive, Norcross, GA, 30093-1877

Tel: (770) 662-3620 Fax: (770) 662-3696

Mfr. analytical instruments.

Micromeritics China, Xi Yuan Hotel, Bldg. 6, Room 5609, Beijing 100046, China (PRC)

MICROSOFT CORPORATION

One Microsoft Way, Redmond, WA, 98052-6399

Tel: (425) 882-8080 Fax: (425) 936-7329 Web site: www.microsoft.com

Computer software, peripherals and services.

Microsoft (China) Co., Ltd., 6/F, Beijing Sigma Ctr.m No. 49, Zhichun Rd., Hai Dian Dist., Beijing, China (PRC) 100080

Tel: 86-10-6261-7711 Fax: 86-10-6253-6630

MILLIPORE CORPORATION, ANALYTICAL PRODUCT DIVISION

80 Ashby Road, PO Box 9125, Bedford, MA, 01730

Tel: (781) 275-9200 Fax: (781) 533-3110 Web site: www.millipore.com

Mfr. flow and pressure measurement and control components; precision filters, hi-performance liquid chromatography instruments.

Millipore China Ltd., Ste. 1101/1106/16, Asia Pacific Bldg., 8 Ya Bao Rd., Chao Yang Dist., Beijing 100020, China (PRC)

MINTEQ INTERNATIONAL INC.

405 Lexington Ave., 19th Fl., New York, NY, 10174-1901

Tel: (212) 878-1800 Fax: (212) 878-1952 Web site: www.mineralstech.com

Mfr./market specialty refractory and metallurgical products and application systems.

Huzhou MINTEQ Refractory Co. Ltd., 118 Beitu, Hangchanguiao, Ximen, Huzhou, Zhejiang, China (PRC) PC 313000

Tel: 86-572-210-2254 Fax: 86-572-210-4571 Contact: Yu Bingquan, Mgr. Emp: 56

MOBIL CORPORATION

3225 Gallows Road, Fairfax, VA, 22037-0001

Tel: (703) 846-3000 Fax: (703) 846-4669 Web site: www.mobil.com

Petroleum and gas exploration and refining, mfr. petroleum products, chemicals and petrochemicals.

Mobil China, China (PRC)

MOLEX INC.

2222 Wellington Court, Lisle, IL, 60532

Tel: (630) 969-4550 Fax: (630) 969-1352 Web site: www.molex.com

Mfr. electronic, electrical & fiber optic interconnection products & systems, switches, application tooling.

Molex Inc., Shilong Town, China (PRC)

MORGAN STANLEY DEAN WITTER & CO.

1585 Broadway, New York, NY, 10036

Tel: (212) 761-4000 Fax: (212) 761-0086 Web site: www.msdw.com

Securities and commodities brokerage, investment banking, money management, personal trusts.

Morgan Stanley Asia Ltd., Ste. 700 B, Shanghai Ctr., 1376 Nanjing Xi Lu, Shanghai 200040, China (PRC)

Morgan Stanley Asia Ltd., No. 1, Jian Guo Men Wai St., Beijing 100004, China (PRC)

Morgan Stanley Asia Ltd., 6 Fu Xing Men Wai Ave., Beijing 1000045 PRC, China (PRC)

MORRISON & FOERSTER

425 Market Street, San Francisco, CA, 94105

Tel: (415) 268-7000 Fax: (415) 268-7522 Web site: www.mofo.com

International law firm.

Morrison & Foerster, Beijing, China (PRC)

MORRISON KNUDSEN CORPORATION

1 Morrison Knudsen Plaza, PO Box 73, Boise, ID, 83729

Tel: (208) 386-5000 Fax: (208) 386-7186 Web site: www.mk.com

Design/construction for environmental, industrial, process, power and transportation markets.

Morrison Knudsen Corp., Beijing, China (PRC)

MOTOROLA, INC.

1303 East Algonquin Road, Schaumburg, IL, 60196

Tel: (847) 576-5000 Fax: (847) 538-5191 Web site: www.mot.com

Mfr. communications equipment, semiconductors and cellular phones.

Motorola China, Locations in Fuzhou & Tianjin, China (PRC)

Motorola China, Innovation Ctr. II, No. 2 S. Dongsanhuan Rd., Jianguomenwai, Chaiyang Dist., Beijing 10022, China (PRC)

Tel: 86-10-6564-1800 Fax: 86-10-6546-1801

MTS SYSTEMS CORPORATION

1400 Technology Drive, Eden Prairie, MN, 55344-2290

Tel: (612) 937-4000 Fax: (612) 937-4515 Web site: www.mts.com

Develop/mfr. mechanical testing & simulation products & services, industry measure & automation instrumentation.

MTS Systems (China) Inc., Xi Yuan Hotel, Ste. 674-5-6 691, Bldg. No. 6, Er Li Gou, Xi Jiao, Beijing, China (PRC)

NATIONAL STARCH & CHEMICAL COMPANY

10 Finderne Ave., Bridgewater, NJ, 08807-3300

Tel: (908) 685-5000 Fax: (908) 685-5005 Web site: www.national starch.com

Mfr. adhesives & sealants, resins & specialty chemicals, electronic materials & adhesives, food products, industry starch.

National Starch & Chemical (Guangdong) Ltd., Nanzha Fifth Industrial Estate, Humen, Dongguan, Guangdong, China (PRC) (Locations: Beijing, Gunagzhou, and Shanghai, China (PRC).)

Tel: 86-769-556-3700 Fax: 86-769-556-3703

NEW BRUNSWICK SCIENTIFIC CO., INC.

44 Talmadge Road, Box 4005, Edison, NJ, 08818-4005

Tel: (732) 287-1200 Fax: (732) 287-4222 Web site: www.nbsc.com

Mfr. research and production equipment for life sciences.

New Brunswick Scientific, Shennan Garden A Bldg. 25D, Shenzhen 518052, China (PRC)

Tel: 86-755-663-1609 Fax: 86-755-663-3731 Contact: Jia Fu, Gen. Mgr.

New Brunswick Scientific, Science & Technology Bldg., Central South Hotel, 288 Wu Luo Rd., Wuchang, Wuhan 430070, China (PRC)

Tel: 86-27-731-2644 Fax: 86-27-731-2655 Contact: Jia Fu, Gen. Mgr.

New Brunswick Scientific, Taicheng Commercial Business Complex, No.8, Da Hui Si Rd., Beijing 100081, China (PRC)

Tel: 86-10-6218-2905 Fax: 86-10-6218-2909 Contact: Jia Fu, Gen. Mgr.

New Brunswick Scientific, No. 1 Lane 590 Wan Ping (S) Rd., Shanghai, 200030 China (PRC)

Tel: 86-21-6481-2658 Fax: 86-21-6481-2665 Contact: Jia Fu, Gen. Mgr.

NORDSON CORPORATION

28601 Clemens Road, Westlake, OH, 44145

Tel: (440) 892-1580 Fax: (440) 892-9507 Web site: www.nordson.com

Mfr. industry application equipment, sealants & packaging machinery.

Nordson Corp. Representative Office, 828 Xin Jin Qiao Rd., Pudong, Shanghai 201206, China (PRC)

Tel: 86-21-5854-2345 Fax: 86-21-5854-9150

NORGREN

5400 S. Delaware Street, Littleton, CO, 80120-1663

Tel: (303) 794-2611 Fax: (303) 795-9487 Web site: www.norgren.com

Mfr. pneumatic filters, regulators, lubricators, valves, automation systems, dryers, push-in fittings.

IMI Norgren Pneumatic (Shanghai) Co. Ltd., 2/F, Block 7, 471 Gui Ping Rd., Shanghai Caohejing Hi-Tech Park, Shanghai 200233, China (PRC)

Tel: 86-21-6485-7935 Fax: 86-21-6495-6042

Norgren Pneumatic Products, Rm 905-907 Jin Ying Hotel, No.19 Bei Jiao Chang Rd., Guangzhou, 510050 China (PRC)

Tel: 86-20-8381-1888 Fax: 86-20-8380-4332

NORTHWEST AIRLINES CORPORATION

2700 Lone Oak Parkway, Eagan, MN, 55121-3034

Tel: (612) 726-2111 Fax: (612) 727-6717 Web site: www.nwa.com

Airline passenger and cargo carrier.

Northwest Airlines, Beijing, China (PRC)

NOVELLUS SYSTEMS INC.

3970 North First Street, San Jose, CA, 95154

Tel: (408) 943-9700 Fax: (408) 943-3422 Web site: www.novellus.com

Mfr. advanced processing systems used in fabrication of integrated circuits.

Novellus Systems Semiconductor Equipment Shanghai Co., Ltd., 603-611 No. 300, Tian-Lin Bldg., Tian-Lin Rd., Shanghai 200233, China (PRC)

Tel: 86-21-6485-3889 Fax: 86-21-6485-1282

OGILVY & MATHER WORLDWIDE

309 West 49th Street, New York, NY, 10019

Tel: (212) 237-4000 Fax: (212) 237-5123

Advertising, marketing, public relations & consulting firm.

Ogilvy & Mather, Shanghai, China (PRC)

OSMONICS INC.

5951 Clearwater Drive, Minnetonka, MN, 55343-8995

Tel: (612) 933-2277 Fax: (612) 933-0141

Mfr. fluid filtration and separation equipment and components.

Osmonics, Shanghai, China (PRC)

OSRAM SYLVANIA CHEMICALS INC.

Hawes Street, Towanda, PA, 18848

Tel: (717) 268-5000 Fax: (717) 268-5157

Chemicals.

Osram Sylvania Chemicals, China (PRC)

OTIS ELEVATOR COMPANY

10 Farm Springs Road, Farmington, CT, 06032

Tel: (860) 676-6000 Fax: (860) 676-5111

Mfr. elevators and escalators.

China Tianjin Otis Elevator Co. Ltd., Jie Fang Nan Lu, Tianjin, China (PRC)

OWENS-ILLINOIS, INC.

One SeaGate, PO Box 1035, Toledo, OH, 43666

Tel: (419) 247-5000 Fax: (419) 247-2839

Largest mfr. of glass containers in the US; plastic containers, compression-molded closures and dispensing systems.

Wuban Owens Glass Container Company, Ltd., Wuhan, China (PRC)

PACCAR INTERNATIONAL

777 106th Ave. NE, Bellevue, WA, 98004

Tel: (425) 468-7400 Fax: (428) 468-8216

Heavy duty dump trucks, military vehicles.

Paccar China Ltd.- Bejing Office, Unit 8-08 Landmark Bldg., Liang Ma Tower & Square, 8 North Dongsanhuan Rd., Beijing, 100004, China (PRC)

Tel: 86-10-6501-6688 Fax: 86-10-6501-1972

PACKARD BELL NEC, INC.

One Packard Bell Way, Sacramento, CA, 95828-0903

Tel: (916) 388-0101 Fax: (916) 388-1109 Web site: www.packardbell.com

Sales/distribution of home computers.

Packard Bell NEC, Shanghai, China (PRC)

PALL CORPORATION

2200 Northern Boulevard, East Hills, NY, 11548-1289

Tel: (516) 484-5400 Fax: (516) 484-5228 Web site: www.pall.com

Specialty materials and engineering; filters & related fluid clarification equipment.

Pall Filter (Beijing) Co., Ltd., 3/F, Bailing Bldg., No. 1 Zuojiazhuang Oianjie, Chaoyang Dist., Beijing 100020, China (PRC)

Tel: 86-10-6464-3232 Fax: 86-10-6464-3838

Pall Gelman Sciences, Asia Games Garden, No. 12 Xiao Ying Dong Rd., Beijing 100101, China (PRC)

Tel: 86-10-6497-4680 Fax: 86-10-6497-4682

Pall Gelman Sciences, Simon Pang Bo, Apt. 8B #2 Bldg., Asia Gambes Garden, No. 12 Xiao Ying Dong Rd., Beijing 100101, China (PRC)

Tel: 86-10-6497-4680 Fax: 86-10-6497-4682

PANDUIT CORPORATION

17301 Ridgeland Ave., Tinley Park, IL, 60477-0981

Tel: (708) 532-1800 Fax: (708) 532-1811

Mfr. electrical/electronic wiring components.

Panduit Corp., 542-1 Jie Fang Bei Rd., Guangzhou 510030, China (PRC)

PARAMETRIC TECHNOLOGY CORPORATION

128 Technology Drive, Waltham, MA, 02154

Tel: (781) 398-5000 Fax: (781) 398-5674 Web site: www.ptc.com

Mfr. CAD/CAM/CAE software.

Parametric Technology Beijing, Room 1716 Beijing Fortune Bldg., No. 5 Dong San Huan Bie Lu, Chaho Yank Dist., Beijing 100 004 China (PRC)

Tel: 86-10-6590-8699 Fax: 86-10-6590-8698

Parametric Technology Guangzhou, Room 714-716, 7/F., Metro Plaza, 183 Tian He Rd. North, Guangzhua 510 620 China (PRC)

Tel: 86-20-8755-4146 Fax: 86-20-8755-4416

Parametric Technology Shanghai, Ste. 2201-2203, 22nd Fl., Super Ocian Finance Bldg., 2168 Yan An Rd. West, Shanghai 200 005 China (PRC)

Tel: 86-21-6278-5080 Fax: 86-21-6278-5086

Parametric Technology Sichuan, Room 2303, Business Bldg., Minshan Hotel No. 55 Section 2, Ren Min Nan Rd. Chengdu, Sichuan 610 021 China (PRC)

Tel: 86-28-553-4010 Fax: 86-28-553-4011

PARKER HANNIFIN CORPORATION

17325 Euclid Ave., Cleveland, OH, 44112

Tel: (216) 896-3000 Fax: (216) 896-4000 Web site: www.parker.com

Mfr. motion-control products.

Parker Aerospace Beijing, Ste. 1B, 5/F, CITIC Bldg., 19 Jianguomenwai Dajie, Beijing 100004, China PRC

Tel: 86-10-6593-1872 Fax: 86-10-6593-1872

Parker Hannifin Hong Kong Ltd., Room 1101, Peregrine Plaza, 1325 Huai Hai Rd. (M), Shanghai 200031, China (PRC)

Tel: 86-21-6445-9339 Fax: 86-21-6445-9717

Parker Hannifin Hong Kong Ltd., Ste. B9-B11, 21/F, West wing, Hanwei Plaza, No.7 Guanghua Rd., Chaoyang Dist., Beijing 100004, China (PRC)

Tel: 86-10-6561-0117 Fax: 86-10-6561-0115

Parker Hannifin Motion & Control (Shanghai) Co., Ltd., D6C-8A, No. 211, Fute Rd., Wai Gao Qia o Free Trade zone, Shanghai 200131 China (PRC)

Tel: 86-21-5866-2672 Fax: 86-21-5866-2990

PARSONS TRANSPORTATION GROUP

1133 15th Street NW, Washington, DC, 20005

Tel: (202) 775-3300 Fax: (202) 775-3422

Consulting engineers.

De Leuw Cather Intl. Ltd., Room 4a-4C, Yan Dang Bldg., Yan Dang Rd., Shanghai, China (PRC)

PAUL, WEISS, RIFKIND, WHARTON & GARRISON

1285 Ave. of the Americas, New York, NY, 10019-6064

Tel: (212) 373-3000 Fax: (212) 373-2268 Web site: www.paulweiss.com

Law firm engaged in American and international law practice.

Paul, Weiss, Rifkind, Wharton & Garrison, Ste. 2201, Scitech Tower, 22 Jianguomenwai Dajie, Beijing, 100004, China (PRC)

Tel: 86-10-6512-3628 Fax: 86-10-6512-3631

PEPSiCO INC.

700 Anderson Hill Road, Purchase, NY, 10577-1444

Tel: (914) 253-2000 Fax: (914) 253-2070 Web site: www.pepsico.com

Beverages and snack foods.

PepsiCo China Ltd., China (PRC)

THE PERKIN-ELMER CORPORATION

761 Main Ave., Norwalk, CT, 06859-0001

Tel: (203) 762-1000 Fax: (203) 762-4228 Web site: www.perkin-elmer.com

Leading supplier of systems for life science research and related applications.

Perkin-Elmer, Beijing, China (PRC)

Tel: 86-10-849-2588 Fax: 86-10-849-2589

PFAUDLER, INC.

1000 West Ave., PO Box 23600, Rochester, NY, 14692-3600

Tel: (716) 235-1000 Fax: (716) 436-9644 Web site: www.pfaudler.com

Mfr. glass lined reactors, storage vessels and reglassing services.

Suzhou Pfaudler Glass-Lined Equipment Company Ltd., Suzhou, China (PRC)

Tel: 86-512-534-1622 Fax: 86-512-534-0870

PFIZER INC.

235 East 42nd Street, New York, NY, 10017-5755

Tel: (212) 573-2323 Fax: (212) 573-7851 Web site: www.pfizer.com

Research-based, global health care company.

Pfizer Pharmaceuticals Ltd., Dalian, China (PRC)

PHARMACIA & UPJOHN

95 Corporate Drive, PO Box 6995, Bridgewater, NJ, 08807

Tel: (908) 306-4400 Fax: (908) 306-4433 Web site: www.pnu.com

Mfr. pharmaceuticals, agricultural products, industry chemicals

Pharmacia & Upjohn Asia Ltd., Rm. 2002-2009, Shui on Plaza, 333 Huai Hai Rd. M, Shanghai 200021, China (PRC)

PHILIPP BROTHERS CHEMICALS INC.

1 Parker Plaza, Fort Lee, NJ, 07029

Tel: (201) 944-6020 Fax: (201) 944-7916

Mfr. industry and agricultural chemicals.

Philipp Brothers Chemicals Inc., PO Box 9028, Intl. Club, Sanlitun Branch, Beijing, China (PRC)

PICTURETEL CORPORATION

100 Minuteman Road, Andover, MA, 01810

Tel: (978) 292-5000 Fax: (978) 292-3300 Web site: www.picturetel.com

Mfr. video conferencing systems, network bridging & multiplexing products, system peripherals.

PictureTel International Corporation, Shanghai Office, Rm#15, 6/F Central Place, Business Centre, No. 16, Henan Rd. South, Shanghai 200002, China (PRC)

Tel: 86-21-6374-0220 Fax: 86-21-6374-8180

PictureTel International Corporation, Beijing Office, Ste. A1203, Full Link Plaza, Chao Yang Men Wai St., Beijing 100020, China (PRC)

Tel: 86-10-6588-102124 Fax: 86-10-6588-1029

PILLAR INDUSTRIES

N92 W 15800 Megal Drive, Menomonee Falls, WI, 53051

Tel: (414) 255-6470 Fax: (414) 255-0359

Mfr. induction heating & melting equipment.

Pillar Industries Shanghai, Jian Lan Bldg. #104, 50 Pu Hui Tang Rd., Shanghai 200031, China (PRC)

PLANET HOLLYWOOD INTERNATIONAL, INC.

8669 Commodity Circle, Orlando, FL, 32819

Tel: (407) 363-7827 Fax: (407) 363-4862 Web site: www.planethollywood.com

Theme-dining restaurant chain and merchandise retail stores.

Planet Hollywood International, Inc., Bangkok, China (PRC)

PPG INDUSTRIES

One PPG Place, Pittsburgh, PA, 15272

Tel: (412) 434-3131 Fax: (412) 434-2190 Web site: www.ppg.com

Mfr. coatings, flat glass, fiber glass, chemicals. coatings.

PPG Nanchang Chemical Technology Development Corp. Ltd., 302 Hung Du North Rd., Nanchang City, Jiangxi Province, 330077, China (PRC)

PRAXAIR, INC.

39 Old Ridgebury Road, Danbury, CT, 06810-5113

Tel: (203) 837-2000 Fax: (203) 837-2450 Web site: www.praxair.com

Produces and distributes industrial and specialty gases.

Beijing Praxair, Inc., Hua Gong Lu Dajiating, Chaoyang Dist., Beijing 100022, China (PRC)

Tel: 86-10-6771-6715 Fax: 86-10-6771-4768

Praxair Shanghai Meishan, Inc., 2nd Fl. of Construction Bank, Shangyixincun, Shanghai Meishan, China (PRC)

Tel: 86-25-6705-665 Fax: 86-25-6703-011

Shanghai Praxair-Baosteel Inc., 3888 Yunchun Rd., Baoshan Dist., Shanghai, 200941 China (PRC)

Tel: 86-21-5693-1234 Fax: 86-21-5693-2650

Shanghai Praxair-Yidian, Inc., 7th Fl., Vanke Plaza, 37 South of Shuicheng Rd. (South), Shanghai, 201103 China (PRC)

Tel: 86-21-6270-2670 Fax: 86-21-6270-4551

PREFORMED LINE PRODUCTS COMPANY

600 Beta Drive, PO Box 91129, Cleveland, OH, 44101

Tel: (440) 461-5200 Fax: (440) 461-2918

Mfr. pole line hardware for electrical transmission lines; splice closures & related products for telecommunications.

Beijing PLP Conductor Line Products Co., Ltd., Liangxiang, Fangshan, Beijing, China (PRC)

PRICEWATERHOUSECOOPERS LLP

1251 Ave. of the Americas, New York, NY, 10020

Tel: (212) 596-7000 Fax: (212) 790-6620 Web site: www.pwcglobal.com

Accounting and auditing, tax and management, and human resource consulting services.

Price Waterhouse Ltd., Hang Tian Bldg., 8th Fl., 222 Cao Xi Rd., Shanghai 200233, China (PRC)

Tel: 86-21-482-8028 Fax: 86-21-482-0688

Price Waterhouse Ltd., Rms. 1802-4, Block A, Shenzhen Tian An Int'l Bldg., Renmin So. Rd., Shenzhen 518005, China (PRC)

Tel: 755-217-7333 Fax: 755-217-7666

Price Waterhouse Ltd., A1, 15/F, Off.Tower A, Guandong Int'l Bldg., GITIC Plaza, 339 Huanshi Dong Lu, Guangzhou 510060, PRC

Tel: 86-20-331-1570 Fax: 86-20-331-1570

Price Waterhouse Ltd., Ste. 2921, China World Tower, China World Trade Ctr., #1 Jian Guo Men Wai Ave., Beijing 100004, PRC

Tel: 86-10-505-1523 Fax: 86-10-505-1026

Price Waterhouse Ltd., Room C404-6 Lufthansa Ctr., Off. Bldg., #50 Liang Ma Qiao Rd., Chaoyang Dist., Beijing 100016, China (PRC)

Tel: 86-10-463-8075 Fax: 86-10-463-7932

PRINCIPAL INTERNATIONAL INC.

711 High Street, Des Moines, IA, 50392-9950

Tel: (515) 248-8288 Fax: (515) 248-8049 Web site: www.principal.com

Insurance and investment services.

Principal Mutual Life Insurance Company - Bejing, Unit B2003, Vantone New World Plaza, 2 Fu Chen Men Wai Ave., West Dist., Beijing, China (PRC) 100037

Tel: 86-10-6803-7818 Fax: 86-10-6803-7838 Contact: Russ Miller, Mgr.

PROCTER & GAMBLE COMPANY

One Procter & Gamble Plaza, Cincinnati, OH, 45202

Tel: (513) 983-1100 Fax: (513) 562-4500 Web site: www.pg.com

Personal care, food, laundry, cleaning and industry products.

Procter & Gamble Guangzhou Ltd.., 2-4 Aether Square, 986 Jie Fang Bei Rd., Guangzhou, China (PRC) 510075 (Locations: Huangpu, Beijing, Chengdu and Tianjin, China (PRC).)

PSDI MAXIMO

100 Crosby Drive, Bedford, MA, 01730

Tel: (781) 280-2000 Fax: (781) 280-0200 Web site: www.psdi.com

Develops, markets and provides maintenance management software systems.

PSDI China, Room 1115, Pine City Hotel, 777 Zhao Jia Bang Rd., Shanghai 200032, China (PRC)

Tel: 86-21-647-49087 Fax: 86-21647-46594 Contact: Sam Ji, Gen. Mgr. Emp: 1

QUAKER CHEMICAL CORPORATION

Elm & Lee Streets, Conshohocken, PA, 19428-0809

Tel: (610) 832-4000 Fax: (610) 832-8682 Web site: www.quakerchem.com

Mfr. chemical specialties; total fluid management services.

Wuxi Quaker Chemical Co., Ltd., 97 Wu Qiao Xi Rd., Wuxi 214044, China (PRC)

Contact: Daniel S. Ma, Mng. Dir.

RADISSON HOTELS INTERNATIONAL

Carlson Pkwy., PO Box 59159, Minneapolis, MN, 55459-8204

Tel: (612) 540-5526 Fax: (612) 449-3400

Hotels and resorts.

Radisson Movenpick Hotel, Xiao Tianzhu Village, Shunyi County, PO Box 6193, Beijing 100621, China (PRC)

RAY & BERNDTSON, INC.

301 Commerce, Ste. 2300, Fort Worth, TX, 76102

Tel: (817) 334-0500 Fax: (817) 334-0779 Web site: www.prb.com

Executive search, management audit and management consulting firm.

Ray & Berndtson, Room 929, 9th Fl., Economical & Trade Consulting Bldg. of MOFTEC, B12 Guang, Hua Rd. Jian Guo Men Wai, Beijing 100020, China (PRC)

Tel: 86-10-505-1119 Fax: 86-10-505-1417 Contact: Jean Seabrook, Mng. Ptnr.

Ray & Berndtson, 321, 3 Fl. Shanghai, International Business Centre No. 2004, Nanjing Rd., Shanghai 200040, China (PRC)

Tel: 86-21-6248-2282 Fax: 86-21-6248-0489 Contact: David S. Seabrook, Mng. Ptnr.

RAYCHEM CORPORATION

300 Constitution Drive, Menlo Park, CA, 94025-1164

Tel: (650) 361-3333 Fax: (650) 361-2108 Web site: www.raychem.com

Develop/mfr./market materials science products for electronics, telecommunications & industry.

Raychem Beijing, Unit 3-4, 4th Fl., China World Trde Centre, 1 Jian Guo Man Wai Ave., Beijing 100004, PRC

Tel: 86-10-6505-3399 Fax: 86-10-6505-4139

Raychem-Shanghai Cable Accessories Ltd., G/F 481 Gui Ping Rd., Cao He Jing Hi-Tech Development Park, Shanghai 200233, China (PRC) (Office: Guangzhou, China)

Tel: 86-21-6485-3288 Fax: 86-21-6485-0361

RAYTHEON COMPANY

141 Spring Street, Lexington, MA, 02173

Tel: (781) 862-6600 Fax: (781) 860-2172 Web site: www.raytheon.com

Mfr. diversified electronics, appliances, aviation, energy and environmental products; publishing, industry and construction services.

Raytheon International, Locations in Beijing, Cuangzhou and Shanghai, China (PRC)

REXNORD CORPORATION

4701 West Greenfield Ave., Milwaukee, WI, 53214

Tel: (414) 643-3000 Fax: (414) 643-3078

Mfr. power transmission products.

Rexnord Shanghai, Conch Bldg., Ste. 627, 1271 Zhongshan Rd., Shanghai, China (PRC) 200051

REYNOLDS INTERNATIONAL INC.

6601 W. Broad Street, PO Box 27002, Richmond, VA, 23261

Tel: (804) 281-2000 Fax: (804) 281-2245

Mfr. aluminum primary and fabricated products, plastic and paper packaging and food service products; gold mining.

Reynolds Aluminum Beijing, Beijing, China (PRC)

RJR NABISCO INC.

1301 Ave. of the Americas, New York, NY, 10019

Tel: (212) 258-5600 Fax: (212) 969-9173 Web site: www.rjrnabisco.com

Mfr. consumer packaged food products & tobacco products.

Nabisco (China) Ltd., Unit 306 Estoril House, No. 2 Jian Tai Rd., Chaoyang Dist. 100016, Beijing, China (PRC)

ROBBINS & MYERS INC.

1400 Kettering Tower, Dayton, OH, 45423-1400

Tel: (937) 222-2610 Fax: (937) 225-3355

Mfr. progressing cavity pumps, valves and agitators.

Robbins & Myers China, Shanghai, China (PRC)

ROCKWELL INTERNATIONAL CORPORATION

600 Anton Boulevard, Costa Mesa, CA, 92626-7147

Tel: (714) 424-4200 Fax: (714) 424-4251 Web site: www.rockwell.com

Products & service for aerospace and defense, automotive, electronics, graphics & automation industry.

Allen-Bradley Enterprise Xiamen Ltd., Flat F, 15/F., Peace World Plaza, 362-266 Huan Schi Dong Rd., Guangzhou 510060, China (PRC) (Locations: Shenyang, Xiamen, Xian, and Wuhan, China (PRC).)

Tel: 86-20-8384-9977 Fax: 86-20-8383-9989

Rockwell Collins International, Inc., Ste. 1310, New Town Mansion, 55 Loushanguan Rd., Shanghai 200335, China (PRC)

Tel: 86-21-6219-5507 Fax: 86-21-6219-9152

Rockwell International Overseas Corp., 4/F, Office Tower 1, Henderson Ctr., 18 Jianguomennei Ave., Dongcheng Dist., Beijing 100005, China (PRC)

Tel: 86-10-6518-2545 Fax: 86-10-6518-2536

Rockwell Semiconductor Systems Worldwide, Inc., LT Square Bldg., Ste. 3002, 500 Shangdu North Rd., Shanghai 200003, China (PRC)

Tel: 86-21-6361-2515 Fax: 86-21-6361-2516

Rockwell-Collins Air Transport Systems, Ste. 1310, New Town Mansion, 55 Loushanguan Rd., Shanghai 200335, China

Tel: 86-21-6219-5507 Fax: 86-21-6219-9152

ROHM AND HAAS COMPANY

100 Independence Mall West, Philadelphia, PA, 19106

Tel: (215) 592-3000 Fax: (215) 592-3377 Web site: www.rohmhaas.com

Mfr. industrial & agricultural chemicals, plastics.

BEHRC - Beijing Plant, No. 143, Bin He Rd., Tong County, Beijing 101149, China (PRC)

Tel: 86-10-6955-0220

Rohm and Haas China,Inc., Ste. 819-825 Beijing Golden Land Bldg., 32 Liang Ma Qiao Lu, Chaoyang Dist., Beijing 100016, PRC (Location: Foshan, Guabgzhou, China (PRC).)

Tel: 86-10-6464-3450-60

Rohm and Haas Shanghai Chemical Inc./BEHRC, Room 602-607, 6/F Metro Tower, #30 Tianyaoqiao Rd., Shanghai 20030, China (PRC)

Tel: 86-21-6426-7500

RUSSELL REYNOLDS ASSOCIATES INC.

200 Park Ave., New York, NY, 10166-0002

Tel: (212) 351-2000 Fax: (212) 370-0896 Web site: www.ressreyn.com

Executive recruiting services.

Russell Reynolds Associates Inc., Room 322, Jintai Bldg., 58 Maoming Rd. South, Shanghai 200020, China (PRC)

Tel: 86-21-6445-0955 Fax: 86-21-6445-1543 Contact: Raymond C.P. Tang

SARA LEE CORPORATION

3 First National Plaza, Chicago, IL, 60602-4260

Tel: (312) 726-2600 Fax: (312) 558-4995

Mfr./distributor food and consumer packaged goods, intimate apparel and knitwear.

House of Sara Lee, China (PRC)

SAS INSTITUTE INC.

SAS Campus Drive, Cary, NC, 27513

Tel: (919) 677-8000 Fax: (919) 677-8123 Web site: www.sas.com

Mfr./distributes decision support software.

SAS Institute (China) Ltd., Shanghai, China (PRC)

Tel: 86-21-6358-2288 Fax: 86-21-6372-5477

SAS Institute (China) Ltd., Beijing, China (PRC)

Tel: 86-10-235-1280 Fax: 86-106-235-1279

SBC COMMUNICATIONS INC.

175 East Houston, PO Box 2933, San Antonio, TX, 78299-2933

Tel: (210) 821-4105 Fax: (210) 351-5034 Web site: www.sbc.com

Telecommunications.

China Telecom, Shanghai, China (PRC)

SCHENKER INTERNATIONAL FORWARDERS INC.

150 Albany Ave., Freeport, NY, 11520

Tel: (516) 377-3000 Fax: (516) 377-3005 Web site: www.schenkerusa.com

Freight forwarders.

Schenker (H.K.) Ltd., Rep. Office, Jiangsu Science & Techno Mansion, Rm. 230237, Guangzhou 210008, China (PRC)

Tel: 86-25-336-9651 Fax: 86-25-335-6468

Schenker (H.K.) Ltd., Rep. Office, 380 Overseas Chinese Hotel, 15 Hu Bin Rd., Hangzhou 310006, China (PRC)

Tel: 86-571-702-3333 Fax: 86-571-706-7360

Schenker (H.K.) Ltd., Beijing Station, 308 Ceroilfood Zing Da Bldg., 19B Ming Wang, He Ping Li Dong Jie, Donchent, 100013 Beijing, China (PRC)

Tel: 86-10-6429-6520 Fax: 86-10-6429-6518

SCIENTIFIC-ATLANTA, INC.

1 Technology Pkwy South, Norcross, GA, 30092-2967

Tel: (770) 903-5000 Fax: (770) 903-2967 Web site: www.sciatl.com

A leading supplier of broadband communications systems, satellite-based video, voice and data communications networks and worldwide customer service and support.

Scientific-Atlanta of Shanghai, Ltd. (JV), 3rd Fl., Bldg. 18, No. 300 Tian Lin Rd., Shanghai 200233, China (PRC)

Tel: 86-21-485-0770 Fax: 86-21-485-0132

Scientific-Atlanta, Inc., No. 3 Lucky Tower, Block B, Ste. 141314, Dong San Huan Bei Lu, Beijing 100027, China (PRC)

Tel: 86-10-6461-5761 Fax: 86-10-6461-5754

SEAGATE TECHNOLOGY, INC.

920 Disc Drive, Scotts Valley, CA, 95066

Tel: (408) 438-6550 Fax: (408) 438-7205 Web site: www.seagate.com

Develop computer technology, software and hardware.

Seagate Technology (Shenzhen) Co. Ltd., 3/F Kaifa Complex, Daitian Rd., Futian Industrial Dist., Shenzhen, China (PRC) 518026

Tel: 86-755-323-3168 Fax: 86-755-323-8819 Contact: Eddie Lui, VP Mng. Dir. Emp: 1,700

Seagate Technology International (Wuxi), Wuxi-Singapore Industrial Park, #106, Xing Chuang Er, Wuxi, Jiangsu, China (PRC) 214028

Tel: 86-510-521-0674 Fax: 86-510-521-9880 Contact: Eddie Lui, VP Mng. Dir. Emp: 2,200

SEALED AIR CORPORATION

Park 80 Plaza East, Saddle Brook, NJ, 07662-5291

Tel: (201) 791-7600 Fax: (201) 703-4205 Web site: www.sealedair.com

Mfr. protective and specialty packaging solutions for industrial, food and consumer products.

Sealed Air Packaging (Shanghai) Co., G/F No. 223, Fu Te North Rd., Waigaoqiao Free Trade Zone, Shanghai 200131 China (PRC)

Tel: 86-21-58-66-2813 Fax: 86-21-58-66-2306

SEAQUIST PERFECT DISPENSING

1160 North Silver Lake Road, Cary, IL, 60013

Tel: (847) 639-2124 Fax: (847) 639-2142 Web site: www.seaperf.com

Mfr. and sale of dispensing systems; lotion pumps and spray-through overcaps.

Aptar Suzhou Dispensing Systems Co., Ltd., Suzhou, China (PRC)

SHEARMAN & STERLING

599 Lexington Ave., New York, NY, 10022-6069

Tel: (212) 848-4000 Fax: (212) 848-7179 Web site: www.shearman.com

Law firm engaged in general American and international financial and commercial practice.

Shearman & Sterling, Ste. #2205, Capital Mansion, No. 6, Xin Yuan Nan Lu, Chao Yang Dist., Beijing 100004, China (PRC)

Tel: 86-10-6465-2299 Fax: 86-10-6465-4532 Contact: Edward L. Turner III, Mng. Ptnr.

SHELDAHL INC.

1150 Sheldahl Road, Northfield, MN, 55057-9444

Tel: (507) 663-8000 Fax: (507) 663-8545 Web site: www.sheldahl.com

Mfr. electrical & electronic components & laminated plastic products/adhesive-based tapes & materials & adhesiveless Novaclad®.

Jiangxi Changjiang Chemical Plant, Juijiang, Jiangxi, China (PRC)

SILICON GRAPHICS INC.

2011 N. Shoreline Blvd., Mountain View, CA, 94043-1389

Tel: (650) 960-1980 Fax: (650) 961-0595 Web site: www.sgi.com

Design/mfr. special-effects computer graphic systems and software.

Silicon Graphics Ltd., Guangzhou Liaison Office, PRC, Guangzhou 510060, China (PRC)

Tel: 86-20-838-78-793 Fax: 86-20-838-78-248

Silicon Graphics Ltd., Shanghai Liaison Office, Units 603-606, Dynasty Business Ctr., No. 457 Wu Lu Mu Qi Rd. (N), PRC, Shanghai, China (PRC)

Tel: 86-21-6249-0680 Fax: 86-21-6249-2512

Silicon Graphics Ltd., Beijing Lisison Office, 7F, Sinochem Bldg., No. A2, Fuxingmen Wai Da Jie, Beijing 100046, China (PRC)

Tel: 86-10-6856-8382 Fax: 86-10-6856-8388

J.R. SIMPLOT CO., INC.

One Capital Center,999 Main Street, Ste.#1300, Boise, ID, 83702

Tel: (208) 336-2110 Fax: (208) 389-7515 Web site: www.simplot.com

Fresh/frozen fruits & vegetables, animal feeds, fertilizers.

Simplot China Inc., Ste. 425, Hua Tong Bldg., No. 19, Chegongzhuang Xi Lu, Haidan Dist., Beining, 100044, China (PRC)

Tel: 86-10-6848-1707 Fax: 86-10-6848-2565

SKADDEN, ARPS, SLATE, MEAGHER & FLOM LLP

919 Third Ave., New York, NY, 10022

Tel: (212) 735-3000 Fax: (212) 735-2000 Web site: www.sasmf.com

American/International law practice.

Skadden, Arps, Slate, Meagher & Flom LLP, East Wing Office, Level 4, China World Trade Centre, No. 1, Jian Guo Men Wai Ave., Beijing, 100004, China (PRC)

Tel: 86-10-6505-5511 Fax: 86-10-505-5522 Contact: E. Anthony Zaloom, Partner

WILBUR SMITH ASSOCS

NationsBank Tower, PO Box 92, Columbia, SC, 29202

Tel: (803) 758-4500 Fax: (803) 251-2064

Consulting engineers.

Wilbur Smith Associates, De Bei Office Bldg., #1, Jianwei Nanlangjianyuan, Chaoyang Dist., Beijing 100022,China (PRC)

Tel: 86-10-6507-1675 Contact: Tai T. Change, Reg. VP

A.O. SMITH CORPORATION

11270 West Park Place, PO Box 23972, Milwaukee, WI, 53224

Tel: (414) 359-4000 Fax: (414) 359-4064 Web site: www.aosmith.com

Auto and truck frames, motors, water heaters, storage/handling systems, plastics, railroad products.

A.O. Smith International Corporation (China), SWSSOTEL Business Ctr., Dong Si Shi Tiao Li Jiao Qiao, Beijing, China (PRC) 100027

Tel: 86-10-6510-2583 Fax: 86-10-6501-2582 Contact: Michael J. Cole, V.P. Asia

Harbin A.O. Smith Fiberglass Products Company Ltd., 32 Gongbin Rd., Xinxiangfang, Xiangfang Dist., Harbin, China (PRC) 150038

Tel: 86-451-532-3761 Fax: 86-451-532-3759 Contact: Jerry Kennedy, Gen. Mgr.

Nanjing A.O. Smith Water Meter Company, Ltd., 14 Fenghuang (W) St., Nanjing, Jiangsu Province, China (PRC) 210029

Tel: 86-25-665-1100 Fax: 86-25-665-1108 Contact: Jerry Kennedy, Gen. Mgr.

SOLECTRON CORPORATION

777 Gibraltar Drive, Milpitas, CA, 95035

Tel: (408) 957-8500 Fax: (408) 956-6075 Web site: www.solectron.com

Provides contract manufacturing services to equipment manufacturers.

Solectron Corporation, Bl. M1-C, 2nd Fl., #5 Xinghan St., China-Singapore Suzhou Industrial Park, Suzhou, China (PRC) 215021

Tel: 86-512-761-2300 Fax: 86-512-761-8430

SONOCO PRODUCTS COMPANY

North Second Street, PO Box 160, Hartsville, SC, 29550

Tel: (803) 383-7000 Fax: (803) 383-7008 Web site: www.sonoco.com

Mfr. packaging for consumer & industrial market and recycled paperboard.

Sonoco Hongwen Paper Company Ltd., No. 243 Xi Tai Lu, Shanghai, China (PRC) 200231

Tel: 86-21-64364431 Fax: 86-21-64700332

SPENCER STUART & ASSOCIATES INC.

401 North Michigan Ave., Ste. 3400, Chicago, IL, 60611

Tel: (312) 822-0080 Fax: (312) 822-0116 Web site: www.spencerstuart.com

Executive recruitment firm.

Spencer Stuart & Associates Inc., Room 718, 7th Fl., Office Tower 3, Henderson Centre, 18 JiangGuoMen Nei Ave., DongCheng Dist., Beijing 100005 China (PRC)

Tel: 86-10-6518-2144 Fax: 86-10-6518-2143 Contact: Henry Chang

Spencer Stuart & Associates Inc., Ste. 2311, Shui On Plaza, 333 Huai Hai Zhong Lu, Shanghai, 200021, China (PRC)

Tel: 86-21-6386-1177 Fax: 86-21-5306-2718 Contact: Anne Ng

STATE STREET BANK & TRUST COMPANY

225 Franklin Street, Boston, MA, 02101

Tel: (617) 786-3000 Fax: (617) 654-3386 Web site: www.statestreet.com

Banking & financial services.

State Street Bank & Trust Co., Beijing, China (PRC)

STOKES VACUUM INC.

5500 Tabor Road, Philadelphia, PA, 19120

Tel: (215) 831-5400 Fax: (215) 831-5420 Web site: www.stokesvac.com

Vacuum pumps and components, vacuum dryers, oil-upgrading equipment and metallizers.

Vacuum Systems Eng- Winstart, I/F, W/A, Hi-tech Industry Village, Sherran Rd, Shenzhen , China (PRC)

Tel: 86-755-663-5800 Fax: 86-755-663-5900 Contact: M.Gu

STONE CONTAINER CORPORATION

150 N. Michigan Ave., Chicago, IL, 60601-7568

Tel: (312) 346-6600 Fax: (312) 580-3486 Web site: www.stonecontainer.com

Mfr. paper and paper packaging.

Stone Container Corporation, Beijing (JV), Shanghai & Dong Guan, China (PRC)

STRUCTURAL DYNAMICS RESEARCH CORPORATION

2000 Eastman Drive, Milford, OH, 45150-2789

Tel: (513) 576-2400 Fax: Web site: www.sdrc.com

Developer of software used in Modeling esting, drafting and manufacturing.

SDRC Ltd., Room 1005, Bright China Chand An Bldg., Beijing 100005, China (PRC) (Office: Shenzhen, China)

Tel: 86-10-6510-2235 Fax: 86-10-6510-2236

SYBASE, INC.

6475 Christie Ave., Emeryville, CA, 94608

Tel: (510) 922-3500 Fax: (510) 922-3210 Web site: www.sybase.com

Design/mfg/distribution of database management systems, software development tools, connectivity products, consulting and technical support services..

Sybase Software (Beijing) Company Ltd., Room 401. 4/F, Sinochem Mansion, A2 Bldg., Fu Xing Men Wai Ave., Beijing, China (PRC) 100046

Tel: 86-10-6856-8488 Fax: 86-10-6856-8489

SYMBOL TECHNOLOGIES, INC.

One Symbol Plaza, Holtsville, NY, 11742-1300

Tel: (516) 738-2400 Fax: (516) 563-2831 Web site: www.symbol.com

Mfr. bar code-driven data management systems, wireless LAN's, and Portable Shopping System™.

Symbol Beijing, Ste. No. 561, Poly Plaza, 14 Dongzhimen Nandajie, Dongcheng Dist., Beijing 100027, China

Tel: 86-10-65011898 Fax: 86-10-65019468

SYSTEM SOFTWARE ASSOCIATES INC.

500 West Madison Street, Ste. 3200, Chicago, IL, 60661

Tel: (312) 258-6000 Fax: (312) 474-7500 Web site: www.ssax.com

Mfr. computer software.

System Software Associates, 11/F, Scite Tower, 22 Jiangoumenwai Ave., Beijing, China (PRC)

Tel: 86-10-6512-3682 Fax: 86-10-6512-3680

TBWA INTERNATIONAL

180 Maiden Lane, New York, NY, 10038

Tel: (212) 804-1000 Fax: (212) 804-1200

International full service advertising agency.

TBWA Lee Davis, Shanghai, China (PRC)

TEAM INC.

1019 S. Hood Street, Alvin, TX, 77511

Tel: (281) 331-6154 Fax: (281) 331-4107 Web site: www.teamindustrialservices.com

Consulting, engineering & rental services.

Team Inc. Asia, Beijing, China (PRC)

Tel: 86-1692-50753 Fax: 86-1692-50761

TECH-SYM CORPORATION

10500 Westoffice Drive, #200, Houston, TX, 77042-5391

Tel: (713) 785-7790 Fax: (713) 780-3524 Web site: www.syntron.com

Electronics, real estate, aeromechanics.

Syntron China, Room 1406 Zhichun Bldg., No. 118 Zhichun Rd., Beijing 100080, China (PRC)

Zhong Hai Syntron (Tianjin) Geophysical Cable Company Ltd., No. 39 Jilin Rd., Tanggu, Tianjin 300451 China (PRC)

Tel: 86-22-2582-3224 Fax: 86-22-2582-3242

TECHNITROL INC.

1210 Northbrook Drive, #385, Trevose, PA, 19053

Tel: (215) 355-2900 Fax: Web site: www.technitrol.com

Mfr. of electronic components, electrical contacts, and other parts/materials.

Pulse Engineering - Electronic Components, ChangAn & Hong Kong, China (PRC)

TEKTRONIX INC.

2660 Southwest Parkway Ave., PO Box 1000, Wilsonville, OR, 97070-1000

Tel: (503) 627-7111 Fax: (503) 627-2406 Web site: www.tek.com

Mfr. test & measure, visual systems/color printing & communications/video and networking products.

, Locations in Shanghai, Chengdu, Guangzhou, Xian & Wuhan, China

Tektronix Electronics (China) Co. Ltd., Room 101, Tong Heng Tower, No.4, Hua Yuan Rd., Haidian Dist., Beijing 100088, China

Tel: 86-10-6235-1230 Fax: 86-10-6235-1236

Yangzhong Tektronix Electronic Instrument Co. Ltd., Yangzhong, China (PRC)

TELLABS INC.

4951 Indiana Ave. 6303788800, Lisle, IL, 60532

Tel: (630) 378-8800 Fax: (630) 679-3010

Design/mfr./service voice/data transport & network access systems.

Tellabs Inc., Beijing, China (PRC)

TENNECO AUTOMOTIVE

500 North Field Drive, Lake Forest, IL, 60045

Tel: (847) 482-5241 Fax: (847) 482-5295

Automotive parts, exhaust systems, service equipment.

Beijing - Monroe Automotive Shock Absorber Company, Yaziqiao Rd. No. 25, Guang an Men Wai, Xuan Wu Dist., 100055 Beijing, China (PRC)

Tel: 86-10-6346-3605 Fax: 86-10-6340-2141 Contact: Willy Pierle, Gen. Mgr. Emp: 623

Dalian Walker-Gillet, Dalian, Liaoning Province, China (PRC)

Tel: 86-411-767-2504 Fax: 86-411-769-2061 Contact: John Zhu, Gen. Mgr. Emp: 141

TENNECO PACKAGING CORPORATION OF AMERICA

1900 West Field Court, Lake Forest, IL, 60045

Tel: (847) 482-2000 Fax: (847) 482-2181 Web site: www.tenneco

Mfr. custom packaging, aluminum and plastic molded fibre, corrugated containers.

Tenneco Packaging, Dongguan, Shaoxing City, China (PRC)

TEXAS INSTRUMENTS INC.

8505 Forest Lane, Dallas, TX, 75243

Tel: (214) 995-2011 Fax: (214) 995-4360 Web site: www.ti.com

Mfr. semiconductor devices, electronic electro-mechanical systems, instruments and controls.

Texas Instruments China Ltd., Locations in Beijing and Shanghai, China (PRC)

Tel: 811-800-800-1450

THERMADYNE INDUSTRIES INC.

101 South Hanley Road, #300, St. Louis, MO, 63105

Tel: (314) 746-2197 Fax: (314) 746-2349 Web site: www.thermadyne.com

Mfr. welding, cutting, and safety products.

Thermadyne-Cigweld, Shanghai, China (PRC)

Tel: 86-21-6566-0066

THERMO BLACK CLAWSON

605 Clark Street, Middletown, OH, 45042

Tel: (513) 424-7400 Fax: (513) 424-1168

Manufactures & specializes in the brown-paper segment of the recycling market

Thermo Black Clawson China, Beijing Kelun Bldg. 12, Guanghua Lu, Chaoyang Dist., Beijing 10020, China (PRC)

Tel: 86-10-659-33011

TRANSAMERICA CORPORATION

600 Montgomery Street, San Francisco, CA, 94111

Tel: (415) 983-4000 Fax: (415) 983-4400 Web site: www.transamerica.com

Life insurance, leasing, and commercial lending services.

Transamerica Corporation, Shanghai, China (PRC)

Tel: 86-21-637-53141 Fax: 86-21-637-53460

TRICON GLOBAL RESTAURANTS INC.

1441 Gardner Lane, Louisville, KY, 40213

Tel: (502) 874-1000 Fax: (502) 874-8315 Web site: www.triconglobal.com

KFC, Taco Bell and Pizza Hut restaurant food chains.

Kentucky Fried Chicken Ltd. - Shanghai, China (PRC) (151 stores)

TRUE NORTH COMMUNICATIONS INC.

101 East Erie Street, Chicago, IL, 60611

Tel: (312) 425-6000 Fax: (312) 425-6350

Holding company, advertising agency.

FCB/MegacoM, Room 509, Osroc Office Bldg., 94 Dongsi Shitiao St., Dongcheng Dist., Beijing, China (PRC) 100007

FCB/MegacoM, 6th Fl., 10 (Ding) Baoqing Rd., Zuhui Dist., Shanghai 200031, China (PRC)

FCB/MegacoM, Room 308, Tianyuan Bldg., 6 Tianta Rd., Nankai Dist., Tianta, China (PRC) 300381

FCB/MegacoM, Room 5A, Holiday Inn City Centre, Huangshi Dong, 28 Guangming Rd., Guangzhou, China (PRC) 510095

UNION CAMP CORPORATION

1600 Valley Road, Wayne, NJ, 07470

Tel: (973) 628-2000 Fax: (973) 628-2722 Web site: www.unioncamp.com

Mfr. paper, packaging, chemicals and wood products.

Guangzhou Zin Li Paper Pakaging Co., Ltd., No. 2 Industrial Zone, Luntou Village, Luntou Rd., Haizhu Distrcit, Guangzhou, China (PRC)

Tel: 86-20-8429-1208 Fax: 86-20-8429-1108

UNION CARBIDE CORPORATION

39 Old Ridgebury Road, Danbury, CT, 06817

Tel: (203) 794-2000 Fax: (203) 794-6269 Web site: www.unioncarbide.com

Mfr. industrial chemicals, plastics and resins.

Union Carbide China Ltd., Beijing & Guangdong, China (PRC)

UNITED PARCEL SERVICE OF AMERICA, INC.

55 Glenlake Parkway, NE, Atlanta, GA, 30328

Tel: (404) 828-6000 Fax: (404) 828-6593 Web site: www.ups.com

International package-delivery service.

UPS - Sinotrans Beijing JV Company, Unit A, 1st Fl., Tower B, Beijing Kelun Bldg., 12A Guanghua Lu, Chaoyang Dist., Beijing 100016 China (PRC) (Locations: Guangzhou, Shanghai)

Tel: 86-10-6593-2932 Fax: 86-10-6593-2941

UNITED TECHNOLOGIES CORPORATION

United Technologies Building, Hartford, CT, 06101

Tel: (860) 728-7000 Fax: (860) 728-7979 Web site: www.utc.com

Mfr. aircraft engines, elevators, A/C, auto equipment, space and military electronic and rocket propulsion systems. Products include Pratt & Whitney, Otis elevators, Carrier heating and air conditioning and Sikorsky helicopters.

UTIO, 19 Jianguo Men Wai, Room 1603, CITIC Bldg., Beijing, China (PRC)

Tel: 86-10-6592 Contact: Richard Latham, Pres.

UNIVERSAL INSTRUMENTS

90 Bevier Street, S. Dock, Binghamton, NY, 13904

Tel: (607) 779-7522 Fax: (607) 779-7971 Web site: www.dover.com

Mfr./sales of instruments for electronic circuit assembly

Surface Mount Technology, Beijing, China (PRC)

Tel: 86-10-6851-5294 Fax: 86-10-6254-5050

VALMONT INDUSTRIES INC.

West Highway 275, PO Box 358, Valley, NE, 68064-0358

Tel: (402) 359-2201 Fax: (402) 359-4948

Mfr. irrigation systems, steel lighting, utility & communication poles.

Valmont SST, 250 Cao Xi Rd., Ste. A802, Shanghai 200233, China (PRC)

VARIAN ASSOCIATES INC.

3050 Hansen Way, Palo Alto, CA, 94304-100

Tel: (650) 493-4000 Fax: (650) 424-5358 Web site: www.varian.com

Mfr. microwave tubes & devices, analytical instruments, semiconductor process & medical equipment, vacuum systems.

Varian China Ltd., Room 907/908 Beijing Yanshan Hotel, 138A Haidian Rd., Beijing, China (PRC)

WACKENHUT CORPORATION

4200 Wackenhut Drive, Ste. 100, Palm Beach Gardens, FL, 33410

Tel: (561) 622-5656 Fax: (561) 691-6736 Web site: www.wackenhut.com

Security systems & services.

Wuhan Larch Wackenhut Security Co. Ltd., 1/F Unit 2, Bldg. 12, Huixi Residential Section, Jiangan Dist., Wuhan Hubei, China (PRC)

Tel: 86-27-262-9604 Fax: 86-27-262-9564

WAHL CLIPPER CORPORATION

2902 N. Locust Street, Sterling, IL, 61081

Tel: (815) 625-6525 Fax: (815) 625-1193

Mfr. hair clippers, beard and mustache trimmers, shavers, pet clippers and soldering irons.

Ningbo Wahl Knives & Scissors Mfg. Co. Inc., Xikou, Fenghua, Zhejiang, China (PRC)

WAL-MART STORES INC.

702 SW 8th Street, Bentonville, AR, 72716-8611

Tel: (501) 273-4000 Fax: (501) 273-8980 Web site: www.wal-mart.com

Retailer.

Wal-Mart Stores Inc., China (PRC)

WARNACO INC.

90 Park Ave., New York, NY, 10016

Tel: (212) 661-1300 Fax: (212) 687-0480 Web site: www.warnaco.com

Mfr./sales intimate apparel and men's and women's sportswear.

Warnaco, Beijing, China (PRC)

WATERS CORPORATION

34 Maple Street, Milford, MA, 01757

Tel: (508) 478-2000 Fax: (508) 872-1990

Mfr./distribute liquid chromatographic instruments and test and measurement equipment.

Waters Associates, China (PRC)

WATSON WYATT & COMPANY

6707 Democracy Blvd., Ste. 800, Bethesda, MD, 20817

Tel: (301) 581-4600 Fax: (301) 581-4937 Web site: www.watsonwyatt.com

Creates compensation and benefits programs for major corporations.

Watson Wyatt & Co., Rm. 606, Gloria Plaza Hotel, No. 2 Jianguomen Nanjie, Beijing 100022, China (PRC)

Tel: 8610-6515-8855 Fax: 8610-6515-8533 Contact: Paula DeLisle

Watson Wyatt Shanghai, 21/F, E2, Shanghai Industrial Investment Bldg., No. 18, Cao Xi North Rd., Shanghai 200030, China (PRC)

Tel: 86-21-6427-1891-4 Fax: 86-21-6427-1889

WATTS INDUSTRIES, INC.

815 Chestnut Street, North Andover, MA, 01845-6098

Tel: (978) 688-1811 Fax: (978) 688-5841 Web site: www.wattsind.com

Designs/mfr./sales of industry valves and safety control products.

Suzhou Watts Valve Co. Inc., 679 Renmin Rd., Suzhou 215001, China (PRC)

Tianjin Tanggu Watts Valve Co. Ltd., 5 Yong Tai Rd., Tanggu Dist., Tianjin 300450, China (PRC)

WAXMAN INDUSTRIES INC.

24460 Aurora Road, Bedford Heights, OH, 44146

Tel: (440) 439-1830 Fax: (440) 439-8678

Assemble/distributor plumbing, electrical and hardware products.

CWI Intl. China Inc., Dan Keng Villalge, Fu Ming County, Guan Lan Town, Bao An, Shenzhen, China (PRC)

Tel: 86-755-801-0919 Fax: 86-755-802-0387 Contact: Alex Huang

WEATHERFORD INTERNATIONAL INC.

5 Post Oak Blvd, Ste. 1760, Houston, TX, 77227-3415

Tel: (713) 287-8400 Fax: (713) 963-9785 Web site: www.weatherford.com

Oilfield services, products & equipment; mfr. marine cranes for oil and gas industry.

Weatherford Intl. Inc., c/o Nan Hai West Oil Corp., Shekou Industrial Zone, Shenzhen, China (PRC) (Office:Beijing)

Tel: 852-2574-6204 Fax: 852-2834-5380

WENDY'S INTERNATIONAL, INC.

428 West Dublin-Granville Roads, Dublin, OH, 43017

Tel: (614) 764-3100 Fax: (614) 764-3459

Fast food restaurant chain.

Wendy's International, China (PRC)

THE WEST COMPANY, INC.

101 Gordon Drive, PO Box 645, Lionville, PA, 19341-0645

Tel: (610) 594-2900 Fax: (610) 594-3014 Web site: www.thewestcompany.com

Mfr. products for filling, sealing, dispensing & delivering needs of health care & consumer products markets.

The West Company, Beijing, China (PRC)

Tel: 86-21-6514-1614

WESTERN ATLAS INC.

10205 Westheimer, Houston, TX, 77251-1407

Tel: (713) 972-4000 Fax: (713) 952-9837 Web site: www.waii.com

Full service to the oil industry.

China Petroleum Logging-Atlas Coop. Service co., 17 Yan Shan Rd., Shekou, Shenzhen, Guangdong Province, China (PRC)

Tel: 86-755-669-2483 Fax: 86-755-669-6206 Contact: K. Gui, Pres. L.C.C.

Western Atlas Export Sales, Lido Park Office Bldg., Beijing Holiday Inn Hotel, Jichang Rd., Jiang Tai Rd.,Beijing 100004, China (PRC)

Tel: 86-10-6437-9858 Fax: 86-10-6437-9856 Contact: Steve Lee, Dir.

Western Atlas Software, Lido Park Office Bldg., Beijing Holiday Inn Hotel, Jichang Rd., Jiang Tai Rd., Beijing 100004, China (PRC)

Tel: 86-10-6437-9858 Fax: 86-10-6437-9857 Contact: John Still, Country Mgr.

Western Geophysical, Lido Park Office Bldg., Beijing Holiday Inn Hotel, Jichang Rd., Jiang Tai Rd., Beijing 100004, China (PRC)

Tel: 86-10-6437-9858 Fax: 86-10-6437-9856 Contact: Zhao Zhi Yong, Mgr.

WHIRLPOOL CORPORATION

2000 N. M-63, Benton Harbor, MI, 49022-2692

Tel: (616) 923-5000 Fax: (616) 923-5443 Web site: www.whirlpoolcorp.com

Mfr./market home appliances: Whirlpool, Roper, KitchenAid, Estate, and Inglis.

Beijing Whirlpool Snowflake Electric Appliance Co. Ltd. (JV), Beijing, China (PRC) (Location: Shunde, China (PRC).)

Shenzhen Whirlpool Raybo Air-Conditioner Industrial Co., Ltd, (JV) Shenzhen, China (PRC)

Whirlpool Narcissus (Shanghai) Co., Ltd. (JV), Shanghai, China (PRC)

Whirlpool SMC Microwave Co. Ltd., Shunde, China (PRC)

WHITING CORPORATION

15700 Lathrop Ave., Harvey, IL, 60426-5098

Tel: (708) 331-4000 Fax: (708) 785-0755 Web site: www.whitingcorp.com

Mfr. EOT cranes, metallurgical & railroad shop equipment.

Zheijiang NAMAG Equipment Manufacturing Co., Ltd., 23 Xiangian Rd., Tongxiang, Tongxiangg, Zheijiang, 314500 China (PRC)

Fax: 86-573-802-1306 Contact: Tim Andersen, Gen. Mgr.

WILBUR-ELLIS COMPANY

PO Box 7454, San Francisco, CA, 94120

Tel: (415) 772-4000 Fax: (415) 772-4011

International merchants and distributors.

Connell Bros. Co. Ltd., 1405 Shanghai Union Bldg., 100 Yanan East Rd., Shanghai, China (PRC)

WINDMERE-DURABLE HOLDINGS, INC.

5980 Miami Lakes Drive, Hialeah, FL, 33014

Tel: (305) 362-2611 Fax: (305) 364-0635 Web site: www.windmere.com

Mfr. fans, electronic housewares.

Durable Electrical Metal Factory Ltd., Wan Seng Village, Shajiang Shenvhen, Guang Dong, China (PRC)

Tel: 852-2-320-4201

WIX FILTRATION PRODUCTS

1301 E. Ozark Ave., Gastonia, NC, 28052

Tel: (704) 864-6711 Fax: (704) 864-1843

Mfr. oil, air and fuel filters.

Tianjin Wix Filter Corp Ltd., Shi Yan Lou Hou Ce, Zhong Shan Men, He Dong Dist., Tianjin 300180, China (PRC)

Tel: 86-22-243-94388 Contact: Gerry Wong, Gen. Mgr. Emp: 300

WM WRIGLEY JR. COMPANY

410 N. Michigan Ave., Chicago, IL, 60611-4287

Tel: (312) 644-2121 Fax: (312) 644-0353 Web site: www.wrigley.com

Mfr. chewing gum.

Wrigley Chewing Gum Company Ltd., Guanzhou, Guangdong, China (PRC)

WUNDERMAN CATO JOHNSON

675 Ave. of the Americas, New York, NY, 10010-5104

Tel: (212) 941-3000 Fax: (212) 633-0957 Web site: www.wcj.com

International advertising and marketing consulting firm.

Wunderman Cato Johnson, c/o DY&R Advertising Co., Room 1115, Office Tower 2, 11th Fl., Henderson Centre, Beijing Junguomannei Ave., Dongcheng Dist., Beijing, 100005, China (PRC)

Tel: 86-10-6518-2888 Fax: 86-10-6518-3980 Contact: Chris Marsh, Gen. Mgr.

XEROX CORPORATION

800 Long Ridge Road, PO Box 1600, Stamford, CT, 06904

Tel: (203) 968-3000 Fax: (203) 968-4312 Web site: www.xerox.com

Mfr. document processing equipment, systems and supplies.

Xerox Shanghai Ltd. (JV), 46 Nan Gu Lu, Minhang, Eco. & Tech. Dev. Zone, Shanghai, 200240, China (PRC)

XTRA CORPORATION

60 State Street, Boston, MA, 02109

Tel: (617) 367-5000 Fax: (617) 227-3173 Web site: www.xtracorp.com

Holding company: leasing.

Xtra International, Shanghai, China (PRC)

YAHOO! INC.

3420 Central Expressway, Santa Clara, CA, 95051

Tel: (408) 731-3300 Fax: (408) 731-3301 Web site: www.yahoo-inc.com

Internet media company providing specialized content, free electronic mail and community offerings and commerce.

Yahoo! Inc., China (PRC)

YOUNG & RUBICAM INC.

285 Madison Ave., New York, NY, 10017

Tel: (212) 210-3000 Fax: (212) 370-3796 Web site: www.yr.com

Advertising, public relations, direct marketing and sales promotion, corporate & product ID management.

Dentsu Young & Rubicam Pte. Ltd., Shanghai, China (PRC)

Colombia

3COM CORPORATION

5400 Bayfront Plaza, Santa Clara, CA, 95052-8145

Tel: (408) 764-5000 Fax: (408) 764-5001 Web site: www.3com.com

Develop/mfr. computer networking products & systems.

3Com Colombia, Carrera 43A No. 15 Sur 15 Ofic. 305, Medellin, Colombia

Tel: 57-4-313-2539 Fax: 57-4-313-4870

3Com Colombia, Calle 114 No. 9-45, Torre B piso 14, Bogotá, Colombia

Tel: 57-1-629-4847 Fax: 57-1-629-4503

3M

3M Center, St. Paul, MN, 55144-1000

Tel: (612) 733-1110 Fax: (612) 733-9973 Web site: www.mmm.com

Mfr. diversified products for industry, health care, imaging, communications, transport, safety, consumer, etc.

3M Colombia SA, Aptdo. Aereo 11091 y 12693, Diagonal 6 No. 5-95, Soacha (Cundinamarca), Bogotá, Colombia

Tel: 57-1-416-1666 Fax: 57-1-416-1677

AEROGLIDE CORPORATION

PO Box 29505, Raleigh, NC, 27626-0505

Tel: (919) 851-2000 Fax: (919) 851-6029 Web site: www.aeroglide.com

Mfr. rotary dryers, dehydrators, roasters, grain & coffee dryers.

Empresa Metalurgica Colombiana SA, Carrera 19 No. 16-75, Bucaramanga, Colombia

AIR EXPRESS INTERNATIONAL CORPORATION

120 Tokeneke Road, PO Box 1231, Darien, CT, 06820

Tel: (203) 655-7900 Fax: (203) 655-5779 Web site: www.aeilogistics.com

Air freight forwarder.

AEI de Colombia S.A., Carrera 103 Bis No. 46A-04, Santafé de Bogotá, Colombia (Locations: Barranquilla, Buenaventura, Cali, Cartagena, Medellin, Pereira)

Tel: 57-1-413-8111 Fax: 57-1-413-9085

ALCOA (ALUMINUM CO OF AMERICA)

Alcoa Bldg., 425 Sixth Ave., Pittsburgh, PA, 15219-1850

Tel: (412) 553-4545 Fax: (412) 553-4498

World's leading producer of aluminum & alumina; mining, refining, smelting, fabricating & recycling.

Alusud Embalajes Colombia Ltda., Bogotá, Colombia

ABC, INC.

77 West 66th Street, New York, NY, 10023

Tel: (212) 456-7777 Fax: (212) 456-6384

Radio/TV production & broadcasting.

Producciones Tecnicas Ltda., Calle 22 No. 6-27, piso 6, Bogotá, Colombia

AMERICAN INTERNATIONAL GROUP INC.

70 Pine Street, New York, NY, 10270

Tel: (212) 770-7000 Fax: (212) 509-9705 Web site: www.aig.com

Worldwide insurance and financial services.

La Interamerica Cia. de Seguros General SA, Apartado Aereo 92381, Bogotá, Colombia

AMERICAN RE-INSURANCE COMPANY

555 College Road East, Princeton, NJ, 08543

Tel: (609) 243-4200 Fax: (609) 243-4257

Reinsurance.

American Re-Insurance Co., Carrera 7 No. 32-33, Bogotá, Colombia

AMERON INC.

245 South Los Robles Ave., Pasadena, CA, 91109-7007

Tel: (626) 683-4000 Fax: (626) 683-4060

Mfr. steel pipe systems, concrete products, traffic & lighting poles, protective coatings.

American Pipe & Construction Intl., Aptdo. Aereo 90087, Bogotá, Colombia

AMMIRATI PURIS LINTAS

One Dag Hammarskjold Plaza, New York, NY, 10017

Tel: (212) 605-8000 Fax: (212) 605-4705 Web site: www.interpublic.com

International advertising agency.

Ammirati Puris Lintas Colombia, Transversal 20, No. 94-25, Santafé de Bogotá, Colombia

Tel: 57-1-257-6859 Fax: 57-1-256-6258 Contact: Jorge Fernando Pabon

ANDERSEN CONSULTING

100 South Wacker Drive, Ste. 1059, Chicago, IL, 60606

Tel: (311) 123-7271 Fax: (312) 507-7965 Web site: www.ac.com

Provides management & technology consulting services.

Andersen Consulting, Carrera 7 Námero 74-09, piso 8, Santafé de Bogotá, D.C., Colombia

Tel: 57-1-345-3300 Fax: 57-1-313-0508

AON CORPORATION

123 North Wacker Drive, Chicago, IL, 60606

Tel: (312) 701-3000 Fax: (312) 701-3100 Web site: www.aon.com

Insurance brokers worldwide; underwrites accident & health insurance, specialty & professional insurance; & provides risk management consultation.

AON Ossa Limitada, Carrera 11A No. 93A-62 Of. 301, Bogotá, Colombia

Tel: 57-1-635-9084 Fax: 57-1-610-7891 Contact: Julian Efren Gomez

AON Previsionales y Personas Ltda. Corredores de Reaseguros, Carrera 11A No. 93A-62 Of. 404, Bogotá, Colombia

Tel: 57-1-635-9084 Fax: 57-1-610-7891 Contact: Mauricio Parra

AON/Saiz Ltda., Carrera 11A No.86-35, Bogotá, Colombia

Tel: 57-1-623-7520 Fax: 57-1-623-7565 Contact: Camilo Saiz, Sr.

ARBOR ACRES FARM INC.

439 Marlborough Road, Glastonbury, CT, 06033

Tel: (860) 633-4681 Fax: (860) 633-2433

Producers of male & female broiler breeders, commercial egg layers.

Avicola Colombiana Ltda., Carrera 74 No. 48-B-7, Medellin, Colombia

ARTHUR ANDERSEN & COMPANY

33 West Monroe Street, Chicago, IL, 60603

Tel: (312) 372-7100 Fax: (312) 507-0123 Web site: www.arthurandersen.com

Accounting & audit, tax & management consulting services.

Andersen Consulting,, Carrera 7 Numero 74-09, piso 7, Santafé de Bogotá, D.C., Colombia

Tel: 57-2-346-0200

Arthur Andersen y Cia Columbia/David, Cheng, Rubio y Cia, Centro Colseguros, Calle 53, No. 45-112, Apartado Aereo 444, Medellin, Colombia

Tel: 57-4-251-4829

Arthur Andersen y Cia Columbia/David, Cheng, Rubio y Cia, Edif. Banco del Comercio, piso 26, Apartado Aereo 4445, Cali, Colombia

Tel: 57-2-883-7027

Arthur Andersen y Cia Columbia/David, Cheng, Rubio y Cia, Numero 74-09 P.3 y P.7, Apartado Aereo 75874, Santafé de Bogotá, D.C., Colombia

Tel: 57-2-346-0200

AVERY DENNISON CORPORATION

150 N. Orange Grove Blvd., Pasadena, CA, 91103

Tel: (626) 304-2000 Fax: (626) 792-7312 Web site: www.averydennison.com

Mfr. pressure-sensitive adhesives & materials, office products, labels, tags, retail systems, Carter's Ink & specialty chemicals.

Avery Dennison Colombia, Colombia

BAKER & McKENZIE

One Prudential Plaza, 130 East Randolph Drive, Ste. 2500, Chicago, IL, 60601

Tel: (312) 861-8000 Fax: (312) 861-2899 Web site: www.bakerinfo.com

International legal services.

Raisbeck, Lara, Rodriguez & Rueda, Calle 35 No.7-25, 4th Fl., (Apartado Aereo No.3746), Santafé de Bogotá, Colombia

Tel: 57-1 285-1400 Fax: 57-1-285-6908

BAKER HUGHES INCORPORATED

3900 Essex Lane, Ste. 1200, Houston, TX, 77027

Tel: (713) 439-8600 Fax: (713) 439-8699 Web site: www.bakerhughes.com

Develop & apply technology to drill, complete & produce oil and natural gas wells; provide separation systems to petroleum, municipal, continuous process & mining industries.

Baker Hughes de Colombia, Baker Tools, World Trade Ctr., Carrera 8A, No.99-51, Torre A, Of. 305, Bogotá, Colombia

Tel: 57-1-218-3706 Fax: 57-1-218-3449

Baker Hughes INTEQ, Carrera 21 #27-45, Yopal, Colombia

Tel: 57-987-556287

Milchem Western Hemisphere Inc., Aptdo. Aereo 9313, Bogotá, Colombia

BANKAMERICA CORPORATION

555 California Street, San Francisco, CA, 94104

Tel: (415) 622-3530 Fax: (415) 622-8467 Web site: www.bankamerica.com

Financial services.

Bank of America - Andean/Central America & Caribbean Region, Carrera 7, No. 71-52, Torre B, piso 4, Santafé de Bogotá, Colombia

Tel: 57-1-312-1681 Fax: 57-1-312-1663 Contact: Roberto Anguizola, SVP

Bank of America NT & SA, Carrera 7, No. 71-52, Torre B, piso 4, Santafé de Bogotá, Colombia

Tel: 57-1-312-1583 Fax: 57-1-312-1645 Contact: Duván Gómez

BANKBOSTON CORPORATION

100 Federal Street, PO Box 1788, Boston, MA, 02110

Tel: (617) 434-2200 Fax: (617) 434-7547 Web site: www.bankboston.com

Banking & insurance services.

BankBoston S.A. - Bogotá, Calle 77 No. 11-19, piso 3 y piso 5, Apartado Aereo 2993, Santa Fe de Bogotá, Colombia

Tel: 57-1-313-3455 Fax: 57-1-313-3536 Contact: William Gambrel, Pres.

BANKERS TRUST COMPANY

280 Park Ave., New York, NY, 10017

Tel: (212) 250-2500 Fax: (212) 250-2440 Web site: www.bankerstrust.com

Banking & investment services.

Bankers Trust Company, CRA. 7 #74-36, piso 4, Bogotá, Colombia

Tel: 57-1-212-7503 Fax: 57-1-217-4374 Contact: Jorge Alberto Jimenez, Global Markets

BATES WORLDWIDE INC.

405 Lexington Ave., New York, NY, 10174

Tel: (212) 297-7000 Fax: (212) 986-0270 Web site: www.batesww.com

Advertising, marketing, public relations & media consulting.

SSA Bates, Calle 96, No. 116-13, Santale de Bogotá, Colombia

Tel: 57-1-616-9296 Contact: Alejandro Sala, Mgr.

BAUSCH & LOMB INC.

One Bausch & Lomb Place, Rochester, NY, 14604-2701

Tel: (716) 338-6000 Fax: (716) 338-6007 Web site: www.bausch.com

Mfr. vision care products & accessories & hearing aids.

Bausch & Lomb de Colombia S.A., Bogotá, Colombia

BAXTER HEALTHCARE CORPORATION

One Baxter Parkway, Deerfield, IL, 60015

Tel: (847) 948-2000 Fax: (847) 948-3948 Web site: www.baxter.com

Pharmaceutical preparations, surgical/medical instruments & cardiovascular products.

Laboratorios Baxter SA, Aptdo. Aereo 2446, Cali, Colombia

BBDO WORLDWIDE

1285 Ave. of the Americas, New York, NY, 10019

Tel: (212) 459-5000 Fax: (212) 459-6645 Web site: www.bbdo.com

Multinational group of advertising agencies.

BBDO Colombia, Bogotá, Colombia

BDO SEIDMAN, LLP

Two Prudential Plaza, 180 N. Stetson Ave., Ste. 2300, Chicago, IL, 60601

Tel: (312) 240-1236 Fax: (312) 240-3329 Web site: www.bdo.com

International accounting & financial consulting firm.

BDO Audit AGE, (Apartado Aéreo 3374), Transversal 21 No. 98-05, Bogotá, Colombia

Tel: 57-1-623-0199 Fax: 57-1-236-8407 Contact: Alfonso Escobar Barrera

BENTLY NEVADA CORPORATION

1617 Water Street, PO Box 157, Minden, NV, 89423

Tel: (702) 782-3611 Fax: (702) 782-9259

Electronic monitoring systems.

Vibran Cia. Ltda., Carrera 9 No. 80-15, Aptdo. Aereo 92077, Bogotá, Colombia

BEST FORM, INC.

136 Madison Ave., New York, NY, 10016

Tel: (212) 696-1110 Fax: (212) 532-5708

Mfr. foundation garments.

Exquisite Form Brassiere de Colombia Ltda., Carrera 34-A No. 7-06, Bogotá, Colombia

BESTFOODS, INC.

700 Sylvan Ave., International Plaza, Englewood Cliffs, NJ, 07632-9976

Tel: (201) 894-4000 Fax: (201) 894-2186 Web site: www.bestfoods.com

Consumer foods products; corn refining.

DISA S.A., Apartado Aereo 92483, Santafé de Bogotá, Colombia

Tel: 57-1-313-1399 Fax: 57-1-348-0147 Contact: Luis Eduardo Marquez, Mgr.

BETZDEARBORN

4636 Somerton Road, PO Box 3002, Trevose, PA, 19053-6783

Tel: (215) 953-2568 Fax: (215) 953-5524 Web site: www.betzdearborn.com

Mfr. water/wastewater and process system treatment chemicals and services.

BetzDearborn Colombia S.A., Calle 20 N. 68D54, Santafé de Bogotá, D.C., Colombia

BOOZ ALLEN & HAMILTON INC.

8283 Greensboro Drive, McLean, VA, 22102

Tel: (703) 902-5000 Fax: (703) 902-3333 Web site: www.bah.com

International management and technology consultants.

Booz Allen & Hamilton Inc., Carrera 12 #79-43, piso 4, Santafe-de Bogotá, Colombia

Tel: 57-1-313-0041 Fax: 57-1-313-0093

BORDEN INC.

180 East Broad Street, Columbus, OH, 43215-3799

Tel: (614) 225-4000 Fax: (614) 220-6453

Mfr. Packaged foods, consumer adhesives, housewares and industrial chemicals.

Cia. Quimica Borden S.A., Calle 15-A, nr. 1-25, Yumbo, Cali, Colombia

Tel: 57-2-669-3000 Fax: 57-2-669-5002

BOYDEN CONSULTING CORPORATION

100 Park Ave., 34th Floor, New York, NY, 10017

Tel: (212) 980-6534 Fax: (212) 980-6147 Web site: www.boyden.com

Executive search.

Boyden/Consultores Ejecutivox Ltda., Carrera 7a No. 67-02 Of. 804, Torre Ejecutiva, Bogotá, Colombia

Tel: 57-1-212-8382

BOZELL WORLDWIDE

40 West 23rd Street, New York, NY, 10010

Tel: (212) 727-5000 Fax: (212) 645-9173 Web site: www.bozell.com

Advertising, marketing, public relations and media consulting.

Silva Publicidad & Cia. Ltda., Calle 93 No. 20-46, Santafé de Bogotá, Colombia

Tel: 57-1-623-2088 Fax: 57-1-257-7599 Contact: Claudia Silva, Mng. Dir.

BRANSON ULTRASONICS CORPORATION

41 Eagle Road, Danbury, CT, 06813-1961

Tel: (203) 796-0400 Fax: (203) 796-2285

Mfr. plastics assembly equipment, ultrasonic cleaning equipment.

RRV Rafael Rengifo Vila, Centro Aereo Intl., Av. Eldorado, Carrera 103 No. 47-85, Aptdo. Aereo 8210, Bogotá, Colombia

Tel: 57-1-612-0917 Fax: 57-3-331-3797

BRISTOL-MYERS SQUIBB COMPANY

345 Park Ave., New York, NY, 10154

Tel: (212) 546-4000 Fax: (212) 546-4020 Web site: www.bms.com

Pharmaceutical and food preparations, medical and surgical instruments.

Bristol Faramaceutica S.A., Calle 34, No. 603, Bogotá, D.E. Colombia S.A.

BUDGET RENT A CAR CORPORATION

4225 Naperville Road, Lisle, IL, 60532

Tel: (630) 955-1900 Fax: (630) 955-7799 Web site: www.budgetrentacar.com

Car and truck rental system.

Budget Rent A Car De Colombia, Av. 15 #107-08, Bogotá, Colombia

Tel: 57-1-612-5040

LEO BURNETT CO., INC.

35 West Wacker Drive, Chicago, IL, 60601

Tel: (312) 220-5959 Fax: (312) 220-6533 Web site: www.leoburnett.com

International advertising agency.

Leo Burnett - Colombia SA, Carrera 13 No. 89-59, Bogotá, Colombia

BURSON-MARSTELLER

230 Park Ave., New York, NY, 10003-1566

Tel: (212) 614-4000 Fax: (212) 614-4262 Web site: www.bm.com

Public relations/public affairs consultants.

Burson-Marsteller Bogota, Calle 93A #2066, Office #304, Santafé de Bogotá, Colombia

Tel: 57-1-621-4550 Fax: 57-1-621-4620

CABOT CORPORATION

75 State Street, Boston, MA, 02109-1807

Tel: (617) 345-0100 Fax: (617) 342-6103

Mfr. carbon blacks, plastics; oil & gas, information systems.

Cabot Colombiana SA, Aptdo. Aereo 14471, Carrera 13 No. 2700, Bogotá, Colombia

Cabot Colombiana SA, Aptdo. Aereo 2903, Edif. Banco de America Latina, Of. 8-05 & 8-06, Cartagena, Colombia

Cabot Colombiana SA, Edif. Seguros Bolivia, Carrera 4A No. 12-41 of 413, Cali, Colombia

CARGILL, INC.

15407 McGinty Road, Minnetonka, MN, 55440-5625

Tel: (612) 742-7575 Fax: (612) 742-7393 Web site: www.cargill.com

Food products, feeds, animal products.

Cargill Cafetera de Manizales SA, Aptdo. Aereo 240928, Bogotá, Colombia

CARRIER CORPORATION

One Carrier Place, Farmington, CT, 06034-4015

Tel: (860) 674-3000 Fax: (860) 679-3010 Web site: www.carrier.com

Mfr./distributor/services A/C, heating & refrigeration equipment.

Carrier Equipprac, Santefe de Bogotá, Colombia

Tel: 57-2-446-4706 Fax: 57-2-446-4697

CENTRAL NATIONAL-GOTTESMAN INC.

3 Manhattanville Road, Purchase, NY, 10577-2110

Tel: (914) 696-9000 Fax: (914) 696-1066

Worldwide sales pulp and paper products.

Central National Andina Ltda., Aptdo. Aereo 14431, Bogotá, Colombia

Tel: 57-1-340-0279 Fax: 57-1340-0269 Contact: Chris Kessler

THE CHASE MANHATTAN CORPORATION

World Headquarters, 270 Park Ave., New York, NY, 10017

Tel: (212) 270-6000 Fax: (212) 622-9030 Web site: www.chase.com

International banking and financial services.

Banco del Commercio (Associated Bank), Calle Trece 8-52/56, Aptdo. Aereo 4749, Bogotá, Colombia

The Chase Manhattan Bank, Representative Office, Carrera 9A No. 99-02, Of. 702, Apartado Aereo 16192, Bogotá, Colombia

Tel: 57-1-618-3008 Fax: 57-1-618-3039

CHEVRON CORPORATION

575 Market Street, San Francisco, CA, 94105

Tel: (415) 894-7700 Fax: (415) 894-2248 Web site: www.chevron.com

Oil exploration & production & petroleum products.

Chevron Petroleum Co. of Colombia, Carrera 13 No. 27-75, Bogotá, Colombia

CHIQUITA BRANDS INTERNATIONAL INC.

250 East Fifth Street, Cincinnati, OH, 45202

Tel: (513) 784-8000 Fax: (513) 784-8030 Web site: www.chiquita.com

Sale and distribution of bananas, fresh fruits and processed foods.

Compania Frutera de Sevilla, Aptdo. Aereo 50309, Medellin, Colombia

Compania Frutera de Sevilla, Aptdo. Aereo 541, Santa Marta, Colombia

THE CHUBB CORPORATION

15 Mountain View Road, Warren, NJ, 07061-1615

Tel: (908) 580-2000 Fax: (908) 580-3606 Web site: www.chubb.com

Holding company: property/casualty insurance.

Chubb de Colombia Campania de Seguros, SA, Carrera 50, #75-161 Local #5, Barranquilla, Colombia

Tel: 57-53-686-117 Fax: 57-53-689-914

CIGNA CORPORATION

One Liberty Place, Philadelphia, PA, 19192

Tel: (215) 761-1000 Fax: (215) 761-5008

Insurance, invest, health care and other financial services.

Cigna Seguros de Colombia SA, Calle 72 No. 10-51, Bogotá, Colombia

Grancol, Asesoramiento y Servicios Ltda., Carrera 13 No. 26-45, Bogotá, Colombia

CISCO SYSTEMS, INC.

170 Tasman Drive, San Jose, CA, 95134-1706

Tel: (408) 526-4000 Fax: (408) 526-4100 Web site: www.cisco.com

Develop/mfr./market computer hardware and software networking systems.

Cisco Systems Colombia, Cra. 18 #86A-14, Santafé de Bogotá, Colombia

Tel: 57-1-296-0067 Fax: 57-1-616-3030 Contact: Isaac Majerowicz

CITICORP

399 Park Ave., New York, NY, 10043

Tel: (212) 559-1000 Fax: (212) 527-2066 Web site: www.citibank.com

International banking and financial services.

Citibank N.A., Carrera 9A No. 99-02, 3rd Fl., Santafé de Bogotá, Colombia

Tel: 57-1-312-1583 Fax: 57-1-312-1645 Contact: Eric Richard Mayer, Pres.

THE CLOROX COMPANY

1221 Broadway, PO Box 24305, Oakland, CA, 94623-1305

Tel: (510) 271-7000 Fax: (510) 832-1463

Mfr. soap & detergents, and domestic consumer packaged products.

Tecnoclor SA, Cali, Colombia

CMS ENERGY CORPORATION

Fairlane Plaza South, Ste. 1100, 330 Town Drive, Dearborn, MI, 48126

Tel: (313) 436-9200 Fax: (313) 436-9225 Web site: www.cmsenergy.com

Independent power plant operator.

CMS Nomeco Colombia Oil Co., Calle 100 No. 8A-49 - Ofc. 705, World Trade Ctr., Torre B, Apartado Aereo 89956, Bogotá, Colombia

Tel: 57-1-226-8285 Fax: 57-1-226-8756

THE COCA-COLA COMPANY

P.O. Drawer 1734, Atlanta, GA, 30301

Tel: (404) 676-2121 Fax: (404) 676-6792 Web site: www.coca-cola.com

Mfr./marketing/distributor soft drinks, syrups & concentrates, juice & juice-drink products.

Industrias Roman Colombia, Colombia - All mail to U.S. address.

COLGATE-PALMOLIVE COMPANY

300 Park Ave., New York, NY, 10022

Tel: (212) 310-2000 Fax: (212) 310-2919

Mfr. pharmaceuticals, cosmetics, toiletries and detergents.

Colgate Palmolive Cia., Carrera 1 No. 40-108 Cali, Colombia

COLUMBIA PICTURES INDUSTRIES INC.

10202 West Washington Blvd., Culver City, CA, 90232

Tel: (310) 244-4000 Fax: (310) 244-2626 Web site: www.sony.com

Producer and distributor of motion pictures.

Fox/Columbia Pictures of Columbia Inc., Carrera 5 No. 22-85, piso 5, Bogotá, Colombia

COMPAQ COMPUTER CORPORATION

20555 State Highway 249, PO Box 692000, Houston, TX, 77269-2000

Tel: (713) 370-0670 Fax: (713) 514-1740 Web site: www.compaq.com

Develop/mfr. personal computers.

Compaq Computer de Colombia S.A., Edif. Banco Union, Carrera 7, No. 71-52 Ofc. 504, Santafe de Bogotá, Colombia

Tel: 57-1-312-0147 Fax: 57-1-312-0614

COMPUTER ASSOCIATES INTERNATIONAL INC.

One Computer Associates Plaza, Islandia, NY, 11788

Tel: (516) 342-5224 Fax: (516) 342-5329 Web site: www.cai.com

Integrated software for enterprise computing and information management, application development, manufacturing, financial applications and professional services.

Computer Associates de Colombia S.A., Av. 81 No. 12-18, Of. 305, Santafé de Bogotá, Colombia

Tel: 57-1-623-7886

COMSAT CORPORATION

6560 Rock Spring Drive, Bethesda, MD, 20817

Tel: (301) 214-3200 Fax: (301) 214-7100 Web site: www.comsat.com

Provides global telecommunications services via satellite and develops advanced satellite networking technology.

COMSAT International, Santafé de Bogotá, Colombia

CONTINENTAL AIRLINES INC.

2929 Allen Parkway, Ste. 1501, Houston, TX, 77019

Tel: (281) 834-5000 Fax: (281) 520-6329

International airline carrier.

Continental Airlines Inc., Colombia

COOPER INDUSTRIES INC.

6600 Travis Street, Ste. 5800, Houston, TX, 77002

Tel: (713) 209-8400 Fax: (713) 209-8995 Web site: www.cooperindustries.com

Mfr./distributor electrical products, tools and hardware and automotive products.

Cooper Hand Tools Div., Cali, Colombia

CORE LABORATORIES

5295 Hollister, Houston, TX, 77042

Tel: (713) 460-9600 Fax: (713) 460-4389

Petroleum testing/analysis, analytical chemicals, laboratory and octane analysis instrumentation.

Core Laboratories, Aptdo. Aereo 80347, Bogotá, Colombia

CORESTATES BANK

1500 Market Street, Philadelphia, PA, 19101

Tel: (215) 973-3100 Fax: (215) 786-8899 Web site: www.corestates.com

Primary international businesses; correspondent banking and trade services.

Corestates Bank, World Trade Ctr., Calle 100 No. #8A-55, Torre C, Of. 613, Santafé de Bogotá, Colombia

CRANE PUMPS & SYSTEMS, INC.

420 Third Street, Piqua, OH, 45356

Tel: (937) 773-2442 Fax: (937) 773-2238

Mfr. water/waste water pumps and systems.

Barnes de Colombia SA, Aptdo. Aereo 12098, Calle 15 No. 41-17, Bogotá, Colombia

CROWN CORK & SEAL COMPANY, INC.

One Crown Way, Philadelphia, PA, 19154-4599

Tel: (215) 698-5100 Fax: (215) 698-5201

Mfr. cans, bottle caps; filling & packaging machinery.

Crown Litometal SA, Aptdo. Aereo 4084, Bogotá, Colombia

CUMMINS ENGINE CO., INC.

500 Jackson Street, PO Box 3005, Columbus, IN, 47202-3005

Tel: (812) 377-5000 Fax: (812) 377-3334

Mfr. diesel engines.

Cummins de Colombia SA, Aptdo. Aereo 90988, Botoga, Colombia

D'ARCY MASIUS BENTON & BOWLES INC. (DMB&B)

1675 Broadway, New York, NY, 10019

Tel: (212) 468-3622 Fax: (212) 468-2987 Web site: www.dmbb.com

Full service international advertising and communications group.

Procesos Creativos, Carrera 9, No.70A-11, Santa Fe de Bogotá, Colombia

Tel: 57-1-211-5511 Fax: 57-1-211-5801 Contact: Christian Toro, Pres.

DANA CORPORATION

4500 Door Street, Toledo, OH, 43615

Tel: (419) 535-4500 Fax: (419) 535-4643 Web site: www.dana.com

Mfr./sales of automotive, heavy truck, off-highway, fluid & mechanical power components.

Dana Corporation, Colombia

DDB NEEDHAM WORLDWIDE INC.

437 Madison Ave., New York, NY, 10022

Tel: (212) 415-2000 Fax: (212) 415-3417

Advertising agency.

DDB Needham Worldwide, Santafé de Bogotá, Colombia

DELOITTE TOUCHE TOHMATSU INTERNATIONAL

PO Box 820, Wilton, CT, 06897

Tel: (203) 761-3000 Fax: (203) 834-2200 Web site: www.u.s.deloitte.com or www.dtti.com

Accounting, audit, tax and management consulting services.

Deloitte & Touche, Carrera 13, #37-37, piso 11, Santafé de Bogotá, D.C., Colombia

Deloitte & Touche, Carrera 43B, #16-80, Officina 501, Medillin, Colombia

DHL WORLDWIDE EXPRESS

333 Twin Dolphin Drive, Redwood City, CA, 94065

Tel: (650) 593-7474 Fax: (650) 593-1689 Web site: www.dhl.com

Worldwide air express carrier.

DHL Worldwide Express, Carrera 13 Nr. 75-74, Santafé de Bogotá, Colombia

Tel: 57-1-217-2200

THE DOW CHEMICAL COMPANY

2030 Dow Center, Midland, MI, 48674

Tel: (517) 636-1000 Fax: (517) 636-3228 Web site: www.atdow.com

Mfr. chemicals, plastics, pharmaceuticals, agricultural products, consumer products.

Dow Colombiana SA, Manonal, Aptdo. Aereo 1651, Cartagena, Colombia

Dow Quimica de Colombia SA, Calle 37 No. 8-47, Bogotá, Colombia

Dow Quimica de Colombia SA, Carrera 56 No. 50-40, Aptdo. Aereo 3715, Medellin, Colombia

DOW CORNING CORPORATION

2220 West Salzburg Road, PO Box 1767, Midland, MI, 48640

Tel: (517) 496-4000 Fax: (517) 496-6080

Silicones, silicon chemicals, solid lubricants.

Dow Corning Latin America Ltd., Aptdo. Aereo 91079, Bogotá 8, Colombia

DRAKE BEAM MORIN INC.

101 Huntington Ave., Boston, MA, 02199

Tel: (617) 450-9860 Fax: (617) 267-2011 Web site: www.dbm.com

Human resource management consulting & training.

DBM Colombia, Calle 98 No. 22-64, Of. 1003, Santafé de Bogotá, D.C. Colombia

Tel: 57-1-623515 Fax: 57-1-623-5599

E.I. DU PONT DE NEMOURS & COMPANY

1007 Market Street, Wilmington, DE, 19898

Tel: (302) 774-1000 Fax: (302) 774-7321 Web site: www.dupont.com

Mfr./sale diversified chemicals, plastics, specialty products and fibers.

DuPont de Colombia SA, Via 40 No. 85-85, Aptdo. Aereo 1386, Barranquilla, Colombia

EASTMAN KODAK COMPANY

343 State Street, Rochester, NY, 14650

Tel: (716) 724-4000 Fax: (716) 724-0663

Develop/mfr. photo & chemicals products, information management/video/copier systems, fibers/plastics for various industry.

Kodak Colombiana Ltda., Aptdo. Aereo 3919, Av. El Dorado 78A-93, Bogotá, Colombia

EATON CORPORATION

1111 Superior Ave., Cleveland, OH, 44114

Tel: (216) 523-5000 Fax: (216) 479-7068

Advanced technical products for transportation & industrial markets.

Eaton Intl. Inc., Aptdo. Aereo 32258, Bogotá, Colombia

J.D. EDWARDS & COMPANY

One Technology Way, Denver, CO, 80237

Tel: (303) 334-4000 Fax: (303) 334-4970 Web site: www.jdedwards.com.

Computer software products.

EDP Ltda., Carrera 54-No. 72-80, Edif. Centro Ejecutivo, Local 12, Barranquilla, Colombia

Tel: 57-53-58-7305 Fax: 57-53-56-3736

EDP Ltda., Transversal 33, Mp 125-19 Tercer piso, Santafé de Bogotá, Colombia

Tel: 57-1-612-6599 Fax: 57-1-612-4823

EFCO

1800 NE Broadway Ave., Des Moines, IA, 50316-0386

Tel: (515) 266-1141 Fax: (515) 266-7970

Mfr. systems for concrete construction.

EFCO, Transversal 22 No. 83-66, Bogotá, Colombia

ENDO LABORATORIES INC.

500 Endo Boulevard, Garden City, NY, 11530

Tel: (516) 522-3300 Fax:

Ethical pharmaceuticals.

Endo Pan American Corp., Aptdo. Aereo 29674, Bogotá, Colombia

ENRON CORPORATION

1400 Smith Street, Houston, TX, 77002-7361

Tel: (713) 853-6161 Fax: (713) 853-3129 Web site: www.enron.com

Exploration, production, transportation and distribution of integrated natural gas and electricity.

Enron International Colombia, Lewis May, Calle 93B #12-28 Office 207, Santa Fe de Bogotá, Colombia

ERNST & YOUNG, LLP

787 Seventh Ave., New York, NY, 10019

Tel: (212) 773-3000 Fax: (212) 773-6350 Web site: www.eyi.com

Accounting and audit, tax and management consulting services.

Ernst & Young, Apartado Aero 092638, Bogotá, Colombia

Tel: 57-1-6210411 Fax: 57-1-6103060 Contact: Pedro Pablo Guaidia

EURO RSCG Worldwide

350 Hudson Street, New York, NY, 10014

Tel: (212) 886-2000 Fax: (212) 886-2016

International advertising agency group.

Procesos Creativos/Euro RSCG, Bogotá, Colombia

EXXON CORPORATION

225 E. John W. Carpenter Freeway, Irving, TX, 75062-2298

Tel: (972) 444-1000 Fax: (972) 444-1882 Web site: www.exxon.com

Petroleum exploration, production, refining; mfr. petroleum & chemicals products; coal & minerals.

Esso Colombiana Ltd., Planta de Lubricantes, Zona Industrial Mamonal, Cartagena, Colombia

Intl. Colombia Resources Corp., Edit. Teusaca, Carrera 7 No. 37-69, Bogotá 1, Colombia

FLINT INK CORPORATION

25111 Glendale Ave., Detroit, MI, 48239-2689

Tel: (313) 538-6800 Fax: (313) 538-3538 Web site: www.flintink.com

Manufacturer of printing inks and pigments.

Flink Ink De Colombia, Cra. 60 No. 48-35 Sur, A.A. 028505, Santafé de Bogotá, Colombia

Tel: 57-1-204-0953 Fax: 57-1-7113-5260 Contact: Jerko E. Rendic, Pres.

FRANKLIN COVEY CO.

2200 W. Parkway Blvd., Salt Lake City, UT, 84119-2331

Tel: (801) 975-1776 Fax: (801) 977-1431 Web site: www.franklinquest.com

Provides productivity and time management products and seminars.

Franklin Covey Colombia, Calle 90, No. 11 A-34, Of. 206, Santa Fe de Bogotá, Colombia

Tel: 57-1-610-0396 Fax: 57-1-610-2723

FRITZ COMPANIES INC.

706 Mission Street, Ste. 900, San Francisco, CA, 94103

Tel: (415) 904-8360 Fax: (415) 904-8661 Web site: www.fritz.com

Integrated transportation, sourcing, distribution & customs brokerage services.

Fritz Companies Inc., Barranquilla, Bogotá, Cali, Cartegena & Medellin, Colombia

H.B. FULLER COMPANY

1200 Willow Lake Blvd., Vadnais Heights, MN, 55110

Tel: (612) 236-5900 Fax: (612) 236-5898 Web site: www.hbfuller.com

Mfr./distributor adhesives, sealants, coatings, paints, waxes, sanitation chemicals.

H.B. Fuller Colombia Ltd., Apartado Aereo 90048, Itagul-Antioguia, Colombia

Tel: 57-4-372-3000 Fax: 57-4-281-0068

GENERAL MOTORS ACCEPTANCE CORPORATION

100 Renaissance Center, Detroit, MI, 48243-7301

Tel: (313) 556-5000 Fax: (313) 556-5108 Web site: www.gmac.com

Automobile financing.

GMAC Colombia SA, Centro Comercial Granahorrar, Calle 100 No. 11A-35, Aptdo. Aereo 28280, Bogotá, Colombia

GENERAL REINSURANCE CORPORATION

695 East Main Street, Stamford, CT, 06904-2350

Tel: (203) 328-5000 Fax: (203) 328-6423 Web site: www.genre.com

Reinsurance services worldwide.

La Colonense Ltda. Corredores de Reaseguros, Calle 119 A No. 22-18, Apartado Aeréo 17 33, Santafé de Bogotá, Colombia

Tel: 57-1-612-4783 Fax: 57-1-612-4931 Contact: Guillermo Sandoval, Mng. Dir.

THE GILLETTE COMPANY

Prudential Tower Building, Boston, MA, 02199

Tel: (617) 421-7000 Fax: (617) 421-7123 Web site: www.gillette.com

Develop/mfr. personal care/use products: blades & razors, toiletries, cosmetics, stationery.

Cali Propiedades SA, Cali, Colombia

Gillette de Colombia SA, Cali, Colombia

THE GOODYEAR TIRE & RUBBER COMPANY

1144 East Market Street, Akron, OH, 44316

Tel: (330) 796-2121 Fax: (330) 796-1817 Web site: www.goodyear.com

Mfr. tires, automotive belts and hose, conveyor belts, chemicals; oil pipeline transmission.

Goodyear de Colombia SA, Aptdo. Aereo 8020, Cali, Colombia

GPU INTERNATIONAL, INC.

300 Madison Ave., Morristown, NJ, 07962-1911

Tel: (973) 455-8200 Fax: (973) 455-8582 Web site: www.gpu.com

Global electric energy company.

GPU International, Bogotá, Colombia

W. R. GRACE & COMPANY

One Town Center Road, 1750 Clint Moore Road, Boca Raton, FL, 33486-1010

Tel: (561) 362-2000 Fax: (561) 561-2193 Web site: www.grace.com

Mfr. specialty chemicals and materials: packaging, health care, catalysts, construction, water treatment/process.

Grace Colombia S.A., Calle 17 #69-18, Bogotá DE, Colombia

Tel: 57-1-411-3875 Fax: 57-1-411-0962

GRACO INC

4050 Olson Memorial Hwy, PO Box 1441, Minneapolis, MN, 55440-1441

Tel: (612) 623-6000 Fax: (612) 623-6777 Web site: www.graco.com

Mfr./sales of infant & juvenile products; services fluid handling equipment & systems.

Milhem Continente S.A., Calle 103, No. 22-24, Santafe de Bogotá, Colombia

Tel: 57-1-623-5393 Fax: 57-1-610-9927 Contact: Eli Milhelm

GREY ADVERTISING INC.

777 Third Ave., New York, NY, 10017

Tel: (212) 546-2000 Fax: (212) 546-1495 Web site: www.giworldwwide.com

International advertising agency.

Esfera Grey, Carrera 5a 5779, Bogotá, Colombia

GRIFFITH LABORATORIES INC

One Griffith Center, Alsip, IL, 60658

Tel: (708) 371-0900 Fax: (708) 597-3294 Web site: www.griffithlabs.com

Industrial food ingredients and equipment.

Laboratorios Griffith de Colombia SA, Aptdo. Aereo 8589, Medellin, Colombia

Tel: 57-4-285-3911 Fax: 57-4-285-0193

GTE CORPORATION

One Stamford Forum, Stamford, CT, 06904

Tel: (203) 965-2000 Fax: (203) 965-2277 Web site: www.gte.com

Electronic products, telecommunications systems, publishing and communications.

GTE Electric SA, Calle 13 No. 46-52, Bogotá, Colombia

HALLIBURTON COMPANY

500 North Akard Street, Ste. 3600, Dallas, TX, 75201-3391

Tel: (214) 978-2600 Fax: (214) 978-2685 Web site: www.halliburton.com

Energy, construction and insurance.

Halliburton Ltd., Calle 99 No. 12-08, Santafé de Bogotá, Colombia

Tel: 57-1-218-7400 Fax: 57-1-623

Halliburton Ltd., Via a Bogotá KM 3, Neiva, Colombia

Tel: 57-88-748-092 Fax: 57-88-740-683

HARCOURT BRACE & COMPANY

6277 Sea Harbor Drive, Orlando, FL, 32887

Tel: (407) 345-2000 Fax: (407) 345-9354

Book publishing, tests and related service, journals, facsimile reprints, management consult, operates parks/shows.

Harcourt Brace Andina, Carrera 16A no. 19-25, Santafé de Bogotá, Colombia

Tel: 57-1-616-0591 Fax: 57-1-616-0592 Contact: José Luis Hernández

THE HARPER GROUP

260 Townsend Street, San Francisco, CA, 94107-1719

Tel: (415) 978-0600 Fax: (415) 978-0692 Web site: www.circleintl.com

Ocean/air freight forwarding, customs brokerage, packing and wholesale, logistics management and insurance.

ACI Cargo, Calle 30, Autopista, Frente Al Nuevo Aeropuerto, Barranquilla, Colombia

Tel: 57-58-423-277 Fax: 57-58-422-030

Celia de Castro, Aueropuerto Crespo, Cartagena, Colombia

Tel: 57-56-666-211 Fax: 57-56-666-211

Circle Freight International de Colombia Ltda., Carrera 43A No. 19-127 Of. 305, Edif. Recife, Medellin, Colombia

Tel: 57-4-262-1448 Fax: 57-4-262-1710

Circle Freight Internationl de Colombia Ltda, Carrera 103, No. 47-85, Of. 306, Edif. Centro Aereo Internacional, Bogotá, Colombia

Tel: 57-1-413-8177 Fax: 57-1-413-8308

Circle Freight Internationl de Colombia Ltda, Calle 25 Norte No. 5N-57, Of. 309-Astrocentro, Cali, Colombia

Tel: 57-2-668-9641 Fax: 57-2-661-4401

HELMERICH & PAYNE INC

1579 East 21st Street, Tulsa, OK, 74114

Tel: (918) 742-5531 Fax: (918) 743-2671

Oil/gas exploration & drilling, real estate, mfr. gas odorants.

Helmerich & Payne (Colombia) Drilling Co., Calle 78B No. 7-46, Aptdo. Aereo 12041, Bogotá, Colombia

HEWLETT-PACKARD COMPANY

3000 Hanover Street, Palo Alto, CA, 94304-0890

Tel: (650) 857-1501 Fax: (650) 857-7299 Web site: www.hp.com

Mfr. computing, communications & measurement products & services.

Hewlett-Packard Colombia SA, Calle 100 No. 8A-49, Torre B, piso 7, Of. 706, Bogotá, Colombia

HILTON HOTELS CORPORATION

9336 Civic Center Drive, Beverly Hills, CA, 90210

Tel: (310) 278-4321 Fax: (310) 205-7880

International hotel chain: Hilton International, Vista Hotels and Hilton National Hotels.

Hilton International Company, Av. 116 (Pepe Sierra), No. 19-65, Apartado Aereo 27533, Bogotá, Colombia

HOUSTON INDUSTRIES INCORPORATED

1111 Louisiana Street, Houston, TX, 77002

Tel: (713) 207-3000 Fax: (713) 207-0206 Web site: www.houind.com

Provides gas and electric services.

NorAM, Colombia

Contact: Pastor Sanjurjo, VP

IBM CORPORATION

New Orchard Road, Armonk, NY, 10504

Tel: (914) 765-1900 Fax: (914) 765-7382 Web site: www.ibm.com

Information products, technology & services.

IBM de Colombia SA, Transversal 38 No. 100-25, Bogotá, Colombia

Tel: 57-1-623-0111 Fax: 57-1-257-9839

InaCom CORPORATION

10810 Farnam Drive, Omaha, NE, 68154

Tel: (402) 392-3900 Fax: (402) 392-3602 Web site: www.inacom.com

Provider of technology management products and services; reselling microcomputer systems, work stations and networking and telecommunications equipment.

InaCom de Colombia, Cra. 13 No. 90-2- Of. 601, Santa Fé de Bogotá, Colombia

Contact: Amparo de Rodriguez, Gen. Mgr.

INFONET SERVICES CORPORATION

2100 East Grand Ave., El Segundo, CA, 90245

Tel: (310) 335-2600 Fax: (310) 335-4507 Web site: www.infonet.com

Provider of Internet services and electronic messaging services.

Infonet Colombia, Av. El Dorado No. 84A-55, Of. 301, Bogotá, Colombia

Tel: 57-1-263-4122 Fax: 57-1-295-4889

INFORMIX CORPORATION

4100 Bohannon Drive, Menlo Park, CA, 95025

Tel: (650) 926-6300 Fax: (650) 926-6593 Web site: www.informix.com

Designs & produces database management software, connectivity interfaces & gateways, and other computer applications.

Informix de Colombia, Teleport Business Park, 11th Fl. Tower B, Calle 114, No.9-45, Bogotá, Colombia

Tel: 57-1-296-0145

INGERSOLL-RAND COMPANY

200 Chestnut Ridge Road, Woodcliff Lake, NJ, 07675

Tel: (201) 573-0123 Fax: (201) 573-3172 Web site: www.ingersoll-rand.com

Mfr. compressors, rock drills, pumps, air tools, door hardware, ball bearings.

Ingersoll-Rand de Colombia, Conjunto Capital Ctr., Av. El Dorado No. 69A-51, Interior 3 - piso 3 - Torre B, Apartado Aereo No. 89655, Bogotá D.E. - Colombia

Tel: 57-1-412-4754 Fax: 57-1-412-4771

INTER-CONTINENTAL HOTELS

1120 Ave. of the Americas, New York, NY, 10036

Tel: (212) 852-6400 Fax: (212) 852-6494 Web site: www.interconti.com

Worldwide hotel and resort accommodations.

Hotel Inter-Continental Medellin, Variante Las Palmas, PO Box 51855 Medelin, Colombia

Tel: 57-4-266-0680 Fax: 57-4-266-1548

INTERNATIONAL ELECTRONICS INC.

427 Turnpike Street, Canton, MA, 02021

Tel: (781) 821-5566 Fax: (781) 821-4443 Web site: www.ieib.com

Manufacture security devices.

Electronic Security International, Bogotá, Colombia

Tel: 57-1-222-6209 Fax: 57-1-221-0084

INTERNATIONAL FLAVORS & FRAGRANCES INC.

521 West 57th Street, New York, NY, 10019-2960

Tel: (212) 765-5500 Fax: (212) 708-7132 Web site: www.iff.com

Design/mfr. flavors, fragrances & aroma chemicals.

International Flavors & Fragrances (Colombia), Bogotá, Colombia

INTERNATIONAL PAPER COMPANY

2 Manhattanville Road, Purchase, NY, 10577

Tel: (914) 397-1500 Fax: (914) 397-1596 Web site: www.ipaper.com

Mfr./distributor container board, paper, wood products.

Productora de Papeles SA, Aptdo. Aereo 4412, Cali, Colombia

INTERNATIONAL SPECIALTY PRODUCTS

1361 Alps Road, Wayne, NJ, 07470

Tel: (973) 628-4000 Fax: (973) 628-3311 Web site: www.ispcorp.com

Mfr. specialty chemical products.

ISP Colombia, Carrera 52 No. 125 A-59, Of. 379, Centro Empresarial Caribe, Blvd. Niza, Santafé de Bogotá, Colombia

Tel: 57-1-624-0687 Fax: 57-1-624-5655

IRRIDELCO INTERNATIONAL CORPORATION

440 Sylvan Ave., Englewood Cliffs, NJ, 07632

Tel: (201) 569-3030 Fax: (201) 569-9237 Web site: www.irridelco.com

Mfr./distributor of the most comprehensive lines of mechanical and micro irrigation; pumps and irrigation systems.

IDC Colombia, Transversal 26 No. 116-19, ApartadoAereo 92164, Bogotá, Colombia

Tel: 57-1-214-9001 Fax: 57-1-612-8759 Contact: German Herrera

ITT CORPORATION

1330 Ave. of the Americas, New York, NY, 10019-5490

Tel: (212) 258-1000 Fax: (212) 258-1297

Design/mfr. communications & electronic equipment, hotels, insurance.

ITT Standard Electric de Colombia SA, Carrera 7 No. 33-92, Bogotá, Colombia

J. WALTER THOMPSON COMPANY

466 Lexington Ave., New York, NY, 10017

Tel: (212) 210-7000 Fax: (212) 210-6944 Web site: www.jwt.com

International advertising and marketing services.

J. Walter Thompson Co., Bogotá, Colombia

JOHNSON & JOHNSON

One Johnson & Johnson Plaza, New Brunswick, NJ, 08933

Tel: (732) 524-0400 Fax: (732) 214-0334 Web site: www.jnj.com

Mfr./distributor/R&D pharmaceutical, health care and cosmetic products.

Janssen-Cilag Farmaceutica SA, Aptdo. Aereo 047303, Bogotá, Colombia

Johnson & Johnson de Colombia SA, Aptdo. Aereo 6530, Cali, Colombia

Johnson & Johnson Medical Colombia S.A., Bogotá, Colombia

S C JOHNSON & SON INC.

1525 Howe Street, Racine, WI, 53403

Tel: (414) 260-2000 Fax: (414) 260-2133 Web site: www.scjohnsonwax.com

Home, auto, commercial and personal care products and specialty chemicals.

S.C. Johnson & Son Colombiana S.A., Calle 93 No. 11-28 3rd Fl., Sante Fe de Bogotá D.C., Colombia

KELLOGG COMPANY

One Kellogg Square, PO Box 3599, Battle Creek, MI, 49016-3599

Tel: (616) 961-2000 Fax: (616) 961-2871 Web site: www.kelloggs.com

Mfr. ready-to-eat cereals and convenience foods.

Kellogg de Colombia SA, Bogotá, Colombia (All inquiries to U.S. address)

KENNAMETAL INC.

State Rte. 981, Latrobe, PA, 15650

Tel: (724) 539-5000 Fax: (724) 539-4710 Web site: www.kennametal.com

Tools, hard carbide & tungsten alloys for metalworking industry.

IMOCOM S.A., Calle 16 No. 50-24, Apdo. Aereo 12287, Santafé de Bogotá, Colombia

Tel: 57-1-262-3800 Fax: 57-1-262-4982 Contact: Luis Alberto Lopez

KIMBERLY-CLARK CORPORATION

351 Phelps Drive, Irving, TX, 75038

Tel: (972) 281-1200 Fax: (972) 281-1435 Web site: www.kimberly-clark.com.

Mfr./sales/distribution of consumer tissue, household and personal care products.

Colombiana Kimberly SA, Locations in Barbosa, Guarne, Pereira and Tocancipa, Colombia

Colombiana Kimberly SA, Carrera 51 No. 50-51, Of. 806, Aptdo. Aereo 51906, Medellin, Colombia

Colombiana Universal de Papeles SA, Pereira, Colombia

KNOLL, INC.

1235 Water Street, East Greenville, PA, 18041

Tel: (215) 679-7991 Fax: (215) 679-3904 Web site: www.knoll.com

Mfr. and sale of office furnishings.

Knoll Muebles y Systemas, Carrera 9 No. 80-15, Bogotá DE, Colombia

Tel: 57-1-312-3394 Fax: 57-1-217-3914 Contact: Maria Isabel Argaez, Gen. Mgr.

KORN/FERRY INTERNATIONAL

1800 Century Park East, Los Angeles, CA, 90067

Tel: (310) 552-1834 Fax: (310) 553-6452 Web site: www.kornferry.com

Executive search; management consulting.

Korn/Ferry International, Carrera 7a No. 74-56, piso 19, Bogotá, Colombia

Tel: 57-1-629-2301 Fax: 57-1-629-2390

KPMG PEAT MARWICK LLP

Three Chestnut Ridge Road, Montvale, NJ, 07645

Tel: (201) 307-7000 Fax: (201) 930-8617 Web site: www.kpmg.com

Accounting and audit, tax and management consulting services.

KPMG Peat Marwick, Carrera 43-A No. 14-109, Office 706, Edif. Novatempo, Medellin, Colombia

KPMG Peat Marwick, Calle 19 Norte No.2-N-29, 31st Fl., Office 31-01-A, Edif. Torre Cali, Cali, Colombia

KPMG Peat Marwick, Calle 90, Nº 21-74, Santafé de Bogotá, D.C., Colombia

Tel: 57-1-616-6100 Fax: 57-1-218-5490 Contact: Alan A. Doig, Ptnr.

LAI WARD HOWELL INTERNATIONAL INC.

200 Park Ave., Ste. 3100, New York, NY, 10016-0136

Tel: (212) 953-7900 Fax: (212) 953-7907 Web site: www.laix.com

International executive search firm.

LAI Ward Howell Intl., Carrera 9A No. 99-02, piso 4, Bogotá, Colombia

LANIER WORLDWIDE, INC.

2300 Parklake Drive, N.E., Atlanta, GA, 30345

Tel: (770) 496-9500 Fax: (770) 621-1535

Specialize in digital copiers and multi-functional systems.

Lanier Colombia, S.A., 2DN #24N-128, No. 25 N 29/31, Cali, Colombia

Tel: 57-2-667-7177 Fax: 57-2-677-2419

Lanier Colombia, S.A., Av. El Dorado No. 100-55, Santafé de Bogotá, Colombia

Tel: 57-1-415-9400 Fax: 57-1-418-5865

LANMAN & KEMP-BARCLAY & CO., INC.

25 Woodland Ave., Westwood, NJ, 07675

Tel: (201) 666-4990 Fax: (201) 666-5836 Web site: www.lanman-and-kemp.com

Manufacturers toiletries, soap and cologne.

Lanman & Kemp-Barclay & Co. of Colombia, Carrera 67 No. 9-30, Aptdo. Aereo 3761, Bogotá, Colombia

Emp: 23

LE TOURNEAU COMPANY

PO Box 2307, Longview, TX, 75606

Tel: (903) 237-7000 Fax: (903) 267-7032

Mfr. heavy construction and mining machinery equipment.

E. McAllister & Cia., Calle 75 No. 11-74, Bogotá, Colombia

LHS GROUP INC.

6 Concourse Pkwy., Ste. 2700, Atlanta, GA, 30328

Tel: (770) 280-3000 Fax: (770) 280-3099 Web site: www.lhsgroup.com

Provides multilingual software for telecommunications carriers.

LHS Colombia, Calle 147, #4-45, Apt. 401, Torre 6, Bogota, Colombia

Tel: 573-229-7953 Fax: 573-229-7954

ELI LILLY & COMPANY

Lilly Corporate Center, Indianapolis, IN, 46285

Tel: (317) 276-2000 Fax: (317) 277-6579 Web site: www.lilly.com

Mfr. pharmaceuticals and animal health products.

Eli Lilly Interamerica Inc., Carrera 4N No. 64N-30, Cali, Colombia

Tel: 57-2-449-4949 Fax: 57-2-449-3729

THE LINCOLN ELECTRIC COMPANY

22801 St. Clair Ave., Cleveland, OH, 44117-1199

Tel: (216) 481-8100 Fax: (216) 486-8385 Web site: www.lincolnelectric.com

Mfr. arc welding and welding related products, oxy-fuel and thermal cutting equipment and integral AC motors.

Lincoln Electric Latin America, Av. Ciudad de Quito, No. 70-A-52 Of. 602, Bogotá, Colombia

Tel: 57-1-630-6589 Fax: 57-1-630-6489 Contact: Fernando Ojeda H.

ARTHUR D. LITTLE, INC.

25 Acorn Park, Cambridge, MA, 02140-2390

Tel: (617) 498-5000 Fax: (617) 498-7200 Web site: www.adlittle.com

Management, environmental, health & safety consulting; technical & product development.

Arthur D. Little de Colombia Ltda., Edif. Premium 98, Diagional 97 No. 17-60, Ofic. 801 y 802 Santafé de Bogotá, Colombia

Tel: 57-1-635-6060 Fax: 57-1-635-6005

LOCTITE CORPORATION

10 Columbus Boulevard, Hartford, CT, 06106

Tel: (203) 520-5000 Fax: (203) 520-5073 Web site: www.loctite.com

Mfr./sale industrial adhesives and sealants.

Loctite Colombia SA, Calle 17 No. 69-66, Bogotá, Colombia

Tel: 57-1-411-4969 Fax: 57-1-411-0912

LOWE & PARTNERS WORLDWIDE

1114 Ave. of the Americas, New York, NY, 10036

Tel: (212) 403-6700 Fax: (212) 403-6710

International advertising agency network.

Lowe & Partners/SSPM, Bogotá, Colombia

THE LUBRIZOL CORPORATION

29400 Lakeland Blvd., Wickliffe, OH, 44092-2298

Tel: (440) 943-4200 Fax: (440) 943-5337 Web site: www.lubrizol.com

Mfr. chemicals additives for lubricants & fuels.

Lubrizol Colombia, Bogotá, Colombia

Tel: 57-1-611-3440

M-I

PO Box 48242, Houston, TX, 77242-2842

Tel: (713) 739-0222 Fax: (713) 308-9503

Drilling fluids.

IMCO Services, Carrera 90A No. 62-37, Bogotá, Colombia

MARSH & McLENNAN COS INC.

1166 Ave. of the Americas, New York, NY, 10036-2774

Tel: (212) 345-5000 Fax: (212) 345-4808 Web site: www.marshmac.com

Insurance agents/brokers, pension and investment management consulting services.

J&H Marsh & McLennan (Colombia) Ltda.- Corredores de Seguros, Carrera 7, 32-33 piso 3, Bogotá, Colombia

Tel: 57-1-281-4300 Fax: 57-1-287-9178 Contact: Rod Fajarado

J&H Marsh & McLennan (Colombia) Ltda.- Corredores de Seguros, Calle 11, No. 3-58, Of. 603, Cali, Colombia

Tel: 57-2-882-3198 Fax: 57-2-882-5770 Contact: N/A

J&H Marsh & McLennan (Colombia) Ltda.- Corredores de Seguros, Carrera 46 No. 52-82 Of. 903, Edif. Camara de Comercio, Medellin, Colombia

Tel: 57-4-511-3734 Fax: 57-4-231-9878 Contact: Rafael Restrepo

MASTERCARD INTERNATIONAL INC.

200 Purchase Street, Purchase, NY, 10577

Tel: (914) 249-2000 Fax: (914) 249-5475 Web site: www.mastercard.com

Provides financial payment systems globally.

MasterCard International Inc., Carrera 7a #71-52, Of. 801, Torre A, Santafé de Bogotá, Colombia

McCANN-ERICKSON WORLDWIDE

750 Third Ave., New York, NY, 10017

Tel: (212) 984-3644 Fax: (212) 984-2629

International advertising/marketing services.

McCann-Erickson Colombia. SA, Calle 22 Norte No. 3-21, Aptdo. Aereo 976, Cali, Valle, Colombia

McCann-Erickson Colombia. SA, Edif. Colgas, Calle 38 No. 8-43, Bogotá, Colombia

McDONALD'S CORPORATION

Kroc Drive, Oak Brook, IL, 60523

Tel: (630) 623-3000 Fax: (630) 623-7409

Fast food chain stores.

McDonald's Corp., Colombia

McKINSEY & COMPANY

55 East 52nd Street, New York, NY, 10022

Tel: (212) 446-7000 Fax: (212) 446-8575 Web site: www.mckinsey.com

Management and business consulting services.

McKinsey & Company, Carrera 12 #84-12, Edif. Corfitolima Of. 501, Santa Fé de Bogotá, Colombia

Tel: 57-1-622-4080 Fax: 57-1-622-2528

MERCK & COMPANY, INC.

1 Merck Drive, Whitehouse Station, NJ, 08889

Tel: (908) 423-1000 Fax: (908) 423-2592

Pharmaceuticals, chemicals and biologicals.

Laboratorios Merck, Sharp & Dohme Quimica de Colombia SA, Calle 30 No. 6-38, piso 6, Bogotá, Colombia

MICROSOFT CORPORATION

One Microsoft Way, Redmond, WA, 98052-6399

Tel: (425) 882-8080 Fax: (425) 936-7329 Web site: www.microsoft.com

Computer software, peripherals and services.

Microsoft de Colombia, Carrera 9a No. 99-02, piso 2, Bogotá, Colombia

Tel: 57-1-618-2245 Fax: 57-1-618-2269

MOBIL CORPORATION

3225 Gallows Road, Fairfax, VA, 22037-0001

Tel: (703) 846-3000 Fax: (703) 846-4669 Web site: www.mobil.com

Petroleum and gas exploration and refining, mfr. petroleum products, chemicals and petrochemicals.

Codi-Mobil, Aptdo. Aereo 052973, Zona 2, Bogotá, Colombia

MOTOROLA, INC.

1303 East Algonquin Road, Schaumburg, IL, 60196

Tel: (847) 576-5000 Fax: (847) 538-5191 Web site: www.mot.com

Mfr. communications equipment, semiconductors and cellular phones.

Motorola Radiocommunicaciones de Colombia Ltd., Torre Banco Ganadero, piso 13, Carrera 7A, #71-52, Of. 1301, Santafe de Bogotá, Colombia

Tel: 57-1-312-2545 Fax: 57-1-312-2523

MULTIWARE

PO Box 907, Brookfield, CT, 06874

Tel: (203) 374-8000 Fax: (203) 374-3374

Mfr. applications development software.

Iris Software, Calle 26 No. 4 N-17, Cali, Colombia

NABORS INDUSTRIES INC.

515 West Greens Road, #1200, Houston, TX, 77067

Tel: (281) 874-0035 Fax: (281) 872-5205

Oil & gas drilling, petrol products.

Nabors Drilling Co. Ltd., Bogotá, Colombia

NALCO CHEMICAL COMPANY

One Nalco Center, Naperville, IL, 60563-1198

Tel: (630) 305-1000 Fax: (630) 305-2900 Web site: www.nalco.com

Chemicals for water and waste water treatment, oil products and refining, industry processes; water and energy management service.

Quimica Nalco de Colombia SA, Aptdo. Aereo 92219, Bogotá, Colombia

Tel: 57-1-623-1103 Fax: 57-1-623-1226

NATIONAL STARCH & CHEMICAL COMPANY

10 Finderne Ave., Bridgewater, NJ, 08807-3300

Tel: (908) 685-5000 Fax: (908) 685-5005 Web site: www.national starch.com

Mfr. adhesives & sealants, resins & specialty chemicals, electronic materials & adhesives, food products, industry starch.

National Starch & Chemical S.A., Calle 3, 25-351 Of. 204, Edif., Belvedere, Medellin, Colombia

Tel: 57-4-317-2667 Fax: 57-1-317-2175

NATIONSBANK CORPORATION

100 North Tryon Street, Corporate Center, Charlotte, NC, 28255

Tel: (704) 386-5000 Fax: (704) 386-1709 Web site: www.nationsbank.com

Banking and financial services.

NationsBank Corp., Bogotá, Colombia

THE NEWELL COMPANY

29 E Stephenson Street, Freeport, IL, 61032-0943

Tel: (815) 963-1010 Fax: (815) 489-8212 Web site: www.newellco.com

Mfr. Hardware, housewares, and office products.

The Newell Company, Colombia

A .C. NIELSEN COMPANY

177 Broad Street, Stamford, CT, 06901

Tel: (203) 961-3000 Fax: (203) 961-3190 Web site: www.acnielsen.com

Market research.

A.C. Nielsen de Colombia SA, Calle 80 No. 5-81, Bogotá 2, Colombia

NORDSON CORPORATION

28601 Clemens Road, Westlake, OH, 44145

Tel: (440) 892-1580 Fax: (440) 892-9507 Web site: www.nordson.com

Mfr. industry application equipment, sealants & packaging machinery.

Nordson Andina Ltda., Unidad Industrial Las Vegas, Carrera 49 No. 48-S-60 Local 108, Envigado-Antioquia, Colombia

Tel: 57-4-332-9111 Fax: 57-4-331-7077

OCCIDENTAL PETROLEUM CORPORATION

10889 Wilshire Blvd., Los Angeles, CA, 90024

Tel: (310) 208-8800 Fax: (310) 443-6690 Web site: www.oxy.com

Petroleum and petroleum products, chemicals, plastics.

Occidental de Colombia Inc., Calle 79 No. 8-70, Bogotá, Colombia

OCEANEERING INTERNATIONAL INC.

11911 FM 529, Houston, TX, 77041

Tel: (713) 329-4500 Fax: (713) 329-4951

Transportation equipment, underwater service to offshore oil and gas industry.

Oceaneering Intl. Inc., Cartegena, Colombia

OFFICE DEPOT, INC.

2200 Old Germantown Road, Delray Beach, FL, 33445

Tel: (561) 278-4800 Fax: (561) 265-4406 Web site: www.officedepot.com

Discount office product retailer with warehouse-style superstores.

Office Depot Colombia, Av. 68 No. 75-A-50, Centro Comercial Metropolis, Local 171, Santafé de Bogotá, D.C., Colombia

Tel: 57-1-311-8088 Fax: 57-1-630-9543 Contact: Ricardo Cortes, Gen. Mgr.

OGILVY & MATHER WORLDWIDE

309 West 49th Street, New York, NY, 10019

Tel: (212) 237-4000 Fax: (212) 237-5123

Advertising, marketing, public relations & consulting firm.

Centrum O&M, Bogotá, Colombia

ORACLE CORPORATION

500 Oracle Parkway, Redwood Shores, CA, 94065

Tel: (415) 506-7000 Fax: (415) 506-7200

Develop/manufacture software.

Oracle Colombia, Calle 100 No. 8A-55, Of. 415, Bogotá, Colombia

OWENS-ILLINOIS, INC.

One SeaGate, PO Box 1035, Toledo, OH, 43666

Tel: (419) 247-5000 Fax: (419) 247-2839

Largest mfr. of glass containers in the US; plastic containers, compression-molded closures and dispensing systems.

Cristaleria Peldar SA, Locations in Envigado and Zipaquira, Colombia

PAN-AMERICAN LIFE INSURANCE CO.

Pan American Life Center, PO Box 60219, New Orleans, LA, 70130-0219

Tel: (504) 566-1300 Fax: (504) 566-3600 Web site: www.palic.com

Insurance services.

Pan-American de Colombia, Cia de Seguros de Vida SA, Carrera 7 No. 75-09, Bogotá, Colombia

Tel: 57-1-212-1300 Fax: 57-1-212-1300 Contact: Enrique Marino, VP & Gen. Mgr. Emp: 88

PARKER DRILLING COMPANY

8 East Third Street, Tulsa, OK, 74103-3637

Tel: (918) 585-8221 Fax: (918) 585-1058

Drilling contractor.

Parker Drilling Co. of South America, Aptdo. Aereo 90027, Carrera 62 #18-14, Bogotá, Colombia

THE PERKIN-ELMER CORPORATION

761 Main Ave., Norwalk, CT, 06859-0001

Tel: (203) 762-1000 Fax: (203) 762-4228 Web site: www.perkin-elmer.com

Leading supplier of systems for life science research and related applications.

Perkin-Elmer de Columbia S.A., Calle 93B, No. 17-25, Of. 401, Santafe de Bogotá, Colombia

Tel: 57-1-621-1300 Fax: 57-1-621-2900 Contact: Rafael Vargas, Gen. Mgr.

PFIZER INC.

235 East 42nd Street, New York, NY, 10017-5755

Tel: (212) 573-2323 Fax: (212) 573-7851 Web site: www.pfizer.com

Research-based, global health care company.

Pfizer SA, Colombia

PHARMACIA & UPJOHN

95 Corporate Drive, PO Box 6995, Bridgewater, NJ, 08807

Tel: (908) 306-4400 Fax: (908) 306-4433 Web site: www.pnu.com

Mfr. pharmaceuticals, agricultural products, industry chemicals

Compania Upjohn SA, Diagonal 45 93-43, Santafe de Bogotá, Colombia

PHILLIPS PETROLEUM COMPANY

Phillips Building, 411 S. Keeler Ave., Bartlesville, OK, 74004

Tel: (918) 661-6600 Fax: (918) 661-7636 Web site: www.phillips66.com

Crude oil, natural gas, liquified petroleum gas, gasoline and petro-chemicals.

Phillips Petroleum Co., Carrera 13 No. 26-49, piso 12, Cali, Colombia

Phillips Petroleum Ventas SA, Carrera 13 No. 26-45, Cali, Colombia

Phillips Petroquimica SA, Calle 11 No. 3-58, Cali, Colombia

Phillips Quimica Ventas Colombia SA, Calle 11 No. 3-58, Cali, Colombia

PRAXAIR, INC.

39 Old Ridgebury Road, Danbury, CT, 06810-5113

Tel: (203) 837-2000 Fax: (203) 837-2450 Web site: www.praxair.com

Produces and distributes industrial and specialty gases.

Oxigenos de Colômbia Efese S.A., Carreta 19A, no. 16-36/26, Santafé de Bogotá, Colombia

Tel: 57-1-360-1977 Fax: 57-1-360-1476

PRICEWATERHOUSECOOPERS LLP

1251 Ave. of the Americas, New York, NY, 10020

Tel: (212) 596-7000 Fax: (212) 790-6620 Web site: www.pwcglobal.com

Accounting and auditing, tax and management, and human resource consulting services.

Price Waterhouse Ltd., Edif. Atlantico, Carrera 53 No 74-16, 4th Fl., Apartado 29, Barranquilla, Colombia

Tel: 57-58-452538 Fax: 57-58-453627

Price Waterhouse Ltd., Edif. la Torre de Cali, Calle 19 Norte No 2-N-29, 7th Fl., Apartado 180, Cali, Colombia

Tel: 57-2-6671260 Fax: 57-2-6671181

Price Waterhouse Ltd., Calle 100 No 11-A-35, 5th Fl., Apartado 60188, Bogotá, Colombia

Tel: 57-1-610-0155 Fax: 57-1-218-8544

Price Waterhouse Ltd., Edif. Colinas del Poblado, Carrera 43A No 14-27, piso 9, Apartado 81164 Envigado, Medellin, Colombia

Tel: 57-4-2662200 Fax: 57-4-2662993

PROCTER & GAMBLE COMPANY

One Procter & Gamble Plaza, Cincinnati, OH, 45202

Tel: (513) 983-1100 Fax: (513) 562-4500 Web site: www.pg.com

Personal care, food, laundry, cleaning and industry products.

Norwich Colombiana SA, Bogotá, Colombia

Procter & Gamble Industries Inextra, Transversal 38 No. 100-25, 2nd Fl., Santafe de Bogotá, Colombia (Locations: Funza & Medellin, Colombia.)

PROCTER & GAMBLE PHARMACEUTICALS

17 Eaton Ave., Norwich, NY, 13815-1799

Tel: (607) 335-2111 Fax: (607) 335-2798

Develop/manufacture pharmaceuticals, chemicals and health products.

Norwich Colombiana, D.E. Transversaal 42B 19-77, Aptdo. Aereo 13902, Bogotá, Colombia

RICE FOWLER

201 St. Charles Ave., 36th Fl., New Orleans, LA, 70170

Tel: (504) 523-2600 Fax: (504) 523-2705

Law firm specializing in maritime, insurance, int'l, environmental, oil/gas, transportation, bankruptcy & reorganization.

Rice Fowler, Carrera 12A #77-41, Of. 502, Bogotá, Colombia

Tel: 57-1-313-4488 Fax: 57-1-313-4677 Emp: 1

ROCKWELL INTERNATIONAL CORPORATION

600 Anton Boulevard, Costa Mesa, CA, 92626-7147

Tel: (714) 424-4200 Fax: (714) 424-4251 Web site: www.rockwell.com

Products & service for aerospace and defense, automotive, electronics, graphics & automation industry.

Rockwell Automation Colombia S.A., Muelle Industrial II Bidega 4, Cr. 98 No. 42A-41, Santafe de Bogotá, Colombia

Tel: 57-1-418-5902 Fax: 57-1-418-5995

ROHM AND HAAS COMPANY

100 Independence Mall West, Philadelphia, PA, 19106

Tel: (215) 592-3000 Fax: (215) 592-3377 Web site: www.rohmhaas.com

Mfr. industrial & agricultural chemicals, plastics.

Rohm and Haas Colombia SA, Calle 72 No. 12-65, Bogotá, Colombia (Locations: Barranquilla, Colombia.)

Tel: 57-1-312-4545

SCHENKER INTERNATIONAL FORWARDERS INC.

150 Albany Ave., Freeport, NY, 11520

Tel: (516) 377-3000 Fax: (516) 377-3005 Web site: www.schenkerusa.com

Freight forwarders.

Schenker Colombia SA Transportes Internacionales, Carrera 13, No. 98-06, Interior 1, PO Box 29312, Santafe de Bogotá, Colombia

Tel: 57-1-63-63000 Fax: 57-1-611-3351

SONOCO PRODUCTS COMPANY

North Second Street, PO Box 160, Hartsville, SC, 29550

Tel: (803) 383-7000 Fax: (803) 383-7008 Web site: www.sonoco.com

Mfr. packaging for consumer & industrial market and recycled paperboard.

Sonoco Colombiana S.A., Carrera 7a. #34-120, Cali, Valle, Colombia

Tel: 57-2-438-4715 Fax: 57-2-444-2746

Sonoco Colombiana S.A., Carretora Panamericana Km 25, Jamundi, Valle, Colombia

Tel: 57-2-553-0892 Fax: 57-2-516-1382

Sonoco Colombiana S.A., Carrera 100 #11-60, Office 618, Holguines Trade Ctr., Cali, Valle, Colombia

Tel: 57-2-353-0892 Fax: 57-2-339-4585

Sonoco Colombiana S.A., Calle 139 No.94-56 Int. 5, Bogotá, D.E., Colombia

Tel: 57-16-81-4530 Fax: 57-16-81-2876

SPENCER STUART & ASSOCIATES INC.

401 North Michigan Ave., Ste. 3400, Chicago, IL, 60611

Tel: (312) 822-0080 Fax: (312) 822-0116 Web site: www.spencerstuart.com

Executive recruitment firm.

Spencer Stuart & Associates Inc., Carrera 9A No. 99-02, Cuarto piso, Bogotá, Colombia
Tel: 57-1-618-2488 Fax: 57-1-618-2317 Contact: Alvaro Cadavid

THE ST. PAUL COMPANIES, INC.
385 Washington Street, St. Paul, MN, 55102
Tel: (612) 310-7911 Fax: (612) 310-8294 Web site: www.stpaul.com
Provides investment, insurance and reinsurance services.
Compania de Seguros La Colmena S.A., Calle 72, No. 10-07, piso 8, Santafe de Bogotá, D.C., Colombia

THE STANLEY WORKS
1000 Stanley Drive, PO Box 7000, New Britain, CT, 06053
Tel: (860) 225-5111 Fax: (860) 827-3987 Web site: www.stanleyworks.com
Mfr. hand tools & hardware.
Herramientas Stanley SA, Aptdo. Aereo 241, Palmira, Colombia

STEPAN COMPANY
22 West Frontage Road, Northfield, IL, 60093
Tel: (847) 446-7500 Fax: (847) 501-2443
Mfr. basic intermediate chemicals.
Stepan Colombiana de Quimicos Ltda., Av. 7 Norte No. 24A-113, Santa Monica Norte, Cali, Colombia

STIEFEL LABORATORIES INC.
255 Alhambra Circle, Ste. 1000, Coral Gables, FL, 33134
Tel: (305) 443-3807 Fax: (305) 443-3467
Mfr. pharmaceuticals, dermatological specialties.
Laboratorios Stiefel Colombia SA, Carrera 12 No. 98-39, Int. 201, Aptdo. Aereo 91492, Bogotá, Colombia

STONE CONTAINER CORPORATION
150 N. Michigan Ave., Chicago, IL, 60601-7568
Tel: (312) 346-6600 Fax: (312) 580-3486 Web site: www.stonecontainer.com
Mfr. paper and paper packaging.
Stone Container Corporation, Bogotá, Colombia

TECHNOLOGY SOLUTIONS COMPANY (TSC)
205 N. Michigan Ave., Ste. 1500, Chicago, IL, 60601
Tel: (312) 228-4500 Fax: (312) 228-4501 Web site: www.techsol.com
Designs computer information systems and strategic business and management consulting for major corporations.
TSC Colombia, S.A., Teleport Business Park, Calle 114 No. 9-45, Torre B, Piso 8, Bogotá, Colombia
Tel: 98-571-629-2881 Fax: 98-571-629-3616 Contact: Jimena Garcia-Calderon

TENNESSEE ASSOCIATES INTERNATIONAL
223 Associates Blvd., PO Box 710, Alcoa, TN, 37701-0710
Tel: (423) 982-9514 Fax: (423) 982-1481
Management consulting services.
TAI Colombia, Carrera 100 No. 11-60, Torre Valle del Lili, Of. 713, Aptdo. Postal 25528, Unicentro, Cali, Colombia

TRUE NORTH COMMUNICATIONS INC.
101 East Erie Street, Chicago, IL, 60611
Tel: (312) 425-6000 Fax: (312) 425-6350
Holding company, advertising agency.
Foote, Cone & Belding, Calle 37 No. 20-24, Carrera 20, No. 37-15, Santafé de Bogotá, Colombia

UNION CARBIDE CORPORATION

39 Old Ridgebury Road, Danbury, CT, 06817

Tel: (203) 794-2000 Fax: (203) 794-6269 Web site: www.unioncarbide.com

Mfr. industrial chemicals, plastics and resins.

Union Carbide InterAmerica, Carrera 13 No. 26-45, piso 11, Aptdo. Aereo 48054, Bogotá, Colombia (Locations: Barranquilla, Cali & Medellin)

UNIROYAL CHEMICAL CO., INC.

World Headquarters, Benson Road, Middlebury, CT, 06749

Tel: (203) 573-2000 Fax: (203) 573-2265

Tires, tubes and other rubber products, chemicals, plastics and textiles.

Uniroyal Croydon SA, Carretera del Sur No. 61-51, Aptdo. Aereo 14509, Apartado National 4980, Bogotá, Colombia

UNITED PARCEL SERVICE OF AMERICA, INC.

55 Glenlake Parkway, NE, Atlanta, GA, 30328

Tel: (404) 828-6000 Fax: (404) 828-6593 Web site: www.ups.com

International package-delivery service.

UPS / T.G. Express, Calle 50, No. #79-54, Interior #10, Santafe Bogotá, Colombia

Tel: 57-1-416-6166 Fax: 57-1-416-1500

UOP INC.

25 E. Algonquin Road, Des Plaines, IL, 60017

Tel: (847) 391-2000 Fax: (847) 391-2253

Diversified research, development & mfr. of industry products & systems management studies & service.

UOP Process Intl., Bogotá, Colombia

WACKENHUT CORPORATION

4200 Wackenhut Drive, Ste. 100, Palm Beach Gardens, FL, 33410

Tel: (561) 622-5656 Fax: (561) 691-6736 Web site: www.wackenhut.com

Security systems & services.

Wackenhut de Colombia SA, Av. 82 No. 7-53, Aptdo. Aereo 4008, Santafé de Bogotá, Colombia (Locations: Barranquilla, Sogamoso Boyaca, Calli, & Medellin, Colombia.)

Tel: 57-1-310-0088 Fax: 57-1-217-4848

WARNER-LAMBERT COMPANY

201 Tabor Road, Morris Plains, NJ, 07950-2693

Tel: (973) 540-2000 Fax: (973) 540-3761 Web site: www.warner-lambert.com

Mfr. ethical and proprietary pharmaceuticals, confectionery and consumer products & pet care supplies.

Chicle Adams SA, Calle 62 No. 1N-80, Cali, Colombia

Parke-Davis & Co., Edif. Colpatria, Calle 72 No. 8-56 , piso 6, Bogotá, Colombia

WATERS CORPORATION

34 Maple Street, Milford, MA, 01757

Tel: (508) 478-2000 Fax: (508) 872-1990

Mfr./distribute liquid chromatographic instruments and test and measurement equipment.

Waters Associates, Colombia

WATSON WYATT & COMPANY

6707 Democracy Blvd., Ste. 800, Bethesda, MD, 20817

Tel: (301) 581-4600 Fax: (301) 581-4937 Web site: www.watsonwyatt.com

Creates compensation and benefits programs for major corporations.

Watson Wyatt Colombia, Diagonal 127A, No. 17-54 Office 503, Apartado 59546, Santa Fe de Bogota, Colombia

Tel: 57-1-615-5034 Fax: 57-1-216-7392 Contact: Uladislao Prieto

WEATHERFORD INTERNATIONAL INC.

5 Post Oak Blvd, Ste. 1760, Houston, TX, 77227-3415

Tel: (713) 287-8400 Fax: (713) 963-9785 Web site: www.weatherford.com

Oilfield services, products & equipment; mfr. marine cranes for oil and gas industry.

Weatherford Intl. Inc., Bogotá & Yopal, Colombia

Tel: 57-1-616-1130 Fax: 57-1-610-8743

THE WEST COMPANY, INC.

101 Gordon Drive, PO Box 645, Lionville, PA, 19341-0645

Tel: (610) 594-2900 Fax: (610) 594-3014 Web site: www.thewestcompany.com

Mfr. products for filling, sealing, dispensing & delivering needs of health care & consumer products markets.

West Rubber de Colombia, Bogotá, Colombia

Tel: 57-1-413-2234

WESTERN ATLAS INC.

10205 Westheimer, Houston, TX, 77251-1407

Tel: (713) 972-4000 Fax: (713) 952-9837 Web site: www.waii.com

Full service to the oil industry.

Western Atlas Logging Services, Calle 42, No. 101-61, FontiBon, Bogotá, Colombia

Tel: 57-1-415-5814 Fax: 57-1-298-8577 Contact: Gary Ryer, Sales Eng.

Western Geophysical, Aptdo. Aereo 91014, Zona 8, Calle 42, No. 101-61, Bogotá, Colombia

Tel: 57-1-413-1799 Fax: 57-1-298-8766 Contact: I. Ortega, Gen. Mgr.

WHITEHALL-ROBINS INC.

1407 Cummings Drive, PO Box 26609, Richmond, VA, 23261-6609

Tel: (804) 257-2000 Fax: (804) 257-2120 Web site: www.ahp.com/whitehall.htm

Mfr. ethical pharmaceuticals and consumer products.

Instituto Medico Tecnico Sanicol SA, Carrera 27 No. 8-46 a 8-70, Bogotá, Colombia

Whitehall-Robins Intl. SA, Carrera 27 No. 8-46 a 8-70, Bogotá, Colombia

WITCO CORPORATION

One American Lane, Greenwich, CT, 06831-2559

Tel: (203) 552-2000 Fax: (203) 552-3070 Web site: www.witco.com

Mfr. chemical and petroleum products.

Witco Colombia Ltda., Aptdo. Aereo 3559, Calle 18A No. 33-15, Santafé de Bogotá, Colombia

WUNDERMAN CATO JOHNSON

675 Ave. of the Americas, New York, NY, 10010-5104

Tel: (212) 941-3000 Fax: (212) 633-0957 Web site: www.wcj.com

International advertising and marketing consulting firm.

Wunderman Cato Johnson, Calle 93 A No. 20-66 Of. 401, Santafé de Bogotá, Colombia

Tel: 57-1-621-4691 Fax: 57-1-622-6725 Contact: Raul Eduardo Pacheco, Gen. Mgr.

XEROX CORPORATION

800 Long Ridge Road, PO Box 1600, Stamford, CT, 06904

Tel: (203) 968-3000 Fax: (203) 968-4312 Web site: www.xerox.com

Mfr. document processing equipment, systems and supplies.

Xerox de Colombia, S.A., Apartado Aereo 12044, Av. 26 No. 61-96, Bogata D. E., Colombia

YOUNG & RUBICAM INC.

285 Madison Ave., New York, NY, 10017

Tel: (212) 210-3000 Fax: (212) 370-3796 Web site: www.yr.com

Advertising, public relations, direct marketing and sales promotion, corporate & product ID management.

Young & Rubicam Bogota, Bogotá, Colombia

Congo

BAKER HUGHES INCORPORATED

3900 Essex Lane, Ste. 1200, Houston, TX, 77027

Tel: (713) 439-8600 Fax: (713) 439-8699 Web site: www.bakerhughes.com

Develop & apply technology to drill, complete & produce oil and natural gas wells; provide separation systems to petroleum, municipal, continuous process & mining industries.

Baker Hughes Tools, Pointe Noire RP, Congo

Tel: 87-1-382-341498 Fax: 87-1-382-341496

DHL WORLDWIDE EXPRESS

333 Twin Dolphin Drive, Redwood City, CA, 94065

Tel: (650) 593-7474 Fax: (650) 593-1689 Web site: www.dhl.com

Worldwide air express carrier.

DHL Worldwide Express, Ave. Foch, Boite Postale 643, Brazzaville, Congo

Tel: 242-83-8525

ERNST & YOUNG, LLP

787 Seventh Ave., New York, NY, 10019

Tel: (212) 773-3000 Fax: (212) 773-6350 Web site: www.eyi.com

Accounting and audit, tax and management consulting services.

Ernst & Young, Tour Arc, B.P. 84, Brazzaville, Congo

Tel: 33-1-46-93-6758 Fax: 33-1-47-67-0106 Contact: Daniel Tapin

EXXON CORPORATION

225 E. John W. Carpenter Freeway, Irving, TX, 75062-2298

Tel: (972) 444-1000 Fax: (972) 444-1882 Web site: www.exxon.com

Petroleum exploration, production, refining; mfr. petroleum & chemicals products; coal & minerals.

Exxon - Exploration & Production, Congo

FRITZ COMPANIES INC.

706 Mission Street, Ste. 900, San Francisco, CA, 94103

Tel: (415) 904-8360 Fax: (415) 904-8661 Web site: www.fritz.com

Integrated transportation, sourcing, distribution & customs brokerage services.

Fritz Companies Inc., Congo

GLOBAL MARINE INC

777 North Eldridge, Houston, TX, 77079

Tel: (281) 496-8000 Fax: (281) 531-1260 Web site: www.glm.com

Offshore contract drilling, turnkey drilling, oil & gas exploration & production.

Global Marine Inc., Pointe Noire, Congo

HALLIBURTON COMPANY

500 North Akard Street, Ste. 3600, Dallas, TX, 75201-3391

Tel: (214) 978-2600 Fax: (214) 978-2685 Web site: www.halliburton.com

Energy, construction and insurance.

Halliburton Ltd., BP #865, Zone Industrielle Luandijili, Point Noire, Congo

Tel: 242-942893 Fax: 242-94-2167

OCCIDENTAL PETROLEUM CORPORATION

10889 Wilshire Blvd., Los Angeles, CA, 90024

Tel: (310) 208-8800 Fax: (310) 443-6690 Web site: www.oxy.com

Petroleum and petroleum products, chemicals, plastics.

Occidental de Congo Inc., Congo

OCEANEERING INTERNATIONAL INC.

11911 FM 529, Houston, TX, 77041

Tel: (713) 329-4500 Fax: (713) 329-4951

Transportation equipment, underwater service to offshore oil and gas industry.

Oceaneering Intl. Inc., Pointe Noire, Congo

PRICEWATERHOUSECOOPERS LLP

1251 Ave. of the Americas, New York, NY, 10020

Tel: (212) 596-7000 Fax: (212) 790-6620 Web site: www.pwcglobal.com

Accounting and auditing, tax and management, and human resource consulting services.

Price Waterhouse Ltd., 32 Ave. du General de Gaulle, (BP 1306) Pointe Noire, Congo

Tel: 242-94-3028 Fax: 242-94-2334

R&B FALCON CORPORATION

901 Threadneedle, Ste. 200, Houston, TX, 77079

Tel: (281) 496-5000 Fax: (281) 496-4363 Web site: www.rbfalcon.com

Offshore contract drilling.

Reading & Bates Exploration Co., c/o Ponteco Socopao, PO Box 1018, Pointe Noire, Congo

WEATHERFORD INTERNATIONAL INC.

5 Post Oak Blvd, Ste. 1760, Houston, TX, 77227-3415

Tel: (713) 287-8400 Fax: (713) 963-9785 Web site: www.weatherford.com

Oilfield services, products & equipment; mfr. marine cranes for oil and gas industry.

Weatherford Intl. Inc., Boite Postale 807, Pointe Noire, Congo

Tel: 242-94-1517 Fax: 242-94-4492

Costa Rica

3COM CORPORATION

5400 Bayfront Plaza, Santa Clara, CA, 95052-8145

Tel: (408) 764-5000 Fax: (408) 764-5001 Web site: www.3com.com

Develop/mfr. computer networking products & systems.

3Com Costa Rica, Ofiplaza del Este, San Pedro Edif. C. piso 2, San Jose, Costa Rica

Tel: 506-280-8480 Fax: 506-280-5859

3M

3M Center, St. Paul, MN, 55144-1000

Tel: (612) 733-1110 Fax: (612) 733-9973 Web site: www.mmm.com

Mfr. diversified products for industry, health care, imaging, communications, transport, safety, consumer, etc.

3M Costa Rica SA, Aptdo. 10119, 1000 San Jose, Costa Rica

Tel: 506-260-3333 Fax: 506-260-3360

AIR EXPRESS INTERNATIONAL CORPORATION

120 Tokeneke Road, PO Box 1231, Darien, CT, 06820

Tel: (203) 655-7900 Fax: (203) 655-5779 Web site: www.aeilogistics.com

Air freight forwarder.

AEI de Costa Roca, c/o Corporacion Cormar S.A., Barrio Tournon, Contiguo A, Edif. de BISCA, San Jose, Costa Rica

Tel: 506-257-6969 Fax: 506-257-2998

AMERICAN & EFIRD INC.

PO Box 507, Mt. Holly, NC, 28120

Tel: (704) 827-4311 Fax: (704) 822-6054

Mfr. industrial thread, yarn & consumer sewing products.

Hilos A&E de Costa Rica SA, Apartado Postal 20.3008, Del Cenada 300 Mts. al Este, Barreal de Heredia, Costa Rica

AMERICAN STANDARD INC.

One Centennial Ave., Piscataway, NJ, 08855-6820

Tel: (732) 980-3000 Fax: (732) 980-6118

Mfr. heating, plumbing & sanitary equipment, china, earthenware.

INCESA, Aptdo. 4120, San Jose, Costa Rica

AMMIRATI PURIS LINTAS

One Dag Hammarskjold Plaza, New York, NY, 10017

Tel: (212) 605-8000 Fax: (212) 605-4705 Web site: www.interpublic.com

International advertising agency.

Publimark S.A., De La Esquina Surcoeste, del ICE en San Pedro, 300 Mts. Sur. Diagonal, a la Price Waterhouse, San Pedro, San Jose, Costa Rica

Tel: 506-283-2356 Fax: 506-224-8224 Contact: Fernando Berger

AON CORPORATION

123 North Wacker Drive, Chicago, IL, 60606

Tel: (312) 701-3000 Fax: (312) 701-3100 Web site: www.aon.com

Insurance brokers worldwide; underwrites accident & health insurance, specialty & professional insurance; & provides risk management consultation.

AON Worldwide / Seguros Continental, PO Box 7969, San Jose, Costa Rica

Tel: 506-257-1155 Fax: 506-257-1170 Contact: Julio Acosta

ASSOCIATES FIRST CAPITAL CORPORATION

250 E. Carpenter Freeway, Irving, TX, 75062-2729

Tel: (972) 652-4000 Fax: (972) 652-7420 Web site: www.theassociates.com

Consumer financial services.

Associates First Capital Corporation, San Jose, Costa Rica

AVIS, INC.

900 Old Country Road., Garden City, NY, 11530

Tel: (516) 222-3000 Fax: (516) 222-4381 Web site: www.avis.com

Car rental services.

Avis Rental Office, Av. Las Americas Sabana Norte, San Jose, Costa Rica

BATES WORLDWIDE INC.

405 Lexington Ave., New York, NY, 10174

Tel: (212) 297-7000 Fax: (212) 986-0270 Web site: www.batesww.com

Advertising, marketing, public relations & media consulting.

IPC Bates, Corresponsal Bates CentroAmerica, Rohrmoser, 100 Mts Oesle del Parque La Amistad, PO Box 5284-1000, San Jose, Costa Rica

Tel: 506-220-1028 Fax: 506-232-3269 Contact: Gerardo Vicente Soteia, Mgr.

BAXTER HEALTHCARE CORPORATION

One Baxter Parkway, Deerfield, IL, 60015

Tel: (847) 948-2000 Fax: (847) 948-3948 Web site: www.baxter.com

Pharmaceutical preparations, surgical/medical instruments & cardiovascular products.

Baxter SA, Aptdo. Postal 1-7052, Parque Industrial, Cartago, Costa Rica

BBDO WORLDWIDE

1285 Ave. of the Americas, New York, NY, 10019

Tel: (212) 459-5000 Fax: (212) 459-6645 Web site: www.bbdo.com

Multinational group of advertising agencies.

Garnier BBDO, San Jose, Costa Rica

BEST WESTERN INTERNATIONAL

6201 North 24th Place, Phoenix, AZ, 85106

Tel: (602) 957-4200 Fax: (602) 957-5740

International hotel chain.

BW Irazu, Box 952, San Jose, Costa Rica 1000

Tel: 506-232-4811

BESTFOODS, INC.

700 Sylvan Ave., International Plaza, Englewood Cliffs, NJ, 07632-9976

Tel: (201) 894-4000 Fax: (201) 894-2186 Web site: www.bestfoods.com

Consumer foods products; corn refining.

Productos Agroindustriales del Caribe, S.A. (PROAGRO), Apartado Postal 104-4050, Alajuela, Costa Rica

Tel: 506-293-4411 Fax: 506-293-4420 Contact: Andres Gutierrez

BOART LONGYEAR CO.

2340 West 1700 South, Salt Lake City, UT, 84104

Tel: (801) 972-6430 Fax: (801) 977-3372

Mfr. diamond drills, concrete cutting equipment and drill services.

Longyear Co., Aptdo. 5235, San Jose, Costa Rica

BOURNS INC.

1200 Columbia Ave., Riverside, CA, 92507

Tel: (909) 781-5500 Fax: (909) 781-5273

Mfr. resistive components and networks, precision potentiometers, panel controls, switches and transducers.

Trimpot Electronics SA, Aptdo. 45, San Antonio de Belen, Heredia, Costa Rica

BRISTOL-MYERS SQUIBB COMPANY

345 Park Ave., New York, NY, 10154

Tel: (212) 546-4000 Fax: (212) 546-4020 Web site: www.bms.com

Pharmaceutical and food preparations, medical and surgical instruments.

Bristol-Myers Squibb Costa Rica, Apartado Postal 10269, 1000 San Jose, Costa Rica

ConvaTec - Costa Rica, San Jose, Costa Rica

BUDGET RENT A CAR CORPORATION

4225 Naperville Road, Lisle, IL, 60532

Tel: (630) 955-1900 Fax: (630) 955-7799 Web site: www.budgetrentacar.com

Car and truck rental system.

Budget Rent A Car, Central Hdqrs., San Jose, Costa Rica

Tel: 506-2554966

LEO BURNETT CO., INC.

35 West Wacker Drive, Chicago, IL, 60601

Tel: (312) 220-5959 Fax: (312) 220-6533 Web site: www.leoburnett.com

International advertising agency.

Leo Burnett-Costa Rica, Aptdo. 2316-1000, San Jose, Costa Rica

CALMAQUIP ENGINEERING CORPORATION

7240 NW 12th Street, Miami, FL, 33121

Tel: (305) 592-4510 Fax: (305) 593-9618

Engineering

Reifi SA, Aptdo. 3156, San Jose, Costa Rica

CENTURY 21 REAL ESTATE CORPORATION

6 Sylvan Way, Parsippany, NJ, 07054-3826

Tel: (973) 496-5722 Fax: (973) 496-5527 Web site: www.century21.com

Real estate.

Century 21 Central American Real Estate, Omni Bldg., St. 3th-5th, San Jose, Costa Rica

Tel: 506-257-1294 Contact: Jose Pablo Montoya, Regional Dir.

CHIQUITA BRANDS INTERNATIONAL INC.

250 East Fifth Street, Cincinnati, OH, 45202

Tel: (513) 784-8000 Fax: (513) 784-8030 Web site: www.chiquita.com

Sale and distribution of bananas, fresh fruits and processed foods.

Compania Palma Tica, Aptdo. Aereo 30, San Jose, Costa Rica

Polymer United SA, Aptdo. Aereo 5123, San Jose, Costa Rica

Unimar SA, Aptdo. Aereo 3657, San Jose, Costa Rica

CISCO SYSTEMS, INC.

170 Tasman Drive, San Jose, CA, 95134-1706

Tel: (408) 526-4000 Fax: (408) 526-4100 Web site: www.cisco.com

Develop/mfr./market computer hardware and software networking systems.

Cisco Sistemas de Redes, S.A., Costa Rica, De las Tunas 100 Metros Norte, 50 Metros Este, Sabana Norte, San José, Costa Rica

Tel: 506-296-1885 Fax: 506-442-4256 Contact: Mauricio Naranjo

CITICORP

399 Park Ave., New York, NY, 10043

Tel: (212) 559-1000 Fax: (212) 527-2066 Web site: www.citibank.com

International banking and financial services.

Citibank N.A., Oficentro Ejecutivo La Sabana, San José, Costa Rica

Tel: 506-296-1494/1496 Fax: 506-296-2458 Contact: Juan Antonio Miro Llort, Pres.

THE CLOROX COMPANY

1221 Broadway, PO Box 24305, Oakland, CA, 94623-1305

Tel: (510) 271-7000 Fax: (510) 832-1463

Mfr. soap & detergents, and domestic consumer packaged products.

American Sanitary Co. SA, San Jose, Costa Rica

THE COCA-COLA COMPANY

P.O. Drawer 1734, Atlanta, GA, 30301

Tel: (404) 676-2121 Fax: (404) 676-6792 Web site: www.coca-cola.com

Mfr./marketing/distributor soft drinks, syrups & concentrates, juice & juice-drink products.

Coca Cola Interamericana Corp., Aptdo. Postal 2749, San Jose, Costa Rica

COLGATE-PALMOLIVE COMPANY

300 Park Ave., New York, NY, 10022

Tel: (212) 310-2000 Fax: (212) 310-2919

Mfr. pharmaceuticals, cosmetics, toiletries and detergents.

Colgate-Palmolive (Costa Rica) SA, Calles 26-28, Av. 3 Bis., San Jose, Costa Rica

COMMUNICATIONS SYSTEMS INC.

213 S. Main Street, Hector, MN, 55342

Tel: (320) 848-6231 Fax: (320) 848-2702

Mfr. telecommunications equipment.

Suttle Costa Rica SA, Parque Industrial Z.F. Alajuela, Alajuela, Costa Rica

Tel: 506-440-2520 Contact: Wualter Soto Emp: 225

CONAIR CORPORATION

150 Milford Road, E. Windsor, NJ, 08520

Tel: (609) 426-1300 Fax: (609) 426-8766

Mfr. personal care & household appliances.

Conair Costa Rica SA, Zona Industrial de Cartago, Cartago, Costa Rica

CONTINENTAL AIRLINES INC.

2929 Allen Parkway, Ste. 1501, Houston, TX, 77019

Tel: (281) 834-5000 Fax: (281) 520-6329

International airline carrier.

Continental Airlines Inc., Costa Rica

CROWN CORK & SEAL COMPANY, INC.

One Crown Way, Philadelphia, PA, 19154-4599

Tel: (215) 698-5100 Fax: (215) 698-5201

Mfr. cans, bottle caps; filling & packaging machinery.

Crown Cork Centro Americana SA, Aptdo. 504, San Jose, Costa Rica

D'ARCY MASIUS BENTON & BOWLES INC. (DMB&B)

1675 Broadway, New York, NY, 10019

Tel: (212) 468-3622 Fax: (212) 468-2987 Web site: www.dmbb.com

Full service international advertising and communications group.

Union Publisitaria/DMB&B, Sabana Sur, do Universal, 100m Sur, 50 Ote, 75 Sur, Apt.244-1005, San Jose, Costa Rica

Tel: 506-231-1002 Fax: 506-232-6978 Contact: Nelson Barraza, Gen. Mgr.

DDB NEEDHAM WORLDWIDE INC.

437 Madison Ave., New York, NY, 10022

Tel: (212) 415-2000 Fax: (212) 415-3417

Advertising agency.

DDB Needham Costa Rica, San Jose, Costa Rica

DELOITTE TOUCHE TOHMATSU INTERNATIONAL

PO Box 820, Wilton, CT, 06897

Tel: (203) 761-3000 Fax: (203) 834-2200 Web site: www.u.s.deloitte.com or www.dtti.com

Accounting, audit, tax and management consulting services.

Deloitte & Touche, (PO Box 3667-1000) Herrero illalta Bldg., Barrio Dent., San Pedro, San Jose, Costa Rica

DHL WORLDWIDE EXPRESS

333 Twin Dolphin Drive, Redwood City, CA, 94065

Tel: (650) 593-7474 Fax: (650) 593-1689 Web site: www.dhl.com

Worldwide air express carrier.

DHL Worldwide Express, Zona Industrial de Pavas, De Ofs. Centrales de Pizza Hut, 500 Mts. Al oeste, San Jose, Costa Rica

Tel: 506-290-3020

DOVER CORPORATION

280 Park Ave., New York, NY, 10017-1292

Tel: (212) 922-1640 Fax: (212) 922-1656 Web site: www.dovercorporation.com

Elevator manufacturer and holding company for varied industries.

COREMSA, Edif. Yale, Carretera Principal, Santa Rosa, Santo Domingo de Heredia, Costa Rica

Tel: 506-244-2828 Fax: 506-244-2226

THE DOW CHEMICAL COMPANY

2030 Dow Center, Midland, MI, 48674

Tel: (517) 636-1000 Fax: (517) 636-3228 Web site: www.atdow.com

Mfr. chemicals, plastics, pharmaceuticals, agricultural products, consumer products.

Dow Quimica de Centro America SA, Aptdo. 10207, San Jose, Costa Rica

DRESSER INDUSTRIES INC.

2001 Ross Ave., PO Box 718, Dallas, TX, 75221-0718

Tel: (214) 740-6000 Fax: (214) 740-6584 Web site: www.dresser.com

Diversified supplier of equipment & technical services to energy & natural resource industrial.

Dresser Industries Inc. - Waukesha Engine Div -, Latin America Reg.Office - De Rest. La Cascada 200 N. 100 Oeste, 10mts Sur Escazu, San José, Costa Rica

Tel: 506-380-1754 Fax: 506-289-8954 Contact: Manuel Chaves

EAGLE ELECTRIC MFG. CO., INC.

45-31 Court Square, Long Island City, NY, 11101

Tel: (718) 937-8000 Fax: (718) 482-0160

Mfr. electrical wiring devices and switchgear.

Eagle Electric of Canada Ltd., 44 Atomic Ave., Etobicoke, ON, Canada M82 5L1, Costa Rica

EATON CORPORATION

1111 Superior Ave., Cleveland, OH, 44114

Tel: (216) 523-5000 Fax: (216) 479-7068

Advanced technical products for transportation & industrial markets.

Cutles Hammes Centro America SA, Aptdo. 10156, San Jose, Costa Rica

EATON CORP/CUTLER HAMMER

4201 North 27th Street, Milwaukee, WI, 53216

Tel: (414) 449-6000 Fax: (414) 449-6221

Electric control apparatus, mfr. of advanced technologic products.

Eaton Controles Industriales SA, Apartado 10156-1000, San Jose, Costa Rica

ECOLAB INC.

Ecolab Center, 370 N. Wabasha Street, St. Paul, MN, 55102

Tel: (612) 293-2233 Fax: (612) 225-3105 Web site: www.ecolab.com

Develop/mfr. premium cleaning, sanitizing and maintenance products and services for the hospitality, institutional, and residential markets.

Ecolab Ltd., San Jose, Costa Rica

Tel: 506-438-1725

J.D. EDWARDS & COMPANY

One Technology Way, Denver, CO, 80237

Tel: (303) 334-4000 Fax: (303) 334-4970 Web site: www.jdedwards.com.

Computer software products.

The Premier Group, 100 E., 100 S. del Colegio de Medicos, Barrio La Salle, Sabana Sur, San Jose, Costa Rica

Tel: 506-290-7494 Fax: 506-290-2698

EFCO

1800 NE Broadway Ave., Des Moines, IA, 50316-0386

Tel: (515) 266-1141 Fax: (515) 266-7970

Mfr. systems for concrete construction.

EFCO, Urb. Los Rosales, Sabanilla, San Jose, Costa Rica

ERNST & YOUNG, LLP

787 Seventh Ave., New York, NY, 10019

Tel: (212) 773-3000 Fax: (212) 773-6350 Web site: www.eyi.com

Accounting and audit, tax and management consulting services.

Marin, Mendez & Co., Apdo. Postal 3301-1000, San Jose, Costa Rica

Tel: 506-257-23-27 Fax: 506-233-53-51 Contact: Mario Marin

FEDERAL-MOGUL CORPORATION

26555 Northwestern Highway, PO Box 1966, Southfield, MI, 48034

Tel: (248) 354-7700 Fax: (248) 354-8983 Web site: www.federalmogul.com

Mfr./distributor precision parts for automobiles, trucks, farm and construction vehicles.

Federal-Mogul de Costa Rica SA, San Jose, Costa Rica

FRITZ COMPANIES INC.

706 Mission Street, Ste. 900, San Francisco, CA, 94103

Tel: (415) 904-8360 Fax: (415) 904-8661 Web site: www.fritz.com

Integrated transportation, sourcing, distribution & customs brokerage services.

Fritz Companies Inc., San Jose, Costa Rica

H.B. FULLER COMPANY

1200 Willow Lake Blvd., Vadnais Heights, MN, 55110

Tel: (612) 236-5900 Fax: (612) 236-5898 Web site: www.hbfuller.com

Mfr./distributor adhesives, sealants, coatings, paints, waxes, sanitation chemicals.

H.B. Fuller - Latin America, 225 metros al oeste de LACSA, La Uruca, PO Box 4178 - 1000, San Jose, Costa Rica

Tel: 506-290-1142 Fax: 506-290-1143

Kativo Chemical Industries SA, 225 metros al oeste de LACSA, La Uruca, PO Box 4178 - 1000, San Jose, Costa Rica (Locations: Centro Colon)

Tel: 506-290-2222 Fax: 506-231-0229

GERBER PRODUCTS COMPANY

445 State Street, Fremont, MI, 49412

Tel: (616) 928-2000 Fax: (616) 928-2723

Mfr./distributor baby food and related products.

Productos Gerber de Centroamerica SA, Aptdo. 1811, San Jose, Costa Rica

THE GILLETTE COMPANY

Prudential Tower Building, Boston, MA, 02199

Tel: (617) 421-7000 Fax: (617) 421-7123 Web site: www.gillette.com

Develop/mfr. personal care/use products: blades & razors, toiletries, cosmetics, stationery.

Gillette de Costa Rica SA, Colimba de Tibas, Costa Rica

Laboratorios Oral-B de Centro America SA, Costa Rica

GREY ADVERTISING INC.

777 Third Ave., New York, NY, 10017

Tel: (212) 546-2000 Fax: (212) 546-1495 Web site: www.giworldwwide.com

International advertising agency.

Jimenez, Blanco & Quiros, San Jose, Costa Rica

GRIFFITH LABORATORIES INC

One Griffith Center, Alsip, IL, 60658

Tel: (708) 371-0900 Fax: (708) 597-3294 Web site: www.griffithlabs.com

Industrial food ingredients and equipment.

Laboratorios Griffith de Centro America SA, Aptdo. 7-2820, 1000 San Jose, Costa Rica

Tel: 506-239-0385 Fax: 506-239-1942

GTE DIRECTORIES CORPORATION

2200 West Airfield Drive, DFW Airport, TX, 75261-9810

Tel: (972) 453-7000 Fax: (972) 453-7573

Publishing telephone directories.

Compania General de Directorios Telefonicos, Aptdo. 5932, San Jose, Costa Rica

HALLIBURTON COMPANY

500 North Akard Street, Ste. 3600, Dallas, TX, 75201-3391

Tel: (214) 978-2600 Fax: (214) 978-2685 Web site: www.halliburton.com

Energy, construction and insurance.

Halliburton Ltd., De Tega 700 mts. Al Oeste Del Parue, 150 mts. Al Sur Casa No. 77, Trejos, Monte Alegre, Escazu, Costa Rica

Tel: 506-289-7480 Fax: 506-289-7480

HARCOURT BRACE & COMPANY

6277 Sea Harbor Drive, Orlando, FL, 32887

Tel: (407) 345-2000 Fax: (407) 345-9354

Book publishing, tests and related service, journals, facsimile reprints, management consult, operates parks/shows.

Harcourt Brace Costa Rica, Urbanizacion La Florita Casa n. 21, Calle Fallas, Desamparados, San Jose, Costa Rica

Tel: 506-259-3675

THE HARPER GROUP

260 Townsend Street, San Francisco, CA, 94107-1719

Tel: (415) 978-0600 Fax: (415) 978-0692 Web site: www.circleintl.com

Ocean/air freight forwarding, customs brokerage, packing and wholesale, logistics management and insurance.

Mudanzas Mundiales (Costa Rica) S.A., 125 MTS Este de la Republic Tobacco, Radial Zapote, PO Box 6540-1000, San Jose, Costa Rica

Tel: 506-224-2525 Fax: 506-253-3390

HOCKMAN-LEWIS LTD

200 Executive Drive, Ste. 320, West Orange, NJ, 07052

Tel: (973) 325-3838 Fax: (973) 325-7974

Export management.

Equigas de Costa Rica SA, Apartado 119-1150, San Jose, Costa Rica

IBM CORPORATION

New Orchard Road, Armonk, NY, 10504

Tel: (914) 765-1900 Fax: (914) 765-7382 Web site: www.ibm.com

Information products, technology & services.

IBM de Costa Rica SA, San Jose, Costa Rica

INFONET SERVICES CORPORATION

2100 East Grand Ave., El Segundo, CA, 90245

Tel: (310) 335-2600 Fax: (310) 335-4507 Web site: www.infonet.com

Provider of Internet services and electronic messaging services.

Infonet Costa Rica, Avenues Central y Segunga, Calle 41, Barrios Los Yoses - San Pedro, San José, Costa Rica

Tel: 506-224-3434 Fax: 506-253-1496

IRRIDELCO INTERNATIONAL CORPORATION

440 Sylvan Ave., Englewood Cliffs, NJ, 07632

Tel: (201) 569-3030 Fax: (201) 569-9237 Web site: www.irridelco.com

Mfr./distributor of the most comprehensive lines of mechanical and micro irrigation; pumps and irrigation systems.

IDC Colombia, Sabanilla de Montes de Oca, San Jose, Costa Rica

Tel: 506-286-0793 Fax: 506-273-3161 Contact: Eduardo Leiva

ITT SHERATON CORPORATION

60 State Street, Boston, MA, 02108

Tel: (617) 367-3600 Fax: (617) 367-5676

Hotel operations.

Sheraton Herradura Hotel & Spa, Aptdo. 7-1880, Ciudad Cariari, San Jose, Costa Rica

J. WALTER THOMPSON COMPANY

466 Lexington Ave., New York, NY, 10017

Tel: (212) 210-7000 Fax: (212) 210-6944 Web site: www.jwt.com

International advertising and marketing services.

APCU Costa Rica, San Jose, Costa Rica

JOHNSON & JOHNSON

One Johnson & Johnson Plaza, New Brunswick, NJ, 08933

Tel: (732) 524-0400 Fax: (732) 214-0334 Web site: www.jnj.com

Mfr./distributor/R&D pharmaceutical, health care and cosmetic products.

Johnson & Johnson de Costa Rica SA, Aptdo. Postal 72-4005, San Antonio de Belen, Heredia, Costa Rica

S C JOHNSON & SON INC.

1525 Howe Street, Racine, WI, 53403

Tel: (414) 260-2000 Fax: (414) 260-2133 Web site: www.scjohnsonwax.com

Home, auto, commercial and personal care products and specialty chemicals.

S.C. Johnson de Centroamerica SA, Aptdo. 4971, 1000 San Jose, Costa Rica

KIMBERLY-CLARK CORPORATION

351 Phelps Drive, Irving, TX, 75038

Tel: (972) 281-1200 Fax: (972) 281-1435 Web site: www.kimberly-clark.com.

Mfr./sales/distribution of consumer tissue, household and personal care products.

Kimberly-Clark Co. de Costa Rica SA, Cartago, Costa Rica

Kimberly-Clark Corporation, San Jose, Costa Rica

KPMG PEAT MARWICK LLP

Three Chestnut Ridge Road, Montvale, NJ, 07645

Tel: (201) 307-7000 Fax: (201) 930-8617 Web site: www.kpmg.com

Accounting and audit, tax and management consulting services.

KPMG Peat Marwick, Amcham Plaza Bldg., Second Fl., 7 Ave., Sabana Norte, San Jose, Costa Rica

Tel: 506-220-1366 Fax: 506-220-0408 Contact: Federico A. Golcher, Sr. Ptnr.

LANIER WORLDWIDE, INC.

2300 Parklake Drive, N.E., Atlanta, GA, 30345

Tel: (770) 496-9500 Fax: (770) 621-1535

Specialize in digital copiers and multi-functional systems.

Lanier de Costa Rica, S.A., Costa Rica - Mail to US: Unit C-101, 1601 NW 97th Ave., PO Box 25216, Miami, FL 33102-5216

LOCTITE CORPORATION

10 Columbus Boulevard, Hartford, CT, 06106

Tel: (203) 520-5000 Fax: (203) 520-5073 Web site: www.loctite.com

Mfr./sale industrial adhesives and sealants.

Loctite de Costa Rica SA, Aptdo. 7, 1007 Centro Colon, San Jose, Costa Rica

Tel: 506-232-2033 Fax: 506-232-6859 Contact: Lic Ruben Carmona Astorga, Mgr.

MAIDENFORM INC.

200 Madison Ave., New York, NY, 10016

Tel: (212) 592-0700 Fax: (212) 686-2087

Mfr. intimate apparel.

Betex SA, Aptdo. 197-2110, Ipis, Guadalupe, Costa Rica

MARRIOTT INTERNATIONAL INC.

1 Marriott Drive, Washington, DC, 20058

Tel: (301) 380-3000 Fax: (301) 380-5181

Lodging, contract food and beverage service, and restaurants.

Costa Rica Marriott Hotel, San Jose, Costa Rica

Tel: 506-298-0000

McCANN-ERICKSON WORLDWIDE

750 Third Ave., New York, NY, 10017

Tel: (212) 984-3644 Fax: (212) 984-2629

International advertising/marketing services.

McCann-Erickson Centroamericana (Costa Rica) Ltda., Autopista General Canas, Contiquo Canal 6, Aptdo. 4505, San Jose, Costa Rica

MERCK & COMPANY, INC.

1 Merck Drive, Whitehouse Station, NJ, 08889

Tel: (908) 423-1000 Fax: (908) 423-2592

Pharmaceuticals, chemicals and biologicals.

Merck, Sharp & Dohme (IA) Corp., Aptdo. 10135, San Jose, Costa Rica

MICROSOFT CORPORATION

One Microsoft Way, Redmond, WA, 98052-6399

Tel: (425) 882-8080 Fax: (425) 936-7329 Web site: www.microsoft.com

Computer software, peripherals and services.

Microsoft de Centroamerica S.A., Costa Rica

MOTOROLA, INC.

1303 East Algonquin Road, Schaumburg, IL, 60196

Tel: (847) 576-5000 Fax: (847) 538-5191 Web site: www.mot.com

Mfr. communications equipment, semiconductors and cellular phones.

Motorola de Centro America SA, Calle Blancos, 1 KM al Este de 6 Esquinas de Tibas, San Jose, Costa Rica

Tel: 506-240-7070 Fax: 506-235-0670

NATIONAL STARCH & CHEMICAL COMPANY

10 Finderne Ave., Bridgewater, NJ, 08807-3300

Tel: (908) 685-5000 Fax: (908) 685-5005 Web site: www.national starch.com

Mfr. adhesives & sealants, resins & specialty chemicals, electronic materials & adhesives, food products, industry starch.

National Starch & Chemical CA, Edif. Agencias Kabat 2, piso, 100 Norte y 225 Este del ICE la Sabana, Costa Rica

Tel: 506-296-8020 Fax: 506-296-8021

OGILVY & MATHER WORLDWIDE

309 West 49th Street, New York, NY, 10019

Tel: (212) 237-4000 Fax: (212) 237-5123

Advertising, marketing, public relations & consulting firm.

Modernoble Publicidad (O&M), San Jose, Costa Rica

PADCO INC.

2220 Elm Street SE, Minneapolis, MN, 55414

Tel: (612) 378-7270 Fax: (612) 378-9388

Mfr. paint sundries.

Padco SA, Parque Industrial Zona Franca, Bodega 35, Apartado 42-7042, Cartago, Costa Rica

THE PERKIN-ELMER CORPORATION

761 Main Ave., Norwalk, CT, 06859-0001

Tel: (203) 762-1000 Fax: (203) 762-4228 Web site: www.perkin-elmer.com

Leading supplier of systems for life science research and related applications.

Analitica de Centro America, SA, Aptdo Postal 5535-1000, Costa Rica

Tel: 506-220-0600 Fax: 506-231-0678 Contact: Javier Vargas, Gen. Mgr.

PFIZER INC.

235 East 42nd Street, New York, NY, 10017-5755

Tel: (212) 573-2323 Fax: (212) 573-7851 Web site: www.pfizer.com

Research-based, global health care company.

Deknatel SA, Costa Rica

Pfizer SA, Costa Rica

PHELPS DODGE CORPORATION

2600 North Central Ave., Phoenix, AZ, 85004-3089

Tel: (602) 234-8100 Fax: (602) 234-8337

Copper, minerals, metals & spec engineered products for transportation & electrical markets.

Conducen SA (COCESA), Autopista General Canas Km. 11.5, Heredia, Costa Rica

PHILLIPS PETROLEUM COMPANY

Phillips Building, 411 S. Keeler Ave., Bartlesville, OK, 74004

Tel: (918) 661-6600 Fax: (918) 661-7636 Web site: www.phillips66.com

Crude oil, natural gas, liquified petroleum gas, gasoline and petro-chemicals.

Phillips Productos Plasticos SA, Aptdo. 271, San Jose, Costa Rica

PRICEWATERHOUSECOOPERS LLP

1251 Ave. of the Americas, New York, NY, 10020

Tel: (212) 596-7000 Fax: (212) 790-6620 Web site: www.pwcglobal.com

Accounting and auditing, tax and management, and human resource consulting services.

Price Waterhouse Ltd./Interamericas Office, Edif. Adriatico, 3rd Fl., Barrio Dent, Apartado 2594-1000, San Jose, Costa Rica

Tel: 506-224-15-55 Fax: 506-253-40-53

PROCTER & GAMBLE COMPANY

One Procter & Gamble Plaza, Cincinnati, OH, 45202

Tel: (513) 983-1100 Fax: (513) 562-4500 Web site: www.pg.com

Personal care, food, laundry, cleaning and industry products.

P&G Costa Rica, Barrio Dent A 100 Mts., San Pedro, Costa Rica

RELIABILITY INC.

PO Box 218370, Houston, TX, 77218-8370

Tel: (281) 492-0550 Fax: (281) 492-0615

Mfr. burn-in/memory test systems, DC/DC converters.

RICR de Costa Rica, Apartado 1-3006, Zona Franca Metropolitana, Barreal, Heredia, Costa Rica

RIVIANA FOODS INC.

2777 Allen Parkway, Houston, TX, 77019

Tel: (713) 529-3251 Fax: (713) 529-1661

Rice & rice by-products & pet foods.

Pozuelo SA, San Jose, Costa Rica (All mail to: Mail Stop SJO 454, PO Box 025216, Miami, FL 33102-5216)

RJR NABISCO INC.

1301 Ave. of the Americas, New York, NY, 10019

Tel: (212) 258-5600 Fax: (212) 969-9173 Web site: www.rjrnabisco.com

Mfr. consumer packaged food products & tobacco products.

Nabisco Royal Inc., Urbanizacion Industrial Rohrmoser, Del Centro Comercial del Oeste, 200 m al sur, Pavas, San Jose, Costa Rica

ROHM AND HAAS COMPANY

100 Independence Mall West, Philadelphia, PA, 19106

Tel: (215) 592-3000 Fax: (215) 592-3377 Web site: www.rohmhaas.com

Mfr. industrial & agricultural chemicals, plastics.

Rohm and Haas Centro America SA (ROHACA), Oficentro Ejecutivo La Sabana, Edif. 2, Primer piso, Sabana Sur, San Jose, Costa Rica

Tel: 506-220-4725

SEA-LAND SERVICE INC.

6000 Carnegie Boulevard, Charlotte, NC, 28209

Tel: (704) 571-2000 Fax: (704) 571-4693 Web site: www.sealand.com

Largest U.S-based containerized transport service; ships, railroads, barge lines and trucking operations.

Colina & Cia. SA, Aptdo. 10259, San Jose, Costa Rica

Sea-Land Service Inc., Aptdo. 10259, San Jose, Costa Rica

G.D. SEARLE & COMPANY

5200 Old Orchard Road, Skokie, IL, 60077

Tel: (847) 982-7000 Fax: (847) 470-1480 Web site: www.searlehealthnet.com

Mfr. pharmaceuticals, health care, optical products and specialty chemicals.

Searle, Division of Monsanto de Costa Rica, Del Colegio de Medicos, 100 Mts. Este Y 75 Mts. Sur, Calle Lang, Sabana Sur, San Jose, Costa Rica, C.A.

Tel: 506-32-5868 Fax: 506-32-7529

STONE CONTAINER CORPORATION

150 N. Michigan Ave., Chicago, IL, 60601-7568

Tel: (312) 346-6600 Fax: (312) 580-3486 Web site: www.stonecontainer.com

Mfr. paper and paper packaging.

Stone Container Corporation, Palmer Norte, Costa Rica

TEXACO INC.

2000 Westchester Ave., White Plains, NY, 10650

Tel: (914) 253-4000 Fax: (914) 253-7753 Web site: www.texaco.com

Exploration/marketing crude oil, mfr. petro chemicals and products.

Texaco Caribbean Inc., Aptdo. 10090, San Jose, Costa Rica

THERMADYNE INDUSTRIES INC.

101 South Hanley Road, #300, St. Louis, MO, 63105

Tel: (314) 746-2197 Fax: (314) 746-2349 Web site: www.thermadyne.com

Mfr. welding, cutting, and safety products.

Thermadyne-Central America/Caribbean, San José, Costa Rica

Tel: 506-383-2578

TRUE NORTH COMMUNICATIONS INC.

101 East Erie Street, Chicago, IL, 60611

Tel: (312) 425-6000 Fax: (312) 425-6350

Holding company, advertising agency.

FCB de Costa Roca SA, De la Pops en la Sabana, 300 mts. Oeste 100 Sur y 100 Este, Apartado 120-1009 Fecosa, San Jose, Costa Rica

UNION CARBIDE CORPORATION

39 Old Ridgebury Road, Danbury, CT, 06817

Tel: (203) 794-2000 Fax: (203) 794-6269 Web site: www.unioncarbide.com

Mfr. industrial chemicals, plastics and resins.

Union Carbide Inter-America Inc., Aptdo. 4364-1000, Edif. Yolanda, San Jose, Costa Rica

UNITED PARCEL SERVICE OF AMERICA, INC.

55 Glenlake Parkway, NE, Atlanta, GA, 30328

Tel: (404) 828-6000 Fax: (404) 828-6593 Web site: www.ups.com

International package-delivery service.

UPS / Union Pak de Costa Rica, S.A., Edif. United Parcel Service, Av. 3 Entre Calle 30 y 32, San Jose, Costa Rica

Tel: 506-257-7447 Fax: 506-257-5343

UNIVERSAL FOODS CORPORATION

433 E. Michigan Street, Milwaukee, WI, 53202

Tel: (414) 271-6755 Fax: (414) 347-4783

Mfr. food products & food ingredients.

Universal Foods Products Intl. Ltd., Calle 1, Avdas. 1/3, Apartado 1670, San Jose, Costa Rica

WACKENHUT CORPORATION

4200 Wackenhut Drive, Ste. 100, Palm Beach Gardens, FL, 33410

Tel: (561) 622-5656 Fax: (561) 691-6736 Web site: www.wackenhut.com

Security systems & services.

Wackenhut S.A., Aptdo. 923, Escazu, San Jose, Costa Rica

Tel: 506-223-8064 Fax: 506-233-8516

WARNACO INC.

90 Park Ave., New York, NY, 10016

Tel: (212) 661-1300 Fax: (212) 687-0480 Web site: www.warnaco.com

Mfr./sales intimate apparel and men's and women's sportswear.

Warnaco, San Jose, Costa Rica

XEROX CORPORATION

800 Long Ridge Road, PO Box 1600, Stamford, CT, 06904

Tel: (203) 968-3000 Fax: (203) 968-4312 Web site: www.xerox.com

Mfr. document processing equipment, systems and supplies.

Xerox de Costa Rica, S.A.., 400 Metros Sur Y 75 Al Oeste, Zona Industrial De Pavas, Apt. 10098, 1000, San Jose, Costa Rica

Tel: 506-220-1033 Fax: 506-231-4867

YOUNG & RUBICAM INC.

285 Madison Ave., New York, NY, 10017

Tel: (212) 210-3000 Fax: (212) 370-3796 Web site: www.yr.com

Advertising, public relations, direct marketing and sales promotion, corporate & product ID management.

Asesores/Young & Rubicam, San Jose, Costa Rica

Croatia

AMP INC.

470 Friendship Road, PO Box 3608, Harrisburg, PA, 17105-3608
Tel: (717) 564-0100 Fax: (717) 780-6130
Develop/mfr. electronic & electrical connection products & systems.
AMP Croatia, Zagreb, Croatia
Tel: 385-41-67-04-46

ARTHUR ANDERSEN & COMPANY

33 West Monroe Street, Chicago, IL, 60603
Tel: (312) 372-7100 Fax: (312) 507-0123 Web site: www.arthurandersen.com
Accounting & audit, tax & management consulting services.
Arthur Andersen d.o.o.Zagreb,, Mesnicka 7, 10000 Zagreb, Croatia
Tel: 385-41-426-523

AVON PRODUCTS INC.

1345 Ave. of the Americas, New York, NY, 10105-0196
Tel: (212) 282-5000 Fax: (212) 282-6049 Web site: www.avon.com
Mfr./distributor beauty & related products, fashion jewelry, gifts & collectibles.
Avon-kozmetika d.o.o., Bijenika cesta 33A, 10000 Zagreb, Croatia
Tel: 385-4680-342 Fax: 385-4680-343

BATES WORLDWIDE INC.

405 Lexington Ave., New York, NY, 10174
Tel: (212) 297-7000 Fax: (212) 986-0270 Web site: www.batesww.com
Advertising, marketing, public relations & media consulting.
S Team Bates Saatchi & Saatchi Advertising, 26, Jadriceva St., 41000 Zagreb, Croatia
Tel: 385-1-482-2797 Fax: 385-1-482-2797 Contact: D. Sakan

BBDO WORLDWIDE

1285 Ave. of the Americas, New York, NY, 10019
Tel: (212) 459-5000 Fax: (212) 459-6645 Web site: www.bbdo.com
Multinational group of advertising agencies.
BBDO Zagreb, Zagreb, Croatia

BUDGET RENT A CAR CORPORATION

4225 Naperville Road, Lisle, IL, 60532
Tel: (630) 955-1900 Fax: (630) 955-7799 Web site: www.budgetrentacar.com
Car and truck rental system.
Budget Rent A Car, Kneza Trpimira 127, Trogir 58220, Croatia
Tel: 385-21881989

DELTA AIR LINES INC.

PO Box 20706, Atlanta, GA, 30320-6001
Tel: (404) 715-2600 Fax: (404) 715-5494 Web site: www.delta-air.com/index.html
Major worldwide airline; international air transport services.
Delta Air Lines Inc., Zagreb, Croatia

DHL WORLDWIDE EXPRESS

333 Twin Dolphin Drive, Redwood City, CA, 94065

Tel: (650) 593-7474 Fax: (650) 593-1689 Web site: www.dhl.com

Worldwide air express carrier.

DHL Worldwide Express, Planinska bb, Zagreb 10000, Croatia

Tel: 385-41-652-9219

GREY ADVERTISING INC.

777 Third Ave., New York, NY, 10017

Tel: (212) 546-2000 Fax: (212) 546-1495 Web site: www.giworldwwide.com

International advertising agency.

Grey Zagrab, Zagreb, Croatia

HALLIBURTON COMPANY

500 North Akard Street, Ste. 3600, Dallas, TX, 75201-3391

Tel: (214) 978-2600 Fax: (214) 978-2685 Web site: www.halliburton.com

Energy, construction and insurance.

Halliburton Ltd., c/o Miso Alfirevic, Zelengai 31, H-1000 Zagreb, Croatia

Tel: 385-49-232459 Fax: 385-51-445-406

IBM CORPORATION

New Orchard Road, Armonk, NY, 10504

Tel: (914) 765-1900 Fax: (914) 765-7382 Web site: www.ibm.com

Information products, technology & services.

IBM Croatia (Hrvatska), Lastovska ulica 23, 10000 Zagreb, Croatia

Tel: 385-41-6124-500 Fax: 385-41-6111-119

KPMG PEAT MARWICK LLP

Three Chestnut Ridge Road, Montvale, NJ, 07645

Tel: (201) 307-7000 Fax: (201) 930-8617 Web site: www.kpmg.com

Accounting and audit, tax and management consulting services.

KPMG, Vlaska 58/III, Zagreb 10 000, Croatia

ELI LILLY & COMPANY

Lilly Corporate Center, Indianapolis, IN, 46285

Tel: (317) 276-2000 Fax: (317) 277-6579 Web site: www.lilly.com

Mfr. pharmaceuticals and animal health products.

Eli Lilly (Suisse) S.A., Trg D. Petrovica 3/18th Fl., 41000 Zagreb, Croatia

Tel: 385-41-301-659 Fax: 385-41-338-847

LOCTITE CORPORATION

10 Columbus Boulevard, Hartford, CT, 06106

Tel: (203) 520-5000 Fax: (203) 520-5073 Web site: www.loctite.com

Mfr./sale industrial adhesives and sealants.

Henkel Croatia d.o.o., Business Unit Loctite, Savska cesta 118, HR - 10000 Zagreb, Croatia

Tel: 385-41-6191-662 Fax: 385-41-6191-663 Contact: Igor Pureta, Mgr.

McCANN-ERICKSON WORLDWIDE

750 Third Ave., New York, NY, 10017

Tel: (212) 984-3644 Fax: (212) 984-2629

International advertising/marketing services.

McCann-Erickson Croatia, Zagreb, Croatia

McDONALD'S CORPORATION

Kroc Drive, Oak Brook, IL, 60523

Tel: (630) 623-3000 Fax: (630) 623-7409

Fast food chain stores.

McDonald's Corp., Zagreb, Croatia

Contact: Alan Perl, Mgr.

MICROSOFT CORPORATION

One Microsoft Way, Redmond, WA, 98052-6399

Tel: (425) 882-8080 Fax: (425) 936-7329 Web site: www.microsoft.com

Computer software, peripherals and services.

Microsoft Hrvatska d.o.o., Croatia

THE PERKIN-ELMER CORPORATION

761 Main Ave., Norwalk, CT, 06859-0001

Tel: (203) 762-1000 Fax: (203) 762-4228 Web site: www.perkin-elmer.com

Leading supplier of systems for life science research and related applications.

Perkin-Elmer, Zagreb, Croatia

Tel: 385-41-191-838 Fax: 385-41-191-840

PHARMACIA & UPJOHN

95 Corporate Drive, PO Box 6995, Bridgewater, NJ, 08807

Tel: (908) 306-4400 Fax: (908) 306-4433 Web site: www.pnu.com

Mfr. pharmaceuticals, agricultural products, industry chemicals

Pharmacia & Upjohn, Srbrnjak 129/C, 10000 Zagreb, Croatia

PRAXAIR, INC.

39 Old Ridgebury Road, Danbury, CT, 06810-5113

Tel: (203) 837-2000 Fax: (203) 837-2450 Web site: www.praxair.com

Produces and distributes industrial and specialty gases.

Montkemija, Senjska cesta b.b., HR-51222 Bakar, Croatia

Tel: 385-5176-1466 Fax: 385-5176-1175

PROCTER & GAMBLE COMPANY

One Procter & Gamble Plaza, Cincinnati, OH, 45202

Tel: (513) 983-1100 Fax: (513) 562-4500 Web site: www.pg.com

Personal care, food, laundry, cleaning and industry products.

Procter & Gamble KTT, Zagreb, Croatia

RONALD E. LAIS, INC.

136 South Imperial Highway, Anaheim, CA, 92807-3943

Tel: (714) 937-1700 Fax: (714) 937-1900

International law firm.

Ronald E. Lais, Inc., Dordijiceva 6, 1000, Zagreb, Croatia

TBWA INTERNATIONAL

180 Maiden Lane, New York, NY, 10038

Tel: (212) 804-1000 Fax: (212) 804-1200

International full service advertising agency.

TBWA Zagreb, Zagreb, Croatia

TRANE COMPANY

3600 Pammel Creek Road, La Crosse, WI, 54601

Tel: (608) 787-2000 Fax: (608) 787-4990

Mfr./distributor/service A/C systems and equipment.

Trane DOO Croatia, Fra. Filipa Grabovca 1, 41000 Zagreb, Croatia

UNITED PARCEL SERVICE OF AMERICA, INC.

55 Glenlake Parkway, NE, Atlanta, GA, 30328

Tel: (404) 828-6000 Fax: (404) 828-6593 Web site: www.ups.com

International package-delivery service.

UPS / Intereuropa d.o.o. Zagreb, P.P. 21 Zagreb Airport, 10150 Zagreb, Croatia

Tel: 385-41-660-1089 Fax: 385-41-660-1085

Cyprus

AIR EXPRESS INTERNATIONAL CORPORATION

120 Tokeneke Road, PO Box 1231, Darien, CT, 06820

Tel: (203) 655-7900 Fax: (203) 655-5779 Web site: www.aeilogistics.com

Air freight forwarder.

AEI Cyprus, c/o Christodoulos G. Mavroudis Ltd., Klimentos & Kleomenous St., No. 7, 2nd Fl., 1513 Nicosia, Cyprus

Tel: 357-2-752039 Fax: 357-2-754801

AMERICAN INTERNATIONAL GROUP INC.

70 Pine Street, New York, NY, 10270

Tel: (212) 770-7000 Fax: (212) 509-9705 Web site: www.aig.com

Worldwide insurance and financial services.

American Home Assurance Co., 30 Grivas Dhigenis Ave., PO Box 1745, Nicosia, Cyprus

AON CORPORATION

123 North Wacker Drive, Chicago, IL, 60606

Tel: (312) 701-3000 Fax: (312) 701-3100 Web site: www.aon.com

Insurance brokers worldwide; underwrites accident & health insurance, specialty & professional insurance; & provides risk management consultation.

AON Worldwide / Care - Cyprus, Maximos Court Leontiou St., Limassol, Cyprus

Tel: 357-5-339-990 Fax: 357-5-339-170 Contact: Antoine Khoury

BDO SEIDMAN, LLP

Two Prudential Plaza, 180 N. Stetson Ave., Ste. 2300, Chicago, IL, 60601

Tel: (312) 240-1236 Fax: (312) 240-3329 Web site: www.bdo.com

International accounting & financial consulting firm.

BDO Minas Ioannou, Galaxias Commercial Ctr., 4th Fl., Office 403, 33 Makarios the III Ave., & 36 Ayias Elenis St., Nicosia, Cyprus

Tel: 357-2-440-979 Fax: 357-2-446-308 Contact: Minas Ioannou

LOUIS BERGER INTERNATIONAL INC.

100 Halsted Street, East Orange, NJ, 07019

Tel: (201) 678-1960 Fax: (201) 672-4284 Web site: www.louisberger.com

Consulting engineers, architects, economists & planners.

Louis Berger International Inc., PO Box 2422, Metropolis Bldg., 2nd Fl., 207 Anthenon St., Limassol, Cyprus

Tel: 357-5-454-338 Fax: 357-5-452-959

M.G.Jordanou & Assoc/Louis Berger International Inc., POBox 2422, Karantokis Bldg., 16 Zenas Kanther Bldg., Fl. 6, Office #19, Nicosia, Cyprus

Tel: 357-2-454-338 Fax: 357-2-452-959

BEST WESTERN INTERNATIONAL

6201 North 24th Place, Phoenix, AZ, 85106

Tel: (602) 957-4200 Fax: (602) 957-5740

International hotel chain.

.Pavemar Hotel, Limassol, Cyprus

BUDGET RENT A CAR CORPORATION

4225 Naperville Road, Lisle, IL, 60532

Tel: (630) 955-1900 Fax: (630) 955-7799 Web site: www.budgetrentacar.com

Car and truck rental system.

Budget Rent A Car, 52 Makarious Ave., Larnaca, Cyprus

Tel: 357-4-629170

DDB NEEDHAM WORLDWIDE INC.

437 Madison Ave., New York, NY, 10022

Tel: (212) 415-2000 Fax: (212) 415-3417

Advertising agency.

Pyramis DDB, Nicosia, Cyprus

DELOITTE TOUCHE TOHMATSU INTERNATIONAL

PO Box 820, Wilton, CT, 06897

Tel: (203) 761-3000 Fax: (203) 834-2200 Web site: www.u.s.deloitte.com or www.dtti.com

Accounting, audit, tax and management consulting services.

Deloitte & Touche, (PO Box 7233) 1, Iasonos St., CY6010 Larnaca, Cyprus

Deloitte & Touche, (PO Box 772) 15 Nicodemou Milona St., Zachariades, Cyprus

Deloitte & Touche, (PO Box 3180) Eftapaton Bldg., 256 Makarios Ave., CY3105 Limassol, Cyprus

Saba & Co./Touche Ross, Saba & Co., (PO Box 8550) Hawaii Nicosia Tower, 6th Fl., 41, Themistocles Dervis St., CY-1066 Nicosia, Cyprus

DHL WORLDWIDE EXPRESS

333 Twin Dolphin Drive, Redwood City, CA, 94065

Tel: (650) 593-7474 Fax: (650) 593-1689 Web site: www.dhl.com

Worldwide air express carrier.

DHL Worldwide Express, 13 Acropolis Ave., PO Box 2002, Nicosia, Cyprus

Tel: 357-2-490450

THE DUN & BRADSTREET CORPORATION

One Diamond Hill Road, Murray Hill, NJ, 07974

Tel: (908) 665-5000 Fax: (908) 665-5524 Web site: www.dnbcorp.com

Provides corporate credit, marketing & accounts-receivable management services & publishes credit ratings & financial information.

Moody's Interbank Credit Service Ltd., PO Box 3205, Aranthi Court, 50 Ayias Zonis St., Limassol, Cyprus

ERNST & YOUNG, LLP

787 Seventh Ave., New York, NY, 10019

Tel: (212) 773-3000 Fax: (212) 773-6350 Web site: www.eyi.com

Accounting and audit, tax and management consulting services.

Ernst & Young, Nicolaou Pentadromos Centre, POBox 123, Limassol (205), Cyprus

Tel: 357-5-362580 Fax: 357-5-365174 Contact: Neophytos Neophytou

EXPEDITORS INTERNATIONAL OF WASHINGTON INC.

999 Throd Ave., Ste. 2500, Seattle, WA, 98104

Tel: (206) 674-3400 Fax: (206) 682-9777 Web site: www.expd.com

Air/ocean freight forwarding, customs brokerage, international logistics solutions.

Expeditors International Service Center, PO Box 896, Larnaca, Cyprus

FRITZ COMPANIES INC.

706 Mission Street, Ste. 900, San Francisco, CA, 94103

Tel: (415) 904-8360 Fax: (415) 904-8661 Web site: www.fritz.com

Integrated transportation, sourcing, distribution & customs brokerage services.

Fritz Companies Inc., Larnaca, Cyprus

GRANT THORNTON INTERNATIONAL

800 One Prudential Plaza, 130 E. Randolph Drive, Chicago, IL, 60601-6050

Tel: (312) 856-0001 Fax: (312) 616-7052

Accounting, audit, tax and management consulting services.

Grant Thornton Costouris, Michaelides & Co., 1 Deligeorgi St., PO Box 3907, CY-1687 Nicosia, Cyprus

Tel: 357-2-477124 Fax: 357-2-474844 Contact: George M. Michaelides

THE HARPER GROUP

260 Townsend Street, San Francisco, CA, 94107-1719

Tel: (415) 978-0600 Fax: (415) 978-0692 Web site: www.circleintl.com

Ocean/air freight forwarding, customs brokerage, packing and wholesale, logistics management and insurance.

Orbit International Forwarders, Artemidos Ave., PO Box 896, Larnaca, Cyprus

Tel: 357-4-622-830 Fax: 357-4-622-833

Orbit International Forwarders, 109 Omonia Ave., PO Box 1773, Limassol, Cyprus

Tel: 357-5-346-568 Fax: 357-5-367-537

Orbit International Forwarders, Artemidos Ave., PO Box 896, Larnaca, Cyprus

Tel: 357-4-622-830 Fax: 357-4-622-833

HILTON HOTELS CORPORATION

9336 Civic Center Drive, Beverly Hills, CA, 90210

Tel: (310) 278-4321 Fax: (310) 205-7880

International hotel chain: Hilton International, Vista Hotels and Hilton National Hotels.

Hilton International Hotels, Archbishop Makarios III Ave., CY 1071, Nicosia, Cyprus

HOBART BROTHERS COMPANY

Hobart Square, 600 W Main Street, Troy, OH, 45373-2928

Tel: (937) 332-4000 Fax: (937) 332-5194

Mfr. arc/automatic welding systems, power systems, filler metals.

Hobart Brothers Co., PO Box 5572, Limassol, Cyprus

HORWATH INTERNATIONAL

415 Madison Ave., New York, NY, 10017

Tel: (212) 838-5566 Fax: (212) 838-3636

Public accountants and auditors.

Horwath P. Kalopetrides & Co., 2 Christ. Sozos St., Eiffel Tower, 3rd & 6th Flrs., Nicosia, Cyprus

IBM CORPORATION

New Orchard Road, Armonk, NY, 10504

Tel: (914) 765-1900 Fax: (914) 765-7382 Web site: www.ibm.com

Information products, technology & services.

IBM SEMEA S.p.A. - Cyprus Branch, 42044 Grivas Dighenis Ave., Nicosia, Cyprus

Tel: 357-2-443949 Fax: 357-2-456372

INFORMATION RESOURCES, INC.

150 N. Clinton St., Chicago, IL, 60661

Tel: (312) 726-1221 Fax: (312) 726-0360 Web site: www.infores.com

Provides bar code scanner services for retail sales organizations; processes, analyzes and sells data from the huge database created from these services.

MEMRB International, MEMRB House, 21 Academias Av., POBox 2098, Postal Code 2107, Nicosia, Cyprus

Tel: 357-233-5333 Fax: 357-233-2533

INTERMEC TECHNOLOGIES CORPORATION

6001 36th Ave. West, PO Box 4280, Everett, WA, 98203-9280

Tel: (425) 348-2600 Fax: (425) 355-9551 Web site: www.intermec.com

Mfr./distributor automated data collection systems.

Intermec Middle East/ A.Y. Samara, Sales & Service, 38 Makarios St., Karaouana Court, Flat 5, CY6017 Larnaca, Cyprus

Tel: 357-4-664-596 Fax: 357-4-664-596

INTRACO CORPORATION

530 Stephenson Hwy., Troy, MI, 48083

Tel: (248) 585-6900 Fax: (248) 585-6920

Export management and marketing consultants.

Intech (USA) Ltd., PO Box 3417, Limassol, Cyprus

ITT SHERATON CORPORATION

60 State Street, Boston, MA, 02108

Tel: (617) 367-3600 Fax: (617) 367-5676

Hotel operations.

Limassol Sheraton Resort & Pleasure Harbour, Amathus Ave., PO Box 1064, Limassol, Cyprus

S C JOHNSON & SON INC.

1525 Howe Street, Racine, WI, 53403

Tel: (414) 260-2000 Fax: (414) 260-2133 Web site: www.scjohnsonwax.com

Home, auto, commercial and personal care products and specialty chemicals.

S.C. Johnson & Son Ltd., 8, Preveza St., Etyk Bldg., 2nd Fl., PO Box 3874, Nicosia, Cyprus

KPMG PEAT MARWICK LLP

Three Chestnut Ridge Road, Montvale, NJ, 07645

Tel: (201) 307-7000 Fax: (201) 930-8617 Web site: www.kpmg.com

Accounting and audit, tax and management consulting services.

KPMG Peat Marwick M/L/S, Berengana Bldg., 25 Spyrou Araouzou St., Limassol 3601, Cyprus

KPMG Peat Marwick M/L/S, Atheneon Bldg., 51 Gr. Dhigenis Ave., Paphus, Cyprus

KPMG Peat Marwick M/L/S, 14 1st April St., Office 4, Paralimni, Cyprus

KPMG Peat Marwick M/L/S, 49 Griva Dhigeni, Larnaca, Cyprus

KPMG Peat Marwick Metaxas, Loizides Syrimis, 10 Mnasiadou St., Nicosia, 1502, Cyprus

Tel: 357-2-448700 Fax: 357-2-365336 Contact: Nicos G. Syrimis, Ptnr.

McCANN-ERICKSON WORLDWIDE

750 Third Ave., New York, NY, 10017

Tel: (212) 984-3644 Fax: (212) 984-2629

International advertising/marketing services.

Gremona McCann-Erickson, Nicosia, Cyprus

MOBIL CORPORATION

3225 Gallows Road, Fairfax, VA, 22037-0001

Tel: (703) 846-3000 Fax: (703) 846-4669 Web site: www.mobil.com

Petroleum and gas exploration and refining, mfr. petroleum products, chemicals and petrochemicals.

Mobil Oil Cyprus Ltd., PO Box 1344, Nicosia 151, Cyprus

NCR (NATIONAL CASH REGISTER)

1700 South Patterson Blvd., Dayton, OH, 45479

Tel: (937) 445-5000 Fax: (937) 445-7042 Web site: www.ncr.com

Mfr. automated teller machines and high-performance stationary bar code scanners.

NCR, 80, Limassol Ave., Nicosia, Cyprus

Tel: 357-2-390-170 Fax: 357-2-424-460 Contact: Adonis Papaconstantinou, VP

OGILVY & MATHER WORLDWIDE

309 West 49th Street, New York, NY, 10019

Tel: (212) 237-4000 Fax: (212) 237-5123

Advertising, marketing, public relations & consulting firm.

Ogilvy & Mather, Nicosia, Cyprus

THE PERKIN-ELMER CORPORATION

761 Main Ave., Norwalk, CT, 06859-0001

Tel: (203) 762-1000 Fax: (203) 762-4228 Web site: www.perkin-elmer.com

Leading supplier of systems for life science research and related applications.

Perkin-Elmer, Nicosia, Cyprus

Tel: 357-2-47-4210 Fax: 357-2-45-2732

PRICEWATERHOUSECOOPERS LLP

1251 Ave. of the Americas, New York, NY, 10020

Tel: (212) 596-7000 Fax: (212) 790-6620 Web site: www.pwcglobal.com

Accounting and auditing, tax and management, and human resource consulting services.

Price Waterhouse Ltd., Pissas Bldg., One Michael Michaelides St., (PO Box 1453) Limassol, Cyprus

Tel: 357-5-367204 Fax: 357-5-372294

Price Waterhouse Ltd., Elpa Bldg., 8 Greg Afxentiou Ave., Larnaca, Cyprus

Tel: 357-4-653878 Fax: 357-4-629008

Price Waterhouse Ltd., Xenios Commercial Centre, Arch Makarios III Ave., PO Box 1687, Nicosia, Cyprus

Tel: 357-2-375577 Fax: 357-2-374473

RAYCHEM CORPORATION

300 Constitution Drive, Menlo Park, CA, 94025-1164

Tel: (650) 361-3333 Fax: (650) 361-2108 Web site: www.raychem.com

Develop/mfr./market materials science products for electronics, telecommunications & industry.

Raychem Technologies Ltd., Mernrb House, 21 Akademias Ave., PO Box 582, Nicosia, Cyprus

THE ST. PAUL COMPANIES, INC.

385 Washington Street, St. Paul, MN, 55102

Tel: (612) 310-7911 Fax: (612) 310-8294 Web site: www.stpaul.com

Provides investment, insurance and reinsurance services.

Laiki Insurance Company Ltd., 6 Evgenias & Antoniou Theodotou St., PO Box 2069, CY-1517 Nicosia, Cyprus

SYBASE, INC.

6475 Christie Ave., Emeryville, CA, 94608

Tel: (510) 922-3500 Fax: (510) 922-3210 Web site: www.sybase.com

Design/mfg/distribution of database management systems, software development tools, connectivity products, consulting and technical support services..

Sybase Solutions Ltd., 1 Lambousa St., PO Box 2119, Nicosia, Cyprus

UNITED PARCEL SERVICE OF AMERICA, INC.

55 Glenlake Parkway, NE, Atlanta, GA, 30328

Tel: (404) 828-6000 Fax: (404) 828-6593 Web site: www.ups.com

International package-delivery service.

UPS Cyprus, City Forum, 27 Themistoclis Dervis Str., 1066 Nicosia, Cyprus

Tel: 357-2-360777 Fax: 357-2-361555

WACKENHUT CORPORATION

4200 Wackenhut Drive, Ste. 100, Palm Beach Gardens, FL, 33410

Tel: (561) 622-5656 Fax: (561) 691-6736 Web site: www.wackenhut.com

Security systems & services.

Wackenhut Security Cyprus, 15 Vasili Michaelides St., 162 Engomi, PO Box 7622, Nicosia, Cyprus

Tel: 357-2-472123 Fax: 357-2-477849

WEATHERFORD INTERNATIONAL INC.

5 Post Oak Blvd, Ste. 1760, Houston, TX, 77227-3415

Tel: (713) 287-8400 Fax: (713) 963-9785 Web site: www.weatherford.com

Oilfield services, products & equipment; mfr. marine cranes for oil and gas industry.

Weatherford Intl. Inc., Nicosia, Cyprus

Tel: 357-2-236-5347 Fax: 375-2-276-5473

XEROX CORPORATION

800 Long Ridge Road, PO Box 1600, Stamford, CT, 06904

Tel: (203) 968-3000 Fax: (203) 968-4312 Web site: www.xerox.com

Mfr. document processing equipment, systems and supplies.

Xerographic Systems Ltd.., 8 Michalakis Karaolis St., Nicosia Town Centre Nicosia, Cyprus

Tel: 357-2-245-1211 Fax: 357-2-245-1436

Czech Republic

3COM CORPORATION

5400 Bayfront Plaza, Santa Clara, CA, 95052-8145

Tel: (408) 764-5000 Fax: (408) 764-5001 Web site: www.3com.com

Develop/mfr. computer networking products & systems.

3Com pobocka Praha, Burzovni Palac, Rybna 14, 110 05 Praha 1, Czech Republic

Tel: 420-2-21845-800 Fax: 420-2-21845-811

3M

3M Center, St. Paul, MN, 55144-1000

Tel: (612) 733-1110 Fax: (612) 733-9973 Web site: www.mmm.com

Mfr. diversified products for industry, health care, imaging, communications, transport, safety, consumer, etc.

3M Cesko spol s.r.o., Vyskocilova 1, 140 00 Prague 4, Czech Republic

Tel: 420-2-61-380-111 Fax: 420-2-61-380-110

ACADEMIC PRESS INC.

6277 Sea Harbor Drive, Orlando, FL, 32887

Tel: (407) 345-2000 Fax: (407) 345-8388 Web site: www.academicpress.com

Publisher of educational & scientific books.

Academic Press, Sokolovska 189/968, Prague 9, 19000, Czech republic

Tel: 420-2-68-49349 Fax: 420-602-294-014

AIR EXPRESS INTERNATIONAL CORPORATION

120 Tokeneke Road, PO Box 1231, Darien, CT, 06820

Tel: (203) 655-7900 Fax: (203) 655-5779 Web site: www.aeilogistics.com

Air freight forwarder.

AEI, c/o Cargoplan, Europska 61, Prague 6, Czech Republic

Tel: 420-2-361024 Fax: 420-2-367933

ALAMO RENT A CAR

110 Southeast Sixth Street, Fort Lauderdale, FL, 33301

Tel: (954) 522-0000 Fax: (954) 220-0120 Web site: www.alamo.com

Car rentals.

Alamo Rent A Car, Prague International Airport, Arrival Hall & Hilton Hotel, Prague, Czech Republic

ALTHEIMER & GRAY

10 South Wacker Drive, Ste. 4000, Chicago, IL, 60606-7482

Tel: (312) 715-4000 Fax: (312) 715-4800

International law firm.

Altheimer & Gray, Platnerska 4, 110 00 Prague 1, Czech Republic

Tel: 420-2-2481-2782 Fax: 420-2-2481-0125

AMERICAN APPRAISAL ASSOCIATES INC.

411 E. Wisconsin Ave., Milwaukee, WI, 53202

Tel: (414) 271-7240 Fax: (414) 271-1041

Valuation consulting services.

American Appraisal Ltd., Podolska 50, 147 00 Prague 4, Czech Republic

AMERICAN EXPRESS COMPANY

American Express Tower, World Financial Center, New York, NY, 10285-4765

Tel: (212) 640-2000 Fax: (212) 619-9802 Web site: www.americanexpress.com

Travel, travelers cheques, charge card & financial services.

American Express s.p.o.l., Czech Republic - All inquiries to U.S. address.

AMERICAN STANDARD INC.

One Centennial Ave., Piscataway, NJ, 08855-6820

Tel: (732) 980-3000 Fax: (732) 980-6118

Mfr. heating, plumbing & sanitary equipment, china, earthenware.

Keramicke Zavody Teplice, Teplice, Czech Republic

AMETEK INC.

4 Station Square, Paoli, PA, 19301

Tel: (610) 647-2121 Fax: (610) 296-3412 Web site: www.ametek.com

Mfr. instruments, electric motors & engineered materials.

Ametek Elektromotory s.r.o., ul. Beloveska 318, Nachod 54701, Czech Republic

Tel: 420-441-23877 Fax: 420-44123111

AMMIRATI PURIS LINTAS

One Dag Hammarskjold Plaza, New York, NY, 10017

Tel: (212) 605-8000 Fax: (212) 605-4705 Web site: www.interpublic.com

International advertising agency.

Ammirati Puris Lintas Czech Republic, Zitná 8, 12000 Prague 2, Czech Republic

Tel: 420-2-24993-100 Fax: 420-2-24993-110 Contact: Ladislav Kopecky, CEO

AMP INC.

470 Friendship Road, PO Box 3608, Harrisburg, PA, 17105-3608

Tel: (717) 564-0100 Fax: (717) 780-6130

Develop/mfr. electronic & electrical connection products & systems.

AMP Czech s.r.o., Brno, Czech Republic

Tel: 420-5-4116-2111

ANDERSEN CONSULTING

100 South Wacker Drive, Ste. 1059, Chicago, IL, 60606

Tel: (311) 123-7271 Fax: (312) 507-7965 Web site: www.ac.com

Provides management & technology consulting services.

Andersen Consulting, Jiraskovo nam. 6, 120 00 Prague 2, Czech Republic

Tel: 420-2-2198-4545 Fax: 420-2-2198-4646

AON CORPORATION

123 North Wacker Drive, Chicago, IL, 60606

Tel: (312) 701-3000 Fax: (312) 701-3100 Web site: www.aon.com

Insurance brokers worldwide; underwrites accident & health insurance, specialty & professional insurance; & provides risk management consultation.

AON Ceská Republika spol s.r.o., Karlovo ná mesti 28, Prague 2, Czech Republic

Tel: 420-2-293-009 Fax: 420-2-298-976 Contact: Jitka Bendová

AON Ceská Republika spol s.r.o., Wanklova 4, Brno, Czech Republic

Tel: 420-5-4321-1580 Fax: 420-5-4324-3760 Contact: Zdenék Koêvara

ARTHUR ANDERSEN & COMPANY

33 West Monroe Street, Chicago, IL, 60603

Tel: (312) 372-7100 Fax: (312) 507-0123 Web site: www.arthurandersen.com

Accounting & audit, tax & management consulting services.

Arthur Andersen & Co.GmbH Wirtsehaftsprufungsgesellschaft,, Husova 5, 110 00 Prague 1, Czech Republic

Tel: 420-2-2440-1300 Fax: 420-2-2491-5111

AUTODESK INC.

111 McInnis Parkway, San Rafael, CA, 94903

Tel: (415) 507-5000 Fax: (415) 507-6112 Web site: www.autodesk.com

Develop/marketing/support computer-aided design, engineering, scientific & multimedia software products.

Autodesk s.r.o., Jeseniova 1, 130 00 Praha 3, Czech Republic

Tel: 420-2-2278-0108 Fax: 420-2-2278-2719

AUTOMATIC SWITCH CO. (ASCO)

50-60 Hanover Road, Florham Park, NJ, 07932

Tel: (973) 966-2000 Fax: (973) 966-2628

Mfr. solenoid valves, emergency power controls, pressure & temp. switches.

Asco/Jouco, S.R.O., Udolni 15, C-140 00 Praha 4, Czech Republic

Tel: 420-2-49-53-83 Fax: 420-2-49-52-80 Contact: M. David

AVON PRODUCTS INC.

1345 Ave. of the Americas, New York, NY, 10105-0196

Tel: (212) 282-5000 Fax: (212) 282-6049 Web site: www.avon.com

Mfr./distributor beauty & related products, fashion jewelry, gifts & collectibles.

Avon Cosmetics spol. s r.o., Hellichova 1, 118 00 Pragua 1, Czech Republic

Tel: 420-2-57007-120 Fax: 420-2-57007-121 Contact: Pavel Maier, Sales. Dir.

BAKER & McKENZIE

One Prudential Plaza, 130 East Randolph Drive, Ste. 2500, Chicago, IL, 60601

Tel: (312) 861-8000 Fax: (312) 861-2899 Web site: www.bakerinfo.com

International legal services.

Baker & McKenzie, Celakovskeho sady 4, 120 00 Prague 2, Czech Republic

Tel: 420-2-2422-7330 Fax: 420-2-2422-2124

BANKERS TRUST COMPANY

280 Park Ave., New York, NY, 10017

Tel: (212) 250-2500 Fax: (212) 250-2440 Web site: www.bankerstrust.com

Banking & investment services.

Bankers Trust Company, Rytirska 8, 110 00 Prague 1, Czech Republic

Tel: 420-2-2423-7300 Fax: 420-2-2423-2077 Contact: Valerie Cox-Polaskova

BATES WORLDWIDE INC.

405 Lexington Ave., New York, NY, 10174

Tel: (212) 297-7000 Fax: (212) 986-0270 Web site: www.batesww.com

Advertising, marketing, public relations & media consulting.

Bates Czech & Slovak Republic, Klimontska 52, 110 00 Praha 1, Czech Republic

Tel: 420-2-231-1334 Fax: 420-2-231-3824 Contact: Jana Kuev, CEO

BAXTER HEALTHCARE CORPORATION

One Baxter Parkway, Deerfield, IL, 60015

Tel: (847) 948-2000 Fax: (847) 948-3948 Web site: www.baxter.com

Pharmaceutical preparations, surgical/medical instruments & cardiovascular products.

Baxter CSFR sro, Dobrovskeho c. 20, 170 00 Prague 7, Czech Republic

BBDO WORLDWIDE

1285 Ave. of the Americas, New York, NY, 10019

Tel: (212) 459-5000 Fax: (212) 459-6645 Web site: www.bbdo.com

Multinational group of advertising agencies.

Mark/BBDO, Klimentska 30, 110 00 Prague 1, Czech Republic

BDO SEIDMAN, LLP

Two Prudential Plaza, 180 N. Stetson Ave., Ste. 2300, Chicago, IL, 60601

Tel: (312) 240-1236 Fax: (312) 240-3329 Web site: www.bdo.com

International accounting & financial consulting firm.

BDO CS s.r.o., Kvestorská 2, 140 00 Prague 4, Czech Republic

Tel: 420-2-499-367 Fax: 420-2-499-365 Contact: Vlastimil Hokr

BECKER & POLIAKOFF, P.A.

Emerald Lake Corporate Park, 3111 Stirling Road, Fort Lauderdale, FL, 33312

Tel: (954) 987-7550 Fax: (954) 985-4176

Law firm; advice & assistance with foreign investments.

Becker & Poliakoff, P.A., Zastoupeni V CR, Apolinarska 06, 128 00, Prague 2, Czech Republic

Tel: 420-2-298-005 Fax: 420-2-296-807

BELL ATLANTIC CORPORATION

1095 Ave. of the Americas, New York, NY, 10036

Tel: (212) 395-2121 Fax: (212) 395-1285 Web site: www.bellatlantic.com

Telecommunications.

EuroTel Praha, Prague, Czech Republic

BEST WESTERN INTERNATIONAL

6201 North 24th Place, Phoenix, AZ, 85106

Tel: (602) 957-4200 Fax: (602) 957-5740

International hotel chain.

City Hotel Moran, CZ-120 00 Praha, Czech Republic

BESTFOODS, INC.

700 Sylvan Ave., International Plaza, Englewood Cliffs, NJ, 07632-9976

Tel: (201) 894-4000 Fax: (201) 894-2186 Web site: www.bestfoods.com

Consumer foods products; corn refining.

Bestfoods CZ, a.s., IBC, Pobrezni 3, 186 00 Prague 8, Czech Republic

Tel: 420-2-218-78111 Fax: 420-2-232-3733 Contact: Alex Van den Winckel, Mgr.

BOYDEN CONSULTING CORPORATION

100 Park Ave., 34th Floor, New York, NY, 10017

Tel: (212) 980-6534 Fax: (212) 980-6147 Web site: www.boyden.com

Executive search.

Boyden Associates Ltd., Nekrasova 2, 16000 Prague 6, Czech Republic

Tel: 420-2-24-22-8446

BOZELL WORLDWIDE

40 West 23rd Street, New York, NY, 10010

Tel: (212) 727-5000 Fax: (212) 645-9173 Web site: www.bozell.com

Advertising, marketing, public relations and media consulting.

Avant Bozell, Cechtická 10, 142 00 Praha 4, Czech Republic

Tel: 420-2-471-6841 Fax: 420-2-471-3313 Contact: Svatopluk Benes, Gen. Mgr.

BRISTOL-MYERS SQUIBB COMPANY

345 Park Ave., New York, NY, 10154

Tel: (212) 546-4000 Fax: (212) 546-4020 Web site: www.bms.com

Pharmaceutical and food preparations, medical and surgical instruments.

ConvaTec Czechoslovakia, ConvaTec SPOL SRO, NA Perstyne 2, 11000 Prague 1, Czech Republic

ConvaTec SRO, Lazarska 6, 12000 Prague 6, Czech Republic

Laboratories UPSA, Soukalova 3355, 14300 Prague 4, Prague, Czech Republic

BROBECK PHLEGER & HARRISON

Spear Street Tower, One Market Plaza, San Francisco, CA, 94105

Tel: (415) 442-0900 Fax: (415) 442-1010

International law joint venture.

Brobeck Hale & Dorr International, Prague, Czech Republic

BUDGET RENT A CAR CORPORATION

4225 Naperville Road, Lisle, IL, 60532

Tel: (630) 955-1900 Fax: (630) 955-7799 Web site: www.budgetrentacar.com

Car and truck rental system.

Budget Rent A Car, Stresovicka 49, Prague 6, Czech Republic

Tel: 420-2-206-10095

LEO BURNETT CO., INC.

35 West Wacker Drive, Chicago, IL, 60601

Tel: (312) 220-5959 Fax: (312) 220-6533 Web site: www.leoburnett.com

International advertising agency.

Leo Burnett Advertising, s.r.o., Ceskomalinska 41, 160 00 Prague 6, Czech Republic

Tel: 420-2-323-029 Fax: 420-2-322-981

BURSON-MARSTELLER

230 Park Ave., New York, NY, 10003-1566

Tel: (212) 614-4000 Fax: (212) 614-4262 Web site: www.bm.com

Public relations/public affairs consultants.

Donath/Burson Marsteller CS, Vaclavske Namesti. 21, 110 11 Prague 1, Czech Republic

Tel: 420-2-2421-1220 Fax: 420-2-2421-1620 Emp: 18

CH2M HILL INC.

6060 South Willow Drive, Greenwood Village, CO, 80111

Tel: (303) 771-0900 Fax: (303) 770-2616

Consulting engineers, planners, economists and scientists.

CH2M Hill, Prague, Czech Republic

Tel: 420-2-643-1750

THE CHASE MANHATTAN CORPORATION

World Headquarters, 270 Park Ave., New York, NY, 10017

Tel: (212) 270-6000 Fax: (212) 622-9030 Web site: www.chase.com

International banking and financial services.

The Chase Manhattan Bank, Representative Office, Karlova 27, Male Namesti, 110 01 Praha 1, Czech Republic

Tel: 420-2-2423-4313 Fax: 420-2-2423-4314

CHESTERTON BINSWANGER INTERNATIONAL

Two Logan Square, 4th Floor, Philadelphia, PA, 19103-2759

Tel: (215) 448-6000 Fax: (215) 448-6238

Real estate & related services.

Blumenauer Immobilien, Novotneho Lavka 5, 116 68 Prague 1, Czech Republic

CISCO SYSTEMS, INC.

170 Tasman Drive, San Jose, CA, 95134-1706

Tel: (408) 526-4000 Fax: (408) 526-4100 Web site: www.cisco.com

Develop/mfr./market computer hardware and software networking systems.

Cisco Systems (Czech Republic) s.r.o., U Uranie 18, 170 00 Prague 7, Czech Republic

Tel: 420-2-8387-1300 Fax: 420-2-8387-0300 Contact: N/A

CITICORP

399 Park Ave., New York, NY, 10043

Tel: (212) 559-1000 Fax: (212) 527-2066 Web site: www.citibank.com

International banking and financial services.

Citibank, a.s. Prague, Evropska 178, 166 40 Prague 6, Czech Republic

Tel: 420-2-264-024 Fax: 420-2-316-4793

COMPAQ COMPUTER CORPORATION

20555 State Highway 249, PO Box 692000, Houston, TX, 77269-2000

Tel: (713) 370-0670 Fax: (713) 514-1740 Web site: www.compaq.com

Develop/mfr. personal computers.

Compaq Computer Spol. s.r.o., International Business Ctr., Pobrezni 3, 18600 Prague 8, Czech Republic

Tel: 420-2-232-8772 Fax: 420-2-232-8773

COMPUTER ASSOCIATES INTERNATIONAL INC.

One Computer Associates Plaza, Islandia, NY, 11788

Tel: (516) 342-5224 Fax: (516) 342-5329 Web site: www.cai.com

Integrated software for enterprise computing and information management, application development, manufacturing, financial applications and professional services.

Computer Associates Intl. GmbH, Donska 9, 10000 Praha 10, Czech Republic

Tel: 420-2-67-20-6360

CULLIGAN INTERNATIONAL COMPANY

One Culligan Parkway, Northbrook, IL, 60062

Tel: (847) 205-6000 Fax: (847) 205-6030 Web site: www.culligan-man.com

Water treatment products and services.

Culligan Czech & Slovak Republic, Hdqtrs., Kosinova 59, 612 00 BRNO, Czech Republic

Tel: 420-5-412-17751 Fax: 420-5-4921-1151

D'ARCY MASIUS BENTON & BOWLES INC. (DMB&B)

1675 Broadway, New York, NY, 10019

Tel: (212) 468-3622 Fax: (212) 468-2987 Web site: www.dmbb.com

Full service international advertising and communications group.

D'Arcy Masius Benton & Bowles Prague, Vodickova 36, 116 02 Prague 1, Czech Republic

Tel: 420-2-2422-6641 Fax: 420-2-2421-3715

DDB NEEDHAM WORLDWIDE INC.

437 Madison Ave., New York, NY, 10022

Tel: (212) 415-2000 Fax: (212) 415-3417

Advertising agency.

DDB Needhan Worldwide, Orlicka 9, 130 00 Prague 3, Czech Republic

Tel: 42-2-274-082 Fax: 420-2-274-801

DELL COMPUTER CORPORATION

One Dell Way, Round Rock, TX, 78682-2222

Tel: (512) 338-4400 Fax: (512) 728-3653 Web site: www.dell.com

Direct marketer & supplier of computer systems.

Dell Computer Czech Republic, Osadni 12a, Prague 7, PSC 17000, Czech Republic

Tel: 420-2-879250 Fax: 420-2-808237 Contact: K. Stastny, Mng. Dir.

DELOITTE TOUCHE TOHMATSU INTERNATIONAL

PO Box 820, Wilton, CT, 06897

Tel: (203) 761-3000 Fax: (203) 834-2200 Web site: www.u.s.deloitte.com or www.dtti.com

Accounting, audit, tax and management consulting services.

Deloitte & Touche, Tynska 12/633, 110 00 Prague 1, Czech Republic
Tel: 420-2-2481-1456 Fax: 420-2-232-5700

IDOM a.s., Tynsky dvur 1049/3, Prague 110 00, Czech Republic

DELTA AIR LINES INC.

PO Box 20706, Atlanta, GA, 30320-6001
Tel: (404) 715-2600 Fax: (404) 715-5494 Web site: www.delta-air.com/index.html
Major worldwide airline; international air transport services.

Delta Air Lines Inc., Prague, Czech Republic

DEWEY BALLANTINE LLP

1301 Ave. of the Americas, New York, NY, 10019
Tel: (212) 259-8000 Fax: (212) 259-6333 Web site: www.deweyballantine.com
International law firm.

Dewey Ballantine Theodore Goddard, Revoluci 13, 110 15 Prague, Czech Republic
Tel: 420-2-2481-0283 Fax: 420-2-231-0983

DHL WORLDWIDE EXPRESS

333 Twin Dolphin Drive, Redwood City, CA, 94065
Tel: (650) 593-7474 Fax: (650) 593-1689 Web site: www.dhl.com
Worldwide air express carrier.

DHL Worldwide Express, Bezecka 1, Prague 6, 16900 Czech Republic
Tel: 420-2-2051-1133

DIGITAL EQUIPMENT CORPORATION

111 Powder Mill Road, Maynard, MA, 01754
Tel: (978) 493-5111 Fax: (978) 493-7374 Web site: www.digital.com
Mfr. network computer systems, components, software and services.

Digital Equipment s.r.o., Na Pankraci 26, 140 00 Prague 4, Czech Republic
Tel: 420-2-611-08111 Fax: 420-2-611-08112

DRG INTERNATIONAL INC.

PO Box 1188, Mountainside, NJ, 07092
Tel: (908) 233-2075 Fax: (908) 233-0758
Mfr./sale/service medical devices, diagnostic kits, clinical equipment.

DRG-CR, Sumavska 33, 612 54 Brno, Czech Republic
Tel: 420-5-4123-5326 Fax: 420-5-4123-5326 Contact: Dr. Pavel Giacintov, Gen. Dir.

THE DUN & BRADSTREET CORPORATION

One Diamond Hill Road, Murray Hill, NJ, 07974
Tel: (908) 665-5000 Fax: (908) 665-5524 Web site: www.dnbcorp.com
Provides corporate credit, marketing & accounts-receivable management services & publishes credit ratings & financial information.

Dun & Bradstreet spol s.r.o., Spalena 17, CR-110 00, Prague 1, Czech Republic
Tel: 420-2-24909-111

EASTMAN CHEMICAL

100 North Eastman Road, Kingsport, TN, 37660
Tel: (423) 229-2000 Fax: (423) 229-1351 Web site: www.eastman.com
Mfr. plastics, chemicals, fibers.

Eastman Chemical B.V., Mala Stepanskia 9, 120 00 Praha 2, Czech Republic
Tel: 420-2-2423-9235 Fax: 420-2-295-781 Contact: Marta Kubeckova

ECOLAB INC.

Ecolab Center, 370 N. Wabasha Street, St. Paul, MN, 55102

Tel: (612) 293-2233 Fax: (612) 225-3105 Web site: www.ecolab.com

Develop/mfr. premium cleaning, sanitizing and maintenance products and services for the hospitality, institutional, and residential markets.

Ecolab Ltd., Prague, Czech Republic

Tel: 420-5-4224-0823

J.D. EDWARDS & COMPANY

One Technology Way, Denver, CO, 80237

Tel: (303) 334-4000 Fax: (303) 334-4970 Web site: www.jdedwards.com.

Computer software products.

BSC Praha spol.s.r.o., U Kreskeho nadrazi 36, CZ 140 00 Praha 4-Krc., Czech Republic

Tel: 420-2-617-11589 Fax: 420-2-617-11588

J. D. Edwards & Company, Libus, Czech Republic, BSC Praha, spol.s.r.o., Satrova 807,808, 14200 Praha 4, Libus, Czech Republic

Tel: 420-2-471-0228 Fax: 420-2-471-4125

ERNST & YOUNG, LLP

787 Seventh Ave., New York, NY, 10019

Tel: (212) 773-3000 Fax: (212) 773-6350 Web site: www.eyi.com

Accounting and audit, tax and management consulting services.

Ernst & Young CS Consulting, Vinohradska 184, 130 52 Praha 3, Czech Republic

Tel: 420-2-6713-3010 Fax: 420-2-6713-3012 Contact: Monika Ruprechtova

EURO RSCG Worldwide

350 Hudson Street, New York, NY, 10014

Tel: (212) 886-2000 Fax: (212) 886-2016

International advertising agency group.

Euro RSCG, Prague, Czech Republic

EXCEL INDUSTRIES, INC.

1120 North Main Street, Elkhart, IN, 46514

Tel: (219) 264-2131 Fax: (219) 264-2136 Web site: www.excelinc.com

Mfg. automotive, heavy truck, RV and bus components.

Schade, Czech Republic

FISHER-ROSEMOUNT

8000 Maryland Ave., Ste. 500, Clayton, MO, 63105-4755

Tel: (314) 746-9900 Fax: (314) 746-9974

Mfr. industrial process control equipment.

Fisher Rosemount, s.r.o., V Olsinach 75, 10097 Praha 10, Czech Republic

FRITZ COMPANIES INC.

706 Mission Street, Ste. 900, San Francisco, CA, 94103

Tel: (415) 904-8360 Fax: (415) 904-8661 Web site: www.fritz.com

Integrated transportation, sourcing, distribution & customs brokerage services.

Fritz Companies Inc., Brno, Jablonec, Olomouc & Prague, Czech Republic

GENERAL ELECTRIC CO.

3135 Easton Turnpike, Fairfield, CT, 06431

Tel: (203) 373-2211 Fax: (203) 373-3131 Web site: www.ge.com

Diversified manufacturing, technology and services.

GE FANUC Automation, c/o GE International Inc., Prague 1, CZ 1100, Czech Republic

Tel: 420-2-24408-57479 Fax: 420-2-24401-286

General Electric Co., Czech Republic - All mail to U.S. address; phone (800) 626-2004 or (518) 438-6500

THE GILLETTE COMPANY

Prudential Tower Building, Boston, MA, 02199

Tel: (617) 421-7000 Fax: (617) 421-7123 Web site: www.gillette.com

Develop/mfr. personal care/use products: blades & razors, toiletries, cosmetics, stationery.

Braun k.s., Prague, Czech Republic

GLENAYRE ELECTRONICS LTD.

1 Glenayre Way, Quincy, IL, 62301

Tel: (217) 223-3211 Fax: (217) 223-3284

Mfr. Infrastructure components and pagers.

Glenayre Electronics, Inc., NaPorici 10/V Celnici 5, 110 00 Prague 1, Czech Republic

Tel: 420-2-2481-3584 Fax: 420-2-2481-5777

GRACO INC

4050 Olson Memorial Hwy, PO Box 1441, Minneapolis, MN, 55440-1441

Tel: (612) 623-6000 Fax: (612) 623-6777 Web site: www.graco.com

Mfr./sales of infant & juvenile products; services fluid handling equipment & systems.

AGS Sport spol. S.r.o., Elisky Premyslovyn 433, 156 00 Praha 5, Zbraslav, Czech Republic

Tel: 420-2-4023187 Fax: 420-2-57921158 Contact: Evzen Prusa

GRAHAM & JAMES LLP

One Maritime Plaza - Ste. 300, San Francisco, CA, 94111-3404

Tel: (415) 954-0200 Fax: (415) 391-2493 Web site: www.gj.com

International law firm.

Graham & James/Haarmann Hemmelradt & Partners, Prague, Czech Republic

GRANT THORNTON INTERNATIONAL

800 One Prudential Plaza, 130 E. Randolph Drive, Chicago, IL, 60601-6050

Tel: (312) 856-0001 Fax: (312) 616-7052

Accounting, audit, tax and management consulting services.

Grant Thornton ACI, Melnicka 13, 150 00 Prague 5, Czech Republic

Tel: 420-2-53-2728 Fax: 420-2-53-4044 Contact: Albert Castro

GREY ADVERTISING INC.

777 Third Ave., New York, NY, 10017

Tel: (212) 546-2000 Fax: (212) 546-1495 Web site: www.giworldwwide.com

International advertising agency.

Grey Prague, Opletalova 55, 111 83 Prague, Czech Republic

THE HARPER GROUP

260 Townsend Street, San Francisco, CA, 94107-1719

Tel: (415) 978-0600 Fax: (415) 978-0692 Web site: www.circleintl.com

Ocean/air freight forwarding, customs brokerage, packing and wholesale, logistics management and insurance.

Circle Freight International, Eliasova 38, 160 00 Praha 6, Czech Republic

Tel: 420-2-243-15554 Fax: 420-2-243-13671

HARRIS CORPORATION

1025 West NASA Blvd., Melbourne, FL, 32919

Tel: (407) 727-9100 Fax: (407) 727-9344 Web site: www.harris.com

Mfr. communications and information-handling equipment, including copying and fax systems.

Avnet EMG, E2000 setron s.r.o., Slevacska 744/1, Hloubetin, CZ-19400 Praha 9, Czech Republic

Tel: 420-2-861142 Fax: 420-2-81861442

HEIDRICK & STRUGGLES INC

Sears Tower, 233 South Wacker Drive, Chicago, IL, 60606

Tel: (312) 496-1200 Fax: (312) 496-1290 Web site: www.h-s.com

Executive search firm.

Heidrick & Struggles Intl. Inc., Lazarska St. 5, 110 00 Prague 1, Czech Republic

Tel: 420-2-2423-6591 Fax: 420-2-2423-6591

HELLER FINANCIAL INC.

500 West Monroe Street, Chicago, IL, 60661

Tel: (312) 441-7000 Fax: (312) 441-7256

Financial services.

Heller Financial Inc., Czech Republic

HERCULES INC

Hercules Plaza, 1313 North Market Street, Wilmington, DE, 19894-0001

Tel: (302) 594-5000 Fax: (302) 594-5400 Web site: www.herc.com

Mfr. specialty chemicals, plastics, film and fibers, coatings, resins, food ingredients.

Hercules XZ s.r.o., Prague, Czech Republic

HEWITT ASSOCIATES LLC

100 Half Day Road, Lincolnshire, IL, 60069

Tel: (847) 295-5000 Fax: (847) 295-7634

Employee benefits consulting firm.

Hewitt Associates, Röttig & Rutkowski, Konevova 141, 130000 Prague 3, Czech Republic

Tel: 420-2-67108-239

HEWLETT-PACKARD COMPANY

3000 Hanover Street, Palo Alto, CA, 94304-0890

Tel: (650) 857-1501 Fax: (650) 857-7299 Web site: www.hp.com

Mfr. computing, communications & measurement products & services.

Hewlett-Packard s.r.o., Novodvorska 82, 142 00 Prague 4, Czech Republic

HILTON HOTELS CORPORATION

9336 Civic Center Drive, Beverly Hills, CA, 90210

Tel: (310) 278-4321 Fax: (310) 205-7880

International hotel chain: Hilton International, Vista Hotels and Hilton National Hotels.

Prague Hilton Atrium, Pobrezni 1, 186 00, Praha 8, Czech Republic

HONEYWELL INC.

PO Box 524, Minneapolis, MN, 55440-0524

Tel: (612) 951-1000 Fax: (612) 951-3066 Web site: www.honeywell.com

Develop/mfr. controls for home and building, industry, space and aviation.

Honeywell Ssro., Budejovicka 1, 140 00 Prague 4, Czech Republic

HORWATH INTERNATIONAL

415 Madison Ave., New York, NY, 10017

Tel: (212) 838-5566 Fax: (212) 838-3636

Public accountants and auditors.

IB Interconsult Praha Himmer, Egger spol, Vaclavske Namesti 64, 110 00 Prague 1, Czech Republic

IBM CORPORATION

New Orchard Road, Armonk, NY, 10504

Tel: (914) 765-1900 Fax: (914) 765-7382 Web site: www.ibm.com

Information products, technology & services.

IBM Czech Republic, Murmanska 4/1475, CZ-10500 Prague 10, Czech Republic

Tel: 420-2-7213-1111 Fax: 420-2-7213-1401

INFONET SERVICES CORPORATION

2100 East Grand Ave., El Segundo, CA, 90245

Tel: (310) 335-2600 Fax: (310) 335-4507 Web site: www.infonet.com

Provider of Internet services and electronic messaging services.

Infonet Czech Republic, Aliatel A.S., Administrativni Centrum, Sokolovska 86, Prague 8, CZ-180 00, Czech Republic

Tel: 420-2-83-03-3312 Fax: 420-2-83-03-3322

INFORMIX CORPORATION

4100 Bohannon Drive, Menlo Park, CA, 95025

Tel: (650) 926-6300 Fax: (650) 926-6593 Web site: www.informix.com

Designs & produces database management software, connectivity interfaces & gateways, and other computer applications.

Informix Software SRO, Praha City Center, Klimentska 46, 110 02 Prague 1, Czech Republic

Tel: 420-2-218-57050

INTER-CONTINENTAL HOTELS

1120 Ave. of the Americas, New York, NY, 10036

Tel: (212) 852-6400 Fax: (212) 852-6494 Web site: www.interconti.com

Worldwide hotel and resort accommodations.

Forum Hotel Phaha, Kongresova 1, 140 69 Prague 4, Czech Republic

Tel: 420-2-611-91-111

INTERGRAPH CORPORATION

One Madison Industrial Park, Huntsville, AL, 35894-0001

Tel: (205) 730-2000 Fax: (205) 730-7898 Web site: www.intergraph.com

Develop/mfr. interactive computer graphic systems.

Intergraph CR, Podbabska 20, Praha 6, Prague, Czech Republic 16046

Tel: 420-2-243-11741 Fax: 420-2-243-11742

INTERNATIONAL RECTIFIER CORPORATION

233 Kansas Street, El Segundo, CA, 90245

Tel: (310) 322-3331 Fax: (310) 322-3332 Web site: www.irf.com

Mfr. power semiconductor components.

International Rectifier - Czech Republic, Novodvorská 994, 14221 Prague 4, Bránuk, Czech Republic

Tel: 420-2-476-2822 Fax: 420-2-476-2542

INTERNATIONAL SPECIALTY PRODUCTS

1361 Alps Road, Wayne, NJ, 07470

Tel: (973) 628-4000 Fax: (973) 628-3311 Web site: www.ispcorp.com

Mfr. specialty chemical products.

ISP Czech Republic spol s.r.o., Trebohosticka 2283, 100 00 Prague 10, Czech Republic

Tel: 420-2-707-8332 Fax: 420-2-707-8305

J.P. MORGAN & CO. INC.

60 Wall Street, New York, NY, 10260-0060

Tel: (212) 483-2323 Fax: (212) 648-5209 Web site: www.jpm.com

International banking services.

J.P. Morgan International Ltd., Mala Stupartska 7, 110 11 Praha 1, Czech Republic

Tel: 420-2-2481-3068

J. WALTER THOMPSON COMPANY

466 Lexington Ave., New York, NY, 10017

Tel: (212) 210-7000 Fax: (212) 210-6944 Web site: www.jwt.com

International advertising and marketing services.

Ark Communications/JWT, Prague, Czech Republic

JOHNSON & JOHNSON

One Johnson & Johnson Plaza, New Brunswick, NJ, 08933

Tel: (732) 524-0400 Fax: (732) 214-0334 Web site: www.jnj.com

Mfr./distributor/R&D pharmaceutical, health care and cosmetic products.

Johnson & Johnson spol. s.r.o., Prague, Czech Republic

S C JOHNSON & SON INC.

1525 Howe Street, Racine, WI, 53403

Tel: (414) 260-2000 Fax: (414) 260-2133 Web site: www.scjohnsonwax.com

Home, auto, commercial and personal care products and specialty chemicals.

S.C. Johnson SRO, Na Kozacce 1/869, 120 22 Prague 2, Czech Republic

JOHNSON CONTROLS INC.

5757 N. Green Bay Ave., PO Box 591, Milwaukee, WI, 53201-0591

Tel: (414) 228-1200 Fax: Web site: www.johnsoncontrols.com

Mfr. facility management & control systems, auto seating, & batteries..

Johnson Controls International spol. S.R.O., Budejoviká 5, 140 00 Praha 4, Czech Republic

Tel: 420-2-61213021 Fax: 420-2-61213023 Contact: Josef Kalina, Gen. Mgr.

JONES LANG WOOTTON

101 East 52nd Street, New York, NY, 10022

Tel: (212) 688-8181 Fax: (212) 308-5199

International marketing consultants, leasing agents and property management advisors.

Jones Lang Wootton, Czech Republic

A.T. KEARNEY INC.

222 West Adams Street, Chicago, IL, 60606

Tel: (312) 648-0111 Fax: (312) 223-6200 Web site: www.atkearney.com

Management consultants and executive search.

A. T. Kearney GmbH, Ovocny trh 8, 110 00 Praha 1, Czech Republic

Tel: 420-2-22-120-111

KENNAMETAL INC.

State Rte. 981, Latrobe, PA, 15650

Tel: (724) 539-5000 Fax: (724) 539-4710 Web site: www.kennametal.com

Tools, hard carbide & tungsten alloys for metalworking industry.

V.H.S.M., 100 10 Praha 10, Czech Republic

Tel: 420-2-67-15-5155 Fax: 420-2-67-15-5155

KIMBERLY-CLARK CORPORATION

351 Phelps Drive, Irving, TX, 75038

Tel: (972) 281-1200 Fax: (972) 281-1435 Web site: www.kimberly-clark.com.

Mfr./sales/distribution of consumer tissue, household and personal care products.

Kimberly-Clark Corp., Jaromer, Czech Republic

Kimberly-Clark Corp., Litovel, Czech Republic

KORN/FERRY INTERNATIONAL

1800 Century Park East, Los Angeles, CA, 90067

Tel: (310) 552-1834 Fax: (310) 553-6452 Web site: www.kornferry.com

Executive search; management consulting.

Korn/Ferry International, Valdstenjska 150/4, 110 00 Prague 1, Czech Republic

Tel: 420-2-5732-0088 Fax: 420-2-5731-1160

KPMG PEAT MARWICK LLP

Three Chestnut Ridge Road, Montvale, NJ, 07645

Tel: (201) 307-7000 Fax: (201) 930-8617 Web site: www.kpmg.com

Accounting and audit, tax and management consulting services.

KPMG Czech Republic, PO Box 189, Vesel 5, Brno 601 00, Czech Republic

KPMG Czech Republic, Riegrova 14, Jablonec, 466 01, Czech Republic

KPMG Czech Republic, PO Box 107, Jana Masaryka 12, Prague, 120 00, Czech Republic

Tel: 420-2-691-0194 Fax: 420-2-691-0480 Contact: Charles J. Randolph III

LAI WARD HOWELL INTERNATIONAL INC.

200 Park Ave., Ste. 3100, New York, NY, 10016-0136

Tel: (212) 953-7900 Fax: (212) 953-7907 Web site: www.laix.com

International executive search firm.

LAI Ward Howell Intl., Vodickova 38, 110 00 Prague, Czech Republic

LEVI STRAUSS & COMPANY

1155 Battery Street, Levi's Plaza, San Francisco, CA, 94111-1230

Tel: (415) 544-6000 Fax: (415) 501-3939 Web site: www.levistrauss.com

Mfr./distributor casual wearing apparel.

Levi Strauss & Company Prague, Na Porici 10, 110 00 Prague 1, Czech Republic

Tel: 420-2-2189-96360 Fax: 420-2-2189-9370

ELI LILLY & COMPANY

Lilly Corporate Center, Indianapolis, IN, 46285

Tel: (317) 276-2000 Fax: (317) 277-6579 Web site: www.lilly.com

Mfr. pharmaceuticals and animal health products.

Eli Lilly s.r.o., Parizska 11, Prague 1, Czech Republic

Tel: 420-2-2189-1111 Fax: 420-2-2189-1891

ARTHUR D. LITTLE, INC.

25 Acorn Park, Cambridge, MA, 02140-2390

Tel: (617) 498-5000 Fax: (617) 498-7200 Web site: www.adlittle.com

Management, environmental, health & safety consulting; technical & product development.

Arthur D. Little International, Inc., Konviktska 24, 100 00 Prague 1, Czech Republic

Tel: 420-2-2423-1963 Fax: 420-2-2423-1829

LOCTITE CORPORATION

10 Columbus Boulevard, Hartford, CT, 06106

Tel: (203) 520-5000 Fax: (203) 520-5073 Web site: www.loctite.com

Mfr./sale industrial adhesives and sealants.

Loctite CZ S.r.o., Vaclavkova ul 10, 160 00 Prague 6, Czech Republic

Tel: 420-2-32-2543 Fax: 420-2-32-5316

LOWE & PARTNERS WORLDWIDE

1114 Ave. of the Americas, New York, NY, 10036

Tel: (212) 403-6700 Fax: (212) 403-6710

International advertising agency network.

Lowe GGK Praha/Brno, Prague, Czech Republic

MANPOWER INTERNATIONAL INC.

5301 N. Ironwood Road, PO Box 2053, Milwaukee, WI, 53201-2053

Tel: (414) 961-1000 Fax: (414) 961-7081 Web site: www.manpower

Temporary help, contract service, training & testing.

Manpower Praha Spol. Sto., 7 Valentinska, 110 00 Prague 1, Czech Republic

Tel: 420-2-232-2793 Fax: 420-2-221-383

MARSH & McLENNAN COS INC.

1166 Ave. of the Americas, New York, NY, 10036-2774

Tel: (212) 345-5000 Fax: (212) 345-4808 Web site: www.marshmac.com

Insurance agents/brokers, pension and investment management consulting services.

J&H Marsh & McLennan Inc., KOVO - Jankovcova 2, 170 88 Prague 7, Czech Republic

Tel: 420-26-678-4000 Fax: 420-26-678-4038 Contact: Zdenekn Tucek

J&H Marsh & McLennan Inc., Janska 1/3, Brno, 620 00, Czech Republic

Tel: 420-5-4221-8126 Fax: 420-5-4221-8125 Contact: Vladimir Nespor

McCANN-ERICKSON WORLDWIDE

750 Third Ave., New York, NY, 10017

Tel: (212) 984-3644 Fax: (212) 984-2629

International advertising/marketing services.

McCann-Erickson Prague, Gorkeho nam. 23, 112 82 Prague 1, Czech Republic

Tel: 420-2-2414-2687 Fax: 420-2-2414-2398

McDONALD'S CORPORATION

Kroc Drive, Oak Brook, IL, 60523

Tel: (630) 623-3000 Fax: (630) 623-7409

Fast food chain stores.

McDonald's Corp., Czech Republic

Contact: Martin Dlough, Mgr.

McKINSEY & COMPANY

55 East 52nd Street, New York, NY, 10022

Tel: (212) 446-7000 Fax: (212) 446-8575 Web site: www.mckinsey.com

Management and business consulting services.

McKinsey & Company, Rimska 15, 120 04 Prague 2, Czech Republic

Tel: 420-2-24-408-222 Fax: 420-2-24-408-200

MERITOR AUTOMOTIVE, INC.

2135 W. Maple Road, Troy, MI, 48084-7186

Tel: (248) 435-1000 Fax: (248) 435-1393 Web site: www.meritorauto.com

Mfr./sales of light and heavy vehicle systems for trucks, cars and speciality vehicles.

Skoda Miada Boleslav, Czech Republic

MICROSOFT CORPORATION

One Microsoft Way, Redmond, WA, 98052-6399

Tel: (425) 882-8080 Fax: (425) 936-7329 Web site: www.microsoft.com

Computer software, peripherals and services.

Microsoft s.r.o., Eltodo Centrum, Novodvorska 1010/14 B, 142 00 Prague 4, Czech Republic

Tel: 420-2-611-97111 Fax: 420-1-611-97100

MOTOROLA, INC.

1303 East Algonquin Road, Schaumburg, IL, 60196

Tel: (847) 576-5000 Fax: (847) 538-5191 Web site: www.mot.com

Mfr. communications equipment, semiconductors and cellular phones.

Motorola Czech Republic S.R.O., Praha City Ctr., Klimentska 46, 110 02 Prague, Czech Republic

Tel: 420-2-2185-2222 Fax: 420-2-2185-2191

NATIONAL STARCH & CHEMICAL COMPANY

10 Finderne Ave., Bridgewater, NJ, 08807-3300

Tel: (908) 685-5000 Fax: (908) 685-5005 Web site: www.national starch.com

Mfr. adhesives & sealants, resins & specialty chemicals, electronic materials & adhesives, food products, industry starch.

National Starch & Chemical, Dobrocovická 54, 10000 Prague 10, Czech Republic
Tel: 420-2-782-2456 Fax: 420-2-781-7404

A .C. NIELSEN COMPANY
177 Broad Street, Stamford, CT, 06901
Tel: (203) 961-3000 Fax: (203) 961-3190 Web site: www.acnielsen.com
Market research.
Nielsen Marketing Research spol sro, Havelkova 22, 130 00 Prague 3, Czech Republic

NORDSON CORPORATION
28601 Clemens Road, Westlake, OH, 44145
Tel: (440) 892-1580 Fax: (440) 892-9507 Web site: www.nordson.com
Mfr. industry application equipment, sealants & packaging machinery.
Nordson CS, spol.s.r.o., Bellova 1, 623 00 Brno, Czech Republic
Tel: 420-5-4722-1955 Fax: 420-5-4722-1977

OGILVY & MATHER WORLDWIDE
309 West 49th Street, New York, NY, 10019
Tel: (212) 237-4000 Fax: (212) 237-5123
Advertising, marketing, public relations & consulting firm.
Ogilvy & Mather, Rasinova nabr. 10, 120 00 Prague, Czech Republic

OTIS ELEVATOR COMPANY
10 Farm Springs Road, Farmington, CT, 06032
Tel: (860) 676-6000 Fax: (860) 676-5111
Mfr. elevators and escalators.
Tranza Otis a.s., Jana Opetala 1279, 690 59 Breclav, Czech Republic

OWENS-ILLINOIS, INC.
One SeaGate, PO Box 1035, Toledo, OH, 43666
Tel: (419) 247-5000 Fax: (419) 247-2839
Largest mfr. of glass containers in the US; plastic containers, compression-molded closures and dispensing systems.
Avirunion A.S., Novo Sedlo, Czech Republic

PARAMETRIC TECHNOLOGY CORPORATION
128 Technology Drive, Waltham, MA, 02154
Tel: (781) 398-5000 Fax: (781) 398-5674 Web site: www.ptc.com
Mfr. CAD/CAM/CAE software.
Parametric Technology (C.R.) s.r.o., Janovskeno 36, 170 00 Prague 7 Czech Republic
Tel: 420-2-6671-2673 Fax: 420-2-6671-2680

PAREXEL INTERNATIONAL CORPORATION
195 West Street, Waltham, MA, 02154
Tel: (781) 487-9900 Fax: (781) 487-0525 Web site: www.parexel.com
Provides contract medical, biotechnology, and pharmaceutical research and consulting services.
PAREXEL/MIRAI-Czechia, Praha 10, Rybalkova 57, 10100, Prague, Czech Republic
Tel: 420-2-71-741-396 Fax: 420-2-71-741-396

PARKER HANNIFIN CORPORATION
17325 Euclid Ave., Cleveland, OH, 44112
Tel: (216) 896-3000 Fax: (216) 896-4000 Web site: www.parker.com
Mfr. motion-control products.
Parker Hannifin Corp., Technometra Praha, Strasnicka 783, 102 22 Prague 10, Czech Republic

THE PERKIN-ELMER CORPORATION

761 Main Ave., Norwalk, CT, 06859-0001

Tel: (203) 762-1000 Fax: (203) 762-4228 Web site: www.perkin-elmer.com

Leading supplier of systems for life science research and related applications.

Perkin-Elmer, Praha, Czech Republic

Tel: 420-2-6122-2164 Fax: 420-1-6122-2168

PHARMACIA & UPJOHN

95 Corporate Drive, PO Box 6995, Bridgewater, NJ, 08807

Tel: (908) 306-4400 Fax: (908) 306-4433 Web site: www.pnu.com

Mfr. pharmaceuticals, agricultural products, industry chemicals

Pharmacia & Upjohn, Pobrezni 1, 18600 Prague 8, Czech Republic

PINKERTON'S, INC.

15910 Ventura Boulevard, Ste. 900, Encino, CA, 91436

Tel: (818) 380-8800 Fax: (818) 380-8515 Web site: www.pinkertons.com

Security solutions.

Pinkerton's of CSFR Ltd., Na Jarove 4, 130 00 Praha 3, Czech Republic

Tel: 420-2-66-026-327 Fax: 420-2-66-026-105 Contact: Emilion Hamernik, Mng. Dir.

PLANET HOLLYWOOD INTERNATIONAL, INC.

8669 Commodity Circle, Orlando, FL, 32819

Tel: (407) 363-7827 Fax: (407) 363-4862 Web site: www.planethollywood.com

Theme-dining restaurant chain and merchandise retail stores.

Planet Hollywood International, Inc., Prague, Czech Republic

PRICEWATERHOUSECOOPERS LLP

1251 Ave. of the Americas, New York, NY, 10020

Tel: (212) 596-7000 Fax: (212) 790-6620 Web site: www.pwcglobal.com

Accounting and auditing, tax and management, and human resource consulting services.

Price Waterhouse Ltd., Vinohradska 10, 121 47 Prague 2, Czech Republic

Tel: 420-2-2421-7438 Fax: 420-2-2421-8024

RADISSON HOTELS INTERNATIONAL

Carlson Pkwy., PO Box 59159, Minneapolis, MN, 55459-8204

Tel: (612) 540-5526 Fax: (612) 449-3400

Hotels and resorts.

Radisson SAS Hotel Praha, Stepanska Ulica 40, CZ-110-00 Praha, Czech Republic

Tel: 420-2-242-353-90 Fax: 420-2-242-353-90

RAY & BERNDTSON, INC.

301 Commerce, Ste. 2300, Fort Worth, TX, 76102

Tel: (817) 334-0500 Fax: (817) 334-0779 Web site: www.prb.com

Executive search, management audit and management consulting firm.

Ray & Berndtson, Klimentska 46, Praha 1 11002, Czech Republic

Tel: 420-2-2185-2253 Fax: 420-2-2185-2099 Contact: Joachim Zyla, Mng. Ptnr.

RAYTHEON COMPANY

141 Spring Street, Lexington, MA, 02173

Tel: (781) 862-6600 Fax: (781) 860-2172 Web site: www.raytheon.com

Mfr. diversified electronics, appliances, aviation, energy and environmental products; publishing, industry and construction services.

Raytheon International, Prague, Czech Republic

RENAISSANCE HOTELS AND RESORTS

1 Marriott Drive, Washington, DC, 20058

Tel: (301) 380-3000 Fax: (301) 380-5181

Hotel and resort chain.

Renaissance Prague Hotel, Prague, Czech Republic

Tel: 420-2-2182-2100

ROCKWELL INTERNATIONAL CORPORATION

600 Anton Boulevard, Costa Mesa, CA, 92626-7147

Tel: (714) 424-4200 Fax: (714) 424-4251 Web site: www.rockwell.com

Products & service for aerospace and defense, automotive, electronics, graphics & automation industry.

Rockwell Automation s.r.o., Americka 22, 120 00 Prague 2 - Vinoohrady, Czech Republic

Tel: 420-2-2-54-6913 Fax: 420-2-250467

SAS INSTITUTE INC.

SAS Campus Drive, Cary, NC, 27513

Tel: (919) 677-8000 Fax: (919) 677-8123 Web site: www.sas.com

Mfr./distributes decision support software.

SAS Institute (Czech Republic), Praha, Czech Republic

Tel: 420-2-22 21 20 64 Fax: 420-2-96 22 06 14

SEA-LAND SERVICE INC.

6000 Carnegie Boulevard, Charlotte, NC, 28209

Tel: (704) 571-2000 Fax: (704) 571-4693 Web site: www.sealand.com

Largest U.S-based containerized transport service; ships, railroads, barge lines and trucking operations.

Sea-Land Service, U pujcovny 9, 111 23, Prague 1, Czech Republic

Tel: 420-2-2421-1309 Fax: 420-2-2421-1491

G.D. SEARLE & COMPANY

5200 Old Orchard Road, Skokie, IL, 60077

Tel: (847) 982-7000 Fax: (847) 470-1480 Web site: www.searlehealthnet.com

Mfr. pharmaceuticals, health care, optical products and specialty chemicals.

SANITAS AS, Cernokostelecka 1621, 251 01 Ricany, Czech Republic

Tel: 420-204-48-111 Fax: 420-204-48-465

Searle European Inc., Krakovska 9, Nove Mesto, 110 00 Prague 1, Czech Republic

Tel: 420-2-21-66-4380 Fax: 420-2-21-66-4388

SEQUENT COMPUTER SYSTEMS INC.

15450 SW Koll Pkwy., Beaverton, OR, 97006-6063

Tel: (503) 626-5700 Fax: (503) 578-9890 Web site: www.sequent.com

Mfr. symmetric multiprocessing technology computers.

Sequent Computer Systems Inc., K. Zizkovu 4, 190 00 Prague 9, Czech Republic

THE SERVICEMASTER COMPANY

One ServiceMaster Way, Downers Grove, IL, 60515-1700

Tel: (630) 271-1300 Fax: (630) 271-2710 Web site: www.svm.com

Management service to health care, school and industry facilities; diversified residential and commercial services.

ServiceMaster, Prague, Czech Republic

SILICON GRAPHICS INC.

2011 N. Shoreline Blvd., Mountain View, CA, 94043-1389

Tel: (650) 960-1980 Fax: (650) 961-0595 Web site: www.sgi.com

Design/mfr. special-effects computer graphic systems and software.

Silicon Graphics, Czech Republic

SPENCER STUART & ASSOCIATES INC.

401 North Michigan Ave., Ste. 3400, Chicago, IL, 60611

Tel: (312) 822-0080 Fax: (312) 822-0116 Web site: www.spencerstuart.com

Executive recruitment firm.

Spencer Stuart & Associates Inc., V Jame 12, CZ-11121 Prague 1, Czech Republic

Tel: 420-2-2422-8217 Fax: 420-2-2422-1730 Contact: Tibor Gedeon

SQUIRE, SANDERS & DEMPSEY

4900 Society Center, 127 Public Square, Cleveland, OH, 44114-1304

Tel: (216) 479-8500 Fax: (216) 479-8780 Web site: www.ssd.com

International law firm.

Squire, Sanders & Dempsey, Vaclavski Namesti 57/813, 110 00 Praha 1, Czech Republic

Tel: 420-2-2166-2111 Fax: 420-2-2166-2222 Contact: Vladimira N. Papirnik

SYBASE, INC.

6475 Christie Ave., Emeryville, CA, 94608

Tel: (510) 922-3500 Fax: (510) 922-3210 Web site: www.sybase.com

Design/mfg/distribution of database management systems, software development tools, connectivity products, consulting and technical support services..

Sybase Czech Republic s.r.o., Tychnova 2, 160 00 Prague 6, Czech Republic

Tel: 420-2-2431-0808 Fax: 420-2-2431-5024

TBWA INTERNATIONAL

180 Maiden Lane, New York, NY, 10038

Tel: (212) 804-1000 Fax: (212) 804-1200

International full service advertising agency.

Grade/TBWA & Mas TBWA, Prague, Czech Republic

TENNECO AUTOMOTIVE

500 North Field Drive, Lake Forest, IL, 60045

Tel: (847) 482-5241 Fax: (847) 482-5295

Automotive parts, exhaust systems, service equipment.

Gillet Lazne Belohrad S.R.O., Dolni Nova Nes 60, 50781 Lazne Belohrad, CR-Bezirk Jicin, Czech Republic

Tel: 420-434-92624 Fax: 420-434-92250 Contact: Bernd Ruser, Mgr. Emp: 38

Monroe Czechia (Ateso), Rychnouska 383, 463 42 Hodkouice n.m. Czechia, Czech Republic

Tel: 420-48-514-5097 Fax: 420-2-4851-45110 Contact: Peter Kancian, Mgr. Emp: 479

TETRA TECH, INC.

670 N. Rosemead Blvd., Pasadena, CA, 91107

Tel: (626) 351-4664 Fax: (626) 351-1188 Web site: www.tetratech.com

Environmental engineering and consulting services.

Tetra Tech - Europe, Janackovo nabrezi 17, 150 00 Prague 5, Czech Republic

Tel: 420-2-5731-3910 Fax: 420-2-5731-3911 Contact: Andrew Johnson

TRANE COMPANY

3600 Pammel Creek Road, La Crosse, WI, 54601

Tel: (608) 787-2000 Fax: (608) 787-4990

Mfr./distributor/service A/C systems and equipment.

Trane Czech Republic, Bldg. RAMMS, Budecska 6, 100 00 Prague 10, Czech Republic

TRUE NORTH COMMUNICATIONS INC.

101 East Erie Street, Chicago, IL, 60611

Tel: (312) 425-6000 Fax: (312) 425-6350

Holding company, advertising agency.

FCB/Praha, s.r.o., Hybemska 8, 110 00 Praha 1, Czech Republic

TYCO INTERNATIONAL LTD.

One Tyco Park, Exeter, NH, 03833

Tel: (603) 778-9700 Fax: (603) 778-7700 Web site: www.tycoint.com

Mfr./sales fire & security systems, sprinkler systems, undersea fiber optic telecommuncations, printed circuit boards, pipe tubing and flow meters.

Keystone Praha, Na Petrinach 55, Praha 6, Czech Republic CR-16100

Tel: 420-2-2061-0379 Fax: 420-236-7846

UNION SPECIAL CORPORATION

One Union Special Plaza, Huntley, IL, 60142

Tel: (847) 669-4345 Fax: (847) 669-3534 Web site: www.unionspecial.com

Mfr. sewing machines.

Unia Special, SRO, Tolsteho 23, 58601 Jihlava, Czech Republic

Tel: 420-66-731-0019

UNITED PARCEL SERVICE OF AMERICA, INC.

55 Glenlake Parkway, NE, Atlanta, GA, 30328

Tel: (404) 828-6000 Fax: (404) 828-6593 Web site: www.ups.com

International package-delivery service.

UPS Czech Republic, Vytvarna 1023/4, Prague 6, 16100, Czech Republic

Tel: 420-2-33003-110

US WEST, INC.

7800 East Orchard Road, PO Box 6508, Englewood, CO, 80155-6508

Tel: (303) 793-6500 Fax: (303) 793-6654

Tele-communications provider; integrated communications services.

Cable Plus, Liberec, Czech Republic

WACKENHUT CORPORATION

4200 Wackenhut Drive, Ste. 100, Palm Beach Gardens, FL, 33410

Tel: (561) 622-5656 Fax: (561) 691-6736 Web site: www.wackenhut.com

Security systems & services.

Wackenhut Czech, Na Porici 6, 110 00 Prague 1, Czech Republic

Tel: 420-2-24-214024 Fax: 420-2-24-214024

WEIL, GOTSHAL & MANGES LLP

767 5th Ave., New York, NY, 10153

Tel: (212) 310-8000 Fax: (212) 310-8007 Web site: www.weil.com

International law firm.

Weil, Gotshal & Manges LLP, Charles Bridge Ctr., Krizonicke Nam 1, 110 00 Prague 1, Czech Republic

Tel: 420-2-2409-7300 Fax: 420-2-2409-7310 Contact: Joseph C. Tortorici, Ptnr.

WHITE & CASE LLP

1155 Ave. of the Americas, New York, NY, 10036-2767

Tel: (212) 819-8200 Fax: (212) 354-8113 Web site: www.whitecase.com

International law firm.

White & Case LLP, Association of Advocates, Staromestske namesti 15, 110 00 Prague 1, Czech Republic

Tel: 420-2-2481-1796 Fax: 420-2-232-5522 Contact: Ivan Cestr

WOODWARD GOVERNOR COMPANY

5001 North Second Street, PO Box 7001, Rockford, IL, 61125-7001

Tel: (815) 877-7441 Fax: (815) 639-6033 Web site: www.woodward.com

Mfr./service speed control devices and systems for aircraft turbines, industrial engines and turbines.

Woodward Governor Czech Republic, VT-C (Woodward), Americka 24, 30135 Plzen, Czech Republic

Tel: 420-19-722-6076 Fax: 420-19-723-6754 Contact: Frank Veinfurt, Mgr.

WM WRIGLEY JR. COMPANY

410 N. Michigan Ave., Chicago, IL, 60611-4287

Tel: (312) 644-2121 Fax: (312) 644-0353 Web site: www.wrigley.com

Mfr. chewing gum.

Wrigley S.R.O., Prague, Czech Republic

XEROX CORPORATION

800 Long Ridge Road, PO Box 1600, Stamford, CT, 06904

Tel: (203) 968-3000 Fax: (203) 968-4312 Web site: www.xerox.com

Mfr. document processing equipment, systems and supplies.

Xerox Corp., Prague, Czech Republic

YOUNG & RUBICAM INC.

285 Madison Ave., New York, NY, 10017

Tel: (212) 210-3000 Fax: (212) 370-3796 Web site: www.yr.com

Advertising, public relations, direct marketing and sales promotion, corporate & product ID management.

Young & Rubicam, Olivova 6, 110 00 Prague 1, Czech Republic

Tel: 420-2-2421-0389 Fax: 420-2-2422-8781

Dem. Rep. of Congo

LOUIS BERGER INTERNATIONAL INC.

100 Halsted Street, East Orange, NJ, 07019

Tel: (201) 678-1960 Fax: (201) 672-4284 Web site: www.louisberger.com

Consulting engineers, architects, economists & planners.

Louis Berger International Inc., c/o Delegation de I'Union Europeenne Unite de Coordination & Gestion de PAR, 16 Ave. de Pumbu, Kinshasa 1 - GOMBE, Dem. Republic of Congo

Tel: 871-682-041-133

Louis Berger International Inc., B.P. 15388, Brazzavulle, Dem. Republic of Congo

CITICORP

399 Park Ave., New York, NY, 10043

Tel: (212) 559-1000 Fax: (212) 527-2066 Web site: www.citibank.com

International banking and financial services.

Citibank N.A., Coin Des Aves, Colonnel Lukusa et Ngongo Lutet, Kinshasa 1, Dem. Rep. Of Congo

Citibank N.A., Dem. Rep. of Congo

Citibank N.A., Kinshasa-Gombe, Rep of Congo, Kinshasa 1, PO Box 9999,Dem. Rep of Congo

CROWN CORK & SEAL COMPANY, INC.

One Crown Way, Philadelphia, PA, 19154-4599

Tel: (215) 698-5100 Fax: (215) 698-5201

Mfr. cans, bottle caps; filling & packaging machinery.

Crown Cork Co., Boite Postale 2684, Lubumbashi, Dem. Rep. of Congo

DHL WORLDWIDE EXPRESS

333 Twin Dolphin Drive, Redwood City, CA, 94065

Tel: (650) 593-7474 Fax: (650) 593-1689 Web site: www.dhl.com

Worldwide air express carrier.

DHL Worldwide Express, Angle des Av. Tchad & Bas-Zaire, Kinshasa Gombe, Dem. Republic of Congo

Tel: 243-12-21526

GENERAL MOTORS CORPORATION

100 Renaissance Center, Detroit, MI, 48243.7301

Tel: (313) 556-5000 Fax: (313) 556-5108 Web site: www.gm.com

Mfr. full line vehicles, automotive electronics, commercial technologies, telecommunications, space, finance.

General Motors Zaire SARL, Boite Postale 11199, Kinshasa, Dem. Rep. of Congo

IBM CORPORATION

New Orchard Road, Armonk, NY, 10504

Tel: (914) 765-1900 Fax: (914) 765-7382 Web site: www.ibm.com

Information products, technology & services.

IBM, Mail: IBM Zaire, Budimex, 11C, rue van Eivck, B-1050 Brussels, Belgium

ITT CORPORATION

1330 Ave. of the Americas, New York, NY, 10019-5490

Tel: (212) 258-1000 Fax: (212) 258-1297

Design/mfr. communications & electronic equipment, hotels, insurance.

ITT Bell Telephone Co., Boite Postale 11210, Kin l, Kinshasa, Dem. Rep. of Congo

ITT SHERATON CORPORATION

60 State Street, Boston, MA, 02108

Tel: (617) 367-3600 Fax: (617) 367-5676

Hotel operations.

Karavia Sheraton, Boite Postale 4701, Lumbumbashi, Dem. Rep. of Congo

MOBIL CORPORATION

3225 Gallows Road, Fairfax, VA, 22037-0001

Tel: (703) 846-3000 Fax: (703) 846-4669 Web site: www.mobil.com

Petroleum and gas exploration and refining, mfr. petroleum products, chemicals and petrochemicals.

Zaire Mobil Oil, 3900 PC Ave. de la Republic du Tchad, Face Au Memling, BP 2400, Kinshasa, Dem. Rep. of Congo

PHARMACIA & UPJOHN

95 Corporate Drive, PO Box 6995, Bridgewater, NJ, 08807

Tel: (908) 306-4400 Fax: (908) 306-4433 Web site: www.pnu.com

Mfr. pharmaceuticals, agricultural products, industry chemicals

Upjohn Intl. Co., 483 Ave. Zinnias Limite, Boite Postale 894, Kinshasa, Dem. Rep. of Congo

PRICEWATERHOUSECOOPERS LLP

1251 Ave. of the Americas, New York, NY, 10020

Tel: (212) 596-7000 Fax: (212) 790-6620 Web site: www.pwcglobal.com

Accounting and auditing, tax and management, and human resource consulting services.

Price Waterhouse Ltd., Galeries Presidentielles, Place du 27 Octobre, BP 10195 Kinshasa 1, Dem. Rep. of Congo

Tel: 243-12-21544 Fax: 243-12-21543

Denmark

3M

3M Center, St. Paul, MN, 55144-1000

Tel: (612) 733-1110 Fax: (612) 733-9973 Web site: www.mmm.com

Mfr. diversified products for industry, health care, imaging, communications, transport, safety, consumer, etc.

3M Denmark A/S, Postboks 1393, Fabriksparken 15, DK-2600 Glostrup, Denmark

Tel: 45-4348-0100 Fax: 45-4396-8596

ACADEMIC PRESS INC.

6277 Sea Harbor Drive, Orlando, FL, 32887

Tel: (407) 345-2000 Fax: (407) 345-8388 Web site: www.academicpress.com

Publisher of educational & scientific books.

Academic Press, Rosenaengets Alle 8, ITH, 2100 Copenhagen 0, Denmark

Contact: Guy Simpson

AIR EXPRESS INTERNATIONAL CORPORATION

120 Tokeneke Road, PO Box 1231, Darien, CT, 06820

Tel: (203) 655-7900 Fax: (203) 655-5779 Web site: www.aeilogistics.com

Air freight forwarder.

AEI - Universal Air Express A/S, 2C Fugelbaekvej, PO Box 109, DK-2770 Kastrup, Copenhagen, Denmark (Locations: Aarhus, Billund.)

ALLEN-BRADLEY COMPANY, INC.

1201 South Second Street, Milwaukee, WI, 53204

Tel: (414) 382-2000 Fax: (414) 382-4444

Mfr. electrical controls & information devices.

Allen-Bradley A/S, Herstedostervej 27-29, DK-2620 Albertslund, Denmark

ALPHARMA INC.

One Executive Drive, 4th Fl., Fort Lee, NJ, 07024

Tel: (201) 947-7774 Fax: (201) 947-5541 Web site: www.alphapharm.com

Development/manufacture specialty human pharmaceuticals & animal health products.

Alpharma Fine Chemicals Division, Copenhagen, Denmark

Dumex Ltd., Dalslandsgade 11, DK-2300 Copenhagen S, Denmark

AMDAHL CORPORATION

1250 East Arques Ave., PO Box 3470, Sunnyvale, CA, 94088-3470

Tel: (408) 746-6000 Fax: (408) 773-0833 Web site: www.amdahl.com

Development/mfr. large scale computers, software, data storage products, information-technology solutions & support.

Amdahl Danmark Computer Systems A/S, Hammerensgade 4, DK-1267 Copenhagen, Denmark

Tel: 45-33-12-25-60 Fax: 45-33-12-25-70

AMERADA HESS CORPORATION

1185 Ave. of the Americas, New York, NY, 10036

Tel: (212) 997-8500 Fax: (212) 536-8390 Web site: www.hess.com

Crude oil & natural gas.

Amerada Hess A/S, Ostergade 26B, DK-1100 Copenhagen K, Denmark

AMERICAN METER COMPANY

300 Welsh Road, Bldg. #1, Horsham, PA, 19044-2234

Tel: (215) 830-1800 Fax: (215) 830-1890

Measure & control services for natural gas industry.

International Gas Apparatus A/S, Anholvej 1, DK-9800 Hjorring, Denmark

AMERICAN TOOL COMPANIES INC.

8400 LakeView Pkwy., #400, Kenosha, WI, 53142

Tel: (847) 478-1090 Fax: (847) 478-1090

Mfr. hand tools, cutting tools & power tool accessories.

American Tool Companies A/S, Industriholmen 15A, DK-2650 Hvidovre, Copenhagen, Denmark

AMERITECH CORPORATION

30 South Wacker Drive, Chicago, IL, 60606

Tel: (312) 750-5000 Fax: (312) 207-0016 Web site: www.ameritech.com

Provides security systems & telecommunications services.

Tele Danmark, Coperhagen, Denmark

AMETEK INC.

4 Station Square, Paoli, PA, 19301

Tel: (610) 647-2121 Fax: (610) 296-3412 Web site: www.ametek.com

Mfr. instruments, electric motors & engineered materials.

Ametek Denmark A/S, Gydevang 32-34, PO Box 30, DK-3450 Allerod, Denmark

Tel: 45-4816-8000 Fax: 45-4816-8080

AMMIRATI PURIS LINTAS

One Dag Hammarskjold Plaza, New York, NY, 10017

Tel: (212) 605-8000 Fax: (212) 605-4705 Web site: www.interpublic.com

International advertising agency.

Ammirati Puris Lintas Denmark, Kobmagergase 60, DK-1500 Copenhagen K. Denmark

Tel: 45-3315-7100 Fax: 45-3313-5400 Contact: Dorthe Arnoldi Brangstrup, Mng. Dir.

Signatur - Denmark, Kobmagergase 60, DK-1500 Copenhagen K. Denmark

Tel: 45-3332-3043 Fax: 45-3393-7710 Contact: Lars Thomsen

AMP INC.

470 Friendship Road, PO Box 3608, Harrisburg, PA, 17105-3608

Tel: (717) 564-0100 Fax: (717) 780-6130

Develop/mfr. electronic & electrical connection products & systems.

AMP Danmark, Gunnar Clausens Vej 36, DK-8260 Vibyj, Denmark

Tel: 45-8629-5055

ANALOG DEVICES INC.

1 Technology Way, Box 9106, Norwood, MA, 02062

Tel: (781) 329-4700 Fax: (781) 326-8703

Mfr. integrated circuits & related devices.

Analog Devices ApS, Horkaer 20, DK-2730 Herlev, Denmark

ANALOGIC CORPORATION

8 Centennial Drive, Peabody, MA, 01960

Tel: (978) 977-3000 Fax: (978) 977-6811

Conceive/design/mfr. precision measure, signal processing & imaging equipment for medical, scientific, industry & communications.

B&K Medical A/S, Sandtoften 9, DK-2820 Gentofte, Denmark

ANDERSEN CONSULTING

100 South Wacker Drive, Ste. 1059, Chicago, IL, 60606

Tel: (311) 123-7271 Fax: (312) 507-7965 Web site: www.ac.com

Provides management & technology consulting services.

Andersen Consulting, Oslo Plads 1, DK-2100 Copenhagen Ø, Denmark

Tel: 45-3342-2000 Fax: 45-3342-7100

AON CORPORATION

123 North Wacker Drive, Chicago, IL, 60606

Tel: (312) 701-3000 Fax: (312) 701-3100 Web site: www.aon.com

Insurance brokers worldwide; underwrites accident & health insurance, specialty & professional insurance; & provides risk management consultation.

AON Denmark A/S, Skanderborgvej 234, DK - 8260 Viby J, Aarhus, Denmark

Tel: 45-8628-8811 Fax: 45-8628-8822 Contact: Lars Grunnet

AON Holdings Scandinavia A/S, Straandgade 4, C DK - 1401 Copenhagen, Denmark

Tel: 45-32-697100 Fax: 45-32-964399 Contact: Niels de Bang

ARTHUR ANDERSEN & COMPANY

33 West Monroe Street, Chicago, IL, 60603

Tel: (312) 372-7100 Fax: (312) 507-0123 Web site: www.arthurandersen.com

Accounting & audit, tax & management consulting services.

Arthur Andersen & Co., Midtermolen 1, PO Box 2662, 2100 Copenhagen 0, Denmark

Tel: 45-35-25-2525

Arthur Andersen,, H.H. Seedorffs Straede 3-5, DK-8000 Arhus C, Denmark

Tel: 45-8619-5555

ASHLAND OIL INC.

1000 Ashland Drive, Russell, KY, 41169

Tel: (606) 329-3333 Fax: (606) 329-5274 Web site: www.ashland.com

Petroleum exploration, refining & transportation; mfr. chemicals, oils & lubricants.

Valvoline Nordisk Biltjeneste ApS, Vejiegardegej 45-47, DK-2665 Vallensbaek Strand, Copenhagen, Denmark

ASSOCIATED MERCHANDISING CORPORATION

1440 Broadway, New York, NY, 10018

Tel: (212) 596-4000 Fax: (212) 575-2993

Retail service organization; apparel, shoes and accessories.

Associated Merchandising Corp., Tornsangerveg 5, DK-3600 Frederikssund, Denmark

ASSOCIATED PRESS INC.

50 Rockefeller Plaza, New York, NY, 10020-1605

Tel: (212) 621-1500 Fax: (212) 621-5447 Web site: www.ap.com

News gathering agency.

Associated Press A/S, Bremerholm 1-3, DK-1069 Copenhagen, Denmark

Tel: 45-33-11-1504

AST RESEARCH INC.

16215 Alton Parkway, PO Box 19658, Irvine, CA, 92713-9658

Tel: (949) 727-4141 Fax: (949) 727-8584 Web site: www.ast.com

Design/development/mfr. hi-performance desktop, server & notebook computers.

AST Denmark, Postboks 120, DK-3450 Allerod, Denmark

Tel: 45-4517-0200

ATTACHMATE CORPORATION

3617 131st Ave. S.E., Bellevue, WA, 98006-1332

Tel: (425) 644-4010 Fax: (425) 747-9924 Web site: www.attachmate.com

Mfr. connectivity software.

Attachmate, Copenhagen, Denmark

Tel: 45-4217-1000

AVERY DENNISON CORPORATION

150 N. Orange Grove Blvd., Pasadena, CA, 91103

Tel: (626) 304-2000 Fax: (626) 792-7312 Web site: www.averydennison.com

Mfr. pressure-sensitive adhesives & materials, office products, labels, tags, retail systems, Carter's Ink & specialty chemicals.

Fasson A/S, Marielundvej 46D, DK-2730 Copenhagen, Denmark

R. Ancker Jorgensen A/S, 18 Topstykket, DK-3460 Birkerod, Denmark

BAKER HUGHES INCORPORATED

3900 Essex Lane, Ste. 1200, Houston, TX, 77027

Tel: (713) 439-8600 Fax: (713) 439-8699 Web site: www.bakerhughes.com

Develop & apply technology to drill, complete & produce oil and natural gas wells; provide separation systems to petroleum, municipal, continuous process & mining industries.

Baker Hughes de Mexico, S. de R.L. de C.V., Haandvaerkervej 2-4, Esbjerg, DK-6710, Denmark

Tel: 45.7515-3866 Fax: 45-7515-4976

BANKERS TRUST COMPANY

280 Park Ave., New York, NY, 10017

Tel: (212) 250-2500 Fax: (212) 250-2440 Web site: www.bankerstrust.com

Banking & investment services.

Bankers Trust Company, Admiralgade 24, DK-1066 Copenhagen K, Denmark

BATES WORLDWIDE INC.

405 Lexington Ave., New York, NY, 10174

Tel: (212) 297-7000 Fax: (212) 986-0270 Web site: www.batesww.com

Advertising, marketing, public relations & media consulting.

Bates A/S, Landemaarket 29, DK-1119 Copenhagen K, Denmark

Tel: 45-33-137913 Fax: 45-33-157126 Contact: H. U. Longhi, CEO

Leise & Company, Landemaeket 19, DK-1119 Copenhagan K, Denmark

Tel: 45-33-33-0077 Fax: 45-33-33-9998 Contact: S. Leise, Dir.

Norgard Mikkelsen Reklamebureau A/S, Vandeveerksvel 18, DK-5100 Odanse C, Denmark

Tel: 45-6614-1480 Contact: Erik Laumand, Dir.

BAUSCH & LOMB INC.

One Bausch & Lomb Place, Rochester, NY, 14604-2701

Tel: (716) 338-6000 Fax: (716) 338-6007 Web site: www.bausch.com

Mfr. vision care products & accessories & hearing aids.

Bausch & Lomb Denmark A/S, Copenhagen, Denmark

BAX GLOBAL CORPORATION

16808 Armstrong Ave., PO Box 19571, Irvine, CA, 92623

Tel: (714) 752-4000 Fax: (714) 852-1488 Web site: www.bax.com

Air freight forwarder.

BAX Global A/S - Denmark, Head Office - Kirstinehoj 47, DK-2770 Copenhagen, Denmark

Tel: 45-32-51-3366 Fax: 45-32-51-2116

BAXTER HEALTHCARE CORPORATION

One Baxter Parkway, Deerfield, IL, 60015

Tel: (847) 948-2000 Fax: (847) 948-3948 Web site: www.baxter.com

Pharmaceutical preparations, surgical/medical instruments & cardiovascular products.

Baxter A/S, Gydevang 30, DK-3450 Allerod, Denmark

BBDO WORLDWIDE

1285 Ave. of the Americas, New York, NY, 10019

Tel: (212) 459-5000 Fax: (212) 459-6645 Web site: www.bbdo.com

Multinational group of advertising agencies.

BBDO Denmark, Copenhagen, Denmark

BDO SEIDMAN, LLP

Two Prudential Plaza, 180 N. Stetson Ave., Ste. 2300, Chicago, IL, 60601

Tel: (312) 240-1236 Fax: (312) 240-3329 Web site: www.bdo.com

International accounting & financial consulting firm.

BDP Scanrevision Aktieselskab, Strandgade 12, 1401 Copenhagen K, Denmark

Tel: 45-32-96-1100 Fax: 45-32-96-1101 Contact: Jens Rye

BEA SYSTEMS, INC.

2315 North First Street, St. Jose, CA, 95131

Tel: (408) 570-8000 Fax: (408) 570-8091 Web site: www.beasys.com

Develops communications management software & provider of software consulting services.

BEA Systems, Emdrupvej 28 C, 2100 Copengagen, Denmark

Tel: 45-3927-0208 Fax: 45-3927-7780

BELLSOUTH INTERNATIONAL

1155 Peachtree Street NE, Ste. 400, Atlanta, GA, 30367

Tel: (404) 249-4800 Fax: (404) 249-4880 Web site: www.bellsouth.com

Mobile communications, telecommunications network systems.

Sonofon Holding A/S, Lyngse Alee 3, DK-2070 Hersholm, Denmark

Tel: 45-38-18-6000 Fax: 45-38-18-6060

BEST WESTERN INTERNATIONAL

6201 North 24th Place, Phoenix, AZ, 85106

Tel: (602) 957-4200 Fax: (602) 957-5740

International hotel chain.

Hellerup Parkhotel, DK-2900 Hellerup, Denmark

Neptun Hotel, KD-1250 Copenhagen K, Denmark

BESTFOODS, INC.

700 Sylvan Ave., International Plaza, Englewood Cliffs, NJ, 07632-9976

Tel: (201) 894-4000 Fax: (201) 894-2186 Web site: www.bestfoods.com

Consumer foods products; corn refining.

CPC Foods A/S, Mileparken 9, DK-2740 Skovlunde, Denmark

Tel: 45-4494-6800 Fax: 45-4494-6171 Contact: Allan Christiansen, Mgr.

BETZDEARBORN

4636 Somerton Road, PO Box 3002, Trevose, PA, 19053-6783

Tel: (215) 953-2568 Fax: (215) 953-5524 Web site: www.betzdearborn.com

Mfr. water/wastewater and process system treatment chemicals and services.

BetzDearborn Denmark A/S, Skt. Pauls Gade 42, DK-8000 Aarhus C, Denmark

BIO-RAD LABORATORIES INC.

1000 Alfred Nobel Drive, Hercules, CA, 94547

Tel: (510) 724-7000 Fax: (510) 724-3167

Mfr. life science research products, clinical diagnostics, analytical instruments.

Bio-Rad Laboratories Inc., Hadsund, Denmark

BLACK & DECKER CORPORATION

701 E. Joppa Road, Towson, MD, 21286

Tel: (410) 716-3900 Fax: (410) 716-2933 Web site: www.blackanddecker.com

Mfr. power tools and accessories, security hardware, small appliances, fasteners, information systems & services.

Black & Decker Denmark, Denmark - All mail to U.S. address.

BOOLE & BABBAGE, INC.

3131 Zanker Road, San Jose, CA, 95134

Tel: (408) 526-3000 Fax: (408) 526-3055 Web site: www.boole.com

Develop/support enterprise automation & systems management software.

Boole & Babbage Europe, Hejrevang 13, DK-3450 Alleroed, Denmark

BORDEN INC.

180 East Broad Street, Columbus, OH, 43215-3799

Tel: (614) 225-4000 Fax: (614) 220-6453

Mfr. Packaged foods, consumer adhesives, housewares and industrial chemicals.

Cocio Chokolademaelk A./S, PO Box 65, 6701 Esbjerg, Denmark

Tel: 45-7512-7788

BOSE CORPORATION

The Mountain, Framingham, MA, 01701-9168

Tel: (508) 879-7330 Fax: (508) 766-7543

Mfr. quality audio equipment/speakers.

Bose A/S, Industrivej 7, DK-2605 Brondby, Denmark

BOSTON SCIENTIFIC CORPORATION

One Scientific Place, Natick, MA, 01760-1537

Tel: (508) 650-8000 Fax: (508) 650-8923 Web site: www.bsci.com

Mfr./distributes medical devices for use in minimally invasive surgeries.

Meadox Surgimed A/S, Gymnasievej 5, 3660 Stenlose, Denmark

Tel: 45-4217-3990 Fax: 45-4217-1955

BOYDEN CONSULTING CORPORATION

100 Park Ave., 34th Floor, New York, NY, 10017

Tel: (212) 980-6534 Fax: (212) 980-6147 Web site: www.boyden.com

Executive search.

Boyden Associates Ltd., 92, Store Kongensgade, DK-1264 Copenhagen K, Denmark

Tel: 45-33-129988

BOZELL WORLDWIDE

40 West 23rd Street, New York, NY, 10010

Tel: (212) 727-5000 Fax: (212) 645-9173 Web site: www.bozell.com

Advertising, marketing, public relations and media consulting.

En Vision Copenhagen, Amager Torv 14, 4, Post Office 2233, 1160 Copenhagen Denmark

Tel: 45-33-30-13-55 Fax: 45-33-30-13-34 Contact: Soren Parup, Dir.

En Vision Grafisk (Arhus) Tegnestue A/S, Postboks 261, Christiansgade 30, DK-8100 Arhus, Denmark

Tel: 45-8619-4455 Fax: 45-8618-4767 Contact: Bent Christensen, Mgr.

BRANSON ULTRASONICS CORPORATION

41 Eagle Road, Danbury, CT, 06813-1961

Tel: (203) 796-0400 Fax: (203) 796-2285

Mfr. plastics assembly equipment, ultrasonic cleaning equipment.

Branson Ultrasonics-Scandinavia, Lojtegardsvej 155, DK-2770 Kastrup, Copenhagen, Denmark

Tel: 45-32-513-233 Fax: 45-32-515-139

BRISTOL-MYERS SQUIBB COMPANY

345 Park Ave., New York, NY, 10154

Tel: (212) 546-4000 Fax: (212) 546-4020 Web site: www.bms.com

Pharmaceutical and food preparations, medical and surgical instruments.

Bristol-Myers Squibb A/B, Wilder Plads, Byning V, 1404 Copenhagen, Denmark

ConvaTec Denmark, Jaegersborgvej 65-66, DK-2800 LYNGBY, Denmark

BUDGET RENT A CAR CORPORATION

4225 Naperville Road, Lisle, IL, 60532

Tel: (630) 955-1900 Fax: (630) 955-7799 Web site: www.budgetrentacar.com

Car and truck rental system.

Budget Rent A Car, Kastrup International Airport 2770, Copenhagen, Denmark

Tel: 45-3252-3900 Fax: 45-3252-5218

LEO BURNETT CO., INC.

35 West Wacker Drive, Chicago, IL, 60601

Tel: (312) 220-5959 Fax: (312) 220-6533 Web site: www.leoburnett.com

International advertising agency.

Leo Burnett Denmark, Vesterbrogade 2B, DK-1620 Copenhagen V, Denmark

BURSON-MARSTELLER

230 Park Ave., New York, NY, 10003-1566

Tel: (212) 614-4000 Fax: (212) 614-4262 Web site: www.bm.com

Public relations/public affairs consultants.

Burson-Marsteller/Public Affairs Group A/S, Blegdamsvej 104, DK-2100 Copenhagen, Denmark

Tel: 45-35-437375 Fax: 45-35-437377

BUSSMANN

PO Box 14460, St. Louis, MO, 63178-4460

Tel: (314) 394-2877 Fax: (314) 527-1405

Mfr. electronic fuses and circuit breakers.

Bussmann, Copenhagen, Denmark

CANBERRA-PACKARD INDUSTRIES

800 Research Parkway, Meriden, CT, 06450

Tel: (203) 238-2351 Fax: (203) 235-1347 Web site: www.packard.com

Mfr. instruments for nuclear research.

Canberra-Pack AB, Greveager 7, DK-2670 Greve AB, Denmark

CATERPILLAR INC.

100 NE Adams Street, Peoria, IL, 61629-6105

Tel: (309) 675-1000 Fax: (309) 675-1182 Web site: www.cat.com

Mfr. earth/material-handling and construction machinery and equipment and engines.

Caterpillar, Inc., Copenhagen, Denmark

THE CHASE MANHATTAN CORPORATION

World Headquarters, 270 Park Ave., New York, NY, 10017

Tel: (212) 270-6000 Fax: (212) 622-9030 Web site: www.chase.com

International banking and financial services.

Chase Manhattan Bank NA, Vognmagergade 10, DK-1120 Copenhagen, Denmark

THE CHUBB CORPORATION

15 Mountain View Road, Warren, NJ, 07061-1615

Tel: (908) 580-2000 Fax: (908) 580-3606 Web site: www.chubb.com

Holding company: property/casualty insurance.

Chubb Insurance Co. of Europe, SA, Marina Park, Sundkrogsgade 4, 2100 Copenhagen, Denmark

Tel: 45-3917-5000 Fax: 45-3917-5970

CIGNA CORPORATION

One Liberty Place, Philadelphia, PA, 19192

Tel: (215) 761-1000 Fax: (215) 761-5008

Insurance, invest, health care and other financial services.

Cigna Insurance Co. of Europe SA/NV, Amargeriorv 24, DK-1160 Copenhagen K, Denmark

Insurance Co. of North America, c/o PFA Skade, Marina Park, Sundkrogsgade 4, DK-2100 Copenhagen 0, Denmark

CINCOM SYSTEMS INC.

2300 Montana Ave., Cincinnati, OH, 45211

Tel: (513) 612-2300 Fax: (513) 481-8332 Web site: www.cincom.com

Develop/distributor computer software.

Cincom Systems Inc., Copenhagen, Denmark

CISCO SYSTEMS, INC.

170 Tasman Drive, San Jose, CA, 95134-1706

Tel: (408) 526-4000 Fax: (408) 526-4100 Web site: www.cisco.com

Develop/mfr./market computer hardware and software networking systems.

Cisco Systems, Vesterbrogade 149, DK-1620 Copenhagen, Denmark

Tel: 45-33-26-5900 Fax: 45-33-26-5901 Contact: N/A

THE COCA-COLA COMPANY

P.O. Drawer 1734, Atlanta, GA, 30301

Tel: (404) 676-2121 Fax: (404) 676-6792 Web site: www.coca-cola.com

Mfr./marketing/distributor soft drinks, syrups & concentrates, juice & juice-drink products.

Coca-Cola Nordic Beverages A/S, Copenhagen, Denmark - All mail to U.S. address

COLGATE-PALMOLIVE COMPANY

300 Park Ave., New York, NY, 10022

Tel: (212) 310-2000 Fax: (212) 310-2919

Mfr. pharmaceuticals, cosmetics, toiletries and detergents.

Colgate-Palmolive A/S, Smedeland 9, DK-2600 Glostrup, Denmark

COLUMBIA PICTURES INDUSTRIES INC.

10202 West Washington Blvd., Culver City, CA, 90232

Tel: (310) 244-4000 Fax: (310) 244-2626 Web site: www.sony.com

Producer and distributor of motion pictures.

Columbia-Fox, C. Hauchsvej 13, DK-1825 Frederiksberg, Denmark

COMPAQ COMPUTER CORPORATION

20555 State Highway 249, PO Box 692000, Houston, TX, 77269-2000

Tel: (713) 370-0670 Fax: (713) 514-1740 Web site: www.compaq.com

Develop/mfr. personal computers.

Compaq Computer A/S, Kongevejen 2, 3460 Birkeroed, Denmark

Tel: 45-4590-4590 Fax: 45-4590-4595

COMPUTER ASSOCIATES INTERNATIONAL INC.

One Computer Associates Plaza, Islandia, NY, 11788

Tel: (516) 342-5224 Fax: (516) 342-5329 Web site: www.cai.com

Integrated software for enterprise computing and information management, application development, manufacturing, financial applications and professional services.

Computer Associates Scandinavia A/S, Ryttermarken 10, DK-3520 Farum, Denmark

COMPUTER SCIENCES CORPORATION

2100 East Grand Ave., El Segundo, CA, 90245

Tel: (310) 615-0311 Fax: (310) 322-9768 Web site: www.csc.com

Information technology services, management consulting, systems integration, outsourcing.

CSC Computer Sciences AB - Scandinavian Division, Copenhagen, Denmark

Contact: Denis Hocking, Pres.

CONAGRA INC.

One ConAgra Drive, Omaha, NE, 68102-5001

Tel: (402) 595-4000 Fax: (402) 595-4595 Web site: www.conagra.com

Prepared/frozen foods, grains, flour, animal feeds, agri chemicals, poultry, meat, dairy products, including Healthy Choice, Butterball and Hunt's.

ConAgra Inc., Copenhagen, Denmark

COOK INC.

925 South Curry Pike, PO Box 489, Bloomington, ID, 47402

Tel: (812) 339-2235 Fax: (812) 339-8206

Instruments for cardiovascular diagnosis.

Willam Cook A/S, Sandet 6, DK-4632 Bjaeverskov, Denmark

COOPER INDUSTRIES INC.

6600 Travis Street, Ste. 5800, Houston, TX, 77002

Tel: (713) 209-8400 Fax: (713) 209-8995 Web site: www.cooperindustries.com

Mfr./distributor electrical products, tools and hardware and automotive products.

Bussmann Division, 5 Literbuen, DK-2740 Skovlunde, Copenhagen, Denmark

Tel: 45-4485-0900 Fax: 45-4485-0901

CROWN CORK & SEAL COMPANY, INC.

One Crown Way, Philadelphia, PA, 19154-4599

Tel: (215) 698-5100 Fax: (215) 698-5201

Mfr. cans, bottle caps; filling & packaging machinery.

Crown Cork Co. A/S, Hoerskaetten 13, DK-2630 Taastrup, Denmark

CUBIC CORPORATION

9333 Balboa Ave., PO Box 85587, San Diego, CA, 92123

Tel: (619) 277-6780 Fax: (619) 505-1523 Web site: www.cubic.com

Automatic fare collection equipment, training systems.

Scanpoint Technology A/S, Vibeholms Alle 22, DK-2605 Brondby, Denmark

Tel: 45-4343-3999 Fax: 45-4343-3940 Contact: George Nora, Mng. Dir.

CURTISS-WRIGHT CORPORATION

1200 Wall Street West, Lyndhurst, NJ, 07071

Tel: (201) 896-8400 Fax: (201) 438-5680

Mfr. precision components and systems, engineered services to aerospace, flow control and marine industry.

Curtiss-Wright Flight Systems/Europe, PO Box 51, DK-7470 Karup, Denmark

D'ARCY MASIUS BENTON & BOWLES INC. (DMB&B)

1675 Broadway, New York, NY, 10019

Tel: (212) 468-3622 Fax: (212) 468-2987 Web site: www.dmbb.com

Full service international advertising and communications group.

DMB&B Reklamebureau A/S, Sankt Knudsvej 41, DK-1903 Frederiksberg C, Denmark

DMM/Ipsen & Parmo A/S, Brostes Gaard, Ovengaden oven Vandet 10, DK-1415 Copenhagen K, Denmark

DATA GENERAL CORPORATION

4400 Computer Drive, Westboro, MA, 01580

Tel: (508) 898-5000 Fax: (508) 366-1319 Web site: www.dg.com

Design, mfr. general purpose computer systems & peripheral products & services.

Data General A/S, Fabriksparken 38, DK-2600 Glostrup, Denmark

DATAWARE TECHNOLOGIES INC.

222 Third Street, Ste. 3300, Cambridge, MA, 02142

Tel: (617) 621-0820 Fax: (617) 494-0740 Web site: www.dataware.com

Multi-platform, multi-lingual software solutions & services for electronic information providers.

Dataware Technologies Scandinavia A/S, Bredgade 36B, DK-1260 Copenhagen, Denmark

DDB NEEDHAM WORLDWIDE INC.

437 Madison Ave., New York, NY, 10022

Tel: (212) 415-2000 Fax: (212) 415-3417

Advertising agency.

DDB Denmark, Montergarden, Gothersgade 49, DK-1123 Copenhagen K, Denmark

DELL COMPUTER CORPORATION

One Dell Way, Round Rock, TX, 78682-2222

Tel: (512) 338-4400 Fax: (512) 728-3653 Web site: www.dell.com

Direct marketer & supplier of computer systems.

Dell Denmark, Slossmarkren 11, Dk-2970 Hoershoim, Denmark

Tel: 45-4517-0100 Fax: 45-4517-0117 Contact: Ulf Sandmark, Mng. Dir.

DELOITTE TOUCHE TOHMATSU INTERNATIONAL

PO Box 820, Wilton, CT, 06897

Tel: (203) 761-3000 Fax: (203) 834-2200 Web site: www.u.s.deloitte.com or www.dtti.com

Accounting, audit, tax and management consulting services.

Deloitte & Touche, H.C. Andersens Blvd. 2, DK 1780 Copenhagen V, Denmark (Locations: Aalborg, Arhus, Esbjerg, & Skovlunde, Denmark.)

DHL WORLDWIDE EXPRESS

333 Twin Dolphin Drive, Redwood City, CA, 94065

Tel: (650) 593-7474 Fax: (650) 593-1689 Web site: www.dhl.com

Worldwide air express carrier.

DHL Worldwide Express, Jydekrogen 14, Vallensbaek 2625, Denmark

Tel: 45-7013-1131

DIGITAL EQUIPMENT CORPORATION

111 Powder Mill Road, Maynard, MA, 01754

Tel: (978) 493-5111 Fax: (978) 493-7374 Web site: www.digital.com

Mfr. network computer systems, components, software and services.

Digital Equipment A/S, Aadalsvej 99, DK-2970 Hoersholm, Denmark

Tel: 45-4576-9666 Fax: 45-4517-3091

WALT DISNEY COMPANY

500 South Buena Vista Street, Burbank, CA, 91521

Tel: (818) 560-1000 Fax: (818) 560-1930

Film/TV production, theme parks, resorts, publishing, recording and retail stores.

Walt Disney Productions A/S, Ostergade 24B, DK-1100 Copenhagen, Denmark

THE DOW CHEMICAL COMPANY

2030 Dow Center, Midland, MI, 48674

Tel: (517) 636-1000 Fax: (517) 636-3228 Web site: www.atdow.com

Mfr. chemicals, plastics, pharmaceuticals, agricultural products, consumer products.

Dow Chemical A/S, Strandvejen 171, DK-2900 Hellerup, Denmark

DRAKE BEAM MORIN INC.

101 Huntington Ave., Boston, MA, 02199

Tel: (617) 450-9860 Fax: (617) 267-2011 Web site: www.dbm.com

Human resource management consulting & training.

DBM International Office - Copenhagen, DK_1263 Copenhagen K, Copenhagen Europe Ctr., Vesterbrogade 149, 1620 Copenhagen V, Denmark (Locations: Kirketorvet, Norregade, Sondergrade.)

Tel: 45-33-79-0803 Fax: 45-7572-3855

THE DUN & BRADSTREET CORPORATION

One Diamond Hill Road, Murray Hill, NJ, 07974

Tel: (908) 665-5000 Fax: (908) 665-5524 Web site: www.dnbcorp.com

Provides corporate credit, marketing & accounts-receivable management services & publishes credit ratings & financial information.

D&B Danmark, Egegaardsvej 39, DK 2610 Rodovre, Denmark

Tel: 45-36-70-5566

EASTMAN CHEMICAL

100 North Eastman Road, Kingsport, TN, 37660

Tel: (423) 229-2000 Fax: (423) 229-1351 Web site: www.eastman.com

Mfr. plastics, chemicals, fibers.

Eastman Chemical B. V., Naverland 2, 11th Fl., KD-2600 Glostrup, Denmark

Tel: 45-7731-7760 Fax: 45-7731-7761 Contact: Jens Michael Poulsen

EASTMAN KODAK COMPANY

343 State Street, Rochester, NY, 14650

Tel: (716) 724-4000 Fax: (716) 724-0663

Develop/mfr. photo & chemicals products, information management/video/copier systems, fibers/plastics for various industry.

Eastman Chemical Intl. AG - Kodak A/S, Dybendal Alle 10, DK-2630 Taastrup, Denmark

Kodak & H-Color A/S, Korsor & Risskov, Denmark

ECOLAB INC.

Ecolab Center, 370 N. Wabasha Street, St. Paul, MN, 55102

Tel: (612) 293-2233 Fax: (612) 225-3105 Web site: www.ecolab.com

Develop/mfr. premium cleaning, sanitizing and maintenance products and services for the hospitality, institutional, and residential markets.

Ecolab Ltd., Copenhagen, Denmark

Tel: 45-36-15-8585

EG&G INC.

45 William Street, Wellesley, MA, 02181-4078

Tel: (781) 237-5100 Fax: (781) 431-4114

Diversified R/D, mfr. & services.

Wallac Danmark A/S, Gydevang 21, DK-3450 Allerod, Denmark

EMC CORP.

35 Parkwood Drive, Hopkinton, MA, 01748-9103

Tel: (508) 435-1000 Fax: (508) 435-8884 Web site: www.emc.com

Designs/supplies intelligent enterprise storage & retrieval technology for open systems, mainframes & midrange environments.

EMC Computer Systems (Denmark), Meterbuer 15 A, 2740 Skovlunde, Meterbuer, Denmark

Tel: 45-7010-6878

EMERY WORLDWIDE

One Lagoon Drive, Ste. 400, Redwood City, CA, 94065

Tel: (650) 596-9600 Fax: (650) 596-7901 Web site: www.emeryworld.com

Freight transport, global logistics and air cargo.

Emery Worldwide, Fuglebaekvej 4A, DK/2770 Kastrup, Copenhagen, Denmark

ERNST & YOUNG, LLP

787 Seventh Ave., New York, NY, 10019

Tel: (212) 773-3000 Fax: (212) 773-6350 Web site: www.eyi.com

Accounting and audit, tax and management consulting services.

Ernst & Young A/S, Tagensvej 86, DK-2200 Copenhagen N, Denmark

Tel: 45-35-82-48-48 Fax: 45-35-82-47-10 Contact: Per Lundbaek Christensen

ESTEE LAUDER INTERNATIONAL INC.

767 Fifth Ave., New York, NY, 10153

Tel: (212) 572-4200 Fax: (212) 572-3941

Cosmetics, perfumes & Aveda hair care products.

Estee Lauder Cosmetics A/S, Norregade 7-A, DK-1165 Copenhagen K, Denmark

EURO RSCG Worldwide

350 Hudson Street, New York, NY, 10014

Tel: (212) 886-2000 Fax: (212) 886-2016

International advertising agency group.

Euro RSCG, Copenhagen, Denmark

EXIDE ELECTRONICS INTERNATIONAL CORPORATION

8521 Six Forks Road, Raleigh, NC, 27615

Tel: (919) 870-3020 Fax: (919) 870-3100 Web site: www.exide.com

Mfr./services uninterruptible power systems.

Exide Electronics AB, Hammerholmen 39 L-M, DK-2650 Hvidovre, Denmark

Tel: 45-3677-7910 Fax: 45-3677-7921

FERRO CORPORATION

1000 Lakeside Ave., Cleveland, OH, 44114-1183

Tel: (216) 641-8580 Fax: (216) 696-5784 Web site: www.ferro.com

Mfr. Specialty chemicals, coatings, plastics, colors, refractories.

Ferro (Holland) B.V., Industrivej 10, Vassingerod, DK-3540 Lynge, Denmark

Tel: 45-4218-8222 Fax: 45-4218-7634 Contact: P. Nielson, Off. Mgr.

FISCHER IMAGING CORPORATION

12300 North Grant Street, Denver, CO, 80241

Tel: (303) 452-6800 Fax: (303) 452-4335 Web site: www.fischerimaging.com

Mfr. x-ray equipment.

Fischer Imaging Europe A/S, Nordkajen 11, DK-7100 Vejle, Denmark

Tel: 45-7572-7766

FISHER-ROSEMOUNT

8000 Maryland Ave., Ste. 500, Clayton, MO, 63105-4755

Tel: (314) 746-9900 Fax: (314) 746-9974

Mfr. industrial process control equipment.

Fisher Rosemount A/S, Hejrevang 11, 3450 Alleroed, Denmark

FLUKE CORPORATION

PO Box 9090, Everett, WA, 98206-9090

Tel: (425) 347-6100 Fax: (425) 356-5116 Web site: www.fluke.com

Mfr. electronic test tools.

Fluke Electronics, Copenhagen, Denmark

FMC CORPORATION

200 E. Randolph Drive, Chicago, IL, 60601

Tel: (312) 861-6000 Fax: (312) 861-6141

Produces chemicals & precious metals, mfr. machinery, equipment & systems for industrial, agricultural & government use.

FMC Litex A/S, Copenhagen, Denmark

FORD MOTOR COMPANY

The American Road, Dearborn, MI, 48121

Tel: (313) 322-3000 Fax: (313) 322-9600 Web site: www.ford.com

Mfr./sales motor vehicles.

Ford Motor Co. A/S, Sluseholmen 1, DK-2450 Copenhagen SV, Denmark

FORT JAMES CORPORATION

1650 Lake Cook Road, Deerfield, IL, 60015

Tel: (847) 317-5000 Fax: (847) 236-3755 Web site: www.fortjames.com

Mfr./sales of consumer paper and packaging products.

Fort James Corporation, Copenhagen, Denmark

FRITZ COMPANIES INC.

706 Mission Street, Ste. 900, San Francisco, CA, 94103

Tel: (415) 904-8360 Fax: (415) 904-8661 Web site: www.fritz.com

Integrated transportation, sourcing, distribution & customs brokerage services.

Fritz Companies Inc., Aalborg, Aahus, Billund, Copenhagen & Odense, Denmark

GENERAL ELECTRIC CAPITAL CORPORATION

260 Long Ridge Road, Stamford, CT, 06927

Tel: (203) 357-4000 Fax: (203) 357-6489

Financial, property/casualty insurance, computer sales and trailer leasing services.

Employers Reinsurance Corp. (ERC), Gronningen 25, DK-1270 Copenhagen K, Denmark

Tel: 45-33-979-593 Fax: 45-33-979-441

GENERAL MOTORS ACCEPTANCE CORPORATION

100 Renaissance Center, Detroit, MI, 48243-7301

Tel: (313) 556-5000 Fax: (313) 556-5108 Web site: www.gmac.com

Automobile financing.

GMAC Finansiering A/S, Klampenborgvej 232, DK-2800 Lyngby, Denmark

GENERAL MOTORS CORPORATION

100 Renaissance Center, Detroit, MI, 48243.7301

Tel: (313) 556-5000 Fax: (313) 556-5108 Web site: www.gm.com

Mfr. full line vehicles, automotive electronics, commercial technologies, telecommunications, space, finance.

General Motors Denmark A/S, Tobaksvejen 22, DK-2860 Soeborg, Denmark

GENERAL REINSURANCE CORPORATION

695 East Main Street, Stamford, CT, 06904-2350

Tel: (203) 328-5000 Fax: (203) 328-6423 Web site: www.genre.com

Reinsurance services worldwide.

General Re Europe Scandinavia, Chr. IX's Gade 10, 3rd Fl., 111 Copenhagen K, Denmark

Tel: 45-3333-7878 Fax: 45-3333-7475 Contact: Kim Schwartz, VP

Kölnische Norden A/S, Chr. IX's Cade 10, 3rd Fl., DK - 1111 Copenhagen K, Denmark

Tel: 45-3333-7878 Fax: 45-3333-7475 Contact: Hans-Kristian Jacobsen, Gen. Mgr.

THE GILLETTE COMPANY

Prudential Tower Building, Boston, MA, 02199

Tel: (617) 421-7000 Fax: (617) 421-7123 Web site: www.gillette.com

Develop/mfr. personal care/use products: blades & razors, toiletries, cosmetics, stationery.

Braun Denmark A/S, Soborg, Denmark

Gillette A/S, Copenhagen, Denmark

GRANT THORNTON INTERNATIONAL

800 One Prudential Plaza, 130 E. Randolph Drive, Chicago, IL, 60601-6050

Tel: (312) 856-0001 Fax: (312) 616-7052

Accounting, audit, tax and management consulting services.

Grant Thornton Denmark Grothen & Perregaard, Stockholmsgade 45, DK-2100, Copenhagen, Denmark

Tel: 45-31-42-4844 Fax: 45-31-42-2911 Contact: J. Frank Jakobsen

GREY ADVERTISING INC.

777 Third Ave., New York, NY, 10017

Tel: (212) 546-2000 Fax: (212) 546-1495 Web site: www.giworldwwide.com

International advertising agency.

Grey Communications Group, Sankt Peders Straede 49A, DK-1453 Copenhagen K, Denmark

HALLIBURTON COMPANY

500 North Akard Street, Ste. 3600, Dallas, TX, 75201-3391

Tel: (214) 978-2600 Fax: (214) 978-2685 Web site: www.halliburton.com

Energy, construction and insurance.

Halliburton Ltd., PO Box 4060, 6715 Esbjerg, Denmark

Tel: 45-7914-5400 Fax: 45-7914-5410

HANDY & HARMAN

555 Theodore Fremd Ave., Rye, NY, 10580

Tel: (914) 921-5200 Fax: (914) 925-4496

Precious & specialty metals for industry, refining, scrap metal; diversified industrial mfr.

Indiana Tube Denmark A/S, Kokbjerg 25, DK-6000 Kolding, Denmark

HARMAN JBL INTERNATIONAL

800 Balboa Boulevard, Nothridge, CA, 91329

Tel: (818) 895-8734 Fax: (818) 893-1531 Web site: www.harman.com

Mfr. audio and video equipment, loudspeakers and sound reinforcement equipment.

Lydig Maraketing A/S, Rugmarken 27A, DK-3520 Farum, Denmark

Lydig of Scandinavia A/S, Vesterled 6-8, DK-6950 Ringkobing, Denmark

THE HARPER GROUP

260 Townsend Street, San Francisco, CA, 94107-1719

Tel: (415) 978-0600 Fax: (415) 978-0692 Web site: www.circleintl.com

Ocean/air freight forwarding, customs brokerage, packing and wholesale, logistics management and insurance.

Circle Leman Airfreight`, Amager Landevej 149, PO Box 110, DK-2770 Kastrup, Denmark
Tel: 45-32-501-322 Fax: 45-32-501-979

Leman Airfreight, Lufthavnsvej 27 D, Billund DK 7190, Denmark
Tel: 45-7533-1233 Fax: 45-7533-2763

Leman Airfreight, H. C. Tvenges VEJ 3-5, Aarhus, DK 8100, Denmark
Tel: 45-8613-4400 Fax: 45-8613-6251

HARRIS CORPORATION

1025 West NASA Blvd., Melbourne, FL, 32919
Tel: (407) 727-9100 Fax: (407) 727-9344 Web site: www.harris.com
Mfr. communications and information-handling equipment, including copying and fax systems.

Independent Elcronic Components, Bernhard Bangs Alle 39, DK-2000 Frederiksberg, Denmark
Tel: 45-38-10-2925 Fax: 45-38-10-2926

HEIDRICK & STRUGGLES INC

Sears Tower, 233 South Wacker Drive, Chicago, IL, 60606
Tel: (312) 496-1200 Fax: (312) 496-1290 Web site: www.h-s.com
Executive search firm.

Heidrick & Struggles Intl. Inc., Oslo Plada 16, DK-2100, Copenhagen, Denmark
Tel: 45-35-43-7044 Fax: 45-35-43-7045

HELLER FINANCIAL INC.

500 West Monroe Street, Chicago, IL, 60661
Tel: (312) 441-7000 Fax: (312) 441-7256
Financial services.

Heller Financial Inc., Denmark

HERCULES INC

Hercules Plaza, 1313 North Market Street, Wilmington, DE, 19894-0001
Tel: (302) 594-5000 Fax: (302) 594-5400 Web site: www.herc.com
Mfr. specialty chemicals, plastics, film and fibers, coatings, resins, food ingredients.

A/S Kobenhavns Pektinfabrik, Ved Banen 16, DK-4623 Lille Skensved, Denmark

HEWLETT-PACKARD COMPANY

3000 Hanover Street, Palo Alto, CA, 94304-0890
Tel: (650) 857-1501 Fax: (650) 857-7299 Web site: www.hp.com
Mfr. computing, communications & measurement products & services.

Hewlett-Packard A/S, Kongevejen 25, DK-3460 Birkerod, Denmark

HONEYWELL INC.

PO Box 524, Minneapolis, MN, 55440-0524
Tel: (612) 951-1000 Fax: (612) 951-3066 Web site: www.honeywell.com
Develop/mfr. controls for home and building, industry, space and aviation.

Honeywell A/S, Lyngby Hovedgade 98, DK-2800 Lyngby, Denmark

HORWATH INTERNATIONAL

415 Madison Ave., New York, NY, 10017
Tel: (212) 838-5566 Fax: (212) 838-3636
Public accountants and auditors.

Askgaard Olesen Horwath, Stoltenbergsgade 9, DK-1576 Copenhagen V, Denmark

HOUGHTON INTERNATIONAL INC.

PO Box 930, Madison & Van Buren Avenues, Valley Forge, PA, 19482-0930
Tel: (610) 666-4000 Fax: (610) 666-1376
Mfr. specialty chemicals, hydraulic fluids & lubricants.

Houghton Danmark A/S, Skodsborgvej 48A, DK-2830 Virum, Denmark

HOWMEDICA INC.

359 Veterans Boulevard, Rutherford, NJ, 07070

Tel: (201) 507-7300 Fax: (201) 935-4873 Web site: www.howmedica.com

Hospital, medical and dental supplies.

Howmedica Denmark, Copenhagen, Denmark

Tel: 45-339-36099

IBM CORPORATION

New Orchard Road, Armonk, NY, 10504

Tel: (914) 765-1900 Fax: (914) 765-7382 Web site: www.ibm.com

Information products, technology & services.

IBM Danmark A/S, IBM Nordic Information Centre, Nymollevej 85, Lyngby, DK-2800 Aarhus, Denmark

Tel: 45-4523-3000 Fax: 45-4593-2420

IKON OFFICE SOLUTIONS

70 Valley Stream Parkway, Malvern, PA, 19355

Tel: (610) 296-8000 Fax: (610) 408-7022 Web site: www.ikon.com

Provider of office technology solutions.

Ikon Office Solutions, Copenhagen, Denmark

INFONET SERVICES CORPORATION

2100 East Grand Ave., El Segundo, CA, 90245

Tel: (310) 335-2600 Fax: (310) 335-4507 Web site: www.infonet.com

Provider of Internet services and electronic messaging services.

Infonet Denmark, Lautruphoej 2-6, DK-2750 Ballerup, Denmark

Tel: 45-4480-1111 Fax: 45-4480-4228

INFORMIX CORPORATION

4100 Bohannon Drive, Menlo Park, CA, 95025

Tel: (650) 926-6300 Fax: (650) 926-6593 Web site: www.informix.com

Designs & produces database management software, connectivity interfaces & gateways, and other computer applications.

Informix Software A/S, Gladsaxevej 342, DK 2860 Soeborg, Denmark

Tel: 45-3966-1110

INGRAM MICRO INC.

PO Box 25125, Santa Ana, CA, 92799

Tel: (714) 566-1000 Fax: (714) 566-7940 Web site: www.ingrammicro.com

Distribute computer systems, software and related products.

Ingram Micro Inc., Denmark

INTEL CORPORATION

Robert Noyce Building, 2200 Mission College Blvd., Santa Clara, CA, 95052-8119

Tel: (408) 765-8080 Fax: (408) 765-1739 Web site: www.intel.com

Mfr. semiconductor, microprocessor and micro-communications components and systems.

Intel Semiconductor (Denmark) Ltd., Copenhagen, Denmark

Emp: 146

INTERGRAPH CORPORATION

One Madison Industrial Park, Huntsville, AL, 35894-0001

Tel: (205) 730-2000 Fax: (205) 730-7898 Web site: www.intergraph.com

Develop/mfr. interactive computer graphic systems.

Intergraph CAD/CAM (Denmark) A/S, Roskildevej 39, DK-2000 Frederiksberg, Denmark

Tel: 45-36-44-5888 Fax: 45-36-44-2070

INTERMEC TECHNOLOGIES CORPORATION

6001 36th Ave. West, PO Box 4280, Everett, WA, 98203-9280

Tel: (425) 348-2600 Fax: (425) 355-9551 Web site: www.intermec.com

Mfr./distributor automated data collection systems.

Intermec Technologies A/S, Gydevang, 21A, 3450 Allerød, Denmark

Tel: 45-4816-6166 Fax: 45-1816-6167

INTERNATIONAL PAPER COMPANY

2 Manhattanville Road, Purchase, NY, 10577

Tel: (914) 397-1500 Fax: (914) 397-1596 Web site: www.ipaper.com

Mfr./distributor container board, paper, wood products.

Horsell Enk A/S, Valjoejs Alle 155, DK-2610 Roedovre, Denmark

Ilford Photo A/S, Gadelandet 18, DK-2700 Bronshoj, Denmark

INTERNATIONAL RECTIFIER CORPORATION

233 Kansas Street, El Segundo, CA, 90245

Tel: (310) 322-3331 Fax: (310) 322-3332 Web site: www.irf.com

Mfr. power semiconductor components.

International Rectifier - Denmark, PO Box 88, Teelfonvej 8, DK-2860 Soeborg, Denmark

Tel: 45-3-957-7150 Fax: 45-3-957-7152

INTRALOX INC.

PO Box 50699, New Orleans, LA, 70150

Tel: (504) 733-0463 Fax: (504) 734-0063

Mfr. plastic, modular conveyor belts and accessories.

Intralox A/S, Egholmverj 3, DK-9800 Hjorring, Denmark

ITT SHERATON CORPORATION

60 State Street, Boston, MA, 02108

Tel: (617) 367-3600 Fax: (617) 367-5676

Hotel operations.

Sheraton Copenhagen Hotel, Vester Sogade 6, DK-1601 Copenhagen V, Denmark

J. WALTER THOMPSON COMPANY

466 Lexington Ave., New York, NY, 10017

Tel: (212) 210-7000 Fax: (212) 210-6944 Web site: www.jwt.com

International advertising and marketing services.

J. Walter Thompson Co., Copenhaen, Denmark

JOHNSON & JOHNSON

One Johnson & Johnson Plaza, New Brunswick, NJ, 08933

Tel: (732) 524-0400 Fax: (732) 214-0334 Web site: www.jnj.com

Mfr./distributor/R&D pharmaceutical, health care and cosmetic products.

Janssen-Cilag, PO Box 149, DK-3460 Birkerod, Denmark

S C JOHNSON & SON INC.

1525 Howe Street, Racine, WI, 53403

Tel: (414) 260-2000 Fax: (414) 260-2133 Web site: www.scjohnsonwax.com

Home, auto, commercial and personal care products and specialty chemicals.

Johnson Wax A/S, Midtager 18, DK-2600 Glostrup, Denmark

A.T. KEARNEY INC.

222 West Adams Street, Chicago, IL, 60606

Tel: (312) 648-0111 Fax: (312) 223-6200 Web site: www.atkearney.com

Management consultants and executive search.

A. T. Kearney A/S, Amaliegade 12, DK-1256, Copenhagen K, Denmark

Tel: 45-33-69-3000

KELLOGG COMPANY

One Kellogg Square, PO Box 3599, Battle Creek, MI, 49016-3599

Tel: (616) 961-2000 Fax: (616) 961-2871 Web site: www.kelloggs.com

Mfr. ready-to-eat cereals and convenience foods.

Nordisk Kellogg's A/S, Svendborg, Denmark (All inquiries to U.S. address)

KELLY SERVICES, INC.

999 W. Big Beaver Road, Troy, MI, 48084

Tel: (248) 362-4444 Fax: (248) 244-4154 Web site: www.kellyservices.com

Temporary help placement.

Kelly Services of Denmark, Inc., Amagertov 11, DK-1160 Copenhagen K, Denmark

Tel: 45-33-117070 Fax: 45-33-115122

Kelly Services of Denmark, Inc., Clemens Torv 17, 8000 Arhuc C, Denmark

Tel: 45-8613-8100 Fax: 45-8620-9043

KENNAMETAL INC.

State Rte. 981, Latrobe, PA, 15650

Tel: (724) 539-5000 Fax: (724) 539-4710 Web site: www.kennametal.com

Tools, hard carbide & tungsten alloys for metalworking industry.

Granaths Hardmetal A/S, DK-7000 Fredericia, Denmark

Tel: 45-7594-2122 Fax: 45-7594-1975

KORN/FERRY INTERNATIONAL

1800 Century Park East, Los Angeles, CA, 90067

Tel: (310) 552-1834 Fax: (310) 553-6452 Web site: www.kornferry.com

Executive search; management consulting.

Korn/Ferry International, Copenhagen, Denmark

Tel: 45-2-525-0090 Fax: 45-35-25-0099

KPMG PEAT MARWICK LLP

Three Chestnut Ridge Road, Montvale, NJ, 07645

Tel: (201) 307-7000 Fax: (201) 930-8617 Web site: www.kpmg.com

Accounting and audit, tax and management consulting services.

Corporate Finance KPMG/C. Jespersen, Sundsmarkvej 12, S Underborg, DK 64, Denmark

Corporate Finance KPMG/C. Jespersen, Torret 10, Nyborg, DK-5800, Denmark

Corporate Finance KPMG/C. Jespersen, Burstenbindervej 6, Odense, DK-5230, Denmark

Corporate Finance KPMG/C. Jespersen, Borups All, Copenhagen, Denmark

Tel: 45-38-183000 Fax: 45-38-183045 Contact: Finn L. Meyer, Sr. Ptnr.

Corporate Finance KPMG/C. Jespersen, Vestre Havnepromenade 1, Aalborg, DK-9000, Denmark

LAMSON & SESSIONS CO

25701 Science Park Drive, Cleveland, OH, 44122

Tel: (216) 464-3400 Fax: (216) 464-1455

Mfr. thermoplastic electrical conduit and related products; products for transportation equipment industry.

Lamson & Sessions APS, Rojrupveg 15, DK-5550 Langeskov, Denmark

LANIER WORLDWIDE, INC.

2300 Parklake Drive, N.E., Atlanta, GA, 30345

Tel: (770) 496-9500 Fax: (770) 621-1535

Specialize in digital copiers and multi-functional systems.

Lanier Denmark A/S, Markaervej 5, 2630 Tastrup, Denmark

Tel: 45-4371-0200 Fax: 45-4371-0221

LEVI STRAUSS & COMPANY

1155 Battery Street, Levi's Plaza, San Francisco, CA, 94111-1230

Tel: (415) 544-6000 Fax: (415) 501-3939 Web site: www.levistrauss.com

Mfr./distributor casual wearing apparel.

Levi Strauss Denmark, Kattesundet 4, DK-1458 Copenhagen K, Denmark

Tel: 45-33-155800 Fax: 45-22-156539

LIFE TECHNOLOGIES INC.

9800 Medical Center Drive, Rockville, MD, 20850

Tel: (301) 840-8000 Fax: (301) 329-8635

Biotechnology.

Life Technologies, Denmark

ELI LILLY & COMPANY

Lilly Corporate Center, Indianapolis, IN, 46285

Tel: (317) 276-2000 Fax: (317) 277-6579 Web site: www.lilly.com

Mfr. pharmaceuticals and animal health products.

Eli Lilly Denmark A/S, Thoravej 4, DK-2400 Copenhagen, Denmark

Tel: 45-38-168600 Fax: 45-38-881733

ARTHUR D. LITTLE, INC.

25 Acorn Park, Cambridge, MA, 02140-2390

Tel: (617) 498-5000 Fax: (617) 498-7200 Web site: www.adlittle.com

Management, environmental, health & safety consulting; technical & product development.

Arthur D. Little International, Inc., Bredgade 56, DK-1260 Copenhagen K, Denmark

Tel: 45-33-32-2555 Fax: 45-33-32-8455

LOCKHEED MARTIN CORPORATION

6801 Rockledge Drive, Bethesda, MD, 20817

Tel: (301) 897-6000 Fax: (301) 897-6652 Web site: www.imco.com

Design/mfr./management systems in fields of space, defense, energy, electronics and technical services.

Lockheed International, LRO Per Udsen Co., Aircraft Industry A/S, Fabrikvej 1, DK-500 Grenaa, Denmark

Tel: 45-8630-0292 Fax: 45-8632-0753

Lockheed International, LRO NEA Lindberg, DK-2250 Ballerup, Denmark

Tel: 45-4497-1311 Fax: 45-4497-1311

LOCTITE CORPORATION

10 Columbus Boulevard, Hartford, CT, 06106

Tel: (203) 520-5000 Fax: (203) 520-5073 Web site: www.loctite.com

Mfr./sale industrial adhesives and sealants.

Loctite Denamrk A/S, Hersvinget 7, DK-2630 Taastrup, Denmark

Tel: 45-4330-1301 Fax: 45-4330-1310 Contact: Per Hansen, Bus. Mgr.

LOWE & PARTNERS WORLDWIDE

1114 Ave. of the Americas, New York, NY, 10036

Tel: (212) 403-6700 Fax: (212) 403-6710

International advertising agency network.

Lowe & Partners, Copenhagen, Denmark

LSI LOGIC CORPORATION

1551 McCarthy Blvd, Milpitas, CA, 95035

Tel: (408) 433-8000 Fax: (408) 954-3220 Web site: www.lsilogic.com

Develop/mfr. semiconductors.

LSI Logic Development Center Ballerup, Lautrupuang 2B, 2750 Ballerup, Denmark
Tel: 45-4486-5555 Fax: 45-4486-5556

M-I
PO Box 48242, Houston, TX, 77242-2842
Tel: (713) 739-0222 Fax: (713) 308-9503
Drilling fluids.
Halliburton Co., Kanalen 1, DK-6700 Esbjerg, Denmark

R.H. MACY & COMPANY INC.
151 West 34th Street, New York, NY, 10001
Tel: (212) 695-4400 Fax: (212) 643-1307
Department stores; importers.
R.H. Macy & Co. Inc., Chr. Winthersvej 5, DK-1860 Copenhagen V, Denmark

MANPOWER INTERNATIONAL INC.
5301 N. Ironwood Road, PO Box 2053, Milwaukee, WI, 53201-2053
Tel: (414) 961-1000 Fax: (414) 961-7081 Web site: www.manpower
Temporary help, contract service, training & testing.
Manpower A/S, Norre Voldgade 19, DK-1358 Copenhagen K, Denmark
Tel: 45-33-69-8000 Fax: 45-33-69-8080

MARSH & McLENNAN COS INC.
1166 Ave. of the Americas, New York, NY, 10036-2774
Tel: (212) 345-5000 Fax: (212) 345-4808 Web site: www.marshmac.com
Insurance agents/brokers, pension and investment management consulting services.
Bonnor Marsh & McLennan A/S, Teknikerbyen 3, 2830 Virum, Denmark
Tel: 45-4595-9595 Fax: 45-4595-9500 Contact: John Bonnon

MASCO CORPORATION
21001 Van Born Road, Taylor, MI, 48180
Tel: (313) 274-7400 Fax: (313) 374-6666
Mfr. home improvement, building and home furnishings products.
Damixa A/S, Ostibirkvej 2, Postbox 50, DK-5240 Odense NO, Denmark
Tel: 45-6610-9700

McCANN-ERICKSON WORLDWIDE
750 Third Ave., New York, NY, 10017
Tel: (212) 984-3644 Fax: (212) 984-2629
International advertising/marketing services.
McCann-Erickson A/S, Toldbodgade 19B, DK-1253 Copenhagen K, Denmark

McDONALD'S CORPORATION
Kroc Drive, Oak Brook, IL, 60523
Tel: (630) 623-3000 Fax: (630) 623-7409
Fast food chain stores.
McDonald's Corp., Denmark
Contact: Jesper Gad Andresen, Mgr.

McKINSEY & COMPANY
55 East 52nd Street, New York, NY, 10022
Tel: (212) 446-7000 Fax: (212) 446-8575 Web site: www.mckinsey.com
Management and business consulting services.
McKinsey & Company, Ved Stranden 14, DK-1061 Copenhagen, Denmark
Tel: 45-33-933030 Fax: 45-33-931621

MEMOREX CORPORATION

10100 Pioneer Boulevard, Santa Fe Springs, CA, 90670

Tel: (562) 906-2800 Fax: (562) 906-2848

Magnetic recording tapes, etc.

MRX A/S, Vallensbaekvej 25, DK-2600 Glostrup, Copenhagen, Denmark

MENTOR GRAPHICS/MICROTEC RESEARCH

880 Ridder Park Drive, San Jose, CA, 95131

Tel: (408) 487-7000 Fax: (408) 487-7001

Develop/mfr. software tools for embedded systems market.

Microtec Denmark, Denmark

MERCK & COMPANY, INC.

1 Merck Drive, Whitehouse Station, NJ, 08889

Tel: (908) 423-1000 Fax: (908) 423-2592

Pharmaceuticals, chemicals and biologicals.

Merck, Sharp & Dohme, Marielundvej 46C, DK-1625 Copenhagen, Denmark

MICROSOFT CORPORATION

One Microsoft Way, Redmond, WA, 98052-6399

Tel: (425) 882-8080 Fax: (425) 936-7329 Web site: www.microsoft.com

Computer software, peripherals and services.

Microsoft Danmark APS, Lautruphoj 1-3, DK-2750 Ballerup, Denmark

Tel: 45-4489-0100 Fax: 45-4468-5510

MILLIPORE CORPORATION, ANALYTICAL PRODUCT DIVISION

80 Ashby Road, PO Box 9125, Bedford, MA, 01730

Tel: (781) 275-9200 Fax: (781) 533-3110 Web site: www.millipore.com

Mfr. flow and pressure measurement and control components; precision filters, hi-performance liquid chromatography instruments.

Millipore A/S, Baldersbven 46, DK-2640 Hedehusene, Denmark

MOBIL CORPORATION

3225 Gallows Road, Fairfax, VA, 22037-0001

Tel: (703) 846-3000 Fax: (703) 846-4669 Web site: www.mobil.com

Petroleum and gas exploration and refining, mfr. petroleum products, chemicals and petrochemicals.

Mobil Oil Danmark A/S, Birkerod Kongevej 64, DK-3460 Birkerod, Denmark

MODINE MANUFACTURING COMPANY

1500 DeKoven Ave., Racine, WI, 53403

Tel: (414) 636-1200 Fax: (414) 636-1424 Web site: www.modine.com

Mfr. heat-transfer products.

Modine Manufacturing Co., Horsens, Denmark

MOOG INC.

Jamison Road, East Aurora, NY, 14052-0018

Tel: (716) 652-2000 Fax: (716) 687-4457 Web site: www.moog.com

Mfr. precision control components & systems.

Moog Buhl Automotson, Topstykkat 24, DK-3460 Birkerod, Denmark

MORRISON KNUDSEN CORPORATION

1 Morrison Knudsen Plaza, PO Box 73, Boise, ID, 83729

Tel: (208) 386-5000 Fax: (208) 386-7186 Web site: www.mk.com

Design/construction for environmental, industrial, process, power and transportation markets.

Morrison Knudsen Corporation, Copenhagen, Denmark

MOTOROLA, INC.

1303 East Algonquin Road, Schaumburg, IL, 60196

Tel: (847) 576-5000 Fax: (847) 538-5191 Web site: www.mot.com

Mfr. communications equipment, semiconductors and cellular phones.

Motorola Storno A/S, Midtager 20, DK-2605 Broendby Denmark

Tel: 45-4345-5544 Fax: 45-4343-4358

NAI TECHNOLOGIES INC.

282 New York Ave., Huntington, NY, 11743

Tel: (516) 271-5685 Fax: (516) 385-0815 Web site: www.naitech.com

Mfr. computers & peripherals, office machines, communications equipment.

Lynwood Scientific Developments Ltd., Tempest Eurpoe A/S, Drejovej 12, DK-3450 Allerod, Denmark

Tel: 45-4052-5540 Fax: 45-48-17-1508 Contact: Jan Engelund

NATIONAL CAR RENTAL SYSTEM, INC.

7700 France Ave. South, Minneapolis, MN, 55435

Tel: (612) 830-2121 Fax: (612) 830-2921

Car rentals.

National Car Rental System A/S, Gammel Kongevej 70, DK-1850 Copenhagen V, Denmark

NATIONAL CHEMSEARCH CORPORATION

2727 Chemsearch Blvd., Irving, TX, 75061

Tel: (972) 438-0211 Fax: (972) 438-0186 Web site: www.nch.com

Commercial chemical products.

National Chemsearch ApS, Industribuen 7E, DK-2635 Ishoj, Denmark

NATIONAL STARCH & CHEMICAL COMPANY

10 Finderne Ave., Bridgewater, NJ, 08807-3300

Tel: (908) 685-5000 Fax: (908) 685-5005 Web site: www.national starch.com

Mfr. adhesives & sealants, resins & specialty chemicals, electronic materials & adhesives, food products, industry starch.

National Starch & Chemical A/S, Tollose, Denmark

NETSCAPE COMMUNICATIONS

501 East Middlefield Road, Mountain View, CA, 94043

Tel: (650) 254-1900 Fax: (650) 528-4124

Mfr./distribute Internet-based commercial and consumer software applications.

Netscape Communications Denmark A/S, Larsbjornsstraede 3, 1454 Copenhagen K, Denmark

Tel: 45-33-337-72-03 Fax: 45-33-37-72-04

A .C. NIELSEN COMPANY

177 Broad Street, Stamford, CT, 06901

Tel: (203) 961-3000 Fax: (203) 961-3190 Web site: www.acnielsen.com

Market research.

A/S Markeds-Data, Strandboulevarden 89, DK-2100 Copenhagen, Denmark

NORDSON CORPORATION

28601 Clemens Road, Westlake, OH, 44145

Tel: (440) 892-1580 Fax: (440) 892-9507 Web site: www.nordson.com

Mfr. industry application equipment, sealants & packaging machinery.

Nordson Danmark A/S, Laehegnet 75, DK-2620 Albertslund, Denmark

Tel: 45-4364-8500 Fax: 45-4364-1101

NORGREN

5400 S. Delaware Street, Littleton, CO, 80120-1663

Tel: (303) 794-2611 Fax: (303) 795-9487 Web site: www.norgren.com

Mfr. pneumatic filters, regulators, lubricators, valves, automation systems, dryers, push-in fittings.

IMI Norgren AS, Vesterlundvej 18, DK-2730 Herlev, Denmark

Tel: 45-4491-4166 Fax: 45-4491-1560

NORTON COMPANY

1 New Bond Street, Worcester, MA, 01606

Tel: (508) 795-5000 Fax: (508) 795-5741

Abrasives, drill bits, construction and safety products and plastics.

Norton BV Holland, Fynsvej 73, DK-6000 Kolding, Denmark

OGILVY & MATHER WORLDWIDE

309 West 49th Street, New York, NY, 10019

Tel: (212) 237-4000 Fax: (212) 237-5123

Advertising, marketing, public relations & consulting firm.

Ogilvy & Mather, Copenhagen, Denmark

OLSTEN CORPORATION

175 Broad Hollow Road, Melville, NY, 11747-8905

Tel: (516) 844-7800 Fax: (516) 844-7022 Web site: www.olsten.com

Staffing, home health care & information technology services.

Olsten Personale AS (Denmark), Radhuspladsen 55, 2.th, Postboks 401, DK-1504 Copenhagen, Denmark

Tel: 45-33-11-3335 Fax: 45-33-11-3364

OSMONICS INC.

5951 Clearwater Drive, Minnetonka, MN, 55343-8995

Tel: (612) 933-2277 Fax: (612) 933-0141

Mfr. fluid filtration and separation equipment and components.

Osmonics, Copenhagen, Denmark

OSMOSE INTERNATIONAL INC.

980 Ellicott Street, Buffalo, NY, 14209

Tel: (716) 882-5905 Fax: (716) 882-5139

Mfr. wood preservatives; maintenance and inspection utility poles, railroad track and marine piling.

Osmose Denmark, Copenhagen, Denmark

OTIS ELEVATOR COMPANY

10 Farm Springs Road, Farmington, CT, 06032

Tel: (860) 676-6000 Fax: (860) 676-5111

Mfr. elevators and escalators.

Otis A/S, Ellekaer 9A, DK-2730 Herlev, Denmark

OWENS-CORNING FIBERGLAS CORPORATION

Fiberglas Tower, Toledo, OH, 43659

Tel: (419) 248-8000 Fax: (419) 248-6227 Web site: www.housenet.com

Mfr. insulation, building materials, glass fiber products.

Dansk-Svensk Glasfiber A/S (Denmark), Denmark

PANAMETRICS

221 Crescent Street, Waltham, MA, 02154

Tel: (781) 899-2719 Fax: (781) 899-1552 Web site: www.panametrics.com

Process/non-destructive test instrumentation.

Houlberg (Panametrics), Myrestien 7, DK-2670 Greve Strand, Denmark
Tel: 45-4390-3181 Fax: 45-4390-3133

PARAMETRIC TECHNOLOGY CORPORATION
128 Technology Drive, Waltham, MA, 02154
Tel: (781) 398-5000 Fax: (781) 398-5674 Web site: www.ptc.com
Mfr. CAD/CAM/CAE software.
Parametric Technology Denmark, Skovbrynet 1, DK-6000 Kolding, Denmark
Tel: 45-7550-0258 Fax: 45-7550-0259
Parametric Technology Denmark A/S, Stationsparken 24 DK-2600 Glostrup, Denmark
Tel: 45-7327-0600 Fax: 45-4343-9099

PARKER HANNIFIN CORPORATION
17325 Euclid Ave., Cleveland, OH, 44112
Tel: (216) 896-3000 Fax: (216) 896-4000 Web site: www.parker.com
Mfr. motion-control products.
Parker Hannifin Danmark A/S, Industribuen 8, Industrigrenen 11, DK-2635 Ishoj, Denmark
Polar Seals ApS, PTFE-Packing Mfg. Operation, Hellebaekvej 57, DK-3000 Helsingor, Denmark

THE PERKIN-ELMER CORPORATION
761 Main Ave., Norwalk, CT, 06859-0001
Tel: (203) 762-1000 Fax: (203) 762-4228 Web site: www.perkin-elmer.com
Leading supplier of systems for life science research and related applications.
Perkin-Elmer A/S, Sjaelso Alle 7A, DK-3450 Allerod, Denmark
Tel: 45-4810-0400 Fax: 45-4810-0401

PFIZER INC.
235 East 42nd Street, New York, NY, 10017-5755
Tel: (212) 573-2323 Fax: (212) 573-7851 Web site: www.pfizer.com
Research-based, global health care company.
Pfizer A/S, Denmark

PHARMACIA & UPJOHN
95 Corporate Drive, PO Box 6995, Bridgewater, NJ, 08807
Tel: (908) 306-4400 Fax: (908) 306-4433 Web site: www.pnu.com
Mfr. pharmaceuticals, agricultural products, industry chemicals
Pharmacia & Upjohn, Overgaden Neden Vandet 7, DK-1414 Kobenhavn K, Denmark

PHILLIPS PETROLEUM COMPANY
Phillips Building, 411 S. Keeler Ave., Bartlesville, OK, 74004
Tel: (918) 661-6600 Fax: (918) 661-7636 Web site: www.phillips66.com
Crude oil, natural gas, liquified petroleum gas, gasoline and petro-chemicals.
Phillips Industri & Handel, PO Box 1919, DK-2300 Copenhagen, Denmark

PLIBRICO COMPANY
1800 N. Kingsbury Street, Chicago, IL, 60614
Tel: (773) 549-7014 Fax: (773) 549-0424
Refractories, engineering and construction.
Plibrico A/S, Cirkelhuset, Christianshusvej 2, DK-2970 Horsholm, Denmark

POLAROID CORPORATION
549 Technology Square, Cambridge, MA, 02139
Tel: (781) 386-2000 Fax: (781) 386-3276 Web site: www.polaroid.com
Photographic equipment & supplies, optical products.
Polaroid A/S, PO Box 9, Blokken 75, DK-3460 Birkerod, Denmark

PREMARK INTERNATIONAL INC.

1717 Deerfield Road, Deerfield, IL, 60015

Tel: (847) 405-6000 Fax: (847) 405-6013 Web site: www.premarkintl.com

Mfr./sale plastic, diversified consumer & commercial products.

Rexall Scandinavia A/S, Rygards Alle 104, DK-2900 Hellerup, Denmark

PRICEWATERHOUSECOOPERS LLP

1251 Ave. of the Americas, New York, NY, 10020

Tel: (212) 596-7000 Fax: (212) 790-6620 Web site: www.pwcglobal.com

Accounting and auditing, tax and management, and human resource consulting services.

Price Waterhouse Ltd., Aboulevarden 70, DK-8000 Aarhus C, Denmark

Tel: 45-8932-0000 Fax: 45-8932-0010

Price Waterhouse Ltd., Tuborg Blvd. 1, (PO Box 129) DK-2900 Hellerup, Denmark

Tel: 45-3947-0000 Fax: 45-3947-0010

PROCTER & GAMBLE COMPANY

One Procter & Gamble Plaza, Cincinnati, OH, 45202

Tel: (513) 983-1100 Fax: (513) 562-4500 Web site: www.pg.com

Personal care, food, laundry, cleaning and industry products.

Procter & Gamble Denmark Forbrugerservice., Postboks 1459, 7500 Holstebro, Denmark

Tel: 45-7012-3839

THE QUAKER OATS COMPANY

Quaker Tower, 321 North Clark Street, Chicago, IL, 60610-4714

Tel: (312) 222-7111 Fax: (312) 222-8323 Web site: www.quakeroats.com

Mfr. foods and beverages.

OTA A/S, Islands Brygge 39, DK-2300 Copenhagen S, Denmark

RADISSON HOTELS INTERNATIONAL

Carlson Pkwy., PO Box 59159, Minneapolis, MN, 55459-8204

Tel: (612) 540-5526 Fax: (612) 449-3400

Hotels and resorts.

Radisson SAS Royal Hotel Copenhagen, Hammerichsgade 1, DK-1611 Copenhagen V, Denmark

Tel: 45-33-42-6000 Fax: 45-33-42-6100

RAY & BERNDTSON, INC.

301 Commerce, Ste. 2300, Fort Worth, TX, 76102

Tel: (817) 334-0500 Fax: (817) 334-0779 Web site: www.prb.com

Executive search, management audit and management consulting firm.

Ray & Berndtson, Nyhavn 63 C, DK-1051 Copenhagen K, Denmark

Tel: 45-33-143636 Fax: 45-33-324332 Contact: Kurt Brusgaard, Mng. Ptnr.

RAYCHEM CORPORATION

300 Constitution Drive, Menlo Park, CA, 94025-1164

Tel: (650) 361-3333 Fax: (650) 361-2108 Web site: www.raychem.com

Develop/mfr./market materials science products for electronics, telecommunications & industry.

Raychem A/S, Formervangen 12-16, DK-2600 Glostrup, Denmark

Raychem A/S, Also in Glostrup & Vejie, Denmark

READER'S DIGEST ASSOCIATION INC.

Reader's Digest Rd., Pleasantville, NY, 10570

Tel: (914) 238-1000 Fax: (914) 238-4559

Publisher of magazines and books and direct mail marketer.

Forlaget Det Bedste A/S, Jagtvej 169B, PO Box 810, DK-2100 Copenhagen, Denmark

REPLOGLE GLOBES INC.

2801 South 25th Ave., Broadview, IL, 60153-4589

Tel: (708) 343-0900 Fax: (708) 343-0923

Mfr. geographical world globes.

Scan-Globe A/S, 23 Ulvevej, DK-4622 Havdrup, Denmark

Tel: 45-4618-5400 Fax: 45-4618-5270 Contact: Per Lund-Hansen

RMS GROUP INC.

43-59 10th Street, Long Island City, NY, 11101

Tel: (212) 684-5470 Fax: (212) 684-6019

Technology-transfer development and sales.

Pak-Item ApS, Fredericiagade 16, DK-1310 Copenhagen K, Denmark

ROCKWELL INTERNATIONAL CORPORATION

600 Anton Boulevard, Costa Mesa, CA, 92626-7147

Tel: (714) 424-4200 Fax: (714) 424-4251 Web site: www.rockwell.com

Products & service for aerospace and defense, automotive, electronics, graphics & automation industry.

Rockwell Automation A/S, Herstedoestervej 27-29, D-2620 Albertslund, Denmark (Location: Silkeborg, Denmark.)

Tel: 45-4346-6000 Fax: 45-4346-6001

RUSSELL REYNOLDS ASSOCIATES INC.

200 Park Ave., New York, NY, 10166-0002

Tel: (212) 351-2000 Fax: (212) 370-0896 Web site: www.ressreyn.com

Executive recruiting services.

Russell Reynolds Associates Inc., Østergade 1, First Fl., 1100 Copenhagen K, Denmark

Tel: 45-33-69-2320 Fax: 45-33-69-2349 Contact: Kai Hammerich

SAS INSTITUTE INC.

SAS Campus Drive, Cary, NC, 27513

Tel: (919) 677-8000 Fax: (919) 677-8123 Web site: www.sas.com

Mfr./distributes decision support software.

SAS Institute (Denmark) Inc., Kobenhavn K., Denmark

Tel: 45-33 96 98 98 Fax: 45-33 96 99 91

SCHENKER INTERNATIONAL FORWARDERS INC.

150 Albany Ave., Freeport, NY, 11520

Tel: (516) 377-3000 Fax: (516) 377-3005 Web site: www.schenkerusa.com

Freight forwarders.

Schenker Albert Nielsen A.S, Park AIIU 350, Copenhagen Brondby, DK-2605, Copenhagen, Denmark

Tel: 45-4363-5544 Fax: 45-4363-1808

SCIENTIFIC-ATLANTA, INC.

1 Technology Pkwy South, Norcross, GA, 30092-2967

Tel: (770) 903-5000 Fax: (770) 903-2967 Web site: www.sciatl.com

A leading supplier of broadband communications systems, satellite-based video, voice and data communications networks and worldwide customer service and support.

Arcodan A/S, Sub. of Scientific-Atlanta, Augustenborg Landevej 7, DK 6400, Søoderborg, Denmark

Tel: 45-7442-2150 Fax: 45-7442-3907

SEA-LAND SERVICE INC.

6000 Carnegie Boulevard, Charlotte, NC, 28209

Tel: (704) 571-2000 Fax: (704) 571-4693 Web site: www.sealand.com

Largest U.S-based containerized transport service; ships, railroads, barge lines and trucking operations.

Sealand Transport, Nyholmsvej 7, DK-2000 Copenhagen F, Denmark

G.D. SEARLE & COMPANY

5200 Old Orchard Road, Skokie, IL, 60077

Tel: (847) 982-7000 Fax: (847) 470-1480 Web site: www.searlehealthnet.com

Mfr. pharmaceuticals, health care, optical products and specialty chemicals.

Searle Scandinavia, Division of Monsanto Danmark A.S., Skelbaekgade , DK-1717 Copenhagen V Denmark

Tel: 45-31-241533 Fax: 45-31-243120

THE SERVICEMASTER COMPANY

One ServiceMaster Way, Downers Grove, IL, 60515-1700

Tel: (630) 271-1300 Fax: (630) 271-2710 Web site: www.svm.com

Management service to health care, school and industry facilities; diversified residential and commercial services.

Merry Maids, Copenhagen, Denmark

SILICON GRAPHICS INC.

2011 N. Shoreline Blvd., Mountain View, CA, 94043-1389

Tel: (650) 960-1980 Fax: (650) 961-0595 Web site: www.sgi.com

Design/mfr. special-effects computer graphic systems and software.

Silicon Graphics A/S, Stationsparken 25, 2600 Glostrup, Denmark

Tel: 45-4343-8600 Fax: 45-4343-8606

THE ST. PAUL COMPANIES, INC.

385 Washington Street, St. Paul, MN, 55102

Tel: (612) 310-7911 Fax: (612) 310-8294 Web site: www.stpaul.com

Provides investment, insurance and reinsurance services.

Topdanmark Forsikring A.S, Borupvang 4, DK-2750 Ballerup, Denmark

STANDARD COMMERCIAL CORPORATION

PO Box 450, Wilson, NC, 27893

Tel: (919) 291-5507 Fax: (919) 237-1109

Leaf tobacco dealers/processors and wool processors.

Leafco A/S, Tordenskjoldsjade 24, DK-1055 Copenhagen, Denmark

THE STANLEY WORKS

1000 Stanley Drive, PO Box 7000, New Britain, CT, 06053

Tel: (860) 225-5111 Fax: (860) 827-3987 Web site: www.stanleyworks.com

Mfr. hand tools & hardware.

Stanley Vaerktoj & Beslag A/S, Generatorvej 6A, DK-2730 Herlev, Denmark

STATE STREET BANK & TRUST COMPANY

225 Franklin Street, Boston, MA, 02101

Tel: (617) 786-3000 Fax: (617) 654-3386 Web site: www.statestreet.com

Banking & financial services.

State Street Bank & Trust Co., Larsbjoernstraede 3, DK-1454 Copenhagen K, Denmark

STORAGE TECHNOLOGY CORPORATION

2270 S. 88th Street, Louisville, CO, 80028-0001

Tel: (303) 673-5151 Fax: (303) 673-5019

Mfr./market/service information, storage and retrieval systems.

Storage Tek A/S, Stamholmen 149, DK-2650 Hvidovre, Copenhagen, Denmark

SYBASE, INC.

6475 Christie Ave., Emeryville, CA, 94608

Tel: (510) 922-3500 Fax: (510) 922-3210 Web site: www.sybase.com

Design/mfg/distribution of database management systems, software development tools, connectivity products, consulting and technical support services..

Sybase Denmark A/S, Lyngbyvej 20, 2100 Copenhagen, Denmark

Tel: 45-3927-7913 Fax: 45-3927-7912

SYBRON INTERNATIONAL CORPORATION

411 E. Wisconsin Ave., Milwaukee, WI, 53202

Tel: (414) 274-6600 Fax: (414) 274-6561

Mfr. products for laboratories, professional orthodontic & dental markets.

Nunc A/S, PO Box 280, DK-4000 Roskilde, Denmark

SYMBOL TECHNOLOGIES, INC.

One Symbol Plaza, Holtsville, NY, 11742-1300

Tel: (516) 738-2400 Fax: (516) 563-2831 Web site: www.symbol.com

Mfr. bar code-driven data management systems, wireless LAN's, and Portable Shopping System™.

Symbol Technologies Denmark A/S, Gydevange 2, 3450 Allerød, Denmark

Tel: 45-7020-1718 Fax: 45-7020-1716

SYSTEM INTEGRATORS INC.

PO Box 13626, Sacramento, CA, 95853

Tel: (916) 929-9481 Fax: (916) 928-0414

Develop/marketing software for publishing and newspapers.

System Integrators, Copenhagen, Denmark

TBWA INTERNATIONAL

180 Maiden Lane, New York, NY, 10038

Tel: (212) 804-1000 Fax: (212) 804-1200

International full service advertising agency.

TBWA Reklamebureau, Copenhagen, Denmark

TEKTRONIX INC.

2660 Southwest Parkway Ave., PO Box 1000, Wilsonville, OR, 97070-1000

Tel: (503) 627-7111 Fax: (503) 627-2406 Web site: www.tek.com

Mfr. test & measure, visual systems/color printing & communications/video and networking products.

Tektronix A/S, Tonsbakken 16-18, Skovlunde DK-2740, Denmark

Tel: 45-4485-0700 Fax: 45-4485-0701

TENNECO AUTOMOTIVE

500 North Field Drive, Lake Forest, IL, 60045

Tel: (847) 482-5241 Fax: (847) 482-5295

Automotive parts, exhaust systems, service equipment.

Walker Denmark A/S, Falstervej 11, DK-5500 Middelfart, Denmark

Tel: 45-6441-4545 Fax: 45-6441-6529 Contact: Aksel Pedersen, Mgr.

TENNECO INC.

1275 King Street, Greenwich, CT, 06831

Tel: (203) 863-1000 Fax: (203) 863-1134 Web site: www.tenneco.com

Mfr. automotive products and packaging materials/containers.

Walker Danmark A/S, Falstersvej, DK-5500 Middelfart, Denmark

TENNECO PACKAGING CORPORATION OF AMERICA

1900 West Field Court, Lake Forest, IL, 60045

Tel: (847) 482-2000 Fax: (847) 482-2181 Web site: www.tenneco

Mfr. custom packaging, aluminum and plastic molded fibre, corrugated containers.

A/S Haustrup-Ekco Aluminium-Emballage, PO Box 929, DK-5000 Odense, Denmark

Omni-Pac ApS, Retortvej 36, DK-2500 Copenhagen Valby, Denmark

TEXACO INC.

2000 Westchester Ave., White Plains, NY, 10650

Tel: (914) 253-4000 Fax: (914) 253-7753 Web site: www.texaco.com

Exploration/marketing crude oil, mfr. petro chemicals and products.

Texaco A/S, Borgergade 13, DK-1300 Copenhagen, Denmark

TEXAS INSTRUMENTS INC.

8505 Forest Lane, Dallas, TX, 75243

Tel: (214) 995-2011 Fax: (214) 995-4360 Web site: www.ti.com

Mfr. semiconductor devices, electronic electro-mechanical systems, instruments and controls.

TI Europe, Copenhagen, Denmark

THERMO ELECTRIC COMPANY

109 North Fifth Street, Saddle Brook, NJ, 07662

Tel: (201) 843-5800 Fax: (201) 843-7144

Mfr. temp/measure control products.

Telemetric Instrument ApS, Gl. Hovedgade 10E, DK-2970 Horsholm, Denmark

TRANTER INC.

1054 Claussen Road, #314, Augusta, GA, 30907

Tel: (706) 738-7900 Fax: (706) 738-6619 Web site: www.tranter.com

Mfr. heat exchangers.

SWEP Danmark A/S, Sofienlystvej 7, Postbox 20, DK-8340 Malling, Denmark

Tel: 45-8693-3633 Fax: 45-8693-3895

TRUE NORTH COMMUNICATIONS INC.

101 East Erie Street, Chicago, IL, 60611

Tel: (312) 425-6000 Fax: (312) 425-6350

Holding company, advertising agency.

Createam, Overgaden Neden Vandet 19, 1414 Copenhagen K, Denmark

TYCO INTERNATIONAL LTD.

One Tyco Park, Exeter, NH, 03833

Tel: (603) 778-9700 Fax: (603) 778-7700 Web site: www.tycoint.com

Mfr./sales fire & security systems, sprinkler systems, undersea fiber optic telecommuncations, printed circuit boards, pipe tubing and flow meters.

Gustaf Fagerberg A/S, PO Box 267, Brondby, Denmark KD-2605

Tel: 45-4363-2666 Fax: 45-4363-2544

UNION CAMP CORPORATION

1600 Valley Road, Wayne, NJ, 07470

Tel: (973) 628-2000 Fax: (973) 628-2722 Web site: www.unioncamp.com

Mfr. paper, packaging, chemicals and wood products.

Bush Boake Allen A/S, Maglebergvej 5A, DK-2800 Lyngby, Denmark

UNISYS CORPORATION.

PO Box 500, Union Meeting Road, Blue Bell, PA, 19424

Tel: (215) 986-4011 Fax: (215) 986-6850 Web site: www.unisys.com

Mfr./marketing/servicing electronic information systems.

Unisys A/S, Biegdamsvej 56, DK-2100 Copenhagen, Denmark

UNITED PARCEL SERVICE OF AMERICA, INC.

55 Glenlake Parkway, NE, Atlanta, GA, 30328

Tel: (404) 828-6000 Fax: (404) 828-6593 Web site: www.ups.com

International package-delivery service.

UPS Danmark A/S - Head Office, Naverland 7, 2600 Glostrup, Denmark (Locations: Kolding, Viby)

Tel: 45-23-8888 Fax: 45-23-8800

UNITED TECHNOLOGIES CORPORATION

United Technologies Building, Hartford, CT, 06101

Tel: (860) 728-7000 Fax: (860) 728-7979 Web site: www.utc.com

Mfr. aircraft engines, elevators, A/C, auto equipment, space and military electronic and rocket propulsion systems. Products include Pratt & Whitney, Otis elevators, Carrier heating and air conditioning and Sikorsky helicopters.

Nielson-Otis Elevator A/S, Hoerkaer 7-9, DK-2730 Harlev, Denmark

UNIVERSAL INSTRUMENTS

90 Bevier Street, S. Dock, Binghamton, NY, 13904

Tel: (607) 779-7522 Fax: (607) 779-7971 Web site: www.dover.com

Mfr./sales of instruments for electronic circuit assembly

Sincotron A/S, Risskov, Denmark

Tel: 45-8621-7744 Fax: 45-8621-7766

URSCHEL LABORATORIES INC.

2503 Calumet Ave., PO Box 2200, Valparaiso, IN, 46384-2200

Tel: (219) 464-4811 Fax: (219) 462-3879

Design/mfr. precision food processing equipment.

Urschel Intl., Pilevej 24, Taulov, Fredericia, Denmark

VARIAN ASSOCIATES INC.

3050 Hansen Way, Palo Alto, CA, 94304-100

Tel: (650) 493-4000 Fax: (650) 424-5358 Web site: www.varian.com

Mfr. microwave tubes & devices, analytical instruments, semiconductor process & medical equipment, vacuum systems.

Varian Electronics APS, Lyskaer 9, DK-2730 Herlev, Denmark

WASTE MANAGEMENT, INC.

3003 Butterfield Road, Oak Brook, IL, 60523-1100

Tel: (630) 572-8800 Fax: (630) 572-3094 Web site: www.wastemanagement.com

Environmental services and disposal company; collection, processing, transfer and disposal facilities.

Waste Management Danmark Miljøservice A/S, Ørnegärdsvej 19, DK-2820 Gentofte, Denmark

WATERS CORPORATION

34 Maple Street, Milford, MA, 01757

Tel: (508) 478-2000 Fax: (508) 872-1990

Mfr./distribute liquid chromatographic instruments and test and measurement equipment.

Waters A/S, Roskildevej 342, DK-2630 Tastrup, Denmark

Waters Associates A/S, Sondre Ringvej 24, DK-4000 Roskilde, Denmark

WEATHERFORD INTERNATIONAL INC.

5 Post Oak Blvd, Ste. 1760, Houston, TX, 77227-3415

Tel: (713) 287-8400 Fax: (713) 963-9785 Web site: www.weatherford.com

Oilfield services, products & equipment; mfr. marine cranes for oil and gas industry.

Weatherford Intl., c/o DOGIS APS, Made Engvej 7, DK-6701 Esbjerg, Denmark

THE WEST COMPANY, INC.

101 Gordon Drive, PO Box 645, Lionville, PA, 19341-0645

Tel: (610) 594-2900 Fax: (610) 594-3014 Web site: www.thewestcompany.com

Mfr. products for filling, sealing, dispensing & delivering needs of health care & consumer products markets.

The West Company Danmark, Fuglevangsvej 51, DK-8700 Horsens, Denmark

Tel: 45-7561-6000 Fax: 45-7562-7028

WEST STAFF SERVICES INC.

301 Lennon Lane, Walnut Creek, CA, 94598-2453

Tel: (925) 930-5300 Fax: (925) 934-5489 Web site: www.westaff.com

Secretarial & clerical temporary service.

Western Service A/S, PO Box 2088, DK-1013 Copenhagen K, Denmark

WITCO CORPORATION

One American Lane, Greenwich, CT, 06831-2559

Tel: (203) 552-2000 Fax: (203) 552-3070 Web site: www.witco.com

Mfr. chemical and petroleum products.

Witco GmbH, Rundforbivej 2, DK-2950 Vedbaek, Denmark

WORLD COURIER INC.

1313 Fourth Ave., New Hyde Park, NY, 11041

Tel: (516) 354-2600 Fax: (516) 354-2644

International courier service.

World Courier Copenhagen, Fuzlebaekvej 3, DK-2770 Kastrup, Denmark

WUNDERMAN CATO JOHNSON

675 Ave. of the Americas, New York, NY, 10010-5104

Tel: (212) 941-3000 Fax: (212) 633-0957 Web site: www.wcj.com

International advertising and marketing consulting firm.

Genesis Marketing, Blegdamsvej 104, DK-2100 Copenhagen, Denmark

Tel: 45-35-43-7777 Fax: 45-35-43-0804 Contact: Claus Pedersen, Mgr.

Wunderman Cato Johnson A/S, Blegdamsvej 104, DK-2100 Copenhagen, Denmark

Tel: 45-35-43-7777 Fax: 45-35-43-0804 Contact: Peter Frederiksen, Mng. Dir.

XEROX CORPORATION

800 Long Ridge Road, PO Box 1600, Stamford, CT, 06904

Tel: (203) 968-3000 Fax: (203) 968-4312 Web site: www.xerox.com

Mfr. document processing equipment, systems and supplies.

Rank Xerox A/S, Borupvang 5C, DK2750, Ballerup, Denmark

Tel: 45-4465-4444 Fax: 45-4465-4813

YAHOO! INC.

3420 Central Expressway, Santa Clara, CA, 95051

Tel: (408) 731-3300 Fax: (408) 731-3301 Web site: www.yahoo-inc.com

Internet media company providing specialized content, free electronic mail and community offerings and commerce.

Yahoo! Inc., Denmark

YOUNG & RUBICAM INC.

285 Madison Ave., New York, NY, 10017

Tel: (212) 210-3000 Fax: (212) 370-3796 Web site: www.yr.com

Advertising, public relations, direct marketing and sales promotion, corporate & product ID management.

Young & Rubicam Copenhagen, Enhjornvagens Bastion, Langebrogade 6V, DK-1411 Copenhagen K, Denmark

Djibouti

DHL WORLDWIDE EXPRESS

333 Twin Dolphin Drive, Redwood City, CA, 94065

Tel: (650) 593-7474 Fax: (650) 593-1689 Web site: www.dhl.com

Worldwide air express carrier.

DHL Worldwide Express, Rue de Geneve, PO Box 81, Djibouti

Tel: 253-35-0642

ERNST & YOUNG, LLP

787 Seventh Ave., New York, NY, 10019

Tel: (212) 773-3000 Fax: (212) 773-6350 Web site: www.eyi.com

Accounting and audit, tax and management consulting services.

Ernst & Young, Boite Poste 2593, Djibouti

Tel: 253-2-725625 Fax: 253-2-716271 Contact: Coutts Otolo

XEROX CORPORATION

800 Long Ridge Road, PO Box 1600, Stamford, CT, 06904

Tel: (203) 968-3000 Fax: (203) 968-4312 Web site: www.xerox.com

Mfr. document processing equipment, systems and supplies.

Dcp La Source Information, BP 2537 rue d'Athenes, Djibouti

Tel: 253-354-347

Dominican Republic

3M

3M Center, St. Paul, MN, 55144-1000

Tel: (612) 733-1110 Fax: (612) 733-9973 Web site: www.mmm.com

Mfr. diversified products for industry, health care, imaging, communications, transport, safety, consumer, etc.

3M Dominicana SA, Aptdo. 103-2, Av. Luperon, Zona Industrial de Herrera, Santo Domingo, Dominican Republic

Tel: 809-530-6560 Fax: 809-537-2344

AIR EXPRESS INTERNATIONAL CORPORATION

120 Tokeneke Road, PO Box 1231, Darien, CT, 06820

Tel: (203) 655-7900 Fax: (203) 655-5779 Web site: www.aeilogistics.com

Air freight forwarder.

AEI de Dominican Republic, c/o Frederic Schad, C. Por A., Jose Gabriel Garcia No. 26, Santo Domingo, Dominican Republic

Tel: 809-685-3275 Fax: 809-688-7696

AMERICAN & EFIRD INC.

PO Box 507, Mt. Holly, NC, 28120

Tel: (704) 827-4311 Fax: (704) 822-6054

Mfr. industrial thread, yarn & consumer sewing products.

Hilos A&E Dominicana SA, Zona Franca, Santiago, Dominican Republic

AMERICAN AIRLINES INC.

4333 Amon Carter Boulevard, Ft. Worth, TX, 76155

Tel: (817) 963-1234 Fax: (817) 967-9641 Web site: www.amrcorp.com

Air transport services.

American Airlines, Aptdo. 1295, El Conde #401, Edif. Copello, Santo Domingo, Dominican Republic

AMERICAN STANDARD INC.

One Centennial Ave., Piscataway, NJ, 08855-6820

Tel: (732) 980-3000 Fax: (732) 980-6118

Mfr. heating, plumbing & sanitary equipment, china, earthenware.

Sanitarios Dominicanos SA, Aptdo. 910, Santiago de Los Caballeros, Dominican Republic

AMMIRATI PURIS LINTAS

One Dag Hammarskjold Plaza, New York, NY, 10017

Tel: (212) 605-8000 Fax: (212) 605-4705 Web site: www.interpublic.com

International advertising agency.

Pia, Apartado Postal 1456, Santo Domingo, Dominican Republic

Tel: 809-567-8281 Fax: 809-549-3822 Contact: Lil Esteva

AON CORPORATION

123 North Wacker Drive, Chicago, IL, 60606

Tel: (312) 701-3000 Fax: (312) 701-3100 Web site: www.aon.com

Insurance brokers worldwide; underwrites accident & health insurance, specialty & professional insurance; & provides risk management consultation.

AON Worldwide / Redondo Llenas SG, S.A., Plazar El Alcazar Calle Manuel de Jesus, Santo Domingo, Dominican Republic

Tel: 809-567-7178 Fax: 809-541-9333 Contact: M.R. Redondo

AVON PRODUCTS INC.

1345 Ave. of the Americas, New York, NY, 10105-0196

Tel: (212) 282-5000 Fax: (212) 282-6049 Web site: www.avon.com

Mfr./distributor beauty & related products, fashion jewelry, gifts & collectibles.

Productos Avon, S.A., Apartado Postal 21727, Santo Domingo, Dominican Republic

Tel: 809-567-5586 Fax: 809-566-9082 Contact: Ada Mena, Sales Mgr.

BATES WORLDWIDE INC.

405 Lexington Ave., New York, NY, 10174

Tel: (212) 297-7000 Fax: (212) 986-0270 Web site: www.batesww.com

Advertising, marketing, public relations & media consulting.

EPI Bates, H. Nunez #41, Urb. Fernandez, Santo Domingo, Dominican Republic

Tel: 809-567-7888 Fax: 809-567-8905 Contact: A.Guerrero, Pres.

BAXTER HEALTHCARE CORPORATION

One Baxter Parkway, Deerfield, IL, 60015

Tel: (847) 948-2000 Fax: (847) 948-3948 Web site: www.baxter.com

Pharmaceutical preparations, surgical/medical instruments & cardiovascular products.

Baxter Laboratorios SA, Aptdo. Postal 21426, Parque Industrial Itabo, Haina, Dominican Republic

Baxter SA, Aptdo. Postal 58, Haina, San Cristobal, Dominican Republic

BESTFOODS, INC.

700 Sylvan Ave., International Plaza, Englewood Cliffs, NJ, 07632-9976

Tel: (201) 894-4000 Fax: (201) 894-2186 Web site: www.bestfoods.com

Consumer foods products; corn refining.

Knorr Alimentaria SA, Calle C #6, Zona Industrial Herrera, Aptdo. Postal 623-2, Santo Domingo, Dominican Republic

BRISTOL-MYERS SQUIBB COMPANY

345 Park Ave., New York, NY, 10154

Tel: (212) 546-4000 Fax: (212) 546-4020 Web site: www.bms.com

Pharmaceutical and food preparations, medical and surgical instruments.

Bristol-Myers Squibb - Dominican Republic, Apartado 1167, Santo Domingo, Dominican Republic

BUDGET RENT A CAR CORPORATION

4225 Naperville Road, Lisle, IL, 60532

Tel: (630) 955-1900 Fax: (630) 955-7799 Web site: www.budgetrentacar.com

Car and truck rental system.

Budget Rent A Car, Las Americas International Airport, Santo Domingo, Dominican Republic

Tel: 809-567-0175

LEO BURNETT CO., INC.

35 West Wacker Drive, Chicago, IL, 60601

Tel: (312) 220-5959 Fax: (312) 220-6533 Web site: www.leoburnett.com

International advertising agency.

Leo Burnett Inc., Prolongacion Arabia 13, Arroyo Hondo, Santo Domingo, Dominican Republic

CALMAQUIP ENGINEERING CORPORATION

7240 NW 12th Street, Miami, FL, 33121

Tel: (305) 592-4510 Fax: (305) 593-9618

Engineering

Calmest SA, Abraham Lincoln, Esquina Modesto Diaz, Aptdo. 1693, Santo Domingo, Dominican Republic

THE CHASE MANHATTAN CORPORATION

World Headquarters, 270 Park Ave., New York, NY, 10017

Tel: (212) 270-6000 Fax: (212) 622-9030 Web site: www.chase.com

International banking and financial services.

Chase Manhattan Bank NA, Av. John F. Kennedy y Tiradentes, Aptdo. 1408, Santo Domingo, Dominican Republic

CIGNA CORPORATION

One Liberty Place, Philadelphia, PA, 19192

Tel: (215) 761-1000 Fax: (215) 761-5008

Insurance, invest, health care and other financial services.

Insurance Co. of North America, Edif. Torre BHD, 2 piso, Av. Winston Churchill/Esq. 27 de Feb., Santo Dom., Dominican Republic

CITICORP

399 Park Ave., New York, NY, 10043

Tel: (212) 559-1000 Fax: (212) 527-2066 Web site: www.citibank.com

International banking and financial services.

Citibank N.A., John F. Kennedy 1, piso 4, Apartado Postal 1492, Santo Domingo, Dominican Republic

Tel: 809-566-5611 Fax: 809-567-2255 Contact: Robert Matthews, Gen. Mgr.

THE CLOROX COMPANY

1221 Broadway, PO Box 24305, Oakland, CA, 94623-1305

Tel: (510) 271-7000 Fax: (510) 832-1463

Mfr. soap & detergents, and domestic consumer packaged products.

Productor del Holgar C por A, Santo Domingo, Dominican Republic

COLUMBIA PICTURES INDUSTRIES INC.

10202 West Washington Blvd., Culver City, CA, 90232

Tel: (310) 244-4000 Fax: (310) 244-2626 Web site: www.sony.com

Producer and distributor of motion pictures.

Columbia Film Trading Corp., Av. Independencia 310, Zona 1, Aptdo. 1459, Santo Domingo, Dominican Republic

CONTINENTAL AIRLINES INC.

2929 Allen Parkway, Ste. 1501, Houston, TX, 77019

Tel: (281) 834-5000 Fax: (281) 520-6329

International airline carrier.

Continental Airlines Inc., Dominican Republic

D'ARCY MASIUS BENTON & BOWLES INC. (DMB&B)

1675 Broadway, New York, NY, 10019

Tel: (212) 468-3622 Fax: (212) 468-2987 Web site: www.dmbb.com

Full service international advertising and communications group.

Staff/DMB&B, Edif. Concordia, Ste. 211, C/Jose A. Soler, Esq. A. Lincoln, Santo Domingo, Dominican Republic

Tel: 809-563-1212 Fax: 809-563-7784 Contact: Jose Rivera, Pres.

DELOITTE TOUCHE TOHMATSU INTERNATIONAL

PO Box 820, Wilton, CT, 06897

Tel: (203) 761-3000 Fax: (203) 834-2200 Web site: www.u.s.deloitte.com or www.dtti.com

Accounting, audit, tax and management consulting services.

Deloitte & Touche, Gomez, Santos. Gonzalez & Asociados, Scotiabank Bldg., Av. J.F.Kennedy, Esq. Lope de Vega, Santo Domingo, DN, Dominican Republic

DEVELOPMENT ASSOCIATES INC.

1730 North Lynn Street, Arlington, VA, 22209-2023

Tel: (703) 276-0677 Fax: (703) 276-0432

Management consulting services.

Development Associates, Inc., Federico Henrique y Carvajal, 11 Gazcue, Santo Domingo, Dominican Republic

Tel: 809-688-7950 Fax: 809-682-4452

DHL WORLDWIDE EXPRESS

333 Twin Dolphin Drive, Redwood City, CA, 94065

Tel: (650) 593-7474 Fax: (650) 593-1689 Web site: www.dhl.com

Worldwide air express carrier.

DHL Worldwide Express, Av. Sarasota 26, Santo Domingo, Dominican Republic

Tel: 809-534-7888

DOVER CORPORATION

280 Park Ave., New York, NY, 10017-1292

Tel: (212) 922-1640 Fax: (212) 922-1656 Web site: www.dovercorporation.com

Elevator manufacturer and holding company for varied industries.

Dalsan C. Por A, Apartado de Correos 751, Ave. Lopez de Vega, Santo Domingo, Dominican Republic

Tel: 809-565-4431 Fax: 809-541-7313

DU BOIS CHEMICAL

255 East 5th Street, Cincinnati, OH, 45202-4799

Tel: (513) 762-6000 Fax: (513) 762-6030

Mfr. specialty chemicals & maintenance products.

Productos Quimicos Industriales, Apt. Postal 529-2, Calle Isabel Aguiar No. 3 (Casi), Eng. 27 De Febrero, Zona Indus. de Herrera, Santo Domingo, Dominican Republic

Tel: 809-530-0303 Fax: 809-530-0545 Contact: Jaime Malla, Pres.

EASTMAN KODAK COMPANY

343 State Street, Rochester, NY, 14650

Tel: (716) 724-4000 Fax: (716) 724-0663

Develop/mfr. photo & chemicals products, information management/video/copier systems, fibers/plastics for various industry.

Kodak Dominicana, Av. Charles Sumner 17, Santo Domingo, Dominican Republic

ERNST & YOUNG, LLP

787 Seventh Ave., New York, NY, 10019

Tel: (212) 773-3000 Fax: (212) 773-6350 Web site: www.eyi.com

Accounting and audit, tax and management consulting services.

Francisco & Asociados, Aptdo 140, Santo Domingo, Dominican Republic

Tel: 809-565-5831 Fax: 809-541-3883 Contact: Ramon Francisco

FEDERAL-MOGUL CORPORATION

26555 Northwestern Highway, PO Box 1966, Southfield, MI, 48034

Tel: (248) 354-7700 Fax: (248) 354-8983 Web site: www.federalmogul.com

Mfr./distributor precision parts for automobiles, trucks, farm and construction vehicles.

Federal-Mogul Dominicana SA, Dominican Republic

FRITZ COMPANIES INC.

706 Mission Street, Ste. 900, San Francisco, CA, 94103

Tel: (415) 904-8360 Fax: (415) 904-8661 Web site: www.fritz.com

Integrated transportation, sourcing, distribution & customs brokerage services.

Fritz Companies Inc., Santo Domingo, Dominican Republic

H.B. FULLER COMPANY

1200 Willow Lake Blvd., Vadnais Heights, MN, 55110

Tel: (612) 236-5900 Fax: (612) 236-5898 Web site: www.hbfuller.com

Mfr./distributor adhesives, sealants, coatings, paints, waxes, sanitation chemicals.

H.B. Fuller Dominicana, S.A., Apartado No.004, Piedra Bianca, Haina, San Cristobal, Dominican Republic

Tel: 809-542-2902 Fax: 809-542-2585

THE GILLETTE COMPANY

Prudential Tower Building, Boston, MA, 02199

Tel: (617) 421-7000 Fax: (617) 421-7123 Web site: www.gillette.com

Develop/mfr. personal care/use products: blades & razors, toiletries, cosmetics, stationery.

Gillette Dominicana SA, Santo Domingo, Dominican Republic

GOYA FOODS, INC.

100 Seaview Drive, Secaucus, NJ, 07096

Tel: (201) 348-4900 Fax: (201) 348-6609 Web site: www.goyafoods.com

Produces canned and packaged Hispanic food products, fruit juices and frozen entrees.

Goya Foods, Inc., Dominican Republic

GREY ADVERTISING INC.

777 Third Ave., New York, NY, 10017

Tel: (212) 546-2000 Fax: (212) 546-1495 Web site: www.giworldwwide.com

International advertising agency.

El Taller Creativo, Santo Domingo, Dominican Republic

GTE CORPORATION

One Stamford Forum, Stamford, CT, 06904

Tel: (203) 965-2000 Fax: (203) 965-2277 Web site: www.gte.com

Electronic products, telecommunications systems, publishing and communications.

Codetel GTE, Santo Domingo, Dominican Republic

THE HARPER GROUP

260 Townsend Street, San Francisco, CA, 94107-1719

Tel: (415) 978-0600 Fax: (415) 978-0692 Web site: www.circleintl.com

Ocean/air freight forwarding, customs brokerage, packing and wholesale, logistics management and insurance.

E. T. Heinsen, C. Por. A., Ave. George Washington 353, PO Box 852, Santo Domingo, Dominican Republic

Tel: 809-221-6111 Fax: 809-689-2177

HOLIDAY INNS WORLDWIDE, INC.

3 Ravinia Drive, Ste. 2900, Atlanta, GA, 30346-2149

Tel: (770) 604-2000 Fax: (770) 604-5403

Hotels, restaurants and casinos.

Holiday Inn, Av. Anacaona, Santo Domingo, Dominican Republic

HORWATH INTERNATIONAL

415 Madison Ave., New York, NY, 10017

Tel: (212) 838-5566 Fax: (212) 838-3636

Public accountants and auditors.

Sotero Peralta y Associados, Aptdo. 355-2, Av. Winston Churchill, Edif. Lama, Dominican Republic

INFONET SERVICES CORPORATION

2100 East Grand Ave., El Segundo, CA, 90245

Tel: (310) 335-2600 Fax: (310) 335-4507 Web site: www.infonet.com

Provider of Internet services and electronic messaging services.

Infonet Dominican Republic, Abraham Lincoln 953, Santo Domingo, Dominican Republic

Tel: 809-220-5114 Fax: 809-220-5286

INTER-CONTINENTAL HOTELS

1120 Ave. of the Americas, New York, NY, 10036

Tel: (212) 852-6400 Fax: (212) 852-6494 Web site: www.interconti.com

Worldwide hotel and resort accommodations.

V Centerario Inter-Continental Santo Domingo, Av. George Washington 218, PO Box 2890, Santo Domingo, Dominican Republic

Tel: 809-221-0000 Fax: 809-221-2020

INTERNATIONAL PAPER COMPANY

2 Manhattanville Road, Purchase, NY, 10577

Tel: (914) 397-1500 Fax: (914) 397-1596 Web site: www.ipaper.com

Mfr./distributor container board, paper, wood products.

Impresora del Yaque C por A, Autopista Santiago Navarrete Km 2.5, Santiago/Navarrete, Dominican Republic

ITT SHERATON CORPORATION

60 State Street, Boston, MA, 02108

Tel: (617) 367-3600 Fax: (617) 367-5676

Hotel operations.

Santo Domingo Sheraton Hotel & Casino, Av. George Washington 365, Aptdo. 1493, Santo Domingo, Dominican Republic

J. WALTER THOMPSON COMPANY

466 Lexington Ave., New York, NY, 10017

Tel: (212) 210-7000 Fax: (212) 210-6944 Web site: www.jwt.com

International advertising and marketing services.

Thompson AIFE MFP, Santo Domingo, Dominican Republic

JOHNSON & JOHNSON

One Johnson & Johnson Plaza, New Brunswick, NJ, 08933

Tel: (732) 524-0400 Fax: (732) 214-0334 Web site: www.jnj.com

Mfr./distributor/R&D pharmaceutical, health care and cosmetic products.

Johnson & Johnson (Dominicana) C por A, Aptdo. Postal 2252, Santo Domingo, Dominican Republic

S C JOHNSON & SON INC.

1525 Howe Street, Racine, WI, 53403

Tel: (414) 260-2000 Fax: (414) 260-2133 Web site: www.scjohnsonwax.com

Home, auto, commercial and personal care products and specialty chemicals.

Ceras Johnson Dominicana SA, Av. San Martin 296, Santo Domingo, Dominican Republic

KPMG PEAT MARWICK LLP

Three Chestnut Ridge Road, Montvale, NJ, 07645

Tel: (201) 307-7000 Fax: (201) 930-8617 Web site: www.kpmg.com

Accounting and audit, tax and management consulting services.

KPMG Peat Marwick, J. F. Kennedy Ave., Santo Domingo, Dominican Republic

KPMG Peat Marwick, Edif. Hache, East Entrance, 1st Fl., 4th Level JFK Ave., Santo Domingo, Dominican Republic

Tel: 809-566-9161 Fax: 809-566-3468 Contact: Juan R. Herrera, Sr. Ptnr.

KPMG Peat Marwick, Apartado Postal 1519, Santiago, Dominican Republic

LANIER WORLDWIDE, INC.

2300 Parklake Drive, N.E., Atlanta, GA, 30345

Tel: (770) 496-9500 Fax: (770) 621-1535

Specialize in digital copiers and multi-functional systems.

Lanier Dominicana, S.A., Av. 27 de Febrero, Esquina Calle H, Zona Ind. De Hererra, Santo Domingo, Dominican Republic

Tel: 809-537-7779 Fax: 809-537-8590

MAIDENFORM INC.

200 Madison Ave., New York, NY, 10016

Tel: (212) 592-0700 Fax: (212) 686-2087

Mfr. intimate apparel.

Elizabeth Needle Craft Inc., Zona Franca de la Romana, La Romana, Dominican Republic

Nicholas Needlecraft Inc., Apdo. Postal 150, Higuey, Dominican Republic

MARSH & McLENNAN COS INC.

1166 Ave. of the Americas, New York, NY, 10036-2774

Tel: (212) 345-5000 Fax: (212) 345-4808 Web site: www.marshmac.com

Insurance agents/brokers, pension and investment management consulting services.

Ros & Asociados S.A., Ave. Winston Churchill, Esq, Jose Brea, Pena, Santo Domingo, Dominican Republic

Tel: 809-567-1021 Fax: 809-562-4764 Contact: N/A

McCANN-ERICKSON WORLDWIDE

750 Third Ave., New York, NY, 10017

Tel: (212) 984-3644 Fax: (212) 984-2629

International advertising/marketing services.

McCann-Erickson Dominicana SA, Moises Garcia 17, Gazque, Santo Domingo, Dominican Republic

MICROSOFT CORPORATION

One Microsoft Way, Redmond, WA, 98052-6399

Tel: (425) 882-8080 Fax: (425) 936-7329 Web site: www.microsoft.com

Computer software, peripherals and services.

Microsoft Dominicana, S.A., Santo Domingo, Dominican Republic

NATIONAL CAR RENTAL SYSTEM, INC.

7700 France Ave. South, Minneapolis, MN, 55435

Tel: (612) 830-2121 Fax: (612) 830-2921

Car rentals.

National Car Rental System Inc., A. Lincoln 1056, Aptdo. 800, Santo Domingo, Dominican Republic

OGILVY & MATHER WORLDWIDE

309 West 49th Street, New York, NY, 10019

Tel: (212) 237-4000 Fax: (212) 237-5123

Advertising, marketing, public relations & consulting firm.

Ogilvy & Mather, Santo Domingo, Dominican Republic

PAN-AMERICAN LIFE INSURANCE CO.

Pan American Life Center, PO Box 60219, New Orleans, LA, 70130-0219

Tel: (504) 566-1300 Fax: (504) 566-3600 Web site: www.palic.com

Insurance services.

Cia de Seguros PALIC SA, Abraham Lincoln esq. Jose Amado Soler, Santo Domingo, Dominican Republic

Tel: 809-562-1271 Fax: 809-562-1825 Contact: Eduardo Tolentino, VP & Gen. Mgr. Emp: 70

THE PERKIN-ELMER CORPORATION

761 Main Ave., Norwalk, CT, 06859-0001

Tel: (203) 762-1000 Fax: (203) 762-4228 Web site: www.perkin-elmer.com

Leading supplier of systems for life science research and related applications.

Inverciones Tecnicas Dominicana SA, Luisa Ozema Pellerano #7, Zona 2, Santo Domingo, Dominican Republic

Tel: 809-688-4927 Fax: 809-682-9506 Contact: Samuel De Mora, Mgr.

PRICEWATERHOUSECOOPERS LLP

1251 Ave. of the Americas, New York, NY, 10020

Tel: (212) 596-7000 Fax: (212) 790-6620 Web site: www.pwcglobal.com

Accounting and auditing, tax and management, and human resource consulting services.

Price Waterhouse Ltd., Ed. Bank of Nova Scotia, Av. John F Kennedy, Esq.de Av. Lope de Vega, POB 1286 Santo Domingo, Dominican Republic

Tel: 809-567-7741 Fax: 809-541-1210

RENAISSANCE HOTELS AND RESORTS

1 Marriott Drive, Washington, DC, 20058

Tel: (301) 380-3000 Fax: (301) 380-5181

Hotel and resort chain.

Renaissance Jaragua Hotel and Casino, Santo Domingo, Dominican Republic

Tel: 809-221-2222

RUSSIN & VECCHI L.L.P.

815 Connecticut Ave. NW, Ste. 650, Washington, DC, 20006

Tel: (202) 822-6100 Fax: (202) 822-6101

Law firm.

Russin Vecchi & Heredia Bonetti, Edif. Monte Mirador, 3ER piso, Calle El Recodo No. 2, Ensanche Bella Vista, Anto Domingo, Dominican Republic

Tel: 809-535-9511 Fax: 809-535-6649 Contact: Luis Heredia Bonetti

Russin Vecchi & Heredia Bonetti, Plaza Turisol, Local 11-A, Puerto Plata, Dominican Republic

Tel: 809-586-5535 Fax: 809-586-5861 Contact: Luis Heredia Bonetti

SEA-LAND SERVICE INC.

6000 Carnegie Boulevard, Charlotte, NC, 28209

Tel: (704) 571-2000 Fax: (704) 571-4693 Web site: www.sealand.com

Largest U.S-based containerized transport service; ships, railroads, barge lines and trucking operations.

Sea-Land Service, Aptdo. 1431, Santo Domingo, Dominican Republic

THE SERVICEMASTER COMPANY

One ServiceMaster Way, Downers Grove, IL, 60515-1700

Tel: (630) 271-1300 Fax: (630) 271-2710 Web site: www.svm.com

Management service to health care, school and industry facilities; diversified residential and commercial services.

Terminix, Santo Domingo, Dominican Republic

TEXACO INC.

2000 Westchester Ave., White Plains, NY, 10650

Tel: (914) 253-4000 Fax: (914) 253-7753 Web site: www.texaco.com

Exploration/marketing crude oil, mfr. petro chemicals and products.

Texaco Caribbean Inc., Aptdo. 779, Santo Domingo, Dominican Republic

TRANS WORLD AIRLINES INC.

505 N. Sixth Street, St. Louis, MO, 63101

Tel: (314) 589-3000 Fax: (314) 589-3129 Web site: www.twa.com

Air transport services.

Trans World Airlines, Santo Domingo, Dominican Republic

TRUE NORTH COMMUNICATIONS INC.

101 East Erie Street, Chicago, IL, 60611

Tel: (312) 425-6000 Fax: (312) 425-6350

Holding company, advertising agency.

Foote, Cone & Belding, Av. Romulo Betancourt Ho. 53, Edif. Plaza Bolivar, 1do piso, Esquina Caonabo, Local No. 205, Santo Domingo, Dominican Republic

Impact, Av. Romulo Betancourt Ho. 53, Edif. Plaza Bolivar, 1do piso, Esquina Caonabo, Local No. 205, Santo Domingo, Dominican Republic

UNITED PARCEL SERVICE OF AMERICA, INC.

55 Glenlake Parkway, NE, Atlanta, GA, 30328

Tel: (404) 828-6000 Fax: (404) 828-6593 Web site: www.ups.com

International package-delivery service.

UPS / Dominican Parcel Service, S.A., Calle Jose Amado Soler, Esq. Abrahan Lincoln, Edif. Progresus, Santo Domingo, Dominican Republic

Tel: 809-563-5639 Fax: 809-565-9561

WACKENHUT CORPORATION

4200 Wackenhut Drive, Ste. 100, Palm Beach Gardens, FL, 33410

Tel: (561) 622-5656 Fax: (561) 691-6736 Web site: www.wackenhut.com

Security systems & services.

Wackenhut Dominicana S.A., Paseo de los Locutores 36, Ensanche Piantini, Aptdo. 1677, Zona 1, Santo Domingo, Dominican Republic (Location: Santiago & Puerta Plata, Dominican Republic.)

Tel: 809-544-3333 Fax: 809-567-4767

WARNACO INC.

90 Park Ave., New York, NY, 10016

Tel: (212) 661-1300 Fax: (212) 687-0480 Web site: www.warnaco.com

Mfr./sales intimate apparel and men's and women's sportswear.

Warnaco, Santo Domingo, Dominican Republic

WARNER-LAMBERT COMPANY

201 Tabor Road, Morris Plains, NJ, 07950-2693

Tel: (973) 540-2000 Fax: (973) 540-3761 Web site: www.warner-lambert.com

Mfr. ethical and proprietary pharmaceuticals, confectionery and consumer products & pet care supplies.

Laboratories Warner-Chilcott/Adams Dominicana SA, Ramon Santana 12, Santo Domingo, Dominican Republic

WENDY'S INTERNATIONAL, INC.

428 West Dublin-Granville Roads, Dublin, OH, 43017

Tel: (614) 764-3100 Fax: (614) 764-3459

Fast food restaurant chain.

Wendy's International, Dominican Republic

WEST CHEMICAL PRODUCTS INC.

1000 Herrontown Road, Princeton, NJ, 08540

Tel: (609) 921-0501 Fax: (609) 924-4308

Sanitary equipment & supplies.

West SA, Aptdo. 428, Santo Domingo, Dominican Republic

WOMETCO ENTERPRISES INC.

3195 Ponce de Leon Boulevard, Coral Gables, FL, 33134

Tel: (305) 529-1400 Fax: (305) 529-1499

Television broadcasting, film distribution, bottling, vending machines.

Operadora Filmica SA, Aptdo. 1396, Av. Bolivar 453, Zona 2, Santo Domingo, Dominican Republic

XEROX CORPORATION

800 Long Ridge Road, PO Box 1600, Stamford, CT, 06904

Tel: (203) 968-3000 Fax: (203) 968-4312 Web site: www.xerox.com

Mfr. document processing equipment, systems and supplies.

Xerox Dominicana C.POR.A., Apartado #40, Ave. Bolivar 1004, Ens. LaJulia, Santa Domingo, Dominican Republic

Fax: 809-541-2762

YOUNG & RUBICAM INC.

285 Madison Ave., New York, NY, 10017

Tel: (212) 210-3000 Fax: (212) 370-3796 Web site: www.yr.com

Advertising, public relations, direct marketing and sales promotion, corporate & product ID management.

Young & Rubicam Damaris C por A, Av. de Los Proceres, Esq. Camino del Oeste, Arroya Hondo, Santo Domingo, Dominican Republic

Ecuador

3M

3M Center, St. Paul, MN, 55144-1000

Tel: (612) 733-1110 Fax: (612) 733-9973 Web site: www.mmm.com

Mfr. diversified products for industry, health care, imaging, communications, transport, safety, consumer, etc.

3M Ecuador CA, Km. 1.5 Via Duran, Tambo, Guayaquil, Ecuador

Tel: 593-4-800-777 Fax: 593-4-802-254

AIR EXPRESS INTERNATIONAL CORPORATION

120 Tokeneke Road, PO Box 1231, Darien, CT, 06820

Tel: (203) 655-7900 Fax: (203) 655-5779 Web site: www.aeilogistics.com

Air freight forwarder.

AEI de Ecuador, c/o Metropolitan Expreso Cia. Ltda., Panamericana Norte KM 3 1/2 y Los Cedros, Quito, Ecuador

Tel: 593-2-475-732 Fax: 593-2-475-730

ABC, INC.

77 West 66th Street, New York, NY, 10023

Tel: (212) 456-7777 Fax: (212) 456-6384

Radio/TV production & broadcasting.

Primera Television Ecuatoriana SA, 9 de Octubre 1200, Casilla 5063, Guayaquil, Ecuador

Primera Television Ecuatoriana SA, Calle Padre Aguirre y Nueva Tola, Casilla 70, Quito, Ecuador

Telesistema del Ecuador SA, Palacio Municipal, Casilla 400, Cuenca, Ecuador

AMMIRATI PURIS LINTAS

One Dag Hammarskjold Plaza, New York, NY, 10017

Tel: (212) 605-8000 Fax: (212) 605-4705 Web site: www.interpublic.com

International advertising agency.

Qualitat S.A., Casilla 189, Guayaquil, Ecuador

Tel: 593-4-882-969 Fax: 593-4-889-334 Contact: Miguel Fitz-Patrick

AON CORPORATION

123 North Wacker Drive, Chicago, IL, 60606

Tel: (312) 701-3000 Fax: (312) 701-3100 Web site: www.aon.com

Insurance brokers worldwide; underwrites accident & health insurance, specialty & professional insurance; & provides risk management consultation.

AON Worldwide / Uniseguros CA, Calle 8, Conominio 2.001 Ciudadela Kennedy, Guayaquil, Ecuador

Tel: 593-4-287144 Fax: 593-4-282952 Contact: Robert E. Cackett

ARBOR ACRES FARM INC.

439 Marlborough Road, Glastonbury, CT, 06033

Tel: (860) 633-4681 Fax: (860) 633-2433

Producers of male & female broiler breeders, commercial egg layers.

Ecuador Farms SA, Casilla 2042, Quito, Ecuador

ARTHUR ANDERSEN & COMPANY

33 West Monroe Street, Chicago, IL, 60603

Tel: (312) 372-7100 Fax: (312) 507-0123 Web site: www.arthurandersen.com

Accounting & audit, tax & management consulting services.

Arthur Andersen & Co.,, Av. Diego de Almagro #1550 y, PO Box 17-11-06465, Quito, Ecuador

Tel: 593-2-545-624

AVIS, INC.

900 Old Country Road., Garden City, NY, 11530

Tel: (516) 222-3000 Fax: (516) 222-4381 Web site: www.avis.com

Car rental services.

Avis Rent A Car System Inc, P. Icaza 425 y Cordova, Guayaquil, Ecuador

AVON PRODUCTS INC.

1345 Ave. of the Americas, New York, NY, 10105-0196

Tel: (212) 282-5000 Fax: (212) 282-6049 Web site: www.avon.com

Mfr./distributor beauty & related products, fashion jewelry, gifts & collectibles.

Productos Avon Ecuador S.A., El Batan #405 y Av. 6 de Diciembre, Frente al Colegio, Benalcazar, Ecuador

Tel: 593-2-259791 Fax: 593-2-259792 Contact: Gladys de Len, Sales Mgr.

BAKER HUGHES INCORPORATED

3900 Essex Lane, Ste. 1200, Houston, TX, 77027

Tel: (713) 439-8600 Fax: (713) 439-8699 Web site: www.bakerhughes.com

Develop & apply technology to drill, complete & produce oil and natural gas wells; provide separation systems to petroleum, municipal, continuous process & mining industries.

Baker Transworld Inc., Av. Amazonas 477 Y Roca, piso 7, Of. 720, Quito, Ecuador

Tel: 593-2-554356 Fax: 593-2-564881

Milchem Western Hemisphere Inc., Casilla 4143, Quito, Ecuador

BAKER PETROLITE CORPORATION

3900 Essex Lane, Houston, TX, 77027

Tel: (713) 599-7400 Fax: (713) 599-7592

Mfr./prod specialty chemical treating programs, performance-enhancing additives & related equipment & services.

Ecuatoriana de Petroquimicos Petrolite SA, Edif. Albatros, Av. de los Shyris 1240 y Portugal, Casilla 11026, Quito, Ecuador

BALSA ECUADOR LUMBER CORPORATION

10 Fairway Court, PO Box 195, Northvale, NJ, 07647

Tel: (201) 767-1400 Fax: (201) 387-6631

Light lumber.

Compania Ecuatoriana de Balsa SA, Robles 301, Casilla 3842, Guayaquil, Ecuador

BATES WORLDWIDE INC.

405 Lexington Ave., New York, NY, 10174

Tel: (212) 297-7000 Fax: (212) 986-0270 Web site: www.batesww.com

Advertising, marketing, public relations & media consulting.

VIP Bates Ecuador, Whimper 777, Casilla 4558-A, Quito, Ecuador

Tel: 593-2-502-024 Fax: 593-2-563-901 Contact: G. Vallejo, Pres.

BDO SEIDMAN, LLP

Two Prudential Plaza, 180 N. Stetson Ave., Ste. 2300, Chicago, IL, 60601

Tel: (312) 240-1236 Fax: (312) 240-3329 Web site: www.bdo.com

International accounting & financial consulting firm.

BDO Stern, Av. Amazonas 540 y Carrión, Edif. Londres, 6° piso, Quito, Ecuador

Tel: 593-2-566-915 Fax: 593-2-504-477 Contact: Rolf Stern

BELCO OIL & GAS CORPORATION

767 Fifth Ave., 46th Floor, New York, NY, 10153

Tel: (212) 644-2200 Fax: (212) 644-2230

Exploration & production of crude oil & natural gas.

Belco Petroleum Ecuador Inc., Cordova 808 y V.M. Rendon, Edif. Torres de la Merced, Guayaquil, Ecuador

BELLSOUTH INTERNATIONAL

1155 Peachtree Street NE, Ste. 400, Atlanta, GA, 30367

Tel: (404) 249-4800 Fax: (404) 249-4880 Web site: www.bellsouth.com

Mobile communications, telecommunications network systems.

BellSouth Ecuador, Edif. BellSouth, Av. Republica Y La Pradera, Esquina, Quito, Ecuador

Tel: 593-2-227-700 Fax: 593-2-227-597

BEST WESTERN INTERNATIONAL

6201 North 24th Place, Phoenix, AZ, 85106

Tel: (602) 957-4200 Fax: (602) 957-5740

International hotel chain.

Best Western Quito, Gonzalez Suarez 2500, Box 2201, Quito, Ecuador

BESTFOODS, INC.

700 Sylvan Ave., International Plaza, Englewood Cliffs, NJ, 07632-9976

Tel: (201) 894-4000 Fax: (201) 894-2186 Web site: www.bestfoods.com

Consumer foods products; corn refining.

S.B. Penick del Ecuador SA, Casilla Postal No. 17-11-6488, Quito, Ecuador

Tel: 593-2-352905 Fax: 593-2-352905 Contact: Hugo Fernandez, Mgr.

BETZDEARBORN

4636 Somerton Road, PO Box 3002, Trevose, PA, 19053-6783

Tel: (215) 953-2568 Fax: (215) 953-5524 Web site: www.betzdearborn.com

Mfr. water/wastewater and process system treatment chemicals and services.

BetzDearborn de Ecuador S.A., Calle Luiz de Gongora, Casa no. 0152, Cjidaleda Oscus, Ambato, Ecuador

SAMUEL BINGHAM COMPANY

127 East Lake Street, Ste. 300, Bloomgindale, IL, 60108

Tel: (630) 924-9250 Fax: (630) 924-0469 Web site: www.binghamrollers.com

Print and industrial rollers and inks.

Industrial Paragraficas Cia. Ltd., Casilla 6540, Guayaquil, Ecuador

BORDEN INC.

180 East Broad Street, Columbus, OH, 43215-3799

Tel: (614) 225-4000 Fax: (614) 220-6453

Mfr. Packaged foods, consumer adhesives, housewares and industrial chemicals.

Cia Borden Ecuatoriana, S.A., Panamericana Sur Km. 14.5, Sector Turubamba, Quito, Ecuador

Tel: 593-2-690-925 Fax: 593-2-690-639

BOZELL WORLDWIDE

40 West 23rd Street, New York, NY, 10010

Tel: (212) 727-5000 Fax: (212) 645-9173 Web site: www.bozell.com

Advertising, marketing, public relations and media consulting.

Bozell Ecuador, Ave. Miguel H. Alcivar, MZ 3V, #3, Guayaquil, Ecuador

Tel: 593-4-395-855 Fax: 593-4-395-865 Contact: Adriana R. de Hernandez, Mng. Dir.

BRISTOL-MYERS SQUIBB COMPANY

345 Park Ave., New York, NY, 10154

Tel: (212) 546-4000 Fax: (212) 546-4020 Web site: www.bms.com

Pharmaceutical and food preparations, medical and surgical instruments.

Bristol-Myers Squibb Company - Ecuador, Mecanos 3ER piso, Guayaquil, Ecuador

Bristol-Myers Squibb Company - Ecuador, Juan Diguja, No. 198 Yvos Andes, Esquina Quito, Ecuador

BUDGET RENT A CAR CORPORATION

4225 Naperville Road, Lisle, IL, 60532

Tel: (630) 955-1900 Fax: (630) 955-7799 Web site: www.budgetrentacar.com

Car and truck rental system.

Budget Rent A Car De Quito, 1408 Y Colon Esquina Ave Amazo, Guayaquil, Ecuador

LEO BURNETT CO., INC.

35 West Wacker Drive, Chicago, IL, 60601

Tel: (312) 220-5959 Fax: (312) 220-6533 Web site: www.leoburnett.com

International advertising agency.

Valencia y Asociados Publicidad, Quito, Ecuador

CALMAQUIP ENGINEERING CORPORATION

7240 NW 12th Street, Miami, FL, 33121

Tel: (305) 592-4510 Fax: (305) 593-9618

Engineering

Calmaquip Engineering del Ecuador SA, Casilla 56, Edif. Torres de Colon, Av. Colon 1346, Quito, Ecuador

CARBOLINE COMPANY

350 Hanley Industrial Court, St. Louis, MO, 63144

Tel: (314) 644-1000 Fax: (314) 644-4617

Mfr. coatings, sealants.

Pinturas Condor SA, 763 Ruiz de Castill, Quito, Ecuador

THE CHASE MANHATTAN CORPORATION

World Headquarters, 270 Park Ave., New York, NY, 10017

Tel: (212) 270-6000 Fax: (212) 622-9030 Web site: www.chase.com

International banking and financial services.

Chase Manhattan Overseas Corp., 18 de Septiembre 332 y Juan Leon Mera, piso 7, Casilla 9439, Sucursal 7, Quito, Ecuador

CHIQUITA BRANDS INTERNATIONAL INC.

250 East Fifth Street, Cincinnati, OH, 45202

Tel: (513) 784-8000 Fax: (513) 784-8030 Web site: www.chiquita.com

Sale and distribution of bananas, fresh fruits and processed foods.

Compania Agricola del Guayas, Aptdo. Aereo 09-01-4245, Guayaquil, Ecuador

CIGNA CORPORATION

One Liberty Place, Philadelphia, PA, 19192

Tel: (215) 761-1000 Fax: (215) 761-5008

Insurance, invest, health care and other financial services.

Cigna Worldwide Insurance Co., Edif. Antisana, 4 piso, Av. Amazonas 3655, Catalina Herrera, Quito, Ecuador

Indi Servicios C Ltda., Av. Eloy Alfaro 939 y Amazonas, Quito, Ecuador

CITICORP

399 Park Ave., New York, NY, 10043

Tel: (212) 559-1000 Fax: (212) 527-2066 Web site: www.citibank.com

International banking and financial services.

Citibank N.A., Juan Leon Mera 130 y Ave. Patria, Edif. CFN, Quito, Ecuador

Tel: 593-2-563-300 Fax: 593-2-566-893

CMS ENERGY CORPORATION

Fairlane Plaza South, Ste. 1100, 330 Town Drive, Dearborn, MI, 48126

Tel: (313) 436-9200 Fax: (313) 436-9225 Web site: www.cmsenergy.com

Independent power plant operator.

CMS Nomeco, Quito, Ecuador

COLUMBIA PICTURES INDUSTRIES INC.

10202 West Washington Blvd., Culver City, CA, 90232

Tel: (310) 244-4000 Fax: (310) 244-2626 Web site: www.sony.com

Producer and distributor of motion pictures.

Productora Filmica Nacional del Ecuador Cia. Ltda., Calle 9 de Octobre 424, Casilla 3445, Guayaquil, Ecuador

COMPAQ COMPUTER CORPORATION

20555 State Highway 249, PO Box 692000, Houston, TX, 77269-2000

Tel: (713) 370-0670 Fax: (713) 514-1740 Web site: www.compaq.com

Develop/mfr. personal computers.

Compaq Computer Ecuador, Republica del Salvador #1082, y Naciones Inidas, Torre Paris, piso 4, Quito, Ecuador

Tel: 593-225-4343 Fax: 593-246-7713

CONTINENTAL AIRLINES INC.

2929 Allen Parkway, Ste. 1501, Houston, TX, 77019

Tel: (281) 834-5000 Fax: (281) 520-6329

International airline carrier.

Continental Airlines Inc., Ecuador

CROWN CORK & SEAL COMPANY, INC.

One Crown Way, Philadelphia, PA, 19154-4599

Tel: (215) 698-5100 Fax: (215) 698-5201

Mfr. cans, bottle caps; filling & packaging machinery.

Crown Cork del Ecuador CA, Casilla 5401 & 8888, Guayaquil, Ecuador

D'ARCY MASIUS BENTON & BOWLES INC. (DMB&B)

1675 Broadway, New York, NY, 10019

Tel: (212) 468-3622 Fax: (212) 468-2987 Web site: www.dmbb.com

Full service international advertising and communications group.

Creacional/DMB&B, Costanera 611 Y Las Monjas, Guayaquil, Ecuador

Tel: 503-4-38-0132 Fax: 593-4-88-5692 Contact: Miguel Loret De Mola, Gen. Mgr.

DELOITTE TOUCHE TOHMATSU INTERNATIONAL

PO Box 820, Wilton, CT, 06897

Tel: (203) 761-3000 Fax: (203) 834-2200 Web site: www.u.s.deloitte.com or www.dtti.com

Accounting, audit, tax and management consulting services.

Deloitte & Touche, Edif. Contemporaneo, Noveno piso, Tulcan 803 y Av. 9 de Octubre, Guayaquil, Ecuador

Deloitte & Touche, Edif. Xerox, Septimo piso, Av. Amazonas 3617 Y Pablo Sanz, Quito, Ecuador

DHL WORLDWIDE EXPRESS

333 Twin Dolphin Drive, Redwood City, CA, 94065

Tel: (650) 593-7474 Fax: (650) 593-1689 Web site: www.dhl.com

Worldwide air express carrier.

DHL Worldwide Express, Av. Republica 396 y Diego de Alamgro, Quito, Ecuador

Tel: 593-2-565059

DOVER CORPORATION

280 Park Ave., New York, NY, 10017-1292

Tel: (212) 922-1640 Fax: (212) 922-1656 Web site: www.dovercorporation.com

Elevator manufacturer and holding company for varied industries.

Celco Cia Ltd., Cordova 10004 Y.P. Ycaza, Guayaquil, Ecuador

Tel: 593-4-431-2987 Fax: 593-4-313-324

THE DOW CHEMICAL COMPANY

2030 Dow Center, Midland, MI, 48674

Tel: (517) 636-1000 Fax: (517) 636-3228 Web site: www.atdow.com

Mfr. chemicals, plastics, pharmaceuticals, agricultural products, consumer products.

Dow Chemical Intl. Inc., Circunvalacion Calle 6a., Urdesa, Casilla 6560, Guayaquil, Ecuador

LIFE (Laboratorios Industriales Faramceuticos Ecuatorianos), Edif. LIFE, Av. Zumaco y de la Prensa, Casilla 458, Quito, Ecuador

LIFE (Laboratorios Industriales Faramceuticos Ecuatorianos), V.M. Rendon 408, Casilla 3783, Guayaquil, Ecuador

DUKE ENERGY CORPORATION

422 South Church Street, Charlotte, NC, 28242

Tel: (704) 594-6200 Fax: (704) 382-3814

Energy pipeliner, oil/gas exploration and production.

Electroquil, Guayaquil, Ecuador

J.D. EDWARDS & COMPANY

One Technology Way, Denver, CO, 80237

Tel: (303) 334-4000 Fax: (303) 334-4970 Web site: www.jdedwards.com.

Computer software products.

E.D.P. ECU, Calle Rumipamba #706 Y, Av. Republica, Edif. Borja Paez P-3, Ofs. 32-33, Quito, Ecuador

Tel: 593-2-263-036 Fax: 593-2-263-037

EFCO

1800 NE Broadway Ave., Des Moines, IA, 50316-0386

Tel: (515) 266-1141 Fax: (515) 266-7970

Mfr. systems for concrete construction.

EFCO, Shyris 2678 y Garpar Villarroel, Edif. El Tablon, piso 60, Casilla 17-15-181-C, Quito, Ecuador

ERNST & YOUNG, LLP

787 Seventh Ave., New York, NY, 10019

Tel: (212) 773-3000 Fax: (212) 773-6350 Web site: www.eyi.com

Accounting and audit, tax and management consulting services.

Ernst & Young, Junin 114Y Malecon, Edis Torres Del Rio, piso 6, Off. 8, (PO Box 09-01-9094) Guayaquil, Ecuador

Tel: 593-4-560-655 Fax: 593-4-562-199 Contact: Cesar R. Holguin

Ernst & Young House, Quito, Ecuador Mail to: PO Box 09-01-9094, Guayaquil, Ecuador

Tel: 593-2-439-383 Fax: 593-2-439-375

EXPEDITORS INTERNATIONAL OF WASHINGTON INC.

999 Throd Ave., Ste. 2500, Seattle, WA, 98104

Tel: (206) 674-3400 Fax: (206) 682-9777 Web site: www.expd.com

Air/ocean freight forwarding, customs brokerage, international logistics solutions.

Leidasa SAC, Faustino Sarmiento 158 y Portete, Quito, Ecuador

Leidasa SAC, Av. Juan Tanca Marengo Km. 1.5, Edif. Sumelec, Primer piso, Ofic. 01, Guyaquil, Ecuador

FEDERAL-MOGUL CORPORATION

26555 Northwestern Highway, PO Box 1966, Southfield, MI, 48034

Tel: (248) 354-7700 Fax: (248) 354-8983 Web site: www.federalmogul.com

Mfr./distributor precision parts for automobiles, trucks, farm and construction vehicles.

Federal-Mogul del Ecuador SA, Quito, Ecuador

FERRO CORPORATION

1000 Lakeside Ave., Cleveland, OH, 44114-1183

Tel: (216) 641-8580 Fax: (216) 696-5784 Web site: www.ferro.com

Mfr. Specialty chemicals, coatings, plastics, colors, refractories.

Ferro Ecuadoriana SA, PO Box 01-01-1188 Cuenca, Ecuador

Tel: 593-7-801288 Fax: 593-7-807042 Contact: Braulio Fernandez, Mng. Dir.

FRITZ COMPANIES INC.

706 Mission Street, Ste. 900, San Francisco, CA, 94103

Tel: (415) 904-8360 Fax: (415) 904-8661 Web site: www.fritz.com

Integrated transportation, sourcing, distribution & customs brokerage services.

Fritz Companies Inc., Guayaquil & Quito, Ecuador

H.B. FULLER COMPANY

1200 Willow Lake Blvd., Vadnais Heights, MN, 55110

Tel: (612) 236-5900 Fax: (612) 236-5898 Web site: www.hbfuller.com

Mfr./distributor adhesives, sealants, coatings, paints, waxes, sanitation chemicals.

Glidden Ecuador, Quito Sales Office, Av. America 4034 y Lallemet, Casilla Postal 01-17-3545, Quito, Ecuador

Tel: 593-2-259418 Fax: 593-2-435545

H.B. Fuller Ecuador SA, Casilla 7441, Guayaquil, Ecuador

Tel: 593-4-25-0588 Fax: 593-4-25-0901

GENERAL MOTORS CORPORATION

100 Renaissance Center, Detroit, MI, 48243.7301

Tel: (313) 556-5000 Fax: (313) 556-5108 Web site: www.gm.com

Mfr. full line vehicles, automotive electronics, commercial technologies, telecommunications, space, finance.

Autos y Maquinas del Ecuador SA, Quito, Ecuador

Omnibus BB Transportes SA, Quito, Ecuador

THE GILLETTE COMPANY

Prudential Tower Building, Boston, MA, 02199

Tel: (617) 421-7000 Fax: (617) 421-7123 Web site: www.gillette.com

Develop/mfr. personal care/use products: blades & razors, toiletries, cosmetics, stationery.

Gillette del Ecuador SA, Guayaquil, Ecuador

GLOBAL SILVERHAWK

1000 Burnett Ave., Concord, CA, 94520

Tel: (510) 609-7080 Fax: (510) 609-7081 Web site: www.globalsilverhawk.com

International moving & forwarding.

Global Transportes Ltda., Bartolome Sanchez #N 71-69, Y J. Guerrero, Quito, Ecuador
Contact: Pablo Calero, Gen. Mgr.

GREY ADVERTISING INC.
777 Third Ave., New York, NY, 10017
Tel: (212) 546-2000 Fax: (212) 546-1495 Web site: www.giworldwwide.com
International advertising agency.
DeMaruri, Guayaquil, Ecuador

HALLIBURTON COMPANY
500 North Akard Street, Ste. 3600, Dallas, TX, 75201-3391
Tel: (214) 978-2600 Fax: (214) 978-2685 Web site: www.halliburton.com
Energy, construction and insurance.
Halliburton Ltd., Calle Japon 123y, Av. Amazonas, Edif. Ferlosant, Quito, Ecuador
Tel: 593-6-880-636 Fax: 593-6-880-639
Halliburton Ltd., Calle Japon 123y, Av. Amazonas, Edif. Ferlosant, Quito, Ecuador
Tel: 593-6-830-447 Fax: 593-6-830-235

THE HARPER GROUP
260 Townsend Street, San Francisco, CA, 94107-1719
Tel: (415) 978-0600 Fax: (415) 978-0692 Web site: www.circleintl.com
Ocean/air freight forwarding, customs brokerage, packing and wholesale, logistics management and insurance.
Poclani S.A., CLDA Kennedy Norte, MZ 103 Atras de Llantera Oso, Guayaquil, Ecuador
Tel: 593-4-281-416 Fax: 593-4-281-818
Poclani S.A., Robles 653 Y Amazonas, 4TO piso Of. 411, Quito, Ecuador
Tel: 593-2-236-440 Fax: 593-2-221-946

H.J. HEINZ COMPANY
600 Grant Street, Pittsburgh, PA, 15219
Tel: (412) 456-5700 Fax: (412) 456-6128 Web site: www.heinz.com
Processed food products and nutritional services.
Star-Kist Foods Inc., Guayaquil, Ecuador

HELMERICH & PAYNE INC
1579 East 21st Street, Tulsa, OK, 74114
Tel: (918) 742-5531 Fax: (918) 743-2671
Oil/gas exploration & drilling, real estate, mfr. gas odorants.
Helmerich & Payne del Ecuador, Av. Republica 1650 y Azuay, Quito, Ecuador

IBM CORPORATION
New Orchard Road, Armonk, NY, 10504
Tel: (914) 765-1900 Fax: (914) 765-7382 Web site: www.ibm.com
Information products, technology & services.
IBM del Ecuador C.A., Diego de Almagro 2054 y Whimper, Quito, Ecuador
Tel: 593-2-565100 Fax: 593-2-565145

InaCom CORPORATION
10810 Farnam Drive, Omaha, NE, 68154
Tel: (402) 392-3900 Fax: (402) 392-3602 Web site: www.inacom.com
Provider of technology management products and services; reselling microcomputer systems, work stations and networking and telecommunications equipment.
InaCom de Ecuador, Borja Lavayen y Juan Pablo Sanz, Edif. Viscaya OF, 4B Quito, Ecuador
Contact: Alan Sanchez, Mng. Ptnr.

INFONET SERVICES CORPORATION

2100 East Grand Ave., El Segundo, CA, 90245

Tel: (310) 335-2600 Fax: (310) 335-4507 Web site: www.infonet.com

Provider of Internet services and electronic messaging services.

Infonet Ecuador, Av. America 3576 y Atahualpa, PO Box 1703398, Quito, Ecuador

Tel: 593-2-444-965 Fax: 593-2-444-966

INGRAM MICRO INC.

PO Box 25125, Santa Ana, CA, 92799

Tel: (714) 566-1000 Fax: (714) 566-7940 Web site: www.ingrammicro.com

Distribute computer systems, software and related products.

Ingram Micro Inc., Bulgaria 146 y Diego de Almagro, #11 Mezzanine, Quito, Ecuador

Tel: 593-2-222-2044 Fax: 593-2-222-3163

IRRIDELCO INTERNATIONAL CORPORATION

440 Sylvan Ave., Englewood Cliffs, NJ, 07632

Tel: (201) 569-3030 Fax: (201) 569-9237 Web site: www.irridelco.com

Mfr./distributor of the most comprehensive lines of mechanical and micro irrigation; pumps and irrigation systems.

IDC Ecuador, 1 ro de Mayo 1006 y Tulcan, 7mo piso, Guayaquil, Ecuador

Tel: 593-4-28-1010 Fax: 593-4-28-1256 Contact: Cristobal Ripalda

ITT CORPORATION

1330 Ave. of the Americas, New York, NY, 10019-5490

Tel: (212) 258-1000 Fax: (212) 258-1297

Design/mfr. communications & electronic equipment, hotels, insurance.

Intl. Standard Electric of New York Ltd., Edif. Banco de Prestamos, 4 piso, Of. D, Casilla 2754, Quito, Ecuador

J. WALTER THOMPSON COMPANY

466 Lexington Ave., New York, NY, 10017

Tel: (212) 210-7000 Fax: (212) 210-6944 Web site: www.jwt.com

International advertising and marketing services.

Norlop Thompson Asociados, Guayaquil, Ecuador

JOHNSON & JOHNSON

One Johnson & Johnson Plaza, New Brunswick, NJ, 08933

Tel: (732) 524-0400 Fax: (732) 214-0334 Web site: www.jnj.com

Mfr./distributor/R&D pharmaceutical, health care and cosmetic products.

Johnson & Johnson del Ecuador SA, Casilla 09-01-7206, Guayaquil, Ecuador

S C JOHNSON & SON INC.

1525 Howe Street, Racine, WI, 53403

Tel: (414) 260-2000 Fax: (414) 260-2133 Web site: www.scjohnsonwax.com

Home, auto, commercial and personal care products and specialty chemicals.

S.C. Johnson & Son (Ecuador) SA., PO Box 09-01-874, Guayaquil, Ecuador

KPMG PEAT MARWICK LLP

Three Chestnut Ridge Road, Montvale, NJ, 07645

Tel: (201) 307-7000 Fax: (201) 930-8617 Web site: www.kpmg.com

Accounting and audit, tax and management consulting services.

KPMG Peat Marwick, Av. Amazonas 1188 y Cordero, Edif. FLOPEC, 6to.piso, Quito, Ecuador

KPMG Peat Marwick, Cdla. Kennedy Norte, Av. Miguel Alcivar, Mz. 302 Solar 7 y 8, Guayaquil, Ecuador

Tel: 593-4-290697 Fax: 593-4-288774 Contact: Leonidas Sánchez, Jr., Sr. Ptnr.

THE LUBRIZOL CORPORATION

29400 Lakeland Blvd., Wickliffe, OH, 44092-2298

Tel: (440) 943-4200 Fax: (440) 943-5337 Web site: www.lubrizol.com

Mfr. chemicals additives for lubricants & fuels.

Lubrizol de Ecuador, Guayaquil, Ecuador

Tel: 593-4-288-538

MANPOWER INTERNATIONAL INC.

5301 N. Ironwood Road, PO Box 2053, Milwaukee, WI, 53201-2053

Tel: (414) 961-1000 Fax: (414) 961-7081 Web site: www.manpower

Temporary help, contract service, training & testing.

Manpower - Quito, Jorge Washington 570 y Juan Leon Mera, Quito, Ecuador

Tel: 593-2-504-867 Fax: 5932--509-517

MARRIOTT INTERNATIONAL INC.

1 Marriott Drive, Washington, DC, 20058

Tel: (301) 380-3000 Fax: (301) 380-5181

Lodging, contract food and beverage service, and restaurants.

Quito Marriott Hotel, Quito, Ecuador

Tel: 593-2-506-366

MARSH & McLENNAN COS INC.

1166 Ave. of the Americas, New York, NY, 10036-2774

Tel: (212) 345-5000 Fax: (212) 345-4808 Web site: www.marshmac.com

Insurance agents/brokers, pension and investment management consulting services.

Tecniseguros Cia. Ltda., Whimper 1210, Casill: 17-21-0433, Quito, Ecuador

Tel: 593-2-250-5655 Fax: 593-2-256-4773 Contact: Francisco Proano-Salvador

Tecniseguros Cia. Ltda., Edif. Tecniseguros, Kennedy Norte, Calle San Rogue y Av. Francisco de Orellana, Guayaquil, Ecuador

Tel: 593-4-468-0700 Fax: 593-4-468-0822 Contact: Pedro Hallon

McCANN-ERICKSON WORLDWIDE

750 Third Ave., New York, NY, 10017

Tel: (212) 984-3644 Fax: (212) 984-2629

International advertising/marketing services.

McCann Erickson Publicidad SA, Malecon 1401, Casilla 5809, Guayaquil, Ecuador

McCann Erickson Publicidad SA, Leonidas Plaza 150, 18 de Septiembre, Casilla 3491, Quito, Ecuador

MERCK & COMPANY, INC.

1 Merck Drive, Whitehouse Station, NJ, 08889

Tel: (908) 423-1000 Fax: (908) 423-2592

Pharmaceuticals, chemicals and biologicals.

Merck, Sharp & Dohme Intl., Carretera al Tingo, Guayaquil, Ecuador

MICROSOFT CORPORATION

One Microsoft Way, Redmond, WA, 98052-6399

Tel: (425) 882-8080 Fax: (425) 936-7329 Web site: www.microsoft.com

Computer software, peripherals and services.

Corporacion Microsoft Del Ecuador S.A., Av. Naciones Unidas 1014 y Av .Amazonas (esquina) Edif. La Previsora Torre A, Officina 1001, Quito, Ecuador

Tel: 593-2-463-090 Fax: 593-2-463-093

MOBIL CORPORATION

3225 Gallows Road, Fairfax, VA, 22037-0001

Tel: (703) 846-3000 Fax: (703) 846-4669 Web site: www.mobil.com

Petroleum and gas exploration and refining, mfr. petroleum products, chemicals and petrochemicals.

Mobil Oil Co. del Ecuador, Casilla 169, Quito, Ecuador

NATIONAL CAR RENTAL SYSTEM, INC.

7700 France Ave. South, Minneapolis, MN, 55435

Tel: (612) 830-2121 Fax: (612) 830-2921

Car rentals.

Natl. Car Rental, Madrid 1471 y 12 de Octubre, Quito, Ecuador

OCCIDENTAL PETROLEUM CORPORATION

10889 Wilshire Blvd., Los Angeles, CA, 90024

Tel: (310) 208-8800 Fax: (310) 443-6690 Web site: www.oxy.com

Petroleum and petroleum products, chemicals, plastics.

Occidental of Ecuador Inc., Ecuador

OGILVY & MATHER WORLDWIDE

309 West 49th Street, New York, NY, 10019

Tel: (212) 237-4000 Fax: (212) 237-5123

Advertising, marketing, public relations & consulting firm.

Veritas/O&M, Guayaquil, Ecuador

ORYX ENERGY COMPANY

PO Box 2880, Dallas, TX, 75221-2880

Tel: (214) 715-4000 Fax: (214) 715-3311 Web site: www.oryx.com

Oil and gas exploration and production.

Oryx Ecuador Energy Co., Av. NN UU 685 y Shyris, Edif. Cordiez, 60 piso, Quito, Ecuador

Contact: Tim Martin, Gen. Dir.

OWENS-ILLINOIS, INC.

One SeaGate, PO Box 1035, Toledo, OH, 43666

Tel: (419) 247-5000 Fax: (419) 247-2839

Largest mfr. of glass containers in the US; plastic containers, compression-molded closures and dispensing systems.

Cristaleria del Ecuador, S.A., Guayaquil, Ecuador

PAN-AMERICAN LIFE INSURANCE CO.

Pan American Life Center, PO Box 60219, New Orleans, LA, 70130-0219

Tel: (504) 566-1300 Fax: (504) 566-3600 Web site: www.palic.com

Insurance services.

Pan-American Life Insurance Co., Av. Republica del Salvador 10-81 y Naciones Unidas, Torre Londres, pisos 10 y 11, Quito, Ecuador

Tel: 593-2-253-490 Fax: 593-2-252-502 Contact: Juan Bustamante, Gen. Mgr. Emp: 54

PARKER DRILLING COMPANY

8 East Third Street, Tulsa, OK, 74103-3637

Tel: (918) 585-8221 Fax: (918) 585-1058

Drilling contractor.

Parker Drilling Co., Av. Amazonas 648, Casilla 3644, Quito, Ecuador

Parker Drilling Co. of South America, Casilla 3644, Quito, Ecuador

THE PERKIN-ELMER CORPORATION

761 Main Ave., Norwalk, CT, 06859-0001

Tel: (203) 762-1000 Fax: (203) 762-4228 Web site: www.perkin-elmer.com

Leading supplier of systems for life science research and related applications.

Distecnica, Av. Los Shyris 1094, Quito, Ecuador

Tel: 593-2-24-3306 Fax: 593-2-46-4844 Contact: E. Montenegro, Sales Mgr.

PETROLEUM HELICOPTERS INC.

2121 Airline Highway, Ste. 400, Metairie, LA, 70001

Tel: (504) 828-3323 Fax: (504) 828-8333 Web site: www.Phihelico.com

Aerial transportation and helicopter charter.

Ecuavia-Oriente SA, Av. 6 de Diciembre 3805 y Noruega, Quito, Ecuador

PFIZER INC.

235 East 42nd Street, New York, NY, 10017-5755

Tel: (212) 573-2323 Fax: (212) 573-7851 Web site: www.pfizer.com

Research-based, global health care company.

Pfizer CA, Ecuador

PHARMACIA & UPJOHN

95 Corporate Drive, PO Box 6995, Bridgewater, NJ, 08807

Tel: (908) 306-4400 Fax: (908) 306-4433 Web site: www.pnu.com

Mfr. pharmaceuticals, agricultural products, industry chemicals

Pharmacia & Upjohn, Edif. Club De Leones, 3 piso, Av. Naciones Unidas 1204, Quito, Ecuador

PHELPS DODGE CORPORATION

2600 North Central Ave., Phoenix, AZ, 85004-3089

Tel: (602) 234-8100 Fax: (602) 234-8337

Copper, minerals, metals & spec engineered products for transportation & electrical markets.

Cables Electricos Ecuatorianos CA (CABLEC), Casilla 1701, 02730 Quito, Ecuador

PRAXAIR, INC.

39 Old Ridgebury Road, Danbury, CT, 06810-5113

Tel: (203) 837-2000 Fax: (203) 837-2450 Web site: www.praxair.com

Produces and distributes industrial and specialty gases.

Praxair Ecuador S.A., Km 2.5, Via Duran Tambo, Via a la Feria, Guayaquil, Ecuador

Tel: 593-4-480-3710 Fax: 593-4-486-2990

PRICEWATERHOUSECOOPERS LLP

1251 Ave. of the Americas, New York, NY, 10020

Tel: (212) 596-7000 Fax: (212) 790-6620 Web site: www.pwcglobal.com

Accounting and auditing, tax and management, and human resource consulting services.

Price Waterhouse Ltd., Av. 12 de Octubre 394, 1st to 6th Fls., Casilla 17-21227, Quito, Ecuador

Tel: 593-2-562288 Fax: 593-2-567096

Price Waterhouse Ltd., Carchi 702, 2nd Fl., Casilla 5820, Guayaquil, Ecuador

Tel: 593-4-280-757 Fax: 593-4-284-153

RENDIC INTERNATIONAL CORPORATION

9100 South Dadeland Blvd., Ste 1800, Miami, FL, 33156

Tel: (305) 670-0066 Fax: (305) 670-0060 Web site: www.flintink.com

Sales of printing inks, press equipment and supplies.

Rendic International Corporation, Centro Comecial Dicentro, Av. Juan Tanca Y Agustin Marengo, Freire Kim #3, Primer piso Of. 27, Guayaquil, Ecuador

RJR NABISCO INC.

1301 Ave. of the Americas, New York, NY, 10019

Tel: (212) 258-5600 Fax: (212) 969-9173 Web site: www.rjrnabisco.com

Mfr. consumer packaged food products & tobacco products.

Nabisco Royal Ecuador, S.A., Ave. 10 de Agosto, 5133 y Naciones Unidas, Edif. Urania, Quito, Ecuador

THE ST. PAUL COMPANIES, INC.

385 Washington Street, St. Paul, MN, 55102

Tel: (612) 310-7911 Fax: (612) 310-8294 Web site: www.stpaul.com

Provides investment, insurance and reinsurance services.

Compania de Seguros Ecuatoriano - Sujiza S.A., Av. 9 de Octobre, PO Box Casilla 397, Guayaquil, Ecuador

SYBASE, INC.

6475 Christie Ave., Emeryville, CA, 94608

Tel: (510) 922-3500 Fax: (510) 922-3210 Web site: www.sybase.com

Design/mfg/distribution of database management systems, software development tools, connectivity products, consulting and technical support services..

InfoPower, S.A., Alpallana 289, Diego de Alnagro, Quito, Ecuador

Tel: 593-2-508-593 Fax: 593-2-500-806

TEXACO INC.

2000 Westchester Ave., White Plains, NY, 10650

Tel: (914) 253-4000 Fax: (914) 253-7753 Web site: www.texaco.com

Exploration/marketing crude oil, mfr. petro chemicals and products.

Lubricantes y Tambores del Ecuador CA (LYTECA), End of Av. Mons. Domingo Comin, Casilla 6071, Guayaquil, Ecuador

Texaco Petroleum Co., Edif. Perez Guerrero, Calle Jorge Washington 715, Esq. de Amazona, Casilla 1006, Quito, Ecuador

TRUE NORTH COMMUNICATIONS INC.

101 East Erie Street, Chicago, IL, 60611

Tel: (312) 425-6000 Fax: (312) 425-6350

Holding company, advertising agency.

Foote, Cone & Belding, Alpallana No. 581, Edif. Pradera II, Quito, Ecuador

UNION CARBIDE CORPORATION

39 Old Ridgebury Road, Danbury, CT, 06817

Tel: (203) 794-2000 Fax: (203) 794-6269 Web site: www.unioncarbide.com

Mfr. industrial chemicals, plastics and resins.

UCAR Polimeros y Quimicos CA SA de CV, Casilla 09-01-5322, Guayaquil, Ecuador (Location: Quito, Ecuador.)

UNITED PARCEL SERVICE OF AMERICA, INC.

55 Glenlake Parkway, NE, Atlanta, GA, 30328

Tel: (404) 828-6000 Fax: (404) 828-6593 Web site: www.ups.com

International package-delivery service.

UPS / Ecuador, Nuñez de Vela 470 e Ignacio San Maria, Edidicio Metropoli, Planta Baja, Quito, Ecuador (Locations: Guayaquil, Cuenca)

Tel: 593-2-460-598 Fax: 593-2-258-270

WACKENHUT CORPORATION

4200 Wackenhut Drive, Ste. 100, Palm Beach Gardens, FL, 33410

Tel: (561) 622-5656 Fax: (561) 691-6736 Web site: www.wackenhut.com

Security systems & services.

Wackenhut del Ecuador SA, Valladolid 936 y Cordero, Casilla 17-11-04791, Quito, Ecuador (Locations: Cuenca, Manta & Guayaquil, Ecuador.)

Tel: 593-2-224-664 Fax: 593-2-225-109

WARNER-LAMBERT COMPANY

201 Tabor Road, Morris Plains, NJ, 07950-2693

Tel: (973) 540-2000 Fax: (973) 540-3761 Web site: www.warner-lambert.com

Mfr. ethical and proprietary pharmaceuticals, confectionery and consumer products & pet care supplies.

Producto Adams, Casilla 2200, Quito, Ecuador

WESTERN ATLAS INC.

10205 Westheimer, Houston, TX, 77251-1407

Tel: (713) 972-4000 Fax: (713) 952-9837 Web site: www.waii.com

Full service to the oil industry.

Western Atlas & Western Geophysical, Av. Orellana 1811 y 10 de Agosto, Edif. El Cid,Officio 201/202, Quito, Ecuador

Tel: 593-2-223-356 Fax: 593-2-223-356 Contact: John Horsey, Bus. Mgr.

WITCO CORPORATION

One American Lane, Greenwich, CT, 06831-2559

Tel: (203) 552-2000 Fax: (203) 552-3070 Web site: www.witco.com

Mfr. chemical and petroleum products.

Witco Ecuador SA, Autopista Manual Cordova Galarza, Km. 10.5, Apartado Postal 1703557, Quito, Ecuador

WORLD COURIER INC.

1313 Fourth Ave., New Hyde Park, NY, 11041

Tel: (516) 354-2600 Fax: (516) 354-2644

International courier service.

World Courier de Ecuador, Elizalde 1194 Pichincha, Of. 404, Guayaquil, Ecuador

World Courier de Ecuador, Robles 653 y Amazonas, Quito, Ecuador

XEROX CORPORATION

800 Long Ridge Road, PO Box 1600, Stamford, CT, 06904

Tel: (203) 968-3000 Fax: (203) 968-4312 Web site: www.xerox.com

Mfr. document processing equipment, systems and supplies.

Xerox del Ecuador, S.A., Ave. Amazonas 3623 Y, Juan Pablo Sanz, Apt. Postal 17-03-174, Quito, Ecuador

Tel: 593-2-439-952 Fax: 593-1-430-994

VOLUME 1

PUBLISHER'S NOTES

Related publications

The 9th Edition
DIRECTORY OF FOREIGN FIRMS OPERATING IN THE UNITED STATES

EDITED & PUBLISHED BY
UNIWORLD BUSINESS PUBLICATIONS, INC.
PUBLISHED 1998

ONE VOLUME • 864 PAGES • PRICE: $200.00 • ISBN: 0-8360-0042-0

COMPREHENSIVE LISTINGS

- 2,050 Foreign Firms
- 4,190 U.S. Affiliates
- 71 Countries

EASY AND FLEXIBLE ACCESS

The firm(s) you are looking for can be found:

- ***by country*** — (Part I)
- ***by name*** — the name of the parent company (Part II)
- ***by affiliate*** — the name of the American based affiliate (Part III)

KEY CONTACT AND LOCATION INFORMATION

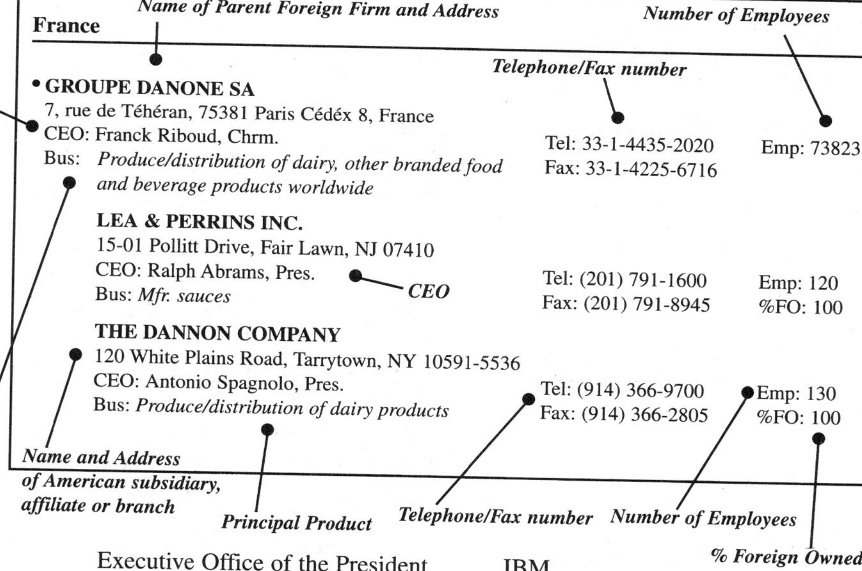

PARTIAL BUYERS LIST

Springfield Library
Harvard University Office of Career Services
Price Waterhouse
US International Trade Commission
Citibank
Heidrick & Struggles
Canadian Embassy
KLM
Emory University Career Services
Executive Office of the President
US Chamber of Commerce
Rochester Public Library
LA Chamber of Commerce
Merrill Lynch
Hitachi Foundation
Johns Hopkins Hospital
Columbia University
CBS
IBM
New York Public Library
University of Texas
Sprint International
Notre Dame University
Stentor International
The Washington Opera
Zagat
Liberty Mutual

Directory of American Firms Operating in Foreign Countries, 15th Edition Country/Regional Editions Softbound

AFRICA $69.00
Algeria, Angola, Benin, Botswana, Burkina Faso, Burundi, Cameroon, Cent. African Rep., Chad, Congo, Dem. Republic of Congo, Djibouti, Egypt, Ehtiopia, Gabon, Gambia, Ghana, Guinea, Ivory Coast, Kenya, Lesotho, Liberia, Libya, Madagascar, Malawi, Mali, Mauritius, Morocco, Mozambique, Namibia, Niger, Nigeria, Reunion, Senegal, Seychelles, Sierra Leone, South Africa, Sudan, Swaziland, Tanzania, Tunisia, Uganda, Zambia, Zimbabwe.

ASIA $149.00
Bangladesh, Brunei, Cambodia, China, Hong Kong, India, Indonesia, Japan, Laos, Macau, Malaysia, Mongolia, Myanmar, Nepal, Pakistan, Philippines, Singapore, So. Korea, Sri Lanka, Taiwan, Thailand, Vietnam

South Asia $49.00
Bangladesh, India, Myanmar, Nepal, Pakistan, Sri Lanka

South East Asia $89.00
Brunei, Cambodia, Indonesia, Laos, Malaysia, Philippines, Singapore, Thailand, Vietnam

Japan & South Korea $69.00

China, Hong Kong $69.00

China, H.K., Singapore, Taiwan $99.00

Near & Middle East $69.00
Bahrain, Cyprus, Iran, Israel, Jordan, Kuwait, Lebanon, Oman, Palestine, Qatar, Saudi Arabia, Syria, Turkey, United Arab Emirates, Yemen

The Arabic Countries $59.00
Algeria, Bahrain, Egypt, Iran, Jordan, Kuwait, Lebanon, Libya, Morocco, Oman, Palestine, Qatar, Saudi Arabia, Sudan, Syria, Tunisia, United Arab Emirates, Yemen

Near & Middle East & Arabic Countries Combined $69.00

AUSTRALIA & Pacific Islands $69.00
Australia, New Zealand, Fiji, French Polynesia, Guam, New Caledonia, Palau, Papua New Guinea, No. Mariana Is., Polynesia, Solomon Islands, Vanuatu

EUROPE All $199.00

EUROPE Western $179.00
Austria, Belgium, Channel Is., Denmark, England, Finland, France, Germany, Gibraltar, Greece, Iceland, Ireland, Isle of Man, Italy, Liechtenstein, Luxembourg, Madeira, Malta, Monaco, Netherlands, No. Ireland, Norway, Portugal, San Marino, Scotland, Spain, Sweden, Switzerland, Wales

British Isles $99.00
England, Scotland, Wales, Gibraltar, Ireland, Isle of Man, Northern Ireland, Channel Islands

EUROPE Western excluding the British Isles $159.00

Belgium	$49.00
France	$59.00
Germany	$69.00
Italy	$49.00
Netherlands	$49.00
Spain	$49.00
Sweden	$39.00
Switzerland	$39.00
Scandinavia (Denmark, Finland, Norway, Sweden)	$69.00

EUROPE Eastern $79.00
Albania, Armenia, Azerbaijan, Belarus, Bosnia-Herzegovina, Bulgaria, Croatia, Czech Rep., Estonia, Georgia, Hungary, Kazakhstan, Latvia, Lithuania, Macedonia, Poland, Romania, Russia, Slovakia, Slovenia, Turkmenistan, Tajikistan, Ukraine, Uzbekistan, Yugoslavia

NORTH AMERICA $99.00
Canada, Greenland, Mexico

Canada	$79.00
Mexico	$59.00

Caribbean Islands $49.00
Anguilla, Antigua, Aruba, Bahamas, Barbados, Bermuda, British Virgin Is., Cayman Is., Domincan Rep., Fr. Antilles, Grenada, Haiti, Jamaica, Neth. Antilles, St. Lucia, Trinidad & Tobago, Turks & Caicos

SOUTH AMERICA $99.00
Argentina, Bolivia, Brazil, Chile, Colombia, Ecuador, Guyana, Paraguay, Peru, Surinam, Uruguay, Venezuela,

Argentina	$39.00
Brazil	$49.00
Argentina, Brazil, Chile	$69.00
Venezuela	$39.00

CENTRAL AMERICA $49.00
Belize, Costa Rica, El Salvador, Guatemala, Honduras, Nicaragua, Panama

Directory of Foreign Firms Operating in the United States, 9th Edition Country/Regional Editions Softbound

AFRICA N/A
Egypt, Ivory Coast, Morocco, Nigeria, South Africa

ASIA $69.00
China, Hong Kong, India, Indonesia, Japan, Malaysia, Pakistan, Philippines, Singapore, South Korea, Taiwan, Thailand

Japan & South Korea $59.00

China, Hong Kong, Singapore, Taiwan $29.00

Near & Middle East & No. Africa $29.00
Bahrain, Cyprus, Egypt, Iran, Israel, Jordan, Kuwait, Lebanon, Morocco, Saudi Arabia, Turkey, United Arab Emirates.

AUSTRALIA $29.00
Australia, New Zealand

NORTH AMERICA $39.00
Canada, Mexico

LATIN AMERICA $39.00
South/Central America & the Caribbean
Argentina, Bermuda, Bolivia, Brazil, Cayman Is., Chile, Colombia, Costa Rica, Dominican Republic, Ecuador, Guatemala, Guyana, Mexico, Panama, Paraguay, Peru, Uruguay, Venezuela

EUROPE $109.00
Austria, Belgium, Czech Republic, Denmark, England, Finland, France, Germany, Greece, Hungary, Iceland, Ireland, Italy, Luxembourg, Monaco, Netherlands, Norway, Poland, Portugal, Romania, Russia, Scotland, Slovenia, Spain, Sweden, Switzerland

British Isles $49.00
England, Ireland, Scotland

EUROPE excluding the British Isles $99.00

France	$39.00
Germany	$49.00
Italy	$29.00
Netherlands	$39.00
Scandinavia	$49.00
Sweden	$39.00
Switzerland	$39.00

EUROPE Eastern N/A
Czech Republic, Hungary, Poland, Romania, Russia, Slovenia

Uniworld Business Publications, Inc.
257 Central Park West, Suite 10A
New York, New York 10024
Tel: (212) 496-2448
Fax: (212) 769-0413
E-mail: uniworldbp@aol.com
WEBsite: http://www.uniworldbp.com

November 30, 1998
Prices subject to change without notice